BREWER'S
BRITAIN
&IRELAND

BREWER'S BRITAIN & IRELAND

COMPILED BY

John Ayto and Ian Crofton

PLACE-NAME CONSULTANT

Dr Paul Cavill

WEIDENFELD & NICOLSON

Weidenfeld & Nicolson
Wellington House
125 Strand, London.WC2R 0BB
www.orionbooks.co.uk

10 9 8 7 6 5 4 3 2 1

First published 2005

Brewer's Trademark registered in Great Britain,
British Patent Application No. 1137780
Brewer's Dictionary of Phrase and Fable first published 1870

British Library Cataloguing-in-Publication Data
A catalogue entry for this book is available from the British Library

ISBN 0 304 35385 X

Typeset in Stone by
Gem Graphics, Trenance, Cornwall
Printed in Finland by WS Bookwell

Contents

Contents

Authors' Preface

Blarney and Killarney, Culloden and Flodden, Shankhill, Swansea and Slough ... Windrush, Windscale, Windsor, and Windermere, Loch Lomond, Loch Ness and Lough Neagh ... Knightsbridge, Neasden, Naseby, the Nore, Cader Idris, Caernarfon and Clun ... Everton, Ealing, Enniskillen and Eton, Dunfermline, Dublin and Duns ... names that most inhabitants of these islands will find, for a whole host of different reasons, full of evocative resonances. Each of us will have in our minds a unique store of responses, depending on background and personal history; but we all have this in common – that the name of a particular place can participate in a web of mental associations as subtle and as far-reaching as any that link our everyday vocabulary. Some names can instantly conjure up an arcadian English countryside (Malmesbury, Malvern, Midsomer Norton); others, marked forever by some terrible event, evoke a much more sombre response (Dunblane, Aberfan, Lockerbie, Drogheda, Rillington Place, Saddleworth Moor); some simply raise a smile (Macgillycuddy's Reeks, the Slug, Auchtermuchty, Tubbercurry, Tavernspite, Netherthong, Wyre Piddle, Effin, Twatt, Pratt's Bottom).

The sheer sound of our place names has been employed to incantatory effect:

> Rime Intrinseca, Fontmell Magna, Sturminster Newton and Melbury Bubb,
> Whist upon whist upon whist upon whist drive, in Institute, Legion and
>   Social Club.
>
> John Betjeman 'Dorset', from *Continual Dew* (1937)

And Michael Flanders and Donald Swann's 'Slow Train', inspired by Dr Beeching's Axe that, in the early 1960s, fell on hundreds of rural railway stations, is essentially a nostalgic litany of names: *Kirby Muxlow and Scholar Green, Dog Dyke and Tumby Woodside, Littleton Badsey and Cheslyn Hay, Somercotes and Pye Hill.* North of the border, the first official Scots makar (national poet), Edwin Morgan, has celebrated the somewhat wirier toponymy of his country in 'Canedolia' (1968), an 'off-concrete Scotch fantasia' that begins:

> oa! hoy! awe! ba! mey!

… then proceeds via a whole range of colourful names,

> from largo to lunga from joppa to skibo from ratho to shona …

… to culminate in the triumphal toast:

> schiehallion! schiehallion! schiehallion!

In *Under Milk Wood* Dylan Thomas has the Rev. Eli Jenkins wax lyrical and extensively over the soft sounds of Wales, albeit with an ironic dig at the Reverend's prolixity:

> By Sawdde, Senny Dovey, Dee,
>
> Edw, Eden, Aled, all
>
> Taff and Towy broad and free,
>
> Llynfant with its waterfall …

In Ireland, Percy French, in his haunting songs of exile, similarly pushes the button of national attachment to place with his invocations of the Twelve Pins, the Mountains of Mourne and the lost Eden of Ballyjamesduff:

> Come back, Paddy Reilly, to Ballyjamesduff,
>
> Come back, Paddy Reilly, to me.

The meanings and associations of our 'ordinary' words are fully expounded in conventional dictionaries, but hitherto the names of our towns and villages, rivers, lakes, islands, hills and moors have for the most part languished in the obscurity of gazetteers and specialized place-name dictionaries or had mere walk-on parts in guidebooks. In contrast to these, *Brewer's Britain and Ireland* – in the great tradition established by the Rev. Dr E. Cobham Brewer when he first published his eponymous *Dictionary of Phrase and Fable* in 1870 – offers a rounded and integrated portrait of the places of these islands and the names our ancestors (and we ourselves) have given them.

Each entry begins with an etymology, i.e. an account of the history and original meaning of the name, where it is known – which, thanks to the work of scholars over the decades, it usually now is. There then follows a description of the place so named, in the case of human settlements touching on its topographical position, its historical development and (if merited) its architectural aspect. If the place has a nickname – for example, the Great Wen (London), Furry Boots City (Aberdeen), Auld Reekie (Edinburgh), Tinopolis (Llanelli), the City of the Tribes (Galway) – this is mentioned, as is any special name given to its inhabitants, from Moonrakers (Wiltshire) to Sandrakers (Redcar), Geordies (Tyneside) to Rosbifs (the English according to the French, with the football-supporting variety more likely to be 'les fuck-offs'), from Dubs (Dublin) to Weegies (Glasgow), and from Mackems (Sunderland) to the Taffia (the Welsh political establishment), not forgetting the trendy metropolitan Ladbroke Groovers.

Events of note and local legends and customs are mentioned, as are well-known people who were born in or who lived in the place. Quotations concerning the place – celebratory or derogatory, prosy or poetical, familiar or obscure – are included, and appearances of the place (in disguise or as itself) in fiction, film or television are noted. Towns and cities beyond these shores that share the place name are listed, and artefacts, creatures, events, etc. that are known by the name are fully covered, often under subheadings: thus you will find, among many others, Arbroath smokie, Downing Street Declaration, Dublin Lockout, Eccles cake, Edinburgh rock, Enfield rifle, Gloucester old spot, Guernsey lily, Harris tweed, Hoxton fin, Manchester School, Millbank Tendency, Monmouth cap, St Kilda wren, strathspey, the Thrilla in Rhylla, the Swan of Usk, Tolpuddle Martyrs, Ulster fry and Wexford Rebellion, not forgetting, of course, Piltdown Man and Worcester Woman.

The bones of fact are also fleshed out with associations and connotations, and with idiomatic expressions that have brought a place's name into the general language: 'fight like Kilkenny cats', 'get off at Paisley', 'Dublin uppercut', 'Glasgow kiss', 'Jeddart justice', 'Staines Massive', 'Tipperary fortune', 'set the Thames on fire', 'normal for Norfolk' and so on. Titles of pieces of music (classical to rock) and works of art and literature (both high and low) that include the name are briefly described, so the reader will come upon *A Glastonbury Romance*, *Emilia di Liverpool*, *The Mousehole Cat*, *On Wenlock Edge*, *The Tailor of Gloucester*, *Heart of Midlothian*, *Bound East for Cardiff*, *Aberystwyth Mon Amour*, *The Cattle Raid of Cooley*, *Dubliners*, *They Came from SW19*, 'Eton Rifles', 'Penny Lane', 'Waterloo Sunset', 'Ye Banks and Braes o' Bonnie Doon' – and a host of others.

Brewer's Britain and Ireland concerns itself with the names of natural features (mountains, hills, uplands, moors, valleys, rivers, lakes, islands and islets, bays, cliffs, headlands, sandbanks, forests) and of humanity's contributions (nations, regions, counties, cities, towns, villages, estates, castles and palaces, gardens, roads, canals, tunnels, bridges, monuments). Most of the places included are real, but a certain number of imagined counties, towns and villages appear too, if their fame has become well enough established (e.g. Ballyslapadashamuckery, Barchester, Barrytown, Casterbridge, Cranford, Grimpen Mire, Loamshire, Llareggub, Midwich, Mummerset, The Shire, Sun Hill, Walford, South Riding. The book does not, of course, attempt exhaustive coverage of all British and Irish places and their names, but all large or significant settlements and topographical features are included, together with a wide selection of others with a name or associations that are of particular interest. This volume could easily have been three times as long, but that might have proved beyond both the art of the bookbinder and the lifting ability of the reader.

The responsibility for what might in the very broadest terms be called the 'Soft' South of England (including as far north as Cheshire, Derbyshire, Nottinghamshire and Lincolnshire) fell to John Ayto; the 'Gritty' North of England was tackled by Ian Crofton, who also spread his net over Ireland, Scotland and Wales. The compilers are greatly indebted to Paul Cavill of Nottingham University (and also Research Fellow of the English Place-Name Society): he oversaw – and in not a few instances created – the material relating to place-name origins, as well as providing the boxed entries on place-name elements, the Introduction ('The Place Names of Britain and Ireland'), the Appendices and the Glossary.

A debt of thanks is also due to Richard Milbank, reference publishing director of Weidenfeld & Nicolson, whose idea this book was, and who planned its shape and structure, as well as making numerous significant contributions to the text. Mark Hawkins-Dady was responsible for the management of a long and complex project; he and Michael Janes edited the text, pulling its disparate elements together and adding many felicitous touches of their own. Rosie Anderson, Martin Bryant, Lydia Darbyshire and Patrick Heenan proofread the book, while Catherine Cleare at Weidenfeld showed her stamina, efficiency and good eye throughout successive correction and proof stages. Gwyn Lewis designed the book's 'look', while Peter Harper created the five maps that give it a visual dimension. Any errors or omissions, however, remain the responsibility of the compilers.

Information for the etymologies has been drawn from a wide range of sources, but we would like specifically to acknowledge the work of David Mills, whose Oxford University Press place-name dictionaries have provided concise and scholarly judgments, and whose opinions we have disagreed with only at risk of controversy. Adrian Room's *Dictionary of Irish Place-Names* and Hywel Wyn Owen's *Place-Names of Wales* also proved invaluable sources of reference.

The compilers would welcome any suggestions for additional material, and indeed for completely new entries, for inclusion in any future editions of *Brewer's Britain and Ireland*. We are in no doubt that our readers have many an untold tale to tell, and we look forward to hearing them: we may be contacted by email at bbi@orionbooks.co.uk or via the publishers' address, which can be found on the copyright page of this book.

John Ayto
Ian Crofton

Introduction

The Place Names of Britain and Ireland

BY PAUL CAVILL

The earliest place names

Some of the names in Britain and Ireland have been around for a very long time indeed. It is not possible to be precise, but when we refer to 'pre-Celtic' or 'Indo-European' we are talking about a language that was in use around 3000 BC, at which time the people speaking it began to migrate and the language itself began to change and develop into the historic languages – Greek, Latin, Old Celtic, Germanic (and others) – that we are more familiar with. The Indo-European language has been studied extensively, and place names are important in that study because they preserve early elements that can be traced back to the parent language. The date of record for these names bears no resemblance to the date at which the names were used. British and Irish names are recorded earliest in Greek and Roman texts of the period either side of the beginning of the 'Common Era', i.e. when BC turned into AD; but the earliest names were in use centuries and possibly millennia before these or any other written records.

One of the interesting features of the place names of the earliest period is that they usually refer to indelible and significant landscape features rather than settlements: rivers, islands and hills rather than towns or villages. When we try to trace some of these names, we simply cannot find a secure meaning in any of the languages we know to have been used in the period. The list of these is disappointingly long. In England and Wales, the river names Allen (Northumberland), Cary (Somerset), Colne (Essex and Hertfordshire), Humber (East Yorkshire), Itchen (Hampshire), Neen (Shropshire), Severn (Powys to Bristol) and Welland (Northamptonshire to Lincolnshire) are among those for which an Old Celtic or pre-Celtic name is suspected, but for which we have no certain meaning. For other names we have at least an idea of the meaning: Nairn (Highland) probably means 'submerging one', Nidd (North Yorkshire) and Welsh Neath reflect an Indo-European river name meaning 'running water', Ouse means 'water', Tees (Cumbria to Durham) possibly means 'surging one' and Tyne (Northumberland to Durham) means 'river'. It is perhaps unfortunate that the names produced by delving so far into the past turn out to be so bland, but no doubt they expressed what was necessary information for the users of the names.

Early names like these have recently been the focus of research, which has revealed that certain names are probably related. The river names Ayr (Ayrshire), Oare (Somerset), Arrow (Warwickshire) and Orwell (Suffolk) have been linked with the French rivers Arve and the Italian Arvo, and are thought to derive from an Indo-European root meaning 'move', and hence mean something like 'rapidly moving river'. Another cluster of names is that comprising the rivers Tamar (Cornwall), Tame (Warwickshire and Staffordshire, and Greater Manchester and Yorkshire), Teme (Powys to Worcestershire), Thame (Oxfordshire, also Dorset), Thames (Gloucestershire to London), Taf (South Wales), and Tavy (Devon). All these probably derive from an Indo-European word meaning 'to melt, flow turbidly', with the Welsh Taf and the Devon Tavy showing the characteristic lenition (a process of smoothing in pronunciation) of *m* to *f* or *v* (*see* the place-name element entry on *bach*) that occurred in the Brittonic strand of Old Celtic, a change that took place by around the 5th century AD.

Greek and Latin texts occasionally preserve early names that were possibly meaningful to the writers, but the significance of which is not always clear to us now. The small and great islands of the British Isles were known to the Greeks: Ireland was *Ierne*, a version of the Old Celtic name later transformed into Latin *Hibernia*; the Orkneys were known as *Orkas*, Latinized as *Orcades*; and Mull was known as *Malaios*. The river and Vale of Avoca (County Wicklow) derive from a re-use of the Egyptian astronomer-geographer Ptolemy's name *Oboka*. York was among the relatively small number of settlements important enough to be recorded by Greek geographers: *Eburakon* probably derives from an Old Celtic word meaning 'place characterized by yew-trees', although it has undergone numerous changes. Winchester's Roman name, *Venta Belgarum*, preserves a pre-Celtic element, *venta*, perhaps meaning 'chief place', along with the tribal name.

Many Roman names contain Old Celtic elements. Among these are several *Isca* names, the Latin version of an Old Celtic element meaning 'water', occurring fairly evidently in Eskdalemuir (on the River Esk, Dumfries and Galloway), Exeter (on the River Exe, Devon), and the River Usk (South Wales). The fort at Caerleon on the latter river was known by the Romans as *Isca Silurum*, but the modern town name preserves another Latin element, *legio* 'legion'. Powys in Wales may derive from Latin *pagus* 'outlying region', and Paisley (Renfrewshire) may, by a roundabout route, be from Latin *basilica* 'church'. Lincoln, as well as having an Old Celtic element *lindo-*, *linn* 'pool', has the Roman *colonia*, essentially a retirement settlement for pensioned soldiers. Anglesey (North Wales) was known in Latin as *Mona* and in Welsh as *Ynys Môn*, but neither version gives any decisive clue as to the etymology.

Speen (Berkshire) may represent an early Latin name *Spinis* 'at the thorn bushes', perhaps overlaid with an Anglo-Saxon reinterpretation that derived it from a word meaning 'wood chip'. There can be no disguising Pontefract (West Yorkshire), Latin for 'broken bridge', though. But it should be noted that many Latin words appearing in names are not necessarily very early: common elements, particularly in English names – like *sub* 'under', *super* 'over, upon', *juxta* 'next to', *cum* 'with', *parva* 'little', *magna* 'big', *superior* 'upper', *inferior* 'lower', *abbas* 'belonging to the abbot or abbess', *regis* 'belonging to the king', *episcopi* 'belonging to the bishop' and *ambo* 'two' – may be old, but most are later than the names that accompany them.

Celtic names

Before the Anglo-Saxons and, earlier still, the Romans, the language spoken throughout these islands was Celtic. In the course of time, the Celtic language divided into the modern languages of Irish, Manx and Scots Gaelic on the one hand, and Welsh and Cornish on the other. These branches are called the Goidelic and the Brittonic respectively. However, that simple division disguises the fact that Brittonic-speaking Celts remained in England and Scotland long after the Anglo-Saxon conquest.

The Old Celtic that is found in English names tends to be Brittonic (*see below*), but the interaction between the various Celtic peoples in Scotland gives a much more complex range of names. The kingdom of Rheged, from Galloway to Cumbria, was Brittonic, and it retained some independence until the 11th century; that of Strathclyde, with its capital in Dumbarton, lasted a similar length of time, and it was also originally Brittonic-speaking. The effective end of the Brittonic kingdom of the Gododdin, based in Edinburgh at the end of the 6th century, is told in the poem *Gododdin* by the Welsh poet Aneirin. But further north, Goidelic-speakers from Ireland were settling in Dalriada (modern Argyll area) from the 3rd century onwards, and their language was to have the most substantial influence on Scottish names.

Pictish was a Brittonic dialect; it has left behind little evidence of its existence, although the east of Scotland is dotted with minor names containing Pictish *pett* 'a portion of land'. Pitlochry (Perth and Kinross), Pittenweem (Fife) and Pittencrieff Glen (Dunfermline) all contain this Pictish element. Other elements of Brittonic origin in Scottish names are more familiar: Perth itself and Narberth (Pembrokeshire) share the element *perth* 'thicket'; Lanark (South Lanarkshire) and Rhosllanerchrugog (Wrexham) share the element *llanerch* 'clearing, glade'. The name Bannockburn (Stirling), so evocative of Scottish nationalism, contains within it the Brittonic legacy of *bannauc* 'peaked hill', which is also found in the Welsh name for the Brecon Beacons, *Bannau Brycheiniog*. The second element of Blantyre (South Lanarkshire), Brittonic *tir* 'land', is the same as that of Pentire (Cornwall) and Gwydir (Conwy). The *penn* element so characteristic of Cornish names such as Penzance, and meaning 'head, end', is also found in Pennan (Aberdeenshire) and Penicuik (Midlothian), as well as in Penn (Buckinghamshire) and Penge (Greater London). Overlap with other Brittonic names in England is evident: Callander (Stirling) derives from the same elements as Calder (West Yorkshire and Cumbria), meaning 'hard water', i.e. fast-flowing stream. These are just a few of many names from the Brittonic source.

Gaelic elements are plentiful in Scotland, and there is considerable overlap with those in Ireland. Topographical features may be represented by Strabane (County Tyrone) and Strathclyde, which both contain Gaelic *srath* 'river valley'. There is the occasional ridge: Drumelzier (Scottish Borders) and Drumcree (County Armagh) and Drumcliff (County Sligo) all begin with Gaelic *droim* 'ridge'. Glens and lochs (*lough* in modern Irish, but *loch* originally) abound in both countries. Settlement and defensive features have similar names, too. Forts are particularly common: Dunbar (East Lothian), Dundee, Dumbarton and Dunkeld (Perth and Kinross) may be compared with Dundalk (County Louth), Dunglow (County Donegal), Dungannon (County Tyrone) and County Down itself – all containing Gaelic *dùn* or Irish *dún* 'fort'. Less secure settlements are also in evidence: Gaelic *bal* 'farm, settlement, village' appears less frequently in Scotland than does its (Irish) equivalent *baile* in Ireland, but plentifully still: Ballater and Balmoral (Aberdeenshire), Ballachulish and Balmacara (Highland), Ballantrae (South Ayrshire), amongst others. And in the local agricultural economy, pigs were valuable, wild or domestic, and we can compare the island of Muck (Inner Hebrides) with Muckross (County Kerry), Slievenamuck (County Tipperary) and Muckish Mountain (County Donegal), all from Gaelic *muc* 'pig' and testifying indirectly to the hardiness of the animal.

There are a good many Irish names that serve to illustrate the idea that the nation is peculiarly sensitive to spiritual influences. The welter of names beginning with *Kil-* 'church' and the number of saints commemorated, among others, express the Christian spiritual legacy. But there are other, more pagan presences, such as the legendary Tuatha Dé Danann. This group was originally a pantheon of pre-Christian gods who were reinterpreted as a powerful historical clan. They figure frequently in names such as Éire itself, Aileach (County Donegal), Bog of Allen and Lough Allen (County Leitrim), Enniskillen (County Fermanagh), Louth, Maynooth (County Kildare) and Moytura (County Mayo;

see the entry on County Mayo for the legend). The name of the Isle of Man is also thought by some to derive its name from this clan: Manannán mac Lir was the ancient Irish sea god, and as well as contributing to Man, he may have had something to do with Ynys Môn, Anglesey, although this is uncertain.

There are fairies in Ireland, too: Sion Mills (County Tyrone) may not be an old name, but it disguises a *sían* 'fairy mound' with a suitably biblical cover. Yew trees were significant in early Celtic legend and religious practice: it may not be coincidence that the name of York changed from focusing on yews under the Celts to boars under the Anglo-Saxon settlers, as boars had a cultic significance for the latter people. Yews appear in the Irish names Youghal (County Cork), Aghadoe (County Kerry), Mayo, Newry (County Armagh) and Emly (Tipperary; *see* the entry for a possible connection with pre-Christian religion).

The Celtic languages in these islands were almost lost in recent centuries because of the desire of those in power to impose linguistic uniformity. It may yet be some time before Cornish revives as a vernacular language giving rise to place names, but Welsh, Irish, Scots and Manx Gaelic are all alive and well, and new names drawing on the ancient stock of Celtic are still being coined.

Old English names

There is almost no overlap between the Celtic languages and the Old English language that came to Britain in the 5th century with the Anglo-Saxon invaders. What the Celts called a *breg* or a *penn*, the Anglo-Saxons called a *dun* or a *hyll*; what the Celts called a *ced* the Anglo-Saxons called a *wudu*. Names show us that the invaders did not understand the Celtic languages, since they added their own name-elements referring to the same features: Bredon (Worcestershire) and Pendle (Greater Manchester) both mean roughly 'hill hill' in terms of etymology, and Chetwode (Buckinghamshire) by the same token means 'wood wood'. On the other hand, the Anglo-Saxons were not unwilling to borrow Celtic elements for new ideas: Eccles (Greater Manchester) represents a frequently-occurring Celtic name element, *eglws* meaning 'church' (*see* the entry on *eccles*), something which the Anglo-Saxons were not familiar with, but which later they were to embrace wholeheartedly and call *cirice* (*see* the entry on *church*).

The Anglo-Saxons invaded from the east, and if Celtic names and Anglo-Saxon names are plotted on a map, it will be evident that the density of Celtic names is greater the further west one goes. On the British mainland, Wales, parts of Devon and Cornwall, and Cumbria were never fully under Anglo-Saxon control. The theory that the Anglo-Saxons wiped out the Celtic populace is disproved not only by the tautological place names mentioned above, but also by the number of Celtic names and elements that survive, which indicate a speech-community using them. In addition, names like Wales, Walton-on-Thames (Surrey), Walton-on-the-Naze (Essex) and Walton-le-Dale (Lancashire), all containing the English element *walh* meaning 'Celt, foreigner, servant', show not only that communities of Celts survived, but that they had their own farms and settlements.

Nevertheless, in terms of naming, the Anglo-Saxon conquest was a revolution. The vast majority of settlements were either renamed or newly founded with English names. Elements borrowed from Latin before the Anglo-Saxons left the Continent, such as *ceaster* 'fort', *funta* 'spring', *stræt* 'paved road', *weall* 'wall' and *wic* 'specialized farm or settlement' were put to good use, and many of the names they formed retained an association with Roman features. Chester, Lancaster and Leicester were all Roman fortified settlements; Cheshunt (Hertfordshire) combines both *ceaster* and *funta* to form 'spring by the Roman fort'; Akeman Street, Watling Street and Stane Street are all Roman roads; the Antonine Wall, Hadrian's Wall and Wallsend refer to Roman walls; and the various Wickhams, and Wickhambreaux (Kent) and Wickham Skeith (Suffolk), have recently been shown to be settlements of Romano-British origin. These are English names, and are clearly used with precision to retain their associations with Roman features.

The great wealth of English names derive from Old English elements. Topographical or landscape features that nowadays we can hardly differentiate appear. The elements *ecg*, *clif*, *hlinc*, *ora*, *ofer* and *hrycg* are among those that refer to ridges, banks and hillsides. Among the places containing these elements are Edge (Shropshire) and Edgehill (Warwickshire); Cliffe (Kent) and Cleeve (North Somerset); Shanklin (Isle of Wight) and Sydling St Nicholas (Dorset); Ore (East Sussex) and Ower (Hampshire); Over (Cambridgeshire, Cheshire, Gloucestershire) and Bolsover (Derbyshire); and Rugeley (Staffordshire) and Longridge (Lancashire). The most comprehensive work on these topographical elements is Margaret Gelling and Ann Cole's *The Landscape of Place-Names* (2000), and the interested reader can find detailed treatment of all these elements there. As their discussion shows, it becomes clear that once again these names are precise and nuanced, referring to features in the landscape for which we do not now have accurate, simple descriptions.

The Anglo-Saxons were often devout (*see* the Appendix on Church and Ecclesiastical Names), but before Christianity, and for long afterwards, the shadows of the old gods and a range of supernatural creatures continued to fall across the land. Woden, the chief of the pre-Christian Anglo-Saxon gods and specialist in war, poetry and drinking, has given his name to various places: Wednesbury and Wednesfield (West Midlands), Wormshill (Kent) and Wansdyke (Berkshire, Wiltshire and Somerset); under his alias, Grim, he also appears in Grim's Dyke

(Greater London and Oxfordshire), Grimspound (on Dartmoor) and Grimes Graves (Norfolk). It is unclear whether these manifestations represent survival of belief, especially when put alongside parallels like the many Devil's names, such as Devil's Dyke (Cambridgeshire and elsewhere) and Devil's Den (Wiltshire). The most probable explanation here is that they refer to impressive land features thrown up, cut out, flattened or dug by ancient and powerful beings; indeed a significant number of the features referred to are ancient man-made earthworks. On the other hand, Thundersley (Essex) probably does represent heathen worship, here in a sacred grove dedicated to Thunor, as do Harrow (Greater London), Wye (Kent) and Weedon Bec (Northamptonshire), which all refer to the presence of a heathen shrine. And of course gods were not the only supernatural beings: Filey (North Yorkshire) possibly refers to the shape of the headland, but the first element means 'sea monster'; and Pokesdown and Pooksgreen (Hampshire) were places thought to be inhabited by goblins.

Alongside a vast array of flora and fauna that we find in the British Isles today, Anglo-Saxon names show us some species that are now extinct: Beverley (East Yorkshire) refers to beavers, and indeed ancient beaver bones have been found in the vicinity; Woolpitt (Suffolk) reminds us that wolves were a problem, and needed to be trapped. Closer to our own times, Elm (Cambridgeshire), Nine Elms and the 'Seven Sisters' of Seven Sisters Road (London) refer to recently lost but magnificent elm trees. The area known as Lyme to the ancient Celts, and found in Ashton-under-Lyne (Greater Manchester), was possibly an area originally noted for its elm trees, and a 'farm with ash trees' (Ashton) was sufficiently different to attract attention.

A feature not immediately apparent from modern versions of Old English names is the number that contain personal names of women. These include Abingdon (Oxfordshire), Abram (Greater Manchester), Alderley Edge (Cheshire), Bamburgh (Northumberland), Beaminster (Dorset), Bibury (Gloucestershire), Binegar (Somerset), Bognor Regis (West Sussex), Homerton (Greater London), Kenilworth (Warwickshire), Quenington (Gloucestershire), Royston (Hertfordshire), Tetbury (Gloucestershire), Wivenhoe (Essex) and Wolverhampton (West Midlands). The women in such cases were powerful landowners, abbesses, saints and queens.

The ordinary people worked the land on their farms (*see* entry on *-ton*), set up homes and settlements (*see* entry on *ham*), built fortifications for defence (*see* entry on *bury*), cleared forest (*see* entry on *-ley*) and grazed their cattle on the open land (*see* entry on *field*). They crossed rivers (*see* entry on *ford*), climbed hills (*see* entry on *down*) and found secluded nooks and hollows (*see* entry on *hale*). The sheer busyness of the Anglo-Saxons, and the breadth of their naming, both imaginative and unimaginative, is impressive: the overwhelming majority of village names in England were given before the time of the Norman Conquest in 1066. They were not all linguistically English names, however, which brings us to the Scandinavians.

Scandinavian names

Old Scandinavian, whether Danish or Norwegian, is a Germanic language, as is Old English. This means that while it is usually possible to distinguish Celtic and Old English elements in English names, it is not always possible to distinguish Old Scandinavian and Old English names and elements from one another. Take, for example, the word *hlith* 'slope', which is the same in both Old English and Old Scandinavian: Leith Hill (Surrey) contains the Old English version, as probably does Lytham St Anne's (Lancashire), although the first element here is the dative plural *hlithum* '(place) at the slopes', which is the same in both languages. We can tell Litherland (Greater Manchester) is Old Scandinavian because the possessive plural form in this name, *hlithar*, is different from the Old English form.

In England, the Scandinavian influence on names is relatively clear: once again, if the names are plotted on a map, the Scandinavian names will be found predominantly in the north and east of the country, along the line of Watling Street from London to Chester. This is because that was the boundary of political power between the English kings of Wessex in the south and west, and the Scandinavian kings of the Danelaw in the 9th and 10th centuries. Viking marauders attacked England from the end of the 8th century, and by the end of the 9th century had conquered substantial areas of England. King Alfred made a treaty with the Scandinavians, dividing the country into his kingdom, with its capital in Winchester, and several Scandinavian kingdoms, based in York and in the Five Boroughs (Derby, Leicester, Lincoln, Northampton and Stamford) in the East Midlands.

From this conquest and the subsequent settlement and colonization, Scandinavian names and elements were introduced in addition to, or combined with, and occasionally replaced, English ones. Whitby (North Yorkshire) and Derby, both with the characteristic Scandinavian *-by* meaning 'farm, village', were the main names changed for which we have clear documentary evidence: originally they were Old English, *Streonaeshalch* and *Northworthy*. It is perfectly possible, however, that names like Coniston (Cumbria) and Conisbrough (South Yorkshire) have had Old Scandinavian *konungr* 'king' substituted for the Old English form that would have given Kingston and Kingsbury. And at the other end of the social scale, the number of names with Old English *-ton* combining with a Scandinavian *karl* 'peasant, free man', as in Carleton Forehoe and Carleton Rode

(Norfolk), and Carlton Curlieu (Leicestershire) and Carlton Scroop (Lincolnshire), might suggest that these could have been Charltons originally. Some of the many Kirbys or Kirkbys might have substituted for other names, with or without Old English 'church' in them, simply because the Scandinavians named or renamed them after a recognizable feature.

Two of the more commonly occurring names, Ashby (many) and Willoughby, as in Silk Willoughby (Lincolnshire) and elsewhere, have the Scandinavian *-by*, but in most cases they appear to have the English tree names 'ash' and 'willow', perhaps suggesting that these trees were not altogether familiar to the settlers, or possibly even that the names were given metonymically, representing some particular feature of the way these two woods were used by the Scandinavians. The process of hybridization of names is not at all uncommon, however. Durham combines the Old English word for a hill, *dun* (*see* the entry on *down*), with the Old Scandinavian word for land surrounded by water, *holmr*. Stixwold (Lincolnshire) combines the Old English word *weald* 'forest' with a Scandinavian personal name; Swadlincote (Derbyshire) does the same with *cot* 'cottage, shed', and so do Somerleyton (Suffolk), Thompson (Norfolk) and Thrumpton (Nottinghamshire), with Old English *-ton*. Somerleyton and the purely Scandinavian Somersby (Lincolnshire) both contain the name *Sumarlithi*, which means 'summer sailor'; in England this was a term used for the Viking sea-borne forces, marauding during the summer months, who augmented the Scandinavian land-based armies. Presumably these men called *Sumarlithi* decided to settle, but they were not amongst the earliest armies.

While Old English has an element *throp*, related to, and confusable with, Old Scandinavian *thorp*, most of the common words for settlements in Old Scandinavian are quite different from those in Old English. The very common element *-by* has already been mentioned, but to that can be added *thveit* 'cleared land', as in Bassenthwaite and Seathwaite (Cumbria), Langthwaite (North Yorkshire) and Slaithwaite (West Yorkshire), and *toft* 'homestead, building plot', as in Lowestoft (Suffolk), Toft (Lincolnshire and Cambridgeshire) and Newton by Toft (Norfolk). The possible confusion of *thorp* and *throp* is more potential than real: there are great numbers of Thorpes in the former Danelaw territories, but only a few *throps* even in southern England. Moreover, *thorp* seems to have replaced *throp* as the normal word for a small hamlet or dependent farm: compare Thorpe (Surrey), a place which has an overwhelming majority of its recorded spellings with *thor-*, which indicates that the word may be of Scandinavian rather than English origin. Of course the Scandinavians in Britain travelled, and Scandinavian personal names also became popular: Thurloxton (Somerset) contains a Scandinavian personal name in an area not normally associated with Scandinavian influence.

The Scandinavians settled in areas that were often similar to those of their homelands: the Danes settled in low and rolling country in the east of England, the Norwegians in high, wild country in the north and west. Perhaps it is unsurprising, then, that the features we associate today with striking beauty often have names of Scandinavian origin. So we have fells, riggs, tarns, forces, dales, ghylls, becks and braes, manifested in, for example, Snaefell (Isle of Man), Nine Standards Rigg and Innominate Tarn (Cumbria), High Force (County Durham), the Yorkshire Dales, Gaping Ghyll (North Yorkshire), Caldbeck Fells (Cumbria) and the Braes (Skye). These examples illustrate the pervasive influence of Scandinavian vocabulary in the north: *brae* became the Scots dialect word for a steepish hillside, *carse*, from Old Scandinavian *kjarr*, became the Scots dialect word for low-lying and well-watered land (as in Carse of Gowrie in Perth and Kinross), and *kirk*, from Old Scandinavian *kirkja*, became the Scots word for church (as in Kirkcudbright in Dumfries and Galloway, Kirkwall in Orkney, and many other names).

We began this section with Scandinavian conquest and settlement. What enabled the Scandinavians to achieve this was their mastery of the sea, and this is proclaimed in a staggering number of coastal and maritime names from the Scillies to the Orkneys. In Ireland, Dalkey Island and Lambay (County Dublin) and the Saltee Islands (County Wexford) are Scandinavian names with *ey*, as are Anglesey and Bardsey Island (Gwynedd), Caldey (Carmarthen), Ramsey (Pembrokeshire) and Swansea. In Scotland and the Isles we might mention Rona (Highland), Gigha (Argyll and Bute) and the Isle of May (Fife); in the Outer Hebrides, Barra, probably Eriskay, and Mingulay and Pabbay; in the Shetlands, Bressay, Foula Mousa and Papa Stour; in the Orkneys, Eday, Papa Westray and Rousay: all these have the Old Scandinavian element *ey* 'island' (*see* the entry on *-ay*).

Many of the names of bays, inlets and headlands are Scandinavian. St Agnes, one of the Scilly Isles, disguises its origin as an Old Scandinavian *nes* name, but others do not, for example Caithness and Durness (Highland), the Minches (Outer Hebrides) and Ness (Lewis). Old Scandinavian *fjorthr* 'fjord, inlet' appears in Strangford (County Down), Waterford and Wexford in Ireland, in Milford Haven (Pembrokeshire) in Wales, and in Moidart, Knoydart (Highland) and Loch Seaforth (Lewis) in Scotland. Bays or names with Old Scandinavian *vik* include Achmelvich, Arisaig and Mallaig (Highland) and Lerwick (Shetland). Point of Ayr (Flintshire) and Point of Ayre (Isle of Man) have the element *eyrr* 'sandbank'.

Practical and capable people as they were, the Scandinavians did not only fight, farm, settle and sail. In the names Dingwall (Highland) and Tynwald Hill (Isle of Man) we have a transferred name from the Scandinavian homelands meaning 'field of assembly', the place where people met to govern themselves, and the Manx Tynwald still retains its right to govern the people.

The Norman influence

Most names of settlements were already given by the time the Normans conquered these islands. That means that the Norman French element is slight in some respects; but in others it is highly significant.

New names included Battle (East Sussex), from Old French *bataille*, Bray (Berkshire), meaning 'marsh', and Camber (East Sussex) meaning 'enclosed area'. Boundaries are a theme, with Devizes (Wiltshire) meaning simply 'boundary', and Malpas (Cheshire), which is on the Anglo-Welsh border, being a 'bad road' because of cross-border banditry. Many religious foundations have French names or contain French elements: examples include Blanchland (County Durham), meaning 'white land', St Bees at Egremont (Cumbria), meaning 'pointed hill', Fountains Abbey (North Yorkshire), Haltemprice (East Yorkshire), meaning 'high enterprise', and Rievaulx (North Yorkshire), meaning 'Rye valley'. Charterhouse (Somerset) was a foundation of Carthusian monks.

The language the Normans used, Old French, added a number of new elements, and here the influence can be seen to run deeper. The element *bel*, *beau* 'beautiful' occurs in several names, and suggests that the French had refined tastes, if not overmuch onomastic ingenuity. Beaulieu (Hampshire), where there was a Cistercian monastery, Bewdley (Worcestershire) and Beauly (Highland) are all 'beautiful places'. Beachy Head (Sussex) is a 'beautiful headland', Belper (Derbyshire) is a 'beautiful retreat', Belsize Park (London) is a 'beautiful seat', and Belvedere (Lincolnshire) and the Vale of Belvoir (Leicestershire and Nottinghamshire) have 'beautiful views'. Belgravia (London) is a little more ingenious than the others: although it means 'beautiful grove', it was renamed from a medieval *Merdegrave* 'weasel grove', which would have had unfortunate connotations for French-speakers since *merde* means excrement.

Chapels and hospitals seem to have been bequeathed by the Normans. Chapel-en-le-Frith (Derbyshire) and Cold Chapel (South Lanarkshire) are names that do not immediately impress, meaning 'chapel in the sparse woodland' and 'chapel in an exposed place', and we can deduce from this that chapels were not imposing, but served a purpose. More impressive was Grampound (Cornwall) 'large bridge'; and at the opposite end of the size range were Petty Cury (Cambridge) and Petty France (London), respectively the street for cooks and the enclave of French merchants. Hospitals or hospices are widely found: Spital (Berkshire and elsewhere; *see* the entry on *spital*) contains the English version of the French element; the Gaelic version, appearing in Spiddal (County Galway), is probably from the same source.

Barras Bridge (Newcastle upon Tyne) contains the element *barras* 'an outwork, fortification', and an element *botavant* with similar meaning is found in Buttevant

(County Cork). In this area of defensive stonework the French contribution was considerable. Castles were built all over the territories conquered by the Normans, and their remains are still impressive and popular with tourists. The Old French word *castel* appears particularly in England and Wales, from Castell Dinas Brân (Denbighshire) to Castle Howard (North Yorkshire), as well as in Castletown (Isle of Man), Castlerigg Fell (Cumbria), Castlebar (County Mayo) and many another name. The last-mentioned example of *castle* may have been assimilated to the English word from an original Irish *caisléan* (derived directly from Latin *castellum*), and this might have happened in many of the Irish castle names; a parallel assimilation to *castle* is found in Castleford (West Yorkshire), which originally had Old English *ceaster* instead of *castle-*.

The French language gave a new name for a hill, *mont*, not apparently a significant addition, since there were at least a dozen other words for 'hill' in the Celtic languages and Old English. Egremont (Cumbria) has already been mentioned, but we can add to the list Montacute (Somerset), Mountsorrel (Leicestershire) and Richmond (North Yorkshire). French also, and much more significantly, gave the generic term *mountain*, a word whose purpose and ubiquity needs no further illustration. Other very common generic elements with a French source include *lake*, *forest*, *river* and *valley*, all widely distributed throughout the corpus of names.

Unassuming French elements also appear in large numbers of place names. These are the definite articles *le* and *la* and the particle *en*. Chapel-en-le-Frith (Derbyshire) has already been mentioned, but there is also Alsop-en-le-Dale in the same county and Stretton en le Field (Leicestershire), as well as many others with the reduced form *le*: Walton-le-Dale (Lancashire), Kirby le Soken and Thorpe-le-Soken (Essex), Thorpe le Fallows (Lincolnshire) and Adwick le Street (South Yorkshire). One of the more interesting names is Kirkby la Thorpe (Lincolnshire), where the name is Frenchified, since it was originally *Kirkby Laythorpe*, with Laythorpe being the name of an adjacent settlement. French influence is similarly apparent in the spelling of a name like Friskney Eaudike (Lincolnshire), and Popham's Eau (Cambridgeshire) disguises the original Old English element *ea* 'river, waterway' under the French spelling *eau* 'water'.

These spellings had no particular effect on the pronunciation of the names; they simply made life difficult for the newcomer to the area. But French influence on spelling and pronunciation was quite pervasive. Nottingham, first recorded as *Snotengaham* 'homestead of the family or followers of a man called Snot', lost the initial *S-* by the end of the 12th century as it became an important city for the Anglo-Norman kings. The principal reason for the change of pronunciation is that French did not have an initial sound *sn-*, and speakers and scribes simply omitted the *S*-. The same happened with Trafford (Greater Manchester), which lost the initial *S*- somewhat later on; but here the change is complicated by the fact that nearby Stretford, containing the same elements *street* and *ford*, needed to be distinguished. This is a change for practical reasons rather than because of an inability to pronounce the sounds, but it was one made by the French administration.

Perhaps the most obvious French influence on place names is in the manorial influence, where ordinary names like Acton or Thorpe are distinguished by the name of the family or person occupying or owning the land. Almost all the family names associated with *Acton* that appear in this book, namely Acton Beauchamp, Acton Burnell, Acton Pigott, Acton Trussell and Acton Turville, are of French origin. Even the exception, Acton Round, is also French, assuming *Round* means 'circular'. Of those names included here that take *thorp* as the first element, Thorpes Arnold, Constantine, Malsor, Morieux, Satchville and Waterville are associated with French family names. These names show how completely the land-owning class of Anglo-Saxon England was replaced by the French influx in medieval times. One has to look further for the French influence in Ireland, Scotland and Wales, at least partly because the vernacular Welsh and Gaelic borrowed far less vocabulary from French; but the Norman castles remain as testimony to the power and prestige of the Norman and Anglo-French rulers.

Modern names

Modern names have a tendency to depart from the established patterns of naming of earlier times. The old pattern typically combines generic elements with specific elements. The generic element is usually a feature like a ford, a village, a river or a hill, and these are then distinguished from other fords, villages, rivers and hills by the specific elements. These latter elements might be physically or visually descriptive, such as 'long' or 'black'; they might be defined by the owner or occupant with a personal or occupational name; they might be floral or faunal characteristics, such as tree species or animal names; or they might be evaluative, such as 'good' or 'bad', 'poor' or 'lush'. Modern names do not add much to the range of generic elements available, although they do use some in a distinctive fashion.

Industrialization has had a significant impact on place names. Coal, the backbone of the Industrial Revolution, gave rise to several modern names, such as Coalisland (County Tyrone), Coalbrookdale (Shropshire), Coalville (Leicestershire), Nantyglo and the adjacent Coalbrookvale (Blaenau Gwent). The Seven Sisters Colliery (Neath Port Talbot) is more typical of modern naming practice, as it was apparently named after the seven daughters of the colliery owner.

An effect of industrialization was the need for places to ship and receive goods, and there is a good range of modern names containing the element *port*. Port Talbot (Neath Port Talbot) and Port Penrhyn (Gwynedd), Ports Erin and St Mary (Isle of Man), Portlaw (County Waterford) and Portstewart (County Londonderry), Ports Charlotte and Ellen (two more sisters here; Argyll and Bute) and Ellesmere Port (Merseyside) all represent the need for shipping facilities.

Some modern names pleasingly evoke and imitate older naming. Peterlee (County Durham) and Telford (Shropshire) are both named after people, but *lee* and *ford* sound sufficiently like place-name elements to satisfy most of those who hanker after tradition. Thamesmead and Queensbury (Greater London), Cambourne (Cambridgeshire), Hartrigg Oaks and Cliftonville (Kent) re-use and re-combine older elements to lend the aura of long-established settlements to essentially new ones. This goes a little further with Jarlshof (Shetland), Sir Walter Scott's 19th-century name for a settlement site that had been occupied for millennia, where he uses historical elements particularly redolent of the Viking era to suggest the historical depth of the place. It has to be said that not all modern names are quite so subtle: Central Lancashire New Town needs no annotation.

There are also some regional patterns of modern naming. In Ireland, the division of the country into townlands (*see* the appendix on Administrative Names) means that there is a good deal of continuity of naming with Irish *baile* and English *-town*. Mitchelstown (County Cork) and Blanchardstown (County Dublin) are 13th-century names, from Anglo-Norman landowners. On the same pattern there are names like Cookstown (County Tyrone), Randalstown (County Antrim), Draperstown (County Londonderry) and Charlestown (County Mayo), among others, from the 17th to 19th centuries. In Wales the growth of Nonconformist Christianity, particularly in the 19th century, led to a range of biblical names being used, often for settlements around chapels: Nebo (Ceredigion, Conwy, Gwynedd and Anglesey), Pisgah (Ceredigion), Bethesda (Gwynedd and Pembrokeshire), Bethania (Ceredigion and Gwynedd), Bethlehem and Horeb (Carmarthen) and Beulah (Powys and Ceredigion) are examples.

Two final strands of modern naming are amongst the most entertaining: names of remoteness and names that derive from pubs and inns. There are many examples of World's End, from Denbighshire to Berkshire. California (Falkirk and Norfolk) and New York (Lincolnshire) invoke the remoteness of the New World. Abyssinia (Argyll and Bute), Egypt and Palestine (Hampshire) represent the distant exoticism of Africa and the Near East. Canterbury (Aberdeenshire), Dunkirk (Kent) and Piccadilly Corner (Norfolk) are also probably remoteness names, although transfer of the names for some other reason cannot be ruled out. Jericho (Oxford) may be a biblical name of remoteness or it may be a hostelry name.

Inn and pub names are not particularly prominent in Ireland, but in England, Wales and Scotland the variety is remarkable. London localities and district names of varying ages derive from inn names: Angel, Elephant and Castle, Fitrovia, Globe Town, Maida Vale, Swiss Cottage, Welsh Harp and White Hart may be cited. The reader is urged to proceed to the entries to learn the origins of Beeswing (Dumfries and Galloway), Craven Arms (Shropshire), Cripplesease (Cornwall), Golden Ball (County Dublin), Horse and Jockey (County Tipperary), Loggerheads (Staffordshire), Nelson (Lancashire), New Invention (Shropshire and West Midlands), Normandy (Surrey), Phoenix Green (Hampshire), Queensbury (West Yorkshire), Star (Pembrokeshire), Staylittle (Powys), Three Chimneys (Kent), Twice Brewed (Northumberland), Waterlooville (Hampshire) and Woolpack Corner (Kent). A wealth of onomastic invention is exhibited here, and there is almost no limit to the future possibilities of naming.

Note on Language Terms

Brewer's Britain and Ireland adopts a minimalist approach to the labelling of the languages given in the etymologies of names. This is partly because of the difficulties associated with precise definition, and partly to offer a readily understandable scheme.

The languages used in English place names can be traced fairly easily. There is a trickle of predominantly Brittonic Old Celtic, which then runs into the main river of Germanic names – Old English, Old Scandinavian, Middle English and Modern English – and an admixture of Latin, Old French and other languages. By and large, the evidence is plentiful and has been recorded and evaluated in depth. The linguistic categories are clearly defined, and the dates are relatively straightforward. Old Celtic is often earlier than Old English, but it survives in Old English names because the Anglo-Saxons re-used names that were already employed by the Celtic-speaking populace. 'Old Celtic', 'Old Scandinavian' and 'Old English' as used in this book – in their abbreviated forms OCelt, OScand and OE – refer to names and elements of names that were in circulation up to about AD 1100. Our custom is to refer to Middle English (ME, up to about 1500) and Modern English (ModE, after 1500) elements only when the record, the spelling, or the pronunciation makes it clear that the name or element originated or was used after 1100.

The evidence relating to the Irish, Scottish, Cornish and Welsh names is more complex for two reasons. First, documentary evidence is scarce before about 1100, which means that although we know of some standard Old Celtic elements, and can reconstruct others, the vast majority of names are found in distinctly modern 'regional' forms, often enough influenced by English-speakers. Moreover, the evidence itself is still in the process of being gathered and assessed, so that the place-name surveys available for Scotland, Ireland and Wales are not so far advanced as that for England. For some names we have only the current form to work with. Where that form gives an obvious meaning we can be reasonably sure of the name, but there are possibilities of confusion that only a range of early (or earlier) spellings will resolve.

The second difficulty is that the languages in these largely Celtic-speaking areas developed in different ways and in discernibly different stages. The long-standing classic work on the Celtic languages of Britain, Kenneth Jackson's *Language and History in Early Britain* (1953), discusses the stages of development of (to take the main example) Welsh from Indo-European through Common Celtic, Brittonic, Early and Late British, Primitive Welsh, and Old, Middle and Modern Welsh, giving dates for each development. While the Goidelic branch of Celtic shares the same early ancestry, the dates of its development into Old Irish and later Irish and Gaelic do not coincide with those for Old and later Welsh. The reader who wishes to discover precisely how the languages developed is directed to Jackson's excellent work.

In relation to the Celtic languages, then, some simplification was desirable for *Brewer's Britain and Ireland*. Names and place-name elements found before about 1100 have been labelled as Old Celtic ('OCelt'), whether of the Brittonic or Goidelic strands. Thereafter, the terms Welsh, Cornish, Gaelic and Irish are used, with elements recorded in the standard spelling of those languages. This pattern, incidentally, explains why Celtic elements are presented with accents where appropriate: these elements are in current use, whereas accents on Old Scandinavian and Old English elements were added by later scholars to indicate pronunciation.

The treatment of the Celtic language family thus parallels that of the Germanic one. They have a common ancestor, Indo-European. Then the stages of language labelled 'Old' reach to about 1100. After that there are modern languages with occasional references to forms of the language that come between the 'Old' stage and strictly modern forms. While this approach may obscure some legitimate scholarly distinctions – such as those between Brittonic and Goidelic, between Old Danish and Old Norwegian, and between the various dialects of Old English, all of which have significance in names – this scheme has the values of consistency, accuracy and clarity: real advantages in a book for general consumption.

Paul Cavill

Guide to the Use of the Dictionary

The A–Z entries are arranged alphabetically in letter-by-letter order, rather than word-by-word order: this means that, for example, 'Greenock' precedes 'Green Park'. Place names beginning 'St' are positioned as if spelt out 'Saint'.

Within the main body of an entry, noteworthy names or phrases that originate from – or are related to – the place in question (e.g. Roman names, nicknames, the names of football teams, or local estates, etc.) are often elevated by way of a bolder type. Also, in traditional *Brewer's* style, the reader may find after the main text of an entry one or more sub-entries on related geographical areas, battles, treaties, events, floral and faunal species, phrases and sayings, inventions, local characters or people of repute – a host of phenomena whose names or titles stem from, or play on, the name of the place. These, too, are listed in alphabetical order (letter-by-letter style).

This scheme means that, for example, 'Salisbury Plain' will be found within the entry on 'Salisbury'. However, an entry such as the 'Pass of Brander' has its own main entry, because there is no place called 'Brander' under which to place it. *Brewer's Britain and Ireland* has numerous 'dummy' entries (e.g. **Great Marlow**. *See* MARLOW) to make navigation painless.

Slightly (although often imperceptibly) off from the alphabetical sequence are a number of boxed entries on 'place-name elements', i.e. commonly occurring word forms (*-ham*, *-ton*, etc.) that contribute to so many of the place names of Britain and Ireland. These are complemented by the Glossary at the back of the book, which gives definitions for a multitude of other elements.

Entries usually begin with an etymology explaining the derivation of the place name, where known. In some cases the story of the name is subsumed (for self-evident reasons) in the main text of an entry. The plus symbol (+) in an etymology normally indicates a conjunction of elements that form a single modern word or name: thus, for example, the modern place Guildford is described as deriving from the original elements *gylde* + *ford*.

In sequences of entries that begin with the *same* name, and have the *same* etymology (e.g. Newton Abbot, Newton Aycliffe, Newton Blossomville), the etymology for the common part (here 'Newton') is given once, at its first appearance, and then normally not repeated for the subsequent names. If the modern names look the same but have *different* etymologies (as is the case with Acton Trussell followed by Acton Turville) then the usual, fuller style is used.

Readers curious to delve more broadly into the history of British and Irish place names should consult the Introduction and Appendices for succinct highlights.

Brewer's Britain and Ireland is extensively cross-referenced, using SMALL CAPITALS. This has not, however, been automatic for *every* mention of a place within entries: too much, of an indiscriminate nature, would have made the book ugly to look at and indigestible to read. Thus, the reader should not assume that a place is absent from the book simply because it is not cross-referenced (rule of thumb: always explore). The main body of an entry usually begins with information to locate the place geographically: here, neighbouring towns, villages, etc. and the counties containing places are usually not rendered as cross-references, except to make linkages between human settlements and the natural landscape, or when there is special significance (e.g. when a town is a county town).

Abbreviations

b.	born
c.	*circa* (= around the time of, approximately)
d.	died
fl.	*floruit* (= flourished, where life dates not known)
ME	Middle English
ModE	Modern English
OCelt	Old Celtic
OE	Old English
OFr	Old French
OScand	Old Scandinavian

Additionally, the phonetic 'schwa' symbol, ə, is used to express the swallowed 'uh' sound in the pronunciation of so many place names (e.g. Balham as 'bal-əm').

THE DICTIONARY

A

A1. *See under* GREAT NORTH ROAD.

A6. An arterial road from Luton to Carlisle, passing through Bedford, Leicester, Manchester and Lancaster.

A6 murder. The shooting of Michael Gregsten and his lover Valerie Storie in their car in a lay-by on DEAD MAN'S HILL, off the A6 between Luton and Bedford in August 1961. Gregsten died, but Storie survived, paralysed from the waist down. James Hanratty, a petty criminal, was convicted of the murder, having been identified by Ms Storie, and was hanged in April 1962. Doubts were widely cast on his guilt, and the case became a *cause célèbre*. Over the following four decades many books were written and many television programmes made seeking to ascertain Hanratty's innocence and propose alternative culprits, and the matter was repeatedly officially reinvestigated. In 2001, DNA evidence established as certainly as such things ever can be that Hanratty was the murderer.

Abbess Roding. *See under* the RODINGS.

Abbeyfeale Irish *Mainistir na Féile* 'abbey of the River Feale'. A small market town on the River Feale in County Limerick, 17 km (11 miles) southwest of Newcastle West. A Cistercian abbey was founded here by Brian O Brien in the 12th century; fragments of it are incorporated into the Catholic church.

Abbeyford Woods *Abbeyford* presumably 'FORD on land owned by the abbey, or on the road to the abbey'; the name is not recorded before the 17th century.

An area of woodland to the north of Okehampton in Devon, on the northern edge of DARTMOOR. The southern part of the 'Tarka Trail', a tourist path exploiting the fame of Henry Williamson's *Tarka the Otter* (1927) (set in north Devon), passes through.

Abbeyleix Irish *Mainistir Laoise* 'monastery in Laois' (Leix is an anglicized version of Laois).

A small town in County Laois, 12 km (7.5 miles) south of Portlaoise. There is nothing left of the Cistercian abbey of De Lege Dei, founded here in 1183, after which the town is named. Abbeyleix was laid out as a model village in the 18th century.

Abbey Road From the medieval priory at Kilburn to which the track led on which the road was based.

A road in ST JOHN'S WOOD, northwest Inner London (NW6, NW8), in the City of WESTMINSTER. It was developed (from an old trackway) in the 19th century. At No. 3 are the recording studios of EMI (originally The Gramophone Company, later HMV), inaugurated in 1931 by Edward Elgar with a recording of his *Falstaff*. Their existence was largely unknown to the general public until 1969, when the Beatles named an album recorded there: *Abbey Road*. Its cover photograph features the four Beatles, including a shoeless Paul McCartney, on a zebra crossing outside the studios. The photograph gave rise to bizarre rumours that McCartney was dead, fanatics claiming that the album's cover image carried clues to that effect. The 'Abbey Road Ghost', a spectral, white-clad female figure, is said to have been observed opening and closing a pair of firedoors inside the studios.

In 1874 the Abbey Road and St John's Wood Mutual Benefit Building Society was founded, in a Baptist chapel in KILBURN. In 1944 it merged with the National Building Society to form the Abbey National Building Society. In 1988 this became a bank, Abbey National PLC (known simply as Abbey from 2003).

Abbey St Bathans From the Cistercian convent and abbey church built here in the 12th century, dedicated to St *Baothen* (or *Baothan*), who succeeded St Columba on Iona on the latter's death in 597.

A small village on the south side of the Lammermuir Hills (*see under* LAMMERMUIRS), 26 km (16 miles) northwest of Berwick-upon-Tweed. It is in Scottish Borders (formerly in Berwickshire).

Abbey Theatre From its location in *Abbey* Street.

The theatre founded in DUBLIN in 1904 by Yeats and Lady Gregory as the home of the Irish National Theatre Society.

It became the focus of the Irish Literary Revival and a bastion of cultural Nationalism. The Abbey presented the premières of the plays of Synge and O'Casey as well as those of Yeats, and received a government grant from 1925, making it the unofficial national theatre of the new state. The original theatre, punningly known as the **Oul' Shabbey**, burnt down in 1951 and the company moved to the Queen's Theatre in Pearse Street until 1966, when it returned to a new building on the original site. In its early decades the Abbey had a reputation of presenting many plays with Irish rural settings, in contrast to the more cosmopolitan Gate Theatre, run by Mícheál Mac Liammóir and his partner Hilton Edwards; these circumstances led one anonymous wit to characterize the Dublin theatre world of the 1940s as 'Sodom and Begorrah'.

Abbotrule 'abbey lands in the valley of the River Rule', OE *abbat* 'abbot' + OCelt river name *Rule*, possibly meaning 'hasty'.

A tiny settlement in Scottish Borders (formerly in Roxburghshire), 8 km (5 miles) south of Jedburgh.

Abbotsbury 'abbot's manor', OE *abbodes* possessive form of *abbod* 'abbot' + BURY; because the place was formerly in the possession of the abbots of GLASTONBURY.

A village in Dorset, at the western end of the narrow lagoon between CHESIL BEACH and the mainland. It is best known for its Swannery, home of a huge colony of swans. In the novels of Thomas Hardy, it is fictionalized as 'Abbotsea'.

Abbotsea. A fictional name for ABBOTSBURY in the novels of Thomas Hardy.

Abbotsford From the nearby FORD across the Tweed used in medieval times by the monks of Melrose Abbey (*see under* MELROSE).

A country house built in the Scots baronial style by Sir Walter Scott. It is in Scottish Borders (formerly in Roxburghshire), on the River TWEED, 3 km (2 miles) west of MELROSE. When Scott bought the estate in 1811, it was occupied by a farm called Clartyhole (Scots *clarty* 'mucky'). Scott proceeded to fill the house with a great collection of antiquities and historical relics, plus an extensive library. Those who stayed with Scott at Abbotsford included William Wordsworth, Washington Irving and Thomas Moore. Scott died at Abbotsford in 1832. The house, which is open to the public, is in the hands of Scott's descendants. *See also* SCOTT'S VIEW.

Abbots Langley *Abbots* denoting manorial ownership in the Middle Ages by the Abbot of St Albans (a more circumstantial local legend has it that the town got its name in 1045 when a Saxon, Ethelwise the Black, and his wife Wynfelda gave it to the monks and monastery of St Albans); *Langley* 'long glade', OE *lang* 'long' + -LEY.

A small town in Hertfordshire, about 8 km (5 miles) north of Watford. It is said to be the birthplace of Nicholas Breakspear, later Pope Adrian IV (1154–9), the only Englishman ever to become Pope in Rome.

See also KINGS LANGLEY.

Aber *See* ABER; the full name of the village is *Abergwyngregyn*, 'mouth of the river of the white shells'.

A village in Conwy (formerly in Caernarvonshire, then in Gwynedd). Llywelyn the Great had a stronghold here in the 13th century, and it was here that Llywelyn ap Gruffydd (also known as Llywelyn the Last) rejected Edward I's demand that he should acknowledge the English king as his overlord.

Aber Falls. A spectacular 30 m (98.5 ft) waterfall south of the village of Aber, on the northwest slopes of the Carneddau. Its Welsh name is **Rhaeadr Fawr**.

Aberaeron 'mouth of the River Aeron', ABER + river name meaning 'goddess of battle'.

A small town on Cardigan Bay, at the mouth of the River Aeron, in Ceredigion (formerly in Cardiganshire, then in Dyfed), 8 km (5 miles) northeast of New Quay. It is the administrative headquarters of the unitary authority of CEREDIGION.

Aberaeron Express. A cable car that formerly crossed the small harbour here. It was constructed in 1885 and ceased functioning in 1932.

Aberaman 'mouth of the River Aman', ABER + name meaning 'pig' or 'pigling'.

A town in Rhondda Cynon Taff (formerly in Glamorgan, then in Mid Glamorgan), 2 km (1.2 miles) southeast of Aberdare.

See also GLANAMAN.

❖ aber ❖

Originally an Old Celtic word meaning 'estuary' or 'confluence', this word was used at two different stages of the Celtic languages, which explains the two main forms of the element in modern place names. Welsh and Scottish names with *aber* derive from the Brittonic form of the word *adbero*, and this appears in such names as ABERDEEN and ABERYSTWYTH.

The other form of the element, Irish *inbhir* and Gaelic *inver*, gives a few Irish names such as Inver (County Donegal) but there are considerably more Scottish ones: INVERNESS, INVERGORDON, INVERCLYDE and so on.

Aberbrothock. Another name for the town of ARBROATH.

Abercarn 'mouth of the Carn', ABER + river name meaning 'cairn'.

A town in Ebbw Vale, Caerphilly (formerly in Monmouthshire, then in Gwent), some 8 km (5 miles) west of Cwmbran.

Aberchirder 'mouth of the dark water', ABER + Gaelic *ciar* 'dark, swart' + *dobhar* 'water'.

A small town in Aberdeenshire (formerly in Banffshire, then in Grampian region), 13 km (8 miles) southwest of Banff. It was founded in 1764 by Alexander Gordon of Auchintool. Its nickname is **Foggieloan** (Scots, 'mossy track').

Aberconwy 'mouth of the Conwy', ABER + CONWY[1].

A former district (1974–96) of Gwynedd county. Aberconwy was also the original name of the town of CONWY[2].

Treaty of Aberconwy (1277). A treaty that ended the war between Edward I and Llywelyn ap Gruffydd ('Llywelyn the Last'), by which the latter's territory was reduced to that part of Gwynedd west of the River Conwy.

Abercynon 'mouth of the River Cynon', ABER + river name *Cynon*.

A town on the River CYNON in Rhondda Cynon Taff (formerly in Glamorgan, then in Mid Glamorgan), some 5 km (3 miles) southeast of Mountain Ash. It was at the southern end of Richard Trevithick's pioneering steam-locomotive track of 1804 (*see* MERTHYR TYDFIL).

Aberdare 'mouth of the River Dâr', ABER + river name possibly meaning 'oak river'. It is sited where the River Dâr joins the River CYNON.

A town (Welsh **Aberdâr**) in Rhondda Cynon Taff (formerly in Glamorgan, then in Mid Glamorgan), 7 km (4.5 miles) southwest of Merthyr Tydfil. It grew around the iron and coal industries in the 19th century, both of which are now long gone. It was the administrative seat of the former Cynon Valley district.

Alun Lewis (1915–44), one of the most celebrated of British Second World War poets, was born in the village of Cwmaman near Aberdare; he was killed in action in Burma.

> From this high quarried ledge I see
> The place for which the Quakers once collected
>   clothes ...
>
>   Alun Lewis: 'The Mountain over Aberdare'

There is an Aberdare Range of mountains in Kenya.

Aberdaugleddau. The Welsh name for MILFORD HAVEN.

Aberdeen 'mouth of the River Don', ABER + river name Don. Scotland's third largest city, a royal BURGH on the coast of northeast Scotland, some 90 km (55 miles) north of Dundee. It straddles the mouths of the rivers DEE[1] and DON[1]. (The Dons – *see under* DON[1] – is the nickname of

Aberdeen FC, founded in 1903.) Aberdeen was formerly the county town of ABERDEENSHIRE, then the administrative centre of GRAMPIAN region, and the City of Aberdeen (taking in some of the surrounding countryside) is now a unitary authority. Aberdeen is known as the **Granite City**, from the stone used in many of its older buildings –

> Howked out of the Rubislaw Quarry's
> Undiamandiferous granite.
>
>   Robert Crawford: from *The Tip of My Tongue* (2003)

(The ornate 19th-century Marischal College building is said by some to be the largest granite building in the world.) Aberdeen is also known as **the City of Bon-accord** (i.e. good will, friendship). The inhabitants of Aberdeen are called **Aberdonians**, and the city and its dialect used to be referred to as **Aberdeen awa**. For some reason, Aberdonians are regarded by some as the most financially prudent of a financially prudent nation. (And the reputation has spread: the inhabitants of PORTADOWN have been called the 'Aberdonians of Ireland'.) Others have taken a different view:

> Bleakness, not meanness or jollity, is the keynote to Aberdonian character ... For anyone passing their nights and days in The Silver City by the Sea ... it is comparable to passing one's existence in a refrigerator.
>
>   Lewis Grassic Gibbon: *Scottish Scene, or the Intelligent Man's Guide to Albyn,* 'Aberdeen' (1934)

Gibbon is perhaps referring strictly to the chilly climate, as many graduates of the University of Aberdeen declare that it has the best student social life of anywhere in Britain. Nevertheless, some fellow Scots persists in being unkind:

> Aberdeen ... the armpit of these islands, moist with a cold drizzle of greed, cant and mendacity.
>
>   Euan Ferguson: *The Observer* (22 September 2002)

Foreigners have also not been as charitable as they might have been:

> I came to hate Aberdeen more than any other place I saw. Yes, yes, the streets were clean; but it was an awful city ... It was only in Aberdeen that I saw kilts and eightsome reels and the sort of tartan tighfistedness that made me think of the average Aberdonian as a person who would gladly pick a halfpenny out of a dunghill with his teeth.
>
>   Paul Theroux: *The Kingdom by the Sea* (1983)

Aberdeen was until 1891 two separate burghs. **Old Aberdeen** on the mouth of the River Don was supposedly founded in 580 by St Machar, a follower of St Columba who had instructed him to establish a church where he found a bend in a river shaped like a shepherd's crook; the bend in the Don here evidently fitted the bill. Old Aberdeen contains the twin-spired Cathedral of St Machar (begun 1424) and the **University of Aberdeen**, the third-oldest university in Scotland, and the fifth-oldest in Britain. It originated as King's College, founded in 1495 by William Elphinstone, Bishop of Aberdeen and Chancellor of Scotland. Its first principal was the historian and humanist Hector Boece. In 1593 was added the avowedly Protestant Marischal College (founded by George Keith, 5th Earl Marischal). When Dr Johnson visited in 1773 with Boswell, he was made a freeman of the city, but was disappointed that the university professors failed to start 'a single mawkin for us to pursue' (a mawkin being a hare, metaphorical or otherwise). There was a well-established medical school, and like others elsewhere it acquired a somewhat sinister reputation, as recalled by an old tinker as recently as 1954:

> I mind once upon a time when ye couldna pass the Marischal College or the King's College, for the students would fairly take a haud o' ye with a cleik [hook] by the leg. They took ye right inside. They wanted fresh bodies.

The two colleges combined to form a single institution in 1860, a merger that resulted in the redundancy from his position of professor of natural philosophy at Marischal College of James Clerk Maxwell, perhaps the most influential physicist of the 19th century.

Other important educational institutions in Aberdeen include the Robert Gordon University and the medieval Grammar School, where Lord Byron was a pupil from 1794 to 1798, as was the novelist Eric Linklater (1899–1974). Linklater went on to study medicine, then English, at the university, where he later taught, and of which he was rector from 1945 to 1948. Other rectors have included the biologist T.H. Huxley ('Darwin's Bulldog') and Sir John (later Lord) Hunt, the leader of the successful 1953 Everest expedition. Notable alumni of the university have included Sir Thomas Urquart (1611–60), the cavalier and translator of Rabelais; Thomas Reid (1710–96), who helped to establish the 'common sense' school of philosophy; the novelist Tobias Smollett (1721–71); and the satirist Peter Pindar (pseudonym of John Wolcot, 1738–1819).

Aberdeen's other original burgh, **New Aberdeen**, started as a fishing and trading centre at the mouth of the River Dee, the site of the present harbour. The Aberdeen Harbour Board claims to be Britain's oldest business, founded in 1136, and the Shore Porters Society of Aberdeen, said to be the world's oldest documented transport company, was founded in 1498. Aberdeen is still an important fishing port, and since the 1970s has been the main onshore base of the North Sea oil industry. This has made **Aberdeen Airport** (at Dyce, north of the city) the world's busiest heliport, taking personnel to and from the rigs. Ferries sail from Aberdeen to Orkney and Shetland.

Despite its relative geographical isolation, Aberdeen has suffered its fair share in Scotland's wars. Aberdeen Castle, a royal residence, was destroyed in 1308 when the local supporters of Robert the Bruce, crying 'Bon Accord' (now the city's motto), evicted the English garrison. The English returned in 1336, and virtually destroyed Old Aberdeen. During the Civil Wars of the 17th century the Covenanting army of the Marquess of Montrose defeated the city's Royalist defenders at the Battle of the Bridge of Dee (*see under* DEE[1]) in 1639. Montrose returned in 1644 as a supporter of Charles I, and this time defeated an army of Covenanters and Aberdonians at the so-called Battle of the Justice Mills (also called the **Battle of Aberdeen**), on 'Black Friday', 13 September. His troops went on to sack the city.

Aberdeen was the birthplace of the noted Philadelphia cabinet-maker Thomas Affleck (1745–95), and of the soprano Mary Garden (1874–1967). The poet John Barbour, author of *The Bruce*, was archdeacon at Aberdeen, and died here in 1395, as, in 1937, did the Austrian psychiatrist Alfred Adler, who originated the concept of the inferiority complex. There are towns called Aberdeen in Australia (New South Wales), Canada (Saskatchewan), Hong Kong, South Africa (Western Cape) and the USA (Idaho, Maryland, Mississippi, North Carolina, Ohio, South Dakota, Washington). There is a Lake Aberdeen in Canada (Northwest Territories).

> Here lie the bones of Elizabeth Charlotte,
> That was born a virgin and died a harlot.
> She was aye a virgin till seventeen –
> An extraordinary thing for Aberdeen.
>
> Anon.: Epitaph, quoted in Donald and Catherine Carswell, *The Scots Week-End* (1936)

See also FURRY BOOTS CITY.

Aberdeen, George Hamilton-Gordon, 4th Earl of (1784–1860). A British statesman who was prime minister from 1852 to 1855, when he was obliged to resign over his misconduct of the Crimean War.

Aberdeen Angus. A breed of hornless black beef cattle.

Aberdeen buttery or **rowie.** The Scottish version of the croissant, being a flaky, crispy, buttery roll, combining a fatty dough and a bread dough.

Aberdeen Press and Journal. The original name of Britain's 'oldest surviving newspaper' (according to the British Library), founded in 1747. It subsequently became simply *The Press and Journal.*

Aberdeen terrier. A former name for a Scottish terrier or Scottie.

'Queenis Progress at Aberdeen, The'. A poem by William Dunbar describing the visit of Margaret Tudor, wife of James IV, to the city in 1511, when she was accompanied by the poet. The piece begins:

> Blyth Aberdeane, thow beriall of all tounis,
> The lamp of bewtie, bountie, and blythnes;
> Unto the heaven [ascendit] thy renoun is

> Off vertew, wisdome, and of worthiness;
> He nottit is thy name of nobilnes.
>
> (*beriall* 'beryl', *He* 'high')

Roull of Aberdeen. A poet of whom little is known apart from his appearance in William Dunbar's (?1456–?1513) elegy for dead poets, *Lament for the Makaris* (1508):

> He has tane Roull of Aberdene
> And gentill Roull of Corstorphin;
> Two bettir fallowis did no man se.
> *Timor mortis conturbat me.*

Aberdeenshire From ABERDEEN + SHIRE.

A former county and current unitary authority of northeast Scotland. The old county was bounded on the north and east by the North Sea, on the northwest by Banffshire, on the west by Inverness-shire, and on the south by Perthshire, Angus and Kincardineshire. In addition to ABERDEEN (the county town), Aberdeenshire included BALLATER, BRAEMAR, FRASERBURGH and PETERHEAD. In 1975 it became part of GRAMPIAN region, but in 1996 it was restored as a unitary authority. The new unitary authority also includes most of the former county of KINCARDINESHIRE (with the towns of STONEHAVEN and LAURENCEKIRK), but excludes the City of Aberdeen. It is bounded on the north and east by the North Sea, by Moray and Highland on the west, and by Angus and Perth and Kinross on the south. The east of Aberdeenshire is mostly agricultural lowland, while in the west are the CAIRNGORM MOUNTAINS.

Aberdour 'mouth of the water', ABER + river name *Dour* from Gaelic *dobhar* 'water'.

A small seaside town in Fife, 9 km (5.5 miles) from the Edinburgh shore across the Firth of Forth (*see under* FORTH). It has a medieval church and castle, and Whitesands Bay makes it a popular resort. It is best known, however, from the anonymous traditional 'Ballad of Sir Patrick Spens':

> Haf owre, haf owre to Aberdour,
> It's fiftie fadom deip:
> And thair lies guid Sir Patrick Spens,
> Wi' the Scots lords at his feit.

Aberdovey 'mouth of the River Dyfi', ABER + DYFI.

A small seaside resort at the mouth of the Dyfi (Dovey) estuary, in Ceredigion (formerly in Cardiganshire, then in Dyfed), 14 km (8.5 miles) north of Aberystwyth. Its Welsh name is **Aberdyfi**. West of the village is the stretch of sand called **Aberdyfi Bar**.

'Bells of Aberdovey, The'. A folk song (Welsh 'Clychau Aberdyfi'), referring to the legend that where Cardigan Bay is today was once the land called Cantref Gwaelod (the Lowland Hundred) until a terrible flood inundated the area, drowning 16 noble cities. It is said that on a still day at Aberdovey, the submerged bells of Cantref Gwaelod can still be heard. The song was popularized in Charles Dibdin's opera *Liberty Hall* (1785).

Aberdulais 'mouth of the River Dulais', ABER + river name *Dulais* meaning 'black stream' (*see* DDU, DUBH).

A village at the junction of the River Dulais and the Vale of Neath, in Neath Port Talbot (formerly in Glamorgan, then in West Glamorgan), 4 km (2.5 miles) northeast of Neath. Nearby are the **Aberdulais Falls**, painted by many artists, including J.M.W. Turner, who visited in 1795. Copper works built here in 1584 used the power of the falls, as did a number of later industries up to the end of the 19th century. The site is now in the care of the National Trust, who have embarked on an archaeological conservation scheme; the waterwheel here is the largest currently used in Europe to generate electricity.

Aberdyfi. The Welsh name for ABERDOVEY.

Aber Falls. *See under* ABER.

Aberfan 'mouth of the River Fan', ABER + river name meaning 'peak' (the Fan joins the TAFF here).

A former mining village in Merthyr Tydfil unitary authority (formerly in Glamorgan, then in Mid Glamorgan), some 6 km (4 miles) south of the town of Merthyr Tydfil. The village became a byword for tragedy after 21 October 1966, when a coal tip subsided on the local school, killing 116 children and 28 adults. The collapse was believed to have been caused by water pouring into the tip from a previously unknown natural spring. The subsequent inquiry blamed the tragedy on the lack of any tipping policy by the National Coal Board.

Aberfeldy ABER + Gaelic *Pheallaidh*, a local river spirit.

A small Highland town at the junction of the Urlar Burn with the River TAY, 10 km (6 miles) east of Loch Tay, in Perth and Kinross (formerly in Perthshire, then in Tayside region). The bridge over the Tay was built in 1733 by William Adam for General Wade, as part of the latter's programme of military road-building in the Highlands after the 1715 Jacobite Rebellion. On one side of the bridge is a monument erected in 1887 to commemorate the various independent units of the Black Watch (originating in 1667) who assembled here in 1739 to form a single regiment.

> Ye sons of Mars, it gives me great content
> To think there has been erected a handsome monument
> In memory of the Black Watch, which is magnificent to see,
> Where they first were embodied at Aberfeldy.
>
> William McGonagall: 'The Black Watch Memorial'
> (This verse is followed by 18 more in the same vein.)

The regiment was given the freedom of the BURGH of Aberfeldy in 1970.

Birks of Aberfeldy, the. The picturesque tree-lined (Scots *birk* 'birch') lower glen of the Urlar Burn, including the Falls of Moness. Burns visited the Birks on 30 August 1787:

> The hoary cliffs are crown'd wi' flowers,
> White o'er the linns the burnie pours,
> And rising, weets wi' misty showers
>> The birks of Aberfeldy.
>>> *Bonnie lassie, will ye go,*
>>> *Will ye go, will ye go,*
>>> *Bonnie lassie, will ye go*
>>>> *To the birks of Aberfeldie?*
>
>> Robert Burns: 'The Birks of Aberfeldy' (1787)

Aberffraw 'mouth of the River Ffraw', ABER + river name meaning 'flood'.
A village on the southwest coast of ANGLESEY (formerly in Gwynedd), 18 km (11 miles) west of Menai Bridge. Between the 7th and the 13th centuries, it was the capital of the princes of Gwynedd. Gwalchmai ap Meilyr (*fl. c.*1140–80) was court poet here, as was his father Gwalchmai and grandfather Meilyr before him. The death at the hands of the English of the last Prince of Gwynedd, Llywelyn ap Gruffydd, in 1282, was commemorated in a contemporary poem ending:

> *Gwir vreinyawl vrenhin Aberffraw*
> *gwenwlat nef boet adef idaw!*
> (True regal king of Aberffraw,
>> may Heaven's white kingdom be his abode!)
>
>> Gruffudd ab yr Ynad Coch: 'The Death of Llywelyn ap Gruffud' (*c.*1282), translated from the Welsh by Gwyn Williams

Aberfoyle 'confluence of the streams', ABER + Gaelic *poll*, possessive *phuill* 'stream'.
A village between LOCH ARD and the LAKE OF MENTEITH, about 30 km (19 miles) northwest of Stirling. It was formerly in Stirlingshire, then in Central Region and is now in the unitary authority of Stirling. It is at the foot of the DUKE'S PASS leading north to the TROSSACHS. It was at the inn in Aberfoyle that Bailie Nicol Jarvie met Rob Roy in Sir Walter Scott's novel *Rob Roy* (1817). Scott described Aberfoyle as a 'clachan' (hamlet), but it is now much larger, and popular with tourists as the 'gateway to the Trossachs'. There is a Rob Roy Roadhouse and an inn called the Bailie Nicol Jarvie.

Abergavenny 'mouth of the River Gafenni', ABER + OCelt river name *Gobannia* 'river of the blacksmiths'.
A town at the junction of the River Gavenny or Gafenni and the Usk, south of the BLACK MOUNTAINS, in MONMOUTHSHIRE (formerly in Gwent), some 15 km (9 miles) north of Pontypool. The Welsh version of the name is **Abergafenni**, but in Welsh it is usually called **Y Fenni**, where the first syllable of the river name has been replaced by Welsh *y* 'the'. Recognizing its strategic siting, the Romans built a fort here called **Gobannium** (after the OCelt river

name, *see above*), and also extracted iron in the locality – it was these iron workings that gave the river its name. The Normans also built a castle here, round which a market town developed. At Christmas in 1176 William de Braose invited a number of local Welsh lords to the castle, and then put them to death in revenge for the slaying of his uncle.

The local hospitality had not improved much by 1802, when the poet Samuel Taylor Coleridge stayed a night at Abergavenny and reported on 'vile supper, vile beds, and vile breakfast'. By a strange coincidence, John Wordsworth, beloved brother of Coleridge's friend William, was captain of a ship called the *Abergavenny*, and drowned when it went down off Portland Bill (*see under* PORTLAND) in 1805. During the Second World War Hitler's deputy Rudolf Hess, who had flown alone to Scotland in 1941 to negotiate a peace, was kept in Abergavenny's lunatic asylum.

Abergele 'mouth of the River Gele', ABER + *gele*, a local dialect version of Welsh *gelau* 'spear, blade'.
A town on the north coast of Wales, in Conwy (formerly in Denbighshire, then in Clwyd), 10 km (6 miles) east of Colwyn Bay. Abergele was one of the first places to pioneer sea-bathing in North Wales, as witnessed by the poet Coleridge:

> Walking on the sea sands, I was surprised to see a number of fine women bathing promiscuously with men and boys – *perfectly* naked! Doubtless, the citadels of their chastity are so impregnably strong, that they need not the ornamental outworks of modesty.
>
>> Samuel Taylor Coleridge: letter to Henry Martin (22 July 1794)

Abergele was the birthplace of Thomas Gwynn Jones (1871–1948), the Welsh-language poet.

Abergele Martyrs, the. The name given to two members of the clandestine Welsh organization Mudiad Amddiffyn Cymru ('movement for the defence of Wales'), William Alwyn Jones and George Francis Taylor, of Abergele, who were killed when the explosive devices they were carrying were accidentally detonated on 1 July 1969, the day of the investiture of the Prince of Wales at Caernarfon Castle (*see under* CAERNARFON). Their deaths were commemorated by several poets, and their graves have become the focus for an annual ceremony.

Aberglaslyn Gorge 'gorge of the mouth of the River Glaslyn', ABER + river name Welsh *glas* 'blue' + *lyn* 'river, lake'.
A narrow defile in Snowdonia, Gwynedd (formerly in Caernarvonshire), through which the **River Glaslyn** rushes between Beddgelert and **Pont Aberglaslyn** ('bridge of Aberglaslyn'), 2 km (1.2 miles) to the south. Up to the 19th century, boats could sail up the Glaslyn as far as Pont Aberglaslyn. The gorge is also known as the **Pass of Aberglaslyn**.

Abergwaun. The Welsh name for FISHGUARD.

Abergwyngregyn. The full name for the village of ABER.

Aberhonddu. The Welsh name for BRECON.

Aberlady ABER + *lady* possibly referring to Our Lady, the Blessed Virgin Mary: all the early forms reflect ME *lauedi* 'lady'.
A small coastal village in East Lothian, on the south shore of the Firth of Forth about 25 km (16 miles) northeast of Edinburgh. It looks out across **Aberlady Bay**, whose sand dunes and mudflats are an important nature reserve for waders and sea birds.

Aberlour 'mouth of the Lour Burn', ABER + Gaelic *labhar* 'the noisy one'.
A large village in Moray (formerly in Banffshire, then in Grampian region), situated where the Lour Burn joins the River SPEY, some 6 km (4 miles) northwest of Dufftown. The present village – notable for its mile-long, tree-lined high street – was laid out in 1812 by Charles Grant of Wester Elchies, and in his honour is formally known as **Charlestown of Aberlour**, although it is popularly known simply as Aberlour, originally the name of the locality. The settlement that preceded Grant's foundation was known as **Skirdustan** ('parish of St Drostan', Gaelic *sgìre* 'slice', 'parish'); Drostan was a local 7th-century abbot, and there is still a Drostan's Well in the grounds of the local distillery.

Abermenai Point 'mouth of the Menai'; *see* ABER and MENAI STRAIT.
The southwestern-most point of ANGLESEY, at the southwest end of the MENAI STRAIT. The area – comprising stretches of sand and dunes – is a bird reserve, but in the Middle Ages, before the sand took over, there was an important anchorage at Abermenai, and it was said that Branwen, one of the legendary children of Llyr, embarked from here with her new husband, the Irish king Matholwch.

> *Dymhunis tonn mor ymerweryt,*
> *o Aber Menai mynych dyllt.*
> (The sea wave with its great roar woke me,
> steadily flowing from Aber Menai.)
>> Gwalchmai: 'Exultation' (12th century), translated by
>> Gwyn Williams

Abernethy[1] ABER + possibly the OCelt river name *Nedd* or *Neithon*.
A village near the confluence of the Earn and Tay, 10 km (6 miles) southeast of Perth, in Perth and Kinross (formerly in Perthshire, then in Tayside region). It was once a Pictish capital and an important ecclesiastical centre. The tapering round tower (22.5 m / 74 ft high) dates from the 9th to the 12th centuries, and is of a type common in Ireland, but only two other examples exist in Scotland. Its purpose was defensive.

> In the years of the Dark Age swan
> And the wolf, on hills like this one,
> A herdsman looked over and down
> On the blue waters in the strath.
>> Douglas Dunn: 'Abernethy', from *Northlight* (1988)

Incidentally, Abernethy biscuits, a type of crisp unleavened biscuit, were probably named not after the village but after Dr John Abernethy (1794–1831), an English surgeon and dietician.

Treaty of Abernethy (1072). An agreement by which Malcolm III Canmore was obliged to do homage to William I of England, although this may have been in respect to lands that Malcolm held in England. The treaty is also sometimes called the **Submission of Abernethy**.

Abernethy[2]. *See under* NETHY.

Aberpennar. The Welsh name for MOUNTAIN ASH.

Abertawe. The Welsh name for SWANSEA[1].

Aberteifi. The Welsh name for CARDIGAN.

Aberteleri. The Welsh name for ABERTILLERY.

Abertillery 'mouth of the Teleri', ABER + name of a stream, itself from a personal name.
A former mining town in Blaenau Gwent (formerly in Monmouthshire, then in Gwent), 7 km (4.5 miles) southeast of Ebbw Vale. In Welsh it is **Abertyleri** or **Aberteleri**.

Abertyleri. An alternative Welsh name for ABERTILLERY.

Aberystwyth 'mouth of the River Ystwyth', ABER + Welsh river name meaning 'winding'.
A university town and holiday resort (pronounced 'aber-ist-with') on Cardigan Bay (*see under* CARDIGAN), in Ceredigion (formerly in Cardiganshire, then in Dyfed), some 30 km (19 miles) northeast of New Quay. The town is at the mouths of the rivers Rheidol and Ystwyth (taking its name from the latter).

An ecclesiastical foundation was established in the 6th century at Llanbadarn Fawr, now a suburb of the town, which was known as Llanbadarn ('church of St Padarn', a companion of St David) until the 15th century. There were also a succession of medieval castles here, which changed hands fairly regularly. The young women of Llanbadarn caused one poet considerable frustration:

> I am one of passion's asses,
> Plague on all these parish lasses!
> Though I long for them like mad,
> Not one female have I had …
>> Dafydd ap Gwilym 'The Girls of Llanbadarn' (mid-14th century), translated from the Welsh by Rolfe Humphries

Aberystwyth is a bastion of Welsh culture, and is the unofficial capital of the Welsh-speaking area of Wales. Cymdeithas yr Iaith (the Welsh Language Society) was founded here in 1963, and Aberystwyth is home to the first college (1872) of the University of Wales, and of the National Library of Wales (1911). There is little now to suggest its industrial past, when it was

> ... a very dirty, black, smoky place, and we fancied the
> people looked as if they lived continually in the coal or
> lead mines.
>
>> Daniel Defoe: *A Tour Through the Whole Island of Great Britain*
>> (1724–6)

Sir Geraint Evans, the operatic baritone, died in Aberystwyth in 1992.

ABER! A 1970s-style Scandopop tribute band from Aberystwyth, who had some considerable success touring the Continent in the later 1990s. The initials of the name stand for the names of the band's members, *A*lun Williams, *B*ertha Llewelyn-Jones (nicknamed 'Rivermouth' by her fans), *E*ustace Richards and *R*aine ('Drops-Keep-Falling-on-My-Head') Davies (stage name of Liz Shotts). ABER!'s songs include 'Austerlitz', 'Moany Moany Moany' and 'Loser Takes F-All'.

aberystwyth. 'A nostalgic yearning which is in itself more pleasant than the thing being yearned for'; the coinage is that of Douglas Adams and John Lloyd in *The Deeper Meaning of Liff: A Dictionary of Things that There Aren't Any Words for Yet* (1992).

Aberystwyth Electric Cliff Railway. 'A conveyance for gentle folk since 1896' to the summit of Constitution Hill (120 m / 394 ft) to the north of the town.

Aberystwyth Mon Amour. A novel (2001) by Malcolm Pryce about a Welsh private eye investigating schoolboy deaths in Aberystwyth. The title parodies that of *Hiroshima, Mon Amour* (1959), the avant-garde film by Alain Resnais. Pryce published a sequel, *Last Tango in Aberystwyth*, in 2003, the title coming from Bertolucci's buttery film *Last Tango in Paris* (1972).

Abhainn Dubh. The Irish name for the river BLACKWATER[2].

Abhainn Mór. An alternative Irish name for the river BLACKWATER[2].

Abhóca. The Irish name for AVOCA.

Abingdon 'Æbba's or Æbbe's hill', OE *Æbban* possessive form of the male personal name *Æbba* or the female personal name *Æbbe* (*see also* -ING) + *dun* (*see* DOWN, -DON).

A town in Oxfordshire (before 1974 in Berkshire), at the confluence of the River THAMES[1] with the River OCK, about 10 km (6 miles) south of Oxford. It has some claim to be considered the oldest continually inhabited town in England: there is believed to have been a settlement here in the Bronze and Iron Ages, and it was a flourishing town during the Roman period. In 675 a monastery, later a Benedictine abbey, was founded here, of which now only the 16th-century Long Gallery, a 15th-century gatehouse and the 14th-century Checker Hall (now restored as an Elizabethan-style theatre) survive.

Until 1870, Abingdon was the county town of BERKSHIRE. Between 1930 and 1980 the town was the home of Morris Garages, where MG cars were made.

There are towns called Abingdon in Illinois and Virginia, USA.

Abinger Originally (1191) *Abingewurd* 'Abba's people's enclosure' or 'enclosure at Abba's place', OE male personal name *Abba* + *-inga-* (*see* -ING) + *-worth* (*see* -WORTH, WORTHY, -WARDINE); the shortened form *Abinger* is first recorded in 1552.

A village (pronounced 'abinjer') in Surrey, about 8 km (5 miles) southwest of Dorking. It is also often called **Abinger Common**.

Abinger Harvest. A book of collected essays by E.M. Forster, published in 1936. He based the title on the village of Abinger, where he inherited a house in 1924.

Abinger Hammer *Hammer* from a former iron foundry here, called the Hammer Mill.

A village in Surrey, about 2 km (1.2 miles) northwest of Abinger.

Ab Kettleby *Ab* denoting the manor owned by a man called Abba; *Kettleby* 'Ketil's farmstead', OScand male personal name *Ketil* + -BY.

A village in Leicestershire, about 5 km (3 miles) northwest of Melton Mowbray.

Abney Park From a former house on the site owned by Sir Thomas Abney (d.1722), one-time Lord Mayor of London.

A cemetery in STOKE NEWINGTON (N16), in the London borough of Hackney. Founded in 1840, and officially named **Prince of Wales Abney Cemetery**, it succeeded BUNHILL FIELDS as the centre of Nonconformist burials in London. Among those interred here is William Booth (1829–1912), founder of the Salvation Army. Booth would probably have taken a dim view of the cemetery's use in the 1980s and 1990s as a gay trysting-place.

go to Abney Park, to. From the late 19th century into the 1920s, a colloquial euphemism for 'to die'.

p.w. abney. A funereal style of hat fashionable 1896–1900, featuring three black, upright ostrich feathers, reminiscent of the three feathers of the Prince of Wales's crest.

Aboyne 'white cow river', Gaelic *abh* 'river' + *bo* 'cattle' + *fhionn* 'white'.

A large village in Deeside, Aberdeenshire (formerly in Grampian region), 44 km (27 miles) west of Aberdeen. Most of the present village dates from the 1880s. Highland Games are held here every September.

Abrahamstead. A facetious nickname given in the 1970s to the North London suburb of HAMPSTEAD (blending the Jewish name *Abraham* with *Hampstead*) on the basis of its large Jewish population.

Abram 'Eadburh's homestead', OE female personal name *Eadburh* + HAM.

A village in Greater Manchester, some 23 km (14 miles) west of the city centre.

Abyssinia Probably a name signifying remoteness.

A remote farm in upper Glen Kinglas, Argyll and Bute (formerly in Strathclyde region), 3 km (2 miles) north of Ben Ime in the Arrochar Alps (*see under* ARROCHAR).

Accrington 'farmstead of the acorns', OE *æcern* 'acorn' + -TON.

An industrial town in Lancashire, 8 km (5 miles) east of Blackburn. It was the birthplace of the composer Harrison Birtwhistle (b.1934).

Accrington Pals, the. The nickname of the 11th (Service) Battalion (Accrington) East Lancashire Regiment. It was formed in the early months of the First World War, and was almost destroyed on 1 July 1916, the first day of the Battle of the Somme. ('Pals battalions' were volunteer units recruited 1914–15 from local communities, factories, sports clubs and other closely knit social groups.)

Accrington Stanley FC. Accrington's football club, whose notoriously up-and-down history has made its name synonymous with footballing failure. The original Accrington Football Club, Th' Owd Reds (as they are known locally), was founded in 1888 but left the Football League after only five seasons in 1893. The team revived in the form of the amateur club Stanley Villa (so named because its founders lived on Stanley Street) which joined the Football League in 1921. Financial difficulties led to its resignation from the League in 1962. The present Accrington Stanley, reformed in 1968, is a non-League club.

Achadh an Iúir. The Irish name for VIRGINIA.

Achadh Dá Eó. The Irish name for AGHADOE.

Achadh na Gréine. The modern Irish name for AUBURN.

Achill Island The early spellings of this name, *aichill*, suggest a meaning 'lamentation'.

Ireland's largest island, 22 km (14 miles) long and 19 km (12 miles) wide, just off the west coast of Mayo. It is linked to the mainland by a bridge built across the 20-m-wide **Achill Sound** in 1888. At its western tip is **Achill Head**. In addition to many beaches, there are also the hills of Slievemore (671 m / 2201 ft) and Croaghaun (665 m / 2181 ft); from nearly the top of the latter descend what are said to be the highest sea cliffs in Europe. In the past the islanders largely survived on fishing for basking sharks, which they harpooned from their curraghs …

> … here where currachs walk on the ocean …
>
> Derek Mahon: 'Achill', from *Collected Poems* (1999)

In 1834 the Rev. E. Nangle of the Church of Ireland founded a Protestant colony on the island, with a view to converting the natives; there was a great deal of hot air and mutual hostility, but little success on the part of the proselytizers. A century and a half later, in 1982, Dom Allum, on board his boat the *QE3*, landed on Achill Island, becoming the first person to row the Atlantic in both directions. What is now the Corrymore House Hotel was once owned by the notorious Captain Boycott, and then, in the 1920s, by the American painter Robert Henri. Earlier, in 1912, another painter, Paul Henry (1877–1958), came here for a two-week holiday. As he recalled 'I felt that here I must stay somehow or another', so he tore up his return ticket and lived on the island until 1919.

> A dog barks, once; far off the sea is breaking
> On an invisible bleached strand, below the hill
> Patterned with ghostly sheep.
> This is the tangible silence of world's end.
>
> Margaret Rhodes: 'Waking in Achill'

Achill Disaster (June 1894). A disaster in which a boat taking 100 migrant workers from Achill Island to the mainland capsized, resulting in the deaths of 23 young men. The disaster happened when the young men all rushed to one side of the boat to see the steamship that was to take them on to Glasgow. There is still a seasonal migration of agricultural labourers from Achill to England and Scotland. **Book of Achill.** An ancient Gaelic legal text, now kept in Trinity College Dublin.

❖ achadh ❖

Perhaps the most common and general name in Ireland for a field is *achadh*, but it rarely appears in major settlement names precisely because of its usefulness as the name for a field. It does, however, appear in many major Scottish names, where it is not so generally used: in Scotland it has a more specific sense, namely 'secondary settlement'. ACHNASHEEN, AUCHINLECK and SLIGACHAN all contain this element.

More specific elements meaning 'field' appear far more frequently in Irish names of settlements. The element *cluain* 'pasture land' is found in CLONES (County Monaghan), CLONFERT (County Galway), CLONMACNOISE (County Offaly), CLONMEL (County Tipperary) and CLONTARF (County Dublin), to mention just the more notable examples. The element *gort* and its common diminutive *gorteen* '(little) tilled field' are equally frequent, but do not feature so often in major names: GORTAHORK in County Donegal is an example of a village with this element in its name. In this pattern of usage, it is possible to see parallels with early English names using *feld* and *æcer* (*see* FIELD).

Achiltibuie Etymology uncertain. The first element is Gaelic ACHADH, and the last is *buidhe* 'yellow'. The middle element may be *allt* 'stream', or *a-tigh* 'of the house', or *a-gille* 'of the young man'.

A small village overlooking the SUMMER ISLES on the southern side of the COIGACH peninsula, in Highland (formerly in Ross and Cromarty), 18 km (11 miles) northwest of Ullapool.

Achmelvich Possibly 'field on the bay with the sandbank', Gaelic ACHADH + OScand *melr* 'sandbank' + *vik* 'bay'.

A small village on the northwest coast of Highland (formerly in Sutherland), 5 km (3 miles) northwest of Lochinver.

Achnasheen 'field of the storm', Gaelic ACHADH + *na* 'of the' + *sian* 'storm'.

A small, remote settlement, little more than a road junction, hotel and railway station on the Kyle of Lochalsh–Inverness line, in Highland (formerly in Ross and Cromarty). It is some 39 km (24 miles) west of Dingwall, and situated on the watershed between LOCH MAREE to the west and Strath Bran to the east.

Acle 'clearing in an oak wood', OE *ac* 'oak' + -LEY.

A village in the Norfolk BROADS, about 16 km (10 miles) east of Norwich.

Acol 'oak wood', OE *ac* 'oak' + *holt* 'wood'.

A village (pronounced 'ak-ol') in the ISLE OF THANET in Kent, about 3 km (2 miles) north of Minster.

Acol system. In the game of bridge, a commonly used system of bidding designed to enable partners with weaker hands to find suitable contracts, the only opening forcing to game being 2 Clubs. It was devised in the 1930s in a house in Acol Road, South Hampstead, London. That road in turn took its name from the Kentish village.

Acton 'oak farmstead', OE *ac* 'oak' + -TON; the reference is probably either to a farmstead or village with oak trees nearby, or to a farm where oak timber was worked (in the Middle Ages London got much of its firewood from Acton).

A district of West London (W3), in the borough of EALING. Surrounding Acton proper, centred on the Uxbridge Road, are **North Acton**, **East Acton** and **South Acton** with, a little to the southeast, **Acton Green**. Formerly an agricultural village, it became built up and industrialized in the second half of the 19th century, and in the 1930s it was claimed that Acton was the largest industrial centre south of Coventry. Around 1900 South Acton, home of 180 laundries, was known familiarly as 'Soapsuds Island'.

Acton Town Underground station, on the District and Piccadilly lines, opened in 1879 (under the name Mill Hill Park). East Acton, on the Central line, opened in 1920, and North Acton and West Acton, on the same line, in 1923. South Acton, on the District line, opened in 1905 but closed in 1959. The pop singer Adam Faith (1940–2003) was born in Acton. There are settlements called Acton in the USA (California, Massachusetts, Montana).

See also IRON ACTON.

Acton Beauchamp *Acton see* ACTON; *Beauchamp* denoting manorial ownership in the Middle Ages by the Beauchamp family.

A village (pronounced 'beecham') in Herefordshire (before 1998 in Hereford and Worcester, before 1974 in Herefordshire), about 17 km (11 miles) southwest of Worcester.

Acton Burnell *Acton see* ACTON; *Burnell* denoting manorial ownership in the Middle Ages by the Burnell family.

A village in Shropshire, about 10 km (6 miles) south of Shrewsbury. Acton Burnell castle, now in ruins, is one of the oldest fortified houses in England. It was reputedly in its barn that the first English parliament to include commoners was held, in 1283. Edward I's chancellor Robert Burnell (d.1292) was born in Acton Burnell, and owned the castle.

Statute of Acton Burnell. A statute passed by the parliament assembled at Acton Burnell, providing for the prompter recovery of debts and removing the staple (exclusive market rights for major exports) from Calais to various towns in Britain.

Acton Pigott *Acton see* ACTON; *Pigott* denoting manorial ownership in the Middle Ages by the Picot family.

A village in Shropshire (pronounced 'piggot'), about 10 km (6 miles) south of Shrewsbury.

Acton Round *Acton see* ACTON; *Round* either from *round* 'circular', or from a folk-etymological analysis of *Arundel* (the village belonged in the Middle Ages to the Earls of Arundel).

A village in Shropshire, about 8 km (5 miles) northwest of Bridgnorth.

Acton Trussell *Acton see* ACTON; *Trussell* denoting manorial ownership in the Middle Ages by the Trussell family.

A village in Staffordshire, about 5 km (3 miles) south of Stafford.

Acton Turville *Acton* 'Acca's farmstead', OE male personal name *Ac(c)a* + -TON; *Turville* denoting manorial ownership in the Middle Ages by the Turville family.

A village in South Gloucestershire (before 1996 in Avon, before 1974 in Gloucestershire), about 14 km (8.5 miles) southwest of Malmesbury.

Adam and Eve. *See under* TRYFAN

Adare Irish *Áth Dara* 'ford of the oak wood'.

A village in County Limerick, 15 km (9 miles) southwest of Limerick itself. The ruined Desmond's Castle dates back to the 13th century, and there are also ruins of a Franciscan friary, founded in 1464.

There is a Cape Adare in Antarctica.

Adare Robbery (7 June 1996). An armed robbery carried

out by the Provisional IRA in which one garda was killed and another seriously injured. The three perpetrators were jailed for manslaughter.

Adelphi From Greek *adelphoi* 'brothers'; because the buildings were designed by the Adam brothers.

A complex of buildings and streets between the western end of the STRAND and the EMBANKMENT in Central London, originally designed and built in the 1770s as a development of 24 terraced houses by the Scottish architects John, Robert, James and William Adam. The sumptuous and imposing neo-classical residences were very fashionable, housing such tenants over the decades as David Garrick, Thomas Rowlandson, Richard D'Oyly Carte, Thomas Hardy and Sir James Barrie. The main block, the Royal Terrace, was demolished in 1936, and very few of the original Adam houses remain.

To accommodate the sloping site, the riverward part of the Adelphi was built on arched vaults. Their tenebrous purlieus, with a strong complement of sex-workers, soon became known as 'the Shades' or, more colloquially, 'the Darkies'.

The **Adelphi Theatre** in the Strand opened in 1806, as the 'Sans Pareil', and changed its name to 'Adelphi' in 1819. In the 1840s it was noted for its 'Adelphi dramas', mostly written by J.B. Buckstone, the best of which were *The Green Bushes* (1845) and *The Flowers of the Forest* (1847); and at the end of the 19th century it became famous for the 'Adelphi melodramas' produced by G.R. Sims, Henry Pettit and Sydney Grundy (e.g. *The Bells of Hazlemere* (1887)).

Adlestrop 'Tætel's farmstead', OE male personal name *Tœtel* + *-throp* (*see* THORPE). The original initial 't' dropped out in the 14th century owing to confusion between *at Tadlestrop* and *at Adlestrop*.

A village in Gloucestershire, about 6 km (4 miles) west of Chipping Norton, in the COTSWOLDS. It owes its fame entirely to the eponymous poem written in 1917 by Edward Thomas. This recalls a moment of summer stillness in the English countryside when, the train having stopped at Adlestrop station (Adlestrop was at that time on the Oxford-to-Evesham line), the song of a blackbird could be heard:

> Yes. I remember Adlestrop –
> The name, because one afternoon
> Of heat the express-train drew up there
> Unwontedly. It was late June.

> The steam hissed. Someone cleared his throat.
> No one left and no one came
> On the bare platform. What I saw
> Was Adlestrop – only the name.

> And willows, willow-herb, and grass,
> And meadowsweet, and haycocks dry,
> No whit less still and lonely fair
> Than the high cloudlets in the sky.

> And for that minute a blackbird sang
> Close by, and round him, mistier,
> Farther and farther, all the birds
> Of Oxfordshire and Gloucestershire.

The poem is inscribed on a metal plate attached to an old railway station bench in the village that was rescued from Adlestrop station before it closed permanently.

Adlington 'Eadwulf's farm', OE male personal name *Eadwulf* + -ING + -TON.

A small town in Lancashire, 5 km (3 miles) southeast of Chorley.

Adur[1] From *Portus Adurni*, the Roman name for PORTCHESTER, misidentified by the 17th-century poet and antiquarian Michael Drayton with Shoreham-by-Sea, which is at the mouth of the Adur.

A river in West Sussex. It rises in eastern WEST SUSSEX and flows 32 km (20 miles) southwards, entering the English CHANNEL at SHOREHAM-BY-SEA.

Adur[2] From the River ADUR[1].

An administrative district of West Sussex in the lower Adur valley between Worthing and Brighton, centred on Shoreham-by-Sea.

Adwalton Moor 'moor on or near Æthelwald's farm', OE male personal name *Æthelwald* + -TON + moor.

A battle site in West Yorkshire, 6 km (4 miles) southeast of Bradford, where, on 29 June 1643, the Duke of Newcastle led the Royalists to victory over the Parliamentarians under the Fairfaxes (Ferdinando and son Thomas).

Adwick le Street 'Adda's dwelling or dairy farm on a Roman road', OE male personal name + WICK + *strœt* (*see* STREET) (in this case, Ermine Street); the last element distinguishes it from the small, nearby village of Adwick upon Dearne.

A small town in South Yorkshire, 7 km (4.5 miles) north-west of Doncaster. The Washington family who occupied Adwick Hall in the 16th and 17th centuries were probably ancestors of George Washington, the first US president.

Ae OScand *a* 'river' (*see* EA-).

A small village in Dumfries and Galloway, about 12 km (7.5 miles) north of the town of Dumfries. It has the shortest place name in Britain (with the OA in Islay being a rival). It was established in 1947 by the Forestry Commission for workers in the surrounding **Forest of Ae**, and both it and the forest take their name from the **Water of Ae**, a tributary of the River ANNAN[1].

For the longest place name in Britain, see either LLAN-FAIRPWLLGWYNGYLLGOGERYCHWYRNDROBWLLLLANDYSILIO-GOGOGOCH or GORSAFAWDDACHA'IDRAIGODANHEDDOGLED-DOLLÔNPENRHYNAREURDRAETHCEREDIGION.

Afan named after a man called *Afan* or *Afen*.

A river in south Wales, approximately 15 km (16 miles)

long, in Neath Port Talbot (formerly in Glamorgan, then West Glamorgan), reaching the sea at Port Talbot (part of which is called **Aberavon**, meaning 'mouth of the Afan'). The village of **Cwmafan** is further up the river, and the attractive river valley, surrounded by the wooded hills of the **Afan Forest Park**, is also called **Cwm Afan** ('valley of the Afan') – although the local tourist board prefers to call it 'Little Switzerland'. The West Glamorgan district of Port Talbot, extant 1974–96, was initially known as Afan.

Affane Irish *Áth Mheadhoin* 'middle ford'.
A tributary of the BLACKWATER[2], County Waterford, which also gives its name to the surrounding area. It was on his father's estate here that Valentine Greatrakes (1629–83), the faith healer known as 'the Stroaker', was born.
Affane cherry. The first cherry tree to be planted in Ireland, brought thither from the Canaries by Sir Walter Raleigh.
Battle of Affane (8 February 1565). A battle in which Black Tom Butler, Earl of Ormond, beat the Fitzgeralds, in the last private aristocratic battle in Ireland. As the wounded Gerald Fitzgerald, Earl of Desmond, was carried from the field on the shoulders of Ormond's men, one of them began to crow: 'Where is the great Earl of Desmond now?' To which Desmond replied, 'Where he belongs – on the neck of the Butlers.'

Affpuddle 'Æffa's estate on the River Piddle', OE male personal name *Æffa* + river name Piddle.
A village in Dorset, on the River PIDDLE, about 11 km (7 miles) northeast of Dorchester.

Affric. *See* GLEN AFFRIC.

Afton Water 'brown stream', Gaelic *abhainn* 'river, stream' (*see* AVON) + *don* 'brown'.
A small tributary of the NITH, about 12 km (7.5 miles) long, in South Ayrshire (formerly in Strathclyde). It rises near WINDY STANDARD, and joins the Nith at New Cumnock. The river inspired Robert Burns's famous song:

Flow gently, sweet Afton, among thy green braes,
Flow gently, I'll sing thee a song in thy praise;
My Mary's asleep by thy murmuring stream,
Flow gently, sweet Afton, disturb not her dream.

Sweet Afton. An Irish brand of cigarettes, dating back to before the Second World War. The slogan on the packet 'It's the sweetest leaf that gives you the taste', inspired the title of Black Sabbath's song 'Sweet Leaf' (1971), a tribute to marijuana.

Agar Town. A former name for the area now occupied by ST PANCRAS in London.

Aggro Corner. *See under* BOGSIDE.

Aghadoe Irish *Achadh Dá Eó* 'field of two yew trees'.

The site of a medieval monastic church in County Kerry, some 5 km (3 miles) west of Killarney.

There's a glen in Aghadoe, Aghadoe, Aghadoe,
There's a green and silent glade in Aghadoe,
Where we met, my love and I, Love's fair planet in the sky,
O'er that sweet and silent glen in Aghadoe.
John Todhunter (1839–1916): 'Aghadoe'

Aherlow, Glen of. *See* GLEN OF AHERLOW.

Ahoghill Irish *Áth Eochaille* 'ford of yew trees'.
A village in County Antrim, 5 km (3 miles) west of Ballymena.
pachal frae Ahoghill, the. A dismissive phrase heard in Ulster, a pachal being a man who combines physical ungainliness, unreliability and laziness. The collocation derives from the fact that pachal rhymes with Ahoghill, a place mocked, like nearby CULLYBACKEY, for its name.

Aileach The feature referred to is a circular stone fort, but it is unclear whether the etymology is *aileach* 'stallion' or '(place, fort) of rock'.
An ancient fortress, reconstructed in 1870, on a mound in County Donegal, 5 km (3 miles) west of Derry/Londonderry, overlooking Lough FOYLE and LOUGH SWILLY. It is also called the **Grianán of Aileach** (Irish *grianán* 'solarium, bower'). It was said to have been built by the Tuatha Dé Danaan (the old gods of Ireland), and to have been the place where three of the sister goddesses divided Ireland between themselves (*see under* ÉIRE). It became the home of the ancient kings of Ulster, and also the name of a separate kingdom when Ulster split up after the 4th century AD. Ptolemy marked the place on his map in the 2nd century AD. In 1101 it was destroyed by Muirchertach Ó Brien, King of Munster. In legend, the ancient warriors of Ireland sleep under Aileach, until they are needed to free their country:

'Tis told in tales of wonder how under Aileach's palace
Kings in countless number lie still as carven stone;
And steeds with them in hiding are reined for warriors' riding
To the last of Erin's battles from the cave of Inish Owen.
Alice Milligan: 'The Horsemen of Aileach', from *We Sang for Ireland* (1950)

Aillte an Mhothair. The Irish name for the CLIFFS OF MOHER.

Ailsa Craig Perhaps 'fairy rock', Gaelic, but unlikely.
A large, pointed rock, 338 m (1109 ft) high, guarding the entrance to the Firth of CLYDE some 16 km (10 miles) west of Girvan on the Ayrshire coast. In *Buile Suibne* (*Sweeney the Mad*), an ancient Irish tale, it was described as

the abode of the seagulls, chilly for its guests … sufficient is the sheer height of its side, nose to the rushing main.

In 1597 Ailsa Craig was held by a group of Scots Catholics on behalf of Philip II of Spain; Alexander Montgomerie, one of the last of the *makaris* (Renaissance poets writing in Scots), was implicated in the plot and disgraced. The rock is home to large numbers of seabirds, and here a special kind of granite – called **ailsite** – was once quarried. This was used to make curling stones, themselves known as **Ailsa Craigs**. The island is also known as **Paddy's Milestone**, the rock being halfway on the sea passage between Belfast and Glasgow. Ailsa Craig also has its meteorological uses, according to the old saying:

> When Ailsa Craig has on its cap, it's sure to be wet, but when its cap is in the sky it's sure to be dry.

Both William Wordsworth and John Keats were impressed enough to write poems on the rock, the latter confessing in a letter to his brother Tom to having been 'a little alarmed' at its appearance.

> Hearken, thou craggy ocean-pyramid,
> Give answer by thy voice – the sea-fowls' screams!
> When were thy shoulders mantled in huge streams?
> When from the sun was they broad forehead hid?
> How long is't since the mighty Power bid
> Thee heave to airy sleep from fathom dreams ...?
> Thou answer'st not; for thou art dead asleep ...
>
> John Keats: 'Sonnet on Ailsa Craig Rock' (1818)

Robert Burns found the rock equally unresponsive, dismissing it in a simile in 'Duncan Gray':

> Meg was deaf as Ailsa Craig.

Apparently the actress Ellen Terry was once heard to exclaim, 'Ailsa Craig – what a magnificent name for an actress!'

Ailsa cock. A 19th-century Scots term for a puffin. Ironically Ailsa Craig's population of puffins was decimated in the 20th century by brown rats. In 2002, the rats having been liquidated, puffins were reported to have successfully bred on the rock for the first time in 50 years.

Ailsa Course. A championship golf course at TURNBERRY, from where Ailsa Craig can clearly be seen. The course first hosted the Open in 1977, and its first hole is called Ailsa Craig.

Ailsworth 'Ægel's enclosure', OE male personal name *Ægel* + *-worth* (*see* -WORTH, WORTHY, -WARDINE).
A village in Peterborough unitary authority, 7 km (4 miles) west of Peterborough.
See also EMMONSAILS HEATH.

Aintree 'lone tree', OScand *einn* 'one, single' + *tre* 'tree'.
A racecourse on the northern edge of LIVERPOOL, Merseyside. Britain's most celebrated horse race, the Grand National steeplechase, is held here every spring. It was inaugurated in 1839 as the Grand Liverpool Steeple Chase,

and adopted its present name in 1847. The taxing Grand National course – it is not unknown for only a handful of starters to complete the race – comprises two circuits totalling 7242 m (4 miles 880 yds), with 30 formidable jumps, the highest of which is the Chair at 1.56 m (5 ft 2 in). Its most famous jump, **Becher's Brook** (pronounced 'beacher'), is named after the jockey Captain Martin Becher (1797–1864), who in 1839, parting company from his horse Conrad, was propelled over the obstacle and into the brook that was to bear his name. He is said to have complained 'how dreadful water tastes without the benefit of whisky'.

The legendary steeplechaser Red Rum (1965–95), three times winner of the Grand National (1973, 1974 and 1977), is buried next to the winning post at Aintree.

In 2003 plans were revealed to hold the Grand National and the Derby on the same weekend in early June, alternating the venue between Aintree and Epsom. Traditionalists were aghast, until BBC Radio 4's *Today* programme admitted that they had put out the story on 1 April.

Aintree also has a motor-racing circuit, where the British Grand Prix was held in 1955, 1957, 1959 and 1961–2.

Aira Force 'waterfall on the gravel bank river', OScand *eyrr* 'gravel bank' + *a* 'river, stream' (*see* EA-) + *foss* 'waterfall'.
A waterfall on Aira Beck river, on the north side of ULLSWATER, in the LAKE DISTRICT, Cumbria (formerly in Cumberland), 5 km (3 miles) north of Patterdale. It was formerly spelt **Airey Force**. Above it is another fall, High Force.

> The higher part of the water, the two streams running athwart each other, is original, but where the wheel-part is broken, it spreads into a muslin apron and the whole waterfall looks like a long-waisted lady-giantess slipping down on her back.
>
> Samuel Taylor Coleridge: journal (16 November 1799)

William Wordsworth set his romantic ballad 'The Somnambulist' here, in which Emma, missing her lover, Sir Eglamore, at the Crusades, sleepwalks into the torrent, waking in time to be held in her lover's arms, only to expire. It was a favourite spot of the poet, and he writes of it again in a late poem:

> – Not a breath of air
> Ruffles the bosom of this leafy glen.
> From the brook's margin, wide around, the trees
> Are stedfast as the rocks ...
>
> William Wordsworth: 'Airey-Force Valley' (1842; written 1836)

Aird Mhór. The Irish name for ARDMORE.

Airdrie 'high slope', Gaelic ARD + *ruighe* 'reach' or 'slope'.
A town about 18 km (11 miles) east of Glasgow, in North Lanarkshire (formerly in Strathclyde region). It once had

important iron and coal industries, but is now more of a residential town for people working in Glasgow. It became a BURGH in 1821. A resident of Airdrie is called (in some quarters) an **Airdrieonian**, as in **Airdrieonians FC** (founded in 1881 and nicknamed the Diamonds or the Waysiders).

Airds Moss Gaelic ARD with English plural + *mos* 'swamp, peat moor'.
A battle site in East Ayrshire (formerly in Strathclyde region), 5 km (3 miles) north of Cumnock, where in July 1680 a small body of Cameronians (extreme Covenanters) were surprised and defeated by a Royalist force. Their leader, Richard Cameron, was killed, and David Hackston of Rathillet, who had been present at the murder of Archbishop Sharp, was captured, mutilated and hanged. Just before the battle Cameron (not realizing that the Almighty is colour-blind) had devised a prayer:

Lord, spare the green and take the ripe.

Aire Possibly from OE *eg* 'island' (*see* -EY, -EA) or *ea* 'river' (*see* EA-), but the spelling suggests influence of OScand *ey, eyjar* 'island(s)' (*see* -AY).
A river, 110 km (68 miles) long, rising in the PENNINES near Malham, North Yorkshire. It flows southeastwards then eastwards through West and East Yorkshire, and joins the River OUSE[2] near Goole.

Airedale is the valley of the Aire in the YORKSHIRE DALES between Skipton and Bradford. Early in its course, the Aire flows through the **Aire Gap**, a natural break in the Pennines in which Skipton is situated. North of the Aire Gap the Pennines are principally limestone, while to the south Millstone Grit predominates. The Gap provides one of the most spectacular parts of the Leeds–Liverpool Canal. Further downstream, below the dye works of Salts of SALTAIRE, the waters used to change colour every few days, from blue to mustard yellow to purple.

Aire and Calder Navigation. A system of rivers and canals linking GOOLE to Leeds, and CASTLEFORD to WAKEFIELD. Construction followed an act of Parliament of 1699.

Airedale terrier. A large breed of terrier with a large, somewhat rectangular muzzle, black-and-tan colouring and a rough coat. Airedale terriers were first bred in the Airedale town of BINGLEY.

Airey Force. A former spelling of AIRA FORCE.

Airgialla Possibly Irish for 'eastern hostage', apparently in origin the name of a king's daughter.
An old Celtic kingdom of central Ulster, which emerged after Ulster split up in the 4th century. It is also spelt **Oirghialla**, and is anglicized as **Oriel**. It broadly took in MONAGHAN, LOUTH and ARMAGH. By the 13th century Airgialla had been reduced to a part of Monaghan ruled by the MacMahons.

Airyhassen 'shieling of the track', Gaelic *airidh* (*see* -ARY) + *casán* 'track, path'.
A village in the MACHARS of Dumfries and Galloway (formerly in Wigtownshire), 10 km (6 miles) southwest of Wigtown.

Akeman Street Probably 'Acemann's Roman road', *Akeman* OE male personal name *Acemann*, although a connection with the Roman British name for Bath, *Aquae Sulis* 'waters of (the goddess) Sulis', has been suggested; *Street see* STREET.
A Roman road running from BATH to ST ALBANS. The individual who gave his name to it was evidently an important and influential personality in the West of England, since in late Anglo-Saxon times **Acemannes ceastre** 'Acemann's (Roman) city' was an alternative name for Bath.
In the 17th century the name Akeman Street was appropriated, probably by a local East Anglian antiquary, to a Roman road running from ERMINE STREET through CAMBRIDGE[1] and ELY[1] to DENVER in Norfolk.

Akenfield. A fictional village in Suffolk, the subject of the eponymous modern classic (1969) by Ronald Blythe, which chronicles the lives of a community of farm people in the mid-1960s. The book was based on the village of Charsfield about 5 km (3 miles) north of WOODBRIDGE, where much of the shooting for the identically titled film version (1974) took place. The film was directed by Suffolk-born (Sir) Peter Hall, and Blythe was credited as a co-writer; most of the dialogue was created by the mainly unknown local cast.

Alba Possibly OCelt *alp* 'rock, crag'. It may or may not be etymologically related to ALBION, but almost certainly is with ALBANY[1].
The kingdom formed in Scotland when in 843 Kenneth MacAlpin united the Scots of DALRIADA (broadly Argyll) with the Picts to the east (eastern Scotland from Fife north to Caithness). After Duncan I had succeeded in extending his rule over Strathclyde, Lothian and Cumbria in the mid-11th century, the term Alba began to fall out of use (although it is still the Gaelic name for Scotland), and the rulers of the expanded kingdom styled themselves 'king of Scots' (first recorded in 1094 as '*Rex Scotie*').

Albany[1] From ALBA.
An ancient Gaelic name for Scotland; variants include **Albin**, **Albyn**, **Albainn** and even **Albania**. The name survives in a number of others: BREADALBANE; Glen Albyn or Glen of Albyn or Glen More Albin (alternative names for GREAT GLEN); and Drum Alban.

Albany herald. One of the heralds in the Lyon Court (the Scottish Court of Heralds).

Duke of Albany. The dukedom of Albany was one of the first two Scottish ducal creations (1398): the 1st Duke was Robert Stewart (1340–1420), the younger son of Robert II and regent of Scotland 1406–20, thought to have been responsible for the death of the other duke, his nephew the Duke of Rothesay (*see under* ROTHESAY). There was another creation of the same title later in the 15th century (*c.*1458). The title was held by the monarch's second oldest son, and the tradition continued after the union of the crowns in 1603, the English Duke of York also bearing the Scottish title.

In September 1787, shortly before he died, his liver prematurely pickled in brandy, Bonnie Prince Charlie declared that his daughter (previously regarded as natural) was legitimate, and styled her Duchess of Albany. In a fit of simpering Jacobitism (Jacobinism fitted him better) Robert Burns was moved by the news to write his ballad 'The Bonnie Lass of Albany', ending:

> We'll daily pray, we'll nightly pray,
> On bended knees most fervently,
> The time may come, with pipe and drum
> We'll welcome hame fair Albany.

The poet somewhat redeems himself by describing the 'usurper' of the title, Frederick, Duke of York (younger brother of the Prince Regent), as 'a witless youth'.

It was after this witless youth that Albany (originally Frederickstown) in Western Australia was named (as was ALBANY[2]). Albany in New York State, USA, was named after an earlier duke, the future James II and VII, the great-grand-father of Burns's 'Lass of Albany'.

Albany[2] From the Duke of York and ALBANY[1].
A block of exclusive flats adjoining Burlington House, Piccadilly, in the West End of London. It was originally built between 1770 and 1774 as a town residence for Lord Melbourne, and named Melbourne House. Shortly afterwards Melbourne exchanged residences with Frederick, Duke of York and Albany, and in 1802 the house was sold to a property speculator, who had it enlarged and converted into bachelor apartments.

It attracted distinguished and wealthy residents, who over the centuries have included Lord Palmerston, Lord Byron, William Gladstone, Lord Macaulay (who wrote his *History of England* (1849, 1855) here), Aldous Huxley, Graham Greene, Terence Stamp, Alan Clark and (after the men-only restriction was lifted) Dame Edith Evans.

It once enjoyed a social cachet akin to an Edwardian gentlemen's club (E.W. Hornung housed his burglarious toff Raffles here), and it used to be a touchstone of U-ness to call it 'Albany' (rather than 'the Albany').

> Walking back along Vigo Street I turned into Albany on impulse and called on Graham Greene.
>
> Evelyn Waugh: diary (21 July 1955)

Albertopolis. An informal name given in the 1850s to the complex of museums, colleges, schools, concert halls and premises for learned societies in SOUTH KENSINGTON that arose in the later part of the 19th century at the behest of Prince Albert, the Prince Consort (1819–61) – who alas did not live to see the realization of his grand vision. The term seems to have lain fallow for many decades, and was revived in the 1990s as the result of an unsuccessful proposal to extend the boundaries of the area.
See also COLEVILLE.

Albert Square. The centre of activity of BBC television's *EastEnders* (*see under* EAST END).

Albert Village From Prince *Albert*, the Prince Consort.
A village in Leicestershire on the Derbyshire border, now effectively a southeastern suburb of SWADLINCOTE. It was developed in the 19th century to service the local coal-mining industry and named in honour of Prince Albert, who was officially appointed consort to Queen Victoria in 1840.

Albion Latin. The traditional explanation of the name is that it is from OCelt *Albio*, which was probably based on *albho-* 'white' (related to Latin *albus* 'white'), in allusion to the white cliffs of the south coast of England, visible from the coast of Celtic Gaul. This is now discredited, but no convincing alternative has been suggested; some etymologists, however, have referred it to OCelt *alp* 'rock, crag'.
An ancient and poetic name for Britain and (latterly) for England. It is of considerable antiquity: the Roman writer Pliny used the term in the 1st century AD, and the Venerable Bede referred in the 8th century to Britain being formerly known as 'Albion'. And writers and poets adopted it with considerable enthusiasm from the 16th to the early 19th centuries: the poet Michael Drayton, for example, gave to his magnum opus, a long topographical poem on England, the name *Poly-Olbion* (1612–22), which is from the Greek for 'having many blessings' but cannot help recalling 'Albion'; Shakespeare frequently invokes Albion ('Is this the fashion of the court of England? Is this the government of Britain's isle, and this the royalty of Albion's king?' asks Queen Margaret in *Henry VI, Part 2* I.iii (1593)); and William Blake often used it as a personification of England, in such works as *Visions of the Daughters of Albion* (1793) and *Jerusalem: The Emanation of the Giant Albion* (1804–20). In more recent times, Michael Horovitz's anthology *Children of Albion: Poetry of the 'Underground' in Britain* (1969) is a tribute to Blake (Horovitz also compiled *Grandchildren of Albion* (1997), featuring the work of younger poets); and following the election of the Labour government in 1997, the magazine *Private Eye* satirized Prime Minister Tony Blair in a cod parish magazine as the 'Vicar of St Albion'. But *Albion*'s highest-profile role in 21st-century Britain is in the name of football clubs (mostly dating from the late 19th or early 20th century): in England, for example, Brighton

and Hove Albion (1901), Burton Albion (1950) and West Bromwich Albion (1879), and in Scotland, **Albion Rovers** (*see below*). Rugby has also got into the act, notably with Bridgwater and Albion RFC.

The name is probably of Celtic origin, but more fanciful stories became attached to it in the Middle Ages. In one version, a giant son of the Roman sea-god Neptune, named Albion, discovered Britain and ruled over it for 44 years. Another legend tells how 50 daughters of the king of Syria (the eldest of whom was named Alba) were all married on the same day and murdered their husbands on their wedding night. They were set adrift in a ship as punishment and eventually reached Britain, where they duly married natives.

There are towns called Albion in the USA (California, Idaho, Illinois, Indiana, Iowa, Michigan, Montana, Nebraska, New York, Oregon, Pennsylvania).

Albion Rovers. A Scottish football team based in Coatbridge, lingering in the Third Division in the early years of the 21st century. It was formed in 1882 by the merger of two local teams, Rovers and Albion, the latter presumably intended as a variant of ALBANY[1], i.e. Scotland.

New Albion. The name under which Sir Francis Drake annexed territory in what is now California in 1579, during his voyage of circumnavigation. He recorded this act by setting up a brass plate. Such a plate materialized near San Francisco in 1936, but scientific tests in 1977 proved it a forgery.

Perfidious Albion. An encapsulation of foreigners' (and particularly French people's) supposed view of Britain as untrustworthy in international affairs. The phrase is a translation of French *la perfide Albion*, which is said to have been first used by the Marquis de Ximenès (1726–1817) (it is prefigured by Jacques Bénigne Bossuet's 'L'Angleterre, ah, la perfide Angleterre' [England, oh, perfidious England], uttered in a sermon on the circumcision preached at Metz in 1652). It attracted no particular attention at the time, and next appears in both a poem by Henri Simon and a song. Its later currency stems from its wide use in the Napoleonic recruiting drive of 1813, and it was well established by the end of the war in 1815. It was quoted by Napoleon as he left England for his final exile on St Helena.

Alcester 'Roman river settlement', from an OCelt river name of uncertain meaning (as in ALNMOUTH) + OE *ceaster* (*see* CHESTER).

A market town (pronounced 'awl-stə') in Warwickshire, at the confluence of the rivers ARROW[1] and ALNE, about 11 km (7 miles) west of Stratford-upon-Avon. It is on the Roman road leading west from Stratford.

Aldborough 'old or disused stronghold', OE *ald* 'old' + *burh* (*see* BURY).

A village in North Yorkshire, 37 km (23 miles) north of Leeds. It is situated on the River URE, on the former site of the Roman town of **Isurium Brigantum**. At the time of the Roman conquest Aldborough was the capital of the Brigantes, a tribe of ancient Britons whose territory covered most of northern England. During the Roman occupation it was the home of the consuls and governors of York, and the remains of their villas can still be seen. The ancient history of Aldborough is mentioned by the antiquary John Leland in his *Itinerary* (an account of his tour of Britain in 1534–43).

Alde A back-formation from ALDEBURGH.

A river in Suffolk. It rises in northern Suffolk, to the north of Framlingham, and flows about 25 km (16 miles) southeast towards ALDEBURGH, where it turns south towards Orford Ness (*see under* ORFORD). There it combines with the River Butley to form the ORE[2].

Aldeburgh 'old or disused stronghold', OE *ald* 'old' + *burh* (*see* BURY).

A fishing village and resort on the Suffolk coast, about 32 km (20 miles) northeast of Ipswich. In former times it was a noted shipbuilding centre: Sir Francis Drake's ships *Pelican* (in which, renamed *Golden Hind*, he circumnavigated the world) and *Greyhound* were both constructed here, and many members of their crews were local men. Its modern fame, however, derives from the **Aldeburgh Festival**, an annual music festival founded in 1948 by the Suffolk-born composer Benjamin Britten (1913–76) and his partner, the singer Peter Pears (1910–86). They lived in Aldeburgh, and both are now buried in the churchyard of the 15th-century church of St Peter and St Paul. Festival performances are held at several venues in the neighbourhood (notably the Maltings at SNAPE), and the renown of its founders has ensured it a rollcall of illustrious international participants over the decades (e.g. Dietrich Fischer-Dieskau, Janet Baker, Sviatoslav Richter and Mstislav Rostropovich). The festival did, however, in Britten's period at the helm, gain something of a reputation as a gay coterie, and the robustly heterosexual English composer William Walton gave it the waspish nickname **Aldebugger**.

The poet George Crabbe (1754–1832) was born in Aldeburgh. There is a statue to him in the parish church. He wrote a collection of poetical tales about Aldeburgh, entitled *The Borough* (1810), one of which forms the theme of Britten's opera *Peter Grimes* (1945).

Elizabeth Garrett Anderson (1836–1917), the first English woman to qualify as a doctor, lived in Aldeburgh. She was elected mayor in 1908, becoming the first woman mayor in Britain.

The scholar and ghost-story writer M.R. James (1862–1936) often stayed in Aldeburgh, and it serves, in the guise of Seaburgh, as a setting for his chilling story 'A Warning to the Curious' (1925).

See also SLAUGHDEN.

Alderley Edge *Alderley* 'Althryth's glade', OE female personal name *Althryth* + -LEY; *Edge* from *edge* 'escarpment'.

A town and a wooded cliff in Cheshire, about 5 km (3 miles) northwest of Macclesfield. The town's original name was simply **Alderley**, and the 198-m (650-ft) pink sandstone escarpment took its name from that. This in turn was transferred to the town in the 19th century.

Numerous legends attach to the place (for example, that knights wait in the Wizard of the Edge cave until called on to come to their country's rescue). Many of them are incorporated into the mythology constructed by Alan Garner (who was born in Alderley Edge in 1934) for his children's novels *The Weirdstone of Brisingamen* (1960) and *The Moon of Gomrath* (1963).

Aldermaston 'nobleman's farmstead', OE *ealdormannes* possessive form of *ealdormann* 'nobleman, chief' + -TON.

A village in Berkshire, about 14 km (8.5 miles) southwest of Reading. The village itself is old and picturesque, but its name is nowadays almost exclusively associated with the nearby Atomic Weapons Research Establishment, where Britain's nuclear bombs and warheads are designed and made. It owes its notoriety largely to the **Aldermaston Marches** (1958–63), organized by the Campaign for Nuclear Disarmament to protest against the British development of nuclear weapons in particular and the policy of nuclear deterrence in general. The first march was from London to Aldermaston, subsequent ones in the opposite direction, culminating in a mass protest rally in Trafalgar Square. Before long, enthusiasm had waned to the point where the marches were discontinued, but by then the name 'Aldermaston' had become almost synonymous with leftish bearded unilateralist protest:

> Every now and then we march from Aldermaston,
> protesting like a ton of bricks ... And then we sit a good
> deal.
>
> P.G. Wodehouse: *Plum Pie* (1966)

The first filling station in Britain was opened in Aldermaston in 1919.

Alderney 'gravel island', OScand *aurinn* 'gravel, mud' + *ey* (*see* -AY).

The northernmost (and third largest) of the CHANNEL ISLANDS, about 35 km (22 miles) northeast of Guernsey. It is approximately 8 sq km (3 sq miles) in area. Its capital is St Anne. It is separated from the coast of Normandy by the perilously swift **Race of Alderney**, which is 16 km (10 miles) wide. Its economy is based on dairy farming and tourism.

Under German occupation in the Second World War

Alderney was entirely evacuated. Four forced labour camps were set up in here in 1942 by the Todt Organization, the Third Reich's labour organization. Slave-workers – many of them Russian – were held on the island in appalling conditions.

Alderney's French name, *Aurigny*, has been appropriated by an airline that since 1968 has operated flights between the Channel Islands themselves and between the Islands and various locations in mainland Britain and Continental Europe.

Alderney. A term applied originally (in the late 18th century) specifically to a type of cattle bred on Alderney, but subsequently used to refer to a range of Channel Island dairy breeds (e.g. Jersey or Guernsey).

Aldersgate Street From *Aldersgate* (a former gate of the City of London), 'gate associated with Ealdred', OE male personal name *Ealdred* + *geat* 'gate'.

A street in the City of London (EC1), running southwards from the Goswell Road past the BARBICAN towards CHEAPSIDE.

The old city gate from which it took its name was originally built by the Romans in the 2nd to 3rd centuries. It was one of London's northern exits and entrances. The medieval gate burnt down in the Great Fire of 1666. It was restored, but eventually dismantled in 1761.

Barbican Underground station, on the Circle and Metropolitan lines, opened in 1865 as 'Aldersgate Street'. Its name was changed in 1910 to 'Aldersgate', in 1923 to 'Aldersgate & Barbican' and finally, in 1968, to 'Barbican'.

Aldershot 'projecting piece of land where alder trees grow', OE *alor* 'alder' + *sceat* 'projecting wood or piece of land'.

A town in northeast Hampshire, about 13 km (8 miles) west of Guildford. In the mid-19th century it was still a village, but the arrival of the British Army, which decided in the 1850s to construct a very large camp here for manoeuvres, prompted a rapid growth in size. Permanent barracks were built, and Aldershot became over the decades the chief garrison town and army training centre in the UK. The local economy depends very much on the military, and army families are strongly represented in the populace (in his 1945 poem 'A Subaltern's Love Song' John Betjeman's adored Miss Joan Hunter Dunn was 'Furnish'd and burnish'd by Aldershot sun').

Aldershot Barracks were bombed by the Official IRA in 1972. A device was placed in the headquarters of the Parachute Regiment on 22 February 1972 (believed to have been in revenge for the Paras' role in the Bloody Sunday killings the previous month), killing seven people: five canteen workers, a (Catholic) padre and a gardener.

Cambridge Hospital, a military hospital founded in Aldershot at the same time as the army camp, pioneered the use of plastic surgery to treat the seriously wounded and disfigured during the First World War. It closed in 1996.

In Thomas Hardy's *Jude the Obscure* (1895) Aldershot is fictionalized as **Quartershot**.

Aldgate Alteration of earlier *Alegate*, from OE *ealu* 'ale' + *geat* 'gate' (probably because ale was sold and consumed nearby); the intrusive *d*, first recorded in the 17th century, is probably due to the influence of other London place names and street names beginning *Ald-*, notably *Aldersgate*.

A street in the City of London (*see under* LONDON), leading from the junction of FENCHURCH STREET and LEADENHALL STREET towards WHITECHAPEL High Street. It takes its name from one of the six original gates of the City built by the Romans, through which led the road to the east and Colchester. This was at first apparently called by the Anglo-Saxons *Æst geat* 'East gate', but *Alegate*, from which the modern form of the name evolved, is recorded as early as 1108. The poet Geoffrey Chaucer lived in rooms above the gate. It was demolished in 1761.

Aldgate Ward, one of the administrative divisions of the City of London, covers the area immediately to the north, south, and west of Aldgate. Aldgate Underground station, on the Circle line, opened in 1876, and Aldgate East, on the District line and the Hammersmith & City line, in 1884.

Aldgate Pump. A stone fountain at the junction of Fenchurch Street and Leadenhall Street in the City of London. A well is recorded on the site in King John's time, and a pump is known to have been here at the end of the 16th century. The present structure, with a brass dog's-head spout, dates from 1871. It no longer dispenses water. In the 18th and 19th centuries, the phrase *a draught on the Aldgate pump* denoted a forged banknote or fraudulent bill of exchange.

Aldminster. The fictional name for GLOUCESTER in Joanna Trollope's novel *The Choir* (1988).

Aldridge 'farm among the alders', OE *alor* 'alder' + *wic* (*see* WICK).

A town in the West Midlands, within the unitary authority of Walsall (before 1974 straddling the Staffordshire/Warwickshire boundary), about 13 km (8 miles) north of Birmingham. To the southwest is BARR BEACON.

Aldwincle 'Ealda's river bend', OE male personal name *Ealda* + *wincel* 'bend, corner'.

A village in Northamptonshire, about 14 km (8.5 miles) east of Kettering. The poet-playwright John Dryden (1631–1700) and the historian Thomas Fuller (1608–61) were born here.

Aldwych From the name of a medieval settlement in the area.

A crescent in Central LONDON, linking the lower end of KINGSWAY with the STRAND. It was constructed at the beginning of the 20th century. Its name was a revival of a term applied in the Middle Ages to a settlement in the area, just to the west of the City of London, first recorded in Latin in 1199 as *Vetus vicus* 'old settlement' and in English in 1211 as *Aldewich* (from OE *ald* 'old' + *wic* '(trading) settlement'). The nearby DRURY LANE was originally known as 'Via de Aldwych'. The trading settlement referred to in the name is almost certainly the one known from the 7th to the 9th centuries in Latin as *vicus Lundonie* and in English as *Lundenwic* (*see under* LONDON).

The street was part of the massive KINGSWAY redevelopment of 1900–5. It has become closely associated with many of the large and imposing buildings it contains, including Australia House, Bush House (home of the BBC World Service), India House, the **Aldwych Theatre** (*see also below*) and the Waldorf Hotel. Aldwych Underground station, on a spur of the Piccadilly Line from HOLBORN, opened in 1907. It is actually situated on The Strand, and was called Strand until 1915, when the name was changed. In the Second World War, the Elgin Marbles were stored in a disused tunnel here. The station closed in 1994.

Aldwych farce. Any of a series of farces by the English playwright Ben Travers (1886–1980) presented at the Aldwych Theatre, Aldwych from the mid-1920s to the early 1930s: *A Cuckoo in the Nest* (1925), *Rookery Nook* (1926), *Plunder* (1928), *A Cup of Kindness* (1929), *A Night Like This* (1931), *Dirty Work* (1932), and *A Bit of a Test* (1933). They combined absurdly improbable situations, eccentric characters and broad humour with social satire. Most were filmed.

Alexandria Named in 1760 after Alexander Smollett, the local MP, a relative of the novelist Tobias Smollett.

A small town in West Dunbartonshire (formerly in Strathclyde), about 3 km (2 miles) south of Loch Lomond.

Alfardisworthy 'Ælfheard's enclosure', OE male personal name *Ælftheard* + *worthig* (*see* -WORTH, WORTHY, -WARDINE).

A village (locally pronounced 'all-zəry') in Devon, in the Hartland Peninsula (*see under* HARTLAND POINT), on the River TAMAR, about 11 km (7 miles) northeast of Bude.

Alford¹ 'old ford', OE *ald* 'old' + FORD.

A market town (pronounced 'awlfəd') in Lincolnshire, about 40 km (25 miles) northeast of Boston and 10 km (6 miles) from the North Sea coast. The political radical Thomas Paine worked in Alford as an excise officer before emigrating to America in 1774. There is also a town called Alford in Florida, USA.

Alford² 'high ford', Gaelic *átha* 'ford' + *aird* 'high'.

A village (locally pronounced 'ah-fəd') in Aberdeenshire (formerly in Grampian region), on the Don, 40 km (25 miles) west of Aberdeen. It is situated in the **Howe of Alford**, a flat, fertile area between the hills.

Battle of Alford (2 July 1645). A victory during the Civil Wars by a Royalist army under James Graham, the Marquess of Montrose (1612–50), over a Covenanting force under General Baillie.

Alfred's Castle. A small Iron Age earthwork, situated on the ASHDOWN Estate in the southwestern corner of Oxfordshire. There is no direct evidence connecting the site to King Alfred. The name of the fort appears to be an 18th-century attempt to romanticize the site by connecting it with King Alfred who had his capital at nearby WANTAGE.

Alfredston. The fictional name for WANTAGE used by Thomas Hardy, as in *Jude the Obscure* (1895).

Alfreton 'Ælfhere's farmstead or village', OE male personal name *Ælfhere* + -TON.
A town in Derbyshire, about 16 km (10 miles) south of Chesterfield. It grew up as a mining town, but its townscape is less obviously industrial than most such.

Alfriston 'Ælfric's farmstead', OE *Ælfrices* possessive form of male personal name *Ælfric* + *tun* (*see* -TON).
A village in the CUCKMERE Valley, in East Sussex, about 10 km (6 miles) northeast of Eastbourne. The 14th-century Clergy House was the first building ever bought by the National Trust, in 1896. The imposing parish church of St Andrew, of similar date, has been called the 'Cathedral of the Downs'.

Allan Water. *See under* BRIDGE OF ALLAN.

All Cannings 'Old Cannings': *All* 'old', from OE *eald* 'old', later assimilated to *all*; *Cannings* '(settlement of) Cana's people', OE male personal name *Cana* +-*ingas* (*see* -ING).
A village in Wiltshire, about 6 km (4 miles) east of Devizes.

Allen An OCelt or pre-Celtic river name, of unknown meaning.
A river of Northumberland, flowing north to meet the South Tyne 13 km (8 miles) west of Hexham. There are two branches: the **West Allen** and the **East Allen**. The area through which the rivers flow is called **Allendale**, and includes the villages of **Allenheads** and **Allendale Town**. Allendale was once a centre of lead mining, and in 1761 many protesting Allendale miners were killed by the Hexham Butchers (*see under* HEXHAM). Every New Year's Eve Allendale Town holds the Tar Barling ceremony, a midwinter fire festival in which the men of the village, dressed in outlandish costumes, parade to the village square with sawn-off tar barrels blazing on their heads.

Wolf of Allendale, the. A creature responsible for a spate of sheep worrying and sheep killing around Allendale in 1904. One man reported that on a dark and stormy night he had seen the clear outline of a huge wolf stalking the fells. He was generally disbelieved, but the killings continued. Then it transpired that a Captain Bain of Shotley

Bridge near Consett had owned a wolf that had recently escaped. He offered a reward for its capture, dead or alive. Scores of hunters scoured the fells, but to no avail. Then news came that a body of a wolf, killed by a train, had been found on the Settle-to-Carlisle line, near Cumhinton. The body was stuffed and displayed in the railway company's headquarters at Derby – and, as a song of the time concluded:

> If thoo dissent believe mi,
> Or think Ah's tellin a lee,
> Just ax for the wolf at Derby,
> It's there for a' to see.

Allen, Bog of. *See* BOG OF ALLEN.

Allendale Town. *See under* ALLEN.

Aller '(place at the) alder tree', OE *alor* 'alder'.
A village in Somerset, about 13 km (8 miles) southwest of Glastonbury.

Allerton 'alder-tree farm', OE *alor* 'alder-tree' + -TON.
A southern suburb of LIVERPOOL. Former Beatle Paul McCartney (b.1942) moved here from SPEKE in the mid-1950s, and his parents' modest house, at number 20 Forthlin Road, is now restored to an appropriate appearance for that period, under the care of the National Trust. John Lennon's childhood home lies less than a mile away in WOOLTON.
See also The DINGLE.

Allhallows 'All Saints'; from the dedication of the local church to All Saints. In the Middle Ages the village was called Hoo All Hallows (*hoo* means 'a spur of land', and is an element in other place names on the Isle of Grain, e.g. St Mary's Hoo and Hoo St Werburgh).
A village in Kent, on the ISLE OF GRAIN, about 13 km (8 miles) northeast of Rochester. Just to the north, on the Thames Estuary coast, is **Allhallows-on-Sea**.

Allihies Irish *Na hAilichí* 'the circular stone forts', from AILEACH.
A village on the western end of the Beara peninsula, West Cork, 8 km (5 miles) west of Castletown Bearhaven. It was here that the Children of Lir were supposed to have come ashore, having spent 900 years as swans (alternatively they landed on the shores of LOUGH DERRAVARAGH). They died shortly afterwards. The nearby copper mines closed in the late 19th century, but at one time the area round Allihies was Europe's biggest source of copper ore.

Allival. An alternative name for HALLIVAL.

Alloa 'rocky place', Gaelic *aileach* 'rocky' or *allmhagh* 'rock-plain'.
An industrial town in Clackmannanshire (formerly in Central region) about 9 km (5.5 miles) east of Stirling, between the FORTH estuary and the OCHIL HILLS. When Clackmannan district was formed in 1975, Alloa became

its administrative headquarters, and remained as such when CLACKMANNANSHIRE was revived in 1996. **Alloa Tower**, a stronghold of the Earls of Mar, was occasionally home to Mary Queen of Scots and her son James VI. It was the birthplace of John Erskine, 6th Earl of Mar (1675–1732), leader of the 1715 Jacobite Rising. There is a village called **South Alloa** on the south side of the Forth, opposite Alloa.

Alloa Athletic FC (nicknamed the Wasps) was founded in 1883 and is based at Recreation Park. Alloa has had a quiet footballing history, the club's moment of glory coming in 1964 when its players took the role of the fictional TANNOCHBRAE team in an episode of *Dr Finlay's Casebook*.

> Ah'll awa tae Alloa,
> And ah'll awa the noo,
> Ah'll awa tae Alloa
> Tae buy a poond o' oo.
>
> Anon.: traditional rhyme (Scots *oo* 'wool')

Alloway 'rocky place', Gaelic *allmhagh* 'rock-plain'.
Formerly a village, now a suburb on the south side of AYR², in South Ayrshire (formerly in Strathclyde). It was the birthplace of the poet Robert Burns (1759–96), who spent his first seven years here. Burns Cottage is preserved, and there is also a classical Burns Monument, not to mention the Burns National Heritage Park and the Tam O'Shanter Experience. Burns's poem 'Tam O'Shanter' arose when he was asked in 1790 by the lexicographer and writer Francis Grose, who was compiling a book entitled *The Antiquities of Scotland*, to provide a poem to go with **Alloway Auld Kirk**. The Kirk – 'Whare ghaists and houlets nightly cry' – was already a ruin in Burns's time, and is where Tam O'Shanter comes across 'Warlocks and witches in a dance', while Auld Nick plays the pipes:

> They reel'd, they set, they cross'd, they cleckit,
> Till ilka carlin swat and reekit,
> And coost her duddies to the wark,
> And linket at it in her sark!

There are several other landmarks from the poem (including Brig o' Doon (*see under* DOON) to be found in and around Alloway.

Keats visited Burns Cottage in Alloway on his 1818 tour, and from the sonnet he wrote here it appears he raised his glass more than once to honour the dead bard:

> My pulse is warm with thine own Barley-bree,
> My head is light with pledging a great soul,
> My eyes are wandering, and I cannot see,
> Fancy is dead and drunken at its goal ...
> Yet can I gulp a bumper to thy name, –
> O smile among the shades, for this is fame!
>
> John Keats: 'Written in Burns' Cottage' (1818)

Almond¹ from Gaelic *amhainn* 'river', cognate with AVON.
A river that flows through West Lothian and Midlothian via **Almondell and Calderwood Country Park** to join the Firth of Forth (*see under* FORTH) at Cramond (which derives from Latin *castrum* 'military camp' + the river name). Its length is approximately 40 km (25 miles).

Almond². A river in Perth and Kinross (formerly in Perthshire, and then in Tayside region), approximately 50 km (30 miles) long. It rises in the hills between lochs Tay (*see under* TAY) and Earn (*see under* EARN), then flows east through **Glen Almond** (the middle north–south section of which is called the SMA' GLEN) to join the Tay just north of PERTH. The area to the east of the Sma' Glen is known as **Logiealmond** (Gaelic *lagaidh* 'hollow'), and this was depicted as 'Drumtochty' in the sentimental 'kailyard' stories of Ian Maclaren (the Rev. John Watson) contained in *Beside the Bonnie Briar Bush* (1894). Trinity College, an Episcopalian public school in the lower glen, is commonly referred to as 'Glen Almond'.

Almondsbury 'Æthelmod's or Æthelmund's stronghold', OE *Æthelmodes* or *Æthelmundes* possessive forms of male personal names *Æthelmod* or *Æthelmund* (the earliest recorded form of the place name (1086) was *Almodesberie*) + BURY.
A village in South Gloucestershire, about 5 km (3 miles) north of Bristol.

Alne From an OCelt river name of uncertain meaning.
A river in Warwickshire, which rises about 16 km (10 miles) south of Birmingham and flows 24 km (15 miles) to join the River ARROW¹ at Alcester.

Alness Probably a pre-Celtic river name meaning 'flowing one'.
A small town in Easter Ross, Highland (formerly in Ross and Cromarty), 5 km (3 miles) west of Invergordon.

Alnmouth 'mouth of the River Aln', OCelt river name *Alaunos*, of unknown meaning, + OE *mutha* 'mouth'.
An attractive small resort and former port at the mouth of the River Aln in Northumbria, some 6 km (4 miles) southeast of Alnwick. Alnmouth has suffered a number of blows over the course of its history: in 1748 the preacher John Wesley condemned the place for its excesses of wickedness; in 1779 the American privateer John Paul Jones bombarded it from his ship, the *Ranger*, aiming for the church but hitting a farmhouse; and on Christmas Day 1806 a great storm changed the course of the river, leading to the silting up of the harbour.

Alnwick 'dwelling by the River Aln', OCelt river name (*see* ALNMOUTH) + WICK.
An appealing market town on the River Aln in Northumberland, some 50 km (31 miles) north of Newcastle. It is pronounced as indicated in the following anonymous limerick:

> There was a mechalnwick of Alnwick

Whose opinions were very Germalnwick.
So when war had begun
He went off with a gun
The proportions of which were Titalnwick.

Every Shrove Tuesday Alnwick holds a wild *mêlée*, a sort of rule-less, mass-participation prototype of football, with the goals set a quarter of a mile apart; immersion of players in the River Aln is not unknown. Despite this, in 2002, Alnwick was voted the town with the best quality of life in England.

Alnwick Castle dates back to the 11th century, although heavily restored in the 18th (by Robert Adam) and 19th (by Antony Salvin). The grounds were laid out by 'Capability' Brown, and have been recently restored to include a central Grand Cascade of fountains and a magnificent Rose Garden, featuring the raspberry-scented **Alnwick Castle Rose**. Since 1309 Alnwick Castle has been the home of the Percy family, earls (from 1377) and (since 1750) dukes of Northumberland. The 15th-century Hotspur Tower (part of the town walls) takes its name from the nickname of Harry Percy (1364–1403), who plays a part in Shakespeare's *Henry IV, Part 1* (1597). The castle has been nicknamed **the Windsor of the North** for its perceived similarity to Windsor Castle when viewed from a distance. *Alnwick Castle* is the title of a once-popular historical romance published in 1822 by the American Knickerbocker poet, Fitz-Greene Halleck. A popular location with film makers, the castle has featured in *Robin Hood: Prince of Thieves* (1991), *Elizabeth* (1998) and in some of the Hogwarts scenes in the *Harry Potter* films (2001 onwards).

Alnwick was the birthplace of the seventh Astronomer Royal, George Airy (1801–92), and of the philosopher Bernard Bosanquet (1848–1923).

Battle of Alnwick (13 November 1093). An English victory over the Scots. The Scottish king, Malcolm III Canmore, was killed; he had paid homage to William I, but under William Rufus asserted his independence, with terminal results.

Battle of Alnwick (13 July 1174). Another English victory over the Scots. The Scottish king, William the Lion, was captured, and was later obliged to sign the Treaty of Falaise, by which he became a vassal of Henry II.

Alresford 'alder-tree ford', OE *alres* possessive form of *alor* 'alder' + FORD.

A town (pronounced 'awlz-fəd') in Hampshire, about 10 km (6 miles) northeast of Winchester. It consists of **New Alresford** and the smaller **Old Alresford**, which are linked by a causeway across a 12th-century reservoir. 'New' Alresford is of considerable antiquity, having been in the possession of the Bishops of Winchester since before the Norman Conquest, and was an important centre of the wool trade, but

it was largely rebuilt in the 17th and 18th centuries after serious fires.

Modern Alresford is noted for its watercress, which inspired the name 'Watercress Line' for the 5-km (3-mile) steam railway line between Alresford and Ropley.

Battle of Alresford. Another name for the Battle of Cheriton (*see under* CHERITON[1]).

Alsager 'Ælle's piece of cultivated land', OE male personal name *Ælle* + *æcer* 'field, acre' (*see* FIELD).

A town (pronounced 'awl-say-jə') in Cheshire, about 5 km (3 miles) east of Crewe. It is now mainly a dormitory for people working in Crewe and Stoke-on-Trent.

Alsatia From Latin *Alsatia* 'Alsace'.

A name given in the 17th and 18th centuries to an area of London between FLEET STREET and the THAMES[1] which was a notorious haunt of criminals, vagabonds and prostitutes. It encompassed the precincts of the former Whitefriars Monastery, whose powers of sanctuary continued to be invoked by the area's low-life inhabitants. In 1580, Elizabeth I declared it to be exempt from the jurisdiction of the City of London (*see under* LONDON), and it became virtually a no-go area for the civil authorities. It was named after Alsace because that much-disputed territory between France and Germany was famous for harbouring the disaffected. Its powers of sanctuary were rescinded in 1697.

Alsop-en-le-Dale *Alsop* 'Ælle's valley', OE *Ælles* possessive form of male personal name *Ælle* + *hop* 'small enclosed valley'; *-en-le-Dale* (1535) 'in the valley' (referring to DOVEDALE[1]), Anglo-French.

A village in Derbyshire, in the PEAK DISTRICT National Park, about 17 km (11 miles) north of Ashbourne.

Altarnun 'altar of Nonn', Cornish *alter* 'altar' + female personal name *Nonne*.

A village in Cornwall, on the edge of Bodmin Moor (*see under* BODMIN) about 11 km (7 miles) southwest of Launceston. The gloomily imposing local church, whose spaciousness has earned it the epithet the **Cathedral of the Moor**, is dedicated to St Nonn, a 6th-century saint who was the mother of St David – hence the name *Altarnun*. The village covers 6077 ha (15,018 acres), and is one of the largest parishes in England.

Althorp 'Olla's farmstead', OE male personal name *Olla* + *thorp* (*see* THORPE).

A mansion (pronounced 'awlthorp' or 'awltrəp') in Northamptonshire, about 10 km (6 miles) northwest of Northampton, which is the ancestral home of the Spencers. The family first settled here in 1486, but the present house is of Elizabethan origin (with many later amendments). It began to register on the national radar screen when a daughter of the family, Lady Diana Spencer, married

Charles, Prince of Wales in 1981. She is now buried on an island in the park, and her brother, Earl Spencer, opened a museum to her memory at Althorp in 1998.

Alton¹ 'farmstead at the source of a river', OE *œwiell* 'river source' + -TON.

A market town in Hampshire, on the PILGRIMS' WAY, about 14 km (8.5 miles) southeast of Basingstoke. The centre of the town has some attractive Georgian buildings. The poet Edmund Spenser (*c*.1552–99) lived in Alton for a time; his cottage can still be seen here. There are four towns called Alton in the USA (California, Illinois, New York, Utah).

Alton² 'Ælfa's farmstead', OE male personal name *Ælfa* + -TON.

A stone-built village in Staffordshire, about 13 km (8 miles) east of Stoke-on-Trent. Its dramatic setting, among beetling wooded crags and with extravagant neo-Gothic buildings (some of them by A.W. Pugin) all around, has been dubbed the 'Rhineland of Staffordshire'.

Alton Towers. A 243-ha (600-acre) pleasure park just to the north of Alton. Since it opened in the 1920s its mixture of roller coasters, cable cars, and other assorted rides and games has made it into the archetypal out-of-town amusement park in England. One of the more notorious events staged here was the ill-advised *It's a Royal Knockout* (1987), a mélange of silly games organized by Prince Edward and participated in (in fancy dress) by various of his relations and other assorted celebrities.

The park takes its name from the mansion in the grounds where it is situated. Once the home of the earls of Shrewsbury, this is now just an empty shell, but its Gothic towers and pinnacles still cut an impressive figure. The 15th earl had it built in the 1830s, replacing the earlier Alveton Lodge.

Alton Pancras *Alton see* ALTON¹; *Pancras* from the dedication of the local church to St Pancras, *compare* ST PANCRAS.

A village in Dorset, about 13 km (8 miles) north of Dorchester.

Altrincham 'homestead of Aldhere's people', OE male personal name *Aldhere* +-*inga*- (*see* -ING) + HAM.

A former market town in Greater Manchester, 12 km (7.5 miles) southeast of the centre. It is pronounced 'Awltring-əm'. The building of a railway link in 1849 turned it into a suburb. Hewlett Johnson (1874–1966), Dean of Canterbury (1931–63), nicknamed 'the Red Dean' for his pronounced leftish political sympathies, was vicar of St Margaret's, Altrincham, from 1908 to 1924.

Alum Bay From the *alum* mined in the area from the 16th century (alum is a sulphate of aluminium, used in the making of leather and paper). The name is first recorded in 1720.

A bay at the western tip of the ISLE OF WIGHT, with the NEEDLES at its southern extremity. Its cliffs are formed from multi-coloured strata, and local souvenirs are made by layering sand from them in transparent containers of various shapes (e.g. lighthouses). At the beginning of the 20th century the radio pioneer Guglielmo Marconi transmitted his first wireless messages from the top of the cliff to a tug moored in the bay.

Alva 'rocky plain', Gaelic *allmhagh*.

A town in Clackmannanshire (formerly in Central region) between the FORTH estuary and the OCHIL HILLS, about 11 km (7 miles) northeast of Stirling.

Alverdiscott 'Alfred's cottage', OE *Ælfredes* 'Alfred's' + *cot* (*see* -COT, COTE).

A village (pronounced as spelt or as 'awlskət') in north Devon, about 6 km (4 miles) east of Bideford.

Alyth 'rugged bank' or 'rocky place', Gaelic *aill* or *ailech*.

A small town 8 km (5 miles) northeast of Blairgowrie, in Perth and Kinross (formerly in Perthshire, and then in Tayside region). Just to the north is the **Hill of Alyth**, while through the town runs the **Alyth Burn**, rising some 11 km (7 miles) to the northwest in the **Forest of Alyth**. In 1651 General Alexander Leslie, commander of Scottish forces, was captured at Alyth by Cromwell's dragoons.

Am Bàsteir Possibly 'the executioner', Gaelic *am* 'the' + *bàsadair* 'executioner', the Bàsteir Tooth having something of the appearance of an axe head. Others, seeing in the shape of the Tooth a hooded priest, have suggested the name means 'one who baptizes'.

A rocky summit (935 m / 3067 ft) in the Cuillin of Skye, some 5 km (3 miles) southwest of Sligachan. Next to the summit is the jagged pinnacle of the **Bàsteir Tooth**.

Amber Valley From the River *Amber*, from a pre-Celtic river name of unknown meaning.

A district in Derbyshire, to the north of Derby, centred on the valley through which the River DERWENT⁴ flows and containing ALFRETON, BELPER and RIPLEY. It is now also a parliamentary constituency.

Amble 'Amma's promontory', OE male personal name *Amma* + *bile* 'promontory'.

A town at the mouth of the River COQUET, on the North Sea coast of Northumberland, 40 km (25 miles) north of Newcastle. It developed as a coal-exporting port in the 1840s, but this trade stopped in 1969, since when the town has transformed itself into a holiday resort.

Ambleside 'summer pasture by the river sandbank', OScand *a* 'river' + *melr* 'sandbank' + *saetr* 'summer pasture'; *Amelseta c*.1095.

A market town in Cumbria (formerly in Westmorland), at the north end of WINDERMERE, 17 km (11 miles) northwest of Kendal. The Romans built a camp here, and called it **Galava**. Ambleside is now one of the main tourist centres of the LAKE DISTRICT.

The best-known building in the town is the tiny Bridge House (late 17th century), built on a small bridge over Stock Ghyll. It is said to have been built by a man too mean to buy land, but was actually a folly for the grounds of nearby Ambleside Hall. The largest of the two rooms measures 13 ft by 6 ft, and in the 1850s the house was home to a Mr and Mrs Rigg and their six children. It is now a National Trust information centre.

William Wordsworth, in his little-known capacity as Distributor of Stamps for Westmorland, had his office in Ambleside. The town has other literary connections: Mrs 'Boy Stood on the Burning Deck' Hemans lived at 'Dove Nest' from 1828 to 1831; 'The Knoll' was home from 1845 to Harriet Martineau, the political writer and author of a famous guide to the Lake District; and 'Fox Howe' was the holiday home of Dr Thomas Arnold, the reforming headmaster of RUGBY School; his son, the poet and critic Matthew Arnold, spent his last years here.

Ambleside also has the grave of the Dadaist poet and artist Kurt Schwitters (1887–1948), who settled in Ambleside in 1942, having fled Nazi persecution in Germany some years before. Schwitters was the creator of *Merz* ('trash'), the term he applied to his elaborate constructions of bits and pieces he picked up from dustbins and gutters. 'I am a painter and I nail my pictures together,' said Schwitters. Near Ambleside, at Chapel Stile in Langdale, he created his third, unfinished *Merzbau* ('*Merz* building'), which is now in the Hatton Gallery in Newcastle. However, to survive, Schwitters was obliged to paint conventional Lakeland views and to offer them for sale on the steps of Bridge House.

On the Saturday nearest to St Anne's Day (26 July), the citizens of Ambleside participate in a rush-bearing ceremony, in which men carry pillars of rush some 2.5 m (8 ft) tall, while children carry various smaller objects made out of rushes.

Ambridge. A fictional rural English village in which the BBC radio soap opera 'The Archers' (1951–) is set. It is in the county of Borsetshire (*see under* BORCHESTER) Among its most notable landmarks are Brookfield Farm, ancestral farm of the Archer family, Grey Gables, the neighbourhood's smart hotel, and the 'The Bull' inn.

Am Buachaille. *See under* SANDWOOD BAY.

Amen Corner Probably from the processional chanting of 'Amen'. Alternatively the name might allude to writers of religious texts working in the vicinity.
A site at the western end of PATERNOSTER ROW in the City of London (EC4), where the clergy of ST PAUL'S[1] Cathedral finished the Paternoster (the Lord's Prayer) on Corpus Christi Day as they went in procession to the cathedral. They began the prayer in Paternoster Row and continued it to the end of the street, and they said Amen at the corner of the Row. On turning down AVE MARIA LANE they began chanting the Hail Mary, then, crossing LUDGATE they entered CREED LANE chanting the Credo.

Amen Corner was destroyed in an air raid on 28 December 1940, but the name was briefly revived in the later 1960s by the Welsh **Amen Corner** rock band, which featured guitarist Andy Fairweather-Low.

Amersham 'Ealhmund's homestead', OE *Ealhmundes* possessive form of male personal name *Ealhmund* + HAM.
A town in Buckinghamshire, about 10 km (6 miles) north of Beaconsfield. The headquarters of the administrative district of CHILTERN are here. Its central part is a conglomeration of thatched cottages, bourgeois Georgian, and ancient inns: in 1959, *The Good Food Guide* commented:

> A lot of olde realle beames in Amersham and a lot of olde phonie cookynge too.

To the northwest, in **Amersham-on-the-Hill**, can be found 'High and Over', one of the first houses in England in the Modernist style, designed in 1929 by Connell and Ward.

The poet and politician Edmund Waller (1606–87) was born in nearby Coleshill.

Amesbury Probably 'Ambre's stronghold' (referring to a nearby Iron Age hillfort known as Vespasian's Camp), OE *Ambres* possessive form of male personal name *Ambre* + *byrig* dative form of *burh* 'stronghold' (*see* BURY); alternatively the first element could represent OE *amer* 'bunting' (as in *yellowhammer*). More circumstantial but fanciful identities have been attributed to 'Ambre': a Roman called Ambrosius, for instance, a descendant of Constantine who became king of Britain, or Ambrius, a British monk who founded a large monastery, later destroyed by the Saxons.
A town in Wiltshire, on Salisbury Plain (*see under* SALISBURY), on the River AVON[3] , about 13 km (8 miles) north of Salisbury. **Amesbury Abbey**, the former home of the dukes of Queensberry, was designed by Inigo Jones. John Gay wrote *The Beggar's Opera* while staying as a guest here in 1727.

Amesbury Archer. The name given by the media to an exceptionally rich early Bronze-Age burial uncovered during archaeological excavation in advance of a housing development in Amesbury in May 2002. The archer, a male between 35 and 45 years old, was buried with the accoutrements of a hunter (including a wristguard to protect his arm from the recoil of a longbow) and symbols of his status. An array of objects, including boars' tusks, pots, flint tools and arrow heads, were found alongside him in the tomb.

Evidence suggests that he may have originally come from the Alps.

The grave is the richest of any found in Britain from the Early Bronze Age (roughly 2400–1500 BC). Because the archer was buried just 3 miles from STONEHENGE, at about the time when the latter was being erected, there has been speculation that he may have been linked to the building of that monument.

A'Mhaighdean Gaelic 'the maiden'.

A graceful mountain (967 m / 3172 ft) in the Northwest Highlands, in the Letterewe Forest, north of LOCH MAREE. Pronounced 'a-vayjun', it is sometimes cited as the most remote Munro (see MUNROS) in Scotland, being some 16 km (10 miles) on foot from the nearest road. This isolation might be thought to account for its name, but it is more likely that it comes from its shape, which resembles a stook of corn: in both Gaelic and Scots a maiden is the name given to last sheaf cut during harvest.

Amlwch 'near the marsh or inlet', Welsh *am* 'near' + *llwch* 'marsh, inlet'.

A small port and resort on the northern coast of ANGLESEY (formerly in Gwynedd), 24 km (15 miles) north of Menai Bridge. In the 18th and 19th centuries, Parys Mountain, just south of Amlwch, was the site of the world's largest copper mine. **Ynys Amlwch** ('isle of Amlwch') is the Welsh name for East Mouse, just offshore (see under MOUSE ISLANDS).

Ammanford 'ford on the River Aman'; the river name derives from Welsh *banw* 'pig' + FORD.

A mining town in Carmarthenshire (formerly in Dyfed), 20 km (12 miles) north of Swansea. It grew up around an inn in the later 19th century. Its Welsh name, **Rhydaman**, was formed by translating the English name. John Cale, the rock musician and member of the Velvet Underground, was born in 1942 at Garnant near Ammanford.

Ampleforth 'ford where dock or sorrel is found', OE *ampre* 'dock, sorrel' + FORD.

A village in North Yorkshire, on the south side of the North York Moors 27 km (17 miles) north of York. In the 19th century, 2 km (1.2 miles) to the east of the village, the Benedictines established a monastery and **Ampleforth College**, a Catholic boys' public school. Cardinal Basil Hume, archbishop of Westminster from 1976 until his death in 1999, was abbot of Ampleforth 1963–76.

Ampney Crucis From *Ampney Brook* local stream name: *Ampney* 'Amma's stream', OE *Amman* possessive form of male personal name *Amma* + EA-; *Crucis* from Latin *crucis* 'of the cross', in allusion to the dedication of the local church to the Holy Rood.

A village (pronounced 'ampny' or 'amny') in Gloucestershire, about 5 km (3 miles) east of Cirencester. Within a radius of a mile or so of Ampney Crucis are the villages of **Ampney St Mary** and **Ampney St Peter** (named for the dedications of their churches).

See also DOWN AMPNEY.

Ampthill 'anthill, hill infested with ants', OE *æmette* 'ant' + *hyll* 'hill'.

A town in Bedfordshire, about 16 km (10 miles) northwest of Luton. The now vanished **Ampthill Castle** was the home of Catherine of Aragon at the time of her divorce from Henry VIII (1533).

The queen was at Ampthill ... having entered on her sad tenancy ... as soon as the place had been evacuated by the gaudy hunting party.

J.A. Froude: *History of England* (1856)

To the north are the ruins of the 17th-century Houghton House, believed to be the original of John Bunyan's 'House Beautiful' in *The Pilgrim's Progress* (1678–84).

An Aird. *See* ARDS PENINSULA[1].

Anale. An ancient name for County LONGFORD.

An Baile Méanach. The Irish name for BALLYMENA.

An Bháinseach. The Irish name for BANSHA

An Bheinn Mhór. The Irish name for FAIR HEAD.

An Bhinn Bhorb. The Irish name for BENBURB.

An Bhlarna. The Irish name for BLARNEY.

An Bhóinn. The Irish name for the River BOYNE.

An Blascaod Mór. The Irish name for Great Blasket Island (*see under* BLASKET ISLANDS).

An Cabhán. The Irish name for CAVAN.

An Caisleán Nua. The Irish name for NEWCASTLE[1].

An Caisleán Riabhach. The Irish name for both CASTLEREA and the local authority CASTLEREAGH[1].

Ancaster 'Roman fort associated with Anna', OE male personal name *Anna* + *ceaster* (*see* CHESTER).

A village in Lincolnshire, about 11 km (7 miles) east of Grantham. During the Roman occupation (when it was known as **Causennae**) it was the last station on ERMINE STREET before LINCOLN. A particular type of limestone, known as **Ancaster stone**, is quarried nearby.

An Cathair. The Irish name for CAHIR.

An Cheathrú Mhór. The Irish name for CARROWMORE.

An Chorr Chríochach. The Irish name for COOKSTOWN.

An Chorrcoill. The Irish name for PROSPEROUS.

An Cionn Bán. The Irish name for WHITEHEAD.

An Claddach. The Irish name for the CLADDAGH.

An Clár. The Irish name for County CLARE.

An Clochán. The Irish name for CLIFDEN.

An Clochán Liath. An alternative Irish name for DUNGLOW.

An Clochar. The Irish name for CLOGHER.

An Cloigeann. The Irish name for CLEGGAN.

An Cnoc. The Irish name for KNOCK.

An Cóbh. The Irish name for COBH.

An Coireán. The Irish name for WATERVILLE.

An Comar. The Irish name for COMBER.

An Creagacha Dubha. An Irish name for the Dublin suburb of BLACKROCK.

Ancrum 'bend in the River Ale', Gaelic *crom* 'bend' + river name *Ale*; the early form *Alnecrumba* points to OCelt sources for the river name and *crom*. The village lies in a bend of the river. A small village in Scottish Borders (formerly in Roxburghshire), about 8 km (5 miles) northwest of Jedburgh. It was the birthplace of Robert Livingston (1654–1728), who went on to found of a wealthy and influential dynasty in New York state.

Battle of Ancrum Moor (27 February 1545). A battle fought a little to the north of Ancrum village, in which a Scots army under Archibald Douglas, 6th Earl of Angus, defeated an English force under Sir Ralph Evers, sent by Henry VIII in pursuit of his desire to marry his son, the future Edward VI, to the infant Mary Queen of Scots – a policy called 'the Rough Wooing'. The site of the battle is also known as Lilliards Edge, supposedly after a young woman who took her slain lover's place in the fight, and was herself killed. She is commemorated on a memorial on the moor thus:

> Fair Maiden Lilliard lies under this stane,
> Little was her stature but muckle was her fame.
> Upon the English loons she laid many thumps
> And when her legs were cuttit off
> She fought upon her stumps.

> (*muckle* 'great', *loons* 'boys')

However, the first written version of the above dates from only 1743, the memorial was built around the same time, and versions of the story of the legless fighting lass are also found in the folklores of various Germanic peoples. It seems likely, therefore, that the heroine acquired her name from the local topography rather than vice versa.

An Currach. The Irish name for the CURRAGH.

An Daingean. The Irish name for DINGLE.

Anderitum. A Roman fort on the site of present-day PEVENSEY.

Andersonstown 'Anderson's town', a name dating from the period of Scottish plantations in Ulster. In Irish it is *Baile Andarsan*, meaning the same.

A working-class Nationalist area of west Belfast, a focus of tension and conflict during the Troubles. It is nicknamed Andytown.

An Dìollaid. The Gaelic name for the SADDLE.

Andover '(place by the) ash-tree waters', OCelt river name *Ann* 'ash-tree stream' (an earlier name for the local River Anton and Pillhill Brook) + *dubras* 'waters' (*see also* DOVER).
A market town in Hampshire, on the River Anton, a tributary of the River TEST, about 19 km (12 miles) northwest of Winchester. It was created a municipal borough in the time of King John, and was important in the medieval wool trade.

Andover has always been situated on important lines of communication. The Roman road known as the PORTWAY passed through here, and coaches en route to Exeter stopped here in the pre-railway era. In the age of steam, Andover had railway stations on both the north–south and east–west lines. Modern Andover expanded considerably after 1961, when a planning agreement with the London County Council nearly doubled the town's population.

There are six towns called Andover in the USA (Maine, New Hampshire, New Jersey, New York, Ohio and South Dakota) and one in Canada (New Brunswick).

Avro Andover. A twin-turbo-prop military transport aircraft, a.k.a. the Avro (post-1963, Hawker-Siddeley) 780, developed from the civilian airliner, the Avro 748, which first flew in 1960. It saw extensive service in the Queen's Flight in the 1960s and 1970s.

An Droichead Nau. The former Irish name for AVOCA.

An Dún. The Irish name for County DOWN.

Andytown. A nickname for ANDERSONSTOWN, Belfast.

An Earagail. The Irish name for ERRIGAL.

An Fheoir. The Irish name for the River NORE.

An Fhiacail. The Irish name for FEACKLE.

Anfield 'sloping ground', ME *hange* 'slope' + *feld* (*see* FIELD). An area of Liverpool on the northern side of the city, which has given its name to the home ground of Liverpool FC (*see under* LIVERPOOL). Anfield stadium was originally the home ground of another celebrated Liverpudlian club, EVERTON, but when Everton left Anfield in 1892 after falling out with their landlord, the latter promptly founded a new club (also initially called Everton) to occupy the ground. This new club soon took the name of Liverpool Assocation Football Club and has remained here ever since. Notable features of the Anfield ground include the KOP, and – on **Anfield Road** – the wrought-iron Shankly Gates dedicated to Bill Shankly, one of Liverpool's most successful postwar managers.

Anfield Iron, the. A nickname bestowed on the Liverpool

footballer Tommy Smith (b.1945). A stalwart of the successful Liverpool sides of the 1960s and 1970s, Smith had the not undeserved reputation of being a footballing 'hard man'.

Angel, the From the *Angel*, a former coaching inn at the southern end of the GREAT NORTH ROAD.

An area in ISLINGTON, North London (N1), centred on the southern end of Islington High Street. The inn from which it takes its name was established in the 17th century, and was the nearest staging post to London on the GREAT NORTH ROAD. It was rebuilt twice in the 19th century, and finally closed around 1960. (In the 21st century there is another pub called 'The Angel' on very nearly the same site.)

The Angel's most salient feature for modern Londoners is the chronic traffic jams that converge on the junction between Islington High Street, Pentonville Road, St John Street and the City Road. Angel Underground station, on the Northern Line (Bank branch), opened in 1901, re-inforcing the name of the area. The Angel is valued at £100 on a Monopoly board (where it is called 'Angel Islington').

Angel of the North, The. *See under* the NORTH[1].

Angel's Peak, the. *See under* the DEVIL'S POINT.

An Gleann Garbh. The Irish name for GLENGARRIFF.

An Gleann Mór. The Irish name for DEVIL'S GLEN.

Anglebury. A fictionalized version of WAREHAM in the novels of Thomas Hardy.

Angler's Retreat Presumably from the name of an inn.

A small, remote hamlet on the shore of New Pool, a little lake among the hills northwest of Plynlimon, in Ceredigion (formerly Cardiganshire, then in Dyfed), 19 km (12 miles) northeast of Aberystwyth.

Anglesey 'Ongull's island', OScand male personal name *Ongull* + *ey* (*see* -AY); the present spelling and pronunciation have been influenced by the name 'Angles' for the English.

A large, low-lying island off the northwest coast of Wales, separated from the mainland by the narrow MENAI STRAIT. It is by far the largest Welsh island. Its Latin name was **Mona**, and its modern Welsh name is **Ynys Môn** ('island of Môn'; the second element is obscure, but perhaps derives from a Celtic word for 'end'). It was once known – when it was covered by trees – by the Welsh name **Yr Ynys Dywell** ('the dark island'), and was also known as **Mam Cymru** ('the mother of Wales'; *see also under* CYMRU), because of its fertility – Daniel Defoe noted that the island 'is very fruit-ful for corn and cattle'.

Anglesey was a county before 1974, with BEAUMARIS as the county town, then with HOLY ISLAND[2] became part of Gwynedd as the Ynys Môn district (with its administrative seat at LLANGEFNI), until becoming a unitary authority as the Isle of Anglesey in 1996.

In ancient times Anglesey was an important centre for the druids, and resisted Roman conquest until AD 78; Tacitus described how on this occasion the natives sought to repel the invaders by 'pouring out frightful curses with their hands raised high to heaven'. The island was subsequently raided by the Irish, Saxons, Vikings and Normans. ABERFFRAW on the southwest coast was the capital of the princes of Gwynedd until Edward I brought the island under English rule at the end of the 13th century.

Anglesey, Henry William Paget, 1st Marquess of (1768–1854). The commander of Wellington's cavalry at Waterloo, where he gave birth to an anecdote:

> *Paget:* By God, sir, I've lost my leg!
> *Wellington:* By God, sir, I believe you have.

For his bravery he was elevated from the earldom of Uxbridge to the marquessate of Anglesey.

Anglesey Abbey Possibly 'island of the Angle' or 'grassy nook island', OE *eg* (*see* -EY, -EA) with *Angle*, a tribal name, or *anger-halh* 'grassy nook' (*see also* HALE, -HALL).

A house and estate in Cambridgeshire, about 10 km (6 miles) northeast of Cambridge. The house was built around 1600 on the site of an Augustinian priory. It has a vast and eclectic collection of furnishings and works of art, assembled by its last private owner, Lord Fairhaven.

Anglezarke Moor 'Anlaf's hill pasture', anglicized OScand male personal name *Olafr* + possessive suffix *-es* + *erg* 'hill pasture' (*see* -ARY).

An area of moorland in Lancashire, some 5 km (3 miles) east of Chorley. Lead and witherite (barium carbonate, used as rat poison and as a coloured glaze for porcelain) used to be mined here, and grouse shot. Among the prehistoric features of the moor are Pike Stones, Devil's Ditch, Round-loaf and Standing Stones Hill; Anglezarke Quarry is popular with rock climbers.

Towerlands Anglezarke. A horse ridden by the showjumper Malcolm Pyrah.

Anglia Latin, from *Anglus* 'Angle', from a prehistoric Germanic base which also produced ModE ENGLAND.

See also EAST ANGLIA.

Anglian. Of or relating to the Angles, or (as a noun) the dialect of Old English spoken by them.

Anglia Television. *See under* EAST ANGLIA.

Ford Anglia. A modest-sized family car produced by Ford at DAGENHAM. It was developed out of the previous Ford Eight in the late 1930s. It appeared in a number of versions over the next thirty years, including, latterly, one with an idiosyncratically backward-slanting rear window (the flying Anglia owned by Ron Weasley's dad in J.K. Rowling's *Harry Potter and the Chamber of Secrets* (1998) was of that model).

By the time the Ford Anglia was withdrawn in 1968, 1,300,000 had been produced Ford also made a simplified version called the Popular, the cheapest car in their range.

Angmering '(settlement of) Angenmær's people', OE male personal name *Angenmær* + *-inga-* (*see* -ING).

A village in West Sussex, about 6 km (4 miles) west of Worthing and 2.5 km (1.5 miles) from the SOUTH COAST.

An Gort. The Irish name for GORT.

Angry Brow A modern name presumably reflecting the potential danger of the sandbank.

An area of sands offshore from Southport, Lancashire.

Angus From a personal name: *Angus* was the son of Fergus, an 8th-century Pictish king.

A former county and current unitary authority in eastern Scotland. The county town was FORFAR (although the main city was Dundee), and the county was once known as **Forfarshire**. Other towns include BRECHIN, KIRRIEMUIR, ARBROATH and CARNOUSTIE. The county of Angus was bounded to the east by the North Sea, to the north by Kincardineshire and Aberdeenshire, to the west by Perthshire, and to the south by the Firth of Tay. The county largely became the district of Angus (within Tayside region) in the reorganization of 1975, and lost Dundee. Angus became a unitary authority in 1996. The Douglas earls of Angus played important parts in Scottish politics in the 16th century.

When Daniel Defoe travelled through Angus he wrote of

> ... the country fruitful and bespangled, as the sky in a clear night with stars of the biggest magnitude, with gentlemen's houses, thick as they can be supposed to stand with pleasure and conveniency.
>
> Daniel Defoe: *A Tour Through the Whole Island of Great Britain* (1724–6)

Angus. Another name for Aberdeen Angus, a breed of hornless black beef cattle.

Angus Glens, the. Four long, beautiful glens that run northwestward into the Grampians from STRATHMORE. They are (from west to east) Glen Isla, Glen Prosen, Glen Clova and Glen Esk.

Angus Herald. Formerly an officer in the Lyon Court (the Scottish Court of Heralds).

Braes of Angus, the. The hillsides marking the southern edge of the Highland Line in Angus, on the northern flank of Strathmore.

Howe of Angus, the. That part of Strathmore in which Forfar is situated.

An Iarmhí. The Irish name for WESTMEATH.

An Life. The Irish name for LIFFEY.

An Líonán. The Irish name for LEENANE.

An Longfort. The Irish name for the town of LONGFORD.

An Lorgain. The Irish name for LURGAN.

An Má. The Irish name for the former MAZE Prison in County Armagh.

An Marchach. The Irish name for HORSE AND JOCKEY.

An Mhainsitir Mhór. The Irish name for MELLIFONT ABBEY.

An Mhí. An Irish name for County MEATH.

An Mhucais. The Irish name for MUCKISH MOUNTAIN.

An Mhuma. The Irish name for MUNSTER.

An Muileann gCearr. The Irish name for MULLINGAR.

An Muileann Iarainn. The Irish name for SWANLINBAR.

An Mullach Mór. The Irish name for MULLAGHMORE.

Annaghdown Irish *Eanach Dhúin* 'marsh of the fort'.

A village on the east shore of LOUGH CORRIB, County Galway, 20 km (12 miles) north of Galway itself. There are the remains of a medieval cathedral, nunnery and priory. St Brendan the Navigator died here in 578.

Annaghdown Tragedy (3 September 1822). On their way by boat down Lough Corrib to a fair in Galway, 19 people were drowned when a sheep put its hoof through the boat's bottom.

> *Má fhaighimse sláinte beidh caint is tráchtadh*
> *Ar an méid a báthadh as Eanach Dhúin*
> (So long as I have health I'll tell the story of the people who drowned at Annaghdown.)
>
> Antaine Ó Raifteirí (*c*.1784–*c*.1835): 'Eanach Dhúin'
> (The poet was celebrated by Yeats as Blind Raftery.)

Annaghmakerrig Irish *eanach* 'marsh' + most likely a surname of the Mac- type.

A house in County Monaghan, 8 km (5 miles) east of Clones. It was the home of the theatre director Sir Tyrone Guthrie and is now a centre for writers and artists, opened by Brian Friel in 1988.

Anna Liffey. A personification of the River LIFFEY.

Anna Livia. A Latinate personification of the River LIFFEY.

Annalong Irish *Áth na Long* 'ford of the ships'.

A small fishing port on the east coast of County Down, 12 km (7.5 miles) south of Newcastle.

Annaly. An ancient name for County LONGFORD.

Annan[1] 'the river' or 'water'. The name is possibly OCelt or pre-Celtic in origin.

A river, about 55 km (34 miles) long, in what was once Dumfriesshire, and is now Dumfries and Galloway. It rises in the DEVIL'S BEEF TUB north of Moffat, flows south through the valley of **Annandale**, and enters the SOLWAY FIRTH at the town of ANNAN[2].

> Annan water's wading deep,
> And my love Annie's wond'rous bonnie;
> And I am laith she should weet her feet,
> Because I love her best of ony.
>
> 'Annan Water' (traditional ballad)

Annan[2]. A royal BURGH (1538) at the mouth of the River ANNAN[1] in Dumfries and Galloway (formerly in Dumfriesshire), about 25 km (16 miles) east southeast of Dumfries. Annan was the site of the defeat of Edward (de) Balliol (son of King John (de) Balliol, and claimant to the throne of Scotland) by Sir Archibald Douglas in 1332. It was the birthplace of Hugh Clapperton (1788–1827), the explorer of West Africa; and Edward Irving (1792–1834), the founder of the Catholic Apostolic Church (the 'Irvingites'). From 1814 to 1816 Thomas Carlyle was a mathematics teacher at Annan Academy, where he met and befriended Irving, who was also a teacher there. In Carlyle's *Sartor Resartus* (1833–4) Annan Academy becomes the 'Hinterschlag Gymnasium', and Carlyle described Annan itself as 'a fine, bright, self-confident little town'. When Daniel Defoe visited in the 1720s he thought the town was 'in a state of irrevocable decay'.

Annandale. The valley of the River ANNAN[1].

Annandale and Eskdale. A district in Dumfries and Galloway region from 1975 until 1996. The administrative seat was at ANNAN[2].

An Nás. The Irish name for NAAS.

Annesley Woodhouse *Annesley* perhaps 'An's glade', OE *Anes* possessive form of the male personal name *An* + -LEY; *Woodhouse* (a 13th-century addition) 'woodland hamlet'.
A village (pronounced 'anzli') in Nottinghamshire, about 10 km (6 miles) northwest of Nottingham.

Annfield Plain A modern name; Annfield might be identical with ANFIELD (and is spelt thus in the earliest reference), but the modern affix *plain* seems to contradict the 'sloping land' meaning of Anfield.
A village in County Durham, 15 km (9 miles) southwest of Newcastle.

An Ómaigh. The Irish name for OMAGH.

An Pasáiste. The Irish name for PASSAGE WEST.

An Pointe. The Irish name for WARRENPOINT.

An Ráth. The Irish name for RÁTH LUIRC.

An Ráth Mhór. The Irish name for RATHMORE.

An Rinn. The Irish name for RINGSEND.

An Ros. The Irish name for both ROSSES POINT and RUSH.

An Sciobairín. The Irish name for SKIBBEREEN.

An Scoil. The Irish name for SKULL.

An Spidéal. The Irish name for SPIDDAL.

An Sráidbhaile. The Irish name for STRADBALLY.

Anster. The alternative local name for the Scottish village of ANSTRUTHER.

An Strath Bán. The Irish name for STRABANE.

Anstruther 'the little stream', Gaelic *an* 'the' + *sruthair* 'rivulet'; the root word *sruth* 'stream, current' can be applied to a sea current.
A village on the south coast of Fife, on the Firth of Forth, some 15 km (9 miles) southeast of St Andrews. It was formerly an important fishing port:

> *Anstraea … ubi nat haddocus in undis,*
> *Codlineusque ingens, & fleucca & sketta pererrant …*
> ('Anstruther, where the haddock swims in the waves,
> And the huge codling, and the fluke and skate wander
>   …')
>
> William Drummond of Hawthornden: '*Polemo-Middinia inter Vitarvan et Nebernam*', translated from the early 17th-century cod Latin by Allan H. MacLaine

It is known as **Anster** to locals (as in William Tennant's poem 'Anster Fair'), and was formerly known in full as **the Royal** BURGH **of Kilrenny, Anstruther Easter and Anstruther Wester** (Kilrenny is just to the northeast of the main village). It was the birthplace of Thomas Chalmers (1780–1847), who led the schism within the Church of Scotland that led in 1843 to the formation of the Free Church of Scotland, of which he was the first moderator.

On a more worldly note, 18th- and early 19th-century Anstruther was the site of the meetings of the Beggar's Benison Club, a gentlemen's club founded in the 1730s by John McNachtane, a minor Highland chief who made a living as a crooked customs officer in the area. Members of the club (including aristocrats, wealthy merchants, and, it has been claimed, the future George IV) drank heavily from phallic drinking-cups (adorned with such toasts as 'May prick nor purse never fail'), and enjoyed an early form of lap-dancing performed by local girls.

> How now? – what's this? – my very eyes, I trow,
>   Drop on my hands their base prosaic scales;
> My visual orbs are purg'd from film, and lo!
>   Instead of *Anster*'s turnip-bearing vales,
> I see old Fairyland's mirac'lous show,
>   Her trees of tinsel kiss'd by freakish gales,
> Her ouphes, that cloak'd in leaf-gold skim the breeze,
> And fairies swarming thick as mites in rotten cheese.
>
> William Tennant: 'Anster Fair' (1812) (*ouphes* 'elves')

An tAonach. The Irish name for NENAGH.

An Teallach 'the anvil', Gaelic *an* 'the' + *teallach* 'anvil, forge, hearth'.

A magnificent mountain (1059 m / 3474 ft) in northwest Highland (formerly in Ross and Cromarty), some 13 km (8 miles) south of ULLAPOOL. It is pronounced 'an tchallach' (with the first 'ch' as in 'cheese', and second as in 'loch'). Its long pinnacled ridge, overlooking mighty precipices on the northern side, comprises a number of summits, the highest of which is Sgùrr Fiona ('white peak', Gaelic *sgùrr* 'peak' + *fionn* 'white', or possibly *fion* 'wine' from its barrel-shaped buttresses). One of the more spectacular pinnacles is Lord Berkeley's Seat, so named from a gentleman who, for a bet, sat on its summit with his legs dangling over the edge into space.

An Teampall Mór. The Irish name for TEMPLEMORE.

Anthrax Island. The nickname for Gruinard Island (*see under* GRUINARD BAY).

An Tiaracht. The Irish name for TEARAGHT ISLAND.

An tInbhear Mór. The Irish name for ARKLOW.

An tIúr. The Irish name for NEWRY.

Antonine Wall, the named after the Emperor *Antoninus* Pius (AD 86–161).
A Roman fortification, also called **Antoninus' Wall**, stretching 58.5 km (36.5 miles) across the Central Belt of Scotland from near Bo'ness on the Firth of Forth to Old Kilpatrick on the Clyde. The wall was built under orders from Lollius Urbicus, governor of Britain, by the II, VI and XX Legions in AD 142 or 143, extending the frontier of the Roman Empire 160 km (99 miles) northwards from HADRIAN'S WALL. The Antonine Wall consisted of a turf barrier built on a stone base, with a ditch on one side and a military road on the other; forts were built along its length every 3 km (2 miles). By the end of the 2nd century the legions had withdrawn back south to Hadrian's Wall. The most visible remains are near Bonnybridge and Falkirk, and the section near Bo'ness is known as **Graham's Dyke**.

Antony 'Anna's or Anta's farmstead', OE male personal name *Anna* or *Anta* + -TON. Later assimilated to the male forename *Anthony*.
A village in eastern Cornwall, about 1.5 km (1 mile) to the west of Torpoint.

An Torc. The Gaelic name for the Boar of Badenoch (*see under* BADENOCH).

An tOspidéal. The Irish name for HOSPITAL.

Antrim Originally OCelt *Oentreb* 'one house', from *aon* 'one, single' + *treabh* 'house', reinterpreted as Irish *Aontroim* 'single ridge' with *droim* 'ridge'.
A market and industrial town in County Antrim, some 20 km (12 miles) northwest of Belfast, where the Six Mile Water enters LOUGH NEAGH. There is a 28-m (92-ft) round tower, all that remains after the 10th-century monastery of Aontreibh (the later spelling of *Oentreb*), after which the

town is named (*see above*). The town was burnt by Scottish Presbyterians in 1643. It gives its name to a local authority district. 'Antrim and BALLYMENA' was a NEW TOWN[1] entity.

Antrim was the birthplace of the evangelist and socialist Alexander Irvine (1862–1941), who remembered his mother and his happy childhood here in *My Lady of the Chimney Corner* (1913). Their poor house in Pogue's Entry is now the Irvine Museum.

Battle of Antrim (7 June 1798). A battle during the Rebellion of 1798 in which a force of United Irishmen (mostly Presbyterians) under the command of Henry Joy McCracken were defeated by British troops. McCracken was later executed in Belfast.

Antrim, County. A county of Northern Ireland, bounded to the south by Down and Armagh, to the west by Tyrone and Londonderry, and to the north and east by the North Channel. The county town is BELFAST, and other towns include ANTRIM, LARNE, CARRICKFERGUS, BALLYMENA and LISMORE[2]. In the northeast are the **Antrim Hills**, rising to 554 m (1817 ft) at Trostan, bisected by the **Antrim Glens**: Glentaisie, Glenshesk, Glendun, Glencorp, Glenaan, Glenballyeamon, Glenariff, Glencloy and Glenarm (*see* the NINE GLENS). These otherwise isolated glens were linked in 1834 with the building of the **Antrim Coast Road**, initially constructed for famine relief and now a popular scenic route with tourists. On the north coast is the GIANT'S CAUSEWAY.

Antrim Glens, the. An alternative name for the NINE GLENS.

An tSeanbhean Bhocht. The Irish name for SHAN VAN VOCHT, a personification of Ireland.

An tSionnainn. The modern Irish name for the River SHANNON.

An tSuca. The Irish name for the River SUCK.

An Tulach. The Irish name for TULLOW.

An Uaimh. The Irish name for NAVAN.

An Urnaí. The Irish name for URNEY.

Anzac-on-Sea From *ANZAC*, acronym from 'Australian and New Zealand Army Corps'.
A former nickname for the East Sussex seaside resort PEACEHAVEN. It alludes to the fact that New Zealand and Australian troops were stationed at the start of the First World War near a site which after the war was to become Peacehaven.

Aonach Beag 'small ridged mountain' Gaelic *aonach* 'ridged mountain' + *beag* 'small'.
The sixth highest mountain in Britain, at 1236 m (4054 ft). It is in Highland (formerly in Inverness-shire), 3 km (2 miles) east of Ben Nevis. Its lower companion to the north is the equally inaccurately named **Aonach Mòr**

('big ridged mountain'), which is a mere 1221 m (4005 ft). It is assumed that the names derived from the fact that Aonach Mòr is closer to the GREAT GLEN, and therefore appears the larger of the two. There is an extensive skiing development (known as Nevis Range) on the northern slopes of Aonach Mòr, first opened in 1990.

Aonach Eagach 'notched ridge', Gaelic *aonach* 'ridged mountain' + *eagach* 'notched'.

As its name suggests, a precipitous notched ridge with many pinnacles, forming what Samuel Taylor Coleridge described as 'a bulgy rifted continuous mountain' (journal, 2 September 1803) along the northern side of GLEN COE in Highland (formerly in Argyll). It is usually pronounced (though not by Gaelic speakers) as 'annoch aiga'. It extends some 4 km (2.5 miles) between Am Bodach ('the old man'; 940 m / 3083 ft) and Sgorr nam Fiannaidh (967 m / 3172 ft). The impressive buttress that Am Bodach flings down towards the road is known (for reasons unknown) as The Chancellor.

Aonach Mòr. *See under* AONACH BEAG.

Apostle's Grove. A punning late 19th- and early 20th-century nickname for ST JOHN'S WOOD.

Apperknowle 'apple-tree knoll', OE *æppel* 'apple(-tree)' + *cnoll* 'knoll'.

A village in north Derbyshire, about 5 km (3 miles) north of Chesterfield.

Appin Gaelic *abthain* 'abbey lands', referring to the old monastery on nearby LISMORE[1].

A mountainous area straddling Argyll and Bute and Highland (formerly in Strathclyde and Highland, and before that entirely in Argyll). It lies to the southwest of GLEN COE, and is bounded on the north by LOCH LEVEN[1], on the west by Loch Linnhe and on the south by Loch Creran. The valley called **Strath of Appin** (*see under* DULL) and the village of **Port Appin** are in the southern part of the area.

Appin Murder, the. The murder of Colin Roy Campbell of Glenure, called 'the Red Fox', in May 1752. He was keeping rule for the government in the Stewart lands of Appin in the wake of the 1745 Jacobite Rising, and was shot by an unknown gunman hiding on the hill above the road between Ballachulish and Duror. James Stewart, known as James of the Glens, was arrested and tried at Inveraray by a Campbell jury and a Campbell judge. He was found guilty and hanged on Gallows Hill at Ballachulish. It is said that the identity of the real killer is known to the Stewarts of Appin, but only one person at a time knows it, and passes this knowledge on to another when they die. The murder is recreated in Robert Louis Stevenson's novel *Kidnapped* (1886), and the hero, David Balfour, is taken for an accomplice and has to flee the scene.

Appin Regiment, the. A Jacobite regiment, the only one to fight at Culloden (*see under* CULLODEN MUIR) and save its colours; all the other regimental flags were burnt by Edinburgh's common hangman. The flag can be seen in Edinburgh Castle.

Appin of Dull. *See under* DULL.

Appleby-in-Westmorland 'apple(-tree) village in WESTMORLAND', OE *æppel* 'apple (tree)' + -BY.

A market town on the River EDEN[1], Cumbria (formerly in Westmorland, of which it was the county town), 33 km (20 miles) northeast of Kendal. The castle dates from Norman times, but was restored by Lady Anne Clifford in the 17th century, who also founded the almshouses that can still be seen. The younger Pitt first entered Parliament in 1781, as MP for Appleby, at the age of 21.

Appleby Horse Fair. A boisterous gathering held every June since 1750 on Gallows Hill, attended by gypsies, tinkers, New Age travellers and other pillars of Middle England.

Applecross 'mouth of the River Crossan', ABER + OCelt river name (meaning 'little cross'). The river here is now called the River Applecross (probably by back-formation). The old Gaelic name for Applecross was *a' Chomraich Abrach* 'the sanctuary (or girth) of the aber', referring to the ancient monastery, the 'girth' of whose lands was apparently marked with stone crosses.

A village in Wester Ross, Highland (formerly in Ross and Cromarty), 18 km (11 miles) north of Kyle of Lochalsh on the west coast of a large mountainous peninsula, also known as Applecross, bounded on the north by Loch Torridon and on the south by Loch Kishorn. Maelrubha (d.722) founded a monastery at Applecross in 673, later destroyed by the Vikings. Until the building of the road around the north tip of the peninsula in the 1970s, the only access to the village was via the high, winding road pass (626 m / 2053 ft) of the BEALACH NA BA.

Appledore[1] '(place at the) apple-tree', OE *apuldor* 'apple-tree'.

A fishing village on the north Devon coast, at the point where the estuaries of the River TAW and the River TORRIDGE[1] meet. Once a shipbuilding centre, it is now a popular sailing resort, and the largest covered dock in Europe, opened nearby in 1970, maintains its maritime tradition.

Appledore[2]. A village in Kent, about 10 km (6 miles) southeast of Tenterden, on the ROYAL MILITARY CANAL.

Appletreewick 'farm by the apple trees', OE *æppel-treow* 'appletree' + WICK.

A village in Wharfedale, North Yorkshire, 6 km (4 miles) north of Bolton Abbey.

Aquae Sulis Latin, 'waters of Sulis' (referring to a pagan goddess).

The Roman name for BATH.

Aran Island Irish *árainn*, dative of *ára* 'loin, kidney', here figuratively suggesting 'ridge, arched back'.

An island off the west coast of Donegal, 70 km (43 miles) west of Derry/Londonderry. It is often called **Aranmore** ('big Aran') to avoid confusion with the ARAN ISLANDS. There was an abbey here in the 6th century, where St Ciaran studied with Abbot St Enda.

Aran Islands Irish *Arainn*; etymology as ARAN ISLAND.

A group of three rocky islands in Galway Bay (*see under* GALWAY), some 40 km (25 miles) from Galway itself. Administratively they are part of County Galway. The islands are INISHMORE (Irish *Inis Mór* 'big island'), Inishmaan (Irish *Inis Meáin* 'middle island') and Inisheer (Irish *Inis Oírr* 'eastern island').

> A dream of limestone in sea-light
> Where gulls have placed their perfect prints.
>
> Derek Mahon: 'Thinking of Inis Oírr in Cambridge, Mass.',
> from *Collected Poems* (1999)

The Aran Islands were settled from the late Bronze Age. In Irish legend it was here that the Firbolgs fled after their defeat at MOYTURA, and it was they who were supposed to have been responsible for DÚN AENGHUS, an Iron Age fort on Inishmore. In the 5th century the first monastery in Ireland was founded here by St Enda. The islands have no native soil, what there is having been built up out of sand and seaweed by the islanders.

In the later 19th century there began a great passion for studying the islanders, because of their use of the Irish language and because of their undiluted traditions and rich oral folklore. The playwright J.M. Synge, encouraged by W.B. Yeats, spent time on Inishmore in 1898, and returned yearly until 1902, learning Irish and absorbing the culture, which he thought of as a last unspoilt relic of a lost civilization. It was these visits (which he wrote about in *The Aran Islands*, 1907) that inspired much of his later work, including *The Riders to the Sea* (1905). In his poem 'Synge on Aran' (1966), Seamus Heaney talks of Synge's pen ...

> the nib filed on a salt wind
> and dipped in the keening sea.

The painter Augustus John visited the islands in 1912, writing:

> The smoke of burning kelp rose from the shores, women and girls in black shawls in red or saffron skirts stood or moved in groups with a kind of nun-like uniformity and decorum. Upon the precipitous Atlantic verge some forgotten people had disputed a last foothold upon the rampart of more than one astonishing fortress.

Today's visitors are sometimes a bit more cynical, as in this observation by Terry Eagleton:

> Rumour has it that the Aran Islands are rolled up when the tourist season ends and towed into Galway, where workmen chip away at the rocks to make them look a bit more rugged.

The writer Liam O'Flaherty (1896–1984) was born on Inishmore, and recalls Aran life in his novel *The Black Soul* (1924). Emily Lawless's novel *Grania* (1892) also concerns life on the islands. The painter Sean Keating (1889–1977) spent half of every year on the islands, painting many portraits of the locals.

aran. Highly patterned knitwear, usually in cream-coloured (originally undyed) wool. In the past, particular patterns were handed down from generation to generation of a particular family on the Aran Islands, and it was said that the body of an otherwise unrecognizable long-drowned fisherman could be identified by his knitwear (such a situation arises in Synge's *Riders to the Sea*, set on Inishmaan).

Man of Aran. A 1934 documentary film by Robert Flaherty portraying the islanders' traditional way of life. In Martin McDonagh's play *The Cripple of Inishmaan* (1997), as Flaherty comes to film on the islands, the eponymous hero, 18-year-old Billy, dreams of escaping to Hollywood.

Aranmore. A name by which ARAN ISLAND is often known.

Arans, the From their principal peaks; *Aran* itself appears to be a river name.

A mountain group in Gwynedd (formerly in Merioneth), some 8 km (5 miles) southwest of BALA Lake. The principal tops are **Aran Fawddwy** or **Aran Mawddwy** (905 m / 2968 ft; *fawddwy* and *mawddwy* are possibly different pronunciations of a regional name deriving from *fawr* or *mawr* 'great') and **Aran Benllyn** (884 m / 2900 ft; *benllyn* is possibly 'lake head').

Aray. *See under* INVERARAY.

Arbeia. A Roman fort on the site of present-day SOUTH SHIELDS.

Arboe. An alternative spelling for the Irish village of ARDBOE.

Arbor Low 'earthwork hill', OE *eorth-burh* 'earthwork' + *hlaw* 'hill, tumulus' (*see* LAW, LOW).

An ancient stone circle in the PEAK DISTRICT of Derbyshire, about 8 km (5 miles) southwest of Bakewell. It dates from around 2000 BC, and consists of 46 recumbent stones within a retaining ditch. It has been called the **Stonehenge of the North**.

Arbroath 'mouth of the Brothock Water', also called

Aberbrothock, Gaelic *Obar Bhrotháig*, from ABER + Gaelic *broth-ach* 'boiling', from *bruth* 'heat'.

A town, fishing port and holiday resort on the North Sea coast of Angus, 26 km (16 miles) northeast of Dundee. (It was in Tayside region from 1975 to 1996.) The once wealthy **Arbroath Abbey** (now a well-preserved ruin) was founded as a priory dedicated to Thomas Becket in 1178 by the Scottish king, William the Lion, and he is buried here. In 1951 the two young Scots nationalists who stole the Stone of Scone (*see under* SCONE) from Westminster Abbey placed it on the high altar of Arbroath Abbey, symbolically remind-ing the world of the **Declaration of Arbroath** (*see below*).

In Sir Walter Scott's novel *The Antiquary* (1816), Arbroath becomes **Fairport**. Arbroath was the birthplace of David Dunbar Buick (1854–1929), the US automobile manufac-turer.

> A two-toothed old man of Arbroath
> Gave vent to a terrible oath.
> > When one tooth chanced to ache
> > By an awful mistake
> The dentists extracted them both.
> > Anon.: limerick

Arbroath smokies. Smoked haddock, a local speciality. In 2004 the Arbroath smokie was granted protected status by the European Commission. The name can be used only to describe haddock smoked in the traditional manner within 8 km (5 miles) of Arbroath.

Declaration of Arbroath. A document signed by the Estates of Scotland meeting in Arbroath in April 1320, by which they declared their loyalty to King Robert the Bruce, and proclaimed Scotland's independence. It is thought to have been drafted by Bernard de Linton, Abbot of Arbroath. The Declaration was delivered to Pope John XXII at Avignon, in an attempt to end Bruce's excommunication, which had followed his murder of the Red Comyn in the church of Greyfriars Monastery in DUMFRIES in 1306. The most famous passage reads (in translation from the original Latin) as follows:

> For so long as but a hundred of us remain alive, we will in no way yield ourselves to the dominion of the English. For it is not for glory, nor riches, nor honour that we fight, but for Freedom only, which no good man lays down but with his life.

O of Arbroath, the. The great rose window of Arbroath Abbey, said in former times to have been lit up to help to guide boats out at sea. Another guide to shipping was the bell placed by order of the abbot on the treach-erous BELL ROCK, 19 km (12 miles) to the southeast of Arbroath.

Archiestown After Sir Archibald Grant, who founded the village *c.*1760. The trend seems to have caught on round here: close by is Robertstown, and nearby ABERLOUR is in full Charlestown of Aberlour.

A village in Moray (formerly in Banffshire, then in Grampian region), 4 km (2.5 miles) west of Aberlour.

Archway From the viaduct that crosses the Great North Road here.

An area of North London, on the GREAT NORTH ROAD, between HIGHGATE to the northwest and HOLLOWAY to the southeast. It was chosen in 1809 as the site of a tunnel to take the Great North Road under Highgate Hill (*see under* HIGHGATE). However, the tunnel collapsed while it was being excavated, leaving a cutting in its stead. A viaduct was needed to carry Hornsey Lane over this, and one was designed by John Nash, in the style of a Roman aqueduct with a single main arch. This was called the **Highgate Archway**, and gave its name to the section of the Great North Road running beneath it: **Archway Road** (opened in 1813). (Nash's viaduct was replaced in 1897 by a cast-iron one, subsequently a favourite launching pad for suicides.) Archway Underground station, on the Northern Line, was opened in 1907, as 'Highgate', and renamed 'Archway' in 1947 (reinforcing the name of the area in general).

See also Hampstead Slopes *under* HAMPSTEAD.

Ardagh Irish *Ardach* 'high field', ARD + ACHADH.

❖ **ard** ❖

This Old Celtic element is a word meaning 'high place', and it can be found throughout Britain and Ireland. It is not common in England, but TOLLARD ROYAL (Wiltshire), and possibly the Warwickshire Forest of Arden (*see under* ARDEN) contain the ele-ment, as well as the Cornish LIZARD.

There are many names in Ireland containing *ard*, but it is not always clear which of the two reflexes, *àrd* 'height' or the variant *aird* 'promontory', is being used: ARMAGH is the 'height of Macha' (*àrd* 'height'), and the ARDS PENINSULA[1] (in County Down) has *aird* 'promontory'. The several examples of Ardagh

(including ARDAGH in County Limerick) mean 'high field'.

The Welsh compound *pennardd* 'high land' is found in the name PENARTH in Glamorgan, and the related Cornish one in Penare (and thus NARE POINT). ARDTORNISH POINT in Mull illustrates the localized development of the element to refer to a piece of high land protruding into the sea, since here it means 'Thorir's promontory'– in fact triply so, with Gaelic *àrd*, Old Scandinavian *nes* (*see* NESS) and English *point* all referring to the same feature: a prominent, protruding landmass.

A village in County Limerick, some 5 km (3 miles) north of Newcastle West.

Ardagh Chalice. An 8th-century chalice found at the ringfort at Ardagh in 1868. It is one of the masterpieces of early Irish religious art, now in the National Museum, and is sometimes used as a symbol of Ireland.

Ard Aidhin. The Irish name for the Dublin suburb of ARTANE.

Ard Bó. The Irish name for ARDBOE.

Ardboe Irish *Ard Bó* 'cow height' or 'cow promontory' (*see* ARD).

A village in County Tyrone, on the western shores of LOUGH NEAGH 15 km (9 miles) east of Cookstown. It is also spelt **Arboe**. There are the remains of an abbey founded by St Colman in 590, near the 10th-century **Ardboe Old Cross**, which towers about 5.5 m (18.5 ft) high on a hillock overlooking Lough Neagh, and is believed to be the first high cross in Ulster. Ardboe was the scene of a reported vision of the Virgin Mary, recalled in Paul Muldoon's poem **'Our Lady of Ardboe'**:

> Just there, in a corner of the whin-field,
> Just where the thistles bloom.
> She stood there as in Bethlehem
> One night in nineteen fifty-three or four.
> The girl leaning over the half-door
> Saw the cattle kneel, and herself knelt.

The village and its surroundings also feature in the stories of Polly Devlin, for example in *The Far Side of the Lough* (1983); she was born here in 1940.

Ardee Irish *Baile Átha Fhirdia* 'town of Ferdia's ford' (*see* FORD). The name refers to the legendary Battle of the Ford, Cuchulain's last battle, said to have taken place here; Ferdia was his opponent in single combat.

A market town in County Louth, 20 km (12 miles) northwest of Drogheda. During his unsuccessful Irish campaign, James II had his headquarters at Ardee.

Arden Perhaps from an OCelt name meaning 'high district'.

A large medieval forest in the West Midlands, originally (according to Michael Drayton's *Poly-Olbion* (1612–22)) extending from the Severn to the Trent, but later restricted to northern WARWICKSHIRE. It no longer exists, but its name survives in the Warwickshire market town of HENLEY-IN-ARDEN.

> The forest often features in romantic literature …

> Where nightingales in Arden sit and sing
> Amongst the dainty dew-impearled flowers

> Michael Drayton: Sonnet 53 (1603)

… and is famous as the setting of Shakespeare's *As You Like It* (1599). Strictly speaking the forest in the play was based on the forest of the Ardennes, in what is now Belgium, but Shakespeare no doubt had his own local Warwickshire forest in mind too. So it is in the **Forest of Arden** that we can visualize Amiens singing:

> Under the greenwood tree
> Who loves to lie with me,
> And turn his merry note
> Unto the sweet bird's throat,
> Come hither.

> *As You Like It* (1599), II.v

Shakespeare's close association with the forest, and the fact that his mother's maiden name was Arden, contributed to the naming of the **'Arden Shakespeare'**, a series of scholarly editions of the plays initiated in 1899 and revised from 1951 onwards.

The original members of the Free Foresters, a noted amateur cricket club, came from the Forest of Arden, and played their first match in 1856 in Rectory Park in nearby SUTTON COLDFIELD.

The American cosmetician **Elizabeth Arden** (1881–1966) was originally called Florence Nightingale Graham. It has been speculated that she took her new name from 'Arden', the name of the vast estate in the Catskills owned by the railroad magnate E.H. Harriman, which in turn may have been inspired by the Shakespearean Arden (an alternative theory is that she was a great fan of Alfred, Lord Tennyson's narrative poem *Enoch Arden* (1864)). There are towns called Arden in the USA (Nevada, North Carolina) and Canada (Manitoba, Ontario).

Forest of Arden. A golf course near MERIDEN in the West Midlands. The British Masters and the English Open are held here.

Arden Hills. *See under* EISCIR RIADA.

Ardfert Irish *Ard Fhearta*, 'height of the grave' (*see* ARD).

A village in County Kerry, 8 km (5 miles) northwest of Tralee. St Brendan the Navigator founded a monastery here in the 6th century, and in the 12th century it became the see of a diocese. There are a number of religious buildings, including a partly restored 12th-century cathedral and the remains of a Romanesque church. Nearby, at McKenna's Fort, Sir Roger Casement was arrested on Good Friday, 1916, having landed at BANNA STRAND.

Ard Fhearta. The Irish name for ARDFERT.

Ardgour Probably 'height of the goat', Gaelic ARD + *obhar* 'goat'.

A mountainous area of the western Highlands, formerly in Argyll and now in Highland. It is bounded on the east by Loch Linnhe (across which it may be accessed via the Corran ferry) and on the west by LOCH SHIEL. To the west lie the areas of SUNART and ARDNAMURCHAN.

Ardingly 'Earda's people's glade', OE male personal name *Earda* + *inga-* (*see* -ING) + -LEY.

A straggling village (pronounced 'arding-lie') in West Sussex, about 4 km (2.5 miles) north of Haywards Heath. It is the permanent home of the South of England Agricultural Show. The local co-educational public school **Ardingly College** was founded in 1858. A little to the north is Wakehurst Place, built by the Culpeper family and dating from 1590. It has extensive woodland and gardens and is managed by the Royal Botanic Gardens.

Árd Macha. The Irish name for the town of ARMAGH.

Ardmeanach. The Gaelic name for the WILDERNESS peninsula.

Ard Mhic Nasca. The Irish name for HOLYWOOD.

Ardmore Irish *Aird Mhór* 'great headland'.

A seaside resort in County Waterford, 10 km (6 miles) east of Youghal, overlooking **Ardmore Bay**. The obscure St Declan is said to have founded a monastery here before the arrival of St Patrick, and his burial place is traditionally at Ardmore. The remains of the 12th-century cathedral include a 29-m (95-ft) high round tower. In 1642 an Irish force took refuge here from the English, and 117 of them were hanged after they surrendered. On 24 May 1954 Ardmore became the first village to benefit from Ireland's rural electrification scheme.

There is a town called Ardmore in the USA (Oklahoma).

Ard na Croise. The Irish name for ARDNACRUSHA.

Ardnacrusha Irish *Ard na Croise* 'height of the cross' (*see* ARD).

The site of a vast hydroelectric plant built on the River SHANNON just north of Limerick in 1925–9. It was the Free State's first major power project, and there was some controversy over its construction by a German firm, Siemens. It was unfairly dubbed, by an anonymous commentator, **Mr McGilligan's White Elephant**, after Patrick McGilligan, Minister for Industry and Commerce (1924–32).

Ardnamurchan Possibly 'promontory of piracy', Gaelic ARD + *muir-* 'sea' + *col* 'sin, wickedness'. This may relate to the story that St Columba, while in Ardnamurchan, prayed that a gang who had robbed one of his companions and escaped in a boat be drowned (the prayer was duly answered). Alternatively, the last two elements may be from *muirchú* 'sea-hounds', i.e. sea otters.

An area of the western Highlands, formerly in Argyll and now in Highland. It comprises a peninsula extending into the Atlantic, west of Sunart and Moidart. **Ardnamurchan Point** at the western tip is the most westerly point in Great Britain. The lighthouse was built in 1849.

Ardnaree Irish *Ard na Ria* 'height of the executions' (*see* ARD),

referring to four brothers supposedly hanged here for the murder of the Bishop of Kilmoremoy.

The name given to that part of BALLINA, County Mayo, on the east side of the River Moy.

Battle of Ardnaree (23 September 1586). A battle in which Sir Richard Bingham, governor of Mayo, defeated a force of redshanks (Scottish mercenaries) brought over by the Burkes of Mayo.

Ard na Ria. The Irish name for ARDNAREE.

Ardoyne 'Eoghan's height or promontory', Irish ARD + a frequently-occurring historical and mythological personal name *Eoghan*, possibly here referring to one of the sons of Niall of the Nine Hostages (as in INISHOWEN).

A Nationalist and Republican area of north Belfast, scene of many confrontations during the Troubles. The first violence here was at Bombay Street, when on 14–15 August 1969 Protestants fired many Catholic homes. When the British Army intervened on the 16th, they were welcomed by Nationalists. The welcome did not last.

Ardrossan 'promontory of the little peninsula', Gaelic ARD + *ros* 'peninsula, cape' + *-an* 'small'.

A coastal town in North Ayrshire (formerly in Strathclyde region), 12 km (7.5 miles) northwest of Irvine. It is a holiday resort, and there is regular ferry service to ARRAN.

Ards Peninsula¹ Irish *An Aird* 'the peninsula' (*see* ARD), with the addition of English *-s*.

A 30-km (19-mile) long peninsula on the east side of STRANGFORD Lough, County Down, separating it from the sea. NEWTOWNARDS is at its northern end. It forms the most easterly part of Ireland, the most eastern point being BURR POINT. It also gives its name to a local authority district.

Ards Peninsula². A peninsula on the north coast of Donegal, between SHEEP HAVEN and Tory Sound (*see under* TORY ISLAND). At its tip is HORN HEAD.

Ardtornish Point 'point of Thorir's point point', Gaelic ARD + *Thoris* possessive of OScand male personal name *Thorir* + OScand *nes* 'promontory' + ModE *point*.

A highly tautological feature on the east coast of Mull, next to FISHNISH. The opening scenes of Sir Walter Scott's poem *The Lord of the Isles* (1815) take place at **Ardtornish Castle**, the ruined remains of which can still be seen.

Treaty of Westminster–Ardtornish (1462). An agreement between Edward IV of England and John Macdonald, Lord of the Isles, his son Donald and James, Earl of Douglas, whereby the boy-king James III was to be overthrown in an English invasion and the Scottish signatories were to divide all of Scotland north of the FORTH between them. The Lord of the Isles (*see under* ISLES, LORDSHIP OF THE) signed the treaty at his castle at Ardtornish, and Edward ratified the treaty at WESTMINSTER on 17 March. Nothing came of the treaty, and by 1493 the power of the

Macdonald Lords of the Isles had been destroyed. The treaty is sometimes known simply as the **Treaty of Westminster** or the **Treaty of London**.

Ardudwy 'region belonging to the Ardud tribe'.

A traditional area of northwest Wales, between the sea and the RHINOGS north of Barmouth on the coast of Gwynedd (formerly in Merioneth). The name is preserved in that of the village of **Dyffryn Ardudwy** 7 km (4.5 miles) north of Barmouth. The medieval Welsh bishop and historian Giraldus Cambrensis (Gerald of Wales) described the area as 'the rudest and roughest of all the Welsh districts'.

Men of Ardudwy, the. In an old folk tale, the men of Ardudwy, finding no suitable women to marry in the neighbourhood, ventured to the Vale of Clwyd and carried off a number of maidens. Infuriated, the men of the Vale of Clwyd followed them and attacked the men of Ardudwy by a lake in the hills near Ffestiniog. The Clwyd maidens had come to love their captors, and when they saw them slaughtered they were so distressed that they cast themselves into the lake, ever after known as Llyn y Morwynion (Welsh, 'lake of the maidens').

Ardverikie Probably 'height of the banner', Gaelic ARD + *mheirghe* 'flag, banner, standard'.

The mountainous area on the south side of LOCH LAGGAN, in Highland (formerly in Inverness-shire), some 25 km (15 miles) southwest of Newtonmore. **Ardverikie House**, set among plantings of exotic conifers on the shore of the loch, was built in the Scottish Baronial style in 1840 by the Marquess of Abercorn. Queen Victoria considered buying the place, but, having spent a very wet holiday there, plumped for BALMORAL instead. The house appears as 'Strathbogle House' in BBC television's drama series *Monarch of the Glen* (2000–), in which the sky is always blue and never a midge is seen. On Binnean Shuas, the craggy mountain southwest of the house, is to be found **Arverikie Wall**, one of the finest rock climbs in Scotland, pioneered by Doug Lang and Graham Hunter in 1967.

Ardvreck Castle Probably 'speckled promontory', Gaelic ARD + *breac* 'speckled'.

A ruined 16th-century castle on a promontory in Loch Assynt (*see under* ASSYNT), Highland (formerly in Sutherland), 32 km (20 miles) north of Ullapool. It was here that Macleod of Assynt held the Marquess of Montrose after his defeat at CARBISDALE in 1650, before handing him over to the authorities for execution.

Areley Kings *Areley* 'wood or glade frequented by eagles', OE *earn* 'eagle' + -LEY; *Kings* because it was part of a royal manor.

A hamlet in Worcestershire (before 1998 in Hereford and Worcester, before 1974 in Worcestershire), about 6 km (4 miles) southwest of Kidderminster.

Arennig Fawr *fawr* 'great', Welsh; *Arennig* is obscure.

A mountain (854 m / 2801 ft) in Gwynedd (formerly in Merioneth), some 8 km (5 miles) northwest of BALA Lake. The group of which it is the highest peak is sometimes called **the Arennigs**; one of the other peaks is called **Arennig Fach** (*fach* 'small', 689 m / 2260 ft). In 1943 a US B-17 Flying Fortress crashed into Arennig Fawr, a tragedy commemorated on a tablet at the summit.

Arennig or **Arennigian series.** In geology, one of the six series into which the Ordovician system is divided in Britain. It is dated at 488 to 478 million years ago.

Arfon *ar Fôn* 'facing Môn (ANGLESEY)', Welsh.

A traditional area of northwest Wales, bordering the MENAI STRAIT, and including the towns of CAERNARFON ('fort in Arfon') and BANGOR[1], and part of SNOWDONIA. From 1974 to 1996 Arfon was a local authority district within the county of Gwynedd.

Argyll 'land, country of the Gaels', OCelt *airer* 'country' + *Gaidheal* 'Gaels' (referring to the Scots immigrants from Ireland); *Arregaithel c.*970. In modern Gaelic it is *Earraghaidheal*.

A former county of western Scotland, bounded on the east by Dunbartonshire and Perthshire, and on the north by Inverness-shire. It included much of the southwestern and western HIGHLANDS, from the ARDNAMURCHAN Peninsula in the northwest to the MULL OF KINTYRE in the south. It also included many of the Inner HEBRIDES – COLL, TIREE, MULL, Colonsay (*see under* COLONSAY AND ORONSAY), JURA and ISLAY. The county town was INVERARAY. **Argyllshire** is an alternative form of the name, although the suffix is otiose, there being no town called Argyll. The name 'Argyll' is still much in use as a geographical designation, and so indented is its shoreline that it is said to have a greater length of coast than France.

Argyll was the first area settled by the Scots, who began to arrive from Ireland possibly as early as the 3rd century AD. They called the area DALRIADA. It was from here that from the 6th century Christianity began to spread across Scotland. Argyll was later ruled by the Norsemen, then the Norse-Celtic Lords of the Isles (*see under* ISLES, LORDSHIP OF THE), and did not come under the Scottish Crown until 1266. The MacDonald Lords of the Isles maintained a semi-independence until they lost their lands in 1493. From the 16th century the Campbells came to dominate the area, their chiefs becoming earls then dukes of Argyll (formerly spelt Argyle); in the 17th and 18th centuries they were leaders of the Presbyterian, anti-Jacobite faction in Scotland (and in the 20th century **Duke of Argylls** became Glaswegian rhyming slang for 'piles', i.e. haemorrhoids). Robert

Burns ventured briefly into their territory, and wrote to a friend from Loch Long:

> I write you this on my tour through a country where *savage* streams tumble over *savage* mountains, thinly overspread with *savage* flocks, which starvingly support the *savage* inhabitants.
>
> Robert Burns: letter to Robert Ainslie (28 June 1787)

The county of Argyll was abolished in 1975, its territory being divided between Strathclyde and Highland regions.

Argyll and Sutherland Highlanders (Princess Louise's), the. A regiment formed in 1881 by the merger of the Argyllshire Highlanders (raised in 1794) and the Sutherland Highlanders (*see under* SUTHERLAND). Their nickname is **the Argylls**.

Argyll Forest Park. A large area of mountains and Forestry Commission plantations on the COWAL peninsula between Loch Fyne and Loch Long.

Argyll's Bowling Green. A remote and rugged – indeed nubbly – peninsula between Loch Goil and Loch Long. Given the topography, the name (coined in the early 19th century) is patently jocular.

Duchess of Argyll, Margaret (1912–93). A noted society beauty and adultress, best remembered as the fellatrix of the mysterious 'Headless Man' (so called because the evidence was captured on an early Polaroid camera, but only torso and waist, and produced in court (1963) by the Duke's divorce lawyers). The Duchess kept her secret; but the recipient of her favours turned out to be neither Duncan Sandys (Defence Minister at the time) nor the Earl of Merioneth (*see under* MERIONETH), but most probably US actor Douglas Fairbanks Jr, a revelation that disappointed many.

'God bless the Duke of Argyle!' In the 19th century, a remark made on observing one's companion shrug their shoulders; the insinuation is that they have lice (from a row of iron posts erected in Glasgow by the contemporary Duke: grateful lice-ridden citizens were able to use them as scratching-posts; another version suggests that the posts were erected around the Duke's various estates, primarily for the benefit of sheep, but adopted by verminous shepherds).

Argyll and Bute. A former district of Strathclyde region, formed in 1975. With some boundary adjustments it became a unitary authority in 1996. It includes much of the former county of Argyll, including all the islands, apart from the northern part of the mainland area. The district also included the islands of Arran and Bute (both formerly in the old county of Buteshire), although in the 1996 reorganization Arran went to North Ayrshire. LOCHGILPHEAD is the administrative seat.

Arisaig 'bay of Aros', OScand *vik* 'bay, inlet', Gaelicized as *-aig* 'bay' + personal name *Aros*; an alternative possibility, perhaps more linguistically consistent, is that the name is 'river-mouth bay', OScand *a* in the possessive form *ar* 'of the river' + *os* 'mouth' + *vik*. The actual bay now has the Gaelic name Loch nan Ceall.

A village in the western Highlands, formerly in Inverness-shire and now in Highland, 10 km (6 miles) south of Mallaig, looking out towards the islands of EIGG and RUM. The name Arisaig is also applied to the surrounding area, one of the supposed birthplaces of the ancient Gaelic bard Ossian (*fl.*3rd century AD). It was at Loch nan Uamh, on the south shore of Arisaig, that Bonnie Prince Charlie arrived on the mainland of Scotland on 25 July 1745, and departed again on 20 September 1746 following the defeat of the Jacobite Rebellion. During the Second World War the Special Operations Executive (SOE) conducted much of its training in the Arisaig area, some of the participants using up spare energy and explosives in poaching salmon from the local rivers. The sandy shore and the views from Arisaig feature much in Bill Forsyth's film *Local Hero* (1983), although the village used was PENNAN, on the northeast coast. The **Sound of Arisaig** is the large sea inlet between Arisaig and MOIDART to the south.

Arkaig Possibly 'little place of difficulty', Gaelic *aerc* 'a difficulty', in the diminutive form *aircéag*; perhaps a reference to the steep slopes of the loch shore.

An area of the western HIGHLANDS, formerly in Inverness-shire, now in Highland, some 16 km (10 miles) northwest of Fort William. It takes its name from the short **River Arkaig**, which links the long **Loch Arkaig** to Loch Lochy. A large amount of Jacobite gold is supposedly buried somewhere in Arkaig (or is at the bottom of the loch); this comprised a hoard of louis coins, plus muskets, musket balls, powder – and brandy. It was sent by the French in a last vain effort to help the Young Pretender after his defeat at CULLODEN MUIR in 1746.

Arkengarthdale 'valley of Arkil's enclosure', OScand personal name *Arkil* + *garthr* 'enclosure' + *dalr* 'valley'; Arkle Beck is a back-formation with OScand *bekkr* 'stream'.

The valley of the **Arkle Beck**, North Yorkshire, which joins the River SWALE[1] 14 km (8.5 miles) west of Richmond. The area is also known as **The Disputes**, from some disputed lead-mining rights in the past. The largest village is LANGTHWAITE.

Arkenholme. An alternative spelling for ARKINHOLM.

Arkinholm Possibly 'raised land of a man called Arnkell', OScand personal name *Arnkell* + *holmr* 'raised land, promontory' (*see* -EY, -EA).

A battle site, also spelt **Arkenholme**, in Dumfries and Galloway (formerly in Dumfriesshire), near Langholm.

Here in 1455 the Black Douglases were finally defeated by James II, marking the beginning of an era of peace for the Scottish Crown.

Arkle Possibly 'ark mountain', OScand *ork* 'chest, ark' + *fjall* 'mountain'; alternatively, the first element may be OScand *orc* 'whale'.

A rocky mountain (787 m / 2581 ft) in the far northwest of Highland (formerly in Sutherland), some 30 km (19 miles) south of Cape Wrath. Like its neighbouring mountain FOINAVEN, it gave its name to a successful race-horse of the 1960s, owned by the Duchess of Westminster (*see also* CHELTENHAM). This in turn provided the nickname of the Nottinghamshire cricketer Derek Randall (b.1951), noted as a fielder for his turn of speed in pursuit of a ball.

Arklow 'Arnkel's meadow', OScand male personal name + *lo* 'meadow'.

A port and resort on the east coast of County Wicklow, 60 km (37 miles) south of Dublin. It is at the mouth of the River AVOCA, which gives it its Irish name **An tInbhear Mór** ('the big estuary'). There is a tradition that St Patrick landed here; it is also said that St Palladius arrived here in 431. Arklow was seized by Oliver Cromwell in 1649.

Battle of Arklow (9 June 1798). A fierce conflict between the British Army and the Wexford insurgents led by Father Murphy. The latter failed to link forces with the United Irishmen.

Arkwright Town From the descendants of the cotton manufacturer Sir Richard *Arkwright* (1732–92), who bought the manor of Sutton here in 1824. Arkwright invented a spinning machine which replaced spinning by hand.

A village in Derbyshire, about 5 km (3 miles) east of Chesterfield.

Arlington. *See* BIBURY.

Armadale[1] 'long valley', OScand *armr* 'arm, wing' (presumably referring to one of the little peninsulas here) + *dalr* 'valley'.

The seat of the Macdonalds of Sleat in southern SKYE, formerly in Inverness-shire, now in Highland, 19 km (12 miles) south of Broadford. The present **Armadale Castle** was completed in 1819. There is a car ferry from Armadale to Mallaig on the mainland.

Armadale[2] From Lord *Armadale*, who founded the town in the 19th century, and who took his title from ARMADALE[1].

An industrial town and former BURGH in West Lothian, 5 km (3 miles) west of Bathgate.

Armagh Irish *Árd Macha* 'height of Macha'; Macha is said to be Macha Mong Ruadh (Queen Macha of the Red Locks), who traditionally founded the city in *c*.370 BC.

A cathedral city and the county town of County Armagh,

55 km (34 miles) southwest of Belfast. It is also the administrative headquarters of Armagh district. The hillfort of Árd Macha was already important by the 4th century, and Armagh has been the religious centre of Ireland since the 5th century, when St Patrick became Archbishop of Armagh and established it as a noted seat of learning.

> I also found in Armagh, the splendid,
> Meekness, wisdom, and prudence blended,
> Fasting, as Christ hath recommended,
> And noble councillors untranscended.
>
>> Anon.: 'Aldfrid's Itinerary through Ireland' (12th century), translated by James Clarence Mangan (The poem was formerly attributed to Aldfrid or Aldfrith, a late 7th-century Northumbrian king. Aldfrid was educated in Ireland, where he was known as Flann Fionn.)

Armagh was the seat of the kings of Ulster for 700 years, and is now the seat of both the Roman Catholic and Protestant primates of Ireland, each of whom bears the title 'Archbishop of Armagh and Primate of All Ireland'. Both **Armagh Cathedrals** are dedicated to St Patrick and date from the 19th century; the Anglican one is on the site of his original church. As Sam Hanna Bell observed in a 1960 radio broadcast:

> Armagh, where two cathedrals sit upon opposing hills like the horns of a dilemma.

One of the more famous Anglican archbishops (1625–56) was James Ussher, who calculated that the world had been created in 4004 BC (he was out by a factor of more than a million). Armagh was the birthplace of St Malachy (1094–1148), who became Archbishop of Armagh and was prominent in the reform of the church in Ireland; the actor Patrick Magee (1922–82); and the Rev. Ian Paisley (b.1926), the militant adversary of the papist Anti-Christ. Another saintly Archbishop of Armagh was St Oliver Plunkett (1629–81).

Armagh Registers. Seven volumes of documents pertaining to the doings of the archbishops of Armagh from the mid-14th to the mid-16th centuries. They are an important source for historians of the period.

Bard of Armagh. In the anonymous ballad, this is 'Bold Phelim Brady':

> It was long before the shamrock our green isle's loved emblem
> Was crushed in its beauty 'neath the Saxon lion's paw
> I was called by the colleens of the village and valley
> Bold Phelim Brady, the Bard of Armagh.

Book of Armagh. A 9th-century Latin manuscript (Latin *Liber Armachus*) compiled by Ferdomhnach at the behest of Abbot Torbach. It includes the *Confessio* of St Patrick and lives of several other saints. The manuscript is in Trinity College Dublin.

Armagh, County. A county of Northern Ireland, bounded on the east by Down, on the south by Louth, on the southwest by Monaghan, on the northwest by Tyrone and on the north by Lough Neagh. The county town is ARMAGH, and other towns include LURGAN and PORTADOWN. It is called **the Orchard of Ireland**, apples traditionally having been grown here since 3000 BC (and St Patrick himself is said to have planted an apple tree near Armagh city). The southern part of the county was known as BANDIT COUNTRY to the British during the Troubles.

Armagh Outrages. An organized Protestant campaign of attacks on Catholics in Armagh and surrounding counties in 1795–6, resulting in the forced departure of some 7000 Catholics to Connacht.

Armagh spade. The same as a Lurgan spade (*see under* LURGAN).

'Boys from the County Armagh, The'. The anthem of Armagh's Gaelic football team, which asserts 'There's only one fair county in Ireland'. The song was given a particularly moving rendition by the team after they had won the All-Ireland championship (for the first time ever) in 2002. The anthem ends:

> Sure my heart is at home in old Ireland,
> In the county of Armagh.

Armitage '(place at the) hermitage' (presumably referring to a former hermitage or oratory here), ME *ermitage* 'hermitage'.
A village in Staffordshire, about 3 km (2 miles) southeast of Rugeley. The pottery founded here in 1817 is the source of Armitage sanitary-ware (the firm merged with Shanks Holding Ltd in 1969 to form the Armitage Shanks Group Ltd).

Armthorpe 'Arnulfr's outlying farm', OScand male personal name *Arnulfr* + THORPE; *Ernulfestorp* 1086.
A village in South Yorkshire, 6 km (4 miles) northeast of Doncaster.

Arncliffe 'eagles' cliff', OE *earn* 'eagle' + *clif* 'cliff'.
A village in Littondale, in the YORKSHIRE DALES, 20 km (12 miles) northwest of Skipton. It was the village of Beckingdale, later Emmerdale, in the television soap *Emmerdale Farm* from 1972 to 1989. Britain's second-longest running soap has been known simply as *Emmerdale* from 1989 onwards.

Arndale Centre *Arndale* after *Arn*old Hagenbach and Samuel Chippin*dale*.
The shopping malls so named arose from the business set up in Bradford in 1931 by Samuel Chippindale (1909–90), an estate agent specializing in shops. This grew into the Arndale Property Trust, taking its name from a blend of Chippindale's own name and the first name of his partner, Arnold Hagenbach. The first Arndale Centre opened in Leeds in 1967, its architecture based on a US design.

The bulldozing of various town centres to make way for the malls horrified many, although the later buildings regained some of the panache of Victorian glass and wrought-iron shopping arcades. Manchester's Arndale Centre, derisively dubbed 'the longest lavatory in Europe' for its expanses of yellow tiling, was destroyed in 1996 by an IRA bomb, which devastated the city centre, but it was revamped and reopened in 1999.

Arnold 'nook of land frequented by eagles', OE *earn* 'eagle' + *halh* (*see* HALE, -HALL).
A town in Nottinghamshire, now effectively a northeastern suburb of NOTTINGHAM[1], at the southern edge of SHERWOOD FOREST.

Arra Mountains Irish *Sliabh Ára* 'mountain of the district of Ára', the name of the river here.
A small range of hills in County TIPPERARY, some 30 km (19 miles) northeast of Limerick. The highest point is Tountinna (460 m / 1509 ft). There is an old legend that Cesair, great-granddaughter of Noah, along with three men and fifty women, came to uninhabited and therefore sinless Ireland to escape the Flood. However, the Flood knew no bounds, and all the women and two of the men were drowned; Fintan, the only survivor, saved himself by climbing up to the top of Tountinna. The hill also features in a later story concerning the wife of Brian Boru, the 11th-century high king. She promised her daughter in marriage to the king of Leinster and so lured him to Tountinna, where he was killed in an ambush. Her furious husband beat her so badly that she ran off to join her Viking enemies.

Arran Possibly related to the ARAN ISLANDS, but the etymology is unknown.
A large island in the Firth of Clyde, in North Ayrshire (formerly in Buteshire, and then in Argyll and Bute district of Strathclyde). At its closest, it is about 16 km (10 miles) from the mainland of Ayrshire. Some regard it as the most southerly of the Inner HEBRIDES, although it is separated from the other islands by the long peninsula of KINTYRE.

The contrast between the mountainous north and the gentler south of the island, and the great variety of scenery, has led to Arran being called **Scotland in Miniature**. The profile of the island when seen from the Ayrshire mainland – what John Keats described as 'the Mountains of Annan [sic] Isle, black and huge over the Sea' (Letter to J.H. Reynolds, 11 July 1818) – has inspired another name, namely **the Sleeping Warrior**, for the fancied resemblance to a knight recumbent on his tomb.

The high jagged hills in the north of the island are formed from a rough granite. The highest peak is GOAT FELL (rising above the main town, BRODICK), while the beautiful CÌR MHÒR dominates the heads of both GLEN ROSA and GLEN SANNOX. Off the east coast is HOLY ISLAND[3], while on the west coast are King's Caves, where Fingal, head of the Fenians in Irish legend, and later Robert the Bruce are supposed to have hidden, the latter being here inspired by the spider (although most authorities believe that RATHLIN ISLAND has a better claim to the latter story). The island came into the possession of the Hamilton family in 1503, who were made earls of Arran. Daniel Macmillan (1813–57), who with his brother Alexander founded the publishing firm of Macmillan, was born on the island.

> Arran of the many stags,
> The sea strikes against her shoulder
> Island where great companies are fed
> And blue spears reddened. …
>
> O, Arran! is delightful at all times.
>
> Anon.: 'Arann' (12th century), from the Ossianic Cycle, based on translations by Standish Haye O'Grady and Kuno Meyer

Arran cheese. A kind of modified DUNLOP cheese.

Arran Chief, Arran Pilot, Arran Banner, Arran Rose. Varieties of seed potato developed on the island by Donald 'Tattie' McKelvie MBE in the early 20th century.

Cock of Arran, the. The most northerly point on Arran, deriving its name from the fact that the hillside here once apparently resembled a crowing cock, but erosion has since altered its appearance. In the early 19th century it was the site of some important geological discoveries regarding stratification and folding.

Arrochar From Latin *aratrum*, an ancient land measure (equivalent to one carucate, or something over 40 ha / 100 acres).
A village at the head of LOCH LONG, about 50 km (31 miles) northwest of Glasgow, in Argyll and Bute (formerly in Strathclyde region). It is on the Glasgow–Fort William railway line.
See also TARBERT.

Arrochar Alps, the. The jagged peaks above Arrochar, including the COBBLER, Beinn Ime and Beinn Narnain. The term was coined by the working-class rock climbers from Clydeside who made this area their playground in the 1930s.

> With hobnail on Ben Narnain
> Or mind on the word's crest
> I'll walk the kyleside shingle
> With scarcely a hark back
> To the step dying from my heel
> Or the creak of the rucksack.
>
> W.S. Graham: 'Since all my steps taken', from *The White Threshold* (1949)

Arrow[1] An OCelt river name, meaning 'stream'.
A river in Warwickshire. It rises to the south of BIRMINGHAM, and flows 18 km (11 miles) southwards, through REDDITCH, to join the River AVON[1] near BIDFORD-ON-AVON.

Arrow[2]. A river in Wales and England, which rises in POWYS and flows 40 km (25 miles) eastwards to join the River LUGG just to the south of LEOMINSTER in Herefordshire.

Arrow[3] From the River ARROW[1], which flows just to the east of the village.
A village in Warwickshire, about 13 km (8 miles) west of Stratford-upon-Avon.

Arsenal From Woolwich *Arsenal*.
A North London football club that plays its home games at **Highbury Stadium** (*see under* HIGHBURY). Nicknamed the Gunners, Arsenal are one of the great club sides of English football, having won the League title on 12 occasions and the FA Cup/League championship 'double' three times. Arsenal dominated English football in the 1930s and 1940s, under the legendary manager Herbert Chapman. Thereafter it went into something of an eclipse (overshadowed by its great North London rival Spurs – *see* TOTTENHAM), but in the 1970s it re-emerged as one of the leading English clubs, which it has remained ever since. Highbury Stadium is a fine Art Deco building. In 2004 a new stadium was under construction, dubbed the 'Emirates Stadium' following a sponsorship deal with the airline.

The club dates back to 1886, when a group of workers at the Woolwich Arsenal Armament Factory (*see under* WOOLWICH) decided to form a football team which they named Dial Square, from the name of one of the workshops at Woolwich Arsenal. The club played as **Royal Arsenal** until 1891 when it turned professional and became **Woolwich Arsenal**. Financial problems forced the club to make a fresh start from a new home in North London in 1913, and the following year Woolwich Arsenal became simply **The Arsenal**. The definite article was dropped in 1927, but is still sometimes used nostalgically by football commentators and club aficionados.

Arsenal Underground station, on the Piccadilly line, opened in 1906 as Gillespie Road. In 1932 it was renamed Arsenal (Highbury Hill) – the name change was proposed to London Transport by Herbert Chapman – and over the years the suffix was gradually dropped, but neither the football club nor the station has ever led to the local area being referred to as 'Arsenal'.

Arsenal Stadium Mystery, The. A film (1939) revolving round the poisoning of a footballer during a match at Arsenal's ground. It stars Leslie Banks.

Artane Irish *Ard Aidhin* 'Aidhean's height'.
A northern suburb of DUBLIN. The industrial school run at Artane by the Christian Brothers was 'home' to orphaned, neglected or illegitimate children, many of whom suffered physical and sexual abuse at the hands of their carers in the 1950s and 1960s. The Artane Boys' Band, founded in

1872, plays at championship matches at CROKE PARK. It is no longer run by the Christian Brothers and now allows girls to join.

Arthur's Seat After King *Arthur*, in the 12th century Giraldus Cambrensis, the chronicler of King Arthur, referred to it as *Cathedra Arturii* (Latin 'Arthur's throne'), and by the 16th century it had become *Arthurissete*. An alternative theory has it that it is Gaelic *Ard na Said*, 'height of the arrows'.

A small but dramatically rocky hill (251 m / 823 ft) within Queen's Park in EDINBURGH. Recalling the shape of a lion *couchant*, it is the remains of an old volcano, and its various features, such as SALISBURY CRAGS, Whinney Hill, Samson's Ribs, Haggis Knowe and the Guttit Haddie ('gutted haddock'), have long proved of interest to geologists. Other features include St Margaret's Well and the ruined St Anthony's Chapel (both 15th century).

> Arthur's Seat shall be my bed,
> The sheets shall ne'er be pressed by me,
> St Anton's well shall be my drink,
> Sin' my true-love's forsaken me.
>
> Anon. 'Old Song', quoted in Sir Walter Scott's *Heart of Midlothian*

Arthur's Seat provides a backdrop to Scott's *Heart of Midlothian* (1818) – both the down-to-earth heroine Jeanie Deans and her silent suitor, the Laird o' Dumbiedikes, live in its shadow. Towards the end of the novel, when the Duke of Argyle invites a homesick Jeanie to admire the vista of the Thames and its surrounding parkland, she replies:

> 'I like just as weel to look at the craigs of Arthur's Seat, and the sea coming in ayont them as at a' thae muckle trees.'
>
> Sir Walter Scott: *The Heart of Midlothian* (1818), chapter 35

Arthur's Seat provides a strange and chilling scene in James Hogg's *The Private Memoirs and Confessions of a Justified Sinner* (1824), in which George Wringhim, the brother of the sinister 'justified sinner' of the title, finds himself, in strange conditions of mist and sunlight, 'haunted by some evil genius in the shape of his brother, as well as by that dark and mysterious wretch himself'.

Arthur's Seat is also the scene of some dark doings in Ian Rankin's Inspector Rebus mystery *The Falls* (2001).

Every May Day, at dawn, there is a service conducted by a Church of Scotland minister on the summit of Arthur's Seat. In recent decades the congregation has had to put up with competition from nearby pagans.

The charming village of DUDDINGSTON (where Scott supposedly sketched out his plan for *The Heart of Midlothian*) is on the south side of Arthur's Seat.

Artney, Glen. *See* GLEN ARTNEY.

Arun A back-formation from ARUNDEL.

A river in West Sussex. It rises in two branches in Surrey and flows 60 km (37 miles) westwards and then southwards, through PULBOROUGH (where it is joined by the ROTHER[1]) and ARUNDEL, into the English Channel at LITTLEHAMPTON. Before the name 'Arun' became established, in the 16th and 17th centuries, the river was known as the 'Tarrant'.

Arundel 'horehound valley', OE *harhune* 'horehound (a plant of the mint family)' + *dell* 'valley'.

A town in West Sussex, about 5 km (3 miles) northwest of Littlehampton, at the point where the River ARUN cuts through the SOUTH DOWNS. It is dominated by **Arundel Castle**, family seat of the Dukes of Norfolk (who are also Earls of Arundel). With its serried turrets, this is the epitome of a medieval fortress – but in fact the present building dates largely from the 18th and 19th centuries (the original was badly damaged by Parliamentary troops during the Civil Wars). The keep, however, goes back to Norman times. The Roman Catholic **Arundel Cathedral** dates from 1869.

Ian Nairn admired the overall effect, but deplored the details:

> Arundel seen from a distance is one of the great town views in England, although very un-English: castle and dramatic pinnacled church at either end of a long ridge, backed by the Downs, with mellow brick buildings

---

❖ -ary ❖

This is the common form of the ending of many minor names in Scotland and northern England that derive from Old Scandinavian *erg*, *ærgi* 'shieling, temporary shelter'. But the element appears in many different modern reflexes.

However, perhaps the two Lancashire names GOOSNARGH and Anglezarke (*see under* ANGLEZARKE MOOR) best illustrate the element's origins. Goosnargh contains the Irish personal name *Gussan*, and Anglezarke the Old Scandinavian personal name *Olafr*, anglicized to *Anlaf*. The element was borrowed by the Scandinavians from the early Gaelic word *áirge*, the ancestor of Irish *àirigh*. They then introduced it to Scotland and northern England, with the practice of transhumance – pasturing animals on the hills in summer. The word refers to either the shieling (the building used by the herdsman or child for shelter), or to the summer hill-pasture itself.

tumbling down to the river Arun. At closer view, however, the two accents are demonstrably c19 and demonstrably mock-medieval, and as soon as this can be seen the views somehow become compromised, a piece of elaborate open-air fancy dress.

The Buildings of England: Sussex (1965)

There is a very attractive cricket ground in the shadow of the castle, where the Duke of Norfolk's XI (the 16th Duke was an enthusiastic supporter of the game, and managed the 1962–3 MCC team in Australia) and latterly Lavinia, Duchess of Norfolk's XI used to play international touring teams near the start of their summer tours.

Arundel marbles. A collection of ancient sculptures acquired at great expense by Thomas Howard, 14th Earl of Arundel (1585–1646) and presented to Oxford University in 1667 by his grandson Henry, 6th Duke of Norfolk. They include the famous *Marmor Chronicon* or *Parian Chronicle* (said to have been executed on the isle of Paros in about 263 BC) which recorded events in Greek history from 1582 to 264 BC, although now incomplete and ending at 354 BC. They are now in the Ashmolean Museum.

Arundel Society. A society, founded in 1848 and dissolved in 1897, for promoting artistic knowledge. It was named after Thomas Howard, 2nd Earl of Arundel (1586–1646). In the 19th and early 20th centuries, the designation 'Arundel' was a familiar one applied to prints, engravings, etc. issued by the Society:

Corridors hung with Arundel prints and faded photographs of cathedrals.

Compton Mackenzie: *Sinister Street* (1914)

Aschled. The anglicized form of BAILE ÁTHA CLIATH, the Irish name for Dublin.

Ascot 'eastern cottage(s)', OE *east* 'east' + *cot* (*see* -COT, COTE). A town in Berkshire, within the unitary authority of WINDSOR AND MAIDENHEAD, about 10 km (6 miles) south-west of Windsor. Its fame rests on the nearby racecourse, **Ascot Heath**, founded by Queen Anne in 1711. The royal connection has continued ever since, notably in **Royal Ascot**, a four- (latterly five-) day race meeting held every June, and forming part of the London 'Season'. It is attended by the Sovereign and assorted members of the royal family, who ride down the course in horse-drawn carriages before the racing starts. Places in the Royal Enclosure are much coveted, and those lucky enough to get one take advantage of the opportunity to dress up: top hat and morning coat for the men, best dresses and elegant-to-outlandish hats for the women. The two main races are the **Ascot Gold Cup** and the King George VI and Queen Elizabeth Diamond Stakes.

Ascot is also the name of a district of Brisbane, Queensland, Australia.

ascot. A broad cravat tied under the chin. Originally called an **Ascot tie**.

Ascot. A type of gas water heater, popular in British homes between the 1930s and 50s, introduced into Britain under the name 'Ascot' by Bernard Friedman. Typically fixed to a wall near the kitchen sink, its reservoir stores water from the tap that it heats via burners thus providing a continual supply of hot water for doing the dishes.

Ascot races. A now largely redundant piece of Cockney rhyming slang for *braces*. Usually reduced to **Ascots**.

Ascott-under-Wychwood. *See under* SHIPTON-UNDER-WYCHWOOD.

Ash '(place at the) ash tree(s)', OE *æsc* 'ash tree'. A village in Kent, about 4 km (2.5 miles) west of Sandwich. It is often known more fully as **Ash-next-Sandwich**, to distinguish it from another, smaller Kentish village called Ash, to the northwest of Maidstone.

Ashbourne[1] 'stream where ash trees grow', OE *æsc* 'ash tree' + *burna* 'stream'. A small town in Derbyshire, on the River DOVE, at the southern edge of the PEAK DISTRICT, about 17 km (11 miles) west of Belper. It is a popular centre for walkers.

St Oswald's Church, with its impressive 65 m (213 ft) spire, has been called the 'Cathedral of the Peak'. James Boswell praised it:

The church of Ashbourne, which is one of the largest and most luminous that I have seen in any town of the same size.

The Life of Samuel Johnson (1791)

and for George Eliot it was 'the finest mere parish church in the kingdom'. Her novel *Adam Bede* (1859) was set in Ellastone, just 6 km (4 miles) to the southwest of the town.

On Shrove Tuesday and Ash Wednesday, Ashbourne is the scene of an annual (and very robust) game of football between teams drawn from the opposite banks of the Henmore Brook in which the goals are 5 km (3 miles) apart (one at Sturston Mill, the other at Clifton Mill). There are few rules and anyone can play.

Ashbourne gingerbread. A distinctive variety of ginger shortbread biscuit, the recipe of which is said to have been introduced to Ashbourne by some of the 300 French prisoners of war billeted here during the Napoleonic Wars.

Ashbourne water. A natural mineral water produced at Ashbourne and sold commercially.

Ashbourne[2] Presumed to be a transferred name from the English Ashbourne (*see* ASHBOURNE[1]). A village in County Meath, 20 km (12 miles) north of Dublin. Its Irish name is **Cill Dhéagláin** ('St Declan's church'). In 1916 Thomas Ashe, the Ashbourne village schoolteacher, led a party of rebels in a skirmish with the Royal Irish Constabulary. Ashe died a year later in Mountjoy

Prison after a hunger strike, his death remembered by Francis Ledwidge in the lines:

> But down the pale roads of Ashbourne
> Are heard the voices of the free.

Ashbrittle *Ash see* ASH + *brittle*, denoting manorial ownership in the early Middle Ages by a man called Bretel.

A village in Somerset, about 14 km (8.5 miles) west of Taunton. A 3800-year-old yew in its churchyard is thought to be Britain's oldest tree.

Ash Bullayne *Bullayne* denoting manorial ownership in the Middle Ages by the Bullayne family.

A village in Devon, about 6 km (4 miles) northwest of Crediton.

Ashburton 'farmstead by the stream where ash-trees grow', OE *æsc* 'ash-tree' + *burna* 'stream' + -TON.

A town in Devon, on the River Yeo (formerly called the Ashbourne), at the southeastern corner of DARTMOOR, about 16 km (10 miles) northwest of Totnes. A pretty town with gable-styled houses typical of the county, it became a Stannary town (*see under* STANNARIES) in 1328 through a charter established by Edward III. The former Mermaid Inn in North Street was a headquarters of General Fairfax (Parliamentary commander-in-chief) during the Civil Wars.

Ashburton is one of a small number of towns in England that retain the old Anglo-Saxon office of 'portreeve', a bailiff-like municipal official with tax-collecting responsibilities (the office is connected to the annual Ale Tasting and Bread Weighing Ceremony, which takes place in Ashburton near the end of July).

Ashby Either 'ash-tree farmstead', OE *æsc* or OScand *askr* 'ash tree' + -BY, or 'Aski's farmstead', OScand male personal name *Aski* + -BY; *see also* COLD ASHBY.

A village in North Lincolnshire (before 1996 in Humberside, before 1974 in Lincolnshire), now a southeastern suburb of SCUNTHORPE.

Ashby by Partney *Partney* 'Pearta's patch of dry ground', OE *Peartan* possessive form of male personal name *Pearta* + *eg* 'island, area of dry ground in a marsh' (*see* -EY, -EA).

A village in Lincolnshire, about 13 km (8 miles) west of Skegness.

Ashby-cum-Fenby *cum* 'with', Latin; *Fenby* 'fen farmstead', OE *fenn* 'fen' + -BY.

A village in North East Lincolnshire (before 1996 in Humberside, before 1974 in Lincolnshire), about 8 km (5 miles) south of Grimsby.

Ashby de la Launde *de la Launde* denoting manorial ownership in the Middle Ages by the de la Launde family.

A village in Lincolnshire, about 19 km (12 miles) southeast of Lincoln.

Ashby-de-la-Zouch *de-la-Zouch* denoting manorial ownership in the Middle Ages by the de la Zuche family.

A town in Leicestershire, about 26 km (16 miles) northwest of Leicester. The de la Zuches, a Breton family, became lords of the manor of Ashby in the 12th century. Their house became the basis of the late-medieval castle, fortified by Edward IV's lord chancellor, Lord Hastings, after he acquired it in 1461. It is now largely in ruins, but the 'Hastings Tower' survives. Mary Queen of Scots was imprisoned there in 1569. Nearby are the fields in which Sir Walter Scott set the tournament scene in his novel *Ivanhoe* (1819).

Ashby Puerorum *Puerorum* from Latin *puerorum* 'of the boys', alluding to a bequest for the support of the choir-boys of Lincoln Cathedral.

A village in Lincolnshire, about 27 km (17 miles) northwest of Skegness.

Ashdown 'hill overgrown with ash trees', OE *æscen* 'ash trees' + *dun* (*see* DOWN, -DON).

A location in Oxfordshire (before 1974 in Berkshire), on the Berkshire Downs (*see under* BERKSHIRE), about 13 km (8 miles) east of SWINDON. The 17th-century **Ashdown House** was built by Lord Craven for Elizabeth of Bohemia, Charles II's sister. It is of unusual, almost 'doll's house' appearance and is now owned by the National Trust. *See also* ALFRED'S CASTLE.

Battle of Ashdown (8 January 871). A battle between the forces of Wessex, under King Æthelred and his brother Alfred, and the Danes (who had camped in READING and started to raid the surrounding countryside). The English prevailed, but failed to follow up their victory. Æthelred died a few weeks after the battle and Alfred became king. The exact location of the battle is unknown.

Ashdown Forest. An area of forest and heathland in the WEALD of East Sussex, to the northeast of Haywards Heath and the southwest of Tunbridge Wells. In late Roman and Anglo-Saxon times it was part of the vast forest called **Anderida** (anglicized as *Andredesweald* – *see* WEALD), which covered much of southeast England (*see also* ST LEONARD'S FOREST). In the Middle Ages it was a royal hunting ground.

The author A.A. Milne lived at Hartsfield, on the edge of Ashdown Forest, and he used the forest as the setting for his Winnie-the-Pooh stories (*Winnie-the-Pooh* (1926), *The House at Pooh Corner* (1928)). (A helpful signpost in the forest directs the most ardent Winnie-the-Pooh pilgrims from a car park to the original 'Poohsticks Bridge'.)

Ashford[1] 'ash-clump ford', OE *æscet* 'clump of ash trees' + FORD.

A town in Kent, about 21 km (13 miles) northwest of Folkestone. Originally a market town, industrialization and enlargement arrived in the 19th century, when it became an important centre for building steam locomotives.

A terminus for the CHANNEL TUNNEL rail link is situated here, resulting in a recent local burgeoning of French culture, especially cafés and food shops.

The writer Frederick Forsyth (b. 1938), author of *The Day of the Jackal* (1971) and *The Odessa File* (1972), was born in Ashford. The French philosopher and writer Simone Weil (1909–43) died in a sanatorium here.

Ashford² Originally (969) *Ecelesford*, perhaps 'Eccel's ford', OE *Ecceles* possessive form of the male personal name *Eccel* + FORD; alternatively the first element may be an old river name *Ecel*. The name evolved to *Ashford* in the early Middle Ages, no doubt under the influence of *Ash-* in other place names.

A town in Surrey (before 1965 in Midlesex), about 5 km (3 miles) east of Egham, to the north of Queen Mary Reservoir.

Ashford Bowdler *Ashford* 'ash-tree ford', OE *æsc* 'ash tree' + FORD; *Bowdler* denoting manorial ownership in the Middle Ages by the de Boulers family.

A village in Shropshire, about 5 km (3 miles) south of Ludlow.

Ashingdon Probably 'hill of the ass', OE *assan* possessive form of *assa* 'ass' + *dun* (*see* DOWN, -DON). Alternatively, the first element could represent the OE male personal name *Assa*; but the author of the 11th-century *Encomium Emmae* ('In Praise of Emma') was in error when he confidently stated that the name meant *mons fraxinorum* ('hill of ash-trees').

A village in Essex, now a northern district of ROCHFORD. Here, on 18 October 1016, was fought the **Battle of Ashingdon** (or **Assandun**), in which the forces of Edmund II (Ironside) were defeated by King Cnut's Danish army. Following the battle the two kings agreed to divide the kingdom (Edmund was to have WESSEX), but Edmund died on 30 November leaving the whole of England in the hands of Cnut. There is some controversy over the battle site, some modern historians believing that the battle may in fact have been fought at a site in Suffolk.

Ashington 'valley of ash trees', OE *æscen* 'place growing with ash trees' + *denu* 'valley'.

A former mining town in Northumberland, just inland from the coast, 22 km (14 miles) north of Newcastle. It was the birthplace of the Newcastle United and England footballer Jackie Milburn (1924–88), affectionately dubbed 'Wor Jackie' (a Geordie rendition of 'Our Jackie') by his fans.

Ashington Group. A group of amateur artists active in Ashington from 1934 to 1984. The group originated when Robert Lyon (1894–1978), an art lecturer at King's College, Newcastle upon Tyne, then part of Durham University, was asked to run an extramural class in Ashington under the auspices of the Workers' Educational Association. Lyon encouraged members to 'paint what you know', and their paintings were mainly of scenes drawn from their working, domestic and social lives.

Ashop 'ash tree valley', OE *æsc* 'ash tree' + *hop* 'valley'.

A river in the PEAK DISTRICT of Derbyshire. It rises to the southeast of GLOSSOP and flows 12 km (7.5 miles) southeastwards into the western arm of LADYBOWER RESERVOIR. **Ashop Manor** is to the south.

See also SNAKE PASS.

Ashover 'ridge where ash-trees grow', OE *æsc* 'ash-tree' + *ofer* 'ridge'.

A village in Derbyshire, in the AMBER VALLEY, about 5 km (3 miles) northeast of Matlock. The spire of the 14th-century local church, 39 m (128 ft) high, is a landmark for miles around. The church bell allegedly cracked while ringing the news of Napoleon's fall in 1814.

Ash Priors *Ash* '(place at the) ash tree(s)', OE *æsc* 'ash tree'; *Priors* from its early possession by the Priors of Taunton.

A village in Somerset, about 6 km (4 miles) northwest of Taunton.

Ashreigney *Ash* '(place at the) ash tree(s)', OE *æsc* 'ash tree'; *-reigney* denoting manorial ownership in the Middle Ages by the de Regny family.

A village in Devon, about 21 km (13 miles) southeast of Bideford.

Ashstead 'place where ash-trees grow', OE *æsc* 'ash-tree' + *stede* 'place'.

A residential town in Surrey, between EPSOM and LEATHERHEAD. A village until the early 20th century, thereafter commuters moved in, doubling the population between the two world wars.

Ashton-in-Makerfield *Ashton* 'ash tree farm', OE *æsc* + -TON; *Makerfield* was an old name for the area, 'open land of ruins', OCelt word meaning 'ruin' + OE *feld* (*see* FIELD), *compare* INCE-IN-MAKERFIELD.

A small town in Greater Manchester, 6 km (4 miles) south of Wigan.

Ashton-under-Lyne Lyne is from *Lyme*, an old name for the area, possibly OCelt for 'elm tree area'; some think the elms were used in the construction of the Roman road across marshy ground from Manchester to York. The names of a farm distinguished by ash trees in an area distinguished by elms illustrate ancient onomastic precision.

An industrial and former mining town on the River TAME² in Greater Manchester, 10 km (6 miles) east of the city centre. It is the administrative centre of TAMESIDE metropolitan borough.

Around 1760 a Newcomen steam engine was installed in the area called Fairbottom, to pump water out of the mines; the engine became known as Fairbottom Bobs; in 1929 it was purchased by Henry Ford and taken as an exhibit to America. In 1882 Ashton Moss Colliery became the deepest pit in the world.

Ashton-under-Lyne was the birthplace of the watchmaker Thomas Earnshaw (1749–1829).

Until the mid-20th century, every Easter Monday Ashton-under-Lyne held the ceremony called Riding the Black Lad. This commemorated the hated Sir Ralph de Assheton (*fl*.15th century), who, dressed in black armour and accompanied by his thugs, would extort fines from the people of Ashton every Easter Monday ('Black Monday') for allowing weeds to grow on their land. The Black Lad of the ceremony was an effigy of Sir Ralph, and was paraded round the town to general derision and catcalls, before being set up for target practice using any missiles to hand.

Early 19th-century Ashton-under-Lyne was the headquarters of the Christian Israelites, a sect led from 1824 by Prophet John Wroe. Publicly circumcised in Ashton in 1824, Wroe declared the town to be the site of the New Jerusalem, and in 1830 reported he had received a divine command 'to take seven virgins to cherish and comfort him'. The virgins, obligingly supplied by members of Wroe's congregation, accompanied the Prophet on a preaching tour, from which one of them returned pregnant. The child was heralded by Wroe as a new Messiah, but when it turned out to be a girl he was turned out of Ashton by his disillusioned followers. The episode formed the subject-matter of Jane Rogers' novel *Mr Wroe's Virgins* (1991, televised 1993).

Asia Minor. A snide nickname applied to the London district of BELGRAVIA in the mid-19th century, on account of the large number of wealthy Jews who lived there. By the end of the century it had transferred northwards, to BAYSWATER and KENSINGTON, favoured areas for retired Indian civil servants to settle. It had largely died out by the time of the First World War.
See also MESOPOTAMIA[2].

Askeaton Irish *Eas Géitine* 'Géitine's waterfall'.
A small market town in County Limerick, 25 km (16 miles) west of Limerick itself. There are the remains of a 14th-century castle built by the Desmonds. In 1579 the English burnt the town and killed its friars, and the next year took the castle. It was seized by Confederate Catholic troops in 1642, but fell to Cromwell ten years later and was dismantled.

Askeaton Affair (August 1821). A fight between a group of Whiteboys (agrarian agitators) and police commanded by the Orangeman Major Richard Going. A number of Whiteboys were killed, and the survivors were ordered to bury the dead in quicklime; it was said that not all those thus buried were actually dead. Going was subsequently removed from his post and later killed.

Askival Probably 'spear mountain', OScand *askr* 'ash(wood)' (standing by synechdoche for a spear) + *fjall* 'mountain'.
The highest mountain (812 m / 2663 ft) of the Cuillin of RUM, Highland (formerly in Inverness-shire). Several other mountains on Rum have the Norse *-val* ending, including HALLIVAL, Trollaval, Barkeval and Ainshval.

Askrigg 'ridge with ash trees', OScand *askr* 'ash' + *hryggr* 'ridge', possibly replacing earlier OE elements *æsc* and *ric*.
A village in WENSLEYDALE, North Yorkshire, 25 km (16 miles) southeast of Richmond. It acted as the village of Darrowby in the television series *All Creatures Great and Small* (1978–90), based on James Herriott's veterinary tales.

Aslackby 'Aslakr's farmstead or village', OScand male personal name *Aslakr* + -BY.
A village in Lincolnshire, about 17 (11 miles) southeast of Grantham.

Asparagus Island Because asparagus grows here in abundance.
A small island in KYNANCE COVE, northwest of Lizard Point in western Cornwall.

Aspatria 'St Patrick's ash tree', OScand *askr* 'ash tree' + OCelt personal name; the order of the elements here is Celtic.
A village on the River Ellen in northwest Cumbria (formerly in Cumberland), 30 km (19 miles) southwest of Carlisle.

Aspley Guise *Aspley* 'aspen wood or glade', OE *æspe* 'aspen' + -LEY; *Guise* denoting manorial ownership in the Middle Ages by the de Gyse family.
A village in Bedfordshire, about 22 km (14 miles) northwest of Luton.

Aspull 'hill of aspens', OE *æspe* 'aspen' + *hyll* 'hill'.
A village in Greater Manchester, 4 km (2.5 miles) northeast of Wigan.

Assynt Probably OScand *asynt* 'visible from afar'.
An area in the Northwest HIGHLANDS, formerly in Sutherland and now in Highland. The main settlement is LOCHINVER, and the mountains include STAC POLLAIDH, CUL MÒR, SUILVEN, CANISP, Glas Bheinn and **Ben More Assynt** ('big mountain of Assynt', 998 m / 3274 ft). ARDVRECK CASTLE is on the shores of **Loch Assynt**.

> … has it come to this,
> that this dying landscape belongs
> to the dead, the crofters and fighters
> and fishermen whose larochs
> sink into the bracken
> by Loch Assynt and Loch Crocach?
>
> Norman MacCaig: 'A Man in Assynt', from *A Man in my Position* (1969)

Aston 'eastern farmstead', OE *east* 'east' + -TON; *see also* COLD ASTON, WHITE LADIES ASTON.

A northeastern suburb of BIRMINGHAM. It is home to King Edward VI Aston School (formerly King Edward VI Grammar School) and to the HP Sauce factory. The **Aston Expressway** runs through the suburb, linking the city centre with the M6.

Two places with which Aston is associated, **Aston Hall** (*see under* BIRMINGHAM) and **Aston University**, are not actually in Aston. The university is in Gosta Green, closer to the centre of Birmingham. When it was founded, from a college of advanced technology, in 1966, it took the name 'Aston' so as to be at the top of the alphabetical list of new universities and so readily catch the eye of the University Grants Committee. Its site is bisected by Aston Street.

Ozzy Osbourne, the former hell-raising heavy-metal star (and ex-lead singer of the rock group *Black Sabbath*) turned television icon, was born in Aston in 1948.

Aston Villa FC. A football club founded in Birmingham in 1874 by members of the Villa Cross Wesleyan Chapel in Aston. It is often referred to simply as Villa (the club's supporters are, inevitably, thus called Villans). Aston Villa joined the Football League in 1897, and moved to its present ground, Villa Park, in 1897. Before the First World War, Aston Villa was one of England's leading clubs, but thereafter success proved elusive until the late 1970s and 1980s brought renewed triumphs, notably victory in the 1982 European Cup final.

Aston Blank. An alternative name for COLD ASTON.

Aston Botterell *Botterell* denoting manorial ownership in the Middle Ages by the Boterell family.
A village in Shropshire, about 13 km (8 miles) southwest of Bridgnorth.

Aston Cantlow *Cantlow* denoting manorial ownership in the Middle Ages by the de Cantilupe family.
A village in Warwickshire, in the valley of the River ALNE, about 8 km (5 miles) northwest of Stratford-upon-Avon. Local tradition has it that William Shakespeare's parents, John Shakespeare and Mary Arden, were married in Aston Cantlow in 1557 – a theory not aided by the church register not starting until 1560. A timbered house here owned by the Shakespeare Birthplace Trust is believed to have been the home of Mary Arden.

Aston Clinton *Clinton* denoting manorial ownership in the Middle Ages by the de Clinton family.
A village in Buckinghamshire, about 5 km (3 miles) southeast of Aylesbury. The Bell Inn here is a celebrated hostelry. The prestigious Aston-Martin sports car owes the first part of its name to a motorsport hill-climb at Aston Clinton (the second part comes from Lionel Martin, one of the progenitors of the car, which was originally (1926) made at Feltham in Middlesex and from 1958 in Newport Pagnell).

Aston Flamville *Flamville* denoting manorial ownership in the Middle Ages by the de Flamville family.
A village in Leicestershire, about 2.5 km (1.5 miles) east of Hinkley.

Aston juxta Mondrum *juxta* 'by, next to, within the bounds of', Latin; *Mondrum* the name of a forest (used as a hunting preserve), 'pleasure', OE *man-dream*.
A village in Cheshire, about 5 km (3 miles) west of Crewe.

Aston le Walls *le Walls* '(within) the walls' (referring to an earthwork nearby), *le* 'the', OFr.
A village in Northamptonshire, about 29 km (18 miles) southwest of Northampton.

Aston Rogers *Rogers* denoting manorial ownership in the Middle Ages by a man called Roger.
A village in Shropshire, about 16 km (10 miles) southwest of Shrewsbury.

Atch Lench 'Ǽcci's hillside', OE male personal name *Ǽcci* + *hlenc* 'extensive hill-slope'.
A village in Worcestershire (before 1998 in Hereford and Worcester, before 1974 in Worcestershire), about 8 km (5 miles) north of Evesham.
See also CHURCH LENCH, ROUS LENCH.

Athboy Irish *Baile Átha Buí* 'town of the yellow ford'.
A small market town on the River Athboy in County Meath, 15 km (9 miles) west-southwest of Navan. It was a stronghold of the English PALE from the 14th to the 16th centuries.

Áth Cinn. The Irish name for HEADFORT.

Áth Dara. The Irish name for ADARE.

Athelney 'island of the princes', OE *æthelinga* possessive plural form of *ætheling* 'prince' + *eg* 'island' (here in the sense 'dry ground in the middle of a marsh') (*see also* -EY, -EA).
A village in Somerset, on the River TONE, about 13 km (8 miles) northeast of Taunton. It inherits its name from the piece of high ground on which it stands, which in Anglo-Saxon and medieval times was the only area of dry land in surrounding marshes. It was here that King Alfred took refuge from Danish invaders in 878, and during his stay the unfortunate incident with the burnt cakes is said to have taken place (the story, not recorded before the 11th century, is that the king, unrecognized, took refuge in a cowherd's hut, and while seated by the fire attending to his equipment, he allowed the housewife's loaves to burn, for which he was soundly scolded). After the defeat of the Danes, Alfred commanded that an abbey be built at Athelney.

The so-called 'Alfred Jewel', one of the most famous objects surviving from Anglo-Saxon England, was found near Athelney in 1693. It is probably the handle of a wand for tracing the words in the reading of books, and bears the inscription 'Alfred commanded me to be made'.

In more recent times the area has had the etymologically tautologous name **Isle of Athelney**.

Athelstaneford 'Athelstan's ford', OE personal name *Athelstan* + FORD.
A small village in East Lothian, about 3 km (2 miles) northeast of Haddington. It was the site of a battle in the early 10th century, in which Athelstan, the king of Wessex and Mercia, was defeated by the Picts and the Scots, so ending his invasion of Scotland. During the battle the victors are said to have been encouraged by the appearance of a white St Andrew's cross in the blue sky, and this subsequently formed the motif for the Scottish flag.

Sir David Lindsay (*c*.1486–1555), Lyon King-of-Arms and author of *Satyre of the Thrie Estaitis* (1540), a morality play in verse, is thought to have been born near the village, and in the 18th century Athelstaneford had two literary ministers. The first was Robert Blair (1699–1746), remembered for his long poem *The Grave* (1743), which helped to establish the 'Graveyard School' of poetry. He was succeeded as minister by John Home (1722–1808), author of the hugely successful play *Douglas: A Tragedy* (1756), who had to resign his living as a result, the theatre being disapproved of by the Kirk.

Athenry Irish *Baile Átha an Rí* 'town of the ford of the king' (*see* FORD).
A town in County Galway, 20 km (12 miles) east of Galway itself. In the 13th century Myler de Bermingham turned the place into an Anglo-Norman stronghold (known as 'Bermingham's Court'), and the remains of a castle, friary and town walls survive.

> The wounded wood-dove lies dead at last:
> The pine long-bleeding, it shall not die!
> – This song is secret. Mine ear it pass'd
> In a wind o'er the stone plain of Athenry.
>
> Aubrey de Vere (1814–1902): 'Song'

Battle of Athenry (10 August 1316). A battle in which the Irish under the O'Connors (chieftains of Connacht) were heavily defeated by an Anglo-Norman force under William de Burgh and Richard de Bermingham. It proved a fatal blow to O'Connor power in the west.

'Fields of Athenry, The'. A ballad written in 1979 by Pete St John, popularized by Paddy Reilly and known in numerous cover versions. It is often played as dance music and is sung by rugby supporters at Irish internationals. The chorus goes:

> Low lie the fields of Athenry
> Where once we watched the small free birds fly.
> Our love was on the wing, we had dreams and songs to
>   sing,
> It's so lonely round the Fields of Athenry.

Athens of Ireland. A nickname given in the early 19th century to CORK, then home to such literati as Thomas Crofton Croker, William Maginn, Richard Milliken and Francis Sylvester Mahony.

Athens of the North, the. A nickname given to EDINBURGH from the later 18th century, when the city was home to many of the leading thinkers of the Scottish Enlightenment, such as David Hume, Joseph Black and Dugald Stewart. More specifically, it reflects the classical architecture of the city's New Town (built in the late 18th and early 19th centuries), in particular the old Royal High School at the foot of CALTON HILL, modelled on the Temple of Theseus in Athens, and the unfinished copy of the Parthenon on the top of the hill, known as Edinburgh's Folly.

> A fine fantasy of the Whig literati
> to build a modern Athens in our frore islands ...
>
> Douglas Young (1913–73): 'Winter Homily on the Calton Hill'

Some have preferred to think of the rather chilly city as ...

> The Reykjavik of the South.
>
> Tom Stoppard: *Jumpers* (1972)

The title 'Athens of the North' was also awarded to itself by BELFAST in the later 18th and early 19th century. The title seemed an appropriate reward to the burgers who had founded the Belfast Reading Society, the Belfast Academical Institution and the Belfast Natural History and Philosophical Society.

> Turn back in thought to when ...
>   ... this city wore the name
> of Northern Athens with no irony
> staining that title ...
>
> John Hewitt: 'Pro Tanto Quid Retribuamus' (Belfast's motto) (1954)

Irony could not be held long at bay, however. When one Belfast boy asked his teacher why the city had deserved its title, the man replied:

> I cannot pronounce on that, but I am certain that Athens was never known as the 'Belfast of the South'.

Áth Eochaille. The Irish name for AHOGHILL.

Atherstone 'Æthelred's farmstead', OE *Æthelredes* possessive form of male personal name *Æthelred* + -TON.
A small market town in Warwickshire, on WATLING STREET[1], about 11 km (7 miles) southeast of Tamworth. A milestone outside the old Red Lion coaching inn here bears the incised words: '100 miles London'. In a custom dating back to the 13th century, an idiosyncratic local form of football is played in the streets on Shrove Tuesday.

Atherton 'Æthelhere's or Eadhere's village', OE male personal name *Æthelhere* or *Eadhere* + -TON.

A small town in Greater Manchester, 7 km (4.5 miles) south-west of Bolton. The Atherton family who held the manor from the early 13th century to 1738 took their name from the place name.

Athlone Irish *Baile Átha Luain* 'town of the ford of Luan' (*see* FORD).

A town in County Westmeath, on the River SHANNON just south of LOUGH REE, where counties Westmeath, Longford and Roscommon meet. It is an important transport hub and is known as 'the capital of the Midlands', while 3 km (2 miles) to the south is the geographical centre of Ireland, marked by a Victorian folly. Athlone's strategic position has meant that it has been fought over since the early 11th century. Parts of the 13th-century castle and town walls (and later defences) survive. The castle was important in the conflicts of the 16th and 17th centuries. It was taken by Cromwell's forces in 1650, and was besieged three times in the Williamite Wars – in 1688, 1690 and 1691. In the last siege, a band of twelve Irish defenders tried to save the town by destroying the strategic bridge over the Shannon, built in 1566. In the process ten of them died:

> O many a year, upon Shannon's side,
> They sang upon moor and they sang upon heath,
> Of the twain that breasted that raging tide,
> And the ten that shook bloody hands with Death!
>
> Aubrey de Vere (1814–1902): 'A Ballad of Athlone'

Their effort was in vain, however, as on 30 June the Williamite general, Godart Ginkell, ordered his men to wade the river and take the town; Ginkell was later created Earl of Athlone. The large army barracks in the town are named after one of the defenders, Sergeant Custume, and the incident is also commemorated in the dance called 'The Bridge of Athlone'.

Athlone was the birthplace of the celebrated tenor John MacCormack (1884–1945). In 1917, at the height of anti-German feeling in Britain, the Prince of Teck (1874–1957), brother-in-law of George V, took the surname Cambridge and the title Earl of Athlone. There is a Lake Athlone in South Africa (Orange Free State).

> A hungry young man of Athlone
> Had a great many reasons to moan.
>   His wife ate the ham
>   And the best leg of lamb,
> So that all that was left was the bone.
>
>   Anon.: limerick

Romance of Athlone, A. An American musical play (1899) by Chauncey Olcott, which includes the well-known song 'My Wild Irish Rose':

> My Wild Irish Rose,
> The sweetest flow'r that grows,
> You may search ev'rywhere,

> But none can compare
> With My Wild Irish Rose ...
> And some day for my sake,
> She may let me take
> The bloom from My Wild Irish Rose.

Áth Mheadhoin. The Irish name for the River AFFANE.

Áth na Long. The Irish name for ANNALONG.

Atholl 'new Ireland', Gaelic *ath* denoting repetition + *Fótla* 'Ireland'; an alternative might be 'ford of *Fótla*', Gaelic *áth* 'ford' + female personal name *Fótla*.

An area of the central HIGHLANDS, southwest of the Cairngorms, in Perth and Kinross (formerly in Perthshire, and then in Tayside region). It is also spelt **Athol**. The area is bounded on the north by the DRUMOCHTER PASS and includes GLEN GARRY[1], GLEN TILT, the **Forest of Atholl** (a now deforested area north of Glen Garry), BEINN A'GHLO, BLAIR ATHOLL (and Blair Castle), the Pass of KILLIECRANKIE, PITLOCHRY, Loch Tummel (*see under* TUMMEL) and Loch Rannoch (*see under* RANNOCH).

Blair Castle at Blair Atholl dates from 1269, and is the seat of the dukes (originally earls) of Atholl; the **mormaership of Atholl with Gowrie** was one of the original Celtic earldoms of Scotland. Blair Castle was the last castle in Britain to be besieged, when in 1746 Lord George Murray and his Jacobites failed to dislodge the Hanoverian troops within. The dukes of Atholl acquired the lordship of Man (*see* ISLE OF MAN) in 1726.

There is a town called Athol in the USA (Massachusetts) and a Cape Athol in northwestern Greenland.

Atholl brose. A mixture of honey, oatmeal and whisky (brose is a Scots dish of oatmeal or peasemeal mixed with hot water or milk and seasoning).

Atholl Crescent. A street in Edinburgh's New Town, and also the informal name for the Edinburgh College of Domestic Science located here from 1891 to 1970.

Atholl Highlanders. Britain's only extant private army. After Queen Victoria visited Blair Castle in 1844 she granted the Duke of Atholl the right to retain a standing army. There is also a traditional tune called 'The Atholl Highlanders'.

Sow of Atholl, the. A mountain (803 m / 2634 ft) on the west side of the Drumochter Pass. It gained its name from its rounded shape and from the proximity of the Boar of Badenoch (*see under* BADENOCH), its orginal Gaelic name being Meall an Dòbhraichean ('hill of the watercress').

Áth Trasna. The Irish name for NEWMARKET[2]

Athy Irish *Baile Átha Í* 'town of the ford of Ae' (*see* FORD), the latter being a Munster chieftain killed here in the 11th century.

A town in County Kildare, 60 km (37 miles) southwest of Dublin, at the junction of the GRAND CANAL and the River

BARROW. The Normans built a castle here, but the present White's Castle, on a bridge over the Barrow, was built by William White in 1575. It was taken by Cromwell in 1650. Some 5 km (3 miles) to the northeast is the Motte of Ardsaill, where in 1315 Edward Bruce defeated Sir Edmund Butler and proceeded to sack the town of Athy.

> While going the road to sweet Athy,
> A stick in my hand and a drop in my eye,
> A doleful damsel I heard cry:
>> 'Och, Johnny, I hardly knew ye!'
>> Anon.: 'Johnny, I Hardly Knew Ye'

Atmospheric Road, the. The name given to an early Irish railway, opened on 29 March 1844, and running the 2.8 km (1.75 miles) between Kingstown (*see under* DÚN LAOGHAIRE) and DALKEY. It was so named because powered by compressed air.

Attenborough 'stronghold associated with Adda or Æddi', OE male personal name *Adda* or *Æddi* + -ING + *burh* (*see* BURY). A village in Nottinghamshire, to the southwest of and now virtually continuous with BEESTON. Henry Ireton (1611–51), one of the signatories of Charles I's death warrant, was born here.

Attingham Park *Attingham* probably 'homestead associated with Eata', OE male personal name *Eata* + -ING + HAM. A Georgian mansion and deer park in Shropshire, 7 km (4 miles) southeast of Shrewsbury, close to the confluence of the River Tern with the River SEVERN. Built in 1785 by George Steuart for the 1st Lord Berwick, and now owned by the National Trust, the house has Regency interiors (including a picture gallery by John Nash) and lies in parkland landscaped by Humphry Repton.

Attleborough 'Ætla's stronghold', OE male personal name *Ætla* + *burh* (*see* BURY). A town in Norfolk, about 24 km (15 miles) northeast of Thetford.

Auburn So named by Oliver Goldsmith, possibly borrowing the name of the village of Auburn near Bridlington in Yorkshire. Its original name was Lissoy, Irish *Lios Uaimhe* 'fort of the cave'. A hamlet in County Westmeath, 10 km (6 miles) northeast of Athlone. Its modern Irish name is **Achadh na Gréine** ('field of the sunny place'). Oliver Goldsmith's father was rector here and it was the poet's childhood home. Goldsmith made **Lissoy**, as it was then known, into the 'Sweet Auburn' of his poem *The Deserted Village* (1770):

> Sweet Auburn! loveliest village of the plain;
> Where health and plenty cheered the labouring swain,
> Where smiling spring its earliest visit paid,
> And parting summer's lingering blooms delayed:
> Dear lovely bowers of innocence and ease,
> Seats of my youth, when every sport could please,
> How often have I loitered o'er thy green,
> Where humble happiness endeared each scene!

Living in England, Goldsmith maintained an enduring affection for his native place:

> ... if I climb Hampstead Hill, I confess it is fine, but then I had rather be on the little mount before Lissoy Gate, and there take in, to me, the most pleasing horizon of nature.

Auchendinny Probably 'field of the fox valley', Gaelic ACHADH + *an-t sionnaighe* 'of the fox valley'. A village in Midlothian, on the River North ESK[3], some 12 km (7.5 miles) south of Edinburgh.

Auchendolly 'field of MacIndoly', Gaelic ACHADH + MacIndoly, the name of a 14th-century owner and rector of the parish. A small settlement formerly in Kirkcudbrightshire, now in Dumfries and Galloway, 6 km (4 miles) north of Castle Douglas.

Auchinleck 'field of the flat stone', Gaelic ACHADH + *na* 'of the' + *leac* 'flat stone'. A village in East Ayrshire (formerly in Strathclyde), about 20 km (12 miles) southeast of Kilmarnock. It was long the seat of the Boswell family, and Alexander Boswell, who took the judicial title Lord Auchinleck on his elevation to the Bench in 1754, built **Auchinleck House** (known locally as Place Affleck) in 1762. Auchinleck was the father of the biographer James Boswell, who brought Samuel Johnson here in 1773. Johnson had such a fierce argument with Lord Auchinleck that his friend was too shocked to record it. Boswell is buried in the family mausoleum by the church. The great Scottish fiddler Neil Gow (1727–1807) composed a strathspey entitled 'Lady Boswell of Auchinleck'.

Auchterarder 'upland of high water', Gaelic *uachdar* 'top' + OCelt ARD + Gaelic *dobhar* 'water'. A town 20 km (12 miles) southwest of Perth, in Perth and Kinross (formerly in Perthshire, and then in Tayside region). Its ruined castle was once a royal residence. The town was burnt by the Earl of Mar's Jacobites after the Battle of Sheriffmuir (*see under* SHERIFF MUIR) in 1715. The folksinger Ewan MacColl (1915–89) was born here, as was the novelist James Kennaway (1928–68), author of *Tunes of Glory* (1956). In 1947 the youthful Kennaway, fresh out of the army, wrote to George Bernard Shaw in rhyme, asking himself to tea:

> I am no fond regarder
>> Of pompous interview
> But I come from Auchterarder
>> And I'd like a chat with you.

To which the aged GBS replied:

> I have not tea enough for you
>> Nor teacakes in my larder

And so send this rebuff to you
        Dear lad from Auchterarder.

Auchtermuchty 'upper pig house', Gaelic *uachdar* 'top'
+ *mucatu* 'pig place'.

A town in Fife, 15 km (9 miles) northeast of Kinross. It is
known to locals as **Muchty**, and to everyone else as the
archetypal joke Scottish place name. The town at one time
had a reputation for rampant holiness:

> ... the people o' the town o' Auchtermuchty grew so
> rigidly righteous, that the meanest hind among them
> became a shining light in other towns an' parishes. There
> was nought to be heard, neither night nor day, but
> preaching, praying, argumentation, an' catechising in the
> famous town o' Auchtermuchty. The young men wooed
> their sweethearts out o' the Song o' Solomon, an' the girls
> returned answers in strings o' verses out o' the Psalms.

> James Hogg: *The Private Memoirs and Confessions of a Justified
> Sinner* (1824)

This state of affairs, according to Hogg, so annoyed the
Devil that he determined to corrupt these God-fearing folk.
He visited the town disguised as a minister, and preached so
inspiringly that the people would have done anything he
said – had not an old man lifted the hem of his long gown
to reveal a tellingly cloven hoof. Since then no Auchtermuchty man will pay much heed to a sermon, 'for he
thinks aye that he sees the cloven foot peeping out from
beneath every sentence'.

In the second television series (1993) of *Dr Finlay's Casebook*, Auchtermuchty played the part of TANNOCHBRAE.

> And as at sicna times am I,
> I wad ha'e Scotland to my eye
> Until I saw a timeless flame
> Tak' Auchtermuchty for a name,
> And kent that Ecclefechan stood
> As pairt o' an eternal mood.

> Hugh MacDiarmid: *A Drunk Man Looks at the Thistle* (1926)

'Wife of Auchtermuchty, The'. An anonymous narrative
poem from *c.*1500, in which the eponymous heroine keeps
her errant husband in order. At the end –

> Quoth he, Dame, I sall hauld my tongue,
> For, and we fecht, I'll get the waur ...

Audenshaw 'Aldwine's copse', OE male personal name
Aldwine + OE *sceaga* 'copse'.

A suburb of MANCHESTER, 8 km (5 miles) east of the city
centre.

Audley End From *Audley End*, a Jacobean mansion in the area.
It was built on land once owned by the Abbey of Walden,
which was given by Henry VIII to Sir Thomas Audley after the
Dissolution of the Monasteries in the late 1530s.

A village in Essex, on the River CAM[2], about 3 km (2 miles)
south of Saffron Walden. The transfer of the house's name

to the village was no doubt reinforced by the presence of
Audley End station (on the Liverpool Street to Cambridge
line) – although when it originally opened, in 1845, the
station was called 'Wendon', after a nearby village.

Aughrim Irish *Eachdroim* 'horse ridge'.

A village in County Galway, 6 km (4 miles) southwest of
Ballinasloe.

Battle of Aughrim (12 July 1691). The final defeat of the
Jacobites in Ireland during the Williamite Wars. The Jacobite commander, Charles Chalmont, Marquis de St Ruth,
was decapitated by a cannonball, and between 7000 and
10,000 of his men killed, many while fleeing. The battle –
the bloodiest ever fought in Ireland – has been called
'the Last Stand of the Gael', and is commemorated in
various pieces of music, such as The Chieftains' lament
'After Aughrim's Great Disaster', as well as in verse:

> Do you remember, long ago,
>   Kathaleen?
> When your lover whispered low,
> 'Shall I stay or shall I go,
>   Kathaleen?'
> And you answered proudly, 'Go!
> And join King James and strike a blow
>   for the Green!'

> Arthur G. Geoghegan (1810–89): 'After Aughrim'

> She said, 'They gave me of their best,
> They lived, they gave their lives for me;
> I tossed them to the howling waste,
> And flung them to the foaming sea.'

> Emily Lawless: 'After Aughrim', from *With the Wild Geese*
> (1902) (The poem and volume title refer to the Wild Geese,
> the Irish soldiers who went into exile on the Continent.)

Auld Reekie. A nickname for EDINBURGH, literally meaning 'old smoky', and so named from the pall of smoke that
formerly hung over the city – as Coleridge witnessed when
he looked down on the city from Arthur's Seat:

> The smoke was rising from ten thousand houses, each
> smoke from some one family.

> Samuel Taylor Coleridge: letter to Robert Southey (13
> September 1803)

It is said that James VI first came up with the epithet, viewing the city across the Forth from the coast of Fife in the
early morning, while the citizens lit their fires. It is unlikely, however, that Edinburgh was any smokier than other
cities of comparable size; it is just that there are many high
or distant viewpoints from which the reek can be viewed.

One of the best known poems of the doomed young
Edinburgh poet Robert Fergusson (1750–74) is a muscular
satire in the vernacular entitled 'Auld Reekie'; this mentions the city's 'stinking air'. Robert Burns talks of 'Auld
chuckie Reekie' (*chuckie* being a Scots term of endearment)

in his epistle 'To William Creech' (1787), while two centuries later Lewis Spence (1874–1955) wrote a poem called 'The Prows o' Reekie', beginning:

> O wad this braw hie-heapit toun
> Sail aff like an enchanted ship,
> Drift owre the warld's seas …

For the English equivalent, *see* the SMOKE.

Aultnapaddock 'stream of the old men', Gaelic *allt* 'stream' + *nam bodach* 'of the old men'.
A small settlement in Aberdeenshire (formerly in Grampian region), 13 km (8 miles) west of Huntly.

Auquhorthies 'field of the pillar stone', Gaelic ACHADH + *choirthe* 'pillar stone', a reference to a stone circle.
A small settlement in the Formartine area of Aberdeenshire (formerly in Grampian region), some 3 km (2 miles) northeast of Old Meldrum.

Avalon Perhaps from an OCelt compound meaning 'island of apples'.
A legendary island: in Celtic mythology the Island of Blessed Souls, and in Arthurian romances the abode and burial place of Arthur, who was carried there by Morgan le Fay. It has been identified with GLASTONBURY (where King Arthur is reputed to be buried), but this is due to a set of etymological misapprehensions: Avalon came to be associated with the paradisal 'Glass Island' of Celtic legend that itself was identified with *Ineswytren*, the Welsh name of Glastonbury, which was popularly but mistakenly translated as 'island of glass'.

There are towns called Avalon in the USA (California, Mississippi and New Jersey), a Lake Avalon in New Mexico, USA and an Avalon Peninsula in Newfoundland, Canada.
See also DERWENT[2].

Avebury Probably 'Afa's stronghold', OE male personal name *Afa* + BURY.
A village in Wiltshire, about 19 km (12 miles) east of Chippenham. It is the site of one of the largest late Neolithic stone circles in Europe, along with STONEHENGE a UNESCO World Heritage Site from 1986. Nearly 1.5 km (1 mile) in circumference, this contains over a hundred sarsens, or standing stones, up to 5 m (16 ft) high and 60 tons in weight. Within it are two smaller, incomplete rings. Other prehistoric sites in the immediate vicinity include SILBURY HILL, WINDMILL HILL and The SANCTUARY.

The antiquarian John Aubrey was the first to rediscover the Avebury stones in the modern era, in 1648, and wrote detailed accounts of them. In the 18th century William Stukely evolved elaborate theories, linking the stones with the druids.

Ave Maria Lane Probably from the processional chanting of *Ave Maria* ('Hail Mary'). Alternatively the name might allude to writers of religious texts working in the vicinity.
A street in the City of London (EC4), running northwards from LUDGATE HILL. In the Middle Ages the clergy of ST PAUL's[1] Cathedral went in procession to the cathedral reciting the Lord's Prayer. They began it in PATERNOSTER ROW, and on turning down Ave Maria Lane they began chanting the 'Hail Mary'. The street was very badly damaged in an air raid on 28 December 1940.

Aviemore 'big pass', Gaelic *agaidh* 'pass' + *mór* 'big'; the first element also means '(rock) face', and while the pass or gap is conspicuous, so also is the face of the hill at Aviemore.
A large village in Strathspey (*see under* SPEY), formerly in Inverness-shire and now in Highland. It turned into a major tourist resort following the construction of the **Aviemore Centre** in the later 1960s, a complex of concrete hotels and leisure facilities in the regrettable architectural style of the period, built by the infamously corrupt architect John Poulson. Aviemore is the main base for the nearby Cairngorm ski slopes, and boasts Britain's first theme park, Santa Claus Land:

> … a miserable municipal world of creosote and bark chippings, where you will find Snow White and seven crudely-renovated garden gnomes lurking beneath a bush, a giant garden shed containing a Christmas tree, a plastic dinosaur, a few yards of model railway and a wire for children to slide up and down on.
>
> George Monbiot: 'Christmas Comes Every Day', in *The Guardian* (7 November 1998)

The German-born singer, composer and conductor Sir George Henschel (1850–1934) died at Aviemore.

Avoca From Ptolemy's name *Oboka*.
The river formed by the confluence of the rivers Avonmore ('big river') and Avonbeg ('little river'), County Wicklow. The name is shared by the village of **Avoca** (Irish *Abhóca*, formerly *An Droichead Nau* 'the new bridge'), which acted the part of BALLYKISSANGEL in the BBC television drama series. The rivers meet in the **Vale of Avoca** at Meeting of the Waters, celebrated in an 1807 song of that name by Thomas Moore, who was visiting friends in the vale. The song is sung to the tune of 'The Old Head of Dennis' and ends:

> Sweet vale of Avoca! How calm could I rest
> In thy bosom of shade, with the friends I love best,
> Where the storms that we feel in this cold world should cease
> And our hearts, like thy waters, be mingled in peace,
> And our hearts, like thy waters, be mingled in peace.

There is an Avoca River in Australia (Victoria).

Avon¹ From an OCelt word meaning 'river' (*see also* AVON).
River Avon thus means etymologically 'river river'.

A river in Northamptonshire, Warwickshire, Worcestershire and Gloucestershire, known in full as the **Upper Avon** or the **Warwickshire Avon**. It rises in Northamptonshire, near NASEBY, and flows about 154 km (95 miles) southwest through STRATFORD-UPON-AVON and EVESHAM to join the River SEVERN at TEWKESBURY.

Bard of Avon. William Shakespeare (1564–1616), who was born in Stratford-upon-Avon and returned to spend the latter part of his life there. The epithet, which is often curtailed to simply **the Bard**, is first recorded in 1881, but the idea behind it is of much greater antiquity: 'For the bard of all bards was a Warwickshire Bard,' David Garrick (1769).

Swan of Avon. A florid and now little used alternative to Bard of Avon (*see above*), conceived by the playwright Ben Jonson in 1623:

> Sweet Swan of Avon! what a sight it were
> To see thee in our waters yet appear,
> And make those flights upon the bankes of Thames.

The idea of comparing a poet with a swan (surely for its beauty of appearance rather than of voice) and associating it with a particular body or source of water goes back to classical antiquity (the Greek poet Pindar was known as the 'Swan of Dirce', Dirce being a fountain near Thebes). It no doubt derives from the legend that the soul of Apollo, Greek god of music and poetry, passed into a swan (whence the Pythagorean fable that the souls of all good poets passed into swans). The conceit is sustained to this day by the large number of swans that populate the Avon at Stratford. The Royal Shakespeare Company's Swan Theatre in Stratford, opened in 1986 in the theatre's former Conference Hall, takes its name from the epithet.

Avon² *see* AVON¹.
A river in South Gloucestershire, Gloucestershire, Wiltshire, Bath and North East Somerset, and Bristol, known in full as the **Bristol Avon** or the **Lower Avon**. It rises in the COTSWOLDS and flows about 120 km (74 miles) south and west through MALMESBURY, CHIPPENHAM, BATH and BRISTOL to enter the SEVERN estuary at AVONMOUTH.
See also BRADFORD-ON-AVON.

Avon Gorge. A scenic steep-sided valley through which the River Avon flows along the western edge of Bristol. It is spanned by the Clifton Suspension Bridge (*see under* CLIFTON). Its sheer limestone walls are popular with rock-climbers. There is a nature reserve on its western bank.

Rolls-Royce Avon. A jet aero-engine developed in the late 1940s. It was the most successful of the early jet engines produced by Rolls-Royce, and powered such British combat aircraft of the 1950s and 1960s as the Hawker Hunter and the English Electric Lightning.

Avon³ *See* AVON¹.
A river in Wiltshire, Hampshire and Dorset, known in full as the **Wiltshire Avon** or the **East Avon**. It rises near DEVIZES and PEWSEY and flows about 96 km (60 miles) south through SALISBURY into the English Channel at CHRISTCHURCH. For much of its lower reaches it forms the boundary between Dorset and Hampshire.
See also NETHERAVON and UPAVON.

Avon Forest. An area of woodland on the western side of the River Avon, close to RINGWOOD.

Avon⁴ *See* AVON¹.
A river in Devon, which rises on DARTMOOR and flows 34 km (22 miles) southwards into the English Channel at Bigbury Bay (*see under* BIGBURY).
See also AVONWICK.

Avon⁵ From Gaelic *abhainn* 'river'. Some think it cognate with the English Avons and Welsh *afon*, which also mean 'river' (*see* AVON).

A river in the northeastern CAIRNGORM MOUNTAINS of Moray (formerly in Grampian region), approximately 65 km (40 miles) long. It is pronounced 'aan'. The Avon has its source in **Loch Avon**, a high loch (*c*.715 m / 2350 ft) in a vast and magnificent corrie between CAIRN GORM and BEN MACDUI, with, at its head, the SHELTER STONE, and surrounded by the great cliffs of Carn Etchachan, Shelter Stone Crag, Hell's Lum (the *lum* or chimney in question being a vertical fissure) and Stag Rocks. The ultimate source of the river is the torrent of Feith Buidhe, rising on the sub-Arctic plateau of Ben Macdui and cascading over red granite slabs down to the loch. Even in summer, the Loch Avon basin can be a wintry place, as witnessed by one early explorer who was caught here in a storm:

> ... the interstices of the tempest-driven clouds only showed us a dreary, winter, Greenland-like chaos of snow and rocks and torrents. It taxed our full philosophy ... to believe that we were still in the United Kingdom ... and that it was the 1st of August.
>
> J.H. Burton: *The Cairngorm Mountains* (1864)

From Loch Avon the river flows eastward through **Glen Avon**, passing the **Fords of Avon** and, just before it turns northward, **Ben Avon** (1171 m / 3842 ft), noted for the granite tors on its summit plateau. These tors are collectively known as the **Bads o' Ben Avon** (Scots *bad* 'tuft'), although individually they have Gaelic names; one of them, Clach Bhan ('stone of the women'), takes its name from the former practice of local women, when pregnant, visiting the tor to bathe in its rockpools, with the expectation that thereby their forthcoming labour would be rendered less arduous. From a distance the tors might be taken for castles or houses in the sky, but this fantasy is bleakly discounted by the Northeast poet Olive Fraser (1909–77):

Yon's nae wife's hoose ayont A'an
In the green lift ava,
Yon's the cauld lums o' Ben A'an
Wha's smeek is snaw.

(*ayont* 'beyond', *lift* 'sky', *ava* 'at all', *cauld* 'cold', *lums* 'chimneys', *smeek* 'smoke', *snaw* 'snow')

The all-year-round wintriness of the hill was witnessed by an earlier traveller (albeit writing in the period known as 'the Little Ice Age'):

There [from Braemar] I saw mount Benawne, with a furr'd mist upon his snowie head instead of a nightcap: for you must understand that the oldest man alive never saw but the snow was on the top of divers of these hills, both in summer, as well as in winter.

John Taylor: *The Pennyles Pilgrimage* (1618), an account of a Thames bargeman's travels in Scotland without a coin in his pocket

Beyond Ben Avon the river turns northward, flowing by Tomintoul and then into the broader valley of **Strath Avon**, until, just after **Bridge of Avon**, the Avon enters the mighty SPEY.

Avon⁶ From the River AVON³.
A village in Hampshire, on the River AVON³, about 8 km (5 miles) north of Christchurch.

Avon⁷ From the River AVON².
A former county in southwest England, on the Bristol Channel (*see under* BRISTOL), formed in 1974 from the county boroughs of BATH and BRISTOL and parts of the counties of Gloucestershire and Somerset. It was abolished in 1996, and its territory distributed between Bath and Northeast Somerset, North Somerset, South Gloucestershire and the City of Bristol. The idea of 'Avon' as a local territorial name survives, however, in the designation of various official bodies (e.g. the Avon and Somerset Police Force).

Avonbeg. *See under* AVOCA.

Avondale A transferred modern name, presumably given by the builder of the house, a Mr Hayes.
A house in County Wicklow, 2 km (1.2 miles) south of Rathdrum and some 15 km (9 miles) southwest of Wicklow.

The house was built in 1779 and was the birthplace and home of the Irish Nationalist leader Charles Stewart Parnell (1846–91). The house is now an agricultural school.
'Blackbird of Avondale, The'. A ballad about Parnell:

Near to Rathdrum in the County Wicklow
This brave defender of Granuaile
First tuned his notes on old Ireland's freedom,
In the lovely woodlands of Avondale.

(*Granuaile*, a personification of Ireland, based on Grace O'Malley, the Queen of Clew Bay (*see under* CLEW BAY))

Avonmore. *See under* AVOCA.

Avonmouth 'mouth of the Avon', AVON² + OE *mutha* 'mouth'.
A town and port in Bristol, on the Bristol Channel (*see under* BRISTOL) at the mouth of the River AVON². Although the name dates back to Anglo-Saxon times, it originally referred simply to the mouth of the river. It did not gain wider significance until the development of the port here in the late 19th century, following the opening of Avonmouth Dock in 1877.

Avonwick *Avon* (*see* AVON⁴) + WICK.
A village in Devon, on the River AVON⁴, about 22 km (14 miles) east of Plymouth. Its original name was Newhouse, which was deliberately changed to Avonwick in the late 1870s.

Awbeg Irish *Abha Bheag* 'little river'.
A tributary of the River BLACKWATER², County Cork, rising in the BALLYHOURA MOUNTAINS and flowing past BUTTE-VANT and DONERAILE. In Edmund Spenser's *Colin Clouts Come Home Againe* (written at Kilcolman Castle on the river in 1591) it becomes the Mulla, derived from Cill na Mallach, the Irish name for Buttevant. The Mulla reappears in Spenser's *Epithalamion* (1595):

Ye nymphs of Mulla, which with careful heed
The silver scaly trouts do tend full well,
And greedy pikes which use therein to feed
Those trouts and pikes all others do excel.

Awliscombe Probably 'valley near the fork of a river', OE *awel* 'awl, fork, grappling-hook' + *-combe* (*see* -COMBE, COOMBE).

❖ avon ❖

This is an Old Celtic word used widely in the place names of Britain and Ireland. From Brittonic *abona*, the English river AVON¹ and names such as Aveton Gifford 'farm on the river Avon' use the word in a characteristically English fashion as a name, not as an element. STRATHAVEN in Lanarkshire, along with the Scottish River AVON⁵, use the element in a similar way.

The same word in Welsh, *afon*, is an element meaning 'the river', and characteristically has a name attached, as in Afon Gwy 'the river WYE¹', Afon Dyfrdwy 'the river DEE²' and BLAENAVON in Torfaen 'headwater of the river'. Gaelic *amhainn* is found in the names of some remote rivers, but Irish *abhainn* is frequent in settlement and river names, most commonly beginning with *owen-*, such as Owenbeg 'little river' and Owenmore 'big river'.

A village (pronounced 'awe-liskəm') in Devon, about 3 km (2 miles) northwest of Honiton.

Awniduff. The anglicized name for the Irish rivers Black-water[2] and Blackwater[3].

Axbridge 'bridge over the Axe', Axe[2] + OE *brycg* 'bridge'.
A small town in Somerset, on the River Axe[2], about 14 km (8.5 miles) west of Wells. It was the base from which Saxon and Norman kings hunted for stags in the nearby Mendip Hills. From the Middle Ages to the 19th century it was a wool town, specializing in the knitting of stockings.

Axe[1] An Indo-European river name, cognate with Exe and Esk[1], from a root meaning 'gush'.
A river in Devon and Dorset. It rises in west Dorset, about 3 km (2 miles) north of Beaminster, and flows 34 km (21 miles) westwards and then southwestwards, through Axminster, before entering the English Channel on the eastern side of Seaton.

Axe[2]. A river in Somerset. It rises in the Mendip Hills, at Wookey Hole, and flows 40 km (25 miles) into the Bristol Channel (*see under* Bristol) at Uphill.

Axholme. *See* Isle of Axholme.

Axminster 'monastery by the Axe' (referring to an early Anglo-Saxon monastery, where some West Saxon princes were buried), Axe[1] + OE *mynster* 'monastery, large church'.
A small market town in Devon, about 14 km (8.5 miles) southeast of Honiton, on the River Axe[1]. It developed at the intersection of the Portway and the Fosse Way. It is famous chiefly as a centre of carpet manufacturing. The industry was founded here in 1755 by Thomas Whitty, but his original business only survived for eighty years. Carpet-making was revived in the town in 1937, and since then **Axminster** (or in full **Axminster carpet**, **Axminster rug**, etc.) has become a generic term for a type of carpet in which pile tufts are inserted into a backing according to a predetermined pattern (in contrast with Wilton carpets, whose pattern is woven with loops of cut or uncut pile).

Aylesbury 'Ægel's stronghold', OE *Ægeles* possessive form of male personal name *Ægel* + bury.
The county town of Buckinghamshire, about 27 km (17 miles) northeast of Oxford. It lies in the **Vale of Aylesbury** (*see below*), north of the Chiltern Hills. Perhaps the gentlest way to summarize Aylesbury would be to say that architectural fragments of its medieval and Tudor past (such as the medieval gateway of the King's Head Hotel) survive amongst much 20th-century redevelopment. The television murder-mystery series *Midsomer Murders* (1997–) is filmed in the town and its environs.

The Radical John Wilkes was a Whig member of parliament for Aylesbury from 1757 to 1764. The composer Rutland Boughton (1878–1960) was born here.

There are towns called Aylesbury in Canada (Saskatchewan) and New Zealand (Canterbury).

Aylesbury case. A legal wrangle concerning voting rights that lasted from 1701 until 1704, leading to a lengthy dispute between the two houses of parliament. Matthew Ashby, an Aylesbury cobbler, sued three local constables for denying him the right to vote in an election despite his being legally qualified to do so. Other 'Aylesbury men' brought similar cases against the constables. The case was referred to the House of Lords who found in Ashby's favour, but the Commons insisted that *it* was the sole arbiter of electoral matters. The dispute was heightened by party feeling, the Whigs being dominant in the House of Lords, the Tories in the Commons.

Aylesbury duck. A large breed of domestic duck with white plumage and a yellow beak. The term is first recorded in 1854. In 20th-century rhyming slang **Aylesbury duck**, or simply **Aylesbury**, was used as a euphemistic substitute for *fuck* in such phrases as 'not give an Aylesbury'. Hence

---

❖ -ay ❖

Most of the names of the islands off the Scottish coast contain the Scandinavian element *ey* 'island', which is testimony to the skill and persistence of the Scandinavians as sailors, navigators and settlers. Not all of the islands were uninhabited when they were named, of course, and the names containing Old Scandinavian *papi* 'monk, priest, hermit', particularly Pabbay[1], Papa Stour and Papa Westray, indicate that Irish monks got there before the Scandinavians. Very ancient remains show that even the Irish were latecomers, however, but little if anything remains of an earlier strand of naming.

Further south, the characteristic -*ay* sound is often lost, some-times altogether as in Barrow-in-Furness (Cumbria), which is a hybrid of Old Celtic *barr* 'promontory' and Old Scandinavian *ey*. More often, though, it becomes the same sound as that which represents Old English *eg* 'island, dry ground in marsh' (*see* -ey, -ea). Anglesey, for example, is pure Scandinavian 'Ongull's island'. Haxey (Lincolnshire) has a Scandinavian personal name, *Hakr* or *Haki*, but the second element could be either *ey* or Old English *eg* 'island, dry ground in marsh' since the place is not coastal, but in the low-lying Isle of Axholme; Axholme itself derives from a combination of Haxey and Old Scandinavian *holmr* 'raised land in marsh'.

also **Aylesbury'ed** (as in 'I'm absolutely Aylesbury'ed after climbing all those stairs').

Aylesbury Vale. An administrative district of Buckinghamshire, based on the Vale of Aylesbury.

Vale of Aylesbury. A broad plain between the CHILTERN HILLS and the COTSWOLDS, which stretches north from Aylesbury and Oxford towards the borders of Northamptonshire. It is rich dairy-farming country, its fields interspersed with woods and the occasional tranquil village.

Aylesford 'Ægel's ford', OE *Ægeles* possessive form of male personal name *Ægel* + FORD.

A small town in Kent, on the River MEDWAY[1], about 5 km (3 miles) northwest of Maidstone. There is a restored Carmelite friary here: it was dissolved by Henry VIII, but the Carmelites came back in 1949. The megalithic monument KIT'S COTY is 3 km (2 miles) to the north.

Aylesham 'Ægel's homestead or enclosure', OE *Ægeles* possessive form of male personal name *Ægel* + HAM.

A town in Kent, approximately 11 km (7 miles) southeast of Canterbury. It was planned in 1926–7 as a coalfield town to house migrant workers from Wales and the northeast of England who were working at nearby Snowdown colliery. However, it never grew to its projected size, and Snowdown colliery closed in 1986.

Aylsham 'Ægel's homestead', OE *Ægeles* possessive form of male personal name *Ægel* + HAM.

A small town in Norfolk, on the River BURE, about 16 km (10 miles) southwest of Cromer. The landscape gardener Humphry Repton (1752–1818) is buried in the local churchyard.

Aynho 'Æga's hill-spur', OE *Ægan* possessive form of male personal name *Æga* + *hoh* 'hill-spur'.

A village in Northamptonshire, about 24 km (15 miles) southwest of Towcester.

Ayot St Lawrence *Ayot* 'Æga's gap or pass', OE male personal name *Æga* + *geat* 'gap, pass'; *St Lawrence* from the dedication of the local church.

A village in Hertfordshire, about 8 km (5 miles) southwest of Stevenage. Its main claim to fame is that the Irish playwright George Bernard Shaw (1856–1950) spent the last 44 years of his life here. He called his house, now owned by the National Trust and open to the public, 'Shaw's Corner'.

Ayr[1] Gaelic *Ar* or *Ad'har*, derived from an OCelt or pre-Celtic river name, possibly meaning 'flowing movement'.

A river flowing east–west for about 50 km (31 miles) in South and East Ayrshire, joining the Firth of Clyde (*see under* CLYDE) at the town of AYR[2]. It was on the banks of the river, at Failford just west of Mauchline, on 14 May 1786 that Robert Burns last saw 'Highland Mary' (Mary Campbell), who died shortly afterwards:

> That sacred hour can I forget
> Can I forget the hallowed grove
> Where by the winding Ayr we met
> To live one day of parting love.

'**The Bonnie Banks of Ayr**' is a traditional fiddle air.

Ayr[2] In Gaelic the town of Ayr is *Inbhir-àir* 'mouth of the Ayr' (*see* ABER).

A town at the mouth of the River AYR[1] in South Ayrshire, some 55 km (34 miles) southwest of Glasgow. Ayr looks out across **Ayr Bay**, and is a royal BURGH (1202), market town and seaside resort. There is also a well-known horse-racing track. It was the county town of the former county of Ayrshire, and the administrative HQ of the former Kyle and Carrick district (in Strathclyde region). **Ayr Academy** was founded in 1233, and was attended by George Douglas Brown (1869–1902), author of *The House with the Green Shutters* (1901).

When Daniel Defoe visited Ayr in the 1720s he found the place 'decaying and declining':

> At present like an old beauty, it shows the ruins of a good face.
>
> Daniel Defoe: *A Tour Through the Whole Island of Great Britain* (1724–6)

Ayr has many associations with Robert Burns, who was born in the village of ALLOWAY, now a suburb of Ayr. The poet described Ayr as unsurpassed 'for honest men and bonnie lasses', and the inn where Burns's Tam O'Shanter got drunk is now a Burns museum. In '**The Brigs of Ayr**' (1786; Scots *brig* 'bridge') the 'Auld Brig' (12th century) holds a dialogue with the 'New Brig' (built 1786–8), in which the 'clishmaclaver' (idle talk) becomes somewhat heated.

Ayr was the birthplace of John Loudon McAdam (1756–1836), the inventor of the 'tarmacadam' road surface. The Labour politician Keir Hardie (1856–1915) lived in Ayr in the 1880s, organizing miners' unions in the county.

Ayr United FC (nicknamed the Honest Men) was founded in 1910 and plays at Somerset Park.

'**The Auld Toon o' Ayr**' is the name of a traditional strathspey (*see under* SPEY).

There are towns called Ayr in Australia (Queensland) and in the USA (North Dakota, Nebraska).

Barns of Ayr, the. In 1297 William Wallace trapped the English garrison in Ayr by burning all the barns round about. The site where Wallace is said to have watched 'the barns o' Ayr burn weil' is marked by the Barnweil Monument. According to the 15th-century poet Blind Harry in his poem *The Wallace*, this was in revenge for a piece of treachery in which 360 Scottish nobles were summoned to a conference by the English in Ayr, but were caught and hanged one by one. However, this part of the story is fictitious, arising from a misunderstanding of an earlier account in which some Scottish nobles are hanged 'in ar' – the reference being to a circuit court or *eyre*.

Ayres, the. *See under* POINT OF AYRE.

Ayrshire From AYR[2] + SHIRE.

A former county of southwest Scotland, bordered to the north by Renfrewshire, to the east by Lanarkshire and Dumfriesshire and to the south by Kircudbrightshire and Wigtownshire. It was traditionally divided into the areas of CUNNINGHAME in the north, KYLE in the centre and CARRICK[1] in the south. In 1975 it was abolished, becoming part of STRATHCLYDE region. With the reorganization of 1996, the new unitary authorities of NORTH AYRSHIRE, EAST AYRSHIRE and SOUTH AYRSHIRE were created. There is a town called Ayrshire in the USA (Iowa).

Ayrshire cattle. A breed of reddish-brown and white dairy cattle originating in the county (and said to have been first bred by the Dunlops of DUNLOP). They are chiefly reared in the UK and North America.

Ayrshire lassie. An opening in the game of draughts devised in the later 19th century.

Ayrshire needlework or **Ayrshire whitework.** A type of fine needlework using white thread on white muslin. Although such work was known from medieval Germany, it became particularly associated with Ayrshire from the later 18th century.

Bard of Ayrshire, the. A sobriquet sometimes given to Robert Burns, a native of the county (*see* ALLOWAY).

Aysgarth 'gap or pass with oak trees', OScand *eiki* 'oak wood' + *skarth* 'gap, pass'.

A village in WENSLEYDALE, North Yorkshire, some 20 km (12 miles) southwest of Richmond. Nearby is the spectacular **Aysgarth Falls** where the River URE hurtles down a narrow gorge over giant steps – a sight that thrilled the aesthetic sensibilities of the poet William Wordsworth, the painter J.M.W. Turner and the art critic John Ruskin. The old mill at Aysgarth (now the Yorkshire Carriage Museum) made the red shirts worn by Garibaldi's Thousand, the liberators of Sicily and Naples in 1860.

Aythorpe Roding. *See under* the RODINGS.

B

Babbacombe 'Babba's valley', OE male personal name *Babba* + *combe* (*see* -COMBE, COOMBE).

A seaside village in south Devon, now a northern suburb of TORQUAY. It is noted for its pottery.

Babbacombe Bay. A bay on the south Devon coast, from Babbacombe in the south to Shaldon in the north. It was the scene of the drowning in a sailing accident of Elizabeth Barrett's much-loved brother Edward in 1840. The South West Coast Path runs along the bay.

Babbacombe Lee. A 1971 concept album by the folk-rock group Fairport Convention, recounting the true story of John 'Babbacombe' Lee, who in 1885, on circumstantial evidence, was sentenced to death for the murder of an elderly woman, Emma Keyse, at Babbacombe. Continuing to protest his innocence, he survived three attempts to hang him and was eventually released from prison in 1907. Fairport's fiddler, Dave Swarbrick, was inspired by an old copy of Lee's autobiography, *The Man They Could Not Hang*, which he found in a junk shop.

Babbinswood 'wood named after Babba', OE male personal name *Babba* + *wudu* 'wood'.

A village in Shropshire, about 3 km (2 miles) east of Oswestry.

Babcary 'Babba's (estate on the River) Cary', OE male personal name *Babba* + CARY.

A village in Somerset, about 11 km (7 miles) southeast of GLASTONBURY.

Bablock Hythe 'landing place at Babba's stream', *Bablock* OE male personal name *Babba* + *lacu* 'stream'; *Hythe* OE *hyth* 'landing place'.

An ancient crossing-point on the River Thames in Oxfordshire, 3 km (2 miles) west of CUMNOR. The Romans are known to have crossed the Thames here. It was a favourite haunt of the poet Matthew Arnold, who famously alludes to it in his pastoral elegy 'The Scholar-Gipsy' (1853, *see quotation under* THAMES[1]). Arnold would almost certainly be unimpressed by the sprawling mobile home park that disfigures the north bank of the Thames near here.

BÁC. An abbreviation of BAILE ÁTHA CLIATH (i.e. Dublin), sometimes used in addresses when writing in Irish.

Bachelor's Walk Possibly from a surname.

A street by the quays on the LIFFEY in Dublin, scene of a violent incident on 26 July 1914 in which a British Army detachment, returning to barracks after failing to intercept 1500 smuggled rifles at HOWTH, opened fire on a hostile crowd, resulting in four deaths. The incident, also known as Bloody Sunday, was commemorated in a 1915 painting by Jack Yeats, entitled *Bachelor's Walk, In Memoriam*.

For other Bloody Sundays *see* CROKE PARK *and* BOGSIDE.

❖ bach ❖

The element represented variously as *bach*, *bychan*, *fach* and *fechan*, meaning 'small', shows some of the sound- and spelling-changes that occur particularly in some elements descended from Brittonic. Scots Gaelic and Irish are relatively uncomplicated: Avonbeg and Avonmore mean small river and big river respectively (*see under* AVOCA), and BALLYBEG and Ballymore are 'small' and 'big town'. But in Welsh and Cornish the sounds change according to variations of age, grammar and context. The paired Welsh mountain names Glyder Fawr and Glyder Fach (*see under* GLYDERS) and Moelwyn Mawr and Moelwyn Bach (*see under* MOELWYNS), with the affixes meaning 'big' and 'small' in each case, show how both *b*- and *m*- could be pronounced *f*-. Cwm Bychan Gwynedd (*see* ROMAN STEPS) and LLANFAIRFECHAN in Conwy illustrate further variants on the form of the word.

Backbone of England, the. A nickname for the PEN-NINES, a range of hills running north–south from the PEAK DISTRICT in Derbyshire and Staffordshire to the CHEVIOTS on the Scottish border.

Backhill of Clackriach Probably 'ridge at the back', OE *bæc* 'back' + *hill* 'ridge'; *Clackriach* distinguishes it from Back-hill, Backhill of Bulwark and Backhill of Trustach, all also in Aberdeenshire.

A tiny settlement in Aberdeenshire (formerly in Grampian region), some 20 km (12 miles) west of Peterhead.

Backlass Etymology unknown.

A tiny settlement in Highland (formerly in Caithness), 16 km (10 miles) west of Wick.

Backs, the. The gardens behind colleges bordering on the River CAM[2] at CAMBRIDGE[1] – Queens', King's, Clare, Trinity Hall, Trinity and St John's. The views of medieval and Tudor magnificence and serenity available from the other side of the Cam have been a magnet for tourists since at least the 1870s, when the term is first recorded:

> You wander through those lovely 'backs' of colleges,
> which might almost be carpeted with poetry.
>
> *London Society* (1871)

Bacon End Originally *Beacon End* '(land in) the area of the beacon' (referring to a fire-signal or possibly to a standing cross or stone, which was among the applications of OE *beacen* 'beacon').

A village in Essex, about 18 km (11 miles) northeast of Harlow.

Bacup 'valley below a ridge', OE *bæc* 'ridge' + *hop* 'secluded valley'.

An industrial town (pronounced 'bay-cup') in Lancashire, 6 km (4 miles) east of Rawtenstall. Bacup is known for its Britannia Coconut Dancers, who every Easter Saturday perform their Nutters' Dance from one side of the town to the other. Some of its old terraced houses (now demolished) were 'back to earth', i.e. built into the hillside.

Badbury Probably 'Badda's stronghold', OE male personal name *Badda* + BURY; alternatively, since the village is the site of an Iron Age hillfort (as at BADBURY HILL and BADBURY RINGS), the element *Bad-* may represent OE *badde* 'evil', referring to a disturbing or 'evil' atmosphere perceived in such places.

A village in Wiltshire, within the unitary authority of SWINDON, about 4 km (2.5 miles) southeast of the town of Swindon.

Badbury Hill *See* BADBURY.

A hill in Oxfordshire (before 1974 in Berkshire), about 3 km (2 miles) west of FARINGDON. It is 158 m (518 ft) high, and surmounted by an Iron Age hillfort. Known locally as **Badbury Clump**, it is owned by the National Trust and

noted for its beech woods and bluebell displays. The beech trees are believed to have been planted by prisoners of war who were stationed nearby during the Second World War. Badbury Hill has wide views over the Berkshire Downs (*see under* BERKSHIRE) and the VALE OF THE WHITE HORSE to the south and the Upper THAMES VALLEY to the north.

Badbury Rings *See* BADBURY.

An Iron Age hillfort 8 km (5 miles) northwest of Wimborne Minster in Dorset. A Roman temple was later built on the site of the hillfort. The dense plantation of trees on the summit dates from the 18th century, when the parkland was fashionably landscaped.

Badbury Rings is identified by some scholars with Mons Badonicus (MOUNT BADON), where, according to the 6th-century chronicler Gildas, the Saxons were defeated around AD 500 (however, BADBURY and BADBURY HILL, amongst other locations, have also been put forward as candidates for the battle site). The battle has come to be associated with King Arthur, but Gildas makes no mention of him.

Badcall 'hazel clump or thicket', Gaelic *bad* 'clump or thicket' + *call* 'hazel tree'.

The name of two small settlements in the far northwest of Highland (formerly in Sutherland), one 2 km (1.2 miles) south of Scourie, the other 2 km east of Kinlochbervie.

Baddesley Ensor *Baddesley* 'Bæddi's glade', OE *Bæddis* possessive form of male personal name *Bæddi* + -LEY; *Ensor* denoting manorial ownership in the Middle Ages by the de Edneshoure family (whose name derived from EDENSOR).

A village in Warwickshire, about 12 km (7.5 miles) north-west of Nuneaton.

Badenoch Apparently 'land subject to flooding', Gaelic *baideanach* 'drowned place'.

A traditional area of the HIGHLANDS, centred on the Upper SPEY Valley, and bounded by the Monadhliath Mountains to the northwest, the Cairngorms to the east and Atholl to the south.

Boar of Badenoch, the. A mountain (739 m / 2424 ft) on the south edge of Badenoch, on the west side of the DRUMOCHTER PASS. Its Gaelic name *An Torc* means 'the boar', and was inspired by its hog's-back shape and the story that it was haunted by a ghostly boar. Just to the south is the similarly porcine Sow of ATHOLL.

Wolf of Badenoch, the. Alexander Stewart, Earl of Buchan. He was the son of Robert II (reigned 1371–90), who gave him the lands of Badenoch. Alexander was excommunicated when he refused to abandon his mistress, and in retaliation he burnt ELGIN Cathedral in 1390 with the aid of 'wild wikkid Hielandmen'. It was said that he died while playing the Devil at chess. His son abducted the widow of the Earl of Mar, and so gained the earldom.

Badenoch and Strathspey. A former district (1975–96) of Highland region, with its administrative seat at Kingussie.

Badger's Drift. A fictional English village, which features in the detective novels of Caroline Graham (adapted for television as *Midsomer Murders* since 1997). Its population, like that of the neighbouring fictional village of **Midsomer Mallow** (*see* MIDSOMER NORTON), suffers from a disconcertingly high homicide rate.

Badgers Mount Probably 'badgers' hill', ModE *badger* + *mount*.
A village in Kent, about 8 km (5 miles) northwest of Sevenoaks, and just inside the M25.

Badgeworthy Water *Badgeworthy* originally *Bicheordin* 'Bicca's enclosure', OE male personal name *Bicca* + *worthign* 'enclosure'; later influenced by the OE male personal name *Bacga* and -*worth* (*see* -WORTH, WORTHY, -WARDINE).
A river (pronounced 'badgery') forming the northern extremity of the boundary between Devon and Somerset. It rises on EXMOOR and flows northwards 7 km (4.5 miles) to join Oare Water, becoming the East Lyn River, which enters the sea at LYNMOUTH.

Badminton 'Baduhelm's estate', OE male personal name *Baduhelm* + -ING + -TON.
The name of a pair of villages, **Great Badminton** and **Little Badminton**, in South Gloucestershire, about 9 km (5.5 miles) east of CHIPPING SODBURY. Between them lies Badminton Park, setting of **Badminton House**, the country seat of the dukes of Beaufort. The park, through which the modest beginnings of the Bristol AVON[2] flow, is the venue of the annual **Badminton Horse Trials**, a demanding three-day event first held in 1949, at the suggestion of the 10th Duke (who had watched with dismay the lack of success of British riders at the 1948 Olympics). But it is the house itself that was the inspiration of two of the more notable topographical eponyms in English:

badminton. A racquet game that involves hitting a shuttlecock back and forth across a high net. An informal version of this, generally known as 'battledore and shuttlecock', had been played since at least the Middle Ages, but it appears to have been at Badminton House in the 1860s or 1870s that the rules of the modern game were codified. It was popularized by army officers in India, where it was played outdoors. The first unofficial All-England championships were held in 1899.

Badminton. A cooling drink consisting of sweetened diluted claret, popular in the middle years of the 19th century and apparently originating in Badminton House.

Badminton Library. A series of volumes (in full, the Badminton Library of Sports and Pastimes), each devoted to a particular sport, its techniques, rules and lore, edited in the late 19th and early 20th centuries by Henry Somerset,

Duke of Beaufort (hence the title) and A.E.T. Watson, and published by Longmans, Green & Co. It covered topics as varied as fishing, yachting, bowls, mountaineering, billiards, coursing and falconry, and (the bestseller) golf.

> *Wisden* will be, as ever, at my side, to say nothing of a collection of Badminton diaries and a long shelf of cuttings-books.
>
> E.W. Swanton: *Following On* (1977)

Badon, Mount. *See* MOUNT BADON.

Bads o' Ben Avon. *See under* AVON[5].

Bae Colwyn. The Welsh name for COLWYN BAY.

Bag Enderby *Bag* perhaps from the name of a manorial owner in the Middle Ages, or alternatively from OE *bagga* 'bag', possibly referring to a local landscape feature; *Enderby* probably 'Eindrithi's farmstead or village', OScand male personal name *Eindrithi* + -BY.
A village in Lincolnshire, about 21 km (13 miles) northwest of Skegness.
See also MAVIS ENDERBY *and* SOMERSBY.

Baggy Point In the 16th century known as *Bag Point*, presumably a reference to the shape (*see also* BAG ENDERBY).
A headland at the northwest corner of Devon, about 12 km (7.5 miles) southwest of ILFRACOMBE. It is at the southern end of Morte Bay (*see under* MORTE POINT) at the northern end of Bideford Bay (*see under* BIDEFORD).

Baginbun Head The etymology is uncertain: Irish *bun* 'end' is normally the first element in a name; the first element here may be related to *bágach* 'contentious' or *bòcan* 'sprite, goblin'.
A headland on the west side of BALLYTEIGE BAY on the south coast of County Wexford.

Battle of Baginbun (1170). A battle between Anglo-Norman adventurers and an army of Vikings and Irishmen. Having landed at the 'Creeke of Bagganbun', the Anglo-Normans under Raymond le Gros, and acting as a vanguard for Strongbow (Richard de Clare, Earl of Pembroke), established a fortified position on Baginbun Head and fought off a much larger force. Subsequently, Strongbow landed in Ireland and made himself king of LEINSTER, establishing the first English presence in Ireland.

> At the creeke of Bagganbun
> Ireland was lost and won.
>
> Quoted in Meredith Hanmer, *Chronicle of Ireland* (1571)

Bagshot 'projecting piece of land frequented by badgers', OE *bagga* 'badger' + *sceat* 'projecting wood or piece of land'.
A town in Surrey, about 10 km (6 miles) northwest of Woking. Its military demographics (there are several army establishments here and its near neighbours are Sandhurst and Camberley), together with the rather truculent sound of its name, have contributed to a certain reputation as the

abode of retired red-faced colonels. **Bagshot Heath**, just to the south, is a Country Park, and a valuable heathland habitat. **Bagshot Park**, formerly the home of the Army Chaplain's Department, was leased to the Earl of Wessex (formerly Prince Edward) in 1997.

Bagshot sand. A type of sand, generally yellow or brownish, originally identified in the Bagshot area.

'You have as many aliases as Robin of Bagshot'. A phrase formerly said to someone who has many different names. It comes from John Gay's *Beggar's Opera* (1728), in which Robin of Bagshot, one of Macheath's gang, was alias Gordon, alias Bluff Bob, alias Carbuncle, alias Bob Booty. He was meant to represent the contemporary Whig politician Sir Robert Walpole.

Baildon 'circle hill', OE *bægel* 'circle' + *dun* (*see* DOWN, -DON). An industrial town in West Yorkshire, 2 km (1.2 miles) north of Shipley.

Baile an Bhiataigh. The Irish name for BETTYSTOWN.

Baile an Bhuinneánaigh. The Irish name for BALLYBUNNION.

Baile an Chaisleáin. The Irish name for BALLYCASTLE and CASTLETOWNSHEND.

Baile an Chollaigh. The Irish name for BALLINCOLLIG.

Baile Andarsan. The Irish name for ANDERSONTOWN.

Baile an Mhóta. The Irish name for BALLYMOTE.

Baile an Phoill. The Irish name for PILTOWN.

Baile an Róba. The Irish name for BALLINROBE.

Baile an Sceilig. The Irish name for BALLINSKELLIGS.

Baile Aodha. The probable Irish name for the beach of BALLYEAGH STRAND.

Baile Átha an Rí. The Irish name for ATHENRY.

Baile Átha an Urchair. The Irish name for HORSELEAP.

Baile Átha Buí. The Irish name for ATHBOY.

Baile Átha Cliath 'town of the ford of the hurdles', Irish *baile* (*see* BAL-, BALL-, BALLY-) + *átha* 'ford' (*see* FORD) + *cliath* 'hurdle'.
The Irish name for DUBLIN, known from at least AD 770. Before there was a bridge over the LIFFEY there was a tidal crossing, probably made more secure by placing a mat of woven saplings on the river bed. The Irish name is sometimes anglicized as **Aschled**, in an attempt to indicate the pronunciation of the last two words of the name. In the context of postal addresses, Baile Átha Cliath is sometimes abbreviated to **BÁC**.

Baile Átha Fhirdia. The Irish name for ARDEE.

Baile Átha hÚlla. The Irish name for BALLYHOOLY.

Baile Átha Í. The Irish name for ATHY.

Baile Átha Luain. The Irish name for ATHLONE.

Baile Átha Troim. The Irish name for TRIM.

Baile Beag. The Irish name for dramatist Brian Friel's 'everyvillage' of BALLYBEG.

Baile Bhlainséir. The Irish name for BLANCHARDSTOWN.

Baile Brigín. The Irish name for BALBRIGGAN.

Baile Chaisleáin Bhéarra. The Irish name for Castletown Bearhaven (*see under* BEARA).

Baile Chathail. The Irish name for CHARLESTOWN[3].

Baile Chinnéidigh. The Irish name for NEWTOWNMOUNTKENNEDY.

Baile Deasumhan. The Irish name for BALLYDESMOND.

Bailegangaire 'town without laughter', Irish.
A fictional town that is the setting of Tom Murphy's 1985 play of the same name. It is a tragi-comedy, telling the stories of three women, and involves a laughing competition.

Baile Locha Riach. The Irish name for LOUGHREA.

Baile Loch Cuan. The Irish name for STRANGFORD.

Baile Mhaodhóg. The Irish name for BOOLAVOGUE.

Baile Mhistéala. The Irish name for MITCHELSTOWN.

Baile Monaidh. One of the two Irish names for BALLYMONEY.

Baile Mór. The Irish name for BALLYMORE HILL.

Baile Muine. One of the two Irish names for BALLYMONEY.

Baile na Croise. The Irish name for DRAPERSTOWN.

Baile na hInse. The Irish name for BALLYNAHINCH.

Baile na Mainistreach. The Irish name for the Belfast suburb of NEWTOWNABBEY.

Baile Nua na hArda. The Irish name for NEWTOWNARDS.

Baile Raghnaill. The Irish name for RANDALSTOWN.

Baile Shéamais Dhuibh. The Irish name for BALLYJAMESDUFF.

Baile Shláine. The Irish name for SLANE.

Baile Uí Dhonnagáin. The Irish name for DUNGANSTOWN.

Baile Uí Mhatháin. The Irish name for BALLYMAHON.

Bailey From the name of submerged sandbanks, Bill *Bailey*'s Bank and Outer *Bailey* Bank.
A sea area in the shipping forecast. It is in the northeastern Atlantic, to the northwest of Scotland, between the sea areas of HEBRIDES to the east and ROCKALL to the south.

Bailieborough 'Bailie's town', ModE personal name *Bailie* + borough (*see* BURY).
A small market town in County Cavan, 38 km (24 miles) southwest of Dundalk. Its Irish name is **Coill an Chollaig** ('wood of the boar').

Bainbridge 'bridge on the River Bain', OScand river name meaning 'short one or useful one' + OE *brycg* 'bridge'.

A village in WENSLEYDALE, North Yorkshire, 25 km (15 miles) southwest of Richmond. Every evening throughout the winter, in a custom of obscure origin, a horn is ceremonially blown in the village.

Bakerloo From *Baker* Street + Water*loo*, the two stations between which the line originally ran.

A line of the London Underground which, when opened in 1906, ran only between BAKER STREET[1] and WATERLOO[1] stations. Hence its portmanteau name, said to have been coined by 'Quex' (G.H.F. Nichols) of the *Evening News*. The line was subsequently extended to Watford Junction in the north and ELEPHANT AND CASTLE in the south (the northernmost section was closed in 1982, leaving Harrow and Wealdstone as the terminus).

Bakers End *Bakers* denoting manorial ownership in the early Middle Ages by John le Bakire.

A village in Hertfordshire, about 4 km (2.5 miles) northeast of Ware.

Baker Street[1] From *William Baker*, who laid it out.

A street in the WEST END[1] of London, in the City of WESTMINSTER (W1, NW1), running between REGENT'S PARK in the north and Portman Square in the south. It was developed from the mid-1750s onwards by William Baker, a speculative builder. It is a broad thoroughfare, linking Marylebone Road (*see under* MARYLEBONE) with OXFORD STREET, and is now mainly lined with shops and offices (including the head office of Marks & Spencer). Number 60 was the headquarters of the Special Operations Executive in the Second World War.

Baker Street's most celebrated resident was a fictional one: Sherlock Holmes. His creator Arthur Conan Doyle lodged the great detective in a first-floor flat at No. 221B, where he was looked after by his housekeeper Mrs Hudson and, in the earlier part of his career, shared his accommodation with the faithful Dr Watson. Among the features of its cluttered interior were a Persian slipper for holding tobacco, a coal scuttle for cigars, and bullet holes in the wall (a result of indoor target practice). A plaque commemorating Holmes can be found on the building now occupying the site where 221B, had it ever existed, would have been – the office of the Abbey National Bank, now known as Abbey (where requests for his help with insoluble mysteries are still regularly received). It is doubtless no coincidence that Conan Doyle, who was a doctor, had his consulting rooms in Devonshire Place, not far from Baker Street.

Baker Street Underground station, on the BAKERLOO, Circle, Jubilee, Metropolitan and Hammersmith & City lines, was opened in 1863.

'Baker Street'. A song (1978) by Gerry Rafferty. Its soaring saxophone riffs and mellow vocals made this evocation of big-city alienation a UK and US No. 1 hit:

> Winding your way down on Baker Street
> Light in your head and dead on your feet
> Well, another crazy day, you'll drink the night away
> And forget about everything.

Baker Street Irregulars. A fictional band of young street urchins, led by a lad called Wiggins, employed by Sherlock Holmes to search for clues, lost articles, etc. Their name was adopted by a society of Sherlock Holmes enthusiasts, founded in 1933.

Baker Street[2] Named after the family of William *Bakere*, known here from 1402.

A village in Essex, about 2.5 km (1.5 miles) northeast of Grays.

Bakewell 'Badeca's spring or stream', OE male personal name *Badeca* + *wella* 'spring, stream'.

A market town in Derbyshire, on the River WYE[2], within the PEAK DISTRICT National Park, about 12 km (7.5 miles) northwest of Matlock. Springs in the area led the Duke of Rutland to plan a spa here in the early 19th century, but little came of the enterprise, and most of the springs have since run dry.

Bakewell tart. A sweet tart containing a layer of jam beneath a topping made from ground almonds, sugar, eggs and butter. The connection with Bakewell is not known for certain, although legend has it that the original was created by accident in the early 19th century, when a chef at the Rutland Arms Hotel, in the centre of the town, made a mistake over a recipe. The 'tart' is a relatively new element. In the 19th century the confection was known as **Bakewell pudding** (the earliest known reference to this is in Meg Dods's *The Cook and Housewife's Manual* of 1826), and the name *Bakewell tart* is not recorded before the 20th century.

Bala Welsh *bala* 'outlet' or 'land between two lakes'; the town is situated at the outlet of the River Dee from Bala Lake (*Llyn Tegid*), but the area of Bala is also situated between the two lakes of Llyn Tegid and Llyn Celyn.

A town in Gwynedd (formerly in Merioneth), some 30 km (18 miles) west-southwest of Llangollen. It is sited at the end of **Bala Lake**. In Welsh, the lake is called **Llyn Tegid**, after Tegid Foel, 'Tegid the Bald', a legendary 5th-century Prince of Penllyn, although George Borrow more poetically suggests it means 'Lake of Beauty'. A heritage steam railway, the Bala Lake Railway, runs for *c*.7 km (4.5 miles) along the lake's southern shore; two of its locomotives once worked in the region's slate quarries.

Bala Lake is the largest natural lake in Wales (6.4 km / 4 miles long and 1.6 km / 1 mile wide), and is the home of a primitive whitefish called the gwyniad (*Coregonus pennantii*), found nowhere else. It is also reputedly the home of a monster called Teggi, and is mentioned both by Spenser in his *Faerie Queen* and by Tennyson:

> And Enid tended on him there; and there
> Her constant motion round him, and the breath
> Of her sweet tendance hovering over him,
> Fill'd all the genial courses of his blood
> With deeper and with ever deeper love,
> As the south-west that blowing Bala lake
> Fills all the sacred Dee.
>
> Alfred, Lord Tennyson: 'Geraint and Edith' (1859), from
> *Idylls of the King*

According to tradition, the original town of Bala lies under the waters of the lake, which will, in time, also cover the present Bala. The lake is also supposedly the last resting place of Charles the Harper, who drowned here some time in the 18th century after making a pact with the Devil, in which his part was to feed communion wafers to the local dogs. Religious practice in Bala stiffened somewhat after another Charles, the noted Calvinist Methodist minister Thomas Charles – **Charles of Bala** – (1755–1814), settled here in 1783, and the town became famous for its revivalist meetings. Bala Calvinist Methodist College was founded some years after Charles's death. In 1865, 153 Welsh colonists, mostly from Bala, set up a model nonconformist settlement called Y Wladfa ('the colony') in Patagonia.

Bala was once famous for its knitwear, and George III wore stockings knitted in the town to alleviate his rheumatism.

> At Bala is nothing remarkable except a lake of eleven miles in circumference.
>
> Samuel Taylor Coleridge: letter to Robert Southey (15 July 1794)

> And every time I set eyes on Lake Bala, particularly when its surface was churned up by the wind in winter, I remembered the story Evan the cobbler had told me, about the two headstreams of Dwy Fawr and Dwy Fach which are said to flow right through the lake, far down in its dark depths, never mingling their waters with its own. The two rivers, according to Evan, said Austerlitz, were called after the only human beings not drowned but saved from the biblical deluge in the distant past.
>
> W.G. Sebald: *Austerlitz* (2001), translated from the German by Anthea Bell

Bala series. In geology, one of the series into which the Ordovician system is sometimes divided in Britain; it is alternatively separated into the Ashgill and Caradoc series. It ended 438 million years ago.

O'r Bala i Geneva. (Welsh, 'From Bala to Geneva'.) The title of a work (1889) by Sir Owen Morgan Edwards, comparing life in Wales with that Abroad.

Balafark Etymology unknown.

A small settlement on the north side of the Gargunnock Hills (*see under* GARGUNNOCK), Stirling (formerly in Central region), 18 km (11 miles) west of Stirling.

Balamory. The fictional name of TOBERMORY in the BBC children's television programme of that name.

Balbriggan Irish *Baile Brigín* 'Brigin's homestead' (*see* BAL-, BALL-, BALLY-).

A coastal town in County Dublin, 30 km (19 miles) north of the capital.

balbriggans. Knitted cotton hosiery, for which the town was once famous.

Sack of Balbriggan (20 September 1920). An incident during the Anglo-Irish War in which Auxiliaries, in retaliation for the nearby killing of Head Constable Peter Burke, burnt down houses and shops in Balbriggan and killed two local men.

Balcombe Street Origin unknown.

A street in the City of WESTMINSTER (NW1), running southwards into Marylebone Road. When it was originally laid out in the late 1820s it was called Milton Street. The change of name dates from 1886, but it is not known what occasioned it.

The street's notoriety rests on what became known as the **Balcombe Street Siege**. In December 1975 four IRA gunmen (Joseph O'Connell, Harry Duggan, Eddie Butler and Hugh Doherty) held a husband and wife hostage at No. 22B for six days. Police surrounded the building, and eventually the men surrendered and gave up the hostages unharmed.

❖ bal-, ball-, bally- ❖

Irish, Scots and Manx Gaelic *baile* is similar in many ways to English -TON, in that it can refer to a farm, a village, a settlement or an estate. Its modern sense in Ireland is 'townland', an administrative district of variable size, and it is one of the most frequently occurring Irish place-name elements. It is easy to confuse with *béal* 'estuary, mouth' and *bealach* 'road': Ballymore could be 'big town' or 'big estuary', depending on whether there is a river nearby; BALLYCLARE (County Antrim) seems to be 'road of the plain', with *bealach*; and BALLYCLARE (County Roscommon) seems to be 'estate of the plain', with *baile*. Many minor settlements or farms on the Isle of Man use this element in its early sense of 'farm'.

Baldock 'Baghdad'. Baldock was founded in the 12th century by the Knights Templar (a crusading order established in 1119 and named after the Temple of Solomon at Jerusalem, where they had their headquarters). The Templars called the new town *Baldac*, this being the OFr form of the Arabian city of Baghdad (now the capital of Iraq).

A town in Hertfordshire, contiguous with Letchworth, about 11 km (7 miles) north of Stevenage. The GREAT NORTH ROAD passed through Baldock, forming part of the town's high street.

Baldons, the. A collective name for MARSH BALDON and TOOT BALDON in Oxfordshire.

Baldwin's Gate From a gate into Madely Park, named after the gatekeeper, ME surname *Baldwin*, known here in the 13th century.

A village in Staffordshire, about 11 km (7 miles) southwest of Stoke-on-Trent.

Bale 'bath glade' (i.e. a woodland clearing where there are springs for bathing in), OE *bæth* 'bath' + -LEY.

A village in North Norfolk, about 22 km (14 miles) southwest of Cromer.

Balfour Bay. *See under* EARRAID.

Balham Probably 'smooth or rounded enclosure', OE *bealg* 'swollen thing' + HAM.

A district (pronounced 'bal-əm') of southwest GREATER LONDON, in the borough of WANDSWORTH (SW12). The original settlement was on STANE STREET[1], the Roman road from London to Chichester. It remained a rural village until the middle of the 19th century, when the arrival of the railway began its transformation into a built-up London suburb. Balham Underground station, on the Northern Line, opened in 1926.

Balham's profile was raised, not altogether positively, by Peter Sellers's 1958 recording of the cod travelogue 'Bal-ham – Gateway to the South' by Frank Muir and Denis Norden (originally written as a radio sketch in the 1940s). It ended with the poetical peroration:

> Broad-bosomed, bold, becalmed, benign
> Lies Balham, foursquare on the Northern Line;
> Matched by no marvel save in Eastern scene,
> A rose-red city half as gold as green.

Ballachulish 'settlement by the narrows', Gaelic *baile* (*see* BAL-, BALL-, BALLY-) + *chaolais* 'narrows'.

A village (pronounced 'balla-hoolish') on the south shore of Loch Leven (see LOCH LEVEN[2], under the slopes of BEINN A'BHEITHIR, formerly in Argyll and now in Highland, 2 km (1.2 miles) west of Glencoe village. The smaller settlement of **South Ballachulish** is 3 km (2 miles) to the west, at the narrows where Loch Leven opens out into LOCH LINNHE. Until the bridge across the narrows was built in 1975, there was a car ferry here for the short crossing to the village of

North Ballachulish. In 1752 James of the Glens, found guilty of the Appin Murder (*see under* APPIN), was hanged on Gallows Hill at Ballachulish.

Ballaghadereen Irish *Bealach an Doirín* 'road of the little oak-wood'.

A small market town in County Roscommon, 33 km (20 miles) west of Carrick-on-Shannon. It has the (undistinguished) cathedral of the Catholic diocese of Elphin.

Ballah. A fictionalized version of the town of SLIGO in the poems of W.B. Yeats.

Ballantrae Gaelic *baile* (*see* BAL-, BALL-, BALLY-) + *an traighe* 'on the shore'.

A small village in South Ayrshire, overlooking **Ballantrae Bay**, some 20 km (12 miles) south of Girvan. It was formerly a noted den of smugglers. Curiously, it was not the setting of Robert Louis Stevenson's *The Master of Ballantrae* (1889), which Stevenson wrote in up-state New York. However, Stevenson had earlier visited the village, where his manner of dress had so offended the inhabitants that they threw stones at him. In Stevenson's novel both the Master and his brother come to bad ends, so the author may have been indulging in some kind of revenge in borrowing the village name.

Ballater An obscure name, but a possible etymology is 'town of the wooded stream', Gaelic *baile* (*see* BAL-, BALL-, BALLY-) 'town' + *challater* 'wooded stream'.

A summer resort in upper Deeside, Aberdeenshire (formerly in Grampian). It is 60 km (37 km) west of Aberdeen. It owes its origins to an old woman who in *c*.1760, supposedly guided by dreams, cured herself of scrofula by immersing herself in a bog at the foot of Pannanich Hill, just to the east of the present town. Hearing of this, Francis Farquharson of Monaltrie, an old Jacobite recently returned from exile, built a spa, from which the town of Ballater eventually grew. The town was given an immense boost following Victoria and Albert's acquisition of BALMORAL CASTLE, further up Deeside, as Ballater was the terminus of the railway (now long gone), Victoria having refused to allow it any closer to her Highland retreat. Ballater was the birthplace of Sir Patrick Geddes (1854–1932), one of the pioneers of town and country planning.

Pass of Ballater, the. A rocky defile about 1 km (0.6 miles) north of Ballater, between the hills of Craigendarroch and Creagan Riach. It was the site of the Battle of Tullich (the name of the local area) in 1654, in which Cromwell's forces routed the Highlanders. It was the last British battle in which the longbow was used. In 1689 the Jacobite John Farquharson of Inverey (who gave his name to the COLONEL'S BED), escaped on horseback from government troops up the craggy north side of the pass.

Ball Hill Probably 'rounded, ball-shaped hill'.

A village in Hampshire, about 8 km (5 miles) southwest of Newbury.

Ballina Irish *Béal an Átha* 'mouth of the ford' (*see* FORD).

A port, fishing and market town at the mouth of the River Moy, County Mayo, 30 km (19 miles) north of Castlebar. It is the largest town in the county, and St Muredach's Cathedral (built in 1829) is the cathedral of the Catholic diocese of KILLALA. The part of town on the east side of the river is called ARDNAREE.

Ballina was the birthplace of Mary Robinson (b.1944), President of Ireland (1990–7), and UN High Commissioner for Human Rights since 1997. There is a town called Ballina in Australia (New South Wales).

Ballinalee Irish *Béal Átha na Lao* 'mouth of the ford of the calves' (*see* FORD).

A village in County Longford, 15 km (9 miles) northeast of Longford itself.

Blacksmith of Ballinalee, the. Seán MacEoin (1894–1973), who was indeed a blacksmith in the village. However, his fame lies in his role as a guerrilla leader in the Anglo-Irish War, during which he launched successful attacks on the Black and Tans in Ballinalee in 1920 and 1921. He later became a general in the Irish Army and was a cabinet minister in three governments.

Ballinamuck Irish *Béal Átha na Muc* 'mouth of the ford of the pigs' (*see* FORD).

A village in County Longford, some 30 km (19 miles) southeast of Carrick-on-Shannon.

Battle of Ballinamuck (8 September 1798). The final defeat for the Irish rising following the French invasion of 1798. The small French force soon surrendered to the British, but the Irish fought on desperately and were shown no quarter.

Ballinasloe Irish *Béal Átha Sluaighe* 'ford-mouth of the gathering', referring to the annual fair (*see* FORD).

A market town on the River SUCK in County Galway, 20 km (12 miles) southwest of Athlone. There is an annual livestock (especially horse) fair, established in the 1730s or even earlier, and held in the week of the second Tuesday of October. It was revived as part of a local festival in the 1950s, and is the largest such fair in Ireland and a major tourist attraction. The local quarries provided building stone for part of New York.

Ballinasloe was the birthplace of the Fenian and Nationalist politician John O'Connor Power (1848–91).

Ballincollig Irish *Baile an Chollaigh* 'homestead or town of the boar' (*see* BAL-, BALL-, BALLY-).

A village in County Cork, 12 km (7.5 miles) west of the centre of Cork itself. **Ballincollig Castle**, now ruined, was built in the reign of Edward III (1327–77).

Ballinrobe Irish *Baile an Róba* 'homestead or town of the River Robe' (*see* BAL-, BALL-, BALLY-).

A small market town in County Mayo, 5 km (3 miles) east of LOUGH MASK. There is an annual racing meet in June.

Ballinskelligs Irish *Baile an Sceilig* 'homestead of the SKELLIGS (sea rocks)' (*see* BAL-, BALL-, BALLY-).

A village in County Kerry, on the Atlantic coast overlooking **Ballinskelligs Bay**, some 60 km (37 miles) southwest of Killarney.

Ballinspittle Irish *Béal Átha an Spidéil* 'ford-mouth of the hospital' (*see* FORD).

A village in County Cork, some 5 km (3 miles) southwest of Kinsale. In 1985 a statue of the Virgin in a nearby grotto was reported to have moved, and the place attracted thousands of pilgrims. Later in the same year the statue was damaged by Christian cultists from California, and has subsequently remained resolutely stationary.

Ballitore Irish *Béal Átha an Tuair* 'mouth of the bleach-green ford' (*see* FORD); a bleach-green was land where cloth was stretched out to dry.

A village in County Kildare, some 10 km (6 miles) northeast of Athy. The Quaker school here was founded in 1726 by Abraham Shackleton, and its most famous pupils were the politician Edmund Burke (1729–97) and Paul Cullen (1803–78), Ireland's first cardinal. Abraham's descendant, the Antarctic explorer Ernest Shackleton (1874–1922), was born at Kilkea House to the south of the village.

Annals of Ballitore, The. An account of life in the village by Mary Leadbetter (1758–1826), including the local fall-out of the 1798 United Irishmen's Rebellion.

Balls Cross. *See* BALL'S GREEN.

A village in West Sussex, about 21 km (13 miles) southwest of Horsham.

Ball's Green *Ball's* denoting land ownership in the late Middle Ages by Rychard *Balle* of Pulborough.

A village in East Sussex, about 6.5 km (4 miles) northwest of Crowborough.

Balls Pond Road From a large pond nearby, *Ball's Pond* (which survived until the early 19th century), named after its 17th-century owner, a man called John *Ball*. It was used for a 'sport' of the time in which dogs hunt a duck whose wings have been pinioned, its only means of escape being to dive to the bottom of a pond (whence arises the pub name 'Dog and Duck').

A road in the North London borough of ISLINGTON. It is at the eastern edge of the borough, leading into HACKNEY; this, together with a certain suggestiveness about its name, made it a favourite of 20th-century comedians wanting a cheap 'Cockney culture' laugh.

Ballybeg Irish *Baile Beag*, 'little town' (*see* BAL-, BALL-, BALLY-).

The dramatist Brian Friel's Irish 'everyvillage', featuring in such plays as *Faith Healer* (1979) and *Translations* (1980).

Ballybunnion Irish *Baile an Bhuinneánaigh* 'homestead or town of Bunion or Buinnéan' (*see* BAL-, BALL-, BALLY-).

A seaside resort on the northwest coast of County Kerry, overlooking the Mouth of the Shannon 25 km (16 miles) north of Tralee. It is also spelt **Ballybunion**. There is a championship golf course (where President Bill Clinton played with Dick Spring, leader of the Irish Labour Party, in 1998), amusement arcades, seaweed baths and, as well as a beach, there are caves in the sea cliffs (one of which was visited by the poet Tennyson in 1842). A ruined castle stands on the nearby headland.

Ballycastle Irish *Baile an Chaisleáin* 'town of the stone fort' (*see* BAL-, BALL-, BALLY-), referring to the castle built here by Sir Randall MacDonnell (d.1682), 2nd Earl of Antrim.

A market town and resort on the north coast of County Antrim, 70 km (43 miles) north of Belfast, on **Ballycastle Bay**. Since 1606, on the last Monday and Tuesday in August, the Lammas Fair has been held, as much a social occasion as a market for livestock, as celebrated in the famous ballad by the local woodcarver John MacAuley:

> Did you treat your Mary Ann
> To dulse and yellow man
> At the ould Lammas fair in Ballycastle-O?

Boats can be taken from Ballycastle to RATHLIN ISLAND, and it was from the town to the lighthouse on Rathlin Island that in 1898 Guglielmo Marconi established a radio link, the first over water.

Battle of Ballycastle (1565). A decisive victory for the Irish patriot Shane O'Neill over Sorley Boy Macdonnell, Scots-Irish chieftain of Ulster, who became O'Neill's captive.

Ballyclare Irish *Bealach Cláir* 'road of the plain'.

A market town in County Antrim, 10 km (6 miles) west of Carrickfergus.

Ballydehob Irish *Béal an Dá Chab* 'mouth of the two openings'.

A picturesque village on ROARINGWATER BAY, County Cork, some 14 km (8.5 miles) west of Skibbereen. The name has become an archetype of pretty, mythy, Irish-misty Éire.

Ballydesmond Irish *Baile Deasumhan* 'town of DESMOND (i.e. south Munster)' (*see* BAL-, BALL-, BALLY-), although it is thought by some to be 'Desmond's village', after Gerald Fitzgerald, 14th Earl of *Desmond* (1533–83), who is said to have hidden nearby during the Desmond Rebellion of 1579–83. The name, however, is modern: the village was built as a model village in 1832, in the reign of King William IV, and it was known as

Kingwilliamstown until 1938, when the villagers opted for the present name.

A village in the SLIABH LUACHRA region of northwest County Cork, 23 km (14 miles) northeast of Killarney. Its original name (*see above*) is celebrated in a well-known ballad:

> My bonny barque bounced light and free
> Across the surging foam,
> Which bears me far from Innisfail,
> To seek a foreign home.
> A lonely exile driven neath
> Misfortune's coldest frown,
> From my loved home and cherished friends
> In dear Kingwilliamstown.

> > Danny Buckley: 'Sweet Kingwilliamstown' (Buckley, a local man, survived the sinking of the *Titanic*, but was killed in France on the last day of the First World War. *Innisfail* is a poetic name for Ireland.)

Ballyeagh Strand Probably Irish *Baile Aodha* 'Hugh's town' (*see* BAL-, BALL-, BALLY-).

A beach in County Kerry, by the mouth of the River Cashen just south of BALLYBUNNION, some 15 km (9 miles) northwest of Listowel. It was the scene of one of the worst of the (largely recreational) faction fights that broke out across southern Ireland in the early 19th century. This particular fight, on the day of the Ballyeagh Races, 24 June 1834, involved some 2500 participants from the Cooleen faction and the Lawlor-Blacks Mulvihills. Some 15 people died, mostly by drowning in the River Cashen.

> And if ye ever ride in Ireland,
> The jest may yet be said:
> There is the land of broken hearts,
> And the land of broken heads.

> > G.K. Chesterton: 'Notes to a Tourist'

Ballygobackwards Irish *baile* 'town' (*see* BAL-, BALL-, BALLY-) + ModE phrase 'go backwards'.

A generic term applied to provincial Irish towns by metropolitan Dubliners.

See also BALLYSLAPADASHAMUCKERY.

Ballygullion Irish *baile* 'town' (*see* BAL-, BALL-, BALLY-) + *goilín*, 'creek, gullet'.

A fictional town in the humorous short stories of Lynn Doyle (pseudonym of Leslie Alexander Montgomery, 1873–1961), based on Doyle's native DOWNPATRICK, part of which is called 'the Gullion'. The first volume of stories, *Ballygullion*, was published in 1908, and an omnibus edition, *The Ballygullion Bus*, in 1957.

Ballyhaunis Irish *Béal Átha hAmhnais* 'ford-mouth of the battle' (*see* FORD); the identity of the battle is unknown.

A small market town in County Mayo, 37 km (23 miles) southeast of Castlebar. It probably developed around the Augustinian friary founded here in 1348, and today claims to have Ireland's only purpose-built mosque.

Ballyhooly Irish *Baile Átha hÚlla* 'town of the ford of the apple trees' (*see* BAL-, BALL-, BALLY- *and* FORD).

A village in County Cork, some 25 km (16 miles) north of Cork itself.

ballyhooly. An Irish slang term for 'bad trouble', dating from the 19th century when the village of Ballyhooly was known for its faction fights. In the early 20th century it acquired a second meaning of 'rubbish, nonsense', expanding on the word *ballyhoo* (a fairground barker's spiel), and **ballyhooly truth** became music-hall argot for a lie.

Ballyhoura Mountains Irish *Bealach Abhradh*, 'pass of Feabhra or Febrat'; it is uncertain who Feabhra was, though some have identified him with Áed Abrat of Irish mythology.

A range of hills on the border between counties LIMERICK and CORK. The highest point is Seefin Mountain (528 m / 1732 ft).

Ballyjamesduff Irish *baile* 'town' (*see* BAL-, BALL-, BALLY-) + *James Duff*, a commander of British forces during the Rebellion of 1798. The name has been translated into Irish as *Baile Shéamais Dhuibh*.

A town in County Cavan, 15 km (9 miles) southeast of Cavan itself. The place was immortalized by Percy French in his haunting song, written in 1912:

> The Garden of Eden has vanished they say,
> But I know the lie of it still,
> Just turn to the left at the bridge of Finea
> And stop when halfway to Cootehill.
> 'Tis there I will find it I know sure enough
> When fortune has come to my call,
> Oh the grass it is green around Ballyjamesduff
> And the blue sky is over it all,
> And tones that are tender and tones that are gruff
> Are whispering over the sea,
> Come back, Paddy Reilly, to Ballyjamesduff,
> Come back, Paddy Reilly, to me.

Paddy Reilly was a real person who had emigrated from the town.

Ballykissangel Irish *baile* 'town' + marketing-executive Oirishry.

A fictional Irish village that gave its name to a BBC-television light drama series (1996–2001). The location work was shot in the village of AVOCA, County Wicklow.

Ballymagash Based on Irish *baile* 'town' with a Mac-type surname.

The fictional rural town featured in RTÉ's satirical series *Hall's Pictorial Weekly* (1971–80), created by Frank Hall (1921–95).

Ballymagraw Based on Irish *baile* 'town' with surname Magraw.

A fictional east Ulster town that featured in BBC Northern Ireland's 1936 variety series, *The Ballymagraw Gazette*.

Ballymahon Irish *Baile Uí Mhatháin* 'homestead of the descendants of Mahon' (*see* BAL-, BALL-, BALLY-).

A village in County Longford, some 30 km (19 miles) west of Mullingar. In 960 Mahon, King of Thomon-Dál gCais, defeated Fergal, son of the King of Bréifne and Connacht, near where the village now stands. The playwright and poet Oliver Goldsmith (1728–74) was born nearby.

Ballymena Irish *An Baile Meánach* 'the middle farm or town', i.e. a farm between two others (*see* BAL-, BALL-, BALLY-).

A town in County Antrim, some 35 km (22 miles) north-west of Belfast. It was founded in the 17th century by William Adair as a Lowland Scots plantation, and its linen industry was established in 1733. In 1798 it was captured by the United Irishmen under Henry Joy McCracken. A children's saying links the town with another in Antrim:

> The people of Antrim are bally mean about bally money.

Another old Ulster joke goes as follows:

> Q: Why are pound notes green?
> A: Because Ballymena folk pick them before they're ripe.

The town is linked with ANTRIM to form a NEW TOWN[1] entity. Ballymena is the administrative centre of a local authority district of the same name.

The actor Liam Neeson (b.1952) was born here. In 2004 the Unionist politician Ian Paisley accepted the Freedom of the town, in which he had grown up.

Ah cud have soaped my behind and slid all the way to Ballymena and back for the time that took ye. An Ulster expression denoting 'That took you a long time.'

Ballymoney Irish *Baile Muine* or *Baile Monaidh* 'town of the thicket' (*see* BAL-, BALL-, BALLY-).

A market town in County Antrim, some 10 km (6 miles) southeast of Coleraine. It is the administrative centre of a local authority district of the same name. Ballymoney was the birthplace of the playwright George Shiels (1886–1949), author of many successful kitchen comedies set in Ulster. *See also* BALLYMENA *and* DRUMCREE.

Armour of Ballymoney. The byname of James Brown Armour (1841–1928), the liberal Presbyterian minister who campaigned for Home Rule.

Ballymore Hill Irish *Baile Mór* 'big farmstead' (*see* BAL-, BALL-, BALLY-).

The site of a famous skirmish on 4 June 1798 near ENNIS-CORTHY in County Wexford. Father Murphy, leading his Wexford rebels, ambushed a small British unit, killed its commander and seized its guns. The incident boosted the morale of the insurgents.

Ballymote Irish *Baile an Mhóta* 'town of the mound' (*see* BAL-, BALL-, BALLY-), referring to a 13th-century motte (earthen castle mound).

A small market town in County Sligo, 20 km (12 miles) south of Sligo itself. The extensive remains of **Ballymote**

Castle, built *c*.300 by Richard de Burgh, can still be seen. The castle changed hands twice during the 14th century, and many times during the upheavals of the 16th and 17th centuries. It was largely dismantled after its capture by Williamite forces in 1690.

Book of Ballymote, The. A manuscript collection compiled in Gaelic *c*.1390 by Maghnus Ó Duibhgeannáin and his helpers. Its contents include versions of Virgil's *Aeneid* and *The Book of the Dun Cow*, together with a key to the ogam alphabet, which has enabled scholars to decipher many early inscriptions. In 1522 the O'Donnells of Tyrconnel were obliged to exchange the manuscript for 140 dairy cows.

Ballynahinch Irish *Baile na hInse* 'town of the island' (*see* BAL-, BALL-, BALLY-).
A small town in County Down, 25 km (16 miles) southeast of Belfast.

Battle of Ballynahinch (12–13 June 1798). One of the last encounters in the north in the 1798 Rebellion, ending in defeat for the United Irishmen under General Munro at the hands of government forces under Colonel Nugent. Munro was subsequently hanged in front of his family.

Ballyporeen Irish *Béal Átha Póirín* 'ford-mouth of the pebbles' (*see* FORD); *póirín* are small round objects from seeds to stones; probably here pebbles in the river.
A village in County Tipperary, between the GALTEE and KNOCKMEALDOWN Mountains, 10 km (6 miles) east of Mitchelstown. With an eye to the Irish-American vote, President Ronald Reagan claimed it as his ancestral home on his visit to Ireland in June 1984. Never content with a teaspoon when a spade would do, the president addressed Balyporeen's good citizens thus:

> I didn't know much about my family background – not because of a lack of interest, but because my father was orphaned before he was 6 years old. And now thanks to you and the efforts of good people who have dug into the history of a poor immigrant family, I know at last whence I came. And this has given my soul a new contentment. And it is a joyous feeling. It is like coming home after a long journey ... I can't think of a place on the planet I would rather claim as my roots more than ... um ...Ballyporeen, County Tipperary.

See also the OULD SOD. (For the visit of President Kennedy to Ireland, *see* DUNGANSTOWN.)

Ballyregan Probably Irish *baile* 'town' (*see* BAL-, BALL-, BALLY-) with surname *Regan*, from *Riagán* 'little king'.
A village in County Cork, 5 km (3 miles) northwest of Kinsale.

Ballyregan Bob. A noted greyhound based at Hove, Sussex, who between 1984 and 1986 won 42 out of 48 races. He is reckoned by *Greyhound Monthly* to be the second-greatest greyhound ever, after Mick the Miller (raced between April 1928 and October 1931). Bob, now stuffed, may be viewed alongside Mick at the Rothschild Zoological Museum in Tring, Hertfordshire.

Ballyshannon Irish *Béal Átha Seanaidh* 'ford-mouth of the hillside' (*see* FORD).
A port and market town at the mouth of the River ERNE, Donegal, 30 km (19 miles) northeast of Sligo. It is also called **Belashanny**, and in the Middle Ages the O'Donnell's had a castle here, where in 1597 Red Hugh O'Donnell defeated the English.

> I sat by Ballyshannon in the summer,
>   And saw the salmon leap,
> And I said, as I beheld the gallant creatures
>   Spring glittering from the deep,
> Through the spray and through the prone heaps striving
>   onward
>   To the calm, clear streams above,
> So seekest thou thy native founts of freedom, Thomas
>   Davis,
>   In thy brightness of strength and love!
>
> > Samuel Ferguson (1810–86): 'Lament for the Death of Thomas Davis' (Thomas Davis (1814–45) was the chief organizer of the Young Ireland movement, and also a poet.)

Ballyshannon was the birthplace of the poet William Allingham (1824–89), best known for his poem 'The Fairies' ('Up the airy mountain, / Down the rushy glen ...'); *see under* SLIEVE LEAGUE.

> Adieu to Ballyshannon! where I was bred and born;
> Go where I may, I'll think of you, as sure as night and
>   morn,
> The kindly spot, the friendly town, where everyone is
>   known,
> And not a face in all the place but partly seems my own
>   ...
> I leave my warm heart with you, though my back I'm
>   forced to turn –
> So adieu to Ballyshannon, and the winding banks of
>   Erne!
>
> > William Allingham (1824–89): 'The Winding Banks of Erne, or, The Emigrant's Adieu to Ballyshannon'

Allingham is buried in the town's Church of Ireland graveyard, and there is a bridge named after him.

Also born in Ballyshannon was the rock guitarist Rory Gallagher (1948–95).

Ballyslapadashamuckery Irish *baile* 'town' + cod Oirishry.
A rural Irish town invented by the comedian Jack Cruise for his satirical sketches performed in the 1960s and 1970s. *See also* BALLYGOBACKWARDS.

Ballyteige Bay Irish *baile* 'town' (*see* BAL-, BALL-, BALLY-) with surname O'Teige.

A bay on the south coast of County Wexford, some 5 km (3 miles) east of Waterford Harbour (*see under* WATERFORD).

Balmacara 'homestead of the *MacAras* or *Macraes*', Gaelic *baile* (*see* BAL-, BALL-, BALLY-) + Scots clan name.

A small village overlooking Loch Alsh and Skye, in western Highland (formerly in Ross and Cromarty), 5 km (3 miles) east of Kyle of Lochalsh. The scenic **Balmacara Estate** is in the care of the National Trust for Scotland.

Balmoral Castle The first two elements are probably Gaelic *baile* (*see* BAL-, BALL-, BALLY-) + *mór* 'big', but the *-al* element is uncertain (OCelt *ial* 'clearing' has been suggested). The earliest record of the name (1484) has it as *Bouchmorale*.

A private royal residence in upper Deeside, in Aberdeenshire (formerly in Grampian region), 12 km (7 miles) west of Ballater. The Balmoral estate includes GLEN MUICK, LOCHNAGAR and Broad Cairn. The original castle dates from the 16th century, and was extended in the earlier 19th century by Sir Robert Gordon. After his death, Queen Victoria and Prince Albert – having had a very wet holiday further west at ARDVERIKIE on Loch Laggan – took the tenancy of Balmoral for four years, finding the more easterly Deeside (*see under* DEE[1]) notably drier. It seems to have been around this time that an old local custom died out, in which, each Hallowe'en, a huge bonfire was lit before the castle, and, accompanied by the skirling of pipes, the effigy of a witch called Shandy Dann was thrown into the flames.

Victoria described Balmoral as 'this dear paradise', and Albert bought the estate for her in 1852. The present castle, designed by William Smith (with input from Albert), was built in 1853–6. It is in the Scottish baronial style, and its interior décor set the fashion for unrestrained tartanry. After Albert's death, Victoria retreated here for long periods, accompanied by her loyal Scottish servant John Brown. Balmoral continues to be used for summer holidays by the present queen.

> Ye lovers of the picturesque, away and see
> Beautiful Balmoral, near by the River Dee;
> There you will see the deer browsing on the heathery hills,
> While down their sides run clear sparkling rills.
>
> William McGonagall: 'Beautiful Balmoral'

There seems to be a certain stringency about life in the castle. According to ex-butler Paul Burrell's memoir, *A Royal Duty* (2003), the servants at Balmoral are not allowed to look out of the windows; and in a jolly touch in the 2004 climate-change movie *The Day after Tomorrow* the royal family freeze to death in the castle (which is notoriously underheated).

There are towns called Balmoral in Australia (Victoria),

Canada (Manitoba) and New Zealand (South Island). A district of Brisbane in Queensland, Australia, is called Balmoral, and there is a tiny Balmoral Island off New Providence in the Bahamas.

Balmoral bonnet. A kind of lopsided Highland bonnet or beret with a bobble on top and a (usually) red-and-white chequered band.

Balmorality. A vaunted love of Scotland that in fact comprises little more than a fondness for tartanry, Balmoral bonnets and other superficial trappings of national identity, rather than a deeper engagement with the people and their problems.

> And O! to think that there are members o'
> St. Andrew's Societies sleepin' soon,
> Wha' to the papers wrote afore they bedded
> On regimental buttons or buckled shoon,
>
> Or use o' England whaur the U.K.'s meent,
> Or this or that anent the Blue Saltire …
>
> Hugh MacDiarmid: *A Drunk Man Looks at the Thistle* (1926)

Beast of Balmoral, the. Not Queen Victoria's hirsute attendant John Brown in kilt and swaying sporran, but rather a big cat allegedly seen in these parts.

Balnamoon 'peat bog homestead', Gaelic *baile* (*see* BAL-, BALL-, BALLY-) + *moine* 'peat bog'.

A small settlement in Angus (formerly in Tayside region), 7 km (4.5 miles) northwest of Brechin.

Balquhidder 'fodder settlement', Gaelic *baile* (*see* BAL-, BALL-, BALLY-) + corruption of OE *fodor* 'fodder'.

A village (pronounced 'bal-whidder') west of Strathyre, just off the Callander–Crianlarich road, at the east end of Loch Voil. It is about 16 km (10 miles) northwest of Callander, and was formerly in Perthshire, then in Central region, and is now in the unitary authority of STIRLING[1]. It is famous as the burial place of the outlaw Rob Roy Macgregor (1671–1734), celebrated in Sir Walter Scott's novel *Rob Roy* (1817). Wordsworth, in the prefatory note to his dreadful 'Rob Roy's Grave' (1803), mistakenly places the outlaw's grave 'near the head of Loch Ketterine [Katrine]'. In Robert Louis Stevenson's novel *Kidnapped* (1886), David Balfour and Alan Breck pass through Balquhidder, and Breck and Rob Roy's son, the vainglorious Robin Oig (executed in 1754), fight a duel on the bagpipes.

Braes of Balquhidder, the. The braes (Scots, 'hillsides') to the west of Balquhidder, on the north side of Loch Voil. In the mid-18th century these were lawless lands, as described by Stevenson:

> At the door of the first house we came to, Alan knocked, which was no very safe enterprise in such a part of the Highlands as the Braes of Balquhidder. No great clan held rule there; it was filled and disputed by small septs, and broken remnants, and what they call 'chiefless folk',

driven into the wild country about the springs of Forth and Teith by the advance of the Campbells.

> Robert Louis Stevenson: *Kidnapped* (1886), xxv

But the Braes by the end of the 18th century had become a more pastoral venue:

> Now the summer's in prime
> Wi' the flowers richly blooming,
> And the wild mountain thyme
> A' the moorlands perfuming,
> To our dear native scenes
> Let us journey together,
> Where glad innocence reigns
> 'Mang the braes o' Balquhither.

> Robert Tannahill (1774–1810): 'The Braes o' Balquhither'

Baltimore 'town of the big house', Irish *baile* 'town' (*see* BAL-, BALL-, BALLY-) + *na* 'of the' + *tighe* 'house' + *mór* 'big'; the current Irish name is different.

A pretty fishing village on the southwest coast of County Cork, 10 km (6 miles) southwest of Skibbereen. Its modern Irish name is **Dún na Séad** ('fort of the treasure'). There are the ruins of an O'Driscoll Castle looking out to SHERKIN ISLAND. In 1537 Baltimore was sacked in a reprisal raid by the men of Waterford, and later became a predominantly English settlement. In 1631 Barbary corsairs carried off 200 of the inhabitants, most of them English (apparently they did not dare take on the native Irish women). The latter incident is commemorated in a ballad, 'The Sack of Baltimore', by Thomas Davis (1814–45):

> All, all asleep within each roof along that rocky street,
> And these must be the lover's friends, with gently gliding feet –
> A stifled gasp, a dreamy noise! 'The roof is in a flame!'
> From out their beds and to their doors rush maid and sire and dame,
> And meet upon the threshold stone the gleaming sabre's fall,
> And o'er each black and bearded face the white or crimson shawl.
> The yell of 'Allah!' breaks above the prayer, and shriek, and roar:
> O blessed God! the Algerine is lord of Baltimore!

The city of Baltimore in Maryland, USA, is named after the Irish village, via the founder of Maryland, Lord Baltimore (1579–1632).

Baltinglass Irish *Bealach Conglais* 'pass or road of Cúglas'.

A small market town in County Wicklow, 55 km (34 miles) southwest of Dublin. There are the remains of Vallis Salutis Abbey, founded in 1148 by Dermot MacMurrough, King of Leinster, and above the town, on **Baltinglass Hill** (383 m / 1258 ft), is Rathcoran, a large hill fort with burial chambers and standing stones.

Baltinglass Rebellion (1580–1). A Catholic rebellion led by Viscount Baltinglass. After initial success against Lord Deputy Grey at Glenmalure, the rebels were crushed and Baltinglass fled to the Continent.

Battle of Baltinglass (1950–1). A figurative battle in which the people of Baltinglass protested at the appointment by James Everett, Minister for Posts and Telegraphs, of one of his supporters, Michael Farrell, as postmaster in Baltinglass, ignoring the rights of the Cooke family who had held the position. The citizens of Baltinglass boycotted Farrell's general store in the town, and Farrell resigned as postmaster in 1951. An anonymous balladeer celebrated the ballyhooly:

> There were bren-guns and Sten-guns and whippet tanks galore
> As the battle raged up and down from pub to gen'ral store.

Balti Triangle *Balti* from the spicy culinary dish; *Triangle* from the shape of the area, and by humorous analogy with the *Bermuda Triangle*, a sea area between Bermuda, Florida and Puerto Rico, said to be a region of danger for anyone venturing into it.

A name applied since the late 1970s to an area centred on Sparkbrook, Balsall Heath and MOSELEY[1], south of BIRMINGHAM city centre, which is home to more than 50 balti houses. Balti, a British Asian variant on traditional Kashmiri and Pakistani styles of cooking, emerged in the 1970s from Birmingham's Kashmiri community. The origins of the word 'balti', in its modern British Asian culinary sense, are uncertain. In Urdu (the official language of Pakistan, and also widely spoken in parts of India) *balti* means a 'bucket' or 'pail'. In balti cooking the food is prepared in a small, two-handled, wok-like pan known as a *karahi*. The ingredients of a balti dish are cooked largely in the same way as those of a conventional curry. During the final stages of cooking, however, fresh spices, herbs and chillis are added to the dish, which is then cooked at a high temperature before being served sizzling in the *karahi* itself. By the 1990s restaurants serving balti dishes had spread throughout England from their original Birmingham base.

> Born in Birmingham, unheard of in India, the balti is a curious mix of entrepreneurialism and the English palate. The balti and Indian restaurant phenomenon tell a tasty tale of cultural integration shaped by market forces.

> 'Birmingham's Balti Triangle', bbc.co.uk

Balubaland. A term used in Ireland of the less savoury parts of some Irish cities. The term derives from the Baluba tribe of the Congo, who in 1960 killed nine Irish soldiers (serving with the United Nations) in an ambush.

Bamburgh 'Queen Bebbe's stronghold', OE personal name *Bebbe* + *burgh* (*see* BURY). Bebbe was the queen of Aethelfrith of Bernicia (reigned 593–617), who slaughtered 1200 Celtic monks before defeating the army of King Cadwallon at Chester in *c*.616.

A village on the coast of Northumberland, 26 km (16 miles) southeast of Berwick-upon-Tweed. The parish church is dedicated to St Aidan, who founded the church here and died at Bamburgh in 651. The church became an Augustinian monastery in 1121, but is now again the parish church, still supposedly incorporating in its structure the wooden post St Aidan leant against as he expired. Bamburgh's Grace Darling Museum commemorates the famous heroine whose gallantry took place off the FARNE ISLANDS, some 5 km (3 miles) out to sea; she is buried in Bamburgh's churchyard.

On a 45-m (150-ft) whin-sill crag above the sea is the massive **Bamburgh Castle**. According to the *Anglo-Saxon Chronicle*, Ida, the king of Bernicia (one of the components of the later kingdom of Northumbria), built a fort at Bamburgh in 547, on a site previously fortified by the Celts. It was for a time the Northumbrian capital, and preserved the head and hand of Oswald, the Northumbrian king who had invited St Aidan from Iona to convert his people; so impressed was the latter by Oswald's deeds of charity that he declared, 'Let this hand never wither nor corrupt.' (The spirit of the good King Oswald was revived in Bamburgh in the 18th century, when Dr John Sharpe's charitable trust provided a free school, infirmary and library, cheap flour, and a coastguard and lifeboat service.)

The great stone keep of Bamburgh Castle dates back to the Norman period. In 1095 Robert Mowbray, Earl of Northumberland, was besieged here by William Rufus and eventually obliged to surrender. Bamburgh was the scene of much fighting in the Anglo–Scottish wars of the 14th century. During the Wars of the Roses it changed hands several times; Henry VI ruled briefly from Bamburgh, but after the Battle of Hexham Levels (*see under* HEXHAM) in 1464 the castle was besieged and fell after a bombardment – the first English castle to fall to artillery. In 1894 the first Lord Armstrong of Cragside, the engineer and arms manufacturer, bought the castle and rebuilt it for private use. It is now open to the public.

Worm of Bamburgh, the. Also known as the Laidley Worm (a worm being a large and dragonlike medieval monster), but in reality the daughter of a Northumbrian king, who had thus been metamorphosed by a wicked stepmother. The Worm devastated the surrounding countryside until the king's son, the Childe of Wynde, not knowing the Worm's true identity, went out to fight it – whereupon it divulged its true nature and thereby broke the spell. The wicked stepmother turned into a toad, who still lives in a cave underneath the castle, hoping that some day her prince will come: the successful candidate must unsheathe the Childe's sword three times, blow his horn three times, and then kiss the toad, whereupon the queen will be restored to human shape.

Banagher Irish *Beannchar* 'place of sharp rocks'; although the element normally refers to 'peaks', it appears that the reference here is to rocks in the Shannon.

A village on the River SHANNON in County Offaly, some 35 km (22 miles) west of Tullamore. Charlotte Brontë's husband, A.B. Nicholls, is buried here. Anthony Trollope worked as a Post Office surveyor in Banagher in 1841, and it was here that he embarked on the writing of novels, such as *The Macdermots of Ballycloran* (1847) and *The Kellys and the O'Kellys* (1848).

> I was to live in a place called Banagher, on the Shannon, which I had heard of because of its once having being conquered, though it had heretofore conquered everything, including the devil.
>
> Anthony Trollope: *An Autobiography* (1883)

That beats Banagher and Banagher beats the band. An expression of surprise at something out of the ordinary. It is said that the expression originates in the fact that Banagher was a noted rotten borough, so that if an MP spoke of his own rotten borough where all the voters were in his employ, it was customary to respond, 'That beats Banagher.' This later became 'That beats Banagher and he [*sic*] beat the Devil.'

Banba. An early name for Ireland; *see* ÉIRE.

Banbridge Irish *Droichead na Banna* 'bridge on the River BANN'.

A town in County Down, 35 km (22 miles) southwest of Belfast. The main street runs along a sunken cutting (excavated in the mid-19th century), the sides of which are joined by a bridge, hence the nickname the **Town With the Hole in the Middle**. Banbridge was the birthplace of Captain Francis Crozier (1796–1848), who was Sir John Franklin's second-in-command on his final, fatal voyage to find the Northwest Passage; and of the sculptor F.E. McWilliam (1909–92). Banbridge is the administrative centre of a local authority district of the same name.

Banbury 'Ban(n)a's stronghold', OE male personal name *Ban(n)a* + BURY.

A market town in Oxfordshire, about 40 km (25 miles) north of Oxford. Nowadays it is most closely associated with its cakes and the nursery rhyme about its cross (*see below*), but in former, more religiously intense centuries it had a strong reputation for zealous Puritanism (reflected also in its support for Parliament during the Civil Wars):

> In my progress travelling Northward,
> Taking my farewell o' the Southward,
> To Banbury came I, O prophane one!
> Where I saw a Puritane-one,

Hanging of his cat on Monday,
For killing of a Mouse on Sunday.

Richard Brathwaite: *Barnabee's Journal* (1638)

Ben Jonson in *Bartholomew Fair* (1614) describes Zeal-of-the-land-Busy as a 'Banbury man', and **Banbury man** became something of a byword for sanctimoniousness between the 17th and 19th centuries. Puritans were known facetiously as **Banbury bloods** in the 17th century.

The Oxford–Banbury canal was built in 1778 and the railway connection was completed in 1850.

Banbury cake. A kind of spiced flaky-pastry cake with a criss-cross pattern on the top, originally made exclusively in Banbury. The earliest known recipe for it dates from 1615, and the town has been proudly selling the cakes ever since (there is a record from 1833 of 'The Original Banbury Cake Shop' in Parsons Street, which reputedly opened in 1638).

A somewhat forced linkage between 'Banbury cakes' and 'tarts' led in the late 19th century to the slang use of the word **banbury** for 'a promiscuous woman'.

Banbury Cross. A market cross celebrated in the nursery rhyme 'Ride a cock-horse to Banbury Cross' (a 'cock-horse' was a toy on which a child pretended to ride like a horse – for example, a stick with a wooden horse's head on it. In the days when the rhyme was composed, *horse* would have rhymed with *cross*):

Ride a cock-horse to Banbury Cross
To see a fine lady on a white horse,
Rings on her fingers and bells on her toes,
And she shall have music wherever she goes.

(The fine lady has been variously identified as Elizabeth I, Lady Godiva and a member of the Fiennes family from Broughton Castle, which is not far away.)

The original cross was destroyed by Puritans in 1602. The present-day one is a replica, erected in 1859. It commemorates the marriage in that year of Queen Victoria's eldest daughter to the Crown Prince of Prussia (from which union sprang Kaiser Wilhelm II).

Banburyshire. A local term applied to the northern part of Oxfordshire plus the nearby parts of Warwickshire and Northamptonshire.

Shepherd of Banbury, the. The ostensible author of a weather guide (published 1744), written by John Claridge, which attained considerable popularity at the time.

Banchory Possibly 'place of the horns', Gaelic *beancharr* 'horn-cast', from the horn-shaped bends in the River Dee. An alternative suggestion is Gaelic *beannachar* 'mountainous'. A town in Aberdeenshire (formerly in Grampian region), 27 km (16.5 miles) west of Aberdeen. It is on the River DEE[1], near where it is joined by the Water of Feugh (locally pronounced 'fuch', with 'ch' as in 'loch', or by the more genteel as 'fee–yuch'). Traditionally St Ternan (or Torannán,

a contemporary of Columba) founded a monastery here in the 6th century.

Banchory was the birthplace of the great composer for the Scottish fiddle, Scott Skinner (1843–1927), who wrote a reel called 'Bonnie Banchory'. Andrew Lang, the collector and writer of fairy tales, died here in 1912.

The **Banchory Morrismen**, established in the 1970s, are the only morris dancers in Scotland, although they claim that the activity is as much a Scottish as an English tradition. In recent years they have faced a recruitment crisis, one of their founder members commenting, 'There's a limit as to how far most Scotsmen are willing to go to make a fool of themselves.'

Bandit Country. A name given to the southern part of County ARMAGH, by the then Labour secretary of state for Northern Ireland, Merlyn Rees, in November 1975. Rees used the name after the shooting by the IRA of three British soldiers at Drummuckavall, near Crossmaglen:

There has never been a cease-fire in South Armagh for a variety of reasons – the nature of the countryside and the nature of the people. It is an unusual area – there is little support for the security forces in South Armagh. The government is not trying to buy off terrorism by the release of detainees as the number of terrorists arrested and charged shows. The release of detainees has nothing to do with the violence of the bandit country of South Armagh. There is wholesale gangsterism there.

The term was resented by Nationalists, who saw it as typical of British efforts to portray as the actions of thugs and outlaws what they regarded as blows for Irish freedom. Some Republicans, however, revelled in it as a badge of honour and as triumphant proof of the effectiveness of the IRA's military strategy in the area. South Armagh is bordered on three sides by the Irish Republic and its largely Catholic population is historically sympathetic to the Republican cause. From the outset of the Troubles it was dominated by the Provisional IRA, who operated here with greater freedom of action than in any other part of Northern Ireland. Attacks by the local brigade of the IRA included the sectarian massacre at KINGSMILLS, near Newry, in January 1976 of 12 Protestants (itself a revenge attack for the slaughter of three Catholics by Loyalists), the ambush and murder of 18 British soldiers at Narrow Water, near WARRENPOINT, in August 1979, and the assassination of Captain Robert Nairac, a maverick Grenadier Guards officer, whose body has never been found. A bestselling book, *Bandit Country* by Toby Harnden (1999), exploited the cliché of South Armagh's lawlessness.

Bandon[1] Irish *Banda*, dative *Bandain*, 'goddess', a frequent designation for rivers in the Old Celtic languages; *see* BANN. A river in County Cork; length 60 km (37 miles). It rises near DUNMANWAY in the Maughanaclea Hills and flows east through the town of BANDON to meet the sea at KIN-SALE Harbour.

> The pleasaunt Bandon crownd with many a wood ...
>
> Edmund Spenser: *The Faerie Queen* (1596), IV, xi

Bandon² Irish *Droichead na Banna* 'bridge on the River BANDON'.

A town on the River Bandon in County Cork, 25 km (16 miles) southwest of Cork itself. Bandon was founded in the early 17th century by Richard Boyle, 1st Earl of Cork, on lands taken from the Irish for the plantation of Protestant English settlers. It has the first Protestant church to be built in Ireland (1610). According to local tradition, on one of the gates in the town's walls was the inscription:

> Turk, Jew or Atheist
> May enter here –
> But not a Papist.

To which a contemporary graffitist apparently added:

> Who wrote it, wrote it well –
> For the same is written in the gates of Hell.

A later visitor to the town, on seeing pigs being herded through the Church of Ireland churchyard, famously remarked:

> Even the pigs are Protestant.

Bandon was the birthplace of Nicholas Brady (1659–1726), who, with Nahum Tate, produced a well-known metrical version of the Psalms. In 1921, during the Anglo-Irish War, the IRA kidnapped the Earl of Bandon and burnt his home, Castle Bernard; Bandon himself was released after a few days.

> There was a young lady of Bandon
> Whose feet were too narrow to stand on.
> She stood on her head,
> 'For my motto,' she said,
> 'Has always been *nil desperandum*.'
>
> Anon.: limerick

BANES. An acronymic name formed from the initial letters of the unitary authority BATH AND NORTH EAST SOMERSET.

Banff 'Place on the River Banff', possibly from *Banba*, an OCelt name for Ireland; *banb* (Gaelic *banbh*) 'sucking pig' is a more likely possibility, and would make sense as an affectionate river name.

A royal BURGH and port on at the mouth of the River Deveron, now in the new unitary authority of Aberdeenshire, 30 km (18.5 miles) west of Fraserburgh, and just across **Banff Bay** from Macduff. It was the county town of the old county of Banffshire, and was then the seat of Banff and Buchan district of the former Grampian region. In the Middle Ages it was a member of the Northern Hanseatic League. There are only ruins left of the old castle, and the present

Banff Castle dates from 1750. The most notable of many fine buildings is Duff House, designed by William Adam for the 1st Duke of Fife and begun in 1735. James Duff, the 4th Duke, recruited José de San Martín to the cause of South American independence, and persuaded the local burgers to make San Martín a freeman of the burgh.

There is a town called Banff in Canada (Alberta), which gives its name to the Banff National Park in the Rockies.

Banff bailies. Big white fluffy clouds in line along the horizon, thought to herald bad weather.

go to Banff! An early 19th-century expression for 'get lost', 'go to hell', etc.

Banff and Buchan From the town of BANFF and the traditional area known as BUCHAN.

A former district (1975–96) of the old Grampian region, in northeast Scotland. It comprised parts of the traditional counties of Banffshire and Aberdeenshire, and is now part of the new unitary authority of Aberdeenshire. The administrative HQ was at BANFF.

Banffshire From the town of BANFF.

A traditional county of northeast Scotland, bounded on the north by the North Sea, on the east and south by Aberdeenshire, and on the west by Inverness-shire and Moray. The county town was BANFF. In 1975 it was incorporated into the districts of Moray and Banff and Buchan, in Grampian region, and in 1996 much of the former county became part of the new unitary authority of Aberdeenshire.

Banglatown Bengali *Bangla* 'Bengali' (as in *Bangladesh*) + ModE *town* (as in *Chinatown*).
See Spitalfields and Banglatown at SPITALFIELDS.

Bangor¹ OCelt *bangor* 'plaited fence', and by extension 'monastery surrounded by a plaited fence'.

A cathedral city in Gwynedd (formerly in Caernarvonshire) on the Menai Strait opposite Anglesey. It was formerly the seat of the old Arfon district. St Deniol founded a church here in the 6th century and Bangor became a centre of Celtic Christianity, long resisting submission to Canterbury. The foundation suffered something of a setback *c.*614, when Æthelfrith defeated the Welsh at Chester and proceeded to massacre the monks of Bangor, who had accompanied their side to the battlefield. According to Bede, 1200 monks were killed, testimony to the size and significance of the monastery at this time. The claim by the monks that they were present merely in a praying role apparently cut no ice with the Saxons.

The medieval **Bangor Cathedral** is dedicated to St Deniol, and some of the medieval Welsh princes are buried here. It was damaged by Owain Glyndwr among others, and described by Daniel Defoe as 'mean looking, and almost despicable' (*A Tour Through the Whole Island of Great Britain*, 1724–6) before its restoration in the 19th century by Gilbert Scott. The University College of North Wales was founded in Bangor in 1884, and is a campus of the federal University of Wales.

> There was an old person of Bangor,
> Whose face was distorted with anger!
>   He tore off his boots
>   And subsisted on roots,
> That irascible person of Bangor.
>
> Edward Lear (1812–88): limerick

'Bangor'. A hymn tune by William Tans'ur, published in *Harmony of Zion* (1734). Bangor in Maine, USA, is said to have been named after the hymn tune by a local clergyman in 1791.

Bangorian Controversy, the. A political and theological dispute that arose following the publication in 1716 of *A Preservative against the Principles and Practices of the Non-jurors both in Church and State* by the Low-Church Bishop of Bangor, William Hoadly, who argued that the Established Church had no divinely sanctioned right to control its members.

blue bangors or **bangor blues.** Now a generic term for traditional grey slates, but originally thick, large slates produced in the quarries around Bangor, weighing 4.5–7 kg (10–15 lb) and measuring 30 cm by 100 cm (1 ft by 3 ft) to 100 cm by 130 cm (3ft by 4 ft).

'Day Trip to Bangor'. An irritating number-one hit for the otherwise under-appreciated folk-rock group Fiddler's Dram in 1979:

> Didn't we have a lovely time
> The day we went to Bangor ...

In response to the suggestion that the song was actually about Rhyl, because it mentioned a pier, one of the members of the band writes:

> Debbie Cook, who wrote the entire song, said Bangor worked because it was two syllables and thereby fitted the tune – the song was supposed to be about mill girls from industrial Lancashire having a day trip to N Wales; 'Rhyl' was too short and 'Llandudno' too long (and sounded like someone expectorating). No other reason.
>
> Ian Kearey, email to the author (6 November 2002)

Bangor² Irish *Beannchar* 'peaked hill'.
A commuter town and seaside resort on BELFAST Lough, County Down, some 15 km (9 miles) east of Belfast. St Comgall founded an abbey here in 555, which subsequently sent out many missionaries, such as St Columban and St Gall. The abbey was first raided by the Vikings in 842, and repeated attacks led to its closure by the end of the century. An Augustinian foundation was established on the site in the early 12th century. It was later taken over by Franciscans, and dissolved in the 16th century by Henry

VIII. It was also used during the Larne Gun Running (*see under* LARNE). Today Bangor is home to the Royal Irish Yacht Club.

> [Bangor:] elderly and respectable and cliffy, and in a tawdry-genteel way it had a comic air of pretension that was rare in Ulster.
>
> Paul Theroux: *The Kingdom by the Sea* (1983)

> Visible from your window the sixth-century
> abbey church of Colum and Malachi,
> 'light of the world' once in the monastic ages,
> home of antiphonary and the golden pages
> of radiant scripture ...
>
> Derek Mahon: 'A Bangor Requiem', from *Collected Poems* (1999)

Antiphonary of Bangor. A prayer book created in Bangor in the 7th century, making it one of the oldest surviving ecclesiastical manuscripts in the world. St Columban (543–615) took it with him to Bobbio in the Apennines, and it is now in the Ambrosian Library in Milan. It contains the hymn 'Sancte, venite'.

Bank. An area in the City of London in the immediate vicinity of the Bank of England (EC2), at the point where the congested thoroughfares of THREADNEEDLE STREET, CORNHILL, LOMBARD STREET and POULTRY meet. To the east of the Bank of England is the Royal Exchange, and to the south stands the Mansion House, official residence of the Lord Mayor of London.

The **Bank of England**, the central bank of England and Wales (founded in 1694, nationalized in 1946 and restored to self-governing status in 1997), has stood on a site here since 1734, but the present monolithic building, designed by Sir John Soane, dates from 1788. The extension of its name to the area around it was strongly promoted by the opening of two Underground stations named 'Bank', on the Waterloo & City line in 1898 and on the Northern line in 1900 (the eastern branch of the Northern line is generally known as the 'Bank' branch).

Banker Chapel Ho. A facetious nickname for the East London district of WHITECHAPEL, current around the turn of the 20th century. It represents an anglicization of cod Italian *bianca capella* 'white chapel' plus the Italianate ending -*o*.

Banking, The Self-explanatory, although it is not clear what the bank was for; ModE *bank*.
A tiny settlement in Aberdeenshire (formerly in Grampian region), 7 km (4.5 miles) north of Old Meldrum.

Bankside '(area) alongside the bank (of the Thames)'.
An area in Central London, on the south bank of the River THAMES¹, in the borough of SOUTHWARK, to the west of Southwark Bridge. The name also belongs specifically to a narrow street along the bank of the Thames at this point.

From earliest times the area had been one to which Londoners went to have fun: drinking in the numerous taverns, cheering the dogs on in the bear-baiting pits, and enthusiastically patronizing the brothels (the area was also known in Tudor times as 'Stews Bank', and prostitutes were often termed 'sisters of the Bank' or **Bankside ladies**). Numerous theatres opened here towards the end of the 16th century, notably the Rose, the Swan and the Globe, where Shakespeare nurtured his talents. Gradually, however, the fun receded, and Bankside's forbidding 19th-century wall of wharves and warehouses made it easy for Londoners to blank out. The area's attractiveness was not enhanced by the erection of **Bankside Power Station**, designed by Sir Giles Gilbert Scott as a smaller, single-chimneyed version of his Battersea Power Station (*see under* BATTERSEA). Bankside opened in 1963 and closed down in 1981.

Renaissance for Bankside came at the end of the 20th century. A working replica of Shakespeare's Globe was opened in 1997, and the disused power station was converted into an art gallery, Tate Modern, which opened in 2000. Bankside's connection to the north bank of the Thames via the new pedestrian Millennium Bridge opened up long-lost vistas of St Paul's Cathedral, and the area now has a thriving cultural and touristic life.

Bann Irish *Banna* 'goddess'; *see* BANDON.

The longest river in Northern Ireland, called by Edmund Spenser 'the fishy fruitful Ban'. It is in two parts. The **Upper Bann** (length 65 km / 40 miles) rises in the MOURNE MOUNTAINS and flows northwest into LOUGH NEAGH on its southern side. The **Lower Bann** (length 64 km / 40 miles) exits Lough Neagh on its northwest side and flows northwest through LOUGH BEG before entering the NORTH CHANNEL near COLERAINE. The Upper Bann forms much of the boundary between counties Antrim and Londonderry, and also between the Unionist east and Nationalist west; 'west of the Bann' is an expression with political implications in Northern Ireland, especially during the 1950s and 1960s when the Stormont government concentrated most of its investment in the east.

> On the banks of Bann water, where first I beheld her
> She appeared like fair Juno or a Grecian queen,
> Her eyes shone like diamonds, her hair softly twining,
> Her cheeks were like roses, or like blood drops in snow.
>
> Anon.: 'The Banks of the Bann' (sung to the tune 'Slane', also used for the hymn 'Be thou my vision')

Bann Valley Exodus, the. The settlement in New Hampshire in 1718 of 200 Presbyterians from the villages of Aghadowey and Macosquin in the valley of the Lower Bann. The biblical element in the phrase is due to the Mosaic words of one of the group's leaders, the Rev. James McGregor:

> Brethren, let us depart, for God has appointed a new country for us to dwell in. It is called New England. Let us be free of these Pharaohs, these rackers of rent and screwers of tithes, and let us go into the land of Canaan.

Do you think I came down the Bann in a bubble? Do you think I was born yesterday?

Banna Strand Irish *banna* 'peaks'.

A long stretch of beach in County Kerry, some 10 km (6 miles) northwest of Tralee. It was here that Roger Casement landed on Good Friday 1916, but he was arrested (at McKenna's Fort) before he could bring ashore the consignment of German arms intended for the Easter Rising.

> 'Twas on Good Friday morning,
> All in the month of May,
> A German ship was signalling,
> Beyond there in the bay,
> We've twenty thousand rifles
> All ready for to land,
> But no answering signal did came from
> The lonely Banna Strand.
>
> Anon.: 'The Lonely Banna Strand' ('May' in the second line is the result of extreme poetic licence.)

Bannau Brycheiniog. The Welsh name for the BRECON BEACONS.

Banner County, the. The nickname of County Clare, due to all the banners displayed at a mass meeting held in 1843 in support for Daniel O'Connell's campaign to repeal the Act of Union.

Bannister Green *Bannister* originally *Bernestey*, perhaps 'Beorn's enclosure', OE *Beornes* possessive form of male personal name *Beorn* + *teag* 'small enclosure'.

A village (pronounced 'bansta green') in Essex, about 8 km (5 miles) southwest of Braintree.

Bannockburn 'stream from the peaked hill', Scots *burn* 'stream' + possibly OCelt *bannauc* 'peaked hill'. In the *Life of St Cadoc*, the hill is referred to as *mons Bannauc*, 'Bannock mountain'.

A town just south of Stirling (of which it is now a part), formerly in Stirlingshire, then in Central region, and now in the unitary authority of Stirling. It takes its name from the **Bannock Burn**, a small tributary of the FORTH that meanders across the plain past the town. On his retreat northward in 1746, Bonnie Prince Charlie stayed for a month at the 17th-century **Bannockburn House**, just south of the town.

Battle of Bannockburn (24 June 1314). A decisive victory in which Robert the Bruce's smaller Scots force, largely consisting of pikemen, defeated a much larger English force under Edward II. This had come to relieve the English garrison in Stirling Castle, whose governor had promised to surrender to the Scots if not relieved by 24 June. Much of the credit for the victory goes to the Scots' use of the local topography, trapping the English in marshy ground between the Forth and the Bannock Burn. The victory secured Scottish independence, and confirmed Bruce's position on the Scottish throne as Robert I.

> we for our lives
> And for our childer and wivis
> And for the freedom of our land,
> Are streinyeit in battale for to stand,
> And they for their micht anerly,
> And forthat they leit of us lichtly,
> And for they wad destroy us all,
> Makis them to ficht …

> John Barbour: Bruce's address to his army before Bannockburn, from *The Bruce* (1376). (*streinyeit* 'constrained', *anerly* 'only', *leit* 'consider')

The victory is also celebrated in Burns's 'Scots, wha hae', in which Bruce encourages his fellow Scots before the battle:

> Now's the day, and now's the hour:
> See the front o' battle lour,
> See approach proud Edward's power –
>   Chains and slaverie!

Every year the Scottish National Party celebrates **Bannockburn Day** by processing to the giant statue of Bruce at the battlefield.

Bansha Irish *An Bháinseach* 'the grassy place'.
A village at the mouth of the beautiful GLEN OF AHERLOW, County Tipperary, 8 km (5 miles) southeast of Tipperary itself.

Bard of Bansha, the. Darby Ryan (1777–1855), remembered for '*Aréir Cois Taoibhe na hAtharlaigh*' ('Last night by the side of the Aherlow River') and for the satirical 'The Peeler and the Goat', based on a true incident in Bansha in 1830 in which a policeman arrested a goat in the main street for 'roistering':

> The Bansha peeler went out one night on duty and patrolling-O,
> He spied a goat upon the road, who seemed to be a strolling-O,
> With bayonet fixed he sallied forth and seized him by the wizen-O,
> Swearing out a mighty oath he'd send him off to prison-O.
> 'Oh mercy! Sir,' the goat replied. 'Pray let me tell my story-O,
> I am no rogue or ribbon man, no croppy, whig or tory-O,
> I'm guilty not of any crime ne'er petty nor high-treason-O,
> And I'm sorely wantin' at this time, for 'tis the rantin' season-O.

Bantry Irish *Beanntraí* '(district of) Beann's people'; Beann was the son of a 1st-century king of Ulster, Conor Mac Nessa.
A port on the southwest coast of County Cork, 70 km (43 miles) southwest of Cork itself. Nearby is the elegant Georgian **Bantry House**, built for Richard White, 2nd Earl of Bantry. The town is at the inner end of **Bantry Bay**, an inlet 40 km (25 miles) long and 6–10 km (4–6 miles) wide. In 1689 a French fleet entered Bantry Bay in support of the deposed James II. A century later, in 1796, the French returned (with Wolfe Tone on board) in support of an unsuccessful rising by the United Irishmen, but their fleet was scattered by storms and returned to Brest.

> As I'm sitting all alone in the gloaming,
> It might have been but yesterday,
> That I watched the fisher sails all homing,
> Till the little herring fleet at anchor lay;
> Then the fisher girls with baskets swinging,
> Came running down the old stone way,
> Every lassie to her sailor lad was singing
> A welcome back to Bantry Bay.

> James Lyman Molloy (1837–1909): 'Bantry Bay'

An oil terminal on Whiddy Island in Bantry Bay closed after an explosion on board the French tanker *Betelgeuse* in 1979.

Bantry Band, the. The nickname of the political machine controlled by Bantry-born Tim Healy (1855–1931), lawyer and Irish Nationalist politician of variable allegiances who opposed Parnell over the O'Shea divorce case and who became the first governor general (1922–8) of the Irish Free State.
See also HEALY PASS.

Bapchild 'Bacca's spring', OE male personal name *Bacca* + *celde* 'spring'.
A village in Kent, about 3 km (2 miles) east of Sittingbourne.

Barbaraville After the local laird's wife.
A small village on Nigg Bay, Easter Ross, Highland (formerly in Ross and Cromarty), 5 km (3 miles) northeast of Invergordon.

Barber Booth 'Barber' s temporary shelter', *Barber* name of a family known here from the 15th century + OScand *both* 'temporary shelter'; the place was known earlier as *Whitemoorley Booth* 'temporary shelter by a copse on bare waste land', OE *hwit* 'white, bare' + *mor* 'waste land' + -LEY.
A village in Derbyshire, in the HIGH PEAK, about 13 km (8 miles) northeast of Buxton.

Barbican From *Barbican*, the name of a former street in the area, which itself was named after an outer fortification of the City of London, possibly a watch-tower, believed to have been demolished in 1267. The word *barbican* itself, a generic term for 'an outer fortification or defence to a city or castle', comes from Old French *barbaquenne*, which is probably ultimately of Arabic origin.

An area in the City of London (EC2), to the northeast of St Paul's[1] Cathedral, consisting of a complex of high-rise apartment blocks and other buildings grouped around the Barbican Centre. It was constructed from the 1950s onwards on a site of 14 ha (35 acres) which had been flattened by bombing in the Second World War. Its northern edge is the line along which the former street called 'Barbican' (which in the 18th century was a centre of the clothing trade) used to run. It is bounded on the west by Aldersgate Street and on the south by London Wall (*see under* London).

The Barbican's apartment blocks, in adventurous modern design and, at 122 m (400 ft), the tallest in Europe at the time of construction, became fashionable places in which to live. Their cultural environment is enriched by the Guildhall School of Music and Drama, the Museum of London, and most notably the **Barbican Centre for Arts and Conferences**, a multi-purpose, ten-level arts complex including a concert hall, a theatre, three cinemas and extensive exhibition space. Designed by Chamberlin, Powell and Bon, it opened in 1982. It is home to the London Symphony Orchestra and was the London base of the Royal Shakespeare Company until the company's withdrawal in 2002.

Barbican Underground station, on the Circle, Metropolitan and Hammersmith & City lines, was originally called Aldersgate Street, then Aldersgate. It opened in 1865. The name was changed to Barbican in 1968.

Barchester. A fictional 19th-century English cathedral city featuring in the 'Barsetshire' novels of Anthony Trollope. It was inspired by a visit to Salisbury, but was modelled mainly on Winchester. Barchester looms especially large in *Barchester Towers* (1857), a tale of clerical intrigues in the cathedral close that buzz around the ineffectual Dr Proudie, Bishop of Barchester.

The name was also appropriated by M.R. James for his disturbing ghost story 'The Stalls of Barchester Cathedral' (1911). James identified his version as 'a blend of Canterbury, Salisbury and Hereford'.

Bardfield Saling *Bardfield* 'open land by a bank or border', OE *byrde* 'bank, border' + *feld* (*see* FIELD); *Saling* from the neighbouring parish of Great Saling.
A village in Essex, about 8 km (5 miles) northwest of Braintree.

Bardsey Island 'Bardr's island', OScand male personal name *Bardr* + *ey* 'island' (*see* -AY).
A small island 3 km (2 miles) across **Bardsey Sound** from the western tip of the Lleyn Peninsula, Gwynedd (formerly in Caernarvonshire). Its Welsh name is **Ynys Enlli** (Welsh, 'island of the currents'), and the Welsh of Bardsey Sound is **Swnt Ennlli** (Welsh *swnt* 'sound').

Bardsey Island was said to have been the site of the earliest religious foundation in Wales, established by St Cadfan in the 5th century, and was for long a pilgrimage destination (three pilgrimages here counted as one to Rome). It is sometimes called **the Island of 20,000 Saints**, owing to the number of monks buried on the island (although since St Dyfrig was exhumed and reinterred in Llandaff Cathedral in 1120, it might more accurately be termed 'the Island of 19,999 Saints').

The remains of St Mary's Abbey, a medieval Augustinian foundation, can still be seen, as can the cowled ghosts of some of the monks, who, according to local tradition, only walk when disaster is imminent. Also resting on the island is Merlin (presumably when not sleeping in his many other pieds-à-terre around Britain). The island is now a bird reserve and a Site of Special Scientific Interest, although it is still used as a religious retreat.

> The Maker who made me will meet me
> In the fair parish of Enlli's faithful.
>
> Meilyr Brydydd: 'Poem on his Death-bed' (early 12th century), translated from the Welsh by Joseph P. Clancy

Saints' Road to Bardsey, the. A nickname for the B4417, running along the north side of the Lleyn Peninsula.

Barfrestone Probably 'Beornfrith's farmstead', OE *Beornfrithes* possessive form of male personal name *Beornfrith* + -TON.
A village in Kent, about 11 km (7 miles) west of Deal. It has a tiny and exceptionally fine 12th-century church, considered to be one of the best examples of Norman architecture in England.

Bargoed Welsh *bargod* 'boundary', from the River Bargoed. The 'e' was mistakenly introduced in the 16th century to make the name appear more Welsh, reflecting the influence of *coed*, 'wood' (*see* CED).
A town on the **River Bargoed** in Caerphilly (formerly in Glamorgan then in Mid-Glamorgan), 15 km (9 miles) west of Pontypool. It developed round a railway junction and station in the 19th century.

Barking '(settlement of) Berica's people', OE male personal name *Berica* + -*ingas* (*see* -ING).
A district in eastern Greater London, in the borough of Barking and Dagenham (until 1965 in Essex). Until the middle of the 19th century fishing was the most important local industry, but after the arrival of the railway in 1854, houses and factories converted the Essex fishing village into a part of the East End cityscape.

The former England footballer Sir Trevor Brooking was born in Barking in 1948.
Barking Creek. The name given to the mouth of the River Roding, which enters the Thames 2.5 km (1.5 miles) south

of Barking. It flows through a bleak landscape of gas- and sewage works.

Barking and Dagenham. A borough in eastern Greater London, on the north bank of the THAMES[1], to the east of Newham. It was formed in 1965 from the districts of BARKING and DAGENHAM.

Barkingside '(place) beside Barking'; from its position on the extreme edge of the former parish of BARKING.

A district in eastern Greater London, in the borough of REDBRIDGE.

See also ILFORD.

Bar-L, the. A nickname for BARLINNIE, the high security prison in the RIDDRIE area of GLASGOW. It is also known, with heavy irony, as the 'Riddrie Hilton'.

Barlavington Probably 'estate associated with Beornlaf', OE male personal name *Beornlaf* + -ING + -TON.

A village in West Sussex, at the foot of the SOUTH DOWNS, about 16 km (10 miles) northeast of Chichester. **Barlavington Down**, to the southwest, is 210 m (689 ft) high.

Barlinnie 'top of the pool', Gaelic *barr* 'head, top' + *linne* 'pool'.

Glasgow's high security prison in the Riddrie area of the city, built in 1880 and known to those on nodding terms with it as **the Bar-L** or **the Riddrie Hilton**. Between 1946 and 1960, ten men were hanged here. In the 1970s a Special Unit was set up at Barlinnie designed to rehabilitate the most hardened of criminals: one such was Jimmy Boyle, a violent gangster, who, butterfly-like, emerged from the Unit as a respected sculptor and author of an admired autobiography, *A Sense of Freedom* (1977). Abdelbaset Ali Mohmed al-Megrahi, convicted of the LOCKERBIE bombing, began his minimum 20-year sentence in Barlinnie in 2002. Like many other British prisons, Barlinnie is severely overcrowded. One MSP (Member of the Scottish Parliament) has commented:

> The slopping out scene at dawn is beyond any degradation I have seen, even in Russia. Steam from the faeces rises up through the halls into the cells where men must eat.

Barmouth The English version, via *Abermouth*, of the Welsh name *Abermaw*, 'mouth of the River Mawddach', Welsh ABER + the original river name *Mawdd,* from a personal name; in the Welsh, *-ach* is a diminutive, thus *Mawddach* is 'Little Mawdd'.

A small seaside resort on **Barmouth Bay** (an inlet of Cardigan Bay), at the mouth of the Mawddach Estuary, in Gwynedd (formerly in Merioneth), 12 km (7.5 miles) west of Dolgellau. In Welsh it is **Abermaw** (*see above*) or **Y Bermo** (a misdivision of *Abermaw*, where *A-* has been taken as the definite article *Y*).

> Fly to the shore, brave brightness,
> And say where I was held fast
> By the mouth, no gentle wave,
> Of rough Bermo, cold foaming,
> In all moods a sorry spot,
> A cold black sea for sailing.
>
> Siôn Phylip: 'The Seagull' (early 17th century), translated from the Welsh by Joseph P. Clancy

Barmouth was an important port in the Middle Ages, and it was here that Jasper Tudor, uncle of Henry VII, reputedly plotted the overthrow of Richard III. Above the town is Dinas Oleu, the first property acquired by the National Trust, in 1895. To the north is the so-called CALIFORNIA OF WALES.

Barnacle Originally (1086) *Bernhanger* 'wooded slope by a barn', OE *bere-œrn* 'barley-house, barn' + *hangra* 'wooded slope'; later assimilated to English *barnacle*.

A village in Warwickshire, about 3 km (2 miles) northeast of Coventry.

Barnard Castle After *Bernard de Balliol*, who built the castle's 13th-century circular tower.

A market town on the River TEES in County Durham, 24 km (15 miles) west of Darlington. The ruined castle, dating from Norman times, is on a rock above the river, and belonged to the Balliol family, claimants to the Scottish Crown in the 13th and 14th century. The town, known as **Barney** to locals, is also home to an extraordinary château, built in the 19th century by John Bowes, businessman and MP, to house his important art collection, and now open to the public as the Bowes Museum. Dickens stayed at the King's Head Inn in Barnard Castle in 1838 while investigating conditions in some of the local boarding schools; one of these, at nearby BOWES, became the basis of Dotheboys Hall in *Nicholas Nickleby* (1839).

Barnard Castle was the birthplace of C. Northcote Parkinson (1909–93), formulator of Parkinson's law.

> The Moon is in her summer glow,
> But hoarse and high the breezes blow,
> And, racking o'er her face, the cloud
> Varies the tincture of her shroud;
> On Barnard's towers, and Tees's stream,
> She changes as a guilty dream …
>
> Sir Walter Scott: *Rokeby* (1813), Canto I. i, opening lines (Part of the action of the poem is set at Barnard Castle; ROKEBY itself is nearby, close to Greta Bridge.)

'Barnard Castle'. A Durham dialect term for a coward. It derives from the Northern Rebellion (*see under* the NORTH[1]) by the Catholic earls in 1569, when Sir George Bowes refused, despite many opportunities, to leave his fortified position in Barnard Castle to engage in battle. Hence also the expression **come, come, that's Barney Castle**, meaning 'that's a pathetic excuse'.

A coward, a coward, o' Barney Castle
Dare na come out to fight a battle.

Barnes '(place by the) barns', OE *bere-œrn* 'barley-house, barn'.
A residential district of West London, on the south bank
of a northerly loop of the River THAMES[1], in the borough
of RICHMOND-UPON-THAMES. By the end of the 20th
century it was the beneficiary of a tide of fashionability
that flowed westwards down the King's Road via Fulham.

Barnes Bridge, a railway bridge built 1846–9 and crossing to Chiswick, is the last bridge that the crews have to
negotiate in the annual Oxford and Cambridge Boat Race.

The pop star Marc Bolan (1947–77) died when the car in
which he was travelling hit a tree on Barnes Common.

Barnet 'land cleared by burning', OE *bœrnet*; from the method
used to clear the dense forests in the area in the early Middle
Ages.
A borough of northwest GREATER LONDON (N2, N3, N10,
N11, N12, N20, NW4, NW7, NW9, NW11), between Enfield
in the east and Harrow in the west. It was created in 1965
from parts of HERTFORDSHIRE and MIDDLESEX and contains,
among other districts, COCKFOSTERS, EDGWARE, FINCHLEY,
GOLDERS GREEN, HAMPSTEAD GARDEN SUBURB, HENDON
and MILL HILL, but at its centre (symbolically – on the map
it is at the northern boundary) is the urban aggregate
known as Barnet (before 1965, in Hertfordshire). This consists of Chipping Barnet and East Barnet, which date back
to Anglo-Saxon times; **High Barnet** (the name was originally an alternative to *Chipping Barnet*, but now refers to a
separate northern part of the town); and the more recent
New Barnet and Barnet Vale. (*See also* FRIERN BARNET.)

Barnet was granted a charter to hold markets in 1199,
and an annual September fair has been held here since the
Middle Ages. In consequence of the resulting necessary
provision of refreshment, Barnet became known as a 'town
of inns'.

The town's position on the GREAT NORTH ROAD contributed significantly to its development. Barnet was the
first staging post on the journey north from London, and in
the 18th and early 19th centuries the coaching trade was
very important to its economy. In modern times, the borough of Barnet contains the southern end of the M1. The
railway arrived in Barnet in the middle of the 19th
century, and its conversion into a fairly anonymous
London suburb began. High Barnet 'Underground' station,
a northern terminus of the bifurcated Northern line, opened
in 1940.

The Middlesex and England left-arm spin bowler Phil
Tufnell (b.1966) was born in Barnet.

barnet. A rhyming-slang term, abbreviated from *Barnet
Fair*, for 'hair' (first recorded in 1857), which was inspired
by the annual merrymaking in Barnet (*see above*).

Battle of Barnet (14 April 1471). A battle in the Wars of

the Roses fought on Hadley Green in MONKEN HADLEY, to
the north of Barnet. The Yorkists defeated the Lancastrians, and the Earl of Warwick was killed while trying to
escape.

Barney. The local nickname of BARNARD CASTLE in County
Durham.

Barnoldswick 'Beornwulf's farm', OE male personal name
Beornwulf + WICK.
A town in Lancashire, 12 km (7.5 miles) southwest of
Skipton.

Barnsley[1] 'Beorn's clearing', OE male personal name *Beorn*
+ -LEY.
A mining and industrial town on the River Dearne, South
Yorkshire, 26 km (16 miles) north of Sheffield. It is the
administrative headquarters of Barnsley metropolitan
borough, and also has the headquarters of the National
Union of Mineworkers.

> ... a town called Black Barnsley, eminent still for the
> working of iron and steel; and indeed the very town looks
> as black and smoky as if they were all smiths that lived in
> it; though it is not, I suppose, called Black Barnsley on
> that account, but for the black hue or colour of the
> moors, which, being covered in heath ... look all black ...
>
> Daniel Defoe: *A Tour Through the Whole Island of Great Britain*
> (1724–6)

Some two-and-a-half centuries after Defoe, a consumer
guide, *The Guinness Book of Top Towns* (1995), ranked the
citizens of Barnsley by adjudging their town the least
desirable place to live in the United Kingdom. Local pub
landlords poured gallons of Guinness down the drain in
protest, and the matter was even raised in the House of
Commons.

Barnsley was the birthplace of the poet Donald Davie
(1922–95) and the left-wing playwright John Arden
(b.1930). Davie commented of his home town:

> Taciturn is the toast
> Hereabouts.
>
> Donald Davie: 'Barnsley, 1966', from *Essex Poems* (1969)

and elsewhere wrote:

> And Bethal and Zion Baptist,
> Sootblack on pavements foul with miners' spittle
> And late-night spew and violence, persist.
>
> Donald Davie: 'Barnsley and District', from *Events and
> Wisdoms* (1964)

Barnsley was also the birthplace of two contemporary
Yorkshire icons: the perennial chat-show host Michael
Parkinson (b.1935), who was educated at the local
grammar school; and Darren ('Dazzler') Gough (b.1970),
the wholehearted Yorkshire and England fast bowler of the
1990s and early 2000s.

Barnsley FC, originally founded as a church team in 1887, is nicknamed the Tykes (see under YORKSHIRE) and plays its home games at Oakwell. The Barnsley team that won the FA Cup in 1912 was dubbed **Battling Barnsley** for its gritty efforts in a long-drawn-out campaign that led up their eventual cup final victory against West Bromwich Albion.

Ken Loach's classic film *Kes*, based on a novel by Barry Hines, was filmed in Barnsley in 1968.

At the beginning of 2003 the world was surprised to learn of plans, devised by the architect Will Alsop, to turn Barnsley into a Tuscan-style hilltop town. 'If we can only make this town beautiful,' said Alsop, 'people will come.'

Barnsley² 'Beornmod's glade', OE *Beornmodes* possessive form of male personal name *Beornmod* + -LEY.

A picturesque village in Gloucestershire, in the COTSWOLDS, about 6.5 km (4 miles) northeast of Cirencester. It was part of an estate owned by a single family until the mid-20th century, which held back commercial development in the village and contributed to its unspoilt character. The *Architectural Review* (in an article called 'Counter-Attack') opined in December 1956:

> Here is a village that has made itself into one of the most memorable places in Britain ... everything is in the right place with the right treatment.

The celebrated gardens of **Barnsley House** (formerly the village Rectory and now a smart country hotel) were designed by Rosemary Verey (1919–2001), one of the great 20th-century gardeners.

Barnstaple 'post or pillar of the battle-axe' (probably denoting the site of a meeting-place), OE *beardan* possessive form of *bearde* 'battle-axe' + *stapol* 'post, pillar'.

A town in Devon, on the estuary of the River TAW, about 45 km (28 miles) northwest of Tiverton. It claims to be the oldest borough in England, its charter dating from 950. Until the Taw estuary began to silt up in the 19th century, it was an important and busy port.

In the 18th century Barnstaple was well known for its pottery, and it also produced metal-ware (in Ireland its name became transformed into *bastable* as a term for a cast-iron pot with a snug-fitting lid used for baking bread).

Locals are known as **Barumites**, from *Barum* 'Barnstaple'. That form of the name may have arisen in the past from its being written in manuscripts as *Bar'*, with a suspension mark over the *r* representing the rest of the name; the conventional expression of this mark in Latin texts was *–um*, which (as in the possibly parallel case of SARUM) could easily have been tacked on to the first part of the English name.

John Gay (1685–1732), writer of *The Beggar's Opera* (1728), was born in Barnstaple.

Barnstaple Bay. Another name for **Bideford Bay** (*see under* BIDEFORD).

Barons Court Probably modelled on *Earls Court*, perhaps also with an allusion to *court-baron*, an ancient term for an assembly held by the lord of a manor.

A district of west London, in the borough of HAMMERSMITH AND FULHAM (W14), to the west of Earls Court. It was laid out in the late 19th century by Sir William Palliser, who gave it its name. This was later reinforced by the opening of Barons Court Underground station on the District and Piccadilly lines in 1905.

Barra 'hill island'. A tradition has it that the name derives from St Barr (*c*.560–*c*.615), Bishop of Cork, to whom there was once a chapel dedicated on Barra (some say he was sent here by Columba after the previous missionary had fallen prey to cannibals). However, the name is actually from an OCelt word *barro* 'hill' (*see* BARRY in Wales and BARRHEAD in Ayrshire for later Celtic forms); OScand *ey* 'island' (*see* -AY) was added in the 12th century. The Gaelic name is *Eilean Barraigh*.

The southernmost of the larger Outer HEBRIDES, Western Isles (formerly in Inverness-shire). It is separated from South Uist by the 6-km (4-mile) wide **Sound of Barra**, and is linked by a causeway to the smaller island of VATERSAY to the south. Barra has ferry links to OBAN and MALLAIG on the mainland, and to LOCHBOISDALE on South Uist. The runway of the island's airport is on a sandy beach, and is washed twice daily by the tide.

Barra, which is still mostly Catholic, was long in the hands of the MacNeils of Barra, whose Kisimul Castle is at the island's main settlement, CASTLEBAY. The MacNeils, who claim descent from Niall of the Nine Hostages, High King of Ireland in the 4th century, were renowned pirates.

> One day on the Misty Mountain
> Rounding up the sheep to get them ...
> 'Twas I myself beheld the vision,
> Seeing thy galley going past me,
> Setting her head to the wide ocean
> From MacNeil of Barra's country,
> Out of Ciosamul's joyful castle ...
>
> Anon.: from J.L. Campbell and F. Collinson (eds.), *Hebridean Folksongs* (3 vols, 1969, 1977, 1981)

The MacNeils were also renowned for regarding themselves as sovereign lords. It is said that after they had finished dining at Kisimul Castle, a herald would proclaim:

> Hear ye, ye peoples and ye nations. The MacNeil of Barra has eaten, and now the princes of the earth may dine.

James Boswell recorded how, having received a letter from MacNeil, the Earl of Argyll complained that his style 'runs as if he were of another kingdom'.

When Bonnie Prince Charlie called at the castle on 22 July 1745 on his way to raise a rebellion on the Scottish mainland, MacNeil was not 'at home'. The MacNeils were forced to sell up in 1838, and were succeeded by some unscrupulous landlords who cleared much of the population. However, in 1937 the 45th MacNeil chief, an American, bought back much of the island.

The novelist Compton Mackenzie lived on Barra during the Second World War, and is buried here. The foundering of SS *Politician* between Barra and ERISKAY on 5 February 1941 inspired his novel *Whisky Galore* (1947). Although the novel is set on Eriskay, the film version (1948) was made on Barra. Fourteen bottles of whisky from the real-life wreck fetched a total of over £12,000 at auction in Glasgow in 1993, although it is said that the liquid is quite undrinkable.

Barra Head. The southernmost point of the Outer HEBRIDES, not on Barra itself, but on the associated islet of BERNERAY[1], 20 km (12.5 miles) to the south. The sea cliffs here are some 190 m (620 ft) high. It gives its name to the **Barrahead Islands**, an alternative name for the BISHOP'S ISLES.

Barrahead Islands. *See* the BISHOP'S ISLES.

Barras Bridge 'bridge of the outwork', OFr *barras* 'barrier, outwork' + ME *bridge.*
A district of NEWCASTLE UPON TYNE, in which the civic centre is situated. It was traditionally the site of the single combat in 1388 between Henry Percy ('Harry Hotspur') and the Earl of Douglas, before the Battle of OTTERBURN.

Barr Beacon OCelt *barro* 'hill', with the later addition of ModE *beacon* 'hilltop used for fire signals'.
A hill, about 225 m (740 ft) high, 3 km (2 miles) southwest of Aldridge in the West Midlands. It affords panoramic views.

Barrhead A tautonym: Gaelic *barr* 'summit' + ModE *head.*
A town 12 km (7.5 miles) to the southwest of Glasgow, in East Renfrewshire (formerly in Strathclyde region). The town is renowned throughout Britain for its production of porcelain sanitary ware. It was the birthplace of the suicidal *fin-de-siècle* poet and playwright John Davidson (1857–1909), author of *Fleet Street Eclogues* (1893).

Barripper 'beautiful retreat', Fr *beau repaire.*
A village in Cornwall, about 2.5 km (1.5 miles) southwest of Camborne.

Barrow Possibly Irish *barra* 'ridge', 'top'.
A river in southeastern Ireland, 190 km (118 miles) long. It rises in the SLIEVE BLOOM MOUNTAINS of County Laois, and flows east then south to enter the sea at Waterford Harbour (*see under* WATERFORD). It is linked to the sea at Dublin by the GRAND CANAL. Its main tributaries are the NORE, which joins it just north of NEW ROSS, and the SUIR, which joins it at Waterford Harbour; together the three rivers are known as the 'Three Sisters'.

> ... the goodly Barow, which doth hoord
> Great heapes of Salmons in his deepe bosome
>
> Edmund Spenser: *The Faerie Queen* (1590), IV, xi, 43

Barrowford 'ford by the small wood', OE *bearu* 'grove' + FORD.
A small town in Lancashire, 7 km (4.5 miles) northeast of Burnley.

Barrow Gurney *Barrow* '(place at the) wood or grove', OE *bearwe* dative form of *bearu* 'wood, grove'; *Gurney* denoting manorial ownership in the early Middle Ages by Nigel de Gurnai.
A village in North Somerset, about 5 km (3 miles) southwest of Bristol.

Barrow-in-Furness 'promontory island in FURNESS', OCelt *barro* 'promontory' + OScand *ey* (*see* -AY).
A large industrial town at the southern end of the FURNESS peninsula, Cumbria (formerly in Lancashire), some 30 km (19 miles) west across Morecambe Bay from Lancaster. It developed in the mid-19th century as a centre of iron working using local ore, and later shipbuilding and ship repairing became the most important industry, using the channel between the town and the ISLE OF WALNEY. The best-known shipbuilding firm, specializing in submarines, was Vickers, which gave its name to the district called Vickerstown. The last steelworks closed in 1983, but VSEL, the successor to Vickers, continues to build nuclear submarines and other warships.

Barry Welsh *barr* 'summit' (referring to the hill here); traditionally but implausibly the town is said to be named after St Baruch, supposedly buried here in the 7th century.
An industrial port on the Bristol Channel (*see under* BRISTOL) coast of Vale of Glamorgan (formerly in Glamorgan, then in South Glamorgan), 12 km (7.5 miles) southwest of Cardiff. Its Welsh name is **Barri** or **Y Barri**. It is the administrative seat of VALE OF GLAMORGAN. There was a Norman castle here (built by the de Barri family), but the town's growth dates from 1889 when big new docks were built to export coal. Sticking out into the Bristol Channel is the small **Barry Island** (Welsh name **Ynys y Barri**; it is not actually an island), popular with holidaymakers who enjoy amusement arcades and funfairs. The poet Dannie Abse recalled childhood daytrips there, where

> The sea crinkled its lace petticoat up the beach ...

Barry is celebrated in athletics circles as the location of the first-ever women's international cross-country event in 1967.

Barrytown. A fictional working-class suburb of north DUBLIN, created by Roddy Doyle in his **Barrytown Trilogy**: *The Commitments* (1987), *The Snapper* (1990) and *The Van* (1991), all involving the Rabbitte family. Doyle's Booker

Prize-winning *Paddy Clarke Ha Ha Ha* (1993) is also set in Barrytown. Barrytown is based on Kilbarrack, where Doyle taught for a time.

Barsetshire. The fictional West Country county in which Anthony Trollope (1815–82) set his series of 'Barsetshire' novels: *The Warden* (1855), *Barchester Towers* (1857), *Doctor Thorne* (1858), *Framley Parsonage* (1861), *The Small House at Allington* (1864) and *The Last Chronicle of Barset* (1867). Apart from the occasional excursion to London, the action of all of them takes place in the rural cottages and country houses of Barsetshire (or **Barset**) or in the almshouses, archdeaconry and episcopal palace of BARCHESTER, its cathedral city. Trollope had the county's whole geography minutely plotted in his mind.

Angela Thirkell (1890–1961) used Barsetshire (and Barchester) as a setting for some of her novels, the first of which (though not intended to be such) was *High Rising* (1993). The name has also been pressed into service in other fictional milieux (e.g. the St Trinian's stories based on Ronald Searle's cartoons).

The soundalike county of 'Borsetshire' is *Archers* country: *see under* BORCHESTER.

Barton Bendish *Barton* 'barley-farm, outlying grange where grain is stored', OE *bere, bær* 'barley' + -TON; *Bendish* 'inside the ditch' (referring to a local defensive earthwork known as the 'Devil's Dyke'), OE *binnan* 'inside' + *dic* 'ditch'.
A village in Norfolk, about 18 km (11 miles) southeast of King's Lynn.

Barton Hartshorn *Hartshorn* perhaps from a local house with a gable decoration of deer horns (*hart* 'stag').
A village in Buckinghamshire, about 6.5 km (4 miles) southwest of Buckingham.

Barton in Fabis 'Barton in the beans' (from the commonness of beans as a local crop), Latin *fabis* ablative plural of *faba* 'bean'.
A village in Nottinghamshire, about 8 km (5 miles) southwest of Nottingham.

Barton in the Beans The second part of the name is from beans as a local crop.
A village in Leicestershire, about 20 km (12.5 miles) west of Leicester.

Barton-under-Needwood From its proximity to NEEDWOOD FOREST.
A small town in Staffordshire, on the western side of the Trent and Mersey Canal (*see under* TRENT[1]), to the southeast of NEEDWOOD FOREST, about 8 km (5 miles) southwest of Burton upon Trent.

Barton-upon-Humber 'barley farm by the Humber'; *Humber see* HUMBER.
A small town in North Lincolnshire (in Humberside 1974–1996 and before that in Lincolnshire), lying at the southern end of the Humber Bridge (*see under* HUMBER). Barton-upon-Humber was the birthplace of Chad Varah (b.1911), the founder of the Samaritans.

Barwick in Elmet. *See under* ELMET.

Baseball Ground. *See under* DERBY.

Basildon 'Beorhtel's hill', OE *Beorhteles* possessive form of OE male personal name *Beorhtel* + *-don* (*see* DOWN, -DON).
A town in southern Essex, about 10 km (6 miles) southeast of Brentwood, and about 10 km (6 miles) northwest of Canvey Island on the THAMES[1] estuary. It is on the railway line between SOUTHEND-ON-SEA and London FENCHURCH STREET, which in the 19th century promoted its expansion from a tiny rural village, but its real growth spurt came after the Second World War, when it was designated a London overspill town and a NEW TOWN[1]. The influx of traditionally Labour-voting East Enders turned into Thatcher supporters in the late 1970s, providing Basildon with its first Conservative MP (Harvey Proctor) and giving rise to the so-called '**Basildon man**', a more narrowly political clone of Essex Man (*see under* ESSEX).

The actress and television presenter Denise Van Outen (b.1974) was born in Basildon.

Basildon Park. *See under* LOWER BASILDON

Basingstoke 'Basa's people's outlying farmstead', OE male personal name *Basa* + *inga* (*see* -ING) + *stoc* 'secondary settlement, outlying farmstead'.
A market town in Hampshire, about 28 km (17.5 miles) northeast of WINCHESTER. The quiet pre-Second World War country town was transformed beyond recognition in the latter part of the 20th century by extensive house-building and the introduction of businesses and light industries.

For Gilbert and Sullivan aficionados Basingstoke is, in the words of *Brewer's Dictionary of Phrase and Fable*, a town whose name 'has come to be regarded as droll or even irresistibly amusing'. The character Mad Margaret in *Ruddigore* (1887) is soothed by sustained bathetic incantation of the word:

> *Mad Margaret*: When I am lying awake at night ... strange fancies crowd upon my poor mad brain, and I sometimes think that if we could hit upon some word for you to use whenever I am about to relapse – some word that teems with hidden meaning – like 'Basingstoke' – it might well recall me to my saner self.

Perhaps its latter-day expansion and homogenization have quelled its drollness, for in the 21st century the name 'Basingstoke' is not one to raise a laugh among non-Savoyards.

Basingstoke was the birthplace of the writer and cricket commentator John Arlott (1914–91), famed for his rich

Hampshire burr. He called his autobiography *Basingstoke Boy* (1990). Thomas Burberry opened his first outfitters shop in Basingstoke in 1856. The town is fictionalized in the novels of Thomas Hardy as '**Stoke-Barehills**'.

Bassenthwaite Lake After the nearby village of *Bassenthwaite*, which means 'meadow of the Bastun family', ME personal name *Bastun* + OScand *thveit* 'meadow, clearing'.

The most northerly lake in the LAKE DISTRICT, Cumbria (formerly in Cumberland), 6 km (4 miles) northwest of Keswick, and overlooked by SKIDDAW. In woodland above the lake is the nest of the first pair of ospreys to breed in England, in 2003.

Bassetlaw Perhaps 'mound or hill of the people living on land cleared by burning', OE *bærnet* 'land cleared by burning' + *sæte* 'dwellers' + *hlaw* (*see* LAW, LOW).

An administrative district in northern Nottinghamshire, comprising WORKSOP and RETFORD and the rural areas surrounding them. It was the home of the Pilgrim Fathers who set sail for Newfoundland in 1620.

Bass Rock, the Origin uncertain; possibly from a personal name Bass, or from Gaelic *bathais* 'forehead' or 'brow'.

A small rocky island in the Firth of FORTH, about 5 km (3 miles) northeast of North Berwick. On most sides it is surrounded by sheer cliffs, up to 107 m (350 ft) high. It is home to the largest colony of gannets (a.k.a. solan geese) in the North Atlantic, hence its description by William Drummond of Hawthornden (1585–1649) as '*soligoosifera Bassa*' (cod Latin, 'solan-goose-bearing Bass Rock'). (The rock supplied the scientific name for the gannet, *Morus* or *Sula bassana*, and also its French and German names, *fou de bassan* and *Basstölpel* respectively.) There is a lighthouse here (unmanned since 1991), and the ruins of a chapel and fortress-prison dating from late medieval times. The chapel was dedicated to St Baldred, an Irish missionary who is said to have lived on the rock in the 6th century. The fortress was used as a prison for Covenanters in the 17th century, and was the last place in Scotland held by the Jacobites after the Glorious Revolution, eventually surrendering in 1694.

In Robert Louis Stevenson's *Catriona* (1893), the hero, David Balfour, is for a time held captive on the Bass. Stevenson describes the rock thus:

> It is just the one crag of rock, as everybody knows, but great enough to carve a city from.

Bastardstown Presumably this means what it says: English for property of an illegitimate son.

A townland (administrative division of a parish) in County Wexford, near Forlorn Point, 17 km (11 miles) south of Wexford itself.

Bàsteir Tooth. *See under* AM BÀSTEIR.

Bath '(place at) the (Roman) baths', OE *bæthum* dative plural of *bæth* 'bath'; from the use of its hot springs for bathing.

A city in southwest England, on the River AVON[2], 16 km (10 miles) to the southeast of Bristol; part of the unitary authority of Bath and North East Somerset. It was previously, between 1974 and 1996, in Avon, and before 1974 in Somerset. Bath owes its fame to its reputedly therapeutic hot springs, claimed as the only ones of their type in Britain, which according to legend were discovered by a Celtic prince called Bladud in 860 BC (he allegedly cured his leprosy by taking a dip, having noted their miraculous effect on the skin tone of some scabrous pigs). The springs have certainly been used for bathing since at least Roman times (when the town was known as **Aquae Sulis**). The Great Roman Bath was rediscovered and excavated in 1880.

In Anglo-Saxon times the town was identified as the place where there were 'baths', and by the 10th century *Bathan* was being used as its name; it also had a Latinized form, *Bathonia*. In late Anglo-Saxon times it was also called *Bathanceastre*, 'Baths-chester', but that name did not survive long. An alternative name dating from the same period was *Acemannes ceastre* (*see* AKEMAN STREET). In the early medieval period, *Bathan* became shortened to *Bathe*, and by the 17th century the modern form *Bath* had become firmly established.

The town waters continued to be used for bathing in the Middle Ages (Robert of Gloucester mentions in his *Chronicle* (1297) the 'water of Bathe ... that ever is yliche [equally] hot ... Suche bathes there beth fele [many] in the close & in the street'), but at that time Bath was also a noted cloth-making centre, its reputation alluded to in Geoffrey Chaucer's description of the **Wife of Bath** in the Prologue to the *Canterbury Tales*: 'In making cloth she showed so great a bent, she bettered those of Ypres and of Ghent...' (Chaucer's character is actually one of English literature's merriest widows: she condemns celibacy in the strongest terms and gives an enthusiastic account of her life with five successive husbands.)

Bath's popularity as a spa began to rise again in the mid-18th century, after Bath Hospital (later famous as the Royal Mineral Water Hospital) opened in 1738 for the treatment of gout (one of its founders was Dr William Oliver, of **Bath Oliver** fame (*see below*); it is now the Royal National Hospital for Rheumatic Diseases). At that time the town was often known as '**the Bath**' or '**the Baths**'. By the end of the century it had become a fashionable centre to which the English upper and upper-middle classes came to take the waters. Fine Georgian streets and squares were laid out (including the world-famous Royal Crescent) and elegant buildings erected (notably the Assembly Rooms, where the celebrated dandy 'Beau' Nash (1674–1762, known as the **King of Bath**) held court, and the Pump Room), largely owing to the enterprise of a local postmaster, Ralph Allen.

Much of the layout of the Georgian city was planned by John Wood and his son, also John. The most famous architect of the late 18th century, Robert Adam, was responsible for Pulteney Bridge, built between 1769 and 1774, which crosses the River Avon. The baths themselves were closed after a young girl caught meningitis from the water in 1978, but after extensive redevelopment (to the designs of Nicholas Grimshaw) they are due for reopening in the early 21st century.

Today, the 'City of Bath' is a UNESCO World Heritage Site.

The balls, routs and intrigues of Bath's high society are reflected in English literature from Tobias Smollett, Henry Fielding, and Fanny Burney to Charles Dickens – in the latter's *Pickwick Papers*, Nathaniel Winkle pays court to Arabella Allen in Bath. However, the pre-eminent chronicler of Bath was Jane Austen (who lived there between 1801 and 1806). The city features or is referred to in many of her novels, and in *Northanger Abbey* (1818) the naive heroine Catherine Morland declares:

> I really believe I shall always be talking of Bath ... I do like it so very much. Oh! who can ever be tired of Bath?

Not everyone took the same rosy view, though: in the 18th century, Smollett described the Bath waters as flavoured with 'sweat and dirt and dandruff'.

Bath Abbey, often called the 'Lantern of the West' because of the huge clear glass windows in its nave and choir, dates in its rebuilt form from the end of the 15th century. The **University of Bath** was founded in 1966 – in time for the students to sample George Perry-Smith's cooking at the Hole in the Wall restaurant, which in the 1960s and 70s was one of the outriders of the late 20th-century English gastronomic renaissance. Plasticine was first made on a large scale in 1900 in an old flour mill near Bath.

C.P. Scott (1846–1932), editor of the *Manchester Guardian* from 1872 to 1929, was born in Bath. Haile Selassie, Emperor of Ethiopia, lived here in exile from 1936 to 1940.

There are towns called Bath in the USA (Illinois, Maine, North Carolina, New York, South Carolina, South Dakota), Canada (New Brunswick), and the West Indies (Jamaica, Nevis).

See also LANSDOWN[2].

Bath and Wells. A diocese of the Church of England coextensive with the county of Somerset. It dates from the 10th century, but the first bishop to take the joint title 'Bath and Wells' was Roger of Salisbury (1244). After the dissolution of Bath Abbey in 1538, the bishop, though retaining the old style, had his seat at WELLS Cathedral alone.

Bath asparagus. A variety of the Star of Bethlehem plant whose young shoots can be eaten and are said to taste like asparagus.

Bath brick. A scouring brick made at BRIDGWATER in Somerset, used for cleaning polished metal, made from sand and clay taken from the River PARRETT, which runs through the town. It probably got its name from its resemblance to Bath stone.

Bath bun. A sweet bun made from white dough and containing candied peel, raisins, etc., originally made in Bath. A forerunner, known as a **Bath cake**, was in existence in the middle of the 18th century, but the first we hear of the bun itself is in 1801, when Jane Austen wrote in a letter of 'disordering my Stomach with Bath bunns'. It came to national prominence in the 19th century (943,691 Bath buns were consumed at the Great Exhibition in 1851).

Bath chair. An early type of wheelchair, typically made of wickerwork and with a hood over one end. The term is first recorded in 1823, and alludes to the large numbers of the infirm who sought relief in the waters of Bath.

Bath chap. The pickled or smoked cheeks of a pig, usually boiled and covered in breadcrumbs and eaten cold. The reason for the specific connection with Bath is not known, although the West Country has always been famous for its charcuterie. *Chap* is probably the same word as *chops*, 'jaws, mouth'.

Bath coating. A type of fabric used in the 18th and 19th centuries for making men's coats, waistcoats, etc.

Bath coup. A tactic in whist or bridge in which a player who holds the ace, jack and another card of the same suit refrains from taking his opponent's king. It is said to have originated at the card tables of Bath in the middle of the 18th century.

Bath Guide. Originally the *New Bath Guide*, a series of verse letters recounting the fictional adventures of Squire Blunderhead and his family in Bath, written by Christopher Anstey and published in 1766; in the 19th century the term became generic for verse of this type.

Bath metal. An alloy like pinchbeck, consisting of copper, zinc, lead and tin.

Bath Oliver. A kind of unsweetened biscuit, today usually eaten with cheese. It was invented by (or named after) Dr William Oliver (1695–1764), founder of Bath's Royal Mineral Water Hospital in 1760 and an authority on gout. He left his biscuit recipe to his coachman, Atkins. The biscuit was originally called simply an **Oliver**; *Bath* does not appear as part of the name until the 1870s.

Bathonian. A term meaning of or relating to Bath; used specifically in geology to denote a subdivision of the Jurassic, of which the formations at Bath are typical.

Bath post. A 19th-century term for a type of writing paper.

Bath Rugby. The name adopted in the professional era by Bath rugby union club (originally founded in 1865). One of

England's most successful rugby union clubs, Bath play their home games at the Recreation Ground.

Bath stone. An attractive but not very durable building stone quarried from limestone formations near Bath. Also known as **Bath oolite**.

Bath water/ Bath waters. The natural hot spring water of Bath, which issues at a temperature of 49°C and is usable for both bathing and drinking. Its effect on the drinker is not invariably curative:

> I had the misfortune to lose a beloved brother in the prime of life, who dropt down dead as he was playing on the fiddle at Sir Robert Throgmorton's, after drinking a large quantity of Bath Waters, and eating a hearty breakfast of spungy hot rolls, or Sally Luns.
>
> P. Thicknesse: *Valetudinarian's Bath Guide* (1780)

Bath White. A rare European butterfly, *Pontia daplidice*. The underside of the Bath White's hind wing is a greenish colour spotted with white.

go to Bath! A 19th-century colloquial euphemism, roughly equivalent to *go to blazes!* An extended version went **go to Bath and get your head shaved!** (alluding to the lunatic's shaven head – Bath had a reputation for attracting eccentrics and madmen). It may have evolved out of an earlier expression meaning 'to take up the life of a beggar', Bath's floating population of the wealthy providing rich pickings for mendicants.

> She may go to Bath, or she may go to Jericho, for me.
>
> W.M. Thackeray: *The Virginians* (1858)

Bath, the Irish. A nickname for the spa-town of MALLOW.

Bath and North East Somerset. A unitary authority in the West Country, formed in 1996 from part of the former county of AVON[7]. By the early 21st century it had acquired the acronymic name BANES.

Bathgate possibly 'wood of the boar', OCelt *baedd* 'boar' + CED.
An industrial town in West Lothian, about 28 km (17 miles) west of Edinburgh. Here James 'Paraffin' Young set up his first commercial refinery in 1851. Bathgate was the birthplace of the obstetrician Sir James Simpson (1811–70), who pioneered the use of chloroform and ether as anaesthetics. The adjacent **Bathgate Hills**, including CAIRNPAPPLE HILL, form a country park. Another of the hills, Torbane Hill, gave its name to the mineral torbanite, also called boghead coal.

Batley 'Bata's woodland clearing', OE male personal name *Bata* + -LEY.
A town in West Yorkshire, 11 km (7 miles) southwest of Leeds. Batley originated the heavy reprocessed cloth known as 'shoddy', and is still a centre for the heavy woollen trade. Oakwell Hall, in nearby Birstall, is a 15th-century manor

house, and was the inspiration for 'Fieldhead' in Charlotte Brontë's novel *Shirley* (1849).

Batsford Originally *Bæccesore* 'Bæcci's hill-slope', OE *Bæcces* possessive form of male personal name *Bæcci* + *ora* 'hill-slope'; the version with FORD is first recorded in 1577.
A village in Gloucestershire, in the COTSWOLDS, about 8 km (5 miles) north of Stow-on-the-Wold. It boasts an arboretum, founded in the late 1880s by Lord Redesdale (father of the Mitford sisters).

Battersea 'Beaduric's island', OE *Beadurices* possessive form of male personal name *Beaduric* + *eg* 'island' (*see* -EY, -EA); in this case 'island' refers to an area of dry ground surrounded by Thames-side marshes.
A district in Central London, on the south bank of the River THAMES[1], in the borough of WANDSWORTH (SW8, SW11), to the north of Clapham. Until the 1830s its main occupation was market gardening (the local asparagus, sold in '**Battersea bundles**', was widely prized), but the coming of the railway turned it inexorably into an identikit INNER LONDON suburb. The land along the bank of the Thames, known as **Battersea Fields**, was once famous for its places of refreshment and entertainment, including a fair held there every Sunday. It proved too rumbustious for mid-Victorian sensibilities, and it was tamed and regularized as **Battersea Park** (opened in 1853). In the 1890s it became a fashionable centre for the new craze of cycling. In 1951 the Festival of Britain Gardens were laid out in the Park, and the site was subsequently occupied by **Battersea Funfair**, not a development universally welcomed:

> It is not only Battersea Park (the enchanted garden of our childhood) that has been turned into a honky-tonk ...
>
> Iona and Peter Opie: *Children's Games* (1969)

Battersea's somewhat depressing reputation for inner-city grime and run-down housing was to some extent abated in the 1980s, when renovators and yuppifiers began to move in. (Pundits began to refer to **Batt-er-sia** (stress on the 'er'), a mangling of the name supposedly engaged in by the area's new wealthy inhabitants in order to distance it as far as possible from its traditional reputation.) Its riverfront is now embellished by a Buddhist Peace Pagoda, erected in 1985.

The original, wooden **Battersea Bridge**, crossing the Thames to CHELSEA, was erected in 1771–2; the present-day bridge replaced it in 1886–90.

Battersea'd. An 18th-century slang term denoting that one's penis had been treated for venereal disease. The underlying allusion is to the curative herbs that grew in the market gardens of Battersea.

Battersea Dogs' Home. An establishment in Battersea Park Road where lost and stray dogs (and a few cats) are taken in and cared for. It was founded in HOLLOWAY in

1860 by Mary Tealby, and she moved the Home to Battersea in 1871. It has become a minor British institution (notably since the Prince of Wales conferred his royal seal of approval on it in 1879), and has provided generations of aspirant dog-owners with a new pet.

Battersea enamel. A description of various types of small articles (e.g. candlesticks, needle cases) ornamented with decorative enamel, as produced in a workshop at York House, Battersea, between 1753 and 1756.

Battersea Power Station. A former coal-fired power station on the south bank of the River Thames, at NINE ELMS, just to the east of Chelsea Bridge. Designed by Sir Giles Gilbert Scott, it opened in 1937. Austere, monolithic and massive, with a towering chimney at each of its four corners, it remains a distinctive outline on the London skyline, despite the fact that it was decommissioned in the early 1980s. At the beginning of the 21st century the power station was still an empty shell, forlornly awaiting 'redevelopment' into a proposed 'housing and leisure complex'. (In 1993 it was sold to a firm of Hong Kong property developers who were hoping to turn it into a theme park before their business collapsed.)

Battersea Shield. A unique Celtic ovoid bronze shield with 27 settings of red enamel, recovered from the Thames near Battersea Bridge.

early Battersea. A snide colloquialism of the 1970s denoting vulgar, tasteless decor (Battersea had not yet started to up and come).

Battle '(place of the) battle', OFr *bataille*; from the dedication of a former church on the site.
A small town in East Sussex, about 10 km (6 miles) northwest of Hastings. It was the scene of the encounter in 1066 between the English and the invading Normans, conventionally known as the Battle of Hastings (more pedantically as the 'Battle of Senlac'). William of Normandy had vowed beforehand that if God granted him victory he would build a church, and he did just that, siting the high altar on the very spot where the English king Harold fell. The church was in due course replaced by a Benedictine abbey, **Battle Abbey**, the remains of which now form part of a school.
See also HASTINGS.

Battlefield 'field of battle'; from the foundation of a college of secular canons there to commemorate the Battle of SHREWSBURY in 1403.
A village in Shropshire, about 5 km (3 miles) north of Shrewsbury.

Battle of the Ford. *See under* ARDEE.

Batt's Corner *Batt's* denoting manorial ownership in the early Middle Ages by the Batt family.

A village in Surrey, about 5 km (3 miles) south of Farnham.

Bauds of Cullen *Bauds* Gaelic *bad* 'a clump' or 'a hamlet'; *Cullen see* CULLEN.
A village in Moray (formerly in Banffshire, then in Grampian region), some 4 km (2.5 miles) west of Cullen.

Baulds Possibly Gaelic *bad* 'a clump' or 'a hamlet'.
A small settlement in Aberdeenshire (formerly in Grampian region), 10 km (6 miles) west-southwest of Banchory.

Bawdsy 'Baldhere's island' (referring to a raised area of land), OE *Baldheres* possessive form of male personal name *Baldhere* + *eg* 'island' (*see* -EY, -EA).
A village in Suffolk, close to the NORTH SEA coast and about 19 km (12 miles) east of Ipswich. The still-standing transmitter block here housed the world's first radar station, crucial to victory in the Battle of Britain.

Bawtry Probably 'ball-shaped tree', OE *ball* 'ball' + *treow* 'tree'.
A town in South Yorkshire, 14 km (8.5 miles) southeast of Doncaster. It is at the extreme southeastern boundary of the county, and the first house on the old GREAT NORTH ROAD, coming from London, is known as 'Number One, Yorkshire'.

Bay or **Bay Town.** The local name for ROBIN HOOD'S BAY.

Bayard's Leap *Bayard* the name of a horse of incredible swiftness, said to have been given by Charlemagne to the four sons of Aymon (Renauld, Alard, Guichard and Richard), and subsequently applied to any valuable or wonderful horse.
A set of three stones, about 27 m (90 ft) apart, 8 km (5 miles) northwest of SLEAFORD in Lincolnshire. According to legend, a horse called Bayard made a mighty leap here to escape from a witch. The stones are said to represent the three horseshoes that he lost in the leap.

Bay of Holland. *See under* STRONSAY.

Bayswater Probably 'watering-place for horses', ME *bayards* '(bay) horses' + *water* (or alternatively 'watering-place belonging to the *Bayard* family').
A district in west London, in the City of WESTMINSTER (W2), at the northwest corner of HYDE PARK. Laid out between the 1820s and the 1860s, it was a very fashionable residential area in the 19th century.

> Lupin ... has taken furnished apartments at Bayswater ... Lupin says one never loses by a good address.
>
> George and Weedon Grossmith: *Diary of a Nobody* (1892)

But in the 20th century it went into a decline (a decline perhaps anticipated by the arrival of Lupin Pooter, the fictional diarist's ne'er-do-well son) and it became known as a district of C-list hotels, down-at-heel boarding houses and bed-sits.

Bayswater Underground station, on the District and Circle lines, was opened in 1868.

Bayswater captain. Late-19th-century slang for a man who scrapes a living in good society by scrounging. The idea was evidently of someone who lived in cheapish lodgings in Bayswater, within easy reach of the WEST END[1] and MAYFAIR.

Bayswater Road. A major thoroughfare in West London, running along the northern edge of Hyde Park. In the era of street prostitution (pre-1959) it was a major pick-up point (nicknamed **the Baze**), but distinctly down-market from Mayfair and PICCADILLY[1].

Beachy Head *Beachy* 'beautiful headland', OFr *beau* 'beautiful' + *chef* 'headland'; the name *Beachy Head* is thus tautological.

A chalk headland 152 m (500 ft) high on the East Sussex coast, about 5 km (3 miles) southwest of EASTBOURNE. At its foot is a lighthouse with a 25-km (16-mile) beam. The cliff's scenic attractiveness has been marred by its sad reputation as a 'Cape Farewell' for suicides, who throw or drive themselves over its edge to the beach below. Its sheer, crumbling face was notably ascended in 1894 by the satanist, unorthodox mountaineer and self-styled 'wickedest man alive', Aleister Crowley. A large section of the cliff collapsed onto the beach in the winter of 2000–1.

G.K. Chesterton pressed the cliff into service as an extreme location in his evocation of England's circuitous byways, 'The Rolling English Road' (1914):

Before the Roman came to Rye or out to Severn strode,
The rolling English drunkard made the rolling English road.
A reeling road, a rolling road, that rambles round the shire,
And after him the parson ran, the sexton and the squire;
A merry road, a mazy road, and such as we did tread
The night we went to Birmingham by way of Beachy Head.

There is also a headland called Beachy Head on the Caribbean island of Barbados.

Battle of Beachy Head (29 June 1690). A naval engagement off Beachy Head following the Glorious Revolution of 1688. The French fleet defeated the English, and gained control of the Channel until the English naval victory two years later at La Hogue.

Second Battle of Beachy Head (September 1916). A week-long episode in which a large number of Royal Navy ships fruitlessly sought three German U-boats operating between Beachy Head and the EDDYSTONE ROCKS. In the seven days concerned the U-boats managed to sink 30 British merchantmen.

Beacon's Bottom Probably a modern name, not known before the 19th century, possibly meaning 'valley near the old beacon hill'.

A village in Buckinghamshire, in the CHILTERN HILLS, about 8 km (5 miles) west of High Wycombe.

Beaconsfield 'open land near a beacon', OE *beacen* 'beacon, signal-fire' + FIELD.

A town (pronounced 'beckonzfield') in Buckinghamshire, in the CHILTERN HILLS, about 10 km (6 miles) southeast of High Wycombe. It grew up at the point where the London–Oxford road crossed the Aylesbury–Windsor road, and its several surviving coaching inns bear witness to its former importance as a staging-post. The old town still has an unmistakable aura of stockbroker-ish wealth, but it shares its urban space with a large swathe of more humble modern housing erected in the 20th century.

A notable local landmark is the small but perfectly formed Bekonscot Miniature Village, modelled on a scale of 1 inch (25.4 mm) to 1 foot (0.305 m).

The Whig politician and writer Edmund Burke (1729–97) was born in Beaconsfield, and the 19th-century British prime minister Benjamin Disraeli (1804–81), who lived nearby at Hughenden Manor (*see under* HUGHENDEN VALLEY), took his title **Earl of Beaconsfield** from the town.

There is a town called Beaconsfield in Tasmania.

Bealach Abhradh. The Irish name for the BALLYHOURA MOUNTAINS.

Bealach an Doirín. The Irish name for BALLAGHADEREEN.

Bealach an Tirialaigh. The Irish name for TYRRELLSPASS.

Bealach Cláir. The Irish name for BALLYCLARE.

Bealach Conglais. The Irish name for BALTINGLASS.

Bealach na Ba 'pass of the cattle', Gaelic *bealach* 'pass' + *na* 'of the' + *ba* 'cattle'.

A high, winding road pass between LOCH KISHORN and APPLECROSS in Wester Ross, Highland (formerly in Ross and Cromarty). The summit is at 626 m (2053 ft), making it the highest public road in Britain.

Béal an Átha. The Irish name for BALLINA.

Béal an Átha Bhuí. The Irish name for the YELLOW FORD battle site.

Béal an Dá Chab. The Irish name for BALLYDEHOB.

Béal an Mhuirtead. The Irish name for the MULLET pensinsula.

Béal Átha an Spidéil. The Irish name for BALLINSPITTLE.

Béal Átha hAmhnais. The Irish name for BALLYHAUNIS.

Béal Átha na Lao. The Irish name for BALLINALEE.

Béal Átha na Muc. The Irish name for BALLINAMUCK.

Béal Átha na Muice. The Irish name for SWINFORD.

Béal Átha Póirín. The Irish name for BALLYPOREEN.

Béal Átha Seanaidh. The Irish name for BALLYSHANNON.

Béal Átha Sluaighe. The Irish name for BALLINASLOE.

Béal Feirste. The Irish name for BELFAST.

Béal na mBláth Irish 'the mouth of flowers'.

A valley in County Cork, between BANDON and MACROOM, notorious in Irish folk memory as the location of the assassination on 22 August 1922 of the Nationalist leader Michael Collins (1890–1922). As commander of the army of the newly created Irish Free State, Collins had travelled to the west of Ireland, where Republican 'irregulars' opposed to the treaty that he had signed with Britain (which had brought the new state into being) were holding out against the forces of the Free State government. Travelling in an armoured convoy, Collins was ambushed and killed in a gun battle with anti-treaty IRA men, plunging Ireland into mourning and exacerbating the bitterness of the civil war. The assassination is graphically and movingly recreated in Neil Jordan's film *Michael Collins*, released in 1996. Collins's near-legendary status in Nationalist Ireland, and the dramatic circumstances of his death, ensured that myth and controversy attached to the events of 22 August. In particular, the presence in the vicinity of Béal na mBláth at the time of Collins's death of Éamon de Valera – Collins's former comrade-in-arms, Republican arch-opponent of the Anglo-Irish Treaty and future Irish prime minister – gave rise to conspiracy theories implicating de Valera in the assassination; but these have long since been discredited.

Shortly after Collins's death, George Bernard Shaw tactlessly (if truthfully) consoled his sister with the following words:

> Let us all praise God that he did not die in a snuffy bed of a trumpery cough, weakened by age, and saddened by the disappointments that would have attended his life had he lived.

Béal Tairbirt. The Irish name for BELTURBET.

Beaminster 'Bebbe's church', OE female personal name *Bebbe* + *mynster* 'large church'.

A town (pronounced 'bemminster') in Dorset, on the River BRIT[1] (which runs alongside the main street), about 21 km (13 miles) northwest of Dorchester. Set among rolling hills and with a full complement of attractive Tudor and Georgian buildings, it is the model of an Old English small country town. Thomas Hardy portrayed it as EMMINSTER, for example in *Tess of the D'Urbervilles* (1891).

Bean Possibly 'hillock shaped like a bean'.

A village in Kent, about 5 km (3 miles) east of Dartford.

Beanacre 'bean-field', OE *bean* + *æcer* 'field' (*see* FIELD).

A village (pronounced 'binnager') in Wiltshire, about 1.5 km (1 mile) north of Melksham.

Beannchar. The Irish name for both BANAGHER and BANGOR[2].

Beanntraí. The Irish name for BANTRY.

Bear. An alternative name for BEARA.

Beara Irish *Béarra*; according to legend, named after his Spanish wife Beara by Owenmore, a 9th-century king of Munster.

A beautiful wild peninsula in southwest Ireland, partly in County Kerry and partly in County Cork, situated between the Kenmare River (*see under* KENMARE) and Bantry Bay (*see under* BANTRY). It includes the SLIEVE MISKISH and the CAHA Mountains (it is sometimes called the **Caha** peninsula), and is, according to the novelist W.M. Thackeray, 'a country of the magnificence of which no pen can give an idea'. Beara is also called **Bear** or **Beare**, and in Irish is **Béarra**. **Bear Island** (or **Beare Island**) is situated off its southern coast, opposite **Castletown Bearhaven** (also called just **Berehaven**, or **Castletown Bere**, and in Irish **Baile Chaisleáin Bhéarra**). Castletown was one of the treaty ports held by the British following the Anglo-Irish Treaty of 1921; it was surrendered to the Irish government in 1938. Castletown was also the birthplace of the novelist Standish James O'Grady (1846–1928). Near Castletown is the site of the stronghold of Donall O'Sullivan Beare, Dunboy Castle, which in 1602, during the Nine Years' War, fell to the English, who proceeded to hang all the defenders.

Cailleach Béara Irish 'the hag of Beara'.

A folk goddess who was associated with extreme longevity, having outlived seven periods of fertility and seven husbands who died of old age.

> The Old Woman of Beare am I
> Who once was beautiful.
> Now all I know is how to die.
>
> Anon.: 'The Old Woman of Beare', translated from the medieval Irish by Brendan Kennelly

The poem '*Mise Éire*' ('I am Ireland') by Patrick Pearse, executed in 1916 for his part in the Easter Rising, begins:

> *Mise Éire – Sine mé ná an Chailleach Béara*
> I am Ireland: I am older than the Old Woman of Beare.

Beare Green *Beare* denoting manorial ownership in the early Middle Ages by the de la Bere family (from OE *bær* 'woodland pasture').

A village in Surrey, about 6.5 km (4 miles) south of Dorking.

Bear Island. *See under* BEARA.

Bearnas na Diallaite. The Irish name for SALLY GAP.

Bearpark 'beautiful retreat', OFr *beau* 'beautiful' + *repaire* 'retreat'; *Beaurepayre* 1267. The name derives from the fact that it was the site of a country residence of the priors of Durham Cathedral.

A village in County Durham, 4 km (2.5 miles) west of Durham itself.

Béarra. The Irish name for BEARA.

Bearsden A modern name, presumably intended to be humorous.

A town (pronounced 'bear's den') 8 km (5 miles) northwest of the centre of Glasgow, in East Dunbartonshire (formerly in Strathclyde region). It is in effect an outer suburb of GLASGOW, teased by 'true' Glaswegians for its gentility. Until the mid-19th century the town was a small village known as **New Kilpatrick** or **New Kirk**.

Bearsden and Milngavie From the towns of BEARSDEN and MILNGAVIE.

A district of the former Strathclyde region, formed in 1975 and abolished in 1996. It is pronounced 'bear's den and mull-guy'.

Beattock Etymology uncertain; possibly 'the pointed hill', Gaelic *beodach* 'sharp-topped'.

A village 3 km (2 miles) south of Moffat, formerly in Dumfriesshire, now in Dumfries and Galloway. The now disused railway station, which served the defunct branch line to MOFFAT, is the setting for a short story, '**Beattock for Moffat**', by R. Cunninghame Graham (1852–1936). Some 11 km (7 miles) northwest is **Beattock Summit**, which, at 315 m (1033 ft), marks the high point on both the M74 and the Glasgow–Euston main railway line.

Beauchamp Place A modern name, probably linked to the *Beauchamp* family.

A street in BROMPTON, in southwest London (SW3), running between Brompton Road and PONT STREET. Until 1885 it was called **Grove Place**. It is full of breathtakingly expensive boutiques for the wives and daughters of the ultra-rich and equally expensive restaurants for the delectation of ladies-who-lunch.

Beauchamp Roding. *See under* the RODINGS.

Beauchief 'beautiful spur (of a hill)', OFr *beau* 'beautiful' + *chef* 'headland'.

A southwestern suburb of SHEFFIELD, South Yorkshire.

Beaulieu 'beautiful place', OFr *beau* 'beautiful' + *lieu* 'place'.

A village (pronounced 'byoo-ly') close to the south coast of Hampshire, on the Beaulieu River.

Beaulieu Abbey. The ruined remains of a Cistercian Abbey near Beaulieu, founded in 1204. Its gatehouse now forms part of Palace House, Lord Montagu's home. The National Motor Museum, which he founded, is in its grounds.

Beaulieu River. A river in Hampshire, which rises near LYNDHURST and flows east and then south across **Beaulieu**

Heath into the SOLENT about 11 km (7 miles) east of LYMINGTON.

Beauly 'beautiful place', OFr *beau* 'beautiful' + *lieu* 'place'.

A village in Highland (pronounced 'byoo-ly'), formerly in Inverness-shire, 14 km (8.5 miles) west of Inverness. It is in the traditional lands of the Frasers of Lovat, originally a Norman family, who may have given the place its name. The village is near where the **River Beauly** enters the **Beauly Firth**, which is the inner, westerly portion of the MORAY FIRTH. The River Beauly itself is formed by the confluence near Struy Bridge of the River Glass and the River Farrar.

The war correspondent and novelist Maurice Baring (1874–1945) died at Beauly.

Beaumaris 'beautiful marsh', Norman French *beau* 'fair' + *marais* 'marsh'; the marsh was drained by the castle's moat.

An attractive small town on the southeast coast of Anglesey (formerly in Gwynedd), where the MENAI STRAIT opens out into Conwy Bay. It is 9 km (5.5 miles) northeast of Menai Bridge, and was the county town of Anglesey until 1974. The Welsh version of the name is **Biwmaris**, pronounced 'bew-marras'.

The fine **Beaumaris Castle** (begun 1295) was built by Edward I after he had captured the island. It was briefly held by Owain Glyndwr in 1404, and during the Civil Wars General Mytton seized it from the royalists. Edmund Ludlow, the radical republican, was for a time imprisoned in the castle owing to his opposition to Cromwell declaring himself 'Lord Protector' in 1653. The castle is now a World Heritage Site.

Beazley End Originally *Baseleymede*, perhaps 'meadow in Basa's glade', OE male personal name *Basa* +-LEY + *mæd* 'meadow', later substituted with ME *end* 'district'; but there may be some connection with the plant name *basil*.

A village in Essex, about 5 km (3 miles) north of Braintree.

Bebington 'estate associated with Bebba or Bebbe', OE male personal name *Bebba* or female personal name *Bebbe* + -ING + -TON.

A town on the east coast of the WIRRAL, to the south of Birkenhead. It has swallowed up PORT SUNLIGHT.

Beccles Probably 'pasture by a stream', OE *bece* 'stream' + *læs* 'pasture'.

A town in Suffolk, on the River WAVENEY[1], about 13 km (8 miles) southwest of LOWESTOFT. Most of its ancient buildings were destroyed in fires in the 16th and 17th centuries, but they were replaced by fine new ones, mainly in red brick.

Becher's Brook. *See under* AINTREE.

Beckenham 'Beohha's homestead', OE *Beohhan* possessive form of male personal name *Beohha* + HAM.

A district in southeast Greater London, in the borough of

BROMLEY (until 1965 in Kent). The 13th-century lychgate in St George's churchyard is claimed to be the oldest one in England.

Beckhampton 'home farm by the ridge', OE *bœc* 'ridge' + *ham-tun* (*see* HAM and -TON); there is a narrow ridge to the west of the village.

A village in Wiltshire, about 2 km (1.2 miles) southwest of Avebury. In the 19th century, the Waggon & Horses inn was an important coach stop on the London–Bath road. It is said to provide the setting for the 'The Bagman's Story' in Charles Dickens's *The Pickwick Papers* (1836–7), a rather odd tale about a man who drinks too much and a talking chair.

Beckindale. A fictional village, based on ARNCLIFFE in the YORKSHIRE DALES, which features in the television soap *Emmerdale Farm* (1972–89), known simply as *Emmerdale* from 1989.

Beckton From Simon Adams *Beck*, governor of the Gas, Light and Coke Company, which opened a very large gasworks here in 1870 + -TON.

A district of East London, in the borough of NEWHAM (E6), to the south of East Ham. Its associations are far from fragrant: it is home to an extensive sewage works, receiving the main northern outfall of the London sewerage system, and the local gasworks became, in time, the world's largest coal-gas works. They ceased operation in 1976, and were subsequently to impersonate a Vietnamese battleground in Stanley Kubrick's 1987 film *Full Metal Jacket*.

Becontree 'Beohha's tree', OE *Beohhan* possessive form of male personal name *Beohha* + *treow* 'tree'; the tree would have marked the place on the local heath where the meetings of the medieval Hundred took place.

A district in East London, in the borough of BARKING AND DAGENHAM. The **Becontree Estate**, built by the London County Council between the First and Second World Wars, was then the largest public-housing estate in the world, covering about 10 sq km (4 sq miles) and providing over 27,000 homes.

Beddgelert 'grave of Celert', Welsh *bedd* 'grave' + personal name *Celert*; *see also below*.

A village at the foot of the GWYNANT VALLEY on the south side of SNOWDON, in Gwynedd (formerly in Caernarvonshire), some 19 km (11.5 miles) south of Caernarfon.

Although Celert, after whom the village is named, was almost certainly a human being (probably a Celtic saint), the village has become associated with Gelert, the faithful hound of Prince Llywelyn the Great (Llewelyn ap Iowerth, *fl.*13th century). According to the story, one day Llywelyn came home to be greeted enthusiastically by Gelert, whose jaws were dripping with gore. Llywelyn rushed inside to see his infant son's cradle spattered with blood, but there was no sign of the child. Assuming the worst, he slew his dog. Only after the dog was dead did he find his son safe beneath the cradle, and the body of a wolf nearby. Sorrowfully, Llywelyn buried his brave dog and raised a great cairn over the grave.

Variations of this story are found across Europe and Asia, and go back to a Sanskrit tale. This version was devised by the enterprising innkeeper David Pritchard, who came to Beddgelert in 1793 as landlord of the Royal Goat Inn. He added substance to the story by building a cairn to mark the spot where 'Gelert' had been buried. People flocked to see it, and to avail themselves of the inn's hospitality in the process. As one disenchanted visitor wrote:

> Pass on, O tender-hearted, dry your eyes.
> Not here a greyhound, but a landlord lies.

George Borrow was less cynical: not only was he moved by the story and the grave (although allowing for the possibility of fraud), but also by the whole setting:

> Truly, the valley of Gelert is a wondrous valley – rivalling for grandeur and beauty any vale either in the Alps or Pyrenees.
>
> George Borrow: *Wild Wales* (1862)

Bedford 'Bieda's ford', OE *Biedan* possessive form of the male personal name *Bieda* + FORD.

The county town of BEDFORDSHIRE, on the River Ouse (*see under* GREAT OUSE), about 27 km (16.5 miles) north of Luton. An important town since the Anglo-Saxon period, in modern times its main activities have been engineering and brick-making.

Its most famous townsman is John Bunyan (1628–88), who was imprisoned in Bedford Gaol for his Nonconformism between 1660 and 1672. He was briefly sent back to prison in 1676, during which period he probably wrote the first part of *The Pilgrim's Progress*.

According to the Panacea Society, Bedford is the site of the Garden of Eden, and Christ will return to Earth here at the Apocalypse (he will live at 18 Albany Road, which has been got ready for him). The Society, whose headquarters are in the town, was founded in 1919 by 'Octavia', reincarnated spiritual daughter of the early 19th-century mystic Joanna Southcott. Another address, 63 High Street, hosted the shop of the fruit-breeding Laxtons (*see under* BEDFORDSHIRE).

Vauxhall Motors Ltd (*see under* VAUXHALL) moved to LUTON in Bedfordshire in 1905, and from 1931 used the trade name 'Bedford' for its vans and trucks.

From the 17th to the early 20th centuries Bedford locals were sometimes known as 'malt-horses' (from the high-quality malt extracted from Bedfordshire barley).

The athlete Harold Abrahams (1899–1978), whose rivalry with the Scottish runner Eric Liddell was the theme of Hugh Hudson's celebrated British film *Chariots of Fire* (1981), was born in Bedford.

There are towns called Bedford in the USA (Indiana, Iowa, Kentucky, New Hampshire, Pennsylvania, Virginia and Wyoming) and Canada (Nova Scotia and Quebec). In Australia, there is a Cape Bedford in Queensland and the Bedford Range of mountains in Western Australia, whilst in Grenada, West Indies, there is Bedford Point.

Bailiff of Bedford. A term for the overflowing of the River Ouse in former times, possibly because it turned people out of their homes.

Bedford College. A former college of London University (*see under* LONDON), founded in 1849 as a women's college. It took its name from the original site in **Bedford Square** (*see below*). Between 1909 and 1985 it was located in REGENT'S PARK. It was then amalgamated with Royal Holloway College in ESHER and its name has now disappeared.

Bedford cord. A clothing fabric with lengthways raised ribs, resembling corduroy.

Bedford Estate. An area of land in BLOOMSBURY, in Central London (WC1), owned by the dukes of Bedford. Their original land-holding, granted to the 1st Earl of Bedford in 1552 for services to the Crown, was in COVENT GARDEN, but this was sold in 1914. The Bloomsbury territory came into the family by inheritance in 1723. Many of the streets and squares in the area perpetuate the family's name (Russell), the names of its subsidiary titles, the names of its relatives and the name of its Bedfordshire seat, WOBURN Abbey: Gower Street, Malet Street, Russell Square, Tavistock Square, Torrington Place, Woburn Place and so on. **Bedford Square**, the only complete Georgian square left in Bloomsbury, was until the 1980s synonymous with book publishing, as many publishers had offices there.

Bedfords. A term for trousers made of Bedford cord.

Bedford Level Named after the Earl of *Bedford*, at whose instigation the work was carried out.

A vast expanse of drained FENS in northern Cambridgeshire, southern Lincolnshire and Norfolk. The work was carried out between 1630 and 1652 by the Dutch land reclamation engineer Cornelius Vermuyden (1595–1683).

New Bedford River. An alternative name for the HUNDRED FOOT DRAIN.

Old Bedford River. A drain (also known as **Old Bedford Delph** – *delph* 'a ditch or drainage canal', ultimately from OE *delfan* 'to dig') cut in the 1630s by Cornelius Vermuyden between two points on the GREAT OUSE river (Earith in Cambridgeshire and Denver in Norfolk). The drain was intended to make a more direct route to the sea and drain the surrounding fens. Winter flooding continued, however, and in 1649 it was supplemented by the parallel HUNDRED FOOT DRAIN.

A 10-km (6-mile) straight stretch of the Old Bedford River was used in the 19th century for rival experiments by flat-earthers and globularists. The flat-earthers claimed (quite reasonably in the circumstances) that the fact that upright objects could be seen through a telescope at this distance in their entirety proved their point, since if the earth were a globe then the curvature should have obscured the bottom metre (3 ft) of said objects. Today scientists realize this effect is caused by the bending of light, and for the most part adhere to the globular theory.

Bedford Park From *Bedford* House, a Georgian villa in the grounds of which Bedford Park was laid out. The house itself was named after the man who built it, in the 1790s, 'John Bedford' (an assumed name – he was originally John Tubbs). A prosperous district to the east of ACTON, in the southeastern corner of the London borough of EALING (W4). It was laid out as a garden suburb in 1875–81, the first of its kind in London, designed by Norman Shaw in Queen Anne architectural style. Many original trees still stand.

Bedford Park appears in G.K. Chesterton's tale of suburban anarchism *The Man Who Was Thursday* (1908) under the name '**Saffron Park**', and was the setting for various escapades in the 1990 comic film *Nuns on the Run*.

Bedfordshire From BEDFORD + SHIRE. The name *Bedfordshire* is first recorded in the 11th century.

A county in south central England, to the northwest of London. Its county town is BEDFORD, and other important centres are BIGGLESWADE, DUNSTABLE, LEIGHTON BUZZARD, LUTON, SANDY and WOBURN. Largely low-lying and agricultural, at 1192 sq km (460 sq miles) it is the smallest county in England (*see also* RUTLAND).

Before the coming of the Romans, the area was part of the kingdom of the ancient British tribe known as the Catuvellauni (*see also* HERTFORDSHIRE). By the end of the 6th century, following the Anglo-Saxon occupation, it had became part of the kingdom of MERCIA.

The borough of **Mid-Bedfordshire** covers an area that includes AMPTHILL, BIGGLESWADE, FLITWICK and Sandy. The district of **South Bedfordshire** covers an area that includes Dunstable, Houghton Regis, Leighton Buzzard and WHIPSNADE.

'Bedfordshire' has been used since at least the mid-17th century as a facetious synonym for *bed*, particularly in the context of going upstairs to sleep at the end of the day:

Faith, I'm for Bedfordshire

Jonathan Swift: *A Complete Collection of Polite and Ingenious Conversation* (1738)

Bedfordshire occupies an important niche in the history of fruit-growing. The experimental grounds maintained in Bedford and Sandy by the Victorian plant breeder Thomas Laxton (1830–93) and his descendants produced such famous apple varieties as Lord Lambourne, Laxton's

Epicure, Laxton's Fortune and Laxton's Superb, together with plums (Laxton's Gage, Early Laxton, Laxton's Supreme) and varieties of pears, gooseberries, raspberries, currants and strawberries.

In cricketing terms Bedfordshire is a 'minor county' (the club was founded in 1899) and plays in the minor counties championship.

Bedfordshire clanger. A tube-shaped pasty made with a suet crust, with a savoury filling at one end and a sweet filling at the other (*see also* Cornish Pasty *under* CORNISH).

Bedlington 'Bedla's estate', OE male personal name *Bedla* + -ING + -TON.

An industrial town on the River Blyth, Northumberland, 6 km (3.5 miles) west of the town of Blyth, in the traditional area known as Bedlington or **Bedlingtonshire**.

Bedlington terrier. A breed of long-legged terrier, usually grey, with a woolly coat, topknot and a somewhat lamb-like appearance. It was bred in 19th century as a badger-hunter. Bedlington–whippet crosses have in recent years become fashionable; the result, although possessed of a certain rough-edged charm, has nothing on the noble perfection of the whippet itself.

Bedlingtonshire. A traditional area of Northumberland, centred on BLYTH[2]. It is also known simply as **Bedlington**.

Bedruthan Steps *Bedruthan* a farm name, 'Rudhynn's dwelling', Cornish *bod* 'dwelling' + male personal name *Rudhynn* (the 'legend' that the rocks were the stepping stones of a giant called Bedruthan was invented in the 19th century). A series of rocks on the north Cornish coast, about 11 km (7 miles) north of Newquay. It consists of massive granite stacks that rise to increasing heights (up to 60 m (200 ft)) from a broad beach (which shares its name).

Beds. The standard written abbreviation of BEDFORDSHIRE.

Bedwas Welsh *bedwos* 'grove of birches'.
A town in Caerphilly unitary authority (formerly in Monmouthshire, then in Gwent), 2 km (1.2 miles) northeast of the town of Caerphilly.

Beech '(place at the) beech-tree', OE *bece* 'beech-tree'.
A village in Staffordshire, about 18 km (11 miles) northwest of Stafford.

Beechingstoke 'outlying farmstead where bitches or hounds are kept', OE *biccena* possessive plural form of *bicce* 'bitch' + *stoc* 'outlying farmstead' (*see* -STOCK, STOCK-, STOKE).
A village in Wiltshire, about 8 km (5 miles) west of Pewsey.

Beecraigs Possibly 'hills frequented by bees', OE *beo* 'bee' + Gaelic *creag* 'hill'.
A country park in West Lothian, some 3 km (2 miles) south of Linlithgow.

Beefstand Hill Etymology unknown.
A hill (561 m / 1840 ft) in the CHEVIOT Hills on the border between Scotland and Northumberland, 14 km (8.5 miles) south of Kirk Yetholm.

Beeny Etymology obscure.
A village on the north coast of Cornwall, north of BOSCASTLE. **Beeny Cliff** is the subject of a poem by Thomas Hardy written in wistful remembrance, after his first wife's death, of happy times he spent there with her:

> … Still in all its chasmal beauty bulks old Beeny to the sky,
> And shall she and I not go there once again now March is nigh,
> And the sweet things said in that March say anew there by and by?
> Nay. Though still in chasmal beauty looms that wild weird western shore,
> The woman now is – elsewhere – whom the ambling pony bore,
> And nor knows nor cares for Beeny, and will see it nevermore.
> Thomas Hardy: 'Beeny Cliff: March 1870–March 1913'

See also ST JULIOT.

Beer '(place by the) grove', OE *bearu* 'grove'.
A fishing village on the south Devon coast, about 11 km (7 miles) east of Sidmouth. To the south of the village is **Beer Head**, the most westerly of the English Channel's chalk cliffs. It has many caves, which were fully exploited in the 18th and 19th centuries by the industrious local smugglers.

Beercrocombe *Beer* '(place by the) grove', OE *bearu* 'grove', or '(place by the) woodland pasture', OE *bær* 'woodland pasture'; *crocombe* denoting manorial ownership in the Middle Ages by the Craucombe family.
A village in Somerset, about 11 km (7 miles) east of TAUNTON.

Beer Hackett *Beer*, *see* BEERCROCOMBE; *Hackett* denoting manorial ownership in the Middle Ages by the Haket family.
A village in Dorset, about 6.5 km (4 miles) southwest of Sherborne.

Beesands Perhaps *Bee-* (from the nearby village of *Beeson* 'Bæde's farmstead', OE male personal name *Bæde* + -TON) + *sands*.
A seaside village in Devon, on Start Bay, about 13 km (8 miles) southwest of Dartmouth.

Beeston 'farmstead where bent-grass (a type of rough grass used for pasture and thatching) grows', OE *beos* 'bent-grass' + -TON. There are other Beestons with the same place-name origin in Bedfordshire, Norfolk and West Yorkshire.
A town in Nottinghamshire, on the River TRENT[1], on the southwestern outskirts of Nottingham. The administrative centre of BROXTOWE, Beeston is dominated by the drugs factories of Boots the Chemist.

Beeswing After the name of the inn built here, itself named after Beeswing, a highly successful racehorse sired by Dr Syntax in 1833, and who herself foaled two classic winners.

A small village in Dumfries and Galloway (formerly in Kirkcudbrightshire), 10 km (6 miles) southwest of Dumfries at the foot of Lotus Hill.

Beginish. *See under* the BLASKET ISLANDS.

Beguildy 'shepherd's hut', Welsh *bugail* 'shepherd' + *dŷ* 'house, hut'.

A village in Powys (formerly in Radnorshire), on the Anglo-Welsh border 12 km (7.5 miles) northwest of Knighton.

Beinn a'Bheithir *Beinn* 'mountain', Gaelic; *Bheithir*, name of an ancient Celtic goddess of winter and death. More generally the Gaelic word *beithir* was used for a variety of destructive phenomena, from a thunderstorm to a sea serpent.

An elegant, triple-peaked mountain, pronounced 'ben a vair', just west of GLEN COE, Highland (formerly in Argyll). The highest point is Sgorr Dhearg ('red peak'; 1024 m / 3359 ft). It is pronounced 'ben a vair'.

Beinn a'Bhùird 'table mountain', *Beinn* 'mountain', Gaelic; *Bhùird*, Gaelic *bùird*, possessive of *bòrd* 'table'.

A massive, remote and lofty mountain (1197 m / 3926 ft) in the CAIRNGORM MOUNTAINS, some 10 km (6 miles) northwest of Braemar. It is mostly in Aberdeenshire, although its northern slopes are in Moray (all of it was formerly in Grampian region). Not surprisingly given his brief, the Rev. Dr George Skene Keith, author of the *General View of Agriculture in Aberdeenshire* (1811), found the mountain 'an immense mass, without beauty or fertility'. Only a few years later William MacGillivray (subsequently Professor of Natural History at Aberdeen University) saw it with very different eyes, noting of the view from the top:

> The scene which presented here I considered at the time as the most noble without exception which I had ever seen.
>
> William MacGillivray: journal (1819)

The mountain also had some less respectable visitors:

> One night I went to Ben-a-Bhuird, my gun intae my hand, Soon there follaed aifter me six keepers in a band ...
>
> W. McCombie Smith: 'The Poacher o Braemar', from *The Romance of Poaching in the Highlands* (1904)

For some even more disreputable stravaigers in these airts, *see below*.

Although the mountain takes its name from the extensive summit plateau, there are spectacularly beautiful crag-lined corries on its eastern and northeastern sides. In the latter is the precipitous 200-m (650-ft) rock feature known as the Mitre Ridge (from its shape), first ascended on the same day by two different routes in 1933; the present author's father was one of the party, all Cambridge undergraduates, and his route is the classic *Cumming-Crofton Route.*

Beinn a'Ghlo 'veiled mountain', *Beinn* 'mountain', Gaelic; *Ghlo*, Gaelic *glo* 'veil, hood', presumably from the frequency with which its tops are in the cloud.

A large, three-peaked mountain (pronounced 'ben a-glaw') in Perth and Kinross (formerly in Perthshire and then in Tayside region), some 13 km (8 miles) north of Pitlochry. The highest of the three summits, at 1121 m / 3677 ft, is Carn nan Gabhar ('peak of the goats'; pronounced 'carn nan gower').

Beinn Alligin *Beinn* 'mountain', Gaelic; *Alligin* from the river name *Ailigin*, of uncertain meaning: one suggestion is Gaelic *àilleagan* 'jewel'; alternatively, *Alligin* may come from *ail* 'rock'.

A craggy mountain in TORRIDON, Highland (formerly in Ross and Cromarty), some 5 km (3 miles) northwest of Liathach. The rocky towers on its summit ridge are called the **Horns of Alligin**.

Beinn Dorain 'peak of the streamlet', *Beinn* 'mountain', Gaelic; *Dorain,* Gaelic *dobhar* 'stream' + *an* 'little'. Alternative suggestions include *dòbhran* 'otter' and *dòrainn* 'anguish', from the tradition that in high winds the mountain makes a keening noise; *Bin Dowran*, 17th century.

A mountain (1074 m / 3523 ft) in the central HIGHLANDS, in Argyll and Bute, 8 km (5 miles) north of TYNDRUM. It is notable for its symmetrical conical shape when viewed from the south, and for the myriad streamlets gouging its flanks. It was the subject of **Moladh Beinn Dóbhrainn** (*The Praise of Ben Dorain,* 1768), one of the greatest poems of the Gaelic poet Duncan Ban Macintyre (Donnchadh Bàn Mac an t-Saoir), who as a young man worked as a forester in the vicinity:

> *An t-urram thar gach beinn*
> *Aig Beinn-dorain,*
> *De na chunnaic mi fo 'n ghrein,*
> *'S I by bhoidhche leam.*
>
> (Praise over every other mountain
> To Beinn Dorain,
> It is the most beautiful mountain
> I have seen under the sun.)

Samuel Taylor Coleridge was also impressed, walking past it northward from TYNDRUM (where, as he confessed, he had been inspired by a bottle of Burton ale for lunch) on his way to the KINGSHOUSE on the far side of Rannoch Moor (*see under* RANNOCH):

> I seemed to think that these high green mountains, so furrowed, delved, and wrinkled with torrents, are still wilder than craggy mountains ... One I shall never forget, in shape resembling a schoolboy's top, or rather presenting to the eye two sides of a spherical triangle.
>
> Samuel Taylor Coleridge: journal (30 August 1803)

Beinn Eighe 'file mountain', *Beinn* 'mountain', Gaelic; *Eighe* 'file' (from its jagged appearance). Other possibilities are *eigh* 'ice', perhaps from the pale quartzite that tops the mountain, and a derivative of *each* 'horse'.

A mountain (1010 m / 3314 ft) on the north side of Glen Torridon (*see under* TORRIDON), in Wester Ross, Highland (formerly in Ross and Cromarty). It is usually pronounced to rhyme with 'hay' (although Gaelic speakers would opt for 'byn ay-a'). There are many tops, the highest of which is Ruadh Stac Mor, and on the northwest side there are the famous and spectacular Triple Buttresses of Coire Mhic Fhearchair, each of which is over 300 m (1000 ft) high and comprises two layers of Torridonian sandstone (*see under* TORRIDON) topped by a layer of quartzite. Towards the northern end of the main ridge are the pinnacles known as the Black Carls. **Beinn Eighe National Nature Reserve**, established in 1951, was the first in Britain.

Beinn Laoigh. *See* BEN LUI.

Beinn Narnain. *See under* ARROCHAR.

Belashanny. An alternative name for BALLYSHANNON.

Belas Knap 'beacon hill', *Belas* OE *bel* 'beacon fire'; *Knap* OE *cnæpp* 'hill'.
A Neolithic barrow on a high ridge of the Cotswolds overlooking WINCHCOMBE in Gloucestershire. Probably originally a shrine built around 2500 BC, it is the best-preserved ancient burial chamber in England, and was used for burials over a period of seven centuries. Belas Knap is 24 m (78 ft) long, 18 m (60 ft) wide and (at its highest point) 4 m (13 ft) high. Extensive excavation of the site in 1863 uncovered 26 burials and other human remains, plus Roman coins and pottery.

The Cotswold Way (*see under* COTSWOLDS) runs past Belas Knap.

Belchamp Otten *Belchamp* probably 'homestead with a beamed roof', OE *belc* 'beamed or vaulted roof' + HAM. *Otten* denoting manorial ownership in the early Middle Ages by a man called Otto.
A village in Essex, about 20 km (12.5 miles) north of Braintree.

Belchford Probably 'Belt's ford', OE *Beltes* possessive form of male personal name *Belt* + FORD.
A village in Lincolnshire, about 13 km (8 miles) southwest of LOUTH[1].

Belfast Irish *Béal Feirste* 'mouth of the sandbank', the sandbank in question being where the small River Farset (also named after the sandbank) enters the River Lagan.
An industrial city, local authority district and port in County Down and County Antrim, situated where the River LAGAN enters the 20-km (12-mile) inlet of the North Channel known as **Belfast Lough**.

> ... the empty freighters
> Sailing forever down Belfast Lough
> In a fine rain, their sirens going ...
>
> Derek Mahon (b.1941): 'My Wicked Uncle'

Belfast became the capital of Northern Ireland at the time of Partition following the Anglo-Irish Treaty of 1921, and is home to STORMONT, where the former Northern Ireland Parliament met and where the Northern Ireland Assembly has convened since the Good Friday Agreement of 1998. Belfast is also home to **Belfast Castle**, built in 1870 for the Donegall family, and to Queen's University (1909; founded as Queen's College in 1849). It is nicknamed **Redbrick City**, because of the many brick-built 19th-century workers' terraces.

The city's original castle was built in 1177 by the Anglo-Norman baron, John de Courcy, on the site of an earlier fort guarding the ford over the River Lagan. However, Belfast remained small until Sir Arthur Chichester received a grant of land here in 1603 and proceeded to build a 'towne of good forme', which received a charter in 1613. During the 17th century, with the plantation of many English and Scots, Belfast became the centre of Ulster Protestantism, a status reinforced in 1685 with the arrival of Huguenot refugees from France, who stimulated the linen industry. After the Act of Union Belfast's industry developed further, taking in shipbuilding (notably Harland and Wolff) and heavy engineering, and Belfast became a city in 1888. In the 18th century it had a reputation for enlightened liberalism, earning it the name the ATHENS OF THE NORTH (a title also claimed by Edinburgh), and it was here that the Society of United Irishmen was founded in 1791. However, in the 19th century Belfast's Presbyterianism turned more hardline, and the city became the centre of Unionist opposition to Home Rule, while still containing a substantial Catholic population.

> With the possible exception of Jerusalem and Mecca, Belfast must be the most religion-conscious city in the world.
>
> Tyrone Guthrie: *A Life in the Theatre* (1959)

With its many working-class ghettoes, Belfast became a hotbed of sectarian violence and bombings during the Troubles, and British troops were sent here in 1969:

> By yesterday morning British troops were patrolling the streets of Belfast. I fear that once Catholics and Protestants get used to our presence they will hate us more than they hate each other.
>
> Richard Crossman: *Diaries*, 17 August 1969

> Buy now while shops last.
>
> Graffito in Belfast, 1970. A lot of plate glass went in the course of the Troubles.

The Troubles increased the geographical polarization within

the city, with west Belfast becoming predominantly Catholic and east Belfast predominantly Protestant (*see also* ANDERSONTOWN, FALLS ROAD *and* SHANKILL ROAD). The military presence has been reduced, but tensions are still very much to the fore, despite the city's renaissance as a centre of Northern Irish cultural life.

Belfast was the setting for Carol Reed's film masterpiece *Odd Man Out* (1946), with James Mason playing a wounded IRA man. Louis MacNeice (1907–63) was born here:

> I was born in Belfast between the mountain and the
>   gantries
> To the hooting of lost sirens and the clang of trams …
>
> Louis MacNeice: 'Carrickfergus' (1937)

Belfast was also the birthplace of the poet William Drennan (1754–1820), first president of the United Irishmen and coiner of the phrase 'the Emerald Isle' for Ireland; the physicist William Thomson (Lord Kelvin; 1824–1907); the poet Joseph Campbell (1879–1944); C.S. Lewis (1898–1963), author of the Narnia books for children; Chaim Herzog (1918–97), president of Israel (1983–93); the novelist Brian Moore (1921–99); the flautist James Galway (b.1939); the Conservative politician Brian Mawhinney (b.1940); the footballer George Best (b.1946); Gerry Adams (b.1948), the Sinn Féin leader; Mary McAleese (b.1951), president of the Republic of Ireland since 1997; and the actor and director Kenneth Branagh (b.1960). The chemist Joseph Black (1728–99), although born in Bordeaux, was educated in Belfast (his father was a native). The novelist Anthony Trollope worked as a surveyor for the Post Office in Belfast in 1853–4, and the writer Samuel Beckett taught here briefly in the 1920s.

> [In Belfast] There is no aristocracy – no culture – no grace – no leisure worthy of the name. It all boils down to mixed grills, double whiskies, dividends, movies, and these strolling, homeless, hate-driven poor.
>
> Sean O'Faolain: *Irish Journey* (1941)

> Belfast … as uncivilized as ever – savage black mothers in houses of dark red brick, friendly manufacturers too drunk to entertain you when you arrive. It amuses me till I get tired.
>
> E.M. Forster: Letter to T.E. Lawrence (3 May 1928)

> Red brick in the suburb, white horse on the wall,
> Eyetalian marbles in the City Hall:
> O stranger from England, why stand so aghast?
> *May the Lord in His mercy be kind to Belfast.*
>
> Maurice James Craig: 'Ballad to a Traditional Refrain' (1938)
> (The refrain comes from a tribute to the city's kind
> treatment of the United Irishmen in 1798.)

The things that happen in the kitchen houses
And echoing back streets of this desperate city

Should engage more than my casual interest,
Exact more interest than my casual pity.

> Derek Mahon: 'Spring in Belfast', from *Collected Poems* (1999)

See also BOG MEADOWS, DUNDONALD *and* NEWTOWNABBEY.

Belfast Agreement. Another name for the Good Friday Agreement of 1998 that led to the establishment of the Northern Ireland Assembly.

Belfast Blitz. The German air raids on Belfast in April–May 1941 during which nearly 1000 people died.

Belfast Boycott. A boycott imposed in 1920 by the Dáil in Dublin of goods from Northern Ireland, in retaliation for attacks on and discrimination against Catholics in the north. The boycott continued for some years.

Belfast Celtic. A former football team, founded in 1891 and supported by Nationalists. Violence with supporters of Belfast's Protestant team, Linfield, led the club to disband itself in 1948.

'Belfast Child'. A chart-topping single by Simple Minds, inspired by the Troubles and released in 1989. It is the second-longest single (after The Beatles' 'Hey Jude') to reach the top of the charts.

> Some say troubles abound,
> Some day soon they're gonna pull the old town down.
> One day we'll return here,
> When the Belfast Child sings again.

Belfast confetti. A collective slang term for materials chucked at the opposition during riots (originally aimed at Catholics by Protestant shipyard workers in the 1920s):

> Suddenly as the riot squad moved in, it was raining exclamation marks, nuts, bolts, nails, car-keys. A fount of broken type. And the explosion itself – an asterisk on the map. This hyphenated line, a burst of rapid fire. I was trying to complete a sentence in my head but it kept stuttering. All the alleyways and side streets blocked with stops and colons.
>
> Ciaran Carson: 'Belfast Confetti', from *Belfast Confetti* (1989)

Belfast cradle. The mode adopted by British soldiers in Northern Ireland of carrying their rifles while on urban patrol.

Belfast Harp Festival (11–14 July 1792). A seminal event in the revival of traditional Irish music. Ten harpers (six of them blind) competed and many melodies were transcribed and preserved.

Belfast News-Letter. The older surviving Irish newspaper, founded in 1737 as a Patriot journal. However, since the early 19th century its position has been Unionist.

Belfast Quasimodo, the. The nickname of the ugly but passionate Nationalist Joe Biggar (1828–90), awarded to Biggar by T.P. O'Connell in the phrase 'The Belfast

Quasimodo to the Irish Esmeralda', referring to the hunchback and beautiful heroine in Victor Hugo's novel *Notre Dame de Paris* (1831).

Belfast Regiment. The old 35th Foot, raised in Belfast in 1701. It later became the 1st Battalion Royal Sussex Regiment and then the 3rd Battalion, the Queen's Regiment.

HMS *Belfast*. A Royal Navy cruiser, commissioned in 1939. During the Second World War it took part in the Battle of the North Cape and in the Normandy landings. Since 1971 it has been moored in the THAMES[1] near Tower Bridge and is open to the public.

Belfry, the Presumably from a church with a belfry, or a building with a feature resembling a belfry.

A golf course to the north of WISHAW[1], in northern Warwickshire. The Ryder Cup competition has been held here four times, most recently in 2002.

Belgravia *Belgrave* name of a Cheshire estate of the Earl Grosvenor + quasi-Latin suffix *-ia*. (The estate's original name was Merdegrave, which etymologically meant 'marten grove' (these animals frequented the place). But the word was taken to be OFr for 'dung grove', so it was changed to the more salubrious Belgrave.)

A district in the WEST END[1] of London, in the City of WESTMINSTER (SW1), to the south of Hyde Park, centring on Belgrave Square and extending from KNIGHTSBRIDGE in the north to VICTORIA[2] and SLOANE SQUARE in the south. It was laid out in the 1820s as a fashionable residential area, largely by Thomas Cubitt (*see also* CUBITTOPOLIS), on land owned by the Earl Grosvenor, later the 1st Marquess of Westminster. Its lavish stuccoed terraces were intended to lure the rich and well-connected south from MAYFAIR, and they succeeded. Today it is still their natural habitat, although Belgrave Square itself now houses more embassies than millionaires.

In the 19th century Belgravia's sizeable population of wealthy Jews earned it the slang nicknames ASIA MINOR, 'the New Jerusalem' and 'Mesopotamia'.

Belgravian. (A person) of or from Belgravia: 'That ineffable Belgravian, Lady Galbraith', *Athenaeum* (1891).

Bellahoe Possibly Irish *Béal Átha* 'mouth of the ford', with an unidentified element.

A river ford on the border between counties Meath and Monaghan, some 25 km (16 miles) southwest of Dundalk. In August 1539 Lord Deputy Grey here defeated an Irish force under Conn O'Neill and Manus O'Donnell, which had been raiding the northern PALE.

Belleek Irish *Béal Leice*, 'flagstone mouth' or 'flagstone ford'. A village on the River ERNE in western County Fermanagh, close to the border with the Irish Republic. In 1858 John Caldwell Bloomfield, a local landowner and keen amateur mineralogist, having established that his land was rich in kaolin and other raw materials necessary for the manufacture of pottery, founded the **Belleek Pottery Works Company**. Ordinary domestic items were the pottery's mainstay for many years, but its name is now synonymous with a kind of Parian porcelain (a fine marble-like porcelain which gets its name from the Aegean island of Paros) which the pottery has manufactured since the late 19th century.

Bell Rock, the From the bell once placed here.

A barely submerged rock in the North Sea, some 18 km (11 miles) southeast of the Angus coast at Arbroath. It is also known as the **Inchcape Rock** (possibly 'basket island', Gaelic *inis* 'island' + Old Scandinavian *skeppa* 'basket'). It has long been a hazard to shipping heading for either the Firth of Tay (*see under* TAY) or the Firth of Forth (*see under* FORTH), and it gained its more commonly used name from the warning bell placed here by an abbot of Arbroath (earlier known as Aberbrothock). This was subsequently removed by a pirate, who, according to John Monipennie's 1633 account, one year later 'perished upon the same rocke, with ship and goodes, in the righteous judgement of GOD'.

This story was the basis of Robert Southey's ballad '**The Inchape Rock**' (written 1796–8, published 1802), in which Sir Ralph the Rover, whose 'mirth was wickedness', decides to 'plague the Abbot of Aberbrothok' by cutting the bell from its float and sending it to the bottom. Some time later he and his men find themselves again in these waters, this time in poor visibility …

> They hear no sound, the swell is strong;
> Though the wind hath fallen they drift along,
> Till the vessel strikes with a shivering shock, –
> 'Oh, Christ! It is the Inchcape Rock!'
>
> Sir Ralph the Rover tore his hair;
> He curst himself in his despair;
> The waves rush in on every side,
> The ship is sinking beneath the tide.
>
> But even in his dying fear
> One dreadful sound could the Rover hear,
> A sound as if with the Inchcape Bell,
> The Devil below was ringing his knell.

The Bell Rock's dangers were considerably reduced in 1811, when work on a lighthouse, begun in 1807, was completed. The lighthouse was the work of John Rennie and Robert Stevenson, the grandfather of Robert Louis Stevenson. Another writer of adventure stories, R.M. Ballantyne, stayed a fortnight in the lighthouse researching his novel *The Lighthouse* (1865).

Bellshill Possibly the surname *Bell* in the possessive + *hill*.

An industrial town in North Lanarkshire (formerly in Strathclyde), 4 km (2.5 miles) northwest of Motherwell. It has an old-established community of Lithuanians, who first came to Scotland as prisoners of war during the Crimean War. It was the birthplace of Sir Matt Busby (1909–94), the manager of Manchester United FC from 1945 to 1969.

Bells Yew Green *Bells* probably from the surname *Bell* + *yew green*; the poisonous berries of yew kept domestic animals away.

A village in East Sussex, about 5 km (3 miles) south of Tunbridge Wells.

Belmarsh Possibly OFr *bel* 'beautiful' + ModE *marsh*.

A high-security prison in GREENWICH, in southeast London. Opened in 1991, its designated number of inmates is 880, with overcrowding currently at 18 per cent. The disgraced author and former Tory chairman Jeffrey Archer provided a grim account of his first 21 days at Belmarsh prison in *A Prison Diary*, published in 2002.

Belmullet. *See under* the MULLET.

Belowda From the local family name *de Boloude* (from Cornish *bod* 'dwelling' + an unknown element).

A village in Cornwall, about 16 km (10 miles) east of Newquay.

Belper 'beautiful retreat', OFr *beau repaire*.

A town in Derbyshire, about 16 km (10 miles) southeast of Matlock. Its profile was raised in the middle years of the 20th century when the colourful Labour MP and minister George Brown represented the Belper constituency between 1945 and 1970. The industrial heritage of the area around it is reconized by UNESCO under the label of the 'Derwent Valley Mills', a World Heritage Site (*see under* DERWENT[4]).

Belsize Park From *Belsize House*, a manor house in the area, rebuilt in the 17th century, and finally demolished in 1854, from *Belsize* 'beautiful seat, beautiful residence', the name of a medieval sub-manor of Hampstead, OFr *bel* 'beautiful' + *assise* 'seat'.

A district of HAMPSTEAD, North London, in the borough of CAMDEN (NW3), centred on Haverstock Hill. It was laid out from the late 1850s onwards in the gardens and grounds of the former **Belsize House**. The opening of Belsize Park Underground station on the Northern line in 1907 helped to establish its name.

Belton. A stately home, and its estate, in Lincolnshire, 5 km (3 miles) northeast of Grantham. It was built in the 1680s, but subsquently remodelled by James Wyatt. Its plasterwork and wood carvings are particularly notable. The commissioning family, the Brownlows, lived in it until the late 20th century, and it now belongs to the National Trust.

Belturbet Irish *Béal Tairbirt* 'mouth of the isthmus'.

A small market town on the River ERNE in County Cavan, 17 km (11 miles) southwest of Clones. On **Turbet Island**, in the River Erne, there is an Anglo-Norman motte.

Belvedere From the name of an 18th-century mansion in the area (since demolished), 'the fine view', from OFr *bel* 'beautiful, fine' + *vedeir* 'to see'.

A district in southeast London, in the borough of BEXLEY (before 1965 in Kent). It was the birthplace of the Kent and England wicketkeeper-batsman Alan Knott (b.1946).

Belvoir. *See* VALE OF BELVOIR.

Bemersyde 'hill-side of the trumpeter', OE *bemere* 'trumpeter' + *side*. It is possible that *bemere* is a bird with a trumpeting call.

The traditional home of the Haig family, 6 km (3.5 miles) east of Melrose, in Scottish Borders (formerly in Berwickshire). The present house dates back to the 16th century, and was improved and extended in the 17th and 18th centuries, although the Haig connection goes back to the 12th century. In the 13th century the seer Thomas the Rhymer prophesied:

> Tyde what may, what'er betyde
> Haig shall be Haig of Bemersyde.

In the 19th century the estate passed to a different branch of the family, but in 1921 a grateful nation raised sufficient funds to buy the house for Field Marshal Earl Haig, British commander-in-chief on the Western Front in the First World War.

Ben ... *See also* the *Beinn* names for mountains better known by the Gaelic.

Ben, The. An alternative name for BEN NEVIS.

Ben A'an. *See* BEN AN.

Ben Alder 'mountain of rock and water', Gaelic *beinn* 'mountain' + *ail* 'rock, cliff' + *dobhar* 'water'.

A large and remote mountain (1148 m / 3766 ft) west of Loch Ericht in the central HIGHLANDS, formerly in Inverness-shire and now in Highland. The nearest road is at RANNOCH Station, 16 km (10 miles) to the southwest, while to the northeast it is 19 km (11.5 miles) to the road at Dalwhinnie. It was described as 'the most eminent of bens' by the 16th-century Gaelic poet Domnhall mac Fhionnlaigh nan Dan.

After the failure of the 1745 Rising, the Jacobite chief, Ewan Macpherson of Cluny, hid in a makeshift shelter on the slopes of the mountain, and this became known as Cluny's Cage. Bonnie Prince Charlie stayed here in September 1746 as he fled the government troops, as did David Balfour and Alan Breck in Robert Louis Stevenson's novel *Kidnapped* (1886):

> Quite at the top, and just before the rocky face of the cliff sprang above the foliage, we found that strange house which was known in the country as 'Cluny's Cage'. The trunks of several trees had been wattled across, the intervals strengthened with stakes, and the ground

behind this barricade levelled up with earth to make the floor. A tree, which grew out from the hillside, was the living centre-beam of the roof. The walls were of wattle and covered with moss. The whole house had something of an egg shape; and it half hung, half stood in that steep, hillside thicket, like a wasp's nest in a green hawthorn.

Kidnapped, Chapter xxiii

There is a Prince Charlie's Cave above Loch Ericht to the south of the mountain, and nearby is the famously haunted **Ben Alder Cottage**, a bothy where otherwise sober and rational people have been terrified out of their wits by unearthly sounds.

Ben An A corruption due to Sir Walter Scott of Gaelic *binnean* 'pointed peak'. The Ordnance Survey give *Binnein* as an alternative name, although it is never now referred to as such.

A small but picturesquely pointed peak (533 m / 1750 ft) in the Trossachs, Stirling unitary authority (formerly in Stirlingshire and then in Central region). It is also spelt **Ben A'n** or **Ben A'an**, and its many small crags are popular with climbers. Ben Venue and Loch Katrine are just to the south:

While on the north, through middle air
Ben-an heaved high his forehead bare.

Sir Walter Scott: *The Lady of the Lake* (1810), Canto I, xiv

Ben Arthur. *See* The Cobbler.

Ben Avon. *See under* Avon[5].

Benbecula Possibly 'hill of the fords', Gaelic *beinn* 'mountain' + *na* 'of the' + *fhaodla* 'fords'.

A flat island in the Outer Hebrides, Western Isles (formerly in Inverness-shire). It is linked by a causeway to Presbyterian North Uist and by a bridge to Catholic South Uist (*see under* the Uists), and its own religious profile is a mixture of the two denominations.

Following his defeat at Culloden, Bonnie Prince Charlie arrived on Benbecula on 26 April 1746. After considerable peregrinations around the Outer Hebrides, on 28 June he set sail once more from Benbecula, disguised as Flora MacDonald's maid, Betty Burke, and headed 'over the sea to Skye'. It was an unpleasantly wet passage, and Flora was in some distress:

To divert her the Prince sung several pretty songs. She fell asleep, and to keep her so, the Prince still continued to sing.

Bishop Forbes: *The Lyon in Mourning* (1746–75)

In 1830 it was reported that the body of a small mermaid, fatally injured by a boy throwing stones, was washed up on the shores of Benbecula. The local sheriff arranged for a seemly burial, but provided no funeral service; he was no doubt sensitively attuned to the island's bi-denominational nature, and presumably concluded that it was not possible to ascertain whether the mermaid was a

right- or left-footer. Today the British Army has a base on Benbecula for the men who run the missile range on South Uist.

In all the Hebrides, Benbecula is the sea's dearest child. That is why the returning tide races so quickly over the sand, hurrying with pouted lips to kiss its shore. And when the night's embraces are over, the sea leaves Benbecula again, like a mother bird going to forage for its young.

Hector MacIver: 'The Outer Isles', in G. Scott-Moncrief, *Scottish Country* (1936)

Benbulben Irish *Binn Ghulbáin* 'Gulban's Peak' or 'beak peak'. A mountain (527 m / 1729 ft) in County Sligo, 10 km (6 miles) north of Sligo itself. It is also spelt **Ben Bulben**. With its long flat top girt with limestone cliffs, below which descend steep grass slopes, it recalls some mysterious Lost World.

It was on Benbulben in Irish legend that Diarmaid, while hunting with the Fianna, was gored to death by the wild boar that was in fact his metamorphosed half-brother. In another version of the story, Diarmaid, after slaying the boar, measured its hide with his bare feet, and was pierced by a bristle in his one vulnerable spot, his heel; the measuring was undertaken on the orders of Finn MacCool, angered by Diarmaid's elopement with Grainne, and in full knowledge of Diarmaid's problem in the Achilles' heel department.

In another story involving Finn, it is at the foot of Benbulben that he finds a naked boy, the son of his lover Sadb, who has been turned into a deer by the Dark Druid. Finn has searched for Sadb for seven years, and when he finds the boy, who has been raised as a deer, he calls him Oisín (Ossian), meaning 'fawn'.

In 561 the base of the mountain became the scene of the Battle of Cúl Dreimhne between the northern and southern Uí Néill clans, possibly a late manifestation of the conflict between Christianity and druidism.

The poet Yeats is buried in the churchyard at Drumcliff to the west of the mountain, having written his own epitaph:

Under bare Ben Bulben's head
In Drumcliff churchyard Yeats is laid.

W.B. Yeats: 'Under Ben Bulben' (1938)

Benburb Irish *An Bhinn Bhorb* 'the rough peak' (referring to the cliff above the river).

A village on the River Blackwater[3] in County Tyrone, 10 km (6 miles) south of Dungannon.

Battle of Benburb (5 June 1646). A battle during the Civil Wars in which the Irish under Owen Rua O'Neill defeated a Scottish army under General Robert Munroe. O'Neill's death three years later has always been bemoaned by

Nationalists, who saw in him a bulwark against the Cromwellian onslaught:

> Weep the Victor of Benburb – Weep him, young men and old;
>
> Weep for him, ye women – your Beautiful lies cold!
>
> We had thought you would not die – we were sure you would not go,
>
> And leave us in our utmost need to Cromwell's cruel blow …
>
> Thomas Davis: 'Lament for the Death of Eoghan Ruadh O'Neill', from *The Poems of Thomas Davis* (1845)

Ben Cruachan 'mountain of the conical hill', *Cruachan* Gaelic *cruach* 'of the stacks' (referring to its several peaks).

A fine, many-peaked granite mountain (1126 m / 3694 ft) 21 km (13 miles) east of Oban, situated between Loch Etive (*see under* ETIVE) and LOCH AWE, in Argyll and Bute (formerly in Strathclyde). The PASS OF BRANDER is at the foot of its southwestern flank.

In one legend, a spring high on the mountain was guarded by a Fenian warrior; in another, this spring was tended by a hag, whose inattentiveness led to the formation of Loch Awe itself. In John Barbour's poem *The Bruce*, a 14th-century epic on the Scottish Wars of Independence, Cruachan is elevated to the highest mountain in Britain:

> Crechinben hecht yat montane
> I trow nocht yat in all Bretane
> Ane heyar hill may fundyne be.

The mountain was described by William Wordsworth, in his 'Address to KILCHURN CASTLE' (1803), as 'yon sovereign Lord, / Huge Cruachan', and indeed the mountain can be seen from great distances in many directions. There is a spectacular hydroelectric scheme in one of its southern corries, with the actual power station buried deep within the mountain. Below are the **Falls of Cruachan**. In the late 1990s a sculptor put forward a proposal to dynamite a 300-m (1000-ft) high statue of a Highland warrior out of the northeastern flank of the mountain, but fortunately this failed to pass through the local planning process. The mountain inspired the war cry of Clan Campbell: **'Cruachan!'**

> Cruachan: the painted people call it the shield-boss of the world.
>
> Rosemary Sutcliff: *The Eagle of the Ninth* (1954)

Benderloch 'mountain between two lochs', Gaelic *beinn* 'mountain' + *eadar* 'between' + *dà* 'two' + *loch* (SEE LAKE).

The peninsula between Loch Creran and Loch Etive (*see under* ETIVE), about 12 km (7.5 miles) northeast of Oban, in Argyll and Bute (formerly in Strathclyde region). On the western coast is a small village also called **Benderloch**.

Bendish 'bean enclosure', OE *bean* 'bean' + *edisc* 'enclosure'.

A village in Hertfordshire, about 8 km (5 miles) southwest of Stevenage.

Benenden 'Bionna's woodland pasture', OE male personal name *Bionna* + -ING + *denn* 'woodland pasture'.

A village in Kent, about 21 km (13 miles) southeast of Tunbridge Wells. **Benenden School**, a girls' private school, which was attended by Princess Anne, was founded in 1923 and moved to its present site here in 1924.

Benfleet. *See* SOUTH BENFLEET.

Ben Hope 'mountain of the bay', *Hope* OScand *hop* 'bay': viewed from the sea, the mountain rises behind the deep inlet of Loch Eriboll.

A mountain (927 m / 3041 ft) in the far north of Highland (formerly in Sutherland), some 34 km (21 miles) southeast of CAPE WRATH, above **Loch Hope**. It is the most northerly of the MUNROS in Scotland. A claim, conceivably not rooted in reality, to a first ascent of the mountain in 1776 was made by a reverend gentleman, Charles Cordiner, in his *Antiquities and Scenery of the North of Scotland* (1780).

Ben Lawers 'mountain of the noisy stream', *Lawers* Gaelic *labhair* 'loud'.

A mountain (1214 m / 3984 ft) on the north side of Loch Tay (*see under* TAY), in Perth and Kinross (formerly in Perthshire, and then in Tayside region). It is the ninth-highest mountain in Britain. Its name probably derives from the noisy **Lawers Burn** that descends on its south flank from Lochan nan Cat ('lochan of the wildcats') to the little village of **Lawers**. The name of this lochan, and the general shape of the Lawers massif, has led some to suggest that the name Lawers derives from Gaelic *ladhar* 'paw'. The mountain is noted for its alpine flora, and is in the care of the National Trust for Scotland. Before the extensive provision of mechanical uplift elsewhere in the Highlands, Ben Lawers was popular with skiers.

Ben Lawers was possibly the first Scottish mountain to be painted for its own sake. In 1741 the Duke of Hamilton commissioned R. Norie (1711–76) to carry out the work. The result raised the Ben to an alpine splendour beyond its actual lumpishness, and Norie also peopled the foreground with classical nymphs and shepherds.

Lady of Lawers, the. A seer who probably lived in the later 17th century. She may have been a Stewart of Appin. In the village of Lawers there are some ruins known as the House of the Lady of Lawers.

Ben Ledi 'mountain of the slope', *Ledi* Gaelic *leitir* or *leathad* 'slope'; this is thought more likely as the Gaelic original than *le dia* 'with God'.

A mountain (879 m / 2883 ft) above LOCH LUBNAIG, about 8 km (5 miles) northwest of CALLANDER in the southern Highlands. It is pronounced to rhyme with 'teddy'. The mountain formerly had a particular significance for the local people, as recorded by James Robertson, minister of Callander, in 1794:

> By reason of the altitude of Ben Ledi and of its beautiful conical figure, the people of the adjacent country to a great distance, assembled annually on its top, about the time of the summer solstice, during the Druidical priesthood, to worship the Deity. This assembly seems to have been a provincial or synodical meeting, wherein all the congregations within the bounds wished to get as near to Heaven as they could to pay their homage to the God of Heaven.
>
> *Old Statistical Account*, vol. XII

On the northern side of the mountain is Lochan nan Corp (Gaelic, 'lochan of the corpses'), so called because long ago a funeral party, attempting to cross its frozen surface, perished when the ice broke – an event commemorated by Sir Walter Scott:

> The moon, half-hid in silvery flakes,
> Afar her dubious radiance shed,
> Quivering on Katrine's distant lakes,
> And resting on Benledi's head.
>
> Sir Walter Scott: 'Glenfinlas' (1801)

The mountain is also mentioned in Robert Burns's poem 'By Allan stream I chanced to rove' (*see under* BRIDGE OF ALLAN).

Ben Lomond 'beacon mountain', *Lomond* OCelt *llumon* 'beacon', or possibly Gaelic *luimean* 'bare hill'.

A mountain (974 m / 3195 ft) some 40 km (25 miles) northwest of Glasgow. It is the most southerly of the MUNROS, and was formerly in Stirlingshire, then in Central region, and is now in the unitary authority of Stirling. It stands halfway up the eastern shore of LOCH LOMOND, to which it gave its name.

Because of its proximity to Glasgow, Ben Lomond has been enormously popular with tourists since the later 18th century:

> In the months of July, August and September, the summit of Ben Lomond is frequently visited by strangers from every quarter of the island, as well as by foreigners.
>
> Charles Ross: *Travellers Guide to Loch Lomond* (1792)

Colonel Peter Hawker, who made an icy ascent in 1812, tells how, in more clement conditions, ladies would take along a piper so that they could dance on the summit. The poet Keats contemplated an ascent in 1818, but thought the price of a guide 'very high'. There is a notable painting of the summit, executed in 1834 by John Knox.

> While winds frae off BEN-LOMOND blaw,
> And bar the doors wi' driving snaw
> And hing us owre the ingle,

> I set me down, to pass the time,
> And spin a verse or twa o' rhyme,
> In hamely, *westlin* jingle.
>
> Robert Burns: 'Epistle to Davie, A Brother Poet'
> (written in January 1785)

> Ben Lomond from the lake rises up, and goes *bounding* down, its outline divided into six great segments, scolloped like many leaves, with five or six small scollops in each great segment, of the same shape.
>
> Samuel Taylor Coleridge: journal (25 August 1803)

In northeastern Tasmania there is a massif called Ben Lomond, which rises to 1573 m (5161 ft) at Legges Tor, the highest point on the island. It was named by the explorer Colonel William Paterson in 1804.

Ben Loyal 'law-hill mountain', *Loyal* OScand *laga* 'law' + *fjall* 'mountain'; in Norse tradition, new laws were proclaimed from the top of hills.

A rocky four-peaked mountain (764 m / 2506 ft) in the far north of Highland (formerly in Sutherland), 8 km (5 miles) south of TONGUE, and just west of Loch Loyal. Its elegant appearance when viewed from the north (and perhaps a misunderstanding of its name) has led to it being dubbed '**Queen of the Scottish Peaks**'.

Ben Lui 'mountain of the calves', *Lui* Gaelic *laogh* 'calf, fawn', possessive plural *laoigh*, probably from the two-pointed summit. In Gaelic it is *Beinn Laoigh*.

A mountain (1130 m / 3707 ft) on the border of Stirling unitary authority and Argyll and Bute (formerly between Argyll and Perthshire, then between Central and Strathclyde regions), 8 km (5 miles) southwest of TYNDRUM. Its most spectacular aspect is that from the east, and the great northeast face (with its classic winter climb, *Central Gully*) usually holds snow well into the spring. The mountain is a nature reserve, and is the ultimate source of the River TAY.

Ben Macdui Probably 'mountain of the MacDuffs', *Macdui* Gaelic *mhac* 'son of' + *dhuibhe* 'the black one', i.e. Duff; the MacDuff family (the earls of Fife) owned much land around here for centuries, until selling out in the 1960s (*see also* DUFFTOWN). A more colourful and popular theory, but less likely, is that it is 'mountain of the black pig', Gaelic *muic* 'pig' + *duibh* 'black'.

The highest mountain (1309 m / 4294 ft) in the CAIRNGORM MOUNTAINS, situated on the border between Moray and Aberdeenshire (formerly in Grampian region), 20 km (12.5 miles) northwest of Braemar. It is the second highest mountain in the British Isles, and until the Ordnance Survey measurements of 1846–7 erected BEN NEVIS to the premier position, it was long thought to be the highest in the British Isles. Somewhat disconcerted, the local landowner, the Earl of Fife, determined on a plan to construct himself a huge burial cairn on the summit to add the necessary 100 ft or so and thus restore glory to the eastern claimant. Happily the plan never came to fruition.

Ben Macdui is a vast and remote mountain, consisting of a high sub-Arctic plateau (one of the few places in Britain that snow buntings find chilly enough to spend the summer) surrounded on many sides by mighty crags such as Carn Etchachan, the SHELTER STONE Crag, Craig na Coire Etchachan and Coire Sputan Dearg, all of which hold long and serious climbs in both summer and winter. More sedately, Queen Victoria reached the summit on a pony in 1859, and her prime minister, Mr Gladstone, on foot in 1884. They, of course, made their ascents in summer; in winter the mountain takes on a polar mantle:

> The scene from the moment we left the Ben Muich Dhui cairn was not one which we shall readily forget … For mountain and rock, loch and stream, were shrouded in ice and snow; not a water-course visible … everything white, except here and there the black top of some great rock. The outlines, storm-formed, were weird and grand … On the top of Ben Muich Dhui we estimated the depth of snow to be six feet, and in the corries often a hundred …
>
> A.I. McConnochie: 'The Cairngorms in Winter', in *The Scottish Mountaineering Club Journal*, vol. 1 (1890)

In April 2001 two US F-15 jets crashed into the mountain.

Grey Man of Ben Macdui, the. A giant shadowy presence that haunts the higher reaches of the mountain. In Gaelic he is referred to as *Am Fear Mòr Liath* ('the Great Grey Man') or more colloquially as *Ferlas Mor*. One of the most famous reports of the Great Grey Man was given many years after the event (and it is thought somewhat reluctantly) by Professor Norman Collie, by then a veteran mountaineer and, what is more, a distinguished scientist with a reputation to lose. He had been nearing the summit on a misty grey day when he heard behind him footsteps heavier than any human would make. When he stopped the steps stopped too. The steps came closer and closer, and then a shadow, far taller than a man, appeared in the mist. Collie fled:

> I was seized with an intolerable fright and I ran my hardest down the mountainside. No power on earth will ever take me up Ben Macdui again.
>
> Norman Collie: speech to the Cairngorm Club (1925)

Other reports (always from solo walkers) speak of the pursuing footsteps occurring only for every two and a half or three of the listener's steps – so an echo may be ruled out, as can the phenomenon known as the Brocken spectre, by which the sun projects the viewer's shadow onto cloud. All agreed that the experience was utterly terrifying. The locals throw no light on the phenomenon, as Alistair Borthwick recounts in *Always a Little Further* (1939), his classic of stravaiging during the Depression:

> Once I was out with a search-party on MacDhui; and on the way down after an unsuccessful day I asked some of the gamekeepers and stalkers who were with us what they thought of it all. They worked on MacDhui, so they should know. Had they seen Ferlas Mor? Did he exist, or was it just a silly story?
>
> They looked at me for a few seconds, and then one said:
>
> 'We do not talk about that.'

Ben Mòr Coigach. *See under* COIGACH.

Ben More[1] 'big mountain', *More* Gaelic *mòr* 'big'.
The 15th highest mountain (1174 m / 3852 ft) in Scotland, and the highest of a cornucopia of Scottish Ben Mores. It is in the unitary authority of Stirling (formerly in Central region, and before that in Perthshire; it is still often referred to as **'the Perthshire Ben More'**). It is joined by a high col to another giant, STOB BINNEIN.

> … before me Ben More or the Huge Mountain, one of the highest in the Highlands, shaped like a haystack, which dallies with the clouds, that now touch, now hide, now leave it.
>
> Samuel Taylor Coleridge: journal (30 August 1803)

> The wildest glen, but this, can show,
> Some touch of Nature's genial glow;
> On high Benmore green mosses grow,
> And heath-bells bud in deep Glencroe …
>
> Sir Walter Scott: *The Lord of the Isles* (1815), Canto III, xiv

Ben More[2]. The highest mountain (966 m / 3169 ft) on MULL, Argyll and Bute (formerly in Argyll, then in Strathclyde region). It is the only MUNRO on a Scottish island apart from those on Skye. It has provided some with quite a challenge:

> In my journeys among the High Alps I never found so much difficulty as here …
>
> Barthelemy Faujas de Saint-Fond: *Travels in England, Scotland and the Hebrides* (1797)

Saint-Fond himself failed to make the summit, complaining of heather, bog and monotonous lavas, but his companion, an American called William Thornton, went on to make the first recorded ascent – in the company of a young local guide called Campbell, who had doubtless been to the top before.

Benmore. The anglicized name for An Bheinn Mhór (*see under* FAIR HEAD.)

Ben More Assynt. *See under* ASSYNT.

Benna Beola. An Irish name for the TWELVE PINS.

Bennachie 'hill of the breast', Gaelic *beinn* 'mountain' + *na* 'of the' + *ciche* 'breast' or 'nipple'; *Benychie*, 1170.

A small but perfectly formed massif of hills (pronounced 'bennahee') in Aberdeenshire (formerly in Grampian region), some 30 km (18 miles) northwest of Aberdeen. They are the most easterly outliers of the distant CAIRN-GORM MOUNTAINS. The highest top is Oxen Craig (528 m / 1733 ft), but the name probably derives from the shape of the neighbouring Mither Tap (518 m / 1698 ft), with its summit granite tor surrounded by an ancient hillfort. On the south side is **Bennachie Forest**. The hills are visible from a long way away in several directions, and fill exiled North-easterners with fond thoughts of home – as evinced by the following lines by the local poet, Charles Murray:

> ... Ben Nevis looms, the laird of a',
> But Bennachie! Faith, yon's the hill
> Rugs at the hairt where you're awa'.
>
> > (*rugs at the hairt* 'tugs at the heart')

The hills also feature in a song by John Imlah (1799–1846):

> O ance, ance mair where Gadie rins,
> Where Gadie rins, where Gadie rins –
> O micht I dee where Gadie rins
> > At the back o' Bennachie.

Sadly, Imlah died not here, but on a voyage to Jamaica.

Bailies of Bennachie, the. A group founded in 1970 to look after the welfare of the hills.

Bennane Head Etymology obscure, but the first element is probably Gaelic *beinn* 'mountain'.

A headland on the South Ayrshire coast (formerly in Strathclyde region), some 5 km (3 miles) north of BALLANTRAE. It was said to have been the haunt of Sawney Bean, the head of a large incestuous family who, in the 15th century, preyed on travellers on this lonely stretch of coast, and then ate them. The king himself led a band to catch them, and traced them to a sea cave, full of pickled body parts and treasure. They were taken to Edinburgh, where, without trial, the men were burned and the women and children had their hands and feet cut off and bled to death.

Ben Narnain. *See under* ARROCHAR.

Ben Nevis 'mountain of the spiteful stream', *Nevis* Gaelic *nibheis* (nee-vash) 'evil, venomous'; *Ben Neevush* 1532. Other theories suggest an origin in the old European root-word *neb*, 'cloud' or 'water', or the Gaelic *nèamh*, 'sky, heaven'.

The highest mountain (1344 m / 4409 ft) in the British Isles, known simply as **The Ben** to climbers. Its summit stands some 7 km (4.5 miles) southeast of Fort William, and the mountain was formerly in Inverness-shire and is now in Highland. The Scottish Tourist Board once tried to promote it as 'the Real Big Ben', but happily this never caught on. Its claim to be the highest was long challenged by BEN MACDUI, until measurements made by Colonel Winzer of the Ordnance Survey in 1846 and 1847 favoured the western claimant. The first recorded ascent of the mountain was made on 19 August 1771 by a Mr James Robertson, a former student of botany who was working for the commissioners of the estates annexed after the failure of the 1745 Jacobite Rising.

From most perspectives Ben Nevis presents itself as a great whaleback; the most spectacular view requires an ascent of the high neighbouring mountain, Carn Mor Dearg. In 1891 an anonymous correspondent suggested to the Scottish Press that the mountain might be improved

> by blasting with dynamite some of the neighbouring hills, where the excavation would not be noticed, and obtaining a supply of ... stones to be piled up to form a more lofty and graceful summit to the hill, bringing it to the full height of 5,000 feet, and giving the British tourist a finer mountain to look at and to ascend; the view would be superb.
>
> > 'Loch-ma-ben': letter to the *Glasgow Herald* (8 May 1891)

Fortunately for the British tourist this plan was never implemented. *Un*fortunately for the British tourist, Ben Nevis is one of the wettest places in Britain, and the top is only clear of cloud on a third of the days in any year. Snow lingers in the northeastern corries all year round, where mighty cliffs extend for some 3 km (2 miles), and rise to well over 300 m (1000 ft) in height, providing challenges to experienced mountaineers in both summer and winter. Tourists use the more gently angled pony track on the western flanks, the route of an annual foot race; this track was long ago ascended by a Model-T Ford. A century before this, on 5 August 1818, the poet John Keats made an ascent with his friend Charles Armitage Brown, together with a guide, a dog and several draughts of whisky (which may explain why he was obliged to tackle some sections of the summit plateau on all fours). Judging from the sonnet he wrote on the summit, Keats experienced fairly typical conditions:

> Read me a lesson, Muse, and speak it loud
> Upon the top of Nevis, blind in mist!
> I look into the chasms, and a shroud
> Vaporous doth hide them, – just so much I wist
> Mankind do know of hell; I look o'erhead,
> And there is sullen mist, – even so much
> Mankind can tell of heaven ...
>
> > John Keats (1795–1821): 'Ben Nevis'

More informally, he wrote to his brother:

> ... yesterday, we went up Ben Nevis, the highest mountain in Great Britain – On that account I will never ascend another in this empire – Skiddaw is no thing to it

either in height or in difficulty ... I am heartily glad it is done – it is almost like a fly crawling up a wainscoat – Imagine the task of mounting 10 Saint Pauls without the convenience of Stair cases.

John Keats: letter to Tom Keats (6 August 1818)

A later ascentionist, following the tricky Northeast Buttress, remarked:

Not even in Skye have I seen rocks so wet. There was quite a respectable waterfall coming off the ridge, and innumerable smaller ones that in England would draw hosts of worshippers.

W. Brown: 'Ascent of Ben Nevis by the N.E. Buttress', *Scottish Mountaineering Club Journal*, vol. III (1895)

An observatory was established on the summit of the mountain in 1883, but abandoned in 1904; some of the stonework can still be seen. The building lent its name to the magnificent *Observatory Ridge*, which plunges 365 m (1200 ft) down the north face straight from the summit. A nearby gully, used for rubbish disposal while the observatory was in occupation, is known as *Gardyloo Gully* – 'Gardyloo' (French *gardez l'eau*, 'beware the water') being the traditional cry in Edinburgh when emptying a chamber pot from a high window into the street. Climbers have kept up the tradition of giving astronomical names to the severe winter routes hereabouts (recorded in the guidebooks and journal of the Scottish Mountaineering Club); examples include *Orion Face*, *Astral Highway* and *Galactic Hitchhiker*.

More prosaically, the Victorians named the main gullies, from left to right, Number One Gully through to Number Five Gully. When the steep ice couloirs to the left of Number One Gully began to attract the attentions of later generations, the mathematical nomenclature was continued with the appropriate logic, yielding Zero Gully, Minus One Gully, Minus Two Gully and Minus Three Gully. A bit of creative accounting was then required to squeeze in Point Five Gully.

Beinn Nibheis that gach aonach
(Ben Nevis towering over mountains)

Sìleas na Capaich (Cicely Macdonald, *c*.1660–*c*.1729): *Alasdair á Gleanna Garadh* (*Alasdair of Glengarry*), translated by Derick Thomson

A horse called Ben Nevis won the Grand National in 1980; for other mountainy mounts *see* ARKLE and FOINAVEN.

See also LOCH NEVIS.

Dew o' Ben Nevis. A slang term for whisky, used in the late Victorian and Edwardian periods.

Glen Nevis. The glen of the short **Water of Nevis**, which curves round the base of the western and southern flanks of Ben Nevis. The glen constricts to a spectacular gorge before opening out into the alpine meadows of Upper Glen Nevis.

It was described by one Gaelic poet as 'A glen on which God has turned his back: the slop-pail of the great world', while another described it as

A long wild waste glen,
With thievish folk of evil habit.

This reputation may explain why glen and ben are called *nibheis* (nee-vash) 'evil' (*see above*).

Nevis Range. The name of the skiing development on Aonach Mòr, just east of Ben Nevis (*see* AONACH BEAG).

Benson 'estate associated with Benesa', OE male personal name *Benesa* + -ING + -TON.

A village in Oxfordshire, close to the River Thames, about 16 km (10 miles) southeast of Oxford. Recent archaeological excavations have established that a settlement has existed here from at least early Saxon times.

RAF Benson was the home of the RAF's Photographic Reconnaisance Unit during the Second World War, but the airfield now operates primarily as a helicopter base. Oxford University Air Squadron has its home there.

Battle of Benson (*c*.777). A battle in which Offa of MERCIA defeated Cynewulf of WESSEX, enabling the former to regain territory south of the River Thames seized by Wessex 25 years earlier.

Ben Stack 'mountain of the steep rock', Stack OScand *stakkr* 'steep rock', borrowed into Gaelic as *stac*.

A mountain (721 m / 2365 ft) in the far northwest of Highland (formerly in Sutherland), some 33 km (20 miles) south of CAPE WRATH. **Loch Stack** is to the east and **Strath Stack** to the south.

Bentley 'clearing with bent grass', OE *beonet* 'bent grass' (*Agrostis tenuis*, grown for hay) + -LEY.

A town in South Yorkshire, 3 km (2 miles) north of Doncaster.

Ben Venue 'small mountain', *Venue* probably Gaelic *mheanbh* (*venav*) 'small'; other suggested meanings for the anglicized 'Venue' include 'caves', 'milk', 'young cattle'.

A mountain (727 m / 2393 ft) rising above the TROSSACHS, 6 km (4 miles) northwest of Aberfoyle, in the southern Highlands. It was formerly in Perthshire, then in Central region, and is now in Stirling unitary authority. The northern aspect, above LOCH KATRINE, is steep and craggy:

High on the south, huge Benvenue
Down on the lake in masses threw
Crags, knolls, and mounds, confusedly hurl'd,
The fragments of an earlier world;
A wildering forest feather'd o'er
His ruin'd sides and summit hoar ...

Sir Walter Scott: *The Lady of the Lake* (1810), Canto I, xiv

Ben Vorlich[1] probably 'mountain of the bays', *Vorlich* Gaelic *mhuir'g* (*mh* is pronounced 'v') 'sack-shaped sea inlets'; *Binvouirlyg* 1650.

A mountain (985 m / 3224 ft) above Loch EARN, in Perth and Kinross (formerly in Perthshire, and then in Tayside region). Sir Walter Scott's poem *Lady of the Lake* begins with a deer hunt below the peak:

> ... when the sun his beacon red
> Had kindled on Benvoirlich's head,
> The deep-mouth'd bloodhound's heavy bay
> Resounded up the rocky way ...

> Sir Walter Scott: *The Lady of the Lake* (1810), Canto I, i

At foot of northern slopes is **Ardvorlich House**, which appears in Scott's novel *The Legend of Montrose* (1819): the hero of the novel, Allan Macaulay, was based on the historical Major James Stewart of Ardvorlich.

Ben Vorlich[2]. A mountain (943 m / 3094 ft) above the west shore of LOCH LOMOND, in Argyll and Bute (formerly in Argyll, and then in Strathclyde region), 15 km (9 miles) southwest of Crianlarich.

Ben Vrackie 'speckled mountain', *Vrackie* Gaelic *breac* 'speckled'.

A mountain (841 m / 2758 ft) in Perth and Kinross (formerly in Perthshire, and then in Tayside region), 5 km (3 miles) north of PITLOCHRY. It is a fine viewpoint and is popular with walkers.

Ben Wyvis 'awesome mountain', *Wyvis* Gaelic *fhuathais* 'of the ghost or goblin', or Gaelic *uais* 'noble, majestic, elegant'.

A great sow's back of a mountain (1046 m / 3431 ft) in EASTER ROSS, Highland (formerly in Ross and Cromarty), some 30 km (20 miles) northwest of Inverness. An early ascent in unseasonal conditions was made in June 1767 by James Robertson, a surveyor for the Commissioners of the Forfeit Estates (estates forfeited after the failure of the 1745 Jacobite Rising):

> On the summit I was whitened by a fall of snow, and in many lower parts of the mountain it lay underfoot to a considerable depth.

> MS no. 2507, National Library of Scotland

Although Robertson's brief was to establish the economic potential (specifically the mineral and botanical resources) of the region, he might have jumped ahead of his time and concluded from this visit that the mountain would be suitable for skiing development – something that has often since been proposed (with all the trappings of rack-and-pinion railways, etc.), but never (to the relief of environmentalists) put into practice. The ability of the mountain to hold snow through the warmer months is attested by the fact that the Mackenzie earls of Cromarty held their lands from the Crown on condition that at any time of year, when demanded, they could pay rent in the form of a snowball gathered from Ben Wyvis.

Little Wyvis (764 m / 2506 ft) is a smaller mountain 6 km (4 miles) southeast of Ben Wyvis.

Bere. An alternative name for BEARA.

Bere Alston Originally *Alphameston* 'Ælfhelm's farmstead', OE *Ælfhelmes* possessive form of male personal name *Ælfhelm* + -TON; *Bere* was adopted (from BERE FERRERS) in the 15th century.

A village in Devon, in the TAMAR Valley, about 15 km (9 miles) northwest of Plymouth.

Bere Ferrers *Bere* 'grove', OE *bearu*, or 'woodland pasture', OE *bær*; *Ferrers* denoting manorial ownership in the Middle Ages by the de Ferers family.

A village in Devon, on the mouth of the River TAVY, about 3 km (2 miles) south of Bere Alston.

Berehaven. *See under* BEARA.

Berepper 'beautiful retreat', Fr *beau repaire*.

A village in Cornwall, about 5 km (3 miles) south of Helston.

Bere Regis *Bere, see* BERE FERRERS; *Regis* 'of the king', Latin *regis* (because Bere Wood, to the east, was once a royal forest).

A village in Dorset, about 16 km (10 miles) northeast of DORCHESTER[1]. In the novels of Thomas Hardy, it is fictionalized as **Kingsbere** or **King's-Bere**.

Berinsfield From St *Berin*, a missionary bishop from Rome who baptized the King of the West Saxons in the River THAME[1] at Dorchester in AD 634, +*field*, from Field Farm on which the village was built.

A village in Oxfordshire, about 8 km (5 miles) south of Oxford. It was designed in the late 1950s and 1960s on the site of an airfield used in the Second World War.

Berkeley 'birch-tree glade', OE *beorc* 'birch-tree' + -LEY.

A small Georgian town (pronounced 'barkly') in Gloucestershire, close to the southeast bank of the River SEVERN and about 26 km (16 miles) northwest of Bristol. It was the birthplace and lifelong home of Edward Jenner (1749–1823), the pioneer of smallpox vaccination.

Berkeley Castle. A 12th-century castle dominating the town of Berkeley, home of the Berkeley family for 800 years. Edward II was brutally murdered here in 1327, on the orders of Isabella of France and Roger Mortimer 'with a hot spit put thro the secret place posterial' – Ranulf Higden, *Polychronicon* (1340s).

Berkeley Hunt. A fox-hunt in the Vale of Berkeley, best known for contributing the rhyming slang for *cunt* to the English language. First recorded in the 1930s, its now barely recognized shortened form *berk* has become a standard colloquialism for 'fool'.

Vale of Berkeley. A 24-km (15-mile) long stretch of flat land on the east bank of the River Severn, in Gloucestershire and South Gloucestershire, approximately between THORNBURY and Frampton on Severn. The COTSWOLDS rise to the east.

Berkeley Square From *Berkeley House*, a mansion in Piccadilly built in 1665 for the 1st Lord *Berkeley* of Stratton, the Royalist commander in the Civil Wars.

A square in MAYFAIR, in the WEST END[1] of London (W1), which is linked to PICCADILLY[1] by Berkeley Street and to OXFORD STREET by Davies Street. It was laid out in the 1730s as a residential square (it is actually oblong, not square), and contained elegant and fashionable town houses (originally on the east and west sides only). However, anonymous office blocks usurped many of the houses in the 20th century and, despite the square's forest of plane trees, there is little to encourage the nightingale of the Eric Maschwitz/Manning Sherwin song ('**A Nightingale Sang in Berkeley Square**', 1940) to sing here today.

Ghosts of Berkeley Square, The. A film comedy (1947) starring Robert Morley and Felix Aylmer as two 18th-century army officers who accidentally kill themselves and are doomed to haunt a Berkeley Square mansion until it is visited by reigning royalty.

Berkhamsted Probably 'homestead on or near a hill', OE *beorg* 'hill' + HAM + *stede* 'homestead'.

A town (pronounced 'berkəmsted') in Hertfordshire, on the GRAND UNION CANAL, about 8 km (5 miles) northwest of Hemel Hempstead. William the Conqueror is said to have accepted the throne of England from the defeated Anglo-Saxons here in 1066. He built a castle here (as was his wont); in a later century the poet Geoffrey Chaucer was its clerk of works.

Berkhamsted was the birthplace of the poet William Cowper (1731–1800), whose father was the local rector; of the novelist Graham Greene (1904–91), whose father was headmaster of **Berkhamsted Collegiate School**, the local public school; and of the actor Michael Hordern (1911–95).

Berks. The standard written abbreviation for BERKSHIRE.

Berkshire *Berk-* from a prehistoric Celtic name meaning 'hilly place' + SHIRE.

A county (pronounced 'barkshire') in central southern England, one of the HOME COUNTIES, to the west of London. It is bounded to the north by Oxfordshire and Buckinghamshire, to the east by London, to the south by Hampshire and Surrey and to the west by Wiltshire. Its northwestern border until 1972 was the Upper THAMES[1], which from LECHLADE in the west to WALLINGFORD in the east separated it from Oxfordshire. In 1972 Berkshire lost a large northern chunk on the south bank of the Thames (including Abingdon, Faringdon, Wallingford and Wantage) to Oxfordshire. Berkshire gained SLOUGH and ETON from Buckinghamshire in 1972 at the same time.

Berkshire is no longer an administrative county, these functions having been dispersed in 1998 among the six unitary authorities which now occupy its territory: BRACKNELL FOREST, READING (the former county town), SLOUGH, WEST BERKSHIRE, WINDSOR AND MAIDENHEAD and WOKINGHAM. Other important centres are ASCOT, Eton, and NEWBURY. The eastern part of its northern boundary continues to be formed by the River Thames.

Before the coming of the Romans, Berkshire was part of the territory of the British tribe known as the Atrebates, who also occupied adjoining parts of Surrey, Wiltshire and Hampshire (*see* SILCHESTER). For much of the Anglo-Saxon period the area was disputed between the kingdoms of MERCIA and WESSEX, the latter finally gaining the upper hand in the early 9th century. It became an important part of Wessex, being the home territory of Alfred the Great (*see* WANTAGE).

The original Berkshire was a quiet farming county of sheep-grazed downland in the west (increasingly prairiefied these days by intensive farming), and more barren heathland in the east. It has always been something of a county for passing through from east to west, either by rail (on the Great Western Railway from the 1830s) or – in the motorway age – by car (along the M4).

In recognition particularly of the royal connections of Windsor and Eton, Berkshire was officially designated '**Royal Berkshire**'.

In cricketing terms Berkshire is a 'minor county' (the club was founded in 1895) and plays in the minor counties championship.

There is a range of hills in western Massachusetts, USA, known as the Berkshire Hills (pronounced 'berkshire', and generally abbreviated to 'the Berkshires').

> It was in 1934 that his lunchtime host asked André Simon, the founder of the Wine and Food Society, for his first reactions to the wines [a range of old clarets]. They 'evoked memories of Berkshire', the 1870 Lafite 'of the Majesty of the Royal Oak'.
>
> Michael Broadbent: *Vintage Wine* (2002)

> All Berkshire women are very silly. I don't know why women in Berkshire are more silly than anywhere else.
>
> Mr Justice Claude Duveen: Reading County Court, July 1972

Berkshire. One of a breed of medium-sized pigs that are black with white markings. They were originally bred in the area around Wantage and Faringdon. Bacon from Berkshire pigs was used to make the local dish of **Berkshire bacon pudding**, a suet roly-poly filled with home-cured bacon and flavoured with sage and onion.

Berkshire Bubs. A nickname for WITTENHAM CLUMPS.

Berkshire Downs. A range of chalk hills in northern Berkshire and southern Oxfordshire, to the south of the VALE OF THE WHITE HORSE. The RIDGEWAY, a prehistoric trackway, runs along the tops. The hills form the northern part of the North Wessex Downs (*see under* WESSEX).

Berkshire hunt. An occasional synonym of the Berkeley Hunt (*see under* BERKELEY).

'Berkshire Tragedy, The'. A 44-verse folk song published in the late 17th century, about a miller's apprentice who makes a girl pregnant and, when pressed to marry her, murders her and throws the body into a river. The song, one of the best-known such 'murder songs' carried around the country by street singers, is also known as 'The Miller's Apprentice', 'The Oxford Miller', 'The Wittam Miller' (Wittam is probably WYTHAM, which was in Berkshire until 1972, *see above*) and, in Ireland, 'The Wexford Miller'.

Bermondsey 'Beornmund's island', OE *Beornmundes* possessive form of male personal name *Beornmund* + *eg* 'island' (*see* -AY); in this case 'island' refers to an area of dry ground surrounded by Thames-side marshes.

A district in southeast London, on the south bank of the THAMES[1], to the east of London Bridge, in the northern part of the borough of SOUTHWARK (SE1, SE16). It was in the past a centre of brewing and leather-making, and in the days when London Docks were still in operation, the 5.5 km (3.5 miles) of wharfs and warehouses along its riverfront made an important contribution to its economy. In 1836, the first passenger railway terminus in London was opened in Bermondsey; it later became London Bridge Station.

As a parliamentary constituency Bermondsey gained brief notoriety as the scene of gay-leftwing-activist Peter Tatchell's first rise to prominence in a 1983 by-election when he succeeded the traditionalist Bob Mellish as Labour candidate amid much controversy (only to be defeated in the by-election by Simon Hughes of the Liberals).

> We are some of the Bermondsey boys,
> We are some of the boys.
> We know our manners, we spend our tanners,
> We are respected wherever we go.
> We go walking down the Old Kent Road,
> All the windows open wide.
> Can't you hear those bobbies shout: blow those bloody
>   Woodbines out?
> We are some of the boys.
>
>   Anon.: 'The Bermondsey Boys'

Bermondsey banger. Late 19th-century slang for:

> ... a society leader among the South London tanneries, who must ... be prepared to hold his own and fight at all times for his social belt ...
>
>   J. Redding Ware: *Passing English of the Victorian Era* (1909)

Banger in this context is both one who 'bangs' his fellows about physically and one who makes a 'bang' in society.

Bermudas, the. A late 18th-century slang name for certain no-go areas of London where criminals hid themselves away and the authorities were not inclined to pursue them. It was applied in particular to the lanes and passageways running near DRURY LANE, COVENT GARDEN, and to parts of SOUTHWARK. It was inspired by the use of the Bermuda islands, in the Atlantic, as a bolt hole to which certain well-connected debtors had fled to avoid their creditors.

Berneray[1] 'bear island' or 'Bjorn's island', OScand *bjorn*, possessive *bjarnar* 'of the bear' or 'belonging to Bjorn' + *ey* (*see* -AY). The Gaelic name is *Bearnaraigh*.

A small island at the southern tip of the Outer HEBRIDES, Western Isles (formerly in Inverness-shire). It is separated from Mingulay to the north by the **Sound of Berneray**, which is only about 750 m (820 yds) wide. The southernmost point is BARRA HEAD. The last inhabitants were the lighthouse-keepers, who left in the late 1970s when the lighthouse was automated. The island is now in the care of the National Trust for Scotland.

Berneray[2]. A small inhabited island (Gaelic *Eilean Bhearnaraigh*) in the Outer HEBRIDES, at the north end of North Uist (*see under* the UISTS), to which it is linked by a causeway.

Berners Roding. *See under* the RODINGS.

Bernicia Latinization of OCelt *Beornica*, later Welsh *Bryneich*, usually associated with the people known by the Romans as *Brigantes*; the name Bernicia might mean 'land of the mountain passes'.

An Anglo-Saxon kingdom founded in the early 6th century by Ida, who built his fortified capital in AD 547 at BAMBURGH. Bernicia extended from the River Tees north to the Forth, and in the 7th century this kingdom, together with the kingdom of DEIRA, which stretched from the Tees to the River Humber, was united to make the kingdom of NORTHUMBRIA.

Berrick Salome *Berrick* 'barley-farm', OE *bere* 'barley' + *wic* (*see* WICK); *Salome* denoting manorial ownership in the Middle Ages by the de Suleham family, presumably later assimilated to *Salome*, the name of the Old Testament temptress who asked Herod for the head of John the Baptist.

A village (*Salome* pronounced 'saləm') in Oxfordshire, about 13 km (8 miles) southeast of Oxford.

Berry Hill A modern coinage.

A village just to the south of Stoke-on-Trent, created in the mid-1990s as a community for those aged 55 and over. The notion of such senior villages, free from the noise of children and the aggravation of teenagers, began in the USA, and Berry Hill was one of the first to be built in Britain.

Berryhillock Possibly OScand *berg* 'hill' with tautological ModE *hillock*.

A small settlement in Moray (formerly in Banffshire, then in Grampian region), 6 km (4 miles) south of Cullen.

Berry Pomeroy *Berry* '(place at the) fortification', OE *byrig*, dative form of *burh* 'fortification' (*see* BURY), *Pomeroy* denoting manorial ownership in the Middle Ages by the de Pomerei family.

A village in Devon, about 1.5 km (1 mile) northeast of Totnes. Nearby is the ruined **Berry Pomeroy Castle**, a Norman fortress containing a great Tudor mansion built by Edward VI's regent, Protector Somerset (*see under* SOMERSET). The castle was badly damaged in the Civil Wars, and subsequently abandoned; it is now in the care of English Heritage.

The wedding of Marianne Dashwood and Colonel Brandon in Ang Lee's film (1995) of Jane Austen's *Sense and Sensibility* was filmed at Berry Pomeroy church.

Berwickshire From BERWICK-UPON-TWEED, now stranded on the wrong side of the English–Scottish border.

A former county of southeastern Scotland. It was bounded on the north by East Lothian, to the northeast by the North Sea, to the south by Northumberland and Roxburghshire, and to the west by Midlothian. The county town was DUNS. In 1975 most of it became the Berwickshire district of Borders region (*see under* the BORDERS), while small parts were attached to ROXBURGH and ETTRICK AND LAUDERDALE districts. Berwickshire district was abolished in 1996 when Scottish Borders unitary authority was formed.

Berwick-upon-Tweed 'barley farm on the River Tweed', OE *bere* 'barley' + WICK; the second part of the name distinguishes it from NORTH BERWICK.

A town in Northumberland, at the mouth of the River TWEED, some 90 km (56 miles) north of Newcastle. It is the most northerly town in England, and the only English town north of the Tweed. There is a legend that when the Devil was tempting Christ and showing him 'all the kingdoms of the world', he kept Berwick under his thumb to preserve it as his own special fiefdom.

Berwick was long disputed between the Scots and the English, changing hands 13 times. When Edward I took it in 1296, he massacred the inhabitants. Despite this instability, the town prospered and was Scotland's richest port; in medieval times it was known as **the Second Alexandria**. Berwick finally ended up in the possession of the English in 1482. Even so, it continued to be exposed to the aggression of both sides until 1551, when it was made a free BURGH by treaty between Edward VI and Mary Queen of Scots.

Fearing a joint Franco-Scottish attack, Elizabeth I spent a fortune on building the town's current artillery-proof fortifications, with their thick walls and bastions. These became irrelevant a few decades later with the Union of the Crowns, and it was at Berwick, 'the little door to the wide House of England', that in 1603 James VI of Scotland entered his new realm to become James I of England. Not happy with the old wooden bridge across which he had been obliged to traverse the Tweed, James spent £15,000 on a new bridge, built between 1611 and 1634 and still in use today. (It was later joined by the 28-arched Royal Border Railway Bridge, built by Robert Stephenson and opened by Queen Victoria in 1850, and by the Royal Tweed Bridge in 1928.) From 1604 to 1611 Berwick became the unofficial capital of Scotland, as the Earl of Dunbar ran Scottish affairs from his palace here (demolished in 1650 to build the town's towerless and steeple-less Holy Trinity Church, one of the few churches in Britain built during the Commonwealth period). Ravensdowne Barracks, based on a design by Nicolas Hawksmoor and among the earliest purpose-built barracks, were constructed between 1717 and 1725, following friction between soldiers and the townspeople upon whom they were billeted.

> It [Berwick] is old, decayed, and neither populous nor rich.
>
> Daniel Defoe: *A Tour Through the Whole Island of Great Britain* (1724–6)

Berwick retained its status as a free burgh until an Act of Parliament of 1885 included it in England, as part of Northumberland (leaving the county of Berwickshire stranded in Scotland). Prior to this, in some official documents 'Berwick-upon-Tweed' was added alongside 'Great Britain and Ireland'; it is said that at the outset of the Crimean War, war was declared against Russia in the name of Great Britain, Ireland and Berwick-upon-Tweed, but when it came to the peace treaty, Berwick's name was omitted – so the town is still technically at war with Russia.

The inhabitants themselves tend to regard themselves as **Berwickers** or Tweedsiders rather than Scots or English. However, the town's football team (**Berwick Rangers FC**, nicknamed the Borderers) plays in the Scottish League, and the Tweed here is classed as a Scottish water, so for fisherfolk rod licences are not required, although permits are.

John Wilkes, the radical politician and debauchee, made his first attempt to enter Parliament by standing for Berwick-upon-Tweed in 1754. Never one to baulk at ethical niceties, Wilkes attempted to block the arrival of a shipload of opposition voters sailing from London by bribing the captain to take them to Norway rather than Berwick. Despite this ruse, he lost the election.

> Berwick is an ancient town,
> A church without a steeple,
> A pretty girl at every door
> And very generous people.
>
> Anon.

A bridge without a middle arch,
A church without a steeple,
A midden heap in every street
And damned conceited people.

Robert Burns (1759–96) (attributed)

Berwick's history is piled layer upon layer in a hot and cold geology of Border misadventure.

Nicholas Crane: *Two Degrees West* (1999)

Duke of Berwick. The title of James Fitzjames (1670–1734), illegitimate son of James II, who awarded Fitzjames the dukedom of Berwick-upon-Tweed in 1687. Berwick fled with his father at the Glorious Revolution, and later, as a Marshal of France, led French forces to a number of victories against the Allies in the War of the Spanish Succession. After he lost his head to a cannonball at the Siege of Philipsburg, his old colleague Marshal Villars, who was dying a painful and lingering death, remarked, 'Ah, Berwick, he always had more luck than me.'

Treaty of Berwick (1357). A treaty by which the Scots paid a 100,000-mark ransom for the return of their king, David II, captured by the English at NEVILLE'S CROSS in 1346.

Treaty of Berwick (January 1560). A treaty by which Queen Elizabeth I of England and the Calvinist Lords of the Congregation in Scotland agreed to an alliance, and the expulsion from Scotland of French troops who were supporting the Catholic regent, Mary of Guise, mother of Mary Queen of Scots.

Treaty of Berwick (July 1586). An agreement between James VI of Scotland and Elizabeth I by which, in return for an English pension of £4000, both sides agreed to maintain their established religions and cooperate in case of an invasion of Britain by Catholic forces.

Treaty of Berwick (18 June 1639). The treaty that ended the first Bishops' War. It is also called the **Pacification of Berwick**. King Charles I agreed with the Scottish rebels that a General Assembly of the Scottish Church, the Kirk, would determine religious matters, and that a parliament would be summoned in Edinburgh; in return they stood down their forces.

Berwyn Mountains Possibly 'foaming', i.e. having white snowy summits, Welsh *berwyn* 'foaming, boiling', the second part from *gwyn* 'white'.

A range rising to the southwest of LLANGOLLEN, in Denbighshire, Wrexham and Powys (formerly in Clywd). The highest point is Moel Sych (827 m / 2713 ft).

There are towns called Berwyn in Canada (Alberta) and the USA (Illinois).

Besses o' th' Barn Thought to have derived from the name of the landlady of a local inn.

An urban area in Greater Manchester, to the south of

WHITEFIELD, Greater Manchester. The **Besses o' th' Barn Brass Band**, one of the oldest and considered by many to be the most famous, traces its origins to 1818.

Bessie Bell and Mary Gray After two heroines of an old ballad.

Two hills in County Tyrone, some 10 km (6 miles) north of Omagh, on either side of the road to Derry/Londonderry. It is said that they were so named by the Duke of Abercorn after two heroines in an old Scottish ballad mentioned by Sir Walter Scott in *Minstrelsy of the Scottish Border* (1802–3), in which the two young women friends are wooed by the same beau, and all three eventually die of plague despite having built themselves a retreat on the hillside. An alternative toponymical account explains that the two women were nannies in the Abercorn household.

Bestwood. A fictional coal-mining village in Nottinghamshire, which is the setting of D.H. Lawrence's autobiographical novel *Sons and Lovers* (1913). It is based on EASTWOOD[1], to the west of Nottingham, where Lawrence was born in 1885.

Bethania[1] After the Biblical town of Bethany, the home of Martha, Mary and Lazarus, where Jesus often stayed (Matthew 21:17, John 11:1). It was probably so named in the early 19th century, at the time of the Evangelical Revival.

A village in Ceredigion (formerly in Cardiganshire, then in Dyfed), 15 km (9 miles) north of Lampeter.

Bethania[2] *See* BETHANIA[1].

A village in Gwynedd (formerly in Merioneth), 3 km (2 miles) south of Blaenau Ffestiniog.

Bethesda From the name of the Nonconformist chapel built here in 1820, which took its name from a pool with healing properties in Jerusalem (John 5:2–9). It was formerly known as *Glanogwen*, Welsh 'bank of the River Ogwen'.

A small town in Gwynedd (formerly in Caernarvonshire), 8 km (5 miles) southeast of Bangor. It grew round the Penrhyn slate quarries in the 19th century (*see under* PENRHYN CASTLE).

Three things of slate in this village:
Work, home, and grave.

Edward Larrissy: 'Bethesda'

There is also a small village called Bethesda in Pembrokeshire. Bethesda, Maryland (USA), is a suburb of Washington DC, and took its name from the Bethesda Presbyterian Church built here in 1820. Appropriately enough, it is a centre of medical research.

Bethlehem After the town in Judah where Jesus was born. It was probably so named in the early 19th century, at the time of the Evangelical Revival.

A village in the Vale of Towy (*see under* TOWY),

Carmarthenshire (formerly in Dyfed), 6 km (4 miles) east of Llandeilo.

Bethnal Green *Bethnal* probably 'Blitha's corner of land', OE *Blithan* possessive form of male personal name *Blitha* + *halh* 'corner of land' (alternatively *Blitha* might be an OE stream name, meaning literally 'the gentle one'); the combination *Bethnal Green* is first recorded in 1443.

An area in East London, in the borough of TOWER HAMLETS (E1, E2, E3), to the northeast of the City of London and to the south of Hackney. Once a pleasant country village, by the middle of the 18th century it had become one of the poorest and most overcrowded areas of London, a network of slums in which people scraped a living working at home (making clothes or shoes, for example) for less than a pittance.

Victorian philanthropy and 20th-century slum clearance improved conditions, but the area's reputation as a dangerous nest of crime has been slow to dissipate (its cause was not helped by the activities of the locally based Kray gang in the 1960s and 1970s). It suffered the first fatalities from a V1 rocket attack in the Second World War, on 12 June 1944.

Bethnal Green Museum, now known as the Museum of Childhood, houses the doll and toy collections of the Victoria and Albert Museum. It opened in 1872, in a building moved from its original site in South Kensington. Nearby York Hall is a notable venue for boxing contests.

Bethnal Green Underground station, on the Central line, opened in 1946. It was the scene of a notable disaster in 1943 when 173 people were crushed or suffocated to death after panic-stricken crowds rushed into the as yet unopened station on hearing noises from the Army's experimental rocket firing in nearby Victoria Park, about which the population had not been informed. The incident was hushed up for morale reasons.

The footballer and manager Terry Venables (b.1943) was born in Bethnal Green.

See also the JAGO.

'Bethnal Green in the Sun'. A facetious nickname for the Spanish seaside resort of Marbella, which is situated on the Costa del Sol. The coastline as a whole was dubbed the 'Costa del Crime' in the 1960s and 1970s, when a significant proportion of the local population seemed to consist of British criminals fleeing justice (abetted by the lack of an Anglo-Spanish extradition treaty). The Bethnal Green fraternity evidently homed in on Marbella.

Betteshanger Probably 'wooded slope by a house or other building', OE (*ge*)*bytle* 'building, house' + *hangra* 'wooded slope'.

A mining village (pronounced 'bets–hanger') in the Kentish coalfield, about 5 km (3 miles) west of Deal. The last mine here closed in 1989.

Bettyhill Named after Elizabeth, 1st Countess of Sutherland, on its foundation in 1820.

A village on the north coast of Scotland, formerly in Sutherland and now in Highland, 12 km (7.5 miles) east of Tongue.

Bettystown Irish *Baile an Bhiataigh* 'homestead of Betagh'.

A small town on the east coast of County Meath, 7 km (4.5 miles) southeast of Drogheda.

Betws-y-coed 'prayer-house in the wood', OE *bed-hus* 'prayer house' + Welsh *y* 'the' + *coed* (*see* CED).

A small town and tourist centre (pronounced 'betoos-ah-coyd') in Conwy (formerly in Caernarvonshire, then in Gwynedd), some 14 km (8.5 miles) northeast of Blaenau Ffestiniog. Nearby are many attractive wooded gorges and waterfalls, including Swallow Falls, Conwy Falls and Fairy Glen.

Beulah¹ From the Biblical term (Hebrew for 'married woman') applied to Israel when blissfully returned to God's favour (Isaiah 62:4). In John Bunyan's *Pilgrim's Progress* (1678, 1684), the Land of Beulah is a land of heavenly joy where the pilgrims wait until they are summoned to the Celestial City. The Congregational chapel was built here in 1822.

A village in Powys (formerly in Brecknockshire), 12 km (7.5 miles) west of Builth Wells.

> Thou shalt no more be termed Forsaken; neither shall thy land any more be termed Desolate: but thou shalt be called Hephzibah, and thy land Beulah: for the Lord delighteth in thee, and thy land shall be married.

Beulah speckled-face sheep. A breed of sheep, with black-and-white speckled faces. They are common in the hills of Mid-Wales.

Beulah² *See* BEULAH¹.

A village in Ceredigion (formerly in Cardiganshire, then in Dyfed), 11 km (7 miles) east of Cardigan.

Beverley Probably 'beaver stream', OE *beofor* 'beaver' + *licc* 'stream'.

A market town in the East Riding of Yorkshire (formerly in Humberside), of which it is the administrative centre. It is 13 km (8 miles) northwest of Hull. An abbey was founded here by **St John of Beverley** (d.721), the archbishop of York who ordained the Venerable Bede. Because of St John's great reputation for sanctity, William the Conqueror spared the town of Beverley when he ravaged the rest of Yorkshire during the Harrying of the North (*see under* the NORTH). St John of Beverley is not to be confused with **John of Beverley** (*fl*.14th century), a Carmelite friar who was a doctor and professor of divinity at Oxford and the author of *Quaestiones in Magistrum Sententiarum* and *Disputationes Ordinariae*; nor with **Robert of Beverley** (*fl*.13th century), one of the architects of Westminster Abbey; nor indeed with St John Fisher (1469–1535), who was born in Beverley. Less easily confused with the above is **Constance of Beverley**, the perjured nun in Sir Walter Scott's *Marmion* (1808), who is discarded by the eponymous hero and walled up alive.

Beverley Minster (13th century) is a fine example of Gothic architecture, as is the church of St Mary's, also 13th century; the carving of the 'Pilgrim's Rabbit' in the latter is said to have been the model for Lewis Carroll's White Rabbit.

The Frithstool in Beverley Minster, dating from the 10th century, was the goal of fugitives, who could claim sanctuary if they reached it. It was King Athelstan (ruled 925–39) who made Beverley a sanctuary, after he had prayed successfully to St John of Beverley to give him victory over the Danes. Fugitives who reached the Frithstool were then offered the possibility of becoming 'Frithmen' if they gave all their property to the Crown and swore to become a servant of the Church and to live in Beverley in perpetuity.

> It is easy to conceive how Beverley became a town from this very article, namely, that all the thieves, murtherers, housebreakers and bankrupts, fled hither for protection ...
>
> Daniel Defoe: *A Tour Through the Whole Island of Great Britain* (1724–6)

There is a story that the reason that William the Conqueror spared the town was because one of his men, pursuing some of the townspeople into the sanctuary, was struck down by a flash of light and his body horribly mutilated.

In the 19th century Beverley was renowned for electoral shenanigans. The novelist Anthony Trollope stood for the seat in the 1870, but lost. After this the constituency was abolished.

On the western side of the town is **Beverley Westwood**, a large area of pastureland that includes the town's racecourse.

There is a town called Beverley in the USA (Massachusetts).

Bewcastle 'shelters at the Roman fort', OScand *buth* 'shelter' + OE *cæstre* (*see* CHESTER).
A village in Cumbria (formerly in Cumberland), 25 km (16 miles) northeast of Carlisle. It is on the site of a Roman fort called **Fanum Cocidi** ('temple of Cocidius', a Celtic war god).

Bewcastle Cross. A fine example of Anglo-Saxon sculpture, dating from the 8th century and similar in style to the Ruthwell Cross (*see under* RUTHWELL).

Bewdley 'beautiful place', OFr *beau* 'beautiful' + *lieu* 'place', *compare* BEAULIEU.
A town in Worcestershire (before 1998 in Hereford and Worcester, before 1974 in Worcestershire), on the River SEVERN, to the east of Wyre Forest, about 5 km (3 miles) west of Kidderminster. Its centre (prone to flooding by the river) is characterized by fine Georgian houses and a three-arched bridge designed by Thomas Telford. It was the birthplace of the British prime minister Stanley Baldwin (1867–1947).

Bewl Water *Bewl* is obscure, though it is found in the 16th century in the form Bewl Bridge, indicating that Bewl was a river name; *water* refers to the reservoir.
A large reservoir in East Sussex, on the Kent border, just to the east of WADHURST. It is the largest inland water in southeast England, 312 ha (770 acres) in extent. It is a popular centre for yachting, windsurfing, canoeing, etc.

Bexhill Originally *Bexley* 'box-tree glade', OE *byxe* 'box tree' + -LEY; the modern form was in existence by the end of the 14th century.
A town and seaside resort in East Sussex, 8 km (5 miles) west of HASTINGS. It was originally an inland village; development of the coastal area into a holiday resort began in the 1880s (the publicists backed it up by inventing the name **Bexhill-on-Sea**). The De La Warr Pavilion on the seafront, designed by Erich Mendelsohn and Chermayeff and built 1933–6, is one of the most notable Art Deco buildings in England.

The novelist Angus Wilson (1913–91) was born in Bexhill, and the comedian Eddie Izzard was brought up here.

> You can't get buried quickly in Bexhill-on-Sea; it's like getting a table at the Caprice.
>
> David Hare: quoted in Richard Eyre, *National Service: Diary of a Decade at the National Theatre* (2003)

Bexley 'box-tree glade', OE *byxe* 'box tree' + -LEY.
A town and borough in southeast Greater London, to the west of Dartford and the east of Greenwich (before 1965 in Kent). The original village, now distinguished by the name **Old Bexley**, was for many centuries an important agricultural centre, but the 20th century brought urbanization and considerable expansion. The borough of Bexley was formed in 1965 by combining the town of Bexley with Crayford, Erith and SIDCUP. Between 1950 and 2001 the former prime minister Edward Heath was MP for Bexley (the constituency was renamed Old Bexley and Sidcup during his tenure).

There is a town called Bexley in the South Island of New Zealand.

Bexleyheath *See* BEXLEY + *heath*; from the heathland originally lying to the north of Bexley.
A residential area of southeast Greater London, in the borough of BEXLEY (before 1965 in Kent). It was laid out from the early 19th century on what had been an open

heath to the north of Bexley. It was originally called **Bexley New Town**, but the name Bexleyheath is recorded from the 1870s.

The **Red House**, a notable example of English domestic architecture built in 1859 by Philip Webb for William Morris, is in Bexleyheath.

In 19th-century rhyming slang *Bexleyheath*, or *Bexley Heath*, stood for 'teeth'.

Bibury 'Beage's stronghold or manor house', OE female personal name *Beage* + *byrig* dative form of *burh* (*see* BURY).

A village in Gloucestershire on the River COLN, about 10 km (6.5 miles) east of Cirencester. William Morris, the moving spirit of the late 19th-century Arts and Crafts movement, considered it the most beautiful village in England. Its peaceful riverside setting, plus an abundance of well-preserved 17th- and 18th-century buildings – the latter testimony to Bibury's former wool-driven prosperity – draw tourists and trippers by the thousand in the summer.

Bibury is in fact a double village, and the more picturesque part of it, on the western bank of the Coln, is strictly speaking **Arlington**. **Arlington Row**, owned by the National Trust, is a photogenic riverside row of cottages, originally a 14th-century sheephouse then converted in the 17th century into cottages for weavers who used the mill stream in front of the cottages to wash and dye their cloth.

Bicester 'warriors' fort' or 'Beorna's fort', OE *beorna* possessive plural form of *beorn* 'warrior' or OE male personal name *Beorna* + *ceaster* (*see* CHESTER).

A market town (pronounced 'bister') in Oxfordshire, at the edge of the Vale of Aylesbury, about 19 km (12 miles) northeast of Oxford. It is in an area that has traditionally been fox-hunting country and provides essential back-up to participants, in the form of stabling, equipment, etc. **Bicester Village** is a 'park' of factory-outlet shops to which people flood in their tens of thousands at weekends from all over the Home Counties.

> There is little to see in Bicester, a small market town which, to judge from its buildings, has never been wealthy.
>
> Jennifer Sherwood and Nikolaus Pevsner: *The Buildings of England: Oxfordshire* (1974)

Bicknoller 'Bica's alder', OE *Bican* possessive form of male personal name *Bica* + OE *alor* 'alder tree'.

A village in northern Somerset, in the QUANTOCK HILLS, about 17.5 km (11 miles) west of Bridgwater. It was the birthplace of Harold Gimblett (1914–78), the heavy-hitting Somerset and England batsman nicknamed the '**Bicknoller Biffer**'. Despite his success, Gimblett's life was troubled psychologically: he committed suicide, thus prompting a

biography entitled *Harold Gimblett: The Tormented Genius of Cricket* (1982) by David Foot.

Biddenden 'Bida's woodland pasture', OE male personal name *Bida* + -ING + *denn* 'woodland pasture'.

A village in Kent, about 26 km (16 miles) east of Tunbridge Wells.

Biddenden Maids, the. The name given to Elizabeth and Mary Chulkhurst, Siamese twins joined at the hip and shoulder, who were born in Biddenden, supposedly around 1135 (an early 16th-century date is more likely). They survived to the age of 34, and died within hours of each other. They left the income from their property to provide bread and cheese for the poor, and this dole is still distributed on Easter Monday morning. By tradition this is known as the **Biddenden Dole**, and the hard biscuits that accompany the bread and cheese are **Biddenden cakes**.

Biddulph '(place) by the quarry', OE *bi* 'by' + *dylf* 'diggings'.

An industrial and former coal-mining town in the Staffordshire moorlands, 11 km (7 miles) north of Stoke-on-Trent, on the edge of the PEAK DISTRICT. Biddulph lies in a valley between the ridges of **Biddulph Moor** (the source of the River TRENT[1]) to the east and MOW COP[1] to the west.

Biddulph Grange garden, a restored Victorian garden originally created by the Bateman family between 1842 and 1871, is now owned by the National Trust.

See also KNYPERSLEY.

Bidean nam Bian Usually said to be 'sharp peak of the mountains', Gaelic *bidean* 'point, peak' + *nam* 'of the' + *beann* 'mountains'; alternatively the last word may be *bian* 'hide, pelt' (possibly referring to the stolen cattle hidden in the Lost Valley of Glen Coe (*see under* GLEN COE)). The difficulty here is that *nam* and *beann* are plural, but *bian* is singular, so linguistically 'of the mountains' is more plausible; but the name is ambiguous.

The highest mountain (1150 m / 3772 ft) in Glen Coe, Highland (formerly in Argyll), some 6 km (4 miles) southeast of Glencoe village. It is actually the highest point of a complex, rugged massif, which also includes the rocky peaks of Stob Coire nam Beith ('peak of the corrie of the birches'), Stob Coire nan Lochan ('peak of the corrie of the lochan'), Stob Coire Sgreamhach ('peak of the horrible or loathsome corrie') and the Three Sisters of Glen Coe (*see under* GLEN COE).

In the northeastern corrie of Bidean the summit rises above the twin buttresses known as Diamond Buttress and Churchdoor Buttress. The latter contains a peculiarly subterranean yet airy rock climb known as *Crypt Route* (1920); this involves in part a long and constricted wriggle through the mountain's dark innards, until one pops out the other end above a not inconsiderable abyss.

Bideford Perhaps 'ford at the River Byd', river name *Byd* (or possibly OE *byd* 'tub') + EA- + FORD.

A town and port in north Devon, close to the mouth of the River TORRIDGE[1], about 13 km (8 miles) southwest of Barnstaple. It is the main town of TORRIDGE[2] administrative district. Trade declined from the 18th century on, but before that it had been an important commercial port, and a considerable maritime centre in general: the naval hero Sir Richard Grenville (*c*.1541–91) was born in Bideford, and he had a Bideford crew aboard his ship the *Revenge* in his battle against overwhelming Spanish odds in the Azores in 1591.

> So Lord Howard passed away with five ships of war
>   that day
> Till he melted like a cloud in the silent summer heaven;
> But Sir Richard bore in hand all his sick men from the
>   land
> Very carefully and slow,
> Men of Bideford in Devon,
> And we laid them on the ballast down below;
> For we brought them all aboard,
> And they blessed him in their pain, that they were not
>   left to Spain,
> To the thumbscrew and the stake, for the glory of the
>   Lord.
>
>   Alfred, Lord Tennyson:'The Revenge' (1878)

Charles Kingsley wrote some of *Westward Ho!* (1855) in the Royal Hotel, Bideford, and it was the book's great success that led to the development of nearby WESTWARD HO!

Bideford Bay. A wide bay (also called Barnstaple Bay) on the North Devon coast. It is about 20 km (14 miles) across from BAGGY POINT in the northeast to HARTLAND POINT in the southwest. The combined mouths of the Rivers TAW and TORRIDGE[1] debouch into it.

Bideford Postman. An epithet applied (from his former occupation and abode) to Edward Capern (1819–94). His subsequent avocation is revealed by his later soubriquet 'the Devonshire poet'. The bell he carried on his postman's rounds still hangs in a niche in his tombstone at HEANTON PUNCHARDON.

Bidford-on-Avon *Bidford* either 'ford at the River Byd' (*see* BIDEFORD) or 'deep ford', OE *bydic* 'trough, deep place' + FORD. A village in Warwickshire, on the Warwickshire AVON[1], about 11 km (7 miles) west of Stratford-upon-Avon. In Roman times a road forded the river here, and in the Middle Ages an eight-arched bridge was built. Shakespeare is said to have frequented the Falcon Inn, and to have referred to the village as 'drunken Bidford'.
See also SHAKESPEARE VILLAGES.

Big Ben From the nickname of Sir Benjamin Hall, Commissioner of Works at the time when the bell was installed.
The original (and, to those of a pedantic turn of mind, still the only correct) application of this unofficial designation was to the 13-ton bell in the clock tower at the northern end of the Houses of Parliament in Westminster, London. This was cast in WHITECHAPEL and installed in 1859 and ever since has rung out the hours after the famous Westminster chimes. Before long the name was also being applied to the tower itself (officially St Stephen's Tower), whose unmistakable outline remains a symbol of British democracy around the world.

Bigbury 'Bica's stronghold', OE male personal name *Bica* + BURY.

A village in Devon, on the estuary of the River AVON[4], about 8 km (5 miles) northwest of Kingsbridge. The seaside village of **Bigbury-on-Sea** is about 2.5 km (1.5 miles) away, at the mouth of the Avon. Its Burgh Island Hotel (1932) is a notable example of English Art Deco architecture.

Bigbury Bay. A bay in south Devon, on the west side of the Kingsbridge peninsula, into which the River Avon flows. *See also* BOLT HEAD.

Bigbury Camp Uncertain, but *see* BURY, here referring to the hillfort, as also does ModE *camp*.

An Iron Age hillfort about 3 km (2 miles) west of Canterbury, constructed by the Belgae tribe. It was the forerunner of the Roman regional centre **Durovernum**, which later became CANTERBURY[1].

Biggar 'field of barley', OScand *bygg* 'barley' + *geiri* 'small or triangular plot of land'.

A royal BURGH (1451) in South Lanarkshire (formerly in Strathclyde region), 17 km (11 miles) southeast of Lanark. It has a strikingly wide main street, the site of a huge bonfire every Hogmanay, a tradition going back hundreds of years. During the Second World War locals kept the tradition going, without attracting the attention of German bombers, by burning a candle in a tin. In the early 1990s, after complaints by incomers, the organizers agreed with the local fire brigade that the fire could be put out at half past midnight. The firemen duly doused the fire, only for the locals to ignite it again with the aid of 30 gallons of diesel; the fire had indeed been put out, so it was felt that the agreement had been honoured. As the saying goes:

> London and Edinburgh are big, but Biggar's bigger.

Another annual ceremony is the crowning of the Fleming Queen in July, in memory of Mary Fleming of nearby Boghall Castle (only a small tower remains). The Flemings were the dominant local family, and Mary was one of the 'Four Marys' (ladies-in-waiting to Mary Queen of Scots).

From 1951 until his death in 1978 the Scots poet Hugh MacDiarmid (C.M. Grieve) lived in a cottage near Biggar.

There is a town called Biggar in Canada (Saskatchewan).

Biggin Hill 'hill with or near a building', ME *bigging* 'building'
+ OE *hyll* 'hill'.

A district in southeast GREATER LONDON, formerly a village
in Kent, about 11 km (7 miles) southeast of Croydon. Its
fame rests with its military airfield. This was already in use
in the First World War (which is when its nickname 'Biggin
on the Bump' was coined), but it really came into its own in
the Second World War, specifically in 1940, when the
Hurricanes of 32 Squadron and the Spitfires of 72, 94 and
610 Squadrons made RAF Biggin Hill a household name
throughout Britain. The RAF station closed after the war,
but there is still a civilian airfield here.

In 1951 Major the Rev. Vivian Symonds was appointed
to the living of St Mark's, Biggin Hill, the church then being
a 50-year-old building that had never been consecrated. In
order to rebuild it he obtained permission to use material
from a war-damaged church, All Saints' in PECKHAM, 27
km (17 miles) away. Standing in a lorry facing All Saints', he
is said to have commanded with military vigour, 'In the
name of Jesus Christ, be thou removed to Biggin Hill.' To
effect this he relied not on divine intervention but on his
own efforts and those of volunteers, by which over the
next three years St Mark's, 'The Moving Church', was
rebuilt.

Biggleswade 'Biccel's ford', OE *Bicceles* possessive form of
male personal name *Biccel* + *wæd* 'ford' (*see* FORD).

A town in Bedfordshire, on the River IVEL, about 15 km
(9 miles) southeast of Bedford, on the GREAT NORTH ROAD
(A1). The nearby Oldwarden (Biggleswade) Aerodrome
houses the Shuttleworth Collection of Historic Aeroplanes
and Cars.

Bignor 'Bicga's hill brow', OE *Bicgan* possessive form of male
personal name *Bicga* + *yfer* 'brow of a hill'.

A village in West Sussex, about 15 km (9 miles) northeast of
Chichester. In the early 19th century a farmer unearthed
a section of Roman mosaic flooring, depicting a dancing
girl, in one of his fields. Excavations, begun in 1811,
gradually uncovered **Bignor Roman Villa**, an extensive and
well-appointed dwelling that was probably occupied
between the 2nd and the 4th centuries AD and contains
some of the finest Roman mosaics ever discovered in Britain
(one, 25 m / 82 ft in length, is the longest on show in
Britain).

Big Pit, the. *See under* BLAENAVON.

Big Red Shed, the. The nickname for the Scottish
Exhibition and Conference Centre, built in the 1980s on
the north side of the Clyde to help make GLASGOW 'miles
better'.

Billericay Probably from Medieval Latin *bellerica* 'dyehouse,
tanhouse'.

A town in southwest Essex, about 8 km (5 miles) north-
east of Brentwood. It shared fully in the post-Second
World War demographic changes in this area (*see under*
ESSEX), epitomized for many by its late-20th-century
MP, the extrovert, anti-European Thatcherite Teresa
Gorman.

'Billericay Dickie'. A song (1977) by Ian Dury whose
characters (a tasty young man and his dubious girlfriends)
seem to prefigure Essex Man and Essex Girl (*see under*
ESSEX). It begins:

> Good evening! I'm from Essex, in case you
>   couldn't tell,
> My given name is Dickie, I come from Billericay,
> And I'm doin' very well.
> 'ad a love affair with Nina
> In the back of my Cortina,
> A seasoned-up hyena
> Could not've been more obscener.

Billingham 'Bill's or Bill's people's homestead', OE male
personal name *Bill* + -*ing*- or -*inga*- (*see* -ING) 'family, followers'
+ HAM.

An industrial town in Stockton-on-Tees unitary authority
(formerly in County Durham, then in Cleveland), 5 km
(3 miles) northwest of Middlesbrough.

Billingsgate 'Billing's gate' (probably referring to a gap in
the Roman riverside wall, giving access to the Thames), OE
Billinges possessive form of male personal name *Billing* + OE
geat 'gate'.

London's principal fish market. From at least the 13th century, fish were landed at a wharf on its site, on the north
bank of the River THAMES[1] to the west of the TOWER OF
LONDON, but it was at first a general market. Its restriction
to fish dates from 1698, and until the 19th century it was
just a collection of sheds. Palazzo-like premises were
provided for it in the 1870s in Lower Thames Street (EC3).

Billingsgate's porters were famous for their characteristic leather hats (said to have been modelled on those of
English archers at Agincourt), on which they carried
unfeasibly tall loads of fish. They also acquired a reputation for vigorous expletives, and from the 17th to the 20th
century **Billingsgate** was a metaphor for abusive language.

The market eventually became too big and far-reaching for its building, and in 1982 it moved to a new site on
the ISLE OF DOGS (still retaining the name 'Billingsgate').

Billy Row *Billy* refers to nearby Billy Hill, OE *billing* 'prominent
hill'; *Row* OE *raw* 'row of houses'.

A village in County Durham, just north of Crook.

Bilston 'farmstead of the dwellers at the sharp ridge', OE *bill*
'sharp ridge' + *sætna* possessive form of *sæte* 'dwellers'
+ -TON.

A town in the West Midlands, about 4 km (2.5 miles) southeast of Wolverhampton (and now a district within the

metropolitan borough of Wolverhampton). **Wolverhampton and Bilston Athletics Club** has to some extent lifted its name from obscurity.

Binegar Probably 'Beage's wooded slope', OE *Beagan* possessive form of female personal name *Beage* + *hangra* 'wooded slope'.

A village (pronounced to rhyme with *vinegar*) in Somerset, in the MENDIP HILLS, about 6.5 km (4 miles) north of Shepton Mallet.

Bingley 'Bynna's people's clearing', OE male personal name *Bynna* + *-inga-* (*see* -ING) 'family, followers' + -LEY.

A woollen-textile and engineering town on the River AIRE in West Yorkshire, 8 km (5 miles) northwest of Bradford. Bingley lies on the Leeds–Liverpool canal, which rises out of the Aire Valley here via the Five Rise Locks. Bingley was granted a manor and a market charter by King John in 1213, and throughout the Middle Ages was an important market town. The Airedale Agricultural Society Show, or **Bingley Show**, founded in 1878, is still held here annually on the first Wednesday in August.

It was in Bingley that the Airedale terrier (*see under* AIRE) was first developed in the mid-19th century. Probably the most celebrated non-canine sons of Bingley, however, are the astronomer and writer Fred Hoyle (b.1915) and the showjumper Harvey Smith (b.1938).

Binn Éadair. The Irish name for HOWTH.

BinnGhulbáin. The Irish name for BENBULBEN.

Binns, The 'the hills', Gaelic *beinn* 'hill' + English plural *-s*.

An old mansion in West Lothian, some 6 km (4 miles) east of Linlithgow. The lands round about have been known as The Binns since at least the 14th century, the name presumably referring to the low hills. The house, dating mostly from the 17th century, was long in the possession of the Dalyell family. General Tam Dalyell (1599–1685), scourge of the Covenanters and victor of RULLION GREEN, raised the Royal Scots Greys here in 1681. He is said by his enemies to have built the towers of the house to prevent the Devil from blowing it away. Another story tells how Dalyell and the Devil were playing cards in the house one night. When Dalyell won, the Devil was so furious that he hurled a marble table at Dalyell. 'Bloody Tam' ducked and the table sailed through a window to land in Sergeant's Pond. The table was found in the pond in 1878, and is now back in the house.

Dalyell's namesake and descendant, the independent-minded Labour MP Tam Dalyell, was Father of the House of Commons from 2001. He still lives in part of The Binns, which is now owned by the National Trust for Scotland.

Binsey 'Byni's island' OE personal name *Byni* + *eg* (*see* -EY, -EA).

A tiny THAMES[1]-side hamlet in Oxfordshire, opposite PORT

MEADOW, 2.5 km (1.5 miles) northwest of Oxford city centre. Any fame that attaches to Binsey (other than its perennially popular pub, The Perch) rests entirely on its being the subject of an environmental elegy by the poet Gerard Manley Hopkins (written 1879, published 1918) bewailing the felling here of a row of poplars by the Thames towpath:

> My aspens dear, whose airy cages quelled,
> Quelled or quenched in leaves the leaping sun,
> All felled, felled, are all felled;
> …
> When we hew or delve:
> After-comers cannot guess the beauty been.
> Ten or twelve, only ten or twelve
> Strokes of havoc únselve
> The sweet especial scene,
> Rural scene, a rural scene,
> Sweet especial rural scene.
>
> Gerard Manley Hopkins: 'Binsey Poplars' (*felled 1879*)

History repeated itself in 2002 when some of the poplars replanted on the site of the trees so loved by Hopkins were felled by Oxford City Council as they had supposedly become dangerous.

Biorra. The Irish name for BIRR.

Birdcage Walk From an aviary for exotic birds in St James's Park known as 'The Bird Cage', originally built by James VI and I in the early 17th century and later enlarged by his grandson Charles II.

A street in Central London, in the City of WESTMINSTER (SW1), running along the south side of St James's Park (*see under* ST JAMES'S). Wellington Barracks are at its western end.

Birdfield Possibly self-explanatory.

A small settlement in Argyll and Bute (formerly in Argyll, then in Strathclyde region), on the northwest shore of LOCH FYNE, 11 km (7 miles) northeast of Lochgilphead.

Birdlip Probably 'steep place frequented by birds', OE *brydd* 'bird' + *hlep* 'steep place'.

A village in Gloucestershire, about 9 km (5.5 miles) southeast of Gloucester.

Birgham-on-Tweed 'homestead by the river-crossing' *Brycgham*, OE *brycg* 'bridge, river-crossing' + HAM.

A small village on the River TWEED, in Scottish Borders (formerly in Berwickshire), 6 km (3.5 miles) west of Coldstream. Birgham is at the southernmost point at which the river forms the border between England and Scotland, and was for long a venue for talks between the two sides.

Treaty of Birgham (1290). An agreement by which Margaret, the infant queen of Scotland, was to marry Edward, Prince of Wales, the son of Edward I of England. Margaret – known as the 'Maid of Norway' – was the granddaughter of Alexander III, by his daughter's marriage to Eric II of Norway. Unfortunately for the relations between the two countries, Margaret died in ORKNEY in September 1290 on her way to Scotland from Norway.

Birkdale 'valley with birch trees'; OScand *birki* 'birch-tree' + *dalr* 'valley'.

A suburb of SOUTHPORT, Merseyside, and home to **Royal Birkdale** golf club. The course was laid out in 1897 (though the club had opened here in 1889). It is now the venue for international championships, including the Open, which has been held here seven times between 1954 and 2000.

Birkenhead 'headland where birch-trees grow', OE *birce* 'birch-tree' + *heafod* 'headland'.

A town and port towards the northeastern corner of the WIRRAL, in the metropolitan area of Merseyside (before 1974 in Cheshire). It is linked by road tunnel – the Mersey Tunnel (*see under* MERSEY) – rail tunnel and ferry with LIVERPOOL, on the opposite bank of the Mersey.

Its historical kernel is **Birkenhead Priory**, a Benedictine house founded in the 12th century. The place remained a quiet hamlet until the early 19th century, when the introduction of the Liverpool ferry encouraged settlement from the other side of the river. William Laird established a small shipbuilding yard here in the 1820s (the first iron vessel in England was built there in 1829) and the first docks were opened in 1847, fuelling Birkenhead's expansion and enrichment in the later 19th and early 20th centuries. The huge Cammell Laird yards produced some of Britain's mightiest ships (such as the liner *Mauretania*, the aircraft-carrier *Ark Royal*, the Second World War battleship *Prince of Wales* and the nuclear submarines *Renown* and *Revenge*). The first public park in Britain was opened in Birkenhead in 1834.

The Boy Scout movement was inaugurated in Birkenhead by Robert Baden-Powell in 1908.

The journalist J.L. Garvin (1868–1947), legendary editor of *The Observer* from 1908 to 1942, and the actress and Labour politician Glenda Jackson (b.1936) were born in Birkenhead, as was the flamboyant Conservative politician F.E. Smith (1872–1930), who took the title **Lord Birkenhead** when appointed lord chancellor in 1919.

> The Union Jacks at our masthead,
> And bosun roars to wake the dead.
> We'll soon be level with Birkenhead –
> Come and get your oats me son.
>
> Anon.: 'Whup Jamboree'

HMS *Birkenhead*. A Royal Navy paddle-steamer which sank off Cape Town on 25 February 1852 while transporting 480 soldiers and 13 women and children. Almost all the soldiers were killed, having been ordered to remain on board until the women and children had been safely got off. The episode was subsequently cited as an example of both heroic courage and needless sacrifice.

Birmingham 'Beorma's people's homestead' or 'homestead associated with Beorma', OE male personal name *Beorma* + *-inga-* (*see* -ING) + HAM.

A city and metropolitan borough in the WEST MIDLANDS (before 1974 in Warwickshire), about 192 km (120 miles) from London and 142 km (89 miles) from Manchester. Until the end of the 18th century it was a modest market town, specializing in the manufacture of cutlery and edged weapons; but two major factors initiated its growth to a major industrialized city by the end of the 19th: a large supply of local labour skilled in metal-working, and equally large local supplies of coal and iron. Factories and works turned out locomotives, machines, weapons (Birmingham's growth in the 18th and 19th centuries was fuelled by small-arms manufacture, and it was a major centre for the making of munitions in the two World Wars) and in due course cars (Birmingham was at the heart of the 20th-century West Midlands automotive industry; *see also* LONGBRIDGE and SOLIHULL); and as the town's economy and its boundaries both steadily expanded, Birmingham became known as both 'the workshop of the world' (appropriating an epithet originally applied to ENGLAND itself) and as England's 'second city' (it was officially granted city status in 1889, a mere 51 years after it had been designated a borough). The downside of its reputation was that it became known as a mass-producer of rather cheap and tatty manufactured goods (trinkets, imitation jewellery and the like), to which the name 'Birmingham', or its alternative BRUMMAGEM, became attached (*see also* the TOYSHOP OF EUROPE). The city's conventional abbreviation is BRUM.

Birmingham supported Parliament in the Civil Wars (it was sacked by the Royalists under Prince Rupert in 1643), and was the main supplier of weapons for Cromwell's armies. A similar spirit of obstinate independence fuelled its rise towards the top of England's municipal tree in the 19th century. It was led then by a number of oustanding local politicians, notable among them Joseph Chamberlain (*see below*). Birmingham was also a centre of Nonconformism in the 19th century (Joseph Priestley, the chemist who discovered oxygen, was a Unitarian who moved to Birmingham in 1780).

Other scientists and engineers associated with Birmingham, aside from Priestley (who fled to America following the **Birmingham Riots**; *see below*), include Matthew Boulton and James Watt, who produced steam engines at their Soho Works at nearby SMETHWICK in the second half of the 18th century, and William Murdock, a Soho employee, who pioneered the use of coal gas for lighting at the beginning of the 19th century.

A key factor in Birmingham's success was always its

excellent transport links. In the 18th century it was canals (more miles, it is said, than Venice, and extensively restored in the latter part of the 20th century; the romantically named Gas Street Basin, hub of the city's canal network, is now a showpiece); in the 19th century, the railway (the main station is New Street); and in the 20th century, roads: Birmingham is at the centre of a network of (often jam-clogged) roads and motorways (*see also* SPAGHETTI JUNCTION). Birmingham Airport is also an important international intersection (hence its designation 'Eurohub').

After the Second World War, the centre of the city was extensively redeveloped, producing a landscape of flyovers, ring roads and tower blocks that many have judged at best anonymous, at worst disorienting and depressing (*see also* BULL RING[1]). Not all Brummies (or outsiders) share that view, and even if they do they can point to such positive alternative features of the city as the **City of Birmingham Symphony Orchestra** (raised to world-class level by Sir Simon Rattle and now housed in the brand-new Symphony Hall), the handsome National Exhibition Centre and International Conference Centre, the **University of Birmingham** (which received its Royal Charter in 1900; *see also* ASTON) and EDGBASTON Cricket Ground. The city's Science Museum has a huge collection of the machines and apparatus produced by Birmingham's science and industry over the centuries.

Nor is Birmingham's earlier architectural and cultural heritage to be sneezed at. Nineteenth-century civic pride was responsible for the imposing Town Hall (1834; designed in classical style by Joseph Hansom (of Hansom cab fame) and closely modelled on the Roman temple in Nîmes), the Council House of 1879 and the redbrick Roman Catholic St Chad's Cathedral (designed by A.W. Pugin). (The Anglican Cathedral of St Philip was originally a parish church, consecrated in 1715. When the diocese of Birmingham was created in 1905, it was raised to cathedral status.)

The **Birmingham Museum and Art Gallery** houses (among many other treasures) a remarkable collection of pre-Raphaelite art, including Dante Gabriel Rossetti's *First Anniversary of the Death of Beatrice* (1849) and Ford Madox Brown's *The Last of England* (1855). Many of Birmingham-born Burne-Jones's (*see below*) most notable works are here, including the *Star of Bethlehem*, one of the largest watercolours ever painted, which was commissioned by the Gallery in 1897. Some of the Museum's collection is now in Aston Hall, just to the north of Aston, one of the finest Jacobean country houses in England, built between 1618 and 1635 by Sir Thomas Holt (1571–1654). Queen Victoria stayed there in 1853.

Lawn tennis was invented in Birmingham. Birmingham's eponymous football club, **Birmingham City FC**

(nicknamed the Blues), was founded in 1875 and plays its home matches at St Andrews. The comedian Jasper Carrott, a club supporter, remarked in 1979 of his side's often undistinguished history, 'You lose some, you draw some.' Birmingham City bucked this trend by being promoted to the Premier League in 2002, but historically speaking greater successes have tended to come the way of Birmingham's other prominent club, Aston Villa (*see under* ASTON).

The writer (and former University of Birmingham professor) David Lodge (b.1935) has memorably recast Birmingham as RUMMIDGE in his comic novels of academic life.

The artist Edward Burne-Jones (1833–98), the writer Rex Warner (1905–86), the comedian Tony Hancock (1924–68) and the theatre critic Kenneth Tynan (1927–80) were all born in Birmingham, as were the political half-brothers Austen (1863–1937) and Neville Chamberlain (1869–1940; prime minister 1937–40). The Chamberlain-family connection with Birmingham ran deep: their father Joseph (1836–1914) made a fortune in the Birmingham screw-manufacturing business, was elected a Liberal MP for Birmingham in 1876, and was three times mayor of the city.

There are towns called Birmingham in the USA (Alabama, Iowa and Michigan) and in Canada (Saskatchewan).

> … full of inhabitants, and resounding with hammer and anvils, for most of them are smiths. The lower part thereof standeth very waterish.
>
> William Camden: *Britannia* (1596)

> One has no great hopes from Birmingham. I always say there is something direful in the sound.
>
> Mrs Elton in Jane Austen: *Emma* (1816)

> [Birmingham is] a disgusting town with villas and slums and ready made clothes shops and Chambers of Commerce.
>
> Evelyn Waugh: diary (1925)

See also BALTI TRIANGLE, BOURNVILLE, CHAD VALLEY, ERDINGTON, GRAVELLY HILL, HANDSWORTH, KING'S NORTON, KING'S OAK, LADYWOOD, MOSELEY[1], NORTHFIELD, PERRY BAR, SAREHOLE, SELLY OAK, SHIRLEY[3] *and* YARDLEY.

anti-Birmingham. A term (also **anti-Bromingham**) applied in the late 17th century to opponents of the anti-Catholic Exclusion Bill of 1680 (for its origin, *see* BRUMMAGEM). Another, almost contemporary nickname for them, 'Tory', has survived a good deal longer.

Birmingham Poet. An epithet given to John Freeth, who died at the age of 78 in 1808. He was a wit, a poet and a publican, who not only wrote the words and tunes of poems, but also sang them.

Birmingham Post, The. A broadsheet newspaper for the Midlands region, founded in 1857, and now owned by the Trinity Mirror Group (which also owns the *Evening Mail*, another Birmingham newspaper).

Birmingham Riots. Anti-revolutionary riots in Birmingham on 14 July 1791, when a mob attacked the house of the scientist Joseph Priestley who was giving a dinner in celebration of the storming of the Bastille in Paris.

Birmingham Six. The six Irishmen who were arrested following the IRA bombing of two crowded Birmingham pubs on 21 November 1974, killing 21 and wounding more than 150. Billy Power, Gerry Hunter, Hugh Callaghan, John Walker, Paddy Joe Hill and Dick McIlkenny were tried in 1975, convicted on 21 murder counts and sentenced to life imprisonment. Subsequent appeals against the sentence failed until 1991, when they were said to have been wrongly convicted, and freed.

Birnam Possibly 'homestead of the warriors', OE *beorn* 'warrior' + HAM.

A village on the south side of the River TAY, opposite Dunkeld, 20 km (12.5 miles) north of Perth. It is in Perth and Kinross (formerly in Perthshire, and then in Tayside region).

Just south of the town rises **Birnam Hill** (404 m / 1324 ft), while 2 km (1.2 miles) to the southwest is the **Birnam Wood** immortalized by Shakespeare. In 1045 the real Macbeth – having assumed the Scottish throne after defeating and killing Duncan in a battle near Elgin (not murdering him in bed) – defeated a rebel army near Birnam. This may account for the mention of Birnam Wood in Shakespeare's *Macbeth*, when the Third Apparition conjured by the witches prophesies:

Macbeth shall never vanquish'd be until
Great Birnam wood to high Dunsinane Hill
Shall come against him.

William Shakespeare: *Macbeth* (1606), IV.i

DUNSINANE Hill (the site of Macbeth's castle in the play) is some 20 km (12.5 miles) to the southeast, and Birnam Hill is visible from there. The remains of a fort on Birnam Hill is called Duncan's Camp, and the rock on the summit is called King's Seat. In Shakespeare's play, the catch in the Third Apparition's prophesy is that Malcolm, 'before Birnam wood', hatches a cunning plan to camouflage his army advancing on Dunsinane:

Let every soldier hew him down a bough
And bear't before him; thereby shall we shadow
The numbers of our host, and make discovery
Err in report of us.

Macbeth, V.iv

The great Scottish fiddler Neil Gow (1727–1807) was born, and died, in Birnam, and lived nearby.

Birr Irish *Biorra* 'stream, watery place'.

A small town in County Offaly, 40 km (25 miles) west of Portlaoise. It is pronounced 'burr' (leading to the jokey suggestion that it is the coldest place in Ireland). **St Brendan of Birr** (d.*c*.573) built a monastery here in the 6th century, but there is nothing left of it. From 1620 until 1922 Birr was known as **Parsonstown**, after Sir Lawrence Parsons, who was granted the estate by James VI and I. The Parsons family, who became earls of Rosse, have lived in Birr Castle ever since (although the castle changed hands a few times in the upheavals of the 17th century). It was here that the 3rd Earl, William Parsons (1800–67), a noted astronomer, installed the **Leviathan of Parsonstown** (also called the Rosse Telescope) a vast 180-cm (72-in) telescope which was, at the time, the largest in the world; with it Parsons discovered many a spiral nebula. The telescope was restored in 1996–7, and visitors to the castle and its fine grounds may view it in action. (It was the 3rd Earl's youngest son, Charles Parsons, who invented the steam turbine engine.) In 1888 Birr was the location of the first All-Ireland hurling championship.

Council of Birr. A gathering in the later 7th century at which St Adamnan introduced a variety of reforms, particularly in relation to women, such as allowing them exemption from military service.

Birreencorragh Etymology unknown.

The highest peak (697 m / 2286 ft) in the NEPHIN Beg Range of County Mayo, some 20 km (12 miles) northwest of Castlebar.

Biscay. A sea area in the shipping forecast. It is in the Bay of Biscay, between FitzRoy to the west and Plymouth to the north.

Biscuitopolis. A 19th-century nickname for READING, the site of a Huntley and Palmer factory.

Bishop Auckland 'land belonging to the bishop at the cliff on the river Clyde', OCelt *allt* 'cliff' + river name *Clut* identical with the CLYDE, and meaning 'cleansing one'; the bishop was the Bishop of Durham, the Clyde a former name of the River Gaunless, OScand *gegn-lauss* 'profitless'.

A town on the River Gaunless, a tributary of the WEAR, in County Durham, 14 km (8.5 miles) southwest of Durham itself. **Auckland Castle** has been the country home of the bishops of Durham since the 12th century, and is now their official residence.

Bishopbriggs 'the fields of the bishop (of Glasgow)', Scots *rigs* 'fields, cultivated ridges'.

A small suburban town in East Dunbartonshire (formerly in Strathclyde) to the north of Glasgow and contiguous with it. The actor Dirk Bogarde spent a miserable period of his childhood here, as described in his memoir *A Postillion Struck by Lightning* (1977). Its other literary association is with the middlebrow publishing firm of Wm. Collins (now Murdoch'd into HarperCollins), whose Scottish editors continue (if in diminishing numbers) to languish on a barren industrial estate on the north side of the town.

Bishop Rock Originally *Maenenescop*, 'the stone of the bishop', Cornish *men* 'stone' + *an* 'the' + *escop* 'bishop', later translated into English.

A rocky islet that is the westernmost of the SCILLY ISLES. At over 48 m (160 ft), its lighthouse is the tallest in England.

Bishops and Clerks Apparently named from the rocks' proximity to the cathedral of ST DAVID'S.

A series of rocks off RAMSEY ISLAND and St David's Head, Pembrokeshire (formerly in Dyfed). One wit noted that:

> They keepe residence better than the rest of the canons of that see [St David's] are wont to do.

> George Owen: notes to his 1602 map, quoted in R. Fenton,
> *A Historical Tour through Pembrokeshire* (1903)

Bishop's Cannings *Bishop's* because in former times it was owned by the bishops of Salisbury; *Cannings* '(settlement of) Cana's people', OE male personal name *Cana* + *-ingas* (*see* -ING).

A village in Wiltshire, about 5 km (3 miles) northeast of Devizes.

Bishop's Caundle *Bishop's* because in former times it was owned by the bishops of Salisbury; *Caundle* of uncertain origin – perhaps from a former local hill name.

A village in Dorset, in the Blackmoor Vale, about 8 km (5 miles) southeast of Sherborne.

See also PURSE CAUNDLE *and* STOURTON CAUNDLE.

Bishop's Cleeve *Bishop's* because in former times it was owned by the bishops of Worcester; *Cleeve* '(place at the) cliff', OE *clife* dative form of *clif* 'cliff, bank'.

A small town in Gloucestershire, about 5 km (3 miles) northeast of Cheltenham. CLEEVE HILL is about 2.5 km (1.5 miles) to the southeast.

Bishopsgate *Bishops* from the tradition that it was rebuilt in the late 7th century by *Eorconweald*, Bishop of London.

Originally, the main northern gate of the Roman city of LONDON, through which ERMINE STREET ran. It was built around AD 200, and its final incarnation was pulled down in 1760.

By then, the name of the gate had been transferred to the road running through it, which goes from just north of LIVERPOOL STREET down to the junction of CORNHILL and LEADENHALL STREET. The ancient and tiny church of St Ethelburga in Bishopsgate, dating from the early 13th century, was destroyed by an IRA bomb in 1993 (it has since been rebuilt). In Elizabethan times the street was lined with fine merchants' houses, and the magnificently carved frontage of Sir Paul Pindar's house is now on display in the Victoria and Albert Museum.

The extensive **Bishopsgate Goods Yard** on the line into Liverpool Street station, which contained some unique examples of early Victorian brick railway arches, was controversially demolished at the beginning of the 21st century to make way for an extension to the East London line (*see under* EAST LONDON). Liverpool Street Underground station on the Metropolitan line was originally called 'Bishopsgate'; the name was changed in 1909.

Bishop's Isles So named because the islands were for a long time in the possession of the church.

A collective name for the small islands forming the tail of the Outer HEBRIDES south of Barra and Vatersay, including SANDRAY, PABBAY[1], MINGULAY and BERNERAY[1]. They are also known as the **Barrahead Islands**, after Barra Head on Berneray, the southernmost tip of the Outer Hebrides.

Bishop's Stortford *Bishop's* because in former times it was owned by the bishops of London; *Stortford* 'ford by the tongues of land', OE *steort* 'tongue of land' + FORD.

A market town in Hertfordshire (close to the county border with Essex), on the River STORT, about 13 km (8 miles) northeast of Harlow. It was a staging-post on the mail-coach routes from London to Cambridge and Newmarket, so there are a lot of old coaching-inns here.

The imperialist and business magnate Cecil Rhodes (1853–1902) was born in Bishop's Stortford.

Bishop's Waltham 'bishop's forest homestead', OE *weald* 'forest' + HAM. The forest in question was held by the bishops of Winchester.

A town in Hampshire, 16 km (10 miles) southeast of Winchester. The town was originally in the see of Winchester, but it is now in the Portsmouth diocese. The Bishop's Palace, built by Bishop Henry de Blois (brother of Stephen of Blois, i.e. King Stephen of England) around 1135, was completely destroyed during the Civil Wars in 1644. The ruins are open to the public.

Bishopwearmouth. *See under* SUNDERLAND *and* WEAR

Bisley[1] 'Byssa's glade', OE male personal name *Byssa* + -LEY.

A village in Surrey, about 5 km (3 miles) west of Woking. It is the home of competitive firearm shooting in Britain, and the site of the National Rifle Association ranges and the National Shooting Centre.

Bisley[2]. A village in Gloucestershire, high up in the COTSWOLDS, about 6 km (4 miles) east of Stroud.

Bitches, the. *See under* RAMSEY ISLAND.

Bitterne Perhaps 'house near a bend', OE *byht* 'bend' + *ærn* 'house'.

A district of SOUTHAMPTON, on the eastern side of the River ITCHEN.

Bix '(place at the) box-tree wood', OE *byxe* 'box-tree wood'.
A village in Oxfordshire, about 5 km (3 miles) northwest of Henley-on-Thames. One of Britain's first dual carriageways (from Henley through the middle of Bix) was built here in the 1930s.

Bla Bheinn 'blue mountain', OScand *bla* 'blue' + Gaelic *beinn* 'mountain'; it is earlier recorded as OScand *Bla Fjall* with the same meaning.
An isolated, rocky peak (928 m / 3044 ft) of the Black CUILLIN of Skye, separated from the main ridge by a deep glen. The spelling is often anglicized to **Blaven**, although the old spelling, **Blaavin**, recalls the name's partially Norse origins. The first recorded ascent, in 1857, was by a pair of radical republican atheists and ardent drinkers, Professor John Nichol of Glasgow University and the flagellatory poet Charles Algernon Swinburne, a fellow Balliol man.

Blaby Probably 'Blar's farmstead or village', OScand male personal name *Blar* + -BY.
A village in Leicestershire, on the southern outskirts of Leicester. Between 1974 and 1992 it was the parliamentary constituency of Nigel Lawson, chancellor of the exchequer from 1983 to 1989: he subsequently took the title 'Baron Lawson of Blaby' on his elevation to the House of Lords.

Blackamore. An old name for the NORTH YORK MOORS.

Blackbird Leys Earlier *Blackford*, a reference to a dark-coloured ford of the Thames near Sandford, with ME *leys* 'pasture, meadow'.
An outer southwestern suburb of OXFORD, mainly taken up by a large housing estate built in the late 1950s and early 1960s by Oxford City Council. Its population is generally low-income, and at the end of the 20th century it acquired a reputation for youthful lawlessness (notably car crime).

Blackboys From the name of the local *Blakeboy* family, known here from the end of the 14th century.
A village in East Sussex, about 5 km (3 miles) east of Uckfield.

Blackburn 'dark stream', OE *blæc* 'black, dark' + *burna* 'stream'.
An industrial city in Blackburn with Darwen unitary authority, of which it is the administrative centre. It was formerly in Lancashire, and is 14 km (8.5 miles) east of Preston. Flemish weavers settled here in the 14th century, and Blackburn later became the centre of the Lancashire cotton-weaving industry until its decline in the mid-20th century. The parish church became a cathedral when the diocese of

Blackburn was created in 1926. The diocese covers most of Lancashire.

Blackburn was the birthplace of the contralto Kathleen Ferrier (1912–53). James Hargreaves (*c*.1720–78), the inventor of the spinning jenny, was born at nearby OSWALDTWISTLE; in 1768 a mob of outraged spinners from Blackburn, threatened by this new invention, destroyed his house and equipment. Blackburn has had some notable MPs, including Philip Snowden, Barbara Castle and Jack Straw.

> I read the news today oh boy,
> Four thousand holes in Blackburn, Lancashire,
> And though the holes were rather small
> They had to count them all,
> Now they know how many holes it takes to fill the Albert Hall.
>
> John Lennon and Paul McCartney: 'A Day in the Life', from *Sergeant Pepper's Lonely Hearts Club Band* (1967)

This verse was inspired by an article in *The Daily Mail*:

> There are 4000 holes in the road in Blackburn, Lancashire, or one twenty-sixth of a hole per person, according to a council survey. If Blackburn is typical, there are two million holes in Britain's roads and 300,000 in London.
>
> *Daily Mail* (17 January 1967)

Blackburn Rovers FC. Blackburn's football club (nicknamed the Blue and Whites) began life as Blackburn Grammar School Old Boys before turning professional in 1880, thereafter becoming one of the most successful teams of the pre-First World War era, and enjoying a keen local rivalry with nearby BURNLEY. Glory returned in 1995, when Blackburn won the Premier League title under the management of Kenny Dalglish. Blackburn Rovers play their home games at Ewood Park.

Blackburn with Darwen. A unitary authority created in 1998 out of part of LANCASHIRE. The administrative centre is BLACKBURN, and the River DARWEN runs through it.

Black Carls, the. *See under* BEINN EIGHE.

Black Country, the. An unflattering name coined in the early 19th century (and first recorded in 1834) for a heavily industrialized area of what is now the WEST MIDLANDS, centred on DUDLEY and including also WALSALL, WEDNESBURY, WEST BROMWICH and WOLVERHAMPTON. The local collieries, blast furnaces, foundries and metal industries blackened the area with soot and smoke, creating a desolate, almost infernal environment.

> By night the Black Country blazes up lurid and red with fires which are never extinguished.
>
> *Daily Telegraph* (1864)

Coal-mining ceased here in 1968, so the area is no

longer as 'black' as it used to be, and in the 21st century its leviathans have largely been replaced by light industries; but even its most loyal inhabitants would not call the Black Country a beauty spot. Its industrial heritage is the subject of the notable **Black Country Museum**, near Dudley.

Black Cuillin. *See under* the CUILLIN.

Black Dog From the name of a local public house.

A village in Devon, about 16 km (10 miles) southwest of Tiverton.

Blackdog Possibly ModE, a fanciful name from the dangerous rock.

A small settlement in Aberdeenshire (formerly in Grampian region), on the coast 8 km (5 miles) north of Aberdeen. Just offshore is **Blackdog Rock**.

Blackdown Hills *Blackdown* 'dark-coloured hill', OE *blæc* 'dark, black' + *dun* 'hill' (*see* DOWN, -DON); the name *Blackdown Hills* is thus tautological.

A range of hills in Somerset and Devon, to the south of TAUNTON. Their highest point is the 315 m (1034 ft) Staple Hill, at their eastern end. They are at the centre of a much larger area now officially designated an Area of Outstanding Natural Beauty, which stretches nearly to CHARD in the east and to HONITON and the A35 in the south.

Black Dwarf's Cottage, the. A cottage near the village of Kirkton in the Manor Valley, some 6 km (4 miles) southwest of Peebles, in Scottish Borders (formerly in Peeblesshire).

It was the home of 'Bowed Davie Ritchie' (d.1811), whom Sir Walter Scott (himself partly lame) visited in 1797, and who became the model for Elshie of the Mucklestanes in Scott's novel *The Black Dwarf* (1816). In Border legend, the Black Dwarf is a malevolent character blamed for all the ills that befall the flocks and herds. Scott's eponymous hero, although a misanthropic recluse, nevertheless intercedes in local affairs to the good. He turns out to be the wealthy Sir Richard Manley. The present cottage dates from 1802, after Scott's visit, and includes a doorway that is only 117 cm (3 ft 10 in) high. Ritchie is buried in Kirkton graveyard, by a rowan tree to ward off the witches.

Blackfriars From the community of Black Friars (another name for Dominicans, who wore black mantles over their white habit) established in the area in 1278.

An area in the City of London, on the north bank of the River THAMES[1] (EC4), opposite BANKSIDE.

In 1600, the Children of the Chapel – a boy theatrical troupe – began performing in the defunct Black Friars' monastery, now converted to the **Blackfriars Theatre**; in 1608 the grown-up King's Men company, to which Shakespeare was attached, acquired the upmarket venue, for well-to-do audiences willing to pay much more than

at their sister theatre, the open-air Globe, and some of the Bard's last plays were performed in the more intimate space.

The original **Blackfriars Bridge**, a road bridge, was built in 1760–9, and the present structure replaced it in 1860-9. A figure of a Black Friar adorns the Black Friar pub at its northern end, on the site of the original Dominican monastery. Also at its northern end, the FLEET[1] River flows into the Thames. From its southern end, **Blackfriars Road** extends about 1 km (0.6 miles) into south London. The paired iron Blackfriars Railway Bridges (the western one subsequently disused) were erected in the second half of the 19th century. **Blackfriars Station**, at the northern end of the eastern railway bridge, was called St Paul's Station until 1937. From it led the line carried by the viaduct that until 1990 obscured the view to the east of St Paul's Cathedral up Ludgate Hill. Blackfriars Underground station, on the District and Circle lines, opened in 1870.

Blackgang 'dark path', *black* + dialect *gang* 'path, track'; first recorded in 1781.

A coastal village on the ISLE OF WIGHT, about 1.5 km (1 m) from the southern tip of the island.

Blackgang Chine. A deep narrow ravine descending to the sea at Blackgang (*chine*, from OE *cinu* 'a crack or fissure', is a characteristic Isle of Wight term for such ravines, which are cut in a cliff by a descending stream). From the clifftop gardens (now adorned by a theme park) it is possible to see all the way along the southwest coast of the island to the NEEDLES.

Black Head. *See under* WHITEHEAD.

Blackheath 'dark-coloured heathland', OE *blæc* + *hæth*.

Originally, an area of windswept heathland (**Black Heath**) in northwestern Kent, to the southeast of London, on the London-to-Dover road. It gave its name to one of the ancient Hundreds (administrative areas) of Kent, whose meetings were held on the heath. In former centuries it was the scene of momentous events, both ominous (Wat Tyler's supporters gathered here during the Peasants' Revolt of 1381) and propitious (the restored Charles II was welcomed here in 1660). An annual fair was held here from 1689. It is traversed by SHOOTERS HILL Road.

The village and district of Blackheath (now in the London borough of Lewisham, SE3) evolved, mainly in the middle of the 19th century, into a solidly elegant suburb for the well-to-do. It has strong sporting associations: the **Royal Blackheath**, founded by James VI and I in 1608, is the oldest golf club in England (its course is now in neighbouring Eltham); and **Blackheath Rugby Club** (1853) is the oldest in Britain.

Denizens of the Heath were often known facetiously in the past as 'Heathens', particularly in sporting contexts:

Blackheath crossed over with a goal to love … The Oxonians … got two goals, while the Heathens were unable to score.

  Pall Mall Gazette (1891)

Battle of Blackheath (17 June 1497). An incident involving Cornish rebels (led by Thomas Flammock and James, Lord Audley) who marched on London, protesting against taxes levied by Henry VII for a campaign in Scotland. They were intercepted at Blackheath and dispersed, and their leaders executed.

Black Isle, the Some say it is named for its appearance, others that the name results from a misreading in which Duthuc, a local saint, was taken for Gaelic *dubh* 'black' (*see* DDU, DUBH). Its Gaelic name is *Ardmeanach* 'middle high land or point', presumably referring to its position between the Moray and Cromarty Firths.

A low-lying peninsula (not an island) in northeast Scotland, formerly in Ross and Cromarty and now in Highland. It is bounded by the Cromarty Firth to the north and the Beauly and Moray Firths to the south, and has much productive farmland.

Black Ladders, the A literal translation of the Welsh name *Ysolglion Duon*; presumably so named from the crag's appearance.

A large cliff on the north side of Carnedd Dafydd in the CARNEDDAU, Snowdonia, Gwynedd (formerly in Caernarvonshire). In Welsh, it is called **Ysolglion Duon** (meaning the same). It is a dank, dark place, shunned by climbers except when it glitters in winter's snow and ice.

Behind the mist
That shifts and stirs, to lap itself again
Round the enduring patience of the crag,
A sheep, somewhere amid old drifts of snow,
Wails out its wet and solitary grief
And gets no answer but the moss's drip.

  E.H. Young: 'Isoglion Duon'

Blackmoor Vale *Blackmoor* 'dark-coloured marshland', OE *blœc* 'dark, black' + *mor* 'marsh'.

A low-lying area in Dorset, running approximately west and southwest from Shaftesbury to the Somerset border. It includes the towns of GILLINGHAM[2], STURMINSTER NEWTON and WINCANTON. It is largely given over to pasturage. Streamside willows and alders and the hanging mists contribute to an almost wetland atmosphere, characterized by the novelist Thomas Hardy as 'the beautiful Vale of Blackmoor … in which the fields are never brown and the springs never dry'. The Vale was central to many of his novels: STURMINSTER NEWTON is 'Stourcastle' in *The Return of the Native*, for instance, and 'Shaston' is SHAFTESBURY in *Jude the Obscure*.

Black Mount A direct translation of the Gaelic name *Am Monadh Dubh* (*see* DDU, DUBH).

A massif between Rannoch Moor and Glen Etive, extending southwestward towards BEN CRUACHAN. It straddles the border between Highland and Argyll and Bute (formerly Highland region and Strathclyde region, and before that entirely in the county of Argyll). The massif contains several MUNROS, including Meall a'Bhuiridh (location of the 'Glen Coe' or 'White Corries' ski area), Stob Gabhar and Ben Starav. For Samuel Taylor Coleridge's appreciation of the fine view of these shapely hills from Rannoch Moor, *see under* RANNOCH.

Black Mountain From the Welsh name: *y* 'the' + *mynydd* 'mountain' + *du* 'black' (*see* DDU, DUBH).

A hill range in Carmarthenshire (formerly in Dyfed), in the western part of the BRECON BEACONS National Park (not to be confused with the plurally named BLACK MOUNTAINS to the east). The Welsh name is **Y Mynydd Du**, and it is sometimes also called **Carmarthen Fan**; this latter name is sometimes applied to the highest point, Fan Foel (804 m / 2639 ft). Made up of limestone, gritstone and old red sandstone, it is a wild, bleak area, full of shake holes, swallow holes, caves, reed-marshes and boulder fields.

Black Mountains. A range of mountains in the northeast of the BRECON BEACONS National Park in Powys. It is not to be confused with the BLACK MOUNTAIN region to the west of the Beacons. The highest peak is Waun Fach (811 m / 2660 ft); also of note is LORD HEREFORD'S KNOB. The Welsh name is **Mynydd y Gader**, Welsh *mynydd* 'mountain' + *y* + *cadeir* 'shaped like a chair'; the earliest references in Welsh and English are singular, and the name must have been applied later to the mountain range.

Black North, the. The name given (especially formerly) by Catholics in the south of Ireland to Presbyterian NORTHERN IRELAND.

Black Pig's Dyke From the folk tale that it was formed by a wizard turned into a pig who dug up the earth as he charged westwards.

An Iron Age earthwork stretching across part of southern ULSTER, between County Longford and County Cavan, and dating from the second half of the 1st Millennium BC. It is also called **Worm's Ditch**, and is said to have been built to protect Ulster's cattle from raiders from LEINSTER to the south. To some it remains as a symbolic barrier, akin to HADRIAN'S WALL; this symbolism is reflected in the title of Vincent Woods's 1992 play, *At the Black Pig's Dyke*, about the love between a Protestant man from the North and a Catholic woman from the South at the time of the Troubles.

Black Pill 'black stream', OE *blœc* 'black' + *pyll* 'stream, tidal creek'; the Welsh name of the river was Afon Dulais, with the same meaning.

A village in Swansea unitary authority (formerly in

Glamorgan, then in West Glamorgan), 2 km (1.2 miles) north of Mumbles.

Blackpool 'dark pool', OE *blæc* 'black, dark' + *pull* 'pool'.

A seaside resort and unitary authority in northwest England, formerly in Lancashire, some 25 km (15 miles) northwest of Preston. It is the biggest and brashest seaside resort in northern England, and, despite the popularity of cheap overseas package holidays, it still attracts millions of visitors every year from all over the north of England and southern Scotland. The main political parties and the TUC also succumb to its lure, regularly holding their conferences at the Winter Gardens here. (New Labour, however, abandoned the Blackpool tradition on the grounds that its hotels 'use winceyette sheets'.) With venues such as Funny Girls (a transvestite cabaret) and The Flying Handbag, Blackpool is also one of Britain's most popular gay resorts.

Features of the town included the Illuminations, autumn light displays along the promenades; the **Blackpool Tower** (158 m / 518 ft high), built in 1894 in homage to the Eiffel Tower; and the Pleasure Beach, a vast amusement park with the largest and fastest rollercoaster in Europe; not to mention a plethora of piers and pleasure gardens, a sea-front tramline and miles of sands and promenades, including the attractions of the **Golden Mile**, once full of waxworks and freak shows, but now a vast 'entertainment' complex – although still holding on to its boisterous, cheeky and fun-loving reputation.

Blackpool first developed as a resort in the 18th century, on the site of the peaty pool that gave the place its name. The coming of the railway in 1846 accelerated its growth, and by the later 19th century workers from all over industrial Lancashire and Yorkshire travelled to Blackpool during their 'Wakes Weeks' holidays. In 1879 the borough became the first in England allowed to spend money on advertising, and more rapid growth followed, with innumerable hotels and boarding houses being built in closely packed terraces.

The place is not to everyone's taste: one local comedian once suggested that the reason the sea goes out so far at Blackpool is because – it doesn't want to come back in again. It is not a place for misanthropes:

> Blackpool was real clutter – the buildings that were not only ugly but also foolish and flimsy, the vacationers sitting under a dark sky with their shirts off, sleeping with their mouths open, emitting hog whimpers. They were waiting for the sun to shine, but the forecast was rain for the next five months … Blackpool was perfectly reflected in the swollen guts and unhealthy fat of its beer-guzzling visitors – eight million in the summer, when Lancashire closed to come here and belch.

> Paul Theroux: *The Kingdom by the Sea* (1983)

Blackpool FC (nicknamed the Seasiders) might not unfairly be said to have a more distinguished past than present. Their finest hour came in the legendary 1953 FA Cup Final, when they defeated Bolton 4–3, Stan Mortensen scoring a unique FA Cup Final hat-trick with the creative assistance of the immortal Stanley Matthews.

Blackpool was the birthplace of Michael Smith (b.1932), winner of the 1993 Nobel Prize for Chemistry for his development of oligonucleotide-based site-directed mutagenesis.

Blackpool. A television musical drama (2004) by Peter Bowker, somewhat in the manner of Dennis Potter. Blackpool reinvents itself as Las Vegas.

Blackpool rock. A long, cylinder-shaped, sugary confection, pink on the outside and white inside, with the letters making up the name 'Blackpool' appearing all the way through it (apparently inserted by hand; no site-directed mutagenesis is required). It was first made in 1887 by Ben Bullock, a sugar boiler from Dewsbury, Yorkshire; rock was first made in Blackpool itself in 1902. It is not to be confused with Edinburgh rock (*see under* EDINBURGH).

The confection was celebrated, with lashings of double entendre, in the George Formby song **'My Little Stick of Blackpool Rock'**; the record sleeve shows the diminutive Formby astride a giant tube of rock, with the shout line 'EEE! What a Whopper'. The largest piece ever made (1987) measured 3.66 m (12 ft) long and 0.4 m (16 in) in diameter.

There is a Country and Western dance called 'Blackpool Rock', choreographed by Jean Thompson.

Blackpool Vanishes. A novel (1979) by Richard Francis in which 'infraterrestrials' in miniature flying saucers abduct the population of Blackpool.

Blackrock A translation of the Irish names, *An Creagacha Dubha* and *Carraig Dubh*.

A southeastern suburb of DUBLIN on the south side of Dublin Bay. In the 18th century it was a fashionable seaside resort and is still a popular bathing place. **Blackrock College** is a boys' school run by the Holy Ghost Fathers and founded in 1860; the future Irish *taoiseach* (prime minister) Éamon de Valera was a pupil here.

Blackrock was the birthplace of John Dillon (1851–1927), who succeeded John Redmond as leader of the Irish National Party in March 1918 before losing his Westminster seat that November.

Blacksod Bay From the small settlement of Blacksod at the southern end of the MULLET peninsula, presumed to be a self-explanatory English name.

A large sheltered inlet of the Atlantic off County Mayo, north of ACHILL ISLAND. The coast here, between Blacksod Bay and the smaller Tullaghan Bay to the east, is where J.M. Synge is said to have set his *Playboy of the Western World* (1907).

Blackstable. A fictionalized version of WHITSTABLE as appearing in Somerset Maugham's *Of Human Bondage* (1915) and *Cakes and Ale* (1930).

Blackstairs Mountains Referring to the colour and jagged nature of the mountains.

A range of hills along the border between County CARLOW and County WEXFORD. The highest point is Mount Leinster (793 m / 2601 ft).

Black Torrington *Black* from the dark waters of the River Torridge; *Torrington see* TORRINGTON.

A village in Devon, on the River TORRIDGE¹, about 16 km (10 miles) northwest of Okehampton.

Blackwall 'black wall', OE *blœc* + *wall*; from an artificial embankment built there to keep out the river.

A district of East London, on the north bank of the River THAMES¹, at the northeastern corner of the ISLE OF DOGS, in the borough of Tower Hamlets (E14). It is in the heart of DOCKLAND, and had its own dock, **Blackwall Basin** (closed in 1987). The area is fictionalized as 'Sun Hill' in the ITV police series *The Bill*, and the firefighters of the television series *London's Burning* (*see under* LONDON) are supposedly based in Blackwall.

Blackwall hitch. A type of rudimentary knot for attaching a rope to a hook. A **double Blackwall hitch** is more secure.

Blackwall Reach. A stretch of the River Thames that curves around the GREENWICH peninsula (home of the Millennium Dome). It was widely used in former times as a mooring place for vessels too large to venture further up the Thames, and was a well-known point of arrival and departure for voyagers overseas. The Virginia Settlers under Captain John Smith, financed by the Virginia Company of London, set sail from here in December 1606 in three small merchant ships, to found the first permanent colony in North America.

Blackwall Tunnel. A road tunnel under the River Thames, between Blackwall in the north and the Greenwich peninsula in the south. The original (now the northbound) tunnel was built in 1891–7 by Sir Alexander Binnie. It is 1345 m (4412 ft) long. The southbound tunnel was added in 1960–7. It is in both directions a notorious traffic congestion point.

In 20th-century rhyming slang, *Blackwall Tunnel* denoted a ship's funnel.

Blackwater¹ 'dark-coloured river', OE *blœc* 'dark, black' + ME *water* 'river'.

A river in Essex, 64 km (40 miles) long. It rises to the east of SAFFRON WALDEN and flows (at first under the name **Pant**) southeastwards through BRAINTREE to MALDON (where it links with the **Chelmer and Blackwater Navigation**, a canal joining Chelmsford to Maldon). Thereafter it

broadens out into a very wide estuary (containing OSEA ISLAND). It flows into the NORTH SEA to the south of Mersea Island (*see under* MERSEA). The river's Romano-British name was **Idumania**.

At the Battle of Maldon (*see under* MALDON) in 991, the commander of the English armies, Byrhtnoth, allowed a Viking force to cross the Blackwater from NORTHEY ISLAND, and was defeated, thus precipitating the habit of buying off the Vikings that prevailed under King Ethelred the Unready.

Blackwater² A direct English translation of the Irish name.

A river of southern Ireland; length 165 km (102 miles). In Irish it is **Abhainn Dubh** ('black river'), anglicized to **Awniduff**.

> Swift Awniduff which of the Englishman
> Is cal' de Blackwater.
>
> Edmund Spenser: *The Faerie Queene* (1590–6) IV, xi, 41

The river is also known in Irish as **Abhainn Mór** ('big river'). The Blackwater initially forms the border between County KERRY and County CORK, then flows east through County Cork and into County WATERFORD, where it turns south to reach the sea at YOUGHAL. An Irishman travelling on the Continent is reported to have described the Rhine as 'Germany's Blackwater'.

Blackwater³. A river of Northern Ireland, rising in the southeast of County Tyrone; length 80 km (50 miles). It shares the various Irish names with its southern namesake (*see* BLACKWATER²). As it flows southeast the Blackwater forms part of the border between County MONAGHAN (in the Republic) and County TYRONE, and then as it flows northeast into LOUGH NEAGH it forms the border between County Tyrone and County ARMAGH. The Battle of YELLOW FORD in 1598 is sometimes called the **Battle of the Blackwater**.

Blackwater⁴. A river in HAMPSHIRE and WILTSHIRE, a tributary of the TEST. For a small part of its 17-km (11-mile) course it forms the boundary between its two counties.

Blackwood From the Welsh *coed* 'trees, wood' (*see* CED) + *duon* plural of 'black'.

A town in Caerphilly (formerly in Monmouthshire, then in Gwent), some 3 km (2 miles) southeast of Bargoed. Its Welsh name is **Coed-Duon**. It was the administrative seat of the former Islwyn district (1974–96).

Black Wood of Rannoch. *See under* RANNOCH.

Bladon A pre-English river name of uncertain meaning; formerly the name of the River EVENLODE².

A village in Oxfordshire, on the edge of the BLENHEIM PALACE estate, about 2.5 km (1.5 miles) south of Woodstock. Sir Winston Churchill (who was born in Blenheim Palace in 1874) is buried in Bladon churchyard.

Blaenafon. The Welsh name for BLAENAVON.

Blaenau Ffestiniog 'the heights of Ffestiniog', *Blaenau* 'heights', Welsh; *Ffestiniog see* FFESTINIOG.

A town in Gwynedd (formerly in Merioneth) 15 km (9 miles) northeast of Porthmadog, and 5 km (3 miles) north of the village of Ffestiniog. There are vast disused slate caverns, and the old steam **Ffestiniog Railway** (*see under* FFESTINIOG) running through them is a popular tourist attraction. During the Second World War, the caverns at Blaenau's Manod slate quarry were used to shelter the National Gallery's masterpieces from German bombing, after their unhappy sojourn at PENRHYN CASTLE. After the war Manod was designated a 'prepared quarry' for securing the nation's art treasures in the event of nuclear conflagration; this policy was abandoned by Mrs Thatcher's government in the 1980s, in favour of restricting protection to the core governmental and military apparatus of the state.

The novelist John Cowper Powys moved to Blaenau in 1955, and died here in 1963.

Blaenau Gwent *See* BLAENAU FFESTINIOG *and* GWENT.

A unitary authority created in 1996 from part of the former county of Gwent. It is bordered on the north by Powys, to the east by Torfaen, and to the south and west by Caerphilly. The administrative seat is at EBBW VALE, and other towns include TREDEGAR and ABERTILLERY.

Blaenavon 'headwater of the river', Welsh *blaen* 'height, headwater' + *afon* (*see* AVON).

A former iron and coal town in Torfaen (formerly in Monmouthshire, then in Gwent), some 9 km (5.5 miles) north of Pontypool. Its Welsh name is **Blaenafon**. It is the site of the Big Pit, operated from 1880 to 1980, and now a tourist attraction. '**Blaenavon Industrial Landscape**' was declared a UNESCO World Heritage Site in 2000.

Blaenavon is the setting of Alexander Cordell's novel *Rape of the Fair Country* (1959), a vivid portrayal of a South Wales mining family in the late 19th century. Cordell's life and work is celebrated in the town's Blaenafon Heritage and Cordell Museum.

Blaina Welsh *blaenau* 'heights'.

A small town in Blaenau Gwent (formerly in Monmouthshire, then in Gwent), 4 km (2.5 miles) southeast of Ebbw Vale.

Blair Atholl *Blair* Gaelic *blàr, blair* 'plain, cleared land'; *Atholl see* ATHOLL.

A village in Atholl, Perth and Kinross (formerly in Perthshire, and then in Tayside region), 9 km (5.5 miles) northwest of Pitlochry. It is the site of the historic **Blair Castle** (*see under* ATHOLL).

Blairgowrie 'plain of Gowrie', Gaelic *blàr* 'plain' + the name of the district, which itself means 'territory of Gabran' (this may refer to a 6th-century king of DALRIADA). Note that this Gowrie is etymologically distinct from the CARSE OF GOWRIE.

A town some 22 km (14 miles) north of Perth, in Perth and Kinross (formerly in Perthshire, and then in Tayside region). With the adjacent settlement of Rattray (Gaelic *ràth* 'circular fort' (*see* RATH) + OCelt *tref* 'settlement'; *Rotreffe* 1291), it forms the BURGH of **Blairgowrie and Rattray**. It is at the centre of a raspberry-growing district. Nearby is Ardblair Castle, birthplace of Lady Carolina Nairne (née Oliphant; 1766–1845), author of many nostalgic Jacobite songs such as 'Charlie is My Darling'.

Blairgowrie was the birthplace of the poet and songwriter Hamish Henderson (1919–2002), best known for 'The Freedom Come All Ye', described as Scotland's *Internationale*.

Blaise Hamlet from *Blaise* of Blaise Castle, possibly the French name *Blois* or ME *blase* 'a torch'.

A tiny village on the **Blaise Castle** estate, about 8 km (5 miles) northwest of Bristol. Built in 1809 to the design of John Nash as accommodation for estate workers and now owned by the National Trust, its small cottages, each architecturally distinct, give an impression of Lilliput.

Blakeney[1] 'dark island' (here probably referring to an area of dry ground in a marsh), OE *blæc* 'dark, black' + *eg* (*see* -EY, -EA).

A small town on the north Norfolk coast, on the estuary of the River Glaven, about 21 km (13 miles) west of Cromer. Until the early 20th century it was a busy port. Its church, St Nicholas, has two (non-matching) towers; the smaller of them used to contain a warning beacon for sailors.

Blakeney Point. A spit of land to the north of Blakeney, enclosing **Blakeney Harbour**. It is an important wildlife habitat, with a bird sanctuary; common seals breed on offshore sandbanks in the summer.

Blakeney[2]. A village in Gloucestershire, at the southeastern edge of the FOREST OF DEAN, about 2.5 km (1.5 miles) from the west bank of the SEVERN estuary.

Blakey Topping. *See under* HOLE OF HORCUM.

Blanchardstown Irish *Baile Bhlainséir* 'Blanchard's town', referring to an Anglo-Norman family.

A northwestern suburb of DUBLIN, with one of the largest shopping centres in Ireland.

Blanchland 'white glade', OFr *blanche* 'white' + *launde* 'woodland glade'.

A village on the River DERWENT[2] in County Durham, 14 km (8.5 miles) west of Consett. Many parts of **Blanchland Abbey** (founded in the later 12th century) can still be seen in the village, including St Mary's Church, the gatehouse and gateway, fishponds and mill. There is a story that when the abbey was about to be attacked by Scottish raiders, the monks were relieved that the invaders became lost in mist on Grey Friars Hill. Such was their joy that the monks rang the abbey bells to celebrate – thus guiding the Scots to their whereabouts, and resulting in the name of the nearby locality: Dead Friars.

Blandford Forum *Blandford* probably 'ford where gudgeon (a type of fish) are found', OE *blægna* possessive plural of *blæge* 'gudgeon' + FORD; *Forum* (first recorded in 1297) from Latin *forum* 'market'.

A market town (commonly referred to simply as **Blandford**) in Dorset, on the River STOUR[1], about 25 km (16 miles) northeast of DORCHESTER[1]. The settlement dates back well into Anglo-Saxon times, but the town was almost completely destroyed by fire in 1731. It was rebuilt with handsome Georgian houses and public buildings. Bryanston School (*see under* BRYANSTON) is nearby.

Blandford Forum is fictionalized in the novels of Thomas Hardy as **Shottsford Forum**.

Blandford fly. A type of biting fly found in the low-lying marshy areas of the Stour Valley. The name has been appropriated to a spicy-tasting ale brewed by the Badger Brewery in Dorset.

Blantyre Perhaps 'border land', from OCelt *blaen* 'edge' + *tir* 'land'.

A town in South Lanarkshire (formerly in Strathclyde region), some 5 km (3 miles) northeast of East Kilbride. It was the birthplace of the missionary-explorer David Livingstone (1813–73), who also worked in the local mills as a boy.

The city of Blantyre in Malawi (formerly Nyasaland) was named in Livingstone's honour; it was founded in 1876 as a mission station by the Church of Scotland.

Blarney Irish *An Bhlarna* 'the small field'.

A village and tourist trap in County Cork, 8 km (5 miles) northwest of Cork itself. The present **Blarney Castle**, with its imposing 26-m (85 ft) keep standing on a granite rock, was built in 1446 by Cormac MacCarthy, and is home to the famous **Blarney Stone** (*see below*). The delights of the 18th-century demesne around the castle were famously celebrated by Richard Alfred Milliken (although he originally wrote his poem as a burlesque of Irish verse rendered into English):

> The groves of Blarney
> They look so charming,
> Down by the purling
>   Of sweet, silent brooks,
> Being banked with posies
> That spontaneous grow there,
> Planted in order
>   By the sweet rock close.

> Richard Alfred Milliken (1767–1815): 'The Groves of Blarney' (1798), sung to the tune 'Castle Hyde' (The song was apparently sung by Italian liberationist Garibaldi's soldiers on their marches.)

blarney. Flattering talk, often with wheedling or flowery turns of phrase. The term comes from the **Blarney Stone** (*see below*). It is sometimes applied more generally to garrulousness, the gift of the gab, a gift thought widespread among the Irish:

> If one could only teach the English how to talk and the Irish how to listen, society would be quite civilized.

> Oscar Wilde: *An Ideal Husband* (1893)

> The Irish equivalent of 'gilding the lily' can be translated as 'rubbing lard on a sow's arse'.

> Niall Toibin: remark

Blarney Stone. A block of rough limestone measuring about 1.2 m (4 ft) by 30 m (100 ft), set high in the battlements of Blarney Castle. Bolder visitors to the castle aim to kiss it and so gain the gift of **blarney** (*see above*). This can only be done by lying on one's back and leaning out over a sheer drop, with a pair of strong arms gripping one's shins. Some say this is a relatively modern 'tradition', geared to the tourist industry and dating from the 18th century, while others say a king of MUNSTER saved an old woman from drowning and in reward she told him that if he kissed the highest stone in the castle he would gain the gift of persuasion. There is also a story that the stone is part of the Stone of SCONE, given to a MacCarthy who had supported the campaign of Edward Bruce.

The most common version of the story, however, is that in 1602, when smooth-talking Cormac MacDermot MacCarthy, Lord of Blarney, was asked by Sir George Carew, Queen Elizabeth's deputy in Ireland, to give up the tradition by which Irish clans elected their chiefs and to transfer his allegiance to the English Crown, MacCarthy constantly procrastinated, until the queen finally exploded: 'Blarney! Blarney! What he says he never means! It's the usual Blarney!'

In 1825 Father Prout, manager of the woollen mills in Blarney, added a verse to Milliken's poem 'The Groves of Blarney' (*see above*) to take account of the stone's prowess:

> There is a stone there,
> That whoever kisses,
> Oh! he never misses
> To grow eloquent;
> 'Tis he may clamber
> To a lady's chamber,
> Or become a member
> Of parliament.
> A clever spouter
> He'll soon turn out, or
> An out-and-outer …

Blasket Islands Etymology unknown.

A group of small islands off the end of the Dingle peninsula, County Kerry (*see under* DINGLE). They are the most westerly part of the British Isles, apart from ROCKALL. The largest island is **Great Blasket Island** (or **the Great Blasket**; Irish *An Blascaod Mór* 'the big Blasket', although known locally as *An tOileán Tiar* 'the western island'). This is separated from the mainland by **Blasket Sound**, which at its narrowest is only 1.6 km (1 mile) wide.

The last inhabitants left Great Blasket in 1953, settling in Springfield, Massachusetts. Before that the island was a mecca for Celtic folklorists, notably Robin Flower, who wrote an account of his experiences in *The Western Isle* (1944). The island's home-grown writers have produced a number of memorable autobiographies: Maurice O'Sullivan's *Twenty Years a-Growing* (1933), Peig Sayer's *Peig* (1936) and Tomás O Crohan's *The Islandman* (1937).

The other islands in the group include Beginish, Inishnabro, Inishvickillane and Inishtooshkert (where, during the Second World War, a German bomber crashed and its crew managed to survive for a time before being rescued). The traditional air 'The Fairies' Tune' is said to have been given to the Inishvickillane man Tomás Ó Dalaigh by a fairy woman (this was in the early 20th century):

> On the most westerly Blasket
> In a dry-stone hut
> He got this air out of the night …
>> Seamus Heaney: 'The Given Note'

More recently, the colourful politician Charles Haughey bought Inishvickillane and on it built an extravagant house in the form of an ancient chieftain's fort.

Blatherwycke Perhaps 'bladder-plant farm', OE *blædre* 'bladder' + *wic* (*see* WICK).
A village in Northamptonshire, about 11 km (7 miles) northeast of Corby.

Blaven. *See under* BLA BHEINN.

Blaydon Probably 'cold hill', OScand *blar* 'cold, comfortless' + OE *dun* (*see* DOWN, -DON).
An industrial town on the River TYNE[1], in Tyne and Wear, 6 km (3.5 miles) west of Newcastle.
'Blaydon Races'. A song written in 1862 by the Newcastle music-hall singer Geordie Ridley, celebrating a day out at the horse races that used to take place at Blaydon. The song has since become the anthem of Tyneside. The chorus goes:

> Oh me lads, you should've seen us gannin
> Passing the folks along the road
> And all of them were stannin'
> All the lads and lasses there
> They all had smilin' faces
> Gannin along the Scotswood Road
> To see the Blaydon races.

The Blaydon Race for runners has taken place annually for over two decades. Its course connects closely to the song, following the route of the revellers and taking place on the same day, 9 June.

Bleaklow 'dark hill', OE *blæc* 'dark' and *hlaw* (*see* LAW, LOW).
A hilly area in the PEAK DISTRICT of Derbyshire, about 8 km (5 miles) northeast of Glossop. Appropriately 'bleak', especially in winter, it is one of the largest areas in England still uncrossed by a road. Many rivers rise here, including the DERWENT[4]. **Bleaklow Hill** is 628 m (2060 ft) in height.

Blean Probably '(place in the) rough ground', OE *blean* dative form of *blea* 'rough ground'.
A village in Kent, about 4 km (2.5 miles) northwest of Canterbury.

Blebocraigs Possibly 'rocks of the meal-sack place', Gaelic *blàtha bolg* 'meal sack' + *carraig* 'rock'.
A small settlement in Fife, 8 km (5 miles) west of St Andrews.

Blencathra 'points of Arthur', OCelt *blain* 'top, point' + an unknown element which became associated with (presumably King) Arthur.
A mountain (868 m / 2847 ft) to the east of SKIDDAW in the northern Lake District, Cumbria (formerly in Cumberland), some 6 km (3.5 miles) northeast of Keswick. It is also known as **Saddleback** (from its shape), and thrusts three striking buttresses down towards the valley, reminiscent of the three great buttresses of Piz Palü in the Bernina Alps.

> On stern Blencartha's [sic] perilous height
>> The winds are tyrannous and strong;
> And flashing forth unsteady light
> From stern Blencartha's skiey height,
>> As loud the torrents throng!
> Beneath the moon, in gentle weather,
> They bind the earth and sky together.
> But oh! the sky and all its forms, how quiet!
> The things that seek the earth, how full of noise and riot!
>> Samuel Taylor Coleridge: 'A Thought Suggested by a View of Saddleback in Cumbria', in his journal (25 August 1800)

> The Boy must part from Mosedale's Groves,
> And leave Blencathra's rugged Coves …
>> William Wordsworth: 'Song at the Feast of Brougham Castle', from *Poems in Two Volumes* (1807)

Blencogo 'summit of the cuckoos', OCelt *blain* 'summit' + *cogow* 'cuckoos'.
A small village in Cumbria, 6 km (4 miles) west of Wigton.

Blenheim Palace Commemorating the victory of the Duke of Marlborough over the French at the Battle of *Blenheim* (pronounced 'blennim') in 1704 (Blenheim is in Bavaria, on the River Danube).

A mansion in Oxfordshire, near Woodstock, about 12 km (7.5 miles) northwest of Oxford, the home of the dukes of Marlborough. Designed by Sir John Vanbrugh, it was presented by a grateful nation to John Churchill, 1st Duke of Marlborough, as a reward for his victory over the French and their Bavarian allies at Blenheim in the War of the Spanish Succession. Building began, in golden Cotswold stone, in 1705, but it was not completed until 1722, after the 1st Duke's death (the Duchess had been strongly opposed to the building and said: 'I mortally hate all gardens and architecture'). Its park was later landscaped by 'Capability' Brown (the trees in the garden are supposedly planted according to the original battle plan at Blenheim). Sir Winston Churchill (1874–1965) was born in the house (*see also* BLADON).

> Under this stone, Reader, survey
> Dead Sir John Vanbrugh's house of clay.
> Lie heavy on him, Earth! for he
> Laid many heavy loads on thee!
>
> Abel Evans (1679–1737): 'Epitaph on Sir John Vanbrugh, Architect of Blenheim Palace'

Blenheim was declared a UNESCO World Heritage Site in 1987.

There are towns called Blenheim in the Marlborough district of South Island, New Zealand, and in Ontario, Canada.

Blenheim Orange. A variety of golden-coloured apple, sometimes also known as the **Blenheim Pippin** or **Woodstock Pippin.**

Blenheim spaniel. A small type of spaniel, similar to a King Charles spaniel.

Blessington An English translation of *baile comaoine* 'town of favour', mistakenly supposed at one time to be the meaning of the Irish name *Baile Coimin*, in which the second element is in fact a personal name, that of the 13th-century Archbishop John Comyn.

A village on the western side of the Wicklow Mountains, County Wicklow, 10 km (6 miles) southeast of Naas. Blessington was called **Burgage** until 1683, when Charles II granted the place a charter and built **Blessington Manor** for the archbishop of Dublin (it was burnt down in the 1798 United Irishmen's Rebellion). Blessington gives its name to the nearby **Blessington Lakes**, a large reservoir complex that supplies Dublin with water and also generates hydroelectricity.

Blessington was the birthplace of the choreographer Dame Ninette de Valois (1898–2001).

Five km (3 miles) from Blessington is Russborough House, designed by Richard Castle and constructed 1741–51 for Joseph Leeson, later Earl of Milltown. Paintings have twice been stolen from the house: in 1974 Rose Dugdale stole 16 paintings to raise funds for the IRA, but all the paintings were recovered; of the paintings stolen by the Dublin criminal Martin Cahill in 1988, only one has been recovered.

Bletchley 'Blæcca's glade', OE male personal name *Blæcca* + -LEY.

A former railway town in the southern corner of the unitary authority of Milton Keynes (formerly in Buckinghamshire).

Bletchley Park. A country house in Bletchley which during the Second World War housed the British Government Code and Cypher School. Some of the acutest minds in the country (perhaps most notably Alan Turing's) were employed in deciphering enemy radio traffic, and in particular material produced by the German 'Enigma' coding machine. Techniques developed here were highly significant in the evolution of the modern computer. Those who worked at Bletchley Park were sworn to secrecy, an undertaking they adhered to with such tenacity that until the 1970s its existence was almost unknown to the general public. Thereafter, however, it became a popular subject for films, plays and novels (e.g. Robert Harris's novel *Enigma* (1995), made into a film (2001) of the same name directed by Michael Apted and starring Kate Winslet).

Blickling '(settlement of) Blicla's people', OE male personal name *Blicla* + -*ingas* (*see* -ING).

A village in Norfolk, about 21 km (13 miles) north of Norwich. Anne Boleyn (1507–36), Henry VIII's second wife, was born and brought up in **Blickling Hall**. The current bearer of that name, however, is a much grander building, a magnificent red-brick Jacobean mansion built in 1619–29 by Henry Hobart, Lord Chief Justice of England, with formal gardens laid out later by Humphry Repton. It has a particularly impressive Long Gallery, lined with books and adorned with ornate ceiling plasterwork, and is now administered by the National Trust.

Blickling Homilies. A 10th-century collection of Anglo-Saxon sermons and saints' lives, preserved in Blickling Hall.

Blighty From Urdu *bilayati* 'foreign', from Arabic *wilayat* 'dominion'.

British slang, originally military, for ENGLAND, especially as a place you are homesick for when serving abroad. It was first picked up by British troops stationed in India, but it really came into its own during the First World War, when thoughts of getting 'back to Blighty' were on the mind of every British 'Tommy' in Flanders. A highly popular song of the period was A.J. Mills, Fred Godfrey and Bennett Scott's **'Take Me Back to Dear Old Blighty'** (1916): 'Take me back to dear old Blighty, put me on the train for London town'.

> As far as ageing romantics are concerned, Dover is the only way to return to good old Blighty.
>
> *The Times* (17 August 1999)

Blighty. A magazine, specializing in pin-ups and cartoons, which was a former favourite with the troops, particularly during and after the two world wars. Its last issue appeared in 1958.

Blighty one, a. In British First World War slang, a wound of (just) sufficient severity to require repatriation to Britain – the ambition of many British soldiers serving overseas. Also known as a plain **Blighty**.

Blindcrake 'summit crag', OCelt *blain* 'summit' + *creig* 'rock'.
A small village in Cumbria, 5 km (3 miles) northeast of Cockermouth.

Blisland *Blis* of unknown origin and significance + OE *land* 'land, estate'. In Domesday Book (1086) the place was called Glustone, from an unknown first element + -TON.
A village in Cornwall, on Bodmin Moor (*see under* BODMIN), about 8 km (5 miles) northeast of Bodmin. In the Middle Ages it was called *Blisland-juxta-Montem* 'Blisland near the Mountain', probably a reference to the nearby BROWN WILLY.

Bliss Gate ModE *gate*, a gate on to Rock Common, with possibly a surname or *bliss* in the sense of 'pleasure'.
A village in Worcestershire (before 1998 in Hereford and Worcester, before 1974 in Worcestershire), to the south of WYRE FOREST, about 5 km (3 miles) west of Bewdley.

Blisworth 'Blith's enclosure', OE *Blithes* possessive form of male personal name *Blith* + *worth* (*see* -WORTH, WORTHY, -WARDINE).
A village in Northamptonshire, about 8 km (5 miles) south-west of Northampton. Just to the south of the village is the northern entrance to the **Blisworth Tunnel** on the GRAND UNION CANAL, the longest navigable tunnel in England at nearly 3 km (1.75 miles). It was constructed in the early 19th century, and before the coming of steam power to the canal in the 1870s, boats were propelled through it by men 'walking' their way along the walls (a practice known as 'legging').

Blo Norton *Blo* probably ME *blo* 'bleak, exposed'; *Norton see* NORTON.
A village in Norfolk, about 11 km (7 miles) west of Diss.

Bloody Bay From the 15th-century battle fought here.
A bay near the northeast tip of MULL, in Argyll and Bute (formerly in Strathclyde), about 3 km (2 miles) north of Tobermory. The name derives from the sea battle fought here in 1439 between the forces of John MacDonald, Lord of the Isles (*see* ISLES, LORDSHIP OF THE), and his son Angus, who was in rebellion against him and who emerged from the battle victorious.

Bloody Foreland Irish *Cnoc Fola* 'hill of blood' (*see* KNOCK-), said to refer to the sunsets visible from here; *foreland* is a headland or promontory.

A headland in County Donegal, 12 km (7.5 miles) northwest of Gweedore, and effectively forming the north-western corner of the island of Ireland.

Bloomsbury 'manor held by the de Blemund family', *Blemund* OFr family name (which probably came from one of two places called Blémont in France) + BURY. First recorded in 1291.
A district in Central London, in the borough of CAMDEN (WC1), between the Euston Road to the north and New Oxford Street and Theobalds Road to the south, and between Tottenham Court Road to the west and Gray's Inn Road to the east, and roughly centring on RUSSELL SQUARE. It first became fashionable in the second half of the 17th century, when many grand houses were erected here (**Bloomsbury Square** was laid out in the early 1660s). In the 1750s the British Museum arrived, in Great Russell Street, and thereafter the area became the abode of writers, intellectuals, lawyers, artists, etc. Large parts of it are now occupied by London University. Enough of its original buildings survive to preserve some of its Georgian character.

Bloomsbury Gang. A Whig party faction that appeared in July 1765, led by the 4th Duke of Bedford (large portions of Bloomsbury are part of the Bedford Estate).

Bloomsbury Group. A group of writers, artists and intellectuals (also sometimes termed the **Bloomsbury Set**) who lived and worked in Bloomsbury from about 1907 to 1930. They included Leonard and Virginia Woolf, Clive and Vanessa Bell, Roger Fry, E.M. Forster, Lytton Strachey, Duncan Grant, David Garnett, Dora Carrington and John Maynard Keynes. They saw themselves as advocates of a new, rational, civilized society, and several of them had Cambridge links. They had many critics, though, who thought them dilettante and élitist, not a few of whom were ready to tar them with the brush of homosexual artiness.

Bloomsburyite. A usually derogatory name for a member or supporter of the Bloomsbury Group.

Bloomsbury Publishing plc. A publishing house set up in 1986 by Liz Calder and Nigel Newton, specializing mainly in fiction and reference. Its coup in securing the 'Harry Potter' books (1997–) made it the envy of other British publishers. Its original offices were in Bloomsbury Square.

Blore Perhaps '(place at the) hill', OE *blor* 'swelling, hill'.
A village in Staffordshire, about 24 km (15 miles) north-east of Stoke-on-Trent, on the southern edge of the PEAK DISTRICT National Park.

Battle of Blore Heath (23 September 1459). A battle in the Wars of the Roses in which the Yorkists triumphed over Lancastrian royalist forces. The Lancastrians had tried to prevent an army under the Earl of

Salisbury linking up with forces led by the Duke of York.

Blorenge A corruption of ModE 'blue ridge'.
A hill (559 m / 1834 ft) in Monmouthshire (formerly in Gwent), 4 km (2.5 miles) southwest of Abergavenny. It is pronounced to rhyme with 'orange' (something that, famously, no word in the English lexicon is able to do).
See also the SKIRRID.

Blubberhouses 'houses by the foaming spring', OE *blubber* 'boiling, foaming' + *hus* 'house'.
A village in North Yorkshire, 14 km (8.5 miles) west of Harrogate.

Blue Anchor[1] Possibly from the name of a local public house.
A village on the Somerset coast, about 8 km (5 miles) southeast of Minehead.
Blue Anchor Bay. A shallow bay on the northern Somerset coast, between MINEHEAD and WATCHET.

Blue Anchor[2] *See* BLUE ANCHOR[1].
A village in Cornwall, about 11 km (7 miles) southeast of Newquay.

Blue Bell Hill From the bluebells growing here.
A hill and village in Kent, at the point where the A229 joins the M2 at Junction 3, to the south of Chatham.

Blue John Cavern From the name of the blue fluorspar found here.
The name given to either of a pair of caves (*see* TREAK CLIFF) in the PEAK DISTRICT, just to the west of Castleton. They are the world's only source of a sparkling fluorspar called **Blue John**. This actually comes in a whole spectrum of colours, ranging from a rich blue through deep red to yellow. Before being cut and polished it is soaked in pine resin. This technique was developed in France, and the name *Blue John* may be a folk-etymological alteration of French *bleu-jaune*, a term descriptive of the mineral's colour-range.

Bluestack Mountains Irish *Cruacha Gorma* 'blue peaks', where *cruach* is the usual word for a haystack or rick.
A range of hills in County DONEGAL, rising to the north of the town of Donegal itself. The highest point is **Blue Stack** (676 m / 2217 ft).
See also LOUGH BELSHADE.

Bluewater From the ring of six lakes which are a feature of its design.
A retail park opened in 1999 in a disused chalk quarry to the east of Dartford in Kent, in the fork between the M25 and the A2. It is the largest shopping centre in Europe.

Blunts Perhaps from a family name.
A village in Cornwall, about 10 km (6 miles) southeast of Liskeard.

Blyth[1] 'the gentle one', OE *blithe*.
A river (pronounced 'blithe') in Suffolk, which rises 8 km (5 miles) north of FRAMLINGHAM and flows eastwards about 24 km (15 miles) through HALESWORTH into the sea at WALBERSWICK. Its estuary is a nature reserve, which acts as a sanctuary for wading birds. Along its course the villages of **Blyford** and **Blythburgh** (once a thriving port) have adopted its name.

Blyth[2] After the River Blyth, OE *blithe* 'the gentle one'; the town was recorded as *Blithemuth* in the 13th century.
A town (pronounced 'blithe') in Northumberland, on the southern side of the mouth of the **River Blyth**, 18 km (11 miles) northeast of Newcastle upon Tyne. It was formerly a coal-exporting port and shipbuilding centre.
The local football club, a non-League side founded in 1899, goes under the battling name of **Blyth Spartans**.

Blyton Probably 'Bligr's farmstead', OScand male personal name *Bligr* + -TON.
A village in Lincolnshire, about 8 km (5 miles) northeast of GAINSBOROUGH.

BMW. In Ireland, as well as denoting flash German automotive engineering, the abbreviation is also used for the less glamorous Border, Midland and Western region, which squats between Ulster and the far west.

Boa Island Irish *Inis Badhbha* 'Badhbh's island'; this could be named after a valkyrie-like figure in early Irish tradition, a (usually evil) supernatural female who attends and finds pleasure in battles.
A long thin island at the north end of Lower Lough ERNE, County Fermanagh. It is linked to the mainland by road bridges at each end.

Boarhills Apparently self-explanatory.
A small village close to the east coast of Fife, 7 km (4.5 miles) southeast of St Andrews.

Boarhunt 'spring of the stronghold or manor', OE *burh* (*see* BURY) + *funta* 'spring' (*funta* was adopted from Latin *font-*, the stem form of *fons* 'spring', and there are Roman remains nearby).
A village in Hampshire, about 4 km (2.5 miles) northeast of Fareham. The rather larger village of **North Boarhunt** is a further 1.5 km (1 mile) to the north.

Boar of Badenoch, the. *See under* BADENOCH.

Boarshead Reputedly from a local rock formation which resembles a boar's head (first recorded in the 16th century).
A village in West Sussex, about 2.5 km (1.5 miles) northeast of Crowborough.

Boar's Hill Possibly from the presence of *boars*.
A hill on the southwestern outskirts of OXFORD, now a sylvan residential district. It has been the home of many poets, including Edmund Blunden, Robert Bridges, Robert

Graves and John Masefield, but it was Matthew Arnold who established its fame when he made it the point from which he saw 'that sweet city with her dreaming spires' (Oxford) in his poem 'Thyrsis' (1865).

At the highest point of Boar's Hill is Jarn Mound, a viewing platform built by unemployed Welsh miners in the 1930s as part of a conservation scheme. 'Matthew Arnold's Field', a pretty meadow, lies near the foot of the mound.

The Open University has its offices here, in turn-of-the-century Foxcombe Hall, nicknamed 'the Kremlin' for the stark brutalism of its architecture.

The composer Lennox Berkeley (1903–89) was born in Boar's Hill.

Boars of Duncansby, the. *See under* DUNCANSBY HEAD.

Boat of Garten Named after the ferry that formerly operated where the small River Garten enters the River SPEY. A village in Strathspey, formerly in Inverness-shire and now in Highland, 8 km (5 miles) north of Aviemore. **Loch Garten**, 3 km (2 miles) east of the village, was the first site where breeding ospreys re-established themselves in Britain, in 1959.

Bobbing '(settlement of) Bobba's people', OE male personal name *Bobba* + *-ingas* (*see* -ING). A village in Kent, now a western suburb of SITTINGBOURNE.

Bodenstown English *town* with the surname *Boden* or *Bowden*. A tiny settlement in County Kildare, some 5 km (3 miles) north of Naas, principally noted for its churchyard, which has the grave of the Irish national hero Wolfe Tone (1763–98), who killed himself in prison after the failure of the 1798 United Irishmen's Rebellion. Padraic Pearse, shot by the British for his part in the Easter Rising (1916), described Bodenstown as 'the holiest spot in Ireland'.

'Bodenstown Churchyard'. A ballad by Thomas Davis (1814–45):

In Bodenstown churchyard there lies a green grave
And wildly around it the winter winds rave;
Small shelter is weaned from the cruel walls there
When the storm clouds blow down on the plains of
    Kildare.

Once I stood on that sod that lies over Wolfe Tone
And I thought how he perished in prison alone,
His friends unavenged and his country unfreed;
Oh pity, I thought, is the patriot's need ...

In Bodenstown churchyard there lies a green grave
And wildly around it let the winter winds rave;
Far better it suits him the wind and the gloom
Until Ireland a nation might build him a tomb.

Bodenstown Sunday. An annual pilgrimage of Repub-

licans to Bodenstown churchyard, held on the second last Sunday in June. Since the 1970s the event has been dominated by Sinn Féin.

Bodiam 'Boda's homestead or enclosure', OE male personal name *Boda* + HAM. A village in East Sussex, about 16 km (10 miles) north of Hastings. Until the 1970s it was an important centre of hop-growing.

Bodiam Castle, on the north bank of the River ROTHER[2], is today only a shell, but its white exterior conforms perfectly with everyone's idea of the medieval fortress: high battlemented walls, massive round towers at each corner, beetling bartizans, all set in the middle of a broad, lake-like moat. It was built in the 1380s, by Sir Edward Dalyngruge, when there were fears of a French invading force coming up the still navigable Rother, but the threat did not materialize. It fell into decay over the centuries, but it was restored by Lord Curzon (of KEDLESTON), who in 1925 bequeathed it to the nation (it is now owned by the National Trust).

The writer Edith Wharton recalled visiting Bodiam Castle with her friend and mentor Henry James in the first decade of the 20th century:

Tranquil white clouds hung above it in a windless sky, and the silence and solitude were complete as we sat looking across at the crumbling towers, and at their reflection in a moat starred with water-lilies and danced over by great blue dragon-flies. For a long time no one spoke; then James turned to me and said solemnly: 'Summer afternoon – summer afternoon; to me those have always been the two most beautiful words in the English language ...'

In 1911 Wharton published, in *Scribner's Magazine*, the poem **'Summer Afternoon (Bodiam Castle, Sussex)'**; but anyone hoping to find evocations of the actual castle amidst the overwrought verse ('Spirals of incense and the amber drip / Of lucid honey-comb on sylvan shrines ...') would be disappointed.

Bodieve 'dwelling of a lord', Cornish *bod* 'dwelling' + *yuv* 'lord'. A village in Cornwall, just to the north of Wadebridge, on the estuary of the River CAMEL.

Bodinnick 'fort dwelling', Cornish *bod* 'dwelling' + *dynek* 'fort'. A village in Cornwall, on the eastern side of the River FOWEY[1] estuary, opposite Fowey.

Bodle Street Green 'Green of Bodle hamlet', with the name of the local *Bothel* family, known in the area from the 13th century; *see also* STREET. A village in East Sussex, about 11 km (7 miles) northwest of Bexhill.

Bodmin Probably 'dwelling by church-land', Cornish *bod* 'dwelling' + *meneghi* 'church-land'.

A market town in Cornwall, about 27 km (17 miles) northeast of Newquay, on the steep southwestern edge of Bodmin Moor. It was the county town of Cornwall between 1835 and 1989, when it was replaced by TRURO. Its church, St Petroc's, is the largest in Cornwall. Every July there takes place the **Bodmin Riding**, a procession on horseback around the town; the origins are medieval, but the custom was abandoned in the 19th century until revived in 1974.

The novelist, poet, anthologist and critic Sir Arthur Quiller-Couch (1863–1944) was born in Bodmin (he wrote about FOWEY[2] as TROY TOWN[1]), as was 'Sapper' (Herman Cyril McNeile, 1888–1937), creator of the Bulldog Drummond stories.

See also JAMAICA INN.

Beast of Bodmin Moor. The nickname for a wild animal, possibly a black panther, that has reportedly attacked sheep and calves on farms in the region of Bodmin Moor since the early 1980s. It was first sighted in 1983, but has still not been captured or even fully identified. Speculation persists that the beast may be a big cat released into the countryside by its former owner when it grew too big to be kept as a pet. Its size and reputation may well owe something to memories of the chilling 'gigantic hound' that haunted DARTMOOR in Arthur Conan Doyle's *The Hound of the Baskervilles* (1902).

Bodmin Moor. A bleak windswept expanse of granite upland to the northeast of Bodmin, officially designated an Area of Outstanding Natural Beauty. It is about 207 sq km (80 sq miles) in area, and the plateau is about 245 m (800 ft) above sea level. Above this rise the heights of BROWN WILLY and ROUGH TOR[1]. The vast reservoir of **Colliford Lake** dominates the centre of the moor, but of more interest, just to its east, is the mysterious DOZMARY POOL: according to legend, it was into this shallow lake that Sir Bedivere threw King Arthur's sword as the king lay dying after the Battle of Camlann. Its lonely waters complement the brooding emptiness of the often mist-shrouded moor.

Bodnant Probably 'house by a stream', Welsh *bod* 'house' + *nant* 'stream, valley'.

A large 32-ha (80-acre) garden in Conwy, 13 km (8 miles) south of LLANDUDNO. It was begun in 1875 and continued under several generations of Lord Aberconways. Its most famous feature is a grand laburnum arch, but it also possesses early 19th-century oaks, cedars and beeches, as well as a large variety of rhododendrons (hybrids of which were the speciality of the 2nd Lord Aberconway). Streams flow through the terraced landscape into the River CONWY[1].

Bodrugan's Leap. A clifftop location on the southern coast of Cornwall, between Gorran Haven and MEVAGISSEY.

It takes its name from the endgame of a local 15th-century feud, which was in turn a manifestation of the Wars of the Roses. During the reign of Richard III, the Cornish Lancastrian Richard Edgcumbe (*see* COTEHELE) escaped the virulent Yorkist thug Henry Bodrugan by, it seems, the decoy of tossing his hat into the River TAMAR – to make Bodrugan believe he had drowned. In 1487, with the Lancastrian-Tudor Henry VII installed on the throne, the newly knighted Edgcumbe obtained a warrant for Bodrugan's arrest. Bodrugan was chased, and:

> ... leapt from the cliff at this point ... landing on a small grassy island whence a waiting boat took him into exile abroad.
>
> Philip Payton: *Cornwall: A History*, 2nd edition (2004)

Bog, the. A nickname for the large prison in PORTLAOISE, a town set midst the peaty purlieus of the Irish MIDLANDS.

Bogbain Uncertain; the first element is Gaelic *bog* 'marsh'.

A small settlement in Highland (formerly in Inverness-shire), 6 km (4 miles) southeast of Inverness.

Bogbuie 'yellow marsh', Gaelic *bog* 'marsh' + *buidhe* 'yellow'.

A small settlement in the BLACK ISLE, Highland (formerly in Ross and Cromarty), 5 km (3 miles) southeast of Dingwall.

Bogfern 'alder bog', Gaelic *bog* 'marsh' + *fearn* 'alder'.

A small settlement in Aberdeenshire (formerly in Grampian region), 8 km (5 miles) north of Aboyne.

Bogfields Gaelic *bog* 'marsh' + ModE *field*.

A small settlement in Aberdeenshire (formerly in Grampian region), 9 km (5.5 miles) north of Aboyne.

Boggeragh Mountains Etymology unknown.

A range of hills in County CORK, some 30 km (19 miles) northwest of Cork itself. The highest point is Musheramore (646 m / 2119 ft).

Boghall Castle. *See under* BIGGAR.

Bogie. *See under* STRATHBOGIE.

Bog Meadows. An area of BELFAST, which, before it was drained, provided a barrier between the Catholic FALLS ROAD and neighbouring Protestant areas. It is now covered by an industrial estate.

Bognor Regis *Bognor* 'Bucge's shore', OE *Bucgan* possessive form of female personal name *Bucge* + *ora* 'shore'; *Regis* 'of the king', Latin *regis*.

A town and seaside resort on the West Sussex coast, about 25 km (16 miles) west of Worthing. Until the end of the 18th century Bognor was a quiet fishing village. It was the arrival in 1787 of Richard Hotham, a London hatter with grand development plans, that presaged its transformation into a salubrious and popular holiday resort.

Its modern reputation as somewhere to sedate the pulse rather than make it race is not new: it has always attracted convalescents, and it was after a stay here to get over an illness that King George V in gratitude bestowed the title 'Regis' on the town in 1929. His private opinion of the place may perhaps be better gauged by his reaction when his private secretary, Lord Stamfordham, relayed to him a request by the burghers of Bognor to rename the town 'Bognor Regis' in honour of his recovery: 'Bugger Bognor!' was the king's alleged retort. Lord Stamfordham silkily transformed this into Royal Assent. (An alternative version of the story is that the remark was made on the King's deathbed, after a courtier had tried to revive his spirits by saying 'Cheer up, your Majesty, you will soon be at Bognor again.')

Since 1979 an annual 'Bognor Birdman' contest has been staged, in which people jump off the pier and attempt to fly. There is a £25,000 prize (as yet unclaimed) for the first to stay aloft for 100 m.

Bog of Allen Irish *Móin Alúine*, meaning the same; *Allen* is possibly from the female personal name Almu, a daughter of the Tuatha Dé Danaan, early pre-Christian settlers in Ireland according to Irish mythology.

A low-lying area of peat bogs in the Irish MIDLANDS between the LIFFEY and the SHANNON, extending through parts of counties Kildare, Offaly, Laois and Westmeath. The peat here has been cut to fuel power stations.

> Yes, the newspapers were right: snow was general all over Ireland. It was falling on every part of the dark central plain, on the treeless hills, falling softly upon the Bog of Allen and, farther westward, softly falling into the dark mutinous Shannon waves ...
>
> James Joyce: from the final paragraph of 'The Dead', in *Dubliners* (1914)

Bog of Plewlands. *See* GORDONSTOUN.

Bogside It was formerly a boggy area.

A staunchly Nationalist area on the west side of DERRY/LONDONDERRY. In the past, Catholics settled here, as they were forbidden to live within the city walls. It became a flashpoint during the Troubles (*see* **Battle of the Bogside** *below*), and it was here – at the Rossville Flats and 'Aggro Corner' (the meeting of William Street and Rossville Street) – that the tragedy of Bloody Sunday took place, when, on 30 January 1972, 13 unarmed demonstrators were killed by British Paratroopers:

> PARAS THIRTEEN, the walls said,
> BOGSIDE NIL.
>
> Seamus Heaney: 'Casualty', from *Field Work* (1979)

Battle of the Bogside (12–14 August 1969). One of the earliest major outbreaks of violence during the Troubles, involving serious rioting by Nationalists, who saw themselves as defending the area from the Royal Ulster Constabulary. It was at this time that the

Bogside declared itself 'Free Derry' (*see under* FREE DERRY CORNER).

Boireann. The Irish name for the BURREN.

Bojewyan Probably 'Uyon's dwelling', Cornish *bod* 'dwelling' + male personal name *Uyon*.

A village (pronounced 'bodge-yewan') at the western tip of Cornwall, about 11 km (7 miles) northeast of LAND'S END.

Boldon 'rounded hill' OE *bol* 'rounded' + OE *dun* (*see* DOWN, -DON).

A town in South Tyneside, Tyne and Wear (formerly in County Durham), 11 km (7 miles) southeast of Newcastle upon Tyne.

Boldre Perhaps from an old name of the river at Lymington, but the etymology is obscure; one suggestion not widely accepted is that the name is OE *boulder* 'bullrush'.

A village (pronounced 'bolder') in Hampshire, about 3 km (2 miles) north of Lymington.

Bolsover Probably 'Boll's ridge', OE *Bolles* (or *Bulles*) possessive form of male personal name *Boll* (or *Bull*) + *ofer* 'ridge'.

A former mining town (locally pronounced 'bozer') in Derbyshire, about 11 km (7 miles) southeast of Chesterfield. The original **Bolsover Castle** was built in the 11th century by William Peveril, who also built Peak Castle near CASTLETON (as in Walter Scott's *Peveril of the Peak*); the present structure dates from the 17th century.

'Beast of Bolsover, the'. The nickname given by parliamentary correspondents to Dennis Skinner (b.1932), the left-wing, decidedly non-New Labour MP for Bolsover since 1970. He is notorious for his forthright and sometimes personally abusive language in the House of Commons. He was expelled from the Chamber in 1980 for refusing to acknowledge the authority of George Thomas, the Speaker, and again in 1992 after he called the Conservative minister John Gummer a 'little squirt' and a 'wart'. Skinner describes himself in *Who's Who* as of 'good working-class mining stock', and he is generally held in public affection, even gaining admiration for his passion, integrity and honesty.

Bolt Head OE *bolt* 'projectile', hence a headland projecting into the sea.

A headland in Devon, at the western tip of the mouth of the KINGSBRIDGE Estuary, about 3 km (2 miles) south of Salcombe. About 8 km (5 miles) to the northwest, at the eastern end of Bigbury Bay (*see under* BIGBURY), is its sister headland **Bolt Tail**.

Bolton 'settlement with a special building', OE *bothl* 'special building' + -TON.

An industrial town and unitary authority in Greater Manchester, 17 km (11 miles) northwest of Manchester itself.

In the 18th century it grew as a centre of cotton spinning; Richard Arkwright (1732–92), the inventor of the spinning jenny, lived and worked in Bolton, while Samuel Crompton (1753–1827), inventor of the spinning mule, was born nearby and is buried in the town.

The Old Man and Scythe is the oldest inn in Bolton, dating from 1251. James Stanley, Earl of Derby, reputedly spent his last night at the inn before being executed by Oliver Cromwell, following a Royalist massacre in the town in 1651 during the Civil Wars.

Bolton was the birthplace of William Lever (1851–1925), the first Lord Leverhulme and founder of the Unilever soap empire; of the Burnley, Everton, Chelsea and Notts County footballer Tommy Lawton (1919–96); and of the fearsome Northamptonshire and England fast bowler Frank Tyson (b.1930).

Bolton Wanderers FC. Bolton's football club (nicknamed the Trotters) was founded in 1874 as a Sunday-school team. They acquired their name in 1877 when, after a disagreement with the local vicar, they severed their church links and found themselves with no permanent home ground, a state of affairs that persisted until 1895. The ground that they moved to, Burnden Park, was the scene of tragedy on 9 March 1946 when, during a home game with Stoke City, overcrowding caused many injuries due to crushing, and 33 people died. Bolton moved from Burnden Park to the new Reebok Stadium in 1997.

One of Bolton's most famous players was the England international Nat Lofthouse (b.1925), who earned the nickname the Lion of Vienna after a tough away win over Austria in 1952; Bolton now has a pub called The Lion of Vienna.

Bolton Abbey From the Augustinian priory here.
A small village on the River WHARFE in North Yorkshire, 8 km (5 miles) east of Skipton. An Augustinian community was established at Embsay, 6 km (4 miles) to the west in 1120 by William de Meschines and his wife Cicely de Romilly. Cicely's daughter Alice moved the community to Bolton Abbey in the 1150s, after her son, the Boy of Egremont (*see under* EGREMONT), had drowned in the nearby STRID. Destroyed in the Dissolution of the Monasteries, the priory is mostly now ruined, although the nave now functions as the parish church. The beautiful Abbey grounds, part of the Devonshire estates, are open to the public.

William Wordsworth based his poem *The White Doe of Rylstone* (1815) on a legend associated with the priory. The tale is set in the early 16th century, and concerns the local house of Norton. The heroine Emily is given a white doe by her brother Francis, who is later murdered following a rebellion. When Emily goes from her home in RYLSTONE to visit her brother's grave at Bolton Priory, the doe comes with her; after her death the doe continues to visit the grave alone.

J.M.W. Turner painted Bolton Priory *c.*1825, and the art critic John Ruskin, moved by its 'sweet peace and tender decay', described the scene as the most beautiful in England.

Boltons, the Probably from the *Bolton* family, which held land in the area from at least the mid-16th century until the mid-19th century, when it was sold for building.
A pair of facing crescents, which, together with neighbouring roads (e.g. **Little Boltons**), form a fashionable residential area in SOUTH KENSINGTON (SW10), in the London borough of Kensington and Chelsea. Several of its mansions approach the palatial, although a large proportion have now been adapted to commercial or institutional use. Past residents include the lyricist W.S. Gilbert, the singer Jenny Lind, the children's author Beatrix Potter and the film star Douglas Fairbanks, Jnr.

Bolton upon Dearne Dearne may be of OCelt origin or from OE *derne* 'hidden'.
A town on the River Dearne in South Yorkshire, 12 km (7.5 miles) southeast of Barnsley.

Bolventor 'bold venture' (alluding to the bravery involved in starting up a farming community on Bodmin Moor in the 19th century; the name is first recorded in 1844).
A village in Cornwall, in the middle of Bodmin Moor (*see under* BODMIN), about 16 km (10 miles) northeast of Bodmin. JAMAICA INN is nearby.

Bomb Alley[1]. In the Second World War, a corridor through Kent and Sussex that was badly damaged by German V-1 flying bombs aimed at London in 1944–5. The hits were caused either by the doodlebugs' notorious inaccuracy or as a result of being shot down by RAF fighters or anti-aircraft fire (out of 9521 launched at southern England, 4621 suffered this fate).
See also HELL'S CORNER.

Bomb Alley[2]. The name formerly given to a sequence of streets in DUBLIN, leading from the city centre to the Portobello Barracks in RATHMINES. It was the scene of many ambushes on British troops during the Anglo-Irish War (1919–21), and was also known as the Dardanelles, after the bloody and unsuccessful campaign in the First World War.

Bo-Mo. An occasional nickname for BOURNEMOUTH, used by the town's younger, trendier inhabitants.

Bonchurch 'Bona's church', OE male personal name *Bona*, perhaps a shortening of *Boniface* (the local church is dedicated to St Boniface) + *cirice* 'church'.
A seaside village on the ISLE OF WIGHT, at the eastern edge of VENTNOR.

The poet A.C. Swinburne (1837–1909) grew up in Bonchurch and is buried in the churchyard (his interment here caused a bit of a local stir because of his *douteux* reputation).

Bond Street From Sir Thomas *Bond*, Comptroller of the Household to Queen Henrietta Maria (widow of Charles I), who was one of the developers of Old Bond Street in the 1680s (*see also* STREET).

A street in MAYFAIR, in the City of WESTMINSTER, running from OXFORD STREET in the north to PICCADILLY[1] in the south. It is actually a street of two parts: the original, southern section, which from the middle of the 18th century has been called **Old Bond Street**, but before then was plain *Bond Street*; and the much longer northern section, from Burlington Gardens to Oxford Street, which dates from the 1720s and is known as **New Bond Street**.

From the beginning it was a street for wealthy shoppers and emulous window-shoppers, and it continues to be a by-word for expensive luxury. Jewellers are thick on the ground (Asprey's, Bentley and Skinner, Cartier, Tessier), couturiers abound (Armani, Donna Karan, Versace), there are art galleries aplenty (or alternatively Sotheby's) for those in search of old masters, and perfumers fragrance the air (in 1894 Max Beerbohm in the *Yellow Book* praised 'the admirable unguentarians of Bond Street'). The cachet of 'of Bond Street' is worth its weight in gold to a firm (e.g. Yardley's of Bond Street).

Bond Street Underground station, on the Central and Jubilee lines, opened in 1900 (its entrances are actually in Oxford Street).

Bond Street is valued at £320 on a Monopoly board.

Bonehill Probably 'hill where bulls graze', OE *bulena* possessive plural form of *bula* 'bull' + *hyll* 'hill'.
A village in Staffordshire, on the western outskirts of Tamworth.

Bo'ness A contraction of Borrowstounness, 'the promontory of Borrowstoun', village name + NESS. Borrowstown is 'farm or village of a man called Beornweard, or the bear-keeper', OE male personal name *Beornweard* in the possessive or ME *bere-ward* 'bear-keeper'. The earliest form is *Berwardeston* and it is unclear whether this is the personal name *Beornweard* or 'bear-keeper'; streets in medieval London, Nottingham, Northampton and Chester were named after bear-keepers.
An industrial town about 28 km (17 miles) west of Edinburgh, on the south shore of the Firth of FORTH. It was formerly in West Lothian, then in the Falkirk district of Central Region, and is now in Falkirk unitary authority. Until the early 19th century it was an important port.

Bonhill Apparently from *buth an uillt* 'house of the stream', Gaelic *buth* 'house, cottage' + *an uillt* 'of the stream', possessive form of *allt* 'stream, river'.

A small town just across the River Leven (*see under* LOCH LEVEN[1]) from Alexandria, in West Dunbartonshire (formerly in Strathclyde region). The family of the novelist Tobias Smollett (1721–71) owned the lands round here.

Bonnybridge 'bridge over the Bonny Water'.
A large village, 6 km (3.5 miles) west of Falkirk, formerly in Stirlingshire, then the Falkirk district of Central Region, and now in Falkirk unitary authority. It takes its name from the small **Bonny Water** (Scots *bonny* 'handsome, attractive') that flows through the village.

Bonnymuir. *See* Carron Ironworks *under* CARRON.

Bonnyrigg 'rounded ridge', Scots *bannock* 'round oat-cake' + *rigg* 'ridge'. An 18th-century record gives this name as *Bannockrig*, which suggests that Scots *bonny* 'handsome' is a red herring.
A small town in Midlothian, 10 km (6 miles) south of Edinburgh.

Booker Possibly 'beech-slope', OE *boc* 'beech' + *ora* 'slope'.
A southwestern suburb of HIGH WYCOMBE, Buckinghamshire.

Boolavogue Irish *Baile Mhaodhóg* 'Maodóg's town'.
A village in County Wexford, 8 km (5 miles) southeast of Ferns. The burning of the Catholic chapel here in 1798 sparked off the Wexford Rebellion (*see under* County WEXFORD), led by Father John Murphy.

> At Boolavogue, as the sun was setting,
> O'er the bright May meadows of Shelmalier,
> A rebel hand set the heather blazing
> And brought the neighbours from far and near,
> Then Father Murphy from old Kilcormack,
> Spurred up the rock with a warning cry
> 'Arm! Arm!' he cried, 'for I've come to lead you
> For Ireland's freedom to fight or die.'
>
>> P.J. McCall (1861–1919): 'Boolavogue' (a song long popular with Republicans)

Boor Etymology unknown.
A tiny settlement on LOCH EWE, northwest Highland (formerly in Ross and Cromarty), about 1.5 km (1 mile) northwest of Poolewe.

Boosbeck 'stream near a cow-shed', OE *bos* 'cow-shed' + OScand *bekkr* 'stream'.
A village in Redcar and Cleveland (formerly in the North Riding of Yorkshire, then in Cleveland), 5 km (3 miles) east of Guisborough.

Bootle 'special building', OE *botl*; *see also* BOLTON.
A large industrial town and port at the mouth of the River MERSEY in Merseyside, north of and contiguous with LIVERPOOL. In 1903 the House of Lords defeated a bill to unite Bootle with Liverpool. During the Second World War Bootle suffered badly in the Blitz; further destruction came

in 1995 when the Inland Revenue demolished its 19-storey office in Bootle owing to sick building syndrome.

Borchester. A fictional town, in the equally fictional West Midland county of **Borsetshire**, in which the BBC radio soap opera 'The Archers' (1951–) is set.

Border, the. Most frequently applied to the Anglo-Scottish border, but also, in Ireland, to the border between the North and the Republic. Those that live near the Anglo–Scottish border are called **Borderers**, and this is also the nickname of Berwick Rangers, the only English team to play in the Scottish League.

See also the DEBATABLE LANDS *and* the MARCHES.

'Blue Bonnets over the Border'. A rousing song by Sir Walter Scott:

> March, march, Ettrick and Teviotdale,
> Why the deil dinna ye march forward in order?
> March, march, Eskdale and Liddesdale,
> All the Blue Bonnets are bound for the Border.

Border ballad. A genre of traditional narrative verse (sometimes sung) from the Scottish BORDERS. Many deal with the darker doings of the Border reivers (*see below*), but they usually end unhappily anyway (for example, *see under* YARROW WATER). Many were collected by Sir Walter Scott in his *Minstrelsy of the Scottish Border* (1802–3).

Borderers, The. The title of a forgotten tragedy by William Wordsworth, set during the reign of Henry III. It was published in 1842, but written some fifty years earlier.

Border Leicester. A breed of sheep originating from a cross of Cheviot (*see under* CHEVIOT) and Leicester (*see under* LEICESTER) sheep.

Border Regiment. A regiment formed in 1881 by the amalgamation of the Cumberland Regiment of Foot and the Westmorland Regiment of Foot. In 1959 the Border Regiment joined with the King's Own Royal Regiment to form the King's Own Royal Border Regiment.

Border reiver. One who in former times conducted raids for plunder and booty across the Anglo–Scottish Border. They were also called 'moss troopers', from the high moorland that was their natural habitat. One of the most famous of the reivers was Kinmont Willie, of the Armstrong clan, who was celebrated in a famous ballad.

King of the Border, the. A nickname of Adam Scott of Tushielaw (executed 1529), a famous Border outlaw and chief.

North of the Border. A phrase meaning, effectively, Scotland. Pedants delight in pointing out that substantial parts of southwest Scotland, in Dumfries and Galloway, are actually *south* of the Border.

Borders, the. The informal name for the large area of southern Scotland on the north side of the BORDER with England, containing the easterly portion of the SOUTHERN UPLANDS. (In former times, the Anglo-Scottish border areas, in addition to the Anglo-Welsh ones, were sometimes called the MARCHES.) It is a land of high, rolling hills (now deforested and sheep-clad, except where the Forestry Commission has planted its exotics) and majestic rivers, among them the TWEED, the TEVIOT, ETTRICK WATER and YARROW WATER. This is above all SCOTT COUNTRY, a land of legend, blood feuds and romance. The area contains the old counties of ROXBURGHSHIRE, BERWICKSHIRE, PEEBLESSHIRE and SELKIRKSHIRE.

In 1975 these counties, together with a part of MIDLOTHIAN, were merged into **Borders** region, comprising the districts of Tweeddale (*see under* TWEED), ETTRICK AND LAUDERDALE, Berwickshire and ROXBURGH. The administrative centre was at NEWTON ST BOSWELLS, and other notable towns (many once famed for their weaving and knitwear) include LAUDER, DUNS, COLDSTREAM, KIRK YETHOLM, KELSO, JEDBURGH, HAWICK, MELROSE, GALASHIELS, SELKIRK, INNERLEITHEN and PEEBLES. In 1996 Borders region was abolished and replaced by the unitary authority called SCOTTISH BORDERS.

The Borders is the traditional heartland of Scottish rugby union. Clubs such as Gala, Hawick, Jed-Forest, Kelso, Melrose and Selkirk have proud histories, but (like the Scottish national side) have struggled in the professional era that arrived in the mid-1990s. A Borders team (based in Galashiels) is one of just three professional Scottish rugby union teams that plays in rugby union's Celtic League alongside other professional teams from Wales and Ireland.

> When I die, bury me low
> Where I can hear the bonnie Tweed flow,
> A sweeter place I'll never know
> Than the rolling hills o' the Borders.
>
> Matt McGinn: 'The Rolling Hills o' the Borders' (song)

Borderer. Someone who lives in the Borders.

> [Of the Borderers] They are not, to put it as tactfully as possible, the most immediately lovable folk in the United Kingdom.
>
> George Macdonald Fraser: *The Steel Bonnets* (1971)

King's Own Scottish Borderers, the. A regiment originally raised in 1689 as the Earl of Leven's or Edinburgh Regiment of Foot. After several changes, it settled on the present name in 1887. Its nicknames include The KOBs, The Botherers, and The Kosbees.

Borehamwood 'wood associated with a homestead or enclosure on a hill', OE *bor* 'hill' + HAM + OE *wudu* 'wood'.

A town in Hertfordshire, on the northwestern outskirts of London, about 8 km (5 miles) southwest of POTTERS BAR. In the golden years of the British film industry there were several studios and associated facilities here, many of which were transformed later in the 20th century to television use.

Bori-congriken gave. The Romany name for YORK, according to George Borrow's *Romano Lavo-Lil* ('word book of the Romany', 1874). The name means 'great church town'.

Borley 'glade frequented by boars', OE *bar* 'boar' + -LEY.

A village in Essex, about 35 km (22 miles) northeast of Saffron Walden, near the Suffolk border. In first half of the 20th century the local rectory had the reputation of being the most haunted house in England. It was the subject of an exhaustive series of 'ghost hunts' conducted between 1929 and 1938 by Harry Price, founder of the National Laboratory of Psychical Research. The manifestations were supposedly in the form of poltergeist activity, with interest in the phenomena first fuelled by the *Daily Mail*. Price himself stayed at the rectory for a year from 1937 and assiduously documented his investigations using remote-control cine-cameras, still cameras, fingerprinting paraphernalia and other equipment. The rectory burned down in 1939, and the following year Price published his sensational account *The Most Haunted House in England*. Critics pointed out, however, that the incumbents of the rectory had not reported any unusual incidents, and Price was accused of having faked or fabricated them. Legends of the hauntings lingered even so, and the site continues to draw the curious.

Boro-gueroneskey tem. The Romany name for NORTHUMBERLAND, according to George Borrow's *Romano Lavo-Lil* ('word book of the Romany', 1874). The name means 'big fellows' country'.

Borough, the ME *borough* 'a suburb, outside the city wall' (in contrast with the walled City of London, on the north bank of the Thames).

A name given to the former London borough of SOUTH-WARK (SE1), and in particular to the area just to the south of **London Bridge** (not to be confused with the much larger modern borough of Southwark). Records of the name 'Southwark borough', which emphasize its status as the southern, extra-mural portion of the entity known as London, go back to the mid-16th century, but the term 'the Borough' on its own is not recorded before the 18th century (there is evidence that in the 17th and 18th centuries it was being applied to **Borough High Street**, which in Roman times was STANE STREET[1]).

In former times the area was the principal gateway from London to southeast England and thence to the Continent. In the Middle Ages numerous taverns sprang up here to cater for travellers' needs, notably the White Hart, the Queen's Head, the George (still extant, and the last-remaining with galleries in London) and the Tabard (where Chaucer's Canterbury pilgrims lodged). The Borough developed a reputation for strong, high-quality beer, brewed locally from Thames water. The area was seriously damaged by bombing during the Second World War, but several attractive Georgian squares survive.

The Victorian criminal underworld in the Borough is brilliantly evoked in Sarah Waters's novel *Fingersmith* (2002).

Borough Market, nestling beneath railway arches at the southern end of London Bridge, has claims to be the oldest wholesale fruit and vegetable market in London: the original one may go back to 1014, and the site of the current one is first recorded on a map in 1542. In the latter part of the 20th century the Borough was a somewhat neglected portion of London, unmodernized and, with its old pubs, workshops and wine vaults, almost a 19th-century time capsule. But in the 1990s trendiness began to catch up with it, new restaurants and shops opened, and the Market, threatened with redevelopment, found a new lease of life as a retail market and foodies' mecca.

Borough Underground station, on the Northern line, opened in 1890.

In the early 19th century inhabitants of the Borough were often referred to as '**boro-onions**', a comical Cockney re-interpretation of **Boro(ugh)nians**.

Boroughbridge 'bridge by the stronghold', OE *burh* (*see* BURY) + *brycg* 'bridge'.

A small market town in North Yorkshire, 26 km (16 miles) northwest of York.

Battle of Boroughbridge (16 March 1322). A battle in which the rebel earls of Lancaster and Hereford were defeated by Edward II's forces. Hereford was killed during the battle, and Lancaster executed after it.

Borrowdale 'valley of the Borrow river', OScand *borgar-a*, 'river of the fort' (*borgar*, possessive of *borg* 'fort' + *a* 'river') + *dalr* 'dale'; the *borg* is a Roman fort at Low Borrow Bridge.

A valley in the northern LAKE DISTRICT, Cumbria (formerly in Cumberland), some 5 km (3 miles) south of Keswick. The village of Borrowdale is towards its southern end. The valley combines fields in its bottom with woods and crags on its steep sides, and leads the visitor from the gentle banks of Derwent Water (*see under* DERWENT[1]) south into the high fells towards SCAFELL PIKE. Coleridge describes a walk in the opposite direction, from Wasdale Head to Borrowdale:

> Brooks in their anger: all the gullies full and white, and the chasms now black, now half hid by the mist, and the waterfalls in them flashing through the mists.
>
> Samuel Taylor Coleridge: journal (15 November 1799)

The wettest place in England is Styhead Tarn, at the head of Borrowdale. It has an average annual rainfall of

4391 mm (172 in). The wettest *inhabited* place in England, the village of SEATHWAITE, is also in Borrowdale.

The novelist Sir Hugh Walpole latterly lived in Borrowdale, and died here in 1941. His historical romance, *The Herries Chronicle* (1930–3), is largely set in Borrowdale.

It was in Borrowdale that an exceptionally pure deposit of graphite (known locally as 'wadd') was discovered in 1564, leading to the development of the modern 'lead' pencil. The area became famous for its pencil manufacture, as commemorated at the Cumberland Pencil Museum at Keswick. The graphite was so valuable that men guarded the mine with blunderbusses, and in 1779 smuggled Borrowdale graphite was fetching 30 shillings a pound on the black market.

Borrowstounness. *See* BO'NESS.

Borstal 'place pledged as security', OE *borg* 'pledge, security, bail' + *steall* 'place'.
A village in Kent, about 3 km (2 miles) southwest of Rochester. In 1902, part of the local prison was converted into what was termed a 'juvenile-adult reformatory'. The methods applied here to young offenders were dubbed in 1908 the **Borstal system**: a person between the ages of 16 and 23 convicted of a criminal offence was sent to the Borstal institution for a period of reformative training, usually three years, and then released subject to future supervision by the Borstal Association. Further such institutions were soon opened, and by the 1920s the term **borstal** was being applied generically to them all. Brendan Behan's *Borstal Boy* (1958) gives a vivid fictionalized autobiographical account of life in such a centre. The name is now fading quietly into the past: in 1982, borstals officially became 'Youth Custody Centres', and were subsequently redesignated 'Young Offender Institutions'.

Borthwick 'castle farmstead', OE *burh* (*see* BURY) + *wic* (*see* WICK).
A small village 9 km (5.5 miles) south of Dalkeith in Midlothian. The well-preserved **Borthwick Castle** dates from the early 15th century. It was here that Mary Queen of Scots and Bothwell came after their marriage in 1567. They were immediately surrounded by their enemies, and were obliged to escape separately, Mary disguised as a page-boy.

Boscastle 'Boterel's castle' (referring to a castle held in the early 14th century by William de Botereus, of which little now remains), OFr surname *Boterel* + *castel* (*see* CASTLE).
A fishing port and holiday resort on the Atlantic coast of Cornwall, 5 km (3 miles) north of CAMELFORD. The young Thomas Hardy came here on 7 March 1870, and met his first wife Emma Gifford at nearby ST JULIOT the same year. In his melancholy poem '**At Castle Boterel**' (*Satires of Circumstance*, 1914), written after Emma's death in 1912 and permeated with his remorse at the souring of their rela-

tionship, Hardy recalls an early cliff-walk taken with Emma at Boscastle. The title of the poem echoes the village's medieval name of *Boterelescastel* (*see above*). The village also features as **Castle Boterel** in Hardy's novel *A Pair of Blue Eyes* (1873).

Boscastle lies in a steep valley where two valleys meet, formed by the rivers Valency and Jordan. On 16 August 2004, 70 mm (nearly 3 in) of rain fell in the hills above the village in just two hours, turning the rivers into a 3-m (10-ft) high torrent of water that devastated Boscastle, damaging numerous buildings and hurling cars and uprooted trees into the sea. 150 stranded villagers had to be airlifted to safety by the RAF. The Boscastle flash flood took place 52 years to the day after the LYNMOUTH flood disaster of 1952.

Most of picturesque **Boscastle Harbour** is owned by the National Trust.

Boscobel House *Boscobel* 'beautiful wood', Italian *bosco* 'wood' + *bello* 'beautiful', with reference to the timbers of which the house was built.
A 17th-century hunting lodge in Shropshire, about 16 km (10 miles) east of Telford. The **Boscobel Oak** or 'Royal Oak' in the grounds is said to be descended from one in which the future Charles II hid from his Parliamentarian pursuers after his defeat at the Battle of Worcester (*see under* WORCESTER) in 1651 (as described by Thomas Blount in his *Boscobel, or, the History of His Sacred Majesties most miraculous preservation after the Battle of Worcester* (1660)). The Pendrell family, who helped the king in his escape, were later granted a royal pension; their descendants continue to receive the (non-index-linked) sum of £1.49.
See also MOSELEY OLD HALL.

Boscombe¹ Probably 'valley overgrown with spiky plants', OE *bors* 'spiky plants' + *combe* (*see* -COMBE, COOMBE).
A village in Wiltshire, on the River Bourne, about 5 km (3 miles) southeast of Amesbury.
Boscombe Down. A Ministry of Defence establishment and RAF station to the northwest of Boscombe. It is home to the Empire Test Pilot School and the RAF Strike/Attack Operational Evaluation Unit.

Boscombe². An eastern coastal suburb of BOURNEMOUTH.

Bosham 'Bosa's homestead or promontory', OE male personal name *Bosa* + HAM 'homestead' or *hamm* 'promontory'.
A harbour town (pronounced 'bozzəm') in West Sussex, on **Bosham Channel**, on a small peninsula of Chichester Harbour (*see under* CHICHESTER). It is reputedly the place where King Cnut (Canute) (1016–35) ordered the waves to retreat, to illustrate not (as is popularly supposed) his presumptuousness, but rather his possession of merely human powers – a reprimand to obsequious courtiers. The

Anglo-Saxon church is said to be the burial-place of Cnut's wife or daughter.

It was from Bosham that Harold Godwineson set sail in 1064 on his ill-fated expedition to France. He was shipwrecked, then entertained by William of Normandy, but ended up being forced to swear a sacred oath to support William of Normandy's claim to the English throne after the death of Edward the Confessor.

In modern times the town is a busy yachting centre.

Boston 'Botwulf's stone' (probably a marker stone for a boundary or meeting-place), OE male personal name *Botwulf* + *stan* (*see* STONE); Botwulf is often identified with St Botulf or Botolph, the 7th-century missionary who is said to have founded an abbey here and to whom the local church is dedicated, but this is unlikely to be so.

A town in Lincolnshire, about 8 km (5 miles) from the WASH. In the Middle Ages it was an important port, on the River WITHAM, and the town became rich on the wool trade with Flanders. However, as the river started to silt up, and trade in the 16th and 17th centuries became increasingly monopolized by western ports, it went into a decline.

In the early 17th century the town was a noted centre of Puritanism and a point of departure for the early Pilgrim Fathers, and in 1630 a band of Puritans set sail from here to found Boston in Massachusetts. There is also a town called Boston in Georgia, USA, and Boston Bays in Jamaica and South Australia.

The poet Elizabeth Jennings (1926–2001) was born in Boston.

Boston Stump. The vertiginous tower – the second highest in the country at 83 m (272 ft) – of the 14th-century St Botolph's Church, Boston. It can be seen for many miles across the FENS, and ships in the Wash use it as a navigational aid.

> Play uppe, play uppe, O Boston bells!
> Play all your changes, all your swells.
>
> Jean Ingelow: 'The High Tide on the Coast of Lincolnshire, 1571' (1863)

Boston Spa *Boston* possibly a family name; *Spa* refers to the mineral spring discovered here in 1744.

A village in West Yorkshire, some 20 km (12 miles) southwest of York. Boston Spa is the British Library's northern site, with as many as 7 million publications in its document supply collection.

Bosworth 'Bosa's enclosure', OE male personal name *Bosa* + *-worth* (*see* -WORTH, WORTHY, -WARDINE).

The site (in full **Bosworth Field**), about 3 km (2 miles) southwest of the village of Market Bosworth and 20 km (12 miles) west of Leicester, of the **Battle of Bosworth**, the last battle of the Wars of the Roses. It was fought on 22 August 1485 between the Yorkist forces of Richard III

and Henry of Richmond's army. Richard was defeated and killed, and Henry became Henry VII, the first Tudor monarch of England.

Botany Bay From *Botany Bay* in Australia, site of an early British penal colony, in allusion to its remoteness.

A village in the north London borough of ENFIELD, just inside the M25.

Bóthar na Trá. The Irish name for SALTHILL.

Bothwell 'shelter by a spring', ME *bothe* 'booth, temporary shelter' + *well* 'spring'.

An industrial village in North Lanarkshire (formerly Strathclyde region) on the River CLYDE, 4 km (2.5 miles) north of Hamilton. **Bothwell Castle**, dating from the 13th century, is one of the largest in Scotland, and changed hands many times.

Battle of Bothwell Brig (22 June 1679). A battle in which the Duke of Monmouth (illegitimate son of Charles II) and James Graham of Claverhouse ('Bonnie Dundee' (*see under* DUNDEE)) routed a force of Covenanters.

Earl of Bothwell. James Hepburn, 4th Earl of Bothwell (*c*.1536–78), was the third husband of Mary Queen of Scots. His stronghold was Hermitage Castle, in the remote fastnesses far to the south of Bothwell. He was implicated in the murder of Mary's second husband, Lord Darnley, and there was general outrage when he subsequently abducted and married Mary (1567). The nobles revolted, and Bothwell was forced to flee to Denmark, where he died insane in a prison dungeon.

Botolph Claydon *Botolph* originally (1224) *Botle*, from OE *botl* 'house, building' – the assimilation to the name of the English saint is first recorded around 1825; *Claydon* 'clayey hill', OE *clǣgig* 'clayey' + *-don* (*see* DOWN, -DON).

A village in Buckinghamshire, about 16 km (10 miles) northwest of Aylesbury.

Botusfleming Cornish *bod* 'dwelling' + an unknown element later assimilated to the surname *Fleming*.

A village in Cornwall, to the west of the TAMAR estuary, about 3 km (2 miles) northwest of Saltash.

Boughton Aluph *Boughton* either 'beech-tree farmstead', OE *boc* 'beech' + *-TON*, or 'farmstead held by charter', OE *boc* 'book, charter' + *-TON*; *Aluph* denoting manorial ownership in the Middle Ages by someone called Alulf.

A village in Kent, about 6.5 km (4 miles) north of Ashford.

Boughton Malherbe *Malherbe* denoting manorial ownership in the Middle Ages by the Malherbe family.

A village in Kent, about 16 km (10 miles) northwest of Ashford.

Boughton Monchelsea *Monchelsea* denoting manorial ownership in the Middle Ages by the de Montchensie family.

A village in Kent, about 5.5 km (3.5 miles) south of Maidstone. The local quarries have been producing Kentish ragstone for building for at least 700 years, and much of the village sits on filled-in workings. The 15th-century lychgate in the local church is claimed as the oldest in England.

Boulby 'Bolli's farm', OScand male personal name *Bolli* + -BY.
A village in Redcar and Cleveland (formerly in the North Riding of Yorkshire, then in Cleveland), 4 km (2.5 miles) east of Loftus. The sea cliffs at nearby **Boulby Head** are the highest in England, at 203 m (666 ft). In **Boulby Mine**, run by Cleveland Potash Ltd, astrophysicists have set up an underground laboratory to detect the mysterious 'dark matter' that apparently fills our universe.

Boulter's Lock From the surname *Boulter* + ModE *lock*.
A lock on the River THAMES[1] at Taplow. Easily the most famous of Thames locks, its late-Victorian heyday is celebrated in Edward J. Gregory's celebrated painting *Boulter's Lock, Sunday Afternoon* (1895), in which trippers down from London disport themselves in punts and launches.

Bourne 'stream', OScand *brunnr*.
A market town in Lincolnshire, about 9 km (14 miles) northwest of Peterborough. An abbey for Augustinian canons was founded here in 1138.

It has a particular association with the early 14th-century cleric and writer Robert Mannyng, who was born here and who is generally known (following the original Scandinavian form of the place name) as **Robert Mannyng of Brunn**. His best-known work is *Handlyng Synne*, a 13,000-line collection of somewhat laboured rhyming couplets intended as an aid to spiritual self-examination prior to confession.

Bourne was also the birthplace of William Cecil, 1st Lord Burghley (1520–98), principal adviser to Elizabeth I.

Bourne End 'end of the stream' (because here the River Wye meets and merges with the Thames), OE *burna* 'stream' + *ende* 'end'.
A village in Buckinghamshire, on the River THAMES[1], about 5 km (3 miles) southwest of Beaconsfield. It is a notable boating centre.

Wooburn Grange in Bourne End played the part of Fawlty Towers Hotel in the eponymous BBC television sitcom (1975–79).

Bournemouth 'mouth of the stream', OE *burna* 'stream' + OE *mutha* 'mouth'.
A town, seaside resort and unitary authority within Dorset (until 1974, in Hampshire), on Poole Harbour (*see under* POOLE), about 39 km (24 miles) southwest of Southampton. It was designated a unitary authority (incorporating BOSCOMBE[2]) in 1997.

At the beginning of the 19th century Bournemouth was little more than a stretch of sandhills at the mouth of a stream called the **Bourne**. Then, in 1812, a certain Captain Lewis Tregonwell built himself a holiday home here. The town's real growth got under way in the 1830s, when a local landowner, Sir George Jervis, laid out a marine village round Tregonwell's house. An eminent physician of the period, Dr Granville, recommended its climate as an aid to recuperation, and in the second half of the 19th century Bournemouth expanded into one of the leading English seaside resorts.

Always at the more genteel, middle-class end of the resort spectrum, Bournemouth (soubriquet: '**The Queen of the South Coast**') offers its visitors spacious clifftop hotels, promenades and gardens, long sandy beaches, a lively musical culture (the **Bournemouth Symphony Orchestra** has achieved an international reputation) and the scent of pines:

> The real Bournemouth is all pines and pines and pines and flowering shrubs, lawns, begonias, azaleas, bird-song, dance tunes, the plung of the racket and creak of the basket chair.
>
> John Betjeman: *First and Last Loves* (1952)

Creeping bourgeois colonization led E.M. Forster to a more jaundiced view, however, in spite of the pines:

> Bournemouth's ignoble coast cowers to the right, heralding the pine trees that mean, for all their beauty, red houses and the Stock Exchange, and extend to the gates of London itself.
>
> *Howard's End* (1910)

Bournemouth's climate has the reputation of being 'relaxing', which makes it an ideal place for nursing and retirement homes and may perhaps exercise a calming influence over those who visit it in its more recent role as a conference venue. On the other hand, in the 1990s Bournemouth developed a lively club 'n' drug scene; somewhat shedding its reputation as a bastion of the COSTA GERIATRICA it has been described as 'the new Faliraki', implying a heady round of clubbing, drugging and copulation, and is referred to by its younger, trendier inhabitants as '**Bo-Mo**'.

The heart of the poet Percy Bysshe Shelley (1792–1822) is buried in Bournemouth. The writer Thomas Hardy fictionalized the town as 'Sandbourne' in several novels, including *Tess of the D'Urbervilles* (1891), *Jude the Obscure* (1895) and *The Well-Beloved* (1897).

See also POKESDOWN.

Bournville *Bourn* (from the River *Bourne*) + French *-ville*.
A southwestern suburb of BIRMINGHAM. It was developed from 1879 by the Quaker chocolate manufacturer George Cadbury as a model estate for his factory workers. His first

intention had been to call it Bournbrook, after a local mansion named **Bournbrook Hall** (which itself took its name from the **River Bourne**). At the last moment, however, he switched his preference to Bournville, apparently on the grounds that it sounded more 'French', and French chocolate had a greater commercial cachet than English. To this day, *Bournville* is used as a brand name for Cadbury's dark chocolate.
See also SELLY OAK.

Bournville boulevard. A contemporary slang term for the anus, with a vulgar play on the colour of the popular dark chocolate.

Bourton-on-the-Water *Bourton* 'farmstead near a fortification' (with reference to the nearby hillfort of Salmonsbury), OE *burh* (*see* BURY) + -TON; *Water*, referring to the River Windrush, distinguishes Bourton-on-the-Water from the village of Bourton-on-the-Hill.
A village in Gloucestershire, in the COTSWOLDS, about 21 km (13 miles) east of Cheltenham, and 12 km (7 miles) south of **Bourton-on-the-Hill**. It is one of the main villages on the Cotswold tourist route, featuring a picture-postcard church and cottages in glowing Cotswold stone and the River WINDRUSH flowing down the main street beneath five low stone bridges and turning an 18th-century watermill. The prominence of the river here is the source of Bourton-on-the-Water's nickname, '**the Venice of the Cotswolds**'.
Bourton lies at the southern end of the Roman road called ICKNIELD STREET.

Bovey A pre-English river name of unknown origin and meaning.
A river (pronounced 'buvvy') in south Devon, which rises on DARTMOOR and flows 20 km (13 miles) southeastwards to join the TEIGN south of BOVEY TRACEY.

Bovey Tracey *Bovey* from the River BOVEY; *Tracey* denoting manorial ownership in the Middle Ages by the de Tracy family.
A small town in Devon, on the River BOVEY, about 8 km (5 miles) northwest of Newton Abbot.

Bovey Beds. A deposit of sands, clays and lignite, 60–90 m (197–295 ft) thick, extending from Bovey Tracey to NEWTON ABBOT. The extracted clay is used for pipe- and pottery-making.

Bovington 'estate associated with Bofa', OE male personal name *Bofa* + -ING + -TON.
An army camp in Dorset, on **Bovington Heath**, about 9.5 km (6 miles) west of Wareham. It houses the Royal Armoured Corps Tank Museum.

Bovium. A Roman fort, possibly on the site of present-day COWBRIDGE.

Bow From the 'bow'-shaped bridge over the River Lea, originally built here in the 12th century.

An area in East London (E3), in the borough of TOWER HAMLETS, on the opposite bank of the River LEA from STRATFORD. It appears to have grown up in the early Middle Ages as an adjunct to Stratford, and its earliest separate identification is as **Stratford-atte-Bow** (Stratford at the Bow) in 1279. It still retained this name a century later:

> And Frenssh she [the Prioress] spak ful faire and fetisly,
> After the scole of Stratford atte Bowe,
> For Frenssh of Parys was to hire unknowe.
>
> Geoffrey Chaucer: *The Canterbury Tales* (1387)

The 'bow' in question was an arched stone bridge over the River Lea, said to have been built at the instigation of Maud, the wife of Henry I. Its present-day successor was built in 1973.
The expansion of London in the mid 19th century brought factories and slums to Bow. The largest of the former was Bryant and May's match factory, scene of the famous match-girls' strike of 1888. Bow Road Underground station, on the District line and the Hammersmith & City line, opened in 1902. In the late 20th century, however, gentrification crept over the area.
The famous '**Bow bells**' of London have no connection with Bow. They were the peal of bells at St Mary-le-Bow, CHEAPSIDE, destroyed by bombing in 1941 ('bow' in this context refers to the arches that supported the steeple of the original church). The notion that a true 'Cockney' is someone born within the sound of Bow bells (the earliest allusions to which date from the beginning of the 17th century: 'All within the sound of Bow Bell are in reproch called cochnies, and eaters of buttered tostes', Fynes Morison, *Itinerary* (1617)) probably comes from the medieval practice of ringing the City of London curfew on them.

Bow. A type of blue-and-white porcelain originally made in the mid-18th century at the Bow China Manufactory in Stratford. The name perhaps refers to early experiments in the technique carried out at Bow. In 1775 manufacture was moved to Derby.

Bow Brickhill *Bow* originally (1198) *Bolle*, from OE male personal name *Bolla* (probably an early tenant); *Brickhill* 'hill called *Brig*', OCelt *brig* 'hilltop' + OE *hyll* 'hill' - the name is thus tautological.
A village in Buckinghamshire, about 6.5 km (4 miles) southeast of Milton Keynes.

Bowd 'curved wood', OE *boga* 'bend, bow' + OE *wudu* 'wood'.
A village in Devon, lying about 3 km (2 miles) northwest of Sidmouth.

Bowen's Court After the *Bowen* family.
A former 18th-century mansion in County Cork, some 40 km (25 miles) north of Cork itself. It was built by the Bowen family on land granted to them in the 17th century by

Oliver Cromwell. The novelist Elizabeth Bowen (1899–1973) was brought up here and lived here after her husband's death in 1952. She later sold the house to a local man, who subsequently demolished it. She herself is buried near the front door of the church at Bowen's Court.

Bowerchalke *Bower* either from OE (*ge*)*bura* 'of the peasants' or from *burh* 'fortified place' (*see* BURY) + -*chalke* (*see* CHALK).

A village in Wiltshire, about 14 km (8.5 miles) southwest of Salisbury.

See also BROAD CHALKE.

Bowes 'the river-bends', OE *boga* in ME plural form *bowes*; the river is the GRETA.

A village in County Durham, 7 km (4 miles) southwest of Barnard Castle, on a crest of the PENNINES known as **Bowes Moor**. Bowes has a ruined 12th-century Norman keep, built on the site of the old Roman camp of **Lavartris**.

Charles Dickens visited Bowes in 1838 while conducting research on the state of private education, and the boarding school owned by William Shaw in Bowes became the basis of Dotheboys Hall in *Nicholas Nickleby* (1839). Shaw himself provided the model for Wackford Squeers.

> … these Yorkshire schoolmasters were the lowest and most rotten round of the whole ladder. Traders in the avarice, indifference or imbecility of parents and the helplessness of children; ignorant, sordid, brutal men, to whom few considerate persons would have entrusted the board and lodging of a horse and dog …
>
> Charles Dickens: *Nicholas Nickleby* (1839), Preface

'Tragedy of Bowes, The'. An anonymous ballad about the young lovers Rodger Wrightson and Martha Railton of Bowes. When Rodger died of a fever in March 1714 or 1715, Martha's heart broke:

> She spent her time in godly prayers,
> And quiet rest did from her fly;
> She to her friends full oft declares,
> She could not live if he did die:
> Thus she continued till the bell,
> Began to sound his fatal knell.
>
> And when she heard the dismal sound,
> Her godly book she cast away,
> With bitter cries would pierce the ground.
> Her fainting heart 'gan to decay:
> She to her pensive mother said,
> 'I cannot live now he is dead.'

And she was as good as her word, dying within hours of her lover's death.

Bowfell Possibly 'curved mountain', ME *bow* 'bent, curved' + OScand *fjall*, 'mountain, fell'.

A mountain (902 m / 2959 ft) at the head of LANGDALE, in the LAKE DISTRICT, Cumbria, 13 km (8 miles) west of Ambleside. The summit is gained from Langdale by a ridge called the Band, and on the north side of the mountain is a pass called the Ore Gap, because of the rich vein of haematite that stains the rocks here.

Bowland, Forest of. *See* FOREST OF BOWLAND.

Bowling Green From a local bowling green (the name dates from the 19th century).

A village in Worcestershire (before 1998 in Hereford and Worcester, before 1974 in Worcestershire), about 5 km (3 miles) southwest of Worcester.

Bowness-on-Windermere. *See under* WINDERMERE.

Bow Street From its layout: it runs in a curving line, in the shape of a bow.

A street in Central London (WC2) running between LONG ACRE in the north and Wellington Street in the south, just to the east of COVENT GARDEN. It was built between 1633 and 1677. It was originally an elegant residential street (Dr Johnson lodged here for a while), but gradually THEATRE-LAND encroached (the first Covent Garden Theatre opened here in 1732, on the site of what is now the Royal Opera House) and by the beginning of the 19th century it had become notorious for its brothels. In 1740 the Bow Street magistrates' office was opened, from which the Bow Street Runners (*see below*) operated. It stood on the site of what is now **Bow Street Magistrates' Court**, where the Metropolitan Chief Magistrate sits.

Bow Street is valued at £180 on a Monopoly board.

See also CHINA STREET.

Bow Street Runner. A member of a London police force based in Bow Street in the late 18th and early 19th centuries. They had their origins in an irregular force set up in the middle of the 18th century by the Bow Street magistrate, the novelist and barrister Henry Fielding (1707–54), to supplement the less than adequate parish constabularies of the time. By the beginning of the 19th century, when the term 'Bow Street Runner' is first recorded, they had been placed on a more regular footing, with a uniform of a blue dress-coat, brass buttons, and a bright red waistcoat (whence their nickname, 'redbreast' or 'Robin redbreast'). They were disbanded in 1839, having been rendered redundant by the new Metropolitan Police.

Box[1] '(place at the) box-tree', OE *box* 'box-tree'.

A village in Wiltshire, about 9 km (5.5 miles) northeast of Bath.

Box Tunnel. A railway tunnel under BOX HILL[2], through which the main line from London to Bath and Bristol runs. It was designed by Isambard Kingdom Brunel. A small adjacent tunnel, now disused, leads to the secret TURN-STILE headquarters (*see under* CORSHAM).

Box[2]. A village in Gloucestershire, about 5 km (3 miles) south of Stroud.

Boxgrove 'box-tree grove', OE *box* 'box-tree' + *graf* 'grove'.
A village in West Sussex, about 5 km (3 miles) northeast of
Chichester. In 1622 six parishioners were prosecuted for
playing cricket in the local churchyard.

Boxgrove Man. An early hominid, half a million years
old, identified from teeth and fragments of a fossilized
shinbone found in a gravel quarry in Boxgrove in 1993.
They were at the time estimated to be the oldest human
remains discovered in Europe, but two years later much
older ones were found in a Spanish cave.

Box Hill¹ From the *box* trees that once grew on it in
abundance.

A steep hill, 183 m (600 ft) high, in Surrey; it is part of
the NORTH DOWNS, about 3 km (2 miles) northeast of
DORKING, overlooking the River MOLE¹. The extensive views
available from its summit have made it a popular spot for
visitors (including small boys, who invent various white-
knuckle methods of descending its precipitous side), and
it has been officially declared an area of outstanding
natural beauty. Along its foot runs an ancient trackway
that may have linked STONEHENGE to the coast. A few of
the hill's original box trees remain, but most of them were
cut down in the 18th century, when boxwood was in much
demand for engraving.

The hill was the destination of the celebrated outing in
Chapter 43 of Jane Austen's *Emma* (1816), in which Emma
is reprimanded by Mr Knightley for making a joke at the
expense of the garrulous old maid Miss Bates. (Reader, she
married him.)

A memorial on Box Hill marks the resting-place of the
18th-century Marines officer Major Peter Labelliere (d.1800),
the eccentric provisions of whose will required that he be
buried upside down on Box Hill in order that 'as the world
has turned topsy-turvy he might come right at last'. Labelliere's will also stipulated that before he was thus interred
his youngest son and the daughter of his landlady should
dance on his coffin.

The village of **Box Hill**, taking its name from the hill, is
just to the northeast.

Box Hill² From Box¹.

A hill a little to the northeast of Box in Wiltshire. Beneath
its summit is the old Bath-stone quarry in which the
British Government's secret Cold War command centre,
codenamed TURNSTILE, was constructed (*see under*
CORSHAM).

Boyle Irish *Mainistir na Búille* 'monastery on the River Boyle';
the river name is possibly from Irish *buille* 'cast of a net', with
reference to the abundance of fish.

A small market town on the River **Boyle**, County Roscommon, 13 km (8 miles) west of Carrick-on-Shannon. The
Cistercian **Boyle Abbey** was founded in 1161 and its

well-preserved ruins can still be seen. They were used as
barracks in the 17th and 18th centuries, and were badly
damaged by Oliver Cromwell's forces.

> I found in the noble district of Boyle …
> … horsemen bold and sudden in fight.
>
> Anon.: 'Aldfrid's Itinerary Through Ireland' (12th century),
> translated by James Clarence Mangan

Boyne Irish *An Bhóinn*, traditionally said to refer to the local
river goddess *Boand*, whose name derives from Irish *bó* 'cow'
+ *bhán* 'white'.

A river of central-eastern Ireland; length 110 km (68 miles).
It rises in the BOG OF ALLEN and flows northeastwards
through NAVAN to meet the Irish Sea just east of DROGHEDA.
In legend the River Boyne was formed when Boann, mother
of Aengus Og, god of love, failed to honour the obligations
associated with the Well of Knowledge, which in retaliation overflowed to drown her, thus forming the river.
A pool in the river also became the home of Fintan, who
took the form of a salmon to survive the Flood; after he
consumes the Nuts of Knowledge he becomes the Salmon
of Knowledge. In another legend, it was on the banks of
the River Boyne that Morrigan, goddess of feuds, made love
to Dagda, father of the gods.

Battle of the Boyne (1 July Old Style 1690). A defeat for
James II and the Jacobite cause, but not, despite its place
in Orange iconography, the final, decisive battle of the
Williamite Wars (that was to come at AUGHRIM the
following year). The battle took place at Oldbridge near
the mouth of the River Boyne, 5 km (3 miles) from
Drogheda. Orangemen celebrate William III's victory every
year on 12 July (New Style) with marches, flutings and
banging of drums.

> July the First, of a morning clear, one thousand six
>   hundred and ninety,
> King William did his men prepare, of thousands he had
>   thirty;
> To fight King James and all his foes, encamped near the
>   Boyne Water,
> He little fear'd, though two to one, their multitudes to
>   scatter.
>
> Anon.: 'The Boyne Water', an old Orange song (Actually,
> William had some 36,000 men, to James's 25,000.)

Boyne Valley. A Bronze Age culture in the valley of the
Boyne in counties Meath and Louth, and also the collective name (in Irish **Brú na Bóinne** 'palace of the Boyne') for
the four great prehistoric sites at NEWGRANGE, KNOWTH
and Dowth on the River Boyne between Slane and
Drogheda, and at FOUR KNOCKS hill 20 km (12 miles) to
the southeast, built between 3100 and 1800 BC. The first
three form a UNESCO World Heritage Site (since 1993) –
under the not very trippingly entitled '**Archaeological
Ensemble of the Bend of the Boyne**' – on the basis that

they constitute 'Europe's largest and most important concentration of prehistoric megalithic art'.

In Irish mythology, Brú na Bóinne is the home of Aengus Og, god of love, and of the goddess Morrigan; it was also the birthplace of the legendary hero Cuchulainn, whom Morrigan later failed to seduce.

> There came a breath of finer air
>   That touch'd the Boyne with ruffling wings,
> It stirr'd him in his sedgy lair
>   And in his mossy moorland springs.
>
> Samuel Ferguson (1810–86): 'The Burial of King Cormac'

'Green Grassy Slopes of the Boyne'. Another Orange song celebrating King Billy's victory:

> On the green grassy slopes of the Boyne
> Where the Orangemen with William did join
> And fought for our glorious deliv'rance
> On the green grassy slopes of the Boyne.

Of course, the Orange Order was not formed for another hundred years.

Bozeat 'Bosa's gate or gap', OE male personal name *Bosa* + *geat* 'gate, gap'.
A village (pronounced 'boazi-at') in Northamptonshire, about 11 km (7 miles) east of Northampton.

Braaid 'place at the pass', Manx Gaelic *brágha* 'gorge, pass', in the dative case *bràghaid*.
A small settlement on the Isle of Man, 6 km (4 miles) west of Douglas.

Brack, the 'speckled (mountain)', Gaelic *breac* 'speckled'.
A craggy mountain (787 m / 2583 ft) in the Arrochar Alps (*see under* ARROCHAR), Argyll and Bute (formerly in Argyll, then in Stratchclyde), 6 km (4 miles) west of Arrochar, guarding the entrance to the REST AND BE THANKFUL Pass.

Brackenbury Village From *Brackenbury Road* in the northern part of the area.
A name invented by estate agents in the early 21st century for an area of HAMMERSMITH (W6) roughly between Goldhawk Road in the north and Glenthorne Road in the south. The rural connotations are designed to make the area sound more attractive to potential house-buyers.

Bracklesham 'Braccol's homestead', OE *Braccoles* possessive form of male personal name *Braccol* + HAM.
A seaside village in West Sussex, about 6.5 km (4 miles) northwest of Selsey Bill.
Bracklesham Bay. A wide shallow sandy bay, about 11 km (7 miles) long, between SELSEY Bill and the mouth of CHICHESTER Harbour.

Bracknell 'Bracca's corner of land', OE *Braccan* possessive form of male personal name *Bracca* + *halh* (*see* HALE, -HALL).
A town in the unitary authority of Bracknell Forest, about 6 km (4 miles) east of Wokingham. It was designated a NEW TOWN[1] in 1998. Until 2004 it was home to the headquarters of the Meteorological Office, which then moved to EXETER.

Bracknell Forest. A unitary authority created in 1998 in the southeastern part of the historic county of Berkshire. It is partly forested. Its administrative headquarters are in BRACKNELL.

Braddock Down 'broad oak down' or 'down in broad hooked piece of land', *Braddock* OE *brad* 'broad' + *ac* 'oak' or *hoc* 'hooked piece of land'; *Down see* DOWN, -DON.
An area of downland to the west of LISKEARD in Cornwall.
Battle of Braddock Down (19 January 1643). A battle of the Civil Wars in which a Royalist army under Sir Ralph Hopton defeated a Parliamentarian force.

Bradenham[1] 'broad homestead or enclosure', OE *bradan* dative form of *brad* 'broad' + HAM 'homestead' or *hamm* 'enclosure' (*see* HAM).
A village in Buckinghamshire, about 6.5 km (4 miles) northwest of High Wycombe.
Bradenham ham. A variety of English cooked ham whose most distinctive feature is its black exterior. This is achieved by extended curing in molasses, with an admixture of juniper berries and spices. Inside, it looks perfectly normal and has quite a delicate flavour. It has been made in CHIPPENHAM, Wiltshire, since the late 18th century. The connection with Bradenham is that the recipe for the curing mixture is said to have been brought to Wiltshire by the butler from **Bradenham Park**.

> This was at one time the home of Disraeli, but whether he was accustomed to Bradenham ham or whether his Jewish origins prevented him enjoying it, we do not know
>
> Jane Grigson: *English Food* (1974)

Bradenham[2]. A village in Norfolk, about 32 km (20 miles) west of Norwich. The writer H. Rider Haggard (1856–1925) was born here.

Bradfield 'broad stretch of open land', OE *brad* 'broad' + *feld* (*see* FIELD).
A village in Berkshire, on the River PANG, about 13 km (8 miles) west of Reading. **Bradfield College**, a co-educational public school, was founded in 1850 by Thomas Stevens, Rector and Lord of the Manor of Bradfield.

Bradfield Combust *Combust* 'burnt' (because local land was cleared by burning); the name appears with the prefix *burne* 'burnt' in the 17th century, but the addition of *Combust* seems to be modern.
A village in Suffolk, about 13 km (8 miles) south of Bury St Edmunds. The villages of **Bradfield St George** (named after the dedication of its parish church) and **Bradfield St Clare** (named after the medieval Seyncler family) lie respectively to the northeast and east. Also to the east, close

to the village of Felsham, are **Bradfield Woods**, one of the oldest examples of coppiced woodland in England. The first records of Bradfield Woods date back to 1252, when they were owned by the abbots of Bury St Edmunds, and the woods have been managed continuously since then. More than 350 plant species have been recorded there.

Bradford 'broad ford', OE *brad* 'broad' + FORD.

An industrial city and metropolitan borough in West Yorkshire, 14 km (8.5 miles) west of Leeds. It was a centre of the woollen industry from the 13th century, and both industry and city greatly expanded in the 19th century, when Bradford became the world's largest producer of worsted cloth, and the seventh largest town in the country. However, the textile industry declined in the 1970s.

In the past, Bradford did not have an altogether favourable press, as witnessed by this 1840 tirade by the German revolutionary poet Georg Weerth (1822–56):

> Every other factory town in England is a paradise compared to this hole. In Manchester the air lies like lead upon you; in Birmingham it's as if you're sitting with your nose in a stove; in Leeds you splutter with the filth as if you had swallowed a pound of Cayenne pepper – but you can put up with all this. In Bradford, however, you are lodged with the devil incarnate ... If anyone wishes to feel how a sinner is tormented in Purgatory, let him travel to Bradford.

Bradford's natives are inclined to be more charitable; one such, J.B. Priestley, lightly disguised Bradford as **Bruddersford** in *The Good Companions* (1929), and also in *Bright Day* (1946):

> Lost in its smoky valley among the Pennine hills ... Bruddersford is generally held to be an ugly city ... but it always seemed to me to have the kind of ugliness that could not only be tolerated but often enjoyed.

Elsewhere Priestley notes that Bradford 'has the good fortune to be on the edge of some of the most enchanting country in England'; more recently, the travel writer Bill Bryson has averred that 'Bradford is here to make everywhere else look better.'

Bradford is home to **Bradford Grammar School** (of medieval foundation; pupils have included the archaeologist Sir Mortimer Wheeler and Denis Healey), **Bradford University** (founded as the Bradford Institute of Technology in 1957 and thus elevated in 1966) and the National Museum of Photography, Film and Television (opened 1983). **Bradford Cathedral** (14th–15th century; elevated to cathedral status in 1919) is home to the National Faith Centre. Bradford has a highly multicultural population, including many people from the Indian Subcontinent, who have, among other contributions, provided the city with

a plethora of notable curry houses. The area of the city called **Little Germany**, full of what were once woollen warehouses, reflects the 19th-century influx of German-Jewish merchants.

Bradford was the birthplace of the composer Frederick Delius (1862–1934); the painter and writer William Rothenstein (1872–1945); the physicist and Nobel laureate Edward Appleton (1892–1965), after whom the Appleton Layer is named; the novelist and playwright J.B. Priestley (1894–1984); the Labour politician Barbara Castle (1911–2002); the novelist John Braine (1922–86); and the artist David Hockney (b.1937). (There is a large collection of Hockney's paintings at the 1853 Gallery at SALTAIRE, on the northwest edge of the city.) Last but not least, the Bradford suburb of Frizinghall was the birthplace of the Surrey and England off-spinner Jim Laker (1922–86), whose feat of taking 19 wickets in a single test match against Australia (at Old Trafford in 1956) has never been equalled.

The Independent Labour Party was founded by Keir Hardie at a conference in Bradford in 1893; the pioneering social worker and educationalist Margaret Macmillan joined the party that same year, when she moved to Bradford (where she was to live and work for a decade). Vic Feather (1908–76), General Secretary of the TUC from 1969 to 1973, was brought up in Bradford, and raised to the peerage in 1974 as Baron Feather of the City of Bradford. The Brontës were born in the western suburb of THORNTON[2].

There are towns called Bradford in the USA (Massachusetts, Pennsylvania).

Bradford. Rhyming slang in West Yorkshire (especially Leeds) for 'cheque', as in *Bradford Beck*, Bradford being 'the city that can't afford a river'.

Bradford Bulls. Bradford's rugby league club, which plays at the Odsal Stadium. **Bradford Rugby Club**, originally founded in 1864, seceded from the Rugby Football Union along with 21 other northern rugby clubs (*see* HUDDERSFIELD) in 1895 to form the Northern Rugby Union (later to become the Rugby Football League). The club split in 1907, some members rejecting the new form of rugby in 1907 to found Bradford Park Avenue football club (*see below*), others creating a new club, **Bradford Northern**. When the rugby league formed a Super League in 1995, Bradford Northern became Bradford Bulls.

Bradford City FC. Bradford's main football club, founded in 1903, is nicknamed the Bantams on account of the supposed resemblance of the club's colours (amber and claret) to those of a bantam chicken. Bradford City's home ground, Valley Parade, was on 11 May 1985 the scene of the horrific **Bradford City Disaster** – 56 people were killed and 200 suffered burns when the main stand was destroyed by a fire, probably started by a discarded cigarette setting light to mounds of rubbish that had accumulated beneath the stand (a newspaper found afterwards in the débris dated from as far back as 1968). Another Bradford football team, **Bradford Park Avenue**, originally founded by disaffected rugby players in 1907 (*see above*), folded in 1974, but was revived in 1988.

Bradford Cities is rhyming slang for 'titties', i.e. the breasts. The usage may date from as recently as the 1990s.

Bradford-on-Avon *See* BRADFORD *and* AVON[1].
A town in Wiltshire, on the Bristol AVON[2], about 9 km (5.5 miles) southeast of Bath. In former centuries it was an important centre for the wool trade. A notable architectural feature is the minute chapel on the 14th-century bridge over the Avon, originally for the use of pilgrims travelling to GLASTONBURY and MALMESBURY, but in the 17th century pressed into more secular service as a lock-up. Of late, many of its former wool-trade buildings have been converted into residential accommodation.

Bradford Peverell *Peverell* denoting manorial ownership in the Middle Ages by the Peverel family.
A village in Dorset, about 5 km (3 miles) northwest of Dorchester.

Brading 'place of those dwelling on the hillside', OE *brerd* 'hillside' + *-ingas* (*see* -ING).
A village on the ISLE OF WIGHT, 6 km (4 miles) south of Ryde, situated at the foot of **Brading Down** (124 m / 407 ft). Brading's 12th-century church is the oldest on the Isle of Wight, and the village has two museums: Osborn-Smith's Wax Museum, which is devoted to the history of the Isle of Wight, and the Lilliput Museum of Antique Dolls and Toys. The remains of a bull-baiting ring and a Roman villa are nearby

Bradley Stoke A modern coinage (1984), from the names of the local *Bradley* Brook and *Stoke* Brook.
A town in South Gloucestershire (before 1996 in Avon), created in the 1980s and 1990s as a northerly suburb of BRISTOL. It has the largest housing estate in Europe.

Bradshaw 'broad wood', OE *brad* 'broad' + *sceaga* 'wood, copse'.
A village in Greater Manchester, 4 km (2.5 miles) northeast of Bolton.

Bradwell-on-Sea '(place at the) broad spring or stream', OE *brad* 'broad' + *wella* 'spring, stream'.
A village in Essex, near the mouth of the BLACKWATER[1] estuary, about 16 km (10 miles) east of Maldon. Its Roman garrison, **Othona**, was part of the defensive network along the SAXON SHORE. The smaller nearby **Bradwell Waterside** is actually closer to the sea. Bradwell nuclear power station produced electricity for 40 years before being closed down in 2002.

Braehead of Lunan 'head of the hill above Lunan', Scots *brae* 'hillside'.
A tiny settlement in Angus (formerly in Tayside region), 5 km (3 miles) south of Montrose. It is close to the settlement of **Lunan**, and both overlook LUNAN BAY.

There are a number of other Braeheads in Scotland: in Moray, Orkney (two) and South Lanarkshire (two).

Braemar 'upper part of MAR', Gaelic *braighe* 'upper part' + *mar*.
A village (also called **Castleton of Braemar**) in upper Deeside, in Aberdeenshire (formerly in Grampian region), 12 km (7.5 miles) west of Balmoral Castle. It is at an altitude of over 300 m (1000 ft), and its inland position, nestled among the high CAIRNGORM MOUNTAINS, makes it the coldest place in Britain, with an annual mean temperature of 6.34°C (43.41°F). Braemar also holds the record for Britain's lowest temperature: on 11 February 1895, and again on 10 January 1982, the temperature fell to –27.2°C (–11.7°F). Despite the inclement weather, the consumptive Robert Louis Stevenson spent a winter here, and began the writing of *Treasure Island*.

In 1715 the Earl of Mar raised the standard for the Old Pretender, King James VIII of Scotland, on a mound in Braemar, so marking the beginning of the ill-fated 1715 Jacobite Rising. (The site is where the Invercauld Arms now stands.) The Earl's seat, **Braemar Castle**, dates from 1628, and was considerably modified and extended by occupying Hanoverian troops after the failure of the 1745 Jacobite Rebellion.

Braemar Gathering, the. The most famous of the Highland Games, held on the first Saturday in September. The Gathering was founded by the Braemar Wrights' Friendly Society in 1832, although it is said that in the 11th century Malcom III Canmore summoned the clans to Braemar for athletic contests, as a means of selecting the strongest men for his army. The royal connection was re-established in 1848, when Queen Victoria first visited, and the Gathering is still patronized annually by royalty.

'Poacher o Braemar, The'. A ballad by W. McCombie Smith, from his classic work, *The Romance of Poaching in the Highlands* (1904):

> I am a roving Highlander, a native o Braemar
> I've often climbed the mountains surrounding
>   Lochnagar ...

Braeriach 'the mottled upland', from its Gaelic name *Am Bràigh Riabhach, am* 'the' + *bràigh* 'upland' (*compare* Scots *brae*) + *riabhach* 'brindled, greyish'.
The third highest mountain (1296 m / 4248 ft) in the British Isles, on the border of Highland and Aberdeenshire (formerly Inverness-shire and Aberdeenshire, then Highland and Grampian), some 7 km (4 miles) southwest of

CAIRN GORM. It is the second highest of the Cairngorm Four-Thousanders (*see under* CAIRNGORM MOUNTAINS). The River DEE[1] rises on its summit plateau, before tumbling into the mountain's cliff-lined Garbh Choire ('rough corrie'), notable in winter and spring for the massive size and baroque curlicues of the snow cornices that hang over its rim. More than one climber has reported an almost irresistible urge, when alone on Braeriach's summit, to hurl himself or herself off this rim into the boulder-strewn depths of the corrie below. As far as is known, all such urges have thus far been resisted.

Braes, The *Scots* braes 'hillsides', from OScand *bra*, literally 'eyelid', but related to English 'brow'.

A crofting township on the east coast of SKYE, in Highland (formerly in Inverness-shire), 10 km (6 miles) south of Portree.

Battle of the Braes (1882). A violent confrontation between crofters threatened with eviction and a contingent of 50 Glasgow policemen. Although the incident resulted in no fatalities, it is sometimes said that this, and not the Battle of Culloden (*see* CULLODEN MUIR), was the last battle on British soil. A Royal Commission followed in 1883, and the Crofter Act passed four years later did much to protect crofters' rights.

Braes of Balquhidder. *See under* BALQUHIDDER.

Braes of the Carse. *See under* CARSE OF GOWRIE.

Brahan Etymology unknown.

An estate once belonging to the Mackenzie earls of Seaforth, in Highland (formerly in Ross and Cromarty), some 3 km (2 miles) southwest of Dingwall. **Brahan Castle** was demolished in 1951, and the old stables became the new **Brahan House**.

Brahan Seer, the. A shady figure, whose prophesies were for long known only in Gaelic oral tradition. He may have been Kenneth Mackenzie (also called *Coinneach Odhar* 'duncoloured Kenneth'), who was born near Uig in Lewis *c*.1650, and who from *c*.1675 worked as a labourer on the Brahan estate. However, there are records from 1577 in which one 'Keanoch Odhar' is to be prosecuted for witchcraft. Among other things, he is supposed to have predicted the Battle of CULLODEN MUIR and the building of the CALEDONIAN CANAL. He also made various predictions about STRATHPEFFER (just north of the Brahan estate), and about the end of the Seaforth Mackenzie line as he died – on the orders of the Countess of Seaforth at Chanonry Point (*see* FORTROSE).

Brain From BRAINTREE.

A river in Essex, which flows 22 km (14 miles) southeastwards through Braintree to join the River BLACKWATER[1] at Witham.

Braintree 'Branca's tree', OE male personal name *Branca* + *treow* 'tree'.

A town in Essex, about 27 km (16.5 miles) west of Colchester. From the Middle Ages to the 19th century it was an important wool-weaving centre. In 1880 Courtaulds opened a factory here for silk production, which spelt the end for wool.

Nicholas Udall, author of *Ralph Roister Doister* (1566), the earliest known English comedy, was vicar of Braintree from 1537 to 1544.

A suburb of Boston, Massachusetts, USA is called Braintree.

Bramblewick. A fictionalized version of ROBIN HOOD'S BAY as appearing in the novels of Leo Walmsley (1892–1966).

Bramham 'homestead or enclosure where broom grows', OE *brom* 'broom' + HAM.

A village in West Yorkshire, 6 km (4 miles) south of Wetherby.

Battle of Bramham Moor (20 February 1408). A battle in which Henry Percy, Earl of Northumberland, was defeated and killed by Sir Thomas Rokeby, Sheriff of Yorkshire, so ending his rebellion against Henry IV.

Brampton 'farmstead where broom grows', OE *brom* 'broom' + -TON.

A market town in Cumbria (formerly in Cumberland), 14 km (8.5 miles) northeast of Carlisle.

Bramshill 'hill where broom grows', OE *brom* 'broom' + *hyll* 'hill'.

A village in Hampshire, about 12 km (7.5 miles) south of Reading. It is the home of the Police Staff College, for the training of senior officers.

Brancaster 'Roman station at Branodunum', a reduced form of the Roman name (itself based on an OCelt name probably meaning 'fort of the raven') + OE *ceaster* (*see* CHESTER).

A village close to the North Norfolk coast, about 11 km (7 miles) northeast of Hunstanton. The Roman garrison here, **Branodunum**, was part of the defensive network built in the late 3rd century AD along the SAXON SHORE.

Brander, Pass of. *See* PASS OF BRANDER.

Brandon Mountain Irish *Cnoc Bréanainn* 'St Brendan's Hill' (*see* KNOCK-), after St Brendan the Navigator (484–577).

A mountain on the DINGLE peninsula, County Kerry, 10 km (6 miles) north of the town of Dingle. It is also called **Mount Brandon**, and at 950 m (3116 ft) it is the second highest mountain in Ireland. South of the main summit of Brandon Mountain is **Brandon Peak** (840 m / 2755 ft), while to the north Brandon Mountain plunges steeply to the sea at the cliffs of **Brandon Head**. Northeast of this is **Brandon Point**, at the western side of **Brandon Bay**; the latter contains a 19-km (12-mile) sandy beach, the longest in Ireland, and also the village of **Brandon**.

> The broad-browed fishers of Brandon,
> torn sails dipped to the foam,
> bid life bold
> for a crust hard won;
> till they spy red gold
> in the Western sun,
> and hunger waits them at home.
>
> Geoffrey Winthrop Young: 'Brandon Bay', from
> *Collected Poems* (1936)

Brandon Bay also contains **Brandon's Creek**, from where in 1976 Tim Severin launched his reconstruction of St Brendan's carrach (coracle); in this he sailed across the Atlantic to show that it was possible that Brendan could have reached America as the legend tells us.

Just below the summit of Brandon Mountain can still be seen the remains of the 6th-century cell, oratory and well of St Brendan the Navigator. On the oratory is a cross made from aluminium spars salvaged from a German bomber that crashed into the mountain during the Second World War. Every 29 June pilgrims climb to the summit following the Saint's Road, which is marked by Stations of the Cross. Brandon Mountain is one of the four holy places in Ireland to which those with a lot of repenting to do must make their way.

> Do you remember Brandon,
> Our mountain in the west:
> Brandon that looks on oceans,
> Brandon of the blessed.
>
> Hamish Brown: 'Brandon'

There are towns called Brandon in Canada (Manitoba) and the USA (Vermont).

Brands Hatch Perhaps 'gate of the steep slope', OE *branc, brant* 'steep' + *hæcc* 'gate'.
A village in Kent, about 13 km (8 miles) northeast of SEVENOAKS. The nearby motor-racing circuit originated in the 1920s as a grass motorcycle track. It opened for Formula 3 racing in 1949, and first hosted the Formula 1 British Grand Prix in 1964. Its full Grand Prix course is 4.2 km (2.65 miles) long.

Branksome Adopted in the 19th century from the name of a large house, *Branksome* Tower, built in the area in 1855 by Charles William Packe. This in turn appears to have been taken from 'Branksome Tower', the setting of Sir Walter Scott's *Lay of the Last Minstrel* (1805), which may have been inspired by Branxholm Castle, near Hawick, Scotland.
A district of Poole, Dorset.

Branodunum. The Roman name for the garrison at BRANCASTER, one of the SAXON SHORE forts built in the 3rd century AD.

Bransdale 'Brandr's valley', OScand male personal name *Brandr* + *dalr* 'valley'.

A valley in the NORTH YORK MOORS, North Yorkshire, some 25 km (16 miles) east of Northallerton. Its river is Hodge Beck.

Brantwood Possibly 'steep wood', OE *brant* 'steep' + OE *wudu* 'wood'.
The home of the art critic and writer John Ruskin from 1872 to 1900. It is on the east side of CONISTON WATER in the LAKE DISTRICT, Cumbria, and is now open to the public.

Braughing '(settlement of) Breahha's people', OE male personal name *Breahha* + *-ingas* (*see* -ING).
A village (pronounced 'braffing') in Hertfordshire, about 11 km (7 miles) northwest of Bishop's Stortford.

Brawl Possibly 'wide valley', OScand *breithr* 'wide, broad' + *vollr* 'valley'.
A small settlement on the north coast of Highland (formerly in Sutherland), some 30 km (18.5 miles) west of Thurso.

Brawlbin Presumably 'Brawl hill', *Brawl see* BRAWL + Gaelic *beinn* 'mountain'.
A small settlement in Highland (formerly in Caithness), some 12 km (7.5 miles) south of Thurso.

Bray[1] Probably OFr *bray(e)* 'marsh'.
A village in Berkshire, on the River THAMES[1], about 5 km (3 miles) northwest of Windsor. It is something of a gastronomic centre, numbering the Waterside Inn and the Fat Duck among its restaurants. (In 2004 both restaurants were awarded three Michelin stars.)

Vicar of Bray, the. The original Vicar of Bray was a 16th-century incumbent of the parish who managed to retain his living during the turbulent religious changes in the reigns of Henry VIII, Edward VI, Mary and Elizabeth I. He was transformed in an anonymous, probably 18th-century song into a symbol of time-serving cynicism:

> And this is the law, I will maintain,
> Unto my dying day, Sir,
> That whatsoever King shall reign,
> I will be the Vicar of Bray, sir!

In late 19th-century card-players' rhyming slang, a *Vicar of Bray* was a 'tray' – that is, a card numbered three.

Bray[2] Irish *Bré* 'hill'.
A seaside resort and commuter town in County Wicklow, 20 km (12 miles) southeast of Dublin. It is one of the oldest seaside resorts in Ireland, largely developed by William Dargan in the 19th century. The promontory on the south side of the town is **Bray Head**. James Joyce lived here as a boy (when on holiday from Clongowes College) from 1888 to 1891, his father having made the move in the hope, as he said, that the train fare would provide an obstacle to visits from his in-laws.

Brazacott 'Broysa's cottage', *Broysa* personal name of unknown origin + OE *cot* (*see* -COT, COTE).

A village in Cornwall, about 11 km (7 miles) northwest of Launceston.

Breadalbane 'high part of Scotland', Gaelic *braghaid* 'upper part' + *Alban* 'Scotland' in the possessive form *Albainn* (*see* ALBA; ALBANY[1]).

A traditional area of the central HIGHLANDS around Loch Tay (*see under* TAY) and BEN LAWERS, incorporating parts of Stirling and Perth and Kinross unitary authorities (formerly all within Perthshire). It is bounded on the north by Loch Rannoch, on the east by Strath Tay, on the south by Loch Earn and Strath Earn, and on the west by the glens linking Crianlarich and Bridge of Orchy. The main settlements are at ABERFELDY, Killin and FORTINGALL.

Earl of Breadalbane. John Campbell, 1st Earl of Breadalbane and Holland (*c.*1635–1717), a Scottish politician who was (possibly unfairly) implicated in the Massacre of Glencoe (*see under* GLEN COE).

Breadstone '(place at the) broad stone', OE *brad* 'broad' + *stan* (*see* STONE).

A village in Gloucestershire, just to the east of the River SEVERN, about 13 km (8 miles) southwest of Stroud.

Breakneckshire. A nickname for Brecknockshire, cited by Daniel Defoe in his *A Tour Through the Whole Island of Great Britain* (1724–6).

Breaky Bottom 'valley overgrown with brushwood', OE *bracu* 'thicket of brushwood' + *botm* 'valley'.

A vineyard on the SOUTH DOWNS in East Sussex, near Rodmell.

Breany. An anglicized version of the medieval Irish kingdom of BRÉIFNE.

Brechin From the personal names *Brachan* or *Brychan* or *Brecon*, the names of various early Celtic princes and nobles, also the origin of BRECON in Wales.

A royal BURGH (1641) 11 km (7 miles) west of Montrose, in Angus (formerly in Tayside region). In the Middle Ages it was an ecclesiastical centre. The small cathedral (mostly 13th century) is now the parish church, and there is also a notable round tower 26.5 m (87 ft) high, dating from the 10th or 11th century, of a type common in Ireland but rare in Scotland. On 10 July 1296, just north of the town, John (de) Balliol handed over the Crown of Scotland to Edward I of England, via the Bishop of Durham. The castle (subsequently the seat of the earls of Dalhousie) resisted an English siege for three weeks in 1303, and the town itself was sacked during the English Civil Wars.

Brechin was the birthplace of Fox Maule Ramsay, the 11th Earl of Dalhousie (1801–74), who was secretary of state for war between 1855 and 1858, and was criticized for his conduct during the latter part of the Crimean War;

and of Sir Robert Watson-Watt (1892–1973), the inventor of radar.

The ambitiously named **Brechin City FC** (Brechin has rather fewer than 10,000 souls) was founded in 1906 and plays at Glebe Park.

Battle of Brechin (1452). A battle in which the Earl of Huntly led James II's forces to victory over the 'Tiger Earl', the 4th Earl of Crawford, who had sided with the Douglases in rebellion against the king. James himself had already (in February) killed Douglas with his own hand at STIRLING[1].

Breckland 'area in which ground has been broken up for cultivation', local dialect ME *breck* 'newly cultivated land' + *land*; the name dates from the 19th century.

A 777-sq km (300-sq mile) area of heathland around THETFORD in southwestern Norfolk. It was cleared and cultivated in the Stone Age, but once the sandy topsoil had blown away it was abandoned to grazing sheep. Large parts of it were replanted in the 20th century by the Forestry Commission. GRIMES GRAVES, Stone Age flint mines now in the care of English Heritage, are in the Breckland.

Brecknock. The former name for BRECKNOCKSHIRE.

Brecknock-Mere. *See* LLANGORSE LAKE.

Brecknockshire An anglicized version of BRYCHEINIOG, the original name of BRECON + *shire*.

A former county of southern central Wales. It was also called **Breconshire**, and its Welsh name is **Sir Frycheiniog**. As **Brecknock** it was a district of Powys between 1974 and 1996, and is now part of POWYS unitary authority. It was bordered by Herefordshire to the east, Radnorshire to the north, Cardiganshire and Carmarthenshire to the west, and Glamorgan to the south. The county town was BRECON, and other towns included BUILTH WELLS.

> Brecknockshire is a mere inland county ... the English jestingly (and I think not very improperly) call it Breakneckshire. 'Tis mountainous to an extremity ...
>
> Daniel Defoe: *A Tour Through the Whole Island of Great Britain* (1724–6)

The mountains Defoe refers to include the BRECON BEACONS.

The medieval Welsh poet Siôn Cent (*c.*1367–*c.*1430) wrote a notable poem in praise of the county, suggesting to some scholars that he may have been born there. Sir George Everest (1790–1866), the surveyor after whom Mount Everest is named, was born in Gwernvale, Brecknockshire.

> Where cider ends there ale begins to reign
> And warms on Brecknock hills the Cambrian swain;
> High on the summit of King Arthur's Chair
> He quaffs his ale, and breathes untainted air;
> Looks down on Hereford with scornful eyes –
> Esteems himself a native of the skies ...
>
> Edward Davies: *Chepstow: A Poem* (1784)

Brecon Welsh 'territory of Brychan', from its original name BRYCHEINIOG.

An attractive old town in Powys (formerly in Brecknockshire, of which it was the county seat), some 22 km (13.5 km) north of Merthyr Tydfil, and the name of a former Marcher Lordship (*see under* the MARCHES). The town is situated where the River USK[1] is joined by the River Honddu, hence the Welsh name **Aberhonddu** (etymology *see* ABER + river name of uncertain meaning, but possibly containing Welsh *hawdd* 'happy').

Although Daniel Defoe commented that 'The most to be said of this town, is ... that it is very ancient', Brecon was, until the Industrial Revolution, one of the most important towns in Wales, thriving on the cloth trade. During the Civil Wars the citizens declared their firm neutrality by demolishing the town walls and most of the Norman castle. In 1923 Brecon became the seat of the new Anglican diocese of Swansea and Brecon, the medieval priory church (where Giraldus Cambrensis [Gerald of Wales] was archdeacon in the 12th century) becoming the cathedral.

Brecon was the birthplace of the actress Sarah Siddons (1755–1831) – the actual building is now the Sarah Siddons pub – and of the actor-manager Charles Kemble (1775–1854).

See also BRECON BEACONS.

Brecon buff. A hardy breed of goose, one of the few originating in Britain. It has pink legs and a pink beak. Bill Wiggin, MP for Leominster, declared a gift of four Brecon buffs in the 2002 Register of Members' Interests.

Brecon Beacons The Welsh name is Bannau BRYCHEINIOG; *Beacons* may merely be a translation of *bannau* 'peaks', without any signalling connotation.

A range of sandstone mountains in Powys (formerly in Brecknockshire), rising on the south side of BRECON. The highest point is PEN Y FAN (885 m / 2904 ft). At one place in the massif, near Llyn Cwm Llwch, there was in legend once a door into the Land of the Fairies, through which mortals could pass on May Day – until one person stole a fairy flower, after which the frontier was closed. The Brecon Beacons were presented to the National Trust in 1965.

Brecon Beacons National Park. A national park designated in 1957. Its Welsh name is **Parc Cenedlaethol Bannau Brycheiniog**. It includes not only the Brecon Beacons themselves, but also the BLACK MOUNTAINS to the east and the similarly named BLACK MOUNTAIN range to the west. The British Army's SAS Regiment does much of its initial training in these areas, including the gruelling endurance test euphemistically known as the 'Fan Dance'.

Breconshire. An alternative name for BRECKNOCKSHIRE.

Brecqhou 'steep island', OScand *brekka* 'steep, precipitate' + *holmr* 'island' (*see* -EY, -EA).

One of the CHANNEL ISLANDS. Only 30 ha (74 acres) in area, it lies off the northeastern corner of Guernsey. Politically it is part of nearby SARK.

The island is now dominated by the fortress-like home built by the secretive multi-millionaire Barclay brothers, who became owners of the *Daily Telegraph* newspaper group in 2004. They bought the island in 1993, and have run a campaign (including the issuing of Brecqhou stamps and designing a Brecqhou flag) for political separation from Sark.

Bredbury 'stronghold made of planks', OE *bred* 'plank' + *burh* (*see* BURY).

A small town in Greater Manchester, 4 km (2.5 miles) northeast of Stockport.

Bredfield 'wide open land', OE *brædu* 'plain' + *feld* (*see* FIELD). A village in Suffolk, about 5 km (3 miles) north of WOODBRIDGE. The poet and translator Edward Fitzgerald (1809–83) was born here.

Bredon 'hill called *Bre*', OCelt *breg* 'hill' + OE *dun* (*see* DOWN, -DON); the name *Bredon* is thus tautological, and *Bredon Hill* doubly so.

A village in Worcestershire (before 1998 in Hereford and Worcester, before 1974 in Worcestershire), about 13 km (8 miles) southwest of Evesham. It has one of the largest tithe barns in England.

The summit of **Bredon Hill**, 5 km (3 miles) to the northeast, is 211 m (692 ft) above sea level, reputedly affording views over 14 counties – a reputation exploited by A.E. Housman in his poem 'Bredon Hill', from *A Shropshire Lad* (1896):

> In summertime on Bredon
> The bells they sound so clear;
> Round both the shires they ring them
> In steeples far and near,
> A happy noise to hear.
>
> Here of a Sunday morning
> My love and I would lie,
> And see the coloured counties,
> And hear the larks so high
> About us in the sky.

Bredwardine Probably either 'broad enclosure' or 'boarded enclosure', OE *brædu* 'broad stretch of land' or *bred* 'board, plank' + *worthign* 'enclosure' (*see* -WORTH, WORTHY, -WARDINE). A village in Herefordshire (before 1998 in Hereford and Worcester, before 1974 in Herefordshire), about 19 km (11.5 miles) northwest of Hereford.

Breffny. An anglicized version of the medieval Irish kingdom of BRÉIFNE.

Bréifne Irish *bréife*, *bréifne* 'loop, ring', possibly with reference to ring forts.

A medieval Irish kingdom, occupying the present counties of LEITRIM and CAVAN. The anglicized version of the name is **Breany** or **Breffny**. It was initially ruled by the O'Rourkes, but later their dominion was confined to the west, while the O'Reillys ruled in the east. Bréifne successfully resisted the Anglo-Normans, and the area was not brought under English rule until the late 16th century.

> And the little roads of Cloonagh go rambling through my heart …
> But the little waves of Breffny have drenched my heart in spray.
>
> Eva Gore-Booth (1870–1926):'The Little Waves of Breffny'

Brendon 'hill where broom grows', OE *brom* 'broom' + *dun* 'hill'.

A village in north Devon, close to the Devon–Somerset border and within about 1.5 km (1 mile) of the sea.

Brendon Hills. A range of limestone hills in northern Somerset, rising to about 420 m (1380 ft) and extending from the eastern edge of EXMOOR eastwards for about 15 km (9 miles). In former times they were mined for their iron ore.

Brent[1] A Celtic river name meaning 'high, holy one', from OCelt *brigantia*, also the name of a goddess (perhaps reflecting a cult of river-worship in prehistoric times – *see also* DEE[2]).

A river in northwest London, rising in south Hertfordshire (where it is known as the 'Dollis Brook') and flowing 32 km (20 miles) southward through BARNET, BRENT[2], EALING and HOUNSLOW to flow into the River THAMES[1] at BRENTFORD. Along its course it has been dammed to form the 'Welsh Harp' Reservoir (also known as **Brent Reservoir**).

> Gentle Brent, I used to know you
> Wandering Wembley-wards at will,
> Now what change your waters show you
> In the meadowlands you fill!
> Recollect the elm-trees misty
> And the footpaths climbing twisty
> Under cedar-shaded palings,
> Low laburnum-leaned-on railings,
> Out of Northolt on and upward to the heights of Harrow hill.
>
> John Betjeman: 'Middlesex' (1954)

Brent[2] From the River BRENT[1].

A borough of northwest London, between Camden to the east and Harrow to the north and west, formed in 1965 by uniting the former boroughs of WEMBLEY and WILLESDEN. Also within the borough are DOLLIS HILL, Harlesden and NEASDEN. Its administrations became well known for their leftward leanings, although there was also a controversial Conservative period in the 1990s. Ken Livingstone was Labour MP for Brent East from 1987 to 2001, before being elected Mayor of London.

National Theatre of Brent. A minimalist comedy theatre company created in the early 1980s by Patrick Barlow. In the persona of Desmond 'Olivier' Dingle he stages productions notable chiefly for their economy of resources (as typified by the NTOB's first effort, a two-man version of the Charge of the Light Brigade; other highlights have included *Zulu* and a television series (1985) called *Mighty Moments from World History*). His best-known coadjutor has been Wallace, played by Jim Broadbent.

Brent Cross. An area in the southern part of the northwest London borough of BARNET, on the River BRENT[1]. It is close to the southern extremity of the M1, and to the intersection of the NORTH CIRCULAR ROAD and the A41 (site of the **Brent Cross Flyover**). It was from this proximity to crossroads (from at least the early 19th century, well pre-dating present-day concrete and tarmac) that it took its name.

Wider renown came with the **Brent Cross Shopping Centre**, opened in 1976. Built on a site of 21 ha (52 acres), its agglomeration of department stores (from John Lewis to Marks & Spencer) became the British prototype for the out-of-town-centre shopping mall aimed at car-driving shoppers.

Brent Cross 'Underground' station, on the Northern line (Edgware branch), opened in 1923, originally under the name Brent. The current name was introduced in 1976.

Brentford 'ford across the Brent', BRENT[1] + FORD.

A district in the West London borough of HOUNSLOW (formerly in MIDDLESEX), at the point where the River Brent flows into the River THAMES[1], on the opposite bank of the Thames to KEW Gardens. It grew up at the point where the main road from London to the west (whose modern manifestations are the A4 and the M4) crossed the River Brent. It is often referred to as the county town of the former county of Middlesex, although its historical and legal entitlement to this distinction is not clear.

James Boswell, in his *Life of Dr Johnson* (1791), records a competitive conversation between his subject and Adam Smith. The Glaswegian economist extolled the charms of his native city at some length. The great lexicographer responded with: 'Pray, Sir, have you ever seen Brentford?'

A strike by the women workers at the Trico-Folberth windscreen-wiper factory at Brentford in the mid-1970s successfully achieved equal pay, under the terms of the 1976 Equal Pay Act (earlier strikes and tribunals elsewhere had failed). It was celebrated in a song called 'The Trico Strike' (1977) by Sam Richards; it begins:

> Now stop what you're doing and listen,

Here's a story I know you will like,
Three hundred women at Brentford,
They spent a long summer on strike.

Brentwood 'burnt wood', ME *brent* 'burnt' + *wood*.

A town in Essex, situated, appropriately, in wooded countryside about 13 km (8 miles) northeast of Romford and just outside the M25.

The new Brentwood Roman Catholic Cathedral, designed in neo-neoclassical style by Quinlan Terry, was built between 1989 and 1991.

Bressay Probably 'breast-shaped island', with OScand *brjost* 'breast' + *ey* 'island' (*see* -AY), but 'Brusi's island', OScand personal name *Brusi*, is possible.

An island off the east coast of Mainland, Shetland, less than 1 km (0.6 miles) across **Bressay Sound** from LERWICK. The Sound itself has had a lively history. It sheltered the invasion fleets of Harald Hardrada in 1066 and of Haakon IV in 1263, both of which expeditions were to meet with disaster (at STAMFORD BRIDGE and LARGS respectively). In 1640 there was a Dutch–Spanish naval battle here, and during the 17th and 18th centuries hundreds of Dutch fishing boats would congregate in the Sound, leading to the saying that Amsterdam was 'built out of the back of Bressay'.

Bretton. A fictional town in Charlotte Brontë's *Villette* (1853), thought to have been based on BRIDLINGTON.

Breydon Water 'place where the River Yare spreads out', *Breydon* OScand *breithing* 'place of broadening'.

A large lake in the Norfolk BROADS, to the west of Great Yarmouth. It is fed by the rivers WAVENEY[1] and YARE. The Romans used it as a harbour.

Brick End A modern name, perhaps from a brick-built area.
A village in Essex, about 11 km (7 miles) northeast of Bishop's Stortford.

Brick Lane From the making of bricks and tiles in the immediate area since the 16th century; the name is first recorded in 1542.

A road in SPITALFIELDS, East London, in the borough of Tower Hamlets (E1, E2), running from beyond Bethnal Green Road in the north to just short of Whitechapel Road in the south. In the late 20th century it became a focus of the Bengali community in the area. The local mosque was originally a church built by Huguenots and later a synogogue.

Brick Lane. A novel (2003) by Monica Ali, set in the Bangladeshi community of London's East End, in which a young Bangladeshi woman, Nazneen, trapped in a loveless marriage, finds an escape from her domestic constraints in a relationship with a young political activist. It was shortlisted for the Man-Booker Prize in 2003.

Bricklehampton 'estate associated with Beorhthelm', OE personal name *Beorhthelm* + -ING + -TON.

A village in Worcestershire (before 1998 in Hereford and Worcester, before 1974 in Worcestershire), about 6 km (4 miles) west of Evesham. At 14 letters, its name has been claimed as the longest place name in England with no repeated letters.

Bridestones Possibly from their 19th-century use as a trysting place.

A series of natural sandstone tors or pinnacles on the NORTH YORK MOORS, North Yorkshire, some 15 km (9 miles) north of Pickering. One of the rocks is called the Pepperpot, while a route on another has been dubbed by climbers *Big Dog's Cock*, giving a graphic idea of the rock's shape. The rocks are in the care of the National Trust.

There are some standing stones near GOATHLAND, a little to the north, called **High Bridestones**, and there is also a Neolithic burial chamber on Biddulph Moor (*see under* BIDDULPH), Staffordshire, called **Bridestones**.

Bridgend From the Welsh name *Pen-y-Bont ar Ogwr*, 'end of the bridge over the River Ogwr (or Ogmore)', Welsh *pen* 'end' + *y* 'the' + *pont* 'bridge' + *ar* 'on' + river name deriving from *og* 'sharp' + an unknown element. The river name is anglicized as Ogmore.

An industrial town and surrounding unitary authority (formerly in Glamorgan, then in Mid Glamorgan), situated on the River OGMORE 31 km (19 miles) west of Cardiff. Its Welsh name is **Pen-y-Bont ar Ogwr**. The town has a Ford motor plant. The unitary authority also includes PORTHCAWL, and is bordered by Rhondda Cynon Taff to the east, Vale of Glamorgan to the southeast, the Bristol Channel to the south and Port Talbot to the west.

Bridge of Allan Probably from an OCelt river name meaning 'flowing water' or possibly 'holy one', like the Aln of ALNWICK in Northumberland.

A residential town 4 km (2.5 miles) north of Stirling, at the west end of the OCHIL HILLS. It was formerly in Stirlingshire, then in Central Region, and is now in Stirling unitary authority. It is on the **Allan Water**, a tributary of the FORTH.

By Allan stream I chanced to rove,
  While Phoebus sank beyond Benledi;
The winds were whispering through the grove,
  The yellow corn was waving ready ...

Robert Burns: 'By Allan stream I chanced to rove' (1793)

Bridge of Avon. *See under* AVON[5].

Bridge of Bogendreip Etymology unknown.

A bridge over the Water of Dye on the CAIRN O' MOUNT road in Aberdeenshire (formerly in Grampian region), 6 km (4 miles) southwest of Banchory.

Bridge of Earn. *See under* EARN.

Bridge of Orchy. *See under* ORCHY.

Bridge over the Atlantic, the. *See under* SEIL.

Bridge Sollers *Bridge* '(place at the) bridge', OE *brycg*; *Sollers* denoting manorial ownership in the Middle Ages by the de Solers family.

A village in Herefordshire (before 1998 in Hereford and Worcester, before 1974 in Herefordshire), on the River WYE[1], about 11 km (7 miles) west of Hereford.

Bridgewater Canal Named after Francis Egerton, 3rd Duke of *Bridgewater* (1736–1803), the pioneer of canal building, who promoted this canal.

England's first industrial canal, between MANCHESTER and RUNCORN. Francis Egerton, on the lookout for a way of transporting coal from his mines in Worsley to Manchester and inspired by the Canal du Languedoc (now the Canal du Midi) in France, which he had seen on his Grand Tour, had the initial 16-km (10-mile) stretch built, with the help of the engineer James Brindley. It opened in 1761, making it the first major project of the great age of canals. An extension of 45 km (28 miles) to link Manchester and Runcorn was added in 1776. It closed to commercial traffic in 1974.

Bridgnorth Originally *Bridge* '(place at the) bridge', OE *brycg*; the suffixed *-north* is first recorded in 1282.

A market town in Shropshire, on the River SEVERN, about 21 km (13 miles) southeast of Telford. It is divided into two parts, known as 'Old Town' and 'New Town', by a 30-m (100-ft) red sandstone cliff. A funicular railway has connected the two for over a century. There are caves in the cliff which until the 19th century were used as dwellings by local people. Bridgnorth's castle (a former Royalist stronghold) was blown up by Parliamentarians following the Civil Wars, but its 12th-century principal tower remains, albeit leaning sharply.

Bridgwater Originally (1086) *Bridge* '(place at the) bridge', OE *brycg*; later (1194) *Bridgewaltier*, denoting ownership by a man called Walter; the modern form of the name is due to assimilation to *water*.

A market town in Somerset, on the River PARRETT, about 13 km (8 miles) northeast of Taunton. It was an important port until the 18th century, when the expansion of Bristol took away much of its trade. It is now an industrial centre. *See also* ALBION.

Bridgwater Bay. A large, almost right-angled bay on the north coast of Somerset, in the Bristol Channel. At the point of its angle is the estuary of the River Parrett.

Bridlington 'Berhtel's farmstead', OE male personal name *Berhtel* + -ING + -TON.

A seaside resort in the East Riding of Yorkshire (formerly in Humberside), 25 km (15.5 miles) southeast of

Scarborough. It overlooks the wide expanse of **Bridlington Bay**. An Augustinian priory was founded here in 1119, and part survives as the nave of St Mary's Church. In the 14th century the prior was **St John of Bridlington**, whose most spectacular miracle was to rescue some sailors in distress off nearby FLAMBOROUGH HEAD by walking across the water and towing their boat to safety.

Subsequently, Bridlington suffered two attacks from the sea: the first was in 1643, when Admiral Batten's Parliamentary ships opened fire on the lodgings of Queen Henrietta Maria; and the second was a bombardment at the hands of the American privateer John Paul Jones in 1779. Since then Bridlington has not always given outsiders the warmest of welcomes; the comedian Les Dawson observed of matinée audiences here:

> You could see the dampness rising from the wet raincoats like mist on the marshes.

Over two centuries earlier, Daniel Defoe was similarly unimpressed:

> There is nothing remarkable upon this side [of the Humber] for above thirty miles together ... Bridlington or Burlington is the only place, and that is of no note ...
>
> Daniel Defoe: *A Tour Through the Whole Island of Great Britain* (1724–6)

Others have found the place more stimulating, albeit in a moist sort of way: when Charlotte Brontë visited in 1839 she was so overwhelmed by her first sight of the sea that she burst into tears and was obliged to find somewhere to sit down. In a later letter to a friend she wrote that the sea's

> glories, changes, its ebb and flow, the sound of its restless waves, formed a subject for contemplation that never wearied either the eye, the ear, or the mind

... while in another letter she wrote

> I should very much like to know how the great brewing-tub of Bridlington Bay works, and what sort of yeasty froth rises now on the waves.

It is thought that the fictional Bretton – a 'clean and ancient town' – in *Villette* is based on Bridlington.

Bridlington was the birthplace of the architect and landscape gardener William Kent (1685–1748).

Bridlington Agreement (1939). An agreement among the trade unions that they would not poach each other's members, and would work to prevent the creation of breakaway unions.

Bridport 'port or market town belonging to Bredy', Long *Bredy* being the name of a village about 11 km (7 miles) to the east (from the River *Bride*, from a Celtic river name meaning 'gushing or surging stream') + PORT.

A town in Dorset, on the River BRIT[1], about 25 km

(15.5 miles) west of Dorchester, and about 3 km (2 miles) from the coast. An ancient town with strong maritime connections, it remains a major centre for rope- and net-making (its characteristic wide pavements were once ropewalks, where new ropes were laid out to be twisted and dried). Bridport was the model for Thomas Hardy's **Port Bredy**, for example in the story 'Fellow Townsmen' (1880), one of his *Wessex Tales*.

There is a town named Bridport in Tasmania.

Bridport dagger. A former euphemistic soubriquet for the hangman's noose.

Brierfield 'field of briars', a 19th-century name influenced by nearby Briercliffe, OE *brer* 'briar'.

A small town between NELSON and BURNLEY, Lancashire, and now conjoint with the two.

Brigadoon. *See under* DOON.

Brigg Originally *Glanford Brigg* 'bridge at the ford where people gather for revelry or games', OE *gleam* 'revelry' + FORD + OE *brycg* 'bridge' (in Scandinavian pronunciation); plain *Brigg* is first recorded in 1681.

A market town in North Lincolnshire, about 11 km (7 miles) east of Scunthorpe.

Brigg Fair. A traditional Lincolnshire folk song ('It was on the fifth of August, the weather hot and fair. Unto Brigg Fair I did repair, for love I was inclined'), which takes its name from the fair held annually at Brigg since 1235. It was brought to a wider public by Frederick Delius's orchestral setting (1907), subtitled 'An English rhapsody'; this consists of a set of variations on the original tune (to which Delius – by no means a member of the so-called English 'Cowpat School' of early 20th-century folk song arrangers — had been introduced by the composer Percy Grainger).

Briggflatts 'level ground at the bridge', ME and Yorkshire dialect *brigg* 'bridge' + *flatt* 'level piece of ground'.

A hamlet just south of Sedbergh, Cumbria. It is the site of one of the oldest Quaker meeting houses in the world, near where George Fox preached the sermon in 1652 that inspired the birth of the movement. The place gave a title to Basil Bunting's long semi-autobiographical poem, *Briggflatts* (1966), which opens:

Brag, sweet tenor bull,
descant on Rawthey's madrigal,
each pebble its part
for the fells' late spring.

Brighouse 'house by the bridge', OE *brycg* 'bridge' + *hus* 'house'.

A textile town in West Yorkshire on the River CALDER[2], 6 km (4 miles) north of Huddersfield. Its local brass band, the **Brighouse and Rastrick Brassy Band**, is over a century old, and is still maintained by public subscription. It is one of the leading brass bands in the UK, winning numerous

championships, inlcuding the first World Championship in 1969. To a wider public, it is best known for its almost chart-topping hit 'The Floral Dance' in 1977 (Paul McCartney's 'Mull of Kintyre' (*see under* KINTYRE), in the top slot, was to blame for the 'almost').

Brighton Originally *Brighthelmstone* 'Beorhthelm's farmstead', OE *Beorhthelmes* possessive form of male personal name *Beorhthelm* + -TON; the reduced form *Brighton* is first recorded in the early 19th century.

A city and seaside resort on the East Sussex coast, about 85 km (53 miles) south of London. Previously a borough, in 1997 it was conjoined as a unitary authority with its long-standing, more staid partner to the west, HOVE, and in 2000 was accorded city status: the new entity's official designation is **Brighton and Hove**.

Until the middle of the 18th century, Brighton – or Brighthelmstone – was a simple fishing village, little different from its neighbours up and down the Sussex coast. Remnants of that era survive in the LANES, an area of narrow streets in the centre of the city now given over largely to antique shops, boutiques and restaurants.

Its projection to star status began in 1754, when Dr Richard Russell took up residence. This popular physician proclaimed the health-giving properties of Brighton's sea-air and the benefits of sea-bathing. His endorsement brought fashionable London society to the south coast to consult **Doctor Brighton** (as Brighton came to be called – one of the Prince Regent's very few *bons mots*). Fanny Burney and Dr Johnson (not together) were early celebrity visitors (the great lexicographer, however, pronounced Brighton 'dull'). By far the most notable and influential enthusiast, though, was that same Prince Regent (later George IV), who loved the place and built himself a villa here (this later, with the spectacular addition of minarets and onion domes in the Mughal style by John Nash, became **Brighton Pavilion**). Elegant Regency squares and crescents followed, which still set the tone of the seaward part of the city. The Brighton of this period was fictionalized as **Sanditon**, and its future development presciently described, by Jane Austen in her unfinished novel *Sanditon* (1817); and Thackeray characterized it, in *Vanity Fair* (1847–8), as 'Brighton, that always looks brisk, gay, and gaudy, like a harlequin's jacket'.

From the middle of the 19th century, the railway progressively reduced the travel time from London to about an hour, turning Brighton into the first, archetypal mass-market seaside resort in the south of England. Most notable of the attractions available to day-trippers and week-long holidaymakers was the Old Chain Pier (1823), England's first pleasure pier. It was swept away by a storm in 1896, but on a nearby site is the 0.5 km (0.3 mile) long Palace Pier, whose funfair rides, slot-machines and video games have kept generations entertained. (Its partner, the West Pier (1866), was reduced to girders by storms in 2004.) It was perhaps the easy accessibility of Brighton that in the early 20th century led to its increasing reputation as a place of illicit sexual liaison, convenient for a 'dirty weekend'. The general air of loucheness was compounded by the frequent use of Brighton's hotels as venues for the staged acts of 'adultery' often required to obtain a divorce at that period. Easy pickings from holidaymakers and race-goers (*see* **Battle of Brighton** and *Brighton Rock*, *below*) attracted the criminal fraternity too, adding to the town's raffishness. Keith Waterhouse described Brighton as having:

> ... the perennial air of being in a position to help the police with their inquiries.
>
> *The Observer* (28 April 1991)

With the growth of foreign travel in the second half of the 20th century, visitor numbers slipped, but Brighton was quick to diversify itself in other directions. It became a successful conference venue, for instance, regularly hosting the annual conferences of the main British political parties; in 1966 it instituted the **Brighton Festival** of the arts; and it attracted language schools, which in the summer swelled its population with thousands of foreign students ostensibly trying to improve their English. In 1961 Sussex University opened nearby at FALMER, just to the northeast of Brighton (it has since been joined by **Brighton University** (1992), formerly Brighton Polytechnic). The town gained itself a reputation for sophistication and cosmopolitanism ('London by the Sea' it was often called; *see also* JERUSALEM-ON-SEA), and by the end of the 20th century had one of the largest gay communities in the country ('the heaving Sodom of the south coast', according to Robert Hanks, *The Independent* (4 April 2001)). An avant-gardish youth culture burgeoned – 21st-century Brighton is seriously groovy. In the meantime, behind the seaside pleasure arcades and the Regency squares, the town's hinterland had steadily grown, and its demography and politics followed suit (in 1964 Brighton's KEMP TOWN became the first Sussex constituency to elect a Labour MP).

Brighton's football club, **Brighton and Hove Albion**, nicknamed the Seagulls, the Shrimps or simply the Albion, was founded in 1901. The club played at the Goldstone Ground until 1997.

The artist Aubrey Beardsley (1872–98), the composer Frank Bridge (1879–1941), the sculptor Eric Gill (1882–1940) and the philosopher Gilbert Ryle (1900–76) were all born in Brighton. So was the diminutive but fiery fast bowler John Wisden (1826–84), founder of the cricketers' almanac that still bears his name (first published in 1864).

The first Body Shop opened in Brighton, in 1976.

There are towns called Brighton in the USA (Colorado, Florida, Illinois, Iowa, Massachusetts – a suburb of Boston – and Michigan), Canada (Ontario) and Australia (South Australia and Victoria: the latter is an upmarket beachside suburb of Melbourne whose past residents have included the composer Percy Grainger, the writers Henry Handel Richardson and Marcus Clarke, and the 'mystery' spinbowler Jack Iverson).

See also NEW BRIGHTON *and* ROEDEAN.

Battle of Brighton. A gangland encounter at Brighton Racecourse in 1936 in which the Sabini brothers of Clerkenwell (in league with the police) outwitted and defeated their rivals, the Hoxton Gang. The incident provided material for Graham Greene's *Brighton Rock*.

Brighton Belle. A luxury train consisting of Pullman carriages which ran between London Victoria and Brighton. The service began in 1934 (succeeding the previous 'Southern Bell', which started in 1908) and its journey time was 55 minutes. Its economic viability was ebbing fast in the 1960s, and British Railways often announced its demise. Supporters, loath to lose its traditional charms (such as kipper breakfasts in the dining car), campaigned to save it. They succeeded for a while, aided no doubt by the influence of such regular users as Lord Olivier, but the service was finally withdrawn in 1972.

Brighton Bomb, the. A shorthand term for the IRA bomb attack on the Grand Hotel on Brighton seafront on 12 October 1984, which killed five people and injured 30. The IRA plan was to eliminate the prime minister, Margaret Thatcher, and her cabinet, many of whom were staying in the hotel for the Conservative Party conference. She had a narrow escape; her bathroom was completely destroyed.

Brighton line. A bingo-callers' rhyme, from the 1940s, for the number *nine*.

Brighton Pier. Generically, a term that covers both the Palace Pier and the West Pier (*see above*), but in the hands of rhyming slangsters it becomes synonymous with 'queer'. At first, in the 19th century, the usage applied to the standard sense 'odd' , and also to 'ill', but since the 1950s it has also assumed gay associations. Often shortened to 'Brighton', it has a certain appropriateness in view of the city's reputation as a gay capital.

Brighton Rock. A novel by Graham Greene (termed by its author 'an entertainment'), published in 1938, which centres on crime and corruption in pre-Second World War Brighton (its name refers to Brighton rock, a sugary pink cylindrical confection with the name 'Brighton' running through its white interior; *compare* Blackpool rock *under* BLACKPOOL). The money circulating at Brighton race meetings encouraged the formation of so-called 'race gangs', in emulation of Chicago hoodlums, who engaged in extortion, protection and general mayhem. The leader of one of these, scarred, babyfaced Pinkie, is the novel's anti-hero. It begins with the memorable line: 'Hale knew, before he had been three hours in Brighton, that they meant to murder him.' In the film version (1947), which successfully recreated the book's seedy but menacing atmosphere, Pinkie was played by Richard Attenborough.

Brighton Run. An annual rally for veteran cars from Hyde Park in London to the promenade at Brighton. It is held on the first Sunday in November and commemorates the so-called 'Emancipation Run' made by 33 motorists between the two towns on 14 November 1896, the day of repeal of the Locomotive Act of 1865 that limited the speed of steam carriages to 6.4 km per hour (4 mph) in the country and 3.2 km per hour (2 mph) in the town. Its most celebrated fictional representation is in the film *Genevieve* (1953).

Brighton School. A group of pioneer film-makers who were based in the Brighton area at the beginning of the 20th century, among them G.A. Smith (1865–1959) and J.A. Williamson (1855–1933). They attached great importance to the close-up and are best remembered for *Rescued by Rover* (1905), a seven-minute drama showing a collie rescuing his master's baby from kidnappers.

Brighton trunk murders, the. A series of murders between the First and Second World Wars in which the victims were secreted in trunks and dispatched to the left-luggage office at Brighton railway station:

> In the 1920s and 1930s it was highly unusual in Brighton for a week to pass without the body of a dead woman turning up in a trunk
>
> William Donaldson: *Brewer's Rogues, Villains and Eccentrics* (2002)

The term is applied particularly to the murder of Violette Kaye, for which Tony Mancini (under whose bed Miss Kaye and her trunk were found) was tried and acquitted in 1933.

Les Vieillards de Brighton. A book ('The Old People of Brighton' (2002)) by Gonzague Saint-Bris, recounting the true story of how the five-year-old Saint-Bris, the son of a French diplomat, was confined to a French old people's home in Brighton because his parents couldn't control him.

Brighton and Hove. *See under* BRIGHTON.

Brightwell Baldwin *Brightwell* 'clear spring', OE *beorht* 'bright, clear' + *wella* 'spring'; *Baldwin* denoting manorial ownership in the Middle Ages by Sir Baldwin de Bereford.
A village in Oxfordshire, about 16 km (10 miles) southeast of Oxford.

Brightwell-cum-Sotwell *Sotwell* probably 'Sutta's spring', OE male personal name *Sutta* + *wella* 'spring'.
A village in Oxfordshire, about 16 km (10 miles) south of Oxford.

Brig o' Doon. *See under* DOON.

Brig o' Turk 'bridge of the boar', Scots *brig o'* 'bridge of'

+ a river name related to Gaelic *torc* 'boar', although the rivers here are the Black Water and the Finglas.
A small village at the foot of GLEN FINGLAS, 4 km (2.5 miles) east of the TROSSACHS. It was formerly in Perthshire, then in Central region, and is now in the unitary authority of Stirling.

Brill Probably 'hill hill', OCelt *breg* 'hill' + later OE *hyll* 'hill', added as a reinforcement when the original meaning had been forgotten.
A hilltop village in Buckinghamshire, about 16 km (10 miles) west of Aylesbury. A local nursery rhyme describes the village as 'Brill on the hill where the wind blows shrill'. Those who care about such things regard Brill as almost certainly the model for the village of Bree in J.R.R. Tolkien's *The Lord of the Rings* (1954–5).

Brimham Rocks 'rocks at Byrna's tree', ModE *rocks* + OE male personal name *Byrna* + *beam* 'tree'; *Bernebeam* 1135.
A series of gritstone outcrops, towers and tors in North Yorkshire in the YORKSHIRE DALES, 13 km (8 miles) northwest of Harrogate. They are in the care of the National Trust, and are popular with visitors and climbers. The rocks, surrounded by heather and birch trees, and with glimpses over the moors, provide a magical setting for occasional outdoor theatrical productions, such as Shakespeare's *A Midsummer Night's Dream*. Some of the rocks have names such as Druid's Altar and Druid's Head, reflecting the former belief that they were the creation of druids. From the top of another rock, known as Lover's Rock, an eloping couple, pursued by an irate father, are said to have jumped. Miraculously, they were unharmed, and were thereupon forgiven by their pursuer.

Bristol Originally *Bristow* 'assembly place by the bridge', OE *brycg* 'bridge' + *stow* 'holy place or asssembly place'; *Bristol*, with a change of *w* to *l* that is characteristic of the regional dialect, is first recorded in the 12th century.
A city, unitary authority and port in the West of England (before 1996 in Avon, before 1974 in Gloucestershire), on the River AVON[2] about 11 km (7 miles) from the estuary of the River SEVERN. Legend has it that it was founded by two shadowy Celtic figures called Belinus and Brennus.

A natural harbour on the Avon was the nucleus from which Bristol developed into a major port in the Middle Ages. At that time its main business was the export of wool, but later, as English merchant venturers extended their reach further and further around the world, it became a key base for their operations (a notable pioneer in the field was the Venetian navigator John Cabot, who sailed from Bristol to the coast of North America in 1497). In the 17th century Bristol's diversification extended to the slave trade, and in the late 17th and 18th centuries it was the largest and wealthiest town in England after London. Its importance as a port shrank after the abolition of the trade in the 19th century, but it continued to make a good living out of the wine trade, and long-established wine merchants such Avery's and Harvey's continue the link into the 21st century (*see* **Bristol Cream** *and* **Bristol Milk**, *below*).

It was in **Bristol Docks** that Isambard Kingdom Brunel constructed two of his great ships, the *Great Western* (1837) and the *Great Britain* (1843), the latter being the first iron-clad propeller-driven ocean liner. Brunel also designed **Bristol Temple Meads** (1840), the city's main railway station. Somewhat suggesting a Tudor castle, it was the first great piece of Victorian railway architecture. (The Temple Mead area takes its name from the old Temple Church.)

The 13th-century church of St Mary Redcliffe is a famous Bristol landmark, described by Elizabeth I as 'the fairest church in England'; and John Wesley's chapel, dating from 1739, is England's earliest Methodist building.

Bristol is a cathedral city (**Bristol Cathedral** is the Abbey Church of St Augustine, founded in 1140 and elevated to cathedral status in 1542 by Henry VIII). It is also a university city: the **University of Bristol** was founded in 1909, with generous donations from the Fry and Wills families, purveyors of those prerequisites of student life, chocolate and cigarettes. **Bristol Zoo** is situated in the elegant and salubrious western suburb of CLIFTON.

The city has two major football clubs: **Bristol City** (founded 1894), whose nickname is 'the Robins' (from its red-and-white strip), and which has found lasting fame as a piece of rhyming slang (*see* **Bristols** *below*) and **Bristol Rovers** (founded 1883), which has two nicknames, 'the Pirates' (from their original 'roving' style without a home base, and for Bristol's fame as a port from which pirates set sail), and 'the Gas' (arising from taunts by fans of deadly rivals City about a gasholder overlooking their ground). But Bristol is also a rugby town, and Bristol's rugby union club (now called **Bristol Shoguns**) has a historical rivalry with nearby Bath (*see* Bath Rugby *under* BATH).

In addition to Thomas Chatterton (*see* **Bristol Boy** *below*), the painter Thomas Lawrence (1769–1830), the poet Robert Southey (1774–1843), the trade-union leader Ben Tillett (1860–1943), the writer Geoffrey Household (1900–88), the publisher Allen Lane (1902–70), the physicist Paul Dirac (1902–84), the actor Cary Grant (1904–84; a statue of him stands on the harbourside), the playwright Christopher Fry (b.1907), the actor Michael Redgrave (1908–85) and the skater Robin Cousins (b.1957) were all born in Bristol.

There are 11 towns called Bristol in the USA (in Colorado, Connecticut, Florida, Georgia, Indiana, New Hampshire, Pennsylvania, Rhode Island, South Dakota, Vermont and Virginia) and two in Canada (New Brunswick, Quebec). There is a Bristol Bay in Alaska and a Bristol Island in Antarctica.

> What do they know of England who do not Bristol know? Its seamen found America; its merchants sent out the first settlers there; and it was Bristol that made the first ship to cross the Atlantic under its own power. It was a Bristol ship that brought home Alexander Selkirk and made Robinson Crusoe possible.
>
> Arthur Mee: *Gloucestershire* (1938)

See also BRADLEY STOKE, FRENCHAY *and* MANGOTSFIELD.

Bristle. A phonetic respelling of 'Bristol', reflecting the strong local accent. The spelling crops up in the titles of a series of books about Bristolian dialect and history by Derek Robinson, including *Krek Waiters peak Bristle* (i.e. The Correct Way to Speak Bristol) (1970) and *Sick Sentries of Bristle* (i.e. Six Centuries of Bristol) (2004).

Bristol. A description applied to a type of porcelain or pottery similar to delftware, made in Bristol.

Bristol Aeroplane Company. An aircraft manufacturer founded (under the name British & Colonial Aeroplane Company) at FILTON, near Bristol, in 1910. At first best-known for its military aircraft (the **Bristol Fighter** of the First World War, the Blenheim and Beaufighter of the Second World War), in the 1940s and 1950s it moved into the civilian market, first with the huge but ill-fated Brabazon, subsequently with the much more successful Britannia (the world's first turboprop airliner). Later, under the umbrella of British Aerospace, it built and flew Concordes at Filton. Between 1947 and 1960, the company also made cars. The Bristol marque became synonymous with high-quality, exclusive and very expensive fast touring cars – a sort of cross between a Rolls Royce and a sports car. In 1960 **Bristol Cars Ltd** became a separate entity.

Bristol board. A stiff drawing paper or fine cardboard, said to have been made first at Bristol. The term is first recorded in 1809. In the 19th and early 20th centuries visiting cards, which were often made of this material, were known colloquially as 'Bristols'.

Bristol Boy, the. An epithet sometimes applied to the poet Thomas Chatterton (1752–70), who was born in Bristol and here wrote his so-called 'Rowley' poems, including his 'Bristowe Tragedie', which purported to be the work of an imaginary 15th-century Bristol monk, Thomas Rowley.

Bristol brick. A siliceous material made in the form of a brick, used in former times for cleaning cutlery.

Bristol Channel. The seaward extension of the estuary of the River SEVERN, westwards from WESTON SUPER MARE on the English bank and Lavernock Point, to the south of PENARTH, on the Welsh bank. It is 137 km (85 miles) long. Its breadth varies from 8 km (5 miles) to 69 km (43 miles) and its depth from 9 m (30 ft) to 73 m (240 ft). The main islands in the Channel are FLAT HOLM, STEEP HOLM and LUNDY.

Bristol Cream. The proprietary name of a brand of sweet sherry, registered by Harvey's of Bristol in 1886.

Bristol diamond. A type of transparent rock-crystal found in the Clifton limestone near Bristol, resembling diamond in brilliancy. Also known as **Bristol stone** or just plain **Bristol**, it has been used since at least the 16th century as a diamond-substitute (in early days it was usually *Bristow*):

> Studded with what was once the vogue, bristow.
>
> *Edinburgh Evening Courier* (1818)

Bristol glass. A type of opaque coloured (usually blue) or white glass made in Bristol.

Bristol hog. An 18th- and 19th-century slang term for a Bristolian.

Bristolian. A person or thing of, or from, Bristol.

Bristol man. In the early to mid-19th century, a slang term for a rogue or villain, the rationale presumably being that such people gravitated towards Bristol – a port, and therefore inevitably full of wickedness.

Bristol milk. An epithet applied to sherry. It dates back to the mid-17th century, when sherry (or rather, at that time, sherry sack) was already being imported into Bristol in large quantities.

Bristol Nails. The name given to the four bronze pillars outside the Exchange building in Corn Street, Bristol. The city's merchants concluded their financial dealings there, so it has been put forward as a source of the expression 'pay on the nail'.

Bristol nonsuch. A garden plant, *Lychnis chalcedonica*, with bright red flower heads. It is more generally known as the 'Jerusalem cross'.

Bristol Riots. Riots in Bristol that erupted on 29 October 1831, following the rejection by the House of Lords of the Second Reform Bill, in which the Mansion House, Customs House and Bishop's Palace were attacked and looted. After two days troops restored order, killing 12 rioters and arresting a further hundred.

Bristols. A British slang term for a woman's breasts, first recorded in 1961. Its success probably owes something to a passing resemblance to *breasts*. It is short for rhyming slang *Bristol Cities = titties*, from the name of one of the city's two major football teams, Bristol City (*see above*).

Bristol water. The water of warm springs at CLIFTON near Bristol, used medicinally.

Hotel Bristol. The name of many hotels in Europe, all named after the 'Earl-Bishop', Frederick Augustus Hervey (1730–1803), Earl of Bristol and eccentric Bishop of Derry (*see* DOWNHILL), who was an inveterate Continental traveller.

'Jolly Bristol Coachman, The'. A traditional rhyme, first recorded in the early 19th century, in which sexual intercourse is transparently euphemized via the metaphor of coach-driving. The canonical version, cleaned up enough to be a nursery rhyme, runs:

> Up at Piccadilly oh!
> The coachman takes his stand,
> And when he meets a pretty girl,
> He takes her by the hand;
> Whip away for ever oh!
> Drive away so clever oh!
> All the way to Bristol oh!
> He drives her four-in-hand.

lady from Bristol. An Australian rhyming-slang term for 'pistol'.

shipshape and Bristol fashion. A nautical expression meaning 'in perfect order'. It alludes to the port of Bristol's reputation for efficiency in the days of sail.

Brit[1] A back-formation from BRIDPORT.

A river in Dorset, which rises to the north of BEAMINSTER and flows 14.5 km (9 miles) southwards into Lyme Bay (*see under* LYME REGIS) just to the south of Bridport.

Brit[2]. A colloquial abbreviation of BRITON, i.e. a BRITISH person. In the plural, it is used particularly in the USA, usually implying some level of affection (somewhat contrasting with its use in Ireland, *see below*). It is also used adjectivally in certain collocations, and an expression of Britishness can be a **Briticism**.

Britart. A media-created label for a group of young British conceptual artists (including Damien Hurst, Rachel Whiteread and Tracey Emin) who rose to prominence during the 1990s with their often deliberately shocking works. Their main patron was the millionaire advertising magnate, Charles Saatchi. Several of these artists' works, owned by Saatchi, went in flames in a 2004 warehouse fire in LEYTON.

Brit Awards. Annual (since 1982) awards made in various categories for British pop and rock music, with 'Brit' both short for 'British' and an acronym of 'British Record Industry'. The first awards were held as the British Record Industry 'Britannia Centenary' Awards in 1977, the winners receiving recognition for their achievements over the previous 25 years. They included the groups Queen and Procul Harum, the cellist Jacqueline du Pré and the singers Cliff Richard and Julie Covington. The formal title 'Brit Awards' was adopted in 1989. In the 1990s the event became much slicker and more high-profile. The awards are colloquially known as **'the Brits'**.

Britpop. British pop music, especially of the type that emerged among the young bands of the mid-1990s such as Oasis and Blur, that was influenced by The Beatles and other 1960s bands.

There is an eagerness to accept that our national culture is exemplified by Britpop, even at a time when the 'Brit' is as meaningless as the pop.

Roger Scruton: in *The Times*, 14 April 1999

'Brits out'. A slogan used by Nationalists during the Northern Ireland Troubles demanding the withdrawal of British troops.

Britain *See* BRITANNIA.

A large island off the northwest coast of mainland Europe, comprising ENGLAND, WALES, SCOTLAND, and also administratively including the many smaller islands surrounding it, apart from the ISLE OF MAN and the CHANNEL ISLANDS. Britain is the largest of the BRITISH ISLES, and forms the main part of the UNITED KINGDOM, for which it is often used as a synonym (although the United Kingdom also includes NORTHERN IRELAND). Conversely, Britain and/or the United Kingdom are often referred to by English people and foreigners as 'England', and vice versa – a confusion that even prime ministers are capable of:

Fifty years from now, Britain will still be the country of long shadows on county grounds, warm beer, invincible green suburbs, dog lovers, and – as George Orwell said – old maids bicycling to Holy Communion through the morning mist.

John Major: speech, 22 April 1993

The name Britain is an anglicized version of the Roman name BRITANNIA. In the 4th century BC the inhabitants were known to the Greeks as Prettanoi or Brettanoi ('figured ones', a reference to their tattoos), and under the Roman occupation they were known as Brittani (BRITONS), although in the 1st century AD Pliny referred to the island as ALBION.

Who the first inhabitants of Britain were, whether natives or immigrants, remains obscure; one must remember we are dealing with barbarians.

Tacitus: *Agricola* (AD 98)

The name GREAT BRITAIN was first officially used in 1604, when James VI of Scotland and I of England was proclaimed 'King of Great Britain', the year following the union of the crowns of England and Scotland. It had been used earlier by some writers, however, to distinguish Britain from *Britannia Minor*, or Brittany, in France (*see* LITTLE BRITAIN). It has been suggested that the term was first coined by the Scottish historian John Major (1469–1550) as the punning title for his history of Britain, *Historia Majoris Britanniae* (1521). After the Act of Union of 1707 abolishing the separate Scottish Parliament, those in favour of the Union referred to Scotland as NORTH BRITAIN, but the term did not last (*see also* WEST BRITON).

Antipodeans refer to Britain as FOGLAND or Pomgolia (*see under* POM).

Battle of Britain (August to October 1940). An air campaign following the Fall of France during the Second World War in which the German Luftwaffe (air force) attempted to destroy the power of the RAF as a prelude to invading southeast England. However, the Hurricanes and Spitfires of RAF Fighter Command, aided by radar (which the Germans did not then possess), defeated the attempt and won universal admiration. The name arose from a speech by Sir Winston Churchill on 18 June 1940:

What General Weygand called the 'Battle of France' is over. I expect that the Battle of Britain is about to begin.

Brain of Britain. A radio quiz show first broadcast in 1967 with often abstruse general-knowledge questions put to selected members of the public. The overall annual winner is deemed 'Brain of Britain'.

Britain. The fourth part (1736) of James Thomson's long poem *Liberty*.

'Britain can take it'. Supposedly morale-boosting words promulgated by the Ministry of Information during the early months of the Second World War. They were regarded as patronizing, however, and as portraying Britons in a humourless 'stiff upper lip' stereotype, and the slogan was soon dropped.

Britain plc. Business jargon for Britain if it is regarded as a unified commercial concern or 'corporation' formed from all its registered companies. UK plc is similarly used. (*Plc* 'publicly limited company', i.e. one floated on the stock exchange.)

Festival of Britain. A grand, government-sponsored celebration staged on an area of derelict ground on London's SOUTH BANK[1] in 1951 ostensibly to mark the centenary of the Great Exhibition of 1851. In reality it was a morale-boosting exercise, a gesture of faith in a brighter future for Britain after the deprivations of the Second World War and the years of austerity that followed. Three of its most striking structures were the Dome of Discovery, the world's largest dome at the time, the Skylon ('sky pylon'), a spindle-shaped filigree spire with no visible means of support, and the Royal Festival Hall, the only permanent building, now one of London's main concert venues.

We believe in the right to strike,
But now we've bloody well got to like
Our own dear Festival of Britain.

Noël Coward: 'Don't Make Fun of the Fair', from *The Lyric Revue* (1951)

'I'm backing Britain'. The slogan of a national campaign to buy British goods in the late 1960s, first coined by workers at a factory in SURBITON.

'Keep Britain tidy'. An enduring anti-litter slogan devised by the Central Office of Information in the 1950s.

Little Britain. *See* LITTLE BRITAIN.

Britannia Etymologically the name derives from the Greek name for the Celtic people here, *Prettanoi* or *Brettanoi* 'figured ones', a reference to their tattoos. After the Roman conquest, Britannia became the name of the province.

The Roman name for the southern part of BRITAIN, broadly comprising what is now ENGLAND and WALES; however, it sometimes denoted the whole island of Britain, as the term does today. The name is also applied to the personification of Britain as a female warrior wearing helmet and breast-plate and carrying a trident and shield. The first depiction of the figure of Britannia dates from the 2nd century AD, on a coin of the Emperor Antoninus Pius (d.161). The figure reappeared on copper coins in 1665, in the reign of Charles II, the model being one of Charles's mistresses, Frances Stuart ('La Belle Stuart'), later Duchess of Richmond. The engraver was Philip Roetier. Britannia continued to appear on pennies until decimalization in 1971, since when she has graced the 50p piece.

> The king's new medal, where, in little, is Mrs Stewart's face ... and a pretty thing it is, that he should choose her face to represent Britannia by.
>
> Samuel Pepys: diary (25 February 1667)

The associated adjective is **Britannic**, as in His or Her Britannic Majesty, an expression familiar from British passports.

> What two ideas are more inseparable than beer and Britannia?
>
> Sydney Smith (1771–1845): quoted in H. Pearson, *The Smith of Smiths* (1934)

Britannia. A sort of *Brewer's Britain and Ireland* of its day, written in Latin by William Camden and first published in 1586 (enlarged edition 1607; English translation by Philemon Holland 1610). It is subtitled *A Chorographicall Description of the Most Flourishing Kingdomes of England, Scotland and Ireland, and the Ilands Adioyning, out of the Depth of Antiquitie*, and comprises a guide to the antiquities, history, topography, etc., of each county. Camden was one of the first to realize that many place names derive from ancient languages.

Other Britannia titles include: *Britannia's Pastorals* (1613, 1616), two books of poems by William Browne of Tavistock; *Britannia Triumphans* (1638), a drama by Sir William Davenant; *Britannia Rediviva* (1688), a long poem by John Dryden; *Britannia* (1729), a long poem by James Thomson; *Britannia* (1729), a drama by David Mallet; *Britannia and Batavia* (1740), a drama by George Lillo; and *Britannia Victrix* (1919), a verse collection by Robert Bridges.

Britannia. The name given to the world's first turboprop airliner, built by the Bristol Aeroplane Company (*see under* BRISTOL).

Britannia Bridge. *See under* MENAI STRAIT.

Britannia coin. Any of a range of gold coins of various denominations (£100, £50, £25 and £10) introduced in Britain for the purposes of investment in 1987.

Britannia metal. An alloy with a low melting point used for decorative purposes; it comprises tin with small amounts of antimony, copper and sometimes some other metals.

Britannia Royal Naval College. See under DARTMOUTH.

Britannicus. The son of the Emperor Claudius by his third wife Messalina (d.AD 48), and so named because of the successful conquest of Britain by his father's legions in AD 43. Claudius's fourth wife, Agrippina, persuaded him to confer the succession not on Britannicus but on her own son, Nero. She is thought to have poisoned Britannicus in AD 55, a year after Claudius had met with a similar fate. Britannicus is the subject of the tragedy *Britannicus* (1669) by the French dramatist Jean Racine.

Cool Britannia. A phrase, punning on '**Rule, Britannia**' (*see below*), briefly in vogue after youthful-looking guitar-playing Tony Blair came to power in May 1997 at the head of a 'New Labour' government. The phrase actually occurred 30 years earlier, in a 1967 send-up of both the traditional song and contemporary British grooviness as recorded by the Bonzo Dog Band:

> Cool Britannia,
> Britannia you are cool (take a trip!),
> Britons ever ever ever
> Shall be hip!
>
> Vivian Stanshall: 'Cool Britannia', from the album *Gorilla* (1967)

The new government in 1997 wooed, and was for a while wooed by, fashionable young artists and musicians (especially of the Britart and Britpop varieties; *see under* BRIT²), and the term suggested a revitalized and rejuvenated Britain after 18 years of Conservative rule. However, as the prime-ministerial coiffure thinned and his government adopted, in the eyes of many, increasingly illiberal policies the inevitable disillusion set in, and Cool Britannia became nothing more than an embarrassing memory.

> When I think of Cool Britannia, I think of old people dying of hypothermia.
>
> Tony Benn: speech to the Labour Party Conference (September 1998)

'Cool Britannia' was briefly a flavour of the Vermont-based Ben and Jerry's ice cream company in the late 1990s. At a Parliamentary Select Committee discussion (20 May 1998) on government culture policy, its chairman opined that it was the 'least edible' of the manufacturer's flavours, a verdict not entirely uninfluenced by political considerations.

Encyclopedia Britannica. The most revered, and most extensive, English-language encyclopedia, which is now, naturally, produced in the USA. It began life in EDINBURGH, where the first edition was published in 1768–71 under the editorship of William Smellie. Over the next 150 years it got bigger as it covered an ever larger number of subject areas, and in 1910–11, now with Cambridge University Press (*see under* CAMBRIDGE[1]), the still-cherished 11th edition appeared in 29 volumes. It (and its price) continued to increase and ownership passed across the Atlantic, to a Chicago company. Possession of a set, with the implication of substantial financial outlay in the cause of polymathic enlightenment, became something of a mark of 'made it' middle-classness. The computer revolution changed all that, but the Britannica company was wise enough to shift emphasis in time. Today, rather than caviar for the general (and for big library budgets) the contents of the continually revised *Britannica* can be had on CD-ROM for the price of a theatre ticket, and an affordable online subscription service is available.

Oceanus Britannicus. A former name for the ENGLISH CHANNEL.

Pax Britannica. The peace formerly imposed by Britain in her colonial empire. The phrase is modelled on the Latin *Pax Romana*, the peace prevailing within the Roman Empire.

'Rule, Britannia'. A patriotic song with words by James Thomson (1700–48), author of *The Seasons* (1726–30), and music by Dr Thomas Arne (1710–78). It first appeared in a masque entitled *Alfred* produced in August 1740 at Cliveden House, near Maidenhead, Berkshire. It was written at the command of the Prince of Wales and performed before him. The original opening was:

> When Britain first, at Heaven's command,
> Arose from out the azure main,
> This was the charter of the land,
> And guardian angels sung this strain:
> 'Rule, Britannia, rule the waves;
> Britons never will be slaves.'

In the Rising of 1745 'Rule, Britannia' was sung by the Jacobites with modifications appropriate to their cause. Today, the song is belted out annually and enthusiastically at the Last Night of the Proms by hordes of flag-waving patriots or young fogeys, depending on one's view. (*See also* Cool Britannia, *above*)

British. As an adjective, relating to BRITAIN, to its people ('Sheep with a nasty side', according to Cyril Connolly) or to the British variety of the English language. As a noun, it denotes the natives of Britain or the ancient Britons (*see* BRITON) or the language of the latter (more usually referred to as Brittonic or Brythonic).
See also BRIT[2].

'British are coming!, The'. The warning famously supposed to have been uttered by American Patriot Paul Revere to those he encountered on his ride from Boston to Concord in 1775. (Apparently he said 'the Regulars are coming', which makes more sense historically – most of his compatriots still thought of themselves as British – but fiction is often better than fact.) The phrase has been invoked many times since, in rather less serious contexts. Actor-writer Colin Welland triumphantly exclaimed it while receiving an Oscar for his screenplay for *Chariots of Fire* (1981): the film gathered a total of four Oscars, and was taken to mark something of a resurgence in the British film industry.

British Broadcasting Corporation (BBC). The British Broadcasting Company, as it was originally called, was formed by six electrical companies and broadcast its first programme, a news bulletin, at 6 p.m. on 14 November 1922 from 2LO, a studio in Savoy Hill, London. Two days later this was followed by the first entertainment programme. It lasted an hour, opening with Leonard Hawke, a baritone, performing 'Duke Goes West' and 'Tick' and concluding with Dorothy Chalmers performing 'Hymn to the Sun' and Schubert's *Rosamunde* on the violin. Its charter expired on 31 December 1926, and the following year it became a corporation. Television was first broadcast from Alexandra Palace in 1936, and foreign broadcasts began the following year. The BBC's television monopoly was broken in 1955 with the airing of the first programme by a commercial channel, and its radio monopoly was similarly lost in the 1970s. The BBC's contribution and finances are governed by royal charter, and its broadcasting is funded by an annual television licence fee. Increasing competition from commercial channels has latterly obliged the BBC to lighten its 'fuddy-duddy' image without losing its long-held respected public-service status.

The most familiar nickname of the BBC is 'the Beeb', but the term 'Auntie' is also used, with the underlying suggestion that the BBC is a conservative or 'nannyish' organization, especially by comparison with the more populist and permissive commercial television.

British bulldog. A symbol of British tenacity, JOHN BULL's dog being of the bulldog breed. In the Second World War, Winston Churchill was said to embody 'the bulldog spirit' (his physical resemblance to the creature reinforced the image).

In the jingoistic days of the early 20th century, British bulldog was also the name given to a team game popular among boys, particularly of the scouting variety (and sometimes among girls, of the guiding variety). Members of one team dashed across a field and attempted to break through a line formed by the other team, who in turn attempted to catch them. A caught player was hoisted off the ground with the cry 'British bulldog!' and then joined the opposing team. The game was still being played in the 1960s and beyond.

British champagne. An early 19th-century slang term for porter or dark ale.

British Commonwealth. A loose association of states (usually known as the Commonwealth of Nations) whose sole common characteristic is that they were once colonies of the British Empire (*see below*). (Mozambique, formerly a Portuguese colony, is an exception.) All member-states accept the British monarch as the symbolic head of the Commonwealth, but not all recognize the monarch as their own head of state.

British disease. An uncomplimentary term used abroad with reference to the prevalence of strikes and other forms of industrial action in Britain during the 1960s and 1970s. In the 1980s the Conservative government of Margaret Thatcher, believing that desperate diseases required desperate remedies, set about the problem through a programme of privatization and employment (including trades-union) reform. The consequences, including the closure of much manufacturing industry, remain controversial.

British Empire. Britain began to build its overseas empire in the later 16th century. It reached its greatest extent at the end of the First World War, encompassing over a quarter of the world's land surface and over a quarter of its population. This was the empire on which the sun never set (allegedly because, as Duncan Spaeth pointed out, 'God wouldn't trust an Englishman in the dark'). Britain's colonies mostly gained their independence in the decades after the Second World War, and by the end of the 20th century the empire was reduced to a few small islands scattered around the globe. Nevertheless, the British monarch continues to dole out honours with names such as the **Member of the Order of the British Empire**, **Companion of the Order of the British Empire**, and so on.

British English. The type of spoken English that is used in Britain and not in the USA or elsewhere.

Britisher. A term for a BRITON used by some foreigners (and especially by actors playing Germans in war films).

British Invasion. The transformation of the US popular music scene by British performers in the 1960s, especially The Beatles and The Rolling Stones. Some acts, such as Chad and Jeremy, were famous in the United States but almost unknown at home. The 'second British invasion' was by punk rock and New Wave in the early 1980s.

Britishism. An idiom, custom or other cultural appurtenance unique to the British. The word is sometimes rendered as **Briticism**.

British Israelites. *See under* TARA.

British Legion. An organization for promoting the welfare of ex-service personnel, especially the aged, sick and disabled. It was founded in 1921 largely through the exertions of Field Marshal Earl Haig (1861–1928), and it became the Royal British Legion in 1971. There are many local branches, and much of the money is raised by the sale of poppy badges in the period leading up to Remembrance Day (11 November).

British Library. The British national library, formed in 1973 from the British Museum library. It opened in new premises at St Pancras, London, in 1998.

British Lion, the. The pugnacity of the British nation, as opposed to JOHN BULL, who symbolizes its solidity and obstinacy. The **British Lions** is the name given to the combined British and Irish rugby team when they tour abroad.

British Museum. This famous institution, housing collections of antiquities and artefacts from different cultures, began in Montague House, Great Russell Street. It resulted from an Act of 1753, and its first collections were purchased from the proceeds of a public lottery. Its library become the core of the **British Library** (*see above*), and in its famous circular Reading Room many famous persons (such as Karl Marx) studied and wrote. Among its more controversial holdings are the Elgin Marbles (*see under* ELGIN).

> A foggy day in London Town
> Had me low and had me down.
> I viewed the morning with alarm,
> The British Museum had lost its charm ...
>
> Ira Gershwin: 'A Foggy Day' (1937) (song)

British Museum is Falling Down, The. A novel (1965) by David Lodge, in which the Catholic hero struggles to give birth to his thesis in the British Museum while struggling to master the rhythm method with his wife at home, in the hope of avoiding a fourth child ('Literature is mostly about having sex and not having children. Life is the other way round ...').

British National Party. A far-right political party, derived from the old National Front. It supports such policies as voluntary repatriation of immigrants and withdrawal from the European Union. Its name is often abbreviated to **BNP**.

Britishness. The state or quality of being British.

British Restaurant. A government-subsidized restaurant operating in Britain in the Second World War. The designation 'Communal Feeding Centre' was originally proposed, but Winston Churchill suggested 'British Restaurant' as more appropriate and attractive.

British roarer. A late 19th-century slang term for the lion that appears alongside the unicorn on the British coat of arms.

British Summer Time. The official time of one hour in advance of Greenwich Mean Time (*see under* GREENWICH) that comes into force between March and October.

British thermal unit. The quantity of heat needed to raise the temperature of 0.45 kg (1lb) of water by 1°F, equivalent to 1055.06 joules.

British Union of Fascists. A British fascist party founded in 1932 out of Sir Oswald Mosley's New Party and a number of other groups. Mosley continued as leader of the anti-Semitic, black-shirted party, which lost its impetus after 1936 when the Public Order Act banned political uniforms and restricted political marches.

British warm. A thick short overcoat worn by army officers.

Great British Public, the. *See under* GREAT BRITAIN.

twist the tail of the British lion, to. A phrase formerly used in the USA meaning to attempt to annoy or goad the British people or to provoke them by abuse or to inflict a rebuff. This was a device used to gain the support of Irish Americans.

British Isles. A geographical rather than a political term, denoting the islands of BRITAIN, IRELAND, ORKNEY, SHETLAND, the HEBRIDES, the ISLE OF MAN, the SCILLY ISLES, the ISLE OF WIGHT, the CHANNEL ISLANDS and many lesser islands around the coast of Britain. In Ireland the term is not generally used, the Republic not having been British for many years, and in preference the Irish talk of THESE ISLANDS or even the Hibernian Archipelago (*see under* HIBERNIA).

Briton. A native of Britain. The **Ancient Britons** were a Celtic people, speaking a language (or group of languages) known as **Brittonic** or **Brythonic**. The Romans conquered southern Britain in the 1st century AD, and, after the usual revolts, suppressions and slaughters ('*Nemo bonus Brito est*' – 'No good man is a Briton' – quipped Ausonius in the 110th of his *Epigrams*), the Romans and Britons rubbed along well enough, the latter buying into the *Pax Romana* and becoming known as **Romano-Britons** (the fabled King Arthur is thought to have been one of these). The withdrawal of the Roman legions in the early 5th century to deal with pressures nearer home left the Britons somewhat defenceless against the waves of Germanic tribes (Angles, Saxons, Jutes and their ilk) arriving in increasing numbers on British shores. Within a century or so the so-called Anglo-Saxons dominated much of what became known, in their honour, as ENGLAND, while the Brittonic-speaking peoples were restricted to CORNWALL, WALES, CUMBRIA and southwest Scotland (*see* RHEGED *and* STRATHCLYDE). Today, WELSH survives as the only Brittonic language still spoken in Britain as a native tongue (although CORNISH, extinct since the late 18th century, has been revived by enthusiasts, and Breton, in Brittany, has similarly been adopted by nationalists).

The idea of being a Briton revived again in the 18th century, after the Act of Union of 1707 joined England with Scotland (or NORTH BRITAIN), and George III, shrugging off his German ancestry, was proud to announce to the House of Lords: 'I glory in the name of Briton.'

Today, the term 'Briton' denotes what we are still obliged to call a 'British subject' (i.e. of Her Britannic Majesty), although there are increasing numbers who would prefer to be citizens.

Britons are variously referred by non-Britons by such names as Brits (*see* BRIT[2]), Britishers (*see under* BRITISH), LIMEYS, POMS, ROSBIFS and John Bull's Bastards (*see under* JOHN BULL).

See also WEST BRITON.

Briton Ferry 'ferry at the settlement with the bridge', OE *brycg* 'bridge, river crossing' + -TON + ModE *ferry*.

A former port and now a part (since 1922) of the town of NEATH[2], on the River NEATH[1], in Neath Port Talbot unitary authority (formerly in Glamorgan and then West Glamorgan), some 3 km (2 miles) south of the town centre. There is no record of an old bridge, but there was once a ferry here across the river.

Britwell Salome *Britwell* probably 'spring or stream of the Britons', OE *Bryt* 'Briton' + *wella* 'spring, stream'; *Salome* denoting manorial ownership in the Middle Ages by the de Suleham family, presumably later assimilated to *Salome*, the name of the Judaean temptress who asked for the head of John the Baptist.

A village (*Salome* pronounced 'sa-lohm' or, locally, 'saləm') in Oxfordshire, about 16 km (10 miles) southeast of Oxford.

Brixham 'Brioc's homestead or enclosure', possessive form of OCelt male personal name *Brioc* + HAM.

A town, fishing port and seaside resort in Devon, at the southern extremity of TOR BAY. The old village is up on a hill, separated from the fishing village below, with its picturesque harbour.

William of Orange landed at Brixham in 1688 on his way to taking up the throne of Britain as William III. He is said to have remarked as he set foot in the country, 'Mine goot people, I mean you goot, I am here for your goot, for all your goots'. He is commemorated by a statue here.

Henry Francis Lyte, who wrote the hymn 'Abide with me' (*c.*1845), was vicar of Brixham in the early 19th century.

Brixton 'Beorhtsige's stone', OE male personal name *Beorhtsige* + *stan* (*see* STONE) (probably referring to the stone which marked the meeting place of Brixton Hundred).

An area of South London, in the borough of LAMBETH (SW2, SW9), to the east of Battersea and to the north of Streatham. London's encroachment on the former Surrey village began in the early 19th century. At first the housing was salubrious and the population relatively well-to-do, but Brixton's demographic profile sank in the course of the 19th century, and by the 20th it was a run-down inner-city area. After the Second World War, the availability of cheap accommodation near the centre of London attracted many West Indian immigrants, notably to the Railton Road area. Racial tension was often a problem, especially between the police and the ethnic population (leading for example to the 1981 **Brixton Riots**), but overall the rainbow mix of blacks, whites and Asians of a myriad nationalities has created a vibrant local culture.

The painter Vincent van Gogh stayed in lodgings in Brixton 1873–5 while working for the family art dealership (in 2002 the National Theatre presented a production of Nicholas Wright's *Vincent in Brixton*).

Brixton Prison opened in 1820 as a Surrey House of Correction. It dates in its present form from 1902.

Brixton Underground station, on the Victoria line, opened in 1971.

Brixton briefcase. A slang term for a ghetto-blaster.

Brixton riot. A 21st-century British rhyming-slang term for *diet* (for the original literal reference, *see above*).

Brixton Deverill 'Beorhtric's estate on the River Deverill' (the former name of the River Wylye): *Brixton*, OE *Beorhtrices* possessive form of male personal name *Beorhtric* + -TON; *Deverill* OCelt river name, meaning 'watery'.

A village in Wiltshire, on the River WYLYE[1], on the West Wiltshire Downs, about 5.5 km (3.5 miles) south of Warminster.

Brixworth 'Bricel's enclosure', OE male personal name *Bricel* + -worth (*see* -WORTH, WORTHY, -WARDINE).

A village in Northamptonshire, 11 km (7 miles) north of Northampton. Much of the exterior of its parish church, including the tower, is Anglo-Saxon ('the original church is probably late 7th century' says Simon Jenkins in his *Britain's 1000 Best Parish Churches*).

> One of our famous places, where there comes to us a solemn sense of the age-old continuity of our island life. Here, gaunt and solitary among farm buildings, stands a church older than King Alfred.
>
> Arthur Mee

Brize Norton *Brize* denoting manorial ownership in the early Middle Ages by a certain William le Brun; *Norton see* NORTON.

A village in Oxfordshire, about 24 km (15 miles) west of Oxford. The RAF has its main strategic transport base here, and many military and humanitarian overseas missions set off from here.

Broad, the. The colloquial name of the wide street in central Oxford, officially called **Broad Street**. It contains Balliol College, Trinity College, the Sheldonian Theatre and Blackwell's bookshop.

Broad Chalke *Broad* 'great, chief', OE *brad* 'broad, great'; the earliest references are to *Magna* or *Grete* (Latin and ME 'great') *Chalke* (*see* CHALK), hence the interpretation of Broad.

A village in Wiltshire, about 12 km (7.5 miles) southwest of Salisbury.

See also BOWERCHALKE.

Broadford 'broad ford', ModE, a translation of Gaelic *Allt a' Mhuillinn*.

A village in SKYE, formerly in Inverness-shire and now in Highland, 11 km (7 miles) west of the bridge linking the island to KYLE OF LOCHALSH. It overlooks **Broadford Bay**.

Broadhalfpenny Down Dialect *broad* 'open space' (from OE *brad* 'broad') and OE *dun* (*see* DOWN, -DON). The significance of *halfpenny* is obscure, but it may refer to the rent (or ironically to the value) of the land.

A domed windswept hilltop 3 km (2 miles) northeast of HAMBLEDON, Hampshire, on which the cricketers of the all-conquering Hambledon team played at the end of the 18th century. After (and possibly during) play they could refresh themselves in the Bat and Ball Inn, on the edge of the ground, of which one of their number, Richard Nyren, was landlord.

Broad Haven There are no known Irish forms, so it is probably ModE, and self-explanatory.

A bay on the northwest coast of County Mayo, between the mainland and the northern part of the MULLET. The **Stags of Broad Haven** are seven rocks 3 km (2 miles) north of Benwee Head on the east side of the bay.

Broadheath '(place at the) broad heath'; originally (1240) *Heath* (OE *hæth*), with later addition of ModE *Broad* (1646) (from OE *brad*).

A village in two parts (**Lower Broadheath** and **Upper Broadheath**) in Worcestershire (before 1998 in Hereford and Worcester, before 1974 in Worcestershire), about 6 km (4 miles) west of Worcester. The composer Edward Elgar was born in Upper Broadheath in 1875. His birthplace is now a museum.

Broadhembury 'great high fortified place' (referring to Hembury Fort), OE *brad* 'broad, great' + *heah* 'high' + *burh* (*see* BURY).

A village in Devon, about 8 km (5 miles) northwest of Honiton. Most of its houses and cottages are thatched. Its vicar from 1768 to 1778 was the Rev. Augustus Toplady, author of the popular hymn 'Rock of Ages' (*see* BURRINGTON).

To the south of the village is **Hembury Fort**, which was inhabited from *c*.200 BC to *c*.AD 75. It has extraordinarily good views over DARTMOOR, in the distant southwest.

Broad Law 'broad rounded hill', from its shape, Scots 'rounded hill' from OE *hlaw* (*see* LAW, LOW).

The second-highest hill (840 m / 2755 ft) in the SOUTHERN UPLANDS, after MERRICK. It is in the Tweeddale Hills (*see under* TWEED), Scottish Borders (formerly in Peeblesshire), 9 km (5.5 miles) west of St Mary's Loch.

Broadmoor OE *brad* 'broad' + *mor* 'moor, barren land'.

A village just to the east of Crowthorne in Berkshire. It is the site of **Broadmoor Hospital**, a hospital for the secure detention and treatment of mental patients with a propensity to violence or criminality. It was established in 1863, and the many notorious murderers and other felons since incarcerated here (including Peter Sutcliffe (the 'Yorkshire Ripper') and Ronnie Kray), have given its name a chill resonance. For most British English-speakers it has become synonymous with 'prison for the criminally insane' (although there are two other such establishments in England – Ashworth and Rampton).

See also The Surgeon of Crowthorne, under CROWTHORNE.

Broads 1787; from *broad* 'a large stretch of fresh water formed by the broadening out of a river', from the adjective *broad*.

A low-lying, roughly triangular area of watery land, approximately 20,000 ha (50,000 acres) in extent, in the southeast corner of Norfolk, between LOWESTOFT, SEA PALLING and NORWICH. Its characteristic feature is the shallow lakes known locally as 'broads' (the term is first recorded from the mid-17th century, but the earliest known use of it as a name for this area is from 1787).

There are 52 such 'Broads', the main ones being Barton, Filby, HICKLING, Ormesby, OULTON and Wroxham. They owe their existence to peat-digging, begun by the Anglo-Saxons in the 9th century. When sea levels rose in the Middle Ages they were flooded, to form, with the rivers that join them (notably the BURE, WAVENEY[1] and YARE), an interconnected 32-km (200-mile) system of reed-bordered waterways. The **Norfolk Broads** (as they are often referred to) became a popular tourist destination in the Victorian period, and sailing and cruising holidays continue to attract many visitors. They are also an important wildlife refuge.

The Broads provide the setting for Arthur Ransome's children's novel *Coot Club* (1934).

Broadstairs 'broad stairway', from the wide set of steps that were cut into the cliff, apparently in the early 15th century, to lead down to the sea.

A town and seaside resort at the northeastern tip of Kent, between MARGATE and RAMSGATE. Its popularity as a holiday destination began in the Regency period, and continued through the 19th century. Charles Dickens liked the place: he wrote *David Copperfield* here in 1849–50, basing Betsy Trotwood's cottage on a local house, and took a holiday home here, which he renamed 'Bleak House'.

Broadstairs has always been decidedly more upmarket and genteel than neighbouring Margate – perfect for the fictional middle-class Pooter family:

Hurrah! at Broadstairs. Very nice apartments near the station. On the cliffs they would have been double the price. The landlady had a nice five o'clock dinner and tea ready, which we all enjoyed, though Lupin seemed fastidious because there happened to be a fly in the butter.

George and Weedon Grossmith: *The Diary of a Nobody* (1892)

The cliff steps from which Broadstairs got its name may have inspired the title of John Buchan's thriller *The Thirty-Nine Steps* (1915). He began the book while staying in Broadstairs in 1914, recuperating from an illness. The original number of oak steps was 78, and a friend is said to have advised him to halve the number for the title. (*See also* KIRKCALDY).

The veteran Conservative politician Sir Edward Heath (b.1916; prime minister 1970–4) was born in Broadstairs.

Broadwas 'broad expanse of alluvial land', OE *brad* 'broad' + *wæsse* 'alluvial land'.

A village in Worcestershire (before 1998 in Hereford and Worcester, before 1974 in Worcestershire), about 10 km (6 miles) west of Worcester, on the River TEME.

Broadway '(place at the) broad road', OE *brad* 'broad' + *weg* 'way, road'.

A village in Worcestershire (before 1998 in Hereford and Worcester, before 1974 in Worcestershire), about 8 km (5 miles) southeast of Evesham, at the foot of the northern end of the COTSWOLDS. The Tudor, Jacobean and Georgian buildings in glowing golden Cotswold stone that line its appropriately broad main street have made it probably the most painted and most photographed of all Cotswold villages and a coach-tour favourite.

To the southeast is **Broadway Hill** (at 312 m / 1024 ft the second highest point on the Cotswold escarpment), on top of which stands **Broadway Tower**, an 18th-century folly with sweeping views of the surrounding countryside. (It is claimed that on a clear day 14 counties can be seen from here.) Once the home of William Morris, founder of the Arts and Crafts Movement, today the tower lies at the centre of an extensive country park.

Above Broadway, the A44 trunk road from Oxford to Aberystwyth descends from the Cotswolds via the exhilarating, brake-testing bends of Fish Hill. The present road layout, with its two wide sweeping curves, was created in 1822, replacing a 'Serpentine Road' dating from the 1770s (which itself had replaced an earlier road that plunged directly down the hill). Before the early 19th century, coaches and wagons had, in winter conditions, sometimes needed as many as 14 horses to reach the top of Broadway Hill.

Broadwoodkelly Originally *Broadwood* 'broad wood', OE

brad + wudu; -kelly (1261) denoting manorial ownership in the Middle Ages by the de Kelly family.

A village in Devon, about 24 km (15 miles) northwest of Crediton.

Broadwoodwidger Originally *Broadwood* (*see* BROAD-WOODKELLY); -*widger* (1310) denoting manorial ownership in the Middle Ages by the Wyger family.

A village in Devon, about 19 km (11.5 miles) southwest of Okehampton.

Brockenhurst Probably 'Broca's wooded hill', OE *Brocan* possessive form of male personal name *Broca* + *hyrst* 'wooded hill'; an alternative explanation of the first element is that it may be from OE *brocen* 'broken, undulating'.

A town in Hampshire, in the NEW FOREST, about 8 km (5 miles) northwest of LYMINGTON. A yew in the local churchyard, 6 m (20 ft) in circumference, is said to be the oldest tree in the New Forest.

Brockholes OE *brocc-hol* 'badger's set'.

A village in West Yorkshire, 6 km (4 miles) south of Huddersfield.

Brocklebridge. Charlotte Brontë's fictional version of TUNSTALL[2], Lancashire, as appearing in *Jane Eyre* (1847).

Brodgar, Ring of. *See* RING OF BRODGAR.

Brodick 'broad bay', OScand *breithr* 'broad' + *vík* (*see* WICK).

The main town and ferry port on ARRAN, halfway up the east coast. It is in North Ayrshire (formerly in Buteshire, then in Strathclyde region). The town is on the east side of the island, overlooking **Brodick Bay**, and itself overlooked by GOAT FELL. At the foot of Goat Fell is **Brodick Castle**, the oldest part of which dates from the 13th century. Robert the Bruce used it as a base for a time during the Scottish Wars of Independence (early 14th century). The building was extended in 1652 and 1844, and it was formerly the seat of the dukes of Hamilton.

Broighter Etymology unknown.

A locality in County Londonderry, some 5 km (3 miles) northwest of Limavady.

Broighter Hoard, the. A collection of prehistoric gold ornaments dug up by a ploughman at Broighter in 1896. The hoard was the subject of a legal dispute over ownership between the Crown (who claimed the pieces as treasure trove) and the British Museum. In 1903 the judge ordered that the hoard be awarded to the National Museum in DUBLIN, where it can still be seen.

Bromborough. *See* BRUNANBURH.

Bromley 'glade where broom grows', OE *brom* 'broom' + -LEY.

A southeastern suburb of LONDON (formerly a market town in northwest Kent), in 1965 designated a London borough, to the south of Lewisham and Bexley, containing BECKENHAM, CHISLEHURST, ORPINGTON and PENGE as well as Bickley, Keston, Petts Wood, Swanley and West Wickham, and Bromley itself.

Bromley was the birthplace of the writer H.G. Wells (1866–1946) and of the cricketer Derek Underwood (b.1945), a left-arm spin bowler for Kent and England. *See also* CAESAR'S CAMP.

Brompton 'farmstead or estate where broom grows', OE *brom* 'broom' + -TON.

A well-to-do area of London to the south of Hyde Park (formerly pronounced 'brumpton', now more usually in accordance with the spelling), between Belgravia to the east and Knightsbridge to the west, in the borough of KENSINGTON AND CHELSEA (SW1, SW3). **Brompton Road** links Knightsbridge to the Fulham Road (there was once a Brompton Road Underground station, on the Piccadilly line, which opened in 1906, but it closed in 1934), and slightly further to the west, the **Old Brompton Road** extends from South Kensington Underground station to **West Brompton**, to the south of Earls Court. **The Royal Brompton Hospital**, in the Fulham Road, opened in 1842, as the 'Hospital for Consumption and Diseases of the Chest'. It now (as part of the Royal Brompton and Harefield NHS Trust) specializes in heart and lung surgery.

Brompton cocktail. A powerful painkiller and sedative consisting of vodka or other liquor laced with morphine and sometimes also cocaine. The preparation is used to relieve pain caused by cancer and is said to have been named after the Brompton Hospital, where it was first applied to this end.

Brompton Oratory. A large and ornate Roman Catholic church, properly designated the London Oratory of St Philip Neri, which stands next to the **Victoria and Albert Museum** on the north side of Brompton Road. It was designed in Baroque style by Herbert Gribble and opened in the mid-1880s. There is a strong musical tradition at the church. In the 1990s it developed a somewhat modish society reputation and attracted 'yuppie' worshippers and agonized former Anglicans.

Brompton stock. A biennial variety of the stock (a sweet-scented garden plant) originally bred in the early 18th century at Brompton Park Nursery.

Brompton Ralph *Brompton* 'farmstead in the Brendon Hills', OE *Bruna* name of the Brendon Hills (literally 'brown hills') + -TON; *Ralph* denoting manorial ownership in the Middle Ages by a man called Ralph.

A village in Somerset, about 16 km (10 miles) northwest of Taunton.

Bromsash 'Breme's ash-tree', OE *Bremes* possessive form of male personal name *Breme* + *æsc* 'ash tree'.

A village in Herefordshire (before 1998 in Hereford and

Worcester, before 1974 in Herefordshire), about 5 km (3 miles) east of Ross-on-Wye.

Bromsgrove 'Breme's grove', OE *Bremes* possessive form of male personal name *Breme* + *graf* 'grove, copse'.

A market town in Worcestershire (before 1998 in Hereford and Worcester, before 1974 in Worcestershire), at the foot of the LICKEY Hills, about 18 km (11 miles) northeast of Worcester. Its industrial specialism has been the production of nails.

Bromsgrove has connections with two very different poets: A.E. Housman (1859–1936) went to school here, and Geoffrey Hill (b.1932), author of *Mercian Hymns* (1971) (*see under* MERCIA), was born here.

Jovial Hunter of Bromsgrove, the. The sobriquet of the legendary Sir Ryalas, who at the behest of a lady in distress slew a huge wild boar that had just killed her husband, only for her to attack him ferociously. Instantly recognizing her as a witch, he split her head in two with his axe. A boar's head now features on Bromsgrove's municipal coat-of-arms, and there is a tomb alleged to be that of Sir Ryalas in the (originally Norman) local church. His deeds are celebrated in an old ballad, the last verse of which runs:

> In Bromsgrove church, the knight he doth lie,
> Wind well thy horn, good hunter;
> And the wild boar's head is pictured thereby,
> Sir Ryalas, the jovial hunter.

Brontë Country. Those parts of Yorkshire associated with the novelists Charlotte (1816–55), Emily (1818–48) and Anne (1820–49) Brontë. Their home was the parsonage at HAWORTH, near Keighley, but Charlotte and Emily spent a period at the harsh school at COWAN BRIDGE (just inside Lancashire), the inspiration for the Lowood Institution in *Jane Eyre*. Later Charlotte worked (unhappily) as a governess at Stone Gappe house in Lothersdale, some 6 km (4 miles) southwest of Skipton, and this experience inspired her to write *Jane Eyre*; the house itself became the model of Gateshead Hall.

On the moor near Haworth is the derelict house of Top (or High) Withins, whose situation (although not its structure) was the inspiration for the Earnshaw house that provides the title of *Wuthering Heights*. The place is described at the beginning of the novel by the narrator Lockwood:

> Wuthering Heights is the name of Mr Heathcliff's dwelling. 'Wuthering' being a significant provincial adjective, descriptive of the atmospheric tumult to which its station is exposed in stormy weather. Pure, bracing ventilation they must have up there at all times, indeed: one may guess the power of the north wind blowing over the edge, by the excessive slant of a few stunted firs at the end of the house; and by a range of gaunt thorns all stretching their limbs one way, as if craving alms of the

sun. Happily, the architect had foresight to build it strong: the narrow windows are deeply set in the wall, and the corners defended with large jutting stones.

When Mrs Gaskell visited Top Withins in 1853, she commented on the contrast between the house's bleak exterior and the 'snugness and comfort' inside. Near to Top Withins is Ponden Hall, where Emily had free run of the library; the house may have been the inspiration for Thrushcross Grange in *Wuthering Heights*.

Compare CONSTABLE COUNTRY, BURNS COUNTRY, HARDY COUNTRY *and* SCOTT COUNTRY.

Brooklands 'marshy land' (by the River Wey), ME *brok* 'marshy land' + *lands*. The Broc or Brok family is known here from the end of the 12th century.

The site of the world's first custom-built motor-racing circuit, near WEYBRIDGE in Surrey. It was the enterprise of Hugh Locke-King, a Surrey landowner, who in 1907 paid £150,000 to build a concrete racetrack in the form of an oval course with heavily banked curves. It was soon widely used by car manufacturers for testing new models. In its first year a record was set up by Selwyn Edge for travelling 2552 km (1582 miles) in 24 hours at an average speed of 106 kph (66 mph), a figure that remained unbeaten for 18 years.

Brooklands was the venue for the first British Grand Prix (then known as the RAC Grand Prix) in 1926. Racing continued there until the Second World War, during which the track was given over to aircraft production. It was not restored subsequently.

Lady Clayton East Clayton [*sic*] met her death at Brooklands in 1933 'while engaged in aviation' (according to her obituary in *The Times*). She was the model for Katherine Clifton in Michael Ondaatje's novel *The English Patient* (1992).

Broom[1] 'place where broom grows', OE *brom* 'broom'.
A village in Bedfordshire, about 3 km (2 miles) southeast of Biggleswade.

Broom[2]. A village in Warwickshire, about 11 km (7 miles) west of Stratford-upon-Avon. Shakespeare is said to have referred to the village as 'beggarly Broom' (*see* SHAKESPEARE VILLAGES).

Broomielaw. 'broom-covered hill', OE *bromig* 'broom-covered' + *hlaw* (*see* LAW, LOW).
A waterfront area of GLASGOW, on the north side of the CLYDE just to the west of the city centre. It was formerly much used by shipping, but has since been redeveloped with no great panache. It is also the name of the main road along the front, often referred to as **the Broomielaw**, as is this stretch of the Clyde itself:

> Nae mair will the bonnie callants
> Mairch tae war when oor braggarts crousely craw,

Nor wee weans frae pit-heid an' clachan

Mourn the ships sailing doon the Broomielaw.

> Hamish Henderson: 'The Freedom Come All Ye' (1947)
> (*callants* 'youths', *crousely craw* 'arrogantly crow', *weans*
> 'young children', *clachan* 'village')

In the past, the Broomielaw was one of the main points of disembarkation for seasonal agricultural workers ('tatie-howkers' or potato pickers) from Donegal, as celebrated in this anonymous song:

> Wha saw the tattie-howkers,
> Wha saw them gang awa,
> Wha saw the tatie-howkers,
> Sailing down the Broomielaw?

Broomie Law. A diminutive Glaswegian lass who featured in a cartoon strip by Cinders McLeod in *The Herald* in the 1990s, acerbically commenting on matters social and political. The strip also included other characters named after Glasgow places, such as Annie Land (a trusting baby-doll; after Anniesland), Hag's Castle (Broomie's cynical handbag), and Mary Hill (a grumpy old lady; after Maryhill).

Brora 'river of the bridge', OScand *bruar*, possessive of *bru* 'bridge' + *a* 'river'.
A small resort town on the northeast coast of Scotland, in Highland, formerly in Sutherland, 18 km (11 miles) northeast of Dornoch. It is sited where the **River Brora**, having flowed through **Strath Brora** and **Loch Brora**, enters the North Sea. Brora boasts Scotland's oldest coal mine, in use since 529, and only closed after the Second World War.

Brothers Water. A small lake in the Lake District, Cumbria, some 3 km (2 miles) south of Ullswater and Patterdale. According to William Wordsworth, it was named:

> From those two Brothers that were drown'd therein.
> William Wordsworth: *The Prelude* (1805–50), Book VIII

His sister Dorothy describes the attraction of the place as stemming from:

> The water under the boughs of the bare old trees, the simplicity of the mountains, and the exquisite beauty of the path.
> Dorothy Wordsworth: journal (16 April 1802)

Brotton 'farmstead by a stream', OE *broc* 'stream' + -TON.
A town in Redcar and Cleveland (formerly in the North Riding of Yorkshire, then in Cleveland), some 20 km (12.5 miles) east of Middlesbrough.

Brough¹ 'fortified place', OE *burh* (*see* BURY).
A village in Cumbria, formerly in Westmorland, about 6 km (4 miles) north of Kirkby Stephen. Brough was the site of the Roman fort of **Verteris**, later the site of a medieval castle.

Brough². A village in the East Riding of Yorkshire, 16 km (10 miles) west of Hull, also known as **Brough-on-Humber** (it stands at the point where Ermine Street crossed the River Humber by ferry). The Romans built the town of **Petuaria** here.

Broughton 'farmstead by a brook', OE *broc* 'brook' + -TON.
A village in Oxfordshire (pronounced 'brawton'), about 5 km (3 miles) southwest of Banbury. **Broughton Castle**, the earliest parts of which date from 1306, is a winningly beautiful medieval moated manor house that has been owned by the Fiennes family for more than 600 years. The Elizabethan Great Hall incorporates the original medieval house. Broughton Castle's picture-postcard qualities brought it an appearance in the film *Shakespeare in Love* (1998); and Joseph Fiennes, the star of the film, is a fourth cousin of the house's present occupiers, Lord and Lady Saye and Sele.

> ... about the most beautiful castle in all England ... for sheer loveliness of the combination of water, woods, and picturesque buildings of the later and more decorative age of military architecture.
> Sir Charles Oman (1860–1946)

Broughton Bay *Bay*, ModE, first recorded 16th century.
A sandy bay on the northwestern side of the Gower Peninsula, in Swansea unitary authority (formerly in Glamorgan, then West Glamorgan).

Broughton Hackett *Hackett* denoting manorial ownership in the Middle Ages by the Hackett family; dates from the 10th century.
A village (pronounced 'brawton') in Worcestershire (before 1998 in Hereford and Worcester, before 1974 in Worcestershire), about 8 km (5 miles) east of Worcester.

Broughton Poggs *Poggs* denoting manorial ownership in the Middle Ages by the Pugeys family; dates from the 11th century.
A village in Oxfordshire, about 13 km (8 miles) southwest of Witney.

Broughty Ferry 'the ferry on the bank of the Tay', *Broughty* is an anglicization of Gaelic *Bruagh Tay* 'bank of the Tay'; *Tay* is an OCelt or pre-Celtic name, possibly meaning 'silent one'.
A ferry crossed the Tay here from the time of Robert the Bruce until after the Second World War.
Formerly a separate BURGH in Angus, but now included in the unitary authority of Dundee, of which it is a suburb. It is on the north shore of the Firth of Tay, and its beaches make it popular with holidaymakers. Broughty Ferry was originally a fishing village, and in the late 18th century there was a plan to make it into Dundee's 'New Town' (on the model of the New Town of Edinburgh), but only the gridiron plan was implemented. Many wealthy 19th-century Dundee industrialists who had made their fortune

from jute or jam built their mansions here, and at one time Broughty Ferry was known as 'the richest square mile in Europe'.

> When the city merchants, cool an' cute,
> Have fortunes made frae jam or jute
> They flee tae scape the smeel an' soot
> Awa tae Broughty Ferry.
>
> Tae 'scape the smeel an' but the tax
> (Oor laws are shuir a trifle lax)
> They tak' the honey, lave the wax
> These Nabobs o' the Ferry.
>
> An' thus we see braw villas stand
> Wi' whigmaleeries on ilk hand
> As raised by some enchanter's wand
> Round bonnie Broughty Ferry.
>
> Anon.: 'Broughty Ferry', in the *City Echo* (1907)

Broughty Ferry has continued to inspire poets, one writing of

> … Broughty Ferry's stone,
> Improved by roselight's neutral flawlessness
>
> Douglas Dunn: 'Broughty Ferry', from *Northlight* (1988)

Broughty Castle, on the sea front, dates from the 15th century. It was captured by the English after the Battle of Pinkie (1547), and recaptured three years later with the aid of French troops. It was restored in 1855, during the Crimean War, to protect the Tay from Russian warships. Today it houses a whaling museum. The castle was unmemorably commemorated by the local 'poet' William McGonnagal (d.1902):

> Ancient Castle of Broughty Ferry
> With walls as strong as Londonderry;
> Near by the sea-shore,
> Where oft is heard and has been heard the cannon's roar
> In the present day and days of yore,
> Loudly echoing from shore to shore.

We're sure you won't want any more …

Brow Head Etymology unknown, though English *brow* in the sense 'front of the head' might be possible.
A headland in southwest County Cork, some 4 km (2.5 miles) east of Mizen Head. Brow Head is marginally further south than Mizen Head, making it the most southerly point on the Irish mainland.

Brown Candover *Brown* denoting manorial ownership in the Middle Ages by the Brun family; *Candover* from an OCelt river name meaning 'pleasant waters'.
A village in Hampshire, about 14 km (8.5 miles) northeast of Winchester.

Brown Clee Hill. *See under* Clee Hills.

Brown Cow Hill ModE, from its rounded shape and heather-clad flanks.

A mountain (829 m / 2719 ft) in the eastern Grampian Mountains of Aberdeenshire (formerly in Grampian region), 6 km (3.5 miles) southwest of Cock Bridge. In most years the largely heather-covered mountain has a crescent of snow that lingers well into the spring, and this is known as the White Calf; even after the snow has melted, a crescent of pale grasses are left behind, as the long period of snow cover prevents heather from growing in this area.

Brownsea Island *Brownsea* 'Brunoc's island', OE *Brunoces* possessive form of male personal name *Brunoc* + *eg* 'island' (*see* -EY, -EA); the name *Brownsea Island* is thus tautological.
An island in the middle of Poole Harbour, in Dorset. Brownsea is 1.5 km (1 mile) long and 1.2 km (0.75 mile) wide, and is home to one of England's few remaining red squirrel colonies. Spiritually, it is the home of the worldwide Scouting Movement, which grew from a Scout camp which Robert Baden-Powell held on the island in 1907.

In the early 20th century the island was bought by the autocratic and somewhat eccentric Florence Bonham Christie, who evicted all the inhabitants, deterred visitors with talk of armed guards and allowed the place to revert to a wilderness. This at least had the advantage of encouraging wildlife, and now, under the ownership of the National Trust, the island is partly a nature reserve.

Brownsea is fictionalized as **Whispering Island** in Enid Blyton's children's stories, and she set her *Five Have a Mystery to Solve* (1962) there.

Brown Willy 'hill of swallows', Cornish *bronn* 'hill' + *gwennili* 'swallows'.
A steep granite tor on Bodmin Moor (*see under* Bodmin), Cornwall. At 420 m (1378 ft), it is the highest point on the moor.

Broxburn 'Brock's burn', probably OE *brocc* or Gaelic *broc* 'badger' + *burna* stream. Strathbrock in the same parish means 'badger valley'.
An industrial town in West Lothian, 5 km (3 miles) northeast of Livingston. It was formerly known as **Easter Strathbrock**, the eastern part of the barony based at Uphall, formerly Wester Strathbrock.

Broxtowe 'Brocwulf's assembly place' (referring to the place where the local wapentake – an administrative district of the shire – met), OE *Brocwulfes* possessive form of male personal name *Brocwulf* + *stow* 'place, assembly place'.
An administrative district of Nottinghamshire, in the valley of the River Trent[1], covering the western suburbs of Nottingham. Its administrative centre is Beeston.

Bruar, Falls of. *See* Falls of Bruar.

Bruce's Cave. *See under* Rathlin Island.

Bruddersford. J.B. Priestley's thinly disguised version of

BRADFORD in his novels *The Good Companions* (1929) and *Bright Day* (1946).

Bruisyard 'peasant's enclosure', OE (*ge*)*bures* possessive form of (*ge*)*bur* 'peasant' + *geard* 'enclosure'.
A village in Suffolk, on the River ALDE, about 6 km (3.5 miles) northwest of Saxmundham. **Bruisyard St Peter** vineyard was a pioneer in the revival of English wine-making in the latter part of the 20th century.

Brum Short for BRUMMAGEM.
A colloquial name for BIRMINGHAM.
Big Brum. A local nickname for the tower of Birmingham Council House, modelled on BIG BEN.
Brum. A live-action television series (since 1990) for young children involving the eponymous yellow kid-sized vintage car, which secretly steals out of its owner's work-shop to have adventures in the Big Town. It is filmed in Birmingham, and the series' name punningly combines a tribute to the city with the 'brrmm' sound that a car engine makes.
Brumbrella. A movable cover for the playing area of Edgbaston Cricket Ground (*see under* EDGBASTON), Birm-ingham, designed to protect the wicket from rain and con-sisting of a huge tarpaulin sheet on a motorized roller. It was installed in 1989, but its use was discontinued in 1999 following a ban on flat wicket-covers.
Brummy, Brummie. (A native or inhabitant, or the dialect) of Birmingham. A less well-known nickname for a native of the city, current in the late 19th and early 20th centuries, was 'hardware bloke' (Birmingham then being famous for the manufacture of pots, pans and other hardware).

Brummagem A dialectal variant of *Birmingham*, with the original *Beorm-* (*see* BIRMINGHAM) changed to *Brom-* or *Brum-* by metathesis of the *r*. It is first recorded in the 15th century. (There is no etymological connection with *Bromwich*, but the proximity of CASTLE BROMWICH and WEST BROMWICH has no doubt led to some interaction between the names.)
An alternative name for BIRMINGHAM. In the local dialect it is neutral, but in wider contexts it has tended in the past to carry associations of showy cheapness and tattiness, which have been carried over into the adjectival use of the word:

> The vulgar dandy, strutting along, with his Brummagem jewellery.
>
> A.K.H. Boyd, *Recreations of a Country Parson* (1861)

This grew mainly out of the city's reputation in the 19th century for mass-producing cheap manufactured goods (trinkets, toys, imitation jewellery and the like), but was also no doubt partly a memory of the counterfeit groats (fourpenny coins) minted here in the 17th century.
These dud coins were also the inspiration for the ironic use of **Brummagems** as an insulting name for

the Protestants (self-proclaimed 'True Protestants') who supported the anti-Catholic Exclusion Bill of 1680, which sought to prevent Charles II's Catholic brother James from succeeding him.
See also BRUM *and* anti-Birmingham *under* BIRMINGHAM.

Brú na Bóinne. The Irish name for 'palace of the Boyne' (*see under* BOYNE).

Brunanburh Known from the OE poem 'The Battle of Brunan-burh', this is 'Bruna's fort', OE male personal name *Bruna* + *burh* (*see* BURY). Since this etymology is that of Bromborough in the Wirral and Bromborough in every way fits the description of the place where the battle was fought in the OE poem (a water feature called *Dingesmere* is mentioned, which probably refers to the mouth of the DEE[2]), Bromborough is the strongest candidate for the site of this encounter.
A battle site in northern England, probably in the WIRRAL, where in 937 an invading army under Constantine III, comprising Scots, Scandinavians from Ireland and men of STRATHCLYDE, were crushingly defeated by the English under Athelstan. Some Icelanders fought on the English side, and the battle is described in the 13th-century *Egils Saga* where it is called the Battle of Vinheith. The English victory is celebrated in a triumph-song in the *Anglo-Saxon Chronicle*:

> Athelstan King,
> Lord among Earls,
> Bracelet-bestower and
> Baron of Barons,
> He with his Brother,
> Edmund Atheling,
> Gaining a lifelong
> Glory in battle,
> Slew with the sword-edge
> There by Brunnanburh,
> Brake the shield-wall,
> Hew'd the linden-wood,
> Hack'd the battle-shield,
> Sons of Edward with hammer'd brands.
>
> Anon.: 'The Battle of Brunanburh', translated by Alfred, Lord Tennyson (1876)

Brundish 'pasture by a stream', OE *burna* 'stream' + OE *edisc* 'pasture'.
A village in Suffolk, about 13 km (8 miles) northwest of Saxmundham.

Bruton 'farmstead on the River Brue', OCelt river name *Brue* 'fast-flowing' + -TON.
A small and picturesque town in Somerset, about 19 km (11.5 miles) east of Glastonbury. It grew up as a centre of textile manufacturing, and one of England's first fulling mills (where cloth is processed) was built nearby in 1290. An attractive feature of the town is its series of narrow alleyways called Bartons – once home to Bruton's

wool-workers – which connect the high street to a riverside walk.

King's School, a public school in Bruton, dates from 1519.

Bruton Baw. A very old and extremely narrow packhorse bridge which crosses the River Brue at Bruton.

Bryanston 'Brian's estate', *Brians* possessive form of Irish male personal name *Brian* + -TON; denoting manorial ownership in the Middle Ages by Brian de Insula.

A village in Dorset, about 1.5 km (1 mile) west of Blandford Forum. **Bryanston School**, a co-educational independent school, was founded in 1928.

Brycheiniog 'territory of Brychan', Welsh *Brychan*, personal name of the 5th-century King Brychan + -*iog* 'territory of'.

The Welsh name for BRECON. It was originally the name of an early medieval Welsh kingdom in southern Powys (formerly southern Brecknockshire), known from at least the 8th century and said to have been founded by the Irish King Brychan in the 5th century. It was dominated by the kingdom of DEHEUBARTH from the 10th century, and conquered by the Normans in the 11th. Under the Normans it became a lordship of the MARCHES, taking the name Brecon. In 1536 it joined with the lordships of Builth (*see* BUELLT *and* BUILTH WELLS), Blaenllynfi and Hay (*see* HAY-ON-WYE) to become the county of BRECKNOCKSHIRE.

Bryher Probably 'the hills', from the plural of OCelt *breg* 'hill'. The most northwesterly of the main SCILLY ISLES (pronounced 'bryə'). It has one significant settlement, Pool. Off its southwest coast is an island called **Castle Bryher**.

The island's name was adopted in 1918 as a pen name by the feminist writer Winifred Ellerman (1894–1983). Under it she wrote, amongst many other things, *The Fourteenth of October* (1954), a novel about the Norman invasion of Britain (the Battle of Hastings was fought on 14 October 1066).

Brynbuga. The Welsh name for USK[2].

Brynmawr 'big hill', Welsh *bryn* 'hill' + *mawr* 'big'.

A former mining and steel town in Blaenau Gwent (formerly in Monmouthshire, then in Gwent), some 3 km (2 miles) northeast of Ebbw Vale.

Bryn Mawr in Pennsylvania, USA, is home to **Bryn Mawr College**, a prestigious women's university founded in 1885.

Buachaille Etive Mór 'the great shepherd of Etive', Gaelic *buachaille* 'shepherd' + river name ETIVE + *mór* 'big'.

'The most splendid of earthly mountains,' according to W.H. Murray (*Mountaineering in Scotland*, 1947), and long a mecca for Scottish climbers. The Buachaille (as it is familiarly known) guards the entrances to both GLEN COE and Glen ETIVE (in Highland, formerly in Argyll). In the classic view from the KINGSHOUSE, the mountain appears as a great rocky pyramid, culminating in the high point, Stob Dearg ('red peak', 1022 m / 3352 ft), although in fact this summit is just the end of a long ridge extending some 4 km (2.5 miles) to the southwest. It is pronounced 'byoochəl ettiv more' (with the 'ch' pronounced as in 'loch'). Many of us, when city-bound, might echo the sentiments of the 18th-century Gaelic poet Duncan Ban Macintyre:

> *Is truagh nach robh mi 'm Buachaill Eitidh*
> *Gu h-aird na sleisde anns an t-sneachd ann …*
> (I would love to be on the Buachaille, thigh-deep in snow)

> Duncan Ban Macintyre (Donnchadh Bàn Mac an t-Saoir): extemporization in Edinburgh. (Macintyre added to his wish that every citizen of that city should follow behind him barefoot.)

The best-known features of the Buachaille are the Crowberry Ridge, which provides a classic rock climb, and to its side Crowberry Gully, which slits the front of the mountain almost from top to bottom, and which, although a rubble chute in summer, provides a fine snow and ice climb in winter. The sunny, red-tinted Rannoch Wall is on the other flank of Crowberry Ridge, overlooking Rannoch Moor (*see under* RANNOCH), while more discreetly tucked away on the opposite side of the mountain is the vertiginous, shady horror of Slime Wall, harbouring much harder routes with names such as *Shibboleth* and *Apocalypse*.

To the west of the Buachaille is its companion, **Buachaille Etive Beag** ('the little shepherd of Etive'; 1022 m / 3352 ft), which anywhere other than Glen Coe would stand out as an impressive hill.

> … 'the keepers of Etive' … seem to frown in solemn sullenness on the puny mortals who venture to encroach on the solitudes over which they have for ages so patiently kept watch.

> Rev. Hugh Fraser: in *National Statistical Account*, Vol. VII (18th century)

Bubbenhall 'Bubba's hill', OE *Bubban* possessive form of male personal name *Bubba* + OE *hyll* 'hill'.

A village in Warwickshire, about 5 km (3 miles) south of Coventry.

Bubwith 'Bubba's wood', OE male personal name *Bubba* + OScand *vithr* 'wood'.

A village in the East Riding of Yorkshire, 10 km (6 miles) northeast of Selby.

Buchan Possibly from OCelt *buwch* 'cow' + -*an*, a diminutive suffix.

A traditional lowland region of northeast Scotland, in northern Aberdeenshire, jutting out into the North Sea, and hence sometimes called the **Northeast Neuk** (Scots *neuk*, 'projecting point of land'), or (because of its chilly position) the **Cold Shoulder of Scotland**. It is bounded on the northwest by the River DEVERON and on the southeast by the River YTHAN. MAR with Buchan was one of the ancient Celtic mormaerships (earldoms) of Scotland. Between 1975 and 1996 the area was part of the Banff and Buchan district of Grampian region. The main towns are FRASERBURGH and PETERHEAD; part of the latter is called Buchanhaven.

There are some other, less important areas known as Buchan in Scotland, for instance that giving its name to DUNGEON OF BUCHAN in Galloway; and there is a River Buchan in Australia (Victoria).

Buchan humlie. A hornless variety of Aberdeen Angus (*see under* ABERDEEN), bred in Buchan from the late 19th century (Scots *hummlied* 'having had the horns removed').

Buchan Ness. A headland (*see* NESS) projecting into the North Sea some 4 km (2.5 miles) south of Peterhead. Some claim it as the most easterly point of mainland Scotland, although Keith Inch in Peterhead just pips it to the post.

> This point of land, called Buchan-Ness, is generally the first land of Great Britain, which the ships make in their voyages home from Arch-Angel in Russia, or from their whale-fishing-voyages to Greenland and Spits-Berghen in the north seas.
>
> Daniel Defoe: *A Tour Through the Whole Island of Great Britain* (1724–6)

Defoe goes on to record how the ship carrying the first ambassadors from Muscovy to Queen Elizabeth I was wrecked here, and how, although the ambassadors were saved, their gifts of sables, ermine and black fox skins were all lost, 'to Her Majesty's great disappointment'.

Bullers of Buchan, the Scots *buller* 'whirlpool', 'bubble'. A narrow sea-filled chasm – described by Dr Johnson as a 'monstrous cauldron' – on the North Sea coast of Aberdeenshire, 9 km (5.5 miles) south of Peterhead. The entrance is guarded by a rock arch, and the cliffs here – some 60 m (200 ft) high – are home to many seabirds. The structure was originally a sea cave, of which the roof has fallen in. After T.E. Lawrence (Lawrence of Arabia) visited, he wrote of

> whole systems of slabby rocks, thrusting into the maddened North Sea which heaves and foams over them in deafening surges.

Howes o'Buchan, the. The hollows between the low ridges that run across Buchan.

'Logie o' Buchan'. A ballad song about the love of the gardener of Logie House, near CRIMOND in Buchan, for the daughter of the house, Isobel Keith. He was sacked, while she went on to marry a farmer and died at the age of 80 in 1826.

Buchlyvie 'hut on a slope', Gaelic *both* 'hut' + Gaelic *slèibhe* 'slope'.

A village in Stirling unitary authority (formerly in Stirlingshire, then in Central region), 21 km (13 miles) west of Stirling.

Buckfastleigh 'Buckfast glade', *Buckfast* name of a nearby village ('bucks' place of shelter', OE *bucc* 'male deer' + *fœsten* 'place of shelter') + -LEY.

A town in Devon, about 19 km (12 miles) west of Torquay. It is in the valley of the River DART, and is the terminus of the Dart Valley railway. **Buckfast Abbey**, 1.5 km (1 mile) to the north, is a Benedictine house, founded in 1018 and abandoned after the Dissolution of the Monasteries in the mid-16th century. It was rebuilt between 1906 and 1932 by French Benedictine monks, and is now a notable tourist attraction. The Abbey's honey and tonic wine are on sale to the public.

Buckhaven 'harbour of the buck', ModE *buck* 'male deer' + *haven* 'harbour'.

A BURGH in Fife, 10 km (6 miles) northeast of Kirkcaldy, on the north shore of the Firth of Forth (*see under* FORTH). It was formed in 1891 by the merger of the original Buckhaven (which came into existence about 1550) and neighbouring Methil (possibly Old Scandinavian *methal* 'middle'). Buckhaven was formerly a coal port, and then built oil platforms.

Buckie Possibly '(place, river) of the buck', Gaelic *bocaidh*, genitive of *boc* 'buck'; the place is named after the river (*see* BANFF).

A fishing port on the north coast of Moray (formerly in Banffshire, and then in Grampian region), some 20 km (12 miles) east of Elgin.

Buckingham 'Bucca's people's river bend land', OE male personal name *Bucca* + -*inga*- (*see* -ING) + *hamm* 'land in a river bend' (*see* HAM).

A market town in Buckinghamshire, on the GREAT OUSE, about 25 km (15.5 miles) northwest of Aylesbury. In 888 Alfred the Great decreed that it should be the county town, an eminence it retained until the 18th century, when Aylesbury took its place (in his *A Tour Through the Whole Island of Great Britain* (1726), Daniel Defoe noted that Aylesbury 'is the principal market town in the county of Bucks; tho' Buckingham, a much inferior place, is call'd the county town' – it had, to be fair, been partly destroyed by fire in 1725).

The **University of Buckingham**, which was granted its royal charter in 1983, is the only independent university in Britain.

The crooked media tycoon Robert Maxwell (1923–91) was Labour MP for Buckingham from 1964 to 1970.

Buckingham Palace From its originally being the residence of the dukes of *Buckingham*.

A palace in the City of WESTMINSTER (SW1), at the

western end of the MALL. It was built in 1703 (to the design of William Winde) for the Duke of Buckingham and Normanby, and was originally called **Buckingham House**. George III bought it in 1762, and had it virtually rebuilt on a much grander scale by John Nash. Since the middle of the 19th century it has been used (with varying degrees of enthusiasm) by British monarchs as their official London residence. The ceremony of Changing the Guard in the palace forecourt is an essential stop on the London tourist route, and the extensive grounds to the rear are the venue for the Buckingham Palace garden parties, at which some 8000 guests have the privilege of taking tea with the sovereign. On such occasions, the facetious nickname **Buck House** (first recorded in 1922) is perhaps best left outside the gates.

In 1993 the palace's State Rooms were first opened to the visiting public, for the summer months (amidst some initial controversy over the entry charge). Recent un-authorized visitors to the palace grounds include a hang-glider pilot and, in 2004, an activist for 'Fathers for Justice' dressed in a Batman costume.

Arthur Ferguson (b.1883), a conman who specialized in selling bits of London to gullible Americans, once secured a down-payment of £30,000 on Buckingham Palace.

See also SAWBRIDGEWORTH.

Buckinghamshire From BUCKINGHAM + SHIRE. The name *Buckinghamshire* is first recorded in the 11th century.

A county in central southern England, one of the HOME COUNTIES, to the northwest of London. It is bounded to the north by Northamptonshire, to the west by Oxford-shire, to the south, where the River THAMES[1] forms part of the county boundary, by Berkshire, and to the east by Greater London, Hertfordshire and Bedfordshire. In the local-government changes of 1972 Buckinghamshire lost SLOUGH and ETON to Berkshire.

The county is divided for administrative purposes into Aylesbury Vale (*see under* AYLESBURY), CHILTERN, SOUTH BUCKS and WYCOMBE, and it also includes the unitary authority of MILTON KEYNES. Its county town is AYLESBURY, and other important centres are AMERSHAM, BEACONSFIELD, BLETCHLEY, BUCKINGHAM, CHESHAM, HIGH WYCOMBE and MARLOW. The CHILTERN HILLS run from southwest to northeast across the county.

In cricketing terms Buckinghamshire is a 'minor county' (the club was founded in 1891) and plays in the minor counties championship.

Buckland 'charter land' (that is, an estate with particular rights and privileges created by an Anglo-Saxon (usually) royal charter), OE *boc* 'book, charter' + *land*.

A village in south Devon, about 8 km (5 miles) northwest of Salcombe. There are also villages called Buckland in Gloucestershire (2 km / 1.2 miles southwest of Broadway);

in Oxfordshire (about 21 km / 13 miles southwest of Oxford); and in Surrey (about 5 km / 3 miles west of Reigate).

The novelist J.R.R. Tolkien adopted the name 'Buck-land' for a village in the SHIRE in *The Lord of the Rings* (1954–5).

See also EGGBUCKLAND.

Buckland Brewer *Brewer* denoting manorial ownership in the Middle Ages by the Briwerre family.

A village in Devon, about 6.5 km (4 miles) southwest of Bideford.

Buckland Filleigh *Filleigh* denoting manorial ownership in the Middle Ages by the de Fyleleye family.

A village in Devon, about 19 km (11.5 miles) northwest of Okehampton.

Buckland Monachorum *Monachorum*, Latin possessive plural 'of the monks', referring to the monks of Buckland Abbey.

A village in Devon, about 6.5 km (4 miles) south of Tavistock. **Buckland Abbey**, a Cistercian house, was built nearby in 1278. The English naval hero Sir Richard Grenville converted it into a house, and another early occu-pant was Sir Francis Drake, who bought it after his return from his round-the-world voyage (1580) and lived in it for the rest of his life. It is the repository of Drake's Drum, which once belonged to the old sea dog and supposedly sounds when England is in peril.

See also SCAPA FLOW.

Buckland-tout-Saints *tout-Saints*, Fr, 'all Saints', denoting manorial ownership in the Middle Ages by the Tuz Seinz family.

A village in south Devon, about 2.5 km (1.5 miles) northeast of Kingsbridge.

Bucklebury 'Burghild's fortified place', OE female personal name *Burghild* + BURY.

A village in West Berkshire, 5 km (3 miles) northeast of Thatcham. **Upper Bucklebury** lies just to the south.

See also the SHIRE.

Bucklerheads Possibly 'hills belonging to the Buckler family', OE *heafod* 'head, hill' + surname *Buckler*.

A small settlement in Angus (formerly in Tayside region), some 8 km (5 miles) northeast of Dundee.

Bucklersbury From a medieval tenement called *Bucklersbury* 'Buckerels' manor house', from *Buckerel* name of an impor-tant and influential London family of the early Middle Ages + BURY (in this context meaning 'manor house').

A street in the City of London (EC4), going southwest from POULTRY and now cut through by Queen Victoria Street. Sir Thomas More lived here at the beginning of the 16th century. It was in those days noted for its apothecaries and herbalists, and Shakespeare makes Falstaff say:

> I cannot cog [flatter], and say thou art this and that, like a many of these lisping hawthorn buds, that come like women in men's apparel, and smell like Bucklersbury in simple-time [time of medicinal herbs].

> *The Merry Wives of Windsor* (1598), III.iii

Bucklers Hard 'Bucklers' landing-place', *Buckler* the name of a local family; *Hard* local dialect 'firm landing-place'. The place name is first recorded in 1789 (earlier in the 18th century the place had been called *Montagutown*, after the Duke of Montagu, who had put forward proposals for developing the site in 1724).

A village near the mouth of the Beaulieu River (*see under* BEAULIEU) in Hampshire, about 9.5 km (6 miles) northeast of LYMINGTON. Today pleasure yachts are the main visitors to the quayside to which it owes the second part of its name, but in the 18th and 19th centuries Bucklers Hard was an important shipyard: many Royal Navy ships were built here, including HMS *Agamemnon*, on which Nelson served in the Mediterranean during 1793–6.

Buckley 'wood of the bucks', OE *bucc* 'buck' + -LEY.
A town in Flintshire (formerly in Clywd), 7 km (4.5 miles) west of Chester. Its Welsh name is **Bwcle**, which is a Welshification of the English name.

Bucks. The shortened form of the name BUCKINGHAMSHIRE. It dates back at least to the mid-17th century. Like other abbreviations of its type, it is widely used in such contexts as postal addresses, but it also (owing in part, no doubt, to the considerable length of *Buckinghamshire*) enjoys a separate career as a less formal alternative to the full name. A salient usage is '**beechy Bucks**', conjuring up the well-ordered sylvanity of the HOME COUNTIES; Benjamin Disraeli (a resident) referred to it in a letter in 1830 ('Our beloved and beechy Bucks'), and it was a favourite of John Betjeman:

> A typical Voysey detail, this pane, which opens to let in the air from beechy Bucks, which is just on the other side of the road

> John Betjeman: in *Metroland*, BBC Television (1973)

See also SOUTH BUCKS.

Buddon Ness 'river-valley headland', OE *botm* 'river-valley' + OE *næss* (*see* NESS).
The sandy headland marking the north side of the mouth of the Firth of Tay (*see under* TAY), in Angus (formerly in Tayside), opposite TENTSMUIR POINT.

Bude Perhaps originally a river name, of unknown provenance and meaning.
A town and resort on the north Cornish coast, at the mouth of the River Neet, about 25 km (16 miles) northwest of LAUNCESTON. It has a small harbour, known as **Bude Haven**. The wide sandy beaches at the foot of the cliffs in Bude Bay (*see below*) face directly westwards, towards the Atlantic, so Bude is a very popular centre for surfers (the first ever Surf Life Saving Club was formed here). In the 19th century, however, Bude's 'thundering shore' (as Tennyson called it) had a more sinister reputation: the locals were notorious 'wreckers' – plunderers of ships that had foundered there in the prevailing westerlies.

Bude Bay. The shallow bay, about 10 km (6 miles) wide, in which Bude is situated, between Lower Sharpnose Point in the north and WIDEMOUTH BAY in the south.

Bude-burner. A gas burner consisting of several concentric rings with cylindrical wicks. It was invented, in the late 19th century, by Sir Goldsworthy Gurney, who lived in Bude – whence the name.

Bude sand. Sand from Bude, used as a dressing for soil.

Budleigh Salterton *Budleigh* from the nearby (*East*) *Budleigh* 'Budda's glade', OE male personal name *Budda* + -LEY; *Salterton*, originally *Saltern* 'building where salt is made or sold', OE *salt-ærn*, from *salt* 'salt' + *ærn* 'building' (from the local salt trade), with -TON first recorded as added in 1667.

A town on the south Devon coast, at the mouth of the River OTTER, about 5 km (3 miles) northeast of Exmouth. It grew up around salt pans at the river mouth. It began to be developed as a holiday resort in the early 19th century.

Sir Walter Raleigh was born just north of Budleigh Salterton in 1552, and the town's sea-wall features in Sir John Everett Millais's celebrated painting *The Boyhood of Raleigh* (1870).

Budmouth. The fictional version given to WEYMOUTH by Thomas Hardy, as in *The Trumpet-Major* (1880).

Buellt 'cow pasture', OCelt *bu* 'cow' + *gellt* 'pasture'.
An early medieval Welsh kingdom, covering parts of north BRECKNOCKSHIRE and RADNORSHIRE (both now parts of Powys). The Normans turned it into a Marcher lordship (*see under* the MARCHES). It is the origin of the name of BUILTH WELLS, and is pronounced 'bilth'.

Bugle From a public house, reputedly named in honour of a bugler, built in the early 19th century; the name is first recorded in 1888.
A village in Cornwall, in the middle of the china-clay mining area, about 6.5 km (4 miles) north of St Austell.

Bugthorpe 'Buggi's outlying settlement', OScand male personal name *Buggi* + THORPE.
A village in the East Riding of Yorkshire, 6 km (4 miles) northeast of Stamford Bridge.

Buildwas An unknown first element + OE *wœsse* 'alluvial land'.
A village (pronounced 'bilwas' or 'bildas') in Shropshire, on the River SEVERN, about 8 km (5 miles) southwest of

Telford. The nearby **Buildwas Abbey**, now an empty shell, was founded in 1135.

> When Severn down to Buildwas ran
> Coloured with the death of man,
> Couched upon her brother's grave
> The Saxon got me on the slave.
>
> > A.E. Housman: from *A Shropshire Lad* (1896)

Builth Wells From the district of BUELLT; *Wells* was added in the 19th century, when the town became a spa.

A town in Powys (formerly in Brecknockshire), in the upper WYE[1] valley, 23 km (14 miles) north of Brecon. It is also known in Welsh as **Llanfair-ym-Muallt** ('church of St Mary in Buallt'). The Normans built a castle here, frequently attacked by the Welsh. Prince Llywelyn ap Gruffydd (also known as Llywelyn the Last) was killed nearby in 1282; the previous night the Welsh garrison of Builth had refused him refuge, and forever after became known as **the Traitors of Buallt**. Llywelyn's death marked the end of major Welsh resistance to the English.

> For the killing of our prop, our golden-handed king,
> for Llywelyn's death, I remember no one.
> The heart is chilled under a breast of fear,
> lust shrivels like dry branches.
>
> > Gruffudd ab yr Ynad Coch: 'The Death of Llywelyn ap Gruffudd' (*c*.1282), translated from the Welsh by Gwyn Williams

The chalybeate (iron salt) springs here led to Builth's development as a spa in the 19th century. The Royal Welsh Showground is just north of the town.

Bulg Gaelic *builg* 'rise, bulge'.

A hill (607 m / 1991 ft) on the south side of Glen Esk (*see under* ESK[1]), Angus (formerly in Tayside region), 17 km (10.5 miles) north-northwest of Brechin.

Bullers of Buchan. *See under* BUCHAN.

Bullring. An open area in WEXFORD, used for bull-baiting in the 17th and 18th centuries. It was here that Cromwell is said to have had the city's inhabitants massacred in 1649 during the Civil Wars, and later, during the 1798 United Irishmen's Rebellion, the Bullring became an armaments factory for the rebels.

Bull Ring[1] From the former bull-baiting venue here (there was a licensed market on the site from the 12th century, and in the 16th century bull-baiting rights were granted to John Cooper).

A multi-level shopping centre in the middle of Birmingham. It is on a 10.5-ha (26-acre) site, and includes markets, car parks, restaurants and a bus station. Long notorious as representing the nadir of postwar town-centre retail 'reconstruction', the Bull Ring was demolished at the beginning of the 21st century and reopened in 2003 after a complete rebuild. It is now dominated by the vast, bloblike Selfridges

building, designed by Future Systems and described by its detractors as looking like 'a blue blancmange with chicken pox'.

Bull Ring[2] From its shape.

See under WATERLOO[1].

Bullslaughter Bay Probably 'rough water bay', an anglicization of Welsh *pwll* 'bay, pool' + Welsh *cletwr* 'rough water'.

A bay a little to the west of St Govan's Head, Pembrokeshire (formerly in Dyfed). It was painted in 1963 by John Piper (1903–92).

Bulwark Possibly originally a defensive work.

A small settlement in Buchan, Aberdeenshire (formerly in Grampian region), 20 km (12.5 miles) west of Peterhead.

Bumble's Green Possibly named from the family of Adam Brichmare, known here in the 13th century (*Brimmer's Green* is an early variant).

A village in Essex, about 6.5 km (4 miles) southwest of Harlow.

Bun Abhann Dalle. The usual Irish name for CUSHENDALL.

Bunbury 'Buna's stronghold', OE male personal name *Buna* + BURY.

A small town in Cheshire, about 14 km (8.5 miles) west of Crewe. Its name is most widely known as that of the imaginary and sickly country-dwelling friend invoked by Algernon Moncrieff in Oscar Wilde's play *The Importance of Being Earnest* (1895) whenever he wished to wriggle out of a tiresome social engagement (a dissimulation known in the play as '**Bunburying**'). There is evidence that Wilde had the town in mind when naming the character.

There is a town called Bunbury in Western Australia, on the coast to the south of Perth.

Buncrana Irish *Bun Cranncha* 'mouth of the River Crana'; the river name is from Irish *crannach* 'abounding in trees'.

A seaside resort and port on the east shore of LOUGH SWILLY in County Donegal, 18 km (11 miles) northwest of Derry/Londonderry.

Buncrana was the birthplace of the playwright Frank McGuinness (b.1953), author of *Observe the Sons of Ulster Marching to the Somme* (1985).

Bun Cranncha. The Irish name for BUNCRANA.

Bun Dobhráin. The Irish name for BUNDORAN.

Bundoran Irish *Bun Dobhráin* 'end, mouth of the little river'.

A seaside resort in County Donegal, 25 km (16 miles) northeast of Sligo.

Bungay Probably 'Buna's people's island', OE male personal name *Buna* + *–inga–* (see -ING) + *eg* (see -EY, -EA).

A town in Suffolk, on the River WAVENEY[1], about 16 km (10 miles) west of LOWESTOFT. Uniquely, its civic leader still holds the ancient office of Town Reeve. The town and surrounding area were once said to be haunted by a monstrous satanic hound called Old Shuck.

Bungay-play. A 19th-century colloquialism denoting various styles of illicit or unskilful play in whist or billiards. The term may be some sort of allusion to the old dialectal expression 'been to Bungay fair and broken both his legs', meaning 'drunk'.

Bungay Stone. A standing stone near the north porch of St Mary's Church, Bungay, said to be 2000 years old.

Bunhill Fields *Bunhill* probably 'heap of bones', from its use as a burial ground.

A former burial ground on the western side of City Road in Finsbury, in the borough of Islington (EC1), just to the north of the City of London. The spectacular deposition here of cartloads of bones from the Charnel House of St Paul's[1] Cathedral is recorded from 1549, but it seems certain that it was being used as a cemetery before that. Amongst its notable monuments are those to John Bunyan (1688), Daniel Defoe (1731), the hymnist Isaac Watts (1748) and William Blake (1827). Also commemorated here is Susannah Wesley (1742), mother of John and Charles: as unconsecrated ground it was much used as a burial place by Nonconformists, and came to be known as 'the Cemetery of Puritan England'. The last burial took place here in 1854.

Bun na Eas. An alternative Irish name for Devil's Glen.

Bunny Probably 'reed island', OE *bune* 'reeds' + *eg* 'island' (*see* -EY, -EA) (here probably denoting reeds growing on an area of drier ground in a marsh).

A village in Nottinghamshire, about 11 km (7 miles) south of Nottingham.

Buntingford 'ford frequented by buntings or yellow-hammers', ME *bunting* + FORD.

A town in Hertfordshire, about 13 km (8 miles) south of Royston, where the River Rib is crossed by Ermine Street.

Bure A back-formation from Briston, earlier *Burstuna*, OE *burh*, possessive *bures* (*see* BURY) + -TON.

A river in Norfolk, which rises about 13 km (8 miles) east of Fakenham and flows southeastwards through the Broads to join the eastern end of Breydon Water at Great Yarmouth.

Burford 'ford by the fortified place', OE *burh* (*see* BURY) + FORD.

A town in Oxfordshire, in the Cotswolds, on the steep banks of the River Windrush, about 11 km (7 miles) west of Witney. Its former prosperity as a wool town is evidenced in the fine medieval and later buildings that line its sloping main street, and also in the sumptuous merchants' tombs in the medieval church of St John. One of them (from the 1560s) carries the first known depiction of a Native

American in England. When William Morris protested against the restoration of the church in the late 19th century, the vicar replied: 'The church, Sir, is mine and if I choose to, I shall stand on my head in it.'

The town had a walk-on role in the Civil Wars: Cromwell's refusal to implement the radical political programme urged by the Levellers (*see* Southwark) led to mutinies by Levellers in the New Model Army; these were suppressed by Cromwell at Burford in 1649, effectively ending the Leveller movement.

Burford is a classic Cotswold honeypot for tourists, and a useful illustration of the piece of local 'folk' advice to avoid – on bank holidays and sunny weekends in summer – places in the Cotswolds beginning with the letter 'B' (Bibury, Bourton-on-the-Water, Broadway, Burford) if one wishes to find peace and quiet away from the hordes of trippers ...

Battle of Burford (*c*.752). A battle in which Cuthred of Wessex defeated Æthelbald of Mercia, allowing Wessex to make short-lived territorial gains north of the River Thames that would last only 25 years until the Battle of Benson (*see under* Benson).

take a Burford bait, to. A 19th-century slang expression meaning 'to get drunk'. It is presumed to have been based on some long-forgotten anecdote relating to Burford. *Bait* at that time could mean 'a pause for refreshment'.

Burgess Hill From a local family called *Burgeys*; first recorded in 1597.

A town in West Sussex, about 13 km (8 miles) north of Brighton. Its modern development can be dated from 1841 and the opening of the London–Brighton railway line, which runs through it. It now functions as a commuter town in respect of both those cities.

burgh The Scottish version of *borough* (*see* BURY), although sometimes early -*burgh* names derive from the sense of 'fortified place'.

In Scotland, a town, usually incorporated by a charter, that possessed certain privileges and some degree of administrative independence prior to the reorganization of local government in 1975. A **royal burgh** was one where the charter, along with trading privileges, had been granted by the Crown. Unsurprisingly, the towns that gained burgh status tended to be royalist in politics and predominantly English-speaking: Perth was one such. Prior to the Union of 1707, the royal boroughs formed a separate estate of the Scottish Parliament.

See also BURY *and* ROYAL BOROUGH.

Burgh by Sands OE *burh* (*see* BURY).

A village in Cumbria (formerly in Cumberland), close to the Solway Firth and 8 km (5 miles) northwest of Carlisle. It is on the line of Hadrian's Wall, and **Burgh Marsh** is to the north. Edward I, 'the Hammer of the Scots', died here in 1307 while advancing north against Robert the Bruce.

Burgh Castle OE *burh*, 'stronghold' (*see* BURY).

A Roman fortress in Suffolk, on the River WAVENEY[1], 5 km (3 miles) west of Great Yarmouth. Built in the 3rd century, the Roman fort of *Gariannonum* was part of the SAXON SHORE defences. Parts of the fortress walls are still standing, and fragments of a later Norman motte-and-bailey castle also remain. A monastery was established here by Fursa, an Irish monk, in the mid-7th century, but no traces of it are now visible.

Burghclere OE *burh* (*see* BURY) + *-clere* probably the original settlement name, perhaps from an OCelt river name meaning 'bright stream'; *see also* HIGHCLERE *and* KINGSCLERE.

A village (pronounced 'ber-clear') in northern Hampshire, about 6 km (4 miles) south of Newbury. The nearby Sandham Memorial Chapel, built by Mr and Mrs J.L. Behrend in 1926 to commemorate a relative who died in the First World War, has some notable Stanley Spencer murals.

Burghead 'headland with the fortification', OE *burh* (see BURY) + ModE *head*.

A fishing port on the north coast of Moray (formerly in Grampian region), on the headland at the northeast end of **Burghead Bay**, 12 km (7 miles) west of Lossiemouth. The village was founded in the early 19th century, and derives its name from the Iron Age and Viking fortifications on the headland. The village holds a notable midwinter fire ceremony known as 'Burning the Clavie', in which half a tar barrel (the clavie) is set alight and carried around on a salmon-fisherman's pole called a spoke.

Burlingjobb 'secluded valley associated with a man called Beorhtel', OE personal name *Beorhtel* + -ING + OE *hop* 'secluded valley'.

A village in Powys (formerly in Radnorshire), on the Anglo–Welsh border 20 km (12.5 miles) east of Llandrindod Wells and 4 km (2.5 miles) south of EVENJOBB.

Burnham 'homestead or village on a stream', OE *burna* 'stream' + HAM.

A town in Buckinghamshire, about 6.5 km (4 miles) northwest of Slough. About 1.5 km (1 mile) to the north is Dorneywood, owned by the National Trust and used as the official residence of the chancellor of the exchequer.

Burnham Beeches. An area of beech-wood, about 2.6 sq km (1 sq mile) in extent, to the north of Burnham. It was part of an ancient forest which once covered the whole of the CHILTERN HILLS. It belongs to the City of London (*see under* LONDON), which bought it in 1879.

Burnham on Crouch *Burnham see* BURNHAM; *Crouch* from the River Crouch.

A town in Essex, on the north bank of the River CROUCH[1],

about 8 km (5 miles) from the point where it enters the North Sea. It is an important yachting centre (it is home to five yacht clubs, including the Royal Corinthian and the Royal Burnham), and it is also famous for its oyster beds.

Caustic lines from Ian Dury's song 'Billericay Dickie' (*see under* BILLERICAY) reflect the town's naffly moneyed aura:

Oh golly, oh gosh, come and lie on the couch
With a nice bit of posh from Burnham on Crouch.

Burnham on Sea *Burnham* 'enclosure by a stream', OE *burna* 'stream' + *hamm* 'enclosure' (*see* HAM).

A seaside resort in Somerset, at the mouth of the River PARRETT, at the corner of Bridgwater Bay (*see under* BRIDGWATER). Its wooden 'lighthouse on legs' is a reminder of its one-time aspiration to be a spa town: a 19th-century local curate had it built, and used the fees from passing ships to finance two wells. The 'spa' idea never worked out, but the town continues to attract holidaymakers.

Burnham Thorpe *Burnham see* BURNHAM ON SEA; *Thorpe* 'outlying farmstead' (*see* THORPE).

A village in North Norfolk, 5 km (3 miles) from the coast, 32 km (20 miles) northeast of King's Lynn. Horatio Nelson (1758–1805) was born here, the son of the local rector.

Burnley 'clearing by the River Brun', OE river name from *brun* 'brown' or *burna* 'stream' + -LEY.

An industrial town, formerly renowned for its cotton mills, in Lancashire, 30 km (20 miles) east of Preston. It is situated on the Leeds–Liverpool Canal, at the confluence of the River Brun and the River CALDER[2], and forms a continuous urban area with BRIERFIELD, NELSON and Colne to the north.

During the Industrial Revolution cotton mills were established beside the River Calder and the Leeds–Liverpool Canal, and by the end of the 19th century the town was the hub of Lancashire's cotton-textiles industry. The 20th century saw the decline of Burnley's traditional manufacturing base, but the town's industrial heritage is celebrated in the weaving sheds, weavers' cottages, foundries and mills that have been preserved in the Weavers' Triangle, and its history is further illustrated at the Canal Toll House Heritage Centre.

Racial disturbances here in the summer of 2001 were exploited by the far-right British National Party, which went on to win a number of council seats.

Burnley was the birthplace of the Labour politician Judith Hart (1924–91) and of the stage and film actor Sir Ian McKellen (b.1939). Burnley's football team, founded in 1881 and nicknamed the Clarets, play at Turf Moor. Alastair Campbell – New Labour's iron-fisted former director of communications – is a prominent supporter of the club, which last won the old First Division trophy in 1960.

Barghest of Burnley, the. A fierce and phantasmagoric dog, whose appearance to a person allegedly heralds their imminent demise.

Burn of Care and Burn of Sorrow. *See under* CASTLE CAMPBELL.

Burns Country. Those parts of southwestern Scotland associated with Robert Burns (1759–96), the country's national bard – in particular that traditional part of South Ayrshire known as KYLE. Among Burns-related places here are ALLOWAY (his birthplace), AYR[2], the River DOON, MAUCHLINE, TARBOLTON and, a little to the south in Carrick, KIRKOSWALD. Also associated with Burns is DUMFRIES (where he is buried) and the valley of the NITH. Bardolators will find themselves well provisioned with tasteful touristical offerings, such as the Burns National Heritage Park or the Tam O' Shanter Experience.

Compare CONSTABLE COUNTRY, HARDY COUNTRY, BRONTË COUNTRY *and* SCOTT COUNTRY

Burnt Houses A modern name, presumably 'houses rebuilt after a fire'.
A village in County Durham, 10 km (6 miles) southwest of Bishop Auckland.

Burntisland Possibly 'Burnet's (or Brand's) land', ME personal name *Burnet* or *Brand* + *land*, or more likely ModE 'burnt island', from the destruction of the fishing settlement by fire some time before 1600, when the name is first recorded; before that it was called Wester Kingorne.
A formerly important port in Fife, 7 km (4.5 miles) southwest of Kirkcaldy, on the north shore of the Firth of Forth (*see under* FORTH). By tradition the Roman general Agricola used the harbour as a base in AD 83, and in 1601 James VI summoned a General Assembly of the Church of Scotland here, away from the Edinburgh mob; it was here that an Authorized Version of the Bible – also to become known as the King James Bible – was first proposed (published 1611).

Burpham[1] 'homestead near the fort', OE *burh* (*see* BURY) + HAM.
A village in Surrey, now a northern suburb of GUILDFORD.

Burpham[2]. A village in West Sussex, about 3 km (2 miles) northeast of Arundel.

Burren, the Irish *Boireann* 'stony place, area'.
A large limestone plateau in northern County Clare, between Galway Bay (*see under* GALWAY) and the Atlantic, where it ends abruptly in the dramatic CLIFFS OF MOHER. The area, characterized by limestone pavement, caves and underground waterways, is the largest limestone area in the British Isles, and has been seen in the past as a barren wilderness (apocryphally, one of Cromwell's surveyors is said to have complained that there was not enough water to drown a man, nor a tree to hang him, nor soil to bury him). Today, however, the Burren attracts not only geologists but also botanists, who recognize it as home to one of the richest varieties of plant life of any area in the British Isles. There are also many prehistoric remains and the POULNABRONE Dolmen, a Neolithic grave, has become a symbol of the area.

Burrington 'farmstead by a fortified place', OE *byrig*, dative form of *burh* (*see* BURY) + -TON.
A village in North Somerset (before 1996 in Avon, before 1974 in Somerset), in the MENDIP HILLS, about 16 km (10 miles) east of Weston-super-Mare.

Burrington Combe. A cave-studded gorge to the southwest of Burrington. An inscription on the rocks tells the pleasing but possibly tall story of how the Rev. Augustus Toplady (then curate at nearby Blagdon), sheltering here from a storm around 1762, was inspired by it to write the hymn 'Rock of Ages'.

Burrow Head Probably 'stony hill headland', OE *beorg* 'stony hill' + ModE *head* 'headland'.
The southernmost tip of the MACHARS of Wigtownshire (now in Dumfries and Galloway), some 20 km (12 miles) south of Wigtown. It extends into the SOLWAY FIRTH, and is the second-southernmost point in Scotland after the Mull of Galloway (*see under* GALLOWAY).

Burr Point Possibly Irish *borr* 'a lump'.
The most easterly point of Ireland. It is situated on the ARDS PENINSULA[1], County Down, 2.5 km (1.5 miles) southeast of the village of Ballyhalbert.

Burry Port 'port of the burrows', from the sand dunes nearby. *Burry* for burrows or sand dunes is common in south Wales, and here gives its name to the local river.
A port on the south coast of Carmarthenshire (formerly in Dyfed), 7 km (4 miles) west of Llanelli. Its Welsh name is **Port Tywyn** (Welsh *tywyn* 'sand-dune, sea shore'). It is at the mouth of the **Burry Inlet**, which extends along the northern side of the GOWER PENINSULA (and is in effect an extension of the Loughor estuary). Burry Point provided the landing site for Amelia Earhart in June 1928 after 21 hours in the air, after she had made the first female flight across the Atlantic.

Bursledon 'hill associated with Beorhtsige', OE *Beorsa* (a diminutive form of the OE personal name *Beorhtsige*) + -*ing*- (*see* -ING) + *dun* (*see* DOWN, -DON).
A village on the river HAMBLE, about 3 km (2 miles) north of Hamble-le-Rice. TARRANT[2], the fictional setting of the BBC television sailing drama *Howard's Way*, was based on Bursledon.

Burslem 'fort-keeper's estate, or Burgweard's estate, in Lyme', OE *burgweardes* possessive form of *burgweard* 'fort-keeper', or OE *Burgweardes* possessive form of male personal name

Burgweard + Lyme OCelt district name probably meaning 'elm-tree region'.

A town in Staffordshire, one of the six towns of the POTTERIES, now a northern suburb of STOKE-ON-TRENT. It is sometimes referred to as the 'Mother of the Potteries'. Josiah Wedgwood (1730–95) was born in Burslem, and opened his first factory here in 1759.

Arnold Bennett, who in his locally set novels finessed the six towns to FIVE TOWNS, fictionalized Burslem as Bursley. The town has a number of plaques identifying various sites that appear in Bennett's works.

Bursley. A fictional name for BURSLEM in the novels of Arnold Bennett.

Burton Joyce Burton 'farmstead of the fortified place or stronghold', OE byrh-tun, from byrh possessive form of burh (see BURY) + -TON; Joyce denoting manorial ownership in the Middle Ages by the de Jorz family.

A village in Nottinghamshire, 8 km (5 miles) northeast of Nottingham.

Burton Latimer Latimer denoting manorial ownership in the Middle Ages by the Latimer family.

A town in Northamptonshire, 5 km (3 miles) southeast of Kettering. The breakfast cereal Weetabix was first made here, in 1932.

Burton Lazars Lazars from the Hospital of St Lazarus for lepers, founded here c.1138.

A village in Leicestershire, 3 km (2 miles) southeast of Melton Mowbray.

Burton-le-Coggles Coggles 'cobble-stones', ME cogel (Burton presumably produced cobble-stones).

A village in Lincolnshire, about 13 km (8 miles) southeast of Grantham.

Burton Pedwardine Pedwardine denoting manorial ownership in the Middle Ages by the Pedwardine family.

A village in Lincolnshire, about 21 km (13 miles) west of Boston.

Burton upon Trent Trent from the River Trent, on which it stands.

A town in Staffordshire, on the River TRENT[1], about 16 km (10 miles) southwest of Derby. In the early Middle Ages it was mainly a cloth-making town, but according to legend, in the 13th century the local abbot realized that Burton's water was suitable for making beer (it does in fact have a high gypsum content, which is useful), and it has never looked back. Brewing on an industrial scale began in the 1770s, when the **Trent and Mersey Canal** was opened. The firm Bass led the way, but was soon followed by the likes of Worthington, Ind Coope and Marston, and **Burton ale** became synonymous with beer (in due course it came to be used as a generic term for any dark-coloured strong ale made with highly roasted malt, whether or not brewed in

Burton). Marmite, a yeast-based savoury spread that is a by-product of the brewing industry, was introduced to the world in Burton upon Trent in 1902.

go for a Burton, to. Originally, Second World War Royal Air Force slang meaning 'to be killed (in battle or in a crash)'. After the war it entered civilian usage, in the sense 'to be broken or ruined'. Its antecedents remain obscure, but one theory that is as plausible as any other is that it was originally short for to go for a Burton ale, a euphemism based on the idea of leaving and being no longer there.

Burwash 'ploughed field by the fort', OE burh (see BURY) + ersc 'ploughed field'.

A village in East Sussex, about 21 km (13 miles) northwest of Hastings. In the 16th and 17th centuries it was the headquarters of the Wealden iron industry. The writer Rudyard Kipling (1865–1936) lived here from 1902 until his death, in a house called 'Bateman's' which had originally belonged to a local ironmaster.

See also POOK'S HILL.

Bury 'stronghold', OE burh (see BURY).

An industrial town and metropolitan borough on the River IRWELL in Greater Manchester, 13 km (8 miles) north of the centre of Manchester. The Irwell was the engine that drove the town's 19th- and early 20th-century industrial prosperity, providing the energy required by the cotton, wool, paper-manufacture and engineering industries that flourished here. A canal linking BURY to BOLTON and MANCHESTER was constructed in 1791, and from 1846 the East Lancashire Railway Company provided a rail link with Manchester.

Bury claims to be the 'capital' of black pudding, a type of sausage made of pigs' blood and binding agents such as cereal, rice and chopped fat. Although also made and appreciated in the Midlands and elsewhere, the black pudding (a stodgier item than its more delicate French equivalent, the boudin noir) is generally seen as a quintessentially down-to-earth Northern foodstuff, and, in the minds of Southerners at least, is often bracketed with such other perceived Northern cultural icons as whippets, cloth caps, pigeon fancying and rugby league.

Bury is the regimental home of the Lancashire Fusiliers (see under LANCASHIRE). The frontline role of the Fusiliers in the Gallipoli campaign of spring 1915 resulted in Bury losing – even by First World War standards – a very large number of its young men. The regiment's wartime history and the traumatic impact on Bury of the losses at Gallipoli are movingly described by the writer Geoffrey Moorhouse in his book Hell's Foundations (1992).

Bury FC, founded in 1885, plays its home games at Gigg Lane. Their interesting-sounding nickname – the **Shakers** – has disappointingly mundane origins in a former chairman's remark that the team would 'shake' their opponents.

❖ bury ❖

The Old English element *burh* is often rendered in modern place names by *borough*, *brough* and (notably in Scotland) *burgh*; even more frequently, the dative *byrig* 'at the stronghold' is found in names ending in *bury*, or in BURY (Lancashire) itself. In the vast majority of cases the *burh* is a fortified place of some kind, from an Iron-Age hillfort, through to a Roman fortified town, to a defensible Anglo-Saxon town or even monastery, to a town or estate, in later times a borough. SALISBURY (Wiltshire) was named from an Iron Age hillfort, CANTERBURY[1] (Kent) from a Roman station and EDINBURGH from a pre-Anglo-Saxon fortress, while PETERBOROUGH was renamed from Medeshamstede after the building of a monastic enclosure in the 10th century, and BLOOMSBURY (London) was an estate named after a William Blemund in the 13th century.

A wide range of elements can be combined with *burh*: the cardinal points of the compass are found in Astbury in Cheshire, WESTBURY (Berkshire), Norbury (Cheshire) and Sudbury (Greater London). ALDEBURGH (Suffolk) and NEWBURY (Berkshire) are among the 'old' and 'new' fortifications; Queniborough (Leicestershire) and Kingsbury (Oxfordshire) belonged to royalty; MALMESBURY (Wiltshire) was named after an Irish abbot, BAMBURGH (Northumberland) after a Northumbrian queen and IRTHLINGBOROUGH (Northamptonshire) after ploughmen. The number of names with OE *thorn* – like Thornbury (Gloucestershire), and including, among others, Thornbrough and Thornborough (Yorkshire) and Thornby (Northamptonshire) – might suggest that the thorns made part of the defences. The common place names Burton (*see* BURTON JOYCE) and Boughton (*see* BOUGHTON ALUPH) combine *burh* and *tun*, but it is not absolutely clear what the compound means, possibly a fortified farmhouse or a farm belonging to a town.

The element is easily confused with OE *beorg* 'hill, mound, tumulus' since a common reflex of that element is *borough*; the Scottish name ROXBURGH, which contains *burh*, may be contrasted with the English Roxborough (Middlesex), which contains *beorg*. The example of Thornby is one of a small group of names where *by* (*see* -BY) and *burh* are confused also.

The earliest Scottish *burghs* were fortified places, notably EDINBURGH and the aforementioned Roxburgh, but in the later Middle Ages, the word came to refer to status. The status of BURGH was originally awarded to towns by royal authority, and with it came trading privileges. The element remained long in use without quite losing the conservative associations of its medieval origins: FRASERBURGH is a late example.

Bury was the birthplace of the Tory prime minister Robert Peel (1788–1850); of Richmal Crompton (b. Richmal Samuel Lamburn; 1890–1969), author of the 'Just William' stories; and of the brothers Gary (b.1975) and Philip (b.1977) Neville, footballers for Manchester United and England. John Kay (1704–80), inventor of the flying shuttle (used to speed up the work of hand-loom weaving), was born nearby.

Bury St Edmunds Originally (1038) *Saint Edmunds Bury* 'town associated with St Edmund' (ModE *St Edmundsbury*), OE *Sancte Eadmundes* possessive form of the name of the 9th-century King Edmund of East Anglia, who was killed after being defeated in battle against the Danes and subsequently canonized; *Bury* from *byrig* dative form of *burh* (*see* BURY). Bury St Edmunds is first recorded in modern times.

A market town in Suffolk, on the River Lark, about 40 km (25 miles) northwest of Ipswich. It had its origins in the shrine of Edmund, last king of the East Anglians, who led his troops against the Danes at Thetford in 869. They were defeated, and Edmund later killed. Probably he was simply executed after the battle, but a more elaborate (and later) version has it that when he refused to share his Christian kingdom with the infidel Danes, they tied him to a tree, shot him full of arrows, and cut his head off.

Martyrdom was followed by sanctification, and around the year 900 his bones were placed in a shrine in a monastery not far from where he was killed.

A Benedictine abbey was founded on the site in 1020. The town was later planned deliberately around it by the Normans: it was the first planned town in Norman Britain, laid out on a grid pattern by Abbot Baldwin (1065–97). On 14 November 1214 (St Edmund's Day) Cardinal Langton, Archbishop of Canterbury, and the barons swore at the high altar of the abbey church to force King John to sign the Magna Carta. The cult of St Edmund became widespread in the Middle Ages, and Bury St Edmunds was a much visited place of pilgrimage. The abbey is now an empty ruin, but the church of St James was designated a cathedral in 1914.

The grammar school at Bury St Edmunds was founded in 1550 by Edward VI. The Nutshell in Bury St Edmunds claims to be the smallest pub in England.

Buscot 'fort-keeper's cottage(s)' or 'Burgweard's cottage(s)', OE *burh-weardes* or *Burgweardes* possessive forms of *burh-weard* 'fort-keeper' or OE male personal name *Burgweard* + OE *cot* 'cottage'.

A village in Oxfordshire, on the River THAMES[1], about 16 km (10 miles) northeast of Swindon. The nearby **Buscot Park** contains a fine neo-classical house dating from the late 18th-century, where Edward Burne-Jones's celebrated 'Briar Rose' series, four large pictures illustrating the story of Sleeping Beauty, can be seen.

Bushey 'enclosure near a thicket, or hedged with box-trees', OE *bysce* 'thicket' or *byxe* 'box-tree' + *hæg* 'enclosure'.
A town in Hertfordshire, to the southwest of and virtually contiguous with WATFORD[1].

Bushmills Irish *Muilleann na Buaise* 'mill on the River Bush'; the river name possibly means simply 'river, stream'.
A village in County Antrim, 12 km (7.5 miles) northeast of Coleraine. The place is celebrated for the products of its **Old Bushmills** distillery (established in 1602), such as Old Bushmills whiskey itself, and the liqueur whiskey **Black Bush**, a brand name that has invited ribaldry.

> The more prosperous a place was in Ulster, the sterner and more forbidding it looked. Bushmills, rich on whiskey, was made of flat rocks and black slates and was cemented to the edges of straight roads.
>
> Paul Theroux: *The Kingdom by the Sea* (1983)

Beast of Bushmills. A puma reported to have been seen in the area of Bushmills, Portballintrae and PORTRUSH in the summer of 2003.

Bushy Park possibly 'bushy enclosure', ME *bush* + *hay*, with ModE *park*.
A Royal Park in the London borough of Richmond upon Thames, constituting the northern, and larger, part of the grounds of Hampton Court Palace (*see under* HAMPTON COURT). It is relatively open and informal compared with the southern section, and deer graze here. Its most striking feature is the Diana Fountain, a large circular pond with a bronze statue of Diana the huntress at its centre, the work of Christopher Wren.

take a turn in Bushy Park, to. A euphemistic 19th-century slang expression meaning 'to have sexual intercourse'.

Bute 'isle of fire' (from signal or ceremonial fires), Gaelic *bod*, *bochd* 'fire'.
An island in the Firth of Clyde (*see under* CLYDE), about 8 km (5 miles) off the North Ayrshire coast. It is in Argyll and Bute (formerly in Buteshire, then in Strathclyde region). The main town, a popular tourist resort, is ROTHESAY. The seat of the marquesses of Bute is the vast Victorian Gothic castle (1877) at Mount Stuart, south of Rothesay. John Stuart, 3rd Earl of Bute and Lord Mount Stuart, a favourite of George III, was prime minister in 1762–3.

Bute pursuivant. Until 1867, one of the pursuivants (officials) of the Lyon Court (the Scottish Court of Heralds).

Kyles of Bute. The narrow curved straits ('kyles' is from Gaelic *caolas* 'narrows', 'straits') between Bute and the deeply indented mainland to the north. At their narrowest the Kyles are only some 400 m (440 yds) wide.

Sound of Bute. The wide channel in the Firth of Clyde between Bute and ARRAN.

Buteshire. A former county, including Bute, ARRAN and the CUMBRAES. The county town was ROTHESAY, on Bute. It was abolished in 1975, becoming part of STRATHCLYDE region.

Butetown After the Marquess of *Bute*.
A small village in Caerphilly unitary authority (formerly in Monmouthshire, then in Gwent), some 2 km (1.2 miles) north of Rhymney town (*see under* RHYMNEY). Its Welsh name is **Drenewydd** (*tre* 'farm, village' + *newydd* 'new'). It was set up in 1802–3 as a model village for his workers by the Marquess of Bute, who had extensive interests in the coalfields and ironworks of south Wales.

Butser Hill *Butser* 'Briht's slope', OE *Brihtes* possessive form of male personal name *Briht* + *ora* 'steep slope', with *Hill* added later.
A hill 270 m (889 ft) high in Hampshire, about 5 km (3 miles) southwest of Petersfield. It is the highest point on the SOUTH DOWNS. On its summit is a prehistoric site, with two round barrows and evidence of ancient Celtic cultivation. At the nearby **Butser Ancient Farm** there is also current cultivation in the Iron Age manner: authentic livestock and crop varieties are maintained amidst reconstructed roundhouses and other ancient farm structures, for purposes of historical research and public education.

Buttercrambe 'good pasture in a river-bend', OE *butere* literally 'butter' but here referring to rich pasture for cows producing the butter + *cramb* 'river-bend'.
A hamlet on the River DERWENT[3], North Yorkshire, 3 km (2 miles) north of Stamford Bridge.

Buttermere 'lake with good pasture', OE *butere* 'good pasture' + OE *mere* 'lake' (*see also* LAKE).
A lake in the western LAKE DISTRICT, Cumbria (formerly in Cumberland), some 12 km (7 miles) southwest of Keswick. The lake gives its name to the village of Buttermere. On either side are high, craggy mountains, such as ROBINSON, HAY STACKS, High Style and Red Pike:

> Conceive an enormous round bason mountain-high of solid stone cracked in half and one half gone: exactly in the remaining half of this enormous bason, does Buttermere lie, in this beautiful and stern embracement of rock.
>
> Samuel Taylor Coleridge: letter to Sara Hutchinson (5 August 1802) (written at the top of Scafell)

Maid of Buttermere, the. The epithet given to Mary Robinson, the beautiful and innocent daughter of the landlord of the Fish Inn, Buttermere. She was also known as **the Beauty of Buttermere** or **Mary of Buttermere**. At the age of 14 she caught the (apparently innocent) eye of one

Captain Joseph Budsworth, who, in *A Fortnight's Ramble in the Lakes* (1792), described her thus:

> Her face was a fine oval with full eyes and lips as red as vermilion, her cheeks had more the lily than the rose ... she looked like an angel, and I doubt not but she is the reigning Lily of the Valley.

In 1802 Mary was deceived into marrying John Hatfield, an unscrupulous impostor posing as the Hon. Alexander Augustus Hope, younger brother of the Earl of Hopetoun. He proved to be a much-married confidence trickster who had served numerous prison sentences. Exposed by Samuel Taylor Coleridge, Hatfield was eventually hanged for forgery in 1803. The story was the subject of numerous songs, ballads and poems of the time, and of a more recent novel, *The Maid of Buttermere* (1987), by Melvyn Bragg, himself of Cumbrian origin.

> I mean, O distant Friend! a story drawn
> From our own ground, – the Maid of Buttermere, –
> And how, unfaithful to a virtuous wife
> Deserted and deceived, the Spoiler came
> And wooed the artless daughter of the hills,
> And wedding her, in cruel mockery
> Of love and marriage bonds.
>
> William Wordsworth: *The Prelude* (1805–50),
> Book VII

Butter Tubs Pass. A high road pass (526 m / 1725 ft) linking WENSLEYDALE and Swaledale (*see under* SWALE[1]) in North Yorkshire, some 30 km (20 miles) west of Richmond. It takes its name from the **Butter Tubs**, a series of deep pot holes with fluted sides, said to resemble butter tubs and allegedly bottomless, or even – according to a local who confided in his cups to the travel writer John Hillaby – 'deeper nor that'.

Butterwick 'butter farm', OE *butere* 'butter' + WICK.
There are several villages of this name in England, including two in North Yorkshire and one in Lincolnshire.

Buttevant Probably Norman French *botavant*, 'defensive outwork, subsidiary fortification', although popularly supposed to derive from *Boutez en avant* 'push forward', the war cry of the Anglo-Norman de Barrys who founded the town.
A small market town on the River AWBEG, County Cork, 11 km (7 miles) north of Mallow. Its Irish name is **Cill na Mallach** ('church of the summits'), and the last element of this name gave Edmund Spenser the name Mulla, which he uses for the River AWBEG in *Colin Clouts Come Home Againe* (written in 1591 at nearby Kilcolman Castle):

> Mulla, the daughter of old Mole so hight
> The nymph which of that water course hath charge,
> That springing out of Mole, doth run down right
> To Buttevant, where spreading forth at large

> It giveth name unto that ancient cittie
> Which Kilnemullah cleped is of old.
>
> (*cleped* 'called')

Buttevant was burnt by the forces of William III in 1691, and could never again aspire to the status of 'cittie' that Spenser had awarded it. Nevertheless, in 1752 it became the scene of the very first steeplechase, the course being from the church at Buttevant to the steeple of St Leger at Doneraile, 7.2 km (4.5 miles) away.

Butt of Lewis. See LEWIS.

Buxted 'place where beech-trees or box-trees grow', OE *boc* 'beech-tree' or *box* 'box-tree' + *stede* 'place'.
A village in East Sussex, in the WEALD, about 3 km (2 miles) northeast of Uckfield. In the 16th, 17th and 18th centuries it was involved in the Wealden iron industry, and in 1543 the first cannon in East Sussex was cast here.

Buxton Probably 'the rocking-stone' (a large boulder so poised on a smaller base that it can be rocked to and fro), OE *bug-* 'bend, move sideways or up and down' + *stan* (*see* STONE).
A spa town in Derbyshire, on the River WYE[1], 305 m (1000 ft) high up in the PENNINES (it is the highest town of its size in England), on the edge of the PEAK DISTRICT National Park, about 27 km (17 miles) southeast of Manchester. Its warm springs have been utilized continuously since at least Roman times:

> By Water-drinking, and Bathing at Buxton, I have procured to my self better Health.
>
> Sir John Floyer: *An Enquiry Into the Right Use and Abuse of Hot, Cold and Temperate Baths* (1697)

However, it was at the end of the 18th century that it first made a major impact on the national scene, when the Duke of Devonshire decided to turn it into a rival to BATH, building the elegant and imposing Crescent. In 1801 H. Skrine eulogized 'Buxton where Hygæa has created her palace-like temple'. To this day it is a name to conjure with when it comes to water (**Buxton Water** is now produced commercially in plastic bottles).

The town continued to attract grand buildings to itself, including the Devonshire Royal Hospital (1859) with its huge dome, and the sumptuous Edwardian opera house; the successful annual **Buxton Festival** features opera but also offers other classical-music and literary events.

> There was a rocky valley between Buxton and Bakewell ... You enterprised a railroad ... you blasted its rocks away ... And now, every fool in Buxton can be at Bakewell in half-an-hour, and every fool in Bakewell at Buxton.
>
> John Ruskin: *Praeterita* (1889)

Buxton bloater. A slang term in the late 19th century for the overweight ('bloated') invalids who were wheeled around Buxton in Bath chairs while they took the medicinal waters.

Buxton limp. A late 19th-century term for the hobbling gait affected by invalids taking the waters at Buxton.

Bwlch y Gordinnan. The Welsh name for the CRIMEA PASS.

Byker 'village by a marsh', OScand -BY + *kjarr* 'marsh'.
An area of NEWCASTLE UPON TYNE, some 3 km (2 miles) east of the centre. It is known for the **Byker Wall**, a long, low housing block, part of a development (1969–80) designed by Ralph Erskine in consultation with the community.

> It's down the pits we'll go me lads,
> And down the pits we'll go me mamms,
> We'll try our will and use our skill,

To cut them ridges down below.
[chorus:]
Byker Hill and Walker Shore,
Collier lads for evermore,
Byker Hill and Walker Shore,
Collier lads for evermore.

> Anon.: 'Byker Hill' (folk song)

Byker Grove. A popular 2000s BBC television teen soap set in a youth centre in Byker, featuring heart-throbs Ant and Dec. The series was created by Andrea Wonfor and Adele Rose.

Byland 'Bega's land', OE male personal name *Bega* + *land*.
A battle site in North Yorkshire, just west of Rievaulx, and near the village of **Old Byland**. Here in October 1322 Robert the Bruce humiliatingly put Edward II to flight.

❖ -by ❖

This Old Scandinavian element, meaning 'farmstead, village, settlement', has been at the centre of a long-running debate about the density of the Viking settlement of England. The places named using *by* are mainly concentrated in the area of the DANELAW, the East Midlands of England controlled by the Danish kingdom of the FIVE BOROUGHS in the 10th century, and further into the north and east in pockets of high density in parts of Norfolk and Yorkshire. In all, there are over 300 place names of this type in Domesday Book in 1086, and many more appear afterwards. This indicates that the element had a long and productive life, being in use in England from probably the 9th century until at least the 14th century: the modern word *byelaw* still uses it. Although in origin the element is Scandinavian, the way it is used, and the length of time it has been used for, shows that it became as much English, in the north and east at least, as other words of Scandinavian origin that were borrowed at the time, such as window, steak and sister.

The name DERBY ('deer farm') replaced an Old English name *Northworthy*, and there are many other place names featuring *by* which use a range of terms denoting features of landscape, flora and fauna. Names like SOWERBY (North Yorkshire) 'farm on sour land' and EARBY (Lancashire) probably 'upper farm' suggest that the land taken by the settlers was not always prime agricultural land, and names like Fenby, Haythby and Thurnby ('fen', 'heath' and 'thorn' farms respectively) might support this.

The huge number of farms containing a personal name and *by* are thought to have been settled by the Scandinavian conquerors breaking up English church and secular estates: examples include ASLACKBY, GRIMSBY, INGOLDSBY and OWMBY, all in Lincolnshire (respectively the farms of Aslakr, Grimr, Ingjaldr and Authunn). Such names are dotted all over the land from Northamptonshire to North Yorkshire. Some are ethnic names, too, interesting in what is implied about the balance of ethnicity in the areas: DANBY (North Yorkshire) and FRISBY ON THE WREAKE (Leicestershire) reflect settlements belonging to Danes and Frisians respectively.

Kirby (*see* KIRBY BELLARS) and KIRKBY (frequently occurring) are Scandinavian names for an English feature, a church. Here, clearly, the name refers to a pre-existing settlement, and not to a farm, and many of these names reveal their origin in the early spellings with English *ch*- forms rather than Scandinavian *k*- forms. A more obviously Scandinavian pattern of naming is found in the large number of places called ASHBY and Willoughby, apparently named after the trees ash and willow, but prompting speculation that these were metonymic for, possibly, spearmen and archers in the Viking armies.

C

Cable Street Probably from the manufacture of ships' cables here; there was a rope-walk running alongside the road from the early 18th century.

A road in SHADWELL (E1), in the EAST END of London, running to the north of and parallel to Ratcliff Highway (*see under* RATCLIFF), from just east of the TOWER OF LONDON to Limehouse Basin (*see under* LIMEHOUSE). It achieved notoriety in the 1930s thanks to the so-called '**Battle of Cable Street**', a clash that took place here between Oswald Mosley's British Union of Fascists and their opponents on 4 October 1936. The fighting lasted for two hours and much blood was spilled.

Cackle Street *Cackle* perhaps OE *coccel* 'tares', a weed growing in cornfields; *Street see* STREET.

A village in East Sussex, about 10 km (6 miles) north of Hastings.

Cadair Idris. The Welsh name for CADER IDRIS.

Cadbury 'Cada's fortified place or stronghold', OE male personal name *Cada* + BURY.

A pair of villages, **North Cadbury** and **South Cadbury**, in Somerset, on either side of the A303, about 16 km (10 miles) northeast of Yeovil.

Cadbury Castle. A prehistoric hilltop earthwork to the southwest of South Cadbury. It covers about 7 ha (18 acres). It dates from Neolithic times, and appears to have been in continuous use as a fortification for 4000 years, until about AD 1000. Legend has it that it was the site of CAMELOT, King Arthur's court, but no evidence for this has been uncovered.

Cader Idris 'chair of Idris', *Cader* Welsh *cadair* 'chair'; *Idris*, a personal name, a legendary giant, or possibly a warrior killed *c.*630 fighting the Saxons.

A mountain massif in the form of an 8-km (5-mile) ridge, extending southwestwards from Dolgellau, Gwynedd (formerly in Merioneth). The Welsh form of the name is **Cadair Idris**. It is in the southern part of the SNOW-DONIA National Park, and the highest point is Penygadair

(893 m / 2929 ft). There are many fine cwms, crags and llyns (among them Llyn y Gadair), and Cader Idris became a National Nature Reserve in 1955.

> ... we saw the famous Kader-Idricks, which some are of opinion, is the highest mountain in Britain ...
>
> Daniel Defoe: *A Tour Through the Whole Island of Great Britain* (1724–6)

The mountain was the subject of a notable early example of 'sublime' landscape painting (*c.*1774) by Richard Wilson. The Rev. Francis Kilvert (*see* CLYRO) recorded an ascent of Cader Idris in his diary:

> Cader Idris is the stoniest, dreariest, most desolate mountain I was ever on ... It is an awful place in a storm. I thought of Moses on Sinai ... It is said that if one spends a night alone on the top of Cader Idris he will be found in the morning either dead or a madman or a poet. Hence Mrs Hemans' fine song 'A night upon Cader Idris'.

Dramatically situated below Cader Idris is Castell-y-Bere, a triangular castle built by Llewelyn the Great in 1221. It fell to Edward I in 1283.

Cadfael Country. An occasional touristic designation for the border county of Shropshire. It derives from Brother Cadfael, the SHREWSBURY-based monk who featured in a popular series of medieval detective stories by Ellis Peters (pen name of Edith Pargeter, 1913–95). The term was first used as the title of a 'coffee-table' book (1990) by Robin Whiteman and Rob Talbot which announced itself as 'an illustrated historical pilgrimage through the wild border county of Shropshire'.

Caer Caradoc 'Caradoc's fortified place', Welsh *caer* (*see* CAHER) + male personal name *Caradoc*. The place name is likely to be the invention of an antiquary rather than a genuine commemoration of the Celtic chieftain Caradoc who fought against the Romans in Shropshire before being taken to Rome as a prisoner in AD 51; this is confirmed by the fact that early spellings give the name as *Cordock*, the etymology of which is obscure, but which has nothing to do with *Caradoc*.

A striking, steep-sided hill in Shropshire, 499 m (1638 ft) in height, lying northeast of CHURCH STRETTON and east of the LONG MYND. The summit of the hill is occupied by an ancient hillfort. According to legend the Cauldron of Di-wrnach, said to contain the treasures of Britain and a sword with magical properties, is hidden in **Caradoc's Cave** on the hill's western face.

Confusingly, Shropshire has two ancient hillforts named Caer Caradoc. The second and smaller of the two (399 m / 1309 ft) lies between CLUN[2] and KNIGHTON in the far south of the county. Claims have been made for both Caer Caradocs as the site of the last stand of the British chieftain Caradoc (Latinized as Caractacus by the Roman historian Tacitus) against the Roman general Ostorius Scapula around AD 50 (but *see above*).

Caerdydd. The Welsh name for CARDIFF.

Caerffili. The Welsh name for CAERPHILLY[1].

Caerfyrddin. The Welsh name for CARMARTHEN.

Caergybi. The Welsh name for HOLYHEAD.

Caerlaverock Possibly 'fort of Llywarch' or 'fort of the elm trees', OCelt *caer* (*see* CAHER) + male personal name *Llywarch*; or the second element may be Gaelic *leamhreaich* 'elm trees' or ME *laverok* 'lark'.

A magnificent triangular castle dating from *c*.1290, on the NITH estuary 12 km (7.5 miles) south of Dumfries. It stands on the north side of the SOLWAY FIRTH, in what was Dumfriesshire and is now Dumfries and Galloway. There are the remains of an older castle nearby, and it may have been the site of a Roman port. The present castle was improved during the Renaissance, but captured and destroyed in 1640 by the Covenanters. Nearby there is an important wetland bird reserve.

Siege de Karlaverok, Le. An anonymous verse-chronicle in Norman French, recounting the siege of the castle in 1300 by Edward I of England.

Caerleon 'fort of the legions', OCelt *caer* (*see* CAHER) + Latin *legionum* 'of the legions'.

A small town on the River USK[1] in Newport unitary authority (formerly in Monmouthshire, then in Gwent), 5 km (3 miles) northeast of Newport, of which it is now a suburb. The Welsh version of the name is **Caerllion**. The Romans built an important fort here called **Isca Silurum** ('Isca' was the Roman name for the Usk, and the Silures were the local tribe vanquished by the Romans). The fort was the headquarters of the 2nd Legion from *c*.AD 75 to the late 3rd century – one of the three permanent legionary bases in Britain (the others being at Chester and York). This gave rise to the town's name (*see above*) and its nickname, the **City of Legions**. Caerleon was said to have been one of King Arthur's strongholds, and was the capital of a Welsh princedom until the Norman Conquest. For the 12th-

century chronicler Geoffrey of Monmouth it was CAMELOT; he has Arthur crowned here, and transmogrifies the Roman amphitheatre into the Round Table. In the 6th century St David presided at Caerleon over the Synod of Victory, which apparently put paid to the Pelagian heresy in Britain.

Attracted by its Arthurian connections, Tennyson stayed at Caerleon while writing *Idylls of the King*, and in the section called 'Geraint and Edith' (1859) he deploys a local simile:

> ... but in scarce longer time
> Than at Caerleon the full-tided Usk,
> Before he turn to fall seaward again,
> Pauses, did Enid, keeping watch, behold ...

Caerleon was the birthplace of the fantasy writer Arthur Machen (Arthur Llewellyn Jones; 1863–1947), author of *The Great God Pan* (1894) and *The Angel of Mons* (1915).

Caernarfon 'fort in Arfon', OCelt *caer* (*see* CAHER) + ARFON, the name of the local area.

A port, market town and tourist resort on the MENAI STRAIT, 14 km (8.5) miles southwest of Bangor. It was the country town of CAERNARVONSHIRE, and is now the administrative seat of Gwynedd. The English version of the name is **Caernarvon**, and the Romans called their fort here **Segontium**. Local legend has it that the Emperor Constantine was born here, and for long the Welsh associated Caernarfon with Constantinople – and once called both **Caer Cystennin** ('fort of Constantine'; the earliest spelling is *Custennin*).

This association with Constantinople is referred to in the design of the magnificent **Caernarfon Castle**, which Edward I built to the west of the town in 1284. The design, by the Savoyard master known as James of St George, deliberately reflects – as a symbol of Edward's new *imperium* in Wales – the walls of Theodosius in Constantinople (modern Istanbul) in its use of polygonal towers topped by eagles and bands of limestone and sandstone in the masonry. There is also an echo of 'The Dream of Macsen Wledig' from the *Mabinogion*, in which Macsen (Maximus, Emperor of Rome and supposedly father of Constantine) falls asleep while out hunting:

> ... And he beheld a great city at the entrance of the river, and a vast castle in the city, and he saw many high towers of various colours in the castle ... And thence he beheld an island in the sea, facing this rugged land.

Macsen dreams of a fair maid in this castle, and eventually journeys to Britain, finding her at Caernarfon, opposite the island of Anglesey, as his dream had told him. According to tradition, her name was Helen, after whom the Roman road SARN HELEN was supposedly named, as was St Helens in Merseyside and the Isle of Wight.

The first Prince of Wales (the future Edward II) was born

at Caernarfon Castle in 1284, and was sometimes known as **Edward of Caernarvon** (for Prince of Wales *see under* WALES). The castle was besieged by Owain Glyndwr in 1402, but, regardless of this expression of Welsh nationhood and the strength of local nationalist sentiment, the future Edward VIII was invested as Prince of Wales at the castle in 1911 (largely owing to the manoeuvrings of David Lloyd George, MP for Caernarfon), as was Prince Charles in 1969, despite the efforts of the Abergele Martyrs (*see under* ABERGELE). Whether abdication is a contingent or necessary concomitant of being invested as Prince of Wales at Caernarfon remains to be seen.

Caernarfon Castle was painted by Richard Wilson (*c*.1713–82), and J.M.W. Turner's visit in 1798 resulted in a large-scale watercolour.

Caernarfon was the birthplace not only of the ill-fated Edward II but also of William Morgan (*c*.1545–1604), the Anglican bishop who translated the Bible into Welsh. Lloyd George was elected MP for **Caernarvon Boroughs** in 1890, and retained his seat for 55 years. Guglielmo Marconi established a long-wave transmission station at Caernarfon, and in 1918 successfully sent a radiotelegraph message from here to Australia. The Welsh-language poet and scholar William John Gruffydd died in Caernarfon in 1954.

> The wind was gentle and the sea a flower,
> And the sun slumbered on Caernarfon tower.
>
> Anon.: 'Night and Morning' (16th–17th century), translated from the Welsh by R.S. Thomas

Caernarfon Bay. The area of the Irish Sea bounded by ANGLESEY to the northeast and the LLEYN PENINSULA to the southeast. The town of Caernarfon is not actually on the bay.

Caernarvon, Lord (1826–1923). The British archaeologist who, with Howard Carter, found the tomb of Tutankhamen in 1922. The next year they broke the seal of the door of the tomb, and the same year Lord Caernarvon died, thus proving to some the efficacy of the so-called 'Curse of Tutankhamen'.

Caernarvonshire From CAERNARFON + SHIRE.

A former county of northwest Wales, bounded to the north by the Menai Strait and Anglesey, to the east by Denbighshire, to the south by Merioneth and to the west by the Irish Sea. It was also spelt **Caernarfonshire**. The county town was CAERNARFON, and the county also included BANGOR[1], the LLEYN PENINSULA and much of SNOWDONIA. It is now in GWYNEDD.

Caerphilly[1] 'fort of Ffili', OCelt *caer* (*see* CAHER) + name of an unidentified person.

A market town in the unitary authority of CAERPHILLY[2] (formerly in Glamorgan, and then in Mid Glamorgan), 11 km (7 miles) north of Cardiff. Its Welsh name is **Caerffili**.

Caerphilly Castle is the second largest castle in Britain after Windsor. It was begun by Gilbert de Clare, Lord of Glamorgan, in 1268, but was destroyed in 1270 by Llywelyn ap Gruffydd. It was subsequently rebuilt, only to be captured again in the early 15th century by Owain Glyndwr. In the 1640s it suffered severe damage at the hands of the Parliamentarians during the Civil Wars; when the poet Tennyson visited in the 19th century he described it as 'a town in ruins'. The castle has subsequently been substantially restored.

Caerphilly was the birthplace of the fezzed comedian and aspirant magician Tommy Cooper (1922–84).

Caerphilly cheese. A mild, crumbly white cheese, made in a number of dairies around Caerphilly. The liking the Welsh have for cheese is proverbial:

> The Welch are said to be so remarkably fond of cheese, that in cases of difficulty their midwives apply a piece of toasted cheese to the *janua vitae* [doorway of life], to attract and entice the young Taffy, who on smelling it makes most vigorous efforts to come forth.
>
> Francis Grose: *A Classical Dictionary of the Vulgar Tongue* (1785)

Whether Caerphilly is necessary for this operation, or whether Cheddar will suffice, Grose does not divulge.

Caerphilly[2]. A unitary authority in South Wales, bounded by Cardiff to the south, Rhondda Cynon Taff and Merthyr Tydfil to the west, Powys to the north, and Blaenau Gwent, Torfaen and Newport to the east. It was created in 1996 from parts of the former counties of MID GLAMORGAN and GWENT. The administrative seat is at HENGOED, and other towns include CAERPHILLY[1], BARGOED, NEWBRIDGE[1] and RHYMNEY.

Caerwent 'the fort of Gwent', OCelt *caer* (*see* CAHER) + GWENT. A village in Monmouthshire (formerly in Gwent), 8 km (5 miles) southwest of Chepstow. It was the site of an important Roman town, **Venta Silurum** ('field or market of the Silures tribe').

Caesaromagus. A Roman settlement on the site of present-day CHELMSFORD.

Caesar's Camp. A name given to various locations where Julius Caesar's troops are said to have camped following the Roman invasion of Britain in 55 BC. One is in the southern part of Wimbledon Common (*see under* WIMBLEDON), and is now occupied by the 6th, 7th, 10th and 11th holes of the Royal Wimbledon Golf Club. Another is in BROMLEY, on Keston Common; its site was once an ancient British encampment.

Caha Mountains Irish *Cnoic na Ceachan* 'hills of showers'. A range of mountains in the BEARA peninsula of counties Kerry and Cork. The highest point (685 m / 2247 ft) is HUNGRY HILL, and the range is divided by the HEALY

❖ **caher** ❖

Names containing the element *caher* are interesting because Irish *cathair* was borrowed from Brittonic, ultimately from Latin *cathedra*, as was *cadair* in Welsh. As the Latin word indicates, the original word meant 'seat, throne', and by extension a high place, such as CADER IDRIS. The word came to be used in some English names like CATERHAM (Surrey) and Catterton (North Yorkshire). But the Irish word has apparently taken over the meaning of Welsh *caer* and Cornish *cair*, 'fortified place', since in most cases there is a stone fort in the vicinity of Irish *caher/cahir*

names: two the Cahers, in the counties Tipperary and Mayo, are examples of where this has occurred. The origin of Welsh *caer* is a little difficult, but it possibly had the same distant ancestor as Old English *ceaster* and Latin *castrum* 'a fort or camp' (*see* CHESTER). The Welsh element *caer* hardly needs illustration, given the importance of the names containing it: CARDIFF, CAERNARFON, CAERPHILLY[1]. The Brittonic element is found quite widely in England and Scotland, where it is associated with Roman forts, such as CARLISLE.

PASS. The Beara peninsula is sometimes called the **Caha** peninsula.

Caher. *See* CAHIR.

Caherbarnagh Irish *An Chathair Bhearnach* 'the stone fort with gaps' (*see* CAHER).

The highest summit (682 m / 2237 ft) in County Cork, in the DERRYNASAGGART MOUNTAINS.

Cahersiveen. *See* CAHIRCIVEEN.

Cahir Irish *An Cathair* 'the stone fort'.

A small market town on the River SUIR in County Tipperary, 15 km (9 miles) west of Clonmel, at the foot of the GALTEE MOUNTAINS. It is also spelt **Caher**. The town's name refers to a castle built in 1142 by the Butlers of Ormond on a rocky island in the River Suir. This castle was known as *Cathair-duna-iascaigh* ('fort of the fortification rich in fish'). The present impressive castle on the same site dates from the 15th century, although it was extensively restored in 1840. A 'bulwark for Munster and a safe retreat for all the agents of Spain and Rome', it fell to the Earl of Essex's artillery in 1599, and surrendered to Oliver Cromwell in 1650. The castle, the largest of its period in Ireland, has appeared in films such as John Boorman's *Excalibur* (1981) and Mel Gibson's *Braveheart* (1995).

Cahirciveen Irish *Cathair Saidhbhín* 'fort of little Sadhbh' (a female personal name).

A small market town in County Kerry, on the northwestern side of the IVERAGH peninsula, on the Ring of Kerry, 50 km (31 miles) west of Killarney. It is also spelt **Cahersiveen**. So remote is it that it was said that in the early 19th century it had better communications with the USA than with Dublin. Daniel O'Connell (1775–1847), the Liberator, was born at nearby Carhan House, now ruined, while the town itself was the birthplace of the top Gaelic footballers Jack (Jacko) O'Shea (b.1957) and Maurice Fitzgerald (b.1970). The poet Sigerson Clifford (1913–85) spent his childhood here, commemorating Cahirciveen in his poem 'The Boys from Barr na Sráide' (i.e. the top of the town):

O the town it climbs the mountain and looks upon the sea,

And sleeping time or waking 'tis there I long to be,
To walk again that kindly street, the place I grew a man,
And the boys of Barr na Sráide went hunting for the wran.

Sigerson Clifford: from *Ballads of a Bogman* (1955)

Cahore Point Possibly 'point of the stone fort', *Cahore* Irish *cathair*, possessive *catharach* 'of the stone fort'.

A low headland on the east coast of County Wexford, 25 km (15 miles) south of Arklow.

Cairlinn. The Irish name for CARLINGFORD.

Cairn Gorm 'blue mountain', *Cairn* Gaelic *càrn* 'mountain, heap of rocks'; *Gorm* 'blue', Gaelic; *Kairne Gorum* 1670.

A mountain (1245 m / 4084 ft) in the CAIRNGORM MOUNTAINS (to which it gave its name), on the border between Highland and Moray, 14 km (8.5 miles) southeast of Aviemore. It is the fifth highest mountain in the British Isles, and the smallest of the four Cairngorm Four-Thousanders (*see under* CAIRNGORM MOUNTAINS). The northern slopes have been heavily developed for skiing since the 1960s, and the mountain made accessible for the unenergetic by the provision of a new road to over 600 m (2000 ft), from where the tourist may take a chairlift (and now a funicular) to within a stone's throw of the summit. These developments have been generally opposed by conservationists and mountaineers.

From two centuries before the crowds arrived here, there is a story that the Jacobite James McIntyre, having rescued his regimental colours from the field of CULLODEN MUIR, thereafter ascended Cairn Gorm every year on the anniversary of the raising of Bonnie Prince Charlie's standard in Glenfinnan in 1745, and unfurled the flag on the summit. Today the summit contains an automatic weather station, which not infrequently records wind speeds in winter in excess of 160 kph (100 mph); the highest surface wind speed ever known in Britain was recorded on the summit on 20 May 1986, when a gust reached 278 kph (172 mph).

There is another mountain of the same name 6 km (4 miles) to the south, which is now known, to distinguish it, as **Derry Cairngorm** (1155 m / 3788 ft), after Glen Derry (Gaelic *doireach* 'wooded') on its eastern side.

cairngorm. A yellowish, grey or brown semiprecious stone consisting of smoked quartz, found on Cairn Gorm and neighbouring mountains. The term dates from the late 18th century, and at the beginning of the 19th century Farquarson of Invercauld in Deeside was charging £200 per year to miners looking for the stones on his land.

Cairngorm Mountains From CAIRN GORM.

A mountain range, also referred to as **the Cairngorms**, in the eastern Highlands, part of the GRAMPIAN MOUNTAINS. The original Gaelic name of the range was *Am Monadh Ruadh* ('the red mountains', from the colour of the granite), but the current name came into widespread usage in the 19th century. In its narrower sense it is applied to the mountains between GLEN FESHIE to the west, the River SPEY to the northwest and the upper River DEE[1] in the south. In a broader sense the name takes in the similar mountains south of the Dee, including LOCHNAGAR, the ATHOLL hills (such as BEINN A'GHLO), the mountains around GLEN SHEE and the head of GLEN CLOVA, and eastward to Mount Keen. The Cairngorms thus straddle Highland, Moray, Angus, Perth and Kinross and Aberdeenshire.

The Cairngorms are generally rounded, with extensive high plateaux cut by craggy corries and steep-sided glens. In the northern Cairngorms are **the Cairngorm Four-Thousanders** (four mountains over 4000 ft): BEN MACDUI, BRAERIACH, CAIRN TOUL and CAIRN GORM itself (after which the range is named). Much of the high plateau here is around 1200 m (4000 ft) and supports a sub-Arctic ecosystem unique in the British Isles, while on the lower slopes and glens there are remnants of the Old Caledonian Forest (*see under* CALEDONIA). This northern area is a National Nature Reserve, and became the Cairngorm National Park – the largest in Britain at 3797 sq km (1466 sq miles) – in 2003; controversially, the new park excluded that part of the range in Perth and Kinross. In winter (which can effectively last from September to May) the Cairngorms are subject to blizzards of Arctic ferocity, in which many have died.

> The sense of our minuteness on these empty wastes became acute. I felt a tiny speck swallowed up in an environment incomprehensibly great, like the flicker of earthly life amid the uncountable galaxies. Here we knew what it meant to be alone, yet to feel distant kinship with the gods.
>
> W.H. Murray: *Mountaineering in Scotland* (1947), 'Cairngorm Blizzard'

The eccentric baronet Sir Hugh Rankin (1899–1988), who converted from Christianity to Islam, and thence to Buddhism, believed that one of the five Bodhisattvas who control the destiny of the world lives in the Cairngorms.

Apparently he conceived of these figures as abominable snowmen, so he may have been lured into this confusion by the story of the Grey Man of Ben Macdui (*see under* BEN MACDUI).

> I shall leave tonight from Euston
> By the seven-thirty train,
> And from Perth in the early morning
> I shall see the hills again.
> From the top of Ben Macdhui
> I shall watch the gathering storm,
> And see the crisp snow lying
> At the back of Cairngorm.
> I shall feel the mist from Bhrotain
> And pass by Lairig Ghru
> To look on dark Loch Einich
> From the heights of Sgoran Dubh.
> From the broken Barns of Bynack
> I shall see the sunrise gleam
> On the forehead of Ben Rinnes
> And Strathspey awake from dream.
> And again in the dusk of evening
> I shall find once more alone
> The dark water of the Green Loch,
> And the pass beyond Ryvoan.
> For tonight I leave from Euston
> And leave the world behind;
> Who has the hills as a lover
> Will find them wondrous kind.
>
> Anon.: lines written on the door of Ryvoan Bothy in the northern Cairngorms (The bothy has since burnt down.)

Cairn o' Mount 'cairn of the mountain', Scotticized version of Gaelic *càrn* 'mountain' (but becoming 'cairn' in English) + *monadh* 'mountain, moorland'. It is also called Cairn o' Mounth; *see* the MOUNTH.

A high road pass, reaching 455 m (1493 ft), in Aberdeenshire (formerly in Kincardineshire, then in Grampian region), by which the B974 links the Howe of the MEARNS to the DEE[1] valley, via Fettercairn, Clatterin Brig, Bridge of Dye and Bridge of Bogendreip. The hills of Clachnaben (with its huge granite tor), Meluncart and Hound Hillock are to the west. The pass is prone to blockage by snow in winter.

> As I rode down by the Brig o' Dye
> And past yon hill o' broom,
> A maiden sang right merrily,
> Just as the sun gaed down.
> 'It's Cairn o' Mount is bleak and bare,
> And cauld is Clochnaben,
> And you will see the snow lie there
> Alang the summer's end.'
>
> Alexander Balfour (1767–1829): 'Cairn o' Mount'

Robert Burns also wrote a poem entitled 'As I Came o'er the Cairney Mount', one of his Victorian editors noting that the poet had supplied new words for 'a very indelicate song, now deservedly forgotten'.

Cairnpapple Hill Possibly 'heap of pebbles', *Cairnpapple* Gaelic *càrn* 'heap, pile' + OE *popel* 'pebble'; *Kernepopple* 1619.
One of the Bathgate Hills, about 3 km (2 miles) north of BATHGATE, West Lothian. At just over 300 m (1000 ft) high, the hill is the lowest high-point of any of the old Scottish counties. It was an important prehistoric ritual and burial site from about 2500 BC. The large cairn (used for burials) dates from the Bronze Age, *c*.1600 BC, and its subterranean hollow interior can be visited.

Cairnryan For origins *see* LOCH RYAN.
A port on the eastern shore of LOCH RYAN, sheltered by the northern arm of the Rhinns of Galloway (*see under* GALLOWAY). It was formerly in Wigtownshire and is now in Dumfries and Galloway. There is a ferry service to LARNE in Northern Ireland, and parts of the mulberry harbours used during the Normandy landings in the Second World War were built here.

Cairnsmore of Carsphairn 'big hill of the valley of the alders', *Cairnsmore* Gaelic *càrn* 'hill' + *mòr* 'big'; *Carsphairn* Gaelic *carse* 'valley' + *feàrna* 'alders'.
A prominent mountain (797 m / 2614 ft) to the northwest of the village of **Carsphairn**, which is 19 km (12 miles) north of New Galloway. It was formerly in Kirkcudbrightshire and is now in Dumfries and Galloway. The mountain is so named to distinguish it from another large Galloway hill, **Cairnsmore of Fleet**.

> There's Cairnsmore of Fleet,
> And there's Cairnsmore of Dee,
> But Cairnsmore of Carsphairn
> Is the highest of the three.
>
> Traditional rhyme

Cairnsmore of Fleet 'big hill on the river or estuary', *Cairnsmore* Gaelic *càrn* 'hill' + *mòr* 'big'; *Fleet see* GATEHOUSE OF FLEET.
A mountain (711 m / 2332 ft) in Dumfries and Galloway, which stands above the headwaters of the **Water of Fleet** (*see under* GATEHOUSE OF FLEET). On the south side of Cairnsmore of Fleet is a pass called **Door of Cairnsmore**, while on the east side there is a projecting, rounded ridge called **Knee of Cairnsmore**.

Cairn Toul 'peak of the barn'; its Gaelic form is *Càrn an t-Sabhail*, *càrn* 'peak' + *an* 'of' + *t-* 'the' + *sabhail* 'barn'; the name comes from the appearance of the mountain, which from some angles looks like a peaked roof.
The fourth-highest mountain (1293 m / 4242 ft) in the British Isles, and the third-highest of the Cairngorm Four-Thousanders (*see under* CAIRNGORM MOUNTAINS). It is in Aberdeenshire (formerly in Grampian region); 3 km (2 miles) south of BRAERIACH, to which it is linked by a high plateau where the River DEE[1] rises. Its two main

subsidiary summits are the Angel's Peak and the DEVIL'S POINT. On its northern side, below the summit pyramid, there is a spectacularly sculpted hanging corrie, in which nestles the small Lochan Uaine ('the green lochan').

Cairnwell, the Possibly 'cairn of the bags', Gaelic *càrn* 'cairn' + *bhalg* 'of the bags', from the shape of the peat hags on its slopes.
A mountain (933 m / 3059 ft) above the GLEN SHEE ski area in Aberdeenshire (formerly in Grampian region). There is a chairlift almost to the summit. The name is also applied to the summit of the A93 road pass below the mountain, north of the DEVIL'S ELBOW, linking Blairgowrie and Braemar.

Caiseal. The Irish name for CASHEL.

Caisleán an Bharraigh. The Irish name for CASTLEBAR.

Caisleán an Chomair. The Irish name for CASTLECOMER.

Caisleán Ghriaire. The Irish name for CASTLEGREGORY.

Caisleán na Mainge. The Irish name for CASTLEMAINE.

Caisleán Uidhilín. The Irish name for CASTLEWELLAN.

Caister-on-Sea *Caister* 'Roman camp or town', OE *ceaster* (*see* CHESTER).
A small town on the east Norfolk coast, about 5 km (3 miles) north of Great Yarmouth. In Roman times it was a port.
   Caister Castle was built in 1432 by Sir John Fastolf, who commanded the English archers at the Battle of Agincourt and whose name was later adapted by Shakespeare as Sir John Falstaff in *Henry IV, Henry V* and *The Merry Wives of Windsor*.

Caithness 'cape of the Cait', OScand name *Katanes* (*see* NESS), from the earlier Pictish province found in OCelt as *Cait* or *Cat*. The first element may reflect the name of an ancient tribe, the *Cataibh*, or 'cat-men', who spread from Caithness into Sutherland (a man from Sutherland is called in Gaelic a *Catach*).
A former county forming the far northeastern corner of Scotland. It was bounded on the east by the North Sea, on the north by the Pentland Firth, and on the west and south by Sutherland. The county town was WICK, and the other important town was THURSO. Other well-known places within its bounds included JOHN O'GROATS, DUNCANSBY HEAD and DUNNET HEAD and the area known as the FLOW COUNTRY. The county became a district of HIGHLAND region (1975–96), and is now in Higland unitary authority.
   Caithness, with SUTHERLAND, was one of the ancient Celtic mormaerships (earldoms) of Scotland, but after the Viking invasions the Norse earls of ORKNEY held the title of Earl of Caithness until 1231. The earldom later came into the hands of the Sinclairs, whose clan land this is, and who gave their name to Sinclair's Bay on the east coast,

some 5 km (3 miles) north of Wick. The earldom was subsequently held by the Campbells of Glen Orchy (*see under* ORCHY).

The novelist Neil Gunn (1891–1973) was born at Dunbeath on the coast of Caithness, and these shores provide the setting for several of his novels, such as *The Silver Darlings* (1941); Dunbeath itself is renamed 'Dunster' in them.

Caithness glass. A type of glassware manufactured at Wick, Caithness.

Ord of Caithness, the Gaelic *òrd* 'hammer' or 'steep rounded hill'.

A steep ridge rising above the North Sea on the route of the A9 in northeastern Highland, 4 km (2.5 miles) beyond Helmsdale. It formerly marked the boundary between the old counties of Sutherland and Caithness. It is supposedly unlucky for a Sinclair from Caithness to pass the Ord on a Monday, as it was on a Monday in 1513 when a force of Sinclairs passed the Ord on the way to FLODDEN and annihilation.

Calcaria. A Roman settlement on the site of present-day TADCASTER.

Caldbeck Fells *Caldbeck* OScand *kaldr* 'cold' + *bekkr* 'stream'; *Fells* OScand *fjall* 'fell, mountain'.

The most northerly outliers of the Lake District, Cumbria (formerly in Cumberland), some 8 km (5 miles) northeast of Skiddaw. The highest point is High Pike (658 m / 2158 ft).

Calder[1] 'violent stream', OCelt *caled* 'hard, violent' + *dufr*, in later Scottish names later Gaelic *dobhar*, 'stream'.

A river in West Yorkshire, rising on HEPTONSTALL Moor in the Pennines northwest of Hebden Bridge. It flows generally eastward for 72 km (45 miles) through HALIFAX and WAKEFIELD before joining the River AIRE near CASTLEFORD. It gives its name to the district of **Calderdale**, of which HALIFAX is the administrative centre, and partially to the **Aire and Calder Navigation**. (*see under* AIRE).

Calder[2]. A river rising in West Yorkshire, less than 1 km (0.6 miles) west of the source of the CALDER[1]. It flows generally westward through Lancashire before joining the River RIBBLE.

> By Calder's dew-pearled marge I wandered
> Through ferns and meadows all alone,
> To Calder's song my heart surrendered, –
> That heart afore was hard as stone.
>
> Josiah Hurstwood: 'Calder River' (*c*.1825)

There are two more northern English Calders: one in central Lancashire (a tributary of the WYRE rising on Calder Fell), and one in Cumbria.

Calder[3]. A river in West Lothian. It has given its name to three villages along its course: **East Calder**, **Mid Calder** (both about 3 km / 2 miles southeast of Livingston) and **West Calder** (some 7 km / 4.5 miles) southwest of Livingston. The A71 heading this way from Edinburgh is often referred to as the **Calder Road**.

Caldercruix 'bends of the River Calder', OCelt river name + Scots *cruix* 'bends'.

A large village in North Lanarkshire (formerly in Strathclyde region), 5 km (3 miles) northeast of Airdrie.

Calder Hall. *See under* SELLAFIELD.

Caldey Island 'cold island', *Caldey* OScand *kald* 'cold' + *ey* 'island' (*see* -AY); 'Caldey' Island is thus tautological.

A small island in Carmarthen Bay (*see under* CARMARTHEN) off the coast of Pembrokeshire (formerly in Dyfed), 4 km (2.5 miles) south of Tenby. It is separated from the mainland by **Caldey Sound**. It is also spelt **Caldy Island**, and its Welsh name is **Ynys Byr** (*ynys* 'island', *Pyr* possibly the name of an early abbot).

A Celtic monastic foundation was established here in the 6th century. Anglican Benedictines built a new monastery in 1906, occupied since 1928 by Trappists from Belgium, who grow herbs from which they make perfume.

Caldicot 'cold hut', OE *cald* 'cold' + -COT.

A town in Monmouthshire (formerly in Gwent), 10 km (6 miles) southwest of Chepstow. **Caldicot Castle** dates from the 12th–14th centuries, and was restored in the Victorian era as a family home. To the southwest are the flat lands of **Caldicot Level**.

Caledonia From the ancient inhabitants of northern Britain, whom the Romans referred to as *Caledones*, possibly meaning 'hard or noisy people'. The original Caledonians were quite a small tribe inhabiting the Perthshire Highlands.

The Roman name for northern Britain, broadly corresponding to modern Scotland. For most of the time the frontier was at HADRIAN'S WALL, although in the 2nd century AD it was pushed north to the ANTONINE WALL. Usage appears to have varied somewhat:

> I am now to enter the true and real Caledonia, for the country to the north of the firth [of Forth] is alone called by that name, and was anciently known by no other.
>
> Daniel Defoe: *A Tour Through the Whole Island of Great Britain* (1724–6)

Later in the 18th century the name was patriotically revived (and often personified) in poetic contexts:

> There was once a day, but old Time then was young,
>   That brave Caledonia, the chief of her line,
> From some of your northern deities sprung,
>   (Who knows not that brave Caledonia's divine?)
> From Tweed to the Orcades was her domain ...
>
> Robert Burns: 'Caledonia' (date unknown)

O Caledonia! stern and wild,
Meet nurse for a poetic child!
Land of brown heath and shaggy wood,
Land of the mountain and the flood ...

> Sir Walter Scott: *The Lay of the Last Minstrel* (1805),
> Canto VI, ii

The Pacific island group of New Caledonia was so named by Captain Cook in 1774, although it later became a French colony.

Caledonian, The. The title given to one of the train services running between London and Glasgow.

Caledonian Antisyzygy, the. A concept first articulated by Gregory Smith in his *Scottish Literature: Character and Influence* (1919) to characterize the antithetical, even paradoxical, nature of the Scottish Muse (an antisyzygy being a yoking together of opposites):

> Though the Scottish Muse has loved reality, sometimes to maudlin affection for the commonplace, she has loved not less the airier pleasure to be found in the confusion of the senses, in the fun of things thrown topsy-turvy, in the horns of elfland and the voices of the mountains ...

The Caledonian Muse's 'sudden jostling of contraries' often involves a certain grim, gallows humour, as in such images as the skeleton at the feast, or the 'grinning gargoyle by a saint' – an image borrowed from Smith by Hugh MacDiarmid in his long poem *A Drunk Man Looks at the Thistle* (1926), a masterpiece that self-consciously embodies the Caledonian Antisyzygy.

Caledonian cream. A dessert consisting of cream cheese, double cream, marmalade, lemon juice, sugar and brandy or rum.

Caledonian Hotel, the. For many years **the Cally** was *the* grand hotel in Edinburgh, situated in the capital's West End. It was built by the Caledonian Rail Company above their Caledonian Station, a rival to Waverley Station at the other end of Princess Street. The station was completed in 1899 and the hotel in 1903. The station was closed down by British Rail in 1965, but the hotel continues as one of Edinburgh's two five-star hotels.

Caledonian MacBrayne. A Scottish shipping line that runs most of the ferries between the mainland and the islands of the Hebrides. It is familiarly known as '**Cal-Mac**'. The company was founded in 1878.

Caledonian Orogeny, the. The mountain-building process that took place in northwest Europe 900 million–400 million years ago. The Caledonian system extends from the west of Ireland through Britain and Scandinavia to the north of Norway.

Caledonian Thistle. The name by which Inverness Caledonian Thistle FC (*see under* INVERNESS) is usually known.

Old Caledonian Forest, the. The forest that once covered much of Scotland, but which has been very much depleted since the Middle Ages. It typically consists of scattered Scots pines, together with some birches, mingled with heather and juniper. Currently the greatest threat to the remaining fragments (many in the Cairngorm Mountains) is from red deer, insufficiently culled on most of the large sporting estates.

> The golden edging of a bough at sunset, its pantile
>   way
> Forming a double curve, tegula and imbrex in one,
> Seems at times a movement on which I might be
>   borne
> Happily to infinity ...

> Hugh MacDiarmid: 'In the Caledonian Forest', from *Stony Limits and Scots Unbound and Other Poems* (1956)

Caledonian Canal. A canal (suitable only for smaller boats) linking the North Sea and the Atlantic via the GREAT GLEN, the fault line that divides northwest Scotland from the rest of the country. The canal was planned by Thomas Telford to enable ships heading from the North Sea to the Atlantic (or vice versa) to avoid the dangerous waters of the PENTLAND FIRTH between northern Scotland and Orkney, and built between 1804 and 1847. There are a total of 29 locks, and the sequence of 8 locks at the southern end is known as **Neptune's Staircase**. The overall length is 97 km (60 miles), but for more than half of this the passage takes advantage of the glen's lochs, LOCH NESS, Loch Oich and LOCH LOCHY.

Caledonian Road From the *Caledonian* Asylum. A road in northern Central London (N1, N7), running southwards from HOLLOWAY to KING'S CROSS. It was built in 1826, and originally called Chalk Road. One of its most notable early buildings was an orphanage for the sons of poor London Scots and of Scots killed on active service. This became known as the **Caledonian Asylum**, and in due course its road was renamed after it. Pentonville Prison (*see under* PENTONVILLE) is on the east side of the road, about halfway along its length. Caledonian Road Underground station, on the Piccadilly Line, opened in 1906.

Caledonian Market. Originally, a general market that grew up beside the Metropolitan Cattle Market in Islington in the second half of the 19th century. It took its name from the Caledonian Road, to which it was adjacent. In the early 20th century, as the concept of 'antiques' took hold, it grew enormously in size: bargain-hunters sifted the junk for elusive masterpieces, fences moved stolen goods around, and the so-called 'Caledonian Silver Kings' enriched themselves. It was closed during the Second World War, and never returned to its original site. A new Caledonian Market was opened south of the Thames, in BERMONDSEY.

Calf, The 'calf', ModE; term often used where a smaller object is beside a larger one, as with a calf by its mother.

A hill (676 m / 2217 ft) in the northwest Pennines, Cumbria, 15 km (9 miles) northeast of Kendal.

Calf of Eday. *See under* EDAY.

Calf of Man *See* The CALF; here the Isle of Man is the bovine mother.
A small rocky island just off the southern tip of the ISLE OF MAN. It is a bird reserve run by the Manx National Trust.

Calgary Possibly 'Kali's triangular plot of land', OScand personal name *Kali* + *geiri* 'triangular piece of land', or alternatively Gaelic *caladh garaidh* 'the haven by the dyke'.
A small village in northwest MULL, 14 km (8.5 miles) west of Tobermory, in Argyll and Bute (formerly in Strathclyde region).
    It gave its name to the city of Calgary in Alberta, Canada, which was originally the North West Mounted Police post of Fort Brisebois. It was renamed Fort Calgary in 1876 by Colonel J.F. Macleod, the commissioner of the Royal North West Mounted Police, who was related by marriage to the owner of the estate in Mull that included Calgary, and who had spent a happy holiday at Calgary House.

California¹ Probably derived from the US state to suggest remoteness.
A village in Falkirk unitary authority (formerly in Stirlingshire, then in Central region), some 4 km (2.5 miles) south of Falkirk.

California² Derived from the name of the US state, and chosen to suggest remoteness. The name was probably conferred in the late 18th century, although not recorded until the early 19th.
A village on the west Norfolk coast, about 8 km (5 miles) north of Great Yarmouth.

California of Wales, the. The area to the north of BARMOUTH, in Gwynedd (formerly in Caernarvonshire), so called because gold has been mined here since Roman times.

Calke '(place on the) limestone', OE *calc* 'limestone'.
A village (pronounced 'kawk') in Derbyshire, on the shores of Staunton Harold Reservoir, about 14 km (8.5 miles) south of Derby. The nearby **Calke Abbey**, an early 18th-century baroque mansion which is the ancestral home of the Harpur Crewe family, has been kept as an almost unchanged time capsule since the death of the last baronet in 1924. It passed to the National Trust in 1985, but only essential repairs have been carried out, to preserve the sense of, as the charity says, 'the English country house in decline'.

Callan¹ Probably 'place where hazels grow', Irish *collán* 'hazel-tree'.
A market town in County Kilkenny, 15 km (9 miles) south-

west of Kilkenny itself. It was founded by William the Marshal at the time of the Anglo-Norman invasion, and heroically stood out against Cromwellian forces in 1650 until not a defender was left alive.
    Callan was the birthplace of James Hoban (c.1762–1831), designer of the US White House.

Battle of Callan (14 September 1407). A battle in which Walter de Burgo and O Carroll of Éile were defeated by James Butler, 4th Earl of Ormonde, and Lord Deputy le Scrope. O Carroll and some 800 of his men were killed.

Callan². A battle site in County Kerry, near Kenmare, where in July 1261 the Irish under Fineen MacCarthy decisively defeated the English under John FitzThomas. After this the MacCarthys dominated southwest MUNSTER.

Callander Gaelic *Callader*, possibly the words that come from OCelt *caled* 'hard' + *dobhar* 'water' (*see* CALDER¹), i.e. a driving, turbulent stream.
A town to the east of the TROSSACHS and 22 km (14 miles) northwest of Stirling, on the very edge of the Highlands, overlooked by BEN LEDI. It was formerly in Perthshire, then in Central region, and is now in the unitary authority of Stirling. Its role as a gateway to the Highlands makes it an important tourist centre. It was originally built after the failed 1745 Jacobite Rising by the Commissioners of Forfeited Estates. In the first television series (1962–71) of *Dr Finlay's Casebook*, Callander played the part of Tannochbrae.

Callanish 'Kali's headland', OScand male personal name *Kali* + -NESS.
A megalithic site in LEWIS, Western Isles (formerly in Ross and Cromarty), some 22 km (14 miles) west of Stornoway. It was built between 3500 and 4000 years ago, long before the arrival of the Celts, and is regarded as the most impressive megalithic monument in Britain, after STONEHENGE. Unlike the latter, which is geared to observations of the sun, the **Standing Stones of Callanish** appear to have been built to reflect the movements of the moon. The layout is broadly cruciform, with a stone circle and burial chamber in the centre, and measures 123 m (405 ft) by 43 m (140 ft). There are some 48 monoliths, and the tallest, in the centre, is 4.5 m (14 ft 9 in) high. The stones were largely submerged in bog until excavated in 1857. In local tradition, they are said to be giants petrified by St Kieran, who was irked by their refusal to convert to Christianity. Alternatively, these *Fir Chreig* (Gaelic 'false men') were petrified by the druids.

Calleva Atrebatum. A Roman settlement on the site of present-day SILCHESTER.

Callington 'farmstead by the bare hill', OE *calu* 'bare hill' + -*ing*- a mistaken rendering of the ending of *calwan* 'by the bare hill' + -TON.
A market town in Cornwall, about 16 km (10 miles) south

of Launceston. It is overlooked by a large hill called Kit Hill (etymologically 'kite hill'), from which it gets its name. Granite quarried nearby was used in the construction of the Thames Embankment (*see under* EMBANKMENT), Blackfriars Bridge (*see under* BLACKFRIARS), and Battersea Bridge (*see under* BATTERSEA) in London.

Calne From a pre-English river name *Calne* of unknown meaning, perhaps the former name of the River Marden, on which Calne and CALSTONE WELLINGTON stand.

A market town (pronounced 'kahn') in Wiltshire, at the foot of the Marlborough Downs (*see under* MARLBOROUGH), about 11 km (7 miles) north of Devizes. It holds a Music and Arts Festival in June.

The poet Samuel Taylor Coleridge lodged with the Morgans in Calne from 1814 to 1816. The writers Charles and (his sister) Mary Lamb also stayed with the Morgans for a month in 1816, and it evidently made a favourable impression on Charles:

> How I would wake weeping, and in the anguish of my heart exclaim upon sweet Calne in Wiltshire!
>
> Charles Lamb: 'Christ's Hospital' in *Essays of Elia* (1823)

The historian Thomas Babington Macaulay was elected MP for Calne in 1830.

Calshot Originally (980) *Celcesoran*, from an uncertain first element (possibly OE *cælic* 'cup, chalice', referring to some element in the local landscape) + OE *ora* 'shore'; later (1011) *Celceshord*, with the original second element replaced by OE *ord* 'point or spit of land'.

A village on the Hampshire coast, on the western side of the mouth of Southampton Water (*see under* SOUTHAMPTON) where it flows into the SOLENT. **Calshot Castle**, on a point of land jutting out into the Solent, was one of Henry VIII's contributions to the defence of the south coast of England.

Calshot Naval Air Station. A base for seaplanes (flying boats) opened near Calshot in 1913, and later renamed RAF Calshot. In operational use during the First and Second World Wars, it was closed in 1961 (though it has been subsequently visited occasionally by surviving flying boats).

Calstone Wellington *Calstone* probably 'farmstead or village by the Calne', *Calnes* possessive form of the river name *Calne* (*see* CALNE) + -TON; *Wellington* denoting manorial ownership in the Middle Ages by the de Wilington family.

A village in Wiltshire, about 4 km (2.5 miles) southeast of Calne.

Calton Hill If the name is Gaelic, then *Calton* is from *caltuinn* 'hazel copse'; but ME 'farm in an exposed place', *cald* 'exposed' + -TON is possible.

A low volcanic hill (100 m / 328 ft) in EDINBURGH, at the east end of PRINCES STREET. On its flanks is the sub-Art Deco edifice of St Andrew's House, centre of government in Scotland, together with the Greek-revival building that once housed the Royal High School, and which was intended as the home of a Scottish assembly should the 1979 referendum on devolution have turned out differently. Around the top of the hill are a number of notable classical buildings, including an observatory, the Burns Memorial, the Nelson Monument and Edinburgh's Folly. There are fine views in all directions; that along Princes Street towards the Castle in particular is endlessly photographed and reproduced. When the one o'clock gun goes off in Edinburgh Castle, a ball on the flagpole on top of the Nelson Monument falls: this is a visual signal of the correct time (with due allowances for the respective speeds of sound and light) to ships anchored in the Firth of Forth.

> These chill pillars of fluted stone
> shine back the lustre of the leaden sky,
> stiff columns clustered on a dolerite hill
> in solemn order, an unperfected vision
> dimly gleaming.
>
> Douglas Young (1913–73): 'Winter Homily on the Calton Hill'

Cam[1] An OCelt river name meaning 'crooked'.

A river in Gloucestershire, which rises near Dursley on the western edge of the COTSWOLDS and flows 8 km (5 miles) westwards into the River SEVERN by way of the Gloucester and Sharpness Canal.

Cam[2] A back-formation from CAMBRIDGE[1].

A river in Cambridgeshire, branches of which rise in Essex and Hertfordshire, which flows 64 km (40 miles) northwards through Cambridge (from which point it is navigable) to join the GREAT OUSE northwest of Soham. It is joined to the south of Cambridge by the River GRANTA, and it formerly shared its name (*see* CAMBRIDGE[1]).

Cam[3] From the River CAM[1], on which it is situated.

A village in Gloucestershire, about 8 km (5 miles) west of Nailsworth. **Lower Cam** is just to the northwest.

Camber 'room, enclosed space', OFr *cambre* (perhaps in reference to the small harbour that once existed here).

A village on the East Sussex coast, about 5 km (3 miles) southeast of Rye. Once it had a small harbour, but the silting up of the ROTHER[2] estuary effectively cut it off from the sea. Today it is a quintessential holiday village, composed largely of a 'mess of bungalows' (Ian Nairn and Nikolaus Pevsner, *Buildings of England: Sussex* (1965)) and a holiday camp.

Camber Castle. An artillery fort built by Henry VIII around 1540 on the far side of the Rother estuary from Camber, to help repel a possible French invasion. It was originally on the seashore, but the sea's retreat has left its remains (it was dismantled in 1642) about 1.5 km (1 mile) inland.

Camber Sands. A stretch of broad sandy beach between Camber and the mouth of the River Rother. At low tide the sea retreats about 0.8 km (0.5 miles). In the 1966 film *Carry On, Follow That Camel*, Camber Sands played the part of the Sahara Desert.

Camberley Originally (1862) *Cambridge Town*, in honour of the 2nd Duke of *Cambridge* (1819–1904), recently appointed Commander-in-Chief of the British Army; changed in 1877 to (at the suggestion of Dr E. Atkinson) *Camberley*, combining the first syllable of *Cambridge* with the common local place-name suffix *-ley* (as in *Frimley*, Surrey). The reason for the change was at least partly that the Post Office was finding that the original caused too much confusion with *Cambridge*.

A town in Surrey, about 13 km (8 miles) west of Woking. Its intimate association with the military goes right back to its beginnings, at the turn of the 19th century, when the Army Staff College was established here, and the Royal Military Academy was relocated to nearby SANDHURST. Developers could see that accommodation would be needed for army families and retired officers, and were happy to build it here, among the sandy heaths and pinewoods of West Surrey.

Camberwell Perhaps 'Cantbeorht's spring' or 'Cantmær's spring', OE male personal name *Cantbeorht* or *Cantmær* + *wella* 'well, spring'.

A district of southeast Inner London, in the boroughs of LAMBETH and SOUTHWARK (SE5). Until the 1820s it was a rustic spot, a place of escape for city-dwellers, famous for its flowers and fruit trees. Since then, though, the houses have choked its fields, and it is largely indistinguishable from neighbouring parts of southeast London. In the middle of the 19th century the **Camberwell Tea Gardens** enjoyed a considerable fashionability.

In the 1960s, Camberwell was the centre of operations of the gang of criminals led by Charlie Richardson, South London's answer to the Kray brothers (*see* BETHNAL GREEN; WHITECHAPEL).

Camberwell was the birthplace of the politician Joseph Chamberlain (1836–1914) and of the wrestler 'Giant Haystacks' (1946–98; real name Martin Ruane).

Camberwell Beauty. A butterfly, *Nymphalis antiopa*, which has blackish-brown wings with a broad yellow border. It was given its name in 1748, when there were still more than enough flowers in Camberwell to attract a myriad butterflies.

Camberwick Green. The fictitious rural setting of the eponymous children's puppet drama series devised by Gordon Murray and first shown on BBC television in 1966. Notable inhabitants of the village, which was located in Trumptonshire (*see* TRUMPTON), included Mrs Dingle the

postmistress (and Packet, the Post Office puppy), Windy Miller, the village gossip Mrs Honeyman, Farmer Bell, Roger Varley the chimneysweep, Mr Carraway the fishmonger, Thomas Tripp the milkman, Peter Hazel the postman, PC McGarry and the soldiers of Pippin Fort.

Camborne 'crooked hill', Cornish *camm* 'crooked' + *bronn* 'hill'.

A town in western Cornwall, about 13 km (8 miles) east of St Ives. From the Middle Ages to the 20th century it was at the centre of Cornwall's tin- and copper-mining industries, but these went into a terminal decline, and it now relies for its livelihood mainly on assorted light industries. The **Camborne School of Mines** began its work training engineers in 1859, and was absorbed into the University of Exeter in 1993.

It is now combined for administrative purposes with its eastern neighbour REDRUTH into a single unit known as **Camborne and Redruth**.

Camborne was the birthplace of Richard Trevithick (1771–1833), who invented the high-pressure steam engine. He drove his first steam-carriage up a hill in Camborne on Christmas Eve 1801.

See also KERRIER.

Cambourne CAM² + ModE *bourne* 'stream'.

A new town in Cambridgeshire, about 15 km (9 miles) east of Cambridge off the A428, developed by a consortium of building firms. The first residents began moving in during August 1999. It is planned to include three 'villages' of Greater, Upper and Lower Cambourne.

Cambria Like CUMBRIA, a Latinized version of CYMRU, or, more precisely, *Cymry*, the land being named after the people.

The medieval Latin name for Wales, as found for example in Giraldus Cambrenis's *Itinerarium Cambriae* of 1191 (*see below*) and David Powel's *The Historie of Cambria* (1584). Thus the adjective **Cambrian** (which also means a Welsh person), and even the abstract noun **Cambrianism**:

> It strikes us as rather a pity that a civilized language should have been allowed to mar the complete Cambrianism of the proce[e]dings.
>
> *The Times*, reporting the National Eisteddfod (1866)

There is a Cambria county in the USA (Pennsylvania).

Cambrian, the. A geological period and rock system, dating from 570–510 million years ago. It was named by the geologist Adam Sedgwick in the 1830s, from the Cambrian rocks he described in Wales, where many such are exposed. The period marked the beginning of the Palaeozoic era, and was characterized by the emergence of many marine invertebrates, including trilobites, graptolites, gastropods and nautiloids. Prior to the Cambrian was the 4-billion-year-long **Precambrian era**.

Cambrian Coast Express, the. The title formerly

given to a train service running between London and Aberystwyth.

Cambrian Mountains. A mountain range in Wales, extending from Dyfed in the southwest to Clwyd in the northeast. The highest peak is Aran Fawddwy (905 m / 2968 ft).

Cambrian Way, the. The longest long-distance walk in Wales, consisting of 438 km (272 miles) of largely remote upland terrain linking Cardiff in the south to Conwy in the north.

Giraldus Cambrensis (*c*.1146–*c*.1220). 'Gerald of Wales', a Welsh historian, known in Welsh as **Gerallt Gymro**. His works include an account of Henry II's invasion of Ireland, and *Itinerarium Cambriae* ('Journey Through Wales', 1191).

Cambridge[1] Originally *Grantabridge*, 'bridge over the River Granta', GRANTA (the former name of the River CAM[2]) + *bridge*; the change to *Cambridge* (by way of *Cantabridge*, first recorded in 1086) is due to Norman influence.

A university city in Cambridgeshire and the administrative headquarters of the county, 82 km (51 miles) north of London. There was probably a settlement on its site, around a ford on the River Cam, in Celtic times. It was the focal point of roads to all parts of England (including AKEMAN STREET and a connecting road to ERMINE STREET) and is the highest navigable point on the Cam (leading via the GREAT OUSE to the port of KING'S LYNN), so the Romans established a town here (called **Durovigutum**) and bridged the river.

Since the 13th century the life and the fabric of the city have been increasingly subsumed by the university (*see below*), which is what 'Cambridge' now means to most people around the world: ancient seat of learning, the view of the colleges from the BACKS, the Festival of Nine Lessons and Carols from King's College Chapel at Christmas, punting on the Cam. These are the heritage features that have put Cambridge firmly on the tourist map. The German guide-book author Karl Baedeker may not have been an enthusiast:

> Oxford is on the whole more attractive than Cambridge to the ordinary visitor; and the traveller is therefore recommended to visit Cambridge first, or to omit it altogether if he cannot visit both.
>
> Karl Baedeker: *Great Britain* (1887)

– but there are many who find Cambridge's mixture of imposing and spacious architectural vistas and (relatively) quiet country town more agreeable than the sometimes aggressively urban bustle of OXFORD.

Nor in truth does the university have a complete monopoly on the city: it is a flourishing regional centre, with a long tradition of agriculture-related industries, such as flour-milling and fertilizers, serving the surrounding farmlands, and a more recently established reputation for research-based scientific and technological enterprise (based ultimately on the University's expertise in these areas and given impetus by the foundation of Cambridge Science Park in 1973 by Trinity College). The latter earned it the nickname **Silicon Fen**, alluding to Cambridge's Fenland setting (*see* FENS) and punning on SILICON GLEN:

> For more than a decade, the Cambridge phenomenon has been illuminating Silicon Fen by spawning a legion of biotechnology and electronics groups originating in the university's laboratories and lecture theatres.
>
> *Sunday Times* (6 June 1999)

Christopher Cockerell (1910–99), the inventor of the hovercraft, the Surrey and England batsman Jack Hobbs (1882–1963, *see* PARKER'S PIECE) and Michael Ramsey (1904–88), 100th Archbishop of Canterbury, were born in Cambridge.

The Cambridge carrier Thomas Hobson (*c*.1544–1631) is commemorated in the expression 'Hobson's choice', meaning no choice at all. He refused to hire out any horse except in its proper turn.

There are towns called Cambridge in the USA (in Idaho, Illinois, Iowa, Kansas, Maryland, Massachusetts (site of Harvard University), Minnesota, Nebraska, New York and Ohio), Canada (in Ontario), New Zealand and Jamaica.

> For Cambridge people rarely smile,
> Being urban, squat, and packed with guile.
>
> Rupert Brooke: 'The Old Vicarage, Grantchester' (1915)

> ... city of perspiring dreams.
>
> Frederick Raphael: *The Glittering Prizes* (1976)

Cambridge Apostles. An exclusive debating society founded at Cambridge University in 1826 by John Sterling, which included dons and undergraduates, many of whom later attained celebrity. Among them were Frederick Denison Maurice, Richard Chenevix-Trench, John Kemble, James Spedding, Richard Monckton Milnes, Alfred, Lord Tennyson and A.H. Hallam. More recent members include Henry Sidgwick, Roger Fry, Bertrand Russell, G.E. Moore, Desmond MacCarthy, Lytton Strachey, Leonard Woolf, J.M. Keynes and Lowes Dickinson. The Apostles have been discredited by such members as the traitors Anthony Blunt, Guy Burgess and Donald Maclean (*see* **Cambridge Spy Ring** *below*).

Cambridge blue. A light blue colour, as adopted by Cambridge University as its symbolic colour (e.g. on sports clothing).

Cambridge cheese. A cow's-milk cheese made in the Cambridge area in the form of a small oblong with a creamy top and an orange central stripe, and sitting on a straw mat.

'Cambridge Chimes'. A bell-tune devised by Joseph Jowett and William Crotch and first employed in 1793 at the

Church of St Mary the Great, Cambridge. It is used for the bells of BIG BEN, and is now more generally known as 'Westminster Chimes'.

> As the 'Cambridge Chimes' at St. Stephen's strike 2 p.m. the King will arrive to open Parliament.
>
> *Daily Chronicle* (1909)

Cambridge fortune. A term applied in the 18th century to a woman who had no wealth of her own and had to rely solely on her personal charms to attract a husband. The somewhat obscure allusion is to two key features of the Cambridgeshire landscape, a windmill and a watermill – that is, she can talk and urinate, but that is all.

Cambridge Footlights. A small theatre group (properly the 'Footlights Club') at Cambridge University, founded in 1883 and maintaining a membership of 80. The Footlights has a peerless record of placing student performers on the professional stage, former members including John Cleese, David Frost, Eric Idle, Clive James, Trevor Nunn, Bill Oddie and Griff Rhys-Jones. The Footlights' modern renown owes much to the mid-20th century success of its satirical revue *Beyond the Fringe*, which was introduced at the 1959 Edinburgh Festival Fringe (hence its name) and then moved to the professional theatre in London (where it ran for six years) and on Broadway. *Beyond the Fringe* launched the careers of its co-writers Jonathan Miller and Alan Bennett, and the comedians Peter Cook and Dudley Moore. The highly successful television series *That Was the Week that Was* and *Monty Python's Flying Circus* also had their roots in Footlights revues.

Cambridge greensand. A bed of greensand (a type of sandstone) lying below the chalk in large parts of Cambridgeshire.

Cambridge Mafia. A term of the early 1990s for a group of senior Conservatives who were at Cambridge University together in the early 1960s and active there in university politics. Five were in John Major's cabinet of 1992: Kenneth Clarke, John Selwyn Gummer, Michael Howard (chosen as Conservative leader in November 2003), Norman Lamont and Peter Lilley. A sixth, Norman Fowler, was then party chairman. Yet another of the group, Leon Brittan, was in the cabinet somewhat earlier (1981–86). A more junior Cambridge alumnus, Michael Portillo, is sometimes included.

Cambridge nightingale. A facetious 18th-century nickname for the frog, whose croaking pervades the Cambridgeshire fens.

Cambridge oak. An 18th-century name for the willow, the characteristic tree of the Cambridgeshire fenlands.

Cambridge Platonists. A group of 17th-century Anglican theologians with close connections with Cambridge University (including Benjamin Whichcote, Provost of King's College, and Ralph Cudworth), who sought to promote a rational form of Christianity in the tradition of Richard Hooker and Erasmus.

Cambridge roller. An agricultural roller consisting of loosely mounted tapering ring segments.

Cambridge sausage. A type of pork sausage seasoned with sage, cayenne and nutmeg.

> The finest breakfast I have ever had ... finnan haddock, Cambridge sausages, York ham.
>
> *Sunday Times Colour Supplement* (1970)

Cambridge Spy Ring. A popular name for the spies recruited by the Soviet NKVD (a forerunner of the KGB) at Cambridge University in the 1930s. The five main agents were Kim Philby (1912–86), Donald Maclean (1913–83), Guy Burgess (1911–63), John Cairncross (1913–95) and Anthony Blunt (1907–83). Most accounts consider the first recruit to have been Blunt, who in turn won over Cairncross, although their Soviet handler, Yuri Modin, in his book *My Five Cambridge Friends* (1994), says that Burgess was the man who recruited Blunt. According to Modin, code names for the five were Söhnchen ('Sonny'), Tom and Stanley for Philby; Mädchen ('Missy') and Hicks for Burgess; Johnson, Tom and Yan for Blunt; and Stuart, Wise, Lyric and Homer for Maclean.

Cambridge Spies, a BBC television drama screened in 2003, followed the espionage careers of Burgess, Maclean, Philby and Blunt.

Cambridge University. Along with Oxford University (*see under* OXFORD) one of the two ancient universities of England (*see also* CAMFORD and OXBRIDGE). It traces its origins back to the first decade of the 13th century, when a group of students decamped from Oxford to take up their studies in Cambridge. The first college, Peterhouse, was founded in 1281, and many others followed over the ensuing 300 years, establishing the pattern of the university as we now know it by 1600. An ongoing increase in student numbers from the early 1800s, including the eventual admission of women, led to the establishment of several more colleges in the 19th and 20th centuries (Girton and Newnham originally, although these now take men too; Lucy Cavendish and New Hall still, for women only). (For a female *Bildungsroman* on Cambridge life, one could turn to Rosamond Lehmann's *Dusty Answer* (1927).)

The principal colleges in chronological order of their foundation are:

Peterhouse 1281 ('Porterhouse' in Tom Sharpe's 1974
　　comic novel *Porterhouse Blue*)
Clare 1338
Pembroke 1347
Gonville & Caius 1348 (*Caius* pronounced 'keez')
Trinity Hall 1350 ('Tit Hall')
Corpus Christi 1352
Magdalene 1428 (pronounced 'maudlin')

King's 1441
Christ's 1442
Queens' 1446
St Catharine's 1473 ('St Cat's')
Jesus 1497
St John's 1511
Trinity 1546
Emmanuel 1584 ('Emma')
Sidney Sussex 1594
Downing 1800
Girton 1869
Newnham 1875
Selwyn 1882
Fitzwilliam 1889 ('Fitz')
New Hall 1954
Churchill 1958
Darwin 1965
Lucy Cavendish 1965
Wolfson 1973
Robinson 1977
St Edmund's 1985

Architecturally the university is, if one takes the traditional first furlong of the tourist route, along King's Parade and Trinity Street, a sumptuous showcase of late medieval, Tudor and neo-classical building, highlighted by King's College Chapel (completed in 1515, its soaring Perpendicular Gothic lines an icon of Cambridge), the imposing Great Court of Trinity College, with its magnificent Renaissance fountain, the confident and opulent Tudor gateway of St John's College, the 'sonorous grandeur' (Nikolaus Pevsner, *Cambridgeshire* (1954)) of Sir Christopher Wren's classical Library at Trinity, and, on a smaller scale, the famous Mathematical Bridge at Queens' College, which was originally built, in 1749, without nails, simply by pegging the parts together, and the Bridge of Sighs, a covered bridge built somewhat on the model of its Venetian namesake in 1831 to link St John's College with its new buildings across the Cam. Further exploration, however, will reveal the colleges' enthusiasm for 20th–century architecture: Sir Basil Spence's Erasmus Building at Queens', for example, or Robert Hurd's Second Hall at Gonville and Caius and King's College Library by MacCormac Jamieson Prichard.

Intellectually, Cambridge has a reputation for austerity, even astringency (perhaps engendered by the notoriously searching wind that is said to blow in across the FENS in a direct unimpeded line from the Siberian tundra). Not for its scholars the lotus-eating sometimes ascribed to Oxford. Its strength in science goes back at least to Isaac Newton (Trinity College). Its philosophy comes with a mathematical tinge (Bertrand Russell), or with a rigour suggestive of mathematics (Ludwig Wittgenstein). In literary studies, too, F.R. Leavis introduced a new rigour, in opposition to

what he saw as the intellectual dilettantism of many earlier scholars in this field. John Betjeman felt this draught, as he noted in the autobiographical *Summoned by Bells* (1960):

> For myself,
> I knew as soon as I could read and write
> That I must be a poet. Even today,
> When all the way from Cambridge comes a wind
> To blow the lamps out every time they're lit,
> I know that I must light mine up again.

Cambridge University numbers many of the world's leading academics amongst its teachers, and has its pick of the most highly qualfied applicants for its undergraduate courses. It regularly occupies top place in the British universities' league table, and its graduates have, like those of Oxford, exerted a huge influence in many areas of national, cultural and scientific life.

Degrees of the university are designated as *Cantab*, which is short for Latin *Cantabrigiensis* 'of Cambridge'.

The university's ancient rivalry with Oxford persists, at a somewhat juvenile level, and is projected on to a wider stage every year in the Oxford and Cambridge Boat Race, a rowing race on the River Thames for which each crew has a nationwide camp of supporters, most of whom have no connection with either university.

Cambridge University Press. The printing and publishing house of the University of Cambridge. Founded on a royal charter granted to the University by Henry VIII in 1534, **CUP** (as it tends to be known within the publishing industry) has been operating continuously as a printer and publisher since it printed its first book in 1584. Like its Oxonian equivalent (*see* Oxford University Press *under* OXFORD), it is a commercial publishing house and one of the world's largest publishers of educational and academic materials. It is controlled by a body of senior scholars known as the Syndicate.

Trip to Cambridge, A. A play written by Christopher Smart while a student at Pembroke College in the 1740s.

Cambridge[2] 'bridge over the River Cam', CAM[1]+ *bridge*.
A village in Gloucestershire, in the Vale of Berkeley, about 16 km (10 miles) southwest of Gloucester.

Cambridgeshire From CAMBRIDGE[1] + *shire*.
A largely agricultural county in eastern England, formed in 1974 by the amalgamation of the former county of Cambridgeshire and Isle of Ely with Huntingdonshire and Peterborough, and modified in 1997 by the creation of the new unitary authority of Peterborough. It is bounded to the east by Norfolk and Suffolk, to the south by Essex and Hertfordshire, to the west by Bedfordshire and Northamptonshire and to the north by Peterborough and Lincolnshire. Its county town is CAMBRIDGE[1], and other

significant centres are ELY[1], HUNTINGDON, MARCH, NEW-MARKET[1], ST IVES[1] and WISBECH.

There is a small enclave of Cambridgeshire in the City of London, at Ely Place, where the bishops of Ely had their London residence from the end of the 13th century to 1772. Under an ancient Act of Parliament, Ely Place is a private road, exempt from the authority of the Lord Mayor. A certain Jade Goody (of *Big Brother* fame) was thus not quite as stupid as she first might have appeared when she confessed:

I thought Cambridge was in London.

The county's chief rivers are the GREAT OUSE (and its tributaries the CAM[2] and the Little Ouse) and the NENE. Lying largely in the FENS, Cambridgeshire's landscape is predominantly flat, only the low uplands of the GOGMAGOG HILLS in the south of the county breaking the topographical monotony. In the east of the county is the earthwork known as the DEVIL'S DYKE[1].

... the Cambridgeshire type of landscape, the England of big villages, few, busy roads, thin hawthorn hedges, windswept brick farms, and ivied clumps of trees in corners of fields; a predictable landscape of wide views, sweeping sameness and straight lines.

Oliver Rackham: *The History of the Countryside* (1986)

In cricketing terms Cambridgeshire is a 'minor county' (the club was founded in 1891) and plays in the minor counties championship.

Cambridgeshire camel. A nickname from the late 17th to the early 19th century for a native or inhabitant of Cambridgeshire. The allusion is to the fen-dwellers who used stilts to make their way round their watery home.

Cambridgeshire Handicap. A horserace run at Newmarket in October. First held in 1839, it forms the first half of the 'Autumn double' with the Cesarewitch.

Cambs. The standard written abbreviation of CAMBRIDGE-SHIRE.

Cambuskenneth 'bay of Cinead or Kenneth', Gaelic *camas* 'bay, creek' + male personal name *Cinead* or *Kenneth*.
A village in Scotland, just north of Stirling. It was the site of an important Augustinian priory, founded by David I in the 1140s. James III, killed at nearby SAUCHIEBURN, was buried here, and the priory was an occasional meeting place for the Scottish Parliament. Little remains today beyond a bell tower.

Cambuslang 'bend of the ship [in the River Clyde]', Gaelic *camas* 'bend' + *luinge* 'of the ship'; *Camboslanc* 1296.
Effectively an area of southeast Glasgow. Although now in South Lanarkshire, it was part of Glasgow district (Strathclyde region) until 1996.

Cambuslang Wark, the. A vast religious revivalist meeting held at Cambuslang in 1742, at which George Whitefield, the English Calvinist behind the 'Great Awakening' in North America, played an important role. The Scots word *wark*, literally 'work', was also applied to such revivalist meetings, particularly this one.

Camden From CAMDEN TOWN.
A borough of northwest Central London, formed in 1965. It is centred on CAMDEN TOWN, but also encompasses BLOOMSBURY, HAMPSTEAD (including Hampstead Heath), HOLBORN, KENTISH TOWN, KING'S CROSS and PRIMROSE HILL (N1, NW1, NW2, NW3, NW5, NW6, WC1). It contains three major London railway terminuses (EUSTON, King's Cross and ST PANCRAS) and also the eastern edge of REGENT'S PARK.

Camden Passage From the Earls (later Marquisses) *Camden* (*see* CAMDEN TOWN).
A street in ISLINGTON, northern Central London, just to the north of the ANGEL. It is famous for its antique shops (including a nearby two-storey 'Mall' in a converted former transformer station for the tramway system), and also hosts an antiques market and a farmers' market.

Camden Town From Sir Charles Pratt (1714–94), 1st Earl *Camden*, who owned the manor of Kentish Town and let land in the southern part of it for building on in 1791. He took his title from Camden Place, a mansion in Chislehurst owned by the great antiquarian William Camden (1551–1623) and subsequently acquired by the Pratt family.
A district in NORTH LONDON, to the northeast of REGENT'S PARK (NW1). It had its genesis in the early 1790s, and its growth continued throughout the 19th century – slowly at first, but the new railways swallowed up large swathes of land in the 1830s and 1840s, and residential building had filled in the rest by 1900. Up to the Second World War it was a fairly poor area, with large numbers of Irish and Greek Cypriot immigrants; but the second half of the 20th century saw a return of the professional classes.

Camden Lock. The location for an open-air market, where Chalk Farm Road crosses the Regent's Canal. Its eclectic range of youth-orientated wares – clothing, jewellery, pottery, antiques, craft products of all kinds – attracts large crowds at weekends.

Camden Town Group. A group of artists formed in 1911 by Walter Sickert (1860–1942), who had painted many of his nude studies in drab boarding-house rooms in Camden Town, then a largely working-class area. In the group's first show he included two such paintings, *Camden Town Murder Series No. 1* and *No. 2*, although the link with any recent murder was more for publicity than for actuality. Other members of the group were Robert Bevan (1865–1925), Harold Gilman (1876–1919), Charles Ginner (1878–1952), Spencer Gore (1878–1914), Augustus John

(1878–1961), Henry Lamb (1883–1960), Wyndham Lewis (1882–1957) and Lucien Pissarro (1863–1944). They had no real identity of style, although most shared Sickert's liking for everyday subjects. In 1913 they merged with others to form the larger and more disparate London Group (*see under* LONDON).

Camel From a Cornish river name, *cam* 'crooked'.
A river in Cornwall, rising to the northeast of CAMELFORD and flowing 48 km (30 miles) south and then west into the sea at Padstow Bay (*see under* PADSTOW).

Camelford 'ford over the (River) Camel', CAMEL + FORD.
A village in Cornwall, on the River CAMEL, at the north-western edge of Bodmin Moor (*see under* BODMIN), about 22 km (14 miles) west of Launceston. It is one of the places identified with King Arthur's CAMELOT.

In 1988 the village was the subject of national news: a driver accidentally poured 20 tonnes of aluminium sulphate into a water treatment works in the area, and 15 years later worries remained about the event's effects on the health of the local population.

Camelot Probably from Celtic *cant* 'circle, edge'.
In British fable, the legendary spot where King Arthur held his court. It has been tentatively located at CAERLEON, at the hillfort known as Cadbury Castle (*see under* CADBURY) in Somerset and at CAMELFORD in Cornwall, near where the Duke of Cornwall resided in his castle of TINTAGEL. The Cadbury site is the most probable, although recent claims have also been made for COLCHESTER in Essex, partly on the grounds that this city's Roman name, Camulodunum, is similar to Camelot and partly because the chronicler Geoffrey of Monmouth's description of the Camelot countryside in *Historia Regum Britanniae* (*c*.1136) fits north Essex better than any of the West Country sites. Camelot is mentioned by, among others, Shakespeare in *King Lear*:

> Goose, if I had you upon Sarum plain,
> I'd drive ye cackling home to Camelot.
>
> William Shakespeare: Earl of Kent in *King Lear* (1605), II.ii

– and Arthurian poet Tennyson in his 'Lady of Shalott' (1832) and *Idylls of the King* (1859):

> On either side the river lie
> Long fields of barley and of rye,
> That clothe the wold and meet the sky;
> And throu' the field the road runs by
> To many-tower'd Camelot.
>
> Alfred, Lord Tennyson: 'The Lady of Shalott' (1832), i

Camford A blend of CAMBRIDGE[1] and OXFORD.
A name invented to suggest an ancient university city, on the lines of the now more familiar OXBRIDGE. Both were used by the novelist William Thackeray in *Pendennis* (1848–50), but Camford also features in Conan Doyle's

story 'The Adventure of the Creeping Man' in *The Case Book of Sherlock Holmes* (1927): here the university is famous for its chair of Comparative Anatomy, held in 1903 by Professor Presbury. Holmes duly reveals the secret of the professor's claim that a man can be transformed into an ape by being injected with monkey serum.

> He was a Camford man and very nearly got the English Prize Poem, it was said.
>
> William Makepeace Thackeray: *Pendennis*, Chapter 3

Campbeltown From the *Campbell* earls of Argyll.
A remote royal BURGH (1700) and resort towards the southern end of the KINTYRE peninsula, on its eastern coast. It is in Argyll and Bute (formerly in Strathclyde region). It was originally called **Dalruadhain**, and was at one time a stronghold of the ancient kings of DALRIADA. It was then named **Kilkerran**, after St Kieran, a 6th-century Irish missionary (*see* KIL-), and then **Kinlochkerran**, later anglicized as **Lochhead**. It received its present name in 1667 when it was awarded as a free burgh of barony to Archibald Campbell, Earl of Argyll. The town – a centre of whisky distilling – is on an inlet of KILBRANNAN SOUND called **Campbeltown Loch** (formerly Loch Kerran), of which the music-hall entertainer Harry Lauder (1870–1950) sang:

> Campbeltown Loch, I wish ye were whisky,
> Campbeltown Loch, och aye,
> Campbeltown Loch, I wish ye were whisky,
> I wad drink ye dry.

The locals refer to their town as 'the nearest place to nowhere'.

Camperdown Presumably after the Battle of Camperdown, a British naval victory over the Dutch in 1797; the battle was itself named after the Dutch village of *Kamperduin*.
A village in Tyne and Wear (formerly in Northumberland), some 8 km (5 miles) north of Newcastle upon Tyne.

Camperdown Park. See under DUNDEE.

Campsie Fells 'crooked mountain', *Campsie* Gaelic *cam* 'crooked' + *sith* 'hill, range of hills'; *Fells* OScand *fjall* 'mountain'; *Camsy* 13th century, with the anglicized 'fells' added much later.
A line of somewhat dull, lava-hearted hills in East and West Dunbartonshire (formerly in Strathclyde region), some 15 km (9 miles) north of Glasgow. The highest point is EARL'S SEAT (578 m / 1896 ft), but this barely breaks the monotony of the flat skyline ridge; the only proper peak is the steep volcanic plug of Dumgoyne at the west end, towering over its eponymous distillery. The **Campsies** (as they are also known) merge to the east with the Kilsyth Hills (*see under* KILSYTH).

Camulodunum. The shortened form of the Romano-

British name for the settlement on the site of present-day COLCHESTER.

Camusfeàrna. *See* SANDAIG.

Canada From the name of the North American country, and chosen to suggest remoteness. The name was probably conferred in the late 18th century, although not recorded until the early 19th.

A village in Hampshire, about 8 km (5 miles) southwest of Romsey.

Canada Water From its proximity to *Canada Dock*, a part of Surrey Docks so named because ships bringing goods from Canada used to berth here.

An Underground station in Rotherhithe, on the Jubilee Line and the East London Line, opened in 1999.

Canary Wharf From *Canary Wharf*, name of a warehouse built in the West India Docks in 1937 to house fruit imported from the *Canary* Islands. Coincidentally, *Canary Islands* – in Spanish, *Islas Canaria* – means etymologically 'islands of dogs', echoing the location of the warehouse.

A commercial property development in the ISLE OF DOGS, East London, on the site of the former West India Docks (E14). It was begun in 1987, originally by a Texan consortium and later by the Canadian developer Olympia and York. Its most notable feature is **Canary Wharf Tower** (No.1 Canada Square), at 260 m (850 ft) the tallest building in Britain and the second tallest in Europe, which symbolizes the Thatcherite 'enterprise culture' of DOCKLAND out of which it arose. Designed by the US architect Cesar Pelli, it has a pyramid-shaped stainless-steel crown.

On 9 February 1996 the IRA signalled the end of their first ceasefire (commencing on 31 August 1994) by detonating a massive bomb at Canary Wharf. Two men were killed, 100 were injured and damage worth more than £85 million sustained.

Canary Wharf Underground station, on the Jubilee Line, opened in 1999.

Candida Casa. *See* WHITHORN.

Canisp Etymology uncertain, although the first element may be Gaelic *can* 'white', from the quartzite crags on the mountain. An elegant, remote mountain in ASSYNT, in the northwest of Highland (formerly in Sutherland), 11 km (7 miles) east of LOCHINVER. Like other mountains around here, it leaps up gloriously and alone out of the low-lying lochan-spattered bogs. Canisp persists in keeping its distance and feminine charms from that marauding beast SUILVEN, 5 km (3 miles) to the west.

Canna Several suggestions have been made for this name, recorded as *Kannay* in the 16th century. The most likely is 'porpoise island', Gaelic *cana* 'porpoise' + OScand *ey* (*see* -AY). The most northwesterly of the Small Isles of the Inner

HEBRIDES, formerly in Inverness-shire and now in Highland. It is 3 km (2 miles) across the **Sound of Canna** from Rum. There is a ferry from MALLAIG on the mainland. In 1938 the island was bought by the Gaelic scholar Dr John Lorne Campbell (1906–96), who lived on the island and helped to maintain a viable community here. In 1981 he donated the island to the National Trust for Scotland.

The Gaelic poet and Jacobite Alasdair MacMaighstir Alasdair (Captain Alasdair MacDonald) was baillie on Canna from 1749 to 1751, and it was here that he composed part of his masterpiece *Birlinn Chlann-Raghnail* (*The Birlinn of Clanranald*; a birlinn is a galley). More recently, the long poem *Eileann Chanaidh* by Kathleen Raine (1908–2003) takes its title from the Gaelic name for Canna:

What are these isles but a song sung by island voices?

Canna also appears in other poems by Raine.

Canning Town Probably either from Sir Samuel *Canning*, an industrialist with local links, or from George *Canning*, an engineer connected with the building of local docks and railways; first recorded in 1848.

A district of EAST LONDON, on the north bank of the River THAMES[1], at the outfall of the River LEA (E16). It was developed from the late 1840s largely to house the workers in the Victoria Docks. It suffered severe damage in Second World War air-raids. **Canning Town Flyover**, on the A13, has a certain reputation as a traffic bottleneck.

Canning Town railway station, originally on the North Woolwich line, dates from the late 1840s; Canning Town Underground station, on the Jubilee Line, opened in 1999.

The BBC television sitcom *Till Death Us Do Part* (1966–75) was set in Canning Town, the home of its author Johnny Speight (1921–98).

Cannock 'small hill, hillock', OE *cnocc*.

An industrial town in Staffordshire, about 16 km (10 miles) northeast of Wolverhampton.

Cannock Chase. A 73-sq-km (28-sq-mile) expanse of forest and heathland in Staffordshire, to the northeast of Cannock. It was originally a royal forest and hunting ground (*chase* once meant 'a tract of land for breeding and hunting wild animals'). Richard I sold it to the Bishop of Lichfield to raise money for a crusade, and it was eventually abandoned by a later bishop. At its northern extremity is SHUGBOROUGH Hall, home of the earls of Lichfield.

Cannon Street Originally (1183) *Candlewright Street* 'street of the candle makers'. The variant *Candlewick Street* is recorded in 1241, and the earliest known apparent phonetic erosion of these originals, *Canning Street*, dates from 1480, but the modern form of the name is not recorded before the 17th century.

A street in the City of London, running east–west between the Monument (*see* Great Fire of London *under* LONDON)

and ST PAUL'S[1] Cathedral (EC4). The western end was badly damaged by bombing during the Second World War.

Cannon Street Station, towards the eastern end of the road, opened in 1866. It was the City terminus of the South Eastern Railway, which arrived via Cannon Street Railway Bridge. Its massive single-span trainshed was a familiar feature of the north bank of the Thames until, following severe wartime bomb damage, it was removed in the late 1950s. The station serves Kent and southeast London. The corresponding Underground station, on the District and Circle lines, opened in 1884.

Canovium. A Roman fort built 6 km (4 miles) south of the town of CONWY[2].

Cantab. *See* CAMBRIDGE[1].

Canterbury[1] Originally *Cantwaraburg* 'stronghold of the people of Kent', an OCelt name (*see* KENT) + OE *-ware* 'inhabitants' + BURY.

A cathedral city in Kent, on the River Stour, about 100 km (60 miles) southeast of London. There were settlements here in pre-Roman times, and when the Romans arrived they established their regional centre here, called **Durovernum**.

In Anglo-Saxon times, it was the capital of Kent. In 602, five years after arriving in Kent to convert England to Christianity, St Augustine founded **Christ Church, Canterbury**, and also an abbey dedicated to the saints Peter and Paul; ever since, Canterbury has been the spiritual and literal home of the Anglican Church and the seat of the Archbishop of Canterbury. The ruins of St Augustine's Abbey are still visible, just outside the medieval city walls.

The building of the present **Canterbury Cathedral** was begun in 1070, by Archbishop Lanfranc. The central bell-tower (known as 'Bell Harry'), a key feature of the cathedral's familiar outline, dates from around 1500. Archbishop Thomas Becket was murdered in the cathedral in 1170 by Henry II's knights: the story of his assassination was retold in T.S. Eliot's verse drama *Murder in the Cathedral* (1935), which was first performed in the cathedral's Chapter House, within yards of the scene of the 12th-century crime. In the Middle Ages Becket's shrine drew tens of thousands of pilgrims to Canterbury (as described in Chaucer's *Canterbury Tales* – *see below*). The shrine was destroyed in Henry VIII's time. The cathedral, which contains the tombs of the Black Prince and Henry IV, was badly damaged by bombing during the Second World War.

St Martin's Church, which probably predates St Augustine's arrival, is said to be the oldest church in England still in use. The church, together with the cathedral and St Augustine's Abbey, were declared a UNESCO World Heritage Site in 1988.

King's School, Canterbury, a leading public school, founded by Henry VIII in 1541, is just to the north of the cathedral. Alumni include the playwright Christopher Marlowe (1564–93), who was born in the city, and the novelists Hugh Walpole (1884–1941) and Somerset Maugham (1874–1965; Canterbury appears metathesized as 'Tercanbury' in Maugham's autobiographical *Of Human Bondage* (1915)).

Canterbury is home to the St Lawrence Ground, headquarters of Kent County Cricket Club. Heavy storms in early January 2005 deprived the ground of its most notable feature, a 200-year-old lime tree. The St Lawrence tree, which was already in place when first-class cricket was first played at the ground in 1847, was the only tree to stand within the boundary of a first-class cricket ground. Special rules were drawn up to accommodate it: a batsman who hit the tree was awarded four runs, and a stroke that cleared it was awarded six runs (a feat that was achieved only three times).

The **University of Kent at Canterbury**, often known as UKC for short, and generally referred to simply as the 'University of Kent', was established in 1965 as part of the general expansion in higher education of that period. It is organized on a collegiate system, the colleges being named Darwin, Eliot, Keynes, and Rutherford.

There is a town called Canterbury in New Brunswick, Canada, and a southwestern suburb of Sydney, New South Wales, Australia, also shares the name. Canterbury Plains, an area of rich grassland in Canterbury Province, in the South Island of New Zealand, are the source of Canterbury lamb, for long a staple of British Sunday lunches.

> To travel in Kent without visiting Canterbury is rather like eating plum pudding without brandy butter.
>
> Lord Clonmore: *Kent* (1935) (Shell Guides)

Archbishop of Canterbury. The Primate of All England and spiritual leader of the Anglican Communion throughout the world. His seat is at Canterbury Cathedral and his London residence at Lambeth Palace (*see under* LAMBETH). He crowns the British sovereign and takes precedence of all non-royals in the realm. He signs himself *Cantuar*, which is short for Latin *Cantuariensis*, 'of Canterbury'. The first holder of the office was St Augustine, appointed in 601; the 104th, Rowan Williams, was appointed in 2002.

canter. A term, dating probably from the late 17th century, for a horse's gait similar to, but slower and smoother than, a gallop. It is short for *canterbury*, which in turn came from such expressions as **Canterbury gallop** and **Canterbury trot**, denoting the pace at which Canterbury pilgrims supposedly rode.

Canterburian. Of or relating to Canterbury, and particularly the archiepiscopal See: a term used especially in the 17th century to imply (excessively) High Anglicanism.

Canterbury. A name applied since the early 19th century

to various pieces of furniture, in particular a stand with light partitions to hold sheet music, magazines, etc. It was supposedly inspired by an Archbishop of Canterbury being the original orderer of such a piece.

Canterbury bell. The cultivated flower campanula (*Campanula medium*), named after the bells on the horses of the pilgrims riding to Canterbury, as described by Chaucer in his *Canterbury Tales*.

Canterbury degree. A degree conferred by the Archbishop of Canterbury. He has held the power to grant such degrees since the 13th century, by virtue of his then office of Legate of the Pope. An alternative name for them is 'Lambeth degree' (they are issued from Lambeth Palace, his London residence).

Canterbury hoe. A type of hoe with three pointed tines at right angles to the handle.

Canterbury Pilgrims, The. A name given to various musical treatments of the theme of medieval pilgrims travelling to the shrine of St Thomas Becket at Canterbury, including an opera (1884) by Charles Villiers Stanford, an opera (1917) by Henry de Koven, and a cantata (1931) by George Dyson.

Canterbury tale. An old term, last heard of in the 18th century, for a long and tedious tale, a shaggy-dog story – inspired, it is to be hoped, by actual pilgrims' narratives rather than Chaucer's masterpiece (*see below*):

> What, to come here with a Canterbury tale of a leg and an eye, and Heaven knows what!
>
> George Colman: *Deuce is in Him* (1763)

Canterbury Tales. A set of stories written *c*.1387 by Geoffrey Chaucer (*c*.1340–1400). Chaucer imagines that he is with a party of around thirty pilgrims setting out from the Tabard Inn at Southwark to pay their devotions at the shrine of St Thomas Becket. They included a reeve, a miller, a pardoner, a knight, a shipman, a canon's yeoman, a nun's priest and the Wife of Bath (*see under* BATH). According to the *Prologue*, Chaucer intended each pilgrim should tell two tales on their way there and two on the way back. Whoever told the best tales was to be treated to a supper on the homeward journey. The work is incomplete, however, and there are none of the tales told on the way back.

Quitclaim of Canterbury (1189). A charter by which William I of Scotland reached agreement with Richard I of England that the Scottish monarch should be released from all obligations imposed by Richard's father, Henry II. Many Scottish rights were restored, and William was recognized as 'master of his own subjects in his own kingdom'. In return William paid Richard 10,000 marks to help with his crusade.

Red Dean of Canterbury, the. The sobriquet of the Rev. Dr Hewlett Johnson (1874–1966), Dean of Canterbury from 1931 to 1963, whose very public espousal of Communism made him a regular butt of the right-wing press in the 1950s. He visited Russia in 1938 and launched his public lauding of Sovietism in *The Socialist Sixth of the World* (1939). In 1951 he was awarded the Stalin Peace Prize. His sobriquet was a self-bestowed title when, during the Spanish Civil War, he said: 'I saw red – you can call me red.'

Canterbury² Possibly a nickname denoting remoteness, or an otherwise fanciful name.

A small settlement in Aberdeenshire (formerly in Grampian region), 7 km (4.5 miles) south of Portsoy.

Cantia. The Roman name for KENT.

Cantref Gwaelod. *See* ABERDOVEY.

Canvey Island *Canvey* perhaps 'Cana's people's island', OE male personal name *Cana +-inga-* (*see* -ING) + -*ey* 'island' (*see* -EY, -EA); the name 'Canvey Island' is thus tautological.

A flat, somewhat featureless island in Essex, close to the north bank of the River THAMES¹, about 8 km (5 miles) southwest of Southend. Until the 17th century it consisted of five separate islands, but reclamation work by the Dutch engineer Cornelius Vermuyden (*see also* the FENS) joined them together. Canvey Island is separated from the mainland by Benfleet Creek, Easthaven Creek and Holehaven Creek, but it is umbilically linked by the A130 and the B1014. **Canvey Point** is at its eastern extremity. Much of it is covered by holiday caravans and bungalows or by oil-industry installations (across the Holehaven Creek are the oil refineries of CORYTON²).

Nearly all of it is below high-tide level, and when it was inundated on the night of 31 January 1953, 58 people were drowned. Flood defences were subsequently provided.

Caoláire. The Irish name for KILLARY HARBOUR.

Cape Clear. A headland on the southern tip of CLEAR ISLAND, County Cork, 22 km (14 miles) southwest of Skibbereen. FASTNET ROCK, 6 km (4 miles) to the southwest, is the most southerly point in Ireland.

Cape Cornwall. *See under* CORNWALL.

Capel Celyn. *See under* LLYN CELYN.

Capel Curig 'chapel of St Curig', *Capel* 'chapel', Welsh; *Curig* personal name of the otherwise obscure St Curig.

A small village in Snowdonia, at the junction of the A5 and the road heading southwest to the Llanberis Pass and Snowdon. It is in CONWY³ (formerly in Caernarvonshire, then in Gwynedd), 8 km (5 miles) west of Betws-y-coed. It is a popular centre for hillwalkers and climbers.

Capel Mount 'mare or colt mountain', *Capel* Gaelic *capall* 'mare, colt'; *Mounth* Gaelic *monadh* 'mountain'.

A hill track from GLEN CLOVA in Angus (formerly in Tayside region) to Glen Muick and BALLATER in Aberdeenshire (formerly in Grampian region). The path reaches a height of 683 m (2239 ft), crossing hills that are part of the range called the MOUNTH.

Capel-y-ffin 'chapel near a boundary', Welsh *capel* 'chapel' + *y* + *ffin* 'the boundary'; the boundary is possibly that between the bishoprics of Llandaf and St David's.

A small village in the BLACK MOUNTAINS of Powys (formerly in Brecknockshire), some 12 km (7.5 miles) south of Hay-on-Wye. In 1870 Father Ignatius (Joseph Leycester Lyne), in an attempt to revive the Benedictine spirit within the Church of England, founded Llanthony Monastery at Capel-y-ffin (not to be confused with the medieval priory at nearby LLANTHONY). His attempt, having been made without any reference to ecclesiastical authority, came to an end after his death. The monastery subsequently fell into disuse until the polysexual sculptor, engraver and typographer Eric Gill obtained the tenancy in 1924 (*see also* DITCHLING) and set up a community of artists and craftsmen and their families, including the painter and poet David Jones (1895–1974).

Cape Wrath 'cape of the turning place', *Wrath* OScand *hvarf* 'turning place', referring to the major change of direction in the coastline here.

The northwestern point (pronounced to rhyme with 'bath') of mainland Scotland, formerly in Sutherland, now in Highland, 16 km (10 miles) northwest of Durness. On the mainland, only DUNNET HEAD to the east is further north. The lighthouse (built in 1828) stands on top of cliffs 113 m (370 ft) high.

> Cape Wrath was unimaginable. It was one of those places where ... every traveller felt like a discoverer who was seeing it for the first time.
>
> Paul Theroux: *The Kingdom by the Sea* (1983)

Capital of the Landsker Borderlands. *See* NARBERTH.

Cappoquin Irish *Ceapach Choinn* 'Conn's plot of land' (this Conn is unknown).

A small market town on the River BLACKWATER[3] in County Waterford, 15 km (9 miles) northwest of Dungarvan. It is an angling centre.

Carberry Hill Possibly 'hedge of trees', *Carberry* Gaelic *craobh* 'tree, branch' + *barrán* 'hedge, palisade'.

A low hill above **Carberry Tower**, about 4 km (2.5 miles) south of Musselburgh in East Lothian. It was the site of a battle in June 1567, in which the forces of Mary Queen of Scots and her third husband the Earl of Bothwell (presumed murderer of her second husband) were defeated by the rebel Scottish lords. Captured after her surrender, Mary was subsequently imprisoned on an island in LOCH LEVEN[1].

Carbisdale Etymology uncertain, although the last element may be OScand *dalr* 'valley'.

A battle site some 13 km (8 miles) south of Lairg, Highland (formerly in Sutherland), where on 27 April 1650 the Marquess of Montrose was finally defeated by a force under Colonel Strachan. Montrose fled northwestward to ASSYNT where he was captured, held in ARDVRECK CASTLE, and then taken to Edinburgh, where he was executed. **Carbisdale Castle**, north of the battle site, was built in 1906–17 as a residence for the Dowager Duchess of Sutherland, and is now a youth hostel.

Carcassonne of Wales, the. A nickname for the old town of CONWY[2], comparing it to the medieval walled city in southern France.

Cardiff 'fort on the River Taff', *caer* (*see* CAHER) + river name *Taff* meaning 'dark' or simply 'river'.

The capital of WALES and seat of the Welsh Assembly. Its Welsh name is **Caerdydd**. It is situated at the mouths of the rivers TAFF, RHYMNEY and ELY[2] where they flow into the Bristol Channel, 40 km (25 miles) west of Bristol. The city and a small surrounding area comprise the unitary authority of Cardiff. The city was the county town of GLAMORGAN until 1974, and the administrative seat of SOUTH GLAMORGAN until the county was abolished in 1996.

There was a Roman fort here, and a Norman castle, but Cardiff's growth originates from the building of the docks for the export of coal and iron in 1839; before that, Cardiff was little more than a fishing village. The city was bombed during the Second World War, but is now the largest city in Wales, and has been the capital since 1955. The Welsh Office was established here in 1964, and the new National Assembly of Wales began to sit in Cardiff in 1999. Other institutions include the National Museum of Wales and University College, Cardiff (more ususally called **Cardiff University**, part of the federal University of Wales), whose alumni include Neil Kinnock, leader of the Labour Party between 1983 and 1992.

The Norman **Cardiff Castle** was built on the site of a Roman fort. Duke Robert II of Normandy, eldest son of William the Conqueror, was imprisoned here until his death in 1134 after his failed attempt in 1106 to take England from his younger brother, Henry I. The castle became a home of the marquesses of Bute in the 18th century (the Butes owned large amounts of land here, and developed the docks in the 19th century). It was given a sumptuous new Gothic interior by the architect William Burges in 1868–85, and was presented to the city in 1947.

Cardiff was the birthplace of the novelist Howard Spring (1889–1965), whose works include *Fame is the Spur* (1940); Ivor Novello (1893–1951), songwriter, actor and playwright; the poet and clergyman R.S. Thomas (b.1913); Hugh Cudlipp (1913–98), the newspaper proprietor who pioneered tabloid journalism at the *Daily Mirror*; the poet and playwright Dannie Abse (b.1923), among whose works is the semi-autobiographical novel *There Was a Young Man from Cardiff* (1991); the popular cabaret diva Shirley Bassey (b.1937; *see also under* TIGER BAY); the poet Gillian Clarke (b.1937); and Brian D. Josephson (b.1940), winner of the 1973 Nobel prize for physics for his work on superconductivity. When he was elevated to the peerage in 1987, former Labour prime minister Jim Callaghan took the title Baron Callaghan of Cardiff, having been MP for South (then Southeast) Cardiff since 1945.

There is a town called Cardiff in the USA (New York), site of the 'discovery' in 1869 of the hoax known as 'the Cardiff Giant', purportedly a 3-m (10-ft) high petrified prehistoric man, but actually carved out of a block of gypsum the previous year.

Cardiff's rugby union club, founded in 1876, has contributed more players to the Welsh national team and the British Lions than any other rugby club in Wales. Its most celebrated player is the scrum-half Gareth Edwards (*see* PONTARDAWE), who is honoured by a statue in Cardiff's St David's shopping centre. In rugby union's professional era, Cardiff has two incarnations: **Cardiff Blues**, a regional team playing in the (professional) Celtic League, and **Cardiff RFC**, playing in the (semi-professional) Welsh premiership. Both Cardiffs play their home games at **Cardiff Arms Park** (*see below*).

Cardiff City FC, founded in 1899, is nicknamed the Bluebirds, the club strip being blue and white; it is said that the nickname may date from 1911, when Maurice Maeterlinck's play for children, *The Bluebird*, was performed in the city. The club plays its home games at Ninian Park, and their traditional rivals are Swansea City.

See also CITY OF DREADFUL KNIGHTS *and* LLANDAFF.

Bound East for Cardiff. A one-act play by the US dramatist Eugene O'Neill, first performed in 1916. It is set in the mid-Atlantic aboard the tramp steamer *Glencairn*.

Cardiff Arms Park. Officially the National Stadium, the Welsh national rugby ground until it was replaced by the new Millennium Stadium in 1999. Its Welsh name was **Parc yr Arfau** ('park of the weapons', Welsh *arfau* 'weapons, arms'). The Millennium Stadium, since the demise of WEMBLEY stadium in London, has hosted more than one FA Cup Final. Club rugby matches are still played on the Arms Park site, on what was originally a cricket ground.

> I went to a Wales–England match at Cardiff Arms Park once, too crowded to move, and at half-time the people on the tier above us pissed on us for being English. I tried to explain I was a fellow Celt, but had to settle for turning my collar up.
>
> Pete McCarthy: *McCarthy's Bar* (2000)

Cardiff Bay. The name increasingly used for the TIGER BAY area of Cardiff, currently undergoing massive redevelopment and gentrification, involving housing, offices, cultural facilities, marinas, etc. Cardiff Bay has also been designated as the site for the new building for the National Assembly of Wales. One of the most striking features is the **Cardiff Bay Barrage** across the Taff estuary (its construction at the expense of the local wading birds scandalized environmentalists). Plans for a striking new opera house, the so-called 'crystal necklace' designed by Zaha Hadid, were abandoned in the mid-1990s in the face of local grumbling.

Cardiff Three, the. Three men – Tony Paris, Yusef Abdullahi and Stephen Miller – wrongly jailed for the murder in 1988 of Lynette White, a Cardiff prostitute. They were sentenced to life imprisonment in November 1990 after the longest murder trial in British legal history. They were released in December 1992, after an appeal court ruled that confessions had been obtained by oppressive means. In 2003, following the emergence of new DNA evidence, Jeffrey Gafoor, a security guard, pleaded guilty to the murder.

Scardiff. A jazzy, hard-edged hip-hop album by local band Which Says What?

Cardigan The anglicized version of the Welsh CEREDIGION. A market town situated at the mouth of the River TEIFI in Ceredigion (formerly Cardiganshire, then part of Dyfed), 24 km (15 miles) northeast of Fishguard. Its Welsh name is **Aberteifi** ('mouth of the River Teifi', ABER + river name *Teifi* of unknown meaning). It was formerly an important port and the county town of CARDIGANSHIRE. The town grew up around the 12th-century castle, site of the first-known national Eisteddfod in 1176, organized by Prince Rhys ap Gruffudd. A battle at Aberteifi was recalled in a poem from this period:

> At Aberteifi they cut through falling spears
> As at Badon Fawr, valiant war-cry.
>
> Cynddel w Brydydd Mawr: 'In Praise of Owain Gwynedd' (12th century), translated from the Welsh by Joseph P. Clancy (the reference is to King Arthur's legendary victory at MOUNT BADON)

Aberteifi / Cardigan also features somewhat more gently in a later poem:

> As I was washing under a span
> of the bridge of Cardigan
> and in my hand my lover's shirt ...
>
> Anon.: 'The Lover's Shirt' (16th century), translated from the Welsh by Gwyn Williams

At the mouth of the Teifi estuary is the small **Cardigan Island**, and the large inlet of St George's Channel bounded to the north by the Lleyn Peninsula and to the south by Pembrokeshire is called **Cardigan Bay**. A district of Prince Edward Island, Canada, is called Cardigan.

cardigan. A knitted woollen jacket, buttoned at the front. It took its name from the 7th Earl of Cardigan (1797–1868), who led the Charge of the Light Brigade in 1854 (and whose commander, Lord Raglan, gave his name to the Raglan sleeve; *see under* RAGLAN).

Cardigan. A breed of large, long-tailed corgi (*see also* PEMBROKE).

Cardigans, The. A Swedish pop group with whom Tom Jones collaborated in the 1990s. Their albums include *Long Gone Before Daylight*.

Cardiganshire From CARDIGAN + *shire*.

A former county of southwest Wales, bounded to the west by Cardigan Bay, to the southwest by Pembrokeshire, to the south by Carmarthenshire, to the east by Brecknockshire, Radnorshire and Montgomeryshire, and to the north by Merioneth. In Welsh it is CEREDIGION or **Sir Aberteifi.** The county town was CARDIGAN, and other towns included NEW QUAY, ABERAERON and ABERYSTWYTH. It became part of the district of Ceredigion within Dyfed in 1974, and Ceredigion became a unitary authority in 1996.

> Cardiganshire ... is the richest county I ever knew, and the one which contains the fewest clever or ingenious people.
>> Lewis Morris: letter to William Morris, 11 February 1742 (complaining that the people of Cardiganshire are failing to maximize the potential of their country's abundant natural resources)

Cardi. A native of Cardiganshire. 'Cardis' are popularly reputed to be clannish, parsimonious and excessively thrifty. Thus, among Welsh people, 'an old Cardi' denotes one reluctant to pay for his round of drinks or a stingy person.

Cardington Probably 'estate associated with Cærda', OE male personal name *Cærda* + -ING- + -TON.

A village in Bedfordshire, on the southeastern outskirts of Bedford. It is still dominated by the huge hangars that in the late 1920s housed the R100 and the R101, two giant airships which it was hoped would be the forerunners of a commercial fleet. The R101 crashed in France in 1930, and further development was cancelled. The reserve collection of the RAF Museum (Hendon) is now kept here.

Cardington was the birthplace of the poet George Gascoigne (*c*.1534–77) and of Samuel Whitbread (1720–96), founder of the brewery that bears his name.

Cardross Possibly 'wooded promontory', OCelt *cardden* 'thicket, wood' + *ros* 'promontory'.

A large residential village in Argyll and Bute, on the north shore of the Firth of Clyde 7 km (4.5 miles) southeast of Helensburgh. It was the birthplace of the novelists Tobias Smollett (1721–71) and A.J. Cronin (1896–1981). Robert the Bruce spent much of his last years at **Cardross Castle**, where he died (possibly of leprosy):

> The gud king gaif the gaist to God for to reid;
> In Cardross that crownit closit his end.
>> Sir Richard Holland (?1420–?85): *The Buke of the Howlat* (Scots *reid* 'judge')

Care and Sorrow, Burns of. *See* CASTLE CAMPBELL.

Carew Castle Possibly 'Rhiw's fort', Welsh *caer* (*see* CAHER) + male personal name *Rhiw*. An alternative explanation with Welsh *rhiw* 'hill' does not match the flat topography of the area.

A well-preserved ruined castle in Pembrokeshire, 8 km (5 miles) east of Pembroke. A Norman castle was built here in the 11th century by Gerald de Windsor, on the site of a much older Iron Age fort. However, most of what can be seen today was the work of Sir Nicholas Carew (d.1311), with additions in the 15th and 16th centuries. The castle changed hands four times in the Civil War, and was finally abandoned in 1686.

Carey Street After Nicholas *Carey*, who had a house in the area in the 17th century.

A street in Central London, to the north of the Law Courts in the STRAND (WC2). It was once the location of the Bankruptcy Division of the Supreme Court, and in early 20th-century colloquial English to be '**in Carey Street**' was to be penniless.

Carfax Via French from Latin *quadrifurcus* 'four-forked'.

A crossroads in the centre of OXFORD, at the meeting-place of four streets (Cornmarket, St Aldate's, High Street (*see* the HIGH) and Queen Street) that formerly ran from the city's north, south, east and west gates. In Thomas Hardy's *Jude the Obscure* (1895), set partly in Christminster (Oxford), Carfax becomes 'Fourways'.

In the Middle Ages *carfax* was a generic term for a four-road crossroads, and it survives also in HORSHAM, East Sussex.

Carham 'place at the rocks', OE *carr* 'rock' in the dative plural *carrum* 'at the rocks' (*see also* HAM).

A village on the south side of the River TWEED in Northumberland, some 5 km (3 miles) southwest of Coldstream.

Battle of Carham (September 1018). A battle in which Malcolm II of Scotland, allied to Owen the Bald, last king of Strathclyde, defeated the Northumbrians, so gaining Lothian. The 12th-century chronicler Simeon of Durham reported that 'the people that dwelt between Tweed and Tees were all but annihilated', but he may have been exaggerating.

Carisbrooke Probably 'the brook called *Cary*', OCelt river name *Cary* + OE *broc* 'brook'.

A village in the centre of the Isle of Wight, on the western outskirts of Newport. Overshadowing it is **Carisbrooke Castle**, built in the 12th century as a disincentive to French raids, in which Charles I was imprisoned for a year

(1647–48) before his eventual execution in London. His daughter Princess Elizabeth died here in captivity in 1650.

> I see Carisbrooke Castle from my window, and have found several delightful wood-alleys … and quiet freshes.
>
> John Keats: letter (1817)

Carkeel Perhaps 'fort on the ridge', Cornish *ker* 'fort' + *kyl* 'ridge'.

A village in Cornwall, on the Tamar estuary, about 1.5 km (1 mile) north of Saltash.

Carleton Forehoe *Carleton* 'farmstead or estate of the freemen or peasants', OScand *karl* 'freeman, peasant' (*see* CHARL-, CHORL-) + -TON; *Forehoe* from the nearby *Forehoe* Hills, from OE *feower* 'four' + OScand *haugr* 'hill'.

A village in Norfolk, about 14 km (8.5 miles) west of Norwich.

Carleton Rode *Rode* denoting manorial ownership in the Middle Ages by the de Rode family.

A village in Norfolk, about 19 km (12 miles) southwest of Norwich.

Carlingford From CARLINGFORD LOUGH.

A small port on the south side of Carlingford Lough, in County Louth, 18 km (11 miles) southeast of Newry. Its Irish name is **Cairlinn** ('rock of the lake'). It was founded by the Vikings and grew in the Norman period. The ruined medieval castle was an important stronghold of the PALE, and changed hands several times in the 17th century.

Carlingford was the birthplace of the Irish patriot and Canadian poet and statesman Thomas D'Arcy McGee (1825–68).

The Carlingford in Margaret Oliphant's series of novels, *The Chronicles of Carlingford* (1863–6), is unrelated, being a fictional country town near London.

Carlingford Lough 'lake by hag bay', *Carlingford* OScand *kerling* 'hag' + *fjorthr* 'fjord, bay'; *Lough see* LOCH, LOUGH. The 'hag' element in the name may refer to the Three Nuns, three hills used by sailors to navigate their way into the lough.

A sea inlet in northeast Ireland, separating counties Down (in Northern Ireland) and Louth (in the Republic). It gives its name to the small port of CARLINGFORD, and is linked to LOUGH NEAGH by the Newry Canal (*see under* NEWRY).

Carlin's Cairn 'cairn of the witch', Scots *carline* 'witch, old woman', from OScand *kerling*.

A mountain (807 m / 2647 ft) in the RHINNS OF KELLS, Dumfries and Galloway (formerly in Kirkcudbrightshire).

There is a top called **Carlin Tooth** on the Scottish side of the border in the ridge of hills extending southwest from CARTER BAR.

Carlin's Loup or **Leap**. *See* CARLOPS *and the* WITCH'S STEP.

Carlisle 'fort of Luguvalos', OCelt *caer* (*see* CAHER) + personal name Luguvalos (or the Celtic god Lugus or Lug). The Romans called it *Luguvallium* 'Luguvalos's place', after the native name *Luguvalio*, and *caer* was added after they left.

A city on the River EDEN[1] in CUMBRIA (of which it is the administrative centre), 90 km (56 miles) north of Lancaster. It was formerly in CUMBERLAND, of which it was the county town (and earlier it was also possibly the capital of the ancient British kingdom of RHEGED). Carlisle is an important transport hub, and its strategic position near the SOLWAY FIRTH and the Scottish Border means that it was frequently fought over.

The Romans founded the civilian settlement of **Luguvallium** here, near the western end of HADRIAN'S WALL, and across the river from the fort at Petriana (Stanwix). St Kentigern (a.k.a. St Mungo) brought Christianity in the 6th century, but the first Bishop of Carlisle was not created until 1133. (The Bishop of Carlisle signs himself with his Christian name followed by 'Carliol'.) **Carlisle Cathedral** dates back to 1093, when it was founded as a priory church, although after fires in the 13th and 14th centuries there is little of the Norman original left.

The Vikings sacked Carlisle, then a Saxon town, in 875, and the Normans built the first castle and city walls. Attacks by the Scots under William Wallace (1297) and Robert the Bruce (1315) were resisted, but the town was taken in 1645 by the Parliamentarians in the Civil Wars, and again exactly a century later in 1745 by Bonnie Prince Charlie, only to be recovered after six weeks by Butcher Cumberland (*see under* CUMBERLAND).

Mary Queen of Scots was kept for a time in the castle in 1568, following her flight from Scotland after the Battle of Langside; her 'stay' is commemorated in the name of Queen Mary's Tower. It was in a cell in Carlisle Castle, also during the reign of Elizabeth I, that William Armstrong of Kinmont, a notorious Border raider, was confined by the English, having, against all usage and custom, been seized on a day of truce. A small band of outraged Scots succeeded in rescuing him from the castle, and rode hell for leather for the Border:

> We scarce had won the Staneshawbank,
> When a' the Carlisle bells were rung,
> And a thousand men, in horse and foot,
> Cam wi' the keen Lord Scrope along.
>
> Anon.: 'The Ballad of Kinmont Willie'

In the nick of time they crossed back into Scottish territory, and entered legend. Another piece of legendary cheek delivered by a Scot to the English at Carlisle is recounted in the ballad of the Lochmaben Harper (*see under* LOCHMABEN).

David I of Scotland died in Carlisle in 1153. The utilitarian philosopher William Paley became archdeacon of Carlisle in 1782. Novelist Sir Walter Scott married Charlotte Carpenter in the cathedral in 1797.

There is a town called Carlisle in Pennsylvania, USA, and it is the seat of Cumberland county.

Settle–Carlisle railway line. *See under* SETTLE.

Statute of Carlisle (1307). A law issued by Edward I's Parliament sitting in Carlisle. It forbade demands for payments of inflated amounts of Peter's Pence by the Pope's tax collectors in England.

Carlops A contraction of *carlin's loups* 'witch's leaps', the name of the prominent rock in the village being Carlin's Loup.

A small village on the south side of the PENTLAND HILLS, just inside Scottish Borders (formerly in Peeblesshire), 8 km (5 miles) southwest of Penicuik. C.T.R. Wilson (1869–1959), Nobel laureate and inventor of the Wilson cloud chamber, died here.

Near Carlops, in the valley of the North Esk, is Habbie's Howe, scene of Allan Ramsay's pastoral, *The Gentle Shepherd* (1725):

Gae farer up the burn to Habbie's Howe,
Where a' the sweets o' spring an' simmer grow:
Between twa birks, out o'er a little lin,
The water fa's an' mak's a singan din;
A pool breast-deep, beneath as clear as glass,
Kisses, wi' easy whirls, the bord'ring grass.

Fairies o'Carlops, the. Supernatural denizens of the village, whom the villagers credited in 1997 with removing a mobile-telephone mast to which they had objected.

Carlow Irish *Ceatharlach* 'four lakes' (of which no trace remains).

The county town of County Carlow, on the River BARROW, 70 km (43 miles) southeast of Dublin. Owing to its strategic position it was an important Anglo-Norman stronghold, and there are the remains of a castle from this period. Carlow was taken by the Irish in 1405 and 1577.

Curse and swear, Lord Kildare,
Feagh will do what Feagh will dare,
Now FitzWilliam, have a care,
Fallen is your star, low.
Up with halberd, out with sword,
On we'll go for by the lord
Feagh MacHugh has given the word:
'Follow me up to Carlow.'

P.J. McCall: 'Follow Me Up to Carlow', from *Irish Fireside Songs* (1911). (The reference is to Feagh MacHugh O'Byrne (*c.*1544–97), who gave the English of the Pale a hard time, until his capture and execution in 1597.)

The town changed hands twice in the Civil War period (1641–53), and resisted the United Irishmen rebels in 1798, the latter suffering a defeat here on 25 May.

The historian Lord Acton was elected MP for Carlow in 1859.

Carlow, County. A county of southeastern Ireland, the second smallest in the country, in the province of Leinster. It is bounded by Laois and Kildare to the north, Wicklow to the northeast, Wexford to the southeast and Kilkenny to the west. The county town is CARLOW. It is generally a flat county, apart from the BLACKSTAIRS MOUNTAINS in the south.

Carlton Curlieu *Carlton see* CARLETON FOREHOE; *Curlieu* denoting manorial ownership in the Middle Ages by the de Curly family.

A village in Leicestershire, about 13 km (8 miles) southeast of Leicester.

Carlton Scroop *Carlton see* CARLETON FOREHOE; *Scroop* denoting manorial ownership in the Middle Ages by the Scrope family.

A village in Lincolnshire, about 27 km (17 miles) south of Lincoln.

Carluke Possibly Gaelic *càrn* 'heap, cairn' or OCelt *caer* 'fort' (*see* CAHER) + unknown element; *Carneluk* 1315.

A town in the CLYDE valley, South Lanarkshire (formerly in Strathclyde region), about 8 km (5 miles) northwest of Lanark. It is in the fruit-growing area of Clydesdale, and is famous for its jam-making industry.

Carmarthen 'fort at the fort by the sea', *caer* (*see* CAHER) + *Maridunum*, the name of the Roman fort established here.

A market town in the unitary authority of Carmarthenshire (of which it is the administrative seat), some 23 km (14 miles) northwest of Llanelli. Its Welsh name is **Caerfyrddin**. Carmarthen was the county town of the old county of Carmarthenshire until 1974, then the administrative seat of the district of Carmarthen (within Dyfed) until 1996.

Carmarthen is at a strategic crossing point on the River TOWY, and the Normans built a castle here. The town became one of the most important in Wales in the Middle Ages. Long before this the Romans had built a large fort and town here, calling it **Maridunum** (derived from a British place name with the elements *mor* 'sea' + *din* 'fort'). Maridunum was the capital of the ancient Welsh tribe known as the Demetae, who were granted a *civitas* (administrative tribal area) here by the Romans around AD 75, and would form the nucleus of the early Welsh kingdom of DYFED. Later, the meaning of the name was forgotten, so *caer* ('fort') was unnecessarily added, and Maridunum became associated with Myrddin, a legendary figure who became known as Merlin. The remains of an old oak tree in the town associated with Merlin are carefully preserved, bearing in mind the old rhyme:

When Myrddin's tree shall tumble down
Then shall fall Carmarthen town.

(In fact this oak was probably the one planted in 1659 when

the town proclaimed Charles II king.) Some of Merlin's prophecies are contained in *The Black Book of Carmarthen* (*see below*), and he is said to be incarcerated within Bryn Myrddin, a hill just east of the town, where he was confined by Vivien.

The poet Coleridge visited the town in 1802, and was surprised by its appearance:

> Caermarthen, a large town all white-washed – the roofs of the houses all white-washed! a great town in a confectioner's shop, on Twelfth-cake-Day, or a huge snowpiece at a distance. It is nobly situated …
>
> Samuel Taylor Coleridge: letter to Sara Coleridge (16 November 1802)

Some 15 km (9 miles) south of the town the Towy flows into **Carmarthen Bay**, a wide inlet of the Bristol Channel between Pembrokeshire to the west and the Gower peninsula to the east.

Carmarthen was the birthplace of Walter Devereux, 1st Earl of Essex (1541–76), the father of Elizabeth I's ill-fated favourite (the 1st Earl's attempt to colonize Ulster by means of massacring the local population proved unpopular and somewhat counter-productive); and of the poet Lewis Morris (1833–1907). Bishop Farrar of St David's was burnt in the market place here in 1555, having declined Mary I's request that he convert to Roman Catholicism. The essayist, playwright and journalist Richard Steele retired to Carmarthen in 1724, and was buried here in 1729.

Carmarthen was the first Westminster seat won by the Welsh nationalist party Plaid Cymru, in a by-election in 1966.

Black Book of Carmarthen, The. The earliest extant Welsh manuscript, dating from *c.*1170–1230, which was held at the Augustinian priory at Carmarthen. Its Welsh title is **Llyfr Du Caerfyrddin**.

Carmarthen Fan. An alternative name for the BLACK MOUNTAIN and its highest point.

Carmarthenshire From CARMARTHEN + SHIRE.

A former county and current unitary authority of south-west Wales. Its Welsh name is **Sir Gaerfyrddin**. The county was bordered to the west by Pembrokeshire, to the north by Cardiganshire, to the east by Brecknockshire and Glamorgan, and to the south by the Bristol Channel. The unitary authority is bordered to the west by Pembrokeshire, to the north by Ceredigion, and to the east by Swansea and Powys. The Bristol Channel remains to the south. The former county town and current administrative seat is CARMARTHEN, and the other main town is LLANELLI.

In early medieval times the area formed part of the ancient kingdoms of DYFED and DEHEUBARTH.

> We found the people of this county more civilized and more courteous, than in the more mountainous parts,

> where the disposition of the inhabitants seems to be rough, like the country.
>
> Daniel Defoe: *A Tour Through the Whole Island of Great Britain* (1724–6)

> *Gadawodd Sir Gâr*
> *Lle na chaif ddwr pibau*
> *A dim ond clawdd*
> *(Neu fwced mewn cwt pren*
> *Ym mhen draw'r ardd*
> *I'r ymwelwyr.)*
> She left Carmarthenshire
> Where there's no indoor plumbing
> Nothing but a ditch
> (Or a bucket in a wooden hut
> At the far end of the garden
> For visitors.)
>
> Bobbi Jones: 'Shop Girl', from *Selected Poems* (1986), translated by Joseph P. Clancy

Carmel Named after the 19th-century Nonconformist chapel that adopted the name of Mount *Carmel* in the Holy Land.

A village in Carmarthenshire (formerly in Dyfed), 18 km (11 miles) north of Llanelli. There are also villages of the same name in Flintshire, Gwynedd and Anglesey.

Carmel Head Presumably from Mount *Carmel* in the Holy Land, which runs into the sea at Haifa; but *see also* CARMEL.

The most northwesterly point on Anglesey, some 15 km (9 miles) west of Amlwch. Its Welsh name is **Trwyn y Gader** (possibly 'promontory of the chair', Welsh *trwyn* 'promontory, tip', *y gader* 'of the chair'; *see* CADER IDRIS).

Carnaby Street From *Karnaby* House, built in 1683 in what soon became Carnaby Street. The ultimate source of the name is probably the village of *Carnaby* in North Yorkshire.

A street in the WEST END[1] of London, to the east of REGENT STREET. It was laid out in the 1680s as a residential street, and many of its first inhabitants were Huguenots. By the 19th century it was a street of small shops, and in the 1960s its boutiques became a magnet for fashion-conscious young people. Carnaby Street was for a while an icon of 'Swinging London' (*see under* LONDON), its name a generic term for the trendy mould-breaking unisex couture of the mid-1960s ('Discothèque-crazed tele personalities jerking in Carnaby plumage' said *The Guardian* in 1966). As such, its fame spread worldwide.

> Everywhere the Carnabytion army marches on
> Each one a dedicated follower of fashion
>
> Ray Davies: 'Dedicated Follower of Fashion' (song, 1966)

The street was then somewhat showily refurbished by Westminster City Council in 1973, but its popularity had declined by 1975 when boutiques in the KING'S ROAD, Chelsea, were attracting this type of custom. Its fame lingers on, and it remains a popular tourist attraction, although much of its stock-in-trade now falls into the plastic policeman's helmet and Union-Jack teeshirt category.

Carndonagh Irish *Carn Domhnach* 'cairn of the church'.

A village in County Donegal, 25 km (16 miles) north of Derry/Londonderry. It is the main marketing centre of the INISHOWEN peninsula.

Carneddau, the Welsh *carneddau* 'cairns, hills', but so named from the word *Carnedd* appearing in the names of the two highest peaks.

The most northerly massif in SNOWDONIA, forming the boundary between GWYNEDD and CONWY[3] (formerly entirely within Caernarvonshire, and the old, larger Gwynedd). **The Carnedds** (as they are also sometimes called) lie some 12 km (7.5 miles) southeast of Bangor. The highest peak is **Carnedd Llewelyn** (1064 m / 3490 ft), and the group contains six other WELSH THREE-THOUSANDERS: **Carnedd Dafydd** (1040 m / 3411 ft), Pen-yr-oleu-wen (978 m / 3208 ft), Foel Grach (976 m / 3201 ft), Yr Wlen or Yr Elen (962 m / 3155 ft), Foel Fras (942 m / 3090 ft) and Garnedd Uchaf (926 m / 3037 ft). Carnedd Llewelyn and Carnedd Dafydd were named after the two princely brothers who resisted the English under Edward I.

> The crests of solitude – the moaning wastes of the
>   Carnedds,
> The frightened curlew flying from a wrecked plane's
>   wing.
> The empty, perfect, peaceful top of Llewellyn.
>
>   Roger A. Redfern: 'A Boy Goes Blind', from *Verses from My
>   Country* (1975)

Carnedd Moel-siabod. *See* MOEL SIABOD.

Carnforth 'ford of the herons', OE *cran* 'heron' + -FORD.

A town in Lancashire, on the east side of Morecambe Bay, 10 km (6 miles) north of Lancaster. Carnforth Station, playing the role of 'Milford Junction', was the setting for the classic romantic tale of temptation and unrequited love, *Brief Encounter* (1945). The station was renovated to its 1945 state in 2003.

Càrn nam Marbh. *See under* FORTINGALL.

Carnoustie The first element is possibly Gaelic *càrn* 'cairn', but the name is of uncertain etymology.

A town on the North Sea coast of Angus (formerly in Tayside region), 17 km (11 miles) east of Dundee. It is the site of a famously difficult championship golf course, which has hosted the Open six times since 1931. (In 1999 the Scottish golfer Paul Lawrie won the Open here with a six-over-par total of 290.) Carnoustie is also a popular holiday centre, being one of the sunniest places in Scotland.

> Scottish golf courses were never pretty things: they were windy and lacked topsoil; they were oddly lumpy,

scattered with rabbit holes and bomb craters; they looked like minefields. Carnoustie was that way – battle-scarred.

>   Paul Theroux: *The Kingdom by the Sea* (1983)

Carnsore Point 'sandy point of the cairn', *Carnsore* Irish *chairn*, possessive of *carn* 'cairn' + OScand *ore* 'sandy point'.

The most southeasterly point in Ireland, in County Wexford, 20 km (12 miles) southeast of Wexford itself. Its Irish name is **Ceann an Chairn** ('headland of the cairn').

Carnwath 'cairn of the wood', OCelt *carn* 'cairn' + *gwydd* 'wood'; *Karnewid* 1179.

A moorland village in South Lanarkshire, on the Edinburgh–Lanark road, about 12 km (7.5 miles) east of Lanark. The Red Hose Race, which has been run annually for the last 500 years, is supposed to be the oldest foot race in Britain.

Carnwath-like. A 19th-century term for awkward or odd-looking.

Carragheen 'moss, growth on rock', Irish *carraigín*, here with reference to the local seaweed.

A village on the coast near Waterford, County Waterford. **carragheen.** *Chondrus crispus*, an edible red seaweed found on rocky shores around the North Atlantic. It is so named because it is found in large quantities along the shores at Carragheen. In Irish it is *cairgein*, and alternative English spellings are *carrageen* or *caragen*; it is also called **Irish moss**. It is used in food and medicines, and as a cattle feed. From it is derived **carrageenin**, a complex carbohydrate used as a food additive

Carraig Dubh. An Irish name for the Dublin suburb of BLACKROCK.

Carraig Fhearghais. The Irish name for CARRICKFERGUS.

Carraig Mhachaire Rois. The Irish name for CARRICKMACROSS.

Carraig na Siúire. The Irish name for CARRICK-ON-SUIR.

Carra Lough. An alternative name for LOUGH CARRA.

Carrantuohill Irish *Corrán Tuathail* 'inverted sickle', referring to the mountain's curved ridge as seen from Killarney, with the curve going the opposite way to that on a sickle.

A great rocky mountain in the MACGILLYCUDDY'S REEKS of County Kerry, 17 km (11 miles) southwest of Killarney. At 1041 m (3414 ft) it is the highest mountain in Ireland. It is also spelt **Carrauntoohil**. It provided the Young Irelander John Mitchel (1815–75) with a metaphor in his *Jail Journal* diatribe on the death of Daniel O'Connell, whom he believed had betrayed the Young Ireland movement:

> Wonderful, mighty, jovial and mean old man! … With the keen eye and potent swoop of a generous eagle of Cairn Tual – with the base servility of a hound and the cold cruelty of a spider!

There is a 'Celtic music group' from Poland called Carrantuohill.

Carreg Cennen Castle 'castle on Cennan's rock', Welsh carreg 'rock' + male personal name Cennan.

A large ruined castle in Carmarthenshire, dramatically situated on a rocky hilltop 7 km (4.5 miles) southeast of Llandeilo. The site was first occupied in prehistoric times, then by the Romans and, according to legend, by Urien Rheged and his son Owain, two of King Arthur's knights. The first castle here was built by the Welsh princes of DEHEUBARTH in the late 12th century; this was seized in 1277 by Edward I, who replaced it with the present castle. Subsequent owners included Hugh le Despenser, John of Gaunt and Henry Bolingbroke; when the latter became king as Henry IV, the castle became crown property. Owain Glyndwr's rebels besieged it in 1403, and in 1462, at the end of the first stage of the Wars of the Roses, the victorious Yorkists destroyed much of the fabric of the building.

Carrick[1] 'rock', Gaelic carraig.

A traditional upland area of AYRSHIRE south of the River DOON, bordered on the north by Kyle and on the south by Galloway. It is now in the south of South Ayrshire, and was formerly in Kyle and Carrick district of Strathclyde region (see KYLE), with MAYBOLE traditionally regarded as its 'capital'.

Robert the Bruce's father, also Robert (1253–1304), became Earl of Carrick by marriage, but resigned the title in favour of his son in 1292. Robert III (c.1337–1406), before he was king, was created Earl of Carrick by David II in 1368. One of his descendants was the poet Walter Kennedy (c.1460–c.1508) – younger brother of John, 2nd Lord Kennedy of Dunure in Carrick – who was abused thus by his fellow poet William Dunbar:

> Thow hes full littill feill of fair indyte:
> I tak on me ane pair of Lowthiane hippis
> Sall fairer Inglis mak, and mair parfyte,
> Than thow can blabbar with thy Carrik lippis.
>
> William Dunbar: *The Flyting of Dunbar and Kennedie* (*feill* 'understanding', *indyte* 'composition')

Carrick pursuivant. One of the heraldic officers of the Lyon Court (the Scottish Court of Heralds).

'King of Carrick'. The nickname given to Gilbert Kennedy, 4th Earl of Cassilis, who was outlawed following the incident in 1570 in which he roasted a certain Alan Stewart at Dunure Castle.

Carrick[2] From CARRICK ROADS.

A central-Cornish local authority created in 1974, which extends between the north and south coasts, and encompasses TRURO (its administrative centre), FALMOUTH, PENRYN, ST MAWES, as well as the eponymous estuary. It replaced the areas formerly covered by the Truro City Council, Falmouth Borough, Penryn Borough, and Truro Rural District councils.

Carrickfergus Irish Carraig Fhearghais 'Fergus's rock'; Fergus McErc was a 6th-century king of Dalriada; in other accounts it commemorates a King Fergus who was shipwrecked here c.AD 320.

A port on Belfast Lough (see under BELFAST), County Antrim, 15 km (9 miles) northeast of Belfast, and the administrative centre of Carrickfergus local authority district. It was Ulster's most important port until overtaken by Belfast in the 18th century. **Carrickfergus Castle**, begun in 1180 by John de Courcy, guards the mouth of Belfast Lough. It was taken by Edward Bruce (brother of the Scottish king) in 1316, but reverted to English hands in 1318 and became an English royal fortress. In 1690 it was taken by the Williamites, and on 14 June William III himself landed at Carrickfergus. In 1760 the French under Commodore François Thurot took both town and castle, but were forced out within a week.

Carrickfergus has a number of literary connections. It was the destination of Clanranald's galley in *Birlinn Chlann-Raghnail*, the masterpiece of the Gaelic poet and Jacobite Alasdair MacMaighstir Alasdair (Captain Alasdair MacDonald, c.1695–c.1770). As a boy William Congreve (1670–1729) lived in Carrickfergus for three years, from 1678 to 1681, his father being a lieutenant at the garrison. The father of the poet Louis MacNeice (1907–63) was rector of Carrickfergus, and MacNeice grew up here (as recalled in his memoirs *The Strings Are False* (1965)).

> The brook ran yellow from the factory stinking of chlorine,
> The yarn-mill called its funeral cry at noon;
> Our lights looked over the lough to the lights of Bangor
> Under the peacock aura of a drowning moon.
>
> Louis MacNeice: 'Carrickfergus' (1937)

Nearby to the town were salt mines; the last one closed in 1938:

> When they said Carrickfergus I could hear
> the frosty echo of saltminers' picks.
> I imagined it, chambered and glinting,
> A township made of light.
>
> Seamus Heaney: 'The Singer's House', from *Field Work* (1979)

'Carrickfergus'. A traditional Irish ballad/lament; it was recorded by pop singer Bryan Ferry in 1978, hot on the heels of Paul McCartney's love song to the Mull of Kintyre (see under KINTYRE):

> I wish I was in Carrickfergus
> Only for nights in Ballygrant …

Carrickmacross Irish Carraig Mhachaire Rois 'rock of the plain of the grove'.

A market town in County Monaghan, 20 km (12 miles)

west of Dundalk. Queen Elizabeth I granted lands here to the Earl of Essex, who built a castle; it was dismantled for building materials in 1780.

Carrickmacross lace. The oldest type of Irish lace, dating to 1820 when the industry was established in Carrickmacross. The technique involves attaching organdie or muslin to a net, cutting away some of the fabric from the net to make the basic pattern, then decorating the exposed net with stitching. Finally the net is removed from the pattern. Roses and shamrocks are popular designs. Carrickmacross lace was used in Princess Diana's wedding dress.

Carrick-on-Shannon Not the usual Irish *carraig* 'rock', but a corruption of the first element of the Irish name *Cora Droma Rúisc* 'weir of the marsh ridge', with the river name Shannon. The county town of County Leitrim, 45 km (28 miles) southeast of Sligo, on the River SHANNON. The Costello Chapel (1877) on the main street is said to be the world's second-smallest chapel.

Carrick-on-Suir Irish *Carraig na Siúire* 'rock on the River Suir'. A town on the River SUIR, in County Tipperary, 23 km (14 miles) northwest of Waterford. There is a ruined 15th-century castle here (said by some to be the birthplace of Anne Boleyn), next to a fortified Elizabethan manor house. Carrick-on-Suir was the hometown of The Clancy Brothers and Tommy Makem, who initiated the Irish folk revival in the USA in the 1950s. It was also the birthplace of Sean Kelly (b.1956), ranked as the world's number-one cyclist from 1984 to 1989.

Carrick Roads 'roadstead of the rocks' (referring to a rock called Black Rock at the entrance to the Fal estuary), *Carrick*, Cornish *carrek* 'rock'; *Roads* 'roadstead' (i.e. a sheltered stretch of water), ModE.

The widest part of the FAL estuary on the southern Cornish coast, which is fed by several rivers, including the Fal, the Percuil and the Truro (*see under* TRURO). FALMOUTH is on the western side of its mouth, and ST MAWES on the east, and to guard the estuary Henry VIII had Pendennis Castle (*see under* PENDENNIS POINT) and St Mawes Castle built. The estuary is the third-largest natural harbour in the world, and its deep waters provide refuge for ocean-going ships undergoing repairs or simply staying out of service. It is also a popular area for recreational sailing.

Carrickstown. The fictional north Dublin suburb where RTÉ's soap opera *Fair City* is set, the title coming from the ballad 'In Dublin's Fair City' (*see under* DUBLIN).

Carron Probably related to Gaelic *carraig* 'rock'.

A river of central Scotland, rising in the CAMPSIE FELLS, flowing through the **Carron Valley Reservoir**, and past Falkirk to enter the Firth of Forth (*see under* FORTH) at GRANGEMOUTH (a distance of some 30 km / 19 miles). It

was formerly in Stirlingshire and West Lothian, and is now in the unitary authorities of Stirling and Falkirk. (Loch Carron is somewhere else.)

> Thou dark winding Carron, once pleasing to see,
> To me thou can'st never give pleasure again;
> My brave Caledonians lie low on the lea,
> And thy streams are deep-ting'd with the blood of the slain.
>
> Robert Tannahill (1774–1810): 'The Lament of Wallace, after the Battle of Falkirk'

There is also a River Carron in Australia (Queensland), which is a tributary of the Norman River.

carronade. A type of light gun that could be quickly reloaded. It was manufactured at the Carron Ironworks (from which it took its name) and adopted by the Royal Navy in 1779. It saw notable service at the Battle of the Saints (1782), and was still in use at Trafalgar (1805).

Carron Ironworks. A pioneering ironworks that started production in 1760 on the banks of the Carron just north of Falkirk. Its founders were the chemist John Roebuck and two businessmen, Samuel Garbett and William Caddell. Roebuck pioneered many technical improvements, and supported the experiments of James Watt in improving the steam engine. Robert Burns visited Carron on 26 August 1787, en route to the Highlands, and was disappointed not to be admitted to the works. That night he wrote the following lines with a diamond pen on a window of the local inn:

> We cam na here to view your warks,
> In hopes to be mair wise,
> But only, lest we gang to hell,
> It may be nae surprise:
> But when we tirl'd at your door
> Your porter dought na hear us;
> Sae may, shou'd we to Hell's yetts come,
> Your billy Satan sair us!
>
> (*yetts* 'gates', *sair* 'serve')

The settlement of Carron grew up round the works, and in 1820, during the riots of the 'Radical War', there was a small battle here (sometimes known as the Battle of Bonnymuir), and subsequently three of the insurgents were hanged. The ironworks made all kinds of products, from bathtubs to manhole covers, from cookers to cannons (the Duke of Wellington would trust no other). Production continued well into the 20th century, but now all that remains of the works is the clock tower.

Carrot Hill Possibly referring to a local crop; the small farming settlement of Carrot is at its foot.

A hill (259 m / 851 ft) in the eastern SIDLAW HILLS, Angus (formerly in Tayside region), 11 km (7 miles) northeast of Dundee.

Carrowdore Irish *Ceathrú Dobhair* 'the quarter of the water' (*quarterland* is a technical term for a subdivision of a townland); *see also* CARROWMORE.

A village in the ARDS PENINSULA[1] of County Down, 25 km (16 miles) east of Belfast. The poet Louis MacNeice (1907–63) is buried here.

Your ashes will not stir, even on this high ground,
However the wind tugs, the headstones shake …

Derek Mahon (b.1941): 'In Carrowdore Churchyard (at the grave of Louis MacNeice)'

Carrowmore Irish *An Cheathrú Mhór* 'the great quarter' (for 'quarter', *see* CARROWDORE).

A megalithic burial site in County Sligo, some 3 km (2 miles) southwest of Sligo itself. It is the largest such site in Ireland, containing some 40 passage graves, the oldest (*c.*4200 BC) dating from the Neolithic, although the site continued to be used in the Bronze Age and Iron Age.

Carrs, The OScand *kjarr* 'marshy water-meadow'.

The flat and low area in the upper reaches of the River DERWENT[3], North Yorkshire, some 20 km (12 miles) east of Pickering.

Carryduff Irish *Ceathrú Aodha Dhuibh* 'Black Hugh's quarter' (for 'quarter', *see* CARROWDORE).

A small town in County Down, 10 km (6 miles) south of Belfast.

Carse of Gowrie 'water meadows of Gowrie', OScand *kjarr* 'alluvial land, water-meadow' with Gaelic *gabhar*, in the possessive *gaibhre*, and referring to the area, 'place of the goat'. Note that this Gowrie is etymologically distinct from that in BLAIRGOWRIE.

An area of low fertile land in Perth and Kinross (formerly in Perthshire, and then in Tayside region) west of Dundee, between the Firth of Tay (*see under* TAY) and the SIDLAW HILLS, the southern slopes of which are called the **Braes of the Carse** (Scots *braes* 'hillsides'). The area is famous for growing soft fruit, especially raspberries, some of which go to Dundee's jam industry.

It is a thousand sunsets since I lay
In many-birded Gowrie, and did know
Its shadow for my soul …

Lewis Spence (1874–1955): 'The Carse'

Carshalton 'farm by the river-spring where watercress grows', OE *cærse* 'cress' + *æwell* 'river-spring' + -TON. The *cress* was added to the original name *Alton* in the 13th century, presumably when commercial exploitation of the plant became important.

A southern suburb of London, in the borough of SUTTON[1], to the west of Croydon (formerly in Surrey). Its name now connotes middle-class commuterdom, but in previous centuries it was a prosperous village with a wide range of trades

and industries, including lavender and mint growing and processing and, not least, watercress growing – the occupation which gave the village its name – in beds beside the River WANDLE.

Carshalton Beeches and **Carshalton on the Hill** lie to the south of Carshalton proper.

The Oaks, one of the English classic horseraces, run at nearby EPSOM, commemorates a house of the same name, owned by the Earls of Derby, which once stood in Carshalton.

The botanist and environmentalist David Bellamy (b.1933) was born in Carshalton.

Carsington Probably 'farmstead where cress grows', OE *cærsen* 'place growing with cress' + -TON.

A village in Derbyshire, towards the eastern edge of the Peak District National Park, about 8 km (5 miles) southwest of Matlock.

Carsington Water. A large reservoir to the south of Carsington, owned by Severn Trent Water, and opened in 1992. It stores excess water from the River DERWENT[4] at times of high rainfall, and its surroundings have been landscaped as a tourist attraction.

Carsphairn. *See* CAIRNSMORE OF CARSPHAIRN.

Carstairs 'castle of a man called Tarres', ME *castel* (*see* CASTLE) + male personal name *Tarres*; *Casteltarres* 1172.

A village in South Lanarkshire (formerly in Strathclyde region), on the Edinburgh–Lanark road, some 6 km (4 miles) northeast of Lanark. Nearby is the village of **Carstairs Junction**, an important railway junction where lines from Edinburgh and Glasgow meet. The State Hospital for the criminally insane at Carstairs (opened 1952) is the Scottish equivalent of BROADMOOR.

There is a town called Carstairs in Alberta, Canada.

Carswell Marsh *Carswell* 'spring or stream where watercress grows', OE *cærse* 'cress' + *wella* 'spring, stream'.

A village in Oxfordshire, about 22 km (14 miles) southwest of Oxford.

Carter Bar Possibly 'top of the pair', Gaelic *caraid* 'a pair' + *barr* 'top'. At Carter Bar the road splits in two, the main branch towards Jedburgh, the southern branch towards Hawick, hence perhaps 'the pair'.

The high pass (418 m / 1371 ft) where the A68 (following the course of an old Roman road) crosses from REDESDALE in England into the BORDERS of Scotland, where the first town is Jedburgh, some 15 km (9 miles) to the north. The summit is a fine viewpoint, and is the site of the Redeswire Fray of 1575, celebrated in Sir Walter Scott's ballad 'The Raid of the Reidswire' (*see under* REDESDALE).

Carterhaugh The first element is uncertain, but the second is Scots *haugh* 'water-meadow' (*see* HALE, -HALL).

A tiny settlement in Scottish Borders, on ETTRICK WATER,

4 km (2.5 miles) southwest of Selkirk. It is famous as the home of Tam Lin in the ballad of that name:

> O I forbid you, maidens a',
> That wear gowd on your hair,
> To come or gae by Carterhaugh,
> For young Tam Lin is there.

The narrator explains that this is because, if they disobey, they will leave Carterhaugh without their rings, their green mantles or their maidenheads. These days Carterhaugh is a quieter, more law-abiding place.

Carterton From William *Carter* + -TON.

A town in Oxfordshire, about 24 km (15 miles) west of Oxford. Its barracks-town brutalism comes as a jolt after the Cotswold prettiness of nearby BURFORD. Carterton was founded in 1901 by William Carter, who had plans to establish a self-sufficient colony of smallholders here. This never really worked out, but the proximity of RAF BRIZE NORTON ensured the on-going prosperity of Carterton.

Cartmel 'rough sandbank', OScand *kartr* 'rough, rocky' + *melr* 'sandbank'.

A village in Cumbria (formerly in Lancashire), 20 km (12 miles) southwest of Kendal. The magnificent Gothic church of **Cartmel Priory** survives. Southwest of the village, at the head of Lancaster Sound in MORECAMBE Bay, are **Cartmel Sands**, while the vast sandbank extending south into the bay is **Cartmel Wharf**.

Cary A pre-Celtic river name, probably meaning 'stony'.

A river in Somerset, rising to the south of CASTLE CARY and flowing 39 km (24 miles) northwest through KING'S SEDGE MOOR (where it is canalized as King's Sedgemoor Drain) to join the River PARRETT to the north of Bridgwater.

Cas-Gwent. The Welsh name for CHEPSTOW.

Cashel Irish *Caiseal* 'round stone fort'.

A town in County Tipperary, 22 km (14 miles) northwest of Clonmel. Above the town rises the dramatic **Rock of Cashel** (109 m / 358 ft), supposedly spat out by the Devil when he bit a chunk out of DEVILS BIT MOUNTAIN. The Rock was the seat of the kings of Munster from the 4th or 5th centuries to 1101, when the kings handed the site over to the Church. It was here that St Patrick had baptized King Aengus of Munster in 450 – hence the alternative name, **St Patrick's Rock**. Cashel became an archdiocese in 1111, controlling the whole of southern Ireland, although its sway was reduced to the southwest of the island in 1152. In May 1224 the Scottish Aristotelian and supposed wizard Michael Scot (who had been orogenically involved with the EILDON HILLS) was appointed Archbishop of Cashel, but he declined the post a month later.

The magnificent remains on the Rock of Cashel include Cormac's Chapel (12th century, regarded as the finest bit of Romanesque building in Ireland), an earlier round tower, and the 13th-century cathedral. Over the centuries these bare ruins on their limestone crag have infused Irish poets with a mordant melancholy and a search for Ozymandiatic comparisons:

> Royal and saintly Cashel! I would gaze
>   Upon the wreck of thy departed powers,
>   Not in the dewy light of matin hours
> Nor the meridian pomp of summer's blaze,
> But at the close of dim autumnal days,
>   When the sun's parting glance, through slanting
>   showers,
>   Sheds o'er thy rock-throned battlements and towers
> Such awful gleams as brighten o'er Decay's
> Prophetic cheek. At such a time, methinks,
>   There breathes from thy lone courts and voiceless
>   aisles
> A melancholy moral, such as sinks
>   On the lone traveller's heart, amid the piles
> Of vast Persepolis on her mountain stand,
> Or Thebes half buried in the desert sand.
>
>   Sir Aubrey de Vere (1788–1846): 'The Rock of Cashel'

> Cashel and Ank'hor Vat
> Are not more ghostly than
> London now, its squares
> Bone-pale in moonlight …
>
>   Derek Mahon: 'One of These Nights', from *Collected Poems* (1999)

Other poets have had more mystical experiences here:

> On the grey rock of Cashel I suddenly saw
> A Sphinx with woman breast and lion paw,
> A Buddha, hand at rest,
> Hand lifted up that blest …
>
>   W.B. Yeats: 'The Double Vision of Michael Robartes', from *The Wild Swans at Coole* (1919)

Cashel blue. A soft, moist, blue cheese, rather like a mild Roquefort, named after the Rock of Cashel and first made in the 1980s by Louis and Jane Grubb on their farm at Fethard, County Tipperary.

Psalter of Cashel, The. A verse chronicle attributed to Cormac mac Culinan (836–908), King of Ireland (901–7) and Bishop of Munster.

Singing Men at Cashel, The. A novel (1936) by the Irish poet Austin Clarke (1896–1974).

Synod of Cashel. A church council (1171) summoned by Henry II shortly after his invasion of Ireland. The reforms introduced by the synod brought the Irish church into complete line with Rome.

Casnewydd. The Welsh name for NEWPORT[1].

Cassencarie Probably 'sheep path', Gaelic *cas* 'path' + *an caora* 'of the sheep'.

A tiny settlement just south of Creetown on Wigtown Bay, Dumfries and Galloway (formerly in Kirkcudbrightshire), 10 km (6 miles) southeast of Newton Stewart.

Castell Dinas Brân 'castle of the fort of the crow', Welsh *castell* (*see* CASTLE)+ *dinas* 'fortress' + *brân* 'crow', but possibly also a personal name.

The ruins of a castle in Denbighshire (formerly in Clwyd), some 300 m (1000 ft) up the hillside on the north side of LLANGOLLEN. The site has been fortified since the Iron Age, but the present bare ruins were originally built by Prince Madog ap Gruffydd Maelor *c*.1236.

> Dinas Bran was a place quite impregnable in the old time, and served as a retreat to Gruffydd, son of Madawg, from the rage of his countrymen, who were incensed against him because, having married Emma, the daughter of James Lord Audley, he had, at the instigation of his wife and father-in-law, sided with Edward the First against his own native sovereign. But though it could shield him from his foes, it could not preserve him from remorse and the stings of conscience, of which he speedily died.
>
> George Borrow: *Wild Wales* (1862)

The castle is the subject of an *englyn* by the early 17th-century bard Roger Cyffyn, here translated by George Borrow:

> Gone, gone are thy gates, Dinas Bran on the height!
> Thy warders are blood-crows and ravens, I trow;
> Now no one will wend from the field of the fight
> To the fortress on high, save the raven and crow.

Dinas Brân is said to have been the home of Myfanwy Fechan (*fl*.1390), beloved of the poet Hywel ap Einion, who, scorned by her, wrote the love poem 'Myfanwy'. It was set to music in the 19th century by Joseph Parry, and is now a favourite of Welsh male-voice choirs and featured in the film *Hedd Wyn* (*see* TRAWSFYNYDD).

Castell-nedd. The Welsh name for NEATH[2]

Castellnewydd Emlyn. The Welsh name for NEWCASTLE EMLYN.

Castell-y-Gwynt. The Welsh name for CASTLE OF THE WINDS.

Casterbridge. The name under which the Dorset town of DORCHESTER[1] appears in the novels of Thomas Hardy. It is most closely associated with *The Mayor of Casterbridge* (1886), the tale of the dissolution of Michael Henchard, who sells his wife and child at a fair: at the height of his career he becomes mayor of Casterbridge, in the equally fictional region of WESSEX, but he ends his life in a miserable hovel on EGDON HEATH.

Castlebar Irish *Caisleán an Bharraigh* 'Barry's castle' (*see* CASTLE).

The county town of County Mayo, some 65 km (40 miles) southwest of Sligo, on **Lough Castlebar**. The castle was in the hands of the de Barry or de Barra family after the Anglo-Norman invasion, but the town itself was founded by John Bingham (an ancestor of the doubly errant Lord Lucan) in the early 17th century.

Castlebar was the birthplace of the poet and folklorist William Larminie (1849–1900) and of the politician Charles Haughey (b.1925), three times *taoiseach* of Ireland (1979–81, 1982, 1987–92).

> Make up your mind; don't be unkind
> And we'll drive to Castlebar.
> To the road I'm no stranger.
> To you there's no danger,
> So hop like a bird on me ould jaunting car.
>
> Anon.: 'Come! Come, beautiful Eileen' (mid-19th century)

❖ castle ❖

Defensible sites were very important in the Middle Ages, and the range of place-name elements that reflect this is large, among them Irish *ràth* and *cathair*, Brittonic and Welsh *caer*, Welsh *din*, *dinas*, Gaelic *dùn*, Irish *dún*, and Old English *burh* and *ceaster* (*see* BURY, CAHER, CHESTER and RATH; *see also* DOWN, -DON). To these was added the element we recognize as 'castle' early in the second millennium AD. It comes ultimately from Latin *castellum*, and most often in Britain and Ireland the element arrived via the Norman Conquest and the Old French word *castel*, though it is possible that Irish *caisleán* is more directly from the Latin word and only appears as *castle* in English translation. The name is given to many of the great Norman and later castles that were built all over these islands, but was also given to earlier defensive structures: MAIDEN CASTLE (Dorset and elsewhere), ROUGH CASTLE (Falkirk) and CASTELL DINAS BRÂN (Denbighshire) refer respectively to Iron Age fortifications, a Roman fort on the ANTONINE WALL, and a ruined 13th-century castle on a site fortified for several millennia.

There is sometimes a sense of awkward novelty in some castle names: several Newcastles (NEWCASTLE UPON TYNE, NEWCASTLE UNDER LYME (Staffordshire), NEWCASTLE EMLYN (Ceredigion), and NEWCASTLE WEST (County Limerick) suggest this. But the word *castle* is used unblushingly to claim superior status for an 18th-century building in PENRHYN CASTLE (Gwynedd), where there is no serious defensive purpose to the pile. And at the CASTLE OF THE WINDS (Snowdonia) there is no castle at all: the name is here applied metaphorically to an impressive natural rock formation.

Races of Castlebar, the or **Castlebar Races** (27 August 1798). A brief encounter at Castlebar during the 1798 Rebellion between a British force under General Gerard Lake and a smaller force of Irish rebels and French troops under General Jean Humbert. The encounter turned into a rout, as the British cavalry fled the scene (hence 'Races'), some ending up as far away as Athlone, over 100 km (60 miles) away.

Castlebay From Kisimul *Castle* in the bay.
The main settlement on BARRA, Western Isles (formerly in Inverness-shire), overlooking **Castle Bay** on the south side of the island. There are ferry links to OBAN and MALLAIG on the mainland, and to LOCHBOISEDALE on South Uist. Kisimul Castle, the seat of the MacNeils of Barra, is on an outcrop jutting into the bay.

Castleblaney After Sir Edward *Blayney* (*see also* CASTLE).
A small market town in County Monaghan, on Muckno Lough 5 km (3 miles) from the border with Northern Ireland. During the reign of James VI and I, Sir Edward Blaney was governor of the county, and built a castle here. This was replaced by a Georgian mansion, Hope Castle, now a restaurant.

Castle Boterel. The fictional name adopted by Thomas Hardy for BOSCASTLE, as in *A Pair of Blue Eyes* (1873).

Castle Bromwich *Castle* from a local 12th-century earthwork (*see* CASTLE); *Bromwich* 'dwelling or farm where broom grows', OE *brom* 'broom' + *wic* (*see* WICK).
A northeastern suburb (pronounced 'brommidge' or, less commonly nowadays, 'brummidge') of BIRMINGHAM. The giant Morris Motors plant here turned out thousands of aircraft (including Spitfires) for the RAF during the Second World War. Jaguar cars are now assembled here.
See also WEST BROMWICH.

Castle Campbell After the *Campbell* earls of Argyll.
A well-preserved and dramatically situated castle ruin standing above the town of DOLLAR in the OCHIL HILLS of Clackmannanshire (formerly in Central region). The castle takes its name from the Campbell family, who acquired it by marriage in the 15th century. At this stage it was known, according to a papal bull of 1466 (the earliest record), as 'a tower of the place of Glowm'. The Campbell Earl of Argyll who built the great tower of the present structure obtained an Act of the Scottish Parliament in 1489 to change the name to Castle Campbell. Further additions to the castle were made over the following two centuries. In 1645 the castle was burned by the Marquess of Montrose, a bitter enemy of the Marquess of Argyll.
The original name of the castle – the **Castle of Glowme** or **Castle Gloom** – appears to have inspired the local topographical nomenclature. The Burn of Care and the Burn of Sorrow meet below the castle, then tumble down a gorge towards Dollar – the name of which romantically inclined visitors have interpreted as deriving from 'dolour'. Overlooking the castle is Gloom Hill, on top of which witches were once supposed to meet, and at its foot is the Wizard's Stone, where it is reputed that a warlock was burnt.

Castle Cary *Castle* from the local Norman CASTLE; *Cary* from the River CARY.
A town in Somerset, near the source of the River CARY, about 16 km (10 miles) southeast of Glastonbury.

Castle Combe *Castle* from the local Norman CASTLE; *Combe* see -COMBE, COOMBE.
A village in Wiltshire, in the wooded valley of the By Brook, about 7 km (4.5 miles) northwest of Chippenham. The conformation of its weavers' cottages in golden Cotswold stone (it was once a weaving centre), its three-arched bridge over the winding stream, its church, its medieval market cross and so forth fit it uniquely for the top of a chocolate box, and in 1962 it was officially designated the prettiest village in England. In 1966 it appeared in the film *Dr Doolittle*, heavily disguised as a seaport. A motor-racing track is situated to the east of the village.

Castlecomer Irish *Caisleán an Chomair* 'castle of the confluence' (referring to the Anglo-Norman castle where a tributary joins the River Dinin); *see also* CASTLE.
A small market town in County Kilkenny, some 20 km (12 miles) west of Carlow. There was an Anglo-Norman castle here, and the area was granted to Sir Christopher Wandesford in 1635. The town expanded when he brought in English settlers to mine the local coalfield (no longer exploited). The castle he built was taken by Confederate Catholics in 1641 at the start of the Civil Wars, but retaken the following year. The town was partly burnt by the 1798 (United Irishmen) rebels.

Castle Donington *Castle* from a former Norman castle here (*see* CASTLE); *Donington* 'estate associated with Dun(n) or Dun(n)a', OE male personal name *Dun(n)* or *Dun(n)a* + -ING + -TON.
A town in Leicestershire, about 10 km (6 miles) northwest of Loughborough, just to the west of the M1. The latter, together with the local motor-racing and motorcycle-racing circuit at **Donington Park** (home of the Donington Collection of historic racing cars) and Nottingham East Midlands airport about 1.5 km (1 mile) to the southeast, put it amongst England's less peaceful localities.

Castle Douglas After Sir William *Douglas*.
A market town formerly in Kirkcudbrightshire, now in Dumfries and Galloway, some 25 km (16 miles) southwest of the town of Dumfries. It was originally called **Causewayend** (from a causeway extending into nearby Carlingwark Loch), then was known as **Carlingwark**, but when it

was bought by Sir William Douglas of Gelston, a wealthy merchant, in 1789, Douglas named it after himself. There is no castle in the town, but nearby is THREAVE CASTLE. Castle Douglas was the home of Joseph Train, the antiquary who was an important source of material for the novels of Sir Walter Scott.

Castle Drogo *Drogo* from a 12th-century landowner, French *Drew* or Latin *Drogo*, whose name was revived by the builder of the house.

A towered and battlemented house in Devon, overlooking the valley of the River TEIGN, on the northeastern edge of DARTMOOR, 1.5 km (1 mile) southwest of DREWSTEIGN-TON. Designed by Sir Edwin Lutyens for the tea magnate Julius Drewe, it was completed in 1930. It sits on a 275-m (900-ft) high granite rock commanding wide views over Dartmoor.

Castleford 'ford by the Roman fort', OE *ceaster* (*see* CHESTER) + FORD.

A former mining town in West Yorkshire, 12 km (7.5 miles) northeast of Wakefield, lying at the confluence of the rivers AIRE and CALDER[2]. The Romans built the fort of **Lagentium** here, on WATLING STREET[1].

Castleford was the birthplace of the sculptor Henry Moore (1898–1986); as a boy Moore was so impressed by the local slag heaps that he compared them to the Pyramids, saying they had 'as big a monumentability as any mountain. Monumentability has always been important to me.'

Castleford's rugby league team, founded in 1926, competes in rugby league's Super League as **Castleford Tigers**.

Castle Gloom. *See* CASTLE CAMPBELL.

Castlegregory Irish *Caisleán Ghriaire* 'Gregory's castle', after *Gregory* Hoare (*see also* CASTLE).

A village on the north side of Dingle peninsula (*see under* DINGLE), County Kerry, 22 km (14 miles) west of Tralee. It was named after Gregory Hoare, who built a castle here in the early 16th century. In 1580 Lord Deputy Grey, accompanied by Sir Walter Raleigh and the poet Edmund Spenser, stayed at the castle, then in the hands of Gregory's son Black Hugh. They were on their way to attack the Spanish and Italians at Fort-del-Oro (Dún an Óir) near SMERWICK, and it is said that Black Hugh's wife, reluctant to give hospitality to the English, knocked the bungs out of all the wine kegs so that her visitors would remain thirsty. Black Hugh flew into a rage and slew her, and died himself the following day.

Castle Hedingham *see* SIBLE HEDINGHAM.

A village in Essex, about 13 km (8 miles) north of Braintree. The rectangular stone keep of **Hedingham Castle** (built *c*.1140 by Aubrey de Vere) is a fine example of Norman military architecture. The village of **Sible Hedingham** lies just to the southwest.

Castle Howard After Charles *Howard*, 3rd Earl of Carlisle, for whom it was built.

A vast and magnificent baroque country house in North Yorkshire, 8 km (5 miles) east of Malton, among the HOWARDIAN HILLS. It was designed by architect and playwright Sir John Vanbrugh with technical assistance from the architect Nicholas Hawksmoor, and was built mainly between 1701 and 1712. The expansive and beautifully landscaped grounds also feature buildings by the two architects. When novelist Horace Walpole (1717–97) first saw the house he was overwhelmed:

> Nobody informed me that at one view I should see a palace, a town, a fortified city, temples on high places.

The house provided a fine setting for a BBC television production of *Twelfth Night* in 1978, and more famously played the part of Brideshead in the 1981 ITV dramatization of Evelyn Waugh's *Brideshead Revisited*.

Castle Island. *See under* LOUGH KEY.

Castleisland Referring to the ruined 13th-century castle (*see also* CASTLE); *see also* ISLE.

A small market town on the River Maine in County Kerry, some 15 km (9 miles) southeast of Tralee. Its Irish name is **Oileán Ciarraí** ('island of Kerry'). Nearby are the stalagtited and stalagmited Crag Caves, discovered only in 1983 and now open to the public.

Castlemaine Irish *Caisleán na Mainge* 'castle of the River Maine' (*see also* CASTLE).

A small town in County Kerry, 12 km (7.5 miles) south of Tralee. There was a Desmond Castle here, destroyed by Cromwellian forces. Just to the west, the River Maine enters the sheltered estuary of **Castlemaine Harbour**, a refuge for wildfowl such as brent geese.

Castlemaine was, according to the ballad, the home of the wild colonial boy, thought to have been an admixture of the 19th-century Irish-born Australian bushrangers Jack Donahue and Jack Dowling:

> There was a wild colonial boy,
> Jack Duggan was his name.
> He was born and bred in Ireland
> In a town called Castlemaine.
> He was his father's only son,
> His mother's pride and joy,
> And dearly did his parents love
> This wild colonial boy.
>
> Anon.: 'The Wild Colonial Boy'

A further Australian connection is the town of Castlemaine in Australia (Victoria), original home of the Castlemaine Brewery, set up in 1859 by Nicholas and Edwin

Fitzgerald, sons of an Irish brewer. The brewery is best known for its XXXX lager.

Castlemilk From the castle beside the River Mylk (possibly meaning 'milky river') on the former Dumfriesshire lands of the Stuart family; when the family moved their main residence here in 1579 they brought the name Castlemilk with them.

An area of southern GLASGOW near Rutherglen. The 13th-century castle was succeeded by Cassilton Tower (begun 1460), where Mary Queen of Scots spent the night in 1568 on the eve of her final defeat at LANGSIDE. Cassilton Tower became the core of **Castlemilk House**, demolished by Glasgow Corporation in 1969, to whom the last Stuart laird had sold the estate in 1938. The area was largely farmland until the Corporation began building a massive housing estate in 1953, with many high-rises being added in the 1960s. The usual decline subsequently set in, although in recent years there has been some major regeneration.

Castle O'er Probably 'grey castle', Gaelic *caisteal odhar*.

A small village in Dumfries and Galloway (formerly in Dumfriesshire), 13 km (8 miles) northwest of Langholm. It is surrounded by the extensive **Castle O'er Forest**, popular with rally drivers.

Castle of Mey. *See under* MEY.

Castle of the Winds. A natural rock formation on the summit plateau of Glyder Fach, Snowdonia (*see under* the GLYDERS), consisting of a collection of large stone spikes, somewhat resembling a fantastical castle. In Welsh it is **Castell-y-Gwynt**.

Castle Point A modern name, possibly from the ruined Hadleigh Castle (*see under* HADLEIGH[1]), which is approximately at the centre of the area, and almost certainly its most interesting feature.

A local authority and parliamentary constituency on the south Essex coast, between Basildon to the west and Southend-on-Sea to the east. Its main centre is BENFLEET.

Castle Rackrent. A fictional big house in Ireland, which provides the title for the best-known novel by Maria Edgeworth, published in 1800. The story concerns the decline in the fortunes of three generations of Rackrents, members of the Protestant Ascendancy, and is narrated by their steward, Thady Quirk. Legally speaking, 'rack-rent' is the annual rent that can reasonably be charged for a property, but colloquially 'rack-rent' is any rent that is 'racked' (i.e. stretched) to an excessively high amount.

Castlerea Irish *An Caisleán Riabhach* 'the grey castle' (nothing of this remains); *see also* CASTLE.

A small market town in County Roscommon, 32 km (20 miles) southwest of Carrick-on-Shannon. It is also spelt **Castlereagh**. Castlerea was the birthplace of Sir William Wilde (1815–76), antiquarian and father of Oscar.

Castlereagh[1] Irish *An Caisleán Riabhach* 'the grey castle' (*see also* CASTLE).

A local authority district taking in some of the suburbs of BELFAST, such as DUNDONALD and Newtonbreda.

Castlereagh[2]. An alternative spelling for CASTLEREA.

Castlerigg Stone Circle 'castle ridge', CASTLE + OScand *hryggr* ME *rigg* 'ridge'. It takes its name from the hill to the south called Castlerigg Fell.

An early Bronze Age stone circle (*c*.5000–4000 BC) in the LAKE DISTRICT, Cumbria (formerly in Cumberland), 2 km (1.2 miles) east of Keswick. There are 38 stones in the outer circle, and a further 10 in an inner rectangle, and it is stunningly situated, surrounded by some of the great peaks of Lakeland, including HELVELLYN, BLENCATHRA and SKIDDAW. It probably had a calendrical function.

Castle Rising *Castle* from the local Norman CASTLE; *Rising* probably '(settlement of) Risa's people', OE male personal name *Risa* + *-inga-* (*see* -ING); alternatively, 'dwellers in the brushwood', OE *hris* 'brushwood' + *-inga-* (*see* -ING).

A town in Norfolk, on the River Babingley, at the southeastern corner of the WASH, about 5 km (3 miles) northeast of King's Lynn. It was once a seaport, but it is now about 6.5 km (4 miles) inland, and KING'S LYNN has displaced it in importance. **Castle Rising Castle**, still largely intact, was built in 1150. Its massive keep is one of the largest ever erected in England. Edward III kept his mother, Queen Isabella, a prisoner here for 30 years for her part in the murder of his father, Edward II. Her ghost may, it is said, still be heard screaming.

Castle Rock of Triermain *Castle Rock* is self-explanatory; *Triermain* is Welsh *tref yr maen* 'house of the rock' (*see* TRE-).

A great crag in the northern Lake District, Cumbria (formerly in Cumberland), just north of Thirlmere and towering above the Penrith road. It features in Sir Walter Scott's poem *The Bridal of Triermain* (1813), recounting the quest of Sir Roland de Vaux, Baron of Triermain, for Gyneth. She is a daughter of King Arthur, who in the poem visits the fairy fortress on Castle Rock. The poem includes the oft-repeated line, 'But answer came there none'; the poet Samuel Taylor Coleridge dismissed the whole thing as a 'sleeping canter'.

Castleton 'farmstead or village by a castle', ME *castel* (*see* CASTLE) + -TON.

A village in Derbyshire, in the HIGH PEAK, in the Hope Valley, about 16 km (10 miles) southeast of Glossop. It is encircled by hills, and overlooked by the ruins of **Peveril Castle**, from which it gets its name. The castle was begun by William I's illegimate son William Peveril, to protect royal hunting rights in the forest, which at that time covered much of the High Peak. The keep was added by Henry II.

It is the scene of Sir Walter Scott's *Peveril of the Peak* (*see under* PEAK DISTRICT).

Beneath and around Castleton are some of the Peak District's best-known caves, including the BLUE JOHN CAVERN, Peak Cavern (*see under* PEAK DISTRICT), SPEEDWELL CAVERN and the TREAK CLIFF Caverns.

On Oak Apple Day (29 May), the villagers of Castleton hold a garland ceremony, in which a 'king' and a 'lady' process on horseback, the king wearing a large bell-shaped garland of wild and garden flowers, made by each of the village's pubs in turn.

Castletown Referring to *Castle* Rushen, which dominates the town (*see also* CASTLE).

A town in the south of the ISLE OF MAN, 14 km (8.5 miles) southwest of Douglas. It was the island's capital from the 12th century to 1869, when DOUGLAS, with its bigger harbour, took over. The well-preserved **Castle Rushen** (13th century) was the home of the Tynwald (the island's parliament) after it left its outdoor gathering-place on TYNWALD HILL, and lieutenant-governors are still installed here. Castletown is home to King William's College, founded in 1833. Every year since 1904 the school has set its pupils a famously obscure and difficult general knowledge quiz, introduced by the apposite Latin words: *Scire ubi aliquid invenire possis, ea demum maxima pars eruditionis est* ('To know where you can find something is the greatest part of learning').

Castletown Bearhaven or **Bere**. *See under* BEARA.

Castletown House. *See under* CELBRIDGE.

Castletownshend From the CASTLE built here in the 17th century by Colonel Richard *Townshend*.

A village in County Cork, 8 km (5 miles) southeast of Skibbereen. Its Irish name is **Baile an Chaisleáin** ('town of the castle'). Castletownshend was the home of Edith Somerville (1859–1949), who collaborated with her cousin Violet Martin (1862–1915) as 'Somerville and Ross' on *Some Experiences of an Irish R.M.* (1899) and *Further Experiences of an Irish R.M.* (1908), tales of foxhunting and goings-on in and around the big house. The two authors are buried side by side in the village.

Castleweary 'west enclosure', Gaelic *caiseal* 'fortification, enclosure' + *iarach* 'west'.

A small settlement in Teviotdale, Scottish Borders (formerly in Roxburghshire), 15 km (9 miles) southwest of Hawick.

Castlewellan Irish *Caisleán Uidhilín* 'castle of Uidhilín' (*see also* CASTLE).

A small town in County Down, 5 km (3 miles) northwest of Newcastle. Nearby **Castlewellan Forest Park** is home to the National Arboretum, centred on the walled Annesley Garden, built in 1740. The forest park also has the Peace

Maze, opened in 2001 and said to be the largest and longest hedge maze in the world.

Castor 'Roman fort' (*see* CHESTER).

A village in Peterborough unitary authority (formerly in Northamptonshire), 5 km (3 miles) west of Peterborough. About 5 km (3 miles) north of the village, between AILSWORTH and HELPSTON, lies **Castor Hanglands** (from ME *hangand*, 'wooded slope' (OE *hangra*)), an area of open heathland managed by English Nature and including four distinct habitats: woodland, grassland, scrub and wetland. Now a National Nature Reserve (NNR), the area was much loved by the poet John Clare (*see* Northamptonshire Poet *under* NORTHAMPTONSHIRE), who knew it as EMMONSAILS HEATH.

Cataractonium. A Roman fort built near the Yorkshire town of CATTERICK.

Cat Bells Etymology unknown; the name is first recorded in the 18th century.

An attractive hill (452 m / 1481 ft) on the ridge on the western side of BORROWDALE, Cumbria (formerly in Cumberland), 3 km (2 miles) southwest of Keswick.

Catbrain '(land with the appearance of) cat-brain', a common, if somewhat gruesome, dialectal term for soil composed of clay mixed with pebbles.

A village in South Gloucestershire, about 6 km (4 miles) north of Bristol.

Catchall *Catch*- perhaps 'a chase, hunting park', ME *cach*, from *cacchen* 'to hunt'.

A village in Cornwall, about 5 km (3 miles) southwest of Penzance.

Caterham Probably 'homestead or enclosure at a hill called Cadeir', OCelt *cadeir* 'chair', metaphorically 'high place' (*see* CADER IDRIS) + OE *ham* 'homestead' or *hamm* 'enclosure' (*see* HAM); alternatively, the first element could represent the OE male personal name *Catta*.

A commuter town in Surrey, just within the M25, about 10 km (6 miles) south of CROYDON. Its full name of **Caterham-on-the-Hill** betrays its topography, as does its etymology.

Catfirth Possibly 'cat bay', OScand *fjorthr* 'firth, bay' + OE *catt* 'cat'.

A small settlement on Mainland, Shetland, 13 km (8 miles) north of Lerwick.

Catford 'ford frequented by wildcats', OE *catt* 'cat' + -FORD.

A district of southeast London, in the borough of LEWISHAM (SE6). Until the first half of the 19th century it was a relatively quiet rural hamlet, but the coming of the railway in 1857 accelerated its envelopment by suburbia. The ford referred to in its name was across the River Ravensbourne, which still runs through the area (there is now a bridge at the site of the original ford).

The Decadent poet Ernest Dowson (1867–1900), whose 'Cynara' (1896) contained the phrase 'gone with the wind', providing the title for Margaret Mitchell's epic novel (1936), died in Catford of a romantic mixture of tuberculosis and absinthe addiction. The cricket writer E.W. Swanton (1907–2000) was born here.

The name 'Catford' seems to have the unfortunate property of conjuring up urban ennui and futility (Spike Milligan, who was brought up in the area, is reported to have exclaimed 'Christ! I must be bored. I just thought of Catford').

Cathair na Mart. The Irish name for WESTPORT.

Cathair Saidhbhín. The Irish name for CAHIRCIVEEN.

Cathedin Possibly 'cats' fort', Welsh *cath* 'cat' + *din* 'fort'.
A village in Powys (formerly in Brecknockshire), some 11 km (7 miles) southeast of Brecon.

Cathleen ni Houlihan. *See* KATHLEEN NI HOULIHAN.

Cat Law Possibly 'hill of the battle' or 'cat hill', *Cat* Gaelic *cath* 'battle' or *cat* 'cat'; *Law* Scots, from OE *hlaw* 'mound, conical hill' (*see* LAW, LOW). An early form *Carnecaithla* (1458) suggests a cairn might have been raised here to commemorate this unknown battle. HILL OF CAT, also in Angus, may have a similar etymology.
A hill (678 m / 2224 ft) between GLEN PROSEN and GLEN ISLA, in Angus (formerly in Tayside), 10 km (6 miles) northwest of Kirriemuir.

Catlowdy 'dirty little stream', ME *cac* 'dung' + *lady* a nickname for a small stream.
A village in Cumbria, just south of the Scottish border, 17 km (11 miles) northeast of Gretna.

Cato Street Named after the Roman statesman *Cato* (234–149 BC), who was the first important Latin prose author (the similarly inspired Homer Street is nearby).
A street in West London (W1), between MARYLEBONE and PADDINGTON, just to the east of the Edgware Road (*see under* EDGWARE).

Cato Street Conspiracy. A plot (led by the radical Arthur Thistlewood) to assassinate Lord Liverpool's cabinet (including the Tory foreign secretary Lord Castlereagh) at dinner at the house of Lord Harrowby on 20 February 1820, and thereafter to set up a provisional government. The plotters were apprehended as they gathered in a stable in Cato Street, and five of them (including Thistlewood) were later hanged. Cato Street was subsequently renamed Horace Street, after another Roman writer, but it has since reverted to its original name.

Catstycam. *See under* HELVELLYN.

Catterick 'waterfall', Latin *cataracta*, although this was apparently a mishearing of an OCelt name meaning 'fort ramparts'.

A village in North Yorkshire, some 8 km (5 miles) southeast of Richmond. Nearby are the remains of the Roman fort of **Cataractonium** (on DERE STREET), and **Catterick Racecourse**. The village gave its name to the vast **Catterick Camp**, 8 km (5 miles) to the west, familiar to generations of troops in training. It was established before the First World War at the suggestion of Lord Baden-Powell, and today the Army claims it as the largest 'military settlement' in Europe.

In 2002 archaeologists reported that they had dug up the body of a 4th-century AD tranvestite eunuch priest of the cult of Cybele at Catterick.

Battle of Catterick (*c*.580–600). A battle in which the Three Hundred, an elite of British warriors who had spent a year feasting and drinking at the court of Mynyddog Mwynfawr at Dineiddyn (Edinburgh), were wiped out by the Anglo-Saxons at Catraeth (Catterick). The battle was celebrated by the contemporary poet Aneirin in *The Gododdin*:

> Of those who met over flowing drink
> Only three escaped from the fury of battle …

The battle continues to resonate down the centuries:

> The Invisible War upon which Earth's greatest issues depend,
> Is still the same war the Britons fought in at Catraeth
> And Aneririn sings.
>
> Hugh MacDiarmid: 'On Reading Professor Ifor Williams's "Canu Aneurin" in Difficult Days', from *A Kist of Whistles* (1947)

See also GODDODIN.

Cauldron Snout Possibly 'funnel into the waterfall pool', ME *cauldron* 'place where water boils' + *snute* 'projecting funnel, nozzle'.
A cataract on the upper reaches of the River TEES, just below Cow Green Reservoir, County Durham, 25 km (16 miles) northwest of Barnard Castle. It is mentioned along with HIGH FORCE in Sir Walter Scott's *Rokeby* (1813).

Caulkerbush Etymology unknown.
A small settlement on the **Caulkerbush Burn**, Dumfries and Galloway (formerly in Kirkcudbrightshire), 20 km (12 miles) south of Dumfries.

Causeway Coast, the. The name devised by the Northern Ireland Tourist Board for the dramatic northern and northeastern coast of County Derry and County Antrim, from Magilligan Point to Larne, and including the resorts of PORTSTEWART and PORTRUSH, plus FAIR HEAD, and, of course, the GIANT'S CAUSEWAY itself. The Northern Ireland Tourist Board would probably not welcome the following fine endorsement:

> I shall never forget the wind
> On this benighted coast.
> It works itself into the mind

Like the high keen of a lost
Lear-spirit in agony …

> Derek Mahon: 'North Wind: Portrush', from *Collected Poems*
> (1999) (For the association of the coast with the Children of
> Lir (or Lear), *see* Sea of MOYLE.)

Cavan Irish *An Cabhán* 'the hollow' or 'the rounded, grassy hill' (both features are apparent).

A market town in County Cavan, of which it is the county town. It is 100 km (62 miles) northwest of Dublin. It is the cathedral town of the Catholic diocese of Kilmore, the cathedral itself dating from 1942. The town was destroyed by the Williamites in 1690.

Cavan Orphanage Fire, the (23 February 1943). A disaster in which 36 children in the care of the Poor Clares died. Although the official inquiry blamed poor fire safety and an inadequate fire service, it was said by many that there was a delay in evacuating the children because the sisters refused to allow them outside in their night attire.

> In Cavan there was a great fire;
> Joe McCarthy came to inquire
>   If the nuns were to blame
>   It would be a shame
> So it had to be caused by a wire.
>
> > Brian O'Nolan: limerick composed in a pub in Cavan.
> > (O'Nolan – better known under his pen name Flann O'Brien
> > – was secretary to the tribunal of the inquiry, of which Joe
> > McCarthy was chairman.)

Cavan, County. A county in the north of the Republic of Ireland, part of the traditional province of Ulster. It is sometimes nicknamed POTHOLE COUNTY. It is bounded on the north by Fermanagh (Northern Ireland) and Monaghan, to the southeast by Meath, to the south by Westmeath, to the southwest by Longford, and to the west by Leitrim. The county town is Cavan, and there are many lakes:

> In Cavan of little lakes,
> As I was walking with the wind,
> And no one seen beside me there,
> There came a song into my mind:
> It came as if the whispered voice
> Of one, but none of human kind,
> Who walked with me in Cavan then,
> And he invisible as wind.
>
> > Alice Milligan (b.1866): 'A Song of Freedom'

Cavan people have a certain reputation as entrepreneurs, especially in the construction and pub trades – the comedian Niall Tóibín has characterized them as being 'odious good at turning a buck'.

Cavendish 'Cafna's enclosure', OE male personal name *Cafna* + *edisc* 'enclosure, enclosed park'.

A village in Suffolk, on the Essex border, about 8 km (5 miles) northwest of Sudbury. The family name of the dukes of Devonshire, Cavendish, originated in the village.

Caversham 'Cafhere's homestead or enclosure', OE male personal name *Cafhere* + HAM.

A northern suburb of READING, to the north of the River THAMES[1]. The BBC's Monitoring Unit, which collates and edits news output and broadcasts from around the world, is based here.

Cawdor 'hard water', Gaelic *caled* 'hard' + *dobhar* 'water' (the names of the rivers Callater and Calder mean the same – *see* CALDER[1]).

A village 7 km (4.5 miles) southwest of Nairn, in Highland (formerly in Nairnshire). Shakespeare makes Macbeth **Thane of Cawdor** (as promised by the witches in Act I scene iii), and although he does not name Macbeth's castle where he kills Duncan it is traditionally taken to be **Cawdor Castle**. However, the present castle dates only from 1454, and there is no evidence of an older structure; furthermore, the real Macbeth killed Duncan in battle (not in bed) near Elgin.

> This castle hath a pleasant seat; the air
> Nimbly and sweetly recommends itself
> Unto our gentle senses.
>
> > William Shakespeare: Duncan in *Macbeth* (1606), I,vi

Cawsand 'sandy beach of the Cow' (probably referring to a large rock by the local beach called 'the Cow'), ME *cowes* possessive form of *cow* + *sand*.

A village in Cornwall, on the western side of Plymouth Sound (*see under* PLYMOUTH). It nestles in **Cawsand Bay**, where the vessel that would carry Napoleon to exile in St Helena anchored for a month in 1815.

Caxton Probably 'Kakkr's farmstead', OScand personal name *Kakkr* + -TON.

A village in Cambridgeshire, about 16 km (10 miles) west of Cambridge.

Caxton Gibbet *Gibbet* from the site of a gallows, a replica of which still stands beside the road here.

A village in Cambridgeshire, about 2.5 km (1.5 miles) northwest of Caxton.

Ceannanas Mór. The Irish name for KELLS[1].

Ceann an Chairn. The Irish name for CARNSORE POINT.

Ceann Caillighe. The Irish name for HAG'S HEAD.

Ceann Ear. *See under* MONACH ISLANDS.

Ceann Iar. *See under* MONACH ISLANDS.

Ceann Léime[1]**.** The Irish name for LOOP HEAD.

Ceann Léime[2]**.** The Irish name for SLYNE HEAD.

Ceann Sléibhe. The Irish name for SLEA HEAD.

Ceann Toirc. The Irish name for KANTURK.

Ceapach Choinn. The Irish name for CAPPOQUIN.

Ceatharlach. The Irish name for CARLOW.

Ceathrú Aodha Dhuibh. The Irish name for CARRYDUFF.

Ceathrú Dobhair. The Irish name for CARROWDORE.

❖ ced ❖

The elements *coed* (Welsh) and *keith* (Gaelic) go back to an Old Celtic source, *ced, ceto-* 'wood'. Several names in England use the original Brittonic element, including Chetwoode (Berkshire) and Cheetwood (Lancashire), to both of which the Anglo-Saxons added the semantically unnecessary Old English element *wudu* 'wood', showing that they did not understand the British word they were using.

Several name-types recur, notably *penno-cet* 'wooded hill' in PENGE (Surrey), Penketh (Lancashire) and Penkhill (Stafford-

shire); and *leto-cet* 'grey wood' in LICHFIELD (Staffordshire) and Lytchett in Dorset (*see* LYTCHETT MATRAVERS).

In Wales, *ced* became *coed*, the normal word for a wood: BETWS-Y-COED and Coed y Brenin (*see* COED Y BRENIN FOREST PARK) most obviously, and HENGOED, and less obviously the anglicized COYCHURCH contain this element. In Scotland, the Gaelic word for a wood or forest is *coille*, but the Brittonic word was used in names such as the various examples of Keith (such as KEITH, Moray) and also DALKEITH and BATHGATE.

Cefn-coed-y-cymmer Possibly 'ridge wood of the river confluence', Welsh *cefn* 'ridge' + *coed* (*see* CED) + *y* 'the' + *cymer* possibly 'confluence'.

A village in Merthyr Tydfil unitary authority (formerly in Glamorgan, then in Mid Glamorgan), 2 km (1.2 miles) northwest of Merthyr Tydfil.

Cefn Sidan Sands 'smooth ridge', Welsh *cefn* 'ridge' + *sedan* 'smooth, silky', with ModE *sands*.

The long stretch of sands extending some 12 km (7.5 miles) southeast from the mouth of the TOWY estuary, in Carmarthenshire (formerly in Dyfed).

Ceinewydd. The Welsh name for NEW QUAY.

Celbridge Irish *Cill Droichid* 'church of the bridge'.

A village on the River LIFFEY in County Kildare, 21 km (13 miles) west of Dublin. **Celbridge Abbey** was the home of Esther Vanhomrigh (1690–1723), Jonathan Swift's 'Vanessa'. She built a bower in the grounds where they met while Swift was in Dublin. Soon after their angry parting in 1723 (occasioned by Swift's relationship to 'Stella' – Esther Johnson), 'Vanessa' died, and is buried at Celbridge.

Nearby is the magnificent Palladian Castletown House, the largest private house in Ireland, built in 1722 by William Connolly, an innkeeper's son who rose to become Speaker of the Irish Parliament.

Celtic Sea From the surrounding *Celtic* areas of Britanny, Ireland, Wales and Cornwall.

An area of the northeast Atlantic formally defined as 'that part of the Continental shelf lying between the 200-fathom contour, southern Ireland, the southwestern tip of Wales, Land's End and Ushant'. The name was first used in 1921 by E.W.L. Holt.

Celtic Tiger. A nickname applied to Ireland owing to its thriving economy in the last decade of the 20th century. The name was modelled on the 'tiger' economies of Southeast Asia.

Central. A former region of Scotland, established in 1975. It incorporated all of the old county of Clackmannanshire, most of Stirlingshire, and parts of Perthshire and West

Lothian. It was divided into the districts of Clackmannan, Falkirk and Stirling. In 1996 it was abolished, and replaced by the unitary authorities of CLACKMANNANSHIRE, FALKIRK[1] and STIRLING[2].

Central Lancashire. A region designated a NEW TOWN[1] in 1970. It includes PRESTON, FULWOOD, Bamber Bridge, LEYLAND and CHORLEY, and together these form the largest area covered by any of the New Towns.

Central Lowlands. A geographer's term for the narrow, heavily urbanized and industrialized lowland belt in central Scotland, between the HIGHLANDS and the SOUTHERN UPLANDS. It is also called the **Central Belt** and more frequently simply the LOWLANDS.

Centre Point. A massive and (at one time) controversial 36-storey office block in the WEST END[1] of London, at the northern end of Charing Cross Road (*see under* CHARING CROSS), on the corner with New Oxford Street. It was built in 1963–7 to the designs of Richard Seifert and Partners. Because of an economic downturn much of it remained empty for several years, contributing to its reputation as a monument to the evils of capitalism. It is now officially listed as a building of architectural importance.

Ceredigion 'land of Ceredig', Welsh personal name *Ceredig* + *-ion*, a territorial suffix. Ceredig was probably a 5th-century leader.

An early medieval kingdom and modern administrative division of west-central Wales. It is pronounced 'kerediggion'. The early medieval kingdom was united with the kingdom of YSTRAD TYWI (Carmarthenshire and West Glamorgan) in the 9th century to form the kingdom of SEISYLLWG, which the following century itself became part of the kingdom of DEHEUBARTH.

Ceredigion anglicized becomes CARDIGAN, one of its constituent towns. Ceredigion became the name of a district (corresponding to the old county of CARDIGANSHIRE, also Ceredigion in Welsh) within Dyfed in 1974, and this district became the unitary authority of Ceredigion in 1996.

Ceredigion is bordered to the south by Carmarthenshire and Pembrokeshire, to the west by Cardigan Bay, to the north by Gwynedd, and to the east by Powys. The administrative centre is at ABERAERON, and other towns include LAMPETER and ABERYSTWYTH.

Ceres A number of theories have been put forward. The least likely is that it is named after Ceres, the Roman goddess of agriculture, as the earliest form is *Syreis*. In the reign of William the Lion (1165–1214) the local landowners were the Syras family, who may have given it their name. Another theory derives it from Gaelic *siar-ais* 'western place'. Yet another holds that it is named after St Cyrus, to whom the church is dedicated.

A village on the **Ceres Burn** in Fife, 4 km (2.5 miles) southeast of Cupar. It somewhat bizarrely claims to have the shortest high street in Scotland, and is home to the Fife Folk Museum.

Cerne From OCelt *carn* 'heap of stones, cairn'.

A river in Dorset, which rises about 3 km (2 miles) north of Cerne Abbas and flows southwards into the River FROME[3] just to the north of Dorchester.

Cerne Abbas *Cerne* from CERNE; *Abbas* from Latin *abbas* 'abbot', with reference to the former local abbey.

A village in Dorset, on the River CERNE, about 11 km (7 miles) north of Dorchester. A Benedictine abbey was founded here in 987. The scholar Aelfric was a monk at the abbey between about 990 and 1005, and wrote his *Catholic Homilies* and *Lives of the Saints*, two outstanding examples of Old English prose, during his time here. The abbey's post-Dissolution ruins can still be seen.

In the novels of Thomas Hardy, Cerne Abbas is fictionalized as **Abbot's-Cernel**.

See also UP CERNE.

Cerne Abbas Giant. An outline figure of a giant, 55 m (180 ft) long, cut into chalk in the side of Giant's Hill, Cerne Abbas. Estimates of his age and identity vary, but the latest evidence points to a 17th-century date rather than any great antiquity. He brandishes a club (suggestive of Hercules) in a manner that counterpoints his no-nonsense erection (suggestive of a fertility cult); but if he is from the 1600s he could plausibly be a mocking reference to contemporary images of Oliver Cromwell. The remains of the local abbey are at the foot of his hill.

Chadderton 'farmstead of Cadeir Hill', OCelt *cadeir* 'chair' (*see* CAHER) + -TON.

A former cotton town in Greater Manchester, on the west side of Oldham.

Chaddesley Corbett *Chaddesley* probably 'glade at the hill called *Cadeir*', OCelt *cadeir* 'chair' (*see* CAHER) + -LEY; *Corbett* denoting manorial ownership in the Middle Ages by the Corbet family.

A village in Worcestershire, about 7 km (4.5 miles) southeast of Kidderminster.

Chad Valley A modern name, not used before 1860 when the Chad Valley toy company was founded; the stream here is Chad Brook, but that might be derived from the company as well. Thus, there is probably no connection with St Chad, the 7th-century bishop and missionary who established the Mercian see of Lichfield.

A district of Birmingham, southwest of the city centre. Its name has been made famous by the toy firm, founded in 1860 by Alfred and Joseph Bunn and who established its premises here in 1897. Soon afterwards it adopted the name 'Chad Valley' as its trademark. It is best known for its teddy bears, first produced in 1915. The name is now the brand for toys produced for Woolworths stores.

Chagford 'ford where broom or gorse grows', OE *ceacga* 'broom, gorse' + FORD.

A small town in Devon, about 14 km (8.5 miles) southeast of Okehampton, near the source of the River Teign on the eastern fringes of Dartmoor. It was a Stannary town (*see under* STANNARIES). A shooting incident in the churchyard here is said to have given R.D. Blackmoor the idea for the shooting of Lorna in his Exmoor novel *Lorna Doone* (1869).

John Endecott (1589–1665), four-times governor of the American colony of Massachusetts, was born in Chagford.

Chaldon Herring *Chaldon* 'hill where calves graze', OE *cealf* 'calf' + DOWN, -DON; *Herring* denoting manorial ownership in the Middle Ages by the Harang family.

A village in Dorset, about 12 km (7.5 miles) northeast of Weymouth.

Chale 'ravine, chine', OE *ceole* 'throat, gorge, ravine'.

A village on the southwest coast of the Isle of Wight, about 3 km (2 miles) from St Catherine's Point.

Chalfont St Giles *Chalfont* 'spring frequented by calves', OE *cealf* 'calf' + *funta* 'fountain, spring'; *St Giles* from the dedication of the local church.

A village in Buckinghamshire, in the Chiltern Hills, about 5 km (3 miles) northeast of Beaconsfield. The poet John Milton came to live here in 1665, to escape the plague in London. He completed his masterpiece, *Paradise Lost*, here, and also wrote *Paradise Regained*. A cottage he lived in is now a museum.

In the 20th century the name of the village took on an unsought new role as rhyming slang, especially in theatrical circles, for *piles* (in the haemorrhoidal sense). It is generally abbreviated in this usage to *Chalfonts*.

Chalgrove 'chalk pit', OE *cealc* 'chalk' + *græf* 'pit'.

A village in Oxfordshire, about 13 km (8 miles) southeast of Oxford. **Chalgrove Field** was the site of a Civil War skirmish on 17 June 1643 in which Prince Rupert defeated a Parliamentary army that was pursuing his Royalist force of 2000 men. The parliamentarian John Hampden, who in the late 1630s had famously refused to pay 'ship money', died later (in THAME[2]) of wounds sustained in the fight.

Chalk '(place on the) chalk', OE *cealc*.

A village in northeastern Kent, close to the THAMES[1] Estuary, now an eastern suburb of GRAVESEND.

Chalk Farm *Chalk* originally *Chalcott* 'cold cottage', OE *ceald* 'cold' + -COT (perhaps referring to a draughty dwelling or one in an exposed location) – *Chalk*, first recorded in 1746, is an eroded form, encouraged by its resemblance to *chalk* (the local soil is clay, not chalky); *Farm* from the 17th- to 19th-century name of two local farms.

A district of northern INNER LONDON, to the north of REGENT'S PARK, adjacent to CAMDEN TOWN, and in the borough of Camden. The process of urbanization began here in the 1820s, and was all but complete by the middle of the 19th century. The London to Birmingham Railway, which opened in the early 1850s, had its terminus here, and the Round House, a huge circular building, was erected to house its turntable. It was relegated to the role of a warehouse for nearly a hundred years. Then, in the 1960s, it opened as a theatre and concert-space championing the avant-garde. It subsequently sank again into desuetude, but at the beginning of the 21st century it was back in business, playing host to, for example, the Royal Shakespeare Company.

Chalk Farm was the scene of a famous non-duel on 15 August 1806, when, in response to being called 'the most licentious of modern versifiers' by Lord Jeffrey in the *Edinburgh Review* (July 1806), the Irish poet Thomas Moore issued a challenge. While their seconds attempted to sort out some technical problems with the two pistols the two adversaries chatted, discovering a mutual admiration that deepened after the Bow Street Runners arrived and put them in a cell together.

Chalk Farm Underground station, on the Northern line (Edgware branch), opened in 1907, reinforcing the designation for the district as a whole.

From the mid-19th to the early 20th century, *Chalk Farm* or *chalk* was a rhyming slang term for 'arm'.

Chancellor, The. *See* AONACH EAGACH.

Chancery Lane 'lane beside the chancellor's office', ME *chauncerie* 'chancellor's office', a reduced form of *chauncelerie*; the Keeper of the Rolls of Chancery had his office here.

A street in Central London, linking HOLBORN in the north with FLEET STREET in the south (WC2). It dates from the early 13th century, when it was called New Street. In the 1230s a house for Jewish converts to Christianity was founded there, which led to the road being renamed Converts Lane. In the 14th century the house was taken over by Edward III for the use of the Keeper of the Rolls of Chancery (the records of the Lord Chancellor's court), and the road came to be known as Chancellor's Lane. The present-day version is first recorded in 1454.

The street is in the heart of London's legal district (the Law Courts and several Inns of Court are in the immediate vicinity) and contains several stationers, outfitters, etc. dedicated to the legal profession, as well as the headquarters of the Law Society. The Public Record Office headquarters were here (in a large mock-Tudor building on the site of the Rolls estate) until its functions were transferred to the PRO's new buildings at Kew in 1996.

Chancery Lane Underground station, on the Central Line, was opened in 1900.

Chanctonbury Ring *Chanctonbury* 'prehistoric earthwork at Chancton (a local farm name)', *Chancton* perhaps 'farm near a thicket of brushwood' (OE *sœngel* 'thicket of brushwood' + -TON) + BURY.

An Iron Age hillfort in West Sussex, beside the South Downs Way, about 9 km (5.5 miles) north of Worthing. A circle of beech trees, planted on its summit in 1760, made a landmark visible from many miles around, but this suffered severely in the autumn gales of 1987.

See also CISSBURY RING.

Chandler's Ford Originally (in the early 10th century) *Searnœgles ford* 'Searnægel's ford', from the OE male personal name *Searnœgel* + FORD (the ford in question carried an important Roman road across Monks Brook). The present-day form, first recorded in 1759, may have been influenced by *Chandler*, the name of a family living in the area from the 14th century.

A town in Hampshire, immediately to the west of Eastleigh.

Channel, the. *See* ENGLISH CHANNEL.

Channel Islands. A group of islands – JERSEY, GUERNSEY, ALDERNEY, SARK, HERM, JETHOU, BRECQHOU and a number of lesser islets – in the ENGLISH CHANNEL, to the west of the Cotentin Peninsula in Normandy, northwestern France. Their French name is *Îles Normandes*, or *Îles Anglo-normandes*. They enjoy a unique status as the only portions of the Dukedom of Normandy that still belong to the British Crown, which has held them since the Norman Conquest. As 'Crown Dependencies' they are associated with, but not technically a part of, the United Kingdom. Neither are they a part of the European Union, although they have a special relationship with it.

The Channel Islands were the only British European territory to come under German occupation in the Second World War. They were liberated on 9 May 1945, the day after VE-Day, and 'Liberation Day' is a bank holiday throughout the Islands. Some aspects of the occupation remain controversial for Channel Islanders, but the occupation and its relics nonetheless constitute a distinctive and significant facet of the the Islands' tourist industry, with museums such as Jersey's Underground Hospital Museum (also known as the War Tunnels) drawing many visitors.

The four main islands (Jersey, Guernsey, Alderney and Sark) have their own legislative assemblies and systems of local administration, as well as their own courts, and they are grouped for this purpose into the two 'bailiwicks' of Jersey and Guernsey.

The islands are a lure for tourists on account of their mild, maritime climate and are a tax haven for residents: Jersey and Guernsey enjoy an income-tax rate of only 20 pence in the pound and there is no tax of any kind in Sark.

Channel Island. Used adjectivally to designate particularly, and collectively, the breeds of dairy cattle originating in Jersey, Guernsey and Alderney, and also their products, especially milk: **Channel Island milk** has a high fat content, usually at least four per cent.

Channel Islander. An inhabitant of the Channel Islands.

Channel Television. A commercial terrestrial television channel serving the Channel Islands. The smallest of the ITV network contractors, it first went on the air in 1962. It is now generally known as CTV.

Channel Tunnel. A set of tunnels linking Britain and France by rail under the ENGLISH CHANNEL. It is 50 km (31 miles) long and runs between Cheriton, just north of Folkestone in Kent, and Fréthun, to the southwest of Calais in France, at depths of up to 46 m (150 ft).

The idea of correcting Nature's oversight in separating Britain from the Continent by 29 km (18 miles) of salt water is by no means new: it was first mooted by a French engineer in 1802, and various projects for a tunnel (or, rather more optimistically, a bridge) reached differing stages of maturity over the following two centuries. William George Tolliday produced detailed plans for a tunnel in 1875 (the year in which the Channel was first swum by Captain Matthew Webb). The financier and railway promoter Sir Edward Watkin took up the project, and digging started near Dover in 1880. The tunnel progressed about 1.6 km (1 mile) out to sea, but then the British government got cold feet, and work was abandoned. The idea did not go away, though: it was in the air again in the early 1920s, for example, and in 1973 Britain and France agreed to back a tunnel. However, in discussions, either the cost, or the technical difficulty, or British fears of the loss of its splendid isolation and the prospect of being overrun by hordes of rabid foxes or Russian soldiers – or all three of these reasons – always derailed the plans.

In the 1980s the wheel turned again, and President François Mitterand of France, who had a penchant for *grands projets*, persuaded the somewhat cooler British prime minister Margaret Thatcher to go ahead with a tunnel. Work began on it in 1989, and it finally opened in 1994,

at an overall cost of about £15 billion. Over 13,000 people were involved in its construction. They produced three tubes, two for rail traffic and a third between the two of them for services and security.

The Channel Tunnel proved popular with travellers, taking away a lot of business from the cross-Channel ferries, but it has not been without its problems: it was closed by a fire for two weeks in 1996, and at the beginning of the 21st century it became a magnet for people trying to gain illegal entry into Britain from the refugee camp at Sangatte near Calais.

> I wish I could go back by Channel Tunnel.
>
> George Bernard Shaw: *London Music* (1889)

See also CHUNNEL.

Chantry Probably 'chantry chapel' (a chapel endowed for the saying of prayers for the soul of the person who endowed it; the name perhaps originally referred to land the income from which paid for the upkeep of the chapel), ME.

A southwestern suburb of IPSWICH, in Suffolk.

Chapel-en-le-Frith 'chapel in the sparse woodland', OFr *chapele en le* 'chapel in the' + OE *fyrhth* 'sparse woodland'.

A town in Derbyshire, on the western edge of the PEAK DISTRICT National Park, about 8 km (5 miles) north of Buxton.

Chapelizod Irish *Séipéal Iosóid* 'chapel of Iseult', referring to the Irish princess of Arthurian legend who was betrothed to King Mark of Cornwall, but who tragically fell in love with Tristan, the knight sent to bring her to Cornwall.

A village in County Dublin, effectively a western suburb of DUBLIN. It is pronounced to rhyme with 'gizzard', and was the birthplace of the press magnate Alfred Harmsworth, Lord Northcliffe (1865–1922).

Chapeltown 'village with the chapel', ME *chapel* + *town*.

A town in South Yorkshire, some 8 km (5 miles) north of Sheffield.

Char From OCelt *carn* 'heap of stones, cairn'.

A river in Dorset, rising to the west of BEAMINSTER and flowing 9 km (5.5 miles) southwards into Lyme Bay at CHARMOUTH.

Chard Perhaps 'building in rough ground', OE *ceart* 'rough ground' + *ærn* 'house, building'.

A town in Somerset, about 11 km (7 miles) west of Crewkerne, at 121 m (400 ft) the highest town in the county. Its narrow and precipitous streets overlook the valley of the River AXE². It evolved in the Middle Ages as a tanning centre, but later turned to weaving and lace-making (in the heyday of the British empire it produced many acres of mosquito-netting).

The notorious Judge Jeffreys held one of his 'Bloody Assizes' of 1685, following the rebellion of the Pretender Monmouth, in Chard's 16th-century courthouse.

Chard was the birthplace of Margaret Bondfield (1873–1953), who in 1929 became Britain's first female cabinet minister.

Charing Probably 'bend (in a road)', OE *c(i)erring* 'turn, bend' (alternatively 'place associated with Ceorra', OE male personal name *Ceorra* + -ING).

A village in Kent, about 11 km (7 miles) northwest of Ashford. The archbishops of Canterbury once had a palace here, but its remains now form part of a farmhouse.

Charing Cross *Charing* 'bend', OE *c(i)erring* 'turn, bend', with reference either to a bend in the River Thames here or (more likely) to the conspicuous westward bend in the old Roman road from London at that point (the derivation from French *chère reine* 'dear queen', as if in an endearing tribute from Edward I to his wife, is appropriate but fanciful); *Cross* from the Eleanor Cross erected here by Edward I.

A location in Central London, in the City of WESTMINSTER (WC2), where the western end of the STRAND meets the northern end of WHITEHALL in TRAFALGAR SQUARE. It is officially at the centre of London: distances from the capital are measured from it. It took its name from its Eleanor Cross, but it relies for its modern identity more on its railway station, and in that context its boundary has migrated southwards from the Strand to the north bank of the River Thames.

The original cross was erected in 1290 in the centre of the ancient village of Charing, which stood midway between the cities of London and Westminster, by Edward I to commemorate his queen, Eleanor. It was the spot at which her coffin was halted for the last time on its way from Harby, Nottinghamshire, to Westminster. (Eleven further crosses were put up at the other stopping places on the route.) The cross was sited where the statue of King Charles I now stands on the south side of Trafalgar Square, but it was destroyed by the Puritans in 1647. The present Gothic cross in the courtyard of Charing Cross Station was designed by Edward Middleton Barry and erected in 1865.

> Fleet-street has a very animated appearance; but I think the full tide of human existence is at Charing-Cross.
>
> Samuel Johnson: (1775) in James Boswell *The Life of Samuel Johnson* (1791)

'By the Statue of King Charles at Charing Cross'. A poem (1893) by the fin-de-siècle poet Lionel Johnson, inspired by the statue of Charles I on the south side of Trafalgar Square ('The saddest of all kings / Crowned, and again discrowned').

Charing Cross Hospital. A major London teaching hospital, opened in 1818, and originally situated to the northwest of Trafalgar Square. It moved to its present site in the Fulham Palace Road in 1973.

Charing Cross Road. A road leading northwards from St Martin's Place (at the northeastern corner of Trafalgar Square) to the eastern end of Oxford Street. Laid out in the 1880s, it is renowned for its bookshops, particularly the large and formerly idiosyncratic Foyle's (founded in 1906) and second-hand ones – a reputation reinforced by Helene Hanff's *84 Charing Cross Road* (1971, film version 1987), a record of her correspondence with Marks & Co.'s bookshop at that address.

See also the ROAD.

Charing Cross Station. A terminus for trains from southeast England, opened in 1864. It was built at the western end of the Strand on the site of the former Hungerford Market. (Phileas Fogg left from here on his journey in Jules Verne's *Around the World in Eighty Days* (1873).) The railway bridge leading to it across the Thames is generally known as HUNGERFORD BRIDGE, but it is also called **Charing Cross Bridge**. The original Charing Cross Underground station, on the District and Circle lines, opened in 1870, but in 1976 was renamed Embankment. Three years later Trafalgar Square Underground station, on the Bakerloo and Northern lines, was renamed Charing Cross.

❖ charl-, chorl- ❖

The Old English word that produces names with these spellings is *ceorl*, modern 'churl'. But the Anglo-Saxon churl was not necessarily ill-mannered, and in fact the word only took the modern derogatory overtones after the Norman Conquest. Under the king (*see* KINGSTON BAGPUIZE and the many *King*-names) there were princes (Old English *ætheling* found in ATHELNEY, Somerset), bishops (*see* BISHOP'S STORTFORD, Hertfordshire, and many other bishop names), thanes (Old English *thegn*, found in Thenford, Northamptonshire), knights (Old English *cniht* 'young man, retainer' or Middle English *knight*, *see* KNIGHTON, Powys) and then the ordinary free men, the churls. The churl farmed his own land and was an independent yeoman, the backbone of the economy and the army. The frequency of his name occurring with -TON, such as CHARLTON (often) and CHURSTON FERRERS (Cornwall), underlines this status; but the churl also held woodland (*see* the CHORLEYS of Lancashire, Cheshire and Staffordshire). Particularly in areas affected by the Danish settlement (*see* DANELAW), the pronunciation of the Old English element *ceorl* is affected by the Old Scandinavian element *karl*, hence many examples of Carlton (such as CARLTON CURLIEU) or Carleton (such as CARLETON FOREHOE).

Charlbury 'Ceorl's fortified place', OE male personal name *Ceorl* (*see also* CHARL-, CHORL-) + ing + BURY.

A small town in Oxfordshire, about 8 km (5 miles) southeast of CHIPPING NORTON. Its railway station, on the London-to-Worcester line, has made Charlbury something of a hybrid of COTSWOLD village and affluent commuter town. There is no denying the attractiveness of its centre, however, where Church Street, lined with imposing 18th-century stone houses, slopes down to the church of St Mary.

Cornbury Park, an estate given to Robert Dudley, Earl of Leicester, by Elizabeth I, lies to the southeast, across the River EVENLODE[2], as do the remaining fragments of WYCHWOOD Forest.

Charlecote 'cottages of the freeman', OE *ceorl* (*see* CHARL-, CHORL-) + *cot* (*see* -COT, COTE).

A village in Warwickshire, 8 km (5 miles) east of Stratford-upon-Avon. Local tradition has it that the young William Shakespeare was caught poaching deer in the grounds of nearby **Charlecote House**. Having been harshly punished by the house's owner, Sir Thomas Lucy (for whom the house was built in the 1550s), Shakespeare is said to have revenged himself by composing a satirical ballad so inflammatory that he was forced to flee to London. There is no contemporary evidence to substantiate this story, however. (Some scholars have interpreted an exchange between the characters Shallow, Slender and Evans in the opening scene of *The Merry Wives of Windsor* as a disparaging reference to the Lucy family.) A more welcome – and reliably attested – visitor to Charlecote was Queen Elizabeth I, who spent two nights here in 1572. Much of the house (which is now owned by the National Trust) dates from the 19th century (when a later Lucy had it radically rebuilt), though the east front still retains much of its Elizabethan form, with gables and octagonal corner turrets.

Charles Perhaps 'rock-court', Cornish *carn* + *lys*.

A village in Devon, on the River Bray, close to the western edge of Exmoor, about 13 km (8 miles) east of Barnstaple.

Charlesfort Named after *Charles* II.

A coastal fortification in County Cork, guarding Kinsale Harbour (*see under* KINSALE). Building began in 1678, and Charlesfort remained as a barracks until handed over by the British to the Irish Free State in 1922.

White Lady of Charlesfort, the. The ghost of Wilful Warender, daughter of Colonel Warender, governor of Charlesfort in the late 17th century. Wilful was betrothed to Sir Trevor Ashhurst, an officer of the garrison, and on the eve of their wedding, as they walked along the battlements, they saw some flowers down below. Sir Trevor asked a soldier to fetch his beloved the flowers, and in return Sir Trevor offered to take the soldier's place on guard duty. Unfortunately Sir Trevor fell asleep while carrying out his

half of the bargain, and was mistakenly shot by Colonel Warender. Wilful, in her distress at the news, threw herself off the battlements, wearing her wedding dress, and to this day can be seen wandering the ramparts.

Charlestown[1] From local entrepreneur *Charles* Rashleigh.

A village and port in Cornwall, on St Austell Bay (*see under* ST AUSTELL). Its original name was Porthmear, but around 1790 a local industrialist Charles Rashleigh (d.1825) provided money for the building of a pier and harbour to exploit the china-clay deposits in the area, and for the widening of the local streets, and by the end of the 19th century the reinvented village (designed by John Smeaton, architect of the Eddystone Lighthouse (*see under* EDDYSTONE ROCKS)) had been renamed after him.

Charlestown has been a favoured location as a backdrop for film and television productions, notably *The Eagle Has Landed* (1976) and the television series *The Onedin Line*.

Charlestown[2] Perhaps from Henry *Charles* Howard (1791–1856), 13th Duke of Norfolk, who was Lord of the Manor of Glossop. The name is first recorded in 1843.

A village in Derbyshire, on the southern outskirts of Glossop.

Charlestown[3] After *Charles* Strickland. The Irish version of its name, *Baile Chathail*, means the same.

A small town in County Mayo, on the border with County Sligo, 45 km (28 miles) west of Carrick-on-Shannon. Charlestown was founded in the 1840s by Charles Strickland, agent for the estates of Lord Dillon, to get back at Lord Knox, who had slighted him. Knox owned lands just over the Sligo border, including the thriving little market town of Bellahy, and Strickland offered large subsidies to anyone who would build on his bogland site of Charlestown. The new town prospered at Bellahy's expense, and the latter is now insignificant. Charlestown itself went into a decline after the Second World War, as recounted in John Healy's book, *Death of an Irish Town* (1968). However, since the building of Knock International Airport, the place has recovered some of its former bustle.

Charlestown of Aberlour. *See* ABERLOUR.

Charleville. A former name for RÁTH LUIRC.

Charlton 'farmstead or estate of the freemen or peasants', *charl-* (*see* CHARL-, CHORL-) + -TON.

A district of southeast London, between GREENWICH and WOOLWICH, in the borough of Greenwich (SE7). It was once famous for its 'Horn Fair', held every October since the Middle Ages, which attracted huge crowds by boat from further up the Thames. Its excesses and frequent riots became too much for the mid-Victorian authorities, and it was done away with in 1872.

The archeologist Sir Flinders Petrie (1853–1942) was born in Charlton.

'Charlton' is the middle name of the character Rodney Trotter in the BBC television sitcom *Only Fools and Horses* (1981–93), set in the neighbouring district of PECKHAM.

Charlton Athletic FC (nicknamed the Valiants, the Robins or, more frequently, the Addicks) was formed in 1905. Its ground is called 'The Valley'.

Charlton Horethorne *Horethorne*, name of a former Hundred (administrative district) of Somerset, 'grey thorn-bush', OE *har* 'grey' + *thyrne* 'thorn-bush'.
A village in Somerset, about 13 km (8 miles) northeast of Yeovil.

Charlton Mackrell *Mackrell* denoting manorial ownership in the Middle Ages by the Makerel family.
A village in Somerset, about 14 km (8.5 miles) north of Yeovil.

Charlton Musgrove *Musgrove* denoting manorial ownership in the Middle Ages by the Mucegros family.
A village in Somerset, about 26 km (16 miles) northeast of Yeovil.

Charmouth 'mouth of the River Char', CHAR + *mouth*.
A seaside village in Dorset, at the mouth of the River CHAR, about 2.5 km (1.5 miles) east of LYME REGIS. It has had an eventful history: Catherine of Aragon stayed in a local hostelry here when she arrived in England, and Charles II turned up here in disguise in 1651 looking for a boat to take him to France following his defeat at the Battle of Worcester. An early dinosaur find, of an ichthyosaurus, took place here, and the local cliffs continue to attract fossil-hunters.

Charney Bassett *Charney* 'island in the River Cern', an OCelt river name (*see* CERNE ABBAS) + OE *eg* (*see* -EY, -EA); *Bassett* denoting manorial ownership in the Middle Ages by the Bass(es) family.
A village in Oxfordshire, in the Vale of the White Horse, about 8 km (5 miles) north of Wantage.

Charnwood Forest *Charnwood* 'wood in rocky country', OCelt *carn* 'rocky country' + OE *wudu* 'wood'.
An ancient craggy woodland in Leicestershire, to the south of Loughborough. It covers 62 sq km (24 sq miles), although much of the original area is no longer forested, thanks to the depredations of mining and quarrying. Its highest point is Beacon Hill (248 m / 814 ft), from which four counties can be seen. It is now being reinvigorated, along with NEEDWOOD FOREST, as part of the NATIONAL FOREST scheme.

Charsfield. *See under* AKENFIELD.

Charterhouse 'a house of Carthusian monks' (a Carthusian priory was founded here in the 13th century), OFr *chartrouse*.
A village in Somerset, in the Mendip Hills, about 11 km (7 miles) northwest of Wells.

Charterville Allotments From the 19th-century 'People's *Charter*'.
A village in Oxfordshire, about 5 km (3 miles) west of Witney. It grew out of a land colony set up in 1847 by the Chartists under Fergus O'Connor. (The Chartists were mid-19th-century political activists, whose demands for democratic reform were based on a six-point 'People's Charter'.)
See also O'CONNORVILLE.

Chartham Hatch *Chartham* 'homestead in rough ground', OE *cert* 'rough ground' + -HAM; *Hatch* 'gate, sluice-gate', OE *hæcc*.
A village in Kent, about 5 km (3 miles) west of Canterbury.

Chartwell Perhaps 'spring in rough ground', OE *cert* 'rough ground' + *wella* 'spring'. Kent has many place names beginning *Chart-*, and this may in fact be a comparatively recent formation modelled on them.
A Victorianized country house of Elizabethan origin in Kent, about 8 km (5 miles) southwest of SEVENOAKS. It was bought in 1922, in somewhat dilapidated condition, by Winston Churchill. He lived here for over 40 years, adding a new wing and making many other alterations (including brick walls of his own construction). It was handed to the National Trust in 1946, and visitors were admitted from 1965.

Charwelton. *See under* CHERWELL.

Chaseborough. The fictional name for CRANBORNE, in Dorset, in the novels of Thomas Hardy.

Chastleton 'farm by a ruined camp', OE *caestel* 'ruined camp' (perhaps referring to an Iron Age hillfort above the village) + -TON.
A hamlet in the far northwest of Oxfordshire, 9 km (5.5 miles) southeast of STOW-ON-THE-WOLD. **Chastleton House**, now in the care of the National Trust, is one of the finest and least altered Jacobean mansions in England. Built in the early 17th century for Walter Jones, a wealthy lawyer, it has a famous barrel-vaulted long gallery. The rules of croquet were codified here in 1865 by Walter Jones-Whitmore, and the grounds contain England's first croquet lawn. According to tradition, in 1651 a Royalist ancestor of Jones-Whitmore's, one Arthur Jones, hid in a secret room at Chastleton House after the Battle of Worcester (*see under* WORCESTER), only escaping the attentions of the pursuing Cromwellians thanks to his resourceful wife slipping a sleeping-draught into the thirsty soldiers' drinks.

Chasty 'path overgrown with gorse', OE *ceage* 'gorse, broom' (*chag* is still the local dialect word for 'gorse') + *stig* 'path'.
A village in Devon, about 27 km (17 miles) northwest of Okehampton.

Chatelherault From the French castle of *Châtelherault*.

A mansion near Hamilton, South Lanarkshire (formerly in Strathclyde), built in 1732 for the Hamilton family by William Adam as a copy of Châtelherault, a château near Poitiers in central France. James Hamilton, 2nd Earl of Arran (c.1517–75), was created Duc de Châtelherault in 1549, following his support for the marriage of the young Mary Queen of Scots to the French dauphin. The dukes of Hamilton have kept the title ever since.

Chatham 'homestead or village in or near a wood', CED + -HAM.

A town (pronounced 'chattam') in Kent, at the mouth of the River Medway, about 50 km (31 miles) southeast of London, and formerly one of the leading naval towns in Britain. It was Henry VIII who turned this former fishing village into a naval base, and in 1588 Elizabeth I established the Royal Dockyard here. Over the next four centuries many hundreds of the Royal Navy's ships were built in the dockyard, including Nelson's HMS *Victory*. It was closed in 1984. Chatham is also the home of the Royal School of Military Engineering, founded here in 1812.

Charles Dickens lived in Chatham in his boyhood, from 1817 to 1821, when his father was working in the naval pay office, and the town features in several of his books, including *Pickwick Papers* (1837) and *David Copperfield* (1850).

There are towns called Chatham in the USA (Alaska, Illinois, Louisiana, Massachusetts, New York, Virginia) and Canada (New Brunswick, Ontario). The Chatham Islands, a New Zealand possession in the southwest Pacific Ocean, were named in honour of the statesman William Pitt (the Elder), 1st Earl of Chatham.

chatham and dover. Late 19th-century rhyming slang for 'give over' (i.e. 'stop, desist').

Chatham Lines. A coastal defence at the time of the Napoleonic Wars, consisting of a series of forts built on a hill east of Chatham.

Chatsworth 'Ceatt's enclosed settlement', OE *Ceattes* possessive form of male personal name *Ceatt* + -*worth* (*see* -WORTH, WORTHY, -WARDINE).

A Baroque mansion, in full **Chatsworth House**, in the PEAK DISTRICT of Derbyshire, about 5 km (3 miles) northeast of Bakewell. It is the principal seat of the dukes of Devonshire. The Chatsworth estate was acquired by their ancestor Sir William Cavendish in the 16th century. The house that his wife, Bess of Hardwick (*see under* HARDWICK HALL), built here was replaced by the present grand palace (known colloquially as **the Palace of the Peak**) in the late 17th century. The grounds were landscaped by 'Capability' Brown in 1760. In the early 19th century Joseph Paxton, creator of the CRYSTAL PALACE, was head gardener here; he designed Chatsworth's striking Emperor Fountain, which shoots jets of water 80 m (260 ft) into the air. Chatsworth is believed to

have been the model for Mr Darcy's **Pemberley** in Jane Austen's *Pride and Prejudice* (1813).

See also EDENSOR *and* WETHERBY.

Chatteris Probably 'Ceatta's raised strip or ridge', OE male personal name *Ceatta* + *ric* 'raised strip or ridge'; alternatively the first element may represent OCelt CED 'wood'.

A small town in the midst of the FENS in Cambridgeshire, about 29 km (18 miles) north of Cambridge. At 7.8 m (26 ft) above sea level it is the highest point in the Fens. It is a regional venue for amateur boxing events.

Cheadle A tautonym, from OCelt CED and OE -LEY, both meaning 'wood'.

An area of Greater Manchester, some 10 km (6 miles) south of Manchester city centre. **Cheadle Hulme** just to the south has the added Old Scandinavian element *holmr* 'water meadow' (*see* -EY, -EA).

Just north of Cheadle (and just south of the M60 motorway) is Abney Hall, a mansion built in the 1840s by the cotton magnate James Watts. Following the marriage of her sister Madge to a scion of the family in 1902, the future detective novelist Agatha Christie spent a number of childhood holidays here, and she also recuperated at Abney Hall in the aftermath of her 'disappearance' in 1926 (*see* HARROGATE). The house duly appears in a number of Christie's novels, notably in *They Do It With Mirrors* (1952), in which two characters drown in its fish pond, and in the introduction to *The Adventure of the Christmas Pudding* (1960), which the novelist dedicated to Abney Hall.

Cheam Probably 'homestead or village by the tree-stumps', OE *ceg* 'tree-stump' + -HAM.

A southwestern suburb of Greater London, in the borough of SUTTON[1] (before 1965 in Surrey). It remained an agricultural village until the early 20th century. It was not until after the First World War that urbanization (and then only of a fairly salubrious kind) reached Cheam. It contains NONSUCH PARK. **East Cheam**, a locality unknown to any modern map (although an *Estcheiham* is recorded as long ago as 1225), was made famous in the 1950s and 1960s as the fictional home of Anthony Aloysius Hancock, lugubrious resident of 23 Railway Cuttings, in the long-running radio and television comedy series *Hancock's Half Hour*.

Cheapside 'district beside the "Cheap" or market', OE *ceap* + *side* (the original name was *Cheap* or (to distinguish it from Eastcheap) *Westcheap*; the combination *Cheapside* is first recorded in 1436).

A street in the City of London (*see under* LONDON), running eastwards from the northeast corner of ST PAUL'S[1] Cathedral (EC2). In the Middle Ages it was the main market of the City, and many of the side-streets leading off it (Bread Street, Milk Street, etc.) are reminders of former subsidiary markets. It suffered severely in the Great Fire of 1666, and again in the Blitz of the early 1940s. The saint and archbishop Thomas Becket (1118–70) was born in Cheapside.

by way of Cheapside. Late 18th-century slang for 'on the cheap, at a bargain price', punning on *cheap* 'inexpensive' (a usage which emerged in the 16th century).

Chaste Maid in Cheapside, A. A play (1613) by Thomas Middleton (1580–1627), now generally considered his finest comedy. Its plot revolves around the attempt of the dissolute Sir Walter Whorehound to pass off his mistress as his niece (the 'Chaste Maid') and marry her off. Its title suggests that in the Jacobean period such a person was an unusual phenomenon.

Cheapside Hoard. A notable collection of early 17th-century jewellery discovered in 1912 by workmen at the junction of Cheapside and Friday Street.

Cheddar Probably 'ravine', OE *ceodor* 'ravine' (with reference to the Cheddar Gorge).

A village in Somerset, in the Mendip Hills, about 13 km (8 miles) northwest of Wells.

Cheddar cheese. A type of hard cow's-milk cheese originally made in and around Cheddar. It dates from at least Elizabethan times. The distinctive feature of its manufacture is a process (known as **cheddaring**) in which the chopped curds are formed into blocks and stacked, so as to coagulate. It is easily the most widely consumed cheese in Britain, and has long since outgrown its original boundaries – much of it nowadays comes from Australia and Canada. In Britain its name has become almost synonymous with cheese itself – a fact recognized in 2002 by a UK supermarket chain which decided to label its Cheddar simply 'Cheese'.

Cheddar club. A club formed by dairies for the purpose of making Cheddar cheese. It was a phenomenon largely of the 17th and early 18th centuries.

Cheddar Gorge. A narrow defile in the Mendip Hills, extending for about 1.5 km (1 mile) to the northeast of Cheddar. Its sheer limestone cliffs rise to over 140 m (460 ft), providing exhilarating views over the surrounding countryside. The gorge is honeycombed with caves, two of which in particular, Cox's and Gough's, contain spectacular stalagmites and stalagtites. The southern end of the gorge is somewhat blighted by commercial development.

Cheddar letter. A humorous 18th-century term for a letter to which a number of people contribute a paragraph each, as a Cheddar cheese is made by the contributions of several dairies.

Cheddar Man. The skeleton of a human being who lived around 9000 years ago, discovered near Cheddar in 1903. It is the oldest complete skeleton found in Britain. DNA tests in 1997 established that one of Cheddar Man's present-day descendants was a local headmaster.

Cheddar pink. A pink (*Dianthus gratianopolitanus*) with solitary flowers of a pale rose colour, found on the limestone cliffs at Cheddar.

Cheddington 'Cetta's hill', OE male personal name *Cetta* + *dun* (*see* DOWN, -DON).

A village in Buckinghamshire, about 8 km (5 miles) northeast of Aylesbury. It was near here, on 8 August 1963, that a well-organized gang hijacked a Royal Mail train travelling from Glasgow to London, escaping with mailbags containing £2.6 million in the form of used banknotes on their way to being destroyed. Twelve of the 15-member gang were caught and convicted, but one of them, Ronnie Biggs, escaped from prison, picked up his share of the haul and made his way to Brazil (with which Britain had no extradition treaty); there he spent the next 35 years, frustratingly out of reach of the Metropolitan Police, before surrendering himself back to the British authorities in ill health. Media accounts dubbed the crime the 'Great Train Robbery', imitating the title of a famous silent American film of 1903.

Chedworth 'Cedda's enclosure', OE male personal name *Cedda* + *worth* (*see* -WORTH, WORTHY, -WARDINE).

A village in Gloucestershire, in the COTSWOLDS, 11 km (7 miles) northeast of Cirencester. **Chedworth Woods** nearby is the site of a large Romano-British villa. The earliest buildings on the site date from the 2nd century AD, and by the 4th century it had developed into a large complex, possibly with a sacred function. Excavation began in 1864, and it is now administered by the National Trust.

Chedzoy 'Cedd's island' (in this context probably an area of dry ground in a marsh), OE *Ceddes* possessive form of male personal name *Cedd* + *eg* (*see* -EY, -EA).

A village in the Somerset Levels (*see under* SOMERSET), about 3 km (2 miles) east of Bridgwater.

Cheesewring, The. A pile of granite slabs on Stowe's Hill, to the north of MINIONS in Cornwall. Their shape, narrowing towards the base, resembles that of a cheese-press (an apparatus for pressing curds – 'cheesewring' was a West Country word for it).

See also the DEVIL'S CHEESEWRING.

Chelmer A back-formation from CHELMSFORD. (The river's original name was *Baddow*, which survives in the local villages Great and Little Baddow; it may be derived from OE *beadu* 'battle'. *Chelmer* is not recorded before the 16th century).

A river in Essex, which rises to the north of THAXTED and flows 56 km (35 miles) southeast through Chelmsford to join the River BLACKWATER[1] just to the west of MALDON.

Chelmsford 'Ceolmær's ford', OE *Ceolmæres* possessive form of male personal name *Ceolmær* + -FORD.

The county town of Essex, 27 km (17 miles) east of Harlow. It was founded in the 1st century AD by the Romans, who called it **Caesaromagus**. Since about 1200 it has been an important market town, the largest in the region for the buying and selling of livestock:

> At Chelmsford the mare would fetch £4 because it was going across the water to be made into meat extract.
>
> *Essex Weekly News* (1901)

The 15th-century church of Sts Mary, Peter and Cedd was raised to the status of a cathedral in 1914. **Chelmsford Cathedral** has always been at the centre of the town's life:

> The churchyard is well planted, the walks gravelled; this is the Mall for the beaux and belles of Chelmsford.
>
> Earl of Oxford: in *Portland Papers* (1737)

However, the town did not rate highly in the view of one famous 19th-century novelist:

> If any one were to ask me what in my opinion was the dullest and most stupid spot on the face of the Earth, I should decidedly say Chelmsford.
>
> Charles Dickens: letter (1835)

Chelmsford has an important place in the history of radio. In 1898 Guglielmo Marconi set up the world's first wireless factory here, and in February 1920 the earliest radio programmes were broadcast from the town, two years before the foundation of the BBC.

Central Chelmsford is now graced by a statue of the Essex and England cricketer Graham Gooch (b.1953).

There is a town called Chelmsford in Massachusetts, USA (which gave its name to **Chelmsfordite**, a type of mineral, a silicate of aluminium), and one in Ontario, Canada.

Chelsea Probably 'landing-place for chalk or limestone', OE *cealc* 'chalk, limestone' + *hyth* 'landing-place'.
A district in southwest London, on the north bank of the River THAMES[1] (SW3, SW10). It became an independent borough in 1900, and in 1965 was amalgamated with Kensington to form the ROYAL BOROUGH of KENSINGTON AND CHELSEA (of which it constitutes the southern part).

In Anglo-Saxon and early medieval times it may (according to one interpretation of its name) have been a landing-place for chalk that was brought up the Thames from Kent: in those days chalk was used for fertilizing clayey fields, as well as being burnt to make lime. It remained a small village through the Middle Ages, but already it was appealing to notables as a place to build a peaceful retreat away from the stresses of London. The trend was confirmed when Sir Thomas More built himself a house here in 1520, to be emulated within the following decades by Henry VIII and many among the nobility.

The drift from nobility to intellect began in the 18th century, when the satirist Jonathan Swift and the essayist Joseph Addison lived here. Chelsea became the home of writers, and later, in the 19th century, of artists (J.M.W.

Turner, Dante Gabriel Rossetti, J.A.M. Whistler, Augustus John and John Singer Sargent among the most notable of them). By the early 20th century they had given the area a somewhat raffish, bohemian reputation. Mounting property prices meant that, in reality, the traditional impecunious artist could no longer afford a CHEYNE WALK address, and Mammon and *Burke's Peerage* began once again to figure strongly in the local population; but there was enough loucheness left to fuel the lively trendiness of the KING'S ROAD in the 1960s.

In the mid-1970s Chelsea was again a centre of youth culture, being the location of the boutique 'Sex' where the designer Vivienne Westwood and the entrepreneur Malcolm McLaren launched the punk rock group the Sex Pistols. (Coincidentally, it was in New York's Chelsea Hotel (*see below*) that John Simon Ritchie (a.k.a. Sid Vicious), the group's bass guitarist, was arrested in 1979 for the murder of his girlfriend Nancy Spungen.)

In 18th- and 19th-century Chelsea, the pleasure grounds of first Ranelagh Gardens (1742–1804) and then Cremorne Gardens (1845–77) were celebrated, and sometimes notorious, places of entertainment for Londoners.

The first **Chelsea Bridge**, crossing the Thames from **Chelsea Embankment** to the eastern edge of Battersea Park, was built in 1851–8. Its replacement, like the original a suspension bridge, was opened in 1934.

Chelsea FC, founded in 1905, is nicknamed the Pensioners (*see below*) or, more frequently these days, the Blues (from the colour of its strip). Stamford Bridge, where the club plays its home games, in fact lies just over the borough boundary in Hammersmith and Fulham (hence the vulgar chanted taunt of Arsenal fans: 'You're just a shit team in Fulham'). Following its acquisition by the Russian billionaire Roman Abramovich in 2003, the club was accorded the somewhat predictable nickname of 'Chelski' by the tabloid press.

There are towns called Chelsea in the USA (Iowa, Michegan, Oklahoma, Vermont), and an area on the West Side of New York City has the name Chelsea (the Chelsea Hotel, on 23rd Street, which opened in 1884, is famous for its past residential clientele of writers, artists and musicians, such as Mark Twain, Eugene O'Neill, Arthur Miller, Andy Warhol (who directed a film called *Chelsea Girls* (1966)), poet-singer Leonard Cohen ('I remember you well in the Chelsea Hotel', from 'Chelsea Hotel No.2' (1971)), Edith Piaf, Janis Joplin and Joni Mitchell. In 1953 a whisky-sodden Dylan Thomas died after collapsing there).

'Chelsea' has also shown some signs, especially in the USA, of moving from places to people, as a female first name – a notable example being Chelsea Clinton (b.1980), daughter of the former US President Bill Clinton.

Chelsea Arts Club. A club founded in the 1890s as a

meeting place for the many artists who, at that period, lived in Chelsea (among the founder members were Whistler, Walter Sickert, Philip Wilson Steer and Frank Brangwyn). It moved to its present premises in Old Church Street in 1902. It sponsored the **Chelsea Arts Ball**, an annual knees-up for the *jeunesse dorée*, latterly held in the Royal Albert Hall. The ball became so rowdy that it was discontinued after 1959, but it was revived in the 1980s.

Chelsea boots. A name given in the 1960s to elastic-sided ankle-high boots for men. Hitherto such footwear would have been worn only by septuagenarian survivors of the Victorian age, but the Swinging Sixties declared it sophisticated and fashionable, and signalled its approval by naming it after the with-it borough.

Chelsea bun. A type of square sweet currant-bun made from a sheet of yeast dough that has been rolled up into a coil. It was originally made at the Chelsea Bun House, a bakery that opened near Sloane Square in the late 17th or early 18th century.

Chelsea Flower Show. An annual summer display organized by the Royal Horticultural Society in the grounds of the Chelsea Royal Hospital (*see below*) since 1913. The exhibits range from prize vegetables through horticultural equipment to whole gardens, all housed on the 4.5 ha (11 acres) of lawn. The opening day is a major occasion, attended by the royal family and other celebrities. The event lasts four days and on the final day a bell is rung at 5 p.m., when remaining exhibits are sold to the public.

Chelsea Girl. A much-used epithet since the 1960s, after which a women's fashion-retail chain (now River Island), an album of songs by *chanteuse* Nico (1968) and a score of other cultural artefacts have been named.

Chelsea Green. An estate agents' name for the southeastern purlieus of SOUTH KENSINGTON, to the north of the King's Road.

Chelsea Harbour. A property development of the late 1980s, constructed beside the River Thames on former railway sidings near Lots Road power station in Chelsea. It consists of blocks of flats, hotels, restaurants, etc. surrounding a yacht harbour, and was, certainly to begin with, über-trendy.

Chelsea Pensioner. The popular name for an inmate of the **Chelsea Royal Hospital** (*see below*). The Pensioners' scarlet summer uniforms (they wear dark blue in winter) remain a head-turning feature of London's streets when their wearers venture forth.

Chelsea Physic Garden. A garden, originally for the cultivation of medicinal plants, established in Chelsea by the Apothecaries' Society in 1676. The first cedar trees in England were planted here (in 1683), and the first English greenhouse was built here in the same decade.

Chelsea porcelain. A type of porcelain ware made at the Chelsea Porcelain Works. This was founded in about 1745 and continued until 1784, when all its operations were removed to Derby. Different periods of production are distinguished by the name of the mark then applied: Triangle (the earliest), for example, and Red Anchor. The most familiar of the factory's output are its figurines.

Chelsea Royal Hospital. A habitation for old or disabled soldiers, founded in Chelsea by Charles II at the instigation of Sir Stephen Fox, the Paymaster General of the Forces (the story that royal mistress Nell Gwynn had a hand in its foundation seems to be apocryphal). Building began in 1682, to designs by Sir Christopher Wren, and it was opened in 1692. Its inmates are known as **Chelsea Pensioners** (*see above*). The **Chelsea Flower Show** (*see above*) is held in its grounds.

Chelsea smile. A slang term, dating from the 1970s, for a knife slash that runs from the corner of the mouth up and across the cheek. It is so named for being inflicted on rival fans by the more violent supporters of **Chelsea FC**.

Chelsea tractor. A derisive early 21st-century nickname for a 4x4 off-road vehicle, designed for rough terrain, as used by the Chelsea set (and their staff) for doing the shopping, taking their children to school, etc. London Mayor Ken Livingstone described their drivers as 'complete idiots'.

Sage of Chelsea. A sobriquet of the essayist and historian Thomas Carlyle (1795–1881). He and his wife Jane moved from Dumfriesshire to No. 5 (now 24) Cheyne Row, Chelsea in 1834, where they lived for the remainder of their lives.

Chelt A back-formation from CHELTENHAM.

A short river in Gloucestershire. Rising near Dowdeswell Reservoir, it is some 17 km (11 miles) in length, and flows through Cheltenham (where it can be seen to good effect in the city's Sandford Park) to join the SEVERN between Gloucester and Tewkesbury.

Cheltenham Probably 'enclosure or water-meadow by a hill called Celte', OE or pre-English hill name *Celte* + HAM.

A spa-town in Gloucestershire, on the River CHELT, at the foot of the Cotswolds, about 12 km (7.5 miles) northeast of Gloucester. Mineral springs were discovered here in 1715 (local legend has it that their health-giving properties were deduced from the sleekness of pigeons observed drinking them). In the early 1780s Captain Henry Skillicorne opened a pump room where people could come to take the waters, and by the turn of the 19th century Cheltenham was a fashionable spa. George III was a frequent visitor, and a further considerable boost to trade was given by the Duke of Wellington's taking the cure here in 1816. The elegant Regency and neo-classical architecture that characterizes the town dates from this period. A notable example is the Pittville Pump Room, built in 1825–30 and named after Sir Joseph Pitt MP.

During the 19th century Cheltenham became a

favourite place of retirement for military officers and colonial administrators whose livers and tempers had suffered the effects of long service in the tropics. The Cheltenham waters seem to have been of little benefit to either, as the town developed a reputation for reactionary crustiness to rival Tunbridge Wells's. Its present-day and rather more serious military connection is the Government Communications Headquarters (GCHQ), the centre of the British government's electronic surveillance operations.

Cheltenham is home to two notable public schools: **Cheltenham College**, which originated in the 1840s as a school for the sons of Indian Army officers (it has been fully co-educational since 1998; its cricket ground, in the shadow of its Gothic pinnacles, hosts Gloucestershire county games); and, perhaps even more notably, **Cheltenham Ladies' College**, established by that formidable Victorian advocate of female education Miss Beale, who, together with her fellow headmistress Miss Buss of the North London Collegiate School, is commemorated in a barbed anonymous late 19th-century quatrain:

Miss Buss and Miss Beale
Cupid's darts do not feel.
How different from us,
Miss Beale and Miss Buss.

As a further string to its educational bow, late 19th-century Cheltenham was home to the Guild of Household Dames, which trained ladies for the rigours of domestic work.

The Cheltenham Festival of Music is held every July and the Cheltenham Festival of Literature every October. The Spring meeting at Cheltenham racecourse is the premier event in the National Hunt season (the principal race is the **Cheltenham Gold Cup**, first run in 1924 – and **Cheltenham Gold**, or **Cheltenham** for short, became rhyming slang for 'a cold'). It attracts Irish aficionados of the turf in large numbers – 50,000 annually, according to one estimate – and it is rumoured that 10% of all the Guinness drunk annually in the UK is consumed in the three days of the festival. The fun was interrupted in 2001, when an outbreak of foot-and-mouth disease forced the cancellation of the meeting.

The stage magician John Nevil Maskelyne (1839–1917), the jockey Fred Archer (1857–86), the composer Gustav Holst (1874–1934), the actor Ralph Richardson (1902–83) and guitarist Brian Jones (1942–69) of the Rolling Stones were all born in Cheltenham (a new road in the town was named Brian Jones Close, but in the face of objections from residents, the developers applied in 2003 to change its name).

Inhabitants of Cheltenham, and present and former pupils of Cheltenham College and Cheltenham Ladies' College, are known as '**Cheltonians**'.

Lord of Cheltenham. A nickname given to the celebrated Irish steeplechaser Arkle (1957–70) on account of his feat of winning the Cheltenham Gold Cup on three successive occasions, in 1964, 1965 and 1966.

Chepstow 'market place', OE *ceap* 'market' + *stow* 'place'. A town on the Welsh side of the River WYE[1], just before it enters the Mouth of the Severn. It is in Monmouthshire (formerly in Gwent), some 22 km (14 miles) north of Bristol. Its Welsh name is **Cas-Gwent** ('castle in Gwent'). The place was fortified from prehistoric times, and **Chepstow Castle** (the first Norman stone castle in Wales, now ruined) was begun in 1067 by William FitzOsbern. It was taken by a Parliamentarian force during the Civil Wars. The regicide Henry Marten, who signed Charles I's death warrant, was imprisoned in Chepstow Castle, and died there in 1680; he has given his name to the castle's Marten Tower. There is a notable painting of the castle by Philip Wilson Steer (1860–1942) in Tate Britain. Chepstow has the largest tidal range in Britain (up to 15 m / 50 ft) and was an important river port until the 19th century.

Chepstow Racecourse, situated to the north of the town, hosts the Welsh National and the Welsh Champion Hurdle, among other races.

Chequers. The official country residence of the British prime minister, in the Chilterns near Wendover, Buckinghamshire. It was presented to the nation for this purpose by Lord Lee of Fareham in 1917 and was first so used by Lloyd George in 1921. The house itself is Tudor in origin but with Victorian additions and substantial remodelling by Lee over the period 1909–12. Its formal name is **Chequers Court** and the Tudor house was built on the site of a 13th-century one owned by Laurence de Scaccario (literally 'chequer'), whose own name probably meant that he was an official of the medieval Court of Exchequer, the court of law that dealt with matters of revenue (the term 'exchequer' derived from the use of a chequer board to calculate income and expenditure). The anglicized form of *Scaccario* was applied to the house. The history of the name is in the event appropriate, since the prime minister is also First Lord of the Treasury.

Cheriton[1] 'village with a church', OE *cirice* 'church' + -TON. A village in Hampshire, about 11 km (7 miles) east of Winchester and 3 km (2 miles) south of Alresford. The source of the River ITCHEN is about 1.5 km (1 mile) to the south. The writer and radical reformer William Cobbett (1763–1835) described Cheriton as a 'hard, iron village' – not a characterization that seems particularly appropriate today. **Battle of Cheriton** (29 March 1644). A battle of the Civil Wars, fought to the north of Cheriton, in which a Royalist army under Sir Ralph Hopton and a Parliamentarian army under Sir William Waller fought for control of Winchester. The Parliamentarians prevailed.

Cheriton[2]. A village in Kent, on the northwestern edge of Folkestone. The CHANNEL TUNNEL emerges here.

Cherry Hinton *Cherry* (1576) from the large number of cherry-trees formerly growing here; *Hinton* 'religious community's farmstead', OE *higna* possessive plural form of *hiwan* 'family, brotherhood' + -TON.

A village in Cambridgeshire, on the southeastern edge of Cambridge. It became familiar to the cliff-starved, fen-bound members of the Cambridge University Mountaineering Club for the **Cherry Hinton Wall**, an exiguous area of exposed chalk on which they exercised their skills.

Chertsey 'Cerot's island', Celtic personal name *Cerot* + OE *eg* (*see* -EY, -EA).

A town in Surrey, on the River Thames, in the angle formed by the M3 and the M25 at Junction 12.

> There was an Old Lady of Chertsey,
> Who made a remarkable curtsey;
> She twirled round and round, till she sunk underground,
> Which distressed all the people of Chertsey.
>
> Edward Lear: *A Book of Nonsense* (1846)

Cherwell 'stream with a curve', OE *cearr* 'curve', 'bend' + *wella* 'stream'.

A river in Northamptonshire and Oxfordshire (pronounced 'charwell'), rising 19 km (12 miles) northeast of BANBURY, close to the village of **Charwelton** ('farm on the river Cherwell'). It flows south in a gentle, winding course for 48 km (30 miles), generally tight against the Oxford Canal between CROPREDY and Kidlington, into the leafy northern suburbs of Oxford, through the University Parks (*see* MESOPOTAMIA[1] and PARSON'S PLEASURE), and under Magdalen Bridge, before joining the THAMES[1] a little south of Oxford city centre. The river lends its name to a council district in north Oxfordshire.

Cherwell is the name of an Oxford University newspaper, first published in 1892 (*see also* ISIS).

Winston Churchill's scientific adviser during the Second World War, Frederick Alexander Lindemann (1886–1957), a German-born Oxford academic, took the title 1st Viscount Cherwell in 1956.

Chesham 'river-meadow by a heap of stones', OE *ceastel* 'heap of stones' + *hamm* (*see* HAM).

A town in Buckinghamshire, on the River CHESS, about 13 km (8 miles) northeast of High Wycombe. Its 'Underground' station (opened in 1889) is a northern terminus of the Metropolitan line.

Arthur Lasenby Liberty (1843–1917), founder of the REGENT STREET store Liberty, was born in Chesham.

Chesham Bois *Bois* from manorial ownership in the Middle Ages by the de Bois family.

A town (pronounced 'chesham boyz') in Buckinghamshire, about 3 km (2 miles) south of Chesham.

Cheshire From CHESTER + SHIRE.

A county in the northwest Midlands of England, bordered to the north by Greater Manchester, to the east and south by Derbyshire, Staffordshire and Shropshire and to the west by Wales. In 1974 it lost a significant northeastern portion of its territory (including STOCKPORT) to GREATER MANCHESTER, and the northern part of the WIRRAL (including BIRKENHEAD and WALLASEY) was merged with MERSEYSIDE. Further territorial erosion followed in 1998 with the creation of the unitary authorities of HALTON and WARRINGTON.

Cheshire's county town is CHESTER, and other important centres are CONGLETON, CREWE, ELLESMERE PORT, MACCLESFIELD, NANTWICH, RUNCORN and WILMSLOW. It is largely a fertile plain used for dairy farming, but the Wirral peninsula and the eastern part of the county are industrialized. Crewe is a historically important railway centre, and Cheshire's salt mines go back to Roman times.

From 1237 Cheshire was a COUNTY PALATINE.

In cricketing terms Cheshire is a 'minor county' (the club was founded in 1908) and plays in the minor counties championship.

There is a town called Cheshire in Massachusetts, USA. *See also* GOLDEN TRIANGLE.

Cheshire acre. A measure of the area of agricultural land formerly used in Cheshire, equal to 8560 sq m (10,240 sq yards) (a standard acre has 4047 sq m).

Cheshire cat. A cat of undetermined breed whose chief distinguishing characteristic is its grin. The concept dates back at least to the late 18th century, and was commonly alluded to in the 19th ('Mr. Newcome says, "That woman grins like a Cheshire cat"', William Thackeray, *The Newcomes* (1855)), but it was Lewis Carroll who famously embodied the myth (albeit in vanishing form) in *Alice's Adventures in Wonderland* (1865):

> 'All right', said the Cat; and this time it vanished quite slowly, beginning with the end of the tail, and ending with the grin, which remained some time after the rest of it had gone.

Cheshire cheese. A type of hard cow's-milk cheese made originally in Cheshire. It comes in two colours: white (actually very pale yellow) and red (an orange colour, achieved with the help of annatto dye). There is also a blue-veined variety. It is mentioned in Domesday Book, making it the oldest known English cheese. **Ye Olde Cheshire Cheese**, an ancient pub off FLEET STREET, London, was frequented by Samuel Johnson and Charles Dickens, among many other literary and journalistic luminaries. As its name suggests, the food was always as important as the drink ('For the perfection of a lark pudding, go to the Cheshire Cheese, in Fleet Street,' E.S. Dallas, *Kettner's Book of the Table* (1877)). In the late 19th century it was the meeting place of the Rhymers Club, a group of poets including W.B. Yeats and Ernest Dowson. Today it is a tourist destination.

Cheshire Show. *See under* KNUTSFORD.

Cheshunt Probably 'spring by the old (Roman) fort', OE *ceaster* 'old fort' (*see* CHESTER) + *funta* 'fountain, spring'.

A town (pronounced 'chessənt') in Hertfordshire, beside the River LEA, about 8 km (5 miles) east of Potters Bar and 2.5 km (1.5 miles) north of the M25. It is home to the headquarters of the Tesco supermarket chain.

Richard Cromwell (1626–1712), son and successor of Oliver as Lord Protector of England, spent the last 32 years of his life in seclusion in Cheshunt, having abdicated as head of state in 1659 and lived the intervening 21 years in exile in France.

Chesil Beach *Chesil* 'shingle', OE *cisel*.

A 27-km (17-mile) bank of shingle on the Dorset coast, at the eastern end of Lyme Bay, running from ABBOTSBURY southeastwards to the Isle of PORTLAND. Chesil Beach (also sometimes known as **Chesil Bank**) has been built up over thousands of years by the action of the sea. The average size of its pebbles increases over threefold from its northwestern end to its southeastern. The long narrow lagoon behind the bank is called the FLEET[2]; it is an important nature reserve.

The small village called **Chesil** on the Isle of Portland was named after it. The classic adventure novel *Moonfleet* (1898) by J. Meade Falkner deals with smuggling along this stretch of coast, and has given its name to a number of tourist-related venues in the vicinity.

Chess A back-formation from *Chesham*.

A chalk-stream river that rises to the north of CHESHAM in Buckinghamshire and flows through the CHILTERN HILLS southeastwards into Hertfordshire.

Chessex A blend of *Chelsea* and *Essex*.

A notional location of the 2000s whose female inhabitants are **Chessex girls**: fashionable neo-Sloane Rangers (*see under* SLOANE SQUARE) from Chelsea who affect some of the flashy glamour of the Essex girl (*see under* ESSEX), such as short denim skirts and white high heels. Victoria Adams, a.k.a. Posh Spice and wife of the former Manchester United footballer David Beckham, is apparently a key style icon for Chessex girls, and the actress and model Liz Hurley is the genre's archetype.

Chessington 'Cissa's hill', OE *Cissan* possessive form of male personal name *Cissa* + *dun* (*see* -DOWN, -DON).

A southwestern suburb of Greater London, in the Royal Borough of KINGSTON UPON THAMES (until 1965 in Surrey). **Chessington Zoo**, originally established in 1931, is now part of the theme park **Chessington World of Adventures**.

Chester 'Roman fort or city', OE *ceaster* (*see* CHESTER).

A city in CHESHIRE and its county town, in a loop of the River DEE[2], about 24 km (15 miles) south of Liverpool.

It was an important settlement in pre-Roman times, when it was called **Deoua**. The Romans occupied it, Latinizing its name to **Deva** (or more fully *Castra Devana* 'camp on the Dee') and encircling it with a wall which still, with many subsequent reconstructions and alterations, maintains a 3-km (2-mile) ring around the old city. It was the headquarters of the famous 20th Legion, a status perhaps reflected in the Anglo-Saxons' name for it, **Legacœstir** 'city of the legions'. By the end of the first millennium this had become worn down to simply *Chester*.

In the Middle Ages Chester was a port of some significance, and trade with Scotland, Wales and further afield in Europe made the city rich, but as the River Dee gradually silted up its importance declined.

The most distinctive features of Chester's cityscape are the Rows, two-tiered medieval shopping arcades, which are unique in England (Daniel Defoe was unimpressed – he thought 'they serve to make the city look both old and ugly', *A Tour Through the Whole Island of Great Britain* (1726)), and the 'magpie' buildings with their bold black-and-white pattern of half-timbering. **Chester Cathedral**, a red sandstone building heavily restored in the 1870s, has its origin in the Anglo-Saxon abbey of St Werburgh. Bishops of Chester sign themselves *Cestr*, which is short for Latin *Cestrensis* 'of Chester'.

Henry James provided a transatlantic perspective on the city at the beginning of his novel *The Ambassadors* (1903), through the eyes of the first of the 'ambassadors', the amiable but meandering Lambert Strether:

> The tortuous wall – girdle, long since snapped, of the little swollen city, half held in place by careful civic hands – wanders in narrow file between parapets smoothed by peaceful generations, pausing here and there for a dismantled gate or a bridged gap, with rises and drops, steps up and steps down, queer twists, queer contacts, peeps into homely streets and under the brows of gables, views of cathedral tower and waterside fields, of huddled English town and ordered English country … Strether rested on one of the high sides of the old stony groove of the little rampart. He leaned back on this support with his face to the tower of the cathedral, now admirably commanded by their station, the high red-brown mass, square and subordinately spired and crocketed, retouched and restored, but charming to his long-sealed eyes and with the first swallows of the year weaving their flight all round it.
>
> Henry James: *The Ambassadors* (1903)

Horse-racing has been staged in Chester since 1540, on a piece of land to the west of the city walls known as the

Roodee. **Chester Zoo** has an international reputation. In popular culture, Channel 4's middle-class teen soap *Hollyoaks* (1995–) is located in a suburb of Chester; in higher-brow culture, the conductor Sir Adrian Boult (1889–1983) was born in the city. There are also royal connections: the title of 'Earl of Chester' is, by tradition, conferred on the oldest son of the British sovereign.

The composer William Lawes (1602–45), a Royalist, was killed in the siege of Chester during the Civil Wars.

Battle of Chester (*c*.616). A battle in which Æthelfryth's Saxons of Northumbria defeated the Britons of Powys, thereby helping to isolate the Britons of Strathclyde in the north from those in Wales in the west. The chronicler Bede wrote a description of it.

Chester Mystery Plays. A set of 25 mystery plays based on Bible stories, performed in Chester in the Middle Ages. Each was staged by a trade (or 'mystery') appropriate to its subject matter: *Noah's Flood*, for instance, was put on by the Water-Leaders (water-carriers) and Drawers in Dee (drawers of water from the River Dee), and *The Harrowing of Hell* by the Cooks and Innkeepers (no doubt inspired by the fiery chaos of their kitchens).

Chester pudding. An early form of lemon-meringue pie, consisting of a pastry case with a lemon-custard filling topped with meringue. It dates from at least the 1860s.

Chesterfield 'open land near a Roman fort or settlement', OE *ceaster* (*see* CHESTER) + FIELD.

A town in northern Derbyshire, about 16 km (10 miles) south of Sheffield. By far its best-known feature is the 84-m (280-ft) twisted octagonal spire of its 14th-century Church of St Mary and All Saints. The distortion is thought to be due either to the effects of temperature change on the spire's lead cladding or to the use of unseasoned timber for building it. (The spire is reflected in the nickname of Chesterfield's professional football team, the Spireites.)

Tony Benn was MP for Chesterfield between 1984 and 2001. The Russian emigré M.D. Osinsky (1885–1951) opened his first draper's shop in Chesterfield in 1904. It bore his adopted name: Montague Burton.

Battle of Chesterfield (15 May 1266). A battle in which the barons (including the Earl of Derby) were defeated by the army of Henry III, which went on to take Derby.

Chesterfield sofa. A high-backed and high-armed button-tufted sofa, usually in leather, and thought to be named after (or even invented by) one of the earls of Chesterfield. The term was in use by the end of the 18th century, and has since come to denote a wide range of related styles, still popular in domestic environments as well as in clubs and hotel lobbies.

Chesterholm OE *ceaster* (*see* CHESTER) + possibly OScand *holm* 'water-meadow'.

The site on HADRIAN'S WALL of the Roman fort of **Vindolanda**, where archaeologists have discovered a large collection of Roman letters and military records.

Chester-le-Street 'Roman camp on the Roman road', OE *ceaster* (*see* CHESTER) + *strœt* (*see* STREET), with OFr *le* 'the', *sur* 'on' having disappeared; the Roman road in question is unnamed, or simply known as 'Street'.

A town in County Durham, 14 km (8.5 miles) south of Newcastle upon Tyne. It was made a diocese in 883 after the LINDISFARNE monks fled the Vikings and brought St Cuthbert's remains here, and subsequently became an important pilgrimage centre until both corpse and diocese moved to DURHAM in 995.

Chester-le-Street's Riverside Ground staged its first first-class cricket match in May 1995, and its first test match (the 2nd test match between England and Zimbabwe) in June 2003, when it became not only the first new test match ground in England since 1902, but also the most northerly test match venue in the world. The picturesque ground is overlooked by Lumley Castle, a well-preserved 14th-century structure.

Chesters OE *ceaster* (*see* CHESTER).

A park on the banks of the North Tyne in Northumberland, which contains the site of the Roman fort of **Cilurnum**. One of the most important forts of HADRIAN'S WALL, Cilurnum is believed to have been a cavalry base. Chesters

---

❖ chester ❖

This Old English element, *ceaster*, is from Latin *castrum* 'camp, fort, town, city', and the majority of names containing it are old Roman stations, many of which became major cities: MANCHESTER, LEICESTER, DONCASTER, LANCASTER, EXETER, GLOUCESTER and CHESTER are obvious examples. Not all are so, however: some are now minor and apparently insignificant places, such as BEWCASTLE and PAPCASTLE in Cumbria, both of which illustrate the substitution of the French element *castel* for *ceaster*, and both of which interestingly have Old Scandinavian first elements, *both* 'booth, shelter' and *papi* 'monk, hermit'. So while many *ceaster* names contain elements showing their Romano-British origins (such as Leicester 'fort of the *Ligore* tribe', Exeter 'fort on the *Isca*, the river Exe' and Manchester 'fort of *Mamucium*') over the centuries some names were adapted: GODMANCHESTER (Huntingdonshire) is named after an Anglo-Saxon Godmund; and several names lost, or never had, any identifying element, leaving CAISTER-ON-SEA (Norfolk), CASTOR (Peterborough unitary authority) and CHESTER.

has been a World Heritage Site since 1987. Remnants of its gateway and streets are visible, and its military bath-house, between the fort and the river, is particularly well preserved.

Chevening Perhaps '(settlement of the) dwellers at the ridge', Celtic *cevn* 'ridge' +-ING.

A village in Kent, about 5 km (3 miles) northwest of Sevenoaks. The local stately home, which shares the village's name, was bequeathed to the nation in 1967 by the 7th Earl Stanhope on condition that it be retained for royal or ministerial use. The Prince of Wales lived here 1974–80, and it now serves as the official residence of the British foreign secretary.

Cheviot, the Etymology unknown.

A great rounded mass of a moorland hill (816 m / 2676 ft) in Northumberland, 30 km (19 miles) west-northwest of Alnwick, just south of the Scottish border. Its conventional pronunciation is *chee*viot. The walk over it forms the last stage of the Pennine Way (*see under* PENNINES), terminating just over the Border at KIRK YETHOLM. Daniel Defoe – like most of his contemporaries, a hater of mountains as fearsome and unproductive – nevertheless agreed to be guided on horseback up The Cheviot on his 1720s tour. Part of the way up he refused to continue, convinced that the summit would be a pinnacle, 'and we should only have room enough to stand, with a precipice every way round us'. However, he was reassured that the summit was broad enough to run a race on, and on achieving the top, was delighted by its flatness and by the views.

> A snowstorm drifting down the Bowmont vale
>   A little hour ago made Cheviot white,
> And left him glistening in his silver mail,
>   The day's last champion in the lists with night.
>
>   Will H. Ogilvie: 'Sunset', from *The Land We Love* (1910)

> Cheviot's white shoulder glistens
> in the sun, too glacial for comfort.
>
>   Christine De Luca: 'Harthope, Spring 1966', from *Wast
>   wi da Valkyries* (1997)

Cheviot. A breed of hardy, hornless, white-faced sheep, originally bred in the Cheviot Hills. During the Highland Clearances, people were removed from the land to make way for the Cheviot and for 'sportsmen' – hence the title of John McGrath's political drama, ***The Cheviot, the Stag and the Black, Black Oil*** (1974).

Cheviot Hills. A range of high, rounded, remote hills along the Anglo-Scottish border, also known as the **Cheviots**. They extend for some 55 km (35 miles), from Wooler to Kielder, and are traversed by only one road, the A68 over CARTER BAR. In addition to the Cheviot itself, other tops include Peel Fell, Hungry Law, Hedgehope Hill, BEEFSTAND HILL and WINDY GYLE. The rivers COQUET,

North TYNE (feeding the KIELDER reservoir), and Rede (*see under* REDESDALE) rise in the Cheviots.

In the 1990s the Council for the Protection of Rural England produced a series of 'tranquillity maps', show-ing those areas of England which, according to certain fixed criteria, could be considered remote from power stations, roads, large towns, industrial areas, main line railways, airport noise and open-cast mining. Along with Shropshire and north Devon, the Cheviot Hills were one of only three extensive areas of tranquillity remaining in England.

Hunting of the Cheviot, the. An alternative name for the Battle of Otterburn (*see under* OTTERBURN).

North Country Cheviot. A variety of Cheviot sheep found in Caithness and Sutherland.

Chevy Chase. See OTTERBURN.

Chew Magna *Chew* from the River *Chew*, an OCelt river name apparently meaning 'young of an animal' and referring to the nature of the Chew as a tributary of the River AVON[2]; *Magna* from Latin *magna* 'great'.

A town in Bath and North East Somerset (before 1996 in Avon, before 1974 in Somerset), on the River Chew, about 8 km (5 miles) south of Bristol. In the Middle Ages it was an important centre of the wool industry. To the south of the town is **Chew Valley Lake**, a vast reservoir, which is used for boating and other water sports, as well as being a haven for birds and plant life. It has been designated a site of special scientific interest.

Chew Stoke 'secondary settlement belonging to Chew (Magna)'; *Stoke* from OE *stoc* 'secondary or dependent set-tlement' (*see* -STOCK, STOCK-, STOKE).

A village in Bath and North East Somerset (before 1996 in Avon, before 1974 in Somerset), about 3 km (2 miles) south-west of CHEW MAGNA.

Chewton Mendip *Chewton* 'estate on the River Chew', an OCelt river name (*see* CHEW MAGNA) + -TON; *Mendip see* MENDIP HILLS.

A village in Somerset, on the River Chew, on the eastern edge of the Mendip Hills, about 7 km (4.5 miles) west of Midsomer Norton.

Cheyne Walk From the *Cheyne* family, late 17th-century lords of the manor of Chelsea.

A road (pronounced 'chainy') in CHELSEA, on the north bank of the River Thames, extending westwards from Chelsea Embankment (SW3, SW10). It was laid out between 1708 and 1720. Its numerous distinguished residents have included the writers Hilaire Belloc, George Eliot, Henry James, George Meredith and Algernon Charles Swinburne, the painters William Dyce, J.M.W. Turner and J.A.M. Whistler, and, mixing the two genres, Dante Gabriel Rossetti (who kept a small private zoo here).

Chichester Probably 'Cissa's Roman town', OE male personal name *Cissa* + CHESTER.

A cathedral city and harbour town on the south coast of England, the county town of WEST SUSSEX, about 30 km (19 miles) west of Worthing and 20 km (12 miles) northeast of Portsmouth.

The site was occupied by the Romans soon after they conquered England, and they laid out the plan of the town (more or less as it exists to this day) within an encircling wall (also still evident in many places). Its Roman name was **Noviomagus Regnensium**. After the Romans had left it became a capital of the South Saxons, reputedly given by King Ælla to his son Cissa (whence its English name).

The old city centre is divided into quarters by four streets at whose intersection stands an early 16th-century octagonal Market Cross, probably Chichester's most familiar landmark. Nearby is **Chichester Cathedral**, begun in the early 12th century. Its 84-m (277-ft) 15th-century spire can be seen from miles around. Bishops of Chichester sign themselves *Cicestr*, which is short for Latin *Cicestrensis* 'of Chichester'.

Chichester Harbour, a many-armed haven, lies to the southwest of the city, bounded on the east by the SELSEY peninsula and on the west by HAYLING ISLAND. It was once important to the corn trade, but is now devoted to recreational seamanship.

The **Chichester Festival Theatre** opened in 1962, under the direction of Laurence Olivier. It has since acquired a reputation for starry if not exactly avant-garde productions: the 'middle to upper-middle brow range that Chichester programmes now generally encompass' according to *Country Life* (1974).

Chichester/Goodwood Airport, to the northeast of the city, is used mainly for light aviation. It was an RAF fighter station during the Battle of Britain. It is encircled by a motor-racing circuit (*see* GOODWOOD).

> I cannot say much for the city of Chichester, in which, if six or seven good families were removed, there would not be much conversation, except what is to be found among the canons, and dignitaries of the cathedral.
>
> Daniel Defoe: *A Tour Through the Whole Island of Great Britain* (1726)

Chichester elm. An alternative name for the American elm, *Ulmus americana*.

Chichester Psalms. A three-part setting for choir and orchestra of Hebrew psalms by Leonard Bernstein. It was commissioned by Walter Hussey, Dean of Chichester Cathedral (a considerable patron of the arts) and first performed there in 1965.

Chiddingly Probably 'Citta's people's glade', OE male personal name *Citta* + -*inga*- (*see* -ING) + -LEY.

A hamlet in East Sussex, about 11 km (7 miles) southeast of Uckfield. Some important examples of medieval and Elizabethan architecture are preserved here.

Chiddingly boar. A late 15th-century silver cap-badge depicting a boar, of a sort thought to have been given by Richard III to his followers as a sign of allegiance. It was discovered in a field at Chiddingly.

Chignall Smealy *Chignall* probably 'Cicca's corner of land', OE *Ciccan* possessive form of male personal name *Cicca* + *halh* (*see* HALE, -HALL); *Smealy* name of a nearby place, 'smooth glade', OE *smethe* 'smooth' + -LEY.

A village in Essex, 8 km (5 miles) northwest of Chelmsford.

Chigwell Perhaps 'Cicca's spring or stream', OE male personal name *Cicca* + *wella* 'spring, stream'.

A town in Essex, at the northeastern edge of Greater London, just to the east of the M11. As the home town of Sharon and Tracey in the BBC television sitcom *Birds of a Feather* (1989–94), it is epicentric to the whole 1980s–90s 'Essex' phenomenon (*see* ESSEX). Chigwell 'Underground' station, on the Central line, was opened in 1948.

Childerditch 'ditch or dyke on the river Chilt or Chelt', OE *dic* 'ditch' with what appears to be a river name, of obscure origin, but having been adapted to resemble the word *child*.

A village in Essex, some 5 km (3 miles) south of Brentford, made more famous than it would otherwise have been by the lines of the poet Edward Thomas (1878–1917), killed in action on the Western Front.

> If I should ever by chance grow rich
> I'll buy Codham, Cockridden, and Childerditch,
> Roses, Pyrgo, and Lapwater,
> And let them all to my elder daughter.

Child Okeford *Child* 'son of a noble family' (probably referring to an early manorial owner), OE *cild* 'child, son of a noble family'; *Okeford* 'oak-tree ford', OE *ac* 'oak' + -FORD.

A village in Dorset, about 8 km (5 miles) northwest of Blandford Forum and 3 km (2 miles) northeast of Okeford Fitzpaine.

Child's Ercall *Child's see* CHILD OKEFORD; *Ercall* perhaps 'muddy hill', OE *ear* 'gravel, mud' + *calu* 'bare hill'.

A village in Shropshire, about 10 km (6 miles) south of Market Drayton.

Chillingham 'Ceofel's people's village', OE male personal name *Ceofel* + -*inga*- (*see* -ING) + -HAM.

A castle in Northumberland, 18 km (11 miles) northeast of Alnwick. The castle grew considerably from the 11th century until the 19th. Its park has been the home, since the 13th century, of the unique **Chillingham cattle**, the only remaining wild herd in Britain. They are white with red ears (according to folk belief the same colouring as fairy cattle), and there is a belief that if you touch one of these shy but fierce beasts it will kill you.

Chiltern From CHILTERN HILLS.

A small administrative district of Buckinghamshire. Its headquarters are in AMERSHAM, and it also includes CHESHAM.

Chiltern Hills Perhaps a derivative of an OE or pre-English word *celte* or *cilte* 'hill-slope'.

A range of chalk hills in south-central England, also known as **the Chilterns**, about 72 km (45 miles) long, extending in a northeastward curve from Berkshire (to the north of Reading) through Oxfordshire, Buckinghamshire and Hertfordshire to Bedfordshire (the Dunstable Downs). Their highest point is HADDINGTON HILL (261 m / 857 ft), near Wendover. Almost as high is nearby COOMBE HILL (260 m / 852 ft). Remnants of the great beech woods that once covered the hills remain a notable feature of the Chilterns, which have been designated an Area of Outstanding Natural Beauty.

Since 1996, **Chiltern Railways** has run services between Birmingham and London's Marylebone station, running through what it describes as the 'M40 corridor'.

Chiltern Gap. A cutting made through the Chiltern Hills to accommodate the M40 motorway. It is close to STOKENCHURCH, whence its alternative name, the 'Stokenchurch Gap'.

Chiltern gentian. A species of gentian (*Gentiana germanica*) with large, dull purple flowers. It grows on chalk land but is rare in Britain.

Chiltern Hundreds. The three Hundreds (ancient county subdivisions) of Stoke, Desborough and Burnham, in Buckinghamshire, over which a steward was originally appointed to suppress the robbers who frequented the thickly wooded Chiltern Hills. The necessity has long since ceased, but the office remains. As a consequence of the Succession Act of 1701 and later Acts, the holding of most non-political offices of profit under the Crown meant resignation from the House of Commons, and after 1750 application for the stewardship of the Chiltern Hundreds was used as a means of relinquishing membership of Parliament (since members cannot resign directly). The stewardships of Old Shoreham (Sussex), East Hendred (Oxfordshire), Hempholme (Yorkshire), Poynings (Sussex) and Northstead (Yorkshire) were also used for this purpose, as were (until 1838) the escheatorships of Munster and Ulster, in Ireland. By the House of Commons Disqualification Act (1957) the stewardship of the Chiltern Hundreds and the Manor of Northstead were retained for this use and their gift remains with the chancellor of the exchequer.

Chilthorne Domer *Chilthorne* perhaps from an unrecorded OE or pre-English *celte* or *cilte* possibly meaning 'hill-slope'; *Domer* denoting manorial ownership in the Middle Ages by the Dummere family.

A village in Somerset, about 5 km (3 miles) northwest of Yeovil.

Chilton Candover *Chilton* 'farm of the young (noble)men', OE *cild* 'child, son of a noble family' + -TON; *Candover see* BROWN CANDOVER.

A village in Hampshire, about 13 km (8 miles) southwest of Basingstoke.

Chilton Cantelo *Cantelo* denoting manorial ownership in the Middle Ages by the Cantelu family.

A village in Somerset, about 6 km (4 miles) north of Yeovil.

Chilton Foliat *Foliat* denoting manorial ownership in the Middle Ages by the Foliot family.

A village in Wiltshire, about 13 km (8 miles) east of Marlborough.

Chilvers Coton 'Ceolfrith's cottages', OE *Ceolfrithes* possessive form of male personal name *Ceolfrith* + ME *coten* 'cottages', or from OE *cot* 'cottage' (*see* -COT, COTE).

A southwestern suburb of NUNEATON, in Warwickshire. The novelist George Eliot (1819–80) was born here.

Chimney 'Ceomma's island' (in this context probably an area of dry ground in a marsh), OE *Ceomman* possessive form of male personal name *Ceomma* + *eg* (*see* -EY, -EA).

A village in Oxfordshire, about 19 km (12 miles) southwest of Oxford.

China Street. A 19th-century nickname for BOW STREET, perhaps alluding to its proximity to COVENT GARDEN, then a market, where 'China oranges' would have been plentiful.

Chinatown. A name applied to that part of a Western city that has a large Chinese population. It appears to have originated on the West Coast of America in the middle of the 19th century, but it crossed the Atlantic in the 1890s, when a noticeable (though never particularly large) Chinese population began to build up in LIMEHOUSE, in the area around the London docks. Most were sailors, and perfectly respectable members of the community, but a small amount of opium-smoking was blown up by the press into a 'Yellow Peril', further sensationalized by Sax Rohmer in his 'Dr Fu-Manchu' mysteries. By the 1960s London's Chinatown had moved westwards (although many street names survive in Limehouse and POPLAR as reminders of its original locality: Oriental Street, Canton Street, Ming Street, Pekin Street). It is now in SOHO, between SHAFTESBURY AVENUE and LEICESTER SQUARE, centring particularly on Gerrard Street. The area abounds in Chinese restaurants and supermarkets (the first Chinese restaurant in Europe opened in Piccadilly Circus in 1908), and the street signs are in Chinese as well as English.

Chingford 'shingle ford', OE *cingel* 'shingle' + -FORD.

A northeastern suburb of Greater London, to the east of the River LEA, in the borough of WALTHAM FOREST (E4). It is dominated by the huge William Girling Reservoir, built beside the River Lea in 1951. Further east the River **Ching** (the name is a back-formation from 'Chingford') flows southwards through Chingford towards Walthamstow and the Lea.

The composer Kaikhosru Shapurji Sorabji (1892–1988; original name Leon Dudley Sorabji) was born in Chingford. His *Opus Clavicembalisticum* (1930) is the longest piano piece ever written: it takes four hours to perform.

Chingford Skinhead or **Chingford Strangler.** Media nicknames (the latter inspired by the 'Boston Strangler', a US serial killer of the 1960s) for Norman (now Lord) Tebbit (b.1931), the rightwing populist Europhobe MP for Chingford from 1974 until his elevation to the peerage in 1992. He is known for his abrasive manner and robust invective and was a leading figure in the cabinets of Margaret Thatcher in the 1980s. He famously told the unemployed to get on their bikes to find work, as his own father had done in the 1930s. The future, if short-lived, leader of the Conservative Party, Iain Duncan Smith, succeeded him in the parliamentary seat.

Chinnor 'Ceonna's slope', OE male personal name *Ceonna* + *ora* 'slope'.
A village in Oxfordshire, in the CHILTERN HILLS, about 6 km (4 miles) southeast of Thame. It is situated on the ICKNIELD WAY.

Chippenham Probably 'Cippa's river-meadow', OE *Cippan* possessive form of male personal name *Cippa* + *hamm* (*see* HAM).
A market town in Wiltshire, on the River AVON², about 30 km (19 miles) southwest of Swindon. One of the largest cattle markets in England is held here every Friday.

Chippenham occupies a melancholy niche in the history of pop music. On 17 April 1960 a Ford Consul taxi carrying the US rock 'n' roll stars Eddie Cochran and Gene Vincent from Bristol to London at the end of a UK tour crashed into a lamp post at Rowden Hill. The 21-year-old Cochran was rushed to St Martin's Hospital, Bath, where he was pronounced dead. Vincent survived the crash. A memorial stone marks the scene of the tragedy, and Cochran is also commemorated in Chippenham's annual Eddie Cochran Rock 'n' Roll weekend.

Lodowicke Muggleton, founder of the Muggletonians, a group of 17th-century radical religious dissidents, is believed to have been born in Chippenham.

Battle of Chippenham (6 January 878). A battle in which King Alfred's West Saxon army was routed in a surprise attack by a Danish force under Guthrum and forced into hiding in the Somerset marshes.

Chipping Campden 'market at Campden', *Chipping* OE *cieping* 'market'; *Campden* 'valley with enclosures', OE *camp* 'enclosure, field' + *denu* 'valley'.

A small market town (pronounced 'kamdən') in Gloucestershire, in the COTSWOLDS, about 16 km (10 miles) northwest of Stow-on-the-Wold. It has a claim to be the most picturesque of the many picturesque towns and villages with which the Cotswolds are studded. Chipping Campden was a centre of the 15th-century wool trade, and evidences of its former prosperity abound: notably the magnificent St James's Church and a rich array of merchants' houses (a dozen of Campden's wool merchants became lord mayors of London).

Dover's Hill, a plateau above Chipping Campden, is the venue of the 'Cotswold Olympicks' (*see under* COTSWOLDS). Chipping Campden played the part of a medieval market town in Pier Paolo Pasolini's 'adult' film version of *The Canterbury Tales* (1971).

Campden Wonder. A historical mystery that has never been satifactorily explained: in August 1660, an elderly Chipping Campden rent-collector called William Harrison disappeared; his bloodstained hat was discovered, and it was assumed he had been murdered; a local youth, John Perry, confessed to killing him and was hanged; two years later Harrison reappeared, claiming to have been kidnapped and sold into slavery in the Near East. The veracity of his bizarre story and the reason for Perry's confession continue to defy establishment.

Chipping Norton *Norton see* NORTON.
A small town in Oxfordshire, in the COTSWOLDS, 16 km (10 miles) northwest of WOODSTOCK. At 200 m (656 ft) above sea-level, it is the highest town in its county.

Like any self-respecting Cotswold 'wool town', Chipping Norton abounds in felicitious honey-coloured stone buildings, evidence of its late-medieval prosperity. In 1549 the sometimes violent upheavals of the English Reformation did for Chipping Norton's parish priest, when Henry Joyce was hanged from the tower of the 15th-century church of St Mary for his role in a local revolt against the replacement of the old Latin service book with the new Anglican Book of Common Prayer.

Prominent on the town's western edge is the imposing Bliss Tweed Mill (built in 1872 and now converted into private flats), whose massive central chimney is set slightly incongruously atop a building that resembles a country mansion.

Chipping Ongar *Ongar see* ONGAR.
A market town in Essex, about 13 km (8 miles) southeast of Harlow.

Chipping Sodbury *Sodbury* 'Soppa's fortified place', OE male personal name *Soppa* + -BURY.
A market town in Gloucestershire, about 13 km (8 miles) northeast of Bristol. The name has frequently been exploited by writers, comedians, etc. for the snigger-value of its second element. The children's author J.K. Rowling

(b.1965), begetter of the Harry Potter phenomenon, was born here.

Chirk 'place at the River Ceiriog', from an OCelt river name meaning 'preferred, honoured'; the name is first recorded in 1295.

A village in Wrexham unitary authority. Its Welsh name is **Y Waun** (*y* 'the' + *gwaun* 'moorland'). The imposing **Chirk Castle**, a grim former outpost of the MARCHES, dates from the 12th and early 13th centuries. Its interiors, often luxurious, are mostly from a later date, and it sits amidst 17th- and 18th-century landscaped grounds. OFFA'S DYKE runs through the park surrounding the castle.

Chislehurst 'gravelly wooded hill', OE *cisel* 'gravel' + *hyrst* 'wooded hill'.

A southeastern suburb of GREATER LONDON, in the borough of BROMLEY (before 1965 in Kent). The French Empress Eugénie and her son came to live here, in Camden Place, after they had been exiled from France in 1870. It may be that Chislehurst inspired *Chiselbury*, the name of the fictitious public school invented by Frank Muir and Denis Norden, of which 'Professor' Jimmy Edwards was head-master in the television sitcom *Whack-O!* (1956–60). Sir Malcolm Campbell (1885–1948), racing driver and breaker of world speed records, was born in Chislehurst.

Chislehurst Caves. A series of underground passages in the western part of Chislehurst, probably originally excavated as chalk mines in Roman times (local legend attributes them to druids, who supposedly used deer-antler picks to dig them out). They were used as air-raid shelters during the Second World War.

Chislet Perhaps 'chestnut copse', OE *cistelet*; alternatively 'chestnut water-conduit', OE *cist* 'chestnut-tree' + (*ge*)*lǽt* 'water-conduit', or 'container water-conduit', OE *cist, cyst* 'chest, container' + (*ge*)*lǽt*.

A village in Kent, about 5 km (3 miles) southeast of Herne Bay.

Chiswick 'farm where cheese is made', OE *ciese* 'cheese' + WICK; *see also* KESWICK.

A western suburb (pronounced 'chizik') of GREATER LONDON, on the north bank of the River THAMES[1] as it loops around the Barnes peninsula, in the borough of HOUNSLOW (W4). Until the middle of the 19th century it was a quiet Middlesex village, but the coming of the railway and then the extension of bus and tram routes brought it within London's orbit. The original headquarters of the London United Tramway Company (later to become London Transport's Stamford Brook Garage) was in Chiswick. The first skid-pan for testing buses was opened there in 1922.

On 8 September 1944 the first German V2 rocket of the Second World War fell on Chiswick. In the mid 1990s a new Russian Orthodox Cathedral was erected in Chiswick,

and its blue onion dome is now a familiar landmark by the elevated section of the M4.

Chiswick Eyot. A narrow island (*eyot*, pronounced like *eight*, is a descendant of OE *iggath* 'islet') close to the Chiswick bank of the River Thames. It is about 250 m (275 yards) long. It is best known for the annual name-checks it receives from television and radio commentators on the University Boat Race, which passes the island in its latter stages.

Chiswick House. A major example of a Palladian villa, built 1725–29, and subsequently inherited by the dukes of Devonshire. It is now administered by English Heritage. As well as being a showcase of Palladian symmetry, Chiswick House was the place of expiry of two celebrated political figures: Charles James Fox (in 1806) and prime minister George Canning (in 1827).

Chittlehamholt 'valley-dwellers' wood', OE *cietel* 'valley' (literally 'kettle, cauldron') + *hǽme* 'inhabitants' + *holt* 'wood'.

A village in Devon, about 32 km (20 miles) northwest of Tiverton.

Chittoe Perhaps from OCelt CED.

A village in Wiltshire, about 8 km (5 miles) southeast of Chippenham.

Chohawniskey tem. The Romany name for LANCASHIRE, according to George Borrow's *Romano Lavo-Lil* ('word book of the Romany', 1874). The name means 'witches' country' (for the Lancashire Witches, *see* PENDLE HILL).

Cholsey 'Ceol's island' (referring to land by the River Thames), OE *Ceoles* possessive form of the male personal name *Ceol* + *eg* (*see* -EY, -EA).

A village in Oxfordshire, about 3 km (2 miles) south of Wallingford. The detective-story writer Agatha Christie, who lived at nearby Winterbrook House in WALLINGFORD, is buried in the churchyard here. Cholsey has a station on the Reading–Oxford railway line, and a preserved single-track line, the **Cholsey and Wallingford Railway**, leads to Wallingford.

Chopwell 'trading place by the spring', OE *ceap* 'trading place' + *wella* 'spring'.

A former mining village in Tyne and Wear, 14 km (8.5 miles) southwest of Newcastle upon Tyne. It became known as **Little Moscow** during the General Strike of 1926, when the miners lowered the Union Jack at the council offices and hoisted the Red Flag, replaced the Bible in the village church with the works of Karl Marx, and renamed the streets after Marx, Engels and Lenin. Nearby **Chopwell Wood** supplied 2000 oaks for the rebuilding of the ship *Royal Sovereig*n in the late 17th century.

Chorley 'the freemen's clearing', OE *ceorl* (*see* CHARL-, CHORL-) + -LEY.

An industrial town in Lancashire, 32 km (20 miles)

northwest of Manchester. The former cotton mills now house other industries.

Chorley was the birthplace of Henry Tate (1819–99), the sugar tycoon who founded the Tate Gallery (*see* MILLBANK); and of the Nobel laureate Norman Haworth (1883–1950), the first to synthesize vitamin C.

Chorley cake. A cake similar to, but somewhat plainer than, an ECCLES cake, featuring pastry, spices, currants and mixed peel.

Chorleywood Originally *Chorley* (*see* CHORLEY); *wood* had been added by the early 16th century.

A town in the southwestern corner of Hertfordshire, on the River CHESS and straddling the M25, contiguous with RICKMANSWORTH in the south. The architect C.F.A. Voysey (1857–1941) lived here, and designed his own house and several others in Chorleywood.

According to government statistics published in 2004, out of 32,482 districts in Britain the inhabitants of Chorleywood West enjoyed the highest quality of life and were the most contented.

See also HERONSGATE.

Chorlton-cum-Hardy 'Ceolfrith's farmstead with the hard island', OE male personal name *Ceolfrith* + -TON + *heard* 'hard' + *eg* (*see* -EY, -EA).

A district of southwest Manchester.

Christchurch Originally *Twynham* '(place) between the rivers' (referring to its situation), OE *(be)tweonan* 'between' + *eam* dative plural of *ea* 'river' (*see* EA-); *Christchurch* (first recorded *c.*1125) 'Church of Christ', OE *Crist* + *cirice*.

A coastal town in Dorset (before 1974, in Hampshire), between the rivers AVON[3] and STOUR[1] (whence its original name **Twynham**, *see above*), and merging in the west into Bournemouth. Its harbour was strategically important in Alfred the Great's defence of England against the Danes in the 9th century.

Christchurch Priory is Britain's longest parish church, at around 90 m (300 ft), and its tower contains the two oldest bells in the country, dating from 1370. Events connected with its building (completed in 1094) led, legend has it, to the town's change of name: building materials kept being moved mysteriously at night to a different site, and on one occasion a beam that had been cut too short was miraculously lengthened; the townspeople decided this was because of Christ's personal intervention, so they dedicated the church to him and renamed the town after it.

Christchurch has the world's biggest maze, covering an area of 6.5 ha (16 acres) and with 14.5 km (9 miles) of paths. It is made of maize, and much of it is in the shape of a lobster.

Christchurch is also the name of a major city on South Island, New Zealand, and of a parish in Barbados.

Christian Malford 'ford by a cross', *cristel-mæl* 'cross' + -FORD.

A village in Wiltshire, about 6.5 km (4 miles) northeast of Chippenham.

Christmas Common From *Christmas Coppice*, the name of a local coppice where holly trees, tradititionally associated with Christmas, grew.

A village in Oxfordshire, in the CHILTERN HILLS, about 21 km (13 miles) southeast of Oxford.

Christmas Pie From *Christmas Pie Farm* (1823), the name of a local farm probably associated with a family called Christmas.

A hamlet in Surrey, to the north of the HOG'S BACK and to the west of Guildford. It is little more than a collection of bungalows, and fails to live up to its intriguing name.

Christminster. The fictional name for OXFORD in Thomas Hardy's novels (*see* WESSEX), notably *Jude the Obscure* (1895). The inspiration for it was Oxford's Christ Church Cathedral.

Christow 'Christian place' (perhaps with reference to the local church), OE *cristen* 'Christian' + *stow* 'place'.

A village in Devon, at the eastern edge of Dartmoor National Park, about 13 km (8 miles) southwest of Exeter.

Chudleigh 'Ciedda's glade' or 'glade in a hollow', OE male personal name *Ciedda* or OE *ceod(e)* 'pouch, hollow place' + -LEY.

A village in Devon, about 8 km (5 miles) north of Newton Abbot.

Chunnel. A colloquial and usually fairly facetious term for the CHANNEL TUNNEL, favoured particularly by journalists. It first cropped up in the 1920s, and was revived whenever a new project for building the tunnel was mooted, but when the tunnel actually materialized it failed to create a secure position for itself in the English language.

It has also been used as a verb:

> A ... consortium devoted to Channel-tunnelling, or 'chunnelling', and hoping to make money out of it. If the Group now actually starts to chunnel ... it will be the first time for 80 years [etc.].
>
> *The Observer* (1963)

Church OE *cirice* 'church'.

A village that is now contiguous with ACCRINGTON, Lancashire.

Churchill[1] 'hill hill', OCelt *crug* (*see* CREECH, CROOK) + OE *hyll* 'hill'.

A village in Oxfordshire, about 19 km (12 miles) northwest of Woodstock. In spite of its proximity to the home of the dukes of Marlborough, BLENHEIM PALACE, it is not the source of their family name, Churchill.

Churchill². A village in Devon, about 8 km (5 miles) north of Barnstaple.

Churchill³. A village in North Somerset (before 1996 in Avon, before 1974 in Somerset), about 13 km (8 miles) east of Weston-super-Mare.

Churchill⁴. A village in Worcestershire (before 1998 in Hereford and Worcester, before 1974 in Worcestershire) about 5 km (3 miles) northeast of Kidderminster.

Churchill Barriers, the Named after Sir Winston *Churchill.* The concrete causeways linking the mainland of ORKNEY with the islands of Burray and South Ronaldsay. They were built on the orders of Winston Churchill after the sinking of the battleship HMS *Royal Oak* in October 1939 by a U-boat that had penetrated the naval anchorage at SCAPA FLOW. The barriers (across which a road was later built) blocked the eastern approaches to Scapa Flow.

Church Langton *Church* presumably indicating the location of the parish church; *Langton see* LANGTON HERRING. A village in Leicestershire, about 17.5 km (11 miles) southeast of Leicester.
See also the LANGTONS.

Church Lench 'church slope', OE *cirice* 'church' + *hlenc* 'extensive hill-slope'.
A village in Worcestershire (before 1998 in Hereford and Worcester, before 1974 in Worcestershire), about 10 km (6 miles) north of Evesham.
See also ATCH LENCH, ROUS LENCH.

Church Minshull *Minshull* 'Monn's sloping land', OE male personal name *Monn* + *scelf* 'shelf, sloping land'.
A village in Cheshire, about 6 km (4 miles) northwest of Crewe.

Church Preen *Preen* from OE *preon* 'brooch, pin', perhaps with reference to some aspect of the local landscape.
A village in Shropshire, 16 km (10 miles) south of Shrewsbury.

Church Pulverbatch *Pulverbatch* from an unknown first element (perhaps an old stream name) + OE *bæce* 'valley of a stream or brook'.
A village in Shropshire, about 11 km (7 miles) southwest of Shrewsbury.

Church Stretton *Stretton see* STRETTON EN LE FIELD (the Roman road implied in the name is one which ran north-eastwards from the River CLUN¹ in the direction of modern SHREWSBURY).
A village in Shropshire, among the STRETTON HILLS and in the shadow of the LONG MYND, about 19 km (12 miles) south of Shrewsbury. In the 19th century it was

a fashionable spa. The writer Mary Webb (1881–1927; author of *Precious Bane* (1924)) spent her honeymoon here, and in her novels it is fictionalized as **Shepwardine**.

Church Village Self-explanatory.
A large village in Rhondda Cynon Taff (formerly in Glamorgan, then in Mid Glamorgan), 4 km (2.5 miles) south of Pontypridd.

Churi-mengreskey gav. The Romany name for SHEFFIELD, according to George Borrow's *Romano Lavo-Lil* ('word book of the Romany', 1874). The name means 'cutlers' town'.

Churn An OCelt river-name of unknown meaning, possibly from the same source as the first part of the name CIRENCESTER. A river in Gloucestershire and Wiltshire, a tributary of the Thames. It rises in the COTSWOLDS near Seven Springs, south of Cheltenham, and flows southeast through **North Cerney** ('northern place on the River Churn'), Cirencester and **South Cerney** ('southern place on the River Churn'), joining the THAMES¹ at Cricklade.

Churston Ferrers *Churston* perhaps 'peasant's farm', OE *ceorles* possesive form of *ceorl* (*see* CHARL-, CHORL-) + -TON; *Ferrers* denoting manorial ownership in the Middle Ages by the Ferrers family.
A coastal village in Cornwall, towards the southern end of Tor Bay.

Churt 'rough ground', OE *cert*.
A village in Surrey, about 7 km (4.5 miles) northwest of Haslemere.

Chute Standen *Chute* 'wood, forest', OCelt CED; *Standen* denoting manorial ownership in the Middle Ages by the Standen family.
A village in Wiltshire, about 19 km (12 miles) southeast of Marlborough.

Chyandour 'cottage of the stream', Cornish *chi* 'house, cottage' + *an dour* 'of the stream'.
A coastal village in Cornwall, on the northern outskirts of Penzance.

Chysauster 'Sylvester's cottage', Cornish *chi* 'house, cottage' + male personal name *Sylvester*.
An Iron Age hilltop village (pronounced 'chezoister') in Cornwall, about 5 km (3 miles) north of Penzance, probably inhabited between 100 BC and AD 300. The out-lines of the houses and what is claimed as the oldest street in England can still be seen. The people who lived here probably worked tin mines in the locality.

Ciarraí. The Irish name for County KERRY.

Cilgerran 'Cerran's nook', Welsh *cil* 'nook, corner of land' + male personal name *Cerran*.
A village in Carmarthenshire, 4 km (2.5 miles) south of

Cardigan. Dramatically situated on a rocky promontory overlooking the River Teifi is **Cilgerran Castle**. There was a castle here in Norman times, but the present ruins date from the 13th–14th centuries. The castle suffered considerable damage during the revolt of Owain Glyndwr, and fell into ruin in the 17th century.

Cill Airne. The Irish name for KILLARNEY.

Cill Ala. The Irish name for KILLALA.

Cill Bheagáin. The Irish name for KILBEGGAN.

Cill Chaoi. The Irish name for KILKEE.

Cill Dalua. The Irish name for KILLALOE.

Cill Dara. The Irish name for KILDARE.

Cill Dhéagláin. The Irish name for ASHBOURNE[2].

Cill Dhuinsí. The Irish name for KILLINCHY.

Cill Fhionnúrach. The Irish name for KILFENORA.

Cillín Chaoimhín. The Irish name for HOLLYWOOD.

Cill Iníon Léinín. The Irish name for KILLINEY.

Cill Mhaighneann. The Irish name for KILMAINHAM.

Cill Mhantáin. The Irish name for WICKLOW.

Cill Mhichíl. The Irish name for KILMICHAEL.

Cill Mocheallóg. The Irish name for KILMALLOCK.

Cill na Mallach. The Irish name for BUTTEVANT.

Cill Orglan. The Irish name for KILLORGLIN.

Cill Rois. The Irish name for KILRUSH.

Cill Ruaidh. The Irish name for KILROOT.

Cill Ruairí. The Irish name for KILRUDDERY.

Cill Tartain. The Irish name for KILTARTAN.

Cill Uird. The Irish name for KILWORTH.

Cilurnum. *See* CHESTERS.

Cinderford 'ford built up with cinders or slag (from iron-smelting)', OE *sinder* 'cinder' + -FORD.
A town in Gloucestershire, in the FOREST OF DEAN, about 21 km (13 miles) southwest of Gloucester in what was once an important coal-mining district. Cinderford was the birthplace of the radio presenter Sir Jimmy Young (b.1921).

Cinque Ports 'five ports', OFr *cink porz*.
The original collective name (pronounced 'sink ports'), from the 11th century, for the five Kent and Sussex seaports of HASTINGS, SANDWICH, DOVER, ROMNEY and HYTHE, which were granted special privileges through their provision of ships and men for the defence of the English Channel. WINCHELSEA and RYE were subsequently added and there were ultimately 32 lesser members of the incorporated body (including DEAL, FOLKESTONE, MARGATE, PEVENSEY and SEAFORD). Their privileges were largely surrendered in 1685, and the harbours of the majority have now silted up (indeed Rye, Sandwich and Winchelsea are some 3 km (2 miles) from the sea). The Lord Wardenship of the Cinque Ports, which by the end of the 19th century had faded to a cipher, was revived as an office of some ceremonial éclat by Lord Curzon in 1903, and has since been held (conjointly with the Governorship of Dover Castle) by, among others, Sir Winston Churchill, Sir Robert Menzies and Queen Elizabeth, the Queen Mother.

Cioch, the Gaelic *cìoch* 'nipple, breast'.
A pinnacle projecting from the middle of the vast 300-m (1000-ft) high rock face of Sròn na Cìche, an outlier of Sgùrr Alasdair, in the Black CUILLIN of SKYE.

The existence of the Cioch was unknown until 1906, when Professor Norman Collie, mountaineer and man of science, noticed its shadow extending across the surrounding slabs as the sun declined. (For a more – metaphorically – petrifying encounter with a shadow on the part of Professor Collie, *see under* BEN MACDUI.) The next day, with his local guide John Mackenzie, Collie set about making the first ascent to this airy eyrie. Many have since followed, and marvelled. (Those of a less energetic bent and/or without a head for heights will recall the magnificence of the place from the film fantasy *Highlander* (1986), in which the eponymous hero waves his broadsword about a bit on the tip of the thing.)

It was in fact Collie's guide, Mackenzie, a Gael, who unblushingly named the Cioch; but he was by no means pushing out the envelope of Victorian permissiveness, as Scotland's mountains had been littered with cìochs, cìches and paps for centuries – to wit the Pap of GLEN COE, the Paps of Jura (*see under* JURA), Sgùrr na Cìche ('peak of the breast') in KNOYDART, and Cìoch na h-Òige ('pap of the maiden') in ARRAN, to name but a handful (so to speak). After the new Cioch was named in turn the massive craggy shoulder on whose flank it hangs – **Sròn na Cìche**, 'nose of the Cioch'. (Gaelic *sròn*, although literally meaning 'nose', had already become a standard name for spurs of mountains; no one, as far as one can assess, was being so silly as to deliberately call the crag 'nose of the nipple'.)

It was a great time for naming in the Cuillin, as the practically minded locals had not hitherto concerned themselves with the lesser protuberances of the upper barrens until the gentleman-mountaineers arrived: thus, both Mackenzie and Collie had peaks named after them, respectively SGÙRR MHIC CHOINNICH and SGÙRR THORMAID.

Cionn an Toir. The Irish name for TORR HEAD.

Cionn Mhálanna. The Irish name for MALIN HEAD.

Cionn tSáile. The Irish name for KINSALE.

Cirencester 'Roman camp or town at a place originally called *Corinion*', *Ciren* a reduced form of the OCelt place name *Corinion*, of unknown meaning + OE *ceaster* (*see* CHESTER).

A market town (formerly pronounced 'sissiter') in Gloucestershire, in the Cotswolds, on the River Churn, about 24 km (15 miles) southeast of Gloucester. Its name is often shortened by inhabitants to '**Ciren**', which in the local accent becomes 'ziren'.The source of the River THAMES[1] is about 5 km (3 miles) to the southwest. In the time of the Romans (who called it **Corinium Dobunnorum** – the Duboni were a local British people) – it was the second most important city in Britain, after London, and stood at the hub of the road system in the western part of the country: the FOSSE WAY, AKEMAN STREET and ERMINE WAY met here.

It shrank back into the shadows after the Romans left (the Saxons took Cirencester after defeating the Britons at DYRHAM in 577), but regained its eminence in the Middle Ages, when its status as one of the largest wool markets in England earned it the sobriquet 'Capital of the Cotswolds'. With its new wealth, its Norman church was expanded into one of the largest in the country, more like a cathedral than a church in appearance (indeed it has been nicknamed the 'Cathedral of the Cotswolds' – or, by Simon Jenkins, the 'cathedral of woolgothic'). Its peal of 12 bells is the oldest in the country.

Cirencester House is best known for its early 18th-century park, which covers about 38 sq km (15 sq miles). There is a famous avenue of chestnut trees. Just to the southwest of the town is the Royal Agricultural College, founded in 1845 and alma mater of generations of gentleman farmers. The town was the birthplace of David Hemery (b.1944), who held the world record (48.1 seconds) for the 400-metre hurdles 1968–72.

> Anno 1670, not far from Cirencester, was an apparition: being demanded whether a good spirit or a bad? returned no answer, but disappeared with a curious perfume and most melodious twang. Mr W. Lilly believes it was a fairy.
>
>   John Aubrey: *Miscellanies* (1696)

Battle of Cirencester (628). A battle fought near Cirencester, in which the forces of Cynegils, King of Wessex, were defeated by those of Penda, King of Mercia.

Cìr Mhòr 'the big comb', Gaelic *cìr* 'comb' + *mhòr* 'big'.

A mountain (798 m / 2618 ft) on the island of ARRAN, presenting – to the delight of climbers – magnificently pinnacled aspects at the heads of GLEN SANNOX and GLEN ROSA. It is pronounced 'keer voar', and was described and misnamed by one early visitor to the island as 'the acute and rocky pyramid of Kid Voe' (Dr John MacCulloch, *Highlands and Western Islands of Scotland*, 1824).

The name of the mountain distinguishes it from the neighbouring, lower, pinnacled ridge of A'Chìr ('the comb'). Some of the granite rock formations around the summit

are described as 'Cyclopean', in allusion to the Cyclopean Walls of Mycenae in Greece, composed of massive irregular blocks and supposedly built by the one-eyed giant the Cyclops.

Cissbury Ring *Cissbury* 'Cissa's hillfort', OE male personal name *Cissa* + -BURY. Cissa (*see* CHICHESTER) was the 5th-century founder of the South Saxon kingdom, but his connection with this hillfort seems to be an invention of 16th-century antiquarians.

An Iron Age hillfort in West Sussex, on the SOUTH DOWNS, about 5 km (3 miles) north of Worthing. It was occupied from the 5th century BC to the 1st century AD, and there is evidence of flint mining here 5000 years ago.

See also CHANCTONBURY RING.

City, the[1]. A shorthand way of referring to the City of London (*see* LONDON), and particularly to the more easterly portion of it, centred on the Bank of England, which concerns itself mainly with business and finance. The usage can be traced back to the early 17th century – a record of House of Commons business in 1621, for instance, notes the comment:

> Though money be wanting in the country yet it is in the City … They of the Citty to lay the riches downe.

The 'City' pages of a newspaper (presided over by the 'City' editor) are where share prices and financial stories and comment are to be found. The **City gent**, with his inevitable accoutrements – bowler hat, pinstripe trousers, tightly furled umbrella – was a familiar sight on the streets of London in the early and middle years of the 20th century, but the more relaxed sartorial conventions of recent times have done away with his uniform, while the increasing competitiveness and internationalization of the City have largely done the same to his gentlemanly reputation. There is still the mystique here, though, the aura of financial temples where arcane calculations are performed by high priests known to puzzled outsiders only as **something in the City** (an expression dating from at least the 1860s):

> The people who are 'something in the City' to-day mostly commute to Sussex and Surrey.
>
>   *Daily Telegraph* (1962)

> The City empty on a July evening,
> All the jam-packed commuters gone, and all
> The Wren and Hawksmoor spires and steeples shining
> In a honeyed light …
>
>   Donald Davie: 'To Londoners' (1982)

City University. A higher-education institution founded in 1966, which has close links with the City of London, although it is actually based just to the north, in Islington. *See also* SQUARE MILE.

City, the² Irish *Cathair Chrobh Dhearg*, 'the city of Red Crobh', Crobh being a pagan god.

A site of pagan and Christian worship at the foot of the PAPS mountains in Co. Kerry. The monument, now partly destroyed, comprised a circular wall 3 m (10 ft) high and 1.8 m (6 ft) thick. Inside the walls there were also a large stone circle with traces of ogam writing and a holy well. The site has been associated with human sacrifice, as witnessed by the names of nearby townlands, Gortdearg ('red field') and Gort na gCeann ('field of the heads'). The great Celtic feast of Bealtaine – May Day – has been observed in the City in living memory as a Catholic devotion.

City of Dreadful Knights. An old nickname for CARDIFF. After the First World War, David Lloyd George, prime minister in the coalition government, made lavish grants of honours in a cynical and blatant fashion. Three people connected with prominent south Wales newspapers were among the recipients of these honours, hence Cardiff was dubbed the 'City of Dreadful Knights', a punning allusion to James Thomson's dark and pessimistic poem *The City of Dreadful Night* (1874).

City of Dreaming Spires. An epithet applied to OXFORD, inspired by lines from Matthew Arnold's *Thyrsis* (1866):

> And that sweet City with her dreaming spires,
> She needs not June for beauty's heightening,
> Lovely all times she lies, lovely today.

The vision is of the spires and towers of Oxford's churches and colleges rising above early-summer morning mists, wrapped in academic reverie, as viewed from BOAR'S HILL – much as Jude, at a different time of day, got his first sight of the fictionalized CHRISTMINSTER from an overlooking hill:

> He now paused at the top of a crooked and gentle
> declivity, and obtained his first near view of the city …
> The buildings now lay quiet in the sunset, a vane here
> and there on their many spires and domes giving sparkle
> to a picture of sober secondary and tertiary hues.
>
> Thomas Hardy: *Jude the Obscure* (1895)

A present-day interpretation might perhaps find a touch of nostalgic torpor in the sobriquet.

In his televison series *The Glittering Prizes*, subsequently novelized (1976), Frederic Raphael sardonically reversed the epithet and applied it to CAMBRIDGE[1]:

> 'So this is the city of dreaming spires,' Sheila said.
> 'Theoretically that's Oxford,' Adam said. 'This is the city
> of perspiring dreams.'

City of Legions, the. *See* CAERLEON.

City of London. *See under* LONDON for main coverage; *see also* the CITY and the SQUARE MILE.

City of St Michael, the. *See* DUMFRIES.

City of the Broken Treaty. A nickname for LIMERICK, because of the supposed gross violation by the English of the terms of the 1691 Treaty of Limerick. In fact, it was the Protestant Parliament in Dublin that introduced the so-called Penal Laws that went against the religiously tolerant spirit of the treaty.

City of the Tribes, the. A former byname for GALWAY, which in the later Middle Ages was dominated by a small number of merchant families ('tribes') of Anglo-Norman and English origin: the Athys, Blakes, Bodkins, Brownes, Darcys, Deanes, Fonts, Frenches, Joyces, Kirwans, Lynches, Martins, Morrises and Skerrets. The principal family were the Lynches, who supplied 84 mayors of Galway between 1485 and 1654. There is an apocryphal story that the word 'lynch', meaning to hang someone without due process, derives from a 15th-century Mayor Lynch of Galway who, in his other role as chief magistrate, was obliged to execute his son for a murder, because no one else would carry out his sentence.

City Road From its providing a route to the *City* of London.

A road in FINSBURY, Central London (EC1), running from the ANGEL Islington in the northwest to Finsbury Square in the southeast. It was opened in 1761. Its name is perpetuated in a familiar 19th-century song:

> Up and down the City Road,
> In and out the Eagle,
> That's the way the money goes –
> Pop goes the weasel!
>
> W.R. Mandale: 'Pop Goes the Weasel' (1853)

The 'Eagle' was a hostelry popular with Londoners in the Victorian era. Next door to it was a place of entertainment called The Grecian Hall, where the music-hall singer Marie Lloyd gave her first public performance in 1886, at the age of 15.

The headquarters of the Honourable Artillery Company (known as the HAC), the oldest regiment in England, are in City Road. On their ground in 1744 one of the first important cricket matches in England was played, between Kent and All England.

City Road Underground station, on what is now the Northern line, opened in 1901, but it was closed down in 1922.

See also BUNHILL FIELDS.

City Road African. A late 19th- and early 20th-century euphemism for a 'prostitute'. It may reflect the perceived exoticism of the City Road for those who normally looked for prostitutes in the WEST END[1].

Cityside. *See under* WATERSIDE.

Clachaneasy 'church of Jesus', Gaelic *clachan* 'hamlet, 'stone house, church' + *Iosa* 'Jesus'.

A tiny settlement in Dumfries and Galloway (formerly

on the border of Wigtownshire and Kirkcudbrightshire), 11 km (7 miles) northwest of Newton Stewart.

Clachanpluck. The former name of LAURIESTON, Dumfries and Galloway.

Clachan Sound. *See under* SEIL.

Clachnaben. *See* CAIRN O' MOUNT.

Clacket Lane Possibly containing OE *clacc* 'hill'.
A service facility on the M25, between junctions 5 and 6, about 2.5 km (1.5 miles) south of Biggin Hill.

Clackmannan 'stone of Manau', Gaelic *clach* 'stone' + name of a Celtic god, or the old name for the area on the north side of the upper Forth. The stone called the Clach of Mannan is in the village, next to the bell tower of the old tolbooth.
A village in Clackmannanshire, formerly in Central region, and before that the county town of the old county of CLACKMANNANSHIRE. It is about 3 km (2 miles) southeast of Alloa. There are associations with the Bruce family, and it was here, in 1787, that Mrs Bruce of Clackmannan knighted Robert Burns with the sword of Robert the Bruce.

Clackmannanshire From CLACKMANNAN + SHIRE.
A former county, the smallest in Scotland, bordered by Kinross-shire to the east, Perthshire to the north, Stirling-shire to the west and Fife to the south. It became the district of Clackmannan (in Central region) in 1975, incorporating a fragment of Perthshire, and with ALLOA as the administrative headquarters. It was revived as the unitary authority of Clackmannanshire in 1996.

Clacton-on-Sea Earlier *Claccingtune*, 'estate associated with Clacc', OE male personal name *Clacc* + -ING + -TON.
A town and seaside resort in Essex, about 19 km (12 miles) southeast of Colchester, just to the east of the Blackwater Estuary. The two villages of **Great** and **Little Clacton** are inland, but in the 1870s the railways brought the nearby long sandy beach within reach of a wider public, and a typical Victorian seaside town was the rapid result: sumptuous hotels were erected, a pier appeared in 1873, and a pavilion soon followed. It continues to cater to the family end of the holiday market.

Clactonian. An adjective designating the Lower Paleolithic culture represented by flint implements found at Clacton-on-Sea. It was apparently originally coined in French, as *Clactonien*, in the late 1920s.

Rinyo-Clacton. *See under* ROUSAY.

Claddagh, the Irish *An Claddach* 'the sea shore'.
An area of the town of GALWAY, formerly a fishing village to which the Irish inhabitants of Galway were confined. The fishermen here claimed exclusive fishing rights over the whole of Galway Bay, and had complex rules as to which days were permissible for fishing. The Claddagh was demolished as part of a redevelopment in the 1930s.

Claddagh ring. A ring showing two hands holding a heart. It is named after the village, and given as a love token.

Clap Gate ME *clapgate* 'self-closing gate'.
A tiny settlement in North Yorkshire, 6 km (4 miles) west of Wetherby.

Clapham[1] 'homestead or enclosure by a hill', OE *clopp* 'hill' + HAM.
A district of southwest Central London, to the south of BATTERSEA and north of BALHAM, in the boroughs of WANDSWORTH and LAMBETH (SW4). It remained a rural backwater until the mid-17th century, when wealthier Londoners fleeing the Plague and the Great Fire (including Samuel Pepys) built homes here, especially to the north of the common (*see below*) and in the road now known as Old Town. Over the next century and a half it became a respectable and desirable residential adjunct to the capital:

> Of all the pretty suburbs that still adorn our metropolis there are few that exceed in charm Clapham Common.
>
> William Thackeray: *The Newcomes* (1853–5)

The arrival of the railways in the middle of the 19th century and the industrial boom in neighbouring Battersea later in the century greatly increased the population of Clapham and the density of its housing. It turned into a typical soot-grimed inner-London suburb, but gentrification reached it towards the end of the 20th century (even the pronunciation of its name was jokingly gentrified, to 'klahm'), and it became a refuge for Sloane Rangers (*see under* SLOANE SQUARE) who could not (yet) afford house prices in their eponymous habitat, they were dubbed 'Soanly Rangers', as they were known to remark of Clapham that '*It's only* ten minutes from Sloane Square':

> [The Duchess of York] was, and is, not so much a Sloane Ranger ... as that slightly lesser breed known as 'Soanly Rangers'.
>
> *The Observer* (1988)

The actress and singer Gertrude Lawrence (1901–52) was born in Clapham.

Clapham Common. An area of open land in Clapham, roughly triangular in shape and 89 ha (220 acres) in extent. Originally it was a wild and lawless place (passengers on London's first stage-coach service, which ran to and from Clapham from 1690, had to run the gauntlet of highwaymen), and although it was extensively drained and replanted in the 1720s its early reputation for nefariousness never quite faded away (in 1998 the Labour minister Ron Davis was robbed after allegedly seeking sexual assignations there, and later had to resign). Clapham Common Underground station, on the Northern line, opened (along with its neighbour Clapham Road) in 1900 (Clapham North

– renamed from Clapham Road – and Clapham South followed in 1926).

Clapham Junction. An important railway junction and multi-platform station in Clapham, to the northwest of the Common. The name originally referred to a crossroads in the area, but the railway arrived in 1838 and soon took it over. The station opened in 1863. Lines from all over south and southwest England pass through it on their way to the various southern London termini, and at one time it was the busiest railway junction in the world (2500 trains per day). By the second half of the century its name had spread to the area around it, which is the major centre of Battersea. Locally it is known familiarly as **'the Junction'**, and its down-at-heel griminess was famously put on public display in Nell Dunn's *Up the Junction*, originally (1963) a novel and later (1965) a controversial television play (directed by Ken Loach).

In December 1988, in what became known as the **Clapham Rail Disaster**, 35 people died as a result of a train crash on the approaches to Clapham Junction.

Clapham Sect. A derisive name given by Sydney Smith to a group of well-to-do early 19th-century evangelical Anglicans, who assiduously pursued philanthropy and campaigned particularly against slavery. Their leading lights (also dubbed 'saints') were William Wilberforce, Zachary Macaulay, Hannah More, James Stephen and Henry Thornton. Several of them lived in the Clapham area – whence the name.

man on the Clapham omnibus, the. The man in the street, the ordinary, representative person. The image of Clapham as a commuter suburb was well enough established by the middle of the 19th century for the clerkly Clapham bus-traveller bound for his desk in the City to be a recognized figure:

> So thoroughly has the tedious traffic of the streets become ground into the Londoner's nature, that ... your dog-collar'd occupant of the knife-board of a Clapham omnibus, will stick on London Bridge for half-an-hour with scarcely a murmur.
>
> *Journal of the Society of Arts* (1857)

By the end of the century he was being used, especially by lawyers, as the type of ordinary average person with average middle-of-the-road ideas and opinions.

Clapham² 'homestead by the noisy stream', OE *clæpe* 'noisy one' + HAM.
A village in North Yorkshire, 9 km (5.5 miles) northwest of Settle.

> Bane ta Claapam town-gate lived an ond Yorkshire tike,
> Who i' dealing i' horseflesh hed ne'er met his like;
> 'Twor his pride that i' aw the hard bargains he'd hit,
> He'd bit a girt monny, but nivver bin bit.
>
> Anon.:'The Yorkshire Horse Dealer'

Clapton 'farmstead or estate on a hill', OE *clopp* 'hill' + -TON.
A district of northeast London, to the north of HACKNEY, in the borough of Hackney (E5). It stands on high ground (whence its name) that slopes down eastwards to the River LEA. The northerly part is **Upper Clapton**, the southerly **Lower Clapton**. Until the early 20th century the former was a highly salubrious middle-class residential area, but by the 21st century both were victims of inner-city blight, with an epidemic of drug-related murders, earning Lower Clapton Road the journalistic title of 'Murder Mile'.

Clapton in Gordano *Gordano* an old district name, probably 'dirty or muddy valley', OE *gor* 'dirty, muddy' + *denu* 'valley'.
A village in North Somerset (before 1996 in Avon, before 1974 in Somerset), about 13 km (8 miles) west of Bristol and close to the south bank of the Severn Estuary.
See also EASTON IN GORDANO.

Clapworthy Perhaps 'enclosure by a hill' or 'muddy enclosure', OE *clopp* 'hill' or dialect *clob* 'clod, mud' + *worthig* (*see* -WORTH, WORTHY, -WARDINE); the earliest spelling is *Clobworthy* and may make the second alternative the likelier.
A village (pronounced 'klappery') in Devon, about 16 km (10 miles) southeast of Barnstaple.

Clár Chlainne Mhuiris. The Irish name for CLAREMORRIS.

Clare¹ Probably Irish *clár* 'plain, level place', referring to the local terrain.
A river in County Galway, flowing southward to join LOUGH CORRIB near its southern end.

Clare² Perhaps from an OCelt river name.
A village in Suffolk, about 21 km (13 miles) southwest of Bury St Edmunds. Its houses include outstanding examples of the type of 17th-century plaster decoration known as 'pargeting' (an East Anglian decorative speciality).

Clare, County Irish *An Clár* 'the level place'; the name comes from the village of *Clare*, now called Clarecastle, 3 km (2 miles) south of Ennis. An alternative account, no longer accepted, is that it was named after Thomas de Clare, the Anglo-Norman baron granted land here in 1276.
A county in the west of Ireland, bordered on the north by Galway, on the east by Tipperary, on the south by the Shannon estuary and Limerick, and on the west by the Atlantic Ocean. The county town is ENNIS, and in the north is the unique limestone landscape of the BURREN. Other features include the CLIFFS OF MOHER and the SLIEVE BERNAGH¹ hills.

Owing to its role in Nationalist politics, Clare is also known as the BANNER COUNTY. Daniel O'Connell was MP for Clare from 1828 to 1831, and Éamon de Valera represented the county from 1917 to 1959.

Grass here bends from the wind of bombs and the thrown
  flame
And white in sunlight stand the bony hills of Clare.

> Teresa L. Gray: 'Memories Across Dead Ground', from *New
> Poetry 5*

There was a young lady of Clare
Who was sadly pursued by a bear.
    When she found she was tired
    She abruptly expired
That unfortunate lady of Clare

> Edward Lear: limerick

Clare hearse. The ten of clubs, a card reputedly foretelling
ill fortune.

West Clare Railway. A narrow-gauge railway which ran
for 86 km (53 miles) from ENNIS to KILKEE in Co. Clare. It
was locally nicknamed Kate Mac, for reasons that are not
altogether clear. The first sod in the construction of the
railway was turned by Charles Stewart Parnell at Miltown
Malbay on 26 June 1885. The closure of the line on 31
January 1961 (by which time the gauge was wholly incompatible with the modern Irish railway network) was a source
of regret not only to the people of West Clare but to tourists
and all those who appreciated the beauty of the scenery
along the line.

Clare Island Irish *clíar*, *cléir* 'clergy, scholars', presumably
referring to a community living on the island; *see also* CLEAR
ISLAND.
A hilly island in CLEW BAY, on the west coast of County
Mayo, some 5 km (3 miles) south of Achill Island. There is
a ruined castle supposedly once belonging to Grace
O'Malley, the Queen of Clew Bay, who is said to be buried
in the ruined abbey.

Claremont. *See under* ESHER.

Claremorris Irish *Clár Chlainne Mhuiris* 'plain of the descendants of Morris'.
A small town in County Mayo, 25 km (16 miles) southeast
of Castlebar. The pilgrimage destination of KNOCK is 10 km
(6 miles) to the northeast.
  Claremorris was the birthplace of the ballad singer Delia
Murphy (1902–71).

Clarkston 'cleric's farm', ME *clerc* 'cleric' + -TON.
A town in East Renfrewshire (formerly in Strathclyde),
effectively a southern suburb of GLASGOW.

Clartyhole Scots *clarty* 'mucky' + *hole*.
The name of the farm that stood on the estate where Sir
Walter Scott had ABBOTSFORD built.

Clashindarroch 'hollow of the oak', Gaelic *clais* 'hollow'
+ *an daraich* 'of the oak'.
A tiny settlement in Aberdeenshire (formerly in Grampian region), some 10 km (6 miles) south of Huntly.

It is in the midst of **Clashindarroch Forest**, a conifer
plantation.

Clatterin Brig 'rattling bridge', OE *clatrung* 'rattling' + Scots
brig; the name refers to an old stretch of road and either the
loose stones or the noise made by conveyances.
A small settlement in Aberdeenshire (formerly in Grampian
region), on the south side of CAIRN O' MOUNT, 10 km
(6 miles) north of Laurencekirk.

Clatteringshaws Possibly 'noisy copse', OE *clatrung*
'clatter, noise' + *sceaga* 'copse'.
A village 9 km (5.5 miles) southwest of New Galloway,
formerly in Kircudbrightshire, now in Dumfries and
Galloway. **Clatteringshaws Loch** was created north of the
village in the 1930s when a dam was built across the Black
Water of Dee, as part of a hydroelectric scheme.

Clatworthy 'enclosure where burdock grows', OE *clate*
'burdock' + *worthig* (*see* -WORTH, WORTHY, -WARDINE).
A village in Somerset, about 16 km (10 miles) northwest
of Taunton. **Clatworthy Reservoir**, immediately to the west,
was constructed in the mid-1960s, and is now a site for
trout fishing.

Clauchanpluck. *See* LAURIESTON.

Claudy Irish *Clóidigh* 'strongly-flowing one', with reference to
the River Faughan.
A village in County Londonderry, 15 km (9 miles) southeast of Derry/Londonderry itself. On 31 July 1972 three
IRA car bombs went off here, resulting in the deaths
of 8 and injuries to 34. The telephone box at nearby Dun-
given, intended to convey a warning, had been put out of
operation by a previous IRA action.

> And Christ, little Katherine Aiken is dead,
> And Mrs McLaughlin is pierced through the head.
> Meanwhile to Dungiven the killers have gone
> And they're finding it hard to get through on the phone.

> James Simmons: 'Claudy', from *West Strand Visions* (1974)

Clavering St Mary. The fictionalized version of OTTERY
ST MARY, as adopted by William Makepeace Thackeray for
his novel *Pendennis* (1848–50).

Clay Cross From a local family called *Clay*. The name is first
recorded in 1734.
A former mining village in Derbyshire, about 10 km (6
miles) northeast of Matlock. It achieved a certain notoriety in 1972 when several of its Labour councillors voted
not to implement the Conservative government's Housing Finance Act, which prevented local councils from providing subsidized housing at low rents. They were
surcharged by the District Auditor and barred from office.

Clayhanger 'clayey wooded slope', OE *clæg* 'clay' + *hangra*
'wooded slope'.
A small town in the West Midlands, about 7 km (4.5 miles)

north of Walsall. Arnold Bennett adopted the name for the family at the centre of his 'Clayhanger' series of novels: *Clayhanger* (1910), *Hilda Lessways* (1911), *These Twain* (1916) and *The Roll Call* (1922).

Clayton-le-Moors 'farm with clay soil on the moors', OE *clæg* 'clay' + -TON + OFr *(sur) le* 'on the' + OE *mor* 'moor'.
An industrial town in Lancashire, 3 km (2 miles) north of Accrington, on the Leeds and Liverpool Canal. The villages of **Clayton-le-Dale** and **Clayton-le-Woods** lie, respectively, 7 km (4.5 miles) to the west and 20 km (12 miles) to the southwest.

Clear Island Irish *clíar*, *cléir* 'clergy, scholars', presumably referring to a community living on the island; *see also* CLARE ISLAND.
An island off the southwest coast of County Cork, some 18 km (11 miles) southwest of Skibbereen. At its southern tip is CAPE CLEAR.

Cleator Moor Possibly 'rock shieling' or 'burdock shieling', OScand *klettr* 'rock, cliff' or OE *clæte* 'burdock' + OScand *erg* 'temporary shelter, shieling' (see -ARY).
A town in Cumbria (formerly in Cumberland), 6 km (4 miles) southeast of Whitehaven. It grew around the old village of **Cleator** as a centre for mining iron ore.

Cleckheaton 'high farmstead at the rounded hill', OE *clacc* (OScand *klakkr*) 'rounded hill' + *heah* 'high' + -TON.
An industrial town in West Yorkshire, 14 km (8.5 miles) southwest of Leeds. It forms part of the conurbation of what has been dubbed CLECKHECKMONDSEDGE. The Vorticist painter Edward Wadsworth (1889–1949) was born here.

Cleckheckmondsedge. A semi-serious portmanteau name for the West Yorkshire conurbation of *Cleck*heaton, *Heckmond*wike and Liver*sedge*, southwest of Leeds.

Cleddau Welsh *cleddau*, plural of *cleddyf* 'sword', the name probably evoking some perceived similarity of the rivers' characteristics to swords (as in shining, bright, thrusting, etc.). The name given to two rivers of Pembrokeshire (formerly in Dyfed), the **Eastern Cleddau** and the **Western Cleddau**, which unite to form the Cleddau estuary (also called the **Daugleddau** (Welsh *dau* 'two') estuary. This in turn feeds into the inlet of MILFORD HAVEN, crossed by the **Cleddau Bridge**, a toll bridge built in the 1970s to link Pembroke Dock and Neyland. In Welsh, the town of Milford Haven is Aberdaugleddau (*see* MILFORD HAVEN).
    In the South Island of New Zealand, the Cleddau is one of the feeder rivers of Milford Sound.

Clee Hills *Clee* probably 'ball-shaped rounded hill', OE *cleo*.
A range of hills in southern Shropshire, between LUDLOW to the west and CLEOBURY MORTIMER to the east. Its highest points are **Brown Clee Hill** (546 m / 1791 ft) and TITTER-

STONE CLEE HILL (533m / 1749 ft). Coal used to be mined here, and a hard rock called Dhu stone, which is used mainly for road metal, is quarried.

Cleethorpes 'hamlets near Clee', *Clee* former name (now *Old Clee*) of a nearby village, from OE *clæg* 'clay' (with reference to the local soil). Cleethorpes itself was originally called *Thorp* 'dependent settlement' (*see* THORPE); *Cleethorpes* (with plural -*s*) and the now obsolete *Cleethorpe* are both first recorded in the 16th century.
A seaside town in North East Lincolnshire (before 1974 in Lincolnshire), at the mouth of the River Humber, just to the south of Grimsby and about 40 km (25 miles) east of Scunthorpe. Its 5 km (3 miles) and more of broad sandy beaches began attracting the holiday trade in the 19th century, and it soon added a 90-m (300-ft) pier to its natural attractions. Several fine houses in the suburbs reflect the wealth earlier produced by Grimsby's fishing industry.

Cleeve '(place) at the cliff or bank', OE *clife* dative form of *clif* 'cliff'.
A village in North Somerset (before 1996 in Avon, before 1974 in Somerset), about 16 km (10 miles) southwest of Bristol.

Cleeve Hill *Cleeve* '(place) at the cliff', OE *clife* dative form of *clif* 'cliff, bank'.
The highest point (330 m / 1083 ft) of the COTSWOLDS, 6 km (4 miles) northeast of Cheltenham and 2.5 km (1.5 miles) southeast of BISHOP'S CLEEVE. Cleeve Hill is part of **Cleeve Common**, an upland area of ancient grassland rich in rare plants (covering 3 sq miles), and the source of the River Isbourne. Prehistoric earthworks on the Hill include an Iron Age hillfort and a wide circular enclosure known as The Ring. On the Hill's northern slope is the village of **Cleeve Hill**. The limestone bluff (326 m / 1040 ft) on its rocky western escarpment is known as **Cleeve Cloud** (OE *clud* '(rocky) hill').
    Stunning views can be had from Cleeve Hill to the north and west, to Bredon Hill (*see under* BREDON) and the MALVERN HILLS, and beyond GLOUCESTER to the FOREST OF DEAN.

Cleggan Irish *An Cloigeann* 'the head, the skull', referring to a rounded hill.
A village overlooking **Cleggan Bay** on the west coast of County Galway, some 10 km (6 miles) northwest of Clifden.

Cleggan Bay Disaster (27–28 October 1927). A disaster resulting from a sudden night-time storm, resulting in the deaths of 45 local fishermen. The incident is recalled in a poem called 'The Cleggan Bay Disaster' in Richard Murphy's 1963 collection *Sailing to an Island*.

Clehonger 'clayey wooded slope', OE *clæg* 'clay' + *hangra* 'wooded slope'; *see also* CLAYHANGER.

A village in Herefordshire (before 1998 in Hereford and Worcester, before 1974 in Herefordshire), about 6 km (4 miles) southwest of Hereford.

Cleish Hills Possibly from Gaelic *clais* 'ditch, furrow, narrow valley'; from some views the hills have a furrowed appearance.

A small range of hills, reaching a height of 379 m (1243 ft), some 7 km (4.5 miles) southwest of the town of Kinross, in Perth and Kinross (formerly in Kinross-shire, then in Tayside region). To the north is the small village of **Cleish**.

Clench Common *Clench* 'hill', OE *clenc*.

A village in Wiltshire, about 5 km (3 miles) southwest of Marlborough.

Clent 'rock, rocky hill', OE *clent*.

A village in Worcestershire (before 1998 in Hereford and Worcester, before 1974 in Worcestershire), about 10 km (6 miles) northeast of Kidderminster. Just to the north are the **Clent Hills**, an area of heathland and woodland on three sandstone ridges, rising to 305 m (1000 ft) above the Midland Plain and offering panoramic views not just of the nearby Birmingham skyline but also as far as the Cotswolds and Welsh Borders. On top of Adam's Hill are the Four Stones, a Victorian folly erected in the 19th century by a former owner of nearby Hagley Hall.

Cleobury Mortimer *Cleobury* 'fortified place or manor near the Clee Hills', *Clee* (*see* CLEE HILLS) + -BURY; *Mortimer* denoting manorial ownership in the Middle Ages by the Mortemer family.

A town (pronounced 'klibbery') in Shropshire, on the River Rea, about 16 km (10 miles) east of Ludlow. Local legend has it that it was the birthplace of William Langland (*c.*1330–*c.*1386), who was the author of the lengthy allegorical poem *Piers Plowman* (which has a West Midlands setting); but modern scholarship casts serious doubt on this.

Nearby is Apley Hall, which has been claimed as the original of Blandings Castle, Lord Emsworth's home in P.G. Wodehouse's comic novels (*but see also* WINCHCOMBE).

Clerkenwell 'scholars' spring', ME *clerken* plural of *clerk* 'scholar, student' + *well* 'well, spring'.

A district of Central LONDON, to the north of the City and to the south of Finsbury (EC1). In the Middle Ages the area abounded with springs and with religious foundations, including the Priory of St John of Jerusalem (headquarters of the Knights Hospitallers) and the Charterhouse (still in Clerkenwell, and now a venerable almshouse). The particular spring or well that seems to have given the place its name was rediscovered in 1924; it was adjacent to the Convent of St Mary and was a venue for performances of medieval miracle plays.

After the Dissolution of the Monasteries in the mid-16th century, Clerkenwell became an elegant and salubrious suburb; but the growth and expansion of London's population following the Napoleonic Wars pushed it sharply downmarket. In the 19th century it had a reputation as a centre of radical dissent ('Clerkenwell has ... become mixed in population and in its political opinions tidal', *Daily News* (1896)), and **Clerkenwell Green** (a reminder of the area's village beginnings) was popular as a venue for political rallies and a starting point for demonstrations (for example, by the Chartists). In the 20th century it became something of a forgotten backwater, populated by small trades and crafts (watchmakers, for example), its drabness set forth by Arnold Bennett in his novel *Riceyman Steps* (1923); but in the 1990s it underwent something of a rediscovery, with new restaurants and loft-conversions suggesting an incipient fashionability.

Clerkenwell was the birthplace of the journalist and politician John Wilkes (1727–97).

Clerkenwell Explosion, the. An explosive incident on Friday 13 December 1867, the result of a Fenian attempt to free one of their number from **Clerkenwell Prison** (or more correctly the House of Detention, built in the 1820s) using 247 kg (548 lbs) of gunpowder. The explosive blew a huge hole in the prison wall, and killed six and maimed and injured others living in nearby tenements in Corporation Road. As with Irish Republican attacks on the British capital more than a century later, it caused outrage and panic. It has been claimed that the pejorative term 'Mick' for an Irishman came into currency following the public hanging at NEWGATE on 26 May 1868 of the Fenian Michael Barrett (the last such in Britain) for his supposed role in the incident.

Clerkenwell Tales, The. A medieval mystery story (2003) by Peter Ackroyd, narrated by characters borrowed from Chaucer's *The Canterbury Tales*.

Clevedon 'hill of the cliffs', OE *clifa* possessive plural of *clif* 'cliff' + *dun* (*see* DOWN, -DON).

A small resort town in North Somerset (before 1996 in Avon, before 1974 in Somerset) on the southern shore of the mouth of the River Severn, about 13 km (8 miles) southwest of Avonmouth. It was developed in the mid-19th century as a seaside getaway for Bristolians. A much-admired pier was built here in 1869; much of it sank beneath the waves in the latter part of the 20th century, but it has since been lovingly restored. The nearby **Clevedon Court**, a National Trust property, dates back, in part, to the 12th century.

Clevedon was the location of a famous poetic honeymoon in 1795: that of Samuel and Sara Coleridge after their marriage in St Mary Redcliffe, Bristol.

Cleveland 'land of cliffs', OE *clifa*, possessive plural of *clif* 'cliff, hill' + *land*.

A traditional area and former county of northeast England.

It derives its name from the sea cliffs along its North Sea shore (those at Boulby, around 203 m / 666 ft high, are the highest in England), or possibly from the outcrops of sandstone in the Cleveland Hills. The county was formed in 1974 from part of southern County Durham and part of the North Riding of Yorkshire. Its administrative centre was at Middlesbrough. In 1996 it was replaced by the unitary authorities of HARTLEPOOL, MIDDLESBROUGH, REDCAR AND CLEVELAND and STOCKTON-ON-TEES.

The **Cleveland Hills** and the village of **Cleveland Tontine** are actually in North Yorkshire, the former forming the northeast edge of the NORTH YORK MOORS.

The city of Cleveland, Ohio, was named, not after the English region, but after Moses Cleaveland, who laid it out in 1796.

Cleveland Matterhorn, the. A nickname for ROSEBERRY TOPPING.

Cleveland Way, the. A long-distance footpath opened in 1969. It goes from Helmsley on the south side of the North York Moors up through the Hambledon and Cleveland Hills to the sea at Saltburn. The route then follows the coast in a southeasterly direction to Filey Brigg. The total length is 176 km (109 miles).

Duchess of Cleveland. The title belonging to Barbara Villiers (1641–1709), mistress of Charles II from 1660 to 1670, and bearer of several of his children. She was an ancestor, via the Duke of Grafton, one of those sons, of Lady Diana Spencer, and thus of the present royal princes William and Harry.

Cleveland Street. A Street in the WEST END of London, built 1745–70 on land owned by Charles Fitzroy, Duke of Southampton, son of the Duchess of Cleveland (*see under* CLEVELAND). It is now occupied mainly by the Middlesex Hospital.

Cleveland Street scandal. A society scandal of 1889, when a male brothel was discovered operating in Cleveland Street. The brothel came to light when police investigating a theft at a London post and telegraph office came across a teenage delivery boy with 18 shillings in his pocket – a larger amount than someone in his position might be expected to carry. When questioned, the boy revealed that he and others had been moonlighting as rent boys from 19 Cleveland Street. It soon emerged that several highly placed men, including Lord Arthur Somerset (supervisor of the Prince of Wales's stables,) and the Earl of Euston, were clients of the Cleveland Street operation. There were rumours that the Duke of Clarence, Prince Albert Victor ('Eddy'), the eldest son of the Prince of Wales, was another client; rumours also connected Eddy to the 1888 Whitechapel murders (*see under* WHITECHAPEL).

Cleveland Tontine *Tontine* is presumed to be derived from the name of the manorial owners.

A village in North Yorkshire, at the foot of the Cleveland Hills (*see under* CLEVELAND) 9 km (5.5 miles) northeast of Northallerton.

Cleveleys Probably after a family called Clevely; there are no records of the name earlier than the early 20th century.

A seaside town in Lancashire, 6 km (4 miles) north of Blackpool). It forms part of the town of **Thornton Cleveleys**, which is contiguous with BLACKPOOL.

Clew Bay Possibly ME *clew* 'a round cluster of things', here referring to the islands in the bay.

A large inlet of the Atlantic off the west coast of County Mayo. There are many small islands in its inner reaches, and the larger CLARE ISLAND and ACHILL ISLAND at its mouth.

Queen of Clew Bay, the. Grace O'Malley (Gráinne Ní Mháille, or Granuaile, 1530–1603), the twice-married, freebooting, piratical chieftain who in her time dominated the CONNACHT coast. She visited Queen Elizabeth in London, and refused gifts from her, claiming to be a prince of equal status. She is said to be buried on Clare Island, and later became a personification of Ireland and its quest for freedom:

See also HOWTH.

Cley next the Sea *Cley* 'place with clayey soil', OE *clæg* 'clay'.

A village (pronounced 'kly') in north Norfolk, at the mouth of the River Glaven, about 11 km (7 miles) west of Sheringham. In the Middle Ages it was an important port, specializing in the export of wool, but silting-up and 17th-century land reclamation have stranded it 1.5 km (1 mile) inland, compromising the second part of its name.

Clifden The name given or transferred to the place by the founder of the town, John Darcy; in Irish it is *An Clochán* 'the little stone' or 'the stepping stone'.

A small market town, fishing port and tourist centre, known as 'the capital of CONNEMARA', County Galway, some 70 km (43 miles) northwest of Galway itself, overlooking the narrow inlet of **Clifden Bay**. It was founded *c*.1812. The Marconi wireless station here was the first transatlantic wireless station in Europe. It was destroyed during the Anglo-Irish War (1919–21).

It was in a bog near Clifden that on 15 June 1919 John Alcock and Arthur Brown ended the first ever non-stop flight across the Atlantic, having left Newfoundland the previous day.

Cliffe '(place at the) cliff', OE *clif* 'cliff, bank'.

A village in Kent, on the peninsula separating the estuaries of the Thames and the Medway, about 10 km (6 miles) north of Rochester. At the beginning of the 21st century the surrounding area of marshland, on the south bank of the Thames, was subject to speculation as a possible site for a new London Airport.

Clifford's Mesne 'forest waste belonging to the Clifford family', *Clifford* family name known in the area from the 13th century + ME *munede* 'forest waste' (later assimilated to *mesne*, a term relating to feudal land-holding).

A village (pronounced 'clifford's meen') in Gloucestershire, about 16 km (10 miles) northwest of Gloucester.

Cliffs of Moher Irish *Aillte an Mhothair* 'cliffs of the ruin', referring to an ancient fort that once stood on HAG'S HEAD at the southern end of the cliffs (now the site of a signal-tower built during the Napoleonic Wars).

Spectacular sea cliffs extending some 8 km (5 miles) along the west coast of County Clare, at the edge of the BURREN, 35 km (22 miles) northwest of Ennis. Rising to a height of 200 m (700 ft), they are said to be the highest vertical sea cliffs in the British Isles, and comprise a limestone base, topped by layers of dark sandstone and black shale.

Clifton 'farmstead on or near a cliff', OE *clif* 'cliff, bank' + -TON.

A district of BRISTOL, on the eastern side of the high and rocky Avon Gorge (*see under* AVON²). Its development began in the late 18th century, as prosperous Bristolians moved out here and began to commission the elegant neo-classical buildings that now distinguish it. **Clifton College**, now a co-educational public school, was founded in 1862. Bristol Zoo (in full, the Zoological Garden of the Bristol, Clifton and West of England Zoological Society) opened on **Clifton Down** in 1836.

Over five late-Victorian afternoons (22, 23, 26, 27 and 28 June 1899), while playing in a junior house match at Clifton College, the 13-year-old A.E.J. Collins made 628 not out, the highest individual score in any form of cricket. Collins carried his bat in a total of 836 all out. The scorer gave his score as '628 – plus or minus 20, shall we say'. Collins also took 11 wickets in the match, which his house won by the unsurprisingly huge margin of an innings and 688 runs.

Clifton Suspension Bridge. A suspension bridge spanning the Avon Gorge at Clifton. It was designed by Isambard Kingdom Brunel (1806–59). He was only 25 when building began, but because of an ongoing shortage of funds and intermittent unrest at Bristol docks the bridge (with its Egyptian-inspired pylons) was not actually completed until 1864. At 214 m (702 ft) it had the longest suspended span in the world at the time.

It has long been popular with would-be suicides, by no means all of them successful: the descent of one Victorian woman was slowed down, parachute-like, by her hooped skirt and her landing softened by a yielding Avon mudbank. She survived. Bungee-jumping is firmly discouraged.

Cliftonville Apparently from the *Cliftonville* Hotel, opened in 1868, whose name may itself have been based on the nearby Clifton Street. The district had previously been named *New Town*, and also *Peel Town*, after the former prime minister Sir Robert Peel (1788–1850), who was a Margate landowner.

An eastern suburb of MARGATE, at the northeasterly tip of the Isle of Thanet, in Kent. It was developed in the middle of the 19th century as a more genteel alternative to the somewhat downmarket seaside resort of Margate. Those who chose its name may have found in it comforting reminders of the eminently respectable CLIFTON in Bristol and the reassurance of the classy 'French' suffix *-ville*.

Climping '(settlement of) Climp's people', OE male personal name *Climp* + -*inqas* (*see* -ING).

A village in West Sussex, 6 km (4 miles) northeast of Bognor Regis and about 1.5 km (1 mile) from the sea.

Clink Street From *Clink* Prison.

A street in London on the south bank of the River Thames, between Southwark Bridge and London Bridge, in the borough of SOUTHWARK (SE1). In the Middle Ages, the surrounding area was the London estate of the bishops of Winchester, which was called 'the Liberty of the Clink'. It contained the bishops' palace, known as Winchester House, and also a small prison, the 'Clink'. The origin of this name is not known for certain, but it may be an allusion to the clanking of prisoners' chains, or of warders' keys. The area had a healthy population of inns and brothels, so the prison is unlikely to have been short of customers. There is now a **Clink Prison Museum** near London Bridge.

The expression '**in (the) clink**', meaning 'in prison', dates back at least to the early 19th century.

Clipstone 'Klyppr's or Klipprr's farmstead', OScand *Klypps* or *Klipps* possessive forms of male personal name *Klyppr* or *Klippr* + -TON.

A village in Nottinghamshire, in SHERWOOD FOREST, about 8 km (5 miles) northeast of Mansfield. It was the site of the Parliament Oak, a tree under which Edward I held a parliament in 1282: the king was hunting when a messenger announced that the Welsh were in revolt under Llywelyn ap Gruffydd; Edward hastily convened his nobles under the oak, and it was resolved to march against the Welsh at once. The tree no longer exists.

Clisham The first element may be from OScand *klif* 'cliff'.

A rocky mountain (799 m / 2622 ft) in Harris, Western Isles, the highest in the Outer Hebrides.

Clitheroe 'hill of loose stones', OE *clyder* 'loose stones' + *hoh* 'hill' or OScand *haugr* 'hill'.

A market town in the RIBBLE Valley, Lancashire, 13 km (8 miles) northwest of Burnley. The Labour politician Judith Hart (1924–91) was educated at Clitheroe Royal Grammar

School. Strangely enough, the diminutive comedian Jimmy Clitheroe (1921–73), perpetual schoolboy star of the radio sitcom *The Clitheroe Kid* (1957–72), did actually come from Clitheroe, and Clitheroe was indeed his real name. A spot near Clitheroe, at Lower Hodder Bridge, is said to be the geographical centre of the island of Britain.

Cliveden 'steeply sloping valley', OE *clif* 'cliff, bank, steep slope' + *denu* 'valley'.

An Italianante mansion (pronounced 'klivden') in Buckinghamshire, in full **Cliveden House**, designed in the mid-19th century by Sir Charles Barry. It was built on a site overlooking the River Thames, about 5 km (3 miles) north-east of Maidenhead, previously occupied by two other houses of that name (one of which was the home of Frederick, Prince of Wales, son of George II; the composer Thomas Arne's *Rule Britannia* (1740) was first performed here). From 1893 it was the family home of the Astors. They included Nancy Astor, Britain's first female MP (1919–45), who was a political hostess of considerable influence in the years before the Second World War (*see below*), and Lord Astor, who in 1961 hosted the Cliveden house party at which John Profumo, the Minister for War, met Christine Keeler, precipitating the so-called 'Profumo scandal' of 1963. By the end of the 20th century Cliveden had become a luxury hotel. It is now owned by the National Trust.

Clifden nonpareil. A large European noctuid moth (*Catocala fraxini*) whose name preserves an earlier spelling of Cliveden, near where it was first observed in the mid-18th century. It is dull in coloration, with a pale blue band on its lower wings (whence its alternative name 'Blue Underwing'). It is now found in England only as a rare immigrant.

Cliveden Set. A collective name (coined by the left-wing journalist Claud Cockburn) for the right-wing politicians and journalists who gathered for weekend parties at Cliveden in the late 1930s. They included Geoffrey Dawson, editor of *The Times* (and self-styled 'secretary-general of the Establishment'), and Lord Lothian. They favoured appeasement with Nazi Germany. It was said that government policy was decided at Cliveden, a proposition with which the members of the set would no doubt have concurred (their self-delusion was conclusively demonstrated when Winston Churchill, rather than their preferred candidate, Lord Halifax, was chosen to succeed Neville Chamberlain as prime minister in 1940). A more derisive name for the set was 'God's Truth Ltd.'

> We talk of … how terrible has been the influence of the Cliveden set.
>
> Harold Nicholson: *Diary* (19 September 1938)

Clivocast Etymology unknown.
A small settlement on the south coast of UNST, Shetland.

Clochán an Aifir. The Irish name for the GIANT'S CAUSE-WAY.

Clochán na bhFomaraigh. *See under* GIANT'S CAUSE-WAY.

Cloch Shiurdáin. The Irish name for CLOUGHJORDAN.

Cloggy. The nickname for Clogwyn d'ur Arddu; *see under* SNOWDON.

Cloghaneely Irish *Cloich Chionnaola* 'Cionnaloa's stone'.
An area of northwestern DONEGAL, between GWEEDORE to the west and the DERRYVEAGH MOUNTAINS to the south.

Clogher Irish *An Clochar* 'the stony place'.
A village in County Tyrone, 32 km (20 miles) west of Dungannon. The diocese of Clogher is said to be the oldest see in Ireland, dating back to the 5th century. Since the Reformation, there have been both Catholic and Protestant bishops here. The Protestant cathedral dates from 1744; almost nothing is left of earlier ecclesiastical buildings.

Clogwyn d'ur Arddu. *See under* SNOWDON.

Cloich Chionnaola. The Irish name for CLOGHANEELY.

Cloich na Coillte. The Irish name for CLONAKILTY.

Cloisterham. The name given to ROCHESTER in *The Mystery of Edwin Drood* (1870) by Charles Dickens.

Clonakilty Irish *Cloich na Coillte* 'stone (fort) of the woods'.
A small market town and resort on **Clonakilty Bay**, on the south coast of County Cork, 27 km (17 miles) southwest of Kinsale. It is famous for its black and white puddings.

Clonakilty was the birthplace of Boss Croker (Richard Croker, 1841–1922), manager of Tammany Hall, the Democratic Party political machine in New York. Michael Collins (1890–1922), leader of the Irish forces during the Anglo-Irish War (1919–21), was born nearby and went to school here. The late Noel Redding, bass player with the Jimi Hendrix Experience, lived in Clonakilty up to his death in 2003, and used to play in a local pub every Friday.

'Clonakilty God help us'. An expression of despair in the face of financial adversity, deriving from the former location in Clonakilty of a large workhouse.

Clonard Irish *Cluain Ioraird* 'Iorard's meadow' (*see* ACHADH); Iorard was probably an early local chieftain.
A village in County Westmeath, 6 km (4 miles) east of Kinnegad. A monastery was founded here in 515 by **St Finnian of Clonard** (d.*c*.549), and it became a notable centre of learning, famous throughout Europe in the Middle Ages (St Columba was one of Finnian's pupils). Despite frequent attacks by Vikings and Anglo-Normans, it survived until the Dissolution of the Monasteries under Henry VIII. Nothing of it now remains.

Clondalkin Irish *Cluain Dolcáin* 'meadow of Dolcán' (*see* ACHADH).

A western suburb of DUBLIN. A monastery was founded here in the 7th century by St Crónán, and a round tower remains.

Clonenagh Irish *Cluain Eidhneach* 'meadow of ivy' (*see* ACHADH).

The site in County Laois, 10 km (6 miles) west of Portlaoise, of a monastery founded in the 6th century by **St Fintan of Clonenagh** (d.603), a disciple of St Columba and a noted ascetic, who apparently thrived on stale bread and muddy water. Of his foundation, only a few mounds survive.

Clones Irish *Cluain Eois* 'meadow of Eos' (*see* ACHADH); the identity of *Eos* is unknown.

A small market town in County Monaghan, near the Northern Ireland border, some 20 km (12 miles) southwest of Monaghan itself. St Tighearnach (d.549) founded a monastery here, and there are the remains of a 12th-century abbey and round tower.

Clones was the birthplace of the novelist Patrick McCabe (b.1955), author of *The Butcher Boy* (1992), and also of the boxer Barry McGuigan, who was known as the **Clones Cyclone**: he won the world bantamweight title in 1985.

Clones lace. A particular kind of crochet lace. Lace-making was introduced to Clones in 1847 as a famine-relief scheme by Cassandra Hand, wife of the local vicar. Clones soon became the lace-making centre of the north of Ireland, with each family closely guarding its own patterns.

Clonfert Irish *Cluain Fearta* 'meadow of the grave' (*see* ACHADH).

A locality in County Galway, 20 km (12 miles) southeast of Ballinasloe. St Brendan the Navigator (also called **St Brendan of Clonfert**) founded a monastery here in 558, which became a centre of learning. There is now a 12th-century church here with a fine Romanesque doorway.

Clonfert is also a Catholic bishopric, although the seat of the bishop is at LOUGHREA. It was the Bishop of Clonfert who became involved in the notorious Affair of the Bishop and the Nightie (1966). This arose from a quiz on Gay Byrne's *Late Late Show* on RTÉ, in which the presenter asked couples questions about one other. One wife, when asked what colour nightie she had worn on her wedding night, answered 'None'. Such sexual recklessness provoked Thomas Ryan, the Bishop of Clonfert, into expressions of outrage, widely reported in the public prints. It remains unclear as to what item of lingerie the good bishop might have considered more seemly. These liberalized, Celtic Tigerish days, the affair all seems a bit of a storm in a D-cup.

Clongowes Wood College Irish *Cluain Gabhamn* 'meadow of the smith' (*see* ACHADH).

A Jesuit boarding school in County Kildare, 30 km (19 miles) west of Dublin, known as '**the Eton of Ireland**' (compare ETON). It was founded in 1814, and one of its most famous pupils was James Joyce, who wrote about his experiences there in *Portrait of the Artist as a Young Man* (1916), including unjust floggings and hell-fire sermons.

> – Get at your work, all of you, cried the prefect of studies from the door. Father Dolan will be in every day to see if any boy, any lazy idle little loafer wants flogging, Every day. Every day.
>
> James Joyce: *Portrait of the Artist as a Young Man* (1916)

Clonmacnoise Irish *Cluain Mhic Nóis* 'meadow of the sons of Noas' (*see* ACHADH); Noas was apparently a son of the local chief.

The site of a monastery, which in the Middle Ages was Ireland's most important ecclesiastical centre after ARMAGH. It is situated on the SHANNON in County Offaly, 10 km (6 miles) south of Athlone. It was founded in 545 by **St Ciarán of Clonmacnoise**, and his feast day, 9 September, is still marked by an annual pilgrimage to Clonmacnoise. The monastery developed as a famous institution of learning, attracting students from Britain as well as Ireland. It was here *c*.1100 that the monks compiled *The Book of the Dun Cow*, a Gaelic miscellany, so called because it was supposedly written on vellum from the hide of a cow belonging to St Ciarán.

From the 9th to the 12th centuries Clonmacnoise was sacked over 30 times by the Vikings, and raided by the Anglo-Normans in 1179. Nevertheless it survived until 1552 when it was finally destroyed by the English. Today the remains include eight churches, two round towers, three high crosses, two holy wells and scores of early gravestones – many of the kings of Tara and of Connacht were buried here, including the last high kings, Turlough O'Connor and his son Rory (although some claim the latter was buried at CONG).

> In a quiet water'd land, a land of roses,
>   Stands Saint Kieran's city fair;
> And the warriors of Erin in their famous generations
>   Slumber there.
>
> T.W. Rolleston: 'The Dead at Clonmacnoise' (1909), apparently a translation of the 14th-century Irish of Angus O'Gillan

The **Clonmacnoise and West Offaly Railway**, a narrow-gauge steam railway for tourists, runs 9 km (5.5 miles) through the local bogs.

Annals of Clonmacnoise. A chronicle of Irish history from the earliest times to 1408, compiled at Clonmacnoise and translated into English in 1627 by Conall Mac Geoghan.

> The annals say: when the monks of Clonmacnoise
> Were all at prayers inside the oratory
> A ship appeared above them in the air.
>
> Seamus Heaney :'Lightenings viii' (1991)

Clonmel Irish *Cluain Meala* 'meadow of honey' (*see* ACHADH). A market town on the River SUIR in County Tipperary, 40 km (25 miles) west-northwest of Waterford. It is the administrative centre of the South Riding of Tipperary, and is surrounded by the Comeragh, Galty and Knockmealdown Mountains. The town may have been founded by Richard de Burgos (d.1243), and a friary was founded here in 1269, but little remains (apart from a certain reputation; *see below*). During the English settlement, Clonmel was purchased by the Earl of Desmond in 1338, and later came into the possession of the earls of Ormond. During Henry VIII's Reformation, the Irish Privy Council summoned Ireland's two archbishops and eight bishops to come to Clonmel to swear an oath recognizing Henry's supremacy in the church; however, only five conformed. Clonmel remained loyal to the English Crown until 1641, when it allowed itself to be garrisoned by Confederate Catholics. These staunchly resisted a Cromwellian assault in 1650, but the defenders ran out of ammunition and were forced to steal away in the night, leaving the townspeople to negotiate a surrender.

Clonmel was the birthplace of the novelist Laurence Sterne (1713–68). The writer George Borrow went to school here for a few months in 1815, and Anthony Trollope lived here in 1844–5, while working as an inspector for the Post Office. It was in Clonmel in 1912 that James Connolly and James Larkin founded the Irish Labour Party.

Clonmel – the 'meadow of honey' (*see above*) – features as the Land of Cockayne in the 14th-century goliardic poem of that name. Here all the appetites are pleasingly catered for by the residents of a monastery and convent, who are summoned to church by the slapping of a girl's bottom, and who swim together naked in warm and pleasant streams.

> Ther is a wel fair abbei
> Of white monks and of gre.
> The beth bouris and halles;
> Al of pasteiis beth the walles,
> Of fleis, of fisse and rich met
> The likfullist that man may et.

'Convict of Clonmel, The'. A poem by Jeremiah Joseph Callanan (1795–1829), beginning:

> How hard is my fortune
>   And vain my repining;
> The strong rope of fate
>   For this young neck is twining!
> My strength is departed,
>   My cheeks sunk and sallow,
> While I languish in chains
>   In the gaol of Clonmala.

Clontarf Irish *Cluain Tairbh* 'bull meadow' (*see* ACHADH). A suburb of DUBLIN on the north side of Dublin Bay.

Although most famous for the battle fought here in 1014 (*see below*), Clontarf reappears in Irish history in October 1843, when it was the site of one of the mass meetings summoned by Daniel O'Connell to agitate for the repeal of the Act of Union. The British called out troops and artillery to suppress the meeting.

Battle of Clontarf (23 April 1014). A battle, which took place on Good Friday, in which the forces of Brian Boru, who claimed the title of high king of all Ireland, defeated a force of Leinstermen (who denied his claim) and Vikings. The king himself, too old to take part in the battle, was killed by Brodir, a Viking fleeing from the battle, and his son was also killed. The battle was for long depicted as a great national triumph, ending Norse power in Ireland, although in reality it was the climax of a dynastic struggle. The deaths of Brian and his son in fact put an end to the possibility of a united Ireland.

Clontibret Irish *Cluain Tiobrad* 'meadow of the well' (*see* ACHADH). A village in County Monaghan, 10 km (6 miles) southeast of Monaghan itself.

Battle of Clontibret (27 May 1595). A battle that marked the open rebellion of Hugh O'Neill against the Crown. O'Neill decisively defeated his enemy Henry Bagenal, and was proclaimed a traitor shortly afterwards.

Clouds Hill Perhaps 'rocky hill', OE *clud* 'rock' + *hyll* 'hill'; alternatively from a personal name. The Dorset cottage, about 1.5 km (1 mile) north of Bovington Camp, owned by the author T.E. Lawrence (1888–1935; 'Lawrence of Arabia'). He acquired it while he was serving with the Royal Tank Corps (under the name T.E. Shaw). He set off from here on 13 May 1935 on his motorbike, swerved to avoid two errand-boys, was thrown off the bike and was hit by a passing car, sustaining injuries from which he later died.

Cloughjordan Irish *Cloch Shiurdáin* 'Jordan's stone (castle)'. A village in County Tipperary, some 55 km (34 miles) northeast of Tipperary itself. It was the birthplace of Thomas MacDonagh (1878–1916), poet and patriot, executed in 1916 for his part in the Easter Rising.

Clough Oughter Castle 'castle at Lough Oughter', Irish *cloch* 'castle' + lough name *Oughter*, which means 'upper', Irish *uachtair*. A Norman fortress on a man-made island in Lough Oughter, County Cavan, some 8 km (5 miles) west of Cavan itself. Although built by the De Lacys, it was for centuries a stronghold of the O'Reillys. In 1649, during the Confederate War, Owen Rua O'Neill died at the castle on his way south to join Ormond's forces. Clough Oughter was the last Irish garrison to surrender to Cromwell's forces (April 1653).

Clova. *See under* GLEN CLOVA.

Clovelly Probably 'Fele(c)'s earthworks' (referring to the ancient earthworks of Clovelly Dykes), OCelt *cloth*, Cornish *cleath* 'dyke, bank' + male personal name *Fele* or *Felec*.
A coastal village in Devon, on Bideford Bay, about 10 km (6 miles) east of Hartland Point. It is notably picturesque, with a fishing harbour and a steep pebble-cobbled street, described as being:

> ... so steep, it's like walking up a knobbly ladder
>
> A.A. Gill: *Sunday Times* (26 January 2003)

Appropriately enough, cars are banned from it. The **Clovelly Dykes**, an Iron Age fort, lie about 0.75 km (0.5 miles) to the south.

Clowne From the River *Clowne*, which rises nearby, and whose name is an ancient pre-English one identical with CLUN[1].
A village in northeastern Derbyshire, about 11 km (7 miles) northeast of Chesterfield.

Cloyne Irish *Cluain* 'pasture' (*see* ACHADH).
A village in County Cork, some 10 km (6 miles) east of Cobh. A monastery was founded here in the 6th century by St Colmán mac Lénéne (d.604), the earliest known Irish poet. Cloyne was both a Catholic and a Church of Ireland diocese. The Protestant diocese has long been joined to that of CORK, although Cloyne still has a small Church of Ireland cathedral. The cathedral of the Catholic diocese is in COBH. The most famous Protestant bishop, who held the post from 1734 to 1753, was the philosopher George Berkeley. A later bishop was the colourful Frederick Augustus Hervey, 4th Earl of Bristol, who held the post until 1768, when he was elevated to the bishopric of DERRY/LONDONDERRY, one of the richest sees in the country (*see under* DOWNHILL). He heard the news while playing leapfrog with his clergy, and famously declared:

> I will jump no more; I have beaten you all, for I have jumped from Cloyne to Derry.

Cluain. The Irish name for CLOYNE.

Cluain Cearbán. The Irish name for LOUISBURGH.

Cluain Dolcáin. The Irish name for CLONDALKIN.

Cluain Eighneach. The Irish name for CLONENAGH.

Cluain Eois. The Irish name for CLONES.

Cluain Gabhamn. The Irish name for Clongowes (*see* CLONGOWES WOOD COLLEGE).

Cluainín. The Irish name for MANORHAMILTON.

Cluain Ioraird. The Irish name for CLONARD.

Cluain Meala. The Irish name for CLONMEL.

Cluain Mhic Nóis. The Irish name for CLONMACNOISE.

Cluain Tiobrad. The Irish name for CLONTIBRET.

Cluanie Ridge From Glen Cluanie, probably from Gaelic *cluain* 'field, pasture' (*see* ACHADH).

A mountain ridge in KINTAIL, Highland (formerly in Inverness-shire), some 30 km (20 miles) southeast of Kyle of Lochalsh. Cluanie is pronounced 'cloony'. The ridge contains a number of MUNROS, the easiest seven to 'bag' in one day in the country; nevertheless, it is still an energetic outing, which will earn the walker an evening's conviviality in the handily placed **Cluanie Inn**. The ridge takes its name from **Glen Cluanie**, the **Cluanie Forest** and **Loch Cluanie** on its northern side.

Clubland. Originally, a collective term for the gentlemen's clubs of the West End of London, and for their members. Concentrated mainly in ST JAMES'S Street and PALL MALL, they include the Athenaeum, Boodle's, Brooks's, the Carlton, the Garrick, Pratt's, the Reform and White's. The oldest of them go back to the late 17th and 18th centuries (White's 1693, Boodle's 1762, Brooks's 1764), but the concept is essentially a late 19th-century one: a male freemasonry of the aristocracy and the professional classes at leisure to dine, converse or even sleep under a newspaper in a large leather armchair, away from the cares of business and in surroundings of somewhat oppressive Victorian luxury.

In the latter part of the 20th century the word took on an additional application: to the entertainment clubs of northern England. They had their genesis in the working men's clubs, where men would gather after a day's work for a drink, a game of darts or snooker, enlivened perhaps by the occasional turn from a comic or singer. As the music halls expired, these clubs became important alternative venues for professional entertainers, and many famous names have cut their teeth on the Clubland circuit.

More recently still the term has come to be applied to the milieu of clubbing teenagers and 20-somethings. It is scarcely localizable, not least because it flourishes in swiftly changing venues (in London at the start of the 21st century HOXTON was hot).

Clubworthy 'muddy mound or fortification', dialect *clob* 'clod, mud' + OE *beorg* 'hill' or *burh* 'fortification' (*see* BURY); the element -*worthy* arose from a misinterpretation of the second part of the name (pronounced '-ery') as derived from OE *worthig* 'enclosure' (*see* -WORTH, WORTHY, -WARDINE).
A village (pronounced 'klubbery') in Cornwall, about 11 km (7 miles) northwest of Launceston.

Clumber Park *Clumber* probably 'hill by the River Clowne', *Clowne* pre-English river name (*see* CLOWNE) + OCelt *breg* 'hill'.
A 1540-ha (3800-acre) estate in Nottinghamshire, in the northern part of Sherwood Forest, in the so-called DUKERIES. Its house, built in the 1770s and much embellished in the 19th century, was the seat of the dukes of Newcastle. It was demolished in the 1930s, but the park remains open to the public.

Clumber spaniel. A type of heavily set spaniel originally bred at Clumber Park. Its coat is mainly white.

Clun[1] A pre-English river name of unknown meaning.
A river in Shropshire, which rises in **Clun Forest**, on the westernmost edge of the county, and flows southeastwards through CLUN[2] and then south to join the River TEME about 11 km (7 miles) east of Knighton. Several settlements in the surrounding area (including Clun) take their name from it – as in this litany by A.E. Housman:

> Clunton and Clunbury,
> Clungunford and Clun,
> Are the quietest places
> Under the sun.

> A.E. Housman: from *A Shropshire Lad* (1896)

Clun. A designation for a breed of sheep originating in the southwestern part of Shropshire, around the River Clun.

Clun[2] From the River *Clun*.
A small town in Shropshire, on the River Clun, about 24 km (15 miles) northwest of Ludlow. Situated only about 10 km (6 miles) east of the Welsh border, it has had a violent past: the British chieftain Caractacus made a determined stand against the Romans here; the Normans built a castle here, on a hill overlooking the river, but this did not deter the Anglo-Saxon guerrilla fighters under Edric the Wild; and four times between 1195 and 1400 the Welsh stormed the castle and burned the town. But now the thunder of history has passed on, and all (as A.E. Housman noted – *see* CLUN[1]) is peaceful.

Cluny's Cage. *See under* BEN ALDER.

Clwyd[1] Welsh 'hurdle', possibly referring to a crossing made from these.
A river (pronounced 'cloo-id') in Denbighshire (formerly part of Clwyd), flowing through the **Vale of Clwyd** northwards for 64 km (40 miles) to meet the sea at RHYL. The hills on the eastern side of the Vale are called the **Clwydian Range**; the high point is Moel Famau (554 m / 1817 ft). In 1874 Gerard Manley Hopkins entered the seminary of St Beuno in the Vale of Clwyd, and the landscape here informs much of his poetry.

Clwyd[2]. A former county of northeast Wales, formed in 1974 from FLINTSHIRE, most of DENBIGHSHIRE and part of MERIONETH. It was bordered to the west by Gwynedd, to the north by the Irish Sea, to the east by Cheshire, and to the south by Shropshire and Powys. The administrative seat was in MOLD, and other towns included WREXHAM[1], DENBIGH, RHYL and COLWYN BAY. In 1996 it was broken up into the unitary authorities of WREXHAM[2], FLINTSHIRE, DENBIGHSHIRE and part of CONWY[3].

Clwyd Theatr Cymru. The principal publicly subsidized theatre company of Wales, based in Mold. It began life in

1976 as **Theatre Clwyd**, and over the next 20 years built a high reputation for its productions. Its premises contain five performing spaces, including the Anthony Hopkins Theatre and the Emlyn Williams Theatre, and its director from 1997 has been ex-Royal Shakespeare Company Terry Hands. Despite the name change wrought in 1998, to tune in with the devolutionary self-confidence symbolized by the new Welsh Assembly, the company still performs mainly in English.

Clwydian Range. *See* CLWYD[1].

Clydach Vale From the common south Wales river name *Clydach*, possibly from an OCelt name meaning 'wild rocky river'.
A small town in Rhondda Cynon Taff (formerly in Glamorgan, then in Mid Glamorgan), 10 km (6 miles) northwest of Pontypridd.

Clyde Probably a primary OCelt river name, possibly a river goddess whose name meant 'cleanser', from the Indo-European root *clou* 'wash' (whence Latin *cloaca* 'sewer'). Tacitus referred to it as *Clota*, AD 1st–2nd centuries; the Gaelic name was *Clutha* (modern Gaelic *Cluaidh*).
Scotland's second longest river (158 km / 98.5 miles long), rising as Daer Water in the LOWTHER HILLS of South Lanarkshire, near the sources of the TWEED and the ANNAN[1], hence the traditional rhyme:

> Annan, Tweed and Clyde
> Rise oot o' ane hillside.
> Tweed ran, Annan wan,
> Clyde fell, and brak its neck owre Corra Linn.

> (Corra Linn is one of the Falls of Clyde; *see below*.)

Daer Water is joined by Potrail Water at a little settlement called Watermeetings, and there forms the Clyde, which at first flows northeastwards towards BIGGAR, between Tinto and the Tweedsmuir Hills (*see under* TWEED):

> Yon wild, mossy mountains sae lofty and wide,
> That nurse in their bosom the youth o' the Clyde …

> Robert Burns: 'Yon Wild, Mossy Mountains' (?1786)

After approaching Biggar the river then flows generally northwestwards past LANARK, CLYDESDALE and HAMILTON[1]:

> How sweet to move at summer's eve
> By Clyde's meandering stream,
> When Sol in joy is seen to leave
> The earth with crimson beam;
> When islands that wandered far
> Above his sea couch lie,
> And here and there some gem-like star
> Re-opes its sparkling eye.

> Andrew Parks: 'The Banks of Clyde'

From here the river flows on to Glasgow and CLYDEBANK, and enters the **Firth of Clyde** at DUMBARTON. The Firth extends west then south past BUTE, the CUMBRAES and ARRAN to AILSA CRAIG, where it joins that part of the Atlantic called the North Channel. The Firth is around 105 km (65 miles) long. The world's first sea-going steamboat, Henry Bell's *Comet*, was launched at PORT GLASGOW on the Firth of Clyde in 1812.

The dredging of the Clyde in the 18th century, enabling ocean-going ships to reach beyond Port Glasgow to the BROOMIELAW in Glasgow itself, opened the city to the New World trade, and was the basis of the city's industry, especially shipbuilding – hence the saying 'the Clyde made Glasgow and Glasgow made the Clyde.'

The river and the city in the dark smoke and fire of the Industrial Revolution were evoked in the poem 'Glasgow' by Alexander Smith (1830–67):

And through thy heart, as through a dream,
Flows on that black disdainful stream;
    All scornfully it flows,
Between the huddled gloom of masts,
Silent as pines unvexed by blasts –
    'Tween lamps in streaming rows,
O wondrous sight! O stream of dread!
O long dark river of the dead!

The shipbuilding is now almost all gone, and Glasgow is no longer a major port, but Glaswegians still make holiday excursions 'doon the watter' on passenger ships, taking them to resorts such as DUNOON and ROTHESAY.

Roamin in the gloamin'
By the bonny banks of Clyde.

Harry Lauder: 'Roamin' in the Gloamin'' (song)

After commanding British troops in India during the Indian Mutiny, General Colin Campbell (1792–1863) was raised to the peerage as Baron Clyde of Clydesdale. There are Clyde rivers in Australia (New South Wales, Northern Territory, Tasmania) and New Zealand (South Island). The River Clutha in New Zealand is named after the Gaelic name for the River Clyde, and a town in its valley is called Clyde.

See also CLYDESIDE, INVERCLYDE *and* STRATHCLYDE.

Ah didnae come up the Clyde on a banana boat. An expression meaning 'I'm not that gullible', 'I'm no fool'; alternative forms of unlikely river transport include a bike, a wheelbarrow and a water biscuit.

Clyde FC. A professional football club founded in 1877 which played its first games on the banks of the River Clyde in Glasgow. Now based in CUMBERNAULD, the club's nickname is the Bully Wee.

Clydes Burn. A small tributary that enters the Clyde in its upper reaches, just west of Beattock Summit. The Clydes Burn rises on the southern flank of **Clyde Law** (545 m /1788 ft), near the source of the Tweed at the head of Tweeddale.

Falls of Clyde. Two mighty waterfalls on the Clyde, just above NEW LANARK, notable more for their width and power than their height, although in this stretch the river falls some 75 m (250 ft) in 6.5 km (4 miles). The falls were visited twice (1801 and 1834) by J.M.W. Turner, who made several paintings of them; other notable visitors included poets Coleridge and the Wordsworths, in 1803. Today the full power of the falls is only seen when water is not being taken off for the local hydroelectric scheme.

He could fall intae the Clyde and come up wi a fish supper. An expression meaning 'he is unusually lucky'.

He's as deep and dirty as the Clyde. An expression meaning 'he is not to be trusted'.

What's that got to do wi' the Clyde navigation? The Glaswegian equivalent of 'What's that got to do with the price of fish?', i.e. 'In what way is that remark pertinent to the subject under discussion?'

Clydebank. A town on the north bank of the Clyde, west of Glasgow itself, but part of the Glasgow conurbation. It was formerly a major shipbuilding centre, and the great liners *Queen Mary*, *Queen Elizabeth* and the *QE2* were all launched here. During the Second World War the poet Hugh MacDiarmid (then in his 50s), worked in a munitions factory in the town, which suffered badly from German bombing in the **Clydebank Blitz** of 1941.

The town's football team, **Clydebank FC**, nicknamed the Bankies, was founded in 1965.

Clydebank an' Kilbooie. Clydeside rhyming slang for 'Shooey', i.e. Hugh.

Clydesdale. A traditional area of South Lanarkshire, comprising the valley of the CLYDE between LANARK and CARLUKE. The area is known for its orchards, and was a district (1975–96) of the former Strathclyde region, with its headquarters at Lanark.

Clydesdale. A breed of draft horse, developed in Clydesdale in the 18th century. They are usually bay, black or dark brown, and have notably shaggy legs.

Clydeside. An informal name for the Glasgow conurbation along both banks of the River CLYDE. Its industries of iron and steel, heavy engineering and shipbuilding have long declined, but are inextricably intertwined in the folk memory.

Clydeside,
Webbed in its foundries and loud blood,
Binds up the children's cries alive.

W.S. Graham: 'The Children of Greenock' from *The White Threshold* (1949)

The term **Red Clydeside** is generally applied to the strongly socialist working-class movement in and around Glasgow, particularly associated with the (now largely defunct) ship-building industry. Revolutionary socialism first appeared on Clydeside during the First World War, when a number of left-wingers were jailed after they called for strike action. Early heroes of the movement included the pacifist James Maxton of the Independent Labour Party, who was one of those imprisoned, and the communist school teacher John Maclean. In January 1919 troops and tanks were deployed in Glasgow in the expectation of an imminent Bolshevik revolution. Red Clydeside again came to national notice in the early 1970s, when workers at one of the shipyards, led by the shop steward Jimmy Reid, staged a work-in to stop the yard being closed down. A right-wing perspective on Red Clydeside unrest in the First World War is to be found in John Buchan's novel *Mr Standfast* (1919).

Clydesiders. A loose association of left-wing MPs representing Glasgow and Clydeside constituencies, who enlivened British politics and Parliament from 1922 until they were much diminished in numbers following the 1931 general election. Notable among them were John Wheatley, of Housing Act fame, Campbell Stephen, Emanuel Shinwell and the aforementioned James Maxton, who became chairman of the Independent Labour Party. They acted as a ginger group for the Labour Party and were noted champions of the poor and unemployed.

Clyffe Pypard *Clyffe see* CLIFFE; *Pypard* denoting manorial ownership in the Middle Ages by the Pipard family.
A village in Wiltshire, about 13 km (8 miles) southwest of Swindon.

Clyro 'district of the river Claer', Welsh *claer* 'clear' + *wy* 'district, area'.
A small village in Powys (formerly in Radnorshire), 2 km (1.2 miles) northwest of Hay-on-Wye. The Romans built a station here, and the Rev. Francis Kilvert was curate of Clyro from 1865 to 1872, beginning his famous diary – describing local people and places – in 1870. Ashbrook House, where Kilvert lodged, is now an art gallery.

> And the grey tower of Clyro Church peeped through the bright red branches. A sack half filled with apples stood under a tree but no one was about. A woodpecker was tapping loud some way down Jacob's Ladder. Partridge shooting on all round.
>
> Francis Kilvert: diary (20 September 1870)

Clyst An OCelt river name probably meaning 'clean stream'.
A river (pronounced 'klisst') in Devon, rising to the northeast of Exeter and flowing into the EXE estuary about 6.5 km (4 miles) southeast of Exeter.

Clyst Honiton *Clyst* from the River CLYST; *Honiton* 'farmstead belonging to a religious community' (in this case Exeter Cathedral), OE *higna* possessive form of *hiwan* 'household, members of a (religious) community' + -TON.

A village in Devon, on the River Clyst, on the western edge of Exeter Airport, about 5 km (3 miles) east of Exeter.

Clyst Hydon *Hydon* denoting manorial ownership in the Middle Ages by the de Hidune family.
A village in Devon, on the River Clyst, about 14 km (8.5 miles) northeast of Exeter.

Cnicht Possibly OE *cniht* 'young man', later 'knight', though what the application might be here is unclear.
A small but perfectly formed mountain (689 m / 2260 ft) standing proudly on its own in southern Snowdonia, some 8 km (5 miles) south of SNOWDON itself. It is in Gwynedd. In the most famous view of the mountain, it forms a perfectly symmetrical cone, but this profile is in fact the end of a long ridge. George Borrow described it in *Wild Wales* (1862) as 'beautiful, but spectral'.

Cnobga. The Irish name for KNOWTH.

Cnocán na Biolraí. The Irish name for WATERGRASSHILL.

Cnoc an Sráidbhaile. The Irish name for the STRADBALLY MOUNTAIN.

Cnoc an Urchaill. The Irish name for SPANCIL HILL.

Cnoc Bréanainn. The Irish name for BRANDON MOUNTAIN.

Cnoc Buidhe. The Irish name for KNOCKBOY.

Cnoc Fiodh na gCaor. The Irish name for VINEGAR HILL.

Cnoc Fola. The Irish name for BLOODY FORELAND.

Cnoc Mhaoldonn. The Irish name for Knockmealdown (*see* KNOCKMEALDOWN MOUNTAINS).

Cnoic na Ceachan. The Irish name for the CAHA MOUNTAINS.

Cnoic na Seithe. The Irish name for the SHEHY MOUNTAINS.

Cnoic Shiofra. The Irish name for the SHEEFRY HILLS.

Coalbrookdale 'valley of the cold brook', OE *cald* 'cold' + *broc* 'brook' + ModE *dale*; later assimilated to *coal*, a substance of major local importance (*see also* COALPORT).
A town in Shropshire, within the unitary authority of Telford and Wrekin, about 6.5 km (4 miles) south of Telford. It is one of the seminal sites of the Industrial Revolution. It was here that Abraham Darby (1677–1717) developed his process for smelting iron ore using coke rather than the more expensive charcoal. In the 18th century he and his successors, and their fellow ironmasters, turned out not just domestic iron utensils but also large-scale machine parts, including in 1761 the first of the huge cylinders around which the steam-engines of the new industrial age would be built. In 1778 Abraham Darby III cast here the components of the world's first iron bridge, which was erected at nearby IRONBRIDGE, and this was followed in 1791 by the world's first iron aqueduct.

Colebrook Dale itself is a very romantic spot ... Indeed ... too beautiful to be much in unison with that variety of horrors art has spread at the bottom: the noise of the forges, mills, &c., with all their vast machinery, the flames bursting from the furnaces with the burning of the coal and the smoak of the lime kilns, are altogether sublime.

Arthur Young: *Tours in England and Wales* (1791)

Coalbrookvale. *See under* NANTYGLO.

Coalcleugh 'cold ravine', OE *col* 'cool, cold' + Northern dialect *cleugh* 'deep gully, ravine'.

A deserted and desolate former lead-mining village in Allendale, Northumberland, 23 km (14 miles) southwest of Hexham. At an altitude of 537 m (1761 ft) it was, when inhabited, the highest village in Britain, and was known as 'the End of the World'.

People say funny things about Coal Cleugh. They say that folk who live there burn cats for fuel; but then the cats are only balls made of clay and powdered coal, so that there is nothing so wonderful in it after all. People also say that Coal Cleugh is the end of the world! Just as if the world had an end like a cow's tail! The world, you know, is round, like an orange, and so has not got an end ...

Old Feg: in *Allendale Christmas Annual* (1871)

Coalisland Irish *Oiléan an Ghuail* 'island of the coal'.

A small town in County Tyrone, 5 km (3 miles) northeast of Dungannon. It is at the centre of the Tyrone coalfield, which has, however, never been profitably exploited.

Coalport From the settlement's former status as a port for shipping coal; first recorded in the 18th century.

A village in Shropshire, within the unitary authority of Telford and Wrekin, on the River Severn, about 3 km (2 miles) southeast of COALBROOKDALE. Both Coalport and Coalbrookdale are in what was a major coal-producing area, and in the 18th century coal-shipping was the main trade on the River Severn between Shrewsbury and Bristol.

Coalport's name is synonymous with the china and porcelain made at the **Coalport China Works**, which was founded in 1795 by John Rose. The factory's products in the gilded style of Sèvres, Meissen and Chelsea became very fashionable in the 1830s.

Coalville 'coal town', ModE *coal* + *ville*, an element borrowed from French *ville* 'town'. It originated as the name of a house, Coalville House, built in the 1820s by the colliery owner William Stenson in what was then a hamlet called Long Lane; the town grew up around the house and by 1841 had taken its name.

A town in the former coal-mining area of Leicestershire, about 19 km (12 miles) northwest of Leicester.

Coast. *See* FIRST COAST, SECOND COAST.

Coat 'cottage(s)', OE *cot* (*see* -COT, COTE).

A village in Somerset, about 10 km (6 miles) northwest of Yeovil.

Coatbridge 'bridge by the cottages', ME *cot* (*see* -COT, COTE) + *bridge*.

An industrial town in North Lanarkshire (formerly in Strathclyde region), 14 km (8.5 miles) east of Glasgow. 'Big Eddie' McAteer (1914–86), Nationalist leader in Northern Ireland in the 1950s and 1960s, was born here.

Cobbler, The So named for its appearance.

A craggy mountain (881 m / 2890 ft) in Argyll and Bute (formerly in Argyll, then in Strathclyde), 17 km (11 miles) east of Inveraray, and the most spectacular peak in the Arrochar Alps (*see under* ARROCHAR). It was a particular favourite with working-class Glasgow climbers in the 1930s and 1940s, as they could reach it by train (to Arrochar), or, more strenuously, by bicycle, and these tough shipyard workers put up some appropriately tough rock climbs here.

The Cobbler has three summits, each a rocky pinnacle: the South Peak (on the left as seen from Arrochar), the Central Peak (the highest) and the North Peak (which, with its beetling overhanging prow, is called the Ram's Head by climbers). To reach the highest point (the Central Peak) it is necessary to go through a window in the summit rock onto an exposed ledge above a big drop, and thence attain the top.

The origin of the name is explained by an 18th-century traveller:

This terrific rock forms the bare summit of a huge mountain, and its nodding top so far overhangs the base as to assume the appearance of a cobbler sitting at work, from whence the country people call it *an greasaiche cróm*, the crooked shoemaker.

John Stoddart: *Local Scenery and Manners in Scotland* (1800)

From this description one might suppose that the North Peak was the best candidate to be the Cobbler himself, but writers on the mountain have allocated the name to both of the other peaks as well, with the consensus in favour of the Centre Peak. Similarly, if two of the other peaks are known respectively as Jean (the Cobbler's Wife) and His Last, there appears to be no agreement as to which is which – although, again, the North Peak appears most like a shoemaker's last.

The mountain is also known (on maps at least) as **Ben Arthur**, although The Cobbler name, originally applied to just one of the peaks, has come to stand for the whole mountain. 'Arthur' is more likely to derive from Gaelic *artaich* 'stony' than from the legendary British king.

Cobh Irish *An Cóbh* 'the cove'; the word is not native Irish, but was borrowed from English *cove*, and is pronounced 'cove'.

A port on Great Island in CORK Harbour, County Cork, 13 km (8 miles) southeast of Cork itself. Its old name was

Cove of Cork, and between 1849 and 1922 it was known as **Queenstown** (after a visit by Queen Victoria):

> We … stepped ashore at Cove, a small place, to enable them to call it Queen's Town; the enthusiasm was immense …
>
> Queen Victoria: letter to Leopold, king of the Belgians (her uncle) (6 August 1849)

There is a cathedral, built 1869–1918 and possessing the largest carillon in Ireland. Cobh's Royal Yacht Club was founded in 1720, and is the oldest in the world. It was from Cobh that the *Sirius* set out in 1838, to become the first steamboat to cross the Atlantic, and the harbour was a major embarkation point for Irish emigrants in the 19th century. The British government maintained rights to use the port as a naval base after the formation of the Irish Free State, but these rights were relinquished in 1938.

The Rev. Charles Wolfe, known only for his wonderful poem 'The Burial of Sir John Moore' (1817), is buried in Cobh, as are many of the victims of the *Lusitania*, sunk off the coast near Kinsale in 1915 (Cobh's other association with maritime disaster lies in the fact that it was the last port of call of the *Titanic*).

In the late 1990s an unemployed man from Cobh won the lottery, bought the building housing the dole office, and doubled the rent.

Cobham¹ 'Cobba's enclosure or homestead', OE male personal name *Cobba* + HAM.

A village in Kent, about 8 km (5 miles) west of Rochester. It was here on 28 August 1843 that Richard Dadd (1817–86), the artist who spent the last 43 years of his life in lunatic asylums, killed his father.

Cobham Hall, an Elizabethan structure with later additions, is one of the largest old houses in Kent, with grounds designed by Humphry Repton; it is now a private school for girls.

Cobham² 'Cofa's enclosure or homestead' or 'enclosure or homestead with a hut or shelter', OE male personal name *Cofa* or *cofa* 'hut, shelter' + HAM.

A town in Surrey, on the River Mole, about 5 km (3 miles) northwest of Leatherhead. The Diggers (or True Levellers), a 17th-century radical sect led by Gerrard Winstanley, which attempted to seize and share out common land, set up communal colonies at St George's Hill near Cobham in April 1649.

Coccium. The Roman name for WIGAN.

Cockayne A name used ironically: the Land of *Cockayne* is an idyllic place of luxury and idleness, based on the French Pays de Cocagne 'land of plenty, land of milk and honey'.

A remote settlement in the NORTH YORK MOORS, 23 km (14 miles) northwest of Pickering. The hill called **Cockayne Ridge** (430 m / 1411 ft) rises to the north.

Cockayne Hatley *Cockayne* denoting manorial ownership in the late Middle Ages by the Cockayne family; *Hatley* probably 'glade on the hill', OE *hætt* 'hill' + -LEY.

A village in Bedfordshire, about 22 km (14 miles) east of Bedford.

Cock Bridge *Cock* from the Allt a'Choilich or Cock Burn (stream) which the bridge here crosses.

A village in Aberdeenshire (formerly in Grampian region), some 18 km (11 miles) northwest of Ballater. It is linked to TOMINTOUL by the high road pass over the LECHT.

Cockburnspath 'Kolbrandr's road', OScand personal name + OE *pæth* 'road, path', frequently appearing in northern dialect as *peth*; Daniel Defoe records that in his time it was 'vulgarly' known as *Cobberspeth*; compare MORPETH; *Colbrandespade* c.1130.

A village on the North Sea coast of Scottish Borders (formerly in Berwickshire), at the foot of the Lammermuir Hills 12 km (7.5 miles) southeast of Dunbar. It is the northeastern terminus of the Southern Uplands Way (*see under* SOUTHERN UPLANDS).

Cock Cairn Possibly a version of Gaelic *càrn coilich*, 'cock hill or cairn'.

A hill (727 m / 2385 ft) in the eastern Grampians, on the border between Angus and Aberdeenshire (formerly Tayside and Grampian regions), 6 km (4 miles) east-north-east of Mount Keen.

Cock Clarks Probably 'land associated with Coke and Clerk' (two local families known in the 14th century); recorded at the time of Henry VIII as *Cokeclarkes*.

A village in Essex, about 11 km (7 miles) southeast of Chelmsford.

Cockenzie Uncertain; possibly Gaelic *Cùil C(h)oinnigh* 'Kenneth's nook'.

A fishing village in East Lothian, 7 km (4.5 miles) northeast of Musselburgh. It is now joined to the neighbouring village of Port Seton, and is dominated by a huge coal-fired power station, built in the 1960s. On Children's Gala Day every June, the Summer Queen sails from Cockenzie harbour to Port Seton, repelling an assault by pirates en route.

Cockermouth 'mouth of the River Cocker', OCelt river name meaning 'crooked' + OE *mutha* 'mouth'.

A small town on the northwest edge of the Lake District, Cumbria (formerly in Cumberland), 17 km (11 miles) northwest of Keswick. It is situated where the River Cocker enters the River DERWENT¹. It was the 'sweet Birthplace' of William (1770–1850) and Dorothy (1771–1855) Wordsworth, and their father's house is now known as Wordsworth House. It was almost demolished in the 1930s to make room for a bus station, but it was saved and presented to the National Trust. Also born in Cockermouth, in 1764, was Fletcher Christian, who was to lead the mutiny on the *Bounty*. John Dalton (1766–1844), the originator of modern atomic theory, was born nearby.

Cockfosters '(house or estate) of the chief forester', early ModE *cock* 'chief, head' + *for(e)ster* 'forester'.

An outer northern suburb of Greater London, in the borough of BARNET (N20) (before 1965 in Hertfordshire). It is at the southwestern tip of the ancient royal hunting forest of Enfield Chase (*see under* ENFIELD) – whence its name.

Cockfosters Underground station, opened in 1933, is the northern terminus of the Piccadilly line.

Cockleton. The fictional name for HARTLEPOOL as used by W.M. Thackeray.

Cock of Arran, the. *See under* ARRAN.

Cockpen 'red hill', OCelt *coch* 'red' + PEN.

A parish southwest of Dalkeith in Midlothian. It is pronounced 'co-pen'. In Robert Burns's poem 'Scroggam', an ale-brewing wife of Cockpen cures the fevers of her daughter and the priest of the parish by having them lie in bed together –

> That the heat o' the tane might cool the tither,
> Sing auld Cowl, lay you down by me.
> Scroggam, my dearie, ruffum!

> (Even the broad-minded *Concise Scots Dictionary* fails to enlighten us as to the meanings of 'scroggam' and 'ruffum')

'Laird o' Cockpen, The'. A song by Lady Carolina Nairne (1766–1845), beginning:

> The Laird o' Cockpen he was proud and he's great
> But his mind was ta'en up wi' the things o' the
>   state
> He's wanted a new wife his braw home tae keep
> But favour wi' wooin' was fashous tae seek

The bumptious laird is thought to have been Mark Carse (*fl*.17th century), and the lady he woos Jean McLeish of Claversha' – who has the good sense to say 'No'.

Cockup. *See under* GREAT COCKUP.

Codda Perhaps 'river source', from a derivative of a Cornish verb meaning 'to arise'; recorded in 1385 as *Stymkodda*, from Cornish *stumm* 'bend', so possibly originally 'bend of the river-source'.

A village in Cornwall, on Bodmin Moor, about 16 km (10 miles) southwest of Launceston.

Coed-Duon. The Welsh name for BLACKWOOD.

Coed Y Brenin Forest Park 'wood of the king', Welsh *coed* (*see* CED) + *y brenin* 'of the king'.

A forest park in Gwynedd (formerly in Merioneth), just north of Dollgellau.

Coffinswell Originally *Well* '(place at the) spring or stream', OE *wella*; *Coffins*- denoting manorial ownership in the early Middle Ages by the Coffin family.

A village in Devon, about 5 km (3 miles) north of Torquay.

Cogges 'hills', OE *cogg* 'hill'.

A village in Oxfordshire (pronounced 'Coggs') on the southern outskirts of WITNEY. **Cogges Manor** and its associated Cotswold stone farm buildings house a museum devoted to Oxfordshire rural life in Victorian times. The village of **High Cogges** lies a mile or so to the southeast.

Coggeshall 'Cogg's nook of land', OE *Cogges* possessive form of male personal name *Cogg* + *halh* (*see* HALE, -HALL).

A small town (pronounced 'kogishəl' or 'kokshəl') in Essex, on the River Blackwater, and situated between Braintree and Colchester on STANE STREET[2]. In the Middle Ages it was a prosperous weaving centre, and some important medieval buildings survive, notably the Grange Barn, one of the oldest timber-framed barns left in Europe, and Paycocke's, a 16th-century merchant's house.

A reputation for foolishness seems unfortunately to have attached itself to the people of Coggeshall over the centuries, and any lame-brained action came to be termed a '**Coggeshall job**'. Examples cited include an attempt to use hurdles to divert the course of a stream, and chaining up in a shed a wheelbarrow that had been bitten by a mad dog, for fear the barrow was now rabid.

Coigach Gaelic *còigeach* 'a fifth share', a land division.

A traditional area of the Northwest HIGHLANDS, formerly in Sutherland and now in Highland. It stretches northwestwards beyond ULLAPOOL to the point called **Rubha Coigeach**. The main mountain is the elegant **Ben Mòr Coigach** ('the big mountain of Coigach', 743 m / 2438 ft).

Coill an Chollaig. The Irish name for BAILIEBOROUGH.

Coillte Mach. The Irish name for KILTAMAGH.

Coirneal Mhé. The Irish name for MAY'S CORNER.

Cois Abhann Dalla. An alternative Irish name for CUSHENDALL.

Coity Welsh *coed* 'wood, forest' (*see* CED).

A village in Bridgend unitary authority (formerly in Glamorgan), 3 km (2 miles) northeast of Bridgend itself. The ruined **Coity Castle** dates back to the 12th century, with considerable 14th-century alterations. There is a story that when the Norman adventurer Sir Payn de Turbeville sought to acquire the castle from the Welsh leader, Morgan Gam, the latter demanded that he either fight him for it or marry his daughter Sybil. Apparently Sir Payn chose the more peaceable course. The castle was abandoned in the late 16th century.

Coketown. A fictional industrial city in northern England, which is the setting of Charles Dickens's *Hard Times* (1854).

Based on Dickens's impressions of PRESTON, its claustrophobic ugliness echoes the general atmosphere of the novel. It is here that Thomas Gradgrind required Facts from his pupils:

> Coketown ... was a triumph of fact; it had no greater taint of fancy in it than Mrs Gradgrind herself ... It was a town of red brick, or of brick that would have been red if the smoke and ashes had allowed it ... It was a town of machinery and tall chimneys, out of which interminable serpents of smoke trailed themselves for ever and ever, and never got uncoiled.
>
> Charles Dickens: *Hard Times* (1854), Chapter 5

> Coketown (the spirit-quenching hideousness of which is hauntingly evoked).
>
> F.R. Leavis: *The Great Tradition* (1948)

Colaton Raleigh *Colaton* 'Cola's farmstead', OE male personal name *Cola* + -TON; *Raleigh* denoting manorial ownership in the Middle Ages by the de Ralegh family.
A village (pronounced 'kollatən rawli') in Devon, about 13 km (8 miles) southeast of Exeter.

Colchester Probably 'Roman town on the River Colne', *Colne* from COLNE[1] + OE *ceaster* (*see* CHESTER). There is no link with 'Old King Cole', despite popular legend.
A town and river-port in Essex, on the River COLNE[1], about 82 km (51 miles) northeast of London. It has been the site of a human settlement for over 3000 years, and is the oldest recorded town in England. Cunobelin (d.*c.*42 AD; Shakespeare's Cymbeline), King of the Catuvellauni, made it his capital around 10 AD. It was taken over by the invading Romans *c.*50 AD as a colony of ex-servicemen. Its Romano-British name was **Colonia Camulodunum** (**Camulodunum** for short), the latter part based on a British name meaning 'fort of the Celtic war-god Camulos' (it is possible that the first syllable of *Colchester* may be a worn-down remnant of *Colonia*).

It became a thriving town and an important administrative centre in Roman times (despite being sacked by the Iceni under Queen Boudicca in 55 AD), and many relics of the Roman presence, including parts of the city walls, can still be seen.

At the end of the 11th century the Normans built the largest castle keep in Europe in Colchester. In the Middle Ages the town developed into a key centre of the cloth trade. There was an influx of Flemish refugees in the 17th and 18th centuries, who brought with them their weaving skills, particularly in the making of baize – originally a type of fine-textured cloth (in 1667 Samuel Pepys made a note in his diary of 'a cloak of Colchester baize'), later a rougher sort of material. The trade's importance had declined by the 20th century, its place in the town's economy largely taken over by light engineering.

As a port, both for trade and for fishing, Colchester's great days are behind it, but one product of the sea and estuary for which it continues to be famous is its oysters. They were acknowledged delicacies in Roman times, and **Colchester natives** (or simply **Colchesters** for short) have been esteemed by gourmets ever since. An early 17th-century manuscript notes 'They [oysters] past for good plump colchesters', and the diarist John Evelyn observed in his *Memoirs* (1656) that 'Colchester is also famous for oysters and Eringo root [the candied root of the sea holly, reputedly – like oysters – an aphrodisiac]'. A distinguishing feature of Colchester oysters in previous centuries – now mercifully abandoned – is that they were put into pits to turn them literally 'green about the gills', a process known as 'greening':

> Your Wall fleet Oysters no man will prefer
> Before the juicy Grass-green Colchester.
>
> Thomas Flatman: *Belly God* (1674)

Colchester Oyster Feast is held in October to celebrate the start of the new season.

The University of Essex, established in 1962, is at WIVENHOE Park, on the southeastern outskirts of Colchester. In George Orwell's futuristic novel *Nineteen Eighty-Four* (1949), an atomic bomb is dropped on Colchester in 1955. William Gilbert (1544–1603), physician to Elizabeth I and James VI and I and a pioneering investigator of magnetism, and the mathematician Roger Penrose (b.1931) were born in Colchester.

There are towns called Colchester in the USA (Connecticut, Illinois and Vermont) and a Colchester county in Nova Scotia, Canada.

weaver's beef of Colchester. A name applied in former centuries to sprats.

Cold Ashby *Cold* 'cold, exposed', OE *cald*; *Ashby see* ASHBY.
A village in Northamptonshire, about 19 km (12 miles) northwest of Northampton.

Cold Aston *Aston see* ASTON.
A village in Gloucestershire, in the Cotswolds, about 10 km (6 miles) southwest of Stow-on-the-Wold. An alternative name for it is **Aston Blank** (*Blank* perhaps from Old French *blanc* 'white, bare').

Cold Blow Self-explanatory: an exposed place subject to strong winds.
A village in Pembrokeshire (formerly in Dyfed), 2 km (1.2 miles) south of Narberth and 6 km (4 miles) west of Tavernspite.

Cold Chapel Probably 'chapel on exposed land', ME *cold* 'cold, exposed' + OFr *chapel* 'chapel'.
A tiny settlement in the upper CLYDE valley, in South Lanarkshire (formerly in Strathclyde region), about 1 km (0.6 miles) north of Abington.

Coldharbour 'cold or exposed lodging-place', ME *cald* 'exposed' + *herberg* 'inn, lodging-place'. In all, there are over 300 examples of this name from all over England, the vast majority close to major roads.

A village in Surrey, to the northeast of LEITH HILL, about 5 km (3 miles) south of Dorking. It lies just to the west of the Roman road STANE STREET[1], and Anstiebury Camp, an Iron Age hillfort, is nearby to the east.

The French painter and designer Lucien Pissarro lived and worked in Coldharbour during the First World War. Another notable artistic resident was the composer Ralph Vaughan Williams.

Coldmeece 'exposed place on Meece Brook', OE *cald* 'exposed (place)' + *Meece* a river name (from OE *meos* 'mossy or boggy place').

A village in Staffordshire, 5 km (3 miles) west of Stone.

Cold Shoulder of Scotland, the. A nickname for BUCHAN, a region in northeast Scotland. It juts into the NORTH SEA.

Coldstream 'cold river', from the deep ford here.

A small town on the north side of the River TWEED, in Scottish Borders (formerly in Berwickshire). It is 20 km (12 miles) southwest of Berwick-upon-Tweed. The name derives from the fact that this was the site of a rather deep ford across the river, which here forms the border between England and Scotland. The ford was mostly used for military purposes; for example, Edward I and his army crossed here in 1296 on their way to besiege BERWICK-UPON-TWEED, and James IV used the ford on his way to annihilation at FLODDEN in 1513. The present stone bridge was built in 1766, and the toll house on the north side was the scene of runaway marriages until 1856 (*see* GRETNA).

Coldstream Guards. A Scottish regiment raised in the 1650s, and initially called General Monck's Regiment. It established its headquarters in Coldstream in 1659, from where it marched to London in 1660 to support the Restoration of Charles II, which was largely engineered by General Monck. It became the 2nd Regiment of Footguards in 1661, and in 1670 was renamed the Coldstream Guards.

Coleford 'ford across which coal or charcoal is transported', OE *col* 'coal, charcoal' + -FORD.

A market town in Gloucestershire, in the FOREST OF DEAN, about 12 km (7.5 miles) northwest of Lydney, in what was once a coal-mining district. The Speech House, now a hotel, still holds the Verderers' Court, where the 'Verderers', an ancient body responsible for forestry and unenclosed land, meet to discuss local land issues.

The television dramatist Dennis Potter (1935–94) was born in Coleford; he drew considerably on his childhhod in his writing.

Coleman Country. The area of south County SLIGO around Killavil (a village 6 km / 4 miles southwest of Ballymote), the birthplace of the famous Irish fiddler Michael Coleman (1891–1946). The area is more generally known for its fine traditional musicians.

Coleraine Irish *Cúil Raithin* 'ferny corner'.

A town on the River BANN, County Londonderry, 75 km (47 miles) northwest of Belfast. It is the administrative centre of the local authority district of the same name, which also includes the towns of PORTSTEWART and PORTRUSH. The county was originally created as the **County of Coleraine** in 1585 during the shiring of Ulster, before being changed to Londonderry. There was an ancient monastery at Coleraine dedicated to St Patrick, but nothing of it now remains. The present town was a 17th-century plantation settlement, and radiates out from the central square known as The Diamond.

The University of Ulster was founded at Coleraine in 1968. The Coleraine campus now boasts a Millenium Arboretum, containing more than 100 tree varieties.

Doyen de Killerine, Le. *The Dean of Coleraine*, a novel by Antoine François Prévost d'Exiles, published 1735–40.

'Kitty of Coleraine'. A poem variously attributed to Edward 'Pleasant Ned' Lysaght (1763–1810), Charles Dawson Shanly (1811–75) or to Anon., in which beautiful Kitty, on seeing the narrator, stumbles and breaks her pitcher of milk:

> I sat down beside her, and gently did chide her
>   That such a misfortune should give her such pain;
> A kiss then I gave her, and before I did leave her
>   She vowed for such pleasure she'd break it again.
> 'Twas the haymaking season – I can't tell the reason –
>   Misfortunes will never come single, 'tis plain!
> For very soon after Kitty's disaster
>   The devil a pitcher was whole in Coleraine.

Coleville. An informal name given in the later part of the 19th century to the complex of museums, colleges, schools, concert halls and premises for learned societies in SOUTH KENSINGTON that arose at that time at the behest of Prince Albert, the Prince Consort. It honours Sir Henry Cole (1808–82), the art expert and administrator who implemented much of Albert's plan and who became the first director of the Victoria and Albert Museum.

See also ALBERTOPOLIS.

Colinton Probably 'Colga's farm', OE male personal name *Colga* + -TON, but the name may be Gaelic or Irish *Colca* or *Colcu*.

A suburb of southwest EDINBURGH on the Water of Leith (*see under* LEITH), formerly a separate village. Robert Louis Stevenson's grandfather was the minister here, and as a young boy Stevenson recalled 'the Witch's Walk' to the manse past the churchyard, where he imagined the ghosts of the dead peering through gaps in the wall. Colinton features in Stevenson's unfinished masterpiece, *Weir of Hermiston*.

The sentimental novelist Henry Mackenzie (1745–1831), author of *The Man of Feeling* (1771), lived in a small cottage in Colinton.

Coll Possibly pre-Celtic, or Gaelic *coll* 'hazel tree'.
An island of the Inner HEBRIDES, some 10 km (6 miles) northwest of Mull, in Argyll and Bute (formerly in Strathclyde). Like its neighbour, TIREE, it is low-lying, but less flat; Dr Johnson deftly described it as 'one continued rock, of a surface much diversified with protuberances'.

In the Midde Ages Coll was in the possession of the MacDougalls, but they were enemies of Robert the Bruce (*see* PASS OF BRANDER and LORNE), and Bruce awarded the island to Angus Og, a Macdonald, some time after 1314. The island was then in the hands of the **Macleans of Coll** for many centuries. Johnson and James Boswell visited Coll inadvertently in October 1773; they had intended sailing from Skye to Mull, but a storm obliged them to seek shelter on Coll, whither they were guided by their companion 'young Coll', Duncan Maclean, the chieftain's heir, whose seamanship saved the day. Johnson was fearfully seasick, but was comforted by 'a greyhound of Coll's at his back, keeping him warm'. Johnson and Boswell were delighted with young Coll, who managed his father's estates in an enlightened manner. Young Coll was drowned the following year, on his way to visit his betrothed, the daughter of Maclean of INCH KENNETH.

The Macleans of Coll did all they could to help the growing population, but, in 1856, after the 1840s potato famine, they were obliged to sell the island, and the new owners, by raising rents, effectively forced many to leave.
Collach. An inhabitant of Coll.
Coll cheese. A much-admired cheese (a particular favourite in the House of Lords) in the later 19th century. It was made by Ayrshire dairy farmers, who were lured to take up tenancies on the island when the successors to the Macleans of Coll realized they had taken depopulation a step too far.

College Green[1]. A small grassy open space in front of Westminster Abbey (*see under* WESTMINSTER), in Central London, favoured by television journalists for conducting interviews with politicians.

College Green[2] Presumably from the law courts that were here in the 17th century.
The location of the old Irish Parliament in DUBLIN, and a metonym for that Parliament. The Irish Parliament first sat here, in Chichester House, in 1661, and in 1739 a new Parliament building was completed. An extension for the Irish House of Lords was begun in 1785, designed by James Gandon. The Parliament became known to Dubliners as

Goose Pie because of its shallow-domed roof, and also in reference to the wisdom of its denizens. The building became redundant with the Act of Union, and in 1802 was bought by the Bank of Ireland. The 1966 statue here by Edward Delaney, of the Young Ireland leader Thomas Davis (1814–45), has been dubbed by Dubliners 'Urination Once Again', after Davis's poem entitled 'A Nation Once Again'.

Collingbourne Ducis *Collingbourne* 'Col's or Cola's people's stream', OE male personal name *Col* or *Cola* + -ING + *burna* 'stream'; *Ducis* denoting manorial ownership in the Middle Ages by the Dukes of Lancaster, Latin *ducis* 'of the duke'.
A village in Wiltshire, at the northeastern corner of Salisbury Plain, about 14 km (8.5 miles) northwest of Andover.

Collooney Irish *Cúil Mhuine* 'nook of the thicket'.
A village in County Sligo, 11 km (7 miles) south of Sligo itself. It was the birthplace of the writer and critic Mary Colum (1884–1957), wife of poet-playwright Padráic Colum.
'Priest of Coloony, The'. A poem about a priest, Father O'Hart (d.1793), from 'penal days', by W.B. Yeats. It is one of his less memorable early productions, published in *Crossways* (1889), and is also called 'The Ballad of Father O'Hart'.

Collyweston *Colly-* denoting manorial ownership in the Middle Ages by Nicholas de Seagrave (the earliest recorded form of the name is *Colynweston*, and *Colin* is a pet-form of the name *Nicholas*); -*weston* 'west farmstead', OE *west* + -TON.
A village in Northamptonshire, just to the east of the River Welland, about 19 km (12 miles) northeast of Corby. The local slate beds produce a particularly fine grade of roofing slates, which are known by the name of the village.

Whether or not because the slates were often laid askew, **colley-west** (or, in America, *galley-west*) came to be used to mean 'crooked, scattered in all directions' or, figuratively, 'contrarily':

> When a Lancashire man is altogether unsuccessful in his schemes, he says that everything goes *colley-west* with him.
>
> *Transactions of the Philological Society*, 229 (1855)

Coln *See* COLNE[1].
A river in Gloucestershire, a tributary of the THAMES[1], rising east of CHELTENHAM and flowing through a pretty Cotswold valley before joining the Thames near LECHLADE. The River Coln gives its name to the idyllic villages of **Coln St Aldwyns** (after the dedication of its church to St Athelwyn), **Coln St Dennis** (after the dedication of its church to St Dennis) and **Coln Rogers** (whose manor was held by Roger of Gloucester in the 11th century) that lie on its banks. The tourist honeypot village of BIBURY and the town of FAIRFORD also lie on the Coln.

Colnbrook '(place by the) cool brook', OE *col* 'cool' + *broc* 'brook' or '(place by the) brook near the River COLNE[2]'.

A village in Buckinghamshire, about 3 kms (2 miles) southwest of where the M4 motorway meets the M25, just to the east of Slough. Colnbrook grew up around coaching inns providing rest and refreshment for travellers along the great Bath Road from London to the West Country (in 1577 there were as many as 10 inns listed here). In the 17th century the landlord of the Ostrich Inn, a man named Jarman, was hanged for robbing and dispatching at least 15 (some say 60) of his wealthier guests whom he dropped into a vat of boiling water through a trap door while they slept.

Mr Cox, a retired Colnbrook brewer, developed the Cox's Orange Pippin apple from the 1820s.

See also Thomas of Reading *under* READING.

Colne[1] A pre-Celtic river name of unknown meaning.

A river (pronounced 'kohn') in Essex, rising near HAVERHILL and flowing 56 km (35 miles) southeastwards through COLCHESTER to join the BLACKWATER[1] Estuary to the east of MERSEA Island. It flows through the **Colne Valley** on its way to Colchester. (There is also a Colne Valley in West Yorkshire, *see* COLNE[3].) The single-track **Colne Valley Railway** runs for about 1.5 km (1 mile) on either side of Castle Hedingham.

See also COLNE ENGAINE, EARLS COLNE *and* WAKES COLNE.

Colne[2]. A river in Hertfordshire and Middlesex, rising near HATFIELD[1] and flowing 48 km (30 miles) southwestwards past UXBRIDGE and WEST DRAYTON to join the River Thames near STAINES.

Colne[3]. A river in West Yorkshire, 21 km (13 miles) long. It rises in the Pennines at Standedge and runs northeast through Huddersfield to join the River CALDER[1] near Mirfield. The **Colne Valley**, not to be confused with its Essex homonym (*see* COLNE[1]), together with the valley of the Calder, provide the locations for many of the novels of Halifax-born writer Phyllis Bentley, such as *Inheritance* (1932) and *Tales of the West Riding* (1974). She also wrote about the local textile industry in *Colne Valley Cloth* (1947).

Colne[4]. A former cotton town in Lancashire, 9 km (5.5 miles) northeast of Burnley, with which, along with BRIERFIELD and NELSON, it makes a continuous urban strip.

Colne Engaine *Colne* from COLNE[1]; *Engaine* denoting manorial ownership in the Middle Ages by the Engayne family.

A village (pronounced 'kohn') in Essex, 11 km (7 miles) northeast of Braintree.

See also EARLS COLNE *and* WAKES COLNE.

Colne Valley. *See under* COLNE[1] (Essex) *and* COLNE[3] (West Yorkshire).

Colney Hatch *Colney* probably a Hertfordshire family name or transferred from LONDON COLNEY; *Hatch* 'hatch, hatch gate'

(referring either to a former gateway of Enfield Chase or to a sluice on a tributary of Pymmes Brook), OE *hæcc*.

A district in northwest London (N12), to the southeast of Barnet (formerly a hamlet in Hertfordshire). Its name became so closely associated with that of a mental hospital built there in 1851 (*see* FRIERN BARNET) that at the end of the 19th century the alternative 'New Southgate' (*see under* SOUTHGATE) was introduced.

> If his relations had wanted him certified – and they'd every reason to – I couldn't have done it. Colney Hatch wasn't on the map; I'd swear to that.
>
> Ronald Knox: 'Solved by Inspection' (1931)

'Colney Hatch' continues in use, though. **Colney Hatch Lane** runs northwards from MUSWELL HILL[1] to Friern Barnet.

The first fatality of the London Blitz occurred in Colney Hatch in late June 1940: a goat.

Coln Rogers. *See under* COLN *and* THANKFUL VILLAGES.

Coln St Aldwyns. *See under* COLN.

Coln St Dennis. *See under* COLN.

Colonel's Bed, the Named after *Colonel* John Farquharson.

A sheltered spot under a rock overhang, in a gorge, on the Ey Burn in Aberdeenshire (formerly in Grampian region), 8 km (5 miles) southwest of Braemar in upper Deeside. It takes its name from 'the Black Colonel', the fiery-tempered John Farquharson of Inverey, a Jacobite who in 1689 took refuge here from government troops as his castle at Inverey, 2 km (1 mile) to the north, burnt to the ground.

Colonia Camulodunum. The Romano-British name for the settlement on the site of present-day COLCHESTER.

Colonsay and Oronsay *Colonsay* (modern Gaelic *Colbhasa*) 'Kolbein's island', OScand male personal name Kolbein + *ey* (*see* -AY); *Oronsay* 'St Oran's island', personal name Oran + *ey* (*see* -AY): St Oran founded the priory here in 563.

Two islands of the Inner HEBRIDES, linked by an expanse of sand called the Strand, which is only covered by the sea at high tide. The islands are situated some 16 km (10 miles) west of Jura, and are in Argyll and Bute (formerly in Strathclyde). It is said that St Columba first landed on Scottish soil at Colonsay, but finding he could still see Ireland from the hill still called Cùl ri Éirinn (Gaelic 'back to Ireland'), he pressed on north to Iona.

The ruins of the Augustinian priory on Oronsay date from *c*.1380, and may be on the site of St Oran's priory, founded in 563. Half way across the Strand is the Sanctuary Cross, which, if reached by any felon from Colonsay, bestowed immunity on him if he stayed on Oronsay for a year and a day. Their mild climate gives the islands a rich and diverse flora, and Kiloran Gardens, towards the north

❖ -combe, coombe ❖

The Old English word *cumb* is a borrowing from Brittonic *cumbo*, and means 'a narrow valley'; the Welsh word with the same origin and meaning is *cwm*. CWMBRAN (Monmouthshire) and FEL-INGWMUCHAF (Carmarthenshire) (where the *-gwm-* is a mutated version of *cwm*) represent two of the many Welsh names containing this element. The English names are very clearly distributed in the south and west of England, and they include: CASTLE COMBE (Wiltshire); DACCOMBE, ILFRACOMBE, SALCOMBE and DOCCOMBE in Devon; MELCOMBE BINGHAM (Dorset); EASTER COMPTON and STINCHCOMBE in Gloucestershire; ENGLISHCOMBE and ODCOMBE in Somerset; LETCOMBE BASSETT (Oxfordshire); and SEDLESCOMBE (Sussex).

of Colonsay, include subtropical species such as palms and bamboos.

Colonsay duck. The local term for eider duck, common around the island.

Coltishall 'Cohhede's or Coccede's nook of land', OE *Cohhedes* or *Coccedes* possessive forms of male personal names *Cohhede* or *Coccede* + *halh* (*see* HALE, -HALL).
A village in Norfolk, about 12 km (7.5 miles) north of Norwich. RAF Coltishall opened in 1940, in time to participate in the Battle of Britain.

Colt Island. *See under* SKERRIES.

Colwyn Bay 'bay on the River Colwyn', Welsh *colwyn* 'young animal'.
A seaside resort in Conwy (formerly in Denbighshire, then in Clwyd), some 7 km (4.5 miles) east of Llandudno. Its Welsh name is **Bae Colwyn**.

Combe Florey *Combe* 'valley', OE *cumb* (*see* -COMBE, COOMBE); *Florey* denoting manorial ownership in the Middle Ages by the de Flury family.
A village in Somerset, about 11 km (7 miles) northwest of Taunton. The witty Reverend Sydney Smith (1771–1845) was its rector from 1829 until his death, and the novelist Evelyn Waugh (1903–66) lived here from 1956.

Combeinteignhead 'Combe in Teignhead', *Combe see* -COMBE, COOMBE + *Teignhead* name of a district so called because it contained 'ten hides' of land (a hide was about 49 ha (120 acres)). The *hide* element became *head* in the 15th century, and the spelling of *ten* was influenced by that of the River *Teign*, just to the north of the district, somewhat later.
A village (pronounced 'koom-in-tinni(d)') in Devon, to the south of the TEIGN estuary, about 5 km (3 miles) east of Newton Abbot.

Combe Martin 'Martin's estate in the valley', OE *cumb* 'valley' (*see* -COMBE, COOMBE) + *Martin*, denoting manorial ownership in the early Middle Ages by the Martin family.
A village in north Devon, about 7 km (4 miles) east of Ilfracombe. Behind the rocky cove of **Combe Martin Bay**, Combe Martin runs for 3 km (2 miles) up the sheltered valley of the River Umber. Its main street, which winds for more than 3 km (2 miles) along the valley, is claimed by

villagers to be the longest of its kind in England. The 17th-century Pack of Cards Inn here has 52 windows (one for each card in the pack), and four floors with 13 doors each.

The year 2000 saw the revival for the first time since 1837 of a local 'hobby horse' ceremony known as the 'Hunting of the Earl of Rone'. The hunt, which takes place over the weekend of Ascension Day, begins with a procession of grenadiers, followed by a scouring of local woodland for the 'lost' earl. When caught, the masked earl is placed backwards on a hobby horse, shot off and then 'revived'. Finally an effigy of the earl is marched down to the beach and – usually watched by a substantial crowd of onlookers – dumped in the sea. The earl's identity is shrouded in mystery: one theory links him with the Gaelic Irish chieftain Hugh O'Neill, 2nd Earl of Tyrone, who fled Ireland in 1607 (*see* LOUGH SWILLY).

Comber Irish *An Comar* 'the confluence'.
A small town in County Down, at the head of Strangford Lough (*see under* STRANGFORD) some 10 km (6 miles) east of Belfast. The Protestant church (1610) stands on the site of a 12th-century Cistercian abbey. Linen was once the main industry, but Comber is now largely a dormitory town for BELFAST.

Comber Letter, the. A forged letter written to a Protestant gentleman in Comber in December 1688 purporting to warn of an imminent Catholic plan to massacre Protestants. It was intended to increase opposition to the Catholic James II.

Combpyne 'Combe of the Pyn family', *Combe see* -COMBE, COOMBE; the land was associated with the Coffin family in the 12th century, but by the late 13th century Sir Thomas de *Pyn* was patron of the local church.
A village in Devon, about 2.5 km (1.5 miles) inland and about 5 km (3 miles) west of Lyme Regis.

Comeragh Mountains Irish *Sléibhte an Chomaraigh*, possibly 'hills of the confederates', perhaps the name of a tribe, or reference to hills held in common by several groups of people.
A range of old red sandstone mountains extending south of CLONMEL, in County Waterford. The highest point is Fauscoum (792 m / 2598 ft), and among the rounded tops

there are some fine twisted ridges and precipitous cliffs, providing some good climbing. Among the many beautiful lakes in the corries of the Comeraghs is Lough Coum Gabthartha, better known as Crotty's Lake, after the highwayman William Crotty who hid out there, and who was executed in 1742. The southern end of the range is known as the MONAVULLAGH MOUNTAINS.

> Here is no mercy to compassionate
> The weak or help the strong. Here on the hill
> Only the indifferent wind may dare to play
> Only the curlew make abiding stay.
>
> Patrick Warner: 'Comeraghs' (1978)

Come-to-Good Etymology unclear; possibly a laudatory (or ironic) field name, subsequently borrowed by the Quakers.
A hamlet in Cornwall, just east of Feock, and about 8 km (5 miles) south of Truro. Its historic Quaker meeting house (1710), the first in southwest Cornwall, is still active, holding services each Sunday. The name of the place invokes the traditional phrase meaning 'see the light' or 'see the error of one's ways'.

> I'll never care what wickedness I do,
> If this man come to good.
>
> William Shakespeare: Second Servant in *King Lear* (1605), III.vii

Commercial End A modern invented name.
A village in Cambridgeshire, about 7 km (4.5 miles) west of Newmarket.

Compton Beauchamp *Compton* 'farmstead or village in a valley', OE *cumb* 'valley' (*see* -COMBE, COOMBE) + -TON; *Beauchamp* denoting manorial ownership in the Middle Ages by the de Beauchamp family.
A village (pronounced 'kom(p)ton or kum(p)ton beecham') in Oxfordshire, in the VALE OF THE WHITE HORSE, at the foot of the North Wessex Downs (*see under* WESSEX), about 13 km (8 miles) east of Swindon. Just to the south, by the RIDGEWAY, are the White Horse of UFFINGTON and WAYLAND'S SMITHY, a Neolithic passage grave.

Compton Dando *Dando* denoting manorial ownership in the early Middle Ages by the de Auno or Dauno family.
A village in Bath and North East Somerset (before 1996 in Avon, before 1974 in Somerset), about 8 km (5 miles) west of Bath.

Compton Pauncefoot *Pauncefoot* denoting manorial ownership in the Middle Ages by the Pauncefote (literally 'fat-paunch') family.
A village in Somerset, about 13 km (8 miles) northeast of Yeovil.

Compton Valence *Valence* denoting manorial ownership in the Middle Ages by William de Valencia, Earl of Pembroke.
A village in Dorset, about 11 km (7 miles) northwest of Dorchester.

Comrie Gaelic name *Cuimrigh*, from *comhrág* 'confluence', from the junction here of the River EARN, the Water of Ruchill and the River Lednock.
A village in Strath Earn, 10 km (6 miles) west of Crieff, in Perth and Kinross (formerly in Perthshire, and then in Tayside region). It is a popular holiday centre, despite its reputation as the earthquake capital of Scotland. This results from its position on the Highland Line (*see under* the HIGHLANDS), and many shocks have been recorded – though none ever resulting in serious damage to life or limb. The railway line (long disused) between here and CRIEFF was constructed in the late 19th century by William Mackay.

Conamara. The Irish name for CONNEMARA.

Condate. A Roman settlement on the site of present-day NORTHWICH.

Cong Irish *Conga* 'isthmus'.
A village on the isthmus between LOUGH CORRIB and LOUGH MASK in County Mayo, 35 km (22 miles) northwest of Galway. There was an Augustinian abbey here, built by the high king Turlough O'Connor, who also commissioned the 12th-century **Cross of Cong** (now in the National Museum in Dublin), which is said to contain a relic of the True Cross. Turlough's son Rory O'Connor, the last high king of Ireland, died in Cong in 1198.

> Clear as air, the western waters
> Evermore their sweet, unchanging song
> Murmur in their stony channels
> Round O'Connor's sepulchre in Cong.
>
> Thomas W.H. Rolleston (1857–1920): 'The Grave of Rury'. (Rolleston appended a note: 'Ruraidh O'Chonchobhar, last High King of Ireland, died and was buried in the monastery of St Fechin at Cong, where his grave is still shown in that most beautiful and pathetic of Irish ruins. All the accounts agree in this, but some have it that his remains were afterwards moved to Clonmacnois by the Shannon.' Today the consensus seems to be that his remains are indeed buried in the cathedral at Clonmacnoise.)

Some of John Ford's *The Quiet Man* (1952), starring John Wayne, was filmed in Cong, which boasts a Quiet Man pub, a Quiet Man coffee shop and a Quiet Man hostel. Oscar Wilde was brought up here, and Cong is now home to The Edge, the guitarist from U2. Cong was the birthplace of the Republican revolutionary and physician Kathleen Lynn (1874–1955): she was one of the first women in Ireland to be awarded a degree in medicine (in 1899), and fought with the Irish Citizen Army during the Easter Rising of 1916.

Congleton Probably 'farmstead at the round-topped hill', OE *cung* 'hillock, protuberance' + *hyll* 'hill' + -TON.
A town in Cheshire, on the Macclesfield Canal, about 17 km (11 miles) northeast of Crewe. In the 16th and 17th centuries it was a noted centre of bear-baiting. Tradition

has it that at some time in the 16th century the town bear died just before the annual wakes week. Money intended to buy a Bible was diverted to the purchase of a new bear: hence Congleton came to be called 'Bear Town' and its inhabitants '**Congleton Bears**'. In the words of an old jingle:

> Congleton rare, Congleton rare,
>
> Sold the Bible to buy a bear.

Little Moreton Hall, an eminent example of a moated manor house (begun in the mid-15th century), lies 6 km (4 miles) to the southwest of Congleton. From the outside it is a bold profusion of black and white half-timbering. The stresses of history are evident, as the slate roof and heavy beams have caused the walls to bulge and the floors to undulate. The hall is a National Trust property.

Congresbury 'fortified place or manor associated with (Saint) Congar', OCelt personal name *Congar* + OE *byrig* dative form of *burh* (*see* BURY).

A village (pronounced 'kongzbəry' or 'koomzbəry') in NORTH SOMERSET (before 1996 in Avon, before 1974 in Somerset), on the River YEO² and overlooked by the MENDIP HILLS, about 11 km (7 miles) east of WESTON SUPER MARE.

Congresbury Yeo. An alternative name for the River YEO².

Coningsby 'king's manor, royal estate', OScand *konungr* 'king' + -BY.

A village in Lincolnshire, about 17 km (11 miles) northwest of Boston. RAF Coningsby opened as a bomber base during the Second World War, and continued in that role subsequently; it is the home of the Battle of Britain Memorial Flight, which includes the only airworthy Lancaster bomber remaining in Britain.

Conisbrough 'the king's fort', OScand *konungr* 'king' + *burh* (*see* BURY).

A town in South Yorkshire, 10 km (6 miles) northeast of Rotherham. **Conisbrough Castle** dates from *c*.1180, and in Sir Walter Scott's *Ivanhoe* (1820) becomes the stronghold of Athelstan.

Coniston 'the king's estate', OScand *konungr* 'king' + -TON, possibly a Scandinavianized version of *Kingston*.

A village in the Lake District, Cumbria (formerly in Lancashire), at the northwest end of CONISTON WATER, 10 km (6 miles) southwest of Ambleside. The art critic and aesthete John Ruskin, who spent his latter years at nearby BRANTWOOD, is buried here, and the philosopher and historian R.G. Collingwood died here in 1943. J.M.W. Turner visited in 1797 and painted *Morning Mist on Coniston Hills*.

Old Man of Coniston, the. A mountain (803 m / 2634 ft) 3 km (2 miles) west of Coniston. It is covered in old copper-mine workings, and on its southern side is Dow Crag,

popular with rock climbers. There is a fine view west to the SELLAFIELD nuclear plant on the Cumbrian coast.

Coniston Cold The affix comes from its bleak(ish) position. A small village in North Yorkshire, 10 km (6 miles) northwest of Skipton.

Coniston Water. A long, narrow lake in the Lake District, Cumbria, extending southwards from CONISTON. Malcolm Campbell broke the world water-speed record here on 19 August 1939, reaching 228.2 kph (141.74 mph). Twenty-eight years later, on 4 January 1967, the lake notoriously witnessed the death of Campbell's son Donald. Donald Campbell already held the world water-speed record of 447 kph (276 mph), but aspired to break the 300 mph (486 kph) barrier. On his first run of the 1-km (0.62 mile) course, he made 481 kph (297 mph). Then, with the magic figure so nearly in his grasp, he turned his boat, *Bluebird K7*, around and set off once more. But he had not given the wake of his first run time to settle, and as he reached 531 kph (328 mph) *Bluebird* became impossibly unstable, rose into the air and somersaulted, before smashing back into the water. Campbell died instantly. The previous evening, playing cards, he had been dealt the ace and queen of spades. Recalling that Mary Queen of Scots had been dealt the same combination the night before her execution, he commented to reporters:

> Someone in my family is going to get the chop. I pray
> God it's not me, but if it is, I hope I'm going ruddy fast at
> the time.

Both Campbell's body and *Bluebird* were retrieved from the bottom in 2001, the former being buried in the cemetery at Coniston.

The lake has also been used as a repository for unlawfully killed bodies, such as that of Mrs Margaret Hogg, deposited here by her husband Peter in 1974. The body was found by an amateur diver in 1985, and was identified owing to the fact that Hogg had failed to remove a ring with her name on it before slipping her into the water. Another so-called 'lady in the lake' was Carol Park, who disappeared from her home in 1976 and whose body, wrapped in bin liners, was found in the lake in 1997. Her former husband Gordon Park was eventually convicted after 29 years.

The small Peel Island in the lake was the inspiration for Arthur Ransome's Wild Cat Island in *Swallows and Amazons* (1930), although Windermere provided the model for the lake in the story.

Less salubriously, Coniston Water appears in a passage of onomastical ribaldry spouted by Keats's friend Brown on their Scottish tour, and recorded by the poet:

> The Lady of the Lake went to Rock herself to sleep on
> Arthur's seat and the Lord of the Isles coming to Press a
> Piece and seeing her Assleap remembered their last
> meeting at Cony stone Water so touching her with one

hand on the Vallis Lucis while the other un-Derwent her Whitehaven ... [*et cetera*]

> John Keats: letter to Tom Keats (17 July 1818) (obsolete slang *cony* 'female genitalia')

Connacht Named after the *Connachta* tribe, who once dominated the region (their name possibly derives from Old Irish *conn*, from *ceann* 'head'). Traditionally, however, the province is said to be named after the legendary 2nd-century king, Conn of the Hundred Battles.

An ancient kingdom and historic province of Ireland, comprising the western counties of LEITRIM, ROSCOMMON, GALWAY, MAYO and SLIGO. It is also spelt **Connaught**. The ancient kingdom, along with the four others (*see under* the FIVE FIFTHS), emerged at the beginning of the Christian era. Connacht came to be dominated by the O'Connors, whose power was later threatened by the Anglo-Norman de Burghs. In the 16th century Connacht was broken up by plantations and divided into shires.

A representative Connacht team plays in rugby union's (professional) Celtic League.

> I found in Connaught the just, redundance
> Of riches, milk in lavish abundance;
> Hospitality, vigour, fame,
> In Cruachan's land of heroic name.
>> Anon.: 'Aldfrid's Itinerary Through Ireland' (12th century), translated by James Clarence Mangan

> When all besides a vigil keep,
> The West's asleep, the West's asleep –
> Alas! and well may Erin weep,
> When Connaught lies in slumber deep.
> There lake and plain smile fair and free,
> 'Mid rocks – their guardian chivalry –
> Sing oh! Let man learn liberty
> From crashing wind and lashing sea.
>> Thomas Davis: 'The West's Asleep', a ballad from the Young Ireland publication, *The Nation* (These days the ballad comes bathetically to grief with the lines 'For often in O'Connor's van / To triumph dashed each Connaught clan.')

See also IAR CONNACHT.

Annals of Connacht, the. Chronicles covering Connacht history from 1224 to 1544, written by members of the Ó Duibhgeannáin family of Kilronan, County Roscommon.

Composition of Connacht, the. An agreement on tax established in 1585 between the lords and commons of Connacht and the Crown.

Connaught Rangers. A former regiment of the British Army, nicknamed the Devil's Own (because they were 'the Devil's own at fighting'). They famously mutinied in India in 1920, protesting at the actions of the Black and Tans in Ireland during the Anglo-Irish War. Private James Daly was shot, and others given long prison sentences.

Gateway to Connacht, the. The strategic bridge over the River Shannon at ATHLONE.

poor as a Connacht man. A late 19th-century expression meaning extremely poor.

They're plucking the geese in Connacht. A fanciful expression meaning that it is snowing.

To Hell or Connacht. A phrase, supposedly coined by Oliver Cromwell himself, to denote the deportation of Old Irish and Norman-Irish landowners (all Catholics) to the west of the River Shannon after Cromwell ended Irish resistance in 1652. Their estates were allocated to Cromwell's soldiers and to those who had financed his campaign (mostly London merchants).

'Vision of Connaught in the Thirteenth Century, A'. A poem by James Clarence Mangan (1803–49), in which the poet evokes a Golden Age in Connacht, in the reign of 'Cáhál Mór of the Wine-red Hand':

> I walked entranced
>> Through a land of Morn;
> The sun, with wondrous excess of light,
>> Shone down and glanced
>>> Over seas of corn
> And lustrous gardens aleft and right ...

Connah's Quay After the *Connahs*, a prominent local family. A town at the mouth of the River DEE[2] in Flintshire (formerly in Clwyd), 12 km (7 miles) west of Chester. It grew up around the eponymous quay, built in 1791.

Connaught. An alternative spelling of CONNACHT.

Connemara Irish *Conamara*, 'sea coast of Conmac', male personal name *Conmac* + *muir* 'sea'; the legendary Conmac was the son of Fergus Mac Roy and Queen Medb (Maeve); alternatively *cuain* 'harbours' + *na* 'of the' + *mara* 'sea'; yet another theory suggests *comnhaicne mara* 'tribe of the sea'. A wide and wild peninsula in the west of County GALWAY, dominated by the mountains known as the TWELVE PINS and by numerous little lakes. The main centre is CLIFDEN, on the west coast. Part of the area comprises the **Connemara National Park**. By a wider definition, Connemara also included JOYCE'S COUNTRY and IAR CONNACHT. The actor Peter O'Toole was born in Connemara in 1932.

Connemara pony. A breed of good-natured pony indigenous to Connemara, no more than 14.2 hands high. Formerly work ponies, they are now used for children's mounts and for jumping.

'Hills of Connemara, The'. A song about the poteenmakers of the area:

> Keep your eyes well peeled today
> The excise men are on their way
> Searching for the mountain tay
> In the hills of Connemara.

Maharajah of Connemara, the. The byname of the famous Indian cricketer, Prince Ranjitsinhji ('Ranji') of Nawanagar (1872–1933), who in 1926 bought Ballynahinch

Castle in County Galway, and spent every summer there until his death.

Connolly Station. One of Dublin's main railway stations, serving lines to the north. It was named in honour of the socialist revolutionary James Connolly (1870–1916), executed for his role in the 1916 Easter Rising.

> MacDonagh and MacBride
> And Connolly and Pearse
> Now and in time to be,
> Wherever green is worn,
> Are changed, changed utterly:
> A terrible beauty is born.
>
> W.B. Yeats: 'Easter 1916', from *Michael Robartes and the Dancer* (1921)

Consett Probably 'headland of Conek hill', OCelt or pre-Celtic *cunaco*, possibly meaning 'hill' + OE *heafod* 'headland'; *Covekesheued* 1183.
An industrial town in County Durham, situated at a height of 260 m (850 ft), 19 km (12 miles) southwest of Newcastle upon Tyne. There was nothing here until an ironworks was built in 1840; initially the place was as lawless as a Wild West town, one witness counting 14 fights taking place at the same time. Later a great steelworks was built, but this closed in 1980. Light industry survives, including the Phileas Fogg company, manufacturers of snacks based on recipes from around the world.

Constable Country. A touristic name given to the area on the Essex–Suffolk border where the artist John Constable (1776–1837) lived and worked. Its spiritual epicentres are EAST BERGHOLT, where Constable was born, and Flatford (*see* FLATFORD MILL), which provided him with scenes to immortalize (as in *Flatford Mill* and *The Haywain*), but it encompasses all of the easterly part of Dedham Vale (*see under* DEDHAM) which follows the course of the River STOUR[2] inland from MANNINGTREE.

Constantine '(church of) St Constantine', from the name of the patron saint of the local church (possibly identical with a 6th-century Cornish king mentioned in extremely unflattering terms by the chronicler Gildas as one of 'five tyrants' whose horrible deeds brought the Saxons upon Britain in judgement from God).
A village in Cornwall, about 6.5 km (4 miles) northeast of Helston.

Constantine's Cave. *See under* CRAIL.

Constitution Hill Origin uncertain. The initial reference (perhaps from the 17th century) was probably to some aspect of law or government, its import now lost. It has been linked with the 'constitutionals' or health-giving walks Charles II reportedly took here, but this is likely to be a later folk-etymology, especially as the term *constitutional* in this sense is not recorded before the mid-19th century.

A road in the WEST END[1] of London, rising from the northern side of BUCKINGHAM PALACE towards Hyde Park Corner (*see under* HYDE PARK). It separates the Palace gardens from GREEN PARK. In spite of its name, it has been the scene of some decidedly unconstitutional goings-on. Three attempts were made on Queen Victoria's life here, in 1840, 1842 and 1849. And in 1850 former prime minister Sir Robert Peel was thrown off his horse here and fatally injured.

Conway. The English name for CONWY[2].

Conwy[1] From an OCelt river name meaning 'reedy one'.
A river in CONWY[3] unitary authority, once forming the border between Caernarvonshire and Denbighshire, then (from 1974 to 1996) wholly in Gwynedd. It rises west of BLAENAU FFESTINIOG in the small lake of **Llyn Conwy** in southern Snowdonia and flows northwards, for approximately 50 km (30 miles), through the **Vale of Conwy** to join the sea north of the town of CONWY[2]. William Wordsworth wrote of 'the Alpine steeps of the Conway', and en route the river pours over the spectacular **Conwy Falls** some 3 km (2 miles) south of BETWS-Y-COED. The Romans built a fort 6 km (4 miles) south of the town of Conwy, and called it **Canovium**, a Latinized version of the ancient British river name. **Conwy Sands** are at the mouth of the river.

Conwy[2]. A port, market town and administrative seat of CONWY[3] unitary authority (formerly in Caernarvonshire, then in Gwynedd) on the estuary of the River Conwy, some 4 km (2.5 miles) south of Llandudno. It was originally known as **Aberconwy**, the name being preserved in Aberconwy House (*c.*1500). The anglicized version, **Conway**, has not been used officially since 1972 (for the Treaty of Conway, *see under* ABERCONWY). The magnificent **Conwy Castle** was rebuilt by Edward I in 1284, and the old town walls still survive, leading to its description as **the Carcassonne of Wales**. The castle, part of Edward's IRON RING, was taken by Owain Glyndwr's rebels in 1401, and by the Parliamentarians in 1646, during the Civil Wars, and was painted by J.M.W. Turner in 1802–3. Thomas Telford's suspension bridge (1826) and Robert Stephenson's tubular railway bridge (1848) span the estuary.

Conwy boasts 'the smallest house in Britain', comprising two rooms, each 2.75 m (9 ft) by 1.5 m (5 ft). (For Britain's *narrowest* house, *see* MILLPORT.) Conwy is also **the Teapot Capital of North Wales**, being home to Teapot World, where a thousand varied teapots may be viewed. Behind the town is the small **Conwy Mountain** (Welsh name Mynydd y Dref).

> *Conwy, rhyd dyffryn cynnes,*
> *cefn y ffrwd lle caf win ffres ...*
> (Conwy, ford of a temperate valley,
> the river's verge where I get pure wine ...)
>
> Tudur Aled :'To Ask for a Stallion' (early 15th century), translated from the Welsh by Gwyn Williams

Wordsworth's 'little cottage girl' has siblings in the town:

> She answered, 'Seven are we,
> And two of us at Conway dwell,
> And two are gone to sea …'
>
> William Wordsworth: 'We are Seven', from *Lyrical Ballads* (1798)

Conwy³. A unitary authority in north Wales, formed in 1996 from parts of GWYNEDD and CLWYD¹, and incorporating parts of the old counties of CAERNARVONSHIRE and DENBIGHSHIRE. The administrative seat is the town of CONWY², and other towns include LLANDUDNO, COLWYN BAY and BETWS-Y-COED. Conwy includes the eastern side of the CARNEDDAU range in Snowdonia.

Conwy Bay. The stretch of sea between southeast ANGLESEY and the mainland of north Wales, formed where the MENAI STRAIT widens out just northeast of Bangor.

Cookham Perhaps 'cook village' (that is, a village noted for its excellent cooks) or 'hill village', OE *coc* 'cook' or *coc(e)* 'hill' + HAM.

A THAMES¹-side village in Berkshire, about 4 km (2.5 miles) north of Maidenhead. The artist Stanley Spencer (1891–1959) was born and lived here, and it provided the background and cast for many of his allegorical religious paintings (e.g. *The Resurrection, Cookham* (1923–7)). His *Last Supper* is in the local church, and the Stanley Spencer Gallery opened in Cookham in 1962.

The Keeper of the Royal Swans is based near **Cookham Bridge**, and the annual ceremony of swan-upping (catching and marking the royal swans) takes place nearby in July. **Cookham Marsh**, by the Thames, provided Kenneth Grahame with inspiration for his children's classic *The Wind in the Willows* (1908).

To the south of Cookham are the settlements of **Cookham Dean** (OE *denu* 'valley') and **Cookham Rise**.

Cookstown After its founder, Allen Cook.

A town in County Tyrone, 50 km (31 miles) west of Belfast. Its Irish name is **An Chorr Chríochach** ('the boundary hill'). Cookstown is the administrative centre (since 1973) of the local authority district of the same name. The town was founded in 1609 as a plantation settlement by Alan Cook, but the present layout was put in place by William Stewart in 1750. This is notable for its 2-km (1.25-mile) main street, which has given rise to the visitors' gibe:

> The longest main street in Ireland and the longer you go the meaner it gets.

(The joke depends on the Ulster pronunciation of 'meaner'.) The town is famous for its sausages, and was the birthplace of the sculptor Oliver Sheppard (1865–1941), whose famous *Death of Cuchulainn* (in the GPO in Dublin) became the memorial to the 1916 Easter Rising.

Coole Park Irish *An Chúil* 'the secluded place'.

A former mansion (razed to the ground in 1941) in County Galway, 3 km (2 miles) east of GORT. It was the home of Lady Augusta Gregory (1852–1932), the folklorist and one of the key figures in the Celtic Revival of the late 19th and early 20th centuries. Among her many literary guests here were W.B. Yeats (a close friend and collaborator), J.M. Synge, George Bernard Shaw, Sean O'Casey and Æ, whose names are carved on the trunk of a huge copper beech in the grounds. Of his hostess Yeats later wrote, in his *Autobiographies*, 'I doubt I should have done much with my life but for her firmness and care.' He entitled a 1917 poem, and the collection in which it appears, *Wild Swans at Coole*, and the house reappears in some of his later poems:

> I meditate upon a swallow's flight,
> Upon an aged woman and her house,
> A sycamore and lime-tree lost in night
> Although that western cloud is luminous,
> Great works constructed there in nature's spite …
>
> W.B. Yeats: 'Coole Park, 1929', from *The Winding Stair and Other Poems* (1933)

> We were the last romantics – chose for theme
> Traditional sanctity and loveliness …
> But all is changed, that high horse is riderless,
> Though mounted in that saddle Homer rode
> Where the swan drifts upon a darkening flood.
>
> W.B. Yeats: 'Coole Park and Ballylee, 1931', from *The Winding Stair and Other Poems* (1933)

Cooley Irish *Cuailnge*, the meaning of which is unknown. However, in legend Cuailnge was the son of Brogan, and the peninsula was named from the place of Cuailnge's death.

A peninsula in County LOUTH, between Carlingford Lough and Dundalk Bay.

Cattle Raid of Cooley, The. An ancient Irish epic (in Irish *Táin Bó Cuailnge*) recounting the struggle between Queen Maeve (Medb) of CONNACHT and King Conchobar of ULSTER for possession of Donn Cuailnge ('the brown bull of Cooley'), who is also at odds with Finnbhenach ('the white-horned bull'). Maeve attacks Cooley to seize Donn Cuailnge, but this Ulster territory is defended by the hero Cuchullain. In the end Donn Cuailnge fights and kills Finnbhenach, rampaging round Ireland with the dead bull on his horns until his heart bursts and he too dies. The epic, also called *The War of the Brown Bull*, is part of the Red Branch or Ulster Cycle.

Coolins, the. *See* the CUILLIN.

Coombe, the Irish *cúm* 'hollow', referring to the now-underground River Poddle.

A street on the south side of the Liffey in central Dublin, in the area known as the LIBERTIES (known for its poverty in the 19th century). Coombe Women's Hospital is the busiest in Ireland.

'Queen of the Coombe, The'. A song written in 1889 for a version of *Aladdin* called *Taladoin*, produced at Dublin's Gaiety Theatre and sung by Richard Purdon as Widow Twankey:

> I'm a dashing young widow that lives in a spot
> That is christened the Dublin Coombe,
> Where the shops and the stalls are all out on the street,
> And my palace consists of one room.
> *Chorus:*
> You may ramble through Clare, and the County Kildare
> And from Drogheda down to Macroom,
> But you never will see a widow like me
> Mrs Twankey, the Queen of the Coombe.

This was adapted with slight changes by Seamus Kavanagh in 1930 as 'The Pride of the Coombe' and sung by Jimmy O'Dea.

Coombe Hill *Coombe see* -COMBE, COOMBE.
A hill just to the west of Wendover in Buckinghamshire. At 260 m (852 ft) it is the second highest point in the CHILTERN HILLS, and it is said that on a clear day ST PAUL'S[1] Cathedral in London can be seen from its summit.

Cooper's Hill From a family name *Cooper*, known in the area since the 17th century.
A hill a little to the east of GLOUCESTER, which is the venue every May of a cheese-rolling event. Large (and heavy) Double Gloucester cheeses are launched down the steep 228 m (250 yard) course, pursued by the human competitors. The winner is the person to reach the foot of the hill first (there is no chance of catching up with the cheeses, which reach speeds of 113 kph (70 mph)). In 1997 there were 18 casualties (including 7 spectators).

Cootehill After the *Coote* family, with the second element not topographic, but rather coming from Charles Coote's bride, one Frances *Hill*.
A small market town in County Cavan, 15 km (9 miles) southeast of Clones. Its Irish name is **Muinchille** ('sleeve'). In the 17th century the lands hereabouts were confiscated from the O'Reillys and granted to Sir Charles Coote, one of Cromwell's generals in Ireland. The Cootes's Palladian villa, Bellamont Forest (1730), is just north of the town. The most famous Coote of Cootehill was Sir Eyre Coote (1726–83), who achieved many victories against the French and against Hyder Ali in India.

Cootehill was the birthplace of Thomas Brady (1752–1827), who became an Austrian field-marshal and governor of Dalmatia. John McGahern (b.1934), author of novels *Amongst Women* (1991) and other novels, grew up in Cootehill.
See also FINNEA.

Coquet From a word that produced Welsh *cochwedd* 'red-coloured'.
A river in Northumberland, pronounced to rhyme with 'poke it'. It rises on Grindstone Law in the Cheviot Hills (*see under* CHEVIOT) (another branch comes down from BEEFSTAND HILL), and flows 64 km (40 miles) eastward to reach the North Sea at AMBLE. Near Rothbury it flows through the scenic sandstone ravine called the Thrum.

> Stones trip Coquet burn;
> grass trails, tickles
> till her glass thrills.
> > Basil Bunting: Second Book of Odes, 10 (1970), from
> > *Collected Poems* (1978)

The tiny **Coquet Island** lies just off the mouth of the river, and is now a bird reserve. A monastery was established here at least as long ago as the 7th century, and was later used by monks from Tynemouth Priory.

> At Coquet-isle their beads they tell
> To the good Saint who own'd the cell ...
> > Sir Walter Scott: *Marmion: A Tale of Flodden Field* (1808),
> > Canto II, viii

The lighthouse dates from 1841, and the brother of Grace Darling (*see* FARNE ISLANDS) was keeper here.

Cora Droma Rúisc. The Irish name for CARRICK-ON-SHANNON.

Corbetts Named after John Rooke *Corbett*.
The collective name given to those Scottish mountains over 762 m (2500 ft) and under 915 m (3000 ft) in height that have a re-ascent of 152 m (500 ft) on all sides. J.R. Corbett was an active member of the Scottish Mountaineering Club between the World Wars, the fourth person to complete all the MUNROS (Scottish mountains over 914.4 m / 3000 ft), and the first to climb every Scottish mountain over 609.6 m (2000 ft).
Compare DONALDS, GRAHAMS, MUROS and MARILYNS.

Corbridge 'bridge at Corstopitum', anglicized Roman name *Corstopitum* + OE *brycg* 'bridge'. Corbridge and Corchester retain the first syllable of the Roman name, which was probably originally *Coriosopitum*.
A town in Northumberland, 6 km (4 miles) east of Hexham. In AD 90 the Romans built a fort here called **Coriosopitum**, at the junction of DERE STREET and the STANEGATE. This was before the erection of HADRIAN'S WALL, which runs 4 km (2.5 miles) to the north. The remains that can be seen today (excavated by Leonard Woolley in the early 20th century) date from around AD 140, and Corstopitum developed into the most northerly town in the Roman Empire.

Corby 'Kori's farmstead or village', OScand male personal name *Kori* + -BY.
A town in Northamptonshire, on the western edge of Rockingham Forest (*see under* ROCKINGHAM), about 30 km (19 miles) northeast of Northampton. It stands on a ridge underlain by the Northampton Sands, an iron-ore-bearing

stratum – a resource to tempt steel-makers. Until 1932 it was just a village, but then a Scottish steel firm had the bold idea of moving their entire operation, including many of their Scottish workers, south and opening a steel-works in Corby. They mined the ironstone and manufactured steel tubes and plates, and Corby grew into a substantial town. In 1950 it was designated a NEW TOWN[1]. It could not, however, buck the general decline in the British steel industry in the 1960s and 1970s, and in 1979 the Corby works, by then owned by the British Steel Corporation, closed down.

Corby Pole Fair. A fair held every 20 years in Corby. All the roads are closed and anyone who wants to pass has to pay a toll; if they refuse they are carried on a pole and put in the stocks. According to legend, the fair was given its charter by Queen Elizabeth I in gratitude for her rescue by locals from a nearby bog.

Corcaguiney Peninsula. An alternative name for the Dingle Peninsula (*see under* DINGLE).

Corcaigh. The Irish name for CORK.

Corfe Castle *Corfe* 'cutting, gap, pass', OE *corf*; *Castle* from the Norman castle.
A village in Dorset, in the Isle of Purbeck (*see under* PURBECK), about 6.5 km (4 miles) west of Swanage. It is dominated by the ruins of the massive Norman **Corfe Castle**, built by William the Conqueror. King John used it as a prison. It met its end as an active fortress after a Cromwellian siege (1645) during the Civil Wars, when it was betrayed by one of its own garrison, who let the Parliamentarian troops in. Now it is administered by the National Trust. The original village of Corfe had been the scene of violent history, though, before even the castle was built: the young Anglo-Saxon king Edward the Martyr was murdered in a hunting lodge here in 978.
Corfe's fortress is the model for the castle in Enid Blyton's *Five on Treasure Island* (1942).

Corfe Mullen *Mullen* 'mill', OFr *molin*.
A village in Dorset, about 5 km (3 miles) southwest of Wimborne Minster.

Corinium Dobunnorum. A Roman settlement on the site of present-day CIRENCESTER.

Cork Irish *Corcaigh* 'marsh'.
The second-largest city in the Republic of Ireland, in County Cork (of which it is the county town), 220 km (130 miles) southwest of Dublin. It has long been an important port: the 18th-century Gaelic poet Eileen O'Leary describes it as 'Cork of the white sails'. It is centred on an island formed by two branches of the River LEE[1], before it enters the inlet known as **Cork Harbour** (in which the port of COBH is situated). Until the 18th century the area occupied by the city was intersected by channels of water:

> We have often heard Cork called the Venice of Ireland, but have never heard Venice called the Cork of Italy.
>
> Anon.: quoted by John Betjeman in a letter to Michael Rose (25 September 1955)

Cork was also once known as the ATHENS OF IRELAND, owing to its many literary natives (*see below*). It was named European Capital of Culture for 2005.

Originally Cork grew around the monastery and school founded on the edge of a marsh in the 7th century by St Finbarr. The settlement that grew up around the monastery was raided by the Vikings in the 9th century; however, the Vikings went on to settle peacefully and Cork developed as a thriving trading centre. The Normans took the place in 1172, and it subsequently became a royal borough. In 1690 Cork fell to William III after a devastating siege. In the following century it developed as an important Atlantic port, although its commerce declined in the 19th century. During the Anglo-Irish War Cork suffered again: in 1920 its lord mayor, Thomas Mac Curtain, was assassinated by the British, and his successor, Terence MacSwiney, died on hunger strike in Brixton Prison; at the end of that year the Black and Tans with the Royal Irish Constabulary Auxiliaries burnt down the city centre, in reprisal for an IRA ambush. During the Irish Civil War (1922–3), it was held for a while by the Republicans. Since the Second World War Cork has attracted much inward investment, and is particularly known for its chemical and pharmaceutical industries (*see under* RINGASKIDDY).

Queen's University Cork was founded in 1845 (it became part of the National University of Ireland, in 1909, and is now known as **University College Cork**). There are two neo-Gothic cathedrals; the Protestant cathedral (1863–78) dedicated to St Finbarr, and the Catholic pro-cathedral (1808) of St Mary and St Finbarr. Older than either is the Protestant St Ann's Church (1722–6), in the area called SHANDON, famous for its bells. The city's rugby club, **Cork Constitution RFC**, was formed in 1892 and its ground is Temple Hill.

The poet Edmund Spenser was made high sheriff of Cork in 1598, having married Elizabeth Boyle (for whom he wrote his *Epithalamion*) here in 1594. Cork was the birthplace of the painter James Barry (1741–1806); the political economist and pioneer socialist William Thompson (*c*.1785–1833); the poet William Maginn (1793–1842), who in 1830 founded *Fraser's Magazine*; the poet Jeremiah J. Callanan (1795–1829); Thomas Crofton Croker (1798–1854), antiquarian and folklorist; the poet and writer Francis Sylvester Mahony ('Father Prout'; 1804–66); the poets Thomas Davis (1814–45) and Edward Dowden (1843–1913); the writer Daniel Corkery (1878–1964); the actor and playwright Micheál MacLiammóir (1899–1978); the novelists and short-story writers Seán Ó Faoláin (1900–91) and Frank O'Connor (pen name of Michael O'Donovan, 1903–66); and the footballer Roy Keane (b.1971).

> I feel at times as if I was among a people as mysterious as the Chinese, a people who have taken hold of the English language and moulded it to their cross-purposes.
>
> Conor Cruise O'Brien: comment on Cork (1994)

Cove of Cork. The old name for COBH.

'Madwoman of Cork, The'. A poem by Patrick Galvin (b.1930):

> *Pray for me*
> *I am the madwoman of Cork.*
> Yesterday
> In Castle Street
> I saw two goblins at my feet ...

Cork, County. A county of southwest Ireland, in the province of Munster. Nicknamed the REBEL COUNTY, it is the largest county in the Republic, bounded on the east by Waterford, on the north by Tipperary and Limerick, on the west by Kerry, and on the south by the Atlantic. The county town is CORK, and other towns include COBH, YOUGHAL, KINSALE, SKIBBEREEN, BANTRY, MALLOW and FERMOY. The main rivers are the BLACKWATER[3] and the LEE[1]. The coastline, particularly in the west, is rugged and heavily indented, and the hills in the west include the BOGGER-AGH MOUNTAINS and CAHA MOUNTAINS.

> As I stray'd o'er the common on Cork's rugged border,
>   While the dew-drops of morn the sweet primrose array'd,
> I saw a poor maiden whose mental disorder,
>   Her quick-glancing eye and wild aspect betray'd.
>
> George Nugent Reynolds (1771–1802): 'Mary le More'

> West Cork ... Today, it's a glamorous destination, a haven for upmarket tourists, English expats, and Dutch cannabis importers, but in the 1950s and 1960s it was the arse end of the back of beyond, and that may be talking it up.
>
> Pete McCarthy: *McCarthy's Bar* (2000)

Great Earl of Cork, the. The English adventurer Richard Boyle, 1st Earl of Cork (1566–1643), who made himself a fortune in southern Ireland and who in 1602 bought Sir Walter Raleigh's extensive estates in Cork, Waterford and Tipperary for £1500, a snip even at that time. One of his sons was the scientist Robert Boyle (1627–91), deviser of Boyle's law governing the volume and pressure of gases.

Corkaguiney Peninsula. An alternative name for the Dingle Peninsula (*see under* DINGLE).

Corn Du. *See under* PEN Y FAN.

Cornhill 'hill where corn is grown or sold', OE *corn* 'corn' + *hyll* 'hill'. Originally the name of a hill (it is at the highest point in the City of London), presumably either where corn was grown within the city walls, or the site of a grain market.

A street in the City of London (*see under* LONDON), leading eastwards from the Royal Exchange to the junction of BISHOPSGATE and Gracechurch Street (EC3). It is lined mainly with the 19th- and 20th-century offices of financial institutions.

London's first coffee house was opened in St Michael's Alley, Cornhill, by Christopher Bowman in 1652.

The poet Thomas Gray (1716–71) was born in Cornhill, and the literary periodical *The Cornhill Magazine* was first published here in 1860, under the editorship of William Makepeace Thackeray.

Cornhill is also the name of one of the wards of the City of London.

Cornish *Corn-* (as in CORNWALL) + *-ish*.
Of or relating to Cornwall. As an adjective the term dates from the 16th century. When applied to dairy products (for example, ice-cream), it suggests a rich, almost yellow creaminess. As a noun it denotes the Celtic language of Cornwall, which is part of the Brythonic group, containing also Welsh and Breton. It became extinct in the late 18th century (its last native-speaker was supposedly Dolly Pentreath (Dorothy Jeffery, 1685–1778)), but campaigners for Cornish devolution or independence, for whom it is an important cultural symbol, encourage its revival. The noun is also the name of an English breed of chickens widely used in crossbreeding with popular commercial breeds for increased meat production.

Cornish Alps. A humorous local nickname for the clay spoil tips that are a prominent feature of the landscape surrounding ST AUSTELL in Cornwall. Viewed on a sunny day they do in fact bear a fanciful resemblance to snow-covered peaks. *See also* West Lothian Alps *under* WEST LOTHIAN.

Cornish chough. A name often applied to the common chough (*Pyrrhocorax pyrrhocorax*), a bird of the crow family with red legs and beak. It was once a common sight on the rocky cliffs of Cornwall, but the last pair bred here in 1952. There are now signs, though, that it may be returning. It is the Cornish 'national' bird.

Cornish diamond. A variety of quartz found in Cornwall, or a single crystal of this quartz.

Cornish duck. A facetious late 19th-century term for a pilchard (devoured in unimaginable quantities by Cornish fishermen).

Cornish engine. A type of single-acting condensing steam-engine used for pumping up water, first used in the Cornish mining industry.

Cornish hug. A type of hold used in **Cornish wrestling** (*see below*) involving an attempt to throttle one's opponent:

> The Cornish are Masters of the Art of Wrestling ... Their Hugg is a cunning close with their fellow combatant; the fruits whereof is his fair fall, or foil at the least. It is

figuratively appliable to the deceitful dealing of such who secretly design their overthrow, whom they openly embrace.

Thomas Fuller: *The History of the Worthies of England* (1662)

Cornish pasty. A small pie with, usually, a savoury filling, baked without a container. It is an item that has caused a certain amount of controversy over the years as to its proper pronunciation ('pasty' or 'pahsty'?), its authentic form (the genuine Cornish one is shaped like a pointed oval, with a crimped seam running along the top – serving, the story goes, as a handle for grubby-handed tin-miners to hold it by) and its contents. As to the last point, minced or diced beef with carrot, swede or other roots vegetables now seem to be canonical, but in the past all sorts of things have gone into Cornish pasties, including mutton, pork, bacon, fish, vegetables alone (when money was tight) and even sweet ingredients. They were the Cornish workman's transportable lunch, and often they would contain two courses: a savoury one at one end, and fruit or jam at the other. The Somerset version of the pasty is called a 'priddy oggy'.

My young man's a Cornishman,
Won't leave me in the lurch,
And one day we shall married be
Up to Trura church …

And I shall give him scalded cream
And starry-gazy pie
And make him a saffron cake for tea
And a pasty for by and by.

Charles Causley (1917–2003): 'My Young Man's A Cornishman' (*Trura church* is Truro Cathedral, and *starry-gazy pie* a fish pie made with pilchards whose heads peep heavenwards through the pastry.)

Cornish pump. A pump worked by a **Cornish engine** (*see above*).

Cornish rex. A breed of cat characterized by a sinuous body, large ears and a short, very soft coat. It originated around 1950.

Cornish Riviera. A touristic name, based on that of the French Riviera, for the southern coast of Cornwall, and in particular MOUNT'S BAY, from Penzance in the west to the Lizard in the east. The coastline here is characterized by sandy coves, picturesque fishing villages and luxuriant subtropical vegetation (courtesy of the Gulf Stream's influence). The name is familiar from the Cornish Riviera express train from Paddington to Penzance. It first ran in 1904, when it was named the Riviera Express by J.C. Inglis, General Manager of the Great Western Railway.

Cornish split. A small round yeast-dough bun of a type made in Cornwall. They are typically split open and filled with clotted cream and strawberry jam.

Cornish stone. Partially decomposed Cornish granite, ground and used with clay to make earthenware.

Cornish Wonder, the. An epithet applied by the satirist Peter Pindar to the Cornish painter John Opie (1761–1801).

Cornish wrestling. A form of wrestling practised in Cornwall in which contestants, wearing loose canvas jackets, try to throw their opponent by grappling, tripping, and other techniques.

Cornish Yarg. A nettle-wrapped semi-hard cheese made near Bodmin. This revival of an old recipe acquired its name through reversing that of its rediscoverers: the Grays.

Cornubian From Medieval Latin *Cornubia* 'Cornwall', which was probably based on OCelt *Cornovja* (*see* CORNWALL).

An adjective meaning 'Cornish', originally favoured by poets:

'Tis heard where England's eastern glory shines,
And in the gulphs of her Cornubian mines [i.e. tin mines].

William Cowper: 'Hope' (1782)

The term has been latterly restricted mainly to geological usage ('the Cornubian granite platform').

cornubianite. A type of hard, dark blue laminated rock found in Cornwall with granite.

Cornubian Shore, the. An exhausted poetical metaphor for 'Cornwall'.

Cornwall '(territory of) the Celts of the Cornovja tribe', OCelt *Cornovja* (which was probably derived from *corn(u)* 'horn', alluding to Cornwall's projecting peninsula) + OE *walas* 'foreigners, Celts'. (The alternative, legendary explanation of the name is that a mythical hero called Corineus – a Trojan, according to Geoffrey of Monmouth – conquered the giant Goemagot, was given the western peninsula of England as his reward and named it 'Corinea' after himself).

A peninsular county (Cornish **Kernow**) in southwest England, the most westerly part of England. It includes the SCILLY ISLES. Its eastern boundary with Devon is mainly formed by the River TAMAR. Its county town (and its administrative headquarters) is TRURO. Other significant centres are BODMIN (the former county town), BUDE, CAMBORNE and REDRUTH, FALMOUTH, HELSTON, LAUNCESTON, NEWQUAY, PENZANCE, ST AUSTELL and ST IVES[2]. Bodmin Moor (*see under* BODMIN) dominates the northeastern corner of the county. Other important rivers, aside from the Tamar, are the CAMEL, the FAL and the FOWEY[1].

Cornwall narrows gradually towards its western tip at LAND'S END. Along its northwestern coast dark cliffs, interspersed with sandy bays, take the full force of the Atlantic rollers. The southern coast, sometimes referred to as the Cornish Riviera (*see under* CORNISH). is altogether milder and more tranquil, basking in the warmth of the Gulf Stream.

Cornwall remained largely British, with a language very close to Welsh and Breton, when the rest of England was absorbed by the Anglo-Saxons (*see* DUMNONIA), and it retains strong elements of its Celtic culture and myth – though there is debate as to what exactly that was. Many places claim association with Arthur, legendary king of the Britons, who fought against the Saxon invaders in the 6th century AD (*see* TINTAGEL). The English Crown afforded Cornwall some measures of consitutional accommodation through the Stannary Parliament (*see under* STANNARIES) and the **Duchy of Cornwall** (*see below*), as a way of pacifying its potentially truculent inhabitants. However, rebellions did break out under the first Tudors, because of tax, religion and language, but the failure of the Prayer Book Rebellion (1549) saw Cornwall more tightly reigned in by the English state. In Elizabethan times Cornwall was at the forefront of the fight against the Spanish and of England's burgeoning naval power, and, given the Duchy's local influence (and an instinctive Cornish hostility to Parliamentarian centralization), was notably Royalist in the Civil Wars. Thereafter, however, it somewhat rejected its past by becoming one of the regions to take Methodism to its heart.

In the 20th century, with its Cornish language extinct (*see under* CORNISH), the culture was in great danger of shrinking to a pixie-led heritage industry, but in the latter part of the century it underwent a revival, and there have been many ready to support a Cornish separatist movement, marching under the banner of St Piran, the county's patron saint (the flag is black with a white St George's cross). The political party *Mebyon Kernow* ('Sons of Cornwall') advocates Cornish independence.

The county's place names are, unsurprisingly, heavily dependent on the Cornish language, and in particular on a small set of distinctive Cornish prefixes: *Pen-* 'head, top' (as in *Penzance*), *Pol-* 'pool' (*Polyphant*), and *Tre-* 'farmstead, hamlet' (*Trebetherick*). Hence the jingle:

By Tre, Pol and Pen
You shall know the Cornishmen.

Equally characteristic, though, is the onomastic contribution made by Cornwall's large number of saints: St Austell, St Just, St Kew, St Minver, St Pinnock, St Veep and so on.

Cornwall has important reserves of tin and copper. Tin was mined here in the Bronze Age, and the Phoenicians came to Cornwall to trade for tin early in the first millennium BC. The county made a living from the metals from the Middle Ages until comparatively recently (*see also* the STANNARIES). Early on, tin was often panned from streams. Then it was dug from trenches known as 'rakes'. At the beginning of the 18th century steam power made deep mining possible, and for the next 200 years Cornwall was one of the main world producers of tin and copper. It is no longer a viable industry, but the tall chimneys of its engine houses still dot the county. Cornwall's other mineral resource is kaolin or china clay, extracted mainly around St Austell. In the 21st century the county's chief industries are tourism, agriculture (including flower-growing) and fisheries.

In cricketing terms Cornwall is a 'minor county' (the club was founded in 1894) and plays in the minor counties championship.

Cornwall has given its name to American towns in Connecticut, Pennsylvania and elsewhere, as well as to a county of Vermont; it is also the name of a county in Jamaica.

In Cornwall it's Saturday before you realize it's Thursday.

Wilfred Pickles

Ah! seaweed smells from sandy caves
And thyme and mist in whiffs,
In-coming tide, Atlantic waves
Slapping the sunny cliffs,
Lark song and sea sounds in the air
And splendour, splendour everywhere.

John Betjeman: 'Cornwall'

Cape Cornwall. A headland at the western extremity of Cornwall, about 8 km (5 miles) north (and just a touch east) of LAND'S END.

cornwallite. A green copper-based mineral resembling malachite, found in Cornwall.

Duchy of Cornwall. A private estate belonging to the eldest son of the British sovereign. It includes land not only in Cornwall but also in Devon, Somerset and other parts of southwest England. The dukedom was created by Edward III in 1337 for his son Edward, the Black Prince. It was a smart political move to attempt to tie in this part of England's Celtic fringe with the fate of the Crown. The institution of the Duchy means that Cornwall historically lacked the usual array of local aristocrats (and their stately piles) typical of other English counties. The current duke, Prince Charles, markets agricultural and other products of the estate under the name 'Duchy Originals'.

National Maritime Museum Cornwall. *See under* FALMOUTH.

Corpusty 'raven's path' or 'Korpr's path', OScand *korpr* 'raven' or male personal name *Korpr* + *stigr* 'path'.

A village in Norfolk, about 27 km (17 miles) northwest of Norwich.

Corran 'a low pointed promontory', the meaning of the Gaelic word *corrán*.

A small settlement 15 km (9 miles) southwest of Fort William on a promontory in ARDGOUR, extending eastward into Loch Linnhe. It was formerly in Inverness-shire, and is now in Highland. There is a car ferry here across the **Corran Narrows**, linking Ardgour with Lochaber.

Corrán Binne. The Irish name for HORN HEAD.

Corrán Tuathail. The Irish name for CARRANTUOHILL.

Corrib. *See under* LOUGH CORRIB.

Corrichie. *See under* HILL OF FARE.

Corriedoo 'black marsh', Gaelic *corrach* 'marsh' + *dubh* (*see* DDU, DUBH).

A tiny settlement in Dumfries and Galloway (formerly in Dumfriesshire), 6 km (4 miles) east of Dalry. Next to it is **Corriedoo Forest**, a conifer plantation.

Corrieshalloch Gorge 'hollow of the willow', Gaelic *coire* 'hollow, corrie' + *seilich* 'of willow'.

A dramatic gorge 18 km (11 miles) southeast of Ullapool, formerly in Ross and Cromarty and now in Highland. The gorge, fed by the Falls of Measach, is 1.5 km (1 mile) long and 60 m (195 ft) deep. It is in the care of the National Trust for Scotland.

Corrieyairack Pass 'pass of the rising corrie', Gaelic *coire* 'corrie' + *eirich* 'rising'.

A high pass (764 m / 2507 ft) between FORT AUGUSTUS on Loch Ness and Speyside to the east. The actual **Coire Yairack** is on the eastern side of the summit, and **Coireyairack Hill** to the north. After the 1715 Jacobite Rebellion, General Wade and his government troops built a military road over the pass as part of the effort to control the HIGHLANDS. Ironically, in 1745 Bonnie Prince Charlie's forces used Wade's road over the pass to advance eastwards.

Corrivorrie Etymology unknown, but possibly includes Gaelic *coire* 'hollow, corrie'.

A small settlement in Strath Dearn, Highland (formerly in Inverness-shire), some 6 km (4 miles) west of Slochd summit on the A9.

Corrour 'dun-coloured corrie', Gaelic *coire* 'corrie' + *odhar* 'grey-brown'.

The remotest rail station in Britain, on the Glasgow–Fort William line. It is situated on the eastern side of Rannoch Moor (*see under* RANNOCH), in Highland (formerly in Inverness-shire), and it is 10.5 km (6.5 miles) southeast to the nearest road, at Rannoch Station, and 12 km (7.5 miles) north to the road at Fersit. It serves the Loch Ossian Youth Hostel, 1.5 km (1 mile) to the east, and Corrour Shooting Lodge another 5 km (3 miles) further on, at the far end of Loch Ossian.

Corryvreckan 'Brecon's cauldron', Gaelic *coire* 'hollow, cauldron' + personal name *Brecon*, or possibly *bhreacain* 'speckled'.

A famous whirlpool in the **Strait** or **Gulf of Corryvreckan**, between the north tip of JURA and the small island of SCARBA, both in Argyll and Bute (formerly in Strathclyde region). According to legend, the ancient Celtic hero Brecon (or a Norse prince, Breacan) died here when his 50 ships were sucked down. When St Columba, a relative of Brecon's, sailed this way, one of Brecon's ribs rose to the surface. In another legend, a hag controls the whirlpool, deciding which boats shall founder and which escape; today the locals still refer to the maelstrom as the Cailleach (Gaelic 'old woman').

The whirlpool is formed by the flow of tides through the narrow strait, in which there is a submarine rock stack some 44 m (144 ft) high and a narrow fissure in the sea bed some 100 m (330 ft) deep. It is said that Corryvreckan's roaring can be heard at Craignish Castle on the mainland, some 8 km (5 miles) away.

> … at mid flood tide I saw, particularly if any wind met the tide, the sea begin to rise a great way below the Coire, and then gradually swell to vast billows rolling on, some white and foaming, others glassy and smooth, still getting higher and higher, till they came to the grand whirlpool, where they burst with an amazing noise, forming hundreds of small whirls in the surf around …
>
> Mrs Sarah Murray: *A Companion and Useful Guide to the Beauties of Scotland* (2nd edition, 1804)

Even today, the *West Coast of Scotland Pilot* warns that 'Navigation is at times very dangerous and no vessel should attempt this passage without local knowledge.'

There is a shot of a tiny boat in peril at the Corryvreckan in the Powell and Pressburger film *I Know Where I'm Going* (1945), in which a headstrong young woman falls for a naval officer while on her way to be married in the Hebrides. George Orwell had a lucky escape in the strait in 1949, during an attempted circumnavigation of Jura where he was then living.

Corserine 'cross of the ridges', Gaelic *crois* or Scots *corse* 'cross' + Gaelic *rinn* 'high point, ridge'.

The highest peak (813 m / 2667 ft) in the RHINNS OF KELLS, Dumfries and Galloway (formerly in Dumfriesshire), 16 km (10 miles) northwest of New Galloway.

Corsham 'Cosa's or Cossa's homestead or village', OE male personal name *Cosa* or *Cossa* + -HAM.

A small town in Wiltshire, about 13 km (8 miles) northeast of Bath. The mellow stone buildings in its centre enable it to preserve something of its COTSWOLD character.

Under nearby BOX HILL[2], in the passageways of an old quarry from which Bath stone was once extracted, was the British government's secret Cold War command centre, codenamed TURNSTILE, to which, in the event of a Third World War, the prime minister and relevant associates would have been spirited away and from which he or she would have given any retaliation orders. It was turned over to RAF use in 1979.

Corstopitum. A Roman fort on the site of present-day CORBRIDGE.

Corstorphine 'Thorfinn's cross', Gaelic *crois* 'cross' + OScand male personal name *Thorfinnr*; the first element may be OScand *kros*.

An area of western EDINBURGH, on the flanks of **Corstorphine Hill**, site of Edinburgh's zoo.

Corstorphine sycamore. A subspecies of sycamore, *Acer pseudoplatanus corstorphinense*. The original tree, long-renowned for its beauty, stood for some four or more centuries by Corstorphine Dovecot, until it was blown down in a gale in 1998. On 26 August 1679 it was the site of the murder of Lord James Forrester by his niece and mistress, Christian Nimmo, whose ghost subsequently haunted the place.

Roull of Corstorphine. A poet of whom little is known apart from his appearance in William Dunbar's (?1456–?1513) elegy for dead poets, *Lament for the Makaris*:

> He has tane Roull of Aberdene
> And gentill Roull of Corstorphin;
> Two bettir fallowis did no man se.
> *Timor mortis conturbat me.*

Coruisk. *See* LOCH CORUISK.

Corwen 'small stone' or 'sanctuary stone', Welsh *côr* 'sanctuary' or *cor* 'small' + *maen* 'stone'.

A small market town and tourist centre on the River DEE[2] in Denbighshire (formerly in Merioneth, then in Clwyd), 13 km (8 miles) west of Llangollen. The BERWYN MOUNTAINS are to the south. It was at Corwen that Owain Glyndwr began his rebellion against Henry IV in the early 15th century. The novelist John Cowper Powys lived here from 1934 to 1955.

Coryton[1] Probably 'farmstead on the River Curi', pre-English river name *Curi* + -TON.

A village in Devon, on the River LYD, just off the western edge of DARTMOOR, about 11 km (7 miles) north of Tavistock.

Coryton[2] *Cory*, from the oil refinery established here in 1922 by Cory & Co. + -TON. The chairman of Cory & Co. at that time was Sir Clifford Cory, son of John Cory.

An industrial village in Essex, on the north bank of the THAMES[1] Estuary, adjacent to Thameshaven. It is dominated by oil refineries and other oil-industry installations.

Cosford Perhaps 'excellent ford', OE *cost* 'excellent' + -FORD.

A village in Shropshire, about 13 km (8 miles) southeast of Telford. The nearby RAF station has an indoor athletics stadium which is used for championships and international meetings, and there is also an Aerospace Museum (a branch of the RAF Museum).

Costa Geriatrica Punningly after *Costa Brava*, *Costa Blanca*, etc. (Spanish *costa* 'coast'), substituting mock-Spanish/Latin *Geriatrica* 'geriatric'.

A blackly humorous nickname coined in the 1970s for the south coast of England, and in particular the Sussex coast, as characterized by retirement homes for the elderly. The bungalows of PEACEHAVEN, the nursing homes of WORTHING and the residential hotels of EASTBOURNE are mockingly evoked.

See also 'Hernia Bay' *under* HERNE BAY.

Costessey 'Cost's island or dry ground in a marsh', OE or OScand *Costes* possessive form of male personal name *Cost* + *eg* (*see* -EY, -EA).

A village in Norfolk, on the River Wensum, about 8 km (5 miles) west of Norwich. **New Costessey** is about 1.5 km (1 mile) to the southwest.

Cotehele 'wood on an estuary', Cornish *cuit* 'wood' (*see* CED for the origin of this element) + *heyl* 'estuary'; however, the name has been reinterpreted as 'cottage on a hill', OE *cot* 'cottage' + *hyll* 'hill'.

A house and estate in Cornwall, on the River TAMAR, 7 km (4.5 miles) southeast of Tavistock. The first parts were built in the late 15th century by local eminence Richard Edgcumbe (*see* BODRUGAN'S LEAP). The Edgcumbes owned it until 1947, when it passed to the National Trust in lieu of death duties, the first exchange of its type. The lush

---

❖ **-cot, cote** ❖

The Old English element *cot*, meaning 'cottage, hut, shed', refers to a dwelling, shelter or workshop at the lower end of the range in terms of status. There are numerous villages called Caldicot, Caldecot, or Caldecote (*see* CALDICOT, Monmouthshire and CHALK FARM, Greater London) and it has recently been suggested that these might have originated in the Anglo-Saxon equivalent of prison camps; at any rate, the first element 'cold' reinforces the downmarket sense of the second element.

The name appears in many different forms. The standard Old English plural of the element, *cotu*, is readily confused with the singular, so in PRESCOT (Merseyside), for example, it is hard to say whether the priests had one hut or cottage, or more. This matter is clarified somewhat when the element appears in a different grammatical gender: the feminine noun (with the same meaning) *cote* has the plural form *cotan*, and FAR COTTON (Northamptonshire) reflects this form. In Middle English, however, the *-s* plural was attached to the word, and matters become a little easier: KEAL COTES and Coates, both in Lincolnshire, simply refer to 'the cottages or huts'.

gardens descend steeply to **Cotehele Quay** on the Tamar, whence, in former times, shipments of ore, such as the copper mined in the region, would travel. The mining declined, however, and the river grew sleepy after the railways took most of the remaining traffic in the early 20th century. The quay also has an offshoot of the National Maritime Museum (*see also under* FALMOUTH).

Coton '(place) at the cottages or huts', OE *cotum* dative plural form of *cot* (*see* -COT, COTE).
A village in Cambridgeshire, about 5 km (3 miles) west of Cambridge.

> Meads towards Haslingfield and Coton
> Where *das Betreten*'s not *verboten*.
>
> Rupert Brooke: 'The Old Vicarage, Grantchester' (1912)

Coton in the Elms From the former abundance of elm trees here.
A village in Derbyshire, now in the NATIONAL FOREST area, about 8 km (5 miles) southwest of Swadlincote.

Cotsall. A old term for the COTSWOLDS.

Cotswold From the COTSWOLDS.
An administrative district, almost wholly within Gloucestershire. Its headquarters are in CIRENCESTER, which in earlier centuries, when it was at the centre of the wool trade, was known as the 'Capital of the Cotswolds'.

Cotswolds, the 'Cod's high forest land', OE *Codes* possessive form of male personal name *Cod* + *wald* 'high forest land'.
A range of limestone hills in the West of England, extending from Bath and Northeast Somerset, just to the east of Bristol, through South Gloucestershire, Gloucestershire and northern Oxfordshire to the eastern edge of Northamptonshire – a total length of some 80 km (50 miles). Near CHELTENHAM, and further north around BROADWAY, they rise to about 300 m (1000 ft) and more (the highest points are CLEEVE HILL at 329 m (1080 ft) and Broadway Hill at 312 m (1024 ft)), but their average height is around 200 m (660 ft).

> A green baize tableland … with jutting prows and pocket coombes, fuzzed with woodlands and chequered with drystone walls.
>
> Kevin Reynolds: *The Cotswold Way* (1990)

In early times the Cotswold hillsides were, as their name suggests, heavily wooded, but from the 14th to the 18th centuries they were extensively grazed by sheep. This brought prosperity to the area, first from the wool trade and later from the making of cloth. The generous size of many of the local churches and their towers bears witness to this former wealth. Now, however, the large long-woolled **Cotswold sheep** are nearly extinct, and the area's agriculture is based on arable and cattle-rearing.

Its modern source of wealth is tourism. The rolling wooded Cotswold countryside close to the Oxfordshire border, with its picturesque villages, their buildings all seeming to be made out of the glowing golden **Cotswold limestone**, seems to strike a rich vein of nostalgia. Combined with the incantatory local place names – STOW-ON-THE-WOLD, BOURTON-ON-THE-WATER, MORETON-IN-MARSH, UPPER SLAUGHTER, LOWER SWELL – it is irresistible to visitors, who come in their droves.

> He plays fast and loose with the average Englishman's sentimental leanings towards God-wottery, drawing his clichés from the Cotswolds where, it is widely believed, lie the typical English villages and the homeland of the picturesque.
>
> *Architectural Review* (1952)

> … the Cotswolds, where everything looks right because man has worked with nature.
>
> Arthur Mee: *Gloucestershire* (1938)

Rural life in the Cotswolds in the early years of the 20th century was beautifully evoked in Laurie Lee's memoir, *Cider with Rosie* (1959):

> I remember, too, the light on the slopes, long shadows in tufts and hollows, with cattle, brilliant as painted china, treading their echoing shapes. Bees blew like cake-crumbs through the golden air, white butterflies like sugared wafers, and when it wasn't raining a diamond dust took over which veiled and yet magnified all things.

Cotsall. An archaic term for the Cotswolds. An inhabitant of the area is a **Cotsaller.**

> *Slender:* How does your fallow greyhound Sir? I heard say he was outrun on Cotsall.
>
> William Shakespeare: *The Merry Wives of Windsor* (1597), I.i

The word also appeared in the libretto (by Harold Child) of Ralph Vaughan Williams's opera *Hugh the Drover* (1924), which is set in the Cotswolds:

> Cold blows the wind on Cotsall
> In winter snow and storm.
> But the heart of England's in Cotsall
> And the heart of England's warm.
> O gentle are the men of Cotsall
> And were since the world began,
> But none will fight for England's right
> Like a true-bred Cotsall man.

Cotswold lion. A humorous name in former centuries for the long-fleeced Cotswold sheep. *See also* Lammermuir lion *under* the LAMMERMUIRS.

Cotswold Olympicks. A festival of open-air games held for the first time on Dover's Hill near CHIPPING CAMPDEN in 1612. The games included horse-racing and coursing, jumping, wrestling, shin-kicking, sword-play, and throwing the sledge-hammer and bar. There were also prizes for playing the pipes, and for singing and dancing. The games were held on the Thursday and Friday of Whit-week for nearly two and a half centuries, before growing rowdiness (the result of increased numbers of visitors from the industrial Midlands) brought them to a close in 1852. Revived in 1963, and held on the first Friday after the spring bank holiday, the games retain, along with shin-kicking, such rural pursuits as tug-o'-war, the sack race, throwing the sheaf, greasy-pole climbing and morris dancing,

The name of the hill where the games are held commemorates the man responsible for their existence, Robert Dover (1582–1652), a genial extrovert who loved pageantry. *Annalia Dubrensia* (1636), a collection of poems in praise of Dover and his achievements, included contributions from Michael Drayton, Ben Jonson and Thomas Heywood.

Cotswold Water Park. A recreational and residential area in the Cotswolds consisting of a network of over 100 artificial lakes created from former gravel pits. The lakes are used by sailing boats and for other water sports, and there are lakeside housing developments.

The Water Park has two foci – one south of Cirencester around the villages of South Cerney and Ashton Keynes (so straddling the Gloucestershire–Wiltshire border), and another between Lechlade and Fairford (solely in Gloucestershire).

Cotswold Way, the. A long-distance footpath 162 km (100 miles) in length, traversing the Cotswolds approximately northeast–southwest from CHIPPING CAMPDEN in the north via WINCHCOMBE, Birdlip, DURSLEY and Wootton-under-Edge to BATH in the south.

King of the Cotswolds, the. A sobriquet applied to Lord Chandos of Sudeley (*c.*1579–1621), who was notorious for his extravagant lifestyle and the lavish parties he used to throw at Sudeley House (*see under* WINCHCOMBE).

Cottesmore 'Cott's moor', OE *Cottes* possessive form of male personal name *Cott* + *mor* 'moor'.

A village (pronounced 'kotsmore') in Rutland (before 1996 in Leicestershire, before 1974 in Rutland), about 8 km (5 miles) northeast of Oakham. It is in the heart of traditional fox-hunting country: the celebrated **Cottesmore Hunt** was originally established at nearby Exton in 1732, but moved to Cottesmore in 1788.

RAF Cottesmore opened as a bomber base during the Second World War, and has continued in that role subsequently.

Cottingham 'Cott's people's homestead', OE personal name + *-inga-* (*see* -ING + -HAM).

A town in the East Riding of Yorkshire, some 7 km (4.5 miles) northwest of HULL, with which it is contiguous.

Cottingley 'woodland glade of Cotta's people', OE male personal name *Cotta* + *-inga-* (*see* -ING) + -LEY.

A village in West Yorkshire's BRONTË COUNTRY, between Saltaire and Bingley.

Cottingley Fairies, the. In 1917 two little girls living at Bingley, Yorkshire, Elsie Wright and her cousin Frances, claimed they had seen fairies in nearby **Cottingley Dell** and said they had even taken photographs of them. The story came to the attention of Sir Arthur Conan Doyle, by then a convert to spiritualism. He believed the girls and vouched for the veracity of the photographs, even taking lantern slides made from them to the USA as part of a lecture tour. In 1983 Frances Griffiths, then aged 76, admitted that the pictures had been faked by photographing cut-outs of fairies from *Princess Mary's Gift Book*, a popular children's book at that time.

Cotton[1] '(place) at the cottages', from OE *cot* (*see* -COT, COTE). A village in Staffordshire, about 16 km (10 miles) east of Stoke-on-Trent.

See also FAR COTTON.

Cotton[2]. A village in Suffolk, about 8 km (5 miles) north of Stowmarket.

Cottonopolis. A nickname given to MANCHESTER in the 19th century, owing to the city's vast cotton industry.

Countess Wear From Isabella de Fortibus, *Countess* of Devon in the 13th century, who in 1282 constructed a weir across the River EXE on her land at TOPSHAM to spite the people of EXETER who had offended her.

A village (pronounced 'weir') in Devon, on the south-eastern outskirts of Exeter.

County ... For Irish counties, *see under* the second element of their names, thus for County Cork *see* CORK, COUNTY, etc.

County Bounds. The scenic and mountainous area along the border of counties CORK and KERRY. The **County Bounds Road** is the N22 from Cork to Killarney.

County Durham. *See* DURHAM, COUNTY.

County Oak Perhaps from the name of an inn. A northern suburb of CRAWLEY, in West Sussex.

County Palatine Latin *palatinus*, 'of the palace'. A county over which an earl or other lord had quasi-royal jurisdiction. Cheshire, Shropshire, Durham and Kent became Counties Palatine after the Norman Conquest as English frontier districts; Lancaster became one in 1351. At one time Pembrokeshire, Hexhamshire and the Isle of Ely were also so designated, but only CHESHIRE, Durham (*see* DURHAM, COUNTY) and LANCASHIRE still retain the title, and the Chancellor of the Duchy of Lancaster (*see under* LANCASTER) is a member of the British government. Their jurisdictions are now vested in the Crown.

Coupar Angus Possibly Gaelic *comhpairt* 'common', i.e. common land, with *Angus* added to distinguish it from the CUPAR in Fife.

A market town some 20 km (12 miles) northeast of Perth, in

Perth and Kinross (formerly in Perthshire, and then in Tayside region) – not, despite its name, in nearby Angus. There is little left of the Cistercian Abbey founded in 1164, but, notable in the history of arboriculture, the 15th-century cellarer of the abbey, William Blair, established the first recorded forestry nursery here. Coupar Angus was the birthplace of Jock Sutherland (1889–1948), the noted American football coach.

Court-at-Street Originally (1530) *Cortopstreet*, apparently '(road at or by) a short piece of enclosed land'.

A village in Kent, just to the north of Romney Marsh, about 14 km (8.5 miles) west of Folkestone.

Courteenhall 'Corta's or Curta's nook of land', OE *Cortan* or *Curtan* possessive forms of male personal names *Corta* or *Curta* + *halh* (*see* HALE, -HALL).

A village in Northamptonshire, about 8 km (5 miles) south of Northampton.

Covent Garden 'monastery garden' (referring to a walled enclosure belonging to the monks of Westminster Abbey), ME *convent* 'monastery, convent' + *garden*.

An open area (pronounced 'kovent' or, especially in former times, 'kuvent') in the WEST END[1] of London (WC2), to the north of the STRAND. It was owned in the Middle Ages by the monks of the Abbey of St Peter at Westminster (whence its name). At the Dissolution of the Monasteries in the late 1540s it was granted to the Earl of Bedford. In the 1630s his successor laid out a splendid arcaded square on the site (the first and archetypal of the many squares with which London is now adorned), designed by Inigo Jones, which soon became a very fashionable place to live. (The arcade came to be known as the 'piazza', a misapplication of the Italian term for 'square', which has taken root.) In the 1650s a few stallholders began setting out their wares in the square, thus beginning Covent Garden's association with one of the two things with which its name is today synonymous: the sale of fruit, vegetables and flowers.

By the middle of the 18th century it was a large and successful market, with many permanent buildings. It was rebuilt and enlarged in the late 1820s. Now it was not only London's most important fruit, vegetable and flower market; it was a colourful and vibrant public space where toffs from the West End rubbed shoulders with the coster-mongers and flower-girls (as epitomized by Bernard Shaw's Eliza Doolittle in *Pygmalion* (1916)). By the middle of the 20th century, however, a market of its size in the middle of London was no longer viable, and in 1974 it was moved (under the name **New Covent Garden**) to a site at NINE ELMS, Battersea. It is the largest fruit, vegetable and flower market in the United Kingdom.

Covent Garden's other thing is opera and ballet. There has been a theatre at the eastern end of the square since the 1730s, and the present-day Royal Opera House (known

to devotees simply as 'the Garden') dates from the 1850s. It was extensively redesigned and modernized in the 1990s, reopening in 1999, but it retains its classical entrance portico in Bow Street. Despite the tribulations of under-funding and recurrent criticism of its artistic standards it remains Britain's flagship opera house, home to the Royal Opera and the Royal Ballet.

The buildings left vacant by the departure of the market were refurbished, and the area was turned into a pedestrian precinct with many small shops of a type calculated to appeal to tourists. Street performers now add to the ambience ('The girls wanted to go back to Covent Garden to watch the punks and body-poppers', *New York Times* (1984)), and the two aspects of Covent Garden merged when a giant screen was set up there showing popular productions from the Opera House. The Inigo Jones-designed St Paul's Church at the western end has long theatrical associations, and the cobbled area in front of it is the main performance venue for outdoor performance groups. The area is now also home to the London Transport Museum and the Theatre Museum.

Today Covent Garden is a reasonably respectable place, but it was not always so. In former centuries it was a veritable hotbed of crime and vice (the anonymous author of *The Whole Life and History of Benjamin Child, Lately Executed for Robbing the Bristol Mail* (1722) described it as 'that receptacle of sharpers, pickpockets and strumpets'). The vice was the main thing: the taverns and pavements teemed with prostitutes, and one enterprising barman, John Harris (*c*.1710–65), spotting a niche market, published lists of the names of these professional women, together with their addresses and details of their physical attributes and special skills (the first, his *List of Covent Garden Ladies* (1758), sold 8000 copies of the first edition). Not surprisingly, a number of semantically related slang expressions incorporating *Covent Garden* evolved: **Covent Garden abbess** 'a madame', **Covent Garden ague** 'venereal disease', **Covent Garden gout** 'venereal disease', **Covent Garden nun** 'a prostitute', **Covent Garden nunnery** 'a brothel'.

Covent Garden Underground station, on the Piccadilly line, was opened in 1907.

Covent Garden. Mid 19th-century rhyming slang for a 'farthing' (at that time in working-class London dialect *farthing* and *garden* would have rhymed).

Coventry 'Cofa's tree', OE *Cofan* possessive form of male personal name *Cofa* + *treow* 'tree'. Like other towns with the 'tree' ending, such as BRAINTREE and OSWESTRY, Coventry may have its roots in being an ancient 'place of assembly', marked by a distinctive tree; alternatively, the 'tree' in question may have been a pole or cross.

An industrial city (pronounced 'koventry' or, especially in former times, 'kuventry') and metropolitan borough in the

WEST MIDLANDS (before 1974 in Warwickshire), about 29 km (18 miles) southeast of Birmingham. In the medieval period Coventry was wealthier than nearby Warwick, and in the 19th century its prosperity continued, thanks latterly to the manufacture of cycles (which began around 1870) and sewing machines. Then, in 1896, the Daimler Company produced Britain's first horseless carriage here, setting Coventry's 20th-century course as a car-manufacturing city (leading local lights have been Jaguar, Riley and Standard).

In modern times, though, it has never really recovered from the German bombing raid of 14–15 November 1940, which killed over 550 people, destroyed over 60,000 buildings, and devasted St Michael's Cathedral. Basil Spence's new **Coventry Cathedral** was completed in 1962, Benjamin Britten composing his *War Requiem* for the consecration of the new building and Graham Sutherland and John Piper designing respectively its huge altar tapestry 'Christ in Glory' and a set of stained-glass windows. The remains of the old church are the venue for a triennial performance of the Coventry Mysteries (*see below*). The city's religious associations have led some to suppose, wrongly, that its name derives from *convent*.

In popular legend, Lady Godiva (or Godgifu; d.*c*.1080), wife of Earl Leofric of MERCIA, was shocked by the poverty she saw around her in Coventry, and begged her husband to abolish the crippling taxes. He said he would accede to her request if she rode naked through the town. She did so, on condition that the townsfolk remain in their houses and bolt their windows. Peeping Tom disobeyed, and was struck blind for his prurience. Leofric, however, kept his word and repealed the taxes. Lady Godiva's ride is re-enacted at the start of the annual Spirit of Coventry Festival. The legend of Lady Godiva is mentioned in Michael Drayton's *The Poly-Olbion* (1612–22) and is also the subject of a poem, 'Godiva', by Alfred, Lord Tennyson.

Coventry University was founded in 1992, based on the earlier Coventry (Lanchester) Polytechnic (founded 1970). The Warwick University campus is near Coventry.

Coventry is said to be the original of Middlemarch, the town at the centre of George Eliot's eponymous novel (1871–2) of provincial life. Coventry was the birthplace of the actress Ellen Terry (1847–1928), of the critic Cyril Connolly (1903–74), of Frank Whittle (1907–96), the inventor of the jet engine, of the poet Philip Larkin (1922–85), whose poem 'I Remember, I Remember' (1954) portrays his Coventry life as an undistinguished blank ('Nothing, like something, happens anywhere'), and of the actor Nigel Hawthorne (1929–2001).

> Coventry disappointed me. It would seem decidedly
> odder if it didn't seem quite so new.
>
> Henry James: Letter to William James (26 April 1869)

See also STIVICHALL.

Coventrate. To destroy a town by aerial bombing and kill large numbers of its people. The usage was the bitter, blackly humorous outcome of the German air-raid on Coventry in November 1940 (*see above*). It appears to have been originally coined in German, as *coventrieren*, which makes it even less palatable. The English language soon adopted it, but understandably it did not survive for very long.

coventry. A name, recorded in the mid 19th century, for a three-cornered jam puff – presumably of a sort first made in Coventry.

Coventry bell. A former name for the flower *Campanula medium*, now known as the Canterbury bell (*see under* CANTERBURY[1]).

Coventry blue. A type of high-quality blue dye. The term originally denoted blue thread formerly made in Coventry, and also gave rise to the expression 'true as Coventry blue'.

Coventry Canal. The Coventry canal runs from Fradley to Coventry and is over 61 km (38 miles) long. It was built at the end of the 18th century to transport coal from the Coventry and NUNEATON pits to the rest of the Midlands.

Coventry Carol. An anonymous English Renaissance carol of haunting and melancholy beauty, mourning the brutality of King Herod's massacre of the Innocents (the male children of Bethlehem) when Jesus was born (Matthew 2:16). The slaughter was depicted in the medieval Pageant of the Shearmen and Tailors, one of the Coventry Mystery Plays.

Coventry City FC. The city's football club, founded in 1883 by workers at the Singers cycle firm, after which the club was originally named (Singers FC). It received its present-day name in 1898. Nicknamed the Sky Blues, Coventry City play their home games at Highfield Road.

Coventry Climax. A Coventry-based engine manufacturing company, founded in 1903 as Coventry Simplex. It is no longer in existence.

Coventry dress tie. A type of bow tie:

> The Coventry dress tie is based on the drawknot or single
> bow. It is the easiest dress tie for the non-adept to master.
> One half of the tie tapers to an end that is stiffened at the
> very tip with a small metal disk which is to be stuck in
> between the collar and neckband, and then pushed
> downward from sight.
>
> Clifford W. Ashley: *The Ashley Book of Knots* (1944)

Coventry Mystery Plays. A set of 42 mystery plays based on Bible stories, supposed to have been performed in Coventry at the festival of Corpus Christi (a church festival on the Thursday after Trinity Sunday) until 1591. Each was staged by a trade appropriate to its subject matter. Although they were called *Ludus Coventriae* 'Play of Coventry' by the noted 17th-century antiquarian and manuscript-collector Sir Robert Cotton, their special connection with Coventry and Corpus Christi is doubtful, and the plays are now more usually referred to as the 'N. town cycle'. Two undoubted Coventry pageants do survive from this period, however: the Pageant of the Shearmen and Tailors and the Pageant of the Weavers.

sent to Coventry, to be. To be shunned or ostracized. Royalist prisoners captured at the Battle of PRESTON (1648), in the Civil Wars, were incarcerated in St John's Church, Coventry. The citizens, who sided with Parliament, refused to speak to them, and this may have given rise to the phrase. Some historians claim, however, that the expression comes from Shakespeare's *Henry IV, Part 1* (1592), when Falstaff says of his motley band of foot-soldiers, 'I'll not march through Coventry with them, that's flat' (IV.ii).

Cove of Cork. An earlier name for COBH.

Cover OCelt *gober* 'stream'.
A river in the YORKSHIRE DALES, North Yorkshire, flowing some 20 km (12 miles) southwest–northeast through **Coverdale** before joining the River URE 6 km (4 miles) southeast of LEYBURN.

Cowal The earliest recorded form is *Congall* and tradition associates the place with *Comgall*, the son of Fergus, the 6th-century Irish settler.
A traditional area of ARGYLL AND BUTE (formerly in Argyll, then in Strathclyde region), comprising the large, heavily indented peninsula between LOCH FYNE to the west and the Firth of CLYDE and LOCH LONG to the east.

Cowan Bridge Earlier *Colling-*, perhaps an OE male personal name meaning 'son of Coll'. The sounds *coll-* and *cow-* were similar in the Middle Ages.
A village in Lancashire, some 3 km (2 miles) southeast of Kirby Lonsdale. The Clergy Daughters' School at Cowan Bridge was attended by Emily and Charlotte Brontë, and was the inspiration for the Lowood Institution, the brutal school attended by Charlotte's fictional heroine Jane Eyre. Here girls were thrashed on the side of the neck with bunches of twigs, and faced with food so foul that 'famine itself soon sickens over it'. Jane's suffering is recalled – 'A lost storm in this temperate place' – in Geoffrey Hill's poem, 'Cowan Bridge, at the site of "Lowood School"', in his 1968 collection, *King Log*.

However, the place had its compensations:

> I discovered ... that a great pleasure, an enjoyment that the horizon only bounded, lay all outside the high and spike-guarded walls of our garden: this pleasure consisted in prospect of noble summits girdling a great hill-hollow, rich in verdure and shadow: in a bright beck, full of dark stones and sparkling eddies ...
>
> Charlotte Brontë: *Jane Eyre* (1847), Chapter 9

Cow and Calf, the. *See under* ILKLEY.

Cowbridge 'bridge for cows'. It may have been the site of the Roman fort called *Bovium*.
A town in Vale of Glamorgan (formerly in Glamorgan, then in South Glamorgan), 12 km (7.5 miles) northwest of Barry. Its Welsh name is **Y Bont-Faen** ('the stone bridge'), and it was at one time also known as **Y-Dref hir yn y Waun** ('the long town on the moors', from the length of its main street). East of the town, according to tradition, Owain Glyndwr defeated Henry IV in 1405.

Cowdenbeath Possibly 'Cowden's property in Beith (i.e. the birch wood)', surname Cowden + Gaelic *beith* 'birch'.
A former mining town in Fife, 8 km (5 miles) northeast of Dunfermline. In Scots rhyming slang, *Cowdenbeath* means 'teeth'. **Cowdenbeath FC**, nicknamed Cowden, was founded in 1881 and plays at Central Park.

Cowes 'cows', from two former sandbanks in the mouth of the River Medina known in the Middle Ages as 'Eastcow' and 'Westcow', from their fancied resemblance to cows.
A town at the northern tip of the ISLE OF WIGHT, on either side of the mouth of the River MEDINA[1] (the smaller eastern part is distinguished as **East Cowes**). The two halves of the town are linked by a floating-bridge ferry.

Cowes is England's foremost yachting centre. The annual **Cowes Regatta** has been held here, under the auspices of the Royal Yacht Squadron, since 1776, and **Cowes Week** (in the first week of August) quickly established itself as part of the high-society 'season' (William Thackeray, in *Vanity Fair* (1848), records how Mrs Bute Crawley and her daughters regularly 'penetrated to Cowes for the raceballs and regatta-gaieties there'). Nowadays it perhaps takes itself a little more seriously, with Olympic crews competing and the Admiral's Cup races providing a severe test of seamanship.

Cowes has the dubious distinction of appearing in perhaps the lamest and hoariest of all question-and-answer jokes: Q: What's brown and steaming and comes out of Cowes? A: The Isle of Wight ferry.

On the outskirts of East Cowes is OSBORNE HOUSE, one of Queen Victoria's favourite residences.

Dr Thomas Arnold (1795–1842), the celebrated headmaster of Rugby School, was born in Cowes.

Cowley 'Cofa's or Cufa's glade', OE male personal name *Cofa* or *Cufa* + -LEY.
A southeastern suburb of OXFORD. In 1912, William Morris (later Lord Nuffield) bought a factory here to manufacture cars (one of his earliest models was called the **Morris Cowley**). His firm prospered, taking over rivals such as Wolseley and Riley, and by 1939 it had produced a million cars. In 1952 it merged with Austin as the British Motor Corporation, and in future years combinations with Leyland and Rover would confirm its position as the largest

and most successful mass automaker of British origin. All this time the Cowley factory, straddling the ring road, was growing and growing, dominating the suburb. Nowadays, owned by BMW, it makes the new Mini.

Cowley Fathers. An informal name given to the Society of St John the Evangelist, a religious order founded in 1866 by the Rev. Richard Meux Benson (1824–1914), the vicar of Cowley. Its headquarters continued to be in Cowley until 1980.

Cowton Moor 'moor of the cattle farm', OE *cu* 'cow' + -TON. A battle site in North Yorkshire, some 12 km (7.5 miles) south of Darlington. Here on 22 August 1138 the **Battle of the Standard** was fought, in which David I of Scotland, seeking to acquire Cumbria and Northumberland from the English, was defeated by the Archbishop of York and the Bishop of Durham, fighting under the banners of St Cuthbert, St Peter of York, St John of Beverley and St Wilfrid of Ripon – hence the name of the battle.

Coxheath 'Cock's heath', surname *Cock* + ME *heath* 'heath'. A village in Kent, about 2.5 km (1.5 miles) south of Maidstone. The first recorded formal game of cricket in England was played here in 1646.

Coxhoe Possibly 'Cocc's spur (of a hill)', OE male personal name *Cocc* + *hoh* 'hill-spur'.
A large former mining village in County Durham, 6 km (4 miles) northeast of Spennymoor. A visitor in the 19th century was shocked by the squalor of the place (perhaps not untypical of many other northern colliery villages), and recorded (anonymously) his impressions in the *Newcastle Weekly Chronicle* of 5 October 1872:

> We pass on up and down more close packed rows, back to back, of squalid, broken roofed hovels, whose walls are rotten and mouldering, whose floors are damp, and the wretchedness of whose interiors, in spite of good furniture in many cases, is only exceeded by the abject misery and foul horrors of the exterior surroundings. The haggard women beset my companion as we pass, and pray to be removed into better houses. Have we come to see about repairs? 'We canna live in oor hoose, measter!' God knows, I do not wonder at it, who but pigs could!

Coxwold. *See* SHANDY HALL.

Coychurch 'wood church', Welsh *coed* 'wood' (*see* CED) + ModE *church*.
A village in Bridgend unitary authority (formerly in Mid Glamorgan), 3 km (2 miles) east of Bridgend.

Crabble Perhaps 'hollow of land where crab apples grow', ME *crabbe* 'crab apple' + OE *hol* 'hollow of land'.
A northwestern suburb of DOVER, in Kent. Its early 19th-century water mill, which is still working, once ground grain into flour for the garrison at Dover Castle.

The Crabble cricket ground, on the coast, used to host Kent county matches.

Crabbs Cross *Crabb* probably a local family name + *cross* 'crossroads' or 'stone cross'.
A southern suburb of REDDITCH, in Worcestershire (before 1998 in Hereford and Worcester, before 1974 in Worcestershire).

Crackleybank Origin unknown, but name first recorded in the 19th century.
A village in Shropshire, about 8 km (5 miles) east of Telford.

Crackpot 'crow's pothole', OScand *kraka* 'crow' + ME *potte* 'rift, deep hole'.
A village in Swaledale, North Yorkshire, 20 km (12 miles) west of Richmond.

Craggy Island. The remote and fictional island off the west coast of Ireland that was the setting for the cult Channel 4 1990s sitcom *Father Ted*. During its three series, Craggy Island was the backwater where long-suffering Father Ted Crilly and his fellow priests, the childlike no-brainer Father Dougal McGuire and ageing dipsomaniac Father Jack 'Drink' Hackett, shared a house under the watchful eye of tea-fascist ('Go on, go on') and housekeeper Mrs Doyle.

Cragside Most likely a Victorian coinage, thus meaning what it says.
A Victorian mansion set in extensive wooded and rhododendron-covered grounds in Northumberland, just east of Rothbury, 17 km (11 miles) southwest of Alnwick. It was designed by Norman Shaw for William Armstrong (1810–1900; later Baron Armstrong of Cragside), the engineer and arms manufacturer, and was the first house in Britain to run on hydroelectricity. Both house and grounds are now in the care of the National Trust.

Craigavon After James *Craig*, Viscount Craigavon (1871–1940), the first prime minister of Northern Ireland (1921–40).
A city in County Armagh, incorporating the towns of LURGAN and PORTADOWN. Craigavon was created as a New Town in 1965, and is a local authority district.

Craig Cwm Silyn 'crag of the valley of Silian', Welsh *craig* 'rock, crag' + *cwm* (*see* -COMBE, COOMBE) + unknown element, possibly a personal name.
A mountain (734 m / 2408 ft) in western Snowdonia, Gwynedd (formerly in Caernarvonshire), 14 km (8.5 miles) south of Caernarfon. It is the highest point on the NANTLLE RIDGE, and the eponymous craggy cwm on the northern side of the mountain offers some classic rock climbs.

Craigenputtock Possibly 'rock of the kite' Gaelic *creag* 'rock' + *puttock* 'kite, buzzard'.
A remote farm up in the moors of Dumfries and Galloway

(formerly in Dumfriesshire), 14 km (8.5 miles) east-north-east of New Galloway. The historian and writer Thomas Carlyle and his diarist wife Jane lived here in the early years of their marriage (1828–34), and here Carlyle wrote contributions to the *Edinburgh Review* and parts of his major work *Sartor Resartus*.

Craig Gogarth 'crag of the promontory', Welsh *craig* 'rock, crag' + *gogarth* 'promontory, hill'.

A spectacular vertical sea cliff, up to 120 m (390 ft) high, on Holyhead Mountain (*see under* HOLYHEAD), Holy Island, Anglesey (formerly in Gwynedd). The first rock climbs here were pioneered in the early 1960s, and in that decade the crag's loose quartzite verticalities were *the* place to be for aspiring tigers; such was the heady ego-led frenzy of the time that one would-be hardman went so far as to claim new routes that he had never climbed, his deceptions being exposed by the *Sunday Times*. The BBC made an outside broadcast of climbers in action here in 1970.

Craiglockhart Probably 'rock or crag of the encampment', Gaelic *creag* 'crag' + *longphort* 'harbour, encampment'.

An area of southwest EDINBURGH, around **Craiglockhart Hill**, an old volcanic plug. Craiglockhart formerly had a mental hospital used for shell-shocked officers during the First World War; it was here that Wilfred Owen momentously met Siegfried Sassoon, and the place features in Pat Barker's novel *Regeneration* (1991). The building is now part of Napier University.

Crail Possibly 'boulder rock', OCelt *carr* 'boulder' + *ail* 'rock'.

A royal BURGH (1310) and fishing port in Fife, 14 km (8.5 miles) southeast of St Andrews, on the north shore of the Firth of Forth (*see under* FORTH). Outside the old church here is a large stone said to have been thrown by the Devil from the ISLE OF MAY, some 9 km (5.5 miles) offshore. There is also another stone, whose deep indentations are said to have been made by the archers of Fife sharpening their arrows while preparing to fight for Robert the Bruce. It was Bruce who awarded the town its royal charter, giving it the right to trade on Sundays. Constantine's Cave on the shore is where King Constantine I is said to have been killed by the Vikings in 877.

Crail capon. A 19th-century Scots term for a kind of dried or smoked haddock.

Cramlington 'farm of the people living by stream with herons', OE *cran* 'crane, heron' + *wella* 'stream' + *-inga-* (*see* -ING) + -TON.

A town in Northumberland, 13 km (8 miles) north of Newcastle.

Cramond 'Roman camp on the River Almond', Latin *castrum* 'military camp' + Gaelic river name.

A picturesque village on the northwest side of Edinburgh,

situated where the River ALMOND[1] enters the Firth of Forth (*see under* FORTH). The Romans had a fort and port here, hence its name. Offshore is the small **Cramond Island**, linked to the mainland at low tide by a causeway.

Cranborne 'stream frequented by cranes or herons', OE *cran* 'crane, heron' + *burna* 'stream'.

A village in Dorset, near the southern edge of Salisbury Plain, about 18 km (11 miles) east of Blandford Forum. **Cranborne House**, a Jacobean manor house that evolved from a hunting lodge built in 1208 for King John, was given by James VI and I to the Cecil family, the marquesses of Salisbury, who still use 'Cranborne' as a subsidiary title.

Cranborne is fictionalized as **Chaseborough** in the novels of Thomas Hardy.

Cranborne Chase. A 260-sq-km (100-sq-mile) expanse of chalk grassland and beechwoods in Dorset and Wiltshire. It was originally a royal forest and hunting ground (*chase* once meant 'a tract of land for breeding and hunting wild animals'); King John was very fond of hunting fallow deer here. By the early 19th century it had become a haven for all sorts of unsavoury outlaws, and in 1830 an act was passed in Parliament bringing it under the jurisdiction of the law of the land (as opposed to the forest laws).

Cranfield 'open land frequented by cranes or herons', OE *cran* 'crane, heron' + -FIELD.

A village in Bedfordshire, about 13 km (8 miles) southwest of Bedford. **Cranfield University**, a science- and business-based university with military connections, had its origins in the College of Aeronautics founded in 1946 close to Cranfield airfield. It became Cranfield Institute of Technology in 1969, and was granted university status in 1993. It has three campuses, at Cranfield, Silsoe (also in Bedfordshire) and Shrivenham (in Oxfordshire).

Cranford. A fictional village (based on KNUTSFORD, Cheshire) on which the action of Elizabeth Gaskell's novel *Cranford* (1853) is centred. The book quietly details the lives of the village's middle-class inhabitants and the small dramas that assail them.

There are real settlements in England called Cranford: in Devon, Greater London (Hounslow) and Northamptonshire (Cranford St Andrew and Cranford St John); here the name meant in Old English 'ford frequented by cranes or herons'.

Cranleigh 'woodland glade frequented by cranes'; OE *cran* 'crane, heron' + -LEY.

A small town in Surrey, about 11 km (7 miles) southeast of Guildford. Until the late 19th century Cranleigh was usually spelt **Cranley**: the change to the present spelling was apparently triggered by the perceived need (in an era before post codes) to distinguish the town from nearby CRAWLEY in handwritten addresses on letters.

Cranleigh's proximity to the iron-rich WEALD made it a centre of the iron industry in the Middle Ages. **Cranleigh School**, a private school, was founded in 1863. The maple trees that line the town's high street were planted by Canadian soldiers billeted here during the First World War.

Cranleigh was the birthplace of the mathematician Godfrey Hardy (1877–1947), who distinguished himself in the field of number theory. Prajadhipok, the last absolute king of Siam (reigned 1925–35) and the 32nd son of King Chulalongkorn, died here in 1941.

Cranmere Pool 'lake frequented by herons', *Cranmere* OE *cran* 'crane, heron' + *mere* 'lake'.

A former pool (long since drained) in the central northern part of Dartmoor, which is traditionally regarded as the central point of the moor. It is an isolated, cheerless and mysterious spot.

In 1854 a Dartmoor guide called James Perrott left an empty jar here. People visiting the pool would put self-addressed cards in the jar to prove they had been here. Others coming along later retrieved the cards and posted them, leaving their own cards in their stead. Thus was begun the system of 'Dartmoor letterboxing' (*see under* DARTMOOR), which now has over 3000 such 'drops'.

Cranwell 'spring or stream frequented by cranes or heron', OE *cran* 'crane, heron' + *wella* 'spring, stream'.

A village in Lincolnshire, about 19 km (12 miles) north-east of Grantham. Just to the west of it is the Royal Air Force College, the world's first military air academy (it opened in 1933). Its most famous graduate is probably the Second World War fighter ace Sir Douglas Bader. The next-door RAF station is home to the Red Arrows formation-flying squadron.

Crapstone *crap* perhaps a southern dialect word meaning 'darnel, rye-grass', or alternatively 'excrement, refuse' + STONE.

A village in Devon, on the southwestern edge of Dartmoor, about 6.5 km (4 miles) south of Tavistock.

Crask of Aigas 'crossing at the place of the chasm', Gaelic *crasg* 'crossing, pass' + *aigeann* 'chasm'.

A small settlement in Highland (formerly on the border of Inverness-shire and Ross and Cromarty), 7 km (4.5 miles) southwest of Beauly. Nearby is **Oldtown of Aigas**.

Craven Possibly an OCelt name meaning 'area, district of garlic'.

A limestone area of the central PENNINES, in the YORKSHIRE DALES, North Yorkshire, bounded on the south by Settle and Skipton and extending north to the sources of the rivers Wharfe and Ribble. The area includes the mountains of INGLEBOROUGH, PEN-Y-GHENT, WHERNSIDE and Great Whernside (*see under* WHERNSIDE). The **Craven Fault** forms the great limestone crags at Malham Cove (*see under* MALHAM) and GORDALE SCAR.

Charlotte Brontë, recalling her brutal schooling at COWAN BRIDGE, and missing the softer gritstone moors by Haworth, wrote of 'the hard, grey hills of Craven'.

Craven Arms From the name of an inn opened here in the early 19th century (itself named after the Earls of *Craven*, lords of the nearby manor of Stokesay). The inn's name was first transferred to the road junction it stood at, then to the newly opened railway station, and finally to the town that developed around the station.

A small town in Shropshire, about 10.5 km (6.5 miles) northwest of Ludlow.

Crawfordjohn 'crow ford belonging to John', OE *crawe* 'crow' + FORD + *John*, with John being the name of the local landowner, son-in-law of the sheriff of Lanark in the 13th century.

A small settlement in South Lanarkshire (formerly in Strathclyde region), 5 km (3 miles) west of Abington.

Crawley 'glade frequented by crows', OE *crawe* 'crow' + -LEY.

A town in West Sussex, about 5 km (3 miles) southeast of GATWICK[1]. In the late 18th and early 19th centuries it was an important staging point on the coaching route between London and Brighton, and in the 20th century it continued to provide a refreshment stop for motorists on the A23. For rail commuters to London there is Crawley station on the Horsham line and THREE BRIDGES on the Brighton line.

In 1946 Crawley was designated a NEW TOWN[1] (the only such to the south of London), and since then it has grown enormously in size, with much light industry providing local employment.

The factory storehouse in which John George Haigh (1910–49), the 'Acid-Bath Murderer', dissolved his victims was in Crawley.

See also COUNTY OAK.

Craw Road, the Scots *craw* 'crow'.

The small road (the B822) that climbs over the CAMPSIE FELLS to a height of 333 m (1092 ft), linking FINTRY (Stirling) and Lennoxtown (East Dunbartonshire). There is also a Craw Road in Paisley, and a novel by the Scottish writer Iain Banks entitled *The Crow Road* (1992), referring to Crow Road in the West End of Glasgow, and something more:

> I asked her if she'd ever heard Grandma Margot use the saying: away the Crow Road (or the Craw Rod, if she was being especially broad-accented that day). It meant dying; being dead. 'Aye, he's away the crow road,' meant 'He's dead.'
>
> Iain Banks: *The Crow Road* (1992)

Crazies Hill Perhaps from the surname *Craze* or *Crass* (from French, meaning 'fat').

A village in Berkshire, about 4 km (2.5 miles) southeast of Henley-on-Thames.

❖ **creech, crook** ❖

Like many Old Celtic elements, *cruc, crug* refers to a landscape feature: a hill, artificial or natural. It is found in Welsh and Cornish names like CRICIETH (Gwynedd) and Crugmeer near Padstow. It was evidently used before the Anglo-Saxons, who subsequently borrowed it, and a remarkable number of names survive using this element: Crook in Devon and Dorset (but not Crook in County Durham), Creech in Dorset and Somerset (*see* CREECH ST MICHAEL), Crich (Derbyshire) and Crutch (Worcestershire).

An intriguing development in the history of this place-name element is the substitution of *church* for *crug*, which in the CHURCHILL[1] names in Oxfordshire, Devon, Somerset and Worcestershire provides evidence that the Anglo-Saxons did not understand the British word they were using. Here, not only did the Anglo-Saxons change the unfamiliar word for a familiar one, they also added the element *hyll* 'hill' to a word already meaning 'hill'.

Crazy Corner Apparently a modern name, possibly referring to a sharp bend in road or river.
A village in County Westmeath, some 5 km (3 miles) north of Mullingar.

Creag Meagaidh 'crag of the bog', Gaelic *creag* 'cliff' + OCelt *mig* 'bog'.
A massive mountain (1130 m / 3706 ft) in Highland (formerly in Inverness-shire), some 35 km (22 miles) northeast of Fort William. There are huge precipices (up to 450 m / 1500 ft high) in its northeastern corrie, noted for their many hard ice climbs in winter; notable among these are the great gully icefalls of the North, Central and South Posts. The whole massif is now a national nature reserve, and efficient culling of red deer and the banishment of sheep has paid dividends in the regeneration of woody vegetation on the lower slopes. To the north of the main summit plateau is a high pass called the Window, through which Bonnie Prince Charlie may have passed in his wanderings after Culloden.

Crediton 'farmstead or estate on the River Creedy', CREEDY + -TON.
A town in Devon, in the valley of the River CREEDY, about 13 km (8 miles) northwest of Exeter. In 909 it became the cathedral city of Devon, but in 1050 it was displaced by Exeter. In the 18th century, when it had reached its peak as a centre of the wool trade, a large part of the town was destroyed by fire.
According to legend Crediton was the birthplace of St Boniface (*c*.675–754), who, for his missionary work among the heathen Germanic tribes, became known as the 'Apostle of Germany' (*see* BONCHURCH; ST BONIFACE DOWN).

Creech St Michael *Creech* 'mound, hill', OCelt *crug* (*see* CREECH, CROOK); *St Michael* from the dedication of the local church.
A village in Somerset, about 5 km (3 miles) east of Taunton. *See also* EAST CREECH.

Creed '(church of) St Cride', from *Cride* , the name of the patron saint of the local church. She was a 7th-century Irish saint, who came to Cornwall with St Finbar.

A village in Cornwall, about 11 km (7 miles) east of Truro.

Creed Lane Probably from the processional chanting of the *Creed*. Alternatively the name might allude to writers of religious texts working in the vicinity. Before the 16th century the street was known as *Spurrier Row* 'row (of houses) occupied by spur-makers'.
A street in the City of London (EC4), running southwards from LUDGATE HILL. In the Middle Ages the clergy of ST PAUL'S[1] Cathedral went in procession to the cathedral reciting prayers. They began in PATERNOSTER ROW, and on reaching Creed Lane they began chanting the Creed.

Creedy An OCelt river name meaning 'the winding river'.
A river in Devon, which rises near Puddington Bottom, to the southwest of Tiverton, and flows 12 km (7.5 miles) southwards to join the River YEO[1] near Crediton.

Cresscombe. The fictional name for LETCOMBE BASSETT adopted by Thomas Hardy, as in *Jude the Obscure* (1895).

Creswell '(place by the) spring where cress grows', OE *cærse* 'cress' + *wella* 'spring, stream'.
A village in Derbyshire, 8 km (5 miles) southwest of Worksop.

Creswell Crags. A limestone gorge on the border of Derbyshire and Nottinghamshire, east of Creswell, honeycombed with caves and fissures that were occupied in the last Ice Age between 50,000 and 10,000 BC. The most significant of the caves are (on the northern side of the gorge) the Pin Hole, the Robin Hood and Mother Grundy's Parlour, and (on its southern side) the Church Hole Cavern. Stone tool and animal remains have been found in the caves. Engravings of bison and birds found on the walls of some of the caves in 2003 are the only known examples of Palaeolithic cave art found in Britain.

Crewe 'fish-trap, weir', OCelt *criu*.
A town in Cheshire, in the borough of Crewe and Nantwich, about 32 km (20 miles) southeast of Chester. Previously a small market town, it was transformed in the 1830s by the coming of the railways. In 1837 the Grand Junction Railway Company opened its Liverpool–Birmingham line,

passing through Crewe, and in 1843 it transferred its railway works here. The company effectively controlled the town until the passing of the Crewe Corporation Act of 1938, and even after then Crewe's symbiotic relationship with trains continued. It built them (British Railways', later British Rail's, chief construction works were here) and it sent them on their way to all parts of Britain: until the 1930s it was the biggest railway junction in the world, and lines still converge on it from all main points of the compass. Most train routes in the northwest Midlands pass through here, and the injunction 'Change at Crewe!' became a familiar one to passengers. For those who have had to wait, advertently or otherwise, for their connections, the name can conjure up bleak recollections:

> I was decanted at Crewe ... and had to wait till six to get a train for Birmingham.
>
> John Buchan: *The Thirty-nine Steps* (1915)

> Oh, mister porter, what shall I do?
> I want to go to Birmingham,
> And they're taking me on to Crewe.
>
> Thomas Le Brun: 'Oh Mister Porter' (1892)

Crewe has not been all trains, though: it is also home to Rolls-Royce and Bentley cars. A Rolls-Royce factory opened here in the Second World War to make aero engines, and after the war moved over to car production. Bentley had transferred from CRICKLEWOOD in 1931.

Abbess of Crewe, The. A novel (1974) by Muriel Spark, in which ecclesiastical and other politics are satirized. It was made into a film as *Nasty Habits* (1977)

Crewe Alexandra. A professional football team based in Crewe, formed in 1877. They originally played on the Alexandra Recreation Ground (whence the name). Their nickname, appropriately enough, is the Railwaymen.

Crewe Train. A novel (1926) by Rose Macaulay, of which the central figure is the silent, anarchic Denham. She shuns the false social world of London in favour of a Cornish cottage, but is eventually sucked back into the capital's vortex.

Crewkerne Probably 'house or building at the hill', OCelt *crug* 'hill' (*see* CREECH, CROOK) + OE *œrn* 'house, building' (although *-erne* may alternatively represent an OCelt suffix). A town in Somerset, about 13 km (8 miles) southwest of Yeovil. It was an important centre in Anglo-Saxon times, when it had the right to mint its own coins. In later centuries its chief industries were flax-weaving and sail-making (HMS *Victory*'s sails were made here).

On Shrove Tuesdays, known in the local dialect as 'Sharp Tuesday', the custom once existed among Crewkerne boys of throwing stones at people's doors.

Crianlarich Possibly 'little place by the ruin', Gaelic *crian* 'little' + *làraich* 'ruined house'.

A Highland village at the junction of three glens – Strath Fillan, Glen Falloch and Glen Dochart. It is about 65 km (40 miles) northwest of Glasgow. It was formerly in Perthshire, then in Central region, and is now in the unitary authority of Stirling. It is on the railway from Glasgow to Fort William, and is where the roads from Glasgow and Edinburgh/Perth meet.

> Crianlarich is the most signposted nowhere on the planet.
>
> Jim Crumley: *Gulfs of Blue Air: A Highland Journey* (1997)

Crib Goch 'red crest', Welsh *crib* 'peak, crest' + *coch* 'red'. A mountain (921 m / 3021 ft) in Snowdonia, Gwynedd (formerly in Caernarvonshire), just to the north of the summit of SNOWDON. Its pinnacled ridge provides a fine scramble as part of the Snowdon Horseshoe, and it is one of the WELSH THREE-THOUSANDERS.

> So high am I upon this lofty chair
> The shouting mountain-torrent's thunderous boom
> Sounds but a murmuring throb upon the air ...
>
> Showell Styles: 'On Crib Goch', from *A Climber in Wales* (1948)

Crib-y-Ddysgl. *See under* SNOWDON.

Criccieth. The English name for CRICIETH.

Crichel Down 'hill called Crichel', *Crichel* 'hill-hill' (OCelt *crug* (*see* CREECH, CROOK) + OE *hyll* 'hill') + OE *dun* (*see* DOWN, -DON); the name is thus triply tautologous.

An area of downland in Dorset, in the parish of Long Crichel, to the northeast of BLANDFORD FORUM, which in the middle of the 20th century was at the centre of a political scandal. In 1938, 293 ha (725 acres) of agricultural land here were compulsorily purchased from three separate owners so that a military airfield could be constructed. After the Second World War the original owners wanted to buy the land back, but the Ministry of Agriculture refused to sell, taking the view that it would be better kept in single ownership. The would-be buyers protested vigorously, there was a judicial enquiry, and in 1954 several named civil servants were blamed for acting incorrectly. The minister, Sir Thomas Dugdale, took the blame on his shoulders and resigned. The case was the basis of the so-called **'Crichel Down rules'**, defining the bounds of ministerial responsibility.

Cricieth 'mound of the captives', Welsh *crug* 'hill' (*see* CREECH, CROOK) + *caith* 'captives' (presumably referring to castle). A small coastal resort on Cardigan Bay in Gwynedd (formerly in Caernarvonshire), 7 km (4.5 miles) west of Porthmadog. The anglicized spelling is **Criccieth**, which offends local nationalists, so most road signs round here have one 'c' painted out. The ruined castle (1230) was captured from the Welsh by Edward I in 1282, and retaken by Owain Glyndwr in 1404. Nearby is Yr Ogof Ddu ('the black cave') where long ago a piper and two fiddlers were lured by the fairies, never to be seen again – although their music is still (apparently) sometimes heard.

Cricieth was the birthplace of Lady Megan Lloyd George (1902–66), younger daughter of the Liberal prime minister, who herself became a Liberal and then a Labour MP.

Crick 'rock, cliff', OCelt *creig*.
A village in Northamptonshire, just to the east of the M1, about 21 km (13 miles) northwest of Northampton.

Cricket Malherbie *Cricket* 'small hill', OCelt *crug* 'hill' (*see* CREECH, CROOK) + OFr *-ette* 'small'; *Malherbie* denoting manorial ownership in the Middle Ages by the *Malherbe* family.
A village (pronounced 'malerbi') in Somerset, about 3 km (2 miles) northeast of Chard.

Cricket St Thomas *St Thomas* from the dedication of the local church.
A village in Somerset, about 5 km (3 miles) east of Chard. It is home to the National Heavy Horse Centre.

Cricket House in Cricket St Thomas played the part of Grantleigh Manor in the BBC television sitcom *To the Manor Born* (1979–81).

Crickhowell 'mound of Hywel', Welsh *crug* 'hill' (*see* CREECH, CROOK) + personal name *Hywel*; it takes its name from a hillfort on Table Mountain to the north of the town.
A small town on the River USK[1], on the south side of the Black Mountains in Powys (formerly in Brecknockshire), 9 km (5.5 miles) northwest of Abergavenny. The Welsh version of the name is **Crucywel**. It is a centre for outdoor activities, including caving, and on May Day there is a leek-throwing contest of cod antiquity. There is also an annual tug-of-war across the River Usk in August.

Crickhowell House in Cardiff was the provisional meeting place of the Welsh Assembly from 1999, before the completion of purpose-built premises.

Cricklade 'river-crossing at the rock or hill' (probably referring to a prominent isolated hill just to the west of the town), OCelt *creig* 'rock' or *crug* 'hill' (*see* CREECH, CROOK) + OE (*ge*)*lad* 'way, passage, river-crossing'.
A town in Wiltshire, on the River Thames, about 11 km (7 miles) northwest of Swindon. The River CHURN joins the Thames here.

Cricklewood 'curved wood, wood with an indented outline', ME *crikeled* 'curved' + *wode* 'wood'.
A northwestern suburb of Greater London, just to the south of the southern end of the M1, in the boroughs of Barnet and Brent (NW2). The fields did not succumb here until the late 19th century, when a wave of house-building wrought a sudden transformation. There is some light industry, which formerly included the manufacture of Bentley motor cars (1920–31). In the 1920s Cricklewood Aerodrome was a London–Paris passenger terminus.

Cricklewood Green was the title of a 1970 album by the fairly heavy metal group Ten Years After, and has since been adopted by an Ohio (USA) lawn maintenance company. The journalist Alan Coren (b.1938), the self-styled '**Sage of Cricklewood**', has regularly woven the idiosyncracies of the suburb into his humorous columns in *The Times* and in publications such as *The Cricklewood Diet* (1982), *A Year in Cricklewood* (1991) and *The Cricklewood Dome* (1998).

The district's fairly large Jewish population earned it in the 1970s the facetious nickname '**Cricklewitch**', featuring an adaptation of the 'Jewish' suffix *-vich* in place of *-wood*.

Crieff Gaelic *craobh* 'place among the trees'.
A town situated above the River EARN, 25 km (16 miles) west of Perth, in Perth and Kinross (formerly in Perthshire, and then in Tayside region). The town was once known as Drummond, from the name of the local landed family. In 1491, to the west of the town, the Drummonds burned alive in a church many Murrays (men, women and children); a mausoleum marks the spot. The Drummonds later became dukes of Perth, but their estates were forfeited after the 1745 Jacobite Rising (the town itself was burned by the Jacobites in the 1715 Rising). In the 19th century Crieff became known as a spa town. On the north side of the town is the hill known as the **Knock of Crieff** (278 m / 911 ft).

Criffel 'split mountain', Old Norse *kryfja* 'to split' + *fjall* 'fell, mountain'.
A round-backed, isolated mountain (569 m / 1866 ft) 15 km (9 miles) south of Dumfries. It stands above the NITH estuary and the Solway Firth, in Dumfries and Galloway (formerly in Dumfriesshire), and can be seen clearly from the northern Lake District hills. William Wordsworth mentions 'Huge Criffel's hoary top' in his poem 'At the Grave of Burns' (1803), and Robert Burns himself features the hill in one of his less memorable pieces, 'The Dumfries Volunteers', a 'patriotic effusion' written in 1795:

> The Nith shall run to Corsincon,
>   And Criffel sink in Solway,
> E'er we permit a foreign foe
>   On British ground to rally!
>
> (Corsincon is a hill near the source of the Nith.)

Crimea Pass After the name of an inn, now long gone.
A pass (385 m / 1263 ft) on the A470 between BETWS-Y-COED and BLAENAU FFESTINIOG, in Gwynedd (formerly in Carnarvonshire). Its Welsh name is **Bwlch y Gorddinan**.

Crimond 'boundary hill or moor', Gaelic *crioch* 'boundary' + *monadh* 'moor, hill'.
A village in northeast BUCHAN, Aberdeenshire (formerly in Grampian region), 13 km (8 miles) northwest of Peterhead. It is notable for having given its name to one of the tunes to which the 23rd Psalm ('The Lord's my Shepherd') is sung,

composed in 1871 by Jessie Seymour Irvine (1836–87), daughter of the minister of Crimond, the Rev. Alexander Irvine. It was at one time credited to a David Grant, but it appears that Jessie wrote the tune and then sent it to Grant, who provided the harmony.

Crinan Canal Etymology unknown.

A canal that crosses the north end of the Kintyre peninsula, in Argyll and Bute (formerly in Strathclyde region). The canal links Loch Fyne and the Sound of JURA, so allowing sailors to avoid a 210-km (130-mile) voyage round the Mull of KINTYRE. It was built in 1793–1801, and extends 14.5 km (9 miles) between Ardrishaig on the east and the village of **Crinan** on **Crinan Loch** on the west. There are 15 locks, and today the canal is mostly used by pleasure boats. In 1847 Queen Victoria was conveyed along the canal in a horse-drawn canal boat, and found the passage of the locks 'tedious', although, as she noted in her journal, 'the views of the hills … were very fine indeed'.

Cripplegate Literally 'creeping-gate', that is, a low gate in a wall, OE *crypel-geat*; later associated with *cripple*.

One of the original gates of the City of London (*see under* LONDON), built by the Romans. It stood at the northern end of Wood Street, in the area of the modern BARBICAN. It was demolished in 1760, but is commemorated in the nearby **Cripplegate Street**.

Its unetymological connection with cripples goes back to the early Middle Ages, by which time the legend had grown up that some cripples had been miraculously cured when the body of Edmund the Martyr (*c*.840–70) was brought through the gate in 1010. The church of St Giles without Cripplegate in Fore Street, which was founded in the 11th century, is dedicated to St Giles, the patron saint of cripples. It was destroyed by bombing in the Second World War, but rebuilt as part of the Barbican development.

Cripplesease From the name of an inn near the top of a long hill; first recorded in the 19th century.

A village in Cornwall, about 3 km (2 miles) south of St Ives.

Crix Named after the *de Creyk* family, known here from the 13th century.

A village in Essex, about 8 km (5 miles) northeast of Chelmsford.

Croagh Patrick Irish *Cruach Phádraig* 'St Patrick's peak'; *cruach* originally meant 'stack' or 'rick'.

A mountain (765 m / 2510 ft) of pyramidal symmetry in County Mayo, rising steeply above the south side of CLEW BAY. It is also familiarly known as **the Reek** ('ridge', 'crest', from English *rick*, a translation of Irish *cruach*, hence Croagh Patrick). On its summit, throughout Lent in the year 441, St Patrick supposedly fasted, holding out for the right to act as defence counsel for the Irish on Judgement Day. It was from here, too, that he is said to have issued his *fatwa*

against all the snakes in Ireland, and to have dealt harshly with a number of demons. To this day, on the last Sunday of July, thousands of pilgrims climb to hear Mass at the oratory at the top, many of the greater sinners walking barefoot over the sharp quartzite screes.

> Here they go clambering for soul's arrears
> As if dog-weariness could blot their tears
> Against the thundering doom that weights the skies
> And threatens every hope to pulverize.
>
> George Brandon Saul: 'Pilgrims of Croagh Patrick', from
> *Adam Unregenerate: Selected Lyrical Poems* (1977)

Croak Park. The punning nickname for Dublin's GLASNEVIN CEMETERY, which is near CROKE PARK stadium. The cemetery is playfully referred to as 'the dead centre of Dublin'.

Croakumshire. A former nickname for NORTHUMBERLAND, whose inhabitants were alleged to speak with a peculiar croak. It was said to be particularly noticeable in Newcastle and Morpeth, where the people were believed to be born with a burr in their throats that prevented them voicing the letter 'r'.

Crofton[1] 'farmstead near a hill', OE *crop(p)* 'hill' + -TON.

An outer suburb of southeast London, in the borough of Bromley (before 1965, in Kent). It contains the remains of a Romano-British villa. To the north, **Crofton Heath** adjoins Bromley Common.

Crofton[2] 'farm with a croft', OE *croft* 'small enclosed field' + -TON; *Scroftune* 1086.

A village in West Yorkshire, 5 km (3 miles) southeast of Wakefield.

Crofton[3] *See* CROFTON[2].

A village in Wiltshire, 9 km (5.5 miles) southwest of Hungerford.

Croft-on-Tees OE *croft* 'small enclosed field' + river name (*see* TEES).

A village on the border between Darlington unitary authority (formerly part of County Durham) and North Yorkshire, 5 km (3 miles) south of Darlington. The father of C.L. Dodgson (Lewis Carroll) was rector at Croft-on-Tees, and the boy spent his school holidays here.

Croghan Mountain Irish *Cruachán* 'little rick or peak'.

An isolated hill (605 m / 1984 ft) on the border of WICKLOW and WEXFORD, 11 km (7 miles) west of Arklow.

Croglin 'torrent with a bend', OE *croc* 'crooked, bent' + *hlynn* 'torrent'.

A village in Cumbria (formerly in Cumberland), 19 km (12 miles) southeast of Carlisle. It is on the **Croglin Water**, beneath **Croglin Fell**.

Bat of Croglin, the. Apparently a vampire that in 1875 attacked a young Australian, Emily Cranswell, who was staying at Croglin Low Hall. One night a human-like creature wearing a great black cloak and smelling of decay broke through Emily's window and bit the terrified woman about the neck and face. On a subsequent occasion, Emily's brothers waited in readiness for the creature, and when it appeared chased it to the churchyard, where it disappeared into a vault. The vault was opened, and inside was the part-decayed body of a man – with fresh blood at his mouth. Needless to say, a stake was promptly produced and driven into the creature's heart.

Crois Mhic Lionnáin. The Irish name for CROSSMAGLEN.

Croit e Caley 'Caley's croft', Manx Gaelic *croit* 'croft' + surname *Caley*.
A village on the Isle of Man, 4 km (2.5 miles) northwest of Castletown.

Croke Park Named after Dr Thomas *Croke*, Archbishop of Cashel and a founder-patron of the Gaelic Athletic Association in 1884.
The national stadium, in the north of DUBLIN, of Ireland's Gaelic Athletic Association. Since the GAA bought the site in 1913, Croke Park has been the venue for the All-Ireland Gaelic football and hurling finals and other championship matches. It is known affectionately to Dubliners as **Croker**.

On 21 November 1920 Croke Park was the scene of the Bloody Sunday massacre, in which Auxiliaries of the Royal Irish Constabulary opened fire indiscriminately during a Gaelic football match between Dublin and Tipperary, killing 13 people, including a member of the Tipperary team (who is commemorated in the stadium's Hogan Stand). The GAA had long been a hotbed of Republicanism, and the shooting followed the assassination that morning by Michael Collins's men of 14 members of British Intelligence active in the city.

The name of the standing terrace at Croke Park known as Hill 16 also commemorates a Republican tragedy: the stand was built using rubble from the devastation wreaked on Sackville Street (now O'CONNELL STREET) during the Easter Rising of 1916; the name may also play on all those numbered hills in Flanders so bloodily fought over on the Western Front during the First World War.
See also CROAK PARK.

'Ghost Train for Croke Park, The'. A 1955 poem by Sigerson Clifford, referring to the midnight 'ghost trains' from the provinces caught by those heading for the All-Ireland Football Championship at Croke Park.

> And we gave the Kerry war-cry as we marched north two by two
> To lep aboard the ghost train for Croke Park.

Cromar Possibly 'sheepfold of Mar', Gaelic *crò* + MAR, the name of the district.
A traditional area north of Aboyne and the River Dee, in Aberdeenshire (formerly in Grampian region).

Cromarty The earliest reference, *Crumbathyn*, in the 13th century, suggests 'crooked sea-place', Gaelic *crom*, *crumb* 'crooked' + a doubtful element, possibly OCelt *bath* 'sea', later influenced by ARD 'height'.
A BURGH and port on the northeastern tip of the BLACK ISLE, formerly in Ross and Cromarty and now in Highland. It is 25 km (16 miles) northeast of Inverness, and was once the county town of the old patchwork county of Cromarty, which became part of ROSS AND CROMARTY in 1889. It was the birthplace of Sir Thomas Urquart (1611–60), the eccentric Royalist and translator of Rabelais; and of Hugh Miller (1802–56), the pioneering geologist.

In the version of *Macbeth* by Andrew of Wyntoun (*c*.1350–*c*.1425), the 'thre werd sisteris' predict that Macbeth will be 'thayne of Crumbaghty', i.e. Cromarty.

Cromarty. A sea area in the shipping forecast. It is situated south of Fair Isle, west of Forties and north of Forth.

Cromarty Firth. The long narrow inlet, fed by the River Conon, on the north side of the Black Isle. It was an important deep-water anchorage in both world wars (*see also* INVERGORDON).

Sutors of Cromarty, the Scots *souter* 'cobbler'.
The two hills above cliffs that guard the north and south sides of the mouth of the Cromarty Firth. The **North Sutor** is 148 m (486 ft) high, and the **South Sutor** is 141 m (463 ft).

Cromdale 'crooked water meadows', Gaelic *crom* 'crooked' + *dail* 'water meadow' (referring to the meanders of the River Spey).
A village on the River SPEY, formerly in Moray and now in Highland, 5 km (3 miles) northeast of Grantown-on-Spey. The **Haughs of Cromdale** is the area of land east of the village (Scots *haugh* 'alluvial land by a river'), and also gives its name to a traditional strathspey.

Battle of the Haughs of Cromdale (1 May 1690). The final rout of the Jacobites in Scotland during the Glorious Revolution. The Highlanders were commanded by General Buchan, and were caught by surprise by Sir Thomas Livingston's government troops.

Hills of Cromdale. A line of hills running southwest–northeast, to the east of the village of Cromdale. The highest point is Creagan a'Chaise (722 m / 2368 ft).

Cromer 'lake frequented by crows', OE *crawe* 'crow' + *mere* 'lake'.
A town and resort on the north Norfolk coast, about 34 km (21 miles) north of Norwich. The town itself is set on a cliff above the extensive sandy beaches that have proved a draw to holidaymakers since Victorian times.

Fishing still carries on, as it did before the tourists came, and Cromer is especially famous for its crabs.

Albert Einstein lived in Cromer for a short time in 1933, having fled Hitler's Germany and before moving on to America.

There was an Old Person of Cromer,
Who stood on one leg to read Homer;
When he found he grew stiff, he jumped over the cliff,
Which concluded that Person of Cromer.

Edward Lear: *A Book of Nonsense* (1846)

Cromer Forest Bed. A series of deposits which outcrops on the coast at Cromer, comprising two freshwater beds that enclose the Forest Bed proper, an estuarine bed of clay containing the transported remains of trees and rich in plant and animal fossils. It was probably deposited during the first interglacial period, in the early Pleistocene.

Cromerian. Of or relating to the Cromer Forest Bed, to the first interglacial period of the early Pleistocene or to an ancient culture or people formerly thought to be represented by remains found in Pliocene deposits near Cromer.

Cromford 'ford by the bend of a river' OE *crumbe* 'bend' + FORD.

A village in Derbyshire, on the River DERWENT[4], 5 km (3 miles) south of Matlock. A cotton-spinning mill, based on water power, was set up here in 1771 by the cotton manufacturer Sir Richard Arkwright, who greatly enlarged the village in order to house his new workforce.

The bold rock opposite this house is now disfigur'd by a row of new houses built under it, and the vales are every way blocked up with mills ... These cotton mills, seven storeys high and filled with inhabitants, remind me of a first-rate man-of-war, and, when they are lighted up on a dark night, look most luminously beautiful.

Col. John Byng: 18 June 1790 (on the Arkwright mill at Cromford)

Cromhghlinn. The Irish name for HILLSBOROUGH[1].

Cronebane Possibly Irish *Crón Bán* 'white hollow', but *Cruadhán* 'hard ground' is also possible.

A former copper mine in Co. Wicklow. It gave its name to a copper coin issued *c*.1790 and worth one halfpenny. In Hiberno-English a cronebane, as in such expressions as 'It's not worth a cronebane', has become the epitome of worthlessness.

Cronk-y-Voddy Possibly 'old man's hill', Manx Gaelic *cronk* 'hill' + *boiddagh* 'old man'.

A village on the Isle of Man, 6 km (4 miles) northeast of Peel.

Crook 'land in a secluded corner', OE *croc* 'bend'; *Cruketona* 1267 (-TON having subsequently been lost).

A town in County Durham, 13 km (8 miles) southwest of Durham. Its name reflects the fact that it lies in the bend of a tributary of the River WEAR.

Crookhaven Irish *An Cruachán*, 'haven of the little hay rick'. Fishing village and holiday resort in County Cork, on MIZEN HEAD peninsula, 14 km (8.5 miles) southwest of Schull. Crookhaven is the most southerly village in Ireland.

Croome Park *Croome* is from an OCelt river name *Cromba*, meaning 'twisting, crooked'.

A landscape park in Worcestershire, 9 km (5.5 miles) west of Pershore, celebrated for being the first complete landscape by 'Capability' Brown. Commissioned by the 6th Earl of Coventry, of nearby **Croome Court**, in 1751, Croome Park established a new style of English garden design incorporating not only natural elements but classical-style buildings and water features (all of which would be widely adopted over the next 50 years). The park includes buildings and other structures by Robert Adam and James Wyatt, including eye-catchers to divert the viewer's attention towards specially designed vistas. The MALVERN HILLS provide a dramatic backdrop to the park. Croome Court is privately owned, but the park is now owned by the National Trust who is restoring the gardens and its buildings.

Croppies Acre After the *Croppies*, the nickname of the insurgents of 1798 who wore close-cropped hair in imitation of the French Jacobins.

An area near the Collins Barracks (formerly the Royal Barracks) in DUBLIN, used as a mass grave for those executed in the wake of the 1798 United Irishmen's Rebellion. It is also called **Croppies Hole**.

No rising column marks this spot,
Where many a victim lies;
But Oh! The blood which here has streamed
To Heaven for justice cries.

Robert Emmet: 'Arbour Hill', a poem about Croppies Acre

Emmet's plea for a monument to the Croppies did not go unheeded. A mere 182 years after his death (1803) a large granite block was raised on the spot, inscribed with a simple '1798'. The Croppies were also, more swiftly, commemorated in a number of ballads entitled '**The Croppy Boy**'.

Cropredy 'Croppa's small stream' or 'small stream near a hill', OE male personal name *Croppa* or *crop(p)* 'hill' + *rithig* 'small stream'.

A village (pronounced 'kropreedy') in Oxfordshire, about 6.5 km (4 miles) north of Banbury, on the Oxford Canal. Cropredy was the birthplace of the Labour politician and diarist Richard Crossman (1907–74).

Battle of Cropredy Bridge (29 June 1644). A battle in the Civil Wars, in which Royalist forces under Baron Henry Wilmot (later the 1st Earl of Rochester) defeated a Parliamentarian army commanded by Sir William Waller. It was a hollow victory for the Royalists, whose northern army was crushed at MARSTON MOOR a few days later.

Crosby 'village of crosses' OScand *krossa* (*see* CROSS) + -BY.

A seaside town in Merseyside (formerly in Lancashire), 9 km (5.5 miles) north of Liverpool. It overlooks the **Crosby Channel** leading south towards the MERSEY.

❖ cross ❖

This element was borrowed by Old Celtic from Latin *crux*, as was the Old English word *cruc*. OE *cruc* produced relatively few names, but is found in, for example, in CROUCH END and CRUTCHED FRIARS (London). The Brittonic word becomes Welsh *croes*, Irish *crois*, elements that are found in, for example, Pen-y-Groes (Gwynedd) and Crossboys (County Sligo). These two names illustrate the two main meanings of the element: Pen-y-Groes is at crossing of two main roads, and here means 'cross-roads', whereas the 'yellow cross' of Crossboys can hardly be other than a standing cross.

In Scotland the element is not infrequently found in names of the form Corsby (Ayrshire) or Corsewall (Dumfries and Galloway), where the *-r-* has swapped places with the *-o-*, a change known as metathesis. Another example is Corserine in the

Rhinns of Kells (Dumfries and Galloway). Here the element is Gaelic *crois* or Scots *corse*.

The monumental sense of 'cross' is predominant in Ireland, and it appears that OE *cros*, with this meaning, was introduced in northern England from Ireland via Old Scandinavian *kross*. It gradually replaced two other OE words for 'cross, crucifix' in names and in ordinary speech: *mæl* as in MALDON (Essex) and NEW MALDEN (Greater London), 'cross on a hill'; and *rod* as in RUTHWELL (Dumfries and Galloway). And in due course it took the 'crossroads' meaning as well, but chiefly in minor names. The Old Scandinavian element is found in numerous names in the north and east of England – various examples of CROSBY (Merseyside), Crostwick (Norfolk) and Croston (Lancashire).

At a by-election here in 1981 the former Labour cabinet minister Shirley Williams overturned a large Conservative majority to win the Crosby parliamentary constituency for the Social Democratic Party, then enjoying its brief salad days. Constituency boundary changes contributed to her losing the seat in the 1983 election, but she would be ennobled as Baroness Williams of Crosby in 1993.

Crosby was the birthplace of the Anglican clergyman Robert Runcie (1921–2000), Archbishop of Canterbury (1980–91), known to *Private Eye* as 'Killer' Runcie from his time as a tank officer in the Second World War.

Cross, The. An alternative name for DRAPERSTOWN.

Crossfarnoge Point. An alternative name for FORLORN POINT.

Cross Fell From the cross raised to disperse the demonic powers once thought to occupy the place.

The highest point (893 m / 2929 ft) in the PENNINES, situated on the Pennine Way in eastern Cumbria, 18 km (11 miles) east-northeast of Penrith. Its wide prospects across Durham, Cumbria and Northumberland have led to it being described as 'Sentinel of three great counties'. It was once known as **Fiends Fell**, until St Paulinus (*fl.*5th century) drove out the demons and raised a cross on the summit (no longer there). There is still, one is happy to report, a Fiend's Fell, 8 km (5 miles) to the northwest. On the flanks of Cross Fell above Kirkland are the ancient cultivation terraces known, for a reason apparently unknown to scholars, as 'the Hanging Walls of Mark Antony'.

Cross Hands[1] Probably a reference to the sign at a cross-roads.

A village in Carmarthenshire (formerly in Dyfed), 14 km (8.5 miles) north of Llanelli.

Cross Hands[2]**.** A village in Pembrokeshire (formerly in Dyfed), 5 km (3 miles) southwest of Narberth.

Cross in Hand First recorded (1547) in Latin as *via cruce manus* 'way (leading) by the cross of the hand'. Local legend has it that the village was a meeting place for Crusaders on their way to embark at Rye for the Holy Land.

A village in East Sussex, about 8 km (5 miles) east of Uckfield.

Crosskeys Named after a public house.

A village in Caerphilly (formerly in Monmouthshire, then in Gwent), 7 km (4.5 miles) southwest of Cwmbran.

Crossmaglen Irish *Crois Mhic Lionnáin* 'cross of the son of Lionnán' (whose identity is unknown).

A village in south Armagh, 22 km (14 miles) southwest of Newry. Deep in so-called BANDIT COUNTRY, the place acquired a certain status during the Troubles as the most Republican of Republican heartlands. It was known as **XMG** to British soldiers serving in Northern Ireland.

Crossmyloof 'cross of Maoldubh', Gaelic *crois* 'cross' + male personal name *Maoldubh*; several saints of this name are known.

An area in the South Side of GLASGOW, once famous for its skating rink. In Glasgwegian rhyming slang *Crossmyloof* means 'poof', i.e. homosexual.

Cross o' th' Hands Perhaps referring to a finger-pointing signpost at a crossroads.

A village in Derbyshire, about 8 km (5 miles) west of Belper.

Crotty's Lake. *See under* COMERAGH MOUNTAINS.

Crouch[1] Probably from a lost place name *Crouch*, from OE *cruc* (*see* CROSS).

A river in Essex, which rises to the south of BILLERICAY and flows 39 km (24 miles) eastwards, broadening out less than halfway along its length into an estuary with many creeks, flats and islands, before entering the North Sea to the north of FOULNESS. BURNHAM ON CROUCH is on its north bank, about 8 km (5 miles) from its mouth.

Crouch² '(place with) a cross', OE *cruc* (*see* CROSS), ME *crouch*.
A village in Kent, about 10 km (6 miles) east of Sevenoaks.

Crouch End 'district around the cross' (probably referring to a wayside cross that once stood at a road junction in the area), ME *crouche* 'cross' (*see* CROSS) + *ende* 'district'.
A northern inner suburb of Greater London (N8), between Highgate and Hornsey, in the borough of HARINGEY. Situated in a hollow below the heights of Highgate, MUS-WELL HILL¹ and Alexandra Palace, it has a self-contained feel, as if semi-detached from the rest of London (it has been nicknamed 'Sleepy Hollow', after Washington Irving's 'The Legend of Sleepy Hollow' (1820)). Over the years it has achieved a certain desirability without giving itself excessive airs.

Other nicknames for it include 'Couch End' (from the inordinate number of psychoanalysts, therapists, etc. per square kilometre) and 'Nappy Valley' (people supposedly move here when they have babies). By contrast, in Will Self's short story 'The North London Book of the Dead' (1991), old people, rather than dying, are found to have moved to Crouch End.

A notable contemporary-music choir, the **Crouch End Festival Chorus**, was founded in 1985 by two residents, and it now records and performs at national venues. Local folklore associates the area with Bob Dylan, who reputedly waited patiently in the suburban front room of a local resident coincidentally named 'Dave', under the mistaken impression that the house belonged to rock-musician Dave Stewart, owner of a Crouch End recording studio.

The actress Jean Simmons was born in Crouch End in 1929.

Crowborough 'hill frequented by crows', OE *crawe* 'crow' + *beorg* 'hill, mound'.
A village in East Sussex, about 11 km (7 miles) southwest of Tunbridge Wells and just to the east of ASHDOWN FOREST.

Groombridge Place, a red-brick Jacobean house about 6 km (4 miles) to the north, is almost certainly the scene of a murder in Conan Doyle's Sherlock Holmes novel *The Valley of Fear* (1915). The house in the book is described as being 'a Jacobean brick house ... on the fringe of the great Weald Forest'.

Crowland 'land at the bend', OE *cruw* 'bend' + *land* 'land, estate'. The name refers to a bend in the River Welland.
A town in the Lincolnshire Fens, on the River WELLAND, 8 km (5 miles) east of Deeping St James. **Crowland Abbey**, founded in 716 by King Æthelbald in memory of St

Guthlac, a fenland recluse, and twice burned in the Middle Ages before its final dissolution in 1539, is now the parish church. Hereward the Wake (*see* Isle of Ely *under* ELY¹) is said to be buried here. In the centre of the town is the curious triangular Trinity Bridge, built between 1360 and 1390, and consisting of three stone arches meeting at an angle of 120 degrees. They originally spanned three streams of the River Welland, but now stand over dry land.

Croyland History, The. A chronicle of medieval church life that was long attributed to Ingulf, abbot of Croyland (Crowland) and secretary to William I (the Conqueror). In the 19th century, however, scholars grew suspicious of some aspects of the History, not least its claim that Crowland's 14th-century triangular bridge was built in the 10th century, and for crediting the monks of the Abbey with implausible longevity – life-spans of 115, 142 and 148 years being cited. In the end the scholars decided that the History was a 15th-century forgery.

Crow Road. *See* the CRAW ROAD.

Crowthorne 'thorn-tree frequented by crows', ModE.
A small town in Berkshire, within the unitary authority of Wokingham, about 16 km (10 miles) southeast of Reading. It grew up in the 1860s following the establishment nearby of Wellington College (royal charter 1853; opened 1859 in memory of the Duke of Wellington) – traditionally the public school chosen by military men for the education of their sons, SANDHURST being just down the road – and BROADMOOR asylum (1863). It inherited the name of an ancient hawthorn tree at a junction of the roads from Bracknell and Wokingham.

Surgeon of Crowthorne, The. A book (1998) by Simon Winchester about the bizarre case of Dr W.C. Minor, former millionaire American Civil War surgeon-turned-lunatic, who had been imprisoned in Broadmoor for murder. Minor devoted much of his time in the asylum to the study of the English language, and he made copious contributions to the *Oxford English Dictionary*, then in course of compilation.

Croxley Green *Croxley* 'Krokr's glade', OScand male personal name *Krokr* + -LEY.
A village in Hertfordshire, on the GRAND UNION CANAL, about 3 km (2 miles) east of Rickmansworth. Croxley Green 'Underground' station, on the Metropolitan line, was opened in 1925; it was renamed Croxley in 1949.

Every summer the **Croxley Green Revels** are held, 'a tradition that stretches back to 1952' (John Betjeman, *Metroland*, BBC TV (1973)).

Croydon 'valley where wild saffron grows', OE *croh* 'wild saffron', *crogen* 'place where wild saffron grows' + *denu* 'valley'.
A town and borough at the southern edge of Greater

London (before 1965 in Surrey). In the Middle Ages it was mainly notable for containing the summer home of the archbishops of Canterbury: **Croydon Palace**, which was probably built in the 13th century. It was sold in 1780, but the archbishops of Canterbury continued their strong connection with Croydon: they were Lords of the Manor (a title originally granted by William the Conqueror to Archbishop Lanfranc), and they used Addington Palace as a residence until the late 19th century (it is now occupied by the Royal School of Church Music).

From Roman times Croydon had been on an important road from London to the south coast. In 1809 it was linked to London by canal. Then, in 1839, the passenger railway arrived. Croydon's position as a communications hub ensured its rapid growth in the 19th century and its population increased 23-fold between 1801 and 1901:

> Croydon is a good market-town; but is, by the funds,
> swelled out into a wen.
>
> William Cobbett: *Rural Rides* (1830)

In the 20th century it expanded yet further, although the writer in the *Architectural Review* who complained in 1939 of 'that universal Croydon towards which the townscapes of England are tending' would have been still more mortified by the late 20th-century mini-Chicago-style skyline of tall office blocks with which Croydon filled in its considerable Second World War bomb damage. In 1999 a new tram system began to run in Croydon – an idea whose time had come round again.

In the first half of the 20th century, Croydon was also an air communications centre. An airfield was opened here in 1915, originally for defence. It was made London's airport in 1920, and it retained that role until after the Second World War, when Heathrow took over from it. Amy Johnson took off from here on her record-breaking flight to Australia in 1930. The airport was closed in 1959.

Sainsbury's opened their first self-service store in Croydon, in 1950.

The sexologist Havelock Ellis (1859–1939), the actress Dame Peggy Ashcroft (1907–91), the film director Sir David Lean (1908–91), the comedian Roy Hudd (b.1936), the singer-songwriter Kirsty MacColl (1959–2000) and the supermodel Kate Moss (b.1974) were born in Croydon. Dame Peggy is commemorated here in the Ashcroft Theatre (1962; part of the Fairfield Halls entertainment complex). The composer Samuel Coleridge-Taylor (whose father was from Sierra Leone) died in Croydon in 1912, as did Karl Popper in 1994.

D.H. Lawrence came to Croydon as a school teacher in 1908.

There are towns called Croydon in Australia (Queens-land and Western Australia) and New Zealand, and a Croydon mountain range in New Hampshire, USA.

croydon. A type of two-wheeled horse-drawn carriage, introduced about 1850, originally of wicker-work, but afterwards made of wood. The reason for it being named after Croydon is not known.

Croydon facelift. A slang expression of the early 21st century for hair that is scraped back so tightly into a ponytail that it pulls back the skin on the wearer's cheekbones – a style apparently favoured by the proles of Croydon.

Cruacha Gorma. The Irish name for the BLUESTACK MOUNTAINS.

Cruachan[1]. The mountain BEN CRUACHAN.

Cruachan[2] In modern form this is Irish for 'little hill', but it is possible that originally it was a female (?) personal name in the possessive, *Cruachain*.

An ancient kingdom of Ireland prior to the introduction of Christianity. It was one of four kingdoms – along with TARA, AILEACH and AIRGIALLA – to emerge in the 4th century after Ulster split up.

Cruach Phádraig. The Irish name for CROAGH PATRICK.

Crucywel. The Welsh name for CRICKHOWELL.

Cruden Bay Possibly from Gaelic *crùidein* 'kingfisher'.
A village on the east coast of Aberdeenshire (formerly in Grampian region), at the north end of **Bay of Cruden**, 11 km (7 miles) south of Peterhead. It is notable as the landfall of the oil pipeline from the North Sea Forties Field, which continues from here south to GRANGEMOUTH. Nearby is SLAINS CASTLE.

Crumlin Road Irish *croimlinn* 'crooked valley'.
An evocative street in BELFAST. The **Crumlin Road Jail** held many paramilitary prisoners until it was decommissioned after the 1998 Good Friday Agreement. The place inevitably featured in Republican balladry:

> We'll keep the fight until the end,
> We know we cannot fail.
> And there's the reason why today,
> They keep our lads in Crumlin Jail.
>
> Anon.: 'Our Lads in Crumlin Jail'

See also the MAZE.

Crummock Water 'crooked lake', OCelt *crumbaco* 'crooked'.
A lake in the northwestern end of the valley of Buttermere, Cumbria (formerly in Cumberland), 12 km (7.5 miles) southwest of Keswick. Above the southwest side of the lake on Scale Beck are the SCALE FORCE falls.

Crutched Friars '(street of the) Friars of the Holy Cross'; *Crutched* from ME *crouched* 'carrying or wearing a cross', from *crouch* (*see* CROSS). The order of Crutched Friars (which was established in Italy in 1169 and arrived in England in 1244) maintained a small friary in the street in the Middle Ages, founded c.1298.

A street in the City of London (EC3), in the area of FENCHURCH STREET station.

Cruwys Morchard *Cruwys* denoting manorial ownership in the Middle Ages by the de Crues family; *Morchard see* MORCHARD BISHOP.

A village (pronounced 'cruise mortchard') in Devon, 9 km (5.5 miles) west of Tiverton.

Crux Easton *Crux* denoting manorial ownership in the early Middle Ages by the Croc(h) family; *Easton see* EASTON IN GORDANO.

A village in Hampshire, about 19 km (12 miles) northwest of Basingstoke.

Crystal Palace From the 'Crystal Palace', a vast glass pavilion erected here in 1854 (the name of the building was originally conferred by *Punch* magazine).

A district in southeast London, between Sydenham and Penge, in the borough of BROMLEY (SE19, SE20). It takes its name from the original 'Crystal Palace', a monumental glass conservatory designed by Joseph Paxton for the Great Exhibition of 1851. This covered an area of 71,737 sq m (772,289 sq ft) and its iron framework weighed 4064 tonnes (4000 tons). After the exhibition it was dismantled and moved from HYDE PARK to a site in SYDENHAM, where it was re-erected in enlarged form. It was the focal point of an entertainment, sports and exhibition complex in **Crystal Palace Park**. Until 1924 the FA Cup Final was played here, and it was a regular venue for spectacular firework displays (known popularly as 'Brock's benefits', from the name of the firework-maker). But in November 1936 it was destroyed by fire.

Its 85-year life was enough to imprint its name on the surrounding area. Crystal Palace railway station opened in 1854, **Crystal Palace FC** (which since 1924 has played its home games at Selhurst Park in Norwood), was founded in 1905, and the National Sports Centre in Crystal Palace Park commonly answers to 'Crystal Palace'. The BBC television transmitter serving London and southeast England is sited at Crystal Palace.

Cuailnge. The Irish name for COOLEY.

Cuan Na gCaorach. The Irish name for SHEEP HAVEN.

Cubittopolis After Thomas *Cubitt* (1788–1855), brother of William (*see* CUBITT TOWN), and the greatest London builder and developer of the early 19th century (with perhaps a pun on *cubit*, an ancient measure of length, often used in connection with buildings) + the suffix *-opolis* 'city'.

A colloquial name applied in the middle of the 19th century to that area of London around Warwick and Eccleston Squares, and hence broadly to PIMLICO. Its eponymous

builder Thomas Cubitt's major creation, backed by his patron the Duke of Westminster, was BELGRAVIA.

Cubitt Town After William *Cubitt* (1791–1863), who developed the area in the 1840s and 1850s to provide homes for workers at the nearby shipyards, factories and docks. Cubitt was Lord Mayor of London 1860–1.

A district in the southeastern corner of the ISLE OF DOGS, in the London borough of TOWER HAMLETS (E14).

Cuckmere Probably 'Cuca's lake', OE male personal name *Cuca* + *mere* 'lake', with the name later transferred to the river.

A river (pronounced 'cook-') in East Sussex. It rises to the south of Heathfield and flows 27 km (17 miles) southwards into the English Channel about 3 km (2 miles) east of Seaford. The bay at its mouth is known as **Cuckmere Haven**.

Cuckold's Point. A promontory on the south bank of the River THAMES[1] in ROTHERHITHE, in the borough of Southwark (SE16). It marks the eastern extremity of the POOL OF LONDON. It was named from the setting up here in 1562 of a pair of cuckold's horns on a maypole (a cuckold – a man whose wife had been unfaithful – was traditionally represented as having horns on his head). As well as being a generalized warning to husbands, this may have had some connection with the Horn Fair at nearby CHARLTON, to which ferry-borne revellers may well have come via the landing place at **Cuckold's Point Stairs**. Local legend says that a miller was granted an estate in the vicinity by King John as compensation for having his wife seduced by the king.

Cuckoo's Nest A 19th-century name, obviously ironic but of uncertain meaning.

A village in Cheshire, about 6.5 km (4 miles) southwest of Chester.

Cudworth 'Cutha's enclosure', OE male personal name + *worth* (*see* -WORTH, WORTHY, -WARDINE); *Cutheworthe* 12th century.

A village in South Yorkshire, 5km (3 miles) northeast of Barnsley.

Cúil an tSúdaire. The Irish name for PORTARLINGTON.

Cuilcagh Irish *Binn Chuilceach* 'chalky peak'.

The highest point (667 m / 2188 ft) of the **Cuilcagh Mountains** of counties Cavan and Fermanagh. Cuilcagh itself is on the border between Northern Ireland and the Republic, 20 km (12 miles) southwest of Enniskillen. Shannon Pot, the source of the SHANNON, is in the Cuilcagh Mountains.

Cuillin, the Etymology uncertain. Those of a romantic disposition have suggested that the range is named after either *Cùil Fhionn*, the hiding place of Finn MacCool (or Fingal, *see* FINGAL'S CAVE), or after another Irish hero, Cuchulain. The latter was Sir Walter Scott's favoured explanation: 'Coolin the

ridge, as bards proclaim, / From old Cuchullin, chief of fame'
(*Lord of the Isles*, Canto III, xv).

A jagged mountain range of almost alpine grandeur in
SKYE, formerly in Inverness-shire and now in Highland.
An anglicized version of the name (now rarely used) is **the
Coolins**. They are also known as **the Cuillin Hills**, although
if any hills in Britain deserve to be called mountains, it is
they:

> The tops of the ridge, apparently inaccessible to human
> foot, were rent and split into the most tremendous
> pinnacles ... and the mountains rose so perpendicularly
> from the water edge, that Borrowdale, or even Glencoe, is
> a jest to them.
>
> Sir Walter Scott: journal (August 1814)

Scott later put his impressions into verse:

> Huge terraces of granite black
> Afforded rude and cumber'd track;
>   For from the mountain hoar,
> Hurl'd headlong in some night of fear,
> When yell'd the wolf and fled the deer,
>   Loose crags had toppl'd o'er ...

He goes on to describe fairly mild weather conditions for
these often rain-drenched peaks:

> The evening mists, with ceaseless change,
> Now clothed the mountain's lofty range,
>   Now left their foreheads bare,
> And round their skirts their mantle furl'd,
> Or on the sable waters curl'd,
> Or on the eddying breezes whirl'd,
>   Dispers'd in middle air.
>
> Sir Walter Scott: *The Lord of the Isles* (1815), Canto III, xv (In
> the poem, unhistorically, Scott has Robert the Bruce
> wandering among the Cuillin.)

Later in the 19th century the range drew the gentlemen-
mountaineers, who explored their mighty crags and secret
summits with a passionate vigour. One such explorer was
Professor Norman Collie (1859–1942), who described the
allure of the Cuillin thus:

> Not the mystery of clearness such as is seen in the Alps
> and Himalaya, where range after range recedes into the
> infinite distance, till the white snow peaks cannot be
> distinguished from the clouds, but in the secret beauty
> born of the mists, the rain, and the sunshine in a quiet
> untroubled land, no longer vexed by the more rude and
> violent manifestations of the active powers of nature.

The name is usually taken to refer to the jagged **Black
Cuillin** (so called because it consists of gabbro with basalt
intrusions), whereas the more rounded and lower **Red
Cuillin** (or Red Hills) to the northeast are largely red granite.
The Black Cuillin comprise a main ridge roughly in the
shape of a horseshoe around LOCH CORUISK, plus the outlying ridge of BLA BHEINN to the east. The main ridge

includes many peaks, including Sgùrr na Ciche (with the
famous CIOCH), SGÙRR ALAISDAIR, SGÙRR MHIC CHOIN-
NICH, the INACCESSIBLE PINNACLE, AM BÀSTEIR, and SGÙRR
NAN GILLEAN. Some of these peaks require rock-climbing
to reach their summits, the only mountains in Britain to
do so, and the traverse of the main ridge in a single day is a
long and serious mountaineering expedition.

> Oh the far Coolins are puttin' love on me
> As step I wi' my cromack to the Isles.
>
> Kenneth MacLeod: 'The Road to the Isles' (1917) (MacLeod
> was a native of Eigg.) (*cromack*, from Gaelic *cromach*
> 'walking-stick')

In 2001 MacLeod of Dunvegan put the Cuillin Hills
on the market, in the hope of raising millions of pounds
to repair the roof of his castle. The proposed sale raised
objections from those who questioned Macleod's ownership, given that in Highland tradition the clan chief holds
land on behalf of his clan, and not solely in his own right.
By 2003 Macleod had failed to find a private buyer,
and entered into negotiation with the John Muir Trust,
Highlands and Islands Enterprise and Highland Council.

The **Cuillin Sound** separates Skye from RUM to the south,
and the craggy mountains of Rum are also called the
Cuillin.

> Beyond misery, despair, hatred, treachery,
> Beyond guilt and defilement; watchful, heroic, the
>   Cuillin is seen
> Rising on the other side of sorrow.
>
> Sorley MacLean: 'The Cuillin', *From Wood to Ridge: Collected
> Poems* (1985)

> Out of the sway of wild flowers
> I turn to the tent
> And the coiled rope
> And the coolness.
> My limbs rest on turf
> And there is only night now –
> Night
> And the Black Cuillin waiting.
>
> Anne B. Murray: 'End of a Day in Skye'

Cúil Mhuine. The Irish name for COLLOONEY.

Cúil na Baice. The Irish name for CULLYBACKEY.

Cúil Raithin. The Irish name for COLERAINE.

Cúirt an Phaoraigh. The Irish name for POWERSCOURT.

Cúl Dreimhne. *See under* BENBULBEN.

Culdrose Etymology unknown, but probably includes
Cornish *ros* 'promontory' or 'moorland'.

A village in Cornwall, immediately to the southwest of
Helston. It is home to **Culdrose Royal Naval Air Station**, an
important helicopter base, which does much air-sea rescue
work.

Culham 'Cula's river-meadow', OE male personal name *Cula* + *hamm* (*see also* HAM).

A village in Oxfordshire, about 10 km (6 miles) south of Oxford. There is an important atomic-energy research laboratory here.

Cullen 'little nook', Gaelic *cùilan*.

An attractive fishing port on the north coast of Moray (formerly in Banffshire, then in Grampian region), 17 km (11 miles) west of Banff. It overlooks the picturesque **Cullen Bay** with its various isolated rocks, such as the Three Kings and the Bow Fiddle. Dr Johnson visited in 1773, and turned down a breakfast of dried haddock. Cullen was the model for the village of 'Portlossie' in George Macdonald's sentimental kailyard novel *Malcolm* (1875).

See also BAUDS OF CULLEN.

Cullen skink. A fish soup involving smoked haddock, onion, mace, cream, milk, parsley and mashed potatoes. 'Skink' does not refer to the small lizard, but is rather an old Scots word for 'shin', 'knuckle' (from the Middle Dutch word *schenke*), which also denoted a soup made from shin of beef. In the coastal village of Cullen, the beef was replaced by fish.

Culloden Muir 'moor at the back of the little pool', Gaelic *cùl lodain*, 'the back of the little pool' + Scots *muir* 'moor'.

The site of the **Battle of Culloden**, the last battle fought on British soil, 8 km (5 miles) east of Inverness, in Highland (formerly in Inverness-shire). It is also (although rarely) called the **Battle of Drummossie Muir**, of which Culloden Muir is a part.

> The lovely lass o' Inverness,
>   Nae joy nor pleasure can she see;
> For e'en and morn she cries, alas!
>   And ay the saut tear blin's her e'e.
> Drumossie moor – Drumossie day –
>   A waeful' day it was to me!
> For there I lost my father dear,
>   My father dear, and brethren three.
>
> Robert Burns: 'The Lovely Lass of Inverness' (published posthumously)

The battle is said to have been predicted by the Brahan Seer (*see under* BRAHAN):

> Oh! Drumossie, thy bleak moor shall, ere many generations have passed away, be stained with the best blood of the Highlands. Glad I am that I will not see that day, for it will be a fearful period: heads will be lopped off by the score and no mercy will be shown or quarter given on either side.

On 16 April 1746, at Culloden Muir, a Hanoverian force of 9000 under William, Duke of Cumberland, routed a Jacobite force of 5000 under Bonnie Prince Charlie. There were few casualties on the government side, but 1000 Jacobites were killed, and a 1000 more in the slaughter that followed the 40-minute battle, earning the Duke his nickname 'Butcher' Cumberland. Although the Jacobite force consisted largely of Highlanders, it was assisted by French troops, while on the government side there were considerable numbers of anti-Jacobite Scots. The battle marked the end of the 1745 Jacobite Rebellion. Prince Charles fled the field, and was pursued by the Redcoats around the Highlands and Islands for five months, before making his escape to the Continent.

The battle inspired Tobias Smollett's best-known poem:

> Mourn, hapless Caledonia, mourn
> Thy banished peace, thy laurels torn.
>
> Tobias Smollett: 'The Tears of Scotland' (1746)

Later poets were also inspired:

> Weep, Albin, to death and captivity led.
> Oh weep, but thy tears cannot number the dead:
> For a merciless sword on Culloden shall wave,
> Culloden, that reeks with the blood of the brave.
>
> Thomas Campbell: *Lochiel's Warning*

> 'Ill-starr'd, though brave, did no visions foreboding
>   Tell you that fate had forsaken your cause?'
> Ah! were you destined to die at Culloden,
>   Victory crown'd not your fall with applause ...
>
> Lord Byron: 'Lachin y Gair' (1807). Byron is addressing his Gordon forefathers.

In contrast, the composer Georg Frideric Handel welcomed Cumberland back to London with 'See the Conquering Hero Comes' (in the 1746 oratorio *Judas Maccabeus*).

The memorial cairn and markers of the clan graves at Culloden were erected in 1881, and the battle site is now in the care of the National Trust for Scotland. Hugh MacDiarmid described the place as 'black as Hell'.

There is a town called Culloden in the USA (Georgia), and a Culloden River in Australia (Queensland).

> ... much later, bards from Tiree and Mull
> would write of exile in the hard town
> where mills belched English, anger of new school ...
>
> Iain Crichton Smith: 'Culloden and After'

Cullompton 'farmstead on the River Culm', OCelt *Culm* river name meaning 'winding stream' + -TON.

A small town in Devon, on the River Culm, about 18 km (11 miles) northeast of Exeter. Cullompton Services on the M5 are just to the east.

Cullybackey Irish *Cúil na Baice* 'nook of the river bend'.

A village in County Antrim, 5 km (3 miles) northwest of Ballymena. Like nearby AHOGHILL, it is sometimes unfairly pilloried on account of its name.

Cullybackey was the birthplace of the 21st president of the USA, Chester Alan Arthur (1830–86).

Cul Mòr A somewhat difficult name, in that Gaelic *cul* means 'back of (something)'; *mòr* 'big' distinguishes it from the neighbouring Cul Beag.

An isolated, twin-peaked bastion of a mountain (849 m / 2785 ft) in northwest Highland, 20 km (12 miles) north of ULLAPOOL. To its south lies the equally craggy **Cul Beag** (769 m / 2523 ft; Gaelic *beag* 'small'), and the two mountains are among several striking eruptions from the hummocked boglands of COIGACH and ASSYNT, others being STAC POLLAIDH, Suilven and CANISP. For Cul Mòr's imagined carryings-on with its neighbour to the north, *see* SUILVEN.

> Wagnerian Devil wrote the Coigach score;
> And God was Mozart when he wrote Cul Mor.
>
> Norman MacCaig : 'Moment Musical in Assynt', from *The White Bird* (1973)

Culross 'holly point', Gaelic *cuillenn* 'holly' + *ros* 'promontory', or possibly OCelt *celyn* 'holly' + *rhos* 'moorland'.

A royal BURGH (1588) in Fife, 9 km (5.5 miles) west of Dunfermline, on the north shore of the Firth of Forth. It is pronounced 'coo-ross'. It was once an important port, and many fine buildings from the 16th and 17th centuries are preserved. It was also formerly famous for its iron girdles (griddles):

> Locks and bars, plough-graith and harrow-teeth! and why not grates and fireprongs, and Culross girdles?
>
> Sir Walter Scott: *The Fair Maid of Perth* (1828), Chapter 2

See also TRAPRAIN LAW.

Culter Fell 'back-land fell', Gaelic *cultir* 'back land' + OScand *fjall* 'fell'.

A hill (748 m / 2456 ft) on the border of South Lanarkshire and Scottish Borders, 9 km (5.5 miles) south of Biggar. To its southwest is the small **Culter Waterhead Reservoir**, from which **Culter Water** flows north down to the village of **Coulter**.

Culver Hole OE *culfre* 'a dove' + *hole*.

A partially man-made cave with a masonry frontage in a fissure in the limestone cliffs just west of PORT EYNON Point in the GOWER PENINSULA, Swansea unitary authority (formerly in Glamorgan and then West Glamorgan). It was said to have provided a refuge from the English for a Welsh prince, and later to have been used by smugglers, and then as a dovecot.

Culzean Castle 'nook of the birds', Gaelic *cuil* 'nook' + *ean* 'of the birds'.

A vast neo-gothic mansion above the cliffs on the coast of South Ayrshire (formerly in Strathclyde), 16 km (10 miles) southwest of Ayr. It is pronounced 'cull-ain'. The present house was built in 1777–90 for the Earl of Cassilis (head of the Kennedy family) by Robert Adam, and was handed over, together with its gardens and grounds (now a country park), to the National Trust for Scotland in 1945. Within the castle is a suite of rooms that was reserved for the use of Dwight D. Eisenhower as a gesture of gratitude for his role as Supreme Allied Commander in Europe in the Second World War.

The Kennedy family had lived at Culzean for centuries before the present house was built, and a number of legends attach to them. One of them is a variation on the Bluebeard story in which the daughter of the laird of Culzean is taken off by either 'false Sir John' or an 'elf knight' who has already murdered seven wives. However, his would-be bride manages to push him off a cliff or stab him while he sleeps. It is also said that when a future head of the Kennedy family is about to marry, ghostly piping is heard on Piper's Brae, a tree-lined avenue in the castle grounds.

Cumberland 'land of the Britons', OE *Cumbre* 'Cumbrian Britons' + *land*; *see also* CAMBRIA, CUMBRIA *and* CYMRU.

A former county of northwest England, incorporating the northern part of the LAKE DISTRICT. It was absorbed into CUMBRIA in 1974. Cumberland was bounded by Scotland and the Solway Firth to the north, Northumberland and County Durham to the east, Westmorland and Lancashire to the south, and the Irish Sea to the west. The county town was CARLISLE, and other towns included KESWICK, WORKINGTON and WHITEHAVEN. Cumberland was surrendered in 1157 by Malcolm IV of Scotland to Henry II of England.

> There's a waterfall I'm leaving
> Running down the rocks in foam,
> There's a pool for which I'm grieving
> Near the water-ouzel's home,
> And it's there that I'd be lying
> With the heather close at hand,
> And the curlews faintly crying
> Mid the wastes of Cumberland.
>
> Nowell Oxland: 'Outward Bound' (Oxland was killed in action at Gallipoli in 1915.)

The writer and broadcaster Melvyn Bragg (b. 1939) was reared in Cumberland, which provides the setting for a number of his novels, including *The Maid of Buttermere* (1978) and *A Time to Dance* (1990).

Despite its administrative demise, Cumberland remains a county in cricketing terms, and plays in the minor counties championship (the club was founded in 1948).

There is a town called Cumberland in the USA (Maryland), near the scenic gorge known as the Cumberland Narrows. There is also a county (Pennsylvania) and a river (Kentucky) called Cumberland. The Cumberland Gap is a pass through the Appalachians, near where Tennessee, Kentucky and Virginia meet (it gave its name to an American folk song, popularized in Britain in 1957 by

Lonnie Donegan). There is a Cumberland House in Canada (the first permanent white settlement in Saskatchewan), and the Cumberland Islands are an archipelago in the Great Barrier Reef, Australia. The Cumberland Sound is an inlet of the Davis Strait penetrating Baffin Island, in the Canadian Arctic, while there is a Cumberland Bay in the South Sandwich Islands in the South Atlantic. Most of these were named after various **dukes of Cumberland** (such as Civil War Royalist leader Prince Rupert, who received the title in 1644; and Butcher Cumberland).

> Exalted by love, in wintry rigours
> Unlikely Cumberland rages
> Thus in my memories.
>
>> Donald Davie: 'Cumberland', from *The Shires* (1974) (Davie had spent his honeymoon in the Lake District in the winter of 1945.)

Butcher Cumberland. The nickname of William Augustus, Duke of Cumberland (1721–65), younger son of George II who led the Hanoverian government forces to victory at the Battle of Culloden (*see under* CULLODEN MUIR) in 1746, and who subsequently dealt savagely with the defeated Highlanders.

Cumberland and Westmorland wrestling. A style of wrestling in which the contestants must grasp each other in a specified way, with arms locked around the other's body and the chin on the opponent's shoulder. The loser is he who first touches the ground with any part of his body apart from his feet, or who loses the specified grip on his opponent. *Compare* Lancashire style (*see under* LANCASHIRE).

Cumberland ham. A dry-cured ham, with added salt and sometimes brown sugar.

Cumberland pig. A now defunct pig breed.

Cumberland rum nickies. An apple-pie variant, which includes rum and dates.

Cumberland sauce. A cold sauce, generally served with cold meat. It is made with port, redcurrant jelly, mustard and shreds of orange peel. It is said to have been named after Ernest Augustus, Duke of Cumberland (1771–1851), a younger son of George III, who became king of Hanover in 1837. The first known reference to it by name is in Alfred Suzanne's *La Cuisine anglaise* (1904); it was subsequently popularized and commercialized by Escoffier.

Cumberland sausage. A long pork sausage, presented curled up, or even in a spiral, and usually cooked whole.

'Old Cumberland Beggar, The'. One of Wordsworth's *Lyrical Ballads* (1798), in which the poet glimpses an element of the divine in the eponymous rustic.

Cumbernauld 'meeting of the streams', Gaelic *comar* 'confluence' + *an* 'of the' + *allt* 'stream'.

A New Town in North Lanarkshire, 19 km (12 miles) north-east of Glasgow. It was formerly the HQ of **Cumbernauld**

and Kilsyth district in the old Strathclyde region (before 1975 it was in an exclave of Dunbartonshire). Cumbernauld was designated as a NEW TOWN[1] in 1956, to take population 'overspill' from Glasgow to the southwest, and was built above the old village of Cumbernauld. Its nickname is **Noddytown**, partly from a play on the last syllable of its name and partly because, as a New Town, it is not a 'real' town. It was the location for Bill Forsyth's hit film comedy, *Gregory's Girl* (1981), and of its sequel, *Gregory's Two Girls* (1999). Cumbernauld was named 'Scotland's most dismal town' in the 2001 Carbuncle Awards.

The professional football club Clyde FC has played at Broadwood Stadium in Cumbernauld since 1994.

Bond of Cumbernauld, the. An expression of loyalty to Charles I signed in August 1640 by a group of Scots nobles, even though some of them (including the Marquess of Montrose) had signed the 1637 Covenant in protest at the king's anti-Presbyterian religious policies.

Cumbraes, the 'islands of the Brittonic Celts', OCelt *Cymri* + OScand *eyjar* 'islands'; *Cumberays* 1264.

Two small islands, **Great Cumbrae** and **Little Cumbrae** to its south, in the Firth of Clyde between Bute and the mainland. They are now in North Ayrshire, but were formerly in the old county of Buteshire, and then in Strathclyde region. Great Cumbrae, whose chief town is MILLPORT, is a popular holiday destination and hosts a Country and Western festival. It is about 2 km (1.2 miles) west of LARGS. The Norwegian King Haakon is supposed to have used the island as his base before his defeat at the Battle of Largs in 1263. Little Cumbrae was a royal deer forest in the 14th century, and now has only a handful of inhabitants. In the 19th century the local minister, the Rev. James Adams, was wont to pray for the people of Great and Little Cumbrae and also 'for the adjacent islands of Great Britain and Ireland'.

> Where Cumray's isles with verdant link
> Close the fair entrance of the Clyde …
>
>> Sir Walter Scott: *The Lord of the Isles* (1815), Canto V, xiii

Cumbria 'land of the Britons', a Latinization from OE *Cumbre* 'Cumbrian Britons'; *see also* CAMBRIA.

An ancient region and modern county of northwest England. The region was Christianized by St Ninian from Scotland in the late 4th century, and came under Northumbrian rule in the 7th century. The northern part was held alternately by Scotland and England until 1157, when it became a permanent part of England – although subject to Scottish raids for some centuries more.

The modern county was created in 1974 out of the former counties of CUMBERLAND and WESTMORLAND, plus a small part of northwest LANCASHIRE. It includes the whole of the LAKE DISTRICT, plus the highest parts of the northern PENNINES. Cumbria is bounded by the Solway Firth and

Scotland on the north, Northumberland and County Durham to the east, Lancashire and North Yorkshire to the south, and the Irish Sea to the west. The administrative headquarters are at CARLISLE, and other towns include WORKINGTON, WHITEHAVEN, KESWICK, AMBLESIDE, BARROW-IN-FURNESS, KENDAL, KIRKBY STEPHEN and APPLEBY-IN-WESTMORLAND.

See also RHEGED.

Cumbrian Ballads. A collection by the Carlisle-born dialect poet Robert Anderson, published in 1805.

Cumbrian Mountains. The name sometimes given in atlases (but by no one else) to the fells of the Lake District.

Cumbrians, the. The nickname of Carlisle United FC.

Cumnock Etymology unknown.

A small BURGH in East Ayrshire (formerly in Strathclyde region), 24 km (15 miles) east of Ayr. The biographer James Boswell (1740–95), who was brought up in nearby AUCHINLECK House, is buried here, and it was the birthplace of Keir Hardie (1856–1915), the first socialist MP. It is sometimes called **Old Cumnock**, to distinguish it from the small town of NEW CUMNOCK, 8 km (5 miles) to the southeast.

Cumnock and Doon Valley. A district of the former Strathclyde region, formed in 1975 and abolished in 1996. It included the towns of CUMNOCK, Muirkirk, DALMELLINGTON and MAUCHLINE, although the district headquarters was in AYR², in the district of Kyle and Carrick.

Cumnor 'Cuma's hill-slope', OE *Cuman* possessive form of male personal name *Cuma* + *ora* 'hill-slope'.

A hilltop village in Oxfordshire, about 6.5 km (4 miles) west of Oxford. Matthew Arnold made the hill, and the view from it, famous in his poem 'The Scholar-Gipsy' (1853):

> And thou hast climbed the hill,
> And gained the white brow of the Cumnor range;
> Turned once to watch, while thick the snowflakes fall,
> The line of festal light in Christ Church hall.

but nowadays **Cumnor Hill** is a residential suburb of OXFORD, between Cumnor and the city centre.

In **Cumnor Place**, now demolished, Amy Robsart, wife of the Earl of Leicester, fell to her death down a staircase in 1560. It was whispered that Leicester had had her killed, so that he could marry Elizabeth I. The story of her death (with fictional embellishments) is told in Sir Walter Scott's *Kenilworth* (1821) – which he had wanted to call *Cumnor Place* until he was overruled by his publisher.

In the novels of Thomas Hardy, Cumnor is fictionalized as **Lumsdon**.

Cunninghame This may be the *Incuneningum* mentioned by Bede in 731, and be an Anglo-Saxon settlement, '(farmstead of) the people of Conna' (or some such name), personal name *Conna* + OE *ingas* (*see* -ING) + -HAM, but the place is perhaps too far north to have been in Anglo-Saxon hands this early, and it may be that Cunninghame is a Gaelic name filtered through English.

A traditional area of northern Ayrshire, north of Kyle and the River Irvine, and including the towns of ARDROSSAN, SALTCOATS, KILWINNING and LARGS. From 1975 to 1996 Cunninghame was a district of Strathclyde region, and expanded to include the island of ARRAN. The administrative seat was at IRVINE. The area is now divided between the unitary authorities of NORTH AYRSHIRE and EAST AYRSHIRE.

Cupar Possibly Gaelic *comhpairt* 'common', i.e. common land.

A royal BURGH (1356) in Fife, 13 km (8 miles) west of St Andrews. It was formerly the county town of Fife, and from 1975 to 1996 was the seat of North East Fife district. Sir David Lindsay (*c*.1486–1555) lived nearby, and his *Satyre of the Thrie Estaitis* – the only complete Scottish morality play to survive – was first performed in Cupar in 1552.

Cupar justice. The Fife version of Jeddart justice (*see under* JEDBURGH), in which the accused is punished first and tried afterwards.

Cougar of Cupar, the. A big cat, possibly a mountain lion (a.k.a. cougar or puma), reportedly seen more than 30 times in this part of Fife. *See also* Beast of Bodmin Moor *under* BODMIN.

He that will to Cupar maun to Cupar. An old Fife expression implying that the strong-willed will have their way.

Curlew Mountains From their distinctive fauna.

A range of low-lying hills on the border between counties Sligo and Roscommon, just north of the town of Boyle. The view from the Curlew Mountains is said to have inspired Thomas Moore's 'The valley lay smiling before me'.

Battle of the Curlew Mountains (5 August 1599). An engagement during the Nine Years' War, in which the Irish under Brian Og O'Rourke defeated an English force under Sir Conyers Clifford, who was killed.

Curr, the Possibly from Gaelic *corr* 'pointed summit'.

A hill (564 m / 1850 ft) on the north side of the CHEVIOT Hills, just on the Scottish side of the Border, some 5 km (3 miles) south of Kirk Yetholm.

Curragh, the Irish *An Currach* 'the racecourse' (although *currach* more usually means 'moor').

An area of open downland in County Kildare, just east of the town of KILDARE. It is also known as the **Curragh of Kildare**. It has been a horse-racing centre since at least the 18th century (races here include the Irish Derby), and has been used for military training since the French Revolutionary and Napoleonic wars. During the United Irishmen's rising of 1798 the rebels suffered a defeat here (29 May).

A permanent military base was established in 1854, and the internment camp here – nicknamed Tintown – was used by the British during the Anglo-Irish War, by the Free State during the Irish Civil War (on one day, 19 December 1922, seven Republicans were executed here for unauthorized possession of firearms), and by the Fianna Fáil government during the Emergency of the 1940s, during which time the writer and IRA-member Brendan Behan was imprisoned at the Curragh for his involvement in a shooting incident involving a policeman.

> The winter it has passed
> And the summer's come at last
> The small birds are singing in the trees
> And their little hearts are glad
> Ah, but mine is very sad
> Since my true love is far away from me
> *chorus:*
> And straight I will repair
> To the Curragh of Kildare
> For it's there I'll find tidings of my dear.
>   Anon.: traditional song

Curragh Incident or **Curragh Mutiny, the.** An incident in March 1914 when a number of officers at the Curragh camp offered their resignations rather than face the possibility of being ordered to act against Ulstermen to impose the Irish Home Rule Bill. They succeeded in obtaining a written assurance from their commander-in-chief that they would not be expected to do this.

Curry Mallet *Curry* from a pre-English river name of unknown origin and meaning; *Mallet* denoting manorial ownership in the Middle Ages by the Malet family.
A village in Somerset, about 11 km (7 miles) east of Taunton.

Curry Rivel *Rivel* denoting manorial ownership in the Middle Ages by the Revel family.
A village (pronounced 'kurri rivl') in Somerset, about 16 km (10 miles) east of Taunton.

Cursitor Street From the Cursitors, 24 clerks of the Court of Chancery whose job was to write out and issue writs, and whose office was in Chancery Lane. The position was instituted in the 1520s and abolished in 1835 (owing to the increasing use of printed forms).
A street in the City of London (EC4), leading eastwards off CHANCERY LANE.

Cury Originally *Egloscuri* 'church of Cury' (*see* ECCLES), Cornish *eglos* 'church' + *Curi* a pet-form of the name of St Corentin, the patron saint of the local church (he was originally a Breton saint and is also patron of Quimper Cathedral in Brittany); the reduced form *Cury* is first recorded in 1473.
A village in Cornwall, about 8 km (5 miles) south of Helston.

Cushendall From the alternative Irish name *Cois Abhann Dalla* 'foot or end of the River Dall'.

A small seaside resort on the northeast coast of County Antrim, at the foot of Glenballyemon, one of the NINE GLENS, 30 km (20 miles) northwest of Larne. Its Irish name is **Bun Abhann Dalle** ('mouth of the River Dall').

Cushendall was the birthplace of Séamus Ó Duillearga (1899–1908), founder of the Irish Folklore Commission. *Cushendall* is also the title of a 1910 collection of musical settings of Irish poems by Charles Villiers Stanford (1852–1924).

Cushendun Irish *Cois Abhann Doinne*, 'foot of the River Dun'. An attractive seaside village in County Antrim, at the foot of Glendun, one of the NINE GLENS, 16 km (10 miles) southeast of Ballycastle. The village was designed by Clough Williams-Ellis (1883–1978) of PORTMEIRION fame, in two stages, 1912 and 1923.

After his defeat at FARSETMORE in 1567, the ULSTER chieftain Shane O'Neill threw himself on the mercy of the MacDonnells at Cushendun; they, however, murdered him at a feast given in his honour on 2 June 1567. Cushendun was the birthplace of the poet Moira O'Neill (Nesta Skrine, 1865–1955), author of the two-volume *Songs of the Glens of Antrim* (1901, 1921).

Cuthberts-Lond, S. *See* DURHAM, COUNTY.

Cwmaman. *See under* ABERDARE.

Cwmbran 'valley of the River Brân', Welsh *cwm* (*see* -COMBE, COOMBE) + river name *Brân* meaning 'raven', or possibly a personal name.
A large NEW TOWN[1], which is also the administrative headquarters of MONMOUTHSHIRE, although itself in the unitary authority of TORFAEN (formerly in the old county of Monmouthshire and then Gwent, of which Cwmbran was also the administrative headquarters). It is 7 km (4.5 miles) north of Newport, and in Welsh it is **Cwm-Brân**. It was designated a New Town in 1949.

Cwm Idwal 'cwm (corrie) of Idwal', *cwm* (*see* -COMBE, COOMBE); *Idwal* is a personal name; local legend tells how Prince Idwal, son of Owain Gwynedd, was drowned in Llyn Idwal by his foster father.
A spectacular cwm on the north side of the GLYDERS in Snowdonia, Gwynedd (formerly in Caernarvonshire), 8 km (5 miles) south of Bethesda. The cwm, situated above the tiny settlement of **Idwal Cottage** in the OGWEN VALLEY, contains the small lake of **Llyn Idwal** (haunted by Prince Idwal, *see above*), and a number of spectacular cliffs, including the DEVIL'S KITCHEN (haunted by Prince Idwal's killer) and the **Idwal Slabs**. The latter offer many easier rock climbs from the early years of the 20th century, notably 'The Three Virtues', *Faith*, *Hope* and *Charity* (and by general consensus the greatest of these is *Hope*).

In the first half of the 19th century Cwm Idwal was once of the first places where geologists recognized evidence of glacial scarring. As well as its geological interest, the cwm holds many rare alpine plants, and was declared Wales's first nature reserve in 1954.

Cymru From *Cymry*, the Welsh word for the Welsh, meaning 'compatriots'. The word now more broadly designates the present-day Brittonic peoples, i.e. Cornish and Bretons as well as Welsh.

The Welsh name for Wales. It is pronounced 'kum-ri'. In the Middle Ages the name was Latinized as both CAMBRIA and CUMBRIA.

Cool Cymru. A collective term dreamt up by recording companies for the resurgent Welsh rock bands (Stereophonics, Super Furry Animals, Catatonia, etc.) of the later 1990s, echoing the birth of 'Cool Britannia' (*see under* BRITANNIA) following New Labour's election victory in 1997.

Cymru am byth! A Welsh-language phrase meaning 'Wales forever!', seen on banners waved by Welsh fans at international rugby matches, on car bumper stickers, etc.

Mam Cymru. An old name for ANGLESEY, meaning 'mother of Wales'. The title was also given to Katheryn Tudor of Berain (d.1591), who married four times and had a large number of descendants. In legend, she married seven times, killing each of her husbands by pouring molten lead into their ears. She is not to be confused with Mrs Wales (*see under* WALES).

Plaid Cymru. 'Party of Wales', the Welsh national party, founded in 1925 with the aim of achieving independence for Wales. It contested elections from 1929, but won its first Westminster seat only in 1966.

Radio Cymru. The BBC's Welsh-language service, which began broadcasting in 1977.

Sianel Pedwar Cymru. 'Channel Four Wales', also called S4C. Established in 1982, it broadcasts many Welsh-language programmes. *S4C Makes Me Want To Smoke Crack* is a 1990s compilation album featuring such artists as Rheinallt H. Rowlands, Ectogram and Catatonia, released by the Welsh-language label Ankst.

Urdd Gobaith Cymru. 'Welsh League of Youth', a Welsh-language youth movement founded in 1922.

See also WALES.

Cynffig. *See* KENFIG.

Cynon Meaning uncertain.

A river of south Wales, in Rhondda Cynon Taff (formerly in Glamorgan, then in Mid Glamorgan). It is about 25 km (16 miles) long, and meets the River Taff near ABERCYNON. The felling of the forest in **Glyn Cynon** (the valley of the Cynon) five centuries ago was lamented by one anonymous poet (who had thus lost his favourite trysting place):

> Many a birch-tree green of cloak
> (I'd like to choke the Saxon!)
> is now a flaming heap of fire
> where iron-workers blacken.
>
>> Anon: 'Glyn Cynon Wood' (16th century), translated from the Welsh by Gwyn Williams

Cynon Valley. A former district of the old county of Mid Glamorgan. The administrative seat was at ABERDARE.

D

Daccombe 'Dæcca's valley', OE *Dæccan* possessive form of male personal name *Dæcca* + *cumb* (*see* -COMBE, COOMBE).

A village in Devon, on the northern outskirts of Torquay.

Dacorum '(Hundred) belonging to the Danes' (apparently referring to the fact that the area had been under Danish overlordship), Latin, possessive form of *Daci* 'Dacians' (an ancient people of southeastern Europe), mistakenly applied in the Middle Ages to the Danes.

An ancient administrative unit of Hertfordshire, in the northwestern part of the county. The name was revived in 1974 for a modern administrative area (somewhat smaller than the original one), which includes the districts of BERKHAMSTED, TRING, and HEMEL HEMPSTEAD (where the borough's administrative headquarters are based).

Daddry Shield 'shelter of the Daudry family', ME *shele* 'shieling, shelter' + family name *Daudry*.

A small settlement in Weardale, County Durham, 11 km (7 miles) west of Stanhope.

Daffy Green Origin uncertain; *Daffy* perhaps from *daffy*, a widespread dialect word for a daffodil.

A village in Norfolk, about 27 km (17 miles) west of Norwich.

Dagenham 'Dæcca's homestead or village', OE *Dæccan* possessive form of male personal name *Dæcca* + HAM.

A district in EAST LONDON (before 1965 in Essex), on the north bank of the River THAMES[1], in the borough of BARK-ING AND DAGENHAM, between Barking to the west and Hornchurch to the east. Until the early 20th century it was a rural village. Urbanization then began to grow, but what really changed Dagenham's life was the arrival of the Ford Motor Company's works in 1931. Over the next 70 years Ford's influence permeated almost every aspect of the district, not least the provision of employment, and its massive factory site (with its own docks and jetties) dominated the townscape between the A13 and the Thames. It was a major blow when car production at the plant ceased in 2001.

Dagenham East and Dagenham Heathway 'Underground' stations, on the District line, opened in 1902 and 1932 respectively. '**Daggers**', a nickname supposedly awarded to prime minister Margaret Thatcher by unsympathetic members of her own cabinet, was not inspired by her 'looking daggers' at them, but was an abbreviation of 'Dagenham' – Dagenham being three stops on (on the District line) from Barking (as in 'barking mad').

The 1966 World Cup-winning England football manager Sir Alf Ramsey (1920–99), the entertainer Max Bygraves (b.1922) and the comedian and film star Dudley Moore (1935–2002) were born in Dagenham.

Dagenham Breach. A small lake within the boundaries of the former Ford Motor Works, Dagenham. It is all that remains of the expanse of water created when the nearby Thames wall was 'breached' (hence the name) in 1707.

'**Dagenham Dave**'. A song (1995) by the mournful balladeer Morrissey (formerly of the pop group The Smiths) concerning an archetypal male working-class inhabitant of Dagenham ('I love Karen, I love Sharon on the windowscreen / With never the need to fight or to question a single thing').

Dagenham Girl Pipers, the. An all-female Scots-style pipe band formed by the Rev. J.W. Graves at Dagenham Congregational Church in Osborne Square between the two world wars to provide wholesome recreation for the young womanhood of the district. Its profile is not as high as it was in its heyday in the 1930s and 1940s, when it entertained the troops and went on world tours, but it is still very much in existence.

Dagenham Yanks. The nickname given to workers in the Ford factory in CORK, Ireland, who in the 1930s were transferred to the company's main works in Dagenham.

Daggons From the Dagon family, known here since the 14th century.

A village in Dorset, close to the Hampshire border, just beyond the northern edge of Ringwood Forest, and about 10 km (6 miles) northwest of Ringwood.

Daglingworth 'Dæggel's or Dæccel's people's enclosure' or 'enclosure associated with Dæggel or Dæccel', OE male personal name *Dæggel* or *Dæccel* + *-inga-* (*see* -ING) or + *worth* (*see* -WORTH, WORTHY, -WARDINE).

A village in Gloucestershire, in the southern Cotswolds, about 5 km (3 miles) northwest of Cirencester.

Daimhinis. The Irish name for DEVENISH ISLAND.

Dairbhre. The Irish name for VALENCIA ISLAND.

Dalbeattie 'field by the birches', Gaelic *dail* 'field, meadow' + *beithe* 'birch trees'.

A town on the Water of URR, near where it joins the SOLWAY FIRTH, 21 km (12.5 miles) southwest of Dumfries. It was formerly in Kirkudbrightshire, and is now in Dumfries and Galloway. It was founded in 1780 to service the great granite quarry across the river, and in the 19th century it was a busy port exporting granite all over the world. It took its name from the nearby farm of Meikle Dalbeattie.

Dales, the. A shorthand term for the YORKSHIRE DALES.

Dalkeith 'field by a wood', Gaelic *dail* 'field, meadow' + OCelt CED 'wood'; alternatively, the second element may refer to Robert de Keith, who was awarded an estate here by Malcolm II in 1010.

A town 10 km (6 miles) southeast of Edinburgh. It is the administrative seat of MIDLOTHIAN. Dalkeith was the birthplace of Archibald Campbell, 9th Earl of Argyll (1629–85), who lost his head for opposing the Catholic James II. It was also the home of one of the most notorious of the Scottish 'prickers' (witch-finders), John Kincaid. Among Kincaid's achievements was the exposure in 1647 of one Janet Peaston, whom he had overheard talking to the Devil. Although she and her neighbours asserted that she frequently talked to herself, when Kincaid pricked her she did not flinch. She was thus clearly a witch, and was 'convict and brynt'.

'Dalkeith House'. A reel for the fiddle by James MacDonald.

Dalkeith Palace. A grand house at the east end of the town, which has its origins in a 12th-century castle. In 1575 this was converted into a palace by James Douglas, 4th Earl of Morton, who was regent (1572–8) for the young James VI; from Morton's fearsome reputation (he was involved in the murders of both Rizzio and Darnley) the palace became known as 'the Lion's Den'. The palace was largely rebuilt *c.*1700 by Sir John Vanbrugh for Anne, Duchess of Buccleuch and Monmouth.

Dalkey 'thorn island', OScand *dalkr* 'thorn' + *ey* 'island' (*see* -AY). Its Irish name, *Deilginis*, has the same meaning.

A seaside commuter town in County Dublin, on the south side of Dublin Bay (*see under* DUBLIN), 14 km (8.5 miles) southeast of the centre of Dublin. Offshore is the small rocky **Dalkey Island**, with its Martello tower. In Dalkey itself are the remains of three castles out of the seven that stood here in the Middle Ages. George Bernard Shaw lived in Dalkey as a boy, from 1866 to 1874, and it was the birthplace of the playwright Hugh Leonard (John Keyes Burn, b.1926).

Dalkey Archive, The. A comic novel (1964) by Flann O'Brien, in which, amongst other things, James Joyce is found not to be dead but to be darning socks for the Jesuits in an undersea grotto. In 1965 the novel was adapted for the stage as *When the Saints Go Cycling In.*

King of Dalkey. In the 18th century the tiny Dalkey Island was jocularly declared an independent state, and a king and archbishop elected, together with an admiral of the Muglins, a group of dangerous rocks to the north.

Dallinghoo 'Dalla's people's hill-spur', OE male personal name *Dalla* + *-inga-* (*see* -ING) + *hoh* 'hill-spur'.

A village in Suffolk, about 16 km (10 miles) northeast of Ipswich.

Dalmadilly 'leafy field', Gaelic *dail* 'field, meadow' + *na duille* 'leafy'.

A small settlement in Aberdeenshire (formerly in Grampian region), 6 km (4 miles) southwest of Inverurie.

Dalmellington 'field of the farm of Mealla's people', Gaelic *dail* 'field, meadow' + OE male personal name *Mealla* + *-inga-* (*see* -ING) + -TON. The Lancashire name Melling 'settlement of the family of Mealla' offers a parallel.

A former mining village at the head of the DOON valley in the south of East Ayrshire (formerly in Strathclyde region), 21 km (12.5 miles) southeast of Ayr. There is a gritty novella by K.L. Burns entitled *The Last Pork Pie in Dalmellington* (1987).

Dalriada Named after its founders, the *Dalriada* clan.

An ancient Gaelic kingdom that included parts of ANTRIM in Northern Ireland and parts of the Inner HEBRIDES and ARGYLL in Scotland. Many Gaels (called Scoti or Scotti) had already migrated from Ireland to Scotland by the time the rulers of Irish Dalriada moved to Scotland in the 5th century AD. Their main seat was at DUNADD, north of Knapdale, but they also had strongholds at Dunolly and CAMPBELTOWN (then called Dalruadhain). Gradually the Scots lost control of the Irish Dalriada, which ceased to have an identity. In 843 Kenneth MacAlpin, the king of Dalriada, brought the Picts, who controlled much of the rest of Scotland, under his rule. The country then became known as ALBA.

In Irish 'Dalriada' becomes **Dál Riata**, the form often being preferred for discussions in the Irish context.

Dalruadhain. The original name of CAMPBELTOWN.

Dalry 'field of heather', Gaelic *dail* 'field, meadow' + *fhraoich* 'heather', or possibly *an rígh* 'of the king'.

A village (pronounced 'Dal-rye') 4 km (2.5 miles) north of

New Galloway, formerly in Kirkcudbrightshire, now in Dumfries and Galloway. The full name of the village is **St John's Town of Dalry**. A rough, chair-shaped block of stone in the village is known as St John's Stone, from the story that John the Baptist once rested on it. However, the real reason for the name is that the land round about was owned by the Knights Templar, whose patron saint is John the Baptist. The village was once also known as **Old Galloway**, to distinguish it from NEW GALLOWAY.

There is another village called Dalry in North Ayrshire, and an area (formerly a village) of Edinburgh is also called Dalry.

Dalston 'Deorlaf's farmstead', OE *Deorlafes* possessive form of male personal name *Deorlaf* + -TON.

A district of northeast London (E8), in the borough of HACKNEY. An annual Clowns' Service is held here at Holy Trinity Church, when a wreath is laid on the memorial to the 19th-century clown Joseph Grimaldi. The area gained an unwelcome reputation at the end of the 20th century as the heartland of Yardie criminal activity in London.

Edith Thompson (1893–1923), the lover of Freddy Bywaters and convicted accomplice in his murder of her husband, and the singer and actress Martine McCutcheon (b.1976) were born in Dalston.

Dalton-in-Furness 'farmstead in the valley in the area of FURNESS', *Dalton* OE *dæl* 'valley' + -TON.

A village in Cumbria (formerly in Lancashire), 5 km (3 miles) north of Barrow-in-Furness. It was the birthplace of the painter George Romney (1734–1802), who is buried here.

Dalveen Pass Etymology unknown.

A high road-pass (277 m / 909 ft) through the LOWTHER HILLS, linking DURISDEER in upper Nithsdale to Crawford in South Lanarkshire. The pass, now crossed by the A702, was once used by a Roman road, and parts of the old track, called the Wall or Wald Path, can still be seen.

There is a town called Dalveen in Australia (Queensland).

Dalwhinnie 'valley of the champions', Gaelic *dail* 'field' + *chuinardh* (possessive plural of *cuingid*) 'of the champions'.

A village 16 km (10 miles) southwest of Newtonmore, in Highland (formerly in Inverness-shire), now by-passed by the A9 Perth–Inverness road. It is notable as the first village north of the DRUMOCHTER PASS, and therefore a welcome sight in winter for those caught in severe conditions; doubly welcome is the sight of its beautiful copper-spired distillery, which produces an equally attractive single malt whisky. Queen Victoria had a less happy experience of the place, reporting of the inn she stayed in:

> Unfortunately there was hardly anything to eat, and there was only tea, and two miserable starved Highland chickens, without any potatoes! No pudding, and no fun!
>
> Queen Victoria: journal (8 October 1861)

Dames' Delight. A female bathing enclosure on the bank of the River CHERWELL in Oxford, the women's equivalent of PARSON'S PLEASURE. It was originally known as the **Ladies' Pool**. It opened in 1934 for family bathing, but closed in 1970 following damage from floods.

Danby 'Danes' village', OScand *Dana*, genitive plural of *Danir* 'Dane' + -BY.

A village in the NORTH YORK MOORS, North Yorkshire, 20 km (12 miles) west of Whitby. It is home to the Moors Centre, and to the north lie **Danby Beacon** and **Danby Low Moor. Danby Castle** was the home of Catherine Parr, last wife of Henry VIII.

Danebury 'hillfort', OE *dun* (see DOWN, -DON) + *burh* (see BURY).

An impressive Iron Age hillfort about 2.5 km (1.5 miles) northwest of NETHER WALLOP in Hampshire. Danebury (sometimes called **Danebury Ring**) dates from the 6th or 5th century BC and appears to have been continuously occupied for 500 years until large-scale habitation ceased around 100 BC. Excavation at the site has revealed numerous storage pits, rectangular four-post granary structures and round houses, as well as evidence of weaving, iron-smelting, and salt and shale distribution. Bronze Age ritual pits discovered here were found to contain the remains of dismembered dogs.

Danelaw. In the 9th, 10th and 11th centuries, that area of northern and eastern England between the THAMES[1] and the TEES that had been settled by Vikings, the border defined by the Roman WATLING STREET[1]. The Danelaw recognized the sovereignty of the kings of England for much of the time (apart from a period as an independent federation in the first half of the 10th century); however, it followed Danish laws and customs. The term 'Danelaw' was not used until the reign of King Cnut (1016–35).

> First concerning our boundaries: up the Thames, and then up the Lea, and along the Lea to its source, then in as straight line to Bedford, then up the Ouse to Watling Street.
>
> Treaty, 889: *English Historical Documents* vol. I (describing the division of England agreed by Alfred the Great and Guthrum after the former's victory at Edington in 878)

Danegeld. The geld (tax) on land originally raised to buy peace from the Danes in the time of Æthelred II (978–1016) and continued as a tax long after it was needed for its original purpose. The word also more generally means appeasement by bribery.

And that is called paying the Dane-geld;
But we've proved it again and again,
That if once you have paid him the Dane-geld
You never get rid of the Dane.

> Rudyard Kipling: 'Dane-Geld' (1911)

Dane's Dyke. *See under* FLAMBOROUGH HEAD.

Danum. A Roman military station on the site of modern DONCASTER.

Darfield 'open space with deer', OE *deor* 'deer' + *feld* (*see* FIELD).

A village in South Yorkshire, 7 km (4 miles) east of Barnsley.

Dark Peak From the dark colour of its gritstone outcrops and of the heather moors.

An alternative name for the HIGH PEAK.

Darley Dale *Darley* 'glade frequented by wild animals or deer', OE *deor* 'wild animal, deer' + -LEY.

A picturesque village in Derbyshire, in the valley of the River DERWENT[4], about 10 km (6 miles) southeast of Bakewell.

Darlington 'Deornoth's farm', OE male personal name *Deornoth* + -ING + -TON.

An industrial town and unitary authority, formerly part of County Durham, some 20 km (12 miles) west-southwest of Middlesbrough. It is on the River Skerne, just above where it joins the River TEES. The unitary authority, formed in 1997, includes a little bit of countryside around the town. In the 1720s Daniel Defoe found here 'nothing remarkable but dirt'.

The world's first passenger railway was opened between Darlington and STOCKTON-ON-TEES on 27 September 1825, with George Stephenson's engine *Locomotion* (now in Darlington's railway museum) travelling at a top speed of 24 kph (15 mph). Subsequently the manufacture of locomotives became a major industry in Darlington, until the works closed in 1966.

The nickname of the town's football club, the Quakers, reflects the historical strength of the Society of Friends in the area.

Oscar Wilde invented a Lord Darlington to be his representative of modern metropolitan wit in *Lady Windermere's Fan* (1892).

Darlington was the birthplace of the publisher Joseph Dent (1849–1926), co-founder of Everyman's Library. There is a town and county called Darlington in the USA (North Carolina).

> When I was a little girl,
>   About seven years old,
> I hadn't got a petticoat
>   To keep me from the cold.
>
> So I went into Darlington,
>   That pretty little town,

And there I bought a petticoat,
  A cloak and a gown …

> Anon.: nursery rhyme

See also HELL'S KETTLES.

Darrowby. The fictional village in the television series *All Creatures Great and Small* (1978–90), based on James Herriot's veterinary tales. It was in fact ASKRIGG in Wensleydale, North Yorkshire.

Dart 'river where oak-trees grow', OCelt.

A river in Devon, 57 km (35 miles) long, rising as two separate streams on DARTMOOR (the **East Dart** and the **West Dart**), which join at DARTMEET and flow from there southeastwards through BUCKFASTLEIGH, TOTNES and DARTMOUTH into the sea at Start Bay (*see under* START POINT[2]). The river is susceptible to sudden rises in level, giving it a dangerous reputation:

> River of Dart, River of Dart,
> Every year thou claimest a heart.
>
> Traditional rhyme

Dartford 'ford on the River Darent', *Darent* OCelt river name meaning 'river where oak-trees grow' + FORD.

A town in Kent (but effectively an eastern suburb of GREATER LONDON, within the M25), about 5 km (3 miles) southeast of Bexley and 4 km (2.5 miles) south of the River THAMES[1]. Local industries include the manufacture of cement, chemicals and paper.

For most of its existence Dartford has been somewhere through which to get to other places. Two thousand years ago there was a ford across the River Darent here (*see above*). The local tunnel (*see below*) now carries M25 traffic below the Thames, and the **Dartford Crossing** was augmented in 1991 by the QUEEN ELIZABETH II BRIDGE, at the time of its opening the longest cable-stayed bridge in Europe, and still a prominent landmark in the flat landscape of the area.

Dartford was the birthplace of the perennial lead vocalist of the Rolling Stones, (Sir) Mick Jagger, and of his co-Stone Keith Richards, both born in 1943.

Dartford Tunnel. A tunnel under the River Thames that joins Dartford with PURFLEET in Essex, on the north bank. It was opened in 1963.

Dartford warbler. A small warbler (*Sylvia undata*) with a characteristic brown-purple breast. Its population is tiny and vulnerable, since it is susceptible to cold winters and also suffers from fires in its heathland habitats. Its name comes from the observation by the naturalist Thomas Pennant of a pair shot near Dartford in 1773.

Dartington 'farmstead on the River Dart', DART + -ING + -TON.

A village in Devon, on the River DART, about 5 km (3 miles) northwest of Totnes. Its worldwide reputation rests on two things: glass and music. Both arose out of **Dartington Hall**, a 14th-century manor house bought in 1925 by Dorothy and Leonard Elmhirst, two rich Americans. They restored it and set up the **Dartington Hall Trust**, with the aim of furthering rural regeneration. It promotes a range of crafts and skills, but it is the glass-making company, with its characteristic, deceptively simple modern glassware (**Dartington Crystal**, now based at TORRINGTON), and the music courses, at which musicians of international repute teach and perform, that have made the name Dartington famous.

The cleric R.H. Froude (1803–36), a prominent member of the Oxford Movement (*see under* OXFORD), and his brother, the historian J.A. Froude (1818–94) were born in Dartington.

Dartmeet. A village in the middle of DARTMOOR, situated in a deep valley some 19 km (12 miles) east of Tavistock. The East Dart and the West Dart rivers meet here – hence the name – to form a single river, the DART. The surrounding wooded valleys are amongst the moor's most beautiful scenery and attract a large number of visitors.

Dartmoor 'moor in the valley of the River Dart', DART + OE *mor* 'moor'.

An expanse of high granite moorland in southwestern DEVON[1], measuring 37 km (23 miles) from north to south and 32 km (20 miles) from east to west. Over half of it is 300 m (1000 ft) or more above sea level, and its highest points are HIGH WILLHAYS (621 m/2039 ft) and YES TOR (618 m/2028 ft). Most of Devon's main rivers, including the AVON[4], BOVEY, DART, PLYM, TAVY, TAW and TEIGN, have their sources on the moor. It is for the most part treeless and fairly bleak, with scattered tower-like outcrops of granite known as 'tors' and the occasional bog. Large areas of northwestern Dartmoor are occupied by Ministry of Defence firing ranges.

Dartmoor is what remains of an ancient volcanic region. There is widespread evidence, in its hut circles (notably the Bronze Age shepherds' settlement at GRIMSPOUND), stone rows and barrows, of its occupation by prehistoric humans. In Anglo-Saxon times it was a royal forest (that is to say, a hunting ground), and the main portion is still termed **Dartmoor Forest**. Since 1337 the central area has belonged to the Duchy of Cornwall (*see under* CORNWALL). In the Middle Ages and through to the Tudor period and beyond lead was extensively mined on the moor. In 1951 the moor, together with various wooded areas around its edge, was declared a National Park. This covers an area of 945 sq km (365 sq miles).

> Dartmoor is the Great Source. Its granite produced the stone for votive columns, propitiatory altars, and sacred avenues; for huts and houses and barns; for burial chambers; for the walls of man's earliest cornfields and cattle pounds; and long afterwards for his soaring church

towers and his Christian tombs, and for London's streets and bridges.

> W.G. Hoskins: *Devon* (1954)

Dartmoor has the reputation, especially when its chilling and impenetrable mists have rolled in, of a cheerless and mysterious place, in which the benighted traveller might vanish forever down an abandoned lead-mine or into a bottomless bog, or fall victim to even more sinister secrets of the moor. The reputation inspired, and now in its turn feeds off, *The Hound of the Baskervilles* (1902), Arthur Conan Doyle's blood-curdling tale based on the supposed legend of a supernatural Dartmoor hound that pursues descendants of the wicked Hugo Baskerville to their death. Mists and bogs figure strongly.

Another element in the moor's forbidding image is **Dartmoor Prison**. This was built between 1806 and 1813, on the initiative of Sir Thomas Tyrwhitt (Lord Warden of the STANNARIES and a friend of the Prince Regent), slightly to the west of the centre of the moor, to house French and American prisoners taken during the Napoleonic wars. Its extreme isolation recommended it as a prison for hardened or dangerous criminals or those given to escape attempts, and it was handed over to civil use in 1850. Its reputation as the ultimate penal deterrent grew rapidly amongst both the public and the criminal fraternity, who knew it simply as 'the Moor':

> He's bin on the Moor and the Island an' in the Ville, but I ain't never heard as he was in *Eton*.

> J. Phelan: *In the Can* (1939)

The town of PRINCETOWN[1] gradually grew up around the prison.

Dartmoor-clip. To cut someone's hair very short, in a **Dartmoor crop**, as (formerly) worn by convicts in Dartmoor prison.

Dartmoor letterboxing. A system of over 3000 'drops' scattered over Dartmoor, boxes into which one may put a (self-)addressed postcard, to be retrieved and posted by the next person to come along, who then puts in his or her own postcard, and so on and on. It began in 1854 at CRANMERE POOL.

Dartmoor pony. Any of an old breed of small shaggy English ponies bred on Dartmoor. Each one is someone's personal property, and every autumn they are rounded up and checked.

Dartmouth 'mouth of the River Dart', DART + OE *mutha* 'mouth'.

A town and port in Devon, on the steep wooded western side of the DART estuary, about 1.5 km (1 mile) from its mouth. It was once a thriving general and commercial port, seeing Richard I's knights off to the Crusades in 1190, trading in cloth and Bordeaux wine, important enough for

Henry VIII to build a castle here, known as Bayards Cove, for its protection. The majority of its shipping now is pleasure yachts, however, and its main modern reputation is as a place of naval education: the Britannia Royal Naval College, alma mater of generations of naval officers, opened in 1905. Later in the 20th century the cooking of Joyce Molyneux at the waterfront Carved Angel restaurant put Dartmouth in the vanguard of the renaissance of British cuisine.

The engineer Thomas Newcomen (1663–1729), who invented the atmospheric steam engine, was born in Dartmouth, as was the 'sporting curate' John ('Jack') Russell (1795–1883), breeder of the eponymous terrier.

There is a town and port called Dartmouth in Nova Scotia, Canada, a town of that name in Massachusetts, USA, a River Dartmouth in Quebec, Canada, and a Lake Dartmouth in Queensland, Australia. (Dartmouth College in Hanover, New Hampshire, one of the US Ivy League schools, was named after the 2nd Earl of Dartmouth.)

Darton 'deer farm, estate', OE *deor* 'deer' + -TON.
A village in South Yorkshire, 4 km (2.5 miles) northwest of Barnsley.

Dartry Mountains *Darty* Irish *Dartraige*, 'territory of Dartaid', *Dartaid* being an ancient tribal leader in the area.
A range of hills in northwest Ireland, spanning counties SLIGO and LEITRIM. Peaks include TRUSKMORE (664 m / 2178 ft) and BENBULBEN (527 m / 1729 ft).

Darú. The Irish name for DURROW.

Darvel Etymology uncertain, but Gaelic *dobhar an bhaile* 'oakwood by the hamlet' is suggested.
A small town in East Ayrshire (formerly in Strathclyde region), 14 km (8.5 miles) east of Kilmarnock.

Darwen[1] OCelt river name meaning 'oak river', *compare* DART, DERWENT[1]; in the 17th century the River Darwen was known by the alternative name of 'Moulding Water'.
A river in Lancashire, 29 km (18 miles) in length, which flows through BLACKBURN, DARWEN[2] and CHORLEY before joining the River RIBBLE near Preston. The bridge over the Darwen at Walton-le-Dale (just south of Preston) was the site of a Civil War engagement on 17 August 1648, when Oliver Cromwell's forces seized it from the Scots under the Duke of Hamilton.

> Cromwell, our chief of men ...
> Hast reared God's trophies, and his work pursued,
> While Darwen stream with blood of Scots imbrued ...
>
>   John Milton: 'To the Lord General Cromwell' (1652)

Darwen[2] After the River DARWEN[1].
A former cotton town on the River DARWEN[1], in the unitary authority of BLACKBURN WITH DARWEN (formerly in Lancashire), 6 km (4 miles) south of Blackburn. The town is dominated by the 92-m (303-ft) brick-built India Mill Chimney, constructed in 1867 to resemble the bell tower in St Mark's Square in Venice. In 1931, when Indian nationalists threatened to boycott imported British cotton, Gandhi was persuaded to visit Darwen to listen to the Lancashire viewpoint.

Darwin Mounds After Charles *Darwin* (1809–82), originator of the theory of evolution by natural selection.
A group of cold-water coral reefs covering an area of 100 sq km (40 sq miles) at a depth of about 1000 m (3300 ft), about 200 km (120 miles) off the northwest coast of Scotland. They were discovered in 1998 and are as rich in marine life as Australia's Great Barrier Reef. However, they are threatened by damage from fishermen's trawl nets.

Daugh of Invermarkie *Daugh* from Gaelic *dabhach*, a land measure equivalent to 192 Scots acres (*see also* DAWYCK); *Invermarkie* 'mouth of the Markie Water', Gaelic *inbhir* 'mouth' + river name (*see also* ABER).
A low hill in Aberdeenshire (formerly in Grampian region), 13 km (8 miles) west of Huntly. Some 7 km (4 miles) to the east is **Daugh of Cairnborrow**, which apparently derives from Gaelic *càrn brutha* and means 'cairn of the dwelling of the fairies'.

Daventry 'Dafa's tree', OE *Dafan* possessive form of male personal name *Dafa* + *treow* 'tree' (*see* COVENTRY).
A town (pronounced 'daventry' or, in former times, 'daintry') in Northamptonshire, about 19 km (12 miles) west of Northampton. Just to the east is Borough Hill, the site of a huge Iron Age hillfort. This was also the position, until 1994, of a major BBC transmitter, whose serried ranks of radio masts were visible from the nearby M1. Just to the south of the town is the source of the River NENE.

Charles I reputedly stayed at the Wheatsheaf Inn in Daventry for a week prior to the Battle of NASEBY.

Dawlish OCelt river name meaning 'dark stream'.
A seaside town on the south coast of Devon, about 5 km (3 miles) southwest of Exmouth. The town itself is perched behind bright red cliffs, and a coast-hugging railway has to be negotiated on the way to the beach. Isambard Kingdom Brunel's original plan was to have a pneumatically powered one, but in the event more conventional means of locomotion prevailed.

Dawlish was a fashionable resort in the 19th century, and boasts a legacy of handsome Georgian and Victorian buildings. Jane Austen mentions the town in her novels, and Charles Dickens made it the birthplace of Nicholas Nickleby. The centre of Dawlish is dominated by a public park called 'the Lawn', through which flows **Dawlish Water** (or 'the Brook'), home to an impressive range of riverine wildfowl such as black swans.
See also PARSON AND CLERK.

'Dawlish Fair'. A poem by John Keats, written in 1818. It ends (with not one of his most inspired rhymes):

> O who wouldn't hie to Dawlish fair
> O who wouldn't stop in a Meadow
> O who would not rumple the daisies there
> And make the wild fern for a bed do.

Dawlish Warren. A sand-dune covered promontory to the northeast of Dawlish, protruding into the estuary of the River EXE opposite Exmouth – the perfect setting for a golf links.

Dawn Welsh *dawn* 'gift, donation'.
A village in Conwy (formerly in Denbighshire, then in Gwynedd), 6 km (4 miles) south of Colwyn Bay.

Dawyck Probably from Gaelic *dabhach*, a land measure equivalent to 192 Scots acres (*see also* DAUGH OF INVERMARKIE), or possibly 'deer farm' OE *da* 'doe, female fallow deer' + *wic* (*see* WICK).
An estate some 12 km (7 miles) southwest of Peebles, in Scottish Borders (formerly in Peeblesshire). It nestles beneath a hill called the Scrape and is the site of **Dawyck Botanical Gardens and Arboretum**, a specialized branch of the Royal Botanical Gardens in Edinburgh. The estate was acquired by the Naesmyth family in 1691, and during the 18th century Sir James Naesmyth, a pupil of the great Swedish naturalist Linnaeus, planted many of the North American conifers that have grown into such giants today. The garden is also noted for its Sino-Himalayan trees and rhododendrons. The present **Dawyck House** dates from the 19th century.

Dawyck beech. A cultivated spire-shaped variety of beech with glossy leaves originally grown in Dawyck before 1850.

Dead for Cauld Scots *cauld* 'cold', presumably a reference to its exposed position.
A hill (575 m / 1886 ft) above the high pass linking the Talla and Megget valleys (*see under* TALLA WATER *and* MEGGET WATER), Scottish Borders (formerly in Selkirkshire), 7 km (4.5 miles) west of St Mary's Loch.

Dead Friars. *See* BLANCHLAND.

Dead Man's Hill Probably 'hill where a corpse was found'.
A hill just to the east of AMPTHILL in Bedfordshire, beside the stretch of the A6 running from Luton to Bedford. In a lay-by here in August 1961 Michael Gregsten was murdered by James Hanratty (*see* A6).

Dead River Etymology unknown.
A tributary of the River SHANNON, rising just inside County Tipperary and flowing northwestwards into County Limerick to join the Shannon just east of LIMERICK itself.

Deadwaters Etymology obscure.
A small settlement in South Lanarkshire (formerly in Strathclyde region), 6 km (4 miles) southeast of Strathaven.

Deal '(place at) the hollow or valley', OE *dæl*.
A town and seaport in Kent, about 11 km (7 miles) northeast of Dover, one of the CINQUE PORTS. It has a natural harbour, guarded offshore by the GOODWIN SANDS, and like Dover it has always been in the Continental firing line. Julius Caesar supposedly landed here on a reconnaissance mission in 55 BC, a year before his invasion, and one-and-a-half millennia later invasion fears were still lively enough to encourage Henry VIII to build a castle at Deal, eight-bastioned, like a Tudor rose, for maximum defensive power (its partner and close neighbour Walmer Castle (*see under* WALMER) is the official residence of the Lord Warden of the Cinque Ports). For nearly 300 years it was a great smuggling centre. The gentry of London and the southeast of England flocked here to get their luxury goods at rock-bottom prices (seldom can a town have been more aptly named).

Such stirring times have now departed, and Deal has reinvented itself as a holiday resort. Until the mid-1990s it was home to the Royal Marines School of Music, whose barracks were severely damaged by a Provisional IRA bomb in September 1989, which killed 10 bandsmen and injured 22.

See also the DOWNS[2].

Dear Green Place. A byname for GLASGOW, being a fanciful translation of the Gaelic *Glaschu*, originally from Old Celtic *glas cau* 'green hollow'. Since the Industrial Revolution, the name has been somewhat ironic, although still somehow pertinent given the large number of public parks in the city.

Debatable Lands, the. The areas on either side of the Anglo-Scottish BORDER that were for centuries claimed by

---

❖ ddu, dubh ❖

These are respectively the modern Welsh and Gaelic forms of an Old Celtic word meaning 'black, dark'. When this element appears first or alone in early names it nearly always refers to water, and is found in England in, for example, the River DOVE (Derbyshire and Staffordshire).

It is difficult to know whether it meant something more specific than simply the colour of the water: certainly DUBLIN (Ireland) and DOUGLAS[2] (Isle of Man) are important places. The particular combination of elements in Douglas, *du-glas* 'black water, dark stream' recurs in DOUGLAS[1] (Lanarkshire and Lancashire), in DAWLISH (Devon) and in Dowlais (Glamorgan; *see under* MERTHYR TYDFIL).

both Scotland and England. The Debatable Lands were long subject to the brutal, plundering raids of the moss-troopers and reivers from either side, until the Union of the Crowns in 1603 largely brought such goings-on to an end. In his poem 'Crossing the Border' (1968), Norman MacCaig meditates on the bloody past as he journeys by train through the region:

> I sit, being helplessly
> lugged backwards
> through the Debatable Lands of history, listening
> to the execrations, the scattered cries, the
> falling of roof-trees
> in the lamentable dark.

See also the MARCHES *and* SCOT'S DYKE.

Deben 'deep one', OE *deop* 'deep'.
A river (pronounced 'debbən' or 'deebən') in Suffolk, which rises just north of **Debenham** (which has adopted its name), about 12 km (7.5 miles) west of FRAMLINGHAM, and flows 48 km (30 miles) southeast and then southwest through WOODBRIDGE (where it is joined by the River Fynn) into the sea just north of FELIXSTOWE. Its lower reaches are very popular with yachtsmen.

Decies From *déisí*; *see* the DÉISE.
A medieval kingdom in WATERFORD and southern County TIPPERARY. In the later Middle Ages the area came under the Fitzgeralds of Desmond.

Dedham 'Dydda's homestead or village', OE male personal name *Dydda* + HAM.
A village in Essex, on the River STOUR², on the Suffolk border, about 10.5 km (6.5 miles) northeast of Colchester. It was once a centre of the Flemish cloth trade.
Dedham Vale. The valley of the River Stour, running inland from MANNINGTREE through Dedham and on westwards. The area up to the point where the Stour turns northwest towards SUDBURY¹ was declared an Area of Outstanding Natural Beauty in 1970. Its characteristic small-scale features – water-meadows, willow-lined streams, water-mills, elm trees – remain (with the unfortunate exception of the elms) much as they were portrayed in the early 19th century against the broad Essex and Suffolk skies by John Constable. His paintings, such as *The Hay Wain* (1821), *Flatford Mill* (1825), *The Leaping Horse* (1825) and *Dedham Vale* (1831), have immortalized this country, and his name is forever associated with it.
See also CONSTABLE COUNTRY and FLATFORD MILL.

Dee¹ Celtic *deva* 'goddess'; *compare* DON¹.
Scotland's fifth-longest river, with a course of 137 km (85 miles). It is entirely within Aberdeenshire (formerly in Grampian region), and is a celebrated salmon river.
The Dee rises at the springs called the **Wells of Dee** on the CAIRNGORM plateau between BRAERIACH and CAIRN

TOUL at a height of 1230 m (over 4000 ft), before plunging eastward over the plateau edge at the **Falls of Dee** into the Garbh Choire, from where it flows into upper **Glen Dee**. Here it is joined by another stream flowing south from the **Pools of Dee**, two little lochans near the summit of the LAIRIG GHRU pass. From this confluence the river flows southeastward to the waterfalls known as the **Chest of Dee**, and then eastward to the **Linn of Dee**, a narrow rocky chasm through which the river rushes in a fierce torrent. (The renowned climber Menlove Edwards, who was later to take his own life, swam through the Linn of Dee in 1931 – not a course of action recommended to the visitor.) From the Linn the course of the river continues eastward through **Deeside**, a beautiful scene of heathery mountains and woodlands, past BRAEMAR, BALMORAL CASTLE and BALLATER (this stretch is also known as **Royal Deeside**, as much of it lies within the royal estate of Balmoral). Eventually the river flows into the coastal lowlands and meets the North Sea at ABERDEEN.

> There was a young lady of Dee
> Went to bed with each man she could see.
> When it came to a test
> She wished to be best,
> And practice makes perfect you see.
>
> Anon.: limerick

Battle of the Bridge of Dee (1639). A battle at the bridge over the Dee on the west side of ABERDEEN, in which the Marquess of Montrose led his Covenanting forces to victory over the Royalists who had held the city.

Dee² *See* DEE¹.
A river that rises in BALA LAKE in Gwynedd, and runs broadly northeastwards for 112 km (70 miles). Its Welsh name is **Afon Dyfrdwy** ('divine river', *afon* 'river', *dyfr* 'water, river' + *dwyf* 'divine'). The river follows a tortuous course, the poet William Wordsworth writing of the 'interesting windings of the wizard stream of the Dee'. In its lower reaches it forms part of the Anglo-Welsh border, then flows briefly into England via CHESTER, before re-entering Wales for a short stretch.
The **Dee estuary** extends some 20 km (12 miles) north-westwards to the Irish Sea, bounded by the Wirral to the east and the coast of Flintshire to the west. The estuary contains the treacherous **Sands of Dee**, revealed at low tide to consist of sand banks, mud flats and quicksands, the crossing of which caused the medieval Welsh bishop and historian Giraldus Cambrensis (Gerald of Wales) some anxiety in 1188. Here also was the site of the drowning in 1637 of Milton's friend Edward King, memorialized by the poet in 'Lycidas' (1638):

> He must not float upon his watery bier
> Unwept, and welter to the parching wind,
> Without the meed of some melodious tear.

More cheery, in a dark sort of way, is the contribution made to the literature of Dee by Edward Lear:

> There was an old man of the Dee
> Who was sadly annoyed by a flea.
> When he said, 'I will scratch it,'
> They gave him a hatchet,
> Which grieved that old man of the Dee.

'Miller of Dee, The'. A lyric by Isaac Bickerstaffe, set to music by Thomas Arne, from the comic opera *Love in a Village* (1762):

> There was a jolly miller once
> Lived on the river Dee
> He danced and he sang from morn till night
> No lark so blithe as he.
> And this the burden of his song
> For ever used to be
> I care for nobody, no, not I,
> If nobody cares for me.

The miller referred to ran the old Dee mill at Chester, which burnt down in 1895. There had been a mill here since the 11th century, and in the time of Henry VIII the independence of the miller of Dee is said to have inspired the envy of the king.

Dee³ Same origin as DEE¹, i.e. 'the goddess'; its source river, the Water of Deugh may possibly be cognate.

A river of Dumfries and Galloway (formerly in Kircudbrightshire), flowing out of LOCH KEN for 61 km (38 miles) and having its disembroguement at KIRKCUDBRIGHT. Its ultimate source is the Water of Deugh, which rises on the border with East Ayrshire, feeds into Kendoon Loch, from whence the Water of Ken flows through a succession of small lochs to Loch Ken.

Deepcut 'deep water-channel', ME *deep + cut* 'water-channel'. The cut is on the Basingstoke Canal, at the head of a series of locks.

A village in Surrey, on the Chobham Ridges, about 2.5 km (1.5 miles) east of Frimley. The local Queen Elizabeth Barracks, headquarters of the Royal Logistics Corps, were the scene of controversy in the early 21st century following the unexplained death of several recruits, officially designated as 'suicide'.

Deep Dale From its high sides.

A PENNINE valley in County Durham, extending west from BARNARD CASTLE. Its stream is **Deepdale Beck**.

Deepdale 'deep valley', OE *deop* 'deep' + *dæl* 'valley'.

A valley in the Lake District, Cumbria, leading southwestward from Patterdale between St Sunday Crag and Hart Crag up towards Fairfield. The upper part of the valley is called **Deepdale Common**, and its stream is **Deepdale Beck**.

Deeping St James *Deeping* 'deep or low place', OE *deoping*; *St James* from the dedication of the local church.

An attractive village in the Lincolnshire Fens, on the River WELLAND, contiguous with MARKET DEEPING.

Deeping St Nicholas *St Nicholas* from the dedication of the local church.

A village in the Lincolnshire Fens, about 7 km (4 miles) southwest of Spalding. **Deeping Fen** lies to the west.

Deer Abbey 'abbey of the grove', *Deer* Gaelic *doire* 'grove'.

A ruined abbey in Aberdeenshire (formerly in Grampian region), 16 km (9.5 miles) west of Peterhead. The original Celtic abbey was founded in the 6th century, by St Columba and/or St Drostan, and the present Cistercian abbey in the 13th century. At the Reformation, the parish was divided into **Old Deer** (the village of this name is just east of the ruins) and **New Deer**, a village some 8 km (5 miles) to the west.

Book of Deer, The. A 9th-century illuminated manuscript including Latin versions of the complete Gospel of St John, and partial versions of the other gospels. There are also 12th-century Gaelic additions (the oldest extant writing in Scottish Gaelic), giving information about contemporary clan organization and land ownership. The manuscript was rediscovered in Cambridge University Library in 1860.

Rabbling of Deer, the (1711). A violent confrontation between Presbyterians and Episcopalians, the culmination of a long dispute between the two factions in Old Deer. The Episcopalians successfully managed to prevent the ordination of the new minister, John Gordon. The fact that Presbyterians came off worse in this encounter may explain why Old Deer, unusually for sabbatarian Scotland, has an annual fair held on a Sunday in July.

Deerhurst 'wood frequented by deer', OE *deor + hyrst* 'wood, wooded hill'.

A village in Gloucestershire on the bank of the River SEVERN, 4 km (2.5 miles) south of Tewkesbury, noted for its scenic cluster of fine Anglo-Saxon ecclesiastical buildings. The Church of St Mary here (the remains of what used to be an important monastery) is one of the finest surviving Anglo-Saxon churches in England, while nearby Odda's chapel, dating from 1056, is one of very few wholly Anglo-Saxon buildings remaining in England.

Deerhurst was the site of a meeting in 1016 between Edmund Ironside and Cnut in the aftermath of the battle of ASHINGDON at which they agreed to divide the kingdom, leaving Edmund in possession of WESSEX. But Edmund died shortly afterwards, leaving the whole kingdom of England in Cnut's hands.

Deheubarth 'southern region of Wales', Welsh *deheu* 'south' + *parth* 'region'.

A medieval kingdom of South Wales established in the 10th

century by Hywel Dda, who created the kingdom to bring together his personal territories – he was king of DYFED (904–50) and of SEISYLLWG (909–50). Dyfed then more or less corresponded to PEMBROKESHIRE, and Seisyllwg took in CEREDIGION, CARMARTHENSHIRE and WEST GLAMORGAN (this last now comprising the unitary authorities of Swansea and Neath Port Talbot). Until the murder of the last king of Deheubarth, Rhys ap Tewdwr, in 1093, most of the rest of South Wales was dependent on Deheubarth. After that South Wales was gradually taken over by the Normans, and a reduced principality of Deheubarth was finally extinguished in 1201.

Deilginis. The Irish name for DALKEY.

Deil's Heid, the Scots 'the Devil's head'.
A grotesquely shaped sandstone stack on the North Sea coast of ANGUS, 3 km (2 miles) east of Arbroath.

Deira Etymology unknown.
An Anglo-Saxon kingdom in what is now Yorkshire, extending from the River TEES south to the HUMBER. Pope Gregory I came to know of Deira c.560 when he asked the origin of some slaves on sale in a Roman market, and thus learnt of the kingdom and its king, Aelle. It is reported that he punned that his missionaries would rescue the Deirans *de ira dei* ('from the wrath of God').

Deira was annexed by the kingdom of BERNICIA to the north in 588, but Aelle's son Edwin returned from exile and defeated the Bernician king to form the united kingdom of NORTHUMBRIA in 616.

Deirgderc. The Irish name for LOUGH DERG[2].

Déise, The From Irish *déisí* 'tenants, vassals', which became the name of a number of ancient Irish tribes and their territories.
The area of the small GAELTACHT (Irish-speaking area) around An Rinn (Ringville) in County Waterford, just south of DUNGARVAN.

Delabole From the name of the early medieval manor *Deliou* (perhaps from a Cornish word meaning 'leaves') + Cornish *poll* 'pit' (referring to the huge quarry here).
A small town in Cornwall, close to the northwestern edge of BODMIN MOOR, and about 19 km (12 miles) north of Bodmin. Many centuries of slate-quarrying have produced here the biggest man-made hole in England: 150 m (500 ft) deep and 3 km (2 miles) in circumference.

Deli From the name of the early medieval manor *Deliou* (*see under* DELABOLE).
A village in Cornwall, about 1.5 km (1 mile) east of Delabole.

De Morgannwg. The Welsh name for SOUTH GLAMORGAN.

Denbigh 'small fort', Welsh *din* 'fort' + BACH.

A town in Denbighshire (formerly part of Clwyd), 18 km (11 miles) west of Mold. In Welsh it is **Dinbych**. It was the county town of the old county of DENBIGHSHIRE. Denbigh was founded as a borough in 1283, but was sacked by Owain Glyndwr in 1402. Nevertheless, during the following two centuries Denbigh was one of the more important towns in Wales. The castle (1282) was dismantled in the 17th century. Denbigh was once noted for its manufacture of fine gloves, and it was at Denbigh in 1775 that John Wilkinson built his machine for the accurate boring of cylinders, a machine that enabled James Watt to build his improved steam engine.

Sir Henry Morton Stanley (1841–1904), African explorer and finder of David Livingstone, was illegitimately born plain John Rowlands here in 1841. The Welsh-language writer Kate Roberts (1891–1985) lived in Denbigh for the last 50 years of her life and died here.

Denbighshire From DENBIGH + SHIRE.
A former county and current unitary authority of North Wales. The old county (created in 1536) was bordered to the east by Flintshire and Cheshire, to the south by Shropshire and Montgomeryshire, to the west by Merioneth and Caernarvonshire, and to the north by the Irish Sea. The county town was DENBIGH, and other towns included RUTHIN, LLANGOLLEN, RHYL and COLWYN BAY. In 1974 it became part of CLWYD[2], and in 1996 it was re-created as a unitary authority, although this is somewhat smaller than the old county. The modern Denbighshire is bordered to the south by Powys, to the east by Wrexham, Flintshire and to the west by Conwy. The administrative seat is RUTHIN.

> There's a river, a hillside and fresh boughs of trees
>> that hide three hinds.
> Today no hunter finds
>> them, or tries their willing flesh.
>
> Anon.: 'Three Hinds of Denbighshire' (17th century),
> translated from the Welsh by Glyn Williams

Denby 'village of the Danes', OE *Dene*, possessive plural *Dena* 'Danes' + -BY.
A town in Derbyshire, 13 km (8 miles) north of Derby. A bed of clay uncovered here in 1806 during the construction of the Denby–Alfreton turnpike was found to be the finest stoneware clay in Europe, and in 1809 **Denby Pottery** began production of its now world-famous stoneware. Under the energetic stewardship of Joseph Bourne, Denby Pottery became the biggest exporter of bottles and jars in Britain by the mid-19th century, its products characterized by a distinctive shiny surface created by the technique of salt-glazing.

John Flamsteed (1646–1719), who became the first Astronomer Royal, was born here.

Denby Dale 'valley of DENBY', *Dale* OE *dæl* 'valley, dale'.

A village in West Yorkshire, 12 km (7 miles) southeast of Huddersfield. Denby Dale is famous for its giant pies, the first baked in 1788 to celebrate George III's (temporary) recovery of his sanity. Others have celebrated Waterloo in 1815 and the birth of royal children in 1964. Ingredients of the pies have included several sheep and scores of birds, and even on one occasion a man called Hinchcliffe, who made such a long speech while cutting the pie that the famished spectators knocked down the supports of his stand and tipped him into the pastry.

Denge Marsh *Denge* probably from OE *dyncge* (Kentish *dencge*) 'manured land'; the name may mean simply 'marsh with manured land', or it could refer to the fertility of the recovered marshland.

An area of marshland in Kent, between LYDD and DUNGE-NESS, forming the southeastern section of ROMNEY MARSH.

Denham 'homestead or village in a valley', OE *denu* 'valley' + HAM.

A village in Buckinghamshire, on the GRAND UNION CANAL, about 5 km (3 miles) east of Gerrards Cross. It is best known for **Denham Studios**, which opened in 1936 and became the leading British film studios of the 1940s. Their guiding spirit was Alexander Korda, whose London Films (*see under* LONDON) was based here. His first production here was *Things to Come* (1936). Laurence Olivier's *Henry V* (1944) was a Denham film, and the first British Technicolor movie was made here. The studios closed in 1953.

Just to the north is **Denham Green**, and there is a small airfield, which during the First World War was a pre-flying training ground school.

The painter Ben Nicholson (1894–1982) was born in Denham.

Denhead 'head of the valley', OE *denu* 'valley' + *head*.

There are settlements of this name in Aberdeenshire (two), Dundee, Fife and Angus – this last sometimes being distinguished as **Denhead of Arbirlot** (Arbirlot being a larger village nearby).

Denholme 'water meadow in the valley', OE *denu* 'valley' + *holmr* 'water meadow' (*see also* -EY, -EA).

A village in West Yorkshire, 10 km (6 miles) west of Bradford.

Denny Possibly 'well-watered land in a valley', OE *denu* 'valley' + -*eg* (*see* -EY, -EA).

A small industrial town on the River CARRON, 8 km (5 milers) west of Falkirk. It was formerly in Stirlingshire, then in Central region, and is now in Falkirk unitary authority.

Denton 'farm in a valley', OE *denu* 'valley' + -TON.

An industrial town in Greater Manchester, 8 km (5 miles) east of the city centre, in the valley of the River TAME[2]. Denton is a very common English place name, and there are further Dentons of the same origin in Cambridgeshire, County Durham, Kent, East Sussex, Lincolnshire, Norfolk, Oxfordshire and North Yorkshire.

The place name has been popularized by television's lugubrious Inspector Frost (played by David Jason), who has cleared up numerous murders for Denton CID since *A Touch of Frost* was first aired in 1992: in this case, the fictional Denton is supposedly near to Bristol.

Denver 'Danes' ford or passage' (perhaps referring to a particular Danish incursion, or (Denver being not far from the GREAT OUSE) to the local waterway as the Danes' main way of getting about), OE *Dena* possessive form of *Dene* 'Danes' + *fær* 'ford, passage'.

A village in Norfolk, about 1.5 km (1 mile) south of Downham Market. There are towns and cities called Denver in the USA (Colorado, Idaho, Indiana, Iowa, Pennsylvania) and a Denver City in Texas.

Deptford 'deep ford' (referring to a ford across the River Ravensbourne), OE *deop* + FORD.

A district (pronounced 'detfəd') in southeast London (SE8, SE14), in the borough of LEWISHAM, to the south of Rotherhithe and to the east of Greenwich. Its main historical associations are maritime. It was the site of the Royal Dock, constructed in 1513 to build and maintain Henry VIII's navy. Elizabeth I knighted Francis Drake here on board the *Golden Hind* in 1581, and Captain Cook's two ships, *Discovery* and *Resolution*, were fitted out here. It was closed in 1869. The Russian emperor Peter the Great stayed in Deptford in 1698 while studying shipbuilding. Trinity House, which has charge of the lighthouses of England and Wales, was originally established at Deptford in 1514.

The playwright Christopher Marlowe (1564–93) was notoriously (and mysteriously) murdered in a Deptford tavern, allegedly following a quarrel over a bill. Four centuries later, the writer Charles Nichol investigated the events surrounding the killing – including Marlowe's apparent involvement in covert intelligence work – in his book *The Reckoning* (1992). The novelist Anthony Burgess was also inspired by the episode, writing a 'Marlowe novel' entitled *A Dead Man in Deptford* (1993).

Deptford pink. A species of the plant pink, *Dianthus armeria*.

Derby 'farmstead or village where deer are kept', OScand *djur* 'deer' + -BY.

A city (pronounced 'darby' or, locally, 'derby') and unitary authority (officially termed **Derby City**) in Derbyshire, on the River DERWENT[4], at the southern end of the Pennines, about 21 km (13 miles) southwest of Nottingham.

There was a settlement on the site in Roman times, called **Derventia**. The Saxons knew the place as **Northworthy** ('north enclosure'), and its present-day name was given to it by the Danes after they captured it in 874 (it became one of the FIVE BOROUGHS, centres of Danish rule in the 10th century, the others being Leicester, Lincoln, Nottingham and Stamford). In its modern history, though, Derby did not begin to make a big impact until the 18th century. Then, in 1717, the local silk industry was boosted with a silk mill, one of Britain's first factories; and in the 1750s William Duesbury started manufacturing porcelain in the town. It was similar to Chelsea and Meissen in style, and was widely admired: George III visited in 1773 and signalled his approval by allowing it to be marked with a crown and call itself 'Crown Derby'; Queen Victoria augmented the accolade in 1890 by permitting '**Royal Crown Derby**'.

On 9 July 1735 the Church of St Werburgh in Derby held and registered the wedding of the lexicographer and author Samuel Johnson to Elizabeth Porter. And in 1745 Charles Edward Stuart (Bonnie Prince Charlie), having invaded England with the help of the Scottish Highlanders, held his final war council in Derby before retreating to Scotland.

In the 19th century the Midland Railway works came to town, and ever since Derby has been an important centre for the manufacture and repair of locomotives and railway equipment. Then in 1908 Rolls-Royce established its car-making factory here – the first major product being the Silver Ghost. After the Second World War car production moved to Crewe, with Derby concentrating on the aero-engine business.

Derby Cathedral is the town's All Saints' Church (which contains the tomb of Bess of Hardwick (*see under* HARDWICK HALL)); it was raised to the status of a cathedral in 1927. In 1977 Derby was declared a city in honour of Queen Elizabeth II's Silver Jubilee.

The city's professional football club, **Derby County FC**, was founded in 1884. Its nickname, the Rams, refers to the mythical Derby ram (*see below*). Derby County's heyday was the 1970s: the club won the League championship in 1972 (under their maverick manager Brian Clough) and again in 1975. From 1895 until 1997, when they moved to Pride Park, Derby County played their home matches at the Baseball Ground. Originally a recreation area for foundry workers, it was so named because the foundry's owner, following a visit to the United States, encouraged his employees to play baseball on the site.

The artist Joseph Wright (1734–97), painter of interior scenes with dramatic lighting effects, and widely known simply as '**Wright of Derby**'), the architect Edward Blore (1787–1879, who as architect to the Crown completed Buckingham Palace and restored Windsor Castle), the philosopher Herbert Spencer (1820–1903) and the theatre director John Dexter (1925–90) were born in Derby.

There are cities and towns called Derby in the USA (Connecticut, Iowa, Kansas, Texas) and Australia (Tasmania and Western Australia).

The earls of Derby (whose actual seat and power base is much further northwest, at Knowsley near Liverpool; such was their local clout in former times that they were known as 'the Kings of Lancashire') have lent the name of 'Derby' to various artefacts and events, most notably of course the annual horse-racing Classic **the Derby** run every June at EPSOM, which was founded in 1780 by the 12th Earl, but also including the **Derby scheme**, a First World War recruitment plan promoted by the 17th Earl (soldiers thus recruited were called '**Derbies**') and the bowler-like hat known, especially in the USA, as a **derby** (pronounced as spelt; here again the 12th Earl was the originator). *See also* SINFIN.

Derby brights. A high-quality small-sized grade of coal. The term has occasionally been used in the past as rhyming slang for *lights*.

Derby cheese. A hard cow's-milk cheese similar to Cheddar, made in Derbyshire.

Derby neck. Another name for a Derbyshire neck (*see under* DERBYSHIRE).

Derby ram. A mythical ram of the Derby area, which was so huge that it covered an acre with every stride, while eagles built their eyries in its horns. It forms the basis of a traditional nursery rhyme:

> As I was going to Derby,
> Upon a market day,
> I met the finest ram, sir,
> That ever was fed on hay.

Each succeeding verse ramps up the animal's prodigiousness still further.

The annual **Derby Tup** plays, with a man dressed as a *tup* (a ram), are performed in Derbyshire on Boxing Day.

Derby red. A red pigment made from the dibasic chromate of lead.

Sage Derby. Derby cheese marbled green with sage juice. Traditionally it was made only at harvest time and Christmas, but recently it has become more widely commercialized.

Derbyshire From DERBY + SHIRE. The name *Derbyshire* is first recorded in the 11th century.

A county in northern central England, bounded to the north by Greater Manchester, West Yorkshire and South Yorkshire, to the east by Nottinghamshire, to the south by Leicestershire and to the west by Staffordshire and Cheshire. It contains the unitary authority DERBY City, and other important towns are BUXTON, CHESTERFIELD, GLOSSOP, ILKESTON and MATLOCK (the administrative headquarters). Its main rivers are the DERWENT[4], DOVE, ROTHER[3] and TRENT[1]. Much of the northern part of the county consists of the PEAK DISTRICT National Park – the DARK PEAK to the north, and to the south the WHITE PEAK, which contains the deeply cut ravines of the **Derbyshire Dales**: DOVEDALE[1], Miller's Dale, Monk Dale and so on. The south and east of Derbyshire is farming country, both arable and (on the hills) sheep. Derbyshire has notable reserves of fluorspar (*see* **Derbyshire spar** *below*).

In cricketing terms Derbyshire is a 'first-class' county. Derbyshire County Cricket Club was founded in 1870 and has played in the county championship since 1895, winning it once. Its home ground is the County Ground, Derby.

Derbyshire cheese. Another name for Derby cheese (*see under* DERBY).

Derbyshire neck. A former name for the swollen neck caused by enlargement of the thyroid gland (goitre). It used to be endemic in parts of Derbyshire where iodine did not occur naturally in the drinking water.

Derbyshire spar. The variety of fluorspar found in Derbyshire. Fibrous and violet-tinted, it has been widely used decoratively over the centuries, and now generally goes under its local name 'Blue John' (*see* BLUE JOHN CAVERN). It used to be known alternatively as **Derbyshire drop**.

Dereham. *See* EAST DEREHAM.

Dere Street 'Roman road of the stags', OE *deora* possessive plural 'of the stags' + STREET.

The Roman road that ran north through NORTHUMBERLAND (the ancient English kingdom of DEIRA, with which the road name has sometimes been associated), crossed the CHEVIOT Hills at Woden Law and the TWEED near Melrose, before heading up Lauderdale (*see under* LAUDER) to meet the Firth of Forth at INVERESK near Musselburgh. Much of the route is followed by the modern A68.

Derravaragh, Lough. *See* LOUGH DERRAVARAGH.

Derry/Londonderry Irish *Doire* 'oak grove'; *London-* was added in 1609 when James VI and I granted the area to London merchants. The original full name was *Doire Calgach* 'oak wood of Calgach', an ancient local pagan chieftain; in the 12th century, under the prestigious abbot Flaithbhertach Ó Brolcháin, the name changed to *Doire Columcille* 'oak wood of Columcille', in honour of the saint regarded as Ó Brolcháin's predecessor (*see below*).

Ulster's second city, situated on the River FOYLE in County Londonderry (of which it is the county town), near where it enters Lough Foyle, 100 km (62 miles) northwest of Belfast. It is also a local authority district. Its name has been a bone of contention between Unionists and Nationalists, the former using **Londonderry** and the latter insisting on

the original **Derry**. A solution has been to use Derry/Londonderry, spoken 'Derry stroke Londonderry'; this in turn has led to the place being referred to as **Stroke City** (said to have been coined by the radio personality Gerry Anderson). It also known as **the Wee City**, from the overuse of the word 'wee' (Ulster-Scots for 'little') by its inhabitants.

Sir Henry Docwra, who captured the city in 1600 (*see below*), compared the topography of the city to a bent bow, 'whereof the bog is the string and the river the bow'. The city was dubbed by the poet Francis Lewidge (1891–1917) as 'Derry of the little hills' (in 'The Blackbirds'). For the seasonal workers from Donegal who came here en route to Scotland in the 19th and 20th centuries, it had a very different image:

> God's choice about the company He keeps and never comes near Derry.
>
> Patrick McGill: *The Rat Pit* (1915)

Despite this apparent aversion, God's representative, St Columba (Columcille), founded a monastery here in 546 – but the place was different then:

> It is for this that I love Derry,
> For its quietness, for its purity;
> All full of angels
> Is every leaf on the oaks of Derry.
>
> Anon.: 'Columcille's Greeting to Ireland' (12th century), once attributed to Columba; translated by William Reeves and Kuno Meyer

In the Middle Ages, Derry was known as **Doire Choluim Cille** ('Columba's oak grove'), and it was from Derry that Columba sailed to Scotland, eventually establishing his monastery on IONA.

Derry successfully resisted attacks by the Vikings and Anglo-Normans, but was captured in 1600 during the Nine Years' War by an English force under Sir Henry Docwra. In 1613 James I presented the borough and its environs to the citizens of London, and many English Protestants settled there. In 1689, as the army of the Catholic James II approached, 13 Derry apprentices and citizens loyal to William of Orange rose against the governor (who was preparing to surrender) and locked the gates, with cries of 'No surrender!' The **Siege of Londonderry** had begun. The defenders held out for 15 weeks against the Jacobites, until they were relieved on 28 July; thousands in the city are said to have died of malnutrition and disease. This sturdy Protestant resistance has long been celebrated in Apprentice Boys' Marches and denigrated by Irish patriots:

> But, for you, Londonderry, may Plague smite and slay Your people! May ruin desolate you stone by stone!
>
> Anon.: 'Farewell, O Patrick Sarsfield' (late 17th century), translated from the Irish by James Clarence Mangan (Sarsfield was the leader of the Irish forces at the surrender of LIMERICK.)

Much of the old city wall still survives, now topped by sculptures by Antony Gormley. The city's resistance to siege earned it the byname **the Maiden City**:

> That hallowed graveyard yonder
> Swells with the slaughtered dead –
> O brothers! Pause and ponder –
> It was for us they bled;
> And while their gift we own, boys –
> The fane that tops our hill –
> Oh! The Maiden on her throne, boys,
> Shall be a Maiden still!
>
> Charlotte Elizabeth Tonna (1790–1846): 'The Maiden City'

The city loomed large in the Troubles, and was the site of the 1972 Bloody Sunday shootings; *see* BOGSIDE *and* FREE DERRY CORNER.

> The unemployment in our bones
> Erupting on our hands in stones …
>
> Seamus Deane (b.1940): 'Derry'

> Some Ulster towns inspired fear the way a man with an ugly face frightens a stranger: their scars implied violence. Derry was a scarred city …
>
> Paul Theroux: *The Kingdom by the Sea* (1983)

Derry/Londonderry was the birthplace of the dramatist George Farquhar (*c*.1677–1707); of the murderous resurrectionist William Hare (*fl*.1820s), who turned king's evidence against his colleague William Burke; and of the novelist Joyce Cary (1888–1957). The arch-reactionary Tory politician Lord Castlereagh succeeded his father as **Marquess of Londonderry** in 1821; he cut his own throat the following year.

There is a Cape Londonderry in Western Australia, and a town called Londonderry in the USA (New Hampshire).

Derry crimson. The colour of the collarettes and other insignia of the Apprentice Boys society, founded in 1814 and named after the town's Protestant heroes (*see above*). The colour commemorates the bloody flag that flew throughout the siege.

'Londonderry Air'. A traditional Irish air, collected by Jane Ross of Limavady, County Londonderry, in 1851, from an itinerant fiddler called MacCormick. It is thought that the air may have originated with the 17th-century harpist Ruairí Dall Ó Catháin. Among the various texts supplied to the tune, by far the best-known is 'Danny Boy', by Fred E. Weatherly (1848–1929), and this has been put forward by some as an alternative, more peaceful national anthem for the Republic, to replace the martial 'Soldier's Song'. In response to proposals to change the official name of Londonderry to Derry, commentators have pointed out that 'Londonderry Air' would be transformed to 'Derry Air', a homophone for *derrière*, a French bottom.

whole of Derry and the half of Strabane, the. A phrase

used in northwestern Ireland to denote a large crowd. STRABANE is some 20 km (12 miles) to the south.

Derry Cairngorm. *See* CAIRN GORM.

Derrynasaggart Mountains Irish *Sléibhte Dhoire na Sagart* 'mountains of the oak-grove of the priests'.
A range of hills in southwest Ireland, spanning counties KERRY and CORK. The highest point (699 m / 2293 ft) is one of the PAPS, while to the east CAHERBARNAGH (682 m / 2237 ft) is the highest summit in Cork.

Derryveagh Mountains Irish *Sléibhte Dhoire Bheitheach* 'mountains of the oak-grove in the birch-tree region'.
A range of hills in County DONEGAL, 50 km (31 miles) west of Derry/Londonderry. The tops include Slieve Snaght (683 m / 2240 ft) and the somewhat detached peak of ERRIGAL (752 m / 2467 ft) to the north, the highest hill in Donegal.

Dersingham 'Deorsige's people's homestead', OE male personal name *Deorsige* + *-inga-* (*see* -ING) + HAM.
A village in Norfolk, close to the southeastern corner of the WASH, about 13 km (8 miles) northeast of King's Lynn. SANDRINGHAM is just to the southeast.

Derventia. A Roman settlement on the site of modern DERBY.

Derventio. A Roman settlement on the site of the North Yorkshire town of MALTON, and the name given to a Roman fort on the River DERWENT[1] at present-day PAPCASTLE.

Derwent[1] Apparently an OCelt river name meaning 'river copiously lined with oak trees'.
A river of Cumbria (formerly in Cumberland), about 50 km (30 miles) long. It rises in BORROWDALE in the Lake District, to the east of the **Derwent Fells**, before entering the beautiful lake of **Derwent Water**:

> … this evening, approaching Derwentwater in diversity of harmonious features, in the majesty of its beauties and in the beauty of its majesty – O my God! and the black crags close under the snowy mountains, whose snows were pinkish with the setting sun and the reflections from the sandy rich clouds that floated over some and rested upon others! It was to me a vision of a fair country. Why were you not with us Dorothy? Why were not you, Mary [Hutchinson]?
>
> Samuel Taylor Coleridge: letter to Dorothy Wordsworth (10 November 1799)

Coleridge was so taken with the lake (he lived at its northern end) that he called one of his sons Derwent. Another child, the five-year-old John Ruskin, visited with his parents, and later recalled as one of his earliest memories the view of Derwent Water from Friar's Crag, 'through the hollows in the mossy roots, over the crag into the dark lake'. One of the small islands on the lake, St Herbert's Island, was the model for Owl Island in Beatrix Potter's *The Tale of Squirrel Nutkin* (1903). It was the beauty of Derwent Water and its surroundings that inspired Canon Rawnsley, Vicar of Crosthwaite, Keswick, and others to found the National Trust in 1895, so that such places should be for ever accessible to all.

> The Approach to Derwent Water is rich and magnificent beyond any means of conception – the Mountains all round sublime and graceful and rich in colour – Woods and wooded islands here and there …
>
> > John Keats: letter to George and Georgiana Keats (28 June 1818)

From Derwent Water the river flows northwest to BASSENTHWAITE LAKE, then west through COCKERMOUTH to the sea.

The Derwent features frequently in the poetry of Wordsworth; for example:

> By Derwent's side my Father's cottage stood,
> (The Woman thus her artless story told)
> One field, a flock, and what the neighbouring flood
> Supplied, to him were more than mines of gold.
>
> > William Wordsworth: 'The Female Vagrant', from *Lyrical Ballads* (1798)

Wordsworth even credits the river (which flowed past his father's house in Cockermouth) with inculcating in him as an infant the soothing (to some, the soporific) rhythms of his adult verse:

> Was it for this
> That one, the fairest of all Rivers, lov'd
> To blend his murmurs with my Nurse's song,
> And from his alder shades and rocky falls,
> And from his fords and shallows, sent a voice
> That flow'd along my dreams? For this, didst Thou,
> O Derwent! travelling over the green Plains
> Near my 'sweet Birthplace,' didst thou, beauteous Stream,
> Make ceaseless music through the night and day
> Which with its steady cadence, tempering
> Our human waywardness, compos'd my thoughts
> To more than infant softness, giving me,
> Among the fretful dwellings of mankind,
> A foretaste, a dim earnest, of the calm
> That Nature breathes among the hills and groves.
>
> > William Wordsworth: *The Prelude* (1805–50), Book I

Less loftily, the poet goes on to recall skinny dipping in the river as boy.

Earl of Derwentwater. The most notable holder of this title was James Radcliffe, 3rd Earl (1689–1716), an English Jacobite. He was one of the leaders of the 1715 Rebellion, and was executed on London's Tower Hill, after his defeat at the Battle of Preston (*see under* PRESTON).

Derwent[2]. A river in northeast England. It rises in the **Derwent Reservoir** 9 km (5.5 miles) east of CONSETT. The reservoir, popular for watersports, has a dam 1 km (0.6 miles) long, and is situated on the border of Northumberland and County Durham. The River Derwent continues to form the boundary for another 20 km (12 miles) or so as it flows generally northeastward, joining the TYNE[1] at NEWCASTLE. **Derwentside** is a district of north-central County Durham.

In the Derwent's upper reaches, west of Allensford, is a place on the river called the Sneep, where hidden hollows open in the rock at the foot of a wooded slope. This is said in local legend to be AVALON –

> Where falls not hail, or rain or any snow …

– and where King Arthur sleeps with his horses and his knights.

Derwent Black Fox, the. A creature sighted intermittently over the years in the woodlands of the lower Derwent valley.

Derwent[3]. A river in Yorkshire, known to Bede in the 8th century as **Deruuentionis fluvii**. It rises in the eastern NORTH YORK MOORS near Fylingdales, flows south parallel to the coast, then cuts westwards away from the coast to MALTON (Roman **Derventio**), then south, forming the boundary between the East Riding and York and North Yorkshire, before joining the OUSE[2]. Its length is 92 km (57 miles). The battle of STAMFORD BRIDGE (1066) was fought on the Derwent, east of York. The floodplains of the river are called the **Derwent Ings** (from the Old Scandinavian word *eng* 'outlying pasture').

Derwent[4]. A river in Derbyshire, which rises in the PEAK DISTRICT and flows 97 km (60 miles) southeastwards through DERBY to join the River TRENT[1] to the west of LONG EATON. For some distance it forms the boundary between Derbyshire and South Yorkshire.

The **Derwent Valley**, south of MATLOCK, is an important site in industrial history, with its preponderance of factory mills for cotton from the early 1900s: much of the area has accordingly been designated by UNESCO the '**Derwent Valley Mills**' World Heritage Site.

Its headwaters fill a succession of three reservoirs which have been made from it along **Derwent Dale** (in what has been dubbed Derbyshire's 'Lake District'): Howden Reservoir, **Derwent Reservoir** and LADYBOWER RESERVOIR. The Dam Busters of 617 Squadron practised bouncing their bombs off the first two before their celebrated raid on German dams in 1943, and most of the flying scenes in the 1954 film *The Dam Busters* were made in the area.

The **Derwent Watershed Walk** is one of the big walks of the HIGH PEAK.

The Derwent has a reputation of dealing harshly with those who treat it lightly; at the beginning of the 20th century a local woman is recorded to have commented on a recent drowning:

> He didna know Darrant, he said it were nought but a brook. But Darrant got 'im … He knows now! Nought but a brook! He knows now!

Derwentside. *See under* DERWENT[2].

Desmond Irish *Des-Muma* 'south MUNSTER'; *compare* ORMOND, THOMOND.

A historic territory (11th–17th centuries) in the southwest of Ireland, broadly corresponding to the counties of CORK and KERRY. Up to the later 12th century, the ruler of Desmond alternated with the ruler of Thomond as king of MUNSTER. The Anglo-Norman Fitzgeralds became earls of Desmond (*see below*) in the 14th century.

Desmond rebellions. Two rebellions against the English by the Fitzgeralds of Desmond (*see below*). The first broke out in 1569 and was led by Sir James Fitzgerald, cousin of Gerald Fitzgerald, the 14th Earl of Desmond. Sir James returned from exile in 1579 to lead another rebellion, but was soon killed. The 14th Earl (known as the Rebel Earl) then took up the struggle himself, until he was killed and the rebellion quelled in 1583, after which Kerry and LIMERICK were subjected to English plantation.

Earl of Desmond. The first Anglo-Norman Earl of Desmond was Maurice Fitzgerald, who obtained the title in 1329. His descendants (until the line died out in 1601) were almost independent rulers and played a significant role in Irish history.

Destitution Road. A road near Dundonnell in Wester Ross (*see under* ROSS AND CROMARTY), rising to 338 m (1109 ft) and commanding spectacular views of AN TEALLACH. Named in memory of the sufferings of the HIGH-LANDS during the potato famines of 1846–7 and 1851, Destitution Road was built as part of a programme of relief through public works, the destitute Highland labourers who built it being paid in food only.

Deugh, Water of. *See* DEE[3].

Deva. The Roman settlement more fully known as **Castra Devana**, on the site of what is now CHESTER.

Devenish Island *Devenish* Irish *Daimhinis* 'ox island' + tautological English addition.

A small island in Lower Lough Erne (*see under* ERNE), County Fermanagh. **St Molaise of Devenish** founded a monastery here in the 6th century. Although it was sacked by the Vikings in the 9th century and again in 1157, it was an important religious site until the 17th century. The remains include a 12th-century round tower (26 m / 85 ft

high) and a 15th-century abbey and high cross. The book shrine called the Soiscél Molaise used to be kept here but is now in the National Museum, Dublin.

Deveron Gaelic *dubh* 'black' (*see* DDU, DUBH) + a pre-Celtic river name, from a root *ara* 'water-course', thought to be the same as that in FINDHORN.

A river of northeast Scotland, rising in the hills of southern MORAY and flowing generally northeastwards for 99 km (61 miles) into Aberdeenshire, to reach the North Sea at BANFF.

Devil's Arrows, the. A line of three (originally five) remarkable Bronze Age standing stones, visible from the A1 near BOROUGHBRIDGE, North Yorkshire. The stones were quarried at KNARESBOROUGH, some 10 km (6 miles) away. They were previously ascribed to the druids (i.e. the later Iron Age) and thus to devildom.

A particular legend tells how the king of the Brigantes asked some Christian missionaries and druids to debate the merits of their respective faiths. The Christians were getting the better of it until a new druid arrived, who was a persuasive debater. However, it was noticed that his feet were demonically melting the stone he stood on; discovered, he formed the molten rock into three bolts with which he flew off to destroy the capital of the Brigantes. Fortunately divine intervention drove the bolts harmlessly to the ground. A simpler story tells how the Devil attempted to fire these stone arrows at the nearby Christian settlement of Aldborough from Howe Hill, but that they fell short, forming a line.

Devil's Arse, the. A nickname for the Peak Cavern (*see under* PEAK DISTRICT).

Devil's Beef Tub, the From its former use as a hiding place for smuggled cattle.

A steep-sided semicircular hollow, about 180 m (600 ft) deep, on the south side of Annanhead Hill, some 8 km (5 miles) north of Moffat. It was formerly in Dumfriesshire, and is now in Dumfries and Galloway.

The Devil's Beef Tub acquired its name at the time of the medieval Border reivers (raiders), when the Johnstone clan used the remote corrie to hide stolen cattle. The corrie is the source of the River ANNAN[1], and on its west side is an ancient road pass (now taken by the A701), linking Annandale with upper Tweeddale (*see under* TWEED).

In a story from the 1745 Jacobite Rising, it is said that a Highlander, MacLaren of Invenenty, retreating northwards escaped his would-be captors by wrapping himself in his plaid and rolling down the steep slopes to the bottom of the Devil's Beef Tub. This incident inspired the passage in Sir Walter Scott's *Redgauntlet* (1824), a novel about an imagined Jacobite revolt some years after that of 1745, in which the Laird of Summertrees makes a similarly daring escape here. In 1831, as commemorated by a monument near the summit of the pass, the driver and guard of the Dumfries-to-Edinburgh mail coach perished near here in a blizzard.

Devils Bit Mountain After the story of Satanic frustration associated with the place.

A hill (479 m / 1571 ft) in County Tipperary, 15 km (9 miles) northwest of THURLES. The source of the River SUIR is on its flanks. The story behind the name is that the Devil, irritated at his inability to collect Irish souls (such was the piety of the land), took a bite out of the mountain, the result being a great cleft. He then spat out his mouthful as the Rock of CASHEL. Pedants among the geological fraternity point out that the mountain is made of old red sandstone whereas the Rock of Cashel consists of limestone, but against this it should be pointed out that creationists have long recognized the fondness of the Devil for manipulating geological evidence (fossils, strata, etc.) to deceive the more gullible members of the scientific community.

Devil's Bridge¹. A small village in Ceredigion (formerly Cardiganshire, then in Dyfed), 16 km (10 miles) east of Aberystwyth. There are three bridges here, one above the other, over the deep gorge of the River Mynach. The Welsh name is **Pontarfynach** ('bridge over the Mynach', Welsh *pont* 'bridge' + *ar* 'over the' + *Mynach* 'monk (river)'; *see below*).

The lowest bridge, the Monk's Bridge, was built by the monks of STRATA FLORIDA Abbey in the 12th century, but according to legend it was the Devil who built the bridge, for an old lady whose cow had become stranded on the other side of the gorge. In return he demanded the first living creature to cross the bridge, but, to outwit him, the old lady threw some bread across the bridge and her dog ran after it – and so acquired a new master. (More or less the same story is told of Devil's Bridge over the River Lune at KIRKBY LONSDALE, Cumbria.) The higher bridges were built in the 18th and 20th centuries.

Devil's Bridge². A medieval (13th century) bridge over the River Lune at KIRKBY LONSDALE, Cumbria. The story behind its name is virtually identical to that told of the DEVIL'S BRIDGE¹ in Wales.

Devil's Cheesewring, the. A mass of eight stones rising to a height of 9.8 m (32 ft) in the VALLEY OF THE ROCKS, Lynton, Devon, so called because it looks like a giant cheesepress ('cheesewring' was a West Country word for a cheesepress).

See also the CHEESEWRING.

Devil's Chimney, the. An outcrop of rock, shaped like a crooked chimney, situated above a disused quarry on the western side of Leckhampton Hill, 1 km (0.6 miles) south of CHELTENHAM, Gloucestershire.

Theories as to its origins abound. Local legend saw it as the home of the Devil, who resides deep in the ground beneath. Its curious shape led one local historian to speculate that it was a 'rude creation of some fanciful shepherd'. Others have speculated that the rock was created in jest by 18th-century quarry-workers. A scientifically more plausible explanation attributes its shape to the effects of differential erosion, which has created a column of harder rock as the softer rock around it has been has been worn away.

Devil's Den, the. A Neolithic passage grave some 5 km (3 miles) east of Avebury, Wiltshire. Only a few megaliths remain of what must once have been an impressive chambered tomb. After the coming of Christianity to Britain, prehistoric remains such as this were frequently associated with the Devil.

The Devil's Den was the subject of a watercolour by the landscape artist John Sell Cotman (1782–1842).

Devil's Dyke¹ *Dyke* 'embankment', OE *dic* 'ditch', later 'bank formed by excavating a ditch'.

An ancient military earthwork (also known as **the Devil's Ditch**) in Cambridgeshire stretching from REACH across Newmarket Heath (*see under* NEWMARKET¹) to Wood Ditton, south of Newmarket, and thought to have been built by the East Anglians as a defence against the Mercians *c.* 6th century AD. On the eastern side it is 5.5 m (18 ft) high.

> The Devil's Dyke, as this barrier is called, is clearly a work of defence against enemies advancing from the Fens; and as a defence to the East Anglians it was of priceless value, stretching as it did from a point where the country became fenny and impassable to a point where the woods equally forbade all access, it covered the only entrance to the country they had won.
>
>   J.R. Green: *The Making of England* (1882)

For much of the Middle Ages it was also known as **St Edmund's Ditch**, and it was supposed to mark the boundary of the land given to the Abbey of BURY ST EDMUNDS's by King Cnut (1016–35) by way of apology to the monks for the savagery of his father, Sweyn, in his campaigns in England in the early years of the 11th century.

Devil's Dyke² *Dyke* 'ditch, trench', OE *dic*.

A deep cleft in the SOUTH DOWNS above the village of Poynings, West Sussex, northwest of Brighton (the Downs at this point are 200 m (700 ft) above sea level and offer breathtaking views northwards to the WEALD). The legend is that St Cuthman, priding himself on having christianized the area and having built a nunnery where the dykehouse was later built, was confronted by the Devil and told that all his labour was vain for he would swamp the whole country before morning. St Cuthman went to the nunnery and told the abbess to keep the sisters in prayer until after midnight and then to illuminate the windows. The Devil came at sunset with mattock and spade and began digging a ditch into the sea, but was seized with rheumatic pains all over his body. He flung down his tools, and the cocks, mistaking the illuminated windows for sunrise, began to crow, whereupon the Devil fled in alarm, leaving his work unfinished.

Devil's Elbow, the From the sharp hairpin bends.

A section of the old road just south of the CAIRNWELL Pass, the pass (655 m / 2148 ft high) between Gleann Beag (commonly called GLEN SHEE) and Glen Clunie, some 16 km (10 miles) south of Braemar. It was so named because of its steep double hairpin bend that proved a challenge for many older motor cars, especially in wintry conditions, although boiling radiators in summer could also halt progress. The new road, although still steep, is straighter.

Devil's Frying Pan, the. A curiously shaped rock basin filled by the sea at high tide, situated near the village of Cadgwith, east of LIZARD Point, Cornwall. In 1906 the *Socoa*, bound for San Francisco in California with a cargo of concrete to help rebuild the city after the disastrous earthquake, foundered in the sea off Cadgwith. The concrete sits on the seabed to this day.

Devil's Glen Probably a reference to the large size of the glen.

A wooded defile in County Wicklow, through which the River Vartry tumbles (one of the falls is about 30 m / 100 ft high). The glen is some 8 km (5 miles) northwest of WICKLOW, to the west of the small village of Ashford. Its Irish name is **An Gleann Mór** ('the big glen') or alternatively **Bun na Eas** ('bottom of the waterfall').

Devil's Half-Acre. The nickname given by Michael Collins, leader of the Irish forces during the Anglo-Irish War (1919–21), to Dublin Castle (*see under* DUBLIN), the headquarters of British rule in Ireland until the creation of the Free State at the end of 1921.

Devil's Head, the. *See* the DEIL'S HEID.

Devil's Hole[1]. A system of trenches in the North Sea about 200 km (120 miles) east of Dundee, with a depth in excess of 230 m (750 ft). It was so named by fishermen who frequently lost their trawler nets on the sides of the trenches.

Devil's Hole[2]. A spectacular blow hole on the coast of JERSEY.

Devil's Kitchen, the. A vertical fissure or 'chimney' in the forbidding crags at the back of CWM IDWAL, on the north side of the GLYDERS in Snowdonia, Gwynedd (formerly in Caernarvonshire). When there was cloud on the mountain above the 'chimney' it was said that the Devil

was cooking – hence the name. The Welsh name is **Twll Du** ('black hole').

Devils Mother From the Irish name *Machaire an Deamhain* 'Devil's plain', with *machaire* 'plain' being rendered in English as *Mother*; there is a story that the original Irish name was *Magairli an Deamhain* 'Devil's Testicles'.

A hill (647 m / 2122 ft) in Joyce Country, on the border of counties Galway and Mayo, some 50 km (31 miles) northwest of Galway itself. It is also spelt **Devilsmother**.

Devil's Nostrils, the. Two vast caverns separated by a huge pillar of natural rock on Mainland, Shetland.

Devil's Point, the A bowdlerized translation of the Gaelic *Bod an Deamhain* 'the Devil's penis'.

A sharply pointed, if not exactly phallic, peak (1004 m / 3293 ft) in the CAIRNGORM MOUNTAINS. It is a subsidiary summit of CAIRN TOUL, 2.5 km (1.5 miles) to the southeast of the main peak, and stands proudly above the southern approach to the LAIRIG GHRU. In the 19th century a pious gentleman, a certain Mr Copland, gave the name **the Angel's Peak** to another subsidiary peak, on the northwest side of Cairn Toul, although this bore no relation to its Gaelic name, Sgòr an Lochain Uaine ('pinnacle of the green lochan').

Devil's Punch Bowl, the[1] Probably a reference to the size and shape of the dell.

A deep dell on the southwest side of HINDHEAD Hill, Surrey, scene of the murder of an unknown sailor in 1786. His assassins, Lonagan, Casey and Marshall, were hanged in chains on nearby Hindhead Common. Overlooking the Devil's Punch Bowl is the 272-m (894-ft) Gibbet Hill, used formerly as its name suggests.

Devil's Punch Bowl, the[2]. A dell on MANGERTON MOUNTAIN, County Kerry, some 10 km (6 miles) south of Killarney.

Devil's Ridge, the. *See under* the MAMORES.

Devil's Staircase, the. The steep section of the old military road from GLEN COE over the shoulder (550 m / 1800 ft) of Stob Mhic Mhartuin, heading for the Blackwater Reservoir and Kinlochleven. When the dam for the reservoir was being built, it was not uncommon for labourers, having overindulged in the bar at the KINGSHOUSE, to lose themselves on the hills and perish while attempting to traverse the Devil's Staircase back to their huts at the dam. The path is now part of the West Highland Way (*see under* the HIGHLANDS).

Devil's Testicles. *See* DEVILS MOTHER.

Devil's Water Originally from the same elements that comprise DOUGLAS[1] and DAWLISH: Welsh *du glas*, Irish *dubh glais* 'dark river' (*see* DDU, DUBH).

A small tributary of the TYNE[1] in Northumberland. It rises near Hangman Hill some 15 km (9 miles) south of

HEXHAM, and flows northward to join the Tyne between Hexham and CORBRIDGE.

Devil's Water. A medium-strength beer manufactured by the Hexhamshire Brewery since 1992.

Devizes '(place at) the boundaries' (referring to the boundary between the Hundreds of Potterne and Cannings, which passed through the Norman castle), OFr *devises* 'boundaries'. (From the 14th to the 17th century the town was often known by the abbreviated name *Vize* or *Vizes*.)

A market town in WILTSHIRE, at the northern edge of Salisbury Plain, about 32 km (20 miles) southwest of Swindon. It grew up around the Norman castle built here by Bishop Roger of Salisbury in the 12th century (the original castle was destroyed by Cromwell's forces – the present-day one is 19th-century). It remains an important market town, and is the oldest manufacturer of snuff in England.

Devizes stands on the Kennet and Avon Canal (*see under* KENNET[1]), which just to the west of the town ascends 72 m (237 ft) up Caen Hill in a flight of 29 locks – the longest in Britain.

The market cross in Devizes bears the following inscription:

> The Mayor and Corporation of Devizes avail themselves of the Stability of this Building, to transmit to future time, the Record of an awful Event which occurred in this Market Place, in the year 1753, hoping that such a Record may serve as a salutary Warning against the Danger of impiously invoking Divine Vengeance, or of calling on the Holy Name of God to conceal the Devices of Falsehood and Fraud.
>
> On Thursday the 25th of January 1753, Ruth Pierce, of Potterne, in this County agreed with three other Women to buy a Sack of Wheat in the Market, each paying her due Proportion towards the same. One of these Women, in collecting the several Quotas of Money discovered a Deficiency, and demanded of Ruth Pierce the Sum which was wanting to make up the Amount; Ruth Pierce protested that She had paid her Share, and said, "*She wished She might drop down dead, if She had not.*" She rashly repeated this awful Wish, when, to the Consternation and Terror of the surrounding Multitude, She instantly fell down and expired, having the Money concealed in her Hand.

Devon[1] '(territory) of the Devonians', OE *Defena* possessive form of *Defnas* 'Devonians', from OCelt *Dumnonii*, the name of a Celtic people (*see also* DUMNONIA). This has been interpreted by some as 'deep ones', suggesting a reference to valley-dwellers. According to legend it comes from *Debon*, the name of one of the heroes who came with Brutus from Troy and was allotted this part of Albion, which was thus 'Debon's share'.

A county of southwest England (also called **Devonshire**), bounded to the west by Cornwall and to the east by Somerset and Dorset, and with the Bristol Channel to the north and the English Channel to the south. At 6562 sq km (2534 sq miles) it is the third-largest English county. It contains the unitary authorities PLYMOUTH and TORBAY, and other important centres are BARNSTAPLE, BIDEFORD, EXETER (its administrative headquarters), EXMOUTH, HONITON, ILFRACOMBE, NEWTON ABBOT, PAIGNTON, TEIGNMOUTH, TIVERTON and TORQUAY. Its main rivers are the DART, the EXE and the TAMAR (which forms the boundary with CORNWALL). Much of the southwest of the county is taken up with DARTMOOR National Park, while its southeastern corner is dominated by the BLACKDOWN HILLS and parts of the southeastern coastline are a UNESCO World Heritage Site (under the label '**Dorset and East Devon Coast**'). In the north it shares EXMOOR with Somerset. The bracing north Devon coast and the rather more relaxing southern riviera (from BRIXHAM around to SEATON) attract holidaymakers in steady numbers, who are often tempted further inland by Devon's uniquely comforting landscape of small rolling hills and cosy valleys. The SOUTH HAMS peninsula has perhaps the mildest climate in mainland Britain.

> The contoured map of Devon makes an intricate picture, one which appears at first sight to defy any reduction to simple statements, with thousands of little streams in their combes, hills tumbling away in all directions, ragged and indented coasts, and a variation of surface every mile or so.
>
> W.G. Hoskins: *Devon* (1954)

Agriculture and tourism are the county's most important present-day money-earners. Its most renowned agricultural products are Devon cider, made from local apples, and Devonshire clotted cream, which together with strawberry jam and scones forms the temptatious triumvirate at the heart of the **Devonshire cream tea**. It can be bought in mail-friendly little drums, and tourists in Devon have always delighted in sending off these cholesterol bombs to their family and friends.

> A feast … of saffron buns, Devonshire cream, and cyder.
>
> Charlotte Yonge: *The Two Guardians* (1852)

Devon's major seaport, Plymouth, looks out towards the Atlantic and the world, and the county has long enjoyed a reputation as a springboard for high-seas adventure and discovery. Both Sir Francis Drake and Sir Walter Raleigh were Devonians, and their exploits became part of English national myth in, for example, the novels of G.A. Henty and the verse of Sir Henry Newbolt: 'Drake he was a Devon man, an' ruled the Devon seas' (*Drake's Drum* (1897)).

With its mild and kindly climate, its gentle pace and the bounty of its fields and seas, there are many who have viewed Devon as a sort of earthly paradise:

When Adam and Eve were dispossessed
Of the garden hard by Heaven,
They planted another one down in the west,
'Twas Devon, glorious Devon!

> Harold Boulton: 'Glorious Devon' (1902)

Not everyone has been so impressed, though:

Devonshire … is a splashy, rainy, misty … floody, muddy,
slipshod County.

> John Keats: letter (1818)

In cricketing terms Devon is a 'minor county' (the club
was founded in 1899) and plays in the minor counties
championship.

The **Duke of Devonshire** (a title dating back to
1694) has his seat not in Devon but in Derbyshire, at
CHATSWORTH.

There are towns called Devon in Canada (Alberta and
Ontario) and the USA (Montana).

Devon. Any of a breed of hardy red beef cattle that
originated in Devon.

Devonian. A term meaning 'of or relating to Devon or its
people', or, as a noun, 'a native or inhabitant of Devon'.
In addition, since the late 1830s the term has been applied
in palaeontology and geology specifically to the prehistoric time period of the Palaeozoic era between the
Silurian and the Carboniferous, when the first land plants
flourished and vertebrates left the water for the first time
(between 395 and 345 million years ago), or to the system
of rocks laid down at that time. The usage was proposed
by Adam Sedgwick and Sir Roderick Murchison, who had
studied such rocks in Devon. **The Devonian** is also the name
of an express rail service running from West Yorkshire to
Paignton in Devon.

Devon rex. A breed of cat characterized by an elfin face,
large ears and a wavy or curly coat. It originated in 1959.

Devon Scot, the. An express rail service running from
Aberdeen to Plymouth in Devon.

devonshire, to. To clear or improve land by paring off
turf, stubble, weeds, etc., burning them and spreading the
ashes on the land. The usage, which dates back at least to
the early 17th century, reflects the prevalence of this form
of land husbandry in Devon. It survived until the late 19th
century, by which time it had been eroded to *denshire* or
denshare:

> The system of densharing or devonshiring old and poor
> pasture had made considerable progress.
>
> James E. Thorold Rogers: *A History of Agriculture and Prices in
> England from 1259 to 1793* (1887)

Devonshire dumpling. A jocular term for a Devon person of roly-poly proportions.

Devonshire poet, the. An epithet accorded to O. Jones,
a journeyman woolcomber, writer of *Poetic Attempts* (1786).

Other Devon poets are John Gay (1685–1732) of BARN-
STAPLE and Edward Capern (1819–94), the postman poet
of BIDEFORD. The bell that Capern carried on his rounds
still hangs in a niche on his tombstone at HEANTON
PUNCHARDON.

Devonshire Quarrendon. An old deep-crimson variety
of apple once common in Devon. The origin of the word
Quarrendon is not known.

Devonshire wainscot. A species of moth, *Leucania
putrescens*, found on the south Devon coast.

'Discontents in Devon'. A poem by Robert Herrick
(1591–1674), who was vicar of the south Devon village of
Dean Prior from 1630 until 1647 when he was ejected from
his living for his support of Charles I. Herrick wrote a
number of poems in praise of the simple pleasures of the
countryside ('I sing of Brooks, of Blossomes, Birds and
Bowers'), but 'Discontents in Devon' shows him exasperated
by the isolation of rural life:

> More discontents I never had
> Since I was born, than here;
> Where I have been, and still am sad
> In this dull Devonshire …

Herrick was delighted to be extirpated from the West
Country (*see* 'His Return to London' *under* LONDON), but
he would be reinstated at Dean Prior in 1660, following
the restoration of Charles II.

Devon² 'black river', Gaelic *dubh* 'black' (*see* DDU, DUBH)
+ *abhainn* 'river'; the Gaelic name is *Duibhe*, possibly derived
from the name of an ancient Celtic goddess; *Dowane* 1521.

A river in central Scotland, in Perth and Kinross, Fife and
Clackmannanshire. Some 45 km (28 miles) long, it rises
on the north side of the OCHIL HILLS, then flows east then
south through **Glen Devon** (which, together with GLEN
EAGLES to the north, forms a passage through the Ochils,
and was formerly much used by cattle drovers). The river
then cuts west across the carse (plain) on the south side
of the Ochil Hills to join the FORTH east of Stirling. The
two **Glendevon Reservoirs** are in upper Glen Devon,
while the village of **Glendevon** is in the lower part of the
glen.

'Fairest Maid on Devon Banks'. Probably the last poem of
Robert Burns, written on 12 July 1796 (he died on 21 July),
and recalling a happy time in 1787 when he whiled away
the hours on the banks of the Devon with Peggy Chalmers
and Charlotte Hamilton.

> Fairest maid on Devon banks,
> Crystal Devon, winding Devon,
> Wilt thou lay that frown aside,
> And smile as thou wert wont to do?

The words were intended to be sung to the tune
'Rothemurche's Rant', a traditional Scottish melody.

Devonport Coined around 1824 from *Devon* and *port*.

A district of PLYMOUTH in Devon, to the west of the city, on the eastern bank of the Tamar, opposite Torpoint. William III established a dockyard and naval base here at the end of the 17th century, but at first it was called '**Plymouth Dock**', or simply '**Dock**' (in the 18th century, the local inhabitants were known as 'Dockers'). The name 'Devonport' dates from around 1824, when the docks were enlarged. It became a separate town in 1837, but in 1914 it was formally amalgamated with Plymouth. It remains an important Royal Navy dockyard.

'Devonport' is the name of one of the parliamentary divisions of Plymouth. Lord (David) Owen, one of the founders of the Social Democratic Party, was its MP between 1974 and 1992.

The Antarctic explorer Captain Robert Falcon Scott (1868–1912) and the spy Guy Burgess (1910–63) were born in Devonport.

There are also Devonports in Tasmania, Australia, and in Auckland, New Zealand.

> I saw two sailors in Devonport City
> Their bones were of shell and their eyes were marine
> 'Never forget,' said the one to the other,
> 'The deeds we have done and the sights we have seen.'
>
> Charles Causley (1917–2003): 'Devonport'

Dewsbury 'Dewi's stronghold', OWelsh male personal name *Dewi* + OE *burh* (*see* BURY).

A textile-manufacturing town in West Yorkshire on the River CALDER[1], 12 km (7 miles) northeast of Huddersfield. According to tradition, Paulinus, first Archbishop of York, preached here in 627. With the aim of fending off a less saintly visitor, every Christmas Eve the parish church (which retains some Saxon elements) peels the 'Devil's Knell', in which the bell is rung once for each year since Christ's birth.

Dhá Chích Danainn. The Irish name for the PAPS.

Dhuhallow The first element is possibly Gaelic *dhu* 'black' (*see* DDU, DUBH), but the second element is obscure.

A small settlement on Loch Mhor, Highland (formerly in Inverness-shire), some 5 km (3 miles) east of Loch Ness.

Dial Post From the name of a local early 18th-century farm. The dial in question may have been part of a clock mechanism or other time-indicator, or the dial 'post' could have been a road-sign shaped like a clock-hand.

A village in West Sussex, about 11 km (7 miles) south of Horsham.

Diamond, the[1] A frequent English name for a crossroads in Northern Ireland.

A crossroads in County Armagh, on the outskirts of LOUGH-GALL, 7 km (4.5 miles) north of Armagh itself.

Battle of the Diamond (21 September 1795). A sectarian encounter in which the Protestant (so-called) Peep of Day Boys, holding a hilltop, successfully fought off an attack by a large force of Catholic Defenders, some 30 of whom were killed. Tradition has it that the first meeting of the Orange Order took place that evening.

> The battle of the Diamond!
> A triumph song we sing;
> Hurrah! We fought it for our faith!
> We won it for our King!
> Our King! Whom Papist fools denied,
> To follow Priest and Pope;
> But fallen, we left them without life,
> And living without hope.
>
> Anon.: 'The Battle of the Diamond' (Orange song)

Diamond, the[2]. The central square in COLERAINE, County Londonderry.

Dibden Purlieu *Dibden* 'deep valley', OE *deop* 'deep' + *denu* 'valley'; *Purlieu* 'outskirts of a forest', ME *purlewe*.

A town in Hampshire, on the eastern edge of the NEW FOREST and about 2.5 km (1.5 miles) from the western shore of Southampton Water. It is effectively merged with HYTHE to the west.

Dibley. A fictionalized version of TURVILLE in the BBC television sitcom *The Vicar of Dibley*.

Dickleburgh Perhaps 'Dicel's or Dicla's stronghold', OE male personal name *Dicel* or *Dicla* + OE *burh* (*see* BURY).

A village in Norfolk, about 5 km (3 miles) northeast of Diss.

Didcot 'Dud(d)a's cottage(s)', OE male personal name *Dud(d)a* + *cot* (*see* -COT, COTE).

A small but growing commuter town in Oxfordshire (before 1974 in Berkshire), about 16 km (10 miles) south of Oxford. It was a peaceful rural village until the Great Western Railway arrived in the 1840s. Its main line approached from London and split at Didcot, one line proceeding north via Oxford and the other turning westwards towards Bristol, Wales and the far South West. It remains an important and busy rail junction (its station is now named **Didcot Parkway**), and the Great Western Society maintains a railway museum here. For all who pass through on the train, though, or view the town more distantly (from the Berkshire Downs to the south, for instance), Didcot's un-ignorable landmark is the huge cooling towers of its power station, the prosaically named '**Didcot A**', built between 1972 and 1975 (a smaller power station, using natural gas to produce electricity and called '**Didcot B**', opened on the same site in 1997).

> He might dilate on the plumbing arrangements at
> Cheltenham or some ripe gossip from the beer tent.
> As a Westcountryman frequently required to journey
> east by train, he was forever getting stranded at Didcot.
>
> From Taunton School's obituary of the cricket writer and
> broadcaster Alan Gibson (1997)

Diddlebury 'Dud(d)ela's stronghold or manor', OE male personal name *Dud(d)ela* + BURY.

A village in Shropshire, to the southeast of WENLOCK EDGE, about 11 km (7 miles) north of Ludlow.

Didling '(land of) Dyddela's people', OE male personal name *Dyddela* + *-ingas* (*see* -ING).

A village in West Sussex, at the foot of the SOUTH DOWNS, about 6 km (4 miles) southwest of Midhurst.

Didsbury 'Dyddi's stronghold', OE male personal name *Dyddi* + BURY.

A district of Greater Manchester, 7 km (4 miles) south of Manchester itself, close to the River MERSEY. For centuries Didsbury was a quiet village of farms and hand-loom weaving, but from the late 18th and early 19th centuries its proximity to a fast-expanding industrial metropolis made it a desirable place of residence for successful merchants, and its future as an affluent dormitory suburb was assured.

Dinas Brân. *See* CASTELL DINAS BRÂN.

Dinas Emrys 'fort of Merlin', *Dinas* 'fort, castle', Welsh; *Emrys* actually Welsh for 'Ambrose', i.e. Ambrosius Aurelianus, the Romano-British leader against the Saxons, but the 12th-century historian Geoffrey of Monmouth conflated Merlin and Ambrosius.

An Iron Age hillfort in the GWYNANT VALLEY of Gwynedd (formerly in Caernarvonshire), 2 km (1.2 miles) northeast of Beddgelert. Dinas Emrys is traditionally the site where King Vortigern attempted to build a castle, which kept falling down. His seers explained that the blood of a boy with no father needed to be scattered on the hilltop. The young Merlin fitted the description, but before he could be sacrificed he prophesied that beneath the hill would be found a pool with two dragons, one white (representing the invading Saxons) and one red (representing the Welsh/Britons). When the lake was drained, the dragons woke up and fought each other, the red dragon putting the white to flight. This is said to be the reason the red dragon became the symbol of WALES.

Dinas Head *Dinas* 'fortress', Welsh.

A headland in Pembrokeshire (formerly in Dyfed), 7 km (4 miles) northeast of FISHGUARD. It as at the tip of **Dinas Island**, which is actually a peninsula, forming the east side of Fishguard Bay.

Dinbych. The Welsh name for DENBIGH.

Dinbych-y-Pysgod. The Welsh name for TENBY.

Dinder Probably 'hill with a fort', OCelt *din* 'fort' + *breg* 'hill'.

A village in Somerset, about 3 km (2 miles) southeast of Wells.

Dingle Irish *An Daingean* 'the fortress'.

A small port and tourist centre in County Kerry, 42 km (26 miles) west-southwest of Tralee, known as the most westerly town in Europe. It overlooks the deep inlet of **Dingle Bay**.

> The sun is sinking o'er the westward,
> The fleet is leaving Dingle shore,
> I watch the men row in their curraghs
> As they mark the fishing grounds near Scellig Mor.
> All through the night men toil until the daybreak
> While at home their wives and sweethearts kneel and
>   pray
> That God might guard them and protect them
> And bring them safely back to Dingle Bay
>
>   Anon.: 'Dingle Bay'

Dingle is on the south side of the **Dingle Peninsula**, the most northerly of the three Kerry peninsulas. It is also called the **Corcaguiney** or **Corkaguiney Peninsula** (Irish *Corc Dhuibhne* 'descendants of Duibhne', Duibhne being a 2nd-century grandson of a king of Ireland). It is a scenic area, including BRANDON MOUNTAIN and the SLIEVE MISH MOUNTAINS, and GARRAUN POINT at its tip is the most westerly mainland point in Ireland and thus in Europe. Beyond it are the BLASKET ISLANDS. David Lean's film *Ryan's Daughter* (1970) was filmed at various places around the Dingle Peninsula, including DUNQUIN harbour, Coumeenoole Bay and Inch Strand, together with the specially built set-village of 'Kirrary'. It was this film that brought a mass of tourists to a previously quiet area, of which the critic Cyril Connolly had earlier observed:

> The whole landscape is expectant and devotional like
> Iona and Delphi.

It was at the town of Dingle that Sir James Fitzgerald landed on 18 July 1579 with a force of Italians and Spaniards to further the Irish Catholic cause. He was killed shortly afterwards, but the rebellion continued until 1583 (*see* Desmond rebellions *under* DESMOND).

Dingle beds. The geologists' name for the strata comprising the mountains in the west of the Dingle Peninsula, including Brandon Mountain.

Dingle dolphin, the. A solitary dolphin that began to appear regularly in Dingle harbour in 1984. He was christened Fungie, and attracted both New Age and mainstream tourists:

> Suddenly Dingle was no longer remote. It became a
> Destination, recommended by all the *Rough* and *Lonely*
> *Guides*, with a marketing strategy, and an increasing sense
> of organized craic.
>
>   Pete McCarthy: *McCarthy's Bar* (2000)

However, Dingle's dingliness did not vanish entirely: McCarthy reported the place has a bicycle shop that doubles as a pub, with a bicycle in the window and a Guinness sign over the door.

Dingle, The ME *dingel* 'a deep hollow'.

A working-class, commercial area of south-central LIVER-POOL, known chiefly for being the birthplace in 1940 (in a small terraced house in Madryn Street) of Richard Starkey, later to metamorphose into Ringo Starr of Beatles fame. For his fellow band members, *see under* ALLERTON, SPEKE and WOOLTON.

Dingley Dell. A fictional village in Kent that forms the backdrop to several memorable scenes in Charles Dickens's *The Pickwick Papers* (1837), for instance the cricket match between Dingley Dell and All Muggleton. It is the home of the hospitable Mr Wardle.

The name has been given to a station on the Lavender Line steam railway in East Sussex.

Dingwall 'place of the parliament', OScand *thing* 'parliament, assembly, meeting' + *völlr* 'field of assembly'.

A town at the inner end of the Cromarty Forth (*see under* CROMARTY), some 18 km (11 miles) northwest of Inverness, in Highland. It was formerly the county town of ROSS AND CROMARTY, and then the administrative seat of Ross and Cromarty district. Macbeth, according to one tradition, was born here. There is a funerary obelisk in the town, upon a mound apparently raised by devoted local womenfolk, memorializing George, 1st Earl of Cromartie (1630–1714), who planned this burial arrangement to thwart his wife's expressed desire to dance upon his grave.

In 1879 a Dingwall man was imprisoned for assaulting an old woman he alleged was a witch. He apparently believed that if he shed her blood he would break the curse she had placed on his fishing boat, a spell that stopped him from landing any fish.

Dingwall boasts a professional football club, Ross County (*see under* ROSS AND CROMARTY).

Dinton 'estate associated with Dunna', OE male personal name *Dunna* + -ING + -TON.

A village in Buckinghamshire, about 5 km (3 miles) southwest of Aylesbury.

Dinton Hermit, the. John Bigg (1629–96), a scholar and recluse who spent the last 30 years of his life in a cave near Dinton. He was provided with food and drink by the local people, and his only additional request was for leather straps, which he would nail to his garments. One of his shoes, made up of 1000 pieces of leather, is in the Ashmolean Museum, Oxford.

Dirty River. *See under* DUNMANWAY.

Díseart Uí Dheá. The Irish name for the early monastic settlement of DYSERT O DEA.

Dishes OScand *dys* 'cairn'; it is unclear whether the English plural *-s* has been added or whether the original form was *dysjar-hus* 'cairn-house'.

A small settlement on STRONSAY, Orkney.

Disputes, the. *See* ARKENGARTHDALE.

Diss '(place at) the ditch or dyke', OE *dic*.

A small market town in Norfolk, on the River WAVENEY[1], about 35 km (22 miles) south of Norwich. It has a fine stock of buildings ranging in date from the Middle Ages to the Victorian era, but its most impressive feature is the large mere, or lake, that dominates its centre. The poet John Skelton (?1460–1529), who was Henry VIII's tutor, was once rector here, but his behaviour was too eccentric and often too scandalous for the good people of Diss: they complained to the Bishop of Norwich that he 'kept a fair wench in his house', who had just had a baby.

The composer John Wilbye (?1574–1638) was baptized in Diss.

Distinkhorn 'steward's hall', OE *disc-thegn* 'steward' + *ærn* 'hall, storehouse'.

A hill in East Ayrshire (formerly in Strathclyde region), some 5 km (3 miles) south of Darvel.

Ditch, the. An abbreviated East London nickname in the late 19th century for the district of SHOREDITCH (whence also the joint name **Ditch and Chapel** for Shoreditch and WHITECHAPEL) and for the street called HOUNDSDITCH.

Ditchling '(settlement of) Dicel's people', OE male personal name *Dicel* + *-ingas* (*see* -ING).

A village in East Sussex, on the edge of the SOUTH DOWNS, about 11 km (7 miles) north of Brighton. The sculptor, graphic designer and engraver Eric Gill set up an arts and crafts commune (the Guild of St Joseph and St Dominic) here in the early 1920s, before moving on to CAPEL-Y-FFIN in Wales in 1924. A permanent collection of Gill's calligraphy designs and woodcuts is housed in the former village school here.

Ditchling Beacon. A 248-m (813-ft) hilltop on the South Downs, just to the south of Ditchling, which offers breath-taking views in all directions. It is surmounted by an ancient earthwork. In 1588 one of a chain of great fires was lit here to warn of the approach of the Spanish Armada.

Divis Flats After Divis Mountain, west of Belfast.

A group of tower blocks in the 'Lower Falls' area of Catholic west Belfast (*see under* FALLS ROAD), known as a centre of hardcore Republicanism, especially of the Irish Republican Socialist Party (IRSP), the political wing of the INLA (Irish National Liberation Army). This has earned the Divis Flats the metathetical nickname of **Planet of the IRPS**, after the 1968 sci-fi film *Planet of the Apes*.

Dobwalls 'Dobb's walls', ME surname *Dobb(e)*, known here from the 14th century + *walls*.

A village in Cornwall, about 4 km (2.5 miles) west of Liskeard. The local miniature steam railway operates on the steepest gradients of their type in England.

The bird-illustrator Archibald Thorburn (1860–1935) lived and worked in Dobwalls in the latter part of his life, and there is now a gallery here displaying his works.

Doccombe 'valley where dock grows', OE *docce* 'dock' + *cumb* (*see* -COMBE, COOMBE).

A village in Devon, at the northeastern corner of DARTMOOR, about 16 km (10 miles) southwest of Exeter.

Dock Green. A fictional Metropolitan Police district in London's DOCKLAND, the setting of the long-running BBC television drama series *Dixon of Dock Green* (1955–76), created by Ted Willis. It starred Jack Warner as the firm but kindly PC George Dixon, whose greeting 'Evening, all' became a catch-phrase of the time.

Dockland. A name (with the alternative form **Docklands**) for the area around the docks of EAST LONDON that emerged around the beginning of the 20th century. It seems to have originated as a journalist's coinage, and it quickly took on board more than its fair share of cliché: crowded back-to-back housing, inhabited by families whose living depended on the vagaries of the docks' casual labour practices; the high prison-like walls of the docks, enclosing warehouses and cellars impregnated with all the exotic smells of the world's trade; the bustling wharves, with their forests of cranes (so memorably lowered as one when Winston Churchill's funeral procession passed down the Thames in 1965); the ships coming and going in the POOL OF LONDON; the fog-horns piercing the river's mists; the destruction wreaked in the Blitz, when Dockland was an obvious and sitting target and many of the premises belonging to the Port of London Authority were destroyed. Nevertheless, one commentator could aver that:

> ... there is glamour even in the mean streets of dockland.
>
> *Weekly Dispatch* (1922)

It was always more of a concept than a geographical district, but any account of its extent would have to pass from Tower Bridge (*see under* TOWER OF LONDON) in the west to BECKTON in the east on the north bank of the Thames, taking in **St Katherine's Dock**, built in 1828 in the shadow of the Tower of London; **London Dock** in Wapping, whose bonded warehouses and vaults bulged with liquor, tobacco, furs, etc.; the **East** and **West India Docks** and the **Millwall Docks** on the ISLE OF DOGS; and furthest east, and most recently built, the vast **Royal Docks**, comprising the **Royal Victoria**, **Royal Albert** and **King George V Docks**; while on the Thames's southern shore were the **Surrey Commercial Docks**, specializing in the importation of timber.

At their commercial apogee, between the two world wars, these wharves and basins covered 285 ha (700 acres) and provided employment for a significant proportion of London's East Enders. Not too long after the Second World War, though, the writing became visible on the wall:

modern merchant ships were becoming too big for the shallow docks, and from the 1960s containerization made traditional cargo-handling techniques redundant. London's port moved downstream to TILBURY, and within twenty years all the docks had closed down.

The end of the docks did not, however, mean the end of Dockland. An energetic programme of redevelopment was set in train in the early 1980s by the **London Docklands Development Corporation**. St Katherine's became a marina, surrounded by housing, shops and restaurants; London Dock was filled in, and its former site occupied by, among others, News International's headquarters, home of *The Times* and the *Sun*; the Isle of Dogs has seen extensive redevelopment (most spectacularly in the shape of CANARY WHARF, leading the drive to relocate London's commercial centre of gravity from the City area eastwards); communication links with central London have been improved, with the Docklands Light Railway (*see below*) and the Jubilee line extension from Westminster to Stratford by way of (among others) Bermondsey, Canary Wharf and Canning Town; and the Royal Docks have given way to London City Airport (*see under* LONDON). Dockland is cool.

Docklands Light Railway. A railway built 1984–7 eastwards from the City of London to the tip of the Isle of Dogs in the south and Stratford in the north. Later extensions took the line to Beckton and (crossing under the Thames) to Lewisham. It is underground in the City, but carried on a viaduct for much of the rest of its length. It was built essentially as a quick fix for the transportation problems of the rapidly developing Dockland area, which it was hoped would attract businesses from the centre of London.

Doc Penfro. *See* PEMBROKE DOCK.

Doctor's Gate The earliest spelling, from the 17th century, names the road through the valley (which is the Roman road from Brough to Melandra Castle) after a Dr Talbot, but he has eluded identification; *Gate* OScand *gata* 'road'.

A narrow moorland valley in the PEAK DISTRICT, to the east of GLOSSOP.

Doddiscombsleigh Originally *Leigh* (Domesday Book *Leuga* (1086)), 'woodland clearing, glade' (*see* -LEY); *Doddiscombs*- denoting manorial ownership in the Middle Ages by the Doddescumb family.

A village (pronounced 'daskəm(z)li') in Devon, about 10 km (6 miles) southwest of Exeter. It has a renowned hostelry known as The Nobody Inn.

Dodman Point From the ME surname *Dodman*, documented in Cornwall from the early 13th century.

A dramatic gorse-covered headland in Cornwall, 9 km (5.5. miles) south of MEVAGISSEY and forming the eastern end of Veryan Bay (*see under* VERYAN). At its highest part, it is 114 m (374 ft). It is also referred to simply as '**the Dodman**', and was the site of an imposing Iron Age fort. In local legend, the cliff was the work of a giant. The headland was donated to the National Trust in 1919, and now forms a section of the South West Coast Path.

The sea around here has been something of a ships' (and sailors') graveyard. In an effort to alleviate the dangers, a churchman of the locality had the granite cross erected (1896) that is now visible on the Point. But it did not do the trick: a couple of warships sank the next year, and shipwrecks continued into the 20th century.

Dodworth 'Dodd's enclosure', OE male personal name + *-worth* (*see* -WORTH, WORTHY, -WARDINE).
A village in South Yorkshire, 3 km (2 miles) west of Barnsley.

Dogdyke 'ditch where docks or water-lilies grow', OE *docce* 'dock, water-lily' + *dic* 'ditch'.
A village in Lincolnshire, about 19 km (12 miles) northwest of Boston.

Dogger Bank Etymology uncertain, but some reference to OE *dogga* 'a dog' may be imagined.
A huge sandbank in the central NORTH SEA, about 115 km (70 miles) off the Yorkshire coast. Its depth is mostly 17–36 m (55–120 ft), but in places it is only 11 m (36 ft) below the surface. It is an important fishing ground. The **Battle of Dogger Bank**, an engagement between British and German naval forces, took place on 24 January 1915. **Dogger** is a sea area in the shipping forecast, east of Tyne, north of Humber and south of Forties.

Dogger bank incident. An incident that took place in the North Sea on 21 October 1904 when the Russian Baltic fleet, bound for the Far East and action in the Russo-Japanese War, fired on and sank a British trawler, believing it to be a Japanese gunboat. The British government, outraged, demanded compensation and the matter was referred to an international commission in The Hague. A kind of rough justice came the following year, when two-thirds of the Russian ships were sunk by the Japanese in the Straits of Tsushima.

Dogmersfield 'open land at Doccanmere', place name *Doccanmere* 'dock pool' (OE *docce* 'dock (the plant)' + *mere* 'pool' (*see also* LAKE)) + OE *feld* (*see* FIELD).
A village in Hampshire, about 16 km (10 miles) east of Basingstoke.

Dog Village Probably so named from an excess of dogs.
A village in Devon, about 6.5 km (4 miles) northeast of Exeter.

Doire. The Irish name for DERRY/LONDONDERRY.

Dolgellau 'water meadow with (monastic) cells', Welsh *dôl* 'water meadow' + *cellau* 'cells'.
A market town in Gwynedd (formerly in MERIONETH, of which it was the county town), 12 km (7 miles) east of

Barmouth, at the foot of CADER IDRIS. It was formerly known as **Dolgelly**, and is pronounced 'dal-gethly'. Traditionally it was where Owain Glyndwr's parliament met. Gold from the nearby Clogau mine has been used to make the rings of royal brides since 1923, but has patently failed in a number of cases to ensure either a happy or a permanent union.

Dolgellau series. In geology, a series of rocks (slates and shales) from the Cambrian period (*see under* CAMBRIA).

Dollar 'arable field', OCelt *dol* 'field' + *ar* 'arable'.
A town at the foot of the OCHIL HILLS in Clackmannanshire (formerly in Central region), some 18 km (11 miles) northeast of Stirling. It was burnt in 1645 by the Marquess of Montrose. The town's Harviestown brewery produces Bitter and Twisted, judged Britain's best beer in 2003. The **Dollar Academy** is a co-educational boarding school founded in 1818.

Dollar Glen. A small glen north of Dollar, leading up into the Ochils. There are many waterfalls, and the river is formed by the confluence of the Burn of Sorrow and the Burn of Care below CASTLE CAMPBELL.

Dollis Hill Probably 'hill associated with the Dalley family'. Although the local section of the River Brent is called the *Dollis Brook*, there appears to be no historical connection between the two names: the riverine *Dollis* came from *Dollis Farm*, probably literally 'the portions or shares of land (in a common field)', ME *doles*. The two no doubt grew to resemble one another by association.
A district in northwestern Greater London (NW2), in the borough of BRENT[2], between Neasden to the west and Cricklewood to the east. As its name suggests, it is relatively high. It was still a small hamlet in the 1890s and did not finally succumb to suburbia until the 1930s. Dollis Hill Underground station, originally on the Bakerloo line and now on the Jubilee line, opened in 1939.

Dolly's Brae Probably Irish *bré* 'hill', or Scots *brae* 'hillside', with a personal name.
The site, near Castlewellan, County Down, of a sectarian skirmish on 12 July 1849. A group of Orangemen, celebrating the Battle of the Boyne (*see under* BOYNE), marched through this Catholic district, and in the ensuing violent encounter with Catholic Ribbonmen houses were burnt and 30 Catholics died. The Party Processions Act of the following year banned such provocative marches, but the event is still celebrated in one or two of the more ecumenical of Orange ballads:

> Come all ye blind-led papists, wherever that ye be,
> Never bow down to priest or Pope, for them they will disown,
> Never bow down to images, for God you must adore,
> Come, join our Orange heroes, and cry Dolly's Brae no more.

Dollywagon Pike The etymology of the first word is obscure; for the second word, OE *pic* 'pointed hill, peak'.

A mountain (857 m / 2810 ft) in the LAKE DISTRICT, Cumbria, at the southern end of HELVELLYN's main north–south ridge. It is effectively a subsidiary top of Helvellyn.

Domhnach Broc. The Irish name for the Dublin suburb of DONNYBROOK.

Domhnach Daoi. The Irish name for DONAGHADEE.

Don[1] Celtic *devona* 'goddess', from the same root as DEE[1], but with a different suffix.

Scotland's sixth-longest river, with a course of 129.5 km (80.5 miles). It is entirely within Aberdeenshire (formerly in Grampian region), and flows generally eastward. It rises at the spring called the **Well of Don** at about 600 m (2000 ft) in the northeast Cairngorms, a little north of Brown Cow Hill. It is initially called the Feith Bhàit, then the Allt Tuileach, before becoming the River Don in the vicinity of COCK BRIDGE. Passing by Inverurie, it eventually reaches the North Sea at **Bridge of Don**, on the north side of ABERDEEN (to which it gives its name). The narrow upper valley of the river is called **Strathdon**, where there is also a village of the same name.

Dons, the. The nickname of Aberdeen FC. However, the etymological link to the river is somewhat uncertain; the name may be simply short for 'Aberdonians' or, alternatively, it may refer to the fact that the founders of the club were teachers.

'Auld Brig o' Don, The'. A fiddle tune by James Henry of Macduff (early 20th century).

Don[2] Celtic river name meaning 'river, water'.

A river in Yorkshire, 112 km (69 miles) long. It rises in the PENNINES and flows through the **Don Valley**, via PENISTONE, SHEFFIELD, ROTHERHAM and DONCASTER (to which it gave its name) to join the OUSE[2] at GOOLE.

Donaghadee Irish *Domhnach Daoi* 'Daoi's church'.

A port and resort in County Down, 9 km (5.5 miles) east of Bangor. There was a ferry service from here to PORTPATRICK in southwest Scotland, a distance of 32 km (20 miles), until 1865, when the service moved to the more sheltered although somewhat longer LARNE–STRANRAER route. Donaghadee and Portpatrick were also linked by the first undersea telegraph cable, laid in 1853. Grace Neill's in Donaghadee, founded in 1611, claims to be the oldest inn in Ireland. The Russian emperor Peter the Great visited it in 1697, during his travels in Western Europe. Donaghadee was also used in the Larne Gun Running (*see under* LARNE).

The chorus of a popular song goes:

> Toora loo, toora lay, oh it's six miles from Bangor to Donaghadee.

Donalds After Percy *Donald*.

The collective name given to those hills in 'Lowland' Scotland over 2000 ft (609.8 m) in height. The highest is MERRICK. The list of such hills was first compiled by Percy Donald, and includes everything south of the Highland Line, mostly in the SOUTHERN UPLANDS, but also including the OCHIL HILLS. There are a total of 133 'tops', 86 of which are considered as separate 'hills'.

Compare CORBETTS, GRAHAMS, MARILYNS *and* MUNROS.

Doncaster 'Roman fort on the River DON[2]' + OE *ceaster* (*see* CHESTER).

An industrial town and metropolitan borough on the River DON[2] in South Yorkshire, 27 km (17 miles) northeast of Sheffield. It is known affectionately to locals as **Donny**.

The Romans built the fort of **Danum** here, recognizing the site's strategic importance on the main route north. By the Middle Ages it had become a significant trading centre, and in the mid-17th century the English diarist John Evelyn described Doncaster as a 'large, fair town', famous for great wax lights and good stockings. Doncaster was an important coaching stop on the GREAT NORTH ROAD – although now bypassed by the A1(M). It is also on the main east coast railway line, and has long been an important centre of railway engineering.

There is a famous racecourse here, home to the Saint Leger, a flat race over 2.8 km (3060 yds) and the last Classic of the flat-racing season. Established by Colonel Barry Saint Leger in 1776, it is England's oldest classic horse race.

Today, 'Sunny Doncaster' – sheltered from wet westerlies by the Pennines, and far enough from the North Sea to avoid Siberian winds and sea fret – has implausibly relaunched itself as 'the Northern Riviera'. Its image was dented at the beginning of the 21st century by the so-called '**Donnygate Scandal**' involving illegal payments to former council employees, a subject made much of in the satirical *Private Eye* magazine.

Edmund Cartwright, the inventor of the power loom, had a factory in Doncaster in the late 18th century, and the town features in Robert Southey's *The Doctor* (1834–47), the fictional memoirs of Dr Daniel Dove.

Doncaster is the birthplace of the actress (Dame) Diana Rigg (b.1938) and is also the home town of the motoring correspondent and would-be bad boy Jeremy Clarkson (b.1960). The location shots from Ronnie Barker's 1970s television sitcom *Open All Hours* were filmed in Lister Avenue in Doncaster.

A gang of young men, who were ordered to plant daffodil bulbs as part of their community service, saw their work come to fruition in Spring 2000. The group had had to plant hundreds of bulbs along one of the main dual carriageways near Rotherham and Doncaster the previous autumn. But when the bulbs sprouted, the blooms spelt

out the words 'BOLLOCKS' and 'SHAG' in letters 1.3
metres wide.

> Donny Online: 'Bizarre Donny'

Donegal Irish *Dún na nGall* 'fort of the foreigners', referring
to the Vikings who used Donegal Bay as an anchorage and
built an earth rampart here.

A market town in County Donegal, some 45 km (28 miles)
northeast of Sligo. It is at the head of **Donegal Bay** (*see under*
County DONEGAL), a wide inlet of the Atlantic. Donegal
was for long the seat of the O'Donnells. The ruined
Donegal Abbey was a Franciscan friary founded in 1474 by
Nuala, mother of Red Hugh O'Donnell, the man who built
Donegal Castle (now ruined) in 1505. Donegal was once
also known as the **Town of the Four Masters**, after the
Annals of the Four Masters compiled at Donegal Abbey
between 1632 and 1636; the *Annals* are an important source
for early Irish history and mythology.

Donegal, County. A county in the northwest of the Republic of Ireland, and part of the traditional province of Ulster.
It is bounded to the east by the Northern Ireland counties
of Londonderry, Tyrone and Fermanagh, to the south
by Leitrim, and to the west and north by the Atlantic.
The county town is LIFFORD, and other towns include
BALLYSHANNON and DONEGAL. The coastline is heavily
indented and craggy, and the interior wild and mountainous. The larger part of the county, apart from the
peninsula of INISHOWEN in the northeast, is known as
TYRCONNELL and was ruled by the O'Donnells until the
17th century.

> Mostly, in West Donegal,
> it is rock and light, and water, but rock above all,
> and rain, to-day it is rain, rain falling softly in veils ...
>
>> Francis Harvey: 'In the Light on the Stones in the Rain',
>> from *In the Light on the Stones* (1978)

> I dreamt we slept in a moss in Donegal
> On turf banks under blankets, with our faces
> Exposed all night in a wetting drizzle ...
>
>> Seamus Heaney: 'Glanmore Sonnets', X, from *Field Work*
>> (1979)

> As ever, the nearby hills were a deeper green
> Than anywhere in the world, and the grave
> Grey of the sea the grimmer in that enclave.
>
>> Derek Mahon: 'Day Trip to Donegal', from *Collected Poems*
>> (1999)

Blind Poetess of Donegal, the. Frances Browne (1816–79),
daughter of the postmaster in Stranorlar. She went blind
in infancy owing to smallpox, but became a prolific author,
best known for the collection of fairytales entitled *Granny's
Wonderful Chair* (1856). She moved to Edinburgh and then
to London, where she died.

Donegal Bay. The large inlet of the Atlantic separating

County Donegal from County Sligo on the west coast of
Ireland. It was in Donegal Bay, off MULLAGHMORE, that
Lord Mountbatten's boat was blown up by the Provisional
IRA on 27 August 1979.

Donegal tweed. A local speciality, also called breadeen.

Doneraile Irish *Dún ar Aill* 'fort on the cliff'.

A village on the River AWBEG in County Cork, some 35 km
(22 miles) north of Cork itself. Doneraile was part of the
estate granted in 1586 to the poet Edmund Spenser, who
lived at nearby Kilcolman Castle, now ruined. The last
hereditary poet of the MacCarthys of BLARNEY, Tadhg Ó
Duinnín (d.1726) was parish priest here, as was, from 1895
until his death, the novelist Canon (Patrick Augustine)
Sheehan (1852–1913), author of *My New Curate* (1900) and
other works. The novelist W.M. Thackeray's mentally unstable wife, Isabella Creagh Shawe, came from Doneraile.

'Curse of Doneraile, The'. A poem by Patrick O'Reilly,
composed *c*.1754, bewailing the loss of his watch, chain
and seal in Doneraile. In the poem O'Reilly heaps
imprecation upon imprecation on the 'thieving town of
Doneraile', and concludes:

> May curse of Sodom now prevail,
> And sink to ashes Doneraile.
> May Charon's boat triumphant sail,
> Completely manned from Doneraile.
> Oh! may my Couplets never fail,
> To find new curse for Doneraile.
> And may grim Pluto's inner jail,
> For ever groan with Doneraile.

In response to the poem, widely circulated at the time in
Ireland, Lady Doneraile sent the poet a new watch and seal,
to which O'Reilly graciously responded with a poem
entitled 'Blessings on Doneraile', beginning

> How vastly pleasing is my tale
> I found my watch in Doneraile ...
> May fire and brimstone ever fail
> To hurt or injure Doneraile.

Doneraile Conspiracy, the (1829). A conspiracy by local
landlords to buy evidence of illegal activity during the
agrarian upheavals of the early 19th century. The conspiracy
culminated in 21 men being brought to trial in Cork before
a packed jury, and on 22 October 1829 four were sentenced
to death. An urgent summons was sent to Daniel
O'Connell, the Liberator, who rode through the night to
appear in court, where, during his cross-examination, the
perjured witnesses were discredited. The death sentences
were commuted to transportation to Australia, and the rest
of the accused were acquitted.

Donibristle Possibly '(place) at the bright hill', Gaelic *dùn*
(*see* DOWN, -DON) + *brisg-gheal* 'bright, clear'.

A village in Fife, 8 km (5 miles) east of Dunfermline. It was here that the Bonnie Earl of Moray (*see under* MORAY) was brutally slain in 1592, as recorded in the famous ballad (*see also* Doune Castle *under* DOUNE).

Donkey Town Origin uncertain, but if not a reference to the animal, then perhaps to the *donk(e)y*, a small steam engine.
A village in Surrey, about 6.5 km (4 miles) northwest of Woking.

Donnington 'estate associated with Dunn', OE male personal name *Dunn* + -ING + -TON.
A village within the unitary authority of Telford and Wrekin, now a northeastern suburb of TELFORD. The British Army has its main storage centre here. Amongst all the armaments and *materiel* kept in the vast sheds there is also metal from Chinese-made Russian guns captured in the Crimea, which is used for making Victoria Crosses.

Donny. The natives' nickname for DONCASTER.

Donnybrook Irish *Domhnach Broc* 'church of St Broc'.
A former village, now a suburb of DUBLIN, best known in the past for its riotous fairs (*see below*).

There is a town called Donnybrook in Western Australia.

donnybrook. A rowdy brawl, taking its name from Donnybrook Fair.

Donnybrook Fair. An annual fair once held at Donnybrook, the Irish equivalent of London's Bartholomew Fair (*see under* SMITHFIELD). It was granted a charter in 1204, but by the 18th century its importance as a market had been superseded and it had become a week of boisterous entertainment.

> Brisk lads and young lasses can there fill their glasses
>   With whisky, and send a full bumper around;
> Jig it off in a tent till their money's all spent,
>   And spin like a top till they rest on the ground.
> Oh, Donnybrook capers, to sweet catgut-scrapers,
>   They bother the vapours, and drive away care;
> And what is more glorious – there's naught more
>   uproarious –
> Huzza for the humours of Donnybrook Fair!
>
> Anon.: 'The Humours of Donnybrook Fair' (18th century)

There is another poem of the same title by Charles O'Flaherty (1794–1828), beginning:

> Oh! 'Twas Dermot O'Nowland McFigg,
> That could properly handle a twig.
>   He went to the Fair,
>   And kicked up a dust there,
> In dancing the Donnybrook Jig,
>   With his twig.
> Oh, my blessing to Dermot McFigg!

All these sorts of goings-on were frowned upon at the dawn of the Victorian era, and in 1855 a killjoy consortium purchased the fair's charter and surrendered it, thus bringing a 650-year tradition to an end.

Doolin Irish *Dúlinn* 'black pool'; *see* DUBLIN.
A fishing village on the west coast of County Clare, 33 km (20 miles) northwest of Ennis. It is also known as **Fisherstreet**, and is famous for its traditional music, O'Connor's Pub on Fisher Street being a famous venue. To the west is **Doolin Point**, and there is a ferry service to Inisheer in the ARAN ISLANDS.

Doon From *Devona*, an OCelt name meaning 'river goddess, holy one'.
A river of East and South Ayrshire (formerly in Strathclyde region), forming the border between the traditional areas of CARRICK[1] and KYLE. Some 30 km (19 miles) long, it rises in **Loch Doon** on the north side of the Galloway Hills and enters the sea just south of Ayr. When the loch was dammed in the 1930s, **Loch Doon Castle** (early 14th century), formerly on an island, was moved to the shore.

> First we stood upon the Bridge across the Doon;
> surrounded by every Phantasy of green in tree, Meadow,
> and Hill, – the Stream of the Doon, as a Farmer told us, is
> covered with trees from head to foot – you know those
> beautiful heaths so fresh against the weather of a
> summers evening – there was one stretching along
> behind the trees.
>
> John Keats: letter to J.H. Reynolds (11 July 1818)

See also CUMNOCK AND DOON VALLEY.

Brig o' Doon. A single-arched medieval (possibly from the 13th century) bridge in ALLOWAY, over the River Doon. It was by riding over the Brig that Tam O'Shanter and his horse Maggie were able to escape the pursuing witches in Robert Burns's 1791 poem. The poet himself explained in a 1793 note:

> It is a well known fact that witches, or any evil spirits,
> have no power to follow a poor wight any farther than
> the middle of the next running stream.

Unfortunately for Maggie:

> Ae spring brought off her master hale,
> But left behind her ain gray tail:
> The carlin claught her by the rump,
> And left poor Maggie scarce a stump.
>
> (*carlin* 'witch', *claught* 'seized')

It is possible that the name 'Brig o' Doon' inspired the title of Lerner and Loewe's Broadway musical *Brigadoon* (1947; film version 1954).

'Ye Banks and Braes o' Bonnie Doon'. A poem written by Robert Burns in 1787. It is sung to the tune 'Caledonian Hunt's Delight' by James Miller, an amateur Edinburgh musician. The poem begins:

> Ye banks and braes o' bonnie Doon,
>   How can ye bloom sae fresh and fair!
> How can ye chant, ye little birds,
>   And I sae weary fu' o' care!

The poem was inspired by the case of a 17-year-old niece of Mrs Gavin Hamilton of Mauchline, who was unfortunate in her choice of lover, a 'Captain M——' of Wigtownshire. Percy Grainger made an arrangement of the tune.

Dorchester[1] 'Roman town of the people of Durn(ovaria)', OE *Dornwaraceaster*, from *Dorn* a reduced form of the settlement's Romano-British name *Durnovaria* (itself based on an OCelt name perhaps meaning 'place with fist-sized pebbles') + *-wara* 'people, inhabitants' (probably influenced by the *-varia* of *Durnovaria*) + *ceaster* 'Roman town' (*see* CHESTER).

A market town in Dorset, and its county town, on the River FROME[3], about 45 km (28 miles) west of Bournemouth. It dates back to Roman times (when it was called **Durnovaria**; *see above*), and the line of the Roman walls can still be traced (it is marked by avenues known as 'the Walks'). It continued to be an important town in the Middle Ages: a royal borough by the time of Domesday Book, with its own castle in the 12th century and a priory by the 14th. Cloth provided much of its wealth from the 16th century, and the beer brewed here has always enjoyed a high reputation. Most of its old buildings were destroyed by 17th- and 18th-century fires, but its eventful past bears witness to its centrality in the life of the region: Judge Jeffreys held some of his Bloody Assizes here (in the Antelope Hotel) following Monmouth's rebellion in 1685 (*see* SEDGEMOOR), and in 1834 the TOLPUDDLE Martyrs were sentenced to transportation at the Old Crown Court.

The ancient earthwork of MAIDEN CASTLE is a little to the southwest, and MAUMBURY RING is just to the south.

The novelist Thomas Hardy (1840–1928) was born at HIGHER BOCKHAMPTON, to the northeast, and lived during the latter part of his life on the outskirts of Dorchester. He fictionalized the town as CASTERBRIDGE, and it figures in one of his best-known novels, *The Mayor of Casterbridge* (1886), the story of Michael Henchard, who sells his wife and child to a stranger at a fair and later becomes mayor of Casterbridge. In it, Hardy vividly portrays the bustle of a 19th-century market town.

There are towns called Dorchester in Canada (New Brunswick) and the USA (Massachusetts, Nebraska, Wisconsin) and Dorchester Counties in the USA (Maryland, South Carolina).

Dorchester Hotel. A luxurious hotel on PARK LANE, London, haunt of film stars and Arab princes. It opened in 1931. It was built on the site of Dorchester House (latterly Hertford House), which got its name when its original owner Joseph Damer was created Earl of Dorchester in 1792.

Dorchester[2] 'Roman town called Dorcic', from an OCelt place name of unknown meaning + OE *ceaster* (*see* CHESTER).

A village in Oxfordshire, on the River THAME[1], just to the north of its confluence with the River Thames (the village is also called **Dorchester-on-Thames**), about 11 km (7 miles)

southeast of Oxford. It was an important military centre in Roman times, on the road between Silchester and Alchester, and in the Anglo-Saxon period it was the cathedral city of WESSEX. It has now dwindled to a (very attractive) village, but **Dorchester Abbey**, begun by the Normans, gives an idea of its former glory. It has an especially fine Jesse window.

Dore 'the waters', OCelt.

A river in Herefordshire (before 1998 in Hereford and Worcester, before 1974 in Herefordshire), which rises to the east of HAY-ON-WYE and flows 20 km (13 miles) southeastwards to join the River MONNOW on the borders of Monmouthshire. In the middle of its course it flows through the GOLDEN VALLEY[1].

Dorking '(settlement of) Deorc's people', OE male personal name *Deorc* + *-ingas* (*see* -ING).

A residential market town in Surrey, on the River MOLE[1], at the edge of the NORTH DOWNS, about 18 km (11 miles) east of Guildford and 36 km (22 miles) southwest of London. BOX HILL[1] is just to the northeast. Dorking was already of importance in Roman times, when it was a posting station on STANE STREET[1], the road from London to Chichester. This was crossed at Dorking by the PILGRIMS' WAY.

At its centre it still has very much the air of an old market town, but its edges have swollen with commuter suburbs serving the metropolis.

Dorking was the birthplace of the economist Thomas Malthus (1766–1834), the actor Laurence Olivier (Lord Olivier; 1907–89) and the surrealist painter Julian Trevelyan (1910–88).

'Battle of Dorking, The'. A futuristic story (1871) by George Chesney that envisages the invasion of Britain by Germany, culminating in decisive defeat for the British at Dorking. It was the precursor of many literary constructions of Anglo-German conflict in the period leading up to the First World War.

Dorking. A breed of poultry which is long and square in form and has five toes.

> The market of Darking [*sic*] is of all the markets in England famous for poultry; and particularly for the fattest geese, and the largest capons, the name of a Darking Capon being well known among the poulterers in Leaden-Hall Market; in a word, they are brought to this market from as far as Horsham in Sussex; and 'tis the business of all the country, on that side for many miles, to breed and fatten them up, insomuch, that 'tis like a manufacture to the country people; and some of these capons are so large, as that they are little inferior to turkeys.
>
> Daniel Defoe: *A Tour Through the Whole Island of Great Britain* (1724–6)

Dorking Thigh, The. A collection (1945) of somewhat macabre ballads by William Plomer (including a title piece of the same name).

Dorneywood. *See under* BURNHAM.

Dornoch 'pebbly place', Gaelic *dornach*, literally 'fist-stones', apparently alluding to the suitability of the local stones for throwing.

An attractive royal BURGH in Highland, formerly the county town of SUTHERLAND, some 46 km (27 miles) north of Inverness. It is situated to the north of the mouth of the **Dornoch Firth**, a 20-km (12-mile) inlet of the North Sea. South of the town is **Dornoch Point**, and to the southeast, beyond Dornoch's famous golf course, is the long stretch of **Dornoch Sands**.

Dornoch Cathedral (now the parish church) was begun in 1224 by Gilbert of Moravia, Bishop of Caithness, and was the burial place of many earls of Sutherland. The town was the site in 1727 of the last burning of a witch in Scotland (a claim disputed by FORTROSE). The victim was one Janet Horne, who was convicted of the not uncommon offence of turning her daughter into a pony and having her shod by the Devil.

Dorset '(territory of) the people around Dorchester', OE *Dorn*, a reduced form of *Durnovaria* (*see* DORCHESTER[1]) + *sǣte* 'dwellers, settlers'.

A county of southern England, on the English Channel coast, bounded to the west by Devon and Somerset, to the north by Wiltshire and to the east by Hampshire. It contains the unitary authorities of BOURNEMOUTH (until 1974 in Hampshire) and POOLE, and other important centres are BLANDFORD FORUM, BRIDPORT, CHRISTCHURCH, DORCHESTER[1] (the county town), LYME REGIS, SHAFTESBURY, SHERBORNE, SWANAGE, WAREHAM, WEYMOUTH and WIMBORNE MINSTER. Its chief rivers are the FROME[3] and the STOUR[1]. Notable features of its landscape are the BLACKMOOR VALE, CHESIL BEACH, Cranborne Chase (*see under* CRANBORNE) and the Isle of Purbeck (*see under* PURBECK).

Many evidences remain of ancient human occupation, but Dorset is no longer especially on the way to anywhere, and it has something of the air of a land apart, forgotten almost – a deep England, of small rolling hills, winding river valleys with willows and cattle grazing, gorsey heaths (where the rare smooth snake still lurks), the chalk uplands of the **Dorset Downs** and a rich harvest of resonant place names:

> Rime Intrinseca, Fontmell Magna, Sturminster Newton
>   and Melbury Bubb,
> Whist upon whist upon whist upon whist drive, in
>   Institute, Legion and Social Club,
> Horny hands that hold the aces which this morning
>   held the plough –

> While Tranter Reuben, T.S. Eliot, H.G. Wells and
>   Edith Sitwell lie in Mellstock Churchyard now.
>
> John Betjeman: 'Dorset', from *Continual Dew* (1937)

Dorset, along with adjacent parts of Wiltshire and Somerset, was occupied during the late Iron Age by the ancient British Durotriges people. In Dorset, at any rate, they appear to have put up stiff resistance to the Romans, archaeological evidence suggesting that their strongholds such as HOD HILL and MAIDEN CASTLE had to be taken by storm.

Dorset is indissolubly linked with the novelist Thomas Hardy (1840–1928), a native of the county. It was at the core of his fictionalized landscape of WESSEX. Dorset itself, in the guise of South Wessex, is the setting of many of his novels, including *Far from the Madding Crowd* (1874), *The Mayor of Casterbridge* (1886) and *Tess of the D'Urbervilles* (1891). By coincidence an earlier Thomas Hardy, the sailor who ministered to the dying Nelson ('kiss me, Hardy') at the Battle of Trafalgar (1805), was also a Dorset man.

In cricketing terms Dorset is a 'minor county' (the club was founded in 1896) and plays in the minor counties championship.

Dorset blue vinney. A type of cow's-milk cheese traditionally produced in Dorset. Reports of old leather harnesses being immersed in the milk to provide the mould for the veins are probably a little exaggerated. It can be made only when conditions are propitious, so it has always been an elusive cheese. *Vinney* comes from OE *fyne* 'mould'.

Dorset Horn. A breed of English sheep with exceptionally large horns

Dorsey Irish *dóirse* 'gates, doors'.

A double line of Iron Age earthworks (*c*.100 BC) in south Armagh. It is also known as **Dursey**, and is regarded as the traditional gateway to ULSTER.

Dottery Origin unknown.

A village in Dorset, about 3 km (2 miles) northwest of Bridport.

Doublebois 'double wood', OFr *double* + *bois* 'wood'.

A village in Cornwall, about 6.5 km (4 miles) west of Liskeard.

Douglas[1] 'black stream', Gaelic *dubh* (*see* DDU, DUBH) + *glais* 'stream'.

A town in South Lanarkshire (formerly in Strathclyde region), about 14 km (8.5 miles) southwest of Lanark, on the **Douglas Water**, a tributary of the CLYDE. It is from this river that the town and the great Douglas family – so powerful in medieval Scotland – get their name. The last **Douglas Castle**, an 18th-century building, suffered subsidence owing to underground coal workings, and had to be demolished in the 1940s. The partly ruined 14th-century St Bride's Church has the tomb of the Black Douglas (*see below*), and here too is buried the heart of Archibald

'Bell-the-Cat' Douglas (*see* LAUDER). The clock on the tower (a gift from Mary Queen of Scots) chimes three minutes before the hour, in accordance with the Douglas motto, 'Never behind'. Nearby is a stone on which are carved scissors and an ear, commemorating an outrage in 1684 when a local tailor had his ears cut off with his own scissors for his Covenanting beliefs.

Black Douglas, the. Sir James Douglas (*c.*1286–1330), Robert the Bruce's loyal lieutenant. The name was given to him by the English because of his successes against them, for example in the capture of ROXBURGH Castle. To his friends he was known as 'the guid Schir James'. He died fighting the Moors in Spain, on his way to the Holy Land (*see* MELROSE).

Douglas groat. A coin minted during the period (1525–8) early in the reign of James V when Archibald Douglas, 6th Earl of Angus, wielded supreme power in Scotland.

Douglas Larder, the. On Palm Sunday, 19 March 1307, during the Scottish Wars of Independence, Sir James Douglas finally recaptured, at the third attempt, his own Douglas Castle from the English. Before destroying the castle, Douglas's men took what foodstuffs they could, scattering the rest across the cellar floor, where they also threw the severed heads of the English garrison. The episode became known as 'the Douglas Larder'. The capture of the castle was the inspiration for Sir Walter Scott's novel *Castle Dangerous* (1831).

Douglas². The capital of the ISLE OF MAN, situated on the east coast of the island, overlooking **Douglas Bay**. The island's parliament, the Tynwald, has met here since 1869, when Douglas replaced CASTLETOWN as the island's capital. There are ferry services from Heysham, Liverpool and Dublin, and the town is popular with holidaymakers. The poet William Wordsworth visited Douglas in 1833 (resulting in the sonnet 'On Entering Douglas Bay, Isle of Man'), and Matthew Arnold holidayed here, resulting in 'To a Gipsy Child by the Sea-shore' (1843).

Doune Possibly Gaelic *dùn* 'fort' (*see* DOWN, -DON); *Downe* 14th century.

A small town (pronounced 'doon') on the River Teith, 11 km (6.5 miles) northwest of Stirling. It was formerly in Perthshire, then in Central region, and is now in the unitary authority of Stirling. It is strategically placed on the routes from Edinburgh to the western Highlands, and from Glasgow to Perth. The bridge over the Teith was originally built in 1535 by Robert Spittal, tailor to James IV, to spite the local ferryman who had once refused to carry him.

Doune Castle. A well-restored 14th-century castle, built by Robert, Duke of Albany (*c.*1340–1420; *see under* ALBANY¹), brother of Robert III. It was appropriated by the Crown in 1425, but was later restored to Albany's descendants, the earls of Moray, who became hereditary constables of the castle, with the title Lord Doune. The castle appeared in the films *Ivanhoe* (1952) and *Monty Python and the Holy Grail* (1975).

> O lang lang will his lady
> Look ower the Castle Doune
> Ere she sees the Earl o' Moray
> Come sounding through the toun.
>
> 'The Bonnie Earl o' Moray' (a traditional ballad referring to James Moray, the 2nd Earl of Moray, brutally killed at Donibristle, Fife, in 1592)

Dounreay 'hillfort', Gaelic *dùn* (*see* DOWN, -DON) + Gaelic *ràth* 'fort' (*see* RATH).

The site of an experimental nuclear-power installation, formerly in Caithness, now in Highland, 13 km (8 miles) west of Thurso. It was set up by the UK Atomic Energy Authority in 1955.

Dove From an OCelt river name meaning 'dark', 'black'.

A river (pronounced 'duv') in the northwest Midlands of England, which rises on Axe Edge in the PEAK DISTRICT, just to the southwest of BUXTON, and flows 65 km (40 miles) southeastwards to join the River TRENT¹ near REPTON. For most of its course it forms the boundary between DERBYSHIRE and STAFFORDSHIRE.

See also DOVEDALE¹.

Dove Cottage. *See* GRASMERE.

Dovedale¹ 'valley of the River Dove', DOVE + OScand *dalr* 'dale'.

A tree-clad twisting limestone gorge, about 3 km (2 miles) in length, through which the River DOVE flows, about 24 km (15 miles) northeast of STOKE-ON-TRENT. It is renowned for the strangely weathered rock formations that line it, with names like the Twelve Apostles, Dovedale Castle, Jacob's Ladder, Lion Rock, Lover's Leap, Viator's Bridge and Tissington. There are also caves, such as DOVE HOLES and Reynard's Cavern.

Dovedale is thought to have been the model for the Happy Valley in Samuel Johnson's *Rasselas* (1759) and Eagle Valley in George Eliot's *Adam Bede* (1859).

Izaak Walton, author of *The Compleat Angler* (1653), delighted to fish for trout in the Dove here with his friend Charles Cotton.

Dovedale² As DOVEDALE¹, though the river in question is a different Dove.

A steep little valley in the LAKE DISTRICT, Cumbria, some 5 km (3 miles) south of Ullswater, rising westwards towards the summit of Hart Crag, an outlier of Fairfield. At the head of the dale is the vertiginous bastion of **Dove Crag** – 'Ill home for bird so gentle', according to William Wordsworth (*The Prelude*, Book VIII). Indeed it is home to some of Lakeland's harder and more thuggish rock climbs, the overhanging *Dovedale Groove*, put up by the legendary

Mancunian duo of Joe Brown and Don Whillans in 1953, being a sign of things to come.

Oddly, the main stream in the dale is, according to the Ordnance Survey, called Harrison Beck, although the old river name is famously recorded by Wordsworth:

> She dwelt among th' untrodden ways
>> Beside the springs of Dove,
> A Maid whom there were none to praise
>> And very few to love.
>
> William Wordsworth: 'Lucy', from *Lyrical Ballads* (1798)

Dove Holes From the name of the caves in DOVEDALE[1], which were originally hollows made in the process of producing quicklime.

A village in Derbyshire, on the western edge of the PEAK DISTRICT, about 5 km (3 miles) north of Buxton.

Dover From a stream here, now called the Dour, an OCelt river name *dubras* meaning 'the waters'.

A town and seaport in southeast Kent, about 24 km (15 miles) southeast of Canterbury. It has long been England's gateway to and from the continent of Europe (to the French it is *Douvres*). It overlooks the narrowest part (34 km / 21 miles) of the English Channel, known as the **Straits of Dover** (in French the *Pas de Calais*), and for many centuries ferries have carried passengers and cargo to and from Calais and other French ports. It is England's main passenger port (at the beginning of the 21st century 16 million passengers and 2 million vehicles passed through it annually). Boat (or once hovercraft) has not been the only method of arriving or leaving, though: Louis Blériot's first cross-channel flight ended near Dover in 1909, and it is a common departure point for cross-channel swimmers (including the first, Matthew Webb, in 1875). And for many Continent-bound travellers of the late 19th and 20th centuries the boat-train journey (perhaps on the 'Golden Arrow') from Victoria to Dover will have formed an essential part of the experience.

There was a pre-Roman settlement here. The Romans (who called it **Portus Dubris**) developed it, building on the cliffs a beacon or 'lighthouse' that is one of the oldest buildings still standing in Britain. It formed part of the defensive SAXON SHORE to keep out invaders. WATLING STREET[1] led from Dover to London and on into the heart of England. The Saxons built a fort here, and the Normans a great castle on the cliffs (**Dover Castle**, its massive keep walls 5–7 m /17–22 ft thick) that still overlooks and protects the harbour (the network of tunnels underneath was used in 1940 as an operations centre for the Dunkirk evacuation and the Battle of Britain). Dover's strategic position has always made it a vulnerable point for would-be and actual invaders to attack: Anglo-Saxons and Vikings availed

themselves of its facilities; there was a lengthy French siege in 1216 (the tunnels dug in the cliffs by the defenders then were used as air-raid shelters in the 1940s); Napoleon was a much feared potential visitor; and during the Second World War, Dover was the most heavily attacked town in Britain after London (*see* HELL'S CORNER). Dover was one of the original five CINQUE PORTS, which took it upon themselves to aid in the protection of the English Channel.

The NORTH DOWNS sweep down to meet the English Channel at the **White Cliffs of Dover**, a line of (somewhat off-white) chalk cliffs that for centuries have symbolized both the promise of home for returning British voyagers and Britain's defiance of foreign foes (and indeed antipathy to anything foreign). They were apotheosized in the sentimental ballad 'The White Cliffs of Dover' (1941) by Nat Burton, a favourite of Second World War audiences, especially as sung by Vera Lynn:

> There'll be bluebirds over
> The white cliffs of Dover,
> Tomorrow, just you wait and see.

Realists have taken other views:

> Since the days of the air, the old frontiers are gone. When you think of the defence of England you no longer think of the chalk cliffs of Dover; you think of the Rhine. That is where our frontier lies
>
> Stanley Baldwin: speaking to the House of Commons (1934)

Nevertheless, although the CHANNEL TUNNEL may have undermined Dover's commercial importance, in people's minds the White Cliffs remain England's bastion.

The cricketer Wally Hammond (1903–65) was born in Dover.

There are towns called Dover in the USA (Florida, Georgia, Kentucky, New Hampshire, New Jersey, North Carolina, Ohio, Oklahoma, Tennessee) and Australia (Tasmania, Western Australia).

See also CRABBLE *and* SHAKESPEARE CLIFF.

Battle of Dover (19 May 1652). A naval battle (also known as the **Battle of Goodwin Sands**) fought in the English Channel, off Dover, between the English under Admiral Robert Blake and the Dutch commanded by Admiral Maarten Tromp. The Dutch withdrew after five hours' fighting. It was the initial engagement of the first Anglo-Dutch War.

Dover. A sea area in the shipping forecast. It is in the English Channel, off the south and east coast of Kent, between Wight to the west (*see under* WIGHT) and Thames (*see under* THAMES) to the north.

'Dover Beach'. A poem (1867) by Matthew Arnold. The sound of the sea prompts melancholy thoughts of the receding tide of religious faith in the modern world. A personal commitment to another human being –'love' – is all we are left with in an insensible universe:

> And we are here as on a darkling plain
> Swept with confused alarms of struggle and flight,
> Where ignorant armies clash by night.

The poem was set to music by Samuel Barber in 1931, for solo voice and string quartet.

Dover Patrol. A naval patrol based in Dover that was formed in the First World War to maintain communications across the English Channel, comprising a varied collection of warships and fishing vessels. Both *Dover Patrol* and *L'Attaque* later became the names of popular board games.

Dover sole. A European flatfish (*Solea solea*) of the sole family. Its firm texture and fine flavour make it much more highly prized culinarily than the other members of its family (which does not include the lemon sole, an interloper), and its name has a place among those foodstuffs whose mention instantly suggests luxury and sophistication. It was bestowed not because the fish congregate in the Straits of Dover, but because the port of Dover was in the past the main source of supply for London markets.

Jack of Dover. Some unidentified eatable mentioned by Chaucer in the Prologue to 'The Cook's Tale'(*c.*1387):

> Many's the Jack of Dover you have sold
> That has been twice warmed up and twice left cold.
>
> Modern translation by Nevill Coghill (1951)

In his edition of Chaucer, W.W. Skeat says that it is 'probably a pie that has been cooked more than once'. Another suggestion is that it is some kind of fish.

Treaty of Dover. A secret treaty concluded by Charles II with France in 1670, in which Charles promised to support French policy in Europe (and, in a protocol, to become a Roman Catholic) in return for money.

Dovercourt Perhaps 'enclosed farmyard by the River Dover', OCelt river name (*see* DOVER) + OE *cort(e)*, perhaps from Latin *cohors* 'enclosure'.

A village in Essex, at the mouth of the STOUR[2] estuary, now forming the southeastern part of HARWICH. In former centuries its name was synonymous with a confused gabble or babel. According to legend, Dovercourt church once possessed a cross that spoke, and John Foxe in his *Book of Martyrs* (1563) says that the crowd in the church was so great 'that no man could shut the door'.

> And now the rood of Dovercourt did speak,
> Confirming his opinions to be true.
>
> *Grim, the Collier of Croydon* (1600) (*rood* 'cross')

Dovercourt also seems to have been noted for its scolds and chattering women:

> When bells ring round and in their order be,
> They do denote how neighbours should agree;
> But when they clam, the harsh sound spoils the
> sport,
> And 'tis like women keeping Dovercourt.
>
> Lines in the belfry of St Peter's, Shrewsbury (?before 1800)
> (*clam* 'crash together')

Dovey. The English name for the River DYFI.

Dow Crag. *See* Old Man of Coniston *under* CONISTON.

Dowlais. *See under* MERTHYR TYDFIL.

Dowlish Wake *Dowlish* from an OCelt river name meaning 'dark stream'(*see also* DAWLISH); *Wake* denoting manorial ownership in the early Middle Ages by the Wake family.

A village in Somerset, about 8 km (5 miles) northwest of Crewkerne.

Down, County Irish *An Dún* 'the fort'.

A county in southeastern Northern Ireland, in the traditional province of Ulster. It is bordered on the west by Armagh, on the north by Antrim, on the east by the North Channel and the Irish Sea, and to the south by Carlingford Lough, across which lies County Louth and the Republic. The county town is DOWNPATRICK, and other towns include BANGOR[2], DUNDONALD, NEWTOWNARDS, NEWRY and BANBRIDGE, together with the eastern outskirts of Belfast. Strangford Lough (*see under* STRANGFORD) and the ARDS PENINSULA[1] are in the east, and the MOURNE MOUNTAINS in the south. Part of the county, around Downpatrick and NEWCASTLE[1], is the local authority district of DOWN.

> Near Banbridge town in the County Down
> One morning in July
> Down the boreen came a sweet colleen
> And she smiled as she passed me by.
> Oh, she looked so neat from her two bare feet
> To the crown of her nut-brown hair,
> Such a winsome elf that I pinched myself
> To be sure I was really there.
>
> Anon.: 'The Star of the County Down' (song)

Battle of Down (14 May 1260). A battle fought at Druimdearg near Downpatrick in which the English of County Down defeated the forces of the Irish king Brian O'Neill (who was killed) and his ally Áed O'Connor, son of the king of CONNACHT.

Down Ampney 'downstream Ampney' (because it is further downstream – on a tributary of the River Thames – than other villages called Ampney), OE *dune* 'further downstream' + *Ampney* (*see* AMPNEY CRUCIS).

A village (pronounced 'ampny' or 'amny') in Gloucestershire, about 8 km (5 miles) southeast of Cirencester. The composer Ralph Vaughan Williams (1872–1958) was born here (his father was the local vicar), and he gave the name

❖ down, -don ❖

It is one of many curiosities in the English language that we call high land 'downs'. The common English place-name elements *down* and *-don* derive from the Old English word *dun*, meaning 'a hill' or 'high open land'. *Dun* generates a large number of place names, and also combines with many other frequently occurring elements, witness Downton (Herefordshire; *see* DOWNTON ON THE ROCK) and DUNTON BASSETT (Leicestershire) – combined with -TON – and Dunham (Cheshire and Nottinghamshire) – combined with HAM. Almost any feature of topography, flora or fauna, as well as man-made features or personal names can be combined with the element: for example, 'mill-stone' is found at Quarndon (Derbyshire),

QUORNDON (Leicestershire) and Quarrington Hill (County Durham).

In Scotland, the Gaelic element *dùn* has some of the same senses as the Old English word, often meaning 'hill' as well as 'fort' (as in DUNBAR, DUNBLANE or DUNDEE) and for this reason even Lowland Scotland has a few examples of the element, such as DUNS. In Ireland the same applies, as in DUNADD, DUNDALK, DUNGANNON and many others. Occasionally in English names there is confusion of Old English *dun* and *denu* 'valley', as in THEYDON BOIS (Essex), where the second element of Theydon is *denu*. And the aforementioned Quarrington Hill is an example of a more frequent confusion of *-don* and *-ton*.

'Down Ampney' to the tune he wrote for the hymn 'Come Down, O Love Divine' (1906).

Downe '(place at the) hill', OE *dun* (*see* DOWN, -DON).
A village in southeastern Greater London (before 1965 in Kent), in the borough of BROMLEY, between Orpington to the northeast and BIGGIN HILL to the southwest. The local **Down House**, in which Charles Darwin lived between 1842 and his death in 1882 and in which he wrote his *Origin of Species by Means of Natural Selection* (1859), preserves an earlier alternative spelling of the village's name.

Downend 'end of the down', OE *dun* (*see* DOWN, -DON) + *ende*.
A village in South Gloucestershire (before 1996 in Avon, before 1974 in Gloucestershire), now a northeastern suburb of BRISTOL. The GLOUCESTERSHIRE and England cricketer W.G. Grace (1848–1915) was born in Downend. His mother Martha, who legendarily if not apocryphally coached him as a young boy in the orchard of their house here, was for many decades the only woman to appear in the 'Births and Deaths of Cricketers' column of *Wisden Cricketers' Almanack*.

Downham Market *Downham* 'homestead on or near a hill', OE *dun* (*see* DOWN, -DON) + HAM; *Market* from the market here since at least the 11th century.
A market town in Norfolk, on the River Ouse (*see under* GREAT OUSE), about 18 km (11 miles) south of King's Lynn. It is an important agricultural market centre for the Fen Country to the west and the heathland to the east. Horatio Nelson went to school here as a child (*see also* BURNHAM THORPE).

> From Lynn, I bent my course to Downham, where is an ugly wooden bridge over the Ouse.
>
> Daniel Defoe: *A Tour Through the Whole Island of Great Britain* (1724–6)

Down Hatherley 'downstream Hatherley', *Down* OE *dune*

'further downstream'; *Hatherley* 'hawthorn glade', OE *haguthorn* 'hawthorn' + -LEY.
A village in Gloucestershire, in the Vale of Gloucester, about 5 km (3 miles) north of Gloucester. It is just to the northwest of Gloucestershire airfield.

Downhill The first element comes from the first element of the Irish name *Dún Bó* 'fort of cows', while the second element, English *hill*, is topographical.
A grand mansion and estate in County Londonderry, perched on cliffs above the sea 15 km (9 miles) northeast of Limavady. The house was built for Frederick Augustus Hervey, 4th Earl of Bristol and Lothario-esque Bishop of Derry from 1768 until his death. Hervey modestly wanted something 'about the size of Blenheim' and building began in 1776. Subsequently Hervey stuffed it with art treasures collected from all over Europe, and delighted in entertaining his clergy here, whom he would oblige to ride in horse races on the sands beneath the house, the winners receiving a better living. Hervey was also wont to sprinkle flour at night on the floors of the servants' quarters, to see who was seeing to whom. Hervey himself died with his mind half lost near Rome in 1803, while his great house lost its entire roof in 1950 and has since become derelict. However, his magnificent domed library, Mussenden Temple, is preserved by the National Trust; Hervey built it for his beautiful young cousin, Mrs Frideswide Mussenden, but she died before it was completed. Hervey allowed its vault to be used for worship by local Catholics.
See also ICKWORTH.

Downing Street From the diplomat and MP Sir George *Downing* (1623–84), who around 1680 financed a building development of terraced houses here.
A cul-de-sac in Central London (SW1), in the City of Westminster, leading westwards off Whitehall. There was probably a road here in medieval times, but Downing Street

as we now know it was the creation of Sir George Downing (*see above*). The brick terraced houses he had built around 1680 continued to attract a good class of tenant in the following century: James Boswell lodged here in 1762, Tobias Smollett tried to start up a surgeon's practice here in 1774, and in 1732 No. 10 was acquired by the Crown. That house has been the official residence and office of the British prime minister ever since. Meetings of the British Cabinet are usually held there. Behind its familiar facade and shiny black door it has undergone considerable expansion and reconstruction over the two-and-a-half centuries since its first occupant, Sir Robert Walpole, moved in. The south side of Downing Street was completely replaced with Sir George Gilbert Scott's Government Offices (now housing the Foreign Office) in the late 1860s, and on the north side only two houses apart from No. 10 remain: No. 11, home of the chancellor of the exchequer, and No. 12, which is occupied by the government chief whip. The entrance to the street via Whitehall was closed off with metal high-security gates in 1989, to guard against terrorist attack (on 7 February 1991 the IRA mounted a mortar attack on No. 10 from a nearby van).

Since at least the late 18th century, '**Downing Street**' (or more specifically **No. 10**) has been used as a metonym for the British prime minister (or those who speak or spin on his or her behalf) or for the British government in general.

Downing Street Declaration. An agreement between the British and Irish governments, formulated in 1993 and intended as the basis of a peace initiative in Northern Ireland. The declaration, issued on 15 December from No. 10 Downing Street by the British prime minister John Major and Irish *taoiseach* Albert Reynolds, was a further step along the road initiated by the Anglo-Irish Agreement of 1985.

Downpatrick Irish *Dún Pádraig* 'St Patrick's fort'; for the connections with St Patrick.

The county town of County Down, near the southwestern arm of Strangford Lough (*see under* STRANGFORD), 33 km (20 miles) southeast of Belfast. It was formerly called **Rathkeltair** (Irish *Ráth Cealtchair* 'Cealtchar's ring fort'), the fort in question having been on the hill where **Downpatrick Cathedral** now stands (the diocese of Down was established in the Middle Ages and is now Protestant). It is possible that Downpatrick's first church may have been built by St Patrick in the 5th century, and St Patrick is said to have begun his mission at SAUL[1], 3 km (2 miles) northeast of Downpatrick (Saul was also traditionally his place of death). However, there is no evidence to support the tradition that the saint – together with Saints Brigid and Columba (Columcille) – is buried at Downpatrick. This tradition is reflected in the Latin verse ascribed to the Anglo-Norman

John de Courci, who took Downpatrick in 1177, and proceeded to build a strong castle here:

> *In burgo Duno tumulo*
> *Tumulantur in uno*
> *Brigida, Patricius*
> *Atque Columba Pius.*
> (In Down three saints one grave do fill,
> Brigid, Patrick and Columcille.)

Downpatrick has a race course, where the annual Ulster Harp National is run.

In 1803 Downpatrick witnessed the hanging of the United Irishman Thomas Russell, executed after the failure of Robert Emmet's rising.

> Then he bowed his head to the swinging rope,
> While I said 'Please God' to his dying hope
> And 'Amen' to his dying prayer
> That the wrong would cease and the right prevail,
> For the man they hanged at Downpatrick gaol
> Was the man from God knows where.
>
> Florence Wilson: 'The Man from God Knows Where' (the sobriquet derived from the time Russell spent travelling Ulster to establish clubs for the Society of United Irishmen)

Downs, the[1] 'hills', OE *dun* (*see* DOWN, -DON).

Used generically, 'the Downs' can refer to any of a number of undulating treeless chalk uplands in southern England (e.g. the Berkshire Downs, the Dunstable Downs, the West Wiltshire Downs), but as a specific term it denotes either or both of the NORTH DOWNS and the SOUTH DOWNS. As a unit they form two scarps, which face each other across the Kentish and Sussex WEALD. In modern times they have been kept closely cropped by sheep, and indeed sheep of breeds originating here are termed 'Downs'.

> The Weald is good, the Downs are best –
> I'll give you the run of 'em, East to West.
>
> Rudyard Kipling: 'The Run of the Downs', from *Rewards and Fairies* (1910)

> Up on the Downs the red-eyed kestrels hover,
> Eyeing the grass.
> The field-mouse flits like a shadow into cover
> As their shadows pass.
>
> John Masefield: 'Up on the Downs' (1917)

Cathedral of the Downs. *See under* ALFRISTON.

Downsman. A native or inhabitant of the (South) Downs. The establishment of the Society of Sussex Downsmen in 1923 raised the profile of the term.

Downs, the[2] So called because they are opposite the point on the coast where the NORTH DOWNS end.

A roadstead (that is, a partly sheltered anchorage) off the East Kent coast, between DEAL and the GOODWIN SANDS, historically a favourite rendezvousing point for ships using the Straits of Dover. Henry VIII built the castles of Deal,

WALMER and Sandown to defend the Downs, each fortress being about 2 km (1.25 miles) apart.

See also the SMALL DOWNS.

Battle of the Downs. Either of two naval battles fought off the East Kent coast: the first in 1639, in which the Dutch defeated the Spanish, and the second in 1666, between the English and the Dutch, from which the English emerged as on balance the losers.

Downside '(land on a) hill-side', OE *dun* (see DOWN, -DON) + *side*.

A village in Somerset, in the eastern foothills of the MENDIP HILLS, about 16 km (10 miles) southwest of Shepton Mallet. In 1814 some English Benedictine monks who had settled in France but been driven out by the Revolution founded a monastery nearby, which in 1899 became **Downside Abbey**. Its massive building, largely to designs of Sir Giles Gilbert Scott and Thomas Garner, evolved between 1880 and 1935. In the next-door village of Stratton-on-Fosse is **Downside School**, a Roman Catholic boys' school.

Down Thomas 'Thomas's down', OE *dun* (see DOWN, -DON) + the name of a 14th-century squire, *Thomas*.

A village in Devon, about 8 km (5 miles) south of Plymouth.

Downton on the Rock *Downton* 'farmstead on or by the hill', OE *dun* (see DOWN, -DON) + -TON; *Rock* 'rock, peak', ME *rokke*.

A village in Herefordshire (before 1998 in Hereford and Worcester, before 1974 in Herefordshire), on the River TEME, about 10 km (6 miles) west of Ludlow.

Dozmary Pool 'pool on Tosmeri hill', *Tosmeri* a name of obscure origin, apparently referring to the surrounding moorland.

A shallow lake on Bodmin Moor (*see under* BODMIN), Cornwall. It is about 1.5 km (1 mile) in circumference. It is fed by the heavy Atlantic rain, which cannot drain away through the underlying granite. According to legend, it was into Dozmary that Sir Bedivere threw King Arthur's sword as the king lay dying after the Battle of Camlann.

Draeighean. The Irish name for DRAINS BAY.

Dragon Hill. A hill on the Berkshire Downs (*see under* BERK-SHIRE), next to White Horse Hill (*see under* UFFINGTON), in Oxfordshire (formerly in Berkshire), where local legend claims St George killed the dragon:

> The well-known tradition, recorded as far back as 1738 by Wise, is that Dragon Hill is where St George slew the Dragon, and the patch of bare chalk on the knoll is where the blood issued from the Dragon's wound, poisoning the ground so that no grass has ever grown there since. This bare patch is just as plain now as it was two hundred years ago,
>
> L.V. Grinsell: *White Horse Hill and the Surrounding Country* (1939)

Some have interpreted the nearby White Horse of Uffington as the dragon.

Drain, the. A nickname for the Waterloo and City line on the London Underground, opened in 1898. The line runs between Waterloo Station (*see under* WATERLOO[1]) and BANK, with no intervening stations. The designation, at first derogatory but latterly almost affectionate, dates from the 1920s and refers to the deep and dingy route. Before its transfer to London Underground in 1994 it was the only Tube line run by British Rail.

Drains Bay Irish *Draeighean* 'blackthorn, sloe' + ModE *bay*.

A small inlet of the NORTH CHANNEL, overlooked by LARNE, County Antrim, at the mouth of Larne Lough.

Drakeland Corner Probably from the *Drake* family, known here from the 14th century.

A village in Devon, on the southern edge of DARTMOOR, about 8 km (5 miles) northeast of Plymouth.

Drakes Broughton *Drakes* denoting ownership of a local farm in the Middle Ages by the Drake family; *Broughton* 'farmstead by a stream', OE *broc* 'brook, stream' + -TON.

A village in Worcestershire (before 1998 in Hereford and Worcester, before 1974 in Worcestershire), about 10 km (6 miles) northwest of Evesham.

Drakes Cross Perhaps 'cross or crossroads on land held by the *Drake* family'.

A village in Worcestershire (before 1998 in Hereford and Worcester, before 1974 in Worcestershire), on the southern outskirts of Birmingham.

Drake's Island After Sir Francis *Drake*.

An island in Plymouth Sound, Devon (*see under* PLYMOUTH). Its original name was **St Nicholas Island** (after the island's chapel of St Nicholas, demolished in 1548), but this was changed around 1590 to honour the Devonian seafarer Sir Francis Drake (*c.*1540–96), who had anchored the *Golden Hind* near the island in 1580 on his return from his round-the-world voyage.

Draperstown From the Drapers Company of London.

A village in County Londonderry, 12 km (7.5 miles) north-west of Magherafelt. The Drapers Company of London acquired land here in the 17th century and built the village in 1830, having named it in 1818. Its Irish name is **Baile na Croise** ('town of the cross') and it is still sometimes referred to as **the Cross**.

Drax OE *dræg*, assimilated to OScand *drag* 'place where boats are pulled out of the water', perhaps referring to a possible portage between the OUSE[2] and the AIRE, although the junction of the two is so close it would hardly be worth the effort.

A village in North Yorkshire, 8 km (5 miles) southeast of Selby. The presence nearby of a vast coal-fired power station – the largest in western Europe, supplying 10 per cent of Britain's electricity – does not detract from the village's charm. The village of **Long Drax** is a little to the north.

Draycott in the Clay *Draycott* probably 'shed where drays or sledges are kept', OE *dræg* 'dray, sledge' + *cot* (*see* -COT, COTE); *Clay* OE *clæg* 'clayey district'.
A village in Staffordshire, about 11 km (7 miles) northwest of Burton upon Trent.

Drayton Parslow *Drayton* 'farmstead near a portage or slope used for dragging down loads, or where drays or sledges are used', OScand *drag* 'portage' or OE *dræg* 'dray, sledge' + -TON; *Parslow* denoting manorial ownership in the early Middle Ages by the Passelewe family.
A village in Buckinghamshire, about 16 km (10 miles) north of Aylesbury.
See also FENNY DRAYTON, MARKET DRAYTON.

Dreish '(hill of the) brambles', Gaelic *dris* 'bramble'.
A mountain (947 m / 3106 ft) in the southern CAIRNGORMS, above the head of GLEN CLOVA, Angus.

Drenewydd. The Welsh name for BUTETOWN.

Dresden From *Dresden* in Germany, centre of porcelain manufacture since the early 18th century.
A southeastern district of LONGTON in Staffordshire, in the POTTERIES within the unitary authority of STOKE-ON-TRENT. It was built on land purchased around 1850 from Sir Thomas Boughey by the Longton Freehold Land Society. Most of the Society's members were in the china business, and their choice of name for their new suburb reflected their preoccupations (as earlier had that of the nearby ETRURIA).
The composer Havergal Brian (1876–1972) was born in Dresden, the son of a potter.

Drewsteignton Originally *Teignton* 'farmstead or village on the River Teign', OCelt river name (*see* TEIGN) + -TON; *Drews-* (from the 13th century) denoting manorial ownership in the Middle Ages by a man called Drew.
A village in Devon, on the northeastern edge of DARTMOOR, on a ridge above the Teign gorge, about 20 km (13 miles) west of Exeter. CASTLE DROGO is about 1.5 km (1 mile) to the southwest.

Driffield 'open land with stubble', OE *drif* 'stubble' (or possibly *drit* 'dirt') + *feld* (*see* FIELD).
A market town in the East Riding of Yorkshire, 30 km (20 miles) north of Hull. It is sometimes called **Great Driffield**, to distinguish it from the adjacent village of **Little Driffield**. Its origins are ancient: Aldfrith, king of Northumbria, died here in 704.

Drift 'the village', Cornish *an trev*, with added -*t* perhaps by analogy with English *drift* 'cattle-drove'.
A village in Cornwall, about 5 km (3 miles) southwest of Penzance. **Drift Reservoir** is about 0.5 km (0.3 miles) to the northwest.

Drinkstone 'Drengr's farmstead', OScand male personal name *Drengr* (or possibly OScand *drengr* 'good fellow') + -TON.
A village in Suffolk, about 11 km (7 miles) southeast of Bury St Edmunds.

Drogheda Irish *Droichead Átha* 'bridge of the ford' (*see* FORD).
A port and industrial town near the mouth of the River BOYNE, County Louth, 43 km (27 miles) north of Dublin. The pronunciation of Drogheda is indicated in the following anonymous limerick:

> A young Irish servant in Drogheda
> Had a mistress who often annogheda.
>> Whereon she would swear
>> With language so rare
> That thereafter no one emplogheda.

St Patrick founded a monastery here in the 5th century, and there are remains of an Augustinian abbey (1206) and a Dominican friary (1224). There were Viking and then Anglo-Norman settlements here, and very strong walls were built around the medieval town. Richard II held a court at Drogheda in 1394, and exactly a century later the Irish Parliament met here and was persuaded to pass the infamous Poynings' Law, which gave control of the Irish Parliament to the English king and council. In 1649 the town was seized by Cromwell, with unpleasant consequences for the inhabitants (*see below*). Drogheda was a county in its own right until 1898. St Peter's Church in Drogheda contains the embalmed head of St Oliver Plunket, martyred in London in 1681.

Drogheda weavers. A phrase used to describe a workman who has run short of some necessary material:

> Idle for want of weft, like the Drogheda weavers.

Drogheda was a noted weaving town in the 19th century, but at times there were more weavers than there was work to give them – hence the expression.

drugget. A word thought to derive from the name Drogheda and indicating a type of cloth woven from wool and flax.

Siege of Drogheda (1649). On 11 September 1649, after three days of artillery bombardment, Cromwell stormed the walls of Drogheda and massacred the garrison, an action that to many Irish has epitomized the English presence in their country. Some 3500 were killed, including 1000 civilians. Cromwell justified his actions by claiming that civilians had been involved in the massacres of 1641 and that by using this terror tactic he could shorten the war by persuading other Irish towns to surrender (however, only a few nearby towns did so).

> It has pleased God to bless our endeavours at Drogheda ...
> I believe we put to the sword the whole number of the

defendants. I do not think thirty of the whole number escaped with their lives. Those that did are in safe custody for the Barbadoes … I wish that all honest hearts may give the glory of this to God alone, to whom indeed the praise of this mercy belongs.

> Oliver Cromwell: letter to the Hon. John Bradshaw, president of the Council of State (September 1649)

In 1690, after the Battle of the Boyne (fought just to the west of the town), the town surrendered to William III.

Droichead Átha. The Irish name for DROGHEDA.

Droichead na Banna. The Irish name for BANBRIDGE and for BANDON.

Droichead na Sionainne. The Irish name for SHANNONBRIDGE.

Droichead Nua. The Irish name for NEWBRIDGE[2].

Droim Mór. The Irish name for DROMORE.

Droitwich 'dirty or muddy saltworks', OE *drit* 'dirt' + *wic* (*see* WICK).

A spa town in Worcestershire (before 1998 in Hereford and Worcester, before 1974 in Worcestershire), about 10 km (6 miles) northeast of Worcester. It lies above considerable deposits of salt, which were first exploited by the Romans. Mining continued in Saxon and Norman times. This mineral wealth was turned to more therapeutic ends in the 19th century, when the businessman John Corbett built the St Andrews Brine Baths and other facilities to assuage the Victorians' passion for healing waters.

Edward Winslow (1595–1655), founder of Plymouth Colony in Massachusetts, was born in Droitwich.

Dromore Irish *Droim Mór* 'big ridge'.

A town in County Down, 25 km (16 miles) southwest of Belfast. A monastery was founded here in the 6th century by St Colman, also known as Mo-Cholmóg, hence the alternative Irish name for Dromore, **Druim Mocholmóg**. There is a Norman motte and bailey called **Dromore Mound**, and the 8th- or 9th-century **Cross of Dromore**. The town was burnt during the rising of 1641. The 17th-century Protestant **Dromore Cathedral** contains the tombs of two notable bishops: Jeremy Taylor (1613–67), author of *The Rule and Exercises of Holy Living* (1650) and *The Rule and Exercises of Holy Dying* (1651); and Thomas Percy (1729–1811), compiler of *Reliques of Ancient English Poetry* (1765) – known as *Percy's Reliques*.

Dromore was the birthplace of the industrialist Harry Ferguson (1884–1960), designer of the Ferguson tractor.

Droop 'outlying farm, dependent settlement', OE *throp* (*see* THORPE).

A village in Dorset, about 13 km (8 miles) west of Blandford Forum.

Dropping Well. *See* KNARESBOROUGH.

Droylsden 'valley of the dry spring', OE *dryge* 'dry' + *wella* 'spring' + *denu* 'valley'.

An eastern suburb of MANCHESTER. The British Communist Party politician Harry Pollitt (1890–1960) was born here.

Southwest of the centre of Droylsden is the Settlement of the Church of the United Brethren – a sect originally established in Moravia (now part of the Czech Republic) in the 15th century. Established in 1785, and consisting of some 50 red-brick cottages, Fairfield Moravian Settlement – as it is usually known – was originally a self-contained and self-governed village.

Druid Possibly Welsh *driwid* 'druid'; there may have been a stone circle or some such here.

A village in Denbighshire (formerly in Clwyd), 18 km (11 miles) west of Llangollen.

Druidston 'Drew's farm', Anglo-Norman personal name + -TON.

A small village, pronounced 'drewstən', just inland from ST BRIDE'S BAY, Pembrokeshire (formerly in Dyfed), 8 km (5 miles) west of Haverfordwest.

Druimceatt OCelt *Druim-Céte*, the first element of which is 'ridge', but the second is obscure.

The site of a meeting held in 575 between Aedan, king of DALRIADA, and Aed, the High King of Ireland, with St Columba (Columcille) – on a rare return visit to Ireland – acting as intermediary. It is said to have taken place on a small hill now called the Mullagh, near Limavady, County Londonderry. The meeting is recorded in the *Annals of the Four Masters* (*see under* DONEGAL), and the discussions seem mostly to have been about dynastic matters, although Columba also prevented the expulsion of the poets from Ireland, whom some had seen as getting above their station. The event is dramatized in the play *Convention at Druim Ceat* (1943) by Roibeárd Ó Faracháin (Robert Farren).

Druim Chliabh. The Irish name for DRUMCLIFF.

Druim Cria. The Irish name for DRUMCREE.

Druim Mocholmóg. The alternative Irish name for DROMORE.

Drum Gaelic *druim* 'ridge'.

A village in Perth and Kinross (formerly in Kinross-shire, and then in Tayside region), 7 km (4 miles) southwest of Kinross.

> The Laird o' Drum is a-wooing gane,
> It was on a morning early,
> And he has fawn in wi' a bonny maid
> A-shearing at her barley.
>
> Anon.: 'The Laird o' Drum' (a ballad)

Drum Alban 'ridge of Scotland', Gaelic *druim* 'ridge' + ALBA or ALBANY[1].

A name sometimes conferred on the mountains forming

the spine of Scotland, marking the watershed between east and west from BEN LOMOND in the south to BEN HOPE in the north.

Drumcliff Irish *Druim Chliabh* 'ridge of baskets'.

A village in County Sligo, 6 km (4 miles) north of Sligo itself. It is at the foot of BENBULBEN, overlooking **Drumcliff Bay**. The poet Yeats's grandfather was rector here from 1811 to 1846, and Yeats expressed a wish to be buried here:

> Under bare Ben Bulben's head
> In Drumcliff churchyard Yeats is laid.
> An ancestor was a rector there
> Long years ago, a church stands near,
> By the road an ancient cross.
>
> W.B. Yeats: 'Under Ben Bulben' (1938)

Yeats died in France on 28 January 1939, but his remains were brought back to Ireland in 1948 and buried in Drumcliff churchyard. His grave is marked by a stone bearing the epitaph Yeats had written for himself in the same poem:

> Cast a cold eye
> On life, on death.
> Horseman, pass by!

The place has since become a quiet place of pilgrimage.

> Rooks flew up from the old gravestones, circled cawing around the old church tower. Yeats's grave was wet, the stone was cold, and the lines which Yeats had had inscribed on his gravestone were as cold as the ice needles that had been shot at me from Swift's tomb: 'Cast a cold eye on life, on death. Horseman, pass by!' I looked up; were the rooks enchanted swans? They cawed mockingly at me, fluttered around the church tower. The ferns lay flat on the surrounding hills, beaten down by the rain, rust-coloured and withered. I felt cold.
>
> Heinrich Böll: *Irish Journal* (translated by L. Vennewitz, 1967). Swift's famous self-written epitaph, referred to by Böll, is '*Ubi saeva indignatio ulterius cor lacerare nequit*' ('where savage indignation can no longer tear his heart').

Drumclog Possibly 'ridge of the stone', Gaelic *druim* 'ridge' + *cloiche* 'stone', or OCelt *clog* 'crag, rock'.

A small village 8 km (5 miles) southwest of Strathaven in South Lanarkshire (formerly in Strathclyde region).

Battle of Drumclog (29 May 1679). An engagement on the moors northwest of the village in which a force of Covenanters repulsed an attack by John Graham of Claverhouse – 'Bonnie Dundee' (*see under* DUNDEE). Shortly afterwards the Covenanters suffered a major defeat at Bothwell Brig (*see under* BOTHWELL).

Drumcree Irish *Druim Cria* 'ridge of the clay'.

A small village near PORTADOWN, County Armagh. By tradition, on the Sunday before the 12 July celebrations, the Portadown Orangemen march to Drumcree parish church for a service and afterwards march back via the

Nationalist Garvaghy Road. This has always been a source of tension, and since 1995 there have been a series of stand-offs – often violent – between Orangemen, Nationalist residents and the security forces. The Orangemen claim that their traditions are under threat, and the Nationalists complain of aggressive Loyalist triumphalism on their front doorsteps. In 1998 the return march was re-routed on the orders of the Parades Commission, leading to considerable Loyalist resentment. This was linked to a firebomb attack in BALLYMONEY in which three Catholic children died, causing some in the Orange Order to pause for thought:

> No road is worth a life, let alone the lives of three little boys.
>
> William Bingham (chaplain of the Armagh Lodge of the Orange Order): quoted in the *Daily Telegraph* (13 July 1998)

Since then the march has continued to be re-routed and tensions remain high.

Drumelzier Said to be 'mound of Merlin', Gaelic *druim* 'ridge' + possibly a corruption of a personal name, although the second element is obscure (but *see* DRYBURGH ABBEY); *Dunmedler* 6th century.

A village by the River TWEED in Scottish Borders (formerly in Peeblesshire), 14 km (8.5 miles) southwest of Peebles. It is one of many reputed burial places of the wizard Merlin, and according to this version of his death he was chased over the bluffs above the Tweed, fell among the salmon nets below, was caught by his feet and, hanging upside down in the water, was drowned. This satisfied his own prophecy that he would die by falling, hanging and drowning.

Drumelzier itself was the subject of a prophecy by the seer Thomas the Rhymer of ERCILDOUNE:

> When Tweed and Powsail meet at Merlin's grave, England and Scotland shall one monarch have.

It is said that when in 1603 James VI of Scotland was crowned as James I of England, the Tweed overflowed here into the nearby River Powsail.

Drumlanrig 'clearing ridge', Gaelic *druim* 'ridge' + OCelt *llanerch* 'clearing'.

The palatial seat of the dukes of Buccleuch and Queensberry, some 3 km (2 miles) northwest of Thornhill in Dumfries and Galloway (formerly in Dumfriesshire). It was built for William Douglas, 1st Duke of Queensbury, and completed in 1691.

> Drumlanrig, like Chatsworth in Darbyshire, is like a fine picture in a dirty grotto, or like an equestrian statue set up in a barn; 'tis environed with mountains, and that of the wildest and most hideous aspect in all the south of Scotland.
>
> Daniel Defoe: *A Tour Through the Whole Island of Great Britain* (1724–6)

Defoe goes on to offer the following lines (almost certainly written by himself):

> Just thus, with horrid desert hills embrac'd,
> Was Paradise on *Euphra's* border plac'd.
> The God of Harmony to grace the view,
> And make the illustrations just and true,
> Strong contraries presented to the eye,
> And circled beauty in deformity.
> The happy discord entertains the sight,
> And as these shew more black, that shews more bright.

Drumly Harry. *See* FALLS OF DRUMLY HARRY.

Drummossie Muir. *See* CULLODEN MUIR.

Drumnadrochit 'ridge of the bridge', Gaelic *druim* 'ridge' + *na* 'of the' + *drochaid* 'bridge'.
A village on the west side of Loch Ness, in Highland (formerly in Inverness-shire), 22 km (13 miles) southwest of Inverness. It houses the Loch Ness Monster Exhibition Centre (*see under* LOCH NESS).

Drumochter Pass 'ridge of the higher place', Gaelic *druim* 'ridge' + *uachdair* 'upper part'.
A bleak pass (424 m / 1391 ft high) that lies 37 km (22 miles) northwest of Pitlochry, linking GLEN GARRY[2] and Strathspey (*see under* SPEY), and carrying both the A9 Perth–Inverness trunk road and the main-line rail link. The pass marks the boundary between HIGHLAND and PERTH AND KINROSS (and formerly marked the boundary between Inverness-shire and Perthshire, then between Highland and Tayside Regions). It is not infrequently blocked by snow in the winter, and even in summer is a dour place.

> *Mi gabhail Sraith Dhruim Uachdair,*
> *'S beag m'aighear anns an uair so:*
> *Tha an latha air dol gu gruamachd*
>   *S' chan e tha buain mo sproc.*
> (As I travel the Strath of Drumochter,
> little my joy at this season:
> the day has turned out grimly
>   and that does not help my gloom.)
> Iain Lom (John Macdonald, *c.*1620–*c.*1710): '*Oran Cumhaidh air Cor na Rìoghachd*' ('A Lament for the State of the Country'), translated by Meg Bateman

Drumsturdy The first element is probably Gaelic *druim* 'ridge'; the second is obscure.
A small settlement in Angus (formerly in Tayside region), some 10 km (6 miles) northeast of Dundee.

Druridge Bay 'dry ridge bay', OE *dryge* 'dry' + *hrycg* 'ridge' + ModE *bay*.
A wide sandy bay on the Northumberland coast, between NEWBIGGIN-BY-THE-SEA and AMBLE.

Drury Lane From *Drury* House, home in the mid-16th century of Sir Thomas Drury.

A street in the WEST END[1] of London (WC2), leading south-eastwards from HOLBORN to the ALDWYCH. In the 16th and 17th centuries it was a fashionable residential street (occupants included Oliver Cromwell and the poet John Donne), but when the actress and courtesan Nell Gwynne (1651–87) took up lodgings here it was a sure sign that things were on the slide (Samuel Pepys records how in 1667 he 'saw pretty Nelly standing at her lodgings in Drury Lane in her smock-sleeves and bodice looking upon one: she seemed a mighty pretty creature'). In the 18th century Drury Lane was as well known for its gin shops, brothels and drunken brawls as for its theatre (*see below*), and by the end of the 19th century it had become one of the vilest slums in London.
The slums were cleared away when KINGSWAY was constructed at the beginning of the 20th century, and over the next hundred years the street was able to establish a more salubrious reputation on the basis of its theatre – the **Theatre Royal, Drury Lane**, commonly referred to as 'Drury Lane' for short (its entrance is actually around the corner in Catherine Street). The original opened in 1663 (Nell Gwynne, whose nickname was **Sweet Nell of Old Drury**, worked as an orange-seller there), but it burned down nine years later. Its successor was designed by Christopher Wren, but was replaced by a new structure in 1794. That also succumbed to fire (the playwright Richard Sheridan, a shareholder in the theatre, consoled himself with a drink while standing opposite the burning building, and when challenged replied: 'A man may surely be allowed to take a glass of wine by his own fire'). The present theatre, designed by Benjamin Dean Wyatt, was opened in 1812. Many well-known actors have appeared at Drury Lane, including David Garrick, Charles Kemble and Edmund Kean. Since the Second World War it has been noted for its musicals.

Druriolanus. A late 19th-century nickname of the Theatre Royal, Drury Lane, originally coined as its telegraphic address (blending *Drury* and Shakespeare's *Coriolanus*) by the theatre's celebrated manager Augustus Harris (1852–96). The name was also applied to Harris himself.

Drury Lane vestal. A euphemism from the mid-18th to the early 19th centuries for the prostitutes who then frequented Drury Lane ('vestal' facetiously from the idea of a Roman vestal virgin). The type of diseases one might have caught off them, particularly gonorrhoea, were correspondingly termed **Drury Lane ague**.

Dryburgh Abbey 'dry fortress', OE *dryge* 'dry' + *burh* (*see* BURY).
A monastery, now ruined, on the River TWEED just east of NEWTON ST BOSWELLS in Scottish Borders (formerly in Roxburghshire). It was founded *c.*1152 as a Premonstratensian house by Hugh de Morville, and was frequently sacked by the English in the Middle Ages. The lands later

came into the possession of the great-grandfather of Sir Walter Scott, but were then lost to the family, who, however, held onto the right to 'stretch their bones' here. Sir Walter Scott was duly buried in the abbey (*see also* SCOTT'S VIEW) as were his son-in-law and biographer J.G. Lockhart, and Field Marshal Earl Haig.

A local tale tells how a woman who lost her beloved during the 1745 Jacobite Rising swore that she would never look on daylight again until he returned. She duly took to living in the vaults of Dryburgh Abbey, where she was reportedly served by a little man called Fatlips. (Curiously, one possibility for the etymology of the second element of DRUMELZIER, further up the Tweed, is Gaelic *meillir* 'blubber-lips'.)

Dryhope Tower. *See under* YARROW WATER.

Dry Street Presumably from a lack of water; *see also* STREET.
A village in Essex, about 3 km (2 miles) southwest of Basildon.

Duart Castle 'black promontory', Gaelic name *Dubhaird*, from *dubh* (*see* DDU, DUBH) + *aird* 'promontory', or *ard* 'height, crag' – both meanings suit the topography (*see also* ARD).
The seat of the Maclean chiefs on a rocky promontory in southeastern MULL, Argyll and Bute (formerly in Strathclyde region). The castle, which guards the southern entrance of the Sound of Mull, dates back to the 13th century, with later additions. The Macleans lost their lands for supporting the Jacobite cause in the late 17th century, but the 26th chief, Sir Fitzroy Maclean, bought back the castle in 1911 and set about restoring it.

A little off shore from the castle is LADY'S ROCK.

Dublin 'black pool', Irish *dubh* 'black' (*see* DDU, DUBH) + *linn* 'pool', referring to the River Liffey.
The capital of the Republic of Ireland and the county town of County DUBLIN. It is also an important port and industrial centre, and nearly a third of the population of the Republic lives in Dublin and its commuter belt. Its official Irish name is BAILE ÁTHA CLIATH ('town of the ford of the hurdles'), reflecting its strategic importance as a river crossing from the earliest times.

> Dublin the beautie and eie of Ireland, hath beene named by Ptolome, in ancient time, Eblana. Some term it Dublina, others Dublinia, manie write it Dublinum, others of better skill name it Dublinium. The Irish call it Ballee er Cleagh, this is, a towne planted upon hurdles. For the common opinion is that the plot upon which the civitie is builded, hath been a marish ground; and for that by the art or invention of the founder, the water could not be voided, he was forced to fasten the quake mire with hurdles, and on them build the citie.
>
> Richard Stanihurst: *De Rebus in Hibernis Gestis*, in Raphael Holinshed's *Chronicles* (1577)

Dublin is situated halfway down the east coast of Ireland at the mouth of the River LIFFEY (essential for the production of Guinness in one of the world's largest breweries, founded in 1759), and overlooks **Dublin Bay**, which has been favourably compared to the Bay of Naples.

> O Bay of Dublin! My heart you're troublin',
> Your beauty haunts me like a fevered dream,
> Like frozen fountains that the sun sets bubblin'
> My heart's blood warms when I but hear your name.
>
> Helen Selina, Lady Dufferin: 'Dublin Bay', from *A Selection of the Songs of Lady Dufferin* (1895)

Natives of Dublin are **Dubliners**, or more informally **Dubs** (a name also applied to Dublin's Gaelic football team) or **Jackeens**. (The latter, in use since the mid-19th century, is sometimes used pejoratively, and there are two theories as to its origin: either it is a gaelicization of JOHN BULL or it derives from the miniature Union Jacks waved by Dublin schoolchildren on the occasion of Queen Victoria's visit in 1900.)

There was a settlement at Dublin by the 2nd century AD, when Ptolemy recorded the name as **Eblana**. Dublin was seized by Vikings of Norwegian descent in 841. It became the capital of a Norse kingdom, and in the earlier 10th century the kings of Dublin were also kings of YORK. By this time the Dublin Norse had become fairly integrated into the Gaelic fabric of Ireland; their influence diminished after their defeat at CLONTARF in 1014, and in 1052 the kingdom of Dublin was taken over by the king of LEINSTER. From this point Dublin became the virtual capital of Ireland. Its last king was executed by the Anglo-Norman invaders in 1171 and thereafter Dublin became the centre of English rule in Ireland, administered from **Dublin Castle** (*see below*). It also became the seat of the Irish Parliament (at COLLEGE GREEN[2]) until it was abolished by the Act of Union of 1800.

The archdiocese of Dublin, covering southeastern Ireland, was created in 1152. There are now both Catholic and Anglican archbishops, and three cathedrals: the Catholic pro-cathedral of St Mary's (1816) and two Protestant cathedrals, St Patrick's (Early English style; the national cathedral) and Christchurch (the cathedral of the diocese of Dublin). Jonathan Swift became dean of St Patrick's in 1713, but had no high regard for the city:

> This town … I believe is the most disagreeable place in Europe, at least to any but those who have been accustomed to it from their youth, and in such a case I suppose a jail might be tolerable.
>
> Jonathan Swift: letter to Knightly Chetwode (23 November 1727)

There was considerable development in the 18th century, when Dublin's cultural life flourished (it was here, for example, that the first performance of Handel's

Messiah was given, in 1742; *see under* FISHAMBLE STREET), and the place regarded itself as the second city of the British empire, or even 'the fourth city in Christendom' (Sir Charles Wogan, letter to Jonathan Swift, 27 February 1732). However, not everyone agreed on its standing:

> *Boswell:* Should you not like to see Dublin, Sir?
> *Johnson:* No, Sir! Dublin is only a worse capital.
>
> James Boswell: *The Life of Samuel Johnson* (1791)
> (conversation on 12 October 1779)

Many elegant streets and squares (most famously Fitzwilliam and Merrion Squares) were built, and other buildings from the period include City Hall (1769–79; formerly the Royal Exchange), the Bank of Ireland (1729–85; the former Parliament building), the Four Courts (1786) and the Custom House (1791).

> Och, Dublin City, there is no doubtin',
> Bates every city upon the say;
> 'Tis there you'll see O'Connell spoutin',
> An' Lady Morgan makin' tay;
> For 'tis the capital of the finest nation,
> Wid charmin' pisintry on a fruitful sod,
> Fightin' like divils for conciliation
> An' hatin' each other for the love of God.
>
> Charles James Lever (1809–72): 'Dublin City'

In the late 19th century Dublin became the centre of the Irish Literary Revival, and the ABBEY THEATRE was established by W.B. Yeats and Lady Gregory to further this cause in 1904. Yeats did, however, despair of Dublin, calling it 'the blind and ignorant town' ('To A Wealthy Man …', from *Responsibilities*, 1914). James Joyce in 1905 – having left Ireland in despair and for good the previous year – called it 'the centre of paralysis', while in 1911 George Bernard Shaw referred to 'that city of tedious and silly derision'. In a later poem Yeats remembers the prosaic life led there:

> I have met them at close of day
> Coming with vivid faces
> From counter or desk among grey
> Eighteenth-century houses.
>
> W.B. Yeats: 'Easter 1916', from *Michael Robartes and the Dancer* (1921)

Dublin to Yeats had been 'where motley is worn'; but the doomed foolhardy courage of the Easter Rising, which took place in Dublin in 1916 (*see* **Dublin Rising** *below*), changed his mind, as it had, in the eyes of many, transformed the participants:

> All changed, changed utterly:
> A terrible beauty is born.

In 1918 many Irish MPs declined to take their seats at Westminster and instead sat in Dublin as the Dáil; during the Anglo–Irish War that followed, the city was the focus of much fighting. Since independence in 1922, Dublin has been home to the Dáil Éireann (House of Representatives) and to the Seanad Éireann (the Senate); they both sit in Leinster House. Dublin is also home to three universities: Trinity College, University College (part of the National University of Ireland), and Dublin City University (formerly a technical college). Trinity College library contains the Book of KELLS[1]. Other notable institutions in the city include the National Library, the National Museum, the National Gallery, the Hugh Lane Municipal Gallery of Modern Art, the Collins Barracks (now part of the National Museum), the Gate Theatre and KILMAINHAM Jail (now a museum).

Dublin flourished in the later years of the 20th century and into the 21st century as the heart of the CELTIC TIGER and also as a thriving cultural centre and a destination for Brits in search of booze-soaked stag weekends. But there are still areas of poverty and deprivation, as depicted in Roddy Doyle's *Barrytown Trilogy*, set in the fictional northern suburb of BARRYTOWN:

> The Irish are the niggers of Europe … An' Dubliners are the niggers of Ireland … An' the northside Dubliners are the niggers o' Dublin – Say it loud. I'm black an' I'm proud.
>
> Roddy Doyle: *The Commitments* (1987)

Dublin was the birthplace of the poet John Denham (1615–69); the poet Nahum Tate (1652–1715); the dramatist Thomas Southerne (1660–1746); the satirist and cleric Jonathan Swift (1667–1745); the essayist, playwright, and politician Richard Steele (1672–1729); the politician and political theorist Edmund Burke (1729–97); the Shakespeare scholar Edward Malone (1741–1812); the playwright and politician Richard Brinsley Sheridan (1751–1816); the Duke of Wellington (1769–1852), army commander and Tory prime minister 1828–30; the Nationalist leader Robert Emmet (1778–1803); the poet Thomas Moore (1779–1852); the Gothic novelist Charles Robert Maturin (1782–1824); the poet and translator James Clarence Mangan (1803–49); the mathematician William Hamilton (1805–65); the mystery writer Sheridan Le Fanu (1814–73); the hymn-writer Mrs Cecil Frances Alexander (1818–95), author of 'All Things Bright and Beautiful'; the writer Dion Boucicault (1820–90), author of *The Colleen Bawn* (1859); Thomas Barnardo (1845–1905), founder of children's homes; novelist and man of the theatre Bram Stoker (1847–1912), the creator of *Dracula* (1897); the composer Charles Villiers Stanford (1852–1924); the writer Oscar Wilde (1854–1900); the dramatist and man of letters George Bernard Shaw (1856–1950); the newspaper proprietor Lord Northcliffe (1865–1922); the poet W.B. Yeats (1865–1939); the Nationalist Arthur Griffith (1872–1922), founder of Sinn Féin; the writer, surgeon and wit Oliver St John Gogarty (1878–1957); the revolutionary Patrick Pearse

(1879–1916), leader of the Easter Rising (1916); the dramatist Seán O'Casey (1880–1964); the politician and revolutionary William Cosgrave (1880–1965), first prime minister of the Free State 1922–32; the pioneer modernist writer James Joyce (1882–1941); the writer James Stephens (1882–1950), author of *The Crock of Gold* (1912); the Fine Gael politician John Aloysius Costello (1891–1976), *taoiseach* (prime minister) 1948–51 and 1954–7; the poet Austin Clarke (1896–1974); the writer Liam O'Flaherty (1896–1984); the novelist Elizabeth Bowen (1899–1973); the novelist Iris Murdoch (1919–99); Fine Gael politician Liam Cosgrave (b.1920), *taoiseach* 1973–7; the writer Brendan Behan (1923–64); Fianna Fáil politician Charles Haughey (b.1925), *taoiseach* 1979–81, 1982 and 1987–92; Fine Gael politician Garret FitzGerald (b.1926), *taoiseach* 1981–2 and 1982–7; the poet Thomas Kinsella (b.1928); the novelist Jennifer Johnston (b.1930); the novelist John McGahern (b.1934); the novelist Maeve Binchy (b.1940); the jailed Tory perjurer Jonathan Aitken (b.1942); Fianna Fáil politician Bertie Ahern (b.1951), *taoiseach* from 1997; and the novelist Roddy Doyle (b.1958).

> This was never my town ...
>
> But yet she holds my mind
> With her seedy elegance,
> With her gentle veils of rain
> And all her ghosts that walk
> And all that hide behind
> Her Georgian facades ...
>
> Louis MacNeice: 'Dublin'

Dublin looms large in a number of literary works; for example, Edna O'Brien's *The Country Girls* (1960) and J.P. Donleavy's *The Ginger Man* (1955); typical of the anarchic sentiments expressed in the latter is the following:

> When I die I want to decompose in a barrel of porter and have it served in all the pubs in Dublin.

Dublin's most celebrated literary manifestation, however, occurs in James Joyce's *Ulysses* (1922), in which Joyce recreates a day in the life of the city (16 June 1904) in enormous detail. While writing his masterpiece in self-imposed exile, he would send many inquiries regarding Dublin topography to friends remaining in the capital and later claimed that if Dublin were to be destroyed it could be recreated from the picture of it embedded in his works.

See also ARTANE, BLACKROCK, BLANCHARDSTOWN, CLONDALKIN, DONNYBROOK, LUCAN, RATHMINES *and* TALLAGHT.

dead centre of Dublin, the. The punning nickname of GLASNEVIN CEMETERY.

Dublin Area Rapid Transport. An electric commuter train, always referred to by the acronym DART, that runs along Dublin Bay from MALAHIDE south as far as GREYSTONES in

County Wicklow, utilizing for much of its length what was originally the Dublin–Kingstown (Dún Laoghaire) track. For many years it provided Dublin's commuters with the city's only reliable, punctual public transport. Because most of the areas served by the DART were salubrious suburbs ('Dortland' in the local pronunciation) there emerged in the public mind a perception of a kind of DORT-speak, popular especially among young women.

Dublin Bay prawn. A large prawn, usually cooked and served as scampi.

Dublin Castle. A building whose construction began in 1204 on the orders of King John, and which was extensively rebuilt after a fire in 1684. Also known simply as **the Castle**, it was for centuries the official residence of the lord deputy or lord lieutenant and synonymous with British rule in Ireland. In the 19th century, a **Castle Catholic** was an Irish Catholic who supported British policies in Ireland.

Dubliners. A collection of short stories by James Joyce, published in 1914. The stories are all set in Dublin and deal with themes of disease, paralysis and death. The final story, 'The Dead', is regarded as one of the finest in the English language.

Dubliners, The. A famous Irish folk group, which traces its origins to The Ronnie Drew Folk Group, formed in 1962. Despite various deaths and changes of personnel, the band, described by one commentator as looking as though they'd been dragged through a hedge backwards and dropped from a great height, is still performing.

Dublin fair. A 20th-centuryAustralian slang term for 'hair'.

Dublin 4. The Ballsbridge area south of the city centre, which in Ireland has become synonymous with metropolitan sophistication.

Dublin Lockout (1913). A bitter industrial dispute in which a group of employers attempted to force their workers to leave the militant Irish Transport and General Workers' Union by threatening them with the sack if they did not. In response, the ITGWU, led by James Larkin, called out other workers on strike. The Irish Citizen Army (*see under* IRISH) was formed to protect workers from the attentions of the Dublin Metropolitan Police, but the strikers had mostly returned to work by early 1914.

'Dublin Made Me'. One of the best-known poems of Donagh MacDonagh (1912–68). It begins:

> Dublin made me and no little town
> With the country closing in on its streets,
> The cattle walking proudly on its pavements ...

The metropolitan poet goes on to deprecate the 'raw and hungry hills of the West', the 'cute self-deceiving talkers of the South', the 'soft and dreary midlands' and the 'arid censure' of the North.

Dublin Mean Time. Formerly the standard time for Ireland, established by the 1880 Time Act. Dublin Mean Time

(DMT) was 25 minutes behind Greenwich Mean Time (GMT; *see under* GREENWICH) and lasted until GMT was extended to Ireland in 1916.

Dublin Mountains. The northern part of the Wicklow Mountains, adjoining Dublin (*see under* County WICKLOW).

Dublin Rising. An occasional name for the Easter Rising of 1916, the most dramatic of the events in the struggle for Home Rule in Ireland. The uprising had been planned by a number of radical Nationalist groups and began with the seizing of the General Post Office in O'CONNELL STREET (then named Sackville Street), on Easter Monday, 24 April 1916. From its pillared portico Patrick Pearse, a leader of the Irish Republican Brotherhood, read out a proclamation announcing the birth of the Irish Republic. British troops soon arrived to put down the rebellion and for almost a week Dublin was paralysed by street fighting. British artillery bombardments compelled Pearse and his colleagues to surrender on 29 April, and he and 14 other leaders of the rebellion were subsequently court-martialled and executed, their martyrdom creating much sympathy for their cause.

Dublin University graduate. A British-English slang term, dating from the 1950s, for an exceptionally stupid person, based on the stereotyped perception of the IRISH as foolish.

Dublin uppercut. The expression is here explained by Brendan Behan:

> I gave him a Dublin uppercut – a kick in the groin.

'In Dublin's Fair City'. The opening line of the famous ballad:

> In Dublin's fair city,
> Where the girls are so pretty
> I first set my eyes on sweet Molly Malone,
> She wheeled her wheelbarrow,
> Through streets broad and narrow,
> Crying, 'Cockles and mussels, alive, alive, oh!'

Scholars are uncertain as to the origin of the song, though some hold that it was written in the late 19th century by James Yorkston, an Edinburgh man. Molly Malone herself (*fl.* late 18th century) is commemorated by a statue in the city, disrespectfully known as 'The Tart with the Cart' or, alternatively, 'The Dish with the Fish'. (For 'The Floozie in the Jacuzzi' and 'The Hoor in the Sewer' *see under* LIFFEY.) *Fair City* has become the title of a long-running RTÉ soap opera, set in the fictional north Dublin suburb of Carrickstown.

kick up Dublin, to. A Glaswegian expression meaning 'to create a hoo-ha', referring to the stereotype of the hot-tempered Irishman.

'Rocky Road to Dublin, The'. A traditional song, beginning:

> In the merry month of May
> From my home I started,

> Left the girls of Tuam
> Nearly broken hearted,
> Saluted father dear,
> Kissed my darlin' mother,
> Drank a pint of beer
> My grief and tears to smother,
> Then off to reap the corn,
> And leave where I was born,
> I cut a stout blackthorn,
> To banish ghost and goblin,
> In a brand new pair of brogues,
> I rattled o'er the bogs,
> And frightened all the dogs
> On the rocky road to Dublin.
>
> *Chorus:*
> One, two, three, four five,
> Hunt the hare and turn her
> Down the rocky road
> And all the ways to Dublin,
> Whack-fol-lol-de-ra.

The Rocky Road to Dublin is also the title of the 1938 autobiography of the prolific writer Seumas MacManus (1869–1960), who died after falling from his nursing-home window in New York.

Treaty of Dublin (28 March 1646). A peace agreement between the Catholic Confederates and the Duke of Ormond, the lord-lieutenant of Ireland. However, the Confederates disowned the treaty when the terms were published in July, claiming that there was insufficient recognition of the Catholic Church.

Dublin, County. A county in eastern Ireland, bounded on the northwest by Meath, on the west by Kildare, on the south by Wicklow and to the east by the Irish Sea. The county town is DUBLIN, and other towns include BALBRIGGAN, SWORDS, MALAHIDE, HOWTH, DÚN LAOGHAIRE and DALKEY. It is the most populous, and the most densely populated, county in the Republic.

Duck End Presumably because ducks frequented the local watercourse (Stebbing Brook).

A village in Essex, about 11 km (7 miles) west of Braintree.

Duddingston 'estate of Dodin', OE male personal name *Dodin* + -TON; Dodin may be derived from an earlier OE personal name *Dodda* or *Dudda* + -*ingas* (*see* -ING).

A charming lacustrine village on the south side of ARTHUR'S SEAT, now wholly within the city of Edinburgh. The fine **Duddingston House** (1762–4) was designed by Sir William Chambers. The village is next to **Duddingston Loch**, a haven for wildfowl and the setting of Henry Raeburn's famous portrait (*c.*1784) of the skating minister, the Rev. Robert Walker.

> Carelessly
> as a whore

raises her shift
his blades brush
the frozen loch.

He's left on a whim,
the yoke
of the sermon
for Sunday –
stern words between
psalm and hymn.

What words, though,
to send his flock
to paradise
if not this sun –
this air and ice?

> Hamish McEwan Hamilton: 'The Rev. Robert Walker Skating
> from Heaven on Duddingston Loch' (1969)

Sir Walter Scott was ordained an elder at Duddingston in 1806, and apparently planned *Heart of Midlothian* (set largely in these parts) in the garden of the manse (*see under* MIDLOTHIAN).

Duddon Etymology unknown.

A river of the southern LAKE DISTRICT, Cumbria (formerly in Lancashire), rising on the southern side of Pike of Blisco above the WRYNOSE PASS, then flowing generally south-westwards to enter a long, wide estuary at **Duddon Sands**, just up the coast from Barrow-in-Furness. It is approximately 25 km (15 miles) long. The beautiful and relatively unfrequented valley of the Duddon is called **Dunnerdale**, as in the hamlet of **Hall Dunnerdale** and the **Dunnerdale Fells** on its southeastern side.

> Thee hath some awful Spirit impell'd to leave,
> Utterly to desert, the haunts of men,
> Though simple thy Companions were and few;
> And through this wilderness a passage cleave
> Attended but by thy own Voice, save when
> The Clouds and Fowls of the air thy way pursue.
>
> William Wordsworth: 'To the River Duddon', from *Poems in
> Two Volumes* (1807)

In 1820 Wordsworth gathered together for publication 33 more sonnets to the River Duddon, written between 1806 and 1820, arranging them in the form of a 'Tour'. The final poem is called 'Afterthought':

> Still glides the Stream, and shall forever glide;
> The Form remains, the Function never dies;
> While we, the brave, the mighty, and the wise,
> We Men, who in our morn of youth defied
> The elements, must vanish; – be it so!

See also MILLOM.

Dudley 'Dud(d)a's glade', OE male personal name *Dud(d)a* + -LEY.

An industrial town and metropolitan borough within the WEST MIDLANDS (before 1974 in Worcestershire), about 16 km (10 miles) west of Birmingham. Ironstone and coal have been mined here since the Middle Ages, and after the Industrial Revolution the effects of its blast furnaces well earned it the title 'capital of the BLACK COUNTRY'. It made a specialism of nail-making, and its modern industries incude metal working, light engineering and clothing manufacture.

Dudley Zoo is in the grounds of the medieval castle, many of whose massive walls are still intact.

Patrick Thomson in his first novel *Seeing the Wires* (2002) described Dudley as:

> … a bleak concrete wasteland inhabited by serial
> murderers, masochists, occultists and freaks.

The Mayor of Dudley was later quoted as believing that Thomson needed psychiatric help.

In 2002 Brick Kiln Lane in Gornalwood, a western suburb of Dudley, was the epicentre of a small earthquake.

The comedian Lenny Henry was born in Dudley in 1958.

There are towns called Dudley in the USA (Georgia, Massachusetts, Missouri).

Dudmaston 'Dudemann's farm', OE male personal name *Dudemann*, possessive *Dudemannes* + -TON.

A late 17th-century mansion (**Dudmaston Hall**) and estate in Shropshire, 7 km (4 miles) southeast of Bridgnorth, now administered by the National Trust. In addition to its gardens (which include a wooded valley known as the Dingle), Dudmaston has an important collection of contemporary British paintings and sculpture. In the early 19th century Dudmaston enjoyed the luxury of an early form of central heating system, devised by the mathematician and inventor Charles Babbage (a man widely regarded as the inventor of the forerunner of modern computers), who married Georgiana Wolryche-Whitmore of Dudmaston in 1814.

Dufftown From James *Duff*, 4th Earl of Fife, who founded the town in 1817.

A town in Moray (formerly in Banffshire, then in Grampian region), 25 km (15 miles) southeast of Elgin. It is at the centre of a great whisky distilling area (the Balvenie and Glenfiddich distilleries are among those close by), hence the rhyme:

> Rome was built on seven hills;
> Dufftown stands on seven stills.

Dúiche Sheoigheach. The Irish name for JOYCE'S COUNTRY.

Dukeries, the. An area of the northern part of SHERWOOD FOREST, in north Nottinghamshire, containing the estates of four dukes. The land was made over by the Crown in the 17th century, when the king was badly in need of cash, and the beneficiaries were the dukes of Portland, Newcastle, Kingston and Norfolk. They created estates at, respectively, WELBECK, CLUMBER, Thoresby and Worksop. The somewhat facetious nickname for this nest of dukes, apparently modelled on *rookery*, seems to have been coined in the first half of the 19th century.

Duke's Pass From the *Duke* of Montrose.
A road pass (243 m / 796 ft high) between ABERFOYLE and the TROSSACHS, through the Queen Elizabeth Forest Park. It was formerly in Stirlingshire, then in Central Region and is now in the unitary authority of Stirling. The road was built by the 5th Duke of Montrose *c.*1810 and opened to the public in 1931 when the Forestry Commission acquired the land.

Dukestown Named after the *Duke* of Beaufort, who owned the land on which the pit was opened in the 19th century.
A former mining village in Blaenau Gwent (formerly in Monmouthshire, then in Gwent), on the north side of Tredegar and 4 km (2.5 miles) east of Princetown.

Dukinfield 'open land of ducks', OE *ducena*, possessive plural of *duca* 'duck' + *feld* (*see* FIELD).
An industrial area in the TAMESIDE borough of Greater Manchester, 10 km (6 miles) east of Manchester city centre.

Dúlinn. The Irish name for DOOLIN.

Dull Probably Gaelic *dail* 'field', but possibly deriving from an earlier Celtic word.
A small village in Perth and Kinross (formerly in Perthshire, and then in Tayside region), 6 km (4 miles) west of Aberfeldy. It was here that St Adamnan, the biographer of St Columba, traditionally founded a monastery, which accounts for the name of the Strath of Appin, also called the **Appin of Dull** (the valley in which Dull sits), in which the Appin element is from Gaelic *apuinn*, earlier Irish *abdaine* 'abbey land'.

Dullborough. The name given to ROCHESTER in *The Uncommercial Traveller* (1860) by Charles Dickens.

Dulwich 'marshy meadow where dill grows' (dill was used as a medicinal herb), OE *dile* 'dill' + *wisc* 'marshy meadow'.
A southeastern suburb (pronounced 'dullidge' or 'dullitch') of London (SE21), in the borough of SOUTHWARK, between Forest Hill to the east and Tulse Hill to the west. Its green spaciousness and substantial villas, islanded village-like amongst the urban terraces of southeast London, owe much to the philanthropy of the successful actor Edward Alleyn. In 1605 he bought the manor of Dulwich, and in 1619 he endowed here the College of God's Gift. This later became the famous boys' public school **Dulwich College**. Alleyn's School, which split off from the College in the late 19th century, is just to the north, in **East Dulwich** (SE22). The Estates Governors, who managed Alleyn's bequest and controlled the development of much of Dulwich, looked askance at the mushrooming suburbs around them and ensured that Dulwich retained its salubriousness. As if to emphasize its rurality, its main street has been known since 1913 as **Dulwich Village**.

Dulwich Picture Gallery is the oldest public picture gallery in England. The basis of its collection is a bequest made by Edward Alleyn in 1626. The building was designed by Sir John Soane.

The writer P.G. Wodehouse, himself a noted Old Alleynian (former pupil of Dulwich College), fictionalized Dulwich as **Valley Fields**. Other Old Alleynians were the film actor Boris Karloff (real name William Pratt), the definitive Frankenstein's monster (who was also born in Dulwich), and the thriller writer Raymond Chandler.

The children's writer Enid Blyton (1896–1968) was born in East Dulwich.

Dumbarton 'fort of the Britons', Gaelic *dùn* (*see* DOWN, -DON) + Gaelic *Breatann*, OCelt *Breatain* 'Britons'.
An industrial town on the north shore of the Forth of CLYDE, in West Dunbartonshire (formerly in Strathclyde region), some 20 km (12 miles) northwest of Glasgow. The shipbuilding industry has declined, but the yards here were responsible for many ships in the past, including *Cutty Sark* (launched in 1869). Dumbarton was reputedly the birthplace of St Patrick (*c.*387–*c.*461) and of St Gildas (*c.*316–370). Dumbarton is traditionally cited as the southwestern terminus of the diagonal Highland Line (*see under* the HIGHLANDS), the northeastern terminus being Stonehaven.

Rising above the shore is the sheer **Dumbarton Rock**, a volcanic plug of black basalt 75 m (240 ft) high. From the 5th to the 8th century the rock was the capital and main stronghold of the kingdom of STRATHCLYDE, whose kings were Britons (rather than Gaels or Picts). They called their capital Alcluith ('hill of the Clyde'), and in 756 they were defeated at Dumbarton by a combined force of Angles and Picts. The Rock was the site of a royal castle in the later Middle Ages, but only fortifications from the 17th–18th centuries survive. These were used as a barracks into the 20th century.

Sir John Menteith, who treacherously captured William Wallace in 1305, was governor of the castle, and the possibility that Menteith brought Wallace here before sending him on to his death in London is reflected in the name of the higher of the two peaks of the rock: Wallace's Seat. The castle was captured in 1571 from the followers of Mary Queen of Scots by Thomas Crawford of Jordanhill, who led his 100 men in a surprise night-time ascent of the sheerest part of the rock using ladders and ropes. Today these cliffs – in places severely overhanging – are home to some of the most difficult rock climbs in Scotland.

Dumbarton FC (nicknamed the Sons) was founded in 1872 and is based at Boghead Park.
See also DUNBARTONSHIRE.

Dumbarton Oaks Conference. The mansion in Washington, D.C., called Dumbarton Oaks played host in 1944 (21 August–7 October) to a conference of Allied powers (China, the Soviet Union, the United States and the United Kingdom) that laid the foundations of what was to become the United Nations. The same mansion gave its name to an orchestral piece by Igor Stravinsky, commissioned by the owners of the house in 1938. The precise connection of Dumbarton Oaks with the Scottish town is not clear.

Dumbarton youth. A jocular term, current in the 19th century, for a person (usually a woman) past her mid-30s.

Dumbarton and Clydebank. A former district (1975–96) of the old STRATHCLYDE region.

Dumble. The name given to MANCHESTER in Mrs Gaskell's novel CRANFORD (1853).

Dumbleton 'farmstead near a shady glen or hollow', OE *dumbel* 'shady glen or hollow' + -TON.
A village in northern Gloucestershire, about 7 km (4 miles) north of Winchcombe, below the COTSWOLD escarpment. **Dumbleton Hill** (168 m / 551 ft), a Cotswold outlier, lies just to the southwest of the village.

Dumfries 'fort of the copse', Gaelic *dùn* (*see* DOWN, -DON) + *phris* 'of the copse' or 'brushwood'; *Dunfres* 1189.
A market town on the River NITH, and the largest town in southwest Scotland, situated 48 km (30 miles) northwest of Carlisle. It was formally the county town of Dumfriesshire and is now the administrative centre for Dumfries and Galloway. It became a royal BURGH in 1186.

A church dedicated to St Michael was founded at Dumfries in around the 7th or 8th centuries (the present parish church of St Michael is an 18th-century structure). This led to Dumfries being dubbed by some as **the City of St Michael**.

It was in the church of the Monastery of Greyfriars in Dumfries that Robert Bruce murdered the Red Comyn (Sir John Comyn, the nephew of John (de) Balliol, Edward I's puppet on the Scottish throne), and so precipitated the Scottish Wars of Independence that were to culminate in the Scottish victory at BANNOCKBURN in 1314. Many years later, during the 1745 Rebellion, Bonnie Prince Charlie held the town to ransom and managed to obtain £2000 and a thousand pairs of shoes.

Robert Burns lived in Dumfries (working as an excise officer) from 1791 until his death in 1796, latterly in Mill Vennel (now renamed Burns Street). His fellow poet William Wordsworth visited his grave in 1803, resulting in an unmemorable poem, 'At the Grave of Burns'. Perhaps the fact that he reported that Burns's grave was 'grass-grown' prompted the building of an inappropriately pretentious mausoleum in St Michael's churchyard in 1815. John Keats also wrote a poem, 'On Visiting the Tomb of Burns', equally unmemorable, on his visit in 1818:

> Burns' tomb is in the Churchyard corner, not very much to my taste, though on a scale, large enough to show they wanted to honour him.
>
> John Keats: letter to Tom Keats (2 July 1818)

As a youth, J.M. Barrie attended Dumfries Academy, and it was while staying at Moat Brae house with its 'enchanted garden' that he first conceived of the idea for *Peter Pan* (1904). The town was the headquarters of the Free Norwegian Forces in the Second World War.

Dumfries's professional football club goes by the evocative name of **Queen of the South** (a nickname for the town itself). Founded in 1919 and nicknamed the Doonhamers, the club plays its home games at Palmerston Park.

'Dumfries Volunteers, The'. A 'patriotic effusion' by Robert Burns, written in 1795. For an extract, *see under* CRIFFEL.

Dumfries and Galloway. A local government region of southwest Scotland formed in 1975, and comprising the former counties of WIGTOWNSHIRE, KIRKCUDBRIGHTSHIRE and DUMFRIESSHIRE. It became a unitary authority in 1996. It is bounded on the east by Scottish Borders, on the north by South and East Ayrshire and South Lanarkshire (all formerly in Strathclyde region), on the west by the North Channel, and on the south by the Solway Firth and Cumbria. The administrative seat is at DUMFRIES, and other towns include STRANRAER, NEWTON STEWART, KIRKCUDBRIGHT, CASTLE DOUGLAS, DALBEATTIE, LOCKERBIE, ANNAN[2] and MOFFAT.

Dumfriesshire. A former county of southwest Scotland, incorporated into DUMFRIES AND GALLOWAY in 1975. It was bordered on the east by Roxburghshire, on the north by Selkirkshire, Peeblesshire and Lanarkshire, on the west by Ayrshire and Kirkcudbrightshire, and on the south by the Solway Firth and Cumberland. The county town was DUMFRIES, and other towns included MOFFAT, LOCKERBIE and ANNAN[2].

Dummer 'pond on a hill', OE *dun* (*see* DOWN, -DON) + *mere* 'pond' (*see also* LAKE).
A village in Hampshire, about 8 km (5 miles) southwest of Basingstoke.

Dumnonia From *Dumnonii*, the name of a Celtic people (*see* DEVON[1] *and* EXETER).
A British kingdom comprising what is now CORNWALL, DEVON[1] and parts of western SOMERSET, with cultural and religious links to Wales, Ireland and Brittany, established after the Roman withdrawal from Britain in the 5th century.

Devon and Somerset were conquered by the West Saxons in the 7th and early 8th centuries, but the geographical isolation of Cornwall allowed it to remain independent until the early 9th century, when it was absorbed into the Anglo-Saxon kingdom of WESSEX by King Egbert. The Dumnonii played an important role in the British settlement of Brittany in the 5th and 6th centuries AD.

Dunadd 'fort on the River Add', Gaelic *dùn* (*see* DOWN, -DON) + name of the local river, possibly a pre-Celtic word meaning 'water course'.

A rocky hillock rising 54 m (176 ft) above the marshland of the Mòine Mhòr some 6 km (4 miles) northwest of LOCHGILPHEAD in Argyll and Bute (formerly in Strathclyde). It was the site of the fortified capital of the ancient Scots kingdom of DALRIADA, *c*.500–850. Some traces of the fortifications can be seen, and there is a rock at the top on which are carved a boar, a bowl-shaped hollow and a human footprint. This may have been where the kings took on royal power, and where St Columba blessed and inaugurated Aidan MacGabrain as king of Dalriada in 574. Tradition says that during such ceremonies the kings sat on the Stone of Destiny, which later went to DUNSTAFFNAGE CASTLE and then to SCONE.

Dún Aenghus Irish, 'fort of Aenghus' (*see* DOWN, -DON), named after a chief of the legendary Firbolgs.

An Iron Age fort on the southwest coast of INISHMORE, the largest of the ARAN ISLANDS. It is dramatically situated on the top of a 60-m (200-ft) sea cliff, and in legend is said to have been built by the Firbolgs, who retreated to the Aran Islands after their defeat at the First Battle of MOYTURA.

Dunamase, Rock of Irish *Dún Másc* 'fort of Másc' (*see* DOWN, -DON); Másc was traditionally an ancestor of the people of Leinster.

A striking 60-m (200-ft) high limestone protuberance in the flat lands of County LAOIS, some 7 km (4.5 miles) east of PORTLAOISE. There was a fort here from ancient times (it was referred to by Ptolemy as Dunum), and the Vikings sacked it in 844. The Rock was presented in the late 12th century to the Anglo-Norman conqueror Strongbow (Richard de Clare) as part of the dowry for the daughter of Dermot McMurrough, and a castle was built. The Anglo-Norman castle was rebuilt and enlarged in the mid-13th century (the keep can still be seen). In 1479 the Rock was taken from the English by the O'Mores, who held it until the Plantation of Laois under Mary I. The castle changed hands twice in the 1640s until destroyed by Cromwell's men in 1650.

Dún an Óir. *See under* SMERWICK.

Dún ar Aill. The Irish name for DONERAILE.

Dunbar 'fort on the summit', Gaelic *dùn* (*see* DOWN, -DON) + *barr* 'top' (probably from OCelt *din bar*).

A royal BURGH (1369), fishing port and seaside resort on the coast of East Lothian, 15 km (9 miles) southeast of North Berwick. The bare ruin on a rock above the harbour is of a castle dating back to the 9th century. It was here that 'Black Agnes', Countess of March, held out against the English for five months in 1338. Mary Queen of Scots made James Bothwell governor of the castle, and it was hither he brought her when he abducted her from Cramond in 1567, prior to their marriage. She visited him again in Dunbar shortly afterwards, riding there disguised as a man to escape her enemies. After Mary's defeat at CARBERRY HILL (still in 1567) the Regent Moray destroyed the castle, largely because of its associations with Mary.

Dunbar was the birthplace of John Muir (1838–1914), the pioneer US conservationist, who is commemorated in the nearby John Muir Country Park. There are towns called Dunbar in the USA (Oklahoma, Utah, Wisconsin, West Virginia) and Australia (Queensland).

> There was an old dame of Dunbar
> Who took the 4:04 to Forfar.
>> But it went to Dundee
>> So she travelled, you see,
> Too far by the 4:04 from Forfar.
>> Anon.: limerick

Dunbar weather or **wether.** A salted herring, a term current from the late 18th to the early 20th century. Earlier in the 18th century Daniel Defoe reported on the smoking of herrings at Dunbar, the products being known locally as 'red herrings'.

Battle of Dunbar (27 April 1296). A battle in which the Earl of Surrey defeated the Scots after John (de) Balliol renounced his homage to Edward I. The battle was fought some 3 km (2 miles) to the south of the town.

Battle of Dunbar (3 September 1650). An overwhelming victory for Cromwell over the Scots under David Leslie, fought a little to the east of the 1296 battle, at the foot of Doune Hill. Cromwell estimated the Scottish dead at 3000, and 10,000 prisoners were taken. These prisoners were treated, according to one historian, 'with callous disregard', and few survived to be sent to the plantations of the New World. Cromwell went on to take Edinburgh and to control all of southern Scotland.

> And Dunbar field resounds thy praises loud …
>> John Milton: 'To the Lord General Cromwell' (1652)

Dunbartonshire From DUMBARTON + SHIRE.

A former county of west central Scotland, with Stirlingshire to the east, Lanarkshire and Renfrewshire to the south, Argyll to the west and Perthshire to the north. The county also had a small exclave to the east of Glasgow, sandwiched between Stirlingshire and Lanarkshire. The current spelling, with an *n* replacing the *m*, was adopted so as to avoid confusion with the county town, DUMBARTON (such a stratagem was not thought necessary in any of the other Scottish counties, however). Dunbartonshire was abolished in 1975, the area then incorporated into Strathclyde region, but the new Dumbarton district was made up of much of the former county. In 1996 the county was reincarnated as two unitary authorities, WEST DUNBARTONSHIRE and EAST DUNBARTONSHIRE, but their combined area is considerably smaller than that of the old county.

Dunblane 'St Blane's fort', Gaelic *dùn* (*see* DOWN, -DON) + personal name; St Blane (or Bláán) was Bishop of Kingarth in Bute who built a church here in the 6th century.

A small town on the River Allan (*see under* BRIDGE OF ALLAN), 4 km (2.5 miles) north of Stirling, on the old road to Perth. It was formerly in Perthshire, then in Central region, and is now in Stirling unitary authority. David I made Dunblane a bishopric *c.*1150, and some of **Dunblane Cathedral** goes back to this date, although most of it is 13th and 15th century. It was restored in the late 19th and early 20th centuries.

> There was an old man of Dunblane
> Who greatly resembled a crane
> But they said, 'Is it wrong,
> Since your legs are so long,
> To request you won't stay in Dunblane?'
>
> Edward Lear (1812–88): limerick

Dunblane Massacre, the. The killing, on 13 March 1996, of 16 young children and their teacher. On that day a lone gunman, Thomas Hamilton, a former Scout leader, entered the local primary school at Dunblane, and killed his victims before turning the gun on himself. The massacre led to the banning of all privately held handguns in Britain.

'Jessie, the Flower of Dunblane'. A poem by Robert Tannahill (1774–1810), the Paisley weaver. It begins:

> The sun has gane down o'er the lofty Ben Lomond
> And left the red clouds to reside o'er the scene,
> While lanely I stray in the calm simmer gloamin'
> To muse on sweet Jessie, the flow'r o' Dunblane.
> How sweet is the brier wi' its saft faulding blossom
> And sweet is the birk wi' its mantle o' green
> But sweeter and fairer and dear to this bosom
> Is charming young Jessie, the flow'r o' Dunblane
>
> (Scots *birk* 'birch')

Duncansby Head 'headland by Dungal's settlement', *Duncansby* personal name *Dungal* + -BY. Dungal may be Dungad, a 10th-century chieftain referred to in the Norse *Orkneyinga saga* (early 13th century).

The most northeasterly point of the Scottish mainland, in Highland (formerly in Caithness), 3 km (2 miles) east of JOHN O'GROATS and 23 km (14 miles) north of Wick. A lighthouse stands on top of the 60-m (200-ft) cliff. To the north are the **Boars of Duncansby**, a reef made doubly dangerous by the fierce tidal rips of the PENTLAND FIRTH, while to the west is another headland, called **Ness of Duncansby**. To the south are the **Stacks of Duncansby**, comprising the Knee, Gibbs Craig, Tom Thumb Stack, Little Stack and Muckle Stack.

Dún Chaoin. The Irish name for DUNQUIN.

Dún Dá Bheann. The Irish name for MOUNT SANDEL.

Dundalk Irish *Dún Dealgan* 'Dealga's fort' (*see* DOWN, -DON); in Irish legend Dealga was the chief of the Fir Bolg.

The county town of County LOUTH, 75 km (47 miles) north of Dublin, just south of the border with Northern Ireland. It is on the River Castletown where it widens to form **Dundalk Harbour**, just before entering the wide expanse of **Dundalk Bay**, scene, in the 10th century, of two naval engagements between Irish and Vikings.

Dundalk was traditionally the birthplace of Cuchulain, the ancient Irish hero. Historically, the town gained an Anglo-Norman castle and royal borough status at the beginning of the 13th century, and, situated as it was on the border of the PALE, it was frequently fought over by English and Irish. More recently, Dundalk has become a Republican stronghold, and it is reputedly the base of the Real IRA.

It was in Dundalk that the pop group The Corrs was formed in 1991.

There is a town called Dundalk in the USA (Maryland).

Battle of Dundalk (14 October 1318). A battle that ended the attempt of Edward Bruce, brother of Robert I of Scotland, to become ruler of Ireland (he had been crowned at Dundalk two years previously). In the battle, which took place at Faughart, near Dundalk, Bruce was defeated and killed by the forces of John de Bermingham.

Dún Dealgan. The Irish name for DUNDALK.

Dundee 'Daig's fort', Gaelic *Dùn Dèagh*, from Gaelic *dùn* (*see* DOWN, -DON) + personal name *Daig* (possibly meaning 'fire'). It has also been suggested that the second element may derive from the River TAY.

A royal BURGH and port in east central Scotland, on the north shore of the Firth of Tay, some 30 km (20 miles) east of Perth. It became a royal burgh in the late 12th century, and was made a city in 1892. It was once in the county of Angus, then the headquarters of the former TAYSIDE region, and is now a unitary authority. The city incorporates BROUGHTY FERRY. The inhabitants of Dundee are known as **Dundonians** (a late 19th-century coinage on the model of Aberdonians, the natives of Aberdeen). The **University of Dundee** was founded in 1881, and was affiliated with the University of St Andrews from 1897 until it became an independent institution in 1967.

Dundee has had a violent past. It was sacked by the English in 1296, 1385, 1547, 1644 and 1651. The town council supported the Jacobite cause in the 1715 Rising, but had changed loyalties by the time of the 1745 Rebellion.

Dundee – described by Paul Theroux as 'an interesting monstrosity' – is traditionally associated with 'jam, jute and journalism'. The jam industry arises from the city's proximity to the CARSE OF GOWRIE, an important area of soft-fruit production, although Dundee is most closely associated with marmalade (see below). The city's jam-makers have, it is hoped, higher standards than the old woman of the nursery rhyme:

> There was an old woman
> Who lived in Dundee,
> And in her back garden
> There grew a plum tree;
> The plums they grew rotten
> Before they grew ripe,
> And she sold them three farthings a pint.

When jute began to be imported from India in the early 19th century, Dundee was already established as a centre of flax and woollen weaving, and also had a large whaling fleet. It was found that jute, when mixed with whale oil, became more flexible and could be woven into sacking and backing for carpets; such was the city's success with the stuff that it became known as **Juteopolis**. Journalism manifests itself in the form of D.C. Thomson & Co. Ltd., publishers of many popular periodicals, such as *The Beano*, *The Dandy*, *The People's Friend* and *The Sunday Post*.

> Dundee – a dark and smart and self-deprecatingly wonderful secret of a city which deserves, in every sense, a better press.
>
> Euan Ferguson: *The Observer* (2 March 2003)

Dundee was the birthplace of: Hector Boece (c.1465–c.1536), Renaissance humanist, author of a history of Scotland and the first principal of Aberdeen University; Admiral Adam Duncan (1731–1804), the victor of the Battle of Camperdown (1797) – the city's Camperdown Park commemorates the battle; Sir William Alexander Craigie (1867–1957), lexicographer, joint editor of the *Oxford English Dictionary* (1901–33); and Will Fyffe (1885–1947), music-hall performer and actor. The national hero William Wallace (c.1270–1305) is said to have attended Dundee Grammar School, as did the doomed poet Robert Fergusson (1750–74), who inspired Robert Burns. Mary Wollstonecraft Shelley (1797–1851), author of *Frankenstein* (1818), lived in Dundee prior to her elopement with Percy Bysshe Shelley. The world's worst poet, William McGonagall (1825 or 1830–1902), worked as a carpet weaver in the city, which he addressed thus:

> There's no other town I know of with you can
>   compare
> For spinning mills and lasses fair …
>
> William McGonagall: 'Bonnie Dundee in 1878'

In 1908 Winston Churchill became MP for Dundee.

Dundee has two senior football clubs: **Dundee FC** (founded in 1893 and nicknamed The Dee or the Dark Blues), who play at Dens Park; and **Dundee United FC** (founded in 1909 as Dundee Hibernian and nicknamed the Terrors), who play at Tannadice Park. The followers of the latter club are known as Arabs, for reasons that are obscure to the present writer.

There are towns called Dundee in the USA (in Kane County, near Chicago) and in South Africa (Natal).

> The streets are waiting for a snow
>   that never falls:
> too close to the water,
> too muffled in the afterwarmth of jute …
>
> John Burnside (b.1955): 'Dundee'

> I thi hovie an thi howd o sleep,
> Whaur Dundee dovirs oan thi rink
> o ma frore-thocht lyk a Michael-
> angelo oan skates …
>
> W.N. Herbert (b.1961): 'The Socialist Manifesto for East Balgillo' (*hovie* 'swelling', *howd* 'rocking', *dovirs* 'dozes')

> There was an old man of Dundee
> Who frequented the top of a tree.
>   When disturbed by the crows
>   He abruptly arose
> And exclaimed, 'I'll return to Dundee.'
>
> Edward Lear (1812–88): limerick

> There was an old man of Dundee
>   Who molested an ape in a tree.
>   The result was most horrid
>   All bum and no forehead
> Three arms and a purple goatee.
>
> Anon.: limerick

Bonnie or **Bonny Dundee.** The nickname of John Graham of Claverhouse, 1st Viscount Dundee (?1649–89), the famous Jacobite leader who led his forces to victory over those of William III at the Battle of KILLIECRANKIE, in which he was fatally wounded. His enemies – who called him **Bloody Clavers** – believed him to possess supernatural powers, and had said he could be killed only with a silver bullet.

> To the Lords of Convention 'twas Claver'se who spoke
> 'Ere the King's crown shall fall there are crowns to be
>   broke
> So let each cavalier who loves honour and me,
> Come follow the bonnet of Bonny Dundee.
>   *Come fill up my cup, come fill up my can,*
>   *Come saddle your horses, and call up your men;*

Come open the West Port, and let me gang free,
And it's room for the bonnets of Bonny Dundee!

Sir Walter Scott: 'Bonny Dundee' (song)

The phrase 'Bonnie Dundee' is also associated with the city itself:

Dundee, a pleasant, large, populous city ... well deserves the title of Bonny Dundee, so often given it in discourse, as well as in song.

Daniel Defoe: *A Tour Through the Whole Island of Great Britain* (1724–6)

dundee. A type of gaff-rigged sailing vessel similar to a ketch, but with a jigger at the stern instead of a mizzen and gaff topsail.

Dundee cake. Originally a type of inexpensive ginger cake, made in the city. It is said that when the Keiller family began to make marmalade in the city (*see below*), Mrs Keiller put the excess peel in the cake mixture, turning it into a fruit cake. In Dundee, there was long a gentlemen's agreement among the bakers that only Keiller's should make Dundee cake, although bakers elsewhere paid no regard to this and applied the term to any rich fruit cake with almonds on top.

Dundee Law. A hill (Scots *law* 'rounded hill') on the north side of the city. It is 174 m (571 ft) high, and there are the remains of an Iron Age hillfort on the summit, as well as the Dundee War Memorial.

Dundee marmalade. A type of dark marmalade including thick chunks of peel. The name was registered as a trademark in 1880 by James Keiller & Son of Dundee.

Dundee rambler. A variety of rambling rose bred in the 19th century.

'Dundee Weaver, The'. A traditional folk song about the undoing of a Dundee lass, containing the lines:

O all you Dundee weavers, tak this advise by me,
Never let a fairlay an inch above your knee.

'From Sweet Dundee'. A sea shanty from Dundee's whaling days, beginning:

From sweet Dundee where we set sail
All with a sweet and a pleasant gale
With our ringtails set all abaft our mizzen peak
For to see my jolly tars how she's scudding o'er the deep.

'Piper o' Dundee, The'. An anonymous 18th-century song, the refrain of which goes:

And wasna he a roguey,
A roguey, a roguey,
And wasna he a roguey,
    The piper o' Dundee?

Dundonald Irish *Dún Dónall* 'Dónall's fort' (*see* DOWN, -DON). An eastern suburb of BELFAST, some 7 km (4.5 miles) from the city centre.

Dún Dónall. The Irish name for DUNDONALD.

Dundrennan 'hill with the thicket', Gaelic *dùn* (*see* DOWN, -DON) + *draigheanan* 'blackthorn, thicket'.
A village in Dumfries and Galloway (formerly in Kirkcudbrightshire), 7 km (4.5 miles) southeast of Kirkcudbright. In 1972 it played the part of Summerisle in the cult horror film *The Wicker Man*, starring Edward Woodward, Britt Ekland and Christopher Lee. It was in the Ellangowan Hotel (which played the Green Man Inn) that Britt Ekland's character danced naked, and the village has become a pilgrimage destination for thousands of 'Wickerfans', perhaps eager to see this feat repeated.

At the nearby Cistercian abbey (now ruined), Mary Queen of Scots spent her last night in Scotland (May 1568).

Dún Droma. The Irish name for DUNDRUM BAY.

Dundrum Bay From the nearby village of Dundrum, Irish *Dún Droma* 'fort of the ridge' (*see* DOWN, -DON).
A wide bay on the east coast of County DOWN. NEWCASTLE[1] is on its southwest side.

Dunedin 'fort at Eidyn', Gaelic *dùn* 'fort' (*see* DOWN, -DON) + an element of obscure origin, believed to be OCelt *eiddyn* 'rock face'.
The old name for EDINBURGH and meaning the same thing. The earliest recorded form of the latter, Anglo-Saxon name is *Edenburge*, dating from 1126. The older name is preserved in the New Zealand city of Dunedin, capital of Otago province, South Island, and in **Duneideann**, the modern Gaelic name for Edinburgh.

Dunfermline Etymology unkown, although the first element may be *dùn* 'fort' (*see* DOWN, -DON).
A royal BURGH (1588) in Fife, some 8 km (5 miles) northwest of the north end of the Forth Bridge. It was the seat of the former Dunfermline district from 1975 to 1996. The name probably applies to an 11th-century castle in a bend of a small burn in Pittencrieff Glen (only a mound and a ruin remain). **Dunfermline Abbey** was founded in *c*.1072 (initially as a priory) by Malcolm III (Canmore), with the encouragement of his wife, Queen (later Saint) Margaret, whom he had married here, and to whom there is a shrine in the abbey. The abbey became the burial place of seven Scottish kings, from Malcolm III to Robert the Bruce (although the latter's heart was buried in MELROSE Abbey). Dunfermline was also a favourite royal residence, as recalled in the old ballad:

The king sits in Dunfermline town,
Drinking the blude-red wine;
'Oh, where will I get a gude skipper
To sail this ship of mine?'

'Sir Patrick Spens'

Many Scottish kings were born here: Edgar, Alexander I, David I, David II, James I and Charles I. But after the

Union of the Crowns in 1603 the glory of Dunfermline faded …

> The houses, the furniture, the clothing of the rich, in a little time, become useful to the inferior and middling ranks of people … The marriage-bed of James the First … was, a few years ago, the ornament of an ale-house at Dunfermline.
>
> Adam Smith: *The Wealth of Nations* (1776)

Earlier in the 18th century Daniel Defoe (quoting Rochester) had found the place 'in its full perfection of decay'.

The great Renaissance poet Robert Henryson (1420/30?–c.1506) was a schoolmaster in Dunfermline. The town was the birthplace of Andrew Carnegie (1835–1919), the US industrialist and son of a handloom weaver (after his death the town benefited considerably from his philanthropy); the ballerina and actress Moira Shearer (b.1926); and the choreographer Kenneth MacMillan (1929–92).

Dunfermline Athletic FC was founded in 1885. Nicknamed the Pars, the club is based at East End Park.

> What Benares is to the Hindoo, Mecca to the Mohammedan, Jerusalem to the Christian, all that Dunfermline is to me.
>
> Andrew Carnegie: *Our Coaching Trip* (1882)

Declaration of Dunfermline, the (1651). A document in support of Presbyterianism in Scotland that Charles II was obliged to sign here in return for the support of the Covenanters against Oliver Cromwell.

Dunfermline College of Physical Education. An institution founded in Dunfermline in 1905 as the Carnegie Dunfermline College of Hygiene and Physical Training. 'Carnegie' was dropped from its name in 1913–14, and in 1931 it became an all-women institution. In 1966 the institution (having also dropped 'Hygiene') moved to Edinburgh, but, to the puzzlement of all, continued to be known as the Dunfermline College of Physical Education until 1987, when male students returned and it was renamed the Scottish Centre for Physical Education, Movement and Leisure Studies.

Dungannon Irish *Dún Geanainn* 'Geanann's fort' (*see* DOWN, -DON); in Irish legend Geanann was the son of Cathbad the druid.

A market town in County Tyrone, 55 km (34 miles) southwest of Belfast. It is the administrative centre of the local authority district of Dungannon. The town was one of the main seats of the O'Neill family, once kings of Ulster, and in 1598 Hugh O'Neill, 2nd Earl of Tyrone (who was born in the town) defeated English forces at the Battle of YELLOW FORD to the south of Dungannon. After the Irish defeat at KINSALE in 1602 Dungannon was destroyed to prevent it falling into the hands of the English. Later in the 17th century it became a Protestant plantation, and in the

sectarian song 'The Ould Orange Flute' it is the home of the eponymous instrument:

> In the county Tyrone, in the town of Dungannon
> Where many a ruckus meself had a hand in
> Bob Williamson lived there, a weaver by trade
> And all of us thought him a stout-hearted blade.
> On the twelfth of July as it yearly did come
> Bob played on the flute to the sound of the drum
> You can talk of your fiddles, your harp or your lute
> But nothing could sound like the Ould Orange Flute.

Conventions of Dungannon (1782–3). A series of three conventions (15 February 1782, 8 September 1782 and 15–16 February 1783) held by the (largely Protestant) Volunteers of Ulster in Dungannon. Among other things, the conventions called for Irish parliamentary independence (a degree of which was subsequently achieved in Grattan's Parliament), electoral reform and the enfranchisement of Catholics.

Dungannon Clubs. A Nationalist movement founded in 1905 by Bulmer Hobson and Denis McCullough, and named in honour of the Conventions of Dungannon of 1782–3 (*see above*). The movement eventually became part of Sinn Féin.

Dungan's Hill Probably 'Donnagán's hill'.

A battle site near TRIM in County Meath where on 8 August 1647 Parliamentary forces under Michael Jones won a victory over the Catholic Confederates, the first step in re-establishing English rule in Ireland.

Dunganstown Irish *Baile Uí Dhonnagáin* 'Donnagan's farm'.

A village in County Wexford, 5 km (3 miles) south of New Ross. It was the site of the homestead from which Patrick Kennedy emigrated to America in 1848. In June 1963 his great-grandson, President John F. Kennedy, returned for a visit, meeting his cousin Mary Ryan. The cottage is now a museum, while Kennedy himself is the subject of a mosaic in the Cathedral of Our Lady Assumed into Heaven and St Nicholas in GALWAY city. He is also commemorated in the John F. Kennedy Memorial Forest Park south of New Ross.

(For the visit of President Reagan to Ireland, *see* BALLYPOREEN *and the* OULD SOD.)

Dún Garbháin. The Irish name for DUNGARVAN.

Dungarvan Irish *Dún Garbháin* 'Garbhán's fort' (*see* DOWN, -DON); St *Garbhán* (or *Garvan*) founded a monastery here in the 7th century.

A town and seaport on the south coast of County Waterford, some 40 km (25 miles) southwest of Waterford itself, overlooking the natural **Dungarvan Harbour**. There is an Anglo-Norman castle dating from 1185 (built for the future King John), which became part of a British Army barracks, destroyed in 1921. When the town surrendered to Oliver

Cromwell in 1649 it is said that the population was spared because an old woman raised a toast to Cromwell at the gate.

Dungarvan was the birthplace of the scientist E.T.S. Walton (1903–95), who shared the 1951 Nobel prize for physics with Sir John Cockcroft for their development of the first particle accelerator.

Dungarvan Prospect. The former name for the crossing of the shallow River Colligan that divides the town. Until the 19th century the crossing had to be made either by ferry or on foot through the shallow waters, the latter mode obliging the local women to hoist up their skirts – this sight forming the (presumably delectable to male eyes) 'Prospect'.

Dún gCloiche. The Irish name for DUNGLOW.

Dún Geanainn. The Irish name for DUNGANNON.

Dungeness 'headland near DENGE MARSH', OE *Denge* + NESS. A shingly headland in Kent, to the south of ROMNEY MARSH and about 8 km (5 miles) south of Romney. Its bleakness is often covered and accentuated by mists, and it has always been a favourite point for shipwrecks – as witness the many lighthouses built here. When the mists lift, they reveal the unlovely forms of **Dungeness 'A'** and **Dungeness 'B'**, two nuclear power stations built in the 1960s, as well as some equally unattractive clusters of holiday chalets.

On a more positive note, there is an important bird reserve nearby at DENGE MARSH, and Dungeness is the southern terminus of the miniature Romney, Hythe and Dymchurch steam railway (*see under* NEW ROMNEY). In 1986 the film-maker Derek Jarman (1942–94) bought an old fisherman's cottage on the beach and constructed a garden on the shingle.

During the first Anglo-Dutch War the English fleet was defeated by a Dutch fleet under Admiral Maarten Tromp in a naval engagement off Dungeness (30 November–10 December 1652).

PLUTO (Pipe Line Under The Ocean), an underwater oil-supply pipe carrying petrol from England to northern France in the wake of the D-Day landings in 1944, had one of its two northern terminals at Dungeness (the other was at SHANKLIN).

Dungeon Ghyll Northern dialect *dungeon* 'cavern', with *ghyll* (OScand *gill*) 'short, narrow valley'.
A steep mountain stream in the LAKE DISTRICT, Cumbria, on the north side of LANGDALE. It rises on the slopes of Langdale Pikes and hurtles down to the valley via the waterfall called **Dungeon Ghyll Force**, described thus by Samuel Taylor Coleridge:

> Into a chasm, a mighty block hath fallen, and made a
> bridge of rock. The gulf is deep below! and, in a basin
> black and small, receives a lofty waterfall.

Coleridge featured Dungeon Ghyll in 'The Idle Shepherd Boys of Dungeon Ghyll':

> In Langdale Pike and witch's lair,
> And Dungeon Ghyll so foully rent,
> With ropes of rock and bells of air,
> Three sinful sextons' ghosts are pent.

The stream gives its name to the famous climbers' inn to the southwest, the **Old Dungeon Ghyll**, the 'Old' to distinguish it from a newer hotel of similar name at the foot of Dungeon Ghyll itself. In Victorian times the visitor's book of the Old Dungeon Ghyll was filled with poetic appreciations by gentlemen-mountaineers, such as this from 'F.G.T.':

> Oh, whence the name of this hotel,
> The awful name of Dungeon Ghyll?
> A fitter name for it would be,
> The house of all who want their tea.

Dungeon of Buchan 'fastness of Buchan', *Dungeon* Gaelic *an daingean* 'the fastness', with BUCHAN.
A craggy hill in Galloway, some 6.5 km (4 miles) northeast of the head of GLEN TROOL.

Dunglow Irish *Dún gCloiche* 'fort of stone' (*see* DOWN, -DON).
A small fishing port and resort on the west coast of County Donegal, on the south side of the ROSSES. It is also spelt **Dungloe** and the *g* is not pronounced. Its alternative Irish name is **An Clochán Liath** ('the grey stepping-stones').

Dunipace Etymology uncertain, but Gaelic *dùn na bais* 'hill of death' (*see* DOWN, -DON), and OCelt *din y pás* 'hill of the pass' have been suggested.
A small industrial town just north of DENNY. It was formerly in Stirlingshire, then in Central region, and is now in Falkirk unitary authority.

Dunkeld 'fort of the Caledonians', Gaelic *dùn* (*see* DOWN, -DON) + *Chailleann* 'Caledonians' or 'Picts'; *Dúin Chaillden* 873.
An attractive cathedral 'city' (really little more than a large village), with many well-preserved 18th-century houses, on the north bank of the River TAY, 22 km (13 miles) north of Perth, in Perth and Kinross (formerly in Perthshire, and then in Tayside region).

Dunkeld was a residence of Pictish chiefs, and a monastery was founded here in the 7th or 8th century. Having united the Scots and the Picts in the mid-9th century, Kenneth MacAlpin made Dunkeld one of his capitals, alongside SCONE. In 850 Kenneth ordered that the relics of St Columba be brought here from Iona, to preserve them from the Vikings, and he made Dunkeld the centre of the Celtic church in Scotland. In the 10th century Dunkeld itself was sacked by the Vikings, and the headquarters of the church moved to St Andrews. However, Dunkeld was made a bishopric in the 12th century. The most notable bishop was the poet and translator of the *Aeneid*, Gavin

Douglas (?1475–1522). The building of **Dunkeld Cathedral**, whose ruins stand beside the Tay, began in the early 14th century and was completed in 1501, only to be destroyed later in the century during the Reformation.

Dunkeld was the birthplace of J.R.R. Macleod (1876–1935), one of the discoverers of insulin, who shared a Nobel prize with Sir Frederick Banting. '**Dunkeld Bridge**' is a reel by the great 18th-century fiddler, Neil Gow, who was born near here.

Battle of Dunkeld (21 August 1689). A defeat for the Jacobites after their recent victory at KILLIECRANKIE, in which their able commander 'Bonnie' Dundee (*see under* DUNDEE) had been killed. Dundee's successor, Colonel Alexander Cannon, led his Highlanders into Dunkeld, where they were met by fierce resistance from the garrison of Cameronians (who were largely Covenanters). When the Cameronians fired the town, the Highlanders were forced to withdraw.

Dunkery Hill *Dunkery* 'hillfort of the crag', OCelt *dun* 'hillfort' (*see* DOWN, -DON) + an earlier form of Welsh *craig* 'crag, rock'.

A large bleak hill on EXMOOR, in the northwestern corner of SOMERSET, now owned by the National Trust. Its summit, **Dunkery Beacon**, is the highest point in Somerset at 519 m (1705 ft). In favourable weather fine views can be had from here across the Bristol Channel and as far as South Wales.

Dunkirk An application, first recorded in 1790, of the anglicized form of the name of *Dunkerque* in northern France (which had been an English possession for a while in the 17th century). It was perhaps intended to suggest remoteness.

A village in Kent, about 6 km (4 miles) west of Canterbury.

Dunk's Green From the local surname *Dunk*.

A village in Kent, about 8 km (5 miles) east of Sevenoaks.

Dún Laoghaire Irish 'Laoghaire's fort' (*see* DOWN, -DON); Laoghaire was a 5th-century Irish king.

A port and town in County Dublin, contiguous with DUBLIN itself, and some 10 km (6 miles) southeast of the city centre. The name was formerly anglicized as **Dunleary**, and between 1821 and 1920 it was known as **Kingstown**, in commemoration of a visit by George IV. The harbour was constructed in the earlier 19th century, and the town grew on the back of its trade with Britain. Today there are car ferries to HOLYHEAD on Anglesey and it is an important yachting centre.

To the east of Dún Laoghaire, at Sandycove Point, is the Martello tower where in 1904 James Joyce briefly stayed with his friend, the wit and medical man Oliver St John Gogarty, who rented the tower from the War Office for £8 per year. Both tower and Gogarty (in the guise of 'Stately, plump Buck Mulligan') feature at the beginning of *Ulysses*, and the tower ('Joyce's Tower') is now a Joyce museum.

Also at Sandycove is the famous 'Forty Foot' bathing pool, where nude bathing is permitted before 8 a.m. The pool once bore the sign 'Forty Foot Gentlemen Only'.

Dún Laoghaire was the birthplace of the Irish Nationalist martyr Sir Roger Casement (1864–1916); and of the rock singer and Third-World activist Bob Geldof (b.1954).

Dunleary. The former anglicized name for DÚN LAOGHAIRE.

Dún Lios. The Irish name for DUNLUCE CASTLE.

Dunloe, Gap of. *See* GAP OF DUNLOE.

Dún Lóich. The Irish name for the GAP OF DUNLOE.

Dunlop Possibly 'fort on the bend in the river', Gaelic *dùn* (*see* DOWN, -DON) + *lùib* 'bend'.

A small village about 11 km (6.5 miles) north of Kilmarnock in East Ayrshire (formerly in Strathclyde region). The local lairds, the Dunlop family, are said to have been the first to breed Ayrshire cattle (*see under* AYRSHIRE), initially known as **Dunlop cattle**. In the late 18th century Mrs Dunlop was a correspondent of the poet Robert Burns.

Dunlop cheese. A full-cream hard cheese made from fresh, untreated milk ('sweet milk'). It was first made by Barbara Gilmour, the wife of a farmer who settled in Dunlop in 1688, and by the end of the 18th century Dunlop-style cheeses were being made in many parts of Ayrshire and Galloway, and also in Lanarkshire and Renfrewshire.

Dunluce Castle Irish *Dún Lios*, 'fortified residence' (*see* DOWN, -DON).

A spectacularly situated ruined clifftop castle on the north coast of County Antrim, 5 km (3 miles) east of PORTRUSH. The castle, the oldest parts dating back to the 13th century, changed hands between the O'Neills and the Mac-Donnells several times in the 16th century, and in 1639 a portion of the building (together with eight servants) fell into the sea when the cliff beneath it collapsed.

Flower of Dunluce. The local name for the blue-flowered meadow cranesbill.

Dunmail Raise 'Dunmail cairn', possibly after *Domhnall*, King of Cumbria + OScand *hreysi* 'cairn'.

The pass (238 m / 782 ft high) between THIRLMERE and GRASMERE in the Lake District, Cumbria. Legend has it that the large cairn at the summit commemorates the victory in AD 945 of Edmund, king of England, over Domhnall, the last king of Cumbria, whose crown was supposed to have been buried under the rocks or thrown into GRISEDALE Tarn.

Dún Mánais. The Irish name for DUNMANUS BAY.

Dunmanus Bay Irish *Dún Mánais* 'Mánas's fort' (*see* DOWN, -DON).

A narrow 25-km (16-mile) long inlet on the west coast of County Cork, between the SHEEP'S HEAD Peninsula and

MIZEN HEAD. It takes its name from the small settlement of Dunmanus on the south side.

Dunmanway Possibly 'fort of the Manmha', Irish *dún* (*see* DOWN, -DON) + a tribal name.

A market town on the little Dirty River (a tributary of the BANDON[1], and with a presumably self-explanatory name) in County Cork, some 50 km (31 miles) southwest of Cork itself.

Dún Másc. The Irish name for the Rock of DUNAMASE.

Dunmow 'meadow on the hill', OE *dun* (*see* DOWN, -DON) + *mawe* 'meadow'.

A market town in Essex, by the River CHELMER, about 11 km (7 miles) west of Braintree. Its full name is **Great Dunmow**, and there is also a **Little Dunmow**, just to the southeast.

Dunmow flitch. A 'flitch' or side of bacon that by tradition is presented to the married couple judged to have lived together most contentedly for the previous year and a day. The origins of the custom are conjecturally traceable back to the 12th century: it is said to have been instituted by Lady Juga Bayard in 1104 and then restored by Robert Fitzwalter in 1244. It was said that any person going to Dunmow and humbly kneeling on two sharp stones at the church door, might claim a side of bacon if he could swear that for twelve months and a day he had never had a household brawl or wished himself unmarried. Allusions to the tradition are frequent in literature from the 17th century and the custom was revived in the second half of the 19th century. Today the Flitch Trials are held at Little Dunmow in mid-June every leap year.

Dún na nGall. The Irish name for DONEGAL.

Dún na Séad. The modern Irish name for BALTIMORE.

Dunnerdale. *See* DUDDON.

Dunnet Head Possibly 'bull fort headland'. *Tarvo* 'the bull' was the original OCelt river name, from which the Roman name *Tarvedunum* 'bull fort' for both Dunnet and THURSO are derived.

The most northerly point of the Scottish mainland, in Highland (formerly in Caithness), 12 km (7 miles) northeast of Thurso. The lighthouse stands on top of cliffs 120 m (400 ft) high. The name applies to the whole headland, and the actual tip is called Easter Head. The headland takes its name from the village of **Dunnet** at the neck of the peninsula, which looks west across **Dunnet Bay**. The cartographer Timothy Pont was minister of Dunnet church from 1601 to 1608.

Dunnose 'promontory of the down', OE *dun* (*see* DOWN, -DON) + *næss* (*see* NESS).

A rocky headland towards the southern tip of the ISLE OF WIGHT, just to the northeast of Ventnor.

Dunoon 'fort of the river', Gaelic name *Dùn Obhainn*, from Gaelic *dùn* (*see* DOWN, -DON) + *abhainn* 'river'.

A town and holiday resort in the COWAL peninsula, about 6 km (4 miles) from Gourock across the Firth of Clyde. It is in Argyll and Bute (formerly in Strathclyde). There is a ferry to GOUROCK, and the town is a popular destination for those sailing on day trips from Glasgow 'doon the watter'. There are the remains of an old castle (13th century), which became a royal castle and in 1471 came under the hereditary keepership of the earls of Argyll. In return, the earls were obliged to pay the monarch a red rose, if asked to do so. When Elizabeth II visited Dunoon in 1958 the Captain of DUNSTAFFNAGE, on behalf of the Duke of Argyll, presented the queen with a red rose, even though no such payment had been requested; some judged that this was taking obsequiousness to excessive lengths.

The town has a statue of 'Highland Mary' – Robert Burns's beloved Mary Campbell, who was born on the nearby farm of Auchnamore and who died of typhus.

> The golden hours, on angel wings,
> Flew o'er me and my dearie;
> For dear to me, as light and life,
> Was my sweet Highland Mary.
>
> Robert Burns: 'Highland Mary' (1792)

Dunottar Castle 'slope-fort', Gaelic *dùn* (*see* DOWN, -DON) + *fothair* 'slope'.

A ruined castle in Aberdeenshire (formerly in Kincardineshire, then in Grampian region), just south of STONEHAVEN. It is dramatically situated on a high rocky promontory extending into the North Sea (what the 15th-century poet Blind Harry called 'a snuk within the se'), with cliffs on the three seaward sides, and a steep defile on the landward side. It was the site of a Pictish fort and an early Christian church, but the present ruins date back to the 14th century, with later additions up to the early 17th century.

Dunottar was besieged in 1297 by William Wallace, who burnt the English garrison in the church, and in 1645 by the Marquess of Montrose, who failed to take it from the 7th Earl Marischal, a Covenanter, so Montrose turned to burning the Earl Marishal's lands round about, which were 'utelrie spoilzeit, plunderit and undone'. One of the Presbyterian ministers accompanying the earl in the besieged castle assured him that 'the reek will be a sweet-smelling incense in the nostrils of the Lord'.

A few years later the castle was held on behalf of Charles II by the governor, Sir George Ogilvy, and the Scottish royal regalia were brought to the castle for safekeeping. However, Dunnottar was besieged by Cromwell's forces from September 1651 to May 1652, when Ogilvy negotiated an honourable surrender. Prior to this, Mrs Grainger, wife of the minister of Kinneff, obtained leave from the besiegers to visit Lady Ogilvy, wife of the governor. When she left, she smuggled out the crown in her skirts, while her maid-servant hid the sceptre and sword in a bundle of flax. The regalia were then buried under the floor of the church at Kinneff until after the Restoration.

In contrast to his Covenanting ancestor, the 10th Earl Marischal supported the 1715 Jacobite Rebellion. After its failure, the earl's possessions were forfeited, and Dunnottar Castle was dismantled.

In Guillaume le Clerc's Arthurian poem *Fergus* (early 13th century), the hero attempts to seize something called the **Shield of Dunnotar**. The 1991 film version of *Hamlet* starring Mel Gibson in the title role was made at the castle.

Dún Pádraig. The Irish name for DOWNPATRICK.

Dunpender. The original name of TRAPRAIN LAW.

Dunquin Irish *Dún Chaoin* 'pleasant fort' (*see* DOWN, -DON). A village at the west end of the DINGLE peninsula, County Kerry, and hence one of the westernmost non-island settlements in Europe. The harbour at Dunquin (where boats may be taken to the BLASKET ISLANDS) appears in David Lean's film *Ryan's Daughter* (1970). In the same year as the film was released Dunquin became the focus for indignation on the part of Irish-language enthusiasts when the Irish government determined to close its school owing to falling pupil numbers. The school was kept going on an unofficial basis until a new government reversed the closure decision in 1973.

Dunrobin Castle *Dunrobin* Gaelic *dùn Robyn* 'Robert's fort', named after the 3rd Earl of Sutherland at the end of the 14th century.

A vast 189-room castle on the northeast coast of Highland (formerly in Sutherland), just northeast of GOLSPIE. Although it is said to be one of Britain's oldest continuously inhabited houses, with parts dating back to the 14th century, most of the structure dates from the mid-19th century and was designed in a Gothic-fantasy style by Charles Barry (also responsible for the Houses of Parliament). It is the traditional home of the earls and dukes of SUTHERLAND, and the present lavish edifice was built in the wake of the cruel Sutherland Clearances carried out by the 1st Duke between 1810 and 1820. The current owner is Elizabeth Janson, Countess of Sutherland (the dukedom having passed to a cousin). The castle was used as a naval hospital during the First World War and as a boys' boarding school between 1965 and 1972

Duns 'fortified place', Gaelic *dùn* 'fort' + English plural -*s*, or perhaps 'hills' from OE *dunas* (*see* DOWN, -DON).

A small BURGH in Scottish Borders, to the south of the Lammermuir Hills, about 16 km (10 miles) north of Coldstream. It was called **Dunse** until 1882, and was the county town of BERWICKSHIRE until 1975 (the more suitable candidate, BERWICK-UPON-TWEED, having been carelessly lost to the English).

Dunse Law. Duns Law (*law* Scots, 'hill') is a hill (218 m / 714 ft) on the north side of Duns, where in 1639 a Covenanting army under Alexander Leslie confronted the army of Charles I, who wished to impose bishops on the Presbyterians of Scotland. The Covenanters managed to force Charles to concede their demands at the so-called Pacification of Berwick (*see under* BERWICK-UPON-TWEED); hence it was said:

> The bishops were discharged in Scotland neither by Canon Law nor by Civil Law, but by Dunse Law.

This gave rise to the Scots saying **Dunse dings a'** ('Duns beats all').

Duns Scotus. John Duns Scotus (*c.*1266–1308) was a prominent Scholastic philosopher of the realist school. His name reflects the fact that he was born in Duns, and because his theories (especially regarding the primacy of the papacy over the rights of kings) offended the reformers of the 16th century, his followers became known as Dunses or Dunsmen, the origin of the modern word 'dunce' for a dull or stupid person. Duns Scotus was more highly regarded in his own time and had a cosmopolitan career. He is buried in Cologne Cathedral, and his epitaph reads:

> *Scotia me genuit, Anglia me suscepit, Gallia me docuit,*
> *Cononia me tenet.*
> (Scotland bore me, England took me, France taught me, Cologne holds me.)

See also 'Duns Scotus's Oxford' *under* OXFORD.

'Lassies o' Dunse, The'. A traditional jig for the fiddle.

Dunsinane Probably 'fort of the fairy knoll', Gaelic *dùn* (*see* DOWN, -DON) + *an* 'of' + *t-sìthein* 'the fairy knoll', but possibly (the hill being conical) 'fort of the breast', Gaelic *sineachan* 'breast'.

A hill (308 m / 1012 ft) in the SIDLAW HILLS, some 13 km (8 miles) northeast of Perth, in Perth and Kinross (formerly in Perthshire, and then in Tayside region). There is a prehistoric fort on the summit, and this was traditionally the site of Macbeth's castle. It is only 20 km (12 miles) southeast of Birnam Wood (*see under* BIRNAM). In Shakespeare's *Macbeth* it is the scene of Macbeth's final defeat, but in reality this may have happened further north, at LUMPHANAN.

Dunstable 'Dun(n)a's boundary post', OE male personal name *Dun(n)na* + *stapol* 'boundary post'. (The etymology offered by the lexicographer Nathan Bailey (d.1742) was more entertaining but wrong: 'of Dunus, a Robber in the Time of King Henry I, who made it dangerous for Travellers, by his continual Robberies'.)

A market town in Bedfordshire, now virtually continuous with the western edge of LUTON (although symbolically separated from it by the M1). It was an important communications centre in Roman times, standing at the crossing-point of WATLING STREET[1] and the ICKNIELD WAY. The Romans called it **Durocobrivis**. A Norman priory was built here in the 1130s, in which Archbishop Cranmer was to give his consent to Henry VIII's divorce from Catherine of Aragon in 1533, but little of it now remains. In the 19th century Dunstable was known for its straw-work, and its name became synonymous with a particular type of straw plaiting, and also with straw bonnets (the *Pall Mall Gazette* in 1885 was advertising 'Fine crème Dunstable straw bonnets, trimmed with crème velvet, and crème aigrettes with crème and gold osprey'). Its modern reputation, though, rests on motor-manufacturing: until 1992, Vauxhall cars were built here.

To the southwest are the **Dunstable Downs**, at the eastern end of the CHILTERN HILLS. Their updraughts make them a popular venue for gliding and hang-gliding. The headquarters of the London Gliding Club were established there in 1930. About 3 km (2 miles) to the south is WHIPSNADE and its Wild Animal Park.

Dunstable larks. Larks for the table, once a highly prized local dish, in the same way as Whitstable oysters. Famed from the 17th century, they were served as a speciality in the inns of Dunstable, which were much patronized by the local gentry.

> The larks … at Dunstable … are usually taken … with trammeling nets.
>
> William Hone: *Every-Day Book* (1826)

Dunstable Road. The stretch of road between London and Dunstable (along the route of WATLING STREET[1]) was famed in an era of muddy winding tracks for its exceptional straightness and evenness, and 'Dunstable road' became proverbial for plainness and directness:

> As plain as Dunstable Road. It is applied to things plain and simple, without welt or guard to adorn them, as also to matters easie and obvious to be found, without any difficulty or direction.
>
> Thomas Fuller: *History of the Worthies of England* (1662)

The epithet 'Dunstable' also came to be applied to anything or anyone plain, straightforward or without frills:

> Your uncle is an odd, but a very honest, Dunstable soul.
>
> Samuel Richardson: *Sir Charles Grandison* (1754)

– and frank speech became known as **'plain Dunstable'** or **'downright Dunstable'**:

> If this is not plain speaking, there is no such place as downright Dunstable in being!
>
> Sir Walter Scott: *Redgauntlet* (1824)

Dunstaffnage Castle Gaelic *dùn* 'fort' (*see* DOWN, -DON) + unknown elements; the last is possibly Gaelic INIS 'island' or OScand NESS 'promontory'.

An impressive ruined castle on a rocky promontory guarding the entrance to Loch Etive (*see under* ETIVE), in Argyll and Bute (formerly in Strathclyde), some 6 km (4 miles) north of OBAN. It dates from the 13th century, but was built on the site of a stronghold of the kings of ancient DALRIADA, and the Stone of Destiny was kept here until Kenneth MacAlpin unified Scotland in the 9th century and moved it and his court to SCONE.

Dunstanburgh Castle 'Dunstan's fort', OE male personal name *Dunstan* + *burh* (*see* BURY), with ME *castel* (*see* CASTLE). A ruined castle on a bare promontory on the coast of Northumberland, 16 km (10 miles) south of BAMBURGH. It was begun in 1314 by Thomas, Earl of Lancaster, and is haunted by Sir Guy the Seeker, who failed to wake a princess who had been put under a spell. The castle appears in Franco Zeffirelli's 1991 film version of *Hamlet*, starring Mel Gibson (*see also* DUNOTTAR CASTLE).

> And next, they cross'd themselves, to hear
> The whitening breakers sound so near,
> Where, boiling through the rocks, they roar
> On Dunstanborough's cavern'd shore …
>
> Sir Walter Scott: *Marmion: A Tale of Flodden Field* (1808), Canto II, viii

Dunster 'Dun(n)'s craggy hilltop', OE *Dun(n)nes* possessive form of male personal name *Dun(n)* + *torr* 'craggy hilltop'. A village in Somerset, on the northern edge of EXMOOR and close to the sea, about 3 km (2 miles) southeast of Minehead. Its concentrated agglomeration of picturesque historical buildings, including a (partly Victorianized) Norman castle, a medieval packhorse bridge, a 17th-century octagonal yarn market (at that time the type of woollen cloth made locally was known as 'Dunster') and an 18th-century water mill, has long proved irresistible to painters, photographers and holidaymakers.

Duns Tew *Duns* denoting manorial ownership in the Middle Ages by someone called Dunn; *Tew* perhaps 'row' or 'ridge', OE *tiewe*. A village in Oxfordshire, about 13 km (8 miles) south of Banbury.
See also GREAT TEW.

Duntisbourne Leer *Duntisbourne* 'Dunt's stream', OE *Duntes* possessive form of male personal name *Dunt* + *burna* 'stream'; *Leer* denoting manorial ownership in the Middle Ages by the Abbey of Lire in Normandy. A village (pronounced 'dunzborn' or 'duntisborn') in Gloucestershire, in the COTSWOLDS, about 8 km (5 miles) northwest of Cirencester.

Duntisbourne Rouse *Rouse* denoting manorial ownership in the Middle Ages by the le Rous family. A village in Gloucestershire, in the Cotswolds, about 6.5 km (4 miles) northwest of Cirencester.

Dunton Bassett *Dunton* 'farmstead on a hill', OE *dun* (*see* DOWN, -DON) + -TON; *Bassett* denoting manorial ownership in the early Middle Ages by the Basset family.

A village in Leicestershire, about 16 km (10 miles) south of Leicester.

Dunton Wayletts *Wayletts* denoting manorial ownership in the early Middle Ages by Gundreda atte Waylete (a surname deriving from OE *weg-gelœte* 'crossroads').

A village in Essex, about 8 km (5 miles) southeast of Brentwood.

Dunvegan Castle Etymology uncertain, but Gaelic *dùn* 'fort' (*see* DOWN, -DON) + *bheagan* 'few, a small number' is possible.

A grim-looking castle in northwest SKYE, Highland (formerly in Inverness-shire), just north of the village of the same name and overlooking **Loch Dunvegan**, a sea loch. It has been the seat of the MacLeods of Dunvegan since the 12th century, but most of the present building is 15th–19th century. It has been described by the Scottish poet Norman MacCaig as

> the grey honeycomb
> Filled with claret and blood.

Dr Johnson and James Boswell visited in September 1773 and were delighted with the civility of their hosts in such a remote and desert place:

> Whatever is imagined in the wildest tales, if giants, dragons, and enchantments be excepted, would be felt by him, who, wandering in the mountains without a guide, or upon the sea without a pilot, should be carried amidst his terror and uncertainty, to the hospitality and elegance of Raasay or Dunvegan.
>
> Samuel Johnson: *A Journey to the Western Islands of Scotland* (1775)

During the course of the visit Boswell sat up all night drinking with some of the younger gentlemen, inflicting on himself a mighty hangover, while Johnson was delighted when a young married woman sat on his knee and kissed him:

> He kept her on his knee some time, while he and she drank tea. He was now a *buck* indeed … To me it was highly comic, to see the grave philosopher … toying with a Highland beauty.
>
> James Boswell: *The Journal of Tour of the Hebrides* (1785)

Dunvegan was the birthplace of the famed Gaelic poet Màiri Nighean Alasdair Ruaidh (Mary, Red Alasdair's Daughter, or Mary MacLeod, *fl.*17th century), and Dunvegan was also the place where she

> Made poems and ladled her snuff
> Into her randy nose.
>
> Norman MacCaig: 'Dunvegan', from *A Round of Applause* (1962)

Dunvegan Cup, the. A wooden drinking bowl decorated with silver (once set with precious stones). Despite the inscription on the cup dating it to 1493, it is said to have belonged to an Irish king who was killed by Vikings in the 9th century, or alternatively to have been stolen from the fairies by the son of a witch who lived on Harris.

'Dunvegan Lullaby, The'. A lullaby sung by a fairy to the infant child of Iain Borb ('surly John'), a 15th-century MacLeod chief. The fairy wrapped the child in the Fairy Flag of Dunvegan (*see below*), and the child's nurse, who was present, remembered the tune and words of the song. It was sung thereafter to all MacLeod heirs by their nurses. One of these nurses, who spent much of her life at Dunvegan, was the famed Gaelic poet Màiri Nighean Alasdair Ruaidh (*see above*).

Fairy Flag of Dunvegan, the. A fragment of brown silk, known in Gaelic as *Bratach Sith*, which probably originated in Syria or Rhodes, possibly as long ago as the 7th century AD. It is preserved in the drawing room of Dunvegan Castle. There are various stories about the origins of the flag. The one that might be nearest to the truth (given the flag's likely provenance) suggests that it was brought back by a MacLeod from crusade in the Near East, having been won from a water spirit or a she-devil (perhaps the material was a saint's relic). The story that gives the flag its name tells how a 14th-century chief married a fairy wife, and when after some years she was forced to return to the Land of Faery (at the place called Fairy Bridge, 4 km / 2.5 miles northeast of the castle at the junction of the A850 and the B886) she wrapped the baby that she was obliged to leave behind in the flag (for a variant of this story *see* Dunvegan Lullaby *above*). Another theory proposes that the flag is Land-Ravager, the flag of Harald Hardrada (from whom the MacLeods claim descent) that guaranteed him victory in battle until his defeat by the English at STAMFORD BRIDGE in 1066. Certainly it is said that the Fairy Flag, if unfurled, will save the MacLeods when under dire threat, but that this will work only three times. There are stories of the flag being unfurled on three occasions when the MacLeods were in danger of decimation by their traditional enemies on Skye, the Macdonalds (in 1490, in 1520 and in 1579), so perhaps its power has been used up – although this did not prevent various MacLeods serving in the Second World War from carrying photographs of the flag as they advanced into battle.

See also MACLEOD'S TABLES.

Dunwich Originally *Domnoc*, an OCelt name perhaps meaning 'deep water'; the present-day form, incorporating OE *wic* 'harbour, trading centre' (*see* WICK), is first recorded in Domesday Book (1086).

A coastal village (pronounced 'dunnidge' or 'dunnitch') in Suffolk, about 19 km (12 miles) north of Aldeburgh.

In Roman and medieval times it was an important and flourishing port, with a bishop's palace and nine churches, but in 1326 a disastrous storm swept away 400 houses and three of the churches. The North Sea has doggedly continued its assault ever since, nibbling the village away bit by bit (the market place was inundated in 1677, and in the 1920s the clifftop All Saints' Church slid into the sea), and now Dunwich is down to a single street. (Its status as a rotten borough was abolished under the Great Reform Act of 1832 because by then it was virtually submerged.)

Sometimes, so legend says, the bells of the nine submerged churches can be heard tolling under the sea, warning the village of an approaching storm.

> Dunwich, with its towers and many thousand souls, has dissolved into water, sand and thin air. If you look out from the cliff-top across the sea towards where the town must once have been, you can sense the immense power of emptiness.
>
> W.G. Sebald: *Rings of Saturn* (1998)

To the consternation of locals, this emptiness was threatened in 2004 when two young German architects won a competition run by the East of England Devlopment Agency with their proposal for a sculptural recreation of Dunwich's vanished churches arising out of the sea. A feasibility study is in hand.

Around the village, **Dunwich Heath** is an important National Trust-administered conservation area.

Dupplin Moor 'black pool moor', *Dupplin* Gaelic *dubh* 'black' (*see* DDU, DUBH) + *linne* 'pool' (*see also* DUBLIN).
A battle site some 11 km (7 miles) southwest of Perth, in Perth and Kinross (formerly in Perthshire, and then in Tayside region). Here, on 12 August 1332, Edward Balliol, claimant to the Scottish throne, defeated with English support a Scots army under the Earl of Mar, who was killed in the battle.

Durdle Door Perhaps 'pierced opening', *Durdle* OE *thyrelod* 'pierced'; *Door* OE *duru* 'door, opening'.
A natural rock arch on the coast of Dorset, at the western end of Lulworth Cove (*see under* LULWORTH). It was formed by the sea gradually wearing its way through an outcrop of Purbeck Marble (*see under* PURBECK).

Durham 'island with a hill', OE *dun* (*see* DOWN, -DON) + OScand *holmr* 'island' (*see* -EY, -EA); *Dunholm* c.1000.
A city in County DURHAM of which it is the administrative headquarters, 22 km (14 miles) south of Newcastle upon Tyne. The magnificent Norman **Durham Cathedral** (1093–1133), built on a prominent sandstone hill in a great loop of the River WEAR, was voted Britain's most-loved building in a BBC Radio 4 poll (and before this was praised in '**Durham**', an Anglo-Saxon poem in alliterative verse

from the late 11th century). It dwarfs the castle next to it, built by William the Conqueror in 1072. Cathedral and castle together comprise a UNESCO World Heritage Site, and their interiors were used to film some of the HOGWARTS classroom scenes in the Harry Potter films (2001 onwards).
Durham University, traditionally a popular choice with Oxbridge rejects, was founded in 1832, becoming England's third seat of learning after Oxford and Cambridge. It has 15 constituent colleges, one of which, University College, is housed in **Durham Castle**. Durham hosts an annual Miners' Gala, having once been at the heart of a great coal-mining area.

Durham's ecclesiastical origins go back to 995, when Bishop Aldhun and his monks, following a girl in pursuit of her lost dun cow, brought the undecomposed body of St Cuthbert (d. 687) here from CHESTER-LE-STREET (whither it had been taken a hundred years before from LINDISFARNE, to save it from the Vikings). Aldhun founded a church at Durham as St Cuthbert's shrine, which became a place of pilgrimage.

> There, deep in Durham's Gothic shade,
> His relics are in secret laid;
> But none may know the place,
> Save of his holiest servants three,
> Deep sworn to solemn secrecy,
> Who share that wondrous grace.
>
> Sir Walter Scott: *Marmion: A Tale of Flodden Field* (1808), Canto II, xiv

The remains of the Venerable Bede were brought to Durham in about 1020 and placed in the Lady Chapel in 1370.

In return for keeping the north of England largely Scotfree, the bishops of Durham were awarded considerable secular powers, which lasted until 1836 (*see* LAND OF THE PRINCE BISHOPS). The castle was the palace of the prince bishops until this date, when it was handed over to the university, the bishops moving their palace to BISHOP AUCKLAND. The bishops of Durham sign themselves with their Christian name, together with *Dunelm*, the Latin version of their see.

The site of the Battle of NEVILLE'S CROSS, where the English thwarted a Scottish invasion in 1346, is on the northern outskirts of the city. During the battle, the monks of the cathedral sang mass from the tower, and the bishop vowed to do this annually should the English be victorious. To this day anthems are sung on top of the tower every 29 May.

Durham was the birthplace of Granville Sharp (1735–1813), the philanthropist and abolitionist; the novelist Robert Surtees (1803–64); C.E.M. Joad (1891–1953), philosopher and member of the BBC Radio *Brains Trust*; the miner-turned-novelist Sid Chaplin (1916–86), author of *The Day of the Sardine*; the Booker-shortlisted novelist

Barry Unsworth (b.1930); and the pop singer Alan Price (b.1942). The poet Elizabeth Barrett Browning (1806–61) was born near the city, and the poet Christopher Smart (1722–71) went to Durham School in the 1730s. There are towns called Durham in the USA (New Hampshire, North Carolina).

> There was a good canon of Durham
> Who fished with a hook and a worrum.
>   Said the Dean to the Bishop
>   'I've brought a big fish up,
> But I fear we will have to inter 'im'.
>
>   Anon.: limerick

Durham Light Infantry. A regiment in the Light Division, founded in 1881 (although the 1st Battalion traces its origins to 1756).

Simeon of Durham (d.*c*.1130). A chronicler of early medieval England, and also choirmaster at Durham. His works include *Historia ecclesiae Dunelmensis*, a history of the see of Durham from 635 to 1096.

Durham, County After DURHAM.

A county of northeast England, extending from the North Sea west to the Pennines between the rivers Tyne and Tees, with the River Wear running in between. County Durham is bounded on the north by Northumberland and Tyne and Wear, on the west by Cumbria, and on the south by North Yorkshire, Stockton-on-Tees and Hartlepool. Its administrative headquarters are at the city of DURHAM, and other towns include CONSETT, BARNARD CASTLE, CHESTER-LE-STREET and BISHOP AUCKLAND. It was once a major coal-mining area (for this reason the population grew ten-fold in the 19th century), and has much post-industrial landscape, as well as wild high moors in the west. The miners of Durham (and of Northumberland) were once known as Pit Yackers.

> ... mostly, visible beauty
> Intruded on a coal-field
> So little, one was not
> Unsettled by its absence.
>
>   Donald Davie: 'County Durham', from *The Shires* (1974)

During the Roman period Durham formed part of the territory of the British tribe known as the Brigantes. After the Romans departed it became part of the Anglo-Saxon kingdom of BERNICIA. From 1071 to 1836 Durham was a COUNTY PALATINE, being run as a fiefdom by the prince bishops from Durham Castle (*see* LAND OF THE PRINCE BISHOPS). In Domesday Book (1086) it was referred to as **S. Cuthberts-Lond**, St Cuthbert being buried in the cathedral at Durham.

County Durham's profile received a welcome boost when, in 1992, it transmogrified from 'minor county' to become the 18th 'first-class' county and compete in cricket's county championship. Durham County Cricket Club was originally founded in 1882, and now has its headquarters at the Riverside Ground in CHESTER-LE-STREET.

Durisdeer Possibly 'entrance to the forest', Gaelic *dorus* 'door, entrance' + *doire* 'oak forest, grove'.

A hamlet on the west side of the DALVEEN PASS, once in Dumfriesshire, now in Dumfries and Galloway, about 8 km (5 miles) north of Thornhill. It is notable for the late 17th-century church containing the magnificent baroque black and white marble monument to the Duke and Duchess of Queensberry (d.1711 and 1709 respectively).
See also QUEENSBURY[3].

Durlas. The Irish name for THURLES.

Durlston Head *Durlston* 'rock with a hole in it', OE *thyrel* 'hole' + *stan* 'stone, rock' (*see* STONE).

A headland at the southeastern corner of the Isle of Purbeck (*see under* PURBECK) in Dorset, about 1.5 km (1 mile) south of SWANAGE. The imposing cliffs are adorned by a remarkable 40-ton Portland-stone model of the world called the Great Globe, which was installed by a local Victorian building contractor called George Burt.
See also TILLY WHIM CAVES.

Durness 'promontory of the deer', OScand *dyr* 'deer' + NESS.

A village on the north coast of Highland (formerly in Sutherland). It is the nearest settlement to CAPE WRATH, 17 km (10 miles) northwest, making it the most north-westerly village in mainland Scotland. **Durness Old Church**, about 2 km (1 mile) to the northwest, had an obelisk commemorating the Gaelic poet Rob Donn (Robert Mackay, 1740–78), who may be buried here.

Durnovaria. A Roman town on the site of the modern-day DORCHESTER[1].

Durocobrivis. The Roman name for what is now the town of DUNSTABLE.

Durovernum. A Roman town on the site of modern CANTERBURY[1].

Durovigutum. A Roman settlement on the site of present-day CAMBRIDGE[1].

Durrow Irish *Darú* 'oak plain'.

The site in County Offaly of a monastery said to have been founded by St Columba (Columcille) in 551. It is 6 km (4 miles) north of TULLAMORE. The abbey was destroyed by Hugh de Lacy in the course of constructing a castle on the site (de Lacy himself died here in 1186). All that is left of the monastic buildings is a high cross.

Book of Durrow, The. An illuminated manuscript of the four Gospels written in Irish script *c*.650. It possibly originated on LINDISFARNE, and may have been taken to

Durrow Abbey to keep it safe from Viking raiders. It is now in Trinity College Library, Dublin.

Dursey. An alternative name for DORSEY.

Dursey Island Irish *dóirse* 'gates' (*see* DORSEY, although the reference is not clear: possibly something to do with the use of the island to keep people captive).

An island just off the west end of the BEARA peninsula, County Cork, 50 km (31 miles) west of Bantry. At its western end is **Dursey Head**, from where, in 1497, John Cabot set his course due west and some time later arrived on the coast of Newfoundland. Dursey Island is said to be the furthest place in Ireland you can get from Dublin. In the Dark Ages the Vikings held captured Irish slaves here for further transportation to Scandinavia or the Iberian Peninsula. The island's tragic history continued in 1602 after the Battle of KINSALE, when the English found that many Irish people had fled to the island for safety and proceeded to slaughter them, as described in this contemporary account by Philip O'Sullivan:

> They shot down, hacked with swords, or ran through with spears, the now disarmed garrison and others, old men, women and children, whom they had driven into one heap. Some rammed their swords up to the hilt through the babe and mother who was carrying it on her breast, others paraded before their comrades little children, writhing and convulsed on their spears, and finally binding all the survivors, they threw them into the sea over jagged and sharp rocks, showering on them shots and stones. In this way perished about three hundred.

Dursley 'Deorsige's clearing', OE male personal name *Deorsige* + -LEY.

An attractive market town in Gloucestershire, about 20 km (12 miles) south of Gloucester, on the wooded southwestern edge of the COTSWOLDS. It was a centre of woollen cloth manufacture from the 15th century.

It may have been a certain dolefulness inherent in the name Dursley that led the Gloucestershire-born children's novelist J.K. Rowling to choose it as the surname of Petunia and Vernon Dursley, Harry Potter's mean-spirited aunt and uncle in her *Harry Potter* sequence of novels (*see also* LITTLE WHINGEING).

Dursley donkey, the. A local nickname for the train that plied the branch line linking Dursley to the Bristol and Gloucester Railway in pre-Beeching days (the line closed in 1968).

Dutchman's Cap. *See under* TRESHNISH ISLES.

Duxford Originally *Duxworth* 'Duc(c)'s enclosure', OE *Duc(c)es* possessive form of male personal name *Duc(c)* + *worth* (*see* -WORTH, WORTHY, -WARDINE); the present-day form is first recorded in Domesday Book (1086).

A village in Cambridgeshire, on the M11, about 13 km (8 miles) south of Cambridge. The local RAF station became famous during the Second World War, largely because of the exploits of the legless fighter pilot Douglas Bader, who was based there during the Battle of Britain. After the war it remained unused until in 1977 the Imperial War Museum moved its collection of aircraft there and put them on public display. The American Air Museum (opened in 1997) is in an 18-m (60-ft) high glass-walled hangar designed by Norman Foster.

Duxford Wing. A combined formation of five RAF fighter squadrons that flew under the leadership of Douglas Bader during the Battle of Britain.

Dwarfie Stane, the. *See* HOY.

Dyce. *See under* ABERDEEN.

Dyfed 'territory of the Demetae', an ancient Celtic tribe.

A medieval kingdom and former county of southwest Wales. The medieval kingdom (more or less corresponding to Pembrokeshire) was founded by the Irish after the withdrawal of the Romans in the 5th century. In the 10th century Hywel Dda, king of Dyfed (904–950), united it with his other kingdom, SEISYLLWG, to form the kingdom of DEHEUBARTH.

The county of Dyfed was created in 1974 from the old counties of CARDIGANSHIRE, CARMARTHENSHIRE and PEMBROKESHIRE. It was bounded to the west by St George's Channel and Cardigan Bay, to the north by Gwynedd, to the east by Powys and West Glamorgan, and to the south by the outer reaches of the Bristol Channel. The administrative seat was at CARMARTHEN. It was abolished in 1996 and replaced by the unitary authorities of CEREDIGION, Pembrokeshire and Carmarthenshire.

Dyffryn. One of the Welsh names for VALLEY.

Dyffryn Tywi. *See under* TOWY.

Dyfi From OCelt *duf* 'dark, black'.

A river of Gwynedd (formerly in Merioneth), which enters Cardigan Bay at ABERDOVEY. The English version of the name is **Dovey**. It is 48 km (30 miles) in length.

Dymchurch Probably 'judge's church', OE *deman* possessive form of *dema* 'judge' + *cirice* 'church'.

A small town and seaside resort on the southeast coast of Kent, on the edge of ROMNEY MARSH, about 15 km (10 miles) southwest of Folkestone. It is about 2 m (7 ft) below sea level at high tide, and is protected by a massive sea wall. In former centuries it had a reputation as a smugglers' port, and it was also the headquarters of the 'Lords of the Level', who governed the local section of Romney Marsh. Nowadays, however, its most striking feature is probably the strings of caravans and holiday chalets that line its sandy beach.

The daring and mysterious Dr Syn in Russell Thorndyke's eponymous novel (1915) leads a double life as vicar of Dymchurch by day and smuggler leader by night, storing contraband in various churches on Romney Marsh. One of his most daring raids is on LYMPNE Castle on the edge of the marsh. There is now an annual 'Day of Syn' at Dymchurch.

The town is one of the stations on the miniature Romney, Hythe and Dymchurch steam railway (*see under* NEW ROMNEY).

Dyrham 'enclosed land with deer', OE *deor* 'deer' + *hamm* (*see* HAM).

A village in South Gloucestershire, 10 km (6 miles) north of Bath. Nearby, set in the hollow of a valley at the end of the Cotswold escarpment, and surrounded by an ancient deer park, is **Dyrham Park**, a baroque country house built between 1691 and 1702 for William Blathwayt, who as secretary at war from 1686 to 1704 served both James II and William III. Now owned by the National Trust, Dyrham Park was used as the setting for the Merchant-Ivory period

drama *The Remains of the Day* (1993), based on a Booker Prize-winning novel (1989) by Kazuo Ishiguro, in which it played the role of Darlington Hall.

Battle of Dyrham (577). A battle fought near Dyrham in which, according to the *Anglo-Saxon Chronicle*, the Saxon king Ceawlin of WESSEX defeated and killed three British kings, going on to take the towns of BATH, CIRENCESTER and GLOUCESTER. Some historians believe that the battle represented a major advance for the Saxons in their conquest of England.

Dysert O Dea Irish *Díseart Uí Dheá* 'hermitage of Ó Dheá'.

The site of an early monastic settlement in County Clare, 8 km (5 miles) northwest of Ennis. St Tola (d.737) founded a hermitage here, and there are the remains of a Romanesque church and round tower and a magnificent 12th-century high cross.

Battle of Dysert O Dea (1318). A battle in which Muirchertach O'Brien defeated Richard de Clare, so halting Anglo-Norman expansion in THOMOND.

E

Eachdroim. The Irish name for AUGHRIM.

Eagle 'wood where oak-trees grow', OE *ac* (later replaced by OScand *eik*) 'oak' + -LEY.

A village in Lincolnshire, about 11 km (7 miles) southwest of Lincoln.

Eaglescliffe A modernized version of neighbouring *Egglescliffe*, with which it merges. The modernized name is based on the natural association of eagles and cliffs, whereas Egglescliffe is probably 'church by the cliff', OCelt *egles* 'church' (*see* ECCLES) + OE *clif* 'cliff', although the OE male personal name *Ecgwulf* is possible for the first element.

A village in the unitary authority of STOCKTON-ON-TEES (formerly in County Durham), 6 km (4 miles) south of the town itself.

Ealing '(settlement of) Gilla's family or followers', OE male personal name *Gilla* + -*ingas* (*see* -ING).

A suburb (W5, W13) and borough (W3, W4, W5, W7, W13, NW10 and parts of Greenford, Northolt and Southall) of West London, to the west of Acton and to the north of the River THAMES[1] at Brentford and Kew. Its rurality was not seriously threatened until the 1870s and 1880s, when middle-class housing development turned it into what its publicists called the **'Queen of the Suburbs'**. The opening of Underground stations on the Metropolitan and District lines (Ealing Broadway and Ealing Common in 1879, South Ealing in 1883 and North Ealing in 1903) and the start of a tram route to Shepherd's Bush in 1901 increased Ealing's attraction for London commuters, and the more intensive residential and commercial development of the early 20th century somewhat compromised its 'queenliness'. The novelist Nevil Shute (1899–1960) was born in Ealing. *See also* PERIVALE.

Ealing comedies. Comedy films produced by the Ealing Studios from the late 1940s to the mid-1950s. They typically feature a downtrodden group rebelling against authority and are regarded as quintessentially 'English'. Among the best are *Passport to Pimlico* (1948; *see under* PIMLICO); *Whisky Galore* (1948), in which a ship with a cargo of whisky is wrecked off a small Scottish island (*see also* BARRA *and* ERISKAY); *Kind Hearts and Coronets* (1949), in which eight members of the aristocratic D'Ascoyne family, all played by Alec Guinness, are murdered by the grudge-bearing Louis Mazzini (Dennis Price); *The Lavender Hill Mob* (1951; *see under* LAVENDER HILL); and *The Ladykillers* (1955), in which a gang of robbers take refuge in a little old lady's house, but end up falling victim to her guilelessness.

Ealing Studios. A film production company based at Ealing film studios, famous for the Ealing comedies. It was founded in 1907 and five years later its studios were the biggest in

---

❖ **ea-** ❖

This Old English element, meaning 'river, stream', undergoes many mutations. Perhaps the most common simple form of the word is found in the many Eatons (*ea* with -TON): *see* EATON CONSTANTINE (Shropshire) and NUNEATON (Warwickshire). Several rivers have this element as their name, for example the Eye (Leicestershire, *see under* MELTON MOWBRAY, and Lincolnshire). The same name is disguised by Middle English spelling in the Berkshire river Ray and several Rea names (*see under* MEOLE BRACE), where the phrase 'at the river', in Middle English *atter ee* or *atter ea*, has been misdivided as *atte ree* or *atte rea*. A peculiarity of the eastern English fenlands is the spelling of this element as if it were French *eau* 'water', in FRISKNEY EAUDYKE and QUADRING EAUDIKE (both in Lincolnshire) and POPHAM'S EAU (Cambridgeshire and Norfolk); this even extends to spelling the Old Scandinavian element *a* 'river' in the same way, as in Long Eau (Lincolnshire). The element has specific reference here to a fen-draining river or channel.

Britain. The company's fortunes began to fail in the 1950s, when tastes were changing, and after releasing *The Ladykillers* it sold its studios to the BBC. Film stages and offices were subsequently rented out for independent productions, and in 1995 the site was sold to the National Film and Television School.

Eamhain Mhacha. The Irish name for NAVAN FORT

Eanach Dhúin. The Irish name for ANNAGHDOWN.

Earby 'upper farm' OScand *efri* 'upper' + -BY.
A village in Lancashire, 16 km (10 miles) northeast of Burnley.

Eardisland Originally *Erleslen* 'nobleman's estate in Leon', OE *eorles* possessive form of *eorl* 'nobleman' + *Leon* OCelt name for the district (*see* LEOMINSTER); the modern form of the name is probably due to the influence of other local place names such as *Eardisley* and *Eardiston*.
A village (pronounced 'erd(i)zland' or, in the local dialect, 'yerzland') in Herefordshire (before 1998 in Hereford and Worcester, before 1974 in Herefordshire), on the River ARROW[2] about 8 km (5 miles) west of Leominster. It contains several outstanding examples of the local architectural speciality: black-and-white timber-framed buildings – for example, Staick House, a yeoman's hall built around 1300. It had been a village in decline, but the VE Day 50th Anniversary celebrations here in 1995 reportedly gave it a boost that set it back on its feet.

Earls Barton 'earl's barley-farm', *barton* 'barley-farm, outlying grange where grain is stored', OE *bere, bær* 'barley' +-TON.
The earl in question was David, Earl of Huntingdon, owner of the manor here in the 12th century.
A village in Northamptonshire, about 7 km (4.5 miles) southwest of Wellingborough. The village is home to one of England's best-known late Saxon churches, the tower of the Church of All Saints here dating from the 10th century.

Earls Colne *Earls* denoting manorial ownership in the Middle Ages by the earls of Oxford; *Colne see* COLNE[1].
A village (pronounced 'kohn') in Essex, in the Colne Valley (*see under* COLNE[1]), 10 km (6 miles) northeast of Braintree. *See also* COLNE ENGAINE *and* WAKES COLNE.

Earl's Court 'earl's manor house'.
A district of West London (SW5), in the Royal Borough of KENSINGTON AND CHELSEA, between Hammersmith to the west and South Kensington to the east. It grew up in the 16th century as a hamlet centred on the house of the earls of Oxford, who were lords of the manor of Kensington (the original manor house – or *court* in 16th-century English – survived until 1886). London's expansion swallowed it up in the 1870s and 80s, and its status as a distinct area was reinforced by the opening of Earl's Court Underground station, on the District and Piccadilly lines, in 1871 (the station was the first to have an escalator installed, in 1911,

and to dispel initial public distrust the railway employed a wooden-legged man, 'Bumper' Harris, to walk up and down it all day). It was and is mainly residential, its original large villas divided up now into flats that have made it quintessential 'bedsitter land'. The mobile population has given the district a lively cosmopolitan feel. A large influx of temporary Antipodean residents in the 1960s earned it the nickname KANGAROO VALLEY.

A site in the area, at the western end of the Old Brompton Road, had been used since the 1880s for public spectaculars (for instance, Buffalo Bill's Wild West Show), and in 1937 the **Earl's Court Exhibition Hall** opened here. At the time it was the largest reinforced-concrete building in Europe. Usually known simply as 'Earl's Court', it has since played host to innumerable shows and exhibitions, from the Boat Show to the Royal Tournament.

Earl's Court has been used as rhyming slang for *salt*, betraying an *l*-less pronunciation of the latter.

Earlsferry. *See under* ELIE.

Earls Park. The fictitious football club that features in the popular ITV melodrama *Footballers' Wives* (2002, 2003 and 2004). The mundanity of the coinage – an apparent West London portmanteau of *Earl's* Court and Queens *Park* Rangers – belies plots so lurid that no less a moral arbiter than the Archbishop of Canterbury was moved to deplore their content. Serial promiscuity is the stock-in-trade of the spouses in question, and the drama's three series have also featured 'mile-high' sex, a hermaphrodite baby, stalking, drug-taking, attempted suicide and murder.

Earl's Seat Probably after the *Earl* of Lennox, who had a castle on the southern slopes.
The highest point (578 m / 1896 ft) in the CAMPSIE FELLS, on the border of Stirling and East Dunbartonshire, 4 km (2.5 miles) north of Strathblane.

Earlston. *See* ERCILDOUNE.

Earn Probably a pre-Celtic river name meaning 'flowing one'.
A river in the southern Highlands, in PERTH AND KINROSS (formerly in Perthshire, and then in Central region). It is 74 km (46 miles) long, and flows eastwards from **Loch Earn** through the valley of **Strath Earn** and then meanders across a wide flat plain to the village of **Bridge of Earn** just south of Perth. It joins the River TAY southeast of Perth, just as it becomes the Firth of Tay. Loch Earn is 10.5 km (6.5 miles) long, is popular with waterskiers, and gave its name to a reel by Nathaniel Gow (b.1763). At its west end is the village of **Lochearnhead**. The loch is overlooked by Ben Vorlich, and on the south side is Ardvorlich House (*see under* BEN VORLICH[1]).

> The twinkling Earn, like a blade in the snow.
>
> John Davidson (1857–1909): 'Winter in Strathearn'

Earraid Etymology unkown.

A small tidal island off the Ross of Mull, just south of Iona, in Argyll and Bute (formerly in Strathclyde region). It is also spelt **Erraid**. In Robert Louis Stevenson's novel *Kidnapped* (1886), the hero David Balfour is shipwrecked on the island, and thinks he is stranded until he realizes that at low tide he can walk across the sands to the mainland of Mull. A beautiful granite-girt sandy bay on the south of the island is known today as **Balfour Bay**. The old coastguard cottages at the north end of the island are used by the Findhorn Foundation (*see under* Findhorn).

Eas a'Chùal Aluinn Possibly 'waterfall of the beautiful secluded place', Gaelic *eas* 'waterfall, cataract' + *cùil* 'secluded place' + *àlainn* 'beautiful'.

The highest waterfall in the British Isles. It is 200 m (658 ft) high, and is in the far northwest of Highland (formerly in Sutherland), 8 km (5 miles) northwest of Ben More Assynt, and close to the head of Loch Glencoul. The second-highest falls are the Falls of Glomach.

Eas Géitine. The Irish name for Askeaton.

Easington 'Esa's farm', OE male personal name *Esa* + -ING + -TON.

A former mining town in County Durham, 14 km (8.5 miles) south of Sunderland. The mines extended far out under the North Sea. The villages of **Easington Colliery** and **Easington Lane** are contiguous with Easington.

The former left-wing firebrand Emanuel ('Manny') Shinwell was Labour MP for Easington from 1950 until he retired in 1970. The cyclist Tommy Simpson (1938–67), who died from the effects of drugs and exhaustion in the 1967 Tour de France, was born here.

Easington is also the name of a local authority district.

Easole Street *Easole* perhaps 'ridges or banks associated with a god or gods', OE *os*, *ese* '(heathen) god(s)' + *walu* 'weal, ridge, bank'; *Street* 'hamlet', ModE (*see* STREET).

A village in Kent, about 13 km (8 miles) southeast of Canterbury.

East Anglia. A region of eastern England roughly corresponding to the bulge of land that extends from the Wash to the Thames[1] estuary. At its core are Norfolk and Suffolk, the counties covering an area that in Anglo-Saxon times constituted the **Kingdom of East Anglia** (the term seems to have been coined by 17th-century antiquarians); one of its early kings was Rædwald (d.*c*.625), the most likely candidate for identification as the man honoured by the elaborate ship burial excavated at Sutton Hoo. In its modern application it is generally also taken to include the northerly part of Essex and the eastern half of Cambridgeshire.

Mountainous it is not. The occasional modest eminence does no more than emphasize the general flatness of the East Anglian landscape, shading into the Fenlands (*see* the Fens) in the northwest, and around the coast reclaimed from a sea constantly seeking to recoup its loss. It is a land of big horizons. In the Middle Ages it grew rich on the trade in wool, which was brought to North Sea ports via East Anglian waterways (the magnificence of local churches such as St Peter and St Paul, Lavenham, and Holy Trinity, Long Melford, attests to the depth of East Anglian merchants' pockets), and reviving trade with Europe in the present era brings in wealth via ports such as Felixstowe and Harwich.

The **University of East Anglia**, founded in 1964, is centred on Norwich. Its motto is 'Do different' (from a local saying, 'People in Norfolk do things different'). Its creative writing course, initiated by Malcolm Bradbury (1932–2000), numbers the novelists Ian McEwan and Graham Swift among its products.

The latter part of the 20th century saw a tendency to dispense with the 'East' element of East Anglia, and treat the historically spurious Anglia as a region in its own right – mainly in the names of organizations, such as the Anglian Water Authority, and **Anglia Television**, an independent televison company serving East Anglia, founded in 1959, with its headquarters in Norwich and now part of Granada Media group. The railway company **West Anglia Great Northern** (WAGN) runs services into the western part of East Anglia, and **Anglia Railways** served East Anglia from London Liverpool Street until their franchise was withdrawn in 2004.

East Anglian. A person or thing of, or relating to, East Anglia.

East Ayrshire *See* Ayrshire.

A unitary authority created in 1996 from two districts of the former Strathclyde region (*see also* Ayrshire). The administrative HQ is Kilmarnock. It is bounded by South Lanarkshire, Dumfries and Galloway, South Ayrshire and North Ayrshire.

East Barming Etymology uncertain: the early spellings suggest the OE elements *bearm* 'edge' + *leah* 'grove, clearing' (*see* -LEY) + -*ingas* (*see* -ING), and a meaning 'dwellers at the outlying clearing'.

A village in Kent, on the western outskirts of Maidstone.

East Bergholt *Bergholt* 'wood on or by a hill', OE *beorg* 'hill' + *holt* 'wood'.

A village in Suffolk, in the Stour[2] Valley, about 13 km (8 miles) northeast of Colchester. Its fame rests on the fact that the painter John Constable (1776–1837), son of a local miller, was born here. The house where he came into the world no longer exists, but enough of the old 16th- and 17th-century village remains to give an idea of what it must have been like in his boyhood. A rebuilt Victorian version of FLATFORD MILL, which he made famous in his 1817 painting, is 1 km (0.6 miles) to the south.

See also CONSTABLE COUNTRY *and* DEDHAM.

Eastbourne Originally *Bourn* '(place at the) stream', OE *burna*; *east* had been added by the 14th century, to distinguish the place from Westbourne in West Sussex (near Chichester).

A town and seaside resort on the East Sussex coast, about 32 km (20 miles) east of Brighton. It was laid out in its essential modern form in the 1850s by the Duke of Devonshire, the lord of the manor and a substantial local landowner. He created a stately classical seafront, dominated by the majestic Grand Hotel (1875). The later Victorians added fine parks and even a pier (1872), but the 5-km (3-mile) esplanade still bespeaks decorum – this is definitely not a resort that has sold out to 'kiss-me-quickery'. Its stereotypical patrons are not so much day-trippers as the aged occupants of residential hotels, who get their music at the bandstand rather than at clubs.

The French composer Claude Debussy stayed in Eastbourne for a while in 1905, taking refuge from the scandal that followed his marriage to his former mistress. While he was here he completed the orchestration of parts of his set of 'symphonic sketches', *La Mer* (1905). The chemist Frederick Soddy (1877–1956), formulator of the theory of isotopes, and the writers Rumer Godden (1907–98) and Angela Carter (1940–92) were born in Eastbourne.

There is a town called Eastbourne on the North Island of New Zealand, opposite Wellington.

East Calder. *See under* CALDER[3].

East Coker *Coker* from the name of a local stream, an OCelt river name meaning 'crooked, winding'.

A village in Somerset, about 4 km (2.5 miles) south of Yeovil. William Dampier (1652–1715), the pirate turned respectable explorer who rescued Alexander Selkirk (*see* LARGS), probable model for Robinson Crusoe, was born in East Coker, as were ancestors of the poet T.S. Eliot (1888–1965), who is buried in the local churchyard. He gave East Coker's name to the second (1940) of his *Four Quartets*, a meditation on time past and time present that draws its imagery from the Somerset village:

> ... In my beginning is my end. Now the light falls
> Across the open field, leaving the deep lane
> Shuttered with branches, dark in the afternoon,
> Where you lean against a bank while a van passes,
> And the deep lane insists on the direction
> Into the village, in the electric heat
> Hypnotised. In a warm haze the sultry light
> Is absorbed, not refracted, by grey stone.
> The dahlias sleep in the empty silence.
> Wait for the early owl...

See also LITTLE GIDDING.

East Creech *Creech* 'mound, hill' (referring originally to the nearby Creech Barrow), OCelt *crug* (*see* CREECH, CROOK).

A village in Dorset, about 5 km (3 miles) south of Wareham.

East Dereham *Dereham* 'homestead or enclosure where deer are kept', OE *deor* 'wild animal, deer' + HAM.

A market town in Norfolk, about 24 km (15 miles) west of Norwich. The poet William Cowper (1731–1800) lived the last four years of his life in East Dereham, and the writer George Borrow (1803–81) was born here. The village of **West Dereham** is about 36 km (22 miles) away to the southwest, near Downham Market.

East Dunbartonshire From DUMBARTON + SHIRE.

A unitary authority created in 1996. It is bounded on the west by West Dunbartonshire, on the north by Stirling unitary authority, on the south by Glasgow, and on the east by North Lanarkshire. It includes the towns of MILNGAVIE, BEARSDEN, BISHOPBRIGGS and KIRKINTILLOCH. *See also* DUNBARTONSHIRE.

East End. The eastern part of INNER LONDON, north of the River THAMES[1], to the east of the City. The term (first recorded in 1846) implies no specific geographical boundaries, although its western edge might be represented by a line drawn northwards from the Tower of London, and its reach encompasses the working-class residential and industrial areas to the east of that whose population density increased so disastrously in the 19th century: WHITECHAPEL and SPITALFIELDS (where Jack the Ripper lurked and pounced in the 1880s), BETHNAL GREEN (the Kray brothers' beat), SHOREDITCH, MILE END, STEPNEY and BOW, the Dockland communities of WAPPING, LIMEHOUSE, POPLAR, MILLWALL and CANNING TOWN, and on out towards STRATFORD, EAST HAM and WEST HAM, PLAISTOW and BECKTON. Those insensitive to local nuances sometimes push its boundaries further east and northeast, but the citizens of DAGENHAM, ILFORD, WANSTEAD and the like tend not to take kindly to this.

In truth its agenda has always been more demographic than geographic (*compare* EAST LONDON): it suggests teeming masses of working people huddled (perhaps whistlingly cheerful, perhaps sullen with potential rebellion) in cramped and verminous tenements; Dickensian squalor; Cockney chirpiness; crime; the grinding poverty and exploitation recorded by Henry Mayhew in his *London Labour and the London Poor* (1849–64) and visualized in the drawings of Gustave Doré. All this had its valid origins in the East London of the 19th and early 20th centuries, but the East End's docks and other industries made it the prime target of the Blitz in 1940–1, and large swathes of it were obliterated. Its inhabitants' mixture of stereotypical resilient cheerfulness and stubborn gloom may well remain the same, but its physical landscape is now one of council estates, tower blocks (a threatened species in the 21st century) and light industry. In the 1980s gentrification (or 'yuppification', as its detractors would have it) began to infiltrate parts of the East End, and the lofts of Limehouse and the postmodern apartments of DOCKLAND are now highly desirable.

The term has always been markedly contrastive too: you cannot have an East End without a WEST END[1]. Two alien cultures, wealthy nobbish West and poverty-stricken East, counterpoint each other, one indeed often validating itself by reference to the other (there was much resentment that the East End was bearing all the brunt of the Blitz, and when Buckingham Palace was bombed in September 1940, Queen Elizabeth memorably remarked 'I'm glad we've been bombed. Now I feel we can look the East End in the face'). A climatic reason has been posited for the relative location of the 'Ends', in both London and GLASGOW (*see also* WEST END[2]): prevailing westerly winds waft the smoke and stench of the nobs over the hoi polloi, rather than vice versa.

East Ender. A native or inhabitant of the East End.

EastEnders. A BBC televison soap opera set in the fictional East End borough of WALFORD (E20), and chronicling in particular the daily lives of the residents of Albert Square. First broadcast in 1985, it was an instant success and has continued to command high viewing figures ever since, in spite of its consistently depressing storylines. Amongst its most memorable characters have been 'Dirty' Den Watts and his wife Angie, the hypochondriac Dot Cotton, the barman 'Wicksy' Wicks and the bullish Grant Mitchell.

Easter Compton *Easter* 'more easterly', OE *easterra* (to distinguish the village from nearby Compton Greenfield); *Compton* 'farmstead or village in a valley', OE *cumb* 'valley' + -TON.

A village in South Gloucestershire (before 1996 in Avon, before 1974 in Gloucestershire), about 8 km (5 miles) northwest of Bristol.

Easter Head. *See under* DUNNET HEAD.

Easterhouse Probably 'eastern dwelling(s)', a modern name from OE *easter(ra)* 'eastern' + *hus* 'house, dwelling'.

A massive 1960s housing estate (or 'scheme') in the far east of GLASGOW, into which the residents of the cleared inner-city slums were herded, but without providing such basic facilities as shops, pubs, etc., so that Easterhouse became a byword for modern urban desolation and multiple deprivation. However, there has been considerable regeneration in recent years.

> Mercy for the rainy
> tyres and the violet
> thunder that bring you

> shambling and shy
> from chains of Easterhouse
>
> Edwin Morgan: 'In Glasgow'

Eastern Association. An association formed by the English counties of Norfolk, Suffolk, Essex, Cambridgeshire, Hertfordshire, Huntingdonshire and Lincolnshire in 1642 and 1643 for their common defence in the Parliamentary cause during the Civil Wars. Their forces were organized by Oliver Cromwell and they provided much of the cavalry for the New Model Army.

Easter Ross. *See under* ROSS AND CROMARTY.

East Fortune *Fortune* probably 'ford-farm or village', OE FORD + -TON.

A small village, also spelt **East Fortoun**, in East Lothian, 6 km (4 miles) northeast of Haddington. The farm of **West Fortune** is nearby. East Fortune was on RAF base (1918–46) and is now home to the Museum of Flight. The R34 airship departed here in 1919 to make the first east–west air crossing of the Atlantic.

East Ginge *Ginge* from the nearby *Ginge* Brook, a river name meaning 'one that turns aside', from the stem of OE *gægan* 'to turn aside' + -ING.

A village in Oxfordshire (before 1974 in Berkshire), on the North Wessex Downs (*see under* WESSEX), just to the north of the Ridgeway, about 5 km (3 miles) southeast of Wantage. It is often called simply **Ginge**. The village of **West Ginge** is a little to the west.

East Grinstead *Grinstead* 'green place' (that is, pasture used for grazing), OE *grene* 'green' + *stede* 'place'.

A market town in West Sussex, about 11 km (7 miles) northeast of Crawley. There are still a number of impressive half-timbered Tudor buildings in its main street. The late 18th-century church of St Swithun has eight bells, the largest peal in Sussex (they were recast in 1982). During the Second World War the town's name became synonymous with the plastic surgery carried out at its Queen Victoria Hospital, where Sir Archibald MacIndoe and his team reconstructed the faces and limbs of burnt and wounded service personnel. Today, though, its main reputation is as the Cult Capital of Britain:

> Funny place, East Grinstead. Nothing remarkable, on the face of it – just masses of Stockbroker Tudor mansions on the outskirts, a messily indeterminate centre, if you can call it that, and then a sprawl of smaller houses fading into industrial estates. Neither charming nor particularly ugly: just a sort of nothing town. And yet … And yet the whole area has been some sort of manna-accumulator as far back as one can trace. The Druids were just the earliest one could be certain of, but we know there were other practitioners long before they were put down by the Romans. Down, but not out … the place was, and

remains, pagan, in any true sense: friendly, in fact, to just about any belief short of orthodox Christianity. Today, you have the great Mormon Church, the Rudolf Steiner school, the Church of Scientology, and more witches than one could shake a broom at.

> George Hay: 'Sleeper' (1995)

East Ham *East* reflecting its location relative to West Ham; *Ham* 'area of dry land bounded by water or marsh' (alluding to the position of East and West Ham between the River LEA to the west, the RODING to the east and the THAMES[1] to the south), OE *hamm* (*see* HAM).

A district of EAST LONDON (E6, E7, E12), in the borough of NEWHAM, between West Ham to the west and Barking to the east. Until the 19th century it was still an agricultural village, but in the latter part of that century its population grew at a phenomenal rate, and it became a major dormitory suburb of London. East Ham 'Underground' station, on the District and Metropolitan lines, opened in 1902.

East Kennett. *See under* WEST KENNETT.

East Kilbride *Kilbride* 'St Bride's church', KIL- + personal name *Bride*. The first part of the name distinguishes it from WEST KILBRIDE, a small town in North Ayrshire. St Bride or St Bridget (d.*c*.523) is Ireland's second patron saint, and is said to have founded the first convent in Ireland. She may not have existed, and she shares some characteristics with Brigit, the pagan Celtic goddess of fire, the hearth and poetry.

A BURGH of west-central Scotland, 13 km (8 miles) south-east of Glasgow, in South Lanarkshire. It was formerly a district of Strathclyde Region, and before that it was in the county of Lanarkshire. In 1947 it was designated a NEW TOWN[1] – the first in Scotland – and has grown from a small village to the sixth largest settlement north of the Anglo–Scottish border. It is nicknamed **Polomint City**, because of its many roundabouts (*compare* LLANTRISANT, 'the Hole with the Mint').

The first meeting of Quakers in Scotland took place in East Kilbride in 1653, and the brothers John (1728–93) and William (1718–83) Hunter , the leading anatomists of the 18th century, were born in the parish, at Long Calderwood. East Kilbride is home to the National Engineering Laboratory.

> There was a young man from Kilbride
> Who fell down a sewer and died.
>   Now he had a brother
>   Who fell down another,
> And now they're interred side by side.
>
> Anon.: limerick

East Knoyle *Knoyle* '(place at the) knuckle-shaped hill', OE *cnugel* 'knuckle'.

A village in Wiltshire, about 8 km (5 miles) north of Shaftesbury. East Knoyle was the birthplace of Sir Christopher Wren (1632–1723), architect of ST PAUL'S[1] Cathedral, whose father was a clergyman here. The village of **West Knoyle** lies to the northwest.

East Langton *Langton see* LANGTON HERRING.

A village in Leicestershire, about 17 km (11 miles) southeast of Leicester.

See also LANGTONS.

Eastleigh 'east wood or clearing', OE *east* + -LEY. Originally it was the name of a wood.

A town in Hampshire, just to the north of SOUTHAMPTON. It originated as a village built around 1850 for workers on the London–Southampton railway, which had arrived some ten years earlier. Its name was borrowed from that of a local farm, which in turn presumably got it from a nearby wood.

The Vickers Supermarine company had its assembly plant at Eastleigh, and the prototype of its Spitfire, most glamorous and effective of British Second World War fighter aircraft, flew from what is now Southampton Airport (officially designated 'Southampton (Eastleigh)') in Eastleigh on 5 March 1936. The airport now handles commercial traffic on a modest scale.

East Linton *Linton* OE *lin* 'flax' + -TON; the first element distinguishes it from WEST LINTON.

A village in East Lothian, 8 km (5 miles) south of North Berwick. Nearby is Preston Mill, a working water mill, and the Phantassie Doo'cot (dovecote), both in the care of the National Trust for Scotland.

The Scottish engineer and bridge-builder John Rennie (1761–1821) was born here at Phantassie farm.

East London. The eastern part of GREATER LONDON, to the east of the TOWER OF LONDON and to the north of the River THAMES[1]. The designation has no clear eastern frontier: it certainly reaches as far as Barking Creek (*see under* BARKING), but thereafter, as E-coded postal districts give way to what was recently Essex, it seems less and less the *mot juste*. It conjures up many of the same images as EAST END, but does not bear the same weight of folkloric baggage.

East London is also the name of an important city and seaport in Eastern Cape Province, South Africa.

East London line. A line on the London Underground system, which runs from SHOREDITCH southwards via the Thames Tunnel (*see under* THAMES[1]) to NEW CROSS and NEW CROSS GATE. It had its beginnings in the late 1860s as the East London Railway. In the early 1930s, with the advent of the London Passenger Transport Board, it was absorbed into the Metropolitan line, but in the 1980s it resumed its own individual identity. At the beginning of the 21st century, plans were approved to extend it northwards via HOXTON to DALSTON.

University of East London. A university formed in 1992 from the **Polytechnic of East London** (previously North East

London Polytechnic). It has campuses at BARKING and DOCKLAND.

East Lothian *See* LOTHIAN.

A former county and present unitary authority in eastern-central Scotland. It was part of Lothian region from 1975 to 1996. It is bounded on the northwest by the Firth of Forth, on the northeast by the North Sea, on the south by Scottish Borders (the part that was formerly Berwickshire), and on the west by Midlothian. The administrative headquarters is at HADDINGTON (the former county was at one time known as **Haddingtonshire**, after its county town), and other towns include MUSSELBURGH (formerly in Midlothian), PRESTONPANS, COCKENZIE and Port Seton, TRANENT, and the seaside resorts of NORTH BERWICK and DUNBAR. There is much rich red agricultural soil, many charming russet-sandstone-and-pantile cottages, and the rolling heathery expanses of the LAMMERMUIRS in the south.

East Malling *Malling* '(settlement of) Mealla's people', OE male personal name *Mealla* + *-ingas* (*see* -ING).

A village (pronounced 'mawling') in Kent, about 6 km (4 miles) west of Maidstone. The **East Malling Research Station** does important work in horticultural science, developing new strains of fruit, cereals, etc. and tackling plant diseases; the name 'Malling' designates a rootstock for fruit trees developed here after the First World War. *See also* TONBRIDGE *and* WEST MALLING.

East Meon. *See under* MEON.

East Midlands. The eastern part of the English MIDLANDS. Unlike the WEST MIDLANDS it is not an area with a modern statutory boundary, but it might with general consent be taken to comprise LEICESTERSHIRE, NORTHAMPTONSHIRE, RUTLAND, the northern part of BEDFORDSHIRE, the southern part of LINCOLNSHIRE and the southern part of NOTTINGHAMSHIRE, with perhaps also the western section of CAMBRIDGESHIRE and the southeastern corner of DERBYSHIRE. Its central swathe, in particular Leicestershire and Northamptonshire, has been quintessential fox-hunting country, otherwise known as the SHIRES. In the first half of the 10th century it was a discrete entity ruled by the Danes, centred on the so-called 'FIVE BOROUGHS', DERBY, LEICESTER, LINCOLN, NOTTINGHAM[1] and STAMFORD.

Although the name has no present-day official status, it does enter into certain conventional or semi-official designations: **East Midland English**, for instance, was an important variety of Middle English, the language of Geoffrey Chaucer and one of the key forerunners of modern English; and the airport serving this area, at CASTLE DONINGTON, to the south of Nottingham, is now called **Nottingham East Midlands Airport**.

All his life he's been a citizen of the East Midlands ... By the metropolis's jeering estimates, of course, these are ... a series of worthy, yes, but oh how meanly parochial dullsvilles.

The Times (5 December 1980)

East Molesey. *See under* MOLESEY.

East Mouse. *See under* MOUSE ISLANDS

East Neuk, the Scots *neuk* 'promontory, peninsula'.

The eastern part of FIFE, which projects into the North Sea between the Firth of Tay (*see under* TAY) and the Firth of Forth (*see under* FORTH). There is a traditional fiddle tune called '**The East Neuk of Fife**'.

Easton in Gordano *Easton* 'east farmstead or village' (that is, one to the east of another settlement), OE *east* + -TON; *Gordano see* CLAPTON IN GORDANO.

A village in North Somerset (before 1996 in Avon, before 1974 in Somerset), on the southwest bank of the River AVON[2], about 3 km (2 miles) from its mouth and 8 km (5 miles) west of Bristol. Gordano Services at Junction 19 on the M5 are just to the west.

Easton Maudit *Maudit* denoting manorial ownership in the early Middle Ages by the Mauduit family.

A village (pronounced 'mordit') in Northamptonshire, about 11 km (7 miles) east of Northampton.

East Renfrewshire From RENFREWSHIRE.

A unitary authority created in 1996 out of the eastern part of the former district of RENFREW. It is bounded on the west by Renfrewshire, to the north by Glasgow, to the east by South Lanarkshire and to the south by East Ayrshire. Its administrative centre is at GIFFNOCK, and other towns include BARRHEAD, CLARKSTON and NEWTON MEARNS.

East Riding of Yorkshire *Riding see* the RIDINGS OF YORKSHIRE; *Yorkshire see* YORKSHIRE.

A current unitary authority and former administrative division of the old county of Yorkshire. The administrative headquarters is at BEVERLEY, and other towns include DRIFFIELD, HORNSEA, WITHERNSEA and BRIDLINGTON. HULL was part of the old East Riding until the reorganization of 1974, when much of the East Riding was swallowed up, to the disgust of Yorkshiremen, in HUMBERSIDE. When this was abolished and the East Riding re-established in 1996, Hull became a separate unitary authority.

The old East Riding was bordered on the north by the North Riding, to the west by the West Riding, to the south by the River Humber and Lincolnshire, and to the east by the North Sea. The current East Riding is bordered on the west by West Yorkshire, York and North Yorkshire, which also bounds it on the north.

East Yorkshire was the territory of the ancient British tribe known as the Parisi. Their main settlement was at Petuaria on the River Humber (*see* BROUGH[2]).

East Sheen *Sheen* 'sheds, shelters' (referring to shepherds' shelters in summer pastures), OE *sceon* plural form of *sceo* 'shed, shelter'. Originally a manorial name designating the settlement now called RICHMOND[2].

A district of southwest London (SW14), in the borough of RICHMOND-UPON-THAMES, to the east of Richmond and to the south of Mortlake.

East Sussex *See* SUSSEX.

A county on the south coast of England, formed in 1974 from the eastern part of the historic county of SUSSEX (which itself had been constituted as a separate administrative unit with its own county council in 1888, also called 'East Sussex', but with a western border somewhat further west than the present East Sussex's). It is bounded to the east by Kent, to the north by Surrey, and to the west by West Sussex. Geographically it includes the unitary authority of Brighton and Hove (*see under* BRIGHTON). Its county town is LEWES, and other main centres are BEXHILL, CROWBOROUGH, EASTBOURNE, HASTINGS, RYE, SEAFORD, UCKFIELD and the port of NEWHAVEN. Its main rivers are the CUCKMERE, the OUSE[3] and the ROTHER[2].

The southern part of the county is dominated by the SOUTH DOWNS, which sweep down to the sea at BEACHY HEAD. To the north are the sandstone hills of the WEALD, including ASHDOWN FOREST, and to the east, levels of reclaimed marshland. The coast has undergone extensive development in the past century and a half, both residential and in the service of the holiday industry on which the local economy has so much depended.

East Wemyss *Wemyss* Gaelic *uaimh* 'cave': there are several along the shore here; *East*, to distinguish it from the small settlement of West Wemyss along the coast and the nearby village of Coaltown of Wemyss.

A village (pronounced 'weemz') in Fife, on the north shore of the Firth of Forth (*see under* FORTH), 7 km (4 miles) northeast of Kirkcaldy. The place gave its name to the Wemyss family and clan, descendants of the Macduff earls of Fife; the ruined Macduff's Castle (originally 11th century, but what remains dates from the 16th) is at the eastern end of the village. In 1633 Sir John Wemyss was created Earl of Wemyss, but in the 18th century the clan chiefdom and the earldom went to different branches of the family. The chief at the beginning of the 21st century, David Wemyss of Wemyss, still has his seat at **Wemyss Castle** (built 1421, restored in the 1950s) between East and **West Wemyss**.

Jimmy Shand (1908–2000), the dance-band leader, was born in East Wemyss.

Wemyss ware. An exuberant and colourful style of pottery, first produced in Fife in 1882 under the patronage of the Wemyss family. In the 1930s manufacture was transferred to Devon, but returned to Fife in the 1980s. Cats, pigs, tableware and tiles are popular products.

East Wittering *Wittering* '(settlement of) Wihthere's family or followers', OE male personal name *Wihthere* + *-ingas* (*see* -ING).

A seaside resort in West Sussex, on Bracklesham Bay (*see under* BRACKLESHAM), near the western end of the SELSEY peninsula, about 10 km (6 miles) southwest of Chichester. Ian Nairn bemoaned its 'bungalows, chalets and caravans near the beach, in an untidy half-grown-up state' in *The Buildings of England: Sussex* (1965). The posher WEST WITTERING is about 2.5 km (1.5 miles) to the west, at the mouth of Chichester Harbour (*see under* CHICHESTER).

Eastwood[1] 'eastern clearing', OE *east* (perhaps reflecting the settlement's location east of the River EREWASH[1]) + OScand *thveit* 'clearing, meadow'.

A former colliery town in Nottinghamshire, 14 km (8.5 miles) northwest of Nottingham. The novelist D.H. Lawrence was born here on 11 September 1885: his birthplace at 8a Victoria Street has been a museum since 1976. He was to fictionalize the town as BESTWOOD.

Eastwood[2] Self-explanatory, though not much of the wood remains.

A former district (1975–96) of the former Strathclyde region, in Scotland's Central Belt. The administrative headquarters were at PAISLEY (outside the district), and the district took in some of the southern suburbs of Glasgow, such as CLARKSTON, NEWTON MEARNS and GIFFNOCK.

Eatanswill. A fictionalized version of SUDBURY[1] in Suffolk, which figures in Charles Dickens's *Pickwick Papers* (1837).

Eaton Constantine *Eaton* 'farmstead by a river', OE EA- + -TON; *Constantine* denoting manorial ownership in the early Middle Ages by the de Costentin family.

A village in Shropshire, about 11 km (7 miles) southeast of Shrewsbury.

Eaton Socon *Socon* 'district with a right of jurisdiction', OE *socn*.

A village in Cambridgeshire, just to the southwest of St Neots, on the Bedfordshire border.

Eaton Square From *Eaton* Hall in Cheshire, the country seat of the Dukes of Westminster.

A 'square' (actually a very elongated oblong) in BELGRAVIA (SW1), in the City of WESTMINSTER, to the west of Victoria Station. It was built in the 1820s as part of the development of the Grosvenor estate, the property of the dukes of Westminster. Its reputation for extreme exclusivity is sustained by the prices its nobbish houses fetch. Residents have included Stanley Baldwin, Lawrence Olivier and Vivien Leigh, Andrew Lloyd Webber and Margaret Thatcher, and the Bellamys in ITV's *Upstairs, Downstairs* (1971–5) lived just round the corner in **Eaton Place**. Nowadays, though, you are just as likely to find an ambassador here as a lord (the Belgian Embassy is in Eaton Square, for example, as is the Bolivian Consulate).

> Then Petra flashed by in a wink.
> It looked like Eaton Square – but pink.
>
> Sir Charles Johnston: 'Air Travel in Arabia', from
> *Poems and Journeys* (1979)

Ebbing and Flowing Well, the. *See under* GIGGLESWICK.

Ebbsfleet Possibly 'Æbb's creek or inlet', OE male personal name + *fleot* 'creek, inlet'.

A location on the North Kent coast, just to the north of SWANSCOMBE. It was here in 449 that Hengist and Horsa landed with their Jutish forces (according to one version, at the invitation of the British ruler Vortigern), the spearhead of the Anglo-Saxon invasion that transformed southern Britain into England. Nearly a century and a half later, in 597, it was the turn of St Augustine to arrive here, on a mission to end Anglo-Saxon paganism. He is supposed to have met King Æthelbert of Kent, and a cross marks the place where he preached his first sermon. There is now a Suffragan Bishop of Ebbsfleet, subordinate to Canterbury.

At the beginning of the 21st century the **Ebbsfleet St Pancras Thames Tunnel** is under construction, which will carry the CHANNEL TUNNEL Rail Link from the north Kent coast under the Thames to THURROCK.

Ebbw Vale 'valley of the River Ebwy'; the name was coined in the 19th century. The river name is from OWelsh *eb* 'horse' + *gwyth* 'anger' or *gwydd* 'wild'.

A former coal and steel town (pronounced 'ebboo') on the River Ebbw in Blaenau Gwent (formerly in Monmouthshire, then in Gwent), some 30 km (19 miles) north of Cardiff. Its Welsh name is **Glyn Ebwy** (*glyn* 'valley'), and it is the administrative seat of BLAENAU GWENT. Aneurin (Nye) Bevan was MP for Ebbw Vale from 1929, and was succeeded after his death by Michael Foot in 1960.

> Can I forget the banks of Malpas Brook
> Or Ebbw's voice in such wild delight,
> As on he dashed with pebbles in his throat
> Gurgling towards the sea with all his might?
>
> W.H. Davies: 'Days That Have Been'

Eblana. Ptolemy's name for DUBLIN.

Eboracum OCelt *eburaco* 'place abounding in yew trees'; Ptolemy called it *Eborakon*.

The Roman name for YORK. The Archbishop of York signs himself with his Christian name plus 'Ebor'.

Ecchinswell Originally (1086) *Eccleswell*, perhaps 'Eccel's stream', OE *Eccles* possessive form of male personal name *Eccel* + *wella* 'stream'; alternatively the first element may be OCelt *egles* 'Romano-British Christian church' (*see* ECCLES).

A village in Hampshire, about 15 km (9 miles) northwest of Basingstoke.

Ecclefechan Possibly 'St Fechan's church', OCelt *eglwys* (*see* ECCLES) + personal name *Fechin,* but more likely to be *bechan* 'little'; *Eggleffychan* 1296.

A village 9 km (5.5 miles) southeast of Lockerbie, formerly in Dumfriesshire, now in Dumfries and Galloway. Its name may commemorate St Fechan, a 7th-century Irish abbot whose followers proselytized in Scotland. The village was the birthplace of the historian and essayist Thomas Carlyle (1795–1881), who is also buried here. The house of his birth is now a museum in the care of the National Trust for Scotland. In *Sartor Resartus* (1833–4) Carlyle depicts the village as **Entepfuhl**.

Before Carlyle's birth, Robert Burns would sometimes stop off at Ecclefechan on his journeys as an exciseman. He described it as 'this unfortunate, wicked little village', and wrote a poem entitled '**The Lass of Ecclefechan**'. The village also makes an appearance in Hugh MacDiarmid's *A Drunk Man Looks at the Thistle* (*see* AUCHTERMUCHTY).

Ecclefechan butter tart. A sweet tart with a filling of melted butter, soft brown sugar, eggs, cider vinegar, chopped walnuts and mixed dried fruit.

Eccles OCelt *egles* 'church' (*see* ECCLES).

An industrial town on the River IRWELL in Greater Manchester, 8 km (5 miles) west of Manchester itself. It gave its name to the **Eccles cake**, comprising dried fruit in a deliciously lardy kind of puff pastry; sadly, the cakes are no

---

❖ **eccles** ❖

Latin borrowed its word for a church, *ecclesia*, from Greek, and it came to Britain with the Roman occupation. When the Anglo-Saxons invaded Britain in the 5th century, they found communities and presumably buildings with a Christian function, and borrowed the word the British used for these in names such as ECCLES (Greater Manchester), Eccleshall, Exhall, Eccleston and Exley, particularly in the northwest of the country. Most of the names containing this element are early: the Scottish Eccles in Berwickshire and in Dumfries and Galloway, and ECCLEFECHAN in the latter county, have the word in its Brittonic form. Many Cornish names have lost the element in their modern forms: CURY, for example, was *Egloscuri*; but EGLOSHAYLE and EGLOSKERRY retain it. In Ireland and Wales, the element became the common word for a church and most names are both minor and of no great antiquity: *eaglais* is found in Aglish (County Kilkenny) and elsewhere as Eglish; and in Wales, *eglws* is found in Eglwys-bach (Clwyd) and Eglwys-fach (Dyfed), both meaning 'small church' (*see* BACH).

longer made in Eccles. Eccles also gave its name to an intellectually challenged innocent in the radio classic *The Goon Show*. The town was the scene of the death by locomotive of William Huskisson, the free-trade politician, at the opening of the Liverpool and Manchester Railway in 1830.

Eccup 'Ecca's small secluded valley', OE male personal name *Ecca* + *hop* 'small secluded valley or enclosed plot of land'.

A village in West Yorkshire, on the small **Eccup Reservoir**, 8 km (5 miles) north of Leeds.

Ecrehous, Les Probably 'island of the skerries', OScand *sker* 'skerry' + *holmr* 'island' (*see also* -EY, -EA). French *Éc-* is a regular pronunciation of *Sk-* (*compare* 'school' and 'école'). The earliest spelling is *Le Skerhou*; the plural definite article *Les* does not occur before the 18th century.

A reef of rocks and small islands about 9.5 km (6 miles) northwest of JERSEY, and within its Bailiwick. At low tide they cover an area of about 10.3 sq km (4 sq miles). At present thay have no permanent human inhabitants, but there have been tiny settlements here in the past, and in the 19th century Philip Pinel, the self-proclaimed 'King of the Ecrehous', lived here for 48 years. They are only 11 km (7 miles) from France, and ownership has been disputed in the past; it was only finally settled in the 1950s. In the 17th century Les Ecrehous were a centre for smuggling between Jersey and the mainland. *See also* Les MINQUIERS.

Edale 'valley with an island', OE *eg* (*see* -EY, -EA) + OScand *dalr* 'dale'.

A village in Derbyshire, in the HIGH PEAK, about 18 km (11 miles) northeast of Buxton. It is a tourist centre for ramblers: the Pennine Way (*see under* PENNINES) starts here. The tautonymous **Vale of Edale** is the upper part of the valley of the River NOE; at its eastern end is the tiny settlement of **Edale End**.

Edale Moor. An area of moorland to the north of Edale. Its highest point is the bleak KINDER SCOUT.

Édan Doire. The Irish name for EDENDERRY[1].

Eday 'isthmus island', OScand *eith* 'isthmus' + *ey* 'island' (*see* -AY). The name derives from the island's narrow waist.

An island in ORKNEY, 20 km (12 miles) north of Kirkwall on Mainland. It is separated from SANDAY to the northeast by **Eday Sound**. In 1725 the inept but compassionate pirate John Gow and his crew were captured on Eday by the local schoolteacher, Mr Fea, and his neighbour Mrs Honeyman. Off the north coast is the small island called **Calf of Eday**.

Eddrachillis Bay 'bay of the place between two narrows', Gaelic *eadar* 'between', *dà* 'two' + *caolas* 'narrows, straits'.

A beautiful, many-islanded bay in the far northwest of Highland (formerly in Sutherland), 40 km (25 miles) north of Ullapool. Eddrachillis is also the name of the local parish.

Eddystone Rocks *Eddystone* probably ModE *eddy* + *stone*, referring to the lethal currents around the rocks (*see* STONE).

A dangerous group of rocks in the English Channel, about 23 km (14 miles) south of Plymouth. The first **Eddystone Lighthouse** (or **Eddystone Light**, as it is often called) was built by Henry Winstanley in 1698. It was a wooden polygon, 30 m (98 ft) high, on a stone base. Winstanley perished in his own edifice when it was washed away by a storm in 1703. The third lighthouse, built by John Smeaton (1759), was the first in which dovetail-jointed stones were used. The present lighthouse replaced it in 1882. It converted to unstaffed automatic operation in 1982.

'Keeper of the Eddystone Light, The'. A folk song illustrating the perils of an isolated posting. The first verse runs:

> Me father was the keeper of the Eddystone Light
> And he slept with a mermaid one fine night.
> From this union there came three:
> A porpoise and a porgy and the other was me!
> Yo ho ho, the wind blows free,
> Oh for the life on the rolling sea!

Eden[1] An OCelt river name meaning 'water'.

A river largely in Cumbria (formerly in Cumberland), rising in the PENNINES just inside North Yorkshire, some 12 km (7.5 miles) south of Kirkby Stephen, in the valley called the MALLERSTANG. It flows 104 km (65 miles) generally northwestward, through APPLEBY-IN-WESTMORLAND and CARLISLE, before entering the SOLWAY FIRTH, and provides the main dividing line between the Pennines and the Lakeland Fells. It gives its name to a local authority district of Cumbria.

According to legend, Uther Pendragon attempted to divert the Eden to fill the moat of his castle at Nateby, but, as the local rhyme has it:

> Let Uther Pendragon do what he can,
> Eden will run where Eden ran.

(The castle was in fact built in the 12th century by Hugh de Morville, one of the knights who killed Thomas Becket.)

William Wordsworth belatedly discovered the pleasures of this fine river:

> Eden! till now thy beauty had I viewed
> By glimpses only, and confess with shame
> That verse of mine, whate'er its varying mood,
> Repeats but once the sound of thy sweet name ...
>
> William Wordsworth: 'The River Eden, Cumberland' (1833)

Eden[2] A back-formation from *Edenbridge*. The name is first recorded in 1577; before that the river seems to have been called *Hedgecourt*, after Hedgecourt (Pond) in Surrey.

A river in Surrey and Kent, which rises near OXTED in Surrey and flows 27 km (17 miles) eastwards through EDENBRIDGE to join the River MEDWAY[1] near PENSHURST.

Edenbridge 'Eadhelm's bridge', OE male personal name *Eadhelm* + *brycg* 'bridge'.

A small town in southwestern Kent, on the River EDEN[2], about 16 km (10 miles) west of Tonbridge.

Edenderry[1] Irish *Édan Doire* 'brow of the hill of the oak wood'.
A village in County Down, just outside Belfast. It is used for the main Orange celebrations on the 12 July.

Edenderry[2]. A small market town on the Grand Canal in the Bog of Allen, County Offaly, 50 km (31 miles) west of Dublin. It was built largely by the 2nd Marquess of Downshire in the later 18th century, on the edge of the Pale, and there are the remains of many castles in the vicinity.

Eden Project From the Garden of *Eden*, the earthly paradise that, according to the Old Testament, existed before the Fall of Mankind.
An extensive botanical exhibition park, situated in a disused claypit at Bodelva, about 5 km (3 miles) northeast of St Austell in Cornwall. The brainchild of Tim Smit, chief executive since 1999, it was designed by Nicholas Grimshaw and Partners. Opened in March 2001, its key feature is the large geodesic domes, known as biomes, inside which artificial climates can be created. This allows the flora of a wide range of habitats to be exhibited, for example tropical rainforests and Mediterranean hillsides. The Humid Tropical Biome is the largest conservatory in the world, 240 m (787 ft) long and 50 m (164 ft) high. It featured as part of the villain's headquarters in the James Bond film *Die Another Day* (2002).

Edensor 'Eadin's sloping bank or ridge', OE *Eadines* possessive form of male personal name *Eadin* + *ofer* 'edge, bank, ridge'.
A village (pronounced 'ensa' or 'enza') in Derbyshire, on the Chatsworth estate, about 3 km (2 miles) northeast of Bakewell, which in the 1830s had the unnerving experience of being moved to a new site. The 6th Duke of Devonshire found that in its existing position it spoilt his view, so he had it pulled down and rebuilt further to the west in 1839. The new village was far grander than the previous one – indeed it has been called 'probably the grandest village in England' (Candida Lycett Green, *England: Travels through an Unwrecked Landscape* (1996)). Laid out by the duke's gardener Joseph Paxton (of Crystal Palace fame), it boasts an extraordinarily eclectic range of architectural styles, from Norman, Tudor and Gothic Revival to Swiss.

Edgbaston 'Ecgbald's farmstead', OE *Ecgbaldes* possessive form of male personal name *Ecgbald* + -TON.
A southern district of Birmingham, one of the city's more leafy and salubrious suburbs, about 4 km (2.5 miles) from the city centre. Its spacious boulevards contain not just a stock of housing ranging from comfortable to desirable, but also Birmingham University (founded in 1900), Birmingham's Botanical Gardens and **Edgbaston Cricket Ground** (headquarters of Warwickshire County Cricket Club and a test match venue since 1902). The novelist Barbara Cartland (1901–2000) was born in Edgbaston.

Edge[1] '(place at the) edge or escarpment', OE *ecg* 'edge'.
A village in Gloucestershire, about 8 km (5 miles) south of Gloucester.

Edge[2]. A village in Shropshire, about 11 km (7 miles) southwest of Shrewsbury.

Edgehill Originally 'the Edge', OE *ecg*, denoting a long ridge passing through three parishes; the *hill* was added in the 17th century.
A ridge in South Warwickshire, about 17 km (11 miles) southeast of Stratford-upon-Avon.
Battle of Edgehill (23 October 1642). The first battle of the Civil Wars, between Royalists under Charles I and Parliamentarians under the Earl of Essex. The result was indecisive.
Edge-hill, or, the rural prospect delineated and moralised. A topographical poem (1767) in four books by the Cornish-born Warwickshire poet Richard Jago (1767–81), describing views from Edgehill at morning, noon, afternoon and evening.

Edgeworthstown From the *Edgeworth* family, who came to Ireland in 1585 and to Edgeworthstown during the reign of James VI and I.
A village in County Longford, 13 km (8 miles) southeast of Longford itself. Its Irish name is **Meathas Troim** ('boundary of the elder-tree'), anglicized as **Mostrim**. The writer Oliver Goldsmith went to school in the village from 1741 to 1745, and Oscar Wilde's sister is buried here. The novelist Maria Edgeworth, author of *Castle Rackrent*, came to her ancestral seat at Edgeworthstown in 1782 with her father Richard Lovell Edgeworth (a noted educationalist, inventor and progressive landlord) and stepmother, and lived out the rest of her life here. She was visited at Edgeworthstown House (a Georgian mansion built by her father, now a nursing home) by Wordsworth, Byron and Sir Walter Scott, and proved herself a notably benevolent landlord during the Great Famine of the 1840s. Another noted Edgeworth (born in Edgeworthstown) was Henry Essex Edgeworth (1745–1807), a Catholic convert who, as chaplain to the French royal family, was present at the execution of Louis XVI in 1793. Of a later generation, also born here, was the noted economist and statistician, Francis Ysidro Edgeworth (1845–1926), who had strong views on such matters as the indifference curve.

Edgware 'Ecgi's weir or fishing-enclosure', OE male personal name *Ecgi* + *wer* 'weir, fishing-enclosure'. The weir in question was apparently at the place where a local stream (now called Edgware Brook) was crossed by Watling Street.
A northwestern suburb of Greater London, in the borough of Barnet, between Stanmore to the west and Mill Hill to the east. Until the early 20th century it was a small Middlesex town, grown to comfortable proportions thanks

to its position on the road from London to the northwest. Then the Northern line arrived (Edgware 'Underground' station, its northwestern terminus, opened in 1924), and since then it has been subsumed into suburbia.

Its main road artery, the A5, follows the line of the old WATLING STREET[1], out towards St Albans and eventually to Chester. Its southern extremity, from ST JOHN'S WOOD to MARBLE ARCH, is known as the **Edgware Road**. It is lined with a largely forgettable array of office blocks and flats, with an outbreak of small shops and Middle Eastern restaurants as it nears Marble Arch. Edgware Road Underground station, on the Bakerloo, Circle, District and Metropolitan lines, opened in 1863.
See also TYBURN[2].

like Edgware Road. A facetious expression applied in the 20th century to tight trousers – because 'they've got no ballroom either'.

Edina. A polite poetic personification of EDINBURGH. Robert Fergusson mentions 'Edina's Roses' in his poem 'Auld Reekie' (*c.*1773), while Robert Burns began his 'Address to Edinburgh' with the line

> Edina! Scotia's darling seat!

– which led one manufacturer of sanitary ware to dub his leading product '**The Edina**'.

There is a town called Edina in the USA (Missouri).

EDINA. The acronym of Edinburgh Data and Information Access, a resource for the UK tertiary education and research community based at Edinburgh University Data Library.

Edinburgh Originally DUNEDIN, 'fort at Eidyn', Gaelic *dùn* 'fort' (*see* DOWN, -DON) + an element of obscure origin, believed to be OCelt *eiddyn* 'rock face'; the first record of the name in its present form, from the 12th century, simply replaces Gaelic *dùn* with English *burh* (*see* BURY) without changing the meaning.

The capital city of Scotland, in the Central Lowlands, situated between the PENTLAND HILLS and the south shore of the Firth of Forth (*see under* FORTH). It is familiarly referred to as EMBRO and poetically personified as EDINA. Edinburgh was at one time the county town of MIDLOTHIAN (in the past known as **Edinburghshire**), then administrative seat of the former Lothian region (of which it was also a district, 1975–96), and is now, as **the City of Edinburgh**, a unitary authority.

It was Robert the Bruce who made Edinburgh Scotland's capital, in 1325, and four years later he made the city a BURGH with its port at LEITH. However, Stirling and Perth continued as rivals, and it was not until the 16th century that Edinburgh became the undisputed capital of the realm. The city was home to Scotland's Parliament until the Act of Union in 1707, and since devolution in 1999 a new Scottish Parliament, albeit one with limited powers, sits

once more in Edinburgh (*see under* HOLYROOD). Even before this, Edinburgh was home to the Scottish Office, the government department devoted to Scottish matters, and the city is also the location of the Court of Session and the High Court of Justiciary, the senior courts administering Scotland's separate system of law and justice. The Palace of Holyroodhouse (*see again under* HOLYROOD) is the sovereign's official residence in Scotland.

Edinburgh has three universities: the University of Edinburgh (1583), particularly noted for its medical school; Heriot-Watt University (1966; founded as a technical college in 1885); and Napier University (1992; previously a polytechnic); Queen Margaret University College (originally the Edinburgh School of Cookery, founded 1875) hopes to achieve full university status in 2005. Other important institutions include the Royal College of Surgeons of Edinburgh (1505; the oldest medical society in the English-speaking world), the Royal College of Physicians of Edinburgh (1681), the Royal Society of Edinburgh (1783), the National Library of Scotland, the National Gallery of Scotland, the Scottish National Gallery of Modern Art and the Royal Scottish Museum. The principal church is St Giles, dating back to 1243 and consecrated as a cathedral in 1633; it is now the high kirk of the Church of Scotland. There is also an Episcopalian cathedral, St Mary's, a fine three-spired example of the 19th-century Gothic revival. Edinburgh is an important financial, insurance and banking centre, and printing and publishing were formerly key industries: the first printing press was set up in 1507, and *Encyclopaedia Britannica* was first published in Edinburgh in 1768–71; bookmen associated with the city include Sir Walter Scott's publisher Archibald Constable (1774–1827), Adam Black (1784–1874), founder of the firm A. & C. Black, Thomas Nelson (1780–1861), and William (1800–83) and Robert (1802–71) Chambers of encyclopedia and dictionary fame. *The Scotsman*, one of Scotland's two national broadsheet newspapers, was founded in Edinburgh in 1817.

The city is dramatically situated, like Rome and Sheffield, among seven hills, all of them the plugs of long-dead volcanoes. **The Seven Hills of Edinburgh**, as they are collectively known, are: Castle Rock (*see below*), CALTON HILL, ARTHUR'S SEAT, CORSTORPHINE Hill, Blackford Hill, the Braid Hills and CRAIGLOCKHART Hill.

> The first sight of Edinburgh after an absence is invariably exciting. Its bold and stony look recalls ravines and quarried mountains, and as one's eye runs up the long line of jagged roofs from Holyrood to the Castle, one feels that these house-shapes are outcroppings of the rocky ridge on which they are planted, methodical geological formations in which, as an afterthought, people have taken to living ...
>
> Edwin Muir: *Scottish Journey* (1935)

Because of its hilly nature, the city has an exceptional number of fine views, complemented by swathes of magnificent historical buildings. The downside is the chill wind that whips around the place, the 'Damned flinty wind' with its 'scraping kiss', in the words of the poet Norman MacCaig, a native of the city; and if it's not the wind it's the haar, the sea mist that can shroud the city for days at a time, leading Alfred, Lord Tennyson to write of

> The bitter east, the misty summer
> And grey metropolis of the North.
> 'The Daisy'

Coleridge thought Edinburgh one of the few things worth going to Scotland to see (along with the islands of Loch Lomond, the Trossachs and the Falls of Foyers, and possibly Glen Coe):

> What a wonderful city Edinburgh is! What alternation of height and depth! A city look'd at in the polish'd back of a Brobdingnag spoon held lengthways, so enormously *stretched-up* are the houses! When I first looked down on it … I cannot express what I felt – such a section of wasps' nests striking you with a sort of bastard sublimity from the enormity and infinity of its littleness – the infinity swelling out of the mind, the enormity striking it with wonder.
>
> Samuel Taylor Coleridge: letter to Robert Southey (13 September 1803)

As Washington Irving commented to Sir Walter Scott on a visit in 1817:

> I don't wonder that anyone residing in Edinburgh should write poetically.

(Indeed, when the poet Thomas Campbell went to Edinburgh in 1797 to study law, he ended up writing *The Pleasures of Hope* instead.)

At the centre of Edinburgh is the great black crag of Castle Rock, on which stands the grey eminence of **Edinburgh Castle** (*see below*). There are traces on Castle Rock of settlements going back to at least the Bronze Age. Around AD 500 the British tribe known to the Romans as the Votadini moved their capital from TRAPRAIN LAW in East Lothian to Castle Rock; in the early 7th century the people holding Castle Rock were referred to by the Welsh poet Aneirin as the Gododdin, and Edinburgh was referred to as Dineiddyn (*see* DUNEDIN). The warriors of the Gododdin were wiped out *c.*580–600 by the Anglo-Saxons at the Battle of Catterick (*see under* CATTERICK), and around 617 the Castle Rock was taken by Edwin of Northumbria. In the 9th century Edinburgh and the whole of Lothian came under Kenneth MacAlpin, king of the Gaelic-speaking Scots of DALRIADA.

In the Middle Ages the settlement around the castle began to spread down the ridge extending east from Castle Rock, along what is now known as the ROYAL MILE. At the bottom end of the ridge, around the Abbey of HOLYROOD founded by David I in the 12th century, there grew up another settlement, Canongate, and the two gradually merged (although not formally so until 1856). The city that evolved along this spine, now known as the **Old Town** (as distinct from the New Town of the later 18th and early 19th century; *see below*), had some of the tallest tenement buildings in Europe, up to ten storeys high, in which aristocrats, merchants and artisans lived more or less cheek by jowl. The Old Town was a stinking place, a warren of vennels, closes and narrow streets, overhung by the higher floors of tenements, from which the residents would empty their chamber pots with cries of 'Gardyloo!' (from French *gardez l'eau* 'beware the water'). At the time of Scotland's first literary Renaissance, William Dunbar (?1456–?1513) wrote a pungent satire addressed to the city, decrying its smells and sounds and general 'laik of reformatioun' and polish:

> May nane pas throw your principall gaittis
> For stink of haddockis and scattis,
> For cryis of carlingis and debaittis,
> For fensum flyttingis of defame:
>   Think ye not schame,
> Befoir strangeris of all estaitis
> That sic dishonour hurt your name?
>
> (*gaittis* 'gates', *scattis* 'skates', *carlingis* 'old women', *debaittis* 'strifes', *fensum flyttingis* 'nauseous quarrels')

Some centuries later James Boswell, accompanying Dr Johnson on his visit in 1773, regretted that he 'could not prevent his [companion's] being assailed by the evening effluvia', while resident poet and roaring boy Robert Fergusson (1750–74) commented 'how snell [sharp] / Auld Reekie [Edinburgh] will at morning smell'. At the end of the century, another visitor was equally impressed:

> No smells were ever equal to Scotch smells. It is the School of Physic; walk the streets, and you would imagine that every medical man had been administering cathartics to every man, woman and child in the town. Yet the place [Edinburgh] is uncommonly beautiful, and I am in a constant balance between admiration and trepidation:
>   Taste guides my eye, where e'er new beauties spread,
>   While prudence whispers, 'Look before you tread.'
> Rev. Sydney Smith: letter (1798)

All this noxiousness was hardly in keeping with the spirit of the Scottish Enlightenment (*see under* SCOTTISH), of which Edinburgh was the brightest beacon (the novelist Tobias Smollett called it 'a hot bed of genius', and during his 1766 visit he met the likes of philosophers Adam Ferguson and David Hume and economist Adam Smith). So, beginning in 1767, development began to the north of the Old Town of a classical **New Town**, with many wide streets linking a pattern of crescents, squares and circuses, carefully planned by James Craig (*see also* PRINCES STREET); other architects involved in the development of the New Town included Robert Adam and William Playfair. The wealthier citizens soon left the teeming slums of the Old Town for the spacious terraces to the north, although Edinburgh's intellectual heart – in the form of the university and the law courts – remained in the Old Town (the magnificent classical Old College of the university, designed by Robert Adam, dates from this time). Much of the original New Town is preserved, and both Old and New Town became a UNESCO World Heritage Site in 1995.

The smoke and stench of the Old Town earned Edinburgh the nickname AULD REEKIE (Scots 'old smoky'), while the classicism of the New Town and the vigorous intellectual life of the city in the 18th century earned it the more complimentary sobriquet of the ATHENS OF THE NORTH. These two contrasting nicknames are archetypically representative of the polarities of the Caledonian Anti-syzygy (*see under* CALEDONIA), as is the split personality of the city itself:

> Edinburgh produces and sustains agonizing tensions of
> life
> – Edinburgh, a blinded giant who has yet to learn
> What the motive spirit behind his abilities really is.

> Hugh MacDiarmid: 'Talking with Five Thousand People in
> Edinburgh', from *Poetry Scotland No. 2* (1945)

Edinburgh is generally thought of as a genteel and rather pursed-lipped city; when Robert Burns came here in 1786 to find a printer for his poems, he found the Edinburgh people generally stuck-up:

> My curse upon your whunstane hearts,
>   Ye E'nbrugh gentry!

> (Scots *whunstane* 'whinstone', i.e. any hard, dark, smooth
> rock)

(He made an exception for Mrs Agnes MacLehose, whom he found more than attentive: she became his 'Clarinda' and the muse of his song 'Ae Fond Kiss'.) Glasgow folk have a pertinent saying:

> You can have more fun at a Glasgow funeral than at an
> Edinburgh wedding.

However, Glaswegians also say that Edinburgh is 'aw fur coat and nae knickers', a sharp insight into the contra-dictions of the city, for Edinburgh's Presbyterian uprightness has a dark flip side, and Auntie Edina from time to time gets blootered (drunk), pulls up her skirts and head-butts anybody in sight. For this is the city of Deacon Brodie, the respectable 18th-century burgher who burgled by night; the city of the 1736 Porteous Riots, so vividly recreated in Sir Walter Scott's *Heart of Midlothian* (1818; *see under* MIDLOTHIAN); the city haunted by James Hogg's Justified Sinner, predestined for salvation whatever crimes he com-mits; the city of Resurrectionists and of the serial murderers

Burke and Hare; the city whose rotten underbelly of drink, drugs and random violence is picked over by writers such as Ian Rankin and Irvine Welsh; the city where, according to Hugh MacDiarmid, 'the dead snatch at the living'. These and others have peered through the veil of respectability and seen where

> … history leans by a dark entry
> with words from his mouth
> that say *Pity me, pity me*
> *but never forgive.*

> Norman MacCaig: 'Old Edinburgh', from *A Man in My
> Position* (1969)

It comes perhaps as no surprise to learn that Robert Louis Stevenson (*see below*), creator of those embodiments of Manichean dichotomy, Dr Jekyll and Mr Hyde, was a native of the city.

For all its dark contradictions, however, Edinburgh can still tug at the hearts of those who have left her, and the view of the city from the peaks of the Pentland Hills is one never to forget, even when exiled to the South Seas:

> The tropics vanish, and meseems that I,
> From Halkerside, from topmost Allermuir,
> Or steep Caerketton, dreaming gaze again.
> Far set in fields and woods, the town I see
> Spring gallant from the shallows of her smoke,
> Cragged, spired, and turreted, her virgin fort
> Beflagged. About, on seaward-drooping hills,
> New folds of city glitter. Last, the Forth
> Wheels ample waters set with sacred isles,
> And populous Fife smokes with a score of towns.

> Robert Louis Stevenson: 'Untitled'

Stevenson was just one of many notables born in Edinburgh, among whom may be numbered: the mathe-matician John Napier (1550–1617), inventor of logarithms (although his birthplace, Merchiston Castle, was then well outside the city); the goldsmith and philanthropist George Heriot (1563–1624), who founded George Heriot's School in Edinburgh and a fund that eventually led to the founda-tion of Heriot-Watt College (now University) in 1885; James VI of Scotland and I of England (1567–1625), in Edinburgh Castle; Archibald Johnston, Lord Warriston (1611–63), the staunch Parliamentarian executed after the Restoration; the physician and satirical poet Archibald Pitcairne (1652–1713), who helped to found the medical school at Edinburgh in 1685; the philosopher David Hume (1711–76); the painter Allan Ramsay (1713–84); the physician James Lind (1716–94), who recommended the consumption of limes and lemons by seamen to prevent scurvy; James Hutton (1726–97), the founder of modern geology; the printer and scientist William Smellie (1740–95), first pub-lisher and editor of *Encyclopaedia Britannica*; the biographer and diarist James Boswell (1740–95); the sentimental novelist Henry Mackenzie (1745–1831), author of *The Man of Feeling* (1771); the poet Robert Fergusson (1750–74); Gilbert Elliot, 1st Earl of Minto (1751–1814), governor general of India (1807–13); the Common Sense philosopher Dugald Stewart (1753–1828), professor of moral philosophy at Edinburgh University; the portraitist Henry Raeburn (1756–1823; he was born in what was the village of Stockbridge, now part of the city); the painter Alexander Nasmyth (1758–1840); the physicist William Nicol (1768–1851), inventor of the Nicol prism for polarizing light; the poet and novelist Sir Walter Scott (1771–1832); the anatomist and surgeon Charles Bell (1774–1842), who gave his name to Bell's palsy; Henry Brougham (1778– 1868), Whig politician and reforming lord chancellor; Tory politician and prime minister Lord Aberdeen (1784–1860); the anatomist Robert Knox (1791–1862), unwitting client of the body-snatchers and murderers Burke and Hare; the topographical painter David Roberts (1796–1864); the Pre-Raphaelite painter and poet William Bell Scott (1811–90); Archibald Tait (1811–82), Archbishop of Canterbury; W.E. Aytoun (1813–65), founder of the Spasmodic School of poetry; the physicist and engineer William Rankine (1820–72), pioneer of thermodynamics; the world's worst poet, William McGonagall (1830–1902); the physicist James Clerk Maxwell (1831–79), pioneer of the theory of electromagnetism; the architect Norman Shaw (1831–1912); the inventor of the telephone, Alexander Graham Bell (1847–1922); the novelist and poet Robert Louis Stevenson (1850–94), in a number of whose novels – such as *Catriona* (1893) – the city features; the colonial administrator Leander Starr Jameson (1853–1917), leader of the notorious Jameson Raid into the Transvaal in 1896; the writer Arthur Conan Doyle (1859–1930), creator of Sherlock Holmes (a character inspired by Joseph Bell, under whom Conan Doyle studied medicine at Edinburgh); Kenneth Grahame (1859–1932), author of *The Wind in the Willows* (1908); the physiologist J.S. Haldane (1860–1936); Field Marshal Douglas Haig (1861–1928); the Irish socialist and revolutionary James Connolly (1870–1916); the painter S.J. Peploe (1871–1935), doyen of the Scottish Colourists (*see under* SCOTTISH); the painter William Russell Flint (1880–1969); the birth-control campaigner Marie Stopes (1880–1958); the writer and activist Naomi Mitchison (1897–1999); the poet Robert Garioch (1908–81); the poet Norman MacCaig (1910–96); the playwright William Douglas-Home (1912–92); the novelist Muriel Spark (b.1918), whose best-known work, *The Prime of Miss Jean Brodie* (1961), is set in Edinburgh; the Pop artist Eduardo Paolozzi (b.1924); the composer Thea Musgrave (b.1928); the actor Ian Richardson (b.1934); Conservative politician and former foreign secretary Malcolm Rifkind (b.1946); Labour prime minister Tony Blair (b.1953); the actor Simon Russell Beale (b.1961); and the 'laureate

of the Chemical Generation', Irvine Welsh (b.1961 in Leith), best known for his novel *Trainspotting* (1993).

Edinburgh's premier football clubs are Hibernian FC (nicknamed Hibs), who are widely supported by the Catholic population and have their stadium at Easter Road; and the Protestant-supported Heart of Midlothian (*see under* MIDLOTHIAN). Edinburgh hosted the 1970 and 1986 Commonwealth Games; legacies of the 1970 games include the elegant Commonwealth Pool and the Meadowbank Stadium (formerly home of Meadowbank Thistle FC – now Livingston FC – and currently of the amateur Edinburgh City FC).

These days Edinburgh is known for its liberal attitude towards the sex industry, and the city's so-called Pubic Triangle is home to a number of brothels, lap-dancing clubs and strip bars. The city is not exactly new to the industry: an 1842 survey found a total of 200 brothels, which were at their busiest during the annual General Assembly of the Church of Scotland. As if not content with Edinburgh's designation as 'Britain's Sex Capital', in 2003 the Scottish Arts Council and the city's Book Festival suggested that UNESCO initiate a City of Literature, with the assumption that Edinburgh should be the first city to be so crowned (apparently on the grounds that WAVERLEY STATION, the city's main railway terminus, is named after a novel); in 2004 UNESCO duly conceded the honour to the city. Another curious cultural bestowal of the city is the multiplex cinema: the first 'triplex' in Britain was created in the ABC in Edinburgh's Lothian Road in 1969.

There is a Mount Edinburgh in Australia (Queensland), a town called Edinboro in the USA (Pennsylvania) and several called Edinburg (Illinois, Indiana, Mississippi, North Dakota, Texas and Virginia). There is a city called Dunedin (Edinburgh's old name) in New Zealand (South Island). *See also* COLINTON, JOPPA, MORNINGSIDE *and* PORTOBELLO.

Blackwood's Edinburgh Magazine. A monthly literary magazine founded by William Blackwood in 1817, as a rival to the *Edinburgh Review* (*see below*). The first editors were John Wilson, writing under the name Christopher North, and Sir Walter Scott's son-in-law J.G. Lockhart. The latter's series of attacks on Keats in the magazine was said to have hastened the young poet's death, prompting the following lines:

'Tis strange the mind, that very fiery particle,
Should let itself be snuff'd out by an article.

Lord Byron: *Don Juan*, XI

Publication continued until 1981.

Duke of Edinburgh. A title awarded to Philip Mountbatten (né Schleswig-Holstein-Sonderburg-Glücksburg, a.k.a. Prince Philip a.k.a. Phil the Greek) on 19 November 1947, the day before his wedding to Elizabeth Windsor, the future Queen Elizabeth II. A recent portrait (2004) of the duke by Stuart

Pearson Wright shows him bare-chested, a few strands of cress growing from his raised finger (to symbolize his siring of heir and spares), and with a fly (a memento mori) on his shoulder. The painting is entitled *Homo sapiens, Lepidium sativum and Calliphora vommitoria*, these being the scientific names of the three species featured. When he first saw the portrait, the duke cried 'Gadzooks!' Asked by the artist whether he had caught a likeness, the duke spluttered 'I should bloody well hope not.'

The Duke of Edinburgh is worshipped as a god by adherents of cargo cults in some parts of the South Seas, but his divine status is not generally recognized in Edinburgh itself. The **Duke of Edinburgh's Award** is a charity aimed at promoting purposeful activity among the young.

Edinburgh Academy. An independent boys' school founded in 1824 by Sir Walter Scott and others, with the intention of turning 'Scots lads into English gentlemen'. Robert Louis Stevenson was a pupil, as was the great physicist James Clerk Maxwell, although for the most part the school has been content to churn out golf-playing, Tory-voting accountants, doctors and lawyers.

Edinburgh Castle. The castle of the city. Although Castle Rock, the crag on which it stands, has traces of prehistoric settlement (*see above*), the oldest structure of the present Edinburgh Castle is St Margaret's Chapel, which dates from the 12th century; other parts mostly date from the 16th century and after. The castle is replete with history, having been held at various times by Scots kings and English invaders. It was fiercely defended on behalf of Mary Queen of Scots by William Maitland and William Kirkcaldy of Grange in 1573, but they were forced to surrender to the Protestant forces of James Morton in June 1573. In neither 1715 nor 1745 did the Jacobites succeed in taking it. It still has a modest garrison, and hosts an annual military tattoo and Scotland's national war memorial.

A particularly bloody episode in the castle's history occurred in November 1440, during the minority of James II, when Chancellor Crichton invited his rival, the youthful Earl of Douglas, and his even younger brother to dinner at the castle; the bringing in of a black boar's head on a platter was a signal to Crichton's henchmen to fall on their guests and slaughter them. The 'Black Dinner' gave rise to the following rhyme:

Edinburgh Castle, towne and toure,
God grant thou sink for sinne!
And that even for the black dinoir
Earl Douglas got therein.

(Historians now believe that the whole thing might have been organized by the boys' uncle, James the Gross, who inherited the earldom.)

Another notable story concerning the castle concerns the Scottish crown jewels, which had been hidden away in a sealed chamber since the Act of Union in 1707; these were dramatically 'rediscovered' by Sir Walter Scott in 1818 and are now on display in the castle.

George Borrow's father was stationed at Edinburgh Castle in 1813, and the place is recalled in *Lavengro* (1851). The castle makes another literary appearance as the setting of Robert Louis Stevenson's novel *St Ives* (1897).

Edinburgh fog. A rich dessert made with double cream, sugar, vanilla essence, blanched almonds and ratafia biscuits.

Edinburgh International Festival. An annual festival of music, drama, opera and art, founded in 1947 by Rudolph Bing and held annually in August–September. It was described by the poet Hugh MacDiarmid as 'another lousy racket', but more amusedly celebrated by his fellow-poet-in-Scots, Robert Garioch, in the poem 'Embro to the Ploy' (Scots 'Edinburgh to the Festival'):

There's monie hartsom braw high-jinks
mixed up in this alloy
in simmer, whan aa sorts foregather
in Embro to the ploy.

(Scots *hartsom braw high-jinks* 'hearty fine carryings-on')

There is also an **Edinburgh Fringe Festival** held at the same time, in which numerous amateur and less established professional individuals and groups take part. Other add-ons include film, book and television festivals, and, as from 2003, a Festival Erotique. Comedy has loomed large since the 1980s, spurred on by the Perrier Award (from 1981) for best comedy show. The bewildering choice facing Fringe Festival-goers often means famously small audiences for individual performances, so there is intense competition for the best slots and the best venues.

Edinburgh Review. A quarterly Whig periodical, subtitled *The Critical Journal*, founded in 1802 by Henry Erskine, Sydney Smith and Francis Jeffrey, and edited by the latter (who was also a judge) until 1829. Contributors in its influential early decades included the jurist Henry Brougham, the politician and economist Francis Horner, the essayist William Hazlitt, the schoolmaster Thomas Arnold, the historian Thomas Carlyle and the historian Lord Macaulay. Publication continued until 1929.

Edinburgh rock. A stick-shaped confection, crumblier than Blackpool rock (*see under* BLACKPOOL) and ridged lengthwise along its surface. It is made from sugar, cream of tartar and water, and comes in a number of flavours and pastel shades.

Edinburgh Rugby. An Edinburgh-based professional rugby union team (one of only three in Scotland) that plays in the Celtic League alongside other professional teams from Wales and Ireland. The team is based at MURRAYFIELD.

Edinburgh's Folly. A pillared edifice on CALTON HILL, looking like an incomplete Parthenon. It is properly known as the National Monument, and is a memorial to the dead of the Napoleonic Wars. Its nickname comes from the story that it was unfinished owing to an absence of sufficient funds forthcoming from the tight-pursed citizenry of Edinburgh. However, the plans of the architect C.R. Cockerell and his assistant William Playfair demonstrate that they intended the unfinished look all along, in deliberate homage to a ruined Greek temple.

Flouers o Edinburgh, The. A satirical play (1947) by Robert MacLellan, focusing on the debate among the gentlemen of Edinburgh in the 18th century as to the relative desirability of using Scots or English in polite conversation.

Honourable Company of Edinburgh Golfers. The oldest golf club in the world, formed on Leith Links in 1744 as the Gentleman Golfers of Edinburgh. They subsequently moved to MUSSELBURGH, and then to MUIRFIELD.

Treaty of Edinburgh (17 March 1328). A treaty by which Edward III of England recognized Robert the Bruce as king of Scotland, thereby temporarily ending decades of conflict.

Treaty of Edinburgh (1474). A brief alliance between James III of Scotland and Edward IV of England by which the former's infant heir was betrothed to Edward's daughter Cecilia. However, the marriage never took place and the traditional hostilities soon resumed.

Treaty of Edinburgh (6 July 1560). Another name for the Treaty of Leith (*see under* LEITH).

Edinburghshire. The former name of MIDLOTHIAN.

Edington 'place by the bare hill', OE *ethe* 'bare' + *dun* (see DOWN, -DUN).

A village in Wiltshire, about 5 km (3 miles) northeast of Westbury. It is believed to be the site of a battle (also called the **Battle of Ethandun**) fought in 878, in which Alfred's Saxons ambushed an army of Danes under Guthrum, scattering and then pursuing them towards Chippenham. The Saxon victory led to the signing of the treaty of WEDMORE.

Edistone 'Ecghere's farm', OE *Ecgheres* possessive form of male personal name *Ecghere* (identifiable from the early 14th-century spelling *Egereston*) + -TON.

A village in Devon, 6 km (4 miles) south of Hartland Point.

Edith Weston *Edith* probably denoting its possession by Queen Eadgyth, wife of Edward the Confessor, in 1086; *Weston see* WESTON BEGGARD.

A village in Rutland (before 1997 in Leicestershire, before 1974 in Rutland), at the southeastern corner of Rutland Water (*see under* RUTLAND), about 8 km (5 miles) southeast of Oakham.

Edmonton 'Eadhelm's farmstead', OE male personal name *Eadhelm* + -TON.

A district in NORTH LONDON (N9, N18), in the borough of ENFIELD, between the River Lea to the east and Palmers Green to the west. The writer Charles Lamb lived and died

here, and John Keats lived here for a while. In the 18th and 19th centuries the Bell Inn at Edmonton was a popular destination for Londoners seeking a drink in the country – John Gilpin's wife got him to take her there to celebrate their wedding anniversary:

> Tomorrow is our wedding day
> And we will then repair
> Unto the Bell at Edmonton
> All in a chaise and pair.
>
> William Cowper: 'John Gilpin' (1785)

The countryside vanished in a sea of cheap working-class housing later in the 19th century.

The entertainer Bruce Forsyth (b.1928) was born in Edmonton. Charles Lamb (1775–1834) died after falling on his face in Edmonton High Street.

Edmonton is also the name of the capital of Alberta, Canada.

Witch of Edmonton, The. A tragi-comedy (1621) based partly on the story of Elizabeth Sawyer, who was hanged as a witch in April 1621. It is the collaborative work of several dramatists, including Thomas Dekker, John Ford, William Rowley and possibly John Webster.

Edvin Loach *Edvin* 'Gedda's fen or marshland', OE male personal name *Gedda* + *fenn*; *Loach* denoting manorial ownership in the Middle Ages by the de Loges family.

A village in Worcestershire (before 1998 in Hereford and Worcester, before 1974 in Worcestershire), about 16 km (10 miles) west of Worcester.

Edwinstowe 'Eadwine's holy place' (referring to St Edwin, 7th-century king of Northumbria), OE male personal name *Eadwine* + *stow* 'holy place'.

A village in Nottinghamshire, in SHERWOOD FOREST, on the River MAUN, about 11 km (7 miles) northeast of Mansfield. There is a chapel here dedicated to St Edwin, but whether this inspired or was inspired by the place's name is not clear.

The nearby Sherwood Forest Country Park is the location of the Major Oak. Said to have been full grown in the time of King John (reigned 1199–1216), the hollow of its trunk will hold 15 people (although new bark has diminished the opening); its girth is 11.3–11.6 m (37–38 ft), and the head covers a circumference of 73 m (239 ft); Robin Hood is said to have hidden in it, and also to have plighted his troth with Maid Marian beneath its boughs. It was originally called the Queen Oak; its present name is said to honour Major Hayman Rooke, an 18th-century local antiquarian, who was particularly fond of it. In 1990 the tree was drenched daily with thousands of gallons of water, because of fears that in the hot dry weather it could be destroyed by fire or drought. In 1992 it was cloned in a test tube so that exact copies will be growing when it dies.

Dr Ebenezer Cobham Brewer, editor of *Brewer's Dictionary of Phrase and Fable*, lived at Edwinstowe vicarage with his eldest daughter, the wife of the local rector, from 1878 until his death in 1897.

Edwyn Ralph *Edwyn* as *Edvin* (*see* EDVIN LOACH), first assimilated to the male personal name *Edwin* in the 16th century; *Ralph* denoting manorial ownership in the Middle Ages by an unidentified person called Ralph.

A village in Worcestershire (before 1998 in Hereford and Worcester, before 1974 in Worcestershire), about 17 km (11 miles) west of Worcester.

Eel Pie Island Originally, in the 15th century, *Goose Eyot* 'Goose Islet', and from the early 17th century *Parish Eyot*. The present name, which is first recorded in Charles Dickens's *Nicholas Nickleby* (1838–9), alludes to the island's 19th-century popularity as a venue for picnicking boating-parties, who here consumed quantities of that (then) Londoners' favourite, eel pie.

An island in the River THAMES[1] at TWICKENHAM, in the London borough of Richmond. It is 500 m (1800 ft) long, with about 50 houses, several houseboats, a footbridge connecting it with the mainland and a bird sanctuary at each end. It has something of a reputation as the home of artists and other bohemians. In 1996 much of its centre was devastated by a serious fire.

Effin Etymology unknown.

A village in County Limerick, near the border with Tipperary. It is the subject of much coarse wordplay.

Egdon Heath. A fictional stretch of heathland situated in Thomas Hardy's 'South Wessex'. It figures as a brooding presence in various of his novels (Michael Henchard's fate in *The Mayor of Casterbridge* (1886), for instance, is to die alone in a wretched hovel on the Heath), but it is most memorably evoked in the first chapter of *The Return of the Native* (1878), a novel into which its influence seeps at every interstice:

> A Saturday afternoon in November was approaching the time of twilight, and the vast tract of unenclosed wild known as Egdon Heath embrowned itself moment by moment … It was at present a place perfectly accordant with man's nature – neither ghastly, hateful, nor ugly: neither commonplace, unmeaning, nor tame; but, like man, slighted and enduring; and withal singularly colossal and mysterious in its swarthy monotony. As with some persons who have long lived apart, solitude seemed to look out of its countenance. It had a lonely face, suggesting tragical possibilities.

Hardy based it on an amalgam of heaths between Bournemouth and Dorchester, including one near his birthplace at HIGHER BOCKHAMPTON. Gustav Holst's tone poem *Egdon Heath* (1927) encapsulates in sound the Heath's vast emptiness and solitude.

Eggardon Hill. *See under* POWERSTOCK.

Eggborough 'Ecga's stronghold', OE male personal name *Ecga* + *burh* (*see* BURY).

A village in North Yorkshire, 6 km (4 miles) east of Knottingley.

Eggbuckland *Egg-* denoting manorial ownership in the early Middle Ages by a man called *Heca* + BUCKLAND.

A village in Devon, now a northeastern suburb of PLYMOUTH.

Egglescliffe. *See* EAGLESCLIFFE.

Egham 'Ecga's homestead or village', OE male personal name *Ecga* + HAM.

A town in Surrey, just to the southwest of Staines. Just west of the M25 and south of the River THAMES[1], it is in effect a southwestern suburb of London, albeit a comparatively spacious and salubrious one. It is home to Royal Holloway, a college of London University: founded as Royal Holloway College by Victorian pill manufactuer Thomas Holloway, it originally educated women only. Bedford College, formerly in REGENT'S PARK, merged with it in the 1980s. Remains of the earliest known river harbour in Britain, dating from the 8th century BC, have been found in Egham.

A prominent 17th-century resident of Egham was Sir John Denham, Surveyor-General and author of the influential pastoral poem 'Cooper's Hill' (1642) (*quoted under* THAMES[1]), which was inspired by the view of the Thames Valley from a local hilltop and would provide a model for Alexander Pope's *Windsor Forest* (1713) (*see under* WINDSOR). Cooper's Hill, which overlooks RUNNYMEDE, is now the site of the Commonwealth Air Forces Memorial.

Pink-bow-tied broadcaster and wit Frank Muir (1921–98) lived in Egham.

> Egham for me is like a comb crossed with a sponge.
>
> Peter O'Toole

Egloshayle 'church on an estuary', Cornish *eglos* 'church' (*see* ECCLES) + *heyl* 'estuary'.

A village in Cornwall, on the estuary of the River CAMEL, about 8 km (5 miles) northwest of Bodmin.

Egloskerry 'church of St Keri', Cornish *eglos* 'church' (*see* ECCLES) + *Keri* name of a saint (reputedly the daughter of Brychan in Cornish legend) who is patron of the local church.

A village in Cornwall, about 6 km (4 miles) northwest of Launceston.

Egremont 'sharp-topped hill', OFr *aigremont* 'pointed hill'.

A small town in western Cumbria (formerly in Cumberland), 9 km (5.5 miles) southeast of Whitehaven. The founding of ST BEES in the 7th century is associated with the lord and lady of **Egremont Castle**, although the present castle dates from *c.*1120 and was largely destroyed in the 16th century. In *Five Rivers* (1944) Norman Nicholson wrote of the castle:

Still the moated dungeons hide
Legends of poverty and pride
And murdered skulls are stuffed with lore
Of pillage, plunder, famine, fear
And dirk has carved upon the bone
'Blood will not show on the red stone.'

Since 1267 the town has held a Crab Fair on the third Saturday of September, in which apples (originally crab apples) are thrown from a cart, and the local youth attempt to climb a 10-m (30-ft) greasy pole. The Crab Fair also hosts the World Gurning Competition, in which the person who can make the ugliest face wins.

The medieval church at Egremont has a notable example of a sheela-na-gig, a sculptured figure of a grotesque naked woman exposing her genitals; this particular sheela-na-gig appears to be about to trim her pubic hair with a pair of shears.

Boy of Egremont, the. William de Romilly, the son of the powerful William Fitzduncan, a nephew of David I of Scotland, and at this time Lord of Egremont (Cumbria was then in the possession of the Scots). He was born in 1145, and was killed in 1157 when attempting to jump his horse across the STRID, a chasm in the River Wharfe in Yorkshire. High hopes had been pinned on the boy, described by the *Orkneyinga Saga* (*c*.1200) as 'William the Noble, whom all the Scots wished to take for their king', and the tale became an enduring tragedy. The story is told, with considerable deviations from historical accuracy, in William Wordsworth's **'The Boy of Egremont'**.

Egremont russet. A firm, rough-skinned dry-fleshed dessert apple, originating in the later Victorian era. It is hardy enough to be grown in Northern gardens.

Horn of Egremont, the. After the death of the Boy of Egremont, Egremont itself passed via his sister's marriage to the Lucy family. In around 1204 Richard de Lucy became Forester of Cumberland, and, the symbol of the forester being a horn, this may be the origin of the legend of the Horn of Egremont. According to the story, the Lord of Egremont was captured for ransom during the Crusades. His younger brother returned home to raise the ransom, but instead took over his brother's position. His brother, having been freed by his captor's besotted daughter, returned home and blew the horn that only the true Lord of Egremont can sound. The two brothers were eventually reconciled. A variation on the tale is told in Wordsworth's **'The Horn of Egremont Castle'** (1806).

Egypt The name probably suggests remoteness.

A village in Hampshire, about 11 km (7 miles) north of Winchester.

Eigg Gaelic *eag* 'notch'; this feature is clearly visible from Rum, running between An Sgurr and An Cruachan. Up to the 16th century the island was called *Eilean Nimban More*, 'island of the powerful women', possibly referring to the warrior women who, it is said, massacred St Donan and his monks in 617.

An island in the SMALL ISLES of the Inner HEBRIDES, in Highland (formerly in Inverness-shire), 11 km (7 miles) west of the mainland area of Arisaig, and 7 km (4.5 miles) southeast of Rum. It is separated from the island of Muck by the **Sound of Eigg**, and its most striking feature is the great basalt prow of the sheer-sided **Sgurr of Eigg** (properly An Sgurr, 'the sharp rock'), which has a height of 393 m (1289 ft). It was likened by the geologist Hugh Miller to:

… a piece of Babylonian wall, or the great Wall of China, only vastly larger, set down on the ridge of a mountain …

Hugh Miller: *The Cruise of the* Betsey (1856)

St Donan established a monastery on Eigg in the early 7th century, and his name is preserved in the settlement of Kildonan on the southeast side of the island. However, he and 67 of his monks were massacred in 617. Eigg later came into the possession of the MacDonalds, arch-enemies of the MacLeods on Skye. It is said that in 1577 the MacDonalds castrated some MacLeods who had come to Eigg a-ravishing, and in revenge the MacLeods returned in force. The MacDonalds hid in a cave but were discovered by the invaders, who lit a fire at the entrance and succeeded in suffocating some 200 of the fugitives. When Sir Walter Scott visited the 'Massacre Cave' in 1814, he found 'numerous specimens of mortality'.

Eigg was the birthplace of Kenneth MacLeod (b.1872), composer of songs such as 'The Road to the Isles' (*see* CUILLIN *and* RANNOCH). In the later 20th century the island came into the possession of a succession of unpopular owners from elsewhere, but in 1997 the crofters of Eigg, with the support of Highland Council and the Scottish Wildlife Trust, formed the Isle of Eigg Heritage Trust and bought the island from a German artist calling himself Maruma.

Eildon Hills Possibly 'cliff fort', Gaelic *ail* 'cliff' + *dùn* (*see* DOWN, -DON); but OE *eald* 'old' and *dun* in the sense of 'hill' could be represented in the name.

A strikingly isolated trio of small hills (the highest is 422 m / 1384 ft) above MELROSE, in Scottish Borders (formerly in Roxburghshire). There is a pre-Roman hill fort on the northern peak, and the Romans also maintained a signal station here (there was a large Roman camp at Newstead, on the Tweed at the foot of the hills). To the Romans the Eildons were known as **Trimontium** ('three mountains'), which gives the lie to the legend that Michael Scot (*c*.1175–1232), the Border wizard and scholar who went on to work at the court of the Holy Roman Emperor, employed a demon to split what was originally one hill into three.

Another story associated with the hills is that Thomas the Rhymer of nearby ERCILDOUNE was led into Elfland under the Eildons by the Queen of the Fairies, and stayed with her there for seven years. The place of his entry on the east side of the hills is marked by the Eildon Tree Stone:

True Thomas lay on Huntly bank;
A ferlie he spied with his e'e;
And there he saw a ladye bright,
Came riding down by the Eildon tree ...

When seven years were come and gane,
The sun blink'd fair on pool and stream;
And Thomas lay on Huntly bank,
Like one awaken'd from a dream.

Anon.: 'Thomas the Rhymer' (*ferlie* 'wonder, marvel')

A more permanent resident under the hills is supposed to be King Arthur, who sleeps here with his knights (presumably when not sleeping at several other locations in Britain claimed as his place of rest).

The Eildons can be seen from quite considerable distances in a number of directions, but they most famously form the backdrop to SCOTT'S VIEW.

Aneath the hills the gigants turn
In their ayebydan dwaum –
Finn under Nevis, the great King
Under Arthur's Seat, True Tammas
Neth the Eildons steers again ...

Sydney Goodsir Smith: '23rd Elegy: Farewell to Calypso', *Under the Eildon Tree* (1948) (*ayebydan dwaum* 'everlasting sleep', *steers* 'stirs').

There is an Eildon Reservoir in Victoria, Australia.

Eilean Donan 'island of St Donan', Gaelic *eilean* 'island' + personal name *Donnan*. St Donan or Donnan (d.617) founded a monastery on EIGG.

A tiny island just offshore in Loch Duich, Highland (formerly in Ross and Cromarty), some 12 km (7.5 miles) east of Kyle of Lochalsh. It is linked to the mainland by a bridge. There has been a castle here since 1230 (and before that there was a vitrified fort), and this was the seat of the Mackenzies of KINTAIL (later, earls of Seaforth). The old castle – occupied by Jacobites and Spanish troops – was heavily bombarded by the Royal Navy during the minor 1719 Rising (*see* GLEN SHIEL). A major renovation was carried out in 1932, and today the castle is one of the most photographed buildings in Scotland. It became familiar to an even wider audience when BBC1 featured it in one of its 'balloon' series of shorts between programmes.

Éire According to legend, from the name of an ancient goddess, but also derived from *Érainn*, the name of an ancient people in Ireland, subsequently sometimes used of all (or some of) the people of Ireland. After the 7th–8th centuries the term came to be used for Ireland itself, and its inhabitants began to be referred to as *Goídel* (Gaels). The Greek form of *Érainn* was *Iernoi* (later *Ierne*), which was transformed into the Latin name for Ireland, HIBERNIA. An alternative etymology suggests *Éire* is related to modern Irish *iarthar* 'west', but this is implausible.

The Irish name for IRELAND, and the official Irish name of Southern Ireland as prescribed in the constitution of 1937, replacing the name Irish Free State (*see under* IRISH). Éire became the Republic of Ireland in 1949, when it left the Commonwealth. The poetical name ERIN is an anglicized version of Éire.

Éire or Eriu was, with her sisters Fodla and Banba, one of the goddesses of the Tuatha Dé Danaan, and when the Milesians arrived in Ireland each of the sisters demanded that the island be named after her; in the event Amergin, chief poet of the Milesians, chose Éire. However, despite Amergin's choice, *Banba* and FÓTLA are both recorded as early names for Ireland, and are supposed by some to appear in the Scottish place-names BANFF and ATHOLL. *Elg* or *Elga*, also perhaps the name of a god or goddess, is another early name for Ireland, possibly occurring in the name ELGIN in Scotland.

When Eire first rose from the dark-swelling flood,
God blessed the green island, and saw it was good;
The emerald of Europe, it sparkled and shone,
In the ring of the world, the most precious stone.
In her sun, in her soil, in her station thrice blest,
With her back toward Britain, her face to the west,
Eire stands proudly insular, on her steep shore,
And strikes her high harp 'mid the ocean's deep roar.

William Drennan: 'Erin' (1795)

Éirne. The Irish name for the River ERNE.

Eiscir Riada 'running ridge', Irish *eiscir* 'eskar' + *riata* 'riding, running'.

A long, wide eskar system running across the centre of Ireland, formed during the last Ice Age. (Eskars or eskers are long winding ridges of sand or gravel deposited by streams running under glaciers or ice sheets.) The name is also spelt **Esker Riada** or **Riata**. In early Christian times, like many of the other eskars typical of the Irish MIDLANDS, it provided a roadway, in this case from TARA west to CONNACHT. It was known as the *Slí Mór* (Irish, 'big way'), and the section to the east of the important early monastic centre at CLONMACNOISE was called the Pilgrim's Road. Today it is used by sections of the N6 from Dublin to Galway. North of Tullamore in County Offaly the Eiscir Riada is called the **Arden Hills**.

Eisenhower Platz *Eisenhower* from Dwight D. Eisenhower; *Platz* 'Place', on the model of German square names (e.g. *Alexander-Platz* in Berlin).

A sardonic nickname given during the Second World War variously to GROSVENOR SQUARE, which was then largely taken up by the headquarters of the American forces in

Europe, commanded by General Eisenhower, and to SHEPHERD MARKET, whose services were extensively employed by American troops in London.

Elan Of uncertain origin, but possibly from Welsh *elain* 'hind, fawn'.

A river in Powys (formerly in Radnorshire), which joins the WYE[1] just south of RHAYADER. Its course, of about 20 km (12 miles), has been dammed to create the four **Elan Valley Reservoirs**, which provide Birmingham with water. Below the reservoirs is **Elan Village**.

Elcho Gaelic *aileach* 'rocky'.

A small settlement in Perth and Kinross (formerly in Perthshire, and then in Tayside region), on the south shore of the TAY, 5 km (3 miles) southeast of Perth. It is dominated by **Elcho Castle**, built in the 16th century by the Wemyss family, and is now in the care of Historic Scotland. The earldom of Wemyss was created in 1633, and the eldest son of the earl traditionally took the title **Lord Elcho**.

Elderslie 'grove of elder trees', OE *elle* 'elder tree' or *alor* 'alder tree' + -LEY.

A small town on the west side of Paisley, in Renfrewshire (formerly in Strathclyde region). It was traditionally the birthplace of William Wallace (1270–1305), the Scots national hero, referred to by the 15th-century poet Blind Harry the Minstrel as '**Knight of Elderslie**'. The Elderslie estate was in the hands of the Wallace family from the 13th century until 1729, but the surviving 'Wallace Mansion' is no older than the 16th century. There is an ancient 'Wallace's Yew' here, and there was a massive 'Wallace's Oak' (in which he and his men are meant to have hidden), but this was almost destroyed by souvenir hunters in the 18th and 19th centuries.

Electric Brae, the Scots *brae* 'hillside'.

A stretch of road on the A719, between TURNBERRY and AYR[1], in South Ayrshire (formerly in Strathclyde region). An inscription on a roadside stone here explains the name:

> The 'Electric Brae', known locally as Croy Brae. This runs the quarter mile from the bend overlooking Croy railway viaduct in the west (286 feet Above Ordnance Datum) to the wooded Craigencroy Glen (303 feet above A.O.D.) to the east. Whilst there is this slope of 1 in 86 upwards from the bend at the Glen, the configuration of the land on either side of the road provides an optical illusion making it look as if the slope is going the other way. Therefore, a stationary car on the road with the brakes off will appear to move slowly uphill. The term 'Electric Brae' dates from a time when it was incorrectly thought to be a phenomenon caused by electric or magnetic attraction within the Brae.

Part IV of the poem 'Exeunt' by Don Paterson (b.1963) is entitled '**The Electric Brae**'. It ends with the lines:

> On an easy slope, his father lets the engine
> cough into silence. Everything is still.
> He frees the brake: the car surges uphill.

Andrew Greig's novel *Electric Brae: A Modern Romance* (1992) has a background of Scottish climbing and politics.

Elephant and Castle From an 18th-century coaching inn in the locality that had a cast model of an elephant with a castle on its back as its sign (an elephant with a castle – a European rationalization of a howdah – on its back was an old heraldic device; it is the badge of the Cutlers' Company). The notion that the name is an alteration of *Infanta of Castile*, the holder of which rank was once engaged to Charles I, is a piece of romantic post-hoc folk-etymologizing.

A locality in SOUTH LONDON (SE1), in the borough of SOUTHWARK, between Lambeth to the west and Walworth to the southeast. It takes its name from a major road-junction in the area, which has formed an important communications hub since at least the 17th century; that in turn was named after a nearby inn (*see above*). The area was severely damaged by bombing in the Second World War, and the overbearing 1960s architecture that now characterizes the paired Elephant and Castle roundabouts is familiar to all who have had to negotiate them.

In the 21st century some estate agents, despairing of the dampening effect of the name 'Elephant and Castle' on the enthusiasm of potential house-buyers, started calling the area '**South City**'. Elephant and Castle Underground station, on the Bakerloo and Northern lines, was opened in 1890.

The actor Michael Caine (b.1933; real name Maurice Micklewhite) was born in Elephant and Castle.

London rhyming-slangsters have noted a (somewhat precarious) rhyme with *arsehole*, and utilized *Elephant and Castle* accordingly.

Elg(a). An early name for Ireland; *see* ÉIRE.

Elgin Possibly 'little Ireland', Gaelic *Eilgín*, diminutive of *Elg*.

A royal BURGH and ancient cathedral city in MORAY (formerly in Grampian region). It was the county town of the old county of Moray, then the administrative seat of Moray district, and now has the same status in Moray unitary authority. There are many fine old buildings, of which the most notable is the ruined **Elgin Cathedral**, which was founded in 1224 and completed by the end of the 13th century. It was known as **the Lantern of the North**. The cathedral, and the town, were burnt down by Alexander Stewart, Earl of Buchan, the Wolf of Badenoch (*see under* BADENOCH), in 1390, the earl having been disgruntled at his recent excommunication. It was in a battle near Elgin that, on 1 August 1040, Macbeth killed his cousin Duncan I and took over the throne.

As the country is rich and pleasant, so here are a great many rich inhabitants, and in the town of Elgin in particular; for the gentlemen, as if this was the Edinburgh, or the court, for this part of the island, leave their Highland habitations in the winter and come and live here for the diversion of the place and plenty of provisions ...

Daniel Defoe: *A Tour Through the Whole Island of Great Britain* (1724–6)

There are towns called Elgin in Canada (Manitoba, New Brunswick) and the USA (Arizona, Illinois, Iowa, North Dakota, Nebraska, Nevada. Oklahoma, Oregon, Texas, Utah). That in Illinois was named after the Scottish hymn tune 'Song of Elgin', while that in Oregon was named after the popular song 'Lost on the Lady Elgin', which commemorated a steamer that sank on the Great Lakes. There is also an Elgin Downs in Australia (Queensland) and an Elgin County in Canada (Ontario). The city of Niagara Falls in Canada (Ontario) was originally called Elgin.

Elgin, Thomas Bruce, 7th Earl of (1766–1841). The diplomat who at the beginning of the 19th century acquired from the Turks the sculptural friezes from the Parthenon in Athens now known as the **Elgin Marbles**. These controversially remain in the British Museum (*see under* BRITISH).

Elie Possibly from Gaelic *ealadh* 'tomb', or from Gaelic *eilean* 'island'.
A seaside village in Fife, some 16 km (10 miles) south of St Andrews, on the north shore of the Firth of Forth (*see under* FORTH). It united with neighbouring Earlsferry in 1929, and is sometimes referred to as **'the Elie'**. Elie is said to derive its name from a once-famous cemetery, while Earlsferry is named after the story that Macduff, the Earl of Fife, hid from Macbeth in 'Macduff's Cave' at nearby Kincraig Point, before being ferried across the Forth to safety. There were ferries from here to Dunbar until the building of the Forth bridges. Today Elie is a popular beach and golf resort.
Earlsferry was the birthplace of the great golfer James Braid (1870–1950), who won the British Open five times.

Eliseg's Pillar From the name of Prince Eliseg of Powys.
A 9th-century stone pillar in Denbighshire (formerly in Clwyd), a few hundred metres north of VALLE CRUCIS ABBEY, which is possibly named after it (although the pillar was not actually a cross). All that remains now is a 2.5-m (8-ft) stump, but it was originally 8 m (26 ft) high. It was erected by one Cyngen (d.854) in honour of his great-grandfather Eliseg, Prince of POWYS. The pillar was badly damaged in the Civil Wars, but in 1696 an antiquary recorded its inscriptions from the remains, so preserving information about the lineage of the princes of Powys.

Elland 'cultivated land by the river', OE *ea* (*see* EA-) + *land* '(newly) cultivated land'.
An industrial town in West Yorkshire, 24 km (15 miles) southwest of Leeds. In LEEDS[1] itself, **Elland Road** has been the home ground of Leeds United FC since 1919.

Ellendun. A 9th-century battle site thought to have been at WROUGHTON.

Ellenfoot. The previous name of the town of MARYPORT.

Ellen's Isle. *See under* LOCH KATRINE.

Ellesmere Port *Ellesmere* because the *Ellesmere* Canal joins the River Mersey at this point. The canal in turn took its name from the Shropshire market town of *Ellesmere* ('Elli's pool', OE *Elles* possessive form of male personal name *Elli* + *mere* 'pool, lake'), from which it ran as an arm of the Shropshire Union Canal. The name *Ellesmere Port* is first recorded in 1796.
A town and port in Cheshire, on the south bank of the River MERSEY, about 13 km (8 miles) south of Liverpool and 11 km (7 miles) north of Chester. It grew up around the tidal basin constructed in the late 18th century by Thomas Telford for the use of shipping passing between the **Ellesmere Canal** and the Mersey estuary. It is now an important site manufacturing petroleum products.

Ellisland. *See under* NITH.

Ellon Possibly from Gaelic *eilean* 'island'.
A town on the River YTHAN, in Aberdeenshire (formerly in Grampian region), 24 km (15 miles) north of Aberdeen. It was once the 'capital' of BUCHAN.

Elm '(place) at the elm-trees', OE *elmum* dative plural of *elm* 'elm-tree'.
A village in Cambridgeshire, about 3 km (2 miles) south of Wisbech.

Elmbridge 'Emel bridge', OE *Emel* former name of the River MOLE[1] + *brycg* 'bridge'.
An administrative district of northern Surrey, encompassing COBHAM[2], MOLESEY, ESHER, LEATHERHEAD, THAMES DITTON, WALTON-ON-THAMES and WEYBRIDGE. It was formed in 1972, taking the name of a Saxon Hundred that had occupied much the same area a thousand years before.

Elmet An OCelt name of unknown meaning.
An ancient Romano-British kingdom in what is now the southwest of Yorkshire. It survived into the 7th century, when it was taken over by the Anglo-Saxon kingdom of DEIRA. The name survives in various place names, e.g. **Barwick in Elmet** (home of a 26-m / 86-ft maypole, the tallest in the country until Ansty in Wiltshire erected one 3 m / 10 ft higher) and **Sherburn in Elmet**, and in the name of a parliamentary constituency. Its capital may have been at PUDSEY.

Remains of Elmet. A volume by Ted Hughes, published in 1979 with photographs by Fay Godwin, recalling his childhood in the Calder Valley, which he describes as 'the last ditch of Elmet'.

Elstree 'Tidwulf's boundary tree', OE *Tidwulfes* possessive form of male personal name *Tidwulf* + *treow* 'tree'; the initial *t* disappeared in the 13th century due to confusion with the end of a preceding *at*.

A town in Hertfordshire, just beyond the northwestern edge of GREATER LONDON, within the M25 and just to the east of the M1, between Barnet to the east and Watford to the west.

It is best known for its film studios, now known as **Elstree Film and Television Studios**. Filming in Elstree dates from 1914, when Neptune Studios opened on a site there chosen for its proximity to London. They closed in 1917 but were succeeded by a sprawling complex of studios soon dubbed 'the British Hollywood'. The first British 'talkie', *Blackmail*, was directed by Alfred Hitchcock at Elstree in 1929, and in the 1930s a stream of thrillers, comedies and musicals poured from the site. Following the Second World War Elstree produced such British classics as *The Dam Busters* (1954) and also attracted American stars like Gregory Peck in *Moby Dick* (1954) and Cary Grant in *Indiscreet* (1957). Its fortunes then flagged, but Stanley Kubrick kept the studios busy with *2001: A Space Odyssey* (1968) and George Lucas even more so with *Star Wars* (1976). Towards the end of the 20th century diversification into television production became necessary, and hit programmes such as *EastEnders* (1985–) and *Big Brother* (2000) came out of Elstree.

Eltham 'homestead or river-meadow frequented by swans' or 'Elta's homestead or river-meadow', OE *elfitu* 'swan' or male personal name *Elta* + *ham* 'homestead' or *hamm* 'river-meadow' (*see* HAM).

A southeastern suburb (SE9) of London (formerly in Kent), in the borough of GREENWICH, between Lewisham to the west and Sidcup to the east. Its name is pronounced 'eltəm'.

It is probably best known for **Eltham Palace**, a royal palace from the days of Edward I (1239–1307). Henry VIII was an enthusiastic visitor early in his reign, but later he tired of it. Later monarchs found little use for it and gradually it fell into disrepair. Of the surviving parts, the most notable is the Great Hall, one of London's few surviving examples of secular Gothic architecture, with the third largest hammerbeam roof in England. Stephen Courtauld took a lease on the palace in the 1930s and built a new house there. An outstanding example of Art Deco design, it is now open to the public.

The comedian Bob Hope (1903–2003) was born in Eltham; and Well Hall House in Eltham (which no longer exists) was the home (1899–1921) of the children's writer E[dith] Nesbit (1858–1924).

Eltham earned an unwelcome notoriety in the 1990s as the scene of the murder in 1993 of the black teenager Stephen Lawrence, the investigation of which raised questions of racism within the Metropolitan Police.

There is a town called Eltham in the North Island of New Zealand.

Treaty of Eltham. A treaty concluded at Eltham on 18 May 1412, under the terms of which Henry IV of England made an alliance with the Armagnaçais against the Burgundians.

Ely[1] 'district where eels can be found', OE *œl, el* 'eel' + *ge* 'district'. (In the 8th century the Venerable Bede recorded that Ely was named after the large number of eels in the surrounding area.)

A cathedral city in Cambridgeshire, on the GREAT OUSE, about 24 km (15 miles) northeast of Cambridge. It grew up on an area of raised ground amid the surrounding FENS. St Etheldreda founded an abbey here in 670. The building of the present **Ely Cathedral** began in the late 11th century, but many parts of it are from a considerably later period, notably the extraordinary Octagon, an eight-sided central crossing-tower topped by a wooden lantern (a glazed structure), which was added in the first half of the 14th century. Ely's splendid isolation ended in the 17th and 18th centuries, when its fenland moat was drained (the land now supports agriculture, notably the growing of sugar beet), but from a distance across the level landscape, or even suddenly glimpsed from closer to, the sight of its cathedral like a great ship on an empty ocean can still take the breath away.

The great English polyphonist Christopher Tye (*c*.1500–73), an innovator in the 16th-century change of musical and liturgical styles from Roman to Anglican, was appointed choirmaster at Ely Cathedral in 1541 or 1542. King's School, Ely was founded in 1543.

There are towns called Ely in the USA (Iowa, Minnesota, Nevada).

Ely Coucher Book, the. A survey of the Bishop of Ely's lands, commissioned by Bishop Hugo de Northwold in 1251, containing detailed descriptions of landed estates, types of land, field names, woods and meadows.

Isle of Ely. Originally, the raised rocky 'island' among the fens on which Ely and its cathedral were built. It is 11 km (7 miles) long and 6 km (4 miles) wide. The only means of access through the surrounding marshes and meres was by boat or causeway. It served as a place of refuge, and Hereward the Wake hid out here during his campaign against the Normans in the 11th century. The name later came to be applied to a much larger area of East Anglia, an administrative unit with Ely as its chief town. It shared boundaries with Norfolk, Suffolk, Cambridgeshire, Huntingdonshire, Holland and the Soke of Peterborough, and its other main town was MARCH. It was absorbed into Cambridgeshire in 1965.

Ely² Etymology unknown.

A river in south Wales, some 45 km (28 miles) long. It rises in RHONDDA CYNON TAFF and flows generally south-eastwards through the VALE OF GLAMORGAN to enter the Bristol Channel (*see under* BRISTOL) at CARDIFF. It gave its name to the former district of TAFF-ELY.

Ely O'Carroll From the name of a historical-legendary king, *Eile*, a descendant of Owen More, and the *O'Carroll* family.

A traditional area comprising much of County OFFALY, dominated by the O'Carroll family until it was planted with English settlers in 1619. The O'Carrolls had their stronghold at the heavily haunted LEAP CASTLE.

Emain Macha. *See under* NAVAN FORT.

Embankment, the. As a general term for a structure confining a river, *embankment* dates from the late 18th century, but in the context of modern London it refers more specifically to what is known in full as the **Thames Embankment**, a 5.5 km (3.5 mile) stretch of retaining wall along the north bank of the River THAMES¹, from VICTORIA² Embankment in the east to CHELSEA Embankment in the west. Built between 1868 and 1874 to the designs of Sir Joseph Bazalgette, it keeps the Thames in check while providing a conduit for drains and sewers. Along most of its length it is topped with a broad thorough-fare, and several attractive gardens have been laid out beyond.

Although 'the Embankment' can apply to all of it (and indeed to the 1.5 km / 1 mile Albert Embankment on the other side of the Thames), for most Londoners the name has a very particular application to the **Victoria Embankment**, site of Cleopatra's Needle, which extends from Black-friars Bridge to Westminster Bridge. The closeness of the association was confirmed in 1976 by the renaming of Charing Cross Underground station as 'Embankment'.

It is a conventional magnet to those down on their luck, and fictional characters contemplating ending it all can often be found trudging along the Embankment, coat clutched tightly against the chilling Thames mist, eye-ing the possibilities of the parapet or a nearby bridge. Non-suicidal down-and-outs opt for a makeshift bed under the arch of Charing Cross Bridge (*see under* CHARING CROSS).

> The fear of the sack like a maggot in his heart. How it eats at them, that secret fear! Especially on winter days, when they hear the menace of the wind. Winter, the sack, the workhouse, the Embankment benches!
>
> George Orwell: *Keep the Aspidistra Flying* (1936)

Embro. The vernacular version of EDINBURGH's name. The form is used, for example, in Robert Garioch's poem about the Edinburgh Festival:

> Furthgangan Embro folk come hame
> for three weeks in the year,
> and find Auld Reekie's no the same,
> fu sturrit in a steir.
>
> > 'Embro to the Ploy' (Scots *furthgangan* 'wandering abroad, absent' (literally 'going forth'), *ploy* 'festival', *Auld Reekie* 'old smoky' (i.e. Edinburgh), *sturrit in a steir* 'stirred up into a confusion')

In Glaswegian, the name is more likely to come out as *Embra*.

Emerald Isle. A once-poetic and now-hackneyed name for IRELAND. Green is Ireland's national colour, reflecting the country's rain-soaked lushness. The name was coined in a poem by Dr William Drennan (1754–1820), first pres-ident of the United Irishmen and a founder of the Belfast Academical Institution:

> Arm of Eire, be strong! but be gentle as brave!
> And, uplifted to strike, be still ready to save!
> Let no feeling of vengeance presume to defile
> The cause of, or men of, the Emerald Isle.
>
> > William Drennan: 'Erin' (1795)

The image soon caught on, as we find in these lines by John Philpot Curran (1750–1817):

> Dear Erin, how sweetly thy green bosom rises!
> An emerald set in the ring of the sea,
> Each blade of thy meadows my faithful heart prizes,
> Thou queen of the West! the world's cushla ma chree.
>
> > 'Cushla ma Chree'

Emerald Isle Express. A title formerly given to one of the train services running between London and Holyhead (from where there is a ferry to Dún Laoghaire).

Emly Irish *Imleach* 'borderland'. The full Irish name is *Imleach Iobhair*, the second element meaning 'yew tree'.

A small village in County Tipperary, 13 km (8 miles) west of Tipperary itself. There was a pre-Christian sanctuary here associated with Ailbhe, a legendary forerunner of St Ailbhe (d.527), who had a church here. Emly was the ecclesiastical centre of MUNSTER before CASHEL rose to prominence in the 12th century, and it continued as the seat of a see until the Reformation. Today it is part of the archdiocese of **Cashel and Emly**, the cathedral of which is at THURLES.

Emmerdale. The name, since 1989, of the television soap based on the village of ARNCLIFFE in the YORKSHIRE DALES. Between 1972 and 1989 the soap was known more fully as *Emmerdale Farm*. *Emmerdale* has also, since the 1970s, been rhyming slang for 'arm'.

Emminster. A fictional name for BEAMINSTER as adopted by Thomas Hardy in *Tess of the D'Urbervilles* (1891). In 1990 Macmillan publishers issued the '**Emminster Edition**' of Hardy's writings, based on the earlier Wessex Edition (*see under* WESSEX).

Emmonsails Heath The etymology of the first word is obscure: since the area is technically in AILSWORTH parish, the second part of the word may derive from the male OE personal name *Ægel*, as in the parish name; *Emmons-* may be a manorial affix.

The former name for an area of heathland between Peterborough and HELPSTON, whose gauntly beautiful winter landscape was evoked in the poem 'Emmonsails Heath in Winter' by John Clare (1793–1864), the 'Northamptonshire Poet' (*see under* NORTHAMPTONSHIRE):

> I love to see the old heaths withered brake
> Mingle its crimpled leaves with furze and ling
> While the old heron from the lonely lake
> Starts slow and flaps his melancholly wing
> And oddling crow in idle motions swing
> On the half-rotten ash trees topmost twig
> Beside whose trunk the gipsey makes his bed

Emmonsails Heath is now known as the Castor Hanglands (*see under* CASTOR). In Clare's day it was in Northamptonshire, but it is now in Peterborough unitary authority.

End of the World, the. Another name for the abandoned village of COALCLEUGH.

Endon 'Eana's hill', or 'hill where lambs are reared', OE male personal name *Eana* or *ean* 'lamb' + *dun* (*see* DOWN, -DON). A village in Staffordshire, about 6 km (4 miles) southwest of Leek. The annual ceremony of well-dressing, in which the local wells are decorated, is held every May.
See also TISSINGTON.

Enfield 'Eana's open land', or 'open land where lambs are reared', OE male personal name *Eana* or *ean* 'lamb' + FIELD. A town and borough in NORTH LONDON (before 1965 in Middlesex), between the River LEA to the east and BARNET to the west. Its origins are pre-Norman Conquest, and it was a prosperous town in the Middle Ages and later (there is a Tudor grammar school, for example). The central urban area, around the former village green, is known as **Enfield Town**. The borough of Enfield embraces EDMONTON as well as the leafier and posher Enfield and Southgate (*see* SOUTHGATE).

A slump in Enfield's fortunes began to be reversed with the coming of the railway in 1849, but before then, in 1819, an event had occurred that was to take the town's name round the world: the opening of the Royal Small Arms Factory. The factory's products came to be identified by the town's name, notably the **Enfield rifle**. This weapon's key feature was the type of rifling inside its barrel. Then in the late 19th century the American J.P. Lee came along with an improved design for the bolt action, and the **Lee-Enfield rifle** was born. Introduced in 1895, it was the British Army's main infantry weapon in the First and Second World Wars. The name is present too, but disguised, in *Bren gun*, the

term for a type of light machine-gun introduced in the 1930s: the gun was originally made in Brno, a Czech town, whence the *Br*, and was later manufactured at the Enfield factory – *Bren*.

The world's first automated cash dispenser came into operation in Enfield, at a branch of Barclay's Bank in June 1967.

The Conservative Defence Secretary Michael Portillo's loss in 1997 of his Enfield Southgate parliamentary seat to New Labour's radiant Stephen Twigg (before 1 May 1997 it was considered a rock-solid suburban Tory stronghold) has entered modern British political folklore, the count of the votes cast and announcement of the final result being witnessed by millions of (mostly) gleeful small-hours viewers on televison and even spawning the title of a book about the 1997 general election, *Were You Still Up for Portillo?*

Saracens rugby union club, originally founded in 1876, was based in Enfield until 1997, when it moved to WATFORD[1] to share Watford FC's Vicarage Road ground.

Sir Joseph Bazalgette (1819–91), the civil engineer who built London's sewerage system and also the Victoria, Chelsea and Albert Embankments, was born in Enfield, and the poet John Keats attended school here while living in Edmonton. There is a town called Enfield in Connecticut, USA.

Enfield Chase. A large expanse of open land to the northwest of Enfield Town which in the Middle Ages was a royal hunting forest (*chase* once meant 'a tract of land for breeding and hunting wild animals'). The southwestern corner of it is now taken up by Trent Park, a country park.

Engine Common *Engine* perhaps referring to a particular agricultural machine, or possibly denoting ownership of land by a public house named 'The Engine'. A village in South Gloucestershire (before 1996 in Avon, before 1974 in Gloucestershire), on the northwestern outskirts of Chipping Sodbury.

England 'land of the Angles' (the name of the Germanic people who settled in England from the late 4th century onwards and who came from Angeln (etymologically an 'angle or corner of land') in what is now Schleswig in northern Germany), OE *Engla* possessive form of *Engle* 'Angles' + *land*. A country (pronounced 'inglənd') in the southern part of BRITAIN, the largest political division of the United Kingdom of Great Britain and Northern Ireland. Its capital is LONDON.

It has borders with WALES to the west and SCOTLAND to the north, and it is separated from the mainland of Europe by the ENGLISH CHANNEL and the NORTH SEA. In the north are uplands and mountainous areas: the PENNINES, the LAKE DISTRICT, the NORTH YORK MOORS, the PEAK DISTRICT. To the southwest are the granite plateaux of DARTMOOR and EXMOOR. Between the two are sandwiched the lowlands of the MIDLANDS, EAST ANGLIA and the SOUTHEAST. The southwestern, western and north-western parts of the country, exposed to the Atlantic and cosseted by the Gulf Stream, tend to be wetter, the north-eastern and eastern parts relatively cool and dry, with south and southeastern counties often recording the highest temperatures. England's chief rivers are the THAMES[1] and the SEVERN.

The majority of the land area is still given over to agriculture, and there is a long history of mineral extraction (its main manifestation, coal-mining, went into serious decline in the second half of the 20th century, but this was to some extent offset by the exploitation of offshore oil and gas supplies). England was the cradle of the Industrial Revolution, and the heavily industrialized areas of YORK-SHIRE, LANCASHIRE, TYNESIDE, Teesside (see under TEES) and the WEST MIDLANDS (now reinventing themselves in a post-industrial world) are its legacy.

The island that the Romans left as BRITANNIA was politically undifferentiated, but certain boundaries did suggest themselves: the mountains of Wales, the crags of Dartmoor and the intransigence of the inhabitants of NORTH BRITAIN. It was up to these limits that the Germanic peoples from northwestern Continental Europe – the Angles, the Saxons, the Jutes – spread out as they settled in the island from the late 4th century. They created their own kingdoms – broadly speaking, the Angles in the Midlands and the north, the Saxons in the west and southwest, the Jutes in the southeast – which remained separate and often hostile entities. Offa, King of MERCIA, came close to uniting them in the 8th century. Most of the country apart from WESSEX came under his sway, and he declared himself **Rex Anglorum** – a title recognized by Pope Hadrian I. His creation fell apart after his death, however, and it was not until the 10th century that Alfred the Great's son Edward and his grandson Athelstan were able to consolidate Alfred's achievement (the repulsion of the Danes – see also DANELAW and the FIVE BOROUGHS – and the re-establishment of an independent and vigorous Wessex) by subduing the Midlands and North of the country and bringing it under a single united rule – as it essentially has been ever since.

In the early part of the Anglo-Saxon period, before the Danish conquest of the 9th century, the generic name for what we now know as England had been **Angel-cynn** (literally 'race of the Angles'). This originally denoted the combined Germanic peoples in the island (presumably with a pragmatic nod to the greater numbers and influence of the Angles), and came to be applied to the territory they occupied. It was a translation of the 8th-century Venerable Bede's *gens Anglorum*, which represented more an aspiration than a description of current reality. At around that time, **Engla-land** (see etymology *above*) does seem to

have been used as the name of the territory occupied by the Angles (as opposed to the Saxons), but from the late 9th century onwards *Engla-land* was England. The earliest record we have of this usage is from the *Anglo-Saxon Chronicle*, recording the year 1014:

> And æfre ælcne Deniscne cyng utlah of Engla lande gecwædon.
>
> ('And they declared every Danish king outlawed from England for ever.')

(Had the Saxons been more territorially dominant than the Angles, England might today be named after them – and indeed in moments of exasperation the Scots refer to the English as 'Sassenachs', their version of *Saxon*, while the Welsh word for 'English' is *Saesneg*.)

According to legend, when the future Pope Gregory the Great (540–604) saw some attractive fair-haired youths in the slave market, he asked where they had come from. He was told that they were Angles and also heathen. '*Non Angli, sed angeli*' ('Not Angles, but angels') was his simpering comment. The boys evidently made a lasting impression, because when Gregory became Pope, he despatched Augustine to England to convert the inhabitants to Christianity (Christianity of a late Roman kind had existed, and of course Celtic Christianity was being spread in the north and west of Britain, but the Anglo-Saxons were 'pagans'). Augustine and his companions landed on the ISLE OF THANET in 597, and he established his see at CANTERBURY[1]. Ever since then, England has been officially a Christian nation (see **Church of England** *below*).

Following the Norman Conquest of 1066, large parts of France were added to the realm of the kings of England. Normandy itself was lost as early as 1204, but other French territories, including Aquitaine and Poitou, were ruled by English monarchs for many centuries more, and not until Calais was retaken by France in 1558 did England revert to being a completely non-Continental fortress.

Wales was subdued in the late 13th century by Edward I, who built a series of great castles (at CAERNARFON, CONWY[2], BEAUMARIS, HARLECH, etc.) to keep the Welsh in their place. There was an uprising in the early 15th century, led by Owain Glyndwr, but it petered out, and the advent of the Welsh-descended Tudor dynasty in England improved relations. By the Act of Union of 1536 Wales was joined to England, with the right of representation at the WESTMINSTER Parliament. The link has always been closer than that between England and Scotland was to be, particularly in legal matters (see *below*), and the quasi-official entity of **England and Wales** evolved, to which laws applied that were passed by the British parliament but which did not cover Scotland (or NORTHERN IRELAND). The name is also used in the titles of certain supranational bodies – for example, the England and Wales Cricket Board (which, however, perhaps significantly, abbreviates itself to simply ECB).

In the Middle Ages England made repeated attempts, both violent and diplomatic, to annex Scotland. Matters looked promising in 1603 when James VI of Scotland ascended the throne of England as James I, but then it was the English who dragged their feet, unwilling to sacrifice centuries of glorious isolation (a tune played again 400 years later over membership of the EEC, the European currency, etc.). The bond was finally made with the Act of Union of 1707, which joined England and Wales with Scotland in a new nation called GREAT BRITAIN. Scotland had representatives at the Westminster parliament, but preserved its own separate legal system.

The British state was to grow further over the ensuing century (Ireland was swallowed up in 1801, to form the UNITED KINGDOM), but thereafter the trajectory of history turned towards separation. Southern Ireland left in 1922, and towards the end of the 20th century Scotland achieved a large measure of devolution, Wales somewhat less. England was close to being on its own again.

Historically, the main territorial division of England has been the county. At the start of the 21st century there are (if the somewhat anomalous Greater London is included) 35 on the traditional model. The largest is NORTH YORKSHIRE, the second largest CUMBRIA, the third largest DEVON[1] and the smallest BEDFORDSHIRE. Reforms of the late 20th century introduced bodies outside of the traditional county structure, including (in the 1970s) metropolitan counties (such as MERSEYSIDE and the WEST MIDLANDS), of which there are presently six, and (in the 1990s) unitary authorities, of which there are 46.

The name 'England' is strongly associated with Britain, and there are many, particularly those from abroad, for whom the distinction is too subtle. It is commonly observed, for example, that Americans often refer to Britain as England. This is especially irksome to the SCOTS and the WELSH, who feel, understandably, that the English are effectively pocketing the credit for Scottish and Welsh achievements.

In the sporting sphere, the 'home countries' have tended each to field their own national team, and when a joint effort is required (as at the Olympic Games) it is made under the banner of Britain or the United Kingdom. As so often, however, cricket does not quite fit the pattern: the British team that plays test matches is called England, and from time to time contains Welsh and Scottish players (there are representative teams called Scotland and Wales, but they do not play at the same level of competition).

The patron saint of England is St George, and it is his red cross on a white ground that adorns the national flag (and often also, in face paint, the visages of England sports fans). In the latter part of the 20th century, the hijacking of the English flag by racist nationalists led to some disquiet over its more general use. When an English, as opposed to British, national anthem is needed, Elgar's *Land of Hope and Glory* is usually pressed into service.

> Oh, to be in England
> Now that April's there,
> And whoever wakes in England
> Sees, some morning, unaware,
> That the lowest boughs and the brushwood sheaf
> Round the elm-tree bole are in tiny leaf,
> While the chaffinch sings on the orchard bough
> In England–now!
>
> Robert Browning: 'Home-Thoughts, from Abroad' (1845)

> And what should they know of England who only
> England know?
>
> Rudyard Kipling: 'The English Flag' (1892)

> There'll always be an England
> While there's a country lane,
> Wherever there's a cottage small
> Beside a field of grain.
>
> Ross Parker and Hugh Charles: 'There'll always be an England' (1939)

> This royal throne of kings, this sceptered isle,
> This earth of majesty, this seat of Mars,
> This other Eden, demi-paradise,
> This fortress built by Nature for herself
> Against infection and the hand of war,
> This happy breed of men, this little world,
> This precious stone set in the silver sea,
> Which serves it in the office of a wall,
> Or as a moat defensive to a house,
> Against the envy of less happier lands,
> This blessèd plot, this earth, this realm, this England.
>
> William Shakespeare: *Richard II* (1595), II.i

Boast of England, the. A name given to the diminutive nursery-tale character Tom Thumb by Richard Johnson, who in 1599 published a 'history of this ever-renowned soldier, the Red-Rose Knight, surnamed The Boast of England'.

Church of England. The institutionalized and established Christian church in England, which dates from 1534, when Henry VIII severed links with Rome. Under the Act of Supremacy of that year, the sovereign was designated 'the only supreme head of the Church' (watered down slightly to 'Supreme Governor' in the Act of 1559). Doctrinal changes were largely effected in the reign of Edward VI (1547–53) and embodied in the Book of Common Prayer of 1549 and the more obviously Protestant version of 1552. Under the title 'Anglican', the Church's communion today spreads around the world. Its primate is the Archbishop of Canterbury.

England expects that every man will do his duty. Lord Nelson's famous signal to his fleet before the Battle of Trafalgar (1805). The intended signal was 'England confides (etc.)', but the signal officer obtained permission to substitute 'expects' in order to save hoisting seven signal flags, as the word 'confides' was not in the signal book. Still today, 'England expects!' is shorthand for 'big effort now needed'.

England, home and beauty. England as the Englishman's and Englishwoman's native land, especially as seen after a time abroad. The phrase comes from John Braham's patriotic poem 'The Death of Nelson' (1812):

> In honour's cause I fall at last.
> For England home and beauty,
> For England, home and beauty.

England, Their England. A novel (1933) by A.G. MacDonell exposing the foibles of the English via the comical misadventures of a young Scotsman, Donald Cameron, in England. It includes a memorable description of a village cricket match. Its title was inspired by W.E. Henley's lines:

> What have I done for you,
> England, my England?
> 'Pro Rege Nostro' (1900)

Englands Helicon. A miscellany of Elizabethan verse, published in 1600, and including pieces by Edmund Spenser, Michael Drayton, Christopher Marlowe and Sir Walter Raleigh.

Little Englander. An uncomplimentary term first applied in late Victorian times to critics and opponents of imperialism and overseas expansion, mostly Radical and Liberal politicians and propagandists of Victorian England who, influenced by the doctrines of laissez-faire and the Manchester School (*see under* MANCHESTER), or from more positive or idealistic motives, opposed imperialism and advocated retrenchment in the colonial field. William Gladstone (1809–98), George Leveson-Gower, 2nd Earl Granville (1815–91), Richard Cobden (1804–65) and John Bright (1811–89) are examples. The term is first recorded in the *Westminster Gazette* (1 August 1895), but 'little England' with a similar connotation is known from over a decade earlier.

In modern usage, the expression implies a blinkered, narrow-minded patriotism, especially suspicious of things Continental.

Merrie England. An opera (1902) by Sir Edward German. Set on May Day in Elizabeth I's reign, its plot revolves around some fairly improbable amorous to-ings and fro-ings involving the queen, Sir Walter Raleigh and the Earl of Essex. The most successful of German's works, it was popular throughout the 20th century with amateur operatic societies, and the song 'The English Rose' and the chorus 'The Yeomen of England' from it are the best remembered of his compositions today.

Merry England. A conceptualized prelapsarian England, generally set in the period from the Middle Ages to the Elizabethan era but sometimes extended in time to the 18th century, when the sun always shone, happy peasants danced around the maypole, English yeomen consumed their roast beef and good ale and a harmonious hierarchy of classes was in place.

The phrase *merry England* is first recorded as long ago as the 13th century, but in those days *merry* meant 'pleasant, agreeable'. It was revived by that great exhumer of medievalisms, Sir Walter Scott, at the beginning of the 19th century, but others who then seized on it were ignorant of its original signification, and turned it into a label for a lost Arcadia. The concept had its adherents in the late 19th and early 20th centuries – members of the Arts and Crafts movement, for instance, and right-wing nostalgists of the Chesterbellocian school – but its essential bogusness was signalled by the 'olde' spelling *Merrie England* with which it was usually embellished. It still had enough legs in the 1950s for Kingsley Amis to think it worth poking fun at in *Lucky Jim* (1954), in which the hero Jim Dixon, inveigled into delivering a lecture on 'Merrie England' by the egregious Professor Welch, pours drunken scorn on the whole idea:

> The point about Merrie England is that it was about the most un-Merrie period in our history. It's only the home-made pottery crowd, the organic husbandry crowd, the recorder-playing crowd, the Esperanto … [the alcohol gets the better of him at this point].

New England. The collective name of the northeastern states of the USA: Connecticut, Massachusetts, Rhode Island, Vermont, New Hampshire and Maine. In colonial days Plymouth and New Haven formed part of the group before they lost their separate identities as parts of Massachusetts and Connecticut respectively. The name was given to the area by Captain John Smith in 1614, and colonization was begun by the Pilgrim Fathers after the Plymouth Company of Virginia had been revived as the Council for New England. During the English Civil Wars (1642–51) a New England Confederation was set up consisting of Massachusetts, Plymouth, Connecticut and New Haven to maintain a common front. James II formed a short-lived Dominion of New England (1687–9), consisting of Massachusetts, Rhode Island, Connecticut, Plymouth, Maine and New Hampshire, to which New York and New Jersey were added.

Old England. A term for England as seen from the point of view of the colonists in New England and their successors.

Our goods are crossing the water to keep alive old England.

Boston Journal (30 December 1884)

More casually, the term is also invoked in the motherland (notably in song), sometimes implying a romantic bygone England (less specifically medieval than **Merry England**, *see above*) or a stoically enduring England, but usually in a way implying affection.

... Sing Oh, the hard times of Old England
In Old England very hard times

song (traditional)

Who do you think you are kidding Mr Hitler,
If you think we're on the run?
We are the boys who will stop your little game.
We are the boys who will make you think again.
'Cos who do you think you are kidding Mr Hitler,
If you think old England's done?

Jimmy Perry and Derek Taverner: 'Who do you think you are kidding Mr Hitler' (1968) (the theme song to long-running sitcom *Dad's Army*, sung by Bud Flanagan)

Speak for England! An adjuration (in full, 'Speak for England, Arthur!') called out across the floor of the House of Commons on 2 September 1939 by the Conservative MP Leo Amery to the Labour deputy leader Arthur Greenwood. Amery's own leader, the prime minister Neville Chamberlain, seemed to be hesitant and uncertain at that fateful moment, with war about to begin, so Amery invited Greenwood to stiffen the national resolve.

Young England. A group of young Tory politicians of the early 1840s who sought to revive a somewhat romantic concept of paternal feudalism and to idealize the functions of the territorial aristocracy. They saw their movement as a safeguard against revolution and the triumph of the laissez-faire doctrines of the Manchester School (*see under* MANCHESTER). Their leaders were John Manners, 7th Duke of Rutland (1818–1906), and George Smythe, 7th Viscount Strangford (1818–57). Benjamin Disraeli, 1st Earl of Beaconsfield (1804–81), also joined their ranks.

Englewood Forest. An alternative spelling of INGLEWOOD FOREST.

English OE *englisc*, from *Engle* 'Angles' (*see* ENGLAND).
As an adjective, meaning of or relating to England or its people, or the English language; as a noun, meaning the English language or (with a plural verb) the English people.

The English language is a member of the West Germanic branch of the Germanic division of the Indo-European family of languages. Historically it is divided into three main stages of development: **Old English** (sometimes called Anglo-Saxon, though the term is now rather dated), from the invasion in the 5th century to *c*.1100, **Middle English** from *c*.1100 to *c*.1450, and **Modern English** from *c*.1450. It is the most widely used language in the world.

Distressing as it may be for the English, *English* is used in colloquial American English to mean 'deceptiveness' or 'duplicity'. This is not quite the national slur it might appear to be, though. It originated in the late 19th century as a billiards term, denoting spin or 'side' put on to the ball with the cue. It presumably reflects English players' skill at this, although one version of the story has it that the Americans were impressed by the play of a visiting Englishman named English.

The supposed sexual predilection of the English (or at least those of them who had been at a boys' public school) for sado-masochism led in the 20th century to *English* acquiring connotations of naughty spanking, relentless dominatrices, quivering canes and rosy bottoms: **English guidance** is the euphemism for discipline and bondage, and **English culture** has the same connotation.

The English, the English, the English are best!
I wouldn't give tuppence for all of the rest!

Michael Flanders: 'A Song of Patriotic Prejudice' (*c*.1963)

Basic English. A fundamental selection of 850 English words designed in the 1920s by C.K. Ogden and I.A. Richards as a common first step in the teaching of English and as an auxiliary language.

Borough English. An ancient custom, finally abolished in 1925, by which real estate passed to the youngest son instead of the eldest. It was of English origin (the *English* in the term is an adjective, and the term refers literally to the part of a town with an English-speaking population), and it was so called to distinguish it from Norman custom. If there were no son, the youngest daughter was sole heiress. Failing a daughter, the youngest brother was the heir. Failing him, the youngest sister and so on. Land held by Borough English was sometimes called 'cradle-holding' or 'cradle-land'. It was found in Kent, Middlesex, Somerset, Surrey and Sussex.

English as she is spoke. A colloquial term applied to ungrammatical or unidiomatic English. The expression originated in an English edition of a book of selections from the French-Portuguese phrasebook *O Novo Guia da Conversação em Frances e Portuguez* by José da Fonseca, published in Paris in 1836. In 1855 one Pedro Carolino added an English column of text to the original French and Portuguese. The English book, published by James Millington in 1883, took its title from a phrase in the section headed 'Familiar Dialogues'. The Portuguese proverb *Por dinheiro baila o perro*, literally 'The dog dances for money', appeared in English as 'Nothing some money nothing of Swiss' and the saying 'Walls have ears' was presented as 'The walls have hearsay'.

English bearer. A slang term in the late 18th century for a drunken man with a red face (the allusion was to the bearing of heraldic arms, in this case the red Cross of St George on the English flag).

English bond. In bricklaying, a bond of brickwork arranged in alternate courses of stretchers (laid with their long side along the face of the wall) and headers (laid at right angles to the face).

English breakfast. A large breakfast typically consisting of cereal, eggs, bacon, toast and tea or coffee. The term was in use in the 19th century, but it really came into its own in the 20th, in the hotel trade. Trenchermen who opt for the 'full English', with all the (cholesterol-clogged) trimmings, are contrasted with those more sophisticated (or effete) who prefer the 'Continental breakfast' (rolls or croissants and coffee). In America the term is also applied attributively to any of various types of black tea, especially congou. (*See also* Ulster fry *under* ULSTER).

English cane. A slang term from the late 17th to the early 18th centuries for a cudgel.

English disease. A term current in continental Europe in the 1960s and 1970s (French, *la maladie anglaise*) to explain the sluggish state of the British economy. The symptoms were seen as strikes, restrictive practices, absenteeism and extended tea breaks. The same term was applied in the 1980s to soccer hooligans and lager louts. Historically 'English disease' was a term current in continental Europe for melancholy or 'spleen', and also for rickets, a disease first identified in 17th-century England.

English Electric. An electrical engineering company founded in PRESTON in 1918. It originally specialized in the manufacture of trams and railway rolling stock and of heavy electrical equipment, and played a leading role in the electrification of the Southern Railway in the 1930s. An aircraft division was established during the Second World War, which went on to produce the Canberra, the world's first successful jet bomber, and the Lightning, the main British interceptor of the 1960s. After the war it became involved in the making of domestic electrical equipment (e.g. fridges). In the early 1960s the aircraft division was subsumed under the British Aircraft Corporation, and the remainder of the company was taken over in 1968 by GEC.

English elm. A species of elm tree (*Ulmus campestris*) that was a common feature of the English countryside (Alfred Tennyson's 'immemorial elms') until Dutch elm disease struck in the 1970s, killing millions of them.

English English. The English language as spoken in England or Britain (as opposed to, for instance, the USA or Australia). It is sometimes referred to as **British English**.

English Heritage. A public body set up in 1983 to look after ancient monuments, historic buildings and other important sites in England.

English horn. The American name for the instrument known in Britain as the cor anglais, the lower-register cousin of the oboe. It is probably a translation of Italian *corno inglese*.

English Journey. A book (1934) by J.B. Priestley in which he recounts a journey through the towns and villages of England in a search for the roots of Englishness.

Englishman. A male adult English person, variously characterized generically as stalwart, taciturn, jovial, xenophobic, fiercely patriotic, mad, etc.:

> When two Englishmen meet, their first talk is of the weather.
>
>   Samuel Johnson: *The Idler* (24 June 1758)

> For he might have been a Roosian,
> A French, or Turk, or Proosian,
> Or perhaps Ital-ian!
> But in spite of all temptations
> To belong to other nations,
> He remains an Englishman!
>
>   W.S. Gilbert: *HMS Pinafore* (1878)

> Mad dogs and Englishmen
> Go out in the midday sun.
>
>   Noël Coward: 'Mad Dogs and Englishmen' (1931)

The national nickname of an Englishman is JOHN BULL (it became established through its use by John Arbuthnot in his satire *Law is a Bottomless Pit* (1712), republished as *The History of John Bull*, although Arbuthnot did not invent it). The old nickname for him in France was 'Goddam', owing to his particular preference for this oath (an uncanny foreshadowing of the late 20th-century French term for British soccer fans and other tourists, *les fuck-offs*).

Englishman's home is his castle, an. A saying generally used to mean that an Englishman is inviolable in his own home. Nowadays, it is less of a 'castle' than it was, as various authorities (e.g. the VAT inspectors) have right of entry under certain conditions. The premises may even be taken over and destroyed as the result of a compulsory purchase order.

English manufacture. Slang from the late 17th to the early 19th centuries for ale, beer or cider (home-made products, as opposed to wine or brandy).

English martini. US gay slang from the 1950s for tea, especially when spiked with gin.

English method. A term amongst US gays from the 1960s for non-penetrative homosexual intercourse involving rubbing the penis between closed thighs.

English Miss. A dismissive or condescending term (especially as employed by a French person or other Continental European) for a young unmarried English woman, implying primness, prudishness, etc.

English muffin. The American name (to distinguish it

from the cakelike American muffin) for a flat round cake of yeast dough cooked on a griddle and eaten reheated with melted butter – the kind that itinerant muffin men used to sell in past times.

In US gay usage from the 1960s the plural **English muffins** has been slang for a boy's buttocks. The national qualification has more to do with the sexual image of the English than with their particular variety of literal muffin.

English National Opera. An opera company (abbreviation: ENO) based at the Coliseum in London. It specializes in producing operas sung in English, a practice it has maintained from its previous incarnation, the Sadler's Wells Opera Company, from which it metamorphosed in 1974.

Englishness. The quality of being English, or of displaying typically English characteristics. Pundits have laboured in vain to pin down the 'Englishness' of English music, and the architectural historian Nikolaus Pevsner wrote a book (1956) on *The Englishness of English Art*.

Most who have tried to encapsulate England in a few phrases have tended towards the nostalgic. A notable recent example is John Major's enumeration of sepia scenes in a speech of 22 April 1993 (the reference is to Britain, but England was what the then prime minister clearly had in mind):

> Fifty years from now, Britain will still be the country of long shadows on county grounds, warm beer, invincible green suburbs, dog lovers and pools fillers and – as George Orwell said – old maids cycling from Holy Communion through the morning mist.
>
> (Major's Orwell quotation – not quite word perfect – was from an essay called 'England Your England', in *The Lion and the Unicorn* (1940).)

Ordinary English people's attitude to their country is no doubt more complex than this, the affection balanced with exasperation. Self-deprecation, mild or vituperative, is very much part of Englishness.

> An ironic attitude towards one's country and a scepticism about one's heritage is a part of that heritage.
>
> Alan Bennett: quoted in the *Daily Telegraph* (February 2000)

English oak. A species of oak tree, *Quercus robur*. The English oak and the sessile oak (*Quercus petraea*) are Britain's two native species of oak. The druids of Celtic Britain held the oak in great veneration, and the wooden warships of the pre-ironclad Royal Navy depended upon it. About 3500 full-grown oaks (or 900 acres of oak forest) were used in selecting the timber for a large three-decker line-of-battle ship. The strength, hardness and durability of the timber, as well as the longevity of the tree, have given the oak a special significance to Englishmen, hence its nickname, the **Monarch of the Forest**.

English Pale, the. The later name for the PALE of Ireland. There was also an English Pale around Calais (1347–1558); and in imperial Russia, from 1792, a notorious Pale or Settlement for the Jews.

English Patient, The. A novel (1992) by Michael Ondaatje (b.1943), which was joint winner of the Booker Prize with *Sacred Hunger* by Barry Unsworth. Set in 1945 in Tuscany, in the last months of the Second World War, it is a study of an intriguing foursome in a battered villa surrounded by unexploded mines. One of them, the 'English patient' (actually a Hungarian aristocrat), has been burned in a plane crash. A glossily romantic film version (1996), with Ralph Fiennes and Juliette Binoche in key roles, was directed by Anthony Minghella.

English rose. A term for a typically attractive light-complexioned English girl, which dates from the turn of the 20th century and is found in Basil Hood's libretto to Edward German's operetta *Merrie England* (1902) (*see under* ENGLAND), in which Sir Walter Raleigh (for it is he) describes a garden ('Dan Cupid's' garden) where 'women are the flow'rs' and in which 'the sweetest blossoms' or 'fairest Queen' is 'the perfect English rose'. The phrase has subsequently been associated with royal princesses, fair-skinned portrait posers and fine-boned film actresses, among others.

> Despite the fiery talk she [dancer Darcy Bussell] is at heart a delicate English rose, unlikely to be stirred by anything other than ballet.
>
> *The Times* (2 October 1999)

Pop stars seem to favour the phrase in their songs (such as Paul Weller's 'English Rose' for The Jam (1978)) and in their books (Madonna published *The English Roses* (2003), a morally instructive tale for children about the badness of envy).

More literally than any of the above uses, **English roses** are those bred recently from old types of garden rose, floribundas and hybrid teas, and characterized by large blooms and a beautiful fragrance.

Englishry. The medieval legal concept of the differentiation between the English and the Normans or between the Anglo-Normans and the Welsh. William the Conqueror introduced the 'murdrum', or fine for murder, to protect his fellow Normans. The fine was payable by the Hundred if the murderer could not be found. If it could be proved Englishry, i.e. that the corpse was English, the Hundred was exempt.

English saddle. The American term for what in England would be considered an ordinary riding saddle, with no horn at the front (as in the American western saddle).

English sentry. US gay slang from the 1960s for an erect penis. The metaphor takes something from the idea of 'standing to attention', and also perhaps from the reputation of guardsmen for homosexual prostitution.

English setter. A breed of gundog with a fairly long white silky coat with tan or greyish flecks or markings.

English sonnet. An alternative name for the 'Shakespearean sonnet' – that is to say, a sonnet of three four-line units and a couplet, with a rhyme-scheme *abab cdcd efef gg*.

English sparrow. The American name for the house sparrow.

English-Speaking Union. A London-based organization (abbreviation ESU) set up in 1918 by Sir Evelyn Wrench to promote friendship and understanding between the English-speaking nations of the world. The Duke of Edinburgh English-Speaking Union Award is granted annually for the most innovative work on the English language.

English Stage Company. A theatre company founded in 1956 by George Devine to present new drama and encourage young playwrights, and based at the Royal Court Theatre in SLOANE SQUARE. In its early years it was particularly associated with the so-called 'kitchen-sink drama' of such writers as John Osborne and Arnold Wesker.

English sunbathing. A derisive term in New Zealand from the 1970s for sitting fully clothed in the sunshine – something that recent English immigrants were apparently prone to do.

English Sunday. A term used while the institution survived (up to the middle of the 20th century) for a sedate Sunday devoted to church-going and improving tasks (as opposed to the frivolous pleasure of the 'Continental Sunday'):

> The grim visage of the traditional English Sunday looks like disappearing quite soon.
>
> *The Guardian* (22 November 1966)

English Traveller, The. A romantic drama (*c*.1624) by Thomas Heywood involving thwarted love and cruel deception. The hero, Geraldine [*sic*], has just returned to England from his travels at the start of the play – whence the title.

English walnut. A species of walnut tree (*Juglans regia*) with a large edible nut and hard richly figured wood that is used for making fine furniture.

Englishwoman. A female adult English person. As a compound (as distinct from a plain, ordinary 'English woman'), the Englishwoman is something of a dying breed, full of old-fashioned genteel (for she is at least middle-class) virtues that create little resonance in the 21st century.

> This Englishwoman is so refined
> She has no bosom and no behind.
>
> Stevie Smith: 'This Englishwoman' (1937)

Estuary English. *See under* THAMES[1].

History of the English-speaking Peoples, A. A four-volume history of, as its name implies, the people of England and their descendants who have spread around the globe (particularly the USA), up to 1900, written by Winston Churchill and published between 1956 and 1958. It is something of a potboiler.

King's English. The name used for the **Queen's English** (*see below*) when a king is on the British throne.

Last of the English, the. The sobriquet of Hereward the Wake, who led the rising of the English at ELY[1] against William the Conqueror around 1070. Charles Kingsley's novel *Hereward the Wake* was published in 1866. *The Wake* means 'the watchful one'.

New English Bible. A translation of the Bible into contemporary English first proposed by the Church of Scotland and directed by a joint committee of the Protestant Churches of Great Britain and Ireland. The New Testament appeared in 1961 and the translations of the Old Testament and the Apocrypha were finished in 1966. The complete Bible was published in 1970.

Oxford English. *See under* OXFORD.

Queen's English. The term applied when a queen is on the British throne to standard or 'correct' Southern English usage, such as the monarch might be expected to employ. The expression occurs (in the form *King's English*) in Shakespeare's *Merry Wives of Windsor* (1600), but it is older and was evidently common. 'Queene's English' is found in Thomas Nashe's *Strange Newes of the Intercepting Certaine Letters* (1593), and 'thou clipst the Kinge's English' in Thomas Dekker's *Satiro-Mastix* (1602). H.W. and F.G. Fowler wrote a book about 'good and bad English' called *The King's English* (1906). The Queen's English Society, a pressure group which campaigns for 'correct' English, was founded in 1972.

Rock English. The mixed patois of Spanish and English spoken by the native inhabitants of Gibraltar, who are colloquially referred to as Rock Lizards or Rock Scorpions.

Wardour Street English. *See under* WARDOUR STREET.

English Bicknor *English* because it is on the English side of the River Wye (in contrast with WELSH BICKNOR, on the 'Welsh' side – actually in Herefordshire); *Bicknor* probably 'ridge with a point', OE *bican* possessive form of *bica* 'point' + *ofer* 'edge, bank, ridge'.

A village in Gloucestershire, between the River WYE[1] and the northern edge of the FOREST OF DEAN, about 8 km (5 miles) south of Ross-on-Wye.

English Channel. An arm of the Atlantic Ocean which, for the past 40 million years or so, has separated England from France. It is about 450 km (280 miles) long, and 180 km (112 miles) wide at its widest, between Land's End and Ushant, and 34 km (21 miles) wide at its narrowest, between Dover and Calais (*see* Straits of Dover *under* DOVER). The French call it *la Manche* 'the Sleeve', in reference to its tapering shape. Its average depth is 40–60 m (131–197 ft), reaching 120 m (394 ft) at the entrance to the Straits of Dover and as much as 180 m (590 ft) at Hurds Deep, 30 km (19 miles) northwest of Guernsey. As the funnel through which ships must pass between the Atlantic and the ports of southern and eastern England and northern Europe, it is one of the busiest shipping channels in the world (*see also* WESTERN APPROACHES).

Its name, which seems to date from the second half of the 16th century, is usually abbreviated: in context, be it steamers, ferries, swimming or tunnelling, everyone knows what '**the Channel**' means (*see also* CHANNEL ISLANDS).

For those of the island race who take a stereotypically isolationist view (as in the alleged newspaper headline 'Fog in Channel – Europe cut off'), the English Channel symbolizes England's cherished independence and is, more practically, the most strategically important part of that 'silver sea' which, in John of Gaunt's words

> ... serves it in the office of a wall,
> Or as a moat defensive to a house,
> Against the envy of less happier lands.
>
> William Shakespeare: *Richard II* (1595) II.i

William Gladstone later took up the same theme:

> Happy England! ... happy ... in this, that the wise dispensation of Providence has cut her off, by that streak of silver sea ... partly from the dangers, absolutely from the temptations which attend upon the local neighbourhood of the Continental nations.
>
> *Edinburgh Review* (1870)

It was this mindset (undisturbed by the events of 1066) that prevailed until the very end of the 20th century against the idea of a cross-Channel link that would allow free passage from Europe to rabies, garlic, Continental morals, French/German/Russian invasion forces (strike out whichever does not apply), ravaging Mongol hordes, etc. (*see* CHANNEL TUNNEL).

> The best thing I know between France and England is – the sea.
>
> Douglas Jerrold: 'The Anglo-French Alliance' (1859)

Those with wider horizons have always viewed the English Channel, and particularly the Straits of Dover, as a means of communication. The Channel is for crossing, and those who find a new mode of conquering it are marked out for fame. A hydrogen balloon designed by the French physicist Jacques Charles made it across in 1785. Louis Blériot did it in a monoplane of his own design on 25 July 1909, rather more quickly than the first swum crossing, by Matthew Webb on 25 August 1875, which took 21 hours and 45 minutes (the current record is 7 hours 17 minutes, set by Chad Hundeby of the USA, and the first person to swim non-stop in both directions was the Argentinian Antonio Abertondo in 1961).

For rhyming slangsters old enough to remember the pre-NHS system of a list of local doctors prepared to treat patients under the 1913 National Health Insurance arrangements, known as 'the panel', the rhyme *English Channel* often served its turn later on for the National Health Service too.

Channel Dash, the. The escape, in the Second World War, of three German warships through British and French waters to Germany in 1942. The battle cruisers *Gneisenau* and *Scharnhorst* and the heavy cruiser *Prinz Eugen* sailed from Brest on 12 February 1942, through the English Channel and NORTH SEA to the security of the River Elbe. The luck of the so-called 'lucky' *Scharnhorst* ran out the following year, when she was sunk in the Barents Sea.

Englishcombe Probably 'Ingel's or Ingweald's valley', OE *Ingles* or *Ingwealdes* possessive forms of male personal names *Ingel* and *Ingweald* + *cumb* (*see* -COMBE, COOMBE).
A village in Bath and Northeast Somerset (before 1996 in Avon, before 1974 in Somerset), on the southwestern outskirts of Bath.

English Frankton *English* from its being further from the Welsh border than Welsh Frankton; Frankton 'Franca's farmstead or village', OE male personal name *Franca* + -TON.
A village in Shropshire, about 16 km (10 miles) east of Oswestry.

English Pale, the. *See* the PALE.

English Riviera On the model of *French Riviera*.
A touristic name sometimes applied to the south DEVON[1] and DORSET coast. It appears to date from the early years of the 20th century:

> Lyme Regis, Dorset. Hotel Alexandra ... The only hotel in its own grounds in the English Riviera.
>
> *Bradshaw's Railway Guide* (1910)

English Town. *See under* LIMERICK.

Enham-Alamein Originally *Knight's Enham*, *Knight's* from the knight's fee held here by Matthew de Columbers in the 13th century; *Enham* 'homestead or enclosure where lambs are reared', OE *ean* 'lamb' + HAM; *Alamein* was introduced in 1945, as a gesture commemorating the Battle of El Alamein (a British desert victory over Germany in North Africa in 1942), and also alluding to the centre for disabled ex-servicemen here, which had been opened after the First World War and was extended thanks to a fund set up in Egypt after the battle.
A village in Hampshire, about 3 km (2 miles) north of Andover.

Ennerdale 'valley of the River Ehen', river name of unknown origin + OScand *dalr* 'dale'; the earliest recorded form, however, *Anenderdale* c.1135, indicates that at this time the first element was an OScand personal name *Anundr* + the possessive -*ar*.
The upper valley of the River Ehen, in the western Lake District, Cumbria (formerly in Cumberland), some 12 km (7.5 miles) east of Whitehaven. The valley encloses

Ennerdale Water and the Forestry Commission's **Ennerdale Forest**. The sides are steep, with the Buttermere fells to the north and the peaks of Pillar and Steeple to the south.

> ... the Lake of Ennerdale ... shaped like a clumsy battledore – but it is, in reality, exactly *fiddle-shaped*.
>
> Samuel Taylor Coleridge: letter to Sara Hutchinson (5 August 1802) (written at the top of Scafell)

Ennis Irish *Inis* 'island', water meadow (*see* INIS).

The county town of County CLARE, on the River Fergus, 30 km (19 miles) northwest of Limerick. There are the remains of a Franciscan friary (founded *c*.1241) and Ennis also has the cathedral of the Catholic diocese of Killaloe (consecrated 1843).

Ennis was the birthplace of the soldier and poet Thomas Dermody (1775–1802), an alcoholic by the age of 10 and notorious for his ingratitude to patrons; and of the painter William Mulready (1786–1863), depictor of sentimental rural scenes. The actress Harriet Smithson (1800–54), with whom the composer Hector Berlioz became infatuated (*vide* his *Symphonie fantastique*) and whom he eventually married (unhappily), was the adopted daughter of the Rev. Dr James Barrett, Rector of Ennis.

Biddy Early (1798–1874), famous in the folklore of County Clare as a healer, prophet and psychic, was charged with witchcraft in a court in Ennis in 1865, but the case against her was dropped for lack of evidence.

On 15 August 1923, during the Irish Civil War, the future Irish *taoiseach* (prime minister) Éamon de Valera was arrested in Ennis under the terms of the Public Safety Act of 1923 and imprisoned until July 1924.

'Siege of Ennis, The'. One of the most popular of Irish céilí dances.

Enniscorthy Irish *Inis Córthaiddh, inis* 'water-meadow' (*see* INIS) + an unidentified element.

A market town in County Wexford, 20 km (12 miles) north of Wexford. It is across the River SLANEY from VINEGAR HILL, scene of the famous battle during the 1798 United Irishmen's Rebellion, after the rebels had captured the town. St Senan founded a monastery here in the 6th century, and the Anglo-Normans built a castle in the 13th century, replaced by the present one in 1586. Edmund Spenser lived in it for a period, Cromwell captured it in 1649, and after the 1798 Rebellion it was used as a prison; it has since been restored. Enniscorthy is the cathedral town of the Catholic diocese of Ferns, the cathedral (1843–8) being designed in Gothic Revival style by A.W. Pugin, who was indignant about the treatment meted out to his building:

> The new bishop has blocked up the tower and stuck altars under the tower! ... It could hardly have been worse if it had fallen into the hands of the Hottentots.

Enniscorthy was the birthplace of the novelist Colm Tóibín (b.1955), author of such works as *The Heather Blazing* (1993) and *Lady Gregory's Toothbrush* (2002).

Enniskillen Irish *Inis Ceithleann* 'Ceithleann's island' (*see* INIS); in Irish legend, Ceithleann, wife of Balor of the Evil Eye, swam here after having mortally wounded the king of the Tuatha Dé Danaan.

The county town of County FERMANAGH, situated between Upper and Lower Lough Erne (*see under* ERNE), 115 km (70 miles) southwest of Belfast. It is also spelt **Inniskilling**. The lands round about were held by the Maguires until the Protestant plantation under James VI and I, when they were granted to William Cole. Enniskillen subsequently became a Protestant stronghold. During the Glorious Revolution only Londonderry (*see* DERRY/LONDONDERRY) and Enniskillen held out against James II, the inhabitants of the latter breaking out to win a victory at NEWTOWN-BUTLER. On 8 November 1987 an IRA bomb exploded at a Remembrance Day service at Enniskillen, killing 11 and injuring 63.

Enniskillen was the birthplace of William Plunkett (1764–1854), prosecutor of Robert Emmet in 1803 and chief spokesman for Catholic Emancipation after the death of Henry Grattan in 1820. Portora Royal School at Enniskillen, founded in 1618, numbers among its alumni Oscar Wilde, Samuel Beckett and the hymn-writer H.F. ('Abide With Me') Lyte (1793–1847).

Royal Inniskilling Dragoons. A former regiment of the British Army, merged in 1992 into the Royal Dragoon Guards. They were nicknamed the Skillingers or Skins, and were originally raised in 1689 as Sir Albert Cunningham's Regiment of Dragoons.

> Fare thee well Enniskillen, fare thee well for a while,
> And all around the borders of Erin's green isle;
> And when the war is over we'll return in full bloom
> And you'll all welcome home the Enniskillen Dragoons.
>
> Anon.: 'The Enniskillen Dragoons'

Royal Inniskilling Fusiliers. A former regiment of the British Army. It became part of the Royal Irish Rangers in 1968, which in turn merged into the Royal Irish Regiment in 1992. It was previously known as the 27th (Inniskilling) Regiment of Foot, and was raised in 1689 as Zachariah Tiffin's Regiment of Foot. Their nickname was the Skins, most probably deriving from Enniskillen, but more colourfully from the story that during the Napoleonic Wars the regiment was bathing in the nude in southern Italy when the French were (falsely) reported to be approaching, obliging the men to rush to arms without a stitch on.

Ennistimon Irish *Inis Díomáin* 'riverside land of Díomán' (*see* INIS).

A small market town in County Clare, 22 km (14 miles)

northwest of Ennis. It grew round a castle built here in 1588 by Turlough O'Brien, whose descendants, the MacNamaras, held land round here into the 20th century.

Ensis 'enclosures' ME *heghenes* (plural form deriving from OE *hegn* 'hedge, enclosure').

A village in Devon, about 10 km (6 miles) east of Bideford.

Entepfuhl. The name given to ECCLEFECHAN by Thomas Carlyle in *Sartor Resartus* (1833–4).

Enterkinfoot Possibly an OCelt equivalent of Welsh *entyrch celyn* 'summit with holly trees' + ME *foot*.

A small settlement in Dumfries and Galloway (formerly in Dumfriesshire), 8 km (5 miles) north of Thornhill.

Eochaill. The Irish name for YOUGHAL.

Epping Probably '(settlement of) the people of the ridge used as a look-out place', OE *yppe* 'raised place, look-out platform', hence 'ridge used as a look-out place' + -*ingas* (*see* -ING).

A market town in Essex, to the northeast of London, about 8 km (5 miles) south of Harlow. Epping 'Underground' station, on the Central line, opened in 1949.

Epping Forest. A 250-ha (618-acre) tract of woodland to the southwest of Epping. It is the largest hornbeam forest in England. Most of it is in Essex, but there is also a small corner in London, in the borough of WALTHAM FOREST (which was the forest's original name). It is a remnant of the vast primeval forest that once stretched all the way from the River Thames to the Wash. In medieval times, when it was a royal hunting ground, it had shrunk considerably, but still extended as far south as Leytonstone and Wanstead. Enclosure and other vicissitudes brought it to its present size by the middle of the 19th century, by which time royal huntsmen had long since lost interest in it (although herds of deer still remain). In 1878 ownership of the Forest was made over to the Corporation of London, which opened it to the public as a place of recreation. East Londoners have flocked there to walk and picnic ever since.

Epping Forest is now also the name of a borough in Essex, covering CHIGWELL, LOUGHTON and WALTHAM ABBEY as well as Epping itself.

Epsom 'Ebbe's homestead or village', OE *Ebbes* possessive form of male personal name *Ebbe* + HAM.

A town in Surrey, now effectively a southwestern suburb of London. It is in the borough of **Epsom and Ewell**, between Chessington to the west and Banstead to the east. It established a name for itself in the 17th century as a spa town, source of that stimulator of sluggish digestions, Epsom salts (*see below*), but its long-term fame had its beginnings on the nearby Downs. The United Kingdom's first automatic telephone exchange was installed in Epsom by the General Post Office in 1912.

Epsom Downs. A hilly area in the southeastern part of Epsom, a northern outpost of the NORTH DOWNS, on which Epsom racecourse is located. Horses have been raced here competitively since the reign of James VI and I, and towards the end of the 18th century two of England's classic horse-races were founded here: the Oaks in 1779 and the Derby in 1780. Since then the Derby in particular, run in early June, has become an English institution, and the traditional sights and sounds of Derby Day are inextricably linked with Epsom Downs: the Cockney punters down from Town on a day trip, the distractions of the funfair, Prince Monolulu's outrageous schtick ('I gotta horse'), the bookies, the touts, the fortune tellers, the jugglers, the chancers, the three-card-tricksters, perhaps even the odd pearly king and queen – oh, and the horses. The meeting formerly lasted four days, beginning with Derby Day on the first Wednesday in June and ending with the Oaks on Saturday. From 1995, however, with falling attendances at the midweek Derby, it was shortened to three days, with the Oaks on Friday, the Derby on Saturday and the final races on Sunday.

epsomite. The name for a naturally occurring magnesium sulphate (*see* **Epsom Salts**).

Epsom races. A now largely redundant piece of Cockney rhyming slang for *braces*.

Epsom salts. Originally, the salt obtained by evaporation of water from a mineral spring at Epsom. The extraction was first performed around 1675. It is mainly magnesium sulphate, and when combined with water molecules ($MgSO_4.7H_2O$) produces a substance with laxative properties. The combination has been marketed as 'Epsom salts' since the 18th century, regardless of the origin of its main ingredient. According to Thomas Fuller's *Worthies* (1662) the mineral spring was discovered by a farmer in 1618, who noticed that, in spite of the drought, his cows refused to drink water from the spring. **Epsom Wells** developed, like TUNBRIDGE WELLS, as a favourite London spa. John Aubrey, Samuel Pepys, Nell Gwyn and Queen Anne's consort, Prince George of Denmark, were among its visitors. Thomas Shadwell's comedy *Epsom Wells* (1672) portrays the loose life of the spa in those times.

marine epsom. A name applied in the 18th and 19th centuries to magnesium sulphate obtained from seawater.

Epworth 'Eoppa's enclosure', OE male personal name *Eoppa* + *worth* (*see* -WORTH, WORTHY, -WARDINE).

A small town in North Lincolnshire (before 1996 in Humberside, before 1974 in Lincolnshire), in the ISLE OF AXHOLME, about 13 km (8 miles) southwest of Scunthorpe. The founding fathers of Methodism, the brothers John (1703–91) and Charles (1707–88) Wesley, were born here.

Érainn. *See* ÉIRE.

Ercildoune 'Ercil's hill', Gaelic personal name *Ercil* + OE *dun* (*see* DOWN, -DON).

The old name for the small town of Earlston in Lauderdale, 7 km (4.5 miles) north of Newton St Boswells, in Scottish Borders (formerly in Berwickshire). It was the birthplace of the seer **Thomas of Ercildoune** (*c.*1220–*c.*1297), also known as Thomas Rymour of Erceldoune or Thomas the Rhymer. To the south of the town are the ruins of Rhymer's Tower, where Thomas is supposed to have lived – apart from the seven years he spent in Elfland (*see* EILDON HILLS). Thomas was the reputed author of a number of poems, including one on Tristram (which Sir Walter Scott believed to be genuine), and is said to have predicted the death of Alexander III at KINGHORN, the Battle of BANNOCKBURN, the accession of James VI to the English throne and other events. Thomas's predictions were first collected in *Romance and Prophecies of Thomas of Erceldoune* (15th century), and Sir Walter Scott included the ballad 'Thomas the Rhymer' in his *Minstrelsy of the Scottish Border* (1802). The Russian poet Mikhail Lermontov (1814–41) claimed to be descended from the seer. In the church wall at Earlston there is an old stone inscribed

> Auld Rhymer's race lies in this place.

Erddig Etymology unclear; possibly from an English name, despite the Welsh appearance.
A house and estate 3 km (2 miles) south of Wrexham. The first house was designed by John Webb in the later 17th century, and enlarged in the next under its owner Simon Yorke. In 1973 the house passed to the National Trust from the Yorkes. The domestic situation at Erddig seems to have defied prevailing class distinctions, with the household and estate staff valued rather more highly than usually was the case (as evidenced in the existence of a series of their portraits, spanning three centuries).

For anyone with a passion about ivy, Erddig is the place to go: it is home to the National Collection.

Erdington 'estate associated with Earda', OE male personal name *Earda* + -ING + -TON.
A northeastern suburb of BIRMINGHAM, about 6 km (4 miles) from the city centre. The Gravelly Hill motorway interchange is just to the southwest (*see* SPAGHETTI JUNCTION).

Erewash[1] Perhaps 'winding stream', OE *irre* 'wandering' + *wisce* 'wet meadow', and hence applied by extension to the river which makes it wet.
A river in central England that for much of its 24-km (15-mile) course forms, together with the **Erewash Canal**, the boundary between DERBYSHIRE and NOTTINGHAMSHIRE.

Erewash[2] From the River *Erewash*.
An administrative area of eastern Derbyshire, encompassing ILKESTON and LONG EATON.

Eriboll. *See under* LOCH ERIBOLL.

Erin From Irish *Éirinn*, the dative of ÉIRE.

A poetic name for Ireland, as used in countless ballads.

> Erin! the tear and the smile in thine eyes
> Blend like the rainbow that hangs in thy skies!
>
> Thomas Moore: 'Erin! the Tear', from *Irish Melodies* (1807–34)

Erin go bragh. A patriotic slogan taken to mean 'Ireland for ever', the last two words being derived from Irish *go bréa* 'fine'.

> There came to the beach a poor Exile of Erin,
> The dew on his thin robe was heavy and chill.
> For his country he sighed, when at twilight repairing
> To wander alone by the wind beaten hill.
> But the day-star attracted his eyes' sad devotion
> For it rose o'er his own native isle of the ocean,
> Where once in the fire of his youthful emotion
> He sang the bold anthem of Erin go bragh.
>
> Thomas Campbell: 'The Exile of Erin' (1842)

Darling of Erin, the. The nickname of the Irish patriot and martyr Robert Emmet (1778–1803), who was executed by the British after an abortive uprising. The name was coined in a ballad by Thomas Maguire (*fl.*1895):

> Bold Robert Emmet, the darling of Erin,
> Bold Robert Emmet will die with a smile;
> Farewell companions both loyal and daring,
> I'll lay down my life for the Emerald Isle.

Harp of Erin, The. The collected poems (1807) of the soldier-poet and alcoholic ingrate, Thomas Dermody (1775–1802), 'Ireland's most erratic genius' (*see also under* ENNIS):

> He who such polish'd lines so well could form
> Was Passion's slave, was Indiscretion's child ...

Sweet roots of Erin. Potatoes, thus dignified by the Rev. John Graham in his *Poems, Chiefly Historical* (1829):

> Sweet roots of Erin, we can't do without them.
> No tongue can express their importance to man.
> Poor Corporal COBBETT knows nothing about them;
> We'll boil them and eat them as long as we can.

The spectre of history here prods us to consider the awful irony of this last line, in the light of the triple failure of the crop between 1845 and 1849.

Eriskay Possibly 'island of the water sprite', Gaelic *ùruisg* 'water sprite' + OScand *ey* 'island' (*see* -AY), but 'Eirikr's island', OScand personal name *Eirikr* (Erik) + *ey* 'island' is equally possible.
A small island in the Outer HEBRIDES, Western Isles (formerly in Inverness-shire), 2 km (1.2 miles) south of South Uist across the **Sound of Eriskay**. There is now a causeway across the sound, opened by the Earl and Countess of Wessex on 11 September 2002. They had refused any other date than the first anniversary of '9/11', which caused some local unhappiness.

Two and a half centuries earlier, it was on the west coast of Eriskay, at Coilleag a' Phrionnsa (Gaelic 'cockleshell strand of the prince') that another prince, Charles Edward Stuart, the Young Pretender, first set foot on Scottish soil, on 23 July 1745.

On 5 February 1941 the SS *Politician*, bound for America, foundered with its cargo of whisky in the Sound of Barra south of Eriskay. Thousands of bottles were selflessly salvaged by the islanders, but HM Customs and Excise were not amused, and 19 islanders ended up serving prison sentences in Inverness. The lighter side of the story became the basis of Compton Mackenzie's novel *Whisky Galore* (*see* BARRA).

'Eriskay Love Lilt, The'. The best-known of many beautiful Gaelic songs originating on Eriskay.

Erith 'muddy or gravelly landing-place', OE *ear* 'mud, gravel' + *hyth* 'landing-place'.

A southeastern suburb (pronounced 'earith') of London, on the south bank of the River THAMES[1], in the borough of BEXLEY (before 1965 in Kent), between Greenwich to the west and Dartford to the east. It grew up at a point at which prehistoric trackways converged on the Thames. Henry VIII founded a naval dockyard here, where warships built at WOOLWICH, including the *Great Harry*, were fitted out. In the early 19th century it became a fashionable place for Londoners seeking a home away from the centre of the city, so that in 1848 the *Illustrated London News* could comment: 'Erith is the prettiest of pretty suburbanities'; but in the following year the railway arrived, and Erith's development henceforth was along the lines of factories and working-class housing.

Ermine Street Originally *Earninga strœt*, 'Earn(a)'s people's Roman road', OE male personal name *Earn* or *Earna* + *-inga-* (*see* -ING) + *strœt* (*see* STREET). The name was probably first applied to a stretch of the road near Arrington ('Earn(a)'s people's farmstead') in Cambridgeshire, and later generalized to the whole road. (The notion that the road was named after Arminius, the Germanic hero who routed Augustus's Roman legions in the Teutoburger Forest in Germany in AD 9, is completely fallacious.)

A Roman road from London to York, built AD 43–50. Exiting London via what is now BISHOPSGATE, it led northwards through SHOREDITCH, STOKE NEWINGTON, TOTTENHAM and EDMONTON towards ROYSTON[1], and from there on through HUNTINGDON, GRANTHAM and LINCOLN, across the HUMBER estuary at Winteringham to BROUGH[2] and on to YORK. Its course can be followed on the modern A1 (*see under* GREAT NORTH ROAD) from Huntingdon to just south of Grantham, and on the A15 to the north of Lincoln.

Ermine Way From ERMINE STREET.

A name given to the northern section (between CIREN-CESTER and GLOUCESTER) of the Roman road from Silchester (in Hampshire) to Gloucester. Its route is followed by the modern A419. The road as a whole passed through NEWBURY and SWINDON on its way to Cirencester.

Erne Irish *Éirne*, after Érne, a legendary princess, or the Erni, an ancient tribe traditionally belonging to the Fir Bolg.

A river in northwestern Ireland. It rises in Loch Gowna on the borders of counties Longford and Cavan, and flows north into FERMANAGH and the many-islanded **Upper Lough Erne** (20 km / 12 miles long). At the northern end of the lough a short meandering section passes through ENNISKILLEN before entering the larger **Lower Lough Erne** (29 km / 18 miles long). The river exits the lough at its northwestern end, from where another short section takes it into County DONEGAL and then the sea near BALLYSHANNON.

> The Erne ... at its highest flood,
> I dashed across unseen,
> For there was lightning in my blood,
> My Dark Rosaleen!
>
> Owen Roe Mac Ward (attributed): 'Dark Rosaleen' (16th century), translated by James Clarence Mangan (Dark Rosaleen (RóISÍN DUBH) represents Ireland.)

> Farewell to Lock Ern where the wild eagles dwell!
>
> George Darley (1795–1846): 'Lay of the Forlorn'

> Yet dearer still that Irish hill than all the world beside;
> It's home, sweet home, where'er I roam, through lands and waters wide.
> And if the Lord allows me, I surely will return
> To my native Ballyshannon, and the winding banks of Erne.
>
> William Allingham (1824–89): 'The Winding Banks of Erne, or, the Emigrant's Adieu to Ballyshannon'

He/she could drink Lough Erne dry. A phrase used of someone who has a great capacity for liquid intake, usually of an alcoholic nature.

Shannon–Erne Waterway. *See under* SHANNON.

Erraid. An alternative spelling of EARRAID.

Errigal Irish *An Earagail* 'the oratory' (presumed to refer to such a feature that once may have stood on the summit).

At 752 m (2467 ft) the highest mountain in County DONE-GAL, 25 km (16 miles) northwest of Letterkenny, on the northern side of the DERRYVEAGH MOUNTAINS. Its pale quartzite rocks and conical shape mark it out as a mountain of some distinction.

> On and up till Errigal I found
> Raising its shrine of quartzite to the sky ...
>
> Patric Stevenson: 'Mist on Errigal', from *Romantic Donegal* (1964)

From the distance, it was almost edible –
the cake of ceremony.
The appearance of virtue's dress.
The clouds veiled its fierceness.

> Mike Jenkins: 'Radharc an Eargail'

Field-Marshal Harold Rupert Alexander (1891–1969), commander-in-chief in North Africa and Italy during the Second World War, took the title Earl Alexander of Tunis and Errigal on his elevation to the peerage.

Erris Head Irish *Iorras* 'promontory'.

The northernmost point of the MULLET peninsula, County Mayo, some 70 km (40 miles) northwest of Castlebar.

Erskine Origin uncertain, but possibly from an OCelt name meaning 'green slope'.

A small town in Renfrewshire (formerly in Strathclyde), on the south bank of the CLYDE some 15 km (9 miles) west of Glasgow. The **Erskine Bridge**, completed in 1971, carries the M898 across the Clyde.

> There once was a lady of Erskine
> Who had remarkably fair skin.
> When I said to her, 'Mabel,
> You look well in sable,'
> She replied, 'I look best in my bearskin.'
>
> Anon.: limerick

Eryri Welsh *eryri* 'highlands', plural of *eryr* 'high ground'.

The Welsh name for the SNOWDON massif, and also for the whole of SNOWDONIA.

> Silence brought by the dark night: Eryri's
> Mountains veiled by mist:
> The sun in the bed of brine,
> The moon silvering the water.
>
> Walter Davies (Gwallter Mechain) (1761–1849): 'Nightfall', translated from the Welsh by Anthony Conran

Esher 'district where ash-trees grow', OE *æsc* 'ash-tree' + *scearu* 'district'.

A southwestern suburb of Greater London (before 1965 in Surrey), in the borough of ELMBRIDGE, on the River MOLE[1], and about 8 km (5 miles) southwest of Kingston upon Thames. This is suburbia of the distinctly up-market variety, with stockbrokerish villas, leafy avenues and abundant golf courses. But not all is typically suburban: Sandown Park Racecourse (*see* SANDOWN PARK) is also situated in Esher, and a little to the south lie the gardens of Claremont, landscaped from 1715 by Sir John Vanbrugh and 'Capability' Brown, among others, and now run by the National Trust.

The designer and entrepreneur Terence Conran was born in Esher in 1931.

Esk[1] OCelt river name meaning 'water' or 'swiftly flowing'.

The name of two rivers in ANGUS. The **North Esk** (length 56 km / 93 miles) rises in Loch Lee at the head of **Glen Esk** (one of the Angus Glens), and flows generally southeastwards to enter the sea north of Montrose. The **South Esk** (length 79 km / 49 miles) rises at the head of GLEN CLOVA and flows southeastward then eastward to enter the sea at the Montrose Basin.

In the 18th century Glen Esk and its environs were apparently enlivened by a certain Alexander Ross, the 'wale [choice] of hearty cocks':

> Lang may thy stevin fill wi' glee
> The glens and mountains of Lochlee,
> Which were right gowsty but for thee,
> Whase sangs enamour
> Ilk lass, and teach wi' melody
>   The rocks to yamour.
>
> James Beattie (1735–1803): 'To Mr Alexander Ross' (Scots *stevin* 'vocal noise', *gowsty* 'desolate', *yamour* 'clamour')

Esk[2]. A river in Dumfries and Galloway. It is formed by the confluence of the **Black Esk** and the **White Esk** at ESKDALEMUIR, from where it flows 35 km (22 miles) generally southward, crossing into CUMBRIA before entering the head of the SOLWAY FIRTH just south of GRETNA. The total length is 93 km (58 miles). The labels 'Black' and 'White' do not literally refer to the colour of the water, but are used as distinguishing labels.

> Wheesht, wheesht, Joyce, and let me hear
> Nae Anna Livvy's lilt.
> But Wauchope, Esk, and Ewes again,
> Each wi' its ain rhythms till't.
>
> Hugh MacDiarmid: 'Water Music' (Scots *till't* 'to it') (Wauchope Water and Ewes Water are tributaries of the Esk, joining it at Langholm, MacDiarmid's native town.)

Esk[3]. A river in east-central Scotland, formed by the confluence of the **North Esk** (length: 35 km / 22 miles) and the **South Esk** (length: 30 km / 19 miles) at DALKEITH, Lothian, from where it flows 8 km (5 miles) to enter the sea at INVERESK. ROSLIN Glen and HAWTHORNDEN are on the North Esk.

On the wooded banks of the North Esk, near Dalkeith, is 'Rizzio's chestnut', a tree traditionally believed to have been planted by David Rizzio, Italian secretary and close companion of Mary Queen of Scots (*see* HOLYROOD), as a token of his love for her. The sweet chestnut survives to this day.

Esk[4]. A river in the western LAKE DISTRICT, Cumbria (formerly in Cumberland). It rises at over 600 m (1970 ft) on the upper slopes of the high pass called **Esk Hause** (759 m / 2490 ft), just northwest of the peak of **Esk Pike** (885 m / 2903 ft), and is approximately 25 km (16 miles) long. Upper **Eskdale** is a wild place, dominated by Scafell (*see under* SCAFELL PIKE) to the west – on whose lower flank rises the rocky bastion of **Esk Buttress** – and by BOWFELL to the east.

Above the collar of crags,
The granite pate breaks bare to the sky
Through a tonsure of bracken and bilberry.

Norman Nicholson: 'Eskdale Granite'

A series of spectacular waterfalls brings the river down from these wild heights to lower Eskdale, through which it wends its pastoral way to the sea near RAVENGLASS.

Eskdale ... the upper part of it the wildest and savagest surely of all the vales that were ever seen from the top of an English mountain, and the lower part the loveliest.

Samuel Taylor Coleridge: letter to Sara Hutchinson (5 August 1802) (written at the top of Scafell)

Esk⁵. A river in North Yorkshire, flowing approximately 40 km (25 miles) east along the north side of the NORTH YORK MOORS to meet the sea at WHITBY. St Hilda (614–80) is said to have rid Eskdale of snakes by driving them to the cliffs at Whitby and decapitating them with a whip; the story probably originated as an explanation of the fossilized ammonites on the shore.

Eskdalemuir 'the moor of the valley of the River Esk', OCelt river name *isca* 'water' + OScand *dalr* 'valley' + Scots *muir* 'moor'.

A village on the White ESK², some 16 km (10 miles) north-west of Langholm, formerly in Dumfriesshire, now in Dumfries and Galloway. Eskdalemuir is best known as the site of the **Eskdalemuir Observatory**, established in 1908 by the National Physical Laboratory, and administered since 1910 by the Meteorological Office. As well as making meteorological observations, there are facilities for geomagnetic and seismological measurements.

Esker Riada. An alternative spelling of EISCIR RIADA.

Essex '(territory of the) East Saxons', OE *east* + *Seaxe* 'Saxons'.

A county in southeast England, one of the HOME COUNTIES, bounded to the north by Cambridgeshire and Suffolk, to the west by Greater London and Hertfordshire, to the south by the River Thames and to the east by the North Sea. It is for the most part low-lying, with a coastline characterized by tidal inlets and islands. It contains the unitary authorities SOUTHEND-ON-SEA and THURROCK, and other main centres are BASILDON, BRAINTREE, BRENTWOOD, CANVEY ISLAND, CHELMSFORD (site of the county's administrative headquarters), CLACTON-ON-SEA, COLCHESTER, GRAYS, HARLOW, RAYLEIGH and SAFFRON WALDEN. It has important ports at HARWICH and TILBURY, and London's third airport is at STANSTED. It contains the former royal hunting ground of Epping Forest (*see under* EPPING). Its main rivers, apart from the THAMES¹, are the BLACKWATER¹, the BRAIN, the CHELMER, the COLNE¹, the CROUCH¹, the LEA, the RODING and the STOUR².

Before the coming of the Romans, Essex (along with Suffolk) was the territory of the British tribe known as the Trinovantes, the seat of whose kings was at Camulodunum (Colchester). The Trinovantes were conquered by the Catevellauni (*see* HERTFORDSHIRE) around AD 10, whereupon Cunobelin, king of the Catevellauni, moved his capital to Colchester. The Romans settled widely in Essex during their occupation, and there are extensive Roman remains at, among other places, Colchester and Chelmsford.

The Saxons arrived in the 5th century. The kingdom they created here by the early 7th century, from which the name Essex originated (see above), was more extensive than the modern county, covering large parts of what later became Middlesex; its main town was London. As the axis of Anglo-Saxon power shifted, first to Mercia, then to Wessex in the 8th and 9th centuries, the East Saxons adjusted their loyalties appropriately. Danes began to settle the area in the later part of the century, and the Anglo-Danish Treaty of Wedmore (878) (*see under* WEDMORE) placed it within the Danelaw. The Saxon Edward the Elder recaptured the area in the early 10th century, but the East Saxons were defeated by the Danes in 991 at the Battle of Maldon (*see under* MALDON). By the time Cnut acceded to the throne of England in the early 11th century, the county had begun to take its modern form and dimensions.

In the modern era Essex is still mainly an agricultural county, with a southern industrial belt. After the Second World War, the southern and eastern parts of the county received an influx of people from EAST LONDON (who by long tradition had disported themselves in Southend and other Thames estuary resorts), exchanging bomb-damaged tenements for the new towns of Basildon and Harlow and other similar developments. In a *quid pro quo*, Essex lost territory west of the River Lea to London in 1965. The **University of Essex**, established in 1962, is at Wivenhoe Park (*see under* WIVENHOE), on the southeastern outskirts of Colchester.

In cricketing terms Essex is a 'first-class' county. Essex County Cricket Club was founded in 1876 and has played in the county championship since 1895, winning it on six occasions. Essex's famous players include Trevor Bailey, Keith Fletcher, Graham Gooch and Nasser Hussain. Its home ground is the County Ground, Chelmsford.

There are counties called Essex in the USA (Massachusetts, New Jersey, New York, Vermont) and towns called Essex (California, Connecticut, Iowa, Montana, New York and Vermont). There is a town called Essex in Ontario, Canada.

Now here in Essex we're as lax as the 18th century. We hunt in any old clothes. Our soil is a rich succulent clay; it becomes semi-fluid in winter, when we go about in our waders shooting duck ... If I wanted to play golf – which I don't, being a decent Essex man – I should have to motor

10 miles into Hertfordshire. This country is a part of the real England – England outside London and outside manufactures. It's one with Wessex and Mercia or old Yorkshire. And it's the essential England still.

H.G. Wells: *Mr Britling Sees It Through* (1916)

Essex board. A type of boarding for constructing ceilings and walls, consisting of sheets of compressed fibre bound together by cement.

Essex calf. Originally, a calf reared in Essex, but in the 16th and 17th century used (especially by Suffolk folk) as a term of mildly amused contempt for the bumpkinish denizens of that county.

Essexed. A term applied in the 17th century to a well-developed calf in a man (*see* **Essex Growth** *below*):

A good Legge is a great grace if it be discreetly essex'd in the calfe, and not too much spindled in the small.

John Taylor: *All the Workes of John Taylor, the Water Poet* (1630)

Essex Girl. A type of unintelligent and materialistic young woman who emerged in the late 1980s as the female (but decidedly apolitical) counterpart to **Essex Man** (*see below*). Her supposed promiscuity and tarty appearance (short skirt, clunking gold jewellery, white stiletto heels) made her the butt of a variety of politically incorrect jokes (sample: 'How does an Essex Girl turn the light on after sex?' 'She kicks the car door open'):

It was soon obvious I had a blue-green algae problem. The stuff spreads faster than an Essex girl joke in a bar full of salesmen.

Practical Fishkeeping (April 1992)

The stereotypical Essex Girl names Sharon and Tracey owed much to the two lead characters in the BBC television sitcom *Birds of a Feather* (1989–94) (Tracey and her husband Darryl lived in a £750,000 neo-Georgian house in Chigwell called 'Dalentrace' – very Essex).

Essex growth. A colloquialism used in the 17th century, when such a thing was fashionably desirable, for a well-developed calf in a man's leg. The pun was based on the term **Essex calf** (*see above*).

You would wish that his puny baker-legs had more Essex growth in them.

Lady Alimony (1659)

essexite. A dark-grey-to-black igneous rock first described in Essex County, Massachusetts, USA.

Essex lion. A 17th- to 19th-century slang term for a calf (Essex was a major source of cattle for the London meat markets). It was also used, especially by Kentishmen, as a contemptuous name for an Essex person.

Essex Man. A type of socially ungraced and culturally deprived Conservative voter, typically a self-made business-man or tradesman, who lives in Essex, or in southeast England generally, and who in the late 1980s worshipped the consumer-oriented gospel of Thatcherism. The coining of the expression is generally attributed to the late 'left-wing' Conservative MP Julian Critchley (who once opined that 'Essex is so right-wing that even the newsagents are white'), although the claim to authorship is contested by the journalist Simon Heffer. But whoever thought of the name, the species was definitively described in an unsigned profile headed 'Mrs Thatcher's bruiser' that appeared in the *Sunday Telegraph* for 7 October 1990:

He [Essex Man] is discovered in his original state and in the greatest abundance in the triangle between Brentwood, Southend and the Dagenham Marshes.

He is a ruthlessly self-interested, philistine, lager-swilling racist and the potential owner of a Rottweiler, if only he had time to walk it. One might add an element of Jack-the-Laddery to the mix. The specific link with Essex is that the south and southwest of the county had been the recipient of a wave of working-class immigrants from East London after the Second World War. Hitherto solid Labour voters, in the 1980s they discovered *en masse* the joys of unfettered capitalism. The Essex town of Basildon reinforced the stereo-type when, in the 1992 general election, it was the first constituency to declare a result that accurately implied a stronger level of Conservative support in the country than polls had predicted. The term itself suggests an anthro-pological label such as Neanderthal Man or Piltdown Man (*see under* PILTDOWN).

Essex Man, one of Britain's most strident class warriors with his mobile phone, Ford Escort XR3i and 'loadsamoney' mentality, is a doyen among consumers.

Greg Hadfield and Mark Skipworth: *Class* (1994)

See also BILLERICAY.

Essex pig. A pig of a type bred originally in Essex. Also called **Black Essex**.

Essex stile. A facetious 18th- and 19th-century term for a ditch (Essex being a low marshy county, there are more ditches than stiles).

Eston 'east farm or village', OE *east* + -TON.

An industrial town in Redcar and Cleveland (formerly in the North Riding of Yorkshire, then in Cleveland), 6 km (4 miles) southeast of Middlesbrough. The discovery of ironstone on **Eston Beacon** in 1850 led to an explosion of iron- and steelworks in the area.

Etive From the local sprite called *Éiteag*, meaning 'the little horrid one'.

A river in Argyll and Bute (formerly in Strathclyde), about 20 km (12 miles) long. It flows from near the head of GLEN COE past the great rocky pyramid of BUACHAILLE ETIVE MÓR (Gaelic, 'the great shepherd of Etive') into **Glen Etive**, and then into **Loch Etive**. The latter is a long narrow sea loch, extending southwestwards for some 26 km (16 miles) between high mountains (including BEN CRUACHAN) to the Firth of Lorne (*see under* LORNE) at the tidal Falls of Lora.

In ancient Irish legend, it was to Loch Etive that the beautiful Deirdre and her lover Naoise fled from the jealous King Conchobar, only to be lured back to Ireland to their deaths. The earliest version of the story is in *The Fate of the Sons of Usneach* (8th or 9th centuries).

> Glen Etive! Glen Etive! where dappled does roam,
> Where I leave the green shieling I first called a home;
> Where with me and my true love delighted to dwell,
> The sun made his mansion – Glen Etive, farewell!

> Anon.: 'Deirdre's Farewell to Alba', from *The Red Branch Cycle* (12th century), translated by Samuel Ferguson

Glen Etive is supposedly the haunt not only of Éiteag, the sprite that gave the river its name (*see* etymology *above*), but also of a *fachan*, a creature with 'one hand out of his chest, one leg out of his haunch, and one eye out of his face'. Most now find both glen and loch peaceful, if somewhat haunted, places:

> The flowers of the flags
> Are like yellow birds, hanging
> Over the secret pool.

> Bryan Guinness (1905–92): 'By Loch Etive'

Etive Slabs. A swathe of shapely granite slabs, pitched at a deceptively easy angle up the southern flank of Beinn Trilleachan (839 m / 2753 ft), above the northwestern end of Loch Etive. The crag provides a range of climbs that depend on friction and a cool head.

Eton 'farmstead by the river', OE *ea* 'river' (*see* EA-) + -TON. A town within the unitary authority of Windsor and Maidenhead (before 1998 in Berkshire), on the north bank of the River THAMES[1], opposite WINDSOR. Its life very much revolves around **Eton College** (*see below*).

Eton and Oxford. Used as a shorthand designation (approving or damning, according to point of view) of a style, a voice, an attitude, etc., taken to typify those who have followed supposedly the most direct route to power and privilege in British society, via Eton College and Oxford University:

> He may be a bit Eton and Oxford, but he's working in your best interests.

> P.G. Wodehouse: *If I Were You* (1931)

Eton blue. A light blue adopted by Eton College as the school colour in the 19th century.

'Eton Boating Song, The'. A song traditionally sung by Eton boat crews, and deeply imbued with the insouciant heartiness of privileged youth. The words (1865) are by William Cory, an assistant master at Eton College. They begin:

> Jolly boating weather,
> And a hay harvest breeze,
> Blade on the feather,
> Shade off the trees.
> Swing, swing together
> With your body between your knees.

(The mysterious 'blade on the feather', incidentally, refers to the 'feathering' of the oar-blades, turning them edgeways as they leave the water.)

Eton collar. A large stiff white collar as worn, originally by boys of Eton College, turned over the edge of a jacket.

Eton College. A boys' public school in Eton, the second oldest in England (after that at WINCHESTER), founded by Henry VI in 1440. He created scholarships for 70 deserving boys, and to this day there are still 70 'King's Scholars' or 'Collegers' appointed each year (their parents now have to pay fees, though). The other boys in the school are known as 'Oppidans' (from Latin *oppidanus* 'of the town'). Its reputation is as the training camp of Britain's ruling classes, to which the offspring of the nouveaux riches are sent to absorb effortless superiority from the scions of the nobility and the landed gentry. The school has produced 20 British prime ministers. Its 15th-century buildings exude academe, but are not luxuriously appointed, despite the extravagant picture painted by the young Molesworth:

> eton is a small paradise in the thames valley. New bugs who arive are met by the maitre d'hotel who sa Welcome sir we have to put you in suite number 2 this is only temporary sir you understand no bathroom no shower your toothpaste will be waiting for you frozen in the wash-basin.

> Geoffrey Willans and Ronald Searle: *How to be Topp* (1954) (all spellings *sic*)

Old boys are apt to play down its intellectual pretensions (against 'Education' in his 1929 entry in *Who's Who*, Sir Osbert Sitwell noted 'in the holidays from Eton'), but the most searching account of its educational methods, Cyril Connolly's *Enemies of Promise* (1938), is not altogether unsympathetic. Prowess at games or fighting might be more the thing. Relevantly to both, the Duke of Wellington is famously supposed to have pronounced that 'the Battle of Waterloo was won on the playing fields of Eton'; it was left to W.C. Sellar and R.J. Yeatman to muddy the waters with:

> [Napoleon] returned just in time to fight on the French side at the battle of Waterloo. This utterly memorable battle was fought at the end of a dance, on the Playing Fields of Eton, and resulted in the English definitely becoming top nation.

> *1066 and All That* (1930)

The playing field on which home cricket matches take place is called 'Agar's Plough'; the annual game against Harrow School (*see under* HARROW), Eton's long-term rival, is played at Lord's. But the school has its own, somewhat idiosyncratic forms of sporting activity as well (*see* **Eton fives** *and* **Eton wall-game** *below*).

Old Etonian Thomas Gray's *Ode on a Distant Prospect of Eton College* (1747) contrasts the innocent happiness of boyhood with the cares and infirmities of later life, but concludes:

No more; where ignorance is bliss,
'Tis folly to be wise.

Eton crop. A short boyish hairstyle, fairly popular among English women in the 1920s, and taking its name from Eton College.

Eton fives. The version of the game of fives played at Eton College. Fives is a court game, similar to squash, but with the ball being hit with the open hand (its name may ultimately be a reference to the five fingers of the hand). The distinctive features of the Eton game lie in the configuration of the three-sided court, which includes a shallow step dividing it into two and a projecting buttress termed a 'pepper-box', and the scoring system.

Etonian. (A pupil) of Eton College. The term (first recorded in the late 18th century) is at its most familiar in combination with 'Old', denoting those alumni who, in the eyes of generations of conspiracy theorists or the merely envious, have wielded a masonic influence at the tip of English society. Should they choose to wear them, they may be recognized by their **Old Etonian** ties (black with Eton blue stripes).

Eton jacket. A short black jacket with an open front and broad lapels, pointed at the back and cut square at the hips, as originally worn by younger pupils at Eton College.

Eton of Ireland, the. An epithet applied to CLONGOWES WOOD COLLEGE.

Eton Ramblers. A peripatetic cricket club for Old Etonians

'Eton Rifles'. A sardonic song (1979) by Paul Weller for the Mod-cum-punk-rock group The Jam, concerning class divisions. It reached No. 3 in the UK singles charts.

Thought you were smart when you took them on
But you didn't take a peep in their artillery room
All that rugby puts hairs on your chest
What chance have you got against a tie and a crest?
Come out and play, what a nice day, for the Eton Rifles,
    Eton Rifles
Come out and play, I hope rain stops play, with the Eton
    Rifles, Eton Rifles

Eton suit. A suit for boys consisting of an Eton jacket with trousers and waistcoat. A version with a skirt for women's wear (often called simply **Etons**) was fashionable before and after the First World War:

Sylvia was wearing Etons at Monckley's suggestion.

Compton Mackenzie: *Sylvia Scarlett* (1918)

Eton wall-game. A mysterious species of football played at Eton College on St Andrew's Day. The name refers to its being played against a wall (the brick wall that divides the Slough Road from the Lower Playing Field) rather than in an open field. It starts off with something resembling a rugby scrum, but the ensuing proceedings defy description or analysis. Authorities assert that no goal has been scored since 1909, although it has been claimed that Eric Blair (George Orwell) scored one in 1921.

Etruria From *Etruria Hall*, the name of a house built by Josiah Wedgwood.

A district of STOKE-ON-TRENT in Staffordshire, just to the northwest of Hanley. It has its origins in a large house built on the local Ridge House Estate in 1769 by Josiah Wedgwood (1730–95) as accommodation for employees in his pottery works. He called it '**Etruria Hall**', using the name of the area of ancient Italy inhabited by the Etruscans. The link is clear – Etruscan pottery – but the details of Wedgwood's precise motivation are somewhat muddied: it may be that he was under the mistaken impression that the Greek vases in Sir William Hamilton's collection, which he copied, were Etruscan, and it has even been suggested that he chose it deliberately to suggest that his wares were real antiques. Whatever the reason, the name had become transferred from the house to the pottery-works and to the area in general before long.

Ettrick and Lauderdale. A former district of the BORDERS, established in 1975 and abolished in 1996. It comprised the old county of SELKIRKSHIRE and parts of BERWICKSHIRE, ROXBURGHSHIRE and MIDLOTHIAN. Lauderdale is the valley of the Leader Water (*see under* LAUDER).

Ettrick Water Possibly a pre-Indo-European river name, of unknown meaning.

A river in Scottish Borders (formerly in Selkirkshire), to the southwest of Selkirk. It rises in the hills east of MOFFAT, then flows northeastwards for about 45 km (28 miles). The YARROW WATER joins it just before Selkirk, and it flows into the TWEED a little beyond the town. The medieval wizard and scholar Michael Scot (*c*.1175–1232) – allegedly responsible for some major engineering works on the EILDON HILLS – lived in a tower in the lower part of the valley. The village of **Ettrick** is on the river's upper reaches.

Ettrick Forest. A wild upland area to the south of Peebles and to the west of Selkirk. It includes ST MARY'S LOCH, Yarrow Water and Ettrick Water, as well as the hills surrounding these valleys. The Ettrick Forest, which was reserved for the royal chase in the 15th century, is so called because it was originally covered in part of the Old Caledonian Forest (*see under* CALEDONIA), but this suffered considerable depredations in the Middle Ages. The area was turned over to sheep in the 16th century, and the result was described by Scott:

> The scenes are desert now, and bare,
> Where flourish'd once a forest fair,
> When these waste glens with copse were lined,
> And peopled with the hart and hind.

Sir Walter Scott: *Marmion* (1808), introduction to Canto II

In recent times the southern part of the area has been extensively planted by the Forestry Commission.

Ettrick Pen. A hill (692 m / 2270 ft) dominating the head of the valley of the Ettrick Water. (Etymology OCelt *pen* 'head, hilltop'.)

Ettrick Shepherd, the. The name given to James Hogg (1770–1835), the Scottish poet and author of *The Private Memoirs and Confessions of a Justified Sinner* (1824), a strikingly modern novel. Hogg was born at Ettrickhall Farm, near the village of Ettick, the son of a shepherd, and was for a time a shepherd himself. He was a friend of Sir Walter Scott.

Eugene Aram's Cave. *See under* KNARESBOROUGH.

Euston Ultimately from *Euston* ('Efe's farmstead', OE *Efes* possessive form of male personal name *Efe* + -TON), the name of a village in Suffolk where the 2nd Duke of Grafton had his seat.

An area in northern Central London (NW1), in the borough of CAMDEN, centred on **Euston Station**. The name *Euston* first arrived here in 1827, applied to **Euston Square**, newly built on land belonging to the lord of the manor of Tottenham Court, the Duke of Grafton (who was also Earl of Euston). In 1837 Euston Station was opened, serving as the terminus for the London and Birmingham Railway. It soon became the main London starting point for the West Coast line to the Midlands, the North and Scotland, and home to the London, Midland and Scottish Railway (LMS). In 1857 the road running in front of it, built in 1756 and originally called New Road, was renamed as the **Euston Road** (it is valued at £100 on a Monopoly board).

Euston Underground station, on the Northern and Victoria lines, opened in 1907. Euston Square Underground station, on the District and Circle lines, opened in 1863 (it was originally called Gower Street; the name was changed in 1909).

Euston Arch. A massive stone portico with four Doric columns built in front of Euston Station in 1838. It was demolished in the early 1960s when the station was redeveloped. The outrage felt at this, and the protest campaign it engendered, were the first skirmish in what became a battle to preserve historic buildings in Britain in the last third of the 20th century.

Euston Road School. A name coined in 1938 by the art writer Clive Bell for a group of British painters centred round the School of Drawing and Painting that opened in a studio at 12 Fitzroy Street, London, in 1937, soon transferring to nearby 316 Euston Road. Founding members were William Coldstream (1908–87), Victor Pasmore (1908–98) and Claude Rogers (1907–79). They advocated a move away from modernist styles to a more straightforward naturalism and laid stress on the training of observation in the teaching of art.

See also FITZROVIA.

Evelix Etymology unknown.

A small settlement in northeast Highland (formerly in Sutherland), 3 km (2 miles) west of Dornoch.

Evenjobb 'enclosed valley associated with Emma', OE personal name *Emma* (it is uncertain whether it is male or female) + -ING + *hop* 'enclosed valley'.

A village in Powys (formerly in Radnorshire), on the Anglo–Welsh border 20 km (12 miles) east of Llandrindod Wells and 4 km (2.5 miles) north of BURLINGJOBB.

Evenlode[1] 'Eowla's water-course or river-crossing', OE *Eowlan* possessive form of male personal name *Eowla* + *(ge)lad* 'water-course, river-crossing'.

A village in Gloucestershire, in the COTSWOLDS, about 5 km (3 miles) northeast of Stow-on-the-Wold.

Evenlode[2] From EVENLODE[1]. The name seems first to have been used in the 16th century; before that, the river was called the 'Bladon' (*see* BLADON).

A river in Gloucestershire and Oxfordshire, which rises in the COTSWOLDS, not far from the village of **Evenlode**, and flows 56 km (35 miles) southeastwards to join the River THAMES[1] to the northwest of OXFORD.

Evercreech -*creech* 'hill', OCelt *crug* (*see* CREECH, CROOK), with an uncertain first element, perhaps OE *eofor* 'wild boar' or an OCelt word meaning 'yew-tree'.

A village in Somerset, about 5 km (3 miles) southeast of Shepton Mallet.

Everton 'wild-boar farm', OE *eofor* 'wild boar' + -TON.

A district of LIVERPOOL, Merseyside. The football club **Everton FC** is one of the great English club sides, having won the League title nine times. Originally founded in 1878 as a church team called St Domingo's, from 1884 to 1892 Everton played its home games at ANFIELD, before settling permanently at Goodison Park. Anfield thereafter became the home ground of another equally proud Liverpudlian club, Liverpool FC, whose record of trophies won is even more impressive than that of Everton, and whose proximity to Goodison Park has added a unique edge to the rivalry between the two clubs.

The **Everton mint**, a mint toffee, gave Everton FC its nickname, the Toffees; before every Everton home game, the famous Toffee Lady, in traditional dress of skirt, hawl and hat, tosses free toffees into the crowd (for this reason, Goodison Park sometimes goes by the nickname **Toffeeopolis**).

In 1909 a group of Anglo-Chileans in Valparaíso, Chile, founded another Everton Football Club (later Corporación Deportiva Everton), the name apparently inspired when one of them took an Everton mint from his pocket (however, that year Everton had toured Argentina and won many victories over Chile's trans-Andean rivals).

There is a town called Everton in Guyana.

Evesham 'Eof's land in a river-bend', OE *Eofes* possessive form of male personal name *Eof* + *hamm* 'land in a river-bend' (*see* HAM).

A market town in Worcestershire (before 1998 in Hereford and Worcester, before 1974 in Worcestershire), on the River AVON[1], about 22 km (14 miles) southeast of Worcester. *See also* MEON HILL.

Battle of Evesham (4 August 1265). A battle fought just to the north of Evesham, in which the future Edward I defeated Simon de Montfort and his barons. De Montfort was killed.

Vale of Evesham. A crescent of rich agricultural land to the southeast of Evesham, watered by the River AVON[1], in the shadow of the COTSWOLDS. It bulges with orchards and market gardens, and is particularly famous for its plums and asparagus.

Ewe, Loch. *See* LOCH EWE.

Ewell '(place at the) river-source' (referring to a stream called the Hogsmill), OE *æwell* 'river-source'.

A town (pronounced 'you-al' or 'yule') in Surrey, in the borough of Epsom and Ewell, at the foot of the North Downs, about 10 km (6 miles) southwest of Croydon. Effectively it is a southwestern suburb of LONDON.

In the northern part of Ewell is NONSUCH PARK, site of Nonsuch Palace, built in 1538 by Henry VIII as a royal hunting lodge and guest house but demolished at the end of the 17th century.

John Everett Millais painted the watery background to his famous picture of Ophelia (1851) by the River Hogsmill at Ewell.

> There was an Old Person of Ewell,
> Who chiefly subsisted on gruel;
> But to make it more spice, he inserted some mice,
> Which refreshed that Old Person of Ewell.
>
> Edward Lear: *Book of Nonsense* (1848)

Ewell Minnis *Ewell see* EWELL (the source referred to here is that of the Dour – *see* DOVER); *Minnis* 'common land', OE *mœnnes*.

A village in Kent, about 5 km (3 miles) northwest of Dover. *See also* TEMPLE EWELL.

Ewyas Harold *Ewyas* 'sheep district', Welsh; *Harold* denot-

ing manorial ownership in the early Middle Ages by a man called Harold.

A village in Herefordshire (before 1998 in Hereford and Worcester, before 1974 in Herefordshire), about 16 km (10 miles) southwest of Hereford, near the Welsh border.

Exe 'the water' or 'swiftly flowing', OCelt *isca* (the source of many English river names, including AXE[1] and ESK[1]).

A river in Somerset and Devon, which rises on Dure Down, EXMOOR, and flows 86 km (53 miles) southeast and then south through TIVERTON and EXETER to join the English Channel at EXMOUTH, to the east of Dartmoor. The **Exe Valley** is just to the north of Tiverton.

> Exe … runneth a long course with his crooked cranks.
>
> Tristram Risdon: *Survey of Devon* (c.1630)

Execution Dock. A dock in WAPPING (E1), in the borough of Tower Hamlets, on the north bank of the River THAMES[1], in which in former times pirates were executed. The prescribed method was hanging, after which the body was cut down from the gallows and hung in an iron cage. This was suspended in the river until the tide had covered it three times. Among those to have met their fate here was Captain Kidd (1701): the hangman needed two goes, as the first rope proved faulty.

Exeter Originally *Exanceaster* 'Roman town on the River Exe', OCelt river name (*see* EXE) + OE *ceaster* (*see* CHESTER); the reduced form *Exeter* is not recorded before 1547, though spellings suggest a pronunciation similar to the modern one at least a century earlier.

A cathedral city in DEVON[1], and its county town. It is situated on the River Exe, about 16 km (10 miles) from its mouth, having grown up around a river-crossing. It is about 30 km (19 miles) north of Torquay and 16 km (10 miles) from the eastern edge of Dartmoor.

The Dumnonii, the local British tribe (*see under* DEVON[1] *and* DUMNONIA), made it their centre. At that time its name was Iscka (*see* EXE). The Romans called it **Isca Dumnoniorum**, and built solid walls around it, parts of which can still be seen. It was an important town in the Anglo-Saxon period too, and was several times sacked by the Danes.

Exeter Cathedral, dedicated to St Peter, was founded in 1133, although the present building dates from the last quarter of the 13th century. It is the hub of an area of historic buildings in the centre of Exeter, which was badly damaged by air raids (part of the so-called 'Baedeker raids') in the Second World War (in the cathedral itself, the Chapel of St James was destroyed, and later entirely rebuilt). Bishops of Exeter sign themselves *Exon*, which is short for Latin *Exoniensis* 'of Exeter'. Miles Coverdale, translator of the Bible into English, was appointed bishop in 1551, but was ejected from the post after the Roman Catholic Mary came to the throne in 1553.

Exeter was an important port in the early Middle Ages until, *c.*1290, the Countess of Devon had a weir built across the Exe to spite the people of Exeter, who had annoyed her (*see* COUNTESS WEAR), thus effectively cutting the port off from the sea. The opening of the Exeter ship canal in 1563 restored trade for a few centuries, but the only remnant now of the town's seafaring past is the Maritime Museum. Exeter is now home to the headquarters of the Meteorological Office, which moved here from BRACKNELL in 2004.

The **University College of Exeter** was founded in 1922, and promoted to full university status in 1955.

Exeter City football club, founded in 1904 by the St Sidwellian Old Boys, has the unusual nickname of the Grecians. The club adopted the name from a centuries-old nickname applied to inhabitants of the parish of St Sidwell's, just outside the city walls. An 18th-century writer speculated that the nickname derived from footballing encounters between St Sidwell's and the city of Exeter: the inhabitants of St Sidwell's, who 'invaded' the city, being the 'Greeks'; the city's inhabitants, who were 'defending' their city, being the Trojans.

The miniaturist Nicholas Hilliard (1547–1619) and William Temple (1881–1944), 98th Archbishop of Canterbury, were born in Exeter. There are towns called Exeter in the USA (California, Missouri, Nebraska, New Hampshire) and in Canada (Ontario).

See also HEAVITREE.

Exeter Book, the. A manuscript collection of Old English poetry, Exeter Dean and Chapter MS 3501, written about 975 and bequeathed to Exeter Cathedral Library (where it is still preserved) by Bishop Leofric (d.1072). It contains riddles and elegies, didactic and liturgical poems, proverbs and legal documents, including *The Wanderer, The Seafarer, Deor, Widsith, Resignation* and *The Ruin,* and longer religious poems such as *Guthlac, Christ, The Phoenix* and Cynewulf's *Juliana. Widsith* is thought to date from the 7th century and thus to be the earliest poem in Old English. It is named from its opening word, which means 'far traveller'. The Exeter or 'Exon' Domesday is also sometimes called the Exeter Book.

Exeter College. A college of Oxford University, founded in 1314 by Walter de Stapeldon, Bishop of Exeter. Alumni include Roger Bannister, Alan Bennett, R.D. Blackmore, Edward Burne-Jones, Richard Burton, William Morris, Hubert Parry and J.R.R. Tolkien.

HMS *Exeter*. A Royal Navy York-Class heavy cruiser that pursued the German pocket battleship *Graf Spee* in 1939 and was badly damaged by the latter in the Battle of the River Plate. The *Exeter* was sunk by Japanese warships in the South Java Sea on 1 March 1942. A later HMS *Exeter*, built in the 1970s, gave its name to the **Exeter Class** of destroyers.

That's Exeter, as the old woman said when she saw Kerton. A Devonshire saying meaning 'I thought my work was done, but I find there is still more to do'. The story is that the woman in question was going to Exeter and, seeing the fine old church of Kerton (CREDITON), supposed it to be Exeter Cathedral. 'That's Exeter', she said, 'and my journey is over', although she still had 13 km (8 miles) to walk.

Exhibition Road So named because the land on which the surrounding cultural complex was built was bought with the profit from the Great Exhibition, held nearby in 1851. The name was chosen by the moving spirit of the site development, Prince Albert.

A road in KNIGHTSBRIDGE and SOUTH KENSINGTON (W2 and SW7), in the City of Westminster and the Royal Borough of Kensington and Chelsea, running southwards from HYDE PARK to the eastern end of the Old Brompton Road (*see under* BROMPTON), at South Kensington Underground station. It is one of the main arteries of the complex of museums, colleges, concert halls, etc. that was built in South Kensington in the second half of the 19th century, at the initial inspiration of Prince Albert. It contains the Science Museum and the Imperial College of Science and Technology, and the Natural History Museum and the Victoria and Albert Museum both have frontages on the road.

Exmoor 'moorland on the River Exe', river name EXE + OE *mor* 'moor'.

An expanse of high sandstone moorland in northwest Somerset and northeast Devon. It covers an area of 686 sq km (265 sq miles). Together with the stretch of Somerset coastline from MINEHEAD to COMBE MARTIN (with their towering cliffs) it was declared a National Park in 1954 – the smallest in England. The rivers Barle (crossed by a famous ancient clapper bridge, 'Tarr Steps') and Exe rise on the moor. Its highest point is Dunkery Beacon (519 m / 1703 ft) (*see under* DUNKERY HILL). Its eastern end merges into the Brendon Hills (*see under* BRENDON).

In ancient times it was extensively forested, but now, although belts of woodland remain in steep-sided valleys where red deer shelter, it is mainly an open expanse of heather, bracken and moorland grass. It has its own austerity, but it is gentler and less bleak than DARTMOOR.

Prehistoric remains, including early stone circles and burial mounds, are situated mainly around the edge of the moor (human settlement of the moor began around 1800 to 1500 BC).

R.D. Blackmore's novel *Lorna Doone* (1869), in which the outlawed Doone family terrorize the surrounding countryside, is set on Exmoor.

❖ -ey, -ea ❖

The Old English element *eg* has the general meaning 'land wholly or partly surrounded by water' and it is extremely common, especially in the southern parts of England; further north, the Old Scandinavian element *holmr* covers some of the inland names and *ey* the maritime names (*see* -AY). These are the two main senses of the word then: 'dry ground in marsh or fen' for the inland names, and 'island' for the maritime names. Typical inland names are LINDSEY (Lincolnshire) and SANDY

(Bedfordshire); quite a number of Eatons (LONG EATON, Derbyshire, for example) as well as Eyton (found in Shropshire; *see* EYTON UPON THE WEALD MOORS) have *eg* as the first element, and are thus easy to confuse with Eatons containing EA- 'river', such as EATON CONSTANTINE (Shrophire). Coastal and river names include Sheppey (Kent, *see under* ISLE OF SHEPPEY), THORNEY (Hampshire), and MERSEA and Canvey (*see* CANVEY ISLAND) in Essex. *See also* ISLE.

> The country [the River Exe] rises in, is called Exmore, Cambden [William Camden, *Britannia* (1607)] calls it a filthy, barren ground, and, indeed, so it is.
>
> Daniel Defoe: *A Tour Through the Whole Island of Great Britain* (1724–6)

Exmoor pony. Any of a breed of small shaggy ponies bred on Exmoor. They are said to be the truest to type of all Britain's native ponies. A pony fair is held at Bampton, just to the south of the moor, every October.

Exmouth 'mouth of the River Exe', river name EXE + OE *mutha* 'mouth'.

A town and seaside resort in Devon, on the eastern shore of the mouth of the River Exe, opposite Dawlish. It is the county's longest-established seaside resort, with many traditional attractions on offer.

Eyam '(place at) the islands, or the pieces of land between streams', OE *egum* dative plural form of *eg* 'island' (*see* -EY, -EA).

A village (pronounced 'eem') in Derbyshire, in the PEAK DISTRICT, about 16 km (10 miles) east of Buxton. Its modern fame rests on a great 17th-century misfortune. In 1665 some cloth ordered by a local tailor from London brought the plague from the capital to Eyam. The rector, William Mompesson, persuaded the local people that the village should be isolated rather than risk spreading the deadly disease to nearby settlements. The quarantine lasted for 13 months and, out of a population of 350, fewer than 100 were left alive at the end of it.

Eyam was the birthplace of the poetess Anna Seward (1747–1809), the so-called Swan of Lichfield (*see under* LICHFIELD), whose work was posthumously published by Sir Walter Scott.

Eye¹ '(place at the) island' (here probably referring to dry ground in a marsh), OE *eg* (*see* -EY, -EA).

A village within the unitary authority of Peterborough (before 1998 in Cambridgeshire, before 1974 in Huntingdonshire). **Eye Green** is just to the north.

Eye² '(place at the) island' (here perhaps referring to the rivers on either side of it)), OE *eg* (*see* -EY, -EA).

A village in Herefordshire (before 1998 in Hereford and Worcester, before 1974 in Herefordshire), about 5 km (3 miles) north of Leominster. The architecturally exuberant local manor house was built in 1681 for a West Indian sugar planter, Ferdinando Gorges.

Eye³ '(place at the) island' (here probably referring to dry ground in a marsh), OE *eg* (*see* -EY, -EA).

A small market town in Suffolk, on the Suffolk–Norfolk border, on the River Dove, about 19 km (12 miles) northeast of Stowmarket. As its name suggests, it was built on high ground in the midst of marshes, and the soaring church tower of St Peter and St Paul, with its intricate flushwork (arches and spaces imitated on a flat surface with alternate flint and stone), can be seen for many miles around.

Eyemouth 'mouth of the Eye Water', OE *ea* 'river' (*see* EA-).

A fishing village on the North Sea coast, in Scottish Borders (formerly in Berwickshire), about 12 km (7.5 miles) north of Berwick-upon-Tweed. It was formerly a notorious centre of smuggling. Its fishing fleet was devastated in a terrible storm in October 1881, when 23 boats sank and 129 men drowned.

Among the honours bestowed on the 1st Duke of Marlborough, victor of Blenheim, was the title of **Baron Eyemouth**. This gave him the right to sit in the Scottish Parliament (although this abolished itself within three years of Marlborough's victory).

> Fish guts and stinkin' herr'n'
> Are bread and milk for an Eyemouth bairn.
>
> Anon.: traditional rhyme (Scots *bairn* 'child')

Eyemouth fish pie. White fish in a white sauce, with tomatoes and hardboiled eggs, topped with mashed potato and grated cheese

Eye Peninsula Possibly OScand *ey* (*see* -AY), Gaelic *aoi* 'island', which would suit the topography. The Gaelic name is *An Rubha* 'the peninsula'.

A peninsula extending off the east coast of LEWIS, Western Isles (formerly in Ross and Cromarty), some 6 km (4 miles)

east of Stornoway. It is joined to the mainland by only the narrowest of isthmuses. At the northeast end is TIUMPAN HEAD.

Eyke '(place at the) oak-tree', OScand *eik* 'oak'.

A village (pronounced 'ayk') in Suffolk, about 18 km (11 miles) northeast of Ipswich.

Eynhallow 'holy island', OScand *ey* 'island' (*see* -AY) + *heilagr* 'holy'.

A small island in ORKNEY, in **Eynhallow Sound**, the channel separating Mainland from ROUSAY. It is pronounced 'eye-n-halloh'. It was said to have been the site of one of the earliest monastic foundations in Orkney, although the ruined church is no older than 12th century. In local tradition the island has a habit of disappearing then appearing again, although whether this is owing to supernatural or meteorological factors is unclear. Be that as it may, the island was once the summer home of the Fin Folk, whose children were mermaids, and who had a habit of taking human lovers to their undersea city to prevent themselves from growing old and ugly. The Fin Folk were eventually expelled from the island by a farmer from Evie on Mainland, whose wife had been taken by them, and thereafter the island was called 'holy island'.

An incident in 1990, however, suggested to some that the Fin Folk might not have been entirely banished. On 14 July of that year a cruise organized by the RSPB and the Orkney Heritage Society landed a large party on the island.

As was their practice, the crew counted the passengers off as they disembarked, coming to a total of 88. But the alarm was raised when only 86 returned to the boat. A massive air and sea search by police and coastguards followed, but no sign of the missing pair was found. In the long, light nights that followed, there was talk that two of the Fin Folk had at last returned to their summer home ... or that the missing pair had been taken as lovers by the Fin Wives to the marvellous undersea city of Finfolkaheem.

Eype 'steep place', OE *geap*.

A village (pronounced 'eep') just inland of the Dorset coast, on Lyme Bay (*see under* LYME REGIS), about 3 km (2 miles) southwest of Bridport. A little to the north, on the coast, is the hamlet of **Eype Mouth**, so called because the small stream also known as the Eype flows through into the bay there.

Eyton upon the Weald Moors *Eyton* 'farmstead in dry ground in a marsh, or in well-watered land', OE *eg* 'island, or well-watered land, or dry ground in a marsh' (*see* -EY, -EA) + -TON; *Weald* 'wild', OE *wilde*; *Moors* 'marshland', OE *mor*.

A village within the unitary authority of TELFORD AND WREKIN in Shropshire, just to the north of Telford. The open moorland to the north of TELFORD, watered by several tributaries of the River SEVERN, contains various named moors (originally marshy areas): one, to the north of Eyton, is called **Eyton Moor** and another, to the northeast, the **Weald Moors**.

F

Faddiley 'Fad(d)a's glade', OE male personal name *Fad(d)a* + -LEY.

A village in Cheshire, about 13 km (8 miles) west of Crewe.

Faeroes From Danish *Faeroerne* 'sheep islands'.

A sea area in the shipping forecast. It is to the northwest of Scotland, centred on the Faeroe Islands (a Danish possession), between FAIR ISLE to the southeast and SOUTH-EAST ICELAND to the northwest.

Fáil. An old name for Ireland (*see* INNISFAIL).

Faill. The Irish name for the River FOYLE.

Failsworth 'fenced enclosure', OE *fegels* 'fence' + *worth* (*see* -WORTH, WORTHY, -WARDINE).

Formerly a separate town between Oldham and Manchester, and now a district of the borough of OLDHAM in Greater Manchester Metropolitan County.

Fairfield Possibly 'beautiful open land', OE *fæger* 'beautiful' + *feld* (*see* FIELD).

A mountain (873 m / 2863 ft) in the Lake District, Cumbria, 4 km (2.5 miles) southeast of Helvellyn. It is particularly craggy on its eastern side, overlooking Deepdale. The **Fairfield Horseshoe**, via Heron Pike, Greatrigg Man, Fairfield, Hart Crag and High Pike, is one of the finest hill walks in the Lakes.

Fairford 'fair or clear ford', OE *fæger* 'fair, clear, beautiful' + FORD.

A town in Gloucestershire, in the Cotswolds, on the River COLN, about 13 km (8 miles) east of Cirencester. Its late 15th-century church, with its stained-glass windows made by Flemish artisans, is particularly fine, but today Fairford is probably best known for its air base, an RAF station currently operated by the US Air Force. Variously over the past four decades an operating base for Concorde development, home to the Red Arrows formation flyers, and venue of an annual International Air Tattoo, it was used to deploy US B-52s on bombing missions against Iraq in the Gulf War and in the 2003 Anglo-American invasion of Iraq.

The poet and cleric John Keble (1792–1866), after whom Keble College, Oxford is named, was born in Fairford (*see* Oxford Movement *under* OXFORD).

Fair Head A part translation, part corruption of an alternative Irish name, *Rinn an Fhir Léith* 'headland of the grey man'.

A spectacular headland rising 194 m (636 ft) above the sea on the north coast of County Antrim, some 7 km (4.5 miles) northeast of Ballycastle. Its Irish name is **An Bheinn Mhór** ('the big hill'), anglicized as **Benmore**. The headland comprises sheer and gloomy dolerite cliffs (frequented by the bolder sort of rock-climber) perched above steep grass slopes and screes descending to the sea. Fair Head is one of the points from which the length of Ireland is measured: from here it is 486 km (302 miles) to MIZEN HEAD in County Cork. The Grey Man's Path (whence the headland's alternative Irish name; *see above*) leads down a gully through the cliffs to the beach. The eponymous Grey Man in one account is a malevolent horse-like creature who lives under nearby Lough Dhu, and who may appear as a man with grey skin and green hair and horse's hooves

It was on the rocks of Carrig Uisneach (Irish, 'rock of Uisneach') beneath Fair Head that in the tragic old tale Deirdre, her lover Naoise and the sons of Uisneach made their landing on their return from Argyll to Ireland, lured thither by false promises of safe conduct by the jealous King Conchobar. The waters below Fair Head, known as the Sea of MOYLE, is the scene of another ancient legend.

Fair Isle The modern form of the name means 'island of sheep', OScand *faar* 'sheep' + *ey* 'island' (*see* -AY); but the earliest form, *Fridarey*, suggests that it was originally different, though what it was is obscure.

A small, remote island between Orkney and Shetland, 39 km (24 miles) southwest of SUMBURGH HEAD on Shetland Mainland. It is owned by the National Trust for Scotland, and is an important bird reserve: 345 bird species have been recorded here – a British record.

Fair Isle. A sea area in the shipping forecast. It is situated east of Hebrides and Faeroes, west of Viking, and north of Cromarty and Forties.

Fair Isle fieldmouse. An indigenous sub-species, *Apodemus sylvaticus fridariensis*.

Fair Isle pattern. A complex multicoloured style of knitting pattern for sweaters, etc., using Shetland wool. According to legend, the pattern was introduced by Spanish sailors when their ship, *El Gran Grifon*, was wrecked here after the Armada in 1588. However, it more probably derives from traditional Nordic designs.

Fair Isle wren. An indigenous sub-species, *Troglodytes troglodytes fridariensis*.

Fairlop Named from the *Fairlop* Oak, site of an annual fair here, which was cut down in 1820. Tradition has it that Daniel Day, the founder of the fair, was buried in 1767 in a coffin made from a branch cut from the tree; the tree continued to flourish and the cut was therefore 'a fair lop'.

A district of northeast London, in the borough of REDBRIDGE, about 1.5 km (1 mile) south of Chigwell. Fairlop 'Underground' station, on the Central line, opened in 1948.

Gypsies visiting the fair gave Fairlop its Romany name *Boro-rukeneskey gav* 'Great tree town'.

Fairport. Sir Walter Scott's fictional version of ARBROATH in *The Antiquary* (1816).

Fair Snape Fell 'beautiful pasture', OE *fæger* 'beautiful' + *snæp* 'pasture', with *fell*.

One of the more prominent tops (520 m / 1706 ft) in the FOREST OF BOWLAND, Lancashire, 10 km (6 miles) east of Garstang.

Fairy Bridge. *See* DUNVEGAN CASTLE.

Fairyhill The name presumably reflects local superstition.

A village in the GOWER PENINSULA, Swansea unitary authority (formerly in Glamorgan, then West Glamorgan), 18 km (11 miles) west of Swansea.

Faithful County, the. A nickname for County OFFALY. The name probably derives from the county's respectable performance both in hurling and in Gaelic football.

Fakenham 'Facca's homestead', OE *Faccan* possessive form of male personal name *Facca* + HAM.

A market town in Norfolk, on the River WENSUM, about 39 km (24 miles) northwest of Norwich. Set in attractive heathland, the town is dominated by the 34.5 m (115 ft) tower of St Peter and St Paul's church. Fakenham racecourse (National Hunt) is nearby.

Fal Origin and meaning unknown.

A river in western Cornwall, which rises a little to the south of Bodmin and flows 40 km (25 miles) through Penryn into the CARRICK ROADS at FALMOUTH.

Fál. An old poetic name for Ireland, originating in the *Fál* or *Lia Fáil*, the stone at TARA associated with the high kings, and which later became known as the Stone of Destiny or the Stone of Scone (*see under* SCONE).

> Sad to fare far from the hills of Fál,
> Sad to leave the land of Ireland!
> The sweet land of the bee-haunted bens,
> Isle of the hoof-prints of young horses!
>
> Gerald Nugent: 'A Farewell to Fál' (*c.*1573), translated by Padraic Pearse

> From my grief on Fál's proud plain I sleep no night,
> And till doom the plight of her native folk hath crushed me ...
>
> Geoffrey Keating (?1570–?1646): 'My Grief on Fál's Proud Plain', translated by Padraic Pearse

The name occurs in that of the political party Fianna Fáil ('band of warriors of Ireland').

See also INNISFAIL.

Falkirk[1] 'speckled church', ME *fawe* 'variegated, speckled' + Scots *kirk* 'church', a translation of the Gaelic name *an Eaglais Bhreac*, itself a translation from OCelt *egles birth*; a Latin version from 1166 is also known, *Varia Capella*.

A royal BURGH (1646) and industrial town some 16 km (10 miles) southeast of Stirling. It was formerly in Stirlingshire, then in Central region (in Falkirk district, of which it was the administrative HQ), and is now in the unitary authority of FALKIRK[2]. Its strategic position is reflected in the fact that the ANTONINE WALL runs through it, and in the two battles that were fought here (*see below*).

Falkirk FC (nicknamed the Bairns) was founded in 1876 and plays its home games at Brockville Park. There is a second Falkirk-based professional football club, by the name of East Stirlingshire (*see under* STIRLINGSHIRE).

Battle of Falkirk (22 July 1298). A battle in which William Wallace's Scottish force was defeated by the English under Edward I. Although Wallace's schiltrons (formations of pikemen) did well against the English knights, they were broken by Edward's archers. Sir Walter Scott described it as

> Falkirk's fierce and fatal fight
>
> Sir Walter Scott: *The Lord of the Isles* (1815), Canto IV, xix

Battle of Falkirk (17 January 1746). The last Jacobite victory of the 1745 Rebellion, in which Bonnie Prince Charlie's forces, under Lord George Murray, defeated the Hanoverian army under General Hawley, which had come to relieve the Jacobite siege of Stirling Castle. Serving with the Hanoverian forces at the battle was the famed Gaelic poet Duncan Ban Macintyre, not to mention Blind Jack of Knaresborough (*see under* KNARESBOROUGH).

Falkirk Triangle. The name given by the press in recent years to the area round Falkirk (especially BONNYBRIDGE) because of the number of UFO sightings reported here. The area is on the flight path for Edinburgh and Glasgow airports, and the sky at night is lit up by the flares and lights of the huge oil refinery at nearby Grangemouth.

Falkirk Tryst. The huge cattle market held at Stenhouse-muir just northwest of Falkirk from 1770 to the late 19th century.

Falkirk Wheel. The world's only rotating boat lift, officially opened in 2002. The structure, which is some 36 m (120 ft) high and which can carry eight or more boats at a time, completes the so-called Millennium Link joining the Forth and Clyde Canal and the Union Canal just west of Falkirk. The two canals were formerly joined by a series of locks, but these were long ago demolished and replaced by housing.

Falkirk². A unitary authority in the Central Lowlands of Scotland, bounded by Stirling to the north, North Lanarkshire to the southwest, West Lothian to the southeast and the Firth of Forth to the North. It was created in 1996 and replaced the district of Falkirk (part of Central region), which had been formed in 1975. The administrative seat is the town of Falkirk¹, and it also includes the towns of Denny, Dunipace, Grangemouth and Bo'ness.

Falkland Possibly 'land held by folk-right', i.e. subject to royal taxes, OE *folc-land*. However, early forms *Falleland* and *Falecklen* suggest that the first element might be OE *falh* 'fallow, newly cultivated' or *fealu* 'yellowish-coloured', with confusion of *land* and *glen* in the second element.

A small royal BURGH (1458) in Fife, some 7 km (4.5 miles) north of Glenrothes, and northeast of the Lomond Hills. There was a medieval castle here, which came into the hands of Robert Stewart, 1st Duke of Albany (*see under* ALBANY¹) and brother of Robert III, in 1371. It was in this castle that Albany imprisoned Robert's eldest son, David, Duke of Rothesay, who died here in March 1402, apparently deliberately starved to death. Robert's other son, James I, had Albany's son executed in 1425, and the castle came into royal hands.

The splendid French-style royal residence of **Falkland Palace** was begun at the end of the century by James IV, and completed by his son, James V, who died here in 1542 shortly after the Scots defeat at Solway Moss and the birth of his daughter, Mary Queen of Scots. Falkland Palace was the birthplace of Elizabeth (1596–1662), the daughter of James VI and the future, short-lived Queen of Bohemia, known as 'the Winter Queen'. Notable features at the Palace are the gardens and the royal ('real') tennis court (1539), one of the few in the country.

> A narrative of grass
> And stone's hierarchical
>   Scottish Versailles
>
> Douglas Dunn: 'At Falkland Palace', from *Northlight* (1988)

Falkland bred. An 18th–19th-century Scots term for well-mannered, alluding to the earlier presence of the Scottish royal court at Falkland.

Falls of Bruar OCelt *brivaros*, 'bridge stream'; there were formerly natural rock arches in the ravine.

A series of three fine waterfalls on the **Bruar Water**, some 6 km (4 miles) west of Blair Atholl, in Perth and Kinross (formerly in Perthshire, and then in Tayside region). Robert Burns visited the Falls in 1787, while staying as a guest of the Duke of Atholl at Blair Castle (*see under* ATHOLL). This resulted in an 'effusion of a half-hour' of which what follows is an extract:

> Here, foaming down the skelvy rocks,
>   In twisting strength I rin;
> There, high my boiling torrent smokes,
>   Wild-roaring oe'r a linn:
> Enjoying large each spring and well
>   As nature gave them me,
> I am, altho' I say't mysel',
>   Worth gann a mile to see.
>
> Would then my noble master please
>   To grant my highest wishes,
> He'll shade my banks with towering trees,
>   And bonnie spreading bushes.
> Delighted doubly then, my Lord,
>   You'll wander on my banks,
> And listen mony a grateful bird
>   Return you tuneful thanks.
>
> Robert Burns: 'The Humble Petition of Bruar Water to the Noble Duke of Atholie' (1787)

In a note of 1793 Burns wrote that the effect of the Falls 'is much impaired by the want of trees and shrubs'. The Duke took the hint, and the editor of the 1896 edition of his works notes 'the banks are now clothed as verdantly as the poet could desire'.

Falls of Drumly Harry Etymology obscure.

A cascade on the Noran Water at the foot of the Angus Braes, Angus (formerly in Tayside region), some 16 km (10 miles) west of Brechin.

Falls of Foyers *Foyers* Gaelic *fothair* 'slope with terraces'.

A set of two falls on the River Foyers, on the east side of Loch Ness in Highland (formerly in Inverness-shire), 32 km (20 miles) southwest of Inverness. The upper fall is 9 m (30 ft) high, and the lower 27 m (90 ft) high. They were once widely admired:

> Among the heathy hills and ragged woods
> The roaring Fyers pours his mossy floods ...
>
> Robert Burns: 'Written with a pencil, standing by the Fall of Fyers, near Loch-Ness' (5 September 1787)

However, the falls were much reduced in volume by the establishment of Britain's first hydroelectric scheme here in 1896, to power the aluminium works (now long abandoned) at the village of **Foyers** at the foot of the falls.

It was a visit to the Falls of Foyers that led to Robert Addams's famous paper on the motion after-effect – also called the waterfall illusion – in 1834:

> Having steadfastly looked for a few seconds at a particular part of the cascade, admiring the confluence and decussation of the currents forming the liquid drapery of waters, and then suddenly directed my eyes to the left, to observe the face of the sombre age-worn rocks immediately contiguous to the water-fall, I saw the rocky surface as if in motion upwards, and with an apparent velocity equal to that of the descending water, which the moment before had prepared my eyes to behold that singular deception.
>
> Robert Addams: 'An account of a peculiar optical phenomenon seen after having looked at a moving body, etc.' in *Philosophical Magazine and Journal of Science* (1834)

Falls of Foyers was the name of a four-masted iron ship built in Port Glasgow in 1883.

Falls of Glomach Etymology unknown.

The second highest (112 m / 367 ft) waterfall in Britain, after EAS A'CHÙAL ALUINN in Sutherland. The falls break the course of the River Elchaig on the remote northern slopes of Sgurr nan Ceathreamhnan (1151 m / 3775 ft) in KINTAIL (formerly in Inverness-shire, now in Highland), and are in the care of the National Trust for Scotland. The mountaineer W.H. Murray describes a visit in his *Undiscovered Scotland* (1951):

> The water came over the cliff in one bound of a hundred feet, hit a crag, and split into two falls, which made the final bound of two hundred and fifty feet. At the bottom a dark, deep cauldron was clouded by grey spray soaring high. The two long leaps of water struck the rock with a roar and rebounded. A fearsome sight …

The Falls are also the subject of a sombre poem by Andrew Young (1885–1971), beginning

> Rain drifts forever in this place …

Falls Road Etymology unknown.

An almost exclusively Catholic working-class street of industrial west BELFAST. A potent element (like the nearby Protestant SHANKILL ROAD) in the sectarian geography of the city, during the Troubles 'the Falls' – the road and its adjacent streets – became synonymous with hard-line Republicanism. The DIVIS FLATS, a flashpoint in the early years of the Troubles, lie in the 'Lower Falls', at its eastern end. The Divis tower blocks were nicknamed Planet of the Irps, punning on the film title *Planet of the Apes* and the transposed initials of the Irish Republican Socialist Party, the political wing of the INLA (Irish National Liberation Army), thought to have been strongly represented in the Divis.

> Up the Falls and down the Shankill
> You'll never see a neater ankle.

The above traditional compliment dates from a time before the Troubles made such an itinerary inadvisable. However, things are beginning to change:

> You know you are getting somewhere when the tourists arrive. I was on the Falls Road the other week and … this bus with about 100 Japanese sightseers appeared round the wall and they all started snapping away.
>
> Gerry Adams: quoted in *The Observer* (9 November 2003)

Falmer Probably 'fallow (i.e. light yellowish brown) pool', OE *fealu* 'fallow' + *mere* 'pool'.

A village on the northeastern outskirts of Brighton. The University of Sussex (opened 1961) (*see under* SUSSEX) is situated here.

Falmouth 'mouth of the River Fal', FAL + OE *mutha* 'mouth'.

A town and port in western Cornwall, on the Cornish Riviera (*see under* CORNISH), at the mouth of the River FAL, about 13 km (8 miles) south of Truro. Its excellent natural harbour, which opens into CARRICK ROADS, has been in use as a port since Tudor times ('It hath many safe and commodious Ports and Havens, as Falmouth vastly spacious' – John Chamberlayne, *The Present State of Great Britain* (1708)); the castles of Pendennis (*see under* PENDENNIS POINT) and ST MAWES were built in 1543 on opposite sides of the estuary to guard the harbour entrance. Fast mail-boats to the Continent were pioneered there in 1688, when it became the Royal Mail Packet Service's first station. In the 17th century it had the name 'Pennycomequick', a reference to the economic flourishing of the town at that time. Vast oil tankers now use the services of its dry dock. Once the Great Western Railway arrived in the mid-19th century it blossomed as a holiday resort.

At the beginning of the 21st century the harbourside area near the docks has begun experiencing regeneration of a gentrified sort: an exclusive marina and new apartments have been built, and a major branch of the National Maritime Museum (*see under* GREENWICH) opened in December 2002. Its innovatively designed building – a mixture of hull-like wood (oak), glass, steel, concrete and slate – evokes the salty life in its look and textures, and its tower affords fine views across the water. The museum's focus is the physics of sail and flotation, and the history of smaller-scale craft, with plenty of hands-on activities to lure small children.

Extending southwards from PENDENNIS POINT to NARE POINT is **Falmouth Bay**. It is alleged to be home to a monster by the name of Morgawr (from a Cornish word for 'sea giant'). The creature is unreliably described as '15 to 18 ft long with a long neck, humped back, a long muscular tail the length of its body and dark brown or black (or mottled grey) skin'. Intermittent sightings have been reported from the 1870s onwards.

In the early morning light Falmouth bay looked as lovely as ever, with its rounded green hills and little fishing boats jilling about under sail off the Manacles.

The Times (18 July 1955)

The former middle-distance runner Sebastian (now Lord) Coe was Conservative Member of Parliament for Falmouth and Camborne from 1992 to 1997.

There are towns and villages called Falmouth in the USA (Kentucky, Massachusetts, Michigan and Virginia), in Canada (Nova Scotia) and in Antigua and Jamaica.

Fanad Irish *Fánaid* 'place on sloping ground'.
A peninsula on the north coast of County Donegal, between Lough Swilly (to the east) and Mulroy Bay (to the west). At its tip is **Fanad Head** (Irish *Cionn Fhanaide*), with its lighthouse.

Fangfoss 'trap ditch', OScand *fang* 'hunting, fishing, trapping' + *foss* 'ditch', possibly a favoured place for catching fish.
A village in the East Riding of Yorkshire, 16 km (10 miles) east of York.

Fannichs, the After Loch *Fannich*, but meaning is obscure.
A range of mountains in Wester Ross, Highland, some 12 km (7 miles) south of the head of Little Loch Broom (*see under* Loch Broom). The highest peak is Sgurr Mor (1110 m / 3641 ft), and there are some fine cliffs in the remote corries of the range. **Loch Fannich** and the **Fannich Forest** (a deer forest) are on the south side of the mountains. Fionn Bheinn, a southern outlier of the Fannichs and, according to the Scottish Mountaineering Club's guide to the Northern Highlands, 'one of the least inspiring tops in Munro's Tables', is the subject of a prophecy of the Brahan Seer (*see under* Brahan):

The day will come when a raven, attired in plaid and bonnet, will drink his fill of human blood on Fionn Bheinn, three times a day, for three successive days.

The hill being such an uninviting lump, its summit has not been visited frequently enough to establish whether this has in fact happened, although most commentators are sceptical about the sartorial aspects of the prophecy.

Far Cotton *Far* to distinguish the village from other places with the same name; *Cotton* 'the cottages or huts', ME *coten* plural of *cot* (*see* -cot, cote).
A village in Northamptonshire, now a southern suburb of Northampton.

Fare, Hill of. *See* Hill of Fare.

Fareham 'homestead where ferns grow', OE *fearn* 'fern' + ham.
A town in Hampshire, on the western side of Portsmouth Harbour, about 10 km (6 miles) northwest of Portsmouth. It was made fashionable in the 18th century by naval officers who (or perhaps whose wives) decided it was a more desirable place to live than Portsmouth. Their

legacy is a number of fine Georgian houses in the High Street.

Farewell 'pleasant spring or stream', OE *fæger* 'fair, pleasant' + *wella* 'spring, stream'.
A village in Staffordshire, about 5 km (3 miles) northwest of Lichfield.

Faringdon 'fern-covered hill', OE *fearn* 'fern' + *dun* (*see* DOWN, -DON); the modern form with -*ing* results from an earlier misunderstanding of spellings such as *Ferendone*, which are also found in the records relating to Farndon, which has the same etymology, and Farrington.
A market town in Oxfordshire (before 1974 in Berkshire), about 27 km (17 miles) southwest of Oxford. Its most notable feature is **Faringdon House**, home of the noted aesthete, composer and eccentric Lord Berners (1883–1950). Visitors to the house in his time were confronted by whippets wearing diamond collars, doves dyed pink and blue, and an antique Rolls Royce with a clavichord built into its rear seat. Berners had **Faringdon Folly**, a 42 m (140 ft) tower, built in 1935 on a nearby hill. It had a sign (prompted by the protest of a do-gooder who thought people might throw themselves from the top) stating, 'Members of the public committing suicide from this tower do so at their own risk.' When the surrealist painter Salvador Dali visited the house he had the grand piano placed in the garden pool and put chocolate eclairs on its black keys: Lord Berners offered to play 'Eclair de lune' on it.

Farnborough¹ 'hill or mound growing with ferns', OE *fearn* 'fern' + *beorg* 'hill, mound'.
A town in Hampshire, about 5 km (3 miles) north of Aldershot. The French emperor Napoleon III (1808–73), who went into exile after France's defeat in the Franco-Prussian War, lived the last years of his life in a mansion called 'Farnborough Hill' near Farnborough, with his wife, Empress Eugénie, and both are buried in the elaborate mausoleum she had built here at St Michael's Catholic Church.

Today, however, Farnborough is much better known for its aeronautical connections. In 1908, the first powered flight by a heavier-than-air aircraft in Britain was made here, by the American aviator Samuel Cody. For many years its airfield was home to the Royal Aircraft Establishment, the UK's main aeronautical research centre. The RAE (now known as QinetiQ) no longer conducts flight tests there, but the airfield continues to be used by such agencies as the RAF Institute of Aviation Medicine and the Air Accident Investigation Branch. And in 1947 the Society of British Aircraft Companies organized the first **Farnborough Air Show**, a now biennial showcase of the British aerospace industry.

T.E. Lawrence, posing as 'Aircraftsman Ross', was found

and exposed by the press at RAF Farnborough in December 1922.

Farnborough was the venue of the first ever international boxing match, on 17 April 1860, in which Tom Sayers of England took on John C. Heenan of the USA. It lasted 42 rounds and ended in a draw.

See also NORTH CAMP.

Farnborough². A southeastern suburb of Greater London, to the southwest of Orpington, in the borough of BROMLEY (before 1965 in Kent).

Farne Islands *Farne* possibly from OE *fearn* 'fern', or from an OCelt name of unknown meaning.

A group of 28 (15 at high tide) small rocky islands in the North Sea, between 2 and 6 km (1.2 and 4 miles) off the Northumberland coast at BAMBURGH. The islands, which are in the care of the National Trust, are an important bird reserve, and the only place on the east coast where Atlantic seals breed.

The largest island is Inner Farne, where St Cuthbert lived between 676 and 684 in a cell surrounded by an embankment so he could only see heaven; he returned to Inner Farne to die in 687, and wanted to be buried here (although he was actually buried on Lindisfarne, then reburied in DURHAM). St Aidan (*c*.600–651), founder of the LINDISFARNE monastery, spent every Lent on Inner Farne. There is a 14th-century chapel. The eider duck, which breeds on the islands, is also known as Cuthbert's duck, in remembrance of the saint's successful efforts to protect these birds.

One of the outermost of the islands is Longstone, site of the lighthouse where Grace Darling's father was keeper. On 7 September 1838, seeing the ship *Forfarshire* wrecked on Big Harcar, the consumptive Grace and her father rowed out in the storm to save nine lives. She was awarded a medal for her bravery, and became a national heroine. Her boat is preserved at the museum in Bamburgh.

Farnham 'river-meadow where ferns grow', OE *fearn* 'fern' + *hamm* 'enclosure, river-meadow' (*see* HAM).

A market town at the western edge of Surrey, in the WAVERLEY district, on the NORTH DOWNS, about 7 km (4 miles) southwest of Aldershot:

> We came to Farnham, of which I can only say, that it is … without exception the greatest corn-market in England, London excepted.
>
>> Daniel Defoe: *A Tour Through the Whole Island of Great Britain* (1724–6)

The town centre, with its fine Tudor and Georgian buildings, is presided over by the ruined keep of the 12th-century castle, which until 1927 served as the palace of the bishops of Winchester.

Waverley Abbey, the first Cistercian house in England

(dating from 1128) lies just to the southeast. Sir Walter Scott is said to have taken the name of the eponymous hero of his novel *Waverley* (1814) from it.

The farmer, radical politician and polemical writer William Cobbett (1763–1835), author of *Rural Rides* (1830), was born in Farnham. His birthplace is now the William Cobbett Inn. Also born in Farnham were the tenor Peter Pears (1910–86) and the diplomat Robert Vansittart (1881–1957), Permanent Secretary at the Foreign Office in the 1930s.

In his 'dictionary of things that there aren't any words for yet', *The Meaning of Liff* (1983), Douglas Adams proposed the word *Farnham* for the sort of feeling you get at four o'clock in the afternoon when you haven't got enough done.

There is a town called Farnham in New York state, USA.

Farnley Tyas 'ferny clearing', *Farnley* OE *fearn* 'fern' + -LEY; *Tyas* denoting manorial ownership in the Middle Ages by the le Tyeis family.

A village in West Yorkshire, 5 km (3 miles) south of Huddersfield.

Farnworth 'enclosure where ferns grow', OE *fearn* 'fern' + *worth* (*see* -WORTH, WORTHY, -WARDINE).

An industrial town in the borough of Bolton, Greater Manchester, 5 km (3 miles) southeast of Bolton itself.

Farrington Gurney *Farrington* 'farmstead where ferns grow', OE *fearn* 'fern' + -TON; *Gurney* denoting manorial ownership in the Middle Ages by the de Gurnay family.

A village in Bath and Northeast Somerset (before 1996 in Avon, before 1974 in Somerset), about 15 km (10 miles) southwest of Bath.

Farsetmore Irish *Fearsad Mór* 'great sandbank'.

A battle site in Donegal, just east of Letterkenny on the Swilly estuary, where, on 8 May 1567, the forces of Shane O'Neill were defeated by Hugh O'Donnell. Within a month Shane O'Neill had been killed.

Faslane Possibly 'camp-place on enclosed land', Gaelic *fas* 'level place on a hillside' + *lann* 'enclosed land'.

A naval port on the GARE LOCH in Argyll and Bute (formerly in Dunbartonshire, then in Strathclyde region), some 50 km (30 miles) northwest of Glasgow. It is here that Britain's nuclear-strike submarines (formerly Polaris, now Trident) are based, attracting frequent anti-nuclear protests.

Fast Castle *Fast* probably OE *fæst* 'secure'.

The ruins of a perilously positioned castle on top of the sea cliffs about 8 km (4 miles) northwest of St Abbs Head. It is the model of Wolf's Crag, the tower of the Master of Ravenswood in Sir Walter Scott's novel *The Bride of Lammermoor* (1819; *see* the LAMMERMUIRS).

Fastnet Rock Possibly an OScand name with *fastr* 'firm, strong'.

A rock in the sea off County Cork, 6 km (4 miles) south of CAPE CLEAR. It is the most southerly point in Ireland. It has a lighthouse, erected in 1854, whose beams are visible for 29 km (17.5 miles).

Fastnet. A sea area in the shipping forecast. It is situated between Shannon (to the west) and Lundy (to the east).

Fastnet Race. One of the best known of ocean yacht races, established in 1925 and held every two years, the winner receiving the **Fastnet Cup**. The course starts at Cowes on the Isle of Wight, follows the coast of southwest England and then heads across the Celtic Sea to the Fastnet Rock, before returning to Cowes – a total distance of 984 km (615 miles). The race has been the final race of the Admiral's Cup since 1957. In 1979 the 303 vessels competing in the race were hit by a violent storm, resulting in the deaths of 17 yachtsmen.

FATDAD. *See* FATLAD.

Fatfield ModE, 'a field producing rich crops'.
A village just south of Washington, Tyne and Wear.

FATLAD. A mnemonic acronym for the six counties of Northern Ireland: Fermanagh, Armagh, Tyrone, Londonderry, Antrim and Down. Nationalists prefer FATDAD, replacing Londonderry with Derry (*see* DERRY/LONDONDERRY).

Faughart. *See under* DUNDALK.

Faversham 'the smith's homestead or village', OE *fæferes* possessive form of *fæfer* 'smith' + HAM.

A market town on the North Kent coast, on a branch of the SWALE[1], to the south of the ISLE OF SHEPPEY, about 8 km (5 miles) southwest of Whitstable. It used to be a flourishing port – it is a 'Corporate Town', having associate status as one of the CINQUE PORTS. Accumulations of silt have robbed it of that role, but its fine array of Tudor, Stuart and Georgian buildings attest to the prosperity of those times. It turned instead to the explosives industry: the Chart Gunpowder Mills were opened in 1760, and from then until the 1930s Faversham was England's gunpowder centre.

Faversham is home to the Shepherd Neame brewery, which has been brewing beer since 1698 and describes itself as 'Britain's oldest brewer'.

Arden of Faversham. A play (1592) of uncertain authorship (it has been attributed to Shakespeare) which tells the story of Mistress Arden, who with her lover hires two assassins (Black Will and Shakebag) to murder her husband.

Feackle Irish *An Fhiacail* 'the tooth'.
A village in County Clare, some 25 km (15 miles) northeast of Ennis. It was the home and burial place of the poet

Brian Merriman (Brian Mac Giolla-Meidhre, d.1805), best known for the bawdy masterpiece *The Midnight Court* (*Cúirt an Mheá-Oíche*, 1780).

Fear Manach. The Irish name for FERMANAGH.

Fearna. The Irish name for FERNS.

Featherbed Moss *Featherbed* ModE, a reference to soft soil, repeated in *moss* from OE *mos* 'marsh'.

The name of two moors on the northern edge of the PEAK DISTRICT, one on the border of Greater Manchester and Derbyshire 8 km (5 miles) northeast of Stalybridge, and the other east of Bleaklow on the border of South Yorkshire and Derbyshire, 12 km (7.5 miles) west of Stocksbridge.

Featherbed Top A modern name: *top* relating to the hill, *featherbed* referring to the soft soil on the hillside.
A hill in Derbyshire, in the HIGH PEAK, about 5 km (3 miles) southeast of Glossop. It is 535 m (1785 ft) in height.

Featherstone 'four stones', OE *feother* 'four' + *stan* (*see* STONE).

A former mining town in West Yorkshire, 18 km (11 miles) southeast of Leeds. In the so-called **Featherstone Disturbance** of 1893, two striking miners were shot dead by soldiers assisting the police during a riot.

Featherstone Rovers rugby league club, formed in 1902, now plays in National League One.

Feldon, the 'field land', OE *feld* (*see* FIELD), where the type of land is distinguished from the local woodland (*see*, for example, ILMINGTON).

An area of rich agricultural clayland in the southeastern part of WARWICKSHIRE, including the STOUR[4] Valley. In the medieval period the Feldon was a corn-growing area, but during the 14th and 15th centuries many local landowners converted the fields into pasture for sheep and cattle.

Felindre 'mill farm', Welsh *felin* 'mill' + *dre* 'farm' (*see* TRE-).
There are three villages of this name in Carmarthenshire, one in Powys and one in Swansea unitary authority.

Felingwmuchaf 'upper mill valley', Welsh *felin* 'mill' + *cwm* (*see* -COMBE, COOMBE) + *uchaf* 'upper'.
A village in Carmarthenshire (formerly in Dyfed), 11 km (6.5 miles) northeast of Carmarthen.

Felixstowe Probably 'Filica's holy place or meeting place', OE male personal name *Filica* + *stow* 'place'. The personal name was later associated with that of St Felix, first bishop of East Anglia.

A town and port on the Suffolk coast, between the mouths of the rivers ORWELL[1] and DEBEN, about 16 km (10 miles) southeast of Ipswich. It owes its commercial status – it is now Britain's largest container port – to a late 19th-century act of revenge: in 1870 the port of HARWICH (on the opposite bank of the STOUR[2] estuary) rejected Colonel George Tomline as its prospective MP, and in a fit of pique

Tomline went off and set about developing Felixstowe (hitherto a quiet seaside village) as a rival to Harwich. It began operations in 1887, and now serves Rotterdam and Zeebrugge. It is also an oil terminal.

Tomline also fitted Felixstowe out as a holiday resort, and M.R. James used it (fictionalized as **Burnstow**) as the setting of his disturbing tale 'Oh, Whistle, and I'll Come to You, My Lad' (1904).

When he was ennobled in 1919, Field Marshal Edmund Allenby (1861–1936) took the title Viscount Allenby of Megiddo and Felixstowe (Megiddo from the battle in which he defeated the Turks in 1918 and Felixstowe because he had close associations with the town).

Frank Whittle, inventor of the jet engine, was a test pilot at the Marine Aircraft Experimental Establishment, Felixstowe (1931–2).

> It is an air-swept place, this sunny Felixstowe.
>
> *Guide to Felixstowe* (1901)

Felling OE *felling* 'clearing in woodland', or *felging* 'fallow land'.

A town east of and contiguous with GATESHEAD, Tyne and Wear (formerly in County Durham).

Felpham 'enclosure with fallow land', OE *felh* 'fallow land' + *hamm* 'enclosure' (*see* HAM).

A seaside village and holiday resort in West Sussex, now effectively an eastern suburb of BOGNOR REGIS.

The poet William Blake lived in a cottage in Felpham for three years from 1800. He described the village as 'sweet Felpham', and referred to the time he spent there as 'three years' slumber on the banks of the ocean':

> Away to sweet Felpham, for Heaven is there;
> The Ladder of Angels descends through the air.

In 1804 Blake was tried in nearby Chichester for sedition and treasonable comments in favour of Napoleon, following an incident in his garden at Felpham in which he tussled with a soldier. He was found not guilty.

Felsted 'place in open land', OE *feld* (*see* FIELD) + *stede* 'place'.
A village in Essex, about 7 km (4 miles) east of Great Dunmow. **Felsted School**, a private school, was founded in 1564.

Fenchurch St Paul. The fictional village in the FENS (based on various actual villages between Huntingdon and King's Lynn, including TERRINGTON ST CLEMENT) that is the setting of Dorothy L. Sayers's campanological detective novel *The Nine Taylors* (1934). In it, Lord Peter Wimsey prangs his car near MARCH (in Cambridgeshire), is obliged to overnight at the rectory of Fenchurch St Paul, finds himself ringing in the New Year on the bells of the local church and is soon plunged into the mystery of the 'Thorpe necklace'.

Fenchurch Street 'street by the church in fenny or marshy ground', *Fenchurch* OE *fenn* 'marsh' + *cirice* 'church' (the marshiness may have been due to the proximity of the Langbourn, a lost river which supposedly ran nearby).
A street in the City of London (EC3), running north-eastwards from Gracechurch Street to Aldgate. **Fenchurch Street Station**, opened in 1841, was the first railway terminus in the City. It now services southern Essex commuterland. It is valued at £200 on a Monopoly board.

Fenland. A local government area in northern Cambridgeshire, including the towns of WISBECH (the administrative centre), CHATTERIS, MARCH and WHITTLESEY. **Fenlands** is another name for the FENS.

Fenny Drayton 'muddy Drayton', *Fenny* OE *fennig* 'muddy, marshy'; *Drayton see* DRAYTON PARSLOW.
A village in Leicestershire, about 9 km (5.5 miles) north-west of Hinckley, near the Warwickshire border. Satellite measurement in 2002 established that a nearby farm is at the precise central point of England (*see also* MERIDEN).

George Fox (1624–91), who founded the Society of Friends (Quakers), was born in Fenny Drayton.

Fenny Stratford 'muddy ford on a Roman road', *Fenny see* FENNY DRAYTON; *Stratford* OE *stræt* (*see* STREET) + FORD.
A village in Buckinghamshire, now incorporated into the southern sector of Milton Keynes.

Fenny Poppers. Six cannon-like devices, which every 11 November are filled with gunpowder and ignited. The resulting *éclat* celebrates the building of the parish church of St Martin's in 1730.

Fens, the OE *fenn* 'marsh'.
A low-lying area (also known as the **Fenlands**) in eastern England, to the west and south of the WASH covering about 6325 sq km (2450 sq miles) in the counties of Cambridgeshire, Lincolnshire, Norfolk and Suffolk. The main Fenland rivers are the GREAT OUSE, the NENE, the WELLAND and the WITHAM, and many smaller watercourses flow through the landscape. Within the overall area are many individually named fens, such as Deeping Fen, Lopham Fen, Redgrave Fen and Wicken Fen (*see under* WICKEN); some of them contain important nature reserves, home to watery creatures as diverse as the otter and the great raft spider.

Originally, as its name suggests (*see above*), this was a land in a continuous state of saturation. The Romans had a go at draining it, but made only a fleeting impact, as did the Normans with a similar attempt in the reign of William the Conqueror; the reeds, the eels, above all the water soon reclaimed their old domain. Modest prominences of solid ground, such as the Isle of Ely (*see under* ELY[1]), where Hereward the Wake held out against the Normans, merely served to emphasize the flatness of this liquid landscape.

Then in 1643 the Earl of Bedford commissioned the Dutch water-engineer Cornelius Vermuyden (1595–1683) to remove the water. He constructed drains and dykes, and created BEDFORD LEVEL, a huge area of peat-rich land in Cambridgeshire and Lincolnshire with considerable agricultural potential (*see also* FORTY FOOT DRAIN, HUNDRED FOOT DRAIN *and* VERMUYDEN'S DRAIN). Unfortunately, as the peat dried it sank. The level of the land dropped, and to counteract the threatened re-inundation by the sea, pumps – powered at first by windmills and later by steam engines – had to be kept constantly in operation.

With these defences in place, the black soil of the Fens produces a cornucopia of cereals, vegetables (notably sugarbeet and potatoes) and (especially around SPALDING) bulbs. But most parts of the Fens are still below sea-level, and outside the stockade the sea is constantly on the prowl, wolflike, looking for a chink.

> To live in the Fens is to receive strong doses of reality. The great, flat melancholy of reality; the wide, empty space of reality. Melancholia and self-murder are not unknown in the Fens. Heavy drinking, madness and sudden acts of violence are not uncommon.
>
> Graham Swift: *Waterland* (1983)

Fen-man. An inhabitant of the Fens.

> ... fen-men, a sort of people (much like the place) of brutish, uncivilized tempers, envious of all others ... and usually walking aloft on a pair of stilts.
>
> William Camden: *Britannia* (1586)

> The Fen-men hold that the Sewers must be kept.
>
> Francis Bacon: *Sylva Sylvarum; or A Natural History* (1626)

Fen-slodger. A local dialect term in former times for a 'Fen-man' (the verb *slodge* meant 'to walk along slouchingly, with your feet dragging'). The name harks back to a time before extensive draining, when the slodgers eked a meagre watery existence from the Fens, making small islands for pasturage and living on wildfowl and fish. They would progress through the watery landscape on stilts, or use vaulting-poles if it were too deep. When drainage began to threaten their way of life in the 15th and 16th centuries they fought back, breaking down the newly created banks and dams, but they could not resist the industrial-scale draining of the 17th century, and by the 18th century the slodgers were no more.

Fen Tiger. A more romantic alternative name for a 'Fen-slodger' (*see above*), alluding to the slodgers' crafty ferocity. The sobriquet 'The Fen Tiger' was adopted by the welterweight boxer Dave 'Boy' Green of CHATTERIS, who was active in the 1970s.

In the Fen Country. A 'symphonic impression' written in 1904 by Ralph Vaughan Williams. It was the composer's first significant orchestral piece. It taps into the idiom of English folk music to evoke the spaciousness and mystery of the Fens.

Fenton 'farmstead in marshland', OE *fenn* 'marsh' + -TON. A town in the POTTERIES, within the unitary authority of Stoke-on-Trent, just to the north of LONGTON (with which it was merged as 'Longshaw' in Arnold Bennett's FIVE TOWNS).

Feock From St *Fioc*, patron saint of the local church. A village in Cornwall, at the northern end of CARRICK ROADS, about 6 km (4 miles) northeast of Falmouth. Trelissick Garden (*see under* TRELISSICK) is just to the northeast.

Fermanagh Irish *Fear Manach* 'men of Monach'; Monach or Monaigh was an ancient tribal leader. A county in the southwest of Northern Ireland. It is bordered to the northwest by Donegal, to the northeast by Tyrone, to the east by Monaghan and to the south by Cavan and Leitrim. Its county town is ENNISKILLEN, and other features include Upper and Lower Lough Erne. Part of it forms the local authority district of Fermanagh.

'dreary steeples of Fermanagh and Tyrone, the'. Winston Churchill's post-First World War description of the Irish Question as it then stood:

> The whole map of Europe has been changed ... The modes of thought of men, the whole outlook on affairs, the grouping of parties, all have encountered violent and tremendous changes in the deluge of the world. But as the deluge subsides and the waters fall short, we see the dreary steeples of Fermanagh and Tyrone emerging once again. The integrity of their quarrel is one of the few institutions that has been unaltered in the cataclysm which has swept the world. That says a lot for the persistency with which Irishmen on the one side or the other are able to pursue their controversies.

Fermoy Irish *Mainistir Fhear Maí* 'monastery of the men of the plain'. A market town on the River BLACKWATER[2] in County Cork, 30 km (20 miles) northeast of Cork itself. Previously a small village, Fermoy was bought in 1791 by John Anderson, formerly a Glasgow labourer. Anderson persuaded the British government to build a barracks here, and developed the town around the trade with the military. Fermoy subsequently thrived, and in the 19th century had twice its present population. The extensive barracks were destroyed in 1921, during the War of Independence.

> There once was a lass of Fermoy
> Gave soldiers the ultimate joy:
>   She'd start with a kiss
>   And finish with bliss
> When they found she in fact was a boy.
>
> Anon.: from *The Big Boys' Book of Bumper Campfire Fun* (1928)

Ferndale 'fern valley', OE *fearn* 'fern' + *dæl* 'valley'.

A small town in the Rhondda, in RHONDDA CYNON TAFF unitary authority (formerly in Glamorgan, then in Mid Glamorgan), 5 km (3 miles) southwest of Mountain Ash. Its Welsh name is **Glyn Rhedynog** ('fern valley', *rhedynog* 'ferny').

Ferndown Originally *Fyrne*, either 'wooded hill', OE *fergen*, or 'ferny place', OE *fierne*, with the later addition of *dun* (*see* DOWN, -DON).

A town in Dorset, about 8 km (5 miles) north of Bournemouth.

Ferns Irish *Fearna* 'elder trees'.

A village in County Wexford, 10 km (6 miles) northeast of Enniscorthy. St Maodhog founded a monastery here in the 6th century, and achieved holiness by daily lying naked on a cold stone slab and reciting the psalms (the 1817 cathedral at Ferns is dedicated to him). Ferns has the remains of an abbey and castle, both dating from the 12th century, at which time, under Dermot MacMurrough, Ferns was the capital of Leinster. The seat of the diocese of Ferns is at WEXFORD.

Ferns Three. Three young men in the diocese of Ferns who when boys were abused by a local priest. When in 2002 they made it known how Brendan Comiskey, Bishop of Ferns, had treated their complaints, he was obliged to resign. In 2003 the church made an out-of-court payment to one of the complainants.

Ferryhill OE *fergen* 'wooded hill', with *hill* tautonymically added later.

A town in County Durham, 8 km (5 miles) northeast of Bishop Auckland.

Feshie. *See* GLEN FESHIE.

Fethard-on-Sea *Fethard* Irish *Fiodh Ard* 'high wood'; the affix distinguishes it from various other Irish villages of the same name.

A village on the Hook Peninsula, County Wexford, 20 km (12 miles) southeast of Waterford.

Fethard-on-Sea Boycott. In 1957 the village became the scene of a bitter sectarian confrontation, in which the Catholics of the village, encouraged by their clergy, boycotted Protestant businesses and professionals. The ill-feeling arose after Sheila Cloney, a local Protestant woman married to a Catholic, refused to have her children educated as Catholics, despite an earlier promise. Instead she took her two young daughters to Northern Ireland, and then to the Orkneys. The couple were eventually reconciled after a year, and the boycott ended. The story is the subject of the film *A Love Divided* (1999).

Fetlar Probably 'bands', OScand *fetill* 'band, girdle'.

An island in the northeast of Shetland, some 48 km (30 miles) north of Lerwick. It can be reached by ferry from Yell and Unst. The island is a noted bird sanctuary, and between 1967 and 1975 snowy owls bred here.

Fettercairn 'wooded slope', from OCelt elements found in Gaelic as *fothair* 'slope' and *carden* 'wood, thicket'.

A village in the MEARNS, at the foot of the CAIRN O' MOUNT, Aberdeenshire (formerly in Kincardineshire, then in Grampian region), 7 km (4 miles) northeast of Laurencekirk. It is affectionately known as **Fetterie** by the locals, and the Fettercairn malt whisky distillery dates from 1824. Kenneth II was killed at Fettercairn in 995, it is said by his own subjects.

Fetterie. The local nickname for FETTERCAIRN.

Fetter Lane 'lane frequented by impostors or cheats', ME *faitour* 'impostor, cheat'.

A road in the City of London (EC4), linking FLEET STREET with HOLBORN (an extension, **New Fetter Lane**, branches off eastwards to Holborn Circus). The aspersions implicit in its name (*see above*) were probably cast not on the lawyers who have operated in this area since the Middle Ages, nor on the preachers who frequented the lane in the 17th century, still less on the journalists who have been more recent denizens (although Maxwell House, Robert Maxwell's headquarters when proprietor of the *Mirror*, was at the top of New Fetter Lane), but on the local vagrants and beggars of medieval times, who specialized in feigning illness in order to elicit sympathy and money.

Feus of Caldhame *Feu* may be from Gaelic *fuachd* 'cold', reinforcing the meaning of ME *Caldhame*, 'cold farm'.

A small settlement in Angus (formerly in Tayside region), 9 km (5.5 miles) northeast of Brechin.

Ffestiniog Either 'land of Ffestin' or an OCelt word meaning 'defensive position'.

A village in Gwynedd (formerly in Merioneth), 5 km (3 miles) south of Blaenau Ffestiniog, in the **Vale of Ffestiniog**. The surrounding area is known as ARDUDWY.

Ffestiniog Railway. The oldest independent railway company in the world, founded by act of Parliament in 1832. It still runs steam trains for tourists from BLAENAU FFESTINIOG to PORTHMADOG.

Fforest Fawr 'great forest', Welsh *fawr* 'great'.

An upland area rising to over 600 m (2000 ft) in the BRECON BEACONS National Park, straddling Powys (formerly Brecknockshire) and Carmarthenshire (formerly Dyfed). It was one of the largest hunting preserves in Wales, and was Crown property from the time of Henry VIII until 1819.

Ffynnon Wenfrewi. *See under* HOLYWELL.

Fiddler and the Maids, the. *See under* STANTON DREW.

Fiddlers Hamlet Probably from a surname *Fiddler*, popular in Essex.

❖ field ❖

Old English *feld*, appearing in Modern English place names as -*field*, confusingly does not usually mean 'field' in the sense of enclosed cultivated or pasture land. This was a development in sense occurring just before the Norman Conquest as a growth in population led to former rough open lands being used for cultivation. The element in early names means 'open land', that is, land cleared of trees, without buildings, and not particularly hilly. Many significant settlements began in places that were originally *feld* land: ENFIELD (Greater London), MACCLESFIELD (Cheshire), SHEFFIELD (Yorkshire) and many examples of Hatfield amongst them (such as HATFIELD[1], Hertfordshire). Hatfield, where *feld* is combined with *hæth* 'uncultivated land', nicely illustrates this early sense of 'open land', with the first element specifying the rough type of area that existed before enclosure and settlement. TURVILLE (Buckinghamshire) and Longville (Shropshire) show the assimilation of Old English *feld* to French *ville*.

In later use, the element seems to have taken over some of the senses of *æcer* 'cultivated land of limited extent'. An acre was originally the area of land that could be ploughed by a team of oxen in a single day, and this specific measurement has become the main sense of the element today. While there are many examples of *æcer* in place names, relatively few became large and flourishing towns: ALSAGER (Cheshire) is one. Nowadays names of the type 'Broad Acre Field' are very common on farms, where neither acre nor field retain much of their original sense.

A village in Essex, about 1.5 km (1 mile) southeast of Epping.

Fiend's Fell. *See* CROSS FELL.

Fife In ancient texts it is *Fib* 'territory of Vip', which may be a personal name. The modern Gaelic name is *Fiobh*. Gaelic *fiamh* 'path' has also been suggested, but is unlikely.

A former county and region, and current unitary authority, of east central Scotland, broadly comprising the wide peninsula projecting into the North Sea between the Firth of Forth and the Firth of Tay.

> Gurlie an gray the snell Fife shore,
> Frae the peat-green sea the cauld haar drives …
>
> Sydney Goodsir Smith: *Armageddon in Albyn*, VII, 'The War in Fife' (*gurlie* 'stormy', *snell* 'fiercely cold', *haar* 'sea mist')

The place seems to have a reputation among poets for its bracing climate:

> This wind from Fife has cruel fingers, scooping
> The heat from streets with salty finger-tips …
>
> Norman MacCaig: 'Double Life', from *Riding Lights* (1955)

The old county was bounded on the west by Perthshire, Kinross-shire and Clackmannanshire. **Fifeshire** is an alternative form of the name, although the suffix is otiose, there being no town called Fife. Fife is still generally referred to as **the Kingdom of Fife**, possibly because it was once – until the mid-9th century – an independent Pictish kingdom, although others attribute the name to Fife's isolated, self-contained and famously independent-minded position – the county resisted incorporation into TAYSIDE region in the local government reorganization of 1975. This spirit may have led to the term **Fifish** for 'eccentric', 'slightly mad'. A native of Fife is called a **Fifer**, the plural form of which is an informal designation for **East Fife FC**. Founded in 1903 as **East of Fife**, the club is based at Bayview Park in Methil on the northern shore of the Firth of Forth (*see also* BUCKHAVEN *and* FORFAR).

> Fifers make the rest of Scotland look like a living sculpture designed to carry across the concepts of optimism, balance, health and good humour. Cold scabby bars, cold sea, cold grey hearts, rampant unemployment, cold grey knife-scars, and that's just from the tourist brochure …
>
> Euan Ferguson: in *The Observer* (13 January 2002)

Others have seen the people of Fife as remarkably normal:

> In a cottage in Fife
> Lived a man and his wife,
> Who, believe me, were comical folk;
> For, to people's surprise,
> They both saw with their eyes,
> And their tongues moved whenever they spoke! [etc.]
>
> Anon.: nursery rhyme

Well, perhaps not *altogether* normal …

> There was an old spinster of Fife
> Who had never been kissed in her life.
> Along came a cat
> And she said, 'I'll kiss that,'
> But the cat meowed, 'Not on your life!'
>
> Anon.: limerick

'Cooper of Fife, The'. A traditional song beginning:

> There was a wee Cooper wha lived in Fife
> Nickety, nackety, noo, noo, noo,
> And he had gotten a gentle wife,
> Hey Willy Wallacky, hoo John Dougal,
> Alane, quo' Rushity, roue, roue, roue.

The wife is too 'gentle' to demean herself on behalf of the cooper (barrel-maker), and refuses to bake or brew, card or spin, wash or wring, until threatened with a beating.

Fife Adventurers, the. A company promoted by James VI

to colonize the Isle of LEWIS, and to extirpate the natives should they prove a nuisance.

Fife Ness. The easternmost point of Fife, some 3 km (2 miles) northeast of Crail.

See also the EAST NEUK *and* NESS.

Fifie. A type of herring drifter built up to the 1930s, and still in use in the 1950s, when herring were more abundant.

Howe of Fife. The wide valley of the River Eden, stretching northeastwards from the Lomond Hills to Eden Mouth north of St Andrews.

'Witch of Fife, The'. A short poem by James Hogg, from his collection *The Queen's Wake* (1813) about Mary Queen of Scots.

> Away, thou bonny witch o' Fife,
>> On foam of the air to heave an' flit.
> An' little reck thou of a poet's life,
>> For he sees thee yet, he sees thee yet.

Fifehead Magdalen *Fifehead* '(estate of) five hides (of land)', OE *fif* 'five' + *hid* 'hide' (one hide was about 120 acres or 48.5 ha); *Magdalen* from the dedication of the local church to St Mary Magadalen.

A village in Dorset, about 19 km (12 miles) northwest of Blandford Forum.

Filey Possibly 'promontory like a sea monster', OE *fifel* 'monster'+ *eg* 'promontory, land protruding into water' (*see* -EY, -EA), referring to Filey Brigg.

A seaside resort in North Yorkshire, 12 km (7 miles) south of Scarborough. It overlooks sandy **Filey Bay**, which is enclosed at its northern end by the headland of **Filey Brigg**. Filey was the site of a Roman signal station, and is noted for its cliff gardens. Prior to turning their town into a polite Edwardian resort, Filey folk were known for their godlessness, and would fling fish at visiting preachers.

> There was an old person of Filey
> Of whom his acquaintance spoke highly.
> He danced perfectly well,
> To the sound of a bell
> And delighted the people of Filey.
>> Edward Lear: limerick

> There was an old woman of Filey
> Who valued old candle ends highly.
> When no one was looking
> She'd use them in cooking –
> 'It's wicked to waste,' she said dryly.
>> Anon.: limerick

Filton 'farm or estate where hay is made', OE *filethe* 'hay' + -TON.

A northern suburb of BRISTOL, in South Gloucestershire (before 1996 in Avon, before 1974 in Gloucestershire). Its fame rests on its airfield, where the British & Colonial Aeroplane Company began operations in 1910. Later, under the more familiar name of the Bristol Aeroplane Company, it developed and built such Second World War aircraft as the Blenheim and the Beaufighter here, and its successor British Aerospace built and flew Concordes at Filton.

Finalty Hill Etymology unknown, but the first element is possibly Gaelic *fionn* 'white'.

A mountain (901 m / 2954 ft) in the southern Cairngorms, 3 km (2 miles) west-northwest of MAYAR.

Finchingfield 'Finc's people's open land', OE male personal name *Finc* + -*inga*- (*see* -ING) + *feld* (*see* FIELD).

A village in Essex, about 16 km (10 miles) southeast of Saffron Walden. It can make a reasonable claim to the title 'England's most photographed village' – its photogenic attractions including an ancient bridge over a slow-flowing stream, ducks on the village green, a pretty church (St John the Baptist, with a Norman tower), a windmill and assorted attractive houses and cottages.

Finchley 'glade frequented by finches', OE *finc* 'finch' + -LEY.

A residential area of northern Greater London (N2, N3, N12), to the northwest of Hampstead Heath (*see under* HAMPSTEAD), in the borough of BARNET. The build-up of housing began here in the 1870s, and before the 20th century was very old Finchley was a sea of modest but salubrious commuter homes. Its middle-middle-class aspirational demographic suited it perfectly to Margaret Thatcher, who was the local MP from 1959 to 1992.

East Finchley 'Underground' station, on the Northern line, was opened in 1939, Finchley Central and West Finchley in 1940.

The comic actor Terry-Thomas (1911–90), the Kent and England wicketkeeper Godfrey Evans (1920–99) and the singer George Michael (b.1963; original name Georgios Panayiotou) were born in Finchley.

'Finchley Central'. A pop song (1967) by British songwriter-producer Geoff Stephens, which enjoyed a degree of chart success in The New Vaudeville Band's version. (*See also* 'Winchester Cathedral' *under* WINCHESTER.)

Finchley Road. A road in North London that runs southwards from the North Circular Road in Finchley through Golders Green and West Hampstead to Swiss Cottage. It was at a point on or just off it, in the vicinity of Swiss Cottage, that the novelist Wilkie Collins and the artist John Everett Millais, walking from Hanover Terrace to Millais's studio in Gower Street one evening in the late 1850s, encountered what Millais's biography described as 'a young and very beautiful woman dressed in flowing white robes that shone in the moonlight. She seemed to float rather than run in their direction, and, on coming up to the … young men, she paused for a moment in an attitude of supplication and terror'. The incident provided Collins with the inspiration for the opening of his 'sensation novel'

The Woman in White (1860), in which a similar apparition appears to one of the book's many narrators:

> I had now arrived at that particular point of my walk where four roads met – the road to Hampstead ... the road to Finchley, the road to West End, and the road back to London. I had mechanically turned in this latter direction and was strolling along the lonely high-road when ... every drop of blood in my body was brought to a stop by the touch of a hand ... on my shoulder from behind me. ... There, in the middle of the broad, bright high-road ... stood the figure of a solitary Woman, dressed from head to foot in white garments, her face bent in grave enquiry on mine, her hand pointing to the dark cloud over London, as I faced her.

March to Finchley, The. A painting (1749–50) by William Hogarth, inspired by the 1745 Jacobite Rising. The scene depicts soldiers setting off from London to take on the rebels, while being distracted by all the temptations of city life (principally drink and whores). When the painting was shown to George II, the king was apparently immune to the anti-Jacobite subtleties of the work, as the following famous exchange indicates:

> 'Pray, who is this Hogarth?' 'A painter, my liege.' 'I hate bainting and boetry too! neither the one nor the other ever did any good! Does the fellow mean to laugh at my guards?' 'The picture, may it please your Majesty, must undoubtedly be considered a burlesque.' – 'What a bainter burlesque a soldier? He deserves to be picketed for his insolence! Take this trumpery out of my sight.'

Findhorn Gaelic *fionn* 'white' + a pre-Celtic river name thought to be the same as that in DEVERON.

A river of northeast Scotland, rising in the MONADHLIATH MOUNTAINS of Highland and flowing northeastward 99 km (61 miles) into Moray to meet the Moray Firth at **Findhorn Bay**, beyond Forres. The village of **Findhorn** is on the northeast side of the bay. The first village here was overwhelmed by drifting sand in 1694, and the second destroyed in a flood in 1701.

On 3 August 1829 the valley of the Findhorn was the site of the so-called 'Muckle Spate' ('big flood'), the most severe flood ever recorded in Britain. Storms in northeast Scotland caused the river to rise by about 15 m (49 ft), sweeping over farmland and small towns. There were few fatalities but the event led to the creation of a national emergency fund. Meteorologists measured the equivalent of 95 mm (3.75 in) of rainfall in 24 hours at the town of Huntly. The River Findhorn also suffered massive flooding in August 1970.

Findhorn Community, the. A famous New Age community established at the village of Findhorn by Peter and Eileen Caddy, who went there in 1962 and had spectacular success in growing plants on the hitherto barren sand dunes.

Findochty 'white piece of land', Gaelic *fionn* 'white' + *dabhach*, a unit of arable land.

A small, attractive fishing port on the north coast of Moray (formerly in Banffshire, then in Grampian region), 5 km (3 miles) northeast of Buckie.

Findo Gask Possibly 'white nook', *Findo* Gaelic *fionn* 'white'; *Gask* Gaelic *gasc* 'nook'.

A small settlement in Perth and Kinross (formerly in Perthshire, and then in Tayside region), 12 km (7 miles) west of Perth. There is the site of a Roman camp at nearby Gask House.

Findon Possibly 'white hill', Gaelic *fionn* 'white' + *dùn* (*see* DOWN, -DON), but the order of elements is unusual.

A small former fishing village, also known as **Finnan**, on the east coast of Aberdeenshire (formerly in Kincardineshire, then in Grampian region), 9 km (5.5 miles) south of Aberdeen.

Finnan haddie. Haddock smoked using peat or green wood.

Finea. An alternative spelling of FINNEA.

Fine Gall. *See* FINGAL.

Finfolkaheem. *See under* EYNHALLOW.

Fingal Irish *Fine Gall* 'tribe or territory of foreigners', referring to the Vikings who settled here.

A new Irish local authority, established in 1994 in the northern part of County Dublin.

Fingal's Cave. A dramatic and much-trumpeted cave, at the southernmost tip of the Hebridean island of STAFFA. At 75 m (245 ft) deep, it is half filled with the ocean's swell, above which the columned walls comprising regular polygonal pillars rise some 20 m (65 ft) to the roof.

Sir Joseph Banks, who visited Staffa in 1772, reported that the locals called the cave 'the Cave of Fingal' (after the ancient Irish hero Fingal, otherwise known as Finn MacCool), although the recorded Gaelic name is **An Uamh Binn** ('the melodious cave'). The scientist was moved to philosophize:

> Compared to this what are the cathedrals or the palaces built by men! mere models or playthings, imitations as diminutive as his works will always be when compared with those of nature. Where now is the boast of the architect! regularity, the only part in which he fancied himself to exceed his mistress, Nature, is here found in her possession, and here it has been for ages undescribed.
>
> Joseph Banks: quoted in Thomas Pennant, *A Tour of Scotland and a Voyage to the Hebrides; MDCCLXXII* (1773)

In the wake of Banks came a host of tourists. The poet Keats visited in 1818, and described Fingal's Cave thus:

Suppose now the Giants who rebelled against Jove had taken a whole Mass of black Columns and bound them together like bunches of matches – and then with immense Axes had made a cavern in the body of these columns ... For solemnity and grandeur it far surpasses the finest Cathedral.

John Keats: letter to Tom Keats (23/26 July 1818)

Keats also attempted a poem to 'This Cathedral of the Seas', which he included in the letter, but apologized (as well he might have) for its poor quality: 'I am sorry I am so indolent as to write such stuff as this', he wrote. Wordsworth, visiting in 1833, was distracted by the crowds, and did little better on the poetic front. J.M.W. Turner took a steamship trip to the island two years earlier, and this resulted in a notable oil painting, but perhaps the most artistically productive visit was that of a horribly seasick Felix Mendelssohn in 1829, a visit that resulted in the concert overture Opus 26 (1832), known in full as *The Hebrides (Fingal's Cave)*. Mendelssohn's companion Klingemann, secretary to the Hanoverian legation in London, wrote that the pillars made the cave:

... look like the inside of an immense organ, black and resounding, and absolutely without purpose, and quite alone, the wide grey sea within and without.

Finisterre Spanish, from Latin *finis terrae* 'land's end'. Cape Finisterre is an Atlantic cape on the northwest coast of Spain, and that country's most westerly point.
The former designation of the sea area FITZROY.

Finnan. Another name for FINDON.

Finnea Irish *Fiodh an Átha* 'wood of the ford' (*see* FORD).
A village on the River Inny in County Westmeath, 28 km (17 miles) north of Mullingar. It is also spelt **Finea**. Percy French uses it to give directions to Ballyjamesduff in his haunting 1912 song, 'Come Back, Paddy Reilly':

The Garden of Eden is vanished they say
But I know the lie of it still;
Just turn to the left at the bridge of Finea,
And stop on the way to Cootehill.

Battle of Finnea Bridge (5 August 1646). An engagement in which the Confederate Catholics under Myles 'the Slasher' O'Reilly defended the strategically important bridge against the Parliamentarians under General Munro. O'Reilly was killed ...

He fell, but the foot of a foeman passed
Not on the bridge of Finea.

Finsbury 'Finn's manor', OScand *Finnes* possessive form of male personal name *Finn* + ME *bury* (*see* BURY).
A district and former borough of northern Central London (EC1), in the borough of Islington, to the east of KING'S CROSS. Before the Great Fire it had been mainly open land,

known as **Finsbury Fields** (*see below*), but in the following hundred years it was extensively built over. The area's first major traffic artery, the City Road, was constructed in 1761 (it was not joined by Rosebery Avenue until 1895), and in the last quarter of the 18th century **Finsbury Circus** and **Finsbury Square** were laid out as part of a new residential suburb, designed by George Dance. The borough of Finsbury was created in 1900, but it was abolished and absorbed into Islington in 1965.

Before the Second World War, Finsbury had a reputation as a hotbed of socialism – it was dubbed '**Little Moscow**' – and during the war a memorial was erected here to Lenin, who had lived and worked in the borough. It was designed by the modernist architect Berthold Lubetkin (also responsible for the ground-breaking **Finsbury Health Centre** in 1938). Even at the height of fraternal feelings with the Soviet Union the memorial was none too popular, and soon after the war it was quietly removed.

John Wesley lived and preached in Finsbury – his chapel (1778), where Margaret Thatcher was married, is in the City Road, just to the north of BUNHILL FIELDS. The southwestern part of Finsbury, merging into Clerkenwell, is home to a sizeable Italian community.

The Indian-born Dadabhai Naoraji (1825–1917) became Liberal MP for Finsbury Central, and the first 'black' British MP, on 6 July 1892.

Finsbury ... seems always to have been a fairly rebelly quarter.

Manchester Guardian (2 July 1959)

See also CITY ROAD.

Finsbury bridge. A late 20th-century slang term, in the context of gay sex, for a man's perineum (the area between the scrotum and the anus). The reason for the application is not known.

Finsbury Fields. A former open area to the north of the City of London, in what is now Finsbury. Originally marshy land, in the 16th and early 17th centuries it was drained and laid out with trees and pleasant walkways. Sober and godly citizens of London would come out in the evenings and at weekends to disport themselves and take the air here – a fact alluded to by Shakespeare when he has Hotspur poke fun at his wife Kate for her mealy-mouthedness:

You swear like a comfit-makers wife ...
And givest such sarcenet surety for thy oaths,
As if thou never walk'st further than Finsbury.
Swear me, Kate, like a lady as thou art,
A good mouth-filling Oath.

Henry IV, Part 1 (1596), III.i (*sarcenet* a kind of thin taffeta)

Finsbury Park. Originally a park opened in 1857, to the south of Hornsey (N8), on a site formerly called Hornsey Wood, and designated for the use of the inhabitants of

Finsbury. The opening of Finsbury Park mainline railway station in 1861 and of the Underground station (on the Piccadilly and Victoria lines) in 1904 reinforced the application of the park's name to the surrounding area. Since 1990 the park has hosted the annual Irish popular-music festival, the Fleadh (pronounced 'flaa'). **Finsbury Park Mosque** achieved notoriety in the early 21st century as a reputed hotbed of militant Islamists, fronted by radical cleric and tabloid hate-figure Abu Hamza.

Fintona Irish *Fionntamhnach* 'bright clearing '.
A village in County Tyrone, 12 km (7 miles) south of Omagh.

Fintry 'the white house', OCelt *gwen*, Gaelicized as *fionn, finn* 'white, fair' + OCelt *tref* (*see* TRE-).
A village some 20 km (12 miles) southwest of Stirling, in the valley between the Campsie Fells to the south and the **Fintry Hills** to the north. It was formerly in Stirlingshire, then in Central region, and is now in the unitary authority of Stirling. The Fintry Hills rise to 512 m (1678 ft) at Stronend, and at their eastern end merge with the GARGUNNOCK Hills. East of the village is the **Loup of Fintry**, a 29 m (94 ft) waterfall on the River Endrick.
See also CRAW ROAD.

Fiodh an Átha. The Irish name for FINNEA.

Fiodh Ard. The Irish name for FETHARD-ON-SEA.

Fionn Bheinn. A southern outlier of the FANNICHS.

Fionnphort 'white harbour', Gaelic *fionn* 'white' + *port/phort* 'harbour'.
A village (pronounced 'finna-fət') at the western extremity of the Ross of MULL, in Argyll and Bute (formerly in Strathclyde). It is from here that the ferry sails to IONA.

Fionntamhnach. The Irish name for FINTONA.

Firle Beacon *Firle* from a local settlement name (the village of West Firle is nearby), 'place where oak-trees grow', OE *fierel*.
A high point on the SOUTH DOWNS, 217 m (713 ft) above sea level, about 8 km (5 miles) north of Seaford. Nearby is **Firle Place**, a Tudor mansion heavily neoclassicized in the early 18th century.

First Coast, Second Coast Etymology unknown.
Tiny settlements on GRUINARD BAY, Highland (formerly in Ross and Cromarty), some 12 km (7 miles) northeast of Poolewe.

Firth of Clyde. *See under* CLYDE.

Firth of Forth. *See under* FORTH.

Firth of Lorne. *See under* LORNE.

Firth of Tay. *See under* TAY.

Fir Tree The name of the local public house.
A small village in County Durham, 3 km (2 miles) southwest of Crook.

Fishamble Street From *fish shambles*; *shamble* is ultimately from OE *sceamol* 'slab, table', used here for the market stalls where meat and fish were sold.
A street in Dublin, the site of a fish market until the end of the 17th century. It subsequently became a residential street, and home to a famous Music Hall where the first performance of Handel's *Messiah* was given on 13 April 1742.

Fishbourne 'fish stream, stream where fish are caught', OE *fisc* 'fish' + *burna* 'stream'.
A village in West Sussex, about 3 km (2 miles) west of Chichester. It is famous for its Roman palace, remains of which were discovered in 1960. Covering 4 ha (10 acres), this must have been one of the most splendid and sumptuous of its type in Northern Europe in the 1st century AD, with its marble-inlaid walls, exquisite floor-mosaics and extensive grounds. It is thought to have belonged to Cogidubnus, British king of the Regni and an ally of Rome.

Fisher From the name of a submerged sandbank, Great *Fisher* Bank.
A sea area in the shipping forecast. It is in the NORTH SEA, to the south of Norway, between South UTSIRE to the north, FORTIES to the west and GERMAN BIGHT to the south.

Fisherstreet. An alternative name for DOOLIN.

Fishguard 'fish yard', OScand *fiskr* 'fish' + *garthr* 'yard'.
A seaport and holiday resort on the Irish Sea in Pembrokeshire (formerly in Dyfed), on **Fishguard Bay**, 24 km (14.5) miles southwest of Cardigan. The Welsh name is **Abergwaun** ('mouth of the River Gwaun'). There is a ferry crossing to Rosslare in Ireland.
The last foreign invasion of British soil took place at Fishguard during the French Revolutionary Wars, when, on 22 February 1797, 1000 French troops, freshly recruited from French prisons, landed here. However, they were quickly rounded up, having over-indulged in brandy from the local hostelries; their American commander, demonstrating greater concern to avoid collateral damage than his more recent successors, explained that he considered it 'unnecessary to attempt any military operations as they would tend only to bloodshed'. Also playing a part in the French downfall was, according to local tradition, one Jemima Nicholas (d.1832), who encouraged her lady friends to don red cloaks and marched them fiercely towards the French. The invaders panicked, taking them for redcoats, and Jemima Nicholas was thereafter celebrated as 'the General of the Red Army'.
The part of the town called **Lower Fishguard** doubled as Llareggub (*see* LAUGHARNE) in the 1971 film of Dylan Thomas's *Under Milk Wood*.

Fishnish 'fish promontory', OScand *fiskr* 'fish' + *nes* (*see* NESS).
A small settlement on the east coast of Mull, Argyll and

Bute (formerly in Argyll, then in Strathclyde region), 20 km (12 miles) southeast of Tobermory. Just to the west is the tautologically named **Fishnish Point**, and west again is **Fishnish Bay**. There is a car ferry from Fishnish to Lochaline on the mainland.

Fishtown of Usan Presumably because it is a fishing port. The meaning of *Usan* is unknown.

A small settlement on the North Sea coast of Angus (formerly in Tayside region), 3 km (2 miles) south of Montrose. It merges with **Seaton of Usan**, just south of Usan House and the farm of **Mains of Usan**.

Fit o' Shapinsay. *See under* SHAPINSAY.

Fitz Originally *Fittesho* 'Fitt's hill-spur', OE *Fittes* possessive form of male personal name *Fitt + hoh* 'hill-spur'.

A village in Shropshire, about 8 km (5 miles) northwest of Shrewsbury.

Fitzrovia From The *Fitzroy* Tavern + the Latinate place-suffix *-ia*. The name is not recorded until well after the area's heyday, in a 1958 article in the *Times Literary Supplement* by the egregious Ceylon-born Fitzrovian J.M. Tambimuttu, publisher of slim volumes of verse and editor of *Poetry London* magazine; there is no evidence that he coined it.

A name for an area of the WEST END[1] of London to the north of Oxford Street and the west of Tottenham Court Road that during the Second World War and into the early 1950s was the haunt of a somewhat louche arty and literary set – a sort of ersatz Quartier Latin.

Its geographical epicentre was suspended magnetically between the twin poles of BLOOMSBURY and London University to the east and PORTLAND PLACE and the BBC to the west, but its spiritual home was dispersed among the pubs in that area. Its original identification was with The Fitzroy Tavern, on the corner of Charlotte Street (whence the name – *see above*), but it was The Wheatsheaf in Rathbone Place that had the most celebrated Bohemian colony, and other favoured watering holes included The Black Horse, The Marquess of Granby and The Highlander. Amongst its habitués were Dylan Thomas, Wyndham Lewis, Augustus John, John Minton, Nina Hamnett and perhaps the archetypal Fitzrovian, Julian Maclaren-Ross, a minorly talented *flâneur* who recorded its intermittent charms. Several of the characters in Anthony Powell's novel sequence *A Dance to the Music of Time* (1951–75) were drawn from it.

Fitzrovian. A denizen of Fitzrovia.

FitzRoy Named in honour of the British vice admiral and meteorologist Robert FitzRoy (1805–65), who captained HMS *Beagle* on the South American expedition in which Charles Darwin took part, and who in the 1850s founded the Meteorological Office.

A sea area in the shipping forecast. It is in the eastern Atlantic, off the west coast of France and the northwestern corner of Spain, between SOLE to the north, BISCAY to the east and TRAFALGAR to the south. The name replaced the former designation FINISTERRE (which was, confusingly, used by Spain for a different sea area) in February 2002.

Fitzwilliam From the *Fitzwilliam* Hemsworth Colliery Company, which established the village at the beginning of the 20th century; the land was owned by Earl Fitzwilliam in the 19th century.

A village in West Yorkshire, 8 km (5 miles) southeast of Wakefield. The otherwise unheralded Fitzwilliam resonates in cricketing folklore as the birthplace of the Yorkshire and England cricketer Geoffrey Boycott (b.1940), an opening batsman of archetypal Yorkshire cussedness, who displayed limpet-like immovability at the batting crease in virtually all of his 108 test matches between 1964 and 1982.

Five Boroughs. A collective term for DERBY, LEICESTER, LINCOLN, NOTTINGHAM[1] and STAMFORD in the time of the DANELAW. This short-lived independent Danish kingdom or federation, founded by treaty between King Alfred and Guthrum sometime around 886, was based on these five fortified towns. A poem in the *Anglo-Saxon Chronicle* under the year 942 celebrates the capture of the Five Boroughs from the Danes by King Edmund I, Alfred's grandson.

Five Fifths, the. The five ancient kingdoms of Ireland that emerged in the early Christian era, known in Irish as **Cuíg Cuígí.** They were ULSTER, MEATH, LEINSTER, MUNSTER and CONNACHT, and, although nominally subject to a high king, they were usually at war with each other. An alternative name for them is the **Five Kingdoms.**

Five Lamps, the. A five-branched 19th-century lamp post that forms a Dublin landmark at the junction of North Strand, Portland Row, Seville Place, Amiens Street and Killarney Street.

Fivemiletown From its approximate distance from Clabby, CLOGHER and Colebrooke.

A small town in County Tyrone, 20 km (12 miles) east of Enniskillen. It provides the title of a poem and of a collection (1987) by Tom Paulin. Here, 'apart from Armagh, Augher and Clogher, presbyters and piddlers should pray for me' (W.R. Rodgers (1909–69), in his unfinished collection of essays, *The Character of Ireland*).

Five Roads From its location at the junction of five roads.

A village in Carmarthenshire (formerly in Dyfed), 5 km (3 miles) north of Llanelli, and 6 km (4 miles) southeast of FOUR ROADS.

Five Sisters of Kintail, the. *See under* KINTAIL.

Five Towns. The towns in the POTTERIES, in Staffordshire, that Arnold Bennett (1867–1931) used as the scene of the best-known of his novels and stories, one of the earliest being *Anna of the Five Towns* (1902). They are: Tunstall[1], Burslem, Hanley (Bennett's birthplace), Stoke-on-Trent, Longton and Fenton. These actually number six, but for artistic purposes Bennett reduced them to five, giving them the respective fictional names of Turnhill, Bursley, Hanbridge, Knype and Longshaw. All are now part of Stoke-on-Trent.

Fladdabister 'flat island farmstead', OScand *flat-ey* 'flat island' (*see* -AY) + *bolstathr* 'farmstead'.
A small settlement on Shetland Mainland, 10 km (6 miles) south of Lerwick.

Flamborough Head From the nearby village of Flamborough, meaning 'Fleinn's stronghold', OScand male personal name *Fleinn* + *burh* (*see* BURY).
A striking headland in the East Riding of Yorkshire, some 8 km (5 miles) northeast of Bridlington. The chalk cliffs rise to a height of 120 m (400 ft) above the North Sea, and on the top beacons were once lit to warn shipping – although in the last three decades of the 18th century these beacons failed to prevent over 150 ships meeting a watery end off the coast here (the current lighthouse does a better job). On 23 September 1779 the American privateer John Paul Jones, on board the *Bonhomme Richard*, captured the British warship *Serapis* off Flamborough Head.

The earthwork called Dane's Dyke (actually the work of the ancient Britons) runs some 3 km (2 miles) across the headland, and is reputedly haunted by a White Lady. The area is also troubled by the ghost of Jenny Gallows, a waif who when disturbed by the games of local children will cry out:

> Ah'll put on mi bonnet
> An tee on mi shoe,
> An if thoo's not off
> Ah'll be after thoo.

Flanders Moss *Flanders* from its topographical similarity to Flanders in the Low Countries; *Moss* Northern dialect from OE *mos* 'swamp, bog'.
A large flat wetland area in the upper FORTH valley, some 20 km (12 miles) west of Stirling. It was in Stirlingshire, then in Central region, and is now in the unitary authority of Stirling. Some of the area was recovered for agriculture in the late 18th and early 19th centuries by stripping off the layer of peat (2–4 m / 6–12 ft deep) to the rich alluvial soil below, and by employing an ingenious drainage system.

Flannan Isles Named after St *Flannan* (fl.7th century).
A remote group of seven little islands, some 30 km (18 miles) west of LEWIS in the Outer HEBRIDES. They are also called **the Seven Hunters**, while in 1549 Dean Munro called them 'the Seven Haley Isles'. St Flannan's 7th-century chapel is on the largest island, Eilean Mór, as is the lighthouse, built in 1899 and automatic since 1971. Crofters

from Lewis grazed their sheep and collected seabirds on the islands until the 1920s.

The lighthouse was the scene of a famous unsolved mystery, when, on Boxing Day 1900 the Northern Lights relief vessel *Hesperus* arrived from Oban to find all three keepers – James Ducat, Thomas Marshall and Donald McArthur – missing. There were notes for the log up until 15 December, the lamp had been prepared for lighting, and the kitchen had been tidied after a meal. All that appeared to be amiss was one knocked-over chair, and the absence of two sets of oilskins. The official report concluded:

> I am of opinion that the most likely explanation of the disappearance of the men is that they had all gone down on the afternoon of Saturday, 15 December to the proximity of the West landing, to secure the box with the mooring ropes, etc and that an unexpectedly large roller had come up on the Island, and a large body of water going up higher than where they were and coming down upon them had swept them away with resistless force.
>
> Robert Muirhead: Official Report of the Superintendent of the Commissioners of Northern Lights, 8 January 1901

The explanation offered in the official report is not entirely satisfactory, as it does not explain why one of the men had gone out without his oilskins in such weather. This curious fact has led to many a wild surmise. However, the Northern Lighthouse Board, on its website concerning the Flannan Isles Mystery, still accepts Muirhead's conclusion as the most likely explanation.

The story also inspired Peter Maxwell Davies's opera *The Lighthouse* (1980).

Flash 'swamp', OScand *flask* 'swamp, swampy grassland'.
A village in Staffordshire, in the PEAK DISTRICT National Park, about 8 km (5 miles) southwest of Buxton. At 455 m (1518 ft) above sea level, it is the highest village in England.

Flatford Mill Etymology probably self-explanatory, for a shallow and level fording-place.
A water mill on the banks of the River STOUR[2] in Suffolk, close to EAST BERGHOLT. At the turn of the 19th century it was owned and operated by John Constable's father, and it features in one of the painter's most famous works, *Flatford Mill* (1817). Constable also painted *The Hay Wain* (1821) here. The present mill, a Victorian reconstruction, is used as a Field Study Centre.

A little way up the Stour is the National Trust's Bridge Cottage, which contains an exhibition about Constable, and which was one of the painter's subjects.

Flat Holm *Flat* OScand *floti* 'fleet of ships'; *Holm* 'island', late OE from OScand *holmr* (*see* -EY, -EA). The island was used as a Viking base in the Middle Ages.
A small island in the Bristol Channel (*see under* BRISTOL), about 7 km (4.5 miles) southeast of Penarth, 10 km (6 miles)

west of Weston super Mare and 5 km (3 miles) north of its neighbour STEEP HOLM. It has a lighthouse.

On 13 May 1897 Guglielmo Marconi made the first wireless transmission across water when he sent a message from Lavernock Point on the Welsh coast to Flat Holm.

Fleet[1] 'stream, inlet, creek', OE *fleot*.

A river in London, which rises on Hampstead Heath (*see under* HAMPSTEAD) and flows 14 km (9 miles) south-eastwards into the River THAMES[1] beneath BLACKFRIARS Bridge. The name was originally applied only to the lower, navigable part of the river, as far upstream as Holborn, where it was (as the name suggests) a tidal inlet, but in due course it came to stand for the whole.

Navigable it may have been in theory, but in practice it was already by the early Middle Ages a noisome sewer, with human and animal excrement being complemented by the effluvia of the various trades carried on on its banks (it was commonly termed the **Fleet ditch**). Various attempts were made to cleanse it, but eventually the authorities gave up, and between the 1730s and the 1760s the lower reaches of the river were covered over (the upper part followed suit in the 19th century). The final part of its course can be followed along Farringdon Road and New Bridge Street to the Thames. It still functions as a storm drain.

Fleet Line. The original name given in the 1960s to the planned new London Underground line which, when it eventually opened in 1979, was called the Jubilee Line. Part of the original proposed route ran beneath FLEET STREET.

Fleet marriage, a. A marriage performed, clandestinely and without a licence, originally in the chapel of the Fleet Prison (the **Fleet Chapel**) and later in any convenient nearby house or tavern. The first such marriage on record took place in 1613. They were generally performed by so-called **Fleet parsons**, clergymen imprisoned in the Fleet, and were recorded in documents known as **Fleet books** or **Fleet registers**. They were declared illegal in 1753, a step which led to the popularity of GRETNA Green as a destination for eloping couples.

Fleet Prison. A prison on the east bank of the Fleet river, just to the north of the foot of LUDGATE HILL, said to have been built shortly after the Norman Conquest and closed in 1842. In the Middle Ages it mostly incarcerated those condemned by the Star Chamber, but after that was abolished in 1640 it served mainly as a debtors' prison, which was the source of its later notoriety. Its regime was no less harsh and corrupt than that of other gaols of its time, and Dickens vividly describes the miseries and indignities of its inmates in the section of the *Pickwick Papers* (1837) where Mr Pickwick is detained in 'the Fleet' (as it was generally termed) following his unfortunate misunderstanding with Mrs Bardell:

Most of our readers will remember that, until within a very few years past, there was a kind of iron cage in the wall of the Fleet Prison, within which was posted some man of hungry looks, who, from time to time, rattled a money-box, and explained, in a mournful voice 'Pray, remember the poor debtors; pray, remember the poor debtors.'

The prison was destroyed in the Great Fire of London (1666), rebuilt and again burned during the Gordon Riots of 1780, and rebuilt again in 1781–2. Its official address was 9 Fleet Market, and it was known colloquially in the early 19th century as 'Number 9'. It was finally demolished in 1846.

Liberties of the Fleet, the. The district immediately surrounding the Fleet Prison, in which prisoners were sometimes allowed to reside but beyond which they were not permitted to go. It included the north side of Ludgate Hill and the OLD BAILEY to Fleet Lane (a turning off the Old Bailey, parallel to Ludgate Hill), down the lane to the old Fleet Market (situated in what is now Farringdon Road), and on the east side of the Fleet river along by the prison wall to the foot of Ludgate Hill.

Fleet[2]. An elongated lake on the Dorset coast, separated from the English Channel by CHESIL BEACH. It is divided into the **West Fleet** and the **East Fleet**, and the village of **Fleet** (which takes its name from the lake) is situated at the mid-point of the north bank.

The village is fictionalized as MOONFLEET in J. Meade Falkner's novel (1898) of the same name, a tale of smuggling along the Dorset coast.

Fleet[3]. A town in northeastern Hampshire, on the Basingstoke Canal, about 17.5 km (11 miles) east of the town of Basingstoke.

See also HART.

Fleet Street 'street leading to the FLEET[1] river'; first recorded in 1272.

A street in the City of London (EC4), leading from TEMPLE Bar in the west to Ludgate Circus (*see under* LUDGATE HILL) in the east. From the late Middle Ages it came to be firmly associated with the printing trade and with booksellers. Amongst early printers to set up here were Wynkyn de Worde (formerly Caxton's assistant; died 1534–5) and Richard Pynson. On 11 March 1702 the first newspaper to be issued here, the *Daily Courant*, was brought out by Edward Mallett, and over approximately the next three hundred years Fleet Street established and consolidated its reputation as the headquarters of British journalism and the British newspaper industry.

Newspaper barons built their great citadels here – the *Daily Telegraph*'s austere edifice, the *Express*'s art deco

'Black Lubyanka' (1932) of chrome and black glass, where Beaverbrook reigned supreme (both now occupied by Goldman Sachs) – in which not only hacks scribbled against deadlines but printers printed their scribblings, on vast whirring hot-metal rotary presses, to be carried out into Fleet Street and England beyond in the small hours of the morning on fleets of vans and lorries. It was as much a community as a place of work, with its own social life, conducted mainly in the generous range of Fleet Street pubs – Mooney's Irish pub, perhaps, or the King & Keys ('a hellhole' – Alan Watkins, *A Short Walk Down Fleet Street* (2000)), or even Ye Olde Cheshire Cheese (Dr Johnson's local when he lived in Gough Square, just to the north; *see* CHESHIRE) – or, for those who preferred the grape to the grain, in El Vino's winebar (patronized by lawyers from the Inns of Court and the Royal Courts of Justice (the 'Law Courts') around the western end of Fleet Street, as well as by journalists). For those in search of more spiritual sustenance there was – and is – Wren's St Bride, the journalists' church, at the Ludgate Circus end of the street (there is still a village pump in its churchyard wall). So close did the association between place and business become that 'Fleet Street' turned into a metonym for the newspapers themselves and their proprietors, editors and reporters:

> Fleet Street is said to be desperate for reliable
> Pekinologists who can churn out a thousand weekly
> words on the Chinese enigma.
>
> *Punch* (2 April 1969)

It richly earned its old nickname 'the Street of Ink', and many would say it equally deserves its more recent sobriquet 'the Street of Shame' (the title of a regular *Private Eye* gossip column about the enormities of the British newspaper industry), inspired by the perceived moral degradation of its product.

Towards the end of the 20th century Fleet Street had for some decades been, as one of its less original journalists might have put it, 'drinking in the last-chance saloon'. The congested city-centre was no longer a viable venue for printing and distributing newspapers, and the print unions, with their enforced overmanning and other restrictive practices, had been steadily signing their own death warrant. In the 1980s the industry, following the example set by Rupert Murdoch and News International, migrated eastwards, to WAPPING and the ISLE OF DOGS, where the new computerized operations necessary for commercial survival could be implemented. Some organizations lingered on (Reuters, for instance, retained offices here at the beginning of the 21st century), and in the absence of any new single focus its name continues to symbolize Britain's national press, but Fleet Street without the newspapers has a strangely unfocused and purposeless air.

It retains, though, its role as a component of London's west–east royal processional route, from WESTMINSTER to ST PAUL'S[1] (entry into the City is watched over by the griffin at Temple Bar (*see under* TEMPLE)), and in 1990 one of its old glories was restored to it: the demolition of the railway viaduct to the north of BLACKFRIARS Station revealed once again the breathtaking view of ST PAUL'S[1] Cathedral from Fleet Street, its great dome and portico looming between the foregrounded buildings of LUDGATE HILL.

Fleet Street is valued at £220 on a Monopoly board.

> The man must have a rare recipe for melancholy, who can
> be dull in Fleet Street.
>
> Charles Lamb: letter to Thomas Manning (15 February 1802)

Bishop of Fleet Street, the. A nickname given to Hannen Swaffer (1879–1962) by his fellow journalists because of his pronouncements on public morality and his sombre, stylized mode of attire.

Demon Barber of Fleet Street, the. The sobriquet of Sweeney Todd, the fictitious barber who murdered his customers in George Dibdin's play *A String of Pearls, or the Fiend of Fleet Street* (1847), later known as *Sweeney Todd, the Demon Barber of Fleet Street*, and later still turned into a successful musical, *Sweeney Todd* (1979), by Stephen Sondheim.

Fleeter-Streeter. A creature identified by J.S. Farmer and W.E. Henley in *Slang and Its Analogues* (1890) as 'a journalist of the baser sort, a spunging prophet (i.e. racing tipster); a sharking dramatic critic; a spicy paragraphist; and so on'. They go on to particularize the sort of English he wrote, **Fleet-Streetese**: 'the so-called English, written to sell by the Fleeter-Streeter, a mixture of sesquipedalians and slang, of phrases worn threadbare and phrases sprung from the kennel; of bad grammar and worse manners ... which is impossible outside of Fleet Street, but which in Fleet Street commands a price, and enables not a few to live'.

Fleet Street dove. A 19th-century euphemism for a 'prostitute' (at that time Fleet Street was good working territory for them). An alternative was **Fleet Street houri** (a houri was originally one of the female virgin attendants in the Muslim paradise, but the suggestion of *whore* was no doubt not accidental).

Fleet, Water of. *See* GATEHOUSE OF FLEET.

Fleetwood After Sir Peter *Fleetwood*.

A port and resort at the mouth of the River WYRE in Lancashire, 11 km (6.5 miles) north of Blackpool. The town was laid out by Sir Peter Fleetwood in 1836, and became one of Britain's most important fishing ports. It forms the northern terminus of what Paul Theroux has described as a 'fourteen-mile fun fair', stretching from LYTHAM ST ANNE'S through BLACKPOOL.

Fleetwood was the birthplace of the linguist C.K. Ogden

(1889–1957), who (with I.A. Richards) devised Basic English.

See also FYLDE.

Fleur-de-lis From the name of the local brewery, which had the fleur-de-lis as its emblem.

A village in Caerphilly unitary authority (formerly in Monmouthshire, then in Gwent), 3 km (2 miles) south of Bargoed.

Flint ME 'hard rock', referring to the rock on which the castle is built.

A town on the Dee estuary, in Flintshire (formerly in Clwyd), 18 km (11 miles) northwest of Chester. In Welsh it is **Y Fflint** ('the hard rock'). It was the county town of the old county of FLINTSHIRE. **Flint Castle** dates from the 13th century, and it was here that in 1399 Richard II surrendered to Henry Bolingbroke (the future Henry IV). One visiting Welsh poet found it excessively full of the inhospitable Englishry:

> A dire mischance I wish indeed
> On slavish Flint and its mean breed …
>
> Anon.: 'The Saxons of Flint' (15th century), translated from the Welsh by Mary C. Llewelyn

There is a city called Flint in the USA (Michigan).

Flintshire From FLINT + SHIRE.

A former county and current unitary authority of northeast Wales. The county (created in 1284) was bordered on the east by Cheshire, on the north by the DEE[2] estuary, and on the west and south by Denbighshire. It also had a small exclave at the point where Cheshire, Denbighshire and Shropshire would otherwise have met. FLINT was the county town. The current unitary authority (of which the administrative seat is at MOLD) is bordered to the east by Cheshire, on the north by the Dee estuary, and on the west by Denbighshire, and on the south by Wrexham. Other towns include HOLYWELL, CONNAH'S QUAY and BUCKLEY.

Flitwick Based on OE *wic* 'dwelling, (dairy) farm' (*see* WICK), with an unknown first element.

A town (pronounced 'flittick') in Bedfordshire, about 15 km (9 miles) north of Luton. It is on the main railway line between London and Bedford.

Flixborough 'Flik's stronghold', OScand *Fliks* possessive form of male personal name *Flik* + OE *burh* (*see* BURY).

A village in North Lincolnshire (before 1996 in Humberside, before 1974 in Lincolnshire), about 5 km (3 miles) north of Scunthorpe. It achieved an unwelcome notoriety in 1974 when, on 1 June, a local chemical plant exploded and burned down, killing 29 people. The plant was reopened in 1979, but eventually closed for good in 1981. It left Flixborough with a small but resonant place in the roll-call of 20th-century industrial catastrophes, alongside Bhopal in India and Chernobyl in the former Soviet Union.

A notable Anglo-Scandinavian archaeological site has recently been exposed at Flixborough by the local sandworks.

Flodden Possibly 'stony hill', OE *floh* 'stones' + *dun* (*see* DOWN, -DON).

A small settlement in Northumberland, 9 km (5.5 miles) southeast of the Scottish Border at Coldstream.

Battle of Flodden (9 September 1513). A massive victory by Thomas Howard, Earl of Surrey, over a 30,000-strong Scots force led by James IV, who was invading England at the behest of the French. On this occasion the Auld Alliance proved even more disastrous than usual for the Scots: the king, along with some 10,000 of his subjects, was killed, and it was said that not a family in Scotland had not lost a father, husband, brother or son. The battle site, sometimes called **Flodden Field**, is just to the southwest of the village of Branxton. Following the battle, the burgers of Edinburgh hurriedly built a defensive wall round the Old Town; parts of this so-called **Flodden Wall** can still be seen; the wall proved ineffective against the Earl of Hertford in 1544, who penetrated it and sacked the city.

Surrey's victory was celebrated in England. John Skelton produced his *Ballade of the Scottyshe Kynge*, while the anonymous *Scottish Fielde* is one of the last examples of alliterative verse in English. The battle also featured in an early example of newspaper journalism, a pamphlet entitled *The Trew Encountre* (September 1513), which gave an eyewitness account of the fighting. Later in the century, around 1590, the playwright Robert Greene wrote *The Scottish Historie of James the fourth, slaine at Flodden* (published 1598).

Two centuries later, Scott used the battle at the climax *Marmion*:

> Tradition, legend, tune, and song,
> Shall many an age that wail prolong:
> Still from the sire the son shall hear
> Of the stern strife, and carnage drear,
>   Of Flodden's fatal field,
> Where shiver'd was fair Scotland's spear,
>   And broken was her shield!
>
> Sir Walter Scott: *Marmion: A Tale of Flodden Field* (1808), Canto VI, xxxiv

But the battle's most memorable literary appearance is in that most famous of Scots laments:

> I've heard them lilting, at the ewe milking,
> Lasses a' lilting, before dawn of day;
> But now they are moaning, on ilka green loaning;
> The flowers of the forest are a' wede awae.
>
> Jane Elliot: 'The Flowers of the Forest' (*c.*1750)

Floozie in the Jacuzzi, the. *See* LIFFEY.

Flore '(place at the) floor', OE *flor(e)* 'floor' (probably with reference to a lost Roman tessellated pavement).
A village in Northamptonshire, just to the west of the M1, about 11 km (7 miles) west of Northampton.

Florence Court From Lord Mount *Florence*.
A grand 18th-century house in County Fermanagh, 10 km (6 miles) south of Enniskillen. It was built for Lord Mount Florence, who became Earl of Enniskilling in 1784; ever since the house has been the home of the earls of Enniskilling, although it is now owned by the National Trust. **Florence Court Forest Park** is adjacent.

Floss. The fictional name given by George Eliot to the tidal River TRENT[1] in her novel *The Mill on the Floss* (1860). The emotional appeal of the twice-daily tidal wave is evident in her description of the River Floss around Dorlcote Mill:

> A wide plain, where the broadening Floss hurries on between its green banks to the sea, and the loving tide, rushing to meet it, checks its passage with an impetuous embrace.

Her description of the Ripple, a 'lively' tributary of the Floss, is equally evocative:

> How lovely the little river is, with its dark changing wavelets!

Flow Country *Flow* possibly OScand *flói* 'marshy place'.
An extensive low-lying wetland area in CAITHNESS, Highland, comprising blanket bog and a myriad small lochs. It is an important habitat for wildlife, especially birds, but much of it has been damaged by forestry and drainage schemes.

Flowers Bottom *Flowers* possibly from the surname Flower; *Bottom* OE *botm* 'valley'.
A hamlet in Buckinghamshire, just to the southwest of SPEEN[2].

Flushing Apparently so named by Dutch settlers who founded the village in the late 17th century, after the port of Flushing (Dutch *Vlissingen*) in the Netherlands.
A village in Cornwall, on the north bank of the estuary of the River Penryn, opposite Falmouth.
There are towns called Flushing in the USA (Michigan and Ohio), which likewise take their name from the Dutch Flushing (*see above*), as does Flushing Meadow, site of the US lawn tennis championships in New York City.

Flyford Flavell *Flyford* from an unknown first element + OE *fyrhth* 'sparse woodland'; *Flavell* a Normalized form of *Flyford*, to distinguish the village from GRAFTON FLYFORD.
A village in Worcestershire (before 1998 in Hereford and Worcester, before 1974 in Worcestershire), about 13 km (8 miles) east of Worcester.

Fobbing '(settlement of) Fobba's people' or 'Fobba's place', OE male personal name *Fobba* + *-ingas* or *-ing* (*see* -ING).
A village in Essex, about 5 km (3 miles) south of Basildon and 2.5 km (1.5 miles) north of the Thames Estuary.

Fochabers 'lake marsh', Gaelic *fothach* 'lake' + *abor* 'marsh'.
A village on the River SPEY in Moray (formerly in Grampian region), 14 km (8.5 miles) east of Elgin. The old village of Fochabers, described by Boswell as 'a poor place', stood to the north, closer to Gordon Castle, but the 4th Duke of Gordon found it 'inconveniently close' and demolished it, beginning the building of the present village in 1776.
Fochabers is a noted centre of Scottish fiddling: it was the birthplace of William Marshall (1748–1833), composer and fiddler, and is home to the famous **Fochabers Fiddlers**, formed in the 1980s.
Fochabers is also home to the family-run firm of Baxters, manufacturers of soups and condiments, some to recipes that are held as family secrets, and all using local products. The business was established in 1868 by George Baxter, who had been one of many gardeners at Gordon Castle.
Fochabers gingerbread loaf. A mildly spicy gingerbread loaf with dried fruit flavoured with beer.

Fockbury 'Focca's fortification', OE male personal name *Focca* + BURY.
A hamlet in Worcestershire (before 1998 in Hereford and Worcester, before 1974 in Worcestershire), about 5 km (3 miles) northwest of Bromsgrove. The poet A.E. Housman (1859–1936) (*see* A Shropshire Lad *under* SHROPSHIRE) was born here.

Fockerby 'Folcward's farmstead or village', Old German male personal name *Folcward* + -BY.
A village in North Lincolnshire (before 1996 in Humberside, before 1974 in Lincolnshire), about 11 km (7 miles) northwest of Scunthorpe and 5 km (3 miles) south of the Humber Estuary.

Fodderletter Uncertain, Gaelic *fothair* 'terraced slope, wood' + *leitir* 'slope', and hence 'wooded or terraced slope', is possible.
A small settlement in Moray (formerly in Grampian region), 13 km (8 miles) southeast of Grantown-on-Spey.

Fódla. An alternative spelling of FÓTLA.

Foggathorpe 'Folcward's outlying settlement', Old German male personal name *Folcward* + THORPE.
A small settlement in the East Riding of Yorkshire, 15 km (9 miles) northeast of Selby.

Foggieloan. The nickname of the town ABERCHIRDER in Aberdeenshire.

Fogland. A meteorologically inspired Antipodean nickname for Britain.

Fogo 'hollow where long grass is found', OE *fogga* 'long grass, aftermath' + *hol* 'a hollow'.

A small village in the MERSE of the former Berwickshire, now in Scottish Borders, 5 km (3 miles) south of Duns. The well-preserved 17th-century Fogo Church has parts that go back to the 13th century. Just to the south is the small settlement of **Fogorig** (Scots *rig* 'ridge').

There is a settlement called Fogo in Canada (Newfoundland).

Fogwatt Etymology unknown.

A small settlement in Moray (formerly in Grampian region), some 5 km (3 miles) south of Elgin.

Foinaven 'wart mountain', Gaelic *foinne* 'wart' + *beinn* 'mountain', said to refer to the pimples along its long ridge, although the more romantic prefer to think that the first element is a corruption of Gaelic *fionn* 'white', referring to its quartzite crags and screes.

An elegant and remote mountain (914 m / 2998 ft) in the far northwest of Highland (formerly in Sutherland), some 25 km (15 miles) south-southeast of CAPE WRATH. It consists of a long, undulating ridge, flanked by massive cliffs and with a number of protuberant tops, the highest of which is Ganu Mor. Despite its lack of Munro status (it is 0.4 m short) and its remoteness, it is well worth the effort of attaining its far-distant heights ...

> For to sit alone on its crest and listen to the falling of its disintegrated quartzite blocks is one of the most eerie experiences in Britain.
>
> W.A. Poucher: *The Scottish Peaks* (1965)

As did ARKLE, its southern neighbour, Foinaven had a famous racehorse named after it, albeit misspelt as **Foinavon**. Despite this orthographical handicap, Foinavon won the Grand National in 1967.

Folkestone Probably 'Folca's stone' (marking a Hundred meeting-place), OE male personal name *Folca* + *stan* (*see* STONE).

A town and port on the Kent coast, about 11 km (7 miles) west of Dover. Originally a 'limb' of Dover, it was granted a licence for its own port in 1629, and became one of the CINQUE PORTS in its own right. It was the arrival of the railway in the 19th century, though, that brought real prosperity to Folkestone, both in establishing it as a major cross-channel port, now with an enormous passenger terminal, but also as a holiday destination in itself. Along the top of its 60 m (200 ft) cliffs (as near white as its neighbour Dover's) are grassy promenades and public gardens known as 'the Leas', and a lift takes one down to the beach. Further east, beyond the old harbour, is the main bathing beach, with all the traditional seaside attractions.

> I did a cheap trip to Folkestone. I spent sevenpence

on dropping pennies into silly automatic machines and peepshows of rowdy girls having a jolly time.

> George Bernard Shaw: *Misalliance* (1910)

Further east still is the Warren, a chalk landslip basin between cliffs, rich in fossils, while to the west, on the cliffs of the suburb Sandgate, was the Shorncliffe military camp, from which troops were sent to France during the First World War.

Folkestone's cross-channel connection continues with the CHANNEL TUNNEL, the British end of which surfaces at Cheriton, just to the north of the town.

The parliamentary constituency of Folkestone and HYTHE has been held by Michael Howard (leader of the Conservative party from 2003) since 1983.

William Harvey (1578–1657), who discovered the circulation of the blood, Sir William Hall-Jones (1851–1936), a carpenter who became prime minister of New Zealand for seven weeks in 1906, the actress Audrey Hepburn (1929–93), daughter of a Dutch baroness, and the short-story writer Alfred Edgar Coppard (1878–1957) were born in Folkestone, and it was also the home of the writer H.G. Wells (1866–1946), who set the main action of his novel *Kipps* (1905) here:

> [Kipps] would sometimes walk up and down the Leas between twenty and thirty times after supper, desiring much the courage to speak to some other person in the multitude similarly employed. Almost invariably he ended his Sunday footsore.

Folkestone also houses the headquarters of Saga, the organization that caters to the needs of the maturer members of the population.

Departure of the Folkestone Boat, The. A painting (1869) by Edouard Manet showing a crowded quayside as the cross-Channel packet is about to depart. It is now in the Philadelphia Museum of Art.

Folla Rule 'shelter by the River Rule', Gaelic *foladh* 'covering, shelter'.

A small settlement in Aberdeenshire (formerly in Grampian region), 12 km (7 miles) north of Inverurie.

Follifoot OE *fola* 'horse' + *feoht* 'fight', referring to a Norse sport presumed to have been practised here (Horse Pond Beck runs through the village).

A village in North Yorkshire, 5 km (3 miles) southeast of Harrogate.

Follyrood. *See* HOLYROOD.

Fonthill Originally (910) *Funtial*; perhaps from a OCelt river name, meaning 'stream in fertile upland'.

The name of two adjacent villages in Wiltshire, about 22 km (14 miles) west of Salisbury: **Fonthill Bishop** (*Bishop* denoting manorial ownership in the Middle Ages by the bishops of Winchester) and **Fonthill Gifford** (*Gifford* denoting manorial ownership in the early Middle Ages by the Gifard family).

Nearby and sharing the villages' name was **Fonthill Abbey**, a huge and sumptuous house built by William Beckford (1759–1844), author of the florid oriental tale *Vathek* (1786), to designs in the Gothic style by James Wyatt at a cost of some £273,000. It took 18 years to complete and was sold in 1822 for £330,000. The essayist and critic William Hazlitt described it as a 'glittering waste of industrious idleness'. Three years later the octagonal tower, 79 m (260 ft) high, collapsed, destroying part of the house. The rest of the mansion was demolished soon after, and the present Fonthill Abbey is the one built in 1859 by the Marquess of Westminster on the same site.

Fontmell Magna *Fontmell* originally an OCelt river name, meaning 'stream by the bare hill'; *Magna* 'great', Latin.
A village in Dorset, to the west of Cranborne Chase (*see under* CRANBORNE), about 6.5 km (4 miles) south of Shaftesbury.
See also MELBURY BUBB.

Foolow Probably 'hill frequented by birds', OE *fugol* 'bird' + *hlaw* (*see* LAW, LOW).

A village in Derbyshire, in the PEAK DISTRICT, which is situated about 13 km (8 miles) northeast of Buxton.

Ford '(place by) the FORD', OE *ford*. The earliest recorded form of the name (*c.*1194) is in the plural.
A village in West Sussex, on the River ARUN, about 6.5 km (4 miles) south of Arundel. It is close to an important railway junction where the South Coast line crosses the main line from London.

Ford, Battle of the. *See* ARDEE.

Fordingbridge 'bridge of the people living by the ford', OE *ford* + *-inga-* (*see* -ING) + *brycg* 'bridge'.
A town in Hampshire, on the River AVON[3], at the western edge of the NEW FOREST, about 17 km (11 miles) south of Salisbury.

Charles Chubb (1779–1845), the original patentee of Chubb locks, was born in Fordingbridge.

Ford of the Biscuits So named in the *Annals of the Four Masters* (*see* DONEGAL) from the supplies scattered in consequence of the fighting; it was previously called Arney Ford.
A battle site on the River Arney near Enniskillen in County Fermanagh, where on 7 August 1594 Cormac O'Neill (brother of Hugh) and Hugh O'Donnell ambushed and defeated an English relief column heading for besieged Enniskillen.

❖ ford ❖

Fords were extremely important in the Middle Ages, especially as bridges were relatively few. Fords on Roman roads were valued by later users and given the names STRATFORD (frequent), STRETFORD (Merseyside). Wide fords were also appreciated as named in BRADFORD (Yorkshire) and BROADFORD (Skye). Some of these passages through rivers were known by the animals that used them, such as OXFORD and HAVERFORDWEST (Pembrokeshire) respectively used by oxen and goats. Ford names are among the earliest recorded in English sources, and the element has continued in use; TELFORD (Shropshire), however, is named after Thomas Telford the engineer, whose surname was from Old French *taille fer* 'iron-shearer', and only adapted in the 19th century to '-ford'.

In the north of England particularly, the 'ford' element was pronounced 'forth', as in, for example AMPLEFORTH (North Yorkshire), CARNFORTH (Lancashire), GARFORTH (West Yorkshire), GOSFORTH (Newcastle upon Tyne) and HORSFORTH (West Yorkshire). But since there is an Irish element, *áth*, with the meaning 'ford', many Irish names which appear in modern spelling as '-ford' are in fact from other elements: CARLINGFORD (County Louth), WATERFORD and WEXFORD all contain Old Scandinavian *fjorthr*, meaning 'inlet' (as, incidentally, does Laxford in Highland); LONGFORD contains Irish *longphort* 'fortified house'.

Fords often needed to be marked, as the difference between a fordable place and a dangerous one might not always be obvious. One of the means of marking a ford was to erect a pillar or tree-trunk, and this practice gives rise to the numerous Stapleford names such as STAPLEFORD TAWNEY (Essex). The first part of SOLWAY FIRTH probably has the same meaning, 'ford marked by a pillar', but this time the elements are Scandinavian *sul* 'pillar' and *vath* 'ford'. The Scandinavian word for a ford also gives us WATH UPON DEARNE (South Yorkshire). Closely related to Old Scandinavian *vath* is another Old English element, *wæd*, also meaning 'ford': this appears in such widely distributed names as BIGGLESWADE (Bedfordshire), IWADE (Kent) and LASSWADE (Midlothian).

It appears that relatively early on, Welsh fords were given English names: we might note GRESFORD (Wrexham) and WHITFORD POINT (Swansea), in addition to Haverfordwest already mentioned. The Old Celtic root *ritu* does, however appear in Welsh names such as RHYD-DDU (Gwynedd), meaning 'black ford'; and this suggests that the Cornish name RETEW is likely to mean the same. The Cornish elements derived from the same root, *rys* and *rid*, appear in REDRUTH, REJERRAH and RELUBBUS. And the English name PENRITH in Cumbria preserves the Old Celtic element, too.

Fords of Avon. *See* AVON[5].

Foreland, the[1] 'the cape, the headland', ME; *see also* NORTH FORELAND, SOUTH FORELAND *and* BLOODY FORELAND.

A promontory on the north Devon coast, about 8 km (5 miles) northeast of Lynton. At its tip is **Foreland Point**, the most northerly headland in Devon. There is a lighthouse here.

Foreland, the[2]. An alternative name for HANDFAST POINT in Dorset.

Forest Gate From a gate leading into Epping Forest, situated in Woodgrange Road. The purpose of the gate was to prevent cattle from straying from the forest on to the main road. It was taken down in 1883.

A district in East London (E7), between Wanstead to the north and West Ham to the south, in the borough of Newham. It marks the former southern extremity of Epping Forest (*see under* EPPING), now long since retreated northwards.

Forest of ... *See under* the second element of the name, if not appearing below.

Forest of Bere *Bere* 'woodland', OE *bær* or *bearu*.

A former royal hunting forest in southeastern Hampshire, to the north of Portsmouth. Once its woodlands stretched from the River TEST in the west to ROWLAND'S CASTLE in the east, but from the late Middle Ages onwards the depredations of both land-hungry farmers and timber-hungry ship-builders rapidly reduced it, and now only its eastern corner remains, a mixed landscape of woodland, open space, heathland, farmland and downland.

Forest of Bowland *Bowland* 'area of bends', OE *boga* 'bend' + *land*; the forest referred to was an old hunting forest.

A large Area of Outstanding Natural Beauty, comprising moorland fells and farming valleys, in northeast Lancashire, some 25 km (15 miles) northeast of Preston. It forms part of the Pennine chain, and is locally pronounced to rhyme with 'Holland'. The highest point is Ward's Stone (560 m / 1837 ft). The **Trough of Bowland** is a river valley and high pass (290 m / 951 ft) on the west side. There is a Bowland College at Lancaster University.

Forest of Dean *Dean* 'valley', OE *denu*.

An oak and beech forest in the western part of Gloucestershire, between the River Wye to the west and the River Severn to the east. It is 91 sq km (35 sq miles) in extent. Its main settlements are COLEFORD, to the west, CINDERFORD, to the north, and LYDNEY, to the south.

Since 1938 it has been a National Forest Park (England's first), but in the Middle Ages it was a royal hunting forest, and many traditional forms and ceremonies survive from those days. It is ruled by a Verderers' Court, that meets every 40 days in Coleford, in a building called the 'Speech House' (now also a hotel). There is coal and iron ore beneath the soil, and they have been mined for 4000 years. Those who would dig in the forest today (and large-scale deep-mining for coal, centred around Cinderford, continued until 1965) must pay a royalty, called a 'gale', to an official known as a 'gaveller'. People who live in the forest, who are termed 'commoners', retain their ancient rights of sheep pasturage.

The Forest of Dean is somewhat cut off by its interfluvial location, and it has to be conceded that, at least in the rest of Gloucestershire, it has a reputation as a hillbilly land whose squat, swarthy, in-bred inhabitants get up to things civilized folk would prefer not to know about.

The television dramatist Dennis Potter (1935–94) celebrated the forest – the backdrop to his childhood – in plays and in prose.

> 4 Sept. 1251. Order to William Luvel and Henry de Candour, the king's huntsmen, that when they have taken 60 bucks in the king's Forest of Dean, as the king ordered, they should go to the king's New Forest and take another 60 bucks there, ... to be salted and transported to London for the forthcoming feast of St Edmund.
>
> Order from the correspondence of Henry III

> ... a wonderful thick forest, and in former times dark and terrible, by reason of crooked and winding ways, as also the grisly shade therein, that it made the inhabitants fierce and bolder to commit robberies.
>
> William Camden: *Britannia* (1596)

Forfar Etymology obscure, but 'wood on a ridge', Gaelic *fothair* 'terraced slope, wood' + *fàire* 'ridge, viewpoint' is possible.

A royal BURGH and traditional textile town 22 km (13 miles) northwest of Arbroath, in Angus (in Tayside region from 1975 to 1996). It is the seat of the unitary authority of Angus and was the county town of the old county of ANGUS (previously known as **Forfarshire**). It is just to the east of the small **Loch of Forfar**.

The castle (long gone) was a residence of the Scottish kings from the 11th to the 14th centuries. In around 1097 a parliament met here, presided over by Malcolm III Canmore, who is said to have bestowed titles and surnames on the Scottish nobility. (The town still has a Canmore Street.) Forfar was held by the English during the Scottish Wars of Independence, but taken by Robert the Bruce in the early 14th century. In the 17th century there were many witchcraft trials here, including that of Helen Guthrie, who allegedly ate babies in an unsuccessful attempt to ward off torture.

Forfar was the birthplace of the 'progressive' educationalist A.S. Neill (1883–1973), the founder of Summerhill School.

Forfar Athletic FC dates from 1885. The euphonic Scottish football result '**Forfar 4 – East Fife 5**' may well be apocryphal (*see also under* FIFE).

Forfar bridie. A semicircular pie consisting of a round piece of pastry folded over meat and onions. The name is said to derive from one Maggie Bridie of GLAMIS, when the county of Angus was known as Forfarshire.

Forfar bridle. An iron gag (preserved in the Town House) worn by the 17th-century Forfar witches on their way to execution.

Forfar rock. A form of confectionery manufactured by Peter Reid (1803–97) of Forfar. The recipe has since been lost, but it was apparently similar to Edinburgh rock (*see under* EDINBURGH). It was also known as **Peter Reid rock**. When children came to his shop and asked for 'A bawbee's worth o' Peter Reid', he would reply, 'Which bit o' him dae ye want?' Reid made a fortune, and donated the money for Forfar's Reid Hall (1871) and Reid Park (1896).

Forfarshire. A former name for the county of ANGUS.

Forfarshire. The name of the imperilled ship from which Grace Darling and her father saved nine lives in 1838; *see* FARNE ISLANDS.

Forlorn Point Irish *Crois Fearnóg* 'elder-tree cross', of which the current name is possibly an anglicization, with *-n-* changing to *-l-*.

A headland on the south coast of County Wexford, 17 km (11 miles) south of Wexford itself. It is also called **Crossfarnoge Point** (from the Irish name, *see above*).

Formartine 'Martin's land', Gaelic *fearann* 'land' + personal name. The area is said to have been named by St Ninian after St Martin of Tours, his spiritual mentor.

A traditional area and ancient thanage (territory of a thane, i.e. nobleman) in Aberdeenshire (formerly in Grampian region), between the rivers DON[1] and YTHAN. North of the Ythan lies BUCHAN.

Formby 'Forni's farm', OScand male personal name *Forni* + -BY.

A seaside town in Merseyside (formerly in Lancashire), 10 km (6 miles) south of Southport. To the west are the large sand dunes known as the **Formby Hills**, and beyond them is **Formby Point**. The music-hall comedian, film star and archetypal Lancastrian cheeky chappie George Booth (1905–61) took his stage name, George Formby, from the stage name of his father, singer James Booth, who in turn took it from the name of the town.

Fornighty Etymology unknown.

A small settlement in Highland (formerly in Nairnshire), 7 km (4 miles) southeast of Nairn.

Forres 'little shrubland', Gaelic *fo* 'under' + *ras* 'shrubland, underwood'.

A royal BURGH in Moray (formerly in Grampian region), 15 km (9 miles) east of Nairn, near the mouth of the River FINDHORN. It was traditionally a royal residence of King Duncan and Macbeth, and several of the scenes in Shakespeare's play are set in or near Forres: it is while en route to Duncan's court at Forres that Macbeth and Banquo meet the three witches (I.iii), traditionally at **Macbeth's Hillock** west of the town. In the town itself is Sueno's Stone, a 7 m (23 ft) high carved stone, thought to commemorate the victory of Sweyn the Viking over Malcolm II in 1008. Near to this is the Witches' Stone, where some early witches were burnt.

Fort, the. An informal name for FORT WILLIAM.

Fort Augustus After William *Augustus*, Duke of Cumberland.

A village at the southern end of Loch Ness, in Highland (formerly in Inverness-shire), 47 km (28 miles) southwest of Inverness. Its original name was **Kilcumein** ('church of Cumein', after a successor of St Columba). As it is in a strategic point in the Great Glen, and also guards the way to the CORRIEYAIRACK PASS and thus to Speyside, the Hanoverian government decided to station a garrison here after the 1715 Jacobite Rebellion. A barracks was built in 1716, and then in 1729–30 General Wade built a fort and named it after William Augustus, Duke of Cumberland (1721– 65), the younger son of George II and later to achieve infamy in the Highlands as 'Butcher' Cumberland. In the 1745 Rising the Jacobites captured the fort, but after the failure of the rebellion it was occupied by government troops up to the middle of the 19th century. Lord Lovat bought the place in 1867, and presented it to the Benedictine Order in 1876 for the foundation of an abbey and school.

Fort-del-Oro. *See* SMERWICK.

Forteviot Gaelic *fothair* 'terraced slope, wood' + an unidentified element *tobacht*.

A village in Strath Earn (*see under* EARN), 8 km (5 miles) southwest of Perth, in Perth and Kinross (formerly in Perthshire, and then in Tayside region). It was a Pictish capital until it was burnt by the Vikings in the 8th century, and the capital subsequently moved to SCONE. Kenneth MacAlpin, who united the Scots and Picts in the mid-9th century, was said by Andrew of Wyntoun (but not by modern historians) to have been the son of the miller of Forteviot's daughter. Kenneth died in Forteviot *c.*858.

Fort George Named after *George II*.

An impressive Hanoverian fort in Highland (formerly in Inverness-shire), on a peninsula on the south shore of the Moray Firth, guarding the approaches up the inner firth to Inverness 15 km (9 miles) to the southwest. It was built in 1748–63 by Robert Adam, and consists of a large irregular polygon with six bastions. It was the base of the Seaforth Highlanders until their amalgamation in 1963 into the Queen's Own Highlanders. Dr Johnson dined with the governor in 1773, and talked of gunpowder with apparent expertise. An earlier Fort George was built in Inverness by General Wade in 1726, but was blown up by the Jacobites in 1746.

Forth The OCelt name was *Foirthe*, possibly from a root meaning 'run'. It was known as *Bodotria* to the Romans (possibly a variant of *Voredia* 'slow, quiet one'), and in the 12th century the Gaelic name was *Froch*, the Welsh name *Gwerid* and the English name *Scottewattre*. This last name reflects the fact that in Anglo-Saxon times the Forth was the boundary between England and Scotland. In the *Anglo-Saxon Chronicle* 1072, the Forth is referred to as *Gewæde* 'the ford', and this must remain a possible etymology, OE *ford* with -*th* for -*d* (*see* FORD).

A river of central Scotland, 103.5 km (64.5 miles) long, flowing west–east. It rises on the eastern slopes of BEN LOMOND, where it is called Duchray Water, and soon reaches a wide flat plain across which it meanders towards Stirling. In the western part of this plain is the undrained peat bog of FLANDERS MOSS, but further east it has been drained. Towards the eastern end of this plain is Stirling, and below Stirling the Forth makes even wider meanders through the **Links of Forth**, an area of rich alluvial soils, which have given rise to the rhyme:

A crook o' the Forth
Is worth an earldom o' the North.

At Alloa the river enters its estuary, called the **Firth of Forth** (ME *frith* 'fjord'). The Firth of Forth is some 77 km (48 miles) long, and soon widens to become more of an inlet of the North Sea than a river estuary; at its mouth it is some 20 km (12 miles) across. There are a number of small islands in the Firth, including INCHCOLM, INCHKEITH, the BASS ROCK and the ISLE OF MAY.

Out over the Forth, I look to the north;
But what is the north and its Highlands to me?

Robert Burns: 'Out over the Forth' (1791)

There is a Forth River in Tasmania.

Forth. A sea area in the shipping forecast. It is situated north of Tyne, west of Forties and south of Cromarty.

Forth and Clyde Canal. A canal built by John Smeaton (who also built the famous Eddystone Light). It was opened in 1790, extending from Glasgow to the Firth of Forth at Grangemouth, so linking the North Sea with the Atlantic. The world's first successful steam-powered boat, the *Charlotte Dundas*, had its maiden voyage on the canal in 1802. The Union Canal, completed in 1822, links Edinburgh with the Forth and Clyde Canal near Falkirk. Neither are now used commercially, although the opening of the Falkirk Wheel (*see under* FALKIRK¹) in 2002 has re-established the link between the two canals. In Glasgow, the canal is referred to as **the Nollie**, from the local pronunciation of canal: *ca-nawl*. It looms large in the 2003 film *Young Adam* (directed by David Mackenzie after a novel by Alexander Trocchi), a grim tale of everyday existential folk set in the early 1950s.

Forth Bridge, the. A rail bridge across the Firth of Forth, between North and South Queensferry. It was built between 1883 and 1890, and at 2.5 km (1.55 miles) long is the largest cantilevered bridge in the world. It carries the railway line north from Edinburgh to Fife, Perth, Inverness, Dundee and Aberdeen. (Mercifully, the bridge seems to have escaped the poetic attentions of William McGonagall, unlike that over the TAY). For most of its history teams of men were continually painting the huge amount of steel involved in the structure of the bridge. As soon as one cycle of painting was finished (on average taking three years), a new cycle would begin, and in each cycle some 32,000 litres (7000 gallons) of special iron-oxide paint was used. Hence the expression **painting the Forth Bridge** is applied to any Sisyphean or otherwise endless task. More recently the development of new materials has meant the bridge does not require constant painting.

Forth Road Bridge, the. A suspension bridge 2.51 km (1.56 miles) long, crossing the Firth of Forth just west of the rail bridge (*see above*). It was completed in 1964, and at that time was the longest suspension bridge in Europe. It led to the demise of the ferry between SOUTH QUEENSFERRY in Midlothian and North Queensferry in Fife, which had operated for some 900 years.

Forties From the name of a submerged sandbank, Long *Forties*. A sea area in the shipping forecast. It is in the North Sea, to the east of Scotland, between VIKING to the north and Dogger (*see under* DOGGER BANK) to the south.

Fortingall Uncertain, but 'church by the wooded hill', Gaelic *fothair* 'terraced slope, wood' + *cill* 'church' (*see* KIL-) is possible. Other possibilities are 'fort church' or 'church of the Verturiones', a Gaelic word deriving from OCelt *gwerth* 'fort' or Gaelic *Fortrenn* 'of the Verturiones' (an ancient tribe) + *cill* 'church'. There may also be a link to the nearby prehistoric hillfort called *an Dùn Geal* 'the white fort' (*see also* DOWN, -DON).

A village at the mouth of GLEN LYON, 12 km (7 miles) west of Aberfeldy, in Perth and Kinross (formerly in Perthshire, and then in Tayside region). It is said to have been the birthplace of Pontius Pilate, his father being an ambassador in these parts; the legend has been embellished to the extent that his mother was supposedly a Menzies or a MacLaren. Possibly of even greater antiquity is the famous yew tree in the churchyard, said to be 3000 years old. In some accounts, Pilate's Pictish mother gave birth to him under its shelter.

> The glade
> of birches shamed his rags, in paroxysms
> he stumbled, toga'd, furred, blear, brittle, grey.
> They told us he sat here beneath the yew
> even in downpours; ate dog-scraps.
>
> Edwin Morgan: 'Pilate at Fortingall', from *Sonnets from Scotland* (1984)

Close to the village is **Càrn nam Marbh** ('cairn' or 'mound of the dead'), said to be the burial place of victims of the Black Death in the 14th century, but in fact a Bronze Age barrow. It played an important part in Fortingall's Hallowe'en celebrations, which were traditionally held on 11 November. Gorse was collected from the surrounding hills and set alight on top of the mound, while the villagers held hands and danced around. As the fire died down the youths of the village would jump over the dying embers. The practice was stopped by the local gamekeeper in 1924, alarmed that the hillsides were being stripped of gorse, depriving his birds of cover.

Fortnum–Mason line From *Fortnum and Mason*, the name of the prestigious PICCADILLY[1] grocer's shop (established in 1707), modelled punningly on the *Mason–Dixon line* that is the boundary between Maryland and Pennsylvania in the USA and, figuratively, the demarcation between the old slave-owning South and the slave-free North.

A facetious name for the imaginary geographical line that marks off the supposed 'lush' south of England from the 'lean' north – or indeed from anywhere 'north of WATFORD[1]'.

Fortriu From *Fortriu* who, according to tradition, was one of the seven sons of Cruithne, king of the Picts.

The Gaelic name for an ancient Pictish territory in Scotland, probably centred on Strath Earn (*see under* EARN) and Menteith (*see* LAKE OF MENTEITH), northwest of Stirling. The kings of Fortriu may have been supreme kings of the Picts. Fortriu disappeared from the scene in the 9th century, suffering incursions by Vikings and then being absorbed into the Scots kingdom of ALBA.

Fortrose 'below the promontory', Gaelic *foter* 'beneath' + *ros* 'promontory'.

A royal BURGH (1592) on the BLACK ISLE, Highland (formerly in Ross and Cromarty), across the Moray Firth from Fort George and 13 km (8 miles) northeast of Inverness. The ruined cathedral was founded by David I for the see of Ross, and Oliver Cromwell took many of its stones to build a fort at Inverness. Fortrose claims to have been the site of the last witch-burning in Scotland, a claim disputed by DORNOCH. At nearby Chanonry Point, the Countess of Seaforth had the Brahan Seer (*see under* BRAHAN) burnt to death in a barrel of tar for telling her that at that very moment the Earl, away in France, was in the arms of another woman. Before he was crisped into silence, the unfortunate prophet predicted that the line of the Seaforths would end with a deaf-and-dumb earl whose sons would die before him; and in 1815 the last Lord Seaforth died 'in paralytic imbecility', according to Sir Walter Scott.

Fortune, East and West. *See* EAST FORTUNE.

Fortuneswell Probably 'lucky well' or 'well where fortunes can be told'; it is first recorded in 1608, when the place was just a cattle-fold with a well.

A town on the Isle of PORTLAND, in Dorset, about 6 km (4 miles) south of Weymouth.

Fort William Named after *William III*.

A BURGH at the head of LOCH LINNHE in Highland (formerly in Inverness-shire), 50 km (30 miles) north of Oban. It is strategically placed at the hub of routes west to Mallaig and the Hebrides, south to Glencoe, east to Speyside and northeast to Inverness through the GREAT GLEN. The first fort was built here in 1655 by General Monck, and this was replaced in 1690 to keep the Jacobite Highlanders under control after William III had taken the throne. At this time the settlement at the fort was called Maryburgh, after William's queen. The fort was dismantled in 1890 and replaced by a railway station. Fort William was the first town in Britain to light its streets using hydroelectric power. Its position at the foot of BEN NEVIS, Britain's highest mountain, gives it the reputation as one of the wettest places in Scotland. It is sometimes referred to simply as **the Fort** or even as **the Bill**.

The Hanging Tree in Fort William was an oak believed to have been a 'joug tree' on which the local chief hanged wrong-doers; it was cut down in 1985 to make way for a new public library.

There is a town called Fort William in Canada (Ontario; now part of Thunder Bay). Fort William, the citadel in Calcutta, India, was named after William III rather than the Scottish town.

> At Fort William they say a Man is not admitted into Society without [a kilt] – the Ladies there have a horror at the indecency of Breeches.
>
> John Keats: letter to Tom Keats (17–21 July 1818)

Forty Foot. *See* DÚN LAOGHAIRE.

Forty Foot Drain Because it was originally 40 ft (12 m) wide. A canal (also called **Forty Foot River**) dug in 1650, linking the Old Bedford River with the River NENE (old course) and constituting one of the major artificial watercourses of the BEDFORD LEVEL in Cambridgeshire. It is 17 km (10.5 miles) long. Its alternative name, **Vermuyden's Drain**, commemorates the Dutch engineer Cornelius Vermuyden (1595–1683) who masterminded the reclamation of the FENS in the 17th century.

See also HUNDRED FOOT DRAIN, RAMSEY FORTY FOOT *and* SIXTEEN FOOT DRAIN.

Fosse Way *Fosse* 'ditch', OE *foss* (because it had a prominent ditch on each side).

A Roman road leading from Exeter via Cirencester and Leicester to Lincoln. It marked the northern limit of the first phase of the Roman conquest of Britain (*c*.47 AD), and at the height of Roman power the point at which it crossed WATLING STREET[1] (to the south of present-day Hinckley in Leicestershire) was effectively the hub of Roman Britain. It was as straight as any Roman road might be expected to be, and remains so in the sections of the A429, B4455, B4114 and A46 which still follow its course today.

> The Romans were masters of surveying … Whoever set out the Foss [sic] Way evidently knew in which direction Lincoln lay from Exeter, to within a fraction of a degree, and also knew that the Somerset Levels and multiple river-crossings in Nottinghamshire were insuperable obstacles to going there direct. Between the two deviations round these obstacles, the middle 150 miles of the Foss Way never depart by more than 6½ miles from the direct line.
>
> Oliver Rackham: *The History of the Countryside* (1986)

Leicester City FC (*see under* LEICESTER) was originally called **Leicester Fosse FC**, as its founders first met in 1884 in a house on the Fosse Way; this gave rise to the nickname the Fossils, changed in 1919 to the Foxes, when the club became Leicester City.

Fotheringhay Probably 'island or well-watered land used for grazing', OE *fodring* 'grazing' + *eg* (*see* -EY, -EA).

A village (pronounced 'fothering-hay') in Northamptonshire, on the River NENE, about 18 km (11 miles) northeast of Corby. Its chief glory today is the imposing Church of St Mary and All Saints, with its octagonal lantern tower reminiscent of ELY[1] Cathedral's.

This quiet limestone village owes its wider reputation, though, to its 14th-century castle, which witnessed momentous events in English history. Richard III was born there in 1452, and in 1586 Mary Queen of Scots was brought there just before her trial for treason. She was pronounced guilty, and in February 1587 she was executed in the castle hall (the beheading did not go well: it took more than one blow, and when the head was finally severed and the executioner tried to pick it up by the hair, he found he had hold of a wig, and the head rolled away under the scaffold). James VI and I, understandably ashamed of what had gone on there, had the castle demolished, and all that remains of it today is a grassy tump.

The folk-rock group **Fotheringay** was formed by Sandy Denny in 1970 when she left Fairport Convention, and took its name from one of the compositions she wrote for that group. It disbanded in 1971.

Fótla From Fodla, one of the three goddesses whose names were to be selected as the name of Ireland; her sister Eriu or ÉIRE was the winner.

An early name for Ireland, also found in the Scottish place name ATHOLL, which means 'new Ireland'. It is also spelt **Fódla**.

> Ah, faithless Fódla, 'tis shame that thou see'st not clearly
> That 'twere meeter to give thy milk to the clustering clan of Mileadh,–
> No drop hath been left in the expanse of thy smooth white breast
> That the litter of every foreign sow hath not sucked!
>
> Geoffrey Keating (?1570–?1646): 'My Grief on Fál's Proud Plain', translated by Padraic Pearse

> *… Ní bhfuil cliar in iathaibh Fódla*
> *Ní bhfuilid aifrinn againn nó orda,*
> *Ní bhfuil baiste ar ár leanaibh óga …*
> (We have no clergy in Fodla's land
> We have neither Mass nor monks
> We have no means to baptize our children …)
>
> Séafraidh Ó Donnchadha an Ghleanna (*c*.1620–78): '*Do chuala scéal do chéas gach ló mé*' ('I heard news that tortures me every day')

Foula 'bird island', OScand *fugl* 'bird, fowl' + *ey* (*see* -AY).

A small island (pronounced 'foola') some 25 km (15 miles) west of Mainland, Shetland. It is perhaps the most remote inhabited island in Britain: Norn (the old Norse dialect of the Northern Isles) was spoken here until 1800, and the islanders still reportedly prefer the old Julian calendar, abandoned by the rest of Britain in 1753. The indigenous sheep (like the red deer on RUM) have developed a taste for snacking on the chicks of seabirds, for whom the island is otherwise an important sanctuary; particularly notable are the great skuas or bonxies. There are massive sea cliffs on the west coast, culminating in the Kame (376 m / 1233 ft).

> When the Kaim o' Foula lifts on the Smew
> My peerie lass I'm aye thinkin' o' you.
>
> Hugh MacDiarmid: 'Off the Coast of Fiedeland', from *A Kist of Whistles* (1947)

Foula field mouse. An indigenous, large-footed sub-species, *Apodemus sylvaticus thuloe*.

'Shaalds of Foula, The'. A traditional fiddle tune (*shaalds* 'shoals') to which the Foula fishermen would dance the **Foula Reel**.

Foulbog Possibly 'marsh frequented by birds', or 'dirty marsh', OE *fugol* 'bird' or *ful* 'dirty' + Gaelic *bog* 'marsh'.

A small, remote settlement in the upper valley of the White Esk, Dumfries and Galloway (formerly in Dumfriesshire), 16 km (10 miles) east of Moffat.

Foul Mile Origin uncertain; *Foul* may be from OE *fugol* 'bird'.

A village in East Sussex, about 16 km (10 miles) southeast of Uckfield.

Foulness 'promontory frequented by birds', OE *fugol* 'bird' + *næss* (*see* NESS).

An island on the Essex coast, at the eastern end of a peninsula bounded by the Thames estuary to the south and the Crouch estuary to the north, about 11 km (7 miles) northeast of Southend. It is the largest island in the estuary. At its northeastern tip is **Foulness Point**, which is effectively the eastern extremity of the north bank of the Thames estuary. Offshore to the northeast are the **Foulness Sands**.

Since ancient times birds have, as its name suggests, taken advantage of the mudflats, creeks and saltings of Foulness. In the 1960s it seemed as though their habitat might be destroyed by a proposed third London airport, to be built on MAPLIN SANDS, off the island's southeastern shore, but the threat passed (STANSTED was chosen instead), and its avian residents and winter visitors – including 10,000 brent geese – graze in peace. Or comparative peace – since 1915 Foulness has been owned by the War Office and then the Ministry of Defence (access is strictly controlled), and the air is regularly rent by explosions from the firing ranges.

Fountains Abbey OFr *fontein*, 'springs', referring to the springs at the site.

A magnificent ruined Cistercian abbey in North Yorkshire, some 5 km (3 miles) southwest of Ripon. The abbey was founded in 1132 as 'the Abbey of the Blessed Virgin Mary at Fountains' by some dissident Benedictines from York, who found their parent house too lax. Fountains was shut down in 1539 during the Dissolution of the Monasteries, and much of its masonry later used to build **Fountains Hall**. The site was incorporated into Studley Royal Water Park, a vast and elegant landscape garden, with lakes and watercourses, in the 18th century, and both are now in the care of the National Trust. The abbey and gardens became a UNESCO World Heritage Site in 1986.

One of the more famous, if almost certainly fictional, brothers from Fountains was Friar Tuck. This tradition may arise from the ballad 'Robin Hood and the Curtal Friar' (who may or may not have been the same as Friar Tuck):

> That curtal friar in Fountains Abbey
> Well can a strong bow draw;
> He will beat you and your yeomen,
> Set them all on a row.

Fountains Abbey at its height had enormous land holdings, giving its name to **Fountains Fell** (668 m / 2191 ft) far to the west, some 10 km (6 miles) north of Settle.

Four Courts. The main courts in DUBLIN, consisting of chancery, king's bench, common pleas and exchequer. They were originally in Dublin Castle, then from 1608 in the precincts of Christ Church Cathedral. Work on a new building north of the River Liffey began in 1776 (to designs by Thomas Cooley and James Gandon). The occupation of this building by anti-Treaty Republicans on 14 April 1922 is generally regarded as marking the beginning of hostilities in the Irish Civil War; after the expiry of a deadline to leave the building on 28 April, Free State forces began to shell the Four Courts, and the occupiers surrendered two days later. The building was subsequently restored, although the Republicans blew up the adjacent Public Records Office, destroying thousands of invaluable historical documents.

Four Courts Press. One of Ireland's leading academic publishers, founded in 1970. It specializes in Celtic studies, history, art, literature, philosophy, theology and law.

Four Gotes A 'gote' (from OE *geotan* 'to pour') is a waterchannel or sluice; this was the meeting-place of the gotes of Wisbech, Leverington, Newton and Tydd St Giles.

A village in Cambridgeshire, in the FENS, about 8 km (5 miles) north of Wisbech.

See also TYDD GOTE.

Four Green Fields. A somewhat sentimental Republican name for a united Ireland, referring to the four provinces of ULSTER, MUNSTER, LEINSTER and CONNACHT. The name comes from the song by Tommy Makem, and the reference to the field in bondage is to Ulster:

> 'What have I now?' said the fine old woman
> 'What have I now?' this proud old woman did say.
> 'I have four green fields,
> One of them's in bondage,
> In stranger's hands, who tried to take it from me.
> But my sons have sons,
> As brave as were their fathers,
> And my fourth green field
> Will bloom once again,' said she.

There are Irish-themed hostelries called Four Green Fields as far apart as Tampa (Florida) and Rome.

Four Knocks An anglicization and misunderstanding of the Irish name *Fuarchnoc* 'cold hill'; the English name refers to the site's four tumuli.

An early Bronze Age megalithic burial site in County Meath, 28 km (17 miles) north of Dublin.

Four Mile Bridge From its location four miles from HOLYHEAD, at the bridge over the channel separating HOLY ISLAND[2] from ANGLESEY.

A village on Holy Island, Isle of Anglesey (formerly in Gwynedd), 6 km (4 miles) south of Holyhead.

Four Ones Church. *See* ULVERSTON.

Fourpenny Possibly a reference to the rent for the land.

A small settlement on the northeast coast of Highland (formerly in Sutherland), 4 km (2.5 miles) north of Dornoch.

Four Roads From its location at the junction of four roads.

A village in Carmarthenshire (formerly in Dyfed), 6 km

(4 miles) northwest of FIVE ROADS, and 11 km (6.5 miles) northwest of Llanelli.

Four Throws 'four trees', OE *feower* 'four' + *treow* 'tree'.

A village in Kent, about 12 km (7 miles) southwest of Tenterden.

Fowey[1] From a Cornish river name probably meaning 'beech-tree river'.

A river (pronounced 'foy') in Cornwall, which rises on Bodmin Moor (*see under* BODMIN) and flows 48 km (30 miles) southwards through LOSTWITHIEL into the English Channel at FOWEY[2].

Fowey[2] From the River FOWEY[1].

A harbour town (pronounced 'foy') on the southern coast of Cornwall, at the mouth of the River Fowey, about 11 km (7 miles) east of St Austell. Its steep streets descend the estuary's hilly western side to the port, which handles large amounts of the china clay quarried at St Austell.

Fowey was once an important seaport which fitted out ships for the Crusades. During the reign of Edward III the town equipped a fleet of 47 vessels and supplied about 800 men for the siege of Calais in 1347, and Fowey's seafarers continued to raid the coast of France throughout the Hundred Years' War. The inhabitants were later convicted of piracy by Edward IV, and deprived of their vessels.

The popular Cornish novelist and critic Sir Arthur Quiller-Couch (1863–1944) fictionalized Fowey as 'TROY TOWN[1]', and gave it a considerable boost as a holiday resort (he was elected the town's mayor in 1937). Its other literary connection is with the novelist Daphne du Maurier (1907–89), many of whose stories have a Cornish setting, and who lived near Fowey in a house called 'Menabilly' (model for the famous and mysterious 'Manderley' in her 1938 novel *Rebecca*).

At the beginning of the 21st century Fowey is, in common with many other places in Cornwall, something of a cult destination for New-Agers, students and trendy youth.

The Parliamentarian preacher Hugh Peter (1598–1660), who was executed as a regicide, and the astrophysicist and Nobel laureate Antony Hewish (b.1936), who discovered pulsars, were born in Fowey.

See also READYMONEY.

Fowlmere 'lake frequented by birds', OE *fugol* 'bird' + *mere* 'mere, lake'.

A village in Cambridgeshire, in a hollow of the GOGMAGOG HILLS, about 14.5 km (9 miles) south of Cambridge. The Fowlmere nature reserve, run by the Royal Society for the Protection of Birds, is an ideal habitat for reed-loving birds.

Foxford Probably 'ford used by foxes'.

A small town in County Mayo, some 20 km (12 miles) northeast of Castlebar. Its Irish name is **Beal Easa** ('ford of the stream', particularly a rapid stream). Foxford is famous for its Providence Woollen Mills, set up by Mother Arsenius of the Sisters of Charity in the 1890s.

Foxford was the birthplace of Admiral William Brown (1777–1857), known as the father of the Argentinian navy.

Foxhole Possibly 'fox valley or hollow', ME *fox* + Scots *haugh* 'valley' (*see* HALE, -HALL) or ME *hole* 'hollow'.

A remote settlement in Glen Convinth, Highland (formerly in Inverness-shire), 16 km (10 miles) southwest of Inverness.

Foxholes OE *fox-hol* 'fox earth'.

A tiny settlement in North Yorkshire, 13 km (8 miles) southwest of Filey.

Foxt 'fox's den', OE *fox* + *wist* 'den'.

A village in Staffordshire, about 13 km (8 miles) northeast of Stoke-on-Trent.

Foyers, Falls of. *See* FALLS OF FOYERS.

Foyle Irish *Faill* 'cliff'.

A river in Northern Ireland, rising as the Strule in County Tyrone and flowing northwards. It is known as the **Mourne** between Newtonstewart and Strabane, and for a stretch forms the border between Northern Ireland and the Republic, before flowing through the middle of DERRY/LONDONDERRY and then entering the large sea inlet of **Lough Foyle** (Irish *Loch Feabhail* 'lake of the lip', referring to the sandbar that almost closes its mouth; Ptolemy called it *Vidua*). Lough Foyle is celebrated for its birdlife.

> When *will* my Luve againe walk close by Me,
> Where Foyle in floode fish-fulle flowes to Sea?
>
> Sir Graham Lindsay: 'The Lover's Retourne' (*c*.1635)

Framingham Pigot *Framingham* 'Fram's people's homestead', OE male personal name *Fram* + *-inga-* (*see* -ING) + HAM; *Pigot* denoting manorial ownership in the Middle Ages by the Picot family.

A village in Norfolk, about 6.5 km (4 miles) southeast of Norwich.

Framlingham 'Framela's people's homestead', OE male personal name *Framela* + *-inga-* (*see* -ING) + HAM.

A market town in Suffolk, about 24 km (16 miles) northeast of Ipswich. It is dominated by the 12th-century **Framlingham Castle**, extensively rebuilt in the 16th century, which for a long time was the seat of the dukes of Norfolk. St Michael's Church contains the tomb of Henry VIII's bastard son, Henry Fitzroy. The local co-educational public school, **Framlingham College**, was founded in 1864.

Frankley 'Franca's glade', OE male personal name *Franca* + -LEY.

A village in Worcestershire (before 1998 in Hereford and Worcester, before 1974 in Worcestershire), effectively now a southwestern suburb of BIRMINGHAM.

Frank Lockwood's Island Named in the late 19th century after Francis *Lockwood*, solicitor general in 1894–5 and the brother-in-law of the 21st Maclean of Duart, the local landowner.

A tiny island just off the south coast of MULL (Argyll and Bute, formerly in Strathclyde region).

Fraserburgh Named after Alexander *Fraser* + *burgh* (*see* BURY).

A large fishing port on the northeast tip of Aberdeenshire (formerly in Grampian region), 24 km (15 miles) north of Peterhead. The sandy **Fraserburgh Bay** lies to the southeast. The town was originally called **Faithlie**, and derived its present name from Alexander Fraser, Laird of Philorth, who built the harbour in the early 16th century, and in reward was granted a charter elevating the town into a free BURGH of barony. The short-lived **University of Fraserburgh** was established in 1597, but foundered after its principal was imprisoned for attending the (Presbyterian) General Assembly in 1605. On the north side of the town is KINNAIRDS HEAD.

Freathy Origin uncertain; recorded as a surname in the 14th century, and perhaps identical with the name *Friday*.

A village on the southern coast of Cornwall, on Whitsand Bay, about 5 km (3 miles) southwest of Torpoint.

Freeby 'Fræthi's farmstead or village', OScand male personal name *Frœthi* + -BY.

A village in Leicestershire, about 5 km (3 miles) east of Melton Mowbray.

Free Derry Corner. A location in the BOGSIDE, Londonderry, so named because in 1969 a gable end here was adorned with the slogan 'You are now entering Free Derry'. That year the Bogside became a no-go area. The house has been demolished, but the gable end has been preserved.

Freezywater Originally the name of a local pond, so called because of its bleak and exposed situation.

A district in the North London borough of Enfield, just inside the M25.

Frenchay Originally *Fromshawe* 'copse on the River Frome', FROME⁴ + OE *sceaga* 'copse'; the present-day form is due to a folk-etymological association with *French*.

A northeastern suburb of BRISTOL, on the River FROME⁴, in South Gloucestershire (before 1996 in Avon, before 1974 in Gloucestershire). It is home to the University of the West of England (*see under* WEST).

Frenchbeer 'woodland of a family called Friendship', family name *Friendship* (first recorded here in the 16th century, and later modified through folk-etymological association with *French*) + OE *bearu* 'woodland'.

A village in Devon, at the northeastern corner of Dartmoor, about 27 km (17 miles) southwest of Exeter.

Frenchman's Creek Etymology self-explanatory, although the identity of the Frenchman is not known.

A side inlet of the Helford River (*see under* HELFORD) in Cornwall. In the eponymous novel (*see below*) it is described as 'still and soundless, surrounded by the trees, hidden from the eyes of men'.

Frenchman's Creek. A novel (1941) by Daphne du Maurier, which tells of a 17th-century aristocratic lady who leaves London – largely to avoid the attentions of her husband's friend – for Cornwall, where she falls in love with a swashbuckling French pirate. It was filmed in 1944, with Joan Fontaine and Basil Rathbone. A remake appeared in 1998.

Frenchpark After Patrick *French*, who in 1656, during the Cromwellian settlement, was granted 6000 acres (2400 ha) here.

A hamlet in County Roscommon, some 20 km (12 miles) west-southwest of Carrick-on-Shannon. It was the birthplace of Douglas Hyde (1860–1949), co-founder of the Gaelic League and professor of modern Irish at University College, Dublin. He retired to Ratra House in Frenchpark, but was recalled to Dublin to become the first president of the Republic of Ireland (1938–45).

Freshwater 'river with fresh water', OE *fersc* 'fresh' + *wæter* 'water'.

A village at the western tip of the ISLE OF WIGHT, on the estuary of the River Yar. The sandy beaches of **Freshwater Bay**, just to the east of TENNYSON DOWN and the NEEDLES, make it a popular holiday destination.

The poet Alfred Tennyson (1809–92) lived here from 1853 to 1869 (he commemorated it in his noble title: Baron Tennyson of Aldworth and Freshwater). The pioneer photographer Julia Margaret Cameron (1815–79) settled here with her family in 1860 (to be near Tennyson), and after she was given her first camera in 1863 she made a studio in a chicken coop and a darkroom in a coal bin.

The scientist Robert Hooke (1635–1703), discoverer of the law of elasticity, was born in Freshwater.

Friar's Gate 'gap or opening (to land) belonging to a family called Fray', *Friar's* from family name *Fray* (known here from the 16th century, and later modified through folk-etymological association with *friar*); *Gate* OE *geat* 'gap, opening, gate'.

A village in East Sussex, about 5 km (3 miles) northwest of Crowborough.

Friday Bridge Alluding to a nearby fishery owned by the monks of Ely, whose mandatory Friday diet was fish.

A village in Cambridgeshire, in the Fens, about 5 km (3 miles) south of Wisbech.

Friday Street¹ *Friday*, perhaps from a name originally given to a local area of barren land or an impoverished settlement, alluding to the negative associations of Friday (the day of

Christ's crucifixion); alternatively perhaps from the surname *Friday*, which is relatively common locally; *Street* OE *stræt* 'hamlet' (*see* STREET).

A village in East Sussex, on the northeastern outskirts of Eastbourne.

Friday Street². A village in Surrey, about 5 km (3 miles) southwest of Dorking. In the 17th century it was a centre of the Wealden iron industry.

Stephen Langton (*c.*1150–1228), the Archbishop of Canterbury who played a leading role in forcing King John to sign the Magna Carta, was born in Friday Street. The local inn is named after him.

Fridaythorpe 'Frigedæg's outlying settlement', OE male personal name *Frigedæg* + THORPE.

A village in the East Riding of Yorkshire, 16 km (10 miles) west of Driffield.

Friern Barnet 'Barnet of the brothers' (referring to the fact that it once belonged to the Knights of St John of Jerusalem), *Friern* ME *freren* possessive plural form of *frere* 'brother, fellow member of a (military) religious order, friar', from OFr.

A district (pronounced 'fry-ern') in northwest London (N11, N12, N20), to the south of Barnet and to the north of Finchley, in the borough of BARNET (before 1965 in Middlesex). From the 13th century to the Dissolution of the Monasteries in the 1530s it belonged to the Knights of St John of Jerusalem – whence its name (*see above*).

Perhaps its most persistent association is with the care of the mentally ill, thanks to the mental hospital opened in 1851 in the southeast of the district. This was originally known as COLNEY HATCH, but since over the decades that unfortunate district's name became firmly linked in the public's mind with madness, the hospital was redesignated in 1937 as Friern Hospital. It finally closed in 1993.

Frimley 'Frem(m)a's glade', OE male personal name *Frem(m)a* + -LEY.

A town in Surrey, about 2.5 km (1.5 miles) south of Camberley. Just to the south is **Frimley Green** (a name imposed by the Post Office around 1868 to avoid confusion with Frimley), where since 1986 the Lakeside Country Club has hosted the World Darts Championship.

Frinton-on-Sea *Frinton* 'Fritha's farmstead' or 'protected farmstead', OE *Frithan* possessive form of male personal name *Fritha* or *frithen* 'protected' + -TON.

A seaside resort on the Essex coast, about 8 km (5 miles) northeast of Clacton-on-Sea. A product of the 1890s, it is far more genteel than its southwestern neighbour – no kiss-me-quick hats in Frinton. In the 1920s it attracted film stars and royalty, and acquired the nickname **'fashionable Frinton'**. The tide of fashion has long since ebbed, but Frinton maintains a loyal if sedate following.

Friockheim A curious name, apparently named after a man

called *Freke* (a ME word meaning 'warrior'), to which was added German *heim* by the owner, John Anderson, who had spent time in Germany, in 1830.

A village in Angus (formerly in Tayside region), 14 km (8.5 miles) east of Forfar.

Frisby on the Wreake *Frisby* 'farmstead or village of the Frisians', OScand *Frisa* possessive plural form of *Frisir* 'Frisian' + -BY; *Wreake* name of the local river (*see* WREAKE).

A village in Leicestershire, on the River Wreake, about 5.5 km (3.5 miles) west of Melton Mowbray.

Friskney Eaudyke *Friskney* 'river with fresh water', OE *ferscan* dative form of *fersc* 'fresh' (with Scand *-sk-*) + OE EA- 'river'; *Eaudyke* 'river embankment', OE *ea* 'river' + *dic* or OScand *dik* 'embankment' (*eau* is an early modern Frenchified variant of OE *ea* (associated folk-etymologically with French *eau* 'water'), and *dyke* is quite possibly a Scandinavianized variant of OE *dic* 'ditch, embankment').

A village in Lincolnshire, in the FENS, about 19 km (12 miles) northeast of Boston.

See also QUADRING EAUDIKE.

Friston Forest From the nearby village of *Friston*, perhaps 'Freo's farmstead', OE *Friges* (pronounced 'frees') possessive form of male personal name *Freo* + -TON.

A forest in East Sussex, on the SOUTH DOWNS, just to the north of the SEVEN SISTERS¹ and about 8 km (5 miles) west of Eastbourne. Planted in 1926, it consists mainly of beech trees.

Frogmore 'pool frequented by frogs', OE *frogga* 'frog' + *mere* 'pool'; the house presumably sits on the site of a former pool.

A house in the Home Park of WINDSOR Castle dating from the late 17th century but extensively remodelled in 1792 by James Wyatt for Queen Charlotte. Prince Albert, the Prince Consort, is buried in the royal mausoleum here. The house was consequently a great favourite of Queen Victoria's, and she in due course joined Albert in the mausoleum. There is also the mausoleum of the Duchess of Kent, mother of Queen Victoria, who lived here for 21 years. Other members of the royal family (including the Duke and Duchess of Windsor) are buried in the small cemetery adjoining the mausolea. The Grim Reaper by royal appointment has not had it all his own way at Frogmore, though: Lord Mountbatten (1900–79) was born here.

There is a town called Frogmore in South Carolina, USA.

Frognal 'nook of land frequented by frogs', OE *froggena* possessive plural form of *frogga* 'frog' + *halh* (*see* HALE, -HALL).

An area of Hampstead (NW3), in the North London borough of Camden. The local railway station on the North London line is called 'Finchley Road and Frognal'.

Frome¹ From an OCelt river name meaning 'fair, fine, brisk'.

A river (pronounced 'froom') in Somerset, that rises to the north of Bruton Forest in the east of the county, near the border with Wiltshire, and flows 32 km (20 miles) northwards through FROME[2] to join the River Avon just to the west of Bradford-on-Avon. A brief section of it forms part of the boundary between Somerset and Wiltshire.

There are rivers called Frome in Jamaica and South Australia.

Frome² From the River FROME[1].

A market town (pronounced 'froom') in eastern Somerset, on the River FROME[1], about 24 km (15 miles) east of Wells. Its medieval centre, with its steep narrow streets, is well preserved (Cheap Street, from OE *ceap* 'market', still has a water-channel running down its centre, and an 18th-century lock-up adorns the bridge over the Frome), but it is a thriving modern town too, with successful light industries. It originally came to prosperity in the 17th century, with the rise of the cloth-making industry:

> Frome is now reckoned to have more people in it, than the city of Bath, and some say, than even Salisbury itself, and if their [the cloth-makers'] trade continues to increase for a few years more, as it has done for those past, it is very likely to be one of the greatest and wealthiest inland towns in England.
>
> Daniel Defoe: *A Tour Through the Whole Island of Great Britain* (1724–6)

The Frome-born Somerset cricketer Colin Dredge (b.1954) – a fast-medium bowler of no great venom, and possessed of an eccentric slinging action – was accorded the affectionate nickname '**the Demon of Frome**'.

There are places called Frome in Jamaica and in Queensland, Australia.

Frome³. A river (pronounced 'froom') in Dorset, which rises near Evershot in the north of the county and flows 56 km (35 miles) south and then east past DORCHESTER[1] and from there into Poole Harbour just to the east of Wareham. It makes appearances under its own name in the WESSEX novels of Thomas Hardy.

Frome⁴. A river (pronounced 'froom') in Bristol and South Gloucestershire, which rises to the west of CHIPPING SODBURY and flows 32 km (20 miles) west and then southwest to join the River AVON[2] in the centre of Bristol.

Frome⁵. A river (pronounced 'froom') in Herefordshire (before 1998 in Hereford and Worcester, before 1974 in Herefordshire), which rises to the north of Bromyard and flows 32 km (20 miles) southwards and southwestwards to join the River LUGG just to the east of Hereford.

Frome⁶. A river (pronounced 'froom') in Gloucestershire, which rises to the northwest of CIRENCESTER and flows

26 km (16 miles) westward through the GOLDEN VALLEY[2] and STROUD to join the River SEVERN to the southwest of Gloucester.

Frongoch 'red hillside', Welsh *fron* (*bron*) 'hillside' + *goch* 'red'.

A village in Gwynedd (formerly in Merioneth), 4 km (2.5 miles) north of Bala. It was in a camp here that Michael Collins, Arthur Griffith and other prominent figures from the Easter Rising in Ireland (*see under* DUBLIN) were interned from May to December 1916. Those who had been sentenced were released the following June.

Fryup Dale. *See* GREAT FRYUP.

Fuarchnoc. The Irish name for FOUR KNOCKS.

Fugglestone St Peter *Fugglestone* 'Fugol's farmstead', OE *Fugoles* possessive form of male personal name *Fugol* (probably based on *fugol* 'bird') + -TON; *St Peter* from the dedication of the local church.

A village (formerly pronounced 'fowlstən') in Wiltshire, about 4 km (2.5 miles) northwest of Salisbury.

Fulford Ings 'muddy ford pastures', *Fulford* OE *ful* 'foul, dirty, muddy' + FORD; *Ings* OScand *eng* 'outlying meadow'.

A battle site in YORK where Harald Hardrada and Tostig of Northumberland beat the Saxons under Earl Morkere and Earl Edwine in 1066 before being defeated themselves at STAMFORD BRIDGE. The battle site, also called **Gate Fulford**, is at one end of the Millennium Bridge over the Ouse.

Fulham 'Fulla's river-bend land', OE *Fullan* possessive form of male personal name *Fulla* + *hamm* 'land in a river-bend' (*see* HAM).

A district in southwest London (SW6), on the north bank of the River Thames to the west of Chelsea and to the east of Barnes, since 1965 incorporated in the borough of HAMMERSMITH AND FULHAM. Until the 19th century it was a fairly countrified area, with nurseries and market gardens interspersed with fine country houses (which included the 16th-century **Fulham Palace**, residence of the bishops of London until 1973), and noted also in the 18th century for carpet manufacture. Then however the land between Fulham Palace Road and the Fulham Road began to fill in with houses, smallish workers' dwellings of a rather humbler sort than in neighbouring districts, and Fulham became a rather dingy, down-at-heel, working-class suburb:

> Servants ... belong to that ... class of people whose public and private lives have no connection with each other ... Publicly and privately their set-ups are as different as Fulham Road and Grosvenor Square.
>
> D. Frome: *The By-Pass Murder* (1932)

Fulham in the 1930s was a dismal district ... It was full of pubs, convents, second-hand clothes shops, bagwash laundries and pawnbrokers. Everything seemed very broken down.

John Osborne: *A Better Class of Person* (1981)

Its fortunes did not begin to revive until the latter part of the 20th century, when gentrification began to seep into it from BARNES and CHELSEA.

Fulham FC was founded in 1879. It plays its home games at a ground on the bank of the Thames known as Craven Cottage (a familiar sight to followers of the annual Oxford-and-Cambridge Boat Race, and source of the team's nickname, the Cottagers). The present Duke of Westminster once had a trial with the club. It was bought in 1997 by the controversial Egyptian entrepreneur, and owner of department store Harrods, Mohamed Fayed.

From 1980 until 1984 Craven Cottage was also home to Fulham rugby league club. **Fulham RLFC** played at other London stadia from 1984, eventually mutating into London Crusaders in 1991, and then into London Broncos in 1996 (*see under* LONDON).

Fulham Broadway Underground station, on the District line, opened in 1880 (originally under the name 'Walham Green').

John Doulton (1793–1873), who gave his name to Royal Doulton porcelain, was born in Fulham.

fulhams. Underworld slang from the 16th to the late 18th centuries for loaded dice, dice that have been weighted on one side so that the thrower can determine how they will fall. The word was also written as *fullams*, and it is not certain that there was originally any connection with Fulham the place – although Fulham was 'once a noted haunt of gamesters' (OED).

Fulham stoneware. Hard ceramic ware, typically brown-glazed, of a type made at **Fulham Pottery** since 1672.

Fulham virgin. An ironic 19th-century euphemism for a prostitute. The name may have been inspired by the proximity of Cremorne Gardens, a 19th-century pleasure garden on the border of Fulham and Chelsea which developed a reputation as 'a nursery of every kind of vice' (in the words of one contemporary Baptist minister).

Fulwood 'foul wood', OE *ful* 'foul, dirty' + *wudu* 'wood'.

A district of northern Preston, Lancashire, formerly a separate town.

Fungle Road, the Etymology obscure; possibly related to Scots *fung* 'to kick, throw violently, fly along at high speed with a buzzing noise'.

A hill track over the MOUNTH south of Aboyne, in Aberdeenshire (formerly in Grampian region). It is popular with mountain bikers.

what do you do?
we foindle and fungle, we bonkle and meigle and maxpoffle …

Edwin Morgan: 'Canedolia: An Off-Concrete Scotch Fantasia' (a poem constructed largely from Scottish place names)

Furness 'headland by the island shaped like a bottom', OScand *futhar*, possessive of *futh* 'rump' + NESS.

A traditional area of south CUMBRIA, mostly in the Lake District, but also including the lowlands on the north side of Morecambe Bay. It is effectively a broad peninsula, and prior to 1974 formed an exclave of Lancashire. The name is found in such place names as BARROW-IN-FURNESS, DALTON-IN-FURNESS and Broughton-in-Furness. The hills round the Old Man of Coniston are called the **Furness Fells**.

The area was important in the Middle Ages because of **Furness Abbey** north of Barrow, founded in 1123 and subsequently becoming one of the richest in England. In 1537 the abbey was the first large foundation to be closed in the Dissolution of the Monasteries. One of the monks here, **Jocelin of Furness**, wrote lives of St Patrick, St Walthe of Melrose, St Kentigern and King David I of Scotland.

Furneux Pelham *Furneux* denoting medieval manorial ownership by the de Fornellis family; *Pelham* 'Peola's homestead or village', OE male personal name *Peola* + HAM.

A village (pronounced 'fernix') in Hertfordshire, about 9 km (6 miles) northwest of Bishop's Stortford. STOCKING PELHAM lies a little to the northeast.

Furry Boots City. A nickname bestowed on ABERDEEN by the *Glasgow Herald* diarist Tom Shields during the 1980s, owing to the propensity of the inhabitants to find out all about you without giving anything away about themselves; thus they would begin the conversation by asking, in the local dialect, 'Fur aboots are ye from?' (i.e. 'Whereabouts do you come from?').

Fylde OE *filde* 'a plain'.

A low coastal plain in Lancashire, extending from the mouth of the RIBBLE north to Morecambe Bay (*see under* MORECAMBE). It became known as 'the Granary of Lancashire' in the 18th century, and became a local goverment district in 1974. It includes the towns of LYTHAM ST ANNE'S, BLACKPOOL and FLEETWOOD.

Fylde's rugby union club, dating from 1919, numbers former England captain Bill Beaumont among its former players.

Fylingdales Moor 'moor of the people of Fygela's valley', *Fylingdales* OE male personal name *Fygela* + *-ingas* (*see* -ING) + ME *dale*.

An eastern section of the NORTH YORK MOORS, North Yorkshire, some 8 km (4 miles) southwest of Robin Hood's

Bay. During the Cold War giant white 'golf balls' on the moor were part of an early-warning radar system linked to similar installations in Greenland and Alaska. There was something of a furore when they were first installed in 1963 (Fylingdales being within a national park), and another one when they were scrapped in the early 1990s – some even suggested that the golf balls be registered as Listed Buildings.

The structure that the RAF built to replace them is a sort of headless concrete pyramid, and is almost, despite being visible from miles around, too secret to mention. However, it can be revealed that it emits high-powered radar pulses that set off the immobilizers in cars such as BMWs and Mercedes within a not insignificant radius.

In January 2003 the Labour government acceded to the US government's request that Fylingdales, along with MENWITH HILL near Harrogate, be made part of the 'son of Star Wars' missile defence system.

G

Gabhra Uncertain; in early Irish, the word seems to mean 'goat' or 'mare', and the name may mean 'place of the goat or mare'.

A hill said to be to the west of Tara. It was the site of the legendary Irish battle recounted in the Fenian Cycle, in which Finn MacCool and the rest of the Fianna are destroyed by the high king; only the bards Oisín (Ossian) and Caoilte survive.

Gadshill 'God's, or a god's, hill', OE *godes* possessive form of *god* + *hyll* 'hill'. The earliest record is from the 13th century, but it is not impossible that the name refers to a heathen site.

A hamlet in Kent, about 3 km (2 miles) northeast of ROCHESTER. That point on the London-to-Rochester road was notorious in Shakespeare's time for robberies, and he uses it as the venue of the set-up in Act II of *Henry IV, Part 1* (1596) in which the would-be highway-robber Falstaff is mugged by Prince Hal and Poins in disguise – an incident which Falstaff later uses as an opportunity for much vainglorious but transparent embroidery. Unfortunately Shakespeare also uses 'Gadshill' as the name of the professional highwayman in the play (misinterpreting a nickname in one of his sources, *The Famous Victories of Henry the Fifth*), occasioning considerable confusion for centuries of inattentive audience members. A real-life denizen of Gadshill nearly a century later was the highwayman Nicholas Nevinson, who made the celebrated ride to York later attributed to Dick Turpin. Charles II granted him a free pardon and called him 'Swift Nicks'.

In 1856, Charles Dickens bought **Gad's Hill Place**, an 18th-century house at Gadshill he had admired since boyhood, and he spent the rest of his life there. *Great Expectations* (1860), *The Uncommercial Traveller* (1860), *Our Mutual Friend* (1865) and the unfinished *Mystery of Edwin Drood* (1870) were written either in the house or in a small Swiss chalet he had built in the garden.

Gaeltacht An Irish term coined in the 20th century.

Any of the areas of Ireland, largely on the west coast, where Irish is the predominant language spoken. Despite official encouragement, the number of native Irish-speakers is steadily declining. The term **Galltacht** is sometimes applied to the English-speaking areas of the country; in Irish *gall* means 'foreigner' (with an imputation of 'oppressive colonialist English'). The satirical term **Jailteacht** has been used of those prisons in Northern Ireland holding Republican prisoners, who while in jail learnt Irish Gaelic (or 'Jailic').

The term Gaeltacht or **Gaidhealtachd** is also applied to the Gaelic-speaking areas of Scotland.

Gaidhealtachd. *See under* GAELTACHT.

Gaillimh. The Irish name for GALWAY.

Gainsborough 'Gegn's stronghold', OE *Gegnes* possessive form of male personal name *Gegn* + *burh* 'stronghold'.

A market town in Lincolnshire, on the River TRENT[1], about 26 km (16 miles) northwest of Lincoln. The Trent is navigable from the sea to Gainsborough, and the town has long been and remains a busy port, its quayside lined by 18th-century warehouses (Daniel Defoe in his *A Tour Through the Whole Island of Great Britain* (1724–6) called it 'a town of good trade, as well foreign as home trade').

The LINDSEY region was a power base for the Danish king Swein when he returned to conquer England in 1013. He died at Gainsborough in February 1014, aged 54, only a few months after being acknowledged as king of England, and his son Cnut (of incoming-tide fame) remained in the town until Easter 1014 as the battles of succession raged.

Gainsborough features in George Eliot's novel *The Mill on the Floss* (1860) (*see under* FLOSS), in which it is fictionalized as St Ogg's. It is also the birthplace of Dame Sybil Thorndyke (1882–1976).

Gair Loch 'short loch', *Gair* Gaelic *geàrr* 'short'; *see also* LOCH, LOUGH.

A sea loch on the northwest coast of Highland (formerly in Ross and Cromarty), between Loch Torridon (*see under* TORRIDON) and LOCH EWE. At its inner end is the village of **Gairloch**, named after it.

Galashiels 'huts on Gala Water', the second element being ME *schele* (OScand *skali*) 'hut'; recorded as *Galcha* 1124. The etymology of *Gala* is unknown.

A town in Scottish Borders (formerly in Selkirkshire), some 45 km (27 miles) southeast of Edinburgh, on **Gala Water**, a tributary of the Tweed. It originally developed to accommodate pilgrims going to the nearby MELROSE Abbey, but developed as a centre of wool-weaving in the 18th and 19th centuries. The town is often referred to simply as **Gala**, reflected in the name Gala Rugby Football Club. Every year, in the Braw Lads' Gathering (Scots *braw* 'handsome'), riders from the town process round the district.

> Braw lads o' Galla Water!
> Bonnie lads o' Galla Water!
> Lothian lads will ne'er compare
> Wi' the braw lads o' Galla Water.
>
> Chorus of a traditional song, sung to a tune that was Haydn's favourite Scottish melody. Robert Burns wrote a new version:
>
> Braw, braw lads on Yarrow braes,
> Ye wander thro' the blooming heather;
> But Yarrow braes, nor Ettrick shaws,
> Can match the lads o' Galla Water.
>
> Robert Burns: 'Galla Water' (1793) (*shaw* 'small wood')

It was while working as a schoolmaster at Galashiels that the geologist Charles Lapworth (1842–1920) made the observations of the local rocks and fossils that led him to propose the Ordovician period (505–438 million years ago).

Galashiels grey. A rough grey woollen cloth, made in Galashiels in the 18th and 19th centuries.

'Soor Plums in Galashiels'. A traditional song, commemorating a victory near the town over a band of English soldiers, who were sampling the local wild plums. On the town's arms is depicted a fabular fox vainly attempting to reach some plums, with the motto 'Soor Plums'.

Galava. A Roman camp on the site of present-day AMBLESIDE.

Gala Water. *See* GALASHIELS.

Galley Hill So named because it was formerly the site of a gibbet used for public executions.

A barrow-topped hill (187 m / 614 ft) in southern Bedfordshire, just north of Luton. Local tradition has it that the site was used to bury the bodies of local witches who were hanged during the 16th and 17th centuries. The ICKNIELD WAY passes nearby.

Gallions Reach *Gallions* denoting manorial ownership of the corresponding area of riverbank in the Middle Ages by the Galyan or Galyon family.

A stretch of the northern side of the River THAMES[1] in the London borough of NEWHAM, from the promontory (**Gallions Point**) where the river turns northwards at the eastern end of the former Royal Docks to the point where it resumes its eastward course, at the outfall of Barking Creek.

The Gallions Reach Shopping Park opened in the autumn of 2003. Gallions Reach station is on the Docklands Light Railway.

Gallions Reach. The first and probably best-known novel (1927) by the Poplar-born writer H.M. Tomlinson, a tale of ships and the sea.

Galloway 'the land of the foreign Gaels', Gaelic *gall* 'stranger' + *Ghàidhil* 'Gaels'. It was the indigenous Gaels who called the Hiberno-Norse settlers of the 9th–10th centuries the 'foreign Gaels'.

A traditional region of southwest Scotland, formerly comprising parts of Wigtownshire and Kircudbrightshire, and now forming the western part of DUMFRIES AND GALLOWAY. Until the late 12th century, Galloway also included CARRICK[1], in southern Ayrshire.

The local inhabitants were known to the Romans as the Novantae. After the Romans left, the region (together with parts of Cumbria) became the Welsh kingdom of RHEGED, whose ruler, Urien, was praised by the poet Taliesin (6th century). Galloway only submitted to the Scottish Crown in the 11th century, and even after that was dominated by powerful families who took little note of the king. Local power was finally broken when James II seized the seat of the Douglases, THREAVE CASTLE, in 1455. In the 17th century Galloway was a centre of hard-core Presbyterianism, and the wilder parts of the region provided a refuge for many Covenanters. A native of the region is known as a **Galwegian**, and Daniel Defoe, in his *Tour Through the Whole Island of Great Britain* (1724–6), despaired of their lack of commercial acumen, though conceded that 'The people of Galloway itself are not perfectly idle ... they are not all stupid.'

See also NEW GALLOWAY.

East Galloway. An old name for the former county of KIRKCUDBRIGHTSHIRE.

Galloway. A breed of black hornless cattle, or a breed of small sturdy horse:

> ... we call all small truss-strong riding horses Galloways. These horses are remarkable for being good pacers, strong, easy goers, hardy, gentle, well broke, and above all, that they never tire, and they are very much bought up in England on that account.
>
> Daniel Defoe: *A Tour Through the Whole Island of Great Britain* (1724–6)

Galloways were also used as pit ponies, as mentioned in these lines by the Chairman of the Yorkshire Dialect Society in the early 20th century:

I went to wark when I were eight yeer old,
I tended galloways an' sammed up coils.
'Twere warm i' t' pit, aboon 't were despert cowd,
An' clothes were nobbut spetches, darns an' hoils.

F.W. Murman: 'Hungry Forties'

Galloway beltie. A breed of beef cattle, also called **belted Galloway**, all black apart from a wide vertical white band or belt down the middle of its body.

Galloway dyke. A form of drystone dyke (wall), in which there is a course of thin flat stones about halfway up, projecting to either side.

Galloway Forest Park. A large forest park, with an area of 620 sq km (240 sq miles), extending from Galloway into Carrick in South Ayrshire. It was formerly known as GLEN TROOL Forest Park. As well as extensive Forestry Commission plantations, the park incorporates lochs, rivers and high hills, including MERRICK, CORSERINE and the RHINNS OF KELLS.

Galloway white. A type of woollen cloth woven in the 17th century.

Mull of Galloway OScand *múli* 'headland'.

A rocky headland 65 m (213 ft) high at the south end of the **Rhinns of Galloway** (*see below*). It is surmounted by a lighthouse, and is the most southerly point in Scotland. It is said (entirely without historical foundation) that the Mull was the site of the final defeat of the Picts by the Scots, and that the last Pict leapt from the cliffs of the Mull into the sea, taking with him the recipe for his people's fabulous heather ale. In local tradition, the notorious late-medieval family of cannibals headed by Sawney Bean is said to have lived in a cave on the Mull, although he is usually located at BENNANE HEAD in Ayrshire.

Rhinns or **Rinns of Galloway, the** Probably OCelt *roinn* 'headland', 'promontory', the origin of Gaelic *rinn* 'sharp point'. The hammer-headed western extension of Galloway. It is joined to the mainland by an isthmus, with LOCH RYAN to the north and LUCE BAY to the south. At the southern tip of the Rhinns is the Mull of Galloway, while at the north end are Milleur Point and Corsewall Point.

Gallow Hill From its former use.

There are several Gallow Hills in Scotland, including those in Aberdeenshire (near Aberchirder), Highland (in Speyside, west of Bridge of Avon), Angus (at the eastern end of the Sidlaw Hills) and Dumfries and Galloway (just north of Moffat). In England, there is a Gallows Hill north of BOVINGTON Camp, Dorset.

The Gallow Hill in Shetland was the scene of the last witch-burning in those islands, as recorded by William J. Tait (1918–91) in his poem 'Gallow Hill':

O cled me, Christ or Deil,
In sic a sark o fire, I burn

Trowe Heevin an Aert an Hell!

(Scots *Deil* 'Devil' *cled* 'clad, clothe', *sic a sark* 'such a shirt', *Trow Heevin an Aert* 'through Heaven and Earth')

Galston Possibly 'foreigners' settlement', Gaelic *gall* 'stranger, foreigner' + OE -TON. The 'foreigners' were the Hiberno-Norse settlers of the 9th–10th centuries.

A small town in East Ayrshire (formerly in Strathclyde region), some 7 km (4.5 miles) east of Kilmarnock.

Upon a simmer Sunday morn,
  When Nature's face is fair,
I walked forth to view the corn,
  An' snuff the callor air.
The rising sun, owre Galston Muirs,
  Wi' glorious light was glintan;
The hares were hirplan down the furrs,
  The lav'rocks they were chantan
    Fu' sweet that day.

Robert Burns: 'The Holy Fair' (1786), opening verse

Galtee Mountains Irish *Na Gaibhlte* 'the mountains of the woods' or 'fortified valleys'.

A range of mountains straddling counties LIMERICK and TIPPERARY, to the south of the GLEN OF AHERLOW. They are also spelt **Galty Mountains**, and are composed of old red sandstone and quartzite. The highest point is Galtymore ('big Galtee', 919 m / 3014 ft) – which gave its name to a famous dance hall in CRICKLEWOOD, north London, popular with Irish construction workers.

There's a high spring on Galtymore
And I've heard young laughter from its slopes
Tripping from green and golden fields
That mile to Tipperary town
Beyond the Vale of Aherlow.

Hamish Brown: 'Ballydavid, by Galtymore'

Edmund Spenser, in his *Two Cantos of Mutabilite* (1594), gave to Galtymore the name **Arlo**, from the adjacent Glen of Aherlow:

That was, to weet, upon the highest heights
Of Arlo-hill (who knows not Arlo-hill?)
That is the highest head in all men's sight.

'Galtee Mountain Boy, The'. A Republican ballad of the Irish Civil War (1922–3), ending:

I bid farewell to old Clonmel that I never more will see,
And to the Galtee Mountains that oft times sheltered me,
The men who fought for their liberty and who died
  without a sigh,
May their cause be ne'er forgotten, said the Galtee
  mountain boy.

Galtymore. *See under* GALTEE MOUNTAINS.

Galway Irish *Gaillimh* 'stony (place, river)'.

A fishing port, cathedral and university town in County

Galway (of which it is the county town), some 200 km (120 miles) west of Dublin. It is at the mouth of the River CORRIB on the north side of the beautiful **Galway Bay** (*see also below*), a long, wide inlet of the Atlantic between counties Clare and Galway, with the ARAN ISLANDS at its mouth. A native of Galway is a **Galwegian**.

Galway is referred to as the **City of the Tribes** (*see below*), as the **Limestone City**, because of the stone used in many of its buildings (*compare* Aberdeen as 'the Granite City'), and as 'the gateway to Connemara'. It is regarded as the unofficial capital of the west of Ireland, and is an important centre of the Irish language: University College (1908, founded as Queen's College *c.*1845) teaches in both Irish and English.

The town of Galway developed following the seizure of the area by the Anglo-Norman Robert de Burgo in the 1230s and 1240s. Galway became a centre of English settlement, and the Irish were confined to the village of CLADDAGH. From the later 14th century Galway thrived as a port, particularly on the trade with Spain (commemorated in the town's Spanish Arch and Spanish Parade), becoming almost an independent city-state under the oligarchy of families of Anglo-Norman or English ancestry – who gained the town the aforementioned nickname 'City of the Tribes'. The Free School (founded 1580) became a magnet for students from far afield, so much so that the Corporation decreed that 'forreigne beggars and poor schollers' be whipped out of town. In 1614 Sir Oliver St John reported:

> The towne is small, but all is faire and statelie buildings, the front of the houses are all of hewed stone, uppe to the top, garnished with faire battlement, in a uniform course, as if the whole town had been built upon one model.

However, this prosperity came to an end when the citizens backed the wrong side in the 17th-century Civil Wars, resulting in the place being razed to the ground after it surrendered to the Parliamentarians under General Charles Coote in 1652. The burgers of Galway also backed the wrong horse during the Glorious Revolution, and in 1691 the town surrendered to the forces of William III, having negotiated the **Articles of Galway**, which guaranteed their property rights and religious freedom. The attitude of the local anti-Jacobites was summed up in 1698 in a letter by one John Dunton of Galway:

> As in the body naturall the crisis of the disease is often made by throwing the peccant humor into the extreme parts, soe here the barbarities of Ireland under which it so long laboured, and with which it was soe miserably infected, are all accumulated.

Galway became pretty much of a backwater in the 18th and 19th centuries.

> I know a town tormented by the sea,
> And there time goes slow,
> That the people see it flow,
> And watch it drowsily.
>
> Mary Davenport O'Neill: 'Galway'

The stagnation extended into the 20th, when Louis MacNeice visited:

> O, the crossbones of Galway,
> The hollow grey houses,
> The rubbish and the sewage,
> The grass grown pier,
> And the dredger grumbling
> All the night in the harbour ...

However, in the latter decades of the 20th century Galway began to thrive again, both culturally and economically. It is now an important tourist centre, proving especially attractive to young people in search of that particularly Irish brew of fun, craic and folk music, for, as the Ulster flautist James Galway (no relation) has observed:

> It is next to impossible, I believe, to toss a brick in the air anywhere in County Galway without it landing on the head of some musician.
>
> James Galway: *An Autobiography* (1978)

Galway was the birthplace of Frank Harris (1856–1931), journalist, biographer and pornographic memoirist, and of the novelist and dramatist Walter Macken (1915–67). It was also the girlhood home of Nora Barnacle (1884–1951), novelist and wife of James Joyce; the house is now a museum. In 1887 the poet Wilfred Scawen Blunt served a spell in Galway gaol for inciting the tenants of Lord Clanricarde to resist eviction; this experience resulted in his sonnet sequence *In Vinculis* (1889); 'Prison has had an admirable effect on Mr Wilfred Blunt as a poet,' remarked Oscar Wilde. US President John F. Kennedy visited Galway in 1963.

See also SALTHILL.

'Galway Bay'. An anonymous traditional song of somewhat forced sentiment:

> If you ever go across the sea to Ireland
> Then maybe at the closing of your day
> You will sit and watch the moon rise over Claddagh
> And see the sun go down on Galway Bay ...
>
> For the breezes blowing o'er the seas from Ireland
> Are perfumed by the heather as they blow
> And the women in the uplands diggin' praties
> Speak a language that the strangers do not know.

Matthew Edwards, inventor of the Dublin Underground Railway, has provided a parody in his online short story, 'Margaret Barry and a Bicycle', in which the heroine sings:

> She could drink her sixty pints of Irish Guinness
> And stagger from the pub and never sway.

If the sea was beer instead of salty water,
She would live and swim and die in Galway Bay.

For further parodies, *see under* LIVERPOOL and RUNCORN.

Galway Races. A three-day annual horse-racing meet held at the end of July, at which a good time is had by all:

It's there you'll see the pipers and the fiddlers competing,
The nimble-footed dancers a-tripping over the daisies,
There were others crying cigars and lights and bills for all
the races
With the colours of the jockeys and the prize and horses'
ages.

Anon.: song 'Galway Races'

Galway, County. A county in the west of Ireland, bounded on the west by the Atlantic, on the north by Mayo, on the east by Roscommon, Offaly and Tipperary, and on the south by Clare. The county town is Galway. The east of Galway is a fertile plain, while the west includes the wilder areas of IAR CONNACHT and CONNEMARA (an important GAELTACHT, or Gaelic-speaking area), together with the MAUMTURK MOUNTAINS and the TWELVE PINS. The SLIEVE AUGHTY MOUNTAINS and part of LOUGH DERG[2] are in the south, and the ARAN ISLANDS in the southwest.

When the landfolk of Galway converse with a stranger,
softly the men speak, more softly the women ...

W.B. Stanford (b.1910): 'Undertone'

Galway Blazers. The nickname of a hunt in central Galway, at its wildest in the Protestant Ascendancy days of the 19th century. The nickname comes from the incident in 1840 in which members of the hunt set fire to Dooley's Hotel in BIRR during the course of a banquet.

Galway hooker. A type of sailing boat once used widely for the transport of freight in the seas around Galway. They come in various sizes, and have a sharp bow and curved sides, suitable for navigation in difficult inshore waters.

Oh! My boat can safely float in the teeth of wind and
weather
And outrace the fastest hooker between Galway and
Kinsale,
When the black floor of the ocean and the white foam
rush together
High she rides, in her pride, like a sea-gull through the
gale.

Anon.: 'Queen of Connemara'

The word 'hooker' comes from the Dutch *hoeker*, a form of vessel; it has nothing to do with ladies of pleasure, for

No milk-limbed Venus ever rose
Miraculous on this western shore.

Seamus Heaney: 'Girls Bathing, Galway, 1965', from *Door
into the Dark* (1969)

'Man for Galway, The'. A paean to the county's Ascen-

dancy hell-raisers (such as the Galway Blazers; *see above*) by Charles James Lever (1806–72):

To keep game cocks, to hunt the fox,
To drink in punch the Solway,
With debts galore, but fun far more;
Oh, that's 'the man for Galway'.

Some of the Galway Anglo-Irish had more rounded talents; W.B. Yeats celebrated one such, the son of his friend Lady Gregory, as a Renaissance man, 'Soldier, scholar, horseman', a skilled painter who rode out boldly:

When with the Galway foxhounds he would ride ...
... his mind outran the horses' feet.

W.B. Yeats: 'In Memory of Major Robert Gregory', from *The
Wild Swans at Coole* (1919)

Gammersgill 'Gamall's shelter', OScand male personal name *Gamall* + *skali* 'shelter, shieling'.
A small settlement in Coverdale in the YORKSHIRE DALES, North Yorkshire, 10 km (6 miles) southwest of Leyburn.

Gangmoor. A former name for that part of Hampstead Heath known as the VALE OF HEALTH.

Gants Hill *Gants* denoting manorial ownership in the Middle Ages by the le Gant family.
A district in northeast London, to the north of Ilford, in the borough of REDBRIDGE (before 1965 in Essex). Gants Hill Underground station, on the Central line, opened in 1947.

Gaoth Doghair. The Irish name for GWEEDORE.

Gaping Ghyll *Ghyll* OScand *gil* 'ravine', with ModE 'gaping'.
A large and famous pothole or swallow hole (sometimes spelt **Gaping Gill**) on the south side of INGLEBOROUGH, North Yorkshire, in the YORKSHIRE DALES. It is over 107 m (350 ft) deep, and the main chamber is 140 m (460 ft) long and 30 m (100 ft high). On the spring and August bank holidays, local caving clubs set up winches by which the public may be lowered by bosun's chair into the void. The descent is free, but the return journey attracts a fee that most are willing to pay.

Gap of Dunloe From the nearby *Dunlo*e Castle, Irish *Dún Lóich* 'fort of the River Loe' (the meaning of the river name is uncertain; possibly 'water').
A craggy defile in County Kerry, 10 km (6 miles) southwest of Killarney, leading between the main massif of MACGILLYCUDDY'S REEKS to the west and the PURPLE MOUNTAIN to the east. It is a very popular with tourists, attracted by its scenic grandeur; cars are generally discouraged, many tourists being transported to the summit by jaunting car (horse-drawn buggy).

At one entrance is the celebrated café and pub known as Kate Kearney's Cottage; Kate herself may have been a poetical invention:

Oh! should you e'er meet this Kate Kearney,
Who lives on the banks of Killarney,
Beware of her smile, for many a wile
Lies hid in the smile of Kate Kearney.

Lady Morgan: 'Kate Kearney', from *Hibernian Melodies* (1801)

Gap of the North. The strategic gap in counties Armagh and Louth, between the hills of the CARLINGFORD Peninsula and SLIEVE GULLION, to the south of Newry. It takes the main A1/NI road, and the Belfast–Dublin railway line.

The train rattled down through the Gap of the North, mystic country, fairy country, turn a stone and uncover a legend or a myth. Cuchullain the demigod to O'Hanlon the Rapparee, and highwaymen giving their ghosts to those moors and mountains and little fields.

Benedict Kiely: *Land without Stars* (1946)

Garbhachadh. The Irish name for GARVAGH.

Garbh Bheinn 'rough mountain', Gaelic *garbh* 'rough' with *beinn* 'mountain'.
The name of several peaks in Scotland, the most notable being Garbh Bheinn of Ardgour (885 m / 2903 ft). Its craggy east face, with its Great Ridge plunging down from its summit, recalls, when viewed at winter dawn from BALLACHULISH, the north face of the Grandes Jorasses with its famous Walker Spur, in the Mont Blanc massif.

Garden, the. *See* COVENT GARDEN.

Garden County, the. A nickname for County WICKLOW.

Garden of England, the. A name given to any area or county of England whose fertile soil and benign climate promotes the growth of flowers and fruit: particularly WORCESTERSHIRE (where the Vale of Evesham (*see under* EVESHAM) is famous for its plums and asparagus), and even more particularly KENT (whose apple orchards and cherry orchards have kept London supplied since the Middle Ages). The term appears to date from the 19th century.

'Yes, sir, Kent's my county, but even in the garden of England they can't grow finer roses than them.'

B. L. Farjeon: *Sacred Nugget* (1885)

Gare Loch *Gare* Gaelic *gèarr* 'short'; *Loch see* LOCH, LOUGH.
A sea loch in Argyll and Bute (formerly in Dunbartonshire and then in Strathclyde region), extending some 12 km (7.5 miles) north from the Firth of Clyde. HELENSBURGH is at its mouth, and on the eastern shore is FASLANE naval base. At its northern end is **Garelochhead**, a popular resort.
Battle of Garelochhead (22 August 1853). An incident in which Sir James Colquhoun of Luss and his keepers, in order to enforce the Sabbath, attempted to prevent Glaswegian day-trippers disembarking at the pier from the paddle steamer *Emperor* on a Sunday. Colquhoun and his men were routed, but the laird later won the battle in the courts, and Sunday trips were made illegal for some years.

Garforth 'Gæra's ford', OE male personal name *Gæra* + FORD, or the first element may be OE *gara* 'triangular plot of land'.
A town in West Yorkshire, some 10 km (6 miles) east of Leeds, for which it acts as a dormitory town.

Gargunnock Uncertain, but 'pointed enclosure', Gaelic *gart* 'enclosure' + *guineach* 'pointed' has been suggested, as has 'enclosure of the rounded hill', Gaelic *garradh* 'enclosure' + *cnuic* 'rounded hill'.
A village some 10 km (6 miles) west of Stirling, formerly in Stirlingshire, then in Central region, and now in the unitary authority of Stirling. Chopin is said to have visited **Gargunnock House** on his 1848 tour of England and Scotland, and to have written the original *Schottische* for the daughter of the house, Miss Stirling. The village nestles at the foot of the craggy northern escarpment of the **Gargunnock Hills**, whose moorland plateau reaches a high point of 486 m (1594 ft) at Carleatheran. At their western end they merge with the FINTRY Hills.
Gargunnock Braes is the name of a fictional Scottish soap opera in Charles Palliser's tricksy postmodernist novel *Betrayals* (1994).

Garioch 'place of roughness', Gaelic name *Gairbheach*, from *gairbhe* 'roughness' + suffix *-ach*.
A traditional area of Aberdeenshire, northwest of Aberdeen and southwest of Formartine. It is often referred to as **the Garioch**, and includes the hills of BENNACHIE, the town of INVERURIE and the hamlet of **Chapel of Garioch**. David of Huntingdon, great-great-grandfather of Robert the Bruce, was Earl of the Garioch.

Garnish Island. *See under* GLENGARRIFF.

Garraí Eoghain. The Irish name for GARRYOWEN.

Garraun Point Irish *Garrán* 'grove'.
The most westerly mainland point in mainland Ireland, and thus in Europe. It is at the tip of the Dingle Peninsula (*see under* DINGLE), County Kerry, overlooking the BLASKET ISLANDS. The most westerly point altogether is Tearaght Island, 12.5 km (8 miles) west of the Dingle.

Toti Iberni, ultimi habitatores mundi
(All of us Irish, inhabitants of the world's edge).

St Columban (*c*.540–615): letter

Garrow Tor *Garrow* originally *Garros*, perhaps 'rough moorland', Cornish *garow* 'rough' + *ros* 'moorland'.
A tor (craggy hilltop rock) on Bodmin Moor (*see under* BODMIN), about 3 km (2 miles) southeast of BROWN WILLY.

Garry. *See* GLEN GARRY[1]; GLEN GARRY[2].

Garryowen Irish *Garraí Eoghain* 'garden of Eoghan or Owen' (whose identity is unknown).
An area of the city of LIMERICK, and home of the Colleen Bawn (*see under* Limerick). It also gave its name to a marching/drinking song, based on a tune called 'Auld Bessy',

associated with the 5th Royal Irish Lancers who were stationed here. The words were supplied in 1807 by Thomas Moore, in which he describes the regimental recreations, largely violent:

We'll beat the bailiffs out of fun,
We'll make the mayor and sheriffs run,
We are the boys no man dares dun
If he regards a whole skin.
chorus:
Instead of spa we'll drink brown ale
And pay the reckoning on the nail
For debt no man shall go to gaol
From Garryowen in glory.

The song was later adopted by the US 7th Cavalry, and was the last tune heard by General Custer's men as they rode off to their deaths at the Little Big Horn in 1876.

Garryowen, via its rugby football club, gave its name to a high kick in rugby, also called an up-and-under. Finally, in James Joyce's *Ulysses* (1922), Garryowen is the name of a 'mangy mongrel', said to be a play on Owen Garry, an legendary 3rd-century king of Leinster.

'Seán South from Garryowen'. A ballad, sung to the tune of 'Roddy McCorley', commemorating the death of Seán South during an IRA raid on the Royal Ulster Constabulary barracks at Brookeborough, County Tyrone, on 1 January 1957:

There were men from Dublin and from Cork, Fermanagh
    and Tyrone
But the leader was a Limerick man, Seán South from
    Garryowen.

Garsdale 'Garthr's valley', OScand male personal name *Garthr* + *dalr* 'dale'.
One of the YORKSHIRE DALES – at least as far as the national park is concerned, although the valley is actually in Cumbria. It is west of Wensleydale and east of Sedburgh, set between Baugh Fell and Knoutberry Haw to the north, and Aye Gill Pike to the south. Down these steep fellsides flow many short streams, such as Liquor Gill, Church Milk Gill and Ringing Keld Gutter, feeding the dale's river, the Clough. Garsdale is sparsely inhabited, with nothing as substantial as a village. At its eastern end is **Garsdale Head**, where there is a railway station on the remote Settle-to-Carlisle line. South of this is **Garsdale Common**, over which a little road reaches a height of 535 m (1755 ft) on its way to Dentdale.

Garsington 'grassy hill', OE *gœrsen* 'grassy' + *dun* 'hill'.
A hilltop village in Oxfordshire, about 5 km (3 miles) southeast of Oxford, whose outlook on the dreaming spires is not wholly enhanced by the presence in the valley below of the Cowley car plant. The Tudor **Garsington Manor** was built on land once owned by the son of the 14th-century poet Geoffrey Chaucer, and was originally called 'Chaucer's'. From 1915 to 1927 it was the home of the indefatigable hostess Ottoline Morrell (1873–1938), captor of political and artistic lions. Since 1990 it has been the venue of the annual summer **Garsington Opera festival**, one of the pioneers of late 20th-century, post-Glyndebourne country house opera in England.

John Aubrey in his 17th-century *Brief Lives* recalls a sermon preached at Garsington Revels by Ralph Kettell (1563–1643), the somewhat eccentric President of Trinity College, Oxford:

Here is Hey for Garsington! and Hey for Cuddesdon! and
Hey Hockley! but here's nobody cries, Hey for God
Almighty!

Garstang 'spear post', OScand *geirr* 'spear' + *stong* 'post'; spear posts were probably markers for meeting places (weapons were not allowed, and it is possible that this was also where they were left); Gearstones in Ingleton, Yorkshire, probably has the same meaning.
A small town in Lancashire, 16 km (10 miles) south of Lancaster.

Garvagh Irish *Garbhachadh* 'rough field'.
A small town in County Londonderry, 16 km (10 miles) south of Coleraine. The present town was founded by George Canning of the London Ironmongers Guild in the early 17th century; his descendant George Canning (1770–1827), noted British foreign minister (1807–10, 1822–7) and briefly prime minister (1827), was born here. Garvagh was also the home of the centenarian harpist Denis O'Hempsey (1695–1807).
Battle of Garvagh (26 July 1813). An affray in which Protestants at a fair in Garvagh opened fire on a group of Catholics who were attacking them, resulting in one fatality. Those convicted of manslaughter served no sentence.

Garvaghy Road. *See under* DRUMCREE.

Garvellachs, the 'rough rocky mounds', Gaelic *garbh* 'rough' + *eileach* 'rocky mound'.
A group of small islands some 10 km (6 miles) north of Jura, in the Inner Hebrides (*see under* HEBRIDES). They are in Argyll and Bute (formerly in Strathclyde region). They take their name from the largest island, **Garbh Eileach**. They are also known as **the Isles of the Sea**. This name derives from the other main island, **Eileach an Naoimh** ('rocky place of the saint'), which is thought to be the *Hinba* ('isles of the sea') mentioned by Adamnan, abbot of Iona in the 7th century. St Brendan of Clonfert founded a monastery on Eileach an Naoimh in 542, two decades before his nephew St Columba arrived in Iona. St Columba also visited the island, and his mother Eithne may be buried here. The

monastery was destroyed in the Viking raids of the 9th–10th centuries.

Gate Fulford. *See* FULFORD INGS.

Gatehouse of Fleet Possibly 'road house of Fleet', ME *gatehouse*, but it is obscure whether the *gate* is OE *geat* 'gate' or OScand *gata* 'road, way'; *fleet* 'stream' is similarly ambiguous in origin, since both OE *fleot* and OScand *fljot* mean 'river', though the OE form more precisely refers to an estuary.

A small town 10 km (6 miles) northwest of KIRKCUDBRIGHT, near the mouth of the **Water of Fleet**. It was formerly in Kirkcudbrightshire, and is now in Dumfries and Galloway. Until the later 18th century there was just one single house on the road, hence its name. It is said that Robert Burns composed 'Scots Wha Ha'e' while walking nearby, and then wrote it down in the Murray Arms Hotel.

Gateshead 'headland or hill of the goat', OE *gat* 'goat' + *heafod* 'headland, hill'.

An industrial port and unitary authority (formerly in County Durham, then in Tyne and Wear), on the south side of the River TYNE[1] opposite Newcastle. Sometimes Newcastle and Gateshead are considered as one city, the two being linked by many bridges, most recently the 'blinking eye' MILLENNIUM BRIDGE. Decline followed Gateshead's 19th-century industrial heyday, but the town is undergoing something of a revival. Notable features include the vast Metro Centre shopping complex (1986), the largest in Britain; Anthony Gormley's giant 1998 sculpture, *The Angel of the North* (*see under* NORTH[1]); the Baltic Flour Mills, reopened in 2002 as the Baltic Centre for Contemporary Art, one of the biggest art spaces in Europe; and the Sage Centre Gateshead (2004) for music, designed by Norman Foster and resembling a silvery trilobite. Newcastle-Gateshead was one of the leading candidates to become European City of Culture in 2008, although pipped at the post by Liverpool.

From an earlier era is Owen Luder's 1960s Treaty shopping centre, a notable example of Brutalist architecture. In the film *Get Carter* (1971), Michael Caine – entering into the spirit of the movement – throws someone off the roof of the Treaty's multi-storey car park.

The wood engraver, Thomas Bewick (1753–1828), lived and died in Gateshead. Gateshead was also the birthplace of the middle-distance runner Steve Cram (b.1960). The Gateshead suburb of Dunston was the birthplace of the gifted but wayward footballer Paul Gascoigne (b.1967), whose impenetrable Geordie patois and ultimately unfulfilled talents were at various times at the disposal of Newcastle United, Tottenham Hotspur, Lazio (Italy), Glasgow Rangers, Middlesbrough, Everton, Burnley and Gansu Tianma (China).

get off at Gateshead, to. To perform *coitus interruptus*, Gateshead being the station before Newcastle upon Tyne.

Gateslack Possibly 'shallow valley by the road', OScand *gata* 'road' + *slakki* 'a shallow valley'.

A small settlement in Dumfries and Galloway (formerly in Dumfriesshire), some 6 km (3.5 miles) north of Thornhill.

Gateway to the Lakes, the. *See* KENDAL.

Gathersnow Hill Presumably so named because it hangs on to snow longer than the surrounding hills.

A hill (690 m / 2263 ft) on the boundary between South Lanarkshire and Scottish Borders (formerly Peeblesshire), 12 km (7 miles) south of BIGGAR. It is one of the Tweedsmuir Hills (*see under* TWEED).

Gatley 'goat cliff', OE *gat* 'goat' + *clif* 'cliff'.

A town in Greater Manchester, 10 km (6 miles) south of the city centre.

Gat Sand *Gat* probably 'goat', OE *gat*, but the reason for the name is unclear.

A sandbank in the WASH.

Gatwick[1] 'farm where goats are kept', OE *gat* 'goat' + *wic* (*see* WICK).

A location in West Sussex (before 1974 in Surrey), between REIGATE to the north and CRAWLEY to the south. Gatwick Farm is recorded here from the 19th century. A racecourse was opened at Gatwick in 1891. The Grand National was run there after AINTREE was taken over by the military in the First World War. It closed in 1940.

Gatwick Airport. An airport (officially **London Gatwick**) in West Sussex, about 5 km (3 miles) north of Crawley. An airfield was opened in the 1930s, but it was between 1956 and 1958 that it was radically upgraded as a second London airport, to relieve pressure on HEATHROW. Its capacity was further enlarged by the addition of the North Terminal in 1988, and it is now second only to Heathrow in terms of aircraft movement numbers. At first Gatwick was mainly associated with charter operations to the Costa Brava and similar holiday destinations, but by the end of the 20th century the majority of its business was with regular scheduled domestic and international flights. It has good transport links with London, 43 km (26.5 miles) to the north, by rail (the **Gatwick Express**) and via the M23.

Gatwick[2]. A hamlet in Surrey, on the NORTH DOWNS, about 7 km (4.5 miles) east of Farnham.

GB. The standard abbreviation for GREAT BRITAIN (*see also* BRITAIN), as used, for example, on car stickers while driving abroad. The unlovely phrase **Team GB** became the favoured term to describe the British Olympic hopefuls of 2004.

Gedney Probably 'Gæda's or Gydda's island or well-watered land', OE *Gædan* or *Gyddan* possessive forms of the male personal names *Gæda* or *Gydda* + *eg* (see -EY, -EA).

A village in Lincolnshire, in the FENS to the south of the WASH, about 22 km (14 miles) southeast of Boston. St Mary

Magdalene's Church, with its massive tower, has been termed 'the Cathedral of the Fens'.

Gedney Marsh. An extensive area of marshland between Gedney and the Wash.

Gelligaer 'fort grove', Welsh *celli* 'grove, copse' + *caer* (*see* CAHER).

A small town in Caerphilly (formerly in Monmouthshire, then in Mid Glamorgan), some 10 km (6 miles) northeast of Pontypridd. The Romans had a fort here.

Gentleman's Cave. *See under* WESTRAY.

Geordie, Geordieland. *See under* TYNESIDE

George Nympton *George* denoting the dedication of the local church to St George; *Nympton* 'farmstead near the river called Nymet' (probably an old name for the River MOLE[2]), OCelt *nimet* 'holy place' + -TON.

A village in Devon, near the southern edge of EXMOOR, on the River Mole, about 3 km (2 miles) southwest of South Molton.

See also KING'S NYMPTON.

Georgia Probably 'broken-down hedge', Cornish *gor-ge*; the Cornish name is known from records at the end of the 17th century before the American state was so named.

A hamlet in West Cornwall, about 5 km (3 miles) southwest of St Ives. Nearby is the equally tiny settlement of **Georgia Bottom**.

Georgium sidus. *See under* SOUTH LONDON.

German Bight *Bight* 'bay', OE *byht* 'bend'.

A sea area in the shipping forecast. It is in the NORTH SEA, in the angle between Denmark and Germany, flanked by FISHER to the north and DOGGER and HUMBER to the west. The name replaced the former designation HELIGOLAND in 1956.

German Ocean A translation of Greek *Germanikos Okeanos*, the term used by Ptolemy, the Egyptian geographer of the 2nd century AD.

A former name for the NORTH SEA. It is first recorded in 1635.

> Essex hath … the German Ocean on the East.
>
> Thomas Fuller: *History of the Worthies of England* (1662)

Germansweek Originally *Wica* 'dwelling, (dairy) farm', OE *wic* (*see* WICK); *Germans-*, denoting the dedication of the local church to St Germanus, which apparently dates from the 15th century. (Germanus was Bishop of Auxerre in modern France, and twice visited Britain in the mid-5th century to purge British Christianity of the heresy of Pelagianism.)

A village in Devon, at the northern end of Roadford Reservoir, about 16 km (10 miles) west of Okehampton.

Gerrards Cross From a local 17th-century family called *Jarrard* or *Gerrard*; first recorded in 1692.

A residential town in Buckinghamshire, about 8 km (5 miles) southeast of Beaconsfield. It was the birthplace of the actor Kenneth More (1914–82).

The headquarters of the British Forces Broadcasting Service are in Gerrards Cross.

Gherkin, the. The nickname for the SWISS RE TOWER in the City of London, paying tribute to its similarity to an outsized, upended form of the vegetable. **Erotic gherkin** is also heard. A doctor writes:

> It is not a gherkin. It is a suppository and the biggest joke ever played on Londoners.
>
> Dr J.V.C. Mitchell: letter to *The Guardian* (19 October 2004)

Giant's Causeway From the story that it was formed by the giant Finn MacCool.

A remarkable geological formation on the north coast of County ANTRIM, 15 km (9 miles) northeast of Coleraine. Its Irish name is **Clochán an Aifir**, apparently a corruption of **Clochán na bhFomaraigh** ('stepping stones of the Fomorians'; *see below*). The 'causeway' is a headland comprising large numbers of polygonal (mostly irregular hexagonal) basalt columns, formed when lava rapidly cooled as it entered the sea some 50–60 million years ago. It has been a popular tourist attraction since the 18th century, and (along with the CAUSEWAY COAST) was declared a UNESCO World Heritage Site in 1986. However, not everyone has been impressed by the prospect:

> *Boswell:* Is not the Giant's Causeway worth seeing?
> *Johnson:* Worth seeing? yes; but not worth going to see.
>
> Conversation on 12 October 1779, quoted in James Boswell, *The Life of Samuel Johnson* (1791) (Boswell was trying – unsuccessfully – to persuade Johnson to visit Ireland.)

The Giant's Causeway has various fancifully named formations, such as the Giant's Grandmother, the Giant's Chair and the Giant's Organ, and the columns are similar to those around FINGAL'S CAVE on STAFFA. According to legend, it was Finn MacCool, the ancient hero associated with Fingal, and later conceived of as a giant, who made the causeway to enable him to reach Scotland, either to fight another giant (at whom he'd already thrown the ISLE OF MAN, scooped out of the hollow now filled by LOUGH NEAGH), or on some more amorous quest. Its Irish name (*see above*) suggests the causeway dates from an earlier period of Irish mythology, the Fomorians being the grotesque semi-aquatic inhabitants of TORY ISLAND defeated at the second Battle of MOYTURA. Before the geologists provided a more rational explanation, one Englishman came up with the idea that the causeway had been built by the Carthaginians.

In the early 19th century the geologists themselves split into two camps: the Neptunists, believing in the Old Testament, claimed that the columns were crystalline formations precipitated out of the sea at the time of the Flood; whereas the Vulcanites (or Plutonians) claimed that the basalt of the columns was an igneous rock, formed by volcanic action long before Genesis suggested the world had been created.

Giant's Causeway, The. A 2000-line lyrical history of Ireland, centred on the Giant's Causeway, published in 1811 by the Unitarian minister William Hamilton Drummond (1778–1865); the poem was accompanied by notes on mythology and earth science. It begins:

> Ye cliffs and grots where boiling tempests wail,
> Ye terraced capes, ye rocks, ye billows, hail!

Later on, Drummond offers a detailed description of the formation:

> Each mighty artist from the yielding rock,
> Hewed many a polished dark, prismatic block:
> One end was modelled like the rounded bone,
> One formed a socket for its convex stone;
> Then side to side and joint and joint they bound,
> Columns on columns locked, and mound on mound
> Close as the golden cells that bees compose …

Giant's Leap. *See under* TOTNES.

Giant's Ring. A large Neolithic structure in County Down, 6 km (4 miles) south of BELFAST city centre. It consists of a circular earthwork 180 m (600 ft) in diameter, with a dolmen covering a passage grave at the centre.

Gibraltar From the name of the British territory on the southern coast of Spain, but the reason for its adoption is not known.

A village in Lincolnshire, at the mouth of STEEPING River, about 5 km (3 miles) south of Skegness. The nearby sandspit of **Gibraltar Point** marks the northern extremity of the WASH. It is a nature reserve with a wide variety of habitats, including offshore sandbanks where seals bask and some of the most extensive salt marshes in Europe.

Gidea Park Originally *Giddyhall Park*, ME *gidi hall* 'foolish or crazy hall', referring to a local house (later known as 'Gidea Hall') in allusion either to its curious design or possibly to the eccentricity of its occupants.

A northeastern suburb of Greater London, in the borough of HAVERING (before 1965 in Essex), to the northeast of ROMFORD. Its original focus was **Gidea Hall**, once the home of Sir Anthony Cooke, tutor to Edward VI. The grounds of the mansion were turned into a garden suburb in 1910, with houses designed by leading architects of the day. Gidea Hall itself was demolished in the 1930s.

Giffnock Possibly 'little ridge' or 'ridge hill', OCelt *cefn* 'ridge' with diminutive suffix *-oc* or Gaelic *cnoc* 'hill' (*see* KNOCK-).

A town in EAST RENFREWSHIRE (of which it is the administrative centre), effectively a southern suburb of GLASGOW.

Giggleswick 'Gikel's farm', OE male personal name *Gikel* + WICK.

A village just west of Settle, North Yorkshire. The limestone cliff of **Giggleswick Scar** is above the village, and nearby is the **Ebbing and Flowing Well**. The explanation for this phenomenon is literary-classical rather than folkloric: a nymph whose virtue was threatened by a pursuing satyr was turned into a spring by the gods, and the ebbs and flows are her still panting breaths:

> At Giggleswick where I a Fountain can you show,
> That eight times in a day is said to ebb and flow.
>
> Michael Drayton: *Poly-Olbion* (1612, 1622)

Giggleswick School (a co-educational public school) was founded in 1512; its alumni have included the theologian and philosopher William Paley (1743–1805) and the drama critic James Agate (1877–1947). Russell Harty (1935–88) was a teacher here before becoming a television presenter.

Gigha 'rift island', OScand *gja* 'rift' + *ey* (*see* -AY), *island of Gug*, 1309.

A small island some 3 km (2 miles) off the west coast of Kintyre, from which it is separated by the **Sound of Gigha**. It is in Argyll and Bute (formerly in Strathclyde region). Gigha is noted for its mild climate, and the garden of Achamore has a famous collection of rhododendrons, built up by Sir James Horlick (manufacturer of the hot drink), who bought the island in 1944 and presented the garden to the National Trust for Scotland in 1962. The island itself has been in community ownership since a 2001 buyout by tenants under the Land Reform (Scotland) Act.

Gighay. *See under* HELLISAY.

Gilberdyke OE *dic* 'dyke' + affix denoting manorial ownership in the Middle Ages by the Gilbert family.

A village in the East Riding of Yorkshire, 27 km (17 miles) west of Hull.

Gilcrux 'nook by a hill', OCelt *cil* 'corner, nook' + *crug* 'hill' (*see* CREECH, CROOK); the original elements were changed to resemble OScand *gil* 'ravine' and Latin *crux* 'a cross' as the OCelt language was lost.

A village in Cumbria, 8 km (5 miles) north of Cockermouth.

Gildingwells 'gushing springs', OE *gyldande* 'gushing' + *wella* 'spring'.

A village in South Yorkshire, about 6 km (4 miles) north of Worksop.

Gillingham[1] 'Gylla's people's homestead', OE male personal name *Gylla* + *-inga-* (*see* -ING) + HAM.

An industrial town (pronounced 'jill-') in Kent, on the MEDWAY[1] estuary, within the unitary authority of MEDWAY[2], just to the east of ROCHESTER and CHATHAM (with which it forms the three 'Medway towns'). Large sections of the former Chatham Naval Dockyard (closed 1984) were in fact in Gillingham.

The nickname of **Gillingham FC** (founded in 1893 as New Brompton F.C. and renamed Gillingham in 1913) is the Gills (pronounced 'Jills').

The navigator William Adams (1564–1620), the first Englishman to visit Japan, was born in Gillingham. He became a samurai warrior, and James Clavell's novel *Shogun* (1975) is based on his exploits.

Gillingham². A town (pronounced 'gill-') in Dorset, about 6 km (3.5 miles) northwest of Shaftesbury. It has a grammar school which was established in 1526. It grew to prosperity in the 18th century thanks to its silk mills, and the arrival of the railway in the mid-19th century brought other industries, such as brick-making and soap manufacture.

Constable's painting *Gillingham Bridge* (1824) now hangs in Tate Britain.

Gillingham brick. A type of brick made and used in Gillingham, of a characteristically aggressively deep red colour.

Gimmer Crag. *See under* LANGDALE.

Ginge. *See* EAST GINGE.

Gipping¹ '(settlement of) Gip's people', OE male personal name *Gip* + *-ingas* (*see* -ING).

A village in Suffolk, about 5 km (3 miles) northeast of Stowmarket.

Gipping² From GIPPING¹.

A river in Suffolk, which rises near the village of Gipping and flows 30 km (19 miles) southeastwards through STOWMARKET to join the ORWELL¹ at IPSWICH.

Gipsy Hill From the gypsies who frequented the area in the 17th, 18th and early 19th centuries.

A district of southeast London (SE19), in the borough of LAMBETH, to the east of NORWOOD and the west of CRYSTAL PALACE. Until the early 19th century the hill and the surrounding area were quite thickly wooded and fairly inaccessible. They were the haunt of the Romanis who gave the hill, and subsequently the district, its name. One in particular is linked by local legend with the naming: Margaret Finch, a popular character, renowned for her fortune-telling, who died in 1760 at the alleged age of 109. Early 19th-century legislation dispersed the Romanis, the mid century saw the arrival of the railway, and by the end of the century all the paraphernalia of suburbia was in place.

Girton 'farmstead or village on gravelly ground', OE *greot* 'grit, gravel' + -TON.

A village in Cambridgeshire, about 5 km (3 miles) northwest of Cambridge. It gave its name to **Girton College**, the oldest Cambridge University college for women (it now takes undergraduates of both sexes), which was founded in HITCHIN in 1869 and moved to Girton in 1873.

Girvan Possibly 'short river', Gaelic *gèarr* 'short' + *abhainn* 'river'. Other suggestions have included 'white thicket', Gaelic *gar, garan* 'thicket' + OCelt *vindos* 'white'; and 'rough stream', Gaelic *garbh* 'rough' + *allt* 'stream'.

A resort town on the South Ayrshire coast (formerly in Strathclyde region), 28 km (17 miles) southwest of Ayr. It looks out to AILSA CRAIG, and is situated at the mouth of the **Water of Girvan**.

> Girvan – a cauld, cauld place. Naebuddy o' ony consequence was ever born there.
>
> Robin Ross: in *The Chiel* (January 1885)

Glacks of Balloch Pass *Glacks* from Gaelic *glac* 'hollow'; *Balloch* Gaelic *bealach* 'mountain pass'.

A pass (365 m / 1197 ft) above GLEN FIDDICH on the A941 in Moray (formerly in Grampian region), 7 km (4 miles) southeast of Dufftown.

Glamis Gaelic *glamhus* 'wide gap, open country'.

A village and castle 8 km (5 miles) southwest of Forfar, in Angus (in Tayside region from 1975 to 1996). It is pronounced to rhyme with 'arms'. The Lyon family were granted lands in the area by Robert II in 1372, but the present castle mostly dates from the late 17th century. In the village is the Angus Folk Museum.

The late Queen Mother (née Elizabeth Bowes-Lyon; 1900–2002) spent much of her childhood at **Glamis Castle**, and here gave birth to Princess Margaret (1930–2002). The denizens of Glamis were not always so favoured by royalty. In 1537 James V had Janet, Lady of Glamis (sister of the rebel Archibald Douglas, 6th Earl of Angus) burnt at the stake, and in the 1580s the 8th Earl of Angus joined the rebellion of the Earl of Mar and the Master of Glamis against James VI.

The historical Macbeth was Thane of Glamis in the 11th century (a thane being one who held lands from the king).

> *First Witch:* All hail, Macbeth! Hail to thee, Thane of Glamis!
> *Second Witch:* All hail, Macbeth! Hail to thee, Thane of Cawdor!
> *Third Witch:* All hail, Macbeth, that shalt be King hereafter!
>
> William Shakespeare: *Macbeth* (1606), I.iii

Shortly after this Duncan awards Macbeth the thaneship of Cawdor, which gives Macbeth faith in the remainder of the witches' prophecy.

A certain Maggie Bridie of Glamis is supposedly the source of the name for the pie known as the Forfar bridie (*see under* FORFAR).

Glamorgan 'the land of Morgan', Welsh *gwlad* 'land' + name of a Welsh prince, Morgan Mwynfawr (d.*c.975*); the name is recorded in the 12th century as *Glwad Forgan*.

A former county of South Wales. Its Welsh name is MORGANNWG (also the name of an early medieval kingdom), and it was sometimes also referred to as **Glamorganshire**. It was bounded to the east by Monmouthshire, to the south by the Bristol Channel, to the northwest by Carmarthenshire and to the north by Brecknockshire. The county town was CARDIFF, and other towns included SWANSEA[1], NEATH[1], PORT TALBOT, MERTHYR TYDFIL, PONTYPRIDD, BARRY and CAERPHILLY[1]. In 1974 it was divided into the new counties of WEST GLAMORGAN, MID GLAMORGAN and SOUTH GLAMORGAN, which were in turn broken up into smaller unitary authorities in 1996.

Glamorgan survives in cricketing terms as a 'first-class' county (but *see also* WALES). Glamorgan County Cricket Club was founded in 1888 and has played in the English county championship since 1921, winning it on three occasions. Its home ground is Sophia Gardens, Cardiff.
See also VALE OF GLAMORGAN.

Glamorganshire Canal. A canal built in 1795, linking Merthyr Tydfil with Cardiff.

Glanaber Terrace Uncertain, but possibly 'confluence bank', Welsh *glan* 'bank' + ABER 'confluence'.
A remote road-end settlement in CONWY[1] (formerly in Caernarvonshire, then in Gwynedd), in the hills 6 km (3.5 miles) east of Blaenau Ffestiniog.

Glanaman '(place on) the bank of the River Aman', Welsh *glan* 'river bank' + river name *Aman* meaning 'piglet'.
A town in Carmarthenshire (formerly in Dyfed), some 20 km (12 miles) north of Swansea.
See also ABERAMAN.

Glanaruddery Mountains Irish *Slîabhte Ghleann an Ridare* 'mountains of the valley of the knight'.
A range of hills in County Kerry, 15 km (9 miles) east of TRALEE, rising to over 300 m (1000 ft).

Glannaventa. The Roman port and fort on the site of present-day RAVENGLASS.

Glaramara '(place, headland, temporary shelter) at the ravines', OScand *gliufrum* dative plural of *gliufr* 'ravine'; the earliest record has the name preceded by OScand *hofuth* 'headland', and the later ones have OScand *erg* 'temporary shelter' added, represented by the *-ara* of the modern name (*see* -ARY).
A mountain (780 m / 2560 ft) at the head of BORROWDALE in the LAKE DISTRICT, Cumbria (formerly in Cumberland), some 5 km (3 miles) northeast of Scafell. On its northern side is one of the finest of the Lake District's many Raven Crags.

> Long ere the mountain-voice was hush'd,
> That answer'd to the knell;
> For long and far the unwonted sound,

> Eddying in echoes round and round,
> Was toss'd from fell to fell;
> And Glaramara answer flung,
> And Grisedale-pike responsive rung,
> And Legbert heights their echoes swung,
> As far as Derwent's dell.

> Sir Walter Scott: *The Bridal of Triermain* (1813), Canto III, vii

See also GREAT GABLE.

Glas Bheinn 'grey mountain', Gaelic *glas* 'grey' (or sometimes 'green') + *beinn* 'mountain'.
The name of a number of mountains in Scotland, such as that in ASSYNT.

Glasgow OCelt *glas cau*, 'green hollow', romantically translated as DEAR GREEN PLACE; in modern Gaelic it is *Glaschu*.
Scotland's second city (after the capital, EDINBURGH), but by far its largest in terms of population. Glasgow is situated on the western side of the Central Belt, on the River CLYDE, just before it opens out into the wide estuary of the Firth of Clyde. Glasgow was formerly part of Lanarkshire, then a district of Strathclyde region, and since 1995 **Glasgow City** has been a unitary authority.

Natives of Glasgow are known as **Glaswegians**, and also as **Keelies** or **Weegies** by other Scots, the latter two terms connoting a certain degree of hooliganism. In the local vernacular, the city is **Glesca** or **Glesga**. Broad Glaswegian (known as the Patter) is one of the trickier dialects for outsiders to penetrate; for example, 'Gie's aw yer patter' means 'Do tell me your news', while 'Ah'm gaunae chib ye, Jimmie' means 'I'm going to slash your face, my man'. (*See also* **Parliamo Glasgow** *below*.)

Glasgow is an important commercial, manufacturing, educational and cultural centre. There are three universities: **Glasgow University** (founded 1451), now centred around George Gilbert Scott's magnificent Gothic Revival building in the city's WEST END[2]; the University of Strathclyde (1964; formerly the Royal Technical College of Glasgow); and **Glasgow Caledonian University** (1993, formed from a merger of Glasgow Polytechnic and The Queen's College, Glasgow). Glasgow Museum and Art Gallery in KELVINGROVE PARK is one of the most popular visitor attractions in Scotland, as is the Burrell Collection in POLLOK COUNTRY PARK, bequeathed by the shipping magnate William Burrell (1861–1958). Glasgow School of Art is housed in Renfrew Street in a notable building by Charles Rennie Mackintosh (1897–1909), and the city is also home to the Citizens' Theatre, Scottish Opera, Scottish Ballet, the Scottish National Orchestra and the Royal Scottish Academy of Music and Drama. The BBC's main Scottish studios are in the West End of the city. Architecturally, Glasgow is said to be one of the finest Victorian cities in Britain; the centre is set out on a grid pattern around George Square, location of the City Chambers, and includes the major shopping streets of Argyle Street, Buchanan Street and SAUCHIEHALL STREET. The city also has many notable Greek Revival buildings by Alexander Thomson, dating from earlier in the 19th century.

Glasgow is home to Scotland's two leading football clubs, **Celtic FC**, supported by the Catholic descendants of Irish immigrants and playing at PARKHEAD, and **Rangers FC**, supported by Protestants and playing at IBROX PARK. (The usage 'Glasgow Rangers', favoured by English commentators to avoid any confusion with the West London club Queens Park Rangers, is incorrect.) Rangers (nicknamed the Gers) were founded in 1873 by a group of rowing enthusiasts from the west of Scotland, and the club soon became a focus for Presbyterian Unionist identity in response to the rallying of the Catholic Irish community around Celtic, founded in 1888. Celtic (nicknamed the Bhoys) had its origins in the soup kitchens that provided sustenance for poor Irish Catholic immigrants in Glasgow's East End. Brother Walfrid Kerins, a Marist priest, organized a football team as a means of raising funds for Glasgow's slum children, and this rapidly attracted the loyalty of Glaswegian Catholics. Celtic and Rangers have dominated Scottish football to an almost embarrassing degree over the years: Rangers have won the Scottish championship (Scottish Premier League since 1976) on 50 occasions (including a nine-in-a-row sequence 1989–97) and the Scottish Cup 31 times; while Celtic have won the Scottish championship 39 times (including a nine-in-a-row sequence 1966–74) and the Scottish Cup 31 times. The greatest moment in Celtic's history came in 1967, under the management of the legendary Jock Stein (a Protestant), when they became the first British club side to win the European Cup. Rangers' sole European success came in 1972, when they won the European Cup Winners Cup. The sometimes bitter and violent rivalry between the supporters of the two clubs reflects the fact that Glasgow is more prone to sectarianism than any other place in the United Kingdom outside Northern Ireland. (Until 1989, when they signed the former Celtic striker Maurice 'Mo' Johnston, Rangers had not signed a single Roman Catholic player in 116 years.) Together, Rangers and Celtic are known as 'the Old Firm'. As the journalist Sandy Strang once observed:

A Glaswegian atheist is a bloke who goes to a
Rangers–Celtic match to watch the football.

Other Glasgow football teams of note include Partick Thistle (*see under* PARTICK) and Queen's Park FC, who play at HAMPDEN PARK, Scotland's national ground.

There was already a settlement on the site of the present city when St Kentigern (a.k.a. St Mungo) arrived in the mid-6th century, intent on converting the Britons of the kingdom of STRATHCLYDE. Kentigern had trained with St Serf, and the story is that he met a holy man called Fergus who told Kentigern he could not die until he had seen the man who would convert Strathclyde to Christianity. Shortly after their meeting Fergus died, and Kentigern put his body on a cart drawn by two wild bulls, intent to build a church and bury Fergus wherever the bulls should stop. Kentigern duly carried out this plan – his church was in fact built on ground consecrated by St Ninian in the previous century – and established a bishopric at Glasgow. The present **Glasgow Cathedral** (mostly dating from the 13th century, and properly called St Mungo's Cathedral) stands on the site of Kentigern's first church, and Kentigern himself is buried here (nearby is Mungo's Well). The motto and devices on Glasgow's coat of arms are all associated with St Kentigern (*see* **Let Glasgow Flourish** *below*). In 1451 the Pope declared a pilgrimage to Glasgow to be equivalent to one to Rome, and in 1492 Glasgow became an archbishopric.

William the Lion made Glasgow a burgh of barony in 1178, and it became a royal BURGH under James VI in 1636, but Glasgow remained a relatively insignificant place until the Clyde was dredged in the 18th century, allowing ocean-going ships to penetrate beyond PORT GLASGOW and reach as far as the docks along Glasgow's BROOMIELAW. This opened up the city to the Atlantic trade, bringing in tobacco, sugar and cotton from the New World. The 'Merchant City' that grew from this wealth impressed one visitor in particular:

Glasgow is, indeed, a very fine city; the four principal
streets are the fairest for breadth, and the finest built that
I have ever seen in one city together … in a word, 'tis the
cleanest and beautifullest, and best built city in Britain,
London excepted.

Daniel Defoe: *A Tour Through the Whole Island of Great Britain*
(1724–6)

Some 18th-century travellers were rather more underwhelmed: when the Glaswegian economist Adam Smith was boasting about the charms of Glasgow to Dr Johnson, the latter responded:

Pray, Sir, have you ever seen Brentford?

James Boswell: *The Life of Samuel Johnson* (1791)

Along with trade, Glasgow thrived on a great shipbuilding industry, and during the Industrial Revolution the city grew into a major manufacturing centre, specializing at first in cotton and later in heavy engineering, the city being close to large resources of both iron and coal. Like other such industrial centres, Glasgow – no longer the DEAR GREEN PLACE of its name – sucked in a mass of people to work in its yards and mills and live in its teeming slums. Among the city-bound migrants were many exiles from the HIGHLANDS, depopulated in the Clearances, and boatloads from rural Ireland, forced to flee by famine and eviction. To many – including the poet Alexander Smith (1830–67), a native of the city – it was a hell hole:

> Black Labour draws his weary waves
> Into their secret-moaning caves;
>   But with the morning light,
> That sea again will overflow
> With a long weary sound of woe,
>   Again to fade in night.
> Wave am I in that sea of woes,
> Which, night and morning, ebbs and flows.
>
> Draw thy fierce streams of blinding ore,
> Smite on a thousand anvils, roar
>   Down to the harbour-bars;
> Smoulder in smoky sunsets …

Alexander Smith: 'Glasgow'

By 1911 Glasgow had a population of over a million and was regarded as the Second City of the Empire. It also became the cradle of Scottish socialism, and in 1919 the authorities deployed tanks in the city centre in anticipation of Bolshevik revolution (*see also* Red Clydeside *under* CLYDE-SIDE). Economic and demographic decline plagued the city through much of the 20th century –

> Glasgow, where decay flourishes in a genuinely impressive luxuriance.

Edwin Muir: *Scottish Journey* (1935)

– and the Thatcherite 1980s sledge-hammered the final nails into the coffins of Glasgow's shipbuilding and heavy-engineering industries. Demolition of inner-city slums from the 1960s and the movement of populations out to vast peripheral housing estates such as Drumchapel and EAST-ERHOUSE (and to New Towns such as CUMBERNAULD and EAST KILBRIDE) did something to improve living standards (there were at least baths and indoor lavatories), but the new 'schemes' – bleak and remote places without amenities – soon developed all the problems of fractured and dislocated communities, such as alienation, violence and substance abuse, exacerbated by poverty and unemployment. Some looked back with nostalgia to the neighbourly closeness of the slums, as in this anonymous rhyme recalling the games children (*weans*) once played in the inner city:

> Whaur's the weans that yince played in the street,
> Wi a jaurie, a peerie an gird wi a cleat,
>   Can they still codge a hudgie or dreep aff the dyke,
> Play haunch cuddy haunch, kick the can an the like?

Meanwhile, large areas of central Glasgow, such as the GORBALS, were left largely depopulated and barren, with occasional remnants of Victorian tenements and shabbily built high-rise blocks interspersed with vacant acres of wasteland. As the comedian Billy Connolly observed:

> The great thing about Glasgow now is that if there's a nuclear attack, it'll look exactly the same afterwards.

Billy Connolly: *Gullible's Travels* (1982), 'Scotland'

Revival was heralded by the renovation and reopening of Glasgow's underground railway in 1979. (Sporting a bright orange livery, the press dubbed it the Clockwork Orange, although Glaswegians themselves call it the Subway; a 'sub crawl' involves having a drink in the nearest pub to each of the fifteen stations.) The early 1980s saw the Lord Provost, Michael Kelly, launch the **'Glasgow's Miles Better'** campaign, which transformed the image of the city both at home and abroad and attracted a large amount of inward investment. The centre was meta-morphosed into a place of wine bars, restaurants and some of the trendiest hairdressers in Europe. In the same decade the opening of the Burrell Collection and the Scottish National Exhibition and Conference Centre (nicknamed the BIG RED SHED), together with the hosting in 1988 of the Glasgow Garden Festival, all contributed to the new image. In 1990 Glasgow became European City of Culture and in 1999 UK City of Architecture and Design.

Glasgow these days has many reasons to be proud, among them the fact that the West End's Gibson Street (a.k.a. Curry Alley a.k.a. the Khyber Pass) has one of the greatest concentrations of top-class curry houses in Britain. In 2003 Glasgow duly retained its title of Curry Capital of Britain (with Bradford and Edinburgh as runners up), and in the same year was European Capital of Sport. In a 2004 survey of the quality of life enjoyed in cities around the world Glasgow came 52nd, just behind Paris (50th) and significantly ahead of London (59th). That year also saw another relaunch, in which trendy weekenders were invited to enjoy the city's 'seductive shopping, achingly hip hotels, ice-cool watering holes', luring them with the slogans **'Glasgow. The New Black'** and **'Glasgow: Scotland with Style'**, accompanied by the following copy:

> There is only one label to lust after. It's called Glasgow.

Commentators were divided as to whether this was all just horribly gauche and cringe-making, or whether in fact it was a ludic display of post-modern irony. The reaction of many *echt*-Glaswegians was 'to boke doon the cludgie' ('throw up down the lavatory').

Although orchards now grow in the Gorbals, Glasgow is still beset by social problems, and has the three poorest constituencies in Britain (Glasgow Shettleston, Glasgow Springburn and Glasgow Maryhill). The city as a whole has the lowest life expectancy in Britain, and that in Shettle-ston is 63.9 years for men, as opposed to the UK average of 77. As Michael Kelly – the originator of the Glasgow's Miles Better campaign in the 1980s – has said, 'You can't tackle this by slogans. There's only a limited amount of wealth generated by visitors that will trickle down into the housing estates.'

Chan eil mo shùil air Calbharaigh
no air Betlehem an àigh
ach air cùil ghrod an Glaschu
far bheil an lobhadh fàis.
(My eye is not on Calvary
Nor on Bethlehem the Blessed,
but on a foul-smelling backland in Glasgow,
where life rots as it grows.)

> Sorley Maclean (1911–96): 'Calvary', translated from the Gaelic by the author

Glasgow maintains a considerable (but not altogether serious) rivalry between itself and EDINBURGH 60 km (37 miles) to the east. The Edinburgh-born poetaster William McGonagall, probably not intending his compliment to be quite so back-handed, apostrophized Glasgow thus:

> ... without fear of contradiction, I will venture to say
> You are the second grandest city in Scotland at the present day.

> William McGonagall: 'Glasgow' (1890)

Glaswegians tend to regard their eastern neighbours as prim and effete snobs (albeit 'aw fur coat and nae knickers'), while the citizens of Edinburgh in their turn are inclined to think of Glaswegians as crude, over-exuberant and excessively familiar (Glaswegians themselves would describe such characteristics as 'down-to earth, vibrant and friendly'). Others again would hurl a curse on both their houses:

> And Edinburgh and Glasgow
> Are like ploomen in a pub.
> They want to hear o' naething
> But their ain foul hubbub ...

> Hugh MacDiarmid: A Drunk Man Looks at the Thistle (1926) (ploomen 'ploughmen')

Binge drinking and random and/or sectarian violence are also part of the regrettable stereotype of the Glaswegian character peddled abroad (Glasgow's infamous gang culture has been traced back to the 1840s), but Glaswegians themselves believe in moderation in all things (apart, perhaps, from moderation), as attested in the old joke:

> A Glaswegian was spotted by his minister leaving a pub.
> 'Tut, tut,' says the minister, 'and I thought you were a teetotaller.'
> 'Aye, I am, minister, but no' a bigotted wan.'

The Glaswegians consider themselves to have a warm and wicked sense of humour, but this means that they have high standards when it comes to professional comedians. When someone was explaining to comedian Ken Dodd the theory of Sigmund Freud that jokes result in elation and relief from tension, he responded:

> The trouble with Freud is that he never played the Glasgow Empire Saturday night.

Glasgow has perhaps fewer literary appearances than Edinburgh, but both the real Glasgow and its imaginary counterpart UNTHANK are brilliantly realized in Alasdair Gray's masterpiece Lanark (1981). Glasgow writers of earlier generations include John Joy Bell, whose Wee Macgreegor (1902) comprises humorous sketches in Glasgow dialect. In an altogether different vein is the anti-sentimental novelist George Blake: Mince Collop Close (1923) evokes the squalor of slum life, while Shipbuilders (1935) is set during the Depression. A suburban perspective on the city is provided in The Setons (1917) by O. Douglas (Anna Buchan). Glasgow also looms large in the raw vernacular tales of James Kelman, such as the Booker-winning How Late It Was, How Late (1994), in Jeff Torrington's Whitbread Book of the Year, Swing Hammer Swing (1995), and in some of the novels of William McIlvanney, such as Laidlaw (1977). Glasgow is celebrated in many poems by Edwin Morgan (the city's first poet laureate, appointed in 1999), for example in the volume From Glasgow to Saturn (1973), which includes the lines:

> A shilpit dog fucks grimly by the close.
> Late shadows lengthen slowly, slogans fade.
> The YY PARTICK TOI grins from its shade
> like the last strains of some lost libera nos
> a malo.

> 'Glasgow Sonnets', ii (shilpit 'puny, thin')

Glasgow was the birthplace of the bishop and statesman William Elphinstone (1431–1514), founder of the University of Aberdeen; James McGill (1744–1813), the founder of McGill University in Montreal; the soldier Sir John Moore (1761–1809), killed during the retreat from La Coruña; the chemist Charles Macintosh (1766–1843), inventor of the method of waterproofing garments with rubber; the lighthouse-builder Robert Stevenson (1772–1850); the poet Thomas Campbell (1777–1844); the publisher John Blackie (1782–1874); the philosopher William Hamilton (1788–1856); the soldier Sir Colin Campbell, later Baron Clyde (1792–1863), commander-in-chief of British forces during the Indian Mutiny; the chemist Thomas Graham (1805–69), originator of Graham's law and known as 'the father of colloid chemistry'; the Conservative politician John Macdonald (1815–91), first prime minister of the Dominion of Canada (1867–73, 1878–91); Sir James McCulloch (1819–93), prime minister of Victoria, Australia (1863–8); the US private detective Allan Pinkerton (1819–84); the Liberal prime minister Henry Campbell-Bannerman (1836–1908); the tea merchant Thomas Lipton

(1850–1931); the anthropologist James Frazer (1854–1941), author of *The Golden Bough* (1890–1915); the Labour politician Arthur Henderson (1863–1935), leader of the party (1914–18) and winner of the Nobel Peace Prize in 1934; the physician William Leishman (1865–1926), discoverer of the protozoan that causes the disease leishmaniasis; the artist Sir Muirhead Bone (1876–1953), who made many etchings and drawings of his native city; the sculptor William Reid Dick (1879–1961); the aviator Sir Arthur Brown (1886–1948), who with John Alcock made the first non-stop flight across the Atlantic; the playwright James Bridie (1888–1951), author of *Tobias and the Angel* and *The Anatomist*; Lord Reith (1889–1971), pioneer of public-service broadcasting at the BBC; the archaeologist Sir Mortimer Wheeler (1890–1976); the organic chemist and Nobel laureate Alexander Todd (1907–97); Edwin Morgan (b.1920), Glasgow's poet laureate since 1999, and appointed the first 'Scots makar' (i.e. Scotland's national poet) in 2004; the composer Iain Hamilton (1922–2000); the author of adventure stories, Alistair Maclean (1922–87); the actor and comedian Rikki Fulton (1924–2004); the comedian Stanley Baxter (b.1926); the architect Sir James Stirling (1926–92); the anti-psychiatrist R.D. Laing (1927–89); the offbeat novelist and graphic artist Alasdair Gray (b.1934); the Labour politician Donald Dewar (1937–2000), Scotland's first first (*sic*) minister following devolution; the ballet dancer Donald MacLeary (b.1937); Alex Ferguson (b.1941), the footballer and manager of Manchester United; the comedian Billy Connolly (b.1942); the film director Bill Forsyth (b.1946), two of whose films, *That Sinking Feeling* (1979) and *Comfort and Joy* (1984) are set in the city; the footballer Kenny Dalglish (b.1951); the poet Carol Ann Duffy (b.1955); and the golfer Colin Montgomerie (b.1963).

The economist Adam Smith was professor of moral philosophy at Glasgow University (1752–63); he was a contemporary at the university of the chemist and physicist Joseph Black, who devised the concept of latent heat. Around the same time, while working as a technician at the university, James Watt invented a key improvement to Newcomen's steam engine. George Birkbeck pioneered workers' education at the university, admitting artisans to his lectures after he was appointed professor of natural philosophy in 1799; he went on to establish what was later called Birkbeck College in London. Joseph Lister was professor of surgery at Glasgow (1860–9) and pioneered antiseptic surgery at Glasgow Royal Infirmary. The university's Hunterian Museum was endowed by one of its alumni, the eminent anatomist and obstetrician William Hunter (1718–83). The physicist William Thomson, later Lord Kelvin (1824–1907), did his pioneering work on thermodynamics while professor at Glasgow.

There is a town called Glasgow in Jamaica and several of the same name in the USA (Kentucky, Missouri, Montana and Virginia), and also two called Glasco (Kansas and New York). There is a New Glasgow in Canada (Nova Scotia) and the city of Scarborough in Toronto was originally called Glasgow.

See also CASTLEMILK, GOVAN, MILNGAVIE *and* NEWTON MEARNS.

City of Glasgow Regiment. *See* Highland Light Infantry *under* the HIGHLANDS.

Glasgow Academy. An independent coeducational school, founded in 1845, and for long a school for boys only.

Glasgow Assembly (1638). A General Assembly of the Scottish church, the first for twenty years. Dominated by Covenanting Presbyterians, the Assembly got rid of the Prayer Book and abolished bishops, paving the way for the first Bishops' War between Charles I and the Covenanters.

Glasgow bailie. A type of salted herring, also known as a **Glasgow magistrate**.

Glasgow Boys, the. A loose association of painters active in the 1880s and 1890s, influenced by the *plein air* landscapes of the French Barbizon Schoool. It was also known as the First **Glasgow School** (*see below*), and its members included E.A. Hornel, James Guthrie, George Henry and John Lavery.

Glasgow coma scale. A 15-point scale devised by Glasgow neurologists to measure the degree of consciousness in brain-damaged patients. It is abbreviated to GCS, initials heard with mind-numbing frequency in hospital soaps.

Glasgow Cross. An important junction in the older part of Glasgow's city centre, marked by the Tolbooth Steeple and the Mercat Cross. The High Street, Gallowgate, London Road, SALTMARKET and Trongate all meet here.

> Where Gallowgate meets London Road
> and the world walks out with his wife,
> umbrellas sail in long flotillas
> through streets you can't cross twice.
>
> Gerald Mangan (b.1951): 'Heraclitus at Glasgow Cross'

Glasgow Glutton, the. Robert Hall (d.1843), a Glasgow vagrant famed for gluttony when any appropriate opportunity presented itself. He was thus memorialized by the city's urchins:

> Rab Haw, the Glesga Glutton,
> Et ten loaves an a leg o mutton.

Glasgow Green. A park on the east side of the city centre, along the north bank of the Clyde. The park includes the fine building of the People's Palace, a museum of Glasgow history. Glasgow Green was favoured by early golfers, and the playing of the game here was thus poetically described in the early 18th century:

> In Winter too, when hoary Frosts o'erspread,
> The verdant Turf, and naked lay the Mead,

The vig'rous Youth commence the sportive War,
And arm'd with Lead, their jointed Clubs prepare;
The Timber Curve to Leathern Orbs apply,
Compact, Elastic, to pervade the Sky:
These to the distant Hole they drive;
They claim the Stakes who thither first arrive.

James Arbuckle: *Glotta* (1721)

The golfers have long gone, and more recently Glasgow Green has been celebrated by the city's poet laureate:

... the beds of married love
are islands in a sea of desire.
Its waves break here, in this park,
splashing the flesh as it trembles
like driftwood through the dark.

Edwin Morgan: 'Glasgow Green', from *The Second Life* (1968)

Glasgow grin. A razor or knife slash in the face. This unpleasant occurrence may be preceded by the assailant asking: 'Kin yer mammy sew?'

Glasgow Herald. The original name of *The Herald*, one of Scotland's national broadsheet newspapers, published in Glasgow since 1783.

Glasgow Highlanders, the. A territorial battalion of the Highland Light Infantry (*see under* the HIGHLANDS). It was formed in 1868 and disbanded in 1973.

Glasgow hoosie. A bat-and-ball game similar to rounders.

Glasgow jock. A type of rope used for binding haystacks.

Glasgow Keelies, the. A nickname for the Highland Light Infantry (*see under* the HIGHLANDS). More generally, a Glasgow keelie is a Glaswegian hard man.

Glasgow kiss or **nod.** A head-butt.

The sound of bygone battles was steel on steel,
Even cannon's roar had some appeal.
There is one thing I'll never miss,
The sickening sound of a Glasgow kiss.

Frank McNie: 'A Glasgow Kiss'

Glasgow Kiss was also the title of a 2000 BBC TV drama series, a love story set in Glasgow.

Glasgow Letter, the. Letter II of the Casket Letters, asserted by the Earl of Morton in 1567 to have been written by Mary Queen of Scots. The Glasgow Letter in particular, if genuine, proves Mary's complicity in the murder of her second husband, Lord Darnley.

Glasgow nod. *See* **Glasgow kiss** *above*.

Glasgow punch. A cold punch made from rum, water, lemons, limes and sugar.

Glasgow Rugby. A Glasgow-based professional rugby union team (one of only three in Scotland) that plays in the Celtic League alongside other professional teams from Wales and Ireland. It plays its home games at Hughenden Stadium.

Glasgow School, the. A term applied to the **Glasgow Boys**

(*see above*), and also to the later Art Nouveau movement in the city, whose star was the architect and designer Charles Rennie Mackintosh (1868–1928). Among his buildings in Glasgow are the Glasgow School of Art (1896–1909) in Renfrew Street, the Willow Tea Rooms (1904) in SAUCHIEHALL STREET, and Queen's Cross Church in Garscube Road (1896–99).

Glasgow screwdriver. A jocular name for a hammer (*compare* PAISLEY screwdriver and IRISH screwdriver).

'I Belong to Glasgow'. A well-known song by the Dundonian music-hall performer Will Fyffe (1885–1947):

I belong to Glasgow, dear old Glasgow town,
But something's the matter with Glasgow
For it's going round and round.
I'm only a common old working chap as anyone here can see,
But when I get a couple of drinks on a Saturday
Glasgow belongs to me.

The song was offered to Harry Lauder, who turned it down on the grounds that he could not sing a song glorifying drink. When it was pointed out to him that he was quite happy singing 'A Wee Deoch an Dorus' (Gaelic *deoch an dorus* 'a drink at the door, a stirrup cup'), he responded that he emphasized the word 'wee'.

Let Glasgow Flourish. Glasgow's motto, deriving from a sermon supposedly delivered by its patron saint, St Kentigern a.k.a. Mungo (*see above*):

Lord, let Glasgow flourish by the preaching of the Word.

The motto is incorporated into the city's coat of arms (created in the mid-19th century), which also includes the emblems of bird, tree, bell and fish, remembered by Glasgow schoolchildren via the following rhyme:

Here's the bird that never flew,
Here's the tree that never grew,
Here's the bell that never rang,
Here's the fish that never swam.

These items are all associated with St Kentigern. The tree, now depicted as an oak, was originally a hazel. When Kentigern was a pupil of St Serf he was put in charge of a sacred fire; the other pupils, jealous of Kentigern's favoured position, put out the fire, but Kentigern broke off some frozen branches from a hazel tree and by the power of prayer caused them to spontaneously combust. The bird was a robin that St Serf had tamed; when it died, Kentigern was blamed, but he again demonstrated the power of prayer by restoring the corpse to life. The ring was a gift of the king of Strathclyde to his queen, who gave it to a knight, who lost it. When the king demanded to see the ring, the knight went to St Kentigern for assistance, and miraculously the ring was found in the belly of a salmon caught in the Clyde (a similar story is told about ST ASAPH). The bell is St Mungo's Bell, endowed by Glasgow's first Lord Provost, John Stewart, in 1450, and rung to remind the citizens to pray for his soul (the bell is now in the People's Palace on **Glasgow Green**; *see above*).

Parliamo Glasgow. A series of sketches by the comedian Stanley Baxter from the later 1960s and early 1970s, in which he taught the world how to speak the Patter – the dense Glaswegian dialect – as in the closing lines of a song from his 1971 *Mother Goose*:

> Anif yuzkin say ramorra
> Orrabest an itznae borra
> Yezkin parliamo Glasgow orratime!
> (And if you can say *ramorra* [tomorrow]
> *Orrabest* [All the best] and *itznae borra* [it's no bother]
> You can speak Glaswegian all the time)

Glas Naíon. The Irish name for Glasnevin (*see under* GLASNEVIN CEMETERY).

Glasnevin Cemetery Irish *Glas Naíon* 'stream of the infant'. Dublin's main cemetery, more properly called **Prospect Cemetery**, and less respectfully known as **Croak Park**, so punningly dubbed because of its proximity to CROKE PARK. Wags also refer to it as 'the dead centre of Dublin'. Among the 1.1 million bodies reportedly interred therein are those of many leading Nationalists, including Daniel O'Connell, Charles Stewart Parnell, Roger Casement, Arthur Griffith, Michael Collins, Maude Gonne and Éamon de Valera.

Glasstown. *See* ST HELENS[1].

Glastonbury 'stronghold of the people living at Glaston', OCelt place name *Glaston*, possibly meaning 'woad place' + *-inga-* (*see* -ING) + OE *byrig* dative form of *burh* 'stronghold'. A market town in Somerset, on the River Brue, about 21 km (13 miles) east of Bridgwater. Its deep and ancient connection with Christianity centres on the Benedictine Abbey of St Mary, which at the time of the Dissolution of the Monasteries was one of the oldest and richest in England. A 13th-century legend traces its origin back to Joseph of Arimathea, the man who according to the New Testament arranged for Christ's burial. He supposedly came to England around AD 63, bringing with him a chalice of Christ's blood and building the first English church, at Glastonbury. An alternative story is that this original church or chapel was built in 166 by missionaries from Rome, at the request of King Lucius, the first Christian king in Britain.

Of its successors, the penultimate was destroyed by fire in 1184, and its magnificent replacement was scarcely complete before Henry VIII had it pulled down. Parts of it remain to be seen. It is said to have contained the tomb of St Patrick, and in 1191 the bones of King Arthur and his queen Guinevere were claimed to have been found in the cemetery. They were eventually reburied in the abbey, near the altar, and the 'discovery' did much to promote the identification of Glastonbury with Avalon, the paradise of Celtic mythology to which Arthur was taken after his final battle.

Pagan and Christian elements combined in Joseph's chalice, which became the 'Holy Grail' of Arthurian legend. This is said to have been hidden by Joseph of Arimathea in the Chalice Well at the foot of **Glastonbury Tor** (*see below*).

St Dunstan (924–88) was born near Glastonbury.

Glastonbury chair. A kind of carved wooden arm-chair, designed in imitation of 'the Abbot of Glastonbury's chair' preserved in the Bishop's Palace at Wells and popular during the mid-Victorians' love affair with Gothic.

Glastonbury Festival. An annual rock festival (in full the 'Glastonbury Festival of Contemporary Performing Arts') held at the end of June on Worthy Farm in the village of Pilton, near Glastonbury. It was the enterprise of a local farmer, Michael Eavis, who in September 1970 leased out his land for a combination of pop festival, country fair and harvest festival. The event has evolved from a fairly primitive affair with rudimentary facilities and an attendance of only 2000 to a highly organized occasion, complete with roads laid specially for the three days, cashpoint machines, retail outlets, proper restaurants and flush lavatories for the convenience of the thousands of hippies, music fans and performers.

Glastonbury Lake Village. An Iron Age settlement near Godney, 5 km (3 miles) northwest of Glastonbury in the **Somerset Levels** (*see under* SOMERSET). Occupied from around 150 BC to AD 50 and sited in the former marshy waters around **Glastonbury Tor** (*see below*), it was constructed on an artificial island of wooden piles.

Glastonbury Romance, A. A novel (1933) by John Cowper Powys (1872–1963), set in Glastonbury. To illustrate his central theme of self-fulfilment, Powys draws on the legend of Joseph of Arimathea and the Holy Grail (*see above*). The attitude to a symbolic grail of each of the main characters is examined. A climax of the narrative is a pageant depicting details from Arthurian legend and the story of the Crucifixion.

Glastonbury thorn. An early-flowering variety of hawthorn, *Crataegus monogyna praecox*, which according to legend originated when Joseph of Arimathea struck his staff into the ground at Glastonbury and it sprang to life. It is said to flower on Christmas Day.

Glastonbury Tor. A steep 158-m (518-ft) hill to the east of Glastonbury. On the top of it stands St Michael's Tower.

Gleann Bolcáin. The Irish name for GLEN BALCAIN.

Gleann Cholm Cille. The Irish name for GLENCOLUMB-KILLE.

Gleann Dá Loch. The Irish name for GLENDALOUGH.

❖ glen ❖

The related elements, Gaelic and Irish *gleann* and Welsh *glyn* refer to a river valley, and this is demonstrated by the fact that many have a second element that is a river name: GLEN AFFRIC and GLEN GARRY[1] (Highland), GLENLIVET (Moray) and GLYNDYFRDWY (Denbighshire) are, respectively, on the rivers Affric, Garry, Livet and Dee. A water feature appears in GLENDALOUGH (Wicklow) – two lakes – and GLEN FINGLAS (Highland) – white or clear stream; but Irish names containing this element are more likely to have personal names attached, as in GLENCOLUMBKILLE (County Donegal), a pilgrimage site dedicated to St Columba.

Gleann Molúra. The Irish name for GLENMALURE.

Glenaan. *See under* the NINE GLENS.

Glen Affric 'glen of the River Affric'; *Affric*, Gaelic *afraic* 'very dappled', from *ath* 'very' + *breac* 'dappled'; the word may have been the name of a river goddess.

The beautiful glen of the **River Affric**, some 30 km (18.5 miles) west of LOCH NESS in Highland (formerly in Inverness-shire). From its head there is a walking route through to KINTAIL. The glen is ringed by high mountains, and there are stretches of Old Caledonian Forest. The two lochs in the glen are the smaller **Loch Affric**, and the enlarged (because of damming elsewhere) Loch Beinn a'Mheadhoin.

The Liberal politician W.E. Gladstone was once taken to see the glen from the foot of Loch Beinn a'Mheadhoin, and was so moved by the view that he raised his top-hat. One of Scotland's greatest mountaineers asserted that before the damming in the glen:

> The scene was the finest of the Scottish glens or indeed any I have seen in the Alps or Himalaya

W.H. Murray: *The Evidence of Things Not Seen* (2002)

The novelist Neil Gunn (1891–1973) made his home in the glen after 1937, and the BBC shot a television serialization of *The Last of the Mohicans* here in the 1970s.

Glen Albyn. *See* GREAT GLEN.

Glen Almond. *See under* ALMOND[2].

Glenariff. *See under* the NINE GLENS.

Glenarm. *See under* the NINE GLENS.

Glen Artney 'Arthur's glen' or 'pebble glen'; *Artney* from a Gaelic diminutive of *Arthur*, or perhaps Gaelic *artein* 'pebble'. A wooded glen in Perth and Kinross (formerly in Perthshire and then in Tayside region), through which the Water of Ruchill flows from the slopes of Ben Vorlich northeastward to join the EARN at COMRIE. On the north side are the now treeless hills of the **Forest of Glenartney**, an ancient hunting forest.

> The stag at eve had drunk his fill,
> Where danced the moon on Monan's rill,
> And deep his midnight lair had made
> In lone Glenartney's hazel shade;
> But, when the sun his beacon red
> Had kindled on Benvoirlich's head,
> The deep-mouth'd bloodhound's heavy bay
> Resounded up the rocky way,
> And faint, from farther distance borne,
> Were heard the clanging hoof and horn.

Sir Walter Scott: *The Lady of the Lake* (1810), Canto I, stanza i

Glen Avon. *See under* AVON[5].

Glen Balcain Irish *Gleann Bolcáin*, possibly 'glen of St Olcan'; alternatively 'Vulcan's valley', or possibly from *bolgán* 'middle, central'.

A glen of uncertain location that features prominently in the 12th- or 13th-century Irish epic *Sweeney the Mad*. Candidates include a site near ARDEE, County Louth, and, more feasibly, Glenbuck in County Antrim near Rasharkin, an area whose patron saint was Olcan or Bolcan; Sweeney himself says '*Suibhne mh'ainm ó Ros Ercáin*' ('I am Sweeney from Rasharkin'). Sweeney, or Suibhne, was a 7th-century king of Dal Araidhe (DALRIADA), who attempted to evict St Ronan Finn from his territory but was cursed by the saint to banishment and madness. (Alternatively he was driven mad by the sight of the carnage at the Battle of MOIRA[1].) In the end Sweeney dies at peace in the arms of St Moling.

> A year have I been on the mountain
> in this form in which I am,
> without food going into my body
> save crimson holly-berries.
> The madman of Glen Balcain am I ...

translated by J.G. O'Keefe

Glenballyeamon. *See under* the NINE GLENS.

Glenboig Possibly 'soft or marshy glen', GLEN + *buige* 'soft, marshy'.

A village in North Lanarkshire (formerly in Strathclyde region), some 4 km (2.5 miles) north of Coatbridge.

Glen Clova Perhaps 'glen of the victory site'; *Clova* possibly 'victory-site', Gaelic *clòth-ach* 'place of a victory'.

One of the Angus Glens (*see under* ANGUS), containing the upper course of the River South Esk. The mouth of the glen is some 6 km (4 miles) north of Kirriemuir. Near the head of the glen there is a bifurcation, the westward branch being Glen Doll. Some 5 km (3 miles) southeast of this junction is the small village of **Clova**, the scene of 'the Start', an incident in 1650 in which Charles II attempted to escape his Presbyterian supporters in Perth. However, they caught up with him here, and Charles was subsequently obliged to sign certain documents in their favour.

Various hill tracks, including JOCK'S ROAD and the CAPEL MOUNTH lead north from Glen Clova over the high plateau of the southern Cairngorms.

Glencloy. *See under* the NINE GLENS.

Glen Coe 'glen of the River Coe'; *Coe* is, in later Gaelic, *Comhann*, which translates as 'narrow glen', but the original meaning of the river name is obscure.

A magnificently rugged glen west of Rannoch Moor, in Highland (formerly in Argyll), some 16 km (10 miles) south of Fort William. Much of it is now in the care of the National Trust for Scotland. The watershed in the middle of the glen is called the **Pass of Glencoe**: to the west is the RIVER COE and to the east is the River Coupall, which feeds the River ETIVE. At the foot of the glen is the village of **Glencoe**, while at the high east end is the ancient hostelry called the KINGSHOUSE. South of the Kingshouse, on the BLACK MOUNT (and not actually in Glen Coe) is the 'Glen Coe' ski area.

Glen Coe has some of the finest mountains in Scotland, and is a mecca for climbers and walkers in summer and winter. On the north side is the DEVIL'S STAIRCASE (a walking route to Kinlochleven), the long and pinnacled AONACH EAGACH ridge and the peak called the **Pap of Glencoe** (Scots *pap* 'breast'; Gaelic name *Sgorr na Ciche*, 'peak of the breast or nipple'). On the south side the peaks include BUACHAILLE ETIVE MÓR and BIDEAN NAM BIAN. From the latter descend the three rocky spurs known as the **Three Sisters of Glen Coe** (the name coming from the title of a famous 19th-century painting of the scene by Horatio McCulloch). The three peaks of the spurs are Beinn Fhada, Geàrr Aonach and Aonach Dubh; high up on the north face of the latter is OSSIAN'S CAVE. The most famous view of the Three Sisters is from the rock platform high up the glen called the Study (Scots *stiddie* 'anvil'), above a picturesque confluence known as the Meeting of Three Waters.

> To my left the lower and grassy half of the mountains was continuous, save only that they were rifted, often to the foundation, but the rifts in general were narrow – though a few wide enough to contain furious waterfalls. The higher and craggy half rose up into separate mountains, turrets, steeples, sugarloaves, and often bulls' brows, brows savager than those of urus or byson.
>
> Samuel Taylor Coleridge: Journal (2 September 1803)

Strangely, the same day he wrote in a letter:

> Glencoe interested me, but rather disappointed me. There was no *superincumbency* of crag, and the crags not so bare or precipitous as I had expected.
>
> Samuel Taylor Coleridge: letter to Sara Coleridge (2 September 1803)

Beyond the cliff-sided notch between Beinn Fhada and Geàrr Aonach lies the **Lost Valley of Glen Coe**, accessible only by a steep scramble up through birch woods and vast fallen boulders. Suddenly one breaks through into a flat-bottomed hanging valley, which the local Macdonalds apparently found ideal for concealing rustled cattle. An intriguing aspect of the place (unusual in a non-limestone area) is that the river – the Allt Coire Gabhail – disappears underground for a good deal of the length of the valley. The name was for long used only by mountaineers, and is probably no older than the early 20th century; the Ordnance Survey do not mark it on their 1:50,000 second series.

> Spring or autumn – for these have greatest charm – a man might come here for a week and be alone. He might pitch a tent on that meadow and be as much out of sight and sound of civilization as if he dwelt on the North Pole.
>
> W.H. Murray: *Mountaineering in Scotland* (1947), 'The Lost Valley and SC Gully' (recalling a visit in March 1939)

Massacre of Glencoe (13 February 1692). A dark passage in Scotland's history. Following the Glorious Revolution, William III offered a pardon to Jacobite Highland chiefs who would swear an oath of allegiance by 31 December 1691. Owing to a number of unfortunate circumstances and a certain innate reluctance, MacIan, chief of the Macdonalds of Glen Coe, did not reach Inveraray to take the oath until 6 January. As a result, the government decided to 'extirpate' the Macdonalds of Glen Coe as an example. A regiment raised by the Earl of Argyll and commanded by another Campbell (traditional enemies of the Macdonalds) was quartered in Glen Coe for some days, then, in the early hours of 13 February the troops turned on their hosts and killed 38 men, women and children. Many more escaped into the winter night, but of these a number died of exposure in the bitter conditions, their homes having been torched.

There was uproar in Scotland, not because of the massacre *per se* – massacring one's neighbours was a regular part of Highland and Island life, indeed almost *de rigueur* (*see*, for example, EIGG or ISLAY) – but because the Campbell guests had abused their hosts' hospitality, a terrible breach of etiquette. An inquiry ordered by the Scottish Parliament in 1695 laid the blame on the secretary of state, Sir John Dalrymple, who was dismissed from his post but charged with no crime. Subsequently the nine of diamonds playing card became known as 'the Curse of Scotland', because of a supposed resemblance to the arms of the Master of Stair – the title held by Sir John.

Many fanciful stories of post-Massacre Campbell–Macdonald hostility have circulated, usually without any foundation, although in the early 1980s a publisher's representative failed to sell a single copy of a well-researched book on the massacre by former *Sunday Times* Insight journalist Magnus Linklater to the gift shop at INVERARAY Castle, seat of the Campbell dukes of Argyll.

The Massacre has largely now become the subject of facile mirth, witness the joke about two hungry Campbells hiking through Glen Coe, when one says to the other 'I could murder a McDonald.'

Glencolumbkille Irish *Gleann Cholm Cille* 'St Columba's glen' (*see* GLEN).

A village in County Donegal, 20 km (12 miles) northwest of Killybegs. It is thought that the ancient monastery here, of which almost nothing is left, may have been founded by St Columba; at any rate, it was here, according to the story, that Columba successfully banished the demons that had avoided St Patrick's attentions on CROAGH PATRICK. On St Columba's saint's day (15 June) a 5-km (3-mile) pilgrimage is still undertaken around the village. Much of the village's present prosperity is due to the efforts of James McDyer, who was curate here from 1951 to 1971, and who did much to revive what had been a dying region, drained of young people by emigration and lacking in many basic amenities.

Glencorp. *See under* the NINE GLENS.

Glendalough Irish *Gleann Dá Loch* 'valley of two lakes' (*see* GLEN *and* LAKE).

A scenic glen in the Wicklow Mountains, County Wicklow, some 35 km (22 miles) south of Dublin. Its name (*see above*) refers to the Upper Lough and the smaller Lower Lough. As well being a centre for hill-walking and rock-climbing, Glendalough is also an ancient religious site. Although the remains visible today (including an impressive round tower and several churches) mostly date from the 10th, 11th and 12th centuries, Glendalough's ecclesiastical origins go back to 545, when St Kevin established a hermitage here. The cave called St Kevin's Bed, on a rock face above the Upper Lough, can still be visited by the daring; the lame Sir Walter Scott managed the course in 1825. (In the 12th century the cave was also used as a retreat by Glendalough's other saint, Lorcán O Toole.) St Kevin's foundation developed into a larger monastery and then into an important 'city' of learning. Although destroyed a number of times by the Vikings and the English, the monastery survived until the 17th century, and still attracts pilgrims – at one time a pilgrimage to Glendalough was worth one to Rome.

'St Kevin: A Legend of Glendalough'. A poem by Samuel Lover (1797–1868), in which prudish young Kevin ungraciously resists the advances of the lovely 'Miss Kate'. An early hagiographer has it that St Kevin, then a handsome young man, was pursued to Glendalough by one Kathleen. In order to subdue his own ardour he flung himself into a bed of nettles – and then gathered some up and proceeded to beat the unfortunate Kathleen with them, 'so that the fire without might extinguish the fire within'. In a later embellishment to the story, he flings Kathleen from his cave into the depths of the lake, and it is to this ungentlemanly conduct that Lover's poem refers:

The saint, in a rage, seized the lass, –
He gave her one twirl round his head, sir,
And, before Doctor Arnott's invention,
Prescribed her a watery bed, sir.
Oh! – cruel St Kevin! – for shame!
When a lady her heart came to barter,
You should not have been Knight of the Bath,
But have bowed to the order of Garter.

The story of Kevin and Kathleen also inspired poems by Gerald Griffin (1803–40) and Thomas Moore (1779–1852). In the latter poem, 'By That Lake, Whose Gloomy Shore', Kevin

with rude repulsive shock
Hurls her from the beetling rock.

The consequences are fatal:

Glendalough, thy gloomy wave
Soon was gentle Kathleen's grave!
Soon the Saint (yet ah! too late,)
Felt her love, and mourn'd her fate.

Glen Devon. *See under* DEVON[2].

Glenduckie Possibly 'glen of sorrow', GLEN + *dubhaiche* 'of sorrow'.

A small settlement in Fife, some 10 km (6 miles) northwest of Cupar. To its north is **Glenduckie Hill** (218 m / 714 ft).

Glendun. *See under* the NINE GLENS.

Glendurgan A modern coinage, combining GLEN with the hamlet of *Durgan*.

A sharply descending valley-garden in Cornwall, on the HELFORD estuary, 2 km (1.2 miles) south of Mawnan Smith. Alfred Fox, of a FALMOUTH-based family of shipping magnates, planted the garden and built the house at the head of the valley in the 1820s–30s. It (and its neighbouring garden Trebah) typifies the kind of tropical and subtropical planting of the warm and moist Cornish estuary environments. To the sides are conifers and a profusion of shrubs, while in the soggy, deep centre of the valley lie bamboo, tree ferns, and the giant rhubarb-like gunnera (*Gunnera manicata*). In addition, children (and the occasional adult) can get lost in a laurel maze.

Where the valley meets the Helford River there is the hamlet of **Durgan**, formerly a small fishing community but today mainly holiday-rental cottages belonging to the National Trust, which also owns the garden.

Glen Eagles 'glen of the church', Gaelic *eaglais* 'church'.

A glen on the north side of the OCHIL HILLS, some 4 km

(2.5 miles) southeast of Auchterarder, in Perth and Kinross (formerly in Perthshire, and then in Tayside region). Over the watershed at the head of the glen is Glen Devon (*see under* DEVON[2]), and the two glens formed part of an old drove road. **Gleneagles House** near the foot of the glen dates from 1624 (replacing a 14th-century castle). The vast and luxurious **Gleneagles Hotel** is actually some 3 km (2 miles) north of the glen. It was built in 1923 and has three famous golf courses.

Gleneagles Agreement (1977). An agreement among the Commonwealth heads of government meeting in Gleneagles Hotel to end all official sporting links with South Africa as a protest against that country's apartheid regime.

Glenelg 'glen of Ireland', GLEN + Gaelic *Elg* 'Ireland'.
A village on the west coast of Highland (formerly in Inverness-shire), opposite SKYE, 10 km (6 miles) southeast of Kyle of Lochalsh as the crow flies – but a very much longer way by road, as the only road access to the village is over the steep windy pass known as the Mam Rattachan (339 m / 1112 ft). It overlooks **Glenelg Bay**, at the north end of which there is a ferry over the narrows to Skye. There are two well-preserved brochs east of the village. Glenelg has one of the few palindromic place names in Britain.

Glen Esk. *See under* ESK[1].

Glen Etive. *See under* ETIVE.

Glen Feshie 'glen of the River Feshie'; *Feshie* 'boggy river meadow', in Gaelic *Féithisidh*, from *féith* 'boggy place'.
The glen of the **River Feshie**, a tributary of the SPEY, in Highland (formerly in Inverness-shire). It is on the west side of the CAIRNGORM MOUNTAINS, and meets the Spey 8 km (5 miles) southwest of Aviemore, just north of the little settlement of **Feshiebridge**.

The glen is notable for its fine remnants of Old Caledonian Forest (*see under* CALEDONIA), and was formerly proposed (by General Wade and Queen Victoria among others) as the route of a possible road link between Speyside and Deeside. Fortunately it has been left in its current wild condition, with only a footpath for the 30 km (18 miles) between the road end at Achlean and Linn of Dee.

Glen Fiddich 'glen of (River) Fiddich'; *Fiddich* from Gaelic personal name *Fiddich*. This is also the name of an ancient division of Pictland, and is possibly derived from *Fidaid*, the name of one of the seven sons of Cruithne, king of the Picts.
A glen in the hills of Moray (formerly in Grampian region). The **River Fiddich** rises near Corryhabbie Hill and Thunderslap Hill and flows northward to DUFFTOWN, where is to be found the **Glenfiddich Distillery**, famous for its single malt, a global brand if not a connoisseur's top choice. In his 'Ballade of Good Whisky' (1960) Norman MacCaig asserts that you may achieve great things

… if you never once supplant
As basis for your commissariat
Glenfiddich, Bruichladdich and Glengrant.

Glen Finglas 'glen of the white stream'; *Finglas* Gaelic *fionn* 'white' + *ghlais* 'stream'.
A small glen above BRIG O' TURK, near the TROSSACHS in the southern Highlands. It used to be known as **Glenfinlas**, as in Sir Walter Scott's early ballad, 'Glenfinlas; or, Lord Ronald's Coronach', set in 'grey Glenfinlas' deepest nook'.

The glen is now largely filled by **Glen Finglas Reservoir**, which has blocked off the magnificent waterfall painted by John Everett Millais in 1853. Millais visited the area in company with John Ruskin (who appears as a figure in the painting) and Ruskin's wife, Effie, whom Millais also painted in Glen Finglas, her hair woven with foxgloves. Ruskin never consummated his marriage to Effie, and two years after the visit to Glen Finglas she was married to Millais.

Glenfinnan 'Fingon's glen', GLEN + male personal name *Fhionghuin* 'Fingon', who was a medieval abbot of Iona.
A village at the northeast end of Loch Shiel, Highland (formerly in Inverness-shire), 22 km (13 miles) west of Fort William. It was here on 19 August 1745 that the Marquess of Tullibardine raised Bonnie Prince Charlie's standard as a signal that the 1745 Jacobite Rebellion was underway. The Young Pretender, who had arrived in Scotland the previous month, initially had few supporters in the HIGHLANDS, but this changed after Cameron of Lochiel, overcoming his misgivings, brought out his 700 clansmen to join the Prince at Glenfinnan, declaring:

I'll share the fate of my Prince, and so shall every man
over whom nature or fortune hath given me any power.

(This was not entirely accurate, as few of Lochiel's men ended their days as the Prince did, debauched and brandy-sodden in Rome.)

The **Glenfinnan Monument** marking the spot was erected in 1815 by Alexander MacDonald of Glenaladale, grandson of the Prince's host at the time the standard was raised. The monument is now in the care of the National Trust for Scotland.

The famous view down Loch Shiel from Glenfinnan provided the backdrop to Hogwarts School in the Harry Potter films (2001–).

Glen Fruin Meaning of this glen unclear; *Fruin* possibly derived from Gaelic *freoine* 'rage', *fraon* 'place of shelter', or from a personal name.
A glen to the west of LOCH LOMOND and some 4 km (2.5 miles) north of Helensburgh, in Argyll and Bute (formerly in Dunbartonshire, and then in Strathclyde region). Its Gaelic name is **Gleann Freoin**. It was here in 1603 that the Macgregors defeated and massacred the

Colquhouns. Later that year the Macgregors were outlawed and their very name proscribed. The massacre subsequently became known as the Slaughter of Lennox (*see under* LENNOX).

> Our silent love
> wanders in Glen Fruin with butterflies and cuckoos ...
> a sparkling burn, white lambs, the blaze of gorse ...
>
> Edwin Morgan: 'From a City Balcony', from *The Second Life* (1968)

Glengarriff Irish *An Gleann Garbh*, 'the rugged valley' (*see* GLEN).

A village in a scenic glen of the same name in County Cork, 10 km (6 miles) northwest of Bantry at the eastern end of the CAHA MOUNTAINS. It was from Glengarriff in 1602, after the Irish defeat in the Nine Years War (1593–1603), that the Gaelic chieftain Donall O'Sullivan Beare set off on his 'Long March' to Leitrim; only 35 out of the 1000 who left with him survived the journey.

Today Glengarriff is a popular tourist destination, noted for its mild climate and lush vegetation. Offshore is the small island of Garnish with its botanic gardens, where George Bernard Shaw wrote the play *St Joan*.

In 1932, as Éamon de Valera and other Fianna Fáil politicians waxed pious at the massive Eucharistic Congress in Dublin, the writer Æ reportedly sat on a rock in Glengarriff during a thunderstorm and invoked the ancient Celtic sea god:

> Oh, come on, come on, Manannan! You can do better than that. All I want you to do is wash out those damned Christian idolaters!

Glen Garry[1] 'glen of the River Garry'; *Garry* 'rough', modern Gaelic *garbh* 'turbulent'.

A glen leading westward from the GREAT GLEN in Highland (formerly in Inverness-shire), some 34 km (21 miles) north of Fort William. The glen contains the dammed **Loch Garry** and the **River Garry**, which flows into Loch Oich near the village of **Invergarry** ('mouth of the Garry' (*see* ABER)). The village is also at the junction of the roads from Inverness and Kyle of Lochalsh. To the south is the ruined **Invergarry Castle**.

glengarry. A kind of Highland bonnet, pointed fore and aft and with flat sides, often with a ribbon or two dangling down the back. It was so called because it was worn by Colonel Alaistair Macdonnell of Glengarry during George IV's 1822 visit to Edinburgh, a notable early outbreak of unrestrained tartanry. Glengarry himself was something of a peacock to judge from Henry Raeburn's famous portrait (*c*.1812), and was the inspiration of Fergus Mac-Ivor in Scott's *Waverley* (1814).

Glen Garry[2]. The long glen of the River Garry on the south side of the DRUMOCHTER PASS, in Perth and Kinross (formerly in Perthshire, then in Tayside). In its lower reaches is the Pass of KILLIECRANKIE.

Gleniffer Braes 'glen of the stream'; *Gleniffer* GLEN + Gaelic *dobhar* 'water, stream'; *Braes* Scots 'hillsides'.

A range of low hills in Renfrewshire (formerly in Strathclyde), some 5 km (3 miles) southwest of Paisley. They play a bleak part in 'The Braes o' Glennifer', a song by the Paisley weaver-poet and eventual suicide, Robert Tannahill (1774–1810):

> Keen blaws the wind o'er the braes o' Gleniffer,
>   The auld castle's turrets are cover'd wi' snaw;
> How chang'd frae the time that I met wi' my lover,
>   Amang the broom bushes by Stanley green shaw:
> The wild flow'rs o' simmer were spread a' sae bonnie,
>   The mavis sang sweet frae the green birken tree;
> But far tae the camp they ha'e marched my dear Johnnie,
>   And noo it is winter wi' Nature and me.
>
> (Scots *shaw* 'show, display', *mavis* 'thrush', *birken* 'birch')

Glen Isla 'glen of the River Isla'; *Isla* is obscure, but the early forms of the glen name, *Glennilef* (1195) and possibly *Hilef* (1165), perhaps suggest the OScand male personal name *Isleifr*.

One of the Angus Glens (*see under* ANGUS), containing the upper course of the **River Isla**. The mouth of the glen is some 10 km (6 miles) west of Kirriemuir, and the River Isla joins the TAY some 6 km (4 miles) west of Coupar Angus. At the head of the glen is the southern Cairngorm plateau, including Glas Maol and the Caenlochan National Nature Reserve.

Glenkens, the 'white glen'; GLEN + *-ken* Gaelic *cain* 'white, clear'.

An area of central DUMFRIES AND GALLOWAY, formerly in Kircudbrightshire, stretching from Carsphairn in the north to Dalry and Balmaclellan in the south (the plural form of the name refers to these parishes). In the north the Water of Deugh feeds into **Kendoon Loch**, from where the **Water of Ken** flows through a succession of small lochs to **Loch Ken**. The area is flanked by mountainous country, including the RHINNS OF KELLS and CAIRNSMORE OF CARSPHAIRN.

It is thought that Mary Queen of Scots fled through the Glenkens to England after her defeat at Langside (May 1568).

Glenlivet 'glen of the River Livet', GLEN + OCelt river name meaning 'full of water, flooding'.

The glen of the **River Livet** and a village of the same name on the north side of the LADDER HILLS in Moray (formerly in Banffshire, then in Grampian region). The village, with its famous whisky distillery, is 10 km (6 miles) north of Tomintoul. The great 19th-century fiddler J.S. Skinner wrote a strathspey entitled '**Glenlivet**' in honour of the single malt.

> Glenlivet it has castles three,

Drumin, Blairfindy and Deskie,
And also one distillery,
More famous than the castles three.

Anon.: verse

Battle of Glenlivet (4 October 1594). A battle in which the Protestant forces of James VI, commanded by the Earl of Argyll, were defeated by pro-Spanish Catholic rebels under the Earl of Huntly.

Glen Lyon The etymology of this glen is obscure; *Lyon* possibly Gaelic *lì omhuinn* 'coloured river' or *lighe* 'flood'.

A long glen running west for some 50 km (30 miles) from near the northeast end of Loch TAY, in Perth and Kinross (formerly in Perthshire, and then in Tayside region). The BEN LAWERS massif forms part of the southern wall of the glen, and near the head of the glen is the dammed **Loch Lyon**. The **River Lyon** joins the River Tay some 6 km (4 miles) west of Aberfeldy. In the **Pass of Lyon**, the narrow defile near the foot of the glen, is MacGregor's Leap, named after Gregor MacGregor of Glenstrae, who in 1565 (according to the story) made an incredible jump over the rocky rapids to avoid pursuing Campbell bloodhounds.

Glenmalure Irish *Gleann Molúra* 'Molúra's glen' (*see* GLEN); the identity of Molúra is unknown.

A wild glen in the Wicklow Mountains, County Wicklow, 40 km (25 miles) south of Dublin. It is surrounded by many high hills, including TABLE MOUNTAIN and LUGNAQUILLA, and its river is the Avonbeg (*see under* AVOCA). Glenmalure was the scene of a number of Irish victories over the English, the most notable of which came in 1580 (*see below*). After the suppression of the 1798 United Irishmen's Rebellion Michael Dwyer and his men hid out in the valley.

Glenmalure was the setting for J.M. Synge's play *In the Shadow of the Glen* (1903), in which an old peasant pretends to be dead to see if his wife will remain faithful.

Battle of Glenmalure (25 August 1580). A battle in the Baltinglass Rebellion (1580–1), in which the Irish under Fiach O'Byrne routed the English under Lord Deputy Grey de Wilton. Nearly two decades later, in 1597, Fiach's hideout in a cave in the glen was betrayed to the English, and he was executed.

Glenmorangie. *See under* MORANGIE.

Glen More 'big glen', *More* Gaelic *mòr* 'big'.

A wide glen on the north side of CAIRN GORM, in Highland (formerly in Inverness-shire). It is now part of **Glen More Forest Park**, which contains both native Old Caledonian Forest (*see under* CALEDONIA) and plantations of non-indigenous conifers. The beautiful Loch Morlich is cradled in the glen. **Glenmore Lodge** is a national training centre for outdoor activities, especially mountaineering. The forest here was formerly the haunt of Lamh Dhearg (Gaelic 'red hand'), a powerful ghost with a bloody hand

and broadsword who would challenge anyone he met to a fight to the death.

Glen More Albin. *See* GREAT GLEN.

Glen Moriston 'glen of the River Moriston'; *Moriston* a Gaelic river name possibly meaning '(river of the) great falls', *mòr* 'great' + *easan* 'cascades, falls'.

A glen west of Loch Ness in Highland (formerly in Inverness-shire), some 6 km (4 miles) north of Fort Augustus. The **River Moriston** flows into Loch Ness at the small village of **Invermoriston** (*see* ABER).

Seven Men of Glen Moriston, the. Seven impoverished outlaws who for some time hid Bonnie Prince Charlie from the pursuing redcoats, despite a reward of £30,000 on the prince's head. The Young Pretender had arrived at their hut, accompanied only by Glenaladale, on 24 July 1746, having been a fugitive for months after the failure of the 1745 Jacobite Rebellion at Culloden. While he hid (at first in the hut, and then in a cave further up the hillside), an Edinburgh merchant called Roderick Mackenzie, travelling through Glen Moriston, had the misfortune to be taken for the prince by some redcoats. Shot and fatally wounded, he entered into the spirit of the occasion by exclaiming 'Alas, you have killed your prince.' When his head was presented to 'Butcher' Cumberland at Fort Augustus, the duke too was convinced, and this made the real prince's escape to France that much easier. There is now a monument to Mackenzie in the glen.

Glen Muick 'glen of the pig', *Muick* Gaelic *muc* 'pig'.

A glen extending southwestward from Ballater, along the eastern side of LOCHNAGAR, Aberdeenshire (formerly in Grampian region). Muick is pronounced 'mick'. Towards the head of the glen is the tiny settlement of **Spittal of Glenmuick**, beyond which is **Loch Muick**. On the shores of the loch is a small hunting lodge, used by royalty when jaded by the voluptuous extravagance of BALMORAL CASTLE down the road.

Glen Nevis. *See under* BEN NEVIS.

Glen of Aherlow Irish *Eatharlach* 'valley'; also the name of the river in the glen.

A fertile and forested glen in County Tipperary, with the GALTEE MOUNTAINS to the south and SLIEVENAMUCK to the north. It was celebrated in the poem 'Aréir Cois Taoibhe na hAtharlaigh' ('Last night by the side of the Aherlow River') by Darby Ryan (1777–1855), the Bard of Bansha (*see under* BANSHA). Edmund Spenser derived the name **Arlo** from Aherlow, and applied it to Galtymore mountain in the Galtee range.

Glen Ogle 'high glen', *Ogle* OCelt *ocel, uchel* 'high'.

A narrow, craggy-sided glen in Stirling unitary authority, taking the A85 (and a disused railway line) over the pass between LOCH EARN and LOCH TAY.

Glen Orchy. *See under* ORCHY.

Glen Prosen Etymology of this glen unknown; *Prosen* possibly Gaelic *brosnach* 'river'.

One of the Angus Glens (*see under* ANGUS), containing the **Prosen Water**, which rises on the slopes of MAYAR. The river joins the South Esk just beyond the mouth of the glen, which is just west of the mouth of Glen Clova. **Glenprosen Village** is about halfway up the glen.

Dr Edward Adrian Wilson, who accompanied Captain Scott to the South Pole in 1912 and perished with him on the return journey, lived in Glen Prosen. Scott planned his last expedition here, and practised Nordic skiing on the surrounding hills. There is a memorial to the two men near the mouth of the glen.

Glenroe. The fictional setting of a rural Irish television soap opera of the same name, broadcast for many years on RTÉ until 2002. It was filmed in Kilcoole, County Wicklow.

Glen Rosa Etymology obscure, but the granite crags in the glen have a pinkish tinge, so possibly *Rosa* is from Gaelic *rosach* 'red, rosy coloured'.

One of the two main glens in the mountains of north ARRAN (the other being GLEN SANNOX). It is in North Ayrshire (formerly in Buteshire, then in Strathclyde region). The river in the glen is called **Glenrosa Water**, or simply the **Rosa**, and has been described by one fisherman as 'one of the most pellucid streams in Britain'. GOAT FELL forms the east side of the glen, and on this flank are the sheets of pink granite known as the **Rosa Slabs**. At the head of the glen is the majestic CÌR MHÒR, near the summit of which is the **Rosa Pinnacle**.

Glenrothes From *Rothes* colliery.

A NEW TOWN in Fife, 10 km (6 miles) north of Kirkcaldy. It became the administrative seat of Fife in 1976, taking over from the old county town, Cupar. The name dates from 1948, when the town was established to house miners working at the nearby Rothes colliery. There is no glen here, however, and the Rothes colliery took its name from the local landowners, the earls of Rothes (originally from Gallic *rath* 'circular stone fort'). The Rothes colliery was soon forced to close, but Glenrothes has since diversified its industries.

Glen Roy Probably 'glen of the red river'; *Roy* Gaelic *ruaidhe* 'red'.

The glen of the River Roy in Lochaber, Highland (formerly in Inverness-shire). At its foot, 18 km (11 miles) northeast of Fort William, is the little village or **Roy Bridge**, a station on the Glasgow–Fort William line, and situated on the main road northeast to Speyside. Close to the village is Keppoch, the scene in 1688 of the last clan battle in Scotland, between the Mackintoshes and the Macdonalds. The glen itself was the route of a famous forced march by the army of the Marquess of Montrose in the winter of 1645, on its way to the Battle of INVERLOCHY.

Parallel Roads of Glen Roy, the. A remarkable geological feature, comprising three parallel terraces contouring round the hillsides on both sides of the glen for some 10 km (6 miles). These mark the varying levels of an ice-age lake that once filled the valley.

Glen Sannox 'glen of the River Sannox'; *Sannox* possibly from Gaelic *sean* 'old', cognate with the River SHANNON in Ireland, and perhaps referring to an ancient river deity.

A glen in the mountains of north ARRAN, in North Ayrshire (formerly in Buteshire, then in Strathclyde region). The glen leads southwestwards up to the fine peak of CÌR MHÒR, to the east of which there is a pass south into GLEN ROSA. At the foot of the glen is the hamlet of **Mid Sannox**, on the little **Sannox Bay**, while a little to the north, and roughly parallel to the main glen, is **North Glen Sannox**.

Glen Shee 'glen of the fairy mound', *Shee* Gaelic *sidhe* 'fairy mound'.

The glen of the **Shee Water**, in Perth and Kinross (formerly in Perthshire, and then in Tayside region). The Shee Water is formed by the junction of two burns some 2 km (1.2 miles) northwest of the hamlet of **Spittal of Glenshee** (Scots *spital*, 'hospice for travellers', from ME *spitel*), at the foot of Gleann Beag. The Shee Water flows south through Glen Shee to join the Ardle at Bridge of Cally, some 7 km (4 miles) north of Blairgowrie.

Confusingly, Gleann Beag is commonly referred to as Glen Shee, because at its head, some 8 km (5 miles) to the north and up the DEVIL'S ELBOW to the Cairnwell Pass, is the **Glenshee Ski Centre**, one of the most important in Scotland, with many chairlifts and tows on the flanks of Glas Maol, Carn Aosda and the CAIRNWELL.

Glenshesk. *See under* the NINE GLENS.

Glen Shiel 'glen of the River Shiel', *Shiel* an OCelt river name meaning 'stream, current'. The earliest reference is from the 7th century, as *Sale*.

A narrow glen between high mountains in KINTAIL, Highland (formerly in Ross and Cromarty), some 20 km (12 miles) southeast of Kyle of Lochalsh. On the north side of the glen are the Five Sisters of Kintail (*see under* KINTAIL), while on the south side is the SADDLE and the CLUANIE RIDGE. Johnson and Boswell travelled through the glen in 1773.

LOCH SHIEL is somewhere else.

Battle of Glen Shiel (10 June 1719). A battle in the minor Jacobite rising of 1719, in which the Earl of Seaforth's Highlanders were defeated by Hanoverian forces. The Jacobites were supported by some 200 Spanish troops, and the mountain on the north side of the battlefield is named in their honour Sgùrr nan Spàinnteach (Gaelic, 'Peak of the Spaniards').

Glens of Antrim. *See* the NINE GLENS.

Glentaisie. *See under* the NINE GLENS.

Glen Tilt 'glen of the River Tilt', *Tilt* a river name of unknown origin.

A long, remote glen in ATHOLL, PERTH AND KINROSS, leading some 20 km (12 miles) northeastward past BEINN A'GHLO. From the head of the glen the walker may continue in the same general direction for another 10 km (6 miles) to the road-end at Linn of Dee (*see under* DEE¹).

Battle of Glen Tilt (1847). A confrontation in which Professor Hutton Balfour of Edinburgh University led his botany students through Glen Tilt in 1847, resisting attempts by the Duke of Athole and his gamekeepers and ghillies to clear them off the duke's land (their resistance principally took the form of jumping over a wall and running). Subsequently the Society for the Protection of Public Rights of Roadways in Scotland took up the case, and established the public's right to walk the old drove road through the glen. The incident and its outcome are regarded as a milestone in the achievement of general access to Scotland's wild places – a right now enshrined in the Land Reform (Scotland) Act of 2003.

Glen Torridon. *See under* TORRIDON.

Glen Trool 'glen of the stream'; *Trool* Gaelic *an t-* 'of the' + *sruthail*, genitive of *sruth* 'stream, current'.

A beautiful and remote mountain glen in western Dumfries and Galloway (formerly in Kircudbrightshire), some 15 km (9 miles) north of Newton Stewart. It is also referred to as **Glen of Trool. Loch Trool** is in its upper reaches, from which flows the **Water of Trool**.

The lower part of the glen is covered with Forestry Commission plantations, and the village of **Glentrool** was built especially for forestry workers. Glentrool Forest is now part of the GALLOWAY Forest Park. The upper part of the glen (known for its population of shaggy and extravagantly horned feral goats) is encircled by high hills, including MERRICK, Craignaw, Rig of the Jarkness (possibly meaning 'ridge of the turbulent waterfall'), Craig Lee and Mulldonoch. Among the many hill lochs above the glen is Loch Neldricken, at the west end of which is the 'Murder Hole'. This name originates in Samuel Rutherford Crockett's historical novel *The Raiders* (1894) – about cattle rustling in the period after the 1715 Rising – as a hiding place for loot and the bodies of the reivers' (raiders') victims. Crockett took the idea from a story of a woman and her son who lived in a remote cottage on the wild road between Bargrennan and Straiton northwest of Glen Trool; the pair would offer hospitality to travellers, then murder them and dump them in a deep boggy pool on the moor.

Battle of Glen Trool (1307). An engagement during the Scottish Wars of Independence in which Robert Bruce's guerrillas defeated a larger English force by hurling rocks down from the heights of Mulldonoch. The battle is commemorated by the Bruce Stone.

Glen Trool Hoard. A hoard of weapons dating from the Bronze Age, found in Glen Trool in 1915 and now in the care of the National Museums of Scotland.

Glesca. A local vernacular version of the name GLASGOW. Its alternative version is **Glesga**.

Glevum. A Roman town on the site of modern GLOUCESTER.

Globe Town From *Globe Road* (earlier (1708) *Globe Lane*), which is a main local thoroughfare (before that the lane was *Theven lane* 'thieves' or robbers' lane'). The lane in turn probably took its name from an inn called *The Globe*.

A district of East London (E1, E2), in the borough of TOWER HAMLETS, between BETHNAL GREEN to the west and BOW to the east.

Glocca Morra. The fictional Irish home of Finian McLonergan in the American musical *Finian's Rainbow* (1947), by Burton Lane, Yip Harburg and Fred Sady. It is the focus of considerable (if geographically wayward) nostalgia:

> How are things in Glocca Morra?
> Is that little brook still leaping there?
> Does it still run down to Donny Cove?
> Through Killybegs, Kilkerry and Kildare?

Glomach, Falls of. *See* FALLS OF GLOMACH.

Gloom Hill. *See under* CASTLE CAMPBELL.

Glossop 'Glott's valley', OE *Glottes* possessive form of male personal name *Glott* + *hop* 'small enclosed valley'.

A town in northern Derbyshire, at the western edge of the PEAK DISTRICT National Park, about 21 km (13 miles) east of Manchester. From Glossop the SNAKE PASS leads up into the PENNINES.

Until the 19th century just a small village (which retains its separate identity as **Old Glossop**), Glossop expanded to its modern dimensions thanks to the cotton boom, and still has some impressive mill buildings to show for it.

Gloucester 'Roman town called Glevum', Latin *Glevum* (from a OCelt place name meaning 'bright place') + OE *ceaster* (*see* CHESTER).

A cathedral city (pronounced 'gloster') in Gloucestershire, and its county town. It is situated on the River SEVERN, between the COTSWOLDS to the northeast and the FOREST OF DEAN to the southwest, and about 53 km (33 miles) northeast of Bristol. It is a port, linked by a 26 km (16 mile) ship canal to Sharpness docks on the Severn estuary.

There was human settlement here in the Iron Age. At the end of the 1st century AD the Romans established a base here for their assault on Wales, taking their name for it, **Glevum**, from a previous Celtic one. A 2nd-century version of the name is **Coloniae Glev**, suggesting that by that time it was a colony for retired legionaries. Gloucester's strategic position commanding the southeastern approaches to Wales (it was at the lowest crossable point on the Severn) made it important for the Anglo-Saxons as well as the Romans.

A magnificent abbey was built here between 1089 and 1260. It was remodelled in the 14th century, and it is now one of the finest examples of Perpendicular Gothic in England (the fan-vaulted cloisters are particularly breathtaking). After the Dissolution of the Monasteries in the reign of Henry VIII, it was designated a cathedral. **Gloucester Cathedral** houses the tomb of Edward II and it also contains the second largest stained glass window in Britain, made around 1350 to commemorate those who died in the Battle of Crécy. The cathedral is one of the hosts of the annual Three Choirs Festival (along with Hereford and Worcester). It was used as a set for the 2001 film *Harry Potter and the Philosopher's Stone*.

Water-borne trade in iron was carried out from Gloucester before the Norman Conquest, and it has continued as an important port ever since. In the Middle Ages the cloth trade was pre-eminent, and in the 21st century local light industry continues to keep the port busy.

Gloucester achieved an unwanted notoriety in 1994 when the murderous activities of Fred and Rose West came to light. The bodies of their 12 known young female victims (including one of their daughters) were found buried at their house at 25 Cromwell Street, Gloucester. The house was subsequently demolished.

Gloucester was the birthplace of writer Jessica Mitford (1917–96); Robert Raikes (1735–1811), founder of the Sunday School movement; John Taylor, self-styled 'Water Poet' (1580–1653); the economist and pioneer socialist Beatrice Webb (1858–1943); the physicist Sir Charles Wheatstone (1802–75; of 'Wheatstone bridge' fame); and the composer and poet Ivor Gurney (1890–1937).

The city was fictionalized by Joanna Trollope as **Aldminster** in her choirstall-based Aga-saga *The Choir* (1988).

Gloucester is in the West Country heartland of English rugby union. Its famous (and passionately supported) rugby union club was founded in 1873 and is fed by a number of rugby-playing grammar schools in the area. Nicknamed the 'Cherry-and-Whites' after its playing colours, **Gloucester RFC** has played its home games at the Kingsholm ground since 1891.

There are towns called Gloucester in the USA (Massachusetts (an important fishing port and maritime centre), New Jersey and Virginia) and Australia (New South Wales).

'Doctor Foster Went to Gloucester'. A popular nursery rhyme. It is not recorded before 1844, but it has been speculated that it refers to a visit to the city by Edward I (1239–1307), whose horse got stuck in the mud there:

> Doctor Foster went to Gloucester
> In a shower of rain;
> He stepped in a puddle,
> Right up to the middle,
> And never went there again.

Double Gloucester. A firm-textured, mellow-flavoured, orange-coloured cow's-milk cheese originally made from the milk of the Gloucester breed of cattle. In its original state it is pale in colour, but gullible townees associated depth of colour with depth of flavour, and the dairymen of Gloucestershire were only too happy to oblige by dying it with carrot juice or saffron (annatto is now usually used). The 'Double' in its name refers to the fact that milk from two milkings is used for making it. There is also a lighter **Single Gloucester** (undyed), for which the milk from one of the milkings is skimmed.

Glorious Glosters, the. A colloquial name for the Gloucestershire Regiment (*see* GLOUCESTERSHIRE). Not the least of the sources of their glory was their participation in the Korean War, and in particular in the Battle of Imjin River, which started on 22 April 1951.

Gloucester Old Spot. A large breed of pig originating in the **Vale of Berkeley** (*see under* BERKELEY) which is predominantly white with a pattern of a few fairly large black spots. Interest in threatened breeds has raised its profile in recent years, and it now provides the filling for upmarket sausages and pork pies.

Robert of Gloucester. The name of the reputed author of a 13th-century book of verse *Chronicle of England* from the days of the legendary Brutus to Henry III. It is actually the work of several hands, but it is believed that all of it was composed in **Gloucester Abbey**.

Tailor of Gloucester, The. A children's story by Beatrix Potter, published at her own expense in 1902. It concerns a tailor (of Gloucester) whose worries over finishing a garment for an important customer because he lacks the requisite cherry-coloured twist (a sort of fine silk thread) are resolved by the mouse population of his house, who complete the work for him. Miss Potter made no concessions to the vocabulary of her young readers:

> In the time of swords and periwigs and full-skirted coats
> with flowered lappets – when gentlemen wore ruffles, and
> gold-laced waistcoats of paduasoy and taffeta – there lived
> a tailor in Gloucester.

Vale of Gloucester. The broad valley of the River SEVERN which runs southwest-to-northeast to the west of the COTSWOLDS, from south of Gloucester to TEWKESBURY.

Gloucestershire From GLOUCESTER + SHIRE. The name *Gloucestershire* is first recorded in the 11th century.

A county in southwest England, bounded to the west by Herefordshire and Monmouthshire, to the north by Worcestershire and Warwickshire, to the east by Oxfordshire and to the south by Wiltshire and SOUTH GLOUCESTERSHIRE. (Before 1974, when Gloucestershire contained the city of Bristol, its southern neighbours were Wiltshire and Somerset. In 1974 the new county of AVON[7] was created, hiving off some of the southwestern part of Gloucestershire, including Bristol. This was abolished in 1996, and part of its territory was re-assigned to South Gloucestershire and to the unitary authority of Bristol.) Its county town is Gloucester, and other important centres are CHELTENHAM, CINDERFORD, CIRENCESTER, LYDNEY and TEWKESBURY. The valley of the River SEVERN bisects the county: to the east are the COTSWOLDS, an important tourist magnet, and to the west the FOREST OF DEAN. The county's other important rivers are the AVON[2], the COLN, the CHURN and the WINDRUSH, and it also contains the source of the THAMES[1] (to the southwest of Cirencester). It is mainly agricultural.

Before and during the Roman occupation, the area (along with parts of Worcestershire, Herefordshire, Wiltshire and Oxfordshire) was the territory of the British tribe known as the Dobunni, who were granted a *civitas* (self-governing tribal area) based on Cirencester around AD 70. The *civitas* of the Dobunni became one of the most prosperous areas of Roman Britain in the 3rd century AD (as the apparent opulence of Roman villas at CHEDWORTH and Woodchester, together with the county's impressive network of Roman roads – AKEMAN STREET, the FOSSE WAY and ICKNIELD STREET – bears witness). After the Romans departed, the area became something of a frontier region: it became part of the kingdom of Wessex following the Saxon victory over the Britons at DYRHAM in 577, but then fell to Penda of MERCIA when the latter defeated the forces of WESSEX at Cirencester in 628. Wessex regained control of the area in the 9th century.

In cricketing terms Gloucestershire is a 'first-class' county. **Gloucestershire County Cricket Club** was founded in 1871. It was a founder member of the county championship when that competition was officially constituted in 1890 but has never won it. Dr W.G. Grace, regarded as the founder of modern batsmanship (*see also* DOWNEND), played for Gloucestershire from 1865 to 1908. Gloucestershire's other famous players include G.L. Jessop (a fearsome hitter nicknamed the 'Croucher'), Wally Hammond, Tom Graveney and the eccentric wicketkeeper 'Jack' Russell. Its home ground is the Phoenix County Ground in Bristol.

The **University of Gloucestershire** was formed in 2001 from the former Cheltenham and Gloucester College of Higher Education. Its headquarters are in CHELTENHAM.

Gloucestershire is almost certainly the polo-playing model of the aptly named 'Rutshire' of Jilly Cooper's horsily priapic series of novels: *Riders* (1985), *Rivals* (1988), *Polo* (1991), etc.

> In the Romantic West of England there is nothing more appealing to the traveller than this fair county of Gloucestershire. We have only to think of the Cotswolds, and the heart of an Englishman is longing to be there. We have only to think of the great Severn Plain and most of us have some delightful memory of its enchantments. We have only to think of two of its cities to remember that each of them has written a unique chapter in the history of our race. ... it may be truly said of the English traveller who comes west to Gloucestershire that he is merely coming home, for nowhere is England more like herself than in this county of the Severn and the Thames.
>
> Arthur Mee: *Gloucestershire* (1938)

as sure as God's in Gloucestershire. Very certainly indeed.

Gloucestershire Regiment. A regiment of the British Army formed in 1881 from the 28th (North Gloucestershire) Regiment of Foot (dating back to 1694) and the 61st (South Gloucestershire) Regiment of Foot (dating back to 1756).

Gloucs. The standard written abbreviation of GLOUCESTERSHIRE.

Gloup OScand *gloppa* 'cave or cleft'.

A village on the north coast of YELL, Shetland, presumably deriving its name from the narrow inlet called **Gloup Voe** (*see* SULLOM VOE) on which it is situated. Just to the north is the headland of **Gloup Ness** (*see* NESS), while a little to the northwest is the islet of **Gloup Holm**. At Gloup there is a memorial to the 58 local fishermen who died in a great storm in 1881.

Gloup, the. An impressive collapsed sea cave on the southeast coast of Mainland, the largest ORKNEY island, 14 km (8.5 miles) east of Kirkwall.

Glyders, the Meaning obscure; Welsh *clydwr* 'protection' has been suggested, perhaps referring to the defensive screen of the range.

A range of mountains in SNOWDONIA, Gwynedd (formerly in Caernarvonshire), to the north of SNOWDON and the Llanberis Pass, and to the south of the Ogwen Valley and the Carneddau. They are also sometimes referred to as **the Glyderau** (-*au* indicating plural in Welsh). They take their name from the two highest peaks, **Glyder Fawr** (999 m / 3278 ft; Welsh *fawr* 'big') and **Glyder Fach** (994 m / 3261 ft; Welsh *fach* 'small'). Near the summit of the latter is the CASTLE OF THE WINDS, while on the northern side of the former is CWM IDWAL and the DEVIL'S KITCHEN. The massif contains three other WELSH THREE-THOUSANDERS: Elidyr

Fawr (923 m / 3027 ft), TRYFAN (917 m / 3008 ft) and Y Garn (946 m / 3103 ft).

> She sits in splendour, great against the sky,
> And broods upon the little ways of men ...
>
>   E.H. Young: 'Y Garn'

In the 1930s most of the range was bought by the Anglo-Canadian Thomas Firbank, who set up as a sheep farmer and memorably recounted his experiences in *I Bought a Mountain* (1941).

Glyncorrwg Welsh *glyn* 'narrow valley' (*see* GLEN) + unknown element(s). Possibly a river name.

A former mining town in Neath Port Talbot unitary authority (formerly in Glamorgan then in West Glamorgan), some 13 km (8 miles) east-northeast of Neath.

Glynde '(place at the) fence or enclosure', OE *glind* 'fence, enclosure'.

A village in East Sussex, at the foot of the SOUTH DOWNS, about 4 km (2.5 miles) east of Lewes.

Glyndebourne 'stream near Glynde', GLYNDE + OE *burna* 'stream'.

A village in East Sussex, about 1.5 km (1 mile) north of Glynde. Since the 1930s its name has been synonymous with opera. John Christie (1882–1962) owned an estate here. He was devoted to opera, and his wife, the singer Audrey Mildmay (1900–53), would welcome a performance venue on her own doorstep, so he decided to add an opera auditorium to the Elizabethan house. Thus in 1934 was born the **Glyndebourne Festival Theatre**, a pioneer in the country-house opera movement which flourished in England in the latter part of the 20th century. It has subsequently built a world-wide reputation and its summer productions now feature many leading singers and conductors.

A new and larger auditorium opened in 1994, but seats are still in short supply, and this, together with a suspicion that many of the black-tie audience are more interested in their alfresco interval supper in the grounds than in the music, has not helped to dispel the elitist image of opera in Britain. Nor has the helipad. For those who prefer their Puccini without a picnic, Glyndebourne Touring Opera visits in theatres around the country in the winter season.

Glyndwr After the Welsh hero Owain *Glyndwr* (*c*.1359–*c*.1416), who mounted a fierce but finally unsuccessful revolt against the English.

A former district (1974–96) of the county of Clwyd, in northeast Wales, bordering England. Ruthin was the administrative seat, and other towns included DENBIGH and LLANGOLLEN.

Glyndwr's Way. A long-distance walk in Wales, in the shape of a horseshoe, from KNIGHTON on the English border westward to MACHYNLLETH, then back northeastwards towards Pontrobert and the border. It is named after Owain Glyndwr (*see* GLYNDWR). On the route are the ruins of the 12th-century abbey at Cwmhir, destroyed in 1401 by Glyndwr because most of the monks were English.

Glyndyfrdwy 'valley of the River Dee', Welsh *glyn* 'valley' (*see* GLEN) + river name *Dyfrdwy* 'Dee'.

A village on the River DEE[2] in Denbighshire (formerly in Clwyd), 6 km (4 miles) west of Llangollen. The estate of Glyndyfrdwy was owned by Owain Glyndwr (who took his name from it), and it was here that on 16 September 1400 the Welsh rebels declared Glyndwr to be the rightful Prince of Wales. A long and ultimately unsuccessful rebellion against King Henry IV of England followed.

Glyn Ebwy. The Welsh name for EBBW VALE.

Glyn Rhosyn. *See under* ST DAVID'S.

Glywysig 'territory of Glywis', Welsh male personal name related to *glyw* 'warrior, chieftain' + territorial affix *-i(n)g*.

An early medieval kingdom of south Wales, covering Mid and South Glamorgan. It later united with GWENT to form MORGANNWG, which was taken over by the Normans by the end of the 11th century.

Goatacre 'field where goats graze', OE *gat* 'goat' + *æcer* 'field' (*see* FIELD).

A village in Wiltshire, about 11 km (7 miles) northeast of Chippenham.

Goat Fell 'hill used for grazing goats'. The form *Goatfieldhill* (from 1628) indicates that *field* and *hill* have been assimilated to the common northern mountain word *fell*.

The highest mountain (874 m / 2866 ft) on the island of Arran, rising up from Brodick Castle and flanked by GLEN ROSA and GLEN SANNOX. An early ascent was made by 'Lugless' Willie Lithgow (1582–1650), an adventurer who travelled widely in Europe and who lost his ears ('lugs') either at the hands of the Spanish Inquisition or had them cut off by the family of a young woman he had debauched. He remarked that from the summit one could see not only Scotland, but also the north of Ireland, the coast of Cumberland and the Isle of Man:

> A larger prospect no Mountaine in the world can show,
> poynting out three Kingdoms at one sight.
>
>   William Lithgow: *Totall Discourse of the Rare Adventures and Painefull Peregrinations of Long Nineteen Years* (1632)

Goathland 'Goda's or good land', OE male personal name *Goda* or *god* 'good' + *land*.

A scenic village in the NORTH YORK MOORS, North Yorkshire, 12 km (7 miles) southwest of Whitby. It has a station on the steam-powered North Yorkshire Moors Railway, which in the Harry Potter films (2001 onwards) plays the part of Hogsmeade, the nearest station to Hogwarts school. Since 1990 the village itself has played Aidensfield in the

ITV Sunday-evening feel-good drama *Heartbeat*, concerning a rural bobby and his community in the 1960s.

Gobannium. A Roman fort on the site of present-day ABERGAVENNY.

Gobbins, the. *See under* ISLAND MAGEE.

Gobernuisgeach Etymology unknown.

A remote bothy in northeast Highland (formerly in Caithness), 3 km (2 miles) northwest of Morven.

Godalming '(settlement of) Godhelm's people', OE male personal name *Godhelm* + -*ingas* (*see* -ING).

A town in Surrey, on the NORTH DOWNS, about 6.5 km (4 miles) southwest of Guildford. It was an important staging point on the coach journey from London to Portsmouth, and several old coaching inns survive (Peter the Great, Czar of Russia, stayed at the King's Arms in 1698). In 1881 Godalming became the first town in Britain to have electric street lighting. The public school Charterhouse, founded in London in 1611, moved to Godalming in 1872. The novelist Aldous Huxley (1894–1963) was born in Godalming, and Terry-Thomas, the comic actor, died here in 1990.

Wise Men of Godalming, The. A satirical print by William Hogarth celebrating the case of Mary Toft of Godalming, who in 1726 claimed to have given birth to rabbits, and fooled many.

Goddodin The Welsh version of the name of the British tribe known to Ptolemy (2nd century AD) as *Otadinoi*, and to the Romans as *Votadini*.

An ancient British kingdom in Lothian, Scotland, taking its name from the Goddodin tribe. They had their capital on TRAPRAIN LAW, but later moved it to Edinburgh (then Dunedin or Dineiddyn). Three hundred of the Goddodin famously came to a sticky, mead-fuddled end at the hands of the Anglo-Saxons at CATTERICK (*c*.580–600). The fragmentary story of the battle is recorded in a poem called *The Goddodin* preserved in a Welsh manuscript of the 13th century; it is attributed to the bard Aneirin, who lived in the second half of the 6th century. Opinions are divided on whether the attribution is authentic, and as to whether the poem has much merit as either poetry or history. In any event, by 638 the Anglo-Saxons had taken Edinburgh, bringing the kingdom of the Goddodin to an end.
See also GWYNEDD.

Godmanchester 'Roman station associated with Godmund', OE male personal name *Godmund* + *ceaster* (*see* CHESTER).

A town (pronounced 'godmənchester', with the stress on the first syllable, and in former times locally pronounced 'gumsister') in Cambridgeshire (before 1974 in Huntingdonshire), just to the south of Huntingdon. It is linked to HUNTINGDON, across the GREAT OUSE, by an early 14th-century bridge, the building of which was started from both banks simultaneously, and which is consequently misaligned. Godmanchester was an important place in Roman Britain, controlling the crossing of ERMINE STREET over the Ouse, and in the 12th century Henry of Huntingdon referred to it as 'once a noble city, and now a pleasant town'.

Godolphin Cross *Godolphin* origin unknown, though the *go*- element may be from a Cornish word meaning 'small'; *Cross* referring to the crossroads in the village.

A village in western Cornwall, about 7 km (4.5 miles) northwest of Helston. Nearby is **Godolphin House**, former home of the Earls of Godolphin. The 2nd Earl (1645–1712), a Whig politician and one of the most powerful men in the country in the early part of Queen Anne's reign, was an enthusiastic importer of racehorses, including the celebrated **Godolphin Arabian** – one of three Arab stallions from which all British thoroughbred racehorses are descended. Godolphin House is privately owned, but the National Trust has owned the surrounding Godolphin estate since 2000. From **Godolphin Hill** (151 m / 495 ft) there are spectacular views of West Cornwall.

Godrevy Island 'island of small farms' *Godrevy* Cornish diminutive prefix *go*- 'small' + TRE-, in the plural.

An island in Cornwall at the eastern end of ST IVES[2] Bay, off **Godrevy Point**. The lighthouse here, constructed in 1859, warns ships of the proximity of a reef called the Stones, extending towards St Ives. Godrevy Lighthouse appears – transposed to a Hebridean setting – in Virginia Woolf's novel *To the Lighthouse* (1927), which draws on Woolf's memories of family holidays in St Ives.

Godstow 'God's place' OE *stow* 'holy place'.

A Thames-side hamlet 3 km (2 miles) northwest of Oxford city centre, just to the north of PORT MEADOW. The meaning of its name reflects **Godstow Abbey**, a Benedictine nunnery founded here in the 11th century, of which only a ruin remains.

Gogmagog Hills From a large representation of the giant *Gogmagog* reputed once to have been carved in the chalk of one of the hills (if it existed, it has now disappeared under the turf). The name is said by William Camden in his *Britannia* (1586) to have been given jokingly by Cambridge University students in the 16th century. Romantically, but somewhat less plausibly, Michael Drayton, in *Polyolbion* (1598–1622), recounts a legend that Gogmagog fell in love with the nymph Granta (*see* GRANTA), but she turned him down, and he was metamorphosed into a hill. Gogmagog was a legendary British giant chieftain who dominated the western horn of England (Cornwall) but who was defeated and killed by Corineus (*see also under* CORNWALL *and* TOTNES, *and below*).

A range of mild hills in Cambridgeshire, 6 km (4 miles) south of Cambridge. They are well supplied with golf courses, and in recent years have attracted the attention of whoever it is that makes crop circles. There are the remains of an Iron Age fort at Wandlebury, on the crest of the hills, and traces of a Roman road. The local nickname for the hills is 'the Gogs'.

Gogmagog's English name is an adaptation of the original Celtic *Goemagot*, strongly under the influence of *Gog* and *Magog*, the names of two attendant powers of Satan in Revelation and other books of the Bible. In due course names and identities merged, and Gog and Magog emerged as two separate British folkloric giants, said to be the sole survivors of a monstrous brood – the offspring of local demons and the 33 infamous daughters of a supposedly Syrian King Diocletian. (These women had already murdered their former husbands.) Gog and Magog were taken as prisoners to London after their siblings had been killed by Brutus (legendary founder of Britain) and his companions, where they were made to do duty as porters at the royal palace, on the site of the Guildhall – their effigies have stood there since at least the reign of Henry V.

Gogmagogs, The. An English music-theatre group active at the beginning of the 21st century. A highlight of their work was the production *Troy Town*, in which a young woman is assaulted by a bull with a three-foot-long penis.

Golborne 'stream with kingcups', OE *golde* 'kingcup' (marsh marigold) + *burna* 'stream'.
A town in Greater Manchester (formerly in Lancashire), 8 km (5 miles) southeast of Wigan.

Golden Ball Probably from a pub name.
A hamlet in County Dublin, some 12 km (7 miles) south of the centre of Dublin.

Goldenbridge Cemetery A locality presumably named after a painted bridge.
A cemetery in Dublin, established in 1829. It was the first Catholic cemetery in Ireland, and the land for it was acquired after a campaign led by Daniel O'Connell.

Golden Cap From the brightly coloured stratum of sandstone at its top.
A cliff overlooking Lyme Bay in Dorset, about 8 km (5 miles) east of LYME REGIS. At 191 m (627 ft), it is the highest cliff on the south coast of England. From it, views can be had inland as far as Dartmoor. It is rich in fossils, and the first ichthyosaur (a prehistoric fishlike reptile) was found here.

Golden Grove Self-explanatory, though precisely what is 'golden' is uncertain; the Welsh name, *Y Gelli Aur*, means the same, Welsh *celli* 'grove', *aur* 'gold'.
A mansion (1824) in Carmarthenshire (formerly in Dyfed), 21 km (12.5 miles) north of Llanelli. It has also given its name to the surrounding hamlet. Jeremy Taylor (1613–67), the Anglican divine and chaplain to Charles I, retired to an earlier mansion called Golden Grove near the present

site as the guest of the Earl of Carberry following the Royalist surrender at Cardigan in 1645. Taylor wrote many of his religious works here, including *The Golden Grove* (1655), a manual of daily prayers. There is a 'Taylor's Walk' on the estate. The name evokes a lost Eden, a golden age, and the image has resonated down the centuries:

> Márgarét, áre you gríeving
> Over Goldengrove unleaving?
>
> Gerard Manley Hopkins: 'Spring and Fall: to a young child' (1880)

Golden Jubilee Bridges. *See* HUNGERFORD BRIDGE.

Golden Mile, the. *See under* BLACKPOOL.

Golden Pot Probably originally a field name, denoting 'field giving a rich yield' (but perhaps applied ironically).
A village in Hampshire, on the NORTH DOWNS, about 3 km (2 miles) north of Alton.

Golden Road, the[1]. *See under* HARRIS.

Golden Road, the[2]. *See under* PRESCELLY MOUNTAINS.

Golden Triangle. A name applied to a geographical area characterized by high productivity or social superiority, most notably and perhaps originally an area of Southeast Asia where most of the world's raw opium is grown. In England it denotes the champagne-soaked residential region of northern CHESHIRE defined by KNUTSFORD, MACCLESFIELD and WILMSLOW, and including ALDERLEY EDGE. Its rise began, with respectable conformity, as southern Manchester's stockbroker belt, but in the latter part of the 20th century the soap stars and footballers moved in, and discreet good taste slipped down the agenda.

> Cheshire's so-called Golden Triangle owes its existence not to mindless materialists but to its better weather and the beautiful countryside unblemished by the industrial revolution.
>
> letter to the *Sunday Times* (31 October 1999)

Golden Vale From the village of *Golden*, an anglicization of Irish *An Gabhailín* 'the little fork'; the English name also refers to the rich agricultural land here.
A wide fertile valley, known for its dairy farming, extending northwest–southeast in counties LIMERICK and TIPPERARY, between the SILVERMINE MOUNTAINS and the GALTEE MOUNTAINS. In Irish it is **Machaire Méith na Mumhan** ('rich plain of Munster'), and its alternative English name is **Golden Vein**, referring to the rivers that run through it, including the SUIR and the DEAD.

Golden Valley[1] 'valley of the River Dore': *Golden* is probably a folk-etymological 'translation' of the river name DORE, taking it as being from OFr *d'or* 'of gold' (it is actually of OCelt origin).
A valley through which the middle reaches of the River DORE flow, in Herefordshire (before 1998 in Hereford and Worcester, before 1974 in Herefordshire), just to the east

of the Welsh border. It is the epitome of the tranquil beauty of the English countryside. It was used as a location for parts of the film *Shadowlands* (1993).

> The hills that encompass it both sides are clothed with woods, under the woods lie corn-fields on each hand, and under those fields, lovely and gallant meadows. In the middle, between them, lies a clear and crystal river.
>
> William Camden: *Britannia* (1596)

There are counties called Golden Valley in the US (Montana, North Dakota), and also towns of that name in the US (Minnesota) and Zimbabwe.

Golden Valley² From the autumnal colour of the beech trees on its slope.
A valley in Gloucestershire, to the southeast of STROUD, through which the River FROME⁶ flows. Like its Herefordshire namesake, it is a noted beauty spot.

Golden Vein. An alternative name for the GOLDEN VALE.

Golders Green Probably 'village green or hamlet associated with a family called *Golder* or *God(y)er*'.
A district in North London (NW11), in the borough of BARNET, to the northwest of HAMPSTEAD Heath. Until the beginning of the 20th century it was among farmland, but in 1905 a tunnel was driven for the Northern line beneath Hampstead Heath, and thereafter it became rapidly built up (Golders Green station, on the Edgware branch, opened in 1907). It gained something of a reputation as a favourite suburb of the wealthy Jewish community (in the 1950s it was given the nickname 'Goldberg's Green').

Golders Green's twin main associations are with entertainment and cremation. The **Golders Green Hippodrome** opened in 1913, initially as a music hall and then, from 1923, as a theatre (the ballerina Anna Pavlova gave her last public performance there). It is now a BBC studio. **Golders Green Crematorium** opened in 1902, following the legalization of cremation in 1885. It houses the ashes of many famous patrons, including Stanley Baldwin, Neville Chamberlain, T.S. Eliot, Kathleen Ferrier, Sir Alexander Fleming, Sigmund Freud, W.S. Gilbert, Sir Henry Irving, Rudyard Kipling, George Bernard Shaw and Ralph Vaughan Williams.

Goldthorpe 'Golda's farm', OE male personal name *Golda* + THORPE.
A town in South Yorkshire, 12 km (7.5 miles) west of Doncaster.

Golspie 'Gold's farm', possibly OScand male personal name *Goldr* + -BY.
A small town on the northeast coast of Scotland, in Highland (formerly in Sutherland), some 10 km (6 miles) north of Dornoch. It was the administrative seat of the former SUTHERLAND district of Highland region.

> I've a lad in Golspie,
> I've a lad at sea,
> I've a lad at Golspie
> And his number is twenty-three.
> I can wash a sailor's shirt,
> And I can wash it clean;
> I can wash a sailor's shirt,
> And bleach it on the green.
>
> Anon.: nursery rhyme

Gometra. *See under* ULVA.

Good Easter *Good* denoting ownership in the Anglo-Saxon period by a woman called *Godgyth* or *Godgifu*; *Easter* '(place at the) sheep-fold', OE *eowestre*.
A village in Essex, about 11 km (7 miles) northwest of Chelmsford.

Goodison Park. *See under* EVERTON.

Goodrich Originally *Castellum Godric* 'Godric's castle' (referring to the former castle here), Latin *castellum* 'castle' + OE male personal name *Godric*.
A village in Herefordshire (before 1998 in Hereford and Worcester, before 1974 in Herefordshire), on the River WYE¹, about 6 km (4 miles) southwest of ROSS-ON-WYE. Its medieval castle, built to guard a ford across the river and the approaches to Wales, was destroyed by Parliamentarian forces in the Civil Wars.

Goodwick An anglicization of Welsh *Gwyddig*, *Gwydig*, now *Wdig* a river name of uncertain meaning.
A fishing village that is now effectively part of FISHGUARD, in Pembrokeshire (formerly in Dyfed), on the west side of Fishguard Bay. Its Welsh name is **Wdig**. According to James Wade (d.1887), a well-known spinner of tall tales, he was fishing one day on the shore at Goodwick when a great bird carried him off to Ireland, where it dropped him down the mouth of a cannon. Wade was woken up next morning by the cannon being fired, which resulted in his swift return to the shore at Goodwick.

Goodwin Sands From Earl *Godwin*.
Sandbanks extending some 16 km (10 miles) northeast and southwest about 9 km (5.5 miles) off the east Kent coast, in the Straits of Dover (*see under* DOVER). They are divided into the North and South Goodwins, between which is the deep inlet of Trinity Bay. They are exposed at low tide, and have been notorious over the centuries for their wrecks.

It is said that at one time the Sands consisted of about 1620 ha (4000 acres) of low land called **Lomea** (the *Infera Insula* of the Romans), fenced from the sea by a wall and owned by Earl Godwin (d.1053), the father of Harold Godwinson, king of England, killed at the Battle of Hastings in 1066. William the Conqueror gave the land to the abbey of St Augustine, Canterbury, but the abbot allowed the sea wall to decay and in 1099 the sea inundated it.

The Battle of Dover (1652) (*see under* DOVER) is sometimes known as the **Battle of Goodwin Sands**.
See also TENTERDEN.

Goodwood 'Godgifu's wood', OE female personal name *Godgifu* (modernized as *Godiva*) + *wudu* 'wood'.
An estate (in full, **Goodwood Park**) to the northeast of Chichester, West Sussex, the property of the Dukes of Richmond and Gordon. It contains **Goodwood House**, and Chichester/Goodwood airfield was a Spitfire and Hurricane base during the Second World War (it has been encircled since 1948 by a motor-racing circuit), but above all it is famous for **Goodwood racecourse**. Horse-racing here dates from 1801, and the present course was laid out under the direction of Lord George Bentinck (1802–48). The Gold Cup, 'Cup Day', was instituted in 1812, the Goodwood Stakes in 1823 and the Stewards' Cup in 1840. There are 18 days' racing there annually, but the best known are the five days of the Goodwood Festival, or '**Glorious Goodwood**', which takes place at the end of July and traditionally marks the end of the 'London season':

> Improvements have been made to meet the requirements of the most enjoyable race-meeting in England, until it has attained the greatest pre-eminence, and is justly known as 'glorious Goodwood'.
>
> John Kent: *Records and Reminiscences of Goodwood* (1896)

Goole ME *goule* 'stream, channel'.
A port and market town in the East Riding of Yorkshire, situated where the OUSE[2] flows into the HUMBER Estuary. It is the westernmost port on the Humber, and the eastern terminus of the Aire and Calder Navigation (*see under* AIRE).

Goonbell 'distant open pasture', Cornish *goen* 'downland, unenclosed pasture' + *pell* 'far, distant'.
A village in Cornwall, just to the southeast of St Agnes Head (*see under* ST AGNES[1]) about 13 km (8 miles) northwest of Truro.

Goonhilly Downs *Goonhilly* probably 'downland used for hunting', Cornish *goen* 'downland' + *helghi* 'a hunt'; *Downs* see DOWN, -DON.
An area of high open land in western Cornwall, on the LIZARD Peninsula, about 8 km (5 miles) southeast of Helston. It is the site of a BT communications satellite transmitting-receiving station, where in 1962 the first transatlantic television transmission was received, via the satellite Telstar. Today its giant saucers are complemented by a stand of wind turbines.
Goonhilly. A name given in former times to a Cornish pony (such as might be found on Goonhilly Downs). Seventeenth-century spellings such as *Gonhelly* and *Gunnelly* suggest a much worn-down pronunciation, once also shared by the place name itself.

Goose Pie. A nickname for the old Irish Parliament in Dublin's COLLEGE GREEN[2].

Goosnargh 'Gussan's summer pasture', OCelt and Irish male personal name *Gussan* + OScand *erg* 'summer pasture' (*see* -ARY).
A village in Lancashire, 8 km (5 miles) north of Preston.
Goosnargh cake. A type of sugary shortbread with caraway seeds.

Gorbals, the The name is first recorded in the 16th century, but the etymology is not clear.
An area on the southside of GLASGOW, once a stylish suburb but later notorious for its tenement slums, until they were cleared in the 1960s to make way for high-rise blocks and acres of wasteland. A native of the Gorbals is a **Gorbalonian**. In recent years there has been considerable regeneration, including new and less socially oppressive housing, and the innovative and cosmopolitan Citizens' Theatre lies in the heart of the area.

The Gorbals was the birthplace of Allan Pinkerton (1819–84) – he of the American detective agency – and grocer Thomas Johnstone Lipton (1850–1931) – he of the tea.
Miracle in the Gorbals. A ballet-cum-morality-play (1944) with music by Arthur Bliss, libretto by M. Benthall and choreography by Robert Helpmann. Moira Shearer danced at the premiere.

Gordale Scar *Gordale* 'dirty valley', OE *gor* 'dirt, filth' + *dœl* 'valley'; *Scar* OScand *sker* 'scar, rocky ravine'.
A dramatic limestone ravine in North Yorkshire, some 1.5 km (1 mile) east of the village of Malham. When the poet Thomas Gray visited the place in the 18th century he found it alarming: 'there are loose stones that hang in the air and threaten visibly some idle spectator with instant destruction'. Despite these apparent dangers, Gordale Scar has attracted many artists, including John Piper in the 20th century (1943) and J.M.W. Turner and James Ward in the 19th; the latter's well-known version (1814) is in Tate Britain. The mighty limestone cliffs of the Scar are popular with rock climbers.

Gordon OCelt *gor* 'great' + *din* 'fort'.
A traditional area to the north of Aberdeen, including the towns of HUNTLY, ELLON and INVERURIE. The latter was the administrative centre of the former district (1975–96) of Gordon, part of the former Grampian region.
Gordon Highlanders, the. A former regiment of the British army, formed in 1881 and merged in 1994 with the Queen's Own Highlanders (Seaforth and Camerons) to form the Highlanders (Seaforth, Gordons and Camerons). Among those who served with the Gordon Highlanders during the Second World War was the poet Alexander Scott (1920–89), who won a Military Cross and subsequently wrote a

'Coronach [lament] for the Dead of the 5/7th Battalion, the Gordon Highlanders'; in it the dead address the poet thus:

> Makar, frae nou ye maun
> Be singan for us deid men,
> Sing til the warld we loo'd
> (For aa that its brichtness lee'd)
> And tell hou the sudden nicht
> Cam doun and made us nocht.
>
> (Scots *makar* 'poet', *maun* 'must', *loo'd* 'loved', *lee'd* 'lied', *nicht* 'night', *nocht* 'nothing')

Gordonstoun Named after himself in 1638 by Sir Robert *Gordon*, who had acquired the estate previously known as 'Bog of Plewlands'.

A public school (now co-educational) in Moray (formerly in Grampian region), some 6 km (3.5 miles) north of Elgin. It was founded in 1934 by the educationalist Kurt Hahn, who had fled Nazi Germany. There is an emphasis on outdoor activities, character development and public service. Princes Philip, Charles and Andrew all attended the school, with varying degrees of pleasure.

Gorebridge 'river-crossing by a triangular piece of land', OE *gara* 'triangular or pointed piece of land' + *brycg* 'river-crossing'. The name of the small River Gore here is probably a back-formation from Gorebridge.

A small town 16 km (10 miles) southeast of Edinburgh, in Midlothian. Camp Wood near the town is associated with 'Camp Meg' an eccentric woman who in the early 19th century left her home and husband to live alone in a hut in the wood. She worked as a horse-doctor and rode in local races dressed as a man.

Gorey[1] Etymology unknown; the second element may be OScand *ey* 'island' (*see* -AY).

A village and holiday resort on the east coast of JERSEY, about 5 km (3 miles) east of ST HELIER. It is overshadowed by Mont Orgueil Castle, on the summit of which are five massive fortifications, built by German occupation forces in the Second World War.

Gorey[2] Irish *Guaire* 'sandbank'.

A market town in County Wexford, 16 km (10 miles) southwest of Arklow. It was laid out in a grid pattern in the 17th century, and captured by the insurgents in the 1798 United Irishmen's Rebellion.

Goring '(settlement of) Gara's people', OE male personal name *Gara* + *-ingas* (*see* -ING).

A town in Oxfordshire, about 16 km (10 miles) northwest of Reading. It stands on the River THAMES[1], which flows here through a gorge between the Berkshire Downs (*see under* BERKSHIRE) and the CHILTERN HILLS called the **Goring Gap**. In ancient times a ford at Goring linked the ICKNIELD WAY to the east with the RIDGEWAY to the west. Nowadays the town is a popular boating centre. It is linked by a bridge to STREATLEY.

Gorllewin Morgannwg. The Welsh name for WEST GLAMORGAN.

Gorsafawddacha'idraigodanheddogleddollôn-penrhynareurdraethceredigion 'the station on the Mawddach with dragon's teeth on the north Penrhyn Drive on the golden Cardigan sands', Welsh.

A halt on the narrow-gauge steam-driven Fairbourne and Barmouth Railway in Gwynedd (formerly in Merioneth), some 2 km (1.2 miles) south of Barmouth. The name was contrived relatively recently in an attempt to eclipse Anglesey's equally contrived but more firmly established LLANFAIRPWLLGWYNGYLLGOGERYCHWYRNDROBWLLL-LANDYSILIOGOGOGOCH. The 'dragon's teeth' in the name are actually concrete anti-tank blocks dating from the Second World War.

Gorseinon 'marsh of Einon', Welsh *cors* 'reeds, marsh' + male personal name *Einon*.

A town in Swansea unitary authority (formerly in Glamorgan and then West Glamorgan), 2 km (1.2 miles) east of LOUGHOR and 8 km (5 miles) northwest of Swansea. It was the birthplace of Michael 'Something of the Night' Howard (b.1941), former Conservative home secretary and (from 2003) leader of the Conservative Party.

Gort Irish *An Gort* 'the cultivated field' (*see* ACHADH).

A small market town in County Galway, 28 km (17 miles) southeast of Galway itself.

Gort cake. A large type of barmbrack (reportedly 'two feet in diameter and eight inches thick') baked in Lady Gregory's kitchens at COOLE PARK near Gort, and sent by her to nourish the fading thespians of the Abbey Theatre. (W.B. Yeats, co-founder with Lady Gregory of the Abbey, also lived for a while near Gort, in the tower of THOOR BALLYLEE.)

Gortahork Irish *Gort an Choirce* 'field of the oats' (*see* ACHADH).

A village and resort on the north coast of County Donegal, 30 km (20 miles) northwest of Letterkenny and 10 km (6 miles) southeast of Bloody Foreland. It is in the heart of the Donegal GAELTACHT, and there is an Irish college here. Irish-language poet Cathal Ó Searcaigh (b.1956) was born here.

Gort an Choirce. The Irish name for GORTAHORK.

Gorumna Island Etymology unknown.

A small, wild island off the west coast of County Galway, some 50 km (30 miles) west of Galway itself. It is linked by road to the mainland via the smaller island of Lettermore.

Gosforth 'ford of the geese', OE *gos* 'goose' + FORD.

A northern suburb of NEWCASTLE UPON TYNE, Tyne and Wear. There is horse-racing at **High Gosforth Park**, where the Northumberland Plate meeting in June is known as 'the Pitmen's Derby', as all the local pits closed for a holiday on that day.

Gosforth rugby union club, originally founded in 1877, changed its name to Newcastle Gosforth in 1990, and became Newcastle Falcons in 1995.

Gospel Oak From *gospel-oak*, a term applied to an oak-tree marking a boundary between parishes, at which a halt would be made on the 'beating-the-bounds' procession at Rogationtide (the three days leading up to Ascension Day) and a passage from the gospels read. The particular gospel-oak in question was on the boundary between Hampstead and St Pancras; it is known to have been in existence between 1761 and 1819, but it was subsequently cut down. A district of northwest London (NW3, NW5), at the southern edge of Hampstead Heath (*see under* HAMPSTEAD), in the borough of CAMDEN. Until the middle of the 19th century the area was mostly open countryside and pastureland, but within two or three decades that was completely obliterated by bricks (many from Gospel Oak's brickfields) and mortar.

> A week of idleness, the salty winds
> Play in her greying hair; the summer sun
> Puts back her freckles so that Alfred Brown
> Remembers courting days in Gospel Oak
> And takes her to the Flannel Dance.
>
> John Betjeman: 'Beside the Seaside' (1948)

In 20th-century rhyming slang, *Gospel Oak* stood for 'joke'.

Gosport 'market town where geese are sold', OE *gos* 'goose' + *port* 'market town' (*see* PORT).
A naval town in Hampshire, on the SOLENT, on the western side of the mouth of Portsmouth Harbour. Although its name derives from a now defunct non-nautical application of the word *port*, it has always been a base for putting to sea. It began as a small fishing hamlet, developed into an important victualling station for the Royal Navy and at the beginning of the 20th century was fitted out as a submarine base. There is now a Submarine Museum here, where the Royal Navy's first submarine, *Holland I* (launched 1901), can be seen. Priddy's Hard, established in Gosport in 1770 as a powder magazine, became the Royal Navy's principal armaments depot. Gosport was a major embarkation port for the D-Day landings of the Second World War.

There is also a town called Gosport in Indiana, USA.
See also HASLAR.

Gosport System. A system of pilot training developed during the First World War by Major Robert Smith-Barry at the Royal Flying Corps School of Special Flying at Gosport. One of its key features was familiarization with dangerous manoeuvres rather than avoidance of them.

Gosport tube. A rubber tube enabling in-flight communication between a trainee pilot and his or her instructor. It was developed at the Royal Flying Corps School of Special Flying at Gosport.

Gotham 'homestead or enclosure where goats are kept', OE *gat* 'goat' + HAM.
A village (pronounced 'goatəm' or 'gottəm') in Nottinghamshire, about 11 km (7 miles) south of Nottingham. Since at least the 15th century *Gotham* has been used as the name of an imaginary village whose inhabitants (referred to ironically as the **Wise Men of Gotham**) are not the sharpest tools in the bag. It is not clear whether the usage originated with the Nottinghamshire village, but over the centuries the two have certainly become closely associated, and tales of stupidity have attached themselves to the real village. One tells how the villagers joined hands round a thorn bush to prevent a cuckoo from flying away (the Cuckoo Bush pub in the village commemorates the occasion).

The origin of the supposed village idiocy is said to date back to the time of King John, who intended to visit the place with the aim of establishing a hunting lodge, but the villagers had no wish to be saddled with the cost of supporting the court. Wherever the royal messengers went, they saw people engaged in some idiotic pursuit, and the king, when told, abandoned his plan. The 'wise men' cunningly remarked: 'We ween there are more fools pass through Gotham than remain in it.' A nursery rhyme says:

> Three wise men of Gotham,
> They went to sea in a bowl,
> And if the bowl had been stronger
> My song had been longer.

A version with more stamina runs:

> There were three men of Gotham,
> As I have heard men say,
> That needs would ride a hunting
> Upon Saint David's day,
> Though all the day they hunting were,
> Yet no sport could they see,
> Until they spied an owl
> As she sat in a tree:
> The first man said it was a goose,
> The second man said nay,
> The third man said it was a hawk,
> But his bells were fallen away.
>
> *Choice of Inventions, or Several Sorts of the Figure of Three* (1632)

Gotham (pronounced 'goathəm' or 'gothəm') also became a byname of New York City. This usage was introduced (satirically) by the writer Washington Irving in his *Salmagundi* (1807), in which are recounted 'the chronicles of the renowned and antient city of Gotham'.

And by extension the writer and artist Bob Kane used **Gotham City** as the name of the dark, crime-ridden city where his creation Batman (debut 1939) lived and operated.

Gotham. A long poem (1764) in heroic couplets by Charles Churchill (1732–64), in which the author pictures himself as the democratic monarch of a free and ideal state. Its title picks up on the fabled simplicity of the villagers of Gotham.

Gotham College. 'An imaginary institution for the training of simpletons' (OED). It is a late 17th-century usage.

Gothamist. A long-defunct term for a fool or simpleton.

Gothamite. A New Yorker.

> The first thing … that a young Gothamite does is to get a horse.
>
> C.A. Bristed: *The Upper Ten Thousand* (1852)

Gott Apparently from OScand *gata* 'way, road'.
A small settlement on Mainland in SHETLAND, 6 km (3.5 miles) northwest of Lerwick.

Gougane Barra. An alternative spelling of GUAGÁN BARRA.

Gourock Gaelic *guireóc* 'pimple', from the hillocks hereabouts.
A resort town (pronounced 'Goo-r'ək') 4 km (2.5 miles) west of Greenock, on the south shore of the Firth of Clyde (*see under* CLYDE) just where it turns south. It is in Inverclyde (formerly a district of Strathclyde region; before that it was in Renfrewshire). There are ferries to Dunoon and Kilcreggan. In the town is Granny Kempock's Stone (probably a prehistoric standing stone), which was the object of good-luck rituals by fishermen and couples about to wed. In 1662 Mary Lamont was burned as a witch for planning to hurl the stone into the sea, and so to cause ships to founder. There is a Gourock Range in Australia (New South Wales).

All to the one side like Gourock. A 20th-century Scottish expression applied to anything lop-sided, apparently from the fact that Gourock is built largely on one side of a hill.

Govan Among the various suggestions are 'dear rock', OCelt *cu* 'dear' + *faen* 'rock', or OCelt *cefn* 'ridge' or Gaelic *gobhainn* 'smith'; none of these is entirely compelling.
A district of GLASGOW on the south side of the CLYDE, once famous for its shipyards, and now largely for its deprivation, although with admirable hutzpah **Govannites** (as they are known) refer to it as '**Sunny Govan**' (with perhaps more self-deprecatory irony than is used by Doncastrians when they call *their* town 'Sunny DONCASTER').

Govan ferry. Glaswegian rhyming slang for 'Merry', i.e. Mary.

Govan kiss. The same as a Glasgow kiss, i.e. a head-butt.

Good God in Govan! A Clydeside ejaculation, relished for its alliteration and general euphony.

What's that got to do with the price o' spam in Govan? A Clydeside expression enquiring as to the relevance of the preceding observation to the conversation in hand. A Govan kiss may be in the offing when one hears this addressed to one.

Gowbarrow Park. *See under* ULLSWATER.

Gower Peninsula, the Welsh *gwŷr* 'curved', possibly relating to the shape of the peninsula, or of the old Welsh kingdom.
A scenic peninsula in south Wales, extending westward from Swansea for some 25 km (15.5 miles). It is in Swansea unitary authority (formerly in Glamorgan and then West Glamorgan), and its Welsh name is **Penrhyn Gwyr** (meaning 'Gower Peninsula', Welsh *penrhyn* 'promontory'). It is often referred to simply as **the Gower**. On the north it is bounded by Burry Inlet, to the south by the Bristol Channel (*see under* BRISTOL) and to the east by the MUMBLES, OYSTERMOUTH and Swansea Bay (*see under* SWANSEA[1]). At the west end is Rhossili Bay (*see under* RHOSSILI) and WORMS HEAD, while on the craggy south coast the features include CULVER HOLE, Oxwich Bay (*see under* OXWICH) and Three Cliffs Bay. The Gower was designated an Area of Outstanding Natural Beauty in 1956, and much of the coastline is owned by the National Trust.

The Gower Peninsula was once part of the much more extensive ancient Welsh kingdom of **Gwyr**, which also included territory to the north. Some of the natives of the Gower trace their ancestry to the Flemings planted in the south and west of the peninsula by Henry I in the 12th century; the area they inhabited became known as **Gower Anglicana** and the remainder, where Welsh-speakers dominated, was called **Gower Wallicana**. Far more ancient than these were the remains of a man from the 17th millennium BC found in 1823 in Paviland Cave …

> where in the sea-slope chamber
> they shovelled aside the shards & breccia …

to find

> … the young *nobilis*
> the first of the sleepers of
> Pritenia, *pars dextralis*, O! aeons & aeons
> before we were insular'd.
>
> David Jones: 'The Sleeping Lord', from *The Sleeping Lord and Other Fragments* (1974)

The poet Vernon Watkins (1906–67) made his home in the Gower, while working in Swansea at a branch of Lloyds Bank. It was a landscape he knew intimately, and loved; as he wrote in 'Taliesin in Gower':

> I have been taught the script of the stones, and I know
> the tongue of the wave.

Gower Street Named in honour of Lady Gertrude Leveson-Gower (pronounced 'lewson-gore'), wife of the 4th Duke of Bedford, who supervised its development.
A street in BLOOMSBURY, Central London (WC1), in the borough of CAMDEN, running northwest–southeast from

the Euston Road to Bedford Square. Some brick terraces from the 1790s survive at its southeastern end, but its northwestern end is dominated by the austere 19th- and 20th-century monoliths of London University, notably University College, the School of Hygiene and Tropical Medicine, and University College Hospital. It it also home to the Royal Academy of Dramatic Arts (RADA), and Secret Intelligence Service (MI6) once had its headquarters near its Euston Road end.

Gowkhall Probably a 'bird hall' name (*compare* Larkhall in Lanarkshire; Gawk Hall, Yorkshire), OScand *gaukr*, Scots *gowk* 'cuckoo' + OE *halh* 'a nook of land' (*see* -HALE, HALL).
A village in Fife, 5 km (3 miles) northwest of Dunfermline.

Goyt 'running water', OE *gyte* 'water course, rush of water'.
A river in Derbyshire and Cheshire, in the PEAK DISTRICT. It rises to the west of BUXTON and flows approximately 32 km (20 miles) northwards across **Goyt's Moss** and through **Goyt Valley** (in which Fernilee Reservoir has been constructed) and the **Dale of Goyt** to join the River TAME[2] at STOCKPORT.

Grafham Water *Grafham* 'home or enclosure in or by a grove', OE *graf* 'grove' + HAM.
A large reservoir in Cambridgeshire (before 1974 in Huntingdonshire), near the village of **Grafham**, about 10 km (6 miles) southwest of Huntingdon. Created in the 1960s, it has a shoreline 16 km (10 miles) long. It is in heavy use for sailing, wind-surfing and other water sports, and is also an important sanctuary for waterfowl.

Grafton Flyford *Grafton* 'farmstead in or by a grove', OE *graf* 'grove' + -TON; *Flyford* from the nearby FLYFORD FLAVELL.
A village in Worcestershire (before 1998 in Hereford and Worcester, before 1974 in Worcestershire), about 11 km (7 miles) east of Worcester.

Grafton Street Named in 1812 after the 2nd Duke of *Grafton* (illegitimate son of Charles II), who was lord lieutenant of Ireland in the early 18th century.
A street in DUBLIN, and the city's main one for shopping. It is on the south side of the River LIFFEY, extending from ST STEPHEN'S GREEN north past Trinity College. It is now a pedestrian zone, and is regarded as more salubrious than its northern extension over the river, O'CONNELL STREET.

> Grafton Street's a wonderland, there's magic in the air;
> There are diamonds in the lady's eyes and gold dust in her hair;
> And if you don't believe me, come and meet me there,
> In Dublin on a sunny summer morning.
>
> Leo Maguire: 'The Dublin Saunter' (1954), the signature song of the actor and comedian Noel Purcell (1900–85)

Grafty Green *Grafty* either 'grass enclosure', OE *gærs* 'grass' + *teag* 'enclosure', or 'enclosure by a pit or grove', OE *græf* 'pit' or *graf* 'grove' + *teag*.

A village in Kent, at the foot of the NORTH DOWNS, about 11 km (7 miles) southeast of Maidstone.

Grahams Named after Fiona Graham.
The collective name given to Scottish hills over 2000 ft (609.8 m) and under 2500 ft (762.2 m) in height. They were originally called Elsies (LCs, for 'Lesser CORBETTS'), but were renamed in memory of Fiona Graham (née Helen Torbett), who published a new list of such hills in 1992. There are 224 Grahams; many are also DONALDS, although quite a number of Donalds are not Grahams but Corbetts. It is safe to say, however, that no Grahams are Corbetts, let alone MUNROS. But it is beyond the capacity of man to determine whether all or any these of these are also MARILYNS.

Grampian From the GRAMPIAN MOUNTAINS.
A former local government region of northeast Scotland, formed in 1975 and abolished in 1996. It was formed from the old counties of ABERDEENSHIRE, KINCARDINESHIRE, BANFFSHIRE and most of Murray (*see under* MORAY). It was bordered by Tayside to the south, Highland to the west and the North Sea to the north and east. The administrative HQ was in ABERDEEN, and other towns included ELGIN, BANFF, FRASERBURGH, PETERHEAD, INVERURIE and STONEHAVEN.

Grampian Mountains Mistakenly derived in 1520 (possibly via a mistranscription) by the historian Hector Boece from the battle of MONS GRAUPIUS recorded by Tacitus, in which, in AD 84, Agricola defeated the Picts somewhere north of the River Tay.
A name (alternatively **the Grampians**) applied variously by poets, cartographers and geographers (but few others) to the whole of the HIGHLANDS south and east of the GREAT GLEN, or to all the mountains (including the Cairngorms) east of the SPEY and north of the TAY, or just to those hills east of the A9 and the Drumochter Pass and south of the Dee. This last area is sometimes known as the MOUNTH.

> My name is Norval. On the Grampian Hills
> It is forgotten, and deserves to be.
> So are the Grampian Hills and all the people
> Who ever heard of either them or me.
>
> Hugh MacDiarmid: *A Drunk Man Looks at the Thistle* (1926) (These lines are adapted from a speech in *Douglas* (1756), a popular sentimental drama by John Home. Old Norval is a shepherd.)

The range gave its name to the former GRAMPIAN region in northeast Scotland, and to the Grampians, an extension of the Great Dividing Range in Victoria, Australia.

Grampound '(place at the) great bridge', OFr *grant* 'great' + *pont* 'bridge'.
A village in Cornwall, on the River FAL, about 10.5 km (6.5 miles) southwest of St Austell.

Granard Possibly 'sandy height', Irish *greanach* 'sandy or gravelly place' + ARD.

A small market town in County Longford, 20 km (12 miles) northeast of Longford itself. In the 1798 United Irishmen's Rebellion many of the insurgents fleeing the field at BALLINAMUCK were slaughtered here.

Granard was the birthplace of the Chartist leader James O'Brien (1805–64).

Granby 'Grani's farmstead or village', OScand male personal name *Grani* + -BY.

A village in Nottinghamshire, in the VALE OF BELVOIR, about 19 km (12 miles) southeast of Nottingham.

The success and popularity of John Manners, Marquess of Granby (1721–70), as a British commander in the Seven Years' War, led in the late 18th century to a profusion of inns named 'The Marquess of Granby', many of which still remain. He was a conspicuously bald man (legend has it that the expression *go at something baldheaded*, meaning 'to act impetuously', was inspired by a cavalry charge led by him at Warburg in 1760), and the inn signs tend to exaggerate this feature.

Grand Canal. The canal linking DUBLIN through the Irish Midlands to the SHANNON. The first section, linking the River BARROW through Dublin to the sea, was completed in 1791, while the long westward extension to the Shannon was completed in 1805. In Dublin 'inside the Canal' and 'outside the Canal' are commonly used geographical indicators.

> O commemorate me where there is water,
> Canal water preferably, so stilly
> Green at the heart of summer. Brother
> Commemorate me thus beautifully …
>
> Patrick Kavanagh: 'Lines Written on a Seat on the
> Grand Canal, Dublin'. (The poet's wish has been
> granted, the resulting memorial to the notably
> cantankerous poet being nicknamed by Dubliners the
> 'Crank on the Bank'.)

Grand Union Canal. A name given in 1929 to a system of canals formed by amalgamating the Grand Junction Canal (running from London via Watford towards the Midlands), the REGENT'S CANAL, and the Warwick and Birmingham, the Warwick and Knapton and the Birmingham and Warwick Junction Canals. In combination, they provide a canal link between London and Birmingham, via Watford, Milton Keynes and Warwick. The Canal divides into two at Bulls Bridge Junction in West London: the Brentford Arm goes southwards and enters the Thames upstream of Brentford; the Paddington Arm continues eastwards, along the Regent's Canal, and ends at LIMEHOUSE Basin.

Grange Hill *Grange* 'outlying farm belonging to a religious house or feudal lord', OFr and ME; in this case the Grange belonged to Tilty Abbey.

A town in Essex, effectively a suburb of northeast London, about 1 km (0.5 miles) south of CHIGWELL. It was lifted from obscurity by the BBC Television children's soap opera *Grange Hill* (1978–), originated by Phil Redmond (creator of *Brookside*), which is set in 'Grange Hill Comprehensive'.

Grange Hill 'Underground' station, on the Central line, was opened in 1948.

Grangemouth 'mouth of the Grange Burn'. The burn, which joins the River Carron here, is named after the nearby Abbot Grange, formerly the possession of the abbot of Newbattle Abbey.

An industrial town and port 4 km (2.5 miles) northeast of Falkirk, on the south shore of the upper Firth of Forth at the mouth of the River CARRON. It was in Stirlingshire, then in Central region, and is now in Falkirk unitary authority. The town is dominated by the oil refinery (the industry began here in 1924) and by chemical plants. The lights and fires that can be seen at night may go some way to explaining the 'Falkirk Triangle' (*see under* FALKIRK[1]). Britain's first container terminal was built at Grangemouth.

Grange-over-Sands *Grange see* GRANGE HILL, the religious house in this case being nearby Cartmel Priory; the second element refers to its position overlooking the sands of Morecambe Bay.

A seaside resort in Cumbria (formerly in Lancashire), on the north side of Morecambe Bay (*see under* MORECAMBE), 18 km (11 miles) southwest of Kendal. Before the arrival of the railway, it was the northern terminus of the old route across the sands of Morecambe Bay from near Lancaster to the Lake District. Until its dissolution in the 16th century, Cartmel Priory provided monks as guides; subsequently guides were appointed by the monarch. One guide – the so called 'sand pilot', Cedric Robinson – still remains to take the adventurous safely across this treacherous passage; he has held this post since 1963.

Granite City, the. A nickname for ABERDEEN, so called because of the dominant building material.

Granta A OCelt river name of unknown meaning.

A river in Essex and Cambridgeshire, which rises to the northeast of Saffron Walden and flows 19 km (12 miles) northwest to join the River CAM[2] at Great Shelford. The name is sometimes also applied to the eastern branch of the Cam, and in former times it referred to the entire river (*see* CAM[2], CAMBRIDGE[1]).

Granta. A journal which started life as a Cambridge University undergraduate periodical in 1889. In the 1950s and 1960s it functioned as a student literary magazine, publishing work by such assorted future luminaries as Peter Cook, Michael Frayn, Ted Hughes, Sylvia Plath, Jonathan

Routh and Nicholas Tomalin. It went into almost terminal decline, but re-emerged in 1979 as an avant-garde literary periodical, from 1983 in book form in association with Penguin Books, edited originally by Bill Buford. It is now published by the independent Granta Publications along with a range of fiction and non-fiction books.

Grantchester Originally *Granteseta* 'settlers on the River Granta', GRANTA + OE *sǣte* 'settlers'; the *-chester* (*see* CHESTER) is first recorded in 1208.

A village in Cambridgeshire, on the River CAM[2] (formerly called the GRANTA), about 4 km (2.5 miles) southwest of Cambridge. It has a fine old church with many interesting features, but it owed its initial modern fame to its associations with the romantically beautiful poet Rupert Brooke (1887–1915), shooting star of the pre-First World War English literary scene. In 1909 he settled at Grantchester, in the Old Vicarage, and in 1912, while travelling in Germany, he eulogized it in 'The Old Vicarage, Grantchester':

> Ah God! to see the branches stir
> Across the moon at Grantchester! ...
> Say, do the elm-clumps greatly stand
> Still guardians of that holy land? ...
> Say, is there Beauty yet to find?
> And Certainty? and Quiet kind?
> Deep meadows yet, for to forget
> The lies, and truths, and pain? ... oh! yet
> Stands the Church clock at ten to three?
> And is there honey still for tea?

Brooke's death in the First World War preserved his dazzling reputation in aspic for many decades, but it was already somewhat in eclipse when in the 1980s a new resident arrived in the Old Vicarage: author, Tory politician and charlatan Jeffrey Archer (b.1940). The frequent appearances of Grantchester on television news bulletins in the run-up to his arrest for perjury in 2000 channelled its public image in a new and less flattering direction.

Grantchester Grind. A comic novel by Tom Sharpe (1995), a sequel to his earlier *Porterhouse Blue* (1974). Like the latter, it is set in the fictional Cambridge college of Porterhouse (*see* Cambridge University *under* CAMBRIDGE[1]).

Grantham Probably 'Granta's homestead or village', OE male personal name *Granta* + HAM. Alternatively, the first element may be from OE *grand* 'gravel'.

A market town in Lincolnshire, on the River WITHAM, about 37 km (23 miles) southwest of Lincoln. It was an important agricultural centre from Saxon times, and in the Middle Ages it grew rich on the wool trade. The spire of the 13th-century St Wulfram's Church, which soars to 86 m (282 ft), has long been a noted local landmark ('His beard is cut like the spire of Grantham steeple' – Thomas Lodge, *Wits Miserie* (1596)).

In the days of the stagecoach, Grantham was an important staging post on the GREAT NORTH ROAD, and some notable coaching inns survive: the Angel and Royal Hotel, dating from the 15th century, is one of England's oldest (in 1483 Richard III signed the Duke of Buckingham's death warrant there); and the 18th-century George Hotel has a part in Charles Dickens's *Nicholas Nickleby* (1839). When the railways arrived, Grantham became an important junction on the East Coast line from London to Scotland.

Sir Isaac Newton was educated at the 15th-century King's School, Grantham, in the 1650s. The town was also the birthplace of the composer Nicholas Maw (b.1935) and of the Conservative politician and prime minister Margaret Thatcher (b.1925). Details of her early life here (daughter of Alfred Roberts, grocer, alderman and later mayor of Grantham, in whose establishment she learnt frugality, industry and practicality; educated at the local girls' grammar school) were carefully woven into the Thatcher legend.

Graham, as both a first name and a surname, derives from a medieval spelling of *Grantham*. It became popular in Scotland when William de Graham took the name north in the 12th century.

Grantham gruel. An extremely thin and meagre form of gruel:

> Thou wilt get naething at night save Grantham gruel,
> nine grots and a gallon of water.

> Sir Walter Scott: *The Heart of Midlothian* (1818)

Grantown-on-Spey Named after Sir James *Grant* and the River SPEY.

A small resort town on the River Spey, in Highland (formerly in Moray), 20 km (12.5 miles) northeast of Aviemore. It was founded in 1766 as a model village by the local laird, Sir James Grant.

Granuaile. A personification of Ireland (*see under* CLEW BAY).

Grasmere As the earliest recorded form is *Gressemere* 1245, it is probably a tautonym, 'grass lake mere', OE *gres* 'grass' + *sǣ* 'lake' + *mere* 'lake' (*see* LAKE).

A small lake in the LAKE DISTRICT, Cumbria, some 4 km (2.5 miles) northwest of Ambleside. It gives its name to the attractive small village of Grasmere just beyond its northern end.

The village is above all else associated with the poet William Wordsworth, who with his sister Dorothy moved into Dove Cottage in 1799, describing the area as 'this fairest spot on earth' (*Memorials of a Tour in Scotland*, 1803). Even before this the valley had appeared in his poetry: in 'Michael', one of the *Lyrical Ballads* of 1798, the eponymous shepherd lives in 'Grasmere Vale'.

In 1808, the poet, now married and with a family,

moved to Allan Bank, at the north end of the lake, while the writer Thomas de Quincey leased Dove Cottage. In 1811 the Wordsworths moved again, to the Parsonage at Grasmere. Wordsworth's final home was nearby Rydal Mount (*see* RYDAL).

Wordsworth's grave is in St Oswald's churchyard, as are those of Dorothy, his wife Mary and sister-in-law Sara Hutchinson. Close by, eight of the yews by the River Rothay were planted by the poet.

> Let him lie there by Rotha without remark.
> Hiding and half disclosing, the veils of rain
> Make a Chinese painting of his ashen lake,
> Of the slopes where woods deciduously mourn
> Another autumn ...
>
> David Wright: 'Grasmere Sonnets', from *To the Gods the Shades* (1976)

Since Wordsworth's day, the village of Grasmere, and Dove Cottage in particular, have become the destination of probably millions of literary pilgrims.

> Mountains, rivers and grand storms,
> Continuous profit, grand customs
> (And many of them): O Lakes, Lakes!
> O Sentiment upon the rocks!
>
> Geoffrey Hill: 'Elegiac Stanzas on a Visit to Dove Cottage', from *For the Unfallen* (1959)

Grasmere has an annual rush-bearing ceremony, held on 5 August, St Oswald's Day (he is the patron of the parish church). Various items made of rushes are carried into the church, after a procession around the village.

Grasmere gingerbread. A type of gingerbread including lemon peel, oatmeal and plenteous quantities of butter, sugar and golden syrup. Pieces of this gingerbread stamped with the image of St Oswald are given to the participants in the aforementioned Grasmere rush-bearing ceremony.

Gravelly Hill Self-explanatory, i.e. a hill with gravel.
A northeastern suburb of BIRMINGHAM, best known as the site of the extremely complex junction between the M6 motorway and the A38(M) and various other roads (*see* SPAGHETTI JUNCTION).

Gravesend '(place at the) end of the grove or copse', OE *grafes* possessive form of *graf* 'grove, copse' + *ende* 'end'.
An industrial town and port in Kent, on the south bank of the Thames estuary, about 13 km (8 miles) east of Dartford and 11 km (7 miles) northwest of Rochester. It is linked by ferry to TILBURY on the opposite bank of the Thames. It is a customs and pilot station for the Port of London, and river pilots are exchanged for coastal pilots here.

The Native American woman Pocahontas (*c.*1595–1617), who married the Virginian colonist John Rolfe and returned to England with him, died off Gravesend when about to return to America. She is buried here in St George's Church.

Gravesend is a place of records. The first German V1 flying bomb to strike Britain in the Second World War landed on a lettuce patch in Gravesend on 13 June 1944, while the highest shade-temperature recorded in the UK was reached here on 10 August 2003: 38.1°C (101°F).

The poet Thom Gunn (1929–2004) was born in Gravesend.

> Gravesend is a little confused Town ... always full of Seamen.
>
> J. Macky: *Journey thro' England* (1714)

The framing narrative of Joseph Conrad's novella *Heart of Darkness* (1902) takes place on a ship anchored off Gravesend (and no doubt Conrad chose the place name because of its morbid resonance):

> A haze rested on the low shores that ran out to sea in vanishing flatness. The air was dark above Gravesend, and farther back still seemed condensed into a mournful gloom, brooding motionless over the biggest, and the greatest, town on earth.

There is a town called Gravesend in New South Wales, Australia, and a Gravesend Bay on Long Island, New York; Gravesend was also the name of one of the original villages (1645) that became absorbed into Brooklyn.

Gravesend bus. Late 19th-century slang for a 'hearse' – with a pun on the idea of the 'grave' being 'at the end of the line'.

Gravesend sweetmeats. A mid-19th-century colloquialism for 'shrimps'.

Gravesend twins. Mid-19th-century slang for 'solid pieces of excrement', inspired by the sewerage outfall at Gravesend.

Gravesham A modern reintroduction of the form of the name *Gravesend* as it appears in Domesday Book (1086).
An administrative district in northern Kent. It mainly covers GRAVESEND, but it also includes sections of the coast to east and west and an area inland as far as the NORTH DOWNS.

Grays Originally *Grays Thurrock* (*see* THURROCK), denoting manorial ownership in the early Middle Ages by the de Grai family; simple *Grays* is first recorded in 1399.
A town in Essex, within the unitary authority of Thurrock (of which it is the administrative centre), on the north bank of the River Thames, about 4 km (2.5 miles) northwest of TILBURY.

Great and Little Skirtfuls of Stones, the. *See under* ROMBALDS MOOR.

Great Blasket Island. *See under* BLASKET ISLANDS.

Great Bolas *Bolas* from OE *wæsse* 'riverside land liable to flood' with an uncertain first element, perhaps OE *bogela* the possessive plural form of *bogel* 'small river-bend or meander'.
A village in Shropshire, on the River Severn, about 17.5 km (11 miles) northeast of Shrewsbury.

Great Britain. A political entity consisting of ENGLAND, SCOTLAND and WALES, which together with NORTHERN IRELAND makes up the UNITED KINGDOM. It came into de facto existence at the beginning of the 17th century, when the crowns of England and Scotland were united under James VI and I (*see below*). From the start many institutions in Scotland (notably the legal system) remained distinct from those in England and Wales, and the devolution of the late 1990s which brought greater powers of self-determination to Scotland and Wales eroded still further the concept of Great Britain as a fully integrated individual state or country.

The abbreviation GB comes in for fairly heavy use (as a national code on motor vehicles, for example), but on the whole people tend not to refer to 'Great Britain' very often – either because 'Great' gives rise to (historically unjustified – *see below*) embarrassment, or simply because the name is too long. In sporting contests, for instance, when the constituent nations of the UK are competing as a single unit, they are formally referred to correctly as the 'United Kingdom' and more casually called just 'Britain'. There are exceptions, however: the national rugby league team (usually consisting entirely of Englishmen) goes under the name 'Great Britain', while in the Olympics the abbreviation GBR is used.

The term 'Great Britain' was used in the Middle Ages to distinguish Britain from Brittany, which was 'Little Britain', but its modern connotations did not appear until the 15th century, when it was applied to the united England and Scotland envisaged by Edward IV. When James I (VI of Scotland) succeeded Elizabeth I in 1603 and the union finally took place, the name was ready to hand, and the new monarch duly had himself proclaimed 'King of Great Britain, France and Ireland'. The English parliament was not disposed to accept this nomenclature, and withheld its consent, but the name started to appear on the coins, and soon became part of the furniture. It was officially ratified by the Act of Union of 1707, which stated that England and Scotland were 'united into one kingdom by the name of Great Britain'.

In this context, 'great' simply denotes a large, all-encompassing unit, without any connotations of grandeur or superiority, but inevitably the latter began to creep into people's perception of the meaning of the name, particularly in the 19th century, with the solidification of Britain's grip on large parts of the globe (advocates – such as the radical politician Sir Charles Dilke – of the term **Greater Britain** for the British empire no doubt had the double entendre in mind). Nowadays this more modest sense of 'Great' is all that remains – thus provoking the chorus of those wishing to 'put the *Great* back into *Britain*' whenever national decline is on the agenda.

See also BRIT[2], BRITANNIA, BRITISH, BRITISH ISLES, BRITON, JOHN BULL, NORTH BRITAIN *and* UNITED KINGDOM.

Great Britain. A huge passenger ship designed by Isambard Kingdom Brunel. Launched in Bristol on 19 July 1843, it was the world's first large iron ship and also its first screw-propelled ship, and it weighed a massive 3270 tons. Initially it did the transatlantic run, and later it worked the route to Australia. It was abandoned in the Falkland Islands in 1886, but in 1970 was brought back to Bristol and restored, and is now on show there.

Great British Public, the. A usually ironic term (first recorded in 1866) for the mass of the British populace, with all its well-known vices and virtues:

> The major achievements of contemporary novelists appear to be unknown even by name to that part of the community journalists call the Great British Public.
>
> Q.D. Leavis: *Fiction and the Reading Public* (1932)

Great Clacton. *See under* CLACTON-ON-SEA.

Great Coates *Coates* 'the cottages or huts', OE *cot* (*see* -COT, COTE).
A village in North East Lincolnshire (before 1996 in Humberside, before 1974 in Lincolnshire), about 4 km (2.5 miles) west of Grimsby.

Great Cockup *Cockup* Possibly either 'hillock valley' or 'secluded valley frequented by woodcock', OE *cocc* 'hillock' or 'wild bird such as woodcock' + *hop* 'secluded valley'.
A hill (515 m / 1690 ft) in the northern fells of the LAKE DISTRICT, Cumbria (formerly in Cumberland), 5 km (3 miles) north of Skiddaw. The 'Great' distinguishes it from **Cockup** (505 m / 1655 ft), a top at the northern end of the Skiddaw massif, 2.5 km (1.5 miles) south of Great Cockup over Dash Beck.

The late Chris Brasher, mountain environmentalist and sports journalist, opined that after the government's handling of the 2001 foot-and-mouth epidemic – which hit Cumbria particularly badly – Great Cockup would be 'a suitable place for a memorial stone to the Department of Agriculture'.

Great Coxwell *Coxwell* 'Cocc's spring', OE *Cocces* possessive form of male personal name *Cocc* + *wella* 'spring'.
A village in Oxfordshire, about 2 km (1 mile) southwest of FARINGDON. **Great Coxwell Barn**, a superb example of a medieval tithe barn (now owned by the National Trust), dates from the 13th century (when it was built by monks from BEAULIEU Abbey in Hampshire who had established a cell there) and is over 45 m (150 ft) long and 15 m (50 ft) high; William Morris described the barn as being 'as noble as a cathedral'.

The village of **Little Coxwell** lies about 1 km (0.5 miles) to the east.

Great Cumbrae. *See* the CUMBRAES.

Great Driffield. *See* DRIFFIELD.

Great Dunmow. *See* DUNMOW.

Greater London. The county that contains LONDON. 'London' was originally just the City of London, encircled and circumscribed by its wall, but in the Middle Ages it was already outgrowing this straitjacket. By Shakespeare's time the City had taken over the jurisdiction of Southwark, and its tentacles were advancing towards Westminster. Elizabeth I issued a proclamation in 1580 attempting to prevent the further expansion of London, but she had even less success than her royal predecessor Cnut (Canute) had with the waves. By slow accretion, surrounding villages and hamlets were swallowed up, and almost imperceptibly the scope of the name 'London' widened.

The notion of an entity called 'Greater London' seems to have emerged in the 1880s, first with specific reference to the area covered by the London police (consisting of the Metropolitan Police and the City Police), and then somewhat more loosely applied to the area covered by the County of London (created 1888).

For town-planners considering the future scope and structure of London, the name 'Greater London' was an attractive option –

> Some name, then, for these city-regions, these town aggregates, is wanted … What of 'Conurbations'? … For our first conurbation the name of Greater London is … dominant.
>
> Patrick Geddes: *Cities in Evolution* (1915)

– and it was officially adopted in the 20th century for census and other purposes.

This 'Greater London Conurbation' formed the basis in 1965 for the **Greater London Council** (the GLC), a successor authority to the London County Council with jurisdiction over 32 London boroughs: BARKING AND DAGENHAM, BARNET, BEXLEY, BRENT[2], BROMLEY, CAMDEN, City of WESTMINSTER, CROYDON, EALING, ENFIELD, GREENWICH, HACKNEY, HAMMERSMITH AND FULHAM, HARINGEY, HARROW, HAVERING, HILLINGDON, HOUNSLOW, ISLINGTON, LAMBETH, LEWISHAM, MERTON, NEWHAM, REDBRIDGE, RICHMOND-UPON-THAMES, the Royal Borough of KENSINGTON AND CHELSEA, the Royal Borough of KINGSTON UPON THAMES, SOUTHWARK, SUTTON[1], TOWER HAMLETS, WALTHAM FOREST and WANDSWORTH. The new territorial entity swallowed up most of Middlesex together with parts of Hertfordshire, Essex, Kent and Surrey. It did not, however, cover quite all of the 'Greater London Conurbation' area (for example, Epsom and Ewell were not included, and neither were Potters Bar and Watford).

The GLC was abolished in 1986 and most of its powers were devolved to the boroughs, but the name and the idea of 'Greater London' are still in wide use. In 2000 the **Greater London Authority** (the GLA) was set up. Its headquarters, and those of the **London Assembly** (*see* LONDON) and the **Mayor of London** (that is, of Greater London; a post whose first incumbent was Ken Livingstone), are in City Hall. This futuristic sub-globular building (designed by Norman Foster and nicknamed 'the Egg') stands at the southern end of **Tower Bridge**.

See also INNER LONDON.

Greater Manchester *See* MANCHESTER.

A metropolitan county of northwest England, created in 1974 out of parts of Lancashire. It is bounded on the north by Lancashire, to the west by Merseyside, to the south by Cheshire and to the east by Derbyshire and West Yorkshire. In 1986 most of the powers of the county council were devolved to metropolitan district councils. As well as Manchester, the county includes BOLTON, BURY, OLDHAM, ROCHDALE, SALFORD, STOCKPORT, TAMESIDE, TRAFFORD and WIGAN.

Great Fryup 'Friga's valley', OE male personal name *Friga* + *hop* 'secluded valley'.

A division of **Fryup Dale**, a valley in the NORTH YORK MOORS to the southeast of Danby. The other branch is **Little Fryup**.

Great Gable Presumably from its resemblance to a gable end. It was originally *Mykelgavel*, OScand *mikill* 'great' + *gafl* 'gable'; in the early 19th century Coleridge sometimes referred to it as Great Gavel (although below as Gable).

A steep-sided, craggy mountain (899 m / 2949 ft) in the LAKE DISTRICT, Cumbria (formerly in Cumberland), 4 km (2.5 miles) north of Scafell. It dominates the heads of three valleys: Ennerdale, Borrowdale and Wasdale.

> The darkness vanished as if by enchantment; far off, far, far off to the south, the mountains of Glaramara and Great Gable and their family appeared distinct, in deepest, sablest blue.
>
> Samuel Taylor Coleridge: letter to Humphry Davy (18 October 1800)

The solo ascent of Napes Needle on Great Gable by W.P. Haskett-Smith in June 1886 is regarded as the foundation of rock climbing as a sport in the British Isles; at the top Haskett-Smith left as a memento his 'handkerchief fluttering in the breeze'. In 1923 a memorial was raised on the mountain to those members of the Fell and Rock Climbing Club (the premier Lakeland climbing club) who had died in the Great War.

> The torn cloth poppies in the summit's wind
> Mark fallen Fell men, Flanders dead,
> Bones in the foreign mud, souls on a dry
> Mountain …
>
> Shirley Toulson: 'Great Gable'

> Then, on a storm-still mountain top I stood
> And on a simple plaque shed poppy blood.

>> Joanne M. Weeks: 'Great Gable, 2949 Feet above Flanders'

Great Glen, the From its size (*see* GLEN).

A major fault-line running diagonally across Scotland from LOCH LINNHE and FORT WILLIAM in the southwest to INVERNESS in the northeast. It is also known as **Glen Mòr** (Gaelic *mòr* 'big') **Glen Albyn** or **the Glen of Albyn** or **Glen More Albin** (ALBANY[1] being an old name of Scotland). To the north and west of the glen are the Northwest Highlands, once separated from the rest of Scotland, but brought together over many millions of years by continental drift. To the east and south are the Grampian Mountains.

There are several freshwater lochs in the glen: LOCH LOCHY, Loch Oich and LOCH NESS. These are linked to each other and to LOCH LINNHE (a sea loch) in the southwest and the Moray Firth in the northeast by the CALEDONIAN CANAL.

> But there's mair nor a roch wind blawin'
> Through the great glen o' the warld the day.

>> Hamish Henderson: 'The Freedom Come All Ye' (1947)

Great Heck *Heck* OE *hæc* 'gate'; *Great* distinguishes this from nearby Little Heck.

A village in North Yorkshire, 14 km (8.5 miles) east of Pontefract.

Great Malvern *Malvern see* MALVERN HILLS.

A spa town (pronounced 'mawlvern') in Worcestershire (before 1998 in Hereford and Worcester, before 1974 in Worcestershire), on the eastern slopes of the MALVERN HILLS, about 11 km (7 miles) southwest of Worcester. In everyday parlance it is generally referred to simply as '**Malvern**'.

Malvern Priory church, now the parish church, has a richly decorated exterior – particularly its tower – and fine stained glass. Charles Darwin's granddaughter, who died in childhood despite being bathed in Malvern water (*see below*), is buried in its churchyard. The church sits among a cornucopia of Victorian architecture, much of it therapeutic in origin, which gives the town its particular flavour (it has been described as a collection of Swiss sanatoria). It was the Victorians who discovered the beneficial qualities of the water that gushes from St Ann's Well, above the town, and bottled it as **Malvern Water**. In an age of a myriad bottled waters it remains the doyen, by appointment to Her Majesty the Queen.

The **Malvern Festival**, an annual festival of music and drama, was founded in 1929 by George Bernard Shaw. Revived in 1977, the music festival is held in early summer and the Almeida drama festival in August. **Malvern College**, a coeducational public school, was founded in 1862, and Morgan sports cars continue to be made in Malvern.

Smaller namesakes surround Great Malvern like satellites: to the north, MALVERN LINK and **North Malvern**; to the south, **Little Malvern** (the composer Edward Elgar is buried nearby in the churchyard of St Wulstan's), **Malvern Common** and **Malvern Wells**; and to the west, **West Malvern**.

The name has also been taken up abroad: there are Malverns in the USA (Arkansas, Iowa, Ohio), in Australia (a suburb of Melbourne, Victoria) and in Jamaica.

Great Marlborough Street. *See* MARLBOROUGH STREET.

Great Marlow. *See* MARLOW.

Great Missenden *Missenden* probably 'valley where water-plants or marsh-plants grow', OE *mysse* 'water-plant, marsh-plant' + *denu* 'valley'.

A small town in Buckinghamshire, about 8 km (5 miles) west of Chesham. The village of **Little Missenden**, birthplace of the car manufacturer Herbert Austin (1866–1941), is about 3 km (2 miles) away to the southeast.

Great Mis Tor. *See under* MIS TOR.

Great North Road. A name in use since at least the 19th century for a major road leading from London northwards, passing through HOLLOWAY, HIGHGATE, BARNET and HATFIELD[1] on its eventual way to York. The route was already established by the 12th century, as an alternative to the much older ERMINE STREET, which left London further east.

At its southern end it is today designated the A1; from FINCHLEY to WELWYN GARDEN CITY it is the A1000, and from there to EDINBURGH it reverts to the A1. The parts that actually bear the name 'Great North Road' now are a short section at the southern end of the A1000, between ARCHWAY Road and Fortis Green, and the A1000 from BARNET northwards.

Great Orme Possibly 'snake headland', OScand *ormr* 'snake' + *hofuth* 'head, headland', *compare* WORMS HEAD.

A rocky limestone hill (207 m / 680 ft) on the northwest side of LLANDUDNO, Conwy (formerly in Denbighshire, then in Gwynedd). The summit can be accessed by cable car or by the **Great Orme Tramway** (1902), and there are copper mines (open to the public) dating from the Bronze Age. At the northwest end is the precipitous headland known as **Great Ormes Head**. On the east side of Llandudno is another rocky headland, called **Little Ormes Head** (141 m / 463 ft).

> *dy goglat gwenyc gwynn Gygreadwdyr Vynynt,*
> *morua rianet Maelgwn nebyt.*
> (the white waves pound under the Great Orme,
> the seashore of Lord Maelgwn's maidens.)

>> Gwalchmai: 'Exultation' (12th century), translated by Gwyn Williams

Great Ormond Street Probably named in honour of James Butler, 1st Duke of *Ormonde*, Royalist commander in the Irish campaigns of the Civil Wars.

A street in Central London (WC1), in BLOOMSBURY, running approximately east-west to the east of RUSSELL SQUARE. It was laid out at the end of the 17th century. It is most famous for, and now virtually synonymous with, the Hospital for Sick Children, England's premier children's hospital, founded in 1851.

Great Ouse *Ouse see* OUSE[2].

A river in Northamptonshire, Buckinghamshire, Bedfordshire, Cambridgeshire and Norfolk, which rises near Silverstone and flows 257 km (160 miles) northeastwards through Brackley, BUCKINGHAM, NEWPORT PAGNELL, BEDFORD, ST NEOTS, HUNTINGDON, ST IVES[2], ELY[1] and across the FENS into the WASH near King's Lynn (before the 13th century it followed a more westerly course near its end, through Wisbech).

Commonly known simply as the **Ouse**, the river has been subjected to much human manipulation over the centuries, both to enhance its navigational potential and to contribute to the drainage of the Fens. In particular, in the mid-17th century the Old Bedford River (*see under* BEDFORD LEVEL) and the New Bedford River (also known as the HUNDRED FOOT DRAIN) were cut between Earith and Downham Market, isolating a large loop of the Great Ouse to the east. This is now known as the **Old River**: it is made up of the **Old West River**, from Earith to the junction with the River CAM[2]; the **Ely Ouse**, from the junction with the Cam to Littleport; and the **Ten Mile River**, from Littleport to where it reconnects with the New Bedford River.

See also LITTLE OUSE.

Ouse Washes. An area of low-lying watery land to the west of the Old Bedford River in Cambridgeshire.

River Ouse. Cockney rhyming slang for *booze*, first recorded in the 1930s. Frequently spelt *Ooze* rather than *Ouse*.

Great Rollright. *See under* ROLLRIGHT.

Great Saling *Saling* perhaps '(settlement of the) people who live among the sallow-trees', OE *salh* 'sallow-tree' + -*ingas* (*see* -ING); alternatively 'places where sallow-trees grow', from the plural of OE *sal(h)ing*.

A village in Essex, near Pods Brook, about 6.5 km (4 miles) west of Braintree.

Great Snoring *Snoring* probably '(settlement of) Snear's people', OE male personal name *Snear* + -*ingas* (*see* -ING).

A village in North Norfolk, on the River STIFFKEY[2], about 5 km (3 miles) northeast of Fakenham.

See also LITTLE SNORING.

Great Sugar Loaf From its conical shape; the first part of the name distinguishes it from its smaller relation, Little Sugar Loaf.

A relatively small but strikingly formed hill (501 m / 1643 ft) in County Wicklow, some 20 km (12 miles) south of Dublin. It is an isolated outlier of the Wicklow Mountains, and is a noted viewpoint. Nearby is **Little Sugar Loaf** (342 m / 1123 ft), a quartz cone.

Great Tew *Tew* perhaps 'a row or ridge', OE *tiewe*.

A village in Oxfordshire, in the COTSWOLDS, about 13 km (8 miles) southwest of Banbury. Surrounded by woods, its cottages of honey-coloured stone, many of them thatched, make it a preternaturally typical Cotswold village. Great Tew is also one of the earliest existing examples of a planned village: its cottages were originally built for estate workers in the 1630s by Lord Falkland, and the subsequent replanning of Colonel Stratton's estate (of which Great Tew was a part) on landscape and ecological principles was carried out in 1808 by John Loudon, the Scottish landscape gardener, writer and architect. The Falklands Arms inn, which occupies a 16th-century thatched building, claims to offer its customers the biggest range of snuff outside the West End of London.

Little Tew lies 1.5 km (1 mile) to the southwest, and DUNS TEW 5 km (3 miles) to the east.

Great Torrington. *See under* TORRINGTON.

Great Tosson *Tosson* is from OE *tot-stan* 'lookout stone', a reference to nearby Burgh Hill.

A village in Northumberland, 3 km (2 miles) southwest of Rothbury. **Tosson Hill** (440 m / 1444 ft) lies to the southwest.

Great Wen, the *Wen* 'wart, tumour', OE.

An opprobrious name applied to London, viewed as a festering, crowded, overpopulated excrescence injurious to the nation on which it feeds. The general metaphorical application of *wen* to a sprawling city dates from at least the 1780s, and was enthusiastically taken up by the polemical writer William Cobbett (1763–1835) (*see* CROYDON). It was he who established the particular application to London:

> But what is to be the fate of the great wen of all? The monster, called … 'the metropolis of the empire'?
>
> William Cobbett: *Rural Rides* (1830)

See also the WEN.

Great West Road On the model of the GREAT NORTH ROAD.

A name given to a main arterial road leading from LONDON to the WEST COUNTRY, and in particular to the stretch of the A4 through BRENTFORD to HOUNSLOW, opened in 1925 and extended back to HAMMERSMITH around 1950. In its early days its unprecedentedly wide straight stretches of concrete proved irresistibly tempting to adventurous drivers, and it became more of a lethal speedway than a public highway:

> And now they had passed Gunnersbury, and had turned up to the right, and were ripping up the wide, smooth,

deserted spaces of the Great West Road. ... Gee! – it was like a racing track – no wonder he put on speed. It was like being in an aeroplane!

Patrick Hamilton: *The Siege of Pleasure* (1932)

See also WESTERN AVENUE *and the* WESTWAY

Great Whernside. *See under* WHERNSIDE.

Great Yarmouth *Yarmouth* '(place at the) mouth of the River YARE', OCelt river name (probably meaning 'babbling brook') + OE *mutha* 'mouth'.

A town and port on the Norfolk coast, at a point where the Rivers BURE, WAVENEY[1] and Yare (whence its name) flow into the North Sea via BREYDON WATER, about 29 km (18 miles) east of Norwich. For centuries it earned its living as one of England's major herring fishery ports, running a thriving trade in cured fish: notably bloaters (whole herrings lightly cured and cold-smoked), but also kippers, bucklings and red herrings:

The Yarmouth red herring is locally sometimes called a 'militiaman'; *per contra*, the vulgar Norfolk term for a militiaman in his red tunic ... was a 'red herring'.

A.M. Samuel: *The Herring* (1918)

Thomas Nashe satirized the town and its smoked herrings in his *Lenten Stuffe* (1599). In the 19th century the Victorians discovered Great Yarmouth's fine sandy beach, and a new career as a seaside resort was launched. It is also an important centre for boating on the Norfolk BROADS.

In Charles Dickens's *David Copperfield* (1849–50), Mr Peggotty and his family (Ham and Little Em'ly), together with Mrs Gummidge, live in a high-and-dry barge on the shore at Great Yarmouth:

I was quite tired, and very glad, when we saw Yarmouth. It looked rather spongy and soppy, I thought, as I carried my eye over the great dull waste that lay across the river; and I could not help wondering, if the world was really as round as my geography book said, how any part of it came to be so flat. But I reflected that Yarmouth might be situated at one of the poles, which would account for it ... Peggotty ... told me it was well known ... that Yarmouth was, upon the whole, the finest place in the universe.

The surgeon Sir James Paget (1814–99), who gave his name to Paget's disease (a disease of the bones), Francis Palgrave (1824–97), compiler of *The Golden Treasury of Best Songs and Lyrical Poems in the English Language* (1861), and Anna Sewell (1820–78), author of *Black Beauty* (1877), were all born in Great Yarmouth.

The town is not to be confused with YARMOUTH[1] on the Isle of Wight.

As I rode down to Yarmouth fair
The birds they sang 'Good day, good day',
And the birds they sang 'Good day!'

Hal Collins: 'Yarmouth Fair' (1924)

go Yarmouth, to. Twentieth-century naval slang meaning 'to go mad', inspired by the Royal Navy hospital at Great Yarmouth.

Greek Street From the Greek Orthodox refugees from Turkish rule that gathered here in the late 17th century.

A street in SOHO, in the West End of London, running roughly north–south between Soho Square and SHAFTESBURY AVENUE. Amongst its legitimate delights are the restaurants 'The Gay Hussar' (purveyor of Hungarian cuisine since 1953 and a favourite of left-wing politicians) and 'L'Escargot', and it is also home to the 'Coach and Horses' pub, where the inebriated *Spectator* columnist Jeffrey Bernard was a fixture in the latter part of the 20th century.

Green Bridge of Wales. *See under* WALES.

Greencastle From the Anglo-Norman castle built here in the 14th century, itself probably so named because of the lush countryside roundabout.

A small resort on the INISHOWEN peninsula, County Donegal, at the mouth of Lough Foyle (*see under* FOYLE). Richard de Burgo built the eponymous castle here in 1305, but shortly afterwards it fell into Irish hands, and remained so until the whole of Inishowen was granted to the planter Sir Arthur Chichester in 1608. The ruins of the castle, together with a Napoleonic-era fort, can still be seen.

There is a town called Greencastle in the USA (Indiana).

Greendale. The fictional Lake District locale for the *Postman Pat* animated children's television series, first aired on the BBC in 1981 and still in production. Here, the lovably bumbling Pat drives his red van, accompanied by his faithful cat Jess, as he attempts (usually with difficulty) to deliver mail to the likes of Reverend Timms, Granny Dryden and the local handyman Ted Glen. The series was inspired by its local creator John Cunliffe's love for his mainly Cumbrian heritage, including LANGDALE.

Greenham Common *Greenham* 'green enclosure or river-meadow', OE *grene* 'green' + *hamm* 'enclosure, river-meadow' (*see* HAM).

A stretch of common land to the south and east of Greenham, a village on the southern edge of Newbury, Berkshire. It was formerly the site of a US airbase which at the beginning of the 1980s was designated as the first UK cruise missile base. From 1981 until its closure in 1991 this was the focal point of a camp of 'peace women' (known at the time as **Greenham women** or **Greenham Common women**), protesting against the presence of such weapons on British soil. At the peak of their protest in December 1982 some 30,000 women encircled the perimeter fence. The camp was not disbanded until 1999. The 'green' place name was coincidentally appropriate for the stance.

Greenholm Possibly 'green island' or 'green water-meadow', OScand *grœnn* 'green' + *holmr* 'island, water-meadow' (*see* -EY, -EA).

A small town in East Ayrshire (formerly in Strathclyde region), 11 km (6.5 miles) east of Kilmarnock.

Greenigo Etymology unknown.

A small settlement on Mainland in ORKNEY, 5 km (3 miles) southwest of Kirkwall.

Greenisland Self-explanatory.

A town in County Antrim, on the north shore of Belfast Lough (*see under* BELFAST), just northeast of Newtonabbey.

Greenock 'sunny knoll', Gaelic *grianág*.

An industrial town on the south shore of the Firth of Clyde (*see under* CLYDE), some 35 km (21 miles) west of Glasgow, in Inverclyde (formerly in Renfrewshire, and then in Strathclyde region). It was formerly an important port and shipbuilding centre. Greenock was the headquarters of the Free French naval forces in the Second World War, and was the location for Ken Loach's controversial film *Sweet Sixteen* (2002). Glaswegians refer to the Greenock–Port Glasgow conurbation as **Wine City**, implying that the inhabitants are more than commonly fond of the less prestigious brands of fortified wine.

Greenock was the birthplace of Captain William Kidd (*c*.1645–1701), the pirate (executed in Wapping (*see under* EXECUTION DOCK)); James Watt (1736–1819), inventor of the double-acting steam engine; the painter Sir James Guthrie (1859–1930), one of the Glasgow Boys (*see under* GLASGOW); the abstract painter William Scott (1913–89); and the poet W.S. Graham (1918–86):

> As for you loud Greenock long ropeworking
> Hide and seeking rivetting town of my child
> Hood, I know we think of us mostly
> At night.
>
> W.S. Graham : 'Greenock at night I find you', from
> *Implements in their Places* (1977)

The novelist John Galt (1779–1839), author of *Annals of the Parish* (1821) and other works, died here, as did Robert Burns's beloved Mary Campbell ('Highland Mary'), in 1786 (*see* DUNOON).

greenockite. A mineral consisting of cadmium sulphide, the only ore of the metal cadmium. It was first found in Renfrewshire when a railway tunnel was being built for the Glasgow–Greenock line, and was identified in 1840 by Professor Jameson of Edinburgh University, who named it after Lord Greenock, the owner of the site.

Greenock Morton FC. Greenock's professional football club, founded in 1874 and so named because the founders of the club lived in Morton Terrace. Nicknamed the Ton, the club is based at Cappielow Park, and is generally referred to as Morton.

Green Park Probably simply from its verdure (apart from spring bulbs, it has very few flowers), but a more circumstantial account of the name's origin has it that the deer in an enclosure that once existed in the upper part of the park kept the grass cropped like a green lawn.

A Royal Park in Central London (SW1), in the City of WEST-MINSTER, 21.5 ha (53 acres) in extent, bounded to the north-west by PICCADILLY[1], to the south by CONSTITUTION HILL and to the east by Queen's Walk (named after Queen Caroline, wife of George II). Buckingham Palace is just to the south. It was originally part of St James's Park (*see under* ST JAMES'S), to the east, but by the middle of the 18th century it was a separate entity. In the 18th and 19th centuries it was a favourite venue for grand and spectacular celebratory events, generally featuring fireworks (the most famous were probably those in 1749 for the Treaty of Aix-la-Chapelle (1748) for which Handel wrote his 'Music for the Royal Fireworks' – the display was spoiled by the weather, and half the fireworks failed to ignite), and also for balloon ascents. Eighteenth-century duellists also patronized it. Between the First and Second World Wars, according to H.V. Morton (*London* (1951)), it was:

> the dormitory of every idle and destitute person in the city. Many of them were tramps, a race that appears to be dying out, some were hard-luck cases, but the majority were known to the park keepers as 'regulars'.

In the 18th and 19th centuries, and into the early 20th, it was customary to refer to the park as '**the Green Park**', but the last adherents of that usage have now died out, and it is universally known simply as 'Green Park'.

Green Park Underground station, on the Jubilee, Piccadilly and Victoria lines, opened in 1906 (originally as 'Dover Street'; it was renamed 'Green Park' in 1933 – which may well have contributed to the dropping of the definite article from the park's name).

Greensted-juxta-Ongar *Greensted* 'green place' (that is, a pasture used for grazing); *juxta Ongar* from its proximity (Latin *juxta* 'near, beside') to CHIPPING ONGAR, just to the east.

A village in Essex, about 8 km (5 miles) east of Epping. It contains one of the few Saxon churches surviving in England, which may date back to around 850.

Greenwich 'green trading settlement or harbour' (perhaps referring to grass or other vegetation), OE *grene* 'green' + *wic* (*see* WICK).

A town and borough (pronounced 'grenidge', 'grenitch', 'grinidge' or 'grinitch') within southeastern Greater London (SE10), on the south bank of the River THAMES[1], between DEPTFORD to the west and WOOLWICH to the east. The borough was formed in 1965 from the former metropolitan boroughs of Greenwich and Woolwich.

Greenwich has important royal connections going back to the Middle Ages. **Greenwich Palace**, built by Henry V's brother Humphrey, Duke of Gloucester in 1427, was the birthplace of Henry VIII, Mary I and Elizabeth I, and it was

Henry VIII's favourite residence. James VI and I gave it to his queen, Anne of Denmark, and it was for her that Inigo Jones designed and built the Queen's House, the first Renaissance building in England. At the end of the 17th century the palace was demolished and replaced by Christopher Wren's spectacular Royal Naval Hospital (framing the Queen's House, which Wren was prevented from pulling down). In 1869 the Hospital, with its pensioners (the Naval equivalent of the Army's Chelsea Pensioners – many of them with peg-legs or piratical eye-patches), moved out, and from 1873 the building was occupied by the Royal Naval College. This closed in 1996. The Queen's House, meanwhile, now houses part of the National Maritime Museum (opened in 1937; *see also under* FALMOUTH). The combined vista of all these buildings from the opposite bank of the Thames is breathtaking:

> ... Greenwich Hospital, which from this point looks exactly like Somerset House with two St Paul's Cathedrals at the back of it and Hyde Park cocked up behind it. I daresay the reader knows ... that Greenwich Hospital is the most beautiful thing on the Thames, and that to approach that lovely piece of riverside architecture, built partly by Inigo Jones and partly by Christopher Wren, is to feel oneself lifted up on the wings of the morning and carried away into those regions of the heavens where the old sea captains of England sing their nautical songs and sturdily refuse to learn any foreign tongue.
>
> Harold Begbie: *The Take of the Thames* (1920)

The royal connection was continued in the 20th century when Prince Philip was given the title 'Baron of Greenwich' in 1947 on the eve of his marriage to the future Queen Elizabeth II.

Greenwich's long association with naval and maritime affairs was symbolized in 1954 when the tea clipper *Cutty Sark* was put on public exhibition in dry dock there. In 1968 it was joined at Greenwich Pier by *Gipsy Moth IV*, the yacht in which Sir Francis Chichester made the first single-handed circumnavigation of the world. In 1997 this whole historic centre of Greenwich, known as 'Maritime Greenwich', was declared a UNESCO World Heritage Site.

In 1675 the Royal Observatory was built on elevated ground in Greenwich Park, to designs by Christopher Wren. The first Astronomer Royal, John Flamsteed, and his successors (including Edmund Halley) have made many notable contributions to astronomy and related sciences, particularly in the fields of navigation and time measurement (*see* **Greenwich Meridian** *below*). Since 1833 a time ball has been dropped on a turret of the Observatory at one o'clock precisely. In the 1950s the Observatory, bedevilled by London's smoke and fog, moved its instruments and staff to HERSTMONCEUX Castle in Sussex. Fictionally, the

Observatory is the first target of the revolutionaries in Joseph Conrad's *The Secret Agent* (1907), but the bomb goes off prematurely, killing the innocent Stevie.

Greenwich Peninsula, to the east of Maritime Greenwich, juts northwards into the Thames. It contains the southern entrance to the BLACKWALL Tunnel, and in 1999 it became home to the MILLENNIUM DOME. North Greenwich Underground station, on the Jubilee line, opened in 1999. The **University of Greenwich** was formed in 1992 from the former Thames Polytechnic.

The thriller writer Edgar Wallace (1875–1932) was born in Greenwich. St Aelfheah, Archbishop of Canterbury, was martyred by the Danes at Greenwich in 1012, after first being bombarded with ox bones. Greenwich parish church is dedicated to him.

There are towns called Greenwich in the USA (Connecticut, Kansas, Ohio and Utah), and the residential district of Greenwich Village in Manhattan, New York City, has a long-standing reputation for bohemianism.

Greenwich barber. An 18th- and 19th-century slang term applied to the people who obtained and sold sand from the Greenwich sandpits. The underlying metaphor is of the sellers 'shaving' the sand for their product.

Greenwich goose. 18th- and 19th-century slang for a pensioner of Greenwich Royal Naval Hospital.

Greenwich Mean Time. The mean solar time of the Greenwich Meridian, used formerly as the reference point for standard time throughout the world. Its usual abbreviation is **GMT**. It was replaced in 1986 by Coordinated Universal Time.

Greenwich Meridian. The meridian passing through the Royal Observatory at Greenwich, officially designated as 0°. In former times most countries treated their own capital as the point through which the zero degree of longitude passed, but at an international conference held in Washington in 1884 it was agreed that everyone would henceforth recognize Greenwich's as the prime meridian, from which degrees to East and West would be measured. The line is now marked at the Observatory by a brass rail set into the ground.

The name *Greenwich* means 'green harbour' and it in turn links with *Valverde*, 'green valley', in the Canary Islands, on a line of longitude which in 1637 Louis XIII of France ordered geographers to take as the 0° meridian. Louis XIV later overturned his father's decree when in 1667 he constructed the Paris Observatory on a new 0° meridian at a site south of (now part of) the city called *Vauvert*, a name also meaning 'green valley'.

Greenwich Park. A park to the rear of the National Maritime Museum, Greenwich, stretching back to BLACKHEATH. It is the oldest of London's Royal Parks, having been originally enclosed in 1433. It was opened to the public in the 18th century. It contains the original Royal Observatory.

Greenwich Theatre. A small theatre that opened in Greenwich in 1969 on the site of a former music hall. Many distinguished actors and musicians have performed there including Tom Courtenay, Michael Gambon, Mia Farrow, Glenda Jackson and Max Wall.

Greenwich Tunnel. A pedestrian tunnel opened at the beginning of the 20th century between Greenwich and the Isle of Dogs, to replace a former ferry.

Treaty of Greenwich. An Anglo-Scottish agreement of 1543 by which the infant Mary Queen of Scots was to marry the future Edward VI. Mary's mother, the Catholic Mary of Guise, abrogated the treaty, resulting in the English attacks known as 'the Rough Wooing' (*see* Ancrum; Pinkie).

Greet 'gravelly place', OE *greote*.
A village in Gloucestershire, on the River Isbourne, at the northwestern edge of the Cotswolds, about 11 km (7 miles) northeast of Cheltenham.

Gresford 'grassy ford', OE *græs* 'grass' + Ford.
A village in Wrexham unitary authority (formerly in Denbighshire, then in Clwyd), 5 km (3 miles) north of Wrexham itself. The bells at Gresford were one of the so-called Seven Wonders of North Wales.

Greta 'stony stream', OScand *grjot* 'stone, gravel' + *a* 'stream'.
A river in County Durham, joining the River Tees near the village of **Greta Bridge**, some 5 km (3 miles) southeast of Barnard Castle. It is approximately 30 km (19 miles) long. The river gave Coleridge the subject of a meditation:

> River Greta near its fall into the Tees: shootings of water threads down the slope of the huge green stone. The *white rose* of eddy-foam, where the stream ran into a scooped or scolloped hollow of the rock in its channel – this shape, an exact white rose, was forever over-powered by the stream rushing down in upon it and, still obstinate in resurrection, it spread up into the scollop by fits and starts, *blossoming* in a moment into full flower. It *is the life* that we live. I hung over the bridge and, musing, considered how much of this scene of endless variety-in-identity was Nature's, how much the living organ's!
>
>   Samuel Taylor Coleridge: journal (28 October 1799)

The bridge at Greta Bridge was the subject of a famous watercolour by John Sell Cotman (1805), and was also painted by Turner. Nearby is the estate of Rokeby, and in a cave near the bridge Sir Walter Scott is said to have begun his poem of that name.

> For louder clamour'd Greta's tide,
> And Tees in deeper voice replied,
> And fitful waked the evening wind,
> Fitful in sighs its breath resign'd.
>
>   Sir Walter Scott: *Rokeby* (1813), Canto V, ii

Gretna 'gravelly projecting piece of land ', OE *greotan* 'gravelly' + *hoh* 'projecting piece of land, hill'; *Gretenho* 1223.
A Scottish village 14 km (8.5 miles) northwest of Carlisle, situated at the most southerly point of the border with England, formerly in Dumfriesshire and now in Dumfries and Galloway. It encompasses the villages of **Gretna Green** and Springfield. The former was for long associated with illicit marriages. Elopers from England, on crossing the border into Scotland, could (until 1856) get legally married without licence, banns or priest; all that was required was a declaration before witnesses of the couple's willingness to marry. This declaration was generally made to a blacksmith, landlord, toll-keeper or other local official.

Gretna Green – where the blacksmith's smithy is preserved as the site of many such marriages – rose to prominence following the Hardwicke Marriage Act of 1753 that sought to abolish the clandestine marriage of minors. By an Act of 1856 residence in Scotland for at least 21 days by one of the parties became obligatory before a marriage was possible. Although marriage by declaration ceased to be legal in July 1940, Gretna Green and other places in Scotland continued to attract young couples because minors over the age of 16 could still marry there without parental consent. Since the act of 1969 that fixed the legal age of majority at 18, however, this no longer applies. Even so, many couples still seek to be married at Gretna Green for the romantic associations. There are references to elopements (or intended elopements) to Gretna Green in Jane Austen's novels *Pride and Prejudice* (1813) and *Mansfield Park* (1814).

> Their town was large, and seldom pass'd a day
> But some had fail'd, and others gone astray;
> Clerks had absconded, wives eloped, girls flown
> To Gretna-Green, or sons rebellious grown …
>
>   George Crabbe: *Tales in Verse* (1812)

> There was an old person of Gretna
> Who rushed to the crater of Etna.
> When they said, 'Is it hot?'
> He replied, 'No it is not,'
> That mendacious old person of Gretna.
>
>   Edward Lear: limerick

Gretna Green Rail Disaster. The United Kingdom's worst-ever rail disaster, which took place on 22 May 1915 and killed 227 people. One minute after the collision of a south-bound troop train with a stationary local train at Quintins-hill, near Gretna Green, a northbound express ploughed into the wreckage, causing a devastating fire which engulfed a further two trains. 214 of the dead were passengers on the troop train.

Gretta Greene. The name mischievously adopted by Nora Barnacle at the time of her marriage to James Joyce in London in 1931, in order to avoid publicity. They had already cohabited for some three decades, their original elopement from Dublin to the Continent having taken place in 1904.

See also Lochmaben Stone *under* LOCHMABEN.

Grey Auld Toon, the. A name by which HAWICK is sometimes known.

Grey Corries, the A literal translation of the Gaelic name *Na Coireachan Lèithe*, and referring to the grey quartzite screes on the flanks of the mountains.

A long, high, remote and many-peaked ridge starting some 5 km (3 miles) east of BEN NEVIS and extending northeastward parallel to Glen Spean for 7 km (4 miles). There are several tops over 1000 m (3280 ft), the highest of which is Stob Choire Claurigh (1177 m / 3861 ft). Combining the Grey Corries, the Aonachs (*see* AONACH BEAG) and Ben Nevis in one day is a sturdy achievement; linking this route, as has been done, with a traverse of the MAMORES within 24 hours, while laudably heroic, would tend to indicate a need for psychiatric treatment.

Greyfriars Kirkyard 'churchyard of the grey friars', i.e. the Franciscans.

A historical cemetery in EDINBURGH's Old Town, to the south of the ROYAL MILE. The Franciscans established a monastery on the site in 1447, and offered medical care here to the poor until the Reformation. Mary Queen of Scots presented the site to the city as an overflow graveyard, and the present church dates from 1620. The National Covenant, signed by many Scots to confirm their allegiance to Presbyterianism, was inaugurated in the churchyard in 1638. In 1679 around 1200 Covenanters captured at the Battle of Bothwell Brig (*see under* BOTHWELL) were imprisoned here in a makeshift prison. Around a hundred were put to death, others died in the appalling conditions, while many survivors drowned when the ship transporting them to the West Indies foundered off Orkney. They are commemorated in the Martyrs' Monument (1771) in the kirkyard, which also holds the 'Black Mausoleum' of Bloody Mackenzie – Sir George Mackenzie, responsible for prosecuting the Covenanters after his appointment as lord advocate in 1677. In 2003 a teenager was arrested for hacking the mummified head off a corpse in the famously haunted Black Mausoleum, putting his fist in its neck and talking to the head 'like a glove puppet'; he was charged with 'violation of a sepulchre'. Needless to say, Greyfriars Kirkyard – and the violently haunted Black Mausoleum in particular – is the star attraction of the city's many ghost tours. It was also used as a location in the 1996 film version of Thomas Hardy's *Jude the Obscure*.

> Cauld blaws the nippin north wi' angry sough,
> And showers his hailstanes frae the Castle Cleugh
> O'er the Greyfriars, whare, at mirkest hour,

> Bogles and spectres wont to tak their tour,
> Harlin the pows and shanks to hidden cairns ...

> Robert Fergusson: 'The Ghaists: A Kirk-Yard Eclogue' (1773)
> (Scots *harlin* 'hauling, dragging', *pows* 'heads')

Greyfriars Bobby. A Skye terrier who was so attached to his master, John Gray, that after the latter died in 1858 the dog guarded his grave in the kirkyard for 14 years, being fed and petted by the local citizenry until he too passed away. Bobby is also buried in the kirkyard, albeit in unconsecrated ground, and there is a statue of him near the front entrance. This sentimental story was seized upon by the Victorian writer Eleanor Atkinson, later filmed as *Challenge to Lassie* in 1949, and by Walt Disney as *Greyfriars Bobby* in 1961. A further film was in production in 2004.

Grey Man's Path. *See under* FAIR HEAD.

Grey Mare's Tail, the Named after its fancied resemblance to the tail of a white ('grey' in horsey-speak) horse.

A striking 60 m (200 ft) high waterfall, formerly in Dumfriesshire, now in Dumfries and Galloway, 8 km (5 miles) southwest of St Mary's Loch. The fall breaks the course of the **Tail Burn** (presumably a back-formation from the name of the waterfall) as it runs down from the high hill loch of Loch Skene to join Moffat Water (*see under* MOFFAT). Scott describes the Tail Burn's descent from 'dark Loch-skene' in *Marmion*:

> Through the rude barriers of the lake,
> Away its hurrying waters break,
> Faster and whiter dash and curl,
> Till down yon dark abyss they hurl.

> Sir Walter Scott: *Marmion* (1808), Introduction to Canto II

There are two smaller waterfalls in southwest Scotland also called the Grey Mare's Tail: one a little southwest of Clatteringshaws Loch (*see under* CLATTERINGSHAWS) and one near THORNHILL.

Greys Green *Greys* denoting manorial ownership in the Middle Ages by the de Gray family (the same family as owned the nearby ROTHERFIELD GREYS).

A village in Oxfordshire, in the CHILTERN HILLS, about 5 km (3 miles) west of Henley-on-Thames.

Greystones Irish *Na Clocha Liatha* 'the grey stones'.

A seaside resort on the east coast of County Wicklow, 5 km (3 miles) south of Bray.

Grianán of Aileach. An alternative name for the Irish fortress of AILEACH.

Griff '(place at the) deep valley or hollow', OScand *gryfja* (there is a quarry nearby known tautologically as *Griff Hollows*).

A village in Warwickshire, about 2.5 km (1.5 miles) south of Nuneaton.

Grimes Graves Perhaps 'Woden's pits', *Grimes* possessive form of OE *Grim* 'Woden (the supreme god of the ancient

Germanic peoples)'; *Graves* OE *grœfas* plural of *grœf* 'pit' (many place names attribute ancient or spectacular sites to gods).

A Neolithic site in Thetford Forest (*see under* THETFORD), in the BRECKLAND of southwest Norfolk, about 8 km (5 miles) northwest of Thetford. It is a prehistoric flint mine – the largest in Europe – consisting of 350 holes in the ground linked by a maze of 9 m (30 ft) deep underground passages. Here 4000 years ago flints for use as arrowheads and axes were extracted with deer-antler picks.

Grimethorpe 'Grimr's outlying farm', OScand male personal name *Grimr* + THORPE; the early forms have the possessive form *Grims*- but the -s- was later lost.

A former pit village in South Yorkshire. The **Grimethorpe Colliery Band**, one of the most famous in the country, was formed in 1917. It has commissioned works from the avant-garde likes of Hans Werner Henze and Harrison Birtwistle, and provided the soundtrack for the 1996 film *Brassed Off* (*see also* HATFIELD²), which tells the story of a fictional colliery band which wins a national competition shortly after the closure of the pit is announced – which is exactly what happened to the Grimethorpe players in 1992.

Grimpen Mire. An extensive area of desolate, treacherous, mist-wreathed DARTMOOR bog, apparently a fictionalized version of GRIMSPOUND Bog. It provides the dark focus of the action in Arthur Conan Doyle's *The Hound of the Baskervilles* (1902). The villain Stapleton kept his 'spectral' hound on an island in the bog, and lost no opportunity to expand on the terrain's flesh-creeping qualities:

> 'This is the great Grimpen Mire,' said he. 'A false step yonder means death to man or beast. Only yesterday I saw one of the moor ponies wander into it. He never came out. I saw his head for quite a long time craning out of the bog-hole, but it sucked him down at last. Even in dry seasons it is a danger to cross it, but after these autumn rains it is an awful place. And yet I can find my way to the very heart of it and return alive.'

In the end, though, his boast proved vain:

> If the earth told a true story, then Stapleton never reached that island of refuge towards which he struggled through the fog upon that last night. Somewhere in the heart of the great Grimpen Mire, down in the foul slime of the huge morass which had sucked him in, this cruel and cold-hearted man is forever buried.

Conan Doyle's creation subsequently enjoyed some limited generic use:

> In a dark wood, in a bramble,
> On the edge of a grimpen, where is no secure foothold.
>
> T.S. Eliot: 'East Coker' (1940)

Grimpo Origin uncertain: the second element is probably from OE *hoh* 'hill-spur'.

A village in Shropshire, about 8 km (5 miles) southeast of Oswestry.

Grimsby 'Grimr's farmstead or village', OScand male personal name *Grimr* + -BY. (According to legend, Grimr was an 11th-century Danish fisherman. In the early 14th-century verse romance *The Lay of Havelock the Dane*, Grimr (or Grim) saves the young Havelock, prince of Denmark, whom he had been ordered to murder, by escaping with him to England. Grimr now figures in Grimsby's seal.)

A town and port in North East Lincolnshire (before 1996 in Humberside, before 1974 in Lincolnshire), on the southern bank of the mouth of the River HUMBER, about 25 km (15 miles) southeast of Hull. It is the administrative centre of North East Lincolnshire.

Grimsby was an important market town in the Middle Ages, but problems with silting ensured that its harbour could operate only on a small scale. When these were solved around 1800 by the diversion of a river, however, the town was well placed to take advantage of the 19th-century discovery of new fishing grounds in the North Sea and the application of steam power to fishing vessels. The rapid spread of the railways meant that unsalted fish could be transported inland before it went off, and as British workers enthusiastically took to fried fish (mainly cod), later fish and chips, as a staple, Grimsby and its near neighbour Hull prospered as England's premier fishing ports. North Sea fish stocks began to decline in the 1890s, but the Grimsby fleet just went further afield for its catch, to Iceland.

The prosperous times lasted until the 1970s, when first the 'Cod Wars' (disputes over territorial limits) led to the closure of the Icelandic fisheries, and then drastic falls in fish stocks (including the near commercial extinction of the cod) resulted in extensive cuts in fishing quotas. At the end of the 20th century the once bustling quays and markets of Grimsby had fallen silent. In 2001 Grimsby's Labour MP, Austin Mitchell, changed his name by deed poll to Austin Haddock, in an effort to promote the fishing industry.

John Whitgift (*c*.1530–1604), Archbishop of Canterbury (1583–1604), was born in Grimsby.

Grimsby docks. Rhyming slang in the 20th century for *socks*.

Grim's Ditch *See* GRIM'S DYKE.

An ancient earthwork in southern Oxfordshire, running to the north of the RIDGEWAY, from southeast of WANTAGE to south of Chilton.

Grim's Dyke 'ditch associated with Grim', OE *Grim* probably a nickname for the heathen god Woden, who the superstitious Anglo-Saxon settlers thought dug the ditch + *dic* 'ditch'.

The remains of a massive 5th-century earthwork which can still be seen in HARROW, PINNER and STANMORE, northwest London.

Grimsdyke House in HARROW WEALD, designed by Norman Shaw in 1872, takes its name from the earthwork. The librettist and poet W.S. Gilbert (1836–1911) lived here, and died of heart failure in the lake in the grounds when trying to rescue a young woman from drowning.

Grimspound 'Woden's, or the Devil's, cattle enclosure', OE *Grimes* possessive form of *Grim* 'Woden (the supreme god of the ancient Germanic peoples, whose name later came to be used as an epithet of the Devil)' + *pund* 'enclosure for stray cattle'.

A Bronze Age walled settlement on DARTMOOR, about 8 km (5 miles) southwest of Moretonhampstead. It contains the remains of over 20 stone hut circles. Its name and location inspired the GRIMPEN MIRE of Arthur Conan Doyle's *The Hound of the Baskervilles* (1902).

Grimsthorpe 'Grimr's outlying farmstead or hamlet', OScand male personal name *Grimr* + THORPE.

A village in Lincolnshire, about 19 km (12 miles) south-east of Grantham. A little to the southwest is **Grimsthorpe Castle**, ancestral home of the earls of Ancaster and the grandest house in Lincolnshire. It is mainly Tudor, though parts of it date back to the 13th century. It stands in the 800 ha (2000 acre) **Grimsthorpe Park**.

Grisedale 'valley of pigs', OScand *griss* 'young pig' + *dalr* 'valley'.

A steep-sided valley on the east side of HELVELLYN, in the LAKE DISTRICT, Cumbria. On the north side is Striding Edge, on the south St Sunday Crag, while along the bottom runs **Grisedale Beck**. This stream has its source in **Grisedale Tarn**, nestled high between Dollywaggon Pike and Fairfield. According to one version of the story, it was into Grisedale Tarn that the golden crown of Domhnall, last king of Cumbria, was thrown after his death at the Battle of DUNMAIL RAISE in AD 945.

> Grisdale Tarn, rolling towards its outlet like a sea. The gust on the broad beck snatching up water made the smooth and level water as full of small breakers and white waves as the rough and steep part.
>
> Samuel Taylor Coleridge: journal (8 June 1802)

On the west side of Fairfield is the pass called **Grisedale Hause**. GRISEDALE PIKE does not belong to this cluster, being situated some 20 km (12.5 miles) to the northwest.

Grisedale Pike 'mountain peak at GRISEDALE', with OScand *pik* 'mountain peak'.

A mountain (790 m / 2591 ft) in the northwestern LAKE DISTRICT, Cumbria (formerly in Cumberland), 8 km (5 miles) west of Keswick. Grisedale itself is not marked on the Ordnance Survey 1:50,000 map, although **Grisedale Gill** flows northwestward down a narrow cwm from the summit. All this is not to be confused with the GRISEDALE on the east side of Helvellyn.

See also GLARAMARA.

Grizedale 'valley of the young pigs', OScand *griss* 'young pig' + *dalr* 'dale'.

A village in the LAKE DISTRICT, Cumbria, 10 km (6 miles) southwest of Ambleside, between WINDERMERE and CONISTON WATER. The surrounding area has been turned into **Grizedale Forst Park**. Here, since 1977, artists have been invited to create sculptures using natural materials. There are now some 80 pieces, including works by Andy Goldsworthy, and they are linked by a 16-km (10-mile) trail called the Silurian Way, named after the geological time period in which the slate and shale rocks of the area were formed.

Grongar Hill *Grongar* possibly 'round fort', Welsh *gron* 'round' + *caer* (*see* CAHER).

A small hill surmounted by a hillfort in the Vale of Towy, in Carmarthenshire (formerly in Dyfed), some 15 km (9 miles) east of Carmarthen. It is the subject of a long poem of the same name by John Dyer (1699–1758), who lived nearby at Aberglasney House, below the village of Llangathen. The poem, which describes the views from the summit (where Dyer sat under a blackthorn tree, now gone), is a notable early example of topographical poetry:

> Gawdy as the op'ning Dawn,
> Lies a long and level Lawn,
> On which a dark Hill, steep and high,
> Holds and charms the wand'ring Eye!
> Deep are his Feet in *Towy's* Flood,
> His sides are cloath'd with waving Wood
> And antient towers crown his brow,
> That cast an awful Look below …
>
> John Dyer: *Grongar Hill* (1726)

Grosvenor Square *Grosvenor* from the family name of the Dukes of Westminster, on whose estate the square was laid out.

A square (pronounced 'grove-ner') in the WEST END[1] of London (W1), in MAYFAIR, to the south of OXFORD STREET and the east of PARK LANE. Laid out in the 1720s, it is the second-largest square in London. For the first two hundred years or so of its existence it maintained a highly exclusive residential status, its rents more than high enough to keep out any riffraff. In the 20th century the aristocrats and financiers have slowly given way to embassies and businesses.

From early on the square had a US connection – John Adams, America's first 'minister plenipotentiary' to Britain, lived here in the 1780s – and this is now embodied in the US Embassy, built in the late 1950s on the west side of the square. During the Second World War, the buildings around the square were so thickly occupied by US military head-quarters that it was nicknamed EISENHOWER PLATZ. (Another nickname for the square is **Little America**.) A statue of F.D. Roosevelt, the USA's wartime president, stands in the centre of the square. On 27 October 1968 the square was the scene of serious rioting, led by Tariq Ali, who brought 5000 demonstrators from an anti-Vietnam-War rally in Hyde Park in a breakaway group to the US Embassy. Opponents of the war continued to make their case there into the 1970s, and not inappropriately **Grosvenor Squares** became a rhyming-slang name for that essential bit of 1970s gear, flared trousers ('flares').

Traffic can no longer circulate the square, following the cordoning-off of the west side (outside the embassy) after the New York terrorist attacks of 11 September 2001. It was the focal point of a two-minute silence in the week after that event, when hundreds of people filed into the square to sign a book of remembrance.

Grovely Wood *Grovely* probably 'clearing of or in the grove', OE *grafa* 'grove, copse' + -LEY.

A wood in Wiltshire, about 5 km (3 miles) northwest of Wilton. In 1603 the people of the nearby village of Great Wishford were granted the right to gather wood for all time from Grovely Wood. Once a year on 29 May by way of confirming the privilege they march to the wood, cut branches and carry them back to the village. They then process through the streets bearing a banner with the words 'Grovely! Grovely! Grovely! and all Grovely! Unity is strength', chanting the words 'Grovely, Grovely and Grovely' as they go.

Grub Street Probably named after an unidentified family called *Grubbe*, but possibly denoting a street infested with caterpillars or worms.

The former name of a street in the City of London (EC2), in the MOORGATE area, now called Milton Street. Since at least the late Middle Ages it seems to have attracted writers (John Foxe, compiler of the *Book of Martyrs*, had a house here in the late 16th century), and by the 17th century it had the reputation of being, as Dr Johnson later put it, 'much inhabited by writers of small histories, dictionaries and temporary poems'. The expression 'Grub Street' is on record as having been used by writers of the time (including Andrew Marvell and Thomas Shadwell) as a metonym for impecunious penny-a-liners, uninspired literary hacks and (in the contemporary idiom) quill-drivers. Quite possibly it was these unflattering connotations that in the 1820s led the residents to insist on a change of name, substituting that of the owner of the building lease.

The name Grub Street has been adopted, with a certain self-deprecating irony, by a London firm of book publishers.

Grub Street Journal, The. A literary newspaper published between 1730 and 1737. It was noted for its barbed attacks on contemporary writers and other journals. The poet and satirist Alexander Pope is said to have had a hand in it, although the connection has never been definitively proved.

Grub Street news. Late-17th- and 18th-century slang for 'rumours' or plain 'lies'.

New Grub Street. A novel (1891) by George Gissing highlighting the economic realities of literary life and the stultifying effect of financial necessity on artistic aspiration.

Gruinard Bay *Gruinard* possibly 'green firth', OScand *groenn* 'green' + -*ard*, contraction of *fjord* (OScand *fjorthr*).

A bay on the northwest coast of Scotland, between LOCH EWE and Little LOCH BROOM, in Highland (formerly in Ross and Cromarty), 20 km (12.5 miles) west of Ulla-pool. It is fed by the **Gruinard River** and the **Little Gruinard River**, which rise in the Fisherfield Forest to the south.

In the bay is the small, uninhabited **Gruinard Island**, nicknamed **Anthrax Island** because during the Second World War it was seeded with anthrax spores as an experi-ment in biological warfare. The contamination persisted for many years, and landing on the island was strictly forbidden until 1990, when the Ministry of Defence declared the island free of anthrax.

Guagán Barra Irish, 'mountain recess of Barra', referring to *Barra* or *Bairre*, alternative names of St Finbarr.

A beautiful valley nestling among the dramatic SHEHY MOUNTAINS of County Cork, some 20 km (12 miles) north-east of Bantry. It is also spelt **Gougane Barra**, and is in the **Guagan Barra Forest Park** (established in 1966). The small **Lake Gouganebarra** is the source of the River LEE[1], and on an island in the lake St Finbarr (patron saint of CORK) founded a monastery in the 6th century. The island subsequently become a place of pilgrimage, and in the 18th century Thomas Crofton Croker reported how St Finbarr's Well was crammed with diseased bodies looking for a cure, while on the shores of the lake the fitter pilgrims drank, danced and brawled. It was near the lake that Tim Buckley (1863–1945) and his wife Ansty (1872–1947) lived; his conversations and stories and her often bawdy interjec-tions were recorded by Eric Cross in *The Tailor and Ansty*, banned by the Irish censor in 1942, but later becoming a classic of Irish folklore.

Guaire. The Irish name for GOREY[2].

Gubbergill The second part is probably OScand *gil* 'ravine'; the first may be a personal name.

A village in Cumbria, 3 km (2 miles) north of Ravenglass.

Gudetown. John Galt's fictional version of his native IRVINE.

Guernsey Origin uncertain: the second element is 'island', from OScand *ey* (*see* -AY), and the first probably represents the possessive form of another OScand word, but the wide range of early spellings (some beginning with *Gu-*, others with *Gr-*) makes it very difficult to interpret.

An island in the ENGLISH CHANNEL, the second largest and most westerly of the CHANNEL ISLANDS, about 48 km (30 miles) west of the Cotentin Peninsula in Normandy, France. Its Roman name was **Sarnia** (the town of Clearwater in Ontario, Canada was originally (1836) named Sarnia, in honour of Guernsey). It is roughly triangular in shape, 62 sq km (24 sq miles) in area, hilly and rugged in the south but low-lying in the north. It has ten parishes: Castel, Forest, St Andrew, St Martin, St Peter Port, St Pierre du Bois, St Sampson, St Saviour, Torteval and Vale. Its capital is ST PETER PORT. The island was occupied by the Germans in the Second World War.

Guernsey is governed (under the British Crown) by a parliament known as the States of Deliberation. Its chief civil officer is the Bailiff, who is in charge of the 'Bailiwick' of Guernsey (this includes ALDERNEY, HERM, JETHOU and SARK as well as the island of Guernsey).

Its mild climate is ideal for the commercial cultivation of tomatoes and flowers and for the attraction of tourists. Its agriculture is dominated by dairy farming (*see* **Guernsey cattle** *below*). In the latter part of the 20th century Guernsey successfully developed the financial sector of its economy.

The French poet and novelist Victor Hugo lived in political exile in St Peter Port from 1856 to 1870.

guernsey. A thick knitted jumper of a type developed on Guernsey, traditionally worn by sailors. It is typically blue. In Australian English the term is applied to the sort of coloured vest worn by Australian Rules footballers; the expression *get a guernsey* means 'to be selected for a team' and hence, by extension, 'to win approval':

> John Stephenson chose a verse entirely preoccupied with lamentation in which the alleged solaces of faith do not get a guernsey.
>
> I. Warden: *Worst Of* (1980)

Guernsey cattle. A breed of cattle developed on Guernsey. They have a fawn and white coat and produce rich creamy milk. They are slightly larger than Jersey cattle (*see under* JERSEY).

Guernsey centaury. A tiny, yellow-flowered member of the gentian family (*Exaculum pusillum*) found in France and the Channel Islands.

Guernsey lily. An elegant plant of the amaryllis family, of probably Japanese or South African origin, with large umbels of deep orange-pink lily-like flowers. It is said to have been naturalized on Guernsey (whence its scientific name, *Nerine sarniensis*, after Sarnia, the Roman name for Guernsey) after bulbs were washed ashore from a wreck of a ship from Japan in about 1659. It inspired a poem by Christopher Smart:

> Ye beauties! O how great the sum
> Of sweetness that ye bring;
> On what a charity ye come
> To bless the latter spring!
> Like strangers on a rainy day.
>
> Christopher Smart: 'On a Bed of Guernsey Lilies' (1764) ('the latter spring' refers to the fact that the plant flowers in autumn)

Guide Post ModE, and presumably a reference to a way-mark of some kind.

A village in Northumberland, 5 km (3 miles) east of Morpeth.

Guildford Probably 'golden (i.e. sandy) ford', OE *gylde* 'yellow, golden' + FORD.

A town (pronounced 'gilfəd') in Surrey, on the River WEY[1], about 40 km (25 miles) southwest of London and 11 km (7 miles) south of Woking. It stands at the northern edge of the NORTH DOWNS, and is overlooked from the west by the HOG'S BACK. It is the county town of SURREY.

Guildford commands a pass through the Downs (the valley of the Wey), and a Norman castle was built here in the 12th century. Only the ruined keep of this survives, but enough fine old Georgian buildings still stand, notably in the High Street, for the centre of the town – seething mass of shopping as it is – to retain at least a hint of a past, more gracious age.

The brick-built cathedral, designed by Sir Edward Maufe, was consecrated in 1961. **Guildford Cathedral** stands on top of Stag Hill, and around its flanks is the campus of the University of Surrey, which was founded in 1966. The Yvonne Arnaud Theatre was opened in the town in 1965.

An inscription over the gate of Guildford's Royal Grammar School attributes its foundation to Edward VI in 1552. The most reliable early evidence of cricket in England is from 1550 when it was being played by schoolboys in Guildford.

The Labour politician John Strachey (1901–63) and the comic writer P.G. Wodehouse (1881–1975) were born in Guildford. Lewis Carroll died here in 1898, and Hilaire Belloc in 1953.

There is a town called Guildford in Western Australia, and there are towns called Guilford in Connecticut and Maine, USA, named after the Surrey Guildford.

> Ah, Guildford – the Tunbridge Wells of Surrey, where Jaguars roam wild and everything stops for gin.
>
> A.A. Gill: *Sunday Times* (2003)

Guildford Four. On 5 October 1974 two IRA bombs killed five people in two Guildford pubs. A month later two more were killed in an IRA bomb attack on a pub in Woolwich. Patrick Armstrong, Gerald Conlon, Paul Hill and Carole Richardson were subsequently arrested, charged with murder in both incidents and sentenced to life imprisonment. Irregularities in police evidence resulted in the release of all four in 1989. *In the Name of the Father*, a 1993 film based on the case, movingly explored the relationship between Gerald Conlon and his sick father, but was described by one critic as 'unashamed Irish myth-making' on account of the inaccuracies of its court-room dénouement.

John of Guildford. The earliest known English writer on heraldry: his *Tractatus de armis* ('Treatise on arms') was produced about 1394. His name was Latinized, with more ingenuity than etymological accuracy, as *Johannes de Bado Aureo* ('John of the Golden Bucket').

Guisborough 'Gigr's stronghold', OScand male personal name *Gigr* + OE *burh* (see BURY).
A market town in Redcar and Cleveland (formerly in the North Riding of Yorkshire, then in Cleveland), 13 km (8 miles) southeast of Middlesbrough.

There was long a belief that an underground tunnel ran from **Guisborough Priory** to a field in the neighbouring parish, and that in this tunnel was a chest of gold guarded by a raven. The treasure was only ever found by one man, but when the raven revealed itself to be the Devil, he fled.

Guiseley 'Gislic's clearing', OE male personal name *Gislic* + -LEY.
A town in West Yorkshire, 14 km (8.5 miles) northwest of Leeds.

Guiting Power *Guiting* originally a river name, 'running stream, stream with a good current', OE *gyte* 'flood, stream' + -ING; *Power* denoting manorial ownership in the Middle Ages by the le Poer family.
A village (pronounced 'guy-ting') in Gloucestershire, in the COTSWOLDS, about 16 km (10 miles) east of Cheltenham. A Festival of Music and Arts is held here every July. The Cotswold Farm Park, where many rare breeds of farm animals are kept, lies 5 km (3 miles) to the northeast. **Guiting Wood** lies to the northwest.
See also TEMPLE GUITING.

Gulland Rock *Gulland* 'land of the gull', ModE.
A rocky islet off the northwest coast of Cornwall, beyond the mouth of the River CAMEL, about 3 km (2 miles) northeast of TREVOSE HEAD.

Gullane Unknown, but possibly Gaelic *gollan* 'little loch', or *gualainn* 'at a shoulder', or *gamhlann* 'fold'.
A small seaside town (pronounced 'gill'ən') in East Lothian, 7 km (4.5 miles) southwest of North Berwick. The village was almost overwhelmed with drifting sand in the

17th century, but revived in the 19th century as a popular holiday and golfing centre (MUIRFIELD is one of its five courses). It is from 'Gillane Sands' that Alan Breck escapes to the Continent in Robert Louis Stevenson's *Catriona* (1893).

Gunn Possibly Cornish *goen* 'downland, heath'.
A village in north Devon, about 8 km (5 miles) east of Barnstaple.

Gunwalloe '(chapel of St) Winwaloe', from the Cornish name of the patron saint of the local church or chapel. Winwaloe is said to have been one of triplets, whose mother grew an extra breast to suckle them; and he healed his sister's eye which had been pecked out and eaten by a goose. Another version of his name appears in TOWEDNACK.
A fishing village on the south Cornish coast, about 12 km (7.5 miles) northwest of the LIZARD.

Gurney Slade *Gurney* referring to an early tenant from Gournay, Seine-Inférieure, France (a Hugo de Gournai is mentioned in Domesday Book); *Slade* perhaps 'valley', OE *slæd*.
A village in Somerset, in the MENDIP HILLS, about 6.5 km (4 miles) north of SHEPTON MALLET. The actor Anthony Newley adopted the name for a Walter Mitty-like character he devised and played in the 1960 television sitcom *The Strange World of Gurney Slade*. The programme's surreality (Slade talked to trees, brought inanimate objects to life, etc.) might be charitably described as ahead of its time.

Gussage All Saints *Gussage* probably 'gushing stream', originally the name of the river here; *All Saints* from the dedication of the local church.
A village in Dorset, about 19 km (11.5 miles) southeast of Shaftesbury.

Gussage St Michael *St Michael* from the dedication of the local church.
A village in Dorset, immediately to the northwest of Gussage All Saints.

Guyo-mengreskey tem. The Romany name for YORKSHIRE, according to George Borrow's *Romano Lavo-Lil* ('word book of the Romany', 1874). The name apparently means 'pudding eaters' country', presumably referring to Yorkshire puddings.

Guyzance An anglicized version of the French name *Guines*, the owners of the estate in the Middle Ages.
A small village on the River COQUET, Northumberland, 6 km (4 miles) west of Amble.

Gweedore Irish *Gaoth Dobhair* 'water inlet'.
A village in County Donegal, some 35 km (21 miles) northwest of Letterkenny. Gweedore is also the name of the rugged area in which the village is situated, forming the northwesternmost part of Donegal and culminating in BLOODY FORELAND. Gweedore was the birthplace of the

Manhattan gangster Vincent 'Mad Dog' Coll (1908–32); and of the musician Enya (b.1961), formerly of Clannad.

Fighting Priest of Gweedore, the. Father James McFadden (1842–1917), also known as *an Sagart Mór* ('the big priest'). McFadden was celebrated not only for keeping his flock on the straight and narrow, using physical force as required, but also for supporting his parishioners in their battles against eviction (witnessing these brutal evictions helped to persuade Maude Gonne of the necessity of war against England). After the death of a police inspector in a scuffle in nearby Derrybeg in 1889, he and 12 others were charged with murder; however, a deal was done with the prosecution that if they all pleaded guilty, there would be no death sentences. Somewhat controversially, McFadden was released, while some of the others got 30 years.

Gweek Either 'village', Cornish *gwig*, or 'hamlet', OE *wic* (*see* WICK).

A village in Cornwall, on the HELFORD estuary, about 5 km (3 miles) east of Helston. There is a Seal Sanctuary nearby.

Gwennap '(church of Saint) Wynup', from the Cornish name of the patron saint of the local church. She may have been one of the 24 children of the 5th- or 6th-century King Brychan of BRYCHEINIOG.

A village in Cornwall, about 5 km (3 miles) southeast of Redruth.

Gwennap Pit. A cavernous amphitheatre that is the result of subsidence caused by the local tin- and copper-mining operations. John Wesley, the founder of Methodism, preached here in 1762, and eventually it was adapted for permanent congregational use. Today it is a Methodist centre.

Gwennap Head *Gwennap* probably from the surname of families who originated in GWENNAP and moved across.

A headland in western Cornwall, about 4.5 km (3 miles) southeast of LAND'S END.

> He had a shit on Gwennap Head,
> It cost him nothing. Now he's dead.
>
> Auberon Waugh:, epitaph for one of 'these repulsive people in caravans', in *Private Eye* (11 June 1976)

Gwent Welsh *gwent*, originally 'field', later 'market place'.

An early medieval kingdom and former county of southeast Wales.

The territorial basis of the kingdom of Gwent was the area occupied by the Silures (*see* SILURIA), an ancient British people of southeast Wales (described by the Roman author Tacitus as being swarthy and curly-haired. The Silures put up stiff resistance to the Romans before being finally subdued in AD 60), after which they were granted a self-governing *civitas* with a capital at Venta Silurum (CAER-WENT). The kingdom of Gwent emerged after the Roman period. It was united in the 8th century with GLYWYSIG to

form MORGANNWG (Glamorgan), and disintegrated following Norman colonization in the reign of William the Conqueror (1066–87).

The county of Gwent was created in 1974 from most of MONMOUTHSHIRE and part of BRECKNOCKSHIRE, and was bounded on the east by Gloucestershire, to the north by Hereford and Worcester and Powys, to the west by Mid Glamorgan, and to the south by the Bristol Channel. The administrative seat was at NEWPORT[1], and other towns included CAERLEON, CWMBRAN, PONTYPOOL, EBBW VALE, ABERGAVENNY, MONMOUTH, USK[1] and CHEPSTOW. In 1996 it was divided into the unitary authorities of Blaenau Gwent, Torfaen, Newport and Monmouthshire.

> I shall go to the midst of Gwent without delaying, to the south I shall go to search, and charge the sun and the moon to seek for him whose hand and eye are gentle.
>
> Anon.: 'He whose Hand and Eye are Gentle' (16th century), translated from the Welsh by Kenneth Hurlstone Jackson

> Can I forget the sweet days that have been,
> When poetry first began to warm my blood;
> When from the hills of Gwent I saw the earth
> Burned into two by Severn's silver flood.
>
> W.H. Davies: 'Days That Have Been'

Newport Gwent Dragons. *See under* NEWPORT[1].

Gwithian '(parish of Saint) Gothian', from the Cornish name of the patron saint of the local church.

A village in Cornwall, on the eastern side of ST IVES[2] Bay. Nearby are the extensive sand dunes of **Gwithian Towans**.

Gwy. The Welsh name for the River WYE[1].

Gwydir Castle Possibly 'low-lying land', Welsh *gwo-* 'low-lying' + *tir* 'land'.

A mansion just south of LLANRWST, Conwy (formerly in Gwynedd and then in Caernarvonshire), some 5 km (3 miles) north of Betws-y-Coed. The present building dates back to the 14th century, but is mostly 16th and 19th century. In 1921 the 17th-century panelling of the dining room was sold to William Randolph Hearst, the US newspaper magnate and model for *Citizen Kane*, but it has now been returned from America and reinstalled.

Nearby is **Gwydir Uchaf Chapel** ('Upper Gwydir Chapel'), dating from 1673 and notable for its painted ceiling. A large area of wooded hills extending from north of Llanrwst south to near Blaenau Ffestiniog is now the **Gwydyr Forest Park**.

There is a Gwydir River and a Gwydir Highway in Australia (New South Wales)

Gwynant Valley *Gwynant* 'shining stream', Welsh *gwyn* 'white, shining' + *nant* 'stream, river gorge'.

An attractive wooded valley on the south side of SNOWDON, in Gwynedd (formerly in Caernarvonshire). In Welsh it is **Nant Gwynant**. The valley extends southwestward from the PEN-Y-GWRYD Hotel down to BEDDGELERT, and includes the lake of **Llyn Gwynant** and the village of **Plas Gwynant**. The valley contains the ancient hillfort of DINAS EMRYS, associated with Merlin and the red dragon of Wales. The southern slopes of the valley were used to represent China in the 1958 film, *The Inn of the Sixth Happiness*, starring Ingrid Bergman as the missionary Gladys Aylward.

Gwynedd 'territory of the *Venedoti*', OCelt tribal name associated with a 5th-century chieftain called *Cunedda* + territorial affix.

A medieval kingdom and modern administrative division of North Wales. It is pronounced 'gwinneth', with the 'th' as in 'bathe'.

The nucleus of the medieval kingdom of Gwynedd was the territory occupied by the Ordovices, an ancient British people who had put up stiff resistance to the Romans for 20 years until they were pacified by Agricola around AD 78. The Ordovices remained under military rule for the entire period of the Roman occupation, then came under attack from Irish pirates in the 5th century AD. According to traditional accounts, the Ordovices accepted Cunedda (*see above*), a prince of the GODDODIN (or Votadini, *see* TRAPRAIN LAW) as their king, and under his leadership repelled the Irish invaders. The kingdom of Gwynedd was founded before 547 by Maelgwn Hir; it included all of North Wales and Anglesey, and had its capital at ABERFFRAW. The possibly legendary 12th-century Prince Madog (or Madoc) of Gwynedd is supposed to have discovered America (although an expedition mounted by the Welsh preacher John Evans in 1792 failed to substantiate stories of Welsh-speaking Indians beyond the Missouri). In the 11th century Gruffydd ap Llywelyn of Gwynedd almost succeeded in extending his dominion over the whole of Wales, but in 1152 Owain Gwynedd submitted to Henry II of England, and assumed the title of prince (rather than king) of Gwynedd. In the following century Llywelyn the Great extended his rule over much of Wales, and in 1258 Llywelyn ap Gruffydd styled himself Prince of Wales. However, in 1277 Edward I of England conquered all of North Wales except for ANGLESEY, and Llywelyn, attempting to take back his principality, was killed in 1282 near BUILTH WELLS, earning the nickname Llywelyn the Last. Edward had taken over the whole of Gwynedd by 1283.

> I love its strand and its mountains,
> its castle near the woods and its fine lands,
> its water meadows and its valleys ...
>
> Hywel ab Owain Gwynedd: 'Exultation' (12th century),
> translated from the Welsh by Gwyn Williams

The former county of Gwynedd, in northwest Wales, was created in 1974 out of Anglesey, Caernarvonshire, Merioneth and part of Denbighshire It was bounded to the east by Clwyd, to the southeast by Powys, to the southwest by Dyfed and to the west and north by the Irish Sea. The administrative seat was at CAERNARFON.

In the reorganization into unitary authorities in 1996, Gwynedd was reduced in size, pretty much to the areas of the old counties of Merioneth and Caernarvonshire, although the northeastern boundary was pulled in from the Vale of Conwy to the ridge of the CARNEDDAU in SNOWDONIA. Gwynedd is now bounded on the south by Ceredigion, and to the east by Powys and Conwy. The administrative seat remains at Caernarfon.

Candle of Gwynedd. The beautiful image (Welsh *canwyll Wynedd*) deployed by the 15th-century poet Llywelyn Goch to describe a dead girl in his famous lament, 'The Death of Lleucu Llywd'.

Castles and Town Walls of King Edward in Gwynedd. A collective term devised to cover the Edward-related sites given UNESCO World Heritage status in 1986.

H

Habbie's Howe. *See under* CARLOPS.

Hackney Probably 'Haca's piece of dry ground in a marsh', OE *Hacan* possessive form of male personal name *Haca* + *eg* 'island, dry ground in a marsh' (*see* -EY, -EA); alternatively the first element may be from OE *haca* 'hook-shaped piece of land'.

A district and borough in northeast London (E5, E8, E9, E15, N1, N16), to the east of Islington and to the west of Tower Hamlets and Newham. The district of Hackney itself is approximately in the middle of the borough, which also contains CLAPTON, DALSTON, HOMERTON, HOXTON, SHOREDITCH and STOKE NEWINGTON.

Until the early 19th century Hackney was a rural Middlesex village. Londoners would make their way out here at weekends or on summer evenings to disport themselves:

> With my wife only to take ayre, it being very warm and pleasant, to Bowe and Old Ford; and thence to Hackney. There light and played at shuffle board, eat cream and good cherries; and so with good refreshment home.
>
> Samuel Pepys: diary (11 June 1664)

Once the railways arrived in the mid-19th century, however, its fields were soon bricked and asphalted over. Population density soared. Small two-up-and-two-downs built for City clerks went down in the world as poorer tenants moved in, crumbling properties' cheap rents sucked in newly arrived immigrants from the Caribbean, South Asia, Cyprus, etc., and by the middle of the 20th century Hackney had the reputation of one of the most impoverished and run-down boroughs in England. Despite some gentrification at the edges, its malaise continued towards the end of the century, with increasing drug-related gun crime and a series of corruption scandals within the council.

In Hackney's more pastoral past, a major local occupation was the keeping and breeding of horses (largely to feed London's insatiable demands). Although the derivation has never been established beyond doubt, it seems more than likely that this lies behind the application of *Hackney* to a number of usages relating to horses and horse transport. As early as the 14th century, *hackney* was being used for an ordinary riding-horse of average size (as opposed to a war-horse, a draught horse or a hunter). It came to be applied particularly to a horse avaliable for hire, and hence *hackney coach* came to denote a coach kept for hire. **Hackney carriage**, first recorded in 1796 as applying to a carriage plying for public hire, is still the official British term for a taxi. Horses that were hired out had the reputation of being inferior, and were often worn out through overwork. That underlies the use of *hackneyed* for anything drained of originality by overuse, and of the abbreviated form *hack* for a writer who produces dull uninspired work for so much per word (and hence, derogatorily, for any journalist) and more broadly for anyone who does dull, routine work.

Hackney is the home of Matchbox Toys: they were first produced here by the Lesney company in 1953.

The penal reformer John Howard (1726–90), the playwright Harold Pinter (b.1930), the entertainer Anthony Newley (1931–2000), the ballet dancer Christopher Gable (1940–98) and the dart-player Eric 'the Crafty Cockney' Bristow (b.1975) were born in Hackney.

Hackney Downs. An area of (now much circumscribed) parkland in Lower Clapton (E5), to the north of Hackney. The nearby railway station has adopted its name.

> Within an hour the Gallant Band
> Were pouring in on every hand,
> From Putney, Hackney Downs and Bow,
> With Courage high and Hearts a-glow
> They galloped, roaring though the Town,
> 'Matilda's House is Burning Down!'
>
> Hilaire Belloc: *Cautionary Tales* (1907) 'Matilda'

Hackney Empire. A theatre (formerly a music hall) in Hackney, built to the design of Frank Matcham and opened in 1901. It was extensively refurbished at the beginning of the 21st century.

Hackney Marsh. A large area of open land (measuring

about 136 ha / 337 acres) to the east of Hackney, beside the River LEA (officially termed 'Hackney Marsh', but more usually known as 'Hackney Marshes'). Originally marshland, it was drained in the 18th century, but it still often flooded, and fishing was a popular pastime here. It was also beset by footpads (18th- and 19th-century muggers), including the young Dick Turpin. Modern drainage is more effective, and Hackney Marsh is now dotted with football and cricket pitches. In Cockney rhyming slang *Hackney Marsh* has been used (with no great phonetic subtlety) for 'a glass (of alcoholic drink)' and, in the plural, for 'glasses, spectacles'.

> Wiv a ladder and some glasses
> You could see to 'Ackney Marshes,
> If it wasn't for the 'ouses in between.
>
> > Edgar Bateman and George Le Brunn: 'If it wasn't for the 'ouses in between' (1894)

Hackney Wick Originally *Wick* 'specialized farm or trading centre' (perhaps alluding to its position on the River Lea), OE *wic* (*see* WICK), the combination with *Hackney* is not recorded before 1822.

A district in northeast London (E9, E15), mainly in the borough of HACKNEY (to the east of the district of Hackney) but partly also in TOWER HAMLETS, on the western bank of the River LEA. Its name sometimes crops up as an alternative to HAMPTON WICK as rhyming slang for *prick*.

Hackpen Hill *Hackpen* perhaps 'hook-shaped hill' (referring to the projecting end of the hill that runs off Monkton Down), OE *haca* 'hook' + OCelt *penn* (*see* PEN). The name *Hackpen Hill* is thus tautological.

A hill in Wiltshire, on the Marlborough Downs, about 8 km (5 miles) northwest of MARLBOROUGH. At 272 m (892 ft) it is the highest point on the RIDGEWAY. On its slopes is a figure of a white horse, which is thought to have been cut in 1838 in honour of Queen Victoria's coronation the previous year.

Haddington 'the farmstead of Hadda's people', OE personal name *Hadda* + *-inga-* (*see* -ING) + -TON.

A market town 26 km (15.5 miles) east of Edinburgh. It was the former county town of East Lothian – a county once known as **Haddingtonshire** – and is still the seat of East Lothian unitary authority. It was made a royal BURGH in the 12th century. Its St Mary's Church is known as the Lamp of the Lothians (*see under* LOTHIAN). Haddington was the birthplace of Alexander II (1198–1249), king of the Scots (1214–49); Walter Bower (1385–1449), author of the *Scotichronicon* (1447), a history of Scotland; John Knox (*c*.1514–72), the key figure of the Scottish Reformation; Jane Welsh Carlyle (1801–66), noted letter-writer, literary hostess and long-suffering wife of Thomas Carlyle; and Samuel Smiles (1812–1904), the author of the best-seller *Self-Help* (1859).

> Alas my native place! That Goddess of dullness has strewed on it all her poppies.
>
> > Jane Welsh Carlyle: letter to Eliza Stoddart (1824)

Treaty of Haddington (7 July 1548). A treaty by which it was agreed that the infant Mary Queen of Scots was to marry the French dauphin. Thus Mary's mother, Mary of Guise, finally rejected the 'Rough Wooing' of the English, who wanted the five-year-old Scottish queen to marry the ten-year-old Edward VI, and to this end sent armies into Scotland, resulting in the battles of Ancrum Moor (1545) (*see under* ANCRUM) and PINKIE (1547). Following the treaty Mary was sent to France, and married the Dauphin ten years later.

Haddington Hill Etymology unknown; possibly as for HADDINGTON + OE *hyll*.

A hill just to the east of Wendover in Buckinghamshire. At 261 m (857 ft) it is the highest point in the CHILTERN HILLS.

Haddingtonshire. A former name of EAST LOTHIAN.

Hadleigh[1] 'clearing in a heath, clearing where heather grows', OE *hæth* 'heath, heather' + -LEY.

A village in Essex, on the north bank of the Thames Estuary, just to the north of Canvey Island, now effectively a western suburb of SOUTHEND-ON-SEA. No fewer than three of Henry VIII's wives – Catherine of Aragon, Anne of Cleves and Catherine Parr – lived in the now ruined 13th-century **Hadleigh Castle**. The latter's somewhat bleak estuarine setting inspired the artist John Constable, whose dramatic representation of the castle (1829), now hanging in the Yale Center for British Art in New Haven, Connecticut, has the full title *Hadleigh Castle, The Mouth of the Thames, Morning After a Stormy Night*.

Hadleigh[2]. A town in Suffolk, about 13 km (8 miles) west of Ipswich. It was once a prosperous centre of the wool trade, as its many fine medieval and Georgian buildings testify.

Hadrian's Wall After the Emperor *Hadrian*.

A defensive stone wall built across the north of England by Roman legions during the reign of the Emperor Hadrian (AD 117–138). The Wall stretches 110 km (66 miles) from Bowness on the Solway to Wallsend near the mouth of the River Tyne. It was also known as **the Picts' Wall**, and was intended to keep the Caledonian tribes out of Roman Britain. In addition to 16 major forts along its length, fortified gateways were built every Roman mile (1480 m / 1618 yards). Between 138 and 161 the Roman frontier moved north to the ANTONINE WALL between the Forth and Clyde, but Hadrian's Wall came back into use after the death of the emperor Antoninus Pius. However, as the Romans gradually withdrew their forces from Britain, the Wall was penetrated on two or more occasions before being finally abandoned *c*.383. Although much of the Wall has since disappeared, there are some spectacular remnants, and Hadrian's Wall was declared a UNESCO World Heritage Site in 1987. The **Hadrian's Wall Path**, following its course, was opened in its entirety in 2003.

> Where the wall was, is the road;
> Still you may see on either side
> Ditch and vallum, each a wound
> Living on the living ground.
> There the vallum, wide and hollow,
> Is windbreak for lamb and ewe ...
>
> David Wright: 'Walking the Wall', from *A View of the North*

See also CHESTERS *and* HOUSESTEADS.

Hafren. The Welsh name for the River SEVERN.

Haggbeck 'stream by a clearing', OScand *hogg* 'clearing' + *bekkr* 'stream'.
A village in Cumbria, 17 km (10 miles) northeast of Gretna.

Haggerston Probably 'Hærgod's boundary stone', OE *Hærgodes* possessive form of male personal name *Hærgod* + *stan* '(boundary) stone' (*see* STONE).
A district of northeast London (E2), in the borough of HACKNEY, between HOXTON in the west and the district of Hackney in the east and northeast.

Edmond Halley (1656–1742), Astronomer Royal and describer of the comet named after him, was born and lived in Haggerston.

Haggisland. A slang term for SCOTLAND, coined in the later 19th century, referring to the Scottish national dish.

Hag's Head Irish *Ceann Caillighe* with the same meaning; the name relates to an episode in the story of Cuchulain, who jumped on to a rock from the headland now called LOOP HEAD when escaping from the hag Mal; she followed and was drowned, her body washed by the sea down to the Cliffs of Moher, the tip of which was named after her. This is also an example of the characterization of rocks or headlands as malevolent women; *compare* CARLINGFORD.
The headland at the southern end of the CLIFFS OF MOHER, County Clare. There was once an ancient fort here, replaced by a Napoleonic-era signal tower.

Hailes From the name of a local stream, which is of OCelt origin and means 'dirty stream'.
A hamlet in Gloucestershire, 14 km (9 miles) northeast of Cheltenham. The historic ruined **Hailes Abbey** was a wealthy Cistercian foundation that went the way of most such places when the ecclesiastical wind changed direction in the 1530s. Local lore has it that Thomas Cromwell watched the abbey being destroyed from a vantage point close to nearby Beckbury Camp (an Iron Age hillfort) in 1539.

In 1270 Edmund, a nephew of Henry III and son of the abbey's founder, presented the abbey with a phial of the Holy Blood. The abbey's custody of the relic ensured that it became a popular destination of medieval pilgrimage. The abbey and its relic are mentioned by Chaucer's Pardoner:

> 'By Goddes precious herte,' and 'By his nayles,'
> And 'By the blood of Crist that is in Hayles,
> Sevene is my chaunce, and thyn is cynk and treye!'
>
> Geoffrey Chaucer: *Canterbury Tales* (1387)

At the Dissolution in the 16th century the relic was denounced as 'but honey clarified and coloured with saffron'.

Alexander of Hailes (*c*.1175–*c*.1245). A scholastic philosopher and Franciscan monk known as the 'irrefragable doctor'. Originally from Hailes, he was the author of the *Summa universae theologiae.*

Hailsham 'Hægel's homestead or enclosure', OE *Hægeles* possessive form of male personal name *Hægel* + HAM.
A market town in East Sussex, on the River CUCKMERE, at the foot of the SOUTH DOWNS, about 11 km (7 miles) north of Eastbourne. About 3 km (2 miles) to the west is MICHELHAM PRIORY.

Hainault Originally *Hineholt* 'wood belonging to a religious community' (referring to a local section of Epping Forest (*see under* EPPING), which in the Middle Ages was owned by the abbey of Barking), OE *higna* possessive plural form of *hiwan* 'household, member of a religious community' + *holt* 'wood'; the spelling *Hainault*, which appears to date from no earlier than the 17th century, stems from a fictitious connection with Philippa of Hainault (1314–69), queen to Edward III.
A district of northeast London (before 1965 in Essex), in the borough of REDBRIDGE, between Fairlop to the south and Chigwell to the northwest. Hainault 'Underground' station, on the Central line, opened in 1948.

Haldon Forest *Haldon* apparently 'hail hill', OE *hagol* 'hail' + *dun* (*see* DOWN, -DON).
A hilly forest in Devon, about 11 km (7 miles) southwest of Exeter. Outstanding views of Dartmoor and Exeter may be had from here.

Hale[1] OE *hale*, dative of *halh* 'corner of land' (*see* HALE, -HALL).
A southwestern suburb of MANCHESTER, some 13 km (8 miles) from the city centre.

Hale[2]. A village in the unitary authority of Halton (formerly in Merseyside) near the head of the Mersey estuary.
Child of Hale, the. John Middleton (1578–1623), a giant supposedly 9 ft 3 in (2.775 m) tall, of whom many equally tall tales were told; perhaps the most likely of these is that he tossed a bull over a hedge by its horns. The Child's thatched cottage can still be seen, as can his grave in the churchyard, and there is now also a Child of Hale pub in the village.

Halesowen *Hales-* 'nooks or corners of land', from the plural of OE *halh* (*see* HALE, -HALL); *-owen* denoting manorial ownership in the Middle Ages by a Welsh prince called Owen.
A town in the West Midlands (before 1974 in Worcestershire), pronounced 'hails-owen', on the fringe of the BLACK

❖ hale, -hall ❖

The Old English element *halh* takes various forms. The most common meaning for the word is 'nook of land, land in a hollow'. On its own it usually manifests itself in the place name HALE[1], occurring in many counties; but Hales or Heales and Hele appear in the south, and Haugh in Scotland and the north. The same applies when *halh* is the first element of names: HALEWOOD (Merseyside), HALIFAX (Yorkshire) and the many Haughtons in the north illustrate this. By far the most common spelling of the element as the final word of names is *-hall*: KNODISHALL, MILDENHALL[1] and RICKINGHALL SUPERIOR (all in Suffolk), COGGESHALL (Essex), Leinthall (Herefordshire, *see* LEINTHALL EARLS and LEIN-

THALL STARKES), and SAUGHALL MASSIE (Cheshire), all show this.

Haugh in the north and Scotland develops the specific sense of 'land in a river-valley, alluvial land, water-meadow' (*see*, for example, PHILIPHAUGH), which is also present in many of the southern names as well. But curiously the element can sometimes mean the opposite of 'land in a hollow', because it undoubtedly also refers to land projecting in some way from the local topography: BRACKNELL (Berkshire) is on a slight hill, and some *halh* names in fenland, such as the Wiggenhall names in Norfolk (*see* WIGGENHALL ST GERMANS), are also on slightly raised ground.

COUNTRY, now effectively a southwestern outer suburb of BIRMINGHAM. In the 19th century it was a noted nail-making centre.

The poet, essayist and landscape gardener William Shenstone (1714–63) and the novelist and poet Francis Brett Young (1884–1954) were born in Halesowen.

Halesworth Probably 'Hæle's enclosure', OE *Hæles* possessive form of male personal name *Hæle* + *worth* (*see* -WORTH, WORTHY, -WARDINE).

A market town in Suffolk, on the River BLYTH[1], about 13 km (8 miles) west of Southwold. It began to prosper after the river was made navigable to barges in 1756.

The botanist Sir Joseph Dalton Hooker (1817–1911), director of Kew Gardens in succession to his father, was born in Halesworth.

Halewood 'wood near the nook of land', OE *wudu* 'wood' + *hale*, dative of *halh* 'nook or corner of land' (*see* HALE, -HALL).

A town in Merseyside, 12 km (7 miles) southeast of Liverpool. It largely comprises modern overspill housing for the city. The name is also commonly used to refer to the town's huge Ford car-manufacturing plant, built in the early 1960s.

Halewood was the birthplace of the pentathlete Mary Peters (b.1939), a gold medal winner for Britain at the 1972 Munich Olympic Games.

Halfpenny Bridge From the toll that was charged until *c*.1916.

An elegant iron footbridge over the River LIFFEY in DUBLIN, of which it has become something of a symbol. It was completed in 1816, and is known to officialdom (but to no one else) as the **Liffey Bridge**. In 1912 there was a proposal to incorporate the bridge into a new gallery (designed by Sir Edward Lutyens) to house Sir Hugh Lane's bequest, but the burgers of 'the blind and ignorant town' (in Yeats's phrase) rejected the whole idea on grounds of cost.

Halfpenny Green *Halfpenny* probably derogatory, implying 'land of little value'.

A village in Staffordshire, on the border with Shropshire, about 13 km (8 miles) southwest of Wolverhampton. It has its own busy airfield (formerly a Royal Air Force station, RAF Bobbington).

Halfway[1] From its being approximately 'halfway' between NEWBURY and HUNGERFORD. There was also a public house called 'Halfway' here.

A village in Berkshire, about 5 km (3 miles) west of Newbury. There are other villages called Halfway in Carmarthenshire, Powys and South Yorkshire, named for similar reasons.

Halfway[2] Because it is halfway between CORK and KINSALE.

A village in County Cork, 11 km (7 miles) northwest of Kinsale.

Halidon Hill *Halidon* 'holy hill', OE *halig* 'holy' + *dun* (*see* DOWN, -DON); the name *Halidon Hill* is thus tautological; John Leland speculated, *c*.1540, that this was the place 'that Bede calleth *Hevenfeld*', the site of Oswald's victory of 634, *see* HEAVENFIELD.

A low hill just north of Berwick-upon-Tweed, Northumberland, close to the Scottish border.

Battle of Halidon Hill (19 July 1333). An engagement in which a Scots force, under Sir Archibald Douglas, was defeated as it attempted to relieve Berwick. The town, held by the Earl of March, was being besieged by Edward III on behalf of his vassal, Edward Balliol (son of King John (de) Balliol), who was in revolt against David II of Scotland. The day after the battle, in which Douglas was killed, Berwick surrendered. Sir Walter Scott wrote an unmemorable dramatic poem entitled *Halidon Hill* (1822).

Halifax 'corner of land with coarse grass', OE *halh* (*see* HALE, -HALL) + *gefeaxe* 'coarse grass'.

An industrial town in West Yorkshire, 10 km (6 miles) northwest of Huddersfield. Halifax was a centre of the cloth trade as early as the 13th century, and by the 15th was making more cloth than anywhere else in Yorkshire. The magistrates of Halifax acquired draconian powers over those stealing cloth or found guilty of other minor offences, the felon's punishment generally being finished off by the **Maiden of Halifax**, a type of guillotine.

> The country people were, it seems, so terrified at the severity of this proceeding, that hence came the proverbial saying, which was used all over Yorkshire, (viz)
>> From Hell, Hull, and Halifax,
>> Good lord, deliver us.
>
> How Hull came to be included in this petition, I do not find; for they had no such law there, as I read of.
>
>> Daniel Defoe: *A Tour Through the Whole Island of Great Britain* (1724–6) (The order of the first line of this beggars' or vagrants' prayer – first recorded by Antony Copley in his *Wits fittes and fancies* (1594) – is usually given as 'From Hull, Hell and Halifax'. The inclusion of Hull that so puzzled Defoe has been explained by the suggestion that in Hull beggars had little chance of getting anything without doing hard labour for it. *See also under* the YORKSHIRE DALES)

The fearful regime in Halifax came to an end in 1650, when the magistrates were faced with open revolt over the execution of two men for stealing two horses and nine yards of cloth.

Halifax's cloth-trading past is reflected in the magnificent Georgian Piece Hall in the town centre. It dates from 1779, when it opened as a market place for 'pieces' of woollen and worsted cloth made by handloom weavers in the area. Over the next 100 years it was used, variously, for religious and political meetings, for fireworks displays and as a market selling fish, fruit and vegetables. The Piece Hall was restored and reopened as an arts, crafts and entertainment centre in 1976.

During the 19th century there was a considerable expansion in the population of Halifax, although at the same time the neighbouring town of Bradford grew to greater importance. Halifax today has the headquarters of HBOS (formerly the **Halifax Building Society**, and now a bank, which merged with the Bank of Scotland in 2001).

Halifax was the birthplace of William Bramwell Booth (1856–1929), eldest son of William Booth, whom he succeeded as General of the Salvation Army; and of the novelist Phyllis Bentley (1894–1977), who wrote sagas set amidst the textile mills of West Yorkshire. The city of Halifax in Canada is the capital of Nova Scotia.

go to Halifax. A euphemism for 'go to hell', derived from the saying quoted by Defoe above.

Handley Page Halifax. A British four-engined bomber that entered service in 1941, and which was subsequently much used in the Second World War, in a variety of roles.

Lord Halifax. Edward Frederick Lindley Wood (1881–1959), Conservative politician, Viceroy of India (1926–31) and an appeasing foreign secretary (1938–40). His piety earned him the mildly punning nickname 'the Holy Fox'.

Hallaig. *See under* RAASAY.

Hallamshire From the Saxon manor of Hallam, OE *halum*, dative plural of *halh* 'nook of land' (*see* HALE, -HALL).

A name for the area of South Yorkshire centred on SHEFFIELD, and also including CHESTERFIELD in Deryshire and ROTHERHAM; in the Anglo-Saxon period Hallamshire was the most southerly shire of the kingdom of NORTHUMBRIA. The name is found, for example, in the name of the Sheffield cutlers' guild, the **Company of Cutlers in Hallamshire in the County of York**; in the **Hallamshire Rifle Volunteers** (raised 1859); and in the present-day **Royal Hallamshire Hospital** in the city. There is also a brewery bearing the name.

Hallival Probably 'ledge mountain', OScand *hjalli* 'ledge' + *fjall* 'mountain', from the level terraces between the cliffs surrounding the summit of the mountain.

A rocky mountain, 721 m (2365 ft) high, in the Cuillin of RUM, Highland (formerly in Inverness-shire), just next to Askival, the highest peak of the range. It is also called **Allival**.

allivalite. A pale form of the igneous rock gabbro, taking its name from the mountain on Rum where it is found.

Halstead 'place of shelter', OE *hald* 'protection' + *stede* 'place'.

A market town in Essex on the River COLNE[1], 9 km (6 miles) northeast of Braintree.

Haltemprice 'noble enterprise', OFr *haut* 'high, noble' + *emprise* 'enterprise', referring to the Augustinian priory established at nearby Cottingham in 1322.

A residential suburb on the west side of Hull, although itself in the East Riding of Yorkshire (formerly in Humberside) rather than in the unitary authority of Kingston upon Hull. Haltemprice was originally the ancient name for the region to the west and north of Hull.

Halton From *Halton*, a village, now an eastern district of Runcorn; 'farm in a nook of land', OE *halh* (*see* HALE, -HALL) + -TON.

A unitary authority at the eastern end of the WIRRAL, on both banks of the River Mersey, created in 1998 from Ditton, RUNCORN, WIDNES (now its administrative centre) and the surrounding area of Cheshire. It is bordered to the west by Merseyside, to the north and east by Warrington, and to the south by Cheshire.

Haltwhistle Possibly 'high confluence', OFr *haut* 'high' + OE *twisla* 'meeting of two streams', perhaps referring to the confluence of Haltwhistle Burn with the South Tyne.

A market town on the South Tyne, Northumberland, south of HADRIAN'S WALL, 23 km (14 miles) west of Hexham. Some reckon it the dead centre of Britain (if including the Northern Isles and Channel Islands).

Halvergate Marshes *Halvergate* from a local village name, perhaps 'land for which a half heriot (a feudal service or payment) is due', OE *half* + *here-geatu* 'heriot'.

An extensive area of marshland in the Norfolk BROADS, just inland of GREAT YARMOUTH, and to the north of Breydon Water.

Ham[1] 'land in a river bend' (referring to its position in a loop of the Thames), OE *hamm* (*see* HAM).

A district of outer southwest London (before 1965 in Surrey), on the east bank of the River Thames opposite Twickenham, in the borough of Richmond upon Thames. A number of fine 18th- and 19th-century houses remain, and it is altogether a most elegant and expensive residential area. **Ham House** itself is a magnificent example of an early 17th-century country house. It was built in 1660 to an H-shaped Jacobean plan. Its contents, including much Elizabethan walnut, lacquered, gilded and silver furniture, are under the care of the Victoria and Albert Museum.

See also EAST HAM, SOUTH HAMS, WEST HAM.

Ham Common. An area of open common land in the southeastern part of Ham, contiguous with Richmond Park (*see under* RICHMOND[2]) to the east.

Ham[2] 'low-lying enclosure', OE *hamm* (*see* HAM).

A village in eastern Kent. It lies, fortuitously, just 2.5 km (1.5 miles) south of Sandwich.

Hamble 'crooked river' (that is, a river with bends in it), OE *hamel* 'crooked' + EA-.

A river in Hampshire, which rises to the west of Bishop's Waltham and flows 15 km (9 miles) southwestwards into Southampton Water (*see under* SOUTHAMPTON) about 8 km (5 miles) southeast of Southampton. Its estuary is popular with yachtsmen.

Hambleden 'crooked or undulating valley', OE *hamel* 'crooked' + *denu* 'valley'.

A preternaturally pretty tree-girt village in Buckinghamshire, in the CHILTERN HILLS, near the River Thames, about 5 km (3 miles) northeast of Henley-on-Thames. Since 1923 it has been owned by W.H. Smith (founder of the bookshop chain) and his descendants (his great-grandson nearly sold it in 2003, but changed his mind at the last minute). It has been used as a setting for numerous films, including *Chitty Chitty Bang Bang* (1968) and *101 Dalmatians* (1996).

The 7th Earl of Cardigan (James Thomas Brudenell; 1797–1868), who led the disastrous Charge of the Light Brigade at the Battle of Balaclava in 1854, was born in the manor house here.

On the River Thames to the south of the village is **Hambleden Lock**, where walkers can cross the river on a series of bridges.

Hambledon 'crooked or irregularly shaped hill', OE *hamel* 'crooked' + *dun* (*see* DOWN, -DON).

A village in Hampshire, about 21 km (13 miles) east of Southampton, famed as the home of both English cricket and English wine. Cricket may or may not have originated as a game played by shepherds on the SOUTH DOWNS in earlier centuries (the legend is romantic but dubious), but it was certainly in this Georgian village in the late 18th century that it began to come of age. The Hambledon Club (founded in the 1760s by a group of London gentlemen and including such heroes as John Small, Richard Nyren, Tom Sueter and William ('Silver Billy') Beldham) took on

---

❖ **ham** ❖

Old English *ham* is the source of Modern English 'home' and the first part of 'homestead', and that represents pretty well what it means. In later usage it refers to more than the original place of settlement, and often means 'estate'. It is among the most common elements in settlement names in England, and its frequency needs no demonstration. Very often it is combined with *tun* 'enclosure with a dwelling' (*see* -TON) to produce the familiar *ham-tun*, generally appearing as '-hampton' as in NORTHAMPTON. Like *tun* it combines with Old English *stede* and *stall*, both meaning 'the site or building of a homestead', although HAMPSTEAD (Greater London), HEMEL HEMPSTEAD (Hertfordshire) and other names with *ham-stede* are more frequent than *ham-stall* (as in HAMSTALL RIDWARE, Staffordshire).

Some names ending in -*ham* may, confusingly, be from *hamm* 'land partially enclosed, land in a river bend'. This basic meaning of *hamm* relates to widely different land features. Many *hamm* names refer to water meadows and enclosures in the flood plain of the lower reaches of rivers, particularly in the South of England. Some however, are slightly more conspicuous: a *hamm* can be a feature jutting out into water, a 'promontory'. When it occurs on its own, Ham (as in HAM[1]) is always from *hamm*, but in other cases it is difficult to be sure, and often the topography is the surest guide to the meaning. Most names ending in -*ham* derive from one of these two elements.

Another confusion arises from miscorrection of pronunciation: CARHAM (Northumberland) does not contain the element *ham* at all, but is the dative plural *carrum* of the dialect word *carr* 'rock', and meaning 'place at the rocks'; over the years the assumed dropping of the -*h*- in the name has been 'corrected', resulting in the spelling -*ham*. Yet another confusion arises from the interaction of Old Scandinavian *holmr* (*see under* -EY, -EA) and *ham*: HUBBERHOLME (North Yorkshire) has replaced the historical *ham* with this Scandinavian element.

and beat the best that the rest of England could offer, and set the pattern the game was to follow thereafter:

> I was born at Hambledon, in Hampshire – the Attica of the scientific art [cricket] I am celebrating. No eleven in England could compare with the Hambledon, which met on the first Tuesday in May on Broad-Halfpenny. So renowned a set were the men of Hambledon, that the whole country would flock to see one of their trial matches.
>
> John Nyren: *The Young Cricketer's Tutor* (1830)

In the 20th century Hambledon was again a trendsetter, when in 1952 Major-General Sir Guy Salisbury-Jones planted here the vineyard that began the revival of English winemaking. He linked the village's past and present in the bat-and-ball motif in the design of his wine label. *See also* BROADHALFPENNY DOWN.

Hambledon Hill *see* HAMBLEDON.

A hill in Dorset, 184 m (604 ft) high, overlooking the STOUR[1] valley, about 8 km (5 miles) northwest of Blandford Forum. On top is an Iron Age hillfort, and nearby a 4500-year-old causewayed camp where Stone Age herdsmen kept their livestock.

Hamble-le-Rice *Hamble* from the River Hamble; *Rice* 'brushwood, undergrowth', OE *hris*.

A village (in everyday parlance simply **Hamble**) in Hampshire, on the northern side of the mouth of the River HAMBLE. Yachting marinas are a mainstay of the local economy.

Hambleton Hills *Hambleton* 'farm by the crooked hill', OE *hamel* 'crooked hill' + -TON.

The hills forming the western escarpment of the NORTH YORK MOORS, North Yorkshire. They rise to over 300 m (1000 ft). The poet William Wordsworth crossed them on the day of his wedding to Mary Hutchinson, 4 October 1802, and wrote a sonnet:

> We were too late at least by one dark hour,
> And nothing could we see of all that power
> Of prospect, whereof many thousands tell.
> The western sky did recompense us well
> With Grecian Temple, Minaret, and Bower;
> And, in one part, a Minster with its Tower
> Substantially distinct, a place for Bell
> Or clock to toll from. Many a glorious pile
> Did we behold, sights that might well repay
> All disappointment! and, as such, the eye
> Delighted in them; but we felt, the while,
> We should forget them: they are of the sky,
> And from our earthly memory fade away.
>
> 'Composed after a journey across the Hamilton [*sic*] Hills, Yorkshire', from *Poems in Two Volumes* (1807)

The hills gave their name to **Hambleton**, a local authority district of North Yorkshire since 1974.

Hambury Tout *Hambury* may be 'fortified enclosure or farmstead' (*see* HAM and BURY); *Tout* 'look-out hill', ME *toot*.

A cliff about 122 m (400 ft) high, 1.5 km (1 mile) to the west of LULWORTH Cove.

Hamdon Hill *Hamdon* perhaps 'river-meadow hill', OE *hamm* 'river meadow, enclosure' (*see* HAM) + *dun* 'hill' (*see* DOWN, -DON); the name 'Hamdon Hill' is thus tautological.

A hill in Somerset, about 8 km (5 miles) west of Yeovil. It is 130 m (426 ft) high. It was fortified by the Ancient Britons, and the Romans, rightly appraising the quality of the stone it is made of, began quarrying it (*see* HAM HILL). *See also* NORTON SUB HAMDON *and* STOKE SUB HAMDON.

Hameldown Tor *Hameldown see* HAMBLEDON.

A tor (high hilltop rock) on the eastern side of Dartmoor, about 5 km (3 miles) northwest of HAYTOR. It is about 530 m (1737 ft) above sea level.

Ham Hill. The name by which HAMDON HILL is known in the context of the yellow limestone – **Ham Hill stone**, or usually more simply **Ham stone** – which is quarried from it. The local village, STOKE SUB HAMDON, is largely made from it, and it adorns many a church and farmhouse in the surrounding area.

Hamilton[1] From the *Hamilton* family; their name is derived from a variant spelling of HAMBLEDON.

A town in SOUTH LANARKSHIRE (of which it is the administrative centre), in the Clyde valley 16 km (10 miles) southeast of Glasgow. It was formerly in Strathclyde region. The area was originally called Cadzow, and it was given to the Hamilton family by Robert the Bruce after the Battle of Bannockburn (1314). In 1445 James II issued a charter changing the name of the place to Hamilton. The Hamiltons became earls of Arran, then marquesses and later dukes of Hamilton, and also dukes of Châtelherault in France (*see* CHATELHERAULT). The town was a coal-mining centre until the mid-20th century, and it was subsidence caused by mine workings that led in the 1920s to the demolition of **Hamilton Palace** (1829), in the grounds of which Rudolf Hess landed in 1941. There is also a racecourse.

Hamilton was the birthplace of Joanna Baillie (1762–1851), poet, dramatist and friend of Sir Walter Scott. There are towns called Hamilton in Australia (Victoria), Bermuda (the capital), Canada (Ontario), New Zealand (North Island) and the USA (Ohio).

> Hamilton is notoriously a dull place; if a joke finds its way into our neighbourhood, it is looked upon with as much surprise as a comet would be.
>
> *The Hamilton Hedgehog* (October 1856)

> What's Motherwell famous for? Coal and steel.
> What's Hamilton famous for? Stealin' coal.
>
> Anon.: saying

Hamilton Academicals. The informal name for **Hamilton Academical FC**, also known as the **Accies**. The club was founded in 1874 by the rector and pupils of Hamilton Academy, but being a former pupil has long ceased to be a necessary qualification for players. The club has had something of a roller-coaster career, having been at various points in the Scottish Premier, First, Second and Third Divisions.

Hamilton High Parks. A part of the Hamilton estate lying to the south of the town. The area includes the ruined Cadzow Castle and the mansion of CHATELHERAULT.

Hamilton Low Parks. The former grounds of the old Hamilton Palace (*see above*), subsequently disfigured by mine workings but now reclaimed as part of Strathclyde Country Park.

Hamilton Mausoleum. An extravagant domed mausoleum built in Hamilton Low Parks in the 1850s by the 10th Duke, who determined to bury his ancestors here as well. The Duke had already outbid the British Museum for an ancient Egyptian sarcophagus in which he wished to be buried, but suffered anxiety owing to the fact that he was significantly taller than the Egyptian princess for whom it had been originally intended. At his death it was found necessary to cut off the Duke's feet, which were placed beside him in the sarcophagus.

A degree of eccentricity has continued in the family. When the wife of the present Duke rescued a turkey bound for the Christmas table, His Grace remarked: 'I couldn't possibly eat any animal that I have been introduced to.'

Hamilton[2]. A former district of the old Strathclyde region (1975–96). It covered the northwestern part of the traditional county of Lanarkshire, and the town of HAMILTON[1] was the administrative HQ.

Hammersmith '(place with a) hammer smithy or forge', OE *hamor* 'hammer' + *smythe* 'smithy'.

A district of West London (W6), in the borough of HAMMERSMITH AND FULHAM, on the north bank of the River Thames, to the west of Earl's Court and to the east of Chiswick. It grew up between two major routes from London to the West, now the A4 and the A4020, so it has always been, and remains today, traffic dominated (the junction at **Hammersmith Broadway**, a roundabout with too many exits to count, is a notorious congestion point, any relief provided by the opening of **Hammersmith Flyover** in 1961 having long evaporated). For those who can fight their way through, though, there are plenty of places of entertainment and other diversions, such as the **Hammersmith Apollo** (for rock concerts), the Lyric Theatre, the Riverside Studios and Olympia exhibition centre. Further north, beyond SHEPHERD'S BUSH, are the BBC Television Centre and the White City radio studios.

Hammersmith Underground station, on the District, Hammersmith & City and Piccadilly lines, opened in 1864.

Hammersmith. A 'Prelude and Scherzo for Orchestra' (Opus 52), written in 1930 by Gustav Holst. Originally a commission for the BBC Military Band, it contrasts the quiet of the Thames at Hammersmith with the bustle of the streets and street-traders. Holst himself taught music at St Paul's School for Girls in Brook Green, Hammersmith.

Hammersmith and City line. A component of the London Underground system, running between Hammersmith in the west and Barking in the east, via Moorgate and Liverpool Street (an early southwestward extension to Richmond was closed in 1906). It began operation in 1863. It was always represented (on maps of the system, for instance) as being part of the Metropolitan line, but although to the east of Baker Street it runs mainly on Metropolitan (and District line) tracks it has always been essentially a separate operation, and this was recognized in 1990 with its official designation as 'Hammersmith and City' (pink on the map).

Hammersmith Bridge. A suspension bridge crossing the River Thames between Hammersmith and Barnes. It is a notable way-point on the annual Oxford–Cambridge Boat Race. Designed by Sir Joseph Bazalgette, it was built in 1887. It replaced an earlier suspension bridge, the first (1827) to be built in London.

Hammersmith Palais. A colloquial name for the 'Palais de Danse', a dance-hall in the Shepherd's Bush Road that opened in 1919. It was the first venue in Britain to present jazz, and caused something of a scandal when it allowed the hiring of dancing partners ('The young man you choose out of a pen at sixpence a time at the Palais de Danse' – *Punch* (1926)). It helped create a fashion for mass dancing to big bands which reached a peak in the Second World War and survived into the rock 'n' roll era.

Hammersmith and Fulham. A West London borough (SW6, W6, W12, W14) created in 1965. It lies between Ealing and Hounslow to the west and Kensington and Chelsea to the east. Apart from FULHAM and HAMMERSMITH it contains PARSONS GREEN, SHEPHERD'S BUSH, West Kensington and WORMWOOD SCRUBS.

Hammoon Originally *Hame* 'enclosure or land in a river-bend', OE *hamm* (*see* HAM); the *-moon* element reflects manorial ownership in the early Middle Ages by the Moion family.

A hamlet in Dorset, on the River STOUR[1], about 11 km (7 miles) southwest of Shaftesbury.

Hamnavoe. George Mackay Brown's fictional version of STROMNESS, Orkney.

Hamoaze 'muddy place by Ham', *Ham* a local place name ('flat low-lying land', *see* HAM) + OE *wase* 'mud, ooze'.

The estuary of the River TAMAR, which flows southwards between Torpoint (in Cornwall) and Devonport (in Devon) into Plymouth Sound (*see under* PLYMOUTH).

Hampden Park Etymology uncertain.

The national football ground of Scotland, situated in GLASGOW. It is also the ground of Queen's Park FC, the only amateur club in the Scottish Division. Building commenced in 1903. By the 1970s it was clear that many of its facilities were tired and outdated, but it was some time before the necessary finances materialized for improvements. Renovations to all four stands took place in the 1990s, and the stadium is now, with IBROX PARK, one of the two Scottish grounds to be deemed worthy of a '5-star' rating from UEFA.Its capacity is 52,000.

Hampden roar. Rhyming slang for 'score', the roar being heard whenever Scotland do this (a sadly rare event).

Hampshire From *Hamtun* (the original name of SOUTHAMPTON), with SHIRE.

A county of southern England, bounded to the west by Dorset and Wiltshire, to the north by Berkshire and Surrey, to the east by West Sussex and to the south by the English Channel. In 1974 its southwestern extremity, including BOURNEMOUTH, was transferred to Dorset. It includes the unitary authorities of PORTSMOUTH and SOUTHAMPTON, and other important centres are ANDOVER, BASINGSTOKE, EASTLEIGH, GOSPORT, HAVANT, LYMINGTON, PETERSFIELD and the administrative centre WINCHESTER. Its two main rivers, the TEST and the ITCHEN, drain (via Southampton Water) into the Solent, which separates the ISLE OF WIGHT (now an independent unitary authority) from the mainland. Other rivers include the Beaulieu, the Lymington, the MEON and, for part of its length, the AVON[3]. Most of the county is undulating lowland, with, in the southwest corner, the NEW FOREST. In the northern and eastern parts are chalk downland. It is mainly an agricultural county, but Southampton and Portsmouth are important ports.

When the Romans arrived in Hampshire, the county's ancient British inhabitants included the Atrebates in the north (*see* SILCHESTER) and the Belgae in the southwest (*see* WINCHESTER). Another group, the Regni, were granted a *civitas* (self-governing tribal area) in the southeast of the county (*see* FISHBOURNE). According to the Anglo-Saxon scholar the Venerable Bede, the New Forest area of Hampshire was later one of the principal locations of settlement of the Germanic invaders known as the Jutes.

The county gave its name to New Hampshire, in New England, an American colony founded in 1623 and a US state from 1788.

In cricketing terms Hampshire is a 'first-class' county. Hampshire County Cricket Club was founded in 1863 and has played in the county championship since 1895, winning it on two occasions. Its famous players include C.P. Mead, the South African Barry Richards, the West Indian Gordon Greenidge (both brilliant opening batsmen) and Robin Smith. Its home ground is the Rose Bowl, Southampton.

Hampshire. An American breed of black pigs with a white belt round the middle and white forelegs

Hampshire or **Hampshire Down.** A British breed of large hornless sheep, which are reared for meat and produce medium-quality wool

Hampshire hog. Originally, the name of a breed of pig for which Hampshire became famous. The term came to be extended first to a dish of boiled bacon and vegetables, and later to an affectionate or more usually derogatory nickname for a Hampshire person:

> She was a Dorset woman, and both she and her husband had a profound contempt for what they called the Hampshire hogs with whom they were condemned to live.
>
> Compton Mackenzie: *My Life and Times* (1963)

Hampshires, the. The colloquial name of the Royal Hampshire Regiment, a regiment of the British Army formed in 1881 as the Hampshire Regiment, with 'Royal' added in 1946. It was joined with The Queen's Regiment in 1992 to form The Princess of Wales's Royal Regiment.

Hampstead 'homestead', OE *ham-stede*. The spelling with *p* is first recorded in the 13th century.

A district in North London (NW3), in the borough of CAMDEN, between **Hampstead Heath** (*see below*) to the north and Swiss Cottage and Primrose Hill to the south and west.

Originally a quiet rural village, Hampstead's rise to prominence began in the early 17th century, when pronouncements about the medical efficacy of its spring waters attracted London society to it. By 1814 John James Park could describe it as 'a select, amicable, respectable and opulent neighbourhood'. It was an early and somewhat unlikely crucible of the Romantic movement in England: it was while living here, in a house known today as Keats House (now a museum), that John Keats heard the nightingale that inspired his 'Ode to a Nightingale' (1819); Leigh Hunt moved to Hampstead in 1815, and there introduced Keats to Shelley; and John Constable lived in Hampstead 1819–24 for the sake of his consumptive wife's health. Other residents from the cream of culture and intellect have included William Pitt 'the Elder', Lord Byron, H.G. Wells, Kate Greenaway, Sigmund Freud, Robert Louis Stevenson, Anna Pavlova, Mary Webb, Henry Moore, John Galsworthy, Enid Blyton, Michael Foot, Glenda Jackson (its MP since 1992), J.B. Priestley, Ridley Scott and Giles Gilbert Scott, amongst many others. It is one of London's most obviously gentrified, and wealthiest, communities – it has more millionaires per head of population than anywhere else in Britain – which may appear to sit paradoxically with its other, latter-day reputation as a haven of leftism and 'radical chic'. In truth, though, its left-wingery has always been of the tweed-jacketed, Fabian variety, not red-bloodedly revolutionary. The term **Hampstead intellectual** has come to be applied with indulgent contempt to those who muse in the abstract on the problems of humanity in their ivory towers on the heights of NW3 (*see also* **Hampstead Set** *below*).

Hampstead Underground station, on the Northern line (Edgware branch), opened in 1907. At 58 m (192 ft), it is the deepest on the Underground system; its access staircase has 306 steps.

The district of **West Hampstead** (NW2) was originally called *West End*. West Hampstead Underground station, originally on the Metropolitan line and now on the Jubilee, opened in 1879.

The novelists Evelyn Waugh (1903–66) and his brother Alec Waugh (1898–1981) were born in Hampstead, as were the barrister and author John Mortimer (b.1923) and the racing driver Damon Hill (b.1960).

There are towns called Hampstead in the USA (Maryland and North Carolina) and Canada (New Brunswick). The first horse-racing trophy to be contested in North America was run for at Hampstead Plain, Long Island, New York, in 1665.

Ham and High. The colloquial name in the locality for the *Hampstead and Highgate Express*, the local rag.

Hampstead donkeys. Nineteenth-century slang for body lice.

Hampstead Heath. A large area of semi-open, semi-wooded land (about 325 ha / 800 acres in extent) on high ground in North London, in the borough of Camden. It is owned and run by the Corporation of the City of London. Originally it was heavily wooded, but in the latter part of the 17th century many of the trees were cut down (for the rebuilding of London after the Great Fire), and its aspect became as it is today. It is a popular resort for walkers, with or without dogs, and provides scope for all manner of other recreations, from kite-flying to alfresco homosexual assignation, and it commands unparalleled vistas of London below. The FLEET[1] river rises in two places on the Heath, and **Hampstead Ponds** to the west and the man-made Highgate Ponds (*see under* HIGHGATE) to the east have been used to store its water. Other notable features of the Heath include KEN WOOD, PARLIAMENT HILL, the VALE OF HEALTH and Jack Straw's Castle, an old coaching inn (rebuilt 1964) named after one of the leaders of the Peasants' Revolt (in 2004 it was, ironically, being turned into luxury flats). Hampstead Heath has also been immortalized as Cockney rhyming slang for *teeth* – usually in the shortened form *Hampsteads*, occasionally in the even further abbreviated *hamps*.

> Foxes are out on the Heath;
> They sniff the air like knives.
> A hawk turns slowly over Highgate, waiting.
> This is the hidden life of London. Wild.
>
> Al Alvarez (b.1929): 'Mourning and Melancholia'

Hampstead Heath sailor. A jocular term for a very poor sailor – i.e. someone who is sick before the ship leaves port. The 'joke' is that, apart from a few bathing pools, the Heath is dry land.

Hampstead Set. A term originally applied in the 1950s to a group of supporters of Hugh Gaitskill (1906–63), leader of the Labour Party (1955–63). The group, opposed by Aneurin Bevan and his followers, lived, like Gaitskill, in Hampstead. It included Anthony Crosland, Denis Healey, Douglas Jay, Roy Jenkins and Frank Pakenham (Lord Longford). Subsequently, journalists have used the term more generally and collectively for liberal and/or left-leaning intellectuals living in and around Hampstead, such as the playwright Harold Pinter (b.1930) and historical biographer Antonia Fraser (b.1932), who have been involved in fashionable causes such as Charter '88 and are deemed a subset of the 'Chattering Classes'.

Hampstead Garden Suburb. A residential district in northwest London (NW11), in the borough of BARNET, to the northwest of Hampstead Heath and the east of Golders Green. Its development began in 1907, at the instigation of the philanthropist Dame Henrietta Barnett and in accordance with the principles of the new Garden City movement, pioneered at LETCHWORTH in 1903. Its principal designers were Raymond Unwin (1863–1940) and Barry Parker, and it also includes several houses and other buildings by Sir Edwin Lutyens (1867–1941). The result was an attractively laid-out and spacious environment, but one in which community spirit never quite developed as the theory said it ought to (a fact perhaps not unconnected with the complete absence of pubs).

It has had something of a reputation as an overspill area for Hampstead leftism (*see* Hampstead Set *under* HAMPSTEAD) – Harold Wilson had a house here for some time, for instance. By the end of the 20th century, though, the Fabians had moved on, and the Suburb basked in an aura of overweening and flaunted wealth.

Hampstead Norreys *Norreys* denoting manorial ownership in the late Middle Ages by the Norreys family.

A village (pronounced 'norris') in Berkshire, about 21 km (13 miles) west of Reading.

Hampton[1] 'farmstead in a river bend' (here referring to its position by a bend in the River Thames), OE *hamm* (*see* HAM) + -TON.

A district of outer southwest London (before 1965 in Middlesex), on the north bank of the River THAMES, opposite Molesey, in the borough of RICHMOND-UPON-THAMES.

There are towns called Hampton in the USA (Arkansas, Florida, Georgia, Iowa, Nebraska, New Hampshire, Oregon, South Carolina, Virginia and Wyoming) and in Canada

(New Brunswick), and 'the Hamptons' is the popular name of the eastern end of Long Island, New York City, where the resort villages of Westhampton, Southampton, Bridgehampton, East Hampton and Hampton Bays are located (the area is a summer retreat for wealthy New Yorkers). *See also* HAMPTON COURT.

Hampton² 'estate on land hemmed in by rivers' (referring to Southampton's situation between the estuaries of the rivers TEST and ITCHEN), OE *hamm* 'land hemmed in by rivers' (*see* HAM) + -TON.

The original name of the place now called SOUTHAMPTON (Shakespeare's Henry V, waiting in Southampton to embark for France, describes how the Earl of Cambridge 'hath, for a few light crowns, lightly conspired to kill us here in Hampton' *Henry V* (1599) II.ii).

Bevis of Hampton. The hero and title of a popular English medieval romance, in places bearing some similarity to the Charlemagne cycle. Bevis seeks to avenge his father's death, which has been contrived by his mother. As a result he is sold to heathen merchants, and after many adventures he marries Josian, daughter of King Ermyn, eventually returning to England to avenge his father. *Hampton* is usually interpreted as Southampton. The English version (14th century) is based on an earlier French version, but it is possible that the story had previous English origins.

Hampton Court From *Hampton Court* Palace.

A residential district on the southwestern edge of London, on the River THAMES, partly in the London borough of RICHMOND-UPON-THAMES (which contains the palace and its grounds) and partly in Surrey. It is dominated by its royal palace, the transfer of whose name to the area was consolidated by the opening of Hampton Court railway station in 1849.

Hampton Court Conference. A conference held in January 1604 at Hampton Court Palace (*see below*) by James VI and I and the High Church party with some of the Puritans in the Church of England. The High Church bishops would make no concessions of importance and their most valuable decision was to sanction a new translation of the Bible, which would become the Authorized Version of 1611.

Hampton Court Palace. A royal palace on the north bank of the River Thames, just over 1.5 km (1 mile) downstream of HAMPTON¹. It is generally known simply as **Hampton Court**, which was the name of the original medieval manor house (ME *court* 'manor house') on the site. Cardinal Wolsey demolished this when he acquired the estate in 1514, and he set about building himself an ostentatious Renaissance mansion. After he fell from favour in 1529, Henry VIII took over the building and turned it into a royal palace (five of his six wives lived here, and the ghosts of Jane Seymour and Catherine Howard are said to haunt its corridors). It

continued in the role of royal residence for 200 years (with significant additions by Christopher Wren at the end of the 17th century), but thereafter kings and queens became no more than occasional visitors (George II was the last monarch to live here), and in the mid-19th century Queen Victoria opened it to the public. In 1986 part of it was seriously damaged by fire.

> Hampton Court, the neatest pile of all the King's houses.
>
> Morgan Godwyn: translation of the Bishop of Hereford's *Annals of England* (1630)

Hampton Court has become a very important tourist attraction, two of its draws being its fine Tudor interiors and its gardens, the latter incorporating the famous Maze, planted in the time of William III (the first published experiment involving a rat in a maze used a scaled down version of that at Hampton Court; however, the maze proved too baffling for even the hungriest rat – as it does to many humans – and simpler mazes were introduced by psychologists). The palace has one of England's few courts for real tennis.

The palace grounds cover 445 ha (1099 acres). The northern, and larger, section is BUSHY PARK. To the south is **Hampton Court Park** (also known as the Home Park), dominated by the Long Water, an ornamental canal flanked by lime trees imported from Holland by William III. In was in this park that the unfortunate William suffered the fall from his horse that resulted in his death. It seems a molehill was to blame, and ever after Jacobites – whether in Scotland, Ireland, Paris or Rome – would raise their glasses to 'The Little Gentleman in Black Velvet'.

It was at Hampton Court that the theft of a lock of Belinda's hair took place, which forms the centrepiece of Alexander Pope's *The Rape of the Lock* (1712):

> Close by those meads, for ever crown'd with
>   flow'rs,
> Where Thames with pride surveys his rising
>   tow'rs,
> There stands a structure of majestic frame,
> Which from the neighb'ring Hampton takes its
>   name.
> Here Britain's statesmen oft the fall foredoom
> Of foreign tyrants, and of nymphs at home;
> Here thou, Great ANNA! whom three realms obey,
> Dost sometimes counsel take – and sometimes
>   Tea …
> For ever curs'd be this detested day,
> Which snatched my best, my fav'rite curl away!
> Happy! ah ten times happy had I been,
> If Hampton-Court these eyes had never seen!

Hampton Lucy *Hampton see* HAMPTON¹; *Lucy* denoting manorial ownership in the late Middle Ages by the Lucy family.

A village in Warwickshire, about 5 km (3 miles) northeast of Stratford-upon-Avon.

Hampton Township *Hampton* presumably as HAMPTON[1].
A newly developed settlement near Peterborough. It is the largest town in Europe built by the private sector. The first residents moved in in 1997.

Hampton Wick 'harbour for (the manor of) Hampton', *see* HAMPTON[1] with OE *wic* (*see* WICK).
A district of outer southwest London, on the west bank of the River Thames, opposite Kingston upon Thames, in the borough of RICHMOND-UPON-THAMES. It is about 6 km (4 miles) downstream of (i.e. closer to London than) Hampton itself, and presumably developed as a landing-place for goods being transported to and from the capital. It is now a prosperous residential suburb, at the eastern end of Bushy and Hampton Court parks.

In the late 19th century, Cockney rhyming slang adopted *Hampton Wick* as a rhyme for *prick*, in the sense of 'penis'. It seems not to have survived, but its abbreviated form *hampton* is still very much in business (as witness the name-pun *Hugh Jampton*). It has been speculated that the second element of the rhyme may be present in the expression *to get on someone's wick* 'to annoy someone'.

The dramatist R.C. Sherriff (1896–1975) was born in Hampton Wick.

Hamstall Ridware *Hamstall* 'homestead', OE *ham-stall* (*see* HAM); *Ridware* probably '(settlement of the) dwellers at the ford', OCelt *rid* 'ford' + OE *-ware* 'dwellers'.
A village in Staffordshire, on the River Blithe, about 10.5 km (6.5 miles) north of Lichfield.
See also MAVESYN RIDWARE *and* PIPE RIDWARE.

Hanbridge. A fictional name for HANLEY in the novels of Arnold Bennett.

Hanbury '(place at the) high stronghold', OE *heah* 'high' + BURY.
A village in Worcestershire, 7 km (4.5 miles) east of Droitwich. Just to the east of here, in a parkland setting, is **Hanbury Hall**, a William-and-Mary period house completed in 1701 – somewhat in the style of Sir Christopher Wren – for Thomas Vernon by William Rudhall. It is now owned by the National Trust.

Handa 'sand island', OScand *sandr* 'sand' + *ey* (*see* -AY).
A small island off the far northwest coast of Scotland, in Highland (formerly in Sutherland), 28 km (17 miles) south of Cape Wrath. It is separated from the mainland by the narrow **Sound of Handa**. Many seabirds nest on the great cliffs on the west and north sides, and the island is a Site of Special Scientific Interest, managed by the Scottish Wildlife Trust. In the Middle Ages the island was used as a burial place by people on the mainland, so that wolves could not dig up the corpses. The island was inhabited until

the onset of the potato famine in 1846, which forced the 12 families living here to leave; prior to this, the inhabitants had, as did the St Kildans, their own 'parliament', and also their own queen, the oldest widow on the island. Off the north coast is the **Great Stack of Handa** (known in Gaelic as Stac an t-Seabhaig), separated from the island by a narrow chasm 100 m (330 ft) deep. This was first crossed in 1876 by a Lewisman, Donald MacDonald, who hauled himself hand over hand along a rope.

Handcross Probably 'cross used as a signpost (with the figure of a pointing hand)', or alternatively 'cross-roads where five tracks meet' (from the five fingers of the hand). First recorded in 1617.
A village in West Sussex, on the main London-to-Brighton road (A23), about 8 km (5 miles) south of Crawley. About 1.5 km (1 mile) to the northeast is Nymans Gardens, with its famous collection of trees, shrubs and other plants from around the world.

Handfast Point *Handfast* perhaps 'rock fortress' (referring to Studland Castle), OE *han* 'rock' + *fæsten* 'fortress'.
A headland in Dorset, on the eastern coast of the Isle of Purbeck (*see under* PURBECK), at the southern end of Studland Bay (*see under* STUDLAND), about 5 km (3 miles) northeast of Swanage. It is also known as 'the Foreland'.

Handsworth 'Hun's enclosure', OE *Hunnes* possessive form of male personal name *Hun* + *worth* (*see* -WORTH, WORTHY, -WARDINE).
A northwestern inner suburb of BIRMINGHAM. With its large immigrant West Indian and Asian population, it was the setting of *Empire Road*, the first black soap opera on British television, which ran on BBC2 between 1978 and 1979. Its message of racial harmony proved excessively optimistic: six years after the programme aired, Handsworth was torn apart by race-based riots.

Hanger Lane Originally *Hanger Hill Lane*, after *Hanger Hill*, a local hill by the River Brent, itself named after a former wood on its slopes, *Hanger Wood* 'wood on a steep slope', OE *hangra* 'steep slope' with *wudu* 'wood'.
A road (A4005, A406) running north–south in the West London borough of Ealing, from the Ealing–Brent boundary to the Uxbridge Road. Near its northern end is the notorious **Hanger Lane Gyratory System**, a multi-layer intersection and roundabout built in the 1970s where the NORTH CIRCULAR ROAD links up with the A40 (WESTERN AVENUE), and where decades of jam-bound commuters have lost the will to live.

Hanger Lane Underground station, on the Central line, opened in 1947.

Not inappropriately, *Hanger Lane* has been used as Cockney rhyming slang for *pain* (usually the metaphorical sort, as in 'a pain in the neck').

Hanging Langford *Hanging* denoting the village's position below a steep hillside; *Langford* 'long ford' (referring to a crossing of the River Wylye), OE *lang* 'long' + FORD.

A village in Wiltshire, on the River WYLYE[1], about 13 km (8 miles) northwest of Salisbury.

See also STEEPLE LANGFORD.

Hanging Walls of Mark Antony, the. *See under* CROSS FELL.

Hanley 'high wood or clearing', OE *hean* dative form of *heah* 'high' + -LEY.

A town in Staffordshire, in the POTTERIES, since 1910 subsumed into Stoke-on-Trent. In common with its neighbours, it has been shaped by the pottery industry that enriched it. The Wedgwood factory at ETRURIA is little more than 1.5 km (1 mile) to the northwest.

The novelist Arnold Bennett (1867–1931) was born in Hanley. In his fictionalization of the FIVE TOWNS it became 'Hanbridge'. Other natives of Hanley were the footballer Sir Stanley Matthews (1915–2000) and R.J. Mitchell (1895–1937), designer of the Spitfire fighter aircraft.

Hanley Child *Child* from OE *cild* 'young monk, noble-born son' (perhaps referring to land given to a monastery as an endowment for the boys' education).

A village in Worcestershire (before 1998 in Hereford and Worcester, before 1974 in Worcestershire), about 16 km (10 miles) northeast of Leominster.

Hanley Swan *Swan* from the Swan Inn here in the 19th century.

A village in Worcestershire (before 1998 in Hereford and Worcester, before 1974 in Worcestershire), about 13 km (8 miles) south of Worcester.

Hants From *Hanteshire*, an early form of *Hampshire*.

The standard written (and occasionally spoken) abbreviation of HAMPSHIRE.

Happisburgh 'Hæp's stronghold', OE *Hæpes* possessive form of male personal name *Hæp* + *burh* (*see* BURY).

A fishing village (pronounced 'hazeborough') on the East Norfolk coast, about 20 km (13 miles) southeast of Cromer. Its red-and-white-striped lighthouse, which warns against offshore sands, is a landmark for many kilometres around.

Harbledown 'Herebeald's hill', OE male personal name *Herebeald* + *dun* (DOWN, -DON).

A village in Kent, now a western district of CANTERBURY[1]. To the west is the ancient hillfort of BIGBURY CAMP.

Hard Knott Pass 'hard craggy hill', *Hard* OScand *harthr* 'hard'; *Knott* OScand *knutr* 'craggy hill'.

A pass (393 m / 1289 ft) in Cumbria (formerly in Cumberland) linking Eskdale with the rest of the Lake District to the east. Like the WRYNOSE PASS, its twin to the east, it is notorious for its hairpin bends and 1-in-3 gradients. On the west side of the pass, spectacularly situated at an elevation of 240 m (800 ft), is the so-called **Hardknott Castle**, in fact the ruins of the legionary fort of **Mediobogdum** …

> nailed by Rome to a granite pass,
> the mountains of a foreign planet heaving
> at black horrendous combes of sky …
>
> Rodney Pybus: 'Hard Knott'

It is said that Roman legionaries in Britain kept their bare legs warm in winter by beating themselves with nettles; if ever nettles were needed it must have been here, as the January westerlies, freighted with sleet, whipped in across the Irish Sea and up the valley of the Esk.

Hardwick Hall From Elizabeth Talbot, i.e. Bess of *Hardwick*; Hardwick originally 'sheep farm', OE *heorde-wic* (*see* WICK).

A grandiose Elizabethan-era house just inside Derbyshire, about 16 km (10 miles) southeast of Chesterfield. It was commissioned by the immensely powerful and wealthy Bess of Hardwick (*see below*), begetter also of the first CHATSWORTH House, and it contains many treasures in the form of furniture, paintings and tapestries, as well as a fine Long Gallery. The house and grounds passed to the National Trust in 1959.

Bess of Hardwick. Elizabeth Talbot, Countess of Shrewsbury (1518–1608), to whose husband's charge Mary Queen of Scots was committed in 1569. The countess treated the captive queen harshly, through real or feigned jealousy of her husband. The daughter of John Hardwick of Derbyshire, she married four times: Robert Barlow (when she was 14), Sir William Cavendish, Sir William St Loe and lastly George Talbot, 6th Earl of Shrewsbury. She was known as 'Building Bess of Hardwick', and in a district straddling the Nottinghamshire–Derbyshire border built not only Hardwick Hall but also mansions at Oldcotes and WORKSOP, as well as restoring Bolsover Castle (*see under* BOLSOVER).

Hardy Country. A touristic name for the areas of DORSET and western Hampshire that feature (under the name WESSEX) in the novels of the Dorset-born Thomas Hardy (1840–1928). It may have made its first appearance as the title of Charles G. Harper's *The Hardy Country* (1904), which was part of a series published by A & C Black that also included *The Burns Country*, *The Dickens Country* and *The Scott Country*.

Compare CONSTABLE COUNTRY, BURNS COUNTRY, BRONTË COUNTRY *and* SCOTT COUNTRY.

Harecastle Possibly 'grey or hares' castle', OE *har* 'grey' or *hara* 'hare' + ME *castel* (*see* CASTLE). Although there is no castle here now, and the name is not recorded before the 17th century, it may have referred to an earthwork now lost.

A location in northwestern Staffordshire, about halfway between KIDSGROVE and TUNSTALL[1]. Nearby **Harecastle Farm** bears its name.

Harecastle Tunnels. A pair of tunnels through which the Trent and Mersey Canal (*see under* TRENT[1]) runs beneath high ground between Kidsgrove and Tunstall. The original tunnel, 2649 m (2897 yds) long, was the work of the canal's originator, James Brindley, in the 1760s and 1770s (it took 11 years to build). That tunnel suffered from subsidence, and the tunnel now in use, designed by Thomas Telford, was opened in 1827. It is 2675 m (2926 yds) long.

Harefield Probably 'open land used by an army' (perhaps referring to a Viking army), OE *here* 'army' + *feld* (*see* FIELD).
A district in northwest Greater London, in the borough of HILLINGDON (before 1965 in Middlesex), about 5 km (3 miles) west of Norwood. Its surroundings are still relatively rural in aspect, but its grand 17th- and 18th-century mansions have either gone or been converted: Belhammonds, for example, is now **Harefield Hospital** (part of the Royal Brompton and Harefield NHS Trust), world-famous for its work on heart and lung transplantation.

Haringey A revival of an early spelling of *Harringay*.
A North London borough (N4, N8, N10, N11,N15, N17, N22) formed in 1965 from the former boroughs of HORNSEY, TOTTENHAM and WOOD GREEN. It also contains CROUCH END, Finsbury Park (*see under* FINSBURY), HIGHGATE and MUSWELL HILL[1], as well as the district of HARRINGAY itself. It lies between Waltham Forest to the east and Barnet to the west.

Harlaw 'grey mound', OE *har* 'grey' (although the word is frequently associated with boundaries and meeting places) + *hlaw* 'hill, mound' (*see* LAW, LOW). There are numerous Hartlaws in Scotland (meaning 'deer hill'), but the absence of spellings with *-t-*, and the play on the colour words (*see below*), indicate that this name has OE *har* rather than *heort* 'deer'.
A battle site in Aberdeenshire (formerly in Grampian region), near **Harlaw House** some 3 km (2 miles) north of Inverurie. The battle, fought in 1411, arose as a consequence of the dispute between the Regent Albany (*see* Duke of Albany *under* ALBANY[1]) and Donald, Lord of the Isles, over the earldom of Ross. Donald, leading an invasion force towards Aberdeen, was stopped by the Earl of Mar at Harlaw. Such was the bloodiness of the battle that it was long commemorated as **'the Reid Harlaw'** (Scots *reid* 'red').

Harlech 'beautiful rock', Welsh *hardd* 'fine, beautiful' + *llech* 'flat stone'.
A small town on Tremadoc Bay, Gwynedd (formerly in Merioneth), 8 km (5 miles) south of Porthmadog. **Harlech Castle** (begun 1263, now ruined) was built by the Savoyard expert, Master James of St George, on behalf of Edward I in 1283. The castle, situated on a prominent rock, was occupied by Owain Glyndwr from 1404 to 1408. It was the last Welsh castle to surrender to the Yorkists, in 1468, during the Wars of the Roses (*see below*), and the last Welsh

castle to surrender to the Parliamentarians, in 1647, during the Civil Wars. In earlier times, the court of Bendigeid Fran at Harlech was the setting for the story of Branwen, daughter of Llyr, in *The Mabinogion*. The Royal St David's Golf Club at Harlech is a championship course.

Richard Hughes, the author of *A High Wind in Jamaica* (1929), died near Harlech in 1976.

Harlech Dome, the. A large and very ancient geological structure to the south of Snowdon, stretching inland from Harlech and including the RHINOGS. It consists of a folded sequence of rocks from the lower Palaeozoic era, comprising the most complete sequences of strata in Europe from the Cambrian, Ordovician and Silurian periods (570 million to 395 million years ago).

'Men of Harlech'. A song of not altogether certain origin that has become something of an unofficial national anthem in Wales. The stirring music, under the title 'The March of the Men of Harlech', was first published in *Musical and Poetical Relicks of the Welsh Bards* (1784). The original men of Harlech were supposedly the Lancastrian defenders, led by the constable, Dafydd ap Ieuan, of Harlech Castle during the Wars of the Roses, who held out (some say for seven years) against the Yorkists, eventually being forced by starvation to an honourable surrender in 1468.

However, the various lyrics that have been supplied for the melody do not on the whole refer to this incident and rather concentrate on non-specific Welsh martial glory. The first words for the tune – in which 'Cambria' or 'Cymru' is set against 'the Saxon foe' – are by 'Talhaiarn' (Welsh) and W.H. Baker (English), and appeared in *Gems of Welsh Melody* (1860) edited by John Owen. This version begins:

> March ye men of Harlech bold,
> Unfurl your banners in the field,
> Be brave as were your sires of old,
> And like them never yield!
> What tho' every hill and dale,
> Echoes now with war's alarms,
> Celtic hearts can never quail,
> When Cambria calls to arms.

The next version, by John Oxenford, appeared in *The Songs of Wales* (1873), edited by Brinley Richards, and more successfully matched the tune. It begins:

> Men of Harlech, march to glory,
> Victory is hov'ring o'er ye,
> Bright eyed freedom stands before ye,
> Hear ye not her call?
> At your sloth she seems to wonder,
> Rend the sluggish bonds asunder,
> Let the war cry's deaf'ning thunder,
> Ev'ry foe appal.

> Echoes loudly waking,
> Hill and valley shaking;

'Till the sound spreads wide around,
The Saxon's courage breaking;
Your foes on ev'ry side assailing,
Forward press with heart unfailing,
Till invaders learn with quailing,
Cambria ne'er can yield.

The song was officially adopted by the South Wales Borderers Regiment in 1881. This was two years after a small unit from the regiment mounted its famous defence at Rorke's Drift in South Africa, recreated in the film *Zulu* (1964), in which Michael Caine and other famous 'Welshmen' movingly sing a version beginning:

Men of Harlech stop your dreaming,
Can't you see their spear points gleaming,
See their warrior pennants streaming
To this battlefield ...

Of the 1344 Victoria Crosses awarded from 1856 until the making of the film, 11 were awarded to the defenders of Rorke's Drift, a record for any one engagement. However, it is thought unlikely that the courage of the historical defenders was in reality steeled by a rendition of the song.

Harlesden 'Heoruwulf's or Herewulf's farmstead or estate', OE *Heoruwulfes* or *Herewulfes* possessive forms of male personal names *Heoruwulf* and *Herewulf* + -TON (the *-den* ending, suggesting 'valley', is unhistorical).
A district of northwest London (NW10), in the borough of BRENT[2], immediately to the north of the great railway junction of Willesden. It was the railway that promoted its growth from rural village to light-industrial suburb in the last quarter of the 19th century.
Harlesden 'Underground' station, on the Bakerloo line, opened in 1917.

In Harlesden there's a waiting list to get mugged. The only time you would go next door was if you were breaking in.

Shane Richie (Alfie Moon in *EastEnders*), who grew up here: quoted in 2003

Harley Street After Edward *Harley*, 2nd Earl of Oxford, who owned the manor of Marylebone until his death in 1741.
A street in Marylebone (W1), in the City of Westminster, running from Marylebone Road (*see under* MARYLEBONE) in the north to Cavendish Square in the south. Laid out between the 1730s and the 1770s, it was at first a fashionable residential street, but in the early 19th century the medical profession began to move in, and by the end of the century its reputation as a street of doctors was firmly established. The 'fashionability' factor remained, however: even after the coming of the National Health Service, Harley Street was, and remains, only for those with the financial resources to consult the 'top' (i.e. most expensive) physicians, dentists and psychiatrists in their professions or to

foot the bill for a stay in one of the street's private nursing homes. Its name has become synonymous with 'top of the medical range': for the final opinion, you go to a 'Harley Street consultant' or a 'Harley Street specialist'.

Harlington 'farmstead or estate associated with Hygered', OE male personal name *Hygered* + -ING + -TON.
An area within the Urban District of **Hayes and Harlington** (*see under* HAYES) in the London borough of HILLINGDON.

Harlow 'mound or hill associated with an army' (perhaps alluding to a Viking army), OE *here* 'army' + *hlaw* (*see* LAW, LOW).
A town in Essex, on the River STORT, about 8 km (5 miles) north of Epping and the M25. Until just after the Second World War it was a rural village, but in 1947 it was declared a NEW TOWN[1], since when it has grown into a sizeable satellite of London, absorbing many thousands of people from the eastern part of the capital. Its geometrical and somewhat unvarying townscape provides little visual nourishment to its inhabitants and can be disorienting for visitors, but its designer, Sir Frederick Gibberd, evidently liked it enough to make his home in the old village (now known as **Old Harlow** to distinguish it from its outsize offspring to the south).

Harmondsworth 'Heremund's or Heremod's enclosed settlement', OE *Heremundes* or *Heremodes* possessive forms of the male personal names *Heremund* and *Heremod* + *worth* (*see* -WORTH, WORTHY, -WARDINE).
A district (pronounced 'harmənzworth' or, locally in former times, 'harmzworth') in West London (before 1965 in Middlesex), just to the north of Heathrow Airport, in the borough of HILLINGDON. Its name is indissolubly linked with that of Penguin Books, which opened its offices here in 1937.

Harpenden Probably 'valley of the harp' (perhaps referring to the shape of the valley), OE *hearpan* possessive form of *hearpe* 'harp' + *denu* 'valley'; alternatively the first element might be from OE *herepæth* 'highway, main road'.
A town in Hertfordshire, just to the east of the M1, about 8 km (5 miles) northwest of St Albans.

The chief attraction of Harpenden is the way in which the High Street has kept its broad, sloping, tree-planted greens in the middle ... Otherwise there is not much interest, only a few old houses of note and a few distinguished recent buildings, as against the hundreds of phoney half-timbered residences of well-to-do Londoners which have grown up in the last fifty years.

Nikolaus Pevsner and Bridget Cherry: *The Buildings of England: Hertfordshire* (1977)

The film director Stanley Kubrick (1928–99) died in Harpenden.
See also ROTHAMSTED.

Harringay From *Harringay* House, a house built in the district in 1729 and named with a by-then obsolete form of the name *Hornsey*, referring to the house's location.

A district in North London (N4, N8), in the southeastern part of HORNSEY, in the borough of HARINGEY. **Harringay Stadium**, a well-known venue for greyhound racing, opened in 1927. It closed 60 years later, but by then a railway station had been named after it.

Harris Either Gaelic *na h-àirdibh* 'the heights', from OScand *hearri* 'higher (than Lewis)', or Gaelic *na h-earaidhi* from OScand *heruth* 'district'. The modern Gaelic name is *Hearadh*, which points to the second alternative as more likely.

The southern part of the island of Lewis with Harris, Western Isles, some 55 km (33 miles) west across the Minch (*see under* the MINCHES) from the mainland of northwest Scotland. Somewhat oddly, Harris is often thought of as a separate island to LEWIS, although the neck of land joining the two is a good 13 km (8 miles) wide. The distinction is principally topographic, Lewis being flat and boggy and spattered with a thousand lochans, while Harris is much more hilly, the highest point being CLISHAM (799 m / 2622 ft). The difference was reinforced in local government terms before 1975: Harris was in INVERNESS-SHIRE, while Lewis was in ROSS AND CROMARTY. Both now come under the WESTERN ISLES authority.

Harris is separated from North Uist (*see under* UISTS) to the south by the **Sound of Harris**, which is 12 km (7 miles) across, and is itself divided at the narrow isthmus at TARBERT between North Harris (Gaelic name *Ceann a Tuath na Hearadh*) and South Harris (*Ceann a Deas na Hearadh*). Down the latter runs the Golden Road, so called because it was so expensive to construct.

> The narrow bay
> Has a knuckle of houses and a nail of sand
> By which the sea hangs grimly to the land.
>
> Norman MacCaig: 'Harris, East side', from *Measures* (1965)

Offshore islands include SCALPAY[1] (joined to Harris by bridge since 1998), Scarp (where in 1934 a Herr Zucker attempted to use a rocket to deliver the mail, which was incinerated as a result) and TARANSAY, of *Castaway* fame.

Harris was traditionally in the hands of the MacLeods of Harris, but in the 19th century it came into the hands of the Earl of Dunmore, who helped to develop the **Harris tweed** industry (*see below*). Lord Leverhulme, the soap manufacturer, bought Lewis and Harris in 1918 and invested large sums in an unsuccessful attempt to develop the fishing industry, abandoned after his death in 1925. He is commemorated in the village name LEVERBURGH in the south of Harris.

Harris tweed. A loosely woven tweed material, manufactured especially on Lewis and Harris. In Gaelic it is called *clò mór* ('big cloth'). Over 4 million metres are produced each year, a goodly proportion of which is on display when the Countryside Alliance marches in London. Harris Tweed was also the name of the tweedy and moustached Extra Special Agent, fantasist and nincompoop created by John Ryan for *The Eagle* comic in the 1950s.

Harrogate 'road with or to the cairn', OScand *horgr* 'heap of stones' + *gata* 'road.

A town in North Yorkshire, some 20 km (12 miles) north of Leeds. It developed as a spa after the discovery of Tewit Well in 1571; subsequently many other mineral springs (saline, sulphurous and chalybeate) were discovered, and it was the most fashionable spa in northern England in the Victorian and Edwardian eras. The waters were not to everybody's taste, however:

> The Sulphur or Stinking Spaw not improperly termed, for the Smell being so strong and offensive that I could not force my horse near the Well.
>
> Celia Fiennes (1662–1741): *The Journeys of Celia Fiennes* (1888)

Despite the decline in the spa business, Harrogate still fancies itself more refined than its rough industrial neighbours to the south, such as Leeds, Bradford and Huddersfield. Today it is an important conference centre, and holds trade fairs, an annual music festival, and agricultural and flower shows, calling itself 'England's floral town'.

It was to Harrogate that in 1926 Agatha Christie famously 'disappeared', subsequently claiming to have lost her memory. She stayed at the hotel now called The Old Swan, and checked in using the name of her husband's mistress.

Sir Edward Hulton (1906–88), publisher of illustrated magazines and comics such as *Picture Post* and *The Eagle*, was born here.

Harrow 'heathen shrine or temple', OE *hearg*.

A district and borough of northwest Outer London (before 1965 in Middlesex). The borough lies between Brent to the east and Hillingdon to the west. As well as the district of Harrow, it includes Hatch End, Kenton, PINNER, RAYNERS LANE, STANMORE and WEALDSTONE. The district of Harrow itself is immediately to the northwest of Wembley.

The original settlement of Harrow, whose full name is **Harrow-on-the-Hill**, developed on top of a 125 m (408 ft) hill. As the name *Harrow* reveals (*see above*), the summit was the site of pagan worship before the Anglo-Saxons were converted to Christianity. The temple there appears to have been used by a tribe called the Gumeningas, of whom nothing more is known. Its place has been taken by the 11th-century church of St Mary.

Harrow's hilltop situation made it a focal point for the country around, and it became an important local centre.

It did not begin its expansion to its current size until the 19th century, however. Its southwestern extension, **South Harrow**, was followed in the 20th century by **North Harrow** and **West Harrow**. By the interwar period, Harrow was a southern outpost of METROLAND, the Hill highly desirable, the spreading outskirts indistinguishably suburban. At the beginning of the 21st century it had a quite multiracial population.

Harrow-on-the-Hill 'Underground' station opened in 1880 (originally as plain 'Harrow'), West Harrow in 1913 and North Harrow in 1915, all on the Metropolitan line. Harrow and Wealdstone on the Bakerloo line opened in 1917.

Sylvia Townsend Warner (1893–1978), the novelist, poet and essayist; Roger Bannister (b.1929), the first man to run the mile in under 4 minutes; Mike Brearley (b.1942), the cerebral and markedly successful England cricket captain of the late 1970s and early 1980s; and Michael Rosen (b.1946), the children's writer, were all born in Harrow. *See also* GRIM'S DYKE.

Harrovian. (A pupil) of Harrow School (*see below*). The term, first recorded in the mid 19th century, is based on a modern Latinization of *Harrow* as *Harrovia*. It is most commonly preceded by the adjective 'Old', denoting former pupils of the school.

Harrow. A term applied to a cricket bat larger than the numbered sizes used by children but smaller than a full-size bat for adults. It presumably comes from *Harrow* School, but the precise details of the derivation are not known.

Harrow drive. A cricket term that seems originally, in the mid-19th century, to have been applied to an off-drive, presumably thought of as a specialism of Harrovian batsmen. Well before the close of the century, however, those inclined to poke fun at the school's pretensions were using it to denote a botched or edged drive, and by the middle of the 20th century it was firmly attached to a stroke that sends the ball accidentally off the inside edge of the bat past the leg stump.

Harrow Rail Disaster, the. A railway accident that took place in Harrow station at 8.18 on the morning of 8 October 1952. An overnight express sleeper travelling from Perth to Euston overshot signals at Harrow and ploughed into a stationary local train waiting in the station. Shortly afterwards a northbound express from Euston ran into the wreckage, causing carnage in a station crowded with rush-hour commuters. In all, 122 people were killed and 150 injured. The Harrow Rail Disaster is second only to the Gretna Green Rail Disaster of 1915 (*see under* GRETNA) in terms of casualties.

Harrow School. A boy's public school in Harrow-on-the-Hill, founded in 1572 by a local farmer, John Lyon. In the public mind it is paired with Eton College (*see under* ETON)

as the most prototypical of public schools. Its old boys include several British prime ministers (Robert Peel, Lord Palmerston, Stanley Baldwin, Winston Churchill) and one Indian one (Jawaharlal Nehru), and such literary figures as Lord Byron, John Mortimer, Terence Rattigan, Richard Sheridan and Anthony Trollope. Its pupils wear distinctive straw hats. It is famous for its school songs, of which the most familiar is 'Forty Years On'. The game of squash is thought to have originated here.

> At Harrow you could have any boy for a box of Cadbury's milk chocolate. But I didn't want boys.
>
> John Mortimer: quoted in the *Daily Telegraph* (24 September 1998)

Harrow Weald 'forest or woodland at Harrow', *Harrow* with OE *weald* 'forest, woodland' (*see* WEALDSTONE).

A district of northwest Outer London, in the borough of HARROW (before 1965 in Middlesex), to the north of the district of Harrow, and to the west of STANMORE. *See also* GRIM'S DYKE.

Hart From the River *Hart*, a tributary of the Thames, the name of which is itself a back-formation from either HARTLEY WINTNEY or the nearby hamlet of *Hartfordbridge* ('bridge at the ford where stags are seen', OE *heorot* 'hart, stag' + FORD + *brycg* 'bridge').

A local government district in northeastern Hampshire, to the south of Reading. Its administrative headquarters are in FLEET[3].

Hartland Point From the town of *Hartland*, originally *Hertiton* 'farmstead or estate on the peninsula frequented by stags', OE *heorot* 'hart, stag' + *eg* 'island, promontory' (*see* -EY, -EA) + -TON; forms with -*land* in place of -*ton* first appear in the 12th century.

A headland in north Devon, at the eastern extremity of Bideford Bay (*see under* BIDEFORD), about 21 km (13 miles) west of Bideford. It is the northwestern tip of Devon. Its dark sheer 100-m (325-ft) cliffs are spectacularly pounded by the Atlantic rollers.

About 5 km (3 miles) inland, in the flat bleak farming country of the **Hartland Peninsula**, is the small town of **Hartland**, and 2.5 km (1.5 miles) south, on the westward-facing coast, is **Hartland Quay**. Three celebrated Elizabethan sailors, Sir Francis Drake, Sir Walter Raleigh and Sir John Hawkins, financed the building of a harbour here in the 16th century, but its quay finally succumbed to the violence of the Atlantic in the late 19th century.

Hart-Leap Well. A spring made famous in a poem of the same name by William Wordsworth (published in 1798 as one of the *Lyrical Ballads*). In his preface to this ballad the poet notes:

> Hart-Leap Well is a small spring of water, about five miles from Richmond in Yorkshire, and near the side of the road which leads from Richmond to Askrigg.

The poem retells how the spring got its name: a hart, pursued all day by a certain Sir Walter, makes three giant leaps down a steep hill, covering an astonishing 'nine roods', but this last great effort to escape is too much for the deer, which expires next to the spring in question. Sir Walter is so impressed that he vows

> I'll build a Pleasure-house upon this spot,
> And a small Arbour, made for rural joy;
> 'Twill be the traveller's shed, the pilgrim's cot,
> A place of love for damsels that are coy.

However, when the poet visits the place he finds these monuments in decay, and, in discussion with a shepherd, concludes that Nature has cursed the place that witnessed such suffering on the part of the panting hart.

Hartlepool 'bay by the hart's headland', OE *heorot* 'hart, stag' + *eg* (*see* -EY, -EA) + *pol* 'pool, bay'.

An industrial port and unitary authority in northeast England (formerly in County Durham, then in Cleveland), 13 km (8 miles) north of Middlesbrough. In the 7th century a monastery was built on the headland on the north side of **Hartlepool Bay**; St Hilda of Whitby (614–680) was abbess here. In the Middle Ages Hartlepool flourished as a market town, and became the port of the bishops of Durham (*see* LAND OF THE PRINCE BISHOPS). The town developed as a coal port and shipbuilding centre in the 19th century, when a new town, **West Hartlepool**, was founded to the south of the docks, and remained administratively independent until 1969. Because of its shipbuilding, Hartlepool became the target of German naval bombardment on 16 December 1914. It fared badly in the Depression of the 1930s, and despite the proximity of extensive sands never quite made it as a seaside resort.

> Even the sea was grim here – not rough, but motionless and oily, a sort of offshore soup made of sewage and poison.
>
> Paul Theroux: *The Kingdom by the Sea* (1983)

The inhabitants of Hartlepool are called **Hartlepudlians**; their nickname of **Monkey Hangers** comes from the time when, during the Napoleonic Wars, a French ship foundered offshore and the people of Hartlepool hanged the only survivor, a monkey that they mistook for a Frenchman. The monkey episode continues to inform the town's present, **Hartlepool FC**'s mascot going by the name of H'Angus the Monkey. H'Angus (actually a young man called Stuart Drummond) became Hartlepool's first elected mayor in 2002, standing on a platform of 'free bananas for schoolchildren'.

W.M. Thackeray fictionalized Hartlepool as **Cockleton**. The novelist and Scottish nationalist Compton Mackenzie (Edward Montague Compton; 1883–1972) was born in theatrical lodgings in West Hartlepool while his father was appearing at the Gaiety Theatre. Ridley Scott (b.1939), the director of such Hollywood successes as *Alien* and *Blade Runner*, grew up in West Hartlepool and attended the town's art college. Hartlepool's MP 1992–2004 was the controversial twice-sacked New Labour cabinet minister, Peter 'Mandy' Mandelson, who resigned his seat for a new post as an EU Commissioner in 2004.

Hartley Wintney *Hartley* 'glade frequented by stags', OE *heorot* 'hart, stag' + -LEY; *Wintney* denoting manorial ownership in the early Middle Ages by the Priory of Wintney, a nunnery in the parish (*Wintney* 'Winta's raised land in a marsh', OE male personal name *Winta* + *eg* 'raised land in a marsh'; *see* -EY, -EA).

A village in Hampshire, 5 km (3 miles) northwest of Fleet.

Hartrigg Oaks A very recent coinage, modelled on OScand *hjartr* 'hart, deer' + *hryggr* 'ridge', hence 'deer ridge oaks'.

A new village near York, one of the first in Britain to ban residence by anyone under 60. It opened in 1998.

Harwell 'spring or stream by the hill called Hara', OE hill name *Hara* 'the grey one' (from *har* 'grey') + *wella* 'spring, stream'.

A village in Oxfordshire (before 1974 in Berkshire), about 8 km (5 miles) east of Wantage. An atomic research centre was built here in 1947, incorporating Britain's first atomic pile.

Harwich 'army camp' (probably referring to that of a Viking army), OE *here-wic* (*see* WICK).

A town and port (pronounced 'haridge' or 'haritch') in Essex, on a small peninsula at the southern edge of the mouth of the River STOUR[2]. It was already an important naval base in the 14th century, and in Elizabethan times Sir Francis Drake and other seafarers fitted out their ships here. Samuel Pepys was MP for the town in the 1670s. To defend the port during the Napoleonic Wars the massive Redoubt was built, a circular fort 60 m (180 ft) in diameter. Today Harwich is Britain's busiest departure port for car ferries to northern Europe. Ships leave Parkstone Quay for Gothenburg, Esbjerg, Hamburg and the Hook of Holland.

> For you dream you are crossing the Channel, and
> tossing about in a steamer from Harwich –
> Which is something between a large bathing machine
> and a very small second class carriage.
>
> W.S. Gilbert: *Iolanthe* (1882)

The Electric Palace, opened in 1911, is Britain's oldest cinema.

There is a town and former whaling port called Harwich (pronounced 'har-witch') in Massachusetts, USA. It is the birthplace of the US cranberry industry.

Harwood Forest *Harwood* OE *har* 'grey' or *hær* 'rocks' or *hara* 'hare' + *wudu* 'wood'.

An extensive Forestry Commission plantation in Northumberland, some 10 km (6 miles) east of OTTERBURN.

Haselbury Plucknett *Haselbury* 'hazel wood or grove', OE *hæsel* 'hazel' + *bearu* 'wood, grove'; *Plucknett* denoting manorial ownership in the early Middle Ages by the de Plugenet family.

A village in Somerset, about 3 km (2 miles) northeast of Crewkerne.

Hasguard Either 'house enclosure' or 'house by the cleft', OScand *hus* 'house' with either *garthr* 'enclosure' or *skarthr* 'cleft, pass'.

A village in Pembrokeshire (formerly in Dyfed), 6 km (4 miles) northwest of Milford Haven.

Haslar 'point of land growing with hazel', OE *hæsel* 'hazel' + *ord* 'point (of land)'.

A southeastern coastal suburb of GOSPORT. It is best known for the Royal Naval Hospital (a psychiatric institution) sited here.

gone to Haslar. Late-20th-century naval slang for 'insane'.
Haslar nurse. Late-20th-century naval slang for a truncheon.

Haslemere 'pool where hazels grow', OE *hæsel* 'hazel' + *mere* 'pool'.

A town in Surrey, about 21 km (13 miles) southwest of Guildford, on the borders of Hampshire and West Sussex. It nestles among woods and hills in an area designated as one of outstanding natural beauty. This is 24-carat stockbroker country, and sumptuous villas abound.

Arnold Dolmetsch (1858–1940), one of the first pioneers of early music, settled in Haslemere, and his descendants still make reproduction early instruments here. The Dolmetsch Early Music Festival honours him every July.

The aircraft designer Sir Geoffrey de Havilland (1882–1965) was born in Haslemere.

Haslingden 'valley growing with hazel trees', OE as *hæsel* 'hazel' + *-en* 'characterized by' (the modern *-ing* was historically *-en*, as in the word 'wooden') + *denu* 'valley'.

A textile town on the River IRWELL, Lancashire, some 3 km (2 miles) west of Rawtenstall. It was the birthplace of the composer Alan Rawsthorne (1905–71).

Hassocks From a field called *Hassocks*, from OE *hassuc* 'clump of coarse grass'.

A village in West Sussex, about 11 km (7 miles) north of Brighton. It grew up around the London-to-Brighton railway line, which opened in 1841, and today contributes commuters to both termini.

Hastings '(settlement of) Hæsta's people', OE male personal name *Hæsta* + *-ingas* (*see* -ING).

A town and resort on the East Sussex coast, about 21 km (13 miles) northeast of Eastbourne. It has been in the invasion firing-line from earliest times. The Romans built a defensive castle not far to the southwest, at PEVENSEY, which is where the Normans landed in 1066. William the Conqueror built a castle at Hastings in 1067, partly to deter copycat invaders. It was originally the chief of the CINQUE PORTS, a Channel defence alliance, but this did not prevent it from being sacked by the French in 1339 and 1377.

The harbour here has long since silted up, but Hastings maintains its coastal fishing activities, and its distinctive 16th-century 'shops', tall wooden sheds for drying nets, can still be seen on the shingle beach. The fishing boats are drawn up the beach by winches, one of the few places in southern England where this occurs.

In the 19th century Hastings developed as a holiday resort, complete with pier (1872) and a 5-km (3-mile) long promenade linking the town with ST LEONARDS to the southwest. Since the 19th century the fortunes of Hastings have somewhat declined, and it is now, with its tatty bedsits full of the impoverished and unemployed, one of the social blackspots of southeast England. An appalling train service has saved it from being gentrified along the lines of Brighton, although this keeps it affordable for the colony of artists (mostly – with the exception of John Bratby (1928–92) – unknown) who live here. It has the second highest divorce rate in the UK.

In Hastings in the early 1920s John Logie Baird performed embryonic experiments in the electronic transmission of simple shadows of geometric shapes, which formed the basis of his eventual pioneering demonstration of true television in SOHO in 1925. His efforts are played up to the hilt on the main sign for Hastings on the A21 from London, which proclaims the town as 'the birthplace of TV'.

In *The Ragged-Trousered Philanthropists* (1914), Robert Tressell fictionalized Hastings (where he was living when he wrote it) as **Mugsborough**.

Hastings was the birthplace of Sophia Jex-Blake (1840–1912), the feminist icon, who successfully battled for women to be trained and to practise as doctors. Archibald Belaney (1887–1937), who masqueraded lucratively as a Native American called Grey Owl, was brought up in the town.

There is a town called Hastings in New Zealand (North Island), and another in the USA (Nebraska), although the latter is named after Colonel Thomas D. Hastings, a railroad contractor.

See also ORE[1].

Battle of Hastings (14 October 1066). A battle at which the invading Normans under Duke William defeated the English under Harold II and established a bridgehead from which they swiftly went on to gain control of England. William made his overnight preparations for the battle at Hastings, but as every schoolboy knows, the battle itself did not take place here. It was fought 10 km (6 miles) inland, at the place now known as BATTLE, close by a stream called Senlac (literally 'sand-brook', OE *sand* + *lacu* 'stream, water-course') – pedants are inclined to refer to the encounter as the 'Battle of Senlac'. The English soldiers, who had just marched about 430 km (270 miles) southwards from a victorious engagement with Scandinavian forces at STAMFORD BRIDGE, fought bravely, but they never really stood a chance against the Normans' cavalry and archers, and when Harold was killed (reputedly by an arrow in the eye), resistance crumbled.

> In the year 1066 occurred the other memorable date in English History, viz. *William the Conqueror, Ten Sixty-six*. This is also called *The Battle of Hastings*, and was when William I (1066) conquered England at the Battle of Senlac (*Ten Sixty-six*).
>
> W.C. Sellar and R.J. Yeatman: *1066 And All That* (1930)

Hastings Day. An eight-day celebration held in Hastings every October since 1968. The event had its genesis in 1966, the 900th anniversary of the town's foundation. The current festivities include music, sports and flag ceremonies, with all in the town contributing. A recent addition is the revival of a bonfire tradition, and a torchlight procession culminates in a bonfire and fireworks, featuring the 'largest Guy Fawkes in England', on the Saturday nearest 14 October.

Haswell 'stream where hazels grow', OE *hæsel*, 'hazel' + *wella*, 'spring, stream'.

A former pit village in County Durham, 14 km (9 miles) south of Sunderland. The folk ballad **'The Haswell Cages'**, published by the Durham broadside printer George Walker around 1839, describes in documentary detail the new practice employed in the colliery here of winding up miners and coal in cages from the coalface to the surface:

> Come all you good people and listen awhile
> I'll sing you a song that will cause you to smile.
> It is about Haswell I mean for to sing
> Concerning the new plan we started last spring.
>
> And the very first thing I will mention,
> Without any evil intention,
> It's concerning this new invention
> Of winding up coals in a cage.

Hatfield¹ 'heathy open land', OE *hæth* 'heath' + *feld* (*see* FIELD).

A market town in Hertfordshire, about 5 km (3 miles) south of Welwyn Garden City, on the GREAT NORTH ROAD ('Hatfield and the North' was a direction that once featured widely on traffic signs in North London, and became the name of a prog-rock band of the 1970s). Immediately after the Second World War it was designated as one of four NEW TOWNS[1] in Hertfordshire (the other three are HEMEL HEMPSTEAD, STEVENAGE and WELWYN GARDEN CITY).

The aircraft manufacturer de Havilland, which started out in EDGWARE, opened its factory in Hatfield in 1934.

Hatfield was the scene of a serious railway accident on 17 October 2000, in which four people were killed and over 100 injured when an intercity train from Kings Cross to Leeds derailed on a broken rail on the east coast mainline. It triggered disquiet over the management of Britain's post-privatization railways.

To the east of the town is **Hatfield House**, the imposing Jacobean mansion that is the ancestral home of the Cecils, the earls of Salisbury. One wing survives of the so-called Old Palace, which it replaced. Elizabeth I (whom William Cecil, Lord Burghley, served as First Minister) spent much of her childhood here.

Hatfield is the site of the University of Hertfordshire (formerly Hatfield Polytechnic).

Hatfield². A former mining village in South Yorkshire, 11 km (7 miles) northeast of Doncaster. The first shaft of **Hatfield Main** colliery, one of the biggest collieries in the South Yorkshire coalfield, was sunk in 1916. The colliery scenes in the feature film *Brassed Off* (1996) – an angry and affecting tale of pit closures and brass bands (*see also* GRIMETHORPE) – were filmed here. Hatfield Main finally ceased production in January 2004.

To the southeast of Hatfield are **Hatfield Moors**, while to the east is **Hatfield Chase**, a former royal hunting forest. Much of it was marshy, but the area was drained in 1626 by the Dutch engineer Cornelius Vermuyden, resulting in good agricultural land.

Hatfield was the birthplace of the mezzo-soprano Dame Janet Baker (b.1933).

Battle of Hatfield Chase (AD 632). A battle in which Cadwallon (or Caedwalla), king of Gwynedd in North Wales, defeated and killed Edwin of Northumbria.

Hatfield Forest. An area of well-preserved medieval forest in Essex, now a recreational area and nature reserve, about 5 km (3 miles) east of Bishop's Stortford, Essex. It is about 4.25 sq km (1.5 sq miles) in extent. Until 1915 part of the Royal Forest of Essex, it has been owned by the National Trust since 1924.

> The best-preserved of all forests is Hatfield ... There are still deer, cattle, coppice woods, seven species of pollards, scrub, timber trees, grassland, fen, and a 17th-century lodge and rabbit warren. It is a unique survival in England and possibly in the world: here alone (and in the twin Forest of Writtle ...) one can step back into the Middle Ages and see what a Forest looked like in use.
>
> Oliver Rackham: *The History of the Countryside* (1986)

Within the forest are Portingbury Rings, a set of earthen enclosures probably dating back to the Iron Age.

Hathersage Probably 'he-goat's ridge', OE *hæferes* possessive form of *hæfer* 'he-goat' (referring to Millstone Edge, a rocky escarpment in the locality, perhaps resembling a goat in outline, or frequented by goats); alternatively the first element may from the OE male personal name *Hæfer* + *ecg* 'edge'.

A small town in Derbyshire, about 19 km (12 miles) southwest of Sheffield. In folkloric tradition, Little John, follower of Robin Hood (*see under* SHERWOOD FOREST), is said to be buried in Hathersage churchyard.

Hatt 'hat' (referring to the shape of a hill in the locality), OE *hætt*.

A village in Cornwall, about 5 km (3 miles) northwest of Saltash.

Hatton 'farmstead or estate on the heath' (referring to the same heath as gave HEATHROW its name), OE *hæth* 'heath' + -TON.

An outer suburb of West London, in the borough of HOUNSLOW, just to the east of Heathrow Airport. **Hatton Cross** in 1975 gave its name (from a local crossroads) to an Underground station on the Piccadilly line (serving the new Heathrow extension).

Hatton Garden From *Hatton* House, the mansion built here in the late 16th century for Elizabeth I's chancellor, Sir Christopher Hatton.

A street in Central London (EC1), in the borough of Camden, linking Clerkenwell Road in the north with Holborn Circus in the south. Laid out in the mid-17th century, until the early 19th it was a residential street of some pretension, but then the jewellers and silversmiths began to move in, and since then it has become virtually synonymous with their trade. Jewellers' shops line the street, especially towards its more southerly end, and it is the centre of the London diamond business.

The American inventor Hiram Maxim created the machine-gun in 1881 in Hatton Garden, where he was living at the time.

Haughs of Cromdale. *See under* CROMDALE.

Haulbowline Island Possibly referring to a way of navigating around it.

A small island in Cork Harbour, County Cork, opposite COBH. The headquarters of the Irish Navy are here.

Havant 'Hama's spring', OE *Haman* possessive form of male personal name *Hama* + *funta* 'stream, spring'.

A town in Hampshire, just to the north of Langstone Harbour (*see under* LANGSTONE), about 11 km (7 miles) northeast of Portsmouth. HAYLING ISLAND is offshore to the south. Until the early 20th century Havant was a centre for the making of parchment – the Treaty of Versailles (1919) was printed on sheets of Havant parchment.

Haven, the Perhaps from OScand *hafn* 'harbour'.

A waterway from BOSTON to the WASH. On its eastern bank is North Sea Camp detention centre (*see under* NORTH SEA).

Haverfordwest 'western goat-ford', OE *hæfer* 'male goat' + FORD + *west*.

A town in Pembrokeshire (formerly in Dyfed), about 11 km (7 miles) north of Milford Haven, on the Western Cleddau River. Its Welsh name is **Hwlffordd**, and it is locally pronounced 'harford'. It was formerly an important port, and is now the administrative seat of PEMBROKESHIRE unitary authority. The castle dates from the 12th century, and was visited by a number of English kings during the Middle Ages. The town was burnt by Owain Glyndwr's men in 1407, and changed hands several times during the Civil Wars.

Haverfordwest was the birthplace of the pirate captain known as Black Barty (Bartholomew Roberts; ?1682–1722), who seized some 400 vessels during his short career. Lucy Walter (?1630–58), mistress of Charles II, was born at Roch Castle near the town.

Haverhill Probably 'hill where oats are grown', OScand *hafri* or OE *hæfera* 'oats' + OE *hyll* 'hill'; an alternative is OE *hæfer* 'male goat' + *hill*.

A small market town in Suffolk, about 30 km (19 miles) southeast of Cambridge. To the southeast are the indistinct remains of an ancient earthwork known as **Haverhill Castle**. The source of the River COLNE[1] is nearby.

Haverhill grew up on the Roman road known as the VIA DEVANA. Most of the town was destroyed by fire in 1665. Extensive housing estates and factories were built in the 1950s to take population overspill from London.

There is a town called Haverhill in the USA (Massachusetts).

Havering From *Havering-atte-Bower* (the name was chosen because most of the borough lies within the bounds of the Royal Liberty of Havering-atte-Bower, granted by charter in 1465).

A borough of outer northeast London, to the east of Redbridge and Barking and Dagenham. It was formed in 1965 from portions of southwest Essex, notably HAVERING-ATTE-BOWER, HORNCHURCH, Rainham, ROMFORD and UPMINSTER.

Havering-atte-Bower *Havering* '(settlement of) Hæfer's people', OE male personal name *Hæfer* + -*ingas* (*see* -ING); -*atte-Bower* 'at the royal residence' (referring to a nearby medieval royal palace), ME *atte* 'at the' + *bour* (OE *bur*) 'bower, royal residence'.

A district (*atte* pronounced 'atti') of outer northeast London, in the borough of HAVERING (before 1965 in Essex), to the north of Romford and to the east of Hainault. It is still relatively village-like, surrounded by parkland and open country. It is situated on a hillside ridge, which in the Middle Ages was dominated by a royal palace (from which the latter part of the district's name comes – *see above*). This was used by most English monarchs from Edward the Confessor to the Stuarts, and it was the official residence of queens of England until 1620. Some of its grounds survive as **Havering Country Park**, and remains of the building are located on the hillside ridge.

Hawarden 'high enclosure', OE *heah* 'high' + *worthign* 'enclosure' (*see also* -WORTH, WORTHY, -WARDINE); it is recorded as *Haordine* in Domesday Book (1086).

A small town in Flintshire (formerly in Clwyd), 9 km (5.5 miles) west of Chester. Its Welsh name is **Penarlâg** ('high ground full of cattle'). **Hawarden Castle** (1752) was for many years the home of the Liberal prime minister, W.E. Gladstone; he had married into the Glynne family, owners of the estate since the Civil Wars. In 1895 he founded St Deiniol's theological library in the town.

Hawarden Kite, the. An 'indiscreet' statement by Herbert Gladstone, the prime minister's youngest son, to a journalist in December 1885 that his father was considering coming out in favour of Home Rule for Ireland, something that the prime minister denied on 17 December. The following year the first Home Rule Bill was introduced.

Hawes OE *hals* 'pass between hills'.

A small market town on the River URE in upper Wensleydale, North Yorkshire, 32 km (19 miles) southwest of Richmond. It has high fells to both north and south, and is itself at an altitude of 240 m (787 ft), making it one of the highest market towns in England. Hawes is home to the Yorkshire Dales National Park Centre. It was formerly a centre of lead mining, and WENSLEYDALE cheese is made here.

Haweswater 'Hæfer's lake', OE male personal name *Hæfer* + *wæter* 'water, lake'.

A lake in the eastern LAKE DISTRICT, Cumbria (formerly in Cumberland), some 12 km (7 miles) northeast of Ambleside. In 1929, despite objections, Parliament passed a bill for the damming of Haweswater to make a reservoir for Manchester. As a consequence, the village of Mardale was drowned, although in dry summers its walls can still be seen.

Haweswater (2002), a novel by Sarah Hall with a 1930s setting, depicts the decline of a Lakeland farming community and the encroachment of industrialization and modernity.

Hawick 'hedge farm', OE *haga* 'hedge' + *wic* (*see* WICK).

A market town (pronounced 'hoik' or 'haw-ik') in Scottish Borders, on the River TEVIOT, 16 km (10 miles) southwest of Jedburgh. It was formerly in Roxburghshire, and was then the seat of the ROXBURGH district until the latter's abolition in 1996. It is also known as **the Queen o' the Borders** and as **the Grey Auld Toon**. The town was very much involved in the constant Border skirmishes up to the 17th century. The Common Riding Day in June, in which the townsfolk ride round the boundaries, celebrates the time in 1514 when the young men (*callants*) of the town captured the 'Hexham pennant' from an English raiding party at Hornshole. The town's famous knitwear industry originated in the late 18th century.

Hawick appears in a traditional folk tale, in which a shepherd on his way to Hawick market meets a fairy who has nothing to keep her baby warm. So the shepherd hands over his own plaid, and in return he makes his fortune at the market, where he finds the prices have dropped so that he can buy several sheep, rather than just one.

Hawick is deep in Borders rugby union country. Its rugby football club, founded in 1873 , has contributed numerous players to the Scottish national side.

Hawick was the birthplace of James Murray (1837–1915), who spoke Latin to cows and edited the *Oxford English Dictionary* from 1878 until he died.

Hawick ba. A ball (Scots *ba*) game played at Shrovetide in the River Teviot until the early 20th century. The name is now given to a locally made boiled sweet, minty in flavour and brown in colour.

Hawick gill. A generous, indeed intoxicating, measure of spirits, equivalent to 0.28 litre (half a pint).

Hawkshead 'Haukr's summer pasture', OScand personal name *Haukr* + *sætr* 'summer pasture'.

An attractive village in the central Lake District, Cumbria (formerly in Lancashire), 7 km (4 miles) southwest of Ambleside. From 1779 to 1787 William Wordsworth attended Hawkshead Grammar School (founded 1585), and visitors may see the desk on which he carved his name. In a memorable poem, Donald Davie meditates on the lost innocence of the vision of 'the Hawkshead poet':

> In such a time, antediluvian,
> We came to Hawkshead. It was long ago,
> In our own youth and in the youth of Man,
> Not long ago in years, but since we know
> At Dachau Man's maturity began …
>
> Donald Davie: 'Hawkshead and Dachau in a Christmas Glass', from *Brides of Reason* (1955)

Haworth 'hedged enclosure', OE *haga* 'hedge' + *worth* (*see* -WORTH, WORTHY, -WARDINE).

A village in West Yorkshire, some 5 k (3 miles) south of KEIGHLEY (of which it is now a part), on the edge of **Haworth Moor** and PENISTONE Hill. The Rev. Patrick Brontë was vicar of Haworth from 1820 until his death in 1861, and Howarth Parsonage was the home of his daughters, the novelists Charlotte, Emily and Anne Brontë; Emily Brontë's *Wuthering Heights*, Charlotte Brontë's *Jane Eyre* and

Anne Brontë's *Agnes Grey* were all written here. The house was taken over by the Brontë Society in 1928 and turned into a museum (Brontë Parsonage Museum), which has become a place of pilgrimage for the thousands of Brontë fans who come to Haworth every year. Charlotte and Emily are both buried in the family vault in the church. Matthew Arnold wrote a poem lamenting Charlotte's death (but assumed she was buried in the churchyard):

> Console we cannot, her ear
> Is deaf. Far northward from here,
> In a churchyard high 'mid the moors
> Of Yorkshire, a little earth
> Stops it for ever to praise.
>
> Where, behind Keighley, the road
> Up to the heart of the moors
> Between heath-clad showery hills
> Runs, and colliers' carts
> Poach the deep ways coming down,
> And a rough, grimed race have their homes –
> There on its slope is built
> The moorland town. But the church
> Stands on the crest of the hill,
> Lonely and bleak; – at its side
> The parsonage-house and the graves.

> Matthew Arnold: 'Haworth Churchyard, April 1855'

Charlotte Brontë (in *Selections from the Literary Remains of Ellis and Acton Bell*) described the landscape round about:

> The scenery of these hills is not grand, it is not romantic; it is scarcely striking. Long low moors, dark little heaths, shut in valleys where a stream waters here or there a fringe of stunted copse. Mills and scattered cottages chase romance from these valleys, it is only higher up, deep in amongst the ridges of the moors, that Imagination can find rest for the sole of her foot; and even if she finds it there she must be a solitude loving raven, no gentle dove.

Charlotte wrote of her sister Emily's delight in the moors, so central to *Wuthering Heights*:

> She found in the bleak solitude many and dear delights; and not the least and best loved was liberty.

See also BRONTË COUNTRY.

Hawthornden 'hawthorn valley', OE *hagu-thorn* 'hawthorn' + *denu* 'valley'.

A hamlet at the east end of Roslin Glen (*see under* ROSLIN), in Midlothian. **Hawthornden House**, dramatically situated above the River North Esk, is medieval in origin, and beneath it are artificial caverns excavated out of the soft red sandstone that is such a feature of Roslin Glen. The house was largely rebuilt in 1638 by the poet William Drummond (1585–1649), known as **Drummond of Hawthornden**. Earlier, in the winter of 1618–19, he had entertained Ben Jonson at the house, the playwright (proud of his Scottish ancestry) having walked from London to Edinburgh. Jonson stayed three weeks, and accounted for considerable quantities of his host's wine. In return, Jonson observed that Drummond's poems 'smelled too much of the Schooles, and were not after the fancie of the tyme'. Drummond is thought to be the first to have coined the term 'metaphysical' in relation to the poetry of John Donne and others; he did so pejoratively. He is buried in the nearby village of Lasswade. Hawthornden House is now used as a retreat for writers.

Hawthornden Prize. The oldest of the major British literary prizes, founded in 1919 by Miss Alice Warrender. It can be awarded to works of non-fiction as well as for poetry, fiction or drama. Winners have included Sean O'Casey (1925) for *Juno and the Paycock*, Siegfried Sassoon (1928) for *Memoirs of a Fox-Hunting Man*, Robert Graves (1935) for *I, Claudius*, Graham Greene (1941) for *The Power and the Glory*, and Alan Sillitoe (1960) for *The Loneliness of the Long Distance Runner*.

Haxey 'Haki's or Hakr's island or dry ground in the marsh', OE *Hakis* possessive form of male OScand personal name *Haki* or OScand male personal name *Hakr* + OE *eg* (*see* -EY, -EA) or OScand *ey* (*see* -AY), both meaning 'island, dry ground in a marsh'.

A village in North Lincolnshire (before 1996 in Humberside, before 1974 in Lincolnshire), about 16 km (10 miles) southwest of Scunthorpe.

Haxey hood game. A medieval game played on 6 January at Haxey. It is overseen by 12 men known as 'Boggans', a 'King' and a 'Fool', all of whom wear colourful costumes. The game begins when a canvas 'hood' is thrown to the crowd. Whoever secures it, eludes the Boggans and takes it to the nearest inn, receives one shilling. After 12 such hoods are thrown a leather one follows. In a general scrimmage, this also reaches a local inn. The game is then over, with free drinks all round. Its origin is in the 13th century, when the hood of Lady de Mowbray blew away as she was riding home from church and was retrieved by 12 labourers. This so amused the lady that she gave a piece of land, still known as the **Hoodlands**, to the village, the rent being a leather hood to be contested for annually by 12 men dressed in scarlet.

Haycock Probably from the shape of the hill, resembling that of a *haycock*.

A mountain (798 m / 2618 ft) in the Lake District, Cumbria (formerly in Cumberland), 6 km (4 miles) west of GREAT GABLE.

> Great God! there are here huge Mountains, shattered and precipitous as if the Devil himself had raised them to perplex Men. They are like the folds of a Frown puzzling

and troubling the land; and scowl darkly down on us from every side. The rude people here, – for they are rough indeed, sheep-tenders and the like, – do call them Pillars and Steeples, and Pikes and Stacks; yea, even, saving your blushes – Cocks!

> Sir Philip Lamington: letter to William Farquhar (18 June 1754) ('penned in the valley of the Wastewater')

Haydock Probably Welsh *heiddiog* 'grain farm'.

An industrial town in Merseyside, 5 km (3 miles) east of ST HELENS[1], of which it now forms a part. **Haydock Park** racecourse is nearby.

Haydock lies in what used to be the southwest Lancashire coalfield. Exploitation of the region's coal began in earnest in the 18th century, the construction in 1757 of the Sankey Brook Canal (linking St Helens to the River MERSEY at Widnes) greatly facilitating the transportation of coal. On 7 June 1878 at Wood Pit 189 local men and boys died in a huge underground explosion.

For reasons that remain obscure, the inhabitants of Haydock refer to themselves as 'Yickers'.

Hayes 'land overgrown with brushwood', OE *hǣs(e)*.

A district of western Outer London, in the borough of HILLINGDON (before 1965 in Middlesex), to the west of Southall and to the north of Heathrow Airport. Between Hayes and Heathrow is the small settlement of HARLINGTON. The two were joined together in 1930 as the Urban District of **Hayes and Harlington**.

The Gramophone Company – later HMV and EMI – opened its offices and studios at Hayes in 1907. Edward Elgar made regular recordings of his music there between 1914 and 1924.

George Orwell lived in Hayes for a while in the 1930s and loathed it. He once described it as:

> ... one of the most god-forsaken places I have ever struck. The population seems to be entirely made up of clerks who frequent tin-roofed chapels on Sundays and for the rest bolt themselves within doors.

He fictionalized it as **West Bletchley** in his novel *Coming Up for Air* (1939).

Hayling Island Originally *Heglingaigæ* 'Hægel's people's island', OE male personal name *Hǣgel* + -*inga*- (*see* -ING) + *eg* 'island' (*see* -EY, -EA); the final element was subsequently replaced with modern English *island*.

A flat island, about 26 sq km (10 sq miles) in area, on the Hampshire coast, between Chichester Harbour to the east and Langstone Harbour to the west. The 5-km (3-mile) long sandy beach along its southern shore provides the basis for a healthy summer holiday trade. It is popular with yachtsmen and windsurfers.

The playwright and diarist Simon Gray (b.1936) was born on Hayling Island.

Haymarket Self-explanatory.

An area in the West End of EDINBURGH.

get off at Haymarket, to. To perform coitus interruptus, Haymarket being the railway station before Edinburgh Waverley when one is coming south from Glasgow.

Haymarket, the From the market for hay and straw that was held here until 1830.

A street in the WEST END[1] of London (SW1), in the City of WESTMINSTER, linking PICCADILLY CIRCUS in the north with PALL MALL in the south. As its name reveals (*see above*), it was once the site of a real 'hay market', probably servicing the nearby Royal Mews, and until the late 19th century had a reputation as a haunt of prostitutes.

Its attractions today still combine commerce and entertainment, but in a more respectable way. It has several shops, cinemas and theatres, notably the Theatre Royal, Haymarket (usually the **Haymarket Theatre** for short), with its elegant John Nash building, which opened in 1821, and Her Majesty's Theatre, dating from 1897. The first theatre hereabouts, designed by John Vanbrugh, opened in 1705 as the Queen's Theatre. It was at the King's Theatre (as the Queen's Theatre became after Queen Anne's death in 1714) that many of the dramatic works of composer George Frideric Handel received their first performances, including his operatic masterpiece *Giulio Cesare in Egitto* (1724) and the massive oratorio *Israel in Egypt* (1739). The **Little Theatre in the Haymarket** opened on the site of the present Theatre Royal in 1720; in the 1730s it hosted Henry Fielding's political satires against the Walpole government, helping to provoke the Licensing Act that censored theatre until the 1960s.

Hay-on-Wye *Hay* OE *hæg*, 'enclosed forest', with the river name *Wye*.

A small town on the River WYE[1], in Powys (formerly in Brecknockshire), just on the border with England, some 27 km (16 miles) west of Hereford. Its Welsh name is **Y Gelli** ('the woodland').

> ... the *castell* these Eingl-Francwyr
> call in their lingua La Haie Taillée
> that the Saeson other ranks
>   call The Hay
> (which place is in the tongue of the land,
> Y Gelli Gandryll, or, for short, Y Gelli)
>
>> David Jones: 'The Sleeping Lord', from *The Sleeping Lord and Other Fragments* (1974) (The *Saeson* are 'Saxons'.)

Hay lies to the north of the Black Mountains, one of the more northerly of which is **Hay Bluff** (677 m / 2221 ft), some 6 km (4 miles) south of the town.

Hay is sometimes called the **Town of Books** because of its many second-hand bookshops. The town holds an annual literary festival (the **Hay Festival**).

King of Hay, the. Richard Booth, who founded Hay's first second-hand bookshop in 1961, and who lives in part of the town's castle. 'King Richard' issued Hay's unilateral declaration of independence in 1977 and continues to rail against the idiocies of central government.

Hay Stacks Earlier called *Hay-rick*, so the name is clearly a reference to its shape.

A mountain (582 m / 1909 ft) in the Lake District, Cumbria (formerly in Cumberland), on the south side of Buttermere. It is also spelt as one word. INNOMINATE TARN is near the summit.

Haytor Origin uncertain: an early form of the name was *Idetor*, of which the second element is presumably *tor*, but the first element is entirely obscure.

A tor (high hilltop rock) in the eastern part of DARTMOOR, about 14 km (9 miles) northwest of Newton Abbot. Also called **Haytor Rocks**, it is a granite outcrop consisting of a succession of rocks of decreasing height, creating a humped effect. It is 450 m (1490 ft) above sea level. Haytor is easily accessible by car, and is therefore one of the better known of the Moor's sights. Nearby is Haytor Granite Tramway, along which stone destined for some of London's most august buildings was hauled by horsepower in the early 19th century.

To the north of the tor is **Haytor Down**, to the south-east the village of **Haytor Vale**.

Haywards Heath Originally *Hayworth* 'enclosure with a hedge', OE *hege* 'hedge' + *worth* (*see* -WORTH, WORTHY, -WARDINE); the addition of *Heath* is first recorded in the 16th century.

A town in West Sussex, about 20 km (13 miles) north of Brighton. It is essentially a product of the railway: it is on the main London-to-Brighton line, and has grown to its present size and status – as a dormitory for both terminal cities – since the trains started to run in 1841. Nikolaus Pevsner summed it up succinctly:

> Large and quite amorphous. Shopping and offices near a main station to London and housing tapering off in all directions.
>
> *The Buildings of England: Sussex* (1965)

Hazel Grove *Hazel* OE *hæsel* 'hazel', with OE *graf* 'grove'.

A southeastern suburb of MANCHESTER.

H-Blocks. The descriptively apt name for the layout of accommodation in the former MAZE PRISON in County Armagh, and a term well known during the period of the Irish Troubles.

Headcorn Perhaps 'Hydeca's tree-trunk' (used as a bridge), OE male personal name *Hydeca* + *hruna* 'tree-trunk'.

A village in Kent, about 24 km (15 miles) east of Tunbridge Wells. John Willes (*c*.1780–1852), the pioneer of roundarm bowling in cricket, was born here.

Headfort Irish *Áth Cinn*, possibly 'chief ford', with *ceann* 'head' in the sense of 'most important'.

A village in County Kerry, 10 km (6 miles) east of Killarney. It is on the railway line from Cork, and there was formerly a junction here with the branch line to Kenmare.

Headfort Ambush (21 March 1921). An engagement in the Anglo-Irish War in which an IRA flying column attacked a train carrying British soldiers, at least 7 of whom were killed (the IRA claimed 20).

Headingley 'Headda's people's clearing', OE male personal name *Headda* + *-inga-* (*see* -ING) + -LEY.

An area of LEEDS[1], some 3 km (2 miles) west of the city centre. **Headingley Cricket Ground** is the headquarters of Yorkshire county cricket club, and has been a test match venue since 1899 (when England and Australia played a three-day game that ended in a draw). For English cricket fans Headingley is synonymous with the celebrated (probably *over*-celebrated) Headingley test match of 1981, when Ian Botham's cavalier 149 not out set up the most unlikely of victories over Australia.

Leeds's two rugby teams, Leeds Rhinos (rugby league) and Leeds Tykes (rugby union), play next door to the cricket ground at **Headingley Stadium**.

Healy Pass After the politician Tim *Healy*.

A dramatic, hairpinned north–south pass (330 m / 1084 ft) through the CAHA MOUNTAINS of the Beara peninsula, linking counties KERRY and CORK. Work on the road was begun during the 19th century in Famine times, and then abandoned until 1928, when the anti-Parnellite Nationalist politician Tim Healy (1855–1931), then governor general of the Irish Free State, urged resumption of construction. The pass was completed in 1931.

Heanor '(place at the) high ridge', OE *hean* dative form of *heah* 'high' + *ofer* 'ridge'.

A town in Derbyshire, about 16 km (10 miles) northwest of Nottingham. Large coal mines once operated in the area, but have long been closed.

Heanton Punchardon *Heanton* 'high (or chief) farmstead', OE *hean* dative form of *heah* 'high' + -TON; *Punchardon* denoting manorial ownership in the early Middle Ages by the Punchardon family.

A village in Devon, on a high ridge to the north of the TAW estuary, about 8 km (5 miles) northwest of Barnstaple. It affords spectacular panoramic views.

Heart of England. A touristic name for the WEST MIDLANDS of England, extending north to Cheshire with its GOLDEN TRIANGLE, west to the Welsh borders, east to SHAKESPEARE COUNTRY and south to the COTSWOLD Hills, the whole presenting an idyllic image of picturesque houses, pubs and churches, despite the presence of industrial Birmingham and Stoke-on-Trent. The implication is that this is the 'essence' of England. Geographically the region lies more or less in the centre of the country, and politically and culturally may even be identified with MIDDLE ENGLAND.

Heather Spa, the. A former name for the town of ILKLEY.

Heathrow From *Heathrow*, the name of a small village, 'row (of houses) on or near the heath' (referring to an area of heathland at the western edge of Hounslow Heath), ME *hethe* 'heath' + *rewe* 'row'.

An airport (in full **London Heathrow**) in West London, in the borough of HILLINGDON (before 1965 in Middlesex), just to the south of the M4 and inside the M25. Before the Second World War, CROYDON had been London's main airport, but a new postwar start was decided on, and in 1944 work was begun at a site to the west of HOUNSLOW (previously occupied by the Fairey Aviation Company's airfield). It was cleared (and the old settlement of Heathrow obliterated), and by the end of May 1946 the new airport was open. Transatlantic services started immediately.

The new airport was officially designated London (Heathrow) Airport, and was generally referred to as **London Airport**. That name still immediately identifies it, but since the opening of alternative London airports at GATWICK[1], and later LUTON, STANSTED and London City (*see under* LONDON), there has been a greater tendency to call it 'Heathrow'.

The airport has two main parallel runways and four terminals (the first of these, and the airport's first permanent building, was the Europa Building, now Terminal 2, opened by Queen Elizabeth II in 1955; the Oceanic Terminal, now Terminal 3, opened in 1962; Terminal 1 was formally opened in 1969, and Terminal 4 followed in 1986). Terminal 5, designed by Richard Rogers, is due to open in 2008. Heathrow is an important hub for transatlantic and other international flights, and for domestic and European routes. At the beginning of the 21st century it handled 380,000 flights a year. An Underground rail service (Heathrow Central, on the Piccadilly line, opened in 1977 (renamed Heathrow Terminals 1,2,3 in 1986), Heathrow Terminal 4 in 1986), complemented in 1998 by a rail express service from Paddington, immeasurably improved communication with Central London.

Such glamour as Heathrow possessed in its early days has long since dissipated beneath its hordes of often frustrated travellers, its disorienting mazes of buildings and its embattlement on the front line of international terrorism and crime (it is now routinely patrolled by police armed with automatic weapons, and at times of crisis the army turns up with its tanks). Today Britain's gateway to the world is:

> … a beached sky-city, half space station and half shanty town.
>
> J.G. Ballard: *Millennium People* (2003)

See also THIEFROW.

Heavenfield. A battle site near HEXHAM, Northumberland, where in 634 Oswald of Northumbria defeated the rampaging Welsh under Cadwallon of Gwynedd. According to legend, Oswald erected a cross on the site before the battle, hence its name. The monks of Hexham later built a church here, and fragments of Oswald's cross were said to have miraculous properties.
See also HALIDON HILL.

Heavitree Perhaps 'head-tree' (referring to a place of execution), OE *heafod-treow*.
An eastern suburb of EXETER, in Devon.

Hebburn 'high burial place', OE *heah* 'high' + *byrgen* 'burial place, tumulus'.
An industrial town in South Tyneside, Tyne and Wear, 7 km (4 miles) east of Newcastle upon Tyne. From the late 18th century to the 1960s Hebburn's history was dominated by coal-mining, shipbuilding and heavy engineering. Large-scale mining began here in the 1790s and in 1815 Humphrey Davy took gas from Hebburn 'B' pit to test – successfully – his new miners' safety lamp.

The influx of shipyard workers from northwest Scotland during the 1850s gave rise to the nickname **Little Aberdeen** for the Hebburn area.

Hebden Bridge 'bridge over the Hebden Water', OE *heope* 'rose hips, brambles' + *denu* 'valley'.
A town at the junction of the **Hebden Water** and the River CALDER[2], West Yorkshire, 10 km (6 miles) west of Halifax. It is the home town of Sir Bernard Ingham, Mrs Thatcher's rebarbative spin-doctor-in-chief. Unrelatedly, it is, according to *The Guardian*, celebrated as 'the sapphic capital of Britain'.

Hebden Black. A docile yet hardy variety of hen, producing dark brown eggs.

Hebrides, the Ptolemy called them *Eboudai*, and Pliny *Hebudes*, of which the Latinate *Hebrides* is presumed to be a misreading; the original meaning remains obscure. The Gaelic name is *Innse Gall*, meaning 'islands of the stranger(s)'.
The collective name for the large number of islands, both great and small, off the west coast of Scotland. They are also called the **Western Islands** or the **Western Isles**, although in administrative terms the latter applies only to the Outer Hebrides (*see below*). The related adjective is **Hebridean**.

The **Inner Hebrides** are closer to the mainland, and include SKYE, RAASAY, the Small Isles (CANNA, RUM, EIGG and MUCK), COLL, TIREE, MULL, IONA, COLONSAY AND ORONSAY, JURA and ISLAY; ARRAN and BUTE are also sometimes included. They were formerly parts of the old counties of Buteshire, Argyll and Inverness-shire, and are now divided between Highland and Argyll and Bute (with Arran in North Ayrshire). Dr Johnson and James Boswell famously visited Skye, Raasay, Coll, Iona and Mull in 1773, writing about their visits in *A Journey to the Western Islands of Scotland* (Johnson, 1775) and *The Journal of a Tour of the Hebrides* (Boswell, 1785).

The **Outer Hebrides**, also called the LONG ISLAND, are separated from the northwest mainland of Scotland by the Minch (or North Minch), from northwest Skye by the Little Minch (*see under* the MINCHES) and from western Skye by the **Sea of the Hebrides**. The Outer Hebrides include LEWIS with HARRIS, North and South Uist (*see* the UISTS), BENBECULA, ERISKAY, BARRA, PABBAY[1], MINGULAY and BERNERAY[1]. The Outer Hebrides were formerly part of the old counties of Inverness-shire and Ross and Cromarty, but since 1975 have been administered by the unitary authority of the WESTERN ISLES.

The Hebrides may have been the home of the ancient British Attacotti. They were said to be a particularly savage people, whose unpleasant habits included cannibalism. Units of Attacotti were recruited into the Roman army, but they are not heard of again after the 4th century AD.

The Hebrides were the subject of Viking raids from the 8th century, and there was a degree of settlement, reflected in many place names (*see*, for example, -AY). The islands were under the rule of the Norwegian Crown until in 1266, following the Scottish victory at the Battle of Largs (*see under* LARGS) in 1263, they were transferred to the Scottish Crown. However, they maintained a good deal of independence in the later medieval period under the Lords of the Isles (*see* ISLES, LORDSHIP OF THE). At the Reformation some islands (for example, Barra and South Uist) clung onto their Catholicism, while in the 19th century many of the other islands adopted a strictly sabbatarian form of Presbyterianism. The population was radically and callously reduced during the Clearances to make way for sheep and sporting estates, and many people were forced into exile.

> Still the blood is strong, the heart is Highland,
> And we, in dreams, behold the Hebrides.
>
> Anon.: 'A Canadian Boat Song'

Things improved for those who remained following the Crofter Act of 1887. Gaelic is still widely spoken, particularly in the Outer Hebrides.

> No sweeter voice was ever heard
> In spring-time from the Cuckoo-bird,
> Breaking the silence of the seas
> Among the farthest Hebrides.
>
> William Wordsworth: 'The Solitary Reaper' (1803)

The New Hebrides archipelago in the Pacific was so named by Captain Cook in 1774. It changed its name to Vanuatu in 1980.

Hebrides. A sea area in the shipping forecast. It is situated north of Malin, east of Rockall and Bailey and south of Faeroes and Fair Isle.

Hebrides, The. A concert overture (effectively a tone poem) by Felix Mendelssohn, opus 26 (1832). The full title is ***The Hebrides (Fingal's Cave)***, and the piece was inspired by the composer's visit to Scotland in the summer of 1829, and particularly to FINGAL'S CAVE on STAFFA. Granville Bantock less memorably wrote a ***Hebridean Symphony*** (1916).

Heckmondwike 'Heahmund's farm', OE male personal name + WICK.

A town in West Yorkshire, 13 km (8 miles) southwest of Leeds. It forms part of the conurbation of what has been dubbed CLECKHECKMONDSEDGE. It was the birthplace of John Curwen (1816–80), popularizer of the tonic sol-fa system of musical education.

Heddon 'heath hill', OE *haeth* 'heath' + *dun* (*see* DOWN, -DON). The name was probably transferred to the river from a hill of this name.

A river in north Devon, rising in the western part of EXMOOR and flowing into the sea at **Heddon's Mouth**, just west of Highveer Point, about 8 km (5 miles) east of COMBE MARTIN. The steep-sided and wooded **Heddon Valley** is owned by the National Trust. Hunter's Inn, 2 km (1 mile) inland from Heddon's Mouth, is a popular watering-hole for hikers.

Heddon-on-the-Wall 'heather hill on Hadrian's Wall', OE *hœth* 'heather' + *dun* 'hill' (*see* DOWN, -DON), with the affix referring to its situation on the course of HADRIAN'S WALL.

A dormitory village in Northumberland, 16 km (10 miles) west of Newcastle upon Tyne. A pig farm at Heddon was pinpointed as the source of the foot-and-mouth outbreak in 2001, which spread across the UK.

Hedgeley Moor 'Hiddi's clearing', *Hiddi's* possessive of OE male personal name *Hiddi* + -LEY.

A battle site in Northumberland, 15 km (9 miles) northwest of Alnwick. Here on 25 April 1464, during the Wars of the Roses, Yorkist forces under Warwick's brother Lord Montagu defeated the Lancastrians under the Duke of Somerset and Sir Ralph Percy, the latter being killed.

Hednesford 'Heddin's ford', OE *Heddines* possessive form of male personal name *Heddin* + FORD.

A northeastern suburb (pronounced 'henzfəd' or 'hedgefəd') of CANNOCK in Staffordshire.

Hedon 'heathery hill', OE *hœth* 'heath, heather' + *dun* (*see* DOWN, -DON).

A town in the East Riding of Yorkshire, 10 km (6 miles) east of Hull. It is one of the oldest boroughs in England, its civic mace dating back to the reign of Henry V (1413–22).

Heisker. Another name for the MONACH ISLANDS.

Helensburgh Named after Lady *Helen* (daughter of William, Lord Strathnaver), the wife of Sir James Colquhoun of Luss, who founded the town in 1776.

A residential town on the north side of the Firth of Clyde, at the mouth of the GARE LOCH, some 35 km (22 miles) northwest of Glasgow. It is in Argyll and Bute (formerly in Dunbartonshire, thereafter in Strathclyde region). Its best-known building is Hill House (1902), designed by the Glaswegian Art Nouveau architect Charles Rennie Mackintosh. Henry Bell (1767–1830), who built the *Comet*, the first sea-going steam vessel (launched 1812), was Provost of Helensburgh in 1807–9. The anthropologist and folklorist Sir James Frazer (1854–1941), author of *The Golden Bough* (1890–1915), went to school in the town, and John Logie Baird (1888–1946), the inventor of television, was born here (*see also* HASTINGS and SOHO).

Helford 'estuary crossing-place', Cornish *heyl* 'estuary' + OE FORD.

A village in western Cornwall, on the southern shore of the Helford River, 10 km (6 miles) east of Helston. A passenger ferry crosses to **Helford Passage** on the north bank. **Helford River.** An estuary in western Cornwall, at the northeastern corner of the LIZARD Peninsula. Its sides are punctuated by numerous creeks (including FRENCHMAN'S CREEK), which have provided discreet cover for smugglers, and several notable gardens, such as GLENDURGAN, run down to its shore. GWEEK is at its western end.

Heligan 'willow-tree', Cornish *heligen*.

The location, about 3 km (2 miles) northwest of Mevagissey in Cornwall, of the **Lost Gardens of Heligan**. In early 1990 a group of entrepreneurs, looking for land in Cornwall to start a rare-breeds farm, stumbled across the remains of an extensive area of gardens and woodland, neglected for half a century. The gardens, occupying some 63 ha (157 acres), were created by the Tremayne family over the years from 1780 to 1914, but the First World War brought ruin following the death of many estate workers, and new tenants after the war could not afford to maintain the grounds. Painstaking restoration and reconstruction, led by Tim Smit, began following the discovery, and by the end of the 20th century the gardens were open in all their re-created glory to the public. During the restoration, an exorcism of part of the grounds was found to be necessary.

Heligoland From the small German island of *Helgoland*, 68 km (42 miles) northwest of Cuxhaven on the North Sea coast of Germany. (It was a British possession 1807–90.)

The former designation for the sea area GERMAN BIGHT.

Helions Bumpstead *Helions* denoting manorial ownership in the early Middle Ages by Tihel de Helion; *Bumpstead* 'place where reeds grow', OE *bune* 'reed' + *stede* 'place'.

A village in northwestern Essex, about 13 km (8 miles) northeast of Saffron Walden.

See also STEEPLE BUMPSTEAD.

Hellfire Club. The name popularly given to a ruined hunting lodge on top of Montpelier Hill south of DUBLIN. The lodge belonged to Tom Conolly, one of the founder-members in 1735 of the original Hellfire Club, which predated its English equivalent (*see* MEDMENHAM) by some 20 years. The club's *raison d'être* was the usual combination of drink, debauchery and diabolism. Although the club mostly met at the Eagle Tavern in Dublin, where they would down large quantities of scultheen (a mixture of whiskey and butter), in the popular imagination Conolly's lodge was the heart of the members' devilish activities, said to involve the sacrifice of cats and at least one dwarf. There is a story that they burnt down the lodge while still inside, in order to gain a foretaste of hell; in another story the fire was started when one of the members, annoyed by a footman, poured brandy over him and set it alight.

For the Limerick Hellfire Club, *see under* LIMERICK.

Hellisay 'cavern island', OScand *helli* 'cave' (possibly referring to the bite taken out of the island to the northeast) + *ey* (*see* -AY).

A small island off the northeast coast of BARRA, in the Outer HEBRIDES. The **Sound of Hellisay** is on its southern side, while on its northern side, across a narrow, sheltered channel (dubbed 'the Blue Lagoon' because of its beauty), is the slightly smaller island of Gighay ('God's island' or 'good island', from OScand *guth* 'God or god' or *gotha* 'good'). Most of the population was cleared from the island in the 1840s, and the last inhabitants left in 1890.

> Just as a glass resonates
> And sings with the pitch the air brings it,
> So I, here on Hellisay –
> Where history accumulates its causes
> As the sea piles stones on the beach –
> Am forced to draw conclusions
> From the mouths of ghosts in the wind.
>> W.B. McGibbin: 'Dialectics in the Hebrides', from *Onward to May Day* (1952)

Hell's Corner. A name given by RAF pilots during the Second World War to a triangle of Kent centring on CANTERBURY[1], which was the recipient of German bombardment from across the English Channel and the scene of much of the fiercest air combat during the Battle of Britain (1940). *See also* BOMB ALLEY[1].

Hell's Glen *Hell's* may be a mistranslation of Gaelic *Aiffrin* 'offering' as if it were *Iffrin* 'hell'.

A steep-sided pass taking the single-track B839 from Loch Goil to LOCH FYNE, Argyll and Bute. Its Gaelic name is **Gleann Beag** ('small glen').

Hell's Kettles. Four deep pools near the confluence of the River TEES and the River Skerne on the outskirts of DARLINGTON. They are filled with somewhat sulphurous waters of a greenish tinge. From these pools the screams of the damned may sometimes be heard, and among those submerged in the pools is a farmer who irreligiously worked on St Barnabas's Day. Anybody who falls into the holes will – according to local tradition – be eaten alive by pikes and eels. The Tudor chronicler Raphael Holinshed records Abbot Brompton of Jervaulx describing the formation of the holes at Christmas 1178:

> The earth lifted itselfe up on high, in appearance like to a mighty Tower, and so it remained from nine of the clock in the morning till the eventide, and then it fell down with an horrible noise.

The probable explanation behind this account is that the underground limestone and sandstone were eroded by water, leaving a layer of clay and gravel at the top, which, if there were heavy rains, could have been lifted upward before collapsing into the pits beneath.

Hell's Lum *Lum* 'chimney', Scots.
A deep fissure or chimney in the great slabby granite crag of **Hell's Lum Crag**, overlooking Loch Avon on the south side of Cairn Lochan, Highland, 2.5 km (1.5 miles) southwest of the summit of CAIRN GORM. The Lum makes a notable winter climb.

Hell's Mouth Perhaps so named because there is a fierce undertow here.
A bay on the south coast of the LLEYN PENINSULA, Gwynedd (formerly in Caernarvonshire), some 15 km (9 miles) southwest of Pwllheli. Its Welsh name is **Porth Neigwl** (*porth* 'harbour' + possibly a personal name). The beach is popular with surfers.

Helmsdale 'valley of Hjalmund', OScand personal name + *dalr* 'valley'.
A village on the far northeast coast of Highland (formerly in Sutherland), 28 km (17 miles) northeast of Dornoch. The ruined **Helmsdale Castle** (1488) was the scene in 1567 of an unfortunate miscalculation by Isobel Sinclair, mother of the Earl of Caithness. She intended to poison her nephew, the 10th Earl of Sutherland, and his pregnant Countess, so that her son might take the title. In this she was only partly successful, as her son also took a draught of the toxic concoction and thus expired. She was subsequently tried, but managed to kill herself before her execution.

The romantic fictioneer Dame Barbara Cartland (1904–2000) spent many holidays in Helmsdale, and there is a pink effigy of her in the local museum.

Helpston 'Help's farmstead', OE *Helpes* possesive form of male personal name *Help* + -TON.
A village in the unitary authority of Peterborough (before 1998 in Cambridgeshire, before 1974 in Huntingdonshire), 10 km (6 miles) northwest of Peterborough. A memorial at the village cross-roads commemorates John Clare (1793–1864), the so-called Northamptonshire Poet (*see under* NORTHAMPTONSHIRE), who was born and buried here.

> I thought of the last days, the old man
> Sitting alone in the porch of All Saints in Northampton,
> And the dead poet trundling home to Helpston.
>
> Charles Causley (1917–2003): 'At the Grave of John Clare'

Helston 'estate at an old court', Cornish *hen-lys* 'old court' + -TON. The legend that the name comes from *Hell's stone* – applied to a boulder said to have been dropped by the Devil when challenged by St Michael and now embedded in the wall of the 500-year-old Angel Hotel – is no more than that.
A market town in western Cornwall, on the LIZARD Peninsula, about 21 km (13 miles) east of Penzance. Its fame rests on its annual Flora Day, on or about 8 May, when St Michael's victory over the Devil (*see above*) is celebrated in the Furry Dance.

Furry, which perhaps derives from Latin *feriae* 'festivals, holidays', or may be related in some way to English *fair*, was incorrectly changed to *Flora* in the 18th century, and in the 19th century the dance was called the 'Floral Dance', as in the well-known song. It is derived from a pre-Christian festivity and is copied in some other towns. In its present form it begins at 7 a.m. with the Early Morning Dance, led by the Mayor. The children then begin their dance at about 10 a.m., and the principal Furry Dance steps out from the Guildhall at noon. Hundreds of dancing couples try to weave in and out of all the houses in the hilly streets, if possible entering and leaving through different doors, as this brings extra luck. At 5 p.m. a free-for-all ball begins.

Less well known than the dance but probably more ancient is the ceremony that precedes it. Known as Hal-an-tow (probably literally 'in the moorland and in the town'), it was originally a crop-fertility ritual. In its older form, young men and girls went into the country in the early morning and returned with green boughs and flowers, with twigs in their hats and caps. Led by an elderly person riding a donkey, they entered the decorated streets singing the 'Morning Song', the chorus of which is:

> Hal-an-Tow, jolly rum-be-low,
> And we were up as soon as any day-O,
> And for to fetch the summer home, the summer and the May-O,
> For summer is a-come-O and winter is a-gone-O.

Helvellyn Probably 'yellow moor', OCelt *hal* 'upland, moor' + *melyn* 'yellow'.
A mountain (949 m / 3113 ft) in the Lake District, Cumbria, some 12 km (7 miles) southeast of Keswick. It is one of the three Lakeland Three-Thousanders (*see under* LAKE

DISTRICT). On its east side is the rocky ridge of Striding Edge (perhaps so named because either 'bestriding', i.e. between two valleys, or because no wider than a stride); Striding Edge is a popular if exposed scramble on which the faint-hearted will be cheered by the memorial to mark the spot where the fox-hunting Roger Dixon fell to his death in 1858. (For other striding Lakeland rocks, as experienced by the youthful William Wordsworth, *see* PATTERDALE.) Less popular than Striding Edge is Swirral Edge, the parallel ridge to the north, rising from the subsidiary top of Catstycam.

> Am now at the top of Helvellyn ... Travelling along the ridge I came to the other side of those precipices and down below me on the left – no – no! No words can convey any idea of this prodigious wildness. That precipice fine on this side was but its ridge, sharp as a jagged knife, level so long, and then ascending so boldly. What a frightful bulgy precipice I stand on and to my right how the crag which corresponds to the other, how it plunges down like a waterfall, reaches a level of steepness, and again plunges!
>
> Samuel Taylor Coleridge: journal (31 August 1800) (Could this be a description of Striding Edge? Coleridge was on his way from Keswick to the Wordsworths at Grasmere, arriving at eleven o'clock at night and staying up chatting until half-past three.)

Near the summit, on a narrow, level-ish part of the ridge, is a plaque commemorating the remarkable feat of John Leeming and Bert Hinkler, who in 1926 landed an aeroplane (an Avro 585 Gosport) here and successfully took off again; it was the first such landing on the summit of a British mountain.

A third memorial near the summit recounts the tragic tale of Charles Gough, a Quaker from Kendal, who on 18 April 1805 fell over the crags above Red Tarn while travelling from Patterdale to Wythburn. His body was not found until 20 July of that year, guarded by his faithful but starving dog Foxie. This incident inspired Wordsworth's poem 'Fidelity', in which the poet describes the scene:

> It was a cove, a huge recess,
> That keeps, till June, December's snow;
> A lofty precipice in front,
> A silent tarn below!
> Far in the bosom of Helvellyn,
> Remote from public road or dwelling,
> Pathway, or cultivated land;
> From trace of human foot or hand.

The incident also inspired a painting by Sir Edwin Landseer and the poem 'Helvellyn' by Sir Walter Scott:

> How long didst thou think his silence was slumber?
> When the wind waved his garment, how oft didst thou start?
> How many long days and long weeks didst thou number?
> Ere he faded before thee, the friend of thy heart?

> And, oh! was it meet, that – no requiem read o'er him –
> No mother to weep, and no friend to deplore him,
> And thou, little guardian, alone stretch'd before him –
> Unhonour'd the Pilgrim from life should depart?

Hembury Fort. *See under* BROADHEMBURY.

Hemel Hempstead *Hemel* 'broken, undulating' (an old district name), OE *hamel*; *Hempstead* 'homestead', OE *hamstede*; *compare* HAMPSTEAD.

A market town in Hertfordshire, on the River Gade, in the CHILTERN HILLS, about 10 km (6 miles) west of St Albans. The GRAND UNION CANAL passes through its southern outskirts. In 1947 it was designated as one of the eight post-Second World War NEW TOWNS[1] in England, so its attractive 18th-century High Street is now at the hub of acres of 1950s housing.

Hemingford Grey *Hemingford* 'Hemma's or Hemmi's people's ford', OE male personal name *Hemma* or *Hemmi* + *-inga-* (*see* -ING) + FORD; *Grey* denoting manorial ownership in the Middle ages by the de Grey family.

A village in Cambridgeshire (before 1974 in Huntingdonshire), on the GREAT OUSE, about 5 km (3 miles) southeast of Huntingdon. Its riverside church, St James, has a truncated spire: the top was blown off in a gale in 1741, a stone from it being hurled 18 m (20 yards) through a window of the house next door. The spire is said now to be at the bottom of the Ouse.

Hemingford Grey's 12th-century moated manor house was the model for Green Knowe in a series of books – from *The Children of Green Knowe* (1954) to *The Stones of Green Knowe* (1976) – by the children's author Lucy Boston.

Hemsworth 'Hymel's enclosure', OE male personal name *Hymel* + *worth* (*see* -WORTH, WORTHY, -WARDINE).

A former mining town in West Yorkshire, some 10 km (6 miles) northeast of Barnsley.

Hen Cloud 'wild hen rock', *Hen* OE *henn* 'wild hen'; *Cloud* OE *clud* 'rock'. There is another name in Derbyshire, *Eniscloud*, which has the same elements.

A solitary, grim-looking hill, one of the ROACHES, in the PEAK DISTRICT, to the southwest of LEEK. There is a striking, vertical gritstone crag on its southern side.

Hendon '(place at the) high hill' (referring to a prominent 85-m (280-foot) hill on which the settlement developed), OE *hean* dative form of *heah* 'high' + *dun* (*see* DOWN, -DON).

A district of northwest Greater London (NW4, NW9), in the borough of BARNET, to the northwest of Golders Green, at the southern end of the M1 motorway. Although it has a long and varied history (it was a haven from the Black Death in the 14th century, and the actor David Garrick was Lord of the Manor at the end of the 18th), its associations are now firmly aeronautical. **Hendon Aerodrome** opened in 1911:

On June 8th will take place, starting from London Aerodrome, Hendon, the first aerial Derby.

Flight (1912)

and in the same year the world's first airmail service was set up between Hendon and Windsor, to celebrate the coronation of George V. After the First World War the new Royal Air Force began an annual series of highly successful air shows at the Aerodrome (the **Hendon Air Displays**), which did much to raise its national and international profile and popularize flying. The last was held in 1937. Hendon is now home to the RAF Museum and the Peel Centre (Metropolitan Police Training Establishment).

The first bicycle race in Britain was held at Hendon, on 1 June 1868 (the day after the world's first bicycle race, held in the park of Saint-Cloud, Paris).

The swashbuckling Middlesex and England batsman Denis Compton (1918–97) was born in Hendon.

Fairey Hendon. A two-engined heavy bomber, one of the first of the new generation of monoplane bombers that eventually produced the Avro Lancaster. It first flew in 1930, but in the event only 14 were built.

Hengistbury Head *Hengistbury* 'Heddin's fortified place', OE *Hednes* possessive form of male personal name *Heddin* + BURY; the present-day form is due to later association with *Hengist*, the name of one of the first Anglo-Saxon invaders of Britain (*see* EBBSFLEET).

A headland on a spur to the south of CHRISTCHURCH harbour, within the unitary authority of Bournemouth. It is rich in archaeological remains and wildlife.

Hengoed 'the old wood', Welsh *hen* 'old' + *coed* (*see* CED).

A town in CAERPHILLY[2] unitary authority, of which it is the administrative seat, 7 km (4 miles) north of the town of CAERPHILLY[1] itself. It was formerly in Monmouthshire, then in Gwent.

Henley-in-Arden *Henley* 'high (or chief) wood or glade', OE *hean* dative form of *heah* 'high' + -LEY; *Arden* from its being originally in the Forest of ARDEN.

A market town in Warwickshire, on the River Alne, about 13 km (8 miles) northwest of Stratford-upon-Avon. It is a picture-postcard town, with attractive timber-framed houses.

Henley-on-Thames. A riverside town in Oxfordshire, on the River Thames, in the CHILTERN HILLS, about 14 km (9 miles) west of Maidenhead. A five-arched 18th-century bridge crosses the Thames here. The centre of the town boasts many fine Georgian buildings, including coaching inns, from the days when it was a stopping place for stagecoaches, and there are sumptuous Victorian and Edwardian villas by the river, from the high summer of its Regatta-led fashionability. Henley's River and Rowing Museum opened in 1998.

Those who arrive in Henley from the northwest, descending from the beech-clad Chilterns on the A4130 from Nettlebed and Bix, have the pleasure of entering the town via a strikingly wide, straight and elegant thoroughfare known as Fair Mile.

As a parliamentary constituency, Henley for some reason seems to attract blonde-coiffed Conservative mavericks: Michael Heseltine, flamboyant pretender to the Tory party leadership, was MP here from 1974 until 2001, when he was succeeded by the shambling Boris Johnson (editor of the *Spectator* since 1999).

Henleyite. A superannuated term for an enthusiast for Henley Royal Regatta.

Henleyites … will be depressed to hear that the Meteorological Office forecasts … rainy and colder weather.

Westminster Gazette (2 July 1901)

Henley Royal Regatta. An annual rowing regatta, more usually known simply as Henley Regatta, held at the beginning of July on a straight stretch of the River Thames between Temple Island and Henley bridge. It had its beginnings in the first Oxford–Cambridge boat race held at Henley in 1829. The Regatta itself dates from 1839, and the title 'Royal' was bestowed on it in 1851. The royal imprimatur secured its place as a high-society venue, where the *haut monde* went not so much to watch the sweating Leander oarsmen as to promenade in, according to sex, their frilly white dresses and parasols or their straw boaters, loud blazers and white ducks (the trousers, not the birds), observing each other closely. As an institution it has survived remarkably well into the 21st century. The actual rowing is more professional, more international, more serious (from 1998, professional rowers were allowed to compete there after the Regatta's stewards had dropped the amateur stipulation from their rules), but the event is still perceived to be part of the 'London season' – and as ever, the boats take a back seat to onshore activities (marred, for traditionalists, by the corporate sponsors' marquees and a certain lack of tone among the spectators).

Henman Hill. An informal name bestowed by tennis journalists on a grassy bank at the All England Lawn Tennis Club at WIMBLEDON in the late 1990s and early 2000s. It was from here that those (mainly female) fans of Britain's number-one tennis player Tim Henman (b.1974) who found themselves without tickets for the show courts have been able to watch the progress of their hero on a large screen. The perennially hopeful Henman, a fine grass-court player with a serve-and-volley style – but more limited on other surfaces – reached the Wimbledon quarter-finals eight times and the semi-finals four times between 1996 and 2004.

Hensbarrow Downs *Hensbarrow* 'hill of the female deer', OE *hind* 'female deer, hind' + *beorg* 'hill, barrow'; the nearby *Cocksbarrow* was named to form a pair under the misapprehension that *Hen-* = 'hen'.

A range of open downland in Cornwall, about 6 km (4 miles) northwest of ST AUSTELL. Its high point is **Hensbarrow Beacon**, 313 m (1025 ft) above sea level. The mountainous spoil heaps of the china-clay industry are a notable feature of the landscape.

Heptonstall 'farmstead with brambles', OE *heope* 'rose hips, brambles' + *tun-stall* 'farmstead'.

A village on the west side of Hebden Bridge, West Yorkshire. To the northwest is **Heptonstall Moor**, source of the rivers CALDER[1] and CALDER[2].

Hereford 'ford suitable for the passage of an army', OE FORD + *here* 'army'.

A cathedral city in HEREFORDSHIRE, on the River WYE[1], about 37 km (23 miles) northwest of Gloucester and within about 25 km (16 miles) of the Welsh border. Hereford was founded in the 7th century as a garrison town, guarding against Welsh incursions, and became capital of the Anglo-Saxon kingdom of West MERCIA.

Hereford Cathedral was begun around 680 by its first bishop, Putta, but it was destroyed by the Welsh in 1055. It was rebuilt in the late 11th and early 12th centuries. It houses the world's largest chained library, containing about 1600 books, many of them over a thousand years old. The cathedral's greatest treasure, though, is the *Mappa Mundi*, a 13th-century map of the world, drawn on vellum, with Jerusalem at its centre; in 1988 the Dean and Chapter caused something of a stir by putting it up for sale to raise funds for the cathedral, but means were eventually found for preserving it. One year in three the cathedral hosts the Three Choirs Festival.

Hereford endured a difficult Civil War: held by the king for most of the duration of the conflict, it suffered several Parliamentary raids from Gloucester, changed hands more than once, and withstood a siege by the Scots in July and August 1645. Today, the Special Forces of the SAS are based here.

The mystical poet Thomas Traherne (1637–74) and the actor David Garrick (1717–79) were born in Hereford, as was, reputedly, Nell Gwynne (1650–87), the actress and Charles II's mistress (hence Gwynn Street in her memory, just in case).

There are towns called Hereford in the USA (Colorado and Texas).

Hereford. An English breed of hardy red beef cattle with white faces and markings, originating in Herefordshire. They are also occasionally called **Herefordshires**.

> The Herefordshire breed of cattle ... may ... be deemed the finest breed of cattle in this island ... In general appearance the Herefordshire cattle resemble very much those of Sussex.
>
> W Marshall: *The Rural Economy of Gloucestershire* (1789)

Hereford. The name given to a hymn tune composed by S.S. Wesley (1810–79), who between 1832 and 1835 was organist at Hereford Cathedral. The hymn 'Oh Thou who camest from above', by his grandfather Charles Wesley, is often sung to it.

Hereford. A name given in British archery to the Ladies' Championship Round. It involves shooting the same number of arrows at distances of 80, 60 and 50 yards (73.15, 54.86 and 45.72 m).

Nicholas of Hereford. A cleric and theologian who in the 1390s became successively chancellor and treasurer of Hereford Cathedral. He was an early advocate of reform within the Roman Church, and collaborated with John Wycliffe on the first complete English translation of the Bible; but he later recanted, and took part in the persecution of reformers. He died around 1420.

Hereford and Worcester. A former administrative county in the West of England, on the Welsh border, formed in 1974 by joining together the counties of HEREFORDSHIRE and WORCESTERSHIRE. Its administrative centre was WORCESTER. It ceased to exist in 1998, when Herefordshire was split off to form a separate unitary authority and Worcestershire reverted to county status.

Herefordshire From HEREFORD + SHIRE. The name *Herefordshire* is first recorded in the 11th century.

A unitary authority and former county in the West of England, bounded to the west by Wales, to the north by Shropshire, to the east by Worcestershire (from which it is separated by the MALVERN HILLS) and to the south by Gloucestershire and Monmouthshire. Its chief centres are HEREFORD, LEDBURY, LEOMINSTER and ROSS-ON-WYE, its main rivers the Arrow, LUGG and WYE[1]. It is overwhelmingly agricultural in character: it is a patchwork of orchards and rich grazing pasture, the former providing the apples for the famous Herefordshire cider (the cider-makers Symonds (of 'Scrumpy Jack' fame) and Bulmers are based in Hereford) and the latter the original home of the red-and-white Hereford cattle (*see under* HEREFORD).

> ... in Essex or Herefordshire we have the England of hamlets, medieval farms in hollows of the hills, lonely moats and great barns in the clay-lands, pollards and ancient trees, cavernous holloways and many footpaths, fords, irregularly-shaped groves with thick hedges colourful with maple, dogwood and spindle – an intricate land of mystery and surprise.
>
> Oliver Rackham: *The History of the Countryside* (1986)

Before the coming of the Romans Herefordshire was part of the territory of the Silures (*see* SILURIA). In the mid-7th century it fell to Penda of MERCIA.

Herefordshire ceased to exist as a separate county in 1974, when it was joined together with Worcestershire to form HEREFORD AND WORCESTER, but its name was revived in 1998 for a newly constituted unitary authority, roughly corresponding to the old county in area.

In cricketing terms Herefordshire is a 'minor county' (the club was founded in 1991) and plays in the minor counties championship.

Hairyfordshire was a 19th-century slang term for the female pudenda.

Herefordshire Beacon. A hill in Herefordshire, in the MALVERN HILLS, about 6 km (4 miles) southwest of GREAT MALVERN. It is 338 m (1110 ft) high. It is topped by a hillfort with the remains of a 13-ha (32-acre) Iron Age settlement, known as the British Camp. This was built around 200 BC and commanded a pass at the southern end of the Malverns. The view from the top is spectacular. Legend has it that Caractacus was captured here by the Romans. Running along the ridge from the British Camp is the 13th-century Red Earl's Dyke, a shire ditch built by Gilbert de Clare, Earl of Gloucester.

Herm Probably from *Sarmia* in the early Antonine Itinerary, but its meaning is unknown.

One of the CHANNEL ISLANDS. Only 1.3 sq km (0.5 sq miles) in area, it lies off the northeastern corner of GUERNSEY, from which it is separated by the 6 km (4 mile) wide Little Russel Channel. It is part of the 'Bailiwick' of Guernsey. The smaller island of JETHOU is just to the south.

In pre-Christian times Herm was used as a burial ground by the people of Guernsey and of nearby Continental Europe – the idea being that the spirits could not escape across the water.

The lease to the island was bought in 1949 by Major Peter Wood, who over the decades that followed developed its infrastructure and introduced some (fairly restricted) facilities for visitors. No cars are allowed.

Herma Ness. *See under* UNST.

Hermitage Castle Named after a nearby medieval hermitage.

An impressive and forbidding castle in a remote part of upper Liddesdale, 18 km (11 miles) south of Hawick, in Scottish Borders (formerly in Roxburghshire). It is situated on **Hermitage Water**, a small tributary of the Liddel Water (*see under* LIDDESDALE). The oldest parts of the castle go back to the 13th century, and there was considerable restoration work in the 19th century.

The castle was initially owned by the Soulis family. One Lord Soulis was, according to local legend, an infamous warlock. Desiring a young lady called May, the beloved of the Laird of Branxholm, he seized the young couple. His familiar, a fanged old man called Redcap, warned him to 'beware the coming tree' and advised him to flee as Branxholm's men were marching on the castle. Soulis ignored this advice, and just as he was about to hang young Branxholm the latter's men appeared, hiding behind the branches they carried. They wrapped Soulis in a sheet of lead and boiled him to death. Centuries later, with the castle abandoned, the local lads would throw stones into the ruins and shout 'Redcapie-dossie, come out if ye dare!'

Later in the Middle Ages the castle was in the possession of the Douglas family. It was here that the Douglases imprisoned Sir Alexander Ramsay in a pit dungeon; he survived for 17 days on grains trickling through from the granary above. The castle came into the hands of the earls of Bothwell in 1492, and it was hither in 1566 that Mary Queen of Scots came to visit her lover and future husband, James Hepburn, 4th Earl of Bothwell, who had been wounded in a Border skirmish. Mary rode over the high moors from Jedburgh and back in a day, a distance of some 65 km (40 miles), and afterwards lay sick for some weeks in Jedburgh, in what has become known as Mary Queen of Scots' House.

> She rode through Liddesdale with a song;
> 'Ye streams sae wondrous strang,
> Oh, mak' me a wrack as I come back
> But spare me as I gang.'
>
> Marion Angus (1866–1946): 'Alas! Poor Queen'

Hermitage Castle was one of the great castles and abbeys painted by J.M.W. Turner on his visit to the Borders in 1832.

Herne, the Perhaps 'angle, corner of land', OE *hyrne*.

A small area of fenland in Cambridgeshire, about 2.5 sq km (1.5 sq miles) in area, about 19 km (12 miles) north of Huntingdon.

Herne Bay From *Herne*, the name of a village about 2.5 km (1.5 miles) inland (now a southern suburb of Herne Bay), '(place at the) angle or corner of land', OE *hyrne*.

A coastal resort in northeast Kent, on the THAMES[1] estuary, about 8 km (5 miles) east of Whitstable. Until the 19th century it was a fishing village, but the Victorians saw its possibilities and transformed it into a seaside holiday destination. Its pier was (until rudely severed by a storm) the second longest in England. Increasingly popular with the retired community, it attracted the nickname **Hernia Bay** at the end of the 20th century (*compare* COSTA GERIATRICA).

Herne Hill *Herne* probably from a former local field name *le Herne* 'angle or corner of land'; alternatively perhaps from a local 17th-century family called *Herne*. The theory that it is connected in some way with herons is without foundation.

The combination with *Hill* (the district lies on rising ground) is first recorded in 1789.

A district of southeast London (SE24), in the boroughs of LAMBETH and SOUTHWARK, between Dulwich to the east and Brixton to the west. In the early 19th century it was a semi-suburban village with spacious villas for the well-to-do (John Ruskin spent his childhood here, and a local park is named after him), but as with so many other places on the then outskirts of London, the coming of the railway in the 1860s precipitated a rash of congested working-class housing.

The athletics club **Herne Hill Harriers** was founded in 1889. **Herne Hill Stadium**, opened in 1891, was one of the earliest bicycle stadiums in the world. It was used for the cycling events in the 1948 Olympic Games. It has also been used for athletics.

The dog-loving literary eccentric J.R. Ackerley (1896–1967) was born in Herne Hill.

Herodsfoot '(land at the) foot of a place called "long ridge"', Cornish *hir-yarth* 'long ridge' + ModE *foot*; the association with Herod, the unpleasant biblical king who ordered the massacre of children, is first found in the 18th century.

A village in Cornwall, about 5 km (3 miles) southwest of Liskeard, set at the meeting-point of four valleys whose streams join the West LOOE[1] river. John Betjeman described it as 'an inland Polperro in a deeply wooded valley'.

Heronsgate Origin obscure.

A village in Hertfordshire, now a southern suburb of CHORLEYWOOD. In the middle of the 19th century its name was changed to O'CONNORVILLE, after Fergus O'Connor, who bought the land, but eventually the novelty wore off and it reverted to Heronsgate.

Herringfleet 'Herela's people's creek or stream', OE male personal name *Herela* + *-inga-* (*see* -ING) + *fleot* 'creek, stream'.

A village in northeastern Suffolk, just to the east of the River WAVENEY[1], about 8 km (5 miles) northwest of Lowestoft.

Herring's Green Probably from the surname of a modern occupier.

A village in Bedfordshire, about 5 km (3 miles) southeast of Bedford.

Herstmonceux *Herst-* 'wooded hill', OE *hyrst*; *-monceux* denoting manorial ownership in the early Middle Ages by the Monceux family.

A village (pronounced 'herstmənsoo' or 'herstmənsyoo') in East Sussex, about 12 km (8 miles) northwest of Bexhill. **Herstmonceux Castle**, a 15th-century fortified manor house, is one of the earliest brick buildings in England. It was extensively restored in the 1930s.

Herstmonceux's profile was considerably raised in 1957 when the Royal Greenwich Observatory (*see under* GREENWICH), driven out of London by air pollution and light pollution, took up residence in the castle. In 1990 the Observatory moved on again, to Cambridge.

Hertford 'ford frequented by stags', OE *heorot* 'hart, stag' + FORD.

A market town (pronounced 'hartford' or, mainly in former times, 'harford') in HERTFORDSHIRE , at the confluence of the rivers LEA, Beane and Rib about 7 km (4 miles) east of Welwyn Garden City. It is the county's administrative centre.

It was a significant centre in Anglo-Saxon times – an important Church Synod was held here in 672. Little now remains of the Norman castle, in which Elizabeth I lived as a child.

Captain W.E. Johns (1893–1968), creator of the – by modern lights – profoundly politically incorrect *Biggles* series of books about a First and Second World War flying ace, was born here.

To the southeast of Hertford, in **Hertford Heath**, is Haileybury College, a public school that opened in 1862 on a site previously occupied by the East India Company College (founded in 1805 to train agents for the British East India Company).

There is a town called Hertford in North Carolina, USA, and Hartford, the capital of Connecticut, USA, was named after the Hertfordshire town.

> In Hertford, Hereford and Hampshire,
> Hurricanes hardly happen.
>
>> Alan Jay Lerner: 'The Rain in Spain' (song), *My Fair Lady* (1956)

Hertford College. A college of Oxford University (*see under* OXFORD), in Catte Street. It was founded in 1740, on the basis of the earlier Hart Hall. It takes its name from Elias de Hertford, the late 13th-century owner of the site on which Hart Hall stood. In 1974 Hertford was one of the first five Oxford men's colleges to admit female undergraduates.

Hertfordshire From HERTFORD + SHIRE. The name *Hertfordshire* is first recorded in the 11th century.

A county in central southern England, one of the HOME COUNTIES, to the northwest of London, bounded to the west by Buckinghamshire, to the north by Bedfordshire and Cambridgeshire, to the east by Essex and to the south by London. Its chief centres are BISHOP'S STORTFORD, BOREHAMWOOD, CHESHUNT, HARPENDEN, HATFIELD[1], HEMEL HEMPSTEAD, HERTFORD (the county town and administrative centre), HITCHIN, HODDESDON, LETCHWORTH, POTTERS BAR, RICKMANSWORTH, ROYSTON[1], ST ALBANS, STEVENAGE, WATFORD[1] and WELWYN GARDEN CITY. It lost some territory (BARNET, for example) to London in 1965, but it also picked up at the same time some of the pieces of the dismembered Middlesex, including POTTERS BAR.

Letchworth was the first of the garden cities, and the county also has four of the eight post-Second World War new towns in England: Hatfield, Hemel Hempstead, Stevenage and Welwyn Garden City.

Most of Hertfordshire lies in the Lower Thames Basin, rising in the northwest to the CHILTERN HILLS. Its main rivers are the LEA, the STORT and the COLNE². It is a mainly agricultural county, with woods and gentle hills, but there is light industry in such centres as Stevenage and Watford, and in the south, near London, are many current and former film studios (such as those at Borehamwood and ELSTREE).

Before the coming of the Romans, Hertfordshire was part of the territory of the British tribe known as the Catuvellauni (*see* ST ALBANS), who also occupied Bedford-shire and Buckinghamshire. It was their attack on the tribe known as the Atrebates (*see* BERKSHIRE), who were Roman allies, that gave the Emperor Claudius the pretext to invade Britain in AD 43.

The University of Hertfordshire was formed in 1992 from the former Hatfield Polytechnic. It is sited in Hatfield.

In cricketing terms Hertfordshire is a 'minor county' (the club was founded in 1876) and plays in the minor counties championship.

> I had forgotten Hertfordshire,
> The large unwelcome fields of roots
> Where with my knickerbockered sire
> I trudged in syndicated shoots; ...
>
> Colour-washed cottages reed-thatched
> And weather-boarded water mills,
> Flint churches, brick and plaster patched,
> On mildly undistinguished hills – ...
>
> One can't be sure where London ends,
> New towns have filled the fields of root
> Where father and his business friends
> Drove in the Landaulette to shoot ...
>
> John Betjeman: 'Hertfordshire' (1954)

Herts. The standard written abbreviation of HERTFORDSHIRE.

Hertsmere *Herts*, the abbreviated form of *Hertfordshire* + obsolete *mere* 'boundary', OE *mære* (denoting contiguity with Greater London). The name was coined when the district was created.
A borough and administrative district in southern Hert-fordshire, on the borders of Greater London, created in 1977. It stretches from Watford in the west to Hatfield in the east, and also includes Potters Bar. BOREHAMWOOD is its administrative centre.

Hessle 'hazel tree', OE *hæsel* 'hazel'.
A town in the East Riding of Yorkshire, at the northern end of the Humber Bridge (*see under* HUMBER), 6 km (4 miles)

west of Hull. It was the birthplace of the architect and designer C.F.A. Voysey (1857–1941).

Heston 'farmstead or estate among the brushwood', OE *hæs* 'brushwood' + -TON.
A western suburb of London (before 1965 in Middlesex), in the borough of HOUNSLOW, between the GREAT WEST ROAD to the south and the M4 to the north.

Its heyday was between 1929 and 1939, the years of **Heston Aerodrome**. It was there that the British prime minister Neville Chamberlain arrived from Munich on 30 September 1938 and told the world: 'This morning I had another talk with the German chancellor, Herr Hitler, and here is the paper which bears his name upon it as well as mine.' Its aeronautical thunder was stolen after the Second World War by HEATHROW, about 3 km (2 miles) to the west.

Nowadays the suburb is best known for the Heston Service Area, between Junctions 2 and 3 on the M4.

Heswall 'spring where hazels grow', OE *hæsel* 'hazel' + *wella* 'spring'.
A residential town in Cheshire, on the western side of the WIRRAL peninsula, overlooking the DEE² estuary. Parkgate, just ot the south, was a busy port before the Dee silted up, with a ferry serving Ireland. Heswall is the birthplace of England's greatest all-round cricketer, Ian Botham (b.1955), a buccaneering batsman and aggressive swing-bowler for Somerset, Worcestershire, Durham and England (*see* HEADINGLEY).

Hetton-le-Hole 'brambly hill in the hollow', OE *heope* 'rose hips, brambles' + *dun* (*see* DOWN, -DON) + OFr (*en*) *le* 'in the' + OE *hol* 'hollow'.
A former mining village in Sunderland unitary authority (formerly in County Durham), about 17 km (10 miles) southeast of Gateshead.

Bob Paisley (1919–96), manager of LIVERPOOL FC from 1974 to 1983, was born here.

Hetty Pegler's Tump So named because it stands on land owned in the 17th century by Henry and Hester (or *Hetty*) Pegler (d.1694); *tump* is a local dialect word for a long barrow.
A Neolithic burial mound in Gloucestershire, 5 km (3.5 miles) northeast of Dursley, also known as ULEY Long Barrow. Hetty Pegler's Tump is 55 m (180 ft) in length and dates from around 3000 BC. Excavations here in the 19th century uncovered the remains of 15 human skeletons, and later burials from the Roman period along with shards of Roman pottery and a silver groat from the time of Edward IV.

Heuston Station. One of DUBLIN's main railway stations, serving lines to the south and west. It was known as **Kings-bridge Station** (and still is, informally) until 1966, when it was renamed in honour of Seán Heuston (1891–1916), executed for his role in the Easter Rising.

Hever '(place at the) high edge or hill-brow', OE *hean* dative form of *heah* 'high' + *yfer* 'edge, hill-brow'.

A village in western Kent, about 10 km (6 miles) southwest of Tonbridge. Nearby is **Hever Castle**, a 15th-century double-moated manor house which was the childhood home of Anne Boleyn. It was bought in 1903 by the American millionaire William Waldorf Astor, who added several extravagant touches, such as a 'Tudor' village for his guests to stay in. More recently, its moat has made it a favoured venue for top-level official meetings where high security is necessary.

Hexham 'warrior's home', OE *hagustald* 'warrior' + HAM; *Hagustaldes ham* 685.

A market town on the South Tyne in Northumberland, 32 km (19 miles) west of Newcastle upon Tyne. It is situated just to the south of HADRIAN'S WALL. Hexham racecourse is to the south of the town, while further south are the moors of **Hexhamshire Common**, source of DEVIL'S WATER.

It was near Hexham, in 634, that Oswald of Northumbria defeated Caedwalla or Cadwallon of Gwynedd (*see* HEAVENFIELD).

An abbey was founded at Hexham in 674 by Wilfrid, Bishop of York, who had been given the manor of Hexham by St Etheldreda in return for his support against her husband King Egfrith (Etheldreda wished for religious reasons to remain a virgin, while Egfrith understandably did not wish his wife to remain so). Wilfrid's foundation was a magnificent one, his biographer (*c.*700) writing

> We have never heard of anything like it this side of the Alps.

The abbey was sacked by the Danes in 876 and replaced by an Augustinian priory in 1114. The Priory Church survives, and in medieval times St Wilfrid's Chair or the Frith Stool became a place of sanctuary.

Hexham was the birthplace of St Ailred (1109–67), historian, mystic and adviser to kings David I of Scotland, Henry II of England and Louis VII of France.

Battle of Hexham Levels (15 May 1464). A battle during the Wars of the Roses, fought some 5 km (3 miles) south of the town. The Lancastrians were defeated, and their commander, the Duke of Somerset, was executed following his capture. A play entitled *The Battle of Hexham* by Barnabe Barnes (?1569–1609) is now lost, although a melodrama (1789) with the same title by George Colman the Younger is preserved.

Hexham Butchers, the. The nickname given to the North Yorkshire Militia following an incident in 1761 when they opened fire on miners who had gathered in the town to protest against new militia recruitment rules. The militia's action resulted in the deaths of 50 people, and 300 were injured.

Heysham 'village in the brushwood', OE *hæs* 'brushwood' + HAM.

A seaside town in Lancashire, just south of MORECAMBE, with which it is contiguous. There is a ferry from here to Douglas in the Isle of Man.

Heywood 'high wood', OE *heah* 'high, chief' + *wudu* 'wood'. An industrial town in Greater Manchester, 2 km (1.2 miles) south of Rochdale.

Hibernia From the Greek *Iernoi* (later *Ierne*), a version of the OCelt word from which *Érainn* (*see* ÉIRE) derives, with perhaps an admixture of Latin *hibernus* 'wintry'.

The Latin name for IRELAND, one part of western Europe that the Romans never conquered. Natives of Ireland are still sometimes poetically referred to as **Hibernians**, an early version of which occurs in a letter of St Columban (*c.*540–615): *toti Iberni, ultimi habitatores mundi* ('all of us Irish, inhabitants of the world's edge'). 'Hibernian' appears in the name of various organizations, such as EDINBURGH's **Hibernian FC** (Hibs), founded by an Irishman, and the Royal Hibernian Academy (*see below*).

Hibernia is also the name of an offshore Atlantic oilfield, to the east of Newfoundland.

Ancient Order of Hibernians. An Irish-American fraternal society, founded in America in 1836, but also active in Ireland and Britain. Because of its sectarian nature, it is nicknamed the Ancient Order of Catholic Orangemen.

Hibernian Archipelago. A term offered by some Irish Nationalists to replace the offensive BRITISH ISLES; a more accurate and yet vaguer alternative, THESE ISLANDS, is more frequently heard.

Hibernici ipsis Hiberniores. Latin for 'more Irish than the Irish', Archdeacon John Lynch's description of the Anglo-Normans who had invaded Ireland in the 12th century and who proceeded to become thoroughly Gaelicized. It comes from his book *Cambrensis Aversus* (1662).

Hibernicus. The pseudonym of the Irish poet, journalist and satirist James Arbuckle (1700–42). His essays on morals and aesthetics were collected in 1729 as *Hibernicus's Letters*. He was a friend of Jonathan Swift, but fell out with the dean after writing an essay on him entitled *Momus Mistaken* (1735).

Hiberno-English. The dialect of English spoken in Ireland, influenced in part by Irish Gaelic; it is at its most distinctive in areas closest to the GAELTACHT.

'per O atque Mac veros cognoscis Hibernos'. 'By O and Mac you will recognize the Irish', a traditional means of distinguishing the native Irish by the forms of their names, quoted in the autobiographical introduction to William Allingham's *Diary* (1907).

Royal Hibernian Academy. An institution based in DUBLIN for the encouragement of the fine arts. It was founded in 1823, and has held annual exhibitions since 1826.

Hickling Broad *Hickling* from a local village name, '(settlement of) Hicel's people', OE male personal name *Hicel* + *-ingas* (*see* -ING).

The largest of the Norfolk BROADS, with about 2 sq km (0.45 sq miles) of open water and extensive areas of reeds, marsh and woodland. It lies about 5 km (3 miles) from the coast and 21 km (13 miles) northeast of Norwich. It is a nature reserve, where such rarities as marsh harriers and swallowtail butterflies may be seen.

Hickstead 'high place', OE *heah* 'high' + *stede* 'place'.

A village in West Sussex, about 16 km (10 miles) north of Brighton, on the A23 London road. Its ancestral obscurity ended in 1960, when Douglas Bunn (b.1928) opened the All-England Showjumping Course here. National and international competitions are held there (including the British Showjumping Derby, first staged in 1961, and since 1992 the Royal International Horse Show), and frequently televised.

Hidcote Boyce *Hidcote* 'Hydeca's or Huda's cottage', OE male personal name *Hydeca* or *Huda* + *cot* (*see* -COT, COTE); *Boyce* denoting manorial ownership in the Middle Ages by the de Bosco or Bois family.

A village in Gloucestershire, in the Cotwolds, about 5 km (3 miles) northeast of Chipping Campden. Nearby is **Hidcote Manor**, which now belongs to the National Trust. It is world-famous for its 'Arts and Crafts' garden, designed by Major Lawrence Johnston, who bought the property in 1907.

High, the. The colloquial name of the street in central OXFORD officially called **High Street**. Stretching in a curve from CARFAX eastwards to Magdalen Bridge, it contains All Souls College, the Queen's College, University College, the Examination Schools and the University Church of St Mary the Virgin. The architectural historian Nikolaus Pevsner described it as 'one of the world's great streets'.

Higham Ferrers *Higham* 'high (or chief) homestead or enclosure' (alluding to its position high above the NENE valley), OE *heah* 'high' + HAM; *Ferrers* denoting manorial ownership in the early Middle Ages by the Ferrers family.

A town in Northamptonshire, about 8 km (5 miles) east of Wellingborough.

Higham Gobion *Gobion* denoting manorial ownership in the early Middle Ages by the Gobion family.

A village in Bedfordshire, about 8 km (5 miles) southeast of Ampthill.

See also YARDLEY GOBION.

High Barnet. *See under* BARNET.

Highbury 'high manor', ME *heghe* 'high' + BURY (referring to the fact that it stands on higher ground than neighbouring Barnsbury and Canonbury).

A district of North London (N5), in the borough of Islington, to the east of Tufnell Park and to the west of Stoke Newington. Suburbanization began here in the 1820s, when the speculative builders first moved in, and today it is a mixed area of solid Victorian red-brick villas and humbler terraces.

ARSENAL FC, which was originally founded in WOOLWICH, moved to Highbury in 1913. Its ground is **Highbury Stadium**. (In 2004 the club announced that it would move to a new stadium in nearby Ashburton Grove in 2006.)

Highbury and Islington Underground station, on the Victoria line, opened in 1968. It is situated at **Highbury Corner**, a busy junction at the southern end of Holloway Road (A1).

Battle of Highbury. The nickname of a so-called friendly football match between England and Italy at Highbury Stadium on 14 November 1934, which England won 3–2. The name alludes to the behaviour of the Italian team, who, promised exemption from military service if they won, resorted to physical confrontation, leaving a number of England players injured and provoking retaliation.

Highbury Fields. A public park in Highbury. It has a long history, and in its time has seen Wat Tyler's rebels and refugees from the Great Fire of London use it as a camp.

Highclere OE *heah* 'high' + *-clere* probably the original settlement name, perhaps from a OCelt river name meaning 'bright stream'.

A village in Hampshire, about 8 km (5 miles) southwest of Newbury and 3 km (2 miles) west of BURGHCLERE. The nearby Victorian Gothic **Highclere Castle** is the ancestral home of the earls of Carnarvon. It contains mementoes of the fifth earl, who, along with Howard Carter, discovered the tomb of Tutankhamun near Luxor in Egypt in 1922.

Highcliffe From a mansion of that name in the vicinity, in the Gothic style, once the home of the Marchioness of Waterford. The earliest known name of the settlement, from the late 16th century, is *New Town*; in 1610 it is recorded as being called *Black Cliff*. The present name dates from the mid-18th century.

A town and seaside resort in Dorset (before 1974 in Hampshire), now effectively an eastern suburb of CHRISTCHURCH.

High Cogges. *See under* COGGES.

High Cup Nick 'nick or indentation at the high rounded depression', *Cup* OE *cuppe* 'cup, rounded hollow'; *Nick* ModE.

A spectacular narrow cleft in the escarpment of the northwestern Pennines in Cumbria (formerly in Westmorland), some 8 km (5 miles) northeast of Appleby-in-Westmorland.

The Pennine Way goes by the Nick to reach the plateau of **High Cup Plain** at about 600 m (2000 ft).

> down from the windswept top
>> where waterfall spray flew up
> in the blast of air from the hillside's hollow cup
>> that serves as a wind-trap.
>
>> Anna Adams: 'Walking Downhill, High Cup Nick'

take a walk off High Cup Nick, to. A local expression meaning 'to go and take a running jump'.

Higher Bockhampton *Bockhampton* probably 'farm of the people living at the charter land', OE *bochœme* 'people living on land granted by charter' or *bocham* 'beech tree farm' + -TON.

A village in Dorset, about 5 km (3 miles) northeast of Dorchester. The novelist and poet Thomas Hardy (1840–1928) was born here, in a small thatched cottage, and lived here for most of the first 30 years of his life. The cottage is described in detail in *Under the Greenwood Tree* (1872), which, along with *Far from the Madding Crowd* (1874), he wrote here. The building is now preserved by the National Trust. The heathland nearby became a component of Hardy's EGDON HEATH.

High Force 'high waterfall', *Force* OScand *foss* 'waterfall'.

A powerful waterfall, split into two channels by a central rock, on the upper River TEES, County Durham, 20 km (12 miles) northwest of Barnard Castle. The rock system over which it falls is the Whin Sill, on which HADRIAN'S WALL is also built. The waterfall was painted by J.M.W. Turner and celebrated by Sir Walter Scott in *Rokeby* (1813) (*see under* TEES).

> … those high fells where the forces
> Fall from the mist like the white tails of horses.
>
>> Andrew Young: 'In Teesdale', from *The White Blackbird* (1935)

Highgate 'high toll gate', ME *heghe* 'high' + *gate* (referring to the area's altitude and to the toll gate set up here on the road to the North in the Middle Ages by the Bishop of London, who was lord of the manor).

A district of North London (N6, N19), to the north of Hampstead Heath, partly in the borough of HARINGEY and partly in CAMDEN, with a corner too in ISLINGTON. It grew up around a toll gate on a hill that at 130 m (426 ft) is one of the highest points of London's Northern Heights. The steep road that approaches the central 'village' of Highgate is **Highgate Hill**. According to legend, it was at the foot of this hill in the late 14th century that Dick Whittington, resting for a while (with his cat) on his way home having failed to find fame and fortune in London, heard Bow Bells chime out

> Turn again Whittington,
> Thrice Lord Mayor of London Town.

The rest is literally history, for Whittington retraced his steps, and the real-life Richard Whittington (*see also* PAUNTLEY) did in fact become Lord Mayor of London (four times, not three). His fateful recall is commemorated by the Whittington Stone at the bottom of Highgate Hill, and his name crops up in many other places in the area, notably the Whittington Hospital (originally a smallpox hospital), whose logo features a small black cat.

An early 19th-century bypass, in the form of the Archway Road (now the A1), relieves the centre of Highgate of excessive traffic, and it is sufficiently cut off from Central London by its height and by Hampstead Heath to retain its own separate identity. It has a varied stock of old (and very expensive) houses, but it has welcomed innovative modern architecture too: Highpoint I (1938), for example, an apartment block by Berthold Lubetkin and the Tecton group.

The original Highgate Underground station, on the Northern line, opened in 1907. Its name was changed to Archway in 1939, and the present Highgate station opened in 1941.

The painter and nonsense versifier Edward Lear (1812–88) and the poet John Betjeman (1906–84) were born in Highgate. The district's poetical connections go back at least to the 17th century, when Andrew Marvell lived here, and a later resident was Samuel Taylor Coleridge, who died here in 1834. Highgate also proved fatal to Sir Francis Bacon, who succumbed here in 1626 to a chill caught while experimentally stuffing a chicken with snow to ascertain whether putrefaction would thereby be delayed. A more recent son of Highgate is John Lydon (Jonny Rotten of the punk group The Sex Pistols; b.1956).

There is a village called Highgate in Jamaica and a district called Highgate in Perth, Western Australia.

Highgate Cemetery. A commercial cemetery established in the southeastern part of Highgate in the 1830s. It has a number of famous occupants: notably Karl Marx, but also including Charles Dickens, George Eliot, Michael Faraday, Christina Rossetti, Elizabeth Siddal (wife of Dante Gabriel Rossetti, who had her clandestinely exhumed in 1869 so that he could retrieve his manuscript poems buried with her), Herbert Spencer and Mrs Henry Wood. Its Victorian gloom can be mitigated by discreet celebrity-spotting.

Highgate Ponds. A series of ponds constructed on the eastern side of Hampstead Heath (*see under* HAMPSTEAD) as reservoirs to harness the supply of the FLEET[1] River; some of them are used for bathing.

Highgate resin. A type of mineral resin found in deposits in the London clay at Highgate.

Highgate School. A co-educational independent school in Highgate, founded in 1565 as a grammar school for boys. Its former pupils include the poets Gerard Manley Hopkins and (at Highgate Junior School) John Betjeman. Another poet, T.S. Eliot, briefly taught French and Latin at the Junior School during the First World War. Another Highgate alumnus, Philip Tufnell, the ragamuffin Middlesex and England left-arm spin bowler, was expelled from the school.

Highgate Wood. An extensive wooded park on the east side of Archway Road, run (like Hampstead Heath) by the Corporation of the City of London, which took it over from the bishops of London in 1886.

sworn at Highgate. Late 18th- and 19th-century slang meaning 'clever, smart':

> A ridiculous custom formerly prevailed at the public houses in Highgate (then a village north of London), to administer a ludicrous oath to all travellers of the middling rank who stopped there. The party was sworn on a pair of horns, fastened on a stick, the substance of the oath was never to kiss the maid when he could kiss the mistress, never to drink small beer when he could get strong, with many other injunctions of the like kind to all of which was added the saving clause of 'unless you like it best'.
>
> Francis Grose: *A Classical Dictionary of the Vulgar Tongue* (1785)

Highgrove Presumably self-explanatory, 'high grove'.

An estate and Georgian house in Gloucestershire, 2.5 km (1.5 miles) southwest of TETBURY, owned since 1980 by Charles, Prince of Wales. Built between 1796 and 1798 (as High Grove) for a local landowner by the name of John Paul Paul (*sic*), it was badly damaged by fire in 1896, after which it was rebuilt and enlarged. Prince Charles purchased the estate in 1980 and transformed the grounds – with the help of such gardeners and garden designers as Lady Salisbury, Rosemary Verey (*see under* BARNSLEY[2]) and Sir Roy Strong – into a much-praised contemporary garden with (amongst other features) a lime avenue, a wildflower meadow, extravagantly topiaried yew trees, a thyme path and a woodland glade.

The garden and adjoining farm are maintained on organic principles, and the farm produces organic foodstuffs from bacon to biscuits sold under the brand name 'Duchy Originals' (*see* Duchy of Cornwall *under* CORNWALL).

High Holborn. *See under* HOLBORN.

Highland. A local authority region of northwest Scotland, formed in 1975 out of the traditional counties of CAITHNESS, SUTHERLAND, ROSS AND CROMARTY (apart from Lewis), INVERNESS-SHIRE (apart from Harris and the rest of the Outer Hebrides), NAIRNSHIRE, part of MORAY and the northern part of ARGYLL. It became a unitary authority in 1996. It is bordered on the west and north by the Atlantic, on the east by the North Sea, Moray and Aberdeenshire, and on the south by Perth and Kinross, and Argyll and Bute. The administrative centre is at INVERNESS, and other towns

include FORT WILLIAM, MALLAIG, KYLE OF LOCHALSH, ULLAPOOL, WICK, THURSO, DORNOCH, DINGLE and NAIRN[1]. It encompasses all of the Northwest HIGHLANDS and part of the GRAMPIAN MOUNTAINS, the GREAT GLEN, SKYE and the Small Isles (RUM, EIGG, MUCK and CANNA).

Highlands, the. The northern, most mountainous part of Scotland, separated from the LOWLANDS by a major geological fault, the **Highland Line**, which stretches southwest–northeast from HELENSBURGH to STONEHAVEN. The Highlands comprise two main areas, that to the south and east of the GREAT GLEN, largely comprising the GRAMPIAN MOUNTAINS, and that to the west and north of the Great Glen, known as the **Northwest Highlands**. The HEBRIDES are often thought of as part of the Highlands, at least culturally, and together they are known as the **Highlands and Islands**. The mainland Highlands and the islands of Mull and Skye contain all of Scotland's MUNROS, and indeed the vast majority of mountains over 3000 ft (914.4 m) in the British Isles, including the highest, BEN NEVIS.

Inhabitants of the Highlands are known as **Highlanders** or, in broad Scots, **Hielenmen**. In Glasgow they are known somewhat disparagingly as **Teuchters** (apparently from the sound of their speech).

> Heelandman, Heelandman, where were ye born?
> Up in the Heelands amang the long Corn.
> And what grows there, Pray! Why, sibees and leeks,
> And lang-legged Heelandmen wanting their breeks!
>
> Anon.: nursery rhyme (Scots *sibees* 'spring onions')

Much of the Highlands was Gaelic-speaking into the 20th century, and although pockets of Gaelic-speakers remain on the mainland, most are now found in the Outer Hebrides.

The landscape of the Highlands was long regarded as savage by people from the gentler south:

> ... it is all one undistinguished range of mountains and woods, overspread with vast, and almost uninhabited rocks and steeps filled with deer innumerable ... [a] frightful country ...
>
> Daniel Defoe: *A Tour Through the Whole Island of Great Britain* (1724–6)

The people were regarded as equally savage, particularly by the (latterly Presbyterian) Lowland Scots, who suffered centuries of raids by (often Catholic) Highland clansmen.

> Als, in the oute Ylis, and in Argyle,
> Unthrift, sweirnes, falset, povertie and stryfe
> Pat polacey in dainger of hir lyfe.
>
> Sir David Lindsay (?1490–?1555): 'The Compleynt of the Comoun Weill of Scotland'

All this came to an end with the failure of the 1745 Rebellion at CULLODEN MUIR, after which fierce laws were passed with the intention of extirpating Gaelic culture, including the banning of those symbols of Highland pride, the bag-pipes and the kilt. Then came the period of the **Highland Clearances**, when the old clan chiefs, forgetting their tra-ditional obligations to their clansmen, either sold up or turned themselves into English-style 'improving' landlords, evicting the people and their black cattle and replacing them with sheep and, later, vast sporting estates for the shooting of deer and grouse.

With the Highlands thus emasculated and depopulated, the place and its people began to be romanticized, especially via the fashionable literary works of Sir Walter Scott, while Queen Victoria at BALMORAL encouraged the fashion for all things tartan:

> Lord Aberdeen was quite touched when I told him I was so attached to the dear, dear Highlands and missed the fine hills so much. There is a great peculiarity about the Highlands and Highlanders; and they are such a chivalrous, fine, active people.

This 'fine, active people' were largely packed off in over-crowded ships to build the empire in North America and the Antipodes, or forced to trudge south to scrape a living death in the industrial slums of GLASGOW. They left behind them empty glens, silent except during the stalking season.

> Every doctor knows it – the stillness of foetal death ...
> Here is an identical silence, picked out
> By a bickering burn and a lone bird's wheeple
> – The foetal death in this great 'cleared' glen
> Where the *fear-tholladh nan tighem* has done his foul work.
>
> Hugh MacDiarmid: 'The Glen of Silence', from *Lucky Poet* (1943) (Gaelic *fear-tholladh nan tighem* 'destroyer of homes')

> *Tha iad fhathast ann a Hallaig,*
> *Clann Ghill-Eain 's clan MhicLeòid,*
> *na bh' ann ri linn Mhic Ghille-Chaluim:*
> *Chunnacas na mairbh beò.*
>
> (They are still in Hallaig,
> MacLeans and MacLeods,
> all who were there in the time of Mac Gille Chaluim
> the dead have been seen alive.)
>
> Sorley MacLean: 'Hallaig', from *From Wood to Ridge: Collected Poems in Gaelic and English* (1989) (Hallaig is a deserted township on the island of Raasay.)

Greater security was afforded by the Crofters' Holding Act of 1886, introduced partly as a result of pressure by the **Highland Land League** (founded in 1882), but the land of the Highlands continued to be mainly divided into a small number of big estates, often with absentee landlords. In the later 20th century land reform became an important political issue in Scotland, and in 2003 the Scottish Parlia-ment brought in the Land Reform (Scotland) Act, which ended the historic legacy of feudal law, gave rural and croft-ing communities the right to buy land in their area, and established the 'right to roam' over most of the landscape

– reflecting the economic importance of tourism (parti-cularly outdoor activities such as hillwalking) to the Highlands.

> Farewell to the mountains high cover'd with snow;
> Farewell to the straths and green valleys below;
> Farewell to the forests and wild-hanging woods;
> Farewell to the torrents and loud pouring floods.
> My heart's in the Highlands, my heart is not here,
> My heart's in the Highlands a-chasing the deer –
> A-chasing the wild deer, and following the roe:
> My heart's in the Highlands, wherever I go.
>
> Robert Burns: 'My Heart's in the Highlands', sung to the tune 'Failte na miosg'

> O to mount again where erst I haunted;
> Where the old red hills are bird-enchanted,
>   And the low green meadows
>   Bright with sward;
> And when even dies, the million-tinted,
> And the night has come, and planets glinted,
>   Lo, the valley hollow
>   Lamp-bestarr'd!
>
> Robert Louis Stevenson: 'In the Highlands'

Highland. An adjective that, in the 18th and 19th cen-turies, denoted a range of characteristics: hospitableness, pride, lack of couth, untrustworthiness and naivety.

Highland cattle. A breed of stocky cattle with long, usually russet, coats and long curling horns.

Highland Chieftain, The. The title given to a train running between London and Inverness.

Highland Donald. A former nickname for a Highlander.

Highland dress. 'Traditional' Highland garb, specifically the kilt or tartan trews, plaid, BALMORAL or glengarry bonnet (*see under* GLEN GARRY[1]), sporran, dirk, etc.

Highlander. A (some would say silly) fantasy film (1986), in which a 14th-century Scottish warrior becomes an immortal and does battle in contemporary New York. The cast included international Scotsman and former James Bond, Sean Connery. There were two more lowly regarded sequels (1990, 1994).

Highlanders (Seaforth, Gordons and Camerons), the. A regiment of the British army, formed in 1994 from a merger of the **Queen's Own Highlanders** (Seaforth and Camerons) and the **Gordon Highlanders** (*see under* GORDON).

Highlanders' Umbrella, the. The nickname given to the railway bridge over Argyle Street in GLASGOW, by Central Station; the sheltered stretch below the bridge was formerly a popular meeting place for people from the Highlands.

Highland fling. A solitary Scottish country dance of considerable vigour.

Highland games. A summer gathering in which con-testants vie with each other in piping, sword-dancing, hammer-throwing, tossing the caber and other traditional Highland activities, such as twisting the four legs off a cow (no longer so popular an attraction as it was in Invergarry in the 1820s). Highland games originated as clan gatherings and were revived by Sir Walter Scott and others in the early 19th century; today they are held in many venues around Scotland and attract large numbers of tourists.

Highland honours. The mass drinking of a toast in which the participants place one foot on a chair or bench and the other on the table top.

Highland Host, the. A force of Highlanders brought into southwest Scotland by the Earl of Lauderdale in 1678 to suppress the local Covenanters. Their sojourn in the area was unpopular, shortlived and unsuccessful.

Highland Laddie, the. Bonnie Prince Charlie (1720–88), the leader of the unsuccessful 1745 Jacobite Rising.

> The bonniest lad that e'er I saw –
> Bonnie laddie, Highland laddie!
> Wore a plaid and was fu' braw –
> Bonnie Highland laddie!
> On his head a bonnet blue –
> Bonnie laddie, Highland laddie!
> His royal heart was firm and true –
> Bonnie Highland laddie!
>
> Robert Burns: 'Highland Laddie'

Highland Lass. Wordsworth's 'Solitary Reaper', observed on his tour of 1803:

> Behold her, single in the field,
> Yon solitary Highland Lass!
> Reaping and singing by herself;
> Stop here, or gently pass!

Highland Light Infantry (City of Glasgow Regiment). A regiment formed in 1881 and largely recruited in Glasgow. It traces its origins to the formation of **McLeod's Highlanders** in December 1777. In 1959 they amalgamated with the Royal Scots Fusiliers to form the **Royal Highland Fusiliers.** They were generally referred to as the HLI (said to stand for Hairy-Leggit Irishmen), and were nicknamed the Glesca Keelies, and the Pig and Whistle Light Infantry.

Highlandman's garters. A local name in northeastern Scotland for ribbon grass, *Phalaris arundinacea*, presumably from its former sartorial use.

Highland Mary. Robert Burns's beloved Mary Campbell, who was born near DUNOON, Argyll, and with whom Burns had planned to elope to the West Indies. This plan was thwarted in 1786 when Mary died of typhus in Greenock.

> O pale, pale now, those rosy lips,
> I aft hae kissed sae fondly!
> And closed for aye the sparkling glance
> That dwelt on me sae kindly:
> And mouldering now in silent dust
> That heart that lo'ed me dearly!

> But still within my bosom's core
> Shall live my Highland Mary.
>
> Robert Burns: 'Highland Mary' (1792)

Highland Park. A single-malt whisky distilled in Orkney since 1798 (legally since 1826). Given that Orkney is not part of the Highlands, the name is something of an oddity. In fact it derives from High Park, the eminence above Kirkwall on which the distillery is situated.

Highland pony. A breed of pony, also called a garron, originating in the Highlands. Its heavy, stocky build made it suitable for work on crofts, carrying deer off the mountains and so on.

Highland pride. A species of vanity in which the possessor has an exaggerated view of the grandeur and nobility of his or her ancestry. The term was current from the later 18th century, and Scott's Fergus Mac-Ivor in *Waverley* is an exemplar.

Highland saxifrage. A low-growing species of saxifrage, *Saxifraga rivularis*, with small, somewhat insignificant white flowers. It prefers wet rocky habitats in the mountains, and is rare in Britain, although less so in Scandinavia.

Highland terrier. A breed of dog, now vanished, thought to have been the ancestor of all the modern terriers.

Highlands and Islands Development Board. An official body set up in 1965 to foment economic activity in the Highlands, Hebrides, Orkney and Shetland. It became **Highlands and Islands Enterprise** in 1992.

Royal Highlander, The. The title formerly given to a train running between London and Aberdeen.

Royal Highland Show. A large agricultural show organized by the Royal Highland and Agricultural Society of Scotland (founded as the Highland Society of Edinburgh in 1784). Since 1960 the show has been held at Ingliston, just west of Edinburgh.

University of the Highlands and Islands. A higher education institution designated as such in 2001, and currently calling itself UHI Millennium Institute. It aims to achieve university status in 2007. Its headquarters are in Inverness, and it has sites scattered across the Highlands, Hebrides, Orkney and Shetland.

West Highland terrier. A breed of small terrier, with a shaggy white coat.

West Highland Way. A long-distance path, leading from MILNGAVIE (just north of Glasgow) via LOCH LOMOND, Rannoch Moor (*see under* RANNOCH) and GLEN COE to FORT WILLIAM. The route is 152 km (95 miles) long.

High Onn *Onn* probably 'ash-trees', Welsh.

A village in Staffordshire, about 13 km (8 miles) southwest of Stafford.

High Peak Originally the name of a Hundred (local administrative area) centred on Buxton, contrasted with *Low Peak*

Hundred to the southeast, centred on Wirksworth; *Peak see* PEAK DISTRICT.

An administrative district of northern DERBYSHIRE, in the northern part of the Peak District. The name also serves as a general term for this area of high moorland plateaux (also known as the **Dark Peak**), intersected by cloughs, groughs and craggy edges, and characterized by gritstone, heather and peat bog. The highest of its hills is KINDER SCOUT.

See also WHITE PEAK.

High Roding. *See under* the RODINGS.

High Seat *Seat* OScand *sǽti* 'lofty place (sometimes in the shape of a seat)'.

A hill (710 m / 2329 ft) in the northwest Pennines, North Yorkshire, 8 km (5 miles) south of Kirby Stephen.

High Street From the Roman road along its summit ridge (*see* STREET).

A mountain (829 m / 2719 ft) in the eastern Lake District, Cumbria, 10 km (6 miles) northeast of Ambleside:

> A mighty fist of earth,
> Knuckled with crag and veined with ice.
>
> Tom Bowker: 'High Street'

The Romans built a road, also called High Street, along the long summit ridge, leading from Troutbeck to Penrith. This road was used by Bonnie Prince Charlie's army in the 1745 Jacobite Rising, and local legend has it that their ghosts can still sometimes be seen here.

High Willhays *Willhays* 'enclosures by a spring', OE *welle* 'spring' + *hæg* 'enclosure'; it is possible that the entire area at the top of the hill was called Willhays, though the second syllable is a later addition (originally *High Wyll* 'high spring').

A tor (high hilltop rock) on the northern part of DARTMOOR, about 5.5 km (3.5 miles) south of Okehampton. At 621 m (2037 ft) it is the highest point on the Moor. YES TOR is about 1.5 km (1 mile) to the north.

Highworth 'high enclosure', OE *heah* 'high' + *worth* (*see* -WORTH, WORTHY, -WARDINE).

A town in Wiltshire, within the unitary authority of SWINDON, about 8 km (5 miles) northeast of the town centre.

High Wycombe *Wycombe* '(place at the) dwellings or settlements', OE *wicum* dative plural of *wic* (*see* WICK); despite appearances, the name has nothing to do with the River Wye.

A town in Buckinghamshire, on the River WYE[1], in a gap in the CHILTERN HILLS, about 8 km (5 miles) northwest of Beaconsfield. It lies just to the north of the M40, and motorists get a good view of the roofs of the town as the motorway climbs into the Chilterns.

Various light industries are now based here, but High Wycombe's traditional connection is with furniture manufacturing. This grew out of the making of chairs from the wood of the beech trees that grow in abundance on the Chilterns. The craft is illustrated in the town's Local History and Chair Museum. The local **Wycombe Wanderers FC** (founded in 1884 and based at Adams Park) are nicknamed the Chairboys. Since 2002 the Causeway Stadium in High Wycombe has played host to one of England's leading rugby union clubs, London Wasps (*see under* LONDON), who play their 'home' matches here.

Nearby, safe beneath the Chilterns, are the multi-storey underground headquarters of RAF Strike Command, which were used as Joint Headquarters during the 1991 Gulf War.

The jazz composer Mike Westbrook (b.1936) was born in High Wycombe.

There is a custom of unknown antiquity in High Wycombe by which the mayor is weighed annually in front of the town hall; if he has put on weight since the previous year he is deemed not to have been putting his shoulder sufficiently to the civic wheel; however, if he has lost weight, he is deemed to have carried out his duties conscientiously.

See also WEST WYCOMBE *and* WYCOMBE.

Hill 16. The standing terrace in Dublin's CROKE PARK stadium, built from the rubble of the 1916 Easter Rising.

Hillfoots, the. The lowland area of CLACKMANNANSHIRE (formerly in Central region) between the OCHIL HILLS and the Firth of Forth. It includes the towns of MENSTRIE, ALVA, ALLOA, TILLICOULTRY and DOLLAR.

Hillingdon 'Hilda's hill', OE *Hildan* possessive form of male personal name *Hilda* + *dun* (*see* DOWN, -DON).

A district and borough of outer West London (before 1965 in Middlesex), to the west of Harrow, Ealing and Hounslow. As well as HAYES, NORTHWOOD, RUISLIP, UXBRIDGE and WEST DRAYTON, the borough contains HEATHROW Airport. The district of Hillingdon itself (once a Middlesex village) is just to the east of Uxbridge.

Hillingdon 'Underground' station, on the Metropolitan and Piccadilly lines, opened in 1923. A new station, of striking modern design (by Cassidy Taggart), opened here in 1994.

Hill of Cat Probably similar to CAT LAW.

A hill (742 m / 2434 ft) in the eastern Grampians, on the border between Angus and Aberdeenshire (formerly Tayside and Grampian regions), 8 km (5 miles) east of Mount Keen.

Hill of Fare 'hill', *Fare* Gaelic *fàire* 'hill, height'; originally called *Fair* in the 16th century, the name lost currency and the tautological 'Hill of' was added later.

A hill (471 m / 1545 ft) in Aberdeenshire (formerly in Kincardineshire, then in Grampian region), 7 km (4 miles) northwest of Banchory. On its eastern side is the Burn of Corrichie, where in 1562 was fought the Battle of Corrichie in which Mary Queen of Scots defeated the rebel Earl of Huntly. Huntly had been encouraged by the witches of STRATHBOGIE, who had assured him that that night he would lie in the Tolbooth of Aberdeen without a wound on his body. During the battle Huntly suffered a stroke and fell dead from his horse, his body later being taken to the Aberdeen Tolbooth. The chair-shaped stone on the hill, from which Mary watched the battle, can still be seen.

Hill of Tara. Another way of referring to the ancient Irish site of TARA.

Hill of Tarvit. *See under* SCOTSTARVIT TOWER.

Hillsborough[1] After Sir Arthur *Hill*.
A small town in County Down, 17 km (10 miles) south of Belfast. Its Irish name is **Cromghlinn** ('winding valley'). Hillsborough was founded by the planter Sir Arthur Hill in 1650, and in the 18th century his descendants built **Hillsborough Castle**, which was the official residence of the governor of Northern Ireland between 1925 and 1973, and since then the residence of the secretary of state for Northern Ireland. On 31 December 1909, in the castle grounds, 'the Mad Mechanic' Harry Ferguson (later famous for his tractors) made the first Irish flight in a heavier-than-air machine, a monoplane of his own design, which took him all of 120 m (130 yards).

Hillsborough was the birthplace of the composer Sir Hamilton Harty (1880–1941), who is also buried here.
'Defenestration of Hillsborough, The'. A poem by Tom Paulin, from *Fivemiletown* (1987), and referring to the Hillsborough Agreement (*see below*):

> … we have a choice:
> either to jump or get pushed.

Hillsborough Agreement (15 November 1985). Another term for the Anglo-Irish Agreement of 1985, signed at Hillsborough Castle by the prime minister Margaret Thatcher and the *taoiseach* Garret Fitzgerald. The agreement provided for joint consultation between the governments of the UK and the Republic of Ireland over matters pertaining to Northern Ireland, and recognized that the province's status could not be changed without the agreement of the majority of its population.

Hillsborough Declaration (1 April 1999). The joint statement in April 1999 by prime minister Tony Blair and *taoiseach* Bertie Aherne at Hillsborough Castle. It proposed a plan to break the impasse in the Northern Ireland peace process by removing any connotations of surrender in the looked-for decommissioning of weapons by the IRA. The latter rejected the plan.

Hillsborough[2] Originally simply *Hill(s)*, with *-borough* being added in the 19th century.
The stadium of Sheffield Wednesday FC (*see under* SHEFFIELD). On 15 April 1989 it was the scene of the

Hillsborough Disaster, in which, at the FA Cup semi-final between Liverpool and Nottingham Forest, 96 Liverpool fans were crushed to death in the overcrowded Leppings Lane stand. Lord Justice Taylor's report into the disaster, which recommended the phasing out by leading English and Scottish football clubs of concrete terraces and the establishing of all-seater stadiums, led to football clubs spending millions of pounds on the development of existing stadia and, in some cases, the construction of entirely new ones.

In the fiction of Charles Reade (1814–84), Hillsborough is the name used to denote Sheffield.

Hinckley 'Hynca's glade', OE male personal name *Hynca* + -LEY.
A town in Leicestershire, about 19 km (12 miles) southwest of Leicester. The Ashby Canal runs just to the west. Also close by is the tiny Sketchley Brook, near which in 1861 was born Alfred Hawley, founder of Sketchley the dry cleaners.

Hindhead Originally a hill name, 'hill frequented by hinds or does', OE *hind* 'hind, doe' + *heafod* 'head, headland, hill'. It was transferred to the town when it began to be developed in the early 20th century. The local legend that the name was coined by Queen Anne's huntsman, because the contour of the hill reminded him of a stag's head, is chronologically implausible.
A small town in Surrey, on the NORTH DOWNS, about 5 km (3 miles) northwest of Haslemere. To the east is **Hindhead Common**, site of the DEVIL'S PUNCH BOWL.

Hindity-mengreskey tem. The very un-politically correct Romany name for IRELAND, according to George Borrow's *Romano Lavo-Lil* ('word book of the Romany', 1874). The name means 'dirty fellows' country'.

Hindley 'clearing of the hinds', OE *hind* 'hind' + -LEY.
An industrial town in Greater Manchester, 4 km (2.5 miles) southeast of Wigan.

Hinkley Point Origin obscure; the name is first recorded in the early 19th century as *Inkley Point*, and the second element of *Hinkley* might be -LEY.
A headland on the north coast of Somerset, 8 km (5 miles) west of the mouth of the River PARRETT. **Hinkley Point A** nuclear power station, an early Magnox station, opened in the 1960s. It is now out of service. **Hinkley Point B**, an advanced gas-cooled reactor, opened in 1976.

Hinton Admiral *Hinton* 'high (or chief) farmstead', OE *hean* dative form of *heah* 'high' + -TON; *Admiral* denoting manorial ownership in the Middle Ages by the Albemarle family.
A hamlet in Hampshire, about 8 km (5 miles) northeast of Christchurch. It has a station on the main line from London to Bournemouth and Poole.

Hinton Ampner *Hinton see* HINTON ADMIRAL; *Ampner* 'almoner', OFr *aumoner*, from its early possession by the almoner of St Swithun's Priory at Winchester.

A village (pronounced 'am(p)nə') in Hampshire, about 13 km (8 miles) east of Winchester. *Lord Halifax's Ghost Book* (1936) carries a lengthy and circumstantial account of the haunting of the former Hinton Ampner House (since demolished) in the late 18th century.

Hinton Blewett *Hinton see* HINTON ADMIRAL; *Blewett* denoting manorial ownership in the early Middle Ages by the Bluet family.

A village in Bath and Northeast Somerset (before 1996 in Avon, before 1974 in Somerset), about 16 km (10 miles) southwest of Bath.

Hinton Charterhouse *Hinton see* HINTON ADMIRAL; *Charterhouse* 'house of Carthusian monks', OFr *chartrouse*, referring to a priory founded in the early 13th century.

A village in Bath and Northeast Somerset (before 1996 in Avon, before 1974 in Somerset), about 6.5 km (4 miles) southeast of Bath.

Hinton Martell *Hinton* 'farmstead belonging to a religious community', OE *higna* possessive plural form of *hiwan* 'household, religious community' + -TON; *Martell* denoting manorial ownership in the early Middle Ages by the Martell family.
A village in Dorset, about 11 km (7 miles) east of Blandford Forum.

Hinton Parva 'Little Hinton' (which is an alternative name of the village): *Hinton see* HINTON MARTELL; *Parva* 'little', Latin.
A village with the unitary authority of Swindon (before 1996 in Wiltshire), about 6 km (4 miles) east of Swindon.

Hinton St George *Hinton see* HINTON ADMIRAL; *St George* from the dedication of the local church.
A village in Somerset, about 5 km (3 miles) northwest of Crewkerne. On the last Thursday of every October, Punky Night is held here. This event, which may be an etiolated version of the ancient Celtic fire festival of Samhain, features children marching round the village carrying lamps called 'punkies', made from hollowed-out mangel-wurzels, and singing the traditional 'punky' song.

H.W. Fowler, co-author (with his brother) of *Modern English Usage* (1926), died in Hinton St George in 1933.

Hinton St Mary *Hinton see* HINTON ADMIRAL; *St Mary* denoting manorial ownership in the Middle Ages by the Abbey of St Mary in Shaftesbury.
A village in Dorset, about 11 km (7 miles) southwest of Shaftesbury. A 4th-century Roman mosaic discovered here in 1963 is the earliest known depiction of Christ in Britain.

Hinton Waldrist *Hinton see* HINTON ADMIRAL; *Waldrist* denoting manorial ownership in the early Middle Ages by the de Sancto Walerico family.

A village in Oxfordshire, about 16 km (10 miles) southwest of Oxford.

Hints[1] '(place at the) roads or paths', Welsh *hynt* 'road, path'.
A village in Shropshire, about 11 km (7 miles) east of Ludlow.

Hints[2]. A village in Staffordshire, about 5 km (3 miles) west of Tamworth.

Hippy Isle. A nickname for PAPA STOUR, Shetland.

Hirta. The principal island of the ST KILDA group.

Histon Perhaps 'farmstead of the sons or young men', OE *hys(s)e* 'son, young man' + -TON.
A small town in Cambridgeshire, now effectively a northwestern suburb of CAMBRIDGE[1].

Hitchin '(place in the territory of the) *Hicce* tribe', OE *Hiccum* dative plural form of *Hicce*, an old tribal name perhaps derived from a OCelt river name meaning 'dry'.
A market town in Hertfordshire, on the River Hiz, about 19 km (12 miles) north of Welwyn Garden City and just to the west of the A1(M). It has a medieval church and several interesting 17th- and 18th-century buildings.

George Chapman (?1559–1634), the poet and translator of Homer, the engineer and inventor Henry Bessemer (1813–98), and Queen Elizabeth the Queen Mother (1900–2002) were born in Hitchin.

Hiz Adopted from the form of the name *Hitchin* as it appears in Domesday Book.
A river in Hertfordshire and Bedfordshire, which rises near HITCHIN and flows about 27 km (17 miles) northwards to join the River IVEL to the south of Biggleswade. For about 5 km (3 miles) it forms the boundary between Hertfordshire and Bedfordshire.

Hockwold cum Wilton *Hockwold* 'wooded area where mallows grow', OE *hocc* 'hock, mallow' + *wold* 'wooded area'; *cum* 'joined with', Latin; *Wilton* 'farmstead or village where willows grow', OE *wilig* 'willow' + -TON.
A village in Norfolk, on the eastern edge of the FENS, about 16 km (10 miles) northwest of Thetford. **Hockwold Fens** are to the west.

Hoddesdon 'Hod's hill', OE *Hoddes* possessive form of the male personal name *Hod* + *dun* (see DOWN, -DON).
A town (pronounced 'hodzdən') in Hertfordshire, about 13 km (8 miles) southeast of Welwyn Garden City. In the days of coaching, it was about one day's journey north of London on the Cambridge road (now the A10), and all the usual appurtenances of an overnight stopping place grew up here. It is on the River LEA, and was one of Izaak Walton's favourite fishing-places.

The Rye House Plot, an abortive attempt (1683) to assassinate Charles II and his brother James, was hatched at Rye House, 1.5 km (1 mile) from Hoddesdon.

Hod Hill *Hod* 'hood, shelter', OE (possibly referring to the local hillfort).

A hill in Dorset, at the southwestern end of Cranborne Chase (*see under* CRANBORNE), between the rivers STOUR[1] and IWERNE, about 5 km (3 miles) northwest of Blandford Forum. On its summit is an Iron Age hillfort, which was overrun in AD 43 by the Romans.

Hognaston Perhaps 'Hocca's grazing farm', OE *Hoccan* possessive form of male personal name *Hocca* + *æfesn* 'grazing' + -TON.

A village in Derbyshire, beside Carsington Water (*see under* CARSINGTON), about 11 km (7 miles) southwest of Matlock.

Hog's Back From its appearance. Since at least the late 18th century *hog's back* has been used as a generic term for a sharply crested hill-ridge.

A chalk ridge from Guildford to Farnham in Surrey, formed by the western end of the NORTH DOWNS. It reaches more than 150 m (492 ft) at its highest point, with panoramic views. The A31 now runs along it.

Hogs Norton An alteration of HOOK NORTON, apparently inspired by the inhabitants' gluttonous reputation.

An imaginary English village made famous in the 1930s by the comedian Gillie Potter (1888–1975), who in his wireless broadcasts described in mock-erudite fashion a long series of unlikely events taking place in the village.

> The humorous corruption to Hogs Norton, recently employed by Mr Gillie Potter, goes back to at least the 16th century, when the village had become proverbial for rusticity and boorishness ... There was evidently a jingle about Hogs Norton, where pigs play on the organ.
>
> Margaret Gelling: *The Place-Names of Oxfordshire* (1954)

Hogspit Bottom Probably 'pig hollow in the valley', *Hogspit* ME *hogg* 'pig' + *pit* 'hollow'; *Bottom* 'valley'. The present spelling might suggest a surname Hogg, but the earliest record is *Hogpits*.

A village in Hertfordshire, about 8 km (5 miles) southwest of Hemel Hempstead.

Hogwarts. The fairy-tale Gothic school in the 'Harry Potter' novels of J.K. Rowling, dedicated to the teaching of Magic and Wizardry. Behind the magic, monsters, and array of beasts and apparitions, Hogwarts is yet another fictional incarnation of the English boarding-school, with its house system, arcane rituals, eccentric masters and mistresses and all-consuming obsession with school sport (in this case Quidditch, played in the air on broomsticks).

> To the delight of the Daily Telegraph, the 'Harry Potter' series is a priceless advertisement for traditional English public schools. Hogwarts is little more than the Rugby of *Tom Brown's Schooldays* with spells added.
>
> Richard Adams :'Quidditch Quaintness' in *The Guardian* (18 June 2003)

Hogwarts is reached by the **Hogwarts Express** from Platform 9¾ at KING'S CROSS. The train traverses a mountainous landscape to reach its destination, and the school's surroundings would appear to locate it in a place topographically similar to the HIGHLANDS of Scotland. The 'Potter' films to date have used as locations for the school scenes ALNWICK Castle, DURHAM Cathedral and Castle, and the Bodleian Library, OXFORD. Hogwarts' local station, **Hogsmeade**, is played by GOATHLAND station in the North York Moors, although to get to it from King's Cross it appears necessary to use the West Highland Line between FORT WILLIAM and MALLAIG: the ROAD TO THE ISLES.

Holbeach 'hollow stream' or 'hollow ridge', OE *hol* 'hollow' + *bece* 'stream in a valley' or locative form of *bæc* 'ridge'.

A small town in Lincolnshire, in the FENS about 13 km (8 miles) south of the WASH. In the Middle Ages it grew rich as a port, exporting wool and also salt, which was extracted from seawater (the 'salterns', where the salt was evaporated, can still be seen). Those prosperous days have gone, but Holbeach remains one of the largest parishes in England.

Holbeach Marsh, an area of marshland, lies to the north of the town.

Holborn Originally a river name (now usually *Holebourne*), 'hollow stream' or 'stream in a hollow', OE *hol* 'hollow' (adjective or noun) + *burna* 'stream'.

A street and a district (pronounced 'hoe-bən') in Central London (EC1, EC4, WC1), the district in the borough of CAMDEN, the street partly also in the City of London.

The street takes its name from a former stream (*see above*), a tributary of the River FLEET[1], whose course it originally followed. Its low-lying eastern end (where the Holebourne once flowed down to meet the Fleet) was raised in the 1860s on to the **Holborn Viaduct**, crossing Farringdon Road, which joins Holborn with Newgate Street. (In the process, the old **Holborn Hill**, along which criminals were taken to be hanged at Tyburn, disappeared.) At the same time **Holborn Circus** was constructed at the junction of Holborn and Holborn Viaduct; for many years the headquarters of Mirror Group Newspapers (later Maxwell House) were there. Holborn climbs towards the west, and beyond the junction with Gray's Inn Road becomes **High Holborn**. This continues westwards, crossing the top of Kingsway (where Holborn Underground station, on the Central and Piccadilly lines, opened in 1906, is situated) to link up with Shaftesbury Avenue.

Both streets are lined with shops and offices, the most distinctive of which are perhaps the red neo-Gothic headquarters of the Prudential Assurance Company in Holborn, designed by Alfred Waterhouse, and the faux-medieval half-timbered shops in High Holborn depicted on packets of 'Old Holborn' tobacco (*see below*). Before commerce took over, however, the streets were at least partly residential. Francis Bacon, Thomas More and Samuel Johnson all lived at various times in Holborn, and John Milton in High Holborn; John Gerard, author of the *Herball or Generall Historie of Plantes* (1597), had his garden in Holborn; it was in his garret in Holborn that the literary hoaxer Thomas Chatterton took arsenic to end his life in 1770; and Charles Dickens wrote *Pickwick Papers* while living in Furnival's Inn, an Inn of Chancery on the site of what are now the Prudential offices.

The district of Holborn lies to the north and south of High Holborn, bounded approximately to the west by Kingsway and Southampton Row and to the east by Chancery Lane and Gray's Inn Road. It contains Lincoln's Inn and Gray's Inn. In the days (before 1965) when London was divided into metropolitan boroughs, Holborn was the smallest of them.

Holborn Empire. A former music hall in High Holborn, opened in 1857 and rebuilt by Frank Matcham at the beginning of the 20th century. The biggest stars of the time appeared here. It was badly damaged by bombing in the Second World War, and demolished in 1960.

Old Holborn. The brand name of a type of loose tobacco for roll-your-own cigarettes. The quaint half-timbered buildings that used to be pictured on the label still exist in High Holborn, and house among others the tobacconists John Brumfit Ltd (opened 1933).

Holcombe Rogus *Holcombe* 'deep valley', OE *hol* 'hollow, deep' + *cumb* 'valley'; *Rogus* denoting manorial ownership in the early Middle Ages by a man called Rogo.

A village in Devon, about 13 km (8 miles) northeast of Tiverton.

Holdenby 'farmstead owned by Halfdan', OScand male personal name *Halfdan* + -BY.

A village in Northamptonshire, about 10 km (6 miles) northwest of Northampton. **Holdenby House**, built from 1583 by Sir Christopher Hatton, a favourite of Elizabeth I, passed to the English Crown in 1605. Following his defeat by the Scots in 1646, Charles I was brought here in January 1647 and handed over to the Parliamentarians. He remained here for five months before being moved to safer custody in June 1647 (*see* NEWMARKET[1]).

Holderness 'yeoman's headland', OScand *holdr* 'high-ranking yeoman' + NESS.

A rich agricultural area in the East Riding of Yorkshire, southeast of the Wolds, between Bridlington Bay on the North Sea and the HUMBER estuary. Its main settlements are HORNSEA and WITHERNSEA. Holderness is mentioned by the Summoner in Geoffrey Chaucer's *Canterbury Tales* as 'mersshy countree called Holdernesse' – although today the marshes are largely confined to the wetlands around

Hornsea Mere. The soft clay cliffs north of SPURN HEAD are prone to considerable depredation by the sea, into which Holderness is gradually being absorbed and then redeposited inside the Humber estuary.

Charles I awarded Prince Rupert of the Rhine the earldom of Holderness in 1644.

Hole in the Wall Perhaps a modern reformulation of an earlier *Turlstane* 'stone with a hole' (OE *thyrel-stan*), possibly referring to a lost megalith.

A hamlet in Herefordshire (before 1998 in Hereford and Worcester, before 1974 in Herefordshire), on the River WYE[1], about 4 km (2.5 miles) north of Ross-on-Wye.

Hole of Horcum *Horcum* 'dirty valley', OE *horh* 'dirty muddy' + *cumb* (*see* -COMBE, COOMBE).

A vast natural amphitheatre in the NORTH YORK MOORS, North Yorkshire, near Levisham. It is some 1.2 km (0.75 miles) wide and some 120 m (400 ft) deep, and was formed over thousands of years by the actions of glaciers and then by springs. However, according to legend the Hole was scraped out by a Saxon giant called Wade, who threw the mighty handful of earth at his wife Bell (*see also* WADE'S CAUSEY). He missed, and the earth landed about a mile to the east, forming the hill of Blakey Topping.

Hole with the Mint, the. A punning nickname for LLANTRISANT.

Holkham 'homestead in or near a hollow', OE *holc* 'hollow' + HAM.

A village (pronounced 'hoakum') in north Norfolk, about 2.5 km (1.5 miles) west of Wells-next-the-Sea. In recent years it has developed something of a niche as an upmarket retro holiday resort. To the south is **Holkham Hall**, a magnificent Palladian mansion built in the 18th century by William Kent for Thomas Coke (great uncle of the pioneering 19th-century agriculturist Coke of Norfolk (*see under* NORFOLK), also known as **Coke of Holkham**). Its park was laid out by 'Capability' Brown.

Holkham Gap. An extensive sandy beach, which penetrates inland in a 1-km (0.6-mile) inlet to the north of Holkham. It is much frequented by bird-watchers.

Holkham Meals. An extended area of sandbanks between Holkham and the coast. *Meal* is a dialectal word for a 'sandbank' or 'sand-dune', from OScand *melr*.

Holland[1] Probably 'district characterized by hill-spurs', OE *hoh* 'hill-spur' + *land*.

A former administrative area of Lincolnshire, called in full the **Parts of Holland**. It covered a large area of the FENS at the southeastern corner of the WASH, and included the towns of Boston and Spalding. It was absorbed into Lincolnshire in 1974 (*see also* KESTEVEN *and* LINDSEY).

South Holland Main Drain. A drainage canal in the Fens in the south of Lincolnshire (before 1974 in the Parts of

Holland), to the south of the Wash. It drains into the River NENE.

Holland² 'high land', OScand *ha-land*, one of many such names in Orkney; Hollandstoun on North Ronaldsay is named for the same reason.

A settlement on STRONSAY, Orkney, overlooking the **Bay of Holland** to the west.

Holland Park From *Holland House*, itself named after the Earls of HOLLAND¹, whose home it once was.

A park and district in West London (W8, W11), in the Royal Borough of Kensington and Chelsea. The park was originally laid out as the grounds of **Holland House**, a Jacobean mansion built for Sir Walter Cope, James I's chancellor of the exchequer, and originally called Cope Castle. This passed into the family of the earls of Holland in 1621, and achieved its greatest renown in the early 19th century as the venue of Lady Holland's lion-filled political and literary *salons*. It was very badly damaged in the Second World War, but some of it is preserved, and the park remains, albeit smaller than in its greatest days. The Commonwealth Institute is at its southeastern end.

In the mid-19th century Lord Holland began to sell off some land for building, and the area around the park and northwards to Holland Park Avenue came to be known as Holland Park – a name reinforced by the opening of Holland Park Underground station, on the Central line, in 1900. One of the more notable monuments of this period is Leighton House, built to his own deign by the painter Frederic (later Lord) Leighton (1830–96) in 1866, with mosaics by Walter Crane and tiles by William De Morgan. It is now a museum and art gallery.

In the latter part of the 20th century the district came to have a certain radical chic: **Holland Park Comprehensive** became the most celebrated school of its type in England, and the BBC television sitcom *Absolutely Fabulous* (from 1992), about PR and fashion folk, was set here. At the beginning of the 21st century its most famous residents were probably the left-wing Labour politician Tony Benn and the film director Michael Winner.

Holloway 'hollow way, road in a hollow' (referring to a section of the GREAT NORTH ROAD – now called Holloway Road – that runs across relatively low-lying ground between Highgate and Islington), OE *hol* 'hollow' + *weg* 'way'.

A district of North London (N7, N19), in the northern portion of the borough of ISLINGTON, between Hampstead and Kentish Town to the west and Highbury to the east. The northern part is **Upper Holloway** and the southern part **Lower Holloway**. Its central artery is the **Holloway Road** – the road that originally gave the area its name (*see above*) – which runs southeastwards from ARCHWAY. Villas and cottages began to accrete around it in the late 18th century,

and by the middle of the 19th it was fairly comprehensively bricked over. It became a steadily more drab and run-down area, and gentrification has yet to have a marked effect on it. Its two best-known residents make an ill-assorted pair: the murderous Dr Crippen, who lived in Hilldrop Crescent, not far from the prison; and the ridiculous Mr Pooter, anti-hero of George and Weedon Grossmith's *The Diary of a Nobody* (1892), who inhabited the fictitious 'The Laurels, Brickfield Terrace'.

Marie Stopes set up her first family-planning clinic in Holloway, in 1921.

Holloway Road Underground station, on the Piccadilly line, opened in 1906.

(Royal Holloway, a college of London University at Egham, Surrey, was founded by the Victorian philanthropist Thomas Holloway, and has no connection with the district of Holloway.)

From the mid-19th century to the 1920s, *Holloway* was a slang term for the vagina, playing on 'hollow way'.

Holloway Prison. A prison in Camden Road, Lower Holloway (N7). It was opened in 1852 as a general prison (it became known in the slang of its time as **North Castle**, from its position in North London and the castellated architecture of its original gateway); but since 1902 it has housed exclusively female prisoners (among its earliest women residents were Emmeline Pankhurst and some of her fellow suffragettes, in 1906). In 1970 it was demolished and completely rebuilt.

Hollywood ME 'holy wood', referring to a wood here, where, according to an early Life, St Kevin of GLENDALOUGH had a hermitage; first recorded in the 13th century as *Sanctus Boscus* (Latin, 'holy wood').

A village in County Wicklow, 15 km (9 miles) south of Naas. Its Irish name is **Cillín Chaoimhín** ('St Kevin's little church').

Holme Pierrepoint *Holme* 'island, dry ground in a marsh, water-meadow', OScand *holmr* (*see* -EY, -EA); *Pierrepoint* denoting manorial ownership in the Middle Ages by the de Perpount family.

A village in Nottinghamshire, on the eastern outskirts of Nottingham, just to the south of the River Trent. It is the home of the National Water Sports Centre, which hosts sailing events, rowing, canoeing and many others.

Holmfirth 'sparse woodland belonging to a place called Holme', OScand *holmr* 'dry ground in a marsh' (*see* -EY, -EA) + OE *fyrhth* 'sparse woodland'.

A small town in West Yorkshire, 8 km (5 miles) south of Huddersfield.

Holsworthy 'Heald's enclosure', OE *Healdes* possessive form of OE male personal name *Heald* + *worthig* 'enclosure' (*see* -WORTH, WORTHY, -WARDINE).

A small market town in north Devon, on the River Deer,

about 16 km (10 miles) east of Bude. It is said to be the last place in England where someone was punished in the stocks (in 1861). About 5 km (3 miles) to the north is the village of **Holsworthy Beacon.**

Holton le Clay *Holton* 'farmstead on a spur of land', OE *hoh* 'spur of land' + -TON; *le Clay* '(in) the clayey district', Fr *le* 'the', OE *clæg* 'clay'.

A village in Lincolnshire, about 6.5 km (4 miles) south of Cleethorpes.

Holyhead 'holy headland', OE *halig* 'holy' + *heafod* 'headland'.

A port on the northern side of Holy Island, off the northwest side of ANGLESEY (formerly in Gwynedd), some 32 km (19 miles) northwest of Menai Bridge. Its Welsh name is **Caergybi** ('fort of Cybi'; *see* HOLY ISLAND[2]). There is a regular ferry service to DÚN LAOGHAIRE in Ireland, and some voyagers have judged that the town has not cheered up much since the early 18th century, when Jonathan Swift described it as 'scurvy, ill-provided and comfortless'.

The bay to the north of the town is called **Holyhead Bay**, and 2 km (1.2 miles) to the west is **Holyhead Mountain** (220 m / 722 ft), from which plunges CRAIG GOGARTH.

Holy Island[1]. *See* LINDISFARNE.

Holy Island[2] From the monastery established here in the 6th century by St Cybi.

An island off the northwest coast of ANGLESEY, to which it is joined by a sandy causeway and by road and rail links. Its Welsh name is **Ynys Gybi** ('Cybi's island'), and it is also sometimes called **Holyhead Island** (the main settlement on the island is the port of HOLYHEAD).

Holy Island[3]. A small island in Lamlash Bay, some 2 km (1.2 miles) off the east coast of ARRAN, in Argyll and Bute (formerly in Buteshire, then in Strathclyde region). The island rises to 314 m (1030 ft) at Mullach Mór. It derives its name from St Molaise (or Mo Las; b.566 and supposedly dying 120 years later), whose cave and well are on the western shore. There is a site of an old monastery at the northwest corner of the island. Since 1991 the island has been in the ownership of the Samye Ling Tibetan Centre, a group of Scottish Buddhists, who have established a community here.

Holy Land Possibly from *holy ground*, an 18th-century slang expression for a criminal slum or red-light district.

A 19th-century slang description of the area around ST GILES in London, including SEVEN DIALS, which at the time was the site of a notorious criminal slum.

See also PALESTINE IN LONDON.

Holy Loch. A small inlet of the Firth of CLYDE, some 2 km (1.2 miles) north of Dunoon, in Argyll and Bute (formerly in Strathclyde region). It derives its name from the story

that here sank a ship carrying earth from the Holy Land to be used in the foundations of Glasgow's medieval cathedral.

In 1960 the loch became a base for US Polaris (and later Trident) submarines.

> Think how here
> missiles like sugared rocks are all incised
> with Alabaman Homer. These defend
> the clattering tills, the taxis, thin pale girls
> who wear at evening their Woolworth pearls
> and from dewed railings gaze at the world's end.
>
> Iain Crichton Smith: 'By the Sea: Dunoon and the Holy Loch'

Holyrood 'holy cross', OE *rood* 'cross'.

A locality in EDINBURGH, at the foot of the ROYAL MILE to the west and ARTHUR'S SEAT to the southeast. David I built the **Abbey of Holyrood** ('holy cross') here in the 12th century in thanksgiving for a lucky escape: when out hunting he fell from his horse and was about to be gored by a stag when, at his prayer, a cross appeared between the deer's antlers. Some remains of the abbey can still be seen, but of more note now is the **Palace of Holyroodhouse** (also called **Holyrood House** or **Holyrood Palace**). The main parts were built by James IV between 1498 and 1503, and there are 18th-century additions. Mary Queen of Scots spent much time here, and it was in the palace that her jealous husband Darnley and his accomplices stabbed to death her favourite secretary, Rizzio (the palace guides used to point gravely at stains on the wooden floor to show tourists the exact spot). In 1829 Felix Mendelssohn visited Mary's chapel in the palace, and wrote:

> I believe I found today in that old chapel the beginning of my Scotch Symphony.

The symphony took many years to complete, and was not performed until 1842.

The palace was one of the main residences of the Scottish monarchs up to the Union of the Crowns in 1603. A century and a half later, Bonnie Prince Charlie stayed here on his doomed expedition south in 1745, and today the palace is the residence of the queen when she is on an official visit to Scotland.

'Holyrood' today to most Scots denotes the **Scottish Parliament** (whose new building opened opposite the palace in 2004), in the same way that 'Westminster' denotes the UK Parliament in London. The building exceeded its budget ten-fold (from an original £40 million), and opened three years late, leading it to be dubbed **Follyrood**. It was designed by Enric Miralles.

Holywell From St Winifred's Well.

A town in Flintshire (formerly in Clwyd), some 24 km (14.5 miles) northwest of Chester. It Welsh name is **Treffynnon** (*tref* 'settlement' + *ffynnon* 'well'). It takes its name from

St Winifred's Well (or St Winefride's Well; **Ffynnon Wenfrewi** in Welsh), a pre-Christian sacred site that is now enclosed by a Gothic chapel (*c*.1500). The story behind the name dates back to the 7th century, when Winifred had her head chopped off by a disappointed and intemperate admirer, Prince Caradoc. Where her head came to rest a spring burst forth. Luckily Winifred's uncle was St Beuno, who managed to restore her head to her body. Ever since, the spring has been visited by pilgrims looking for a cure, and Holywell has became known as **the Lourdes of Wales**. It was listed among the SEVEN WONDERS OF NORTH WALES. There is a big procession through the town every St Winifred's Day (the Sunday nearest to 22 June), in which pilgrims follow a relic in the form of one of the saint's thumbs.

> The stories of this Well of S. Winifred are, that the pious virgin, being ravished and murthered, this healing water sprung out of her body when buried; but this smells too much of the legend, to take up any of my time; the Romanists indeed believe it, as 'tis evident from their thronging hither to receive the healing sanative virtue of the water ...
>
> Daniel Defoe: *A Tour Through the Whole Island of Great Britain* (1724–6)

> At Holywell I bathed in the famous St Winifred's Well – it is an excellent cold bath.
>
> Samuel Taylor Coleridge: letter to Henry Martin (22 July 1794)

The poet Gerard Manley Hopkins (a convert to Roman Catholicism) wrote an unfinished verse drama about St Winifred's Well.

Holywood As HOLLYWOOD, referring to the church founded in the 7th century by St Laisrén.

A town on the southeast side of Belfast Lough, County Down, some 5 km (3 miles) northeast of Belfast. Its Irish name is **Ard Mhic Nasca** ('height of Mac Nasca'). It developed in the 19th century following the building of the railway line from Belfast.

Home Counties, the. A collective term (first recorded in 1837) for the counties surrounding London. It originally applied to SURREY, KENT, ESSEX and the now defunct MIDDLESEX, but BERKSHIRE, BUCKINGHAMSHIRE and HERTFORDSHIRE are usually included today, and some would also admit SUSSEX, despite its lack of contiguity. The term *home* is here being used in the sense 'surrounding or appertaining to a main property' (as in 'home farm').

The images conjured up by the expression are not altogether positive: this is the land of safeness and 'niceness', of commuterly comfort and stockbrokerish prosperity, buffered from the chill economic winds that from time to time blow over the rest of the United Kingdom (although at the end of the 20th century the wind began to find some cracks), of conformity and clipped lawns, of soft, undramatic landscapes, of unadventurousness, perhaps even of dullness. Its poet laureate is John Betjeman.

Home for Fallen Buildings, the. A nickname for PORTMEIRION, where many threatened old buildings were reconstructed by Clough Williams-Ellis.

Home of Lost Causes. An epithet conferred on OXFORD by the poet and essayist Matthew Arnold (1822–88):

> Oxford ... adorable dreamer ... Beautiful city! so venerable, so lovely, so unravaged by the fierce intellectual life of our century, so serene! ... whispering from her towers the last enchantments of the Middle Ages ... Home of lost causes, and forsaken beliefs, and unpopular names, and impossible loyalties!
>
> *Essays in Criticism* (1865)

Arnold's underlying criticism of Oxford University (at which he was Professor of Poetry at the time) for its failure to engage with the 19th century and its self-indulgent solipsism may not yet have lost all its appositeness.

Homer Perhaps 'marsh of stones' or 'cocks' marsh', OE *han* 'stone' or *hana* 'cock' + *mor* 'marsh'.

A village in Shropshire, about 11 km (7 miles) southwest of Telford.

Homerton 'Hunburh's farmstead', OE female personal name *Hunburh* + -TON.

A district in northeast London (E9), in the borough of HACKNEY, between Hackney to the west and Stratford to the east, and just to the west of the River LEA. It contains Sutton House, a rare surviving example of Tudor domestic architecture in London, and, as a resource of rather more immediate relevance, the large and modern Homerton Hospital.

Homerton College was founded in Homerton in 1695 as an educational institution for Protestant Dissenters. It began teacher-training in the mid-1900s, and moved to CAMBRIDGE[1] in 1894, developing links with the University of Cambridge. In 2001 it achieved the status of consitutent college, and added a range of the usual academic degrees to its teacher-training core.

Hom Green *Hom* perhaps 'low-lying pasture land, land in a river bend', OE *hamm* (*see* HAM).

A village in Herefordshire (before 1998 in Hereford and Worcester, before 1974 in Herefordshire), about 3 km (2 miles) southwest of Ross-on-Wye.

Homildon Hill *Homildon* probably 'crooked hill', OE *hamel* 'crooked' + *-don* (*see* DOWN, -DON); the tautological *Hill* was added later.

A battle site in Northumberland, just to the northwest of Wooler. Here on 14 September 1402 an army of Scots raiders under Archibald, Earl of Douglas (son of Archibald the

Grim) was defeated by an English force under Henry Percy ('Harry Hotspur') and the Earl of March.

> The Earl of Douglas is discomfited:
> Ten thousand bold Scots, two and twenty knights,
> Balk'd in their own blood, did Sir Walter see
> On Holmeldon's plains; of prisoners, Hotspur took
> Mordake, Earl of Fife and eldest son
> To beaten Douglas; and the Earl of Athol,
> Of Murray, Angus and Menteith.
> And is not this an honourable spoil?
> A gallant prize? Ha, cousin, is it not?
>
> William Shakespeare: *Henry IV, Part 1* (1597), I.i

Honeyborough 'manor house producing honey', OE *hunig* 'honey' + *burh* (*see* BURY); the honey may be a product or a complimentary reference to the quality of the land.

A village in Pembrokeshire (formerly in Dyfed), 6 km (4 miles) east of Milford Haven.

Honister Pass *Honister* possibly 'Huni's place', OScand male personal name *Huni* + *stathr* 'place'.

A steep road pass (358 m / 1174 ft) linking BORROWDALE and BUTTERMERE in the Lake District, Cumbria (formerly in Cumberland). On the southwest side of the pass are the dramatic remains of slate mining on **Honister Crag**.

Honiton 'Huna's farmstead', OE male personal name *Huna* + -TON.

A town (pronounced 'hunitən' or 'honitən') in Devon, on the River OTTER, about 24 km (15 miles) northeast of Exeter, for long (before a bypass was opened in the 1960s) notorious as a bottle-neck point on the main A30 road into Devon.

From the 16th to the 19th century it was an important lace-making centre (the industry was introduced by Flemish settlers during the reign of Elizabeth I), and the term **Honiton lace** came to have a particular application, to a type of pillow lace consisting of floral sprigs, either hand-sewn on to fine net or joined by bars of other lace-work.

Honley 'woodcock clearing', OE *hana* 'woodcock' (or 'stone clearing' OE *han* 'stone, rock') + -LEY.

A small town in West Yorkshire, 5 km (3 miles) south of Huddersfield.

Honour of Richmond, the. *See under* RICHMOND[1].

Hoo '(place at the) spur of land', OE *hoe* dative form of *hoh* 'spur of land'.

A village (in full **Hoo St Werburgh**, after the dedication of the local church) within the unitary authority of MEDWAY[2], in Kent, close to the north bank of the MEDWAY[1] estuary, about 5 km (3 miles) north of Rochester.

See also ST MARY'S HOO.

Hooe[1] For etymology *see* HOO.

A village in Devon, just to the south of Plymouth, on the southern bank of the mouth of the River PLYM.

Hooe[2] *See* HOO.

A village in East Sussex, about 5 km (3 miles) northwest of Bexhill.

Hook[1] '(place at the) hook of land, or bend in a river or hill' (perhaps referring to the local River Whitewater), OE *hoc* 'hook'.

A small town in Hampshire, about 10 km (6 miles) north-east of Basingstoke.

Hook[2] '(place at the) hook-shaped piece of land' (perhaps referring to a local topographical feature, or to the shape of the parish, which is elongated north–south with a curved northern tip), OE *hoc* 'hook'.

A district at the southwestern edge of Greater London (before 1965 in Surrey), in the borough of KINGSTON UPON THAMES, just to the north of Chessington.

Hook Head From the shape, but also from a mistaken translation of the Irish name *Rinn Dúain* 'St Dubhán's headland', taking the saint's name to be *dubhán* 'hook'.

A low headland on the south coast of County Wexford, on the east side of the mouth of Waterford Harbour (*see under* WATERFORD). The first lighthouse here was built in the 12th century (before that, the local monks tended a flame), and the current lighthouse was automated in 1996.

Hook Norton Originally *Hocneratune*, perhaps 'farmstead of the Hoccanere tribe', OE tribal name *Hoccanere* (literally '(people at) Hocca's hill-slope', *Hoccan* possessive form of male personal name *Hocca* + *ora* 'hill-slope') + -TON.

A village in Oxfordshire, about 13 km (8 miles) southwest of Banbury. Its name has been made famous by the eponymous local independent brewery, which has been producing fine beers for over 150 years.

See also HOGS NORTON.

Hoor in the Sewer, the. A nickname for the *Anna Livia Plurabelle* statue in Dublin (*see under* LIFFEY).

Hoo St Werburgh. *See* HOO.

Hooton Levitt 'farmstead on a spur of a hill', *Hooton* OE *hoh* 'hill-spur' + -TON; *Levitt* denoting manorial ownership in the Middle Ages by the Livet family.

A village in South Yorkshire, just west of Maltby. There are two other Hootons in South Yorkshire, **Hooton Pagnell** (west of Adwick le Street) and **Hooton Roberts** (southwest of Conisbrough), their affixes also denoting manorial ownership in the Middle Ages.

Hope[1] 'small secluded valley, enclosed plot of land', OE *hop*.

A village in Derbyshire, in the HIGH PEAK, in the **Hope Valley** (through which flows the River NOE), about 16 km (10 miles) northeast of Buxton. A signpost in the neighbouring village of Castleton bears the Bunyanesque legend 'Public Footpath to Hope'.

The pale, sky-piercing eyesore of the Hope Cement Works is carefully situated so that it can be seen from nearly every hill and edge in the High Peak.

Hope Brink. A steep escarpment on the eastern side of Hope Valley.

Hope Forest. A large area of high moorland to the north of Hope and to the east of Glossop, intercut with conifer forests.

Hope². A coastal village in Devon, at the southern end of Bigbury Bay (*see under* BIGBURY), about 7 km (5 miles) southwest of Kingsbridge. It is a two-part village, consisting of **Inner Hope** and **Outer Hope**. Both nestle in **Hope Cove**.

Hope³. A village in Shropshire, about 18 km (11 miles) southwest of Shrewsbury.

Hope Bagot *Bagot* denoting tenantship in the Middle Ages by Roger Bagard.
A village in Shropshire, about 8 km (5 miles) east of the town of Ludlow.

Hope Bowdler *Bowdler* denoting manorial ownership in the early Middle Ages by the de Bulers family.
A village in Shropshire, in the Stretton Hills, about 21 km (13 miles) south of Shrewsbury.

Hope Mansell *Mansell* denoting manorial ownership in the early Middle Ages by the Maloisel family.
A village in Herefordshire (before 1998 in Hereford and Worcester, before 1974 in Herefordshire), about 5 km (3 miles) south of Ross-on-Wye.

Hope's Nose Probably 'promontory of Hope', *Hope* name of a nearby village + OE *nœss* (*see* NESS).
A promontory on the south Devon coast, at the northeastern extremity of TOR BAY.

Hopetoun House After Lord *Hopetoun*.
A vast but elegant classical mansion above the Firth of Forth, some 5 km (3 miles) west of South Queensferry in Midlothian. It was built by Sir William Bruce for the Hope family in 1696, and it was extended and modified in the following century by William Adam and his sons John and Robert. Earlier in the 17th century Sir James Hope had been appointed as a judge, taking the title Lord Hopetoun – hence the name of the house.

Hopton Wafers *Hopton* 'farmstead in a small enclosed valley or enclosed plot of land', OE *hop* 'small enclosed valley, enclosed plot of land' + -TON; *Wafers* denoting manorial ownership in the early Middle Ages by the Wafre family.
A village in Shropshire, about 13 km (8 miles) east of Ludlow.

Hopton Wood 'wood belonging to Hopton', where *Hopton* is 'farm in a valley' (*see* HOPTON WAFERS).
A wood just to the west of WIRKSWORTH in Derbyshire. It has given its name to a type of pale brownish- or greyish-white limestone quarried nearby, which is used for building or decorative purposes.

Hopwas 'marshy or alluvial land near an enclosure', OE *hop* 'enclosure (in a marsh or moor)' + *wæsse* 'riverside land liable to flood'.
A village in Staffordshire, about 3 km (2 miles) northwest of Tamworth.

Horbury 'stronghold on muddy land', OE *horu* 'muddy land', *byrig*, dative of *burh* 'stronghold' (*see* BURY).
A small town in West Yorkshire, 4 km (2.5 miles) southwest of Wakefield. It was the birthplace of the novelist Stan Barstow (b.1928), author of *A Kind of Loving* (1960).

Horeb From the alternative name for the biblical Mount Sinai, probably so named in the 19th century.
A village in Carmarthenshire (formerly in Dyfed), 5 km (3 miles) north of Llanelli.

Horley Probably 'glade in a horn-shaped piece of land', OE *horna* 'horn' + -LEY.
A commuter town in Surrey, on the main railway line between London and Brighton, about 3 km (2 miles) north of Gatwick.

The car and speedboat enthusiast Donald Campbell (1921–67) was born here (*see under* CONISTON).

Hornblotton Green *Hornblotton* 'hornblowers' or trumpeters' farmstead', OE *horn-blawere* 'hornblower' + -TON.
A village in Somerset, about 11 km (7 miles) southeast of Glastonbury.

Horncastle Originally *Horncastre* 'Roman station or fortification on a horn-shaped piece of land', OE *horna* 'horn, horn-shaped piece of land' + *ceaster* 'Roman station or fortification' (*see* CHESTER); the form with *-castle* is first recorded in 1360.
A market town in Lincolnshire, on the River Bain, about 30 km (19 miles) east of Lincoln. As its name reveals, it was once a Roman garrison, and traces of Roman occupation remain. More recently, until the 20th century Europe's largest horse-fair was held here, a four-day affair every August. The fair, with its gypsy horse-dealers, is vividly described in George Borrow's picaresque semi-autobiographical novel *The Romany Rye* (1857).

Hornchurch 'church with horn-like gables' (probably referring to a church with gables of unusual width and size; the figure of a bull's head with horns at the east end of St Andrew's Church appears to be a late 18th-century inspiration), OE *horn* 'horn' or *hornede* 'horned' + *cirice* 'church'.
A district of eastern Outer London (before 1965 in Essex), in the borough of HAVERING, to the south of Romford and to the west of Upminster. During the Second World War, RAF Hornchurch was an important Battle-of-Britain fighter base.

Hornchurch 'Underground' station, on the District line, opened in 1902.

Horn Head A name describing its shape.

A headland and fine viewpoint on the north coast of Donegal, on the west side of SHEEP HAVEN. Its Irish name is **Corrán Binne** ('cresent of the peak').

Hornsea 'lake at a horn-shaped peninsula', OScand *horn* 'horn' + *nes* (*see* NESS) + *sær* 'lake'.

A seaside resort in HOLDERNESS, East Riding of Yorkshire, 20 km (12 miles) northeast of Hull. **Hornsea Pottery** is particularly known for its 1950s and 1960s styles. On the southwest side of Hornsea is **Hornsea Mere**, Yorkshire's largest freshwater lake, now a bird reserve.

Hornsea was the birthplace of Edward John Eyre (1815–1901), the explorer of Australia after whom Lake Eyre is named.

Hornsey Probably 'Hæring's enclosure', OE *Hæringes* possessive form of male personal name *Hæring* + *hæg* 'enclosure'; alternatively the first element might be descended from OE *haring* 'grey wood', in which case the name would mean 'enclosure in or by the grey wood'. A version of the name apparently without the possessive ending -*es* evolved into HARRINGAY, which came, via a house name, to be used as the name of a neighbouring district; and an earlier form of it, HARINGEY, has been adopted as a borough name.

A district (and former borough) of North London (N8), in the borough of HARINGEY, to the east of Highgate and to the west of South Tottenham. The original village lay to the north of CROUCH END; the borough took in the eastern end of the heights on which Hampstead and Highgate are built. The late 19th and early 20th centuries endowed the area with its present covering of Victorian and Edwardian housing.

Horse, the Etymology unknown.

An imposing cliff to the northwest of KYNANCE COVE in West Cornwall.

Horse and Jockey From the name of an inn here.

A village in County Tipperary, some 5 km (3 miles) south of Thurles. Its Irish name is **An Marchach** ('the jockey').

Horse Bank Possibly a reference to the shape of the sands, or an area suitable for riding.

A vast area of sands at Southport, Merseyside (formerly in Lancashire), just north of ANGRY BROW.

Horseleap From the story that Hugh de Lacy, who built nearby Ardnurcher Castle in 1192, jumped his horse over the castle's moat.

A hamlet in County Westmeath, some 15 km (9 miles) northwest of Tullamore. Its Irish name is **Baile Átha an Urchair** ('homestead of the ford of the throw').

Horsforth 'ford for horses', OE *hors* 'horse' + FORD.

A residential town in West Yorkshire, 8 km (5 miles) northwest of Leeds.

Horsham 'homestead or village where horses are kept', OE *hors* 'horse' + HAM.

A market town in West Sussex, on the River ARUN, at the centre of the western WEALD, about 15 km (9 miles) southwest of Crawley. Its most notable physical feature is a cul-de-sac called the Causeway, which contains a variety of interesting old buildings culminating in a 12th-century church. Horsham also has a CARFAX, which, unlike the rather better-known one in Oxford, does not live up to its name as a cross-roads, but is a sort of market place.

Christ's Hospital, a co-educational public school founded in 1552, is in Horsham, as are the headquarters of the Royal Society for the Protection of Animals (RSPCA).

Two rather different writers first saw the light of day here: the poet Percy Bysshe Shelley (1792–1822) and the thriller-writer Hammond Innes (1913–98).

There are towns called Horsham in the USA (Pennsylvania) and Australia (Victoria).

> The burgher's wives of Horsham go as fine as they do in other places.
>
> Daniel Defoe: *English Tradesmen* (1727)

Horwich '(place of) grey wych-elms', OE *har* 'grey' + *wice* 'wych-elm'.

A town in Greater Manchester, 8 km (5 miles) west of Bolton. The construction here of a large locomotive works by the Lancashire & Yorkshire Railway company in the late 19th century transformed what had been a small village into a sizeable town.

The railways left their imprint on the name of Horwich's football club, **Horwich RMI**, founded in 1896 ('RMI' stands for Railway Mechanics Institute). In 1995 Horwich RMI became Leigh RMI (*see under* LEIGH).

Hose 'spurs of land', OE *ho(h)as* plural form of *hoh* 'spur of land'.

A village in Leicestershire, about 11 km (7 miles) north of Melton Mowbray.

Hospital Irish *An tOspidéal* 'the hospital' (*see also* SPITAL), referring to the hospice founded here by the Knights Hospitallers in 1215.

A village in County Limerick, 25 km (15 miles) southeast of Limerick itself. There are the remains of the Hospitallers' church here.

Hot and Cold Corner. A nickname given to the corner of Kensington Gore in London (*see under* KENSINGTON) where the Royal Geographical Society is located. The nickname was inspired by the adjacent statues of David Livingstone and Sir Ernest Shackleton, who made their names in the Tropics and the Antarctic respectively.

Houghton Conquest *Houghton* 'farmstead on or near a ridge or hill-spur', OE *hoh* 'ridge, hill-spur' + -TON; *Conquest* denoting manorial ownership in the early Middle Ages by the Conquest family.

A village in Bedfordshire, about 8 km (5 miles) south of Bedford.

Houghton-le-Spring *Spring* denoting manorial ownership by the Spring family in the 14th century; the name has been adapted to other names with *en le* as if it meant 'in the copse', ME *spring* 'copse, plantation'.

A former mining town in Tyne and Wear (formerly in County Durham), 10 km (6 miles) southwest of Sunderland. Bernard Gilpin (1517–83), the 'Apostle of the North', was rector here and founded the grammar school; he is buried in the church.

Hound Hillock. *See under* CAIRN O' MOUNT.

Houndsditch Perhaps 'ditch frequented by (wild or stray) dogs', OE *hundes* possessive form of *hund* 'dog' + *dic* 'ditch'; alternatively the first element may be descended from the OE male personal name *Hund*. There appears to be little evidence to support the 16th-century antiquary John Stow's assertion that the name came from the dead dogs people used to throw into the ditch.

Originally, a ditch forming part of the moat outside the city walls of London. It was filled in in the 16th century, and the road built along its course inherited its name. It runs from Bishopsgate (just to the south of Liverpool Street Station) southeastwards to ALDGATE (EC3). In the 19th century it was still as insalubrious as its name suggests (it was an old clothes market, and home to many dubious characters). It moved up in the world in the 20th century as the City's banks and institutions took it over, and in 1927 a group of local businessmen, taking offence at the earthiness of its name, petitioned the City Corporation to have it changed. They were quite rightly turned down.

Hound Tor Probably 'dogs' tor', *Hound* OE *hund* 'dog'; there is a Fox Tor nearby.

A tor (high hilltop rock) in the eastern part of DARTMOOR, about 2.5 km (1.5 miles) north of HAYTOR. It is 448 m (1470 ft) above sea level. On the summit is a deserted village, consisting of three or four farmsteads dating from the Bronze Age, abandoned in the Middle Ages.

Hounslow 'dog's mound or tumulus' or 'Hund's (burial) mound', OE *hundes* or *Hundes* possessive forms of *hund* 'dog' and male personal name *Hund* + *hlaw* 'hill, mound, tumulus' (*see* LAW, LOW).

A district and borough of western Outer London (before 1965 in Middlesex), between Hillingdon to the northwest and Richmond-upon-Thames to the east. The borough contains BRENTFORD, Feltham, HESTON and ISLEWORTH. The district of Hounslow itself is to the west of Isleworth.

In Anglo-Saxon times Hounslow was the meeting place for Isleworth Hundred, which may have been how it came by its name – meeting places were often given the name of a conspicuous landmark (such as a burial mound – *see above*) by which they were situated. From at least the Middle Ages Hounslow has earned its money from the travel business. The road from London to Exeter and the West Country passes through it, and from the 17th century the stagecoaches stopped here. They had to cross **Hounslow Heath** (at that time 1620 ha / 4000 acres in extent), which became a popular lurking place for highwaymen. The town also made gunpowder from the 17th century.

The coming of the Great Western Railway in the middle of the 19th century dented Hounslow's prosperity, but things seemed to be looking up again in the early 20th century when, in 1919, the first civil airport in Britain opened on Hounslow Heath. It survived for only a year before being closed in favour of CROYDON, but HEATHROW, opened a little further west after the Second World War, has brought good business to Hounslow.

In the 19th century, *Hounslow Heath* was used as Cockney rhyming slang for 'teeth'. By the 20th, it had largely been supplanted by *Hampstead Heath* (*see under* HAMPSTEAD).

Hounslow East, Central and West 'Underground' stations, on the Piccadilly line, opened in the 1880s (originally on the District line, under the names of, respectively, Hounslow Town, Heston-Hounslow and Hounslow Barracks).

Housesteads Probably OE *hus-stede* 'site of a house' in the plural.

The site on HADRIAN'S WALL of the Roman fort of **Vercovicium**, situated dramatically atop the Whin Sill 16 km (10 miles) west-northwest of Hexham, Northumberland. The grooves worn in the stone paving at the East Gate are 1.4 m (4 ft 8½ in), the standard railway gauge used in Britain. It was said that George Stephenson, the pioneer locomotive engineer and a local boy, was inspired by the grooves at Housesteads to come up with this gauge. Unfortunately for the story, the fort had not then been excavated – although 1.4 m was the traditional axle span of farm carts, presumably since Roman days.

Hove 'hood-shaped hill' or 'shelter', OE *hufe*.

A town and seaside resort in East Sussex, immediately to the west of and contiguous with BRIGHTON, and since 1998 part of (and administrative centre of) the unitary authority (and, since 2000, city) of Brighton and Hove. The two names go together in many things local (the local football team, for instance, is **Brighton and Hove Albion**), and Hove has always been judged very much in the context of its nextdoor neighbour. The impression is of a slightly starchy dowager who has seen better days, looking with some disapproval at a rakish and sometimes disreputable nephew and often, it seems, trying to pretend that they are not related at all. The apartheid is symbolized by a change in the colour of the road surface along the esplanade from black in Brighton to red in Hove (with positively no political subtext). As a resort it offers nothing more sensational than seafront gardens and boating pools, but it is also a comfortable residential town, with broad boulevards and Edwardian villas.

Hove's County Ground is the headquarters of the SUSSEX County Cricket Club.

The composer Roger Quilter (1877–1953) and the violinist Nigel Kennedy (b.1956) were born in Hove.

Howardian Hills After CASTLE HOWARD, itself named after Charles Howard, 3rd Earl of Carlisle.

A range of low rolling hills marking the southern boundary of the Vale of PICKERING, North Yorkshire. Castle Howard is at the eastern end of the range.

Howden '(place in the) valley near the headland', OE *heafod* 'headland' + *denu* 'valley'. At some point during the century before the Norman Conquest, a time of Danish settlement in the area, OE *heafod* was replaced by OScand *hofuth* ('headland'), creating the modern form of the name (*see also* HOWTH).

A historic market town in the western part of the East Riding of Yorkshire (formerly in Humberside), 7 km (4 miles) north of GOOLE. In 1080 William the Conqueror granted the manor and church of what the Domesday Book describes as *Hovedene* to the bishopric of Durham (*see* LAND OF THE PRINCE BISHOPS). The wealth that flowed from the link with the bishopric is reflected in the mainly 14th-century Church of St Peter (better known as **Howden Minster**), established as a collegiate church in 1267 and lavishly re-appointed thereafter, and in the medieval Bishop of Durham's Manor House, a stopping-place for the prince bishops on their frequent journeys between Durham and London. The house belonged to the bishops of Durham until 1836. The Minster's majestic tower is a landmark for travellers on the nearby M62 motorway.

Howe of Fife. *See under* FIFE.

Howes o' Buchan. *See under* BUCHAN.

Howgill Fells, the 'fells by the deeply cut ravine', *Howgill* OE *hol*, OScand *holr* 'hollow, cut' + OScand *gil* 'ravine', with OScand *fjall* 'fell'.

A northwestern section of the PENNINES, in Cumbria (formerly in Westmorland), some 15 km (9 miles) north-east of Kendal. These shapely rolling hills include the Calf (676 m / 2217 ft; the name probably indicates a smaller hill beside a larger one) and Simon's Seat (587 m / 1925 ft; OScand *sæti* 'seat, hilltop' with the name of a prominent landowner). The lovely views of their western slopes are

familiar to travellers on the M6 and the Glasgow–Euston railway line as they speed through the Tebay Gorge.

Howling. A fictional SOUTH DOWNS village in Stella Gibbons's comic rural novel *Cold Comfort Farm* (1932). The Starkadders' farm is close by. Its real-life models may have been the villages of Fulking and Poynings, to the north-west of Brighton.

Howth OScand *hofuth* 'headland'.

A resort in County Dublin, on the peninsula forming the north side of Dublin Bay, and part of DUBLIN itself since 1942. In Irish it is called **Binn Éadair** ('Éadar's peak', he being a legendary figure associated with the place); the Irish name refers to the **Hill of Howth** (169 m / 554 ft), at whose foot Howth lies. On the summit is a cairn purporting to be the burial place of Criffan or Crimthan, a 1st-century high king of Ireland; Aidín, widow of the legendary Fianna warrior Oscar, was also said to have been buried here by her father-in-law Oisín. H.G. Wells described the view from here as 'one of the most beautiful in the world'.

> Delightful to be on the Hill of Howth
> Before going over the white-haired sea:
> The dashing of the wave against its face,
> The bareness of its shores and of its border.
>
> Anon.: 'Columcille's Greeting to Ireland' (12th century), once attributed to Columcille (St Columba, who evangelized Scotland); translated by William Reeves and Kuno Meyer

Howth Castle (1654; restored by Edwin Lutyens in 1910) incorporates a 1564 keep and other earlier buildings. It has been the seat of the St Lawrence family since the 16th century, and there is a story that Grace O'Malley, the pirate Queen of Clew Bay (*see under* CLEW BAY), having found the gate closed to her at dinner time, kidnapped the St Lawrence heir and agreed to surrender him only in return for a promise that hungry travellers would never again be barred from Howth Castle. It is said that to this day the St Lawrences always lay an extra place at dinner; however, the castle is not open to visitors. It features in the opening words of one of the classics of modern Irish literature:

> riverrun, past Eve and Adam's, from swerve of shore to bend of bay, brings us by a commodious vicus of recirculation back to Howth Castle and Environs.
>
> James Joyce: *Finnegans Wake* (1939) ('Howth Castle and Environs' – HCE – is an avatar of the novel's 'hero', Humphrey Chimpden Earwicker.)

> ... look, across
> dark waves where bell-buoys dimly toss
> the Baily winks beyond Howth Head
> and sleep calls from the silent bed ...
>
> Derek Mahon: 'Beyond Howth Head', from *Collected Poems* (1999)

Garland of Howth, the. A medieval illuminated manuscript of the Gospels, made on IRELAND'S EYE, just off the coast at Howth. The manuscript is now in the library of Trinity College, Dublin.

Howth Gun-Running (26 July 1914). An incident in which the Irish Volunteers successfully landed some 1500 German rifles at Howth from Erskine Childers' yacht *Asgard*, in response to Edward Carson's open arming of Ulster Unionists (*see* LARNE). Soldiers sent to seize the arms got hold of only a few, and on their return to barracks were involved in an ugly incident in BACHELOR'S WALK, Dublin.

Hoxne Perhaps 'hock-shaped spur of land', OE *hohsinu*.

A village in Suffolk, about 6 km (4 miles) southeast of Diss. Nearby, St Edmund (*c.*840–870), King of East Anglia, was captured and martyred by the Danes. According to later tradition he hid under a bridge, Goldbrook Bridge, to escape them, but the glint of his spurs gave him away, and they put him to death for refusing to renounce Christianity. Somewhat petulantly for a saint, he put a curse on the bridge, which presumably remains in force. (The less exciting truth seems to be that he made no attempt to run away, and there is no firm evidence that the Anglo-Saxons had spurs.)

A 4th-century treasure hoard was discovered in Hoxne in 1992. It consisted of 200 gold and silver objects (including a silver jug handle in the shape of a tigress) and 15,000 Roman coins.

Hoxton 'Hoc's farmstead or estate', OE *Hoces* possessive form of male personal name *Hoc* + -TON.

A district in East London (N1), in the borough of HACKNEY, about 1.5 km (1 mile) north of Liverpool Street Station. It was rapidly urbanized in the 19th century, and by 1900 it was one of the worst parts of London for poverty, overcrowding and lawlessness:

> Hoxton is the leading criminal quarter of London, and indeed of all England.
>
> Charles Booth: *Life and Labour of the People of London* (1889–90)

In the early part of the 20th century it was also a hotbed of gangland activity: the Hoxton gang controlled many of the race meetings in southern England, and their showdown with the Sabini gang of Clerkenwell was an inspiration for Graham Greene's *Brighton Rock* (1938). Despite this, it was a great place for entertainment: the first theatres in England had been built in the area in the 1570s (*see* SHOREDITCH), and in the 19th and early 20th centuries Hoxton was famous for its music halls – notably the Britannia and MacDonald's (both in Hoxton Street) and the Varieties. In the years before and after the Second World War, Gainsborough Studios in Hoxton, beside the REGENT'S CANAL, were one of the major centres of the British film industry; Alfred Hitchcock directed there before moving to Hollywood.

Following severe bomb damage in the Second World War, the second half of the 20th century did nothing to rescue Hoxton's down-at-heel reputation – until the early 1990s, when young designers, artists and the like moved into the area in search of low-rent, live-in studios. Cheap but increasingly trendy eating places began to follow around 1996, and by the end of the millennium Hoxton had London's 'hippest and most happening bar and club scene' (*Time Out Eating and Drinking 2003*).

St Leonard's Hospital in Hoxton was at one time run by James Parkinson (1755–1824), original describer of the eponymous disease; and Edith Cavell (1865–1915), shot by the Germans for helping Allied soldiers to escape from Belgium, had worked as a nurse there.

The artist and book-illustrator Kate Greenaway (1846–1901) and the music-hall entertainer Marie Lloyd (1870–1922) were born in Hoxton.

Hoxton fin. A men's hairstyle consisting of a gelled crest running from front to back across the middle of the head, briefly fashionable at the beginning of the 21st century. Such a style was sported for a time – and its popularity boosted – by the footballer and fashion icon David Beckham (b.1975).

Hoy 'high island', OScand *ha* 'high' + *ey* (*see* -AY).

The second largest (and the hilliest) island in ORKNEY, about 5 km (3 miles) across **Hoy Sound** from Stromness on Mainland.

> Today on Hoy Sound random blossoms unfurl
> Of feather and rust, a harlequin spring.
>
>   Tomorrow
> The wave will weep like a widow on the rock,
> Or howl like Lear, or laugh like a green child.
>
>   George Mackay Brown (1921–96): 'December Day, Hoy Sound'

The most notable antiquity on the island is the Dwarfie Stane (*c.*3000 BC), a rare northern European example of a prehistoric rock-cut tomb; it features in Sir Walter Scott's novel *The Pirate* (1821), in which it is described by Norna of the Fitful-head as:

> This extraordinary dwelling, which Trolld, a dwarf famous in the northern Sagas, is said to have framed for his own favourite residence.

In the northwest of the island is St John's Head, the highest perpendicular cliff in Britain (350 m / 1140 ft), first ascended over several days by Ed Drummond and partner in 1970. They named their climb the *Longhope Route*, in memory of the crew of Hoy's Longhope lifeboat, all eight of whom had perished in 1969 attempting to assist the *Irene*, a Liberian cargo ship. Better known to a wider public is the nearby sea stack, **the Old Man of Hoy** (137 m / 450 ft high), first climbed by Tom Patey, Rustie Baillie and Chris Bonington in 1966, and the subject of an outside-broadcasting extravaganza in 1967. One Malcolm, a 19th-century Orkney poet, described the Old Man thus:

> See Hoy's old man, whose summit bare
> Pierces the dark blue fields of air.
> Based in the sea his fearful form
> Glooms like the spirit of the storm.

Stevie's Ferry to Hoy. A piano piece (1976) by the composer Peter Maxwell Davies, a resident of Orkney.

Hoylake From *Hyle Lake*, the name of a former roadstead off the northern coast of the Wirral (*Hyle* 'hillock, sandbank', presumably referring to a sandbank that bounded the tidal lake of the roadstead, OE *hygel*), first recorded in 1687; this was re-applied to a small hamlet on the coast, and subsequently to the newly developed resort.

A town and seaside resort in Cheshire (before 1996 in Merseyside, before 1974 in Cheshire), at the northwest corner of the WIRRAL peninsula, about 11 km (7 miles) west of Birkenhead. Its beginnings can be traced to the 1790s, when the Royal Hotel was opened near a hamlet here, for those who wanted to take advantage of the broad sandy beaches and the sea-bathing. Over the course of the 19th century it developed considerably in size. Its grassy sandhills make excellent golf links country: Hoylake is home to the Royal Liverpool Golf Club, which held 10 British Open Championships between 1867 and 1967.

Hoyland 'cultivated land by a ridge', OE *hoh* 'ridge, hill spur' + *land*.

A former mining town in South Yorkshire, 6 km (4 miles) south of Barnsley.

Hubberholme 'Hunburh's homestead', OE female personal name *Hunburh* + HAM.

A village in Langstrothdale, North Yorkshire, at the head of Wharfedale. The writer (and Yorkshireman) J.B. Priestley (1894–1984) – who thought it 'one of the smallest and pleasantest places in the world' – is buried here. The George at Hubberholme was also his favourite pub and is the scene of an annual meeting, held every New Year's Eve, at which the vicar and churchwardens sit in one room, called the House of Lords, and the local farmers sit in another, the House of Commons, and negotiate rents for a piece of land called Poor's Pasture – the money raised going to the needy of the village.

Hucknall 'Hucca's nook of land', OE *Huccan* possessive form of male personal name *Hucca* + *halh* (*see* HALE, -HALL).

A former mining town in Nottinghamshire, about 8 km (5 miles) north of Nottingham. Newstead Abbey (*see under* NEWSTEAD), the ancestral home of the poet Lord Byron, is about 5 km (3 miles) north of here. Byron

himself is buried in the family vault in St Mary Magdalen's Church, Hucknall.

Hucknall was the birthplace of the composer Eric Coates (1886–1957).

Huddersfield 'Hudræd's open land', OE male personal name (or possibly *huder* 'shelter') + *feld* (*see* FIELD); *Odersfelt* 1086. An industrial town on the River COLNE³, West Yorkshire, some 25 km (15 miles) southwest of Leeds. Huddersfield had become a major centre of woollen manufacturing by the end of the 18th century, and continued to expand in the 19th (the development of the town's textile industry is illustrated in the Tolson Memorial Museum).

It was at Huddersfield's George Hotel on 29 August 1895 that there took place a historic meeting of 22 northern rugby clubs that resulted in their breakaway from the Rugby Football Union (*see under* RUGBY) and the foundation of the Northern Rugby Union (later to become the Rugby Football League).

The **University of Huddersfield** (formerly Huddersfield Polytechnic) was established in 1992; its origins lie in the Young Men's Mutual Improvement Society, founded in 1841. The town hosts an annual festival of contemporary music, and has a famous choral society (*see below*).

Huddersfield was the birthplace of the film actor James Mason (1909–84), the Labour prime minister Harold Wilson (1916–95) and the poet Simon Armitage (b.1933).

Huddersfield Choral Society. A choir founded in Huddersfield in 1836 and initially recruiting its members from the mixed choirs of local Nonconformist churches. In 1942 the choir started performing and recording with professional orchestras. It has become particularly associated with performances of Handel's *Messiah*.

Huddersfield Giants. Huddersfield's rugby league club, originally founded in the 1860s. Huddersfield was one of the rugby clubs that defected from the Rugby Football Union in 1895 (*see above*) to found the Northern Rugby Union. Huddersfield Giants now play in rugby league's Super League, playing their home matches at the Alfred McAlpine Stadium.

Hughenden Valley *Hughenden* 'Huhha's valley', OE *Huhhan* possessive form of male personal name *Huhha* + *denu* 'valley'. The name *Hughenden Valley* (*Valley* is probably a 19th-century addition) is thus strictly tautological.

A village (pronounced as in the forename Hugh) in Buckinghamshire, about 5 km (3 miles) north of High Wycombe. Nearby is **Hughenden Manor**, a large and elaborate mansion once the home of Benjamin Disraeli (the Earl of Beaconsfield; 1804–81), Conservative politician, novelist and twice prime minister (1868 and 1874–80). It now belongs to the National Trust. He is buried in Hughenden churchyard, which also contains a monument to him erected by Queen Victoria, who famously preferred

'Dizzy' to his great Liberal rival W.E. Gladstone (*see under* HAWARDEN*).

Hugh Seat After *Hugh* de Morville + OScand *sæti* 'seat, hilltop'.
A top (689 m / 2260 ft) on MALLERSTANG Edge in the Pennines, on the border between Cumbria and North Yorkshire. It takes its name from a local landowner, Hugh de Morville, one of the knights who murdered Thomas Becket in Canterbury Cathedral in 1170 (*see under* CANTERBURY[1]). Near the summit is Lady's Stone, a boundary raised in 1664 by a later owner, Lady Anne Clifford.

Hugh Town *Hugh* 'hill-spur' (referring to a nearby hill on which Star Castle stands), OE *hoh*.
The capital of the SCILLY ISLES, situated on the largest island, ST MARY'S. Overlooking it is a hill called the Garrison, on which stands Star Castle, a fort built on an eight-pointed plan at the time of the Spanish Armada (and now a hotel).

Hugmore 'wasteland for pigs', ME *hogge* + *more* 'wasteland, marshy land'.
A village in Wrexham unitary authority (formerly in Denbighshire, then in Clwyd), 5 km (3 miles) east of Wrexham.

Huish Champflower *Huish* 'measure of land that would support a family', OE *hiwisc*; *Champflower* denoting manorial ownership in the Middle Ages by the Champflur family.
A village (pronounced 'hewish') in Somerset, to the east of Exmoor and to the south of Clatworthy Reservoir (*see under* CLATWORTHY), about 16 km (10 miles) northwest of Taunton.

Huish Episcopi *Episcopi* 'bishop's', Latin, referring to early ownership by the Bishops of Wells.
A village in Somerset, on the River PARRETT, about 22 km (14 miles) east of Taunton. Its 14th-century church, St Mary's, has a particularly fine tower, which in 1972 featured on a 9p stamp.
   Huish Episcopi was reputedly the model for the fictional village of **Plumstead Episcopi** in Anthony Trollope's novel *The Warden* (1855).

Hull In full, *Kingston upon Hull* 'king's estate on the River Hull', OE *cyning* 'king' + -TON with OScand river name meaning 'deep one' or OCelt river name meaning 'muddy one'.
An industrial city, port and unitary authority on the north bank of the Humber Estuary in northeast England (formerly in the East Riding of Yorkshire, then in Humberside), 55 km (33 miles) southeast of York. Its full and official name is **Kingston upon Hull**, although few refer to it as such. It was elevated to city status in 1897.
   Cistercian monks established a settlement called *Wyke* here in the 12th century. In 1293 Edward I acquired the area, and its name changed to its present form. Not all later monarchs were so welcome: in 1642, during the Civil Wars,

the citizens of Hull shut out Charles I, went on to suffer two Royalist sieges, and in 1659 elected the Parliamentary poet Andrew Marvell as their MP.
   Hull has been an important seaport since the Middle Ages. In the 18th century Defoe was writing:

> I believe there is more business done in Hull than in any town of its bigness in Europe.
>
>   Daniel Defoe: *A Tour Through the Whole Island of Great Britain* (1724–6). Defoe also has Robinson Crusoe depart on his fateful voyage from Hull.

By 1800, Hull was the third busiest port in Britain, after London and Liverpool. In the Second World War the city's extensive docks made it a target for German bombers, and the city suffered much damage. Today, as well as handling large volumes of cargo, the port has ferries to Rotterdam and Zeebrugge, although its fishing industry has declined.
   The **University of Hull** was founded in 1927 as University College Hull; the city's other university is the University of Humberside (*see under* HUMBERSIDE).
   Hull City FC (founded in 1904 and nicknamed the Tigers), played at Boothferry Park from 1945 until 2002, when they moved to the brand-new KC ('Kingston Communications') stadium. Hull's history of footballing underachievement (for such a well-populated place) may have something to do with its being first and foremost a rugby league town. There are two major professional clubs here. **Hull FC**, founded in 1865, was one of the 22 northern rugby clubs that broke away from the Rugby Football Union at HUDDERSFIELD in 1895; Hull played their home games at the Boulevard until 2003, when they too moved to the KC stadium (*see above*). They now play in the Super League. **Hull Kingston Rovers**, the younger of Hull's two rugby league clubs, originally founded as Kingston Amateurs in 1883, are based at Craven Park on the eastern side of Hull.
   Hull was the birthplace of the anti-slavery campaigner William Wilberforce (1759–1833), who was also MP for the town (the 17th-century merchant's house where he was born is now a museum); John Venn (1834–1923), the logician who devised the Venn diagram; the movie mogul J. Arthur Rank (1888–1972); the poet Stevie Smith (1902–71); the aviatrix Amy Johnson (1903–41); the comic actor Ian Carmichael (b.1920); the stage and screen actor Tom Courtenay (b.1937); and the comic actress and writer Maureen Lipman (b.1946). John Prescott, deputy prime minister in Tony Blair's New Labour government since 1997, is MP for Hull East.
   The poet Philip Larkin (1922–1985) was a librarian at the University of Hull for nearly all his adult life. The Scottish poet Douglas Dunn was more briefly a librarian there (1969–71), but he drew much material for his earlier verse from the working-class life of the city:

There is no grass in Terry Street. The worms
Come up cracks in concrete yards in moonlight.

> Douglas Dunn: 'A Removal from Terry Street', from *Terry Street* (1969)

In a letter to Robert Conquest (24 July 1955) Larkin was more succinct about the city:

It's a frightful dump.

Larkin's jaundiced perception of Hull appears to have been shared by the authors of *Crap Towns* (2003), which placed it at the top of a list of the 50 least desirable places to reside in Britain.

From Hull, Hell and Halifax ... *See under* HALIFAX.

Humber An OCelt or pre-Celtic river name of unknown meaning.

A long estuary in northeast England, separating Yorkshire from Lincolnshire. In Anglo-Saxon times it marked the frontier between NORTHUMBRIA and MERCIA, and it has continued to mark an important cultural boundary, despite the foolish period (1974–96) when government came up with the bastardized notion of HUMBERSIDE.

Some 12 km (7 miles) east of Goole the Trent flows into the OUSE[2] to form what John Hillaby has described as 'the Brown Windsor waters of the Humber Estuary'. The estuary extends 60 km (40 miles) east to enter the North Sea at SPURN HEAD, at which point it is some 10 km (6 miles) wide. This lower section is called **Mouth of the Humber**. The Humber is an important waterway for ocean-going vessels, and along its shores are the major ports of GRIMSBY and HULL. Just west of Hull it is crossed by the **Humber Bridge**, completed in 1981. Its main span of 1410 m (1542 yards) was the longest in the world at the time; its total length is 2220 m (2427 yards).

> Thou by the Indian Ganges' side
> Shouldst rubies find: I by the tide
> Of Humber would complain.

> Andrew Marvell (1621–78): 'To His Coy Mistress' (Marvell was MP for Hull from 1659, so the Humber was pretty much his home river.)

There are rivers called Humber in Canada (Newfoundland, Ontario). The estuary also gave its name to a marque of cars produced from 1899 to 1976; models included the Humber Hawk and the Humber Super Snipe.

Humber. A sea area in the shipping forecast. It is situated south of Tyne and Dogger, west of German Bight, and north of Thames.

Humberside. A former county of northeast England, created in 1974 out of the northern part of LINCOLNSHIRE and parts of the East and West Ridings of YORKSHIRE. Much to the relief of stateless Yorkshiremen, this mongrel creation was dismantled in 1996 and distributed among the new unitary authorities of EAST RIDING OF YORKSHIRE , HULL,

NORTH EAST LINCOLNSHIRE and NORTH LINCOLNSHIRE. The name survives, however, as a geographical designation, like Clydeside and Tyneside.

Humberside Polytechnic, in HULL, became the **University of Humberside** in 1992.

Hundred Foot Drain So called because it was originally 100 ft (30.5 m) wide.

A drain cut in 1649 by the Dutch engineer Cornelius Vermuyden (1595–1683) between two points on the GREAT OUSE river (Earith in Cambridgeshire and DENVER in Norfolk), making a more direct route to the sea and also serving to drain the surrounding fens. It is about 27 km (17 miles) long and virtually in a straight line. Also called the New Bedford River, it is parallel to the Old Bedford River (*see* BEDFORD LEVEL), which was cut 12 years before but proved not to be effective.

See also FORTY FOOT DRAIN.

Hundred House The reason for the name is uncertain, but it may be an ironic reference to the diminutive size of the settlement.

A hamlet centred on the **Hundred House Inn**, in Powys, 8 km (5 miles) northeast of Builth Wells.

Hungerford Literally 'hunger ford', that is to say, a ford leading to infertile or unproductive land, OE *hungor* 'hunger' + FORD. As if this were too simple, local tradition has come up with two ingenious alternative accounts: the name is said to have been originally *Ingleford* 'ford of the Angles', on the grounds that the Roman road crossing the Kennet marked the boundary between the Angles and the Saxons; and it has also been connected with the 9th-century Danish leader Hingwar, who supposedly drowned while crossing the Kennet here.

A small town in Berkshire, on the River KENNET[1] and the Kennet and Avon Canal, about 16 km (10 miles) west of Newbury. Every year at Hocktide (just after Easter) the granting of fishing rights to the town by John of Gaunt in the 14th century is celebrated in a ceremony involving 'tutti-men' (an old term for tithe-collectors).

Charles Portal (1893–1971), commander-in-chief of the Royal Air Force during the Second World War, was born in Hungerford. He took the title Lord Portal of Hungerford.

There is a town called Hungerford in Queensland, Australia.

Hungerford Massacre, the. The shooting of 28 people, of whom 13 died, by an unbalanced gunman, Michael Ryan, in Hungerford on 20 August 1987. Ryan, whose victims included his own mother, ended his killing spree by shooting himself.

Hungerford Bridge From *Hungerford Market*, a former market (demolished in 1860) on the site of Charing Cross Station, which was set up in 1682 by Sir Edward Hungerford. A railway bridge across the River THAMES in Central

London, carrying tracks to and from CHARING CROSS Station on the north bank. It was built in 1864, to the design of Sir John Hawkshaw, replacing the original Hungerford Suspension Bridge, a footbridge designed by Isambard Kingdom Brunel. At the end of the 20th century the bridge was refurbished, the somewhat makeshift footbridge on its downstream side was removed and a pair of new footbridges, known as the **Golden Jubilee Bridges** (so named to mark the Golden Jubilee of Queen Elizabeth II), were built on each side. They were opened in 2002.

Hungerford Bridge is also known as **Charing Cross Bridge**.

Hungry Hill Presumably a name reflecting the barrenness of the hill.

The highest (685 m / 2247 ft) of the CAHA MOUNTAINS in the BEARA peninsula, West Cork. It gave Daphne du Maurier a title for her novel *Hungry Hill* (1943), an account of the history of the Puxleys (although the author changed their name), a local family who owned copper mines in Beara.

Hungry Law 'barren hill', *Hungry* ModE *hungry*, being a disparaging reference to the barrenness of the place; *Law* OE *hlaw* (see LAW, LOW).

A hill (501 m / 1644 ft) in the CHEVIOT Hills, on the Anglo-Scottish border 5 km (3 miles) east of Carter Bar.

Hunny Hill *Hunny* 'honey', OE *hunig* 'wild honey'.

A village on the ISLE OF WIGHT, just to the north of Newport.

Hunstanton 'Hunstan's farmstead', OE male personal name *Hunstan* + -TON.

A seaside town (pronounced 'hunstantən' or, locally, 'hunstən') on the North Norfolk coast, on the eastern side of the WASH, about 23 km (14 miles) north of King's Lynn. It was developed as a tourist resort in the Victorian period. It is now an archetypal old-fashioned mid- to down-market British seaside resort, well provisioned with arcades. Among its more individual attractions are a long sandy beach and chalk cliffs striped white, red and brown. On top of the cliffs are the ruins of a chapel dedicated to St Edmund, who is said to have landed here in 850.

It was badly hit by the 1953 storm surge, and 32 inhabitants died.

Huntingdon 'huntsman's hill', or 'Hunta's hill', OE *huntan* or *Huntan* possessive form of *hunta* 'huntsman' or male personal name *Hunta* + *dun* (see DOWN, -DON).

A town in Cambridgeshire (before 1974 in Huntingdonshire), on the GREAT OUSE river, about 27 km (17 miles) northwest of Cambridge. It was founded by the Anglo-Saxons, on the route of the Romans' ERMINE STREET, and it rapidly grew in size and prosperity as a bridging point on the Ouse. It continued to prosper in the age of coaching (it is on the GREAT NORTH ROAD and the Cambridge-to-

Birmingham road), and it retains many fine Georgian buildings from the period of its pre-eminence. It was once the county town of HUNTINGDONSHIRE, and it remains an important centre for the surrounding fertile agricultural country.

Huntingdon lies cheek by jowl with GODMANCHESTER, to which it is connected by an old six-arched bridge dating from 1332.

Oliver Cromwell (1599–1659) was born in Huntingdon and was educated at the grammar school here (founded 1565), as was another local boy, Samuel Pepys. Cromwell was MP for the town in the Parliament of 1628–9, a position later held from 1979 until 2001 by John Major (Conservative prime minister 1990–97).

There are towns called Huntingdon in the USA (New York, Pennsylvania and Tennessee) and in Canada (Quebec). *See also* VENANTODUNUM.

Henry of Huntingdon. A medieval cleric and chronicler (?1084–1155) who compiled the *Historia Anglorum* (covering the history of England from the coming of the Romans to the accession of Henry II). He was archdeacon of Huntingdon from around 1110.

Huntingdonshire From HUNTINGDON + SHIRE The name *Huntingdonshire* is first recorded in the 11th century.

An administrative district of Cambridgeshire, formerly a county (also officially designated **Huntingdon and Peterborough**) of central eastern England, but in 1974 absorbed into Cambridgeshire. As an independent county it was bounded to the west by Northamptonshire, to the north by Lincolnshire, to the east by Cambridgeshire and the Isle of Ely and to the south by Bedfordshire. Its main centres were GODMANCHESTER, HUNTINGDON (the county town), ST IVES[1] and ST NEOTS, and it also contained the Soke of Peterborough (*see under* PETERBOROUGH). The northeastern part of the county was in the FENS. The new administrative district of Huntingdonshire was set up in 1996.

Pre-Roman Huntingdonshire was border country between the territory of the Iceni tribe of East Anglia and the Catuvellauni tribe of HERTFORDSHIRE. In the Anglo-Saxon period it became part of the kingdom of EAST ANGLIA before falling to MERCIA. Danes overran the area in the later part of the 9th century.

'Anthology of Huntingdonshire Cabmen'. A surreally plain list of bizarre and banal names (examples: Fodge, S.; Nurthers, P.L.; Whackfast, E.W.) supposedly belonging to Huntingdonshire cabmen, compiled by 'Beachcomber' (J.B. Morton). It was mesmerizingly read by Michael Redgrave in the 1969 BBC television series based on the Beachcomber column.

Huntingtower. A castle on the northwest outskirts of PERTH, formerly the seat of the Ruthven family (pronounced 'riven'), who were earls of Gowrie. The castle consists of two 15th-century towers joined by a narrow, late 17th-century addition. Before this addition, there was a 2.9-m (9.5-ft) gap, known as the 'Maiden's Leap', so named from the story that a daughter of the house leapt across it to avoid compromising herself and her lover.

Prior to 1600 the castle was called **Ruthven Castle**. The reason for the change of name lies in two violent incidents involving the Ruthven earls of Gowrie and King James VI. The first of these was the infamous Ruthven Raid of 1582, in which the Earl of Gowrie, together with the Earl of Mar and other nobles, seized the 16-year-old James VI of Scotland and held him at the castle in an attempt to reassert their influence on the terrified young king. James managed to escape the following year, and Gowrie lost his head shortly afterwards.

The second incident was the so-called 'Gowrie Conspiracy' of 1600, in which John Ruthven, 3rd Earl of Gowrie, and his brother Alexander were killed in their house in Perth in the presence of the king. James alleged that he had been lured up into a turret by the Ruthvens and attacked, but no motivation for a conspiracy has been established, and James's account of the incident was widely disbelieved. Whatever lay behind it all, James proscribed the very name of Ruthven, so Ruthven Castle became Huntingtower, and all that is left of the village of Ruthven is a stone marking the spot in a housing estate to the west of Perth.

Huntingtower was the birthplace of Lord George Murray (1694–1760), one of the ablest Jacobite generals in the 1745 Rising, and is the focus of John Buchan's adventure novel *Huntingtower* (1922; Buchan himself was born in nearby Perth). The castle also gave its name to a traditional ballad:

Blair Atholl's mine, Jeanie,
Little Dunkeld's mine, lassie,
St Johnston's bower, and Huntingtower,
And all that's mine is thine, lassie.

'Huntingtower'

Huntly 'huntsman's wood', OE *hunta* 'huntsman' + -LEY.
A town in STRATHBOGIE in Aberdeenshire (formerly in Grampian region), 54 km (32 miles) northwest of Aberdeen. The name originated in Berwickshire, and was brought north by the powerful Gordon family (who became earls, then marquesses of Huntly). The Gordons lived in **Huntly Castle** (now ruined) from 1376 to 1752, and were responsible for the laying out of the town in the 18th century (before this the BURGH round the castle was called the Raws of Strathbogie).

Huntly was the birthplace of George Macdonald (1824–1905), the writer of sentimental 'kailyard' novels (*Alec Forbes of Howglen* is set in Huntly) and of books for children such as *At the Back of the North Wind*.

There is a town called Huntly in New Zealand (North Island).

'Huntly Lodge'. The title of an air for the fiddle by William Marshall and of a strathspey by Nathaniel Gow.

Huntsman's Leap. A fissure in the cliffs a little to the west of ST GOVAN'S HEAD, Pembrokeshire (formerly in Dyfed). The eponymous huntsman who is said to have made the leap died of fright shortly afterwards.

Hurds Deep. *See under* the ENGLISH CHANNEL.

Hurlers, the. A group of three stone circles dating from around 1500 BC, situated just outside MINIONS, on the southeastern edge of Bodmin Moor (*see under* BODMIN), in Cornwall. Their original purpose is unclear, but they owe their name to the local legend that the uprights represent men turned to stone for playing the game of hurling on the Sabbath.

Hurn '(place at the) angle or corner of land', OE *hyrne*.
A village in Dorset (before 1974 in Hampshire), about 5 km (3 miles) northeast of Bournemouth. Its airport, now known as Bournemouth (Hurn), was a military airfield during the Second World War and now handles a wide range of commercial operations.

Hurst Castle *Hurst* OE *hyrst*, here a reference to sandbank rather than, as is more usually the case, a wooded hill.
A coastal fortification in Hampshire, about 6 km (4 miles) south of LYMINGTON, at the mouth of the western arm of the SOLENT. Situated at the end of a 1.5-km (1-mile) long shingle spit, it was originally built by Henry VIII between 1541 and 1544 in response to the threat of invasion posed by the European Catholic powers. Charles I was imprisoned here for three weeks in December 1648, during the Civil Wars. Hurst Castle was further fortified during the Napoleonic period.

Hurst Point lighthouse indicates the line of approach for vessels passing through the Needles Channel.

Hurst Green 'green at the wooded hill', OE *hyrst* 'wooded hill'; *Green* ModE.
A village in the RIBBLE Valley, Lancashire, about 5 km (3 miles) southwest of Clitheroe. Nearby is the former mansion of **Stonyhurst** where Oliver Cromwell stayed in 1648 on his way to the Battle of Preston (*see under* PRESTON). The building is now Stonyhurst College, a Roman Catholic boarding and day school. Unlike the better-known Ampleforth, Stonyhurst is not attached to a religious order. The five academic years at Stonyhurst are called Lower Grammar, Grammar, Syntax, Poetry and Rhetoric. Sir Arthur Conan Doyle (1859–1930) was a pupil of the school and the poet Gerard Manley Hopkins (1844–89) taught classics there between 1882 and 1884 after his ordination. Another classics teacher was J.R.R. Tolkien's son Michael, who taught there in the late 1960s and 1970s. The Ribble Valley around

Stonyhurst is said to have provided inspiration for Tolkien's *The Lord of the Rings* (1954–5).

Hurstpierpoint Originally *Herst* 'wooded hill', OE *hyrst*; *-pierpoint*, first recorded in the 13th century, denotes manorial ownership in the early Middle Ages by the de Pierpoint family.

A small commuter town in West Sussex, about 10 km (6 miles) north of Brighton. **Hurstpierpoint College**, an independent school, was founded in 1849.

Hurstpierpoint was the birthplace of the actor Paul Scofield (b.1922).

Husbands Bosworth *Husbands* probably 'of the farmers or husbandmen', from late OE *husbonda*; *Bosworth* probably 'Bar's enclosure', OE *Bares* possessive form of male personal name *Bar* + *worth* (*see* -WORTH, WORTHY, -WARDINE).

A village in Leicestershire, about 11 km (7 miles) south-west of Market Harborough.

Huyton 'farm with a landing place', OE *hyth* 'landing place' + -TON.

A suburb of LIVERPOOL, Merseyside, 10 km (6 miles) east of the city centre. It is sometimes referred to as **Huyton-with-Roby**.

Harold Wilson (Labour prime minister 1964–70 and 1974–76) was MP for Huyton from 1950 until 1976. The novelist Barbara Pym (1913–80) was educated at Huyton College, and Huyton was the birthplace of the actor Rex Harrison (1908–90).

Hwlffordd. The Welsh name for HAVERFORDWEST.

Hy-Brasil Irish *Í Brasáil* 'the island of Breasal', *Breasal* being the king of the place.

A mythical land lying to the west of Ireland, beyond the ARAN ISLANDS, depicted variously as the isle of the blest, the land of eternal youth, or the last refuge of the legendary Tuatha Dé Danann. It is said that if any mortal sees it when it arises from the waters of the Atlantic every seven years, they will surely die. In the Middle Ages it was marked on maps, and it is said that when European navigators reached the most easterly part of South America they called it Brazil, believing they had found the lost land.

> Men thought it a region of sunshine and rest
> And they called it Hy-Brasail, the isle of the blest.
>
> Gerald Griffin: 'Hy-Brasail – The Isle of the Blest' (*c*.1830)

Hyde OE *hid* 'hide', an ancient term denoting a portion of land around 49 ha (120 acres). One hide was regarded as the minimum necessary for a peasant to support his family: one hide could be ploughed in a single season by one team of oxen.

A small industrial satellite town in Greater Manchester, some 11 km (6.5 miles) east of the city centre. It was here in 1992 that Dr Harold Shipman, Britain's (and possibly the world's) most prolific mass murderer, set up his one-man medical practice. Shipman was convicted on 31 January 2000 of murdering 15 elderly female patients in his care (including a former mayoress of Hyde) by injecting them with a lethal dose of the painkiller diamorphine. The first report of the public inquiry into the killings (2002) found that Shipman had killed a staggering total of 215 of his patients, with suspicion over a further 45 deaths.

Hyde Park From *Hyde*, a former sub-manor in the area, itself from *hide*, an ancient term denoting a portion of land around 49 ha (120 acres), OE *hid*.

A park in Central London, situated in the City of Westminster (W1, W2, SW7) and bounded to the north by the Bayswater Road, to the east by PARK LANE, to the south by KNIGHTSBRIDGE and to the west by Kensington Gardens (*see under* KENSINGTON). MARBLE ARCH is at its northeastern corner. It is the largest of London's Royal Parks, covering an area of over 138 ha (340 acres).

Henry VIII kept it as a deer park, but Charles II opened it to the public. It was at first rather dirty and disreputable, but by the 18th century had become much as it is now, the 'lungs of London' and a favourite place of relaxation for city workers. Before the First World War it was the place where fashionable society performed its courtly promenade, and in those days Hyde Park was simply 'the Park'. Its role as a venue for large public events reached its apogee in 1851 when the Great Exhibition was held here, in the CRYSTAL PALACE, but it has continued to host open-air events for large audiences, such as 'Proms in the Park' and the 'Three Tenors' show. It has also become associated with free speech and mass meetings, the former because of SPEAKERS' CORNER at its northeastern corner, the latter through its size and central location, which make it a useful assembly point for marches and demonstrations:

> As for the meetings inside the Park, they are one of the minor wonders of the world. At different times I have listened there to Indian Nationalists, Temperance reformers, Communists, Trotskyists, the S.P.G.B. [Socialist Party of Great Britain], the Catholic Evidence Society, Freethinkers, vegetarians, Mormons, the Salvation Army, the Church Army, and a large variety of plain lunatics, all taking their turn at the rostrum in an orderly way and receiving a fairly good-humoured hearing from the crowd … On the platform, or in certain recognized open-air spaces like Hyde Park, you can say almost anything.
>
> George Orwell: 'Freedom of the Park', *Tribune* (1945)

Hyde Park's two most familiar topographical features are the lake called the SERPENTINE and ROTTEN ROW, a road running along its southern edge. The Princess Diana Memorial Fountain, an annular water feature designed by Kathryn Gustafson, 210 m (192 yards) in circumference, was inaugurated in Hyde Park in 2004.

The French artist Claude Monet painted the park in

1871 (the result can be seen in Philadelphia Museum of Art).

The story goes that *nosy parker* as a term for a prying person originated as the nickname of a man who used to spy on courting couples in Hyde Park in the early years of the 20th century.

In former times *Hyde Park* was used as London rhyming slang for *nark*, that is, 'an informer'.

There are towns called Hyde Park in the USA (Massachusetts, New York and Vermont). The one in New York State, by the Hudson River, was the birthplace and home of President Franklin D. Roosevelt (1882–1945). It was not named after the London park.

Hyde Park Barracks. *See* Knightsbridge Barracks *under* KNIGHTSBRIDGE. Two soldiers and seven horses from the barracks were killed when the IRA exploded a nail bomb in Hyde Park on 20 July 1982 (the **Hyde Park bomb**).

Hyde Park Corner. The road junction at the southeastern corner of Hyde Park, at the point where Park Lane meets Piccadilly and Knightsbridge, not to mention Grosvenor Place. In former times there was a toll gate there, for those entering Westminster from the west (the first house you came to on entering was Apsley House, the Duke of Wellington's residence, which hence became known familiarly as 'Number 1, London'). There is now a large and extremely busy roundabout (a calculation in the late 20th century clocked over a hundred vehicles every three minutes), with Constitution Arch on a grassy plot in its centre. Hyde Park Corner Underground station, on the Piccadilly line, opened in 1906.

Hyde Park orator. A dismissive term for a loquacious tub-thumper of the sort who likes to give the world the benefit of his or her opinions at SPEAKERS' CORNER, Hyde Park.

Hyde Park railings. Late 19th-century slang for a breast of mutton, alluding to the rib bones' resemblance to the park's fencing.

Hythe 'landing-place or harbour', OE *hyth*.

A seaside town on the southeast coast of Kent, about 12 km (8 miles) southwest of Folkestone. It was one of the original CINQUE PORTS, but its superannuated port is now cut off from the town by the ROYAL MILITARY CANAL, which terminates there. Hythe's other terminal role is as the northeastern end of the Romney, Hythe and Dymchurch Light Railway. Its MP (also of FOLKESTONE) has been, since 1983, Michael Howard, leader of the Conservative Party from 2003.

About 1 km (0.5 miles) to the north is Saltwood Castle, latterly the home of Lord Clark (Sir Kenneth Clark) and of his diarist son Alan Clark MP, where the knights who murdered Thomas Becket in Canterbury Cathedral (*see under* CANTERBURY[1]) in 1170 met up on the night before their dark deed.

I

Iar Connacht Irish 'west CONNACHT'.

An area of County Galway, between the town of GALWAY to the east and CONNEMARA to the west. It is a wild and unpopulated place, scattered with little lakes, and up to the 18th century was one of the last bastions of the old Gaelic social order. Sometimes the name is applied to a larger area, also including Connemara and JOYCE'S COUNTRY.

Ible 'Ibba's hollow(s)', OE male personal name *Ibba* + *hol* 'hollow'.

A village (pronounced 'ibbəl') in Derbyshire, in the PEAK DISTRICT, about 6 km (4 miles) southwest of Matlock.

Í Brasáil. The Irish name for the mythical Atlantic land of HY-BRASIL.

Ibrox Park 'badger ford', *Ibrox* Gaelic *áth* 'ford' + *broc* 'badger'.

The site in GLASGOW of the stadium of Glasgow Rangers FC. As one of the nicknames of Rangers (and their supporters) is the Teddy Bears (or just Bears; rhyming slang for the Gers, i.e. the second element of Ran*gers*), the area round Ibrox is known as Teddy Bear Country. On 22 January 1971, 66 football supporters died in what became known as the **Ibrox Tragedy**, when the steel barriers on Stairway 13 gave way. As a result, the stadium was rebuilt as an all-seater venue, and has since garnered a '5-star' rating from UEFA, a status it shares in Scotland with HAMPDEN PARK. Its capacity is just over 51,000.

McDiarmid Park, home ground of St Johnstone in PERTH since 1989, is sometimes nicknamed **Mini-Ibrox** for being modelled on Ibrox Park.

Ibstock 'Ibba's outlying farmstead or hamlet', OE male personal name *Ibba* + *stoc* (*see* -STOCK, STOCK-, STOKE).

A small town in Leicestershire, about 8 km (5 miles) north of Market Bosworth. William Laud (1573–1645), later Archbishop of Canterbury and chief adviser to Charles I, was once rector here.

Ickenham Earlier *Tickenham* 'Ticca's homestead or village',

OE *Ticcan* possessive form of male personal name *Ticca* + HAM. The initial *t* was lost in the 13th century owing to a mistaken analysis of such phrases as *at Tickenham*.

A district of outer West London, in the borough of HILLINGDON (before 1965 in Middlesex), between Northolt to the east and Ruislip to the north. It was a rural village until after the First World War, when suburbia began to creep up on it. Ickenham 'Underground' station, on the Metropolitan and Piccadilly lines, opened in 1905.

Icknield Street Originally (in the 12th century) called *Icknield Way*; later changed to *Icknield Street*, in conformity with the names of other Roman roads (*see* STREET).

A Roman road that runs from BOURTON-ON-THE-WATER in Gloucestershire to Templeborough near ROTHERHAM. An alternative form of its name is RYKNILD STREET.

Icknield Way Origin unknown. A similarity to *Iceni*, the name of an ancient British people who lived along part of its course, has been noted, but no verified link with them has been established.

A prehistoric trackway leading from the WASH in Norfolk to the source of the River KENNET[1] in Wiltshire, passing through CAMBRIDGE[1], LETCHWORTH, TRING and along the top of the Berkshire Downs (*see under* BERKSHIRE) and the North Wessex Downs (*see under* WESSEX). It crosses the Thames near GORING (the section to the west of this is generally known as the RIDGEWAY). It follows high ground. Part of it in East Anglia became a Roman road. In the 18th and 19th centuries it was used as a drovers' road.

Ickworth 'Icca's enclosure', OE male personal name *Icca* + *worth* (*see* -WORTH, WORTHY, -WARDINE).

A house and estate in Suffolk, 5 km (3 miles) southwest of Bury St Edmunds. The Italianate **Ickworth House**, with its central rotunda and curving wings, was built in 1795 by Frederick Augustus Hervey, 4th Earl of Bristol – a Church of Ireland bishop who combined eccentricity with aesthetic acquisitiveness – to house the treasures that he had collected from all over Europe. Paintings by Titian,

Gainsborough and Velázquez and a magnificent Georgian silver collection are on display in the house, which is now owned by the National Trust. The house is set in 'Capability' Brown parkland with woodland walks, deer enclosure, vineyard, Georgian summer house, church, canal and lake. *See also* DOWNHILL.

Icolmkill. *See* IONA.

Ide Perhaps an old river name of pre-English origin.
A village in Devon, on the southwestern outskirts of Exeter.

Idle Probably from OE *idel* 'slow' or even 'useless', but may be pre-English and, if so, of unknown meaning.
A river in Nottinghamshire, which flows 48 km (30 miles) northwards from the confluence of the rivers MAUN and Meden through RETFORD to join the TRENT[1] northwest of Gainsborough.

Idumania. The Roman name for the River BLACKWATER[1] in Essex.

Idwal. *See* CWM IDWAL.

Iffley Probably 'glade frequented by plovers', OE *gifete* 'plover or similar bird' + -LEY.
A village in Oxfordshire, now effectively a suburb of southeast OXFORD but retaining much of its village character. St Mary's Church, a well-preserved Norman structure, dates from the 1170s. During the 13th century a cell beside the church was home for nine years to a mysterious anchoress (female religious recluse) by the name of Annora.

On the **Iffley Road**, the beginning of the old road from Oxford to London via Henley, is the University Sports Centre and the running track on which Roger Bannister became the first person to run a mile in under 4 minutes (3 minutes, 59.4 seconds) on 6 May 1954.

Ightham 'Ehta's homestead or village', OE male personal name *Ehta* + HAM.
A village in Kent, about 6 km (4 miles) southeast of Sevenoaks. Nearby is **Ightham Mote**, a 14th-century moated manor house.

Ilchester 'Roman town on the River Gifl or Ivel' (former name of the River Yeo), OCelt river name *Gifl* 'forked river' + OE *ceaster* (*see* CHESTER).
A small town in Somerset, on the River YEO[1], about 8 km (5 miles) northwest of Yeovil. During the Roman occupation (when it was known as **Lindinis**) it was an important military station on the FOSSE WAY. There was a royal mint here between the 10th and 12th centuries. From the 14th to the 19th century, it was Somerset's administrative centre.

Ilchester is traditionally believed to be the town called 'Ischalis' mentioned by the 1st-century Egyptian geographer Ptolemy. Ilchester is also the birthplace of the scholar Roger Bacon (?1214–94).

Ilchester cheese. A cheese made by mixing beer and garlic into Cheddar cheese. It was invented in the early 1960s by a local hotelier, Ken Seaton. It was originally sold in pots.

Ilford 'ford over the River Hyle' (former name of the River Roding below Ongar), OCelt river name *Hyle* 'trickling stream' + OE FORD.
A district of outer East London, in the borough of REDBRIDGE (before 1965 in Essex), to the east of Wanstead and to the north of Barking. It is the highest commercially navigable point on the River RODING, a position which brought Ilford much of its business until after the First World War, but by then its housing estates had begun to mushroom (it was one of the earliest dormitory suburbs to the east of London), and it is now mainly residential.

Ilford Films, founded in Ilford in 1879, were in the 1950s and 1960s the main British commercial rival to Kodak as makers and suppliers of photographic film. The first (Dr) Barnardo's homes for children were opened in Ilford in 1870, and the organization's headquarters remain nearby at BARKINGSIDE.

The jazz trumpeter Kenny Ball (b.1930) and the actress Dame Maggie Smith (b.1934) were born in Ilford. John Logie Baird (1888–1946) lived here in the 1920s.

Ilfracombe 'valley associated with Ælfred', OE male personal name *Ælfred* + -ING + *cumb* (*see* -COMBE, COOMBE).
A coastal town and seaside resort in north Devon, about 16 km (10 miles) north of Barnstaple. Between the 14th and 16th centuries it was an important trading port, and it was twice besieged during the Civil Wars. Thereafter Ilfracombe rather sank back into obscurity as a fishing village, but the arrival of the railway in 1874 opened the town up to holidaymakers, and sent Victorian villas and hotels climbing in terraces up the steep surrounding hills. It is the main departure point for LUNDY Island.

In 1792 a large treasure ship, captured from the Franco-Spanish fleet, was sunk just off the coast here, and gold and silver coins from it still turn up on local beaches.

Anna Parnell (1853–1911), feminist, land agitator and estranged sister of the Irish parliamentary leader Charles Stewart Parnell, was drowned off the Tunnels Beaches at Ilfracombe.

Ilkeston 'Ealac's hill', OE *Ealaces* possessive form of male personal name *Ealac* + *dun* (*see* DOWN, -DON).
A market town in eastern Derbyshire, on the western slopes of the EREWASH[1] valley, about 13 km (8 miles) northeast of Derby. It grew to its present size mainly in the 19th century, on the back of its iron industry. The other major local product is lace.

Ilkley 'Illica's clearing', OE male personal name *Illica* + -LEY.
A pleasant town in Wharfedale (*see under* WHARFE), West Yorkshire, 23 km (14 miles) northwest of Leeds. The Brigantes had a settlement at Ilkley during the Iron Age,

and the Romans built a fort here called **Verbeia** (their name for the River Wharfe; it was once thought that the name of the Roman fort was **Olicana**, but this was the result of a scribal error). In the 18th and 19th centuries Ilkley developed as a spa town. It became known as the **Heather Spa**, referring to the vegetation on the surrounding moors, on the edge of which stand the White Wells spa buildings, the oldest of which dates back to 1690.

The world-famous **Ilkley Moor** (rising to 402 m / 1319 ft), with its great gritstone rocks known as the Cow and Calf, is on the south side of the town. It is said that the song **'On Ilkla Moor baht 'at'** (dialect *baht 'at* 'without a hat') – which has become the unofficial 'national anthem' of Yorkshire – was improvised by a church choir on an outing from Halifax while picnicking by the rocks.

Wheear 'as tha binn since ah saw thee?
  On Ilkla Moor baht 'at
Wheear 'as tha bin since ah saw thee?
Wheear 'as tha bin since ah saw thee?
  On Ilkla Moor baht 'at,
  On Ilkla Moor baht 'at,
  On Ilkla Moor baht 'at.

The relevant lines in the subsequent verses are:

Tha's bin a coortin' Mary Jane ...
Tha's bahn t' catch thi death o' cowd ...
Then we shall ha' to bury thee ...
Then t' worms 'll cum an' eat thee up ...
Then t' ducks 'll come an' eat up t' worms ...
Then we shall come an' eat them ducks ...
Then we shall all 'av etten thee ...
... On Ilkla Moor baht 'at.

The television gardener Alan Titchmarsh (b.1949) was born in Ilkley.

Ill Bell 'round hill', *Ill* OE *hyll* 'hill'; *Bell* tautological OScand *bjalli* 'round hill'.
A mountain (755 m / 2477 ft) in the Lake District, Cumbria, 3 km (2 miles) south of HIGH STREET.

Illogan Named in honour of *St Illogan*, to whom the local church is dedicated.
A village (pronounced 'ilowgən') in Cornwall, about 3 km (2 miles) northwest of Redruth.

Ilmer Probably 'pool where leeches are found', OE *il* 'leech' + *mere* 'pool'.
A village in Buckinghamshire, about 11 km (7 miles) southwest of Aylesbury.

Ilmington 'hill with elm trees', OE *ylme* 'elm wood' + *dun* (*see* DOWN, -DON).
A brick- and stone-built village in southern Warwickshire, in the northernmost part of the COTSWOLDS, about 8 km (5 miles) northeast of Chipping Campden. **Ilmington Downs** reach a height of 260 m (854 ft) above the village.

The area of Warwickshire known as the FELDON lies to the north and east.

George V made the first royal Christmas broadcast to the nation from **Ilmington Manor**, a gabled Elizabethan house here, in 1934.

Ilminster 'large church on the River Isle', river name *Isle* + OE *mynster* 'large church'. The name is found in a late copy of an 8th-century charter, but the present church is apparently 15th-century, presumably a reconstruction of an original (Saxon) church on the same site.
A market town in Somerset, on the River ISLE, at the foot of the BLACKDOWN HILLS, about 16 km (10 miles) southeast of Taunton. The church (St Mary's) from which it gets its name is in its present-day form a 15th-century building. It was endowed as a collegiate foundation by Sir William Wadham. There is a brass inside to his 16th-century descendants Nicholas and Dorothy Wadham, who founded Wadham College, Oxford (*see under* OXFORD).

Imber 'Imma's pool', OE male personal name *Imma* + *mere* 'pool'.
A derelict village in Wiltshire, on Salisbury Plain (*see under* SALISBURY), about 10 km (6 miles) northeast of Warminster. Its inhabitants were turfed out at 47 days' notice in 1943 so that it could be used as a training ground for the US military, and they have never been allowed back in. The blacksmith, Albie Nash, died a few weeks later, reportedly of a broken heart on hearing that his smithy had been demolished.

Imleach. The Irish name for EMLY.

Immingham 'Imma's people's homestead', OE male personal name *Imma* + *-inga-* (*see* -ING) + HAM.
A town and port in North East Lincolnshire (before 1996 in Humberside, before 1974 in Lincolnshire), on the southwestern bank of the HUMBER estuary, about 8 km (5 miles) northwest of its sister port GRIMSBY. The town, which until the early 20th century was just a tiny hamlet, is about 1.5 km (1 mile) inland. It expanded hugely after the Great Central Railway Company opened a dock on the coast in 1912, to relieve the congestion in the docks at Grimsby. More recently, deep-sea oil and coal terminals have been established here.

Inaccessible Pinnacle, the. A peak (978 m / 3208 ft) in the Black CUILLIN of Skye, in the form of an 18-m (60-ft) rock pinnacle on the ridge of Sgurr Dearg. It has the reputation as being the trickiest of the MUNROS to attain, the easiest route – that of the first ascent on 18 August 1880 by the brothers C. and L. Pilkington – being a moderate rock climb. The peak is informally known as the **In Pin**. The noted mountaineer Harold Raeburn recalled an attempted winter ascent around the turn of the last century:

The writer has a vivid recollection of being spread-eagled, and clinging with every available portion of his anatomy to the ice-covered 'easy' ridge of the 'Inaccessible', while the level hail drove fiercely past, expecting every moment to see his legs raised in the air, his hobnailers crack together once or twice like the tails of a pennon, and then, converted into icicles like the crew of the *Hesperus*, along with his three companions, to be hurled away into Coruisk on the wings of the Arctic blast.

> Quoted in Steeple, Barlow, MacRobert and Bell (eds.), *Island of Skye* (1923)

Ince 'island', OCelt INIS.

A village in Cheshire, now effectively an eastern suburb of ELLESMERE PORT, just to the south of the Manchester Ship Canal.

Ince-in-Makerfield OCelt INIS 'island' + *macer* 'wall, ruin' + OE *feld* (*see* FIELD).

A town on the south side of Wigan, Greater Manchester. Its growth in the 19th century was largely due to the building of the Leeds–Liverpool Canal.

Inchcape Rock, the. An alternative name for the BELL ROCK in the North Sea; which features in Robert Southey's ballad of the same name.

Inchcleraun Irish *Inis Clothrann*, 'island of Clothra', *Clothra* being a sister of Queen Maeve.

One of the islands in LOUGH REE, central Ireland. It has the remains of seven churches, and was home to St Diarmaid (*fl.*6th century). In an earlier epoch the island witnessed the end of the legendary Queen Maeve (Medb) of CONNACHT, killed in an unchivalrous fashion as she bathed, the cause of death being a slingshot flung from the mainland by Forbaí (an Ulster chieftain and son of her former husband Conchobhar) in revenge for the death of Cuchulain. The queen is said to be buried under the great cairn on the summit of KNOCKNAREA, near Sligo.

Inchcleraun is also called **Quaker Island**, after a Quaker who settled here in the 19th century, building his house with the stones of an old church – which resulted in his being cursed and his departure soon after.

Inchcolm 'St Columba's island', Gaelic INIS + personal name *Colum* 'Columba'.

A tiny island in the Firth of FORTH, 3 km (2 miles) off the Fife coast at Aberdour. St Columba apparently visited the island *c.*567; before this it was known as *Emona*. In the 12th century a hermit who lived on Inchcolm helped Alexander I, who was shipwrecked on the island while crossing the Forth, and in gratitude the king founded a priory (later an abbey) here in 1123, whose well-preserved ruins remain. It was already regarded as a holy place, and was favoured as a burial ground by many notable people. The island is referred to near the beginning of *Macbeth*, when Ross reports to Duncan the victory of Macbeth and Banquo over the Norwegian king, Sweno, who then seeks terms:

> Sweno, the Norways' king, craves composition;
> Nor would we deign him burial of his men
> Till he disbursed, at Saint Colme's Inch,
> Ten thousand dollars to our general use.

> William Shakespeare: *Macbeth* (1606), I.ii

The place can still have a powerful effect on visitors:

> As sun lowers, symbol
> upon symbol unfolds:
> rose petals, stone,
> old as the hills, old
> as resilience, fragility.

> Christine De Luca: 'Inchcolm Abbey',
> in *Wast wi da Valkyries* (1997)

Inchkeith 'Keith's island', Gaelic INIS + personal name *Keith*, from Robert de Keith, who was awarded the island by Malcolm II in 1010. Alternatively, the second element may be from OCelt CED 'wood'.

A small island in the Firth of FORTH, 7 km (4 miles) southeast of Burntisland in Fife. The island was taken by the English in 1547 and retaken by a Franco-Scots force two years later, on 29 June, the French *Fête Dieu*, prompting Mary of Guise, mother of the infant Mary Queen of Scots, to dub it *L'île de Dieu*. In 1564 the queen herself visited, and carved 'M.R.' and the date on a rock (now built into a wall by the lighthouse).

The island was used for quarantine purposes from the 15th century to the end of the 18th century, and its isolation also prompted James IV to conduct an experiment to prove his theory that man's innate language is Hebrew. He confined a foundling with a dumb nurse in isolation on the island, but unfortunately for his theory, when the child was brought back to the mainland some years later, it could do no more than babble nonsensically – although it is said that James believed the child was speaking Hebrew. In other versions this experiment took place on the tiny island of Inchmickery, also in the Firth of Forth, 3 km (2 miles) southwest of Inchcolm.

Inch Kenneth 'Kenneth's isle', *Inch* Gaelic INIS; *Kenneth* personal name *Cainnech* or *Caioneach*.

A small island at the entrance to LOCH NA KEAL on the west side of Mull, in Argyll and Bute (formerly in Strathclyde). The island was named after St Kenneth (*c.*520–*c.*600; called St Canice in Ireland), a friend of St Columba who with monks from Iona set up a community here in the 6th century. Johnson and Boswell visited the impoverished laird, Sir Allan Maclean, in 1773, and Johnson remarked on his host's 'high birth, polished manners, and elegant conversation', while noting that the floor of his bedroom 'was wet, in consequence of the windows being broken, which let in the rain'. Both visitors were moved to piety by the remains of the ancient chapel and Celtic cross, Johnson penning some devout Latin verses ('Insula Sancti Kennethi'), while, somewhat uncharacteristically, Boswell slipped out in the dark to pray at the old cross.

Inchmahome. *See under* LAKE OF MENTEITH.

Inchmickery. *See under* INCHKEITH.

Inchtuthil 'water-meadow lying crosswise', Gaelic INIS 'water-meadow, island' + *tuathal* 'lying crosswise, across something'.

The site near Dunkeld, Perth and Kinross, of a legionary fortress established by Agricola after his victory over the Caledonians at MONS GRAUPIUS.

Indian Queens From the name of an early 19th-century inn, earlier called The Queen's Head. It is possible that the fame of Pocahontas, the daughter of a Native American chief who saved the English settler John Smith from her father's warriors in the early 17th century, may have contributed to the adoption of 'Indian Queen' names.

A village in Cornwall, about 11 km (7 miles) southeast of Newquay.

Ingatestone 'Ing at the stone' (referring to a Roman milestone), *Ing* a local manor name '(settlement of the) people of the district', OE *ge* 'district' + *-ingas* (*see* -ING) + ME *atte* 'at the' + *ston* (*see* STONE).

A town in Essex, about 10 km (6 miles) southwest of Chelmsford. **Ingatestone Hall**, an Elizabethan manor house, was a refuge for Roman Catholic priests during the Protestant Reformation of the 16th century.

Ingestre Perhaps 'narrow place', OCelt *engyst*, possibly also with the river name TRENT[1].

A village (pronounced 'ing-gestray') in Staffordshire, in the TRENT[1] Valley, about 5 km (3 miles) northeast of Stafford. The late 17th-century church is said to be by Sir Christopher Wren (if it is, it is his only one outside London).

Ingleborough 'fort on a peaked hill', OE *ingel* 'peaked hill' + *burh* 'fortification' (*see* BURY).

A mountain (724 m / 2375 ft) in North Yorkshire, in the YORKSHIRE DALES, some 14 km (8.5 miles) northwest of Settle. It is one of the THREE PEAKS. There is a massive Iron Age hillfort on the flat summit plateau, built by the Brigantes:

❖ -ing ❖

This is amongst the most common English name elements, but also one of the most difficult to summarize as it appears in numerous forms. We can distinguish three basic types of *-ing* elements with various meanings.

The first type is where *-ing* means something like 'place characterized by' a given feature: so THROCKING (Hertfordshire) probably means 'place where beams of wood are cut or made', and DEEPING ST JAMES (Lincolnshire) means 'the church of St James in a place that is deep or in a hollow'.

The second type of *-ing* is where the element refers to an association between a place or feature and a person. There are many of these, and we often render them as 'X's farm', 'X's estate' or similar, because the *-ing-* has the function of representing possession. BADMINTON (Gloucestershire), BARLAVINGTON (Sussex) and BOVINGTON (Dorset) were farms associated with men called Baduhelm, Beornlaf and Bova respectively. (Etymologies in this book giving the form *-ing* imply this second type as most likely.)

The third type is a plural form *-inga-* (possessive) or *-ingas* (nominative) or occasionally *-ingum* (dative). Once again there are many of these, and among them are some of the most important place names. The *-ing* element here represents a group name and means 'descendants or dependants of' the named person. BIRMINGHAM and NOTTINGHAM[1] are the homesteads of Beorma's and Snot's families respectively, and the names originally contained *-inga-*. A similarly large number of names originally contained *-ingas*: DORKING (Surrey), READING (Berkshire), Snoring (Norfolk, *see* GREAT SNORING and LITTLE SNORING) and EALING (Greater London) are the settlements of, or districts occupied by, the families or followers of Deorc, Reada, Snearr and Gilla respectively. HASTINGS (East Sussex) is one of the relatively few places that retains the plural ending in the modern name. A variation on this type is the group name that specifies the sort of place that people live in, rather than the person to whom they trace their origin. EPPING (Essex) means 'settlement or district of the people who live on the ridge', the *yppingas*, where *yppe* means 'high land, a ridge'; BRADING (Isle of Wight) is 'settlement of the people who live on a hillside, where *brerd* means 'a hillside'.

It is not always clear which of the types of *-ing* element is operating in a name: STEYNING (Sussex) is an example. In the early spellings it is plural in the form *staningas*, so it could be 'places characterized by stones' with *-ing* (type one); or 'district of the people who live in a stony place', or indeed 'settlement of the family or followers of a man called *Stan*', with *-ing* (type three). And then there are numerous ways of obscuring the *-ing* element or making an *-ing* form that was not present originally. CLACTON-ON-SEA (Essex) simply misses out the *-ing* of the original spelling, *Claccingtune*. ABINGDON (Oxfordshire), originally 'Æbbe's hill', makes an *-ing* form out of the Old English possessive *-an*, so *Æbbandun* is transformed into Abingdon. GARSINGTON (Oxfordshire) was originally *Gærsentun* 'grassy farm', but has become an *-ing* name in the modern spelling.

The last Brigantes hung to that flat, bare waste –
the losers, the betrayed. Boulders were walls, huts to hold
   out
gales crueller than Roman sword ...

   Colin Speakman: 'Three Peaks: I, Ingleborough', from *That
   Bleak Frontier* (1978)

Stones from the fort were pillaged in 1830 for a tower built
on the top by the new landowner, but his hubris did not
last long as on its opening day the tower was demolished by
drunken visitors. The show cave of **Ingleborough Cavern**
replete with spectacular stalacites and stalagmites and
the awesome pothole of GAPING GHYLL are on the south
side of the mountain. Ingleborough is part of the Three
Peaks Walk, which also takes in WHERNSIDE and
PEN-Y-GHENT.

Inglewood Forest 'forest of the Angles', *Inglewood* OE *Engle*
'the Angles' + *wudu* 'wood'; the area was fought over by the
Angles of Northumbria and the British of Strathclyde for most
of the Anglo-Saxon period.
A traditional (largely unwooded) area between Carlisle and
Penrith, Cumbria (formerly in Cumberland), bisected by
the M6. An alternative spelling is **Englewood Forest**. It was
a hunting forest of the Scottish kings until 1237, when
Alexander II surrendered it to Henry III. An ancient oak on
Wragmire Moss was known, until it collapsed of old age in
1823, as 'the last tree of Inglewood Forest'.
   There is a town (effectively a suburb of Los Angeles)
called Inglewood in the USA (California), and another in
New Zealand (North Island).

Ingoldsby 'Ingjaldr's farmstead or village', OScand *Ingjalds*
possessive form of male personal name *Ingjaldr* + -BY.
A village in Lincolnshire, about 11 km (7 miles) southeast
of Grantham.
Ingoldsby Legends, The. A collection of verse tales, entitled
in full *The Ingoldsby Legends, or Mirth and Marvels*, by
'Thomas Ingoldsby esquire', which originally appeared
from 1837 in *Bentley's Miscellany* and *The New Monthly
Magazine* and was published as a book in 1840. Most of
them are quirky retellings of medieval stories, the best-
known being the tale of 'The Jackdaw of Rheims', who
stole the archbishop's ring. They were written by the Rev.
R.H. Barham (1788–1845), who used 'Thomas Ingoldsby'
as his pseudonym.

Ingon Origin uncertain: there may be some connection with OE
ing 'hill'.
A village in Warwickshire, about 3 km (2 miles) north of
Stratford-upon-Avon.

Ingrow 'corner of land in the meadow', OScand *eng* 'meadow'
+ *vra* 'corner of land'.
A district in the south of KEIGHLEY, West Yorkshire.

Ingst Perhaps 'narrow place', OCelt *engyst*.

A village in South Gloucestershire (before 1996 in Avon,
before 1974 in Gloucestershire), about 2.5 km (1.5 miles)
from the eastern end of the Severn Road Bridge.

Inis Arcáin. The Irish name for SHERKIN ISLAND.

Inis Badhbha. The Irish name for BOA ISLAND.

Inis Bó Finne. The Irish name for INISHBOFIN.

Inis Cathaigh. The Irish name for SCATTERY ISLAND.

Inis Ceithleann. The Irish name for ENNISKILLEN.

Inis Clothrann. The Irish name for INCHCLERAUN.

Inis Córthaiddh. The Irish name for ENNISCORTHY.

Inis Díomáin. The Irish name for ENNISTIMON.

Inis Eoghain. The Irish name for INISHOWEN.

Inis Faithlenn. The Irish name for INISHFALLEN.

Inis Fraoigh. The Irish name for INNISFREE.

Inishark. *See under* INISHBOFIN.

Inishbofin Irish *Inis Bó Finne* 'island of the white cow'(*see*
INIS).
A small inhabited island in County Galway, some 5 km
(3 miles) off the northwest coast of CONNEMARA. Off the
west coast of Inishbofin is the smaller uninhabited island of
Inishark.
   After his defeat at the hands of the Roman faction at
the Synod of Whitby (664), St Colman of Lindisfarne
retreated to Inishbofin with some 30 English monks, but
soon fell out with the Irish brethren, and set up an alternative monastery at MAYO. More recently, the island
became the home of the poet Richard Murphy (b.1927)
and features in a number of his poems; before he moved
to the island, Murphy used to ferry tourists here on his
Galway hooker, and among his passengers were Ted Hughes
and Sylvia Plath. A number of other poets have visited and
been inspired, including Cecil Day Lewis, Louis MacNeice,
Joseph Brodsky, Seamus Heaney and Theodore Roethke. It

❖ **inis** ❖

Originally a Britonnic word, this element is found in some
English names as well as in Celtic ones: INCE-IN-MAKERFIELD
(Greater Manchester) is the best-known of the English ones.
An observation that naturally arises from the situation of INCE
(Cheshire) is that though *inis* usually refers to an island, it
can refer to an inland water-meadow and also to a peninsula.
So Ynys Môn (i.e. ANGLESEY), INISHBOFIN (County Galway),
INISHMORE (the largest Aran island), INISHARK and INISHTURK
(County Mayo), and INCHCOLM and INCHKEITH (both in the
Firth of Forth) are all islands, but INISHOWEN (County Donegal)
is a very substantial peninsula, and the various examples of
Ballynahinch (such as BALLYNAHINCH, County Down) are all
inland water-meadows.

is said that the island once promoted itself with advertisements headed 'Pure Boredom – Nothing to Do'. Visitors came in droves.

Inisheer. *See under* ARAN ISLANDS.

Inishfallen Irish *Inis Faithlenn* 'Fathlenn's island' (*see* INIS). A small island in Lough Leane, the larger of the KILLARNEY lakes, County Kerry. It is also spelt **Innisfallen**. St Fionán Lobhar founded a monastery here in the 6th or 7th century, and there are the remains of a Romanesque church on the island. *Inishfallen* is also the title of a play (1862) by Edmund Falconer (for a quotation, *see under* KILLARNEY).

Annals of Inishfallen. A medieval manuscript recording events in Munster up to 1326. It was begun at EMLY in County Tipperary, but ended up at the monastery on Inishfallen. It is now in the Bodleian Library, Oxford.

Inishmaan. *See under* ARAN ISLANDS.

Inishmore Irish *Inis Mór* 'big island' (*see* INIS). The largest of the ARAN ISLANDS. It has the spectacular clifftop fort of DÚN AENGHUS and was the birthplace of the novelist Liam O'Flaherty (1896–1984), author of *The Informer* (1925), and of his nephew, the writer Breandán Ó hEithir (1930–90), author of, amongst other things, *The Begrudger's Guide to Irish Politics* (1986).

'Leaving Inishmore'. A poem by Michael Longley (b.1939), beginning:

Rain and sunlight and the boat between them
Shifted whole hillsides through the afternoon …

Lieutenant of Inishmore, The. A play (2001) by Martin MacDonagh, set in the 1990s. The publisher's blurb explains (in relation to the death of a cat):

Who knocked Wee Thomas over on the lonely road on the island of Inishmore, and was it an accident? 'Mad Padraig' will want to know when he gets back from a stint of torture and chip-shop bombing in Northern Ireland: he loves that cat more than life itself.

Inishnabro. *See under* the BLASKET ISLANDS.

Inishowen Irish *Inis Eoghain* 'island of Eoghan' (*see* INIS); *Eoghan* (anglicized as Owen) was a son of Niall of the Nine Hostages; his other son, Conall, was awarded the rest of Donegal, since known as Tyrconnel (Irish *Tír Chonaill* 'land of Conall').
A large peninsula in northeast Donegal, between LOUGH SWILLY and Lough Foyle (*see under* FOYLE). MALIN HEAD at its tip is the most northerly point on the Irish mainland, and Inishowen is itself sometimes referred to as 'Ireland in miniature'. The scenic road around it (beginning and ending at Letterkenny) is known as the **Inishowen 100**, from its length in miles. **Inishowen Head** is the most easterly point, at the mouth of Lough Foyle. Inishowen

was the territory of the O'Dohertys until granted in 1605 to the planter Sir Arthur Chichester, whose family took the title Donegall.

Inishtooshkert. *See under* the BLASKET ISLANDS.

Inishtrahull Irish INIS 'island' + possibly *traigh* 'beach, strand'. A tiny island 10 km (6 miles) north of the coast of Donegal. It is the northernmost point in Ireland.

The moon shines on the Isle of Inishtrahull,
Bejewelling nuptial tinted herring-gull,
May-fly dancing on the balmy air,
And moth returning to its daylight lair.
D.J. O'Sullivan (b.1906): 'Dawn at Inishtrahull'

Inishturk Irish *Inis Toirc* 'island of the boar' (*see* INIS). A small island some 10 km (6 miles) off the west coast of County Mayo, between INISHBOFIN and CLARE ISLAND.

Inishvickillane. *See under* BLASKET ISLANDS

Inis Mac Neasáin. The Irish name for IRELAND'S EYE.

Inis Meàin. The Irish name for Inishmaan (*see under* ARAN ISLANDS).

Inis Mór. The Irish name for INISHMORE.

Inis Oírr. The Irish name for Inisheer (*see under* ARAN ISLANDS).

Inis Toirc. The Irish name for INISHTURK.

Inkberrow Originally *Intanbeorgas* 'Inta's hills or mounds', OE *Intan* possessive form of male personal name *Inta* + *beorgas* plural of *beorg* 'hill, mound'.
A village in Worcestershire (before 1998 in Hereford and Worcester, before 1974 in Worcestershire), about 13 km (8 miles) east of Worcester. The local pub, The Old Bull, where Shakespeare stayed in 1582, was the model for The Bull inn in Ambridge, in the BBC radio soap opera *The Archers*.

Inkpen Probably either 'enclosure or fold on a hill' or, tautologically, 'hill hill', OE *ing* 'hill, peak' + *penn* 'enclosure, fold' or Celtic *penn* 'hill' (*see* PEN).
A village in Berkshire, on the North Wessex Downs (*see under* WESSEX), about 11 km (7 miles) southwest of Newbury. To the southwest the possibly doubly tautologous **Inkpen Hill** (also known as **Inkpen Beacon**) is, at 291 m (954 ft), the second-highest chalk hill in England (it is linked by a ridge walk with the highest, WALBURY HILL). The summit offers fine views, if you can ignore Combe Gibbet, the macabre replica of a late 17th-century gibbet that stands there.

The eastern end of WANSDYKE is nearby.

There are some heights in Wessex, shaped as if by a
    kindly hand
For thinking, dreaming, dying on, and at crises when I
    stand,

Say, on Ingpen Beacon eastward, or on Wylls-Neck
    westwardly,
I seem where I was before my birth, and after death
    may be.

    Thomas Hardy: 'On Wessex Heights' (1896)

Inner Hebrides, the. *See under* the HEBRIDES.

Innerleithen 'confluence of the River Leithen', Gaelic *inbhir*
'confluence' (*see* ABER) + OCelt river name meaning 'moist'.
A woollen town some 38 km (24 miles) south of Edinburgh,
situated where the **Leithen Water** flows into the River
Tweed, in Scottish Borders (formerly in Peeblesshire). In
the 19th century it was known as a spa resort, its mineral
water – noted for its effectiveness against skin and eye complaints – coming from St Ronan's Wells above the town.

Innerleithen was the setting for Sir Walter Scott's novel
St Ronan's Well (1823). Unusually for Scott, the novel has
a contemporary setting and a satirical touch, and the author
unfavourably depicts the facile but fashionable society that
gathers at the spa. Prior to publication the spring was
known as Doo's or Dow (Gaelic *dubh* 'black') Well, and it
was Scott who associated it with the 8th-century saint, who
was Bishop of Kilmaroren in Lennox. According to legend,
St Ronan visited the Innerleithen area to drive out the Devil,
a feat celebrated annually by the townspeople in the
'Cleikum ceremony'.

Inner London. As a general term, 'Inner London' merely
denotes the central, most profoundly urban part of the
capital, in contrast with OUTER LONDON, with its whiff of
suburbia. In the context of London government, however,
it has a specific application. When the Greater London
Council was set up in 1965 (*see* GREATER LONDON), 12
boroughs, plus the City of London, were designated as
constituting 'Inner London': they were CAMDEN, GREEN-
WICH, HACKNEY, HAMMERSMITH, ISLINGTON, KENSINGTON,
LAMBETH, LEWISHAM, SOUTHWARK, TOWER HAMLETS,
WANDSWORTH and WESTMINSTER. At the same time the
Inner London Education Authority (ILEA) was set up to
oversee education within this area. Despite being a constant
target of the right-wing press on account of its egregiously
politically correct policies, ILEA survived the death of the
GLC in 1986, but was itself abolished in 1990, responsibility
for education passing to the individual boroughs.

Innisfail Irish *InisFáil* 'the island of Fál or Ireland' (*see* INIS);
Fáil is often mistakenly translated as 'destiny', but is in fact an
old name of Ireland, originating in the FÁL or Lia Fáil, the stone
at TARA associated with the high kings of Ireland (later known
as the Stone of Destiny or the Stone of SCONE).

A name for Ireland first found in 10th-century poetry, and
widespread in that of the 19th:

Oh, once the harp of Innisfail
Was strung full high to notes of gladness;

But yet it often told a tale
Of more prevailing sadness.

    Thomas Campbell: 'O'Connor's Child'

Adieu! – the snowy sail
Swells her bosom to the gale,
And our bark from Innisfail
Bounds away,
While we gaze upon the shore
That we never shall see more
And the blinding tears flow o'er ...

    Richard D'Alton Williams: 'Adieu to Innisfail' (1842)

Innisfail is also the title of a long 1863 poem by Aubrey
Thomas de Vere, cataloguing Ireland's misfortunes and
sorrows.

There is a town called Innisfail in Australia
(Queensland).

Innisfallen. The Irish name for INISHFALLEN.

Innisfree Irish *Inis Fraoigh* 'island of heather' (*see* INIS).
One of the smallest islands in LOUGH GILL, County Sligo.
It is known around the world from one of W.B.Yeats's most
popular poems, 'The Lake Isle of Innisfree', in his collection
The Rose (1893):

I will arise and go now, and go to Innisfree,
And a small cabin build there, of clay and wattles made:
Nine bean-rows will I have there, a hive for the honey-
    bee,
And live alone in the bee-loud glade ...

Yeats wrote the poem in London after being inspired by
the sound of a fountain in a shop window. Later, Yeats's
sister predicted that the island would be covered in signs
such as 'The cabin is private' and 'Do not eat the beans'.

Inniskilling. The Irish name for ENNISKILLEN.

Innominate Tarn Local tradition has it that this was Loaf
Tarn, named after the shape of the clumps of peat, but that
the name Innominate Tarn was given by a writer in the *Fell
and Rock Climbing Club Journal* for undisclosed reasons, but
possibly because the local name had disappeared.

A tiny tarn (miniature mountain lake, from OScand *tjorn*
'tear', 'dewdrop') near the summit of HAY STACKS, above
the head of ENNERDALE, in the Lake District, Cumbria
(formerly in Cumberland). It is one of the most attractive
spots in the Lake District, and features in the foreground
of innumerable photographs of GREAT GABLE, Green Gable
and PILLAR. The ashes of the famous Lakeland guidebook
writer and illustrator Alfred Wainwright were scattered here
after his death in 1991 (*see* WAINWRIGHTS).

International Date Line, the. A nickname given during the 1940s and 1950s to Belfast's Bank Buildings (a
department store), the location of a popular trysting place
amongst the segregated students of the time.

Inveraray 'mouth of the River Aray', Gaelic *inbhir* 'confluence' (*see* ABER) + ancient river name, cognate with AYR[1] and meaning simply 'river'.

A small town at the foot of **Glen Aray**, where the **River Aray** enters LOCH FYNE, some 70 km (43 miles) northwest of Glasgow. It is in Argyll and Bute (formerly in Strathclyde region), and was the county town of the traditional county of Argyll. It was the seat of the powerful Campbells of Argyll, became a royal BURGH in 1648, and was rebuilt by the 3rd Duke of Argyll in the 18th century. The home of the dukes, **Inveraray Castle**, a somewhat forbidding edifice, was built in the 1740s. Robert Burns visited in 1787, and was not impressed by either the duke or his seat:

> Whoe'er he be that sojourns here,
>   I pity much his case,
> Unless he come to wait upon
>   The Lord their God – his Grace.
>
> There's naething here but Highland pride,
>   And Highland scab and hunger;
> If Providence has sent me here,
>   'Twas surely in an anger.
>
>   Robert Burns: 'Epigram at Inveraray' (1787)

Keats, in 1818, thought the castle 'very modern magnificent', but was pained by a piper nearby – 'nothing could stifle the horrors of a solo on the Bag-pipe – I thought the Beast would never have done'.

Neil Munro (1864–1930), creator of the character Para Handy, was born here.

See also GLEN COE.

Inverbervie 'mouth of the River Bervie', *Inver-* (*see* ABER) + an OCelt or pre-Celtic river name, possibly meaning 'boiling, turbulent'.

A small town on the east coast of Aberdeenshire (formerly in Kincardineshire, then in Grampian region), 12 km (7.5 miles) east of Laurencekirk.

Inverclyde 'mouth of the CLYDE', *Inver-* (*see* ABER) + river name. The name was coined when the local authority unit was created.

A unitary authority formed from the northwestern part of the old county of Renfrewshire. It is bounded on the north by the upper reaches of the Firth of Clyde. It includes GREENOCK (the administrative HQ) and PORT GLASGOW. Inverclyde was created in 1975 as a district of Strathclyde region, and became a unitary authority in 1996.

Inveresk 'mouth of the Esk', Gaelic *inbhir* 'river mouth' + *Esk*. A village just south of MUSSELBURGH (now in East Lothian), near the mouth of the River ESK[3]. The Romans had a fort, port and settlement here. Oliver Cromwell used **Inveresk House** as his headquarters in 1650.

Inverewe. *See* LOCH EWE.

Invergarry. *See under* GLEN GARRY[1].

Invergordon Something of a nonsense coinage, in that the *gordon* element comes from the 18th-century founder, Sir William *Gordon*, rather than a river name as is usually the case with names beginning *Inver-* (Gaelic *inbhir*, 'river mouth', *see* ABER). Sir William changed the name from *Inverbreakie* (Gaelic *breac* 'speckled river').

A port on the north shore of the Cromarty Firth, Highland (formerly in Ross and Cromarty), 19 km (12 miles) northeast of Dingwall. It was an important Royal Navy base during the First World War, and the base remained open until 1956.

Invergordon Mutiny (1931). A mutiny by sailors at the Royal Navy's Invergordon base in response to pay cuts introduced by the National Government in an attempt to deal with the economic crisis. The sailors returned to duty when the cuts were somewhat modified. The ringleaders were discharged from the Navy.

Inverkeithing 'river mouth of the Keithing Burn', Gaelic *inbhir* 'river mouth' (*see* ABER) + OCelt CED; the *-ing* may be a form of the diminutive, hence 'little wooded stream'.

A royal BURGH (1165) in Fife, just east of the FORTH bridges. In June 1651 Oliver Cromwell sent a force across the River Forth, which defeated Charles II and the Scots near Inverkeithing. The town was the birthplace of Samuel Greig (1735–88), who established a navy for Catherine the Great of Russia.

Inverlochy 'mouth of the River Lochy', Gaelic *inbhir* 'river mouth' (*see* ABER) + river name (*see* LOCH LOCHY).

A village, now absorbed into the north end of FORT WILLIAM, in Highland (formerly in Inverness-shire). The romantic ruins of **Inverlochy Castle** date from the 13th century and are the subject of a famous painting by Horatio McCulloch (1857).

Battle of Inverlochy (1431). A battle resulting from the imprisonment by James I of Alexander, Lord of the Isles. Alexander's cousin, Donald Balloch, raised a force against the king, and at Inverlochy defeated a royal army commanded by the Earl of Mar and the Earl of Caithness.

Battle of Inverlochy (2 February 1645). A victory for the Marquess of Montrose, at the head of a Royalist army, over the Covenanting forces of the Marquess of Argyll.

Invermoriston. *See under* GLEN MORISTON.

Inverness Gaelic name *Inbhir Nis*, 'mouth of the River Ness', *Inver-* (*see* ABER) + river name (*see* LOCH NESS).

A large town, often called 'the capital of the HIGHLANDS', situated on the River Ness where it enters the Moray Firth at the northeast end of the Great Glen, some 120 km (74 miles) northwest of Perth. It is the administrative seat of Highland, and before that it was the county town of INVERNESS-SHIRE, and then the administrative seat of

Inverness district (1975–96), which comprised the northern part of the old county. It is at the node of many important transport routes in northern Scotland. The people of Inverness are said to speak the clearest, purest English in Britain (Daniel Defoe unconvincingly credited this reputation to the garrison stationed here by Cromwell in the 17th century, but denied that the inhabitants spoke better English than did the people of London).

Inverness was the capital of King Brude, who was converted by St Columba in *c*.565, allegedly after Columba's friend Kenneth had paralysed the hostile Picts with the sign of the cross. In the 11th century Macbeth may have lived in a castle here, and in some editions of Shakespeare's play the editors place Duncan's murder at this castle (although according to another tradition, this took place at CAWDOR; and in reality Duncan was killed in battle near Elgin). A later castle was captured from the English by Robert the Bruce in 1307, and destroyed; its successor was taken in 1562 by Mary Queen of Scots from supporters of the rebel Earl of Huntly. Two centuries later, in 1745, the castle was blown up by Bonnie Prince Charlie. The present castle dates from the 19th century and contains law courts and local government offices. In 1921 the British Cabinet met in Scotland for the first time, in Inverness Town Hall, to ponder the Anglo-Irish Treaty.

Many stories are associated with the wooded knoll called Tomnahurich (Gaelic 'hill of the yews') on the southwest side of the town. Apparently the Queen of the Fairies still holds court inside the hill, and long ago two fiddlers were invited to play for her one night – only to find when they left at dawn that a hundred years had passed. The place was visited by the Irish hero Finn MacCool, whose dog Bran helped him to escape a magic spell by herding two of every species of animal round the knoll. The seer Thomas the Rhymer (*see under* ERCILDOUNE) supposedly sleeps under the mound with his men and white horses, awaiting the time when Scotland needs his services again. Tomnahurich is now the site of a cemetery, and the old mental hospital is just 1.5 km (1 mile) to the west.

The first ever concrete pavement using Portland cement was built in Inverness in 1865. Gavin Maxwell, the naturalist and author of *Ring of Bright Water*, died in Inverness in 1969; as did Sir Robert Watson-Watt, the inventor of radar, in 1973. There are Inverness counties in Canada (Nova Scotia and Cape Breton Island). Darien in Georgia, USA, was founded as New Inverness in 1736, while Cheboygan in Michigan was also formerly known as Inverness.

Inverness Caledonian Thistle. Inverness's Scottish League football team. In 2000 they achieved a giant-killing victory over Celtic in the Scottish Cup, prompting the classic *Sun* headline:

> Super Cally Go Ballistic, Celtic Are Atrocious

Apparently this was a reworking of a headline in the *Mirror* from the 1970s, celebrating Ian Callaghan's part in Liverpool's victory over Queen's Park Rangers:

> Super Cally Goes Ballistic, QPR Atrocious

Inverness cape. A heavy tweed coat with a detachable cape, as favoured by Sherlock Holmes and others in the late 19th century. It is sometimes known as simply as an Inverness.

'Lovely Lass of Inverness, The'. *See under* CULLODEN MUIR.

Treaty of Inverness (29 October 1312). A treaty by which Robert the Bruce reaffirmed with Haakon V of Norway the terms of the 1266 Treaty of Perth (*see under* PERTH), whereby Scotland had obtained the Hebrides and the Isle of Man.

Inverness (district). *See under* INVERNESS-SHIRE.

Inverness-shire From INVERNESS + SHIRE.

A traditional county of northern Scotland, bounded on the north by Ross and Cromarty, on the east by Nairnshire, Moray, Banffshire and Aberdeenshire, on the south by Perthshire and Argyll. The county town was INVERNESS, and it included the islands of SKYE and the SMALL ISLES in the Inner Hebrides, and all of the Outer HEBRIDES apart from Lewis. It was absorbed into Highland region in 1975, the northern part of the old county forming the district of Inverness.

Inverpolly. *See under* STAC POLLAIDH.

Inversnaid 'mouth of the Allt na Snàthaid', Gaelic *inbhir* 'river mouth' (*see* ABER) + *snàthaid* 'needle' (*Allt na Snàthaid* is 'burn of the needle').

An isolated settlement some 20 km (12 miles) northwest of Aberfoyle, at a road end on the otherwise roadless upper east shore of LOCH LOMOND. It was formerly in Stirlingshire, then in Central region, and is now in the unitary authority of STIRLING². The tourist steamer on Loch Lomond calls at the pier here. The barracks (built *c*.1720) at Inversnaid Garrison above Inversnaid were burnt down by the MacGregors in the first action of the 1745 Jacobite Rising. William Wordsworth came here in 1803, and wrote of

> ... these gray Rocks; this household Lawn;
> These Trees, a veil just half withdrawn;
> This fall of water, that doth make
> A murmur near the silent Lake;
> This little Bay ...
>
> > William Wordsworth: 'To a Highland Girl (at Inversneyde, upon Loch Lomond)' (1803)

The 'fall of water' referred to by Wordsworth ends in a waterfall straight into the loch, as described by a later poetical visitor:

> This darksome burn, horseback brown,
> His rollrock highroad rolling down,

In coop and in comb the fleece of his foam
Flutes and low to the lake falls home.

> Gerard Manley Hopkins: 'Inversnaid' (not published until
> after Hopkins's death in 1889), first verse

Inverurie 'mouth of the River Urie', Gaelic *inbhir* 'river mouth'
(*see* ABER) + river name of obscure meaning.
A town in Aberdeenshire (formerly in Grampian region),
24 km (15 miles) northwest of Aberdeen, at the junction
of the Rivers Urie and Don. Arthur Johnstone (1587–1641),
the Latin poet and 'Scottish Ovid', was born at Caskieben
Castle to the east of the town. It has been suggested that
the Battle of MONS GRAUPIUS (*c*.AD 84) may have been
fought near Inverurie.

Battle of Inverurie (1307). A battle in which Robert the
Bruce defeated John Comyn, Earl of Buchan, cousin of the
'Red Comyn' whom Bruce (or his followers) had killed in
Dumfries the previous year.

Iona The oldest recorded forms of the name of the island
include *Ia*, *Hy* and *Ioua*. St Adamnan, in his life of Columba,
refers to it as 'Iova Insula', and the Old Norse *hiöe* 'island of
the den of the brown bear' has been suggested as a meaning. However, as Adamnan was writing in the 7th century,
some two centuries before the Viking raids, a Norse origin
seems unlikely. In fact the name derives from the Old Celtic
word for 'yew tree' and is found in Irish as *éo*. The change
from 'Iova' to 'Iona' was apparently the result of a mistranscription (*n* and *u* or *v* are written with two similar
pen-strokes) and is found as early as 1100, though it took
much longer for this to become the standard spelling. A reason
for the name catching on is perhaps that 'Iona' is a version of
Hebrew *jonah* 'dove', Columba's own name, which is Latin
for dove.
A small island in the Inner HEBRIDES, in Argyll and Bute
(formerly in Strathclyde region). It is separated from the
western tip of the Ross of MULL by the **Sound of Iona**,
which is about 1.5 km (1 mile) across. It was here that
St Columba (or Columcille) arrived from Ireland in 563
to establish a monastery, and to begin the conversion
of the Scots and the Picts. Apparently he missed his
homeland:

> And on Iona Columcille sought ease
> By wearing Irish mould next to his feet.

> Seamus Heaney: 'Gravities', from *Death of a Naturalist* (1966,
> 1991)

Up to the end of the 18th century the island was often
referred to as **Icolmkill**, a combination of the ancient name
'Hy' with the personal name *Columcille*, a distinguishing
variant of *Columba* meaning literally 'church-pigeon' (*see*
KIL-). The name of the place continues to cause a degree of
confusion, as in the following conversation overheard in
an Edinburgh bookshop:

> *American customer:* Do you have a map of Ten en a?
> *Bookseller:* Ten en a, sir? Where is that?
> *American customer:* Well, it's a little island off the west
> coast of Scotland …

> Quoted in Bent's Notes, in *The Bookseller* (17 January 2003)

The island is regarded as the cradle of the faith in
Scotland, and was described by William Wordsworth
as 'this Glory of the west'. St Columba set up an enduring foundation on the island. Apparently discipline was
strict, for when in 1772 Thomas Pennant visited the
bay where Columba landed, he was told a story of 'a vast
tract' nearby, 'covered with heaps of stones of unequal
sizes':

> … these, as is said, were the penances of monks who were
> to raise heaps, of dimensions equal to their crimes: and to
> judge by some, it is no breach of charity to think there
> were among them enormous sinners.

> Thomas Pennant: *A Tour of Scotland and a Voyage to the
> Hebrides* (1773)

From 795 Iona suffered two centuries of Viking attacks,
and the body of St Columba, together with the famous
Book of Kells (probably begun in Iona), were moved to
KELLS[1] in Ireland in 849, after the slaughter of 68 monks
at Martyrs' Bay. The monastery revived in the 11th century,
and a Benedictine establishment was founded in 1203.
Along with the other Hebrides, Iona was in the possession
of the kings of Norway until 1266. Being so far west, and
thus so near to heaven, in the Middle Ages Iona became
the burial place of Scottish (as well as Irish and Norwegian)
kings, and it is said that the bones of all the kings
of Scotland from Kenneth MacAlpin (d.*c*.858) to
Macbeth (d.1057) lie here. In *Macbeth*, when Ross asks what
has happened to the murdered Duncan's body, Macduff
replies:

> Carried to Colmekill,
> The sacred storehouse of his predecessors
> And guardian of their bones.

> William Shakespeare: *Macbeth* (1606), II.iii

In the 18th century the poet William Collins mused upon
the burials at Iona:

> beneath the show'ry west,
> The mighty kings of three fair realms are laid:
> Once foes, perhaps, together now they rest,
> No slaves revere them, and no wars invade:
> Yet frequent now, at midnight's solemn hour,
> The rifted mounds their yawning cells unfold,
> And forth the monarchs stalk with sovereign power,
> In pageant robes, and wreath'd with sheeny gold,
> And on their twilight tombs aerial council hold.

> William Collins: 'Ode on the Popular Superstitions of the
> Highlands' (1784)

The Lewis-born poet Iain Crichton Smith wrote a poem 'For the Unknown Seaman of the 1939–45 War Buried in Iona Churchyard', which ends

> They fell from sea to earth from grave to grave
> and, griefless now, taught others how to grieve.

In 1994, John Smith, the Scottish leader of the Labour Party, who died of a heart attack, was buried on Iona.

The monastery was suppressed at the Reformation, and the abbey building became a ruin. In 1899 the 8th Duke of Argyll gave it to the Church of Scotland, which set about its restoration, and in 1910 the abbey (or cathedral) again became a place of worship.

Johnson and Boswell visited the island in 1773 and were profoundly moved:

> That man is little to be envied, whose patriotism would not gain force upon the plain of *Marathon*, or whose piety would not grow warmer among the ruins of *Iona*!
>
> Samuel Johnson: *A Journey to the Western Islands of Scotland* (1775)

In contrast, Sir Walter Scott found the place 'desolate and miserable'. The island was also visited by John Keats (1818), who was not moved to verse, and by William Wordsworth (1835), who (regrettably) was. A more recent literary visitor reported:

> Topheavy carrion gulls gape
> as they scoop up shite in their beaks
> and peck at seapink sanitary towels
> in the orange light.
>
> Tom Buchan: 'Iona', from *Dolphins at Cochin* (1969)

He then has a vision in which the Moderator of the General Assembly of the Church of Scotland

> waltzes the minute figure of Ernie Finnie
> across the dead water.

Iona Community. A group within the Church of Scotland founded in 1938 by the Rev. George MacLeod (later Lord MacLeod of Fiunary), minister in the working-class Glasgow area of Govan. MacLeod wanted to revitalize the faith by combining the material with the spiritual, and he and his companions began to work on the restoration of the ancient buildings around the abbey on Iona. Members of the Community today – and many other visitors, of many denominations – spend part of the summer on the island, undertaking restoration work and participating in prayers and Bible study.

Statutes of Icolmkill. A ceremony of 1609 in which the Hebridean chiefs swore loyalty to King James VI and I and his successors.

IoW. The standard written abbreviation of ISLE OF WIGHT.

Ippikin's Rock From the male personal name *Ippikin*.

A cliff just to the south of the highest point of WENLOCK EDGE in Shropshire. It is penetrated by a cave in which, according to local legend, there once lived a robber called Ippikin. He is said to have been buried alive in the cave with his ill-gotten gains by a landslide. Anyone incautious enough to stand outside it and shout 'Ippikin! Ippikin! Keep away with your long chin!' is reputedly in danger of being pushed off the cliff by his ghost.

Ipplepen 'Ipela's fold or enclosure', OE male personal name *Ipela* + *penn* 'fold, enclosure'.

A village in Devon, about 8 km (5 miles) northwest of Torbay.

Ipswich 'Gip's harbour or trading centre', OE *Gipes* possessive form of male personal name *Gip* (*see also* GIPPING[1]) + *wic* 'harbour, trading centre' (*see* WICK).

The county town of Suffolk, situated at the point where the River GIPPING[2] meets the ORWELL[1] estuary, about 72 km (45 miles) southeast of Cambridge. From Anglo-Saxon times until the 17th century it was a busy port, vital to the East Anglian cloth trade. It then went into something of an economic decline, but the introduction of light industry in the 19th century began to reverse its fortunes, and its docks are now busy again too.

Dickens used the Great White Horse Hotel in Ipswich as the scene of some of Mr Pickwick's misadventures in *Pickwick Papers* (1837): Pickwick, having pursued the egregious Jingle to Ipswich, inadvertently enters the bedroom of a middle-aged lady at night, and ends up in front of the magistrate.

Thomas Wolsey (Cardinal Wolsey; 1475–1530), the son of an Ipswich butcher, the writer V.S. Pritchett (1900–97), and the theatre and film director Sir Trevor Nunn (b.1940) were born in Ipswich. A US newspaper reported Ernest Simpson's divorce proceedings in Ipswich against the future Duchess of Windsor with the headline: 'King's Moll Reno'd in Wolsey's Home Town'.

Ipswich Town FC is closely associated with the two most famous (and successful) England football managers in history. (Sir) Alf Ramsey managed Ipswich Town from 1955 to 1963, taking them from the old Third Division to the First Division (and winning the League title in 1962) before becoming England manager. Bobby Robson (England coach 1982–90) was manager of Ipswich Town between 1969 and 1982, and turned the East Anglian club into one of the best sides in England, winning the FA Cup in 1978 and the UEFA Cup in 1982. Ipswich Town players are nicknamed the Tractor Boys, referring to the agricultural milieu of the city.

There are towns or cities called Ipswich in the USA (Massachusetts, South Dakota), Australia (Queensland) and Jamaica.

See also CHANTRY.

Ireland 'land of ÉIRE'.

The westernmost of the larger British Isles, or, as the Irish prefer to call them, THESE ISLANDS or (with admirable chutzpah) the Hibernian Archipelago (*see under* HIBERNIA). It is, according to the scholar John Pentland Mahaffy (1839–1919), 'a country in which the probable never happens and the impossible always does'. Ireland's patron saint is St Patrick, and its symbols are the harp and the shamrock, the latter being the three-leaved clover with which Patrick explained the nature of the Trinity to the Irish people.

Ireland has many ranges of hills, mostly around its edges, while in the centre is the Midlands (*see* MIDLANDS, THE IRISH), a large boggy lowland area. There are a number of very large inland lakes (the largest being LOUGH NEAGH), and the longest river, linking several of these lakes, is the SHANNON. The northern and western coasts are heavily indented, and the islands off these coasts include RATHLIN ISLAND, ACHILL ISLAND and the ARAN ISLANDS.

In Irish the whole island is called ÉIRE, and this is also the official Irish name for the **Republic of Ireland** (informally also known as the Irish Republic, Southern Ireland, the South and the Republic). The Republic started life as the **Irish Free State** (*see under* IRISH) following the Anglo-Irish Treaty of 1921 that ended the Anglo-Irish War (or War of Independence); it adopted the name Éire under the constitution of 1937 and became a republic in 1949 when it left the British Commonwealth. The Anglo-Irish Treaty of 1921 had partitioned the island of Ireland, the southern TWENTY-SIX COUNTIES gaining dominion status within the Commonwealth and the northern SIX COUNTIES becoming NORTHERN IRELAND, with self-rule within the UK. Those in favour of a united Ireland prefer to refer to the THIRTY-TWO COUNTIES. Northern Ireland is sometimes referred to as ULSTER, but the traditional province of Ulster also includes three of the counties now in the Republic; nevertheless, Northern Ireland is often referred to as 'the Province'. If the reader is still with us, he or she may be agreeing with Ezra Pound's observation in 1920:

> There is no topic ... more soporific and generally boring than the topic of Ireland *as Ireland, as a nation*.

But there's more. In ancient Greek, Ireland was *Iernoi* (later *Ierne*), and in Latin HIBERNIA; confusingly, some Latin texts refer to it as *Scotia* (the Scots originally coming from Ireland). In Classical times the place had a bit of a reputation:

> Its inhabitants are more savage than the Britons, since they are man-eaters as well as heavy eaters, and since, further, they count it an honourable thing, when their fathers die, to devour them, and openly to have

intercourse, not only with other women, but also with their mothers and sisters; ... but ... I have no trustworthy witness for this ...

> Strabo: *Geography* (1st century BC)

Ancient Irish names for Ireland include FÓTLA, *Banba* and *Elg* or *Elga* (*see under* ÉIRE). *Ierne*, favoured by medieval geographers, comes from *Éirinn*, the dative case of *Eriú*, also related to Éire. Alternative poetic names include *Clár Conn* ('plain of Conn'), *Gort Gaedheal* ('field of the Gaels'), FÁL, INNISFAIL and ERIN. The island has also been referred to as the FIVE FIFTHS (from the number of ancient kingdoms), the EMERALD ISLE (from the effect of the copious pluvial effusions on the vegetation), the LAND OF IRE, the MOST DISTRESSFUL COUNTRY, the ISLAND OF SAINTS AND SCHOLARS, John Bull's Other Island (*see under* JOHN BULL) and, by sentimental Republicans, as the FOUR GREEN FIELDS (referring to the four traditional provinces). In personified form, Ireland is often portrayed as an old woman or a young woman, or both, and in this guise is usually given the name KATHLEEN NI HOULIHAN, RÓISÍN DUBH, the SHAN VAN VOCHT or Granuaile (*see under* CLEW BAY). The country is also sometimes weepily called the OULD SOD.

Historically and officially, in medieval times, and as an English dominion, the country was the **Lordship of Ireland**: the title 'lord of Ireland' was first used in 1177, when Henry II granted it to his son John. The name **Kingdom of Ireland** was officially adopted for the country by an Act of the Irish Parliament in 1541. The Parliament came to an end in 1800, following the insurrection of 1798 (the United Irishmen's Rebellion), when the Act of Union created the **United Kingdom of Great Britain and Ireland**, with representation of the Irish at WESTMINSTER rather than DUBLIN.

According to George Borrow, the Romany name for Ireland is HINDITY-MENGRESKEY TEM ('dirty fellows' country'). In English slang, Ireland has derogatorily been referred to as Paddyland, Murphyland and PATLAND. The English, who behaved in a quite appalling manner in Ireland for centuries, have continued to assert their right to be rude about the country:

> Of my Nation? What ish my Nation? Ish a villain, a bastard, a knave and a rascal.
>
> William Shakespeare: Macmorris in *Henry V* (1599), III.ii

> The bane of England, and the opprobrium of Europe.
>
> Benjamin Disraeli: speech (9 August 1843)

> And if ye ever ride in Ireland,
> The jest may yet be said:
> There is the land of broken hearts,
> And the land of broken heads.
>
> G.K. Chesterton: *Notes to a Tourist*

> The *Big Issue* seller of Europe
>
> A.A. Gill

The Rev. Sydney Smith offered some kind of explanation:

> The moment the very name of Ireland is mentioned, the English seem to bid adieu to common feeling, common prudence, and to common sense, and to act with the barbarity of tyrants, and the fatuity of idiots.
>
> Sydney Smith: *Letters of Peter Plymley* (1807)

The Irish themselves have also availed themselves of the opportunity to be critical, Thomas Moore calling it 'A beautiful country ... to live out of!'

> I reckon no man is thoroughly miserable unless he be condemn'd to live in Ireland.
>
> Jonathan Swift: letter to Ambrose Philips (1709)

> Hapless Nation! hapless Land
> Heap of uncementing sand!
> Crumbled by a foreign weight:
> And by worse, domestic hate.
>
> William Drennan: 'The Wake of William Orr' (1797)

> Ireland is the old sow that eats her farrow.
>
> James Joyce: *A Portrait of the Artist as a Young Man* (1916) (the words are spoken by Stephen Dedalus)

> Men have been dying for Ireland since the beginning of time and look at the state of the country.
>
> Frank McCourt: *Angela's Ashes* (1996)

Since joining the European Union the Republic has thrived, turning itself into the CELTIC TIGER, or, as scholar Terry Eagleton has put it:

> Ireland is a modern nation but it is modernized only recently and at the moment it is behaving rather like a lavatory attendant who has just won the lottery.

New Ireland is an island in the Bismarck Archipelago, Papua New Guinea, named Nova Hibernia by Philip Carteret in 1767.

See also IRELAND'S EYE.

Aberdonians of Ireland. An unflattering name for the residents of PORTADOWN, who (like the people of ABERDEEN) apparently have a reputation for meanness.

Church of Ireland. The largest Protestant church in Ireland, part of the worldwide Anglican Communion. It became the established church in Ireland in 1537, and by the 1801 Act of Union became united 'for ever' with the Church of England; this eternal unity came to an end in 1870, when the Church of Ireland was disestablished.

fair maid of Ireland. Another term for the phenomenon known as ignis fatuus (Latin 'foolish fire') or will-o'-the-wisp, a flame-like phosphorescence (caused by the spontaneous combustion of gases from decaying vegetation) that flits over marshy ground and traditionally deludes people who attempt to follow it.

'Give Ireland Back to the Irish'. A protest song (1972)

released as a single by Paul McCartney, which, together with John Lennon's products of the same year (*see under* IRISH) amounted to a double-whammy of musical anti-Englishness from these ex-Beatles with, as their names suggest, Irish heritages. The song was banned from the BBC's airwaves.

'God Save Ireland'. A ballad (1867) by Timothy Daniel Sullivan, which became the anthem of Irish Nationalists. It was written in tribute to the Manchester Martyrs (*see under* MANCHESTER), three Fenians who had been executed that year. The title was inspired by the shout of defiance made from the dock by Edward Condon, the fourth man, who, as a US citizen, was reprieved:

> 'God Save Ireland!' said the heroes;
> 'God Save Ireland!' said they all;
> 'Whether on the scaffold high
> Or the battlefield we die,
> O, what matter when for Erin dear we fall!'

Government of Ireland Act (1920). The Act passed by the Westminster Parliament that established Home Rule in the six counties of Northern Ireland; it also provided for a Home Rule parliament in the southern twenty-six counties, but elections for this were boycotted and the Anglo-Irish War continued until the Anglo-Irish Treaty was signed in December 1921 (*see above*).

Hidden Ireland, The. An influential book by the Nationalist scholar Daniel Corkery published in 1924. It sought to recover the reputations of the great Irish poets of the 18th century, whose merits had been obscured during the period of the Protestant Ascendancy.

Ireland Act (1949). An Act passed by the Westminster Parliament in response to Southern Ireland declaring itself a republic. The main substance of the Act was to state that Northern Ireland would stay within the United Kingdom unless the Parliament of Northern Ireland decided otherwise.

Ireland of the Welcomes. A bi-monthly magazine produced by Bord Fáilte (the Irish tourist board) since 1952, referring to the ubiquitous Irish slogan *céad mile fáilte* ('a hundred thousand welcomes').

Republic of Ireland Act (1948). The Act by which Ireland declared itself a republic and withdrew from the British Commonwealth.

Uncrowned King of Ireland, the. A nickname for Charles Stewart Parnell (1846–91), leader of the Irish Nationalists from 1880 to 1890, when his party split after he was cited in the O'Shea divorce case. The sobriquet was coined by Tim Healy, one of Parnell's most ardent supporters before the rupture. Parnell died only four months after marrying Kitty O'Shea in 1891.

> Mr Casey, freeing his arms from his holders, suddenly bowed his head on his hands with a sob of pain.

– Poor Parnell! he cried loudly. My dead king! He sobbed loudly and bitterly.

Stephen, raising his terrorstricken face, saw that his father's eyes were full of tears.

James Joyce: *A Portrait of the Artist as a Young Man* (1916)

The death of Parnell also haunts Joyce's story 'Ivy Day at the Committee Room' (in *Dubliners*, 1914). Towards the end, one of the protagonists recites a ballad called 'The Death of Parnell':

He is dead. Our Uncrowned King is dead,
O, Erin, mourn with grief and woe
For he lies dead whom the fell gang
Of modern hypocrites laid low.

Young Ireland. A Nationalist movement of the 1840s. The most significant figure was Thomas Davis, who emphasized the importance of an Irish cultural renaissance, but his death in 1845 (together with the onset of the Great Famine) robbed Young Ireland of some of its momentum. The movement fizzled out after the humiliating failure of William Smith O'Brien's 1848 rebellion, dubbed WIDOW MCCORMICK'S CABBAGE PATCH (the reluctant O'Brien had always regarded himself as a 'Middle-Aged Irelander').

Ireland's Eye From an early Irish name, *Inis Ereann* 'Eria's island' (she was said to have built a church here in the 7th century), but *Ereann* was taken to be the genitive of *Éire* (Ireland), while *Eye* came from OScand *ey* 'island' (*see* -AY); the English name is somewhat reinforced by the topography. A rocky islet in Carriggen Bay off the east coast of County DUBLIN, about 1 km (0.6 miles) north of Howth. Its Irish name is **Inis Mac Neasáin** ('island of the sons of Neasán'), referring to the brothers Diucaill, Mo-Nissu and Neslug, who founded a monastery here in the 7th century. All that remains is their chapel, St Nessan's Church or Kilmacnessan ('church of the sons of Neasán'); it has been restored, excessively in the view of some.

Irish From IRELAND.
A term that is both an adjective and a noun. As an adjective it means of, or relating to, Ireland; or, offensively, it can mean illogical and/or ludicrous, from the racial stereotype of Irish stupidity or topsy-turvyness. As a noun it means either the Irish language – **Irish Gaelic** (*see below*), or, sometimes, Hiberno-English (*see under* HIBERNIA) – or, in 19th-century US slang, it can mean 'temper'. In the form **the Irish** it means the people of Ireland (also referred to as **the Irishry**, or by St Columban in the 7th century as *Iberi, ultimi habitatores mundi* – 'the Irish, denizens of the world's edge'). In English slang the Irish are referred to, usually pejoratively, as *Pats*, *Paddies* or *Micks* (all from the common Irish male Christian names Patrick and Michael), hence also the rhyming slang *Shovel and Picks*. They have also been called *Boghoppers*, *Boglanders* and *Bogtrotters*. At one

time they were also called *Teaguelanders*, from *Teague*, a Catholic. A recent innovation for a particular brand of Irishman is *Nipplie* – New Irish Patriot Permanently Living In Exile. The Irish have come in for more than their fair share of derision over the centuries – mostly (but not always) from the English, and often focused on racial stereotyping involving poverty, hot temper, violence and stupidity (as in many of the phrases listed at the end of this entry).

A servile race in folly nursed,
Who truckle most when treated worst.

Jonathan Swift: 'Verses on the Death of Dr Swift' (1739)

The Irish are difficult to deal with. For one thing the English do not understand their innate love of fighting and blows. If on either side of an Irishman's road to Paradise shillelahs grew, which automatically hit him on the head, yet he would not be satisfied.

Alfred, Lord Tennyson: quoted in *Alfred, Lord Tennyson: A Memoir* (1897)

The Irish people do not gladly suffer common sense.

Oliver St John Gogarty: comment in 1935

Charming, soft-voiced, quarrelsome, priest-ridden, feckless and happily devoid of the slightest integrity in our stodgy English sense of the word.

Noël Coward: diary (1960)

Sure God help the Irish, if it was raining soup, they'd be out with forks.

Brendan Behan: *Brendan Behan's Island* (1962)

The Irishman, now, our contempt is beneath –
He sleeps in his boots and he lies in his teeth.
He blows up policemen, or so I have heard,
And blames it on Cromwell and William the Third.

Michael Flanders (with Donald Swann): 'A Song of Patriotic Prejudice', from *At the Drop of Another Hat* (1964)

The problem with Ireland is that it's a country full of genius, but with absolutely no talent.

Hugh Leonard: interview in *The Times* (August 1977)

Anglo-Irish Agreement. Another name for the Hillsborough Agreement (*see under* HILLSBOROUGH[1]).
Anglo-Irish Treaty (6 December 1921). The treaty that ended the **Anglo-Irish War** (*see below*) and set up the **Irish Free State** (*see below*); it also provoked the **Irish Civil War** (*see below*).
Anglo-Irish War (1919–21). The War of Independence in Ireland. The fighting – between the Irish Republican Army on the one side and the Royal Irish Constabulary, Black and Tans and Auxiliaries on the other – was relatively small-scale, with just over 1300 deaths (combatants and civilians). Peace negotiations began in mid-1921,

culminating in the **Anglo-Irish Treaty** (*see above*) at the end of the year.

buggered for the want of an Irish king. A New Zealand expression suggesting that the speaker is without some vital item.

Irish acre. A unit of land measurement, nearly twice the size of an English acre.

Irish ague. A disease – probably typhus – prevalent in Ireland in the 16th and 17th centuries.

Irish ambulance. An early 20th-century US slang term for a wheelbarrow. Alternatives include **Irish baby buggy** and **Irish chariot.**

Irish apple. A slang term for a potato, in use since the 18th century. Alternatives include **Irish apricot / football / grape / lemon / root.** It is not to be confused, however, with an **Irish cherry** (*see below*).

Irish banjo or **spoon** or **fan.** Some 20th-century slang terms for a spade. (An **Irish toothpick** is a pickaxe.)

Irish bar. A type of theme pub – with all the ersatz commercial 'tradition' that that term implies – that spread around Britain and Europe (and even back to Ireland) in the last two decades of the 20th century.

Irish bouquet. An American slang term, dating from the 1960s, for a thrown projectile. An earlier expression is **Irish confetti** (*see also* Belfast confetti *under* BELFAST).

Irish Box. A name applied, especially in fishing contexts, to all the waters around Ireland.

Irish Brigade, the. A name used of a variety of military units fighting in foreign wars over the centuries, such as the Irish brigades fighting on both sides during the American Civil War, and the Irish Brigade that fought for Franco in the Spanish Civil War. Above all, it refers to the Wild Geese, the thousands of Irish soldiers who, after the surrender of Limerick in 1691, fought for Catholic France and the Jacobite cause:

> They fought as they revelled, fast, fiery and true,
> And though victors they left on the field not a few;
> And they who survived, fought and drank as of yore,
> But the land of their hearts' hope they never saw more;
> For in far foreign fields from Dunkirk to Belgrade
> Lie the soldiers and chiefs of the Irish Brigade.
>
> Thomas Davis: 'The Battle-Eve of the Brigade' (1843)

In the 1850s the name 'Irish Brigade' was adopted by a group of Catholic Irish MPs at Westminster; they were known to their adversaries as the Pope's Brass Band.

Irish bull. A term first coined in the early 17th century by the English in Ireland for any statement regarded by them as stupid or ludicrous, but usually reflecting the fact that the Irish were attempting to speak in a language that was not their native tongue. These days the term is labelled in some dictionaries as 'offensive'. Etymologists have failed to explain the reasons for 'bull', although, as the noted provost of Trinity College Dublin, Sir John Pentland Mahaffy (1839–1919), pointedly remarked: 'An Irish bull is always pregnant.'

Irish cabbage. A meal of corned beef, cabbage and potatoes, traditionally eaten on St Patrick's Day in the USA and also known as **Irish turkey.** However, **Irish chicken** is pork, while **Irish goose** is a meal of cod.

Irish cherry. A slang term for a carrot.

Irish Citizen Army. The socialist militia formed by the Irish Transport and General Workers' Union on 23 November 1913 during the Dublin Lockout (*see under* DUBLIN). It took part in the 1916 Easter Rising, after which its commandant, James Connolly, was executed.

Irish Civil War. A bitter conflict (1922–3) that broke out shortly after the formation of the Irish Free State, created following the Anglo-Irish Treaty of December 1921. Anti-treaty Republicans fought the forces of the Free State, objecting to the partition of Ireland and to the fact that the British monarch remained head of state.

Irish cloak. A full-length hooded woollen cloak worn by Irishwomen up to the early years of the 20th century.

Irish clubhouse. An Edwardian-era slang term for a police station.

Irish coffee. The result of coffee to which Irish whiskey has been added; it is usually served after dinner, with cream on top, thus resembling a pint of porter. The origin is said to go back to 1942, when, on a cold winter's night, the American passengers on a seaplane landing on the west coast of Ireland were heartened by the spirited coffee served by the chef, Jim Sheridan.

> Only Irish coffee provides in a single glass all four essential food groups: alcohol, caffeine, sugar and fat.
>
> Alex Levine

Irish colleges. A type of seminary on the Continent for training Irish priests, first set up during the Counter-Reformation. The first Irish college was founded in Salamanca, Spain, in 1592. The only one to survive today as a seminary is that in Rome.

Irish comics / funnies. The obituary columns in the newspapers, with an implied slur on Irish literacy.

Irish Confederation. A movement formed in 1847 as a result of a split in the Young Ireland movement (*see under* IRELAND). In 1848 the Confederation reunited with the supporters of Daniel O'Connell to form the **Irish League** (*see below*), while also planning the abortive rebellion of that year.

Irish Convention (July 1917–April 1918). A convention of Irish politicians summoned by Lloyd George to resolve the issues surrounding Home Rule. It was boycotted by Sinn Féin and failed to come to any effective conclusion.

Irish disease. A name sometimes given to tuberculosis during the 19th and early 20th centuries. In the 17th century the term was applied, according to Thomas Dineley's *Tour of Ireland* (1681), to 'a dysenteria or bloody flux', for which spirituous liquor was recommended as a cure.

Irish elk. An extinct giant deer, *Megaloceros giganteus*, found across Eurasia during the last Ice Age. It had an antler span of up to 4 m (13 ft).

Irish eyebright. A species of eyebright, *Euphrasia salisburgensis*, subtly different from the standard issue *E. officinalis*.

Irish Famine. The **Great Hunger** or **Great Famine** of 1846–51, in which 1 million people died following the failure of successive potato crops (the staple of the Irish peasantry) when they was decimated by *Phytophthora infestans*, potato blight. A further 1 million Irish emigrated. At this time, Ireland was a net exporter of wheat. The failure of the British government to intervene early enough or fully enough remains a highly contentious political and historical issue. Ireland's population still remains below pre-Famine levels.

Irish favourite. A 1920s US slang term for an emerald (Ireland being the EMERALD ISLE).

Irish flag. A US slang term for a nappy.

Irish fleabane. A composite plant, *Inula salicina*, with a yellow dandelion-like flower.

Irish fortune. A 19th-century euphemism for the vagina.

Irish Free State. The name for Southern Ireland from 1921 to 1937; officially it was known by the Irish name *Saorstát Éireann*. The Irish Free State was formed following the signing of the **Anglo-Irish Treaty** (*see above*) that ended the **Anglo-Irish War** (*see above*). The treaty gave Southern Ireland dominion status within the British Commonwealth, while NORTHERN IRELAND remained within the UK. The **Irish Civil War** (*see above*) soon broke out between the Free State government and anti-treaty Republicans. In 1937 the country changed its name to ÉIRE, and in 1949 became the Republic of Ireland (*see under* IRELAND).

Irish Fright, the (December 1688). A week-long panic that swept England during the Glorious Revolution, sparked by rumours that the Irish troops brought over to support James II were about to embark on a campaign of massacre and rapine. The panic resulted in many attacks on Catholics, real or suspected.

Irish Gaelic. The Irish form of Gaelic, which belongs to the Goidelic group of the Celtic branch of languages. It is often referred to simply as **Irish**. Native speakers of Irish Gaelic are largely confined to the GAELTACHT of the west, although the language has been, since the later 19th century, an emblem of Irish Nationalism, and it is compulsory for all schoolchildren in the Republic to learn it. Although conceived of as a tool for liberation from the English, the turning of the language into a shibboleth has been seen as stultifying by some:

> It seems to me you do not care what banality a man expresses so long as he expresses it in Irish.
>
> James Joyce: *Stephen Hero* (published posthumously in 1944)

Irish Guards. A regiment of the British Army, raised in 1900 in honour of the Irish regiments who had fought in the Anglo-Boer War. They are nicknamed the Micks, or Bob's Own – their first colonel was Lord Roberts of Kandahar.

Irish harp. A small diatonic harp with a hollow wooden soundbox. Its exponents were at one time frowned upon:

> Hang the harpers wherever found.
>
> Elizabeth I: proclamation of 1603

Irish hoist. A slang term for a kick up the arse.

Irish hurricane. A flat calm.

Irish in Us, The. A comedy film (1935) about a New York Irish family, starring James Cagney and Olivia de Haviland.

Irishism. An Irish idiom or custom; when these are regarded as affected, they may be described as **Oirish**.

Irish jig. A characteristic Irish folk dance; it is also rhyming slang for either a wig or a cig (i.e. a cigarette).

Irish joke. A joke turning on the racial stereotype of the Irish as stupid, for example:

> Seamus and Sean start work at a sawmill. After an hour Seamus lets out a big yell. 'Help, Sean, I lost me finger!'
> Sean says, 'Now how did you go about doing that?'
> 'Sure I just touched the big spinning job here, just like thi– Feck! There goes another one!'

It should be pointed out that as the English have Irish jokes, so the Irish have Kerryman jokes (*see under* County KERRY).

Irish lace. A 19th-century term for a spider's web (with a dig at Irish poverty), in addition to its straightforward definition.

Irish lady's tresses. A white-flowered member of the orchid family, *Spiranthes romanzoffiana*, favouring boggy habitats.

Irish lasses. A rhyming-slang term for 'glasses'.

Irish Legion. A military unit founded in 1803 by Bernard MacSheehy, comprising United Irishmen (*see below*) exiled in France after the 1798 rising. Its aim was to participate in a Franco-Irish invasion of Ireland, which did not, however, take place. The legion was disbanded in 1815.

Irish Literary Renaissance, the. The flowering of Irish literature that took place in the late 19th and early 20th centuries. It was inspired by Irish Nationalism and by the rediscovery of traditional Irish culture, especially legends and folklore. Leading figures included W.B. Yeats, Lady Augusta Gregory, Æ (George Russell), George Moore and J.M. Synge.

Irishman's coat of arms. An 18th- and 19th-century expression for a black eye, or, more spectacularly, two black eyes and a bloody nose.

Irishman's necktie. A US slang term for a rope, dating from the late 19th century.

Irishman's nightingale. US slang for a bullfrog, in use in the early 20th century.

Irish mantle. A type of fringed woollen cloak that was a standard item of dress in Ireland from medieval times up to the end of the 17th century. It was worn day and night, despite being banned by Henry VIII, and was described as:

> ... a fit house for an outlaw, a meet bed for a rebel, and an apt cloak for a thief.
>
> Edmund Spenser: *A View of the Present State of Ireland* (1596)

Irish Melodies. Thomas Moore's collection of lyrics for traditional (although somewhat meddled-with) Irish airs, published in ten volumes between 1808 and 1824. The songs included 'The Harp that Once through Tara's Halls', 'Love's Young Dream', 'The Minstrel Boy' and 'The Last Rose of Summer'.

Irish mile. A unit of distance that goes all over the place, and thus appears longer than normal.

Irish Mist. A liqueur made from TULLAMORE Dew whiskey, honey and herbs. It was the first Irish liqueur, launched in 1948, and claims kinship with heather wine, tipple of the ancient Gaels.

Irish moss. Another term for carragheen (*see under* CARRAGHEEN).

Irish needle lace. A type of lace made with a needle, based on 17th-century Venetian patterns. It was developed as a cottage industry during the 1840s, as a Famine-relief measure.

Irish porridge. The dismissive description (in Latin '*pultes Scottorum*') made by critics of *De Praedestinatione* (851) by John Scottus Eriugena, an Irish *doctus* at the court of Charles the Bald.

Irish potato. A term, heard mostly in the USA, for a potato.

Irish Question, the. The puzzle as to what to do with Ireland that so troubled its British rulers from the 19th century:

> Consider Ireland ... You have a starving population, an absentee aristocracy, and an alien Church, and in addition the weakest executive in the world. That is the Irish Question.
>
> Benjamin Disraeli: speech to the House of Commons (16 February 1844)

The German chancellor Otto von Bismarck proposed a solution – displaying an uncharacteristic vein of humour (or was he being serious?):

> You've got to exchange the populations of Holland and Ireland. Then the Dutch will turn Ireland into a beautiful garden and the Irish will forget to mend the dikes and will all be drowned.

The poet Tennyson, meanwhile, querulously asked:

> Couldn't they blow up that horrible island with dynamite and carry it off in pieces – a long way off?
>
> Quoted in William Allingham, *Diary*, 19 September 1880

In the 20th century historians thought they'd at last understood the evasive nature of the beast:

> Gladstone ... spent his declining years trying to guess the answer to the Irish Question; unfortunately, whenever he was getting warm, the Irish secretly changed the Question.
>
> W.C. Sellar and R.J. Yeatman: *1066 and All That* (1930)

Irish rats. It was once the practice in Ireland to do away with rats by anathematizing them in verse or by metrical charms:

> I will not wish unto you ... to be rimed to death, as is said to be done in Ireland.
>
> Sir Philip Sidney: *The Defence of Poetry* (written 1579–80)

> I was never so be-rhymed since Pythagoras' time, that I was an Irish rat.
>
> William Shakespeare: *As You Like It* (1599), III.ii

Irish Republic, the. The Republic of Ireland (*see under* IRELAND).

Irish Republican Army, the. A guerrilla force largely created out of the **Irish Volunteers** (*see below*) by Michael Collins to fight British forces during the **Anglo-Irish War** (*see above*). It then proceeded to fight the government of the Irish Free State in a civil war lasting until 1923. The IRA continued to exist as an underground organization, and, although it was proscribed in 1936, it made occasional raids into Northern Ireland, its aim now being to establish a united Irish republic. It became much more active after the beginning of the more recent Troubles, beginning in 1968: the pro-military-action **Provisional IRA** (nicknamed **Provos**) split from the Official IRA to become the leading group and it mounted a terrorist campaign in Northern Ireland and mainland Britain. There was a ceasefire from 1994 to 1996, and another has been in place since 1997, allowing the Good Friday Agreement to be reached.

Irish Republican Brotherhood. The Irish branch of the Fenians, an anti-British secret society founded in New York in 1858 by John O'Mahony and in Ireland by James Stephens. Revolutionary and separatist in intent, in 1913 the IRB helped to found the **Irish Volunteers** (*see below*).

Irish rise. A slang term for either a pay cut (also **Irish promotion**) or the collapse of an erection; when fully functioning, an erection was, in the 19th century, called **Irish toothache** (*see below*).

Irish R.M., The. A compendium (1956) of stories by

E.O. Somerville (1858–1949) and her cousin Martin Ross (pen name of Violet Martin; 1862–1915), consisting of *Some Experiences of an Irish R.M.* (1899), *Further Experiences of an Irish R.M.* (1908) and *In Mr Knox's Country* (1915). The R.M. (resident magistrate) is Major Sinclair Yeates, appointed to Skebawn, County Cork, where he meets robust and ingenious opposition to his application of the law, while occasionally turning the tables on his tormentors.

Irish rose. A 20th-century rhyming slang term for 'nose', or, in 1930s American slang, a term for a thrown stone.

Irish St John's wort. A small-flowered St John's wort, *Hypericum canadense*.

Irish saxifrage. A white-flowered saxifrage, *Saxifraga rosacea*, not entirely dissimilar to mossy saxifrage, *S. hypnoides*.

Irish screwdriver. A slang term for a hammer (*compare* PAISLEY screwdriver and GLASGOW screwdriver).

Irish Sea. That part of the north Atlantic between Ireland and England, with the NORTH CHANNEL to the north and ST GEORGE'S CHANNEL to the south. (It is also a sea area used in the shipping forecast.) It is also sometimes known as the **Irish Channel**, and it provided a convenient invasion route for the Vikings:

> Since tonight the wind is high,
> The sea's white mane a fury
> I need not fear the hordes of Hell
> Coursing the Irish Channel.
>
> Written in the margin of the 9th-century St Gall manuscript,
> translated from the Irish by Frank O'Connor

Irish Channel is also Edwardian-era slang for the throat, a 'channel' for alcohol.

Irish setter. Another name for red setter, a breed of dog with a silky reddish-brown coat originating in Ireland.

Irish spurge. A small spurge, *Euphorbia hyberna*, as inconsequential in appearance as many a northern euphorbia and as toxic as all of its kin. Can it have been this plant that was etymologically responsible for the POISONED GLEN of Donegal?

Irish stew. A stew of mutton with potatoes (hence Irish), usually also containing onions and sometimes (although purists might decry it) other vegetables, such as carrots. In Depression-era America, it was known as **Irish caviar**. Irish stew is also rhyming slang for blue, and, as in the phrase **too Irish stew**, for true.

Irish terrier. A largish breed of terrier originating in Ireland, with a wiry coat, either wheaten or reddish in colour.

Irish Times, The. One of Ireland's leading national newspapers, founded in 1859. Once the voice of the Protestant Ascendancy, in the latter half of the 20th century it adopted a liberal voice in debates about Irish society.

Irish toothache. A 19th-century euphemism for pregnancy (also known as **Paddy's toothache**), and also for an erection.

Irish Volunteers. A Nationalist military organization founded in 1913, in response to the formation by Unionists earlier that year of the Ulster Volunteer Force. Although the **Irish Revolutionary Brotherhood** (*see above*) were involved, the Volunteers also drew on a much wider constituency, although on the outbreak of the First World War the majority followed John Redmond's call to form the National Volunteers. The more radical remainder of the Irish Volunteers took part in the Easter Rising in 1916, and it was from this group that the **Irish Republican Army** (*see above*) developed.

Irish wager. A rump of beef and a case of claret, which, in the later 18th century and early 19th century, was a popular bet among Protestant Ascendancy hell-raisers.

Irish wake. A description for any lively social gathering (including wakes).

Irish War of Independence. An alternative term for the **Anglo-Irish War** (*see above*). Historically, it is not a term that has been accepted by those who feel that Irish independence remains incomplete without the six counties of NORTHERN IRELAND.

Irish wash. A convenient method of reversing a garment to conceal stains rather than washing it.

Irish water spaniel. A breed of spaniel originating in Ireland and favoured by shooters of wildfowl. Its coat consists of liver-coloured dreadlocks.

Irish way. A slang term for heterosexual anal intercouse; the phrase is presumed to come from the belief that Irish Catholics use this method to avoid conception.

Irish wedding. An obsolete slang term for a 'donnybrook' (*see under* DONNYBROOK).

Irish whiskey. The type of whisky distilled in Ireland, generally sweeter than Scotch whisky.

Irish wolfhound. A big shaggy hound first bred in Ireland in ancient times. It is the tallest breed of dog – males are at least 78 cm (31 in) tall at the shoulder.

'Luck of the Irish, The'. A protest song (1972) by John Lennon (note his Irish name) and Yoko Ono, from the highly politicized album *Some Time in New York City*. It laments the long history of Irish oppression at English hands.

> If you had the luck of the Irish,
> You'd be sorry and wish you were dead
> You should have the luck of the Irish
> And you'd wish you was English instead!

The album also contained 'Sunday Bloody Sunday' excoriating British troops for their activities on that day. Lennon's ex-colleague Paul McCartney also weighed into this arena with his own protest song (*see under* IRELAND).

Royal Irish Constabulary. The centrally controlled and

armed police force of Ireland, formed in 1836 and disbanded in 1922 following the **Anglo-Irish War** (*see above*), in which over 400 members were killed, and the formation of the Irish Free State. It became 'Royal' in 1867.

Royal Irish Fusiliers. A regiment of the British Army, whose origins go back to 1793. They are nicknamed the Faughs, from their motto Faugh-a-Ballagh (Irish *Fág an bealach* 'clear the way'), first shouted by the Fusiliers during a bayonet charge in 1811 during the Peninsular War. In 1968 they (and the **North Irish Brigade**) formed the **Royal Irish Rangers**, which in turn became part of the **Royal Irish Regiment** along with the Ulster Defence Regiment in 1992.

United Irishmen. A society formed by Wolfe Tone in 1791 after the publication of his pamphlet *An Argument on Behalf of the Catholics of Ireland*. Its first headquarters were in Belfast, and its objects were to secure a representative national parliament and to unite all Irishmen against British influence. Membership included both Protestants and Catholics. The movement soon became revolutionary and was largely responsible for the rebellion of 1798, which is often known as the **United Irishmen's Rebellion** or the **1798 Insurgency**.

'When Irish Eyes Are Smiling'. A now-ubiquitous sentimental ballad (1912) written by the Americans Ernest R. Ball and Rida Johnson Young:

> When Irish eyes are smiling
> Sure it's like a morning spring.
> In the lilt of Irish laughter,
> You can hear the angels sing.

wild Irishman. Another name for matagouri or tumatakuri, a thorny thicket-forming bush from New Zealand. Its scientific name is *Discaria toumatou*.

Irish Bath, the. A nickname for the spa-town of MALLOW.

Irish Republic, the. *See under* IRELAND.

Irish Town. *See under* LIMERICK.

Irlam 'homestead on the River IRWELL', river name + HAM.
A town in Greater Manchester, 12 km (7.5 miles) southwest of the city centre.

Iron Acton *Iron* referring to old iron-workings in the vicinity; *Acton see* ACTON.
A village in South Gloucestershire (before 1996 in Avon, before 1974 in Gloucestershire), about 13 km (8 miles) northeast of Bristol.

Ironbridge From the iron bridge built here.
A town in Shropshire, within the unitary authority of TELFORD AND WREKIN, on the River SEVERN, about 8 km (5 miles) south of Telford. Between 1778 and 1781 the world's first cold-cast iron bridge was built here, crossing the steep and wooded **Ironbridge Gorge** (a UNESCO World Heritage Site) with a bold and simple central span that still impresses today. It was designed by Thomas Farnolls Pritchard, a Shrewsbury architect, and cast by Abraham Darby III at his nearby foundry at COALBROOKDALE. It weighs 386 tonnes (380 tons) and is 60 m (196 ft) long. These days only pedestrians are allowed to use it. It forms the centrepiece of the Ironbridge Gorge Museum. As the town spread up the sides of the gorge, it adopted the name of its most salient feature.

Iron Cross *Iron* perhaps 'corner of land', OE *hyrne*; *Cross* denoting a crossroads.
A village in Warwickshire, about 15 km (9 miles) west of Stratford-upon-Avon.

Iron Mountains From their former status as a source of iron ore; the last attempt to mine it was in 1765.
A range of hills in County Leitrim, rising to the east of LOUGH ALLEN. The highest point is Slieve Anierin (586 m / 1922 ft), said to have been the place where the mythical Tuatha Dé Danann arrived in Ireland on their magical ships. It was later a hunting ground of the Fianna. The elusive legendary figure of the Goban Saor supposedly exploited the iron ore but kept his techniques secret.

Iron Ring, the. Edward I's network of castles in North Wales, each a day's march from the next. They are at HARLECH, CAERNARFON, CONWY[2] and BEAUMARIS on Anglesey, and were built in the last two decades of the 13th century following the defeat of Llywelyn ap Gruffyd's rebellion of 1282. They were designed by the Savoyard master, James of St George, and incorporated the concept of the bastide (fortified town).

Ironville From the ironworks built here by the Butterley Iron Company. The name appears to have been coined in the late 1830s.
A village in Derbyshire, about 10 km (6 miles) northeast of Belper. It grew up in the middle of the 19th century around the ironworks that inspired its name.

Irthlingborough Probably 'ploughmen's fortified manor', OE *erthling, yrthling* 'ploughman' + *burh* 'fortified manor' (*see* BURY).
A small town in Northamptonshire, on the River NENE, about 5 km (3 miles) northeast of Wellingborough.
    Rushden and Diamonds FC (*see* RUSHDEN) play their home matches at Nene Park, Irthlingborough.

Irvine Possibly an ancient river name made up of Celtic elements meaning 'fresh river'; the second element is that which comes into Gaelic as *abhainn* (*see* AVON).
A medieval royal BURGH some 40 km (25 miles) southwest of Glasgow, on the North Ayrshire coast (formerly in Strathclyde region). It was designated a NEW TOWN[1] in 1967. It takes its name from the River Irvine, which enters the Firth of Clyde at **Irvine Bay**.

Every August since the 12th century the town has played host to the Marymass Fair, originally linked to the local church of St Mary, but since the visit of Mary Queen of Scots to the town in 1563 the Queen of the Fair has been dressed to look like her. The Bogside racecourse at Irvine (1806) is one of the oldest in the country.

Irvine was the birthplace of the novelist John Galt (1779–1839), author of *Annals of the Parish* (1821) and other works (in which Irvine became **Gudetown**); and Alexander Macmillan (1818–96), the younger of the two brothers who founded the publishing firm of Macmillan & Co.

Treaty of Irvine (1297). A capitulation to the English by the erstwhile supporters of William Wallace, including Robert the Bruce and Sir William Douglas. Wallace was obliged to flee northwards in an effort to raise more allies.

Irwell 'winding stream', OE *irre* 'winding' + *wella* 'stream'.
A river in Lancashire, with a length of 48 km (30 miles). It rises in the Forest of Rossendale (*see under* ROSSENDALE) south of Burnley, and some 6 km (4 miles) from the centre of Manchester flows into the Manchester Ship Canal (*see under* MANCHESTER), which itself feeds the Mersey. It was known as 'the most hard-worked river in the world' in the 19th century, when its waters were used by a host of cotton mills. As a result it also became one of the filthiest rivers in the world, although it is much cleaner today.

Isamnium. The name given by Ptolemy to NAVAN FORT.

Isca. The Roman name for the River USK[1].

Isca Silurum. *See under* CAERLEON.

Isis From *Tamesis*, an early form of the name *Thames*, based on the misapprehension that it was made up of the river name THAME[1] + *Isis* (with the Egyptian goddess, sister and wife of Osiris, in mind).
A name sometimes applied at OXFORD and further upstream to the River THAMES[1]. The antiquary John Leland is on record as using it around 1535, and it appeared officially in a statute of George II in 1751.

The name has been transferred to an Oxford University magazine, first published in 1892, whose contributors are mainly undergraduates and whose tone and political orientation have veered about considerably over the decades; and to the second-string Oxford University rowing crew, which races against Cambridge University's 'Goldie' before the main Boat Race.

In Max Beerbohm's novel *Zuleika Dobson* (1911), the undergraduate population of Oxford drowns itself in the Isis after being rejected by the eponymous heroine.

Swifter, Isis, Swifter Flow. A court ode (subtitled 'A Welcome Song in the Year 1681 for the King') composed by Henry Purcell and dedicated to Charles II. Purcell's biographer Jonathan Keates believes that it may have been written to welcome Charles II back to London on 28 March

1681 after Parliament had finished a session held in Oxford (Charles had invoked an old law that allowed him to summon the Lords and Commons to assemble in a place of the sovereign's choosing – and he cleverly chose Royalist Oxford).

Island, the[1]. A colloquial name for the ISLE OF WIGHT.

> She thinks of nothing but the Isle of Wight, and she calls it *the Island*, as if there were no other island in the world.
>
> Jane Austen: *Mansfield Park* (1814)

Island, the[2]. The local name for Queen's Island, BELFAST, especially of the shipyard sited there.

Island Magee Irish *Oileán Mhic Aodha* 'island of Mac Aodha'.
A north–south peninsula in County ANTRIM lying parallel to the main coast between Larne Lough (*see under* LARNE) and the NORTH CHANNEL. It is also spelt **Islandmagee**. The basalt cliffs on the east side are called the Gobbins (Irish *na Gobáin* 'the peaks'). The peninsula was noted for witchcraft, and in 1711 several local women were imprisoned following the last witchcraft trial in Ireland; a century later, in 1808, another local woman was charged with witchcraft, but the charge was dismissed. The discovery of mysterious paraphernalia in a cave in the Gobbins in 1961 renewed speculation about the continued practice of the Dark Arts on Island Magee.

Island Magee Massacre. A much disputed event, in which it was said that in 1641 or 1642 Scots and English soldiers carried out a massacre of local Catholics and cast their bodies over the Gobbins cliffs. In 1936 John Hewitt wrote a dramatic poem about the massacre entitled *The Bloody Brae*.

Island of 20,000 Saints, the. A name for BARDSEY ISLAND, referring to the number of monks supposedly buried on the island.

Island of Saints and Scholars. A description of Ireland, possibly coined by Archbishop John Healy in 1893. He claimed that the phrase went back to medieval times, but in fact only 'Island of Saints' appears to be of this antiquity (*Hibernia insula sanctorum*, according to Marianus Scottus in 1083). However, the 'scholars' claim is certainly justified, given the role that Irish *docti* played in the intellectual history of medieval Europe.

Islay 'swelling island', Old Celtic *ili*, which seems to be cognate with an earlier element *il*- 'swift (i.e. swelling) river'. In Adamnan's *Life of Columba* (*c*.690) the name is given as *Ilea*, and it is likely that the modern -AY derives from OScand *ey* 'island' by analogy with Oronsay and others, and the *Isl*- by analogy with 'island'. The modern Gaelic name is *Ìle*.
A large island (pronounced 'aye-lay' or 'aye-lə') at the southern edge of the Inner Hebrides, in Argyll and Bute (formerly in Strathclyde region). It is about 25 km (16 miles)

west of the KINTYRE peninsula, and is separated from JURA to the north by the narrow **Sound of Islay**, which is less than 1 km (0.6 mile) across. The island, sometimes referred to as the **Queen of the Hebrides**, is celebrated for its whisky (*see below*). It was once renowned for rearing horses, and there was a saying that

> An Islay man will carry a bridle and saddle for a mile in order to ride half a mile.

In the later Middle Ages Islay was the seat of the Macdonald Lords of the Isles (*see* ISLES, LORDSHIP OF THE); their headquarters were at a castle (now ruined) on an island in Loch Finlaggan. In 1598 Maclean of Duart (*see* DUART CASTLE) invaded the island with 400 men in pursuit of a territorial claim; nearly all were killed by the local Macdonalds in a fierce battle at the head of Loch Gruinart. The Macdonalds were apparently aided by Du-sith, a black elf, and they capped their victory by burning down the church in which 30 Maclean survivors had taken sanctuary.

Islay herald. One of the heralds of the Lyon Court (the Scottish Court of Heralds).

Islay malts. Malt whiskies known for their smoky quality. There are eight distilleries on Islay, each producing its own distinctive malt. These are: Ardbeg, Bowmore, Bruichladdich, Bunnahabhain, Caol Ila, Lagavulin, Laphroaig and Port Ellen.

> What do I remember? A litany of whiskies:
> Lagavulin, Laphroaig, Talisker, Aberlour,
> The Macallan – the hot sweet smoked malt
> that I burned of and for you …
>
> Sarah Maguire (b.1957): 'Uisge Beatha'

In 2003 the Bruichladdich distillery came under the scrutiny of the shadowy US Defence Threat Reduction Agency: apparently its agents had been surfing the Web, and on finding the distillery's site, found that with 'just a small tweak' its facilities could be converted to the production of chemical weapons.

Rinns of Islay Probably OCelt *roinn* 'headland', 'promontory', the origin of Gaelic *rinn* 'sharp point'.

❖ isle ❖

This word is derived ultimately from Old English *egland* 'island'; the *-s-* was apparently added in the Early Modern period by analogy with Latin *insula*, which also means 'island'. Not surprisingly given this etymology, isle shares many of the senses that *eg* has (*see* -EY, -EA). The water-surrounded islands include the ISLE OF MAN and the ISLE OF WIGHT; partially surrounded isles, which protrude into water, include the ISLE OF THANET and the ISLE OF GRAIN (both in Kent); inland islands of dry ground in marshland include the ISLE OF ELY (Cambridgeshire) and the ISLE OF AXHOLME (Lincolnshire).

A southwestward-pointing peninsula on the west side of Islay. Its most southerly point is **Rinns Point**.

Isle An OCelt river name of uncertain meaning.

A river in Somerset, which rises near CHARD and flows 24 km (15 miles) northeastwards through ILMINSTER to join the River PARRETT to the south of Langport.

Isle Abbotts *Isle* from the River ISLE; *Abbotts* denoting manorial ownership in the Middle Ages by the nearby Muchelney Abbey.

A village on an isolated mound in the Somerset Levels (*see under* SOMERSET), about 13 km (8 miles) southwest of Taunton. The tower of its church, St Mary's, is unusually imposing.

Isle Brewers *Brewers* denoting manorial ownership in the Middle Ages by the Briwer family.

A village in the Somerset Levels (*see under* SOMERSET), about 15 km (9 miles) southwest of Taunton.

Isleham 'Gisla's homestead', OE male personal name *Gisla* + HAM.

A village in Cambridgeshire, about 16 km (10 miles) southeast of Ely. **Isleham Fen** is to the northwest.

Isle Maree. See under LOCH MAREE.

Isle of Anglesey. *See* ANGLESEY.

Isle of Athelney. *See under* ATHELNEY.

Isle of Axholme *Axholme* 'raised land in a marsh belonging to Haxey', *Haxey see* HAXEY + OScand *holmr* 'raised land in a marsh' (*see* -EY, -EA); the introduction of ISLE, also denoting 'raised land in a marsh', is hence tautological.

An area in North Lincolnshire, about 2000 ha (500 acres) in extent, centred on the small town of EPWORTH, to the southwest of Scunthorpe. It is bounded by the rivers Don, IDLE, Torne and TRENT[1]. The FENS were drained in the early 17th century by the Dutch water engineer Cornelius Vermuyden (*see also* BEDFORD LEVEL, FORTY FOOT DRAIN, HUNDRED FOOT DRAIN *and* CANVEY ISLAND), and it is now good agricultural land. A form of medieval-style open-field strip farming is still practised here.

Isle of Dogs Probably 'peninsula frequented by (wild or stray) dogs'. The name (first recorded in 1520) may well originally have been applied facetiously, with more decorous models such as *Isle of Man* ironically in mind. (A.D. Mills in his *Dictionary of London Place Names* (2001) speculates that perhaps it was suggested by the Spanish island of Canary, etymologically the 'isle of dogs', wines from which were no doubt landed at the Isle of Dogs in the early days.) The idea that it might be an allusion to kennels on the peninsula where royal hunting dogs were kept when the king (some specify Edward III) was at Greenwich is not implausible but has never been substantiated. Other more far-fetched theories – that the name is an alteration of *isle of docks* or *isle of ducks* (from the wealth of wild fowl that once grazed on it), or that it alludes to dead dogs washed up on the left bank of the peninsula – have little beyond entertainment value to recommend them.

A low-lying peninsula in East London (E14), in the borough of TOWER HAMLETS, formed by a southern loop of the River THAMES[1], between LIMEHOUSE and Blackwall Reaches (*see under* BLACKWALL) and opposite GREENWICH. It contains the districts of MILLWALL and POPLAR.

Flat, cheerless and marshy, it remained largely unused and uninhabited until the 19th century. It then became a home for the expansion of London's docks: first the West India Docks in 1802, then the East India Docks in 1806, and later, in the 1860s, Millwall Dock. Houses built for the dock workers to live in, and the area soon bred its own communities.

> The working men of the Isle of Dogs number some 15,000, engaged in the numerous factories and shipyards; for whose recreation has been formed a Free Library, to provide them with amusement for evenings too often spent in dissipation.
>
> John Timbs: *Curiosities of London* (1867)

The docks were the main engine of the peninsula's economy until the last third of the 20th century, when they quickly ceased to be commercially viable (*see* DOCKLAND). By 1980 they were all closed, and in the succeeding two decades extensive redevelopment took place on the Isle of Dogs (most spectacularly in the shape of CANARY WHARF), leading the drive to relocate London's commercial centre of gravity from the City eastwards.

In *Eastward Hoe* (1605), a comedy by George Chapman, Ben Jonson and John Marston, the less deserving characters are shipwrecked on the Isle of Dogs.

> The river sweats
> Oil and tar
> The barges drift
> With the turning tide
> Red sails
> Wide
> To leeward, swing on the heavy spar.
> The barges wash
> Drifting logs
> Down Greenwich reach
> Past the Isle of Dogs.
>
> T.S. Eliot: *The Waste Land* (1922)

Isle of Dogs, The. A lost satirical comedy by the author and dramatist Thomas Nashe (1567–1601). It was sufficiently inflammatory to get Nashe into trouble with the authorities.

Isle of Ely. *See under* ELY[1].

Isle of Grain *Grain* 'gravelly or sandy ground', OE *greon*; *Isle see* ISLE.

A promontory on the north coast of Kent, on the western side of the mouth of the MEDWAY[1] estuary, opposite SHEERNESS. The village of Grain is at its northeastern corner. When it got its name (first recorded in 1610) it was literally an island, but sand, mud and silt have since conspired to join it on to the mainland.

The Isle of Grain power station was, when it opened in the 1950s, the largest oil-fired power station in Europe.

Isle of Harty *Harty* 'island frequented by stags', OE *heorot* 'hart, stag' + *eg* 'island' (*see* -EY, -EA); the introduction of ISLE, also denoting 'island', is hence tautological.

The southeastern corner of the ISLE OF SHEPPEY, off the north coast of Kent.

Isle of Man Traditionally derived from *Manannán mac Lir* ('Mannanan, son of the land of promise'), an ancient Irish sea god who ruled an island paradise. Another theory was mooted by Richard of Cirencester (d.*c*.1401), who wrote 'Midway between the two countries [Britain and Ireland] is the island called Monoeda, but now Monavia', i.e. deriving from Gaelic *menagh* or *meanagh* 'middle'. Supporters of this theory point out that a circle drawn with Man to Land's End or John O'Groats as the radius will almost exactly encircle the British Isles; however, they assume very accurate cartography on the part of the first namers.

A large island in the Irish Sea, some 50 km (31 miles) west of the Cumbrian coast, and a similar distance from the coasts of Scotland and Ireland. The capital is DOUGLAS[2], and other towns include CASTLETOWN (the former capital), PEEL and RAMSEY[2]. The beaches round the otherwise rocky coast make it a popular tourist destination, and there are hills inland, the highest being SNAEFELL (621 m / 2037 ft). In Irish legend, it was formed when a giant (possibly Finn MacCool) scooped up a chunk of Ulster (so creating LOUGH NEAGH) and hurled it across the sea at the Scottish giant Fingal (who was possibly the same person as Finn, but not in this account).

The Isle of Man is also spelled **Isle of Mann**; in Manx it is **Ellan Vannin** or **Mannin** (both variants meaning 'island of Mann'), in Irish Oileán Mhanannán ('Manannán's Isle'), while the Romans called it **Mona** (as they did Anglesey) or **Monapia**.

> Snaefell, Tynwald, Ben-my-Chree,
> Fourteen ships have sailed the sea.
> Each one bearing a Manx name,
> But there's one will never again.
> *Oh Ellen Vannen,*
> *Of the Isle of Man Company,*
> *Oh Ellen Vannen,*
> *Lost in the Irish Sea.*
>
> Hughie Jones: 'The *Ellen Vannen* Tragedy' (The *Ellen Vannen*

was an Isle of Man steam packet lost in a storm in 1909; Hughie Jones was a member of the now disbanded folk group The Spinners.)

The Isle of Man has been occupied since the end of the last Ice Age. Irish missionaries came here in the 5th and 6th centuries, and around 800 the Vikings arrived – despite what William Wordsworth wrote:

> Bold words affirmed, in days when faith was strong,
> And doubts and scruples seldom teazed the brain,
> That no adventurer's bark had power to gain
> These shores if he approached them bent on wrong ...

William Wordsworth: 'At Sea off the Isle of Man' (1833)

The island was under Norwegian rule until 1266, when it passed to the Scottish Crown. In 1341 it came under English control, its feudal lords beings styled first 'kings' then 'lords of Mann'. The lordship of Mann passed to the dukes of Atholl in 1736, and the island's sovereignty was purchased by the British Parliament in 1765 (in order to suppress smuggling); the dukes' final rights were surrendered in 1828.

Technically, the Isle of Man is not a part of the UK, but rather a dependency of the Crown, and Westminster laws do not apply to it unless specifically stated. Thus the island has became a haven for sundry fat cats wishing to avoid UK tax, and for those yearning for a less tolerant past (homosexuality was illegal until 1992, and capital and corporal punishment were not abolished until 1993 – prior to this, birching of young offenders was a popular pastime). The island has its own parliament, the Tynwald, comprising the Lord of Mann (appointed by the sovereign), the Legislative Council and the representative House of Keys. Although the island uses sterling, it mints its own coins and notes; in 2002 it issued a series of six 25p coins featuring scenes from the film of J.K. Rowling's *Harry Potter and the Chamber of Secrets*.

The island used to have its fair share of native magic: however, it was said that when the railways arrived in the 19th century, the fairy folk (including sundry goblin-types such as bugganes and glashans) left the island, for, according to the saying, 'cold iron is death to the People of the Hills'. A wave of new residents arrived during the Second World War, when the Isle of Man was used for the internment of 'enemy aliens', mostly Italians and German Jews; the members of the Amadeus Quartet met while confined in one of the camps on the island.

The islanders, known as **Manxmen**, used to speak a Celtic language called **Manx**, related to Scottish Gaelic, but this began to die out in the 19th century and officially became a dead language when its last native speaker died in 1971 – although it is now being taught in the island's schools, and appears on dual-language road signs. The island is also responsible for the tailless

Manx cat. There is a novel called *The Manxman* (1894) by Sir Hall Caine, who settled on the island and sat in the House of Keys.

The island's best-known poet, often writing in Manx dialect, was T.E. Brown (1830–97); he wrote the following lines while in England:

> I wonder if in that far isle
> Some child is growing now, like me
> When I was child: care pricked, yet healed the while
> With balm of rock and sea.

T.E. Brown: 'Braddan Vicarage'

Another littérateur from the island is Nigel Kneale (b.1922). In his alarmingly prescient television play *The Year of the Sex Olympics* (1968) a television producer has the brainwave of putting a man, woman and child alone on an island (in fact, the Isle of Man), watching them 24 hours a day, and then making things more interesting by adding a murderer to the mix.

> The Manxman is never wise till the day after the fair.

Traditional Manx saying

See also SODOR AND MAN.

Isle of Man cabbage. A hairless crucifer, *Rhynchosinapis monensis*. It is a member of the cabbage family, with yellow flowers and an almost leafless stem.

Isle of Man TT (Tourist Trophy). An annual motorbike race around the island's winding, hilly roads, involving six laps of 60 km (37.5 miles) and, not infrequently, a number of fatalities. It was first run in 1911, and despite being the most famous motorcycle race in the world, ceased to be a world-championship event in 1976.

Isle of May 'gull island', OScand *mar* 'seagull' + *ey* (*see* -AY); the name *Maeyar* was first recorded in the 13th century.

A small cliff-girt island that guards the entrance to the Firth of FORTH, some 8 km (5 miles) off the coast of Fife. It is an important breeding ground for sea birds and is a National Nature Reserve.

In the period of the Viking raids, St Adrian, Bishop of St Andrews, tried to take refuge here but was caught and murdered (*c*.870). Subsequently the island became a place of pilgrimage and was given by King David I (reigned 1124–53) to the Benedictines of Reading in England, and a priory was built. The island later returned to Scottish ownership, and a small hermitage replaced the ruined priory. In the early 17th century the island's then owner, John Cunynghame of Barnes, built a lighthouse on the island, and the Scottish Parliament granted him the right to levy a tariff on shipping. The island was sold to the Commissioners of Northern Lights (the lighthouses authority) in 1815, and it remains in their possession.

See also TRAPRAIN LAW.

Isle of Oxney *Oxney* 'island where oxen are kept', OE *oxena* possessive plural form of *oxa* 'ox' + *eg* 'island' (*see* -EY, -EA); the introduction of ISLE, also denoting 'island', is hence tautological.

An area of land in Kent, to the west of ROMNEY MARSH. As its name suggests, it was originally dry land surrounded by marshes.

Isle of Portland. *See* PORTLAND.

Isle of Purbeck. *See under* PURBECK.

Isle of Sheppey *Sheppey* 'island where sheep are kept', OE *sceap* 'sheep' + *eg* 'island' (*see* -EY, -EA) (*compare* FAIR ISLE); the introduction of ISLE, also denoting 'island', is hence tautological.

An island in Kent, on the south bank of the Thames Estuary, at the mouth of the River MEDWAY[1], in the administrative district of SWALE[3], about 4 km (2.5 miles) north of Sitting-bourne. It is about 16 km (10 miles) long by 8 km (5 miles) wide. It is separated from the mainland by the River SWALE[2], and joined to it by a bridge (Kingsferry Bridge, completed in 1960) that can be raised to allow the passage of boats. Its main settlements are MINSTER[1] and SHEERNESS. In keeping with its name, sheep still graze here, on pastures reclaimed from the Swale.

Isle of Thanet *Thanet* an OCelt name possibly meaning 'bright island' (perhaps with reference to a beacon).

A promontory at the northeastern tip of Kent, edged with chalk cliffs. It contains the three seaside towns of BROAD-STAIRS, MARGATE and RAMSGATE, and to its south is Pegwell Bay (*see under* PEGWELL).

It was the front door to England for the Romans (*see* RICHBOROUGH), and by tradition it is the place where the Saxons first landed on their fateful cross-Channel excursions (*see* EBBSFLEET). At that time, Thanet was cut off from the mainland by the Rivers STOUR[3] and Wantsum.

Isle of Walney 'killer whale island', OScand *vogn* 'killer whale' + *ey* 'island' (*see* -AY); the introduction of ISLE, also denoting 'island', is hence tautological.

A long, thin island just west of Barrow-in-Furness, Cumbria (formerly in Lancashire), between the DUDDON estuary and MORECAMBE Bay. It is connected to Barrow by a bridge. On its southeastern side it encloses the inlet where Barrow's shipbuilding industry is based.

Isle of Wight *Wight* an OCelt name perhaps meaning 'place of the division' (referring to the island's position between the two arms of the Solent).

A rhomboidal island and unitary authority off the Hampshire coast, opposite Southampton Water (*see under* SOUTHAMPTON). Known also simply as 'the ISLAND', it is separated from the mainland by a channel called the SOLENT. It is 381 sq km (147 sq miles) in area. It was known

to the Romans as **Vectis**, and according to the Anglo-Saxon scholar the Venerable Bede was one of the principal locations of settlement of the Germanic invaders known as the Jutes. Technically, the Isle of Wight is part of the historical county of Hampshire, but it has always had an independent spirit. In 1890 it was designated as an administrative county in its own right, and in 1995 it was declared a unitary authority (the first such to be created). Its administrative headquarters are in NEWPORT[2], and other important towns are COWES, RYDE, SANDOWN, SHANKLIN, VENTNOR and YARMOUTH[1].

It is mainly open downland, whose chalk (it has the thickest bed of chalk in the British Isles) makes itself most spectacularly known in the NEEDLES, at the island's western tip. Its extensive sandy beaches (not to mention its mild and sunny climate) have made it a much visited holiday destination. Ferries serve it from Lymington, Portsmouth, Southampton and Southsea.

The island's popularity received a boost in the 19th century from two high-profile residents: Queen Victoria, for whom OSBORNE HOUSE, near Cowes, was a favourite residence (she died there), and the poet Alfred, Lord Tennyson, who lived near FRESHWATER from 1853 to 1869; he wrote to the Christian Socialist F.D. Maurice:

> ... come to the Isle of Wight;
> Where far from noise and smoke of town,
> I watch the twilight falling brown
> All round a careless order'd garden
> Close to the ridge of a noble down.

A more reluctant temporary royal resident was Charles I, who was imprisoned in CARISBROOKE Castle, 1647–8. The tradition of incarceration (backed up by 5 km / 3 miles of open sea) is continued in Parkhurst Prison, near Newport.

> It appears scarcely credible that the Isle of Wight should be selected as a depot for the worst offenders of England. It is unfortunate enough for the island to be the home for the consumptives of England. It is foolish enough that for a petty economy we try to fill the island asylum with lunatics from other countries. It is bad enough that the Isle of Wight at Parkhurst should have been selected as a penal station for the convicts of other parts of England. And now, forsooth, another convict prison is to be erected in Parkhurst forest (one of the loveliest of England) for the internment of habitual criminals. What is the Isle of Wight County Council about?
>
> Admiral Sir Algernon de Horsey, Joint Deputy Governor of the Isle of Wight: letter to *The Times* (15 August 1908)

Not surprisingly, the Isle of Wight has strong links with the sea. Boatbuilding is economically important, and Cowes, headquarters of the Royal Yacht Squadron, hosts a world-famous annual regatta. A trophy presented by the Squadron in 1851 for a race around the island was won by the New York schooner *America*, and subsequently became known as the 'America's Cup'.

In the late 1960s the Island grooved to an annual rock festival, which was revived in 2002. The scientist Robert Hooke (1635–1703), Dr Thomas Arnold (1795–1842), celebrated headmaster of Rugby School, and the polar explorer Sir Vivian Fuchs (1908–99) were born on the island.

In the 20th century, *Isle of Wight* was used as rhyming slang for 'light', 'all right' and 'tight' (in the sense of 'mean').

There is an Isle of Wight county in Virginia, USA.

Of all the southern isles [Wight] holds the highest place,
And ever since hath been the great'st in Britain's grace.

> Michael Drayton: *Poly-Olbion* (1612–22)

Seen from the west, the Wight is beautiful beyond all laws of beauty. It is as if a fragment of England floated forward to greet the foreigner – chalk of our chalk, turf of our turf, epitome of what will follow.

> E.M. Forster: *Howards End* (1914)

Isle of Wight disease. A disease of bees caused by the parasitic mite *Acarapis woodsi*. It was first identified on the Isle of Wight in 1904.

Isle of Wight vine. An alternative name for the climbing plant bryony or black bryony.

Isles, Lordship of the. The title 'Lord of the Isles' is an ancient one. It was originally held by the Norse rulers of the HEBRIDES, and then passed to the Macdonalds, whose seat was in ISLAY. Although notionally vassals of the Scottish kings, the Lords of the Isles were in fact supreme in their fiefdom. James IV ended this situation in 1493, when he forfeited the title, which later become one of the titles borne by princes of Wales. Sir Walter Scott's long narrative poem *The Lord of the Isles* (1815) is set at the time of the Scottish Wars of Independence in the early 14th century. Lord Ronald is the eponymous Lord of the Isles, beloved of the lovelorn Edith of LORNE.

Isles of Scilly. *See* SCILLY ISLES.

Isles of the Sea. *See* the GARVELLACHS.

Isleworth 'Gislhere's enclosed settlement', OE male personal name *Gislhere* + *worth* (*see* -WORTH, WORTHY, -WARDINE).
A district (pronounced 'eye-zəlworth') of outer West London, on the west bank of the River THAMES[1], in the borough of HOUNSLOW (before 1965 in Middlesex), to the north of Twickenham and to the west of Richmond. Van Gogh taught painting here in the 1870s. In the 20th century its former fields were covered over with houses and the huge West Middlesex Drainage Works. The composer E.J. Moeran (1894–1950) was born in Isleworth, and today the headquarters of Sky TV are here.

Isleworth Ait. A long, narrow island in the River Thames opposite Isleworth.

Islington 'Gisla's hill', OE *Gislan* possessive form of male personal name *Gisla* + *dun* (*see* DOWN, -DON).
A district and borough of North London (N1, N5, N7, N19, EC1), to the north of the City of London and to the west of Hackney. The present borough was formed in 1965 by the amalgamation of the former metropolitan boroughs of Islington and FINSBURY. As well as those areas, it includes Finsbury Park, HIGHBURY, HOLLOWAY, TUFNELL PARK and part of HIGHGATE.

When Islington was still a rural hilltop village it was a popular resort for Londoners to take the air and recreate themselves – and especially, from the late 17th century onwards, to sample the medicinal springs and associated delights of nearby SADLER'S WELLS. It used to be known as 'merry Islington':

Thus all through merry Islington
These gambols he did play.

> William Cowper: *John Gilpin* (1782)

But in the early 19th century it became covered over with brick – the yellowish-grey London stock-brick – and by the 20th century it had developed a reputation as one of the poorer and less desirable areas of London (in the game of Monopoly, the ANGEL Islington rates only £100).

In the 1960s its run-down but elegant and cheap squares and terraces – Barnsbury Square, for instance, and Gibson Square – began to attract middle-class residents back into the area, setting in train the process of gentrification – yuppies on the march, squads of builders' skips in every road – that Islington came to exemplify. By the end of the 20th century it combined radical chic with mega-trendiness: successful maturing Leftish baby-boomers lived here, and it was the natural birthplace of New Labour (Chris Smith, Labour MP for Islington South and Finsbury since 1983, was the first openly gay cabinet minister); and the offspring of the baby-boomers generated a youthful café culture that transformed the centre of Islington (Upper Street, its main artery, is almost wall-to-wall restaurants and bars, relieved only by the occasional estate agent). The political and culinary tendencies combined most memorably in the legendary meeting at the 'Cal-Ital' inspired Granita restaurant (now closed) on Upper Street at which Tony Blair and Gordon Brown resolved the ticklish question as to which of them should become the leader of the Labour Party. Beneath the gloss, however, Islington remains a relatively poor borough, with many social problems.

The artist William Heath Robinson (1872–1944), inventor of fantastical machinery, was born in Islington.
'Bailiff's Daughter of Islington, The'. A ballad given in

Percy's *Reliques* (1765) on the popular theme of a pair of lovers, a squire's son and a bailiff's daughter, separated by differences of social rank. It begins:

> There was a youth, and a well-beloved youth, and he was
>   a squire's son,
> And he loved the bailiff's daughter fair that lived in
>   Islington.

Some doubt has been cast on whether the Islington referred to is the one in London. An alternative settlement in Norfolk has been suggested (there is a Tilney cum Islington just to the southwest of KING'S LYNN, and an Islington Hall Farm and an Islington Lodge are nearby). There is little or nothing in the text to suggest one location rather that the other, however. In American versions of the story, Islington has appeared as 'Ireland Town' and 'Hazelington Town'.

Islington Man. A middle-class socially aware person of (fairly) left-wing views, regarded as typical of Islington, a usage that is more jibe than compliment.

> Just as Essex Man ... represented the 1980s, Islington Man
> – more properly Islington Person – may turn out to be the
> most potent composite of the late 1990s.
>
>   Cal McCrystal: *Independent on Sunday* (17 July 1994)

Islip 'slippery place by the River Ight' (former name of the River Ray), *Ight* pre-English river name of uncertain meaning + OE *slæp* 'slippery place'.
A village (pronounced 'eye-slip') in Oxfordshire, on the River Ray, about 8 km (5 miles) north of Oxford. King Edward the Confessor (*c*.1003–66) was born here.

Itchen A pre-Celtic river name of unknown origin and meaning.
A river in Hampshire. It rises about 13 km (8 miles) northeast of Winchester and flows 40 km (25 miles) southwards through WINCHESTER and EASTLEIGH into SOUTHAMPTON Water. Its chalk stream is the natural habitat of the trout, and along with the TEST it is one of the two great fly-fishing rivers of Hampshire. It found great favour with Izaak Walton, author of *The Compleat Angler* (1653):

> The Itchen is a lovely stream, full of trout and grayling.
> Walton would have hunted them with worm or minnow
> or grasshopper, as the season directed; but no doubt he
> fished the natural mayfly when the big ephemera was up,
> dapping it skilfully over the deep pools, wafting it ahead
> of him on the wind over the shallows.
>
>   Roderick Haig-Brown: 'Izaak Walton: his friends and his
>   rivers', from *The Steelheader Salmon and Trout News*

The watermeadows by the Itchen were the inspiration for John Keats's ode 'To Autumn' (1820) ('Season of mists and mellow fruitfulness ...').

Itchland. A slang term for both WALES and SCOTLAND, in use from the later 17th century until the early 19th century,

presumably because early travellers found these countries flea-ridden, or possibly because they found the inhabitants highly sexed. Scotland also has the honour of the alternative nickname **Scratchland**.

Iveagh Etymology unknown.
A traditional area of County DOWN. In early times the petty kings of Iveagh had their seat at RATHFRILAND, and Iveagh later became a barony. The brewer Edward Guinness (1847–1927), great-grandson of the first Arthur Guinness, took the title **Earl of Iveagh**, and on his death he left his collection of 18th- and 19th-century paintings to the nation; the **Iveagh Bequest** (especially noted for its Gainsboroughs) may be viewed at Kenwood House (*see under* KEN WOOD) on Hampstead Heath, London.

Ivel 'forked stream', OCelt.
A river in Bedfordshire, rising to the north of Luton and flowing 48 km (30 miles) northeast and north through BIGGLESWADE to join the GREAT OUSE near Tempsford (just to the south of ST NEOTS).

Iver '(place by the) brow of a hill or tip of a promontory', OE *yfer*.
A village in Buckinghamshire, about 6 km (4 miles) east of Slough. A little to the north is **Iver Heath**, location since 1936 of Pinewood Film Studios, founded by J. Arthur Rank in partnership with a wealthy local builder called Charles Boot. The studies merged with Shepperton Film Studios (*see under* SHEPPERTON) in 2001.

Iveragh Possibly 'territory of the Iverni', Irish *uibh* 'grandson' and by extension 'tribe' + tribal name *Iverna*, perhaps Ptolemy's *Ivernoi*.
A wide peninsula in southwestern County Kerry, between the DINGLE and BEARA peninsulas. It includes the MACGILLYCUDDY'S REEKS, and is circled by the Ring of Kerry (*see under* County KERRY).

Ivinghoe 'Ifa's people's hill-spur', OE male personal name *Ifa* + *-inga-* (*see* -ING) + *hoh* 'hill-spur'.
A village in Buckinghamshire, about 14 km (8.5 miles) east of Aylesbury, at the northern end of the main ridge of the CHILTERN HILLS. The nearby **Ivinghoe Beacon**, 232 m (761 ft) high, is a frequent recreational destination for northward-venturing London suburb-dwellers and kite-flyers. It is at the northern end of the Ridgeway National Trail (*see under* RIDGEWAY).

Ivybridge 'ivy-covered bridge', OE *ifig* 'ivy' + *bricg* 'bridge'.
A town in Devon, on the River Erme, on the southern fringes of Dartmoor, about 16 km (10 miles) east of Plymouth.

Ivy Todd Probably 'bush or mass of ivy', *Ivy* OE *ifig* 'ivy'; *Todd* 'overgrown mass', OE.
A village in Norfolk, about 8 km (5 miles) east of Swaffham.

Iwade 'ford or crossing-place where yew-trees grow' (referring to a crossing-place from the mainland to the Isle of Sheppey), OE *iw* 'yew' + (*ge*)*wæd* 'ford, crossing-place' (*see* FORD).

A village (pronounced 'eye-wade') in northern Kent, about 5 km (3 miles) north of Sittingbourne. The crossing to the nearby ISLE OF SHEPPEY alluded to in the name is now accomplished by a modern bridge.

Iwerne An OCelt river name, possibly meaning 'yew river' or referring to a goddess.

A river (pronounced 'yew-ən' or 'yew-ern') in Dorset, a tributary of the River STOUR[1]. It joins the Stour about 6.5 km (4 miles) northwest of Blandford Forum. It is about 8 km (5 miles) long.

Iwerne Courtney *Iwerne* from the River Iwerne; *Courtney* denoting manorial ownership in the Middle Ages by the Courtenay family. (Its alternative name is *Iwerne Shroton*. The second element is 'sheriff's estate', OE *scir-refa* 'sheriff' + -TON.)

A village in Dorset, on the River IWERNE, at the western end of Cranborne Chase (*see under* CRANBORNE), about 8 km (5 miles) south of Shaftesbury.

J

Jacobstow 'holy place of St James', from the dedication of the local church to St James, Latin *Jacobus* 'James' + OE *stow* '(holy) place'.

A village in north Cornwall, about 11 km (7 miles) south of Bude.

Jacobstowe For origin *see* JACOBSTOW.

A village in Devon, about 6.5 km (4 miles) north of Okehampton.

Jago, the. A fictionalized version of a 19th-century East London slum off SHOREDITCH High Street, known in real life as 'the Nichol'. Its portrayal in the novel *A Child of the Jago* (1896) by Arthur Morrison (1863–1945) brought the area's appalling conditions to public notice, and it was credited as a major influence on the decision to clear the slums.

Jailteacht. *See* GAELTACHT.

Jamaica Inn. A hotel in the middle of Bodmin Moor (*see under* BODMIN), near the village of Bolventor, on the A30. In earlier centuries it was a coaching inn, and its romantically isolated position inspired Daphne du Maurier to make it the focus of her historical romance *Jamaica Inn* (1936). In the story the inn is the centre of the activities of a gang of smugglers, while divided loyalties inform the romantic aspects of the plot. A film version (1939), starring Charles Laughton and Maureen O'Hara, was directed by Alfred Hitchcock.

James's Street After the old St *James's* Church here, still extant in the 16th century.

The street in DUBLIN where the Guinness brewery is situated. The street was also once the site of a famous foundling hospital, and in the 18th century it formed part of the course of a whipping run for the punishment of wrongdoers.

James's Street! A euphemistic expletive used in Ireland.

Jarlshof 'chieftain's house', OScand *jarl* 'chieftain, nobleman' + *hof* 'temple, hall'. The name is not old, however: it was devised by Sir Walter Scott in his novel *The Pirate* (1821); Scott had visited the site in 1816.

A remarkable archaeological site in the very south of Mainland, Shetland, some 33 km (20 miles) south of Lerwick. There are the remains of Bronze Age, Iron Age, Norse and later medieval settlements.

Jarrow 'land of the Gyrwe', a tribal name from OE *gyr* 'mud, marsh', referring to the *Jarrow Slake* (a corruption of Jarrow Lake), an area of the Tyne estuary east of the town.

A town in Tyne and Wear (formerly in County Durham), on the south bank of the TYNE 8 km (5 miles) east of Newcastle upon Tyne. A monastery was founded here in 681, and this became the home of the Venerable Bede from *c*.682 until his death in 735; it was here that he wrote his *Historia Ecclesiastica Gentis Anglorum*, and the town now has a visitor attraction called Bede's World. From the 19th century it became a major shipbuilding centre and produced the world's first oil tanker, but the Palmer's shipyard closed in 1933, leading to extensive unemployment.

Jarrow was the birthplace of Catherine Cookson (1906–98), writer of popular novels in the clogs-and-shawls mode; and of the Labour politician and former cabinet minister Jack Cunningham (b.1939).

Jarrow Crusade, the (1936). The last of a series of 'hunger marches' on London in the 1920s and 1930s to protest against poverty and high unemployment. Organized by the local MP, 'Red Ellen' Wilkinson, 200 people marched from Jarrow to London, where they met with the prime minister, Stanley Baldwin, and other ministers. The march gained much public sympathy, but little practical action.

In the 1980s Mrs Thatcher's policies saw the return of high unemployment to the NORTH[1], and in 1986, the 50th anniversary of the crusade, a second **Jarrow march** took place.

Jedburgh 'burgh on the River Jed', OCelt river name *Jed* + OE *burh* (*see* BURY); earlier *Jedworth*, OE *worth* 'enclosure' (*see* -WORTH, WORTHY, -WARDINE); recorded as *Geadwearde* in the 8th century.

A royal BURGH and textile town in Scottish Borders, formerly the county town of Roxburghshire. It is about 16 km (10 miles) southeast of Melrose. An old name for Jedburgh was **Jeddart** or **Jethart**, which still appears in a number of phrases (*see below*).

For those crossing into Scotland via the A68 and CARTER BAR, Jedburgh is the first Scottish town they will come to, and the centre, with its old houses gaily repainted, offers a welcoming prospect. Unfortunately this impression is somewhat undermined by the notice greeting travellers on the door of the first café they will encounter in the Canongate:

> PLEASE NOTE We DO NOT offer, sell or give-away TAP WATER Thank you

This policy is rigorously enforced, even if one is attempting to deal with the place's thirst-inducing speciality, 'crispy coated haggis'.

The well-preserved ruins of **Jedburgh Abbey**, which was established in the 12th century, stand on the site of a 9th-century church. Alexander III was married to his second wife, the French noblewoman Yolande of Dreux, in the abbey in 1285 (at the subsequent feast the appearance of a skeletal spectre that pointed at the king was taken as an omen of the king's death, which took place at KINGHORN in the following year). The abbey suffered considerable damage at the hands of the English in the early 16th century, and the foundation was suppressed in 1559.

The building today called **Jedburgh Castle** was actually erected in 1832 as a prison, but it was built on the site of a medieval castle, also dating from the 12th century. In 1195 Malcolm IV died in the old castle, which was eventually demolished in 1409 at the request of the burgers, as it had proved such a magnet for English invaders.

Mary Queen of Scots stayed in Jedburgh in 1566 to preside over the local courts, and it was during her stay that she made her exhausting ride to see Bothwell in HERMITAGE CASTLE. The building where she stayed in Jedburgh is preserved as Mary Queen of Scots' House. Other noted visitors have included Robert Burns (1787) and William and Dorothy Wordsworth (1803), while Sir Walter Scott made his first appearance as an advocate here, at the trial of a sheepstealer (1793); he won the case. Jedburgh was the birthplace of Sir David Brewster (1781–1868), the physicist who did pioneering work on polarized light.

Jedburgh has a well-known rugby union club (known as **Jed-Forest**, after the local area), but unique to the town is the game of handba', played every winter all around the streets between two sides, known as 'the Uppies' and 'the Doonies'. The leather ball is stuffed with hay, and represents an Englishman's head. The annual Redeswire Ride commemorates the Redeswire Fray (*see under* REDESDALE)

of 1575 in which the citizens of Jedburgh played an important part.

Jeddart justice. Precipitate justice, in which a man is hanged first and tried afterwards. The phrase appears to have arisen from a single local example.

Jeddart snails. A kind of toffee made in the town.

Jeddart staff. A type of halberd with which the men of Jedburgh defended their town at the time of the English invasions in the Middle Ages. The Jeddart staff features on the town's coat of arms.

Jeddart. An old name for JEDBURGH.

Jemimaville Named, like nearby POYNTZFIELD, after *Jemima* Poyntz, Dutch wife of the local laird, who founded it as an estate village in 1822.

A small settlement on the north coast of the BLACK ISLE, Easter Ross, Highland, 7 km (4.5 miles) west of Cromarty.

Jericho From a former area of land in the vicinity known as *Jericho* Gardens. There was also an inn nearby called Jericho. The ultimate origin of these names was no doubt the biblical city of Jericho, famously demuralized by Joshua, which was often taken as exemplifying remoteness (the area was outside Oxford's city wall). The idea that the district's name commemorates the *jerry*-builders who constructed it is *ben trovato* but not *vero*.

A district of western Oxford, between Walton Street and the Oxford Canal. Built in the 19th century, it was Oxford's first suburb. It consists mainly of small artisans' cottages, inhabited to begin with largely by workers at Oxford University Press's (*see under* OXFORD) nearby printing works, but latterly, as with much of the rest of Oxford, let out to students. Gentrification is encroaching.

In Thomas Hardy's *Jude the Obscure* (1895), Jude Fawley lodged in Jericho when he was in CHRISTMINSTER (Oxford).

Dead of Jericho, The. A detective novel by Colin Dexter (1981), set in Jericho and featuring the Oxford-based Inspector Morse. It was the first of the Morse novels to be adapted for television (1987).

Jermyn Street From Henry *Jermyn*, Earl of St Albans, on whose land (granted by Charles II) it was built.

A street in the WEST END[1] of London (SW1), running parallel with and to the south of PICCADILLY[1], between St James's Street (*see under* ST JAMES'S) in the west and the HAYMARKET in the east. It was laid out between the 1660s and the 1680s. It is now an elegant and superior (in both the positive and negative senses of the term) shopping street for those for whom price is not the first consideration. It specializes in the paraphernalia of gentlemanly living – notably fine hand-made shirts – but also manages to fit in a royal-warranted cheesemonger.

Thomas Wall (1846–1930), purveyor of the sausages

that (along with ice-cream) bear his and his father's (identical) name, was born in Jermyn Street.

> Your habit of referring to distinguished writers by their Christian names, as if they were personal friends, really irritates me. It makes you sound like an occasional essayist in a middlebrow weekly rather than a trader in fine wines with a whiff of Jermyn Street about him.
>
> William Donaldson: *I'm Leaving You Simon, You Disgust Me* (2003)

Jersey 'Geirr's island', OScand male personal name *Geirr* + *ey* (*see* -AY).

The largest and most southerly of the CHANNEL ISLANDS, lying about 29 km (18 miles) to the southeast of GUERNSEY, about 33 km (21 miles) west of the Cotentin Peninsula in Normandy, France. Its Roman name was **Caesarea**. It covers 115 sq km (44 sq miles), but this area doubles when the tide is out. The island's capital is ST HELIER. Jersey is divided into 12 parishes: Grouville, St Brelade, St Clement, St Helier, St Lawrence, St Martin, St Peter, St Saviour, St Ouen, St Peter, St Mary and Trinity.

The island is governed (under the British Crown) by a parliament known as the **States of Jersey**. Its chief civil officer is the Bailiff, who is in charge of the 'Bailiwick' of Jersey (which also includes the tiny islets of the ECREHOUS, 9.5 km / 6 miles to the northwest of the island, and the MINQUIERS, 19 km / 12 miles to the south). The Crown's representative in the island is the Lieutenant-Governor.

Jersey's official language is French (it is the language of the island's Norman-based legal system as well as of most of its place names), but old Jersey French (**Jerriais**), a dialect of Norman French, is now spoken only by a declining few. English (its onward march accelerated by increasing numbers of English immigrants) is now the everyday language of the island. There has also been an influx of several thousand (Madeiran) Portuguese in recent years. Many now live permanently here, having come originally as seasonal farm workers.

Jersey's main sources of income are tourism, banking and agriculture – notably dairy farming (**Jersey cattle** (*see below*) are world-famous, and **Jersey cream** and **Jersey milk** are particularly rich and delicious) and the production of vegetables, fruit and flowers.

Traditionally there is little love lost between the inhabitants of Jersey and those of nearby Guernsey: inhabitants of the two islands refer to one another respectively as *crapauds* (French, toads) and *ânes* (French, donkeys).

Jersey Zoo was founded in 1959 by the writer and naturalist Gerald Durrell. It was a pioneer in the use of zoos for safeguarding endangered species. It is based in Les Augres manor.

The Jersey-set BBC television detective series *Bergerac*

(1981–91), with John Nettles as DS Jim Bergerac, greatly increased the island's profile and visitor numbers.

The golfer Harry Vardon (1870–1937), six times winner of the Open, was born in Jersey. In a rather earlier era, the Anglo-Norman chronicler Wace (*c*.1100–*c*.1175) is believed to have been born here.

The US state New Jersey, to the south of New York state, was named after Jersey. Jersey City faces New York City across the Hudson River.

Battle of Jersey (6 January 1781). A battle fought when a French force under Baron De Rullecour landed and reached the island's capital, St Helier. Major Peirson, the senior British military officer present, rallied the militia and garrison forces, forcing the French to surrender. It proved to be the last attempt by the French to seize Jersey by force. Peirson's death at the very moment of victory was the subject of a painting by John Singleton Copley (*The Death of Major Peirson*, 1783), which has become something of an icon for islanders. It hangs in the Tate Britain gallery, London.

Beast of Jersey. A journalistic nickname for E.J.L. (Ted) Paisnel, convicted of 13 sex offences against children in Jersey and sentenced to 30 years' imprisonment in 1971. The name was applied to him during the 11 years in which he evaded arrest on the island.

jersey. Originally, going back to the 16th century, used to refer to a sort of knitted woollen fabric made on Jersey and to garments, particularly stockings, manufactured from it. For a long time this was a staple industry of Jersey. The term has become generic for plain machine-knitted fabric made of wool (or nylon, or other yarn), especially as used for making clothing. In the early to mid-19th century it began to be applied more specifically to a woollen garment for the upper body, especially as worn by participants in sports or by sailors.

Jersey cattle. A breed of small short-horned dairy cattle that originated in Jersey. They are typically yellowish-brown or fawn in colour, and they are noted for their rich milk.

Jersey elm. A variety of elm tree (*Ulmus stricta* var. *sarniensis*) that grows with a more upright habit than the standard elm.

Jersey Lily, the. The sobriquet of Emily Charlotte Langtry (1852–1929), known as Lillie (or Lily) Langtry, who was born on the island. She was already known as a society beauty before she made her début on the professional stage in 1881. A one-time intimate of the Prince of Wales (later Edward VII), she was the wife of Edward Langtry and daughter of W.C. Le Breton, Dean of Jersey. After Edward Langtry's death she married Sir Hugo Gerald de Bathe in 1899. The Jersey Museum at St Helier, Jersey, has a three-quarter-length portrait of her by John Everett Millais, painted in 1878, in which she holds a lily in one hand – whence, apparently, the nickname.

Jerseyman. A native or inhabitant of Jersey.

> There is an independence of character in a Jerseyman.
>
> *Guide to the Island of Jersey* (1842)

Jersey royal. A variety of potato grown on Jersey, typically harvested early and sold as 'new potatoes'.

Jersey tiger. A type of tiger moth, *Euplagia quadripunctaria*, that occurs on Jersey.

Jerusalem-on-Sea. A nickname given in the 1950s to BRIGHTON, which then and afterwards was known for its large Jewish population.

Jervaulx Abbey 'abbey in the valley of the River Ure', OCelt or pre-Celtic river name of unknown meaning + OFr *val*, valley. The remains of a 12th-century Cistercian abbey in the valley of the River URE, North Yorkshire, about 8 km (5 miles) northwest of Masham. The last abbot of Jervaulx was hanged for his role in the Pilgrimage of Grace, a Catholic rebellion against Henry VIII in the 1530s. The unfortunate abbot's involvement in the rebellion ensured that Jervaulx suffered a more extreme fate than other Yorkshire abbeys during the Dissolution of the Monasteries. Only fragments of the abbey's original walls are still visible, but wild flowers grow in profusion in its ruined nave.

Jervaulx is the original source of Wensleydale cheese (*see under* WENSLEYDALE).

Jethart. An old name for JEDBURGH.

Jethou 'island of goats', OScand *geit* 'goat' + *holmr* 'island' (*see* -EY, -EA).
One of the CHANNEL ISLANDS. An almost circular hump-shaped mass of granite only 0.18 sq km (0.069 sq miles) in area, it lies off the southern tip of HERM. It is within the Bailiwick of GUERNSEY. It is occupied by a private tenant, and is not accessible to visitors.

Jinney-mengreskey gav. The Romany name for MANCHESTER, according to George Borrow's *Romano Lavo-Lil* ('word book of the Romany', 1874). The name means 'sharpers' town'.

Jock's Road In this context *Jock* may be the Scottish Everyman.
A high-level path (formerly a drove road) in the southern CAIRNGORM MOUNTAINS, leading from GLEN CLOVA via Glen Doll and past Tolmount (958 m / 3143 ft) to Loch Callater, Glen Callater and thence to BRAEMAR.

Jodrellbank Originally *Jodrell Bank* 'bank or hillside belonging to the Jodrell family' (the Jodrells owned land in the area in the 19th century).
A village in Cheshire, in the foothills of the PENNINES, about 11 km (7 miles) southwest of Macclesfield. A little to the north is the **Jodrell Bank Science Centre**, site of the Nuffield Radio Astronomy Laboratories of Manchester University, which opened (as the **Jodrell Bank Experimental Station**) in 1951. It achieved fame in the late 1950s and 1960s under its first director, Sir Bernard Lovell, when its 76.2 m (250 ft) radio-telescope dish, installed in 1957, kept a high-profile track of US and Soviet spacecraft as well as identifying non-man-made objects in deep space.

jodrell. A rhyming-slang contraction from the 1950s meaning 'an act of masturbation, (*Jodrell Bank* = *wank*), and by extension **Jodrell Banker** ('wanker') connoted a 'tired-out old prostitute'.

John Bull. A personification of England and/or Britain, usually accompanied by a bulldog: hence 'British bulldog' (*see under* BRITISH). He was popularized (but not invented) by John Arbuthnot, in *The History of John Bull* (1712), an allegory of the War of the Spanish Succession, in which John Bull appears as a successful trader; in later manifestations he was often a farmer. Arbuthnot contrasts this figure with the bullying Lewis Baboon (the French) and the bamboozling Nicholas Frog (the Dutch).

> Bull, in the main, was an honest plain-dealing fellow, cholerick, bold, and of a very unconstant Temper ... no man kept a better House than John, nor spent his Money more generously.
>
> John Arbuthnot: *The History of John Bull* (1712), Part 1, Chapter 5

John Bull was also the title of a jingoistic magazine established in 1906 by the arch-fraudster and politician Horatio Bottomley (1860–1932), largely with the intention of furthering his own dubious business ventures.

> [In a war 'in a good cause'] John Citizen is transformed into John Bull with a completeness which regularly confounds our enemies and surprises our friends; instead of the strong conscience keeping the strong aggression in check, the two, in the literal as well as the metaphorical sense of the word, join forces and shape the world.
>
> Geoffrey Gorer: *Exploring English Character* (1955)

John Bull's Bastards. An Irish term for the English or the British.

John Bull's Other Island. A term for IRELAND, with an ironic reference to its English rulers. The phrase originates in Leon Paul Blouet's *John Bull et son île* ('John Bull and His Island', 1883), and became the title of George Bernard Shaw's play *John Bull's Other Island*, written in 1904 at the request of W.B. Yeats.

John o'Groats From the local ferry operator, *Jan de Groot*.
The site of a legendary house in the far northeast of Scotland, in Highland (formerly in CAITHNESS). It is supposedly the northernmost point in mainland Britain, although this honour actually belongs to DUNNET HEAD.

It is, however, only 3 km (2 miles) west of the most north-easterly point in mainland Britain, DUNCANSBY HEAD, hence the traditional contrast with LAND'S END in the southwest.

The name originates in that of a Dutchman, Jan de Groot, or John o'Groat, who with his two brothers Malcolm and Gavin came here during the reign of James IV (1488–1513) to run the ferry to Orkney. There came to be eight families of the name, and they met annually to celebrate, but on one occasion a question of precedence arose. Consequently John o'Groat built an eight-sided house with a door to each side, and within which he placed an octagonal table, so that all were 'head of the table'. This house came to be known as John o'Groat's House. It is no longer here, but next to the mound and flagpole marking the site is a 19th-century hotel with an octagonal tower.

From Land's End to John o'Groats. A phrase meaning from end to end of Britain. The distance by road between John o'Groats and Land's End is 1397 km (873 miles), and walking, running or cycling the route is a popular means of raising money for charity. In January 2004, Steve Gough, a campaigner for the right to appear naked in public, completed the route in nothing but walking boots, hat and backpack, his attempt being periodically interrupted by arrests and spells in custody.

Groatie buckie or **John o'Groat's buckie.** The local name for the European cowrie shell.

John o'Groat. A rhyming-slang term for 'coat'. More interestingly, in the plural, **John o'Groats** is rhyming slang for 'oats', as in 'Are yer gettin' yer John o'Groats?', i.e. 'Are you having carnal knowledge on a regular basis?'.

Johnstone 'John's town', ME personal name *John* + -TON.
An industrial town some 6 km (4 miles) west of Paisley in Renfrewshire (formerly in Strathclyde region). It was founded in 1781 by George Houston, laird of Johnstone, on the site of a small village of the same name. The composer Frédéric Chopin stayed at **Johnstone Castle** in 1848, during his tour of England and Scotland, the year before his death.

Johnstone was the birthplace of Sir George Houston Reid (1845–1918), prime minister of Australia (1904–5).

Joppa After the biblical seaport of Palestine, about 50 km (31 miles) west of Jerusalem.
An eastern suburb of EDINBURGH, on the Firth of Forth. There is another Joppa in South Ayrshire.

Jordan Gap. *See* PILLAR.

Jordans Perhaps a shortening of an earlier *Jourdemayns*, from the local family name *Jourdemayn*. First recorded in 1766.
A village in Buckinghamshire, about 4 km (2.5 miles) east of Beaconsfield. It has important Quaker connections: nearby

is the late 17th-century brick-built Friends' Meeting House, which has been described as the 'Quaker Westminster Abbey'; and William Penn (1644–1718), founder of Pennsylvania, USA, is buried in the local churchyard with his two wives (an attempt to exhume him and take him back to America was frustrated).

Jorvik. The Viking name for YORK.

Joy, the. A nickname amongst its residents for Dublin's MOUNTJOY PRISON.

Joyce's Country Irish *Dúiche Sheoigheach* 'Joyce's country', from the *Joyces* who came here from Wales in the 13th century.
A wild area of County GALWAY, between CONNEMARA to the west and Loch Corrib (*see under* CORRIB) to the east, and including the MAUMTURK MOUNTAINS. It is also called **Joyce Country**.

Joyce's Tower. *See under* DÚN LAOGHAIRE.

Jubilee River Named in honour of the Golden *Jubilee* of Queen Elizabeth II in 2002.
An 11.5 km (7.5 mile) artificial river constructed between MAIDENHEAD and WINDSOR as a diversion of the River Thames near Staines, to alleviate flooding in the Maidenhead, Windsor and Eton areas.

Jump ModE *jump* 'a steep incline'.
A village in South Yorkshire, 6 km (4 miles) southeast of Barnsley.

Juniper Hill. *See* LARK RISE.

Jura 'Doraid's island', Gaelic male personal name *Doraid* + *eilean* 'island'; *Doirad Eilinn*, 7th century; the name was reinterpreted by the Scandinavians as 'deer island', OScand *dyr* 'deer' + *ey* (*see* -AY).
A large, thinly inhabited island in the Inner HEBRIDES, in Argyll and Bute (formerly in Strathclyde region). It is separated from ISLAY to the south by the narrow Sound of Islay, and from the mainland of KNAPDALE by the **Sound of Jura**, which is some 7 km (4 miles) wide. At its northern tip is the whirlpool of CORRYVRECKAN. George Orwell lived on Jura from 1946 to 1949 and wrote *Nineteen Eighty-Four* here. He left the island to go into hospital in London, where he died of tuberculosis.

Paps of Jura Scots *pap* 'breast'; *Papes of Ijura* (*sic*) 1600.
A trio of peaks in the southern half of the island, all over 700 m (2400 ft) in height; the highest, Beinn an Oir, is 785 m (2575 ft). They can be seen by seafarers and hill-walkers from great distances in many directions – from where they indeed appear breast-like in shape, if not in number. Here an early ascensionist recalls his efforts:

> After a walk of four miles, reach the Paps ... there are three: Beinn-a-chaolois, or, the mountain of the sound; Beinn-sheunta, or the hallowed mountain; and Beinn-an-òir, or, the mountain of gold. We began to scale the last; a

task of much labor and difficulty; being composed of vast stones, slightly covered with mosses near the base, but all above bare, and unconnected with each other. The whole seems a cairn, the work of the sons of Saturn.

Thomas Pennant: *A Tour of Scotland and a Voyage to the Hebrides* (1773)

It was while hunting on Beinn an Oir, according to a local story, that in old age Fair-haired Murdo of the Deer took aim at a stag, which promptly turned into a fairy. The fairy proceeded to make uncomplimentary remarks about his white hair, whereupon Murdo flummoxed the little pagan by saying that God could make him young again, which God duly did. Later, Beinn an Oir was the site of an 1812 experiment to demonstrate that the boiling point of water is in inverse proportion to altitude.

More recently, the Paps were the subject of a poem by Andrew Young (1885–1971), who, like others, found the hills more challenging than their distant soft outline would suggest:

Now, climbing, I clasp rocks
Storm shattered and sharp-edged …

Andrew Young: 'The Paps of Jura', from
The White Blackbird (1935)

Juteopolis. A former nickname for DUNDEE, awarded because of its jute industry.

Juvlo-mengreskey tem. The Romany name for SCOTLAND, according to George Borrow's *Romano Lavo-Lil* ('Word Book of the Romany', 1874). The name means 'lousy fellows' country', a reputation also found in various former slang names for the country, such as LOUSELAND, ITCHLAND and SCRATCHLAND.

K

Kangaroo Valley Alluding to the symbolical Australianness of the *kangaroo*.

A nickname given in the 1960s to the EARL'S COURT area of West London. At that time there was a large number of temporary or permanent Australian immigrants living here.

Kangaroo Valley is also the title of a comic drama (2003) by Toby Farrow, exploring the mental disintegration of an Australian professional swimmer after he checks into a seedy Earl's Court hostel.

Kanturk Irish *Ceann Toirc* 'headland or promontory of the boar' (perhaps referring to the shape of a local hill).

A small market town in County Cork, 18 km (11 miles) west-northwest of Mallow, at the confluence of the Dalua and Allow rivers (both of which feature in Edmund Spenser's *The Faerie Queene* (1590–6)). There is a ruined MacDonagh castle dating from the early 17th century; it was never finished, as the local English settlers complained that it was 'much too large for a subject', and the Privy Council forbade MacDonagh to complete it.

Kate Kearney's Cottage. *See under* GAP OF DUNLOE

Kathleen ni Houlihan. A personification of IRELAND as a woman, as the Marianne is of France and Britannia is of Great Britain. The figure originates in the Jacobite poets of the 18th century.

> If you want to interest him [an Irishman] in Ireland, you've got to call the unfortunate island Kathleen ni Hoolihan and pretend she's a little old woman.
>
> George Bernard Shaw: *John Bull's Other Island* (1904)

In Yeats's play *Cathleen ni Houlihan* she is a mysterious wandering old woman who inspires Michael, who is about to be married, to join the uprising of the United Irishmen in 1798. When last seen, according to one of the other characters, she has transmogrified into 'a young girl, and she had the walk of a queen'. In the first production in 1902 the title role was played by the ardent Nationalist Maud Gonne, with whom Yeats was for long fruitlessly in love. The play had a big impact on Irish revolutionary

sentiment, and later, long after the failed Easter Rising of 1916, Yeats was to wonder:

> Did that play of mine send out
> Certain men the English shot?
>
> W.B. Yeats: 'The Man and the Echo', in *Last Poems* (1939)

Keal Cotes *Keal* 'ridge of hills', OScand *kjolr* 'a keel', by extension 'a keel-shaped ridge'; *Cotes* 'cottages, sheds', OE *cot* (*see* -COT, COTE).

A village in Lincolnshire, in the FENS, about 21 km (13 miles) west of Skegness.

Kedleston 'Ketill's farmstead', OScand male personal name *Ketill* + -TON.

A mansion in the Palladian style, and its estate, 8 km (5 miles) northwest of Derby. It was commissioned by the Curzon family (*see also* BODIAM) and built in 1756–65. In the words of its National Trust owners, it contains 'the most complete and least-altered sequence of Robert Adam interiors in England'. The medieval village of Kedleston is now identifiable only by All Saints' Church in the grounds.

The Curzons' presence remains strong, in particular that of the statesman **Marquis Curzon of Kedleston** (i.e. Lord Curzon, 1859– 1925), whose collection of orientalia is on display: he was Viceroy of India from 1898 to 1905, until resigning after disagreements with Kitchener.

Keele 'hill where cows graze', OE *cy* 'cows' + *hyll* 'hill'.

A western suburb of NEWCASTLE UNDER LYME, in Staffordshire. **Keele University** opened in 1962. It was born out of the earlier University College of North Staffordshire (1949). Keele Services are between Junctions 15 and 16 on the M6.

Kegworth Perhaps 'Cægga's enclosure', OE male personal name *Cægga* + *worth* (*see* -WORTH, WORTHY, -WARDINE).

A village in Leicestershire, about 10 km (6 miles) north-west of Loughborough. It is immediately to the east of the M1, opposite East Midlands Airport, and in 1989 was the scene of a crash when a landing Boeing 737 ploughed into the motorway embankment.

Keighley 'Cyhha's clearing', OE male personal name *Cyhha* + -LEY; *Chichelai* 1086.

A town in West Yorkshire, 13 km (8 miles) northwest of Bradford. It is pronounced 'keithly'. HAWORTH, the home of the Brontës, is now part of Keighley. The **Keighley and Worth Valley Railway** runs steam trains for tourists, and featured in the film of *The Railway Children* (1970). The town's rugby league team is the **Keighley Cougars**.

Keighley was the birthplace of the Labour politician Denis Healey (b.1917).

Keinton Mandeville *Keinton* 'royal manor', OE *cyne-* 'royal' + -TON; *Mandeville* denoting manorial ownership in the Middle Ages by the Maundevill family.

A village in Somerset, about 11 km (7 miles) southeast of Glastonbury.

Keith OCelt CED 'wood'.

A small town in Moray (formerly in Banffshire, and then in Grampian region), about 25 km (15 miles) southeast of Elgin.

Kells[1] An anglicization of Irish *na cealla* 'the churches', with addition of English plural *-s*.

A market town in County Meath, 15 km (9 miles) northwest of Navan. Its Irish name is **Ceannanas Mór** ('big residence'), anglicized as **Kenlis**. A monastery was founded here by St Colum Cille (Columba) in the 6th century, and the town also has an ancient round tower, carved stone crosses and a two-storey 9th-century building called St Colum Cille's house.

Book of Kells, The. An 8th-century illuminated manuscript of the Gospels from the monastery at Kells. One of the finest examples of its kind, it was probably written on IONA and brought to Kells for safety after the commencement of the Viking raids. The manuscript is now in Trinity College Library, Dublin.

Synod of Kells (1152). An ecclesiastical gathering at Kells, which reorganized the Irish church into four archdioceses: Armagh, Cashel, Tuam and Dublin.

Kells[2]. A village in County Kilkenny, 13 km (8 miles) south of Kilkenny itself. There was an ancient monastery here, founded by St Ciarán of Seir, and this was replaced *c*.1193 by a large, fortified Augustinian priory, whose remains can still be seen (the many towers inspired the local name for the priory, the Seven Castles). The priory and the town were built by Geoffrey fitz Robert de Monte, the motte of whose castle survives.

In 1327 the lord of the manor, Arnold de Poer, provoked the wrath of Maurice, 1st Earl of Desmond, by calling him an 'Irish poet'. In retaliation, Kells was burnt to the ground.

Kelmscot 'Cenhelm's cottage(s)', OE *Cenhelmes* possessive form of male personal name *Cenhelm* + *cot* (*see* -COT, COTE).

A village in southwestern Oxfordshire (before 1974 in Berkshire), on the River Thames, about 29 km (18 miles) southwest of Oxford. It owes its fame largely to the poet, designer, printer and socialist William Morris, who lived here, at **Kelmscott Manor** (a gabled Elizabethan house), from 1871 (when he took a joint tenancy with his fellow Pre-Raphaelite, Dante Gabriel Rossetti) until his death in 1896.

Kelmscott Press. A printing enterprise founded by William Morris in Hammersmith in 1890. He named it after his Hammersmith home, **Kelmscott House**, which in turn was named after Kelmscott Manor (*see above*). It specialized in fine design and typography, and Morris himself created the fonts and the ornamental letters and borders. It issued 52 books, many of them Morris's own, but also several medieval texts.

Kelso 'chalk hill', OE *calc* 'chalk' + *hoh* 'hill spur' (originally OCelt *Calchvynydd*, meaning the same); the name *Calkou* is recorded in the 12th century, and part of the town is still known as *Chalkheugh*.

A market town (locally pronounced 'Kelsie') at the confluence of the rivers TEVIOT and TWEED, in Scottish Borders (formerly in Roxburghshire), some 20 km (12 miles) east of Melrose. Its importance developed after the destruction of the nearby town of ROXBURGH in 1460. There was a ford over the Tweed here, and a ferry, but …

> … the Tweed is so dangerous a river, and rises sometimes so suddenly, that a man scarce knows, when he goes into the water, how it shall be ere he gets out at the other side; and it is not very strange to them at Kelso, to hear of frequent disasters, in the passage, to men and cattle.
>
> Daniel Defoe: *A Tour Through the Whole Island of Great Britain* (1724–6)

The lack of a bridge was remedied in 1800 by the Scottish engineer John Rennie, whose structure at Kelso was the model for his 1811 Waterloo Bridge (*see under* WATERLOO[1]) in London (demolished 1935); two of the lamps on the Kelso bridge come from Waterloo Bridge.

Kelso Abbey was founded by David I in 1128 (when the Benedictines moved here from Selkirk), and ruined by the English in 1545.

Sir Walter Scott spent much of his childhood at his grandfather's farm, Sandy-Knowe, between Kelso and Melrose, and described the former as 'the most beautiful, if not the most romantic village in Scotland'.

There is a town called Kelso in the USA (Washington state), and the racehorse called Kelso had considerable success in America in 1960–1, ridden by Eddie Arcaro.

Kelsae laddie. The leader of Kelso's annual riding of the marches, in which the locals ride round the burgh boundaries.

Kelvin Possibly 'narrow water', Gaelic *caol* 'narrow' + *abhainn* 'water, river' (*see* AVON).

A river in west central Scotland, about 35 km (20 miles) in length. It rises in Dullatur Bog near the hamlet of **Kelvinhead**, east of Kilsyth in North Lanarkshire, and joins the Clyde in Glasgow.

See also KELVINGROVE PARK; KELVINSIDE; STRATHKELVIN.

Lord Kelvin. William Thomson (1824–1907), the Belfast-born physicist who helped to pioneer the new science of thermodynamics. He was professor of natural philosophy at Glasgow University and took the title 1st Baron Kelvin of Largs in 1892. The degree in the absolute scale of temperature is named the **kelvin** in his honour.

Kelvingrove Park. A largely formal park in the West End of GLASGOW, through which the River KELVIN flows. **Kelvingrove Gallery** is the informal name for the Glasgow Art Gallery and Museum, located in the park. The park was subjected to some Victorian whimsy in a song by Thomas Lyle (to the tune of 'O the Shearin's No' for You'):

Let us haste to Kelvin grove, bonnie lassie, O,
Through its mazes let us rove, bonnie lassie, O:
Where the rose in all her pride,
Paints the hollow dingle side,
Where the midnight fairies glide, bonnie lassie, O.

Kelvinside From the River KELVIN.

A middle-class residential area in the west end of Glasgow. **Kelvinside accent.** An affectedly 'refained' Scottish accent; the Glasgow equivalent of a MORNINGSIDE accent.

Kemble '(place at the) border' (probably referring to a tribal territory), from an OCelt word meaning 'edge, border'.

A village in Gloucestershire, about 8 km (5 miles) south-west of Cirencester. Thames Head, the source of the River THAMES[1], lies 3 km (2 miles) to the west. Kemble's attractive railway station, built in 1882, is a larger and grander affair than one might expect from a south Cotswold village. It owes its size to Kemble's former status as a railway junction: the Swindon–Gloucester line (built by Brunel between 1845 and 1850) was joined here by the (now defunct) branch lines to Cirencester and Tetbury. The railway tunnel south of the station was dug at the insistence of the then owner of **Kemble House**, who baulked at the idea of the line crossing his land.

RAF Kemble, used principally as a maintenance unit for aircraft during and after the Second World War (and home to the Red Arrows air display team from the 1960s), ceased its military function in 1992.

Kempston 'farmstead at the bend' (referring to a large bend in the River Ouse (*see under* GREAT OUSE)), from a derivative of OCelt *camm* 'crooked' + -TON.

A town in Bedfordshire, about 3 km (2 miles) southwest of Bedford.

Kempton Park. *See under* SUNBURY-ON-THAMES.

Kemp Town Named after Thomas Read *Kemp* (1781?–1844), who designed and built the area in the 1820s.

An area of BRIGHTON, close to the seafront and to the east of the Palace Pier. It gives its name to one of the two Brighton parliamentary constituencies, which in 1964 was the first in Sussex to be won by the Labour Party.

Brighton Racecourse is located on the hills above here.

Kendal 'valley of the River Kent', OCelt river name of unknown meaning + OScand *dalr* 'dale'. However, early forms, such as *Kirkabikendala c.*1095, were prefixed by two further elements, OScand *kirkju* 'church' + -BY.

A town on the River Kent in Cumbria (formerly in Westmorland), some 30 km (18 miles) north of Lancaster. It is sometimes known as the **Gateway to the Lakes**, being on one of the main tourist routes into the LAKE DISTRICT. Woollen manufacture has been important since John Renne, a Flemish weaver, settled here in 1331, and the town's Latin motto, *Pannus mihi panis*, is often translated as 'Wool is my bread'.

The ruined **Kendal Castle** is said to have been the birthplace of Catherine Parr, Henry VIII's sixth and last wife (*see also* Sudeley Castle *under* WINCHCOMBE), but it seems the place was already a ruin at the time of her birth in 1512. Kendal was the birthplace of the astrophysicist Sir Arthur Eddington (1882–1944), and home to Alfred Wainwright, the Lakeland guidebook writer (*see* WAINWRIGHTS), who was borough treasurer of the town. The adventures of Postman Pat, by John Cunliffe, were inspired by the sub-post office at Beast Bank near Kendal (closed in 2003); Kendal itself is depicted as Pencaster, while nearby LONG SLEDDALE, with a lake added, becomes Greendale.

In Kendal parish church, behind the door, there used to hang a hat that was said to have belonged to Robin the Devil – the Cavalier Sir Robert Philipson. According to legend he lost it when he led his men into the church during Sunday-morning service in search of his enemy, the Parliamentary magistrate of Kendal, Colonel Briggs. The incident provides the basis for a passage in Sir Walter Scott's *Rokeby* (1813). The hat disappeared sometime in the 1870s.

The Heights of Kendal, that dreary Moor ...

William Wordsworth: *The Prelude* (1805–50), Book IV

Kendal green. A type of green woollen cloth, formerly worn by foresters and archers, and originating in Kendal in the 14th century. The dye was a mixture of woad (blue) and broom (yellow).

... as the devil would have it, three misbegotten knaves in Kendal green came at my back and let drive at me ...

William Shakespeare: Falstaff in *Henry IV, Part 1* (1597), II.iv

Sir Walter Scott has Kendal green as the traditional garb of minstrels:

His garb was fashion'd, to express
The ancient English minstrel's dress,
A seemly gown of Kendal green,
With gorget closed of silver sheen ...

> Sir Walter Scott: *Rokeby* (1813), Canto V, xv

Kendal Mintcake. A peppermint-flavoured sugary confection, in the form of a bar, much favoured by Lakeland fell-walkers, and manufactured in Kendal since at least the mid-19th century. It proudly boasts to having been consumed during the first ascent of Mount Everest.

Kenfig From the River Cynffig, the meaning of which is unknown.

A medieval village and castle that once stood near the mouth of the small River Cynffig, which enters the Bristol Channel some 6 km (4 miles) northwest of Porthcawl. The river now forms part of the border between the unitary authorities of NEATH PORT TALBOT and BRIDGEND (formerly in Glamorgan, then West Glamorgan). The village was overwhelmed by sand in the 16th century, and the area of sand dunes stretching south from here (now a National Nature Reserve) are called **Kenfig Burrows**, behind which is a small freshwater lake called **Kenfig Pool**.

Kenilworth ('Cynehild's enclosure', OE female personal name *Cynehild* + *worth* (*see* -WORTH, WORTHY, -WARDINE).

A town in Warwickshire, about 8 km (5 miles) southwest of Coventry. To the northwest is the 12th-century **Kenilworth Castle**, whose massive Norman keep and 14th-century Great Hall (added by John of Gaunt) survive. In 1563, Elizabeth I gave it to Robert Dudley, Earl of Leicester (who added a gatehouse).

Il castello di Kenilworth ('Kenilworth Castle'). An opera (1829) by Gaetano Donizetti, based on Sir Walter Scott's novel (*see below*).

Kenilworth. A novel (1821) by Sir Walter Scott, telling the (highly elaborated) story of Amy Robsart, wife of the Earl of Leicester. There was a scandal in 1560 when she was found at the bottom of a staircase at Cumnor Place, Oxfordshire (*see* CUMNOR), with her neck broken. It was rumoured, without any evidence, that Leicester was responsible, so that he could pursue his suit to the queen. Elizabeth, however, rejected him. In Scott's novel Amy is the victim of a complex plot of deceit by the villain, Varney. At the end of the novel, while Leicester entertains Elizabeth at Kenilworth, Varney engineers Amy's death at Cumnor Place, where she falls through a trapdoor. Scott had originally wanted to call the novel *Cumnor Place*, but his publisher, Archibald Constable, insisted on *Kenilworth*. The novel includes vivid descriptions of the entertainments laid on at Kenilworth Castle by Leicester for Elizabeth I.

Kenilworth. A cantata (1864) by Sir Arthur Sullivan with a libretto by H.F. Chorley, based on Sir Walter Scott's novel.

Siege of Kenilworth (July 1265–December 1266). A siege in which Simon de Montfort's supporters were pinned down in Kenilworth Castle by forces loyal to Henry III after the Battle of Evesham (*see under* EVESHAM). In October 1266 Henry offered an amnesty, known as the **Dictum of Kenilworth**, but the barons held out until December.

Kenlis. An anglicization of the Irish name for KELLS[1].

Kenmare An anglicization of Irish *ceannmara* 'sea head', reflecting the town's position at the highest tidal point on the River Kenmare.

A small market town and tourist centre in County Kerry, 20 km (12 miles) southwest of Killarney. Its Irish name is **Neidín** ('little nest'). The town was founded by Oliver Cromwell's surveyor-general in Ireland, William Petty, and in 1775 his descendant, the 1st Marquess of Lansdowne, designed the original town plan.

Kenmare is situated at the head of the long sea inlet called the **Kenmare River**, which separates the IVERAGH and BEARA peninsulas. The marquesses of Lansdowne called it a 'river' in legal documents so that they could protect their fishing rights.

Kenmare was latterly the home of the English composer E.J. Moeran (1894–1950; *see also* County KERRY). On 1 December 1950 he was seen to fall from the pier at Kenmare during a heavy storm. When his body was recovered it was found that he had had a cerebral haemorrhage following a heart attack.

> Caha to the south, MacGillycuddy to the north,
> This bay lies, a giant bowl
> Of blue water, held reverently
> Between enormous palms.
>
> John Montague: 'Kenmare Bay', from *Poisoned Lands* (1977)

Nun of Kenmare, The. A volume of autobiography (1888) by Margaret Anna Cusack (1822–99), who as a nun in the Poor Clare order was sent to Kenmare in 1861 to set up a convent, and spent many years there helping the poor. She was often at odds with the Catholic hierarchy, and is regarded as something of an early feminist. Late in life she reverted to her original Anglican faith.

Kennet[1] An OCelt river name of uncertain meaning.

A river in Wiltshire and Berkshire, which rises on the Marlborough Downs (*see under* MARLBOROUGH) and flows 71 km (44 miles) south and then east through Avebury, Marlborough and Newbury to join the Thames at Reading. The section upstream of Avebury used to be known as the Winterbourne. The **Kennet and Avon Canal**, joining the Kennet to the River AVON[2] and thereby providing a navigable link between London and Bristol, was opened in 1810. It was designed by the Scottish engineer John Rennie. It was closed in 1951, and reopened in 1990.

See also WEST KENNETT.

Kennet² From the River KENNET¹.

A large administrative district (971 sq km / 375 sq miles) of western WILTSHIRE. It includes the Vale of Pewsey (*see under* PEWSEY), significant portions of the North Wessex Downs (*see under* WESSEX) and Salisbury Plain (*see under* SALISBURY). Its main towns are DEVIZES and MARLBOROUGH.

Kennington 'farmstead or estate associated with Cena', OE male personal name *Cena* + -ING + -TON.

A district of South London (SE11), in the borough of LAMBETH, to the east of Vauxhall and to the northwest of Camberwell. In the Middle Ages it was a royal manor, and the Black Prince (1330–76) had a palace here. Parts of it still belong to the Duchy of Cornwall (*see under* CORNWALL). A large area of common land, part of which is now **Kennington Park**, was once Surrey's main place of execution; the last hanging took place there in the early 19th century. (The park also saw a demonstration by 15,000 Chartists in 1848.) Road upon road of mainly 19th-century houses now cover Kennington's former fields, with at their centre a suitably oval road called **Kennington Oval**, surrounding the OVAL Cricket Ground. Over the 20th century the area became considerably run down and impoverished.

Kennington Underground station, on the Northern line, opened in 1890.

The optician Peter Dolland (1730–1820), inventor of the triple achromatic lens, was born in Kennington.

Kennington Lane, the name of a road in Kennington leading from Vauxhall to the Elephant and Castle, has been used as Cockney rhyming slang for *pain*.

Kensal Green *Kensal* 'king's wood or thicket' (the identity of the king is not known), OE *cyninges* possessive form of *cyning* 'king' + *holt* 'wood, thicket'. The addition of *Green* 'village green' is not recorded until the 16th century.

A district of northwest London (NW10), in the borough of BRENT², to the west of Maida Vale and to the southeast of Willesden. It grew up around **Kensal Green Cemetery**, which opened in 1832. It was the first of the large 19th-century commercial necropolises designed to alleviate problems of churchyard overcrowding in London. It contains the tombs of many notable 19th-century figures, including the Duke of Sussex (sixth son of George III) and his sister, the Princess Sophia, plus Thomas Hood, Sydney Smith, Isambard Kingdom Brunel, Leigh Hunt, William Thackeray, Anthony Trollope, Wilkie Collins and the tightrope-walker Blondin.

> For there is good news yet to hear and fine things to be seen,
>
> Before we go to Paradise by way of Kensal Green.
>
> G.K. Chesterton: 'The Rolling English Road' (1914)

To the northeast is the district of **Kensal Rise**, built on rising ground, and to the southeast (in the borough of Kensington and Chelsea and the City of Westminster) **Kensal Town**, a mid 19th-century development.

Kensal Green Underground station, on the Bakerloo line, opened in 1916.

Kensington 'farmstead or estate associated with Cynesige', OE male personal name *Cynesige* + -ING + -TON.

A district of West London (W8, W10, W11, W14, W5, SW7, SW10) between Notting Hill in the north, Hyde Park and Knightsbridge in the east and West Brompton in the south. One of the old metropolitan boroughs of London, it was granted the status of a 'royal borough' by Edward VII in 1901, in recognition of the fact that Queen Victoria had been born and lived as a child in Kensington Palace. The accolade was retained in 1965 when Kensington combined with Chelsea to form the **Royal Borough of Kensington and Chelsea** (*see under* KENSINGTON AND CHELSEA).

Central Kensington, appropriately enough, has long had associations with royalty and prosperity. No less well heeled than its civic partner Chelsea, it is more staid and respectable. **Kensington Gardens**, a 111-ha (275-acre) public park at the western end of Hyde Park containing the Round Pond, the Broad Walk (a north–south pedestrian road), the Albert Memorial and Sir George Frampton's statue of Peter Pan, and famous in times past for its battalions of nursemaids and nannies perambulating the infant offspring of the gentry, was in the 17th and 18th century the garden of **Kensington Palace**. Converted from an earlier house by Christopher Wren, this has been a royal residence since 1689, when William and Mary moved there from Whitehall Palace. Subsequent occupants have included Queen Anne (who conducted her *ménage à deux* with the Duchess of Marlborough in the palace, and later died there of a fit of apoplexy brought on by overeating), George I, Queen Caroline, Queen Victoria (*see above*), Princess Margaret and Diana, Princess of Wales. Princess Mary of Teck (1867–1953), later Queen Mary, consort of George V, was born in the palace. Royal occupation has proved more controversial in the 21st century, the subsidized rents charged to some tenants (such as Prince Michael of Kent) coming in for criticism from several quarters.

Kensington Palace Gardens, formerly nicknamed 'Millionaires' Row' for its wealthy residents, is a private road to the west of the Palace where many embassies are located. **Kensington High Street** is a venue for serious shopping; big-name stores include Barker's and the now defunct Derry and Toms, with its (still surviving) roof garden.

> The Joneses, when their father was induced to move from Shepherd's Bush to Kensington, showed their gratitude to their mother by hyphening her name with their own …
>
> 'The Misses Robinson-Jones'.
>
> S. Mostyn: *Curatica* (1891)

To the south, wealth and rank give way to the arts and sciences in SOUTH KENSINGTON, while West Kensington, merging into EARL'S COURT, and North Kensington, beyond the A40(M) and to the east of WORMWOOD SCRUBS, are decidedly bedsitterland.

High Street Kensington Underground station, on the District and Circle lines, opened in 1868, West Kensington, on the District line, in 1874 (originally under the name North End (Fulham)), and Kensington (Olympia), on the District line, in 1946.

The artist Paul Nash (1889–1946) was born in Kensington.

There is a New Kensington in the USA (Pennsylvania), and also four towns called Kensington (California, Connecticut, Kansas and Minnesota). The last gave its name to the 'Kensington Stone', a large stone slab with runic inscriptions that is said to have been unearthed nearby in 1898 and has been claimed as evidence of a Viking presence in North America in the 14th century. Kensington is also the name of a suburb of Sydney, Australia, known familiarly to locals as 'Kenso', and of a district of Bridgetown, Barbados: Kensington Oval is the high citadel of Caribbean cricket, where the West Indies remained unbeaten between 1935 and 1994.

Far Cry from Kensington, A. A novel (1988) by Muriel Spark; it is essentially a fictionalized autobiographical account of her days in the bedsitter world of 1950s London and her beginnings as a writer.

Kensington Gore Originally *Gore* 'wedge-shaped or triangular plot of land', OE *gara*. Between the 13th and the 17th centuries it was referred to as *King's Gore*, indicating that it was an estate owned by a king (it is not known who the original royal owner was).

A section of Kensington Road (SW7) between Queen's Gate and Alexandra Gate on the southern edge of Kensington Gardens. The Albert Memorial is to the north, and to the south are the Royal Albert Hall, the Royal College of Art and the Royal College of Organists.

The name is used in theatrical slang as a punning term for stage blood.

Kensingtonian. (A native or inhabitant) of Kensington. The word often connotes snootiness or hauteur, especially as betrayed by speech:

> Superior Margery Seymour, with her Kensingtonian 'mothah and brothah'.
>
> *Times Literary Supplement* (27 June 1936)

Kensington-on-Sea. A nickname for the resort of SAL-COMBE in south Devon.

Kensington stitch. A needlework stitch (called in full **Kensington outline stitch**) formed by putting the needle into the material from the front and returning it some way back while splitting the thread.

Princess of Kensington, A. A light opera (1903) by Sir Edward German, with a libretto by Basil Hood. It failed to live up to the considerable success of its predecessor, *Merrie England* (1902).

Kensington and Chelsea. A borough of southwest London (more formally and in full the **Royal Borough of Kensington and Chelsea**) formed in 1965 by combining the existing boroughs of KENSINGTON and CHELSEA. As well as its two named constituents, this contains BROMPTON, EARL'S COURT, HOLLAND PARK and NOTTING HILL.

As one of the safest Conservative parliamentary constituencies in the country, it has been represented lately by a colourful series of MPs: Nicholas Scott (1974–96), deselected after a series of alcohol-related embarrassments, Alan Clark (1997–9), the famously philandering diarist, and Michael Portillo (in a 1999 by-election following Clark's death), the former Thatcherite and once-mighty leader-in-waiting. In February 2004 the former Conservative Foreign Secretary Sir Malcolm Rifkind was selected to be the consituency's next parliamentary candidate, following Portillo's anouncement that he would not be seeking re-election to Parliament.

Kent An ancient Celtic name, often explained as 'coastal district', but alternatively perhaps 'land of armies'.

A county in the southeast corner of England, one of the HOME COUNTIES, bounded to the west by London, Surrey and East Sussex, to the north by the Thames Estuary, and to the south and east by the English Channel. Its Roman name was **Cantia**. Its chief centres are ASHFORD[1], CANTERBURY[1], CHATHAM, DEAL, GILLINGHAM[1], GRAVESEND, MAIDSTONE (the county town and administrative centre), ROCHESTER, SEVENOAKS, SITTINGBOURNE, TONBRIDGE, TUNBRIDGE WELLS, WHITSTABLE, the port towns of DOVER, FOLKESTONE and SHEERNESS and the seaside resorts of BROADSTAIRS, HERNE BAY, MARGATE and RAMSGATE. It lost some territory to London in 1965 (BROMLEY, for example, and ORPINGTON), and in 1998 Rochester, Chatham and the surrounding area became the unitary authority of MEDWAY[2].

It is mainly a lowland county, relieved in the north by the NORTH DOWNS, which sweep down to chalk cliffs around Dover, and further south by the WEALD. It is one of the country's main fruit-growing areas (whence its sobriquet 'the GARDEN OF ENGLAND'), and hops are a historically important crop:

> Kent, sir – everybody knows Kent – apples, cherries, hops, and women.
>
> Charles Dickens: *Pickwick Papers* (1837)

> Now hopping is all over, all the money spent,
> And don't I wish I never went a-hopping down in Kent.
>
> Anon.: 'Hopping Down in Kent'

ROMNEY MARSH is an important sheep-farming area. Aside

from the Thames, the county's main rivers are the Darent, the MEDWAY[1] and the STOUR[3].

It is the closest part of England to the Continent of Europe (*see* ENGLISH CHANNEL), and over the millennia its southeastern and eastern coast has been a point of arrival and departure. The arrivals have by no means always been welcome ones: since Julius Caesar landed in 55 BC, invaders from Europe have taken the shortest route (*see also* ISLE OF THANET), and the CINQUE PORTS banded together for protection; a more durable invader, Christianity, found its first English foothold in Kent, and the See of Canterbury gives the county a central position in the Anglican Communion. In the 21st century the ferries from Dover and Folkestone have stiff competition from the CHANNEL TUNNEL, which is also a Kentish resource.

According to the Anglo-Saxon scholar the Venerable Bede, Kent was one of the principal locations of settlement of the Germanic invaders known as the Jutes, and tradition has it that Hengist and Horsa (*see under* EBBSFLEET), the two brothers who founded the **Kingdom of Kent** in the 5th century AD, were Jutish. Whatever the exact ethnic identity of the newcomers, by the late 6th and early 7th century, under King Æthelbert (reigned 560–616), the kingdom of Kent had achieved a position of overlordship over all Germanic settlers in England south of the River Humber. Later in the 7th century Kent would lose its dominant position to the Kingdom of EAST ANGLIA.

In cricketing terms Kent is a 'first-class' county. Kent County Cricket Club, founded in 1859, was a founder member of the county championship when that competition was officially constituted in 1890, and has won the competition on seven occasions. Kent's famous players include Frank Woolley, Les Ames, Colin Cowdrey, Derek Underwood and Alan Knott. Its home ground is the St Lawrence Ground, Canterbury. Kent has the distinction of having taken part in the earliest county cricket match on record, on 29 June 1709, playing Surrey at Dartford Brent.

Barn of Kent, the. A nickname for the outsized St Michael's church in SMARDEN.

Fair Maid of Kent, the. An epithet accorded to Joan (1328–85), Countess of Kent, wife of the Black Prince, and only daughter of Edmund Plantagenet, Earl of Kent. The prince was her second husband.

Kentish. Of or relating to Kent. As a noun the word is also used to refer to the English spoken in Kent, particularly during the Old English period.

Kentish cob. A variety of filbert (which is actually a different species from the native cobnut or hazelnut). It was first raised by a Mr Lambert of Goudhurst in Kent in 1830.

Kentish cousins. Distant relations.

Kentish crow. An alternative name for the hooded crow, *Corvus cornix*.

Kentish fire. Originally, rapturous applause or 'three times three and one more'. The expression probably came from the protracted cheers given to the No-Popery orators in 1828–9 in Kent. Lord Winchelsea, proposing the health of the Earl of Roden on 15 August 1834, said: 'Let it be given with the Kentish fire!' It subsequently came to be applied to prolonged slow-handclapping or 'the bird', but in both usages it is now decidedly superannuated.

Kentish Glory. A species of large moth, *Endromis versicolor*. One would be hard put to it to find one in Kent today.

Kentish Knock. A sandbank near the mouth of the River Thames. Generally called simply 'the Knock'.

Kentish long-tails. An expression alluding to the old belief that people from Kent had tails – according to legend, as a punishment for the murder of Thomas Becket. The satirical poet 'Peter Pindar' fastened the story on to the town of STROOD.

Kentishman. A native of Kent, and specifically of West Kent, born west of the River Medway. The distinction from a 'Man of Kent' (*see below*) seems not to be recorded before the 19th century.

Kentish nightingale. An alternative name for the blackcap.

Kentish plover. A type of ringed plover, *Charadrius alexandrinus*, that is a rare migrant to Britain. It was named by the naturalist John Latham, who was sent specimens from Sandwich in Kent in 1802.

Kentish rag. A dark hard compact limestone found in Kent, used for paving and building.

Kentish Suite, A. An orchestral suite (1935) by Hubert Clifford (1904–59), evoking Kent in the 17th century.

Kentish tern. An alternative name for the Sandwich tern (*see under* SANDWICH).

Maid of Kent, the. The sobriquet of Elizabeth Barton (*c*.1506–34), a servant girl who incited Roman Catholics to resist the Reformation and who believed that she acted under inspiration from God. Having denounced Henry VIII for his intention to divorce Anne Boleyn, she was hanged at Tyburn.

Man of Kent. A native of Kent, and specifically of East Kent, born east of the River Medway (as distinct from a 'Kentishman' – *see above*). Legend tells how the Men of Kent went out with green boughs to meet William the Conqueror and were consequently able to obtain confirmation of their ancient privileges.

See also OLD KENT ROAD.

Kentish Town Originally *Kentishton* 'estate held by a family called (le) Kentish', ME surname *Kentish* 'man of Kent' + -TON. A district of North London (NW5), in the borough of CAMDEN, to the north of Camden Town. Until the late 18th century it was a pleasant village by the River FLEET[1], but the 19th century obliterated the fields, first with houses and then, from the 1860s onwards, with railway tracks and sidings. Karl Marx lived here from 1856 until his death in 1883.

Kentish Town Underground station, on the Northern line (High Barnet branch), opened in 1907.

The first branch of Sainsbury's opened in Kentish Town, in 1873.

Kentish Town has been used in Cockney rhyming slang as a synonym for *brown*, an old slang term for a penny.

> Brickish Kentish Town seen through the leaves of
> Highgate.
>
> John Betjeman: *Summoned by Bells* (1960)

Kent's Cavern Perhaps from the surname *Kent*.

A limestone cave at TORQUAY, Devon, about 1.5 km (1 mile) east of the harbour, formerly known as **Kent's Hole**. Apart from the fascination of its natural features, including the beauty of its stalagmite grotto, it is of major importance to archaeologists. Many relics, human and animal, have been found, including those of the mammoth and sabre-toothed tiger. Excavation was begun in the 1820s by a Roman Catholic priest, but he could not publish his results until much later because they clashed with contemporary religious belief.

Ken Wood Perhaps 'canons' wood' (referring to its ownership in the 16th century by the Prior of Holy Trinity, Aldgate, a house of Augustinian canons), ME *canoun* 'canon' + *wode* 'wood'. The spelling of the nearby *Caen Wood Towers Farm* is due to the influence of the French place name *Caen*.

A wooded area in the northeastern corner of Hampstead Heath (*see under* HAMPSTEAD). In the northern part of it is **Kenwood House**, designed by Robert Adam, which dates from 1767–9. Now the property of English Heritage, it contains the IVEAGH Bequest, a collection of pictures by Van Dyck, Rembrandt, Reynolds, Gainsborough, Turner and many others. During the summer an open-air stage is erected in the grounds on which public performances are given.

The area has no connection with Kenwood food mixers, which are named after their inventor Kenneth Wood (1916–97).

Kernow. The name for CORNWALL in the now defunct Cornish language.

Kerrera Possibly 'brushwood island', OScand *kjarr* 'brushwood' + *ey* 'island' (*see* -AY), but the earliest forms have a *-b-* after the first syllable, which is not accounted for in this etymology; it may therefore be a personal name.

An island in the Firth of Lorne (*see under* LORNE), just offshore from Oban, Argyll and Bute. It is separated from the mainland by Oban Bay (*see under* OBAN) and the **Sound of Kerrera**. In July 1249 Alexander II's fleet anchored off Kerrera, as the king prepared an attack against the Norwegian rulers of the HEBRIDES. In a dream, so the king related, St Columba came to him and warned him to return

home. However, Alexander ignored this advice and landed on the island, where he stumbled and fell, dying shortly afterwards of his injuries.

Kerrier From the name of a local Hundred, perhaps '(place of) rounds' (referring to a particular type of hillfort), Cornish *ker* 'fort, round'.

A local government area covering the western tip of Cornwall. Its administrative headquarters are in CAMBORNE.

Kerry, County Irish *Ciarraí* '(land of the) descendants of Ciar'; the legendary *Ciar* was a son of King Fergus and Queen Maeve.

A county in the far southwest of Ireland, bounded on the west by the Atlantic, on the north by the mouth of the River SHANNON, on the east by County Limerick and on the east and south by County Cork. It has a heavily indented coastline, including the DINGLE, IVERAGH and part of the BEARA peninsulas. Except in the north, it is generally mountainous –

> All acclivity and declivity, without the intervention of a
> single horizontal; the mountains all rocks, and the men
> all savages.
>
> Thomas Moore: journal (6 August 1823)

Kerry's mountains include part of the CAHA MOUNTAINS, MANGERTON MOUNTAIN, MACGILLYCUDDY'S REEKS (which has Ireland's highest peak, CARRANTUOHILL), the SLIEVE MISH MOUNTAINS and BRANDON MOUNTAIN. The islands off the coast include the SKELLIGS, VALENCIA ISLAND and the BLASKET ISLANDS. The county town is TRALEE, and other towns include KILLARNEY, LISTOWEL and DINGLE. There are GAELTACHTS (Irish-speaking areas) in the western parts of the county.

Kerry is renowned for the success of its Gaelic footballers, and in the context of sport (and tourism) it is sometimes referred to as **the Kingdom** – as in *Kingdom Come*, the title of a book about Kerry's successful football team published in 1989. As the writer and Kerryman John B. Keane once said,

> Kerry people say there are only two kingdoms, the
> kingdom of Kerry and the kingdom of God.

The nickname is said to derive from a remark by the judge and orator John Philpot Curran (1750–1817) that the magistrates of Kerry were a law unto themselves.

> In pleasant Kerry lives a girl,
> A girl whom I love dearly;
> Her cheek's a rose, her brow's a pearl,
> And her blue eyes shine so clearly!
>
> Anon.: 'The Roving Worker' (18th century), translated
> from the Irish by George Sigerson

> As I was going over the far famed Kerry Mountains
> I met with Captain Farrell and his money he was
> counting.

I first produced my pistol and then produced my rapier

Saying 'Stand and deliver! For I am the bold deceiver!'

Anon.: 'Whiskey in the Jar' (traditional song)

Kerry bog pony. A small breed of pony, little bigger than a Shetland, originally bred for working in wet bogland, where greater size and weight would be a disadvantage.

Kerry blue. A breed of terrier with a dense, wavy coat, a mixture of silver, grey (or black) and blue hairs – the last supposedly deriving from a blue-grey spaniel that swam ashore in Kerry from one of the wrecked ships of the Spanish Armada. They are used for hunting small game, retrieving and, according to one breeder writing in 1924, for 'taking the pants off Irishmen' (he did not elaborate).

Kerry Cousins. A collective term for a number of inter-connected Protestant Ascendancy families – including the Dennys, the Blenerhassets and the Crosbies – who formed political dynasties in the 18th century.

Kerry cow. A small breed of cow, now rare, but once widely reared across southwest Ireland. They are black and have downward-pointing horns. The expression **the Kerry cow knows Sunday** derives from the days when for most poor families a Sunday treat would consist of bleeding the cow and mixing the result with oatmeal to make a pudding.

'Kerry Dance, The'. A poem by James Lyman Molloy (1837–1909), beginning:

O, the days of the Kerry dancing, O, the ring of the piper's tune!

O, for one of those hours of gladness, gone, alas! like our youth too soon …

Kerrygold. A brand of butter, and one of Ireland's best-known exports.

Kerry Head. A headland in County Kerry, at the tip of the next peninsula north of Dingle.

Kerry lily. A low member of the lily family, *Simethis planifolia*, with small white flowers. It is not to be confused with the Lily of Killarney (*see under* KILLARNEY).

Kerryman jokes. The Irish equivalent of Irish jokes (*see under* IRISH), for example:

Did you hear about the Kerryman who had a brain transplant? The brain rejected him.

Kerry security. An early 19th-century term for a worthless pledge; similarly derogatory is the expression **Kerry witness**, for an individual who will swear to anything.

Kerry slide. A movement in the six-movement traditional Irish polka set, involving fast and fancy footwork.

Festival of Kerry, the. An annual festival held in Tralee every August since the 1950s. At its heart is the Rose of Tralee contest (*see also* TRALEE).

Four Kerry Poets, the. A succession of Kerry poets who, according to their memorial erected (1940) in Killarney,

stood 'for all that is heroic in Irish history'. They were Pierce Ferriter (d.1653), Geoffrey O'Donaghue (d.1677), Aodhgan O'Rahilly (d.1728) and Ruadh O'Sullivan (d.1784).

'In Kerry'. A poem by J.M. Synge (1871–1909), beginning:

We heard the thrushes by the shore and sea,

And saw the golden stars' nativity …

Knights of Kerry. A cadet branch of the Desmond family, who collected the Desmonds' rents in the county.

Ring of Kerry. A very popular tourist drive around the Iveragh peninsula and through Killarney. In summer, so congested is the road that there is a one-way system for tourist coaches.

Songs from County Kerry. The title of settings of Kerry folk-songs by the Isleworth-born (and KENMARE-died) composer and Hibernophile E.J. Moeran (1894–1950). He began work on the collection in 1934, and finished it in the spring of 1948 while living in the tents of a group of tinkers (gypsies).

Kersey 'raised land where cress grows', OE *cærse* 'cress' + *eg* (*see* -EY, -EA).

A village in Suffolk, about 16 km (10 miles) west of Ipswich. It seems likely that the village gave its name to **kersey**, a type of heavy ribbed woollen cloth with a short nap, worn by English working men from the Middle Ages until well into the 19th century. The cloth name dates back to at least the 14th century.

Kershope Forest *Kershope* either 'cress valley' or 'grass valley', OE *cærse* 'cress' or *gærs* 'grass' + *hop* 'secluded valley'.

An extensive Forestry Commission plantation in the far northeast of Cumbria. Its northern boundary is marked by the **Kershope Burn**, which also provides part of the border with Scotland. At the foot of the burn is the settlement of **Kershopefoot**.

Kesh, the. An abbreviated form of Long Kesh, i.e. the former MAZE Prison in County Armagh.

Kesteven Probably 'woodland meeting-place', OCelt CED + OScand *stefna* 'meeting-place'.

A former administrative area (in full, the **Parts of Kesteven**) of Lincolnshire, in the FENS, in the southwestern part of the county. It was based in SLEAFORD, and also included GRANTHAM. It was absorbed into Lincolnshire in 1974, but its name lived on in the administrative districts of **North Kesteven** and **South Kesteven**.

When she was ennobled in 1992, Margaret Thatcher (Grantham-born) took the title Baroness Thatcher of Kesteven.

See also HOLLAND[1] *and* LINDSEY.

Keswick 'cheese-making farm', OE *cese* 'cheese' + WICK; *see also* CHISWICK.

A town in the LAKE DISTRICT, Cumbria (formerly in Cumberland), 25 km (15 miles) west of Penrith. It is situated at the northern end of Derwent Water, and overlooked by the grand masses of SKIDDAW and BLENCATHRA. Keswick is an important tourist centre, and was formerly known for its manufacture of 'lead' pencils, using the high-quality graphite from nearby BORROWDALE. Today, only the factory that owns the Cumberland Pencil Museum is still in operation.

Greta Hall, just west of Keswick, was shared by the poets and brothers-in-law Robert Southey and Samuel Taylor Coleridge and their families. Coleridge moved here in 1800, and Southey in 1802, but Coleridge left for London in 1803, leaving his family behind. Southey stayed until his death in 1843. Coleridge had initially moved to the Lakes to be near Wordsworth, and had been thrilled by the place, writing to a fellow recreational drug user:

> My dear fellow, I would that I could wrap up the view from my house in a pill of opium, and send it to you!
>
> Samuel Taylor Coleridge: letter to Humphry Davy (15 July 1800)

However, one of the reasons for Coleridge's departure was the weather. In 1802 he wrote to Sara Coleridge from South Wales, saying there was nowhere in Britain to match the **Vale of Keswick**, but adding:

> O Heaven! that it had but a more genial climate!

Before he left the Lakes, Coleridge was visited by the essayist William Hazlitt, whose behaviour did not go down too well in the town: his advances being refused by a young woman, he grabbed hold of her, and, according to Wordsworth (who heard about the incident later), 'because she refused to gratify his abominable and devilish propensities, lifted up her petticoats and smote her on the bottom'. An angry crowd forced Hazlitt's swift departure.

Kettering '(settlement of) Cytra's people', OE male personal name *Cytra* + *-ingas* (see -ING).
A town in Northamptonshire, about 21 km (13 miles) northeast of Northampton. It came to prosperity mainly via the making of boots and shoes, and of cloth. It was also the original place of manufacture of Weetabix in Britain, in the 1930s.

To the northeast is Boughton House, a 15th-century monastery which ended up, in the hands of the Duke of Montagu, as a palatial late 17th-century mansion in the French taste.

There is a town called Kettering in Ohio, USA.

Kettlebaston 'Ketilbjorn's farmstead', OScand male personal name *Ketilbjorn* with the English possessive ending *-es* + -TON.
A village in Suffolk, about 19 km (12 miles) southeast of Bury St Edmunds.

Kettle Ness 'Ketil's headland', OScand male personal name *Ketil*, with *nes* (see NESS).
A headland on the North Sea coast of North Yorkshire, 8 km (5 miles) northwest of WHITBY. The peninsula is scarred by old alum mines, formerly worked by the people of the village of **Kettleness** just inland; the first village fell into the sea in 1829. Down below the old village, in caves by the sea, lived the **Kettleness Boggles**, a species of goblin who were heard doing their washing on a weekly basis, although no one ever saw them.

Ketton From the former name of the river now called the Chater, and ultimately perhaps from an OCelt tribal name meaning 'old wood' (see CED).
A village in Rutland (before 1997 in Leicestershire, before 1974 in Rutland), about 5 km (3 miles) southwest of STAMFORD.

Robert of Ketton. An English scholar from Rutland who is thought to have lived around 1140. He organized the translation of the Koran into Latin, the first such undertaking in Christian Europe.

Kew Probably 'key-shaped spur of land', OE *cæg* 'key' + *hoh* 'spur of land'; alternatively 'spur of land with a quay', with a first element from ME *key* 'quay, landing-place'.
A district of West London (before 1965 in Surrey), on the southern bank of the River THAMES, in the borough of RICHMOND-UPON-THAMES, in a northward bulge of the Thames to the north of Richmond. The elegant houses around the Green date from the 18th century.

The Public Record Office (now designated as the centre of the National Archives) moved to new premises in Kew in 1996.

> I am his Highness' dog at Kew;
> Pray, tell me sir, whose dog are you?
>
> Alexander Pope: 'Epigram engraved on the Collar of a Dog which I gave to his royal highness' (1738)

Kew Gardens. A botanical park and research institution (officially named the **Royal Botanic Gardens**) in Kew. Originally part of Richmond Park, the gardens were separated off in the 18th century. A special botanic garden was created there in 1759 by Augusta, Dowager Princess of Wales. It was handed over to the nation in 1841. In addition to the extensive and varied displays of plants, there are numerous interesting buildings in the Gardens' 149 ha (368 acres), including the Pagoda, constructed to William Chambers's design in the 1760s; the Palm House, a huge glasshouse built in the 1840s; and **Kew Palace**, a small Jacobean mansion (until the 1730s called the Dutch House) which was a royal residence until the early 19th century. The Gardens were declared a UNESCO World Heritage Site in 2003. Kew Gardens 'Underground' station, on the District line, opened in 1877.

Keynsham 'Cægin's land in a river bend' (referring to a bend in the River Avon), OE *Cægines* possessive form of male personal name *Cægin* + *hamm* 'enclosure' (*see* HAM).

A town (pronounced 'kane-shəm') in Bath and North East Somerset (before 1996 in Avon, before 1974 in Somerset), on the AVON[2] midway between Bristol and Bath. Its name became famous in the 1950s and 1960s thanks to the Bristol entrepreneur Horace Batchelor, who advertised his patent method of winning the Football Pools on Radio Luxembourg and invited listeners to write to him for details at Keynsham. The surreal and satirical Bonzo Dog Band entitled one of its albums *Keynsham* (1969) in dubious honour of the town.

Kibworth Beauchamp *Kibworth* 'Cybba's enclosure', OE male personal name *Cybba* + *worth* (*see* -WORTH, WORTHY, -WARDINE); *Beauchamp* denoting manorial ownership in the Middle Ages by the de Beauchamp family.

A village (pronounced 'beecham') in Leicestershire, about 14 km (9 miles) southeast of Leicester. The Roman Catholic priest and author Ronald Knox (1888–1957) was born here.

Kibworth Harcourt *Harcourt* denoting manorial ownership in the Middle Ages by the de Harewecurt family.

A village in Leicestershire, contiguous with KIBWORTH BEAUCHAMP but on the other (northeastern) side of the A6.

Kidderminster 'Cydela's monastery', OE male personal name *Cydela* + *mynster* 'monastery'.

A town in Worcestershire (before 1998 in Hereford and Worcester, before 1974 in Worcestershire), in the WYRE FOREST district, on the River STOUR[5] and the Staffordshire and Worcestershire Canal, about 22 km (14 miles) north of Worcester and 24 km (15 miles) southwest of Birmingham.

Kidderminster prospered in the late Middle Ages thanks to the Flemish weavers who brought their skills here in the 13th and 14th centuries, but it was in the 18th century that it branched out into the trade that was to make its name: carpet-making. By the 19th century, 'Kidderminster' was a recognized type of carpet, made from yarn that is dyed before being woven. The term even became common enough to be abbreviated colloquially to '**Kidder**'.

Sir Rowland Hill (1795–1879), who introduced the pre-paid penny post, was born in Kidderminster.

The town's most high-profile MP (Conservative; 1950–64) was Sir Gerald Nabarro (1913–73), whose booming voice, quivering mustachios and pompous sentiments were a regular media diversion of the 1950s and early 1960s.

> Kidderminster is a tricksy borough. Its people have a knack of taking their own way.
>
> *Morning Star* (21 May 1862)

Kidderminster Shuttle. The local newspaper of Kidderminster, its name celebrating the shuttles used in carpet looms. It was founded by Unitarians in the 19th century, and is now part of the Newsquest Media Group.

Kidsgrove Probably 'Cyda's grove', OE male personal name *Cyda* + *graf* 'grove, copse'. Early forms suggest an alternative from a dialect form *kidcrew* 'pen, sty for young animals'.

An industrial town in Staffordshire, about 14 km (9 miles) northwest of STOKE-ON-TRENT. The Harecastle tunnels (*see under* HARECASTLE) begin here.

Kidwelly Welsh *Cydweli* 'land of Cadwall' (this Cadwall has not been identified).

A town on the estuary of the River Gwendraeth in Carmarthenshire (formerly in Dyfed), 13 km (8 miles) south of CARMARTHEN. The Welsh version of the name is **Cydweli**. There is a ruined Norman castle, which in 1136 came under attack by Gruffydd ap Rhys ap Tewdwr. His princess, Gwenllian, lost her head in the battle, at a place ever since called Maes Gwenllian ('field of Gwenllian'). Apparently her headless ghost haunted the area for many years, until

---

❖ kil- ❖

Many of the *kil-* names in Scotland and Ireland were given to churches dedicated to the saints, indicating both ancient and modern connections with the men and women who were venerated in these areas. There was a good deal of sharing of saints, and Irish saints were particularly active in the conversion of Scotland: so, in Scotland, KILMACOLM and KILMARNOCK are dedicated to the Irish saint Columba and possibly his uncle; KILMAURS is the church of St Maurus, a French saint. In Ireland, local and international saints are found: KILMICHAEL (County Cork) and KILLALOE (counties Clare and Kilkenny) were dedicated respectively to St Michael the Archangel and St Dalua or Molua. The *kil-* element seems to have replaced very early names with *domnach* in Ireland, perhaps as small monastic cells and hermitages grew up; but in due course, the name became the ordinary word for a church, especially one with a burial ground. That is not to say that the other elements in these names are without significance: KILDARE 'church of the oak tree' reputedly refers to the establishment of a cell, and subsequently a church and monastery, by St Brigid in a pagan oak grove.

The number of names containing the element *kil-* from *ceall*, dative *cill*, 'church' is augmented by those containing other elements. The *kil-* in the Scottish names KILCHURN CASTLE and KILBRANNAN SOUND, both in Argyll and Bute, represents Gaelic *caol* 'strait, narrows'; but in KILKEEL (County Down), both elements are found in 'church of the strait'. KILLIECRANKIE (Perth and Kinross) is a Scottish representative of a confusion very common in Ireland, where the first element is Gaelic *coill* 'a wood'.

someone eventually found her skull and placed it with the rest of her remains.

Kielder From the name of a small river here, an OCelt river name meaning 'rapid stream'.

A small settlement in Northumberland, 26 km (16 miles) west of Otterburn, near the Scottish Border and at the southwestern end of the CHEVIOT Hills. It is just beyond the head of **Kielder Water**, the largest artificial lake in England (created 1982). Kielder Water is the source of the North Tyne (*see under* TYNE[1]), and is much used for water sports. The lake is at the centre of the extensive **Kielder Forest Park**, including the largest Forestry Commission plantation in England.

Kilbarchan 'St Barchan's church', KIL- + personal name *Barchan* or *Berchan*, an Irish saint.

A small town 8 km (5 miles) west of Paisley in Renfrewshire (formerly in Strathclyde region). William Fitzalan founded the church of St Barchan here in the 12th century. The town was once known for its weavers, and the National Trust for Scotland has preserved a weaver's cottage with its hand-loom.

'Life and Death of the Piper of Kilbarchan, The'. An elegy by Sir Robert Sempill of Beltrees (?1595–?1660) for Habbie Simpson, a famous piper of the early 17th century:

> Kilbarchan now may say alas!
> For she hath lost her game and grace,
> Both Trixie, and the Maiden Trace:
>   But what remead?
> For no man can supply his place,
>   Hab Simson's dead.

Kilbarrack. The Dublin suburb that provides the inspiration for Roddy Doyle's fictional BARRYTOWN.

Kilbeggan Irish *Cill Bheagáin* 'church of St Beagán' (*see* KIL-); he founded a monastic church here, possibly in the 7th century.

A village in County Westmeath, some 10 km (6 miles) north of Tullamore. St Beagán's monastery here was succeeded in 1200 by a Cistercian foundation, of which nothing remains. Kilbeggan is at the terminus of a branch of the Grand Canal. The noted orator and judge, John Philpot Curran, represented Kilbeggan in the Irish Parliament from 1783.

Kilbirnie 'church of St Brendan', KIL- + Irish saint's name Brendan, possibly the friend of St Columba.

A town in North Ayrshire (formerly in Strathclyde region), 19 km (11.5 miles) southwest of Paisley.

Kilbrannan Sound 'strait of St Brendan', *Kilbrannan* Gaelic *caol* 'strait, kyle' (*see also* KIL-) + saint's name *Brendan* (*see* KILBIRNIE).

The sound between ARRAN and the KINTYRE peninsula. At its narrowest it is some 6 km (4 miles) across.

Kilburn Perhaps 'Cylla's stream', OE male personal name *Cylla* + *burna* 'stream'. Early forms such as *Kyneburna* suggest an alternative 'cows' stream', with an initial element from OE *cuna* or *cyna*, the possessive plural of *cu* 'cow'.

A district of northwest London (NW6), in the borough of BRENT[2], to the southwest of Hampstead. It is situated on the Edgware Road (*see under* EDGWARE), and a number of venerable local taverns attest to its historical role in refreshing the thirsty traveller. The arrival of the railway in the mid 19th century was swiftly followed by urbanization, and by the early 20th century Kilburn was a fairly run-down working-class area, with a large Irish population. By the end of the 20th century a certain amount of creeping gentrification was in progress.

The 4000-seater Gaumont State Cinema (1937) on **Kilburn High Road**, with its Italian Renaissance-style interior, was once the largest cine-variety theatre in England. It is now a bingo hall. The road itself inspired the early 1970s rock band **Kilburn and the High Roads**, who featured the soon-to-be-famous lead singer Ian Dury.

Kilburn Underground station, originally on the Bakerloo line, now on the Jubilee, opened in 1939, originally under the name Kilburn and Brondesbury, shortened to Kilburn in 1950. (A Kilburn and Brondesbury station also operated on the Metropolitan line between 1879 and 1940.) Kilburn Park Underground station, on the Bakerloo line, opened in 1915; the Underground's first so-called 'passimeter', an automatic ticket machine that also counted the number of passengers, was installed at this station in 1921.

Kilchurn Castle 'narrows of the cairn', *Kilchurn* Gaelic *caol* 'narrows' (*see also* KIL-) + *a' chuirn* 'of the cairn'.

An imposing castle beneath BEN CRUACHAN, built in 1440 by Sir Colin Campbell of Glenorchy in a marsh (then an island) at the northeast end of LOCH AWE, in Argyll and Bute (formerly in Strathclyde region). However, by tradition (as mentioned by the poet William Wordsworth), 'the castle was built by a lady during the absence of her lord in Palestine'. Additions were made in the late 17th century, and the top of one of the towers was blown off in the same storm that destroyed the TAY Bridge in 1879 with such loss of life. Wordsworth visited in 1803 and apostrophized the castle – then, as now, a well-preserved ruin – thus:

> Child of loud-throated War! the mountain Stream
> Roars in thy hearing; but thy hour of rest
> Is come, and thou art silent in thy age;
> Save when the winds sweep by and sounds are
>   caught
> Ambiguous, neither wholly thine nor theirs.
>
> William Wordsworth: 'Address to Kilchurn
> Castle Upon Loch Awe' (1803)

Kilcolman Castle. See under DONERAILE.

Kilconquhar 'church of Conchobar', KIL- + Irish saint's name Conchobar, of whom nothing is known.

A village in Fife, 2 km (1.2 miles) north of Elie. It is pronounced 'kinnuchar'. In the past, the witches of the East Neuk of Fife were drowned in the small **Kilconquhar Loch** next to the village. **Kilconquhar Castle**, originally a 16th-century tower house, was modified and extended in the 19th century.

Kildare Irish Cill Dara 'church of the oak' (see KIL-).

A town in County Kildare, 50 km (30 miles) southwest of Dublin. St Brigid, one of the patron saints of Ireland, founded a monastic settlement here in 470, in what had been a pagan grove associated with love – hence the name (see above); she died here in c.524/528. The Protestant St Brigid's Cathedral incorporates a 10th-century round tower and the ruins of a 13th-century church. Despite the ecclesiastical superstructure, relics of pagan fire-worship survived in Kildare up to the 15th century, in the form of a sacred fire that was always kept burning.

Kildare Place Society. A philanthropic society founded in Dublin in 1811, and more properly known as the Society for Promoting the Education of the Poor. By 1820 Catholic opinion had turned against it, suspicious of its Protestant evangelizing. It was replaced by the national school system in 1831.

Kildare Poems, The. A group of poems dating from the 1330s. They are in Middle English and of unknown authorship, although one is entitled '**Song of Michael of Kildare**', and the poems are known to have come from the Kildare area. The manuscript is in the British Library (Harley 913).

Kildare Rebellion (1534–5). A rebellion against Henry VIII, and in particular his 1534 Act of Supremacy, led by the deputy governor of Ireland, Thomas Fitzgerald, 10th Earl of Kildare, nicknamed Silken Thomas. Fitzgerald eventually surrendered to Sir Leonard Grey, who guaranteed his safety. Despite this, Fitzgerald was hanged, drawn and quartered at Tyburn in 1537.

Kildare side. The right-hand side, a phrase of unknown origin.

Earl of Kildare. In the later Middle Ages the earls of Kildare dominated the government of Ireland. Most powerful of all was the 8th Earl, Garret More, whom Henry VII made lord deputy, saying, 'Since all Ireland cannot rule this man, this man must rule all Ireland.'

'Satire on the People of Kildare'. An anonymous poem from the early 14th century, attacking the town's clergy, monks, nuns, merchants and tradesmen – tailors, cobblers, skinners, brewers, bakers and all:

> Hail be ye bakers with your loaves small
> Of white bread and black, full many and fale!

> Ye pinch on the right weight against God's law,
> To the fair pillory, I rede, ye take heed.

> Modernish version by St John Seymour (*fale* 'numerous', *pinch on the right weight* 'give short weight')

Kildare, County From KILDARE.

A county in eastern Ireland, bounded on the north by Meath, on the east by Dublin and Wicklow, on the south by Carlow, and on the west by Laois and Offaly. It is generally low-lying, with the BOG OF ALLEN in the northwest. The county town is NAAS, and other towns include ATHY, KILDARE and MAYNOOTH. County Kildare – nicknamed the **Thoroughbred County** – is the centre of the Irish horse world: the CURRAGH of Kildare has long been used for racing, the national stud is at Tully, and there are many horse-training establishments.

> – Can you answer me this one? Why is the county of Kildare like the leg of a fellow's breeches?
> Stephen thought what could be the answer and then said:
> – I give it up.
> – Because there is a thigh in it, he said. Do you see the joke? Athy is the town of the county Kildare and a thigh is the other thigh.
> – O, I see, Stephen said.

> James Joyce: *Portrait of the Artist as a Young Man* (1916)

Chair of Kildare. A limestone outcrop on the top of Grange Hill (227 m / 745 ft), County Kildare, overlooking the flat expanse of the Bog of Allen.

Kildonan. See under EIGG.

Kilfenora Irish Cill Fhionnúrach 'church of Fionnúir' (see KIL-); Fionnúir was the legendary son of King Oillil Ólum of Munster and Queen Maeve (Medb).

A village in County Clare, 27 km (17 miles) northwest of Ennis. There are the remains of a 12th-century cathedral here, incorporated into the Protestant church, and several high crosses.

Kilkee Irish Cill Chaoi 'church of St Caoi' (see KIL-).

A small seaside resort on the west coast of County Clare, 10 km (6 miles) northwest of Kilrush. As well as a sandy beach, there are a number of intriguing geological formations. Formerly a fishing village, Kilkee developed as a resort in the 19th century (when it was visited twice by Alfred, Lord Tennyson). The following limerick by Tennyson was found among his papers after his death, but fortunately was burnt before posterity could get wind of it:

> There once was a girl from Kilkee
> Who was stung on the bum by a bee
> It hurt like high hell
> So over she fell
> Into the soothing cold swish of the sea.

Kilkee was the birthplace of the Antarctic explorer Sir Ernest Shackleton (1874–1922).

Kilkeel Irish *Cill Chaoil* 'church of the narrow place' (*see* KIL-); *see also* KYLE.

A fishing port and resort on the southeast coast of County Down, at the foot of the MOURNE MOUNTAINS 35 km (21 miles) southwest of Downpatrick.

Kilkenny Irish *Cill Chainnigh* 'church of St Cainneach' (*see* KIL-); St *Cainneach* (Canice or Kenneth) founded a monastery here in the 6th century; he also gave his name to the Hebridean isle of INCH KENNETH.

The county town of County Kilkenny, 30 km (20 miles) southwest of Carlow. It is an attractive place, with many well-preserved old buildings, including the 13th-century cathedral and castle (the latter formerly the seat of the Earls of Ormond). It is known as **Marble City**, because of the marble quarrying in the area. The substantial Kyteler's Inn was the home of Alice Kyteler (*c.*1280–1330), accused by her stepchildren of having done away with her first three husbands by witchcraft; she escaped to England to avoid the stake, a fate that her serving woman did not escape. In the Middle Ages the Irish Parliament sometimes met at Kilkenny, one of these passing the **Statute of Kilkenny** (*see below*), while in the 1640s an independent parliament, the **Confederation of Kilkenny** (*see below*), met here.

The Protestant College of St John (now **Kilkenny College**) was founded in 1666; its former pupils include a clutch of late 17th-century / early 18th-century notables: the dramatists William Congreve and George Farquhar, the philosopher George Berkeley and the satirist-churchman Jonathan Swift.

> This soil for genius has creative power
> And dreads not a degenerating hour;
> Here Berkeley, Congreve, Swift, in days of yore,
> Lisped the first accents of their classic lore.
>
> > Anon.: epilogue for Kilkenny's Private Theatre,
> > which closed in 1819

It was at the Private Theatre that John Gay's *Polly*, his follow-up to *The Beggar's Opera*, was first performed in 1729, having been banned in England because of its supposedly political content. The poet Thomas Moore appeared on the stage in 1808–10, and here fell in love with his future wife, the 16-year-old actress Bessy Dyke. Kilkenny was the birthplace of two more noted writers: the brothers John (1798–1842) and Michael (1796–1874) Banim, authors of *Tales by the O'Hara Family* (1825–7), one of the first fictional narratives to deal with Irish peasant life and agrarian unrest. It was also the birthplace of the Fenian and founder of the Irish Republican Brotherhood (*see under* IRISH), James Stephens (1824–1901). Today, Kilkenny is a noted centre

for crafts and design, and is home to the Crafts Council of Ireland.

> Oh! the boys of Kilkenny are brave roaring blades
> And whenever they meet with the dear little maids,
> They kiss them and coax them and spend their money
> > free.
> And of all towns in Ireland, Kilkenny's for me,
> And of all towns in Ireland, Kilkenny's for me!
> *Fal de ral de ral de ral de ral lal ra la la lo*
>
> > Anon.: song (early 19th century)

Confederation of Kilkenny. The alliance of Irish Catholics (known as the Confederate Catholics) that fought the forces of the English Parliament from 1642 in the so-called Confederate War (or Civil Wars or Eleven Years' War), until defeated by Cromwell in 1653. The supreme council of the Confederation met in Kilkenny from 1642 to 1648.

fight like Kilkenny cats, to. A phrase meaning to fight until both sides have lost or are destroyed. The story is that during the 1798 United Irishmen's Rebellion Kilkenny was garrisoned by a troop of Hessian soldiers, who amused themselves by tying two cats together by their tails and throwing them across a clothesline to fight. When an officer approached to stop the 'sport' a trooper cut the two tails with a sword and the two cats fled. When asked to explain the two bloody tails, the trooper explained that two cats had been fighting and devoured each other, all but the tails.

County Kilkenny's hurling team are nicknamed the Cats, or the Kilkenny Cats.

> There once were two cats of Kilkenny
> Each thought there was one cat too many.
> > So they quarrelled and fit,
> > They scratched and they bit,
> > Till barring their nails
> > And the tips of their tails,
> Instead of two cats there weren't any.
>
> > Anon.: quasi-limerick

Statute of Kilkenny (1366). A law passed by the Irish Parliament meeting in Kilkenny. Its purpose was to govern relations between the English and the native Irish in the PALE, the latter being regarded as 'enemies'. Among other things the law forbade Englishmen to marry Irishwomen or to listen to Irish musicians or poets, and prevented the Irish from advancing in the Church, or from entering religious houses. Its aim of preventing the Gaelicization of the English settlers was a failure. The law was repealed in the Parliament of 1613–15.

Kilkenny, County From KILKENNY.

A county of southeastern Ireland, bordered on the south by Waterford, on the west by Tipperary, on the north by

Laois, and on the east by Carlow and Wexford. The county town is KILKENNY.

Killala Irish *Cill Ala* 'St Ala's church' (*see* KIL-); nothing is known of this saint.

A small town in County Mayo, 50 km (30 miles) west of Sligo. St Patrick founded a church here, and Killala became a bishopric in the 12th century. The Protestant cathedral dates from 1670, while the cathedral of the Catholic diocese of Killala is in BALLINA. The village overlooks the deep inlet of **Killala Bay**, where the French landed in 1798 in support of the Irish rising (the United Irishmen's Rebellion); they went on to victory at CASTLEBAR, and then defeat at BALLINAMUCK. These events form the basis of Thomas Flanagan's novel *The Year of the French* (1979), dramatized by RTÉ in 1987.

> Forlorn indeed Hope on these shores,
> White-breeched, under a tricorne, shouting orders
> Into the wind in a European language
> *La gloire* against the Atlantic.
>
> Donald Davie: 'Killala', from *New and Selected Poems* (1961)

Killaloe Irish *Cill Dalua* 'church of St Dalua' (*see* KIL-); *St Dalua* (or *Molua*) founded a monastery here in the 6th century.

A small town in County Clare, situated where the SHANNON leaves LOUGH DERG[2], 20 km (12 miles) northeast of Limerick. It was the seat of the high king Brian Boru (*c*.941–1014), and his residence KINCORA is said to have stood on the site of the Catholic church. The cathedral (now Protestant) dates from the 12th century, and was built on the site of the original church founded here in the 6th century by St Molua.

> When Reynard was started he faced to the hollow,
> Where none but the hounds and footmen could follow;
> The gentlemen cried, 'Watch him, watch him, what shall we do?
> If the rocks do not stop him he will cross Killaloe!'
> *Tally-ho hark-away, Tally-ho hark-away* [etc.]
>
> Anon.: 'Reynard the Fox' (a song celebrating the 'Great Hunt' of 1793, in which Reynard traverses much of Ireland)

Killarney Irish *Cill Airne* 'church of the sloes' (*see* KIL-).

A town in County Kerry, some 25 km (15 miles) southeast of Tralee. It has been one of Ireland's principal tourist destinations since the later 18th century, the hordes (including politician Charles James Fox; writers Maria Edgeworth, Sir Walter Scott, Percy Bysshe Shelley, W.M. Thackeray, and Alfred Lord Tennyson; and Queen Victoria) coming for the spectacularly Romantic scenery – the Lakes of Killarney (*see below*), with their islands and their wooded shores, MANGERTON MOUNTAIN and PURPLE MOUNTAIN (all within the **Killarney National Park**), and beyond them the GAP OF DUNLOE and MACGILLYCUDDY'S REEKS. However, opinions have varied as to whether the town itself is a beauty spot:

> A hideous row of houses informed us that we were at Killarney.
>
> W.M. Thackeray (as Michael Angelo Titmarsh): *Irish Sketch-Book* (1843)

> Angels fold their wings and rest
> In that Eden of the west
> Beauty's home, Killarney,
> Heaven's reflex, Killarney.
>
> Edmund Falconer: lyric from his play *Inishfallen* (1862)

> If you took all the visitors away, you'd be left with a beautiful and virtually intact eighteenth and nineteenth-century country town, unvandalized by planners and developers.
>
> Pete McCarthy: *McCarthy's Bar* (2000)

> … very commercial, very spoilt and of little interest …
>
> Brendan Lehane: *The Companion Guide to Ireland* (2001)

But it is the three **Lakes of Killarney** and their environs that the visitors come to see (if they can see them at all for all the other visitors). The Upper Lake is beneath the Gap of Dunloe and the celebrated Ladies' View. From it leads the wide wooded channel known as the Long Range, past the prominence known as the Eagle's Nest, where, in the 19th century, the locals fired cannon and sounded bugles to produce a multiple echo. It was this that inspired Tennyson's famous lyric:

> The splendour falls on castle walls
> And snowy summits old in story:
> The long light shakes across the lakes,
> And the wild cataract leaps in glory.
> Blow, bugle, blow, set the wild echoes flying,
> Blow, bugle; answer, echoes, dying, dying, dying.
>
> Alfred, Lord Tennyson: song added in 1850 to *The Princess* (1847)

The Long Range feeds into Muckross Lake (*see also under* MUCKROSS), as does (a little to the east) the Torc Cascade (which was almost certainly Tennyson's 'wild cataract'). The name Muckross (Irish *mucros* 'pigs' wood') refers to the narrow strip of land separating Muckross Lake from the larger Lower Lake, also called Lough Leane (apparently named after Lean of the White Teeth, a legendary craftsman who had a forge on the shore). On a peninsula (Irish *ros*) on the east shore of Lough Leane is the 15th-century Ross Castle; it is possible that Shelley stayed in Ross Cottage in the castle grounds during his 1813 visit (when he completed *Queen Mab*). On a small island in the lake is INISHFALLEN Abbey.

> By Killarney's lakes and fells,
> Emerald isles and winding bays,
> Mountain paths and woodland dells,
> Memory ever fondly strays;
>
> Edmund Falconer: 'By Killarney's Lakes and Fells'

One Paddy Doyle lived near Killarney,
    And loved a maid called Betty Toole;
His tongue, I own, was tipped with blarney,
    Which seemed to him a golden rule.

Anon.: 'Doran's Ass' (19th century)

There is a village called Killarney in Canada (Ontario), which has given its name to the Killarney Provincial Park.

Killarney Minstrel, the. The blind fiddler James Gandsey (1767–1857), whose mother was a local girl and whose father was an English soldier stationed at Ross Castle.

Lily of Killarney, The. An opera (1862) by Sir Julius Benedict with a libretto by John Oxenford (pseudonym of William Arthur Dunkerley), based on Dion Boucicault's melodrama *The Colleen Bawn* (1860; Irish *cailín bán*, 'fair-haired girl'), itself inspired by Gerald Griffin's novel *The Collegians* (1829). The real Colleen Bawn had nothing to do with Killarney; she was one Ellen Hanley, murdered by her husband in Limerick in 1819. However, Boucicault transferred the action to a more scenically pleasing location, and provided a happy ending: the attempt by Danny Mann, the manservant, to drown his mistress in the lake (believing his master has tired of her) is thwarted by the intervention of 'that poaching scoundrel', Myles-na-Coppaleen. Touristically entrepreneurial Killarney locals have cashed in on the story, and by the shore of Muckross Lake you will find the Colleen Bawn Rock, the Colleen Bawn Caves and the ruined Danny Mann's Cottage.

Songs of Killarney. A collection of verse (1872) by Alfred Perceval Graves, father of the better-known Robert.

Killary Harbour *Killary* Irish *Caoláire* 'narrow sea inlet'.
A long (13-km / 8-mile), narrow inlet on the west coast of Ireland, marking part of the boundary between counties MAYO and GALWAY. The Mweelrea Mountains (*see under* MWEELREA) are to the north, while LEENANE is near the inner end. Killary Harbour was formerly a station of the Royal Navy's Atlantic Fleet.

Killiecrankie 'wood of aspens', Gaelic *coille* 'wood' (*see* CED) + *critheann* 'aspen tree'.
The wooded gorge of the River Garry, just before it meets the River TUMMEL, in Perth and Kinross (formerly in Perthshire, and then in Tayside region). It is some 4 km (2.5 miles) north of Pitlochry, and is also sometimes referred to as the **Pass of Killiecrankie**. It is in the care of the National Trust for Scotland.

Battle of Killiecrankie (27 July 1689). A battle in which the Jacobite supporters of James II (James VII of Scotland) under Bonnie Dundee (*see under* DUNDEE) defeated William III's government troops under Major-General Mackay, despite being outnumbered two to one. Dundee's Highlanders broke the government line with a broadsword charge, but suffered around 1000 casualties. Dundee

himself was fatally wounded during the battle, and the Jacobites lost the subsequent Battle of Dunkeld (*see under* DUNKELD). The **Soldier's Leap** in the gorge commemorates an airborne retreat by one Donald MacBean, a Williamite soldier. The battle is commemorated in a poem by the 17th-century Gaelic poet Iain Lom (John Macdonald), and also by William Wordsworth:

    Like a whirlwind came
    The Highlanders, the slaughter spread like flame;
    And Garry thundering down his mountain-road
    Was stopp'd, and could not breathe beneath the
        load
    Of the dead bodies.

William Wordsworth: 'October 1803, in the Pass of
Killicranky' (1803)

Killinchy Irish *Cill Dhuinsí* 'church of St Dúinseach' (*see* KIL-); nothing is known of this saint.
A village in County Town, on Strangford Lough, 15 km (9 miles) north of Downpatrick.

Killinchy muffler. An embrace with the arms around the neck, rather than the shoulders, back or waist. It is not a move mentioned in *The Perfumed Garden*, and its relation to the village is equally obscure.

Killiney Irish *Cill Iníon Léinín* 'church of the daughters of Léinín' (*see* KIL-); nothing is known of *Léinín*.
A seaside resort in County Dublin, contiguous with DALKEY to the north. It overlooks **Killiney Bay**, while above it **Killiney Hill** is a fine viewpoint.

    Out on Killiney Hill that night, you said
    'Remember how we promised to come up here
    When snow is lying under a full moon?'
    And I made no reply – to hide my sadness ...

Richard Kell (b.1927): 'Spring Night (for Muriel)'

Killorglin Irish *Cill Orglan* 'church of Forgla' (*see* KIL-); nothing is known of *Forgla*.
A small town in County Kerry, 20 km (12 miles) west-north-west of Killarney. It is famed for its Puck Fair (or Puck), an annual livestock fair, now largely an occasion for revelry, dancing and cashing in on the tourists. During the three days of the fair in August, a white billy-goat (or puck-goat, from Irish *poc* 'he-goat') is crowned 'King Puck'. Although probably a piece of residual paganism, the tradition is said to date from the 17th century, when a herd of wild goats charged through the village, thus warning the locals of the imminent arrival of Cromwellian forces (generally regarded as bad news in Ireland). The town itself is sometimes referred to as Puck.

Killybegs Irish *Na Cealla Beaga* 'the small churches' (possibly referring to monastic cells; *see* KIL-) + English plural *-s*.
A fishing port and tourist centre in County Donegal, 20 km (12 miles) west of Donegal itself. It has an annual

sea-angling festival. It was here in 1849, while serving as a customs official, that William Allingham wrote 'The Fairies' ('Up the airy mountain, / Down the rushy glen ...').

> One fateful night in the wind and the rain
> We set sail from Killybegs town,
> There were five of us from sweet Donegal
> And one from County Down,
> We were fishermen who worked the sea
> And never counted the cost
> But I never thought 'ere that night was done
> That my fine friends would all be lost.
>
> Anon.: 'Donegal Danny'

Killykeen Forest Park Probably Irish *cill* 'church' (*see* KIL-) or *coille* 'wood' + male personal name *Cian* (of whom there are several in history and legend).

A scenic area around Lough Oughter, County Cavan.

Kilmacolm 'church of my Columba', KIL- + Gaelic *mo* 'my' + *Colum* 'Columba'. The *mo* is an expression of affection towards the saint.

A residential town some 25 km (15 miles) west of Glasgow, in Inverclyde (formerly in Renfrewshire, then in Strathclyde region).

Kilmahog 'church of my Cùg', KIL- + saint's name variously spelt *Cùg*, *Chug* or *Hog*, of whom nothing is known.

A small village in Stirling unitary authority, 2 km (1.2 miles) northwest of Callander.

Kilmainham Irish *Cill Mhaighneann* 'church of Maighne' (*see* KIL-), with the ending of the Irish name anglicized to HAM. *Maighne* is an unknown figure.

A district in the west of Dublin. **Kilmainham Jail**, now a historical museum, was built in 1792. Here the Irish Nationalist leader Charles Stewart Parnell was imprisoned in 1881–2, until the **Kilmainham Treaty** (*see below*):

> It was the tyrant Gladstone and he said unto himself,
> 'I nivir will be aisy till Parnell is on the shelf,
> So make the warrant out in haste and take it by the mail,
> And we'll clap the pride of Erin's isle into cold
>   Kilmainham Jail.
>
> Anon.: contemporary ballad

Kilmainham Jail also witnessed the executions of the leaders of the 1916 Easter Rising, shot by the British.

Kilmainham look. What this might be may be divined from the famously ribald late 18th-century ballad, 'The Night Before Larry Was Stretched':

> Then the clergy came in with his book,
>   He spoke him so smooth and so civil;
> Larry tipped him a Kilmainham look,
>   And pitched his big wig to the devil;
> Then sighing, he threw back his head
>   To get a sweet drop of the bottle,

And pitiful sighing, he said:
> 'Oh, the hemp will be soon round my throttle
> And choke my poor windpipe to death.'

Kilmainham Treaty (April 1882). The rejection by Charles Stewart Parnell and the Land League of prime minister William Gladstone's 1881 Land Act had led to the Irish leader's incarceration in Kilmainham Jail. Renewed negotiations between the parties resulted in an agreement, whereby Parnell would be released, the provisions of the Act extended and tenants helped with rent arrears in return for Parnell's condemnation of agrarian violence.

Kilmallock Irish *Cill Mocheallóg* 'church of St Mocheallóg' (*see* KIL-); St Mocheallóg (d.639/656) founded the monastery here.

A small market town in County Limerick, some 30 km (20 miles) southeast of Limerick itself. A monastery was founded here in the 7th century, and Kilmallock became an important town in the later Middle Ages – until its sacking in 1570 by Sir James Fitzmaurice *et al.* left it 'a receptacle and abode of wolves'. It suffered further batterings at the hands of the forces of Oliver Cromwell and William III, and never really recovered. There are the remains of a Norman castle and a 13th-century Dominican friary here.

Kilmallock was the birthplace of the soldier Sir Eyre Coote (1726–83), who led many successful campaigns in India.

Kilmarnock 'church of my Ernóc', KIL- + *Mo-Ernóc*. There are some 20 known saints who could be called *Mo-Ernóc* including St Ernán, St Ernín and St Erníne. The *mo* (Gaelic 'my') is an expression of affection towards the saint, and the *-oc* is a diminutive, hence 'my little Ern'.

An industrial town some 30 km (18 miles) southwest of Glasgow, on **Kilmarnock Water** in EAST AYRSHIRE (of which it is the administrative headquarters). It was formerly in Strathclyde region. Kilmarnock is known for the manufacture of textiles and other industries – including whisky blending, established in 1820 by a local grocer by the name of Johnny Walker. There are many connections with Robert Burns, who lived at nearby Mauchline and described 'the streets an' neuks of Killie' (*see also* **Kilmarnock Edition** *below*). **Kilmarnock FC**, founded in 1869 and nicknamed Killie, is the second oldest football club in Scotland.

> Kilmarnock, a grimy, tumble-down place with an air of general slatternliness, but full of character ...
>
> Edwin Muir: *Scottish Journey* (1935)

However, if you desire instant wealth, statistics suggest you should move to Kilmarnock: by September 2004 it had garnered the highest per-capita number of National Lottery millionaires in Britain.

I'm not going to move, I like where I am, I like my
neighbours and my wee house.

> Rosemary Ferguson, unemployed cleaner and Lottery
> millionaire, as quoted by the BBC (21 September 2004)

Boyd of Kilmarnock. Robert Boyd, 1st Lord of Kilmarnock
(d.*c*.1471), a nobleman who briefly held power in Scotland
(1466–9) during the minority of James III.

Kilmarnock bonnet. A wide, flat woollen bonnet.

Kilmarnock Edition, the. The name given to Robert
Burns's *Poems, Chiefly in the Scottish Dialect*, printed in July
1786 by the Kilmarnock publisher John Wilson. The volume contains such well-known poems as 'The Twa Dogs',
'To a Mouse', 'To a Louse', 'An Address to the Deil' and
'The Cotter's Saturday Night'. It earned the poet £20 and
immortal fame.

Kilmarnock hood. A conical woollen cap, formerly worn
as a nightcap or by those working inside.

Kilmarnock shot. In football and other ball games, an
early 20th-century term for any unsporting shot, such as
putting the ball deliberately out of play.

Kilmarnock and Loudon. A former district (1975–96)
of Strathclyde region. The administrative seat was at
KILMARNOCK.

Kilmaurs 'church of St Maurus', KIL- + *Maurus*, a 6th-century
French saint, who also gave his name to the French Benedictine
community of St Maur.

A small town 3 km (2 miles) north of Kilmarnock in East
Ayrshire (formerly in Strathclyde region). It was the
birthplace of the nutritionist John Boyd Orr (1880–1971),
the first director of the UN Food and Agriculture Organization (1945–8), who won the Nobel Peace Prize in 1949.

sharp as a Kilmaurs whittle. An Ayrshire expression for
'sharp-witted' (Scots *whittle* 'knife'; Kilmaurs was once
known for its manufacture of cutlery). In the town itself
they have a saying:

> A Kilmaurs whittle can cut an inch afore the point.

Kilmichael Irish *Cill Mhichíl* 'St Michael's church' (*see* KIL-).
A village in County Cork, 25 km (15 miles) northwest of
Clonakilty.

Kilmichael Ambush (28 November 1920). A famous action
in the Anglo-Irish War, in which an IRA unit led by Tom
Barry accounted for the deaths of 15 Auxiliaries. Some of
the details of Barry's own account of the action have been
subject to scrutiny by revisionist historians, with the
suggestion that some of the Auxiliaries may have been
killed after they had surrendered. Nevertheless, the ambush
has become a part of Republican lore.

'Boys of Kilmichael, The'. A popular ballad celebrating the IRA victory in the Kilmichael Ambush, possibly
written by a local schoolteacher Jeremiah O'Mahoney:

> Whilst we honour in song and in story

> The memory of Pearse and McBride
> Whose names are illumined in glory
> With martyrs that long since have died,
> Oh forget not the boys of Kilmichael
> Who feared not the ice and the foe,
> Oh the day that they marched into battle
> They laid all the Black and Tans low.

Kilnsey Probably 'kiln by the marsh', OE *cyln* 'kiln' + *sæge*
'marsh'.

A village in Wharfedale, North Yorkshire, 16 km (10 miles)
north of Skipton. It appears in the film *Calendar Girls* (2003;
see also RYLSTONE). Nearby is the great overhanging limestone mass of **Kilnsey Crag**, which reminded one Chinese
traveller of the massive stone animals guarding the tombs
of the Ming emperors in Nanking. There is a traditional
challenge whereby new visitors attempt (usually unsuccessfully) to hit the crag with stones thrown from the road.
The brightly clad rock-climbers frequently seen muscling
up the crag's improbable angles may not necessarily
appreciate the continuation of this custom.

Kilrenny. *See* ANSTRUTHER.

Kilroot Irish *Cill Ruaidh* 'church of the red land' (*see* KIL-).
A village in County Antrim, 4 km (2.5 miles) east along the
coast from Carrickfergus. Churchman-writer Jonathan Swift
had his first living here (1695–6), and here wrote *A Tale of
a Tub* (1704).

Kilruddery Irish *Cill Ruairí*, possibly 'church of the wanderers' (*see* KIL-) or alternatively the second word may be a
personal name.

A locality in County Wicklow, between Bray Head (*see under*
BRAY[2]) and GREAT SUGAR LOAF. It is the ancestral home of
the earls of Meath (the present Kilruddery House is Tudor
revival, but there are 17th-century gardens).

'Kilruddery Hunt, The'. A celebration by Thomas Mozeen
(1709–87) of an epic day out with the Earl of Meath's hunt.
It begins:

> In seventeen hundred and forty-four
> The fifth of December, I think 'twas no more,
> At five of the morning by most of the clocks,
> We rode from Kilruddery in search of a fox.

It is five hours and ten minutes later that the fox eventually
meets its end.

Kilrush Irish *Cill Rois* 'church of the wood or peninsula' ('wood'
seems topographically more likely); *see also* KIL-.

A port and market town on the south coast of County
Clare, overlooking the Mouth of the SHANNON some 60 km
(37 miles) west of Limerick. Kilrush is famous for its horse
fairs, and there is a marina and also ferries to nearby
SCATTERY ISLAND.

Kilsyth Possibly 'church of St Syth', KIL- + personal name,
although no local St *Syth* is known. The early form *Kilvesyth*

(1210) confirms the dedication to St Syth, because the -ve- is a form of the *mo* (Gaelic 'my') endearment found in KILMA-COLM and KILMARNOCK.

A town in North Lanarkshire (formerly in Stirlingshire, then in **Cumbernauld and Kilsyth** (*see under* CUMBERNAULD) district of Strathclyde region), 18 km (11 miles) northeast of Glasgow. It was near Kilsyth that the first potatoes in Scotland were grown, in 1739.

Kilsyth Hills. A range of moorland hills with a steep southerly escarpment. They lie to the northwest of Kilsyth, and rise to 570 m (1870 ft) at Meiklebin. They are effectively an eastward extension of the CAMPSIE FELLS.

Battle of Kilsyth (15 August 1645). An engagement in which the Royalist forces of the Marquess of Montrose defeated the anti-Royalist Marquess of Argyll. The battle took place to the east of the town. The following month the tables were turned at PHILIPHAUGH.

Kiltamagh Irish *Coillte Mach* 'woods of the plain'.

A village in County Mayo, 20 km (12 miles) east of Castlebar. It is pronounced 'kulchimah', whence is derived the Hiberno-English word **kulchie**, meaning a person of inexpressible cunning, deviousness and greed.

Kiltartan Irish *Cill Tartain* 'church of Tartan' (*see* KIL-); *Tartan* is an unknown figure.

A locality in County Galway, some 3 km (2 miles) north of Gort. There is a ruined medieval Gothic church here.

> Going to Mass by the heavenly mercy,
> The day was rainy, the wind was wild;
> I met a lady beside Kiltartan
> And fell in love with the lovely child ...
>
> Antaine Ó Raifteirí (*c*.1784–*c*.1835): 'Mary Hynes',
> translated from the Irish by Frank O'Connor

Kiltartan is near COOLE PARK, the home of Lady Gregory, and gave its name to the Hiberno-English idiom she used in her prose-writing and plays, in which the so-called **Kiltartan infinitive** is a recurring feature, for example: 'The poor man to be deserted by his own wife ...' (This sort of thing was sent up by Gerald MacNamara in his 1909 play entitled *The Mist that Does Be on the Bog*.) Kiltartan features in the titles of a number of Lady Gregory's works: *The Kiltartan History Book* (1909), *The Kiltartan Wonder Book* (1910), *The Kiltartan Molière* (1910) and *The Kiltartan Poetry Book* (1918).

Kiltartan also appears in the works of Lady Gregory's friend W.B. Yeats:

> My country is Kiltartan Cross,
> My countrymen Kiltartan's poor,
> No likely end could bring them loss
> Or leave them happier than before.
>
> W.B. Yeats: 'An Irish Airmen Foresees His Death', from
> *The Wild Swans at Coole* (1919) (The dead airman was
> Lady Gregory's son, Major Robert Gregory, killed in the
> First World War.)

Kilwinning 'St Wynin's church', KIL- + personal name, probably the Welsh saint Gwynnion. However, the Gaelic name *Cill Dingean* indicates that some at least derive the name from St Finnén, alias St Findbar of Moyville, the Irish saint mentioned below.

A town in North Ayrshire (formerly in Strathclyde region), some 30 km (20 miles) southwest of Paisley. A church was first built here by the Irish missionary St Wynin in the 6th century. In 1150 an abbey was founded on the site, and it is said that the masons from mainland Europe who came to work on it brought Freemasonry with them; Kilwinning is still regarded by Freemasons as the 'Mother Lodge' in Scotland.

Another old tradition is that of the **Ancient Society of Kilwinning Archers**, founded possibly as long ago as 1483. Every year the Archers hold a competition to shoot a papingo (a wooden bird or popinjay) hung on the abbey tower (a replacement tower was completed in 1816).

Kilworth Irish *Cill Uird* 'church of the order', where *órd*, possessive *úird*, can mean order in most senses – ritual ('the order of the Mass'), monastic, even numerical; *see also* KIL-.

A village in County Cork, 5 km (3 miles) north of Fermoy. To the north are the hills called the **Kilworth Mountains**, the western, lower end of the KNOCKMEALDOWN MOUNTAINS and once the haunt of the highwayman Willie Brennan (executed in 1840):

> 'Tis of a famous highwayman a story I will tell,
> His name was Willie Brennan and in Ireland he did
> dwell.
> 'Twas in Kilworth Mountain he commenced his wild
> career,
> Where many a gallant gentleman before him shook in
> fear.
>
> Anon.: 'Brennan on the Moor', an old ballad that was
> popularized in the 1960s by the Clancy Brothers

Kimmeridge 'convenient track or strip of land' or 'Cyma's track or strip of land', OE *cyme* 'convenient' or male personal name *Cyma* + *ric* 'track or strip of land'.

A village in Dorset, on the Isle of PURBECK, about 11 km (7 miles) west of Swanage. On the nearby coast the low dark cliffs exhibit sedimentary deposits whose exceptional development and exposure has lent the name Kimmeridge (and the adjective **Kimmeridgian**) to the division of the Upper Jurassic (about 150–135 million years ago) from which they date. A productive oil-well was sunk on top of the cliffs in 1959.

Kimmeridge clay. A type of fossil-bearing clay which contains black bituminous shale. Deposits of it occur across much of southern England and parts of Europe.

Kimmeridge coal. Bituminous shale from Kimmeridge clay which can be burnt as fuel.

Kimmeridge coal money. Discs of shale found near

Kimmeridge, popularly supposed to have been used as coins by the ancient inhabitants.

Kincardine 'at the head of the thicket', Gaelic *ceann* 'head', dative *cinn* 'at the head' + *cardden* 'thicket'.

A town in the very southwest of Fife, 17 km (10 miles) west of Dunfermline, on the north shore of the Firth of Forth (it is sometimes called **Kincardine-on-Forth**). It was once an important port, and was the birthplace of Sir James Dewar (1842–1923), who invented the double-walled vacuum flask. The town is best known today for the **Kincardine Bridge**, built in 1936 across the Firth of Forth. Until the Forth Road Bridge was opened in 1964, this was the only crossing for motor vehicles below Stirling, apart from the ferry between South and North Queensferry.

Kincardine and Deeside. A district of the former Grampian region, formed in 1975. In 1996 it was absorbed into the new unitary authority of Aberdeenshire.

Kincardine O'Neill. A village in Deeside in Aberdeenshire, 12 km (7 miles) west of Banchory. The village was in the patrimony of the ancient monastery of Torannan, itself belonging to descendants of the semi-legendary Irish king Niall of the Nine Hostages (hence the second element of its name).

Kincardineshire. A former county of northeastern Scotland, also called the MEARNS, whose county town was STONEHAVEN. It was bounded on the east by the North Sea, on the north by Aberdeenshire and on the west and south by Angus. It took its name from the ancient town of Kincardine (also referred to as **Kincardine in the Mearns**), some 3 km (2 miles) east of Fettercairn, of which only the mound of Kincardine Castle remains. James Graham, 1st Marquess of Montrose (1612–50), the great soldier of the Civil War period, was also Earl of Kincardine. The county disappeared in the 1975 reorganization.

Kincora Irish *Ciann Coradh* 'head of the weir'.

The palatial stronghold of the high king Brian Boru (*c*.941–1014) in or near KILLALOE, County Clare – its exact site is unknown (it was utterly destroyed by Turlough O'Connor in 1119), although it possibly stood where the Catholic church is now situated.

Remember the glories of Brian the brave,
Tho' the days of the hero are o'er;
Tho' lost to Mononia and cold in the grave,
He returns to Kinkora no more!

Thomas Moore: 'Remember the Glory of Brian the Brave', from *Irish Melodies* (1808–24)

Kincora Boys' Home Scandal. A scandal involving sex abuse in a boys' home in Belfast in the 1970s, in which it was said that the British government tried to mount a cover-up because of the alleged links of those involved with Loyalist groups and British intelligence.

Nevertheless, three care-workers at the home were convicted in 1981.

Kinder Scout *Kinder* perhaps '(place) with wide views', OCelt *com* 'with' + an OCelt word related to Greek *derkomai* 'to see'; *Scout* 'projecting cliff', OScand *skuti*.

A mountain (pronounced 'kin-də') in the PEAK DISTRICT, in Derbyshire. It is in the northern part of the District, about 8 km (5 miles) southeast of Glossop. Its bleak table-top summit is 637 m (2088 ft) high – the highest point in the Peak District.

Kinder Mass Trespass (24 April 1932). An action by several hundred ramblers, mostly from Manchester, in which they fought with gamekeepers trying to keep them off the privately owned grouse moors of the Kinder plateau. Several of the leaders, including the young Communist Benny Rothman, were subsequently arrested, but this and other similar actions paved the way for the creation of the Peak District National Park after the Second World War. However, it was not until the 21st century that the right to roam on mountain and moorland in England was established in statute.

He [a keeper] called me a louse and said 'Think
    of the grouse,'
Well, I thought but I still couldn't see,
Why old Kinder Scout and the moors round about
Couldn't take both the poor grouse and me.

Ewan MacColl: 'The Manchester Rambler' (1963)

Kingdom, the. A byname of County KERRY.

Kingdom whose Summits are Lower than the Waves, the. The English translation of a Gaelic nickname for TIREE.

Kingham 'homestead of Cæga's people'. OE male personal name *Cæga* + *inga-* (*see* -ING) + HAM.

A straggling village in Oxfordshire, in the COTSWOLDS, about 9 km (6 miles) southwest of Chipping Norton. Situated on the London-to-Worcester railway line, Kingham has become, like nearby CHARLBURY, something of a commuter village for long-distance London professionals.

It is not so much a village as an extension of the A40 from Ladbroke Grove ... I even got a cab.

Alex Neate James (bass guitarist of Blur and Kingham resident), quoted in *The Times* (11 November 2004)

Kinghorn 'at the head of the bog', Gaelic *ceann* 'head', dative *cinn* 'at the head' + *gronn* 'bog, marshy ground, mossy moor'.

A royal BURGH (early 12th century) in Fife, some 4 km (2.5 miles) east of Burntisland, on the north shore of the Firth of Forth. On 19 March 1286 Alexander III was killed when his horse stumbled over a cliff just south of the town, as he hurried from Edinburgh to rejoin Yolande de Dreux, his wife of one year. His death precipitated many years of conflict over who should rule Scotland – a conflict that was finally resolved at BANNOCKBURN in 1314. To many, the king's death seemed fated, as in the previous year his marriage feast in JEDBURGH had been interrupted by the appearance of a skeletal spectre. Just the day before the king's death, Earl Patrick of Dunbar had challenged the famous seer, Thomas the Rhymer of ERCILDOUNE, to prophesy the morrow's events, and had received the reply:

> Alas for the morrow, day of misery and calamity! Before the hour of noon there will assuredly be felt such a mighty storm in Scotland that its like has not been known for long ages past. The blast of it will cause nations to tremble, will make those who hear it dumb, and will humble the high, and lay the strong level with the ground.

As the morning was fair, Earl Patrick was inclined to mock – until, just before noon, a messenger brought news of the king's death.

In the 1720s Daniel Defoe noted that the men of Kinghorn occupied themselves with the shooting of porpoises, boiling the fat into oil.

Kingsbere. A fictional name for the Dorset village of BERE REGIS in the novels of Thomas Hardy (an alternative spelling of **King's-Bere** is also used).

Kingsbridge 'the king's bridge' (denoting that the upkeep of the bridge (one of the customary duties of local landowners) was the responsibility of the Crown), OE *cyninges* possessive form of *cyning* 'king' + *brycg* 'bridge'.

A market town in Devon, in the SOUTH HAMS, at the head of the **Kingsbridge Estuary**, about 5 km (3 miles) north of SALCOMBE (which is near the mouth of the estuary). It is built on a hill, and its steep narrow streets include the Shambles (a late 16th-century shopping arcade) and Squeezebelly Lane.

William Cookworthy (1705–80), who discovered china clay in Cornwall and made the first porcelain in England, was born in Kingsbridge.

Kingsclere *Kings-* denoting royal manorial ownership in the Middle Ages + *-clere* probably the original settlement name, perhaps from an OCelt river name meaning 'bright stream'.

A village in Hampshire, on the edge of the North Wessex Downs (*see under* WESSEX) about 11 km (7 miles) southeast of Newbury. BURGHCLERE and HIGHCLERE are a little to the west.

King's Coughton *King's* denoting manorial ownership in the Middle Ages by the king; *Coughton* probably 'farmstead near the hillock', OE *cocc* 'hillock' (or possibly 'woodcock') + -TON.

A village in Warwickshire, about 13 km (8 miles) northwest of Stratford-upon-Avon.

King's Cross Previously, and until the early 19th century, *Battlebridge* (a 17th-century alteration of the earlier *Bradford-*

bridge 'bridge at the broad ford', and despite local legend the place was never the site of a battle between Boudicca (Boadicea) and the Romans); *King's Cross* 'king's crossroads', from a road-junction in the area, where Euston Road meets Gray's Inn Road and Pentonville Road, which itself was named after a statue of George IV that stood here, 1830–45.

A district of Central London (N1, NW1), in the boroughs of CAMDEN and ISLINGTON, between Bloomsbury to the south, REGENT'S PARK to the west and Camden Town to the north. The change in the area's nomenclature (*see above*) was confirmed, and reinforced, when in 1852 a new station was opened by the crossroads, at the eastern end of Euston Road, on the site of the former London Smallpox Hospital, and was called King's Cross. It formed the London terminus of the Great Northern Railway, and was at the time the largest station in England. The building, designed by Lewis Cubitt, has a plain brick facade composed of two impressive arches, at present partially obscured by excrescences perpetrated in the 1960s to accommodate a new booking hall and concourse. It is somewhat overshadowed by the Gothic dignity of St Pancras Station and the Midland Grand Hotel just to the west. **King's Cross Station** is now the London terminus for the east-coast main line to northeast England and eastern Scotland (in the days of steam, *The Flying Scotsman* left from here) and for some East Anglian services, and also for northeastern suburban services. One of the many alleged burial places of the British queen Boudicca (Boadicea) is beneath Platform 10 – perilously close to the Platform 9¾ from which Harry Potter's Hogwarts Express (*see under* HOGWARTS) departs. King's Cross is valued at £200 on a Monopoly board.

King's Cross St Pancras Underground station opened in 1863. It originally served the Inner Circle (now the Circle line), and was called simply King's Cross. It was given its present name in 1933, and five lines now use it (more than any other London Underground station). Its worst moment came in November 1987, when 31 people were killed in a fire on the escalators and in the booking hall.

The area around the main-line station, which shares its name, has never been a prosperous one, and in the latter part of the 20th century it became decidedly seedy. In contemporary slang it is known as **the Cross**. Prostitutes ply for hire in front of the station (there is no shortage of new recruits arriving by train), and behind it there was a notorious meat-rack. At the start of the 21st century a 23.5 ha (58 acre) site to the north of the station, a wilderness of Victorian industrial archaeology, is undergoing extensive long-term redevelopment. It will be known as **King's Cross Centre**. The area's distinctive colonnaded gasholders are to survive among the new houses and offices.

The comic actor Kenneth Williams (1926–88) was born in King's Cross.

There is also a district called King's Cross in Sydney, Australia, in the suburb of Darlinghurst, about 3 km (2 miles) east of the city centre. Its reputation is broadly comparable to London's SOHO. Locals call it 'the Cross'.

King's Delph 'the king's drainage ditch', *Delph* 'drainage ditch', OE *delf* 'trench, ditch, quarry'; the king in question might be Cnut, ruler of England (1016–35).

An area of navigable waterway and fenland, about 5 km (3 miles) southeast of Peterborough, near WHITTLESEY. It is also known as **King's Dyke** or **Cnut's** (Canute's) **Dyke**, although the waterway's origins are unclear and may even be Roman. The nearby **King's Dyke Pit**, from a brickworks, has yielded fossils.

King's Forest of Geltsdale After the small River Gelt (OCelt *geilt* 'madman'), a tributary of the EDEN[1].

An old royal hunting forest in the far northwestern PENNINES, on the border between Cumbria and Northumberland. The highest point is Cold Fell (621 m / 2037 ft).

Kingshouse, the Some say it derives its name from the time when there was a royal hunting forest here (the Ordnance Survey still marks the adjacent area as 'Royal Forest'). Others say the name comes from the time it was used as a barracks for George II's soldiers after the failure of the 1745 Jacobite Rebellion.

A remote hotel on the northwest edge of Rannoch Moor (*see under* RANNOCH), close to the upper ends of GLEN COE and Glen Etive (*see under* ETIVE), Highland (formerly in Argyll), 29 km (18 miles) north of Tyndrum. It was built in the 17th century on the drove road from Skye to the Falkirk Tryst (*see under* FALKIRK[1]), and is one of the oldest licensed inns in Scotland.

Early travellers were not particularly impressed. Dorothy Wordsworth visited with William in 1803 and recorded in her journal:

> Never did I see such a miserable, such wretched place, – long rooms with ranges of beds, no other furniture except benches, or perhaps one or two crazy chairs, the floors far dirtier than an ordinary house could be if it were never washed. With length of time the fire was kindled and after another hour of waiting, supper came, a shoulder of mutton so hard that it was impossible to chew the little flesh that might have been scraped off the bones.

Coleridge was also of the party, and, having walked all the way from Tyndrum, failed to appreciate an evening of jollity:

> This Kingshouse, from the rancid moorland peat, smells like a dirty macquerel with bilge-water. Nine miles every way from all dwelling. Vile troop of drovers, with fiddle and dancing, and drinking, kept it up all night, one clamour like a crew of pirates that 'house on the wild sea with wild usages'.

> Samuel Taylor Coleridge: journal (1 September 1803)

The facilities had improved considerably by the early 20th century, when the Kingshouse became a favourite haunt of gentlemen-mountaineers, not least because of its spectacular view of BUACHAILLE ETIVE MÓR. In 1941, just before leaving to join the British forces in Egypt, W.H. Murray made one last visit, to climb Crowberry Gully on the Buachaille:

> We drove up to the Kingshouse Inn at two o'clock in the morning of 1st February. A quilt of new snow covered the ground, the sky was heavy-burdened, and large flakes fell twisting through the beam of the car's head-lamp. After our long drive through snowstorms on Rannoch moor, the old inn looked like a true outpost of civilization. Nor, despite the unearthly hour and the profitless trouble we had caused her in past years, did Mrs Malloch fail us. A fire, hot tea, food, and beds – all were waiting for us …

> W.H. Murray: *Mountaineering in Scotland* (1947)

Kings Langley *King's* denoting royal manorial ownership in the Middle Ages; *Langley see* ABBOTS LANGLEY.

A village in Hertfordshire, about 6 km (4 miles) northwest of Watford. It was here that William the Conqueror received the submission of London in the autumn of 1066. In the Middle Ages there was a royal palace here, the residence of English sovereigns from Henry III to Richard II.

> Ralph holds Langelei [Langley] from the Count. It answers for 1½ hides. Lands for 16 ploughs. In lordship, none, but 2 possible. 1 Frenchman with 4 villagers and 5 smallholders have 2 ploughs; 12 ploughs possible. 2 mills at 16s; 2 slaves; meadow for 3 ploughs; pasture for the livestock; woodland; 240 pigs. Total value 40s; when acquired £4; before 1066 £8. Thorir and Seric, two of Earl Leofwine's men, held this manor.

> > Domesday Book (1086), entry for Kings Langley (The count from whom Ralph held the manor was Count Robert of Mortain, half-brother of William the Conqueror. Before the Norman Conquest the place had been held by two men in the service of Earl Leofwine of Kent, a younger brother of King Harold.)

King's Lynn *King's* from the town's appropriation by Henry VIII after the Dissolution of the Monasteries in the 16th century (before that, its name had been *Bishop's Lynn*, from its connection with the see of Norwich); *Lynn* OCelt *linn* 'pool'.

A market town and port in Norfolk, at the southeastern corner of the WASH, on the GREAT OUSE. Locals usually refer to it simply as **Lynn**. It was already an important port by the 14th century, handling large quantities of wool and cloth, but its greatest prosperity came with the corn-shipping trade of the 18th century.

King's Lynn was once a walled town, but only a small part of the wall and its south gate (1520) remain. The town's mercantile past has endowed it with a legacy of fine commercial buildings, including Hampton Court, originally a 14th-century warehouse; the Hanseatic Warehouse

(1428), a depot used by the German Hanseatic League; the Greenland Fishery House (1605), a former merchant's house, now a museum; and the Dutch-style Custom House (1683) on the quay. Notable municipal buildings include St George's Guildhall, dating from the early 15th century (now restored as a theatre and arts centre), the oldest example in England of a medieval Merchant Guild's house. The octagonal Red Mount Chapel (1485) originally served as a stopping-place for pilgrims on their way to the shrine at WALSINGHAM.

The historian John Capgrave (1393–1464) and the novelist and diarist Fanny Burney (1752–1840) were born in King's Lynn, as was the navigator George Vancouver (1757–98). Vancouver Island in Canada was named after him, and he himself named the Lynn Canal, a fjord on the Alaskan coast, in honour of his birthplace.

The 15th-century mystic Margery Kempe lived in King's Lynn, and Robert Walpole, Britain's first prime minister, was the town's MP from 1702 to 1742.

The royal residence SANDRINGHAM House is about 11 km (7 miles) to the northeast of King's Lynn.

Lynn Channel. A navigable channel through the shallow waters at the southern end of the WASH, forming an outlet from the mouth of the GREAT OUSE. Further out, beyond the sandbanks, and a little to the west, is the much wider **Old Lynn Channel**; and to the southwest of this, the anchorage of **Old Lynn Roads**.

Lynn Deeps. A wide deep-water channel at the northern end of the WASH.

Kingsmarkham. A fictional market town in southern England which serves as the backdrop of the 'Chief Inspector Wexford' *romans policiers* of Ruth Rendell. It is based on MIDHURST in West Sussex.

> Ruth Rendell's Kingsmarkham, nominally in Sussex but vague enough to be anywhere, not quite rural, not quite urban, and anachronistic enough to produce a local evening paper, delivered door-to-door. Rendell's crime contours conform to what Americans call the English Cosy. The occasional modern reference apart, Kingsmarkham remains technophobic and as traditional as Agatha Christie.
>
> Chris Petit: *The Guardian* (9 November 2002)

Kingsmills This may be similar to Kingsmill in Tyrone, 'mills of a man called King', though a reference to royal ownership is also possible.

A locality in south ARMAGH, scene of a sectarian massacre of ten Protestant workers on 5 January 1976 by a group of Republicans, in retaliation for the killing of five local Catholics the day before.

King's Norton *King's* denoting manorial ownership in the early Middle Ages by the Crown; *Norton see* NORTON DISNEY.

A southern suburb of BIRMINGHAM, just to the southeast of Bournville.

King's Nympton *King's* from its status as a royal manor in 1066; *Nympton see* GEORGE NYMPTON.

A village in Devon, near the southern edge of Exmoor, to the east of the River MOLE[2], about 8 km (5 miles) southwest of South Molton.

See also QUEEN'S NYMPTON.

King's Oak A blend of *King's Heath* or KING'S NORTON and SELLY OAK, the names of genuine Birmingham suburbs.

A fictional suburb of BIRMINGHAM that forms the setting of the ATV/Central soap opera *Crossroads*, originally shown 1964–88 and revived (very temporarily) in 2002.

King's Pyon *King's* denoting manorial ownership in the early Middle Ages by the Crown; *Pyon* 'island infested with gnats or other insects', OE *peona* possessive plural of *pie* 'gnat' + *eg* (*see* -EY, -EA).

A village in Herefordshire (before 1998 in Hereford and Worcester, before 1974 in Herefordshire), about 13 km (8 miles) northwest of Hereford.

King's Road 'road belonging to the king'.

A road in Chelsea (SW3, SW6, SW10), in the London borough of KENSINGTON AND CHELSEA, running southwestwards from Sloane Square to Walham Green. (A continuation towards Putney Bridge is called **New King's Road**.) It was constructed in the early 17th century, originally as part of a royal route between WHITEHALL and HAMPTON COURT. It was not opened for public use until 1830.

It came to prominence in the 1960s, when it suddenly became an epicentre of London youth culture, with an admixture of CHELSEA bohemianism. It was awash with boutiques and bistros. The original impulse petered out in the 1970s into a fag-end of punkery, but the reputation, and fleeting hints of the 60s aura, remain.

> No finer honour can be bestowed on a man down the King's Road than to be called a together cat.
>
> *Daily Mirror* (27 August 1968)

King's Sedge Moor Originally 'the king's marsh', OE *cyninges*, possessive form of *cyning* 'king' + *mor* 'marsh', with *king's* denoting royal ownership; the *sedge* element was added later, presumably when the land was drained and sedge started to grow in abundance. In the 17th century there was a *Queen's Sedge Moor* nearby, and *East* and *West Sedge Moor* also.

An area of fenland in SOMERSET, to the southeast of Bridgwater and the southwest of Glastonbury. Very low-lying, it was once covered by the sea, and now offers rich grazing for cattle. It is bisected from northwest to southeast by the River CARY.

See also SEDGEMOOR.

King's Stag *Stag* 'boundary post', OE *staca* 'stake, boundary post'; the stake is at the meeting point of three parish boundaries, and *King's* may refer to the marker being established by royal authority.

A village in Dorset, in the BLACKMOOR VALE, about 17.5 km (11 miles) northwest of Blandford Forum.

Kingston 'the king's manor or estate', OE *cyninges* possessive form of *cyning* 'king' + -TON.

A conventionally abbreviated way of referring to KINGSTON UPON THAMES.

There are numerous towns and cities called Kingston throughout the rest of the English-speaking world, most of them named in colonial times in honour of a British monarch. Among the most notable are those named for Charles II (New York, Pennsylvania and Rhode Island, USA), for William III (Jamaica (the capital) and perhaps Massachusetts and New Hampshire, USA) and for George III (Ontario, Canada).

Kingston Bagpuize *Bagpuize* denoting manorial ownership in the early Middle Ages by the de Bagpuize family.

A village (pronounced 'bagpyooz') in Oxfordshire (until 1972 in Berkshire), about 13 km (8 miles) southwest of Oxford. Kingston Bagpuize is contiguous with the village of Southmoor. On 1 April 1971 the two villages merged into one civil parish of **Kingston Bagpuize-with-Southmoor**, but the somewhat ponderous new name is rarely used.

Kingston Bagpuize House, a red-brick manor house with stone facings, in an attractive parkland setting, dates from the 1660s.

Kingston Blount *Blount* denoting manorial ownership in the early Middle Ages by the le Blund family.

A village (pronounced 'blunt') in Oxfordshire, in the CHILTERN HILLS, between the ICKNIELD WAY and the RIDGEWAY, about 19 km (12 miles) southeast of Oxford.

Kingston Deverill *Deverill see* BRIXTON DEVERILL.

A village in Wiltshire, on the River WYLYE[1], on the West Wiltshire Downs, about 10 km (6 miles) southwest of Warminster.

See also MONKTON DEVERILL.

Kingston Lacy *Lacy* from the *de Lacy* family, earls of Lincoln, who owned the estate from the 13th century.

A house and estate in Dorset, 3 km (2 miles) northwest of WIMBORNE MINSTER. The house was originally built by the architect John Webb for Sir Ralph Bankes in the 1660s, using designs bequeathed by Inigo Jones. Radically altered in the 19th century by Sir Charles Barry, the house, along with its garden and surrounding estate, is now owned by the National Trust. The estate is dominated by the Iron Age hillfort of BADBURY RINGS, lying just to the northwest.

Kingston New Town. An early name for SURBITON.

Kingston upon Hull. The complete and technically correct (but rarely used) name for HULL.

Kingston upon Thames. A town and royal borough in southwest London (before 1965 in Surrey), on the River THAMES (whence the latter part of its name, usually discarded in everyday usage in favour of simply **Kingston**). The borough lies between Richmond-upon-Thames to the west and Merton to the east, the town between Richmond Park to the north and Surbiton to the south. The present-day borough, one of the Greater London boroughs, contains, in addition to Kingston itself, CHESSINGTON, Coombe Hill, NEW MALDEN and SURBITON.

The estate belonged to the Crown in Anglo-Saxon times (it is the earliest recorded of all the English 'Kingstons', whose name denotes royal ownership – *see* KINGSTON), and it is the oldest royal borough in England. Edward the Elder was crowned here in 899, as were all the succeeding Saxon kings (apart from Edgar) down to Ethelred II in 979. It was an important market town in the Middle Ages, and a bridge is recorded here, crossing to HAMPTON WICK on the west bank of the Thames, in the early 13th century (the present **Kingston Bridge** opened in 1828). Until the middle of the 18th century this was the first crossing place of the Thames upstream of London Bridge (*see under* LONDON).

In the 19th and 20th centuries Kingston gradually expanded, inexorably filling in most of the gaps between itself and its neighbours with houses – though sufficient green spaces remain (notably as golf courses) to counteract any tendency towards claustrophobia.

The air pioneer Thomas Sopwith set up a factory in Kingston to produce aircraft, including the legendary First World War fighter, the Sopwith Camel. It later became the Hawker factory, and aeroplanes such as the Hurricane and the Hunter were made here.

The **University of Kingston** was formed in 1992 from the former Kingston Polytechnic.

The photographic pioneer Eadweard Muybridge (1830–1904) and the novelist and dramatist John Galsworthy (1867–1933) were born in Kingston. The historian Edward Gibbon (1737–94) attended school here.

Kingston Bypass. A road, now part of the A3, bypassing Kingston to the south and east. Opened in the early 1920s, it was one of Britain's earliest urban bypasses. Its fast conditions encouraged amateur racing drivers, and it fairly soon attracted a reputation as something of a death-trap. It was decidedly a road for showing off:

> Give me the Kingston By-Pass
> And a thoroughly 'posh' machine
> Like a Healey three-litre

All complete with heater

Or a shiny grey Chevrolet Limousine.

> Noël Coward: *The Globe Revue,* 'Give me the Kingston By-Pass' (1952)

Kingstown. A former name for Dún Laoghaire.

King Street Named in honour of Charles I.

A street in Central London (WC2), linking Garrick Street with Covent Garden. It was built in the 1630s. Between 1920 and 1980 the headquarters of the Communist Party of Great Britain Executive Committee were at No. 16, and for a while *King Street* became a metonym for the party or its leaders or members:

> One version of events is that 'King Street' had decided the miners wouldn't end the strike unless they were given 25 per cent.

> *The Observer* (8 October 1972)

The composer Thomas Arne (1710–78) was born in King Street, and the Garrick Club was founded here in 1831.

The first permanent premises of Moses Moses, whose firm later became the outfitters and suit-hirers Moss Bros, were in King Street, where they remain a century and a half later.

There is also a King Street in St James's, London SW1 (the headquarters of the auctioneers Christie's are there) and one in Sydney, Australia (the hearing of bankruptcy cases in the Supreme Court there gave rise to the expression *up King Street* for 'in financial difficulty').

Kingsway Named in honour of Edward VII, who performed the opening ceremony.

A road in Holborn, Central London (WC2), in the borough of Camden, joining High Holborn (*see under* Holborn) in the north with the Aldwych in the south. It was a key component in a late-Victorian traffic management scheme, intended to relieve the congestion that had been building up in the latter years of the 19th century. A collaterally beneficial effect was that its construction involved the demolition of some particularly noxious slums in the Drury Lane area. It was opened in 1905. A tram tunnel was opened beneath the road in 1906; its southern end is still in use as a traffic underpass.

Kingsway Hall, a former place of worship at the northern end, was for many years a highly rated recording venue. The London School of Economics is close to the southern end of the road, on the east side.

Kington 'royal manor', OE *cyne-* 'royal' (later replaced with *cyning* 'king') + -TON.

A market town in Herefordshire, on the River Arrow[2], about 30 km (19 miles) northwest of Hereford, near the Welsh border. It disputes with Church Stretton the claim to England's highest golf course.

Kingussie '(at) the headland of the pines', Gaelic *ceann* 'head, headland' + *giùthseach* 'pine tree'.

A small town on the River Spey, in Highland (formerly in Inverness-shire), some 5 km (3 miles) northeast of Newtonmore. It is pronounced 'kin-you-ssie', with the stress on the second syllable. The present layout was planned by the Duke of Gordon in the 18th century. The town is known as the 'capital' of Badenoch, and was the administrative seat of the former district of Badenoch and Strathspey (1975–96).

Across the Spey are the ruins of Ruthven Barracks, built on the site of Ruthven Castle, the seat of the Wolf of Badenoch (*see under* Badenoch). The barracks were built in 1718 following the 1715 Jacobite Rising, but captured and destroyed by the Jacobites in the 1745 Rebellion. The remnants of the Highland clans rallied here after the disaster at Culloden Muir, but the Young Pretender ordered them to disperse.

The little village of Ruthven was the birthplace of James Macpherson (1738–96), the famous forger of the 'Ossianic' epics.

Kingwilliamstown. A former name for Ballydesmond.

Kinlochbervie 'head of Loch Bervie', Gaelic *ceann* 'end, point' + non-extant loch name *Bervie.*

A fishing port on the shore of Loch Inchard in the far northwest of Scotland, in Highland (formerly in Sutherland), some 19 km (11.5 miles) south of Cape Wrath.

Kinlochewe. *See under* Loch Ewe.

Kinlochleven. *See under* Loch Leven[2].

Kinlochmoidart. *See under* Moidart.

Kinloch Rannoch. *See under* Rannoch.

Kinnairds Head 'tip or end of the high land', *Kinnairds* Gaelic *ceann* 'end, point' + *aird* 'height, promontory, cliff' (*see* ARD).

A headland on the north side of Fraserburgh, in Aberdeenshire (formerly in Grampian region), marking the most northeasterly point of this part of Scotland. It rises some 18 m (60 ft) above the sea. The tower on the headland was built in 1574 by Sir Alexander Fraser, the grandson of the Alexander Fraser after whom the town is named. The lighthouse dates from 1787.

Kinross 'head of the promontory', Gaelic *ceann* 'head' + *ros* 'promontory'.

A town in Perth and Kinross, some 22 km (13 miles) south of Perth. It was formerly in Kinross-shire (of which it was the county town), and then in Tayside region. It takes its name from the promontory that extends into Loch Leven (*see* Loch Leven[1]) to the east of the town. On this peninsula is **Kinross House** (1692), designed by Sir William Bruce. It was much admired by Daniel Defoe, who dubbed Bruce 'the Kit [i.e. Christopher] Wren of North Britain'.

Kinross-shire From the county town of KINROSS.

A former county of Scotland, the second smallest after CLACKMANNANSHIRE. It was bounded on the north by Perthshire, on the east and south by Fife and on the west by Clackmannanshire. The county included KINROSS (the county town), LOCH LEVEN[1] and the CLEISH HILLS. It became part of PERTH AND KINROSS in 1975.

Kinsale Irish *Cionn tSáile* 'head of the salt water', i.e. the highest point that the sea water reaches.

An attractive harbour town on the south coast of County Cork, 22 km (14 miles) south of Cork itself. It is on the River BANDON[1], near its mouth, before it enters **Kinsale Harbour**, a natural inlet once guarded by CHARLESFORT. The peninsula extending south from the west side of Kinsale Harbour culminates in the **Old Head of Kinsale**, where there is a lighthouse, a ruined castle and a Napoleonic-era watchtower. It was off the Old Head of Kinsale that the *Lusitania* was torpedoed and sank with the loss of 1500 lives in 1915, contributing to the USA's eventual entry into the First World War.

Kinsale had its origins in Anglo-Norman times, but was of little note until the **Battle of Kinsale** in 1601 (*see below*). Subsequently it became an English town: neither Irish nor Catholics were allowed to live here until the end of the 18th century. In 1649, during the Civil Wars, Prince Rupert was blockaded in Kinsale Harbour by the Parliamentarian navy, and in 1689 James II landed here in his unsuccessful campaign to reclaim the Crown; he left Ireland by the same route the following year, after his defeat at the Boyne. Kinsale was an important naval base until the end of the 18th century, but has been quite quiet since – although from that time it became a popular venue for sea-bathing, promoting itself (anonymously) thus:

> Then take my advice, if you've got boil or colic,
> Only try what our baths and pure air will avail.
> Or if you're in health, just come here for the frolic.
> And abundant amusement you'll find in Kinsale.

(Kinsale's airs and waters did no good to the Jacobean dramatist Cyril Tourneur, author of *The Atheist's Tragedy* and possibly of *The Revenger's Tragedy*, who was put ashore here to die with other sick men in 1626, on the return voyage from an unsuccessful raid on Cadiz.) Today, the town is popular with yachtsmen and sea anglers, and the place has gained something of a reputation as a gastronomic centre: Kinsale Gourmet Week is held every August.

Kinsale cloak. A type of Irish cloak (*see under* IRISH), with an elaborately worked hood.

Battle of Kinsale (24 December 1601). The decisive engagement of the Nine Years War. In September 1601 a Spanish force under Don Juan de Aguila landed in Kinsale, in support of the rebellion of the Ulster lords, notably Hugh

O'Neill and Red Hugh O'Donnell. The English lord deputy, Lord Mountjoy, besieged the Spanish in Kinsale, and O'Neill and his allies marched down from Ulster to encircle Mountjoy's men. The planned attack by O'Neill was betrayed to the English, and the Irish were routed. The Spanish surrendered and the English retook Kinsale on 2 January. O'Neill's nine-year rebellion was eventually crushed in 1603. It has been said that the Battle of Kinsale heralded the destruction of the whole Gaelic fabric of Ireland.

> Does history, exhausted, come full cycle?
> It ended here at a previous *fin de siècle*
> though leaving vestiges of a distant past
> before Elizabeth and the Tudor conquest –
> since when, four hundred years of solitude,
> rainfall on bluebells in an autumn wood …
>
>> Derek Mahon: 'Christmas in Kinsale', from *Collected Poems* (1999)

Kintail 'head of the salt water', Gaelic *ceann* 'head' + *an t-* 'of the' + *sàile* 'salt water'.

A mountainous area of the Northwest HIGHLANDS, around the head of Loch Duich (a sea loch) and GLEN SHIEL. It is some 20 km (12 miles) southeast of Kyle of Lochalsh, in Highland (formerly in Ross and Cromarty). Much of Kintail – including the spectacular FALLS OF GLOMACH and the Five Sisters of Kintail (*see below*) – is in the care of the National Trust for Scotland.

> Say farewell but greet kindly Kintail of the cows,
> where once I was reared at the time I was young.
> There were brown-haired young gallants all ready to dance,
> and girls with long curls and cheeks like the rose.
>
>> Ian Mac Mhurchaidh (John MacRae, d.*c*.1780): 'Dèan Cadalan Sàmhach' ('Sleep Softly', translated from the Gaelic by Derick Thomson)

Five Sisters of Kintail, the. A group of five pointed peaks – or rather a ridge with five summits – on the north side of Glen Shiel. The name may have been coined as recently as the early 20th century, probably after the model of the English SEVEN SISTERS[1]. Before that the peaks were known collectively in Gaelic as Beinn Mhòr ('the big mountain'). The names of the individual peaks are (from northwest to southeast) Sgurr na Mòraich ('mighty peak'), Sgurr nan Saighead ('peak of the arrows'), Sgurr Fhuaran (possibly 'peak of the springs'; at 1068 m / 3503 ft, this is the highest of the Sisters), Sgurr na Carnach ('rocky peak') and Sgurr na Cist Duibhe ('peak of the black chest'). The next peak along the ridge is Sgurr nan Spainteach ('peak of the Spaniards'; *see* Battle of GLEN SHIEL).

Kintyre 'head of the land', Gaelic *ceann* 'head' + *tìr* 'land'.

A long peninsula in western Scotland, with the Atlantic Ocean to the west and the Firth of Clyde to the east. It is in Argyll and Bute (formerly in Strathclyde region). The northern end of the peninsula is called KNAPDALE, and from the north end of Knapdale, at Lochgilphead, to the most southerly point is a distance of nearly 90 km (54 miles). The main town is CAMPBELTOWN, towards the southern end.

> Round Scotland's shores and by Cantyre
> A mountainous surging chaos glooms.
>
> Rumann son of Colman (attr.): 'Storm at Sea' (8th century), translated from the Irish by Frank O'Connor

Kintyre pursuivant. One of the heraldic officers in the Lyon Court (the Scottish Court of Heralds).

Mull of Kintyre, the OScand *múli* 'headland' (literally 'snout').

The southernmost point of Kintyre. It gave its name to a No. 1 single (1977) by Paul McCartney, who owns property on the peninsula. It has been said that punk rock boomed in reaction to the song's saccharine qualities. Others saw some merits in it:

> Mull of Kintyre may not be Paul McCartney's finest but at least it fended off the Floral Dance by the Brighouse and Rastrick Brass Band ...
>
> Dorian Lynskey: 'Near Hits' in *The Guardian* (7 May 2004)

(For the brass band in question, *see under* BRIGHOUSE.)

Kinver From OCelt *breg* 'hill', with an unidentified first element.

A town in southern Staffordshire, about 6 km (4 miles) west of Stourbridge. **Kinver Edge** is a wooded sandstone ridge to the south of here. Five ranges of hills can be seen from the top, including the Cotswolds and the Malverns. Caves carved out of the hillside as homes over 2000 years ago were still in use as recently as the 1950s.

Kipping's Cross Probably 'crossroads on land belonging to the Kipping family'.

A village in Kent, about 5 km (3 miles) east of Tunbridge Wells.

Kirby Bellars *Kirby* 'village with a church', OScand *kirkju-by* (*see* -BY); *Bellars* denoting manorial ownership in the early Middle Ages by the Beler family.

A village in Leicestershire, about 5 km (3 miles) west of Melton Mowbray.

Kirby Cane *Kirby see* KIRBY BELLARS; *Cane* denoting manorial ownership in the early Middle Ages by the de Cademo or de Cham family (originally from Caen in France).

A village in Norfolk, about 21 km (13 miles) southeast of Norwich.

Kirby le Soken 'Kirby in the Soke (a local administrative area)': *Kirby see* KIRBY BELLARS; *le* 'the', OFr; *Soken* 'administrative area, soke', OE *socn*.

A village in Essex, about 3 km (2 miles) west of Walton on the Naze.

Kirby Muxloe *Kirby* 'Kærir's farmstead or village', OScand male personal name *Kærir* + -BY; *Muxloe* denoting manorial ownership in the Middle Ages by the Muxloe family.

A village in Leicestershire, now almost a western suburb of LEICESTER but separated from it by the M1. **Kirby Muxloe Castle** is a fine 15th-century brick manor house.

Kirkby 'village with a church', OScand *kirkja* 'church' + -BY.

A town in Merseyside, 10 km (6 miles) northeast of Liverpool, for which it developed as an overspill town after the Second World War. It is pronounced 'curby'.

Kirkby-in-Ashfield *Ashfield* an old district name, literally 'open land where ash-trees grow', OE *æsc* 'ash-tree' + FIELD.

A town in Nottinghamshire, about 19 km (12 miles) north of Nottingham.

See also SUTTON-IN-ASHFIELD.

Kirkby la Thorpe Originally *Kirkby Laythorpe*, where *Laythorpe* (OScand, 'Leithulfr's secondary settlement') was the village across The Beck; the change to *Kirkby la Thorpe*, based on a mistaken analysis of *Laythorpe* as 'the secondary settlement' (*la* 'the', OFr; *Thorpe* 'secondary settlement', OScand *thorp*), is relatively recent.

A village in Lincolnshire, about 2.5 km (1.5 miles) east of Sleaford.

Kirkby Lonsdale *Lonsdale* '(in the) valley of the River LUNE[1]'.

A small market town in Cumbria, 16 km (10 miles) southeast of Kendal. At Kirkby Lonsdale the 13th-century DEVIL'S BRIDGE[2] spans the LUNE[1], which here, according to Ruskin, forms

> one of the loveliest scenes in England. Whatever hill and sweet river and English forest foliage can be at their best is gathered here ... I do not know in all my own country, still less in France and Italy, a place more naturally divine.

Ruskin's view from the eminence called the Brow (87 steps up from behind St Mary's Church) is now known as Ruskin's View.

In Charlotte Brontë's *Jane Eyre* (1847), Kirkby Lonsdale becomes Lowton.

Kirkby Mallory *Mallory* denoting manorial ownership in the early Middle Ages by the Mallory family.

A village in Leicestershire, about 14 km (9 miles) west of Leicester. Nearby is the Mallory Park motor-racing circuit.

Kirkbymoorside 'village with a church by the moor', OScand *kirkja* 'church' + -BY; the affix refers to its position on the south side of the NORTH YORK MOORS.

A small market town in North Yorkshire, 10 km (6 miles) west of Pickering. The politician and occasional playwright George Villiers, 2nd Duke of Buckingham, died here in 1687.

Kirkby Overblow *Kirkby see* KIRKBY; *Overblow* OE *or-blawere* 'iron-ore smelter'.

A village in North Yorkshire, 7 km (4 miles) south of Harrogate.

Kirkby Stephen *Kirkby see* KIRKBY; *Stephen* denotes the saint to whom the church is dedicated.

A small market town on the River EDEN[1] in Cumbria, some 30 km (20 miles) northeast of Kendal.

Kirkcaldy 'fort at the hard hill', OCelt *caer* 'fort' (*see* CAHER) + *caled* 'hard' + *din* 'hill' (*see* DOWN, -DON); *Kircalethyn* 1150.

An ancient port and royal BURGH in Fife, on the north shore of the Firth of FORTH, Scotland, 24 km (15 miles) north of Edinburgh across the Forth. The name is pronounced 'ker-coddy'. Kirkcaldy is known as 'the Lang Toun' originally for its High Street and now for its esplanade, extending 6.5 km (4 miles) along the Firth of Forth. The town is celebrated for its Links Market, held every April and said to be the longest street fair in Europe. It began as a feeing (hiring) fair in 1305.

Sir Walter Scott set the story of 'lovely Rosabella' in the *Lay of the Last Minstrel* (1805) in Kirkcaldy. The steps that flank the ruins of nearby 15th-century Ravenscraig Castle are said to have been the inspiration for John Buchan's spy thriller *The Thirty-Nine Steps* (1915); but *see* BROADSTAIRS.

Kirkcaldy was the birthplace of the architect brothers Robert Adam (1728–92) and James Adam (1730–94), and of the economist and philosopher Adam Smith (1723–90), author of *The Wealth of Nations*. Thomas Carlyle was a school-teacher here from 1816 to 1819, and Gordon Brown (b.1951), the Labour chancellor of the exchequer since 1997, was a pupil at Kirkcaldy High School.

Kirkcaldy stripe. A striped pattern found in cloth manufactured in Kirkcaldy in the later 19th century.

Kirkconnel 'Conguall's church', Scots *kirk* 'church' + OCelt personal name Conguall (Irish *Conall*); *Kyrkconwelle* 1347. The most famous saint of this name was a disciple of St Mungo or Kentigern (d.c.612).

A village in upper Nithsdale, Dumfries and Galloway (formerly in Dumfriesshire), 5 km (3 miles) northwest of Sanquar. There is also a **Kirkconnel Tower** (16th–18th century) 8 km (5 miles) south of Dumfries, near the estuary of the Nith.

'Helen of Kirkconnel'. A traditional ballad, in which the heroine has died for the sake of the narrator:

> I wish I were where Helen lies,
> Night and day on me she cries;
> O that I were where Helen lies
> On fair Kirkconnel lea!

Kirkcudbright 'St Cuthbert's church', probably Gaelic *cille* 'church' (*see* KIL-) replaced by Scots *kirk* 'church' + personal name *Cudbert* (the Gaelic variant of Cuthbert).

A town and royal BURGH (pronounced 'kerr-coo-brie') some 40 km (25 miles) southwest of Dumfries. It is sited where the River DEE[3] enters **Kirkcudbright Bay**, an inlet of the Solway Firth. Kircudbright received its royal charter in 1455. It was the county town of the former Kirkcudbrightshire, then in 1975 became the seat of the Stewartry district of Dumfries and Galloway (*see under* KIRKCUDBRIGHTSHIRE); it lost this role in the reorganization of 1996.

Kirkcudbright gets its name from the story that the body of St Cuthbert (d.687; Gaelic *Cudbert*) rested here for a time after it was exhumed from LINDISFARNE in 875 to preserve it from the Vikings (it was eventually buried in Durham Cathedral *c*.999). When Daniel Defoe visited in the 1720s he was impressed by the piety of the populace, but not by their indolence in the matter of commerce:

> Here is a harbour without ships, a port without trade, a
> fishery without nets, a people without business ...
>
> Daniel Defoe: *A Tour Through the Whole Island of Great Britain*
> (1724–6)

John Paul Jones (1747–92), the naval hero of the American Revolution, was once imprisoned in the tolbooth at Kirkcudbright, and the churchyard contains a monument to Billy Marshall, king of the Galloway tinkers, who died in 1790, supposedly at the age of 120. One of his seven wives, Flora Marshall, is thought to have been the model of Meg Merrilies in Sir Walter Scott's novel *Guy Mannering* (1815) (for an alternative model, *see* KIRK YETHOLM). In 1795 Robert Burns wrote a ballad on that year's Kirkcudbright by-election, beginning:

> Fy, let us a' to Kirkcudbright,
>   For there will be bickerin' there ...

Kirkcudbright has long been a favourite haunt of painters, and the studio of E.A. Hornel (1864–1933), one of the Glasgow Boys (*see under* GLASGOW), is a museum.

'Kirkcudbright Grace, The'. A grace attributed to Robert Burns, and sometimes called 'The Selkirk Grace', as it was spoken at the table of the Earl of Selkirk on his 1793 tour through Galloway:

> Some hae meat and canna eat,
>   And some wad eat that want it;
> But we hae meat, and we can eat,
>   And sae the Lord be thanket.

Stewartry of Kirkcudbright, the. *See under* KIRKCUD-BRIGHTSHIRE.

Kirkcudbrightshire From KIRKCUDBRIGHT + SHIRE.

A former county of southwest Scotland, also once known as East Galloway. It was bordered on the east by Dumfriesshire, on the south by the Solway Firth, on the west by Wigtownshire and on the north by Ayrshire. Its county town was KIRKCUDBRIGHT. In 1975 it was incorporated into DUMFRIES AND GALLOWAY.

The county was also referred to as **the Stewartry of Kirkcudbright**, or simply **the Stewartry**. Here 'stewartry' is a generic alternative to 'county', where an area came under a steward – as happened in the early 14th century when the lands of the Balliols in eastern Galloway were removed from their overlordship and placed under a royal steward. ORKNEY and SHETLAND were also a 'stewartry' from the late 18th to the early 20th century. From 1975 to 1996 **Stewartry** was a district of Dumfries and Galloway region, formed out of the central part of Kirkcudbrightshire.

Kirkie. An informal name for KIRKINTILLOCH.

Kirkintilloch 'fort at the top of the hillock', OCelt *Caerpentaloch* 'fort at the head of the eminences', *caer* 'fort' (*see* CAHER) + *pen* 'head' (*see* PEN) + Gaelic *tulaich* 'hillock, eminence'. The Gallicized name has assimilated *caer-ceann* to *kirkin* and replaced *pen* with *ceann* 'at the head'; it is probable that Gaelic *tulaich* also replaces an earlier OCelt element, but the change had already taken place when the name was first recorded in the 10th century.

A town 10 km (6 miles) northeast of Glasgow, in East Dunbartonshire (formerly in Strathclyde region). A Roman fort was built here in AD 142, as part of the ANTONINE WALL. The town is informally known as **Kirkie**.

Kirklees 'clearing(s) belonging to the church', OScand *kirkja* 'church' + -LEY.

The area around HUDDERSFIELD in West Yorkshire, of which it is a local-government district (borough). The area includes, in addition to Huddersfield, the towns of MIRFIELD, HECKMONDWIKE, CLECKHEATON, DEWSBURY and BATLEY. It takes its name from **Kirklees Hall** (17th century) in **Kirklees Park** near BRIGHOUSE, the reputed burial place of Robin Hood. The story is that Robin, when old and ill, was taken in by the prioress of the Cistercian nunnery founded here in the 12th century. She was possibly his aunt, but nevertheless locked him up and bled him almost to death. With virtually his last breath Robin blew his horn to summon Little John, and requested that he be buried wherever his last arrow landed. A mound still marks the spot.

Kirk Michael 'church of St Michael', *Kirk* OScand *kirkja* 'church'.

A village on the west coast of the Isle of Man, 16 km (10 miles) northwest of Douglas.

Kirk o' Shotts 'church of the steep slopes', Scots *kirk* 'church' + OE *sceot* 'steep slope'.

A hamlet 8 km (5 miles) southeast of Airdrie, in North Lanarkshire (formerly in Strathclyde region). It is a little north of the village of SHOTTS, and is best known for the nearby BBC television tower, 230 m (750 ft) high.

Kirkoswald 'church of St Oswald', OScand *kirkja* 'church' + saint's name *Oswald*, the 7th-century Northumbrian king and martyr.

A village in South Ayrshire, some 6 km (4 miles) southwest of Maybole. Robert Burns went to school here, and the models for his Souter Johnnie and Tam O'Shanter – namely John Davidson (the village souter or cobbler) and Douglas Graham – are buried here. John Davidson's cottage is now open to the public as Souter Johnnie's Cottage, with much Burnsiana on display, including life-size statues of Tam, Souter Johnnie, the innkeeper and his wife.

Kirkstone Pass 'church stones', OScand *kirkja* 'church' + *steinn* (*see* STONE) later anglicized to -*stone*; there are several Kirkstone names, and stone or stones were probably thought to be the rubble of, or derive from ancient churches. A pass (454 m / 1489 ft) between ULLSWATER and WINDERMERE in the Lake District, Cumbria. In past centuries the old **Kirkstone Pass Inn** at the summit must have provided a welcome relief for horses and passengers alike after the effort of ascent. Even today, with efficient motor transport, the inn's warm hospitality provides a happy break in this wild place –

> Where the coarse rushes to the sweeping breeze
> Sigh forth their ancient melodies.
>
> William Wordsworth: 'Ode, Pass of Kirkstone' (1820)

Kirkwall 'church bay', OScand *kirkja* 'church' + *vagr* 'bay'. The capital of ORKNEY, on the north side of the narrow waist that links the eastern and western parts of Mainland. It is a royal BURGH (1486) and sea port, with ferries to several of the other Orkney islands, as well as to Invergordon on mainland Scotland. The town dates from the 11th century, and grew in importance after the building of St Magnus Cathedral, erected in the 12th century by Earl Rognvald to commemorate his martyred uncle, St Magnus. Some 20 years earlier, in *c*.1117, Magnus's cousin Earl Haakon Paulsson had killed him by cleaving his skull with an axe. In 1919 a cleft skull and some other bones were found within one of the pillars of the cathedral.

Other historic buildings include the Bishop's Palace (12th century) and the Earl's Palace (16th century).

King Haakon of Norway died in Kirkwall after his defeat at the Battle of Largs (*see under* LARGS) in 1263, as did the former leader of the Liberal Party, Jo Grimond, in 1993. The poet Edwin Muir went to school in Kirkwall.

Kirkwhelpington 'church by Hwelp's farm', OScand *kirkja* 'church' + OE male personal name *Hwelp* + -ING + -TON. A small village on the River WANSBECK, Northumberland, 20 km (12 miles) west of Morpeth. The church dates from the 13th century, and Sir Charles Parsons (1854–1931), inventor of the steam turbine, is buried in the churchyard.

Kirk Yetholm 'the village by the pass with the church', *Yetholm* OE *geat* 'pass' + HAM, with Scots *Kirk* 'church' to distinguish the village from Town Yetholm.

A small village in Scottish Borders (which was formerly in

Roxburghshire), 12 km (7 miles) southeast of Kelso. It is on the north side of the CHEVIOT, just inside the Scottish border, and is the northern terminus of the Pennine Way (*see under* PENNINES), which begins some 400 km (250 miles) to the south, in Derbyshire. Across the Bowmont Water is the village of **Town Yetholm** and the two are sometimes referred to as the 'twin village' of Yetholm.

For centuries Kirk Yetholm was the main centre for the Scottish gypsies, and the 'kings' of the gypsies, the Faa family, held court in the village. An early king, John Faa, was described by James V in 1540 as 'lord and earl of Little Egypt'. The 'king of the gyptians' in Philip Pullman's 1995 novel *Northern Lights* (1995) is called Johnny Faa, and Sir Walter Scott based the character of the old gypsy Meg Merrilies in *Guy Mannering* (1815) on Jean Gordon (d.1745), wife of Patrick Faa (for an alternative model, *see* KIRKCUDBRIGHT).

There is a cottage in Kirk Yetholm called the Gypsy Palace, built on land given to the gypsies by Bennet of Grubbit and Marlefield, the local laird, whose life had been saved by a Scottish gypsy at the Battle of Namur in 1695. One of the most famous inhabitants of the Gypsy Palace was Queen Esther Faa Blyth (d.1883), who famously described the village thus:

> Yetholm is sae mingle-mangle that ane might think it was built on a dark night or sown on a windy day.

She was succeeded by her son, Charles Faa Blyth, the last king, who was crowned on the village green in 1898, and who died in 1902. Former US president Bill Clinton and the yachtsman Sir Chay Blyth are thought to be descendants of the Faa Blyth clan.

Kirriemuir 'the big *ceathramh*', Gaelic *ceathramh*, a land measure + *mòr* 'big'. The *ceathramh* was equal to a quarter of a davoch, itself equal to 4 ploughgates or 20 pennylands or 32 oxgangs, sometimes reckoned at 192 Scotch acres.

A town in Angus (in Tayside region from 1975 to 1996), 8 km (5 miles) northwest of Forfar. It was the birthplace of the creator of Peter Pan, J.M. Barrie (1860–1937), and of the film actor David Niven (1909–83).

Barrie's birthplace at 9 Brechin Road is in the care of the National Trust for Scotland; also preserved behind the house is the wash-house (the original Wendy House) that served as his first theatre. Kirriemuir features as 'Thrums' in some of Barrie's early work, such as *Auld Licht Idylls* (1888), *A Window in Thrums* (1889) and *The Little Minister* (1891) – the manse of the eponymous minister is opposite Barrie's birthplace; there is also a strathspey by J.S. Skinner entitled 'The Laird o' Thrums'. (The Scots word *thrums* is applied to bits of waste thread; Barrie's father was a weaver.) In reaction to Barrie's parochial 'kailyard' (cabbage patch)

sentimentalism, Hugh MacDiarmid wrote a poem entitled 'Frae Anither Window in Thrums' (1930), replete with references to Dostoevski, Proust, Rimbaud and Nietzsche.
Kirriemuir gingerbread. A type of rich gingerbread, also known as 'starry rock', which includes cinnamon and other spices as well as ginger, muscavado sugar, golden syrup, treacle and buttermilk.

Kishorn. *See* LOCH KISHORN.

Kitley Caves *Kitley* 'kite grove', OE *cyta* 'kite (bird of prey)' + -LEY.
A group of limestone caves near YEALMPTON in south Devon, about 11 km (7 miles) southeast of Plymouth. Uncovered by quarrying activity in the early 19th century, they contain the remains of various Stone Age mammals, including bears, hyenas and mammoths.

Kit's Coty Perhaps 'Kit's house', *Kit* male personal name; *Coty* is likely to be from OE *cot* 'house' (*see* -COT, COTE); the name is taken from *Kit's Coty House*.
A hamlet in Kent, about 5 km (3 miles) north of Maidstone. Just to the south of it is the tautonymously named **Kit's Coty House**, the remains of a prehistoric burial chamber consisting of three upright sarsen stones crossed by a single capstone. It supposedly got its name from a shepherd called 'Kit' who once took shelter in it. Local legend has it that it is the tomb of the local British chieftain Catigern, who was killed in personal combat with Horsa, leader of the Jutes, in AD 455; their spirits are said to re-enact the battle from time to time.

Knapdale 'dale of hillocks', OScand *knappr* 'hillock'+ *dalr* 'dale'. The area is indeed covered with many nubbly little hills.
An area of the southwest Highlands, Argyll and Bute (formerly in Strathclyde), comprising the northern end of the KINTYRE peninsula. It is bounded by the Crinan Canal in the north, and West Loch Tarbert in the south.

Knapp Probably 'hilltop', OE *cnæpp* 'top, hilltop'.
A village (pronounced 'nap') in Somerset, about 8 km (5 miles) east of Taunton.

Knaresborough 'Cenheard's stronghold', OE male personal name *Cenheard* + *burh* (*see* BURY).
A market town on a gorge of the River NIDD, North Yorkshire, 5 km (3 miles) northeast of Harrogate. The ruined castle largely dates from the 14th century; Richard II was imprisoned here in 1399, prior to his murder at Pontefract the following year. However, the first castle was built around 1070, and it was here that the knights who murdered Thomas Becket hid for three years. Knaresborough also has what claims to be England's oldest pharmacy (1720).

There are a number of interesting geological features around Knaresborough. MOTHER SHIPTON'S CAVE was supposedly the home of the prophetess, while the Dropping Well next to it has petrifying qualities, as described by John Leland in the early 16th century:

> ye water is so cowled and of such a nature that, what thyng soever faulith out of the rockes and is touchid of the water, growith ynto stone.
>
> John Leland: *The Itinerary of John Leland* (ed. L. Toulmin Smith, 1907)

St Robert's Cave, carved out of the rock above the River Nidd, was the home of a local hermit, **St Robert Flower of Knaresborough** (allegedly 1116–1218; feast day 24 September). It is sometimes called Eugene Aram's Cave, as this is where the Knaresborough schoolteacher, philologist and murderer Eugene Aram (celebrated in Bulwer-Lytton's 1832 novel of that name) hid the corpse of Daniel Clark in 1745. Nearby is the chapel of Our Lady in the Crag.

Blind Jack of Knaresborough. John Metcalf (1717–1810), who became blind from smallpox at the age of six, but went on to fight on the Hanoverian side at Falkirk and Culloden in 1746. Subsequently he ran a stagecoach between Knaresborough and York, and built some 300 km (200 miles) of turnpike road. He is regarded as the first of Britain's modern road builders.

Knave's Mire 'Knorr's marsh', *Knave* OScand male personal name *Knorr*; *Mire* OScand *myrr* 'marsh'; the association with 'knave' developed in the 16th century, possibly as a result of the use of the place for executions.

An expanse of open ground in York, south of the city centre. It is now home to York's racecourse, but was formerly the site of the city's gallows, which saw off, among many others, Dick Turpin, the highwayman; Eugene Aram, the murderous schoolteacher of KNARESBOROUGH; and Mary Bateman, the Witch of Leeds (*see under* LEEDS[1]). To the west is another open space, Hob Moor, site of York's medieval plague pits.

Knebworth 'Cnebba's enclosure', OE male personal name *Cnebba* + *worth* (*see* -WORTH, WORTHY, -WARDINE).

A town in Hertfordshire, about 3 km (2 miles) south of Stevenage. The nearby **Knebworth House** originated as an early Tudor mansion, built for one of Henry VII's favourites, Robert Lytton. His descendant, the flamboyant and dandyish novelist Sir Edward Bulwer-Lytton, remodelled it in the 1840s in Victorian High Gothic style. Latterly it has branched out into a new career as a pop-concert venue (Oasis attracted an audience of 250,000 over two nights in 1996).

> Has God played Knebworth recently?
>
> Noel Gallagher (of Oasis): quoted in *The Independent* (12 July 1997)

Knee, the. *See under* DUNCANSBY HEAD.

Knighton 'farm of the follower, young man, retainer', OE *cniht* 'follower' (the origin of 'knight') + -TON; earlier forms of its name are *Chenistetone* (1086) and *Cnicheton* (1193).

A town in Powys (formerly in Radnorshire), on the English–Welsh border, 23 km (14 miles) west of Ludlow. Its Welsh name is **Trefyclo** ('settlement on the dyke', *tref* 'farm', 'settlement' + *y* 'the' + *clawdd* 'dyke', from the fact that it straddles OFFA'S DYKE).

Knightsbridge 'bridge of the young men or retainers' (referring to a road bridge crossing the WESTBOURNE Brook; the underlying allusion may simply be to the bridge as a place where young lads hung out, or more specifically to an 11th-century guild of retainers, signifying some sort of limit of jurisdiction; a more romantic but unsubstantiated version has it that two knights fought to the death on the bridge), OE *cnihta* possessive plural form of *cniht* 'young man, military servant of the king or other person of rank in the feudal system' + *brycg* 'bridge'.

A street and district in southwest London (SW1, SW7), in the City of WESTMINSTER. It was a village (renowned for its taverns) in the Middle Ages, having developed around the bridge from which it took its name (*see above*). The street called Knightsbridge runs along the southern edge of HYDE PARK, from Hyde Park Corner westwards to Kensington Road. Its notable landmarks such as the French Embassy, the palatial Hyde Park Hotel and the upmarket department store Harvey Nichols drop broad hints as to the tone of the surrounding neighbourhood, to which the street has given back its name: this is the land of conspicuous consumption, of wealth untrammelled by taste, of über-shopping (check out the designer-name showrooms in Sloane Street, a turning off Knightsbridge), of yesterday's upper crust. Iconic, but now almost a parodic Knightsbridge theme-park, is the mega-emporium Harrods (actually in the Brompton Road (*see under* BROMPTON); it originated when the Essex-born Charles Henry Harrod took over the running of a small grocery shop in Knightsbridge in the 1840s).

Knightsbridge Underground station, on the Piccadilly line, opened in 1906.

During the North African campaign in the Second World War, the nickname 'Knightsbridge' was given by British forces to a crossroads in the desert south of Tobruk. There were fierce tank battles there in May–June 1942 prior to the German advance to Alamein.

'Knightsbridge'. A march, the last of the three movements of the *London Suite* (1932) by Eric Coates. It was used as the signature tune of *In Town Tonight*, a popular radio and television programme of the 1940s and 1950s in which celebrities currently visiting London were interviewed.

Knightsbridge Barracks. A barracks (also know as **Hyde Park Barracks**) in Kensington Road which accommodates the Household Cavalry and their horses. The original barracks was built in the late 18th century; the current building was designed by Sir Basil Spence in 1960, but not completed until 1970.

Knightsbridge of the North. A nickname for the town of WILMSLOW.

Knights Town. *See under* VALENCIA ISLAND.

Knill '(place at the) hillock', OE *cnylle*.

A village in Herefordshire (before 1998 in Hereford and Worcester, before 1974 in Herefordshire), just to the east of OFFA'S DYKE, about 32 km (20 miles) northwest of Hereford.

Knock Irish *An Cnoc* 'the hill' (*see* KNOCK-).

A village in County Mayo, some 25 km (15 miles) southeast of Castlebar. Here in 1879 villagers witnessed an apparition of the Virgin Mary (more were to follow), and the place developed as a Marian shrine, attracting thousands of pilgrims annually, many of them looking for a cure. The pilgrimage business was given a great boost by the efforts of Father James Horan (1912–86), who became parish priest in 1967: the Basilica of Our Lady, Queen of Ireland, seating 12,000, was opened in 1976, and **Knock International Airport** (some 15 km / 9 miles to the north, and also known as Horan International Airport) was opened in 1986 by Charles Haughey, then leader of the Opposition (the government not having interested itself in Horan's vision). Horan also set up a pilgrims' hostel and a centre for invalids, and further put Knock on the map by establishing, in 1968, the **Knock Marriage Introductions Bureau**, whose services were intended for maturer people of the rural persuasion. In 1979 Pope John Paul II – during the first visit of a Pope to Ireland – celebrated Mass at Knock on the anniversary of the first apparition.

Knockainy. *See under* LOUGH GUR.

Knockando 'market hillock', Gaelic *cnoc* (*see* KNOCK-) + *cheannachd* 'of commerce, of the market'.

A village on the River SPEY in Moray (formerly in Grampian region), 8 km (5 miles) west of Aberlour. It is famous for its whisky distillery, producing a single malt of the same name.

Knockboy Irish *Cnoc Buidhe* 'yellow hill' (*see* KNOCK-).

A mountain (705 m / 2312 ft) in the BEARA peninsula, on the border of Kerry and Cork, between the CAHA MOUNTAINS to the west and the SHEHY MOUNTAINS to the east.

Knockdoe Irish *Cnoc Tuagh* 'hook or axe hill' (*see* KNOCK-).

A low hill near the town of Galway, and the site of the **Battle of Knockdoe**, fought on 19 August 1504. It was the largest-scale battle ever fought between Irishmen, with 10,000 taking part (although many of them were gallowglasses – Hebridean mercenaries). Knockdoe was a crushing victory for the lord deputy Garret More, Earl of Kildare, over his great rival (and son-in-law) Ulick Burke, who had seized GALWAY city and, furthermore, mistreated Kildare's daughter. Following his victory at Knockdoe, the earl received the Garter from the king.

Knockdown Probably 'hillock-hill', OE *cnocc* (*see* KNOCK-) + *dun* (*see* DOWN, -DON).

A village in Wiltshire, in the COTSWOLDS, about 10 km (6 miles) west of Malmesbury.

Knockin 'little hillock', OCelt *cnoccin* (*see* KNOCK-).

A village in Shropshire, near the Welsh border, about 19 km (12 miles) northwest of Shrewsbury.

Knockmealdown Mountains From the highest peak, *Knockmealdown*, in Irish *Cnoc Mhaoldonn* 'hill of Maoldomhnach or Maol Duin' (*see* KNOCK-); this may refer to a supernatural being, but this is not certain.

A range of quartzite and old red sandstone hills along the border between County TIPPERARY and County WATERFORD. The highest summit is **Knockmealdown** (793 m / 2601 ft). The north–south road pass through the range is called the Vee. It was in the Knockmealdowns that the last wolf in Ireland was slain in 1770 (or the second-last wolf, if Carlow's 1786 claim is to be believed).

> Here, between Knockshanahullion and Farbreaga,
> Lungs bursting, ribs but a cage for shrivelled guts,
> The old dog-wolf lay down, begging in his look as the
>   light went
> The huntsman deliver him with one clean shot.

❖ knock- ❖

This Old Celtic element is perhaps most common in Ireland, where *cnoc* is the usual word for a hill or mountain: it is found in the many examples of Knock (such as KNOCK, County Mayo) as well as in the KNOCKMEALDOWN MOUNTAINS (County Waterford).

Outside of Ireland, the word is restricted to generally smaller and lower land features. In Scotland, Knock also appears on its own, as do names such as KNOCKANDO (Moray). The Old Welsh version of this word, *cnucc*, appears in the English names Knock (Wiltshire) and KNOCKIN (Shropshire). The Irish element appears in NOCTORUM (Cheshire), where it is treated as if it were Latin *nox* 'night', possessive plural *noctorum*, rather than *cnocc tírim* 'dry hillock'. The Old English element *cnocc*, found in names such as KNOCKDOWN (Wiltshire), may be borrowing from Old Celtic as it has an approximately similar meaning, but this is uncertain.

It was as he wished, and his grey ghost merged with the western clouds.

An hour later, at moonrise, there was no sound.

No moon since in Ireland has been sung to.

> J.P. Macardle: 'The Knockmealdown Wolf ', from *Retracings* (1954)

On 10 April 1923, during the Irish Civil War, the Knockmealdown Mountains witnessed the death in action of the hardline Republican leader, Liam Lynch.

Knocknagree Irish *Cnoc na Graí* 'hill of the stud of horses' (*see* KNOCK-).

A village in County Cork, on the Kerry border some 20 km (12 miles) east of Killarney. It is famous for its traditional music and dancing, and for its fairs.

Knocknarea Irish *Cnoc na Riabh* 'hill of the executions' (*see* KNOCK-). Many hills near settlements were used for this purpose: witness the large number of GALLOW HILLS in Scotland and elsewhere.

An isolated hill (330 m / 1082 ft) in County Sligo, 5 km (3 miles) west of Sligo itself. On its summit is Miscaun Meadhbh, a large cairn 24 m (80 ft) high, supposedly the grave of the legendary Queen Maeve (Medb) of CONNACHT (slain on INCHCLERAUN), but probably pre-Celtic in origin.

> The wind has bundled up the clouds high over Knocknarea,
> And thrown the thunder on the stones for all that Maeve can say.
>
> W.B. Yeats: 'Red Hanrahan's Song About Ireland', from *In the Seven Woods* (1904)

Knodishall 'Cnott's nook of land', OE *Cnottes* possessive form of male personal name *Cnott* + *halh* (*see* HALE, -HALL).

A village in Suffolk, about 6.5 km (4 miles) northwest of Aldeburgh.

Knole OE *cnoll* 'knoll, top of a low hill'.

A house in Kent, about 1.5 km (1 mile) southeast of SEVENOAKS, and one of the largest private houses in England. It was created in the mid-15th century as the Archbishop of Canterbury's palace and was for 400 years the home of the Sackville family. It is set in a park of about 405 ha (1000 acres) and now belongs to the National Trust.

The writer Vita Sackville-West (1892–1962), daughter of the 3rd Baron Sackville and later the creator of the gardens at SISSINGHURST, was born and grew up in the house. She wrote *Knole and the Sackvilles* (1922) describing her ancestral home and family. Both Knole itself and Sackville-West (who had an affair with Virginia Woolf) are celebrated in Virginia Woolf's novel *Orlando* (1928), a kind of time-travelling biography of house and Vita.

Knook Probably 'hillock' (referring to a local tumulus), OCelt *cnucc* (*see* KNOCK-).

A village (pronounced 'nook', rhyming with *look*) in Wiltshire, on the River WYLYE[1], about 24 km (15 miles) northwest of Salisbury.

Knotting Probably '(settlement of) Cnotta's people', OE male personal name *Cnotta* + *-ingas* (*see* -ING).

A village in Bedfordshire, about 16 km (10 miles) north of Bedford.

Knottingley 'Cnotta's people's clearing', OE male personal name *Cnotta* + *-inga-* (*see* -ING) + -LEY.

A town on the River AIRE in West Yorkshire, 5 km (3 miles) northeast of Pontefract.

Knotty Ash The original village took its name from the gnarled old ash tree around which it grew in the late 17th or early 18th century.

An area of LIVERPOOL, some 7 km (4 miles) east of the centre. The comedian Ken Dodd (b.1927) grew up here, and in his imagination it is peopled with diminutive Diddymen (Liverpudlian dialect *diddy* 'tiny'), who make their living working in the local Jam Butty Mines. It is regarded by some as a highly desirable area:

> Perhaps one day we'll have a splash, when Littlewoods provides the cash,
> We'll get a house in Knotty Ash, and buy yer dad a brewery.
>
> Anon.: 'Liverpool Lullaby'

Knowsley 'Cynewulf's clearing', OE male personal name *Cynewulf* + -LEY.

A village in Merseyside, 11 km (7 miles) northeast of Liverpool. It gave its name to one of the borough councils to which many of the powers of Merseyside were devolved in 1986.

Knowsley Hall, home of the earls of Derby, was originally a medieval hunting lodge, and was remodelled in the 18th and 19th centuries. In the 1830s Edward Lear was commissioned by Lord Stanley to paint the birds and animals in his menagerie here. Since 1971 it has been a safari park.

Knowth Irish *Cnobga*, of uncertain meaning.

A townland (administrative division of a parish) in County Meath, 5 km (3 miles) southeast of Slane. It is the site of a vast Neolithic tomb, some 4000 years old, in the form of giant cairn, some 15 m (50 ft) high, within which have been discovered two long passages. It is part of the Boyne Valley site (*see under* BOYNE), also including NEWGRANGE.

Knoydart 'Cnut's inlet', OScand personal name *Cnut* + Gaelic *-art* from OScand *fjorthr* 'fjord, inlet'. Cnut is probably King Cnut (Canute), king of England 1016–35, who invaded Scotland in 1031.

A mountainous peninsula in the Western HIGHLANDS, bounded by Loch Hourn to the north and LOCH NEVIS to the south. It is in Highland (formerly in Inverness-shire).

It is a wild and largely uninhabited area, often referred to as **the Rough Bounds of Knoydart**. The only road is along the western coast, linking the main settlement of Inverie with the smaller settlement of Airor to the northwest. However, this road has no connections with other roads, Inverie's main link to the outside world being by mailboat to Mallaig. Knoydart contains Scotland's most westerly mainland Munro, the magnificent Ladhar Bheinn (1020 m / 3346 ft; it is pronounced 'larven', and is Gaelic for 'forked mountain').

Knoydart is now a National Scenic Area. In 1983 there was a threat that the Army might purchase the area, but after widespread objections this came to nothing. The northern part was purchased by the John Muir Trust in 1987, and in 1999 the Knoydart Estate itself (including Inverie) came under community ownership in the form of the Knoydart Foundation.

Knutsford Probably 'Knutr's ford', OScand *Knuts* possessive form of male personal name *Knutr* + OE FORD. Local legend associates the name with the fording of a stream here by King Cnut (Canute), king of England (1016–35).
A town in Cheshire, about 16 km (10 miles) northwest of Macclesfield and 19 km (12 miles) southwest of Stockport. It lies amongst the fat fields of Cheshire stockbrokerland. The streets of its old centre are narrow, and it has its fair share of typical Cheshire black-and-white 'magpie' houses. Knutsford holds large-scale May Day celebrations involving hundreds of locals parading in costume, and in June in each year the town hosts the Cheshire Show.

The novelist Elizabeth Gaskell spent her childhood in Knutsford (she is buried behind the Unitarian chapel), and she based the village of CRANFORD on it in the novel (1853) of the same name. Knutsford also figures as **Hollingford** in her *Wives and Daughters* (1866).

Knutsford Services are just south of Junction 19 on the M6.
See also TATTON DALE.

Knype. A fictionalized version of STOKE-ON-TRENT, as portrayed as one of the FIVE TOWNS, in the novels of Arnold Bennett. The name was adapted from KNYPERSLEY.

> If Knype drop into the Second Division ... it'll be all up with first-class football in the Five Towns!
>
> Arnold Bennett: *The Matador of the Five Towns* (1912)

Knypersley Perhaps 'Cnibba's glade', OE male personal name *Cnibba* + -LEY.
A village in Staffordshire, now a southern suburb of BIDDULPH, about 11 km (7 miles) north of Stoke-on-Trent.

Kop, the From the Boer War battle of *Spion Kop* (Afrikaans for 'lookout hill'), fought on 24 January 1900.
A former terrace at the southern end of the ANFIELD stadium, the home ground of LIVERPOOL FC. It was opened on 1 September 1906 and within weeks was dubbed the Spion Kop, or simply the Kop, after the Boer War battle of that name (*see above*) in which many Merseysiders were killed or injured. It was roofed in 1928 and became the largest covered terrace in Britain, with room for 28,000 people. It was demolished following the club's final home match of the 1993–4 season on 30 April 1994 against Norwich City and a concert on 1 May featuring many Merseybeat bands of the 1960s, such as Gerry and the Pacemakers and The Searchers. It was replaced by a new stand seating 12,000 and housing a club shop and a branch of McDonald's, the first in a sports stadium in Britain.

The initiator of the original nickname is said to have been Ernest Edwards, sports editor of the *Liverpool Daily Post*. The name was also in use elsewhere, as at Arsenal's former Plumstead ground and Birmingham's former ground at Tilton Road. Bradford City's Valley Parade ground had a 'Nunn's Kop', named after one of the club's founders.

Kuggar Apparently named after a local stream, an OCelt river name meaning 'winding'.
A village (pronounced 'kugə') in western Cornwall, on the LIZARD Peninsula, about 13 km (8 miles) southeast of Helston.

Kyle 'territory of Coel Hen', from the Brittonic chieftain *Coel Hen* who is thought to be the 'Old King Cole' of the nursery rhyme; the *Hen* element of his name means 'old'.
A traditional area of AYRSHIRE, comprising the plain in the centre of the former county, between the Rivers Irvine and Doon. It includes the towns of AYR[1], PRESTWICK, TROON and MAUCHLINE. It is bordered on the north by Cunninghame and on the south by Carrick. From 1975 to 1996 it was part of **Kyle and Carrick** district (Ayr was its administrative headquarters) in Strathclyde region, and it is now divided between the unitary authorities of East and South Ayrshire.

Kyle is very much 'Burns Country', the poet having been born in ALLOWAY (now a suburb of Ayr); the poet's 'Rantin', Rovin' Robin' (referring to himself) begins

> There was a lad was born in Kyle ...

On his Scottish tour of 1818 the poet John Keats described the area in a letter to J.H. Reynolds:

> I had no Conception that the native place of Burns was so beautiful – the Idea I had was more desolate, his rigs of Barley seemed always to me but a few strips of Green on a cold hill – O prejudice! it was rich as Devon ...

Kyleakin 'strait of Haakon', Gaelic *caol* 'strait' + OScand personal name.
The village on SKYE at the southwest end of the bridge (and before that the ferry) from KYLE OF LOCHALSH on the mainland. It is in Highland (formerly in Inverness-shire). It takes

its name from the strait crossed by the bridge, **Kyle Akin**, whose name in turn commemorates the fact that in 1263 King Haakon IV of Norway sailed through here en route to defeat at the Battle of Largs (*see under* LARGS).

Kyle and Carrick. *See under* KYLE.

Kyle of Lochalsh 'the strait of Loch Alsh', *Kyle* Gaelic *caol* 'strait'; *Lochalsh* the name of a sea loch, possibly Gaelic *aillseach* 'foaming'.

A small town on the mainland opposite SKYE, in Highland (formerly in Ross and Cromarty), at the mouth of Loch Alsh, a sea loch. It is the main point of departure from the mainland to Skye, formerly by ferry and now by the new road bridge across to KYLEAKIN. It is also the terminus of the railway line from Inverness.

Kyle of Tongue. *See under* TONGUE.

Kylesku 'narrow straits', Gaelic *caolas* 'straits' + *cumhann* 'narrow'.

A small settlement on the coast of northwest Highland, on the south side of the spectacularly situated narrows between Loch a'Chairn Bhain and lochs Glendhu and Glencoul. There was a ferry here linking Kylesku with KYLESTROME on the north shore until 1984, when it was replaced by the **Kylesku Bridge**. The ferry was established in the 19th century, and saved the traveller a 160-km (100-mile) diversion

via LAIRG. During the Second World War the waters here were used for training in miniature submarines.

Kyles of Bute. *See under* BUTE.

Kylestrome Gaelic *caolas* 'straits' + unknown element.

A small settlement on the coast of northwest Highland, on the north side of the narrows traversed by the Kylesku Bridge (*see under* KYLESKU).

Kyloe Hills 'clearing for cows', *Kyloe* OE *cu* 'cow', plural *cy* + -LEY.

A range of low hills in Northumberland, some 8 km (5 miles) inland from Holy Island. The sandstone outcrops of **Kyloe Crag** and **Kyloe in the Woods** are popular with rock-climbers.

Kyme Eau *Kyme* from the name of two local settlements, *North Kyme* and *South Kyme*, '(place at the) hollow', OE *cymbe*; *Eau* OE *ea* 'watercourse' (*see* EA-).

An artificial watercourse in Lincolnshire, in the FENS, linking the River SLEA with the River WITHAM.

Kynance Cove *Kynance* Cornish *cow-nans* 'ravine'.

A small bay at the southeastern end of the LIZARD Peninsula in western Cornwall. The spectacular grey-black cliffs are streaked with green, red, yellow and white from the serpentine rock. The Cove is now in the care of the National Trust.

L

Lach Dennis *Lach* 'boggy stream', OE *lece*; *Dennis* 'Danish' (alluding to a Dane called Colben who owned the manor in the late 11th century), ME *danais*.

A village in Cheshire, about 6 km (4 miles) east of Northwich.

Lacock 'small stream', OE *lacuc* (*see* LAKE).

A village in Wiltshire, on the River AVON², about 5 km (3 miles) south of CHIPPENHAM. Preternaturally picturesque, its buildings form a harmonious jigsaw of architectural styles and materials (brick, stone, half-timbering) from the Middle Ages to the 19th century (none more recent). Almost all are now owned by the National Trust. Among present-day residents is Camilla Parker-Bowles, consort of the Prince of Wales.

Beside the Avon is **Lacock Abbey**, a 13th-century foundation converted into a house after the Dissolution of the Monasteries in the 16th century. By the 18th century it had come into the possession of the Talbot family and in the 1830s it was the venue for some of the earliest experiments in photography, by William Fox-Talbot.

Lactodunum. A Roman settlement on the site of present-day TOWCESTER.

Ladbroke Grove *Ladbroke* from a family called Ladbroke, which owned land here from the 17th to the 19th century + *grove* 'secluded area, small wood'.

A road in West London (W10, W11), in the borough of KENSINGTON AND CHELSEA. It was laid out in the late 1840s. It is the central thoroughfare of North KENSINGTON and NOTTING HILL, running from the Harrow Road in the north, under the Westway, to Holland Park Avenue in the south. Its annual high spot is the Notting Hill Carnival. Its trendier denizens are known to the press as **Ladbroke Groovers**.

> Saw you walking down by Ladbroke Grove this morning
> Catching pebbles for some sunny beach –
> You're outa reach.
>
> Van Morrison: 'Slim Slow Slide' (song), from *Astral Weeks* (1969)

Ladbroke Grove Underground station, on the Hammersmith & City line, opened in 1864 (originally as Notting Hill; it did not take its present name until 1938). Further north Ladbroke Grove crosses the mainline railway from PADDINGTON, and this was the scene in 1999 of a rail crash in which 31 people were killed.

> It is perhaps through sheer taciturnity that the English swallow half of every word, and then the second half they somehow squash; so it is difficult to understand them. I used to travel every day to Ladbroke Grove; the conductor would come and I would say: 'Ledbruk Grröv.' '…?? Eh?' 'Ledbhuk Ghöv!' '… ??? Eh?' 'Hevhuv Hev!' 'Aa, Hevhuv Hov!' The conductor would rejoice and give me a ticket to Ladbroke Grove. I shall never learn this as long as I live.
>
> Karel Čapek: *Letters from England* (1924)

Ladder Hills Possibly a literal translation of Gaelic *Monadh an Àraidh*, 'hills of the ladder', or alternatively from Gaelic *leitir* 'slope'.

A range of remote moorland hills on the border of Moray and Aberdeenshire, extending northeastward from the LECHT. The highest point is Carn Mor (804 m / 2637 ft).

Ladhar Bheinn. *See under* KNOYDART.

Ladies' Mile, the. An alternative name for ROTTEN ROW, first recorded in a novel by the 19th-century writer Mary Elizabeth Braddon.

Ladybower Reservoir ModE *lady* + *bower* 'shady retreat'.

A large reservoir on the River Derwent, just to the south of Derwent Reservoir (*see under* DERWENT⁴), in the PEAK DISTRICT of Derbyshire. Its construction, completed in 1945, involved the submerging of the villages of Derwent and Ashopton (a church spire was visible for a while whenever the water level was low, but it was demolished for safety reasons).

Lady's Rock. A small rock in the sea off DUART CASTLE on the east coast of MULL. It takes its name from the wife of the 11th Maclean chief, who at the end of the 15th century was abandoned here by her husband after he had grown dissatisfied with her. When she disappeared, apparently washed away by the tide, Maclean reported her death, as if an accident, to her brother, the Earl of Argyll. When Maclean next visited the Earl in Inveraray he was astonished to be confronted with his wife, alive and well. It seems she had been rescued by fishermen, but not a word was said about the matter. Many years later Maclean died at the hands of an unknown murderer.

Lady's View. *See under* KILLARNEY.

Ladywood ModE *lady* + *wood*, presumably owned or used by a lady.

A western inner suburb of BIRMINGHAM. Clare Short, former Secretary of State for International Development (1997–2003), has been the Labour MP for the Ladywood parliamentary constituency since 1983.

Lagan Irish *Abhainn an Lagáin* 'river of the low-lying area or hollow'.

A river in Northern Ireland, rising in County Down, near LURGAN, and flowing 40 km (25 miles) northeastwards through BELFAST into Belfast Lough.

> Where Lagan stream sings lullaby
> There blows a lily fair,
> The twilight gleam is in her eye,
> The night is on her hair,
> And like a love-sick lennan-shee
> She has my heart in thrall,
> Nor life I owe nor liberty
> For love is lord of all.
>
> Seosamh Mac Cathmaoil (Joseph Campbell): 'My Lagan Love', from *Songs of Uladh* (1904)

The river gave its name to *Lagan*, an annual Ulster literary magazine edited by John Boyd and published from 1942 to 1945; it included contributions from the likes of Louis MacNeice and Michael McLaverty.

> O the bricks they will bleed and the rain it will weep,
> And the damp Lagan fog lull the city to sleep;
> It's to hell with the future and live on the past:
> *May the Lord in His Mercy Be Kind to Belfast.*
>
> Maurice James Craig: 'Ballad to a Traditional Refrain' (1938)

Lag an Choile. The Irish name for LEGACURRY.

Lagavulin. *See* Islay malts *under* ISLAY.

Lagentium. A fort built by the Romans on the site of modern-day CASTLEFORD.

Laggan. *See under* LOCH LAGGAN.

Laighin. The Irish name for LEINSTER.

Lairg Gaelic *lorg* 'shank' (i.e. shin) or 'track'. By a bizarre coincidence Lairg is on LOCH SHIN, whose meaning is something else entirely.

A village at the southeast end of LOCH SHIN, in Highland (formerly in Sutherland), 27 km (16 miles) northwest of Dornoch. From here roads lead south, west, northwest, north and east, and there is also a station on the Inverness–Wick railway line. This features in Norman MacCaig's poem 'Back again, Lairg station' (in *The White Bird*, 1973).

Lairig Ghru, the 'gloomy pass', Gaelic *làirig* 'pass', with *ghrù* 'gloomy'.

A high walkers' pass through the Cairngorm Mountains, linking Deeside and Speyside, a distance of 30 km (19 miles). It is in Highland (formerly in Inverness-shire). The summit of the pass at 833 m (2733 ft) is 13.5 km (8.5 miles) southeast of Aviemore, and forms a distinct 'V' cleft through the hills, visible from many miles away. Near the summit are the Pools of Dee (*see under* DEE[1]), and on either side are three of the four Cairngorm Four-Thousanders: BRAERIACH and CAIRN TOUL to the west, and BEN MACDUI to the east (with the fourth, CAIRN GORM, close by but not adjacent). The more attractive route at the south end is via Glen Luibeg and Derry Lodge, rather than following the course of the Dee. At the north end is the Rothiemurchus Forest. Norman MacCaig's poem 'Another incident' (from *The White Bird*, 1973) is set in the Lairig Ghru. It begins:

> In the pass between
> the four great bens of the Cairngorms
> an ant
> climbed down a pinetree.

Láithreach Cora. The Irish name for LARACOR.

Lake County, the. A nickname for WESTMEATH, a county of many lakes, including Lough Leane (*see under* KILLARNEY), LOUGH DERRAVARAGH, Lough Iron, Lough Owle, Lough Ennell and part of LOUGH REE. The name is used particularly in the context of the county's Gaelic football team.

Lake District, the From the plethora of lakes here. The name is first recorded in the early 19th century.

A scenic area of northwest England, all now in Cumbria, but formerly divided between CUMBERLAND, WESTMORLAND and LANCASHIRE. It is also known as **Lakeland** or simply **the Lakes**, and its inhabitants are known as **Lakelanders**. The main centres are KESWICK, AMBLESIDE and WINDERMERE. The area contains England's largest lakes (including WINDERMERE, CONISTON WATER, WAST WATER, ENNERDALE Water, CRUMMOCK WATER, BUTTERMERE, BASSENTHWAITE LAKE, Derwent Water (*see under* DERWENT[1]), THIRLMERE, ULLSWATER and HAWESWATER) and most of its highest mountains, including the three highest, **the Lakeland Three-Thousanders**, SCAFELL PIKE, HELVELLYN and SKIDDAW – the only mountains in England over 3000 ft (914.6 m), if one counts Scafell itself as but a subsidiary

---

❖ lake ❖

The modern word *lake*, which appears in the LAKE DISTRICT and many another place name, is derived from Latin *lacus* through French *lac*, and related to Gaelic and Irish LOCH, the anglicized LOUGH, and to Cornish *logh*. *Lake* in its current sense is first found in the 13th century in England, and before that by far the most common English element signifying 'lake' was *mere*, found in REDMARLEY D'ABITOT (Gloucestershire) and DOGMERSFIELD and DUMMER (Hampshire), as well as in SEMER WATER (Yorkshire) and in WINDERMERE, BUTTERMERE and GRASMERE in the Lake District.

However, the Old English elements *lacu* 'stream' and *lacuc* 'small stream' give some modern spellings that can easily be confused with the later element *lake*. These most obviously appear in such names as LAKENHEATH (Suffolk) and MORTLAKE (Greater London), but also in slightly disguised form in Senlac (East Sussex, *see under* HASTINGS) and LACOCK (Wiltshire).

---

top. These three mountains form the course of the annual THREE PEAKS Race.

The Lake District consists of a number of valleys radiating out like the spokes of a wheel from a hub. Communication between these valleys is often only by small roads clambering over steep, high passes, such as HARD KNOTT, HONISTER, WRYNOSE and KIRKSTONE. The area has a unique scenic combination in which rugged crags and fells rise above lush, pastoral valleys, filled with lakes and fields and woods.

The scenic grandeur of the Lake District has proved a honeypot for visitors since the later 18th century; particular spurs were Thomas Gray's tour of 1769 and subsequent publication of his *Journal*, and the publication in 1786 of John Gilpin's *Observations on Cumberland and Westmorland*. But it was William Wordsworth – a native Lakelander (born in COCKERMOUTH, schooled at HAWKSHEAD and settled at GRASMERE) – who, through his poetry, really drew the nation's attention to the area's beauties. Wordsworth's presence in the Lakes lured his friends Samuel Taylor Coleridge and Robert Southey to live here (these two shared Greta Hall at KESWICK), and together the trio became known as the **Lake Poets** or the **Lake School** – referred to disparagingly by Byron as 'all the Lakers'.

> Wordsworth went to the lakes, but he was never a lake poet. He found in stones the sermons he had already hidden there.
>
> Oscar Wilde: 'The Decay of Lying' (1891)

Prior to the Lake Poets, visitors tended to view the district's mountains as lumps of savage beastliness and inutility:

> Nor were these hills high and formidable only, but they had a kind of unhospitable terror in them. Here were no rich pleasant valleys between them, as among the Alps; no lead mines and veins of rich ore, as in the Peak; no coal pits, as in the hills about Halifax, much less gold, as in the Andes, but all barren and wild, of no use or advantage either to man or beast.
>
> Daniel Defoe: *A Tour Through the Whole Island of Great Britain* (1724–6)

By 1769, when Thomas Gray toured the Lakes, sensibilities were beginning to shift – a little:

> In climes beyond the solar road
> Where shaggy forms o'er ice-built mountains roam
> The Muse has broke the twilight-gloom
> To cheer the shivering native's dull abode.

But it was Coleridge and Wordsworth who were the first great celebrators of mountains as things of grandeur and beauty, and these two partisans of Lakeland's charms favourably compared their mountains with those elsewhere in Britain:

> Their forms are endlessly diversified, sweeping easily or boldly in simple majesty, abrupt and precipitous, or soft and elegant. In magnitude and grandeur they are individually inferior to the most celebrated of those in some other parts of this island; but, in the combinations which they make, towering above each other, or lifting themselves in ridges like the waves of a tumultuous sea, and in the beauty and variety of their surfaces and their colours, they are surpassed by none.
>
> William Wordsworth: *Topographical Description of the Country of the Lakes in the North of England* (1810, 1820)

> I know of no mountain in the north equal to Snowdon, but then we have an encampment of huge mountains, in no harmony perhaps to the eye of the mere painter, but always interesting, various and, as it were nutritive.
>
> Samuel Taylor Coleridge: letter to William Godwin (8 September 1800)

It was not only Lakeland's mountains that Wordsworth preferred to those elsewhere in Britain, but also its lakes, which he thought better arranged than those in Scotland (especially LOCH LOMOND):

> It is much more desirable, for the purposes of pleasure, that lakes should be numerous, and small or middle-sized, than large, not only for communication by walks and rides, but for variety, and for recurrence of similar appearances.
>
> William Wordsworth: *Topographical Description of the Country of the Lakes in the North of England* (1810, 1820)

Coleridge and Wordsworth were both great fell walkers, again among the first to undertake this activity for pleasure. Coleridge's journals in particular are full of joyous walks among the hills (see, for example, HELVELLYN) and in 1802 he made, while descending Scafell (see SCAFELL PIKE), the first recorded rock climb for pleasure in Britain – although the birth of British rock climbing as a sport is usually dated to W.P. Haskett-Smith's solo ascent of Napes Needle on GREAT GABLE in June 1886. The Lake District has been a mecca for fell walkers and rock climbers, as well as coach-bound tourists, ever since. It now constitutes the **Lake District National Park** (created in 1951), and many parts are in the care of the National Trust.

A more traditional pastime in the Lakes has been fox hunting, which in this mountainous area has always been carried out on foot. The most famous Lakeland huntsman was, of course, John Peel (1776–1854; see SKIDDAW), who is buried at Caldbeck.

To some, the Lake Poets, especially Wordsworth, ended up institutionalizing the area, but the raw experience may still be had:

> Am I
> To see in the Lake District, then,
> Another bourgeois invention like the piano?
> Well, I won't. ...
>
> W.H. Auden: 'Bucolics: 3. Mountains'

For other writers, the visitors' Lakeland is a travesty, or at least a mask drawn over the harsher realities of impoverished and debased rural life:

> Here [vice] is flagrant beyond anything I could have looked for: and here while every justice of the peace is filled with disgust and every clergyman with (almost) despair at the drunkenness, quarrelling and extreme licentiousness with women – here is dear good old Wordsworth for ever talking of rural innocence and deprecating any intercourse with towns, lest the purity of his neighbours should be corrupted.
>
> Harriet Martineau: letter from the Lake District to Elizabeth Barrett (1846)

A century and a half later this grim underside was depicted in the 1990s television mini-series *The Lakes* by Jimmy McGovern, featuring rape, murder, fisticuffs and adultery. However, for many people Lakeland is still the home of Beatrice Potter's Jemima Puddleduck and Mrs Tiggywinkle, while Arthur Ransome's Swallows and Amazons will for ever sail in an evening breeze as the sun declines over Windermere.

Lakeland. Another name for the LAKE DISTRICT.
Lakeland Fells, the. The hills of the LAKE DISTRICT.
Lakeland puffties. A type of dumpling fried in bacon fat.
Lakeland terrier. A breed of terrier, rather like a small Airedale (see under AIRE), stocky in build and black and tan in colour, which has been used for hunting foxes and otters. They are also called Patterdale terriers.

Lakeland Three-Thousanders, the. See LAKE DISTRICT.

Lakenheath 'landing-place of the people living by streams', OE *lacu* 'stream' (see also LAKE) + *-inga-* (see -ING) + *hyth* 'landing-place'.
A small town in Suffolk, on the western edge of the BRECKLAND, where it merges into the FENS, about 8 km (5 miles) north of MILDENHALL[1]. Its church, St Mary's, contains a remarkable survival of medieval wall-painting, but the Stars and Stripes hanging in a side aisle are a reminder of modern Lakenheath: since 1948 it has been home to one of the largest USAF bases outside the USA. The air strikes by F-111s against Libya in April 1986 were conducted from Lakenheath.

Lakenheath Warren. A 930-ha (2300-acre) area of open land to the southeast of Lakenheath. During the First World War it was one of the first tank training areas in Britain. In the Second World War an RAF base was built here, which in 1948 was handed over to the USAF (see *above*).

Lake of Menteith *Menteith* is 'moor of the River Teith', OCelt root producing Welsh *mynydd*, Gaelic *monadh* 'high ground' + river name Teith (etymology obscure). For *Lake* in this context, *see below*.
A small loch 8 km (5 miles) southwest of Callander, just to the west of FLANDERS MOSS. It was formerly in Perthshire, then in Central region, and is now in the unitary authority of Stirling. It is the only loch in Scotland to be called a lake. There is a story that the English word is used because it was Sir John Menteith who treacherously captured William Wallace in 1305; in fact 'lake' is a corruption of the Gaelic *laicht* 'low-lying land'. **Strath Earn and Menteith** was one of the original mormaerships (Celtic earldoms) of Scotland, and the earls once had their castle here.

The island in the loch, Inchmahome, has the ruins of a priory founded in *c*.1238 by Walter Comyn, Earl of Menteith. At the age of five Mary Queen of Scots was sent here for safety after the Battle of PINKIE (1547), before leaving for France, and there are the remains of a monastic garden that has become known as 'Queen Mary's Bower'. There is a ferry to the island from **Port of Menteith**, a small village on the northeast shore of the loch.

On those rare occasions when the Lake of Menteith freezes over and the ice reaches a thickness of 17.5 cm (7 in), the Royal Caledonian Curling Club calls a Bonspiel or Grand Match, in which thousands of players participate.

Menteith Hills. A small range of hills north of the Lake of Menteith, reaching a high point of 426 m (1396 ft) at Beinn Dearg.

Lake of Shadows. A nickname for LOUGH SWILLY.

Lakes, the. Another name for the LAKE DISTRICT.

Lake Vyrnwy Named from the River *Efyrnwy*, possibly meaning 'milky stream'.

A reservoir in Powys, 12 km (7 miles) south of Bala. It is pronounced 'verny' and in Welsh it is **Llyn Efyrnwy**. The dam that created the lake (which provides water for Liverpool) was built in the 1880s. The creation of the reservoir, which gathers the waters of the **River Vyrnwy** (a tributary of the Severn), resulted in the submersion of the village of Llanwyddyn, which was rebuilt at the southeast end of the lake.

Lamancha A name given *c.*1736 by Admiral Cochrane, who had lived in the *La Mancha* area of Spain.

A village in Scottish Borders, 9 km (5.5 miles) south of Penicuik.

Lamas 'loam marsh', OE *lam* 'loam' + *mersc* 'marsh' (probably influenced folk-etymologically by *Lammas*, the name of a church festival on 1 August).

A village in Norfolk, in the BURE Valley, about 13 km (8 miles) north of Norwich.

Lambay Island 'lamb island', OScand *lamb* + *ey* (*see* -AY); to add 'Island' is thus tautological.

A small island some 5 km (3 miles) off the east coast of County Dublin. Its Irish name is **Rechrainn** (meaning unknown). St Columba founded a monastery here in the 6th century, and there are the remains of a 15th-century castle, incorporated into a house designed by Edwin Lutyens. After the Battle of AUGHRIM during the Williamite Wars, some Irish prisoners were abandoned on the island to starve. The island is now a bird reserve.

Lamb Corner Earlier a field name, *Lambcroft Pictell* 'small enclosure for lambs'.

A village in Essex, about 8 km (5 miles) northeast of Colchester.

Lambeg Irish *Lann Bheag* 'little church'.

A village in County Antrim, some 10 km (6 miles) southwest of Belfast city centre.

Lambeg drum. A large, loud drum, nearly 1 m (3 ft) in diameter, hung from the shoulders and enthusiastically battered during the course of Orange Order marches. The first such drum was played in 1871 at an Orange demonstration in Lambeg, hence the name.

Lamberhurst 'wooded hill where lambs graze', OE *lambra* possessive plural form of *lamb* + *hyrst* 'wooded hill'.

A village in Kent, in the WEALD, on the River Teise, about 8 km (5 miles) southeast of TUNBRIDGE WELLS. It used to be a centre for the Wealden iron industry, but its modern fame rests on its vineyards. Lamberhurst wines were among the more notable commercial successes of the revived English wine industry in the late 20th century.

A little to the south is Scotney Castle, a ruined 14th-century moated castle with a 17th-century house attached.

Lambeth 'landing-place for lambs' (referring to a harbour from or to which lambs were shipped), OE *lamb* + *hyth* 'landing-place'.

A district and borough of Inner London. The district (SE1, SE11) lies on the south bank of the River Thames, opposite the City of Westminster, to which it is joined by **Lambeth Bridge**, a road bridge originally constructed in 1861, as well as by Hungerford, Vauxhall, Waterloo and Westminster Bridges. In 1965 the district was united with Brixton, Streatham, Tulse Hill, Vauxhall, Waterloo and parts of Clapham and Kennington to form the borough of Lambeth (SE1, SE5, SE11, SE24, SE27, SW2, SW4, SW8, SW9, SW16), between Southwark to the east and Wandsworth to the west.

Originally the area by the river was mostly marshland and fields, interspersed with the occasional human settlement. The spaces began to be filled in with houses in the 18th century, and in the 19th century Lambeth developed into a densely populated slum district. Despite 20th-century slum clearance, it remains one of the poorest boroughs in England.

At the southern end of Lambeth Bridge is **Lambeth Palace**, the London residence of the archbishops of Canterbury (*see under* CANTERBURY[1]) since the 12th century. The oldest part is the chapel built by Archbishop Boniface in 1245, and the buildings have been steadily added to and modified over the centuries. Originally called **Lambeth House**, it came to be called Lambeth Palace *c.*1658 owing to the decay of the palace at Canterbury. It is the Archbishop's principal residence, but he now has another palace at Canterbury. The name 'Lambeth Palace', or even simply 'Lambeth', has come to be used as a metonym for the Archbishop of Canterbury, or for the Church of England in general:

> It is the duty of Lambeth to remind Westminster of its responsibility to God; but this does not mean that Westminster is responsible to Lambeth.
>
> William Temple: *Citizen and Churchman* (1941)

Immigrant Dutch potters set up in Lambeth in the 17th century, bringing with them the techniques of their native Delft, and the sort of glazed and painted earthenware they made there up until the 19th century came to be known as **Lambeth delftware**. The ceramics manufacturer now known as Royal Doulton was founded in Lambeth in 1815 by John Doulton.

Among the borough's notable landmarks are the SOUTH BANK[1] arts complex, County Hall, Waterloo Station, the

OVAL cricket ground, the ELEPHANT AND CASTLE traffic junction, the Old Vic theatre and Brixton Prison. It also once had a well-known public bath-house, and in late 19th-century slang to *Lambeth* was 'to wash'.

Lambeth North Underground station, on the Bakerloo line, opened in 1906.

The poet Edward Thomas (1878–1917) was born in Lambeth.

Lambeth Articles, the. A set of doctrinal statements promulgated in 1595 by the then Archbishop of Canterbury, John Whitgift (*c.*1530–1604). They were strongly Calvinistic, upholding the view that each individual soul is predestined to salvation or damnation.

Lambeth Books, the. A name sometimes given to the symbolic poems that William Blake wrote and etched while living in Lambeth (1790–1800). They include *America*, *Europe* and *The Song of Los*.

Lambeth Conference. An assembly of the archbishops and bishops of the Anglican Church from around the world, held every ten years under the presidency of the Archbishop of Canterbury. From 1867 to 1958 it was held in Lambeth Palace, in 1968 at Church House, Westminster and in 1978, 1988 and 1998 at the University of Kent at Canterbury. An increasingly wide range of issues has been discussed, and the 1998 conference voted overwhelmingly in favour of a motion condemning homosexuality as incompatible with biblical teaching. The resolutions of Lambeth conferences, though not binding, are nevertheless regarded by member churches as significant.

Lambeth degree. A degree in divinity, arts, law, medicine, music or other subjects, conferred *honoris causa* by the Archbishop of Canterbury, who was empowered to do so by a statute of 1533.

Lambeth quadrilateral, the. The four points suggested by the Lambeth Conference of 1888 as a basis for Christian reunion: the Bible, the Apostolic and Nicene Creeds, two Sacraments (baptism and the eucharist) and the historic Episcopate.

Lambeth Walk. A street in Lambeth (SE11) leading from Black Prince Road to the Lambeth Road. It gave its name to a Cockney song and dance featured by Lupino Lane (from 1937) in the musical show *Me and My Gal* at the Victoria Palace, London, and very popular during the Second World War:

> Any time you're Lambeth way,
> Any evening, any day,
> You'll find us all
> Doin' the Lambeth walk.
>
> Douglas Furber and Arthur Rose: 'Doin' the Lambeth Walk' (1937)

The dance has couples strutting forwards, arms linked, then strutting back and jerking their thumbs in the air to the exclamation 'Oi!' Many council estates now have a Lambeth Walk as a memento. The term has also been used in Cockney rhyming slang for *chalk* (as used in billiards and snooker).

Liza of Lambeth. A novel (1897) by W. Somerset Maugham, his first, based on his own experiences of slums and Cockney life as an obstetric clerk.

Lambourn From the river name *Lambourn*, probably 'stream where lambs are washed', OE *lamb* + *burna* 'stream'.

A small town in Berkshire, within the unitary authority of WEST BERKSHIRE, on the River Lambourn, about 19 km (12 miles) northwest of Newbury. A little further upstream to the northwest is **Upper Lambourn**, and just to the north are the **Lambourn Downs**, part of the North Wessex Downs (*see under* WESSEX), noted for their racehorse gallops.

> Leathery limbs of Upper Lambourne,
> Leathery skin from sun and wind,
> Leathery breeches, spreading stables,
> Shining saddles left behind –
> To the down the string of horses
> Moving out of sight and mind.
>
> John Betjeman: 'Upper Lambourne' (1940)

Lamlash 'St Molaise's island', Gaelic *eilean* 'island' + personal name *Molaise* (the final consonant is pronounced 'sh'), the 6th-century saint who lived as a hermit on HOLY ISLAND[3] across the bay. The OScand *Hacon's Saga* calls it *Molasey* with the same meaning, but with OScand *ey* 'island' (*see* -AY) for Gaelic *eilean*.

A village on the east coast of ARRAN, 5 km (3 miles) south of Brodick, in North Ayrshire (formerly in Buteshire, then in Strathclyde region). It looks out across **Lamlash Bay** to HOLY ISLAND[3], and it was from Lamlash that pilgrims sailed to the island. It was in Lamlash Bay that King Haakon IV's Norwegian fleet took shelter before their defeat at the Battle of Largs (*see under* LARGS) in 1263.

Lammermuirs, the 'waste land of the lambs', OE *lamb* 'lamb', possessive plural *lambra* 'of the lambs' + *mor* 'waste land'; *Lombormore* 10th century. The present spelling has assimilated the OE *mor* to Scots *muir* 'moor'.

A range of rolling hills running southwest–northeast in East Lothian, with their southern slopes in Scottish Borders (the part of it that was formerly Berwickshire). They meet the North Sea at FAST CASTLE and ST ABBS Head. The highest point is Meikle Says Law (535 m / 1755 ft), just pipping **Lammer Law** (528 m / 1732 ft). The range is sometimes called the **Lammermuir Hills**, and the area, including the lower ground to the north and south of the range, is sometimes called simply **Lammermuir**.

Bride of Lammermoor, The. A novel by Sir Walter Scott, published in 1819. The 'bride' is Lucy Ashton, who kills her husband and goes mad. The novel is perhaps not as well-known as Donizetti's operatic version, *Lucia di Lammermoor* (1835; libretto by Salvatore Cammarano), with its famous 'mad scene'.

Lammermuir lion. A jocular Scottish expression for a sheep in the 18th and 19th centuries, the Lammermuirs being given over almost entirely to sheep farming. *Compare* Cotswold lion (*see under* COTSWOLDS).

Lampeter 'church of St Peter', from Welsh *llan* 'church site' + personal name *Pedr*.

A town on the River Teifi in Ceredigion (formerly in Cardiganshire, then in Dyfed), 33 km (20 miles) northeast of Carmarthen. The Welsh name is **Llanbedr Pont Steffan** ('church of St Peter by Stephen's bridge', the latter being an old stone bridge over the Teifi). Lampeter is home to St David's University College, Wales's oldest (and most remote) university, founded as a theological college in 1822. It has been part of the University of Wales since 1971.

> Lampeter … A city that stays awake all night staring at the ceiling.
>
> Linda Smith: *A Brief History of Time-Wasting*, BBC Radio 4 (2002)

In the 17th century one of the leading families of Lampeter were the Lloyds of Maesyfelin. When Elen Lloyd became engaged to Samuel Pritchard of Llandovery, her brothers took against the arrangement. They tied Samuel upside down on his horse and ran it all the way back to Llandovery (a distance of some 25 km / 15 miles), with fatal consequences for Samuel – and also for Elen, who shortly after died of grief. The dead boy's father happened to be Rhys Pritchard, the Vicar of Llandovery (*see under* LLANDOVERY), who was both a priest and a poet, and thus well-qualified to place a curse on the house of Maesyfelin, which duly burnt to the ground a few months later. In addition, the eldest Lloyd brother killed the others and then hanged himself.

Lampeter Velfrey 'church of St Peter in Efelfre', *see* LAMPETER; the meaning of the district name, *Efelfre*, is obscure, but may be related to *gefel* 'pincers'.

A village in Pembrokeshire (formerly in Dyfed), 5 km (3 miles) east of Narberth.

Lanark 'glade, clearing', OCelt *llanerch*.

A market town and royal BURGH (1140) above the River Clyde, South Lanarkshire (formerly in Strathclyde region), some 35 km (20 miles) southeast of Glasgow. It was the county town of the traditional county of LANARKSHIRE, and then the administrative headquarters of the former district of CLYDESDALE. Even before it became a royal burgh it was important enough for Kenneth II to hold a parliament here in 978. By tradition, it was here that William Wallace married, and, after his wife was killed by the English, Wallace embarked on his revolt in 1297 by attacking

Lanark's English garrison. Lanark has a racecourse, and the Silver Bell (late 16th century), awarded for a 1.5 mile (2.4 km) race each September, is possibly the world's oldest horse-racing trophy. The granting of the royal charter is commemorated every June with the Lanimers (Scots for 'boundaries of burgh land') festival, which includes a riding of the marches.

Another Lanark festival is Whuppity Scourie (from Scots *whippitie*, diminutive of 'whip' + *scour* 'rush about'), in which, every 1 March, schoolchildren run round the church three times, swinging balls of paper to put winter to flight. There is also a local folk tale (similar to the story of Rumplestiltskin) about a farmer's wife whose pig falls sick. A fairy cures the pig but claims the woman's baby unless she can guess the fairy's name. Later the farmer's wife overhears the fairy chanting in the woods:

> Little kens our guid dame at hame
> That Whuppity Stoorie is my name.

When the fairy comes to claim her fee, the woman calls her by her name, thus putting her to flight.

There are towns called Lanark in Canada (Ontario) and the USA (Illinois and Florida). Alasdair's Gray's novel *Lanark* (1981) is not set in Lanark, but in an alternative Glasgow called Unthank; Lanark is the hero's name.

See also NEW LANARK.

Lanark weight. The Scots Troy system of weight, the standard of which was entrusted to the safekeeping of the burgh of Lanark from the 17th to the early 19th century.

Third Lanark. *See under* LANARKSHIRE.

Lanarkshire From LANARK + SHIRE.

A traditional Scottish county, largely coinciding with the catchment area of the River CLYDE. It was bounded on the west by Renfrewshire and Ayrshire, on the south by Dumfriesshire, on the east by Peeblesshire, Midlothian and West Lothian, and on the north by Dunbartonshire and Stirlingshire. The county town was LANARK. It was absorbed into Strathclyde region in 1975, but in 1996 was re-incarnated as two unitary authorities: heavily urban and industrial NORTH LANARKSHIRE and the more rural SOUTH LANARKSHIRE. It was once a great coal-mining area, but no more:

> Lanarkshire's wheels
> Unwind men underground and me under
> The flowering bings of my own shire …
>
> W.S. Graham : 'The Lost Other', from *The White Threshold* (1949) (Scots *bings* 'slag heaps')

Lanarkshire's local politics are as tough and uncompromising as its post-industrial landscape:

> In the dirty business of politics, the linen doesn't wash much dirtier than in Labour's Scottish heartland of

Lanarkshire. In recent years the grim Scottish shire has become synonymous with corruption, sectarianism, nepotism, bitter grudges and in-fighting.

Gerard Seenan: *The Observer* (20 October 2002)

Third Lanark. A football club founded in 1872 as the 3rd Lanarkshire Volunteer Rifles Football Club, based in Strathbungo, on the south side of Glasgow (then in Lanarkshire). The team later became one of the original members of the Scottish Football Association, and won the championship in 1904 and the Scottish Cup in 1889 and 1905. It stayed in the First Division until the end of the 1964–5 season, when it was relegated, having lost 30 out of 34 matches. Two years later the club went bankrupt and ceased to exist. Its nicknames were the Thirds and the Hi Hi.

Lancashire From LANCASTER; *Lancastreshire* is recorded in the 14th century.

A county in northwest England, bounded on the west by the Irish Sea, on the north by Cumbria, on the east by North and West Yorkshire, and on the south by Merseyside and Cheshire. The standard abbreviation of Lancashire is **Lancs**. In the 1974 reorganization the county lost territory to MERSEYSIDE, CUMBRIA and GREATER MANCHESTER, and in 1998 BLACKPOOL and BLACKBURN WITH DARWEN became separate unitary authorities. Until 1974 the county town was LANCASTER; then the administrative headquarters moved to PRESTON. Other Lancashire towns include ACCRINGTON, BURNLEY, FLEETWOOD, HEYSHAM, MORECAMBE and SOUTHPORT. In the east of the county is part of the PENNINES, including the FOREST OF BOWLAND, and its rivers include the RIBBLE, the WYRE and the LUNE[1]. Formerly Lancashire was the world centre for the manufacture of cotton textiles, but the industry declined after the advent of foreign competition.

The county badge of Lancashire is the red rose, the badge of the House of Lancaster (*see under* LANCASTER), and much of the county is part of the royal Duchy of Lancaster (*see under* LANCASTER). Natives of Lancashire are known as **Lancastrians**. Its name in Romany, according to George Borrow, is **Chohawniskey tem** ('witches' country'), an association also reflected in Harrison Ainsworth's novel *The Lancashire Witches* (*see under* PENDLE HILL).

In 1351 Lancashire became a COUNTY PALATINE, but its rights as a palatinate subsequently passed to the sovereign in his capacity as Duke of Lancaster. Historically a somewhat remote county, Lancashire is rich in historical associations with the 'old faith' of Roman Catholicism. It was a hotbed of recusancy during the reign of Elizabeth I, when its numerous safe houses were used by priests sent from the Catholic English seminary at Douai in northern France to conspire against Elizabeth I's Reformation settlement.

The county has produced some famous singers, including the opera singer and concert artist Kathleen Ferrier, the archetypal Northern lass Gracie Fields and George Formby. Formby's songs were largely locally inspired, thus such titles as 'The Man From Lancashire', 'The Lancashire Scotsman', 'Lancashire Hot Pot Swingers', 'Lancashire Romeo', 'Lancashire Toreador', 'Mr Wu in Lancashire', 'A Lad from Lancashire' and 'The Emperor of Lancashire'.

Little boy, little boy, where wast thou born?
Far away in Lancashire under a thorn,
Where they sup sour milk in a ram's horn.

Anon.: nursery rhyme

In cricketing terms Lancashire is a 'first-class' county. Lancashire County Cricket Club was founded in 1864, was a founder member of the county championship when that competition was officially constituted in 1890, and has won the competition on eight occasions. Lancashire's famous players include A.C. Maclaren, S.F. Barnes (*see also* STAFFORDSHIRE), Brian Statham, Clive Lloyd, Michael Atherton and Andrew Flintoff. Its home ground is at OLD TRAFFORD in Manchester. Lancashire's traditional rivalry with YORKSHIRE is played out in the 'Roses match'.

Lancashire's relegation ensures late cheer.

Headline in the *Yorkshire Post*

Granary of Lancashire, the. A nickname for FYLDE, the low coastal plain between the River RIBBLE and MORECAMBE Bay.

Lancashire cheese. A mild, white cheese, moist yet crumbly.

Lancashire Fusiliers, the. A regiment that traces its origins to Sir Richard Peyton's Regiment of Foot, founded in 1688; it acquired its current name in 1881. The Lancashire Fusiliers sustained particularly heavy losses in the Gallipoli campaign in the First World War, more than half of the regiment's officers and men falling to Turkish machine-gun fire during the ill-fated '**Lancashire Landing**' at W Beach on 25 April 1915 (*see also* BURY).

Lancashire hotpot. A stew made from lamb and onions, with thinly sliced potatoes crisped on top. Purists insist that it be made with plain water; any further additions are regarded as southern frippery.

A billboard for the sex shop chain Ann Summers has been banned after complaints that it was degrading to women, the Advertising Standards Authority said. The ad, shown in the northwest, showed the back of a handcuffed woman's torso with the words: 'Lancashire hotbot … for fashion, passion whip along to your local store.'

The Guardian (9 April 2003)

Lancashire lass. A rhyming-slang term, dating from the late 19th century, meaning 'glass' (and reflecting the local pronunciation of the latter). Thus the plural of the term, **Lancashire lasses**, means 'glasses' in the sense of spectacles.

Lancashire style. A style of wrestling, little seen since the 1930s, in which one may grab hold of any part of one's opponent's body (*see also* NEATH[1]). It is more commonly known as catch-as-catch-can; *compare* Cumberland and Westmorland wrestling (*see under* CUMBERLAND).

> This is not a game of catch-as-catch-can.
>
> Hans Blix (chief UN weapons inspector in Iraq):
> speech (January 2003)

Lancashire Witches, The. A historical novel (1849) by Harrison Ainsworth about the witches of PENDLE HILL.

Lancastria. A troop ship used in the evacuation of British forces from France following Dunkirk. On 17 June 1940 it was sunk off the mouth of the River Loire, resulting in the deaths of some 5000 men, the worst maritime disaster in British history. The event was hushed up for the sake of morale, Churchill commenting 'The newspapers have got quite enough disaster for today at least.'

Queen's Lancashire Regiment, the. A regiment resulting from the amalgamation in 1970 of the Lancashire Regiment and the Loyal Regiment (North Lancashire). They are nicknamed 'the Queen's Last Resort'.

Lancaster 'Roman fort on the River LUNE[1]', OE *ceaster* (*see* CHESTER) + OCelt river name.

A city near the mouth of the River LUNE[1] in Lancashire, 32 km (19 miles) north of Preston. Lancaster was the county town of Lancashire until 1974, when PRESTON became the administrative centre. In the 11th century the Normans built a castle on the site of the old Roman fort that gave Lancaster its name, and also founded a priory here. The town that grew up round the castle received its first charter in 1193, and the castle was much enlarged two centuries later by John of Gaunt, Duke of Lancaster (*see below*). The castle was a Parliamentary stronghold in the Civil Wars, and now serves as a court and prison (it was at their trial here that the Birmingham Six (*see under* BIRMINGHAM) were subjected to a notorious miscarriage of justice in 1974). By the early 18th century the town had gone into something of a decline:

> The town is ancient; it lies, as it were, in its own ruins, and has little to recommend it but a decayed castle, and a more decayed port ...
>
> Daniel Defoe: *A Tour Through the Whole Island of Great Britain* (1724–6)

The later 18th century witnessed a revival, as Lancaster flourished as an important port for the West Indies trade; however, this profitable trade ended as the estuary of the Lune began to silt up.

The **Lancaster Royal Grammar School** was founded in the 13th century, and the **University of Lancaster** in 1964.

Lancaster was the birthplace of the iron-master Henry Cort (1740–1800), the inventor of the puddling process;

Richard Owen (1804–92), the pioneer palaeontologist and opponent of Darwin; the poet Laurence Binyon (1869–1943), largely known for his elegy 'For the Fallen' (1914); and the linguistic philosopher J.L. Austin (1911–60).

There are towns called Lancaster in the USA (California, Ohio, Pennsylvania, South Carolina). Lincoln, the capital of Nebraska, was called Lancaster until 1867.

Avro Lancaster. A four-engined bomber, the last and most successful to enter RAF service in the Second World War, beginning operations in 1942.

Duchy of Lancaster. A valuable estate held by the British monarch, occupying much of the county of Lancashire. The **Chancellor of the Duchy of Lancaster** is a post held by a cabinet minister without specific departmental responsibilities, i.e. a minister without portfolio. The Chancellor is obliged to accompany the monarch when he or she visits Lancashire; on such occasions, regardless of gender, the monarch is described in the county as the Duke of Lancaster.

House of Lancaster, the. An English royal dynasty, a branch of the Plantagenets. Henry III's younger son Edmund became Earl of Lancaster in 1267. The earldom was converted into a duchy in the mid-14th century, and in 1362 passed to John of Gaunt, whom Shakespeare calls 'time-honoured Lancaster' (*see below*). John's son seized the throne as Henry IV in 1399, and was succeeded by two more kings of the House of Lancaster, Henry V and Henry VI. The latter's incompetent rule led to a rival claim to the throne by Richard Plantagenet, Duke of York (descendant of one of John of Gaunt's brothers). This resulted in the Wars of the Roses between **Lancastrians** and Yorkists – so called because the former sported the badge of a red rose, and the latter a white rose (*see under* YORK).

King's Own Royal Regiment (Lancaster), the. A regiment founded in 1680 as the 2nd Tangier Regiment of Foot; it became The King's Own (Royal Lancaster Regiment) in 1881, and acquired its present name in 1921.

Lancaster House Agreement (September 1979). An agreement reached at Lancaster House, London, that paved the way for Rhodesia to become independent as Zimbabwe, with a black majority government, in 1980. Lancaster House, originally called York House in the early 19th century, was acquired in 1912 by Lord Leverhulme, who named it after his native county and presented it to the nation the following year.

Lancaster Sound. A channel between the low-tide sands in Morecambe Bay (*see under* MORECAMBE), extending south from near ULVERSTON.

Time-honoured Lancaster. Old John of Gaunt, Duke of Lancaster (*c*.1340–99), so called by Shakespeare (*Richard II*, I.i (1595)) because his memory had been honoured by Time. His father was Edward III, his son Henry IV and his nephew Richard II, and through his great-granddaughter, Margaret Beaufort, he is the ancestor of all British sovereigns from Henry VII, Margaret's son. Shakespeare calls him 'old', but he was only about 59 at his death.

Lancing '(settlement of) Wlanc's people', OE male personal name *Wlanc* + *-ingas* (*see* -ING).

A village on the WEST SUSSEX coast, about 14 km (9 miles) west of Brighton. It is dominated, from a hill next to the River ADUR[1], by the soaring 19th-century Gothic chapel of **Lancing College**, a co-educational public school founded in 1848 (the novelist Evelyn Waugh was a pupil). The chapel has an internal height of 28.5 m (94 ft), exceeded in England only by Westminster Abbey, York Minster and Liverpool Cathedral.

Lancs. The standard abbreviation for LANCASHIRE.

Landbeach 'low ridge by dry land' (contrasting it with WATERBEACH), OE *land* 'dry land' + *bæc* 'low ridge'.

A village in Cambridgeshire, about 6 km (4 miles) northeast of Cambridge.

Land beneath the Waves, the. The English translation of a Gaelic nickname for TIREE.

Land of Cakes, the. An old term for SCOTLAND, famous for its oatmeal cakes.

> That garret of the earth – that knuckle-end of England – that land of Calvin, oatcakes and sulphur.
>
> Sydney Smith: quoted in Lady Holland, *A Memoir of Sydney Smith* (1855)

Land of Ire. A punning nickname for IRELAND, coined by Elizabeth I's exasperated minister Sir Robert Cecil, in a letter of 8 October 1600.

Land of My Fathers. WALES, so called from the song *Hen Wlad fy Nhadau*, 'Land of My Fathers', which has become the unofficial national anthem of Wales. Written in 1856, it was first sung at the Llangollen Eisteddfod in 1858 and first published in 1860. The song is probably best known to a wider audience from the emotional renditions of it by Welsh rugby fans before and during rugby union internationals at Cardiff's Millennium Stadium (*see under* CARDIFF Arms Park).

The Welsh words, invoking a romanticized Wales of bards and patriots, are by Evan James (1809–93) and the melody by his son James James (1833–1902). The first verse and its chorus are as follows:

> Mae hen wlad fy nhadau yn annwyl i mi
> Gwlad beirdd a chantorion, enwogion o fri
> Ei gwrol ryfelwyr, gwladgarwyr tra mad
> Tros ryddid collasant eu gwaed.
> *Gwlad, gwlad, pleidiol wyf i'm gwlad*
> *Tra mor yn fur i'r bur hoff bau*
> *O bydded i'r heniaith barhau.*

> (The land of my fathers is dear unto me,
> Old land where the minstrels are honoured and free;
> Its warring defenders so gallant and brave,
> For freedom their life's blood they gave.
> *Home, home, true am I to my home,*
> *While seas secure, the land so pure,*
> *O may the old language endure.*)
>
> (English versification by W.S. Gwynn Williams)

The Welsh poet Dylan Thomas offered a characteristically jaundiced perspective on the hallowed lines:

> The land of my fathers – my fathers can have it.
>
> Dylan Thomas: quoted in *Adam* magazine, December 1953

'Land of My Fathers' is also sung as an anthem in Brittany, in a Breton version by J. Taldir.

Land of the Mountain and the Flood. A characterization of SCOTLAND by Sir Walter Scott in *The Lay of the Last Minstrel* (1805); *see* CALEDONIA for the relevant quotation. *Land of the Mountain and the Flood* was adopted as the title of an overture written in 1887 by the youthful Scottish composer Hamish MacCunn (1868–1916). Long popular in Scottish concert halls, MacCunn's overture became known to a wider audience as the theme music of the BBC television series *Sutherland's Law* (1973–6).

Land of the Prince Bishops. The local tourist board's description of County DURHAM. The bishops of Durham became known as prince bishops after 1071, when they were awarded virtual rights of kingship in their 'County Palatinate'; these rights included the administration of law, and the rights to recruit their own army, mint money, create barons and license markets. These rights were awarded because of the county's strategic position as a buffer against the Scots – whom they generally managed to turn back in the invasions of the 12th, 13th and 14th centuries. The bishops built the castle and the great cathedral at DURHAM and had their country palace at BISHOP AUCKLAND, their port at HARTLEPOOL and a hunting forest in Weardale (*see under* WEAR). They also held lands in Northumberland and Yorkshire. Their rights (which became increasingly vestigial over the centuries) finally came to an end in 1836, William van Mildert being the last Bishop of Durham (1826–36) to hold them.

Land's End The etymology is self-explanatory. It is first recorded in 1337.

A slight promontory at the tip of CORNWALL that is the most westerly point on the English mainland. Burger stalls, souvenir shops and a huge theme park do their best to detract from the solemnity of the scene, but its grandeur is restored by the sight of Atlantic rollers crashing against the bare granite cliffs (about 18 m / 60 ft high). The LONGSHIPS lighthouse is 2.5 km (1.5 miles) offshore.

Its Cornish name is Pedn-an-Laaz, which means literally 'headland of land' (*see also* PENWITH). There are parallel formations in Welsh (*Penbro*, the Welsh name of PEMBROKE) and in Brittany (*Finistère*) and Spain (Cape *Finisterre*), both from Latin *finis terrae* 'end of the land'. The unity of name may suggest a westward drive of some kind in the past.

The use of the expression **from Land's End to John o'Groats** (or 'from Land's End to John of Gaunt', as the Rev. W.A. Spooner reportedly once put it) to mean 'from one end of Britain to the other' (*see* JOHN O'GROATS) dates from at least the second half of the 19th century. Its familiarity received a boost from the 1960s with the increasing number of walks undertaken between the two places, usually with Land's End as the destination. A pioneer walker was Dr Barbara Moore.

Land's End/St Just Airfield, about 5 km (3 miles) to the northeast, serves the Scilly Isles (as long as it is not too foggy), but its main users are members of the local flying club.

> I might take up many sheets in describing the valuable curiosities of this little *chersonese* [peninsula], or neck land, called the Land's End, in which there lies an immense treasure, and many things worth notice, I mean besides those to be found upon the surface: but I am too near the end of this letter.
>
> Daniel Defoe: *A Tour Through the Whole Island of Great Britain* (1724–6) (Defoe refers to underground tin deposits)

Landshipping 'long cowshed', OE *lang* 'long' + *scipen* 'cowshed'.

A village on the Cleddau estuary (*see under* CLEDDAU), Pembrokeshire (formerly in Dyfed), 7 km (4 miles) southeast of Haverfordwest.

Landsker Line, the OE *land-scearu*, ME *landsker* 'boundary'.
The boundary that once divided the Welsh in the north of PEMBROKESHIRE from the Vikings and later the Anglo-Normans who settled in the south of the county, the latter area becoming known as LITTLE ENGLAND BEYOND WALES. The line was marked by more than a dozen castles, such as those at Haverfordwest and Narberth. South of the line the place names are English or heavily anglicized (e.g. Newton Mountain, Loveston, Stepaside, Saundersfoot, Cold Blow, Tavernspite, Red Roses), while to the north the place names are largely Welsh. The division is still reflected in political allegiances, the south tending to favour the unionist Conservatives, and the north the nationalist Plaid Cymru. The area around the boundary is sometimes called the **Landsker Borderlands**.

Lanes, the. An area of narrow streets in the centre of BRIGHTON, now given over largely to antique shops, boutiques and restaurants. It occupies the original plan of old Brighthelmstone, but most of the buildings are late 18th-century at the earliest.

Langdale 'long valley' OE *lang* 'long' + *denu* 'valley' replaced by OScand *dalr* 'dale'.

A two-branched valley in the Lake District, Cumbria, starting some 5 km (3 miles) west of Ambleside. The northerly branch is **Great Langdale** (although usually called simply Langdale), while the southerly branch is **Little Langdale** (also the name of a hamlet in the valley). Langdale was once known as **Suicide Valley**, its former isolation apparently leading some of its inhabitants to terminal depression. At Chapel Stile in Langdale the Dadaist Kurt Schwitters created his third and final *Merzbau* (*see under* AMBLESIDE).

The craggy peaks known as **Langdale Pikes** are on the north side of Great Langdale; they are Pike o' Stickle (708 m / 2323 ft), Harrison Stickle (736 m / 2415 ft) and PAVEY ARK (698 m / 2288 ft). Just west of the summit of Pike o' Stickle the scree is thought to be the leftovers of a Neolithic axe factory, while on its south side is **Gimmer Crag**, home to many classic rock climbs, including *Kipling Groove*, so named by its first ascensionist, Arthur Dolphin, in 1948 because it was 'ruddy 'ard'. DUNGEON GHYLL descends to Langdale between Pike of Stickle and Harrison Stickle, while the head of the valley is blocked by the great mass of BOWFELL.

> Wi' Langdl' red, 'n' Kendal grey,
> It's bound to make a gey fine day.
>
> Local weather lore

> Dark are the shrouded hills, and vague, and the rain,
> as the wind changes,
> halts, and clouds over the fells
> drift, and the Pleiades drown.
>
> Michael Roberts: 'Langdale: Nightfall January 4th', from *Collected Poems* (1958)

Langford Budville *Langford* 'long ford', OE *lang* 'long' + FORD; *Budville* denoting manorial ownership in the Middle Ages by the de Buddevill family.

A village in Somerset, about 11 km (7 miles) west of Taunton.

Langholm 'long stretch of low land', OE *lang* 'long' + *holm*, from the OScand word *holmr* 'island, low-lying land by a river' (*see* -EY, -EA).

A town and BURGH on the River ESK[2], in the southeast of Dumfries and Galloway (formerly in Dumfriesshire), near the English border, some 22 km (13 miles) east of Lockerbie. The town lies at the heart of Armstrong country, that clan being notoriously unlawful Border reivers (raiders). Neil Armstrong, the US astronaut who was the first person to set foot on the moon, was made a freeman of the town when he visited Langholm in 1972. Thomas Telford (1757– 1834), the builder of the Menai Suspension Bridge, the Caledonian Canal and many other marvels of engineering, was born a little further up the Esk. The town was the birthplace of the great Scots poet, nationalist and communist, Hugh MacDiarmid (C.M. Grieve; 1892–1978), who subsequently drew on various aspects of **the Muckle Toon** (as it is known to its natives), such as the winding path called the Curly Snake, which features, somewhat transmogrified, in the collection of linked poems called *To Circumjack Cencrastus* (1930), in which a snake or serpent is the central symbol.

Langholm's Common Riding ceremony occurs every year on the last Friday in July. It is one of the oldest of the common ridings of the Border burghs, and involves a ride round the burgh boundaries, asserting the burghers' rights to cut peat and bracken on the surrounding common land. The ceremony is recalled in MacDiarmid's greatest poem:

> A' as it used to be, when I was a loon
> On Common-Ridin' Day in the Muckle Toon.
> The bearer twirls the Bannock-and-Saut Herrin',
> The Croon o' Roses through the lift is farin',
> The aucht-fit thistle wallops on hie …
>
> > Hugh MacDiarmid: *A Drunk Man Looks at the Thistle* (1926)
> > (*loon* 'boy', *lift* 'sky', *aucht-fit* 'eight-foot')

The standards referred to are a wooden fish nailed to a bannock (a round, flat unsweetened cake), a giant crown woven out of roses and a giant thistle woven out of many actual thistles.

Langside Scots (from OE) *lang* 'long' + *side*, a word applied to land extending along a feature such as a hill or river.
A former village in Lanarkshire, now an area of south Glasgow.
Battle of Langside (13 May 1568). An engagement, largely fought in the main street of the old village, in which Mary Queen of Scots met her final defeat at the hands of the rebel lords led by the Regent Moray, after which she fled to England. There she was imprisoned and eventually executed (in 1587) by her cousin Elizabeth I. There is now a Battlefield Road and a Battle Place in Langside.

Langstone 'long (or tall) stone' (perhaps referring to an unidentified marker stone), OE *lang* 'long' + *stan* (*see* STONE).
A village on the Hampshire coast, just to the south of Havant and to the north of Hayling Island.
Langstone Harbour. A large harbour, about 1900 ha (4700 acres) in extent, formed by PORTSEA ISLAND to the west and HAYLING ISLAND to the east, whose southern tips are only about 250 m (0.15 miles) apart.

Langstrothdale 'long tract of marshy ground in a valley', OE *lang* 'long', *strod* 'marshy ground, land overgrown with brushwood' + *dæl* 'valley'.
The valley of the upper River WHARFE, North Yorkshire, extending some 12 km (7 miles) west from the village of HUBBERHOLME (J.B. Priestley's heaven on earth) to the river's source on Cam Fell. The valley together with the fells on either side is known as **Langstrothdale Chase**.

Langthwaite 'long clearing', OScand *langr* 'long' + *thveit* 'clearing'.
A village in ARKENGARTHDALE, North Yorkshire, 17 km (10 miles) west of Richmond. It was formerly known for its lead mines, and, according to local legend, provided Jerusalem with roofing material in the days of King Herod.

Langthwaite featured in the opening credits of BBC TV's long-running vet drama, *All Creatures Great and Small* (1978–80, 1988–90).

Langton Herring *Langton* 'long farmstead or estate', OE *lang* 'long' + -TON; *Herring* denoting manorial ownership in the Middle Ages by the Harang family.
A village in Dorset, just inland from CHESIL BEACH and about 6.5 km (4 miles) northwest of Weymouth.

Langton Matravers *Matravers* denoting manorial ownership in the Middle Ages by the Mautravers family.
A village in Dorset, on the Isle of PURBECK, about 1.5 km (1 mile) west of Swanage.

Langtons, the *See* LANGTON HERRING; but *see also* TUR LANGTON, which has a different origin.
A group of villages in southeast Leicestershire: CHURCH LANGTON, EAST LANGTON, THORPE LANGTON and TUR LANGTON.

Lang Whang, the Scots 'the long whip' or 'whack'.
The traditional name for what is now the A70 Edinburgh–Lanark road. The name dates from coaching days and refers to the long straight stretch across the moors north of the PENTLAND HILLS. The name is also given to individual holes on a number of golf courses in Scotland and northern England.

> But the far-flung line o' the Lang Whang Road,
> Wi' the mune on the sky's eebree,
> An' naething but me an' the wind abroad,
> Is the wuss that's hauntin' me.
>
> > Hugh Haliburton (J. Logie Robertson, 1846–1922):
> > 'The Lang Whang Road' (Scots *wuss* 'wish, desire')

Lann Bheag. The Irish name for LAMBEG.

Lansdown[1] Etymology uncertain, although the second element is OE *dun* (see DOWN, -DON).
A village in BATH AND NORTH EAST SOMERSET (before 1996 in Avon, before 1974 in Somerset), about 5 km (3 miles) northwest of BATH. Nearby **Lansdown Hill** is 248 m (814 ft) high.

Lansdown is the home of Bath Racecourse, the highest in England.
Battle of Lansdown (5 July 1643). A battle of the Civil Wars, in which Sir Ralph Hopton's Royalist forces bested Sir William Waller's Parliamentarians, driving them from the top of Lansdown Hill.

Lansdown². A hilly and well-heeled northwestern suburb of BATH, centred on Lansdown Road (which leads eventually to LANSDOWN¹) and the S-shaped **Lansdown Crescent**. It is the location of Kingswood School, a Methodist foundation.

A little along Lansdown Road to the north is Beckford's Tower, built in 1827 for the writer and eccentric William Beckford.

Lansdowne Road. The location in DUBLIN of Ireland's national rugby stadium. It is due to be expanded and developed by 2008, following the demise of the proposal for an 80,000-seat national sports stadium in Abbotstown, in the north of County Dublin. The *taoiseach* Bertie Ahern gave the latter his vigorous personal support (and it had been nicknamed the Bertie Bowl), but funding did not materialize.

Laoighis. An alternative spelling for LAOIS.

Laois After *Lugaid Laígne* or *Laeighseach*, who drove out invaders from Munster in the 3rd century AD and was subsequently granted land here. He was apparently a follower of Cormac Mac Airt, but the story is a bit hazy.

A county in south-central Ireland. It is also spelt **Laoighis**, and its name was formerly anglicized as **Leix**, while from 1556 to 1920 it was called **Queen's County**, in honour of Mary I, in whose reign the plantation of the area got under way (neighbouring OFFALY was called King's County in honour of Mary's husband Philip II of Spain). Laois is bounded to the east by Kildare and Carlow, to the south by Kilkenny, to the west by Tipperary, and to the north by Offaly. The county town is PORTLAOISE. Apart from the SLIEVE BLOOM MOUNTAINS in the northwest, the county is generally flat and full of bogs, giving rise to a peat industry.

Laphroaig. *See* Islay malts *under* ISLAY.

Laracor Irish *Láithreach Cora* 'place of the weir'.
A village in County Meath, some 2 km (1.2 miles) south of Trim. Churchman-writer Jonathan Swift held the living here from 1700 until his death, although he was often away, and from 1713 he was Dean of St Patrick's Cathedral in Dublin, and rarely returned to Laracor. While he was here, he wrote his *Argument to Prove the Inconvenience of Abolishing Christianity*; also during his sojourn, his friend Stella (Esther Johnson) came to live in the village, and it was to her, while he was in London (1710–12), that he wrote his *Journal to Stella*.

Largo Gaelic *leargach* 'steep sloping field'.
A village in Fife, some 15 km (9 miles) southwest of St Andrews, on the north shore of the Firth of Forth. It is divided into **Upper Largo** and **Lower Largo**, and looks out over **Largo Bay**. It was formerly an important fishing

port, and is now a popular resort. It was the birthplace of Alexander Selkirk or Selcraig (1676–1721), who was marooned on Juan Fernández island west of Chile in 1704, and not rescued until 1709. He was the prototype of Daniel Defoe's Robinson Crusoe, and a statue of Selkirk thus garbed stands outside the cottage in Largo where he was born. The hill of **Largo Law** (290 m / 951 ft) above the village is a notable landmark.

> From Largo Law look down,
>   moon and dry weather, look down
>   on convoy marshalled, filing between mines.
>
>   Basil Bunting: *The Spoils* (1951)

'Largo's Fairy Dance'. A reel for the fiddle by Nathaniel Gow (b.1763).

Largs Gaelic *learg* 'hillside' + English plural *-s*.
A resort town in North Ayrshire, on the Firth of Forth (*see under* FORTH) facing Great Cumbrae (*see under* CUMBRAES), some 30 km (19 miles) west of Paisley. It was the birthplace of the soldier and astronomer Sir Thomas Brisbane (1773–1860), after whom the Australian city is named. When the physicist William Thomson (1824–1907) was elevated to the peerage in 1892, he took the title Baron Kelvin of Largs. He died at his estate of Netherhall, near Largs.

> Went to Mass early, in black darkness and fog, and took
> the morning train to Largs. A smug, substantial, modern
> pleasure resort – or rather pleasure as the Scots conceive
> it – with a superb view across the water to Cumbrae and
> Arran.
>
>   Evelyn Waugh: diary (13 November 1940)

Battle of Largs (2 October 1263). An engagement that ended Norwegian domination in the western Highlands and Islands. The Scottish kings Alexander II and Alexander III had been mounting aggressive expeditions against the Norse power in Argyll and Skye, and in response King Haakon IV of Norway arrived with a large fleet in the Firth of Clyde. This was badly damaged in a storm, and when a party landed at Largs, it was decisively defeated by a Scots army under Alexander III. Three years later, by the Treaty of Perth, the Norwegians conceded the Hebrides to the Scottish kings. Referring to the Norsemen, Burns wrote:

> O'er countries and kingdoms their furies prevail'd,
>   No arts could appease them, no arms could repel;
> But brave Caledonia in vain they assail'd,
>   As Largs well can witness, and Loncartie tell.
>
>   Robert Burns: 'Caledonia' (date unknown) (Luncarty near
>   Perth was the scene of a battle between Scots and Danes in
>   the 10th century.)

Larkhall Probably 'nook of land frequented by larks', OE *lawerce* 'lark' + *halh* 'nook of land' (*see* HALE, -HALL). There are several bird-name + *-hall* names in Scotland and the north of

England, most unconnected with buildings and hence unlikely to mean 'hall'.

A town in South Lanarkshire (formerly in Strathclyde region), in the Clyde valley 7 km (4 miles) southeast of Hamilton.

Larkhill 'hill frequented by larks', OE *lawerce* 'lark' + *hyll* 'hill'.

A large village in Wiltshire, at the southeastern corner of Salisbury Plain (*see under* SALISBURY), about 3 km (2 miles) northeast of Stonehenge. It stands in the middle of a large military training area, and many generations of squaddies have passed through **Larkhill Camp**. It is home to the Army School of Artillery.

Lark Rise. A fictitious hamlet on the borders of Oxfordshire and Northamptonshire that features in the writings of Flora Thompson (1876–1947). It first appeared in *Lark Rise* (1939) and subsequently in the omnibus volume *Lark Rise to Candleford* (1945). It is a lightly concealed version of Juniper Hill, a hamlet in the northeastern corner of Oxfordshire in which the author was born. It forms the focus of the late 19th-century agricultural community that she lovingly recreates.

> We will call [the hamlet] Lark Rise because of the great number of skylarks which made the surrounding fields their springboard and nested on the bare earth between the rows of green corn.
>
> *Lark Rise* (1939)

Larling '(settlement of) Lyrel's people', OE male personal name *Lyrel* + *-ingas* (*see* -ING).

A village in Norfolk, about 13 km (8 miles) northeast of Thetford.

Larne Irish *Latharna* 'descendants of Lathar'; Lathar was a pre-Christian prince.

A port on the east coast of County Antrim, 28 km (17 miles) northeast of Belfast, at the mouth of the long, narrow sea inlet called **Larne Lough**, which is itself fed by the short **Larne River**. There are ferry services to Scotland (STRANRAER and CAIRNRYAN). Larne is the administrative centre of the local authority district of the same name, created in 1973.

> The returning Ulster people who had been on the boat train stood silently at the rail, gazing upon Larne like mourners.
>
> Paul Theroux: *The Kingdom by the Sea* (1983)

Larne Gun-Running (24–25 April 1914). The landing of large quantities of German rifles and ammunition in Larne, DONAGHADEE and BANGOR[2] by the Ulster Volunteer Force, with the aim of offering armed resistance to Home Rule. The Howth Gun-Running (*see under* HOWTH) was a response by the Irish Volunteers.

Larnian industry. A prehistoric technology named after the type site at Larne, dating either from the Mesolithic

period (starting *c.*6000 BC) or the Neolithic (starting 3000 BC in Ireland).

Lasswade 'the ford by the meadow', OE *læs* 'meadow' + *gewaed* 'ford' (*see* FORD).

A village 9 km (5.5 miles) south of Edinburgh, on the River North Esk. Buried here are the poet William Drummond (1585–1649) of nearby HAWTHORNDEN, and 'King Harry the Ninth' – Henry Dundas, 1st Viscount Melville (1742–1811), who, holding various cabinet posts, was the despotic ruler of Scotland from 1775 until 1805 and who built nearby Melville Castle. Sir Walter Scott and his new wife Charlotte Carpenter spent their summers at **Lasswade Cottage** from 1798 to 1804, and the village may be the model for the village of Gandercleugh in the series 'Tales of My Landlord' (1817–31). From 1840 until his death in 1859 Thomas de Quincey mostly lived at Mavis Bush Cottage, a little way up the North Esk at Polton.

Latharna. The Irish name for LARNE.

Lauder 'wash-place river', from OCelt roots *lou* (*compare* French *laver* 'to wash') + *dubro* 'river'. *Lauder* is etymologically unconnected with the *Leader Water* on which it is situated: compare consistent spellings such as *Lawedir*, 1250, for the former with equally consistent spellings *Leder, Ledre*, 12th century, for the latter.

A royal BURGH in Scottish Borders (formerly in Berwickshire), 37 km (22 miles) southeast of Edinburgh. The Leader Water rises in the Lammermuir Hills, and flows south through the valley of **Lauderdale** to join the Tweed a little east of Melrose. (Fort Lauderdale in Florida, USA, was named after a Major William Lauderdale, who commanded the original fort there in 1838.)

The most famous incident associated with Lauder took place in 1482, when James III's disaffected nobles met in Lauder church. They were meant to be repelling an invading English army, but were infuriated that the king had made favourites of architects and masons (one of these, Cochrane, had been made Earl of Mar). Lord Grey asked 'Who will bell the cat?' Archibald Douglas, 5th Earl of Angus (d.1514) replied 'I shall,' and seized and hanged six of the favourites from a nearby bridge in the presence of the king. Thereafter Douglas was known as 'Bell-the-Cat'. The actual location of the bridge has not been identified.

See also ETTRICK AND LAUDERDALE.

Laugharne An abbreviated form of the Welsh name *Talacharn*, of which the first element is probably *tâl* 'end', although the meaning of the rest is uncertain.

A village in Carmarthenshire (formerly in Dyfed), on the western shore of the estuary of the River Taf (formed by the confluence of the Cynin, the Dewi Fawr and the Cywyn), 14 km (8.5 miles) southwest of Carmarthen. It is usually pronounced 'larne', and was described by the poet

Vernon Watkins as 'a fishing village at the end of the world'. There is a ruined 13th-century castle.

The poet Samuel Taylor Coleridge visited Laugharne during his tour of South Wales in 1802, and described in his journal the 'great river of greenish water taking one bend among fieldy hills'. The following century Dylan Thomas and his wife Caitlin were encouraged to move here by Richard Hughes, the author of *A High Wind in Jamaica*. They settled for a while in 1937, made some further visits, then moved here permanently in 1949. Thomas remarked of the village that

> Its literary values are firmly established: Richard Hughes lives in a castle at the top of the hill; I live in a shed at the bottom.

(From 1949 the Thomases lived in The Boathouse, at the bottom of the cliff, where Thomas worked in the garden shed; the house was bought for them by the wife of the historian A.J.P. Taylor.)

Elsewhere Dylan Thomas described Laugharne as:

> This timeless, mild, beguiling island of a town, with its seven public houses, one chapel in action, one church, one factory, two billiard tables, one St Bernard (without brandy), one policeman, three rivers, a visiting sea, one Rolls-Royce selling fish and chips.

Thomas almost certainly based the village of his verse drama *Under Milk Wood* on Laugharne (although Vernon Watkins detected a smattering of NEW QUAY, and the 1971 film of the play was made at FISHGUARD). Thomas called his village **Llareggub** (this being a backwards spelling of 'bugger all'):

> Outside, the sun springs down on the rough and tumbling town. It runs through the hedges of Goosegog Lane, cuffing the birds to sing. Spring whips green down Cockle Row, and the shells ring out. Llareggub this snip of a morning is wild fruit and warm, the streets, fields, sands and waters springing in the young sun.

> Dylan Thomas: *Under Milk Wood* (1954)

Thomas is buried at Laugharne, in the graveyard of the 14th-century Church of St Martin, his grave marked by a white wooden cross.

South of the village are the dunes of **Laugharne Burrows**, and beyond them the expanse of **Laugharne Sands**.

> ... the mussel pooled and the heron
> Priested shore

> Dylan Thomas: 'Poem in October' (1946)

Launceston 'estate near the church-site of St Stephen', Cornish *lann* 'church-site' + saint's name + -TON.
A town (pronounced 'lawnston', 'lahnston' or 'lahnson') in Cornwall, between Bodmin Moor (*see under* BODMIN) to the west and DARTMOOR to the east, about 18 km (11 miles) northwest of TAVISTOCK. It is in a strategically important position, within 1.5 km (1 mile) of the River TAMAR and the Devon border, and guarding the main route into Cornwall (now the A30). Until 1838 it was the Cornish capital. The remains of a 13th-century castle (besieged during the Civil Wars) survive.

In Arthurian romance, Castle Terabil (or Terrible) stood in Launceston. It had a steep keep surrounded by a triple wall. It is also known as Dunheved Castle.

In 1577 St Cuthbert Mayne was martyred in Launceston. He was one of the 'Forty Martyrs of England and Wales' canonized by Pope Paul VI in 1970.

According to local children's lore, a stone successfully lodged on the back of the granite figure of Mary Magdalene on the east wall of Launceston parish church will bring good luck.

Launceston (pronounced 'lawnseston') is also an important industrial port in Tasmania, Australia. It, too, is on a river called the Tamar.

Laurencekirk 'church of St Laurence', Scots *kirk* 'church' + personal name. It was originally called Kirkton of St Laurence, its church having been dedicated to St Laurence of Canterbury (d. 619), one of St Augustine's companions.
A small town in Aberdeenshire (formerly Kincardineshire, then in Grampian region), 13 km (8 miles) north of Montrose. The modern town dates from the later 18th century and is the main town of the Howe of the MEARNS.

Laurieston 'Laurie's town', from personal name + -TON.
A village 9 km (5.5 miles) west of Castle Douglas, formerly in Kirkcudbrightshire, now in Dumfries and Galloway. Its original name was **Clachanpluck**, but this was not sufficiently dignified for William K. Laurie, who bought the estate in the 18th century and renamed it after himself. There is a memorial to the 'kailyard' ('cabbage patch' i.e. sentimental) novelist, Samuel Rutherford Crockett (1859–1914), whose works include *The Raiders* (1894; *see* GLEN TROOL), and who was born a little to the north of the village.

Lavartris. A Roman camp on the site of present-day BOWES.

Lavender Hill From the *lavender* that was once cultivated in market gardens to the north of the road.
A steep road in BATTERSEA (SW11), in the London borough of WANDSWORTH, rising westward towards Clapham Junction (*see under* CLAPHAM[1]). It was a well-used route in coaching days, but since the 1860s it has passed between houses rather than open fields. Its name has spread from the road itself to the area around it.

Lavender Hill Mob, The. A film (1951), one of the Ealing Comedies (*see under* EALING), written by T.E.B. Clarke and directed by Charles Crichton. It concerns a mild-mannered civil servant (Alec Guinness) who decides to use his inside knowledge of bullion transport to steal a million pounds' worth of gold and then spirit it out of the country with his right-hand man (Stanley Holloway) after melting it down into miniature Eiffel Towers. The ludicrous notion that such a retiring, dull individual could pull off this breath-taking crime is underlined by the film's title, which cheekily conveys the unlikelihood of hardened criminals hailing from such a respectable part of London as Lavender Hill.

Lavenham 'Lafa's homestead', OE *Lafan* possessive form of male personal name *Lafa* + HAM.

A small market town in Suffolk, about 16 km (10 miles) southeast of Bury St Edmunds. In the late Middle Ages the cloth trade brought it great wealth, evidence of which can still be seen all around, from the magnificent late 15th-century church of St Peter and St Paul, with its massive tower, a cathedral in miniature, to the inordinately picturesque contemporary timbered houses, inns and other buildings (notably the fine Tudor Guildhall of Corpus Christi, now owned by the National Trust). It was known in those days particularly for its fine blue cloth stamped with a fleur-de-lys.

Laverstock 'outlying farmstead or hamlet frequented by larks', OE *lawerce* 'lark' + *stoc* (*see* -STOCK, STOCK-, STOKE).

A village in Wiltshire, about 1.5 km (1 mile) northeast of Salisbury.

Laverstock Panda, the. The figure of a panda carved into the chalk of a hillside near Laverstock. It was perpetrated in 1970 by a group of students from the University College of North Wales, BANGOR[1]. When discovered, it was at first supposed that the cutting celebrated the meeting of the two pandas Chi-Chi and An-An in London Zoo (*see under* LONDON). In fact it was a rag week stunt, the panda being Bangor's rag symbol, while the particular location was chosen because one of the instigators lived nearby and knew that the site would be suitable. The outlines of the artwork are still faintly visible.

Lawers. *See under* BEN LAWERS.

Laxey 'salmon river', OScand *lax* 'salmon' + *a* 'river'; the settlement took it name from the river.

A village on the east coast of the Isle of Man, 10 km (6 miles) north of Douglas.

Laxton 'estate associated with Leaxa', OE male personal name *Leaxa* + -ING + -TON (an earlier form of the name, *Lexington*, which survived into the 19th century, is the origin of the *Lexington* in Massachusetts, USA).

A village in Nottinghamshire, to the east of SHERWOOD FOREST, about 16 km (10 miles) northwest of Newark. Having somehow managed to avoid the effects of the 18th-century Enclosure Acts, it is the only place in England where medieval-style open-field strip farming is still practised (though now on a fairly minimal scale).

Lea Probably either 'bright river' or 'river dedicated to the god Lugus [Lugh]', from an OCelt root *lug-* meaning 'bright, light' but also forming the base of the name of the god Lugus. *See also* LEYTON and LUTON.

A river (also spelt **Lee**) in Bedfordshire, Hertfordshire, Essex and East London, which rises in southern Bedfordshire and flows 74 km (46 miles) southeast and then south via LUTON, WELWYN GARDEN CITY, CHESHUNT, LEYTON and Hackney Marsh (*see under* HACKNEY) to join the River Thames at CANNING TOWN. In former times it formed the boundary between MIDDLESEX and ESSEX.

The Lea has been an important route since at least Roman times, and canalization schemes are almost as ancient. Today the **River Lea Navigation** runs from HERTFORD virtually to the Thames. Beside the river are several huge reservoirs, which furnish a sixth of London's water supply. In 1967 the **Lea Valley Regional Park** was constituted, which supervises the provision of a wide range of recreational facilities, from sailing and windsurfing on the lakes and reservoirs to fishing and bird-watching. The joys of fishing on the Lea were already familiar in the 17th century to Izaak Walton, and it figures prominently in *The Compleat Angler* (1653).

> Without the Lea Valley, East London would be unendurable … The Lea is nicely arranged, walk as far as you like then travel back to Liverpool Street from

---

❖ law, low ❖

The Old English element *hlaw* meaning 'rounded hill' became the common word for a naturally occurring feature of no particular significance in Scotland. But in a range of names from further south, where rounded hills were perhaps rarer, the element referred to a feature of local importance. The mound or hill was where people met for legal and other business; HARLOW (Essex) seems to have been a meeting place for Viking armies, and BASSETLAW (Nottinghamshire) was the place where the local court and administrative meetings were held in the Middle Ages.

Sometimes the mounds were artificial, being burial mounds or mounds otherwise created or set aside for a purpose. Several English names containing the element *hlaw* were burial mounds, and an association with ancient Neolithic settlement features is found at several locations, such as ARBOR LOW (Derbyshire) and TRAPRAIN LAW (East Lothian). But sometimes they were simply hills, as in FOOLOW (Derbyshire) and LUDLOW (Shropshire) are associated with natural features (birds and a river).

any one of the rural halts that mark your journey. Railway shadowing river, a fantasy conjunction; together they define an Edwardian sense of excursion, pleasure, time out.

> Ian Sinclair: *London Orbital* (2002)

River Lea. Nineteenth-century rhyming slang for both *tea* and *sea*.

Leadenhall Street From *Leadenhall* (the name of a nearby lead-roofed mansion, originally belonging to the 13th-century nobleman Hugh Neville, presented to the City in 1445 by Simon Eyre and destroyed in the Great Fire of 1666), 'hall or large house with a lead roof', OE *leaden* 'of lead' + *hall*.

A street in the City of London (EC3), leading west-to-east from CORNHILL to ALDGATE. Between 1648 and 1861 it contained the headquarters of the East India Company, and its name came to be used as a metonym for the company itself:

> It showed, how the elegant mothers of Leadenhall Street, might, with the greatest gentleness, strain their young ones to bosoms equally *soft*, while they themselves were nourished by the *blood* and sweat of the unhappy peasant of Bengal.
>
> J. Boaden: *Life of Mrs Jordan* (1831)

Just round the corner in Gracechurch Street is **Leadenhall Market**. This traces its origins back to the 14th century, when it was adjacent to the original 'Leadenhall' (*see above*), but it perished with the house in 1666. It was soon reconstructed, and was rebuilt again in high Victorian style in 1881. It was noted in its heyday for poultry and game, but by the beginning of the 21st century most of the shops and stalls had been replaced by city eateries of various speeds.

Leaden Roding. *See under* the RODINGS.

Leadhills from the lead formerly mined in the hills here.

A village in South Lanarkshire (formerly in Strathclyde), 20 km (12 miles) north of Thornhill. It is at an altitude of 412 m (1350 ft) in the LOWTHER HILLS, and is, like its neighbour WANLOCKHEAD, one of the highest villages in Scotland. It gained its name from the lead mines in the surrounding hills, also known as **the Leadhills**. These were worked from the 13th to the 20th centuries. Gold has also been found in the neighbourhood.

Leadhills was the birthplace of the poet Allan Ramsay (1686–1758), author of *The Gentle Shepherd* (1725), who in 1741 presented the village with Britain's first circulating library; and of William Symington (1763–1831), the builder of the first practical steamboat, the *Charlotte Dundas* (1801). The mathematician James Stirling (1692–1770) – also called Stirling the Venetian – became manager of the Scots Mining Company at Leadhills in 1735.

Leam Either 'elm river' or 'marshy river', OCelt.

A river (pronounced 'leem' or sometimes 'lem') in Northamptonshire and Warwickshire, which rises to the west of DAVENTRY and flows 42 km (27 miles) northwards and then westwards through LEAMINGTON SPA to join the River AVON[1] to the east of WARWICK.

Leamhcán. The Irish name for LUCAN.

Leamington Spa Leamington 'farmstead on the River Leam', OE *Leomenan* possessive or dative form of *Leomen(a)* 'LEAM' + -TON; by the 16th century the middle syllable had become -*ing*-, by analogy with other -*ington* names (*see also* LYMINGTON and -ING).

A town (pronounced 'lemmington') in Warwickshire, on the River LEAM and the GRAND UNION CANAL, contiguous with and to the east of WARWICK. Its iron and salt springs began to attract visitors in the late 18th century. Not everyone approved ('In Borrowdale there is a well which, I dare be sworn, will out-stink Leamington water,' wrote the poet Robert Southey in a letter of 1808), but over the following hundred years Leamington bloomed, adding 'Spa' to its name and accumulating the legacy of elegant Georgian, Regency and early Victorian architecture characteristic of English spa towns of its era. The culminating accolade came in 1838 when, following a most satisfactory visit, Queen Victoria condescended to designate it **Royal Leamington Spa**. Its waters were not so much in demand in the 20th century, and its Royal Pump Room, built in 1814, closed in 1990.

Three km (2 miles) to the west of the town is the 900-year-old Midland Oak, claimed (far from uniquely) to mark the central point of England (*see also* FENNY DRAYTON and MERIDEN).

Another local claim is that Leamington Spa is the birthplace of lawn tennis, the game having first been played here in the 1870s.

> She died in the upstairs bedroom
> By the light of the ev'ning star
> That shone through the plate glass window
> From over Leamington Spa.
>
> John Betjeman: 'Death in Leamington' (1932)

Leap Castle Irish *Léim ui Bhanain*, 'leap of the O'Bannons' (the first owners of Leap). Most Leap names are associated with stories of prodigious jumps, but the legend here is lost.

A castle on top of a cliff in County Offaly, some 6 km (4 miles) east of Birr on the edge of the SLIEVE BLOOM MOUNTAINS, guarding the route to Munster. It is pronounced 'lepp'. The keep dates from the 14th or 15th century, and was a stronghold of the O'Carrolls (the area is traditionally known as ELY O'CARROLL). One room in the castle is called the Bloody Chapel, as here in 1532, after the death of the old chief, one O'Carroll murdered his brother and rival, a priest who was saying Mass at the time. Beneath the Bloody Chapel was an oubliette (from French *oublier* 'forget'), a dungeon into which the O'Carrolls' prisoners were dropped; if they failed to impale themselves on the waiting spike, they slowly died of starvation. When workmen were hired to clear out the room around the turn of the 20th century, they found piles of human skeletons, and three carts were needed to remove the remains.

Needless to say, all this horror has resulted in Leap Castle being the most haunted castle in Ireland. In 1909 Mildred Darby, the then chatelaine and a dabbler in magic, reported a horrific experience to the *Occult Review*:

> I was standing in the Gallery looking down at the main floor, when I felt somebody put a hand on my shoulder. The thing was about the size of a sheep. ... Its face was human, to be more accurate inhuman. Its lust in its eyes which seemed half decomposed in black cavities stared into mine. The horrible smell one hundred times intensified came up into my face, giving me a deadly nausea. It was the smell of a decomposing corpse.

The castle was burnt down in 1922 during the Irish Civil War, and in the 1970s the ruins were purchased by an Australian, who brought over a white witch from Mexico to exorcise the place. She reported that the spirits agreed to behave themselves if they were allowed to remain. The present owner restored the castle in the 1990s, and says that the agreement is holding up well, the spirits being particularly appreciative of the family's music-making.

Leath Cathail. The Irish name for LECALE.

Leatherhead 'grey ford' (alluding to a crossing place on the River Mole where it cuts through the North Downs), OCelt *led* 'grey' + *rid* 'ford'.

A town in Surrey, on the River MOLE[1], about 16 km (10 miles) northeast of GUILDFORD and just to the south of the M25. Its key position commanding passage through the NORTH DOWNS has made it an important settlement since Anglo-Saxon times, and the days of the stage-coach have bequeathed it a number of fine inns. It appears in Jane Austen's *Emma* (1816) in the guise of 'Highbury'.

Bishop Samuel ('Soapy Sam') Wilberforce (1805–78), early opponent of Darwinism, died in Leatherhead, as did the archaeologist Sir Mortimer Wheeler (1890–1976) and the aeronautical engineer Sir Barnes Wallis (1887–1979), designer of the Dam Busters' 'bouncing bomb'.

Leather Lane Probably 'Leofrun's lane', OE female personal name *Leofrun* + ME *lane*.

A street in CLERKENWELL, Central London (EC1), in the borough of CAMDEN, leading south from Clerkenwell Road, parallel to and to the west of HATTON GARDEN. It has its own market, selling food and general goods. It seems always to have had a reputation for low-quality wares, and in the 19th century 'leather-lane' was slang for 'poorly made', 'shoddy' or 'second-rate'.

leather lane. Nineteenth-century slang for 'vagina'. A pun on the street's name, inspired by *leather* 'vagina' (a usage dating back to the mid-16th century).

Leaves Green Earlier *Lese Green* 'Leigh's Green', family name *Leigh* + ME *grene* 'village green'.

A village in southeastern Outer London (before 1965 in Kent), in the borough of BROMLEY, just to the north of BIGGIN HILL.

Lecale Irish *Leath Cathail* 'Cathal's half (i.e. share, territory)'; Cathal was an 8th-century chief.

A rich farming area around Downpatrick, in County Down. It comprises a wide, blunt peninsula between DUNDRUM BAY and the mouth of Strangford Lough (*see under* STRANGFORD). At its southern tip is St John's Point.

Lechlade Probably 'river-crossing near the River Leach', OE river name, literally 'boggy stream', OE *læc(c)*, *lece* + *gelad* 'river-crossing'.

A small town in Gloucestershire, at the point where the River THAMES[1] is united with its headstreams, including the Leach, and where the three counties of Gloucestershire, Oxfordshire and Wiltshire meet. It is the highest navigable point on the Thames, and used to be a centre for water-borne transport (stone for use in building St Paul's Cathedral was taken to London from here). Upstream of Lechlade, the Thames is often referred to as the ISIS.

> A little hamlet called Kelmscott, the nearest town to which is Lechlade, – that being however but a 'one-eyed' town as the Yankees say.
>
> Dante Gabriel Rossetti: letter (1871)

Percy Bysshe Shelley's poem **'A Summer Evening Churchyard, Lechlade'** (1815) was inspired by a river-trip in a rowing-boat from Windsor in the company of Thomas Love Peacock.

Lecht, the 'cairn', Gaelic *leacht*.

A high road pass (637 m / 2089 ft) by which the A939 links COCK BRIDGE and TOMINTOUL. The summit is on the border between Aberdeenshire and Moray (formerly Banffshire). No main road in Britain is more frequently blocked with snow than the Lecht, and the slopes on either side have been developed for skiing. The line of the LADDER HILLS extends to the northeast.

Ledbury Probably 'fortified place on the River Leadon', OCelt river name, literally 'broad stream' + OE *byrig* dative form of *burh* (*see* BURY).

A small market town in Herefordshire (before 1998 in Hereford and Worcester, before 1974 in Herefordshire), to the west of the MALVERN HILLS, about 18 km (11 miles) east of Hereford. Its centre, of narrow streets lined with half-timbered buildings, is still redolent of the 16th and 17th centuries. The area roundabout is hop- and apple-growing country.

The poet John Masefield (1878–1967) was born in Ledbury.

Lee[1] Irish *Laoi*, possibly meaning 'water'.
A river in County Cork; length 80 km (50 miles). It rises in Lake Gouganebarra (*see under* GUAGÁN BARRA) on the Kerry border and flows eastwards to the city of CORK, where it divides into two channels before entering Cork Harbour. There is an important hydroelectric scheme between MACROOM and Inniscarra.

> The spreading Lee, that like an island fayre
> Encloseth Corke with his divided flood.
>
> Edmund Spenser: *The Faerie Queene* (1590–6), IV.ii

> Then too, when the evening sun's sinking to rest
> Sheds its golden light over the sea
> The maid with her lover the wild daisies pressed
> On the banks of my own lovely Lee
>
> Dick Forbes and J.C. Flanahan: 'The Banks of My Own
> Lovely Lee'

Lee[2]. An alternative spelling for the River LEA.

Leeds[1] Originally *Ladenses*, a OCelt name meaning 'people by the fast-flowing river'; *Loidis* 731, *Ledes* 1086.
An industrial city and metropolitan borough on the River AIRE in West Yorkshire, 35 km (21 miles) southwest of York. Domesday Book (1086) records that Leeds then possessed 'a priest, a church, and a mill', and that 35 farming families lived here at this time. Local monks began the wool trade in the 12th century, and in the 14th century Flemish immigrants introduced weaving. Major expansion came with the Industrial Revolution, Leeds being located at the heart of major coal and iron fields. Pottery was also an important industry: in the 18th century the Leeds factory rivalled that of Wedgwood. The building of the **Leeds–Liverpool Canal** (1816) and the Aire and Calder Navigation (*see under* AIRE) linking the city to the HUMBER contributed to the city's growth, and Leeds later became a hub of many railway lines. Charles I granted the first charter in 1626, and in 1893 Leeds became a city. The **University of Leeds** was founded in 1904, joined in 1992 by **Leeds Metropolitan University**, the former Leeds Polytechnic.

Leeds is perhaps the cultural centre of Yorkshire. It is home to Opera North, the Leeds International Piano Competition, the Leeds Music Festival and the City of Leeds Open Brass Band Championships. The Leeds City Art Gallery was founded 1888; next to it is the Henry Moore Institute (1993), a large sculpture gallery. In 1996 the Tower of London's national collection of arms and armour was moved to the Royal Armouries Museum in Leeds. Armley

Mill (once the largest textile mill in the world) now houses Leeds Industrial Museum. HEADINGLEY cricket ground is the Yorkshire county ground (*see also* **Leeds Rhinos** *and* **Leeds United** *below*).

A native of Leeds is called a **Loiner**, possibly from *Loidis*, an early form of the name Leeds (*see above*). Others say that the word comes from the 19th century, when the back entrances to yard and closes around Briggate were called 'low-ins' or 'loins', or from the lanes in this area, locally pronounced 'loins', where men, thus dubbed 'loiners', would gather to gossip.

Leeds was the birthplace of: the industrial reformer Richard Oastler (1789–1861), known as 'the Factory King'; the poet laureate Alfred Austin (1835–1913); Arthur Ransome (1884–1967), author of *Swallows and Amazons* and other adventure stories for children; the painter Patrick Heron (1920–99); Keith Waterhouse (b.1929), the novelist and journalist, author of *Billy Liar*, adapted for stage and screen by fellow-Loiner Willis Hall (b.1929), author of *The Long and the Short and the Tall*; the romantic novelist Barbara Taylor Bradford (b.1933), who set her best-selling *A Woman of Substance* (1979) partly in the city; the playwright Alan Bennett (b.1934); the miners' leader Arthur Scargill (b.1938); the poet-professor Tom Paulin (b.1949); and the television journalist Jeremy Paxman (b.1950). The playwright William Congreve (1670–1729) was born near Leeds, as were the chemist and Unitarian minister Joseph Priestley (1733–1804) and the pioneering civil engineer John Smeaton (1724–92).

Thomas Chippendale set up his furniture-making business in Leeds. Another famous business had its origins here, when Michael Marks, a Polish-Jewish refugee, set up a market stall in Leeds with the sign 'Don't ask the price, it's a penny'; in 1884 he set up the company that, after he was joined ten years later by Thomas Spencer, was to become one of Britain's best-known brands. Mr Marks may well have been inspired by Samuel Smiles, who had edited the *Leeds Times* (1838–42), and whose lectures to the young men of the city were turned into book form as *Self-Help* (1859), the bible of Victorian values.

It was on Leeds Bridge that the Frenchman Louis le Prince filmed what is thought to be the first moving picture, in October 1888, but he disappeared mysteriously shortly thereafter, allowing Thomas Edison in the USA to claim credit for the invention. However, the University of Leeds has adopted the Frenchman's name for its school of cinema.

The actor Peter O'Toole grew up in Leeds, and the sculptors Henry Moore, Barbara Hepworth and Kenneth Armitage all studied at the art school there. Hugh Gaitskell, leader of the Labour Party from 1955 until his death in 1963, was MP for Leeds South, and Denis Healey, deputy leader (1980–3), was MP for Leeds Southeast.

Duke of Leeds. Thomas Osborne (1632–1712), Charles II's chief minister from 1673 to 1679, created Earl of Danby in 1674. He later helped William of Orange to the English throne during the Glorious Revolution of 1688, and became 1st Duke of Leeds in 1694.

Leeds Intelligencer. *See* the *Yorkshire Post under* YORKSHIRE.

Leeds Mercury. *See* the *Yorkshire Post under* YORKSHIRE.

Leeds Rhinos. The city's rugby league team, from 1890 until 1997 just plain **Leeds RFC**. The novelist David Storey played briefly for it after leaving school, an experience that informed *This Sporting Life* (1960). Leeds Rhinos play at HEADINGLEY stadium, as do **Leeds Tykes**, their sister team in the rugby union code.

Leeds United FC. Leeds's professional football club, nicknamed the Peacocks or simply United, and based at Elland Road. Football took a little longer to establish itself in Leeds than it did in other northern cities during the late 19th century. Leeds United was founded in 1919, two earlier Leeds clubs, **Leeds Albion** and **Leeds City**, having respectively folded and been expelled from the Football League. After nearly half a century of provincial obscurity Leeds enjoyed a golden era in the late 1960s and early 1970s under the managership of Don Revie, winning the league championship in 1969 and 1974. Leeds won another league title in 1992, but in 2004 – mired in debt – were relegated from the Premier League.

Witch of Leeds, the. Mary Bateman (1768–1809), a thief, liar, supposed healer and confidence trickster, also known as the Yorkshire Witch. Among other feats she persuaded spectators to pay a penny per peep to see her hen that laid eggs bearing the slogan 'Christ is coming'. In the guise of a fortune-teller she also extorted money out of poor women on the basis that terrible things would happen to them otherwise. She was generally thought to have gone too far when, having set up as a healer, she fed one of her clients, Rebecca Perigo, a poisoned pudding. After being hanged in York, she was suspended from a gibbet in Leeds, where the populace, some of whom continued to believe in her unusual powers, stripped her flesh to the bone. Her skeleton may still be viewed in the medical school at Leeds.

Leeds² Perhaps from a local stream name, 'the loud one', OE *hlyde*.

A village in Kent, about 6 km (4 miles) east of Maidstone.

Leeds Castle. A castle about 1.5 km (1 mile) east of Leeds. Constructed towards the end of the 12th century, it was bought by Edward I in 1278 for his queen, Eleanor of Castile. It went on to house many other royal ladies, including Margaret (Edward's second wife), Philippa of Hainault (Edward III's wife), Catherine de Valois (Henry V's wife), Catherine of Aragon and the future Elizabeth I (who was imprisoned here for a while). Its most striking feature is its

situation: half on an island in the middle of a lake, and half on the mainland. It is now a hotel and conference centre.

Leedstown From the Duke of *Leeds*, who founded the village in the 19th century.

A village in Cornwall, about 8 km (5 miles) southwest of Camborne.

Leek '(place at the) brook', OScand *lœkr* 'brook'.

A town in Staffordshire, on the western edge of the PEAK DISTRICT, on the River Churnet, about 13 km (8 miles) northeast of Stoke-on-Trent. It came to prosperity as a silk-weaving centre, from the 17th to the 19th centuries.

To the northeast are the spectacular millstone-grit formations of HEN CLOUD and the ROACHES.

Leekshire. A slang name for WALES, contemptuously treating the entire country as a minor English county. It was in use in the 18th and 19th centuries, and derives from *leek*, an early 18th-century slang term for a Welshman, which in turn refers to the Welsh national symbol.

The origin of the leek as the Welsh national symbol is found in the story that St David, on one occasion, caused his countrymen under King Cadwaladr to distinguish themselves from their Saxon foes by wearing a leek in their caps. Shakespeare suggests the origin lies in the Battle of Poitiers (1356), the Black Prince's victory over John the Good of France:

> If your Majesty is remember'd of it, the Welshmen did good service in a garden where leeks did grow, wearing leeks in their Monmouth caps; which your Majesty know to this hour is an honourable badge of the service; and I do believe your Majesty takes no scorn to wear the leek upon Saint Tavy's day.
>
> William Shakespeare: Fluellen in *Henry V* (1599), IV.vii

In Romany, according to George Borrow, Wales is *Porrum-engreskey tem*, meaning 'leek-eaters' country'.

Leenane Irish *An Líonán* 'the shallow sea-bed'.

A beautifully situated village in County Galway, some 40 km (25 miles) southwest of Castlebar, at the head of the long fjord-like inlet of KILLARY HARBOUR. It is also spelt **Leenaun**. It was the location for the screen version (1990) of John B. Keane's play *The Field*, about a farmer dangerously obsessed with the land that his family has farmed for generations.

Beauty Queen of Leenane, The. A darkly comic play (1996) by Martin McDonagh, about the relationship between a plain middle-aged woman and her manipulative mother. The same author also wrote a trilogy known as **'the Leenane Trilogy'** (first staged 1997), comprising *The Cripple of Inishmaan*, *A Skull in Connemara* and *The Lonesome West*.

Leenaun. An alternative spelling of LEENANE.

Lee-on-the-Solent Originally *Lee* '(place at the) wood or woodland clearing', OE *leah* (*see* -LEY); the suffix, denoting its proximity to the Solent, was not added until the late 19th century, once the place had begun to develop as a seaside resort.

A town and seaside resort in Hampshire, on the SOLENT, on the eastern side of the mouth of Southampton Water (*see under* SOUTHAMPTON) and about 5 km (3 miles) north-west of Gosport. It was converted from unsuspecting village to holiday destination in the late 1880s by the local property developer Sir John Robinson, and its new and rather grand name followed soon after. The *the* departs from the usual pattern of such names and often gets dropped, much to the dismay of local pedants (the nearby airfield, for instance, now disused but once a Fleet Air Arm base, is very firmly called '**Lee-on-Solent**').

Leestown. A fictional village in County Kilkenny, the setting for RTÉ's long-running Sunday-night rural soap opera *The Riordans* (1965–80).

Legacurry Irish *Lag an Choire* 'hollow of the cauldron'; *compare* TUBBERCURRY.

Several villages in Ireland boast this name.

Leicester 'Roman town of the Ligore people', tribal name *Ligore*, from OCelt river name *Ligor* of unknown origin and meaning + OE *ceaster* 'Roman town' (*see* CHESTER).

A city (pronounced 'lester') and unitary authority within Leicestershire, on the River SOAR and the GRAND UNION CANAL, about 40 km (25 miles) south of Nottingham and 62 km (39 miles) west of Peterborough. It is just to the east of the M1 (**Leicester Forest East** services are between junctions 21 and 21A).

Leicester was an important settlement in Roman times, situated as it was at the point where the FOSSE WAY crossed the Soar. Its name then was **Ratae Coritanorum**. Sections of the forum and baths survive, as does the so-called 'Jewry Wall'. Leicester was one of the FIVE BOROUGHS during the period of Danish occupation in the late 9th and early 10th centuries.

The body of Richard III was brought to Leicester for burial after he was killed at the Battle of BOSWORTH in 1485. Later it was said to have been dug up and thrown into the Soar.

Leicester grew to prosperity after the Middle Ages thanks to the hosiery business, and in the 19th century it added the manufacture of footwear to its repertoire. The exploitation of Leicestershire's coalfields led to increasing industrialization. In the early 1950s Leicester was adjudged to have the highest average family income of any city in Europe (thanks largely to the high number of women working in the hosiery trade). The second half of the 20th century saw a significant amount of Commonwealth immigration, particularly from the Indian subcontinent and from Uganda.

Leicester's Jain Centre contains one of the very few Jain temples in Europe.

St Martin's Church became **Leicester Cathedral** in 1927, and in 1957 the local university college, founded in 1918, became the **University of Leicester**. **De Montfort University** was created in 1992 from the former Leicester Polytechnic.

BBC Radio Leicester, which began broadcasting in 1967, was the first local radio station in Britain.

Leicester is home to Britain's National Space Centre and to the world's largest crisp factory (Walkers – the firm was founded in 1948 by Leicester butcher Henry Walker, inventor of the cheese-and-onion flavoured crisp).

In 1997 Leicester was reconstituted as a unitary authority, under the name **Leicester City**. It remains the administrative centre of Leicestershire (Leicester County Council is based in Glenfield, on the outskirts of the city).

Were football less obsessively supported, the relatively modest historical achievements of **Leicester City FC** (founded in 1884 and nicknamed the Foxes or, historically, the Filberts, from their former ground at Filbert Street, next door to the club's current headquarters, the Walkers Stadium) would have been entirely overshadowed by those of the city's mighty rugby union club, officially known as **Leicester Football Club**. Founded in 1880, and nicknamed the Tigers (possibly from the chocolate-and-yellow shirts worn by the team in the 1880s, or from the connection with the local regiment which was nicknamed the Tigers after service in India), Leicester has spawned a host of England internationals, including Martin Johnson, England's glowering World Cup-winning captain of 2003. The club plays its home games at the Welford Road ground.

The naturalist H.W. Bates (1825–92), Joseph Merrick, the so-called 'Elephant Man' (1862–90), the scientist and novelist C.P. Snow (1905–80), the novelists Simon Raven (1927–2001), Colin Wilson (b. 1931) and Julian Barnes (b. 1946), the playwright Joe Orton (1933–67), the comedian and Monty Python pioneer Graham Chapman (1941–89) and the footballer and pundit (and ambassador for Walkers Crisps) Gary Lineker (b.1960) were born in Leicester.

> In his *Guide to England*, Mr Muirhead, in his comfortable fashion, calls [Leicester] 'a busy and cheerful industrial place, for the most part built of red brick,' and for some hours after I had arrived there I found it impossible to improve upon that description and difficult even to amplify it ... The town seemed to have no atmosphere of its own. I felt I was quite ready to praise it, but was glad to think I did not live in it.
>
> J.B. Priestley: *English Journey* (1934)

Border Leicester. *See under* the BORDER.

Leicester. A breed of white-faced meat-producing English sheep with a long and exceptionally fine white fleece.

In Australia and New Zealand it is generally known as **English Leicester**.

Leicester cheese. A hard cow's-milk cheese made using a process similar to Cheddar. It is dyed with annatto, whence its more usual name **Red Leicester**.

Leicestershire From LEICESTER + SHIRE. The name *Leicestershire* is first recorded in the 11th century.

A county in central England, in the EAST MIDLANDS, bounded to the west by Staffordshire and Warwickshire, to the north by Derbyshire and Nottinghamshire, to the east by Lincolnshire and Rutland, and to the south by Northamptonshire. It contains the unitary authority of Leicester City (*see under* LEICESTER), and its other main centres are ASHBY-DE-LA-ZOUCH, COALVILLE, HINCKLEY, LOUGHBOROUGH, MARKET HARBOROUGH and MELTON MOW-BRAY. RUTLAND was absorbed into Leicestershire in 1974, but restored as a unitary authority in 1997. The county's chief rivers are the SOAR and the WREAKE. CHARNWOOD FOREST separates Leicester and Loughborough.

Ancient Leicestershire was part of the territory of the British tribe known as the Coritani, who were granted a *civitas* (self-governing tribal area) by the Romans around AD 75, with Leicester as its administrative centre. In the late 9th century the county came under Danish control (*see* FIVE BOROUGHS). It was divided into 'wapentakes' (rather than the Anglo-Saxons' Hundreds), and acquired many Scandinavian-based place names (e.g. Ashby, Oadby, Osgathorpe, Sileby).

Leicestershire is chiefly agricultural, but there are coal reserves in the western and northeastern parts of the county. Its hilly areas are known as 'wolds'. East Leicestershire and the VALE OF BELVOIR have been fox-hunting country, very much part of the SHIRES, with a number of well known hunts to its name, notably the Belvoir and the Quorn (*see under* QUORNDON). The county's symbol is the running fox (it appears on the caps of the county cricket team, *see below*), but some of its representatives (the Leicestershire Regiment, Leicester's rugby union club) have preferred the more ferocious guise of 'Tigers' (*see under* LEICESTER).

In cricketing terms Leicestershire is a 'first-class' county. Leicestershire County Cricket Club was founded in 1879 and has played in the county championship since 1895, winning it on three occasions. The former England captain David Gower played for the county. Its home ground is the County Ground, Grace Road, Leicester.

> Leicestershire ... yeeldeth great abundance of Peas and Beans ... insomuch that there is an old by-word ... Leicestershire Bean-Belly.
>
> Edward Leigh: *England described; or the several counties & shires thereof briefly handled* (1659)

Leicester Square Originally (late 17th century) *Leicester Fields*, from its adjoining Leicester House, a mansion built in the 1630s by Robert Sidney, 2nd Earl of Leicester. *Leicester Square* is first recorded in 1708.

A square in the WEST END[1] of London (WC2), in the City of WESTMINSTER, to the west of Charing Cross Road (*see under* CHARING CROSS) and the south of SHAFTESBURY AVENUE. It was laid out in the mid-1670s. In the 18th century it was a fashionable residential square (its residents included William Hogarth and Joshua Reynolds), but by the second half of the 19th century it was essentially a place of public entertainment, blending the roles of THEATRELAND and SOHO. Theatres such as the Alhambra and Daly's were replaced in the 20th century by cinemas like the Odeon (the largest in Europe), the Empire and the Warner Village West End (star-studded film premières in Leicester Square became familiar sights on newsreels and television) and night-clubs (notably the Talk of the Town, which flourished at the northeastern corner of the Square in the 1960s and 1970s). The Square contains statues of, amongst others, William Shakespeare and Charlie Chaplin. It is valued at £260 on a Monopoly board.

Leicester Square Underground station, on the Northern and Piccadilly lines, opened in 1906.

In the 20th century *Leicester Square*, or plain *Leicester*, came to be used as rhyming slang for 'chair'.

See also County TIPPERARY.

Leics. The standard written abbreviation of LEICESTERSHIRE.

Leifear. The Irish name for LIFFORD.

Leigh OE *leah* 'woodland clearing, glade' (*see* -LEY).

An industrial town in Greater Manchester, 14 km (8.5 miles) west of Salford. Leigh was the scene of the arrest in 1641 of the LANCASHIRE-born priest St Ambrose Barlow (canonized 1970), who lived secretly in the area from 1617, ministering to local Catholics. Apprehended – after preaching Easter mass – by the vicar of Eccles (assisted by local toughs), the hapless Barlow was taken to Lancaster Castle where he was incarcerated and eventually tried for treason and hanged, drawn and quartered.

Leigh's rugby league club, now known as **Leigh Centurions**, was one of the founder members of the breakaway Northern Rugby Union in 1895 (*see* HUDDERSFIELD). **Leigh RMI**, the town's football club, was formerly known as Horwich RMI (*see under* HORWICH).

James Hilton (1900–54), author of *Goodbye, Mr Chips* and *Lost Horizon*, was born in Leigh.

Leigh-on-Sea *See* LEIGH.

A fishing village and resort on the Essex coast, at the genteel, western end of SOUTHEND-ON-SEA. The cobbled High Street helps to preserve a sense of history. The novelist John Fowles (b.1926, *see also* LYME REGIS) and the Essex and England cricketer Trevor Bailey (b.1931) were born here.

Leighton Buzzard *Leighton* 'leek or garlic enclosure, herb garden', OE *leac-tun*; *Buzzard* denoting manorial ownership in the Middle Ages by the Busard family.

A market town in Bedfordshire, on the GREAT OUSE, about 16 km (10 miles) west of Bedford. It still has some buildings from the Middle Ages (for example, the 14th-century Golden Bells Inn and the Market Cross).

Mary Norton (1903–92), creator of the Borrowers series of classic children's books set in and around the town, was born here.

Léim an Bhradáin. The Irish name for LEIXLIP.

Léim an Mhadaidh. The Irish name for LIMAVADY.

Leinster Irish *Laighin*, after the Lagin (or Lageni) tribe said to have come to Ireland in the 3rd century BC, with the addition of -*ster* (as in Munster and Ulster), possibly a combination of OScand possessive -*s* + Irish *tír* 'land, territory'. Traditionally the name of the Lagin tribe is associated with *laigean* 'spear', and members of the tribe are said to have colonized the Lleyn Peninsula in North Wales, and to have given it their name.

One of the traditional provinces of Ireland, comprising the eastern and southeastern counties of CARLOW, DUBLIN, KILDARE, KILKENNY, LAOIS, LONGFORD, LOUTH, MEATH, OFFALY, WESTMEATH, WEXFORD and WICKLOW. In the early historical period Leinster extended from the SHANNON to the BOYNE, but it was somewhat reduced from the 6th century. The MacMurroughs were kings of Leinster until 1171, when Dermot MacMurrough died, passing on his kingdom to his son-in-law, the Anglo-Norman Richard de Clare, Earl of Pembroke (nicknamed Strongbow), who had helped to restore the exiled king to his throne. Strongbow's assumption of the kingship of Leinster prompted Henry II to invade Ireland, and Leinster then came under the English Crown. However, in reward for his services, in 1173 Henry granted Strongbow the lordship of Dublin, Waterford and Wexford, which became the core of the PALE, the area of Anglo-Norman settlement in Ireland. Further English settlement of Leinster occurred in the 16th and 17th centuries.

A representative Leinster team plays in rugby union's (professional) Celtic League.

> I found in Leinster the smooth and sleek,
> From Dublin to Slewmargy's peak;
> Flourishing pastures, valour, health,
> Long-living worthies, commerce, wealth.
>
> Anon.: 'Aldfrid's Itinerary through Ireland' (12th century), translated by James Clarence Mangan

Book of Leinster. A 12th-century manuscript collection, put together at GLENDALOUGH, and comprising genealogies, poems and legendary histories. Most of the folios are now in the library of Trinity College, Dublin.

Leinster House. An elegant neo-classical building in Dublin, designed in 1745 by Richard Castle as the town house of the Duke of Leinster. The Dáil (the lower house of the Irish parliament) has sat here since 1922, and the building also now houses the Senate.

Leinster Regiment. A former British Army regiment, tracing its origins to 1760. They were nicknamed the '**Forty-Tens**', from the hungover soldier on parade, who, when ordered to dress-off by numbers, called 'forty-ten' instead of 'fifty'.

Mount Leinster. The highest point (793 m / 2601 ft) in the BLACKSTAIRS MOUNTAINS.

Leinthall Earls *Leinthall* 'nook of land by the River Lent', OCelt river name *Lent* 'torrent, stream' + OE *halh* (*see* HALE, -HALL); *Earls* denoting manorial ownership in the Middle Ages by an earl.

A village in Herefordshire (before 1998 in Hereford and Worcester, before 1974 in Herefordshire), about 11 km (7 miles) southwest of LUDLOW.

Leinthall Starkes *Starkes* denoting manorial ownership in the Middle Ages by a man called Starker.

A village in Herefordshire (before 1998 in Hereford and Worcester, before 1974 in Herefordshire), about 2.5 km (1.5 miles) north of LEINTHALL EARLS.

Leiston Perhaps 'farmstead near a beacon-fire', OE *leges* possessive form of *leg* 'beacon-fire' + -TON.

A town (pronounced 'laystən' or 'laysən') in Suffolk, about 6.5 km (4 miles) northwest of Aldeburgh. The SIZEWELL nuclear power stations are nearby.

Leith From the Water of *Leith*, probably an OCelt name meaning 'dripping'.

The port of EDINBURGH, on the Firth of FORTH, at the mouth of Edinburgh's small, meandering river, the **Water of Leith** – a stream notable for having inspired one of the world's more unfortunate epitaphs:

> Erected to the memory of
> John MacFarlane
> Drowned in the Water of Leith
> By a few affectionate friends.

The port of Leith was formerly separate from the capital, but is now conjoined both geographically and administratively (the latter since 1920). Leith has been an important port since the Middle Ages. In 1559–60 it was occupied and fortified by French troops, come to support Mary of Guise, the Catholic regent and mother of Mary Queen of Scots, against the Protestant Lords of the Congregation, who in turn had sought English help. An Anglo-Scots force began a long siege of the French in Leith; at one point during the siege an English scout lost his head (literally) to a group of young ladies from Leith, who turned out to be cross-dressed French soldiers exercising their Gallic sense of humour. The siege ended with the **Treaty of Leith** (*see below*), and the following year Mary Queen of Scots herself landed at Leith, on her return to Scotland from France. The port's genuine ladies of pleasure make an appearance in the hisetorical record in 1639, when they are reported to have carried rubbish to help rebuild the port's fortifications, at a time when Charles I threatened the Covenanters. Although parts of Leith were gentrified in the last two decades of the 20th century, Leith still had sufficient edge to make it an appropriate setting for *Trainspotting* (1993), Irvine Welsh's upbeat tale of drugs and deprivation, in which, at the long-disused Leith Central Station

> an auld drunkard ... lurched up tae us, wine boatil in his hand ... 'What yis up tae, lads? Trainspottin, eh?' he sais, laughing uncontrollably.

Leith was the birthplace of the playwright John Home (1722–1808), best known for the once-popular *Douglas* (1757), and of Irvine Welsh (b.1961), 'laureate of the Chemical Generation' (*see above*).

Leith Links. Up to the later 18th century, one of the most famous of golf courses. It had only five holes, so the emphasis was on hitting for distance. The world's first golf club, the Honourable Company of Edinburgh Golfers, was formed (as the Gentleman Golfers of Edinburgh) on Leith Links in 1744. The club later flew from the *hoi polloi* to MUSSELBURGH, and thence to MUIRFIELD.

'Leith Races'. A poem by Robert Fergusson (1750–74), celebrating the now defunct races once held at Leith:

> Whan on LEITH-SANDS the racers rare,
> Wi jockey louns are met,
> Their orro pennies there to ware,
> An droun themsels in debt ...

From the same period comes the true story of the noted eccentric James Duff (*c*.1720–88), who entered himself as a runner at the races. He came in last, despite flogging himself round the course with a switch.

Concordat of Leith (1572). An agreement between the government of James VI and the church whereby the Crown reserved the right to appoint bishops, with the approval of the church. The agreement was rejected by Scottish Presbyterians, who loathed both bishops and control by the Crown.

Treaty of Leith (1560). The treaty that ended the first phase of the Wars of Religion in Scotland (*see above*). The treaty required both the French and English to withdraw, but did not deal with the religious dispute.

Leith Hill Leith 'steep slope', OE *hlith*; the fairly tautologous *Hill* is first recorded in the 17th century.
A hill in Surrey, towards the southern edge of the NORTH DOWNS, about 7 km (4.5 miles) southwest of Dorking. At 294 m (965 ft) it is the highest point in southeast England, and it is augmented by a 20 m (64 ft) tower folly built on top of it in 1766 by Richard Hull (and now in the care of the National Trust).

The views from the hilltop are spectacular, as John Evelyn noted in his diary at the end of the 17th century:

> Leith Hill, one of the most eminent in England for the prodigious prospect to be seen from its summit.

On a clear day, St Paul's Cathedral and the English Channel can be seen.

Leitir Ceannain. The Irish name for LETTERKENNY.

Leitir Fraic. The Irish name for LETTERFRACK.

Leitrim, County Irish *Liatroim* 'grey ridge'; the county takes its name from that of a village near the Shannon.
A county in the northwest of Ireland, bordered on the north by Donegal and Fermanagh, on the east by Cavan, on the south by Longford and Roscommon, and on the west by Sligo. The county town is CARRICK-ON-SHANNON. There are hills in the north, including TRUSKMORE and the IRON MOUNTAINS, and many lakes, including LOUGH ALLEN. It is the least populated county in Ireland, and is so remote that it has been described as 'one step beyond the back of beyond'. It is also one of Ireland's poorest and wettest counties, Sean O'Faolain comparing it to a lovely woman always weeping.

Leix. An anglicization of LAOIS.

Leixlip 'salmon leap', OScand *leax* 'salmon' + *hlaup* 'leap', from the waterfall on the River Liffey that used to be here (now replaced by a hydroelectric dam and a specially built salmon ladder).
A town in County Kildare, 15 km (9 miles) west of the centre of Dublin. In Irish it is **Léim an Bhradáin** ('salmon leap'). It was founded by the Danes in AD 915. Two towers of the 12th-century Anglo-Norman castle are incorporated into a later house, which was owned by the Guinness family, and it was here that Arthur Guinness brewed his first pint of porter in 1752 (the brewery moved to Dublin in 1759).

> Leixlip, though about seven miles from Dublin, has all the sequestered and picturesque character that imagination could ascribe to a landscape a hundred miles from, not only the metropolis but an inhabited town.
>
> Charles Maturin: 'Leixlip Castle', published posthumously in *The Literary Souvenir* (1825) (The story is a Gothic tale of insanity.)

Lelant 'church site of Anta', Cornish *lann* 'church site' + *Anta* the name of a woman who had a chapel nearby.
A hamlet on the coast of north Cornwall, about 5 km (3 miles) southeast of ST IVES[2].
See also PENWITH.

Lennox Gaelic *Leamhnacht*, from *leamhanach* 'covered in elm-trees', and possibly related to Leven, the old name for LOCH LOMOND.
An ancient territory surrounding Loch Lomond, extending broadly from LOCH LONG in the west to FLANDERS MOSS in the east, and incorporating what later became DUNBARTONSHIRE. The earldom of Lennox was one of the older

earldoms in Scotland, and various Stewart/Stuart earls (and later dukes) of Lennox played their parts in Scottish history. They gave their name to the little town of **Lennoxtown**, which grew up in the late 18th century at the foot of the CAMPSIE FELLS in East Dunbartonshire.

Slaughter of Lennox, the. The raid on the Colquhouns of Luss in GLEN FRUIN in 1603, which got the Clan MacGregor outlawed and their name banned (*see* ORCHY). During the course of the raid the MacGregors took off with 600 head of cattle, 800 sheep and 200 horses. In addition, with the aid of …

> hagbuttis, pistolettis, murrionis, mailzie-coittis, pow-
> aixes, twa-handit swoirdis, bowie, darloches, and utheris
> wappones invasive, in contraire the tenuour of the Actis
> of Parliament

… as the subsequent indictment of MacGregor of Glenstrae put it, they massacred:

> Peter Naper of Kilmahew, Johnne Buchannane of
> Buchlyvie, Tobias Smallet, bailzie of Dumbarten, David
> Fallesdaillis, his sons, Walter Colquhoun of Barnehill,
> Johnne Colquhoun, fear thairof, Adame and Johnne
> Colquhones, sones to the Laird of Captstradden, Johnne
> Colquhoun of Dalmure, and dyverss utheris persones, our
> soverane lordis leigis, to the number of sevin scoir
> personis or thairby.

Lennoxlove From Frances, the Duchess of Richmond and *Lennox*.

An old house (14th–17th century) some 3 km (2 miles) south of Haddington, East Lothian. It was originally owned by the Maitland family, but was acquired in 1682 by the Duke of Richmond and Lennox. The house had always been known as Lethington, but the name was changed in 1704 in honour of Frances, Duchess of Richmond and Lennox, 'La Belle Stuart', who had been mistress of Charles II but who eloped with the duke in 1667.

Leominster 'church in Leon', OCelt district name *Leon* (literally 'at the streams') + OE *mynster* 'church'.

A town (pronounced 'lemstər') in Herefordshire (before 1998 in Hereford and Worcester, before 1974 in Herefordshire), at the junction of the Rivers Pinsley and Lugg, about 17.5 km (11 miles) south of Ludlow. Its narrow streets and timber-framed buildings bespeak its importance in medieval times. Until the 18th century it made its living from sheep and wool: a fine wool known as **Lemster ore** (a word of unknown origin) was particularly prized:

> A bank of mosse … farre more Soft then the finest
> Lemster ore …
>
> Robert Herrick: *Hesperides, Oberon's Palace* (1648)

Now, however, the sheep's place has been taken by the red Herefordshire cattle that graze in the lush Leominster pastures.

5 km (3 miles) north of Leominster is Berrington Hall, a Georgian house built 1778–81 by Henry Holland. Set in parkland designed by 'Capability' Brown, it is now owned by the National Trust.

There is a town called Leominster (pronounced 'leminster') in Massachusetts, USA.

Leonard Stanley *Leonard* denoting the former dedication of the local church to St *Leonard*; *Stanley* 'stony glade', OE *stan* (*see* STONE) + -LEY.

A village in Gloucestershire, about 5 km (3 miles) southwest of Stroud.

Lepe 'leaping place' (referring to a fence to keep domestic animals out of a deer park, jumpable by a deer but not by cattle, sheep, etc.), OE *hliep*.

A village on the Hampshire coast, on the eastern side of the mouth of the BEAULIEU River, about 13 km (8 miles) northeast of Lymington, and opposite Cowes on the Isle of Wight.

Lerwick 'mud bay', OScand *leirr* 'mud' + *vik* 'bay'. With uncalled-for levity, some commentators have observed that the name might be interpreted as meaning 'shit creek'.

The main town and administrative seat of SHETLAND, halfway up the east coast of Mainland. It took over the role of Shetland's 'capital' from SCALLOWAY in the later 18th century. It owes its importance to its sheltered position on Bressay Sound (*see under* BRESSAY), and developed servicing the Dutch fishing fleets that anchored in the Sound. Today it is a base for the North Sea oil industry, and there are also ferries to Out Skerries, Stromness in Orkney, Aberdeen on the Scottish mainland, Bergen in Norway, and Thorshavn in the Faeroes (Lerwick is actually closer to Bergen than to Aberdeen). On the last Tuesday of January is held Up-Helly-aa, a Viking midwinter fire festival, involving the burning of a longship.

Lerwick was the birthplace of Sir Robert Stout (1844–1930), Liberal prime minister of New Zealand from 1884 to 1887. Norman Lamont (b.1942), Shetland-born Tory chancellor of the exchequer (1990–3), was raised to the peerage in 1998 as Baron Lamont of Lerwick.

When John Paul Jones, the American patriot and privateer, called at Lerwick in 1778 during the American War of Independence, he mistook the red petticoats of the local girls for redcoated British soldiers, and promptly sailed away.

> It would be difficult to find any place where the citizens
> are more class conscious – though not in a Marxian sense
> – more purse-proud, more snooty towards their supposed
> inferiors.
>
> Hugh MacDiarmid: *Lucky Poet* (1943)

Les Ecrehous. *See* ECREHOUS, LES.

Les Minquiers. *See* MINQUIERS, LES.

Letchworth Probably 'enclosure that can be locked', OE *lycce* 'lock' + *worth* (*see* -WORTH, WORTHY, -WARDINE).

A town in Hertfordshire, on the A1(M), about 11 km (7 miles) north of Stevenage. It was the world's first 'garden city', the brainchild of the town planner Ebenezer Howard (1850–1928). He had set out his concept of the ideal spacious suburb, counteracting the evils of overcrowding that had beset the industrial towns and cities of Britain, in his book *Garden Cities of Tomorrow* (1902), and he put it into practice the following year in what had been hitherto the modest Hertfordshire village of Letchworth: on 29 August 1903 *The Times* announced 'The Garden City Pioneer Company (Limited) has acquired about 4,000 acres of land near Hitchin on which to build the first garden city'. The original village remained, but around it Howard set wide roads lined with comfortable villas, plentiful open spaces and unintrusive light-industrial areas (including a factory that produced the first tabulating machines), all with ready access to the Hertfordshire countryside. Initially Letchworth had something of a reputation for attracting an odd assortment of anarchists, theosophists, free lovers and other radical Edwardian misfits, but now it is an eminently respectable commuter town.

Howard's ideas were subsequently realized also in HAMPSTEAD GARDEN SUBURB (1908) and WELWYN GARDEN CITY (1920), as well as in many towns in Europe and around the world (the Australian capital Canberra, for instance), and set the pattern for the English post-Second World War NEW TOWNS[1] (*see* HARLOW, HATFIELD[1], HEMEL HEMPSTEAD, STEVENAGE, *and also* Merton Park *under* MERTON).

There is a Letchworth State Park in New York State, USA.

Letcombe Bassett *Letcombe* 'Leoda's valley', OE male personal name *Leoda* + *cumb* (*see* -COMBE, COOMBE); *Bassett* denoting manorial ownership in the Middle Ages by the Bassett family.

A village in Oxfordshire (before 1974 in Berkshire), on the Lambourn Downs (*see under* LAMBOURN), just to the north of the RIDGEWAY, about 5 km (3 miles) southwest of Wantage.

Thomas Hardy fictionalized it in *Jude the Obscure* (1895) as **Cresscombe**, a name inspired by the village's watercress beds.

Leth Cuinn and Leth Moga Respectively 'Conn's half' and 'Mug Nuadat's (or Eóghan's) half'.

The traditional names for the two halves of IRELAND, respectively the north and the south, said to originate in prehistoric times. The dividing line ran from DUBLIN to GALWAY. Although the Uí Néill dynasty dominated the north, the division does not appear to have reflected the political realities of medieval Ireland, as the kings of MUNSTER rarely achieved dominance over LEINSTER.

Letheringsett Probably 'Leodhere's people's dwelling or fold', OE male personal name *Leodhere* + *-inga-* (*see* -ING) + (*ge*)*set* 'dwelling, fold'.

A village in north Norfolk, on the River Glaven, about 11 km (7 miles) southwest of Sheringham. Until the late 20th century it was owned by the Cozens Hardy family, whose monuments remain in profusion in Letheringsett Church.

> But when, Lord Cozens Hardy,
>   November stars are bright,
> And the King's Head Inn at Letheringsett
>   Is shutting for the night,
> The villagers have told me
>   That they do not like to pass
> Near your curious mausoleum
>   Moon-shadowed on the grass
> For fear of seeing walking
>   In the season of All Souls
> That first Lord Cozens Hardy,
>   The Master of the Rolls.
>
> John Betjeman: 'Lord Cozens Hardy' (1954)

Leth Moga. *See under* LETH CUINN AND LETH MOGA.

Letterfrack Irish *Leitir Fraic* 'hillside of Fraic', possibly referring to the hero of *Táin Bó Fraích*, supposedly a divinely handsome young man.

A prettily situated village in Connemara, County Galway, 8 km (5 miles) north of Clifden. It was founded in the 19th century as a Quaker mission and was the location of a notorious industrial school run by the Christian Brothers.

Letterkenny Irish *Leitir Ceannainn* 'hillside of Uí Chanáin' (an unknown figure) or 'hillside of the white top'.

The joint county town (with LIFFORD) of DONEGAL, situated at the head of LOUGH SWILLY, 25 km (16 miles) west of Londonderry. There is a Gothic Revival cathedral dating from the late 19th century. The Irish patriot and rebel Shane O'Neill was routed here in 1567 by the O'Donnells, and was killed shortly afterwards.

Lettermore Island. *See under* GORUMNA ISLAND.

Letters Gaelic *leitir* 'hill slope'; the -*s* appears to be the English plural.

A scattered settlement on the southwest side of LOCH BROOM, Highland, 8 km (5 miles) southeast of Ullapool.

Leuchars Possibly 'place of rushes', Gaelic *luachair* 'rushes' + English plural -*s*.

A village in northeast Fife, 7 km (4 miles) northwest of St Andrews. The railway station here is reputed to be the windiest in Britain, and a branch line used to lead from here to St Andrews. It is said that after a St Andrews man returned from a world tour he remarked that 'It was fine, once I got past Leuchars.' Today, Leuchars is best known for its major RAF base, home also to mountain and air-sea rescue teams. The first airfield was built in 1917 by the Royal Navy Fleet Training School, and the base is now an important part of Britain's defence system.

Leven. *See under* LOCH LEVEN[1].

Leven, Loch. *See* LOCH LEVEN[1], LOCH LEVEN[2] *and* LOCH LOMOND.

Leven, River. The name of two rivers flowing out of LOCH LEVEN[1] and LOCH LOMOND.

Levens 'Leofa's headland', OE male personal name *Leofa* + NESS. The 'headland' in question is likely to be land between two nearby rivers, the Kent and the Gilpin.

A village in Cumbria (formerly in Westmorland) 7 km (4 miles) south of Kendal. **Levens Hall**, an Elizabethan mansion built around a 13th-century pele tower by the Bellingham family, lies just to the south of here. Most of the present structure dates from the late 1690s. Levens Hall is celebrated for its topiary gardens, laid out from 1694 by Guillaume Beaumont, who had trained under Le Nôtre at Versailles and designed the gardens at HAMPTON COURT. Legend has it that a secret recipe for 'Morocco Ale' was buried in the garden here during the Civil Wars. Every spring until 1877, the unique spiced ale (matured for 21 years) was served at a feast, and new guests were required to stand on one leg and empty in a single draught a tall glass of the ale while pledging 'Luck to Levens whilst t'Kent [a local river] flows'.

Leverburgh After Lord *Leverhulme*.

A small fishing port on the south coast of HARRIS, Western Isles (formerly in Inverness-shire), 20 km (12 miles) south of Tarbert. It was selected as the site of a major fishing development by Lord Leverhulme, the soap manufacturer, who bought Lewis and Harris in 1918 (and in 1922 somewhat presumptuously styled himself 'Viscount Leverhulme of the Western Isles'). The original name was **Obbe** (Gaelic *An T-ob* 'the creek'), but Leverhulme didn't like it, and Leverburgh was suggested instead. Leverhulme's plans fizzled out after his death in 1925, and the Gaelic name is now returning into use.

Leverton Outgate *Leverton* probably 'farmstead where rushes grow', OE *læfer* 'rushes' + -TON; *Outgate* 'road leading out (of the town)', OScand *ut-gata*.

A village in southern Lincolnshire, about 11 km (7 miles) northeast of BOSTON and 2.5 km (1.5 miles) from the western shore of the WASH.

Lew '(place at the) mound or tumulus', OE *hlœwe, hlaw* (*see* LAW, LOW).

A village in Oxfordshire, about 5 km (3 miles) southwest of Witney.

Lewes Probably 'burial mounds', OE *hlœwas* plural form of *hlœw, hlaw* 'burial mound' (*see* LAW, LOW).

The county town of EAST SUSSEX, on the SOUTH DOWNS and on the River OUSE[3], about 12 km (8 miles) northeast of BRIGHTON. It was already an important settlement in Anglo-Saxon times, and around 1100 William de Warenne built a castle here, whose keep still dominates the surrounding countryside from its hilltop site (its former tilting-ground is now a bowling green). The characteristic aspect of the town, though, is a very well-preserved Georgian.

Every Guy Fawkes Night (5 November) there are spectacular torch-lit processions through the streets, and bonfires and firework displays on the surrounding Downs, organized by the town's traditional bonfire societies (a memory of Lewes's 17th-century Protestant martyrs).

Daniel Defoe was not impressed by the quality of the local roads:

> Going to church at a country village, not far from Lewis [*sic*], I saw an ancient lady, and a lady of very good quality, I assure you, drawn to church in her coach with six oxen; nor was it done in frolic or humour, but mere necessity, the way being so stiff and deep, that no horses could go in it.
>
> Daniel Defoe: *A Tour Through the Whole Island of Great Britain* (1724–6)

There is a town called Lewes in Delaware, USA.

Battle of Lewes (14 May 1264). A battle in which the forces of Henry III were defeated by the barons under Simon de Montfort. Henry was captured, but the barons' rebellion was broken with de Montfort's death and defeat at the Battle of Evesham (*see under* EVESHAM) the following year.

Lewesdon Hill The first element is obscure, but is probably an OE personal name; the second is from OE *dun* 'hill' (*see* DOWN, -DON).

A beech-clad hill (272 m / 892 ft) in Dorset, about 7 km (4 miles) west of Beaminster. PILSDEN PEN lies a short distance to the west of here.

In the late 18th century Lewesdon Hill inspired William Crowe, a former rector of the nearby village of Stoke Abbott, to write a laudatory eponymous poem. His 524 lines of topographical verse were admired by Wordsworth and Coleridge:

> Up to thy summit, Lewesdon, to the brow
> Of yon proud rising, where the lonely thorn
> Bends from the rude South-east with top cut sheer
> By his keen breath, along the narrow track,
> By which the scanty-pastured sheep ascend
> Up to thy furze-clad summit, let me climb, –
> My morning exercise, – and thence look round
> Upon the variegated scene, of hills
> And woods and fruitful vales, and villages
> Half hid in tufted orchards, and the sea
> Boundless, and studded thick with many a sail.
>
> William Crowe: *Lewesdon Hill* (1788)

Lewis A name of pre-Celtic origin and unknown meaning, since interpreted as a Gaelic name, *Eilean Leodhais*: *eilean* 'island' + name derived from Gaelic *leogach* 'boggy'.

The flatter, moorland northern part of the island of LEWIS WITH HARRIS, Western Isles (formerly in Ross and Cromarty). It is sometimes called the **Isle of Lewis**, although it is not a distinct island in itself. From TIUMPAN HEAD on the Eye Peninsula it is some 40 km (24 miles) across the Minch to the mainland of northwest Scotland. The northernmost point of the island – the tip of the area called NESS – is called the **Butt of Lewis** (Gaelic name *Rubha Robhanais*, possibly meaning 'peninsula or point of robbers'); Butt of Lewis is also the name of a coastal station providing information for the shipping forecast. The remote and largely uninhabited peninsula in the southeast, separated from Harris by Loch Seaforth, is called Park (Gaelic *Pairc*, meaning 'park', 'enclosure'). The main town of Lewis is STORNOWAY. For the distinctions between Lewis and Harris, *see* HARRIS.

Like the rest of the HEBRIDES, Lewis was until 1266 under Norse rule, then part of the virtually independent fiefdom of the MacDonald Lords of the Isles. It subsequently came under the Macleods. Later, James VI (in anticipation of his plantations in ULSTER) encouraged a group known as the Fife Adventurers to colonize Lewis, suggesting that they ethnically cleanse the indigenous Gaels with all necessary force, such as

> ... slauchter, mutilation, fyre-raising, or utheris inconvenieties.

Although the Macleods successfully resisted the rampaging Fifers, in 1610 James handed over Lewis to the Mackenzies of Kintail, who later became earls of Seaforth (*see* LOCH SEAFORTH). The Seaforths proved not to be particularly benevolent, although things improved to an extent under different owners in the 19th century. In 1918 Lord Leverhulme bought Lewis and Harris (*see under* HARRIS).

The people of Lewis largely follow a strictly sabbatarian form of Presbyterianism, and many speak Gaelic as a first language.

Lewis seaweed, turned into alginate, was used to fireproof the notepads of US astronauts, and thus found its way to the moon.

Lewisian gneiss. A form of the metamorphic rock gneiss found in Lewis and other islands of the Outer Hebrides, of which it forms the main geological constituent. It is also found in the Northwest HIGHLANDS, and is the oldest rock in Britain, dating back 2.4–2.6 billion years.

Lewisham 'Leofsa's homestead or village', OE male personal name *Leofsa* + HAM.

A district and borough of southeast Inner London. The district (SE13) lies between GREENWICH to the north and CATFORD to the south. In 1965 it was amalgamated with BLACKHEATH, Brockley, CATFORD, DEPTFORD, Forest Hill and NEW CROSS to form the borough of Lewisham (SE4, SE6, SE8, SE12, SE13, SE14, SE23, SE26).

Until the middle of the 19th century, Lewisham was a small but prosperous town on the River Ravensbourne, on the far outskirts of London. The railway arrived in 1849, transforming it gradually into a salubrious middle-class suburb. Over the course of the 20th century it has declined in social profile but become a livelier, more cosmopolitan place.

H.G. Wells, who was born in next-door BROMLEY, no doubt had Lewisham at the back of his mind when naming the hero of his semi-autobiographical novel *Love and Mr Lewisham* (1900).

Lewis with Harris. The largest and northernmost island of the Outer HEBRIDES, divided into LEWIS in the north and HARRIS in the south. With an area of 2225 sq km (859 sq miles), it is also the third largest island in the British Isles after Britain and Ireland themselves.

Lewknor 'Leofeca's hill-slope', OE *Leofecan* possessive form of male personal name *Leofeca* + *ora* 'hill-slope'.

A village in Oxfordshire, in the Chiltern Hills, near the point where the M40 crosses the RIDGEWAY, about 19 km (12 miles) southeast of Oxford.

Lewtrenchard Originally *Lew*, from the name of a local river, a Celtic river name meaning 'bright one'; *-trenchard* denoting manorial ownership in the Middle Ages by the Trenchard family.

A village (pronounced 'lutrenshəd') in Devon, close to the western edge of Dartmoor and about 11 km (7 miles) north of Tavistock.

Leyburn Possibly 'shelter by the stream', OE *hleg* 'shelter' + *burna* 'stream'.

A small town in the heart of WENSLEYDALE, North Yorkshire, just north of the River URE, 12 km (7.5 miles) southwest of Richmond. From **Leyburn Shawl**, a grassy terrace, there are attractive views of Wensleydale.

Leyburn is linked to the nearby town of Middleham, south of the Ure, by an iron girder bridge built by public subscription in 1850.

Leyland 'estate of uncultivated land', OE *læge* 'uncultivated land' + *land* 'estate'.

An industrial town in Lancashire, 7 km (4 miles) south of Preston.

British Leyland. A former giant motor-manufacturing company. It owed the origins of its name to James Sumner of Leyland, who in 1884 built a steam-driven wagon and went on to set up a business that was to become **Leyland Motors Ltd** in 1907. The company concentrated on building buses and lorries, until it acquired Triumph in 1961. In 1966 it merged with Rover and in 1968, after a merger with the British Motor Corporation (the company that

❖ -ley ❖

This Old English element, *leah*, is distributed very widely over England, particularly in areas that were once predominantly wooded. The names Lee and Leigh occur in Essex, Hampshire, Kent, Lancashire, London, Oxfordshire, Shropshire, Somerset, Surrey and Worcestershire. Although this distribution so far leaves out areas such as Cheshire, Leicestershire, Nottinghamshire, Sussex and Yorkshire, which were in parts densely wooded in the Middle Ages, it nevertheless gives an indication of the spread of the element. It is clear that *leah* has to do with woodland, particularly managed woodland. In these wooded areas, the usual meaning is 'cleared land in a wood', and from this derives the later meaning of 'pasture land'. The animals frequenting the land often feature in the name: domestic sheep were often grazed on it, witness the many examples of Shipley (such as SHIPLEY, West Yorkshire). But wild animals also benefited: HARTLEY WINTNEY (Hampshire) is one of many Hartleys, meaning 'glade frequented by harts or stags', and

likewise BUCKLEY (Welsh Bwcle) in Flintshire refers to the buck.

The general sense of managed woodland is supported by the range of tree names that accompany *-ley*. EAGLE (Lincolnshire), BERKELEY (Gloucestershire) and many examples of Willey (such as WILLEY[2], Shropshire) contain the elements oak, birch and willow respectively. But since these names are not all in densely wooded areas, and the wood of the trees was useful for various domestic applications, it is likely that *-ley* here may have the sense of 'copse or grove of trees preserved for particular purposes'; this sense is also found in Yardley (such as the Birmingham suburb of YARDLEY) 'copse where rods are cut', and in STALYBRIDGE (Greater Manchester) 'bridge by the copse where staves are cut'.

One purpose for groves or clearings, known from ancient sources, is heathen worship: THUNDERSLEY (Essex), Wensley (Derbyshire) and Tuesley (Surrey) were groves dedicated to the worship of Thunor, Woden and Tiw respectively.

---

owned Morris, Austin, MG, Jaguar and Daimler), became British Leyland. The company was partially nationalized in 1975 and has since been largely dismembered, although **Leyland Trucks** continues to have its headquarters in the town of Leyland.

Leyton 'farmstead or estate on the River Lea', LEA + -TON (*see also* LUTON).
A district of northeast London (E10), on the River LEA, in the borough of WALTHAM FOREST, to the east of Hackney Marshes (*see under* HACKNEY).

The local professional football club (founded 1881) is called **Leyton Orient FC** (nicknamed, with a great leap of the imagination, the O's). In its early days, the team attracted players from the Orient shipping line and became known as the Orient Football Club in 1888. At various times since it has also been known as Clapton Orient or simply Orient.

Before it was swallowed up by London, Leyton was in Essex, and the county cricket club staged matches at the Leyton ground. It was here in 1932 that Percy Holmes and Herbert Sutcliffe set the then world-record first-wicket partnership of 555, playing for Yorkshire v. Essex.

On 24 May 2004 Leyton was the scene of a mysterious warehouse fire, which engulfed a significant number of works by Tracy Emin and other contemporary artists associated with the Britart movement (*see under* BRIT[2]).

Leyton 'Underground' station, on the Central line, opened in 1947.

Leytonstone Originally *Leyton atte Stone* 'Leyton at the STONE' (referring to the 'High Stone', which is said to be on the site of a Roman milestone).

A district of northeast London (E11), in the borough of WALTHAM FOREST (previously in Essex), between LEYTON to the southwest and WANSTEAD to the northeast. The Roman road from London to Epping Forest (*see under* EPPING) led through Leytonstone.

Leytonstone 'Underground' station, on the Central line, opened in 1947.

The poet and dramatist John Drinkwater (1882–1937), the film director Alfred Hitchcock (1899–1980), the Essex and England cricketer Graham Gooch (b.1953) and the Manchester United, Real Madrid and England footballer David Beckham (b.1975) were born in Leytonstone.

Liathach Gaelic *liath-ach* 'greyish one', referring to the quartzite of its upper ramparts.

The noblest mountain in that glen of noble mountains, Glen TORRIDON, in the Northwest HIGHLANDS (formerly in Ross and Cromarty). Its pronunciation baffles most, but experts variously proffer 'lyee'ahoch' or 'lee'agach'. Liathach dominates the glen like some ancient dreadnought, its tiers of Torridonian sandstone capped by a sharp, many-peaked and -pinnacled ridge of quartzite, whose traverse (some 8 km /5 miles long) offers an energetic and serious mountain expedition in summer and, especially, in winter. In *Lucky Poet* (1943) Hugh MacDiarmid wrote of the mountain's north face:

Its grandeur draws back the heart.

Liberties, the So named because the area was outside the jurisdiction of the medieval city.

An area of central DUBLIN, south of the River LIFFEY. Many Huguenots came here in the late 17th century, but by the

19th century it was known for its appalling slums. One commentator, the US physician James Johnson, visited the place in 1844 and ironically remarked of its name:

> ... winds and rain have *liberty* to enter freely through the windows of half the houses – the pigs have *liberty* to ramble about – the landlord has *liberty* to take possession of most of his tenements – the silk weaver has *liberty* to starve or beg.

The Liberties contained the COOMBE.

Lichfield 'open land near Letocetum', Romano-British place name *Letocetum*, literally 'grey wood' + OE *feld* (*see* FIELD).

A cathedral city in Staffordshire, about 21 km (13 miles) southeast of Stafford and 21 km (13 miles) northeast of Wolverhampton. Most of the compact city centre preserves its Georgian character, but it is dominated by the medieval red sandstone of **Lichfield Cathedral** (dedicated to St Chad (d.672), who as Bishop of the Mercians had his see at Lichfield), whose trio of graceful spires (unique in England) are known as the 'Ladies of the Vale'.

The 18th century was Lichfield's golden age. It had a vigorous intellectual life, and numbered among its residents such luminaries as the actor David Garrick, the poet Anna Seward (1747–1809), who was known as the **Swan of Lichfield**, and the botanist and inventor Erasmus Darwin, grandfather of Charles, who (together with Josiah Wedgwood and the inventors Matthew Boulton and James Watt) founded here the Lunar Society, which met on brightly moonlit nights. Easily its most famous son, though, is the author and lexicographer Samuel Johnson (1709–84), who was born here and lived much of his life here until he moved to London in 1737. He remembered it afterwards as a town where 'all the decent people got drunk every night and were not the worse thought of', but this does not seem to have reduced the esteem in which he held it:

> I lately took my friend and showed him genuine civilized life in an English provincial town. I turned him loose at Lichfield that he might see for once real civility.

The antiquarian Elias Ashmole (1617–92), whose benevolence to Oxford University created the Ashmolean Museum (*see under* OXFORD), was born here.

> Lichfield ... a nice, dull little place in glazed salmony Midland brick.
>
> V.S. Pritchett: in *Why do I Write?* (1948)

Lichfield has a number of surviving folkloric traditions. The Court of Array descends from a medieval body instituted to ensure men had proper military equipment and training; today it restricts itself to inspecting some old suits of armour and testing the local ale. The annual Sheriff's Ride involves the sheriff and many others making a horseback inspection of the civic boundaries, while the Greenhill Bower (held in May) is a big carnival parade, and derives from the meeting of the city's guilds in a temporarily erected bower at Greenhill.

Lichfield Gospels, the. An 8th-century manuscript text of the gospels, kept at Lichfield cathedral.

Lickey Perhaps 'vegetable enclosure in a woodland', OE *leac* 'vegetable, leek' + (*ge*)*hæg* 'woodland enclosure'.

A village in Worcestershire (before 1998 in Hereford and Worcester, before 1974 in Worcestershire), about 8 km (5 miles) northeast of Bromsgrove, on the southwestern outskirts of Birmingham. The nearby **Lickey Hills** (the area became a designated Country Park in 1971) are a popular recreational destination for the citizens of Birmingham and the Black Country. Their highest point is Beacon Hill (297 m / 975 ft), with excellent views across the city.

Lickey End Possibly 'the end of land belonging to LICKEY'.

A village in Worcestershire (before 1998 in Hereford and Worcester, before 1974 in Worcestershire), about 2.5 km (1.5 miles) southwest of LICKEY, near the junction of the M5 and the M42.

Liddesdale 'valley of the loud river', OE *hlud*, *hlyde* 'noisy one' + *dæl* 'valley'.

The long, remote valley of the **Liddel Water** in the southwest of Scottish Borders. Before it joins the ESK[2], the Liddel Water forms a stretch of the border with England. Liddesdale was long part of the DEBATABLE LANDS: in 603 it was the probable site of the Battle of Degsanstan or Degsastan, in which Æthelfrith of NORTHUMBRIA defeated Aidan of DALRIADA. In the Middle Ages Liddesdale was reivers' (raiders') territory, the base of the notorious Armstrongs, and features in a number of Border ballads. In 'Jock o' the Side', the men of Liddesdale rescue their compatriot from a Newcastle jail:

> Then they ha' rid tae Liddesdale
> Just as fast as they could ride,.
> And when they cam' tae Liddesdale
> They cast the chains frae Jock o' the Side.

In 'The Ballad of Hobie Noble' (Hobie being one of Jock's rescuers) the action takes place in the area between Liddel and Tyne, and begins:

> Foul fa' the breast first treason bred in!
> That Liddesdale may safely say:
> For in it there was baith meat and drink,
> And corn unto our geldings gay.

Lion of Liddesdale, the. The sobriquet given by James Hogg (*see under* ETTRICK) to the moss-trooper Jock Elliot, whose home was at Larriston in Liddesdale.

> Lock the door Lariston, lion of Liddesdale,
> Lock the door Lariston, Lowther comes on,
>   The Armstrongs are flying,
>   Their widows are crying,
> The Castleton's burning, and Oliver's gone ...
>
> 'Lock the Door, Lariston'

Liffey Irish *An Life*; the meaning is obscure, although the 17th-century *Annals of the Four Masters* attributes its origins to a 3rd-century king, Cairbre Liffeachair.

A river in eastern-central Ireland, about 130 km (80 miles) long. It rises in the Wicklow Mountains near the SALLY GAP, then flows west into County KILDARE, by NEWBRIDGE[2], then northeast to DUBLIN, which it divides into two (pedestrians can join them up via the famous HALFPENNY BRIDGE), before flowing into the sea at Dublin Bay. The **Liffey Plain** has the lowest rainfall in Ireland. In 2001 the name **Liffey Valley** was given to a new retail complex to the west of Dublin.

The Liffey has long been personified as **Anna Liffey** (or, in Latinate form, **Anna Livia**), *Anna* deriving from Irish *abha* 'river', and in the past the term has been used in legal documents, as well as in songs and literature.

'Twas down by Anna Liffey my love and I did stray.
There in the good old slushy mud the seagulls sport and
    play.
We got a whiff of fish and ships and Mary softly sighed,
'Yerra John, come on, for a one and one, down by the
    Liffey side.'

Peadar Kearney (1883–1942): 'Down by the
Liffey Side' (song)

where Anna Livia, breathing free,
weeps silently into the sea,
her tiny sorrows mingling with
the wandering waters of the earth.

Derek Mahon: 'Beyond Howth Head', from
Collected Poems (1999)

For James Joyce the river was **Anna Livia Plurabelle**, and this was the title he used in 1925 for a section of his 'Work in Progress', a work that was eventually to become *Finnegans Wake*. In the latter, Anna Livia Plurabelle, as well as being all the rivers of the world and a symbol of womanhood and eternal renewal, is the wife of Humphrey Chimpden Earwicker.

O
Tell me all about
Anna Livia! I want to hear all
About Anna. Well, you know Anna Livia?
Yes, of course, we all know Anna Livia. Tell me all.

James Joyce: *Finnegans Wake* (1939), Book 1, Chapter 8

In 1988, for Dublin's millennium, a fountain entitled *Anna Livia Plurabelle* was commissioned from Sean Mulcahy and Eamonn O'Doherty. The work featured a reclining female figure in a watery setting, earning it the nickname 'The Floozie in the Jacuzzi', or, when it was used as a receptacle for litter, 'The Hoor in the Sewer'.

Liffey Swim, the. An annual 1.9-km (2000-yard) swimming race in the Liffey, held since 1919 (there is a 1923 painting of the event by Jack B. Yeats). The surgeon and wit Oliver St John Gogarty won it several times, and, on being congratulated on one occasion, replied (with reference to the river's once polluted state), 'I was just going through the motions.' There are races for men and women, with more than 100 taking part in each.

Liffey water. Rhyming slang for 'porter', with Guinness very much in mind – Liffey water supposedly being one of that brew's unique ingredients.

Lifford Irish *Leifear* 'side of the water'.

The joint county town (with LETTERKENNY) of DONEGAL. It is on the River Foyle (*see under* FOYLE), opposite Strabane.

Lilleshall 'Lill's hill', OE *Lilles* possessive form of male personal name *Lill* + *hyll* 'hill'.

A village (pronounced 'lily-shawl') in Shropshire, about 6.5 km (4 miles) northeast of Telford, within the unitary authority of Telford and Wrekin. The nearby Heath Hill provides a fine view of the WREKIN.

The 12th-century **Lilleshall Abbey** never recovered from the ravages of a Parliamentarian siege in the 1640s, but in its grounds is **Lilleshall Hall**, once the Duke of Sutherland's country retreat and now home to the **Lilleshall National Sports Centre**, where many of England's top sportsmen and -women, including the national football team, train.

Lilliard's Edge. *See under* ANCRUM.

Lilliesleaf The second element is OE *clif* 'bank, cliff'; the first may be a male personal name *Lil*.

A small village in Scottish Borders, 8 km (5 miles) southeast of Selkirk.

Lillingstone Dayrell *Lillingstone* 'Lytel's people's boundary stone', OE male personal name *Lytel* + *-inga-* (*see* -ING) + *stan* (*see* STONE); *Dayrell* denoting manorial ownership in the early Middle Ages by the Dayrell family.

A village in Buckinghamshire, about 5 km (3 miles) north of Buckingham.

Limavady Irish *Léim an Mhadaidh* 'dog's leap', originally applied to the site of the O'Cahan castle overlooking the River Roe, 5 km (3 miles) to the south, and referring to a local legend in which a dog leapt across the rocky gorge bearing a message from O'Cahan requesting help.

A market town in County Londonderry, 20 km (12 miles) southwest of Coleraine. It was founded as **Newtonlimavady** in 1610 by an Englishman, Thomas Phillips. It is the administrative centre of the local authority district of the same name.

Limavady was the birthplace of Sir William Massey (1856–1925), prime minister of New Zealand from 1912 until his death. It was also here that Jane Ross first wrote down the tune of the Londonderry Air (*see under* DERRY/LONDONDERRY). Nearby is the possible site of DRUIMCEATT.

'Sweet Peg of Limavady'. Some verses by W.M. Thackeray in honour of the local barmaid at the inn he stayed at in Limavady in 1842, while working on his *Irish Sketchbook*:

This I do declare
  Happy is the laddy
Who the heart can share
  Of Peg of Limavaddy;
Beauty is not rare
  In the land of Paddy,
Fair beyond compare
  Is Peg of Limavaddy.

Lime Grove Etymology unkown, perhaps 'grove of lime trees'. A street in SHEPHERD'S BUSH (W12), in the borough of HAMMERSMITH AND FULHAM. Film studios were opened here in 1915. They were the Gaumont-British company's centre of operations. In 1949 they were sold to the BBC, which used them as television studios.

The Grove Family, the first authentic British television soap opera, screened on the BBC from 1954 to 1957, centred on the domestic and social concerns of a lower middle-class family from Hendon whose name was borrowed from the Lime Grove studios.

Hunchfront of Lime Grove, the. A nickname given to the generously endowed starlet known as Sabrina (b.1938 as plain Norma Sykes), who appeared silently but decoratively on Arthur Askey's television show *Before Your Very Eyes*, made at the Lime Grove studios in the early 1950s.

Limehillock Possibly self-explanatory, with *lime* referring to the tree species.
A village in Moray (formerly in Grampian region), 12 km (7.5 miles) north of Huntly.

Limehouse 'lime kilns', OE *lim* 'lime' + *astas* plural form of *ast* 'oast, kiln'.
A district (pronounced 'lime-house' or, in former times, 'lime-əs') of the EAST END of London (E14), in the borough of TOWER HAMLETS, on the north bank of the River Thames, between STEPNEY to the west and CANNING TOWN to the east.

In the Middle Ages it was, as its name suggests (*see above*), a centre for the burning of lime: chalk or limestone was brought up the Thames from Kent and processed in the kilns of Limehouse into lime for various domestic and industrial uses. By the 18th century Limehouse had moved on to the building of ships. For a while it was one of the most important shipbuilding areas of London, and lifeboats continued to be made here up to the end of the 19th century, but by that time it had been firmly drawn into the orbit of London's DOCKLAND. CHINATOWN established itself here, adding opium and the 'Yellow Peril' to the area's already rapidly descending social profile. Its reputation as tough, crime-ridden and often violent territory ('I opened

a tourist bureau. Trips to the London underworld. Limehouse and all that' – Graham Greene, *The Basement Room* (1935)) was not helped in the early 20th century when its choice by the obstreperous Liberal politician David Lloyd George as the venue in 1909 for a particularly rough-house speech led to its name becoming synonymous with invective oratory (Eric Partridge in his *Dictionary of Slang* (1937) defined the verb *Limehouse* as 'to use coarse, abusive language in a speech').

By the end of the 20th century that usage had largely been forgotten, and as Dockland lost its docks and pockets of middle-class intelligentsia penetrated Limehouse, suggesting the possibility of a Hampstead-on-Thames, a new political connection was made: one of the founders of the now defunct Social Democratic Party, David Owen, lived in Limehouse, and since many of the meetings of its formative caucus (Owen plus Roy Jenkins, William Rodgers and Shirley Williams) took place there in the early 1980s, they became known as the **Limehouse Four**, and their embryonic manifesto for their new party (issued on 25 January 1981) as the **Limehouse Declaration**.

The Labour prime minister Clement Attlee (1883–1967) once joked that if he were raised to the peerage he would take the title of 'Lord Love-a-Duck of Limehouse' (he was the local MP between 1922 and 1950); in the event, in 1955 he became Earl Attlee of WALTHAMSTOW.

The early 18th-century church of St Anne's, Limehouse, designed by Nicholas Hawksmoor, figures in the novel *Hawksmoor* (1985) by Peter Ackroyd (it is one of a mystic pattern of churches at which murders are committed). It has the highest church clock in London.

The riverside Grapes pub in Limehouse was fictionalized as the Six Jolly Fellowship Porters by Charles Dickens in *Our Mutual Friend* (1865).

Dan Leno and the Limehouse Golem. A novel (1994) by Peter Ackroyd that revolves around serial murders in late 19th-century East London committed by the 'Limehouse Golem' (in Jewish legend, a golem is a human figure brought supernaturally to life). Real-life characters such as the writer George Gissing and the music-hall comedian Dan Leno are woven into the plot.

Limbs of Limehouse, the. A gang of rowdies from Limehouse of sufficient contemporary notoriety to rate a mention by the porter in Shakespeare's *Henry VIII*:

These are the youths that thunder at a playhouse ... that no audience but the tribulation of Tower Hill, or the Limbs of Limehouse, their dear brothers, are able to endure.
  William Shakespeare: *Henry VIII* (1613), V.iv

Limehouse Basin. A canal basin in which the GRAND UNION CANAL is joined by the Limehouse Cut before debouching into the Thames.

Limerick

Limehouse Cut. A canal about 2.5 km (1.5 miles) long joining the River LEA to the GRAND UNION CANAL at Limehouse. In the past its name has been used as Cockney rhyming slang for *gut*, usually with reference to the size of someone's paunch.

Limehouse Reach. The stretch of the River Thames opposite Limehouse, extending down the western side of the ISLE OF DOGS.

Limekilns From the *lime kilns* formerly operated here.
A village in Fife, on the north shore of the Firth of FORTH, 3 km (2 miles) west of Rosyth. It was an important port in the Middle Ages, servicing DUNFERMLINE. In Robert Louis Stevenson's novel *Kidnapped* (1886), David Balfour comes to Limekilns towards the end of his adventures:

> This is a place that sits near in by the waterside, and looks across the Hope [ST MARGARET'S HOPE[1]] to the town of Queensferry. Smoke went up from both of these, and from other villages and farms upon all hands. The fields were being reaped; two ships lay anchored, and boats were coming and going on the Hope. It was altogether a right pleasant sight to me; and I could not take my fill of gazing at these comfortable, green, cultivated hills and busy people both of the field and sea.

Limerick Irish *Luimneach* 'bare ground'.
Ireland's fourth-largest city, and the county town of County Limerick. It is 85 km (50 miles) north of Cork, at the head of the SHANNON estuary – 'Limerick's grey-green mouth', according to the 8th-century poet Rumann, son of Colman. The city is the cathedral town of both the Protestant and Catholic dioceses of Limerick. There are three main parts of the city: English Town, the old city on King's Island (Inis Ubhdain, or Sibtonn) in the Shannon; Irish Town; and Newtown Pery, the centre of the city today. English Town and Irish Town were segregated thus by legislation in the 13th and 14th centuries, while Newtown Pery was largely laid out in the 18th. The National Institute for Higher Education (1972) at Limerick is part of the National University of Ireland.

Limerick goes back to before the time of the Vikings, who sacked a settlement here in 812. In 922 the Danes built a stronghold on King's Island, which was sacked in 967 by the Irish under Brian Boru. Limerick continued as a Norse trading centre, however, and in the 12th century became the seat of the kings of THOMOND, who styled themselves *Rex Limricensis*. The Anglo-Normans took over at the end of the 12th century, and built the well-preserved King John's Castle on King's Island; the castle was inaugurated by the king himself in 1210. King's Island is also the site of the Protestant cathedral, dating from 1168.

Limerick became an English mercantile centre, trading with France and Spain up to the end of the 17th century. During this period the city changed hands various times,

being taken, for example, by the Confederate Catholics in 1642 and by Cromwellian forces under General Ireton in 1651 (Ireton died at Limerick after the siege). After the Battle of the Boyne (1690) William of Orange failed to take the city in the face of Patrick Sarsfield's stout defence. However, the Williamites returned to besiege the city in 1691, a siege that ended in the Jacobite surrender on the terms of the **Treaty of Limerick** (*see below*) – terms that were soon violated, earning Limerick its byname, CITY OF THE BROKEN TREATY.

> To the heroes of Limerick, the City of the Fights,
> Be my best blessing borne on the wings of the air!
>
> Anon.: 'Farewell, O Patrick Sarsfield' (late 17th century), translated from the Irish by James Clarence Mangan

Limerick in the 20th century acquired a certain reputation for bleak poverty – as depicted in Frank McCourt's memoir of the Depression era, *Angela's Ashes* (1996; film version 1999) – and for criminal gangs and violence, the latter earning it the unfortunate nickname of **Stab City**. Many of the good citizens of Limerick have been incensed by these degrading aspersions cast on their fair city.

> Dublin and Limerick are cities beautiful to me not only with some of the most superb and most neglected architecture in Europe but with a compelling litany, a whole folklore, of tragic and heroic associations.
>
> Brigid Brophy: 'Am I an Irishwoman?', from *Don't Never Forget* (1966),

Limerick was the birthplace of the writer Gerald Griffin (1803–40), author of *The Collegians* (1829), a novel based on the true story of a Limerick woman, Ellen Hanley, murdered by her husband in 1819. It became the basis of Dion Boucicault's melodrama *The Colleen Bawn* (1860; *see under* GARRYOWEN) and Sir Julius Benedict's opera *The Lily of Killarney* (*see under* KILLARNEY). One of the numbers in Boucicault's play is called 'Limerick is Beautiful':

> Limerick is beautiful,
> As everybody knows;
> The river Shannon full of fish,
> Through that city flows.

Limerick was also the birthplace of Lola Montez (1818–61), the 'Spanish' dancer famous for her affair with King Ludwig I of Bavaria; of the novelist and playwright Kate O'Brien (1897–1974), in whose novel *Without My Cloak* (1931) Limerick is fictionalized as **Mellick**; and of the broadcaster Terry Wogan (b.1938).

> The rain drove us into the church – our refuge, our strength, our only dry place ... Limerick gained a reputation for piety, but we knew it was only the rain.
>
> Frank McCourt: *Angela's Ashes* (1996)

acquitted by a Limerick jury. An expression denoting that the accused may have friends among the jurors. The phrase originated with Richard Adams, a Limerick county-court judge in the 1880s and 1890s.

limerick. A five-line humorous verse, in which the first, second and fifth lines rhyme, as do the third and fourth. It originated in England *c*.1820, and the name is said to come (without any firm evidence) from the chorus 'Will you come up to Limerick', which at one time followed each verse as it was improvised by each member of a convivial party. The form was popularized by Edward Lear in his *Book of Nonsense* (1846).

Limerick Hellfire Club. A group of 18th-century dissolutes and rakes, who apparently specialized in rioting in theatres. Unlike the Dublin HELLFIRE CLUB or that in England (*see* MEDMENHAM), the club had a female member, a certain Celinda Blennnerhasset.

Limerick Junction. A major railway junction in County Tipperary, 5 km (miles) northwest of Tipperary itself. Here lines for Limerick and Waterford branch off the main Dublin–Cork line.

Limerick lace. A style of lace involving embroidery on an open fabric. There are two varieties: tambour lace (worked with a hook) and needlerun lace (worked with a needle).

Limerick Soviet, the. A workers' soviet set up on 14 April 1919 after the Limerick United Trades and Labour Council declared a general strike. This was in response to the British imposition of martial law on the city during the Anglo-Irish War. It lasted until 25 April.

Treaty of Limerick (3 October 1691). A treaty, supposedly signed on the Treaty Stone, a large limestone slab on the Thormond Bridge, by which Jacobite forces under Patrick Sarsfield surrendered the city to General Ginkel, leader of the Williamite army that had been besieging Limerick since 4 September. The Irish soldiers were allowed to go into exile in France, where they formed the Irish Brigade (*see under* IRISH) – the Wild Geese. The treaty also promised toleration of Catholics. However, in 1695 the Irish Parliament introduced the so-called Penal Code, which, among other things, deprived Catholics of the rights of citizenship and the right to own property – hence Limerick's byname, the City of the Broken Treaty, and the saying 'The treaty was broken before the ink was dry.'

'Walls of Limerick, The'. One of the most popular of Irish céilí dances, choreographed by Bean uí Chorráin, secretary of the Limerick branch of Conradh na Gaeilge.

Limerick, County. A county of southwestern Ireland, in the traditional province of Munster, bounded on the north by the Shannon and County Clare, to the east by Tipperary, to the south by Cork, and to the west by Kerry. The county town is LIMERICK. Limerick is hilly in the south (the MULLAGHAREIRK and the GALTEE MOUNTAINS), and low-lying and generally fertile elsewhere (especially in the GOLDEN VALE).

Limestone City, the. A nickname for GALWAY.

Lime Street The etymology is uncertain, but there are three possibilities: it was named after lime kilns (making lime for mortar was an important medieval industry); or after lime fruit as part of the diet of sailors; or that it refers to *Lyme*, the ancient district name of Lancashire, found in ASHTON-UNDER-LYNE and other names.

A street in central Liverpool that has given its name to the city's main railway station. The expression 'to get off at Edge Hill' means to perform coitus interruptus, Edge Hill being the station before Lime Street. The area does indeed have a certain notoriety:

> Nellie worked for thirty years,
> In Tetley's pubs selling wines and beers;
> Thirty years in a Lime Street bar –
> You'd think she'd know what sailors are!
>
> Joe Orford: 'Liverpool Ladies'

> A Lime Street girl drew up to me and offered me a bed,
> But when I awoke on the next day's morn with me watch and me money she'd fled,
> And as I walk the streets about the whores they all do roar,
> 'There goes young Jack the sailor lad he must go to sea once more.'
>
> Anon.: 'Jackie Brown'

> Oh, Maggie, Maggie May,
> They have taken her away,
> And she'll never walk down Lime Street any more.
> Oh, she robbed those lime juice sailors,
> And the captains of the whalers,
> That dirty robbing no-good Maggie May.
>
> Anon.: 'Maggie May' (Maggie May was a notorious operator on Lime Street in the 1890s, along with the likes of Jumping Jenny, Cast Iron Kitty and The Battleship; her fame was spread worldwide by The Beatles' snippet of the folk song (on *Let It Be*, 1970) and by Rod Stewart's hit (with Martin Quittenton) 'Maggie' (1971): 'Wake up Maggie, I think I've got something to say to you / It's late September and I really should be back at school')

Limey From the *limes* consumed by British sailors from the 18th century to ward off scurvy.

An originally Australian and now mostly American term for a BRITON. The Australians also call the British **lime-juicers**.

Limpley Stoke Originally *Hangingstoke* 'outlying farmstead or hamlet below a steep hillside', OE *hangende* 'hanging, below a steep hillside' + *stoc* 'outlying farmstead or hamlet' (*see* -STOCK, STOCK-, STOKE); the affix *Limpley*, first recorded in 1585, relates to the dedication of a former chapel here to 'Our Lady of Limpley' in 1578, but the origin of Limpley, perhaps a surname, is unknown.

A village in Wiltshire, about 5 km (3 miles) west of BRADFORD-ON-AVON.

Lincoln Originally *Lindon* 'pool' (referring to the broad pool in the River Witham here), from the OCelt stem *lindo-*. Its Romano-British name was *Lindum colonia* 'Roman colony (for retired legionaries) at Lindon', and this eventually became eroded into *Lincoln*.

A cathedral city (pronounced 'linkən') in Lincolnshire, on the River WITHAM, about 56 km (35 miles) northeast of Nottingham and 64 km (40 miles) west of Skegness. It is the administrative centre of LINCOLNSHIRE. A fort on its hilltop site (60 m (200 ft) above sea level) commanded the surrounding flat countryside in pre-Roman times, and it became a strategic centre of some importance during the Roman occupation, at the intersection of the FOSSE WAY and ERMINE STREET. It now possesses the only Roman city gate in Britain still used by traffic. During the period of Danish rule it was one of the FIVE BOROUGHS.

By the late Middle Ages Lincoln was one of the most important towns in England. The medieval street pattern at its heart survives, together with many original buildings, notably the 12th-century 'Jew's House' (relic of a period when Jews were being encouraged by the Normans to settle in English towns, to provide investment for trade) and **Lincoln Cathedral**, begun in 1075 and described by John Ruskin as 'the most precious piece of architecture in the British Isles'. Its many-statued west front is Norman, but the building was devastated by an earthquake in 1185, and most of the rest of it, including the three towers visible for many miles around, is later medieval (the central tower, completed in 1307–11 to a height of 82 m / 269 ft, is one of the tallest in England).

> Few things in this island are so breathlessly impressive as Lincoln Cathedral, nobly crowning its hill, seen from below … There, it seems, gleaming in the sun, are the very ramparts of Heaven.
>
> J.B. Priestley: *English Journey* (1934)

The cathedral's great glory is the Angel Choir (1260), so called from the 30 figures of angels that adorn its triforium arches. The cathedral also has one of the four original copies of the Magna Carta. At 6923 sq km (2673 sq miles) the diocese of Lincoln is the largest in England.

The biggest name in medieval Lincoln was that of Robert Grosseteste (*c.*1169–1253), scholar and bishop, who is credited by some with founding the study of philosophy at Oxford. He was Bishop of Lincoln from 1235 to his death, and is buried in the cathedral transept.

By the end of the 16th century Lincoln's great days had passed (Daniel Defoe called it an 'old dying, decay'd, dirty city' in his *A Tour Through the Whole Island of Great Britain* (1724–6) and quoted an old saying: 'Lincoln was, London is, and York shall be'), and it now has the role of a relatively modest country town.

The composer William Byrd (1543–1623), the conductors Reginald Goodall (1901–90) and Neville Marriner (b.1924) and the actor Jim Broadbent (b. 1949) were born in Lincoln.

There are several towns and cities called Lincoln in the USA (notably Lincoln, the capital of Nebraska), but they are named after Abraham Lincoln (1809–65) rather than the English city.

Battle of Lincoln (2 February 1141). A battle in the civil war that followed the Angevin invasion of England in 1139, led by Matilda, Henry I's daughter and designated heir. The 'usurper', King Stephen, was captured.

Battle of Lincoln (20 May 1217). A battle in which supporters of Louis, dauphin of France, who were besieging Lincoln castle, were attacked and dispersed by forces loyal to the boy king Henry III.

Devil looking over Lincoln, the. A vitriolic critic or a backbiter. Thomas Fuller in *The History of the Worthies of England* (1662) says the phrase may allude either to 'the stone picture of the Devil which doth or lately did, overlook Lincoln College [in Oxford]', or to a grotesque sculpture at Lincoln Cathedral (no doubt the Lincoln Imp: *see below*).

Great Tom of Lincoln. A bell at Lincoln Cathedral weighing 5.7 tonnes (5.5 tons).

Lincoln. A breed (also called **Lincoln Longwool**) of long-woolled meat-producing sheep that originated in Lincolnshire. They are larger and heavier than the Leicester (*see under* LEICESTER).

Lincoln College. A college of Oxford University, in Turl Street, founded in 1427 by Richard Fleming, Bishop of Lincoln. Its alumni include the poet Edward Thomas, the cartoonist Osbert Lancaster, the children's author Theodor Geisel ('Dr Seuss') and the thriller writer John Le Carré.

Lincoln green. Originally, a type of green cloth first made at Lincoln (the city was for a long time an important centre of the cloth industry). Later, the term came to be applied to the bright green colour of the cloth. Its famous connection with outlaws (it was the fabric of choice for Robin Hood and his merry men) is first recorded in the early 16th century.

> The lichens and mosses, earth's first mercies, shine forth
> – The dusk of Lincoln green warming the ragged tree-bole
>
> Hugh MacDiarmid: 'On Reading Professor Ifor Williams's "Canu Aneuri" in Difficult Days', from *A Kist of Whistles* (1947)

Lincoln Handicap, the. A flat race run over 1 mile (about 1.5 km) at the DONCASTER course in March. It is the first major race of the flat-racing season. Until 1964 it was known as the **Lincolnshire Handicap** (*see under* LINCOLNSHIRE).

Lincoln Imp, the. A grotesque carving of a small gnome-like creature in the Angel Choir of Lincoln Cathedral. He has weird and prominent ears, and nurses his right leg crossed over his left. According to legend, he was turned to stone as a punishment for his misdeeds. He has become something of a symbol of the city (**Lincoln City FC** is nicknamed the Imps) and of the county of Lincolnshire.

Lincoln judgement, the. A judgment made in 1890 by Edward Benson, Archbishop of Canterbury, which codified liturgical ritual and helped to resolve areas of dispute within the Church of England over the proper form of worship. The case arose out of charges made against the then Bishop of Lincoln of improper ritualism.

Lincoln Red. A breed of red shorthorn dairy and beef cattle that originated in Lincolnshire.

Lincoln, Rutland and Stamford Mercury. A newspaper, one of the oldest in England, said to have been established in 1695.

Lincoln say. A type of fine serge material formerly made in Lincoln.

Lincoln twine. (A cloth woven from) a type of thread formerly made in Lincoln.

Little St Hugh of Lincoln. A nine-year-old boy (1245–55) whose body was found in a well in Lincoln. Twenty local Jews were accused of killing him and were hanged. Miracles were associated with him and he was canonized. He figures in Chaucer's 'Prioress's Tale'. *See also* St William of Norwich *under* NORWICH.

St Hugh of Lincoln. A French-born saint (*c*.1140–1200) who from 1186 until his death was Bishop of Lincoln. He was the first Carthusian to be canonized. It was he who undertook the rebuilding of the cathedral after it was nearly destroyed in an earthquake (*see above*).

Lincolnshire From LINCOLN + SHIRE. The name *Lincolnshire* is first recorded in the 11th century.

A county in eastern England. At 5921 sq km (2286 sq miles) it is the fourth-largest county in England. It is bounded to the east by the NORTH SEA, to the south by Leicestershire, Rutland, Cambridgeshire, Norfolk and the WASH, to the west by Nottinghamshire and South Yorkshire, and to the north by the HUMBER estuary. Before 1974 it was divided up into the three administrative regions of HOLLAND[1], KESTEVEN and LINDSEY. In 1974 it was unified into a single structure, but its northern part was hived off into the new county of HUMBERSIDE. In 1996 Humberside was abolished and its territory south of the Humber transformed into the two new unitary authorities of NORTH LINCOLNSHIRE, centred on Scunthorpe, and NORTH EAST LINCOLNSHIRE, centred on GRIMSBY and CLEETHORPES.

In addition to those towns, the main centres in Lincolnshire are LINCOLN (its administrative centre), BOSTON, GRANTHAM, LOUTH[1], SLEAFORD, SKEGNESS, SPALDING and STAMFORD. Its chief rivers, aside from the Humber, are the Bain, the NENE, the WELLAND and the WITHAM. It is for the most part flat, and much of the south is taken up with the FENS, but it does manage to raise itself at least on to an elbow in two places, the **Lincolnshire Edge** (known locally as 'the Heights' or 'the Cliff'), a limestone escarpment running east to west on which the city of Lincoln is situated, and the **Lincolnshire Wolds**, a range of chalk hills running northeast–southwest in the eastern part of the county. It is overwhelmingly agricultural (and horticultural): the county supplies Britain with a cornucopia of vegetables, from potatoes to asparagus and virtually everything in between; its pigs are famous, as are their products – **Lincolnshire sausages**, made with sage and thyme, and **Lincolnshire chine**, a cut of cured pork from between the shoulder blades, stuffed with green herbs; and a large proportion of the bulbs and other plants grown in British gardens come from Lincolnshire. There is, though, industrial development in the northern part (in the former Humberside), and coastal resorts such as Skegness, MABLETHORPE and Cleethorpes bring in tourist income. During the Second World War the county was dotted with RAF bomber bases from which raids on Germany were launched.

At the time of the Roman occupation of Britain, Lincolnshire was part of the territory of the British tribe known as the Coritani (*see also under* LEICESTERSHIRE). In the late 9th century AD, when the area fell under Danish control (*see* FIVE BOROUGHS), it was divided into 'wapentakes' (rather than the Anglo-Saxons' Hundreds). Lincolnshire's Danish heritage is evident in the plethora of Scandinavian-based place names in the county, including many ending in -BY.

Lincolnshire has a reputation for remoteness and mysteriousness, for being somehow semi-detached from the rest of England and not quite in the swing of modern life, a place where old ways are preserved and old secrets kept. Inhabitants of the county, especially its more southerly, fenny part, are known as **yellowbellies**, perhaps from the eels that abound there, or the yellow-stomached frog. The term dates from the late 18th century. Another nickname for a denizen of Lincolnshire, used in the 19th century and again reflecting the county's fenland associations, is a **web-foot**.

In cricketing terms Lincolnshire is a 'minor county' (the club was founded in 1906) and plays in the minor counties championship.

> Lincolnshire may be termed the aviary of England, for the wild fowl therein.
>
> Thomas Fuller: *The History of the Worthies of England* (1662)

> Lincolnshire is … singularly beautiful and … a separate country. I would like to see it with its own flag and needing passports to get in.
>
> John Betjeman: speech to the inaugural meeting of the Lincolnshire Association (1963)

Lincolnshire Curly Coat. An extinct Lincolnshire breed of pig with a curly woolly coat.

Lincolnshire Handicap, the. A flat race first run at Lincoln racecourse in 1853. In 1964 its venue was moved to DONCASTER, and its name was changed to Lincoln Handicap (*see under* LINCOLN).

Lincolnshire limestone. A bed of oolitic limestone of Upper Jurassic (Bajocian) age, extensively developed in Lincolnshire and adjoining counties.

Lincolnshire Longwool. Another name for the Lincoln Longwool breed of sheep (*see under* LINCOLN).

'Lincolnshire Poacher, The'. A traditional English folk song displaying the sunny disposition of a Lincolnshire apprentice turned poacher and his companions, who love all the world except uncorrupted gamekeepers. Benjamin Britten wrote a well-known arrangement for voice and piano.

> When I was bound apprentice in famous Lincolnshire,
> Full well I served my master for more than seven
>   year,
> Till I took up poaching as you will quickly hear;
> O 'tis my delight on a shining night, in the season
>   of the year.

One of the nicknames of the Royal Lincolnshire Regiment is 'the Poachers'.

Lincolnshire Posy. A suite for wind band (1937) by Percy Grainger, punningly described by its composer as a 'bunch of musical wildflowers', and based on folk melodies he had collected in Lincolnshire in 1905 and 1906.

Lincolnshire Red. Another name for the Lincoln Red (*see under* LINCOLN).

Lincoln's Inn Fields From *Lincoln's Inn*, an Inn of Court in Holborn that adjoins the square and whose students were using the area as a playing field as long ago as the 14th century. Lincoln's Inn itself was originally a house (*inn* in this context means 'residence') belonging to one Thomas de Lincoln, and the name was reinforced in the 1420s when new premises were taken (on the present site) near a former house of the Earl of Lincoln, by tradition a patron of the Society of the Inn. A square in Central London (WC2), in the borough of CAMDEN, to the south of High Holborn (*see under* HOLBORN) and to the east of KINGSWAY. It is the largest square in London. **Lincoln's Inn**, one of London's four surviving ancient Inns of Court (associations of lawyers with the right of conferring the rank of 'barrister'), is on its eastern side. Its transformation from a relatively open field into a residential square took place in the 1630s. It retained that character into the early 20th century, and still contains many fine 18th- and 19th-century houses (notably the one inhabited by Sir John Soane's Museum). In 1894 its gardens were opened to the public, and in the 20th century most of its buildings passed into institutional and commercial use. In the 1980s it became a favourite resting place for vagrants and the homeless.

Since the mid-19th century *Lincoln's Inn* has been a rhyming slang usage for 'fin', i.e. the hand.

Lincs. The standard written abbreviation of LINCOLNSHIRE.

Lindinis. The Roman name for ILCHESTER.

Lindisfarne This name is often interpreted as 'island of the travellers from LINDSEY' (part of Lincolnshire), OE *Lindisfara* 'Lindsey traveller' + *eg* 'island' (*see* -EY, -EA); but some connection with the FARNE ISLANDS seems possible, with the first element being OCelt *linn* 'pool', referring to the waters that cut the island off at high tide.

An island about 1.5 km (1 mile) off the coast of NORTHUMBERLAND, to which it is connected by a causeway covered at high tide. It is also known as **Holy Island**. King Oswald of Northumbria presented the island to St Aidan, who founded a monastery here in 635. In 661 **St Colman of Lindisfarne** (*c*.605–676) became abbot. He subsequently led the Celtic party at the Synod of Whitby (*see under* WHITBY) and returned to his base at Iona after the Synod went against him (and then went on to INISHBOFIN, off the west coast of Ireland). St Cuthbert was prior from 664 to 676, after which he lived as a hermit on the FARNE ISLANDS to the south; however, he was briefly Bishop of Lindisfarne prior to his death in 687. Despite his wish to be interred on Inner Farne, his body was brought back to Lindisfarne for burial, and the latter island became a place of pilgrimage. The journey of his uncorrupted corpse was far from over, however: Viking raids (foreshadowed by storms and celestial fiery serpents) forced the monks to take Cuthbert's body to the mainland in 875; it was eventually buried in DURHAM in 995. The saint's connection with the island is not forgotten, in that fossilized crinoids washed up on its shores are called St Cuthbert's beads, while offshore is the tiny St Cuthbert's Island (accessible at low tide), to which the saint would sometimes retreat.

Monks from Durham returned to the island in 1082 to establish a Benedictine priory, and it was they who renamed it Holy Island. The workmen who built the priory are said to have had miraculous help, in that they lived on bread made from air and drank wine from a never-emptying cup. There are some remains of the Benedictine priory, but none of the earlier establishment.

After the Dissolution of the Monasteries in the 16th century, the priory buildings were used as a quarry for the building of **Lindisfarne Castle**. In 1902 the castle was bought by Edward Hudson, founder of *Country Life* magazine, and interestingly adapted for use as a private house by the architect Edwin Lutyens. It is now in the care of the National Trust. The castle features in Roman Polanski's film *Cul de Sac* (1966), and also appears in the same director's film version of *Macbeth* (1972).

Lindisfarne. A Geordie folk-rock group popular in the 1970s. Their biggest hit was 'Fog on the Tyne' (*see under* TYNE[1]).

Lindisfarne Gospels, the. An illuminated manuscript, similar in decorative splendour to the later Book of Kells (*see under* KELLS[1]), produced in the early 8th century at the island's monastery, possibly to commemorate the translation of St Cuthbert's relics. The text is in Latin, with English glosses added *c*.960. The manuscript is now in the British Library.

Lindores 'pool of the stream', Gaelic *linn* 'pool' + *dobhar* 'water, stream' + English plural *-s*.

A village in Fife, 3 km (2 miles) southeast of Newburgh, and next to the small **Lindores Loch**. In the Middle Ages the now-ruined **Lindores Abbey**, dating from 1178, was an important Benedictine foundation. The Duke of Rothesay, who died mysteriously at FALKLAND Castle, was buried here in 1402.

Lindow Moss *Lindow* 'spur of land with lime trees', OE *lind* 'lime tree' + *hoh* 'hill, spur of land'; *Moss* 'swamp, bog', OE *mos* or OScand *mosi*.

An area of boggy land about 2.5 km (1.5 miles) west of WILMSLOW in Cheshire. Peat is now harvested here, and it was while cutting this in 1984 that workers discovered the well-preserved, 2000-year-old remains of a human-being. Officially designated **Lindow Man**, he became more popularly known as 'Pete Marsh'. He almost certainly died from blows to the head and garrotting, but the reason he received this treatment is not known. He now lives in a perspex box in the British Museum. The area where he was found is still treacherous enough in places to entrap unwary walkers; there are occasional stories in the local paper of unfortunate people being rescued by the fire brigade.

To the south is the village of **Lindow End**.

Lindsey Probably 'island, or dry ground in marsh, of the Lindes tribe', OCelt tribal name *Lindes* 'people of Lincoln or of the pool' (*see* LINCOLN) + OE *eg, ig* 'island' (*see* -EY, -EA).

A former administrative area (in full, the **Parts of Lindsey**) of LINCOLNSHIRE, covering the northern part of the county. The largest of the three such areas (*see also* HOLLAND[1] *and* KESTEVEN), its headquarters were in LINCOLN. In 1974 its northern part became the southern half of the new county of HUMBERSIDE, and the rest was absorbed into Lincolnshire.

Lindum. The Roman name for the settlement on the site of modern-day LINCOLN.

Lingfield Probably 'open land of the dwellers in the glade', OE *leah* (*see* -LEY) + *-inga-* (*see* -ING) + FIELD.

A small town in Surrey, about 13 km (8 miles) southeast of Reigate. **Lingfield Park** racecourse has been staging horse races, both on the flat and over the jumps, since 1894.

In this place [Lingfield] the Inhabitants are very fond of Ghirlands, or Garlands, made of Midsummer Silver, a little Herb, which continues all the Year of a bright Ash Colour, and have crowded the Church and their own Houses with them.

> John Aubrey: 'Perambulation of Surrey' (before 1697)

Linlithgow 'lake in the damp hollow', OCelt *llyn* 'lake' + *llaith* 'damp' + *cau* 'hollow'; *Linlidcu* 1138.

A royal BURGH (12th century) 26 km (16 miles) west of Edinburgh. It was formerly the county town of WEST LOTHIAN – which itself was once known as **Linlithgowshire**. Next to the town is **Linlithgow Loch** and on a low promontory extending into the loch is the well-preserved ruin of **Linlithgow Palace**. There was a royal residence here from the 12th century, but the present building dates back to the 15th century – Mary of Guise said she had never seen 'such a princely palace'. James V was born in the palace in 1512, the year his father James IV saw a ghost in Linlithgow's St Michael's Church, which warned him of his impending death. The following year James led a huge army over the border into England, but king and army were annihilated at FLODDEN. Mary Queen of Scots was also born in the palace, in 1542, reportedly prompting her dying father to predict of the Stuart line: 'It cam' wi' a lass, and it'll gang wi' a lass.' The palace was badly damaged by fire when it was occupied by Hanoverian forces during the 1745 Jacobite Rising.

Linlithgow measures. The old standard Scottish dry measures (for measuring dry goods such as grain). They were entrusted to the safekeeping of the burgh of Linlithgow from 1617 to 1824.

Linney Head Possibly from Welsh *llyn* 'pool'.

A headland on the south coast of Pembrokeshire (formerly in Dyfed), some 10 km (6 miles) west-northwest from St Govan's Head.

Linton. *See* EAST LINTON; WEST LINTON.

Linwood 'lime-tree wood', OE *lind* 'lime tree' + *wudu* 'wood'.

A village 4 km (2.5 miles) west of Paisley in Renfrewshire (formerly in Strathclyde). In 1963 a vast automobile-assembly plant was established here by Rootes (Scotland) Ltd, and it was here that the first fully Scottish mass-production car was made – leading one poet to write of Scotland as:

> ... land of the millionaire draper, whisky vomit
> and the Hillman Imp
>
> > Tom Buchan: 'Scotland the Wee', from *Dolphins at Cochin* (1969)

The Linwood plant later came under the ownership of Chrysler, and closed in the early 1980s.

Lios an Daill. The Irish name for LISSADELL.

Lios Dúin Bhearna. The Irish name for LISDOONVARNA.

Lios Mór. The Irish name for LISMORE[2].

Lios Tuathail. The Irish name for LISTOWEL.

Lios Uaimhe. The Irish name for AUBURN.

Liphook Probably 'angle of land by the deer-leap or steep slope', OE *hliep* 'leap, leaping-place' + *hoc* 'angle of land'.
A town in Hampshire, about 5.5 km (3.5 miles) west of Haslemere. As a stopping-place on the old London–Portsmouth road it had a number of coaching inns, notably the 17th-century Royal Anchor Hotel, where Queen Victoria stayed. The nearby Waggoners Wells, a series of ponds originally dug for the iron industry, are now a beauty spot.

Lisburn Etymology uncertain: the first element comes from the Irish name *Lios na gCearrbhach* 'enclosure or ring fort of the gamblers' (gambling apparently took place at the sites of old forts near the town). The Irish name was first anglicized as *Lisnagarvey*, and in 1663 the name *Lisburn* was adopted, the second element traditionally said to refer to the siege of 1641, when town and castle were burnt by the native Irish during the rising of that year.
A town on the River LAGAN in County Antrim, 10 km (6 miles) southwest of Belfast. It is the administrative centre of the local authority district of the same name, created in 1973. In 1609 James VI and I granted Lisburn to Sir Fulke Conway, who planted it with English, Scottish and Welsh settlers. A castle was built in 1627, and both town and castle were burnt during the rebellion of 1641. Huguenot refugees arrived at the end of the 17th century and helped to develop the linen industry. The Protestant cathedral (1625) has a memorial to the writer and high-church prelate Jeremy Taylor (1613–67), who lived in Lisburn when he was Bishop of Down and Connor (1661–7), in which role he had a number of run-ins with the local Presbyterians, or 'Scotch spiders' as he preferred to call them.

Lisburn was the birthplace of General Henry Munro (1758–98), hanged in the town for his role in the Rebellion of 1798; of General John Nicholson (1821–57), a hero of the Indian Mutiny; and of the eminent Victorian courtesan Laura Bell, London's 'Queen of Whoredom', who later found God and became 'God's Ambassadress'.

Lisdoonvarna Irish *Lios Dúin Bhearna* 'enclosure of the gapped fort'.
A spa and resort in the BURREN of County Clare, some 30 km (20 miles) northwest of Ennis. It is celebrated for annual matchmaking festival, billed as 'Europe's Largest Singles Event', and for the annual music festival held here (1978–83), which played host to artists such as Jackson Browne, Emmylou Harris, Van Morrison, Rory Gallagher and Planxty, whose Christy Moore wrote the song '**Lisdoonvarna**' celebrating the festival:

> Clannad were playin' Harry's Game
> Christy was singin' Nancy Spain
> Mary O'Hara and Brush Shields

> Together singin' The Four Green Fields
> Van the Man and Emmylou
> Moving Hearts and Planxty too.

The festival became known as 'Grandson of Woodstock', and was revived in 2003, although Clare County Council refused to grant a site licence so the event had to be held in DUBLIN.

Liskeard Probably 'Kerwyd's court', Cornish *lis* 'court' + male personal name *Kerwyd*.
A hilltop market town (pronounced 'liskard') in Cornwall, to the south of Bodmin Moor and about 19 km (12 miles) east of BODMIN. In former times it was one of the Cornish stannary towns (*see under* STANNARIES) where the purity of the locally mined tin was tested. Its church is the second-largest in Cornwall.

> Our task is the defence of Liskeard. None of us can quite make out why anyone should want to attack it. Even the CO says he cannot rid himself of a sense of unreality.
>
> Evelyn Waugh: *Diaries* (17 July 1940)

There is a town called New Liskeard in Ontario, Canada.

Lismore[1] 'big enclosure' or 'big garden', Gaelic *lios* 'enclosure' (or 'residence, garden, fort, palace') + *mòr* 'big'.
A long thin island some 12 km (7.5 miles) north of Oban, at the entrance to LOCH LINNHE, in Argyll and Bute (formerly in Strathclyde). A monastery was founded here *c*.561–4 by the Irish missionary St Moluag. According to the legend, St Moluag and his rival St Mulhac agreed to a boat race across Loch Linnhe to Lismore, with the first to touch the island being entitled to found a monastery there. On the verge of losing, St Moluag cut off one of his fingers and threw it to the shore, thereby winning. (This is a variation on a not uncommon Celtic tale; *see*, for example, the Red Hand of Ulster *under* ULSTER.) The place where he established his monastery is called Kilmoluaig (Gaelic, 'Moluag's church').

In the 13th century Lismore became the seat of a separate diocese of Argyll at the request of John the Englishman, Bishop of Dunkeld and Argyll, who could not get his tongue round the Gaelic. The new bishops were called *Episcopi Lismorenses* until their seat was moved in the early 16th century. Part of the small cathedral has been restored as the parish church.

There is a town called Lismore in Australia (New South Wales), thought to have been named after the Scottish island rather than the Irish town.

Book of the Dean of Lismore, The. A collection of Scottish and Irish Gaelic poetry compiled in 1512–26 by Sir James MacGregor (*c*.1480–1551), Dean of Lismore, and his brother Duncan. The poems date from the 14th to the 16th centuries, and the poets represented include Fionnlagh Ruadh, Giolla Coluim mac an Ollaimh, Giolla Críost Brúilingeach,

Aithbhreac Inghean Coirceadail and Isabella, Countess of Argyll.

Lismore² Irish *Lios Mór* 'big enclosure'.

A market town on the River BLACKWATER² in County Waterford, some 30 km (19 miles) southwest of Clonmel. A monastery was founded here by St Cárthach (d.637/8), reaching the height of its fame under **St Colmán of Lismore** (d.*c*.702), who became abbot here in 689. The monastery survived sackings by the Vikings to take part in the reforms of the 12th century. In 1185 the future King John built a castle here, which became the bishops' residence until the 14th century; it later came into the hands of the Boyle family, who were earls of CORK, and the renowned scientist Robert Boyle (1627–91) was born here. In 1748 the castle was acquired via marriage by William Cavendish, later Duke of Devonshire and prime minister (1756–70). Fragments of the castle are incorporated into the present 19th-century building.

Lismore was also the birthplace of the travel writer Dervla Murphy (b.1931), and gave its name to a famous range of Waterford glass (*see under* WATERFORD).

Book of Lismore, The. A 15th-century compilation of saint's lives together with secular material, found in a wall of Lismore Castle in 1814. It is not to be confused with the *Book of the Dean of Lismore* (*see under* LISMORE¹).

Liss 'court, chief house in a district', OCelt *lis*.

A town in Hampshire, on the main road (A3) and railway from London to Portsmouth, about 5 km (3 miles) northeast of Petersfield.

Lissadell Irish *Lios an Daill* 'enclosure of the blind man or seer'; the story behind the name is unknown.

An area of County SLIGO, part of the peninsula on the north side of Sligo Bay, some 10 km (6 miles) northwest of Sligo itself. Lissadell was home to the Gore-Booth family for some 400 years, and the present **Lissadell House**, an imposing neo-Grecian edifice, dates from the 1830s. It was home to Eva (1870–1926) and Constance Gore-Booth (1868–1927); the former was a suffragette and poet, while the latter, as Countess Markievicz, became a noted Irish revolutionary and the first woman MP ever to be elected to Westminster (although, being a Sinn Féiner, she refused to take her seat; *see also under* ST STEPHEN'S GREEN). W.B. Yeats visited them here in their youth, and remembered them after their deaths in a poem:

> The light of evening, Lissadell,
> Great windows open to the south,
> Two girls in silk kimonos, both
> Beautiful, one a gazelle.

> W.B. Yeats: 'In Memory of Eva Gore-Booth and Con
> Markiewicz [*sic*]', from *The Winding Stair and Other
> Poems* (1933)

Another poet also paid his homage:

> Child running wild in woods of Lissadell:
> Young lady from the Big House, seen
> In a flowered dress gathering wild flowers …

> Cecil Day-Lewis: 'Remembering Con Markievicz'

The Gore-Booths sold the house in 2003.

Lissoy. The former Irish name for AUBURN.

Listowel Irish *Lios Tuathail* 'enclosure or ring fort of Tuathal'.

A town on the River Feale in County Kerry, 23 km (14 miles) northeast of Tralee. Listowel Writers' Week has been held here every May since 1970, and the Listowel races are held in the third week of each September

Listowel was the birthplace of the writer John B. Keane (b.1928), author of the play *The Field* (1965, film version 1990); Lord Kitchener (1850–1916), the British field marshal, was born near the town.

Litherland 'sloping fields', OScand *hlithar*, possessive of *hlith* 'slope' + *land* 'cultivated land'.

A northern suburb of LIVERPOOL, Merseyside (formerly in Lancashire), 3 km (2 miles) north of Bootle.

Little Aberdeen. A nickname for the area around HEBBURN, motivated by the high numbers of shipyard workers here.

Little America. A nickname for GROSVENOR SQUARE.

Little Barbary From the *Barbary* Coast of North Africa, a haunt of pirates between the 16th and 18th centuries.

A colloquial nickname in the 17th and 18th centuries for WAPPING, at that time a tough port area where robbery and mugging were endemic.

Littleborough 'small stronghold', OE *lytel* 'small' + *burh* (*see* BURY).

A town in Greater Manchester, 6 km (4 miles) northeast of Rochdale.

Little Britain Originally *Bretonstreet*, after Robert le Bretoun, a local 13th-century landowner. *Little Britain*, first recorded in the early 17th century, may indicate that the street was in an area lived in by people from Brittany, France (Little Britain is an old name for Brittany). The dukes of Brittany had a house here before the 16th century.

A street in the City of London (EC1), leading southwestwards from SMITHFIELD to ALDERSGATE STREET. It was noted from the 16th to the 18th centuries for its booksellers, and the *Spectator* magazine was first produced here in 1711. The offices of Mr Jaggers, the lawyer in Dickens's *Great Expectations* (1861), are in Little Britain.

> Little Britain may truly be called the heart's core of the city, the stronghold of true John Bullism.

> Washington Irving: 'Little Britain', in *The Sketch Book*
> (1819–20)

Little Britain is also the title of an offbeat BBC Radio 4 comedy-sketch series (2003) 'exploring British life in Britain as it is lived by Britons today in Britain'. The show was subsequently transferred to television, with great success.

Little Clacton. *See under* CLACTON-ON-SEA.

Little Cumbrae. *See* CUMBRAES.

Little England Beyond Wales. A name given to the southwestern part of PEMBROKESHIRE since the Middle Ages, when many English immigrants settled here.
See also LANDSKER LINE.

Little Germany. A nickname for a part of BRADFORD once associated with German-Jewish merchants working in the textile trade.

Little Gidding *Little* in contrast with Great Gidding, a village about 1.5 km (1 mile) to the northwest; *Gidding* probably '(settlement of) Gydda's people', OE male personal name *Gydda* + *-ingas* (*see* -ING).
A hamlet in Cambridgeshire (before 1974 in Huntingdonshire), about 16 km (10 miles) northwest of Huntingdon. The poet T.S. Eliot gave its name to the last part (1942) of his *Four Quartets*. It takes as its inspiration the religious community established here in 1625 by Nicholas Ferrar (1592–1637) and broken up by Puritans in 1646.

> You are here to kneel
> Where prayer has been valid …
> We shall not cease from exploration
> And the end of all our exploring
> Will be to arrive where we started
> And know the place for the first time.
>
> T.S. Eliot: 'Little Gidding' (1942)

See also EAST COKER.

Littlehampton Originally *Hampton* 'home-farm, homestead', OE HAM + *tun* (*see* -TON). The *Little-*, first recorded in the late 15th century, may have been added to distinguish the place from SOUTHAMPTON.
A town and seaside resort on the WEST SUSSEX coast, at the mouth of the River ARUN, about 10 km (6 miles) west of Worthing. In the past it was a small but important port, importing Caen stone from Normandy for church- and castle-building, and offering a passenger service to and from France, but in the early 19th century it cashed in on the seaside craze and turned itself into a small-scale, low-profile version of Brighton.

The poet Samuel Taylor Coleridge holidayed in Littlehampton for a month in 1817, and wrote 'Fancy in the Clouds: A Marine Sonnet' – on a piece of seaweed. The strip of poetical algae sold for £7770 at Christie's in 2004.

Anita Roddick, founder of the Body Shop, was born in Littlehampton in 1942.

> Come harum scarum collier lads for 'Hampton town we steer,

> We face all kinds of weather and we likes a drop of beer.
> Some people say how rough we are but merrily are we,
> The money we earn so hard at sea we spend on land so free.
>
> Anon.: 'Littlehampton Collier Lads' (about the men on the coal barges that sailed from Newcastle to Littlehampton)

Little Hautbois *Hautbois* originally *Hobbesse*, probably 'marshy meadow with tussocks or hummocks', OE *hobb* 'tussock, hummock' + *wisc, wisse* 'marshy meadow'; later Frenchified, perhaps influenced by French *hautbois* 'tall trees'.
A village (pronounced 'hoe-bis' or 'hobbis') in Norfolk, in the BURE Valley, about 13 km (8 miles) north of Norwich.

Little Lever *Lever* OE *læfer* 'rushes'; *Little* distinguishes it from the (now smaller) village of Darcy Lever nearby.
A town in Greater Manchester, 4 km (2.5 miles) southeast of BOLTON, with which it is virtually contiguous. It was formerly a mining area, the first recorded pit here dating from 1370.

Little London Perhaps so named as humorous references to the rate of house-building in these areas.
The name given to three villages – in East Sussex (about 10 km / 6 miles southeast of Uckfield), Hampshire (about 5 km / 3 miles northeast of Andover) and southern Lincolnshire (about 19 km / 12 miles east of Spalding, south of the WASH). It is also the name of a southwestern suburb of SPALDING, and of a village on the Isle of Man, 8 km (5 miles) northeast of Peel.

Little Minch, the. *See under* the MINCHES.

Little Missenden. *See under* GREAT MISSENDEN.

Little Mis Tor. *See under* MIS TOR.

Little Moreton Hall. *See under* CONGLETON.

Little Moscow. A nickname given to CHOPWELL in Tyne and Wear, MAERDY in South Wales and FINSBURY in London, because of their socialist (or communist) associations at various times.
See also MOSCOW.

Little Ormes Head. *See under* GREAT ORME.

Little Ouse *Ouse see* GREAT OUSE.
A river in Suffolk and Norfolk, which rises to the west of DISS and flows 37 km (23 miles) westwards through THETFORD and then northwards to join the GREAT OUSE about 12 km (7.5 miles) south of DOWNHAM MARKET. For much of its course it marks the boundary between SUFFOLK and NORFOLK.

Little Rollright. *See under* ROLLRIGHT.

Little Snoring *Snoring see* GREAT SNORING.
A village in north Norfolk, about 3 km (2 miles) south of GREAT SNORING. There is an airfield to the northeast.

Little Solsbury Hill The etymology of *Solsbury* is obscure; the first element may be OE *sol* 'mud' or a personal name; the second is likely to be OE *burh* 'stronghold' (*see* BURY).

A hill in Bath and North East Somerset, 4 km (2.5 miles) northeast of Bath, between Swainswick and Batheaston. From its flat hill-top (190m / 624 ft), which covers 9 ha (22 acres) and has the remains of an early Iron Age camp, there are extensive views over the AVON[2] valley, the city of Bath, and five counties. Solsbury Hill has belonged to the National Trust since 1930.

> Climbing up on Solsbury Hill
> I could see the city light
> Wind was blowing, time stood still
> Eagle flew out of the night
>> Peter Gabriel: 'Solsbury Hill' (1977) (song)

Little Sparta. The large garden of the cottage of Stonypath near the village of Dunsyre, South Lanarkshire, created out of bare moorland by the concrete poet and artist Ian Hamilton Finlay (b.1925). The artist moved to Stonypath in 1966, and the garden features many of his sculptures and poems inscribed on stone and wood. The name of the garden reflects the strong Classical influences behind Finlay's work. Sir Roy Strong has called Little Sparta 'the only really original garden made in this country since 1945'.

Little Switzerland. A nickname used widely in the UK for areas of valley, gorge and mountain, such as for DOVEDALE[1], the Afan Forest Park (*see under* AFAN) and (perhaps ironically) part of the HUMBER foreshore.

Little Tew. *See under* GREAT TEW.

Little Venice Coined apparently in the period between the two world wars, although in the 19th century both Lord Byron and Robert Browning had noted a resemblance to the canal-dominated cityscape of Venice.

A small area of West London (W2) around the GRAND UNION CANAL, in the City of Westminster. Just to the north of the A40(M) and bisected by Warwick Avenue, its leafy limpid charm makes it a haven in this somewhat unpre-possessing part of London. Its tone has been moderately artistic and bohemian (musicians and painters such as Lennox Berkeley, Lucien Freud and Feliks Topolsky made it their home, and Lady Diana Cooper was also a resident).

Little Wenlock. *See under* MUCH WENLOCK.

Little Whernside. *See under* WHERNSIDE.

Little Whingeing. In the *Harry Potter* novels of J.K. Rowling, a fictional Surrey village that is the home of Petunia and Vernon Dursley, the aunt and uncle who bring up Harry after his parents are murdered by Voldemort. The Dursleys live at 4 Privet Drive, an address amply redolent of the suburban narrowness that is their hallmark. *See also* DURSLEY.

Liverpool 'muddy pool', OE *lifer* 'thick, muddy' + *pol* 'pool, creek'.

A city, port and metropolitan borough on the Mersey in Merseyside (formerly in Lancashire), 50 km (31 miles) west of Manchester. An inhabitant of Liverpool is a **Liverpudlian** or a **Scouse or Scouser** (*see below*), and the city is sometimes nicknamed **the Pool**.

In 1207 King John issued a charter for a new town on the site of the present city. Liverpool developed as a port in the Middle Ages, serving the trade with Ireland, and also dispatching troops thither. The growth of the American trade from the later 17th century was the real impetus for the growth of Liverpool, the port making enormous profits from the slave-based Golden Triangle, also called the **Liverpool Triangle** (*see below*). In the 1720s Defoe found the place much enlarged since his first visit in 1680:

> Liverpoole is one of the wonders of Britain ... The town has now an opulent, flourishing and increasing trade, not rivalling Bristol ... but is in a fair way to exceed and eclipse it ... there is no town in England, London excepted, that can equal Liverpoole for the fineness of the streets, and beauty of the buildings ...
>> Daniel Defoe: *A Tour Through the Whole Island of Great Britain* (1724–6)

Later in the 18th century, Liverpool became linked to the industrial heartlands of Lancashire and Yorkshire by a series of canals. By 1801 Liverpool had outstripped Bristol in size, and by 1901 its population had increased tenfold – partly due to massive immigration from Ireland, especially during the Great Famine of 1845–8. Liverpool was also one of the main ports out of which hundreds of thousands of poor emigrants sailed to the colonies.

> It's not the leaving of Liverpool that grieves me,
> But my darling when I think of you ....
>> 'The Leaving of Liverpool', traditional song, arranged by Stan Kelly (1961)

Spiritually as well as physically the city has always faced outward to the sea, turning its back on LANCASHIRE. Its business was in commerce on the high seas, not in manu-facturing (hence the saying 'the Liverpool gentleman and the Manchester man'), and in the 19th century it became perhaps the most multicultural city in Britain, populated not only by the Irish, but by Lascars, Africans, Black Amer-icans, Jews and Chinese. In 1907 an official civic book described Liverpool as 'a city without ancestors'.

The 20th century saw a decline in Liverpool's fortunes and population. During the Second World War Liverpool's Blitz was second only to that of London, and after the war the clearance of inner-city slums was accompanied by the mass movement of people out to peripheral estates.

> A feller from the Corpy, just out of planning school,
> Has told us that we've got to move right out of Liverpool.

They're moving us to Kirkby, to Skelmersdale and Speke,
But we want to stay where we used to play in Back
    Buchanan Street.

    Anon.: 'Back Buchanan Street'

Although Liverpool is still Britain's busiest Atlantic port, with ferries to the Isle of Man, Belfast and Dublin, the city has suffered from industrial decline and social impoverishment, and by the 1990s was regarded by many outsiders as the basket case of British cities. The city and its earthy inhabitants have certainly attracted their fair share of metropolitan disdain:

The folk that live in Liverpool, their heart is in their
    boots;
They go to hell like lambs, they do, because the hooter
    hoots.

    G.K. Chesterton: 'Me Heart'

In your Liverpool slums, in your Liverpool slums
You look in the dustbin for something to eat,
You find a dead rat and you think it's a treat,
In your Liverpool slums.

    English football song (aimed at fans of Liverpool FC,
    sung to the tune 'My Liverpool Home', 1980)

Do you know, if you wear a flat heel in Liverpool, they
think you're a lesbian?

    Isabella Blow, the Fashion Director of *Tatler*: quoted
    in *The Guardian* (27 November 2002)

The novelist Linda Grant, a native of the city, has written of the

... venomous derision for Liverpudlians that condemns
them as soon as they open their mouths as thieves and
scallies, rob-dogs and whiners.

    Linda Grant: in *The Guardian* (5 June 2003)

Against this one might place the view of a fellow-Northerner, the Barnsley-born poet, Donald Davie:

            More
Human warmth ...
Is possible or common
In Liverpool than in
Some spick-and-span, intact,
Still affluent city.

    Donald Davie: 'A Liverpool Epistle', from
    The Battered Wife & Other Poems (1982)

The 21st century has brought something of a revival in Liverpool's image: in 2004 'Liverpool – Mercantile Maritime City' became a UNESCO World Heritage Site, and the year before, in 2003, Liverpool beat several other British cities, including Oxford, to be nominated as European Capital of Culture in 2008. The nomination still failed to budge entirely the jokes about the stereotypically light-fingered Scouser:

Did you hear about the Pool becoming European Capital
of Culture? Now when they nick your wheels you find
your car standing on a set of library books.

One of the main prestige projects for the Year of Culture was to add a 'Fourth Grace' to the **Three Graces of Liverpool** (*see below*); but it was scrapped in 2004. The historic waterfront, especially Albert Dock, is visited every year by many thousands of tourists, attracted by the Merseyside Maritime Museum, Tate Liverpool and The Beatles Story, celebrating Liverpool's four most famous sons, who put the city on the international cultural map in the 1960s. The National Trust now cares for the houses in WOOLTON and ALLERTON where John Lennon and Paul McCartney respectively grew up. Lennon has also been honoured in the renaming of Liverpool's airport as **Liverpool John Lennon Airport** (*see also* Mersey Beat *under* MERSEY).

Other cultural institutions of the city include the Walker Art Gallery, the Royal Liverpool Philharmonic Orchestra and the Liverpool Everyman Theatre. The **University of Liverpool** was founded in 1903, while **Liverpool Polytechnic** became John Moores University in 1992. In 1984 Liverpool hosted Britain's first International Garden Festival.

AINTREE, a suburb of Liverpool, hosts the annual Grand National steeplechase, but Liverpool is above all a football-obsessed city, whose loyalties are divided principally between the two major clubs whose grounds lie at opposite ends of the city's Stanley Park: **Everton FC** (*see* EVERTON), who traditionally play in blue; and **Liverpool FC**, who traditionally play in red (hence their nickname 'the Reds'; *see also* ANFIELD). The rivalry between the two clubs, while keenly felt, does not have the combustible intensity of that between Rangers and Celtic in GLASGOW. Both Liverpudlian clubs have outstanding domestic records, Everton having won the League championship on 9 occasions and Liverpool on 18, and the latter excelled in European club competitions in the 1970s and early 1980s under such managers as Bill Shankly, Bob Paisley and Kenny Dalglish. In the 1960s Liverpool's supporters adopted as their club anthem the song 'You'll Never Walk Alone' (originally a 1963 hit for the Merseyside pop group Gerry and the Pacemakers). Since then its dirge-like cadences have drifted skywards from the mouths of what football commentators like to refer to as 'the Anfield faithful' – and especially from those gathered at the end of the ground known as the KOP.

Liverpool was the birthplace of the artist George Stubbs (1724–1806); the poet Felicia Dorothea Hemans (née Browne; 1793–1835), known especially for 'Casabianca' ('The boy stood on the burning deck ...'); the Liberal prime minister W.E. Gladstone (1809–98); the poet Arthur Hugh Clough (1819–61); the electrical engineer Sebastian Ziani de Ferranti (1864–1930); the Liberal politician Herbert Samuel (1870–1963), the first high commissioner for

Palestine, who later took the title Viscount Samuel of Mount Carmel and of Toxteth (**Liverpool 8**; *see below*); the Irish labour leader James Larkin (1876–1947); Walter Citrine (1887–1983), General Secretary of the TUC (1926–46); the Conservative politician Selwyn Lloyd (1904–78), the foreign secretary during the Suez Crisis of 1956; the actor Sir Rex Harrison (1908–1990); the novelist Nicholas Monsarrat (1910–79), author of *The Cruel Sea*; the Labour politician Eric Heffer (1922–91), who represented Liverpool Walton from 1963 to 1991; the comedian Ken Dodd (b.1927; *see* KNOTTY ASH); the novelist Beryl Bainbridge (b.1934); the poet Roger McGough (b.1937); the Beatles John Lennon (1940–80), Paul McCartney (b.1942), George Harrison (1943–2001) and Ringo Starr (formerly Richard Starkey, b.1940); the actress Rita Tushingham (b.1940); the singer and television presenter Cilla Black (b.1943); the singer-songwriter Elvis Costello (b.1955); and the conductor Sir Simon Rattle (b.1955). The liberal Tory statesman George Canning was MP for Liverpool (1812–22).

Liverpool was also the setting for the soap opera *Brookside* (devised by Phil Redmond), a long-running staple of Channel 4's programming from the channel's inception in 1982 until it was axed in 2003. Liverpool was also the location of *Z-Cars* in the 1960s (*see* NEWTOWN[2]).

There is a town called Liverpool in Canada (Nova Scotia), and another called East Liverpool in the USA (Ohio). The Liverpool Range in Australia is part of the Great Dividing Range in New South Wales, and forms the southern boundary of the Liverpool Plains.

> If you ever go across the sea to Liverpool
> Then maybe at the closing of your day,
> You can see the moon rise over Garston Gasworks
> And watch the sun go down on Dingle Bay.
>
> Anon.: 'If You Ever Go Across the Sea to Liverpool' (to the tune of 'Galway Bay' (*see under* GALWAY))

See also the DINGLE, HUYTON *and* LITHERLAND.

Emilia di Liverpool. An opera by Donizetti, first performed in 1824. The anonymous libretto is based on Vittorio Trento's *Emilia di Laverpaut*, itself after a play by Stefano Scatizzi. Emilia, having been betrayed by her fiancé, is now working penitentially in a hermitage in the 'Lancashire Mountains' that in the librettist's mind adjoin Liverpool. By coincidence, fiancé and irate father (Claudio di Liverpool, *naturellement*) turn up on the same day. A bloody outcome seems likely, but love wins out and Emilia gets her guy. The opera is also known as *L'eremitaggio di Liverpool*.

Liver bird. A fanciful bird, pronounced to rhyme with 'fiver', that first appeared on Liverpool's coat of arms around the 13th century, and two of which adorn the twin towers of the Royal Liver Exchange Building (one of the **Three Graces of Liverpool**; *see below*). Tradition holds that these curious creatures first lived by Liverpool's original 'pool',

but probably they resulted from an artist's not very skilled attempt to give a rendition of the eagle of St John the Evangelist, the patron saint of the city.

Subsequently 'Liver bird' has become a term for any young woman from Liverpool, especially when working- or lower-middle-class. The name puns on 'bird' as a colloquialism for a young woman. The term was popularized by Carla Lane's television sitcom *The Liver Birds* (1969–79; 1996) about the exploits of two of the type.

> Our Liverpool ladies will hug and kiss men,
> But a true virgin lady you'll find now and then,
> We know who is who from our perch up on high,
> And we flap our great wings every time she goes by.
> *Liver Birds are the best, tra-la-la,*
> *Liver Birds are the best; tra-la-la,*
> *Venice has pigeons, that's all that they've got,*
> *London has sparrows that cough quite a lot,*
> *We've got the best that the others have not,*
> *Our Liver Birds are the best.*
>
> Gerry Jones: 'Song of the Liver Birds' (sung to the tune of 'My Liverpool Home')

Liver Building, the. *See* **Liver bird** *above*; and **Three Graces of Liverpool** *below*.

Liverpool and Manchester Railway. A line opened on 15 September 1830, the first railway to carry both passengers and freight, and the first to link two major cities. *See also* RAINHILL.

Liverpool Bay. An area of the Irish Sea bounded on the south by North Wales and the Wirral and on the east by Lancashire (now part of Merseyside). It is fed by two major river estuaries, the DEE[2] and the MERSEY.

Liverpool Cathedral. Liverpool has two 20th-century cathedrals. The Anglican Cathedral was designed in a conventional Gothic style by George Gilbert Scott; although work began in 1904, the building was not completed until 1980. The strikingly modern crown-shaped Roman Catholic Metropolitan Cathedral of Christ the King – also known as **'Paddy's Wigwam'** or the **'Mersey Funnel'** (punning on the Mersey Tunnel and referring to its shape, somewhat like an inverted funnel) – was designed by Frederick Gibberd and consecrated in 1967. Edwin Lutyens had previously partly designed a new Catholic cathedral for Liverpool, but his plans were incomplete at his death in 1944.

> In my Liverpool home, in my Liverpool home
> We speak with an accent exceedingly rare …
> If you want a cathedral, we've got one to spare
> In my Liverpool home.
>
> Stan Kelly: 'My Liverpool Home' (sung by The Spinners; *see also* **Liverpool Resurgent** *below*)

Liverpool delft. A type of pottery produced in Liverpool between c.1710 and c.1760. The decorative motifs were often in a Chinese style.

Liverpool 8. The postal designation of TOXTETH, a district of Liverpool that has gained a certain notoriety for lawlessness.

'Liverpool Ladies'. A song by Joe Orford, celebrating a variety of Liver birds (*see above*):

> How I love the Marsh Lane girls,
> Mascara'd eyes and peroxide curls
> I love to kiss those greasy lips,
> Just to get the flavour of the curry and chips.
>> *Liverpool Ladies, Liverpool Ladies, Liverpool Ladies,*
>> *You're loved the whole world over.*

'Liverpool Lullaby'. An anonymous song, beginning with the following verse:

> Oh you are mucky kid, dirty as a dustbin lid,
> When he hears the things you did, you'll get a belt
>> off your dad.
> Oh you have your father's nose, so crimson in the
>> dark it glows,
> If you're not asleep when the boozers close,
>> you'll get a belt from your Dad.

Liverpool Oratorio. The former Beatle Paul McCartney's first venture into classical music (and some hoped it would be his last: it wasn't). Its première was in 1991, at the city's Anglican Cathedral (*see above*).

Liverpool Poets, the. A group of Liverpool writers who came to prominence in the 1960s. Their poetry is in the same playful, colloquial mode as the lyrics of The Beatles, and was often intended for public performance, sometimes with a musical accompaniment. They were also known as the **Merseyside Poets**. The best-known of the group are Brian Patten (b.1946), Roger McGough (b.1937) and Adrian Henri (1932–2000). Henri, in homage to James Ensor's painting *The Entry of Christ into Brussels*, wrote a poem entitled '**The Entry of Christ into Liverpool**' and painted a large painting with the same title. The poem begins:

> City morning. dandelionseeds blowing from
>> wasteground.
> smell of overgrown privethedges. children's voices
> in the distance. sounds from the river …

Liverpool porcelain. A type of soft-paste porcelain made in various factories in Liverpool from 1756 to 1800. Most of it was exported. Characteristics include octagonal plates, biting-snake handles and 'sticky blue' enamel.

Liverpool Resurgent. A once-controversial statue of a naked man by Jacob Epstein that towers above the entrance to Lewis's department store in Ranlegh Street. It is popularly referred to, for visibly apparent reasons, as 'Dickie Lewis', and the area below it is a popular meeting place for Liverpudlians:

> We meet under a statue exceedingly bare …
> In my Liverpool home.
>> Stan Kelly: 'My Liverpool Home' (sung by The Spinners)

Liverpool Triangle, the. A three-part trading system, also called the Golden Triangle, that developed in the later 17th century and continued to bring merchants in Liverpool and elsewhere great profits until Britain abolished the slave trade in 1807. Manufactured goods (such as Lancashire cotton textiles) were shipped from Liverpool and other British ports (such as Bristol) to West Africa, where they were traded for slaves. The slaves were taken in appalling shipboard conditions to the West Indies and the Carolinas, where they were in turn traded for plantation goods such as sugar, spice and cotton, intended for the British market.

'Long-Haired Lover from Liverpool'. An emetic number-one hit in 1972 for James ('Jimmy') Osmond, the youngest, cutest and for some the most loathsome member of the singing siblings The Osmonds. The title is no doubt a reference to the Fab Four, and if so it is a toe-curling one, as 'Little' Jimmy claims he himself will be the eponymous hirsute Lothario.

Lord Liverpool. Robert Banks Jenkinson, 2nd Earl of Liverpool (1770–1828), a Tory politician who as prime minister from 1812 to 1827 oversaw a period of rabid reaction in Britain (*see also* LIVERPOOL STREET).

Pool of Love, the. The analyst Carl Gustav Jung's description of Liverpool. Although he never visited the place, in 1927 it featured in the most significant of his 'big dreams', in which a magnolia tree with red flowers (clearly a supporter of Liverpool FC rather than Everton) grew on an island in the city square. This apparently represented the development of consciousness, and from the dream Jung acquired 'a sense of the goal of life that lay behind the crisis in Western culture'.

Scouse or **Scouser.** A nickname for an inhabitant of Liverpool, so called from lobscouse, a sailor's stew formerly popular as a local dish (and also recorded in northern Lancashire and Cumbria). Lobscouse is probably Baltic in origin: the Germans have *Labskaus*, and the Danes *skipperlabskovs*. The Liverpudlian version contains dripping, onion, carrots, turnip, potatoes and beef or lamb; some insist on either ship's biscuit or pearl barley, while in the Arctic bear or walrus may be substituted. *Lob-* may be linked to dialect *lob* 'to bubble while boiling', or 'to eat in a slurping fashion'; *-scouse* may be a word for 'soup' or 'stew'.

> Half a Leg, Half a Leg, Half a Leg of Mutton,
> Into the Pan of Scouse rolled the six Onions.
>> Anon.: Liverpool street chant, parodying Tennyson's
>> 'Charge of the Light Brigade'

The word *Scouse* also serves for the form of English spoken in Liverpool. Characteristics of this are the pronunciation of words such as *fair* and *spare* as 'fur' and 'spur', the separate sounding of the 'g' in 'long' (as normally in 'longer'), and the sounding of 't' as 'r' in words such as *matter*, giving 'marrer'. In a publicity drive for the

Liverpool 'clean streets campaign' litter was described as 'norra lorra fun'. The voice quality of the Scouse-speaker is markedly adenoidal, a feature that has puzzled phoneticians. Others, such as Alan Bennett, have just been irritated:

> There is a rising inflection in it, particularly at the end of a sentence, that gives even the most formal exchange a built-in air of grievance.

Another nickname for a native of Liverpool, obsolete since the 19th century, is **Dicky Sam**, a Lancashire dialect term.

Three Graces of Liverpool, the. The three fine Edwardian buildings on the Pier Head at Liverpool: the Port of Liverpool Building (1907), the Royal Liver Exchange Building (1911) and the Cunard Building (1916). It was planned to add a fourth Grace, a futuristic building called the Cloud, a ten-storey irregular globe designed by Will Alsop, which was to function as an exhibition space and conference centre. The project was scrapped in July 2004.

Liverpool Street Named in honour of Lord *Liverpool*, prime minister from 1812 to 1827 (*see under* LIVERPOOL).
A short street in the City of London (EC2), a turning to the west off BISHOPSGATE. The first edition of the Communist Party Manifesto was printed here in 1848.

In 1874 **Liverpool Street Station** was opened here, on the site of the former Bethlem Hospital, as the new London terminus of the Great Eastern Railway. Serving Essex and East Anglia, it is the busiest of the London railway termini. Liverpool Street Underground station, on the Central, Circle and Hammersmith & City lines, opened in 1875 (originally under the name Bishopsgate). It is valued at £200 on the Monopoly board.

When the mainline station opened, Liverpool Street was already home to another railway terminus, Broad Street Station, which opened in 1865. It served North London and DOCKLAND. It closed in 1985 and was demolished. Its name lives on, to some extent, in the Broadgate development of office towers to the west of Liverpool Street Station.

Liversedge 'Leofhere's ridge', OE male personal name + *ecg* 'edge, ridge'.
A town in West Yorkshire, 10 km (6 miles) southeast of Bradford. It forms part of the conurbation of what has been dubbed CLECKHECKMONDSEDGE.

Livingston 'Leving's town', personal name from OE *Leofing* (meaning approximately 'darling') + -TON; *Levingstone* 1301–2. Leving and his son Thurstan appear in charters of David I (reigned 1124–53).
A NEW TOWN[1] in West Lothian, between Broxburn and Bathgate, some 20 km (12 miles) west of Edinburgh. It was just a village until designated in 1962 as an overspill town for Glasgow.

Livingston FC, created in 1995 from the former Edinburgh club Meadowbank Thistle, plays at Almondvale Stadium.

Lizard, the 'court on a height', Cornish *lys* 'court' + *ardh* 'high' (*see* ARD).
A promontory (also known as **Lizard Point** or **Lizard Head**) in western Cornwall, at the eastern end of MOUNT'S BAY. It is the most southerly point in England. Just to the north is a village called **Lizard**. The projecting area of land to the south of the HELFORD River, of which the Lizard forms the tip, is known as the **Lizard Peninsula**. Its coastal scenery is spectacular, particularly at KYNANCE COVE.

The Spanish Armada was first sighted by the English off Lizard Point on 29 July (19 July, Old Style) 1588.

> The Lizard being the farewell Cape to most Ships that sail out of the British Seas.
>
> Samuel Sturmy: *The Mariner's Magazine* (1669)

> The Point itself, where England ends, has ... that vertiginous sense of the world falling away to nothing, the earth torn free of some speculative mooring.
>
> Mathew Lyons: *There and Back Again* (2004)

lizardite. A type of mineral, a basic silicate of magnesium, which is a variety of serpentine. It was so named (in 1956) because it is found in cliffs on the Lizard.

Llanarth Possibly 'hill church': the first element is Welsh *llan* 'church-site', the second may be *garth* 'hill'.
A village in Monmouthshire (formerly in Gwent), 8 km (5 miles) southeast of Abergavenny.

'To the Gentlewoman of Llanarth Hall'. A poetical lambasting. In the 18th century, the mistress of Llanarth Hall made the mistake of imprisoning the goat of the poet Evan Thomas (*c*.1710–*c*.1770), the goat having browsed too near her mansion. The injustice resulted in this tirade, the opening of which follows (translated by Gwyn Jones):

> You black-mained, horse-haired, long-faced creature,
>   What have you done to the goat, your sister?

Llanbadarn. *See* ABERYSTWYTH.

Llanbadrig. *See under* MOUSE ISLANDS.

Llanbedr Pont Steffan. The Welsh name for LAMPETER.

Llanberis 'church of St Peris', Welsh *llan* 'church-site' + name of an 11th/12th-century saint, also commemorated in the little village of Nant Peris further up the valley.
A village in SNOWDONIA, Gwynedd (formerly in Caernarvonshire), 10 km (6 miles) southeast of Caernarfon. It is a tourist centre, popular with walkers and climbers, and home to the Welsh Slate Museum (there are vast disused quarries nearby). The **Llanberis Lake Railway** runs along the side of the adjacent Llyn Padarn, and the Snowdon Mountain Railway also runs from here.

At the head of the valley in which Llanberis lies is the spectacular defile of the **Llanberis Pass** or **Pass of Llanberis**, cutting between the GLYDERS and SNOWDON. Its flanks hold a number of fine crags, and to rock-climbers it is known simply as the Pass. At the summit of the pass (356 m / 1168 ft) is the small settlement of PEN-Y-PASS.

Llanberis was the birthplace of Marged vch Ifan (1696–c.1801, reputedly), the strongest woman in Wales, who at the age of 70 could still out-wrestle all comers. The notable Welsh landscape painter Richard Wilson (1714–82) retired to live near Llanberis.

Llandaff 'church on the River Taff', Welsh *llan* 'church-site' + river name TAFF.

A town now incorporated into CARDIFF, lying some 3 km (2 miles) northwest of Cardiff's city centre. In Welsh it is spelt **Llandaf**. St Teilo (*see* LLANDEILO) established a religious foundation here in the 6th century, although Daniel Defoe reported that in his time

> they boast that this church was a house of religious worship many years before any church was founded in England, and that the Christian religion flourished here in its primitive purity, from the year 186 …
>
> Daniel Defoe: *A Tour Through the Whole Island of Great Britain* (1724–6)

The construction of the present **Llandaff Cathedral** began in 1120, when the body of St Dyfrig (*c*.450–546) was brought here from BARDSEY ISLAND to be reinterred. Building work continued through the medieval period, but by the end of the 17th century the cathedral had fallen into disrepair. It was restored in the 19th century (with input from Edward Burne-Jones, Dante Gabriel Rossetti and William Morris), only to suffer considerable bomb damage in the Second World War. Renewed restoration was completed by 1960, and the cathedral now houses stained glass designed by John Piper and Jacob Epstein's sculpture *Christ in Majesty* on an arch of reinforced concrete.

Geoffrey of Monmouth, the chronicler of the doings of King Arthur, was appointed archdeacon of Llandaff *c*.1140. Among the bishops of Llandaff have been William Morgan (1545–1604), the translator of the Bible into Welsh, and Francis Godwin (1562–1633), author of *The Man in the Moon* (1638), possibly the first work of science fiction in English. In 1772 the squire of Llandaff, Thomas Mathews, was obliged to fight two inconsequential duels with the playwright Richard Brinsley Sheridan over the favours of the latter's future wife, Elizabeth Ann Linley. Llandaff was the birthplace of Roald Dahl (1916–90), the writer of books for children, and his own childhood is described in his autobiographical *Boy*.

Llandandras. The Welsh name for PRESTEIGNE

Llandegley Welsh *llan* 'church-site' + unknown element (presumably the name of a saint).

A village in Powys, 8 km (5 miles) east of Llandrindod Wells. In 2002 a large notice appeared on the A44 near Crossgates proclaiming

> Llandegley International Airport 2½ miles

As the area round Llandegley is not only remote but also fairly mountainous, the idea of an international airport here puzzled many. The sign turned out to be an artistic gesture by Nicholas Whitehead of Newport, who hired the advertising hoarding for one year.

Llandeilo 'church of St Teilo', Welsh *llan* 'church-site' + personal name *Teilo*.

A small market town on the River TOWY in Carmarthenshire (formerly in Dyfed), 22 km (14 miles) east of Carmarthen. St Teilo (6th century) was born in Penalun, become Bishop of LLANDAFF, and died in Llandeilo. After his death the churches at these three places all fervently claimed his body. To resolve the difficulty, the monks embarked on a night of prayer, and by the morning the problem had been solved by the miraculous triplication of the corpse.

Llandeilo or **Llandeilan series.** In geology, one of the six series into which the Ordovician system is divided in Britain. It is dated between 468 million and 458 million years ago.

Llandinabo 'Iunapui's church-site', Welsh *llan* 'church-site' + male personal name *Iunapui*.

A village in Herefordshire (before 1998 in Hereford and Worcester, before 1974 in Herefordshire), about 10 km (6 miles) northwest of ROSS-ON-WYE.

Llandovery The anglicized version of the Welsh name *Llanymddyferi*, 'church by the waters', Welsh *llan* 'church-site'+ *am* 'near' + *dyfri* 'waters'.

A town near the confluence of the Brân and the TOWY, in Carmarthenshire (formerly in Dyfed), 28 km (17 miles) west of Brecon. Its Welsh name is **Llanymddyferi** (*see above*).

Llandovery series. In geology, the earliest of the four series into which the Silurian system is divided in Britain. It is dated between 438 million and 428 million years ago.

Vicar of Llandovery, the. Rhys Prichard (1579–1644), the poet-priest and author of *Canwyll y Cymry* ('the Welshman's candle', a version of the Gospels in Welsh quatrains), whose son met an awful (but appropriately avenged) fate on the road from LAMPETER.

Llandrindod Wells 'church of the Trinity', Welsh *llan* 'church-site' + *trindod* 'trinity'; *Wells* was added in the 19th century when the town became a spa.

A town in Powys (formerly in Radnorshire), 10 km (6 miles) north of Builth Wells. It is the administrative seat of POWYS. Llandrindod's chalybeate (iron salt) springs brought it popularity as a spa in the 19th century. The spa closed in the 1960s but reopened in 1983, and today Llandrindod is very much a Victorian heritage town (the railway station was 'revictorianized', according to a plaque there, in 1990).

Llandudno 'church of St Tudno', Welsh *llan* 'church-site' + personal name of a 6th-century saint.

A seaside resort on the North Wales coast in Conwy (formerly in Caernarvonshire, then in Gwynedd), some 8 km (5 miles) northwest of Colwyn Bay, situated between the GREAT ORME (on which St Tudno, after whom the town is named, built a cell) and the Little Orme.

The town developed as an up-market sea-bathing venue in the second half of the 19th century. Visitors included Matthew Arnold, Gladstone and Disraeli (careful to avoid each other), Napoleon III and Bismarck (when not at war with each other), Queen Elizabeth of Romania, and Dean Liddell and his daughters, one of whom was the model for Lewis Carroll's Alice. A family friend of the Liddells, Sir William Richmond, said that Carroll (C.L. Dodgson) visited and wrote part of *Alice in Wonderland* in Llandudno, although there appears to be considerable uncertainty about this – hence the title of the runner-up in the Diagram Prize for the Oddest Title of the Year in 2000, Michael Senior's *Did Lewis Carroll Visit Llandudno?* Whatever the truth of the matter, in 1933 the town erected a statute of the White Rabbit checking his watch on the Western Promenade, and nearby are two rocks named the Walrus and the Carpenter (but *see also* WHITBY); there is also an Alice in Wonderland Centre in the town.

> Llandudno was the sort of place that inspired old-fashioned fears of seaside crime. It made me think of poisoning and suffocation, screams behind closed doors, creatures scratching at the wainscotting. I imagined constantly that I was hearing the gasps of adulterers from the dark windows ...
>
> Paul Theroux: *The Kingdom by the Sea* (1983)

Llandudoc. The Welsh name for ST DOGMAELS.

Llanelli 'church of St Elli', Welsh *llan* 'church-site' + personal name of the possibly legendary 5th-century saint *Elli*, a daughter of King Brychan (who gave his name to BRECON), another of whose daughters may have given her name to MERTHYR TYDFIL.

An industrial town and former port on Burry Inlet, in Carmarthenshire (formerly in Dyfed), 17 km (10 miles) west of Swansea. Tin plate has traditionally been an important industry, and the town was formerly dubbed **Tinopolis**. The tin-plate industry is reflected in Llanelli's civic emblem, a saucepan, and red tin saucepans also top the goal posts of 'the Scarlets', the town's celebrated rugby union club (who beat the All Blacks in 1972 and will not let you forget it). Founded in 1872 or 1876, **Llanelli RFC** has played its home games at Stradey Park since 1904. A host of celebrated Welsh international rugby players have played for the club,

including Carwyn James, Delme Thomas, Phil Bennett, Barry John, Derek Quinnell, Ray Gravell, Ieuan Evans and Scott Quinnell. In rugby union's professional era Llanelli has two rugby-playing incarnations: the **Llanelli Scarlets**, playing in the (professional) Celtic League; and Llanelli RFC, playing in the (semi-professional) Welsh premiership.

The rugby song '*Sosban Fach*' (Welsh, 'little saucepan') is particularly associated with the town:

> Lionel Jospin's socialism is popular in Wales: in Llanelli they sing Jospin Fach.
>
> Rhodri Morgan: the Welsh Labour leader was thus quoted in *The Times* (11 February 2000)

Stepney Street in Llanelli gave its name to the Stepney wheel (*see under* STEPNEY).

Llanelli was the birthplace of the musician Donald Swann (1923–94), who formed a successful comedy partnership with the lyricist Michael Flanders. Swann's place of birth did not prevent him from singing such lines as

> The Welshman's dishonest, he cheats when he can,
> And little and dark – more like monkey than man.
> He works underground with a lamp in his hat,
> And he sings far too loud, far too often, and flat.
>
> Michael Flanders (with Donald Swann): 'A Song of Patriotic Prejudice', from *At the Drop of Another Hat* (1964)

Although Llanelli is generally a law-abiding town, in 2002 it was reported that a number of its citizens were substituting cooking oil at 32p per litre for diesel at 73p a litre in their cars and vans. The practice came to light when the local Asda conducted a stock-taking operation, and found that sales of cooking oil had rocketed. Once this came to the attention of HM Customs and Excise, a special police 'Frying Squad' was set up to track down duty-dodgers. Vehicles whose exhaust fumes smelt of fish-and-chip shops were stopped, and a number of convictions resulted.

Llanelwy. The Welsh name for ST ASAPH.

Llanerchaeron 'clearing by the river Aeron', Welsh *llanerch* 'clearing, glade' + river name *Aeron*.

A house and estate in Ceredigion, 4 km (2.5 miles) east of ABERAERON. In a good state of preservation, it passed to the National Trust in 1989, and represents a good example of John Nash's early style: it was built in 1794–6. Its former agricultural and dairy self-sufficiency has today translated into an organic farm.

Llanfairfechan 'little church of St Mary', Welsh *llan* 'church-site' + *Maire* 'Mary' + *bechan* 'little'.

A small seaside resort on Conwy Bay, facing Anglesey, in Conwy (formerly in Caernarvonshire), 11 km (6.5 miles) northeast of Bangor.

Llanfair PG. A more convenient form for Llanfairpwllgwyngyllgogerychwyrndrobwllllandysiliogogogoch.

Llanfairpwllgwyngyllgogerychwyrndrobwllllan-dysiliogogogoch Welsh 'St Mary's Church in the hollow of white hazel near a rapid whirlpool and the Church of St Tysilio near the red cave'.

A tiny village in ANGLESEY (formerly in Gwynedd), little more than a train station, about 1 km (0.6 miles) west of Menai Bridge. It is widely vaunted as the longest place name in Britain, although the proprietors of the Fairbourne and Barmouth Railway attempted to outdo it with a halt named GORSAFAWDDACHA'IDRAIGODANHEDDOGLEDDOLLÔNPEN-RHYNAREURDRAETHCEREDIGION, while in 2004 the villagers of Llanfynydd in Carmarthenshire came up with the temporary LLANHYFRYDDAWELLLEHYNAFOLYBARCUDPRINDAN-FYGYTHIADTRIENUSYRHAFNAUOLE. The name of the Anglesey village (more conveniently referred to as **Llanfair PG**) was originally no more than the first five syllables until the 1880s, when a tailor from Menai Bridge – with the tourist trade in mind – added the rest. Britain's first Women's Institute was founded here in 1915.

For the shortest place name in Britain, *see* AE.

Llanfair Waterdine 'St Mary's church in the watery (or wet) valley', Welsh *llan* 'church site' + *Mair* 'Mary' + OE *wæter* 'water' + *denu* 'valley'.

A village in Shropshire, on the Welsh border, to the west of OFFA'S DYKE, about 29 km (18 miles) west of Ludlow.

Llanfihangel 'church of the Archangel Michael', Welsh *llan* 'church-site'+ *Mihangel*, Welsh for Michael the Archangel.

There are two score or more places of this name in Wales, and to distinguish them a suffix is usually supplied, e.g. **Llanfihangel uwch-gwili** (Carmarthenshire; '... above the River Gwili'), **Llanfihangel-Tal-y-llyn** (Powys; '... at the head of the lake'), and **Llanfihangel-y-pennant** (Gwynedd; '... at the head of the valley') A variant is **Llanmihangel** (Vale of Glamorgan).

Llanfyllin 'church of St Myllin', Welsh *llan* 'church-site' + personal name of the 7th-century Irish saint *Myllin*.

A small market town in Powys (formerly in Montgomeryshire), 14 km (8.5 miles) northwest of Welshpool. The Well of St Myllin (after whom the town is named) has reputedly curative properties.

Llanfynydd. *See* LLANHYFRYDDAWELLLEHYNAFOLYBAR-CUDPRINDANFYGYTHIADTRIENUSYRHAFNAUOLE.

Llangattock-Vibon-Avel 'church of St Cadog', Welsh *llan* 'church-site' + personal name of the 6th-century saint *Cadog*; the remaining elements are obscure.

A village in Monmouthshire (formerly in Gwent), 6 km (4 miles) northwest of Monmouth.

Llangefni 'church on the River Cefni', Welsh *llan* 'church-site' + river name of unknown meaning but possibly from *cafn* 'a hollow'.

A town in the middle of ANGLESEY, of which it is the administrative seat (it was formerly in Gwynedd). It is 10 km (6 miles) northwest of Menai Bridge.

Llangollen 'church of St Collen', Welsh *llan* 'church-site' + name of the 7th-century saint *Collen*.

A town on the River DEE[2] in Denbighshire (formerly in Clwyd), 15 km (9 miles) southwest of Wrexham. It is in the narrow and picturesque **Vale of Llangollen**, which cuts between the BERWYN MOUNTAINS to the south and Eglwyseg Mountain to the north. The 14th-century bridge at Llangollen is listed among the SEVEN WONDERS OF NORTH WALES. The town has an annual international music festival or eisteddfod, and during the 2002 festival it became possible for a week to use the new European currency in Llangollen, making the town the first part of Britain to join the euro zone. Earlier Continental European visitors (including some whose judgment should be respected) were less enthusiastic about Llangollen's musical charms:

> Here I am in Wales ... a harpist sits in the lobby of every inn of repute playing so-called folk melodies at you – i.e. dreadful, vulgar, fake stuff, and *simultaneously* a hurdy-gurdy is tootling out melodies ... it's even given me a toothache.
>
> Felix Mendelssohn: letter to Zelter from Llangollen (8 August 1829)

Llangollen was probably the birthplace of Huw Morus (1622–1709), one of the finest Welsh poets of the 17th century.

Just to the north of the town are VALLE CRUCIS ABBEY, ELISEG'S PILLAR and CASTELL DINAS BRÂN.

Ladies of Llangollen, the. Lady Eleanor Butler (?1738–1821) and Miss Sarah Ponsonby (?1748–1831), a famous cross-dressing (but apparently chaste) couple who defied their families to settle together at Plas Newydd near Llangollen in the 1770s. 'Living', according to one scholar, 'the Gothic Pastoral Romance', they there ran a model farm for some 50 years, assisted by Flirt the dog and Mrs Tatters the cat. Many curious celebrities called by, including Edmund Burke, William Wordsworth (who wrote them a sonnet), Robert Southey, the Duke of Wellington, Thomas De Quincey, Sir Walter Scott and the Darwins. Scott, who saw them in their twilight years, described them as 'a couple of hazy or crazy old sailors' dressed like 'two respectable superannuated clergymen'. The Swan of LICHFIELD, Anna Seward, wrote *Llangollen Vale* (1796) in memory of her visit:

> Now with a Vestal lustre glows the Vale,
> Thine, sacred Friendship, permanent as pure;
> In vain the stern Authorities assail,
> In vain Persuasion spreads her silken lure,
> High-born, and high-endow'd, the peerless Twain,
> Pant for coy Nature's charms 'mid silent dale,
> and plain.

Llangollen Canal. A canal extending from Llangollen northeastward to join the Shropshire Union Canal near Nantwich, Cheshire. Near the town of Llangollen is Pont Cysylltau, the longest aqueduct in Britain (19 spans), designed by Thomas Telford to carry the canal over the River DEE[2].

Llangorse Lake 'church in the marsh', Welsh *llan* 'church-site' + *cors* 'reeds, marsh'.
A lake in Powys (formerly in Brecknockshire), 8 km (5 miles) east of Brecon. It was formerly known to the English as **Brecknock Mere**:

> Here we saw Brecknock-Mere, a large or long lake of water, two or three miles over. They take abundance of good fish in this lake, so that as is said of the river Thysse in Hungary; they say this lake is two thirds water, and one third fish. The country people affirm, there stood a city once here, but, that by the judgement of Heaven, for the sin of its inhabitants, it sunk into the earth, and the water rose up in the place of it.
>
> Daniel Defoe: *A Tour Through the Whole Island of Great Britain* (1724–6)

Llangrove 'long grove or copse', OE *lang* 'long' + *graf* 'grove' (the *Ll*-spelling was introduced, possibly at the instigation of the Post Office, in the 19th century, as being appropriate in an area with many place names of Welsh origin beginning with *Llan*-).
A village in Herefordshire (before 1998 in Hereford and Worcester, before 1974 in Herefordshire), near the Welsh border, about 10 km (6 miles) southwest of ROSS-ON-WYE.

Llangurig 'church of St Curig', Welsh *llan* 'church-site' + name of a saint, *Curig* Llwyd ('the holy'), Bishop of Llanbadarn Fawr in the early 8th century (so probably not the same saint commemorated in CAPEL CURIG).
A village in Powys (formerly in Montgomeryshire), 7 km (4 miles) southwest of Llanidloes. Into the early 20th century the neighbourhood of Llangurig was known for its 'white witches', who would charge 7 shillings per year per farmer to protect their stock from supernatural damage at the hands of any local 'black witches'.

Llanhilleth Possibly 'church of Hillet', Welsh *llan* 'church-site' + name of an unknown person.
A former mining village in Blaenau Gwent (formerly in Monmouthshire, then in Gwent), some 6 km (4 miles) west of Pontypool. In 2002 former miners' houses were being sold off at £100 each.

Llanhyfryddawellehynafolybarcudprindanfygythiadtrienusyrhafnauole Welsh 'a quiet beautiful village, a historic place with rare kite under threat from wretched blades'.
The name adopted for one week in 2004 by the village of Llanfynydd in Carmarthenshire as a protest against the proposal by Gamesa Energy UK to build a windfarm nearby. The name is longer (although less enduring) than the more famous LLANFAIRPWLLGWYNGYLLGOGERYCHWYRNDROBWLLLLANDYSILIOGOGOGOCH in Anglesey.

Llanidloes 'church of St Idloes', Welsh *llan* 'church-site' + name of the saint *Idloes* about whom little is known.
A small market town on the River Severn (Hafren) in Powys (formerly in Montgomeryshire), 37 km (22 miles) east of Aberystwyth. There is a notable half-timbered market hall (1600).

Llanrothal Welsh *llan* 'church-site', probably with a personal name.
A village in Herefordshire (before 1998 in Hereford and Worcester, before 1974 in Herefordshire), about 14.5 km (9 miles) southwest of Ross-on-Wye.

Llanrumney 'church on the River Rhymney', Welsh llan 'church-site' + river name RHYMNEY.
A town in Cardiff unitary authority (formerly in Glamorgan, then South Glamorgan), 6 km (4 miles) northeast of the centre of Cardiff.

Llanrwst 'church of St Gwrwst', Welsh *llan* 'church-site' + personal name of the saint *Gwrwst*, about whom little is known.
A town in the Vale of Conwy, Conwy (formerly in Denbighshire, then in Gwynedd), 5 km (3 miles) north of Betws-y-coed. The bridge over the River Conwy (early 17th century) may have been designed by the architect Inigo Jones (1573–1652), who is said to have spent some of his early life here (although he was born in London).
   William Salesbury (*c*.1520–*c*.1584), who translated the New Testament into Welsh and produced a Welsh-English dictionary, lived most of his life at Llanrwst.

Llansantffraed 'church of St Ffraid', Welsh *llan* 'church-site' + the Welsh name *Ffraid* for the Irish saint Brigid.
A village on the River USK[1] in Powys (formerly in Brecknockshire), 10 km (6 miles) southeast of Brecon. It was the birthplace of the poet Henry Vaughan (1622–95), and also his home for most of his life. He called himself 'the Silurist', after the Silures tribe that anciently inhabited this area (*see* SILURIA).
See also TOR Y FOEL.

Llanthony 'church of St Dewi on the River Hoddni', from the Welsh version of the name *Llanddewi Nant Hoddni* ('church-site in the valley of the River Hoddni'), the river name derived from *hawdd* 'gentle'.
A small village in Powys (formerly in Monmouthshire), on the east side of the BLACK MOUNTAINS, 25 km (15 miles) east of Brecon. A priory was built here in the 12th century, but was badly damaged in the revolt of Owain Glyndwr in the early 15th century. In 1807 the wealthy writer Walter Savage Landor bought the property and planned to restore

it, but he soon became embroiled in bitter disputes with the locals. He complained in a letter to Robert Southey:

> The earth contains no race of human beings so totally vile and worthless as the Welsh. I have expended in labour, within three years, nearly eight thousand pounds amongst them, yet they treat me as their greatest enemy.

After another three years Landor gave up and left for Italy, but still fondly recalled the place (if not the people):

> I loved thee by thy streams of yore,
> By distant streams I love thee more ...

For the confusingly named Llanthony Monastery, *see* CAPEL-Y-FFIN.

Llantrisant 'church of three saints', Welsh *llan* 'church-site' + *tri* 'three' + *sant* 'saint'; the saints in question are Illtud (*see* LLANTWIT MAJOR), Gwyno, and Dyfod.

A town in Rhondda Cynon Taff (formerly in Glamorgan, then in Mid Glamorgan), some 16 km (10 miles) west of Cardiff. The Royal Mint moved here from Tower Hill in 1967, prompting employees of the old Mint in London to dub Llantrisant **the Hole with the Mint** (playing on the Polo advertising tag, 'the mint with the hole'). Many centuries earlier, some of the men of Llantrisant fought for the Black Prince at the Battle of Crécy in 1346, and thereafter other Welshmen have scorned the men of Llantrisant as 'the Black Army', whose ancestors fought for the English.

In the centre of the town there is a statue to the flamboyant druidic eccentric and former Chartist agitator Dr William Price (1800–93), who on 13 January 1884 tested the law as it then stood by attempting to cremate his infant son Jesu Grist at Caerlan Fields, Llantrisant. The police intervened, but when Price appeared before Cardiff assizes he successfully demonstrated that cremation breached no existing law, and in March 1884 he successfully cremated his son's body on Caerlan Fields. The Cremation Act of 1902 followed.

Llantwit Major 'the most important church of St Illtud', from the Welsh name *Llanilltud Fawr*, Welsh *llan* 'church-site' + personal name of the 6th-century saint *Illtud* who founded a monastery here + *mawr* 'major', to distinguish it from various other churches of St Illtud in south Wales.

A small town on the south coast of Vale of Glamorgan (formerly in Glamorgan, then South Glamorgan), 14 km (8.5 miles) west of Barry. The Welsh form of the name is **Llanilltud Fawr**. The monastery founded here by St Illtud *c*.500 was an important early centre of learning in post-Roman Britain; both St David and St Patrick were probably educated here, and it was from here that St Patrick was supposedly seized by pirates and taken to Ireland.

Llantydewi. The Welsh name for ST DOGWELLS.

Llanwern. *See under* NEWPORT[1].

Llanwrtyd Wells *Llanwrtyd* from the nearby village of Llanwrtyd, meaning 'church of Gwrtud', Welsh *llan* 'church-site' + name of an unknown person (the church here is actually dedicated to St David).

A small spa town in Powys (formerly in Brecknockshire), 17 km (10 miles) west-southwest of Builth Wells. It developed in the 18th century, after the local vicar noted a particularly perky frog jumping from Ffynon Droellwyd ('stinking well'), a sulphurous spring.

Llanyblodwel 'the church at Blodwell', Welsh *llan* 'church-site' + an older English name *Blodwell* 'blood spring or stream' (alluding to the colour of the water, or to some other quality or superstition).

A village in Shropshire, on the Welsh border, to the west of OFFA'S DYKE, about 8 km (5 miles) southwest of Oswestry.

Llanymddyfri. The Welsh name for LLANDOVERY.

Llanymynech 'monks' church-site', Welsh *llan* 'church-site' + *mynach* 'monk'.

A village in Shropshire, on the Welsh border, to the west of OFFA'S DYKE, about 9.5 km (6 miles) south of Oswestry.

Llareggub. The fictional Welsh village ('bugger all' reversed) in Dylan Thomas's verse play *Under Milk Wood* (1954), probably based mainly on LAUGHARNE, though sometimes credited to NEW QUAY.

Lleyn Peninsula The Welsh *Llŷn* is possibly from the name of the Lageni, an Irish tribe who came from Leinster; *Leinster* and *Lleyn* both apparently derive from this tribal name.

A peninsula in Gwynedd (formerly in Caernarvonshire) that extends some 40 km (24 miles) southwestwards into the Irish Sea, between Caernarfon Bay and Cardigan Bay. In Welsh it is **Llŷn**, and it is also referred to just as **the Lleyn**. In the northeast are the mountains known as the RIVALS, and the coast, which is designated as a National Heritage Coastline, an Area of Outstanding Natural Beauty and an Environmentally Sensitive Area, includes dramatic sea cliffs and sandy bays. Off the southwest end of the Lleyn is BARDSEY ISLAND, the 'Island of 20,000 Saints', and to the east of this is HELL'S MOUTH. Resorts include PWLLHELI and CRICIETH.

The peninsula is a bastion of the Welsh language and the heartland of Welsh nationalism, Plaid Cymru having been founded at a meeting in Pwllheli in 1925. It is also home to Britain's only herd of Wagyu cattle, a Japanese breed that produces the world's most expensive meat ('Kobe beef'), 20-oz burgers of which sell for more than $40 each in New York; part of the secret is, apparently, to massage the cows.

Lleyn. A breed of white-faced sheep resident on the peninsula.

Lliwedd Etymology unknown. As one writer, Harold Drasdo, has observed, 'Local hill farmers think hard for a minute of two, then give a studied answer, often interesting but never the same thing twice.' The Welsh word *lliwedd* means 'army, nation', but it is unclear how this might apply here.

A mountain (898 m / 2946 ft) in Gwynedd (formerly in Caernarvonshire), some 2 km (1.2 miles) southeast of the main summit of Snowdon, and forming part of the Snowdon Horseshoe (*see under* SNOWDON). In Welsh it is **Y Lliwedd**. Its northeast face, some 300 m (1000 ft) high, is the largest cliff in SNOWDONIA, and holds many classic rock climbs, mostly dating from the earlier 20th century. Possibly the first pioneer of the crag, however, was King Arthur, who, along with his knights, supposedly sleeps in some hidden crevice among ...

> ... those grey cliffs, streaked with the rain of hills,
> Bare of all verdure save where, here and there,
> A tuft of heather grows within the slits
> Of riven stone ...
>
> E.H. Young: 'The Lliwedd Raven'

Llŷn. The Welsh name for the LLEYN PENINSULA.

Llyn Brenig Possibly 'stagnant lake', Welsh *llyn* 'lake' + *breinig* 'putrid', though Welsh *breiniog* 'royal, privileged' might be kinder.

A reservoir on the border between Denbighshire and Conwy (formerly in Clwyd), 15 km (9 miles) east of Ruthin. Completed in 1976, it is used to control the water level of the River DEE[2].

Llyn Brianne Welsh *llyn* 'lake' + possibly a personal name.

A reservoir where the borders of Ceredigion, Carmarthenshire and Powys meet, 25 km (15 miles) west of Builth Wells. It was built in the 1970s to supply Swansea.

Llyn Celyn The name of the lake and the drowned village of Capel Celyn may be from Welsh *celyn* 'holly', or a personal name Celyn.

A reservoir in Gwynedd (formerly in Merioneth), 6 km (4 miles) northwest of Bala. It was completed in 1965, and supplies Liverpool. Under its waters lies the Tryweryn valley and the drowned village of **Capel Celyn**.

> There are places in Wales I don't go:
> Reservoirs that are the subconscious
> Of a people, troubled far down
> With gravestones, chapels, villages even;
> The serenity of their expression
> Revolts me, it is a pose
> For strangers ...
>
> R.S. Thomas: 'Reservoirs', from *Not That He Brought Flowers* (1968)

Llyn Clwedog 'lake of the River Clwedog', Welsh *llyn* 'lake' + river name possibly from Welsh *clywed* 'to hear', and meaning 'noisy'.

A reservoir in Powys (formerly in Montgomeryshire), 5 km (3 miles) northwest of Llanidloes. It was completed in 1968, and helps to control the levels of the SEVERN (Hafren). Its dam, 72 m (237 ft) high, is the highest in Britain.

Llyn Efyrnwy. The Welsh name for LAKE VYRNWY.

Llyn Ogwen. *See* OGWEN VALLEY.

Llyn Padarn 'lake of St Padarn', Welsh *llyn* 'lake' + a 6th-century monk and bishop, also known as Paternus of Wales.

A lake beside LLANBERIS in Gwynedd (formerly in Caernarvonshire), 6 km (4 miles) northwest from the summit of Snowdon. The **Padarn Inn** in Llanberis is a legendary climbers' pub, where Joe Brown, Don Whillans and their colleagues would meet in the 1950s.

Llyn Tegid. The Welsh name for BALA Lake.

Llyn Trawsfynydd. *See under* TRAWSFYNYDD.

Llyn y Gadair. *See under* RHYD-DDU and CADER IDRIS.

Llyn y Morwynion. *See under* ARDUDWY.

Loamshire *loam* (a kind of particularly fertile soil) + *-shire*.

An imaginary county of rural England, used as a setting by writers of fiction to avoid identification with actual towns and villages. Its earliest exponent on record is George Eliot:

> Transome Court was a large mansion ... with a park and grounds as fine as any to be seen in Loamshire.
>
> *Felix Holt* (1866)

The eponymous town of her novel *Middlemarch* (1872) is set here. The title of the aristocratic employer of the perfect butler in J.M. Barrie's play *The Admirable Crichton* (1902) was Lord Loam.

Latterly the use of the name has become somewhat derogatory, suggesting a rustic backwardness and comicality of speech scarcely a rung above MUMMERSET, or denoting a type of fiction or drama whose concerns are remote from modern urban reality:

> Look about you; survey the peculiar nullity of our drama's prevalent genre, the Loamshire play.
>
> Kenneth Tynan: *The Observer* (31 October 1954)

Used in the plural ('the Loamshires') the term denotes an equally fictitious regiment of the line.

Loanhead Probably 'head of the lane', Scots *loan* 'lane or narrow road' + *head* 'upper end'.

A town in Midlothian, 9 km (5.5 miles) south of Edinburgh. It was a coal-mining town from the 16th century until the closure of the huge Bilston Glen colliery in 1989.

Lochaber 'loch of the confluence or river mouth', *loch* (*see* LOCH, LOUGH) + ABER.

An area of the Western HIGHLANDS broadly centred on FORT WILLIAM, which was the administrative centre of the former

❖ loch, lough ❖

The element *loch* derives from an Old Celtic word, and forms of it can be found in Irish, Gaelic, Cornish and Welsh. It is not particularly common in Welsh, perhaps because of the predominant terrain, but Welsh *llwch* 'lake' may be present in AMLWCH (Anglesey), perhaps referring to a sea inlet here. The same meaning applies in the Cornish LOOE[1], from the element *logh*, and refers to the inlet of the River Looe.

The great majority of examples of the element *loch*, however, are found in Scotland and Ireland. English has borrowed few Gaelic words, but *loch* is one of them (as well as *whisk(e)y*, of course). In Irish the element is *loch* despite the fact that it has been consistently anglicized to *lough*. The term covers both sea inlets and landlocked lakes: the great sea inlets of Lough Foyle (*see under* FOYLE) and LOUGH SWILLY, and Belfast Lough (*see under* BELFAST) and CARLINGFORD LOUGH, may be compared with LOUGH NEAGH, or any of the loughs of landlocked County Westmeath, including Lough Lene, Lough Derravaragh, Lough Iron, Lough Owle, Lough Ennell (*see* LAKE COUNTY). In Scotland and the Isles the same is true: the western coast of Scotland is notched with sea lochs, from LOCH FYNE to LOCH ERIBOLL, as well as having such great freshwater lakes as LOCH NESS and LOCH LOMOND.

district of Lochaber (which also included the SMALL ISLES). The district was abolished in 1995, when HIGHLAND region became a unitary authority.

> Loquabre ... is indeed a frightful country full of hideous desert mountains and unpassable, except to the Highlanders who possess the precipices.
>
>> Daniel Defoe: *A Tour Through the Whole Island of Great Britain* (1724–6)

In Far Lochaber. The title of a novel (1888) by the Scottish writer William Black (1841–98).

Lochaber axe, the. A long-handled axe for lopping off heads, now carried only by those attending Edinburgh's Lord Provost in a ceremonial capacity. In the 18th century it seems to have been used for dealing with drunks:

> Jock Bell gaed furth to play his freaks,
> Great cause he had to rue it,
> For frae a stark Lochaber aix
> He gat a clamihewit ...
>
>> Robert Fergusson: 'Hallow-Fair' (1773) (Scots *clamihewit* 'heavy blow')

'Lochaber No More'. A song by Allan Ramsay (1686–1757) to a tune thought to be by the Irish harpist Thomas Connellan (*c*.1640–98), possibly based on a tune by his compatriot and contemporary, Myles O'Reilly. The tune is often played on its own on the pipes.

> Then glory, my Jeanie, maun plead my excuse;
> Since honour commands me, how can I refuse?
> Without it, I ne'er can have merit for thee;
> And losing thy favour, I'd better not be.
>
> I gae then, my lass, to win honour and fame:
> And if I should chance to come glorious hame,
> I'll bring a heart to thee with love running o'er.
> And then I'll leave thee and Lochaber no more.

Loch Ard 'high loch' (*see* LOCH, LOUGH) + ARD.
A small loch south of the TROSSACHS and BEN VENUE, and 3 km (2 miles) west of Aberfoyle. It was formerly in Perthshire, then in Central region, and is now in Stirling.

Loch Arkaig. *See under* ARKAIG.

Loch Avon. *See under* AVON[5].

Loch Awe 'loch of the river' (*see* LOCH, LOUGH), *Awe* Gaelic *abha*, genitive of *abh* 'river'. This interpretation matches the story below about the origin of the loch, while an alternative suggestion, Gaelic *átha* 'ford', seems topographically inappropriate.

A long narrow loch in Argyll and Bute (formerly in Strathclyde), between Oban and Inveraray. At 39 km (24 miles) it is the longest loch in Scotland. KILCHURN CASTLE is at the end of the northeast arm, and the PASS OF BRANDER at the end of the northwest arm (where there is a low dam). BEN CRUACHAN dominates the northern end of the loch, which is popular with fly fishermen.

> We walked 20 miles by the side of Loch Awe – every ten steps creating a new and beautiful picture.
>
>> John Keats: letter to Tom Keats (17–21 July 1818)

The loch was supposedly created when the Cailleach Bheur, the hag of ridges and guardian of the spring on Ben Cruachan, fell asleep one evening having failed to place a rock over the spring as was her wont. The result was a terrible flood in which all the people below drowned, and the glens filled with a new loch.
See also NEWYORK.

Loch Bél Séad. The Irish name for LOUGH BELSHADE.

Lochboisedale *Boisedale* is an OScand name, with an obscure first element + *dalr* 'valley', later made into a Gaelic name, *Loch Baghasdail*, the name of the sea loch on which the village is situated.

The main settlement on South Uist (*see under* UISTS), Western Isles (formerly in Inverness-shire). It is on the southwest of the island, and there are ferries to CASTLEBAY on Barra and MALLAIG on the mainland.

Loch Broom 'loch of the rain' (*see* LOCH, LOUGH), *Broom* Gaelic *braon* 'rain, raindrop'.

A sea loch in the northwest of HIGHLAND (formerly in Ross and Cromarty). ULLAPOOL is on its northern shore, while **Little Loch Broom** is a smaller, parallel sea loch to the west.

Loch Carron Possibly 'loch of the River Carron' (*see* LOCH, LOUGH), *Carron* Gaelic river name 'of the rocks, rocky'.

A sea loch in Wester Ross, Highland (formerly in Ross and Cromarty), some 15 km (9 miles) northeast of Kyle of Lochalsh. On the north shore is the village of **Lochcarron**, whose inhabitants were once celebrated for their swarthy complexions and were known as *Fithich dhubha Loch Carrann* (Gaelic 'black ravens of Lochcarron'). In local folklore, a wise woman who lived at the head of the loch was particularly adept at dealing with the effects of the evil eye, but in so doing always became desperately ill herself.

Loch Cé. The Irish name for LOUGH KEY.

Loch Ceara. The Irish name for LOUGH CARRA.

Loch Coirib. The Irish name for LOUGH CORRIB.

Loch Con. The Irish name for LOUGH CONN.

Loch Coruisk 'loch of the water corrie' (*see* LOCH, LOUGH), *Coruisk* Gaelic *coire* 'corrie' + *uisge* 'water'. The loch takes its name from Coir-uisg, the corrie at its northwestern end.

A remote and spectacularly situated freshwater loch cradled in the rugged arms of the vertiginous Black CUILLIN of Skye. It is a difficult 10 km (6 mile) walk north along the coast from Elgol to the loch, and the pedestrian must negotiate the infamous 'Bad Step', a rocky passage above the sea. From Loch Coruisk the short but furious Scavaig River leads down and south to a sea loch, Loch Scavaig.

Sir Walter Scott visited the loch in August 1814, aboard the cutter *Pharos*, and was duly impressed:

It is as exquisite a savage scene as Loch Katrine is a scene of romantic beauty ... Upon the whole, though I have never seen many scenes of more extensive desolation, I have never witnessed any in which it pressed more deeply upon the eye and the heart than at Loch Corriskin.

Sir Walter Scott: journal (1814)

Scott commented on 'the precipitous sheets of naked rock, down which the torrents were leaping in a hundred lines of foam': the immense wetness of the place may explain its Gaelic name. Scott reported that 'the lake was popularly called the Water-kettle' by the locals.

Scott later used Coruisk for the setting of one of Robert the Bruce's adventures in *The Lord of the Isles*:

Such are the scenes, where savage grandeur wakes
An awful thrill that softens into sighs;
Such feelings rouse them by dim Rannoch's lakes,
In dark Glencoe such gloomy raptures rise:
Or farther, where, beneath the northern skies,

Chides wild Loch-Eribol his caverns hoar –
But, be the minstrel judge, they yield the prize
Of desert dignity to that dread shore,
That sees grim Coolin rise, and hears Coriskin roar.

Sir Walter Scott: *The Lord of the Isles* (1815), Canto IV, i

A later, equally romantic visitor was J.M.W. Turner, who executed a wildly atmospheric water-colour sketch of the scene in 1831. But in spring Coruisk can also be a place of grass and flowers and calm:

Here I speak from the first of light
On Loch Coruisk's crying shore.
Each bare foot prints the oystercatching
Sand ...

W.S. Graham : 'Sgurr na Gillean Macleod: For the Makar & Childer', from *Implements in their Places* (1977)

Loch Cuan. The Irish name for Strangford Lough (*see under* STRANGFORD).

Loch Dairbhreach. The Irish name for LOUGH DERRAVARAGH.

Loch Dearg. *See* LOUGH DERG[1] *and* LOUGH DERG[2].

Loch Doon. *See under* DOON.

Loch Earn. *See under* EARN.

Lochearnhead. *See under* EARN.

Loch Eriboll 'loch by the farm on the gravel bank' (*see* LOCH, LOUGH), *Eriboll* OScand *eyri* 'gravel bank' + *bol* 'settlement'.

An inlet on the north coast of Scotland, in Highland (formerly in Sutherland), some 24 km (14.5 miles) southeast of CAPE WRATH. It takes its name from the tiny settlement of **Eriboll** on the eastern shore, a little north of which is a well-preserved broch (Iron Age tower). The loch was used as a deep-water naval anchorage during the Second World War. The place impressed Sir Walter Scott with its wildness; for the relevant quotation, *see* LOCH CORUISK.

Loch Etive. *See under* ETIVE.

Loch Ewe *Loch see* LOCH, LOUGH; *Ewe* possibly from the word that in Irish is *éo* 'yew tree' (*see* IONA).

A sea loch in northwest Highland (formerly in Ross and Cromarty), some 25 km (15 miles) north of Torridon. In it is the small **Island of Ewe**. At the head of the loch is the village of **Poolewe** (OScand *bol* 'settlement'), and just north of this is **Inverewe House** (for *Inver-* *see* ABER), with its famous gardens (in the care of the National Trust for Scotland). The sea loch is linked by the short (3 km / 2 miles) **River Ewe** to the northwest end of LOCH MAREE, which was also once known as Loch Ewe – the village at the further, southeast end is called **Kinlochewe** and there is a small settlement called **Letterewe** (Gaelic *leitir* 'hillside') on the north shore. Loch Ewe was an important naval anchorage during both world wars.

Loch Fyne 'loch of the River Fyne' (*see* LOCH, LOUGH), *Fyne* Gaelic river name *fion* 'wine'.

A long sea loch in the southwest of Argyll and Bute (formerly in Argyll, then in Strathclyde region), extending some 65 km (40 miles) northwards from the Firth of CLYDE, between the KINTYRE and COWAL peninsulas. It is joined to the Atlantic by the Crinan Canal near LOCHGILPHEAD, and near its northern end is INVERARAY, seat of the dukes of Argyll. The loch was once so renowned for its herring fishery that its name was given to the herring themselves. Its name has been spread across the UK since the late 1980s by the 23-strong (in 2004) **Loch Fyne** chain of fish restaurants, which is sister to the **Loch Fyne Oyster** company: the company owns a smokehouse and restaurant on the loch's shores.

Loch Garman. The Irish name for the port of WEXFORD.

Loch Garten. *See under* BOAT OF GARTEN.

Loch gCál. The Irish name for LOUGHGALL.

Lochgelly Possibly 'white loch' or 'bright loch', Gaelic *loch* (*see* LOCH, LOUGH) + *geal* 'white', *geallaidh* 'the shining one'. A former mining town in Fife, 3 km (2 miles) northeast of Cowdenbeath. It takes its name from **Loch Gelly**, a small loch nearby, which is now an important centre for water skiing.

The town itself was revealed in a 2004 survey to be the last place in Britain people want to live, in that its house prices are the lowest in the country.

> Lochgelly became a byword for gloom. Shops are boarded up; houses lie derelict. Only undertakers and deep-fried food dealers appear to thrive. It is the Scottish mining town they forgot to shut up.
>
> Stephen Khan: *The Observer* (25 January 2004)

However, with Edinburgh only 40 minutes drive away, prices are on the up and there are rumours of good times just around the corner.

Lochgelly. A tawse (a leather strap with thongs). These were manufactured in Lochgelly, and used in Scottish schools as an instrument of corporal punishment until the later 20th century.

Lochgilphead 'head of Loch Gilp', Gaelic *loch* (*see* LOCH, LOUGH) + possibly *gilp* 'chisel'.

A resort town 30 km (20 miles) southwest of Inveraray, on Loch Gilp, an inlet of LOCH FYNE, in Argyll and Bute, of which it is the administrative centre. It was formerly in Strathclyde, and is near the CRINAN CANAL.

Loch Hourn *Loch see* LOCH, LOUGH; *Hourn* possibly from Gaelic *iutharn* 'hell' or *sòrn* 'furnace'.

A remote and beautiful sea loch in the Highland (formerly in Inverness-shire), bounded by the Sound of Sleat (*see under* SLEAT) to the west and KNOYDART to the south. The only access roads are at CORRAN on the north shore and at **Kinloch Hourn** ('head of Loch Hourn') at the eastern end of the loch.

Lochinvar 'loch on the summit', Gaelic *loch* (*see* LOCH, LOUGH) +*an* 'on the' + *bharra* 'summit'.

A small, remote hill loch 5 km (3 miles) northeast of Dalry, beneath Hog Hill, in what was Kircudbrightshire, and is now Dumfries and Galloway. On a tiny island there are the ruins of a castle, the reputed home of Sir Walter Scott's dashing hero, who carries off his beloved from the altar before she can wed another:

> O young Lochinvar is come out of the West,
> Through all the wide border his steed was the best;
> And save his good broadsword, he weapons had none,
> He rode all unarm'd, and he rode all alone.
> So faithful in love, and so dauntless in war,
> There never was knight like the young Lochinvar.
>
> Sir Walter Scott: *Marmion* (1808), Canto V

In parodies Lochinvar comes out of the West, 'wearing his shirt and his Sunday vest'.

The Gordons of Lochinvar were a local noble family, based at Kenmure Castle near New Galloway. After her defeat at LANGSIDE (1568), Gordon of Lochinvar helped Mary Queen of Scots by supplying her with a disguise as she fled towards England.

The local writer S.R. Crockett wrote a novel entitled *Lochinvar* (1897), and there is a Lochinvar National Park in Zambia.

Lochinver 'loch at the mouth of the river', Gaelic *loch* (*see* LOCH, LOUGH) + *inbhir* 'confluence' (*see* ABER).

A small but important fishing port on the far northwest coast of Scotland, in Highland (formerly in Sutherland), some 30 km (18 miles) north of Ullapool. Norman MacCaig, who spent many holidays in these parts, wrote a poem entitled 'Midnight, Lochinver' (in *A Common Grace*, 1960).

Loch Katrine 'loch of the wood of Eriu' (*see* LOCH, LOUGH), *Katrine* OCelt CED + *Eriu*, probably a river name.

A loch adjoining the TROSSACHS, in the southern Highlands, 13 km (8 miles) west of Callander. It was formerly in Perthshire, then in Central region, and is now in the unitary authority of Stirling. William Wordsworth and his sister Dorothy took a boat trip on the lake in 1803, and William wrote the poem 'Stepping Westward' after an evening walk beside the loch:

> The dewy ground was dark and cold;
> Behind all gloomy to behold;
> And stepping westward seem'd to be
> A kind of *heavenly* destiny ...

Samuel Taylor Coleridge, who accompanied them on this tour, granted that it was 'a fine body of water', but, missing the fields and cottages of the LAKE DISTRICT, complained that 'the mountains were all too dreary'. However, after some further and more intimate exploration, his enthusiasm for the loch's wild environs increased.

Loch Katrine's popularity as a tourist destination followed the publication in 1810 of Sir Walter Scott's long poem set in the 16th century, *The Lady of the Lake*. Scott's publisher, Robert Cadell, remarked of the poem's immediate success:

> Crowds set off to the scenery of Loch Katrine, till then comparatively unknown; and as the book came out just before the season for excursions, every house and inn in that neighbourhood was crammed with a constant succession of visitors.

In Scott's poem the 'lake' is first seen by a hunter pursuing a stag:

> And thus an airy point he won,
> Where, gleaming with the setting sun,
> One burnish'd sheet of living gold,
> Loch Katrine lay beneath him roll'd,
> In all her length far winding lay,
> With promontory, creek, and bay,
> And islands that, empurpled bright,
> Floated amid the livelier light,
> And mountains, that like giants stand,
> To sentinel enchanted land.
>
>   Canto 1, stanza 14

Soon afterwards the Lady of the Lake herself, Ellen Douglas, appears rowing a skiff. Rossini's opera *La donna del lago* (1819) is based on Scott's poem. One of the small islands in the loch is called **Ellen's Isle** (where the MacGregors hid their stolen cattle), and the tourist steamer that has for many years plied its trade on Loch Katrine is called SS *Sir Walter Scott*.

Between 1855 and 1860 an aqueduct 40 km (25 miles) long was built from Loch Katrine to reservoirs at Milnagavie, north of Glasgow, to provide the city's main water supply. It was the first such scheme in Britain.

'Athole Highlanders' Farewell to Loch Katrine, The'. A march tune by W. Rose.

Loch Ken. *See under* DEE[3] *and the* GLENKENS.

Loch Kishorn 'loch of Kishorn' (*see* LOCH, LOUGH), etymology obscure, although it has been suggested that the first element of *Kishorn* is OScand *keis* 'jutting out'.

A sea loch in Wester Ross, Highland (formerly in Ross and Cromarty), some 12 km (7 miles) north of Kyle of Lochalsh, and forming the northerly branch of LOCH CARRON. It is fed by the short **River Kishorn**, and because of its great depth was selected in the 1970s as the site for the construction of oil-rig platforms for the North Sea. The construction workers were known for their toughness:

> We're the Kishorn Commandos way up in Wester Ross,
> We've never had a gaffer, we've never had a boss,
> But we'll build the biggest oil-rig you've ever come across,
> Remember we're the Kishorn Commandos.

> Gordon Menzies: 'The Kishorn Commandos' (as sung by Gaberlunzie, who noted 'Kishorn Commandos was written after a 9 a.m. session of singing with the men working at the Howard Dorris construction camp on Loch Kishorn. They are a very special breed, and we are proud that they have adopted this song as something of an anthem.')

The Kishorn workers also feature in a short story by James Kelman, in his collection *Not Not While the Giro* (1983). The site was closed down and tidied up in the 1990s.

Loch Laggan 'loch of the little hollow' (*see* LOCH, LOUGH), *Laggan* Gaelic *lagan*, diminutive of *lag* 'hollow'.

A loch in the central HIGHLANDS, now enlarged by a dam, on the route between FORT WILLIAM and Speyside (*see under* SPEY). It is in Highland (formerly in Inverness-shire), some 21 km (13 miles) southwest of Newtonmore. At the northeast end of the loch is the small settlement of **Kinloch Laggan**, while a further 10 km (6 miles) to the northeast is the settlement of **Laggan** itself. Sir Edwin Landseer painted a portrait of Queen Victoria sketching by Loch Laggan, during her stay at Ardverikie House on the south side of the loch, which is also the location of the BBC television drama series *Monarch of the Glen* (*see under* ARDVERIKIE).

Goodwife of Laggan, the. A witch who features in a story from the 17th century. She was an apparently virtuous resident of the village of Laggan, but was exposed by a local hunter and witch-finder, whose hounds tore her flesh until she was obliged to turn into a raven to escape. The Goodwife was subsequently lynched by her fellow residents.

Lochlea. *See under* MAUCHLINE *and* TARBOLTON.

Loch Leven[1] Probably 'elm water' (*see* LOCH, LOUGH), *Leven* from an OCelt river name *Lemona* found in many other places in Britain, and coming into Gaelic as *leamhain* 'elm water'.

A loch in Perth and Kinross (formerly in Kinross-shire, and then in Tayside region), just east of the town of Kinross. It is nearly round, and at its widest is some 5 km (3 miles) across. It is the source of the **River Leven**, which flows eastward through Fife for some 20 km (12 miles), entering the Firth of Forth at the little town of **Leven**, once an important port, just to the northeast of Buckhaven and Methil.

Loch Leven is noted for its fishing and for its wildfowl. There are several islands. The largest, St Serfs, has the ruins of a priory, which may date back to the 9th century. The chronicler Andrew of Wyntoun (*c*.1350–*c*.1423) was prior here until his retirement in 1421. On a smaller island is a 14th-century castle where Mary Queen of Scots was imprisoned on 17 June 1567 after her defeat at CARBERRY HILL, and was here forced to abdicate on 24 June by James

Douglas, 4th Earl of Morton, who became regent for Mary's son, the infant James VI. Mary escaped on 2 May 1568 with the help of a (very likely love-struck) pageboy, Willie Douglas, who managed to get hold of the castle keys, locked up Mary's jailers and threw the keys in the loch – where they were found some 300 years later. Mary met her final defeat shortly afterwards at LANGSIDE. These events appear in Sir Walter Scott's novel *The Abbot* (1820).

General Alexander Leslie (c.1580–1661) was created 1st Earl of Leven by Charles I in 1641. Despite this, Leslie led the Scottish army on the Parliamentarian side in 1644–6, and handed over Charles to Parliament in 1647. However, in 1650–1 he led the Scots in resisting Cromwell's invasion.

Gentle Poet of Lochleven, the. The byname of the poet Michael Bruce (1746–67). He was born in the village of Kinnesswood near the eastern shore of the loch, and spent much of his boyhood herding sheep on the adjacent Lomond Hills. Later, as a young schoolmaster dying of consumption at Forrest Mill near Alloa, he recalled this time in his long poem *Lochleven*, which closes thus:

> Thus sung the youth, amid unfertile wilds
> And nameless deserts, unpoetic ground!
> Far from his friends he stray'd, recording thus
> The dear remembrance of his native fields,
> To cheer the tedious night, while slow disease
> Prey'd on his pining vitals, and the blasts
> Of dark December shook his humble cot.

Lochleven trout. A subspecies of brown trout, *Salmo trutta*, which has been introduced to many other parts of the world.

Loch Leven[2]. A sea loch extending some 16 km (10 miles) east from LOCH LINNHE, in Highland unitary authority. Near its mouth a car ferry once crossed the loch, linking North and South BALLACHULISH, but this was replaced by a bridge in 1975. The loch passes the mouth of GLEN COE, and at the head of the loch is the village of **Kinlochleven**, which grew up around the aluminium works built here in 1908. At the village the **River Leven** joins Loch Leven, having as its source the Blackwater Reservoir, some 5 km (3 miles) east of the village. Kinlochleven is on the West Highland Way (*see under* the HIGHLANDS), and is linked to Glen Coe by the DEVIL'S STAIRCASE.

Loch Leven[3]. The old name for LOCH LOMOND.

Loch Linnhe 'pool loch' (*see* LOCH, LOUGH), Gaelic *linne* 'pool'. A long sea loch in Argyll and Bute (formerly in Argyll, then bordering Strathclyde and Highland Regions), at the southern end of the GREAT GLEN and the CALEDONIAN CANAL. It stretches some 55 km (33 miles) from the Firth of LORNE in the southwest to FORT WILLIAM at its north-eastern end.

Loch Lochy From the River Lochy (*see also* LOCH, LOUGH), *Lochy* from Gaelic *lòchaidh* 'dark one'. St Adamnan in his *Life of St Columba* refers to the river as *Nigra Dea* (Latin, 'black goddess'), evidently deriving it from OCelt *loch* 'black' + *dea* 'goddess'.

A freshwater loch near the southwest end of the GREAT GLEN, Highland (formerly in Inverness-shire), 13 km (8 miles) northeast of Fort William. It forms part of the CALEDONIAN CANAL. The short **River Lochy** flows southwest from Loch Lochy to meet LOCH LINNHE near INVERLOCHY. There is reputedly a monster (dubbed 'Lizzie') in Loch Lochy, with sightings reported in 1929, 1930 and 1960.

Loch Lomond From BEN LOMOND.

A loch in the southern HIGHLANDS, some 26 km (16 miles) northwest of the centre of Glasgow. The boundary between Argyll and Bute and the unitary authority of Stirling runs down the middle of the loch, and the southern shore is in West Dunbartonshire. It was formerly in the county of Dunbartonshire, and then in Strathclyde region.

Loch Lomond was earlier known as **Loch Leven** (possibly from a Brittonic word for 'flood', although it is more likely to do with elms, as in LOCH LEVEN[1]):

> *De magno lacu Lummonu, qui Anglice vocatur Lochleuen in regione Pictorum.*
> (Of the great lake Lummonu, which is in English called Loch Leven, in the region of the Picts.)
> Nennius (*fl.*769): *Historia Brittonum*, chapter heading

The outflow from the loch is the River Leven, which joins the Firth of Clyde at Dumbarton. In the 18th century the novelist Tobias Smollett, whose family lived nearby, addressed the river thus:

> On Leven's banks, while free to rove,
> And tune the rural pipe to love,
> I envied not the happiest swain
> That ever trod the Arcadian plain.
> Pure stream! in whose transparent wave
> My youthful limbs I wont to lave;
> No torrents stain thy limpid source,
> No rocks impede thy dimpling course,
> That sweetly warbles o'er its bed,
> With white, round, polish'd pebbles spread.
> 'To Leven Water'

At 71 sq km (28 sq miles) Loch Lomond is Britain's largest lake by area although a mere puddle compared to Ireland's LOUGH NEAGH. There are many wooded islands, mostly in the wider southern half of the loch, while shapely mountains ring the northern half. However, the loch failed to impress one visitor from the Lake District:

> Who ever travelled along the banks of Loch-Lomond, variegated as the lower part is by islands, without feeling that a speedier termination of the long vista of blank

water would be acceptable; and without wishing for an interposition of green meadows, trees, and cottages, and a sparkling stream to run by his side?

> William Wordsworth: *Topographical Description of the Country of the Lakes in the North of England* (1810, revised 1820)

Coleridge (who travelled with the Wordsworths up Loch Lomond-side in 1803) more succinctly agreed, remarking:

> Every where there is a distressing sense of local unrememberableness.
>
> Samuel Taylor Coleridge: journal (25 August 1803)

Keats, on the other hand, experienced a different kind of disappointment at this 'blue place among the mountains':

> Steam Boats on Loch Lomond and Barouches on its sides take a little from the Pleasure of such romantic chaps as Brown and I.
>
> John Keats: letter to Tom Keats (17 July 1818) (However, he did note that 'the north End of Loch Lomond [is] grand in excess'.)

The West Highland Way (*see under* the HIGHLANDS) follows the (largely roadless) eastern shore, passing under Ben Lomond and by INVERSNAID towards the north end of the loch. South of Inversnaid there is Rob Roy's Prison; it is said that he extracted information from his captives by ducking them into the loch on the end of a rope. There is also a Rob Roy's Cave north of Inversnaid, where Robert the Bruce may have hidden in 1306.

The **Loch Lomond and the Trossachs National Park**, Scotland's first, opened in July 2002, and takes in the loch and its shores, including Ben Lomond.

See also TARBERT.

'Bonnie Banks of Loch Lomond, The'. An old Jacobite song, the words of which were polished by Lady John Scott (1810–1900). The chorus goes:

> Oh, ye'll tak the high road and I'll tak the low road,
> And I'll be in Scotland afore ye,
> But wae is my heart until we meet again
> On the bonnie, bonnie banks of Loch Lomond.

It is supposedly sung by a captured Jacobite soldier sentenced to be executed in the wake of the failed 1745 Rising, whose spirit will arrive home before his companion. A variant of the third line is 'But me and my sweetheart will never meet again'.

Loch Long 'long loch' (*see* LOCH, LOUGH), named for its considerable length.

A sea loch extending northwards for 27 km (17 miles) from the Firth of Clyde to ARROCHAR, in Argyll and Bute (formerly in Strathclyde).

See also TARBERT.

Loch Lubnaig 'sinuous loch' (*see* LOCH, LOUGH), *Lubnaig* Gaelic *lùb* 'bend, curve', with diminutives *-an* and *-aig*.

A loch in the southern HIGHLANDS, 5 km (3 miles) northwest of Callander, and overlooked by BEN LEDI. It was formerly in Perthshire, then in Central region, and is now in the unitary authority of Stirling. In Sue Townsend's *The Secret Diary of Adrian Mole Aged 13¾* (1982), Adrian stays in one of the Forestry Commission holiday chalets on the western shore.

Lochmaben 'loch of Mabon', Gaelic *loch* (*see* LOCH, LOUGH) + early OCelt personal name.

A small town and royal BURGH (1298) 6 km (4 miles) west of Lockerbie, on the road to Dumfries. It was formerly in Dumfriesshire, and is now in Dumfries and Galloway. A succession of castles have stood here, guarding the route north from England into Annandale (*see under* ANNAN[1]). Local tradition has Lochmaben as the birthplace of Robert the Bruce (the other claimant is TURNBERRY in South Ayrshire); certainly the town was long associated with the Bruce family.

'Lochmaben Harper, The'. A ballad telling how the 'silly blind Harper' goes to play for King Henry in Carlisle, and manages to trick him out of his stallion and a goodly sum of money. A version appears in Sir Walter Scott's *Minstrelsy of the Scottish Border* (1802–3).

'Lochmaben Hornpipe, The'. A traditional fiddle tune.

Lochmaben Stone See LOCHMABEN.

A Neolithic standing stone (in the form of a hefty lump of granite) overlooking the sea near GRETNA, at the head of the SOLWAY FIRTH (whose Norse name, meaning 'inlet of the pillar ford', refers to the Lochmaben Stone). It dates from *c*.3000 BC, and is also called the **Clochmabon Stone** (Gaelic *cloch Mabon* 'stone of Mabon'). In the Middle Ages it was a standard meeting place for the Wardens of the MARCHES from both sides of the English–Scottish border, where they would exchange prisoners and try to settle disputes peacefully.

Lochmaddy 'loch of the dogs' (*see* LOCH, LOUGH), from the sea loch on which it stands: *Loch na Maidhean*, Gaelic *na* 'of' + *madadh* 'dog', plural *maidhean*, from the dog-shaped rocks guarding its entrance, colloquially known as 'the Maddies'.

The main settlement on North Uist (*see under* the UISTS), Western Isles (formerly in Inverness-shire). It is situated in the northeast of the island, and there is a ferry service to UIG on Skye.

Loch Maree 'Loch of (St) Maree' (*see* LOCH, LOUGH); the Gaelic name is *Loch Ma-Ruibhe*, from St *Maree* or *Maelrubha* (d.722), founder of the monastery at APPLECROSS in 673, who is said to have become a hermit on Isle Maree (*Eilean Ma-Ruibhe*) and to be buried there. Before this, the loch was called Loch Ewe, which explains the name of the village of Kinlochewe at the southeastern end of the loch.

A long, beautiful loch in the Northwest HIGHLANDS, some 50 km (30 miles) north of Kyle of Lochalsh. It is in Highland (formerly in Ross and Cromarty). Impressive mountains such as SLIOCH[1] and BEINN EIGHE rise on either side, and the many wooded islands form the **Loch Maree Islands Nature Reserve**. As recently as the mid-19th century the locals participated in pre-Christian rituals on **Isle Maree**, St Maree or Maelrubha (*see above*) having become conflated with the old Celtic god Mourie. The rituals centred on a sacred well and tree: offerings of milk and sacrifices of bulls were made, and coins were inserted in to the bark of a sacred tree – a tradition upheld by Queen Victoria on her visit in 1877. Some of the rituals were conducted in order to cure the insane, and even as recently as 1868 a successful result was claimed in the case of a madman.

> Loch Mulruy [Maree] is ... compassed about with many fair and tall woods as any in the west of Scotland ... All thir bounds is compas'd and hemd in with many hills, but thois beautiful to look on, thair skirts being all adorned with wood even to the brink of the loch.
>
> Timothy Pont (attrib.): *Noates and Observations on Dyvers Parts of the Hielands and Isles of Scotland* (17th century)

The **Loch Maree Hotel** gained a certain notoriety in August 1922, when eight people – fishing guests and their ghillies – mysteriously died. After a major investigation, it was established that all had eaten the same duck paste in their sandwiches on Monday 14 August and that the paste was contaminated with the deadly microbe *Clostridium botulinum*, the cause of botulism. It was the first such outbreak recorded in Britain (although the bacterium had been notoriously rampant among German sausages in the previous century).

Loch Moidart. *See under* MOIDART.

Loch Morar Possibly 'big water' (*see* LOCH, LOUGH), *Morar* Gaelic *mòr* + OCelt *dobhar* 'water'.

A long narrow loch in the Western HIGHLANDS, formerly in Inverness-shire and now in Highland, some 4 km (2.5 miles) southeast of MALLAIG. It is the deepest freshwater lake in the British Isles, with a maximum depth of 309 m (1017 ft), its nearest rival being Loch Ness (228 / 751 ft); it is also the second deepest lake in Western Europe. The thought of such a dark and unfathomed abyss may have inspired tales of a Loch Morar monster, which had a certain vogue in the late 1960s and early 1970s (the first recorded sighting was in 1887). 'She' was dubbed Morag, and was assumed to be a relative of 'Nessie' (*see under* LOCH NESS); the excitable pondered the possibility of 50-km (30-mile) underground tunnels linking the two lochs. Whether these reports (typically from anglers out in their boats) reflected genuine sightings of a plesiosaur (thought long-extinct by palaeontologists), or resulted from the enjoyment of a hip flask at twilight, is left to the reader to judge.

Loch Morar is separated from the sea at its western end by a narrow isthmus, through which flows the short **River Morar**, and on which is situated the village of **Morar**. On the south shore of the loch is a little settlement called **Lettermorar** (Gaelic *leitir* 'hillside'), and at the eastern end is another called **Kinlochmorar**. The areas of low, nubbly hills and lochans to the north and south of the loch are called **North Morar** and **South Morar** respectively.

Lochnagar Possibly 'loch of the noise', Gaelic *loch* (*see* LOCH, LOUGH) + *na* 'of the' + *gàire* 'noise, laughter', although this interpretation may have been influenced more by Byron (*see below*) than the original elements of the name.

A mountain (1155 m / 3791 ft) in the southern Cairngorms, on the south side of Deeside, in Aberdeenshire (formerly in Grampian region). It is within the royal Balmoral estate, and is some 9 km (5.5 miles) south of Balmoral Castle. It is pronounced 'loch-na-garr' (with the stress on the final syllable), and is normally climbed from Glen Muick. Queen Victoria wrote of her ascent in 1848:

> On the summit there was a thick fog, it was cold, wet and cheerless and the wind was blowing a hurricane.

The old Gaelic name of the mountain was Beinn nan Cìochan ('mountain of the breasts'), after the various tors such as the Meikle Pap (Scots, 'big breast'). It was also known by its old Scots name, the White Mounth (Scots, 'white mountain'), snow surviving here well into the summer, while the actual summit tor is Cac Carn Beag ('slope of the little cairn'). Lochnagar was originally the name of the lochan in the spectacular, cliff-ringed northeastern corrie, but from the 18th century it was increasingly applied to the mountain itself (the name the White Mounth is now restricted to the southern slopes; but *see also* the MOUNTH). The fate of the older names was sealed following Byron's poem:

> Years have roll'd on, Loch na Garr, since I left you,
> Years must elapse ere I tread you again:
> Nature of verdure and flow'rs has bereft you,
> Yet still are you dearer than Albion's plain.
> England! thy beauties are tame and domestic
> To one who has roved o'er the mountains afar:
> O for the crags that are wild and majestic!
> The steep frowning glories of dark Loch na Garr.
>
> Lord Byron: 'Lachan y Gair' (1807)

Byron explained in his note to the poem 'Near Lachan y Gair I spent some of the early part of my life, the recollection of which has given birth to these stanzas.' The influence of the mountain on the young poet is also recalled in *The Island* (1823):

> The infant rapture still survived the boy,
> And Loch-na-gar with Ida look'd oe'r Troy,
> Mix'd Celtic memories with the Phrygian mount
> And Highland linns with Castalie's clear fount.
>
> Canto I, xii

Byron's 'crags that are wild and majestic' – with their gullies, towers and ridges of red granite – are a mecca for climbers, particularly in winter. There is a song sung by Aberdeen climbers that includes the lines:

Gasherbrum, Masherbrum, Distighil Sar,
They're very good training for Dark Lochnagar.

The mountains in the first line are Himalayan giants, and there is some justice in the boast, as the northeastern corrie of Lochnagar holds some of the hardest 'mixed' winter routes in the world.

Lochnagar Crater. The site of a First World War explosion, and one of the most visited locations on the Western Front in France. It is situated at La Boiselle, and was formed on 1 July 1916, the first day of the Battle of the Somme, by British sappers, who let off two charges under German lines. The explosion, along with 16 others, went off two minutes before the Allied attack began at 7.30 a.m. Its name derives from the fact that the sappers who dug the mine were based in 'Lochnagar', the name of the home trench of the 51st Highland Division.

Old Man of Lochnagar, The. An illustrated story for children by Prince Charles.

Royal Lochnagar. A single-malt whisky, made at the distillery at the foot of the mountain since 1845. The name derives from the fact that the distillery, close to Balmoral, supplied Queen Victoria with whisky, which she is said to have mixed with claret – a gustatory crime for which she should have been exiled from Scotland forever.

Loch Na Keal 'loch of the churches' (*see* LOCH, LOUGH), *Na Keal na* 'of the' + *ceall*, possessive plural of *cill* (*see* KIL-).
A sea loch on the west side of MULL, almost bisecting the island. It is in Argyll and Bute (formerly in Strathclyde region). The islands of Ulva and INCH KENNETH, where a colleague of St Columba set up a monastic community in the 6th century (hence the name), guard the mouth of the loch. In Thomas Campbell's poem 'Lord Ullin's Daughter' Loch Na Keal becomes 'Lochgyle' (*see* ULVA).

Loch nan Uamh. *See under* ARISAIG.

Loch nEathnach. The Irish name for LOUGH NEAGH.

Loch Ness 'loch of the River Ness' (*see* LOCH, LOUGH), *Ness* 'roaring' or possibly 'wet' river, from a pre-Celtic element *ned*. A long, narrow loch at the northeastern end of the GREAT GLEN, in Highland (formerly in Inverness-shire). It is 8 km (5 miles) south of Inverness, to which it is linked by the short **River Ness**. It is 39 km (24 miles) long, never more than 2 km (1.2 miles) wide, and, with a maximum depth of 240 m (788 ft), it is the second deepest freshwater loch in the British Isles, after LOCH MORAR (also reputedly the home of a monster; *see below*). It forms part of the CALEDONIAN CANAL linking the North Sea to the Atlantic.

In September 1953 John Cobb was killed making an attempt at the world water speed record on Loch Ness. His jet-engined boat, *Crusader*, broke up at a speed of 330.9 kph (206.8 mph) when it hit the wake of another boat. The wreckage of the *Crusader* was found in September 2002, but was left in the loch as a mark of respect. In 2003 Lloyd Scott spent 12 days walking along the bottom of the loch wearing an old-fashioned diver's suit, to raise money for children with leukaemia.

Loch Ness. A forgettable romantic film comedy (1995), starring Ted Danson and Joely Richardson, about an American scientist who travels to Scotland intending to debunk the myth of the Loch Ness Monster (*see below*).

Loch Ness Monster, the. The holy grail of cryptozoologists, known more familiarly to the general public as **Nessie** (or to Gaels as **an Niseag**). On 22 July 1933 a grey monster some 1.8 m (6 ft) long was spotted crossing a road near Loch Ness. A rash of 'sightings' followed in the 1930s, and the scholarly recalled that St Adamnan, in his life of St Columba, had mentioned that the loch was the home of an *aquatilis bestia*. Descriptions of the beast varied: in 1935 it was reported to be nearer 6 m (20 ft) and its appearance a cross between a seal and a plesiosaur, with a snake-like head at the end of a long neck and two flippers near the middle of its body. From then on, Loch Ness and its mysterious resident became continual objects of media attention. Investigations showed no substantial evidence of the supposed monster, but more recent observations have increased the belief (in some quarters) in its existence; for example, in 1987 a sonar scan of the loch revealed a moving object some 181 kg (400 lb) in weight, which scientists could not identify. The ornithologist Sir Peter Scott dubbed the creature *Nessiteras rhombopteryx*, after its appearance on a photograph taken by some Americans. The name was taken to mean 'Ness monster with the diamond-shaped fin', but crossword puzzlers pointed out that the Latin name was in fact an anagram of 'monster hoax by Sir Peter S'. More recently, experiments have shown that eager searchers readily interpret a straight fence post stuck in the water as having the curved profile of a long-necked, plesiosaur-like creature.

A visitor once to Loch Ness
Met the monster, who left him a mess.
They returned his entrails
By the regular mails
And the rest of the stuff by express.

Anon.: limerick

Sssnnnhuffffll?
Hnshuffl hhnnwfl hnfl hfl?
Gdroblbobhobngbl gbl gl g g g g glbgl.

Edwin Morgan: 'The Loch Ness Monster's Song', opening lines

Loch Nevis *See* BEN NEVIS.

A sea loch some 40 km (25 miles) to the northwest of Ben Nevis, near Mallaig. The name is thought to share the same meaning as its mountainous namesake, i.e. 'evil lake'.

Loch Quoich Possibly 'loch in the hollow', Gaelic *cuach* 'cup, bowl' (from which is derived the Scots word *quaich* for a shallow cup out of which whisky is tasted).

A loch in western Lochaber, Highland (formerly in Inverness-shire), some 30 km (20 miles) northwest of Fort William. The loch was considerably extended when it was dammed, the dam itself being the longest rock-filled dam in Britain, 38 m (126 ft) high by 320 m (1050 ft) wide. **Glen Quoich** is actually at right angles to the main part of the present loch. It was in Glen Quoich that Sir Edwin Landseer painted his famous portrait of a red deer stag, *Monarch of the Glen* (1850).

Loch Rannoch. *See under* RANNOCH.

Lochranza Possibly 'loch of the rowan river'; *Lockransay* (1433) suggests the OScand *reynir* (possessive *reynis*) 'rowan-tree' + *a* 'river'.

A village on the coast of northwest Arran, in North Ayrshire (formerly in Buteshire, then in Strathclyde region). It is on a little inlet of Kilbrannan Sound called **Loch Ranza**, and there is a ferry across the Sound to KINTYRE.

> On fair Loch-Ranza stream'd the early day,
> Thin wreaths of cottage-smoke are upward curl'd
> From the lone hamlet, which her inland bay
> And circling mountains sever from the world.
>
> Sir Walter Scott: *The Lord of the Isles* (1815), Canto V, i

Loch Rí. The Irish name for LOUGH REE.

Loch Ryan *Loch see* LOCH, LOUGH; the etymology of *Ryan* is obscure, but the name may have a root that means 'swift stream'.

A sea loch separating the northern part of the Rhinns of GALLOWAY from the mainland. At its head lies the port of STRANRAER. On the eastern shore is the port of CAIRNRYAN. **'Annie of Lochryan'.** A traditional ballad, in which the heroine meets a sad end:

> O cherry, cherry was her cheek,
> And golden was her hair;
> But clay-cauld were her rosy lips –
> Nae spark of life was there.

Loch Seaforth *Loch see* LOCH, LOUGH; *Seaforth* 'sea fjord', OScand *saer* 'sea' + *fjorthr* 'fjord, inlet'.

A sea loch separating North HARRIS from the Park peninsula of LEWIS, Western Isles. It contains **Seaforth Island**, and at its head is the village of **Seaforth Head** (Gaelic *Ceann Loch Shiphoirt*). The Mackenzies of Kintail who took over Lewis in 1610 were later made **Earls of Seaforth**, a line whose end was predicted by the Brahan Seer (*see* FORTROSE).

Seaforth Highlanders, the. A regiment founded by the Earl of Seaforth in 1777–8 as the 78th (Highland) Regiment of Foot. It was amalgamated with the Queen's Own Cameron Highlanders in 1961 to form the Queen's Own Highlanders, which in turn, in 1994, was amalgamated with the Gordon Highlanders.

Loch Shiel 'loch of the River Shiel' (*see* LOCH, LOUGH), *Shiel* a pre-Celtic river name meaning 'stream, flowing water', emerging in Gaelic as *seile*. Adamnan (*c.*700) refers to the river as good for salmon.

A long narrow loch between ARDGOUR and MOIDART, in Highland (formerly in Inverness-shire and Argyll), some 25 km (15 miles) west of Fort William. At the northeast end of the loch is GLENFINNAN, where Bonnie Prince Charlie raised his standard in the 1745 Jacobite Rebellion; the night before he had stayed with MacDonald of Glenaladale, halfway down the loch. Towards the southwest end is Dalelia House, birthplace of the Gaelic poet and Jacobite Alasdair MacMaighstir Alasdair (Captain Alasdair MacDonald, *c.*1695–*c.*1770), whose works include *Birlinn Chlann-Raghnail* (*Clanranald's Galley*).

Loch Shiel has its very own monster, long-necked and triple-humped. There have been half a dozen sightings since the first in 1874, the most recent in June 1998.

GLEN SHIEL is in an entirely different place.

Loch Shin The loch's name derives from a pre-Celtic river name meaning 'river' and cognate with SHANNON; *see also* LOCH, LOUGH.

A long narrow loch stretching 28 km (17 miles) diagonally across the far north of Scotland. It is in Highland (formerly in Sutherland), and LAIRG at its southeastern end is some 60 km (40 miles) north of Inverness.

Loch Stack. *See under* BEN STACK.

Loch Súill. The Irish name for LOUGH SWILLY.

Loch Sunart. *See under* SUNART.

Loch Tay. *See under* TAY.

Loch Thom 'Thom's loch' (*see* LOCH, LOUGH), *Thom* after Robert *Thom*, who created the reservoir in 1827.

A reservoir in the hills south of Greenock in Inverclyde (formerly in Renfrewshire, and in Strathclyde).

> The heather-edges of the water held
> Between the hills a boyhood's walk
> Up from Greenock.
>
> W.S. Graham: 'Loch Thom', from *Implements in their Places* (1977) (Graham was born and brought up in Greenock.)

Loch Torridon. *See under* TORRIDON.

Loch Trool. *See under* GLEN TROOL.

Loch Tummel. *See under* TUMMEL.

Lockerbie 'Locard's settlement', OScand personal name *Locard* + -BY.

A town 17 km (10 miles) east of Dumfries, in lower Annandale. It was formerly in Dumfriesshire, and is now in Dumfries and Galloway.

Lockerbie has become synonymous with a terrorist outrage that shocked the world, when, on the night of 21 December 1988, a Boeing 727 aircraft, Pan Am Flight 103, en route from London to New York, was blown up by a bomb as it passed high over the town, killing all 259 passengers on board and 11 people on the ground. Two Libyan suspects were named in 1991 and brought to Europe in 1999 for trial by a Scottish court at Camp Zeist in the Netherlands in 2000. One was acquitted and the other convicted (upheld on appeal in 2002).

Lockerbie lick. An old slang term for a cut or wound on the face, from the habit of the local Johnstones of slashing the faces of their defeated enemies – who tended to be Maxwells. The two clans competed for the upper hand in Annandale (*see under* ANNAN[1]) in the 16th and 17th centuries, and many of their fights took place at Lockerbie.

Loddon An OCelt river-name meaning 'muddy stream'.

A river in Hampshire and Berkshire, which rises near BASINGSTOKE and flows about 32 km (20 miles) northeastwards to join the THAMES[1] just to the north of TWYFORD[1].

Loddon lily. A flowering plant (*leucojum aestivum*) that takes its name from the River Loddon, where it was reputedly first identified and categorized. Also known as the summer snowflake or giant snowflake, the Loddon lily favours bogs, wet woodland and damp meadows.

Lodore Apparently 'low door', OScand *lagr* 'low' + OE *duru* 'door', a reference to the gap through which Watendlath Beck flows.

A waterfall in BORROWDALE, in the Lake District, Cumbria (formerly in Cumberland), just south of Derwent Water. It was celebrated enthusiastically by all three Lake Poets:

> His wizard coarse where hoary Derwent takes
> Thro' craggs, and forest glooms, and opening lakes,
> Staying his silent waves, to hear the roar
> That stuns the tremulous cliffs of high Lodore ...
>
> William Wordsworth: *An Evening Walk* (1793)

> Lodore is the Precipitation of the fallen Angels from Heaven, flight and Confusion, and Distraction, but all harmonized into one majestic Thing by the genius of Milton, who describes it. Lodore is beyond all rivalry the first and best thing of the whole Lake Country. Indeed (but we cannot judge from prints) I have seen nothing equal to it in the prints and sketches of the Scotch and Swiss Cataracts.
>
> Samuel Taylor Coleridge: letter to Sara Hutchinson (25 August 1802)

In Robert Southey's poem 'The Cataract of Lodore' (*c*.1823), he answers his little boy's question as to how the water comes down at Lodore with an ever-increasing accumulation of present participles, climaxing in the stuffed-to-bursting last verse:

> Retreating and beating and meeting and sheeting,
> Delaying and straying and playing and spraying,
> Advancing and prancing and glancing and dancing,
> Recoiling, turmoiling and toiling and boiling,
> And gleaming and streaming and steaming and beaming,
> And rushing and flushing and brushing and gushing,
> And flapping and rapping and clapping and slapping,
> And curling and whirling and purling and twirling,
> And thumping and plumping and bumping and
>   jumping,
> And dashing and flashing and splashing and clashing;
> And so never ending, but always descending,
> Sounds and motions for ever and ever are blending
> All at once and all o'er, with a mighty uproar,
> – And this way the water comes down at Lodore.

Loegria From Welsh *Lloegr* 'England', which may be related to *Ligore*, the name of the Celtic tribe from which LEICESTER derives its name.

The name used for England (south of the HUMBER) by the 12th-century chronicler Geoffrey of Monmouth (*see under* MONMOUTH) in his *Historia Regum Britanniae*. Geoffrey himself says that it was derived from *Locrine*, the name of the eldest son of Brutus, mythical first king of BRITAIN, who after his father's death ruled the middle part of the island.

See also LOGRES.

Lofthouse OScand *loft-hus* 'house with a loft'.

A village in West Yorkshire, 9 km (5.5 miles) southeast of Leeds. In March 1973 seven miners were killed in the Lofthouse pit when water and rubble from an old mine closed a century earlier broke through:

> A hundred years of coal-black water
> Waiting to be a miner's tomb,
> Trapped in the silent earth and waiting,
> A hundred years of rubble and stone.
>
>   Sam Richards: 'The Lofthouse Colliery Disaster' (1973) (song)

Many felt that if the maps of the old workings had been studied, the tragedy could have been avoided.

Loftus OScand *loft-hus* 'house with a loft'.

A small town in Redcar and Cleveland (formerly in the North Riding of Yorkshire, then in Cleveland), 23 km (14 miles) east of Middlesbrough.

The town of Junee (Aboriginal 'speak to me') in Australia (New South Wales) was originally called Loftus.

Loggerheads Possibly from the name of a public house (the present hostelry is called 'The Three Loggerheads').

A village in Staffordshire, about 24 km (15 miles) northwest of Stafford. The Battle of Blore Heath (*see under* BLORE) was fought nearby on 23 September 1459.

Logiealmond. *See under* ALMOND[2].

Log na Coille. The Irish name for LUGNAQUILLA.

Logres From LOEGRIA.

The name used for England, as in the kingdom of Arthur, in medieval romance from the 12th century onwards. Edmund Spenser in his *Faerie Queene* (1590–6) used the spelling *Logris*.

> Now ridez this renk thurgh the ryalme of Logres
> Sir Gauan, on Godez halue, thagh hym no gomen thoght.
> (Now rides this knight through the realm of Logres,
> Sir Gawain, God knows, though him no joy it gave.)
>
> Anon: *Sir Gawain and the Green Knight* (*c*.1375)

See also LOEGRIA.

Lombard Street From the *Lombard* merchants (from Lombardy in North Italy) who established banks and money-lending operations here in the late 13th century.

A street in the City of London (EC3), running southeast-wards from BANK to Gracechurch Street. It remains a street of bankers (no longer particularly Italian), and in its time has hosted the head offices of Barclays Bank and of Lloyd's. So strong is the financial connection that its name has become a virtual metonym for the City's banking sector:

> Trade then shall flourish, and ilk art
> A lively vigour shall impart
> To credit languishing and famisht,
> And Lombard-street shall be replenisht.
>
> Allan Ramsay: *Rise and Fall of Stocks* (1721)

There is a street in Paris called Rue des Lombards, which has the same origin as London's Lombard Street.

Lombard Street to a China orange. Unfeasibly long odds, the wealth of Lombard Street being infinite compared to the value of a China orange (an ordinary sweet orange – they originally came from China). In other words, the thing referred to is virtually certain. The expression appears to date from the early 19th century.

> If you didn't already know … then it's most of Lombard Street to a China Orange you'd never find out.
>
> *The Times* (30 November 1974)

Alternative formulations that have not stood the test of time are **Lombard Street to a Brummagem sixpence** (Brummagem being an old name of BIRMINGHAM), **Lombard Street to an eggshell** and **Lombard Street to ninepence**.

Lomond, Ben. *See* BEN LOMOND.

Lomond, Loch. *See* LOCH LOMOND.

Lomond Hills Possibly related to LOCH LEVEN[1], above which they rise.

A range of hills in Fife, to the east of LOCH LEVEN[1]. The most prominent points are **East Lomond** (425 m / 1394 ft) and the highest peak, **West Lomond** (522 m / 1712 ft). This pair were compared by John Buchan in *The Free Fishers* – with a perkiness surprising in a man of his generation – to twin breasts – a form they take when viewed across the Forth from the south. (However, one might observe that anatomical accuracy would require the extent of the cleavage to be reduced considerably from the present disproportionate gulf.)

Londinium. The Roman city that would become LONDON.

London Perhaps 'place at the navigable or unfordable river' (referring to a settlement downstream of the lowest fordable point on the River Thames, at Westminster), from two pre-Celtic (pre-Indo-European) roots with added Celtic suffixes. The theory that the name was based on an OCelt male personal name *Londinos*, meaning literally 'the wild or bold one', is no longer generally accepted. The notion that it comes from King *Lud*, legendary rebuilder of London, which seems to have been first put forward by the 12th-century chronicler Geoffrey of Monmouth (*see under* MONMOUTH), is attractive but quite false (*see* LUDGATE HILL).

The capital city (pronounced 'lundən') of ENGLAND and of the UNITED KINGDOM, in southeast England on the River THAMES[1]. It is one of the world's foremost financial, commercial, industrial and cultural centres. In the 19th and 20th centuries it was the administrative capital of the British Empire. It covers an area of 1579 sq km (610 sq miles) and at the turn of the 21st century had an estimated population of 7,285,000 (it had peaked at about 8,700,000 in the late 1930s).

London was founded on a naturally protected site at the lowest bridging point and highest navigable point for sea shipping on the Thames, the principal entry into England from mainland Europe. There is evidence (for example, the BATTERSEA shield) of Celtic settlement in areas of what is now INNER LONDON, but the first to establish themselves in what would become the **City of London** were the Romans, shortly after they arrived in England in AD 43. The city they built, which they called **Londinium**, was centred on the area of modern CORNHILL and LUDGATE HILL. It quickly became an important trading centre. In AD 60 the original Roman settlement was burned by Boudicca (Boadicea), the queen of the native Iceni people, but Londinium was soon rebuilt, and continued to grow in wealth and importance over the next 300 years. A permanent bridge over the Thames had been built before the end of the 1st century AD, near the site of the present **London Bridge** (*see below*), and between about 190 and 225 a substantial wall was erected around the city. Londinium became the fifth-largest conurbation in the western world.

It was the hub of Roman Britain's road system and its financial centre.

The Romans withdrew in 410 (the most notable survival of their period is the Temple of Mithras (*see under* WALBROOK[1])), and London's political status and influence waned over the succeeding centuries. It remained, however, a significant international port in the Anglo-Saxon period, and an important trading centre grew up to the west of the walled town, known as *Lundenwic* (OE, 'London trading settlement'; *see also* ALDWYCH) – the first strand in the link that would one day join London with WESTMINSTER. The old town itself – where St Æthelbert, king of Kent, founded the church of ST PAUL'S[1] in 604 – had become in anglicized form *Lundene* and also, with assorted OE suffixes, *Lundenburg* 'fortified town of London', *Lundenceaster* 'Roman town of London' and *Lundentun* 'village or estate of London'. It was sacked by the Viking Danes in 842 and 851, and had become their winter quarters by 871, but in 886 Alfred the Great recaptured the city and repaired its walls.

The Danish Cnut, king of England from 1016 to 1040, made London his capital in preference to WINCHESTER, and although Edward the Confessor subsequently moved the royal seat to Westminster, after the Norman Conquest William I designated London his joint capital with Winchester. He also built the White Tower of the TOWER OF LONDON, to protect and dominate the city.

Over the course of the Middle Ages the importance of Winchester declined, and London became the sole capital of England. But increasingly the king and court came to prefer Westminster and its palace, leaving London and its administration in the hands of its powerful merchants (their autonomy is symbolically re-enacted today whenever the sovereign wishes to enter the City of London, and has to stop at Temple Bar (*see under* TEMPLE) to receive official authorization).

Trade associations known as 'guilds' began to flourish in London from the 12th century onwards, and they came to play a more and more central role in the government of the city – for example, in nominating civic officials. The most important of these was, and is, the **Lord Mayor of London**, who is the head of the Corporation of London. The first known holder of the office was Henry Fitzailwyn, who was mayor from 1192 until his death in 1212 (the title 'Lord Mayor' was not formalized until the mid-16th century); the best-known was undoubtedly Richard (Dick) Whittington, mayor four times at the turn of the 15th century (*see* HIGHGATE). Many of the guilds (now known as 'livery companies', after the livery they wear) still survive – the Cordwainers' Company, for instance, the Fishmongers' Company and the Merchant Taylors' Company (there are some new ones too, like the Air Pilots' and Air Navigators' Guild and the Insurers' Company). Their guildhalls remain storehouses of wealth and tradition, and they continue to participate in the government of the City.

Thanks to the feverish economic activity of these guilds' members, and of the merchants who did their business via its port, London grew and prospered during the Middle Ages. Its population increased from about 20,000 at the end of the 11th century to around 80–100,000 in the 1340s. This was halved by the Black Death in 1348–9. It had recovered only to about 50,000 by 1500, but in the 16th century it spurted ahead, reaching 200,000 in 1600. London, through which about 90 per cent of England's overseas trade was done, was benefiting from the opening of new markets in America, Africa and Asia, and its increasing bureaucratic role as the country's capital was also a source of prosperity. Meanwhile, as the spaces between surrounding settlements began to fill up and the aristocracy sited their mansions to the west, along the STRAND, strengthening the link with Westminster, the physical extent of London burgeoned (laws passed in the 16th and 17th centuries to limit its growth seem to have had little effect).

During the Civil Wars, the City of London was a centre of nonconformity and gave its backing to Parliament, its support being a large factor in the defeat of Charles I (who was executed on a scaffold outside the Banqueting Hall in WHITEHALL). Disenchantment with Oliver Cromwell's regime soon set in, however, and London too welcomed the Restoration of Charles II in 1660. It soon suffered two severe setbacks: the Great Plague of 1665, which killed over 80,000 people, about one-sixth of its population; and the following year the **Great Fire of London** (*see below*). The opportunity opened up by the second of these to transform London from a squalid disease-ridden slum into a classically proportioned serene-vistaed 17th-century city was largely squandered, although its bequest to the future remains in the many surviving Wren churches of the 1670s and 1680s. The merchants of London were more interested in making money than in spending it on extravagant new townplanning schemes. It was at this time that many of the institutions that characterize the CITY as a financial centre had their beginnings: Edwin Lloyd opened his coffee house, precursor of **Lloyd's of London** and scores of other insurance houses, in 1688, and in 1694 the Bank of England was founded. By 1700 London was the largest city in western Europe, with a population of around 575,000. Significantly, only 200,000 of them lived in the City. London's expansion was gathering pace. During the 18th century the WEST END[1] became the fashionable place to live, and elegant residential streets and squares were built here, while to the east of the City the need for labour for the rapidly developing docks sowed the seeds of the EAST END. To the north, London swallowed up more and more villages and hamlets in Middlesex and Essex, establishing the pattern of GREATER LONDON as a mosaic of individual communities. Improved cross-Thames communication (the river was bridged four times in the London area in the 18th century) increasingly brought parts of Surrey and Kent within London's orbit too (joining the BOROUGH, which since at least the mid-16th century had been regarded an extramural piece of the City of London across the river).

> Perhaps the Briony who was walking in the direction of Balham was the imagined or ghostly persona. This unreal feeling was heightened when, after half an hour, she reached another High Street, more or less the same as the one she had left behind. That was all London was beyond its centre, an agglomeration of dull little towns. She made a resolution never to live in any of them.
>
> Ian McEwan: *Atonement* (2001)

> I thought of London spread out in the sun,
> Its postal districts packed like squares of wheat.
>
> Philip Larkin: 'The Whitsun Weddings' (1964)

By 1800 the population of London was well past the 1 million mark, and it continued to grow exponentially in the 19th century (6,586,000 in 1901). A major factor from the 1830s onwards was the railways: their tracks seemed to attract housing like a magnet, and within fifty years the suburbs of what is now Inner London (CAMBERWELL, CATFORD and CLAPHAM[1], CAMDEN TOWN, KENTISH TOWN and HACKNEY, EALING, EDMONTON and ENFIELD – the list goes on) had been filled in with modest dwellings for the new lower middle class of clerks and shop assistants. This rapidly growing urban organism needed a higher degree of control and management than had hitherto sufficed: the Metropolitan Police force was established in 1829; the Metropolitan Board of Sewers was set up in 1848, to help deal with the appallingly low level of public health and sanitation in the capital, followed in the 1860s by the construction of a new London sewer system by Joseph Bazalgette; and in 1855 the whole fabric of local government was overhauled, with a much smaller grouping of parishes and districts overseen by the Metropolitan Board of Works.

The nomenclature – 'Metropolitan' referring to London as a whole, not just the City – reveals the extent to which by the early 19th century the concept of an all-encompassing entity called 'London' had taken hold. 'Metropolitan' implies some sort of urban status, but before the century was over it had become apparent that London was too huge and unwieldy to be treated as a mere town. It was in many ways more analogous to a county – and accordingly in 1888 the Metropolis of London (at that time covering 303 sq km/ 116 sq miles) was officially designated a county, under the aegis of the **London County Council** (the LCC) (of which the headquarters, County Hall, designed by Ralph Knott

and erected piecemeal on the SOUTH BANK[1] between 1909 and 1933, are now home to a hotel, an aquarium and an art gallery). In 1899 the existing parishes and districts were regrouped into 28 metropolitan boroughs, excluding the City of London.

The CITY, covering an area of about 274 ha (677 acres; *see also* SQUARE MILE) continues to guard its independent status jealously – as well it might, since its financial institutions contribute handsomely to the wealth of the capital and of the country as a whole. It is governed by the Lord Mayor and the **Corporation of London**, a body that can trace its origins back to Anglo-Saxon times, and it has its own separate police force, the **City of London Police**, distinct from the Metropolitan Police (its caps have red-and-white chequered bands). Parliamentarily, though, it has joined forces with its neighbour to the west: the Central London constituency is the **Cities of London and Westminster**.

The 19th century saw the griming of London: coal smoke from millions of domestic and industrial fires smothered the capital in a blanket of soot and gloom, contributing its own sombre note to the squalor of Dickensian London.

> That great foul city of London there … rattling, growling, smoking, stinking … a ghastly heap of fermenting brickwork, pouring out poison at every pore.
>
> John Ruskin: *The Crown of Wild Olives* (1866)

The 20th century brought lethal smogs, and although the Clean Air Act (1956) returned a sparkle to London's atmosphere, its buildings remained blackened for decades afterwards – and traffic fumes soon made up for the absence of coal smoke.

London got off relatively lightly in the First World War (870 people were killed by German bombs), but in the Second it suffered grievously, both in the Blitz, which started on 7 September 1940, and later in the V1 and V2 rocket attacks. In some parts, such as the City and POPLAR, a third of the buildings were destroyed, and about 30,000 people were killed in the Greater London area. Postwar reconstruction saw communities, particularly from the East End, moved out wholesale to new towns outside London, such as HARLOW and STEVENAGE, and those that remained housed in tower blocks (then in vogue – they turned out to be social and environmental disasters, and many had been demolished by the end of the 20th century).

London seems always to have been too small for the traffic attempting to pass through it. It had been the congestion of horse-drawn vehicles in the capital that led to the development of the world's first underground steam railway in 1863, later to develop into the **London Underground**, better known as the **Tube**. But it was the advent of the motor vehicle in the 20th century that really began to fur up the city's arteries. The ring road constructed between the two world wars (*see* NORTH CIRCULAR *and* SOUTH CIRCULAR) and the M25 of the 1980s proved at best temporary palliatives, and at the beginning of the 21st century a new attempt was made to stave off gridlock by introducing a charge (the Congestion Charge) for the use of roads in the centre of the city. Exemptions are accorded to two monarchs of the London streets: the red bus, whose colour goes back to the London General Omnibus Company's original B-type bus of 1910, and has continued through the faithful Routemaster (from 1959) to the latest 'bendy buses' (an attempt to change it was seen as potentially disastrous for tourism, and vetoed); and the black cab (many now black in name only, their sides mobile advertisement hoardings, but their drivers as sterotypically opinionated and loquacious as ever).

Until well after the Second World War, London was still the UK's major port (*see also* POOL OF LONDON). Its docks covered 285 ha (700 acres) and provided employment for a significant proportion of London's East Enders. But they were too shallow for the new generation of merchant ships, and could not cope with containerization, and within a few years in the 1960s and early 1970s they had vanished. They were replaced in the 1980s by a shining new development on the Thames to the east of London, a postmodern extravaganza of housing and office building designed to offer an alternative commercial focus to the City (*see* DOCKLAND). The docks moved down the Thames to TILBURY. The 1980s, meanwhile, chimed in very nicely with London's main long-term concern – making money:

> Dear, old-fashioned, leisurely, traditional, eccentric London is a legend we have successfully sold to foreigners – even to ourselves. London fails to look splendid because it is a hard place, as hard as nails.
>
> V.S. Pritchett: *London Perceived* (1962)

The notion of London as a county had a good run, but it never really caught on (there was a **London County** cricket team, of which the star turn, lured from Gloucestershire, was W.G. Grace, but it was not admitted to the County Championship and it petered out in 1908). London continued *de facto* to swallow up portions of the HOME COUNTIES beyond its notional boundary, and in the 1960s an accommodation to the new reality was made: the LCC was abolished and a new body, the **Greater London Council** (GLC) (*see under* GREATER LONDON), covering a far larger area, was set up in its stead in 1965. However, under Labour control this managed to provoke the hostility of Margaret Thatcher's Conservative government, and in 1986 it was in its turn abolished, and most of its powers were devolved to its 32 constituent boroughs. At the beginning of the 21st century some measure of city-wide democracy was restored with the establishment of the **London Assembly** (*see below*), which works in concert with the **Mayor of London** (a new

executive post, distinct from the City's Lord Mayor, whose first incumbent was former GLC leader Ken Livingstone).

Throughout its history London has attracted those seeking political or religious freedom, a pot of gold at the rainbow's end, or simply a living. In the late 17th century French Huguenots and immigrants from the Low Countries came in large numbers (bringing their skills in weaving, brewing, glass-making, etc.). Migration from Ireland grew dramatically during the famines of the 1840s and 1850s, and in the late 1880s thousands of Jewish immigrants took up residence in the SPITALFIELDS area to escape the Russian pogroms. The shipbuilding area of LIMEHOUSE became London's first CHINATOWN. Post-Second World War labour shortages brought an influx from the Caribbean and the Indian subcontinent, and the latter part of the 20th century saw the build-up in London of communities from sources as varied as Eastern Europe, Nigeria, Korea, Cyprus, Turkey and Kurdistan (one London primary school was recorded as having pupils from 78 countries).

London in the 21st century is a world city and a collection of villages, with a vibrant and bracing social and ethnic mix; a financial and commercial powerhouse; seat of Britain's legislature and of England's highest courts of law; a richly endowed cultural centre; a magnet for tourists (whose spending provides a significant amount of its income); and a repository of the history and traditions of the English, and British, people. Ugly and beautiful, wealthy and poor, soul-sapping and stimulating, it is no less various than it was when in the 18th century Dr Johnson declared that 'there is in London all that life can afford'.

> … London, that great sea, whose ebb and flow At once is deaf and loud, and on the shore Vomits its wrecks, and still howls on for more.
>
> P.B. Shelley: 'Letter to Maria Gisborne' (1820)

> London is the grandest and most complicated monstrosity on the face of the earth.
>
> Felix Mendelssohn: letter (25 April 1829)

> For one who takes it as I take it, London is on the whole the most possible form of life.
>
> Henry James: *Notebooks* (1881)

> England is a small island. The world is infinitesimal. But London is illimitable.
>
> Ford Madox Ford: *The Soul of London* (1905)

There are towns called London in the USA (Arkansas, Kentucky, Ohio, Texas) and in Canada (Ontario), and towns called New London in the USA (Iowa, Minnesota, Missouri, Ohio, Wisconsin). East London is an important city in Eastern Cape Province, South Africa.

See also EAST LONDON, INNER LONDON, NORTH LONDON, OUTER LONDON *and* SOUTH LONDON.

American Werewolf in London, An. A surprise cinematic hit (1981), directed by John Landis, in which a young American tourist, to his disgust, becomes transformed into a werewolf. Its combination of gruesome horror scenes and witty dialogue brought it a cult status, and the special effects depicting the tourist's lupine transmogrification were much admired.

City of London Cemetery. A cemetery in the East London borough of NEWHAM (E12), to the southeast of WANSTEAD. It was founded (in 1856) and is administered by the City of London. It is the largest municipal cemetery in Europe.

City of London School for Boys. A public school in BLACKFRIARS, in the City, founded in 1837.

City of London School for Girls. A public school in the BARBICAN, in the City, founded in 1894.

Cockney. A working-class Londoner, and particularly an East Ender born and bred. In the Middle Ages the word meant 'cock's egg', and it was used to refer to a small or misshapen hen's egg that was not of much use. On the analogy of the 'runt of the litter' that needs special care and attention, *cockney* came to be applied to an indulged or molly-coddled mother's boy, and by the 16th century we find it being used to refer to a town-dweller (probably on the grounds that people who live in towns are used to soft, easy living, like spoilt children). From the start of the 17th century there is evidence of it being applied specifically to Londoners, and it is then that we first hear of the convention of a Cockney being someone born within the sound of Bow bells (*see under* BOW); the birth-qualifications have tacitly been expanded considerably since then, to allow for the growth of the East End.

Our present-day notion of Cockney culture (the chirpy but combative Londoner, the life of street markets and costermongers, music-hall songs and beery knees-ups, flat caps and mufflers) is essentially a 19th-century one, and its icons are now heritage properties: the Pearly Kings and Queens, for instance, their garments weighed down with many thousands of shimmeringly patterned pearl buttons, who were once coster-community leaders but now function mainly as charity fund-raisers; and perhaps pre-eminently that great linguistic museum-piece, Cockney rhyming slang (*apples and pears* 'stairs', *skin and blister* 'sister', and so on), in which usages that have not passed the lips of a genuine East Ender for a hundred years are lovingly polished and preserved. Which brings us to 'Cockney' speech patterns: the 'dropped' *h* (''Arry'), the *f* or *v* in place of *th* ('your bruvver's got finner'), the ubiquitous glottal stop. Again the stereotype – connived at by such models as George Bernard Shaw's ludicrously exaggerated Eliza Doolittle in *Pygmalion* (1916) and Dick Van Dyke's tortured vowels in *Mary Poppins* (1963) – has become preserved in amber. The speech of London working people evolves, as all language does. The interchange of *v* and *w*, which Dickens made familiar ('a wery remarkable circumstance'), was well on the way out by the time Dickens referred to it. By the end of the 20th century many of the phonetic features of London English had spread far and wide via the vector of Estuary English (*see under* THAMES[1]), and far from being looked down on as 'common', as in former years, Cockney was the lingo to give street-cred, adopted (in an approximate form satirized as '**Mockney**') by trend-setters born many leagues from Bow bells.

Down and Out in Paris and London. An early and part-autobiographical narrative (1933) by George Orwell, in retreat from his Etonian and imperial background, concerning life at the bottom of the social scale in these two cities.

Great Fire of London, the. A conflagration in 1666 that destroyed 187 ha (463 acres) of the City of London, including Old ST PAUL'S[1] Cathedral, the Guildhall, the Royal Exchange, 87 churches and 13,200 houses. Only 20 people were killed, however. It started in the early hours of 2 September in Farryner's baking shop in PUDDING LANE, near London Bridge. It is commemorated by the Monument, a 60.5 m (202 ft) pillar topped with a flaming gilt-bronze urn, erected near the site of the outbreak in 1677. The fire also spawned the well-known round '**London's Burning**' (*see below*).

'His Return to London'. A distinctly pro-London (and anti-West Country) poem by Robert Herrick (1591–1674), celebrating rapturously the poet's return to the capital in 1647 following his removal from a rural living in Devon (*see* 'Discontents in Devon' *under* DEVON[1]):

> From the dull confines of the drooping West,
> To see the day spring from the pregnant East,
> Ravished in spirit, I come, nay more, I fly
> To thee, blest place of my nativity! ...
>
> London my home is: though by a hard fate sent
> Into a long and irksome banishment;
> Yet since called back; henceforward let me be,
> O native country, repossessed by thee!
> For, rather than I'll to the West return,
> I'll beg of thee first here to have mine urn.

Illustrated London News. An illustrated newspaper, first published in 1842 (when such illustration was exceptional).

John o' London's Weekly. A lower-middlebrow literary magazine published between 1919 and 1954. It took its title from the pen-name of its original editor, Wilfred Whitten (d.1942).

London Airport. *See under* CROYDON, GATWICK[1], HEATHROW, HOUNSLOW, LUTON, STANSTED; *see also* **London City Airport** *below*.

London Arena. An exhibition centre and concert venue in London's DOCKLAND, opened in 1989 beside the former Millwall Dock (*see under* MILLWALL), on the site of a former fruit and veg warehouse.

London Assembly, the. A scrutinizing body containing 25 members, elected by the voters of Greater London at the same time as they vote for the Mayor. It was established in 2000, and meets in City Hall, a futuristic sub-globular building (designer Norman Foster; it is nicknamed 'the Egg') at the southern end of Tower Bridge. For electoral purposes, London is divided into 14 Assembly constituencies, consisting of two or more boroughs: BARNET and CAMDEN, BEXLEY and BROMLEY, BRENT[2] and HARROW, City and East London (BARKING AND DAGENHAM, City of London, NEWHAM, TOWER HAMLETS), CROYDON and SUTTON[1], EALING and HILLINGDON, ENFIELD and HARINGEY, GREENWICH and LEWISHAM, HAVERING and REDBRIDGE, LAMBETH and SOUTHWARK, MERTON and WANDSWORTH, North East (HACKNEY, ISLINGTON, WALTHAM FOREST), South West (HOUNSLOW, KINGSTON UPON THAMES, RICHMOND-UPON-THAMES), West Central (HAMMERSMITH AND FULHAM, KENSINGTON AND CHELSEA, WESTMINSTER).

London Assurance. A play (1841) by the Irish dramatist Dion Boucicault. Hovering somewhere between Restoration-style comedy and Oscar Wilde, it recounts the triumphs and disasters of various interwoven amorous intrigues.

'London' Bach, the. J.C. Bach (1735–82), son of Johann Sebastian Bach and a musician and composer of note in his own right. His sobriquet reflects his 25-year residence in London, where he became music master to the family of George III.

London Belongs To Me. A film (1948), directed by Sidney Gilliatt, which revolves around a young man (Richard Attenborough) charged with murder and the support he receives from his fellow lodgers in a South London boarding house. Alastair Sim steals many scenes as a fraudulent medium.

London Bridge. Any of a succession of bridges spanning the River Thames between the City of London and SOUTHWARK. The first one was probably made of wood and built during the Roman occupation. It was deliberately burnt down in 1014 to frustrate Danish invaders, an event celebrated by a contemporary Norse poet with verses beginning

> London Bridge is broken down,
> Gold is won and bright renown.

By the 17th century this had been transformed into the nursery rhyme now more familiar to us in the form

> London Bridge is falling down,
> London Bridge is falling down,
> London Bridge is falling down,
> My fair lady!

widely used in a children's singing game. The first stone bridge was begun in 1176. Over the centuries it acquired an accretion of houses, shops and other buildings, some as much as seven storeys high. It formed the final leg of the journey from DOVER to London, and many notable triumphant crossings were made – by Henry V on his return from Agincourt, for instance, and by Charles II at the Restoration. Latterly, it has been more a conduit for City commuters:

> A crowd flowed over London Bridge, so many,
> I had not thought death had undone so many.
>
> T.S. Eliot: *The Waste Land* (1922)

More gruesomely, from the early 14th century to the late 17th it was the custom to display the heads of executed traitors here. The houses were removed in the mid-18th century. A new bridge, with five arches, was opened slightly upstream of the old one in 1831. This survived until 1967, when it was dismantled and sold for $1.8 million to the McCulloch Oil Corporation, USA, which re-erected it to span an inlet on the Colorado River at Lake Havasu City. It was long rumoured that the company thought it was buying Tower Bridge, a canard hotly denied by the company chairman, George McCulloch. The present-day London Bridge, of three spans, was built in 1967–72.

London Bridge station opened in 1836 as the terminus for the first steam railway to run into London (from DEPTFORD). Its present building was begun in the 1840s. It carries lines from southeast London, Kent and the south coast. London Bridge Underground station, on the Northern and Jubilee lines, opened in 1900.

Freemen of the City of London retain the right to drive sheep across the bridge.

London broil. An American dish, unknown to Londoners, consisting of a large beef steak grilled and then cut in thin slices for serving.

London Broncos. A London-based rugby league club, created in 1994 when the Australian rugby league club Brisbane Broncos acquired the **London Crusaders** (formerly FULHAM rugby league club). The London Broncos play in the Super League. They have led a peripatetic existence, playing their home games at a number of different grounds, including the Stoop, home of Harlequins rugby union club.

London Calling. The title of a song and album (1979) by the literate and politicized punk-rock group The Clash, which evoke the generational, racial and political troubles at the beginning of the Thatcher era. (The album was released in 1980 in the USA, and *Rolling Stone* magazine later voted it 'album of the decade'.)

> London calling to the faraway towns
> Now war is declared – and battle come down
>
> Joe Strummer: 'London Calling' (1979)

London City Airport. An airport situated to the east of the City of London, in the borough of NEWHAM and close to the north bank of the River Thames. Its runway occupies the land separating the former King George V and Royal Albert Docks. It opened in 1987, and serves mainly European destinations.

London clay. Clay that forms an extensive layer in southeast England, dating from the lower Eocene period between 58 and 52 million years ago.

London Clinic. A private hospital situated in Devonshire Place, MARYLEBONE. It opened in 1932. The Chilean former dictator Augusto Pinochet was arrested there in 1998 while undergoing treatment for a bad back.

London Coliseum, the. A theatre in St Martin's Lane (WC2), opened in 1904 to the designs of Frank Matcham. It was originally a variety theatre, and in 1961 it was converted into a cinema. In 1968 it became the home of the Sadler's Wells Opera Company (now the English National Opera, *see under* ENGLISH). Its most instantly recognizable external feature is the globe with which it is surmounted; this used to revolve, but Westminster City Council put a stop to such frivolity.

London Cuckolds, The. A farcical sub-Restoration-style comedy (1682) by Edward Ravenscroft, which used to be performed on Lord Mayor's Day in the 18th century, and is occasionally revived today.

London Dock. *See* DOCKLAND.

London Dungeon, the. A horror museum situated in the vaults beneath London Bridge station (*see above*). It was opened in 1975.

Londoner. A native or inhabitant of London. The word is first recorded in the 15th century.

> Maybe it's because I'm a Londoner
> That I love London so.
> Maybe it's because I'm a Londoner
> That I think of her wherever I go.
> I get a funny feeling inside of me
> Just walking up and down.
> Maybe it's because I'm a Londoner
> That I love London Town.
>
> Hubert Gregg: 'Maybe It's Because I'm a Londoner' (1947)

London Eye, the. A big wheel (more fully, with a nod to its sponsor, the British Airways London Eye, and also known as the **Millennium Wheel**) erected on the SOUTH BANK[1] site by the River Thames in 2000 to celebrate the Millennium. Designed by David Marks and Julia Barfield, it is, at 135 m (442 ft) high, the world's tallest observation wheel. Its 32 glass capsules complete one revolution every half an hour, giving their occupants (a maximum of 25 apiece) an unparalleled array of often surprising London vistas. Itself visible across the rooftops from many parts of the capital, it has quickly become a London landmark, and

its originally brief life has been extended for another 20 years.

London Fields. An area of former grazing land, about 11 ha (27 acres), in the borough of HACKNEY. In the 19th century it acquired a poor reputation on account of it being the resort of various members of the criminal classes.

London Fields. A satirical novel (1989) by Martin Amis, revolving around a love triangle concocted by the soon-to-die female protagonist, in which London is protrayed as a socially disintegrating city.

London Film Festival, the. An annual festival of film held in London. It was founded in 1958 by Derek Prowse and Dilys Powell.

London Films. A film production company formed in the mid-1930s by Alexander Korda. Its headquarters were at Denham Studios (*see under* DENHAM).

London fog. A smoke-laden fog, or smog (the blend is first recorded in 1905), of the sort that enveloped and asphyxiated London from the early 19th century until the Clean-Air Acts of the mid-20th century. It killed thousands of people, and entered popular folklore. It insinuated itself into songs ('A foggy day in London Town / Had me low and had me down', Ira Gershwin (1937)); it turned into rhyming slang (for *dog*); and Australians even used its name for a manual worker who does not do his share of the work (i.e., like a London fog, he 'will not lift').

London Gateway. A blander and less disconcerting name latterly applied to the former Scratchwood Service Area (*see* SCRATCH WOOD) on the M1.

London Gazette. The official organ of the British government and the appointed medium for all official announcements of pensions, promotions, bankruptcies, dissolutions of partnerships and similar events. It appeared first as the *Oxford Gazette* in 1665, when the Court was at Oxford, and Henry Muddiman (b.1629) started it as a daily newsletter or newspaper. It was transferred to London in 1666 and is now published five times a week. A corresponding journal is published in Edinburgh, and the *Iris Oifigiúil* ('official journal'), formerly the *Dublin Gazette*, founded 1922, is the Irish equivalent.

London gin. A type of dry gin to which the flavouring substances are added during rather than after distillation.

London Group, the. A still-surviving society of artists founded in 1913 by an amalgamation of the Camden Town Group (*see under* CAMDEN TOWN) with various small groups and individuals. The first president was Harold Gilman (1876–1919) and apart from other former Camden Town artists there were those who would subsequently be associated with Vorticism, including David Bomberg (1890–1957), Jacob Epstein (1880–1959), C.R.W. Nevinson (1889–1946) and Edward Wadsworth (1889–1949). Its aim was to break away from academic tradition and to draw inspiration from

French Post-Impressionism. Today, it is essentially an umbrella group of artists with a catholic range of styles and themes.

London Guildhall University. A university in the City of London and East London, founded as a polytechnic in 1970. In 2002 it was combined with the University of North London (*see under* NORTH LONDON) to form **London Metropolitan University** (*see below*).

London Irish. A rugby union club, founded in 1898 by a group of London-based Irish exiles. The club was based at Sunbury-on-Thames (with a short period at Blackheath in the late 1940s and 1950s) from 1931 until 2001, when the club moved its base to the Madejski Stadium in READING.

London ivy. A late 19th-century slang term applied to both 'dust' and 'fog' – in each case because it tends to obscure what it 'grows on'. The expression is first recorded in Charles Dickens's *Bleak House* (1852), in which the fogs of London are a pervasive presence.

> A very severe cold caught by nine hours' contact with London ivy.
>
> *Sporting Life* (4 January 1889)

London Labour and the London Poor. A group of articles by journalist Henry Mayhew (1812–87), collected under this title in 1851. It became a classic work of Victorian urban reportage, and, along with the work of Dickens, has shaped modern conceptions of the urban poor in the 19th century.

London Library, the. A library in St James's Square, in Central London, the largest subscription library in London, with a collection of over a million books. Its titles centre on the humanities, and it has no books on law, medicine, science or technology. It was founded by Thomas Carlyle (1795–1881) in 1841 and has had many distinguished writers among its members, who in 2004 were paying an annual subscription of £170.

London Magazine, The. A name given to several periodicals published in London over the past 300 years, of which the most distinguished are one that appeared 1820–9, edited by John Scott, essentially a literary miscellany that featured the work of new young writers and poets such as William Wordsworth, John Keats, William Hazlitt and Thomas Carlyle, and one founded in 1954 by John Lehmann, which covers a broad spectrum of the arts.

London Marathon. A marathon race run annually in London. It was founded by Chris Brasher and John Disley, and first run in 1981. It is now sponsored by margarine manufacturer Flora. A notable feature of it is the large number of charity runners dressed in outlandish costumes.

London Merchant, The. An important play historically, performed at the Theatre Royal, DRURY LANE (1731), and written by George Lillo. It is regarded as reflecting the increasing middle-class tastes of the changing London audiences. Characters moralize along such lines as 'business,

the youth's best preservative from ill, as idleness his worst of snares' (II.iv), apparently without irony.

London Metal Exchange, the. A commodity market in London for trade in metals, incorporated in 1881. With the Commodity Exchange of New York, it is the world's most important for copper, nickel and zinc. It also trades in futures, and organizes the storage of metals. It was originally established in LOMBARD STREET, and later moved to Whittington Avenue (EC3).

London Metropolitan University. A university in London formed in 2002 from a merger of the University of North London (*see under* NORTH LONDON) and **London Guildhall University** (*see above*). Its main campus, in the Holloway Road, is enlivened by the gravity-defying, zigzagging Graduate School designed by Daniel Libeskind, which opened in 2004.

London Museum. A former museum of London's history. Housed in Kensington Palace, it was founded in 1911 and in 1975 was merged with the Guildhall Museum and relocated to form the **Museum of London** (*see below*).

London ordinary. Mid 19th-century slang for Brighton beach.

London Overture, A. A concert overture (1936) by John Ireland. Mainly perky and ebullient in mood, it incorporates a theme suggested by a bus conductor's cry of 'Dilly! Piccadilly!'

London Palladium, the. A theatre in Argyll Street (W1), a turning to the south off OXFORD STREET. It opened in 1910 (as simply 'the Palladium') as a music-hall. It staged revues in the 1920s, and after the Second World War it became known for its variety shows and pantomimes. The variety programme *Sunday Night at the London Palladium* (1955–67), originally compered by Tommy Trinder, was a key ingredient in the early success of ITV. The Palladium has often hosted the Royal Variety Performance, to which members of the ruling family have been annually subjected.

London particular. A colloquial term used in the 19th and early 20th centuries for a **London fog** (*see above*). The sulphurous coal smoke of the period gave London smogs a yellowish tinge (whence the name '**pea-souper**', after soup made from yellow split peas rather than fresh green peas), and it may be that the term was inherited from a variety of Madeira wine of similar colour, so called because it was imported 'particularly' for London merchants.

> 'This is a London particular'. I had never heard of such a thing. 'A fog, miss', said the young gentleman.
>
> Charles Dickens: *Bleak House* (1852)

London Pavilion. A place of entertainment on the north side of PICCADILLY CIRCUS. It opened in 1885 as a theatre. It later became a cinema, and now houses Rock Circus, a museum of rock and pop music.

London Philharmonic Orchestra. A symphony orchestra founded in London in 1932 by Sir Thomas Beecham.

London Pianoforte School. A group of composer-pianists working in London at the turn of the 19th century. They pioneered the Romantic style of keyboard playing, based on a legato touch, and began to develop a more complex harmonic language that ultimately replaced the Classical style. The group included Muzio Clementi, Jan Dussek and John Field.

London plane. A plane tree, *Platanus* x *hybrida*, which is regarded as being a hybrid of the American and the oriental planes. Its flaking bark makes it resistant to pollution and it is widely planted in towns and cities, including London.

London pride. A name applied to various flowering plants. In the 17th century it chiefly denoted the sweet william, whose flowers were reportedly very much sought out by Londoners for their beauty, but nowadays it is the name of a pinkish-white-flowered plant of the saxifrage family, *Saxifraga umbrosa*, which can be found growing in many London gardens. Bishop Walsham How (1823–97) wrote a poem addressed to the flower, rebuking it for possessing the sinful attribute. A lady called his attention to the fact that the name did not mean that the plant was proud, but that London was proud of it, whereupon the bishop wrote a second poem apologizing to it. The literal meaning of the term was exploited by Noël Coward in his patriotic song 'London Pride' (1941), designed to boost Londoners' morale during the dark days of the Second World War:

> London Pride has been handed down to us.
> London Pride is a flower that's free.
> London Pride means our own dear town to us,
> And our pride it for ever will be.

London Regiment, the. A regiment formerly consisting of two regular battalions of the City of London Regiment (Royal Fusiliers) and a number of Territorial battalions, including the London Rifle Brigade, Kensingtons, Artists' Rifles and London Scottish. It is now a wholly Territorial regiment.

London Review of Books, the. A bi-weekly cultural periodical, founded 1979, and inspired in its look and coverage by the *New York Review of Books*, within which its very early editions appeared. Unapologetically high-brow, its contents tend to be more spikily provocative than the otherwise comparable *Times Literary Supplement*; some anti-American views expressed in it after the 11 September (2001) terrorist incidents prompted a high-profile intellectual spat, which spilled out into the popular press. Bucking populist trends, the **London Review Bookshop** was established in BLOOMS-BURY in 2003 to sell serious books and host events.

> There aren't many magazines that can boast that half their readers have a higher degree.
>
> 'Literary Criticism', *The Guardian* (3 December 2001)

London rocket. A plant, *Sisymbrium irio*, of the cabbage family, with very small yellow flowers. It got its name when, according to the contemporary naturalist John Ray, it sprang up in profusion in waste places in the wake of the Great Fire of London in 1666. It is actually a native of the Mediterranean area, but it is an enthusiastic colonizer of patches of devastation anywhere: the ruins around St Paul's Cathedral were covered with it after the Blitz of the Second World War.

'London's Burning'. The title of an old round about the **Great Fire of London** (1666; *see above*): 'London's burning, / Look yonder, / Fire, fire, / And we have no water'. It was subsequently taken up as the title for a television play (1986) and then series about the fictional firefighters of Blue Watch B25, BLACKWALL, first broadcast by **London Weekend Television** (*see below*) in 1988. The series dwelt as much on the fighters' heroics in the many spectacular conflagrations as on their domestic problems.

London School of Economics. A constituent college of **London University** (*see below*), founded in 1895. As its full name, the **London School of Economics and Political Science**, suggests, it specializes in economics and politics, but it also covers the full spectrum of the social sciences and some other disciplines. Its first chairman was the economist and socialist Sidney Webb (1859–1947). Many influential figures in the political and economic establishments of Britain and other countries have studied here. It formerly had a reputation for radicalism, and many of its undergraduates took leading roles in the student unrest of the late 1960s, but in the 1980s it embraced Thatcherism.

London Scottish. A rugby union club originally founded in 1878 by a group of London-based Scots exiles. Based in Richmond, the club enjoyed a distinguished history in rugby union's amateur period up until 1995, contributing numerous players to the Scottish national side. London Scottish failed to survive as a professional club, however, and was disbanded in 1999 (when it was nominally merged with Richmond and London Irish, *see above*).

London Season. A somewhat superannuated term for a period of time, originally tied in with the ceremonial presentation of debutantes at court, when aristocratic and fashionable society resided in London and attended, in addition to a numbing round of balls, dinner parties, etc., a range of public or semi-public events at which it was *de rigeur* to see and be seen. It covered the months of May, June and July and included such fixtures as the Chelsea Flower Show (*see under* CHELSEA), the Royal Academy Summer Exhibition, the Fourth of June (speech day at Eton College; *see under* ETON), Henley Royal Regatta (*see under* HENLEY-ON-THAMES), Cowes Week (*see under* COWES) and the Eton–Harrow match at LORD's. When August arrived, the exhausted protagonists would retire gratefully to their county seats. Latterly, the notion of '**the Season**' has come to encompass events unkown to Victorian and Edwardian high society, many of them a good distance from London, such as the EDINBURGH and GLYNDEBOURNE festivals.

London smoke. A late 19th-century high-society slang term for a yellowish colour, like the polluted London smogs.

London Stone, the. A stone set into the wall of No. 111 Cannon Street (EC4). It is an ancient relic of uncertain history. The antiquary William Camden thought it to be the point from which the Romans measured distances but another theory is that it is an Anglo-Saxon ceremonial stone. According to Holinshed's *Chronicles* (1577), the 15th-century rebel Jack Cade struck it with his sword when proclaiming himself master of the city, and the incident is mentioned in Shakespeare's *Henry IV, Part 2*, IV.vii (1590). The stone was placed against the wall of St Swithin's Church in 1798 as a safeguard against its destruction, but in 1960 it was moved to its present position.

London symphonies, the. A collective name given to the last 12 symphonies (Nos 93–104) of Josef Haydn. He wrote them in the early 1790s at the instigation of the London impresario Salomon, who commissioned them for his Hanover Square concerts (they are occasionally also called the 'Salomon symphonies'). They include many of Haydn's best-known symphonies, including the 'Surprise', the 'Military', the 'Clock' and the 'Drum Roll', not to mention the 'London Symphony' (*see below*).

London Symphony, A. A symphony by Ralph Vaughan Williams, his second. It was completed in 1913, but Vaughan Williams subsequently made substantial revisions to it, and the standard version played today dates from the 1930s. The original version was not recorded until 2000. Although not programmatic (the composer himself preferred to refer to it as a 'Symphony by a Londoner'), it does incorporate some London sounds, such as the Westminster chimes and shipping on the Thames.

London Symphony, The. A symphony in D (1795) by Josef Haydn. It is number 104 in the standard edition of his symphonies, and the 12th of his so-called 'London symphonies' (*see above*). There is no particular justification for the name.

London Symphony Orchestra. A symphony orchestra founded in London in 1904 by breakaway members of Henry Wood's Queen's Hall Orchestra. It is the oldest surviving orchestra in London. Elgar conducted it in many of his recordings of his own music. It is now based in the Barbican Arts Centre.

London taxi. A Cockney rhyming-slang term for *jacksie*, which in turn is slang for *anus*. It is also, of course, an alternative description of the typical black-bodied cab seen in the capital.

London to a brick. An Australian expression denoting the longest possible odds, a dead cert. It dates from the 1960s.

London Transport. A body (abbreviation LT) responsible for public transport in Greater London. It had its origins in the London Passenger Transport Board, set up in 1933 to coordinate bus, tram and tube services. This was superseded in 1948 by the London Transport Executive. In 2000 it was reinvented as Transport *for* London (T*f*L). Its familiar circle-and-bar logo, designed by Edward Johnston (1872–1944), originated on the Underground.

> That big six-wheeler
> Scarlet-painted
> London Transport
> Diesel-engined
> Ninety-seven horse power
> Omnibus!
>
> Michael Flanders and Donald Swann: 'A Transport of Delight' (*c*.1956)

London University. A London-based federal university, the oldest in England after OXFORD and CAMBRIDGE[1], and the largest for full-time students in the UK. Its original institution was University College, founded in 1828. This was followed the next year by King's College. These, together with some hospital medical schools, were combined as the University of London in 1836. Its other constituents now include Birkbeck College, the Courtauld Institute of Art, Goldsmiths' College, Imperial College of Science, Technology and Medicine, the **London Business School**, the **London School of Economics** (*see above*), the **London School of Hygiene and Tropical Medicine**, Queen Mary (an amalgamation of the former Queen Mary College and Westfield College), the Royal Academy of Music, Royal Holloway (an amalgamation of the former Royal Holloway College (*see under* EGHAM) and Bedford College) and the School of Oriental and African Studies (SOAS), as well as an array of (post)graduate-level research centres administered as the School of Advanced Study, such as the Warburg Institute and Institute of Historical Research. It opened all its degrees to women in 1878, the first British university to do so (Royal Holloway and Westfield colleges, although originally outside the university, were founded as women's colleges). Its administrative headquarters, the imposing Senate House in BLOOMSBURY, which also contains its central library, were built in the 1930s.

London Wall. A street in the City of London (EC2). It runs east to west from Broad Street to Aldersgate Street, crossing MOORGATE and following the line of the original City wall.

London Wasps. A rugby union club originally founded as plain 'Wasps' in 1867 (there being a vogue for naming sports clubs after insects, birds and animals in the Victorian period) and based at SUDBURY[2] in north London from 1923.

When rugby union turned professional in the 1990s the club played its home matches first at Loftus Road (*see under* QUEEN'S PARK) and then, from 2002, at the Causeway Stadium in HIGH WYCOMBE. The club has contributed many players to the England national side, including Roger Uttley, Nigel Melville, Rob Andrew and Lawrence Dallaglio.

London Weekend Television. An independent television company (abbreviation **LWT**, latterly its official name), which in 1967 won the ITV franchise for broadcasting to the London area at weekends. It first went on the air on 2 August 1968. Among its notable successes were the period drama series *Upstairs, Downstairs*, the arts magazine *The South Bank Show* and the firefighting soap opera *London's Burning* (*see above*). In 2002 it was swallowed up by ITV and lost its separate identity, but it continues to make programmes for the network.

London weighting. Additional pay attached to a London-based job to compensate for the higher cost of living there.

London Welsh. A rugby union club, originally founded in 1895 by a group of London-based Welsh exiles.

London Zoo. A zoo in the northern part of REGENT'S PARK. It was opened in 1828 under the aegis of the Zoological Society of London. Among its most famous and crowd-pulling animals have been Tommy the chimpanzee (1830s), Jumbo the elephant (1870s), the polar-bear cub Brumus (1950s) and the giant panda Chi-Chi (1960s). Its architecture is almost as varied as its animal collection, ranging from the 'Raven's Cage' (1829), through the Mappin Terraces (1913), an artificial mountain-range for goats, bears, etc. (now disused), Lubetkin's futuristic penguin pool (1936) and the Snowdon Aviary (1963–4) to the Millennium Conservation Centre (1999), which houses the BUGS biodiversity exhibit. After 170 years of exhibiting elephants, the zoo lost its contingent to its sister WHIPSNADE Wild Animal Park after they crushed their keeper to death in their confined and outdated living area during 2001.

Mother London. A socially panoramic history novel (2000) by Michael Moorcock. It moves around the capital in the latter half of the 20th century, allowing a wide range of voices to be heard via its conceit of giving its three central characters – all from a mental hospital – abilities to 'hear' conversations in their minds.

Museum of London, the. A museum of London's history. It was created in 1975 by an amalgamation of the former Guidhall Museum (Roman and medieval) and London Museum (Tudor and later; *see above*) and is housed in a building at the junction of **London Wall** (*see above*) and Aldersgate, near the BARBICAN.

Nine Worthies of London, The. A chronicle history in mixed verse and prose of nine prominent citizens of London, published in 1592 by Richard Johnson, later author of *The Seven Champions of Christendom* (1597). None of the worthies' names strikes a chord nowadays, with the possible exception of Sir William Walworth, a late 14th-century Lord Mayor of London who stabbed the rebel leader Wat Tyler. But the notion of the classical and historical 'Nine Worthies' (nine heroes) to which Johnson's chronicle alludes was as prevalent in the Middle Ages and Renaissance as that of the Seven Wonders of the World.

Polytechnic of Central London. An educational establishment formed in 1966 by combining Regent Street Polytechnic (*see under* REGENT STREET) with the Holborn College of Law, Language and Commerce. In 1992 it became the **University of Westminster** (*see under* WESTMINSTER).

Port of London Authority. A statutory body set up in 1909 to take charge of the tidal part of the River Thames (from TEDDINGTON to its mouth) and the docking activities along its banks. Since the closure of the docks within London (*see* DOCKLAND) its main responsibilities have been at TILBURY. It also has charge of the **Thames Barrier** (*see under* THAMES[1]).

Royal London Hospital. A hospital in the Whitechapel Road (E1), founded in 1740 as the **London Hospital**. It is one of London's major teaching hospitals, and moved to its current site in the late 1750s. It was able to add 'Royal' to its name in 1990, and in 1994 it was combined with St Bartholomew's Hospital (Barts).

'Streets of London'. A seemingly ubiquitous folk song (1969) by Ralph McTell, which became a hit for him in 1974 and subsequently served as the title for his 1980s television series and his 'greatest hits' album. The song recommends sympathetic observation of the lifestyles of London's down-and-outs as an antidote to feelings of loneliness or dissatisfaction.

Swinging London. A phase that London went through in the mid-1960s, when it presented itself as the last word in fashionability, uninhibitedness, unconventionality, liveliness and hipness. It was the era of CARNABY STREET, The Beatles, The Stones, Mary Quant, Biba and the (contraceptive) Pill, and hitherto grey, stuffy London suddenly found itself, much to its surprise, fixed in the world's gaze at the centre of the youth-culture revolution. The expression 'swinging London' seems to have originated with Diana Vreeland, editor of the fashion magazine *Vogue*, and it was popularized by *Time* magazine in 1966.

Treaty of London. Any of a wide range of international agreements concluded in London, dating back to the 14th century. Among the more notable have been the Treaty of 1518, forming an alliance with France (cemented at the Field of the Cloth of Gold in 1520), the Treaty of 1604, in which James VI and I made peace with Spain, the Treaty of 1831, in which the independence and neutrality of the newly formed Belgium were guaranteed, and the secret Treaty of 1915, in which Italy agreed to come into the First

World War on the side of the Triple Entente (Britain, France and Russia).

London Apprentice Probably from an inn name.

A small village in Cornwall, about 1 km (0.6 miles) southeast of Polgooth and 3 km (2 miles) south of St Austell.

London by the Sea. A late-20th-century nickname for BRIGHTON, reflecting the town's sophisticated and cosmopolitan atmosphere (and perhaps the number of former Londoners who decamp there).

London Colney *London* from its situation on the main road to London; *Colney* 'island in the River Colne', pre-English river name *Colne* + OE *eg* (*see* -EY, -EA).

A village in Hertfordshire, on the River COLNE[2], on the route of WATLING STREET[1] and immediately to the north of the M25, about 3 km (2 miles) south of ST ALBANS.

Londonderry[1]. *See* DERRY/LONDONDERRY.

Londonderry[2] A modern place name, presumably derived from a connection with the Irish place.

A village in North Yorkshire, 9 km (5.5 miles) southwest of Northallerton.

Londonderry, County. A county in Northern Ireland, bounded on the north by the Atlantic, to the west by Donegal, to the south by Tyrone and to the east by Lough Neagh, the Lower Bann and County Antrim. The county town was DERRY/LONDONDERRY. The county, initially known as the **County of Coleraine**, was created in 1585, and plantation by English and Scottish Protestants began in the early 17th century. In 1973 the county was divided into the districts of LIMAVADY, Londonderry and MAGHERAFELT, and parts of COLERAINE and COOKSTOWN.

Londrix Perhaps from Fr *Londres* 'London'.

A mid-19th-century slang name for LONDON.

Long Acre 'long narrow strip of agricultural land' (referring to a strip of ground once belonging to the monks of Westminster Abbey), *Acre* OE *æcer* 'plot of cultivated or arable land' (*see* FIELD).

A street in the COVENT GARDEN area of Central London (WC2), in the City of Westminster, running from DRURY LANE in the northeast to just short of LEICESTER SQUARE in the southwest. Various trades have lodged in it over the centuries: in the 17th it was a centre of coachbuilding; in the 18th it had moved on to cabinet-making and furniture design (Thomas Chippendale had a workshop here); and in the 19th and 20th it was a street of publishers and booksellers. It is now essentially part of the boutique and bistro culture of Covent Garden, the travel-book and map sellers Stanfords being a notable exception. On 30 September 1929, John Logie Baird broadcast the first television programme in Britain from a building in Long Acre.

In the mid-19th century the road's name was Cockney rhyming slang for 'baker'.

Longbenton 'bean farm', OE *bean* + -TON, with later addition of *long* denoting 'stretched out'; the middle element may alternatively be OE *beonet* 'bent-grass'.

A town in Tyne and Wear (formerly in Northumberland), 4 km (2.5 miles) northeast of Newcastle upon Tyne. It was the birthplace of the physician Thomas Addison (1793–1860), who identified Addison's disease (a hormonal disorder).

Longbridge A coinage of the early 19th century, referring to a long road bridge over the River Rea.

A southwestern outer suburb of BIRMINGHAM, on the River Rea. Since the early 20th century it has been synonymous with car manufacture. Austin opened its first car factory here in 1905, and it grew rapidly into one of the largest in Europe (latterly under the banner of the British Motor Corporation and British Leyland (*see under* LEYLAND)). Other car-makers associated with Longbridge were Standard and Rootes.

Longdendale 'dale of the long valley', OE *lang* 'long' + *denu* 'valley' + OScand *dalr* 'dale'.

A valley in Derbyshire and Greater Manchester, much of it within the PEAK DISTRICT National Park. The River Etherow flows through it, but it is now largely taken up with reservoirs. Historically it formed part of an important trade route across the PENNINES, and salt from Cheshire was transported along it.

Long Eaton *Long* referring to the length of the original village; *Eaton* 'farmstead on dry ground in a marsh, or on well-watered land', OE *eg* (*see* -EY, -EA) + -TON.

A town in Derbyshire, in the TRENT[1] valley, on the Nottinghamshire border, and about 11 km (7 miles) southwest of Nottingham.

Longford Irish *An Longfort* 'the fortress', from *longphort* 'housefort' (*see* PORT).

The county town of County Longford, 110 km (68 miles) northwest of Dublin. The O'Farrells had their main castle here and founded a Dominican friary in 1400; nothing remains of either. It is the cathedral town of the Catholic diocese of Ardagh and Clonmacnois, and the cathedral itself, begun in 1840, is in Italian Renaissance style.

Longford was the birthplace of the poet and dramatist Padraic Colum (1881–1972).

Earl of Longford. The best-known holder of this title was Frank Pakenham, 7th Earl (1905–2003), but to most people simply **Lord Longford**. He served in Clement Attlee's and Harold Wilson's Labour governments, and later campaigned for prison reform (including the release of Myra Hindley, *see under* SADDLEWORTH MOOR) and against pornography, earning himself the nickname of 'Lord Porn'.

Longford, County. A county in central Ireland, in the province of Leinster, bounded on the north by Leitrim and Cavan, on the east and south by Westmeath, and on the west by Roscommon. The county town is LONGFORD, and LOUGH REE is in the southwest of the county. Its ancient name was **Annaly** or **Anale**, and it was the territory of the O'Farrells until the 12th century, when Henry II granted it to Hugh de Lacy. It became a shire in the 16th century.

Longformacus 'church on Maccus's slope', Gaelic *lann* 'church' + *fothair* 'slope' + male personal name *Maccus*; Maccus was the name of a king of the Isles (*inter alia*) in the 10th century.

A village on the south side of the Lammermuir Hills (*see under* the LAMMERMUIRS), Scottish Borders (formerly in Berwickshire), 10 km (6 miles) northwest of Duns.

Longframlington 'Framela's straggling village', OE *long* 'long, straggling' + male personal name *Framela* + -ING + -TON. It became the surname of Walter de Framlington, who built the church of St Mary the Virgin here *c*.1190.

A village in Northumberland, 16 km (10 miles) northwest of Morpeth. Locally it is known as **Langfram** or simply **Fram**.

Longhope. *See* HOY.

Long Island, the. A name sometimes applied to the whole chain of the Outer HEBRIDES, from the northern tip of Lewis to Mingulay and Berneray in the south (a distance of some 200 km / 124 miles), or sometimes just to the island of LEWIS WITH HARRIS (which is 95 km / 59 miles long).

Long Kesh. The name of the RAF base that originally stood on the site of the former MAZE Prison in County Armagh.

Long Lartin etymology unknown.

A high-security men's prison situated about 6 km (4 miles) northeast of Evesham in Worcestershire. It opened in 1971.

Longleat 'long stream or channel' (reputedly referring to a channel bringing water to a nearby mill), OE *lang* 'long' + *(ge)læt* 'stream, channel'.

An Elizabethan mansion (in full **Longleat House**) in Wiltshire, about 6.5 km (4 miles) west of Warminster. It is the seat of the Marquess of Bath. It was built in 1570s, to the design of Robert Smythson, on the site of a former convent (near which was a mill-stream that supposedly gave the site its name, *see above*). It was extensively altered in the early 19th century. In 1949, under the auspices of the 6th Marquess, it became the first major 'stately home' to be opened to the public, but it made its biggest splash in 1966 with its pioneering Safari Park (brainchild of circus-owner Jimmy Chipperfield (1912–90)), where large beasts of the African savannah roamed 'Capability' Brown's pleasances. '**The Lions of Longleat**' were a must-see (the 7th Marquess (b.1932), notorious for his many 'wifelets', became punningly known as the '**Loins of Longleat**').

Long Load 'long watercourse', *Load* 'watercourse, drainage channel', OE *lad*.

A village in Somerset, on the River YEO[1], about 13 km (8 miles) northwest of Yeovil.

Long Meg and Her Daughters. A stone circle about 1 km (0.6 miles) north of Little Salkeld, Cumbria (formerly in Cumberland), some 9 km (5.5 miles) northeast of Penrith. It probably dates from between 2500 and 1500 BC, in the Bronze Age. It is in the shape of an ellipsis, around 110 m by 90 m (360 ft by 300 ft), and is the third largest stone circle in Britain, after those at AVEBURY and STANTON DREW. It consists of 59 stones, plus some outliers, including Long Meg herself, who is made of red sandstone and, at 4.5 m (12 ft), is much taller than her rhyolite 'daughters' in the ring.

There are various local legends attached to the ring, one being that the stones were a coven of witches surprised and petrified by a saint or wizard. Another says that the stones are uncountable or that you can never count the same number twice (a belief also associated with other such circles), while a third holds that if Long Meg is damaged she will bleed.

There is another, smaller stone circle about 0.5 km (0.3 miles) to the northeast called **Little Meg**.

The poet William Wordsworth was impressed, but as his fellow poet John Keats found with AILSA CRAIG, rocks are rather backward at coming forward with the speeches poets seem to expect of them:

> A weight of Awe not easy to be borne
> Fell suddenly upon my spirit, cast
> From the dread bosom of the unknown past,
> When first I saw that family forlorn;
> Speak Thou, whose massy strength and stature scorn
> The power of years – pre-eminent, and placed
> Apart, to overlook the circle vast.
> Speak Giant-mother! tell it to the Morn,
> While she dispels the cumbrous shades of night;
> Let the Moon hear, emerging from a cloud,
> At whose behest uprose on British ground
> That Sisterhood in hieroglyphic round
> Forth-shadowing, some have deemed the infinite
> The inviolable God that tames the proud.

> William Wordsworth: 'The Monument Commonly Called Long Meg' (1822)

Long Melford *Long* reputedly from the length of its main street, about 3 km (2 miles); *Melford* probably 'ford by a mill', OE *myln* 'mill' + FORD.

A village in Suffolk, about 5 km (3 miles) northwest of SUDBURY[1]. From the late 15th century local wool merchants poured wealth into it, and the result is an impressive array of Tudor domestic architecture (including two notable mansions, one being the National Trust's **Melford Hall**) and the Church of the Holy Trinity, considered by many to be the finest of all Suffolk's 'wool' churches.

The name 'Long Melford' was in times past applied to a type of long stocking purse formerly carried by country people. And in boxing, a 'Long Melford' was, according to George Borrow, a straight right-handed punch:

> 'Now, will you use Long Melford,' said Belle, picking me up. 'I don't know what you mean by Long Melford,' said I, gasping for breath. 'Why, this long right of yours,' said Belle, feeling my right arm.
>
> George Borrow: *Lavengro* (1851)

Long Mynd, the 'long mountain', *Mynd* Welsh *mynydd* 'mountain'.

A rounded ridge (pronounced to rhyme with *tinned*) in Shropshire, about 518 m (1700 ft) high and 11 km (7 miles) long, and about 16 km (10 miles) southwest of Shrewsbury. CHURCH STRETTON is just to the east. Most of the ridge is heather moorland. Along the top runs PORT WAY, a track used 3500 years ago by prehistoric axe traders.

Longmyndian. A geological term for a thick series of non-fossil-bearing sedimentary rocks in the west Midlands, now believed to be of Precambrian age, whose main outcrop forms the Long Mynd. It is first recorded in 1888.

Longpuddle. A fictional version of the Dorset village of PIDDLEHINTON in the novels of Thomas Hardy.

Long Range. *See under* KILLARNEY.

Longridge 'long ridge', OE *lang* 'long' + *hrycg* 'ridge'; *Langrig* 1246.

A former textile town in Lancashire, now a dormitory town for Preston, which is 10 km (6 miles) to the southwest. There is an apocryphal story that the town got its name from Oliver Cromwell, who is said to have exclaimed, on his way to the Battle of PRESTON in 1648, 'What a long ridge it is.'

Longships Probably '(rocks looking like) long ships'; first recorded in the 16th century.

A set of jagged granite rocks about 2 km (1.25 miles) west of LAND'S END in Cornwall. The three largest are named Meinek, Carn Brâs and Tal-y-Maen. A lighthouse stands on one of them.

Long Sleddale *Sleddale* 'flat valley land', OE *slæd* 'flat land' + OScand *dalr* 'valley'.

A valley in the southeast LAKE DISTRICT, Cumbria. Its southern end is some 6 km (4 miles) north of Kendal, and it extends northwestward for some 10 km (6 miles). It includes the tiny settlement of SADGILL.

Long Sleddale was the inspiration for GREENDALE, where Postman Pat has his round.

Longton 'long farmstead or estate', OE *lang* 'long' + -TON.

A town in Staffordshire, within the unitary authority of STOKE-ON-TRENT, on the southeastern edge of Stoke. It is

a large producer of pottery, the manufacture of bone china being concentrated here. In Arnold Bennett's FIVE TOWNS it becomes 'Longshaw'.

Longwood Warren Perhaps from the name of a former owner.

An area of high open downland in Hampshire, about 5 km (3 miles) southeast of WINCHESTER. Once scrubby land, home to rabbits, it is now largely arable. It has become a favourite target for whoever creates crop circles.

Lonmay 'marsh on the plain', Gaelic *lon* 'marsh' + *maigh* 'plain'.

A small village near Fraserburgh in northeast Aberdeenshire that leapt to worldwide fame in 2004 when it was revealed as the ancestral home of Elvis Presley, a certain Andrew Presley having married Elspeth Leg here in 1713. The manager of the village's hotel bar commented: 'I am not a fan of Elvis – not at all. I wish it had been Jimi Hendrix.'

Looe[1] 'pool, inlet' (probably originally referring to the pool or inlet at the mouth of the river), Cornish *logh*.

Either of a pair of rivers (the **East Looe** and the **West Looe**) in Cornwall, which rise to the south of Bodmin Moor (*see under* BODMIN) and flow southwards to join in a common estuary just to the north of LOOE[2].

Looe[2] From the River LOOE[1].

A coastal town in Cornwall, about 16 km (10 miles) east of Fowey. It is a town in two parts (**East Looe** and **West Looe**) on either side of the LOOE[1] estuary. They were originally quite separate entities, but the building of a bridge in 1883 eventually brought about a merging of identities in a single Looe. In the past a busy pilchard-fishing port, it is now the shark-fishing centre of England.

The town is near the southern end of a curve of shore known as **Looe Bay**. A short way offshore is St George's Island, also called **Looe Island**. Now an unassuming bird sanctuary, Looe Island had the misfortune to be bombed during the Second World War, a German pilot mistaking it for a warship.

Loop Head 'leap head', OScand *hlaup* 'leap' + ModE *head*, a translation of the Irish name *Ceann Léime*; the reference is to Cuchulain's superhuman leap to escape from Mal (*see also* HAG'S HEAD).

A headland in County CLARE, at the west end of the peninsula forming the north side of the Mouth of the SHANNON.

Loose '(place at the) pig-sty', OE *hlose* 'pig-sty'.

A village in Kent, about 3 km (2 miles) south of Maidstone.

Lord Berkeley's Seat. *See under* AN TEALLACH.

Lord Hereford's Knob A modern name, from the name of the local landowner with ModE *knob* 'protuberance'.

An eminence (690 m / 2264 ft) on the northern rim of the BLACK MOUNTAINS, Powys, 8 km (5 miles) south of Hay-on-Wye. Its Welsh name is **Twmpa** ('mound, protuberance').

Lord's After Thomas *Lord*, its founder.

A cricket ground in ST JOHN'S WOOD (NW8), in northwest Central London, to the west of REGENT'S PARK. It was opened in 1814 by the Yorkshireman Thomas Lord (1757–1832). Over the nearly two centuries since then it has become the premier cricket ground in England, and it is regarded by many enthusiasts around the world as the spiritual home of cricket. It hosts test matches and important domestic matches (notably the finals of one-day competitions), and since 1877 has been the home ground of MIDDLESEX County Cricket Club. It is the headquarters of its owners, the Marylebone Cricket Club (*see under* MARYLEBONE), and of the England and Wales Cricket Board and the International Cricket Council. Its architecture is eclectic, the stately redbrick Victorian pavilion (with its famous 'Long Room') at the southwestern end balanced to the northeast by the uncompromisingly modernistic Media Centre (the glass frontage of which, arguably reminiscent of a huge grinning mouth, was dubbed 'Cherie Blair's mouth' by a cruel hack in the late 1990s). Beyond the Centre is the 'Nursery End', a large grassed area that doubles as practice ground and the site of nets. The Grace Gates at the southwestern corner commemorate the greatest of English cricketers, W.G. Grace, and the Warner, Allen and Compton and Edrich Stands celebrate notable Middlesex cricketers of the past – respectively Sir Pelham ('Plum') Warner, G.O.B. ('Gubby') Allen, and the buccaneering batsmen Denis Compton and Bill Edrich (the latter being partners in merriment as well as batting, and known affectionately as the 'Middlesex twins' (*see under* MIDDLESEX)). And over all presides the weather-vane figure of Father Time, symbol of Lord's, in the act of removing the bails at the close of play.

For all its chanting crowds on cup-final days, there is undeniably an establishment sheen about Lord's (in contrast with its more plebeian cousin south of the Thames, the OVAL). Within living memory the Eton-and-Harrow match played here was part of the 'London Season' (*see under* LONDON), and it maintains its air of tree-girt gentility in spite of the giant television screens and the painted advertising logos on the sacred turf.

> On the day Hitler invaded Poland I was in the Long Room at Lords. There were balloons in the sky, but although a game was being played there were no spectators in the stands. As I watched the ghostly movements of the players outside, a beautifully preserved member of Lords, with spats and rolled umbrella, stood near me inspecting the game. He did not speak, of course; we had not been

introduced. Suddenly two workmen entered the Long Room in green aprons and carrying a bag. They took down the bust of W.G. Grace, put it in a bag and departed with it. The noble lord by my side watched their every move, then he turned to me. 'Did you see that, sir?' he asked. I told him I had seen. 'That means war,' he said.

> Neville Cardus: *A Cardus for All Seasons*, edited by Margaret Hughes (1985)

Lord's briefly had its own Underground station: when the new St John's Wood station was opened on the Bakerloo line in 1939, the old one on the Metropolitan line was renamed 'Lord's', but it was closed in November of that year.

> Cricket, lovely cricket,
> At Lord's where I saw it;
> Cricket, lovely cricket,
> At Lord's where I saw it;
> Yardley tried his best
> But Goddard won the test.
> They gave the crowd plenty fun;
> Second Test and West Indies won.

> Egbert Moore ('Lord Beginner'): 'Victory Calypso' (1950)

There was once also a cricket ground called Lord's in Durban, South Africa, which staged four test matches in the early part of the 20th century.

'At Lord's'. A poem by Francis Thompson (1859–1907) evoking the image of an exiled Lancastrian watching a cricket match at Lord's, but seeing in his mind's eye a different match, played elsewhere many years ago.

> For the field is full of shades as I near the shadowy coast
> And a ghostly batsman plays to the bowling of a ghost,
> And I look through my tears on a soundless-clapping host
>   As the run-stealers flicker to and fro,
>   To and fro: –
> O my Hornby and my Barlow long ago!

> (Albert Hornby and Dick Barlow were Lancashire cricketers of the late 19th century)

Lord's Taverners, the. An association of cricket-lovers founded in 1950 by Martin Boddey. It stages matches and other events to raise funds for charity. There is a large 'stage-and-screen' element in its membership and its patron is the Duke of Edinburgh. Its name commemorates the Tavern, a hostelry to the right of the pavilion that was demolished in the early 1960s (the Tavern Stand now occupies its site).

Lorn. An alternative spelling of LORNE.

Lorne 'land of Loarn'; Loarn was a Celtic prince here in the 6th century.

A traditional area of ARGYLL, bounded on the west by the Atlantic, on the southeast by LOCH AWE and on the north by the PASS OF BRANDER. It is also spelt **Lorn**. The main town is OBAN, which looks across the **Firth of Lorne** to the southeast side of MULL. The view was familiar to the Oban teacher and poet Iain Crichton Smith:

> In the cold orange light we stared across
> to Mull and Kerrara and far Tiree.
> A setting sun emblazoned your bright knee …
>
> Iain Crichton Smith: 'At the Firth of Lorne', from
> *The Law and the Grace* (1965)

Lorne sausage. A square-shaped slice of sausage meat. If properly cooked, it will have the texture, taste and appearance of a carpet tile.

Lorne shoe. A kind of shoe dating from the later 19th century, named after the Marquess of Lorne.

Brooch of Lorne, the. A fine silver disc of Celtic design, ornamented with filigree work and a large rock crystal, and with a cavity for holding sacred relics. It has been in the possession of the MacDougalls of Lorne for centuries. The explanation of how it came into their care is provided by Sir Walter Scott in a footnote to his passage about the brooch in *The Lord of the Isles* (1815):

> After his defeat at Methven, [Robert the] Bruce, with a remnant of his forces, was attacked by the Lord of Lorn on attempting to retreat into Argyllshire. Two of Lorn's vassals, in the close fight that ensued, seized Bruce by the mantle. He killed them with his battle-axe, but was obliged to leave his mantle, with its brooch, in their dying grasp. The incident is recounted with great spirit by Barbour [in his 14th-century epic, *The Brus*].

In his own poem Scott speculates on the ultimate origin of the brooch:

> Whence the brooch of burning gold,
> That clasps the Chieftain's mantle-fold,
> Wrought and chased with rare device,
> Studded fair with gems of price,
> On the varied tartans beaming,
> As, through night's pale rainbow gleaming,
> Fainter now, now seen afar,
> Fitful shines the northern star?
> Gem! ne'er wrought on Highland mountain,
> Did the fairy of the fountain,
> Or the mermaid of the wave,
> Frame thee in some coral cave?
> Did, in Iceland's darksome mine,
> Dwarf's swart hands thy metal twine?
> Or, mortal-moulded, comest thou here,
> From England's love, or France's fear?

The brooch was kept in the MacDougalls' Gylen Castle on the island of KERRERA until 1647, when, during the Covenanting Wars, General Leslie seized the castle and massacred the garrison. The MacDougalls thought the brooch lost after this, but in 1825 it transpired that it had been taken by one of Leslie's officers, Campbell of Inverawe, whose descendant, General Sir Duncan Campbell, returned the brooch to MacDougall of Dunollie in that year.

'Hills of Lorne, The'. An air for the fiddle by C. Hunter.

Maid of Lorn, the. Edith, the heroine of Scott's poem *The Lord of the Isles* (1815), who has to live up to the following sycophancy:

> O wake, while Dawn, with dewy shine,
> Wakes Nature's charms to vie with thine!
> She bids the mottled thrush rejoice
> To mate thy melody of voice;
> The dew that on the violet lies
> Mocks the dark lustre of thine eyes;
> But, Edith, wake, and all we see
> Of sweet and fair shall yield to thee!

Lossiemouth 'mouth of the River Lossie', *Lossie* Gaelic *uisge lossa* 'water of herbs'.

A fishing port in Moray (formerly in Grampian region), 8 km (5 miles) north of Elgin, sited where the **River Lossie** enters the Moray Firth. Ramsay Macdonald (1866–1937), Britain's first Labour prime minister, was born in a two-room cottage here. RAF Lossiemouth claims to be 'the largest and busiest fast-jet base in the Royal Air Force'.

Lost Valley, the. *See under* GLEN COE.

Lostwithiel 'tail-end of the woodland', Cornish *lost* 'tail' + *gwydhyel* 'forest'.

A town in Cornwall, on the River FOWEY[1], about 8 km (5 miles) north of FOWEY[2]. In former times it was the capital of Cornwall and an important centre of the tin trade; the place where the Stannary Court (*see under* STANNARIES) was held, regulating the trade's affairs, can still be seen. Now, Lostwithiel makes most of its money by being a base for tourists. Restormel Castle (*see under* RESTORMEL) is a little to the north.

The essayist Joseph Addison was MP for Lostwithiel between 1708 and 1719.

Battle of Lostwithiel (31 August 1644). A battle of the Civil Wars, in which the Royalists under the Earl of Forth defeated the Parliamentary army under the Earl of Essex. It was the last major Royalist victory of the war.

Lothian Said to be named after one *Leudonus*, an ancient person of considerable obscurity; *Loonia* c.970, *Lodoneo* 1098, *Louthian* c.1200, *Lowden* 16th century. The present form dates from the 17th century. It has also been identified as the origin of the Arthurian LYONESSE, via OFr *Loonois*.

An ancient kingdom and former region of east-central Scotland, on the south shore of the Firth of Forth (*see under* FORTH). In Roman times and after, it was the territory of the Votadini, a Celtic tribe, who had their capital first at TRAPRAIN LAW and then on the Castle Rock in EDINBURGH (*see also* GODDODIN). The Anglo-Saxons began to settle the area in the 5th–6th centuries, and Lothian came under the domination of NORTHUMBRIA until the 9th century, when it was taken by Kenneth MacAlpin, king of the Gaelic-speaking Scots of DALRIADA.

Eventually Lothian was divided administratively into the counties of WEST LOTHIAN (originally Linlithgowshire), MIDLOTHIAN (originally Edinburghshire) and EAST LOTHIAN (originally Haddingtonshire). These were abolished in 1975 and subsumed into the new Lothian region, with Edinburgh as its administrative centre. Lothian was bordered on the south by Borders region, and on the west by Strathclyde and Central regions. Lothian region in turn was abolished in 1996, and the three former counties were resurrected as unitary authorities (Edinburgh also became a unitary authority at this time).

Lamp of the Lothians, the. A name given to St Mary's Church in HADDINGTON, built in the 14th century out of brightly coloured red sandstone. This may be the origin of the name, although the tower once carried an open masonry crown or 'lantern', like that on St Giles in Edinburgh.

Loudon Hill Possibly 'beacon hill', OScand *log* 'flame' + Scots *doun* 'hill' (*see* DOWN, -DON), with later tautonymous *hill*.
A small craggy hill in East Ayrshire (formerly in Strathclyde), some 18 km (11 miles) east of Kilmarnock.

> Loudoun's bonnie woods and braes
> Ha'e seen our happy bridal days,
> And gentle Hope shall soothe thy waes
> When I am far awa', lassie.
>
> Robert Tannahill: 'Loudon's Bonnie Woods and Braes' (1807)

Battle of Loudon Hill (10 May 1307). A battle in which Robert the Bruce defeated an English army under the Earl of Pembroke.

Lough Allen Probably from *Almu*, a daughter of the Tuatha Dé Danann; *see also* BOG OF ALLEN *and* LOCH, LOUGH.
A lake in northwest Ireland, mostly in County LEITRIM. It forms part of the course of the SHANNON. The IRON MOUN-TAINS – with their associations with the Tuatha Dé Danann and the Fiana – rise above the eastern shore. Isaac Weld described the lake and its environs in 1832:

> ... in the general scene bogs, heather and rocks predominate and the aspect of the country is one of wildness.

Lough Beg Irish 'small lake' (*see* LOCH, LOUGH), i.e. small compared to its neighbour.
A small, shallow lake on the border between counties Antrim and Londonderry. It is on the course of the Lower BANN, which links it by a short channel to LOUGH NEAGH, 2 km (1.2 miles) to the south. With the Strand, an area of wet grassland on the western shore, it is an important wintering ground for waterfowl, and is a National Nature Reserve.

> Like a dull blade with its edge
> Honed bright, Lough Beg half shines under the haze.
>
> Seamus Heaney: 'The Strand at Lough Beg', from *Field Work* (1979)

Lough Belshade Irish *Loch Bél Séad* 'lake of the jewel mouth' (*see* LOCH, LOUGH), from the legend associated with it.
A small lake on the south side of the BLUESTACK MOUN-TAINS, County Donegal. Above it are some fine granite crags, with some good rock climbs. The reason for its name lies in an old legend:

> Coerabar boeth, the daughter of Etal Anbuail of the fairy mansions of Connaught, was a beautiful and powerfully gifted maiden. She had three times fifty ladies in her train. They were all transformed every year into three times fifty beautiful birds and restored to their natural shape the next year. These birds were chained in couples by chains of silver. One bird among them was the most beautiful of the world's birds having a necklace of red gold on her neck, with three times fifty chains depending from it, each chain terminating in a ball of gold. During their transformation into birds they always remained in Loch Crotta Cliath [Lake of Cliath's harps] wherefore the people who saw them were in the habit of saying: 'Many is the Séad at the mouth of Loch Crotta this day. And hence it is called Loch Bél Séad [Lake of the Jewel Mouth].'
>
> Robert Lloyd Praeger: *The Way That I Went* (1937) (*Séad* 'gem, jewel or other precious artefact')

Loughborough 'Luhhede's fortified house', OE male personal name *Luhhede* + *burh* (*see* BURY).
A town (*Lough*- pronounced 'luff-') in Leicestershire, on the River SOAR, about 16 km (10 miles) northwest of Leicester. Historically, it is a town of bells – bell-founding has been its business since the mid-19th century (Great Paul, St Paul's Cathedral's massive bell, was cast here; *see* ST PAUL'S[1]) – and it was also known for lace-making until the Luddites smashed the machines in the early 19th century; but in the 21st century it is best known for its educational associations. **Loughborough College** was founded in 1909, and became famous for its sporting prowess and its serious attitude to sports studies. In 1966 it became **Loughborough University of Technology**. Among its alumni are the runners Sebastian Coe and David Moorecroft, the javelin-thrower Steve Backley, England's 2003 World Cup-winning rugby coach Sir Clive Woodward, and generations of school PE teachers.

Loughborough has long had links with the railway and with rail travel. The first public railway company was insti-tuted here, in 1789, and in 1841 Thomas Cook organized what is believed to have been the first publicly advertised excursion train in England, which conveyed a temperance outing between Leicester and Loughborough. Today Lough-borough Central Station, a terminus of the Great Central Railway (a private steam line), houses a railway museum.

Loughborough Junction From Henry Hastings, 1st Baron *Loughborough* (c.1609–67), who had a house nearby and gave his name also to some roads in the area.

A railway junction and station in southwest London (SW9), in the northeastern part of BRIXTON, in the borough of LAMBETH. The junction, which links the line running south-wards from BLACKFRIARS with east–west lines via a complex of viaducts, was completed in 1872.

Lough Bran After the legendary hound; *see also* LOCH, LOUGH.

A small lake in County Leitrim, 6 km (4 miles) northeast of Carrick-on-Shannon. In legend, Bran, the hound of the hero Finn MacCool (*see under* GIANT'S CAUSEWAY *and* FINGAL) was drowned here.

Lough Carra Irish *Loch Ceara* 'weir lake' (*see* LOCH, LOUGH).

A small lake in County Mayo, just northeast of LOUGH MASK. It is also called **Carra Lough**. The novelist George Moore (1852–1933) was born on its shores, and Lough Carra features in his novel *The Lake* (1905), in which a priest denounces a pregnant schoolteacher and later fakes his own drowning in the lake. Moore's ashes were buried on Castle Island (also called Moore's Island) in the lake. At his funeral the poet Æ (George Russell) gave the oration:

> If his ashes have any sentience, they will feel at home here, for the colours of Lough Carra remained in his memory, when many of his other affections had passed.

Lough Conn Irish *Loch Con*, possibly 'pure lake' or 'lake of the dog' (*see* LOCH, LOUGH).

A lake in County Mayo, some 5 km (3 miles) south of Ballina. It was here that Ireland's largest ever pike was landed, weighing in at 24 kg (53 lb), and the lake is said to hold a million trout.

Lough Corrib Irish *Loch Coirib*, a much altered version of 'Oirbsiu's lake' (*see* LOCH, LOUGH); *Oirbsiu* is a name of Manannán mac Lir, the sea god.

A large lake in County Galway. Its southern tip is joined to GALWAY city by the 5-km (3-mile) stretch of the **River Corrib**, while its northwestern end extends into the mountains of JOYCE'S COUNTRY. Both St Fursey (c.567–c.650) and Roderic O'Connor (d.1198), last high king of Ireland, were born near the lough. Oscar Wilde's father, Sir William Wilde, wrote an account of the antiquities of the area, first published in 1867 as *Lough Corrib, Its Shores and Islands*; it has been reprinted as *Wilde's Lough Corrib*.

> Within
> The crook of tutelary arm that cradled
> The Corrib's urn, the subcutaneous waters
> In their still blue as bright as blood shone out …
>
> Donald Davie: 'Corrib. An Emblem', from *A Winter Talent and Other Poems* (1957)

Inis Feenish ('island of Feenish') in the lough is the sup-posed burial site of Feenish, the mare of the legendary hero Macnamara.

Lough Derg[1] Irish *Loch Dearg* 'red lake' (*see* LOCH, LOUGH), apparently so called from the blood of a monster slain here by the hero Finn MacCool.

A small lake in County Donegal, some 12 km (7 miles) east of Donegal town. It is a remote place, which one local parson in the 18th century described as 'Siberia'. According to tradition, St Patrick fasted for 40 days on a small island in the lake and in a cave was granted a vision of Purgatory and Hell; some say that Dante was inspired by the legends associated with the place. Since the Middle Ages, Lough Derg has been Ireland's most important pilgrimage destin-ation, with people even coming from abroad. Despite being banned by two popes, Alexander VI (the Borgia Pope) and Pius III, the pilgrimage remained popular, and pilgrims continue to visit, fast and keep vigil in their thousands every summer. Not all pilgrims have found themselves in the right frame of mind:

> Pity me on my pilgrimage to Loch Derg!
> O King of the churches and the bells –
> bewailing your sores and your wounds,
> but not a tear can I squeeze from my eyes …
> … pity me on my pilgrimage to Loch Derg
> and I with a heart not softer than a stone!
>
> Donnchadh Mor O'Dala (attributed): 'At Saint Patrick's Purgatory' (13th century), translated by Sean O'Faolain

Later poets have also been driven to cynicism:

> From Cavan and from Leitrim and from Mayo,
> From all the thin-faced parishes where hills
> Are perished noses running peaty water,
> They come to Lough Derg to fast and pray and beg
> With all the bitterness of nonentities …
>
> Patrick Kavanagh: 'Lough Derg' (1942)

Another poet, Denis Devlin (1908–59), also wrote about the pilgrims:

> The poor in spirit on their rosary rounds,
> The jobbers with their whiskey-angered eyes,
> The pink bank clerks, the tip-hat papal counts,
> And drab, kind women their tonsured mockery tries …
>
> Denis Devlin: 'Lough Derg', from *Collected Poems* (1964)

Lough Derg[2] Irish *Loch Dearg* 'red lake' (*see* LOCH, LOUGH); also called *Deirgderc* in Irish, meaning 'of the red eye', a reference to its dedication to the sun-god Éochaid.

A large, long lake in western Ireland, forming the boundary between counties CLARE, GALWAY and TIPPERARY. The lake constitutes part of the course of the SHANNON.

Lough Derravaragh Irish *Loch Dairbhreach*, 'lake with a wood of oak-trees' (*see* LOCH, LOUGH).

A lake in County Westmeath, some 10 km (6 miles) north of Mullingar. It is here that, in the Irish legend, the Children of Lir spent their last 300 years as swans, until the arrival of Christianity and the tolling of a monastery bell restored them to aged human form, allowing them to be baptized before they died. Alternatively, they finally landed at ALLIHIES, in County Cork.

Lough Erne. *See under* ERNE.

Lough Foyle. *See under* FOYLE.

Loughgall Irish *Loch gCál* 'Cál's lake' or 'cabbage lake'.
A village in County Armagh, 7 km (4.5 miles) north of Armagh itself. On its outskirts was fought the Battle of the Diamond (*see under* DIAMOND) in 1795, and in 1987 it was the scene of an SAS ambush, in which eight members of an IRA active-service unit were killed, along with a passing motorist.

The poet W.R. Rodgers (1906–69) was minister at Loughgall and is buried here, and the poet and playwright Richard Rowley (1877–1947) also died here.

Lough Gill Irish *Loch Gile* 'lake of brightness' (*see* LOCH, LOUGH).
A small lake in County Sligo, just east of Sligo itself. One of its islands is INNISFREE, immortalized poetically by W.B. Yeats.
Wild Rose of Lough Gill, The. A historical novel (1883) by Patrick G. Smyth. It has given its name to one of the tourist boats on the lake, and the nearby Manorhamilton holds an annual Wild Rose Festival, a beauty contest. The novel itself is set during the wars of the 17th century, and the eponymous rose is Kathleen Ny Cuirnin, beautiful granddaughter of the local teller of tales. She survives many adventures and ends up in Spain with the Irish Brigade (the so-called Wild Geese; *see under* IRISH), among them her true love, Don Edmundo O'Tracy.

Lough Graney Possibly 'gravelly lake' (*see* LOCH, LOUGH), *Graney* Irish *greanach*, but there is a tradition that the name refers to *Gráinne*, the daughter of Cormac mac Airt whose story is told in *Tóraigheacht Dhiarmada agus Ghráinne* ('the pursuit of Diarmait and Gráinne').
A small lake in County Clare, some 35 km (21 miles) north of Limerick.

> When I looked at Lough Graney my heart grew bright,
> Ploughed lands and green in the morning light,
> Mountains in rows with crimson borders
> Peering above their neighbours' shoulders.
>
>> Bryan Merryman (1747–1805): *The Midnight Court* (written 1780–1), translated from the Gaelic by Frank O'Connor

Lough Graney is said to have a monster in the form of a giant eel.

Lough Gur Etymology unknown; but *see* LOCH, LOUGH.
A small lake in County Limerick, some 15 km (9 miles) southeast of Limerick city. The area is rich in prehistoric remains, of enormous interest to archaeologists, and the earls of Desmond had a powerful castle here.

There is a story that the spirit of the last of the Desmonds, Gerald Fitzgerald, the 'Rebel' 15th Earl, killed when his revolt was crushed in 1583, is doomed to sleep under Lough Gur, riding out over the surface of the waters every seventh year until his horse's silver shoes are worn out, at which point he will be restored to life. In other versions the sleeper is an earlier Gerald Fitzgerald, the son of the 3rd Earl of Desmond and Aine, a fairy queen whom he had seduced at Lough Gur; or the sleeper may be, who knows, an even earlier earl, Gearoid Iarla, who was noted as a magician. Aine herself lives at the hill of Knockainy (Irish *Cnoc Aine* 'hill of Aine') 5 km (3 miles) southeast of Lough Gur; in the past, straw was burnt in her honour at the summer solstice.

In another legend, Gearoid Iarla is turned into a swan, which is why there are so many swans on Lough Gur.

Lough Key Irish *Loch Cé* 'lake of the quay' (*see* LOCH, LOUGH), although it has been suggested that the name refers to Cé, a druid killed at the second Battle of MOYTURA, and buried here.
A lake in County Roscommon, 10 km (6 miles) northwest of Carrick-on-Shannon. It is beautifully situated, with the low Curlew Mountains rising on the west; the area now comprises the **Lough Key Forest Park**. Among the many wooded islands on the lake is Castle Island, where in the 1890s Yeats and Maud Gonne hoped to turn the ruined castle into a 'Castle of Heroes' for a planned 'Celtic Order of Mysteries'.
Annals of Loch Cé. A 16th-century chronicle of the history of CONNACHT from the 11th to the 16th centuries, compiled at the abbey (now ruined) on Trinity Island, Lough Key.

Lough Leane. *See under* KILLARNEY.

Lough Mask Etymology unknown; but *see* LOCH, LOUGH.
A large lake mainly in County Mayo, with its southern end just inside County Galway. The Partry Mountains (*see under* PARTRY) rise to the west. Water flows from Lough Mask to LOUGH CORRIB to the south via an underground river through the limestone (this river can be accessed at various places, notably at the Pigeon Hole). During the Great Famine a canal was built between the two as a famine-relief scheme, but because of the porous nature of the rock the canal remains dry to this day.

Lough Mask has its very own monster, the Dhobar-Chu, described as half wolf, half fish, and termed 'the Irish crocodile' in the following account, recalling an incident that had happened some ten years previously:

> The man was passing the shore just by the waterside, and spied far off the head of a beast swimming, which he took to be an otter, and took no more notice of it; but the beast

it seems lifted up his head, to discern whereabouts the man was; then diving swam under the water till he struck ground: whereupon he run out of the water suddenly and took the man by the elbow whereby the man stooped down, and the beast fastened his teeth in his pate, and dragged him into the water; where the man took hold of a stone by chance in his way, and calling to mind he had a knife in his jacket, took it out and gave a thrust of it to the beast, which thereupon got away from him into the lake.

> Roderick O'Flaherty: *A Description of West Connaught* (1684)

It was near here in 1880, during a period of agrarian disturbance and conflict between landlords, the authorities and tenants, that Captain Charles Cunningham Boycott, land agent for the County Mayo estates of Lord Erne, became the first victim of the Land League's policy of social and economic ostracization, or 'boycotting'.

Lough Neagh Irish *Loch nEathnach* 'Eochu's lake' (*see* LOCH, LOUGH); in legend, *Eochu* or *Eochaid*, of which it is a diminutive, was either a horse-god who ruled the otherworld under the lake, or a prince who drowned when the Bann flooded to form the lake.

The largest lake in Ireland, and, at 396 sq km (153 sq miles), bigger by a factor in excess of five than anything Britain has to offer. It is surrounded by five of the six counties of Northern Ireland: Londonderry, Antrim, Down (just), Armagh and Tyrone. The main river feeding it is the Upper BANN, and its only drain is the Lower Bann. According to legend, where Lough Neagh is now was once just the narrow stream of the Bann, which had to be controlled by a stone placed over the source; however, one day the guardian of the source nodded off and the river flooded the plain, drowning people and villages (a similar story is told of the formation of LOCH AWE in Argyll). Another explanation has it that the giant Finn MacCool, doing battle with a Scottish giant (sometimes said to be Fingal, who may or may not have been the same fellow as Finn), scooped up a chunk of Ireland to lob at his foe – so forming the ISLE OF MAN and Loch Neagh (revisionists also claim a ricocheting pebble formed ROCKALL); the GIANT'S CAUSEWAY was a further geomorphological result of this spat. There are two other beliefs regarding the lough:

> The lough will claim a victim every year.
> It has virtue that hardens wood to stone.
>
> Seamus Heaney: 'A Lough Neagh Sequence', from *Door into the Dark* (1969)

Despite its size, its legends and its vast numbers of eels and wintering waterfowl, it has to be said that Lough Neagh is a plain place, with plain shores and few islands or indentations to lend enchantment to the view.

Loughor 'bright one', Welsh *llychwr* 'brightness'.

A river in south Wales, about 20 km (12 miles) long. Its Welsh name is **Llwchwr**. The Loughor rises on the southwest side of BLACK MOUNTAIN, and forms the boundary between Swansea unitary authority and Carmarthenshire (formerly between West Glamorgan and Dyfed). The small town of **Loughor** stands where the Loughor estuary opens out into Burry Inlet, next to GORSEINON. In Welsh it is **Casllwchwr** ('castle on the River Loughor'): there was a Roman fort here (called **Leucarum**) and a medieval castle.

Loughrea Irish *Baile Locha Riach* 'town of the grey lake' (*see* BAL-, BALL-, BALLY- *and* LOCH, LOUGH).

A market town in County Galway, 15 km (9 miles) southeast of Athenry, on the small **Lough Rea** from which it gains its name. An Anglo-Norman castle and Carmelite priory were built here *c.*1300 by Richard de Burgo, and Loughrea has the cathedral (1897) of the Catholic diocese of CLONFERT.

Lough Ree Irish *Loch Rí* 'lake of the king' (*see* LOCH, LOUGH).

A large, long lake on the course of the SHANNON in central Ireland, forming part of the boundary between counties Westmeath, Longford and Roscommon. It is a lake of many bays and numerous islands, several of them (including INCHCLERAUN) with ancient monastic remains – which perhaps explains the superstition that it is dangerous for a woman (or indeed any female animal) to land on any of the islands. On 18 May 1960 three priests saw a monster in the lough, although, with appropriate modesty, they did not report its gender; earlier sightings were made in 1950, AD 600 and … 300 BC.

> Lough Ree, oh Lough Ree, where the three counties meet,
> Longford, Westmeath and Roscommon,
> As I stroll round her banks, by the heather and peat
> They're the memories I've never forgotten.
>
> Anon.: 'Where the Three Counties Meet' (song)

Lough Swilly Irish *Loch Súill* (*see* LOCH, LOUGH), from the River Swilly that enters it, in Irish *An tSúileach*, 'the one with eyes'.

A narrow sea inlet on the north coast of Ireland. It is 40 km (25 miles) long, and separates INISHOWEN from the rest of County DONEGAL. It is sometimes called the **Lake of Shadows**, because of the play of light upon its waters. Lough Swilly was the site of an important Royal Navy anchorage to which Britain retained rights until 1938. It was from Rathmullan on the western shore that in 1607 the Flight of the Earls took place, an episode in which Hugh O'Neill, Earl of Tyrone, and Rory O'Donnell, Earl of Tyrconnell, left Ireland for ever, leaving Ulster open to Protestant plantation. In September 1798, revolutionary Wolfe Tone sailed into Lough Swilly on board a French ship, too late for the crushed United Irishmen's Rebellion, and was captured.

He cut his throat with a penknife on 12 November as he awaited his execution; it took him seven days to die.

> Proudly the note of the trumpet is sounding,
> Loudly the war-cries arise on the gale;
> Fleetly the steed by Lough Swilly is bounding,
> To join the thick squadrons in Saimear's green vale.
>
> Michael Joseph McCann (1824–83): 'O'Donnell Aboo'

Loughton 'estate associated with Luca', OE male personal name *Luca* + -ING + -TON.
A town (*Lough*- rhyming with *how*) in Essex, on the River RODING, to the east of Epping Forest (*see under* EPPING), about 5 km (3 miles) northeast of Chingford.

Loughton 'Underground' station, on the Epping branch of the Central line, opened in 1948.

The tennis player Christine Truman (b.1941; married name Christine Janes) was born in Loughton.

Louisburgh So named by Henry Browne, the uncle of the 1st Marquess of Sligo, after *Louisburg* in Nova Scotia; Browne had been present at the capture of the latter from the French in 1758.
A small town in County Mayo, 20 km (12 miles) west of Westport. Its Irish name is **Cluain Cearbán** ('meadow of Carbán').

Loup of Fintry. *See under* FINTRY.

Lourdes of Wales, the. A nickname for HOLYWELL in Flintshire.

Louseland. A 17th-century nickname for Scotland, a name that gave way in the following century to SCRATCHLAND and ITCHLAND. The causes of the itching were referred to as Scots Greys or simply Scotchmen. In Romany, according to George Borrow, Scotland is *Juvlo-mengreskey tem*, meaning 'lousy fellows' country'.

Louth[1] Named after the River *Lud*, on which it stands, from OE *Hlude* 'the loud one, the noisy stream'.
A town in Lincolnshire, on the River Lud and on the Greenwich 0° Meridian, about 48 km (30 miles) northeast of Lincoln, on the eastern edge of the Lincolnshire Wolds. Its centre is largely Georgian, but it is dominated by the 15th-century church of St James, whose steeple is, at 90 m (295 ft), the tallest on an English church.

It was in Louth that the Pilgrimage of Grace, a Catholic rebellion against Henry VIII, began in 1536.

Alfred Tennyson attended Louth Grammar School, as did the explorer John Franklin, who was lost in 1847 looking for the Northwest Passage. Jeffrey Archer was the local MP between 1969 and 1974, when huge financial losses forced him to resign and turn his hand to novel-writing.

Louth[2] Irish *Lughmhaigh*, 'Lugh plain'; the first element may refer to *Lugh* Lámfhota, a chief of the Tuatha Dé Danann.
A village in County Louth, to which it gives its name. It is 13 km (8 miles) southwest of Dundalk. St Patrick is reputed to have built the first church here, and there exist here the remains of a medieval church and abbey.

Louth, County. A generally low-lying county in northeastern Ireland, in the province of Leinster. It is the smallest county in the Republic, and is bounded to the east by the Irish Sea, to the north by Armagh and Carlingford Lough, to the northwest by Monaghan and to the southwest by Meath. The county town is DUNDALK, and other towns include DROGHEDA and ARDEE. Louth was annexed by the future King John in 1185 from the ancient kingdom of AIRGIALLA (Oriel), and in the 14th century became part of the PALE.

Louth Mower, the. A nickname for John Foster (1740–1828), an Irish chancellor of the exchequer and the last Speaker of the Irish House of Commons before that institution expired under the Act of Union (1800). The belittling sobriquet derived from rumours that his grandfather had been no more than a (*whisper it*) common farmer.

Love Clough 'Luha's ravine', *Love* OE male personal name *Luha*; *Clough* OE *cloh* 'ravine'.
A village in the Forest of ROSSENDALE, Lancashire, 6 km (4 miles) south of Burnley.

Lover Origin unknown, perhaps a corruption of *Low Ford*.
A village in Wiltshire, about 13 km (8 miles) southeast of Salisbury.

Lower Basildon *Basildon* 'Bæssel's valley', OE male personal name *Bœssel* + *denu* 'valley' (and thus dissimilar to BASILDON in Essex).
A village in Berkshire, within the unitary authority of West Berkshire, about 4 km (2.5 miles) northwest of Pangbourne. To the southwest is the much larger NEW TOWN[1] of **Upper Basildon**. The agriculturalist Jethro Tull (1674–1741), inventor of a seed drill, was born here.

Basildon Bond. A brand of writing paper, so named because the directors of the stationery company that first produced it were staying in Basildon when deciding whether to introduce it in 1911. By the end of the 1920s it was Britain's best-selling brand. It is now produced by John Dickinson.

Basildon Park. A National Trust-owned mansion and estate to the south of Lower Basildon, built 1776–83, and designed in the Palladian style by John Carr for the wealthy imperialist Francis Sykes. It boasts an Octagon Room, among other attractions.

Lower Dicker 'ten lower down', *Dicker* 'ten' (probably alluding to a plot of land for which the sum of ten iron rods – enough to make two horse-shoes – was paid in rent), ME *dyker* (ultimately from Latin *decuria* 'company or parcel of ten').
A village in East Sussex, about 1.5 km (1 mile) north of UPPER DICKER.

Lower Peover *Peover* from the River *Peover*, an OCelt river name meaning 'the bright one'.
A village in Cheshire, about 5 km (3 miles) southwest of KNUTSFORD.

Lower Slaughter *Slaughter* probably 'muddy place', OE *slohtre*.
A picturesque village in Gloucestershire, on the River Eye (a stream that purls along the main street), in the COTSWOLDS, about 1.5 km (1 mile) southeast of UPPER SLAUGHTER.

Lower Swell *Swell* 'rising ground or hill', OE *swelle*.
A village in Gloucestershire, in the COTSWOLDS, about 1.5 km (1 mile) south of UPPER SWELL.

Lower Upham *Upham* 'upper homestead or enclosure', OE *upp* 'upper' + HAM.
A village in Hampshire, about 8 km (5 miles) east of EASTLEIGH. It is not, though, in the vicinity of UPPER UPHAM.

Lowestoft 'Hlothver's homestead', OScand *Hlothvers* possessive form of male personal name *Hlothver* + *toft* 'homestead'.
A town and port on the north Suffolk coast, at the eastern end of OULTON BROAD, about 16 km (10 miles) south of Great Yarmouth. It is said to have originated as a Danish settlement on **Lowestoft Ness**, a promontory (*see also* NESS) just to the north of the Inner Harbour that is the most easterly point in the United Kingdom. It still has a small but active fishing fleet (keeping the large nearby Bird's Eye factory busy), and is famous for its herrings and kippers. The steep narrow alleyways of the old town are known as 'Scores'.

Soft-paste porcelain wares were made here from 1757, and they are known by the designation 'Lowestoft':

'But what a terrible teapot.'... 'It's old Lowestoft.'

Compton Mackenzie: *Carnival* (1912)

The writer Thomas Nashe (1567–1601) and the composer Benjamin Britten (1913–76) were born in Lowestoft, as were, closer to our day, the members of the rock group The Darkness (Justin Hawkins, his brother Dan Hawkins, Frankie Poullain and Ed Graham).

Battle of Lowestoft (3 June 1665). A sea battle during the Second Dutch War (1665–67) in which the English fleet, commanded by the Duke of York (later James II) defeated the Dutch. Samuel Pepys, at that time secretary to the Navy Board, described it as 'a great victory, never known in the world'.

Loweswater 'leafy lake', OScand *lauf* 'leaf' + *sœr* 'lake', with the tautonymous addition of OE *water* 'lake'.
A small lake in the western Lake District, Cumbria (formerly in Cumberland), some 6 km (4 miles) northwest of Buttermere. The village of **Loweswater** is between the lake and CRUMMOCK WATER, while **Loweswater Fell** is to the south.

Lowland Hundred, the. *See under* ABERDOVEY.

Lowlands, the. The low-lying central belt of Scotland, confined between the SOUTHERN UPLANDS and the HIGHLANDS. It contains most of Scotland's population. Until post-Jacobite sentimentality seeped in and the Highlanders seeped out (during the Clearances), the English-speaking, industrious and Protestant Lowlanders traditionally regarded themselves as a superior race to the wild, dangerous and frequently Catholic Gaelic-speakers to the north. For their part, the Highlanders referred to the Lowlanders disparagingly as the SASSENACH.

Lowland lassie, wilt thou go
Where the hills are clad with snow,
Where, beneath the icy steep,
The hardy shepherd tends his sheep?
Ill nor wae shall thee betide,
When row'd within my Highland plaid.

Robert Tannahill: 'O Row Thee in My Highland Plaid'

Lallans. The form of the Scots dialect formerly spoken in the Lowlands of Scotland, and revived by Hugh MacDiarmid and others in the Scottish Literary Renaissance of the earlier 20th century. The term derives from *lawland* 'lowland'.

Lowther Hills Etymology obscure.
A range of high rounded hills on the border between South Lanarkshire and Dumfries and Galloway. The highest point is **Green Lowther** (732 m / 2401 ft); on its summit is a radio mast for aircraft navigation. The second-highest peak is **Lowther Hill** (725 m / 2378 ft), which forms the highest point on the Southern Upland Way (*see under* SOUTHERN UPLANDS). The range is traversed by two high road-passes: that which passes through LEADHILLS and WANLOCKHEAD, and the DALVEEN PASS.

Lowton. The fictional version of KIRKBY LONSDALE in Charlotte Brontë's *Jane Eyre* (1847).

Loxley 'Locc's glade', OE *Locces* possessive form of male personal name *Locc* + -LEY.
A village in Warwickshire, about 6 km (4 miles) southeast of Stratford-upon-Avon.

Lucan Irish *Leamhcán* 'place of elm-trees'.
A western suburb of DUBLIN, formerly a village, some 10 km (6 miles) west of the centre.

Lucan was the birthplace of the Jacobite Patrick Sarsfield (d.1693), one of the principal leaders of the resistance to William III in Ireland. James II made him Earl of Lucan in 1691, but this title was recognized only by the Jacobites. Other notable **Lord Lucans** include George Charles Bingham, 3rd Earl of Lucan (1800–88), commander of the cavalry at the Battle of Balaclava, where he sent the Light Brigade into the 'Valley of Death'; and John Bingham, 6th

Baron 'Lucky' Lucan (1934–?), the gambler who in 1974 (probably) killed his children's nanny in mistake for his wife, and then disappeared.

Luce Bay *Luce* Gaelic *lus* 'herb, plant'.

A wide bay between the Rinns of Galloway (*see under* GALLOWAY) and the MACHARS of Wigtownshire, in Dumfries and Galloway. It is about 30 km (20 miles) deep by 30 km (20 miles) wide. Along its inner shore are the extensive **Sands of Luce**, and the bay is fed by the **Water of Luce**, itself fed by the **Main Water of Luce** and its tributary, the **Cross Water of Luce** (quite why it is so irritated remains a mystery). The villages of **New Luce** and **Glenluce** are on the course of the river.

Ludford 'ford by the noisy stream', OE *hlude* 'noisy stream' (referring to the River Teme) + FORD.

A village in Shropshire on the south bank of the River Teme, just south of LUDLOW.

Ludford Bridge, Battle of (12–13 October 1459). A Lancastrian rout of Yorkist forces during the Wars of the Roses. Richard, Duke of York, had joined forces with the Earl of Salisbury in a retreat to his home at Ludlow Castle. Confronted by a larger Lancastrian army across the River Teme at Ludford Bridge, Richard's army disintegrated. The Lancastrians went on to sack Ludlow, and Richard fled to Ireland with his son, Edward. The battle is sometimes referred to as the **Battle of Ludlow Bridge**.

Ludgate Hill *Ludgate* from the former city gate of that name, 'back gate or postern', OE *ludgeat*. From early times the name was associated with King Lud, who, according to a legend promulgated in the 12th century by the chronicler Geoffrey of Monmouth (*see under* MONMOUTH), rebuilt the City of London.

A hill and street in the City of London (EC4), rising from Farringdon Street (along the line of the River FLEET[1]) eastwards towards ST PAUL'S[1] Cathedral. At its foot was once **Ludgate** (*see above*), the old western gateway to the City of London. This was built by the Romans around AD 200, but legend has given it to King Lud (*see above*). He is said to have erected it in 66 BC, and statues of him and his sons used to stand on the gate. From the time of Richard II there was a prison above the gateway, for debtors and petty criminals; in 17th- and 18th-century slang it was known as 'Lud's bulwark'. The gate was demolished in 1760.

Ludgate Circus, at the junction of Ludgate Hill, Farringdon Street and FLEET STREET, was laid out in 1864. The following year a railway viaduct was thrown across the street, providing access to the now defunct Ludgate Hill station and ruining the striking view of St Paul's from Fleet Street. It was demolished in 1990.

In the 18th and 19th centuries the London Coffee House, on the north side of Ludgate Hill, provided secure overnight accommodation for OLD BAILEY juries that had been unable to reach a verdict.

Ludgate bird. Seventeenth-century slang for someone imprisoned for debt or bankruptcy (the inmates of Ludgate prison (*see above*) were mainly debtors).

Ludgershall[1] 'nook of land with a trapping-spear', OE *lute-gar* 'trapping-spear' (a spear set up to impale animals chased onto it) + *halh* (*see* HALE, -HALL).

A village (pronounced 'luggershawl') in Buckinghamshire, near the Oxfordshire border, about 17.5 km (11 miles) northwest of Aylesbury.

Ludgershall[2]. A small town in Wiltshire, about 21 km (13 miles) southeast of Marlborough.

Ludgvan Perhaps 'place of ashes, burnt place', Cornish *lusow*, *ludw* + a suffix.

A village (pronounced 'ludge-ən') in western Cornwall, about 5 km (3 miles) northeast of Penzance.

Ludlow 'hill or tumulus by the noisy stream' (referring to the River Teme), OE *hlude* 'noisy stream' + *hlaw* (*see* LAW, LOW).

A town in Shropshire, close to the Herefordshire border, about 40 km (25 miles) south of SHREWSBURY. It stands on a steep hill by the confluence of the Rivers Corve and TEME. Its strategic position close to the Welsh border made it an important place during the Middle Ages. It was the seat of the Lord President of the Council of the MARCHES, and its Norman castle, now in ruins, was headquarters of the powerful Mortimer family. Between 1461 and 1552 the castle was a royal palace, and the future Henry VIII's brother Arthur (then heir apparent) died there in 1502. Milton's masque *Comus* was first performed there in 1634.

Several ancient inns and taverns survive, most notably the Feathers Hotel of 1603, with its elaborately carved wooden facade. A pleasing medley of half-timbering and Georgian stucco fills in the town's original 12th-century grid pattern, and all is dominated by the 41 m (135 ft) tower of the 15th-century cathedral-like St Laurence's Church. The ashes of A.E. Housman (1859–1936), SHROPSHIRE poet *par excellence*, are buried in the churchyard.

After its medieval glories Ludlow retreated into the borderland mists, but its profile rose again somewhat towards the end of the 20th century, when it became something of a gastronomic centre, blessed with several notable restaurants and food shops (the restaurant critic Jonathan Meades described the town in 2003 as 'the exception that proves the rule of provincial Britain's gastronomic backwardness').

There are towns called Ludlow in the USA (California, Colorado, Illinois, Massachusetts, Pennsylvania, South Dakota, Vermont) and Canada (New Brunswick).

> Oh, come you home of Sunday
> When Ludlow streets are still

And Ludlow bells are calling
To farm and lane and mill,
Or come you home of Monday
When Ludlow market hums
And Ludlow chimes are playing
'The conquering hero comes',
Come you home a hero,
Or come not home at all,
The lads you leave will mind you
Till Ludlow tower shall fall.

A.E. Housman: 'The Recruit', from *A Shropshire Lad* (1896)

Ludlovian. A term applied by geologists to the latest of the three divisions of the Silurian period, rocks from which have been found in the Ludlow area. It is based on *Ludlovia*, a Latinization of the town's name.

Ludlow Town. A song cycle (1920) by E.J. Moeran, setting four poems from A.E. Housman's *A Shropshire Lad* (1896) (*see under* SHROPSHIRE).

Lugg 'bright stream', OCelt.

A river in Powys and Herefordshire, which rises in the Radnor Forest (*see under* RADNORSHIRE) and flows 64 km (40 miles) southeastwards through PRESTEIGNE, LEOMINSTER and HEREFORD to join the River WYE[1] to the south of Hereford.

Lughmhaigh. The Irish name for LOUTH[2].

Lugnaquilla Irish *Log na Coille* 'hollow of the wood'.

The highest peak (925 m / 3034 ft) in the Wicklow Mountains of County WICKLOW, some 25 km (16 miles) west of Wicklow itself. **Lugnaquillia** is a variant of the name. In the wake of the 1798 United Irishmen's Rebellion Michael Dwyer and his men are supposed to have hidden in a cave on Lugnaquilla, but this has never been found. The US-born composer Robert A. Diebold (b.1924), resident in Ireland since 1972, has written a piece called *Lugnaquilla Variations* (1998) for string quartet.

Lug Walk, the. A 50-km (30-mile) north–south walk over the Wicklow Mountains, covering 17 peaks, the last being Lugnaquilla.

Luguvallium. The Roman name for their settlement on the site of modern CARLISLE.

Luimneach. The Irish name for LIMERICK.

Luing Gaelic *long, luing* 'ship'.

A small island (pronounced 'ling') in the Inner HEBRIDES, some 20 km (12 miles) south of Oban, in Argyll and Bute (formerly in Strathclyde region). It is among a group of small islands close to the mainland, including SCARBA, SEIL and the GARVELLACHS. The **Sound of Luing** separates it from the island of Lunga to the west. The slate that was formerly quarried on the island was used for the restored roof of IONA Cathedral.

Lulworth 'Lulla's enclosure', OE male personal name *Lulla* + *worth* (*see* -WORTH, WORTHY, -WARDINE).

Either of a pair of villages in Dorset, about 17 km (11 miles) east of Weymouth. **West Lulworth** is near the coast, **East Lulworth** about 1.5 km (1 mile) inland. To the west of the latter are the remains of **Lulworth Castle** (destroyed by fire in 1929). The surviving late 18th-century Rotunda was the first Roman Catholic church permitted to be built in England after the Reformation – George III is said to have agreed to it as long as it did not look like a church.

Large areas of land to the east of Lulworth are used by the Army as firing ranges, and are closed to the public (*see also* TYNEHAM).

Lulworth Cove. A small horseshoe-shaped bay on the Dorset coast, just to the south of West Lulworth. To the rear are chalk cliffs, and it is nearly encircled by arms of Purbeck marble and Portland stone spectacularly patterned with folded strata. It is fictionalized in the novels of Thomas Hardy as **Lulwind Cove**. (*See also* DURDLE DOOR *and* HAMBURY TOUT).

Lulworth skipper. A small brown butterfly (*Thymelicus acteon*) found only in the grasslands around Lulworth. It was discovered in 1832 by the eminent lepidopterist J.C. Dale.

Lumphanan 'St Finan's church', OCelt *lann* 'church' + personal name. This St Finan was abbot of LINDISFARNE in the mid-7th century.

A village in Cromar, Aberdeenshire (formerly in Grampian region), 15 km (9 miles) northwest of Banchory. Just north of the village is **Macbeth's Cairn**, traditionally marking the spot where, on 15 August 1057, Macbeth was killed in battle by Malcolm Canmore. Another tradition places his death just south of the village, but whichever is the precise spot, the historical Macbeth died at Lumphanan rather than at DUNSINANE, where, in Shakespeare's play, he is killed by Macduff.

Lumsdon. The fictional name for CUMNOR in the novels of Thomas Hardy.

Lunan. *See under* BRAEHEAD OF LUNAN.

Lunan Bay *Lunan* possibly Gaelic *lunnan* 'waves' or OCelt root meaning 'healthy'.

An indentation of the North Sea on the east coast of Angus (formerly in Tayside region), 5 km (3 miles) south of Montrose. It takes its name from **Lunan Water**, which rises near Forfar and enters the North Sea here. The settlements of **Lunan** and BRAEHEAD OF LUNAN are on the bay.

Lundy 'puffin island', OScand *lundi* 'puffin' + *ey* (*see* -AY).

A rocky island at the entrance to the Bristol Channel (*see under* BRISTOL), about 19 km (12 miles) northwest of HARTLAND POINT in Devon. Vertically long and thin in shape, it is 5 sq km (2 sq miles) in area and surrounded by granite cliffs. Its highest point is 142 m (466 ft) above sea level. In former times Lundy was a stronghold of pirates and smugglers. In 1925 it was bought (for £16,000) by the English financier M.C. Coles, self-styled '**King of Lundy**', who issued illegal currency (1 puffin = 1 UK penny) with his own portrait on it and was fined for his pains. Now, however, under the ownership (since 1969) of the National Trust, it is a sanctuary for nothing more dangerous than seabirds – notably the puffins that gave it its name and which appear on its stamps and unofficial (legal) 'currency'.

The pyramid-shaped Shutter Rock, on the island's southwest tip, features in Charles Kingsley's *Westward Ho!*:

> Then a hundred yards of roaring breaker upon a sunken shelf, across which the race of the tide poured like a cataract; then, amid a column of salt smoke, the Shutter, like a huge black fang, rose waiting for its prey; and between the Shutter and the land, the great galleon loomed dimly through the storm.
>
> Charles Kingsley: *Westward Ho!*, Chapter 32 (1855)

Local consternation was caused in 2003 when EU statisticians ruled that because its population (then 19) was below 50, Lundy could not be officially classed as an island.

In 1986 the seas around Lundy were designated the first Marine Nature Reserve. The island has also given its name to a shipping-forecast area.

See also RAT ISLAND.

Lune[1] An OCelt river name probably meaning 'pure, healthy'. A river in northwest England. It flows 72 km (45 miles) west then south from near Newbiggin in eastern Cumbria through KIRKBY LONSDALE into Lancashire, where it runs through LANCASTER before entering an estuary that disgorges into the Irish Sea.

Crook o' Lune. A beauty spot on the river, 6 km (4 miles) northeast of Lancaster, made famous by the painter J.M.W. Turner.

Lune[2]. A small river, about 20 km (12 miles) long, in County Durham. It rises on the slopes of Mickle Fell in the treeless **Lune Forest**, and flows east through **Lunedale** before entering the TEES 10 km (6 miles) northwest of Barnard Castle.

Lurgan Irish *An Lorgain* 'the ridge'.
A town in County Armagh, 30 km (20 miles) southwest of Belfast. It is nicknamed **Spade Town** (*see below*). In 1610 James VI and I granted Lurgan to John Brownlow for an English plantation. Lurgan later flourished as a linen town.

> There is a bonnie wee lass
> In my own country
> And her I will go and see,
> But if she's dead or wed
> I'm at my liberty.
> If ever I chance to go that way

> As I suppose I may
> I will call and see the lass I loved
> Who lived on Lurgan Braes
>
> Anon.: ballad 'Lurgan Braes' (*braes* 'hillsides')

Lurgan was the birthplace of James Logan (1674–1750), who was secretary to William Penn and later presided over the ruling council of Pennsylvania from 1702 to 1747 (there is a town called Lurgan in that state); the poet and essayist Æ (George Russell, 1867–1935); and Sir John Greer Dill (1881–1944), chief of the Imperial General Staff in 1940–1.

Lurgan enjoys a certain rivalry with its close neighbour to the west, PORTADOWN (both were lumped together into the new town of CRAIGAVON in 1965):

> Once again Portadown has beaten Lurgan in the 'quality of life' index, published yesterday by the Northern Ireland Social Trends Survey. Lurgan was officially ranked 'Worst town in Northern Ireland', while Portadown retained its coveted title of 'Worst town in Northern Ireland (excluding Lurgan)'
>
> Following a series of extensive interviews, questionnaires and RUC undercover operations, Lurgan people are revealed to be consistently uglier, nastier, less intelligent and more inbred than their Portadown counterparts, according to the authoritative report.
>
> *The Portadown News*, a satirical online newssheet (March 2001)

have a face like a Lurgan spade, to. An expression meaning 'to look miserable'. It originated in the late 19th century, and apparently derives from the Irish *lorgán spáid* 'spade handle'.

Lurgan spade. A spade with a long, slim blade, and now more commonly referred to as an Armagh spade.

Luss Said by some to be from Gaelic *lus* 'plant', while the more romantic adhere to OFr *luce* 'lily'. The latter theory derives from the story of Baroness MacAuslin, who died during the Siege of Tournai, and whose body was brought back to Luss for burial covered with flowers, especially *fleurs-de-luce*; these grew up through her grave 'and became miraculously efficacious in staying a pestilence then raging through the countryside'.

A village on the west shore of Loch Lomond, Argyll and Bute. To its west **Glen Luss** extends into the **Luss Hills** (highest point Doune Hill, 734 m / 2408 ft). The village is used as the setting for the television soap opera *Take the High Road*, while in the pre-television age the **Colquhouns of Luss** (the local clan) took a notable hammering at the hands of the MacGregors during the course of the Slaughter of Lennox (*see under* LENNOX).

Lustleigh Probably 'Leofgiest's glade', OE male personal name *Leofgiest* + -LEY.

A preternaturally pretty village in Devon, full of thatched cottages, on the eastern edge of DARTMOOR, about 19 km

(12 miles) southwest of Exeter. Lustleigh's annual May Day celebrations are said to have been revived by the author Cecil Torr (*see* WREYLAND).

Lustleigh Cleave. A rough bare slope, which rises steeply from the Lustleigh side of the River BOVEY, working its way up to Hunters Tor, Ravens Tor, Harten Chest and Sharptor. The whole valley tends to be loosely referred to as 'the Cleave' (*cleave* means 'cleft').

Luton 'farmstead on the River Lea', LEA + -TON (*see also* LEYTON).

A town and unitary authority within Bedfordshire, on the River LEA and the M1, at the northern end of the Chilterns, about 45 km (28 miles) northwest of London and 17.5 km (11 miles) west of Stevenage. Until the end of the 19th century it was a small place, which specialized in straw-plaiting and lace-making and was famous for its straw hats (**Luton Town FC**, founded in 1885, is nicknamed the Hatters). But then the motor car arrived, in the shape of Vauxhall Motors Ltd (*see under* VAUXHALL), which established itself in Luton in 1905, and it dominated the town's industrial landscape during the 20th century. (The automotive connection is onomastically acknowledged in the generic application of the term '**Luton**' to a coachbuilt motor-caravan body-shape that extends over the cab.)

The **University of Luton** was formed in 1993 from the former Luton College of Higher Education.

Luton has never exactly been a place to set the pulses racing, and in a 2004 poll it replaced HULL as Britain's 'crappest' town.

> A recent Nasa probe revealed that Mars has more of an atmosphere than Luton town centre on a Saturday night.
>
> Sarfraz Mazoor (a native of Luton): *The Guardian* (29 September 2004)

To the southeast of the town, **Luton Airport** developed rapidly in the latter part of the 20th century, much of its business coming from holiday charter operations. It is now effectively London's fourth airport, designated 'London Luton'. Its fame received a boost from a 1970s television advertisement for Campari, devised by Vernon Howe, in which, in a reply to the suave inquiry whether she had 'truly wafted in from paradise', beautiful-yet-Estuary-sounding actress Lorraine Chase replied 'nah, Luton Airport' – and thereby established a catch phrase.

Just to the north of Luton is GALLEY HILL. To the south is **Luton Hoo**, a very large and treasure-filled Robert Adam mansion built in 1762.

> I remember Luton
> When I'm swallowing my crouton.
>
> John Hegley (b.1953): 'Luton'

Lutterworth 'enclosure on the River Lutter' (the former name of the river now known as the Swift), OE river name *Hlutre*

'clear one' (from *hluttor* 'clear, bright') + *worth* (*see* -WORTH, WORTHY, -WARDINE).

A small town in Leicestershire, on the River Swift, about 10 km (6 miles) northeast of Rugby. The religious reformer John Wycliffe (*c*.1329–84) spent the last years of his life here, working on his translation of the Bible into English. When his work was condemned, some thirty years after his death, his body was dug up, burnt and thrown into the Swift. St Mary's Church contains his pulpit and assorted alleged 'relics'.

The Cambridge-based **Lutterworth Press**, which began as the Religious Tract Society in the 18th century, describes itself as Britain's oldest independent publishing company, and used to issue the *Boy's Own Paper* and the *Girl's Own Paper*.

Luxulyan 'chapel of Sulyen', Cornish *log* 'chapel' + personal name *Sulyan*.

A village in Cornwall, about 5 km (3 miles) northeast of St Austell, on the side of an exceptionally picturesque wooded valley.

Lybster 'sheltered farm', OScand *hle* 'lee, shelter' + *bolstathr* 'farm'.

A village in northeastern Highland (formerly in Caithness), on the North Sea coast, 19 km (12 miles) southwest of Wick. There is a harbour in the small **Lybster Bay**, which during the 19th-century herring boom was home to Scotland's third-largest fishing fleet. There is a small settlement called Lybster near the north coast of Highland, 40 km (25 miles) to the northwest.

Lyd 'noisy stream', OE *hlyde*.

A river in Devon, which rises on Dartmoor and flows 21 km (14 miles) westwards through LYDFORD to join the River TAMAR to the east of LAUNCESTON.

Lydd Probably '(place at the) gates', OE *hlidum* dative plural form of *hlid* 'gate'.

A town in Kent, at the southern edge of ROMNEY MARSH, about 13 km (8 miles) east of Rye. It was once on the coast (it is one of the CINQUE PORTS), but now it is 5 km (3 miles) inland. The 40-m (132-ft) tower of the 14th-century Church of All Saints, known as the 'Cathedral of Romney Marsh', still dominates the flat surrounding landscape, despite Second World War bomb damage.

Lydd Airport was developed after the Second World War as a base for car-transporter aircraft flying to the Continent, but their tiny capacity proved no match for the giant cross-Channel ferries, and the service was discontinued after 1978.

On the coast, about 5 km (3 miles) to the east, is **Lydd-on-Sea**. The Romney, Hythe and Dymchurch Light Railway (*see under* NEW ROMNEY) passes through on its way to and from DUNGENESS.

lyddite. A high explosive composed of picric acid and guncotton, and used in artillery shells. It takes its name from Lydd, where it was tested on the artillery ranges in 1888.

Lydford 'ford across the River Lyd', the river name Lyd + FORD.

A village in Devon, on the River LYD, on the western edge of DARTMOOR, about 13 km (8 miles) north of Tavistock. In the days when tin was mined in the area, it was an important centre. It was one of the four 'stannary' towns of Devon (*see* STANNARIES). The now ruined 12th-century castle was the venue for the Stannary Court, which administered the mining laws, and below were dungeons so loathsome and dreary that prisoners often died there before they could be brought to trial. As a result, the principle of 'punish first and try afterwards' came to be known as **Lydford law**. (*See also* Jedart justice *under* JEDBURGH) Although its status is now much reduced, Lydford remains one of the largest civil parishes in England, covering most of Dartmoor.

Lydford Gorge. A deep wooded ravine to the southwest of Lydford, through which the River Lyd flows. It contains the 30-m (98-ft) high White Lady waterfall and the Devil's Cauldron whirlpool.

Lydiard Millicent *Lydiard* perhaps 'grey ridge', OCelt *led* 'grey' + *garth* 'ridge, hill'; *Millicent* denoting manorial ownership in the Middle Ages by a woman called Millicent.

A village in Wiltshire, about 6 km (4 miles) west of Swindon, and about 1.5 km (1 mile) northwest of LYDIARD TREGOZE.

Lydiard Tregoze *Tregoze* denoting manorial ownership in the Middle Ages by the Tresgoz family.

A village in Wiltshire, within the unitary authority of Swindon, about 1.5 km (1 mile) southeast of LYDIARD MILLICENT.

Lydney 'Lida's island or river-meadow' or 'sailor's island or river-meadow', OE *Lidan* or *lidan* possessive forms of male personal name *Lida* or of *lida* 'sailor' + *eg* (*see* -EY, -EA).

A town in Gloucestershire, on the west bank of the River Severn, at the southern tip of the FOREST OF DEAN, about 26 km (16 miles) southwest of Gloucester. The choral composer Herbert Howells (1892–1983) was born here.

Nearby **Lydney Park**, an estate owned by the Bathurst family since 1719, contains prehistoric and Romano-British remains on a site occupying five acres on the top of Camp Hill. First inhabited in the 1st century BC, the site not only includes a hillfort and the only Roman iron workings extant in Britain (one of the 'mines' reaches 50 ft into the earth), but also the remnants of a pagan Roman temple. The latter dates from the 4th century AD and is dedicated to an obscure deity called 'Nodens'. The archaeologist Sir

Mortimer Wheeler and his wife examined Lydney Park in the late 1920s; J.R.R. Tolkien, then a professor of Anglo-Saxon at Oxford, also visited the site and contributed a chapter on the possible origin and meaning of the god's name to the Wheelers' report.

Lyford 'ford near a place where flax is gown', OE *lin* 'flax' + FORD.

A village in Oxfordshire (before 1974 in Berkshire), 2 km (1 mile) east of CHARNEY BASSETT and just south of the River OCK. It was at **Lyford Grange**, on 17 July 1581, that Edmund Campion, the English Jesuit propagandist, was captured after celebrating Mass. He was executed at Tyburn on 1 December 1581 and canonized in 1970.

Lyke Wake Walk 'funeral feast for a corpse', *Lyke* OE *lic* 'dead body'; *Wake* ME 'funeral feast'.

A long walk in North Yorkshire, extending some 65 km (40 miles) from Osmotherley, northeast of Northallerton, across the CLEVELAND Hills and NORTH YORK MOORS to the coast at RAVENSCAR. The walk was devised in 1955 by Bill Cowley, a Cleveland farmer, to link a number of traditional lychways or 'corpse roads' – paths or tracks used only for the carriage of the dead, a tradition going back perhaps to prehistoric times. The challenge of the walk is to complete it in under 24 hours. It is associated with a traditional Yorkshire funeral dirge:

> This ae nighte, this ae nighte,
> – *Every nighte and alle,*
> Fire and fleet and candle-lighte,
> *And Christe receive thy saule.*
>
> Anon.: 'Lyke-Wake Dirge' (dialect *fleet*, corruption of *flet* 'house-room')

Lyme Green *Lyme see* NEWCASTLE UNDER LYME.

A village in Cheshire, about 2.5 km (1.5 miles) south of MACCLESFIELD.

Lyme Park. An estate and country house in Cheshire, about 10 km (6 miles) southeast of STOCKPORT. It was begun in the 16th century as a relatively modest Elizabethan house, but was turned into a grand home in the Italianate style by Leoni, a Venetian architect, in the early 18th century. Its gardens are many and varied, from a formal Dutch garden to a 'ravine garden', and they and the house sit amidst an extensive (566-ha / 1400-acre) deer park. The exterior of the house and its gardens played the part of PEMBERLEY, Mr Darcy's home, in the 1995 BBC television adaptation of Jane Austen's *Pride and Prejudice*; and it was into Lyme Park's 'reflection lake' that the diaphanously shirted Darcy (actor Colin Firth) dived for a quick swim, a moment of erotic frisson notably absent from the literary original (*see also* SUDBURY HALL).

Lyme Regis '(settlement on the River) Lim', *Lyme* an OCelt river name meaning 'stream'; *Regis* 'of the king', Latin (the suffix, first recorded in the late 13th century, reflects the royal charter granted by Edward I in 1284).

A harbour town and seaside resort in Dorset, close to the Devon border, at the mouth of the River Lim, about 14 km (9 miles) west of BRIDPORT. The elegant Georgian buildings lining the steep streets of its centre are a reminder of the beginnings of its popularity as a resort, in the late 18th century. It was famously visited by Louisa Musgrove in Jane Austen's *Persuasion* (1818 – written in Lyme), who falls and is badly injured when she is 'jumped down' by Captain Wentworth from the Cobb (as the curving mole or pier of Lyme Regis harbour is known – perhaps in reference to the large round stones from which it was originally made). Its literary connections were reinforced when it figured as the main setting of John Fowles's novel *The French Lieutenant's Woman* (1969). Fowles is Lyme's most celebrated current resident; he characterized the Cobb as:

> ... primitive yet complex, elephantine but delicate; as full of subtle curves as a Henry Moore or a Michelangelo.

The photogenic mole made its mark in the film version (1980; script by Harold Pinter) of the novel when Meryl Streep walked along it in a battering storm. Charles Smithson, a central character in the novel, is an amateur palaeontologist, which forms a link with Lyme Regis's prehistoric past: the fragile limestone cliffs that line Lyme Bay (*see below*) are packed with fossils, and ever since the 12-year-old Mary Anning found the petrified bones of an ichthyosaurus there in 1811 they have been a mecca for fossil-hunters.

The philanthropist Thomas Coram (1668–1751) was born here. Joseph Lister (1827–1912), pioneer of medical asepsis, became Baron Lister of Lyme Regis in 1897.

See also the UNDERCLIFF.

Lyme Bay. A wide bay on the Devon and Dorset coast ('that largest bite from the underside of England's outstretched southwestern leg', according to John Fowles *The French Lieutenant's Woman*, 1969), curving from the east of SEATON eastwards for about 25 km (15 miles). James, Duke of Monmouth landed here, just to the west of Lyme Regis harbour, in 1685, at the start of his ill-fated rebellion against James II.

Lymington Probably 'farmstead on the River Limen', OCelt river name *Limen*, literally 'elm-wood river' or 'marshy river' + -TON (*see also* LEAMINGTON SPA).

A market town and port in Hampshire, on the SOLENT, at the mouth of the Lymington River, about 23 km (14 miles) southwest of Southampton. In the Middle Ages and up until the 19th century its main source of income was salt refining, and the old salt-pans, or 'salterns', can still be seen here. Now it is a major yachting centre, and car ferries cross to YARMOUTH[1] on the Isle of Wight. HURST CASTLE is about 6 km (4 miles) to the south.

Lymm 'noisy stream or torrent', OE *hlimme*.

A town in Cheshire, within the unitary authority of WARRINGTON, on the BRIDGEWATER CANAL, about 7 km (4 miles) east of the town of Warrington.

Lympne Either 'elm-wood place' or 'marshy place', an OCelt place name related to *Limen*, the former name of the river now called the East Rother, literally 'elm-wood river' or 'marshy river' (*see* LYMINGTON).

A village (pronounced 'lim') in Kent, to the north of ROMNEY MARSH, about 5 km (3 miles) west of Hythe. In former times it was by the sea; the Romans built a coastal-defence fort here (its ruins – called Studfall Castle – can still be seen), and it became part of the SAXON SHORE. Over the centuries, however, the sea has receded, and it is now about 2.5 km (1.5 miles) inland.

To the west is a mansion called **Port Lympne**. It stands in 6 ha (15 acres) of grounds, which are now home to the Port Lympne Zoo Park and Gardens, established by the gambler and animal-rights enthusiast John Aspinall (1924–2000).

Lymport. The fictional name used by the novelist George Meredith for PORTSMOUTH (his birthplace) in *Evan Harrington* (1860).

Lyn 'torrent', OE *hlynn*.

Either of two rivers in Devon and Somerset, the **East Lyn** and the **West Lyn**, which rise on EXMOOR and flow 8 km (5 miles) westwards and 6 km (4 miles) northwards respectively to join at LYNMOUTH, where they enter the BRISTOL Channel.

See also WATERSMEET.

Lyndhurst 'wooded hill growing with lime-trees', OE *lind* 'lime-tree' + *hyrst* 'wood, wooded hill'.

A small town in Hampshire, in the midst of the NEW FOREST, about 15 km (10 miles) southwest of Southampton. The Verderer's Court, which administers the forest's laws, meets here six times a year, and it also contains the forest's Visitor Centre. Its mid-19th-century church of St Michael and All Angels is an astonishing gallery of Pre-Raphaelite art, containing murals and stained glass by Morris, Burne-Jones and Lord Leighton. In the churchyard is buried Alice Hargreaves, who as Alice Liddell had been the inspiration for Lewis Carroll's Alice.

Lyneham 'homestead or enclosure where flax is gown', OE *lin* 'flax' + HAM.

A village in Wiltshire, about 11 km (7 miles) northeast of CHIPPENHAM. It is best known for the nearby RAF station, which opened in 1940. It is mainly used for transport operations, and is the home of the entire RAF Hercules fleet. Its closure by 2012 was announced in 2003.

Lynmouth 'mouth of the River Lyn', LYN + OE *mutha* 'mouth'.

A seaside village and resort on the north Devon coast, at the point where the conjoined East LYN and West Lyn rivers flow into the Bristol Channel. It is overlooked by its larger neighbour LYNTON, to which it is joined by a water-powered cliff railway.

The poet Percy Bysshe Shelley stayed here with his 16-year-old bride Harriet Westbrook on their nine-week honeymoon in 1812.

In August 1952 Lynmouth was very badly damaged by a flood caused by a freak storm over EXMOOR (believed by some to have been triggered by an RAF cloud-seeding experiment). A wall of water in the East and West Lyn rivers killed 34 people, uprooted trees, swept away 28 bridges, destroyed 93 buildings and deposited 130 cars in the Bristol Channel.

> Farewell to unpaintable Lynmouth.
>
> Charles Kingsley: *Miscellany* (1849)

Lynn Channel. *See under* KING'S LYNN.

Lynn Deeps. *See under* KING'S LYNN.

Lynton 'farmstead on the River Lyn', LYN + -TON.
A seaside resort on the north Devon coast, on a 183-m (600-ft) cliff overlooking its smaller twin LYNMOUTH. As its situation suggests, spectacular views are to be had in the vicinity. The publication in 1869 of R.D. Blackmore's melodramatic *Lorna Doone*, which is set in nearby parts of EXMOOR, provided a considerable boost to tourism.

Lyon. *See under* GLEN LYON.

Lyonesse An anglicization of the Breton district name *Léonais* (from the town of *St Pol-de-Léon*, known to the Romans as *Castellum Leonense* 'Leo's castle'). Compare LOTHIAN, from which it is said to derive.
A rich tract of land, fabled to stretch between LAND'S END and the SCILLY ISLES, on which stood the City of Lions and some 140 churches. It figures largely in Arthurian romance and mythology: Sir Thomas Malory identified it as the birthplace of Sir Tristram, and according to Tennyson (in 'The Passing of Arthur' (1869)) King Arthur died here.

The writer Thomas Hardy occasionally used the name 'Lyonesse' in his poetry to designate the northern part of Cornwall that he visited (and loved) as a young man (*see also* BOSCASTLE and ST JULIOT):

> When I set out for Lyonnesse,
> A hundred miles away,
> The rime was on the spray,
> And starlight lit my lonesomeness
> When I set out for Lyonesse
> A hundred miles away.
>
> Thomas Hardy: 'When I Set Out for Lyonesse'
> (written 1870, published 1914)

Tristram of Lyonesse. A poem (1882) in heroic couplets by Algernon Charles Swinburne, telling the story of Tristram's love for and marriage to Iseult, and his death.

Lytchett Matravers *Lytchett* 'grey wood', OCelt *led* 'grey' + CED; *Matravers* denoting manorial ownership in the early Middle Ages by the Maltrauers family.
A village in Dorset, about 8 km (5 miles) northwest of Poole.

Lytham St Anne's 'the church of St Anne's at the dunes', *Lytham* OE *hlithum*, dative plural of *hlith* 'sand dune, slope'.
A resort town on the RIBBLE estuary in Lancashire, 8 km (5 miles) south of Blackpool. It came into being in 1922 when **Lytham** (pronounced 'lithəm'), a former fishing village, and **St Anne's** (officially named **St Anne's on Sea**), a seaside resort town originally built next to Blackpool in the 1870s, were formally amalgamated.

Lytham St Anne's was the original home of Premium Bonds, launched in November 1956, and for some years premium-bond holders receiving official-looking letters with a Lytham St Anne's postmark were thus alerted about their winnings.

For many the town is synonymous with its championship golf course: **Royal Lytham St Anne's** has hosted the Open on eight occasions since 1926 (on one of these, in 1969, the winner was a Briton, Tony Jacklin).

M

M1. A motorway running between London and LEEDS[1] (where it links up with the A1). Opened in 1959 with what passed then for razzmatazz by Ernest Marples, the Minister of Transport, it was the first major motorway in Britain (it was beaten to the finishing line by a motorway stretch of the Preston Bypass, which opened in 1958). It is 304 km (189 miles) long. Its route goes via LUTON, MILTON KEYNES, NORTHAMPTON, LEICESTER, NOTTINGHAM[1] and SHEFFIELD. It has 48 junctions and 12 motorway service areas (the best-known of which are probably NEWPORT PAGNELL, Watford Gap (*see under* WATFORD[2]) and Scratchwood (now renamed 'London Gateway') (*see under* SCRATCH WOOD)).

M25. London's orbital motorway, at 188 km (117 miles) the longest city ring road in the world. The first section opened in September 1975, using the A1(M) and the A111. The last section, from Micklefield (Hertfordshire) to SOUTH MIMMS, was opened by Prime Minister Margaret Thatcher on 29 October 1986. By the end of 1986 the M25 was carrying 113,000 vehicles a day, rising to 186,000 in 1998 and about 200,000 by 2003; already clogged by the extra traffic its multiple lanes had so predictably created, it had become a scorned exemplar of the stresses and frustrations of car travel. It has 33 junctions and there are 234 bridges and other crosses over and under the motorway.

In 1996, Kenneth Noye, a well-known criminal, stabbed a young man to death in a road rage incident on an M25 slip road. The murder became known as the **M25 Murder**. Noye was sentenced to life. The M25 also forms part of another notorious label. Kent railway worker Antoni Imiela sexually assaulted women and girls over a 12-month period between 2001 and 2002. He became known as the **M25 Rapist** because his victims were attacked within the vicinity of the M25 motorway. He was given seven life sentences in 2004.

Iain Sinclair's *London Orbital* (2002) describes a walk around the M25:

> As soon as the M25 was opened, swans lifting from the Thames at Staines mistook the bright silver surface for water; there were several nasty accidents. A report in the *Evening Standard* … described the trauma suffered by a man, on his way to visit a retired rock star in the Surrey stockbroker belt, when a large white bird crashed onto the bonnet of his car.

Maamtrasna. An alternative name for MAUMTRASNA.

Mabe Burnthouse *Mabe* originally *Lavabe* 'church-site of Mab', Cornish *lann* 'church-site' + personal name *Mab* – *Mabe* on its own is not recorded (in the form *Mape*) before 1549; *Burnthouse*, presumably referring to a house fire, is first recorded in the 19th century.
A village in Cornwall, about 5 km (3 miles) northwest of Falmouth.

Mablethorpe 'Malbert's outlying farm', OGerman male personal name *Malbert* + THORPE.
A town and seaside resort on the Lincolnshire coast, about 24 km (15 miles) north of Skegness. It has 10 km (6 miles) of sandy beaches, and at low tide the dead stumps of a forest engulfed by the sea are visible. The seafront was almost entirely reconstructed after serious floods in January 1953.

D.H. Lawrence had a holiday here as a boy, and recreated it in *Sons and Lovers* (1913).

Macbeth's Cairn. *See under* LUMPHANAN.

Macbeth's Hillock. *See under* FORRES.

MacCaig's Folly. *See under* OBAN.

Macclesfield Probably 'Maccel's open country', OE *Maccles* possessive form of male personal name *Maccel + feld* (*see* FIELD).
A hilltop market town in Cheshire, by the River Bollin, about 24 km (15 miles) south of Manchester. From the middle of the 18th century until the middle of the 20th century it was an important centre of the English silk industry (the local football team, Macclesfield Town, is nicknamed the Silk Men).

The 27-km (17-mile) **Macclesfield Canal**, constructed in the 1820s, links the Trent and Mersey Canal (*see under* TRENT[1]) and the Peak Forest Canal. It passes through some scenically beautiful countryside close to the western edge of the PEAK DISTRICT.

The blues singer John Mayall (b.1933) was born here. The town's other contributions to popular music include the pop groups Joy Division and the Mac Lads.

Macclesfield tippler. A type of tumbler pigeon, which does backward somersaults in the air.

Macduff 'son of Duff'. The old village of Doune or Down was renamed in honour of his father in 1783 by James Duff, the Earl of Fife.

A fishing port in Aberdeenshire (formerly in Banffshire, then in Grampian region), 2 km (1.2 miles) across BANFF Bay from Banff.

Macems. The nickname for inhabitants of SUNDERLAND.

Macgillycuddy's Reeks *Macgillycuddy* from the *Mac Gillycuddy* clan sept (division), who used the mountains as a refuge; *Reeks* means 'ridges', from English *rick*, as in hay rick. A range of craggy, sharp-crested old red sandstone mountains in Kerry, some 15 km (9 miles) southwest of Killarney. They include Ireland's highest mountain, CARRANTUOHILL (1041 m / 3414 ft), and are familiarly known as **the Reeks**. The Irish name for the range is **Na Cruacha Dubha** ('the black peaks').

> The names are built, tower on tower, battlement-linked, moated, buttressed, defended by storm …
> Knocknapeasta, Cummeennapeasta, Cruach Mhor,
> Caher and Beenkeragh, Carrauntoohil, Curraghmore …
> You need good lungs for that lot, and powerful legs,
> and no fear of heights.
>
> James Macmillan: 'MacGillycuddy's Reeks'

Macgregor's Leap. *See under* GLEN LYON.

Machaire an Deamhain. The Irish name for DEVILS MOTHER.

Machaire Fíolta. The Irish name for MAGHERAFELT.

Machaire Méith na Mumhan. The Irish name for the GOLDEN VALE.

Machaire Rátha. The Irish name for MAGHERA.

Machars, the Gaelic *machair* 'low-lying plain'. A broad peninsula in Dumfries and Galloway (formerly in Wigtownshire), extending into the SOLWAY FIRTH between LUCE BAY and WIGTOWN Bay. The main settlement is WHITHORN, site of St Ninian's *Candida Casa*, thus making the Machars one of the earliest centres of Christianity in Britain.

Machrihanish. An alternative spelling of MACRIHANISH.

Machynlleth 'plain of Cynllaith', Welsh *ma* 'low-lying ground' + name of an unidentified person.

A small town on the River DYFI in Powys (formerly in Montgomeryshire), 25 km (16 miles) northeast of Aberystwyth. It is pronounced 'ma-hun-cleth'. Owain Glyndwr summoned a parliament here in 1402, which helped the town to the shortlist of prospective capitals of Wales in the 1950s (Cardiff won). Today it is the home of the Centre of Alternative Technology, established in 1975 to research renewable sources of energy.

Mackinnon's Cave. A large sea cave, some 30 m (100 ft) high at its entrance and 180 m (590 ft) deep, on the west coast of MULL opposite INCH KENNETH. The cave, which can only be entered at low tide, was visited by Boswell and Johnson in 1773. There is a story that a piper (presumed to be the eponymous Mackinnon) entered the cave with his dog, possibly with the intention of outdoing the local fairies in the piping stakes; however, only the dog, rendered hairless by some subterranean exercise of the Dark Arts (*see under*, for example, SMOO CAVE), ever emerged; the hubristic piper was never seen again. Similar tales are told of other Hebridean caves, and indeed of other dogs and other pipers.

Maclean's Nose 'Maclean's headland', *Maclean* probably a surname; *Nose* OScand *nes* (*see* NESS).

A rugged headland on the south side of ARDNAMURCHAN, Highland, guarding the entrance to Loch Sunart (*see under* SUNART).

Macleod's Tables From the story involving the chief of Clan Macleod.

Two flat-topped hills in Skye, some 5 km (3 miles) southwest of DUNVEGAN CASTLE. They are formed from horizontal terraces of basalt. The lower one, at 468 m (1535 ft), is Healaval Mhor (OScand *hellyr* 'flagstone' + *mòr* 'big'; its plateau is larger than that of the other), while the higher, at 488 m (1601 ft) is Healaval Bheag (Gaelic *beg* 'small').

The story behind the name tells how when he was being entertained in Edinburgh by James V, the Macleod chief boasted that he could offer the king a finer table than this in Skye. When the king repaid the visit, Macleod took him up at dusk to the great plateau of Healaval Bheag, which the chief had had spread with a mighty banquet, while all about his clansmen bearing torches stood in for candles; to top it all, above them, finer than any ceiling painting, the Milky Way sparkled across the vault of heaven.

History does not relate whether the king was also offered the favours of **MacLeod's Maidens**, a cluster of sea stacks at Idrigill Point, some 6 km (4 miles) south of Healaval Bheag. The stacks do indeed resemble (at least to sailors too long at sea) young women in crinolines.

Macmerry Etymology unclear, but the first part is probably Gaelic *magh* 'plain'.

A former mining village in East Lothian, 3 km (2 miles) east of Tranent.

McPhail's Anvil. *See under* TORRAN ROCKS.

Macphee's Hill. *See under* MINGULAY.

Macrihanish The first element is Gaelic *machair* 'plain'; the second is unclear, but may possibly be a type of grass, *sanas*. A village and holiday centre on the west coast of the KINTYRE peninsula, Argyll and Bute, 8 km (5 miles) west of Campbeltown. It is also spelt **Machrihanish**. It overlooks sandy **Macrihanish Bay**. There is a famous links golf course, dating from 1876.

Macroom Irish *Maigh Chromtha* 'plain of the crooked ford'. A town in County Cork, some 35 km (22 miles) west of Cork itself. It was a seat of the MacCarthys until Cromwell handed it over in 1654 to William Penn, father of the founder of Pennsylvania; it was, however, returned to the family after the Restoration. It seems that guidebook writers cannot avoid calling the place ugly.

Macroom was the birthplace of the 'doyen of the Munster realists', the playwright T.C. Murray (1873–1959), remembered particularly for *Autumn Fire* (1924).

Madchester. An occasional modern nickname for MANCHESTER.

Mad Wharf A modern name apparently meaning 'mad sandbank', with *wharf* in the sense 'sandbank'; *mad* may refer to the unstable nature of the sand.
The sands north of Formby Point (*see under* FORMBY), Lancashire.

Maerdy The usual explanation is 'house of the steward', Welsh *maer* 'steward' + *dŷ* 'house'; *maerdy* 'summer house', i.e. something akin to a shieling for cattle graziers, has also been suggested.
A small town in the Rhondda, in RHONDDA CYNON TAFF unitary authority (formerly in Glamorgan, then in Mid Glamorgan), 5 km (3 miles) south of Aberdare. For many years the council was dominated by the Communist Party, earning the town the nickname **Little Moscow**.

Maes Howe The second element is OScand *haugr* 'mound, cairn', but it is uncertain what the first is.
A megalithic monument on Mainland in ORKNEY, 13 km (8 miles) west of Kirkwall. It is the largest chambered cairn in Britain, and dates from *c*.2000 BC. It was pillaged by the Vikings, who left a large number of intriguing runic graffiti, such as 'Thorny got laid'. Nearby are other impressive megalithic monuments, the STONES OF STENNESS and the RING OF BRODGAR.

Maesteg 'beautiful field', Welsh *maes* 'field', *teg* 'fair'.
A former mining town in the unitary authority of Bridgend (formerly in Glamorgan, then in West Glamorgan), 11 km (7 miles) east of Port Talbot. It was the birthplace of the poet Vernon Watkins (1906–67).

Maesyfed. The Welsh name for NEW RADNOR.

Magairli an Deamhain. The Irish name for Devil's Testicles (*see under* DEVILS MOTHER).

Magdalen Laver *Magdalen* from the dedication of the local church to St Mary Magdalen; *Laver* 'water passage or crossing', OE *lagu* 'water, water-course' + *fær* 'passage, crossing'.
A village (pronounced 'magdəlin layvə') in Essex, about 5 km (3 miles) east of Harlow.

Maggieknockater 'fuller's plain', Gaelic *magh* 'plain' + *an fhucadair* 'of the fuller', with reference to the cloth-finishing process of fulling.
A small settlement in Moray, 6 km (4 miles) northwest of Aberlour.
Bees of Maggieknockater, The. A Scottish country dance, to the tune of 'Forres Country Dance' or 'Holyrood House'.

Magharee Islands. An alternative name for the SEVEN HOGS.

Maghera Irish *Machaire Rátha* 'plain of the ring fort'.
A small town in County Londonderry, 10 km (6 miles) northwest of Magherafelt.

Magherafelt Irish *Machaire Fíolta* 'plain of Fíolta'.
A market town in County Londonderry, 5 km (3 miles) west of the northwestern corner of LOUGH NEAGH. It is the administrative centre of the local authority district of the same name. The town was laid out in the 17th century on land granted to the London Salters Company during the plantation of Ulster.

Magh Tuireadh. The Irish name for MOYTURA.

Maghull 'nook where mayweed grows', OE *mægthe* 'mayweed' + *halh* (*see* HALE, -HALL).
A town in Merseyside (formerly in Lancashire), 12 km (7.5 miles) north of Liverpool.

Magna Carta Island. A small island in the River THAMES[1], about 3 km (2 miles) northwest of Staines. King John is said to have landed here before crossing to RUNNYMEDE to seal the Magna Carta in 1215.

Maida Vale From the local 'Hero of *Maida*' inn, which itself was inspired by the Battle of *Maida* in southern Italy, where British forces under General Sir John Stuart defeated the French under General Régnier in 1806. The section of road by the inn was originally called *Maida Hill* (first recorded in 1817; its name is now *Maida Avenue*). Houses were built along the road at the foot of Maida Hill, whence the name *Maida Vale* (first recorded in 1868) – although it is scarcely a valley in the accepted sense.
A road and district in West London (W9), in the City of WESTMINSTER. The road is a northward continuation of the Edgware Road (*see under* EDGWARE) (A5), linking up with Kilburn High Road. The surrounding area became built-up in the 19th century, and the opening of Maida Vale Underground station, on the Bakerloo line, in 1915 confirmed the transfer of the road's name to the district. It lies

between Kilburn to the northwest, St John's Wood to the northeast and Paddington to the south. It boasts some fine Victorian mansions in its more northerly part, but most are now divided into flats, and the area now has a deracinated air.

The actor Alec Guinness (1914–2000) was born in Maida Vale.

A suburb of Perth, Western Australia, is called Maida Vale.

Maiden Castle Perhaps 'castle that has never been taken by an enemy' or 'castle so impregnable as to be defendable by young women'. The term is first recorded in 1639 (with reference to Edinburgh Castle), but it is not known as a name of ancient earthworks until a later date. German has a parallel name in *Magdeburg*.

A name given to various prehistoric fortifications in England, and in particular to a 48.5-ha (120-acre) Iron Age fortress on Fordington Hill, about 2.5 km (1.5 miles) southwest of Dorchester in Dorset. This in turn was built on the site of a Neolithic settlement that may date back to 2000 BC. The fortress was captured by the Romans in AD 43 and abandoned around AD 70. The site was extensively excavated by the archaeologist Sir Mortimer Wheeler in the mid-1930s.

Maiden Castle. A novel (1936) by John Cowper Powys. Set in Dorset against a backdrop of excavations of the fort of Maiden Castle, it explores the intense and interlocking relationships of a group of couples.

Maiden City, the. A name by which DERRY/LONDONDERRY is sometimes known.

Maidenhead 'landing-place of the maidens' (either implying that it was a particularly easy place to land, or denoting that it was a place frequented by girls), OE *mægden* 'maiden' + *hyth* 'landing-place'.

A town in Berkshire, on the River Thames, within the unitary authority of WINDSOR AND MAIDENHEAD, about 8 km (5 miles) northwest of Windsor. It was once an important staging post on the road from London to Bath (its seven-arched road bridge dates from 1777), and its 19th-century railway bridge, designed by Isambard Kingdom Brunel (with two of the widest brick spans in the world), is metamorphosed in Turner's painting *Rain, Steam and Speed*, but it is the river that dominates the town. It became more accessible to London in the latter part of the 19th century, and its heyday was probably the 1890s and the Edwardian era, when boatered and blazered oarsmen and their parasolled ladies amused themselves around BOULTER'S LOCK. It soon, though, gained a reputation as a haunt of the vulgar and the *nouveaux riches*:

> Maidenhead itself is too snobby to be pleasant. It is the haunt of the river swell and his overdressed female companion. It is the town of showy hotels, patronized chiefly by dudes and ballet girls. It is the witch's kitchen from which go forth those demons of the river – steam-launches. The *London Journal* duke always has his 'little place' at Maidenhead; and the heroine of the three-volume novel always dines there when she goes out on the spree with somebody else's husband.
>
> Jerome K. Jerome: *Three Men in a Boat* (1889)

In 2003 a confidential social profile used by the Department of Work and Pensions described it (much to the fury of the locals) as 'somewhat spoiled by the gin and Jag brigade'.

The dramatist George Etherege (*c*.1635–92) and the writer Hugh Lofting (1886–1947), creator of 'Dr Dolittle', were born in Maidenhead.

Maidenhead Thicket. A small area of woodland immediately to the west of Maidenhead. Once part of Windsor Forest (*see under* WINDSOR), it is now preserved by the National Trust.

Maiden Pap *Pap* 'breast', Scots.

A shapely hill (484 m / 1588 ft) in northeast Highland (formerly in Caithness), 4 km (2.5 miles) east of MORVEN.

Maiden Way 'road to Maiden Castle', OE *mægden* 'maiden' + OScand *gata* 'road', later replaced by OE *weg* 'way'; Maiden Castle in Kirkby Thore is known from documents, but now lost, though the name was also given to a place in Dorset (*see* MAIDEN CASTLE).

The Roman road through the PENNINES from CATTERICK in North Yorkshire northwestwards past HADRIAN'S WALL to the Scottish border. Parts of the route are shared by the A66 and A696.

Maids Moreton *Maids* from the tradition that the local church was built by two maiden ladies in the 15th century; *Moreton see* MORETON CORBET.

A village in Buckinghamshire, about 3 km (2 miles) north of Buckingham.

Maidstone Probably 'stone of the maidens' (referring to a stone at which maidens gathered as a group), OE *mægth*, *mægden* 'maiden' + *stan* (*see* STONE).

A town in Kent, on the River MEDWAY[1], at the foot of the NORTH DOWNS, about 40 km (25 miles) west of Canterbury. It is the county's administrative centre. It was an important town in Anglo-Saxon times, and a notable judicial inquiry took place there in 1076 relating to the king's authority to settle land disputes. The nave of its parish church, All Saints, is said to be the widest in England.

Maidstone has always been a key collecting-point and market for the agricultural products (including hops) of the surrounding area of Kent. In the past it was an important cloth-making centre; in more recent years paper has taken the place of cloth.

Allington House just outside Maidstone was the home of the poet Sir Thomas Wyatt (1503–42), who introduced the Petrarchan sonnet to England.

Maidstone appears in the guise of **Muggleton** in Dickens's *Pickwick Papers* (1837), where Dingley Dell plays All-Muggleton in a memorable cricket match.

The essayist and critic William Hazlitt (1778–1830) was born in Maidstone, as was Richard (later Lord) Beeching (1913–85), who reduced the mileage of Britain's railway system. The artist Tracey Emin (b.1963), of 'Unmade Bed' fame, studied fine art at Maidstone College of Art.

There is also a town called Maidstone in Saskatchewan, Canada.

Battle of Maidstone (1 June 1648). A battle of the Civil Wars, at which General Fairfax crushed the Royalist forces (Maidstone supported the Royalist cause during the war).

HMS *Maidstone*. A ship of the Royal Navy, which was pressed into service as a prison ship following the reintroduction of internment in Northern Ireland in 1971. It had been used for a similar purpose during the Second World War. Conditions on the ship, anchored in Belfast Lough (*see under* BELFAST), were so appalling that after a 13-day hunger strike it ceased to be used as a holding centre. Before this, seven prisoners escaped by jumping over the side and swimming ashore.

Maidstone jailer. A 19th-century rhyming-slang term for 'tailor'.

Maigh Bhile. The Irish name for MOVILLE.

Maigh Chromtha. The Irish name for MACROOM.

Maigh Eo. The Irish name for MAYO.

Maigh Nuadhat. The Irish name for MAYNOOTH.

Maigh Rath. The Irish name for MOIRA[1].

Mainistir Bhuithe. The Irish name for the ancient site of MONASTERBOICE.

Mainistir Eimhín. The Irish name for MONASTEREVIN.

Mainistir Laoise. The Irish name for ABBEYLEIX.

Mainistir na Búille. The Irish name for BOYLE.

Mainistir na Corann. The Irish name for MIDLETON.

Mainistir na Féile. The Irish name for ABBEYFEALE.

Mainland (Orkney). *See under* ORKNEY.

Mainland (Shetland). *See under* SHETLAND.

Mainland, the. The term used by Ulster Unionists for the island of Britain (comprising England, Scotland and Wales); it is a term never used by Irish Nationalists.

Mala. The Irish name for MALLOW.

Malahide Irish *Mullach Idé* 'Idé's hilltop'.
A coastal dormitory town at the mouth of the Broad Meadow Water, County Dublin, some 12 km (7.5 miles)

northeast of the centre of Dublin itself. The oldest parts of **Malahide Castle** date from 1174, and the building (added to over the centuries) was home to the Talbot family for 800 years until they gave it to the state in 1973. In the 1920s and 1930s the private papers of James Boswell, Dr Johnson's biographer, were found in the castle, revealing that he was just as interesting a character as his subject.

Malden. *See* NEW MALDEN.

Maldon 'hill with a crucifix', OE *mæl* 'crucifix' + *dun* (*see* DOWN, -DON).
A hilltop town in Essex, on the BLACKWATER[1] estuary, about 16 km (10 miles) east of Chelmsford. The 13th-century All Saints Church has the only triangular tower in England.

The tidal estuary provides the town with two important sources of livelihood: salt, which has been panned in Maldon for centuries and now enjoys a high culinary reputation; and yachting, which attracts many visitors.

The town has important American connections: it was home to an ancestor of George Washington, to the captain of the *Mayflower*, which carried the Pilgrim Fathers across the Atlantic, and to Joseph Hills, who founded the town of Maldon in Massachusetts and named it in honour of his home town. Horatio Gates (1728–1806), the American commander who forced the British to surrender at the Battle of Saratoga (1777), was born here.

There is an old gold-mining town called Maldon in Victoria, Australia.

Battle of Maldon (11 August 991). A battle, fought to the east of Maldon, in which invading Danish forces defeated the local English. It is the subject of a 325-line Old English poem now called *The Battle of Maldon* (preserved only in a 17th-century copy of an incomplete original version), which was probably written at the end of the 10th century. The poem focuses in the first half on the figure of Byrhtnoth, leader of the English, and his headstrong heroism, and in the second on the loyalty of his followers.

Maldwyn. A Welsh name sometimes used for the former county of MONTGOMERYSHIRE.

Malham From OScand *malgum*, dative plural of *malgi* 'gravelly place'.
A village in the YORKSHIRE DALES, North Yorkshire, 14 km (8.5 miles) northwest of Skipton. North of the village is **Malham Moor** and, at a height of about 370 m (about 1200 ft), **Malham Tarn**, an important nature reserve. Among the visitors at the 19th-century Malham Tarn House, home of the local MP, were John Ruskin, Charles Darwin and Charles Kingsley. Kingsley wrote *The Water Babies* (1863) while staying at the house, and no doubt imagined his creations playing in the clear streams hereabouts.

Nearby are the impressive limestone cliffs of **Malham Cove**, a natural rock amphitheatre popular with painters (including Turner) and rock-climbers. The black streaks on the limestone were caused, Kingsley lightly suggested, by a sweep's boy falling over them (something that happens to Tom in the book). From the foot of the cliff face a beck of mysterious origins emerges; it was once thought that this was the source of the AIRE, but experiments with dyes have disproved this. At the head of the Cove are some fine examples of limestone pavement, and the whole area features in most geography and geology text books. The US writer Bill Bryson lived for several years in **Malhamdale**, and in *Notes From a Small Island* (1995) wrote of the 'serene, cupped majesty' of the place.

Malin Head Irish *Cionn Mhálanna* 'headland of the brow'.
The headland at the tip of the INISHOWEN peninsula, County Donegal. It is generally cited as the most northerly mainland point in Ireland, but some pedants insist that the most northerly point is actually an unnamed headland 2 km (1.2 miles) to the northeast. (The absolute most northern point is the little island of INISHTRAHULL.) At Malin Head there is a coastal station providing information for the shipping forecast, in which **Malin** is a sea area bounded by the sea areas of IRISH SEA to the southeast, HEBRIDES to the north and ROCKALL to the west. The village of Malin is 12 km (7.5 miles) southeast of Malin Head, on Trewbreaga Bay.

Mall, the Apparently from PALL MALL.
A road (pronounced 'mal') in the West End of London (SW1), in the City of WESTMINSTER, linking TRAFALGAR SQUARE with BUCKINGHAM PALACE. It was created around 1660, at the instigation of Charles II, as an alley in St James's Park for playing the then-popular game of pall-mall (replacing PALL MALL). By the 1740s the game had gone out of fashion, but high society continued to use the alley as a promenade.

It underwent radical alterations (designed by Aston Webb) at the beginning of the 20th century, when a much wider road was built in parallel just to the south, forming a royal ceremonial route from Admiralty Arch (designed by Webb in 1910 and taking its name from the nearby Royal Navy headquarters) to the Victoria Memorial. The original Mall survives as a horse ride. It is the familiar starting and finishing point for royal processions to and from Westminster Abbey, Parliament and ST PAUL'S[1] Cathedral. At its northeastern end is the Citadel, a sinister-looking blockhouse and bunker built at the start of the Second World War to provide bomb-proof accommodation for Admiralty communications; it has gun-slits covering the Mall.

In 1974 Princess Anne narrowly escaped an attempt to kidnap her in the Mall as she was returning to Buckingham Palace.

Mallaig Possibly 'seagull bay', OScand *mar* 'seagull' + *vik* 'bay'.
An important West Highland fishing and ferry port, north of Arisaig and Loch Morar, in Highland (formerly in Inverness-shire). It is the terminus of a railway line from FORT WILLIAM (a line that intermittently comes under threat from bureaucrats and accountants), and there are ferries to SKYE, BARRA, South Uist (*see under* UISTS) and the remote settlement of Inverie in KNOYDART.

Mallerstang, the Probably 'marker post on the hill called Moel-fre', OCelt *moel-fre* 'bare hill' + OScand *stong* 'pole post', probably a marker of some sort.
A valley on the route of the Settle-to-Carlisle railway in the northwest Pennines, straddling Cumbria (formerly Westmorland) and North Yorkshire. The Mallerstang runs north–south between high fells – WILD BOAR FELL to the west and High Seat and **Mallerstang Edge** to the east – and the whole area is called **Mallerstang Common**. Hell Gill Beck in the Mallerstang is the source of the River EDEN[1].

Past owners of the manor of Mallerstang have included Lady Anne Clifford, Countess of Dorset and Pembroke, who raised a boundary stone (Lady's Pillar) on the Edge dated 1664; and Hugh de Morville, one of the knights who murdered Thomas Becket in Canterbury Cathedral (his name is commemorated in the hill called HUGH SEAT on Mallerstang Edge).

> de Morville restless one full Easter night
> Sought out the rising blackness of Wild Boar
> Found Becket's profile there and fled for France.
>
> Michael Ffinch: 'Wild Boar Fell', from *Westmorland Poems*

Mallory Park *Mallory see* KIRKBY MALLORY.
A motorcycle racing circuit just to the west of KIRKBY MALLORY in Leicestershire. Opened in 1956, it is 2.17 km (1.35 miles) long. In 1958 it began staging the 'Race of the Year', at that time the richest motorcycle road-race in the country.

Mallow Irish *Mala*, 'plain of the Ealla', from *magh* 'plain' + *Eala* or *Allow*, the local name for the Blackwater.
A town in the valley of the River BLACKWATER[2] in County Cork, 30 km (19 miles) north of Cork itself. It was founded in the 13th century by the Desmond Geraldines, and there are the remains of a 16th-century castle. Mallow developed as a fashionable spa in the 18th century and became known as **the Irish Bath**, although by the time Sir Walter Scott visited in 1825 its reputation had somewhat declined. The hell-raisers, bucks and blades who seasonally visited the town were celebrated in the anonymous song, **'The Rakes of Mallow'**:

> Living short but merry lives;
> Going where the devil drives;

Having sweethearts, but no wives,
　Live the rakes of Mallow ...

Then to end this raking life
They get sober, take a wife,
Ever after live in strife,
　And wish again for Mallow.

Mallow was the birthplace of the Young Ireland leader Thomas Davis (1814–45); of the Nationalist leader William O'Brien (1852–1928); and of the novelist Patrick Sheehan (1852–1913). Anthony Trollope lived in Mallow (1845–51) while working for the Post Office.

Mallow Defiance, the (11 June 1843). A speech made in Mallow by Daniel O'Connell, the Liberator, calling for the repeal of the Act of Union. In the speech he likened Robert Peel and the Duke of Wellington to Oliver Cromwell (top bogeyman for Irish Catholics; *see under* DROGHEDA), and suggested that the Irish would respond in an appropriate fashion to any Cromwellian-like behaviour.

Malltraeth 'bad beach', Welsh *mall* 'bad, unhealthy' + *traeth* 'beach'.
A small village on the west coast of Anglesey (formerly in Gwynedd), 15 km (9 miles) west-southwest of Menai Bridge. The village overlooks the estuary of the River Cefni and the extensive **Malltraeth Sands**, leading out into **Malltraeth Bay**. For over 30 years this area was the haunt of the bird painter Charles Tunnicliffe, until his death in 1979.

Malmesbury 'Maeldub's stronghold', OCelt and Irish male personal name *Maeldub* (literally 'black prince') + OE *byrig* dative form of *burh* 'stronghold' (*see* BURY) (Bede knew it in the 8th century as *Maildubi Urbs* 'Maeldub's town').
A hilltop market town in Wiltshire, on the River AVON[2], about 24 km (15 miles) west of Swindon. It is one of the oldest boroughs in England, having been granted its charter by Alfred the Great in AD 880.

Malmesbury is dominated by the gaunt ruins of the former Benedictine abbey. This was founded in the 7th century by (according to the chronicler William of Malmesbury – *see below*) an Irishman called Maeldub (*see above*). The spire of its 12th-century church was as high as that of Salisbury Cathedral. It contains the tombs of King Athelstan (d.939), grandson of Alfred the Great, and of the scholar and riddle-writer St Aldhelm, who was abbot in the 8th century. It is thought that the great Irish scholar John Scottus Eriugena (*c*.840–*c*.877) became Abbot of Malmesbury after the death of his patron Charles the Bald, grandson of Charlemagne; however, the story that his pupils here stabbed him to death with their pens 'because he made them cogitate' is no doubt apocryphal. In 1110 England's first aviator, a monk called Elmer, reportedly attached wings to his hands and feet and attempted to fly from one of the abbey's towers; he ended up on the ground directly below

with two broken legs. The abbey escaped some of the worse post-Dissolution depredations suffered by other English monastic buildings thanks to a local businessman called Stumpe, who turned it into a weaving factory. The truncated remains of the nave now serve as the parish church.

Manufacture of the Dyson vacuum cleaner (launched in 1993) was originally based in Malmesbury (it moved to Malaysia in 2002, much to local disgust).

The philosopher Thomas Hobbes (1588–1679) was born at Westport within the parish of Malmesbury (there is a cottage in the town that proclaims itself to be 'Hobbes' cottage').

There is a town called Malmesbury in South Africa (Western Cape Province); the local version of the Afrikaans accent is reputedly exceptionally strong.
See also the Tamworth Two *under* TAMWORTH.

William of Malmesbury. A monk and a historian (*c*.1095–1143) who was librarian of Malmesbury Abbey. He was the first major writer of history in England since the Venerable Bede (8th century). His main work is *Gesta Regum Anglorum* ('Deeds of the English Kings'), a history of England from 449 to 1120.

Malpas[1] 'difficult passage', OFr *mal* 'bad, difficult' + *pas* 'passage' (according to tradition, the difficulty was caused by marauding Welsh tribesmen who harrassed travellers along the road that formed the English–Welsh border).
A village (pronounced 'mawlpəs' or 'mawpəs') in Cheshire, on the Welsh border, about 24 km (15 miles) southeast of Chester. It has a picturesque mixture of timbered and Georgian houses.

Malpas[2] In this case the 'difficult passage' (*see* MALPAS[1]) was probably an unpleasant river-crossing.
A village (pronounced 'mowpəs') in Cornwall, on the southern outskirts of TRURO, on the eastern side of the Truro River. In the story of Tristram and Iseult, Iseult crosses the water here by ferry.

Maltby 'Malti's or malt farm', OScand male personal name or OE *malt* + -BY.
A mining town in South Yorkshire, 10 km (6 miles) east of Rotherham.

Malton 'village where the assembly is held' or 'middle village', OE *mæthel* 'assembly' or OScand *methal* 'middle' + -TON.
A market town in North Yorkshire, 12 km (7.5 miles) south of Pickering. It is on the River DERWENT[3], and its Roman name was **Derventio**. In the time of the Anglo-Saxon kingdom of DEIRA there was a royal palace here. Old Malton was burnt down in the 12th century, and New Malton largely dates from the early 18th century, when the town flourished as a river port. The Tory politician and thinker Edmund Burke became MP for Malton in 1781, and the Irish patriot Henry Grattan was returned as Malton's MP

in 1805. Just north of the town is Eden Camp, a former prisoner-of-war camp that is now a museum of everyday life in the Second World War.

Malvern. *See* GREAT MALVERN and MALVERN LINK.

Malvern Hills *Malvern* 'bare hill', OCelt *moil* 'bare' + *brinn* 'hill'.

A range of hills (pronounced 'mawlvən') running north to south on the Worcestershire–Herefordshire border, approximately 105 sq km (40 sq miles) in extent. They are not exceptionally high (the highest point is Worcestershire Beacon (*see under* WORCESTERSHIRE), at 425 m (1394 ft), and another notable eminence is Herefordshire Beacon (*see under* HEREFORDSHIRE)), but the way in which they rise out of the surrounding plain gives them a commanding presence. They provide what the 17th-century diarist John Evelyn described as 'one of the goodliest views in England'.

William Langland, the author of the 14th-century *Piers Plowman*, probably lived in the area of the Malvern Hills, and it was while walking 'on a May morning on Malvern hills' that the narrator fell asleep and had the vision of the 'field full of folk' which is the starting point of the poem.

A later artist to find inspiration in the Malvern Hills was the Worcester-born composer Edward Elgar. He had wandered the hills from boyhood, and knew their every contour and mood. Their spirit entered into his music.

There is a namesake range of Malvern Hills in Queensland, Australia, and a Malvern Hill in Virginia, USA, site of a Civil War battle (1 July 1862) in which the Unionists resisted Robert E. Lee's attack.

Malvern Hill. A painting (c.1809) by John Constable, one of his earliest major works. It is in Tate Britain.

Malvernian. Of or relating to Malvern or the Malvern Hills. As an adjective it is chiefly a geologists' word, referring either to the type of Precambrian plutonic rocks of which the hills are largely composed or to their characteristic north–south orientation; as a noun it often denotes a present or former pupil of Malvern College (*see* GREAT MALVERN).

Malvern Water. *See* GREAT MALVERN.

Malvern Link *Link* 'ridge, bank' (referring to the lower slopes of the Malvern Hills), OE *hlinc*.

A village in Worcestershire (before 1998 in Hereford and Worcester, before 1974 in Worcestershire), now effectively a northern suburb of GREAT MALVERN. It has a railway station thus named on the London–Worcester–Hereford line.

Mamble Probably a derivative of OCelt *mamm* 'breastlike hill'.

A village in Worcestershire (before 1998 in Hereford and Worcester, before 1974 in Herefordshire), about 12 km (7.5 miles) west of Stourport.

Mam Cymru. A former Welsh name for ANGLESEY. *See also under* CYMRU.

Mamores, the Possibly 'big breasts', Gaelic *mam* 'breast' + *mòr* 'big'.

A range of mountains in the central HIGHLANDS, some 10 km (6 miles) southeast of Fort William. They form the southern wall of Glen Nevis, while BEN NEVIS provides the northern rampart. The main ridge and its spurs contain ten Munros, the highest of which is Binnein Mor (1128 m / 3700 ft), and includes several fine, narrow sections such as the so-called Devil's Ridge (leading to Sgùrr a' Mhaim). The entire traverse in a day is a feasible, if demanding, excursion; combining this with the traverse of the GREY CORRIES, the Aonachs (*see* AONACH BEAG) and Ben Nevis has also been done within 24 hours.

Mam Rattachan. *See under* GLENELG.

Mám Toirc. The Irish name for the MAUMTURK MOUNTAINS.

Mam Tor 'breastlike hill', *Mam* from OCelt *mamm* 'breast'. The earliest recorded version of the name is *Manhill*.

A high craggy hill in the HIGH PEAK of Derbyshire, about 13 km (8 miles) northwest of Buxton. It is 517 m (1696 ft) above sea level. Its steep eastern face is known for its landslips, one of which, in the 1970s, led to the destruction and permanent closure of the A625 between Castleton and Chapel-en-le-Frith (cars must now use the little and very steep WINNATS PASS road just to the south of Mam Tor). The western side is a gentle slope, and a road goes up this to near the summit.

It is the most visited of all outdoor National Trust sites, attracting a quarter of a million people a year.

Mám Trasna. The Irish name for MAUMTRASNA.

Mamucium. The name of a Roman camp on the site of MANCHESTER.

Man, Isle of. *See* ISLE OF MAN.

Manacles, the Origin uncertain. The name may simply be the English word *manacles*, meaning a trap for shipping, referring to the dangerous nature of the rocks here. Alternatively, it may derive from Cornish *men* 'stone' + *eglos* 'church' (*see* ECCLES) and have the meaning 'church stones' (referring to the landmark of St Keverne Church, visible from the rocks). If the latter is the case, then the name would have later assimilated to the English word *manacles*.

A group of rocky islets (also known as **Manacle Rocks**) off the east coast of the LIZARD peninsula in Cornwall. Essentially a partly submerged reef, they have wrecked thousands of ships over the centuries. The nearby headland is called **Manacle Point**.

Manchester A reduced form of an OCelt name (possibly *mamm* 'breast') + OE *ceaster* 'Roman fort' (*see* CHESTER).

A city and metropolitan district in GREATER MANCHESTER (formerly in Lancashire), on the River IRWELL, 50 km (31 miles) east of Liverpool. Manchester is on the site of a

Roman camp called **Mamucium**; a version of this name, **Mancunium**, was the result of a mistranscription, but nevertheless gave us the word **Mancunian** for an inhabitant of the city (sometimes informally shortened to **Manc**). The Romany name for Manchester, according to George Borrow, is **Jinney-mengreskey gav** ('sharpers' town').

In the Middle Ages Manchester became a centre for the wool trade, and its moist climate and the water power provided by the rivers coming down from the Pennines to the east suited Manchester for the cotton industry, which grew up here from the 16th century. In the 18th century a network of canals, and in the 19th century a network of railways, linked Manchester with the rest of England, especially the ports of Merseyside. Manchester's Victoria Station, which predates London's (*see under* VICTORIA[2]), still has its George Stephenson-designed train-sheds from the mid-19th century. By the 19th century – when cotton textiles were Britain's biggest export – Manchester had become known as **Cottonopolis**.

> From this foul drain the greatest stream of human industry flows out to fertilize the whole world. From this filthy sewer pure gold flows. Here humanity attains its most complete development and its most brutish; here civilization makes its miracles, and civilized man is turned back almost into a savage.
>
> Alexis de Tocqueville: description of Manchester in *Journeys to England and Ireland* (1835)

In 1819 the city – with a population in excess of 84,000 but no representation in Parliament – became a centre of radical politics, and, on 16 August that year, 60,000 peaceful protestors demanding parliamentary reform gathered at St Peter's Fields:

> Come lend an ear of pity while I my tale do tell.
> It happened at Manchester, a place you know right well.
> For to address our wants and woes reformers took their ways,
> A lawful meeting being called upon a certain day.

However, soldiers came to disperse the crowd and 11 people were killed. The incident became known as the **Peterloo Massacre** (satirically playing on St Peter's Fields and Waterloo):

> The soldiers came unto the ground and thousands tumbled down,
> And many armless females lay bleeding on the ground.
> No time for flight was gave to us, still every road we fled.
> There were such heaps were trampled down, some wounded and some dead.
>
> Anon.: 'The Meeting at Peterloo' (sung to the tune of 'The Loyal Lover')

Subsequently Manchester became a centre of Liberal free-trade ideology opposed to the Corn Laws (*see* **Manchester School** *below*). It was at a Liberal Party meeting in Manchester in 1905 that the suffragette campaign was initiated, when Christabel Pankhurst unfurled a banner reading 'Votes for Women' – for which she was sent to jail.

Cotton made some rich – but the workers in Blake's 'dark satanic mills' lived in the most appalling conditions, as described by Friedrich Engels, who managed his family's cotton factory in Manchester for much of his life:

> Masses of refuse, offal and sickening filth lie among standing pools in all directions; the atmosphere is poisoned by the effluvia from these, and laden and darkened by the smoke of a dozen tall factory chimneys. A horde of ragged women and children swarm about here, as filthy as the swine that thrive upon the garbage heaps and in the puddles ... The race that lives in these ruinous cottages, behind broken windows, mended with oilskin, sprung doors, and rotten door-posts, or in dark, wet cellars, in measureless filth and stench, in this atmosphere penned in as if with a purpose, this race must really have reached the lowest stage of humanity.
>
> Friedrich Engels: *The Condition of the Working Class in England* (1845)

So that they need not be affronted by such sights, the middle classes moved out of the centre, especially to the non-industrial suburbs to the south, such as Withington, Fallowfield and DIDSBURY.

An exception to this exodus was the novelist Mrs Gaskell, author of *Cranford* (in which Manchester is 'Dumble'; elsewhere she calls it 'Milton'), who after her marriage in 1832 to a Unitarian minister from Manchester, spent much time helping the destitute in the city's slums. She was visited here by Charles Dickens, who shared her passion for social reform. Mrs Gaskell's novels *Mary Barton* (1848) and *North and South* (1855; *see under* NORTH) are both set in Manchester.

By the end of the 19th century Manchester had become part of a conurbation, with a population of over 2 million. Since the Second World War the cotton industry has declined, as has the population, and Manchester's economy has become more service-based. But towards the end of the 20th century the place began to revive, both economically and culturally. Its lively music and club scene in the later 1980s and 1990s earned it the nickname **Madchester** (with a reference to MDMA, i.e. the drug ecstasy), and Manchester bands from this period included The Smiths, The Stone Roses, Happy Mondays and Oasis. The recent proliferation of museums, such as the Lowry Centre at Salford Quays and Imperial War Museum North, has resulted in another nickname, **Museumchester**. In a slightly different league, one of the city's most popular tourist attractions is the set for *Coronation Street*, ITV's long-running soap, set in the fictitious suburb of Weatherfield. (Apparently Manchester taxi drivers are not infrequently asked by visitors to take them to Weatherfield.)

Manchester is also the setting of two other popular television series of the 1990s/2000s, *Cracker* and *Cold Feet*. That classic of British kitchen-sink realism, *A Taste of Honey* (1961), was filmed in Manchester's Salford docks (and in Blackpool), as was *Billy Liar* (1963), although Bradford and Baildon were also used.

In June 1996 a huge IRA bomb destroyed Manchester's ARNDALE CENTRE in the biggest explosion on mainland Britain since the Second World War. Planners took the opportunity to embark on a major redevelopment in the city, taking in Manchester's hosting of the 2002 Commonwealth Games (the city has been less successful in its bids to hold the Olympics). Manchester is, like Leeds to the east, a great musical centre, being home to the Hallé Orchestra and the Royal Northern College of Music. The Royal Exchange Theatre is Britain's largest theatre-in-the-round.

Another kind of theatre, football, obsesses and divides the city. **Manchester City**, originally founded as Ardwick FC in 1887 and nicknamed the Blues after their traditional light blue colours, played at Maine Road from 1923 until 2003, when they moved to the **City of Manchester Stadium**. Manchester City have had their moments (they won the first division title in 1968), but they have a habit of yo-yoing regularly between divisions. Their position vis-à-vis Manchester's other major football team is neatly summed up by the title of Manchester City fan Colin Shindler's best-selling memoir *Manchester United Ruined My Life* (1999). The club that would become the global brand that is **Manchester United** began life as a railway workers' team called Newton Heath in 1878, joined the Football League in 1892 and took its current name in 1902. Under the managership of Sir Matt Busby, who built three great teams in the 1950s and 1960s (the second included the so-called 'Busby Babes', eight of whom died in the 1958 Munich Air Crash, while the third was adorned by such legends as George Best, Bobby Charlton and Denis Law), Manchester United not only enjoyed success in domestic and European competitions (they won their first European Cup in 1968, the first English club side to do so), but also assumed a high-profile glamour and a worldwide appeal that they have never really lost. Nicknamed the 'Red Devils', Manchester United have won the league title on 15 occasions (second only to their great rivals LIVERPOOL), including 3 league and cup 'doubles', all of the latter under Sir Alex Ferguson, their manager from 1986. Since 1910 they have played most of their home games at OLD TRAFFORD (they were obliged to share Maine Road with Manchester

City between 1941 and 1948, two German bombs having made a mess of Old Trafford's main stand). Old Trafford is also the name of the home ground of Lancashire County Cricket Club close by; it has been used for county matches since 1865 and for test matches since 1884.

Manchester is an important centre of higher education, with the original **University of Manchester** having been joined by **UMIST** (the University of Manchester Institute of Science and Technology), the University of Salford and **Manchester Metropolitan University**. The highly regarded **Manchester Grammar School** dates back to 1515.

Manchester was the birthplace of the poet John Byrom (1692–1763), who also invented a form of shorthand; Samuel Crompton (1753–1827), inventor of the 'spinning mule'; the writer and opium-eater Thomas de Quincey (1785–1859); the historical novelist Harrison Ainsworth (1805–82; *see* PENDLE HILL); Frances Hodgson Burnett (1848–1924), author of *Little Lord Fauntleroy* (1886) and *The Secret Garden* (1911); J.J. Thomson (1856–1940), the discoverer of the electron; the suffragette leaders Emmeline (1858–1928) and Christabel Pankhurst (1880–1958); David Lloyd George (1863–1945), Liberal prime minister (1916–22); the humorist Ian Hay (1876–1952); the drama critic James Agate (1877–1947); the painter L.S. Lowry (1887–1976), who celebrated the industrial landscapes of Manchester and Salford; the novelist, composer and critic Anthony Burgess (1917–93), author of *A Clockwork Orange* (1962; set in Manchester and in 1971 made into a film by Stanley Kubrick); the playwright Robert Bolt (1924–95); the sports commentator (and unwitting progenitor of the sports commentator's gaffes known as 'Colemanballs') David Coleman (b.1926); the journalist Harold Evans (b.1928), former editor of *The Sunday Times*; the Lancashire and England cricketer Brian Statham (1930–2000); the playwright Jack Rosenthal (1931–2004); the comedian Les Dawson (1934–93); the composer Peter Maxwell Davies (b.1934); the architect Sir Norman Foster (b.1935); the playwright Trevor Griffiths (b.1935); the cricketer Michael Atherton (b.1968), captain of England from 1993 to 1998; the rock singer-songwriter Badly Drawn Boy (real name Damon Gough, b.1970); and the Yorkshire and England cricketer Michael Vaughan (b.1974), who captained England from 2003.

Peter Mark Roget came to work in Manchester as a physician in 1802, and after he retired in 1840 devoted himself to compiling his *Thesaurus*. It was in Manchester that John Dalton (1766–1844) worked out the basis of modern atomic theory, and his student James Joule (1818–89) pioneered the science of thermodynamics, running a steam engine in his house to work out the mechanical equivalent of heat until the neighbours complained. In the 1900s Manchester University was an important centre for nuclear research, with Rutherford, Bohr, Geiger and Chadwick all working here; in the 1940s it was home to a pioneering computer, partly developed by Alan Turing. Mr Rolls and Mr Royce set up business together in Manchester in 1906, but moved production of their motor cars to Derby in 1908.

There are towns called Manchester in the USA (Connecticut, New Hampshire, Vermont), and one called North Manchester (Indiana).

> The shortest way out of Manchester is notoriously a bottle of Gordon's gin.
>
> > William Bolitho: *Twelve Against the Gods*, 'Caliogstro and Seraphina' (1930)

> I looked out of the train window and all I could see was rain and fog. 'I know I'm going to love Manchester,' I told Jim, 'if I can only see it.'
>
> > Mae West: *Goodness Had Nothing To Do With It* (1959)

> He chose to live in Manchester, a totally incomprehensible choice for any free human being to make.
>
> > Sir Melford Stevenson: English judge, quoted in the *Daily Telegraph*, 11 April 1979

See also DROYLSDEN, HALE[1], HAZEL GROVE, MOSS SIDE *and* STRANGEWAYS.

'Manchester Angel, The'. A folk song, known in print from the 1770s, referring both to an inn and to the heroine. It begins:

> It's coming down to Manchester
> To gain my liberty,
> I met a pretty young doxy
> And she seemed full of glee.
> Yes, I met a pretty young doxy,
> The prettiest ever I see.
> At the Angel Inn in Manchester,
> There is the girl for me.

Manchester Arena. The largest indoor arena in Europe, opened in 1995 and capable of holding up to 21,000 people.

Manchester Barghest, the. In the folklore of northern England a barghest is a fierce supernatural hound that appears only at night. Those that see it clearly will soon die, while those that only glimpse it may linger on for a few months. The Manchester Barghest is distinguished from other barghests by its headlessness.

Manchester Guardian, The. The original name of the liberal *Guardian* newspaper, first published in Manchester in 1821 to 'advocate the cause of reform'. The paper changed its name to *The Guardian* in 1959, as the majority of its readers by this stage lived outside Manchester. The satirical weekly *Private Eye* consistently refers to it as *The Grauniad* on

account of the newpaper's predisposition to misprint. In 1964 the editorial staff moved to London.

'Guardian reader' has come to denote a holder of the type of liberal-left views espoused by leading articles in *The Guardian* newspaper. The term is often used unflatteringly by Conservatives to ridicule those on the left whose feckless do-goodery – in their opinion – threatens the traditions and institutions that they cherish. *Guardian* readers are often perceived to belong to the 'chattering classes' (*see also* HAMPSTEAD, ISLINGTON *and* NORTH LONDON). A female *Guardian* reader would be unlikely to hit it off with an Essex Man (*see under* ESSEX), but a male one might fantasize furtively about Essex Girls (*see also under* ESSEX).

Manchester Martyrs, the. The Irish Republican name for the Fenians William P. Allen, Michael Larkin, and Michael O'Brien, who were hanged in Manchester in 1867 for their part in a raid to rescue two fellow Fenians that resulted in the death of a policeman. Their deaths inspired the ballad 'God Save Ireland' (*see under* IRELAND).

Manchester Massacre, the. Another name for the Peterloo Massacre (*see above*).

Manchester Poet, the. The long-forgotten Charles Swain (1801–74), also an engraver and printer.

Manchester poplar. An occasional alternative name for the black poplar tree (*Populus nigra*), which is widespread in the north of England.

Manchester pudding. A type of queen of puddings made with breadcrumbs. You would be hard put to find it on the menu of any Manchester restaurant these days.

'Manchester Rambler, The'. A 'folk' song written by Ewan MacColl in 1963, celebrating the dedication of the city's working classes to rambling over the PENNINES. The well-known chorus goes:

> I'm a rambler, I'm a rambler from Manchester way,
> I get all my pleasure the hard, moorland way,
> I may be a wage slave on Monday,
> But I am a free man on Sunday.

Manchester Regiment. A regiment established in 1881, and part of the King's Regiment (Manchester and Liverpool) since 1958.

Manchester School. A group of political economists, notably John Bright and Richard Cobden, who campaigned for the repeal of the Corn Laws and supported a pacific, non-imperial foreign policy in the first half of the 19th century. They were so named, derisively, by Benjamin Disraeli in 1848. The name has also been applied to a group of avant-garde composers who studied at the Royal Manchester College of Music in the 1950s; the leading figures were Harrison Birtwistle, Peter Maxwell Davies, Alexander Goehr and John Ogdon.

Manchester Ship Canal. A waterway for smaller ocean-going vessels that links the city with the Mersey and thus to the Irish Sea and the Atlantic. It was opened in 1894, and for many decades its terminus at Salford Quays made Manchester one of the busiest ports in Britain. However, trade declined and the docks closed in 1982.

Manchester Sonatas. A set of 12 sonatas for violin and basso continuo by the 18th-century Italian composer Antonio Vivaldi, so named because they were discovered amongst a collection of uncatalogued works in Manchester Central Library by the musicologist Michael Talbot in 1973.

Manchester terrier. A medium-sized terrier with a smooth black-and-tan coat, a long neck and a narrow, deep chest. The earliest record of the breed is an illustration in a 15th-century book of hours, and it gained its present name in 1860, Manchester being a noted breeding centre. In the mid-19th century they were cross-bred with greyhounds to produce that finest of hounds, the whippet.

Mancunium. A Roman camp on the site of present-day MANCHESTER.

Mangerton Mountain Etymology uncertain, but possibly Irish *a'mBeannchair* 'at the peaked hill', with another element.
A mountain (837 m / 2745 ft) in County Kerry, rising on the south side of the Lakes of Killarney (*see under* KILLARNEY).

Mangotsfield 'Mangod's open land', OGerman *Mangodes* possessive form of male personal name *Mangod* + OE *feld* (*see* FIELD).
A northeastern suburb of BRISTOL, now in South Gloucestershire, before 1996 in Avon, before 1974 in Gloucestershire.

Manifold Probably '(river with) many folds or turnings', ME *manifold* 'many turnings', but there may also be some reference to the appearance and disappearance of the river.
A river in Staffordshire, within the PEAK DISTRICT National Park, which rises near FLASH and flows 28 km (17 miles) southwards to join the River DOVE near Ilam. In places, where its bed is porous, it disappears underground (via openings known as 'swallow holes') in periods of dry weather.
The southern section of the **Manifold Valley** is spectacular, with dramatic precipices and enticing caverns, such as THOR'S CAVE.

Mankinholes 'hollow of Mancán', Irish male personal name *Mancán* + OE *hol* 'hollow'; the *-s* was added later.
A village in West Yorkshire, 14 km (8.5 miles) west of Halifax.

Manningford Bohune *Manningford* 'Manna's people's ford', OE male personal name *Manna* + *-inga-* (*see* -ING) + FORD; *Bohune* denoting manorial ownership in the Middle Ages by the Boun family.
A village (pronounced 'boon') in Wiltshire, in the Vale of Pewsey, about 3 km (2 miles) southwest of Pewsey.

Manningford Bruce *Bruce* denoting manorial ownership in the Middle Ages by the Breuse family.
A village in Wiltshire, in the Vale of Pewsey, about 2 km (1.2 miles) southwest of Pewsey.

Manningtree 'many trees' or 'Manna's tree', OE *manig* 'many' or male personal name *Manna* + *treow* 'tree'.
A small market town in Essex, on the southern bank of the STOUR[2] estuary, about 11 km (7 miles) northeast of Colchester. Its annual fair in former centuries would no doubt have included the roasting of a whole ox, which probably inspired Prince Hal's description of Falstaff as 'that roasted Manningtree ox with a pudding in his belly' (Shakespeare, *Henry IV, Part 1* (1596), II.iv).
In the 1640s Manningtree was the headquarters of Matthew Hopkins, who set himself up as an inquisitorial witch-hunter.

Manorhamilton After Sir Frederick *Hamilton*.
A small town in County Leitrim, 20 km (12 miles) east of Sligo. Its Irish name is **Cluainín** ('little meadow'; *see* ACHADH). Sir Frederick Hamilton was granted lands here by Charles I and there are the ruins of his baronial mansion (1638).

Mansell Gamage *Mansell* probably 'hill of the gravel ridge', OE *malu* 'gravel ridge' + *hyll* 'hill'; *Gamage* denoting manorial ownership in the Middle Ages by the de Gamagis family.
A village in Herefordshire (before 1998 in Hereford and Worcester, before 1974 in Herefordshire), about 13 km (8 miles) west of Hereford.

Mansfield 'open land by the River Maun', MAUN + OE *feld* (*see* FIELD).
A market town in Nottinghamshire, on the River MAUN, about 21 km (13 miles) north of Nottingham. Once a woodland town, surrounded by SHERWOOD FOREST, it became industrialized in the 19th century and was an important centre of the Nottinghamshire coalfield. It boasts ancient cave-dwellings cut into sandstone cliffs, which were still inhabited at the end of the 19th century.
There are towns called Mansfield in the USA (Georgia, Illinois, Louisiana, Massachusetts, Missouri, Ohio, South Dakota, Texas, Washington) and in Australia (Victoria).

Mansfield Woodhouse 'woodland settlement near Mansfield': *Woodhouse* 'woodland settlement', OE *wudu* 'wood' + *hus* 'house, hamlet'.
A town in Nottinghamshire, about 2.5 km (1.5 miles) north of Mansfield. Two Roman villas were discovered nearby in 1786.

Mansion House From early ModE *mansion-house* 'official residence' (originally applied particularly to one belonging to the benefice of an ecclesiastic). To modern ears the term sounds vaguely tautologous, but it would not originally have done so.

A large building in the City of London (EC2), opposite the Bank of England, which is the official residence of the Lord Mayor of London for his or her year of office. It was built, to the Palladian designs of Charles Dance, in the middle of the 18th century, and opened in 1752.

Mansion House Underground station, on the District and Circle lines, opened in 1871. Its entrance is in Cannon Street, at some distance from the Mansion House itself.

Manston 'Mann's farmstead', OE *Mannes* possessive form of male personal name *Mann* + -TON.

A village in Kent, about 3 km (2 miles) west of Ramsgate. The local airfield was once an RAF station, which played an important role in the Battle of Britain.

Manx. *See under* ISLE OF MAN.

Maol. The Irish name for the Sea of MOYLE.

Mapledurham 'homestead where maple-trees grow', OE *mapuldor* 'maple-tree' + HAM.

A picturesque village (pronounced 'maypldurəm') in the far southeastern corner of Oxfordshire, on the River Thames, about 6 km (4 miles) northwest of Reading. **Mapledurham House**, a fine red-brick Elizabethan mansion, was the model for Soames Forsyte's country house in John Galsworthy's *The Forsyte Saga* (1906–21).

Maplin Sands *Maplin* origin unknown: the area is recorded as *Mablynge Swene* in the 15th century, where the second element is OE *swin* 'creek', but the first part of the name is obscure.

An area of sandbanks off the southeast Essex shore, from SHOEBURYNESS to the mouth of the River CROUCH[1]. In the 1960s it was the subject of a feasibility study for a new London Airport, but (in the face of considerable nimbyish fury) the plans came to nothing.

During the Second World War an anti-submarine net was stretched across the Thames estuary, to prevent German incursions, and the boom to which its northern end was attached can still be seen at Maplin.

Mappowder '(place at the) maple-tree', OE *mapuldor* 'maple-tree'.

A village in Dorset, about 16 km (10 miles) west of Blandford Forum.

Mar 'Mar's land', a tribal district controlled by an otherwise unknown *Mar* or *Marsos*.

A traditional district in western Aberdeenshire, taking in the area between the upper parts of the rivers DON[1] and DEE[1]. The Victorian hunting lodge of **Mar Lodge** is in the **Mar Forest**, a former royal hunting ground (from the 12th century) that takes in part of the CAIRNGORMS and some of Scotland's best remnants of Old Caledonian Forest (*see*

under CALEDONIA); the estate is now owned by the National Trust for Scotland. The name Mar also gave rise to the name BRAEMAR, and to the titles of two fiddle tunes: 'The Braes o' Mar', a traditional strathspey, and 'Mar Castle' by J.S. Skinner.

See also BUCHAN.

Earl of Mar. The most famous holder of this title (one of Scotland's older earldoms) was John Erskine, the 11th Earl (1672–1732), who was the leader of the 1715 Jacobite Rising and nicknamed 'Bobbing John' because of his wandering allegiances. He went into exile in France after the indecisive engagement at SHERIFF MUIR.

Marazion 'little market', Cornish *marghas* 'market' + *byghan* 'little'.

A small coastal town and port (pronounced with the stress on the third syllable) in Cornwall, about 5 km (3 miles) east of Penzance. It was attacked and burnt down by the French in 1513 and 1549. It is linked to ST MICHAEL'S MOUNT, just offshore, by a narrow cobbled causeway. It was also known in the past as MARKET JEW.

Marble Arch From the material of which the arch is made.

A triumphal arch in Central London (W1), at the northeastern corner of HYDE PARK, at the top of PARK LANE and the western end of OXFORD STREET. Designed by John Nash (in the style of the Arch of Constantine in Rome) and built in 1827 in Italian marble, it was intended to commemorate Nelson's and Wellington's victories. It originally stood in front of Buckingham Palace, but it was moved to its present site, close to that of the old TYBURN[2] gallows, in 1851, and in 1908 it was incorporated into a traffic island.

Marble Arch Underground station, on the Central line, opened in 1900.

Marble City. A nickname for KILKENNY.

March '(place at the) boundary' (perhaps referring to the limit of safe, habitable land in the Fens), OE *mearc* 'boundary'.

A market town in Cambridgeshire, in the FENS, on the old course of the River NENE, about 24 km (15 miles) east of Peterborough. Formerly it was part of the Isle of Ely (*see under* ELY[1]). It is now an important railway junction. Its town hall (1900) is described by Pevsner in *The Buildings of England: Cambridgeshire* (1970) as 'hideous'.

The ceiling of the church of St Wendreda boasts a spectacular host of carved angels on the wing (118 in all).

Marches, the 'boundary areas', Fr *marche* 'boundary, frontier' (related to OE *mearc* 'mark, boundary' – *see* MERCIA).

The lands in the vicinity of the English–Welsh border and extending at times deep into Wales (in full, the **Welsh Marches**), which from Anglo-Saxon times until the late Middle Ages were the scene of constant skirmishing, as the English attempted to assert their supremacy in the face of Welsh resistance.

Between the late 11th century and the mid-13th century the majority of southern and eastern Wales had come under Anglo-Norman suzerainty, and it was called the **March of Wales** (in Medieval Latin, the *Marchia Wallia*, as opposed to the Welsh kingdoms, collectively known as *Pura Wallia*; *see* WALLIA). Those areas where Anglo-Norman law prevailed over Welsh law were collectively known as the 'Englishry' (confusingly, a term also applied to those of non-Norman stock).

Control of the Welsh Marches was in the hands of the **Marcher lords** (or **Lords Marchers**, to give them their historical title). They had exclusive quasi-royal jurisdiction over the conquered territories, and they guarded the Welsh Marches at HEREFORD, SHREWSBURY and CHESTER. One of the most powerful of the Marcher lord families was the Mortimers: Roger Mortimer (*c*.1287–1330) was created 1st Earl of March in 1328. The lords' power waned in the 15th and early 16th centuries, in the period leading up to the union of Wales and England in the 1530s. Most of the lordships were taken over by the Crown (the last, BRECON, in 1521), and they were formally united with England in 1536, a process known as the **shiring of the Marches**.

The term *Marches*, or *March* in the singular, was applied also to Anglo-Scottish border areas (*see* **Wardens of the Marches** *below*, and *see also* BORDERS, the DEBATABLE LANDS *and* SCOT'S DYKE).

A territorial and historic division of Italy is called the Marches (in Italian, *Marche*). It is in central Italy, and includes the towns of Ancona (the capital), Pesaro and Urbino.

Council in the Marches. A royal court with jurisdiction over Wales and the Marcher lordships, established in 1473 and abolished in 1641.

Marcher. An inhabitant of the Marches.

ride the marches, to. A Scottish expression equivalent in meaning to 'beating the bounds' of an English parish (i.e. establishing the parish boundaries by processing round them), but in Scotland applied to BURGH boundaries.

Wardens of the Marches. Officials (often local nobles) appointed from the 14th century on each side of the Anglo-Scottish border, which was divided into the East, Middle and West Marches. The job of the Wardens on either side was to settle disputes and keep the peace via regular meetings, but sometimes their tête-à-têtes could degenerate into violence – as happened at the Redeswire Fray (*see under* REDESDALE) of 1575. The wardenships were abolished after England and Scotland united under James VI and I in 1603.

Marchia Wallia. *See under* WALLIA.

Marcle Hill *Marcle see* MUCH MARCLE.

A hill in Herefordshire (before 1996 in Hereford and Worcester, before 1974 in Herefordshire), about 1.5 km (1 mile) west of Much Marcle. Legend has it that at 6 p.m.

on 17 February 1575 the hill 'roused itself with a roar, and by seven next morning had moved 40 paces'. It kept on the move for three days, carrying all with it. It overthrew Kinnaston chapel and diverted two roads a distance of at least 180 m (about 200 yards) from their former course. Altogether, 10.5 ha (26 acres) of land are said to have been moved 360 m (about 400 yards). The site is known locally as 'The Wonder', and is marked as such on modern Ordnance Survey maps ('The Wonder. Landslip AD 1575').

> Marcle Hill … the scene of a remarkable landslip in 1575, which continued for three days (Feb. 17 to 19), resulting in the complete displacement of the hill, which in its progress carried with it and overturned trees, hedges, and sheepcotes, and destroyed a chapel; the movement was accompanied by loud subterranean noises, and was at the time supposed to be caused by an earthquake; it has, however, been shown by Sir R. Murchison and others that the phenomenon was due to a landslip, depending on the geological structure of the district, and similar to that which occurs not infrequently in the Alps.
>
> *Cassell's Gazetteer of Great Britain and Ireland* (1896)

Maree, Loch. *See* LOCH MAREE.

Margaret Roding. *See under* the RODINGS.

Margaretting Originally *Ginga* '(settlement of the) people of the district', OE *ge* 'district, region' + *-ingas* (*see* -ING); the addition of *Margaret* (first recorded in the 13th century) refers to the dedication of the local church.

A village in Essex, about 8 km (5 miles) southwest of Chelmsford.

Margate Probably 'gate or gap leading to the sea, or by a pool', OE *mere* 'sea, pool' + *geat* 'gate, gap'.

A town and seaside resort at the northeastern tip of Kent, in the ISLE OF THANET, about 5 km (3 miles) northwest of Broadstairs. It is one of the CINQUE PORTS. It was a pioneer in the business of promoting the coast as a leisure destination: a local glovemaker called Benjamin Beale invented the covered bathing machine in 1753, and crowds flocked. In the 19th century Margate became virtually the Kentish equivalent of SOUTHEND-ON-SEA, attracting thousands of working-class Londoners in the summer, and its downmarket (and nowadays slightly down-at-heel) image is a legacy of those days. Trippers continue to be drawn to Margate, though, by its 15 km (9 mile) sandy beach, its pier (known to locals as 'the Jetty') – and no doubt by the Scenic Railway (Britain's only listed amusement-park ride) in the Dreamland theme park (opened 1920, but now scheduled for closure).

In 1387 there was a sea battle off Margate, in which the English under the Earl of Arundel defeated the French and their allies.

T.S. Eliot stayed in next-door CLIFTONVILLE in 1921, and completed parts of *The Waste Land* in a shelter overlooking Margate Sands.

> On Margate sands
> I can connect
> Nothing with nothing.
>
> T.S. Eliot: *The Waste Land* (1922)

The artist Tracey Emin (of 'Unmade Bed' fame) was bought up in Margate, and some of her art is based on the town.

> Margate, that brick-and-mortar image of English Protestantism.
>
> Matthew Arnold: *Essays in Criticism* (1865)

> Margate the shrimpy, Ramsgate the asinine, Canterbury the ecclesiastical.
>
> George Sala: *Twice Round the Clock* (1859)

> There's no money in Margate. Eye contact has replaced it as the root of all evil and, yes, this town's as ripe as ever for a low-budget remake of *Brighton Rock*: the joyless amusement arcades, the facial scars ...
>
> David Seabrook: *All the Devils Are Here* (2002)

Margate sands. An early 20th-century rhyming-slang term for 'hands'.

Maridunum. The Roman name for their large fort and settlement at CARMARTHEN.

Marilyns Named after Marilyn *Monroe*.

The collective name for all the mountains and hills in Britain with a drop of at least 150 m (492 ft) on all sides. The original list was compiled by Alan Dawson in his book *The Relative Hills of Britain* (1992). Dawson explains:

> A flippant item in a recent *Scottish Mountaineering Club Journal* suggested using the term 'Mungo' for all the millions of hills over 300 feet high. I have decided to use the more distinguished and appropriate term 'Marilyn', and I therefore officially define a Marilyn as any hill that has a drop of at least 150 metres on all sides, regardless of distance, absolute height or topographical merit. At the last count there were 1542 of them.

'Mungo' is a play on Munro, the name given to Scottish mountains over 3000 ft (*see* MUNROS), and it is clear that it is the well-bosomed Marilyn Monroe after whom Dawson has named his myriad mounds.

See also CORBETTS, DONALDS, GRAHAMS, MURDOS *and* WAINWRIGHTS.

Market Bosworth *Bosworth see* BOSWORTH.

A small market town in Leicestershire, about 19 km (12 miles) west of Leicester. The **Battle of Bosworth** was fought nearby. In the 18th century Samuel Johnson was an usher (a sort of assistant master) at the local grammar school.

Market Deeping *Deeping see* DEEPING ST JAMES.

A former coaching town in the Lincolnshire Fens, on the River WELLAND, about 11 km (7 miles) north of Peterborough. Its 14th-century rectory is the oldest inhabited parsonage in England. It is contiguous with Deeping St James. The village of **West Deeping** lies to the southwest.

Market Drayton *Drayton see* DRAYTON PARSLOW.

A market town (alternatively named **Drayton-in-Hales**) in Shropshire, on the River Tern, about 24 km (15 miles) north of Telford. Its market dates from the time of Edward I. The centre of the town has many fine examples of the black-and-white half-timbered buildings characteristic of Shropshire.

The soldier and administrator Robert Clive ('Clive of India'; 1725–74) was born in Market Drayton, and attended the local grammar school.

Market Harborough *Harborough* probably 'hill where oats are grown', OScand *hafri* or OE *hœfera* 'oats' + OScand *berg* or OE *beorg* 'hill'. Alternatively the first element may be OE *hœfer* or OScand *hafr* 'male goat'.

A market town in Leicestershire, about 24 km (15 miles) southeast of Leicester. Its market dates from the end of the 12th century. Its church, about a century younger, has a particularly fine 49 m (161 foot) tower and spire, from which, every November, the bells are rung to celebrate the rescue of a merchant who had lost his way on the nearby Welland Marshes in 1500. Its early 17th-century half-timbered grammar school is raised on wooden pillars that were once home to a butter market.

The manufacture of the liberty bodice, a vest-like undergarment for women and children, was pioneered in Market Harborough in the 1910s, by the firm of R. & W.H. Symington. Production ceased in the 1960s.

> Am in Market Harborough. Where ought I to be?
>
> G.K. Chesterton: in a telegram to his wife (She cabled the answer 'Home'. Various other places have been quoted as his location, notably WOLVERHAMPTON, but Market Harborough is the version given in his *Autobiography* (1936).)

Market Jew 'Thursday market', Cornish *marghas* 'market' + *yow* 'Thursday'.

A former name of MARAZION.

Market Rasen *Rasen* '(place at the) planks' (referring to a bridge made from planks), OE *rœsn* 'plank', here in the dative plural.

A market town in Lincolnshire, on the River Rase, about 24 km (15 miles) northeast of Lincoln. It has a well-known National Hunt racecourse:

> Seldom do we find Irish raiders at the Market Rasen track, but trainer Moore has sent two over in a bid for a winning double.
>
> *Daily Record* (Glasgow) (4 December 1976)

Market Weighton *Weighton* was *Wicstun* in 1086; *see* WICK and -TON.

A town in the East Riding of Yorkshire, 15 km (9 miles) west of Beverley. Every year near the town the Kipling Cotes Derby is held. It dates back to 1519 and is said to be the oldest flat race in England.

Markinch 'water meadow of the horse', Gaelic *marc* 'horse' + INIS.

A small town in Fife, 2 km (1.2 miles) east of Glenrothes. General Alexander Leslie – *see under* LOCH LEVEN[1] – lived in nearby Balgonie Castle, and was buried in Markinch in 1661.

Mark Lane Originally *Marthe Lane*, probably reflecting either the female personal name *Martha* (OFr *Marthe*) or OE *mearth* 'marten' (the valuable fur of which may have been sold in the street in early times). The present form of the name is first recorded in 1481.

A street in the City of London (EC3), near the Tower of London. Previously the haunt of wine importers, it was very badly damaged during the Blitz.

The former Mark Lane Underground station was renamed **Tower Hill** (*see under* TOWER OF LONDON) in 1946.

Marlborough 'Mærla's (burial) mound' or 'hill where gentian grows', OE male personal name *Mærla* or *meargealla* 'gentian' + *beorg* 'hill, mound' (the first element has no historical connection with *Merlin*, the name of the magician in Arthurian legend whose tomb is said to lie beneath Castle Mound – also known as 'Merle Barrow' – in the grounds of Marlborough College).

A market town (pronounced 'mawl-' or 'mahl-') in Wiltshire, on the River KENNET[1], about 16 km (10 miles) south of Swindon. Its High Street, lined with distinctive colonnades, is one of the widest in England.

Marlborough College, a co-educational public school, was founded in 1843. Among its former pupils were the designer and writer William Morris, the poets Siegfried Sassoon, John Betjeman (Betjeman recalled his school days here in *Summoned by Bells* (1960)) and Louis MacNeice, the novelist William Golding, the politician R.A. Butler, the actors James Mason and James Robertson Justice and the art historian and spy Anthony Blunt.

There are towns called Marlborough in Australia (Queensland) and Guyana and, with a change of spelling to 'Marlboro', in the USA (Massachusetts, New Hampshire). The district of Marlborough on the South Island of New Zealand developed a highly successful wine-growing industry in the latter part of the 20th century.

Duke of Marlborough. A title conferred by Queen Anne in 1702 on John Churchill (1650–1722) in recognition of his success as a military commander in the Low Countries during the War of the Spanish Succession (and also no doubt of his personal support for her in the past against her sister, Queen Mary). He appears to have chosen it on account of a connection on his mother's side with the Ley family, earls of Marlborough, whose title had become extinct some years previously. Two years later he was further rewarded with BLENHEIM PALACE for his victory in the battle of that name in 1704. Subsequent holders of the title have been less distinguished, though the 7th Duke (1822–83) did manage to produce Winston Churchill as a grandson.

Marlborough Downs. An area of downland to the north of Marlborough. It is part of the North Wessex Downs (*see under* WESSEX). The RIDGEWAY runs across it. Like many other chalk downs, it has its own White Horse, on the slopes of HACKPEN HILL.

Marlborough House. A mansion in PALL MALL, in the West End of London (SW1). It was built for Sarah, Duchess of Marlborough (1660–1744) in 1709–11. In 1817 it reverted to the Crown, and its most famous resident thereafter was the Prince of Wales (later Edward VII). During his occupancy it became the centre of fashionable society and the Prince's inner circle became known as the **Marlborough House Set**. In 1959 it was given to the Government for use as a Commonwealth Centre.

Marlburian. A person educated at Marlborough College.

Statute of Marlborough (1267). A piece of legislation, still current, which was enacted during Henry III's parliament in Marlborough. It confirmed provisions of Magna Carta and protected sub-tenants' possessions from unauthorized seizure.

Marlborough Street Named in honour of John Churchill, 1st Duke of *Marlborough* (1650–1722).

A street (in full, **Great Marlborough Street**) in the West End of London, leading eastwards off REGENT STREET. It was built at the beginning of the 18th century. It is now probably best known for its Magistrates' Court:

> A sex-change Kiss-a-Gram girl stepped into the Marlborough Street dock yesterday clad in a see-through bra, black knickers, and fishnet stockings with suspender belt.
>
> *Daily Telegraph* (30 October 1984)

The street is valued at £180 on the Monopoly board.

Marlow 'land remaining after the draining of a pool', OE *mere* 'pool' + *laf* 'remains'.

A town (also known in the past as **Great Marlow**) in Buckinghamshire, on the River Thames, about 6 km (4 miles) northwest of Maidenhead. Mary Wollstonecraft finished *Frankenstein* while living at Albion House in West Street in 1817–18 with her future husband, the poet Shelley. The highwayman Dick Turpin is said to have been a regular at the Crown Hotel.

There are towns called Marlow in the USA (New Hampshire, Oklahoma) and Australia (Queensland).

Marmalade Country. A slang term for SCOTLAND, coined in the music halls of the late 19th century, referring to the popularity of Scottish marmalade (especially that made in DUNDEE).

Marple 'boundary pool or stream', OE *gemære* 'boundary' + *pyll* 'pool, stream'.

A largely residential town in Greater Manchester, 15 km (9 miles) southeast of the city centre. **Marple Hall**, which during the Civil Wars was owned by the brother of one of the regicides, is supposedly haunted by a headless Charles I. There is a town called Marple in the USA (Pennsylvania).

Marsden 'boundary valley', OE *mercels* 'boundary' + *denu* 'valley'.

A small former textile town on the River COLNE[3] in West Yorkshire, 11 km (7 miles) southwest of Huddersfield. It is the home of the Huddersfield-born poet Simon Armitage. In 1812 it was the scene of Luddite violence, including the fatal shooting of a Marsden mill owner. Marsden's annual Cuckoo Day celebrates the time when the people of Marsden identified the arrival of the cuckoo with the coming of pleasant spring weather, so in order to keep spring forever they built a tower round the cuckoo. Unfortunately, the cuckoo escaped by flying over the top of the wall, which, according to the legend, 'were nobbut just a course too low'. Although the people of Marsden thus acquired a reputation for low intelligence, the same cannot be said for the local sheep, who have found a novel way of crossing cattle grids so that they can raid the gardens of Marsden: as a local councillor explains, 'They lie down on their side, or sometimes their back, and just roll over and over the grids until they are clear.'

Marsh Baldon *Marsh* '(place at the) marsh', OE *mersc* 'marsh'; *Baldon* 'Bealda's hill', OE male personal name *Bealda* + *dun* (*see* DOWN, -DON).

A village in Oxfordshire, about 6 km (4 miles) southeast of Oxford. Marsh Baldon and the nearby TOOT BALDON are known collectively as The BALDONS.

Marsh Gibbon *Gibbon* denoting manorial ownership in the early Middle Ages by the Gibwen family.

A village in Buckinghamshire, about 21 km (13 miles) northwest of Aylesbury.

Marske-by-the-Sea OE *mersc* 'marsh'.

A seaside town in Redcar and Cleveland (formerly in the North Riding of Yorkshire, then in Cleveland), 16 km (10 miles) east of Middlesbrough.

Marston Moor *Marston* 'farm by a marsh', OE *mersc* 'marsh' + -TON; *mor* 'waste or marshy land'.

An area of barely raised ground in the flats of the Vale of YORK, North Yorkshire, some 11 km (7 miles) west of York.

Battle of Marston Moor (2 July 1644). One of the most decisive engagements in the Civil Wars, in which the Royalists under Prince Rupert and the Earl of Newcastle were defeated by the Parliamentarians under the Earl of Manchester and Lord Fairfax and their Scots allies under Lord Leven. It was Cromwell's cavalry on the left wing who won the day, after Fairfax's right wing had been routed. After the battle, York, which Rupert had come to relieve, fell to the Parliamentarians, along with much of the North. The elite of the Royalist army was destroyed, making final victory to Parliament a near certainty.

> Wouldst hear the tale? – On Marston heath
> Met, front to front, the ranks of death;
> Flourish'd the trumpets fierce, and now
> Fired was each eye, and flush'd each brow;
> On either side loud clamours ring,
> 'God and the Cause!' – 'God and the King!'
> Right English all, they rush'd to blows,
> With nought to win, and all to lose.
>
> Sir Walter Scott: *Rokeby* (1813), Canto I, xii

Although the area is said to be haunted by the ghosts of Cavaliers (three were spotted on the nearby A59 in the late 1970s), these are more likely to be members of the Sealed Knot battle re-enactment society having a bit of a giggle.

In 1655 Marston Moor was the scene of a limp attempt at a Royalist rebellion against Cromwell, led by Henry Wilmot, 1st Earl of Rochester. On its collapse the earl fled the country.

Marston Moretaine *Moretaine* denoting manorial ownership in the Middle Ages by the Morteyn family.

A village in Bedfordshire, about 10 km (6 miles) southwest of Bedford.

Marston Trussell *Trussell* denoting manorial ownership in the Middle Ages by the Trussel family.

A village in Northamptonshire, about 5 km (3 miles) southwest of Market Harborough.

Martin Hussingtree Originally two separate manor names: *Martin* 'farmstead near a boundary or by a pool', OE *(ge)mære* 'boundary' or *mere* 'pool' + -TON; *Hussingtree* 'Husa's tree', OE *Husan* possessive form of male personal name *Husa* + *treow* 'tree'.

A village in Worcestershire (before 1998 in Hereford and Worcester, before 1974 in Worcestershire), about 7 km (4.5 miles) northeast of Worcester.

Martyr Worthy *Martyr* denoting manorial ownership in the Middle Ages by the le Martre family; *Worthy* 'enclosure(s)', OE *worthig* (*see* -WORTH, WORTHY, -WARDINE).

A village in Hampshire, about 5 km (3 miles) northeast of Winchester.

Marwell Park *Marwell* originally a local stream name, 'boundary stream', OE (*ge*)*mære* 'boundary' + *wielle* 'stream'.
A zoo (in full **Marwell Zoological Park**) in Hampshire, about 8 km (5 miles) southeast of Winchester. It opened in 1972, and has over 40 ha (100 acres) of spacious enclosures.

Maryborough. The former name for PORTLAOISE.

Maryculter. *See under* PETERCULTER.

Mary Gray. *See* BESSIE BELL AND MARY GRAY.

Marylebone Originally *Maryburn* '(place by St) Mary's stream' (referring to the dedication of the local church, built in the 15th century, and to the local TYBURN[1] stream), *Mary* + ME *burne* 'stream'; the medial *-le-*, first recorded in the 17th century, has no intrinsic meaning, and was probably introduced on the analogy of church names such as *St Mary-le-Bow* (*see* BOW), where the infix reflects Fr *le* 'the'. (Before the 15th century the area was known as TYBURN[2].)
A district (pronounced 'marrylebone' or 'marlibon') in northwest Central London (NW1, W1), in the City of WESTMINSTER, between BLOOMSBURY in the east and PADDINGTON in the west, extending southwards to OXFORD STREET, and including REGENT'S PARK. It is sometimes known more fully as **St Marylebone**.

Until the 18th century it was largely open country, but then the landowners (including the Portman Estate, still a major landlord in the area) began to build. The process continued until by the middle of the 19th century most of Marylebone (with the exception of Regent's Park) was covered with the mixture of offices and residences that adorn it today. The area around **Marylebone High Street** (W1) manages to retain something of a villagey feel.

At the end of the 19th century the Great Central Railway carved its way through the northern part of the district and built itself a terminus here, **Marylebone Station**. Opened in 1899, it was the last railway terminus to be constructed in London until the Eurostar terminal at Waterloo (1991–3). It is valued at £200 on a Monopoly board. Marylebone Underground station, on the Bakerloo line, opened in 1907, originally under the name 'Great Central'; it was changed to 'Marylebone' in 1917. The stations are situated on the north side of the **Marylebone Road**, a busy thoroughfare which links the A40(M) Westway via the **Marylebone Flyover** with the Euston Road and forms part of the northern boundary of the London Congestion Zone.

Marylebone Cricket Club. A cricket club (abbreviation MCC) founded in 1787 by members of the old White Conduit Club of Islington, with which it later merged. In 1814 it moved to LORD's cricket ground, which it bought in 1866 and which is still its headquarters. By the middle of the 19th century it was generally recognized as the premier club in the game, its decisions deferred to in matters of interpretation of the rules. By the 20th century it was virtually the ruling body of cricket in England (with wide influence on world cricket to boot), and until the 1970s the England team toured abroad under the banner of the MCC. By then, though, its image as an exclusive men's club (bolstered by the stereotype of the ancient and potentially apoplectic MCC member, complete with assertive red-and-yellow-striped tie (sometimes known as the 'bacon-and-egg tie'), slumbering in front of Lord's pavilion) was widely thought to be inappropriate to a ruling body of a national sport, and it devolved most of its powers to other organizations, of which the latest incarnation is the England and Wales Cricket Board (ECB). The MCC retains, however, its responsibility for the laws of cricket and their interpretation and revision. In 1998 it admitted female members for the first time in its 211-year history.

Maryport After *Mary* Senhouse.
A port at the mouth of the River Ellen on the northwest coast of Cumbria (formerly in Cumberland), some 40 km (25 miles) southwest of Carlisle. It was originally one of the many Roman forts and settlements called **Alauna**, then a small fishing village called **Ellenfoot**, until it was developed as a port to export coal by Humphrey Senhouse, the lord of the manor, who renamed it after his wife Mary in 1756, the name being confirmed by act of Parliament in 1791. The last local coal mine closed in the 1960s.

Writers Charles Dickens and Wilkie Collins and engineer George Stephenson all stayed at The Golden Lion Hotel in Maryport, and Thomas Ismay (1836–99), founder of the White Star Line, was born here.

Mary Tavy *Mary* from the dedication of the local church; *Tavy* from the River TAVY.
A village in Devon, on the western edge of Dartmoor, about 5 km (3 miles) north of Tavistock.
See also PETER TAVY.

Maserfield Etymology uncertain, but possibly 'open land of the titmouses', OE *masra*, possessive plural of *mase* 'titmouse' + FIELD.
A battle site (also spelt **Maserfeld** or **Maserfelth**) of uncertain location where in 642 Penda, the pagan king of Mercia, defeated and killed the Christian Oswald of Northumbria, cutting off his head and hands and placing them on top of stakes – thus ensuring Oswald's future status as saint and martyr. Maserfield may have been near Oswestry in Shropshire, or closer to the Northumbrian–Mercian border.

Masham 'Mæssa's village', OE male personal name *Mæssa* + HAM.
A market town above the River Ure, North Yorkshire, on the edge of the Yorkshire Dales, 20 km (12 miles) southwest

of Northallerton. It is pronounced 'massəm', and is famed for its beer, being the home since 1827 of the Theakston Brewery (makers of the devastating Old Peculiar) and of the more recent Black Sheep Brewery, established on the site of the old Lightfoot Brewery.

Massingham Heath *Massingham* 'homestead of Mæssa's people', OE male personal name *Mæssa* + *-inga-* (*see* -ING) + HAM.

An area of heathland in Norfolk, to the east of King's Lynn. It is crossed by PEDDAR'S WAY. The villages of **Great Massingham** and **Little Massingham** are just to the east.

Matfield 'Matta's open land', OE personal name *Matta* + *feld* (*see* FIELD).

A village in Kent, on the edge of the WEALD, about 7 km (4.5 miles) southeast of Tonbridge. The poet Siegfried Sassoon (1886–1967) lived here as a boy, and it is fictionalized as **Butley** in his *Memoirs of a Fox-Hunting Man* (1928).

Matlock 'oak-tree where meetings are held', OE *mæthel* 'meeting' + *ac* 'oak'.

A spa town in DERBYSHIRE (of which it is the administrative headquarters), on the River DERWENT[4], at the southeastern edge of the PEAK DISTRICT, about 15 km (9 miles) southwest of Chesterfield. To the southeast, between Matlock and BELPER, lie the historically important mills of the Derwent Valley.

It is a town of many parts. Matlock proper consists of **Matlock Bridge**, on the site of the original settlement, and **Matlock Bank**, on the hillside above, which developed around a source of tepid spring water. This had been discovered in the 1690s, but it was the hydrotherapy centre opened by John Smedley in 1853 that brought the Victorians flocking, so seeding urban growth. The centre is now council offices.

About 1.5 km (1 mile) south down the A6 is **Matlock Bath**, which also throve as a spa in Victorian times. It is dominated by the approximately 300-m (1000-ft) 'Heights of Abraham', so named by an officer who had fought with General Wolfe on the original 'Heights of Abraham' in Quebec in 1759. They can be ascended by cable car.

There is a Mount Matlock in Victoria, Australia.

> Mr. Thrale particularly vexes lest you should not see Matlock on a moon-light night.
>
> Hester Thrale: letter to Dr Johnson (1770)

matlockite. A yellowish oxychloride of lead discovered near Matlock in the 1840s.

Mauchline 'field of the pool', Gaelic *magh* 'field' + *linne* 'pool'.

A village 13 km (8 miles) southeast of Kilmarnock, in East Ayrshire (formerly in Strathclyde region). It is closely associated with Robert Burns, who in the period 1777–89 lived at nearby **Lochlea** farm and then at **Mossgiel**. Burns

fell in love with Jean Armour, the daughter of a local master mason:

> When first I came to Stewart Kyle,
>   My mind it was na steady;
> Where'er I gaed, where'er I rade,
>   A mistress still I had aye:
> But when I came roun' by Mauchline town,
>   Not dreadin' onie body,
> My heart was caught before I thought –
>   And by a Mauchline lady.
>
> Robert Burns: 'The Mauchline Lady' (sung to the tune of 'I had a horse, and I had nae mair')

Jean's father forbade the match, but Burns eventually married her in Mauchline in 1788, and four of Burns's children are buried in the graveyard. The village is the setting for Burns's poem 'The Holy Fair'; and Poosie Nansie's Tavern, where his cantata 'The Jolly Beggars' is set, is still open as a public house.

'Belles of Mauchline, The'. A short poem by Robert Burns:

> In Mauchline there dwells six proper young belles,
>   The pride of the place and its neighbourhood a';
> Their carriage and dress, a stranger would guess,
>   In Lon'on or Paris they'd gotten it a':
> *Miss Miller* is fine, *Miss Markland*'s divine,
>   *Miss Smith* she has wit, and *Miss Betty* is braw;
> There's beauty and fortune to get wi' *Miss Morton*;
>   But *Armour*'s the jewel for me o' them a'.

Maud Possibly Gaelic *madaidh* 'place of the dog'.

A village in Buchan, Aberdeenshire, 20 km (12 miles) west of Peterhead. It is an agricultural centre and has a livestock market.

Maumbury Ring *Maumbury* probably 'ancient earthwork on chalky or sandy soil', OE *mealm* 'chalky or sandy soil' + *burh* 'pre-English earthwork' (*see* BURY).

A prehistoric circular earthwork towards the southern edge of Dorchester, in Dorset, dating from the late Neolithic (New Stone Age) or early Bronze Age (about 1800 BC). Excavations between 1908 and 1913 revealed that the original structure was an earthen circle containing an interior ditch cut by shafts 10 m (33 ft) deep.

Maumtrasna Irish *Mám Trasna* 'mountain pass or crossing'.

A plateau-like mountain, at 673 m (2207 ft) the highest point in the PARTRY MOUNTAINS of JOYCE'S COUNTRY, on the borders of Galway and Mayo. The settlement of Maumtrasna (or **Maamtrasna**) is at its southeastern foot, overlooking an inlet of LOUGH MASK.

Maamtrasna Murders (8 August 1882). A notorious case in which John Joyce of Maamtrasna and four members of his family were murdered, possibly as a result of a local feud involving secret societies. Ten men were arrested, apparently on the basis of perjured evidence, and two of them turned Queen's Evidence, with the result that three men were hanged and five sentenced to life imprisonment.

Maumturk Mountains Irish *Mám Toirc* 'pass of the boars'.
A range of beautiful quartzite mountains in JOYCE'S COUNTRY, County Galway, extending westwards from the northwest end of LOUGH CORRIB. The highest point is Binn Idir an Dha Log ('mountain between two loughs'; about 700 m / 2300 ft). The Maumturks are said to mark the westernmost point of St Patrick's travels around Ireland, and where he spent the night before turning back (at the spot known as St Patrick's Bed) a spring of holy water appeared. St Patrick's Bed is at a pass called Mam Ean, on the south side of the range, and is the destination of an annual pilgrimage.

Maun From the name of a hill about 6 km (4 miles) away, *Mammeshead* 'headland of Mam', from OCelt *Mam*, from *mamm* 'breast, breastlike hill'.
A river in Nottinghamshire, which rises to the west of Mansfield and flows 30 km (19 miles) northeastwards through SHERWOOD FOREST towards RETFORD. Before it arrives there it is joined by the River Meden and its name changes to IDLE.

Maund Bryan *Maund* perhaps '(place at the) hollows', OE *magum* dative plural form of *maga* 'stomach' (used in a topographical sense); alternatively *Maund*, which is also a district name, may represent a survival of an OCelt name *Magnis*, probably 'the rocks'; *Bryan* denoting manorial ownership in the Middle Ages by someone called Brian.
A village in Herefordshire (before 1998 in Hereford and Worcester, before 1974 in Herefordshire), about 11 km (7 miles) northeast of Hereford.

Mavesyn Ridware *Mavesyn* denoting manorial ownership in the early Middle Ages by the Malvoisin family (OFr 'bad neighbour'); *Ridware see* HAMSTALL RIDWARE.
A village (pronounced 'mavvisən' or 'maysən') in Staffordshire, on the River Blithe, about 8 km (5 miles) north of Lichfield.
See also PIPE RIDWARE.

Mavis Enderby *Mavis* denoting manorial ownership in the Middle Ages by the Malebisse family; *Enderby see* BAG ENDERBY.
A village in Lincolnshire, about 21 km (13 miles) west of Skegness.

> Gill Foot remembers [John Betjeman's] glee on encountering a signpost on the Spilsby–Boston road which read 'To Mavis Enderby and Old Bolingbroke'. Someone had scrawled underneath '– the gift of a son'.
>
> Bevis Hillier: *John Betjeman – New Fame, New Love* (2002)

Mawla Origin unknown.
A village in Cornwall, about 4 km (2.5 miles) north of Redruth.

Mawnan Smith *Mawnan* '(church of Saint) Maunanus', after the dedication of the local church to the mysterious St Maunanus, a 6th-century Welsh missionary; *Smith* perhaps from the smithy that stood in the village from the 16th century.
A village in Cornwall, just to the north of the HELFORD estuary, about 5 km (3 miles) southwest of Falmouth.

Maxey 'Maccus's island', OScand male personal name *Maccus* + OE *eg* (*see* -EY, -EA).
A village in Cambridgeshire, within the unitary authority of PETERBOROUGH, about 8 km (5 miles) northwest of the city of Peterborough.

Maxwelton House Named after the *Maxwell* family.
An old country house, built in 1641 near the New Galloway road, 8 km (5 miles) southwest of Thornhill, in Dumfries and Galloway (formerly in Dumfriesshire). Although the Maxwells were a prominent local family (the village of Maxwelltown near Dumfries was named in 1810 after Marmaduke Maxwell), Maxwelton House was until relatively recently in the possession of the Laurie family. Its most famous inhabitant was Annie Laurie (born sometime in the 1680s), to whom William Douglas of Fingland, a fiery Jacobite, addressed his famous love song, known either as 'Bonnie Annie Laurie' or as '**Maxwelton Braes'** (Scots *braes* 'hillsides'):

> Maxwelton's braes are bonnie
> Where early fa's the dew
> And 'twas there that Annie Laurie
> Gave me her promise true.
> Gave me her promise true
> Which ne'er forgot will be
> And for bonnie Annie Laurie
> I'd lay me doon and dee.

Despite their mutual promises, Douglas (by this time a soldier of fortune) married an heiress, Elizabeth Clerk of Glendroth, in 1706, while Annie later married Alexander Ferguson of Craigdarroch, a neighbour and relative of Douglas. The tune of the song was actually composed much later, by Alicia Spottiswoode (d.1900), the daughter-in-law of the Duke of Buccleuch, and the most widely known version of the words was written in 1835 by Lady John Scott.

May, Isle of. *See* ISLE OF MAY.

Mayar Possibly 'high plain' (which suits its wide summit plateau), Gaelic *magh* 'plain' + ARD. A more flighty but altogether less likely suggestion is Gaelic *m'aighear* 'my darling'.
A mountain (928 m / 3043 ft) in the southern CAIRNGORMS, Angus, above the head of GLEN CLOVA. There are snow and ice climbs in its northeastern corrie.

Maybole Probably 'kinswoman's dwelling', OE *mæge* 'kinswoman, maiden' + *bothl* 'dwelling'; *Maybothel* 1189.
A small town 12 km (7.5 miles) south of Ayr in South

Ayrshire (formerly in Strathclyde region). The first church was built here in 1193, and Maybole became the 'capital' of the traditional area of CARRICK[1]. It also became a seat of the Kennedy earls of Cassilis, whose town house or 'castle' (17th century) still stands. It was in this building that a 16th-century Countess of Cassilis was reputedly imprisoned for life by her husband, John Kennedy, 6th Earl of Cassilis, after she had run off with Johnny Faa, the 'king' of the gypsies (*see under* KIRK YETHOLM). In the 18th century the Countess became associated with the old ballad 'Gypsy Laddie':

> Oh, what care I for a goosefeather bed
> With the sheet turned down so bravely-o,
> Oh, what care I for my new wedded lord,
> I'm off with the raggle-taggle gypsies-o.

However, the story appears to be apocryphal.

Mayfair From the 'May fair', a fair held in May on an area of open land near TYBURN[2] called Brookfield (on the site of present-day Hertford Street, Curzon Street and SHEPHERD MARKET). There was an annual fair in HAYMARKET from the reign of Edward I, called St James's Fair, which began on the eve of St James the Less (30 April) and was suppressed in 1664. It was renewed by James II to commence on 1 May, and in 1686–8 it was transferred to Brookfield. By the beginning of the 18th century it had become a hotbed of drinking, gambling and whoring; it was temporarily suppressed in 1708 and was finally abolished in 1760.

A fashionable district in the WEST END[1] of London (W1), in the City of WESTMINSTER, bounded to the west by PARK LANE, to the east by REGENT STREET (though conceptually, for many, by BOND STREET), to the north by OXFORD STREET and to the south by PICCADILLY[1].

Building began in the area around the 'May fair' (*see above*) in the first decade of the 18th century, and it seems to have inherited the name *Mayfair* by at the latest the 1750s. Construction (much of it under the auspices of the Grosvenor Estate) was largely of grand residences for the nobility and gentry, and the district quickly acquired a reputation as a nobs' ghetto that has never entirely left it. Until well into the 20th century its squares and boulevards – BERKELEY SQUARE, GROSVENOR SQUARE, Curzon Street, South Audley Street and so on – housed a large proportion of the English aristocracy during the London season, and the name 'Mayfair' was both a shorthand identifier of a social class and its habits of behaviour, speech and dress ('Miss Grosvenor … wailed in a voice whose accent was noticeably less Mayfair than usual', Agatha Christie, *A Pocket Full of Rye* (1953)) and a conferrer of borrowed commercial cachet (as in 'Bendicks of Mayfair'; a long-standing brand of cigarette has taken the name too). After the First World War, however, as aristocratic incomes fell and servants priced themselves out of the market, many of the grand houses were demolished, and the area was given over more to commerce, with a sprinkling of luxury hotels.

At £400 Mayfair is the most valuable property on a Monopoly board.

Mayfair. A 'top-shelf' magazine for men, first published in the 1960s.

Mayfair mercenary. A young woman whose indeterminate social class is transcended by her beauty and her ambition to climb in society, often the mistress of a successful wealthy man. The term originated in *Harpers and Queen* magazine around 1980.

Maynooth Irish *Maigh Nuadhat* 'plain of Nuadu' (king of the legendary Tuatha Dé Danaan and ancestor of the people of Leinster).

A town in County Kildare, 25 km (16 miles) west of Dublin. It has became synonymous with the Catholic seminary here, properly St Patrick's College, set up in 1795 by the **Maynooth Grant** given by Parliament in 1795. This aroused considerable opposition, and when the Conservative prime minister Sir Robert Peel tried to increase the grant in 1845 it led to a split in his party and the resignation from the government of W.E. Gladstone. The college has been part of the National University of Ireland since 1910, and a secular college was founded in 1966. There are some notable Gothic Revival buildings by Pugin, dating from the mid-19th century, and by the college gates are the ruins of the medieval Fitzgerald castle. The Irish bishops have for many years met at Maynooth to issue their spiritual and moral edicts.

About one mile from Maynooth is Carton House, a handsome Palladian mansion designed by Richard Castle in the 1730s for the 19th Earl of Kildare. In 1747 James, 20th Earl of Kildare (from 1766 1st Duke of Leinster), married Lady Emily Lennox, who was responsible for the landscaping of the estate. It remained in the possession of the Fitzgerald family until the 1920s, when the future 7th Duke, then the third in line of succession to the title, mortgaged his birthright to pay off a gambling debt.

Maynooth pardon. During the Kildare Rebellion (*see under* KILDARE), 'Silken' Thomas Fitzgerald, Earl of Kildare, left his castle at Maynooth in the hands of the constable, Christopher Paris, who betrayed it to Sir William Skeffington, the lord lieutenant, in return for silver. However, when Skeffington took possession on 23 March 1535 he had Paris and 25 others executed, so a 'Maynooth pardon' has come to denote any such perfidy. Fitzgerald himself suffered a similar fate, being hanged, drawn and quartered at Tyburn in 1537 after having received a guarantee of safe conduct.

Mayo Irish *Maigh Eo* 'plain of the yews'.

A hamlet that gives its name to County Mayo. It is 5 km (3 miles) south of Balla. It was here in the 7th century that

St Colman of Lindisfarne founded a monastery after his falling-out with the Irish monks on INISHBOFIN – hence the place's original Irish name Maigheó na Sacsan ('Mayo of the Saxons'). In the following century the great English educator Alcuin wrote from the court of Charlemagne to the monks, encouraging them with some fairly typical English sentiments vis-à-vis the Irish:

> Let your light shine among that barbarous nation like a
> star in the western skies.

The monastery continued in existence (latterly as a house of Canons Regular of St Augustine) until the Dissolution. There is very little left to be seen.

> Mayo. Is this where mayo comes from? Like, tuna mayo?
>
> Unnamed American tourist: quoted in Pete McCarthy,
> *McCarthy's Bar* (2000)

Mayo, County. A county in the west of Ireland, bounded on the northeast by Sligo, on the east by Roscommon, and on the south by Galway, while its rugged western and northern shores face the Atlantic. It is a wild area of lakes (including LOUGH CONN and LOUGH MASK) and mountains (including the NEPHIN Beg Range, MWEELREA and the PARTRY Mountains), but there is a low-lying area in the centre and east. Off the heavily indented west coast there are many islands, including ACHILL ISLAND and CLARE ISLAND. The county town is CASTLEBAR, and other towns include BALLINA and WESTPORT. Before tourism and European subsidies arrived, the phrase 'Mayo, God help us' was often to be heard.

> … in Mayo the tumbledown walls went leap-frog
>   Over the moors,
> The sugar and salt in the pubs were damp in the casters
>   And the water was brown as beer …
>
> Louis MacNeice: 'County Sligo'

'County of Mayo, The'. A poem by George Fox, about whom little is known apart from the fact that he emigrated to America in 1848. The poem laments his leaving:

> On the deck of Patrick Lynch's boat I sat in woeful plight,
> Through my sighing all the weary day and weeping all
>   the night.
> Were it not that full of sorrow from my people forth I go,
> By the blessed sun, 'tis royally I'd sing thy praise, Mayo.

'Tailor That Came From Mayo, The'. A terrible piece of old Oirishry by Denis A. McCarthy (1871–1931), including such lines as:

> For 'twas he that could talk, in those days, with the best;
> And you'd laugh at his jokes till you'd fear for your vest.
> And you'd never grow tired of the wonderful flow
> Of the language that came from the man from Mayo.

Maypole Presumably from some local tradition relating to a maypole.

A village in Kent, about 2.5 km (1.5 miles) south of Herne Bay.

May's Corner Irish *Coirneal Mhé*, meaning the same; the identity of May is unknown.

A crossroads with a post office in County Down, 10 km (6 miles) southeast of Banbridge.

Maze, the Irish *An Má* 'the plain'.

A former prison in County Armagh, near Lisburn. It was originally an RAF base called **Long Kesh** (Irish *ceis* or *cís* 'wicker causeway'), a name still used by Republicans (often abbreviated to **the Kesh**). It was turned into a prison camp with the introduction on 9 August 1971 of internment without trial in Northern Ireland, and many suspected of political violence were held in Nissen huts here, 'behind the wire'.

> Armoured cars and tanks and guns
> Came to take away our sons
> But every man will stand behind
> The men behind the wire.
>
> Paddy McGuigan: chorus from the song
> 'The Men Behind the Wire'

The huts were subsequently replaced by new accommodation, the famous **H-Blocks** (named from their H-shaped layout), surrounded by zones known as inertias and steriles.

Although internment without trial was abandoned, the Maze still held paramilitary prisoners (of both persuasions) who maintained that their actions had been politically motivated. In the late 1970s Republican inmates, demanding they be recognized as political prisoners, began a 'blanket protest' in which they refused to wear prison uniform and would only wear blankets.

> So I'll wear no convict's uniform
> Nor meekly serve my time
> That Britain might brand Ireland's fight
> Eight hundred years of crime.
>
> Anon.: chorus from 'The H-Block Song'

Some prisoners went on to mount a 'dirty protest', smearing their cell walls with excrement. In 1981 a number of Republican prisoners embarked on a hunger strike: Bobby Sands (who during his protest was elected as an MP) was the first of ten to die. Although the British government refused to grant political status to the prisoners, the hunger strikes led to a surge in support in the Nationalist community for the IRA and its political wing, Sinn Féin. In 1983 the Maze witnessed the biggest breakout in UK prison history, when 38 IRA inmates hijacked a lorry and smashed their way out; only 19 were recaptured. Subsequently conditions were relaxed, and prisoners were housed according to their paramilitary affiliation, different groups controlling different H-Blocks. After the Good Friday

Agreement of 1998 those paramilitary prisoners whose groups had agreed to a ceasefire were gradually released, and the Maze was closed down in 2000. In 2003 it was proposed to turn the site into a sports stadium, although there has been controversy about this and other proposals, such as that the site be made into a museum of the Troubles. Meanwhile, nature is gradually taking the place back.

Mddx. The standard written abbreviation of MIDDLESEX.

Meare '(place at the) pool or lake', OE *mere* 'pool, lake'.

A village in the Somerset Levels, about 6 km (4 miles) northwest of Glastonbury. As its name reveals, it was once a lake village, raised on piles above the Somerset swamps.

Mearns, the Gaelic *mhaoirne* 'area controlled by a steward'.

A traditional low-lying agricultural area south of Aberdeen, formerly comprising much of the old county of KINCAR-DINESHIRE, for which it was sometimes used as a synonym. The vale of the **Howe of the Mearns** (Scots *howe* 'hollow'), by LAURENCEKIRK, together with the village of Arbuthnott (Kinraddie in the books) provide the setting for Lewis Grassic Gibbon's trilogy *A Scots Quair* (1932–4), comprising *Sunset Song*, *Cloud Howe* and *Grey Granite*:

> ... you'd waken with the peewits crying across the hills, deep and deep, crying in the heart of you and the smell of the earth in your face, almost you'd cry for that, the beauty of it and the sweetness of the Scottish land and skies.
>
> Lewis Grassic Gibbon: *Sunset Song* (1932)

James Leslie Mitchell (Gibbon's real name) had lived for some years in Arbuthnott and is buried there.

Meath Irish *Midhe* or *An Mhí* 'the middle', i.e. between Ulster and Leinster.

A county in eastern Ireland, in the province of LEINSTER, and one of the original FIVE FIFTHS, the five kingdoms into which Ireland was divided in the early Christian era. Today it is bounded to the north by Louth, Monaghan and Cavan, to the west by Westmeath, to the south by Kildare and to the east by County Dublin and the Irish Sea. The county town is NAVAN, and other towns include ATHBOY, KELLS[1] and TRIM; the main river is the BOYNE. It is sometimes called **Royal Meath**, because it is the location of TARA, seat of the ancient high kings. Subsequently it became part of the Anglo-Norman PALE. Meath is a generally low-lying and fertile area, often celebrated as such by Ireland's poets:

> The songs and minstrelsy of the plain of Meath,
> Plain of the noblest companies!
>
> Gerald Nugent: 'A Farewell to Fál' (*c.*1573), translated by Padraic Pearse

> ... let you go off till you'd find a radiant lady with droves of bullocks on the plains of Meath
>
> J.M. Synge: *The Playboy of the Western World* (1907)

> the hushed fields
> Of our most lovely Meath ...
>
> F.R. Higgins (1896–1941): 'Father and Son'

Meath Gaeltacht. Two areas of County Meath settled in the 1930s with Gaelic speakers from the west and southwest of Ireland.

Meathas Truim. The Irish name for EDGEWORTHSTOWN.

Meavy From the nearby River *Meavy*, probably an OCelt river name meaning 'lively stream'.

A village in Devon, on the western edge of Dartmoor, about 10 km (6 miles) southeast of Tavistock. The **Meavy Oak**, standing in front of the lych-gate of the parish church here, is some 7.6 m (25 ft) in circumference, and in the hollow nine people are once reputed to have dined; according to tradition it dates back to Saxon times.

Medina[1] 'the middle one' (referring to the way in which it divides the island into roughly two halves), OE *medume* 'middle'.

A river in the Isle of Wight, which rises in the high southern part of the island and flows 19 km (12 miles) northwards, beyond NEWPORT[2] in a wide estuary, into the SOLENT at COWES (whose two parts flank its mouth).

There is also a river called Medina in Texas, USA.

Medina[2] From MEDINA[1].

An admininstrative district of the Isle of Wight. Encompassing the northeastern part of the island, it includes COWES, NEWPORT[2] (the administrative centre) and RYDE.

Mediobogdum. *See* HARD KNOTT PASS.

Medmenham 'middle or middle-sized homestead or enclosure', OE *meduman* dative form of *medume* 'middle' + HAM.

A village in Buckinghamshire, on the River Thames, about 5 km (3 miles) southwest of Marlow. **Medmenham Abbey**, a 13th-century foundation now in ruins, was the meeting place of the Hellfire Club (also known as the Franciscans), a notorious 18th-century coterie founded (in imitation of the original HELLFIRE CLUB in Dublin) about 1755 by Sir Francis Dashwood, afterwards Baron Le Despencer (1708–81). Its 13 members conducted their lurid satanic rituals in the former Cistercian abbey, which Dashwood owned. Among these so-called **Monks of Medmenham** were the radical politician John Wilkes, the satirist Paul Whitehead (who was secretary and steward), the politician George Bubb Dodington, Charles Churchill and the Earl of Sandwich. The motto of the club was *Fay ce que voudras* ('Do as you would wish' – originally the motto of the Abbey of Thélème in Rabelais's *Gargantua* (1534)).

Medway[1] Based on an ancient pre-English river name *Wey* of unknown origin and meaning, probably combined with OCelt or OE *medu* 'mead' (referring to the colour or sweetness of the water).

A river in Kent and Sussex, which rises in the WEALD to the southwest of TUNBRIDGE WELLS and flows 121 km (75 miles) northwards and then eastwards through TONBRIDGE, MAIDSTONE and ROCHESTER to join the estuary of the River THAMES[1] at SHEERNESS. It has been an important transport route from earliest times, and remains so to this day.

The Roman general Vespasian (before becoming emperor) made a name for himself in the crossing of the Medway near Rochester at the head of the Legio II Augusta during the invasion of Britain in AD 43; it was here that the British under Togodumnus and Caractacus had made a stand.

The Dutch shamed the English in June 1667 when they sailed up the Medway and destroyed much of the Royal Navy.

Traditionally, the Medway separates 'Kentishmen', born to the west of the river, from 'Men of Kent', born to the east.

Medway towns. A collective term for CHATHAM, GILLINGHAM[1] and ROCHESTER, three towns close to the mouth of the River Medway. The first and third of them have a naval history going back to Henry VIII's time.

Medway[2] From the River MEDWAY[1].

A unitary authority in Kent covering the area around the mouth of the River MEDWAY[1] and including CHATHAM, GILLINGHAM[1], Rainham, ROCHESTER and the ISLE OF GRAIN. It was created in 1998. Its administrative centre is STROOD.

Meeting of the Waters. *See under* AVOCA.

Megget Water *Megget* uncertain, but OCelt *mig* 'swamp' has been proposed.

A small upland river in Scottish BORDERS (formerly in Selkirkshire). It rises on the south slopes of BROAD LAW and flows for approximately 10 km (6 miles) generally eastwards via the **Megget Reservoir** before disemboguing into ST MARY'S LOCH. The **Megget Stone** marks the watershed between the valleys of the Megget and the TALLA WATER, formerly the border between Selkirkshire and Peeblesshire, and at the west end of the reservoir is the tiny settlement of **Meggethead**.

Meikle Says Law. *See under* the LAMMERMUIRS.

Meiklour Probably 'big yew tree'; the place was called *Ure* (Gaelic *iubhar* 'yew tree') in the 13th century, and OE *mycel*, Scots *meikle* 'large' was added later – perhaps the tree had grown ...

A village in Perth and Kinross (formerly in Perthshire, and then in Tayside region), some 16 km (10 miles) north of Perth. Nearby, flanking the A93 Perth–Blairgowrie road, is the **Meiklour Beech Hedge**, which extends for 530 m

(580 yards), and is maintained at a height of some 27 m (90 ft), making it the tallest hedge in the world. Clipping is undertaken every ten years by a team of four men, who take six weeks over the job. The hedge was planted in 1745 by Jean Mercer and her husband Robert Murray Nairne, who was killed at Culloden the following year.

Melbourn Perhaps 'stream where orach grows', OE *melde* 'orach, wild spinach' + *burna* 'stream'; there is no evidence that orach was unusually abundant here, and the OE plant name seems to have been fairly elastic in application.

A village in Cambridgeshire, about 5 km (3 miles) northeast of Royston.

Melbourne Probably 'mill stream', OE *myln* 'mill' + *burna* 'stream'.

A small town in Derbyshire, about 11 km (7 miles) south of Derby. The travel agent Thomas Cook (1808–92) was born here; he is commemorated in a General Baptist Mission Hall with the curious inscription 'Memorial House of Call for Mr Cook and Invited Friends, 1891'.

Nearby Melbourne Hall, an 18th-century mansion, was home to two English prime ministers: Lord Melbourne (1779–1848), from whom Melbourne, the capital of the Australian state of Victoria, got its name; and Lord Palmerston (1784–1865).

Melbourne cat. A carved animal of feline aspect – possibly a lion – in the Norman church of St Michael with St Mary in Melbourne.

Melbury Abbas *Melbury* probably 'multi-coloured fortified place', OE *mæle* 'multi-coloured' + OE *byrig* dative form of *burh* (*see* BURY); *Abbas* originally *Abbatisse* 'abbess', Latin *abbatissa*, denoting early possession by Shaftesbury Abbey.

A village in Dorset, about 3 km (2 miles) south of Shaftesbury. Thomas Hardy may have used the name for Grace Melbury, a leading character in *The Woodlanders* (1887).

Melbury Bubb *Bubb* denoting manorial ownership in the Middle Ages by the Bubbe family.

A village in Dorset, about 8 km (5 miles) northwest of Cerne Abbas.

> Rime Intrinseca, Fontmell Magna, Sturminster Newton
>   and Melbury Bubb,
> Whist upon whist upon whist upon whist drive, in
>   Institute, Legion and Social Club.
>
>   John Betjeman: 'Dorset', from *Continual Dew* (1937)

Melbury Osmond *Osmond* denoting manorial ownership in the Middle Ages by a man called Osmund.

A village in Dorset, about 1.5 km (1 mile) northwest of Melbury Bubb.

Melbury Sampford *Sampford* denoting manorial ownership in the Middle Ages by the Saunford family.

A village in Dorset, about 1.5 km (1 mile) west of Melbury Bubb.

Melchester. A fictional English town. It appeared as a version of SALISBURY in the novels of Thomas Hardy (*see under* WESSEX), and re-emerged in a strikingly new guise in the mid-20th century as the setting for the cartoon strip 'Roy of the Rovers' (1954–83) in the comic *Tiger*, whose eponymous hero is centre forward for **Melchester Rovers**.

Melcombe Bingham *Melcombe* 'milk valley' (alluding to rich, fertile grazing land in the valley of the River Wey), OE *meoluc* 'milk' + *cumb* (*see* -COMBE, COOMBE); *Bingham* denoting manorial ownership in the Middle Ages by the Bingham family.
A village in Dorset, about 13 km (8 miles) southwest of Blandford Forum. Just to the southeast is a hamlet called **Bingham's Melcombe**.

Melksham Perhaps 'homestead or enclosure where milk is produced', OE *meoluc* 'milk' + HAM.
A town (pronounced 'melkshəm' or, locally, 'melshəm') in Wiltshire, on the River AVON[2], about 11 km (7 miles) west of Devizes. It is a low-key sort of place – it once aspired to be a spa town but little came of it.

Mellick. Kate O'Brien's fictionalized version of the city of LIMERICK in her novel *Without My Cloak* (1931).

Mellifont Abbey *Mellifont* 'source of honey', Latin *fons* 'source, fount' + *mellis* 'of honey'.
A ruined Cistercian abbey in County Louth, 9 km (5.5 miles) west-northwest of Drogheda. Its Irish name is **An Mhainsitir Mhór** ('the big monastery'). It was founded by St Malachy of Armagh in 1142 and was the first Cistercian house in Ireland. The abbey was suppressed in 1539 during the Reformation and was turned into a fortified residence by the Moore family.
Conspiracy of Mellifont. A period of schism in the early 13th century between the Irish Cistercians affiliated to Mellifont and the General Chapter of the order, the former apparently ignoring important aspects of observance.
Treaty of Mellifont (1603). A treaty that ended the Nine Years War between Hugh O'Neill and the English. O'Neill had been staying with his friend Sir Garret Moore at Mellifont, and here was starved into surrender. By the treaty, however, O'Neill was pardoned for his rebellion and retained his lands.

Mellon Charles *Mellon* 'little hill', Gaelic *meallan*, diminutive of *meall* 'hill'. The same first element is found in the nearby village of Mellon Udrigle: it is assumed that *Charles* and *Udrigle* are the names of (untraced) historical owners.
A little village on the northwest side of Loch Ewe, in Highland (formerly in Ross and Cromarty).

Mells 'mill(s)', OE *myln*.
A village in Somerset, about 5 km (3 miles) west of Frome. The manor was for many centuries owned by the Horner family, who obtained much of their wealth from rich local mineral workings (often said, falsely, to be the original of the 'plum' pulled out of the Christmas pie by Jack Horner in the nursery rhyme). Their artistic patronage in the late 19th and early 20th centuries gave the village and its church works by Edward Burne-Jones, Edwin Lutyens, Eric Gill and Alfred Munnings.

Mellstock. A fictitious village that appears in Thomas Hardy's novel *Under the Greenwood Tree* (1872). Aspects of the novel's gently humorous plot reflect Hardy's boyhood experiences as a singer in the church choir of the real-life Dorset village of STINSFORD, on which Mellstock is based. The name 'Mellstock' has an appropriately rustic flavour, '-stock' deriving from OE *stoc* 'outlying farmstead or hamlet'. The village also features in Hardy's poems 'A Church Romance' (1835) and 'Afternoon Service in Mellstock' (1850).

Melplash Probably 'multi-coloured pool', OE *mæle* 'multi-coloured' + *plæsc* 'pool'.
A village in Dorset, about 5 km (3 miles) north of Bridport.

Melrose 'bare moor', OCelt *mailo-* 'bare' + *ros* 'moor'; *Mailros* 8th century.
A small town on the River Tweed, 5 km (3 miles) southeast of Galashiels, in Scottish Borders (formerly in Roxburghshire). The EILDON HILLS lie just to the south. The town grew up from a small village called Fordel, and derived its present name from **Melrose Abbey**. The original monastery (7th century) was at **Old Melrose** to the east, on a bare promontory in the River Tweed. St Cuthbert, who had been a shepherd until he had a vision in 651, entered the monastery that same year. The great Cistercian abbey at Melrose itself was founded by David I in 1136, and, like the other Border abbeys, suffered considerably at the hands of the English, particularly in 1544. Daniel Defoe gloried in its ruin:

> … the pomp and glory of Popery is sunk now into the primitive simplicity of the true Christian profession … So I leave Mailross with a singular satisfaction, at seeing what it now is, much more than that of remembering what it once was.
>
> Daniel Defoe: *A Tour Through the Whole Island of Great Britain* (1724–6)

A century later attitudes had changed. Restoration work on the abbey was carried out in 1822 under the supervision of Sir Walter Scott, who had used the abbey as the model for the monastery of Kennaquhair in his novel *The Monastery* (1820).

Alexander II (d.1249) was buried in the abbey, as by tradition was the heart of Robert the Bruce; the rest of his body is in DUNFERMLINE Abbey. Bruce died in 1329, before he could go on crusade, so his friend James Douglas took his heart in a casket with him on his way to the Holy Land.

En route, Douglas fought in Spain against the Moors, and finding himself in a hopeless situation threw the casket into the midst of the enemy and charged after it. Douglas was killed but the casket found its way back to Scotland. In 1920 an embalmed heart was found in a casket in the abbey and reburied. Also reputedly buried in the abbey is Michael Scot (*c*.1175–1232), the scholar and wizard; there is a vivid (fictional) account of his burial, and of the opening of his grave, in Sir Walter Scott's *Lay of the Last Minstrel* (1805), Canto II, xiii–xxii.

The game of rugby football is enthusiastically followed in Melrose, as in other Border towns, and it was here, at the Greenyards ground, that the seven-a-side version of the game was first played, in 1883.

There are towns called Melrose in the USA (Massachusetts, New Mexico), and there is a Melrose Boulevard in West Hollywood.

Meltham 'village where smelting is carried out', OE *melt* 'melt, smelt' + HAM.

A town in West Yorkshire, 8 km (5 miles) southwest of Huddersfield.

Melton Constable *Melton* perhaps 'farmstead with a crucifix', OE *mæl* 'crucifix' + -TON; *Constable* denoting ownership by the constable of the Bishop of Norwich in the early Middle Ages.

A village in Norfolk, about 32 km (20 miles) northwest of Norwich.

Melton Mowbray *Melton* 'middle farmstead', OE *middel* 'middle' (replaced by OScand *methel*) + -TON; *Mowbray* denoting manorial ownership in the Middle Ages by the de Moubray family.

A market town in Leicestershire, in the borough of Melton, on the River Eye, about 24 km (15 miles) northeast of Leicester. Situated in the open rolling countryside of east Leicestershire, it is a noted foxhunting centre, with three celebrated hunts – the Belvoir, Cottesmore and Quorn – in the vicinity. (The expression 'paint the town red' is alleged to have originated in Melton in 1837, when hunt celebrations got out of hand to the extent of literally coating The White Swan inn and other buildings with red paint.)

> The hunting fraternity are notoriously lascivious and, in the season, the night air of Melton Mowbray is loud with the sighs of adulterers.
>
>   Paul Johnson: *New Statesman* (12 July 1963)

Melton Mowbray has two notable gastronomic connections: first, with the production of fine pork pies, for which it is justly famous; and second, with STILTON cheese, the only English cheese whose name has legal protection – it must be made from milk produced in the area of Leicestershire and Nottinghamshire centred on

Melton Mowbray (with a special extra dispensation for part of Derbyshire).

Meltonian. A term used in former times to refer to someone who hunted foxes around Melton Mowbray, or more generally to any inveterate foxhunter. **Meltonian cream** is the trade name of a type of boot polish, traded on the image of gleaming hunting boots.

Melton jacket. A type of jacket worn in former times by hunters of the fox.

Melton pad. A hernia truss specially designed to be worn on horseback (as when chasing foxes).

Menabilly Perhaps 'stone of colts', Cornish *men* 'stone' + *ebelyow* plural form of *ebel* 'colt'.

A village in Cornwall, towards the eastern end of St Austell Bay. The house in which the writer Daphne du Maurier (1907–89) lived was the model for Manderley, the setting for her novel *Rebecca* (1938).

Menai Bridge After Thomas Telford's 1826 suspension bridge across the MENAI STRAIT.

A small town on the southeast coast of Anglesey (formerly in Gwynedd), just across the Menai Strait from Bangor. In Welsh it is **Porthaethwy** ('ferry of Daethwy', the latter being a tribe on Anglesey).

Menai Strait Etymology obscure, but may denote a powerful current.

The narrow strait between the mainland of northwest Wales and the Isle of ANGLESEY. Its 22-km (14-mile) length links CONWY BAY to CAERNARFON Bay, and at the southwest end is ABERMENAI POINT. At its narrowest the strait is no more than 200 m (656 ft) across, and here it is majestically spanned by Thomas Telford's 1826 **Menai Bridge**, the world's first large-scale iron-built suspension bridge (to keep it from rusting, Lewis Carroll's White Knight suggests boiling it in wine). A second (railway) bridge across the strait – the Britannia Bridge – was built by Robert Stephenson in 1850. The original tubular design was badly damaged by fire in 1970, and was rebuilt with a road carriageway above the railway line. Prior to the building of the bridges, there were various unreliable ferries, and sometimes attempts were made to cross on foot at low tide, linking sandbar to sandbar – a hazardous undertaking, as, if any delay is experienced, the tidal race can reach eight knots. Tides, currents and shifting sandbars make the Strait famously treacherous to shipping, particularly in the section called the Swellies. In the opinion of Nelson,

> Whoever could navigate a sail ship here could sail any sea in the world.

Safe on dry land, the views from Anglesey across the Strait to the mountains of Snowdonia are stunning.

> On Menai shore the hush of heaven lay …
>
>   Anon.: 'Night and Morning' (16th–17th century), translated from the Welsh by R.S. Thomas

Mendip Hills *Mend-* probably 'mountain, hill', OCelt *monith;* *-ip* perhaps 'upland, plateau', OE *yppe.*

A range of hills in northern Somerset, also known as the **Mendips**, extending 40–48 km (25–30 miles) north and west from Wells. The limestone of which they are made is honeycombed with caves (the best known is WOOKEY Hole) and sliced through by deep gorges (notably CHEDDAR Gorge). They are the source of the rivers AXE² and YEO². Their highest point, at 325 m (1065 ft), is Black Down. **Mendip Forest** is at the northern end of Cheddar Gorge.

Lead and calamine have been mined in the Mendips, and the hills are also renowned for their edible snails, a much prized delicacy (they are known locally as wallfish).

mendipite. A term applied in the 19th century to oxychloride of lead, found in white masses in the Mendips.

Menevia. *See under* ST DAVID'S.

Menstrie 'plain settlement', OCelt *maes-dref* (*see* TRE-).

A small town in Clackmannanshire, 4 km (2.5 miles) west of Alva. It is in the HILLFOOTS (the area at the foot of the Ochil Hills). The attractive **Menstrie Castle** (16th-century) was the birthplace of the statesman and poet William Alexander (c.1576–1640), 1st Earl of Stirling, founder of Nova Scotia; and of the soldier Ralph Abercromby (1734–1801), who led the 1801 campaign against Napoleon's forces in Egypt and was mortally wounded at the Battle of Alexandria.

> O Alva hills is bonny,
> Tillicoultry hills is fair,
> But to think on the Braes o' Menstrie
> It maks my heart fu' sair.
>
> Anon.: lyric (*fu' sair* 'full of pain', i.e. longing)

Menteith. *See* LAKE OF MENTEITH.

Mentmore 'Menta's moor', OE male personal name *Menta* + *mor* 'moor'.

A village in Buckinghamshire, in the CHILTERN HILLS, about 5 km (3 miles) south of Leighton Buzzard. **Mentmore Towers**, a ponderous Victorian mansion designed by Joseph Paxton (of Crystal Palace fame), was once the home of Baron Meyer de Rothschild. It was the subject of a high-profile sale in 1977, when it was acquired on behalf of the Maharishi Mahesh Yogi's World Government of the Age of Enlightenment movement.

Menwith Hill *Menwith* 'common woodland', OE *(ge)mœne* 'commom' + OScand *vithr* 'wood'.

An early-warning and intelligence-gathering station in North Yorkshire, some 11 km (7 miles) west of Harrogate, replete with a range of dishes, masts and golf balls of various sizes. It is officially an RAF station, but is operated by US and GCHQ personnel. Outside the facility, in a lay-by on the A59, is a women's peace camp.

Meole Brace *Meole* from *Meole Brook*, the old name for the nearby Rea Brook, which may come from OE *melu, meolu* 'meal', perhaps applied metaphorically to a stream with cloudy water; *Brace* denoting manorial ownership in the Middle Ages by the de Braci family.

A village (pronounced 'meel') in Shropshire, now a south-western suburb of SHREWSBURY. The novelist Mary Webb lived here before her marriage in 1912.

Meon An OCelt river name of uncertain origin and meaning, perhaps 'swift one'.

A river in Hampshire, which rises in the SOUTH DOWNS just to the south of the picturesque village of **East Meon** (whose Norman church has a magnificent 12th-century black marble Tournai font) and flows 32 km (20 miles) westwards through **West Meon** (where Thomas Lord, originator of LORD'S cricket ground, is buried) and then southwards down the attractive **Meon Valley** into the SOLENT just to the north of LEE-ON-THE-SOLENT.

Meon Hill *Meon* is probably from the name of a nearby watercourse, related to MEON in Hampshire, but of unclear meaning.

A hill in south Warwickshire, 194 m (636 ft) in height, about 9 km (5.5 miles) south of Stratford-upon-Avon. The most northerly point of the COTSWOLDS, Meon Hill is topped by an Iron Age hillfort that overlooks the Vale of Evesham (*see under* EVESHAM).

Local tradition has it that Meon Hill was created by the Devil, who threw a huge rock at Evesham Abbey from the top of nearby Ilmington Downs (*see under* ILMINGTON). The prayers of the abbey's monks, however, diverted the missile, which landed short of its target, thereby creating Meon Hill itself. Rather more troubling to modern sensibilities was the discovery on 14 February 1945, on the hill's lower slopes, of the body of Charles Walton, a farm labourer from the nearby village of Lower Quinton, who had been pinned to the ground with his own pitchfork. Slashes on Walton's head and chest led to rumours of ritual sacrifice, which were fuelled by the discovery that a similar murder had taken place at the nearby village of Long Compton in 1875. His killer was never found.

Meopham 'Meapa's homestead or village', OE male personal name *Meapa* + HAM.

A village (pronounced 'meppəm') in Kent, about 8 km (5 miles) south of Gravesend. The neighbouring settlement of **Meopham Station**, which has grown up around the railway station to the north, is now virtually identical in size.

The naturalist and plant-collector John Tradescant (1608–62) was born in Meopham.

Mercia A Latinized form of OE *Merce, Mierce* 'people of the march, borderers', from *mearc* (*see* the MARCHES).

A kingdom of Anglo-Saxon England, occupying an area broadly corresponding to the modern MIDLANDS. Its boundaries varied over the centuries, but its general orientation was between DEIRA to the north, WESSEX to the south, EAST ANGLIA to the east and the Welsh border to the west (whence its name, which in the early Middle Ages was often re-anglicized to 'the March (of Wales)').

Under the kingship of Penda (*c.*634–55) it became a major power in England, and its influence was extended still further under Offa (757–96; *see* OFFA'S DYKE), who controlled all of England south of the River Humber. In Offa's time Mercia completed its absorption of the old Anglo-Saxon kingdom of the Hwicce, which became **West Mercia**. After Offa Mercia's power declined, and in the 9th century it disappeared into a united England under the control of Wessex.

In modern times the name 'Mercia' has been revived and applied to various bodies and organizations within its area: the policing of the western Midlands, for instance, is in the hands of the **West Mercia Police**, based in Worcester. *See also* TAMWORTH and LICHFIELD.

Mercia Movement. A marginal left-wing group, founded in August 1993, that campaigns for Mercian devolution from the British state and a return to the laws and social structures of Anglo-Saxon England before the Norman Conquest.

Mercian. The dialect of Old English spoken in Mercia. It belonged to the Anglian (as opposed to the Saxon) division of the language. It is the dialect from which modern standard English is mainly descended.

Mercian Hymns. A collection of prose poems (1971) by Geoffrey Hill, celebrating the historical figure of Offa, 'a presiding genius of the West Midlands'.

Meriden 'pleasant valley' or 'valley where merry-making takes place', OE *myrge* 'merry' + *denu* 'valley'. The notion that the name is linked with *meridian*, although *ben trovato* in view of the village's position, is not *vero*.

A village in the West Midlands (before 1974 in Warwickshire), approximately halfway between Birmingham and Coventry. About 150 km (93 miles) from the Wash, the Irish Sea and the Bristol Channel, Meriden is one of a dozen or so places (*see*, for example, NASEBY) claiming to be the exact centre of England, the precise spot being supposedly marked by an old cross on the little village green (satellite measurement has established the actual centre as being a farm near FENNY DRAYTON in Leicestershire).

There is a Meriden in the USA (Connecticut).

Merioneth 'seat of Meirion', Welsh personal name *Meirion*, a grandson of Cunedda (*see* GWYNEDD), + *ydd*, a territorial affix.

A traditional area and former county in northwest Wales. In Welsh it is **Meirionnydd**, and the area was part of the

medieval kingdom of Gwynedd, until Edward I made it a shire in 1284. The county, also known as **Merionethshire** (Welsh **Sir Feirionnydd**), was bordered on the north by Caernarvonshire and Denbighshire, to the southeast by Montgomeryshire and to the south by Cardiganshire. The county town was DOLGELLAU, and Merioneth's many mountains include the RHINOGS, ARENNIG FAWR and CADER IDRIS. In the reorganization of 1974 it was absorbed into the new county of Gwynedd, and in the 1996 reorganization it remained part of the smaller Gwynedd unitary authority.

Merioneth has inspired many poets through the ages:

I love the sea-coast of Meirionnydd,
   where a white arm was my pillow.

> Hywel ab Owain Gwynedd: 'Exultation' (12th century),
> translated from the Welsh by Gwyn Williams

Low ye hills in ocean lie,
That hide fair Meiron from my eye;
One distant view, Oh! let me take,
Ere yet my longing heart shall break.

> Richard Llwyd: 'My Heart is in Merioneth' (?1837), based on
> a Welsh folk verse from the 16th–17th century

Living paradise of flowers, land of honey, land of violets
   and blossoms, land rich in crops, land of nut-bushes,
   and dear land of hills.

> John Machreth Rees: 'Merioneth' (*c.*1900), translated from
> the Welsh by Kenneth Hurlstone Jackson

In Merioneth, over the sad moor
   Drives the rain, the cold wind blows;
   Past the ruinous church door,
The poor procession without music goes.

Lonely she wandered out her hour, and died.
   Now the mournful curlew cries
   Over her, laid down beside
Death's lonely people: lightly down she lies.

In Merioneth, the wind lives and wails,
   On from hill to lonely hill:
   Down the loud, triumphant gales,
A spirit cries *Be strong!* and cries *Be still!*

> Lionel Johnson (1867–1902): 'Dead'

Irritatingly for this most Welsh of counties, Philip Mountbatten (né Schleswig-Holstein-Sonderburg-Glücksburg) was raised to the earldom of Merioneth on the eve of his wedding to Elizabeth Windsor in 1947. In November 2002 the Earl of Merioneth denied having called his former daughter-in-law, Diana Spencer, 'a harlot and a trollop'.

Merlin's Bridge 'bridge of Maudlen', named after the local chapel dedicated to St Mary Magdalene. Several Merlin names in the area have the same origin, and have changed through association with the Arthurian legends, the change being evident from the early 19th century.

A village in Pembrokeshire (formerly in Dyfed), now effectively a southern suburb of HAVERFORDWEST.

Merrick 'branched' or 'fingered', Gaelic *meurach*, from *meur* 'finger'; *Maerack Hill* 17th century.

The highest hill (843 m / 2766 ft) in southwest Scotland, formerly in Kirkcudbrightshire, now in Dumfries and Galloway. It stands 6 km (4 miles) north of GLEN TROOL in the Galloway Forest Park. The name, suggesting the spread-out fingers of a hand, reflects the fact that Merrick is the highest of a succession of westward-leading ridges descending from a long north–south ridge, culminating in the summit of Merrick itself; these 'fingers' include Shalloch on Minnoch, Tarfessock, Kirriereoch Hill, Kirriemore Hill and Benyellary. Collectively this massif is sometimes referred to as **the Awful Hand**, presumably in reference to its somewhat bleak and remote situation. When Daniel Defoe visited the area in the 1720s he was told the hill was 'two miles high'.

Merry Maidens. A Bronze Age stone circle just to the west of Penzance in Cornwall. Its 19 uprights are, according to legend, local maidens turned to stone for dancing on Sunday.

Merrymeet 'pleasant meeting-place', ModE; first recorded in 1699.

A village in Cornwall, about 3 km (2 miles) northeast of Liskeard.

Merry Men of May, the. *See under* MEY.

Merse, the 'flat alluvial land beside a river', Scots *mersk* 'marshland', from OE *mersc* 'marsh'.

The band of flat fertile land south of the LAMMERMUIRS and north of the TWEED in Scottish Borders. The area was formerly in Berwickshire, and the name was sometimes given to the whole county.

Mersea 'island of the pool', OE *meres* possessive form of *mere* 'pool' + *eg* (*see* -EY, -EA).

A low-lying island in Essex, on the northern side of the mouth of the BLACKWATER[1] estuary, about 11 km (7 miles) west of Clacton-on-Sea.

Mersey 'boundary river', OE *mæres*, genitive of *mære* 'boundary' + EA-.

A river of northwest England, with a length of 112 km (69 miles). It originates in the confluence of the GOYT and the TAME[2] at STOCKPORT, south of Manchester, then it is largely canalized as part of the Manchester Ship Canal (*see under* MANCHESTER), flowing through WARRINGTON (from where it is tidal) and entering the Mersey estuary at RUNCORN. Its tributaries include the IRWELL and the WEAVER. The Mersey estuary is some 25 km (16 miles) long, and at its widest is

over 4 km (2.5 miles) across. However, it narrows between WALLASEY and BIRKENHEAD on the southwestern shore (the WIRRAL peninsula), and LIVERPOOL on the northeastern shore (the name Mersey has virtually become synonymous with Liverpool). There are two road tunnels here, the first, the **Mersey Tunnel**, built in 1934 and the second, the Kingsway Tunnel, in 1971. Beyond Wallasey, the Mersey opens out into Liverpool Bay, part of the Irish Sea.

The Mersey has been a major artery of communication and trade since the 18th century. In the 1720s Defoe observed:

> The Mersey is a noble harbour, and is able to ride a thousand sail of ships at once …

But by the later 20th century, business had somewhat declined:

> The eerily unfrequented,
> Once so populous, Mersey.
>
> > Donald Davie: 'A Liverpool Epistle', from *The Battered Wife & Other Poems* (1982)

The area on either side of the Mersey estuary is known as MERSEYSIDE, which became a metropolitan county in 1974, formed out of parts of Lancashire and Cheshire. Before that, the Mersey formed the boundary between the two counties, and, in Anglo-Saxon times, between the kingdoms of Mercia and Northumbria.

'Ferry 'Cross the Mersey'. A hit song from 1964 by Gerry Marsden of Gerry and the Pacemakers (*see* Mersey Beat *below*). The name of the song was subsequently chosen as the title of a film about the combo by Tony Warren.

> So ferry 'cross the Mersey 'cause this land's the place I love …

Mersey Beat. A term (alternatively **Mersey Sound**) for the vibrant version of American rhythm and blues coming out of Liverpool in the early 1960s, as performed by such bands as Gerry and the Pacemakers, The Swinging Blue Jeans and The Beatles – and indeed **The Merseybeats**. Some have attributed Liverpool's pre-eminence at this time to sailors bringing home from the USA the records of the likes of Muddy Waters, Howlin' Wolf and Big Bill Broonzy. Merseyside continues to produce musical talent in the form of bands such as The Stans and The Coral. Punningly, *Merseybeat* is the title of a 2000s BBC television police series.

Mersey Funnel. A nickname for Liverpool's Roman Catholic Cathedral (*see under* LIVERPOOL).

Merseyside. The area either side of the Mersey estuary, and the name of a metropolitan borough formed in 1974 out of parts of Lancashire and Cheshire. This incorporates most of the WIRRAL peninsula on the southwest side, including the towns of WALLASEY and BIRKENHEAD, and on the northeast side incorporates LIVERPOOL, BOOTLE, CROSBY, FORMBY and SOUTHPORT. It is bounded on the east by Lancashire and Greater Manchester, Warrington and Halton, and on the south by Cheshire. In 1986 much of the county's powers were devolved to the metropolitan borough councils of the Wirral, Sefton, Liverpool, Knowsley and St Helens. Merseyside has aquired a certain reputation for theft and violence:

> *Mersey-cide:* killing Scousers.
>
> Tim Brooke-Taylor: spoof definition offered on BBC Radio 4's *I'm Sorry I Haven't a Clue* in 2002

In 2003, after Liverpool was nominated as European Capital of Culture 2008, there was considerable discussion in the region as to whether to replace the name 'Merseyside' (regarded by some as uncharismatic) with something with more international resonance, like 'Greater Liverpool'. Peter Mearns, marketing director of the North West Development Agency, opined that

> Liverpool is the sizzle that sells the sausage ...

... the 'sausage' being the rest of Merseyside.

Merseyside Poets. Another name for the Liverpool Poets (*see under* LIVERPOOL).

Merthyr Mawr Warren. *See under* PORTHCAWL.

Merthyr Tydfil 'grave of St Tudful', Welsh *merthyr* 'grave of a saint' + personal name of an obscure saint, possibly a daughter of King Brychan (5th century) who, according to legend, was martyred here; another of Brychan's daughters probably gave her name to LLANELLI.

An industrial town and the administrative seat of **Merthyr Tydfil** unitary authority (formerly in Glamorgan, then in Mid Glamorgan), at the head of the TAFF valley, some 35 km (22 miles) north of Cardiff. In Welsh it is **Merthyr Tudful**, and is often referred to simply as **Merthyr**. It is a heavily industrial town, leading the poet David Jones to write of 'the black pall of Merthyr'.

Merthyr developed as a centre of iron working and coal mining in the 18th century, and its key position in the Industrial Revolution was emphasized when in 1804 Richard Trevithick built the world's first steam railway – the **Merthyr Tramway** – from Merthyr to ABERCYNON. In 1831 Merthyr had a population of 60,000, making it by far the largest town in Wales, and by the mid-19th century the Dowlais Ironworks were the largest in the world, employing 10,000 people.

At the same time, Merthyr became a centre for Radicalism, and in 1831 rioters in Merthyr dipped their standard in the blood of a calf, making the first Red Flag. Keir Hardie, who had become the first socialist MP (for West Ham) in 1892, was elected MP for Merthyr in 1900.

The pits declined, and the last of Merthyr's ironworks closed in the 1930s. It was at the derelict Dowlais works that Edward VIII famously if somewhat feebly announced (as quoted by the *Western Mail*, 19 November 1936):

These works brought all these people here. Something should be done to get them at work again.

Three years later a Royal Commission delivered its report, helpfully suggesting that Merthyr be abandoned and the inhabitants moved to the coast, where new steelworks were being built near the ports that imported iron ore.

> The tramway climbs from Merthyr to Dowlais,
> Slime of a snail on a heap of slag;
> Here once was Wales, and now
> Derelict cinemas and rain on the barren tips ...
>
> Saunders Lewis: 'The Deluge 1939', translated from the Welsh by Gwyn Thomas

Since the Second World War, Merthyr's industry has revived, and it is once more a lively, thriving place.

Merthyr was the birthplace of the composer Joseph Parry (1841–1903), the son of an ironworker (his cottage can still be visited). Lady Charlotte Guest, the translator of the *Mabinogion* (1893), was the wife of the owner of the Dowlais Ironworks.

Merthyr was also home to the ex-miner and satirical poet Charles Horace Jones (1906–98), who for some five decades distributed his poems (such as his 1955 collection, *A Dose of Salts*) on the streets of the town. He was assaulted on more than one occasion by outraged citizens, and took to carrying a knuckleduster and to standing next to a lamppost so that he could only be attacked from one side at a time. He publicly criticized the local council for wasting public money on printing his 1966 collection, *The Challenger*.

Merthyr Tydfil district was created as part of the county of Mid Glamorgan in 1974, and in 1996 it became a unitary authority. It is bounded by Powys to the north, Caerphilly to the east and south, and Rhonnda Cynon Taff to the west. The foothills of the Brecon Beacons are in the north.

The wooded hill to the southwest of Merthyr is called **Mynydd Merthyr** ('Merthyr mountain'), and there is a village 8 km (5 miles) down the valley called **Merthyr Vale**.

Dial M for Merthyr. A compilation album (1995) featuring a number of soon-to-be-huge Welsh bands, including Manic Street Preachers, Catatonia, Stereophonics and Super Furry Animals. The title puns on Hitchcock's classic thriller film *Dial M for Murder* (1954).

Merton 'farmstead or estate by the pool' (probably referring to a pool in or by the River WANDLE, used as a watering place by travellers crossing the river on the old Roman road from London to Chichester), OE *mere* 'pool' + -TON.

A district and borough of southwest London. In the Middle Ages it was best known for **Merton Abbey**, a large Augustinian priory founded in 1114. Thomas Becket and Walter de Merton (founder of Merton College, Oxford) were educated there. After the Dissolution of the Monasteries the building was demolished, and the stones were used to build Henry VIII's Nonsuch Palace (*see under* NONSUCH PARK) in Cheam.

Lord Nelson lived in Merton with Sir William and Lady Hamilton from 1801 to 1805. The comedian Paul Merton (b.1957) was brought up here (not coincidentally: his original surname was Martin, and he changed it to Merton).

To the southwest of Merton proper is **Merton Park**, a residential area laid out over the last three decades of the 19th century by John Innes, a local businessman. It lays claim to being the forerunner of the Garden Suburb. The local Rutlish School was attended by John Major (prime minister 1990–7).

The borough of Merton (SW19, SW20) was created in 1965 from Merton, MITCHAM, MORDEN, RAYNES PARK and WIMBLEDON. It is bounded to the south by Sutton, to the west by Kingston upon Thames, to the north by Wandsworth and to the east by Croydon.

Statute of Merton. A statute enacted at Merton Abbey in 1236, stating causes of baronial opposition to the king. It is the earliest statute on record in England.

Mesopotamia[1] From *Mesopotamia*, literally (in Greek) 'between the rivers', originally the name of the territory between the Rivers Euphrates and Tigris in modern Iraq.

A strip of land in Oxford, between the River CHERWELL and a small offshoot of the river, to the east of the University Parks.

In the late 1950s *Mesopotamia* was the title given to a satirical Oxford undergraduate magazine, founded by Peter Usborne, to which Richard Ingrams, Willie Rushton and Paul Foot (and many others who were later connected with the satirical bi-monthly *Private Eye*) contributed.

See also PARSON'S PLEASURE.

Mesopotamia[2]. A nickname in the mid-19th century for the London district of BELGRAVIA, which at that time was known for its sizable population of wealthy Jews.

See also ASIA MINOR *and* NEW JERUSALEM.

Messing '(settlement of) Mæcca's people', OE male personal name *Mæcca* + *-ingas* (*see* -ING).

A village in Essex, about 16 km (10 miles) southeast of Braintree.

Metal Man, the. A giant sculpture at TRAMORE Bay.

Methil. *See under* BUCKHAVEN.

Methven Apparently 'mead stone', OCelt *medd* 'mead' + *faen* 'stone'; alternatively the first element may be OCelt *medd* 'middle'.

A village in Perth and Kinross (formerly in Perthshire, and then in Tayside region), 9 km (5.5 miles) west of Perth. Margaret Tudor, widow of James IV, died in Methven Castle in 1540.

Battle of Methven (19 June 1306). A battle in which Robert the Bruce was defeated shortly after his coronation at Scone (27 March) by the Earl of Pembroke. The English hanged all the lay prisoners they took.

Methwold 'middle forest', OScand *methal* 'middle' + OE *wold* 'forest'.

A village in Norfolk, about 16 km (10 miles) southeast of Downham Market. **Methwold Fens** are to the west.

Metroland A fusion of *Metro* from the Metropolitan Railway and *land*.

A name adopted in 1915 by the Metropolitan Railway for the area of Outer London, Middlesex and Hertfordshire through which it ran – countryside tamed and newly available to the workers of Central London and the inner suburbs, with neat new houses for their wives and fields and fresh air for their children (so ran the publicity). *Metro-Land* was the title of the Railway's guidebook, issued annually from 1915 to 1932, the last full year of its existence as an independent company:

> Metro-Land is a country with elastic borders which every visitor can draw for himself, as Stevenson drew his map of Treasure Island.
>
> *Metro-Land* (1932)

This region to the northwest of London was lovingly evoked in John Betjeman's poem 'The Metropolitan Railway' (1954):

> Then out and on, through rural Rayner's Lane
> To autumn-scented Middlesex again.

and further explored in his BBC television programme *Metro-land* (1973).

Lady Metroland, née Margot Beste-Chetwynde, is the wife of Lord Metroland, né Humphrey Maltravers, Minister of Transportation in Evelyn Waugh's *Decline and Fall* (1928), while Julian Barnes drew on memories of his suburban childhood in his first novel, *Metroland* (1980; filmed under the same name in 1997).

Mevagissey 'Meva and Issey', from *Meva* and *Issey*, the names of the patron saints of the local church, joined by Cornish *hag* 'and'. Issey was one of the 24 sons and daughters of King Brychan of BRYCHEINIOG; nothing is known of Meva other than that he was Welsh.

A coastal village and port in Cornwall, about 8 km (5 miles) south of St Austell. Its picturesque fishing harbour (speciality: pilchards and, in former times, smuggling), surrounded by traditional slate and cob cottages, attracts many tourists.

Mew Stone *Mew* OE *mæw* 'seagull'.

A rocky islet to the east of the mouth of the River DART in Devon.

Mey Gaelic *magh* 'plain, flat place'.

A village in the far northeast of Highland (formerly in

Caithness), 10 km (6 miles) west of John o' Groats. The nearby **Castle of Mey** was originally built in the 16th century but has been restored. It was a residence of the late Queen Mother, who bought it in 1952 and changed its name from Barragill Castle. Her elder daughter inscribed the following verse in the visitors' book:

> Although we must leave you,
> Fair Castle of Mey,
> We shall never forget,
> Nor could ever repay,
> A meal of such splendour,
> Repast of such zest,
> It will take us to Sunday,
> Just to digest.
> To leafy Balmoral,
> We are now on our way,
> But our hearts will remain
> At the Castle of Mey.
> With your gardens and ranges,
> And all your good cheer,
> We will be back again soon
> So roll on next year.

When this *vers d'occasion* was drawn to the attention of Mr Andrew Motion, the Poet Laureate, he obligingly commented: 'It is very cheering to know that the Queen has such a strong and good sense of rhythm.'

The village of **East May** is some 3 km (2 miles) northeast of Mey. Off the north coast, in the PENTLAND FIRTH, the **Merry Men of May** (so called long before being exposed to the cheering royal verse) is a reef with a spectacular tidal race.

Michaelston-le-Pit 'holy place of St Michael', personal name of St *Michael* the archangel + OE *stow* 'holy place, meeting place' + Fr definite article *le* 'the' + ME *pit* 'hollow, pit'; the Welsh name Llanfihangel-y-pwll is found much later than the English, and *pwll* appears to have the sense 'pit', rather than 'pool'.

A village in Cardiff unitary authority (formerly in Glamorgan, then in South Glamorgan), 5 km (3 miles) south of Cardiff.

Michaelston-y-Fedw 'holy place of St Michael', personal name of St *Michael* the archangel + OE *stow* 'holy place, meeting place' + Welsh definite article *y* 'the' + *fedw*, possibly a Welsh version of English 'meadow'.

A village in Newport unitary authority (formerly in Monmouthshire, then in Gwent), 8 km (5 miles) west of Newport.

Micheldever Originally *Mycendefr* (recorded in the 9th century), named after a local stream, probably an OCelt name meaning 'boggy waters', the second element of which was *dubras* (see DOVER); by the 11th century the first element had become confused with OE *micel* 'great'.

A village (pronounced 'mitcheldevver') in Hampshire, about 11 km (7 miles) northeast of Winchester.

Michelham Priory *Michelham* originally '(farm in the) big river-bend', OE *micel* 'large' + *hamm* 'land in a river-bend' (*see* HAM).

A Tudor manor house (pronounced 'mickleham') in East Sussex, on the CUCKMERE River, about 3 km (2 miles) west of Hailsham. It was built on the remains of an Augustinian priory, founded in 1229.

Mid Calder. *See under* CALDER[3].

Middle Britain. An early (first recorded in 1973) and more broadly representative equivalent of MIDDLE ENGLAND:

> 'Middle Britain' is easy to make fun of, but it constitutes most of the nation, does most of the work, pays most of the taxes, and mans the organizations which knit the country together.
>
> *The Times* (21 September 1999)

Middle England. The middle classes in England outside London, regarded as representing a conservative political viewpoint. They are self-reliant in their outlook, hold national values higher than international, dislike change and aspire to self-improvement. It was essentially Middle England that brought New Labour into power in the 1997 general election, having finally been prised from its attachment to the Conservative party.

> While Middle England is in vogue with politicians, research suggests that the traditional values it is seen as espousing may be under threat.
>
> *Sunday Times* (4 October 1998)

The term is sporadically recorded from the early 20th century in a geographical sense (corresponding approximately to the MIDLANDS), but this political usage probably dates from the 1970s. It was modelled on a similar application of *Middle America*, first recorded in 1968.
See also HEART OF ENGLAND.

Middlemarch. The fictional provincial town in LOAMSHIRE in which George Eliot's eponymous novel (1872) is set. It is based on COVENTRY.

Middle Mouse. *See under* MOUSE ISLANDS

Middlesbrough 'the middle stronghold', OE *midlest* 'middlemost' + *burh* (see BURY).

An industrial town, port and unitary authority on the south side of the TEES estuary opposite Stockton, 22 km (14 miles) northeast of Darlington. Until 1996 Middlesbrough was in CLEVELAND (and before that in Yorkshire), of which it was the administrative headquarters. Middlesbrough was no more than a tiny village until the 19th century, and is said to be the first town in England to owe its existence to the coming of the railway (in 1830). The new town was set out on a grid pattern, and grew as a centre of steel-making, taking advantage of local coal and iron ore and the natural harbour of the Tees estuary, spanned by the unique Transporter Bridge. By 1900 the population had reached over 100,000 – the result of 'a vast dingy conjuring trick', according to J.B. Priestley. Iron and steel and shipbuilding have now gone, and Middlesbrough's most obvious industry is chemicals, the plants pumping stuff into the air all around the town – as a result the inhabitants are known by their neighbors as **Smoggies**.

Middlesborough FC, founded in 1876 (following discussions over a tripe supper at the Corporation Hotel the previous year), is nicknamed Boro or the Ironsides (after the area's heavy industry). The club moved its home ground from Ayresome Park to the state-of-the-art Riverside Stadium in 1995.

Middlesbrough (or at least the village of Marston, now a suburb) was the birthplace of the explorer Captain James Cook (1728–29). The maverick football manager Brian Clough (1935–2004) and the pop balladeer Chris Rea (b.1951) were also born here.

Middlesborough is home to the University of Teesside (1992), formerly Teesside Polytechnic.

There is a town called Middlesboro in the USA (Kentucky).

Middlesex '(territory of the) Middle Saxons', originally a tribal name, OE *middel* 'middle' + *Seaxe* 'Saxon'.
A former English county, one of the HOME COUNTIES, to the north and northwest of London. It was bounded to the north by Hertfordshire, to the west by Buckinghamshire and Berkshire, to the south by Surrey (the River Thames forming the boundary) and London and to the east by Essex.

It was originally the territory of the Middle Saxons (so called because they were roughly in the middle between the East Saxons of Essex, the South Saxons of Sussex and the West Saxons of Wessex), which included much of Hertfordshire as well as the later Middlesex. It became a shire in the 10th century, and was much reduced in area by the Local Government Act of 1888. Its official existence was finally terminated in 1965, when most of it was absorbed into GREATER LONDON (Staines and Sunbury-on-Thames were inherited by Surrey, and Hertfordshire got Potter's Bar).

The demise of the county was far from universally popular with its residents, and they at least have the consolation that it survives for postal address purposes, in the 'Middlesex station' (the option closer to the north bank of the River Thames for the crews in the Oxford and Cambridge Boat Race), and as a participant in cricket's 'first-class' county structure. Middlesex County Cricket Club was founded in the London Tavern, BISHOPSGATE, on 2 February 1864, was a founder member of the county championship

when that competition was officially constituted in 1890, and has won the competition on 12 occasions. Its famous players include E.H. ('Patsy') Hendren, Denis Compton, Bill Edrich (*see* **Middlesex Twins** *below*), Mike Brearley, Mike Gatting, Angus Fraser and Phil Tufnell. It plays most of its home games at LORD'S. **Middlesex University** was formed in 1992 from the former Middlesex Polytechnic (*see also under* WHITE HART LANE).

The legacy of Middlesex is the suburbia of northwest London. Squire Bramble in Tobias Smollett's *Humphry Clinker* (1771) was already noting the creeping building blight ('If this infatuation continues for half a century I suppose the whole county of Middlesex will be covered with brick'), but until the early years of the 20th century large parts of the county were still essentially rural, little changed from the landscape that had inspired John Keats – if not quite the 'lost Elysium' celebrated by John Betjeman:

> With a thousand Ta's and Pardon's
> Daintily alights Elaine;
> Hurries down the concrete station
> With a frown of concentration,
> Out into the outskirts edges
> Where a few surviving hedges
> Keep alive our lost Elysium – rural Middlesex again.
>
> John Betjeman: 'Middlesex' (1954)

Betjeman's poems contain a litany of former Middlesex villages and hamlets that are now just bits of London – Greenford and Harrow-on-the-Hill, Isleworth, Perivale and Ruislip – all swallowed up long since by southern METROLAND.

One of the counties in Jamaica is called Middlesex.

> An acre in Middlesex is better than a principality in Utopia.
>
> Lord Macaulay: *Essays Contributed to the Edinburgh Review* (1843)

Middlesex. A novel (2002) by American writer Jeffrey Eugenides. It is described by the author as 'a 500-page novel about a Greek family told by a hermaphrodite' (hence the punning title). It won the 2003 Pulitzer Prize for fiction.

Middlesex clown. A slang expression from the mid-17th to the early 19th centuries for a native or inhabitant of Middlesex. Equally disrespectful and roughly contemporary was **Middlesex mongrel**.

Middlesex Hospital. A hospital in Central London, in Mortimer Street (W1). It was founded in 1745 as the Middlesex Infirmary, and moved to its present site in the 1750s. It is one of the major London teaching hospitals. (The **North Middlesex Hospital** is on the NORTH CIRCULAR ROAD, in EDMONTON. The **West Middlesex Hospital** is in ISLEWORTH, since 2003 in a brand-new building.)

Middlesex Sevens. A seven-a-side rugby tournament played annually at TWICKENHAM at the end of the rugby season, with a variety of British and international teams invited to take part.

Middlesex Twins. A nickname given to the Middlesex and England batsmen Denis Compton (1918–97) and Bill Edrich (1916–86), who enjoyed record-breaking success in the 1947 English cricket season, both men scoring over 3000 runs and often batting together. They gave every sign of enjoying life to the full.

Middlesex Street Because it formed the boundary between the City of London and the ancient county of *Middlesex*.
A street in the City of London (E1), leading southeastwards off BISHOPSGATE towards ALDGATE. It received its name around 1830, replacing the earlier PETTICOAT LANE, which survives as the name of a market held here.

Middleton 'middle farm', OE *middel* 'middle' + -TON.
A largely residential town in Greater Manchester, 8 km (5 miles) north of the city centre.

Middleton Scriven *Scriven* probably denoting manorial ownership in the Middle Ages by the Scriven family.
A village in Shropshire, about 8 km (5 miles) southwest of Bridgnorth.

Middle Wallop *Middle* indicating its position between OVER WALLOP and NETHER WALLOP; *Wallop* perhaps 'valley with a spring or stream', OE *wella, wœlla* 'spring, stream' + *hop* 'valley', or alternatively the first element may represent OE *weall* 'wall' or *walu* 'ridge, embankment'.
A village in Hampshire, on the Wallop Brook (*see under* the WALLOPS), about 10 km (6 miles) southwest of Andover. It is part of the military training complex at the southeastern corner of Salisbury Plain, and Middle Wallop airfield is a busy Army helicopter training base. The Museum of Army Aviation is nearby.

Middlewich 'middlemost saltworks' (referring to the town's position between NANTWICH and NORTHWICH; *see also* WICHES), OE *midlest* 'middlemost' + *wic* 'saltworks' (*see* WICK).
A town in Cheshire, at the junction of the Trent and Mersey Canal (*see under* TRENT[1]) and the Shropshire Union Canal (*see under* SHROPSHIRE), about 11 km (7 miles) north of Crewe. As its name suggests, it has earned its living over the centuries from the production of salt.

Middlezoy Originally *Soweie* 'island on the River Sow', a lost pre-English river name *Sow* of unknown meaning + OE *eg* (*see* -EY, -EA); the prefixed *Middle-* is first recorded in the 13th century.
A village in the Somerset Levels (*see under* SOMERSET), about 3 km (2 miles) southeast of WESTONZOYLAND.

Mid Glamorgan *See* GLAMORGAN.
A former county of south Wales, created in 1974 out of part of the old county of Glamorgan. Its Welsh name was **Morgannwg Ganol** ('Mid Glamorgan'). It was bounded to the south by South Glamorgan, to the west by West Glamorgan, to the north by Powys and to the east by Gwent. The administrative headquarters were in CARDIFF, and other towns included MERTHYR TYDFIL, ABERDARE, PONTYPRIDD and CAERPHILLY[1]. In 1996 it was divided among the unitary authorities of RHONDDA CYNON TAFF, Merthyr Tydfil, BRIDGEND and VALE OF GLAMORGAN.

Midhe. An Irish name for County MEATH.

Midhurst 'middle wooded hill', OE *midd* 'middle' + *hyrst* 'wooded hill'.
A market town in West Sussex, on the River ROTHER[1], about 19 km (12 miles) north of Chichester. The writer H.G. Wells was a pupil at the local grammar school in 1881 and later taught there; he disguised the town in his sardonic novel *Tono-Bungay* (1909) as **Wimblehurst**. The Spread Eagle inn at Midhurst was a favourite watering hole of Hilaire Belloc's. The town is also fictionalized as KINGSMARKHAM in the 'Chief Inspector Wexford' novels of Ruth Rendell.

Charles James Fox (1749–1806) was MP for Midhurst. He was first elected at the age of 19 (below the legal limit).

About 1.5 km (1 mile) to the east is Cowdray Park, a venue for polo. It contains the ruins of Cowdray House, an Elizabethan mansion which burnt down in 1793.

Midlands. A term applied to the central part of England. The Midlands have no fixed official boundary, and indeed people's view of what the name encompasses varies with their own location (Tynesiders are often heard to claim that Yorkshire is in the Midlands). The most watertight definition is perhaps a negative one: anywhere in England that is not the NORTH, the SOUTH, the WEST or EAST ANGLIA. And the Midlands do rather suffer from a negative reputation – for a flat, featureless landscape, where people speak with flat accents, and excitement is seldom stirred:

> When I am living in the Midlands
> That are sodden and unkind ...
> And the great hills of the South Country
> Come back into my mind.
>
> Hilaire Belloc: 'The South Country' (1910)

Belloc was, however, strongly biased towards the South; so, to strike a more positive note, the core constituent counties of the Midlands can be confidently identified as LEICESTERSHIRE, LINCOLNSHIRE, NORTHAMPTONSHIRE, OXFORDSHIRE, RUTLAND, STAFFORDSHIRE and WARWICKSHIRE. To these one can add at least the southern parts of Cheshire, Derbyshire and Nottinghamshire, the western part of Cambridgeshire, the northern parts of Bedfordshire and Buckinghamshire, and probably also HEREFORDSHIRE, SHROPSHIRE and WORCESTERSHIRE (although in some people's mental map these last three are verging on 'West').

... in most of the English Midlands, hedged fields are derived from the Enclosure Acts of the 18th and 19th centuries, before which the land had been farmed in great open prairie farming fields. This landscape, laid out hurriedly in a drawing-office at the enclosure of each parish, has a mass-produced quality of regular fields and straight roads. It may have medieval woods, Anglo-Saxon hedges and ancient trees, but only as isolated antiquities that the enclosure commissioners failed to destroy. This is Planned Countryside.

> Oliver Rackham: *The Illustrated History of the Countryside* (1994)

A more specific usage, but one that has now faded from currency, identifies 'Midlands' with the foxhunting counties of central England – the SHIRES, as we would now probably call them: Leicestershire, Northamptonshire and the flat, open parts of Warwickshire, Nottinghamshire and Derbyshire suitable for chasing foxes.

It may be that successive reorganizations of local government in the last quarter of the 20th century, and the abolition and reappearance of many traditional counties, have rendered the concept of 'the Midlands' vaguer still. We now perhaps feel more accustomed to specifying the EAST MIDLANDS or the WEST MIDLANDS.

In an American context, the term Midland is applied to the central part of the USA, roughly between Tennessee, the Mississippi, the Great Lakes and the Atlantic coast, and particularly to the variety of American English spoken there. *See also* MIDLANDS, THE IRISH.

Midlander. A native or inhabitant of the English Midlands, or of the American Midland.

Midland hawthorn. A species of hawthorn (*Crataegus oxyacanthoides*) found in southern England on heavy soils and in woodlands. It is much less widespread than the common hawthorn (*Crataegus monogyna*), and is usually found as a tree rather than as a hedge plant. Red-blossomed garden cultivars of the Midland hawthorn (often hybrids between the common and the Midland hawthorns) are a frequent sight in English suburbs.

Once Upon a Time in the Midlands. A film (2003) parodying spaghetti westerns, set in Nottingham and starring Robert Carlyle. The title echoes that of Sergio Leone's 1969 spaghetti western *Once Upon a Time in the West*.

Midlands, the Irish. The central, low-lying region of the Republic of Ireland, centred on OFFALY and LAOIS, and also taking in all or part of CAVAN, LOUTH, MEATH, WESTMEATH, LONGFORD, ROSCOMMON and KILDARE. It is the antithesis of the English Midlands, being rural and boggy.

> The soft and dreary midlands with their tame canals
> Wallow between sea and sea, remote from adventure ...
>
> Donagh MacDonagh (1912–68): 'Dublin Made Me'

> Through the midlands of Ireland I journeyed by diesel,
> And bright in the sun shone the emerald plain.
>
> John Betjeman: 'A Lament for Moira McCavendish' (1966)

> I pedalled on towards Athlone through slashing rain
> across brown miles of harvested bog – looking like a
> child's dream of a world made of chocolate.
>
> Dervla Murphy: *A Place Apart* (1978)

Midleton ModE 'middle settlement'; it is approximately midway between Carrigtohill and Castlemartyr.
A market town in County Cork, 20 km (12 miles) east of Cork itself. Its Irish name is **Mainistir na Corann** ('monastery of the weir'), referring to a Cistercian monastery founded here in 1180. The town was founded *c.*1670 by the Brodrick family, later earls of Midleton. **Midleton College**, a grammar school, was founded in 1696 by William III's mistress Elizabeth Villiers, and among its alumni was the noted judge and orator John Philpot Curran (1750–1817). Midleton is a noted centre of whiskey distilling, and also produces gin and vodka.

Midlothian *See* LOTHIAN; *Mid-* distinguishes it from EAST LOTHIAN and WEST LOTHIAN.
A former county and present unitary authority (administrative headquarters in EDINBURGH) of eastern-central Scotland. It is bounded on the west by South Lanarkshire and West Lothian, on the north by Edinburgh, on the east by East Lothian and on the south by Scottish Borders (formerly by Berwickshire, Roxburghshire, Selkirkshire and Peeblesshire). The former county included Edinburgh and was originally known as **Edinburghshire**.

Heart of Midlothian, The. Now perhaps the most highly regarded, and most often read, of the novels of Sir Walter Scott (1771–1832). It was published in 1818. The 'Heart of Midlothian' was the nickname of the old Edinburgh Tolbooth, the city's prison. This is explained in the first chapter:

> 'Then the tolbooth of Edinburgh is called the Heart of Midlothian?' said I.
> 'So termed and reputed, I assure you.'

The significance of the Tolbooth in Scott's novel is twofold. A highlight of the early part of the novel is a vivid description of the true events of the Porteous Riots (1736), which broke out in the wake of the hanging of a popular smuggler. After the execution there was some disturbance from the crowd and John Porteous, captain of the city guard, ordered his men to fire, resulting in several deaths. Porteous was convicted of murder and sentenced to hang, but was reprieved for six weeks by Queen Caroline. A furious crowd assembled, dragged Porteous from the Tolbooth where he was being held and lynched him. The second role of the prison in the novel is as the place of incarceration of Effie Deans, who is accused of murdering her child. Her sister, Jeanie Deans, determines to walk to London, where she eventually succeeds in obtaining a pardon for the erring Effie. Many readers have interpreted the title of the novel as referring to Jeanie, who is a figure of simple virtue and kindness. This story is again modelled on a real case, involving one Isobel Walker and her sister Helen.

The Tolbooth was demolished in 1817, and today the place – near the High Kirk of St Giles on Edinburgh's Royal Mile – is marked by red paving stones in the shape of a heart; it was once the custom to spit here, but the health educationists have thankfully had their way. The name is also memorialized in the full name of Hearts, one of EDINBURGH's football teams: **Heart of Midlothian FC** (nicknamed the Jam Tarts), which was founded in 1874 and play at TYNECASTLE. 'Heart of Midlothian' was also the title formerly given to one of the train services running between London and Edinburgh.

Midlothian Campaign. Gladstone's famous campaign in 1879–80 to win the Edinburghshire (as it then was) parliamentary seat, standing against the Tory Lord Dalkieth. In all he made 21 speeches attacking the policies of Disraeli's government and, Gladstone being such a noted orator, the speeches were reported nationally. As a result of his success, Gladstone was invited to form his second administration.

Midsomer Norton *Midsomer* commemorating the festival of St John the Baptist, patron saint of the local church, on Midsummer Day; *Norton see* NORTON DISNEY.

A small town in Bath and Northeast Somerset (before 1996 in Avon, before 1974 in Somerset), about 13 km (8 miles) southwest of Bath. In the past it was a mining town in the now unproductive Somerset coalfield.

The idyllically rural-sounding *Midsomer* was the inspiration for the fictional rustic killing-ground that features in the detective novels of Caroline Graham, adapted for television since 1997 as *Midsomer Murders*. Among the homicide-prone villages featured is **Midsomer Mallow**.

Midwich. A fictional village of indeterminate location in the South of England, in the equally fictional county of Winshire. It is the setting of John Wyndham's chilling science-fiction novel *The Midwich Cuckoos* (1957) in which, following an apparently extraterrestrial intervention, a number of golden-eyed children with strange coercive powers are born to local women. It has been filmed three times, as *Village of the Damned* (1960, by Wolf Rilla; the part of the village was played by Letchmore Heath near Borehamwood in Hertfordshire), as *Children of the Damned* (1964, by Anton Leader) and again (by John Carpenter) as *Village of the Damned* (1995).

Milby. George Eliot's fictional version of NUNEATON in her *Scenes from Clerical Life* (1858).

Mildenhall[1] 'middle nook of land' or 'Milda's nook of land', OE *middel* 'middle' or *Mildan* possessive form of male personal name *Milda* + *halh* 'nook of land' (*see* HALE, -HALL).

A market town in Suffolk, on the River Lark and on the southwestern edge of the BRECKLAND, about 19 km (12 miles) northwest of Bury St Edmunds. The nearby airfield has been operated by the US Air Force since the Second World War. **Mildenhall Fen** is to the northwest.

Mildenhall Treasure. A cache of 4th-century Roman silver tableware discovered by a ploughman in a field at Thistley Green near Mildenhall in 1942. Consisting of 34 pieces in all, it included a great dish showing Bacchus and Hercules and was presumably buried for safety during the troubled days of the Anglo-Saxon invasions. Its importance was not immediately realized by its discoverer, and for four years it remained unreported. It is now in the British Museum.

Mildenhall[2] 'Milda's nook of land', OE *Mildan* possessive form of male personal name *Milda* + *halh* 'nook of land' (*see* HALE, -HALL).

A village (pronounced locally 'my-nəl') in Wiltshire, about 1.5 km (1 mile) east of Marlborough. Its church, St John's, probably of Saxon origin, has a remarkable Regency interior; John Betjeman described visiting it as like walking 'into a church of a Jane Austen novel'. It was used in 1996 for filming the church scenes for the ITV television production of Jane Austen's *Emma*.

The name of the village is sometimes alternatively spelt, following the local pronunciation, as **Minal**.

Mile End '(hamlet) a mile away' (referring to its position on the old London-to-Colchester road, about 1.5 km (a mile) distant from Aldgate), ME *mile* and *ende*.

A district in East London (E1, E2), in the borough of TOWER HAMLETS, to the east of BETHNAL GREEN and to the west of Bow. In the Middle Ages it was largely open land, and it was on Mile End Green during the Peasants' Revolt of 1381 that the men of Essex met Richard II and made their demand for the abolition of serfdom. Then and for some centuries more it was viewed as a distant outpost, but in the 19th century it was swallowed up in the outward growth of London. It was never such an overcrowded and poor area as many in the EAST END, but William Booth began his Salvation Army work here, in the late 1860s, and the first Dr Barnardo's Home for orphans opened here in 1870. The 'Siege of SIDNEY STREET' took place in Mile End in 1911. The area suffered badly in the Blitz.

Mile End Road (the A11) is the area's main artery. On its north side is Queen Mary, a college of London University.

Mile End Underground station, on the Central and District lines, opened in 1902.

Milford Haven 'harbour of the sandbank inlet', OScand *melr* 'sandbank' + *fjorthr* 'fjord, inlet' + ME *haven* 'harbour'; the name was refashioned early to resemble 'mill ford'.

A port in Pembrokeshire (formerly in Dyfed), 11 km (7 miles) south of Haverfordwest, on the estuary of the Eastern and Western CLEDDAU rivers. Its Welsh name is **Aberdaugleddau** ('mouth of the two Cleddaus', ABER + *dau* 'two' + CLEDDAU). The long deep-water estuary is itself referred to as **Milford Haven**, and it is this that gave the port its name. The estuary is an important deep-water anchorage, rated by Nelson as one of the finest natural harbours in the world.

> ... some say, a thousand sail of ships may ride in it, and not the topmast of one be seen from another ...
>
> Daniel Defoe: *A Tour Through the Whole Island of Great Britain* (1724–6)

Defoe adds in qualification: 'this last, I think, merits confirmation', although as far as history records no one has tried the experiment. The Haven is now much used by oil tankers supplying the town's oil refineries and oil pipeline to Llandarcy near Swansea.

The town of Milford Haven itself was founded in 1793 by Quakers from Nantucket in Massachusetts, USA, as a whaling centre, and later a naval dockyard was built (moving to PEMBROKE DOCK in 1814). Milford Haven was an important naval base in both world wars, and began its development as Britain's biggest oil port in 1957.

Somewhat surprisingly to those who associate Milford Haven with the modern oil industry, the place features in Shakespeare's *Cymbeline*. When the heroine, the British princess Imogen, receives a letter from her Roman husband Posthumus telling her he is at Milford Haven, she responds:

> O, for a horse with wings! Hears't thou, Pisanio?
> He is at Milford-Haven: read, and tell me
> How far 'tis thither ...
> To this same blessed Milford. And by th' way
> Tell me how Wales was made so happy as
> T'inherit such a haven.
>
> William Shakespeare: *Cymbeline* (1610), III.ii

Although it is not certain whether it was used by the Romans, Milford Haven was the point of embarkation for military expeditions to Ireland under Henry II and King John. In 1407, in support of Owain Glyndwr's rebellion, 12,000 French mercenaries disembarked here, and, on 7 August 1485, Henry Tudor, Earl of Richmond and the future Henry VII, landed at Milford to take on Richard III – as Shakespeare has Catesby report to his master:

> My liege, the Duke of Buckingham is taken –
> That is the best news. That the Earl of Richmond
> Is with a mighty power landed at Milford
> Is colder tidings, but yet they must be told.
>
> William Shakespeare: *Richard III* (1594), IV.iv

In 1917 Prince Louis of Battenberg (who had been forced to resign as First Lord of the Admiralty because of anti-German feeling) was made **Marquess of Milford Haven**, and in the same year he changed the family name to Mountbatten; he is also known to have accumulated the most comprehensive library of sadomasochistic pornography in Europe. Coincidentally, Milford Haven was the birthplace of the *fin de siècle* poet Arthur Symons (1865–1945), a noted Decadent.

There is a town called Milford in Connecticut, USA, on Long Island Sound, and a Milford Sound in Fiordland, South Island, New Zealand, which, like its Welsh namesake, is fed by a River Cleddau.

Milk Street 'street where milk is sold' (referring to the milk market held here in the Middle Ages).

A street in the City of London (EC2), running north to south between Gresham Street and POULTRY. The statesman and author Sir Thomas More (1478–1535) was born here.

Millbank From the *mills* (owned by Westminster Abbey) along the *bank* of the River Thames (the last of them was demolished in the 1730s).

A road along the north bank of the River Thames, in the City of WESTMINSTER, extending from Vauxhall Bridge to just short of the Houses of Parliament. It is home to the original Tate Gallery (since 2000 known as 'Tate Britain'), built in the 1890s to the designs of Sidney R.J. Smith. Its other significant building is Millbank Tower, an office block erected in 1960–3. From 1997 to 2002 it housed the headquarters of the Labour Party, and in a period when New Labour spin ruled, the metonym 'Millbank' took on connotations of thought-control and amorality that sometimes verged on the sinister. In 2002 the party moved to the sedater Old Queen Street, to the west of PARLIAMENT SQUARE.

Joseph Duveen (1869–1939), a successful and influential art dealer who donated the money for the Duveen Wing of the Tate Gallery, took the title of Baron Duveen of Millbank when he was raised to the peerage in 1933.

Millbank Penitentiary. A prison opened in 1821 on a low-lying, marshy site beside the River Thames at Millbank. It embodied the philosopher Jeremy Bentham's ideas for a 'panopticon', in which prisoners housed around the circumference of the building could be kept under constant observation by someone stationed in the centre. The resulting structure was shaped like a six-pointed star. It was never a great success, and was closed and demolished in the 1890s. The Tate Gallery was built on its site.

Millbank Tendency. A contemptuous nickname coined by adherents of 'Old Labour' for the New Labour apparatchiks whose tentacles spread over the Labour party from their headquarters in Millbank Tower. The term was based on 'Militant Tendency', the name of the Trotskyite group that infiltrated the Labour Party in the 1980s.

Millennium Bridge. A name bestowed in honour of the millennium (strictly speaking a bimillennium) on three bridges intended to be opened in the year 2000 (providing yet another opportunity for pedants to point out that the millennium was in 2001).

In London, it denotes a footbridge over the River THAMES[1], linking BLACKFRIARS with SOUTHWARK. Built to the design of Norman Foster, the bridge was opened by Queen Elizabeth II on 10 June 2000, but had to be closed almost immediately when it was discovered that large numbers of people walking across it made it sway alarmingly. After the necessary adjustments had been made, it was reopened on 22 February 2002. The northern approach to the bridge opens up a new vista of ST PAUL'S[1] Cathedral, and a 180° turn offers an imposing view of Tate Modern (formerly Bankside Power Station (*see under* BANKSIDE)).

On Tyneside, the Millennium Bridge links Newcastle and Gateshead. It was opened to the public on 17 September 2001 and officially by the Queen on 7 May 2002. It is a tilting span bridge (the world's first) over the TYNE[1], which pivots to allow ships to pass. It is for cyclists and pedestrians only. Its outline is somewhat eye-shaped – whence its local nickname, the **Blinking Eye**.

The Millennium Bridge in York also opened tardily in 2001 (although no doubt this pleased the millennium pedants). It is a foot and cycle bridge over the River OUSE[2], and its design is described as 'offset suspension'.

Millennium Dome. A circular structure with a shallow domed roof, designed by Richard Rogers and built, at a cost of over £800 million, on a tract of previously derelict land on the GREENWICH Peninsula (SE10) as the central venue for London's official millennium celebrations on 31 December 1999 and to house the Millennium Experience exhibition. At 49 m (160 ft) in height and over 0.75 km (over half a mile) in circumference, it is easily the largest dome in the world. The exhibition, designed to celebrate the millennium of 2000, was divided into 14 exhibition zones, each sponsored by a well-known company: Body, Faith, Home Planet, Journey, Talk, Learning, Living Island, Mind, Money, Work, Play, Rest, Self Portrait and Shared Ground. It was opened by Queen Elizabeth II on 31 December 1999 but disappointed many of its visitors, who endured long waits to see poorly explained or even malfunctioning exhibits.

The **Dome** (as it is usually called for short) closed on 1 January 2001, having made a heavy financial loss and proved something of an embarrassment to Tony Blair and the New Labour government who had supported it (although it had been initiated by their Tory predecessors). In 2003 permission was granted to turn it into a 20,000-seater arena.

The Dome is served by a purpose-built Underground station (the largest in Europe) at North Greenwich on the Jubilee line (opened in 1999).

> The Millennium Dome … the Teflon meteorite on Bugsby's Marshes.
>
> Iain Sinclair: *London Orbital* (2002)

Dome Secretary. A punning nickname (based on *Home Secretary*) for those New Labour ministers with responsibility for the Millennium Dome (Peter Mandelson was initially in charge of the project, until he was succeeded by Lord Falconer in 1998).

Millennium Spire. *See under* O'CONNELL STREET.

Millennium Stadium. The replacement stadium for Cardiff Arms Park (*see under* CARDIFF).

Mill Hill 'hill with a windmill' (referring to a former mill in the area, near St Mary's Abbey, of which the house still survives). A residential suburb of North London (NW7), on the old RIDGEWAY, in the borough of BARNET between FINCHLEY and the M1. Its status as a named suburb was promoted by Mill Hill station on the Great Northern Railway line, which opened in 1867; this was renamed Mill Hill East in 1928, and began to be used by Underground trains, on a spur of the Northern line, in 1941.

Mill Hill School, a co-educational public school, was founded in 1807 by non-conformist merchants who decided to place the school outside London to avoid the 'dangers both physical and moral, awaiting youth while passing through the streets of a large, crowded and corrupt city'. James Murray, editor of the *Oxford English Dictionary* from 1873 till his death in 1915, taught here between 1870 and 1885. Denis Thatcher, late husband of Britain's first woman prime minister, attended the school as a boarder in the late 1920s and early 1930s.

Millhillian. A present or former pupil of Mill Hill School.

Millom 'at the mills', OE *mylnum*, dative plural of *myln* 'mill'. A small town on the DUDDON estuary, southwest Cumbria (formerly in Cumberland), some 12 km (7.5 miles) north of Barrow-in-Furness. It was formerly a centre of iron-ore mining and smelting, and was the birthplace and home of the Lakeland poet Norman Nicholson (1914–87), who celebrated the town and its surroundings in much of his verse – for example:

> You and I know better, Duddon.
> For I who've lived for nearly 30 years
> Upon your shore have seen the slagbanks slant
> Like screes in the sand.

Millport Named after the mill that used to stand above the harbour.

A resort and the main town on the south coast of the Firth of Clyde island of Great Cumbrae (*see under* the CUMBRAES), North Ayrshire (formerly in Buteshire and then in

Strathclyde region). It is the location of Britain's smallest cathedral, the Episcopal Cathedral of Argyll and the Isles (completed 1886). Also in the town is Britain's narrowest house, called 'the Wedge'. At the front it is little more than the width of a door, and there are two wedge-shaped rooms and a bathroom. For another contender for the title of Britain's smallest house, see CONWY[2].

Milltown Malbay 'mill town (at) Mal Bay'.

A small market town and resort in County Clare, overlooking **Mal Bay**, 28 km (17 miles) west of Ennis. Its Irish name is **Sráid na Cathrach** ('village of the stone fort').

Millwall 'wall with mills' (referring to mills which stood on the marsh walls in the 17th and 18th centuries).

A district in East London (E14), on the western side of the ISLE OF DOGS, in the borough of TOWER HAMLETS. Until the 19th century it was a low-lying, fairly desolate area, its marshland kept drained by the mills from which it gets its name. This began to change when John Scott Russell opened his shipyard on the banks of the Thames (the mills disappeared in the process). Isambard Kingdom Brunel's *Great Eastern*, the largest ship built in Britain until the 1890s, was launched from here in 1859. In 1868 **Millwall Dock** opened, to the south of the West India Docks (*see under* ISLE OF DOGS). It specialized in the Baltic grain trade. It was closed in 1980. The surrounding district was no less plagued by poverty and overcrowded housing conditions than the rest of DOCKLAND, and it suffered heavily during the Blitz, but redevelopment since the 1980s has transformed the area.

Millwall FC was founded in 1885. In 1910 it moved to NEW CROSS, where it plays at a ground known as 'the Den' (whence the club's nickname, the **Lions**). In the latter part of the 20th century its supporters gained an above-average reputation for truculence.

Millwall Chainsaws. The name of a punk rock group founded in the late 1970s which developed into Pogue Mahone, later known as The Pogues, the hybrid punk-Irish folk band fronted by the singer and songwriter Shane McGowan.

Millwall Reserves. A football-derived rhyming-slang term – also plain **Millwalls** – from the 1950s, meaning 'nerves' (as in 'get on someone's Millwalls').

Milngavie Gaelic *muilleann gaoithe* 'windmill'.

A BURGH – effectively an outer suburb of GLASGOW – in East Dunbartonshire, some 10 km (6 miles) northwest of Glasgow city centre. Milngavie is pronounced, to the bafflement of many, 'mull-guy', and mocked by *echt*-Glaswegians for its air of social superiority. It is certainly above BISHOPBRIGGS in the pecking order, but whether it outranks BEARSDEN is a question that might be set to fret the socially anxious.

Milnrow 'mill with a row of houses', OE *myln* 'mill' + *raw* 'row of houses'.

A former cotton town in Greater Manchester, 3 km (2 miles) east of Rochdale.

Milton Abbas *Milton* 'middle farmstead or estate', OE *middel* 'middle' + -TON; *Abbas* 'of the abbot', Latin *abbatis*, referring to its ownership by the local abbey.

A village in Dorset, about 11 km (7 miles) southwest of Blandford Forum. The nearby **Milton Abbey** was founded by King Athelstan in 938. In the 18th century it was converted into a house by Joseph Damer, later Earl of Dorchester. He found that Milton Abbas, then a small market town, spoilt his view, so he had it flattened and built in its place the neat village of 'model' cottages which now exists. The abbey is now a public school.

Milton Damerel *Damerel* denoting manorial ownership in the early Middle Ages by Robert de Albemarle.

A village in Devon, about 16 km (10 miles) southwest of Bideford.

Milton Ernest *Ernest* denoting manorial ownership in the Middle Ages by a man called Erneis.

A village in Bedfordshire, about 8 km (5 miles) northwest of Bedford.

Milton Keynes *Keynes* denoting manorial ownership in the early Middle Ages by the de Cahaignes family.

A town (pronounced 'keenz') and unitary authority in Buckinghamshire, on the M1, about 19 km (12 miles) northeast of Buckingham. For most of its life it has been a small (and quite picturesque) village. Then, in 1967, it was designated a NEW TOWN[1], and underwent massive and transformative growth. It is now an important population centre, with thriving commerce and light industry. The headquarters of the Open University were established here in 1971.

However, as with most new towns, the planned geometricality of its townscape can leave an impression of soullessness and sterility, and the name Milton Keynes came to be used as a byword for bland uniformity. For the unwary motorist the large number of roundabouts is a particular stumbling block. The town's PR cause was not helped by a small herd of concrete cows placed in a field here in 1978 to foster an air of rural tranquillity.

Milton Keynes unitary authority, created in 1997, includes the towns of BLETCHLEY, NEWPORT PAGNELL, STONY STRATFORD, Winslow and WOLVERTON.

In 2004 Milton Keynes officially acquired its own professional football club: Wimbledon FC (*see under* WIMBLEDON), under financial duress, relocated its ground here in 2003, and finally gave in to reality by renaming itself **Milton Keynes Dons** (the Dons being the former Wimbledon nickname).

The new town did not have to wait long to attract the attention of rhyming slangsters. Already by the end of the 1960s its name was being used for 'baked beans' and for 'a male homosexual' (*Keynes* rhyming with *queens*).

Milton Malsor *Malsor* denoting manorial ownership in the early Middle Ages by the Malsor family.

A village in Northamptonshire, about 5 km (3 miles) south of Northampton.

Minal. An alternative form of the name for MILDENHALL[2].

Móin an Mhullaigh. The Irish name for the MONA-VULLAGH MOUNTAINS.

Minches, the Probably 'great headland', OScand *megin* 'great' + *nes* (*see* NESS).

The channels separating the Outer HEBRIDES from the rest of Scotland, sometimes just called **the Minch**. The **North Minch** lies between LEWIS and the northwest part of the Scottish mainland, and is between 35 and 50 km (22 and 31 miles) wide. The **Little Minch** lies between the southern Outer Hebrides and the Inner Hebrides (particularly SKYE), and is on average 20 km (12 miles) wide.

Blue Men of the Minch, the. Legendary beings who haunt the Minch, occasionally bothering sailors. They are either kelpies or fallen angels, and are reputed to drag mariners to the bottom of the sea if they fail to answer questions in rhyming couplets (in Gaelic, naturally). The Rev. John Campbell, minister of Tiree, reported that his boat had been followed by such a creature, 'a blue-covered man' half out of the water; despite this pagan vision, the good minister kept his living on Tiree for 30 years, from 1861 to 1891.

Minchinhampton Originally *Hampton* 'high farmstead', OE *hean* dative form of *heah* 'high' + -TON; the prefix *Minchin-* 'of the nuns', OE *myncena*, refers to ownership by the nunnery of Caen in the 11th century (granted by William I at the instigation of his wife Matilda).

A small market town in Gloucestershire, on a high ridge of the Cotswolds, about 5 km (3 miles) southeast of Stroud. In the Middle Ages it was a centre of the wool trade. It has a curious 17th-century market hall, raised on an impressive array of pillars.

Mincing Lane 'lane of the nuns' (probably alluding to the existence of a community of nuns here, or to property owned by nuns), *Mincing* OE *myncena* possessive plural form of *myncen* 'nun'.

A street in the City of London (EC3), running southwards from FENCHURCH STREET. For a long time it was the centre of the tea trade, for which its name was formerly often used as a generic term:

> Mincing Lane is pretty confident of higher prices for

Africans [i.e. African teas] by the end of the first quarter of this year.

> *East African Standard* (Nairobi) (23 January 1970)

Minehead *Mine-* from a pre-English hill name, perhaps OCelt *monith* 'mountain'; *-head* 'projecting hill-spur', OE *heafod*.

A town and seaside resort on the Somerset coast, to the northeast of Exmoor, about 37 km (23 miles) northwest of Bridgwater. It is a town of two parts. The original section, known as Quay Town, was once an important port for fishing and for cargo, but in the late 18th century the harbour began to silt up and the herring shoals disappeared. The coming of the railway in the mid-19th century gave Minehead the chance to restore its prosperity, which it did by rebuilding itself as a holiday resort. Its sandy beach is 0.8 km (0.5 miles) wide when the tide is out. It has a Butlin's holiday camp (discreetly placed) dating from the 1960s.

Every May Minehead holds a hobby-horse parade somewhat similar to that held at PADSTOW.

The science-fiction writer Arthur C. Clarke was born in Minehead in 1917.

Minera Etymology unkown.

A village in Wrexham unitary authority (formerly in Denbighshire, then in Clwyd), 7 km (4.5 miles) west of Wrexham.

Mingulay 'big island', OScand *mikill* 'big' + *ey* 'island' (*see* -AY). The modern Gaelic name is *Miughalaigh*.

A small uninhabited island in the Outer HEBRIDES, the second southernmost in the chain. It is in Western Isles (formerly in Inverness-shire), 14 km (8.5 miles) south of BARRA, and is separated from PABBAY[1] to the north by the **Sound of Mingulay**. The inhabitants (the last of whom left in 1912) largely lived on seabirds. Mingulay is now owned by the National Trust for Scotland.

> Not far had men's hands to raise from the stony ground
> Blocks the ice and rain had hewn.
> The dry-stone walls of the houses of Mingulay still stand
> Long after the sheltering roof is gone.
> Not far had the heather thatch to blow back to the moor.
>
> Kathleen Raine: 'Deserted Village on Mingulay', from *The Oval Portrait* (1977)

Macphee's Hill in the north of the island is named after MacNeil of Barra's rent collector who long ago landed on the island to find everyone dead of a 'plague'. Hearing of this, the boatmen who had brought him sailed off, leaving Macphee to his fate. The castaway frantically signalled every passing boat from his eponymous hill, but a whole year passed until he was rescued.

'Mingulay Boat Song, The'. A famous but inauthentic 'folk song', based on a tune from the Western Highlands and with words by Hugh S. Robertson, written in 1938 for his Glasgow Orpheus Choir.

Heel yo ho, boys; let her go, boys;
Bring her head round, into the weather,
Hill you ho, boys, let her go, boys,
Sailing homeward to Mingulay.

Minions From a nearby tumulus called *Minions Mound*. *Minions* perhaps from early ModE *minion* 'lover'; alternatively the first syllable may represent Cornish *men* 'stone'.

A village in Cornwall (at over 300 m (985 ft), the highest in the county), at the southeastern edge of Bodmin Moor (*see under* BODMIN), about 6.5 km (4 miles) north of Liskeard. It grew up in the 19th century as a mining village. Nearby are three Bronze Age stone circles known as the HURLERS (legend has it that they are made up of men turned to stone for playing the game of hurling on the Sabbath); and to the north is the CHEESEWRING.

Minnigaff 'moor of the smith', Gaelic *moine* 'moor' + *gobha* 'of the smith'.

A village in Dumfries and Galloway (formerly in Kirkcudbrightshire), just northeast across the River Cree from NEWTON STEWART, of which it is virtually a part.

Minories, The Originally *Minorie Street* 'street of the minoresses' (referring to a former abbey of the Poor Clares here), ME *menouresse* 'nun of the second order of St Francis, known as Poor Clares'.

A street in the City of London (EC3), running southwards from ALDGATE to Tower Hill (*see under* TOWER OF LONDON). In 1294 a nunnery, the abbey of the Franciscan nuns or Minoresses of St Clare (Poor Clares) was established here, giving the street its name. It was dissolved in 1538. From the 16th to the 18th centuries the street was noted for its gunsmiths' shops.

Minquiers, Les Possibly 'sanctuary', Breton *minihi* (Breton is closely related to Cornish).

A reef of rocky islets about 19 km (12 miles) south of JERSEY, and within its Bailiwick. They were subject to an ownership dispute between Britain and France in the 1950s, largely because France wished to build a tidal power station here, but the matter was settled in favour of Britain. (*See also* Les ECREHOUS.)

There are currently no human inhabitants, but there are some buildings here, including cottages put up for the use of stone-quarriers in the 18th and 19th centuries, and a lavatory on the main islet, Maitresse Isle, which has the distinction of being the most southerly building in the British Isles.

Minsmere The second element is from OE *mere* 'lake', but the first is obscure.

A lake on the Suffolk coast, about 11 km (7 miles) north of Aldeburgh. Since 1948 the surrounding area of freshwater marsh, heathland and beach has been an important bird reserve. It is noted in particular for its avocets, but many other endangered species have prospered here, including bitterns and nightjars. The domes of SIZEWELL nuclear power station loom in the distance.

During the Second World War the cliffs near Minsmere became the site for one of the first radar stations.

Minster[1] '(place by the) monastery or large church' (referring to a 7th-century nunnery here), OE *mynster*.

A village in Kent, on the ISLE OF SHEPPEY, about 4 km (2.5 miles) east of Sheerness. It is often designated more fully **Minster-in-Sheppey**, to distinguish it from MINSTER[2].

The earliest Christian missionaries to England passed this way, in the 7th century, and Minster contains one of England's oldest surviving places of worship, the church of St Mary and St Sexburga. This is actually a double church: the older part is what survives of a nunnery originally founded here in 664 by Sexburga, Queen of Kent, destroyed by the Danes and rebuilt for Benedictine nuns in the 12th century; the newer part is a parish church built in the 12th century.

Minster[2]. A village in Kent, in the ISLE OF THANET, about 6 km (4 miles) west of Ramsgate. It is often designated more fully **Minster-in-Thanet**, to distinguish it from MINSTER[1].

Like MINSTER[1], it owes its name to a nunnery founded here in the earliest years of English Christianity – this one by Domneva, niece of King Egbert. The church, St Mary's, was massively expanded by the Normans.

One of the church's more colourful vicars was the 17th-century Richard 'Blue Dick' Culmer, an enthusiastic iconoclast who is said to have torn the cross from the top of the steeple with his bare hands, and became so unpopular with his parishioners that he did not dare turn up here to collect his tithes.

Minster Lovell *Minster see* MINSTER[1] (referring to a former Benedictine priory here); *Lovell* denoting manorial ownership in the Middle Ages by the Lovell family.

A village in Oxfordshire, on the River WINDRUSH, about 5 km (3 miles) west of Witney. Nearby are the ruins of the 15th-century Minster Lovell Hall. In 1708, workmen uncovered a man's skeleton seated at a table in a hidden chamber here. It is generally supposed to have been that of Francis Lovell (known to his enemies as 'Lovell the Dog'), supporter of the losing causes of Richard III and Lambert Simnel. He went into hiding in the house, and is said to have starved to death when the only servant who knew his whereabouts died.

Mirfield 'pleasant open land', OE *myrge* 'pleasant' (or alternatively *myrgen* 'festivities') + *feld* (*see* FIELD).

A town on the River Calder in West Yorkshire, 7 km (4.5 miles) northeast of Huddersfield. The Brontë sisters attended Miss Wooler's School here at Roe Head for a while, and Charlotte returned to the school in 1835 as a teacher, while

Anne worked (1839–40) as a governess at Blake Hall, for local squire and magistrate Joshua Ingham.

Mis Tor 'misty tor', OE *mist* + *tor*.
Either of a pair of hills on DARTMOOR, about 8 km (5 miles) east of Tavistock: **Great Mis Tor** is 539 m (1768 ft) high and **Little Mis Tor** 488 m (1600 ft) high.

Misty Isle, the. A byname of SKYE.

Mitcham 'large homestead or village', OE *micel* 'large' + HAM.
A district in southwest London, in the borough of MERTON (before 1965 in Surrey), between Croydon to the east and Merton to the west. It appears to have originated as an armed camp in the earliest years of Anglo-Saxon occupation, and an Anglo-Saxon cemetery dating from the 5th and 6th centuries was excavated here at the beginning of the 20th century. In Elizabethan and Stuart times it was a popular country retreat for London courtiers.

From the mid-18th to the late 19th centuries Mitcham was famous for the cultivation of lavender and medicinal herbs.

Mitchelstown 'Mitchel's homestead', Anglo-Norman personal name *Mitchel* + -TON; first recorded in the 13th century as *Villa Michel*, medieval Latin 'land, settlement of Mitchell', referring to the Anglo-Norman landowner Mitchel Condon; in Irish it is *Baile Mhistéala*, meaning the same.
A market town in County Cork, 30 km (19 miles) northeast of Mallow, between the KILWORTH and GALTEE mountains. It was laid out in the 19th century and is noted for its creamery industry.

Mitchelstown was the birthplace of the novelist and short-story writer William Trevor (b.1928). John O'Mahony (1816–77), founder of the US branch of the Fenian brotherhood, was born nearby.

The **Mitchelstown Caves**, 12 km (7.5 miles) to the east, just over the border in Tipperary, comprise the Old Caves (known for centuries and used as a hiding place by the Earl of Desmond in 1601) and the New Caves, accidentally discovered by men quarrying rock in 1833.

Mitchelstown Massacre (9 September 1887). An incident that occurred at a Land League meeting in the town, when an angry crowd gathered in support of two local MPs, William O'Brien and John Mandeville, who had been summoned to appear before magistrates because of their involvement in the campaign of tenant resistance. Ordered to take a hard line by Chief Secretary Arthur 'Bloody' Balfour, the Royal Irish Constabulary fired into the crowd, killing three people. Thereafter **'Remember Mitchelstown'** became a catch phrase among Nationalists.

Mither Tap. *See under* BENNACHIE.

Mitre Ridge, the. *See under* BEINN A'BHÙIRD.

Mizen Head Presumably a sailing term; the mizen or mizzen mast on a sailing ship is the one aft of or behind the main mast; here Mizen Head is 'aft' of Brow Head.
A headland of sandstone cliffs in County Cork, some 35 km (22 miles) southwest of Bantry. It is almost the most southerly mainland point in Ireland, but BROW HEAD just to the east beats it by a head, while FASTNET ROCK is the most southerly point altogether. Nevertheless, the length of Ireland is conventionally measured from Mizen Head to FAIR HEAD, a distance of 486 km (302 miles). There is another **Mizen Head** in County Wicklow, 15 km (9 miles) south of Wicklow itself.

Mobberley 'clearing at the fortification where meetings are held', OE *mot* 'meeting' + *burh* 'fortification' (*see* BURY) + -LEY.
A village in Cheshire, about 3 km (2 miles) northeast of Knutsford.

Moccas 'moor where pigs are kept', Welsh *moch* 'pig' + *rhos* 'moorland'.
A village in Herefordshire (before 1998 in Hereford and Worcester, before 1974 in Herefordshire), on the River WYE[1], about 13 km (8 miles) from the Welsh border and 16 km (10 miles) west of Hereford.

Model County, the. A nickname for County WEXFORD, on account of the progressive farming techniques carried out here in the 19th century. The name is mostly used in the context of hurling championship matches.

Moel Hebog 'bare hill of the hawk', Welsh *moel* 'rounded or bare hill' + *hebog* 'hawk'.
A mountain (782 m / 2565 ft) in Gwynedd (formerly in Caernarvonshire), 3 km (2 miles) southwest of Beddgelert in SNOWDONIA. It is the highest point on a ridge that also includes the peaks of **Moel Lefn** and **Moel yr Ogof**. The latter means 'hill of the cave', and is so named because Owain Glyndwr hid here in 1404 – and the cave is still hard to find.

Moel Siabod *Siabod* probably a personal name.
An isolated peak (872 m / 2860 ft) in SNOWDONIA, some 10 km (6 miles) east of Snowdon. It is pronounced 'mole shabodd', and is also known as **Carnedd Moel-siabod** (*carnedd* 'cairn'). The mountain is in Conwy (formerly in Caernarvonshire, then in Gwynedd).

> I ... was soon in a wide valley on each side of which were lofty hills dotted with wood, and at the top of which stood a mighty mountain, bare and precipitous, with two paps like those of Pindus opposite Janina, but somewhat sharper. It was a region of fairy beauty and of wild grandeur. Meeting an old bleared-eyed farmer I inquired the name of the mountain and learned that it was called Moel Siabod or Shabod.
>
> George Borrow: *Wild Wales* (1862)

Moel Sych. *See under* the BERWYN MOUNTAINS.

Moelwyns, the 'white bare hills', Welsh *moel* 'bare, rounded hill' + *wyn* 'white'.

The collective name for two peaks in Snowdonia, **Moelwyn Mawr** (770 m / 2526 ft; *mawr* 'great') and **Moelwyn Bach** (711 m / 2332 ft; *bach* 'little'), some 5 km (3 miles) southwest of Blaunau Ffestioniog, in Gwynedd (formerly in Caernarvonshire). The literalness with which Welsh mountains and other features have come by their names is illustrated in the following exchange between George Borrow and a local peasant, recorded in *Wild Wales* (1862):

> 'And what is the name of yonder hill ... rising like one big lump?'
>
> 'I do not know the name of that hill, sir, further than that I have heard it called the Great Hill.'
>
> (*Mynydd Mawr*, an alternative name then in use for Moelwyn Mawr)

(An onomastician notes: Just as there is many a Mynydd Mawr in Wales, so there is a plethora of Ben Mores in Scotland.)

Moffat 'long plain', Gaelic *magh* 'plain' + *fada* 'long', referring to the river valley of Annandale (*see under* ANNAN[1]).

A town in the northeast of Dumfries and Galloway (formerly in Dumfriesshire), nestling under the hills at the head of Annandale some 30 km (about 20 miles) north of Lockerbie. Moffat is at the hub of some important routes: from here roads head northwest to Glasgow, north by the DEVIL'S BEEF TUB to Edinburgh, and northeast through the steep-sided valley of **Moffat Water** towards ST MARY'S LOCH and the Yarrow valley (*see under* YARROW WATER).

After the discovery of springs containing chalybeate (iron salts) in the 17th century, Moffat developed as a popular spa-town; in the later 19th century the Empress Eugénie of France, the wife of the deposed Napoleon III, was a frequent visitor. James Macpherson (1736–96), forger of the notorious Ossianic fragments, worked as a tutor here. John Loudon McAdam (1756–1836), the inventor of the 'tarmacadam' road surface, is buried in Moffat; and Lord Hugh Dowding (1882–1970), air chief marshal and head of Fighter Command during the Second World War, was born here.

Moffat measure. A generous measure, deriving from the fact that the town once brewed copious quantities of beer.

Mogerhanger *Moger-* origin unknown; *-hanger* 'wooded slope', OE *hangra*.

A village in Bedfordshire, about 10 km (6 miles) east of Bedford.

Moher, Cliffs of. *See* CLIFFS OF MOHER.

Moidart 'Mundi's fjord', OScand personal name + Gaelic *-art* from OScand *fjorthr* 'fjord', *compare* KNOYDART.

An area of the Western HIGHLANDS, bounded by Morar on the north (*see under* LOCH MORAR) and LOCH SHIEL and

SUNART on the south. It is in Highland (formerly in Inverness-shire). It takes its name from **Loch Moidart**, a sea loch from which the water empties at low tide, leaving sand. At the head of the loch is the little settlement of **Kinlochmoidart**, at the foot of **Glen Moidart**. A road was constructed along the previously remote western shore of Moidart in the 1960s.

Seven Men of Moidart, the. The seven men who accompanied Bonnie Prince Charlie from France when he landed in Scotland in 1745. His first landing on the mainland was actually a little to the north, in ARISAIG, but he then waited at Kinlochmoidart for the clans to gather, then travelled through Moidart on his way to GLENFINNAN, where he raised his standard. The seven men have been described by one historian as 'a motley entourage of adventurers', but nevertheless entered Jacobite legend, and in the early 19th century a row of seven beech trees known as the Seven Men of Moidart were planted on the north side of Loch Moidart. Only five survive, and they are none too well.

Móin Alúine. The Irish name for the BOG OF ALLEN.

Móin Rátha. The Irish name for MOUNTRATH.

Móinteach Mílic. The Irish name for MOUNTMELLICK.

Moira[1] Irish *Maigh Rath* 'plain of the ring forts' (*see* RATH).

A town in County Down, 25 km (16 miles) southwest of Belfast. It gave its name, via the Earl of Moira, to the village of MOIRA[2] in Leicestershire.

Battle of Moira or **Mag Roth** (24 June 637). A battle between Domnall II, the high king of Ireland, and the Dalriadans of Ulster and their allies from Argyll (Scottish DALRIADA). King Sweeney or Suibhne of Dalriada was driven mad at the scale of the bloodshed, and thereafter wandered Ireland singing sad songs and woeful stories:

> Over the plain of Moyra
> Under the heels of foemen
> I saw my people broken
> As flax is scutched by women.
>
> Anon.: 'The Sweetness of Nature', a song of the mad King Sweeney from a 12th-century romance, translated by Frank O'Connor

Moira[2] Named in honour of the Earl of *Moira*, whose title was taken from MOIRA[1].

A village in Leicestershire, about 5 km (3 miles) west of Ashby-de-la-Zouch. Coal was discovered here at the end of the 18th century, on land owned by the 2nd Earl of Moira (1754–1826), and the village grew up in the early part of the 19th century around the pits dug to exploit it.

Molash 'speech or assembly ash-tree', OE *mal* 'speech, legal assembly' + *œsc* 'ash-tree'.

A village in Kent, on the NORTH DOWNS, about 13 km (8 miles) southwest of Canterbury.

Mold 'high hill', a contraction of Norman French *mont* 'hill' + *hault* 'high'.

A market town and administrative seat of Flintshire (and formerly the administrative seat of Clwyd), 17 km (11 miles) west of Chester. Its Welsh name is **Yr Wyddgrung** ('the burial mound', *yr* 'the' + *gwydd* 'tomb', 'cairn' + *crug* 'mound' (*see* CREECH, CROOK)). The Normans built a castle here in the 12th century, round which the town grew. Much more recently, the town's name has had resonance because of its major resident theatre company, Clwyd Theatr Cymru (*see under* CLWYD²).

Mold was the birthplace of John Blackwell ('Alun'; 1797–1840), 'the father of the modern Welsh secular lyric'; and of Daniel Owen (1836–95), 'the father the Welsh novel'.

Mole¹ A back-formation from MOLESEY. (The notion that the river got its name because it occasionally disappears underground is ingenious but completely unfounded.) Its former name was *Emel* – *see* ELMBRIDGE.

A river in Surrey and Sussex, which rises to the northeast of CRAWLEY and flows 48 km (30 miles) northwards through DORKING, LEATHERHEAD and THAMES DITTON to join the River THAMES¹ at East Molesey (*see under* MOLESEY).

Its valley has given the name **Mole Valley** to an administrative district of West Surrey (main towns, Dorking and Leatherhead). It enjoyed some limited temporary celebrity in the 1980s thanks to Mole Valley Valves, the employer of the irritating Martin Bryce (played by Richard Briers) in the BBC television sitcom *Ever Decreasing Circles* (1984–9).

Mole² A back-formation from *Molton* (its earlier name was *Nymet* – *see* GEORGE NYMPTON).

A river in Devon and Somerset, which rises on EXMOOR and flows 26 km (16 miles) southwestwards via SOUTH MOLTON to join the River TAW near KING'S NYMPTON.

Molehill Green The early form *Moringesgrene* suggests 'marsh green', OE *moring* 'marshland' with *grene* 'green, village green', later changed by folk-etymology to *Molehill Green*.

A village in Essex, about 8 km (5 miles) northeast of Bishop's Stortford.

Molesey 'Mul's island or dry ground in a marsh', OE *Mules* possessive form of male personal name *Mul* + *eg* (*see* -EY, -EA).

A town in Surrey, on the south bank of the River THAMES¹, in the borough of ELMBRIDGE, to the west of Kingston and to the east of Sunbury. It is divided into **East Molesey** (the larger portion, virtually opposite HAMPTON COURT) and **West Molesey**. The River MOLE¹ flows into the Thames at East Molesey.

Molesworth 'Mul's enclosure', OE *Mules* possessive form of male personal name *Mul* + *worth* (*see* -WORTH, WORTHY, -WARDINE).

A village in Cambridgeshire (before 1974 in Huntingdon and Peterborough), about 16 km (10 miles) west of Huntingdon. Its name was inherited by the anarchic schoolboy character Nigel Molesworth, invented by Geoffrey Willans and Ronald Searle, who appeared in such classics as *Down with Skool!* (1953) and *How to be Topp* (1954).

Mona. The Latin name for ANGLESEY.

Monach Islands Gaelic *monach* 'monk'.

A group of small islands, also called **Heisker** (OScand, 'bright skerry'), some 12 km (7.5 miles) across the **Sound of Monach** from the west coast of North Uist, Western Isles (formerly in Inverness-shire). It was once possible to cross on foot to North Uist at low tide, until a storm shifted the sands in the 16th century. There are two main islands, **Ceann Ear** (Gaelic 'east head') and **Ceann Iar** ('west head').

In the Middle Ages there was a convent on Ceann Ear, and a monastery on the tiny western island of **Shillay** where the monks maintained a light for mariners. A lighthouse was built on Shillay in 1864, but the keepers were withdrawn in 1942. From 1732 to 1734 Lady Grange was held prisoner on the Monachs (*see under* ST KILDA).

The people of the Monachs lived mostly by fishing, and there are a number of Gaelic boat songs that originated on the islands. For example, the following lines end a song sung by Rachel, daughter of Alexander, in the 1750s:

> So, little laddie, sing your song;
> Though many waves will strike her planking;
> The next tack we take with her,
> Puts Currachag to our windward.
>
> (Currachag is a dangerous off-shore rock.)
>
> *O hi u i ho u bho*
> *Let's raise a tune and sing a boat song;*
> *Trim the lines of the boat*
> *That's coming today from Heisgeir;*
> *O hi u i ho u bho.*

The last of the permanent inhabitants left the islands in 1931.

Monadhliath Mountains 'grey mountain', Gaelic *monadh* 'mountain, moorland' + *liath* 'grey'; the name contrasts with the Monadh Ruadh ('red mountains') – the granite Cairngorms across the Spey.

A great swathe of dull, rounded mountains lumbering along between the GREAT GLEN and the upper SPEY valley, in Highland (formerly in Inverness-shire). The River FINDHORN rises here. There are a number of Munros, the highest of which is Carn Dearg (945 m / 3100 ft).

Monaghan Irish *Muineachán* 'place of thickets'.

The county town of County Monaghan, 20 km (12 miles) southwest of Armagh. It is also the cathedral town of the Catholic diocese of CLOGHER, and **Monaghan Cathedral**

(St Macartan's) is a noted example of 19th-century Gothic Revival style.

Monaghan was the birthplace of the Young Ireland leader Charles Gavan Duffy (1816–1903), founder of *The Nation*, who was later prime minister of Victoria, Australia.

Monaghan, County. A county in the north of the Republic of Ireland, bordering Northern Ireland. It is part of the traditional province of Ulster, and is bounded on the southeast by Louth, on the south by Meath and Cavan, on the west by Fermanagh, on the north by Tyrone, and on the northeast by Armagh. The county town is MONAGHAN, and other towns include CLONES. The land is generally low, rolling and agricultural, and is celebrated in a bathetic poem entitled 'Monaghan' by Sir Shane Leslie (1885–1971):

> Monaghan, mother of a thousand
> Little moulded hills,
> Set about with little rivers
> Chained to little mills …
>
> Silvered o'er with sunshine, or by
> Night with shimmering fog,
> Where thy sloping cornland meets
> Beauteous fields of bog.

An altogether more robust response to the place is to be had from an altogether more robust poet:

> O stony grey soil of Monaghan
> The laugh from my love you thieved;
> You took the gay child of my passion
> And gave me your clod-conceived.
>
> Patrick Kavanagh: 'Stony Grey Soil', from *A Soul for Sale* (1947). (Kavanagh was born in Inniskeen, County Monaghan.)

Monasterboice Irish *Mainistir Bhuithe* 'monastery of St Buite'. An ancient monastic site in County Louth, 10 km (6 miles) northwest of Drogheda, said to have been founded by St Buite in the 5th century. There are some notable early crosses – including the elaborately carved, 5-m (17-ft) high Muireadach's Cross, and the even higher 6.5-m (21-ft) West Cross – and the highest (albeit topless) round tower in Ireland (33 m / 108 ft).

Monasterevin Irish *Mainistir Eimhín* 'monastery of St Eimhín' (*fl.*5th century; he was related to the kings of Munster). A village in County Kildare, 10 km (6 miles) west of Kildare itself. The poet Gerard Manley Hopkins (1844–89) lived here for a while, as did the celebrated tenor John McCormack (1884–1945), the latter in the 18th-century Gothic Moore Abbey. In 1975 the Republican kidnappers of the Dutch industrialist Tiede Herrema were besieged by the Gardaí for 21 days in a house in Monasterevin, until Herrema was released unharmed.

Angels of Monasterevin. The nickname of the 700 Irishmen who, with the support of the Catholic Church, went to Spain to fight for Franco's Nationalists in the Spanish Civil War (1936–9). They were led by General Eoin O'Duffy, head of the quasi-fascist Blueshirt movement in Ireland, and in Spain became part of the XV Bandera Irlandesa del Tercio of the Spanish Foreign Legion.

Monavullagh Mountains Irish *Móin an Mhullaigh* 'bog of the summit'. A range of mountains in County Waterford, comprising a southern extension of the COMERAGH MOUNTAINS. The highest point is Seefin (725 m / 2378 ft).

Moniaive Obscure, but the first element seems to be Gaelic *mòine* 'moor'. A village 11 km (7 miles) southeast of Thornhill on the New Galloway road. It was formerly in Dumfriesshire and is now in Dumfries and Galloway. It was the birthplace of James Renwick (1662–88), leader of the extreme 'Renwickite' faction, who was the last of the prominent Covenanters to be martyred. Near Moniaive is MAXWELTON HOUSE, home of 'Bonnie' Annie Laurie.

Monifieth 'peat bog', Gaelic *mòine* 'peat, peat bed, moss' + *féithe* 'bog'. A resort and residential town in Angus (formerly in Tayside), on the north shore of the Firth of TAY, 10 km (6 miles) east of Dundee.

Monken Hadley 'monks' Hadley', *Monken* possessive plural form of ME *monk* 'of the monks' (referring to its ownership in the Middle Ages by Walden Abbey); *Hadley* 'heath or heather clearing' (*see* HADLEIGH[1]). A northern suburb of London, in the borough of BARNET (before 1889 in Middlesex, before 1965 in Hertfordshire). It is the highest point on the GREAT NORTH ROAD between London and York. The Battle of Barnet (*see under* BARNET) was fought here.

Monklands The land belonging to the monks of Newbattle Abbey, Dalkeith, from the 12th century. A former district (1975–96) of the former Strathclyde region, in Scotland's Central Belt. The administrative headquarters were at COATBRIDGE, and the other main town was AIRDRIE. The area in now in North Lanarkshire.

Monkokehampton Originally (in Anglo-Latin) *Monacochamentona* 'monks' estate on the River Okement' (referring to its ownership in the Middle Ages by Glastonbury Abbey), OE *munuc* 'monk' + an OCelt river name perhaps meaning 'swift stream' + -TON (*see* OKEHAMPTON). A village in Devon, on the River OKEMENT (a tributary of the TORRIDGE[1]), to the north of Dartmoor, about 16 km (10 miles) southeast of Torrington and 11 km (7 miles) north of Okehampton.

Monkshaven. A fictional version of WHITBY in Elizabeth Gaskell's novel *Sylvia's Lovers* (1863).

Monksilver Originally *Silver*, probably from an old river name based on OE *seolfor* 'silver', hence 'clear or bright stream'; the prefix *Monk-*, from OE *munuc* 'monk', reflects ownership in the Middle Ages by Goldcliff Priory.

A village in Somerset, in the Brendon Hills (*see under* BRENDON), about 13 km (8 miles) southeast of Minehead.

Monk Soham *Monk* denoting ownership in the Middle Ages by the Abbey of Bury St Edmunds; *Soham* 'homestead by a pool', OE *sœ* or *sa* 'sea, lake, pool' + HAM.

A village in Suffolk, about 8 km (5 miles) west of Framlingham.

Monkton Deverill *Monkton* 'farmstead of the monks', OE *munuc* 'monk' + -TON; *Deverill see* BRIXTON DEVERILL.

A village in Wiltshire, on the River WYLYE[1], on the West Wiltshire Downs, about 8 km (5 miles) southwest of Warminster.

See also KINGSTON DEVERILL.

Monkwearmouth. *See under* SUNDERLAND *and* WEAR.

Monmouth 'mouth of the River Mynwy (or MONNOW)', Welsh river name + OE *mutha* 'mouth'; *Munwi Mutha* (11th century).

A market town in Monmouthshire (formerly in Gwent), at the confluence of the Rivers WYE[1] and MONNOW (Mynwy) near the English border, some 33 km (20 miles) west of Gloucester. Its Welsh name is **Trefynwy** ('settlement on the River Mynwy'). Monmouth is now most commonly pronounced 'monn-məth', although 'munn-məth' still survives among the landed and would-be uncommon. It was the county town of the pre-1974 county of Monmouthshire, and the diocese of Monmouth was created in 1921 (the pro-cathedral is actually in Newport). There are the remains of a 12th-century castle, where Henry V was born in 1388 – hence the name of Agincourt Square in the centre of the town. In Shakespeare's *Henry V* Fluellen calls Henry **'Harry of Monmouth'**, and compares his birthplace with that of 'Alexander the Pig [Great]':

> There is a river in Macedon; and there is also moreover a river in Monmouth; it is call'd Wye at Monmouth, but it is out of my prains what is the name of the other river; but 'tis all one, 'tis alike as my fingers is to my fingers, and there is salmons in both.
>
> William Shakespeare: *Henry V* (1599), IV.vii

The town was also the birthplace of Charles Rolls (1877–1910), co-founder of Rolls-Royce. There are towns called Monmouth in the USA (Illinois and New Jersey).

Duke of Monmouth. James Scott, 1st Duke of Monmouth (1649–85), the illegitimate son of Charles II and his mistress Lucy Walter (a Welsh person). A Protestant, he led an unsuccessful rebellion – **Monmouth's Rebellion** – in 1685 against his Catholic uncle, James II, and was executed. He has given his name to many a public house.

Geoffrey of Monmouth (*c.*1100–54). A chronicler of the early history of Britain, including the semi-legendary stories of King Arthur. It is possible that he was a monk at the medieval priory at Monmouth.

Monmouth cap. A type of flat, round cap or stocking cap, once worn by soldiers and sailors. They are first mentioned in *Henry V*, when Fluellen is recalling the Welsh role in the Black Prince's victory at Poitiers in 1356:

> If your Majesty is remember'd of it, the Welshmen did good service in a garden where leeks did grow, wearing leeks in their Monmouth caps …
>
> William Shakespeare: *Henry V* (1599), IV.vii

They appear to have gone out of fashion in the 18th century.

Monmouth cock. A jaunty upward tilt of the hat favoured by soldiers in the late 17th century, and probably named after the **Duke of Monmouth** (*see above*).

Monmouth's Rebellion. That led by the **Duke of Monmouth** in 1685 (*see above*).

Monmouth Street. A street in London's Soho, once noted for its second-hand clothes shops; hence the expression **Monmouth Street finery** for tawdry, pretentious clothes.

Monmouthshire From MONMOUTH + SHIRE.

A former county and current unitary authority of southeast Wales. Its Welsh name is **Trefynwy**, also the Welsh name of Monmouth (*see* MONMOUTH for the etymology). The pre-1974 county was bordered to the east by Gloucestershire (the River WYE[1] forming part of the border), to the north by Herefordshire and Brecknockshire, to the west by Glamorgan and to the south by the Bristol Channel. The county town was Monmouth. In 1974 the county was absorbed into Gwent, but in 1996 became a unitary authority. The administrative seat is at CWMBRAN (in the neighbouring authority of Torfaen), and other towns include CHEPSTOW, CALDICOT and ABERGAVENNY. Monmouthshire is now bordered to the west by Powys and Torfaen.

Pre-Roman Monmouthshire was part of the territory of the Silures (*see* SILURIA). The impact of the Romans on the county is evident in the remains of the legionary fortress at CAERLEON and the town of CAERWENT. After the Romans left, the area was subsumed first into the kingdom of GWENT, then into the kingdom of DEHEUBARTH. The Normans colonized the region and divided it up into marcher lordships (*see* the MARCHES) to defend it from Welsh incursions. With the advent of the (Welsh) Tudor dynasty, the area was incorporated into England as the new county of Monmouthshire, the Act of Union of 1536 creating the county out of 'divers Lordships Marchers within the said Country or Dominion of Wales'. Later in the Tudor period it was brought under the jurisdiction of the courts of Westminster in certain matters, while separate courts were provided for the rest of Wales. It has been included in Wales since 1964, when the description **Wales and Monmouthshire** was dropped.

Monmouthshire Regiment, the. A volunteer regiment formed as the Monmouthshire Volunteer Rifle Corps in 1859. It became the Monmouthshire Regiment in 1908, and part of the Royal Regiment of Wales in 1971.

Monnow From the Welsh name *Mynwy*, possibly meaning 'fast-flowing'.

A river of western England and southeast Wales, approximately 50 km (31 miles) long. Its Welsh name is **Mynwy**. The Monnow rises on the eastern slopes of **Hay Bluff** (*see under* HAY-ON-WYE), on the Herefordshire flanks of the BLACK MOUNTAINS. For a while it forms the border between England and Wales, before joining the WYE[1] at MONMOUTH (to which it gives its name). At Monmouth , the town and suburb of **Overmonnow** are linked across the river by the 13th-century **Monnow Bridge**, the only surviving fortified bridge in Britain where the gate tower stands on the actual bridge. This tower, called the **Monnow Gate**, dates from the early 14th century.

Mons Badonicus. *See* MOUNT BADON.

Mons Graupius Latin *mons* 'hill', but *Graupius* remains obscure. The name is the origin of that of the GRAMPIAN MOUNTAINS.

A battle site somewhere north of the Tay in which the Romans under Agricola defeated the Caledonians (*see under* CALEDONIA) in AD 84, breaking resistance in the HIGHLANDS and gaining control of the LOWLANDS. The battle is mentioned by Tacitus, but no definite location has been established – some believe it was fought near INVERURIE in Aberdeenshire. Tacitus gives Calgacus, the native chief, a rousing speech before the battle, including this famous condemnation of Roman imperialism:

> *Solitudinem faciunt pacem appellan.*
>
> (They make a wilderness and call it peace)
>
> Tacitus: *Agricola*, chapter 30

Montacute 'pointed hill', OFr *mont* 'hill' + *aigu* 'pointed'.

A village in Somerset, about 5 km (3 miles) west of Yeovil. The nearby **Montacute House** is an Elizabethan mansion, built in 1590 from the locally quarried golden Ham stone of which most of the village's humbler houses are also made. It contains a large Long Gallery, and featured in Ang Lee's film adaptation (1995) of Jane Austen's *Sense and Sensibility* and also in Shekhar Kapur's *Elizabeth* (1998). The National Trust now administers it.

Montervary. An alternative name for SHEEP'S HEAD, County Cork.

Montgomery Named by Roger de Montgomery, 1st Earl of Shrewsbury, who built the first castle here in the late 11th

century, after his castle of Montgommery [*sic*] in Normandy (French *mont* 'mountain' + Germanic personal name *Gumaric*).

A small market town in Powys (formerly in Montgomeryshire, of which it was the county town) close to the English border, 30 km (19 miles) southwest of Shrewsbury. It was formerly pronounced 'munt-gummәry', but the 'munt-' has been largely displaced by 'mont-'. Its Welsh name is **Trefaldwyn**, meaning 'settlement (*tref*) of Baldwin'; Baldwin de Bollers acquired the first castle in 1102, and the new castle built by Henry III in 1223 was named after this Baldwin; little of this second castle survives.

Edward Herbert, 1st Lord Herbert of Cherbury (1583–1648), the philosopher and diplomat, spent part of his life in Montgomery, and surrendered the castle to the Parliamentarians in 1644 in return for his library, which had been requisitioned. (The castle was subsequently dismantled.) Cherbury's brother, the poet George Herbert (1593–1633), was born in the castle. John Donne was a friend of their mother, and visited the castle in 1613, on the way composing his meditation, 'Good Friday, 1613, Riding Westward'. He also wrote (possibly on an earlier visit) 'The Primrose, being at Montgomery Castle upon the hill, on which it is situate'.

In the USA there is a city called Montgomery (Alabama) and a small town of that name (Vermont).

Montgomery Canal. A canal extending from the Llangollen Canal (*see under* LLANGOLLEN) east of Oswestry southwestwards through Welshpool to Newtown. It was constructed in three stages, in 1796, 1797 and 1821.

Treaty of Montgomery (25 September 1267). An agreement by which Henry III recognized the right of Llywelyn ap Gruffydd of Gwynedd to bear the title 'Prince of Wales' (which he had assumed in 1258), and to receive the fealty and homage of the Welsh lords; *see* Prince of Wales *under* WALES.

Montgomeryshire From MONTGOMERY + SHIRE.

A former county of eastern Wales, created in 1536 when Henry VIII took over the Marcher lordships in the area (*see under* MARCHES). In Welsh it is **Sir Drefaldwyn** ('shire of Trefaldwyn', the latter being the Welsh name for the town of MONTGOMERY) or sometimes **Maldwyn** (from an erroneous belief that *-faldwyn* derived from this supposed personal name). The county town was Montgomery, and other towns included LLANIDLOES, NEWTOWN[1] and WELSHPOOL. It was bordered by Denbighshire to the north, Merioneth to the northwest, Cardiganshire to the southwest, Radnorshire to the south, and Shropshire to the east. In 1974 it became a district of Powys, but the district disappeared in 1996 when Powys became a unitary authority.

> In passing Montgomery-shire, we were so tired with rocks and mountains, that we wished heartily we had kept

close to the sea shore … The River Severn is the only
beauty of this county …

> Daniel Defoe: *A Tour Through the Whole Island of Great Britain*
> (1724–6)

Monto From *Montgomery* Street (now Foley Street).

The former nickname of an area of Dublin to the east of
O'CONNELL STREET, once notorious for its ladies of the
night, the area being close to British Army barracks and
the docks. The main focus for vice was not Montgomery
Street itself, but rather Mecklenburgh Street Lower (now
Railway Street) and the lanes round about it (such as Little
Martin's Lane, interestingly renamed Beaver Street). Among
Monto's more illustrious clients was the future Edward VII,
and the illegitimate consequences of such liaisons were
known as **Monto Babies**. The Legion of Mary largely did
for Monto in the 1920s, leaving in its wake reform schools
and Magdalene laundries.

> When the Czar of Rooshia, and the King of Prooshia
> Landed in the Phoenix in a big balloon,
> They asked the Garda band to play 'The Wearin' o' the
> Green'
> But the buggers in the depot didn't know the tune,
> So they both went up to Monto, Monto, Monto …
>
> Anon.: song 'Take Me Up to Monto' (the reference is to
> Dublin's Phoenix Park)

Montrose 'moor of the promontory', Gaelic *monadh*
'moorland' + *ros* 'promontory'.

A royal BURGH, resort and port in Angus (in Tayside region
from 1975 to 1996), on the North Sea coast 18 km (11
miles) north of Arbroath. It is situated at the mouth of the
South Esk (*see under* ESK[1]), behind which is the large tidal
lagoon of the **Montrose Basin**. It was at Montrose that John
(de) Balliol surrendered the kingdom of Scotland to Edward
I of England in 1296, and from here that the Old Pretender
left Scotland for ever (4 February 1716), following his brief
visit during the doomed 1715 Jacobite Rebellion. The
hamlet of **Old Montrose** – the birthplace of the **Marquess of
Montrose** (*see below*) – is on the inner side of the basin. The
poet Hugh MacDiarmid (C.M. Grieve) worked as a journalist
in Montrose in the 1920s:

> An in the toon that I belang tae
> – What tho'ts Montrose or Nazareth? –
> Helplessly the folk continue
> To lead their livin' death! …
>
> Hugh MacDiarmid: *A Drunk Man Looks at the Thistle* (1926)

Montrose was the birthplace of Robert Brown (1773–
1858), the botanist who first described Brownian motion.
There are towns called Montrose in the USA (Colorado,
New York, Pennsylvania); the name of the Colorado
Montrose was inspired by Sir Walter Scott's novel *A Legend
of Montrose* (*see below*).

Montrose FC, founded in 1879 and nicknamed the
Gable Endies, plays at Links Park.

Duke of Montrose. Scots rhyming slang for 'nose'.

Marquess of Montrose, the. James Graham, 5th Earl and
1st Marquess of Montrose (1612–50), the celebrated Scottish
soldier. Montrose had, in 1637, signed the Covenant by
which he swore to defend the Presbyterian religion against
Charles I's attempt to impose episcopacy on Scotland.
However, when the Scottish Covenanters invaded England
in 1644 during the Civil Wars on the side of Parliament,
Montrose's loyalty to the king led him to raise an army of
Highlanders on his behalf. Montrose went on to win a
succession of brilliant victories in that year against the anti-
Royalist armies led by Archibald Campbell, 1st Marquess
of Argyll. It is this campaign that provides the setting for
Sir Walter Scott's novel *A Legend of Montrose* (1819). Later
the tide of war turned, and Montrose was forced to flee
abroad. He returned to Scotland on behalf of the exiled
Charles II in 1650 with only 1200 men. He was defeated
at CARBISDALE in Sutherland, betrayed, and hanged in
Edinburgh.

> He either fears his fate too much,
>   Or his deserts are small,
> That dare not put it to the touch,
>   To win or lose it all.
>
> James Graham, Marquess of Montrose: 'My Dear and Only
> Love'

Mooncoin. *See under* SUIR.

Moonfleet. A fictionalized version of the village of FLEET[2]
in Dorset, which serves as a setting for J. Meade Falkner's
eponymous novel (1898), a tale of smuggling along the
Dorset coast. The nomenclature was no doubt intended to
suggest romantic moonlight as a backdrop to nocturnal
smuggling. The film *Moonfleet* by Fritz Lang (1955) was
based on Falkner's novel.

Moor, the. A colloquial abbreviation of DARTMOOR, used
particularly in the context of the prison.

Moorfields 'fields in marshy ground', ME *moor* 'marshy
ground' + *fields* (*see* FIELD).

Originally an area of marshy ground outside the northern
wall of the City of London, approximately in the area of
the modern BARBICAN (the first known named reference
to it dates from the mid-16th century). It was drained
in 1527, and thereafter it was used for a variety of recreational pursuits (e.g. archery), and also as an area for cloth-
drying. It began to be built over after the Great Fire of
London.

Its name was subsequently applied to a road in the
vicinity (EC2), which runs north–south parallel to
MOORGATE.

A nonsense nursery rhyme probably dating from the
17th century begins:

As I was walking o'er little Moorfields,
I saw St Paul's a-running on wheels,
With a fee, fo, fum.

Moorfields Eye Hospital. A hospital for the treatment of the eyes, situated in the CITY ROAD in the City of London (EC1). It was founded in 1805 under the name of the London Dispensary for the Relief of the Poor Afflicted with Diseases of the Eye and Ear. In the 1820s it moved to new premises in Moorfields, charitably shortening its name to the Royal London Ophthalmic Hospital. Because of its location it was generally known as 'Moorfields Hospital', but this did not become its official name until 1956. It moved to its present site in 1899.

Moorfoot Hills 'moor clearing', OScand *morr* 'moor, rough land' + *thveit* 'clearing', with OE *hyll*.

A line of gently rounded hills on the border between Midlothian and Scottish Borders, representing the first ramparts of the SOUTHERN UPLANDS in these parts. The highest point (point hardly being the correct word) is Blackhope Scar (651 m / 2135 ft).

Moorgate 'gate to the marshy ground' (*see* MOORFIELDS), ME *moor* 'marshy ground' + *gate*.

Originally a postern gate in the city wall of London leading to an area of marshy ground to the north of the city (*see* MOORFIELDS). It was built in 1415.

The gate was demolished in 1762, but its name was revived in the 1840s for a new road built in the City (EC2), running north–south from Finsbury Circus (*see under* FINSBURY) to the Bank of England (*see under* BANK) and designed to give better access to the new **London Bridge**.

Moorgate Underground station, on the Circle, Metropolitan and Northern lines, was opened in 1865 (originally under the name 'Moorgate Street'). Forty-three people were killed in a train crash here in 1975. Moorgate is also the southern terminus of the West Anglia Great Northern line serving suburban Hertfordshire.

Moor of Rannoch. Another name for Rannoch Moor (*see under* RANNOCH).

Moor Park¹ *Moor* 'marshy land', OE *mor*; *Park* ModE.

An estate in Hertfordshire, about 5 km (3 miles) southeast of Rickmansworth. Its fine classical mansion, built around 1727 for Lord Elbury, is now the club-house for Moor Park Golf Club, whose course has hosted many important competitions. Merchant Taylors' School is nearby, having moved from Charterhouse Square, London in 1933.

Moor Park 'Underground' station, on the Metropolitan line, opened in 1910. It was originally called Sandy Lodge; the present name was introduced in 1950.

Moor Park² Originally *Moorhouse* 'house on the moorland', OE *mor* 'wasteland, moorland' + *hus* 'house'; it was renamed Moor Park in the 18th century.

A house on the River WEY¹ in Surrey, about 3 km (2 miles) from FARNHAM. In the late 17th century it was the home of the diplomat Sir William Temple. The writer Jonathan Swift was a member of his household: here he first met Esther Johnson, who became his muse 'Stella', and wrote *A Tale of a Tub* (1704) and *The Battle of the Books* (1704).

Morangie 'extensive meadows', Gaelic *mòr* 'big' + *innse* 'water meadows' (*see* INIS).

A small settlement just northwest of Tain, Easter Ross, Highland. It is dominated by the distillery producing **Glenmorangie** single malt whisky. To the west is **Morangie Forest**.

Morar. *See under* LOCH MORAR.

Moray 'sea settlement', OCelt *mori-tref* (*see* TRE-).

An old kingdom, former county and current unitary authority in northeast Scotland. It is pronounced 'murry', and was formerly sometimes spelt **Murray**. An inhabitant of Moray is called a **Morave**.

The **Kingdom of Moray** – stretching from the SPEY in the east to the west coast, and from the River OYKEL in the north to the GRAMPIANS in the south – was established by an alliance of Scots and Norsemen in the 9th century, who took the area from the Picts. Macbeth was ruler of Moray and took over the Scottish throne in 1040 after killing Duncan I; in the version of *Macbeth* by Andrew of Wyntoun (*c*.1350–*c*.1425), he overhears the three weird sisters:

The first he herd say gangand by:
'Lo, yonder the thayne of Crumbaghty!'
The tother sister said agane:
'Off Murray yonder I see the thayne.'
The third said: Yonder I se the king.'

(*Crumbaghty*, 'Cromarty')

Although Moray had lost its identity as a separate kingdom by the end of the 11th century, the Scottish kings did not really manage to subdue the area until the 13th century.

The county of Moray (or **Morayshire**), absorbed into GRAMPIAN region in 1975, was bounded on the west by Nairnshire, on the north by the MORAY FIRTH (an inlet of the North Sea), to the east by Banffshire and to the south by Inverness-shire. The county town was ELGIN. The unitary authority of Moray (larger than the old county) was created in 1996, with Elgin as its administrative centre; other towns include FORRES, BUCKIE and LOSSIEMOUTH. It is bounded to the west by Highland, to the north by the North Sea, and to the east and south by Aberdeenshire. The CAIRNGORM MOUNTAINS in the south gradually slope down to the coastal lowlands in the north, where much barley is grown for the many local whisky distilleries. The River Spey flow through Moray to the sea.

Murray is, indeed, a pleasant country, the soil fruitful, watered with fine rivers, and full of good towns, but especially of gentlemen's seats, more and more remarkable than could, indeed, be expected by a stranger in so remote a part of the country.

Daniel Defoe: *A Tour Through the Whole Island of Great Britain* (1724–6)

'Bonnie Earl of Moray, The'. A well-known ballad about James Moray (or Murray), the 2nd Earl of Moray, brutally killed at Donibristle, Fife, in 1592. It is possible that his assassins resented the fact that he was a favourite of Anne, queen consort of James VI.

> Ye Highlands and ye Lawlands,
> O where hae ye been?
> They hae slain the Earl of Murray,
> And hae laid him on the green.
>
> He was a braw gallant,
> And he rid at the ring;
> And the bonny Earl of Moray,
> O he might hae been a king!
>
> O lang will his Lady
> Look owre the Castle Downe,
> Ere she see the Earl of Moray
> Come sounding through the town!

Laich of Moray. A coastal plain in the north of Moray, whose sandy loam is ideal for the growing of vegetables such as carrots, turnips, leeks and potatoes -- many of which find their way into the soups created locally by Baxters at FOCHABERS.

Morayshire apple crumble. A crumble with hazlenuts and oatmeal in the topping, underneath which are to be found apples cooked with cloves.

Regent Moray. James Stuart, 1st Earl of Moray (1531–70), an illegitimate son of James V and one of the leaders of the Reformation in Scotland. He became regent of Scotland in 1567, following the deposition of his half-sister Mary Queen of Scots, and kept that position until his assassination at the hands of Mary's supporters. An earlier Regent Moray was Thomas Randolph, 1st Earl of Moray (d.1332), a nephew of Robert the Bruce, in whose cause he fought and after whose death he became regent (1329–32) during the minority of David II.

Moray Firth. A long inlet of the North Sea in northeast Scotland, with Easter Ross (*see under* ROSS AND CROMARTY) and the BLACK ISLE to the north, and MORAY and part of Highland to the south. East of Inverness it becomes the BEAULY Firth. The south shore has many sandy beaches, and the area has a surprising reputation as one of the sunnier spots in Britain. It was in the Moray Firth that scientists first came across evidence of un-PC behaviour on the part of dolphins, who were found to have been bullying their smaller brethren, the porpoises. Dolphin-lovers around the world promptly responded that human activity (such as low-flying jets from RAF LOSSIEMOUTH and

North-Sea-oil shenanigans) must be to blame for this dysfunctionality, despite the positive vibes so obviously emanating from the FINDHORN Community.

Morchard Bishop *Morchard* 'great wood or forest', OCelt *mor* 'great' + CED; *Bishop* denoting its ownership by the Bishop of Exeter in the early Middle Ages.

A village in Devon, to the northeast of Dartmoor, and about 11 km (7 miles) northwest of Crediton.

Morda From the River *Morda*, 'big Taf', Welsh *mor* 'great, big' + river name *Taf*.

A village in Shropshire, on the River Morda, about 1.5 km (1 mile) southwest of Oswestry.

Morden 'hill in marshland' (referring to rising ground between the valleys of the Beverley Brook and the River WANDLE), OE *mor* 'marshland' + *dun* (*see* DOWN, -DON).

A southwestern dormitory suburb of London (before 1965 in Surrey), in the borough of MERTON, to the east of New Malden and to the west of Mitcham. The arrival of the Northern line (of which it is the southern terminus) in 1926 was the catalyst for the absorption of this formerly rural village into bourgeois commuterland:

> I ... had enough to put down on a bungalow in Morden. Do you know South London at all? ... It's a very nice place where we live: doctors and that live there, well-to-do people. It's so convenient to London, you see.
>
> Len Deighton: *Declarations of War* (1971)

Ameliorating this somewhat is the 50-ha (125-acre) **Morden Hall Park**, described by its National Trust owners as an 'oasis in the heart of suburbia', whose grounds feature hay meadows, a rose garden and craft workshops, and through which the River Wandle twists its way.

More 'marsh', OE *mor*.

A village in Shropshire, to the west of the LONG MYND, about 27 km (17 miles) southwest of Shrewsbury. Its near neighbours to the north are, appropriately in view of its name, The Bog and The Marsh.

Morebath 'bathing place in marshy ground', OE *mor* 'marsh' + *bæth* 'bath'.

A village in Devon, to the southeast of Exmoor, about 13 km (8 miles) north of Tiverton.

Morecambe An OCelt name recorded as *Morikambe* c.AD 150, and meaning 'curved inlet', referring to the estuary of the LUNE[1], and revived for the name of the town in 1889; *see also* MORICAMBE.

A seaside resort in Lancashire, 5 km (3 miles) northwest of Lancaster and contiguous with HEYSHAM to the south. At the end of the late 18th century people began to visit the seaside villages here, which expanded with the coming of the railway: it brought thousands of holidaymakers from Lancashire mill towns (hence the nickname **Bradford by the Sea**) and provided a means of trading the area's shrimps and mussels. As the villages developed into a town, it adopted the name of Morecambe (1889), and has since been a thoroughly bucket-and-spade, kiss-me-quick kind of place. However, its attempt to rival BLACKPOOL in the early 1990s by erecting a theme park called Blobbyland failed miserably. As one *Mitteleuropäische* visitor has commented, the town has 'all the virtues of Buda, and all the vices of Pest'.

Morecambe (its inhabitants are **Sandgrown'uns**) was the home town of the comedian John Eric Bartholomew (1926–84), who, when he embarked upon his partnership with Ernie Wise, adopted the stage name Eric Morecambe. The town has reciprocated the gesture by erecting a statue to the great man, with leg uplifted in the duo's trademark 'Give Me Sunshine' dance. Morecambe was also the birthplace of the actress Thora Hird (1911–2003).

The town overlooks **Morecambe Bay**, a 15-km (9-mile) wide inlet of the Irish Sea between the FURNESS peninsula of Cumbria and the northwest coast of Lancashire. At low tide it is possible to walk across the bay to GRANGE-OVER-SANDS, but the route is treacherous, so the journey should only be undertaken in the company of the one remaining professional guide. The position of Queen's Guide to the Sands has been by royal appointment since the 14th century, and the current 'sand pilot' of Morecambe Bay has been, since 1963, Cedric Robinson, who in his book *Sand Walker: A Lifetime on Morecambe Bay* (2000), describes the place as 'the wet Sahara', and advises:

> There's only two people you can put your trust in when crossing these sands: God and the sand pilot.

Morecambe Bay potted shrimps are highly regarded.

Hazards include not only tides that come in faster than you can walk, cutting off the unwary, but also hidden holes called melgraves covered by a firm-looking skin but concealing quicksands 3 m (10 ft) or more deep, which can set around you like concrete. On 5 February 2004 these dangers were illustrated when 21 Chinese cocklepickers were drowned after they were cut off by rising tides.

Moreton Corbet *Moreton* 'farmstead in moorland or marshy ground', OE *mor* 'marsh, moor' + -TON; *Corbet* denoting manorial ownership in the Middle Ages by the Corbet family. A village in Shropshire, about 13 km (8 miles) northeast of Shrewsbury. The empty shell of the 17th-century castellated mansion belonging to the Corbet family, local lords of the manor, can still be seen here.

Moretonhampstead Originally *Moreton* (*see* MORETON CORBET); *-hampstead*, added in the late 15th century, may have been a family name, or alternatively from a nearby place, 'homestead' (*see* HAMPSTEAD).
A town in Devon, on the northeastern edge of Dartmoor, about 19 km (12 miles) southwest of Exeter.

Moreton-in-Marsh The suffix was originally *Henmarsh*, an old district name meaning 'marsh frequented by wild hen-birds' (e.g. moorhens), OE *henn* 'hen' + *mersc* 'marsh'. (The identification of *Marsh* with *march* 'boundary' is without foundation).
A small market town in Gloucestershire, in the COTSWOLDS, about 7 km (4.5 miles) north of STOW-ON-THE-WOLD. It stands on the route of the FOSSE WAY, and its wide main street is lined with fine old houses and coaching inns. Nearby to the southwest is Sezincote House (*see under* SEZINCOTE), an early 19th-century country house built in Indian style. To the southeast is Chastleton House (*see under* CHASTLETON), one of the finest Jacobean mansions in England.

Moreton Jeffries *Jeffries* denoting manorial ownership in the Middle Ages by someone called Geoffrey.
A village in Herefordshire (before 1998 in Hereford and Worcester, before 1974 in Herefordshire), about 13 km (8 miles) northeast of Hereford.

Moreton Morrell *Morrell* originally a distinct place name, 'boundary-hill', OE (*ge*)*mære* 'boundary' + *hyll* 'hill'. The two names were first combined in the 13th century.
A village in Warwickshire, just to the west of the FOSSE WAY, about 11 km (7 miles) south of Warwick.

Moreton on Lugg *Lugg* a river name.
A village in Herefordshire (before 1998 in Hereford and Worcester, before 1974 in Herefordshire), on the River LUGG, about 5 km (3 miles) north of Hereford.

Moreton Pinkney *Pinkney* denoting manorial ownership in the Middle Ages by the de Pinkeny [*sic*] family.
A village in Northamptonshire, about 21 km (13 miles) southwest of Northampton.

Moreton Say *Say* denoting manorial ownership in the Middle Ages by the de Sai family.
A village in Shropshire, about 5 km (3 miles) west of Market Drayton.

Moreton Valence *Valence* denoting manorial ownership in the Middle Ages by the Valence family.
A village in Gloucestershire, about 11 km (7 miles) southwest of Gloucester and close to the east bank of the SEVERN Estuary.

Morgannwg 'the land of Morgan', *Morgan*, name of a Welsh prince, Morgan Mwynfawr (d.*c*.975) + *-wg*, a territorial affix. The Welsh name for GLAMORGAN, and also the name of an early medieval kingdom, formed from the union of GWENT and GLYWYSIG. It was taken over by the Normans by the end of the 11th century, and became a lordship of the MARCHES.

Morgannwg Ganol. The Welsh name for MID GLAMORGAN.

Moricambe From the same OCelt name as MORECAMBE.

An inlet or bay on the south (Cumbrian) side of the SOLWAY FIRTH, some 10 km (6 miles) west of Carlisle. It is fed by the rivers Waver and Wampool.

Mork Origin unknown.

A village in Gloucestershire, between the FOREST OF DEAN and the Welsh border, about 8 km (5 miles) northwest of Lydney.

Morley 'clearing by or in the moor', OE *mor* 'moor, marsh' + -LEY.

A town in West Yorkshire, 7 km (4.5 miles) southwest of Leeds. The Liberal politician H.H. Asquith (1852–1928), prime minister (1908–16), was born here, as was the woollen manufacturer and philanthropist Titus Salt (1803–76) (*see* SALTAIRE).

Morningside Probably originating as the name of an estate here in the 17th century, 'side' referring to the hillside.

A southern suburb of EDINBURGH, known far and wide for its bourgeois respectability. Its late Victorian mansions, now much desired and commanding London-like prices, were not always so admired:

> Day by day, one new villa, one new object of offence, is added to another; all around Newington and Morningside, the dismalest structures keep springing up like mushrooms ... They belong to no style of art, only to a form of business much to be regretted.
>
> Robert Louis Stevenson: *Picturesque Notes on Edinburgh* (1879)

Morningside accent. A refined (or *refaned*) Scottish accent, affected by the denizens of this most middle-class of Edinburgh suburbs. According to the good people of Morningside, *sex* are what you put coal in.

Mornington Crescent Named in honour of the Earl of *Mornington*, who was related by marriage to the Fitzroy family on whose estate the road was built.

A residential street in Central London (NW1), to the east of REGENT'S PARK, in the borough of CAMDEN. It was built in 1821. In the 19th century it was known as a favourite residence of artists and writers.

Mornington Crescent Underground station, on the Northern line (Charing Cross branch), opened in 1907.

The name 'Mornington Crescent' has been given to an improvised parlour game played by panel members on the BBC Radio 4 programme *I'm Sorry I Haven't a Clue* (1972–). The ostensible 'aim' of the game is to move from station to station around the London Underground system according to a set of obscure and indeterminate rules and conventions (about which the players argue and on which they learnedly digress), and to be the first to get to Mornington Crescent station (a task even more surreally

difficult from 1992 to 1998 when the actual station was closed).

> I acted so tragic the house rose like magic,
> The audience yelled 'You're sublime!'
> They made me a present of Mornington Crescent,
> They threw it a brick at a time.
>
> W.F. Hargreaves: 'The Night I Appeared as Macbeth' (1922)

Mo Róisín Dubh. *See under* RÓISÍN DUBH.

Morpeth 'path that was the scene of a murder', OE *morth* 'murder' + *pœth* 'path'.

A town in Northumberland (of which it is the administrative centre), 22 km (14 miles) north of Newcastle. There are some fine old buildings, including the remains of a 15th-century castle and a town hall designed by Sir John Vanbrugh. The 14th-century St Mary's Church has the grave of Emily Davison, the suffragette who threw herself under the king's horse at the Derby in 1913, with fatal consequences.

Morpeth was the birthplace of William Turner (?1508–68), the 'father of English botany'. Basil Bunting's poem, 'The Compaint of the Morpethshire Farmer' (1930) laments the poverty forcing the farmer to emigrate to Canada. There are towns called Morpeth in Australia (New South Wales) and Canada (Ontario).

See also WANSBECK.

Morpeth Rant. A popular country dance.

Morriston After Sir John *Morris*.

A small town in Swansea unitary authority (formerly in Glamorgan, then West Glamorgan), some 5 km (3 miles) northeast of Swansea. It was built to house the workers on the estate of Sir John Morris, an 18th-century landowner; the Welsh name **Treforys** also means 'Morris's town'.

Mort Bank *Mort* possibly 'a salmon in its third year', early ModE.

An extensive sandbank in Morecambe Bay (*see under* MORECAMBE), between BARROW-IN-FURNESS and Lancaster Sound (*see under* LANCASTER).

Morte Point *Morte* OE *mort* 'stump'.

A headland at the northwest corner of Devon, about 8 km (5 miles) west of Ilfracombe. It is at the northern end of **Morte Bay** (the corresponding headland to the south is BAGGY POINT).

Off Morte Point is the rock called **Mortstone**. The ironic old Devonshire saying '**He may remove Mortstone**' was applied incredulously to husbands who pretended to be masters of their wives, and it also meant 'If you have done what you say, you can accomplish anything.'

Mortimer's Cross 'Cross or crossroads of a man called Mortimer', ModE surname + *cross*.

A village in Herefordshire (before 1998 in Hereford and

Worcester, before 1974 in Herefordshire), about 10 km (6 miles) northwest of Leominster.

Battle of Mortimer's Cross (12 February 1461). A battle of the Wars of the Roses in which Edward, eldest son of Richard, Duke of York, defeated the Lancastrian army. He then marched on London, where he was crowned Edward IV about a month later.

Mortlake Probably 'small stream in which young salmon are found' (referring to a small local tributary of the River THAMES[1], now lost), OE *mort* 'young salmon or other fish' + *lacu* 'small stream' (*see also* LAKE).

A district in West London (SW14), on the south bank of the River Thames, in the borough of RICHMOND-UPON-THAMES (previously in Surrey), between BARNES to the east and RICHMOND[2] to the west. It is known for three things: its brewery (beer has been brewed in Mortlake since the 15th century; the brewers Watney established themselves here in 1889, and the brewery now produces Budweiser beer); its tapestry works, at which between 1619 and 1703 Flemish weavers produced the distinctive **Mortlake tapestry** (recognizable by the mark of a white shield with a red cross); and its status as the finishing point of the annual Oxford and Cambridge Boat Race.

Morton Bagot *Morton* 'farmstead in moorland or marshy ground', OE *mor* 'moor, marsh' + -TON; *Bagot* denoting manorial ownership in the Middle Ages by the Bagod family. A village in Warwickshire, about 14 km (8.5 miles) northwest of Stratford-upon-Avon.

Mortstone. *See* MORTE POINT.

Morvah 'grave by the sea', Cornish *mor* 'sea' + *bedh* 'grave'. A village on the northwest coast of Cornwall, about 13 km (8 miles) northeast of Land's End.

Morval Origin uncertain: the first element probably represents Cornish *mor* 'sea'. A village in Cornwall, about 5 km (3 miles) north of Looe.

Morven 'big mountain', Gaelic *mòr* 'big' + *beinn* 'mountain'. An isolated peak (706 m / 2316 ft) in northeast Highland (formerly in Caithness, in which it was the highest point), 13 km (8 miles) north of Helmsdale. It can be seen from as far away as the CAIRNGORMS, 120 km (74 miles) to the south.

Morvern 'sea gap', Gaelic *mor* 'sea' + *bhearn* 'gap'. The Gaelic name *A'Mhorbhairn* was originally applied to Loch Sunart, on the north side of Morvern. A remote area of the Western Highlands, formerly in Argyll and now in Highland. It is bounded on the north by Loch SUNART and on the south by the Sound of MULL, across which a ferry runs between Lochaline and FISHNISH on Mull. Morvern is occasionally used as a girl's name.

Morwenstow 'holy place of St Morwenna', *Morwenna* name of the female saint (one of the 24 sons and daughters of King Brychan of BRYCHEINIOG) to whom the local church is dedicated + OE *stow* '(holy) place'.

A village on the cliff-bound northeastern Cornish coast, about 10 km (6 miles) north of Bude. It is best known for its somewhat eccentric mid-19th-century vicar, the Reverend Robert Hawker (1803–75), who wrote poetry inspired by Cornwall and its landscape and legends. The piece he is now mainly remembered for is 'The Song of the Western Men'. Sabine Baring-Gould's *The Vicar of Morwenstow* (1875) is an account of his life.

Mosborough 'stronghold of the moor', OE *mor* 'moor' + *burh* (*see* BURY).

A small town in South Yorkshire, 8 km (5 miles) southeast of Sheffield.

Moscow 'plain of the hazel', OCelt *magos*, which comes into Welsh as *maes* 'open field, plain' + *collen* (or Gaelic *coll*) 'hazel tree'.

A village in East Ayrshire (formerly in Strathclyde), 6 km (4 miles) east of Kilmarnock. Some sources suggest that the village is on a burn called the Volga, although the consensus among scholars is that someone has been having their little joke.

For **Little Moscow**, *see under* CHOPWELL *and* MAERDY.

Moseley[1] 'Moll's glade', OE *Molles* possessive form of male personal name *Moll* + -LEY.

A leafy, salubrious southeastern inner suburb of BIRMINGHAM. It has a well-known rugby club, and lies within Birmingham's BALTI TRIANGLE.

Moseley[2] 'glade infested with mice', OE *mus* 'mouse' + -LEY. A village in Worcestershire (before 1998 in Hereford and Worcester, before 1974 in Worcestershire), about 8 km (5 miles) northwest of Worcester.

Moseley Old Hall *Moseley see* MOSELEY[1]. A 16th-century manor house (much renovated in the 19th century), 6 km (4 miles) north of Wolverhampton. It belongs to the National Trust, but was the home of the Whitgreave family until 1925. In 1651 they – Catholics and Royalists – accommodated the fleeing Prince Charles (or plain 'Charles Stuart' as the Parliamentarians' 'Wanted' poster had him) following the Battle of Worcester in 1651 (*see under* WORCESTER). The priest hole in which the fugitive hid, and the (rather more comfortable) four-poster bed in which he slept, may be viewed. *See also* BOSCOBEL HOUSE.

Mossgiel. *See under* MAUCHLINE *and* TARBOLTON.

Mossley 'clearing by the bog', OE *mos* 'bog' + -LEY. A town in Greater Manchester, some 15 km (9 miles) northeast of the city centre. The world's first fish and chip shop opened here in 1863.

Moss Side 'place beside the marsh', OE *mos* 'marsh, bog' + *side*.

An area of Manchester. Along with Hulme and Longsight, it forms the city's so-called 'murder triangle', notorious from the early 1990s for gang-related gun crime – to the extent that the national press speculated why the shooting events in the 2002 Manchester Commonwealth Games weren't held in Moss Side.

See also NORTH, THE[1].

Most Distressful Country, the. A common sobriquet for Ireland, due to its many historical tragedies (generally inflicted by the English). The phrase comes from an anonymous early 19th-century ballad, written in the wake of the suppression of the United Irishmen's Rebellion of 1798:

'Tis the most distressful country that you have ever seen
For they're hanging men and women for the wearing of the green.

Mostrim. The anglicized form of the Irish Meathas Troim, the name for EDGEWORTHSTOWN.

Mostyn 'village by a swamp', OE *mos* 'swamp' + -TON.

A small industrial port on the Dee estuary (*see under* DEE[2]) in Flintshire (formerly in Clwyd), 5 km (3 miles) northwest of Holywell. In Welsh it is **Tremostyn** ('Mostyn village', strictly a tautonym). **Mostyn Bank** is the name of a sandbank in the estuary.

Mostyn was the birthplace of the actor and playwright Emlyn Williams (1905–87).

Mother Dunch's Buttocks. A nickname for WITTENHAM CLUMPS.

Mother Shipton's Cave. A popular tourist attraction in KNARESBOROUGH, North Yorkshire. Mother Shipton (1488–1561) was born Ursula Southeil, her mother giving birth to her in the eponymous cave during a thunderstorm, before dying to the accompaniment of strange and terrible noises. As Ursula grew up the house she lived in was subject to many supernatural goings-on of a *poltergeistische* nature. In 1512 she married Toby Shipton near York, and thereafter, owing to her ability as a fortune-teller, she became known as Mother Shipton. Her irregular features gained her a reputation as a witch, and it was said that she had made a pact with the Devil to gain the gift of prophecy. Brought before the magistrates, she was only saved from the usual fate of witches by the intervention of a dragon, on whose back she flew away.

It turns out that many of Mother Shipton's recorded pronouncements were made up by a man called Hindley in 1871. This explains her predictions of the Armada and the Great Fire of London, but she wasn't always bang-on – for example with this one:

The World to an end will come
In Eighteen Hundred and Eighty-One.

Motherwell 'mother's well, well of Our Lady'; there was a healing well dedicated to the Virgin Mary, the 'Holy Mother', in Ladywell Road.

An industrial town 18 km (11 miles) southeast of Glasgow, in North Lanarkshire (formerly in Strathclyde). It amalgamated with neighbouring WISHAW[1] in 1920. It was for a long time an iron and steel centre, and had the largest steelworks in Britain before the First World War. The giant Ravenscraig steel strip mill established in 1958 closed in 1992. The former district of Motherwell (of which Motherwell was the HQ) included the towns of BELLSHILL, Wishaw and SHOTTS.

The poet and playwright Liz Lochhead (b.1947) was born in Motherwell.

Motherwell FC, founded in 1886 and nicknamed the Well, play their home matches at Fir Park.

Mottisfont 'spring near a river-confluence' or 'spring where meetings are held', OE *motes* possessive form of *mot* 'meeting' + *funta* 'spring'.

A village in Hampshire, on the River TEST, about 6 km (4 miles) northwest of Romsey. **Mottisfont Abbey**, originally an Augustinian priory, has been a private house since the Dissolution, although it now belongs to the National Trust. Its grounds have a notable collection of old-fashioned roses as well as what is supposedly the largest plane tree in Britain.

Mottram St Andrew *Mottram* perhaps 'speakers' place' or 'place where meetings are held', OE *motere* 'speaker' or *mot* 'meeting' + *rum* 'place'; *Andrew* probably denoting manorial ownership in the Middle Ages by someone called Andrew (the *St* is a later addition).

A village in Cheshire, about 4 km (2.5 miles) southeast of Wilmslow.

Moulton 'Mula's farmstead' or 'farmstead where mules are kept', OE male personal name *Mula* or *mul* 'mule' + -TON.

A village in Lincolnshire, in the FENS, about 6 km (4 miles) east of Spalding. It possesses the tallest windmill in England. Built in the 1820s by a local miller called Robert King, it is 29 m (97 ft) high. Its sails blew off in 1895, but corn continued to be ground there by other means until 1995.

Moulton Seas End Perhaps 'the part of Moulton nearest the Fens', OE *sæ* 'marsh, lake'.

A village in Lincolnshire, in the FENS, about 4 km (2.5 miles) northeast of MOULTON.

Mound, the. *See under* PRINCES STREET.

Mountain Ash From the name of an inn here (*mountain ash* is another name for the rowan).

An industrial town in Rhondda Cynon Taff (formerly in

Glamorgan, then in Mid Glamorgan), 8 km (5 miles) south of Merthyr Tydfil. The Welsh name is **Aberpennar** ('mouth of the Pennar', a small tributary of the Cynon named after the hill Cefn Pennar, *cefn* 'cliff' + *pennardd* 'height'). The town's development almost entirely occurred after the middle of the 19th century.

Mountain Water OFr *mountaine* 'low hills, heath land'; there are numerous areas and minor places in Wales called 'Mountain'.

A village in Pembrokeshire (formerly in Dyfed), some 13 km (8 miles) south of Fishguard.

Mount Badon Latin *Mons Badonicus*.

The scene of a battle traditionally associated with King Arthur. The battle, probably fought between Saxons or Jutes and native Britons somewhere in southern England around AD 500, is first recorded by the 6th-century historian Gildas in his *De Excidio et Conquestu Britanniae* ('On the Ruin and Conquest of Britain'), but he makes no reference to Arthur. A later source, the 10th-century Welsh *Annales Cambriae*, mentions Arthur and gives the date of the battle as 518. Geoffrey of Monmouth (*see under* MONMOUTH) located Badon at Bath, while others have identified it with BADBURY RINGS in Dorset. Whatever the uncertainty about its date and location, and about who commanded the opposing forces, Mount Badon appears to have been an important battle, and one that halted the advance of the Anglo-Saxons until later on in the 6th century.

See also CARDIGAN.

Mount Brandon. An alternative name for BRANDON MOUNTAIN.

Mounth, the Gaelic *monadh* 'low ridge, mountain mass'.

A name for the GRAMPIAN MOUNTAINS east of the Drumochter Pass and south of the Dee. The name is found in the **White Mounth**, the name for the higher southern slopes of LOCHNAGAR (the whole mountain was once known as the White Mounth), and in the names of some passes, such as CAIRN O' MOUNT and CAPEL MOUNTH.

Mountjoy Prison Named after Charles Blount, 8th Lord *Mountjoy* (1562–1606), lord deputy of Ireland, and victor of the Battle of KINSALE.

Dublin's main prison, dryly known to its clients as **the Joy**. It was built in 1850 and was used, along with KILMAINHAM Jail, by the British, and then by the Free State, for the imprisonment and execution of rebels – most famously the 18-year-old Kevin Barry, hanged for his part in an ambush on an armed convoy in Dublin in 1920.

> In Mountjoy jail one Monday morning
> High upon the gallows tree
> Kevin Barry gave his young life
> For the cause of liberty.
>
> Anon.: ballad 'Kevin Barry'

In 2001 the remains of Barry and others executed by the British at Mountjoy during the Anglo-Irish War were reburied in the Republican plot in GLASNEVIN CEMETERY.

Mountjoy also saw the incarceration for a while of the writer and epic boozer Brendan Behan, sentenced for his involvement in an IRA shooting incident in 1942; a hanging in Mountjoy Prison became the theme of his first play, *The Quare Fellow* (1954).

The women's prison in Mountjoy is nicknamed the **Rasherhouse**, from slang *rasher* 'sexual intercourse'.

Mount Leinster. *See under* LEINSTER.

Mountmellick Irish *Móinteach Mílic* 'bog of the water meadows'.

A market town in County Laois, 11 km (7 miles) northwest of Portlaoise. It was founded by Quakers in the 17th century and became a centre of linen spinning.

Mountmellick embroidery. A type of whitework, i.e. embroidery using white thread on a white fabric background. It originated in the early 19th century and the designs are characteristically floral.

Mount Pleasant The meaning is literal (it is a steep road), but the naming was ironical: the road was once just a country track leading to the FLEET[1] river, and the name (first recorded in 1732) was inspired by the heaps of cinders and other refuse dumped at the end of it, by the river bank.

A road in Clerkenwell, in Central London (WC1, EC1), linking Grays Inn Road with Rosebery Avenue. At its northern end is **Mount Pleasant Sorting Office**, one of the largest postal sorting offices in the world.

US president Ulysses S. Grant (1822–85) was born in Mount Pleasant, Ohio.

Mountrath Irish *Móin Rátha* 'bog of the ring fort'; the anglicized *Mount-* is a corruption of *Móin*.

A small market town in County Laois, 10 km (6 miles) southwest of Port Laoise. In the 17th century Cromwell's general Sir Charles Coote was granted land here, and his son became Earl of Montrath. The Coote family set up the linen industry that flourished here in the 17th and 18th centuries.

Mount Sandel *Sandel* possibly from Irish *Kill Santain* 'church of Samthann', an 8th-century female saint commemorated in several early sources. Its Irish name today is *Dún Dá Bheann* 'fort of the two peaks'.

A prehistoric site in County Londonderry, on a bluff on the east bank of the Lower BANN, near Coleraine. It is the site of the earliest human settlement in Ireland, comprising a group of wooden huts dating from *c*.7000 BC, in the Mesolithic period following the last Ice Age.

Mount's Bay From ST MICHAEL'S MOUNT.

A bay in western Cornwall, enclosed to the east by the Lizard Peninsula (*see under* the LIZARD) and to the west by the peninsula that concludes at LAND'S END. Around its arc are (inter alia) MARAZION, MOUSEHOLE, NEWLYN, PENZANCE, PORTHLEVEN and ST MICHAEL'S MOUNT.

Mountsorrel 'sorrel-coloured hill' (referring to the pinkish-brown local stone), OFr *mont* 'hill' + *sorel* 'sorrel' (a pinkish-brown colour).

A village in Leicestershire, on the River SOAR, in foxhunting country, about 11 km (7 miles) north of Leicester. The pinkish-brown **Mountsorrel granite**, from the local quarries, was extensively used in the past for road surfacing.

Mount Stewart From Robert *Stewart*, Lord Castlereagh.

The seat of the marquesses of Londonderry, in County Down, 10 km (6 miles) south of Newtownards, on the east shore of Strangford Lough (*see under* STRANGFORD). It was the birthplace of Lord Castlereagh (1769–1822), Tory foreign secretary from 1812 until his suicide in 1822 (the year after he succeeded to the Londonderry title). The core of the present house dates from the early 19th century, though it was subsequently enlarged. The magnificent gardens were planted in the 1920s and include the Temple of the Winds (1780). Mount Stewart is in the care of the National Trust and has been nominated a World Heritage Site.

Mount Tabor A 19th-century name referring to the biblical mountain, the scene, according to one tradition, of the Transfiguration (Mark 9:2–8).

A village in West Yorkshire, 4 km (2.5 miles) northwest of Halifax.

Mourne Mountains From the *Mughdhorna* tribe.

A range of quietly craggy granite mountains in the south of County Down, overlooking CARLINGFORD LOUGH to the south and the Irish Sea to the east. The highest peak – and the highest mountain in Northern Ireland, and indeed in the whole of Ulster – is SLIEVE DONARD (850 m / 2788 ft). The mountains are designated an Area of Outstanding Natural Beauty, and have been compared by Paul Theroux to 'a naked giantess lying in a green sleeping bag'. The **Mourne Wall** is a drystone wall that extends for 35 km (22 miles) in a horseshoe shape along the main ridge, linking many of the summits; it was built 1904–22 to mark the catchment area of the reservoirs in the SILENT VALLEY.

> the cupped peace of these aloof
> Uncertain hills …
>
> Roy McFadden: 'Letter from the Mournes', from *Flowers for a Lady* (1945)

Apollo in Mourne. A verse play (1926) by Richard Rowley, founder of the Mourne Press and author of *Ballads of Mourne* (1940). The play throws the Greek god Apollo – banished from Olympus – in among the peasantry of County Down. As Jove predicts:

> There shall you wander
> Amidst a barbarous people, harsh of speech

> And of fierce aspect, dwelling in huts of stone,
> Seeing the sun but seldom, eating strange meats,
> And never tasting wine, or fruits, or oil.

Mountains of Mourne. A 20th-century rhyming slang term for 'horn', i.e. the erect penis.

'Mountains of Mourne, The'. A haunting song of exile by Percy French (1854–1920), written in 1896 after French had seen the Mournes one day from Dublin, distant on the northern horizon.

> Oh, Mary, this London's a wonderful sight
> With people here working by day and by night.
> They don't sow potatoes, nor barley, nor wheat
> But there's gangs of them digging for gold in the streets –
> At least when I asked them that's what I was told
> So I just took a hand at this diggin' for gold,
> But for all that I found there I might as well be
> Where the Mountains of Mourne sweep down to the sea …
>
> There's beautiful girls here, oh, never you mind,
> With beautiful shapes nature never designed
> And lovely complexions all roses and cream,
> But O'Loughlin remarked with regard to the same
> That if at those roses you ventured to sip
> The colours might all come away on your lip.
> So I'll wait for the wild rose that's waitin' for me
> Where the Mountains of Mourne sweep down to the sea.

Mousa 'moss island', OScand *mor* 'moor' + *ey* (*see* -AY).

A small island (pronounced 'moosa') off the southeast coast of Mainland (*see under* SHETLAND) some 17 km (11 miles) south of Lerwick. It is noted for having the best-preserved Iron Age broch (large circular dry-stone tower) in Britain.

Mouse, East, West and Middle. *See* MOUSE ISLANDS.

Mousehold Heath A modern name, perhaps deriving from the many caves made here by chalk-diggers, i.e. 'mouseholed heath'.

An elevated recreational open space in NORWICH, northeast of the city centre, with attractive views of the city and its churches. Passed by the dean and chapter of Norwich Cathedral to Norwich Corporation in 1880, it was dedicated to the free use of the people of Norwich in 1886.

In the summer of 1549, Mousehold Heath became the focal point of the popular uprising known as Kett's Rebellion. In response to an unpopular act of Edward VI, which allowed landowners to fence off their land to prevent poor people from gathering wood or farming, Robert Kett, a radical landowner from nearby WYMONDHAM, raised an army of 12,000 which marched on Norwich (then the second town in England), camped on Mousehold Heath, and occupied the city. The rebels withstood the first attempt by Protector Somerset (*see under* SOMERSET) to dislodge them and held Norwich for more than a month before being finally defeated at nearby Dussindale by the Duke of Northumberland in August.

Tradition has it that Kett established a court of justice on Mousehold Heath under the so-called 'Oak of Reformation', and that nine of the rebellion's ringleaders were hanged on this tree when the uprising was stamped out (in reality Kett was hanged from the wall of Norwich Castle).

Mousehole From the name of a local sea-cave (just south of the harbour), OE *mus* 'mouse' + *hol* 'hole'.

A coastal village (pronounced 'mowzle') in southwest Cornwall, about 4 km (2.5 miles) south of Penzance. In 1595 it was burnt to the ground by invaders from the Spanish Armada who had eluded the English fleet.

In its days as a fishing port its main catch was pilchards. A particular local speciality is stargazy pie, a fish pie with pilchards' heads poking out around the circumference; it is made at the Ship Inn in Mousehole on 23 December every year, Tom Bawcock's Eve, in memory of the fisherman who saved the village from a hungry Christmas one stormy winter (*see below*).

Dylan Thomas, who spent his honeymoon at the Lobster Pot guesthouse in Mousehole in 1937, said it was 'really the loveliest village in England'.

The Mousehole Cat. An illustrated children's book (1990) by Antonia Barber. In it Old Tom (i.e. the Mousehole hero Tom Bawcock), the only fisherman without dependants, braves the storm with his cat Mowzer, to catch fish for the starving village. Mowzer lulls the Great Storm-Cat with her singing, and the fish are safely brought home as everybody in the village puts a candle or lantern in their window to guide Old Tom back to the harbour out of the dark and the storm. It has been made into an animated film.

Mouse Islands From their appearance, OE *mus* 'mouse'.

Three small rocky islets off the north coast of Anglesey (formerly in Gwynedd), named by compass points. In Welsh **West Mouse** is **Maen y Bugael** ('the shepherd rock', *maen* 'rock, stone' + *bugael* 'shepherd'). St Patrick was saved, via divine intervention, from a shipwreck on **Middle Mouse** (in Welsh **Ynys Badrig** meaning 'isle of Patrick'), and in thanks founded a church at Llanbadrig ('church of St Patrick'), on the shore of Anglesey facing the rock. (The church was restored in a somewhat Islamic style in 1884 by Lord Stanley, the local landowner and a Muslim.) **East Mouse** – in Welsh **Ynys Amlwch** ('isle of Amlwch') – is just offshore from the town of AMLWCH.

Moville Irish *Maigh Bhile* 'plain of the old or sacred tree'.

The site in County Down, just northeast of Newtownards, of a famous abbey founded in the 6th century by **St Finnian of Moville** (d.579), who, having retreated from the amorous advances of a girl in Scotland, turned Moville into a centre of biblical study and missionary activity.

Mow Cop¹ Originally *Mowel* 'heap hill', OE *muga* 'heap' + *hyll* 'hill', with the later addition of *Cop* 'hilltop', OE *copp*.

A hill on the Cheshire–Staffordshire border, at the southern end of the PENNINES. It is 300 m (984 ft) high.

On 31 May 1807 it was the scene of an open-air religious meeting which is generally reckoned to have been the starting-point of Primitive Methodism (a fundamentalist-revivalist offshoot of Wesleyan Methodism which specialized in open-air camp meetings).

Mow Cop Castle, a folly, was built in 1754 by local stone masons.

Mow Cop². A village on the Cheshire–Staffordshire border, about 6 km (4 miles) south of Congleton, close by MOW COP¹.

Moy¹ Irish *Muaidhe* 'stately one'.

A river of County Mayo, running south to north and entering the sea just below BALLINA. It gave its name to an ancient kingdom:

> The son of the King of Moy
> Found a girl in a green dell,
> Of the rich abounding fruit
> She gave him his fill.
>
> Anon.: 'The Son of the King of Moy', translated
> from the medieval Irish by Brendan Kennelly

Moy² Gaelic *moigh* 'on level ground'.

The traditional seat of the Mackintosh of Mackintosh, in Highland (formerly in Inverness-shire), by the small **Loch Moy**, just off the A9 some 15 km (9 miles) southeast of Inverness. The present house dates from the 1950s.

Rout of Moy (16 February 1746). An incident during Bonnie Prince Charlie's stay at Moy Hall. Reports of the Prince's presence having reached Inverness, a Hanoverian force of some 1500 men was dispatched to Moy. As the soldiers approached in the dark, half a dozen Moy men started firing, shouting, calling on the great Highland commanders and generally raising such a brouhaha that the redcoats were convinced they had stumbled on the entire Jacobite army, and promptly fled back to Inverness.

Moyle, Sea of Irish *Maol* 'bare hill', possibly referring to FAIR HEAD.

Another name, particularly from the Irish perspective, for the NORTH CHANNEL, the straits between Antrim and southwest Scotland. It is also called the **Waters of Moyle**, and prominent landmarks on the Irish side include Fair Head and RATHLIN ISLAND. It was in the Sea of Moyle that in the old legend the children of Lir were first turned into swans by their jealous stepmother, and where they spent their second period of three hundred years.

> Silent, O Moyle! be the roar of thy water,
> Break not, ye breezes, your chain of repose,

While murmuring mournfully, Lir's only daughter
> Tells to the night-star her tale of woes.

> Thomas Moore: 'The Song of Fionnuala', from *Irish Melodies*
> (1808). Fionnuala was Lir's daughter.

The Sea of Moyle gave its name to **Moyle**, a local government district in northeastern Antrim. The administrative headquarters are at BALLYCASTLE.

Moytura Irish *Magh Tuireadh* 'plain of the towers'.

The name of the sites of two mythical battles, looming large in early Irish literature. The first was near CONG in County Mayo, and was fought between the Firbolgs and the Tuatha Dé Danaan, who had come from across the sea to take Ireland; the second was near Lough Arrow in County Sligo, and was fought between the Tuatha Dé Danann and the Fomorians, hideous creatures from under the sea (or from TORY ISLAND). In the latter battle King Lugh of the Danaan deployed a novel weapon of mass destruction:

> … saith Lugh to his poet, 'What power can you wield in
>   battle?'
> 'Not hard to say,' quoth Carpre … 'I will satirize them, so
>   that through the spell of my art they will not resist
>   warriors.'

> Anon.: *The Second Battle of Moytura*, translated from the Irish
> by W. Stokes

Said satirizing has the effect of producing three blisters on the target's cheek, whereupon the victim dies of shame.

Muaidhe. The Irish name for the River MOY[1].

Much-Binding-in-the-Marsh *Binding* from Second World War RAF slang *bind* 'to complain' (an activity associated with service life on a remote RAF station).

A fictitious English village, venue of the RAF station in the eponymous BBC radio comedy series which ran from 1947 to 1953. It was written by and starred Kenneth Horne (1907–69) and Richard Murdoch (1907–90), who had met in the Air Ministry during the Second World War, and was supposedly set in an RAF station doubling as a country club.

Muchelney '(at the) big island', OE *miclan* dative form of *micel* 'big' + *eg* (see -EY, -EA).

A village in the SOMERSET Levels, on the River ISLE, about 13 km (8 miles) northeast of Ilminster. In Anglo-Saxon times it was, as its name reveals, on an island surrounded by marshes. A monastery was established nearby around 697, the second earliest in Somerset (Glastonbury was the first).

Much Hoole 'big hovel', *Much* OE *mycel* 'great'; *Hoole* OE *hulu* 'hovel, shed'.

A village in Lancashire, 8 km (5 miles) southwest of Preston.

Much Marcle *Marcle* 'wood or clearing on a boundary', OE *mearc* 'boundary' + -LEY.

A village in Herefordshire (before 1998 in Hereford and Worcester, before 1974 in Herefordshire), about 16 km (10 miles) southeast of Hereford, in cider-making country. **Little Marcle** is about 5 km (3 miles) to the north.

The rapist and serial killer Fred West (1941–95) (*see under* GLOUCESTER) was brought up in Much Marcle. *See also* MARCLE HILL.

Muchty. A local nickname for AUCHTERMUCHTY.

Much Wenlock *Much* 'great', OE *mycel* (distinguishing it from Little Wenlock); *Wenlock* perhaps 'enclosure by the white place' (possibly referring to a monastery near the limestone hill of Wenlock Edge), from the first part of the OCelt place name *Wininicas* perhaps 'white place' (from OCelt *winn* 'white') + OE *loca* 'enclosed place'.

A market town in Shropshire, about 19 km (12 miles) southeast of Shrewsbury. The long limestone ridge of WENLOCK EDGE stretches away to the southwest. Nearby is the village of **Little Wentlock**. Coal and iron were formerly mined in the area.

It still preserves much of the air of an old English market town, dotted with Tudor, Jacobean and Georgian buildings ('unfailingly quaint', *The Rough Guide to England* (2002)). To the south are the ruins of the 11th-century Abbey of St Mildburga.

Muck From the Gaelic name *Eilean nam Muc* 'isle of pigs', *eilean* 'island' + *nam* 'of' + *muc* 'pig'. In 1582 it was referred to in Latin as *Insula Porcorum*. It is possible that the name originates in the porpoises that are seen round the shores, as the Gaelic for porpoise translates literally as 'sea-pig'.

The smallest of the SMALL ISLES of the Inner Hebrides. It is in Highland (formerly in Inverness-shire), 4 km (2.5 miles) southwest of Eigg. The island's name has been the subject of many poor jokes, and the occasional cause of embarrassment. Just as the laird of COLL was known simply as 'Coll', so the laird of Muck was by convention known as 'Muck'. However, when Johnson and Boswell visited in 1773 the laird insisted his title was 'Monk', as the first laird (he alleged) had been a monk from Iona.

Mucking '(settlement of) Mucca's people' or 'Mucca's place', OE male personal name *Mucca* + *-ingas* or *-ing* (see -ING).

A village in Essex, close to the north bank of the River THAMES[1], about 6 km (4 miles) northeast of Tilbury.

Muckish Mountain Irish *An Mhucais* 'ridge of the pig', hence 'Pig's Back' *below*.

An isolated mountain (670 m / 2198 ft) in the northwest of County DONEGAL, some 12 km (7.5 miles) south of HORN HEAD. On the western top is Meskan Mave, a prehistoric cairn associated with the legendary Queen Maeve (Medb).

> Muckish, greatest pig in Ulster's oakwoods,
> Littered out of rock and fire,

Deep you thrust your mottled flanks for cooling
Underneath the peaty mire.

> Sir Shane Leslie (1885–1971): 'Muckish Mountain
> (The Pig's Back)'

Muckle Flugga 'big cliffs', *Muckle* OScand *mikill* 'large'; *Flugga* OScand *fluga* 'cliffs, precipices'.

A tiny rocky island about 0.5 km (0.3 miles) north of UNST, Shetland. Until the lighthouse (built in 1858) on Muckle Flugga was automated in 1995, it was the most northerly inhabited island in the British Isles. The most northerly part of Britain, however, is the rock called Out Stack, about 1 km (0.6 miles) further north; it has been described as 'the full stop at the end of Britain'. There is no land between Out Stack and the North Pole.

> … a flicker of names
> that come out of geography but emerge, too,
> from myth – Muckle Flugga, Taransay, Sule Skerry,
> the Old Man of Hoy.

> Norman MacCaig: 'Centre of Centres', from *The
> White Bird* (1973)

Muckle Long Hill *Muckle* 'big', Scots.

A hill (391 m / 1283 ft) in Aberdeenshire, 7 km (4.5 miles) southwest of Huntly.

Muckross Irish *Mucros* 'pigs' wood', referring to the narrow wooded strip of land between Muckross Lake and Lough Leane. A village in Kerry, 3 km (2 miles) south of Killarney. To the southwest is **Muckross Lake**, one of the three Lakes of Killarney (*see under* KILLARNEY). Beside the lake are the remains of the 15th-century Muckross Friary –

> The prettiest little bijou of a ruined abbey ever seen.

> W.M. Thackeray (as Michael Angelo Titmarsh): *Irish Sketch-
> Book* (1843)

It was finally suppressed by Cromwell's men in 1652, and is said to be the burial place of the Four Kerry Poets (*see under* KERRY).

The old **Muckross House** in 1794 was the scene of the death of Rudolph Eric Raspe, the mining engineer, conman and author of *The Adventures of Baron Münchhausen* (1785); Raspe had came to Muckross from Scotland somewhat hurriedly, having been well rewarded for his finds of mineral ores – ores that he had in fact planted himself. The current house, a mock-Tudor affair, dates from 1843, and in 1861 played host to Queen Victoria; the visit bankrupted its owners, whose hope of a title was stymied by the death of Prince Albert.

Mucros. The Irish name for MUCKROSS.

Mudchute 'slope of a spoil-heap down which unwanted material is tipped' (referring to piles of silt dredged during the excavation of the Millwall Docks in the mid-1860s) ModE *mud* + *chute*.

A locality on the ISLE OF DOGS (E14), in CUBITT TOWN, to the east of the former MILLWALL Docks, in the London borough of TOWER HAMLETS. Mudchute station on the Docklands Light Railway opened in 1987.

Mude From MUDEFORD.

A river in Hampshire and Dorset, which rises to the southwest of the NEW FOREST and flows 10 km (6 miles) west and south into CHRISTCHURCH harbour.

Mudeford Probably 'mud ford', ME *mode, mudde* 'mud' + FORD.

A village (pronounced 'muddy-ford') on the Dorset coast, on the northeastern side of Christchurch harbour and now effectively an eastern suburb of CHRISTCHURCH.

Mudfog. The name given to ROCHESTER in *The Mudfog Papers* (1837–8) by Charles Dickens.

Muggleswick 'Mucel's farmstead', OE male personal name + WICK; however, in Potterish terms, the village is almost certainly inhabited entirely by Muggles.

A village on the River DERWENT[2] in County Durham, 7 km (4.5 miles) west of Consett. **Muggleswick Common** to the south was the scene of an extraordinary affair in 1662, when word got to the Prince Bishop of Durham that a great army of Dissenters was massing on the moor there, intent on pulling down all the churches and murdering the bishops, the aristocracy and the gentry. The prince bishop promptly led a strong force of men to Muggleswick, only to find a complete absence of revolting rabbles. Apparently one Joe Hopper had been seen riding home across the moor, and somehow he had become amplified into a great army by the time the rumour reached Durham.

Muggleton. Charles Dickens's fictionalized version of MAIDSTONE.

Mugsborough. The fictional name under which HASTINGS appears in Robert Tressell's novel *The Ragged Trousered Philanthropists* (1914).

Muileann an tSiáin. The Irish name for SION MILLS.

Muilleann na Buaise. The Irish name for BUSHMILLS.

Muinchille. The Irish name for COOTEHILL.

Muineachán. The Irish name for MONAGHAN.

Muirfield Probably a modern name, 'moor field', Scots *muir* 'moor' + ModE FIELD.

A championship golf course at the seaside resort of GULLANE in East Lothian. It has been the home since 1891 of the Honourable Company of Edinburgh Golfers, founded in 1744 on LEITH Links, and later based in MUSSELBURGH. The British Open has been held at Muirfield 15 times between 1892 and 2000.

Mull Possibly Gaelic *muileach* 'highly favoured'; *Malaios* 2nd century AD.

The second-largest island (after SKYE) of the Inner Hebrides, about 10 km (6 miles) west of Oban, in Argyll and Bute (formerly in Strathclyde region). The long peninsula in the southwest is the **Ross of Mull** (Gaelic *ros* 'headland'), terminating opposite IONA. (The beautiful pink granite found in the west of the Ross was used to build the Holborn Viaduct, Blackfriars Bridge and the Albert Memorial in London.) Mull is separated from the mainland of Morvern by the **Sound of Mull**, at its narrowest about 2 km (1.2 miles) wide. There are many hills, the highest being Ben More (966 m / 3169 ft), making Mull the only Scottish island apart from Skye to have a Munro (*see under* MUNROS).

Mull was known to the Greeks, and the Alexandrian geographer Ptolemy (2nd century AD) referred to it as *Malaios*. Through its history the island was dominated in turn by Picts, Scots, Norwegians, MacDougalls, MacDonalds, Macleans (*see* DUART CASTLE) and Campbells. Johnson and Boswell visited the island in 1773, and sailed along the coast from INCH KENNETH to Iona: 'If this is not *roving among the Hebrides*,' Johnson remarked, 'nothing is.' In 1795 the poet Thomas Campbell (1777–1844) went to work as a tutor in Mull, where he wrote 'The Exile of Erin' and 'Lord Ullin's Daughter' (*see* ULVA). In 1818 John Keats and his friend Charles Armitage Brown walked across Mull to Iona:

> The road through the Island, or rather the track is the most dreary you can think of – between dreary Mountains – over bog and rock and river with our Breeches tucked up and our Stockings in hand.

> John Keats: letter to Tom Keats (23 July 1818)

Muilleach. An inhabitant of Mull.

mullite. A mineral consisting of aluminium silicate. It was first discovered on the island of Mull in the form of elongated white crystals. It is used in the manufacture of ceramics.

Mull Little Theatre. Probably the smallest professional theatre in the world. It is in the village of Dervaig in the north of the island and seats 38.

Mullach an Aitinn. The Irish name for MULLAGHANATTIN.

Mullach an Radhairc. The Irish name for the MULL-AGHAREIRK mountain.

Mullach Idé. The Irish name for MALAHIDE.

Mullach Maistean. The Irish name for MULLAGHMAST.

Mullaghanattin Irish *Mullach an Aitinn* 'hilltop of the gorse'. A mountain (771 m / 2529 ft) in the IVERAGH peninsula of County Kerry, some 10 km (6 miles) southwest of MAC-GILLYCUDDY'S REEKS.

Mullaghareirk Mountains After the highest point, Mullaghareirk, which in Irish is *Mullach an Radhairc* 'hilltop of

the lookout'; in times of conflict the hills provided important observation points for the MacAuliffe clan.

A range of low hills straddling the borders of counties LIMERICK, KERRY and CORK. The highest point is Mullaghareirk (406 m / 1332 ft).

Mullaghcarn. *See under* TYRONE.

Mullaghmast Irish *Mullach Maistean* 'hilltop of Maiste' (the identity of *Maiste* is unknown).

A hill (172 m / 563 ft) in County Kildare, some 7 km (4.5 miles) east of Athy. On its top is the **Rath of Mullaghmast** (Irish *rath* 'fort'), the traditional meeting place of the council of Leinster chieftains. In legend, the rath is associated either with Garret Og, Earl of Kildare and a noted wizard, or with another wizard earl, the Desmond Gearoid Iarla; whichever earl it is, he sleeps with his fully armed men under the rath, awaking every seven years to ride out, the earl himself on his silver-shod horse. (A very similar story is told of LOUGH GUR.) On 1 October 1843 on the hill of Mullaghmast Daniel O'Connell, the Liberator, held one of his 'monster meetings' calling for the repeal of the Act of Union.

Massacre of Mullaghmast (1 January 1577). The slaughter of some 40 Irishmen (including local chieftains) at the hands of English soldiers commanded by the soldier-settlers Sir Francis Cosby and Robert Hartpole. The Irish had been summoned to Mullaghmast to a conference to discuss an alliance, and the massacre is supposed to have taken place in a deep hollow called the Bloody Hole. Only one man, Henry O'Lalor, is supposed to have escaped.

Mullaghmore Irish *An Mullach Mór* 'the big hilltop'.

A small seaside resort in Co. Sligo, 20 km (12 miles) north of Sligo itself. It is on a sandy bay, and **Mullaghmore Head**, just to the north, is a fine viewpoint. The place was deathlessly and breathlessly immortalized by Percy French in a poem he wrote for his periodical *The Jarvey* (1889–90):

> Of all bewcheous situations
> For tourists' recreations
> (I make these observations
> As I walk along the shore;)
> The finest naval cinther
> The Atlantic waves can inther,
> In summer or in winther,
> Is lovely Mullaghmore.

Mullet, the Irish *Béal an Mhuirtead* 'sea loop opening'; Mullet derives from the last element.

A remote hammer-headed peninsula in northwest Mayo, vaguely reminiscent in plan view of the hairstyle of the same name favoured by footballers in the 1970s. The 'handle' of the hammer (the southern arm of the peninsula) encloses Blacksod Bay, and at the village of **Belmullet** (another version of the Irish name) a narrow isthmus extends eastwards to join the Mullet to the mainland. The population declined to about one-thirtieth of its former level after the Great Famine, and an attempt by the Norwegians to set up a whaling station here ended in 1922. The writer T.H. White spent much time here and recalled his adventures in his book *The Godstone and the Blackymor* (1959).

Mullingar Irish *An Muileann gCearr* 'the crooked mill'.
The county town of County WESTMEATH, situated on the Royal Canal 75 km (47 miles) west-northwest of Dublin. **Mullingar Cathedral** is the Catholic cathedral (1939) for the diocese of Meath. Round about are many lakes, earning the area the name 'the country of the waters'.

> And then there's Main Street,
> That broad and clean street
> With its rows of gas lamps that shine afar.
> I could spake a lecture on the architecture
> Of the gorgeous city of Mullingar.
>
>   W.J. Rankine: 'Ode in Praise of the City of Mullingar' (1874)

> At the Fleadh Cheoil in Mullingar
> There were two sounds, the breaking
> Of glass, and the background pulse
> Of music. Young girls roamed
> The streets with eager faces
> Shoving for men. Bottles in
> Hand they rowed out a song:
> Puritan Ireland's dead and gone,
> A myth of O'Faolain and O'Connor.
>
>   John Montague: 'The Siege of Mullingar' (1963) (A *fleadh cheoil* is a music festival (originally a drinking feast), and the last lines parody Yeats's 'Romantic Ireland's dead and gone, / It's with O'Leary in the grave' from 'September 1913'.)

beef to the heels like a Mullingar heifer. An unflattering description applied to the sturdier sort of female. It derives from an anonymous 19th-century ballad:

> There was an elopement down in Mullingar,
> But sad to relate the pair didn't get far,
> 'Oh fly!' said he, 'darling, and see how it feels.'
> But the Mullingar heifer was beef to the heels.

like waiting for a train in Mullingar. Stephen MacKenna's description of fighting for the Greeks against the Turks in 1897. MacKenna went on to win fame for his fine translation of the *Enneads* of Plotinus.

Mull of Galloway. *See under* GALLOWAY.

Mull of Kintyre. *See under* KINTYRE.

Mull of Oa. *See under* the OA.

Muma. An alternative name for MUNSTER.

Mumbles Obscure, but OScand *muli* 'headland, promontory' with an uncertain preceding element is possible; French *mamelles* 'breasts', referring to two small islands off the coast, has also been suggested. In Welsh it is Mwmbwl.

A seaside resort at the southeastern end of the GOWER PENINSULA in Swansea unitary authority (formerly in Glamorgan, then West Glamorgan), 6 km (4 miles) southwest of Swansea. It is also known as **The Mumbles**. The name was originally only applied to the two small offshore islands off **Mumbles Head**, and the settlement itself was known as OYSTERMOUTH.

> ... the Mumbles lighthouse
> Turns through gales like a seabird's egg.
>
>   Vernon Watkins: 'Ode to Swansea'

> There's a place in Wales called the Mumbles
> That is filled with groans and grumbles.
>   The locals complain
>   Of constant cold rain,
> Which produces a coastline that crumbles.
>
>   Anon.: limerick

Mumbles Mile, the. A famous pub crawl along Mumbles's hospitable seafront. Formerly, one of the best-known pubs was The Mermaid, where Dylan Thomas drank as a young man. It was regrettably renamed Dylan's Tavern, and was subsequently, by some stroke of poetic justice, consumed by fire.

Mummerset *mummer* 'actor' + Somer*set*.
An imaginary county in the West Country. The term is first recorded in 1951 (in J.B. Priestley's *Festival at Farbridge*, but it is not clear whether he coined it), and it has been mainly used over the decades to guy the broad, slow-witted, 'r'-filled drawl often assumed by actors portraying all-purpose West Country yokels.

> Nowadays you can't be sure if they *are* eggs, even when somebody on television says they are in B.B.C. Mummerset.
>
>   Compton Mackenzie: *Paper Lives* (1966)

See also LOAMSHIRE.

Muncaster Castle 'Muli's fortification', *Muncaster* OScand male personal name *Muli* + OE *ceaster* (*see* CHESTER).
A castle at the foot of Eskdale, Cumbria (formerly in Cumberland), 26 km (16 miles) southeast of Whitehaven. John Ruskin described it as 'the gateway to Paradise', as from here one may follow the course of the ESK[4] into the heart of the Lake District. The oldest part of the castle (which has always belonged to the Pennington family) is a pele tower (small fortified tower) built in the 14th century on the site of a Roman tower; the site is near RAVENGLASS, which was the Roman port of Glannaventa. Additions to the pele tower were made in the 15th and 19th centuries. In the early 17th century the Penningtons' jester was one Thomas Skelton, commemorated (at least according to local tradition) in the expression 'tomfoolery'; he was a friend of William Shakespeare, and was known as 'the late fool of

Muncaster'. The castle and its landscaped grounds, maze and owl centre are a popular tourist attraction, and nearby is the restored **Muncaster Mill**.

Northeast of the castle is **Muncaster Fell** (231 m / 758 ft). There is a story that during the Wars of the Roses, after the Battle of Hexham Levels in 1464 (or the Battle of Towton in 1461), Henry VI became lost on Muncaster Fell until he was rescued by a shepherd and given shelter in the castle. In return he is said to have presented the Penningtons with the **Muncaster Luck**, an enamelled and gilded glass bowl. A few other 'lucks' are found in the Lake District, and are generally supposed to be luck-bringing gifts from the fairies. In the case of the Muncaster Luck, the good fortune it brings is that the castle will never lack a male heir.

Mundesley 'Mul's or Mundel's glade', OE *Mules* or *Mundeles* possessive forms of male personal names *Mul* or *Mundel* + -LEY. A modest seaside resort in Norfolk, about 13 km (8 miles) southeast of Cromer. PASTON is about 3 km (2 miles) to the south.

Munros After Sir Hugh *Munro*.
The collective name given to those Scottish mountains over 3000 ft (914.4 m) in height. The first list of such mountains was published in 1891 by Sir Hugh Munro of Lindertis (1856–1919), a bearded person, and the original *Munro's Tables* included 283 such mountains. Munro himself died with two still to climb: the tricky INACCESSIBLE PINNACLE, and Cloich-mhuillin, the Munro nearest his home which he had intended to be his final ascent.

Refinements in the surveyor's and cartographer's arts have subsequently led to revisions in Munro's list, with a number of additions to and deletions from the original. What constitutes a separate mountain, and thus what tops warrant Munro status, is a Byzantine business best left to the inner cabal of the Scottish Mountaineering Club that rules on such matters. Broadly speaking the criteria are that there should be either a distance of at least 1 mile (1.6 km) between a summit and the next Munro, or a re-ascent of at least 500 ft (152.4 m). Currently there are 284 Munros, plus 227 'Tops', which are distinct summits over 3000 ft but which, according to the men with pipes, do not achieve separate-mountain status. A refinement that allows many of the Tops the dignity of a generic name is the list of mountains known as MURDOS.

The first person to climb all the Munros was the Rev. A.E. Robertson, who achieved the first 'compleation' (as it is quaintly styled) on the top of Meall Dearg in GLEN COE in 1901. Initially, there was no tremendous enthusiasm for **Munro-bagging**, but in the last two decades of the 20th century a passion for ticking spread across the land (aficionados included the Labour politicians John Smith and Chris Smith), and as the years rolled towards the year 2000 so the number of compleaters also approached that

figure. Facial hair, too, is no longer a prerequisite for bagging, as witnessed by elfin Muriel Gray's book, *The First Fifty: Munro Bagging without a Beard* (1992). One person with (one assumes) particularly sturdy calves has climbed all the Munros ten times, while in the late 1970s Hamish Brown (with his beard, and also his dog) made the first non-stop ascent of all the Munros, linking them on foot.

The passion for compiling lists and then ticking them has, since Sir Hugh's day, generated many other classes of hill and mountain, such as CORBETTS, DONALDS, GRAHAMS, WAINWRIGHTS and MARILYNS. Film buffs may be interested to learn that not all Munros are Marilyns, and many a Marilyn is not a Munro.

Munster Irish *An Mhuma*, named after the Mumu tribe; it is also called *Muma*; the ending, as with Leinster, appears to be OScand possessive -*s* + Irish *tir* 'territory'.
One of the four provinces of Ireland, comprising the southern counties of WATERFORD, CORK, KERRY, CLARE, LIMERICK and TIPPERARY. It was one of the ancient FIVE FIFTHS or kingdoms of Ireland. Later in the Middle Ages, Munster comprised the two kingdoms of DESMOND and THOMOND, whose rulers took it in turn to be king of Munster.

> I found in Munster unfettered of any,
> Kings and queens, and poets a many –
> Poets well skilled in music and measure,
> Prosperous doings, mirth and pleasure.
>
> Anon.: 'Aldfrid's Itinerary through Ireland' (12th century),
> translated by James Clarence Mangan

Anglo-Norman infiltration began under Henry II, and powerful families such as the Butler earls of ORMOND and the Geraldine earls of Desmond became increasingly Gaelicized and independent.

A representative Munster team plays in rugby union's (professional) Celtic League.

'Dirge of the Munster Forest'. A poem by Emily Lawless (1845–1913), in which the ancient forest of Munster faces its doom in 1591:

> The axe is sharpened to cut down my pride:
> I pass, I die, I leave no natural heirs,
> Soon shall my sylvan coronals be cast;
> My hidden sanctuaries, my secret ways,
> Naked must stand to the rebellious blast;
> No Spring shall quicken what this Autumn slays.

'God's Blessing on Munster'. An anonymous poem of the 9th century, formerly attributed to St Patrick. It begins:

> God's blessing on Munster
> Men, boys, women!
> Blessing on the land
> That gives them fruit!
>
> Translated from the ancient Irish by Whitley Stokes

Micher from Munster, the. A term of abuse applied to Kerry-born Daniel O'Connell, the Liberator (1775–1847), by Biddy Moriarty, a notoriously rude Dublin street-trader:

> May the divil fly away with you, you micher from Munster, and make celery-sauce of your rotten limbs, you mealy mouthed tub of guts.
>
> (A *micher* is one who plays truant from school.)

The young O'Connell, urged on by his friends, riposted with a blast of oratorical nonsense, culminating in:

> 'Tis with the devil you will fly away, you porter-swiping similitude of the bisection of a vortex!

… a sally that was followed by a swift retreat in the face of Biddy's deployment of an iron saucepan.

Munster Plantation, the (1583). The granting of large estates in Munster following the failure of the Desmond rebellion to English soldiers and administrators serving in Ireland, among whom were Sir Walter Raleigh and the poet Edmund Spenser. At the end of the century, during the Nine Years War (which ended in 1603), the Irish took back many of the estates, but after the Battle of KINSALE in 1601 the English returned, finally ending the Gaelic ascendancy.

> The heart within my breast tonight is wild with grief
> Because, of all the haughty men who ruled this place,
> North Munster and South Munster to the wave beneath,
> None lives, and where they lived lives now an alien race.
>
> Egan O'Rahilly (1670–1726): 'A Sleepless Night', translated from the Irish by Frank O'Connor

Munster plums. A jocular term for potatoes.

Royal Munster Fusiliers. A former regiment of the British Army, tracing its origins to the 1760s and disbanded in 1922. Its nickname, the Dirty Shirts, dates from the regiment's service during the Indian Mutiny (1857), during which the Munsters dyed their shirts khaki with tea (and subsequently insisted that the word khaki, far from being Urdu for 'dusty', was from Irish *cac* 'shit').

Silver Tongue of Munster, the. A sobriquet of the Irish poet and Jacobite sympathizer Seán Ó Coileáin (*c*.1754–*c*.1816), born near Clonakilty, County Cork, and known for such poems as '*An Buachaill Bán*' ('the white-haired boy') and '*Machtnamh an duine dhoilíosaigh*' ('musings of a melancholy man').

Where Finbarr taught, let Munster learn. The motto of University College Cork and also the title of its anthem. The reference is to Cork's patron saint, St Finbar, Finbarr or Findbar (*see also under* GUAGÁN BARRA).

Muntervary. An alternative name for SHEEP'S HEAD in County Cork.

Muraisc. The Irish name for MURRISK.

Murder Hole, the. *See under* GLEN TROOL.

Murdos After *Murdo* Munro.

The collective name given to all mountains in Scotland over 3000 ft (914.4 m) with a drop of at least 30 m (98.4 ft) on all sides of the summit. The list, compiled by Alan Dawson, was first published in 1995. As the blurb explains:

> The time has come for walkers to expand their horizons beyond Munros … This is good news for radical hillwalkers; instead of following a long-dead military knight [Sir Hugh Munro], they can now worship at the feet of a more modern and fashionable guru – Murdo Munro, anti-hero of *The Angry Corrie*, Scotland's hillwalking fanzine: a sheepish man with sheepish friends, a man who was so scared of climbing the Bhasteir Tooth that he designed a list of hills which excludes it.

There are 444 Murdos, a daunting prospect for tickers compared to the mere 284 MUNROS. However, as the blurb reassuringly continues:

> If you believe there are already too many lists and we should stop messing with the existing ones, Murdo Munro has a simple message for you:
> • You *are* allowed to climb summits not listed in this booklet.
> • You do not *have* to climb a summit just because it's listed here …
> On the other hand, once you've started you might as well finish …

Murphyland From *Murphy*, a slang term for an Irishman, Murphy being a common Irish surname.

A moderately offensive name for Ireland, used in the USA from the mid-19th century to the 1940s.

Murray. A former spelling of the old Scottish kingdom of MORAY.

Murrayfield Named after Archibald *Murray*, Lord Henderson, who bought land here in the 18th century.

A residential area of western EDINBURGH, which also gives its name to Scotland's national rugby stadium, the scene of all too little glory of late.

Murrisk Irish *Muraisc* 'sea marsh'.

A village in County Mayo, 8 km (5 miles) west of Westport on the south side of CLEW BAY. There are the remains of an Augustinian priory (1457), the traditional starting point for the pilgrimage up CROAGH PATRICK. The village has Ireland's National Famine Monument (1997), in the form of a sculpture by John Behan of a coffin ship with skeleton bodies.

Murrisk is also the name of the broad peninsula between Clew Bay to the north and KILLARY HARBOUR to the south, including the mountains of Croagh Patrick and MWEELREA.

Múscraí. The Irish name for MUSKERRY.

Museumchester. *See under* MANCHESTER.

Musheramore. *See under* BOGGERAGH MOUNTAINS.

Mushroom Green Presumably self-explanatory.

A district (since 1970 a conservation area) in DUDLEY, in the West Midlands. It used to be a 'chainmakers' hamlet' (originally, in the 18th century, a settlement of nailmakers). It is now an amalgam of terraced houses, cottages and open spaces.

Muskerry Irish *Múscraí* 'the descendants of Cairbre Músc' (he was the legendary ancestor of the local people).

A Gaeltacht (Gaelic-speaking area) in West Cork, around Ballingeary, GUAGÁN BARRA and Ballyvourney.

Our Muskerry Sportsman. Timothy 'Thady' Quill (1860–1932), an itinerant labourer of great strength and legendary reputation, as celebrated in a well-known ballad, 'The Bould Thady Quill', by his contemporary Johnny Tom Gleeson (b.1853):

> For ramblin' and rovin', for gamblin' and courtin',
> For drainin' a bowl e'en as fast as you'd fill,
> In all your days roamin' you'll find none so jovial
> As our Muskerry sportsman, the Bould Thady Quill.

Musselburgh 'mussel town', OE *musele* 'mussel' + *burgh* (*see* BURY).

A town on the Firth of Forth (*see under* FORTH), on the eastern edge of EDINBURGH, at the mouth of the River ESK[3] in East Lothian (formerly in Midlothian). It was once known for the excellence of its mussels (which feature in the town's coat of arms), and indeed its oysters, but since the 1960s the eating of local mussels has been advised against because of pollution.

> At Musselburgh, and eke Newhaven,
> The fisher wives will get top livin,
> When lads gang out on Sunday's even
>   To treat their joes,
> And tak of fat pandours a prieven,
>   Or mussel brose …
>
> Robert Fergusson (1750–74): 'Caller Oysters' (*joes* 'sweethearts'; *pandours* 'Prestonpans oysters'; *prieven* 'taste'; *brose* 'oatmeal broth')

Musselburgh became a BURGH of barony in 1315–28, while Edinburgh was only made a burgh in 1329: hence the traditional song, popular locally:

> Musselburgh was a burgh
> When Edinburgh was nane,
> And Musselburgh will be a burgh
> When Edinburgh's gane.

Musselburgh became known as **the Honest Toun** in 1332 when the Earl of Moray, nephew of Robert the Bruce and regent for David II, died here, and the citizens surrendered their right to a reward for honouring his body.

Golf has been played on **Musselburgh Links** (Scots *links* 'area of turf-covered sandy ground') for hundreds of years,

and Musselburgh was the home of the Honourable Company of Edinburgh Golfers until they moved to Muirfield in 1891. The Links is also the site of the well-known horse-racing track.

Near to Musselburgh were fought the battles of PINKIE (1547; formerly also known as the **Battle of Musselburgh**) and CARBERRY HILL (1567).

Mussenden Temple. *See under* DOWNHILL.

Muswell Hill[1] *Muswell* 'mossy or boggy spring' (referring to an ancient spring here on land owned by the Priory of St Mary at Clerkenwell), OE *meos* 'moss, marsh, bog' + *wella* 'spring'; the combination *Muswell Hill* is first recorded in the 17th century.

A hill, road and district in NORTH LONDON (N10), in the west of the borough of HARINGEY. The district, between Highgate and Crouch End to the south and Southgate to the north, was quietly rural until the late 19th century, with a scattering of country houses. In 1873 one large estate, between the hill itself and WOOD GREEN, made way for Alexandra Palace ('Ally Pally'), the so-called 'People's Palace' and its park. The district's development as a residential suburb happened relatively quickly, between the 1890s and the 1910s, resulting in a striking homogeneity of architectural style – solid brick-built terraced Edwardian villas.

It used to be connected to the City of London (*see under* LONDON) by a rail line that closed in the 1950s, making Muswell Hill something of a backwater again. It retains a certain remoteness from London's centre because of its hilltop location and lack of an Underground station; but in the later 1980s it began rapidly re-gentrifying itself and joined HAMPSTEAD and HIGHGATE as a desirable North London residential locale, favoured by well-to-do families, actors and liberal media types. Such associations have given it the nickname of '**Muesli Hill**'.

In 1899 Robert Paul set up in Muswell Hill what appears to have been the first film studio in England.

In the early 1980s the serial killer Dennis Nilsen lured his young male victims to his home in Cranley Gardens, Muswell Hill. The journalist Sir William Connor (1909–67), who contributed the 'Cassandra' column to the *Daily Mirror* for many years, was born in Muswell Hill. Vivian Stanshall (1944–95), leader of the surreal and satirical 1960s Bonzo Dog Band, died in a fire in his Muswell Hill home.

> I've been driving in my car, it don't look much but I've been far;
> I drive up to Muswell Hill, I've even been to Selsey Bill.
>
> Madness: 'Driving In My Car' (song, 1986)

Muswell Hillbillies, The. The title of an album and song from it (1972) by The Kinks, the pop group formed in the early 1960s by local resident siblings Ray and Dave Davies.

Muswell Hill² As Muswell Hill¹.

A prominent hill about 1.5 km (1 mile) northwest of Brill. It is a familiar northwest Buckinghamshire landmark.

Mweelrea Irish *Sléibhte Cnoc Maol Réidh* 'mountain of the round bare grey hill' (*see* KNOCK-).

A mountain (817 m / 2680 ft) in southwest County Mayo, on the north side of Killary Harbour. It is the highest mountain in Connacht. The massif of which it is part is sometimes called the **Mweelrea Mountains**.

> September grew to shadows on Mweelrea
> Once the lambs had descended from the ridge
> With their fleeces dyed, tinges of sunset,
> Rowan berries, and the bracken rusting.
>
>> Michael Longley: 'On Mweelrea', from *The Echo Gate* (1979)

Mynwy. *See* Monnow.

Mynydd Carn 'mountain of the rocks', Welsh *mynydd* 'mountain' + *carn* 'rocks, cairn'.

A battle site near St David's in Pembrokeshire where in 1081 a number of Welsh princes fought each other, with Gruffydd ap Cynan of Gwynedd and Rhys ap Tewdr of Deheubarth coming out on top.

Mynydd Eppynt 'mountain with a horse-path', *Eppynt eb* 'horse' + *hynt* 'way, path'; a personal name *Epint* is also possible.

A range of hills in Powys (formerly in Brecknockshire), rising to the southwest of Builth Wells. The highest point is Drum-ddu (474 m / 1555 ft). The area is used by the army for live firing exercises.

Mynydd Mawr 'big mountain', *Mawr* 'big', Welsh.

A hill (534 m / 1752 ft) in the southern Berwyns, Powys, 15 km (9 miles) west of Oswestry. There are many other hills of the same name in Wales.

> We fought, and were always in retreat,
> Like snow thawing upon the slopes
> Of Mynydd Mawr …
>
>> R.S. Thomas: 'Welsh History'

Mynydd Preseli. The Welsh name for the Prescelly Mountains.

Mynydd y Gader. The Welsh name for the Black Mountains.

Mynyw. The early Welsh name for St David's.

Mytholmroyd 'clearing at the river mouths', OE *mythum* dative plural of *mythe* 'river mouth' + *rod* 'clearing'.

A village in West Yorkshire, 8 km (5 miles) west of Halifax. It was the birthplace of the poet Ted Hughes (1930–98), and home to 'King David' Hartley, leader of the Cragg Vale Coiners, a notorious gang of local coin-clippers and counterfeiters active in the 1760s.

Myton-on-Swale 'farm at the confluence of two rivers', *Myton* OE *gemythe* 'meeting of rivers' + -TON.

A village near the confluence of the Swale¹ and the Ouse² in North Yorkshire, 14 km (8.5 miles) southeast of Ripon.

Battle of Myton (20 September 1319). A battle in which the Scots under Sir James Douglas defeated an English force under William Melton, Archbishop of York. Melton had had to raise his army in great haste, and the fact that it included a large number of clerics led to its nickname – the **Chapter of Myton**. Douglas's success obliged the English to lift their siege of Berwick, taken by Robert the Bruce in 1318.

N

Naas Irish *An Nás* '(place of) the assembly'.

The county town of County Kildare, 30 km (20 miles) southwest of Dublin. It was the seat of the ancient kings of Leinster and the North Mote in the town is said to have been one of their strongholds – although it is more likely that it was built by the Anglo-Norman adventurer Maurice Fitzgerald, who was granted lands here by Strongbow in the 12th century. Naas prospered in the Middle Ages, but it was sacked in 1316 and 1577, and was taken by Cromwellian forces in 1650. Naas has a racecourse, and there is a steeplechasing course at nearby Punchestown.

Na Beanna Beola. An Irish name for the TWELVE PINS.

Nab Head, the *Nab* ME *nabb* 'promontory, headland'; the name 'Nab Head' is thus tautological.

A headland in Pembrokeshire (formerly in Dyfed), 9 km (5.5 miles) north of ST ANN'S HEAD and 12 km (7 miles) northwest of Milford Haven.

Na Cealla Beaga. The Irish name for KILLYBEGS.

Na Clocha Liatha. The Irish name for GREYSTONES.

Na Cruacha Dubha. The Irish name for MACGILLYCUDDY'S REEKS.

Nadder An OCelt river name, probably from the same ultimate ancestor as Latin *natare* 'to swim'. (R. Colt Hoare's suggestion in his *History of Modern Wiltshire* (1822–44) that the river got its name 'from its numerous windings', as if it were an adder, is entertaining but misplaced.)

A river in Wiltshire, which rises to the north of SHAFTESBURY and flows 30 km (19 miles) eastwards through Wilton to join the River AVON[3] to the south of SALISBURY. The **Nadder Valley** is a notable beauty spot, with attractive villages (*see* TEFFONT EVIAS) and lush farmland.

Na Gaibhlte. The Irish name for the GALTEE MOUNTAINS.

Nagles Mountains Presumably named after the local *Nagle* family; Nano Nagle (1728–84) was the founder of the Presentation order of nuns and a general benefactress.

A range of hills in County Cork, rising between MALLOW and FERMOY, on the south side of the BLACKWATER[2]. The highest point is Knocknaskagh (428 m / 1404 ft).

Nail in the Pale, the. A nickname for the Millennium Spire in Dublin's O'CONNELL STREET.

Nailsea 'Nægl's island or dry ground in a marsh', OE male personal name *Nægl* + *eg* (*see* -EY, -EA).

A village in North Somerset (before 1996 in Avon, before 1974 in Somerset), about 13 km (8 miles) southwest of Bristol. Between the late 18th century and the 1870s it was the place of manufacture of a particular type of decorative coloured glassware, now known as **Nailsea glass**. It specialized in ornamental flasks, and also such items as walking sticks, bells and so-called 'witch-balls' (hollow glass balls used as charms against witchcraft).

Nailsworth 'Nægl's enclosure', OE male personal name *Nægl* + *worth* (*see* -WORTH, WORTHY, -WARDINE).

A town in Gloucestershire, in the COTSWOLDS, about 19 km (12 miles) west of Cirencester. It made its money in the wool trade in the late Middle Ages and the early modern period, and contains reminders of its prosperity in some fine Georgian buildings. The **Nailsworth Ladder** is a nearby hill, with a 1 in 3 gradient, which is used for car-testing.

Nairn[1] After the River *Nairn*, which is from an Indo-European root *ner* 'to submerge'. The earliest reference is from the 12th century, *Inuernaren*, which confirms that the place is named after the river.

A royal BURGH on the Moray Firth (*see under* MORAY), in Highland, 25 km (15 miles) northeast of Inverness. It was formerly in Nairnshire, of which it was the county town, and from 1975 to 1996 was the seat of Nairn district (Highland region), which occupied the same territory as the old county. It is a popular seaside resort, being known as **the Brighton of the North**, although it has not yet achieved a reputation equivalent to BRIGHTON's as 'the heaving Sodom of the south coast'.

James VI remarked that the inhabitants of one end of Nairn (who spoke English) did not understand those at the other end (who spoke Gaelic), and Nairn was long thought of as marking the boundary between the HIGHLANDS and the LOWLANDS. It was here that Dr Johnson first heard Gaelic on his 1773 tour, although the tongue has long since disappeared from the area.

David Thomson's autobiographical *Nairn in Darkness and Light* (1987) – winner of the 1987 McVitie's Prize for Scottish Writer of the Year – recalls his boyhood in Nairn, whither he had been sent to stay with his grandparents following an eye injury.

Nairn was the birthplace of James Augustus Grant (1827–92), co-discoverer with John Hanning Speke of the source of the Nile in Lake Victoria. Grant also died in his home town. The Conservative politician William Whitelaw (1918–99), home secretary (1979–83), was born here.

There is a town called Nairn in Canada (Ontario), and a Mount Nairn in Western Australia.

Nairn². A former district within the old Highland region of Scotland (*see under* NAIRNSHIRE).

Nairnshire. A former small county of northeast Scotland, bounded on the north by the Moray Firth (*see under* MORAY), on the east by Moray and on the south and west by Inverness-shire. The county town was NAIRN¹. It became the district of **Nairn** in the new Highland region in 1975, and in 1996 became part of the unitary authority of Highland.

Nancecuke Probably 'blind valley', Cornish *nans* 'valley' + *cuic* 'blind, empty'.

A site close to the north coast of Cornwall, about 4 km (2.5 miles) northwest of REDRUTH, which for most of the Cold War was home to a Chemical Defence Establishment. (It is also called **Nancekuke**.) Opened in 1951 on the site of RAF Portreath, it closed in 1978 when Britain gave up chemical and biological weapons.

Nant Ffrancon. *See* OGWEN VALLEY.

Nant Gwynant. The Welsh name for GWYNANT VALLEY.

Nantlle Ridge, the After the little village of *Nantlle* on the north side of the range, Welsh *nant* 'narrow valley, stream' + *lle* 'locality, place'.

A ridge of mountains in SNOWDONIA, Gwynedd (formerly in Caernarvonshire), some 6 km (4 miles) northwest of Beddgelert. The summits include Y Garn (634 m / 2080 ft), Trum Y Ddysgl (709 m / 2326 ft), CRAIG CWM SILYN (the highest point, 734 m / 2408 ft) and Garneddgoch (700 m / 2296 ft).

Nantwich Originally *Wich* 'saltworks', OE *wic* (*see* -WICK); the first element, ME *named*, 'renowned, famous' was added in the 12th century; *see also* WICHES.

A market town in Cheshire, on the River WEAVER, about 6 km (4 miles) southwest of Crewe. Its fame, fortune and name were built on salt. Rock salt has been mined and otherwise extracted here from earliest times, and it came to be effectively the capital of Cheshire's salt industry, so widely known that it boastfully incorporated the epithet 'famous' into its name. Most of the town was burned down in 1583, but so vital was its salt production that Elizabeth I launched a nationwide appeal for funds to rebuild it, contributing £1000 herself.

A 17th-century writer described one of the methods of obtaining the salt:

> The manner of boyling the Brine into Salt at Namptwich. They boyl it in Iron Pans, about 3 foot square, and 6 inches deep; their Fires are made of Staffordshire Pit-Coles, and one of their smaller Pans is boiled in 2 hours time. To clarify and raise the Scum, they use Calves, Cows and Sheeps blood, which is said to give the Salt an ill flavour.
>
> John Collins: *Salt and Fishery, Discourse Thereof* (1682)

The herbalist John Gerard (1545–1612) was born in Nantwich, as were the surgeon and histologist Sir William Bowman (1816–92), after whom Bowman's capsules in the kidneys are named, and David (later Earl) Beatty (1871–1936), commander of the British Grand Fleet after the Battle of Jutland.

The clergyman and chemist Joseph Priestley, discoverer of oxygen, taught at a day school here from 1758 to 1761, supply-ing his pupils with various scientific instruments for experiments.

Battle of Nantwich (24 January 1644). A battle of the Civil Wars, in which Irish Royalist forces led by Lord Byron, which had been laying siege to Nantwich, were defeated and put to flight by the Parliamentarian army under Sir Thomas Fairfax and Sir William Brereton.

Nantyglo 'valley of the coal or charcoal', Welsh *nant* 'valley' + *y* 'the' + *glo* 'charcoal, coal'.

A small town in Blaenau Gwent (formerly in Monmouthshire, then in Gwent), 3 km (2 miles) east of Ebbw Vale. There was once a well-known ironworks here. In 1839 Chartists held a secret meeting here, prior to a disastrous advance on NEWPORT¹. Just to the south is the similarly named (but in English) village of Coalbrookvale.

Nant-y-Moch Reservoir Named after a chapel drowned when the dam was built, Welsh *nant* 'valley' + *y* 'the' + *moch* 'pig'.

A reservoir in Ceredigion (formerly in Cardiganshire, then in Dyfed), 16 km (10 miles) northeast of Aberystwyth. The dam was constructed in the 1960s as part of a hydroelectric scheme.

Napes Needle. *See* GREAT GABLE.

Nappa Possibly OE *hnæpp* 'bowl-shaped hollow' + *hæg* 'enclosure'.

A settlement in Ribblesdale, North Yorkshire, 10 km (6 miles) southeast of Settle.

Narberth 'place by the wood', Welsh *yn* 'at' + *ar* 'near' + *perth* 'hedge, wood' (the place developed at the edge of Narberth Forest).

A town in Pembrokeshire (formerly in Dyfed), 15 km (9 miles) east of Haverfordwest. Although 'Narberth' is Welsh, the form now used in Welsh is **Arberth**, the form Narberth having derived from the name 'Castell yn Arberth' ('castle at Arberth'). Traditionally, 'Narberth' was the site of the court of Pwyll, legendary Prince of Dyfed in the Welsh literary masterpiece the *Mabinogion*. Today it calls itself the '**Capital of the Landsker Borderlands**' (*see under* Landsker Line).

It was while writing a letter in the White Hart inn in Narberth during his Welsh tour of 1802 that the poet Samuel Taylor Coleridge was surprised by a large sheepdog crashing through a closed window and landing on his back. He took the incident in good humour.

Nare Head Originally Cornish *penn-ardh* (*see* -ARD).

A headland on the south coast of Cornwall, at the eastern end of Gerrans Bay, about 8 km (5 miles) northeast of St Mawes.

Nare Point. A headland on the south coast of western Cornwall, on the Lizard Peninsula, on the southern side of the mouth of the HELFORD River, about 6.5 km (4 miles) south of Falmouth. It forms the southern extremity of Falmouth Bay (*see under* FALMOUTH).

Na Rosa. The Irish name for the ROSSES.

Ná Sailtí. The Irish name for the SALTEE ISLANDS.

Na Scealaga. The Irish name for the SKELLIGS.

Na Sceirí. The Irish name for SKERRIES.

Naseby Originally *Nasebury* 'Hnæf's stronghold', OE *Hnæfes* possessive form of male personal name *Hnæf* + *byrig* dative form of *burh* (*see* BURY); the second element was replaced by -BY in the 12th century. The idea that the name originated in the village being considered the central point or 'navel' (OE *nafela*) of England (in the same way as Delphi in Greece was thought of as the 'navel of the world') is fanciful.

A village in Northamptonshire, about 19 km (12 miles) northwest of Northampton.

Battle of Naseby (14 June 1645). A battle in the Civil Wars, fought about 2.5 km (1.5 miles) north of Naseby, in which Parliamentarian forces under Oliver Cromwell and Sir Thomas Fairfax decisively defeated the Royalists, led by Prince Rupert. The Royalists lost about 1000 killed and 5000 were taken prisoner, together with all their artillery. Perhaps of more long-term moment than the defeat, though, was the seizure of several letters from Charles I seeking help from foreign powers; their disclosure severely damaged the king's support.

Na Solláin. The Irish name for SALLINS.

Nass, the 'headland', OE *næss* (*see* NESS).

A sandy promontory on the Essex coast, at the northern extremity of the mouth of the River BLACKWATER[1].

Nasty '(place at the) east enclosure', OE *east* + *hæg* 'enclosure'; the N comes from a misanalysis of early ME *atten asthey* 'at the east enclosure'.

A village in Hertfordshire, about 10 km (6 miles) east of Stevenage.

National Forest, the. A 'forest' established in the English MIDLANDS in the late 20th century, to the north of Birmingham, combining CHARNWOOD FOREST and NEEDWOOD FOREST into a single forest park. Covering about 520 sq km (200 sq miles), it spans Derbyshire, Leicestershire and Staffordshire, and the main towns within it are ASHBY-DE-LA-ZOUCH, BURTON UPON TRENT and SWADLINCOTE. Very little of it is at present actually forested (only six per cent at the turn of the 21st century, which is below the national average), but there are plans to plant 30 million trees. It is billed as the first new forest in Britain for 1000 years.

Naunton Beauchamp *Naunton* 'new farmstead or estate', OE *niwan* dative form of *niwe* 'new' + -TON; *Beauchamp* denoting manorial ownership in the early Middle Ages by the Beauchamp family.

A village (pronounced 'beecham') in Worcestershire (before 1998 in Hereford and Worcester, before 1974 in Worcestershire), about 11 km (7 miles) southeast of Worcester.

Navan Irish *An Uaimh* 'the cave'; this was its official name until the citizens voted to return to the more easily pronounced anglicized form (Irish *mh* is pronounced *v*).

The county town of County Meath, at the confluence of the BOYNE and the BLACKWATER[2], 45 km (28 miles) northwest of Dublin. There is an Anglo-Norman motte, and Navan was an important stronghold in the PALE. Its monastery was destroyed by Cromwell.

> The Boyne at Navan swam with light,
> Where children headlong through the trees
> Plunged down the sward, and nicked the bright
> Precarious evening with unease.
>
> Donald Davie: 'Evening on the Boyne', from *Brides of Reason* (1955)

Navan Fort Irish *Eamhain Mhacha*; the meaning of the first word is unknown, but Macha was a goddess or legendary queen. The anglicized *Navan* derives from *Eamhain* (Irish *mh* is pronounced *v*), with the addition of Irish *an* 'the'.

A great circular earthwork dating from the late Bronze Age, in County Armagh, 3 km (2 miles) west of Armagh itself.

It is almost certainly the site of **Emain Macha**, the seat of the ancient kings of Ulster for some 600 years, until the 4th century AD. In legend Emain Macha was the seat of King Conchobar and his Knights of the Red Branch, and it was here that the hero Cuchulain spent his youth. It features as **Isamnium** in Ptolemy's *Geography* (2nd century AD).

Navax Point *Navax* perhaps Cornish *an havek* 'the summerland' (referring to land used for summer grazing).
A headland on the north coast of western Cornwall, at the eastern end of St Ives² Bay.

Naver. *See under* STRATHNAVER.

Nayland '(place at the) island' (referring to land in a bend of the River Stour), OE *eg-land* 'island'. The initial *N-* (first recorded in the 13th century) came from a misinterpretation of ME *atten eiland* 'at the island' as *atte neiland*.
A village in Suffolk, in CONSTABLE COUNTRY, on the River STOUR², close to the Essex border, about 13 km (8 miles) southeast of SUDBURY¹. Its church has an altar painting by Constable: *Christ Blessing the Bread and Wine* (1809)
See also STOKE-BY-NAYLAND.

Naze, the 'headland', OE *næss* (*see* NESS).
A headland in Essex, at the southeastern extremity of Hamford Water, about 24 km (15 miles) east of Colchester. It consists mainly of salt marshes, which are now a nature reserve. Just to the south is WALTON-ON-THE-NAZE.

Near Sawrey *Sawrey* OScand *saurar* 'muddy grounds'; *Near* distinguishes it from the village of Far Sawrey, 1 km (0.6 miles) to the east.
A little village in the LAKE DISTRICT, Cumbria (formerly in Lancashire), 3 km (2 miles) southeast of Hawkshead. Beatrix Potter stayed in the village with her parents, and at the age of 39 bought Hill Top Farm with the royalties from *The Tale of Peter Rabbit* (1900). The house and village appear in several of her subsequent tales, such as *The Tale of Tom Kitten* and *The Tale of Samuel Whiskers*. After she married William Heelis in 1913, she moved to nearby Castle Cottage, and gave up writing and illustrating for farming. When she died in 1943, she left several thousand acres of land she had acquired round about to the National Trust, which now also looks after Hill Top.

> It [Near Sawrey] is as nearly perfect a little place as I ever lived in.
>
> Beatrix Potter: *The Journal of Beatrix Potter, 1881–1897* (1966)

Neasden 'nose-shaped hill', OE *neosu* 'nose' + *dun* (*see* DOWN, -DON).
A district of northwest London (NW2, NW10), in the borough of BRENT², between Cricklewood to the east and Wembley to the west. It failed signally to hit the headlines in the first thousand years or so of its history (it was a small hamlet until the late 19th century, and it was the coming of the NORTH CIRCULAR ROAD in the 1920s that finally sucked it into suburbia), which is no doubt one reason why the satirical magazine *Private Eye* homed in on it in the 1960s as the eminently mockable epitome of suburban futility. The name 'Neasden' seems to possess a certain nasal narrowness that fits it well for the role. Central to *Private Eye*'s Neasden saga is the spectacularly unsuccessful local football club, created by the magazine's Peter Cook and Barry Fantoni, with its cast of grotesques: the manager, tight-lipped, ashen-faced Ron Knee; the heavy-scoring centre forward Pevsner (all own-goals, unfortunately); and the fan club (Sid and Doris Bonkers).

Neasden now has a sizable ethnic South Asian population, and is home to the Sri Swaminarayan Mandir (1995), the first traditional Hindu temple built outside India. It consumed 2000 tons of Italian marble and nearly 3000 tons of Bulgarian limestone.

Neasden 'Underground' station, originally on the Metropolitan line, now on the Jubilee, opened in 1939.

The model Twiggy (b.1949; real name Lesley Hornby; now known as Twiggy Lawson) was born in Neasden, as was Rolling Stones drummer Charlie Watts (b.1941).

> Neasden,
> You won't be sorry that you breezed in,
> The traffic lights and yellow lines,
> And the illuminated signs,
> All say welcome to the borough that everyone's pleased in.
>
> Willie Rushton: *Neasden*

Neath¹ An anglicization of the Welsh name *Nedd*, which is, like the River NIDD in Yorkshire, an Indo-European river name meaning 'running water'.
A river in south Wales, called **Nedd** in Welsh. It rises in the Brecon Beacons in Powys (formerly in Brecknockshire) and flows for approximately 40 km (25 miles) southwestwards through the **Vale of Neath** in Neath Port Talbot (formerly in Glamorgan, then in West Glamorgan), past the town of Neath, to meet the sea at Swansea Bay.

Neath² From NEATH¹.
An industrial town on the River NEATH¹ in Neath Port Talbot unitary authority (formerly in Glamorgan and then West Glamorgan), 10 km (6 miles) east of Swansea. Its Welsh name is **Castell-nedd** ('castle on the River Neath'). The Romans built a fort here in AD 70–80, and called it **Nidum**, the Latinized version of the Celtic river name, Nedd. **Neath Castle**, originally built in the 13th century, was sacked by Llywelyn ab Iowerth (the Great) in 1231, and was badly damaged again in 1321, after which it was rebuilt; its remains can be seen standing forlornly in the corner of the Safeway car park. The remains of the 12th-century **Neath Abbey** can be found standing, equally

forlornly, in an industrial estate on the edge of town; it was here that a monk betrayed Edward II and his lover Hugh Le Despenser to the Earl of Lancaster in 1326. BRITON FERRY, at the mouth of the River Neath, has been part of the town since 1922.

Neath RFC, founded in 1871 and nicknamed the Welsh All Blacks (from its dark playing strip), plays its home games at The Gnoll. More than 70 Neath players have been capped by Wales, including Paul Thorburn, Jonathan Davies and Gareth Llewelyn. The club has a formidable reputation, as the poet Dylan Thomas (a native and supporter of neighbouring SWANSEA[1]) observed:

> In the game there were at least five instances of people being grabbed by the testicles. Neath is the bag-snatching capital of Wales.

Neath RFC now plays in the (semi-professional) Welsh premiership, and is a feeder club to the **Neath-Swansea Ospreys** (a regional team representing West Glamorgan), which plays in the (professional) Celtic League.

There is a town called Neath in Pennsylvania, in the USA.

Neath Port Talbot. A unitary authority in south Wales, created in 1996 from part of the former county of West Glamorgan. It is bounded to the south by the Bristol Channel, to the west by Swansea, to the north by Powys, and to the east by Rhondda Cynon Taff and Bridgend. Its administrative seat is at PORT TALBOT, and the other main town is NEATH[2].

Nebo The name given in Deuteronomy 32:49 and 34:1 to PISGAH[1], on the summit of which Moses died after having had his first sight of the Promised Land.

There are villages of this name in Ceredigion, Conwy, Gwynedd and Anglesey.

> And Moses went up from the plains of Moab unto the mountain of Nebo, to the top of Pisgah, that is over against Jericho. And the Lord shewed him all the land of Gilead, unto Dan …
>
> Deuteronomy 34:1

Nechtansmere 'Nechtan's lake', OE *mere* 'lake' with the Pictish male personal name Nechtan. Nechtan (also Naiton, Neiton, Nechton and other variants) was the name of a succession of Pictish kings: Nechtan IV sent an embassy to Bede's abbot, Ceolfrith, at the monastery of Wearmouth-Jarrow, to find out about the Roman celebration of Easter. The Celtic Church had different practices, and this led to controversy between Celts and Saxons in the 7th century (*see* WHITBY).

A battle site in Angus, where in 685 Brude, son of Bile and king of the Picts, annihilated the invading Northumbrians and killed their king Egfrith, so ending the overlordship that Northumbria had for a time exercised in the north.

The battle is believed to have been fought at Dunnichen, around 6 km (4 miles) east of FORFAR.

Necropolis, the Greek *nekros* 'dead' + *polis* 'city'.

A large cemetery in the centre of GLASGOW, on a hill to the east of the cathedral. The hill is dominated by a monument to John Knox (1825), and the cemetery itself was opened in 1832, modelled on Paris's Père Lachaise. The Necropolis, a very heaven for Goths, contains some of the most sumptuous mausoleums in the country, and many splendid examples of Victorian graveside statuary. South of the river, in the GORBALS, is the **Southern Necropolis** (1840).

> Here row on row of rank
> and rotting dead
> lie in their mansions,
> merchants, surgeons, soldiers all gone
> for ever inside the iron gates to sleep
> in neo-Greek or Gothic glory …
>
> I.D. Feint: 'In the Gardens of the Necropolis' (1979)

Nedd. The Welsh name for the River NEATH[1].

Nedging Tye Originally *Nedging* 'place associated with Hnydda', OE male personal name *Hnydda* + -ING; *Tye* 'common pasture', OE *teag*, is a later affix.

A village in Suffolk, about 16 km (10 miles) northwest of Ipswich.

Needles, the From their (relatively) sharply pointed tips. The name is first recorded in a modern form in a 15th-century Anglo-French document, '*La terre deuaunt les nedeles del Isle de Wight*' ('the land before the needles of the Isle of Wight').

A group of three large chalk rocks at the western tip of the ISLE OF WIGHT, at the southern end of ALUM BAY. They reach 30 m (98 ft); the highest of them was once 36m (118 ft), but it collapsed in a storm in 1764. Their distinctive serrated outline, like snow-covered alps or a set of dangerous teeth, has become an icon of the island, regularly featured in coverage of Cowes Week yacht races (*see under* COWES). They are a potential hazard to shipping and a lighthouse stands on the outermost rock.

Needwood Forest *Needwood* 'poor wood' or 'wood resorted to in need (as a refuge)', OE *ned* 'need' + *wudu* 'wood'.

An area of (largely former) woodland in Staffordshire, about 8 km (5 miles) west of Burton upon Trent. Trees remain in patches. The Swilcar Oak is said to be between 600 and 700 years old. It is now being replanted, along with CHARNWOOD FOREST, as part of the NATIONAL FOREST scheme.

Neen Savage *Neen* an OCelt or pre-Celtic name for the river now called the Rea; *Savage* denoting manorial ownership in the Middle Ages by the le Savage family.

A village in Shropshire, on the River Rea, about 16 km (10 miles) east of Ludlow.

Neen Sollars *Sollars* denoting manorial ownership in the Middle Ages by the le Solers family.

A village in Shropshire, on the River Rea, about 5 km (3 miles) south of Neen Savage.

Neidín. The Irish name for KENMARE.

Neidpath Castle Probably 'cattle track', OE *neat* 'cattle' + *pæth* 'track'.

A castle above the River TWEED on the west side of PEEBLES, in Scottish Borders (formerly in Peeblesshire). The oldest part is 14th century, but there were many alterations in the 17th century. It was besieged and eventually taken by Cromwell during the Civil Wars, and much restored in the 20th century. It was owned by the Frasers and then the Hays, and later by 'Old Q', the 4th Duke of Queensberry (1725–1810), whom the poet William Wordsworth referred to as 'Degenerate Douglas' because he had levelled:

> … with the dust a noble horde,
> A brotherhood of venerable Trees,
> Leaving an ancient Dome, and Towers like these,
> Beggared and outraged!
>
> William Wordsworth: 'Sonnet (composed at [Neidpath] Castle)' (1803)

'Maid of Neidpath, The'. A ballad by Sir Walter Scott, in which the eponymous heroine dies of lovesickness. There is also a ballad of the same title and with the same theme by Thomas Campbell.

Nelson After the local inn name, the Lord *Nelson*, itself named after the naval hero.

An industrial town in Lancashire, north of and contiguous with BURNLEY. It was founded in the early 19th century.

Nelson's Column. *See under* TRAFALGAR SQUARE.

Nelson's Pillar. A former erection in Dublin whose subject was described by James Joyce in *Ulysses* (1922) as 'the onehandled adulterer'; *see under* O'CONNELL STREET.

Nelson Village A modern name commemorating Admiral *Nelson*.

A village in Northumberland, 13 km (8 miles) north of Newcastle.

Nempnett Thrubwell Originally two separate places: *Nempnett* originally *Emnet* '(place at the) level ground', OE *emnet* 'level ground' – the *N* comes from a misanalysis of early ME *atten emnet* 'at the level ground'; *Thrubwell* from OE *wella* 'spring, stream', with an uncertain first element.

A village in Bath and North East Somerset (before 1996 in Avon, before 1974 in Somerset), near Blagdon Lake, about 13 km (8 miles) south of Bristol.

Nenagh Irish *An tAonach* 'the place of assembly'.

A market town in County Tipperary, 36 km (22 miles) northeast of Limerick. The Anglo-Norman castle, with its fine circular keep, dates from *c*.1200 (with 19th-century castellations). It was a stronghold of the Ormonds (*see under* ORMOND), and changed hands several times. Nenagh also has the ruins of a 13th-century Franciscan friary, destroyed by the Cromwellians.

Nene An OCelt or pre-Celtic name of unknown meaning.

A river (pronounced 'neen' or 'nen') in Northamptonshire, Peterborough, Cambridgeshire and Lincolnshire, which rises about 21 km (13 miles) west of Northampton and flows approximately 170 km (105 miles) eastwards and northeastwards through NORTHAMPTON, OUNDLE, FOTHERINGHAY, PETERBOROUGH and WISBECH into the NORTH SEA at the WASH. It is navigable for its last 145 km (90 miles).

The **Rolls-Royce Nene** was an early turbojet engine, first built in 1944.

Nent OCelt *nant* 'valley'.

A small tributary of the South TYNE[1] in Northumberland, rising some 25 km (15 miles) southwest of Hexham. Its upland valley includes the villages of **Nenthead** and **Nenthall**, developed during the lead-mining boom of the 18th and 19th centuries, which had dreadful environmental consequences:

> The little valley of the Nent was once a fairy land, and had its flowery meadows, and wild shaws, and bosky brays, … till the wealth of mining speculations began to improve and enlarge the narrow stripe of enclosed land that fringed the margins of its crystal stream; and blotch its gemmed and emerald fields with the rubbish of its mines and levels, and gutter its head and sides, and poison its sweet water.
>
> Rev. John Hodgson: *History of Northumberland* (1840)

Nephin Etymology unknown.

A somewhat lumpish, isolated mountain (806 m / 2644 ft) in Mayo, 20 km (12 miles) north of Castlebar, to the west of LOUGH CONN and to the north of **Glen Nephin**. To the west, across the R312, rising above a roadless, unpeopled wilderness comprising the largest area of blanket bog in Ireland, are the quartzite peaks of the **Nephin Beg Range**, taking their name from **Nephin Beg** (Irish *beg* 'little'), which at 627 m (2057 ft) is not actually the highest in the range; that honour goes to Birreencorragh (697 m / 2286 ft).

Neptune's Staircase. *See under* CALEDONIAN CANAL.

Ness OScand *nes*, Gaelic *neas* 'promontory' (*see* NESS).

The northernmost part of LEWIS, coming to a point at the Butt of Lewis. Near the tip is the village of **Port of Ness** (Gaelic *Port Nis*), from where once a year the men would sail to remote SULA SGEIR to catch young gannets.

Ness, Loch. *See* LOCH NESS.

❖ ness ❖

This is a Germanic word meaning 'promontory, headland', and the names containing the element are fairly neatly divided between north and south. In the north, the Old Scandinavian *nes* is found in FURNESS (Cumbria), HOLDERNESS (Yorkshire), SKEGNESS (Lincolnshire), the former county of CAITHNESS and DURNESS (Highland), CALLANISH (Lewis), STROMNESS (Orkney)

and BO'NESS (Falkirk). It is worth noting that INVERNESS does not contain this element, but that HORNSEA (East Riding of Yorkshire) does, both despite appearances. In the south, names from Old English *næss* appear both in simple names such as the NAZE (Essex) and in compound names such as DUNGENESS and SHEERNESS (Kent) and FOULNESS and SHOEBURYNESS (Essex).

Netheravon '(place) lower down the Avon' (relative to UPAVON), OE *neotherra* 'lower' + river name *Avon*.

A village in Wiltshire, on the river AVON[3], in the north-eastern part of SALISBURY Plain, about 20 km (12 miles) north of Salisbury. It is in military country, surrounded by firing ranges and tank-exercising grounds.

Nether Stowey *Nether* indicating its position relative to the village of Over Stowey, further up the slope; *Stowey* 'stone way', OE *stan* 'stone' (*see* STONE) + *weg* 'way'.

A village in Somerset, in the QUANTOCK HILLS, about 14 km (9 miles) northwest of Bridgwater. The poet Samuel Taylor Coleridge lived here from 1796 to 1798, housed in a cottage by his friend Thomas Poole, a local man. Coleridge wrote many of his most celebrated poems during this period, including 'The Rime of the Ancient Mariner' (1798), in which Nether Stowey church can be identified. William Wordsworth moved to Alfoxton nearby, enabling them to conceive and collaborate on the *Lyrical Ballads* (1798).

Netherthong 'lower narrow strip of land', OE *thwang* 'narrow strip of land' + *neotherra* 'lower'; sadly, the name has nothing to do with skimpy undergarments. The affix distinguishes it from nearby Upperthong.

A village in West Yorkshire, 7 km (4.5 miles) south of Huddersfield.

Nether Wallop *Nether* indicating its position downstream of OVER WALLOP and MIDDLE WALLOP; *Wallop* (*see* Middle Wallop).

A village in Hampshire, on the Wallop Brook (*see under* the WALLOPS), about 11 km (7 miles) southwest of Andover. The London-born conductor Leopold Stokowski (1882–1977) died here. It has been the village's fate to be the butt of schoolboyish jokes for the perceived suggestiveness of its name. The hillfort of DANEBURY lies to the northwest.

Nethy An OCelt river name meaning 'flowing one'.

A river in Highland, rising on the eastern side of CAIRN GORM and flowing down **Strathnethy** ('valley of the Nethy') between **Abernethy Forest** ('mouth of the Nethy') and the **Braes of Abernethy** ('hillsides of Abernethy') before joining the SPEY just north of the village of **Nethy Bridge**. *See also* ABERNETHY[1].

Netley Earlier *Latley* 'glade where laths are obtained', OE *lætt* 'lath' + -LEY.

A village in Hampshire, about 5 km (3 miles) southeast of Southampton. The Royal Victoria Military Hospital, nicknamed SPIKE ISLAND[1], was opened here to care for soldiers after the Crimean War.

Nettlebed 'plot of ground overgrown with nettles', OE *netele* 'nettle' + *bedd* 'bed (of ground, for growing plants)'.

A village in Oxfordshire, in the CHILTERN HILLS, about 8 km (5 miles) northwest of Henley-on-Thames.

Neuk, East. *See* the EAST NEUK.

Neuk, Northeast. *See under* BUCHAN.

Nevern From a Welsh river name of unknown meaning.

A village in Pembrokeshire, 5 km (3 miles) northeast of NEWPORT[5]. Its Welsh name is **Nanhyfer** (Welsh, *nant* 'stream, valley' + *Nyfer*, a river name of unknown meaning). The church of St Brynach, built on the site of one of the earliest Christian places of worship in Wales was formerly a stopping place for pilgrims on the way from HOLYWELL to ST DAVID'S. The churchyard here contains an impressive line of ancient cypress and yew trees, including the so-called **Bleeding Yew of Nevern**. Various theories have been advanced to explain the blood-like liquid that exudes from its trunk. A patriotic theory holds that the tree will bleed until a Welshman holds Nevern Castle again (*see below*); another, more ghoulish, that the blood of all those buried in the graveyard of St Brynach's is drawn up by the tree's roots and 'bleeds' out of its trunk.

The ruined **Nevern Castle** was originally a native Welsh stronghold, but was seized in the early 12th century by the Norman Robert Fitzmartin. Recaptured by the Welsh in 1191, the castle was abandoned after 1197 and fell into ruin.

Neville's Cross Named after the cross set up by Lord Ralph *Neville* to commemorate the English victory at the battle, originally called the Battle of Redhills.

A battle site on the western side of the city of DURHAM, County Durham. In 1346, following the diktats of the Franco-Scottish Auld Alliance, David II led a Scots army into England to distract Edward III from his siege of Calais. Edward had, however, left a strong force in the north, and on 17 October it defeated the Scots at Neville's Cross (with the help of the monks of Durham, who sang mass from the top of the cathedral's tower). David II was captured, not to be released until 1357, and the whole of southern Scotland was occupied by the English.

Nevis Range. *See* BEN NEVIS.

New Abbey. *See* SWEETHEART ABBEY.

Newark 'new fortification or building' (referring to the Norman castle, in contrast to the old Roman fort, the 'Old-wark' at *Margidunum* (East Bridgford)), OE *niwe* 'new' + *weorc* 'fortification, building'.

A market town and river port in Nottinghamshire, on the River Trent (its full name is **Newark-on-Trent**), about 32 km (20 miles) northeast of Nottingham. It is on the East Coast main railway line and on the A1 (in coaching days it was a major staging post, but the road now bypasses it). Newark's cobbled market place is overlooked by a Georgian town hall and by the church of St Mary Magdalene, one of the most imposing parish churches in England.

King John (1167–1216) died – after over-indulging in, possibly poisoned, peaches and cider – in **Newark Castle**. Only a partial shell now remains of this, as it was pounded to rubble by besieging Parliamentarian forces in 1644 during the Civil Wars. Charles I surrendered in Newark on 5 May 1646 to General Alexander Leslie, Earl of Leven, commander of Scots Covenanting forces, who handed him over to Parliament in January 1647.

William Gladstone, the future prime minister, was MP for Newark from 1832 to 1845. The actor Donald Wolfit (1902–68) was born here, and the composer John Blow (1649–1709) was baptized here.

There are towns called Newark in the USA (Arkansas, California, Delaware, Illinois, Nebraska, New Jersey, New York, Ohio). Newark, New Jersey, is part of the Greater New York Metropolitan Area, and an important focus of air, road and rail routes.

Newark Siege. A piece of music for viol consort by John Jenkins (1592–1678), inspired by the Civil War siege.

Newark Castle. *See under* YARROW WATER.

New Ash Green A modern coinage, based on the name of the nearby village of ASH.

A village in Kent, on the NORTH DOWNS, about 10 km (6 miles) southwest of Gravesend. It was created by the Span development company in the 1960s as a self-sufficient community. Facilities are provided on the principle of the 'neighbourhood unit' (a unit consisting of a primary school, a small shopping centre, a church and a pub, with about half of the area left as open space).

New Bedford River. *See* HUNDRED FOOT DRAIN.

Newbiggin-by-the-Sea *Newbiggin* 'new building', OE *niwe* 'new' + ME *bigging* 'building, house'; the affix distinguishes it from other Newbiggins in Cumbria, County Durham and Northumberland.

A seaside town in Northumberland, just east of Ashington and 24 km (15 miles) north of Newcastle.

Newbold Pacey *Newbold* 'new building', OE *niwe* 'new' + *bold* 'building'; *Pacey* denoting manorial ownership in the Middle Ages by the de Pasci family.

A village in Warwickshire, about 10 km (6 miles) northeast of Stratford-upon-Avon.

Newbold Verdon *Verdon* denoting manorial ownership in the Middle Ages by the de Verdun family.

A village in Leicestershire, about 16 km (10 miles) west of Leicester.

New Bolingbroke. *See* OLD BOLINGBROKE.

Newbridge¹ 'new bridge', OE *niwe* 'new' + *bridge*.

An industrial town in Caerphilly unitary authority (formerly in Monmouthshire, then in Gwent), 14 km (8.5 miles) northwest of Newport.

Newbridge² Irish *Droichead Nua* 'new bridge'.

A town on the River LIFFEY in County Kildare, 10 km (6 miles) southwest of Naas. It was a garrison town under the British. Nearby is the CURRAGH racecourse.

New Brighton Named after BRIGHTON.

A holiday district of WALLASEY, at the northeastern tip of the WIRRAL. It was developed in the early 1830s by a Liverpool merchant called James Atherton, who saw the potential of the extensive sands and heathland as a seaside resort and named it after the already well-established holiday town on the Sussex coast.

Newburgh 'new burgh' OE *niwe* 'new' + *burgh* (*see* BURY).

A royal BURGH (1266) in Fife, on the south side of the Firth of TAY, some 14 km (8.5 miles) southeast of Perth. It was founded as a 'new burgh' beside LINDORES Abbey.

Newburn 'new stream', OE *niwe* 'new' + *burna* 'stream'.

A suburb of NEWCASTLE UPON TYNE, Tyne and Wear (formerly in Northumberland), some 6 km (4 miles) west of the city centre.

Battle of Newburn Ford (28 August 1640). A battle on the Tyne just west of Newburn during the Bishops' Wars in which an army of invading Scots Covenanters defeated the forces of Charles I. The Scots went on to occupy Newcastle, and Charles was obliged to sign the Treaty of Ripon (*see under* RIPON).

Newbury 'new market town or borough', OE *niwe* 'new' + *byrig* dative form of *burh* (*see* BURY).

A market town in Berkshire, on the River Kennet and the Kennet and Avon Canal, about 25 km (16 miles) southwest of Reading. It is the adminstrative centre of WEST

BERKSHIRE. It grew to prosperity in the 15th, 16th and 17th centuries on the back of the cloth trade. Nowadays it specializes in high-tech industries, and also makes money from horse-racing: there has been a racecourse here (to the east of the town) since 1905, and there are many training stables nearby.

The building of Newbury A34 bypass in the late 1990s sparked off major protests and civil disobedience by environmentalists, including sit-ins in trees and the digging of underground tunnels. A burrower nicknamed 'Swampy' achieved national celebrity.

GREENHAM COMMON is just to the southeast, and ALDERMASTON and HARWELL, with their atomic research establishments, are not far away, so Newbury during the Cold War cannot have been a comfortable place to live in.

Richard Adams (b.1920), author of the novel *Watership Down* (1972, *see under* WATERSHIP DOWN), was born here.

Newbury is home to the International Seismological Centre. There are towns called Newbury in the USA (Massachusetts, New Hampshire).

Battle of Newbury, First (20 September 1643). A battle during the Civil Wars in which the Royalists, attempting to cut off a Parliamentarian army under the Earl of Essex, ran out of ammunition and had to withdraw. A poignant incident in the battle was the death of the idealistic young Royalist Lucius Cary, the 2nd Viscount Falkland: appalled by the civil strife of the war, he rode deliberately to his death in a hail of bullets.

Battle of Newbury, Second (27 October 1644). A battle during the Civil Wars in which the Royalists, briefly on the up, got the better of a Parliamentarian army under the Earl of Manchester.

Jack of Newbury. The sobriquet of John Winchcombe, alias Smallwood (d.1520), a wealthy clothier in the reign of Henry VIII (1509–47). He was the hero of many chapbooks (the late medieval equivalent of the tabloids) and is said to have kept 100 looms in his own house at Newbury and to have equipped at his own expense 100–200 of his men to aid the king against the Scots at the Battle of Flodden in 1513. He appears in *Jack of Newburie* (*c.*1597), a work of prose fiction by Thomas Deloney.

See also SPEENHAMLAND.

Newcastle¹ Irish *An Caisleán Nua* 'the new castle', referring to a 16th-century castle demolished in the 19th century. A seaside resort on DUNDRUM BAY, County Down, 15 km (9 miles) southwest of Downpatrick. The MOURNE MOUNTAINS rise to the south.

Newcastle². A village in County Dublin, just to the west of the city. There was an Anglo-Norman castle here.

Newcastle Emlyn *Newcastle* 'new castle', *new + castel* (*see* CASTLE), referring to the castle built here in the 13th century to replace an earlier Norman castle; *Emlyn* was the name of the local area, meaning 'around the valley', Welsh *am* 'around' + *glyn* 'valley'.

A small market town on the River Teifi in Ceredigion (formerly in Cardiganshire, then in Dyfed), 14 km (8.5 miles) southeast of Cardigan. The Welsh name is **Castellnewydd Emlyn** (meaning the same as the English name).

Newcastle under Lyme *Newcastle* referring to a castle built here in the mid-12th century by Ranulf de Gernons, Earl of Chester ('new' in relation to the one at nearby Chesterton); *Lyme* an OCelt district name, probably meaning 'elm-tree region'.

An industrial town in Staffordshire, in the POTTERIES, about 5 km (3 miles) west of Stoke on Trent. It earns its living mainly from the making of bricks and tiles, clothing, paper and machinery. It is the main conurbation adjacent to KEELE University. Only a single wall remains of the castle from which it got its name.

The novelist Arnold Bennett (1867–1931) and the Imagist poet T.E. Hulme (1883–1917) both went to school in Newcastle under Lyme. Thomas Pelham-Holles, prime minister from 1754 to 1756 and from 1757 to 1762, was Duke of both Newcastle under Lyme and NEWCASTLE UPON TYNE.

Newcastle upon Tyne *Newcastle*, the earliest recorded form is the Latin *Novem Castellum* 1130; *Tyne see* TYNE¹.

A city and metropolitan borough of Tyne and Wear, about 115 km (70 miles) north of York. It was formerly in Northumberland, of which it was the county town until 1974. It is on the north bank of the River TYNE¹, opposite GATESHEAD, to which it is linked by many bridges. The two are sometimes considered as a single city; for example, Newcastle–Gateshead was one of the leading candidates to become European City of Culture in 2008, although the designation in the end went to Liverpool. Newcastle is the largest city in northeast England and serves as virtual capital of the region; the diocese of Newcastle upon Tyne was created in 1882. The name is locally pronounced 'New-cassle' (to rhyme with 'hassle', with the stress on the second syllable), a pronunciation increasingly heard on the BBC. The inhabitants of Newcastle (and of Tyneside more generally) are known as Geordies (*see* TYNESIDE), and to Geordies Newcastle is simply **the Toon**. In Romany, according to George Borrow, Newcastle is **Wongareskey gav**, meaning 'coal town' (for Newcastle's coal associations, *see below*).

> Newcastle is a spacious, extended, infinitely populous place; 'tis seated upon the River Tyne, which is here a noble, large and deep river ...
>
> Daniel Defoe: *A Tour Through the Whole Island of Great Britain* (1724–6)

The Romans built a bridge here and on the northern side they established the settlement of **Pons Aelius**. The Normans built a bridge on the same site, and next to it a castle (1080), replaced by a new structure in 1172–7 by Henry II (parts can still be seen). **Newcastle Cathedral**, originally the parish church, is largely 14th–15th century (it would have been destroyed by Scots artillery during the Civil Wars had not the mayor filled it with Scottish prisoners). The town that grew around castle and church was walled from the 13th century to the 18th. Newcastle was an important military base during the frequent wars with the Scots, who held it in 1640 and 1644–7.

Newcastle also developed as an important regional trading centre. The coal trade began in the 13th century, coal being shipped to towns down the North Sea coast, and to London (hence the expression 'to carry coals to Newcastle'; *see below*). The **Newcastle Hoastmen** (merchants) had a monopoly of the coal trade until the 18th century. Shipbuilding also developed as a major industry, and in 1826 George Stephenson built an ironworks, which produced the first engine to run on the Stockton-to-Darlington railway. There was one final industrial product for which Newcastle was famous, as reflected in the old saying:

> In every corner of the world you will find a Scot, a rat and a Newcastle grindstone.
>
> Quoted by John Gibson Lockhart, *Memoirs of the Life of Sir Walter Scott* (1837–8)

The city underwent extensive redevelopments in the early 19th century and in the 1960s and 1970s (largely at the hands of the untalented and notably corrupt local architect, John Poulson, in cahoots with local political bigwig T. Dan Smith), and the city now has an underground railway, the Tyneside Metro. Both the coal trade and shipbuilding declined in the 1980s, and most employment is now in the public and service sectors:

> The Newcastle that made a living by getting its hands dirty has been allowed to die.
>
> Tony Parsons: *Daily Mirror* (1997)

In recent years the waterfront – which the poet Sean O'Brien has called 'the furnished banks of the coaly Tyne' – has undergone a trendy facelift, with many bars, cafés and clubs offering a lively nightlife.

The **University of Newcastle** dates back to the foundation in 1937 of King's College, which was part of the University of Durham until 1963. The city also has the University of Northumbria (1992). The Royal Grammar School dates back to 1525. There are many museums and art galleries, including the visitor centre at Newcastle Brewery, where the famous **Newcastle Brown Ale** (locally known as 'Dog') is made. Dark-coloured and sweet-tinged, 'Broon' (as it is also referred to locally), has been so closely

associated with Newcastle since it first appeared in 1927 that the European Union has given it special status to protect its production (alongside such products as Parma ham and Armagnac).

There is horse-racing north of the city at High Gosforth Park (*see under* GOSFORTH). Another competitive activity, 'The Blond and Brunette Beauty Show', was held in Newcastle on 23 December 1905; it was the first-ever British beauty contest.

Newcastle United FC, pride of the Tyne, was founded in 1881 and has played at St James' Park in the centre of the city since 1892. Its black-and-white strip has given the team the nickname the Magpies. Its famously passionate supporters (known as 'the Toon Army'; for 'the Toon', *see above*) have not had a League championship to celebrate since 1927 (the most recent in a total of four to date). Many Newcastle fans were far from pleased when Freddie Shepherd, a director of the club, was reported to have pronounced that 'Newcastle girls are all dogs'. Newcastle's professional rugby union club **Newcastle Falcons** (*see* GOSFORTH) is based at Kingston Park.

Newcastle was the birthplace of the composer and writer on music Charles Avison (1709–70); the poet Mark Akenside (1721–70); the engineers and railway pioneers George (1781–1848) and Robert (1803–59) Stephenson (the former's name may have inspired the term 'Geordie' for a Tynesider); William Armstrong (1810–1900), the engineer and arms manufacturer; the Imagist poet T.E. Hulme (1883–1917); the famously tactful Conservative cabinet minister Nicholas Ridley (1929–93), sacked for his comments about the Germans; the journalist and broadcaster Brian Redhead (1929–94); the thriller-writer Jack Higgins (b.1929); the pop singer (and former member of The Police) Sting (Gordon Sumner, b.1950); the comedian Rowan Atkinson (b.1955); and the Southampton, Blackburn Rovers, Newcastle United and England footballer Alan Shearer (b.1970). The wood engraver Thomas Bewick (1753–1828), although born in Cherryburn, spent much of his life in Newcastle. Arthur Henderson (1863–1935), leader of the Labour Party during the First World War, was brought up in Newcastle, although a Scot by birth.

Newcastle has had a number of intriguing visitors – not counting Queen Victoria, who, as she approached the city on the royal train, drew down the blinds. Among the temporary inhabitants from overseas have been José Maria de Eça de Queirós, 'the Portuguese Dickens', who wrote his masterpieces while ostensibly working as a diplomat at the Tyneside consulate from 1874 to 1879; the Russian novelist Yevgeni Zamyatin, who during the First World War oversaw the construction of Russian naval icebreakers in the Newcastle yards, and who satirized the inhabitants of Newcastle's middle-class area of Jesmond in two of his novels;

and the Austrian-born philosopher Ludwig Wittgenstein, who in 1943 worked as a porter in the Royal Victoria Infirmary, and who spent his lonely evenings mostly at the cinema.

See also NEWBURN.

carry coals to Newcastle, to. To do what is superfluous. The expression derives from the fact that Newcastle was formerly the port through which most of eastern Britain obtained its coal.

Duke of Newcastle. Thomas Pelham-Holles, 1st Duke of Newcastle (1693–1768), who was prime minister 1754–6 and 1757–62. (*See also* NEWCASTLE UNDER LYME.).

Newcastle disease. Another name for fowl pest, a dangerous disease of poultry and other birds. It was first identified in Newcastle in 1926.

Newcastle Hoppings. The largest travelling fair in the country, which takes place on Town Moor in the last week in June. It originated in the 19th century as a temperance festival.

Newcastle Programme, the. The political programme presented by W.E. Gladstone to a meeting of the National Liberal Federation at Newcastle in 1891. In it he reiterated his support for Irish Home Rule and proposed a number of important domestic reforms, including further parliamentary reform, and the disestablishment of the churches in Scotland and Wales.

Newcastle Propositions, the. A series of demands issued on 14 July 1646 to Charles I by representatives of Parliament and the Scots Covenanters. The terms included the abolition of bishops, the reform of religion and the right of Parliament to oversee foreign affairs and the army for a period of 20 years. Charles prevaricated, and the Scots, tired of waiting for his decision, turned the king over to Parliament and retreated back north.

Treaty of Newcastle (1244). A treaty by which Alexander II of Scotland pledged allegiance to Henry III of England; it also reaffirmed the terms of the Treaty of York (*see under* YORK).

Newcastle West. A market town in County Limerick, some 40 km (25 miles) southwest of Limerick itself. There is a ruined castle, built by the Knights Templar in 1184 and later in the possession of the earls of DESMOND.

New Costessey. *See* COSTESSEY

New Cross *Cross* probably from a crossroads on the former Kent–Surrey border where the road from Dartford to London was joined by the road from Lewisham and the south. (The coaching inn called the 'Golden Cross', which once stood nearby, is almost certainly later, and so could not have been the source of the name, as has sometimes been claimed.)

A district of southeast London (SE14), in the borough of LEWISHAM, to the west of Blackheath and to the east of Peckham. The opening of New Cross station on the South Eastern Railway in 1876 promoted both the residential development of the area (much of it initially undertaken by the Haberdashers' Company) and its separate identity as 'New Cross'. The adjacent Underground station, on the East London line, opened in 1884.

The socialist anthem 'The Red Flag' was reputedly written in the course of a 15-minute train journey between Charing Cross and New Cross by James Connell in 1889. Connell later recounted that the song was inspired by the London dockers' strike that year.

The poet Robert Browning lived in New Cross in the 1840s, in a house he described as 'resembling a goose pie'.

New Cross Gate *Gate* from the toll gate set up on New Cross turnpike road (at the junction of the present Queens Road and New Cross Road) in 1718 (the gate was taken down in 1865).

A district of southeast London (SE14), at the northwest corner of NEW CROSS, in the borough of Lewisham. It was originally called Hatcham, from the name of the local manor.

The first 'semaphore'-style railway signals were used at New Cross Gate junction, on the London & Brighton Railway, in 1841. New Cross Gate station, on the East London line, opened in 1869, originally under the name New Cross; it was renamed New Cross Gate in 1923. In the early part of the 20th century New Cross Gate was home to one of the largest tram depots in London.

New Cumnock The first element distinguishes it from nearby CUMNOCK, the etymology of which is unknown.

A small town in East Ayrshire (formerly in Strathclyde region) 8 km (5 miles) to the southeast of Cumnock.

New Deer. *See* DEER ABBEY.

New Forest From its being 'newly' created as a hunting ground in the 11th century.

A wooded area in Hampshire, occupying much of the land between the River Avon and SOUTHAMPTON Water. It is about 336 sq km (130 sq miles) in extent. The main towns within the Forest are LYNDHURST (the 'capital' of the Forest) and BROCKENHURST.

Animals had been hunted in the area since ancient times, but in the first millennium AD large parts of it were deforested and turned over to agriculture. This all changed, however, with the arrival of the Normans. They were very fond of hunting, and in 1079 William I requisitioned the forest as a game reserve (with its full panoply of draconian medieval game laws). His son William II was killed with an arrow shot by Walter Tirel ('a French gentleman, remarkable for his skill in archery', William Butler, *Chronological, Biographical, Historical and Miscellaneous Exercises*, 1846) while hunting here – assassinated on the orders of his brother, thenceforward Henry I, according to one theory; an obelisk marks the spot.

Over the centuries the game laws were relaxed and much of the land was gradually returned to private ownership (some still belongs to the Crown), but the Forest's history has left it with a legacy of unique institutions and customs. Its affairs are ordered by the Court of Verderers, which meets in Lyndhurst. The inhabitants of the Forest enjoy five privileges: of estover (the right to cut firewood); of marl (the right to improve the soil); of pannage (the right to let pigs forage – they hoover up the acorns that would be poisonous to the ponies); of pasturage (the right to graze livestock); and of turbary (the right to cut turf for fuel). Between the 17th and 19th centuries, the Forest was important as a source of timber for the building of ships.

Today the Forest, most of which is now managed by the Forestry Commission, consists largely of oak and beech woodland, with sizable conifer plantations and extensive areas of open heathland. The area is noted for its extensive flora, including many rare species. In spite of the Normans' depredations, lots of deer still live here. It attracts about eight million visitors every year. In 2004 it was designated a National Park.

The great Scottish geologist Charles Lyell (1797–1875), originator of the modern theory of uniformitarianism, was brought up in the New Forest, and there developed his interest in natural history.

Children of the New Forest, The. A children's historical novel (1847) by Frederick Marryat ('Captain Marryat'). It is about four childen left orphaned after their father's death while fighting on the Royalist side in the Civil Wars. They are sheltered by an old forester, who saves them from detection by the Roundheads and teaches them various forest skills. The children come into their inheritance at the Restoration, and – striking a conciliatory political note – one of them even marries a 'moderate Cromwellian'.

New Forest cicada. A cicada (*Cicadetta montana*) discovered in the New Forest in 1812. The only British member of the cicada family, it is extremely rare. It was thought to be extinct in 1961, but another one turned up in 1992.

New Forest pony. A breed of pony native to the New Forest. It has had various inputs over the centuries (legend has it that it is descended from small horses that came ashore from wrecked Spanish Armada ships), and the ponies vary in size and shape. They are semi-wild, but if broken-in make good children's mounts. Much of their grazing land is unfenced and managed as common land.

Newgale Obscure, but ME *newe* 'new' + *goule* 'channel, stream' might be suggested.

A small resort on the west coast of Pembrokeshire (formerly in Dyfed), 14 km (8.5 miles) southeast of St David's Head. It is at the north end of the extensive **Newgale Sands**.

New Galloway *Galloway see* GALLOWAY.

A small town some 35 km (20 miles) west of Dumfries, at the north end of Loch Ken, formerly in Kirkcudbrightshire, now in Dumfries and Galloway. It obtained a royal charter in 1633 and developed somewhat at the expense of DALRY (also known as 'Old Galloway') to the north.

Newgate From *Newgate*, the name of a former gate in the wall of the City of London. Originally built by the Romans around 200, it was the main entrance to the city from the west, and was referred to in Anglo-Saxon times as the 'West Gate'. *Newgate*, presumably alluding to a rebuilding of the gate in the late Anglo-Saxon or early Norman period, is first recorded in the late 13th century. The gate, which stood at the northern end of Old Bailey, was demolished in 1767.

A former prison at the northern end of OLD BAILEY, in the City of London (EC4). There had been a prison on the site, by the city gate called Newgate, since at least the 12th century. It was refurbished in 1422 and again at the end of the 16th century, but it was destroyed in the Great Fire of London, and completely rebuilt in 1672. Its reputation as a hellhole solidified in the course of the following century, during which its more high-profile inmates included the novelist Daniel Defoe (1660–1731), whose fictional heroine Moll Flanders was famously born here; Titus Oates (1649–1705), the perpetrator of the Popish Plot, a hoax plan to murder Charles II; William Penn (1644–1718), Quaker and founder of Pennsylvania; and the notorious robber Jack Sheppard (1702–24), whose escapes were dramatically recounted by Harrison Ainsworth (*see* **Newgate novel** *below*). The prison's most famous theatrical incarnation is from this period, as it forms the setting for many of the scenes in John Gay's satire of Italian opera, social hypocrisy and contemporary politics, *The Beggar's Opera* (1728), a 'Newgate pastoral':

> Murder is as fashionable a crime as a man can be guilty of. How many fine gentlemen have we in Newgate every year, purely upon that article!
>
> John Gay: Peachum in *The Beggar's Opera* (1728), I.iv

Newgate was pulled down and rebuilt again in the 1770s, but the new prison soon fell victim to the Gordon Riots of 1780, which left it a shell; Charles Dickens vividly described the destruction in *Barnaby Rudge* (1841). Its replacement (one of whose first customers was Lord George Gordon, instigator of the riots) continued as a prison until 1881, no less vile and insanitary than its predecessors: it is said that its floors were so infested with insects that they crunched when walked on. It was the last of the line: it was finally demolished in 1902, and the site is now occupied by the Central Criminal Court (the 'Old Bailey').

Over the centuries the stories of the horrors within Newgate's grim fortress (amplified and sensationalized as they often were – but the truth was bad enough) gave the place a terrible fascination. Nor were things necessarily any better just outside: in the 1780s London's place of public execution was moved from TYBURN[2] to a space in front of Newgate prison, and huge crowds would gather there to be entertained; the last public victim was a Fenian, Michael Barrett (*see* Clerkenwell explosion *under* CLERKENWELL), executed by William Calcraft in 1868; shortly afterwards the scaffold was moved inside the walls.

From its prominence, Newgate came to be used as a general term for gaols, and Thomas Nashe, in *Pierce Pennilesse, his Supplication to the Divell* (1592), says it is 'a common name for all prisons, as homo is a common name for a man or woman'.

In 19th-century underworld slang *Newgate* became, with the canting suffix *-mans*, *Newman's* (or *Numan's*): the prison was, with exquisite irony, *Newman's college*, *Newman's hotel* or *Newman's tea-garden*, and *Newman's lift* was the gallows.

The name's only living legacy now is Newgate Street, which runs west to east between the top of Old Bailey and CHEAPSIDE.

Newgate bird. A slang term between the 17th and 19th centuries for a prisoner, especially one who had been a confidence trickster.

Newgate Calendar, The. A biographical record of the more notorious criminals confined at Newgate. It was begun in 1773 and continued at intervals for many years. In 1824–8 Andrew Knapp and William Baldwin published, in four volumes, *The Newgate Calendar, comprising Memoirs of Notorious Characters*, partly compiled by George Borrow, and in 1886 C. Pelham published his *Chronicles of Crime, or the New Newgate Calendar* (two volumes). Another such 'calendar' was published in 1969. The term is often used as a comprehensive expression embracing crime of every sort.

Newgateer. A 17th-century slang term for a prisoner in Newgate.

Newgate fashion. The way in which things are done in Newgate gaol:

> *Falstaff*: Must we all march?
> *Bardolph*: Yea, two and two, Newgate fashion.
>
> Shakespeare: *Henry IV, Part 1* (1592)

Newgate fringe. A 19th-century term for a beard worn under the chin – so called because it occupied the position of the rope round the neck of a man about to be hanged. Contemporary synonyms were **Newgate collar** and **Newgate frill**.

Newgate gaol. The 20th-century Cockney rhyming-slang term for *tale*, especially in the sense of 'hard-luck story'.

Newgate hornpipe. An early 19th-century slang term for a hanging (victims would 'dance' as they jerked to death – gallows humour at its most literal).

Newgate knocker. A 19th-century term for a lock of hair shaped like the figure 6 and twisted from the temple back towards the ear (the implication seems to have been that those who sported such a style tended to criminality). These racy embellishments were much favoured by costermongers.

Newgate novel. A somewhat dismissive term for a genre of 19th-century English fiction that features the lives of criminals in sensationalized and sentimentalized form, with the noose dangling balefully at the end. William Harrison Ainsworth's *Rookwood* (1824), featuring Dick Turpin, and *Jack Sheppard* (1839) were typical examples, and the school also included Edward Bulwer-Lytton and Charles Whitehead. William Thackeray, who satirized the genre in his *Catherine* (1839–40), liked to include Charles Dickens among their number.

Newgate ring. A tonsorial adornment from the mid-19th century, featuring a moustache and beard but no side-whiskers. The motivation of the coinage was similar to that of Newgate fringe (*see above*).

Newgate saint. An 18th-century slang term for a prisoner under sentence of death.

Newgate solicitor. A term around the turn of the 18th and 19th centuries for a second-rate lawyer who hung around Newgate prison in the hope of picking up work.

Newgrange Its Irish name is *Sí an Bhrú* 'fairy mound of the palace'; the English name rather prosaically means 'new outlying farm'.

A spectacular megalithic passage tomb in the valley of the Boyne, County Meath, 8 km (5 miles) west of Drogheda. It dates from about 3100 BC, and has been interpreted as the world's oldest astronomical observatory: the inner chamber is illuminated by the Sun only at the winter solstice. It is part of the megalithic complex known as **Brú na Bóinne** (*see under* BOYNE).

New Grub Street. *See under* GRUB STREET.

Newham *new* + *ham* (as in EAST HAM and WEST HAM; *see also* HAM).

A London borough (E6, E7, E12, E13, E15, E16) formed in 1965 by combining the former county boroughs of East Ham and West Ham, and including BECKTON, CANNING TOWN, FOREST GATE, North Woolwich, PLAISTOW, SILVERTOWN and STRATFORD. It lies between Tower Hamlets to the west and Barking and Dagenham to the east, and is bounded on the south by the River THAMES[1].

In its early days it was earnestly hoped by officialdom that its name would be pronounced with full value given to each letter, and as if it were two separate words, but the *h* has been decisively dropped, and it is now almost universally 'newəm'.

Newhaven Originally *Meeching* '(settlement of) Mece's people', OE male personal name *Mece* (meaning 'sword')

+ *ingas* (*see* -ING); it acquired the name *Newhaven* 'new harbour' in the 17th century, under circumstances described below.

A town and port on the East Sussex coast, at the mouth of the River OUSE[3], about 15 km (9 miles) southeast of Brighton. It was once a small and relatively obscure village (named **Meeching**), but its life was changed in the 1570s when a violent storm sealed up with shingle the mouth of the River Ouse at SEAFORD, about 3 km (2 miles) to the southeast. The course of the river shifted westwards, and it created a new outfall for itself at Meeching. A port was established here, initially serving the barge trade up the Ouse to LEWES, and it was called *Newhaven*: 'new harbour', to distinguish it from the 'old harbour' at Seaford. The new name is first recorded in 1587. By the 17th century the name had become attached to the adjoining settlement, and 'Meeching' was no more.

A ferry service began operating from Newhaven to Dieppe in France in 1847, and the following year it received its first royal passenger – the French king Louis-Philippe, fleeing from the 1848 Revolution. The modern harbour was essentially constructed between 1860 and 1900, and through the 20th century Newhaven was one of the main conduits for ferry traffic between Britain and the Continent. **Newhaven Fort**, built as a defence against Napoleon, now contains a museum.

> Newhaven is spot and rash and pimple and blister; with the incessant cars like lice.
>
> Virginia Woolf: diary (1921) (Woolf lived nearby)

New Haw 'newly enclosed land'; *Haw* from OE *haga* 'hedge, enclosure'.

A village in Surrey commuter country, on the River WEY[1], about 2.5 km (1.5 miles) north of Byfleet (with whose name it is combined in the local railway station) and 6.5 km (4 miles) northeast of Woking.

Newington Bagpath *Newington* 'new farmstead', OE *niwan* dative form of *niwe* 'new' + -TON; *Bagpath* perhaps 'track used by animals suitable for trapping', OE *bagga* 'bag' + *pæth* 'path, track'.

A hamlet in Gloucestershire, in the COTSWOLDS, about 6.5 km (4 miles) west of Tetbury.

Newington Butts *Newington* from the district in which it is situated; *Butts* from the site of the old archery 'butts' (practice targets) here.

A short road in the South London borough of SOUTHWARK, linking the ELEPHANT AND CASTLE with Kennington Lane. In Cockney rhyming slang 'Newington Butts' (or usually '**Newingtons**' for short) stands for 'guts' (as in 'a pain in the Newingtons').

New Invention[1] From a local public house of that name (itself with a punning reference to *inn*).

A village in Shropshire, just to the east of OFFA'S DYKE and about 5 km (3 miles) north of Knighton.

New Invention[2] Probably from a local public house of that name (*see* NEW INVENTION[1]), but there are other possibilities: it could celebrate the invention of some new contrivance used in the local clay-mining industry (a water-pump has been proposed as a candidate); it has been suggested that it refers to a new sort of clay chimney pot developed in the area; and a local story has it that it is an ironic reference to a man who stuffed a hawthorn bush into the top of his chimney and proudly proclaimed it to anyone who would listen as a wonderful new invention to stop the chimney smoking. The name is first recorded in 1663.

A northwestern district of WALSALL in the West Midlands.

New Jerusalem. A mid-19th century nickname for the London district of BELGRAVIA, which at that time was known for its sizable population of wealthy Jews. *See also* ASIA MINOR; MESOPOTAMIA[2].

New Lanark *Lanark see* LANARK.

A mill village established in 1786 by David Dale on the banks of the CLYDE below LANARK. In 1800 Dale's son-in-law, the Welsh-born Robert Owen (1771–1858), became manager of the mills and set about turning the village into a model community, improving working conditions and housing. In 1816 he set up the first infant school in Britain. New Lanark became one of UNESCO's World Heritage Sites in 2001.

Newlands 'new lands (for the plough)', OE *niwe* 'new' + *land*.

A valley in the northwestern LAKE DISTRICT, Cumbria (formerly in Cumberland), some 5 km (3 miles) southwest of Keswick, and lying roughly parallel with and west of DERWENT[1] Water and Borrowdale. There is a hamlet of the same name in the valley, along whose bed runs **Newlands Beck**. At the head of the valley is the high road pass over **Newlands Hause** to Buttermere. The valley is full of old mine workings, first exploited by Bavarian miners in the reign of Elizabeth I. The miners retrieved copper, lead, graphite, barytes and even a little gold and silver.

> Newlands is indeed a lovely place – the houses, each in its little shelter of ashes and sycamores, just under the road, so that in some places you might leap down on the roof, seemingly at least – the exceeding greenness and pastoral beauty of the Vale itself, with the savage wildness of the mountains, their coves, and long arm-shaped and elbow-shaped ridges – yet this wildness softened down into a congruity with the Vale by the semicircular lines of the crags, and the bason-like concavities.
>
> Samuel Taylor Coleridge: letter to Sara Hutchinson (5 August 1802) (written at the top of Scafell)

The Newlands valley is home to Beatrix Potter's Mrs Tiggy-Winkle.

Newlyn Originally *Lulyn*, probably 'pool for a fleet of boats', Cornish *lu* 'fleet of boats' + *lynn* 'pool'; by the 14th century *Lu-* had become *New-*, under the influence of other place-names beginning thus, including NEWLYN EAST.

A deep-sea fishing port in MOUNT'S BAY, on the south coast of Cornwall. It has now been almost absorbed by PENZANCE, just to the north (the local rugby club is called Penzance/Newlyn), but it maintains its own fishy profile (it holds a Fish Festival every August, and 'Newlyn cod' is on the menu of many a local pub).

The Ordnance Datum adopted by the Ordnance Survey for expressing height on its maps is based on the mean sea level at Newlyn.

In the late 19th and early 20th centuries Newlyn was popular enough with artists to give rise to what was called the **Newlyn School**, founded by Stanhope Forbes (1857–1947). Its adherents sought to capture the evanescent impressions of wind, sun and sea in paint. Some of their work can be viewed at the Passmore Edwards gallery.

The Chartist leader William Lovett (1800–77), drafter of the People's Charter of 1838, was born in Newlyn.

Newlyn East *Newlyn* '(church of St) Niwelina', from the patron saint of the local church, said to have been martyred nearby by her father, a king; *East* was added in the 19th century to distinguish it from the other, larger Newlyn.

A village (also called **St Newlyn East**) in northwest Cornwall, about 5 km (3 miles) south of Newquay. The **Newlyn Downs** lie to the south of the village.

New Malden *Malden* 'hill with a crucifix', OE *mæl* 'crucifix' + *dun* (*see* DOWN, -DON).

A suburb of southwest London, in the borough of KINGSTON UPON THAMES (before 1965 in Surrey), to the east of Kingston and to the west of Morden. It was developed in the middle 19th century, after the coming of the railway, to the north of the original settlement of Malden (now called **Old Malden**). It is now relatively featureless commuterland, with a burgeoning Korean community.

The sculptor Sir Anthony Caro (b.1924) was born in New Malden.

Newmarket[1] 'new market town' (the first record of the name, around 1200, is in the Latin form *Novum Forum*).

A market town in Suffolk, on the Cambridgeshire border, about 21 km (13 miles) east of Cambridge. Its townscape postdates 1683, when most of the existing buildings were destroyed by fire.

Newmarket is situated on open heathland, ideal for high-speed horse-riding, so its evolution into the administrative and spiritual home of British horse-racing is no surprise. The first race took place here, on **Newmarket Heath**, in 1619. James VI and I, who had built a palace nearby, was an interested spectator, but it was his grandson Charles II who really made Newmarket's name: he was so enthusiastic that he actually rode in some of the races, and he brought his court (including Nell Gwynn) here twice a year.

> The diversions the king followed at Newmarket were these:– Walking in the morning till ten o'clock. Then he went to the cockpit till dinner time. About three he went to the horse races. At six to the cockpit for an hour. Then to the play, though the comedians were very indifferent. So to supper. Next to the duchess of Portsmouth's till bedtime, and then to his own apartment to bed.
>
> Sir John Reresby (22 March 1684) (a *cockpit* was a place where cockfights took place)

Newmarket has two racecourses (one, the 'Rowley Mile', was named after one of Charles II's horses, Old Rowley, a particularly productive stallion in the royal stud whose name was also applied to Charles himself). Several important flat races are run on them every season, including two of the English classics, the One Thousand Guineas and the Two Thousand Guineas, in the spring, and the Cesarewitch (first run in 1839) and the Cambridgeshire (*see* CAMBRIDGE-SHIRE) in October. Newmarket is the home of the National Stud and of the ruling body of the Turf, the Jockey Club, which moved here from London in 1752 and has elegant Georgian premises on the High Street. There are dozens of racing stables and stud farms in the vicinity, and horse sales are regularly held. A bookmaker who is 'warned off Newmarket Heath' is banned from all British racecourses. The ghost of the 19th-century jockey Fred Archer is said to ride across the Heath.

During the Civil Wars King Charles I was brought here from HOLDENBY in Northamptonshire by Cornet Joyce as a prisoner of the New Model Army in June 1647.

There are also towns called Newmarket in Jamaica, in Australia (New South Wales), in Canada (Ontario) and in the USA (New Hampshire and, in the form New Market, Iowa and Virginia). Newmarket is also the name of a district of Brisbane in Queensland, Australia.

Newmarket. The name applied in the 19th century (presumably in tribute to the gambling in the town) to the card game previously known as, among other things, 'Pope Joan'. In this game players bet on matching cards in their hands against four court cards taken from a second pack.

Newmarket coat. A term applied to a type of men's close-fitting coat used for riding. It was subsequently used for any outdoor coat of similar design, for women as well as men, and in the days of the coat's fashionability (the 19th century) was often shortened to simply 'Newmarket':

> A brown velvet Newmarket, which completely covered her short satin gown.
>
> Mary Elizabeth Braddon: *Phantom Fortune* (1883)

Newmarket Heath commissioner. An ironic 19th-century slang term for a highwayman, reflecting the Heath's lawlessness in those days.

See also DEVIL'S DYKE[1].

Newmarket[2] ModE 'new town with market rights'.

A small market town in County Cork, 50 km (31 miles) northwest of Cork itself. Its Irish name is **Áth Trasna** ('ford crossing'), and it was founded by the Aldsworth family in the reign of James VI and I.

Newmarket was the birthplace of the judge and orator John Philpot Curran (1750–1817), who lived here for a period at the Priory. He defended many of the 1798 rebels and opposed the Union, but when he found out that his daughter Sarah was secretly engaged to Robert Emmet, the hopeless rebel of 1803, he turned her out of the house. After Emmet was arrested Curran refused to defend him, and the young man was hanged and beheaded. Sarah later married an Englishman, but died in 1808, and her sad story is commemorated in a not entirely accurate poem by Thomas Moore:

> She is far from the land
> Where her young hero sleeps,
> And lovers are round her, sighing;
> But coldly she turns
> From their gaze, and weeps,
> For her heart in his grave is lying.

New Mills From a local mill of that name, operating from the 16th century.

A town in Derbyshire, on the western edge of the HIGH PEAK, on the rivers Goyt and Sett, about 24 km (15 miles) east of Manchester.

Newmilns 'new mills', OE *niwe* 'new' + *myln* 'mill'.

A small town in East Ayrshire (formerly in Strathclyde region), some 7 km (4 miles) east of Kilmarnock.

New Milton *Milton see* MILTON ABBAS. The designation 'New' arose after the opening of the railway station here in 1888. It was named 'Milton' from the nearby village, but apparently this caused confusion with the Milton that is now a district of Portsmouth. The local postmistress, a Mrs Newhook, suggested that it should be renamed 'New Milton'. The original Milton is now known as 'Old Milton'.

A small town in Hampshire, about 8 km (5 miles) northeast of Christchurch. It grew up around the railway station from which it took its name.

Newport[1] 'new market town' OE *niwe*, ME *newe* 'new' + PORT 'market town'.

An industrial port at the mouth of the River USK[1], and the administrative seat of Newport unitary authority (formerly in Monmouthshire), 17 km (11 miles) northeast of Cardiff. Its Welsh name is **Casnewydd** ('new castle', referring to the 12-century castle as opposed to the old Roman fort at nearby CAERLEON). St Woolos's Church, which has its origins in the Saxon period, became the cathedral of the diocese of Monmouth in 1921. Newport was the scene of large-scale Chartist rioting in 1839, sometimes referred to as the **Newport Rising**. The Llanwern steelworks, built in 1959 to the east of the town, closed in 2001. The town also contains a campus of the federal University of Wales (*see under* WALES).

Newport's rugby union club, nicknamed the Black and Ambers, was founded in 1874 and plays its home games at Rodney Parade. **Newport RFC** now plays in the (semi-professional) Welsh premiership and is a feeder club to the **Newport Gwent Dragons**, a regional team that plays in the professional Celtic League.

Newport was the birthplace of the poet W.H. Davies (1871–1940), author of *The Autobiography of a Super Tramp* (1908).

Newport and its surrounding area formed a county borough until 1974, when it became a district of Gwent. It became a unitary authority in 1996.

Newport[2]. The administrative centre of the ISLE OF WIGHT, on the River MEDINA[1], about 8 km (5 miles) south of Cowes and just to the north of the centre of the island. There is ample evidence of Roman occupation here, including the Cypress Road Roman Villa. In the Middle Ages the area was subject to frequent French raids, and the nearby CARIS-BROOKE Castle was built as protection against them.

Treaty of Newport. A treaty (September 1648) negotiated with the Parliamentarians in the town hall at Newport by Charles I, who was imprisoned at Carisbrooke Castle from 1647 to 1648. He made concessions on the episcopacy and on militias, but later said he had done so 'merely in order for my escape'.

Newport[3]. A small market town in Shropshire, within the unitary authority of Telford and Wrekin, about 10 km (6 miles) northeast of Telford. Most of it was destroyed by fire in 1665, and its present townscape of handsome red-brick houses postdates that.

The lowest temperature ever recorded in England, -21.6°C (-15°F), was registered at Newport in 1982.

Newport[4]. A village in Essex, on the River CAM[2], about 5 km (3 miles) southwest of Saffron Walden. It has a station on the main line from London to Cambridge. Its many attractive old timbered houses put it in the picturesque category.

Newport[5]. A small coastal town in Pembrokeshire, 11 km (7 miles) east of Fishguard. Its Welsh name is **Trefdraeth** (Welsh, 'settlement by the shore'). **Newport Castle** was founded towards the end of the 12th century by William Fitz Martin, then taken by Llywelyn the Great in the

13th century and later in the same century by Llywelyn the Last. The remains date from the 13th century, and consist of towers, a gatehouse, a crypt and a dungeon.

Newport-on-Tay *Tay see* TAY.

A town in Fife, 3 km (2 miles) south across the Firth of TAY from Dundee. The second part of the name derives from the ferry across the Tay to DUNDEE, which operated from at least the 12th century until the opening of the Tay Road Bridge in 1966.

Newport Pagnell *Pagnell* denoting manorial ownership in the early Middle Ages by the Paynel family.

A town within the unitary authority of Milton Keynes. Its main claim to fame is Newport Pagnell Services, between junctions 14 and 15 on the M1.

In 1958 the production of Aston-Martin cars moved to Newport Pagnell from Feltham, Middlesex.

New Quay *Etymology self-explanatory.*

A small resort town on Cardigan Bay, in Ceredigion (formerly in Cardiganshire, then in Dyfed), 25 km (15 miles) northeast of Cardigan. Its Welsh name is **Ceinewydd** ('new quay'). On the north side of the town is **New Quay Head**, and to the east **New Quay Bay**. Like its Cornish single-worded namesake, New Quay is popular with surfers.

The poet Dylan Thomas lived in New Quay during the latter part of the Second World War, and it has been suggested (by Thomas's friend the poet Vernon Watkins, among others) that New Quay, rather than LAUGHARNE, was the inspiration for the village of Llareggub ('bugger all' backwards) in Thomas's *Under Milk Wood*. Thomas did not have an entirely smooth sojourn in the town, as he had a bit of a run-in with a commando officer on home leave. The man had come to the conclusion that his wife had been participating in three-in-a-bed romps with Thomas and his wife Caitlin, and the upshot was that the jealous husband peppered the Thomases' bungalow with a machine gun. Luckily no harm was done, and the man was acquitted of attempted murder.

Newquay *From the 'new quay' built here in the mid-15th century. Its Cornish name was, and is, Towan Blistra, from towan 'sand dune' and an unknown second word.*

A town and resort on the north Cornish coast, about 17 km (11 miles) north of Truro. In former times it earned its living from pilchard fishing ('huers' – the word may come from French *huer* 'to hoot' – would keep watch for the shoals from huts perched on top of the cliffs). The pilchards have moved on, and nowadays the town relies on the attractions of the sandy beaches of **Newquay Bay**, which provide good bathing and excellent surfing (top surfing beaches: Fistral and Watergate), along with a host of family-orientated tourist activities. Newquay is now the capital of British

surfing and Cornwall's main clubbing centre. ST MAWGAN Airfield serves as Newquay's airport.

For those in flight from the daytime summer crowds and the night-time alcohol-fuelled revelry, more sedate pleasures can be had 5 km (3 miles) southeast at Trerice, a compact Elizabethan manor house (1571) with fine plasterwork and panelling. Now administered by the National Trust, it also boasts, unusually, a lawnmower museum.

The novelist William Golding (1911–93) was born in St Columb Minor, on the northeastern outskirts of the town.

New Radnor *Radnor see* OLD RADNOR.

A large village in Powys (formerly in Radnorshire) 4 km (2.5 miles) northwest of Old Radnor, and some 10 km (6 miles) southwest of Presteigne. In Welsh it is **Maesyfed** ('Hyfaidd's field', after an unidentified person), and this gave rise to **Sir Faesyfed**, the Welsh name for Radnorshire. Although in 1064 New Radnor was given rights to administer the surrounding district, the county town of the old county of Radnorshire was PRESTEIGNE.

New River. An artificial waterway constructed in the early 17th century to bring water from Hertfordshire to London, a distance of 61 km (38 miles). It was built by Hugh Myddleton, a rich entrepreneur. Its London end was the **New River Head** at CLERKENWELL, from which clean water (or cleaner than that available from the Thames or Fleet) was distributed to those willing to pay for it. The waterway was largely rebuilt in the 19th century. Until the late 20th century the **New River Estate** owned large areas of ISLINGTON.

New Romney *New* to distinguish it from OLD ROMNEY.

A town (pronounced 'romny' or 'rumny') in Kent, at the southern corner of ROMNEY MARSH (of which it is the unofficial 'capital'), about 2.5 km (1.5 miles) from the sea and about 21 km (13 miles) southwest of Folkestone. **Old Romney** is a further 3 km (2 miles) inland to the west.

Romney was one of the original CINQUE PORTS, and had the status of 'lead' port: its merchants had the right of carrying the canopy over the monarch at his coronation, and of sitting at his side at the coronation banquet. At this time, in the early Middle Ages, it was a prosperous town, but then, in 1287, came the Great Storm. It engulfed Romney, and shifted the mouth of the River ROTHER[2], on which the town and port were situated, many miles to the west, to RYE. Marooned inland, Romney went into a long-term decline.

Its main claim to fame nowadays is as an important stop on the **Romney, Hythe and Dymchurch Railway**, a private steam railway with a 15-inch-gauge line and locomotives that are one third of the normal size. Built in the 1920s as a tourist attraction, its 22-km (14-mile) track threads its way between Romney Marsh and the coast. There is a Toy and Model Train Museum at New Romney station.

New Ross Irish *Rhos Mhic Thriúin* 'wood of the sons of Treon'; *New* refers to Pembroke's foundation (*see below*).

A market town on the River BARROW in County Wexford, some 20 km (12 miles) northeast of Waterford. It was founded in 1204 by William the Marshal Earl of Pembroke, and his wife Isabella de Clare, and in the Middle Ages was an important port. It was much fought over up to the 16th century, and again in 1798 (*see below*); it surrendered to Cromwell in 1649. President John F. Kennedy's great-grandfather emigrated to America from his nearby homestead (*see under* DUNGANSTOWN), and the president paid a return visit in June 1963 (some 5 km / 3 miles south of the town is the John F. Kennedy Memorial Forest Park).

Battle of New Ross (5 June 1798). One of the last battles – and the biggest – of the 1798 United Irishmen's Rebellion, in which the rebels under Bagenal Harvey tried to seize the town (much of which was burnt in the process). They were successfully driven off after a ten-hour defence by the outnumbered garrison under General Henry Johnston. In all some 2000 died in the fighting.

> It was one more last
> Intemperate effort,
> A cry from the past,
> Desperate, undisciplined,
> Pitchforks and hoes
> Splintered by grapeshot,
> Fruitless against rows
> Of men with muskets –
>
> One last heave
> Of the tortured beast,
> Thousands to grieve
> At the blood feast.
>
> J. Donough O'Coughlin: 'An Old Song at New Ross', from *Pity the Brute* (1987)

'Fairies in New Ross, The'. An anonymous early 19th-century poem:

> When moonlight
> Near midnight
> Tips the rock and waving wood;
> When moonlight
> Near midnight
> Silvers o'er the sleeping flood;
> When yew-tops
> With dew-drops
> Sparkle o'er deserted graves;

> 'Tis then we fly
> Through welkin high,
> Then we sail o'er yellow waves.

Newry An anglicized pronunciation of the Irish name *An tIúr* 'the yew tree'.

A town (city from 2002) in Counties Armagh and Down, 55 km (34 miles) southwest of Belfast. A Cistercian abbey was built here in 1153 and a de Courcy castle in 1177, but nothing remains of either. The land hereabouts was granted in the 16th century to Nicholas Bagenal. St Patrick's Church – the first purpose-built Church of Ireland church in Ireland – incorporates a tower built by Bagenal in 1578.

Newry's strategic position in the GAP OF THE NORTH made it vulnerable to attack: it was destroyed by Edward Bruce in 1315, by Shane O'Neill in 1566 and by the Duke of Berwick's Jacobites in 1689. When Jonathan Swift visited a few years later, all that was left of St Patrick's Church was the steeple, inspiring his lines:

> High church, low steeple,
> Dirty streets, proud people.

Newry became a hotspot during the Troubles, being the scene of considerable civil rights activity in the later 1960s and of many IRA operations thereafter.

Newry was the birthplace of the footballer Pat Jennings (b.1945), who kept goal for Northern Ireland between 1964 and 1986.

Newry Canal. A canal linking LOUGH NEAGH and CARLING-FORD LOUGH via Newry. It was commenced in 1742, making it the first inland canal to be built in the British Isles.

Newry and Mourne. A local authority district in southeast Northern Ireland. The administrative centre is at NEWRY.

New Scotland Yard. *See* SCOTLAND YARD.

Newstead 'new monastic site' (referring to the abbey), OE *niwe* 'new' + *stede* 'place, (monastic) site'.

A village in Nottinghamshire, in SHERWOOD FOREST, about 15 km (9 miles) northwest of Nottingham. A little to the east is **Newstead Abbey**, built by Henry II in 1170 to atone for the murder of Thomas Becket at Canterbury. At the Dissolution of the Monasteries Henry VIII handed it over to Sir John Byron. He converted it into a family home, which in 1798 was inherited (now in a fairly dilapidated state) by George, the poet of the family. The mercurial Lord Byron never exactly settled down there: he stayed for a while in 1802 (when he probably first met his half-sister Augusta, who later became his lover), and he lived in the Abbey from time to time between 1808 and 1816, but then he sold up and left England for good. Visitors to the house may view his bedroom.

New Tipperary. *See under* TIPPERARY.

Newton Abbot *Newton* 'new farmstead, estate or village', OE *niwe* 'new' + -TON; *Abbot* referring to its possession by Torre Abbey in the early Middle Ages.

A market town in Devon, at the head of the TEIGN estuary, about 21 km (13 miles) southwest of Exeter. William of Orange was first proclaimed king here in 1688.

Newton Abbot has grown considerably since the arrival of the railway in the mid-19th century, which turned it into an important junction.

Newton Abbot racecourse (National Hunt) is the most westerly in England.

Newton Aycliffe *Aycliffe* denotes 'clearing among oaks', OE *ac* 'oak' + -LEY; *Aclea c.*1085.

A town in County Durham, 8 km (5 miles) southeast of Bishop Auckland. It was designated a NEW TOWN[1] in 1947, and took the second part of its name from the nearby village of Aycliffe.

Newton Blossomville *Blossomville* denoting manorial ownership in the Middle Ages by the de Blosseville family.

A village within the unitary authority of Milton Keynes, about 11 km (7 miles) northeast of Newport Pagnell.

Newton Burgoland *Burgoland* denoting manorial ownership in the Middle Ages by the Burgilon family.

A village in Leicestershire, about 24 km (15 miles) west of Leicester.

Newton by Toft *Toft* 'building plot, homestead', OScand.

A village in Lincolnshire, about 19 km (12 miles) northeast of Lincoln and 1.5 km (1 mile) southeast of the village of **Toft next Newton**.

Newton Ferrers *Ferrers* denoting manorial ownership in the Middle Ages by the de Ferers family.

A town in Devon, on the western side of the estuary of the River Yealm, about 8 km (5 miles) southeast of Plymouth.

Newton Flotman *Flotman* denoting manorial ownership in the Middle Ages by a sailor or Viking (OE *flotmann*).

A village in Norfolk, about 11 km (7 miles) south of Norwich.

Newton-le-Willows *le-Willows* 'in the willow-trees'.

An industrial town in Merseyside (formerly in Lancashire), 8 km (5 miles) east of St Helens.

Newton Mearns 'new town of the steward', Gaelic *maor* 'steward'.

A genteel outlying suburb of GLASGOW, in East Renfrewshire, some 10 km (6 miles) south of the city centre.

Newtonmore 'new town on the moor', ModE.

A small resort town in Speyside, Highland (formerly in Inverness-shire), 5 km (3 miles) southwest of Kingussie.

Newton Poppleford *Poppleford* 'pebble ford', OE *popel* 'pebble' + FORD.

A village in Devon, on the River Otter, about 13 km (8 miles) east of Exeter. The 'pebbles' alluded to in the name are round stones known locally as 'Budleigh pobbles'.

Newton Purcell *Purcell* denoting manorial ownership in the early Middle Ages by the Purcel family.

A hamlet in Oxfordshire, about 8 km (5 miles) northeast of Bicester.

Newton St Boswells *St Boswells* from the village of St Boswells.

The administrative seat of SCOTTISH BORDERS (formerly in Roxburghshire), 4 km (2.5 miles) southeast of Melrose. It was little more than a village until the local government reorganization of 1975. It takes its name from the nearby village of **St Boswells**, named after St Boisil, a 7th-century abbot of Old MELROSE just to the west, who also taught and preached with St Cuthbert. **St Boswells Green** was formerly the site of the largest livestock fair in southern Scotland. DRYBURGH ABBEY is nearby.

Newton St Cyres *St Cyres* from the dedication of the local church to St Ciricius.

A village (pronounced 'sires') in Devon, on a small tributary of the River YEO[1], about 8 km (5 miles) northwest of Exeter.

Newton Stewart *Stewart* after William Stewart.

A market town 10 km (6 miles) north of Wigtown, on the River Cree, shortly before it flows into Wigtown Bay. It was formerly in Wigtownshire, and is now in Dumfries and Galloway. It was founded in the later 17th century by William Stewart, third son of the Earl of Galloway, hence its name. The town and surrounding land were bought in the 1770s by Sir William Douglas, who attempted to apply the name Newton Douglas to his new purchase, but the name never caught on. He had more lasting success when he bought and named CASTLE DOUGLAS.

Newton Tony *Tony* denoting manorial ownership in the Middle Ages by the de Toenye family.

A village in Wiltshire, on the River Bourne, about 13 km (8 miles) northeast of Salisbury. Its most notable resident was Celia Fiennes (1662–1741), who was probably born here. She was one of England's first travel writers. Her journals, not published in full until 1947, are filled with an infectious enthusiasm for the things she saw in her travels through all the counties of England, and enlivened by her idiosyncratic spelling.

New Town[1]. The designation given to a type of town established as a new settlement with the aim of relocating populations away from large cities. The first new towns in Britain were inspired by the 'Garden City' concept (*see under* LETCHWORTH), formulated at the end of the 19th century. They were proposed in the **New Towns Act** of 1946, and 12 were designated in England and Wales over the next four years, with a further two in Scotland. Each had its own development corporation financed by the government. Further New Towns were set up in the 1960s. Many are based on existing towns or villages. The general tally is: *England*: BASILDON (Essex), BRACKNELL, CENTRAL LANCASHIRE, CRAWLEY, HARLOW, HATFIELD[1], HEMEL HEMPSTEAD, STEVENAGE, WELWYN GARDEN CITY, NEWTON AYCLIFFE, CORBY, MILTON KEYNES, NORTHAMPTON, PETERBOROUGH, PETERLEE, REDDITCH, RUNCORN, SKELMERSDALE, TELFORD, WARRINGTON, WASHINGTON[1]

Wales: CWMBRAN, NEWTOWN[1]

Scotland: CUMBERNAULD, EAST KILBRIDE, GLENROTHES, IRVINE, LIVINGSTON

Northern Ireland: ANTRIM and BALLYMENA, CRAIGAVON, DERRY/LONDONDERRY

All New Towns, technically, have ceased to exist, the responsibilities of their development corporations having passed to local authorities and other bodies in 1992–6.

New Town[2]. *See under* EDINBURGH.

Newtown[1] Etymology self-explanatory.

A former textile town on the River SEVERN (Hafren) in Powys (formerly in Montgomeryshire), 17 km (10 miles) northeast of Llanidloes. In Welsh it is **Y Drennewydd** ('the new town', *y* 'the' + *tref* 'settlement' + *newydd* 'new'). Despite its name, the town's first charter dates from 1280; in 1967 it was officially re-designated as a NEW TOWN[1].

Newtown was the birthplace of Robert Owen (1771–1858), who contributed to the development of the cooperative movement (*see also* NEW LANARK). W.H. Smith, a retail name now visible in a thousand British high streets, set up his first shop here in 1792, with sets of scurrilous Rowlandson prints being displayed on the top shelf.

Newtown[2]. The fictional modern development patrolled by the police in the long-running 1960s television series *Z Cars*. They also covered the older district of Seaport. Both were thinly disguised bits of Liverpool.

Newtownabbey A modern coinage, partially deriving from the fact that it is a new town development (1958), and partially from one of its constituent settlements, Whiteabbey.

A northern suburb of BELFAST, on the west shore of Belfast Lough. Its Irish name is **Baile na Mainistreach** ('town of the abbey'). It is the administrative centre of the local authority district of the same name.

Newtownards The last element refers to the ARDS PENINSULA[1], at the neck of which the town was founded in the early 17th century by Sir Hugh Montgomery.

A town at the head of STRANGFORD Lough, County Down. Its Irish name is **Baile Nua na hArd** ('new town of the promontory'). There are the remains of a Dominican friary (1244), but most of the older buildings date from the plantation period. (*See also* MOVILLE.)

Newtownbutler After a 17th-century settler called *Butler*. A village in County Fermanagh, 8 km (5 miles) west of Clones. It is also spelt **Newtown Butler**.

Battle of Newtownbutler (31 July 1689). A victory for Williamite forces under Colonel Wesley, who broke out of the siege of ENNISKILLEN to defeat a Jacobite force under General MacCarthy.

Newtownmountkennedy After Sir Robert *Kennedy*, granted land here in the later 17th century.

A village in County Wicklow, 10 km (6 miles) south of Bray. Its Irish name is **Baile Chinnéidigh** ('Kennedy's town').

Newtown Pery. *See under* LIMERICK.

Newtown Unthank *Newtown* self-explanatory; *Unthank* from the name of a family known here from the 15th century.

A village in Leicestershire, about 10 km (6 miles) west of Leicester.

Newyork. A tiny hamlet on the western side of LOCH AWE, south of Dalavich, Argyll and Bute (formerly in Strathclyde region). It was named by the York Buildings Company (*see under* YORK), which operated here in the 18th century.

New York[1] Perhaps from a local field name, bestowed to indicate remoteness. Alternatively, it may have been suggested by the proximity of BOSTON – indeed, it could have been named by Bostonians when they were reclaiming fenland in the area in the 18th century. Both of these explanations depend, of course, on a direct and deliberate allusion to *New York* City (or New York State) in the American colonies (originally *New Amsterdam* – it was renamed *New York* in 1664, after the Duke of York, who had just captured it for the English). On a different tack, it may have been named by the builder who started to develop the place, in honour of his native YORK. The name is first recorded in 1824.

A hamlet in Lincolnshire, on the edge of WILDMORE FEN, about 13 km (8 miles) northwest of BOSTON. Local signposts are on record with the somewhat disorienting combination of Boston and New York.

New York[2] A modern name connoting remoteness.

A village in Tyne and Wear, 3 km (2 miles) northwest of North Shields.

Neyland ME *atten eyland* 'at the island' misdivided as *atte neyland*; ME *eyland* here refers to a dry ground in marsh.

A small port on the north side of the CLEDDAU Bridge across Milford Haven, in Pembrokeshire (formerly in Dyfed), 2 km (1.2 miles) north of Pembroke Dock. It was the main trading link with southern Ireland until the ferry service moved to FISHGUARD in 1906.

Nidd An Indo-European river name cognate with Welsh NEATH[1], meaning 'running water'.

A river in North Yorkshire, rising in the Dales on the slopes of Great and Little WHERNSIDE and flowing southeastwards through the beautiful **Nidderdale** in the YORKSHIRE DALES past Pately Bridge to KNARESBOROUGH, and then eastwards across the Vale of York to join the OUSE[2], 10 km (6 miles) northwest of YORK itself. Its length is approximately 80 km (50 miles).

Nidum. A Roman fort on the site of present-day NEATH[1].

Nigg 'the bay', Gaelic *an* 'the' + *uig* 'bay', from OScand *vik* .
A village overlooking the **Sands of Nigg** and **Nigg Bay**, on the northeast side of the CROMARTY Firth, Highland (formerly in Ross and Cromarty). To the east is the low **Hill of Nigg**. Nigg is some 30 km (20 miles) northeast of Inverness. The place was transformed in the 1970s when it became a site for the construction of North Sea oil platforms.

Nine Ashes Probably from a stand of nine ash trees.
A village in Essex, about 13 km (8 miles) southeast of Harlow.

Nine Elms Probably from a farm in the vicinity called *Nine Elms Farm*, no doubt close to a stand of nine elm trees.
An area of BATTERSEA (SW8), in the London borough of WANDSWORTH, on the opposite bank of the Thames from Pimlico. It was an early beneficiary of, or sufferer from, the railway age: the London terminus of the London and Southampton Railway opened here in 1838, and over the next hundred years the area filled up with tracks, sidings, etc. The townscape was completed by a gasworks and eventually, in 1937, by Battersea Power Station. After the Second World War the area fell prey to neglect, but it was revived by the placing of the New Covent Garden market (*see under* COVENT GARDEN) here in 1974.

Nine Glens, the. Nine scenic glens in County Antrim, also known as the **Antrim Glens**. The northern two, Glentaisie and Glenshesk, run south–north towards Ballycastle Bay (*see under* BALLYCASTLE), while the rest – from north to south, Glendun, Glencorp, Glenaan, Glenballyeamon, Glenariff, Glencloy and Glenarm – run southwest–northeast towards the NORTH CHANNEL.
The origins of the names are not altogether certain. **Glentaisie** (Irish *Gleann Taise*) is taken to mean 'Taise's glen', referring to a semi-legendary princess, daughter of the king of Rathlin; it is also known as **Glentow**, after the river that flows through it. The Tow joins the river of **Glenshesk** just east of Ballycastle; Glenshesk is *Gleann Seische* 'glen of sedges', although *Gleann Seisc*, possibly 'barren glen', also fits most of the early spellings of the name. (The **Virgin of Glenshesk** is St Bronach (*fl.*6th century), a patron saint of seafarers.) **Glendun** (*Gleann Doinne*) is the 'glen of the Dun', the river that meets the sea at CUSHENDUN. **Glencorp** (*Gleann Corp*) is 'glen of the bodies', almost certainly in memory of some ancient battle. **Glenaan** (*Gleann Athain*) may mean 'glen of the burial chamber', and **Glenballyemon**

(*Gleann Bhaile Éamainn*) is 'glen of Ballyemon', the name of a settlement. The remarkably beautiful **Glenariff** (*Gleann Airimh*), the queen of the nine, is 'glen of the arable land'. **Glencloy** is *Gleann Claidhe* ('glen of fenced enclosures'), *Gleann Cloíche* ('glen of the megalith'), *Gleann Claí* ('glen of the ditch') or *Gleann Claíomh* ('glen of the sword'). **Glenarm** (*Gleann Arma*), the most southerly, is 'glen of the weapons', and the village of the same name was the site of a find of prehistoric flint tools.

Songs of the Glens of Antrim. A two-volume poetry collection (1901, 1921) by Cushendun-born Moira O'Neill (Nesta Skrine, 1865–1955).

Nine Mile Burn Possibly from its distance from the edge of Edinburgh, or alternatively a reference to the length of the stream invoked.
A hamlet on the south side of the PENTLAND HILLS, 6 km (4 miles) southwest of Penicuik.

Nine Standards Rigg *Rigg* OScand *hryggr* in the later dialect form *rig* 'ridge'; the *nine standards* were boundary markers between Winton and Hartley, *stander* early ModE 'pillar'.
A hill (662 m / 2171 ft) in the northwest PENNINES of Cumbria, 6 km (4 miles) southeast of Kirkby Stephen, just by the border with North Yorkshire.

Nith From an OCelt name meaning 'new one'.
A river in southwest Scotland, 112 km (69 miles) in length. It rises in East Ayrshire, 6 km (4 miles) east of DALMELLINGTON, flows briefly northwards to NEW CUMNOCK, then east into Dumfries and Galloway and southeast through **Nithsdale** past THORNHILL and through DUMFRIES to meet the SOLWAY FIRTH. (Nithsdale was the name of a local government district in the former Dumfries and Galloway region between 1975 and 1996.)

> This is an interesting valley, the Nith a rough rocky
> stream, the rocks like those on a low but savage sea coast.
>
> Samuel Taylor Coleridge: journal (18 August 1803)

In 1788 Robert Burns acquired the farm of Ellisland, on the banks of the Nith near Dumfries. The farm was not a success and he moved to Dumfries in 1791 to work for the excise full-time. The river itself appears in a number of his poems:

> The Thames flows proudly to the sea,
>   Where royal cities stately stand;
> But sweeter flows the Nith, to me,
>   Where Cummins ance had high command:
> When shall I see that honor'd land,
>   That winding stream I love so dear!
> Must wayward fortune's adverse hand,
>   For ever – ever keep me here?
>
> Robert Burns (attrib.): 'The Banks of Nith' (as if
> written from exile in London)

True-hearted was he, the sad swain o' the Yarrow,
   And fair are the maids on the banks o' the Ayr,
But by the sweet side o' the Nith's winding river,
   Are lovers as faithful, and maidens as fair …

   Robert Burns: 'Young Jessie' (1793)

Burns also polished a Nithy poem by a friend of his, Mrs Maria Riddel, written c.1795:

To thee, lov'd Nith, thy gladsome plains,
   Where late with careless thought I rang'd,
Though prest with care and sunk in woe,
   To thee I bring a heart unchang'd.

I love thee, Nith, thy banks and braes,
   Though Memory there my bosom tear;
For there he rov'd that broke my heart,
   Yet to that heart, ah! still how dear.

After meditating on the death of Burns in Dumfries, Wordsworth turned his thoughts to the poet's riparian life by the Nith:

Let us beside this limpid Stream
   Breath hopeful air.

   William Wordsworth: 'Thoughts suggested … on
   the Banks of Nith, near the Poet's Residence' (1803)

Nithsdale measure. The Nithsdale measure, together with the Nithsdale peck and the Nithsdale pint, were about a tenth again more generous than the standard Scots liquid measures. Sadly, they died out in the early 19th century.

Nitshill 'nuts hill', Scots dialect *nit* 'nut' (OE *hnut*) + *hill*.
A southwestern district of GLASGOW. It developed in the 19th century around local coal mines. *The Angel of Nitshill Road* (1993) is a book for children by Anne Fine.

Noah's Ark[1] Apparently from the name of a house in the vicinity. First recorded in 1819.
A village in Kent, about 4 km (2.5 miles) northeast of SEVENOAKS.

Noah's Ark[2] Perhaps alluding to a local abundance or diversity of animals.
A village in Hertfordshire, about 2.5 km (1.5 miles) northeast of WARE.

Noah's Green Probably from the personal name of an owner.
A village in Worcestershire (before 1998 in Hereford and Worcester, before 1974 in Worcestershire), about 6 km (4 miles) southwest of Redditch.

Nob End Possibly 'area by the hill', *Nob* OScand *knappr* 'hill, hillock'; *End* ME *ende* 'area, end'.
A district of LITTLE LEVER, Greater Manchester, on the Manchester, Bolton and Bury Canal (*see under* BURY).

Nobottle 'new building', OE *niwe* 'new' + *bothl* 'building'.
A village in Northamptonshire, about 8 km (5 miles) west of Northampton.

Nob's Crook Etymology unknown.
A hamlet in Hampshire, about 4 km (2.5 miles) northeast of EASTLEIGH.

Noctorum '(place on a) dry hill' (alluding to its original situation as dry land rising above marshland), OCelt *cnocc* (*see* KNOCK-) + *tirim* 'dry'; the modern form of the name apes Latin *noctorum* 'of the nights', the possessive plural of *nox* 'night'.
A western district of BIRKENHEAD, in the WIRRAL.

Nodding Hull. A nickname for NOTTING HILL.

Noddytown. A nickname for CUMBERNAULD.

Noe A pre-English river-name, possibly from an Indo-European root meaning 'valley, trough'.
A river in Derbyshire, in the PEAK DISTRICT, which rises to the south of KINDER SCOUT and flows 14 km (9 miles) southeastwards to join the River DERWENT[4] to the south of LADYBOWER RESERVOIR.
See also EDALE and HOPE[1].

Noke '(place at the) oak-tree', OE *ac* 'oak'; the *N* comes from a misanalysis of early ME *atten oke* 'at the oak'.
A village in Oxfordshire, on the edge of OTMOOR, about 11 km (7 miles) north of Oxford.

Noltland Castle. *See under* WESTRAY.

No Man's Heath[1] 'heath that no one owns', ME *nan-man* 'no one', with *heth* 'heath'.
A village in Cheshire, about 14 km (8.5 miles) southwest of Nantwich.

No Man's Heath[2]. A village in Warwickshire, about 21 km (13 miles) north of Nuneaton, close to the point where the boundaries of Derbyshire, Leicestershire, Staffordshire and Warwickshire converge.

Nomansland[1] From its not being within a specified parish.
A village in Devon, about 11 km (7 miles) west of Tiverton.

Nomansland[2]. A village in Wiltshire, on the Hampshire border, about 16 km (10 miles) southeast of Salisbury.

Nonsuch Park From *Nonsuch* Palace: when it was built, there was intended to be *none such* (i.e. it was 'without equal, unique').
A park (pronounced 'nunsuch') in CHEAM, Surrey. It is the location of the former **Nonsuch Palace**, built by Henry VIII from 1538, sold by 'Bloody Mary', reacquired by Elizabeth I in 1592, owned by Henrietta Maria (wife of Charles I) in the 17th century, never definitively completed and finally demolished in 1682.

Treaty of Nonsuch (20 August 1585). A treaty between England and the United Provinces of the Netherlands, under the terms of which Queen Elizabeth I sent 7000 troops under Robert Dudley, Earl of Leicester, to the Netherlands to help the Dutch rebels in their struggle against Philip II of Spain.

Norbiton 'northern grange or outlying farm' (referring to its location relative to SURBITON, likewise a grange of the royal manor of KINGSTON), OE *north* + *bere-tun* 'grange, outlying farm'.

A residential district of southwest Outer London (before 1965 in Surrey), between KINGSTON to the west and NEW MALDEN to the southeast, in the borough of KINGSTON UPON THAMES. Kingston Hospital is situated here.

Norbiton was the (quintessentially suburban) home of Reginald Iolanthe Perrin (played by Leonard Rossiter) in the BBC television sitcom *The Fall and Rise of Reginald Perrin* (1976–79), created by David Nobbs.

Nore Irish *An Fheoir* 'the border stream'.

A river in southeastern Ireland, rising in the SLIEVE BLOOM MOUNTAINS of Laois, and flowing southeastwards through KILKENNY to meet the BARROW just north of NEW ROSS. It is one of the so-called THREE SISTERS, along with the Barrow and the SUIR.

Nore freshwater pearl mussel. A species of mussel, *Margaritifera durrovensis*, unique to the river. A breeding programme was set up in 1991 to save it from extinction.

Nore, the Probably '(place) at the sandbank', ME *atten ore* 'at the sandbank' (from Latin *ora* 'shore, coast') being misdivided as *atte nore*.

A sandbank in the estuary of the River THAMES[1], off SHEERNESS. In 1732 the first lightship in English waters was anchored here. The nearby area was extensively used by the Royal Navy as an anchorage during the Dutch Wars of the 17th and 18th centuries:

> Up about 5 a-clock ... and to sail again down to the *Sovereign* at the buoy of the Nore – a noble ship, now rigged and fitted and manned.
>
> Samuel Pepys: *Diaries* (18 August 1665)

In the Second World War seven towers were erected near the Nore as part of the Thames defences. They were demolished in the late 1950s. Until 1961, the naval command area for eastern England was known as 'the Nore'.

Nore Mutiny. A mutiny against bad conditions of service staged at the Nore by a number of sailors in 1797. It lasted from 12 May to 16 June, and its leader Richard Parker and 29 other mutineers were afterwards hanged.

Norfolk '(territory of the) northern people' (referring to the northern East Anglians, as contrasted with the southern East Anglians of Suffolk), OE *north* + *folc* 'people'.

A county in East Anglia, forming the northern part of the great bulge of land from the Thames Estuary to the Wash. It is bounded to the west by Lincolnshire and Cambridgeshire, to the south by Suffolk, and to the north and east by the North Sea. In the local government reorganization of 1974 it gained a small portion of northeastern Suffolk. Its administrative centre is NORWICH;

other towns of note include CROMER, DISS, DOWNHAM MARKET, GREAT YARMOUTH, HUNSTANTON, KING'S LYNN, NORTH WALSHAM, SHERINGHAM, SWAFFHAM and THETFORD. Its chief rivers are the BURE, the GREAT OUSE, the WAVENEY[1] (which forms part of the border with Suffolk), the Wensum and the YARE. It has little in the way of undulations ('Very flat, Norfolk', Noël Coward, *Private Lives*, 1930), and is mainly level agricultural land. To the west are the FENS and the heath and scrub of the BRECKLAND, and inland of the east coast are the lakes, waterways and reedbeds of the **Norfolk Broads** (*see* BROADS). The county contains many large estates, including SANDRINGHAM, favourite of successive British monarchs in the 20th century:

> Spirits of well-shot woodcock, partridge, snipe
> Flutter and bear him up the Norfolk sky.
>
> John Betjeman: 'Death of King George V' (1937)

Norfolk was part of the territory of the ancient British Iceni tribe and later on part of the Saxon kingdom of EAST ANGLIA. From the late Anglo-Saxon period and through the Middle Ages it was one of the wealthiest and most heavily populated areas of England, thanks to the wool trade. Since those high days it has slipped down the leagues, and now has a backwatery image. It earns its living mainly from tourism, arable farming and the intensive breeding of turkeys, for which the county has long been famous (the headquarters of Bernard Matthews Foods Ltd, purveyor of truckloads of frozen turkeys, are in Norwich).

Duke of Norfolk. England's premier duke and the hereditary Earl Marshal of England. The dukedom was created in 1397 for Thomas Mowbray (*c*.1366–99), but since the 15th century has (with gaps) been held by the (Roman Catholic) Howard family. The best-known was the 3rd Duke (1473–1554), who was a powerful statesman under Henry VIII. The ducal seat is a long way from Norfolk, at Arundel Castle in West Sussex.

In cricketing terms Norfolk is a 'minor county' (the club was founded in 1876) and plays in the minor counties championship.

> Norfolk, they say, is flat. Well, have it so:
> These undulations never rise so high
> They reach the dignity of hills – but, oh,
> Range upon range, the mountains of the sky!
>
> F. Pratt Green (1903–2000): 'Skyscape'

There are towns called Norfolk in the USA: Arkansas, Connecticut, Nebraska (where it is a re-imaging of the original name 'North Fork'), Virginia (an important seaport and naval base on Hampton Roads) and also a county called Norfolk (Massachusetts). Norfolk Island, an external territory of Australia in the southwest Pacific Ocean, was named after a duke of Norfolk. The town of New Norfolk, in Tasmania, was so named because Norfolk Islanders were resettled there.

Jockey of Norfolk. A nickname applied to Sir John Howard (*c*.1430–85), the first Howard to be Duke of Norfolk, and a firm adherent of Richard III. It is said that on the night before the Battle of BOSWORTH, where he was killed, he found in his tent the warning couplet:

> Jockey of Norfolk, be not too bold,
> For Dickon thy master is bought and sold.

Norfolk Broads. *See* BROADS.

Norfolk capon. A name humorously applied in the 19th century to a (literal) red herring (a salted herring that has been smoked until it is bright red).

Norfolk dumpling. A standard plain dumpling, made of bread dough. The name reflects the fact that Norfolk is generally credited as its place of origin. Observation of its effect on the waistline led to its use in the 18th century as a mocking term for a Norfolk person. G.K. Chesterton's Father Brown was described by his creator as having 'a face as round and dull as a Norfolk dumpling'.

Norfolk four-course system. A four-year crop-rotation system involving no fallow year. It was developed in Norfolk in the late 17th century, was in fairly general use in Britain by the end of the 18th century and spread widely in Continental Europe in the 19th century.

Norfolk howard. Nineteenth-century slang (often abbreviated to **n.h.**) for a bedbug. It apparently commemorates an unfortunate personage called Joseph (or Joshua) Bug, who was so embarrassed by his name that he changed it to 'Norfolk Howard' (presumably in emulation of the dukes of Norfolk, family name Howard), despite popular derision at what was seen as affectation.

Norfolk jacket. A type of men's loose-fitting belted single-breasted tweed jacket with box pleats and plentiful pockets. The name and the fashion date from the 1860s (both apparently fostered by the Duke of Norfolk's wearing of such a coat), and from then until well into the 20th century the Norfolk jacket was well nigh indispensible apparel for gentlemanly country pursuits such as fishing, bicycling and the slaughtering of large numbers of pheasants and partridges (a frequent occurrence on the large landed estates of Norfolk). It became an item of general informal wear, and young boys were often clad as simulacra of their fathers in small Norfolk jackets. The jacket's standard partner was knee-breeches (*see* Norfolk suit, below).

Norfolk plover. An alternative name for the stone curlew (*Burhinus oedicnemus*).

Norfolk reed. A name for the common reed, *Phragmites australis*, as grown in East Anglia for use as thatching material.

Norfolk Rhapsodies. A set of orchestral pieces (1905–6) by Ralph Vaughan Williams, based on Norfolk folk tunes. He wrote three, but he withdrew the last two shortly after their premiere. The score of No. 3 no longer exists, but No. 2 was unearthed and recorded for the first time in 2002.

Norfolk spaniel. A name used in the 19th century for the English springer spaniel, a breed once associated with the estates of the Duke of Norfolk.

Norfolk suit. A men's suit consisting of a Norfolk jacket and knee-breeches. In the period of its fashionability, in the late 19th and early 20th centuries, its name was often simplified to **Norfolks**:

> A giant little boy – in Norfolks like my brother's.
>
> E. Nesbit: *Five Children and It* (1902)

Norfolk terrier. A breed of dog similar to a Norwich terrier (*see under* NORWICH) but with ears that flop over.

Norfolk turkey. An opprobrious 19th-century nickname for a person from Norfolk (a county famed for its turkey production):

> I shall … shew them the difference of a highly-educated person, and the boorish manners of those Norfolk turkeys.
>
> Amelia Beauclerc: *Ora and Juliet* (1811)

normal for Norfolk. A decidedly non-politically correct doctors' categorization of patients whose behaviour or intelligence level are accounted for by the sort of inbred backwardness stereotypically attributed to country areas like Norfolk. Usually euphemistically disguised as *NFN*.

> This is Norfolk. You get applause for standing up straight.
>
> Sue Townsend: *Adrian Mole: The Cappuccino Years* (as dramatized on BBC television, 2001)

Six Folksongs from Norfolk. A collection (1924) of Norfolk folksongs set to piano accompaniment by the composer E.J. Moeran. The settings include 'Down by the Riverside', 'Lonely Waters' and 'The Oxford Sporting Blade'. An avid collector of folksongs, Moeran later published a similar collection of settings of folksongs from Suffolk (*see under* SUFFOLK).

Norham 'northern homestead or water meadow', OE *north* + HAM.

A village in Northumberland, on the south side of the River TWEED (which here forms the border with Scotland), 12 km (7.5 miles) southwest of Berwick-upon-Tweed. It is pronounced 'nor-əm'.

The magnificent ruins of **Norham Castle** overlook the Tweed, where they guard a once-important ford. The castle was the northernmost stronghold of the prince-bishops of Durham, and the area around it, known as **Norhamshire**, was in those days part of County Durham rather than Northumberland. The castle was the scene of a number of important events. It was here that in 1209 William the Lion, King of Scotland, agreed to pay tribute to King John, and that on 10 May 1291 Edward I declared that Robert the Bruce and John (de) Balliol were his favoured candidates for the throne of Scotland, but that he himself was 'paramount king' (Balliol won Edward's casting vote at Berwick in the following year). James IV captured the castle in 1513, en route to annihilation at FLODDEN. The ruins were often painted by J.M.W. Turner, and provide the setting for the opening of Scott's *Marmion*:

> Day set on Norham's castled steep,
> And Tweed's fair river, broad and deep,
>   And Cheviot's mountains lone:
> The battled towers, the donjon keep,
> The loophole grates, where captives weep,
> The flanking walls that round it sweep,
>   In yellow lustre shone …
>
> Sir Walter Scott: *Marmion: A Tale of Flodden Field*
> (1808), Canto I, i

One of the castle's gates is known as the Marmion Gate.

Norlands 'north open lands' (referring to its location to the north of Kensington parish), ME *north* + *lands*.
A small residential area in West London (W11), to the northwest of HOLLAND PARK, in the borough of Kensington and Chelsea. Three of the local roads have Norland in their name, but it is Norland Place that has spread its fame far and wide, for it was here in 1892 that Mrs Walter Ward opened the **Norland Institute** (later the **Norland Nursery Training College**) for training young women as nursery nurses. Over the next century and more the **'Norland nanny'** became an essential adjunct to the English upper-middle-class family, providing the gold standard of childcare.

Nor Loch, the. *See under* PRINCES STREET.

Normanby-by-Spital *Normanby* 'farmstead or village of the Northmen or Norwegian Vikings', OE *Northmen* + -BY; *by Spital* from its proximity to SPITAL IN THE STREET.
A village in Lincolnshire, about 17 km (11 miles) north of Lincoln.
See also OWMBY-BY-SPITAL.

Normandy Probably from an inn in the locality called 'The Duke of Normandy' (i.e. William I). The name is first recorded in 1656, but this has not deterred proud locals from seeking to link it and the village in some way with the Norman Conquest.
A village in Surrey, north of the HOG'S BACK and about 8 km (5 miles) west of Guildford. The writer William Cobbett (1763–1835) lived the last four years of his life here.

Norman's Bay Probably from a surname *Norman*.
A small coastal village in East Sussex, about 3 km (2 miles) northeast of Pevensey. The nearby railway station shares its name.

Normanton 'farmstead of the Norsemen', OE *Northman* 'Norseman' + -TON.
A town in West Yorkshire, 6 km (4 miles) northeast of Wakefield. There is also a Normanton in South Australia.

North, the[1]. The northern counties of England, constituting everything north of the Midlands. There is some uncertainty as to exactly how far north the MIDLANDS extend, but it is safe to say that Merseyside, Yorkshire, Lancashire, County Durham, Cumbria and Northumberland are all very definitely the North. Cheshire, Derbyshire and Nottinghamshire are also candidates for inclusion, as is, perhaps, the northern part of Staffordshire. The area is also known as the **North Country**:

> A North Country maid up to London had strayed,
> Although with her nature it did not agree.
> She wept and she sighed, and so bitterly she cried,
> How I wish once again in the North I could be!
>
> *Oh the oak and the ash, and the bonny ivy tree,*
> *They flourish at home in my own country.*
>
> Anon.: ballad 'The Oak and the Ash' (traditional
> Northumbrian ballad)

In the clichéd view of Southerners, the North is a place of bleak post-industrial cities mired in poverty and despair, while **Northerners** are gritty plain-speaking folk in cloth caps (the men, anyway), who own whippets and who will not stand for any nonsense or frippery.

> Northerners are far too busy breeding pigeons, eating deep-fried chip butties and executing drive-by shootings on Moss Side to dally over the new Sebastian Faulks.
>
> Hildy Johnson: in *The Bookseller* (9 March 2001)

> People in the North die of ignorance and crisps.
>
> Edwina Currie: speaking as junior health minister (September 1986) (Currie is herself from Liverpool.)

But the North is also a land of cathedrals and minsters and ruined abbeys, of choral societies and brass bands, and of wide tracts of beautiful fells and dales. There are even, here and there, a few constituencies that return Conservative members to Parliament.

> … bright and fierce and fickle is the South,
> And dark and true and tender is the North.
>
> Alfred, Lord Tennyson: song added in 1850 to *The Princess* (1847)

Angel of the North, The. A huge sculpture of an angel with outstretched wings by Antony Gormley (b.1950). It was erected on a hillside next to the A1 at Gateshead in 1998. The angel is 20 m (66 ft) high, and its wingspan is 54 m (177 ft). The structure – erected with the help of major engineering firms – celebrates the region's industrial past (the wings are those of an early aeroplane), while the angel element echoes the area's importance in early Christianity, the northeast being the land of St Cuthbert (c.635–687) and the Venerable Bede (c.673–735). Gormley has said of his work:

The hilltop site is important and has the feeling of being a megalithic mound. When you think of the mining that was done underneath the site, there is a poetic resonance. Men worked beneath the surface in the dark. Now in the light, there is a celebration of this industry.

Gateshead Council's only Conservative member commented: 'I think it is ruining a piece of nice countryside.' Despite such objections, the Angel itself showed its partisan pride when Newcastle United last appeared in the FA Cup Final, when it was seen to don a giant version of the Magpies' black-and-white strip.

Council of the North. A council originating in the 15th century that implemented the king's policies in the counties of Yorkshire, Cumberland, Durham, Northumberland and Westmorland. It was re-established by Henry VIII in 1537 following the Pilgrimage of Grace, a northern rebellion against his religious reforms (see LOUTH[1]), and oversaw the introduction of Protestantism in the region. It was finally abolished in 1641.

Harrying of the North, the. The brutal suppression (1069–70) by the Normans of an Anglo-Saxon rebellion, led by Edgar the Ætheling. Large areas of the North, as recorded in Domesday Book, were completely devastated – but the Harrying had the sought-after effect of deterring any further rebellion.

Lantern of the North, the. The name given to WHITBY Abbey, founded by St Hilda in 657.

North and South. A novel (1854–5) by Elizabeth Gaskell, first published in Charles Dickens's magazine *Household Words*. The title refers to the industrial North of England and the rural South, and the book deals with the contrasts between the two, mainly in terms of poverty versus affluence.

North Country compliment. A late 19th-century slang term for a valueless gift, treasured by neither giver nor receiver. The expression refers to the supposed meanness of Northerners.

North–South divide. An economic division that some hold pertains in Britain between the wealthy South (especially southeast England) and the poor North, especially since the decline of the North's heavy industries from the 1980s. Critics of the concept point to impoverished inner-city areas in the South.

Northern Rebellion. A rising (1569–70) during the reign of Protestant Elizabeth I, led by the Earl of Westmorland and the Earl of Northumberland. Its aim was to secure the English succession for the Catholic Mary Queen of Scots. It is also called the **Rising of the North.** The Spanish promised support, but did nothing, and the rising was suppressed.

The earls fled to Scotland, and 400 of their followers were executed.

Northern soul. A collective term applied to a variety of 1970s and 1980s soul bands from the North, such as Sweet Sensation from Manchester and The Real Thing from Liverpool, and even Scotland's Average White Band.

Our Friends in the North. A play by Peter Flannery, subsequently revised as an award-winning nine-part BBC television series, about the fortunes of a group of Geordie friends from Tyneside between 1963 and 1995. The series, broadcast in 1996, covered local government corruption in the Newcastle of the 1960s, with figures similar to T. Dan Smith and John Poulson (see NEWCASTLE UPON TYNE), and also featured the corrupt involvement by some members of the London vice squad with the Soho sex trade in the 1970s.

North, the[2]. NORTHERN IRELAND, as seen from the Republic, particularly by those who do not recognize its separate existence. It is also known as the BLACK NORTH or the **Wee North**, the latter from the supposed overuse of the word 'wee' (Ulster-Scots for 'little') by many of its inhabitants.

Northallerton 'Ælfhere's farm', OE male personal name *Ælfhere* + -TON, with *North* added in the 13th century.
A market town in North Yorkshire (of which it is the administrative centre), 45 km (28 miles) north of York. Near the town is COWTON MOOR, the site of the Battle of the Standard (1138). Daniel Defoe records that the area of Yorkshire around the town was then (1720s) known as **North Allertonshire**.

In 18th- and 19th-century slang a *Northallerton* denotes a spur, the town then being famous for its production of high-quality spurs.

Northampton Originally *Hamtun* 'home farm, homestead', OE HAM + *tun* (see -TON); the prefix *North-* (first recorded in the 11th century) was added to distinguish the place from SOUTHAMPTON (whose name has a different origin).
A town in Northamptonshire, on the River NENE, about 24 km (15 miles) north of Milton Keynes. It is the administrative centre of the county. It was designated a NEW TOWN[1] in 1968. It has a long history (it received its first charter in 1189), but it was severely damaged by fire in 1675, and almost all of its more imposing buildings postdate that event. Its market square is said to be the largest in England. It has an Eleanor Cross, and also a 19th-century Roman Catholic cathedral, designed by A.W. Pugin.

The town's celebrated connection with boot- and shoemaking dates back to the Middle Ages, but the celebrity was probably the product of the Civil Wars period, when footwear for Cromwell's army was made here. Charles II was sufficiently miffed to have Northampton's walls and the Norman **Northampton Castle** demolished after his restoration, but Northampton later came back into official favour, and the British Army's boots were made here during the Napoleonic Wars. The town still manufactures shoes (and its football team, **Northampton Town** (founded 1897), is nicknamed the Cobblers), but since the 1950s on a much smaller, more specialized scale; light engineering and food production are now its main money-earners.

Rather higher-flying than its footballers are Northampton's rugby union players. **Northampton RFC** was founded in 1880 by Rev. Samuel Wathen Wigg, curate of St James's Church (hence the club's nickname, the Saints), as a suitably muscular means for high-spirited adolescent boys to let off steam. The club, which plays its home games at Franklin's Gardens, has contributed a number of distinguished players to the England national team, including Dickie Jeeps and Matt Dawson.

Anne Bradstreet (1612–72), the Massachusetts-based Puritan poet; Alban Butler (1710–73), author of *Lives of the Saints* (1756–9); the composers Edmund Rubbra (1901–86), William Alwyn (1905–85) and Malcolm Arnold (b.1921); Francis Crick (b.1916), Nobel-Prize-winning co-discoverer of the structure of DNA and the actress Joan Hickson (1906–98) were born in Northampton.

John Clare (1793–1864), the Northamptonshire-born 'peasant poet', having been certified insane, spent the last 23 years of his life as an inmate of St Andrew's Asylum in Northampton (*see below*). The comic novelist Jerome K. Jerome (1859–1927) also died in Northampton.

There are towns called Northampton in the USA (Massachusetts) and Australia (Western Australia), and a county of that name in the USA (Pennsylvania).

Assize of Northampton. A group of ordinances relating mainly to the duties of judges, agreed by Henry II at Northampton in 1176. A somewhat draconian response to a contemporary crime wave, they added new offences to the list of those that judges were to enquire into (among them, arson and forgery) and laid down severe punishments, including the loss of the right hand.

Battle of Northampton (April 1264). An encounter in the Barons' War involving the besieging of Simon de Montfort's supporters in Northampton Castle by Henry III. De Monfort attempted to ride to the rescue, but on 6 April the castle fell and his son (also called Simon) was captured.

Battle of Northampton (10 July 1460). A battle of the Wars of Roses in which Yorkist forces under Richard Neville, Earl of Warwick, defeated the Lancastrians and captured Henry VI. It paved the way for Richard of York to be recognized as successor to Henry (as Richard III).

Treaty of Northampton. An Anglo-Scottish peace treaty (May 1328) by which Edward III recognized Robert the Bruce as king of Scotland, and by which Bruce's infant son, the future David II, was betrothed to Joanna, Edward's sister.

'Written in Northampton County Asylum'. A poem written by John Clare, the Northamptonshire Poet (*see under* NORTHAMPTONSHIRE), while he was confined in the asylum (1841–64). It has the celebrated opening lines:

> I AM! yet what I am who cares, or knows?
> My friends forsake me like a memory lost.
> I am the self-consumer of my woes;
> They rise and vanish, an oblivious host,
> Shadows of life, whose very soul is lost.

Northamptonshire From NORTHAMPTON + SHIRE. The name *Northamptonshire* is first recorded in the 11th century.

A county in the Midlands of England. It is bounded to the north by Leicestershire and Rutland, to the west by Oxfordshire and Warwickshire, to the south by Buckinghamshire and the unitary authority of Milton Keynes, and to the east by Bedfordshire, Cambridgeshire and the unitary authority of Peterborough (the historical county of Northamptonshire included the Soke of Peterborough, which was hived off with its own county council in 1888). Its administrative centre is NORTHAMPTON, and other towns of note are CORBY, DAVENTRY, KETTERING, RUSHDEN and WELLINGBOROUGH. Its chief rivers are the NENE and the WELLAND. In its northeast corner is Rockingham Forest (*see under* ROCKINGHAM).

It merges into the FENS in the east and the COTSWOLDS in the west, but for the most part its landscape is quintessential rolling English Midlands: acre upon acre of quiet pastoral land, great estates and parks, its dreams of a bygone rural England deepened rather than disturbed by the regular passage of men and horses in pursuit of foxes – the epitome of the SHIRES (it has been termed the 'County of Squires and Spires'). It is not all bucolic charm, though. Agriculture may be its main business, but the **Northampton Sands**, in the low hills between the Nene and the Welland, bear low-grade iron ore, and Corby was long a centre of steel production on the strength of it.

Roman-era Northamptonshire was part of the territory of the British tribe known as the Coritani. In Anglo-Saxon times it was part of the kingdom of MERCIA. The area around Northampton fell to the Danes in the early part of the 10th century, but the Saxon king Edward the Elder recaptured it shortly afterwards.

In cricketing terms Northamptonshire is a 'first-class' county. Northamptonshire County Cricket Club was founded in 1878 and has played in the county championship since 1905. It has never won the county championship. Its home ground is the County Ground, Northampton.

Northamptonshire Poet, the. An epithet sometimes applied to the 'peasant poet' John Clare (1793–1864), who was born and is buried in Northamptonshire. Clare worked in his native village of HELPSTON as a hedge-setter and day labourer, publishing the successful collections *Poems Descriptive of Rural Life and Scenery* (1820), *The Village Minstrel* (1821) and *The Shepherd's Calendar* (1827). A move from Helpston to Northborough in 1832 appears to have destabilized him, however, and he was admitted to an asylum at High Beech, near Epping, in 1837. Clare escaped in 1841, walking from Epping Forest back to Northamptonshire in the mistaken hope that he would be reunited with his first love, Mary Joyce. The route that he followed, via Enfield, Stevenage, Baldock, Stilton and Peterborough, covered nearly 161 km (100 miles) and took him four days, during which time he subsisted on grass. Declared insane once again, Clare spent the remainder of his life in the County Lunatic Asylum in NORTHAMPTON, where a liberal regime allowed him to continue to write poetry.

Northants *-hants see* HANTS.

The standard written abbreviation of NORTHAMPTONSHIRE. It is also widely used in colloquial spoken English.

North Atlantic Archipelago, the. A term occasionally used by historians and others who wish to refer to the British Isles without causing offence to the Irish.

See also THESE ISLANDS; Hibernian Archipelago (*under* HIBERNIA).

North Ayrshire From AYR[2] + SHIRE.

A unitary authority created in 1996. It includes IRVINE (the administrative centre), KILWINNING, ARDROSSAN, LARGS, the CUMBRAES and ARRAN. It is bounded on the north by Inverclyde, on the east by Renfrewshire and East Ayrshire, and to the south by South Ayrshire.

North Berwick *Berwick* 'barley farm', OE *bere* 'barley' + WICK. A royal BURGH on the Firth of Forth, in East Lothian, some 30 km (20 miles) northeast of Edinburgh. With its sandy beaches and golf courses it has long been a popular holiday centre. At the new Scottish Seabird Centre visitors can manipulate cameras transmitting back live CCTV pictures from the nearby BASS ROCK.

North Berwick Law. A steep conical hill (*see* LAW, LOW 'rounded hill') behind the town. It is 187 m (613 ft) high, and on the top there is a watchtower from the Napoleonic period and an arch made of whales' jawbones.

North Berwick Witches, the. In 1590 a number of people were accused of holding a coven in the Auld Kirk of North Berwick, where the Devil presided over their supposed conspiracy to kill James VI at the behest of Francis Hepburn, Earl of Bothwell. The witches were said to have attempted the sinking of the king's boat as he sailed up the Firth of Forth on the way back from Norway with his new wife, Anne of Denmark. Their method was to throw a live cat into the waters, to whose paws were tied lumps of flesh from the body of a hanged man. Luckily for the king, the wrong ship foundered. All this came out under extreme torture, the king himself (called 'the wisest fool in Christendom') taking part in the interrogations. Of the accused, Dr John Fian (a schoolteacher), Agnes Sampson

(a midwife) and Euphemia Maclean (daughter of Lord Cliftonhall) were all executed. Bothwell fled to Italy.

North Boarhunt. *See under* BOARHUNT.

North Britain. A name for SCOTLAND that was encouraged by the government following the Act of Union in 1707, which joined the two kingdoms into the single entity known as Great Britain. England became South Britain. However, the names never really caught on, except in a scurrilous way in Wilkes's *North Briton*. A long-surviving relict was the **North British Hotel**, a grand Edwardian edifice above Edinburgh's WAVERLEY STATION. It took its name from the North British Railway Company, which grew to have the greatest mileage of any railway company in Scotland, and became part of the London and North Eastern Railway in 1923. The hotel changed its name to The Balmoral in 1991.

North Briton, The. A periodical founded by the radical John Wilkes in 1762 to air his animosity against George III's minister, Lord Bute, and the Scottish nation as a whole. 'Number 45' is the edition (23 April 1763) in which the King's Speech referring to the Treaty of Paris of that year as 'honourable to my Crown and beneficial to my people' was held to be a lie. Wilkes escaped a charge of libel by pleading parliamentary privilege. The North Briton was also the title formerly given to a train service running between Leeds and Edinburgh.

See also WEST BRITON.

North Camp Originally *The Camp*, a hutted army training encampment opened at the time of the Crimean War to the north of Aldershot. This was subsequently extended to the south, and the original camp was renamed *North Camp*. The name was subsequently allocated to a nearby railway station on the Guildford to Reading line, and inherited by the settlement that grew up around the station.

A southeastern suburb of FARNBOROUGH[1], on the Hampshire–Surrey border.

North Cave Probably from OE *caf* 'quick', referring to a local stream now called Mires Beck.

A village in the East Riding of Yorkshire, 16 km (10 miles) southwest of Beverley. The village of **South Cave** is 4 km (2.5 miles) to the southeast.

North Cerney. *See under* CHURN.

North Channel *North* as opposed to ST GEORGE'S CHANNEL, which links the southern end of the Irish Sea to the Atlantic.

The sea channel linking the northern end of the Irish Sea to the Atlantic. It lies between Northern Ireland to the west and the Mull of KINTYRE, the Firth of CLYDE and the Rhinns of GALLOWAY to the east. It is sometimes nicknamed the SHEUGH.

North Circular Road. A road, the A406, which runs in a 50 km (30 mile) semicircle from CHISWICK in the west through NORTH LONDON to London City Airport (*see under* LONDON) in the east, and together with the SOUTH CIRCULAR ROAD forms an annular traffic artery through the inner suburbs of London.

Unlike its southern companion, which utilizes existing roads, the **North Circular** is purpose-built. The section from Chiswick to SOUTHGATE was planned and built in the 1920s and 1930s, to provide a dedicated east–west link that would relieve the mounting pressure of traffic on roads not originally designed for cars and lorries. The route from WOODFORD to the WOOLWICH Ferry followed the existing A104, A114, A116 and A117, but a new purpose-built section of the A406 superseded this.

As is the fate of roads designed to relieve traffic, it attracted increased numbers of road-users, and today the artery of the North Circular is fairly comprehensively clogged at rush hours. The M25 has taken on its burden of relief. Meanwhile the suburbs that grew up around it (e.g. NEASDEN) seem to have had some of the life sucked out of them by the traffic fumes.

See also HANGER LANE.

North Creake *Creake* 'rock, cliff', OCelt *creig*.
A village in North Norfolk, about 8 km (5 miles) southwest of Wells-next-the-Sea. SOUTH CREAKE is about 2.5 km (1.5 miles) to the south.

North Curry *Curry see* CURRY MALLET.
A village in Somerset, to the north of Curry Mallet and about 11 km (7 miles) east of Taunton.

North Down. A local authority district in Northern Ireland, formed from part of northern County Down. The administrative centre is at BANGOR[2].

North Downs, the *Downs see* DOWN, -DON.
A range of low rolling chalk hills in southern England, extending from West Surrey (near FARNHAM) eastwards and then southeastwards via the Surrey Hills and the Kent Downs to the Kent coast between FOLKESTONE and DOVER, where they end in spectacular chalk cliffs (the northern extremity of which is marked by the SOUTH FORELAND). The North Downs rise to 294 m (965 ft) at LEITH HILL. The best-known beauty spot on the Downs is BOX HILL[1].

Part of the route of the PILGRIMS' WAY, from Winchester to Canterbury, runs along the North Downs, and a more modern footpath along which the hills can be traversed is the 227-km (141-mile) long **North Downs Way**.

The North Downs form an important strategic barrier to the south of London, and the points at which they are penetrated by rivers became centres of settlement (notably DORKING and LEATHERHEAD by the River Mole and GUILDFORD by the Wey).

See also the DOWNS *and* the SOUTH DOWNS.

Northeast, the. A common designation for that part of

the NORTH[1] of England encompassing the counties of NORTHUMBERLAND, TYNE AND WEAR, County Durham (*see* DURHAM, COUNTY) and much of YORKSHIRE. The PENNINES split it from its neighbour, the NORTHWEST. In particular the description is applied to the coastal industrial conurbations of HUMBERSIDE (around HULL) and, further north, Teeside (*see under* TEES), around MIDDLESBROUGH, and TYNESIDE (around NEWCASTLE UPON TYNE). In 2004 the people of the Northeast (excluding Yorkshire) voted by a large majority against having a regional assembly.

North East Lincolnshire *See* LINCOLNSHIRE.
A unitary authority in eastern England created in 1996 from part of the former county of HUMBERSIDE (and before that part of Lincolnshire). Its administrative headquarters are at GRIMSBY and its other main towns are CLEETHORPES and IMMINGHAM.

Northern Ireland. A constituent part of the United Kingdom that came into formal existence with the Government of Ireland Act in September 1920. The partition of IRELAND into Northern Ireland and the Irish Free State (now the Republic) was de facto recognized by the Anglo-Irish Treaty of 1921. Northern Ireland comprises the counties of ANTRIM, DOWN, ARMAGH, LONDONDERRY (or Derry), TYRONE and FERMANAGH – hence it is acronymically sometimes dubbed FATLAD or FATDAD. It is also referred to as ULSTER, or the Province, but the traditional province of Ulster also contains three additional counties that are in the Republic. To some Catholics in the South it is the BLACK NORTH, while Republicans will not use the term Northern Ireland, as it implies an acceptance of partition, and talk instead of the SIX COUNTIES (the other TWENTY-SIX COUNTIES of the THIRTY-TWO COUNTIES are in the Republic as currently constituted), the North of Ireland (NoI) or simply the NORTH. As a Belfast citizen commented in 1970:

> Anyone who isn't confused here doesn't really understand what's going on.

For local government purposes the 6 counties are now divided into 26 districts. The capital of Northern Ireland is BELFAST.

The partition of Ireland came about because the Protestant majority in Northern Ireland, although accepting their own parliament at STORMONT, wished to remain part of the United Kingdom. The fact that most of the Catholics in Northern Ireland wanted to be part of a united Ireland, and the fact that they were discriminated against by the dominant Protestant community in such areas as jobs and housing, led to continual tensions, culminating in the civil rights agitation of the later 1960s and the subsequent Troubles, in which thousands lost their lives. As the Northern Ireland Tourist Board so diplomatically put it in 1969:

> For generations, a wide range of shooting in Northern

Ireland has provided all sections of the population with a pastime which ... has occupied a great deal of leisure time. Unlike many other countries, the outstanding characteristic of the sport has been that it was not confined to any one class.

For many years British politicians failed to grapple with the politics of the place, seeking instead a military or alcoholic solution. One such was Edward Heath's home secretary:

> For God's sake, someone bring me a large Scotch. What a bloody awful country.
>
> Reginald Maudling: reported comment on a flight back to London, 1 July 1970, after a visit to Northern Ireland in the early years of the Troubles

But, as an unnamed Irishwoman once said,

> They say the situation in Northern Ireland is not as bad as they say it is.

Northern Isles, the. A collective name for ORKNEY, SHETLAND and FAIR ISLE.

Northern Riviera, the. An unlikely touristic designation for DONCASTER.

North Esk. *See* ESK[1] *and* ESK[3].

Northey Island *Northey* 'north island', OE *north* + *eg* (*see* -EY, -EA), with tautological ModE *Island*; its original name was *Sigeric's Island*.
An island at the western end of the BLACKWATER[1] Estuary in Essex, about 3 km (2 miles) east of Maldon and 3 km (2 miles) west of Osea Island. It has an area of 133 ha (330 acres). It is the cynosure of yachts and dinghies in the summer, a trend going back at least a millennium to the Viking fleet that defeated the Anglo-Saxon nobleman Byrhtnoth at the Battle of Maldon in August 991 landed and encamped there (*see under* MALDON). It is now owned by the National Trust.

Northfield 'open land to the north', OE *north* + *feld* (*see* FIELD).
A southern suburb of BIRMINGHAM, to the north of King's Norton. Survivals from an earlier era, such as the Great Stone Inn and the village pond, enable it to preserve something of its pre-suburban character.

Northfleet 'northern (place by the) stream' (referring to a creek of the Thames), OE *north* + *fleot* 'stream'.
A town in Kent, on the south bank of the River Thames, contiguous with Gravesend to the east and opposite Tilbury. The Thameside cement industry developed here, using chalk and clay dug from local riverside pits.

North Foreland. A chalk promontory at the northeastern tip of the ISLE OF THANET in Kent, just to the north of Broadstairs. It is in effect the eastern extremity of the south bank of the THAMES[1] Estuary, and the point to be rounded by shipping approaching the Thames and London from the Straits of DOVER. It is guarded by a lighthouse.

Battle of the North Foreland (25 July 1666). A sea battle (also known as the **Battle of St James's Day**) in the Thames Estuary between the English and Dutch fleets, the former having the better of it. News of the victory did not reach Samuel Pepys (at that time an official in the Navy Office) until the 29th. At first he was elated, but by evening a more sober view prevailed:

> The *Resolution* burned; but, as they say, most of her men and commander saved. This is all; only, we keep the sea; which denotes a victory, or at least that we are not beaten. But no great matters to brag on, God knows. So home to supper and to bed.
>
> Samuel Pepys: *Diaries* (29 July 1666)

North Lanarkshire *See* LANARKSHIRE.
A unitary authority created in 1996. It is a largely industrial area bounded on the west by Glasgow, on the north by Stirling, on the east by Falkirk and West Lothian, and on the south by South Lanarkshire. Its towns include CUMBERNAULD, COATBRIDGE, MOTHERWELL and AIRDRIE.

Northleach 'northern estate on the River Leach', OE *north* + *Leach* 'stream flowing through boggy land' (OE *læc(c)*, *lece*).
A village in Gloucestershire, in the Cotswolds, on the River Leach, about 19 km (12 miles) southeast of Cheltenham. In the 15th century it was an extremely prosperous wool town, the most important in the COTSWOLDS, its wool fetching the highest prices in Continental markets. All that remains of its former glory today is the magnificent church of St Peter and St Paul.

> Northleach, lying in 'a wrinkle' of the still dreary hills.
>
> Richard Le Gallienne: *Travels* (1900)

North Lincolnshire *See* LINCOLNSHIRE.
A unitary authority in eastern England created in 1996 from part of the former county of Humberside (and before that part of Lincolnshire). Its administrative headquarters are at SCUNTHORPE, and other towns are BRIGG and EPWORTH. It contains the ISLE OF AXHOLME.

North London. The northern part of GREATER LONDON. It has no official geographical status, but a reasonably accurate picture of its extent can be gauged from the postal districts prefixed 'N' and the more easterly of those prefixed 'NW': so, BELSIZE PARK, CAMDEN TOWN, CHALK FARM, CROUCH END, FINCHLEY, FINSBURY Park, FRIERN BARNET, GOSPEL OAK, HAMPSTEAD, HARRINGAY, HIGHBURY, HIGHGATE, HOLLOWAY, HORNSEY, ISLINGTON, KENTISH TOWN, MILL HILL, MUSWELL HILL[1], Palmers Green, SOUTHGATE, STOKE NEWINGTON, TOTTENHAM, TUFNELL PARK, WOOD GREEN.

But, beyond geography, there is a more numinous North London, whose heart is in Hampstead and that radiates out through Highgate and Camden Town and into Muswell Hill, Crouch End and Upper Holloway: its essence derives in part from its select status as suburbia for the wealthy bourgeoisie in the 18th and 19th centuries, partly from its view of itself as the home of the liberal, the cultured and the *bien-pensant*. The 'culture' part of it, certainly in the guise of fashionable youth culture, has now brought Islington within the charmed boundary too (the comic strip 'It's Grim Up North London' in the satirical magazine *Private Eye* leaves us in no doubt that it is set in Islington).

The **University of North London** existed briefly between 1992 and 2002, based in the Holloway Road. It was formed from the **North London Polytechnic**, which itself resulted from a merger of the Northern Polytechnic Institute and the Northwestern Polytechnic in the 1970s. It merged with Guildhall University to form London Metropolitan University in August 2002. The **North London Collegiate School** was founded as a model school for girls in Camden Town in 1850. It is now in Edgware.

North London line. An above-ground railway line, which runs from Richmond in the west in a broad arc through North London to North Woolwich in the east.

North Minch, the. *See under* the MINCHES.

North of Ireland. A term used by Nationalists in preference to NORTHERN IRELAND, as use of the latter implies an acceptance of Partition.

Northolt Earlier *Northall* 'northern nook of land' ('northern' to distinguish it from SOUTHALL 'southern nook of land'), OE *north* + *halh* (*see* HALE, -HALL); the *-t*, first recorded in the 17th century, comes from an association of the name with *holt* 'wood, thicket'.

A district of West London, in the borough of EALING (before 1965 in Middlesex), between Wembley to the east and Uxbridge to the west. Until the end of the 19th century it was largely agricultural land; suburban development, astride the A40 (Western Avenue), did not begin on any scale until after the First World War.

A little to the west (actually in the borough of Hillingdon) is **Northolt Aerodrome**, opened in 1915. During the Second World War it was an RAF Fighter Command station, and afterwards it served for a while as London's airport while HEATHROW was being built nearby. It is still used for royalty and other VIPs who require a speedy and discreet entry to or exit from London. The body of Diana, Princess of Wales, was brought back to Britain via Northolt after her death in Paris in 1997.

> But wilt thou not from London town
> Journey some day to Northolt down,
> Song to obtain, O sweet reward,
> And walk the garden of the Bard?
>
> > Goronwy Owen: 'The Invitation' (1745), translated from the Welsh by George Borrow. (The poem was sent in 1745 to William Parry, Deputy Comptroller of the Mint; Owen – rated as one of the better Welsh poets of the 18th century – was at that time a curate in Northolt.)

North Oxford. *See under* OXFORD

North Piddle *Piddle* from the local *Piddle* Brook, from OE *pidele* 'marsh, fen' (*compare* PIDDLE).

A village in Worcestershire (before 1998 in Hereford and Worcester, before 1974 in Worcestershire), about 11 km (7 miles) east of Worcester.

See also WYRE PIDDLE.

North Queensferry *See* SOUTH QUEENSFERRY.

A small town in Fife, between the two FORTH Bridges on the north side of the Firth of Forth, 8 km (5 miles) southeast of Dunfermline.

North Riding *See* the RIDINGS OF YORKSHIRE.

A former division of the county of YORKSHIRE. It was bordered on the north by County Durham, on the east by the North Sea, on the south by the East Riding, and on the west by the West Riding and Westmorland. The county town was NORTHALLERTON. In 1974 it was absorbed into the new, larger county of NORTH YORKSHIRE.

North Riding Forest Park. A forest park in the southeastern part of the North York Moors.

North Rona *Rona* possibly 'rough island', OScand *hraun* 'rough' + *ey* 'island' (*see* -AY), or alternatively named after St *Ronan*.

A small, remote island, 70 km (43 miles) north of Lewis. It might be considered the most northwesterly part of the UK (the rock of SULA SGEIR, 18 km / 11 miles to the west-southwest might vie for the title, but unlike North Rona it has never been permanently settled). North Rona was inhabited from at least the 8th century, when St Ronan is supposed to have built his chapel here. Which St Ronan out of the several early medieval ones this was is unknown, but he may have been the abbot of Kingarth in BUTE who proselytized in the Hebrides and who died in 737. Whatever his identity, his chapel is one of the oldest structures of the Celtic Church in Britain.

In the 16th century Dean Monro reported that the inhabitants were 'simple people, scant of ony religione'. In the following century the inhabitants were wiped out by an invasion of rats. The island was later resettled, but by the 19th century only a shepherd and his family remained, and the last person left the island in 1844 – apart from two Lewismen who went to the island in 1884 following a dispute with their minister (they died within the year). Today, shepherds from Lewis pay an annual visit to sheer the sheep they keep on the island. It is a National Nature Reserve.

Rona Cross, the. A semi-pagan cross dating from the 7th or 8th centuries, which once stood in the graveyard of North Rona, reputedly marking the grave of St Ronan. The figure of a naked man is cut into the granite, with a hole under each armpit and another in the neck. The cross is now displayed in northern Lewis.

Rona Stone, the. A smooth, rounded piece of green serpentine marble found near the altar of St Ronan's Chapel on North Rona in 1939. It is said that the monks of Iona took such special stones with them when they left the island to evangelize.

North Ronaldsay *Ronaldsay* etymology is uncertain, possibly 'Ringan's island' (where Ringan is a byname of St Ninian) + OScand *ey* (see -AY). SOUTH RONALDSAY has a different etymology.

The most northerly island in ORKNEY, 51 km (32 miles) northeast of Kirkwall on Mainland. It is separated from SANDAY to the south by the **North Ronaldsay Firth**, the scene of a medieval sea battle between Earl Einar and Halfdan Highlegs, son of King Harfagr or Finehair of Norway. The island has its own variety of sheep, who live off seaweed, and whose ownership is regulated by the island's Sheep Court. The sheep are kept on the shore, and off the farmers' crops, by the Sheep Dyke that rings the island. After this was badly damaged by storms in 1993, the Royal Navy was called in to help repair it.

North Sea In Anglo-Saxon times the name was used for the Bristol Channel (*see under* BRISTOL), and in the Middle Ages it also denoted the Baltic Sea; the present-day application is first recorded in the late 13th century, and is apparently derived from Dutch (Dutch sailors distinguished this tract of water from the 'south sea', the *Zuider Zee*).

A section of the Atlantic Ocean off the coast of Northwest Europe, between the British Isles and the continent of Europe to the north of the Straits of Dover (*see under* DOVER). France, Belgium, the Netherlands, Germany, Denmark and Norway form its southern and eastern seaboard: in French its name is *Mer du Nord*, in Dutch *Noordzee*, in German *Nordsee*, in Danish *Nordsö*. In Britain it was more commonly known as the **German Ocean** until jingoism intervened in the early years of the 20th century. In his preface to *The Marble Faun* (1859, 1860), Nathaniel Hawthorne recalls revising his text 'on the broad and dreary sands of Redcar, with the grey German Ocean tumbling in upon me, and the northern blast always howling in my ears'.

> ... the violet rim of the German Ocean appeared over the green edge of the Norfolk coast.
>
> Arthur Conan Doyle: 'The Dancing Men' (1905) (a Sherlock Holmes story)

Its area is 523,000 sq km (202,000 sq miles). Its floor, which does not extend beyond the continental shelf, has an average depth of 300 m (984 ft). Its deepest point, off the Norwegian coast, is 660 m (2165 ft).

It is a heavily exploited fishing ground, especially for cod and haddock, and in the latter part of the 20th century accounted for 5 per cent of the world's catch; but concern over plummeting stocks of these fish led, at the beginning of the 21st century, to extremely stringent restrictions, which threatened the survival of North Sea fishing fleets.

Deposits of oil and natural gas were discovered under the North Sea in the late 1960s. The oil field was divided up into sectors that were allocated for exploitation to Britain, West Germany, Norway, Denmark and the Netherlands, and the northern part of the North Sea came to be dotted with oil production platforms. Drilling began in 1975, and by the mid-1980s the UK was producing 125 million tonnes of **North Sea oil** a year, and in the quarter century up to 2000 the British Treasury profited enormously from oil-based tax revenues. The supply of gas as a fuel was also transformed in the UK, as coal gas was rapidly phased out in the 1970s and replaced with natural gas.

At the end of May 1916 the North Sea was the venue for the Battle of Jutland between the British and German fleets, off the Jutland coast of Denmark. Both sides suffered significant losses, and claimed victory, but the battle had the effect of diminishing Germany's (already smaller) naval effectiveness for the remainder of the First World War.

See also CALEDONIAN CANAL, DOGGER BANK, GERMAN OCEAN, SULLOM VOE *and* the WASH.

North Sea Camp. A detention centre beside the Haven in Lincolnshire, at the southwestern corner of the Wash, about 6 km (4 miles) southeast of Boston. Its best-known 21st-century inmate has been the novelist Jeffrey Archer.

North Shields *Shields* ME *schele* 'temporary shelter'; *North* distinguishes it from South Shields across the Tyne.

An industrial town and fishing port in Tyne and Wear (formerly in Northumberland), 12 km (7 miles) east of Newcastle. It is on the north side of the River Tyne, near its mouth, opposite SOUTH SHIELDS, and is the administrative headquarters of NORTH TYNESIDE unitary authority. There are ferries to several destinations in Norway and Sweden, and to Amsterdam. There is a Fish Quay Festival every May.

North Somerset. A unitary authority created in 1996 from the southwestern part of the county of AVON[7]. It lies between the City of Bristol to the north and SOMERSET to the south, and contains the western end of the MENDIP HILLS. It has a coast at the mouth of the River Severn, from the mouth of the River AVON[2] down to WESTON SUPER MARE (its administrative centre). Other towns include CLEVEDON and PORTISHEAD.

North Tyneside. A metropolitan borough in Tyne and Wear, east of Newcastle upon Tyne. Its administrative headquarters are at NORTH SHIELDS.

North Uist. *See under* the UISTS.

Northumberland 'land of the Northhymbre', *Northhymbre* OE tribal name for those living north of the Humber + *land*.

A county in northeastern England, forming part of what was the Anglo-Saxon kingdom of NORTHUMBRIA. It is bordered on the east by the North Sea, on the north by Scotland, on the west by Cumbria and on the south by County Durham. Its administrative centre is MORPETH, but until the creation of Tyne and Wear in 1974 the county town was NEWCASTLE UPON TYNE. Other towns include HEXHAM, BLYTH[2], ASHINGTON, ALNWICK and BERWICK-UPON-TWEED. In the east are low rolling hills, while further to the west, culminating in the CHEVIOT, are the higher moorlands and fells of the northern PENNINES, including the great reservoir of Kielder Water (source of the North Tyne). Much of this Pennine area is included in the **Northumberland National Park**, considerable areas of which have been taken over, with somewhat depressing irony, by army firing ranges. Off the coast are the FARNE ISLANDS and LINDISFARNE (Holy Island), while across the county runs the line of HADRIAN'S WALL. The county was formerly nicknamed CROAKUMSHIRE, and Northumbrians are sometimes referred to as Geordies, although more often this term is restricted to Tynesiders (*see under* TYNESIDE). Those who worked in the coal mines of Northumberland (and Durham) were referred to as **Pit Yackers**. In Romany, according to George Borrow, Northumberland is known as **Boro-gueroneskey tem** ('big fellows' country').

In cricketing terms Northumberland is a 'minor county' (the club was founded in 1895) and plays in the minor counties championship.

Duke of Northumberland. A title held by the Percy family (*see* ALNWICK) since 1750, prior to which they were earls of Northumberland (from 1377). The most notable earlier Duke of Northumberland was John Dudley (*c.*1502–53), who ruled England during the minority of Edward VI and attempted to place his Protestant daughter-in-law Lady Jane Grey on the throne at Edward's death. However, both Lady Jane and the Duke lost their heads as the Catholic Mary I took the Crown and her revenge.

Northumberland arms. A 17th- and 18th-century term for a black eye, referring to the arms of the Percy family (earls then dukes of Northumberland), in which there is a red and black badge resembling spectacles.

Northumbria From the *Northhymbre*, the Anglo-Saxons living north of the Humber.

An Anglo-Saxon kingdom in northeast England and southeast Scotland, extending from the HUMBER to the FORTH – and thus much larger than the present county of NORTHUMBERLAND. At its peak it also extended west to the Irish Sea. It was formed in the 7th century by the unification of the kingdoms of BERNICIA (stretching from the Forth to the Tees) and DEIRA (from the Tees to the Humber). Under a series of influential rulers – including

Edwin (d.633), Oswald (reigned 633–41) and Oswy (reigned 642–70) – Northumbria was a dominant force in English political life. Northumbria was also an important early centre for Celtic Christianity, brought here from Iona. It accepted the nominal supremacy of Wessex in 827, but went on to suffer badly from Viking attacks. It was occupied by the Danes at the end of the 9th century, and was not brought under the control of the English Crown until 1069–70, when William the Conqueror unleashed the Harrying of the North (*see under* the NORTH[1]).

The Northumbrian dialect of Old English formed the basis of the modern English dialects of northern England and Scotland.

Northumbrian pipes. A small type of bagpipe in which the bag is filled by a bellows held under the arm. It produces a more mellow sound than its cousin over the border in Scotland.

North Walsham *Walsham* 'Walh's homestead or village', OE *Walhes* possessive form of male personal name *Walh* + HAM.

A market town in Norfolk, about 24 km (15 miles) north of Norwich and 8 km (5 miles) from the coast. Its cousin, the village of **South Walsham**, is about 19 km (12 miles) to the southeast. The centrepiece of North Walsham's sloping market place is a 16th-century three-tiered market cross. Its church, St Nicholas, is one of the largest in Norfolk, but its tower is no longer what it was: its top half crashed down on a stormy night in 1724.

Horatio Nelson attended the local Paston School from 1768 to 1771.

North Warnborough *Warnborough* perhaps 'stream where criminals were drowned', OE *wearg* 'criminal' + *burna* 'stream'; alternatively *wearg* might here have an earlier meaning 'wolf', hence 'stream frequented by wolves'.

A village in Hampshire, just to the south of Junction 5 on the M3, about 10 km (6 miles) east of Basingstoke. **South Warnborough** is about 5 km (3 miles) further south.

North Weald Bassett *Weald see* WEALD; *Bassett* denoting manorial ownership in the Middle Ages by the Basset [*sic*] family.

A village in Essex, about 8 km (5 miles) southeast of Harlow. Its companion, **South Weald**, is about 13 km (8 miles) away to the southeast.

A little to the west, by the M11, is **North Weald** airfield, formerly an RAF station. During the Second World War it was a Battle of Britain airfield, and subsequently much of the film *Battle of Britain* (1969) was shot there. Later it was the home of the 'Black Arrows', 111 Squadron's aerobatics team, which flew Hawker Hunters.

North Weald 'Underground' station, on the Central line, opened in 1949. It was closed in 1994.

North Wessex Downs. *See under* WESSEX.

Northwest, the. A common designation for that part of the NORTH[1] of England encompassing the counties of LANCASHIRE, GREATER MANCHESTER and CUMBRIA, with perhaps a smattering of CHESHIRE. The PENNINES separate it from the NORTHEAST. Its southerly portion, in the triangle defined by MANCHESTER, LIVERPOOL and PRESTON, is as urban and industrial as its north, embracing the Cumbrian Mountains and the LAKE DISTRICT, is rural and ruggedly scenic.

Northwich 'northern saltworks', OE *north* + *wic* (*see* WICK, *see also* WICHES).

A town in Cheshire, on the rivers WEAVER and Dane, about 20 km (12 miles) northwest of Crewe. The Roman settlement was called **Condate**, a Celtic name meaning '(place at the) confluence (of the rivers Weaver and Dane)'. As its modern name suggests, salt is its *raison d'être* – its motto is *Sal est Vita* ('salt is life'), and it even has its own Salt Museum. The local underground deposits of rock salt have been exploited since Roman times, originally by panning (a technique still in use at the Lion Salt Works, the only surviving open-pan salt works in Britain), and now by pumping to nearby chemical works. So much salt has been extracted that it causes problems of subsidence. Processed salt was transported along the Trent and Mersey Canal, and to link this with the River Weaver the spectacular Anderton Boat Lift was constructed in 1875. It can raise craft of up to 100 tonnes to a height of 15 m (50 ft).

The name of the local football team, **Northwich Victoria** (founded 1874, and known to its fans as the Vics), honours that monarch.

The runner Paula Radcliffe (b. 1973) was born in Northwich.

Northwood 'northern wood' (referring to an area of woodland to the north of Ruislip).

A district of West London (before 1965 in Middlesex), in the borough of HILLINGDON, to the west of Pinner. It was agricultural land until the 1880s, when the coming of the Metroplitan Railway (Northwood station opened in 1887) secured it a niche in METROLAND (Northwood Hills station, the next stop on the line just to the southeast, opened in 1933).

The Royal Navy's command and control centre, from which Britain's nuclear submarines are directed, is sited at Northwood. Much of the direction of British forces in the Falklands conflict (1982) emanated from here.

Merchant Taylors' School, a boys' public school founded in 1561, is in Northwood.

The film-maker Derek Jarman (1942–94) was born in Northwood.

North York Moors. A scenic upland area of NORTH YORKSHIRE, east of the Vale of York (*see under* YORK) and north of the Vale of Pickering (*see under* PICKERING). Its western and northwestern escarpments are known as the HAMBLETON HILLS and the Cleveland Hills (*see under* CLEVELAND). On its eastern side the moors end in a line of sea cliffs between WHITBY and SCARBOROUGH. The area is incorporated in the **North York Moors National Park**. The old name for the moors was **Blackamore**, from the colour of the heather when not in bloom. The **North Yorkshire Moors Railway** is a steam line for tourists, running from Pickering in the south to Grosmont in the north, via Goathland. It opened in 1973, the British Railways service on the route having been ended by Lord Beeching in 1965.

See also GOATHLAND.

North Yorkshire *See* YORKSHIRE.

A county – England's largest – formed in 1974 from most of the North Riding and part of the West Riding of YORKSHIRE. In 1996 the city of YORK became a separate unitary authority. North Yorkshire is bounded on the north by Cumbria, County Durham and Redcar and Cleveland, on the south by the East Riding of Yorkshire, South Yorkshire and West Yorkshire, and on the west by Lancashire. Its administrative centre is at NORTHALLERTON, and it also includes WHITBY, SCARBOROUGH, the NORTH YORK MOORS, MALTON, PICKERING, RICHMOND[1], KNARESBOROUGH, HARROGATE, SKIPTON, SETTLE and the YORKSHIRE DALES.

Norton 'north village', OE *north* + -TON.

A small town in North Yorkshire, on the River Derwent opposite Malton. It is famous for its racing stables.

Norton Disney *Disney* denoting manorial ownership in the early Middle Ages by the de Isney family (the family gave its name to a field in Usselby, known in 1386 as *Disneyland*, some years before those in Florida and Paris; Walt, creator of Mickey Mouse and Donald Duck, was a descendant of a junior branch).

A village in Lincolnshire, on the River Witham, about 16 km (10 miles) southwest of Lincoln.

Norton Fitzwarren *Fitzwarren* denoting manorial ownership in the Middle Ages by the Fitzwarren family.

A village in Somerset, in the Vale of Taunton, on the Halse Water, now virtually a northwestern suburb of TAUNTON.

Norton-Juxta-Twycross *Juxta* Latin 'next to'; *Twycross see* TWYCROSS.

A village in Leicestershire, about 2.5 km (1.5 miles) northwest of Twycross.

Norton Malreward *Malreward* denoting manorial ownership in the Middle Ages by the Malreward family.

A village in Bath and North East Somerset (before 1996 in Avon, before 1974 in Somerset), about 8 km (5 miles) south of Bristol.

Norton Mandeville *Mandeville* denoting manorial ownership in the Middle Ages by the Maundevill family.

A village in Essex, about 13 km (8 miles) southeast of Harlow.

Norton Subcourse *Subcourse* denoting manorial ownership in the Middle Ages by the Subcourse family.

A village in Norfolk, about 21 km (13 miles) southeast of Norwich.

Norton sub Hamdon *sub* 'below', Latin; *Hamdon see* HAMDON HILL (referring to a local hill).

A village in Somerset, about 8 km (5 miles) west of Yeovil. *See also* STOKE SUB HAMDON.

Norwich 'northern harbour or trading centre', OE *north + wic* (*see* WICK).

A cathedral city (pronounced 'norridge' or 'norritch') in Norfolk, on the River Wensum, about 160 km (100 miles) northeast of London. It is the administrative centre of NORFOLK. It has more than 1100 years of history behind it (its irregular street plan is a Saxon legacy), and in the Middle Ages it was one of the most prosperous and important provincial cities in England (rivalled only by Bristol and York). Its Provision Market, dating from the 11th century, is the largest open-air market in England. Norwich owed its wealth to its status as an entrepôt for the highly profitable East Anglian wool trade, and also to local textile production (*see also* WORSTEAD), manned to a large extent by Flemish weavers who were initially brought to the city by Edward III in 1336 and continued coming until the late 16th century. By 1700 Norwich was the second richest English city after London, but thereafter, as the Industrial Revolution took hold in the North, its economic status was steadily eroded. No longer rich and not on the way to anywhere, it came to have a backwaterish, provincial quality – ruthlessly exploited by Steve Coogan in his television persona as Alan Partridge, small-hours DJ for Radio Norwich in the dry BBC sitcom *I'm Alan Partridge* (1997 and 2002).

Building work began on **Norwich Cathedral** (more properly, the Cathedral of the Holy and Undivided Trinity) in 1096. Its 96-m (315-ft) 15th-century octagonal spire is the second highest in England after Salisbury's. It contains the tomb of Nurse Edith Cavell, who was executed by the Germans in 1915. The Bishop of Norwich signs himself 'Norvic'. In all, the city centre has 32 medieval churches, more than in any other British town.

Norwich also has a well-preserved 12th-century Norman castle, now a museum and art gallery. Its foursquare outline was once familiar from the labels of the local Colman's mustard (*see below*).

The University of East Anglia (*see under* EAST ANGLIA), founded in 1964, is based in Norwich, and the town's

independent school, **Norwich School**, has a history dating back to the 15th century.

> Swan-eating was popular for a long time in the Norwich area and local hotels were formerly supplied with meat by the Norwich Swan Pit. Historically, the City Corporation, the Great Hospital, the bishop and the dean all had their own marks and associated rights to the birds on the River Wensum and nearby Broads.
>
> Stefan Buczacki: *Fauna Britannica* (2002)

Another bird associated with the city is the canary: Norwich was once famous as a centre for the breeding and exhibition of canaries and other cage birds (originally brought by the immigrant Flemish weavers), and there is a variety of canary called the '**Norwich**'. **Norwich City FC** (founded 1902; the television cook Delia Smith is a director) has the Canaries as its nickname and an appropriate yellow and green strip.

> Delia Smith's a brilliant cook
> She feeds our whole team porridge
> She makes a cracking steak au poivre
> But that don't rhyme with Norwich!
>
> Fans' chant for Norwich FC

Yellow is also a nod to the city's main post-medieval commercial success story: Colman's mustard, produced by the firm founded by Jeremiah Colman in 1823. Its 'Old Mustard Shop' is now a tourist attraction, where the once familiar yellow oval tubs of yellow mustard powder can be viewed.

Norwich's Maddermarket Theatre, built in 1921 on the site of a medieval market where madder, a plant that produces a red dye, was sold, is a replica of an Elizabethan playhouse.

Norwich was the birthplace of Julian of Norwich (*see below*); the composer Thomas Morley (1557–1602); the painters John Sell Cotman (1782–1842) and John Crome (1768–1821), leading lights of the **Norwich school** (*see below*); the philanthropist and prison reformer Elizabeth Fry (1780–1845); the pamphleteer and playwright Robert Greene (1558–92); the botanist William Hooker (1785–1865) and the writer Harriet Martineau (1802–76).

> There was an old woman of Norwich,
> Who lived upon nothing but porridge;
>   Parading the town,
>   She turned cloak into gown,
> The thrifty old woman of Norwich.
>
> *The History of Sixteen Wonderful Old Women* (1820)

> Am surprised to realise that anybody ever goes to, lives at, or comes from, Norwich, but quite see that this is unreasonable of me.
>
> E.M. Delafield: *Diary of a Provincial Lady* (1930)

There are towns and cities called Norwich in the USA (Connecticut – birthplace of the traitor Benedict Arnold

(1741–1801) and of the writer E. Annie Proulx (b.1935) – Kansas and New York) and in Canada (Ontario). Norwich University in Vermont (founded 1819) is the oldest private military college in the USA.

Julian of Norwich. A Christian recluse and visionary (1342–after 1416) whose *Sixteen Revelations of Divine Love* is one of the best known works of English medieval devotional literature (its latterday celebrity owes more than a little to T.S. Eliot's quotation from it in 'Little Gidding' (1942): 'Sin is behovely; but all shall be well and all shall be well and all manner of thing shall be well'). Her thatched monastic cell can be seen by St Julian's Church in Norwich.

NORWICH. An acronym based (phonetically) on the initial letters of 'knickers off ready when I come home', one of the more lubricious of such initialisms, for which there was a craze in the mid-20th century. They usually appeared on the envelopes of love letters (a less steamy example was SWALK 'sealed with a loving kiss'), and the fashion for them probably got going among servicemen overseas in the Second World War.

Norwich Crusade. A military venture of 1383 undertaken for a murky mix of motives – clerical, business and political – in which Henry Despenser, Bishop of Norwich, invaded Flanders with the support of Pope Urban VI as part of the latter's campaign against the rival Avignon Pope Clement VII. Despenser took some coastal towns, but backed off when the Duke of Burgundy's forces hove into view. Thus he was unable to loosen the Burgundian hold on the Flemish wool market – another aim of the 'crusade'.

norwicher. A mid-19th-century slang term for 'more than one's fair share', applied especially to someone who drank more than half a shared tankard before passing it on. Eric Partridge suggested it might have been based on a stereotype of Norwich behaviour, as in the rhyme 'Essex stiles, Kentish miles, Norwich wiles, many men beguiles'.

Norwich school. An English school of landscape painting active in and around Norwich in the first half of the 19th century. It had its beginnings in the **Norwich Society**, founded in 1803 by John Crome, one of the leading exponents of the school. Its other major figure was John Sell Cotman.

Norwich terrier. A breed of small, thickset, red or black-and-tan, rough-coated terrier with pricked ears, developed in East Anglia. In North America the name is also applied to the lop-eared variety, now known in Britain as the Norfolk terrier (*see under* NORFOLK).

Norwich ware. A type of earthenware, similar to delft, associated with Norwich. Its earliest exponents seem to have been two Flemish potters who emigrated to Norwich from Antwerp in 1576, and it reportedly continued in production until the end of the 17th century, but very little of it is now known to exist.

St William of Norwich. A 12-year-old skinner's apprentice of Norwich (1132–44). According to Thomas of Monmouth, a monk of Norwich, he was abducted by a strange man who promised he would become kitchen-boy to the archdeacon. Instead he was allegedly gagged, shaved, lacerated with a crown of thorns and crucified by Jews during the Passover. It was said at the time that it was part of Jewish ritual to sacrifice a Christian child every year; *compare* Little St Hugh of Lincoln (*see under* LINCOLN).

Norwood 'north wood' (referring to a tract of woodland of that name, to the north of Croydon, part of which remained intact in the early 19th century), OE *north* + *wudu* 'wood'.

A district of SOUTH LONDON, to the north of Croydon. South Norwood and Upper Norwood are in the borough of CROYDON (SE19, SE25), and West Norwood is in the borough of LAMBETH (SE27).

There are towns called Norwood in the USA (Massachusetts, New York, North Carolina) and Canada (Ontario).

'Adventure of the Norwood Builder, The'. A story by Arthur Conan Doyle, included in *The Return of Sherlock Holmes* (1905) (originally published in *The Strand Magazine*, 1903–4). It concerns Mr Jonas Oldacre, a rich builder of Lower Norwood (as West Norwood was called until the end of the 19th century), who fakes his own murder in order to evade his creditors.

Noss Mayo *Noss* 'headland' (referring to land between two streams), OE *nœss* (*see* NESS); *Mayo* denoting manorial ownership in the Middle Ages by a man called Matheu (*Mayo* is a form of the OFr version of English *Matthew*).

A village in Cornwall, on the western side of the estuary of the River Yealm, about 8 km (5 miles) southeast of Plymouth.

Noth. *See under* TAP O' NOTH.

Nottingham¹ Originally *Snottingham* 'Snot's people's homestead', OE male personal name *Snot* + *-inga-* (*see* -ING) + HAM. The *S-* was lost in the 12th century because of Norman influence.

A city and unitary authority (officially named **Nottingham City**) in Nottinghamshire, about 53 km (33 miles) southeast of Sheffield. Set on a sandstone hill commanding a crossing-point of the River TRENT¹, it was established by the Anglo-Saxons in the 6th century. It was one of the FIVE BOROUGHS of the Danelaw. In 1068 William the Conqueror built a castle on a crag on the other side of the river. During Richard I's absence from England on the Crusades his brother John commanded **Nottingham Castle**, and it was from here that his villainous lackey, the legendary **Sheriff of Nottingham**, is said to have sallied forth in his fruitless pursuit of Robin Hood (there is a statue of the outlaw-hero by the castle gateway; *see also* SHERWOOD FOREST).

In 1642 Charles I raised his standard over the castle, signalling the start of the Civil Wars (the hill on which it stands is now called Standard Hill). Its reward was to be partially demolished by Oliver Cromwell in 1651. It was heavily restored in the 19th century, and in 1878 it opened as the UK's first provincial art gallery and museum. A picture of the castle long featured on packets of cigarettes produced by John Player Ltd, one of the triumvirate of Nottingham's most high-profile employers in the past hundred years – the other two being Boots the Chemist (which originated in a chemist's shop in Goose Gate taken over by Jesse Boot in 1877) and the bicycle manufacturer Raleigh.

In the Middle Ages Nottingham was a prosperous market town. The famous **Nottingham Goose Fair**, which is still held every October (now with added funfair), dates from around the end of the 13th century. Also of medieval origin is 'The Trip to Jerusalem', built into the side of a cliff, which claims to be the oldest inn in England. In the 14th and 15th centuries alabaster carving was a notable local industry.

Then, in the second half of the 18th century, the Industrial Revolution hit Nottingham. The budding hosiery and lace industries increased the population fivefold, and the city became infamous for desperate overcrowding (the slum alleys were not cleared until the 20th century). By the end of the 18th century Nottingham had become something of a centre of radicalism. Disaffected framemakers, who in 1811, under the leadership of the possibly mythical Ned Ludd, destroyed labour-saving machinery, gave the English language the term 'Luddite'. (Newstead Abbey, family home of the Byrons, is close by, and in February 1812 the poet Byron made his maiden speech in the House of Lords in defence of Nottingham weavers who had rioted and who were being subjected to harsh Tory repression.) It was the collapse in demand for lace after the First World War that finally saw off the industry, but **Nottingham lace** (also known as **Nottingham net**) remains world-renowned, and its name has become generic for a type of machine-made flat lace, guardian of a million windows:

> Some of us still think of machine-made lace as 'Nottingham' and equate it with soot-soiled curtains in back streets.
>
> *The Guardian* (3 July 1967)

Nottingham is also famous for its young women, said to be the handsomest in England, and (rather less so) for **Nottingham stoneware** (or **Nottingham earthenware**), a type of stoneware produced here up to the end of the 18th century.

The headquarters of Nottinghamshire County Cricket Club are at the test-match ground Trent Bridge (*see under* TRENT[1]). Of the city's two Football League clubs, the more

successful, **Nottingham Forest**, is probably still best remembered for its outspoken manager Brian Clough, who held sway from 1975 to 1993 (during which time – implausibly perhaps for posterity to grasp – Forest twice won the European Cup). Founded in 1865, the club was originally called Forest FC. (*see also* NOTTS.).

The **University of Nottingham** was founded in 1948. It was based on the former university college, which had been founded in 1881 and in 1928 moved to a new site on land donated by the ubiquitous Jesse Boot (D.H Lawrence was a student here 1903–06; he had previously attended Nottingham High School 1898–1901). **Nottingham Trent University** was founded in 1992; it was based on **Nottingham Polytechnic** (1970), which before that had been Trent Polytechnic.

William Booth (1829–1912), founder of the Salvation Army; the writer Alan Sillitoe (b.1928), whose *Saturday Night and Sunday Morning* (1958) powerfully evokes post-Second World War working-class Nottingham; the satirist John Bird (b.1936); the mass-murderer Dr Harold Shipman (1946–2004; *see* HYDE); and the ice-skaters Jayne Torvill (b.1957) and Christopher Dean (b.1958) were all born in Nottingham.

> Nottingham, that dismal town.
>
> D.H. Lawrence: 'Nottingham's New University'

Nottingham flycatcher. A white-flowered perennial herb (*Silene nutans*), which has sticky upper parts and soft hair on its leaves and stems.

Nottingham reel. A fishing-rod reel made of wood rather than the more usual substance (brass, at the time when the term was in vogue).

Nottingham system. A contract-bridge system that originated in Nottingham (called more fully the **Nottingham one-club system**).

Nottingham white. A name used in the 19th and early 20th centuries for white lead paint, used as an artists' colour.

Nottingham[2] Presumably so named because of a connection with the English town.

A small settlement in northeastern Highland (formerly in Caithness), 21 km (13 miles) southeast of Wick.

Nottinghamshire From NOTTINGHAM[1] + SHIRE. The name *Nottinghamshire* is first recorded in the 11th century.

A county in the northeastern Midlands of England, to the east of the Pennines. It is bounded to the north by North Lincolnshire and South Yorkshire, to the west by Derbyshire, to the south by Leicestershire and to the east by Lincolnshire. It includes the unitary authority of NOTTINGHAM[1] City, and other major centres are ARNOLD, HUCKNALL, KIRKBY-IN-ASHFIELD, MANSFIELD, NEWARK, RETFORD, SUTTON-IN-ASHFIELD, WEST BRIDGFORD (seat of the county's administrative headquarters) and WORKSOP. Its main rivers are the TRENT[1], which forms part of its northeastern boundary with Lincolnshire; the EREWASH[1], which divides it from Derbyshire; and the SOAR, which divides it from Leicestershire.

According to the Tudor historian William Camden, Nottinghamshire was part of the territory of the British tribe known as the Coritani (*see also under* LEICESTERSHIRE). The area was heavily settled by Danes in the second half of the 9th century (*see* FIVE BOROUGHS). Like neighbouring Leicestershire, it was divided into 'wapentakes' (rather than the Anglo-Saxons' Hundreds), and acquired many Scandinavian-based place names (e.g. *Granby, Thrumpton*).

Large parts of the county are given over to agriculture, but its relatively infertile central section is covered by the remnants of SHERWOOD FOREST (*see also* the DUKERIES). The Nottinghamshire coalfield, in the northern part of the county, was once a major contributor to Britain's fuel resources, and a leading source of employment in the county: D.H. Lawrence, born in Eastwood, to the west of Nottingham, the son of a miner, portrayed the life of Nottinghamshire mining families in his *Sons and Lovers* (1913) (*see* BESTWOOD); and it was once said that Nottinghamshire County Cricket Club had only to whistle down a coal-mine for a world-class fast bowler to emerge – Harold Larwood, famed for his intimidating bowling on the infamous 'bodyline tour' of Australia (1932–3) being the proof cited.

During the 1984–5 miners' strike most of the miners of Nottinghamshire (where proposed pit closures were fewer in number than in Yorkshire) refused to join the national strike called by Arthur Scargill, fiery Marxist leader of the National Union of Mineworkers (NUM). As a result the Nottinghamshire pits became a particular target for pickets from neighbouring South Yorkshire. The Nottinghamshire branch of the NUM eventually broke away to form the core of the Union of Democratic Mineworkers, an organization viewed as a strike-breaking association by many miners outside the county.

In cricketing terms Nottinghamshire is a 'first-class' county. Nottinghamshire County Cricket Club, founded in 1841, was a founder member of the county championship when that competition was officially constituted in 1890, and has won it on four occasions. In addition to Larwood (*see above*) its famous players include Alfred Shaw, Arthur Shrewsbury, Larwood's fast-bowling partner-in-crime Bill Voce, and the great West Indian all-rounder Sir Garfield Sobers. Its home ground is at Trent Bridge (*see under* TRENT[1]).

Nottinghamshire boasts one of the most notorious and vilified local-government officials in English history: the legendary Sheriff of Nottingham of Richard I's time, ever in vain pursuit of Robin Hood (*see* SHERWOOD FOREST).

> The idea I gave Lord Rickingham of this county [Nottinghamshire] was four dukes, two lords, and three rabbit warrens, which, I believe, takes in half the county in point of space.
>
> Sir George Savile (1769)

Notting Hill Originally (in the mid-14th century) *Knottinghill*, 'hill at Knotting'; *Knotting* probably either an old hill name formed from OE *cnotta* 'knot, lump' or a place name, 'Cnotta's place', OE male personal name *Cnotta* + -ING.

A district of West London (W11), in the borough of KENSINGTON AND CHELSEA, to the north of Kensington and the west of Bayswater. Its main thoroughfares are LADBROKE GROVE and PORTOBELLO ROAD. It was built up in the middle of the 19th century on land hitherto largely rural, and from the beginning contained a mix of luxurious housing for the well-to-do and humbler dwellings. It was the latter that attracted attention as over the decades they mouldered and descended into slums. Rapacious landlords and Commonwealth migrants moved in, and in the late 1950s Notting Hill saw Britain's first serious race riots. By the end of the 20th century, however, most of the crumbling houses had been done up and gentrified, and Notting Hill had become a fashionable place to live. A certain sleepiness, though (outside of Carnival time, *see below*), has earned it the nickname **Nodding Hull**.

The music-hall entertainer Albert Chevalier (1861–1923) was born in Notting Hill.

Napoleon of Notting Hill, The. A futuristic fantasy (1904) by G.K. Chesterton, in which Auberon Quin, an obscure government official, finds himself elected as king and, in a London that is a bizarre Chestertonian mixture of the medieval and the postmodern, goes on to win a famous victory over the armies of South Kensington at the Battle of Notting Hill.

Notting Hill. A film (1999), written by resident Richard Curtis, about a celebrated US film actress who falls for a humble British bookshop manager while on a visit to London. It stars Julia Roberts and Hugh Grant as the hesitant lovers, who first meet in Grant's bookshop in Notting Hill, the area where most of the action takes place (with the consequence that the district eagerly looked forward to a flood of tourists inspecting the locations used in the film).

Notting Hill Carnival. A street festival held annually in Notting Hill on the last (bank holiday) weekend of August as a celebration of the Caribbean way of life. It had its origins in a street party held in 1964 for the children of Trinidadian immigrants who had settled in the area. Two years later the party evolved into a regular event, with steel bands providing the music, and food and drink donated by local traders. In due course the colour and extravagance of costume, the volume and variety of music, and the originality and ingenuity of the floats rivalled the panache of New Orleans, Port of Spain or Rio de Janeiro, and a huge amount of trade was generated. The carnival was dogged by violence and disorder for many years, notably in 1976, when Black youths clashed with police, but in the 1990s and the early 21st century it was mostly peaceful.

Notting Hill set. A description in the summer of 2004 by the Conservative MP Derek Conway of certain younger members of the parliamentary party (*The Guardian* called them 'a coterie of young turks surrounding [the Tory party leader] Michael Howard'), whom Conway accused of mounting a whispering campaign against older Tory MPs and, specifically, of suggesting that the latter were preventing younger Tories from standing for Parliament:

> This is what we call the Notting Hill Tory set. They sit around in these curious little bistros in parts of London, drink themselves silly and wish they were doing what the rest of us are getting on with. They'll just have to be a little more patient.
>
> Derek Conway, MP for Old Bexley and Sidcup (July 2004)

Notting Hill Gate From a turnpike gate at NOTTING HILL (removed in 1864) on the road to Oxford (now the Bayswater Road, A40). The area was earlier called *Kensington Gravel Pits*; the name *Notting Hill Gate* does not seem to have attached itself until the 19th century.

A road (a stretch of the A40) and area in West London (W11) at the southeastern corner of Notting Hill, to the northwest of Kensington Gardens. The name was reinforced by the opening of Notting Hill Gate Underground station in 1868, which serves the Central, Circle and District lines. The area is now a magnet for restaurateurs.

The writer Wyndham Lewis lived in Notting Hill Gate in the 1940s, and titled his 1951 critique of decaying England *Rotting Hill*.

Notts. The standard written abbreviation of NOTTINGHAM-SHIRE. It is also widely used in colloquial spoken English. It features prominently in the names of Nottingham's two football clubs: Notts County (founded 1862) and Notts Forest (an abbreviation of the full name, Nottingham Forest; *see* NOTTINGHAM[1]).

Noviomagus Regnensium. A Roman settlement on the site of present-day CHICHESTER.

Nox From a certain Richard *Nocks*, who kept a tavern here in the 16th century.

A village in Shropshire, about 10 km (6 miles) west of Shrewsbury.

Nuffield Originally *Tocfeld*, probably 'tough open land', OE *toh* 'tough' + *feld* (*see* FIELD); the change to initial *N-* began in the 14th century probably by misdivision of ME *atten tocfeld* to *at nuffeld*, but there is no certainty.

A village in Oxfordshire, in the CHILTERN HILLS, about 7 km (4 miles) southeast of Wallingford. William Morris (1877–1963), the car manufacturer and philanthropist, was born here, and in 1938 took its name as part of his title (Viscount Nuffield). He founded **Nuffield College**, Oxford, the **Nuffield Institute for Medical Research** at Oxford University, the **Nuffield Trust** and the **Nuffield Founda-tion**. The Jodrell Bank Experimental Station (*see* JODRELL-BANK) is now known as the **Nuffield Radio Astronomy Laboratories**.

Number One, Yorkshire. A nickname given to the first house on the old Great North Road passing through BAWTRY.

Nunburnholme Recorded as *Brunha* in Domesday Book (1086), from OScand *brunnr* 'spring, stream' in the dative plural *brunnum*, *burnum* 'at the streams', erroneously interpreted as *burn-holm*, with the later addition of the ME prefix *nunne*, reflecting the presence of a Benedictine convent here in the Middle Ages (there are the remains of fish ponds).

A small settlement in the East Riding of Yorkshire, 8 km (5 miles) northwest of Market Weighton.

Nuneaton Originally *Eaton* (*see* EATON CONSTANTINE; *see also* EA-); the prefix *Nun-*, first recorded in the 13th century, denotes a Benedictine nunnery founded here in the 12th century (now ruined).

A town in Warwickshire, on the River Anker and the Coventry Canal, about 13 km (8 miles) north of Coventry. It makes its living by manufacturing textiles, cardboard boxes, bricks and hats, but it used to be a coal-mining centre.

The novelist George Eliot (1819–80) was born on the Arbury Hall estate, just to the southwest of Nuneaton in CHILVERS COTON. She fictionalized the town as **Milby** in her *Scenes of Clerical Life* (1858).

Nuneham Courtenay *Nuneham* 'new homestead or village', OE *niwan* dative form of *niwe* 'new' + HAM; *Courtenay* denoting manorial ownership in the early Middle Ages by the Curtenai family.

A village in Oxfordshire, about 8 km (5 miles) south of Oxford. In the 18th century the antiquarian and leading courtier Simon, 1st Earl Harcourt, newly returned from the Grand Tour and finding the landscape around his house at STANTON HARCOURT insufficiently picturesque and classical, decided to relocate to Nuneham Courtenay, where he built an entirely new house (a Palladian mansion), church and village (removing existing cottages because they spoiled his view). The newly built Georgian cottages of this 'model village' still line the Oxford–Wallingford road in neat pairs. The enterprise provided Oliver Goldsmith (who strongly disapproved of what he saw as the depredations wrought by the Earl) with the inspiration for his poem *The Deserted Village* (1770; *see also* AUBURN).

The University of Oxford Arboretum (Harcourt Arboretum) is located in Nuneham Courtenay.

Nunney Probably 'Nunna's island or dry ground in a marsh', OE male personal name *Nunna* + *eg* (*see* -EY, -EA); alternatively, the first element may be from OE *nunne* 'nun'.

A village in Somerset, about 5 km (3 miles) southwest of Frome.

Nursling 'nutshell place' (probably denoting a small dwelling or settlement), OE *hnutu* 'nut' + *scell* 'shell' + -ING.

A village in Hampshire, on the northwestern outskirts of Southampton.

Nutwood. The fictional village in which the cartoon character Rupert Bear (1920–) lives. At the Ruper Bear Museum in Canterbury one can 'explore Nutwood places'. Apart from its surreal population of anthropomorphized animals (Algy Pug, Edward Trunk, the plus-foured Podgy Pig *et al.*):

... it is not unusual in twentieth-century Nutwood to find people from the Middle Ages wandering around attracting not the faintest surprise from the present populace ... Nutwood is not only a place where time stands still – the village retains much the same sort of life it had in Mary Tourtel's [Rupert's originator's] day, a schoolhouse, a branch line railway station, a general shop, and Rupert and his friends still wear the boy's clothing of the Twenties.

George Perry: *Rupert – A Bear's Life* (1985)

Nymet Rowland *Nymet* 'holy place' (probably also an old name of the River Yeo), OCelt *nimet*; *Rowland* denoting manorial ownership in the early Middle Ages by a man called Roland.

A village in Devon, on the River YEO[1], about 16 km (10 miles) northwest of Crediton.

Nymet Tracey *Tracey* denoting manorial ownership in the Middle Ages by the de Trascy family.

A village in Devon, about 8 km (5 miles) south of Nymet Rowland.

O

Oa, the Possibly OScand *haugr* 'rounded hill or cairn'.

The southernmost peninsula of ISLAY, culminating in the rocky headland known as the **Mull of Oa** (OScand *múli* 'headland'). It is pronounced 'oh'. The American Memorial on the Mull commemorates the dead of two troop ships that were sunk off Islay in 1918: HMS *Tuscania*, torpedoed off the Mull on 5 February, and HMS *Otranto* which sank off the west coast of Islay on 6 October after colliding with HMS *Kashmir*.

Oake '(place at the) oak-trees', OE *acum* dative plural form of *ac* 'oak-tree'.

A village in Somerset, about 8 km (5 miles) west of Taunton.

Oakham 'Oc(c)a's homestead or enclosure', OE male personal name *Oc(c)a* + HAM.

A market town in Rutland (before 1997 in Leicestershire, before 1974 in Rutland), in the VALE OF CATMOSE, just to the east of RUTLAND Water and about 27 km (17 miles) east of Leicester. It is the county town of Rutland.

By ancient tradition, every royal or noble personage who passes through the town has to present it with a horseshoe – hence the impressive array of such artefacts now on show on the walls of the aisled hall, virtually all that now remains of the 12th-century castle. In the nearby market square the ancient octagonal buttercross shelters the town's medieval stocks.

Oakham School, a co-educational public school founded in 1584, is also situated on the market square.

Titus Oates (1649–1705), instigator of the alleged Popish Plot (1678), was born in Oakham. Robert Cawdrey, who produced what is now generally recognized as the first English dictionary, *A Table Alphabeticall* (1604), was a schoolmaster here in the 1580s.

Oare From the name of a local stream, now called *Oare Water*. It comes from a pre-Celtic river name, which is also the precursor of the River AYR[1] in Scotland.

A hamlet in Somerset, on the northern edge of EXMOOR, about 8 km (5 miles) southeast of Lynton.

In R.D. Blackmore's *Lorna Doone* (1869), a melodramatic tale of Exmoor outlaws, Lorna is married to John Ridd in Oare's tiny moorland church. The villainous Carver Doone shoots her on the altar steps, but mercifully she recovers.

Oath Probably 'oath' (perhaps denoting land promised for some purpose as a vow), OE *ath*.

A village in the Somerset Levels (*see under* SOMERSET), about 16 km (8 miles) east of Taunton.

Oban 'little bay', Gaelic *òb* + diminutive *-an*. The full Gaelic name is *an t-Òban Latharnach* 'the little bay of Lorne'.

A port and tourist centre on the west coast of Argyll and Bute (formerly in Strathclyde), some 95 km (60 miles) northwest of Glasgow. It overlooks the sheltered **Oban Bay**, the island of KERRERA and the Firth of Lorne (*see under* LORNE) beyond. Oban was founded in the later 18th century as a fishing village. There are ferry services to the islands of MULL, COLONSAY, LISMORE[1], COLL, TIREE, BARRA and South Uist (*see under* UISTS), and the town has been called 'the Gateway to the Hebrides'. There is a certain tartan tawdriness about some of the delights Oban has to offer the visitor:

> Words cannot express how horrible Oban is ... tacky beyond belief, full of disgusting shops selling Highland dancer dolls.
>
> Tom Morton: *Spirit of Adventure* (1985)

On top of **Oban Hill** above the town is an unfinished Coliseum-like structure known as MacCaig's Folly. It was initiated by a local philanthropist, John Stewart MacCaig, in 1897, to provide employment, and the idea was to fill the niches with statues of MacCaig and his family. However, the project was abandoned after MacCaig's death. On the sea front is the Dog Stone, to which, in legend, the hero Fingal (a.k.a. Finn MacCool) tied his dog Bran.

There is a town called Oban in Canada (Saskatchewan), and Halfmoon Bay on Stewart Island, the most southerly settlement in New Zealand, was formerly called Oban.

Ochil Hills *Ochil OCelt uchel 'high'; Cindocellun 700, Sliab Nochel 850, Oychellis 1461, Ocelli Montes 1580.*
A range of smooth, round-topped hills in Stirling, Clackmannanshire and Perth and Kinross. They have steep southern slopes overlooking the HILLFOOTS and the inner estuary of the FORTH, and the range extends (declining in height) northeastwards from BRIDGE OF ALLAN towards PERTH. The highest point is Ben Cleuch (720 m / 2362 ft).

> What hills are like the Ochil Hills?
> There's nane sae green tho' grander.
> What rills are like the Ochil rills?
> Nane, nane on earth that wander.
>
> Anon.

Ock From an OCelt word for 'salmon', borrowed into OE as *eoccen.*
A river in Oxfordshire (before 1974 in Berkshire), which rises to the southeast of FARINGDON and flows 24 km (15 miles) eastwards via STANFORD IN THE VALE into the Thames at ABINGDON.

Ockham *See* OAKHAM.
A village in Surrey about 5 km (3 miles) east of Woking. It was here that the Franciscan scholastic philosopher **William of Occam** (1285–1349), celebrated for the philosophical principle known as **Occam's razor**, was born (Occam being the Latinized form of the place name). According to Occam's razor, all unnecessary facts or constituents in the subject being analysed should be eliminated.

Ocle Pychard *Ocle 'oak-tree glade', OE ac 'oak-tree' + -LEY; Pychard denoting manorial ownership in the Middle Ages by the Pichard family.*
A village in Herefordshire (before 1998 in Hereford and Worcester, before 1974 in Herefordshire), about 11 km (7 miles) northeast of Hereford.

O'Connell Street *After Daniel O'Connell.*
The main street in Dublin on the north side of the River LIFFEY. These days O'Connell Street has a somewhat seedy reputation – its architectural style has been described as 'neon-classical', and others have decried the proliferation of tacky souvenir shops and fast-food outlets, not to mention the street's late-night aura of booze-fuelled threat.

O'Connell Street was originally called Drogheda Street, and then **Sackville Street**, after Lionel Cranfield Sackville, 1st Duke of Dorset, who was lord lieutenant of Ireland 1730–1 and 1750–5 – hence the title of Oliver St John Gogarty's volume of memoirs *As I Was Going Down Sackville Street* (1937). It is the location of the General Post Office, headquarters of the rebels in the 1916 Easter Rising, and the GPO was one of the few buildings in the street to survive the fighting. Much of the street was rebuilt in the 1920s, with somewhat undistinguished results.

Dublin Corporation had wanted to change the name of the street to O'Connell Street in 1884, but local residents took out an injunction against them. However, in 1924 the name was officially changed, in honour of the Liberator, Daniel O'Connell (1775–1847), who had campaigned successfully for Catholic Emancipation – and unsuccessfully for the repeal of the Union.

For many years the street contained statues not only of O'Connell, but also of Charles Stewart Parnell and Lord Nelson – 'three of history's best-known adulterers', as W.B. Yeats wryly observed. Other statues along the street include those of William Smith O'Brien, the Young Irelander; James Larkin, the trade-unionist; and Father Theobald Matthew, the temperance campaigner (the latter is presumably a popular target for furtive micturition after the pubs close). The landscape of the street was transformed again when on 9 March 1966 the IRA blew up Nelson's Pillar; being 41 m (134 ft) high it had been a popular jumping-off place for suicides, although the demolition team's motivation is thought to have been more political than theological. In 2003 the Pillar was replaced by a very tall (120-m / almost 400-ft) pointy thing, known as the Millennium Spire (sometimes called the Spike), although it arrived a bit late for the occasion. Dubliners had mixed feelings as the erection proceeded, some seeing it as Dublin's Eiffel Tower, but others as a folly – 'a brightly lit needle attracting every junkie in the city', in the words of one citizen quoted in *The Irish Examiner*. With their usual contempt for monumental pretension, Dubs have come up with a number of replacement names for the Millennium Spire, including 'the Stiletto in the Ghetto' and 'the Nail in the Pale', thus continuing that great Dublin tradition that embraces 'the Floozie in the Jacuzzi' and 'the Hoor in the Sewer' (*see under* LIFFEY), not to mention 'the Tart with the Cart' and 'the Dish with the Fish' (*see under* DUBLIN). On the day of the unveiling of the Spire, one wag was heard to comment: 'Well, at least if we can't have the Bertie Bowl [*see under* LANSDOWNE ROAD] we're getting the Bertie Pole.'

O'Connorville *From the name of the Irish Chartist leader Fergus O'Connor (1794–1855), who bought an estate in the area to be let to members of the Chartist Cooperative Land Company.*
An alternative name for the Hertfordshire village of HERONSGATE. First recorded in the mid-19th century, it is nowadays seldom encountered.

Odcombe *Probably 'Uda's valley', OE male personal name Uda + cumb (see -COMBE, COOMBE).*
A village in Somerset, about 5 km (3 miles) west of Yeovil.

Odstock *'Od(d)a's outlying farmstead or hamlet', OE male personal name Od(d)a + stoc (see -STOCK, STOCK-, STOKE).*

A village in Wiltshire, about 3 km (2 miles) south of Salisbury. **Odstock Down** is just to the south; to the north, stretching towards Salisbury, is the large **Odstock Hospital**.

Offaly Irish *Uíbh Fhailí* 'the descendants of Failge', the legendary ancestor of the people of Offaly.

A Midland county of Ireland, in the province of LEINSTER. It was known as **King's County** until 1920, having been so named in 1556 in honour of Philip II of Spain, husband of Mary I (neighbouring LAOIS was called Queen's County). (The former county town of King's County was called Philipstown, now known as Daingean.) In sporting circles it is nicknamed the FAITHFUL COUNTY.

Offaly is bounded on the north by Westmeath and Roscommon, to the east by Meath and Kildare, to the south by Laois and Tipperary and to the west by Galway. The county town is TULLAMORE, and other settlements include BANAGHER, BIRR and EDENDERRY[2]. Offaly is mostly low-lying, with the BOG OF ALLEN and the GRAND CANAL in the north and the SHANNON in the west, but in the southeast are the SLIEVE BLOOM MOUNTAINS.

brown gold of Offaly, the. Peat, the extraction of which is an important industry in the county.

> For the brown gold of thy boggery may the gored lord make us offaly thankful. Ah moan, she says and bares her eden derrière.
>
> Jacques Der Joost: *Flannaganslumber* (1947)

Offa's Dyke Named after *Offa*, king of Mercia from *c*.757 to *c*.797; in archaeology, a *dyke* is a linear earthwork consisting of a line of bank and ditch.

A long defensive earthwork built about AD 785 by King Offa of MERCIA along the Welsh–English border (the present-day border crosses the dyke many times). Offa had ousted the Welsh rulers of POWYS from what were to become HEREFORDSHIRE, WORCESTERSHIRE and SHROPSHIRE, and the earthwork represented the new frontier. It extended 240 km (150 miles), all the way from the mouth of the DEE[2] in the north to the mouth of the SEVERN in the south. Some 130 km (80 miles) of the dyke can still be seen.

> There was in Mercia ... a certain vigorous king called Offa, who terrified all the neighbouring kings and provinces around him, and who had a great dyke built between Wales and Mercia from sea to sea.
>
> Asser: *Life of King Alfred* (*c*.893), chapter 14

> 'There was a time,' said my companion, 'when it was customary for the English to cut off the ears of every Welshman who was found to the east of the dyke, and for the Welsh to hang every Englishman whom they found to the west of it. Let us now be thankful that we are now more humane to each other.'
>
> George Borrow: *Wild Wales* (1862) (Borrow's companion was speaking before the advent of the Five Nations rugby championship.)

The authors of *The Rough Guide to Wales* (3rd edition, 2000) suggest that Border Women, a lesbian network in Mid Wales, 'should surely have called themselves Offa's Dykes'.

Offa's Dyke Path. A long-distance footpath opened in 1971 that broadly follows the line of Offa's Dyke, although there are some scenic diversions. Purists insist on putting their feet in the sea at either end: at PRESTATYN in the north and at Sedbury Cliffs near CHEPSTOW in the south.

Offord Cluny *Offord* 'upper ford', OE *upp(e)* 'upper' + FORD; *Cluny* denoting manorial ownership in the Middle Ages by the monks of Cluny Abbey in France.

A village in Cambridgeshire (before 1974 in Huntingdonshire), on the Great Ouse, about 26 km (16 miles) northwest of Cambridge.

Offord Darcy *Darcy* denoting manorial ownership in the Middle Ages by the Dacy (or le Daneys) family.

A village in Cambridgeshire (before 1974 in Huntingdonshire), to the south of, and now continuous with, Offord Cluny.

Ogbourne Maizey *Ogbourne* 'Occa's stream', OE male personal name *Occa* + *burna* 'stream'; *Maizey* denoting manorial ownership in the Middle Ages by Robert de Meysey.

A village in Wiltshire, about 2.5 km (1.5 miles) north of Marlborough.

Ogmore Welsh *og* 'sharp, fast' + an unknown element, possibly English 'moor'; a personal name *Ocmur* has been suggested.

A river in south Wales, flowing through BRIDGEND unitary authority (formerly Glamorgan, then Mid Glamorgan) for approximately 25 km (15 miles). In Welsh it is **Ogwr**, as in **Pen-y-bont ar Ogwr** ('end of the bridge over the Ogmore'), the Welsh name for the town of Bridgend; from 1974 to 1996 Ogwr was also the name of a district in Mid Glamorgan.

The river has also given its name to the settlements of **Ogmore Vale**, **Glynogwr**, **Ogmore** itself (near the mouth) and **Ogmore-by-Sea** (the birthplace of the Welsh rugby union fullback J.P.R. Williams, b.1949).

At Ogmore are the ruins of the 12th-century **Ogmore Castle**, whose hidden treasure is guarded by a ghostly white lady known as Y Ladi Wen. The river itself is also associated with treasure, in that it is said to be haunted by the ghosts of misers who never revealed the whereabouts of their hidden hoards. However, if such a hoard is found and thrown in the river, its former owner will be freed from his ghostliness.

> ... does grimed Ogwr toss on a fouled ripple his broken-heart flow ... ?
>
> David Jones: 'The Sleeping Lord', from *The Sleeping Lord and Other Fragments* (1974)

Ogwen Valley From the River *Ogwen*, meaning uncertain, although the elements could be *og* + *wen* 'white harrow'.

A valley in Snowdonia, between the ranges of the CAR-NEDDAU and the GLYDERS, straddling Gwynedd and Conwy (formerly in Caernarvonshire, then entirely in Gwynedd). The valley, which takes its name from the River Ogwen, includes the small lake of **Llyn Ogwen**, and a little below this is the **Rhaeadr Ogwen** (Ogwen Falls). The lower part of the valley of the River Ogwen is called **Nant Ffrancon** ('valley of the beavers', although traditionally linked to Adam de Francton, the man said to have killed Llywelyn the Last near BUILTH WELLS). The small town of BETHESDA was formerly called **Glanogwen** (Welsh 'bank of the River Ogwen').

Ogwr. The Welsh name for the River OGMORE.

Oiléan an Ghuail. The Irish name for COALISLAND.

Oileán Ciarraí. The Irish name for CASTLEISLAND.

Oileán Mhic Aodha. The Irish name for the ISLAND MAGEE peninsula.

Oirghialla. Another spelling of the name of the old Ulster kingdom of AIRGIALLA.

Okeford Fitzpaine *Okeford see* CHILD OKEFORD; *Fitzpaine* denoting manorial ownership in the Middle Ages by the Fitz Payn family.

A village in Dorset, about 11 km (7 miles) northwest of Blandford Forum and 3 km (2 miles) southwest of Child Okeford. A little to the southeast is **Okeford Hill**.

Okehampton 'farmstead on the River Okement', OKEMENT + -TON; later remodelled on the analogy of other place-names ending in -*hampton*.

A market town in Devon, on the River OKEMENT, at the northern edge of Dartmoor, about 35 km (22 miles) west of Exeter. It grew to prosperity in the Middle Ages on the strength of the wool trade. Its castle, overlooking the river, has never been the same since Henry VIII turned his unfavourable attention to it.

From the south, the heights of HIGH WILLHAYS and YES TOR loom over the town. To the north are ABBEYFORD WOODS.

Okement An OCelt river name, perhaps meaning 'swift stream'.

A river in Devon, rising on Dartmoor, on the slopes of **Okement Hill**, and flowing about 24 km (15 miles) northwards through Okehampton to join the River TORRIDGE[1] to the northwest of MONKOKEHAMPTON.

Okraquoy The *quoy* in Orkney is 'untaxed pasture', from OScand *kvi* 'cattle fold'; the first element here is obscure.

A small settlement on Mainland, Shetland, 10 km (6 miles) southwest of Lerwick.

Old '(place at the) woodland or forest', OE *wald* 'wood, forest'.

A village in Northamptonshire, about 16 km (10 miles) northeast of Northampton.

Old Bailey *Old* 'old', ME; *Bailey* 'outwork or defensive rampart on the outside of the City wall', ME *baille*.

A street in the City of London (EC4) (*see under* LONDON), running north–south between NEWGATE Street and LUDGATE HILL. It follows the line of London's ancient city wall between Ludgate and Newgate. The former Newgate prison was situated at its northern end.

The Old Bailey, with the definite article, is an informal name for the Central Criminal Court, which is situated at the northern end of Old Bailey, on the site formerly occupied by Newgate prison (whence its 20th-century nickname 'the Old Start', 'the Start' being an ancient slang term for a prison). It has jurisdiction over the City of London and (approximately) the Greater London area.

The first courthouse in the street was built in 1539, next to Newgate prison (it is recorded in 1555 as 'le Justice Hall in le Olde Bailie'). It was replaced by a new building in 1774. The present court building was opened, by Edward VII, in 1907. The statue of Justice on its dome, blindfolded and holding a sword and a pair of scales, has become an icon not only of the building but of the impartial administration of the legal process. Almost as famous is the motto above the main door: 'Defend the children of the poor and punish the wrongdoer.' An extension was added to the building in 1972.

In exceptional circumstances, cases from outside its London jurisdiction are tried at the Old Bailey. Among the more notorious murderers to have stood trial at The Old Bailey are Dr Crippen (1910), George 'Brides-in-the-Bath' Smith (1915), John Christie, of the 10 RILLINGTON PLACE murders (1953) and Peter Sutcliffe, the 'Yorkshire Ripper' (1981; *see under* YORKSHIRE).

In the everyday parlance of those who work there, or are brought there against their will, the Old Bailey is '**the Bailey**', a name familiarized by **Rumpole of the Bailey**, the eccentric barrister created by John Mortimer in the 1970s and played on television by Leo McKern.

Old Bedford River. *See under* BEDFORD LEVEL.

Old Bolingbroke *Bolingbroke* probably 'brook at Bola's or Bula's place', OE male personal name *Bola* or *Bula* + -ING + *broc* 'brook'.

A village in Lincolnshire, about 35 km (22 miles) east of Lincoln. 10 km (6 miles) southeast is **New Bolingbroke**.

Oldbridge. *See under* BOYNE.

Oldbury 'old fort' (there is no record of such a structure in the locality), OE *eald* 'old' + *burh* (*see* BURY).

A town in the West Midlands, in the metropolitan borough of Sandwell, on the Birmingham Canal, about 8 km

(5 miles) northwest of Birmingham. It became part of the conurbation of WARLEY in 1966.

Old Dart, the. An Australian and New Zealand slang term for England or Britain, first recorded in 1892. In this context *dart* is thought to be dialect for 'dirt', so the expression is analogous to the OULD SOD, an informal name for Ireland.

Old Deer. *See* DEER ABBEY.

Old Dungeon Ghyll. *See* DUNGEON GHYLL.

Old Fletton *Fletton* 'farmstead on a stream', OE *fleot* 'stream' + -TON.

A district within the unitary authority of Peterborough (before 1996 in Cambridgeshire, before 1974 in Huntingdonshire), now effectively a southern suburb of the city. **New Fletton** is just to its north. The area once boasted the Fletton United football team (*see under* PETERBOROUGH).

fletton. A 20th-century generic term for a type of brick made by a semi-dry process, very commonly used in housebuilding: the Oxford clay found in the vicinity has long been used for brick-making.

Old Galloway. *See* DALRY.

Oldham Possibly 'old promontory', OE *eald* 'old' (or alternatively an OCelt word meaning 'hill') + OScand *holmr* 'promontory, island' (*see* -EY, -EA).

An industrial town and unitary authority in Greater Manchester, 12 km (7 miles) northeast of Manchester city centre. It was the birthplace of the composer William Walton (1902–83); the comedian Eric Sykes (b.1923); and the theologian Don Cupitt (b.1934). The parliamentary seat of Oldham was held after the 1832 Reform Act by the Radical politician William Cobbett, and was the first seat won by Winston Churchill (1900). More recently, following racial tension in the town, the British National Party polled strongly in the 2001 general election. It was in Oldham that the electrical engineer Sebastian Ziani de Ferranti set up his first company, in 1896.

Oldham Athletic FC, nicknamed the Latics, was founded in 1895 as Pine Villa. The club is based at Boundary Park.

There is an Oldham County in Kentucky, USA.

Old Head of Kinsale. *See under* KINSALE.

Old Jewry 'district formerly occupied by Jews'.

A street in the City of London (EC2) (*see under* LONDON), running north to south from Gresham Street to POULTRY. It lay within an area in which many Jews lived in the 12th and 13th centuries, but they were expelled from it on the orders of Edward I in 1290 – whence its name.

Old Kent Road From the direction in which it takes the traveller, and in contrast with *New Kent Road* (laid out from 1751), which links the northern end of the Old Kent Road with the ELEPHANT AND CASTLE.

A road (A2) in southeast London (SE1, SE15), in the borough of SOUTHWARK, running from WALWORTH in the northwest towards NEW CROSS in the southeast. A southern continuation of Tabard Street, which in the Middle Ages was known as Kent Street, it follows the line of the old road towards Canterbury and Dover, WATLING STREET[1].

After this part of London became clogged with houses and people in the 19th century, the road ran through a fairly tough working-class area, and a famous music-hall song (1894) by Albert Chevalier ensured it a place in the pantheon of Cockney culture:

> 'Wot cher!' all the neighbours cried,
> 'Who yer gonna meet, Bill
> Have yer bought the street, Bill?'
> Laugh! I thought I should 'ave died
> Knock'd 'em in the Old Kent Road!
>> (*knocked* in this context means 'filled them with astonishment and admiration')

The Old Kent Road, lined with pubs and costermongers' stalls, became synonymous with the South London version of beery Cockney conviviality:

> What wonderful winkles we had at that stall at chucking-out time in the Old Kent Road.
>> *The Guardian* (8 May 1970)

It rates a mere £60 on the Monopoly board.

Old Man of Coniston, the. *See under* CONISTON.

Old Man of Hoy, the. *See under* HOY.

Old Man of Stoer, the. *See under* STOER.

Old Radnor *Radnor* 'the red hillside', OE *read* 'red' + *ora* 'bank'.

A village in Powys (formerly in Radnorshire, to which it gave its name), close to the English border, 8 km (5 miles) southeast of Presteigne. Harold Godwinson, who became King Harold I and was subsequently killed at the Battle of Hastings, had a castle here. It became 'Old Radnor' in 1064 when NEW RADNOR was established 4 km (2.5 miles) to the northwest.

Old Romney *Romney see* ROMNEY MARSH.

A village in Kent, at the southern corner of ROMNEY MARSH, about 3 km (2 miles) west of NEW ROMNEY. In former times it was a port, but the sea has long since retreated, and it is now 6 km (4 miles) to the east.

Old Sarum *Old* in contrast with *New Sarum*, an old name for the nearby city of Salisbury; *Sarum see* SARUM.

An Iron Age hillfort about 3 km (2 miles) north of Salisbury in Wiltshire. In the period of the Roman occupation it was known as **Sorviodunum**, a name which lies behind SALISBURY and ultimately also Sarum itself.

An important early medieval town grew up on the hilltop site, and it inherited the name 'Sarum'. In the 13th century, however, a rival centre was established just to the south (*see* SARUM), and this was initially known as 'New Sarum'. The original town came to be called 'Old Sarum'.

By the end of the 18th century it had shrunk to a mere hamlet, with only ten registered voters – making it one of the notorious 'rotten boroughs' that were abolished under the Reform Act of 1832. It was also a 'pocket borough', a parliamentary constituency whose votes were, in effect, controlled by a single patron. In the case of Old Sarum this was the Pitt family, and in 1735 it returned its scion William Pitt ('the Elder', 1708–78, prime minister 1766–8) as MP.

All that can now be seen of medieval Old Sarum are remains of its cathedral and castle, and a few traces of its surrounding wall.

Old Sarum. A large watercolour of the Old Sarum hill-fort under a dark, moody sky, by John Constable, exhibited at the Royal Academy in 1834. It is now in the Victoria and Albert Museum, London.

Old Sod, the. *See* the OULD SOD.

Old Steine ModE *old* + *Steine* 'stony place' (in 1823, large blocks of stone were dug out of the common here), OE *stæne* (*see* STONE).

A triangular open space (pronounced 'steen') at the heart of BRIGHTON, its base facing the Palace Pier and the open sea, with the Prince Regent's Royal Pavilion along part of its western side, and other Regency and Victorian buildings scattered around it. It was originally a common, with a stream running down it, but after the Pavilion was built in 1793 the stream was banished underground, and the centre is now filled with ornamental gardens.

Old Town. *See under* EDINBURGH.

Oldtown of Aigas. *See* CRASK OF AIGAS.

Old Trafford *See* TRAFFORD.

An area of MANCHESTER, southwest of the city centre. It is home to two sports grounds of the same name. The football stadium (opened 1910) is the home ground of Manchester United FC (*see under* MANCHESTER), whose marketing people like to call it 'the Theatre of Dreams'. The cricket ground (1857), more properly if prosaically called the 'City Cricket Ground', has hosted test matches since 1884. It was here that the England and Surrey off-spinner Jim Laker took 19 wickets in the fourth test match against Australia to help England retain the Ashes in the summer of 1956.

Old Wives Lees Formerly *Old Wood Lees* 'common pasture by the old wood', OE *eald* 'old' with *wudu* 'wood' and Kentish dialect *lees* 'common pasture'; the modern name is first recorded in the 17th century.

A village in Kent, about 8 km (5 miles) southwest of Canterbury.

Olicana. *See* ILKLEY.

Olney 'Olla's island, or dry ground in a marsh', OE *Ollan* possessive form of male personal name *Olla* + *eg* (*see* -EY, -EA). A small market town within the unitary authority of MILTON KEYNES (before 1996 in Buckinghamshire), on the GREAT OUSE, about 16 km (10 miles) west of Bedford. Its present-day fame rests largely on its annual Shrove Tuesday pancake race, said to date back to the 15th century. Competitors must successfully toss their pancakes three times on their way from the Market Place to the imposing 14th-century church of St Peter and St Paul.

The poet William Cowper (1731–1800) lived and worked for many years in Olney.

Olney Hymns. A collection of hymns (1779) written by William Cowper and his friend, the local curate John Newton. Cowper's contribution included 'God moves in a mysterious way' and 'Oh, for a closer walk with God'; Newton's, 'Glorious things of Thee are spoken'.

Olympia From *Olympia* in Greece, in the Peloponnese, where in ancient times the Olympic Games were held.

An exhibition complex in West London (W14), in the Hammersmith Road, in the borough of HAMMERSMITH AND FULHAM. The original building, erected in 1884, was called the National Agricultural Hall. It was not until two years later, when the first circus (the 'Paris Hippodrome') was staged here, that it received its present name, chosen for its grandiloquence. Olympia subsequently became famous for its circuses, and also for a wide variety of exhibitions, shows and sporting events, including the Motor Show, the *Daily Mail* Ideal Home Exhibition, Crufts and the equine International Show Jumping Championships.

Kensington (Olympia) Underground station, on a spur of the District line, opened in 1946, but did not offer a regular service until 1986. The station also serves the section of mainline that links Willesden Junction with Clapham Junction and Loughborough Junction to the south of the Thames.

Omagh Irish *An Ómaigh* 'the virgin plain' (the first element is *Óg-* 'complete, untouched').

The county town of County Tyrone, 35 km (22 miles) northeast of Enniskillen. It is the administrative centre of the local authority district of the same name. Omagh town was laid out in the 17th century, and is (meteorologically) the gloomiest spot in Ireland, with an average of only 3 hours 20 minutes sunshine per day.

Omagh was the birthplace of the Irish Nationalist poet Alice Milligan (1886–1953) and of the playwright Brian Friel (b.1929). The writer Benedict Kiely (b.1919) grew up here and used Omagh as the setting for his early novels *Land without Stars* (1946) and *In a Harbour Green* (1949).

Omagh Bomb (15 August 1998). The worst single atrocity in the Troubles, in which a car bomb placed by the Real

IRA (a splinter group who did not recognize the main Provisional IRA ceasefire) killed 29 civilians and injured more than 300 others. The effect, if anything, was to accelerate the peace process. Addressing the relatives of the victims, President Bill Clinton declared:

> It is high time to stop the lilt of laughter and
> language being drowned out by bombs and guns
> and sirens.

Ompton 'Alhmund's farmstead', OE male personal name *Alhmund* + -TON.

A village in Nottinghamshire, to the east of Sherwood Forest, and approximately 29 km (18 miles) northeast of Nottingham.

Once Brewed. *See under* TWICE BREWED.

Onchan 'dog or wolf head', Gaelic *conchenn*; the initial *c-* was lost by assimilation of the two parts of the district name, Kirk Conchan.

A town on the east coast of the Isle of Man, just north of Douglas.

Ongar 'pasture land', OE *anger*.

A twin urban entity consisting of the market town CHIPPING ONGAR and, a little to the east, the much smaller **High Ongar**. It is in Essex, about 13 km (8 miles) southeast of Harlow.

Ongar 'Underground' station, formerly the eastern terminus of the Central line, opened in 1949. It was closed in 1994.

Orchard '(place) beside the wood', OCelt *ar* 'beside' + CED.

A village in Dorset, about 8 km (5 miles) southwest of Shaftesbury.

Orchard of Ireland, the. A nickname for County ARMAGH.

Orchard Portman *Orchard* 'garden, orchard', OE *orceard*; *Portman* denoting manorial ownership in the late Middle Ages by the Portman family.

A village in Somerset, beside the M5, on the southeastern outskirts of Taunton.

Orchy Gaelic name *Urchaidh*, possibly from early OCelt *are-cet-ia* 'stream near the wood'.

A river in Argyll and Bute (formerly Strathclyde region), flowing south from Loch Tulla at the foot of RANNOCH Moor, then southwest through **Glen Orchy** (known as **Strath of Orchy** in its lower reaches) past Dalmally to LOCH AWE. Its length is approximately 25 km (15 miles). Some 3 km (2 miles) south of Loch Tulla is the small settlement and railway station of **Bridge of Orchy**, at a remote spot on the road and railway from the south to FORT WILLIAM. All this area was once MacGregor land, before the clan was proscribed in the 17th century.

> Glen Orchy's proud mountains,
> Coalchuirn and her towers,
> Glenstrae and Glenlyon no longer are ours;
> We're landless, landless, landless, Grigalach!
>> Sir Walter Scott: 'MacGregor's Gathering' (1816)

Much earlier than that, Glen Orchy was a haunt of the ancient Irish heroine Deirdre and her lover Naoise during their idyll in Scotland (*see* ETIVE):

> Glen Urchy! Glen Urchy! where loudly and long
> My love used to wake up the woods with his song,
> While the son of the rock, from the depths of the dell,
> Laughed sweetly in answer – Glen Urchy, farewell!
>> Anon.: 'Deirdre's Farewell to Alba', from *The Red Branch Cycle* (12th century), translated by Samuel Ferguson

Ord of Caithness. *See under* CAITHNESS.

Ore¹ '(place at the) hill-slope or ridge', OE *ora* 'hill-slope, ridge'.

An eastern suburb of HASTINGS in East Sussex. Its station is the terminus for trains from London Victoria to Hastings; the **Ore Tunnel** is on a single-track line leading northeastwards through RYE.

Ore² A back-formation from ORFORD.

An estuarine river in Suffolk formed by the confluence of the rivers ALDE and Butley, just to the south of Orford. About 4 km (2.5 miles) long, it is separated from the sea by Orford Ness (*see under* ORFORD).

Ore Gap. *See under* BOWFELL.

Orford Perhaps 'ford near the shore', OE *ora* 'shore' + FORD.

A village in Suffolk, about 8 km (5 miles) southwest of Aldeburgh and 3 km (2 miles) from the sea. In the Middle Ages it was on the coast, and an important port – Henry II had a massive castle built to protect it, of which only the tower remains. Today, the village has a high reputation for its **Orford oysters** and contains two fish smokehouses.

The 14th-century church of St Bartholomew has served as a venue for the ALDEBURGH Festival, and saw the premieres of Benjamin Britten's *Noye's Fludde, Curlew River, The Burning Fiery Furnace* and *The Prodigal Son*.

George Crabbe gave the name **Ellen Orford** to the stoical eponymous heroine of one of the tales in his lengthy poem *The Borough* (1810), a thinly disguised portrayal of Aldeburgh life. Britten incorporated her into his *Borough*-based opera *Peter Grimes* (1945), as the faithful friend and supporter of the embattled Grimes.

Robert Walpole (1676–1745), the first British prime minister, was created Earl of Orford.

Orford Ness. A narrow spit of shingle, 10 km (6 miles) long, opposite Orford. Behind it, at its northerly end, are flat, drained marshes. In front of its southern, narrower end is **Orford Beach**, and at the point where the River ORE² disgorges into the North Sea, is **Orford Haven**. Assorted weaponry – including Britain's first atomic bomb – was developed and tested on Orford Ness, as was radar. It is now owned by the National Trust.

Orgreave 'ore-pit', OE *ora* 'metal ore' + *græf* 'pit'.

A village in South Yorkshire, about 6 km (4 miles) south of Rotherham and 13 km (8 miles) east of Sheffield. A sleepy place, centered on **Orgreave Hall**, its modern coal-village life began with the establishment of a colliery in 1820 on the Hall grounds, and in the 1920s a coking plant.

Battle of Orgreave. One of the bitterest and bloodiest clashes between police and miners during the miners' strike of 1984–5. It took place outside Orgreave coking plant on 18 June 1984, and thousands were involved on either side. There were 72 policemen injured and 51 pickets (although probably many more did not seek medical attention for fear of arrest). The battle was re-created using some of the original participants in 2001 by Jeremy Deller and filmed by Mike Figgis.

Oriel. The anglicized form of the name of the old Ulster kingdom of AIRGIALLA.

Orkney The islands were known to classical writers as the *Orcades* (the name is mentioned by the Roman geographer Mela in the 1st century AD, and before that there is a Greek reference to *Orkas* in 330 BC), and their inhabitants were known as *Orcs* to the ancient Irish. The name may be pre-Celtic in origin, but if it is Celtic it might mean 'boar', hence 'people of the boar', presumably a totemic symbol. The name was assimilated by the Norsemen to OScand *orkn* 'seal' + *ey* 'island' (*see* -AY).

A group of some 70 islands (around 20 of which are inhabited) to the north of the Scottish mainland. The group is also referred to (but not by the inhabitants) as **the Orkneys** or **the Orkney Islands**. Orkney is separated from mainland Scotland by the Pentland Firth, which at its narrowest is only 10 km (6 miles) across. Orkney was formerly a county, and in 1975 became a unitary island authority. The main town and administrative seat is KIRKWALL, and the other main town is STROMNESS. The inhabitants are known as **Orcadians** or **Orkneymen**, and generally do not consider themselves Scottish – historically, linguistically or culturally. The Scots themselves have sometimes found these distant northern isles both foreign and bleak:

> Upon the utmost corners of the warld,
> and on the borders of this massive round,
> quhaire fates and fortoune hither has me harld,
> I doe deplore my greiffs upon this ground;
> and seeing roring seis from roks rebound
> by ebbs and streames of contrair routing tyds,
> and phebus chariot in there wawes ly dround …
>
> William Fowler (1560–1612): 'Sonet in Orknay'

Despite the climate, the rich soil of Orkney means that the islanders have never been so reliant on the sea as the people of SHETLAND to the north, hence the saying:

An Orcadian is a farmer with a boat, while a Shetlander is a fisherman with a croft.

In Orkney a good harvest was once thought to be assured by smearing the plough with urine before cutting the first furrow of the spring. Since the 1970s another liquid, North Sea oil, has also been important to the economy.

The largest island, on which both Kirkwall and Stromness are situated, is called Mainland (OScand *meggenland*) – to Orcadians the Scottish mainland is simply Scotland. The Old Norse name was actually *Hrossey* ('horse island'). The alternative name **Pomona** (the name of the Roman goddess of fruit) originated in a cartographic error in the 17th century, and was never used by Orcadians. The Mainland is linked to the islands of Burray and SOUTH RONALDSAY by the CHURCHILL BARRIERS. There are also ferry links to SCRABSTER, INVERGORDON and ABERDEEN on the Scottish mainland, to many of the other islands, and to LERWICK in Shetland. The largest islands apart from the Mainland are HOY, South Ronaldsay, SHAPINSAY, ROUSAY, EDAY, STRONSAY, SANDAY, NORTH RONALDSAY, WESTRAY and PAPA WESTRAY. In local folklore there are also islands, such as Hether Blether, that mysteriously appear only to disappear again.

There are many important prehistoric sites on Orkney, for example at SKARA BRAE, the '**Heart of Neolithic Orkney**' which has been designated as a World Heritage Site by UNESCO (1999). Norse raids began in the 8th century, and from the 9th century the islands were under Norse control, becoming the base for Norse rule of the HEBRIDES and parts of mainland Scotland. Although Celtic missionaries had been active from the 7th century, Christianity was officially adopted only in 995. It was in Orkney that Margaret, the Maid of Norway, died in 1290 on her way to assume the Crown of Scotland. The islands remained under notional Scandinavian rule until 1472, when Orkney and Shetland were taken over by the Scottish Crown in lieu of cash payment as part of the dowry of Margaret of Denmark, when she married James III. At this point the language spoken in Orkney was Norn, descended from Old Norse. Norn eventually died out in the 18th century, although some words survive in Orkney dialect. It was replaced by Scots (Gaelic was never spoken in Orkney).

Among the earls (or princes) of Orkney was Henry St Clair of ROSLIN, who in 1398 is said to have reached Nova Scotia in the company of Antonio Zeno of Venice and 300 colonists. Mary Queen of Scots awarded her third husband, James Hepburn, 4th Earl of Bothwell, the title of Duke of Orkney and Shetland when they married in 1567. Thirteen years later he died insane and alone in a Danish dungeon.

Orkney was the birthplace of the writers Edwin Muir (1887–1959), Eric Linklater (1899–1974) and the former's pupil (at Newbattle Abbey College), George Mackay Brown (1921–96). Linklater's early novels *The Men of Ness* (1932) and *Magnus Merriman* (1934) are both set in Orkney, and Linklater returned during the Second World War to command the islands' defences. Brown was a more permanent resident, and his poetry, short stories and novels – such as *Greenvoe* (1972) – are firmly rooted in the islands. He also collaborated with the composer Peter Maxwell Davies (who has lived in Orkney for many years) on works such as the opera *The Martyrdom of St Magnus* (1976). The denouement of Sir Walter Scott's novel *The Pirate* (1821) takes place in Orkney.

Lord Kitchener, war minister during the First World War, died when the ship taking him to Russia hit a mine off the west coast of Orkney's Mainland, on 5 June 1916. Jo Grimond, leader of the Liberal Party from 1956 to 1967, was MP for Orkney, and died in Kirkwall in 1993.

The South Orkney Islands are in the South Atlantic, north of the Weddell Sea, and form part of British Antarctic Territory.

Orcadian oatmeal soup. A creamy soup with oatmeal, milk, carrots and swede.

Orkney chair. A type of chair with a high back made of straw.

Orkney cheese. A type of cheese made using the DUNLOP method, dating back to the 18th century. It was popular at funeral feasts, and at one time was acceptable currency for paying university tuition fees.

Orkneyinga Saga, the. A Norse saga, written *c*.1200, recounting the doings of the earls of Orkney in the 10th, 11th and 12th centuries.

Orkney Saga. An ongoing musical project by the composer Peter Maxwell Davies (an Orkney resident), intended eventually to comprise 14 works. The project embodies the composer's responses to George Mackay Brown's words on a series of tapestries in St Magnus Cathedral in Kirkwall, dealing with the involvement of Orkney men in the Crusades. *Orkney Saga I* was first performed in 1997.

Orkney Tapestry, An. A collection of verse and prose (1969) by the Orkney poet George Mackay Brown.

Orkney vole. An endemic subspecies, *Microtus arvalis orcadensis*, of the common vole.

Orkney Wedding, with Sunrise, An. An orchestral work by Peter Maxwell Davies, first performed in 1985. The piece parodies Scottish country dances, and mimics the descent of the band into a boozy stupor. The sunrise is heralded by the bagpipes.

Pirate of Orkney, the. John Fullarton, an 18th-century pirate, whose bloody career was ended when after he boarded the *Isabella* out of Leith and killed the captain, he was shot through the temple by the captain's wife, one Mary Jones.

Ormes Head. *See* GREAT ORME.

Ormond 'east Munster'; related to DESMOND and THOMOND, with -*mond* relating to *Muma*, an Irish name for MUNSTER.

An ancient territory of eastern Munster, broadly corresponding to the present counties of WATERFORD and TIPPERARY.

> From a Munster vale they brought her
> From the pure and pleasant air;
> An Ormond peasant's daughter,
> With blue eyes and golden hair.
> They brought her to the city
> And she faded slowly there –
> Consumption has no pity
> For blue eyes and golden hair.
>
> Shamrock (Richard D'Alton Williams): 'The Dying Girl' (1842)

Earl of Ormond. A title first taken by the Anglo-Norman Butler family in 1329. In the 15th century the 3rd and 4th Earls of Ormond were effectively rulers of Ireland, as the king's lieutenants. In the 17th century the 12th Earl, a Royalist, was also lord lieutenant of Ireland and was created 1st Duke of Ormond in 1661.

Ormskirk 'Ormr's church', OScand male personal name + *kirkja* 'church'.

A market town in Lancashire, 18 km (11 miles) north of Liverpool. The street market may date back to the 13th century. The Labour politician and future prime minister Harold Wilson won the parliamentary seat of Ormskirk, then a marginal seat, in the 1945 general election.

Oronsay. *See* COLONSAY AND ORONSAY.

Orpington 'estate associated with Orped', OE male personal name *Orped* (from *orped* 'active, brave') + -ING + -TON.

A southeastern suburb of London (before 1965 in Kent), in the borough of BROMLEY, between Chislehurst to the north and Sevenoaks to the south. Until the early years of the 20th century it was a rural village, but the advance of commuterdom was swift once it began.

In the late 19th century a local farmer developed a breed of poultry that has become known by the name 'Orpington'. The most widely recognized variety is probably the **Buff Orpington**. (An Australian variety bred from the original Black Orpington became known as the 'Australorp'.)

Orpington's greatest moment of fame came in 1962, when the Liberal candidate Eric Lubbock took the 'safe' parliamentary seat from the Conservatives at a by-election, further discomfiting Harold Macmillan's already shaky government.

Orrell 'hill of ore', OE *ora* 'ore' + *hyll* 'hill'.

A town in GREATER MANCHESTER, 6 km (4 miles) west of Wigan.

Orwell¹ 'Or stream', *Or* ancient pre-Celtic river name (recorded in the 11th century in the form *Arewan*) of uncertain meaning + OE *wella* 'stream'.

An estuarine river in Suffolk, essentially the tidal section of the River GIPPING², to the southeast of Ipswich. It is 19 km (12 mile) long, and at its mouth joins waters with the River STOUR².

The writer George Orwell (1903–50), whose parents were Suffolk people, took his pen name from the river. His original name was Eric Blair.

Orwell² 'spring by a pointed hill', OE *ord* 'pointed hill' + *wella* 'spring'.

A village in Cambridgeshire, about 13 km (8 miles) southwest of Cambridge. There are towns called Orwell in the USA (New York, Ohio, Vermont).

Osborne House *Osborne* probably 'stream at the sheepfold', OE *eowestre* 'sheepfold' + *burna* 'stream'.

A house on the Isle of Wight, 1.5 km (1 mile) southeast of East COWES. It was built in the late 1840s in Italian Renaissance style to the designs of Prince Albert and Thomas Cubitt. It was Queen Victoria's favourite residence. After Albert's death in 1861 she spent as much time as she could here, and she died here in 1901. Edward VII, for whom the house had no appeal, turned it into a naval college and convalescent home (among the cadets at the naval college were the future kings Edward VIII and George VI, and also Jack Llewelyn Davies, one of the Llewelyn Davies brothers who as boys had inspired J.M. Barrie's *Peter Pan* (1904); the expulsion in 1908 of one of the college's cadets, George Archer-Shee, for allegedly stealing a postal order formed the basis of Terence Rattigan's play *The Winslow Boy* (1946); it was merged with the Britannia Royal Naval College at DARTMOUTH in 1921).

Offshore to the northeast is **Osborne Bay**.

Osea Island *Osea* 'Ufi's island', OE *Ufes* possessive form of male personal name *Ufi* + *eg* (*see* -EY, -EA), with tautological ModE *island*.

An island in the middle of the BLACKWATER¹ Estuary in Essex, about 6 km (4 miles) east of Maldon and 3 km (2 miles) east of Northey Island. It has an area of 133 ha (330 acres). A road linking it with the north bank of the Blackwater is passable only at low tide.

Osgodby 'Asgautr's farmstead or village', OScand male personal name *Asgautr* + -BY.

A village in Lincolnshire, about 3 km (2 miles) northwest of Market Rasen. There are also two villages called Osgodby in North Yorkshire.

Osmotherley 'Asmundr's clearing', OScand male personal name *Asmundr* + OE *leah* (*see* -LEY). According to legend, it was named after a Saxon prince called Osmund, who, warned by a soothsayer that he would drown on a certain day,

removed himself to ROSEBERRY TOPPING; unfortunately, a fountain of water flooded out of the summit of the hill and drowned the prince, who was taken to Osmotherley for burial. A village in North Yorkshire, on the western side of the Cleveland Hills (*see under* CLEVELAND), 10 km (6 miles) northeast of Northallerton. **Osmotherley Moor** is to the east.

Nearby lies what is left of the stately 14th-century Mount Grace Priory, a significant relic of the Carthusian order.

Osney 'Osa's island', OE *Osan* possessive form of male personal name *Osa* + *eg* (*see* -EY, -EA).

A district of West OXFORD, on low-lying land by the River Thames, and including an island in the river. To the north is **New Osney**, just to the south of Oxford railway station.

Osney Abbey, an Augustinian foundation of the 12th century, briefly became Oxford Cathedral after the Reformation, but from 1546 a process of gradual dismantling began, and hardly any of it survives today.

Osraighe. The Irish name for the ancient kingdom of OSSORY.

Ossian's Cave From the bard *Ossian*, an important poet of early Irish legend.

A dark slit, high on the precipitous north face of Aonach Dubh, one of the Three Sisters of GLEN COE. It is said to have been the home or even the birthplace of the ancient Gaelic bard Ossian, although the 'floor' of the cave rises at an undomestic angle of 45 degrees. It is a rock climb to reach the mouth of the cave, and the first recorded ascent was made by a local shepherd, Neil Marquis, in the summer of 1868. The route is called *Ossian's Ladder*, is graded 'difficult', and is not to be attempted by other than experienced rock climbers.

Ossian's Stone. *See under* the SMA' GLEN.

Ossory Irish *Osraighe*, named after a Munster tribe who settled here.

An ancient kingdom of LEINSTER, in the southeast of Ireland, which lasted from the 2nd century AD up to the 12th century. Broadly speaking, it covered most of the present county of KILKENNY and part of western LAOIS, with the River BARROW bounding it on the east and the River SUIR to the south. The name is preserved in various place names, such as **Borris-in-Ossory**, in the Catholic diocese of Ossory, and in the Anglican diocese of Cashel and Ossory.

Osterley 'sheepfold glade', OE *eowestre* 'sheepfold' + -LEY.

A district of West London (before 1965 in Middlesex), in the borough of HOUNSLOW, between Brentwood to the east and Heston to the west. In the northern part of the district is **Osterley Park**, a large open space bisected by the M4. At its centre is **Osterley Park House**, an Elizabethan manor remodelled into an 18th-century villa by Robert Adam. It now belongs to the National Trust.

Osterley 'Underground' station, on the Piccadilly and (before 1964) District lines, opened in 1883, under the name 'Osterley & Spring Grove'. The present name was introduced in 1934.

Oswaldtwistle 'Oswald's confluence', OE male personal name *Oswald* + *twisla* 'meeting of rivers'.
A former cotton town in Lancashire, 2 km (1.2 miles) southwest of Accrington. It was here that James Hargreaves invented his spinning jenny in 1764. The place came to wider attention in March 2003 when a lady from Oswaldtwistle was offended by a nurse at the local hospital addressing her as 'cock'. Correspondence in the national press concluded that all would have been well if she had been addressed as 'chuck'.

The inventor of the spinning jenny (and thus accelerator of the Industrial Revolution), James Hargreaves (1720–78), was born in Oswaldtwistle.

Oswestry 'Oswald's tree', OE *Oswaldes* possessive form of male personal name *Oswald* + *treow* 'tree'. Legend links 'Oswald's tree' with the death of Oswald, King of Northumbria (St Oswald, *c*.605–42): he was defeated in battle against the heathen King Penda of MERCIA at Maserfelth, and according to later tradition was subsequently crucified; but the identification of *Maserfelth* with Oswestry has never been established for certain.
A market town in Shropshire, close to the Welsh border (it did not officially become English until 1535), about 27 km (17 miles) northwest of Shrewsbury. An Iron Age hillfort known as **Old Oswestry** is just to the north of the town.

The poet Wilfred Owen (1893–1918) and the novelist Barbara Pym (1913–80) were born in Oswestry.

Otford 'Otta's ford', OE male personal name *Otta* + FORD.
A village in Kent, on the River Darent, about 3 km (2 miles) north of Sevenoaks.

Battle of Otford (*c*.776). An Anglo-Saxon battle of uncertain outcome. The 11th-century historian Henry of Huntingdon says that the Mercians defeated the army of Kent, whose kings were chafing at the growing power of Mercia. But other historians describe a Kentish victory and the continuation of Kentish independence.

Othona. The Roman name for the garrison at BRADWELL-ON-SEA, one of the Saxon Shore forts built in the 3rd century AD.

Otley 'Otta's clearing', OE male personal name + -LEY.
A town on the River Wharfe in West Yorkshire, 13 km (8 miles) north of Bradford. It was the birthplace of the furniture maker Thomas Chippendale (1718–79).

Otmoor 'Otta's marshy ground', OE male personal name *Otta* + *mor* 'marshy ground'.

An area of open fenny land about 11 km (7 miles) to the north of Oxford. It is rather a bleak place for southern England – legend has it that the Romans were put off because they did not like the feel of it (they built roads across it nevertheless). There is now an army firing range here. Several rare species of bird and plant thrive on the moor.

Otter 'stream frequented by otters', OE *oter* 'otter' + *ea* 'river' (see EA-).
A river in Somerset and Devon, which rises in the BLACKDOWN HILLS and flows 39 km (24 miles) southwestwards and then southwards through HONITON and OTTERY ST MARY into the English Channel at BUDLEIGH SALTERTON. It is a noted trout stream.

Otterburn 'otter stream', OE *oter* 'otter' + *burna* 'stream'.
A village in Redesdale, Northumberland, on the edge of the CHEVIOT Hills some 45 km (28 miles) northwest of Newcastle upon Tyne. North of the village is the vast **Otterburn Camp**, which services the army firing ranges that add so much to the amenities of this part of the Northumberland National Park.

Battle of Otterburn (15 August 1388). A battle in which a Scottish force under James, Earl of Douglas, defeated a superior English army under Henry Percy ('Harry Hotspur').

> It fell upon the Lammas tide,
> When the muir-men win their hay,
> The doughty Douglas bound him to ride
> Into England, to drive a prey.
>
> Anon.: 'The Battle of Otterbourne' (ballad)

Douglas was killed in the battle, an event that the balladeer has him anticipate:

> But I hae dream'd a dreary dream,
> Beyond the Isle of Skye;
> I saw a dead man win a fight,
> And I think that man was I.

When Douglas was mortally wounded, he ordered his followers to hide his body in a stand of bracken, and it was to this stand of bracken that Hotspur formally conceded the battle.

The battle is also called the **Hunting of the Cheviot** or **the Battle of Chevy Chase**. The latter provided the title for a 15th-century ballad, which recounts the long-standing rivalry between Douglas and Percy, and Percy's declaration that he would hunt for three days on the Scottish side of the border. This presumption is displeasing to Douglas:

> Show me, said he, whose men you be
> That hunt so boldly here
> That, without my consent do chase
> And kill my fallow deer?

Douglas goes on to swear that one of the two will die, and the ballad proceeds to give an account of the battle. (Ben

Jonson said that he would rather have written 'Chevy Chase' than all his poetry and plays, and in 1711 Joseph Addison devoted two essays to the ballad in *The Spectator*.)

Chevy Chase was the name of an old hunting ground, taking its name from a hill in the vicinity, a name that may relate to the CHEVIOT. The ballad inspired the name Chevy Chase for a suburb of Washington, D.C., and this in turn gave a stage name to the US comic actor Chevy Chase (b.1943), born Cornelius Crane Chase. Incidentally, 'chevy chase' was rhyming slang for 'face' from the mid-19th century to the 1950s.

Otter Rock. *See under* TORRAN ROCKS.

Ottery St Mary *Ottery* 'River Otter', OTTER + OE *ea* (*see* EA-); *St Mary* from the dedication of the local church.

A small town in Devon, on the River OTTER, about 17 km (11 miles) east of Exeter. It is remarkable chiefly for its church, St Mary the Virgin (from which it gets the second half of its name), which looks like a miniature cathedral. It was originally a dependency of Rouen Cathedral in Normandy, and in 1335 it was bought by Bishop Grandison of Exeter. He embarked on a considerable programme of improvement and enlargement, using his new cathedral at Exeter as a model.

On Bonfire Night the men of Ottery parade around the town with flaming barrels of tar on their shoulders, and on the same date devices called 'rock cannons' are filled with gunpowder and let off with satisfactorily loud bangs.

The poet Samuel Taylor Coleridge (1772–1834) was born in Ottery St Mary. Nearby Escot Grange was the 'Fairoaks' of Thackeray's *Pendennis* (1848–50), and he fictionalized the town itself as 'Clavering St Mary'.

See also UPOTTERY *and* VENN OTTERY.

Oughtershaw 'Uhtred's shieling', OE male personal name *Uhtred* + OScand *skali* 'shieling, shelter' later assimilated to ME *shaw* 'copse'.

A small settlement in the YORKSHIRE DALES, North Yorkshire. It is in the dale of **Oughtershaw Beck**, the headwater of the River WHARFE. The north slopes of the dale are known as **Oughtershaw Side**, while **Oughtershaw Moss** is on the less steep southern side.

Ould Sod, the. A sentimental reference to Ireland. The term may lead to the possibility of misunderstandings, as recorded by Dominic Cleary:

> When President Reagan came to Ireland, he was greeted with a beautifully ambiguous banner which read 'Welcome to the Ould Sod'.

Oul' Shabbey, the. A nickname for the original ABBEY THEATRE in Dublin.

Oulton Broad *Oulton* the name of a nearby village (now a suburb of Lowestoft), 'Ali's farmstead' or 'old farmstead', OScand male personal name *Ali* or OE *eald* 'old' + -TON.

The most southerly of the BROADS, it lies just to the west of Lowestoft. It is a popular yachting and powerboating centre. It is linked to the River WAVENEY[1] by **Oulton Dyke**.

The writer George Borrow, author of *Lavengro* (1851), *Romany Rye* (1857) and *Wild Wales* (1862), lived in the village of Oulton (1840–66).

Oulton Park *Oulton* probably '(place at) the old farm', OE *eald* 'old' + -TON.

A motor-racing circuit in Cheshire, about 19 km (12 miles) east of CHESTER.

Oundle '(settlement of the tribe called) Undalas', OE tribal name *Undalas*, perhaps meaning 'undivided' or 'those without a share' (from OE *dal* 'a share' or *dœlan* 'to divide, deal out').

A market town in Northamptonshire, in a loop of the River NENE, about 16 km (10 miles) east of Corby. In its centre it retains much of the atmosphere of an old country town, its 17th- and 18th-century buildings intersected by narrow lanes.

Oundle School, a co-educational public school, was founded in 1556 by a wealthy grocer, Sir William Laxton, who went on to become Lord Mayor of London.

Oundle was the birthplace of the musicologist Ebenezer Prout (1835–1909).

Ousden 'owl valley', OE *uf* 'owl' + *denu* 'valley'.

A village in Suffolk, about 10 km (6 miles) southeast of Newmarket.

Ouse[1]. *See* GREAT OUSE.

Ouse[2] OCelt or pre-Celtic river name meaning 'water'.

A river in Yorkshire, with a length of 87 km (54 miles). It is formed by the confluence near Boroughbridge of the rivers SWALE[1] and URE, then flows generally southeastwards through YORK to join the TRENT[1] east of Goole, thus forming the HUMBER. Its many tributaries include the AIRE, DERWENT[3], DON[2], NIDD and WHARFE.

> There must be dales in Paradise
> Where Wharfe and Aire and Swale
> Fulfil their several destinies
> And tell their various tale:
> Flinging themselves just when they choose
> Into the honest arms of Ouse!
>
> A.J. Brown: 'Dales in Paradise'

Ouse[3] Earlier *Midewinde* 'middle winding' (perhaps referring to the way the river cuts Sussex in half as it winds towards the sea), OE *midd* 'middle' + *winde* 'winding'; *Ouse*, first recorded in the early 17th century, may come from the Sussex place name *Lewes* (in the late 13th century the river is referred to as *aqua de Lewes* 'Lewes water'), or alternatively it could be descended from OE *wase* (ModE *ooze*) 'estuarine mud'.

A river in West and East Sussex, which rises in the WEALD, between Horsham and Cuckfield, and flows 48 km

(30 miles) east and south through LEWES into the English Channel at NEWHAVEN. (Its original mouth was at SEAFORD, but this was blocked by a great storm in the 1570s.)

The novelist Virginia Woolf (1882–1941) drowned herself in the Ouse near Rodmell (where she lived), about 5 km (3 miles) southeast of Lewes.

Outer Hebrides, the. *See the* HEBRIDES *and the* WESTERN ISLES.

Outer London. A collective term for the suburban parts of London, broadly corresponding with the areas that were added to the capital in 1965 to form GREATER LONDON. It contrasts explicitly with INNER LONDON.

Out Skerries *Out* OScand *ut* 'out, outer'; *Skerries* OScand *sker* 'skerry', i.e rocky island.
A group of small rocky islands 15 km (9 miles) off the east coast of Mainland, SHETLAND, and some 35 km (21 miles) northeast of Lerwick. There are three main islands: Housay (OScand *hus ey* 'house island'), Bruray (OScand *bruar ey* 'island of the bridge') and Grunay (OScand *grœnn ey* 'green island'). Housay and Bruray, which are linked by a bridge, are well-populated (a total of 85 in 1991), and there is an air strip and ferry links to LERWICK and Vidlin on Mainland. Bruray boasts the smallest secondary school in Britain. The islands have been a graveyard for many ships over the years, and it is said that after the wreck of the Dutch ship *Kennermerland* in 1664 the islanders were drunk for weeks on its cargo of spirits.

Out Stack. *See under* MUCKLE FLUGGA.

Oval, the From the 'Kennington *Oval*', on which it was built.
A cricket ground in KENNINGTON (SE11), in the South London borough of Lambeth. It has a spectator capacity of over 23,000. It was built in 1845 on an approximately oval area of open land called **Kennington Oval** belonging to the Duchy of Cornwall, which had previously been a market garden (the road which surrounds the ground preserves the name 'Kennington Oval'). Ever since then it has been the headquarters of Surrey County Cricket Club, which was founded in the same year. The first test match in England was staged here, in 1880 (between England and Australia – England won by five wickets). In the past it has been associated with various other activities, sporting and otherwise – most FA Cup finals between 1870 and 1892 were played here, during the Second World War it was a prisoner-of-war camp, and in 1971 it hosted its first pop concert – but nowadays the playing area is reserved largely for cricket. At 170 m (558 ft) by 150 m (492 ft) it has the largest area of any cricket ground and the gasholders on its northeastern side have become an Oval icon. Its name lends itself to puns and other word-play – as in the (no doubt apocryphal) newspaper placard 'ENGLAND BOWLER'S MAGNIFICENT OVAL FEAT'.

The ground's name (latterly expanded to 'Foster's Oval' thanks to a beer company's sponsorship, then to 'AMP Oval', name-checking a pensions sponsor, and in 2004 to 'Brit Oval') has been borrowed by other similarly shaped cricket grounds elsewhere in the world: the Adelaide Oval in Australia, for instance, and Kensington Oval in Bridgetown, Barbados.

Oval Underground station, on the Northern line, opened in 1890 (originally as 'The Oval'; it was renamed in 1894).

Over[1] '(place at the) ridge or slope', OE *ofer* 'ridge, slope'.
A village in Cambridgeshire, about 16 km (10 miles) northwest of Cambridge.

Over[2]. A hamlet in Cheshire, now a northwestern suburb of WINSFORD[1], about 13 km (8 miles) northwest of Crewe.

Over[3]. A village in South Gloucestershire (before 1996 in Avon, before 1974 in Gloucestershire), on the northwestern outskirts of Bristol.

Overton[1] 'higher farmstead' (probably indicating a location further upstream), OE *uferra* 'higher' + -TON.
A small town in Hampshire, on the River TEST, about 13 km (8 miles) west of Basingstoke. It was once a busy and prosperous town, with coaches passing through and a market and sheep fair, but today it slumbers peacefully.

Overton[2] 'bank farmstead', OE *ofer* 'bank, ridge' + -TON; the town is on a bend in the River Dee.
An attractive village in Wrexham unitary authority (formerly in Denbighshire, then in Clwyd), 9 km (5.5 miles) south of Wrexham itself. It is renowned as the home of one of the SEVEN WONDERS OF NORTH WALES, namely an ancient grove of yew trees round the church, which may be 3000 years old.

Over Wallop *Over* indicating its position upstream of MIDDLE WALLOP and NETHER WALLOP; *Wallop see* MIDDLE WALLOP.
A village in Hampshire, on the Wallop Brook (*see under* WALLOPS, THE), about 11 km (7 miles) southwest of Andover.

Ower '(place at the) bank or slope', OE *ora* 'bank, slope'.
A village in Hampshire, by Junction 2 on the M27, about 11 km (7 miles) northwest of Southampton.

Owermoigne Originally *Ogre*, probably 'wind-gap' (referring to gaps in the chalk hills that funnel winds off the sea), OCelt *ogrodrust-* + *moigne* denoting manorial ownership in the late Middle Ages by the Moigne family.
A village (pronounced 'ormoyn' or 'owermoyn') in Dorset, about 10 km (6 miles) southeast of Dorchester and 5 km (3 miles) from the sea.

Owlswick 'Wulf's farm', OE *Wulfes* possessive form of male personal name *Wulf* (later influenced by the OScand equivalent *Ulfr*) + *wic* (*see* WICK).

A village in Buckinghamshire, about 8 km (5 miles) southwest of Aylesbury.

Owmby Probably 'Authunn's farmstead or village', OScand male personal name *Authunn* + -BY; alternatively, the first element could be OScand *authn* 'uncultivated land, deserted farm'.

A village near the northern edge of Lincolnshire, about 8 km (5 miles) southeast of Brigg.

Owmby-by-Spital *Owmby* perhaps as OWMBY, or alternatively the first element may reflect the OScand male personal name *Aunn*; *Spital* from its proximity to SPITAL IN THE STREET.

A village in Lincolnshire, about 17 km (11 miles) north of Lincoln.

See also NORMANBY-BY-SPITAL.

Owslebury 'Osla's stronghold' or 'stronghold frequented by blackbirds', OE male personal name *Osla* or *osle* 'blackbird' + *byrig* dative form of *burh* (*see* BURY).

A village in Hampshire, about 8 km (5 miles) southeast of Winchester. Marwell Zoo is just to the south.

Oxborough 'fortified place farming oxen', OE *oxa* 'ox' + BURY.

A village in Norfolk, 11 km (7 miles) southwest of Swaffham and 11 km (7 miles) southeast of Downham Market. **Oxburgh House**, a moated manor house, has been lived in by the Bedingfeld family since 1481: their Catholic heritage means that the house comes complete with priest's hole, Catholic chapel and – more unusually – some embroidery by Mary Queen of Scots. It is administered by the National Trust.

Oxbridge A blend of *Oxford* and *Cambridge*.

A name invented (like its mirror image CAMFORD) to suggest an ancient university city. Both are first recorded in W.M. Thackeray's *Pendennis* (1848–50):

> Repeated differences with the university authorities caused Mr Foker to quit Oxbridge in an untimely manner.

But while *Camford* has rather faded out, *Oxbridge* went on to a successful career in the 20th century as a portmanteau term for the two universities, especially as opposed to the 'redbrick' universities, and as a vehicle for their joint connotations: educational excellence, educational privilege, training ground of the Establishment, etc.

> One characteristic that Whitehall does have in common with other *élite* groups is its overwhelmingly Oxbridge character.
>
> Samuel Brittan: *The Treasury under the Tories* (1964)

In the latter part of the 20th century '**Oxbridge reject**' became a term for a recognized category of academically challenged upper-middle-class student who had expected to get into Oxford or Cambridge on the basis of his or her background, but found it did not outweigh lack of intellectual qualifications. The species, often Sloaney in aspect, may be observed at other, almost-Oxbridge universities – Durham, for example, or Bristol.

Emergency – Ward 10, the first medical soap opera on British television, screened on ITV from 1957 to 1967, was set in the (fictitious) Oxbridge General Hospital.

Oxen Craig. *See under* BENNACHIE

Oxford 'ford used by oxen', OE *oxena* possessive plural form of *oxa* 'ox' + FORD.

A university city in OXFORDSHIRE and the administrative headquarters of the county, 90 km (56 miles) northwest of London. It is situated on the River Thames (called the ISIS in and around Oxford) and its tributary the CHERWELL. It grew up here in Anglo-Saxon times at the point (perhaps just to the south of Folly Bridge) where farmers drove their cattle from one water-meadow to another across a shallow part of the river (whence its name).

In 1002 Oxford was the scene of an early attempt at 'ethnic cleansing'. King Æthelred 'the Unready' ordered the slaughter of all Danish men in his kingdom on St Brice's Day, 13 November, on the grounds that they were plotting to kill him. In Oxford, the only place where the massacre is known to have been attempted, the Danish people fled for sanctuary to the monastery of St Frideswide's, and bolted themselves inside its church. Having failed in the attempt to break down the doors, the mob outside burned down the church with its occupants. The king made generous provision for the rebuilding and restocking of St Frideswide's.

After the Norman Conquest further religious foundations were established here, the seeds of the university were planted and by Henry III's reign Oxford was a walled city. It has since been caught up in the tide of history from time to time, as the external world has impinged on it – in Mary I's reign the Protestant martyrs Cranmer, Latimer and Ridley were tried and burned to death here (they are commemorated by the Martyrs' Memorial in ST GILES'); during the Civil Wars it was Charles I's headquarters for three years (the fall of the city to the Parliamentarians on 25 June 1645 marked the end of the first Civil War); and in 1665, during the Great Plague of London, the Court and Parliament removed themselves smartly to Oxford – but for the most part its identity has been fixed and its image shaped by the university that inhabits it and that constitutes much of the physical fabric of its centre (*see below*). This is the Oxford of the well-worn 'dreaming spires' (*see* CITY OF DREAMING SPIRES): ancient buildings of mellow golden stone, secluded ivy-clad courtyards and quadrangles, Gothic pinnacles, gowned dons, bicycling undergraduates, and so on. Add a dash of Inspector Morse (the cerebral Oxford-based detective invented by Colin Dexter, whose televised incarnation (1987–2000), set against picturesque Oxford backdrops, was a worldwide hit), and you have a neatly packaged heritage product that attracts very large numbers of tourists from around the world.

As with CAMBRIDGE[1], Oxford University's, and thus the city's, status as a channel through which so many of the country's cultural, political, and intellectual elite have traditionally passed has given it a pervasive, if not always overt, influence in national life. Fictional incarnations of the city and university are legion. Among the more famous literary versions of 'the Oxford experience' are Thomas Hardy's *Jude the Obscure* (with an Oxford metamorphosed into CHRISTMINSTER) (1895); Max Beerbohm's *Zuleika Dobson* (1911, subtitled *An Oxford Love Story*), in which the unattainability of the eponymous heroine, niece of the warden of the fictional Judas College, leads to a mass suicide of lovelorn undergraduates by drowning in the Isis; Dorothy L. Sayers's *Gaudy Night* (1935), a golden-age detective story set in the fictional Shrewsbury College during its gaudy (commemorative feast for former college members), featuring the aristocratic sleuth Lord Peter Wimsey; Evelyn Waugh's *Brideshead Revisited* (1945), set in Christ Church (*see below*), whose television adaptation (1981) made *faux* pre-war aristocratic effeteness fashionable (in Waugh's earlier novel *Decline and Fall* (1928), the hero Paul Pennyfeather is sent down from the fictional Scone College for 'indecent behaviour'); and Philip Larkin's *Jill* (1946), examining a northern working-class boy's wartime encounter with traditional Oxonian privilege. Gervase Fen, a donnish predecessor of Inspector Morse, created by the novelist Edmund Crispin, appears in such Oxford-based whodunnits as *The Case of the Gilded Fly* (1944) and *The Moving Toyshop* (1946). In addition to the Morse novels, recent literary evocations of Oxford appear in J.I.M. Stewart's Anthony Powell-esque novel quintet *A Staircase in Surrey* (1974–79; *see under* SURREY); in the Kate Ivory mysteries of Veronica Stallwood (including *Oxford Exit*, 1994); and in Philip Pullman's much-celebrated fantasy trilogy *His Dark Materials* (1995–2002) (*see* **Lyra's Oxford** *below*).

The 'dreaming spires' are not the whole picture, however. There is an industrial side to Oxford, too (disappointedly dubbed by John Betjeman 'Motopolis') – Britain's first mass-produced cars came from the car-plants of COWLEY, in southeastern Oxford, in the 1920s – and the city has a more worldly, cosmopolitan air than its academic twin city, Cambridge. And deprivation is in evidence in BLACKBIRD LEYS.

The diocese of Oxford is the fifth largest in England (5752 sq km / 2221 sq miles), but its cathedral (the 12th-century Christ Church Cathedral, which doubles as Christ Church's college chapel) is the smallest. The Bishop of Oxford signs himself 'Oxon'.

The English kings Richard I (1157–99) and John (1167?–1216) were born in Oxford, as were the composer Orlando Gibbons (1583–1625); the geneticist and philosopher J.B.S. Haldane (1892–1964); the physicist Stephen Hawking (b.1942); the detective-story writers Dorothy L. Sayers (1893–1957) and P.D. James (b.1920); and the tennis player Tim Henman (b.1974). The writer Rose Macaulay (1881–1958) and the actress Maggie Smith (b.1934) are alumnae of **Oxford High School for Girls**, the city's leading sub-university-level educational establishment. J.R.R. Tolkien wrote *The Lord of the Rings* (1954–5), mostly in the small hours of the morning, in his house in Northmoor Road, while he was Merton Professor of English Language and Literature in Oxford. He and a group of friends, including C.S. Lewis, writer of the Narnia books, met regularly at the Eagle and Child pub (familiarly known as 'The Bird and Baby') in ST GILES', and this has become a site of pilgrimage for Tolkien and Lewis enthusiasts.

There are towns called Oxford in the USA (Alabama, Idaho, Indiana, Iowa, Kansas, Maine, Maryland, Massachusetts, Michigan, Mississippi, Nebraska, New York, North Carolina, Ohio, Wisconsin), Canada (Nova Scotia) and New Zealand.

See also JERICHO, IFFLEY, OSNEY, OXON, SUMMERTOWN.

Airspeed Oxford. A twin-engined aircraft used by the RAF to train bomber crews during the Second World War. It first flew in 1937. In RAF slang it became known as the 'Oxbox'. The aviator Amy Johnson (1903–41) was piloting an Oxford when she met her death.

Chump at Oxford, A. A feature film (1940) starring Stan Laurel and Oliver Hardy, in which the comic pair are former road-sweepers now aspiring to be undergraduates. The title parodies the 1937 *A Yank at Oxford* (*see below*).

'Duns Scotus's Oxford'. A poem (1879) by Gerard Manley Hopkins, which is both a celebration of the town and a lament for the inroads made by encroaching industrial modernity:

> Towery city and branchy between towers;
> Cuckoo-echoing, bell-swarmèd,
>   lark-charmèd, rook-racked, river-rounded.

Great Tom of Oxford. A bell in the great gate of Christ Church, Oxford, tolled 101 times every night at 9.05 to signify the original number of scholars at the college. It weighs 7.5 tonnes and is celebrated in the old round:

> Great Tom is cast
> And Christ Church bells ring one
> Two, three, four, five, six
> And Tom comes last.

Lyra's Oxford. A tale (2003) by the Oxford-based children's novelist Philip Pullman, featuring the character of Lyra from the author's earlier award-winning Miltonic trilogy of novels, *His Dark Materials* (1995–2002). The Oxford of the title (depicted in a foldout map) is an alternative-reality version of the city, situated in one of the parallel worlds between which the action of Pullman's trilogy moves. *Northern Lights*, the first novel of the trilogy, opens in the hall of the fictional Jordan College. In the second novel, *The Subtle Knife*, a door between two of Pullman's parallel worlds is located in a hornbeam-lined avenue in North Oxford (in real life Sunderland Avenue, part of the Oxford ring road (A40), which links the top of the Woodstock and Banbury roads, *see below*).

Morris Oxford. A motor car, the first to be produced by Morris Motors. It was announced in 1912 by William Morris's company, WRM Motors Ltd of Oxford, as the 'Morris–Oxford light car'. It was one of the 'bullnose' Morrises. The name remained a favourite with the Morris company (long after it disappeared into the British Motor Corporation in 1952), and it was inherited by many later models until 1971. One of them was produced under licence in an Indian version called the 'Ambassador', which virtually monopolized the roads of the subcontinent in the second half of the 20th century.

North Oxford. A northern central section of Oxford, extending northwards from St Giles' towards SUMMERTOWN, and hugging the Woodstock and Banbury roads, the twin arteries by which traffic enters the town from the north. Its physical boundaries are imprecise, but its visual character is instantly recognizable: monumental and often gloomy-looking villas, tall and gabled, encircled by dark laurels, exhale the spirit of High Victorian Oxford. The offspring of William Butterfield's Keble College (at the southern end of North Oxford), one could almost imagine they were the **Oxford Movement** (*see below*) realized in brick. The area's development began around the Norham Gardens estate in the 1830s, and it has a serious claim to be the first 'planned' suburb in England. It was not until the 1870s, though, when the university's dons were for the first time permitted to marry, that its peculiar demography began to evolve – an extramural enclave of the university, almost, in which dons' wives (excluded from college life) entertained, distinguished or eccentric professors held court, and the airs of academia pervaded the lush shrubberies. After the Second World War many of the villas were split up into flats or turned over to institutional use (there is a plethora of language schools trading on Oxford's linguistic associations to teach EFL to foreign students).

Oxfam. A British humanitarian aid organization. It was founded in Oxford in 1942 as the **Oxford Committee for Famine Relief**, to raise funds for the feeding of hungry children in Greece. After the Second World War it concentrated on providing aid to refugees and in the 1960s broadened its scope to help improve agriculture and food production in Third World countries. More generally it provides emergency aid for areas stricken by natural disasters such as droughts, floods and earthquakes. In the light of its rising profile it shortened its name in the late 1950s to the more manageable 'Oxfam'. The first of its permanent shops, selling items donated by the public, opened in Oxford in 1948, and since then they have proliferated to such an extent that **Oxfam shop** has become almost a synonym for 'charity shop'.

Oxford. US Black slang of the 1940s for a particularly dark-skinned person. It was inspired by the brandname of a shoe polish.

Oxford accent. A term in use since the late 19th century to denote an 'educated' English accent, of the type employed by those who attended or had attended Oxford University. From the beginning it was two-edged: for some it stood for a standard to be aspired to; for others it evoked the strangulated effete drawl of the upper-middle-class intellectual (or booby):

> Surely it is permissible to suggest the Oxford Bleat by writing down the directions given me the other day as 'past a whaite house, between the water-tah and the pah station'.
>
> *The Spectator* (5 January 1934)

In the 21st century, when the prestige model has moved on, it seems something of a historical relic.

Oxford bags. Trousers with very wide legs, as typically worn by Oxford undergraduates in the 1920s and 1930s.

> Instead of the wasp-waisted suits with pagoda shoulders and tight trousers affected by the dandies, I wore jackets with broad lapels and broad pleated trousers. The latter got broader and broader. Eventually they were imitated elsewhere and were generally referred to as 'Oxford bags'.
>
> Harold Acton: *Memoirs of an Aesthete* (1948)

Oxford bath. An alternative name for a hip-bath.

Oxford blue. A dark blue colour, as adopted by Oxford University as its symbolic colour (e.g. on sports clothing).

Oxford Blues. A film (1984) in which a Los Angeles casino worker earns enough to finance an Oxford education. Essentially it is a sexed-up version of *A Yank at Oxford* (*see below*).

Oxford Blues, the. A nickname given in 1690 to the Royal Horse Guards, from the Earl of Oxford, their commander, and the blue uniform, which dates from 1661. The nickname was later shortened to 'the Blues' and was incorporated into the regiment's title as the Royal Horse Guards (The Blues). In 1969 the regiment amalgamated with the Royal Dragoons (1st Dragoons) to form the Blues and Royals (Royal Horse Guards and 1st Dragoons).

Oxford Brookes University. A university, created in 1992 from the former Oxford Polytechnic, based at the top of Headington Hill and with other campuses in South Hinksey and Wheatley. Its name commemorates J.H. Brookes, who became principal of the Schools of Technology, Art and Commerce (as the institution was then called) in 1934.

Oxford chair. A type of armchair, popular in the middle of the 19th century, the seat of which extends beyond its padded arms, to which it is attached by turned wooden supports.

Oxford chrome. A name formerly given to a type of yellow ochre used as a colouring material and an artists' pigment, which until the 1930s was extracted from the ground at SHOTOVER near Oxford (traditionally the bodies of Oxfordshire wagons were yellow).

Oxford clay. A deposit of stiff blue clay underlying the coral rag of the Middle Oolite in the Midlands, especially Oxfordshire.

Oxford cloth. A name, now used particularly in the USA, for a type of heavy cotton fabric in which two yarns are woven as one in the warp (also for a similar fabric made partly or wholly from artificial fibre). It is used especially for shirts (*see* **Oxford shirting**, *below*).

Oxford comma. A comma before the *and* or *or* in a listing, as in 'bread, butter, cakes, and jam', so called as the house style of Oxford University Press. It is also the standard North American style, but, in spite of (or perhaps because of) its lesser scope for ambiguity, it is mostly not favoured by the British, who would normally write 'bread, butter, cakes and jam'.

Oxford corners. A term used in printing to denote border lines enclosing printed text that intersect and go beyond each other at the corners, like an **Oxford frame** (*see below*).

Oxford Down. A breed of sheep produced by crossing Cotswold and Hampshire Down sheep, developed by Samuel Druce at Eynsham in Oxfordshire about 1830.

Oxford Elegy, An. A setting (1947–49) by Ralph Vaughan Williams for speaker, choir and orchestra of lines from Matthew Arnold's *The Scholar Gypsy* and *Thyrsis*.

Oxford English. Originally, from the early 20th century, a term virtually synonymous with **Oxford accent** (*see above*):

> In the spoken word the traditional currency was, till recently, Oxford English.
>
> *ITV Evidence to the Annan Committee* (1975)

More recently the term has come to be used by Oxford University Press as a virtual trade name for books and other materials designed to help people learning English as a foreign language.

Oxford English Dictionary. A large, unabridged historical dictionary of the English language (usually abbreviated to *OED*), published by Oxford University Press. Planned in the 1850s, it was compiled over a period of 70 years (over half of them under the editorship of James Murray) and published part by part between 1884 and 1928 (originally under the title *A New English Dictionary on Historical Principles*). A second edition was published in 1989, in 20 volumes, and a third (with online access) is being compiled. It now contains about half a million entries. It has been the progenitor of a whole family of smaller dictionaries, notably the two-volume *Shorter Oxford English Dictionary* and the one-volume *Concise Oxford Dictionary*.

Oxford frame. A picture frame, the sides of which cross each other at the corners forming a cross-like projection. It was once much used for photographs of college groups.

Oxford grey. *See* **Oxford mixture** *below.*

Oxford Group. The original name (first adopted in South Africa and in use until the late 1930s) for the followers of the US evangelist Frank Buchman. It reflected the significant support his movement received at Oxford University in the 1920s and 1930s. The movement was relaunched as Moral Rearmament in 1938. It was evangelical in character and also became concerned with many social, industrial and international questions.

Oxford hollow. A bookbinders' term for a flattened paper tube inserted between the spine of a book and its cover, to strengthen the spine and allow the book to be opened flat more easily.

Oxfordian. Of or relating to Oxford or Oxford University; but more specifically, as a geological term (as which it was originally coined in French, in 1830, as *oxfordien*), being a division of the Upper Jurassic in Britain (containing, inter alia, **Oxford clay**) that lies just below the Kimmeridgian.

Oxfordianism. The literary conceit that the works of William Shakespeare were in fact written by Edward de Vere, 17th Earl of Oxford (1550–1604). The theory was propounded in 1920 by J. Thomas Looney, a schoolmaster, on the basis of four main points: (1) that the few facts known about Shakespeare's life give little indication of poetic or literary activity (despite the fact that to Ben Jonson he was the 'Sweet Swan of Avon' – *see under* AVON[1]); (2) that the many details of Oxford's life show him to have been a poet, a playwright and a patron of writers and actors; (3) that the works themselves are full of references to exclusively aristocratic pastimes and sports, with 36 of the 37 plays set in courtly or wealthy society; (4) that the noble sentiments expressed in the works could only have proceeded from a nobleman's heart. The popularity of Oxfordianism lies in its romantic and nostalgic appeal especially to a war-disoriented generation, who yearned for a return to the class-based hedonism of the Edwardian era.

Oxfordism. An archaic term for the principles and practices of the **Oxford Movement** (*see below*).

Oxford John. A dish of olden times the main ingredient of which was mutton.

Oxford marmalade. A type of thick-cut marmalade originally made in the 1870s at 84 High Street, Oxford. The name, registered as a trademark in 1908 and 1931 by the manufacturers, Frank Cooper, is redolent of the archetypal genteel English breakfast.

Oxford mixture. A type of dark grey woollen cloth, also known as **Oxford grey**. The term dates from the early 19th century.

> The servile squad rises up and marches away to its basement, whence, should it appear to be a gala day, those tall gentlemen at present attired in Oxford mixture, will issue forth with flour plastered on their heads, yellow coats, pink breeches, sky-blue waistcoats, silver lace, buckles in their shoes, black silk bags on their backs, and I don't know what insane emblems of servility and absurd bedizenments of folly.
>
> W.M. Thackeray: *The Newcomes* (1855)

Oxford Movement. A High Church revival movement in the Church of England 'started and guided' by Oxford clerics, especially John Keble (1792–1866), John Henry Newman (1801–90), Richard Hurrell Froude (1803–36) and Edward Bouverie Pusey (1800–82), after whom the movement is sometimes known as Puseyism. They were dissatisfied with the decline of church standards and with the rise of liberal theology, and they feared that the Catholic Emancipation Act of 1829 endangered the English Church. The movement began in 1833 with Keble's sermon against the suppression of ten Irish bishoprics. It was published under the title *National Apostasy*. Three tracts setting forth their views were published in 1833, and many *Tracts for the Times* followed, hence the movement's other alternative name, Tractarianism. They stressed the historical continuity of the Church of England, and the importance of the priesthood and the sacraments. The hostility of both mainstream Protestants and the Evangelical churches was aroused, especially after Newman's reception into the Roman Catholic Church in 1845, but in spite of much official opposition the movement had a lasting influence on the standards and ceremonial of the church.

Oxford Parliament. Either of two parliaments held in Oxford. The first, of 1258, promulgated the **Provisions of Oxford** (*see below*). The second was summoned by Charles II in April 1681 for the purpose, successfully accomplished, of outmanoeuvring his Whig opponents and securing the succession of his brother James, Duke of York.

Oxford ragwort. A plant (*Senecio squalidus*) of the Compositae family, with heads of bright yellow flowers. It is an escapee from the Oxford Botanic Garden, to which it was brought from southern Italy. Some seeds apparently found their way to Oxford station, and from there it proliferated in the 20th century all over the railway system of England and Wales. It also thrived in Second World War bomb sites.

Oxford sausage. A type of fresh, uncooked British sausage. The traditional recipe stipulates pork, veal and beef suet along with sage, nutmeg, pepper and sometimes other herbs.

Oxford Sausage, The. An anthology (1764) of Oxford University verse, compiled by Thomas Warton (1728–90), who at that time was professor of poetry at the university. He later became Poet Laureate.

Oxford scholar. Rhyming slang for 'dollar' – that is, the sum of 5 shillings (25 pence) (it dates from the late 19th century, when the exchange rate was 4 US dollars to the pound sterling). So, **half an Oxford** or a **half-Oxford** was 'half-a-crown' (2/6 or 12.5 pence). An alternative rhyming use for 'Oxford scholar' was for 'collar'; it is of the same period, when most shirt-collars were detachable.

Oxford School. The (people belonging to the) school of thought within the Church of England that favoured the **Oxford Movement** (*see above*).

Oxford shirt. A shirt made from Oxford shirting.

Oxford shirting. Oxford cloth (*see above*) used for making shirts.

Oxford shoe. A style of shoe that is laced over the instep. Often abbreviated to simply 'Oxford':

> He rocked on his hand-lasted Oxfords.
>
> Len Deighton: *The Ipcress File* (1962)

Oxford Symphony, The. A symphony by Josef Haydn, number 92 in the standard edition of his symphonies. It was composed in 1788 and performed in 1791 when the composer was in Oxford to receive the honorary degree of doctor of music.

Oxford Tracts. A name given to the *Tracts for the Times* published 1833–41 (*see* **Oxford Movement** *above*).

Oxford Union. An Oxford University debating society founded in 1825. Its well-appointed Gothic chambers, with murals by Dante Gabriel Rossetti and William Morris, are in St Michael's Street. It has traditionally attracted undergraduates anxious to hone their debating and greasy-pole-climbing techniques for a future career in politics (five British prime ministers have been president of the Union – William Gladstone, Lord Salisbury, H.H. Asquith, Harold Macmillan and Edward Heath), but the more recent appearance of such guest speakers as the late comedian Frankie Howerd and the pop superstar Michael Jackson (the singer Madonna was invited, but she refused) suggest that its members may now have other preoccupations. Its most high-profile debate was held in 1933, when the motion 'that this House will in no circumstances fight for its King and Country' was carried by 275 votes to 153, to nationwide consternation.

Oxford unit. A unit of penicillin originally adopted at the Sir William Dunn School of Pathology in Oxford University in the early 1940s, being the amount that, when dissolved in 1cc of water, gives the same inhibition as a certain partly purified standard solution.

Oxford University. Along with Cambridge University (*see under* CAMBRIDGE[1]) one of the two ancient universities of England (*see also* CAMFORD *and* OXBRIDGE); it traces its origins back to the early 12th century. At that time Oxford was a royal residence, and it appears that the presence of the 'Scholar King', Henry I, attracted students to the town. Their numbers were swelled by English students who had been expelled from the Sorbonne in Paris in 1167, and the university was well-established by the beginning of the 13th century. There were seven non-monastic colleges by the end of the 14th century, all essentially ecclesiastical institutions with a curriculum heavily weighted towards theology. The university's reputation grew and, despite the religious upheavals that impinged on it in the 16th century, it was becoming the place to which the rich sent their sons to turn them into gentlemen. After a lengthy period in the doldrums in the late 17th and 18th centuries, the university had its socks pulled up by the Victorians in the 19th, and it reclaimed its place as one of the world's leading academic institutions. Female students were first admitted in 1878, although they were not allowed to matriculate and take degrees until 1920.

The principal colleges in chronological order of their foundation are:

St Edmund Hall 1190s (not officially a college until 1957; nicknamed 'Teddy Hall')
University 1249 (nicknamed 'Univ')
Balliol 1263
Merton 1264
Worcester 1283 (as Gloucester College)
Exeter 1314
Oriel 1326
The Queen's College 1340
New College 1379
Lincoln 1427
All Souls 1438
Magdalen 1458
Brasenose 1509 (nicknamed 'BNC')
Corpus Christi 1517 (its alumni are referred to informally as 'Corpuscles')
Christ Church 1546 (referred to by its alumni as 'the House')
Trinity 1555
St John's 1555
Jesus 1571
Wadham 1612
Pembroke 1624
Keble 1868
Hertford 1874
Lady Margaret Hall 1878 ('LMH')
Somerville 1879

Mansfield 1886
St Hugh's 1886
St Hilda's 1893 (the only remaining all-female college; its members are nicknamed 'Hildabeests')
Ruskin 1899
Nuffield 1937
St Peter's 1947 (nicknamed 'Pot Hall')
St Anthony's 1950
St Anne's 1952
Regent's Park 1957
Linacre 1962
St Catherine's 1962
St Cross 1965
Wolfson 1966
Green 1979
Manchester 1990
Kellogg 1994

The university's buildings, which virtually define Oxford's visual aspect, range from the medieval 'cottages' of Worcester's quad, through the High Gothic of Magdalen, the sumptuous Baroque of Queen's and the elegant Classicism of Christopher Wren's Sheldonian Theatre, to the Victorian Gothic of William Butterfield's Keble. Most of it is in the mellow golden Cotswold stone that gives the city its tone, relieved here and there (particularly as one approaches **North Oxford**, *see above*) by Victorian polychrome brick.

The university's Bodleian Library is the largest in the UK after the British Library in London (it has over 5 million books), and its Ashmolean Museum, which dates back to 1683 and is named after the 17th-century antiquary Elias Ashmole, is the UK's oldest public museum.

While never exactly a sybaritic retreat, Oxford does not share Cambridge's reputation for intellectual asceticism. The arts have always held a higher position there vis-à-vis the sciences than at its sister institution, and its greater connectedness with the world outside its walls has ensured that those who pass through its system into the Establishment are not only cultivated but also seldom lacking in self-assurance:

One can tell an Oxford man ... almost at a glance. He is full of opinions and of the ability to defend them. He sets his mind at yours with a conscious briskness which seems to foreknow victory. He uses his culture like a weapon always drawn – with a flourish wonderfully easy and graceful ... His trim dress and carefully poised voice, his brisk movements and the precise elaboration of his speech, all seem deliberately and yet easily accomplished, all part of his armoury, weapons fit for his confident attack upon the universe. Not even the world-old traditions, the crumbling towers and quiet quadrangles of his own city, have succeeded in luring him into the past.

Not even the study of Literae Humaniores has seduced him into abstraction; not even the rich seclusion of the Thames Valley has availed to enervate him: he has pressed all into the service of his own ambition.

Charles Tennyson: *Cambridge from Within* (1913)

There are those who detect today an element of complacency within the university, an inclination to think itself the best in the world while the rest of the world gallops past. And not everyone has been impressed in the past either:

To the university of Oxford I acknowledge no obligation; and she will as cheerfully renounce me for a son, as I am willing to disclaim her for a mother. I spent fourteen months at Magdalen College; they proved the fourteen months the most idle and unprofitable of my whole life.

Edward Gibbon: *Memoirs of my Life* (1796)

You will hear more good things on the outside of a stagecoach from London to Oxford than if you were to pass a twelvemonth with the undergraduates, or heads of colleges, of that famous university.

William Hazlitt: *Table Talk* (1821)

Today Papa has gone to Oxford to see how Bertie [the future Edward VII] is getting on in that old monkish place which I have a horror of.

Queen Victoria: (remark, 31 October 1859)

The clever men at Oxford
Know all that there is to be knowed.
But they none of them know one half as much
As intelligent Mr Toad!

Kenneth Grahame: *The Wind in the Willows* (1908)

Yet there can be no doubt that its reputation ensures it the pick of the brightest students from Britain and around the world (over 16,000 from 130 different countries at the start of the 21st century) – a far cry indeed from the flaneurs and deadheads portrayed in fictions such as Cuthbert Bede's *The Adventures of Mr Verdant Green* (1853–7), Max Beerbohm's *Zuleika Dobson* (1911), the archetypal Oxford novel, or Evelyn Waugh's *Brideshead Revisited* (1945).

Oxford University Press. A commercial publishing house that is officially a department of Oxford University, controlled by a body of senior scholars known as the Board of Delegates. **OUP** (as it tends to be known within the publishing industry) can trace its origins back to the early 17th century (or even, with slightly greater latitude, to the late 15th century), but its expansion into a large-scale business did not begin until the latter part of the 19th century. Publication of the *Oxford English Dictionary* (*see above*) provided it with the springboard from which it maintained a stranglehold over the British dictionary market for many decades, and the success of its English Language Teaching publishing

helps it to continue to publish academic books that might otherwise never see the light of day.

Once the Oxford University Press claimed to be the custodian of the English Language. Its 1995 American edition of the New Testament omitted 'darkness' (as a synonym for evil or ignorance) to avoid offending blacks; 'The right hand of God', to appease left-handers; and was reluctant to mention 'The Lord', an editor explaining that '"Lord God" doesn't cut it these days because we don't have Lords'.

Peter Vansittart: *In Memory of England* (1998)

Oxford weed. A name given to the ivy-leaved toadflax (*Cymbalaria muralis*), because, according to Geoffrey Grigson in *An Englishman's Flora* (1958), it favours the old walls of Oxford colleges.

Provisions of Oxford. A set of measures introduced to limit the power of Henry III by the parliament that met at Oxford in 1258. (This parliament has come to be known as the 'Mad Parliament', but the name seems to have arisen not as a comment on its composition or decisions but through error, probably a substitution of *insane* for *insigne* ('famous') in a contemporary description.) The king's freedom of action was to be constrained by an advisory council of 15 barons, which would reform the machinery of government in England. Only three years later, however, the Pope absolved Henry from his promise to adhere to the Provisions, and this led to the Barons' War.

Siege of Oxford. A siege instituted against Oxford in the Civil Wars by Parliamentary forces under Sir Thomas Fairfax in May 1646. The city surrendered after a month.

University of Oxford. *See* **Oxford University** *above*.

Yank at Oxford, A. A film (1937), directed by Michael Balcon, about a cocky young American who comes to Oxford University and finds himself a fish out of water. It stars Robert Taylor and Vivien Leigh. Three years later it was parodied by Laurel and Hardy in *A Chump at Oxford* (*see above*).

Oxford Circus *Oxford* from OXFORD STREET, on which it is situated (it was originally called *Regent Circus*); *circus* 'open space, usually circular'.

An open space and traffic crossing at the junction of OXFORD STREET and REGENT STREET in the WEST END[1] of London (W1). The identical buildings at its four corners, which give it its particular character, were put up in the 1920s. Its central position, on what is effectively the UK's biggest High Street shopping area, means that it is often clogged with pedestrians.

Oxford Circus Underground station, on the Bakerloo, Central and Victoria lines, opened in 1900. Such is the volume of human traffic attempting to use it that at weekday rush-hours its entrances are regularly closed to would-be travellers.

Oxfordshire From OXFORD + SHIRE. The name is first recorded in the 11th century.

A county in the southern Midlands of England. It is bounded to the north by Northamptonshire and Warwickshire, to the west by Gloucestershire and Swindon, to the south by Berkshire, Reading and Wiltshire and to the east by Buckinghamshire. A large portion of northwestern Berkshire was added to it in 1974. Its county town is OXFORD, and other important centres include ABINGDON, BANBURY, BICESTER, DIDCOT, HENLEY-ON-THAMES and THAME[2].

In the southeastern part of the county are the CHILTERN HILLS, in the northwest the northeastern tip of the COTS-WOLDS. Between these two ranges of hills runs the broad THAMES VALLEY, mainly agricultural land, with the VALE OF THE WHITE HORSE to its south. Other significant rivers in the county, besides the Thames, are the CHERWELL, the EVENLODE[1] and the WINDRUSH.

Geographically and culturally, the county sits somewhat schizophrenically on a cusp: it combines MIDLANDS (Banbury), the HOME COUNTIES (Henley certainly is), and the beginnings of the WEST COUNTRY (BURFORD and the WIND-RUSH Valley). This uncertainty of identity has historical roots in the Saxon era, when control of the area yoyo-ed between WESSEX and MERCIA. Wessex held the region in the early 7th century, then lost it, then regained it after the Battle of Burford (752), then lost it again following the Battle of BENSON (777), then finally recaptured it in 825 when King Egbert of Wessex defeated Beornwulf of Mercia at the Battle of Ellendun (*see under* WROUGHTON).

Roman-era Oxfordshire was part of the territory of the British tribe known as the Dobunni (*see under* GLOUCESTER-SHIRE).

In cricketing terms Oxfordshire is a 'minor county' (the club was founded in 1921) and plays in the minor counties championship.

Oxford Street Probably from a combination of its being the road by which one travelled from London to Oxford (so referred to in the 1680s) and the (coincidental) ownership of land to the north of the street by the earl of Oxford (*see also* STREET).

A street in the WEST END[1] of London (W1), in the City of Westminster, running east to west between St Giles Circus (*see under* ST GILES) and MARBLE ARCH.

Its route was an important exit from London to the West in Anglo-Saxon times, and from the Middle Ages until the late 18th century it was the road along which condemned felons were taken on the last part of their journey from NEWGATE to the gallows at TYBURN[2]. Land to the north of the street was acquired in 1713 by the 2nd Earl of Oxford, and building development started. Oxford Street became a residential street, with a fair sprinkling of theatres and other places of entertainment. Then, in the 19th century, it began to turn into a shopping street. Large department stores began to arrive: the now defunct Dickens & Jones led the way in 1833, followed in the 20th century most notably by Selfridge's in 1909 and Marks & Spencer (at Marble Arch) in 1930. In 1921 Sir Edward Elgar opened the HMV record shop, at the time the largest in the world. By the end of the 20th century it had become *the* London shopping destination, for Britons and foreign tourists alike: perhaps a little tacky in places (especially so towards its junction with TOTTENHAM COURT ROAD), but always swarmingly busy and with something of an air of festivity – be it from the dodgy watch sellers and purveyors of the three-card trick, always on the look-out for the police, or the Christmas lights (an annual attraction since 1959, with an interlude in the late 1960s), or the bagpiper outside Selfridge's, or the saffron-robed Krishna devotees chanting their way through the crowds, or Stanley Green (1915–94), who regularly carried a placard up and down the street for 25 years denouncing the evils of meat-eating (his message: 'Less passion from less protein'). The road weighs in at a hefty £300 on the Monopoly board.

New Oxford Street, an extension of Oxford Street to the east, was laid out in the late 1840s, to link Oxford Street with HOLBORN.

Ox Mountains. An alternative name for the SLIEVE GAMPH range of hills in County Sligo.

Oxon An abbreviation of *Oxonia*, a Latinized form of *Oxford*, and of *Oxoniensis* 'of Oxford'.

A term with various Oxfordian functions: it is the standard shortened form used in writing in place of OXFORDSHIRE; it designates degrees of Oxford University, and their holders; and the Bishop of Oxford uses it to sign his name.

Oxonian. A native or inhabitant of Oxford, or a member of Oxford University.

> I'm privileged to be very impertinent, being an Oxonian.
>
> George Farquhar: *Sir Harry Wildair* (1701)

Oxshott 'Ocga's projecting piece of land', OE male personal name *Ocga* + *sceat* 'projecting piece of land'.

A commuter village in Surrey, on the southwestern borders of Greater London, about 3 km (2 miles) south of Esher.

Oxted 'place where oak-trees grow', OE *ac* 'oak' + *stede* 'place'.

A large and affluent commuter village in Surrey, about 13 km (8 miles) east of REDHILL. In among the mock Tudor development dating from the 1920s and 1930s are a 13th-century parish church and some old houses of note.

Oxwich 'ox farm', OE *oxa* 'ox' + *wic* 'specialized farm' in producing (in this case) oxen (*see* WICK).

A village on the south coast of the GOWER PENINSULA in Swansea unitary authority (formerly in Glamorgan, then

West Glamorgan), 12 km (7 miles) west of Mumbles. It overlooks the sandy **Oxwich Bay** (at the east end of which is
Three Cliffs Bay, so named for obvious reasons) and the
freshwater and salt marshes of the Oxwich nature reserve.
The western enclosing arm of the bay ends at **Oxwich Point**.

Oykel Possibly from OCelt *uchel* 'high', a reference to its source.
A notable salmon river in northern Highland (formerly
Sutherland), whose ultimate source is the Dubh Loch Mòr
('big black loch') high on the steep southern slopes of Ben
More Assynt (*see under* ASSYNT). From here, after dropping
over a waterfall, it flows southeastwards into **Glen Oykel**
to **Oykel Bridge**, then through **Strath Oykel** to Bonar Bridge,
where it enters the Dornoch Firth (*see under* DORNOCH)

Oystermouth From the original Welsh name *Ystumllwynarth*,
from *ystum* 'a bend' + *llwyn* 'a grove' + *garth* 'a hill', and presumably meaning 'hill copse on a bend'; it was corrupted by
the Normans to *Osterlaf*.

The name of the original settlement at MUMBLES, in Swansea
unitary authority. The remains of the Norman **Oystermouth
Castle** still stand above the town.

Ozleworth 'enclosure frequented by blackbirds' or 'Osla's
enclosure', OE *osle* 'blackbird' or male personal name *Osla*
+ *worth* (*see* -WORTH, WORTHY, -WARDINE).
A village in Gloucestershire, in the Cotswolds, about 8 km
(5 miles) southwest of Nailsworth.

> This is smart Cotswolds. Cedars glide across terraced
> lawns. Pheasants strut past horse-boxes and look
> disdainfully at King Charles spaniels. Ozleworth,
> hidden away in its secluded valley above Wotton-under-
> Edge, is beautiful. It is one of the corners of England
> whose occupants have used their wealth to grant
> themselves a respite from ugliness, despite a microwave
> tower just over the horizon.
>
> Simon Jenkins: *England's Thousand Best Churches* (1999)

P

Pabbay[1] 'hermit's island', OScand *papi* 'priest, hermit', genitive *papa* + *ey* 'island' (*see* -AY). The modern Gaelic name is *Pabaigh*. A small uninhabited island near the southern tip of the Outer HEBRIDES, Western Isles (formerly in Inverness-shire), 10 km (6 miles) south of Barra. It is separated from the island of Sanday to the north by the **Sound of Pabbay**. In the early Middle Ages a Christian hermit lived here, hence the island's name. On 1 May 1897 most of the men of the island drowned in a storm while fishing, and the last inhabitants left in 1911.

Pabbay[2]. A small uninhabited island in the Sound of HARRIS, Western Isles (formerly in Inverness-shire), 8 km (5 miles) west of South Harris. It was an important Mac-Leod stronghold until the 16th century, and most of the population were cleared to make way for sheep in 1846.

Padarn Lake. *See* LLYN PADARN.

Paddington 'farmstead or estate associated with Padda', OE male personal name *Padda* + -ING + -TON.
A district of western Central London (W2, W9, W10), in the City of WESTMINSTER, to the southwest of Marylebone. Its original nucleus was **Paddington Green**, now an area of stunted grass to the north of the WESTWAY best known for its high-security police station and for **Pretty Polly Perkins of Paddington Green**, a maidservant who was courted by the milkman in the traditional ballad but ended up marrying the 'bandy-legged conductor of a twopenny bus':

> She was beautiful as a butterfly and as proud as a queen,
> Was pretty little Polly Perkins of Paddington Green.

(In the 21st century a latterday and transexual Pretty Polly Perkins was the high point in a BBC television fly-on-the-wall documentary series entitled *Paddington Green*.) Paddington Green was the location of the last thatched house in Central London, demolished in the 1890s.

Paddington remained a country village until the 19th century, but then it expanded rapidly and became absorbed into London. The catalyst for this was **Paddington Station**, the London terminus of the Great Western Railway. The original station opened in 1838, but the present, much grander structure, designed by Isambard Kingdom Brunel, opened on a nearby site in 1854. It is now the main London terminus for rail services to the West and to Wales, and since 1998 a dedicated non-stop service to Heathrow Airport has also run from there. Paddington Underground station, on the Bakerloo, Circle, and Hammersmith & City lines, opened in 1863 (the original station was named Paddington (Bishop's Road) until 1933; the Circle line station was Paddington (Praed Street) until 1948).

The area has some elegant streets, but a certain seediness takes over as one approaches the station (*see also* PRAED STREET). Much of the Victorian housing quickly descended into slums, and exploitable post-Second World War Commonwealth settlers provided easy meat for rapacious landlords such as Peter Rachman in the late 1950s. Paddington became a byword for overcrowding, poverty and vice (not for nothing were eyebrows raised when it was a Paddington off-licence that the Conservative chancellor of the exchequer Norman Lamont allegedly visited in unexplained circumstances in 1992, to buy wine and cigarettes). The area was sliced in half in the late 1960s by the building of the Marylebone Flyover and the raised section of the A40(M). At the beginning of the 21st century a massive new steel-and-glass office development sprang up to the northwest of the station, West London's answer to CANARY WHARF. Called **Paddington Basin**, it takes its name from the local canal basin, which had to be drained while it was being built. This terminates the **Paddington Arm**, a major stretch of canal branching off the GRAND UNION CANAL at Hayes (Bull's Bridge Junction) (*see also* LITTLE VENICE).

A wholesome antidote to Paddington's somewhat seedy image is its contribution to children's literature: **Paddington Bear**. Created by Michael Bond in the late 1950s (the first story was *A Bear Called Paddington* (1958)), he was discovered at Paddington Station by Mr and Mrs Brown, having been sent from Peru as a parcel. To him was tied a label saying 'Please look after this bear.' He wears a sou'wester, wellington boots and a duffel coat, and his favourite food is marmalade. A Paddington Bear concession stall now graces the station concourse. In 1999 the original Paddington story was published in a Latin version by Michael Needham under the title *Ursus nomine Paddington*. When prime minister Tony Blair purchased a £3.6 million house not far from Paddington in autumn 2004 (at 29 Connaught Square), he was predictably dubbed 'Paddington Blair' in some sections of the media.

The singer Elvis Costello (real name Declan McManus; b.1954) was born in Paddington, as was Alan Turing (1912–54), the father of computing.

Near mournful, ever weeping Paddington.

William Blake: *Jerusalem* (1815)

Paddington is also the name of a hilly inner suburb of Sydney, Australia, known colloquially as 'Paddo'. It is now a highly gentrified area of Victorian villas.

dance/do the Paddington frisk. A macabre 17th- to 19th-century slang expression meaning 'to be hanged'. The allusion is to the location of TYBURN[2], London's main gallows until the late 18th century, within the boundaries of Paddington. (A 'frisk' in this context is a caper or jig.)

4.50 from Paddington. A detective novel (1957; in USA as *What Mrs McGillicuddy Saw*, 1957; as *Murder She Said*, 1961) by Agatha Christie, featuring her spinster sleuth Jane Marple. From the 4.50 train from London's Paddington Station, Elspeth sees a man strangling a woman in a compartment in another train that is running alongside hers. Then the other train draws away. A disappointing film version, *Murder She Said* (1961), directed by George Pollock, was not even saved by a gallantly British Margaret Rutherford as Miss Marple.

Paddington Fair day. Gallows-humour between the late 17th and early 19th centuries for 'execution day' (for the reason, *see* 'dance/do the Paddington frisk' above). There was a genuine Paddington Fair, which made the pun grimmer.

'Paddington' Pollacky. The nickname of Ignatius Pollacky, a celebrated late 19th-century private detective with an office on Paddington Green, whose exploits, and surname, earned him temporary entry into the English language in the euphemistic exclamation 'O Pollaky!', meaning 'Nonsense! Rubbish!' W.S. Gilbert also found room for him in a lyric, 'the keen penetration of Paddington Pollaky' (*Patience*, 1881).

Paddington spectacles. A late 18th-century slang term for the hood that was pulled over a condemned felon's head before hanging.

Paddock Wood *Paddock* 'small enclosure', OE *pearroc*.
A town in Kent, about 6 km (4 miles) northeast of Tunbridge Wells. It evolved in the 19th century around the local railway junction, where the line from Reigate to Ashford is joined by the line from Maidstone, and took its name from an area of woodland in the vicinity.

Paddy's Milestone. A nickname for AILSA CRAIG.

Paddy's Wigwam. The nickname of the Roman Catholic Metropolitan Cathedral of Christ the King in LIVERPOOL.

Padstow 'St Petroc's holy place' (referring to the dedication of the local church to the 6th century St Petroc, Cornwall's most famous saint), *Petroc* + OE *stow* '(holy) place'; the *a* in the name probably arose by association with St Patrick.
A coastal town and fishing port in Cornwall, on the south side of the estuary of the River CAMEL, about 15 km (10 miles) northeast of Newquay. It faces **Padstow Bay**. The picturesqueness of its old narrow streets, which wind their way down to the harbour, attracts the tourists, and their numbers have been swelled in the latter part of the 20th century by foodies lured by the reputation of the television chef Rick Stein's Seafood Restaurant.

Every May Day, Padstow resounds to the 'Obby 'Oss parade (first recorded in the 19th century, but no doubt of earlier origin), in which an outlandishly costumed hobby horse dances through the streets, preceded by men clad in white called 'teazers' and accompanied by an enthusiastic retinue, in a dim and degraded version of ancient rites of death and rebirth.

Another, and to modern politically correct sensibilities less amiable, Padstow tradition is Darkie Day, in which fishermen and their wives black up their faces and sing slave songs on Boxing Day and New Year's Day. The custom is said to date from an incident in the 17th century when a slave ship sheltered in the port and its human cargo escaped to (implausibly) chant and caper on the quayside.

Padstow Lifeboat, The. A march (Opus 94) composed in 1967 by Malcolm Arnold to mark the inauguration of the new Padstow lifeboat. It features a very effective ostinato off-key imitation of a foghorn.

Paignton Probably 'estate associated with Pæga', OE male personal name *Pæga* + -ING + -TON. The present-day spelling, with its unjustified *g*, was introduced in the 19th century by the local railway company, probably under the influence of the nearby TEIGNMOUTH.
A town and seaside resort (pronounced 'payntən') within the unitary authority of TORBAY, to the south of Torquay. Once a fishing village, its small harbour now shelters pleasure craft. It has a sizable and well-reputed zoo. It is the northern terminus of the **Paignton and Dartmouth Steam Railway**, run on a disused section of the old Great

Western line. Gilbert and Sullivan's *Pirates of Penzance* was premiered in Paignton in 1879.

The tennis-player-turned-sports-presenter Sue Barker (b.1956) was born in Paignton.

Pailís. The Irish name for PALLAS.

Painswick Originally *Wick* 'dwelling, dairy farm', OE *wic* (*see* WICK); the later affix *Pains-*, first recorded in the 13th century, denotes manorial ownership by Pain Fitzjohn.

A town in Gloucestershire, on the edge of the Cotswolds, about 8 km (5 miles) south of Gloucester. It made its money in the Middle Ages from wool, and there is still evidence of past prosperity in the fine old Cotswold-stone buildings of its centre.

It is firmly on the tourist map for the unique 18th-century Rococo Garden at **Painswick House** and for the churchyard of St Mary's church, which contains an impressive array of 18th-century table-tombs and 99 boldly topiarized yew trees (it is said that if another one is planted, to make the round 100, one will die). A large chunk of the spire was detached during a thunderstorm in 1883.

At the beginning of the 20th century the old custom of 'clipping', or 'embracing', was revived at Painswick. Every September, on **Painswick Feast Sunday**, the churchyard is encircled by a ring of children holding hands. Afterwards the locals have a traditional feast of 'puppy-dog pie' (a cake with a china dog in it).

> Beggarly Bisley, strutting Stroud,
> Mincing Hampton, Painswick proud.
>
> Traditional rhyme

Paisley The Gaelic name *Paislig* may be from Latin *basilica* 'church', via Middle Irish *baslec*. The suggested alternatives – 'plain of the pasture', OCelt *pasgell* 'pasture' + *lledh* 'plain', or 'Pælli's pasture', OE personal name + -LEY – do not accord with the medieval spellings of the name.

A large town 12 km (7.5 miles) west of Glasgow, on the White Cart River, in Renfrewshire (formerly in Strathclyde region). It is the administrative headquarters of RENFREW-SHIRE. The first church was built here in the 6th century by St Mirin (commemorated in the name of one of the Paisley football clubs, St Mirren FC, founded in 1877, and known as the Saints). William Fitzalan founded **Paisley Abbey**, a Cluniac house, in 1163. This was burned down by the English in 1307, but a new abbey was completed in 1484. This suffered at the Reformation, but was restored between the 18th and 20th centuries. Since the 18th century, Paisley has been a spinning and weaving town, in which the Coats family (notable local philanthropists) played an important part. Paisley College of Technology became **Paisley University** in 1992.

Paisley was the birthplace of the Rev. John Witherspoon (1723–94), one of the signatories of the American Declaration of Independence; the poet and pioneering American ornithologist Alexander Wilson (1766–1813); the weaver-poet Robert Tannahill (1774–1810), who drowned himself in the Paisley mill stream now known as Tannahill's Pool; and the critic John Wilson (1785–1854), who, as Christopher North, was the author of the majority of the *Noctes Ambrosianae* in *Blackwood's Magazine*.

get off at Paisley, to. An expression for the practice of coitus interruptus, Paisley being the last railway station before Glasgow on the West Coast line.

he couldnae get a wumman in Paisley. Something that may be said of a physically unappealing man. Apparently the expression casts no aspersions on the women of Paisley, but rather refers to the days when the town was full of cotton mills manned (so to speak) by women, creating an unusual preponderance of single girls.

Paisley bodie. A term for a native of Paisley, known since the 17th century.

paisley pattern. An intricately detailed curvilinear pattern, notably featuring a motif shaped like a comma, copied in Paisley from Kashmiri shawls sent back by Scottish soldiers serving in India *c*.1800. The pattern is Mogul in origin.

Paisley screwdriver. A hammer, implying that Paisley people are too lazy to use a screwdriver to insert a screw (*compare* GLASGOW screwdriver and IRISH screwdriver).

paisley shawl. A machine-woven shawl made of soft fine wool, cashmere or silk, and featuring the paisley pattern (*see above*). They were manufactured in Paisley in the 19th century, and are now highly valued by collectors.

Paiteagó. The Irish name for PETTIGO.

Palatinate, the After the Rhenish Palatinate.

The informal name of an area of northwestern County Limerick, around RATHKEALE. It derives its name from the 1200 German Protestants settled here by Lord Southwell in 1709, after they had been evicted from their native Rhenish Palatinate. Southwell's aim was to strengthen the Protestant presence in the region. For long the immigrants kept themselves apart from the native Irish, but by the end of the 19th century they had all either become assimilated or emigrated to North America. However, a few German names, such as Bovenizer, Switzer and Teskey, remain.

Pale, the ME *pale* 'fence of stakes', referring to a ring of defensive forts and in particular their *palisades*.

In the Middle Ages, the territory in central-eastern Ireland, centred on Dublin, that was under the firm (rather than nominal) rule of the English Crown after the Anglo-Norman invasion under Henry II in the 12th century. It was later known as the **English Pale**. At its greatest extent, in the 14th century, it comprised large areas of LOUTH, MEATH, KILKENNY and KILDARE, but notional efforts to keep the Pale English in language and culture, such as the Statute of Kilkenny, were not effective, and by 1500 the Pale had shrunk to an area of only 80 by 50 km (50 by 31 miles). The plantation of Ireland, beginning in the mid-16th century and accelerating in the 17th, obliterated the concept of the Pale.

beyond the Pale. An expression denoting anything beyond conventional boundaries of morality, decency or taste, originating in the traditional English loathing for, and lack of understanding of, the native Irish.

'Nail in the Pale, the'. A nickname for the Millennium Spire in O'CONNELL STREET, Dublin. An alternative name is 'the Stiletto in the Ghetto'.

Palestine Probably signifying remoteness (the village is almost exactly halfway between Andover and Salisbury).

A village in Hampshire, about 13 km (8 miles) southwest of Andover.

Palestine in London *See* HOLY LAND.

A 19th-century slang term for the area around ST GILES in Central London.

Pallants, the Apparently from Latin *palantia* 'palace' and, by extension, 'land over which a lord (in this case, the Archbishop of Canterbury) had special "palatine" or semi-regal rights'.

The central section of CHICHESTER in East Sussex, which forms a sort of Georgian city-within-the-city. It is quartered by four streets: **East Pallant, South Pallant, West Pallant** and **North Pallant**. The last contains **Pallant House**, a fine early 18th-century building nicknamed 'Dodo House' from the comical stone birds on its gateposts.

Pallas Irish *Pailís* 'palisade'.

A village in County Longford, 4 km (2.5 miles) west of Ballymahon. It is the probable birthplace of the playwright and poet Oliver Goldsmith (1728–74).

Pall Mall From *pall-mall*, a game involving hitting a ball through a ring. The name comes from obsolete Fr *pallemaille*, which itself came from Italian *pallamaglio*, from *palla* 'ball' + *maglio* 'mallet'.

A street (pronounced 'pal mal') in the WEST END[1] of London (SW1), in the City of Westminster, running southwest to northeast from the bottom of St James's Street (*see under* ST JAMES'S) to the bottom of the HAYMARKET. It owes its name and its existence to a craze that began in the late 1640s in fashionable society for a croquet-like game imported from France and Italy: pall-mall. This involved striking a boxwood ball down a long alley with a mallet in an attempt to get it through an iron ring suspended above the ground: the player who did so in the lowest number of strokes won. It was popular among the highest in the land:

> To St. James's Park, where I saw the Duke of York playing at Pelemele, the first time that ever I saw the sport.
>
> Samuel Pepys: diary (2 April 1661)

One of the earliest alleys in England was just to the north of St James's Park, and in 1661 this was converted into a road (because dust from the existing road nearby was blowing on to the king's new pall-mall alley in the Park – *see* the MALL). The road was originally called Catherine Street, in honour of Catherine of Braganza, Charles II's queen, but the colloquial name Pall Mall soon stuck and became official.

Not surprisingly, given its origins and location, Pall Mall was from the beginning a most desirable street, lined with the mansions of the rich and titled and fashionable shops. One of the earliest experiments in gas street-lighting took place here, in 1807. It also had several coffee-houses, and many of these developed into the sort of Victorian gentlemen's clubs that were to turn Pall Mall into one of the two main thoroughfares of London's CLUBLAND. Clubs that still have their august premises here include the Athenaeum, the Reform, the Travellers', and the United Oxford and Cambridge University Club.

Pall Mall rates only £140 on the Monopoly board.

not care/give a Pall Mall, to. A late 19th-century slang expression meaning 'not to care at all, not give a damn'. It depends on the rhyme of 'Pall Mall' with 'gal' (*see below*), the allusion being to the series of articles by W.T. Stead, editor of the *Pall Mall Gazette* (*see below*), on London prostitution, which were called 'The Maiden Tribute of Modern Babylon' (1885) – the 'gals' were presumably seen, punningly, as 'damned'.

pall mall. Late 19th-century Cockney rhyming slang for *gal* (i.e. *girl*).

Pall Mall Gazette. A London evening newspaper founded in 1865 by Frederick Greenwood (1830–1909) and George Smith (1824–1901). It combined features of a conventional newspaper with those of a literary review. It changed to a more sensational tack in 1883 when W.T. Stead (1849–1912) took over as editor. It was folded into the *Evening Standard* in 1923.

Palmer's Green From a village green here, named after a family called *Palmer*. The name is first recorded in the early 17th century.

An area of North London, above the NORTH CIRCULAR ROAD, in the borough of ENFIELD. The writer and poet Stevie Smith (1902–71) lived much of her life here with an eccentric aunt.

Pancrasweek 'hamlet with a church dedicated to St Pancras', *Pancras* (*see* ST PANCRAS) + OE *wic* (*see* WICK).

A village in Devon, about 10 km (6 miles) east of Bude.

Pang A back-formation from PANGBOURNE.

A river in Berkshire, which rises on the North Wessex Downs (*see under* WESSEX) and flows 21 km (14 miles) southwards, eastwards and then northwards to join the THAMES[1] at Pangbourne.

Pangbourne 'Pæga's people's stream', OE male personal name *Pæga* +-*inga*- (*see* -ING) + *burna* 'stream'.

A town in Berkshire, at the confluence of the rivers Pang and Thames, about 8 km (5 miles) northwest of Reading. It was the gentle riverside country around Pangbourne that inspired Kenneth Grahame in the writing of *The Wind in the Willows* (1908) (he lived in Pangbourne for the last eight years of his life). E.H. Shepherd also drew on it for his illustrations to the book. The town has a more recent literary connection in the form of the novel *Running Wild* (1988), a typically dystopian novel by J.G. Ballard, which features the massacre of adults and kidnapping of children in the exclusive Pangbourne Village housing estate.

In the independent school **Pangbourne College** (formerly Pangbourne Nautical College (founded 1917), and still retaining strong Navy associations) there is a memorial chapel dedicated to soldiers killed in the Falklands War. The film director Ken Russell (b.1927) and the writer Jeffrey Bernard (1934–97) attended the college.

> Pangbourne, the sylvan haunt of the Thames angler, the summer retreat of the Saturday-to-Monday punter.
>
> *Daily News* (16 September 1906)

Pant 'valley', Welsh *pant*.

A village in Shropshire, about 7 km (4.5 miles) southwest of Oswestry.

Pantiles, the From the flat tiles with which it was paved (strictly speaking a misnomer – true 'pantiles' are curved roof-tiles – but the term has been used in this context since the late 18th century).

A street in TUNBRIDGE WELLS. Begun in 1700, it is the oldest surviving street in the town. It is lined with an elegantly colonnaded parade of shops. The paving tiles from which it takes its name (said to have been laid after the future Queen Anne threatened never to return after her son had slipped over on the original walkway) have now mostly been replaced with flagstones.

Papa Stour 'big priest island'; *Papa* OScand *papi* 'hermit, priest', genitive *papa* + *ey* 'island' (*see* -AY); *Stour* OScand *storr* 'great'.

A small island 2 km (1.2 miles) across the **Sound of Papa** from the western coast of Mainland, Shetland. There are some spectacular sea caves, and the island is a Site of Special Scientific Interest.

Papa Stour has been used in the past as a place of confinement. In the 14th century Lord Tirval Thoresson confined his daughter to a house on top of a sea stack off the east coast to keep her from her beloved, a poor fisherman; she nevertheless managed to elope with him, and the stack is still known as Maiden Stack. Some 500 years later Earl Balcarres, the father of the Hon. Edwin Lindsay, an officer in the Indian Army, declared his son insane after he had refused a challenge, and kept him on the island for 26 years until he was freed by a lady missionary in 1835; there is a spring on the island still known as Lindsay's Well.

In the early 1970s a decline in population led to an advertisement being placed in *Exchange and Mart*, offering a croft and five sheep to anyone willing to settle on the island. The place subsequently became known as **Hippy Isle**.

Papa Westray 'priest's island by WESTRAY', *see* WESTRAY.

An island in ORKNEY, 38 km (24 miles) north of Kirkwall on Mainland. It is separated from Westray to the west by **Papa Sound**, and the flight across this – a distance of about 2.5 km (1.5 miles) – is said to be the shortest scheduled air service in the world.

At the Knapp of Howar on the west of the island are two stone-built houses dating from *c.*3700 BC, thought to be the oldest houses still standing in northern Europe. In the south are the Loch of St Tredwell and St Tredwell's Chapel, both named after a local maid said to have become the object of burning desire on the part of Nechtan, King of the Picts. Instead of surrendering her body to Nechtan, however, the pious girl plucked out her eyes and gave him those instead. She was later canonized, and her shrine at the chapel became a pilgrimage destination for those with eye problems.

Papcastle 'Roman fort inhabited by a hermit', OScand *papi* 'priest, hermit' + OE *ceaster* (*see* CHESTER) (the fort in question, on the River DERWENT[1], being called DERVENTIO by the Romans).

A village in Cumbria, just north of Cockermouth.

Pap of Glencoe. *See* GLEN COE.

Papplewick 'dwelling or (dairy) farm in the pebbly place', OE *papol* 'pebbly place' + *wic* 'dwelling, (dairy) farm' (*see* WICK).

A village in Nottinghamshire, about 11 km (7 miles) north of Nottingham. It is remarkable for its cast-iron and stained-glass Victorian pumping station, opened in 1884 to improve Nottingham's water supply.

Paps, the Irish *Dhá Chích Danainn*, 'the two breasts of Dana', Dana being a Celtic mother goddess.

A pair of mountains in County Kerry, some 15 km (9 miles) southeast of KILLARNEY. The higher of the two is 699 m (2293 ft). At the foot of the Paps is the ancient religious site known as the CITY.

Paps of Jura. *See* JURA.

Papworth Everard *Papworth* 'Pappa's enclosure', OE male personal name *Pappa* + *worth* (*see* -WORTH, WORTHY, -WARDINE); *Everard* denoting manorial ownership in the early Middle Ages by the Evrard family.

A village in Cambridgeshire, about 17.5 km (11 miles) west of Cambridge. **Papworth Hospital**, which occupies the early

19th-century Papworth Hall, is famous for its pioneering heart surgery. The UK's first heart valve was inserted into a patient here in 1962 and its first permanent pacemaker in 1967.

Par Probably '(place with a) cove or harbour', Cornish *porth* (*see* PORT).

A coastal village in Cornwall, about 5 km (3 miles) east of St Austell. The somewhat clayey sands of **Par Sands** are over 0.5 km (0.3 miles) across at low tide.

Paradise A tribute to the pleasantness of the locality; ME *paradis*.

A hamlet in Gloucestershire, about 2 km (1.25 miles) north of Painswick. It has an inn appropriately named The Adam and Eve.

Parallel Roads of Glen Roy, the. *See under* GLEN ROY.

Park. *See under* LEWIS.

Parker's Piece After Edward *Parker*, who had been farming it as a tenant of Trinity College before it became common land.

A large tree-lined common near the centre of CAMBRIDGE[1]. Previously owned by Trinity College, it was given over to common pasture in 1613. Cricket has been played here in the summer since the 1830s, and the Cambridge-born Surrey and England batsman Jack Hobbs learned his cricket on its pitches (the Hobbs Pavilion was constructed in 1930).

Parkhead Presumably self-explanatory.

An area of Glasgow, some 3 km (2 miles) east of the city centre, that has become synonymous with the stadium of Celtic FC, also known as **Celtic Park**. It was formerly also used for international matches. The once-terraced stand which Celtic's most vocal supporters made their own is known as the Jungle (possibly via rhyming slang 'Jungle Jim' from 'Tim', Glasgow slang for a Catholic).

Parkheid smiddies. Glasgow rhyming slang for 'titties'. The 'smiddies' (smithies) presumably refers to the Beardmore engineering works that once stood in Parkhead.

Parkhurst 'wooded hill in the hunting park' (referring to a royal hunting forest established in the late 11th century), ME *park* + OE *hyrst* 'wooded hill'.

A village on the ISLE OF WIGHT, about 3 km (2 miles) north of Newport. To the west are the remains of **Parkhurst Forest**, to which it is indebted for the first part of its name. Nowadays it is best known for **Parkhurst Prison**, which opened in 1838. It was chosen for the difficulties facing any escaped prisoner who tried to get off the island, but it experienced several embarrassingly successful break-outs in the late 20th century. In an unusual sideline, two prison officers opened a **Parkhurst Prison Heritage Museum** in the 1990s.

Park Lane From its proximity to Hyde *Park*.

A road in the WEST END[1] of London (W1), extending down the eastern side of HYDE PARK from MARBLE ARCH to Hyde Park Corner and forming the western boundary of MAYFAIR. It was built in the middle of the 18th century, but its reputation as the home of the seriously wealthy and exceptionally bred did not begin to develop until the 19th century. The nobility looked out over the park from their grand houses (Londonderry House, Grosvenor House, Dorchester House and so on) and sallied forth into it in their carriages and on horseback to see and be seen – a scene captured many times in the novels of Thackeray, Trollope and their contemporaries. In the 20th century Park Lane remained for a long time at the centre of fashionability, and its name still evokes a tiara-and-white-tie glamour (the Monopoly board values it second only to Mayfair at £350), but the houses were giving way to hotels – the Dorchester (*see under* DORCHESTER[1]), the Grosvenor House, the Inn on the Park, the Hilton – and in the early 1960s the street itself was transformed into a dual carriageway, severing the intimate link between its occupants and the park.

Spring in Park Lane. A romantic comedy film (1948), directed by Herbert Wilcox, in which the niece (Anna Neagle) of a diamond dealer is enamoured of a footman (Michael Wilding), who handily turns out to be an aristo. It was followed up by an even worse sequel entitled *Maytime in Mayfair*.

Park Royal From its origins as a site for the Royal Agricultural Show Ground.

A district of West London, in the borough of BRENT[2] (NW10) (before 1965 in Middlesex), straddling the A40 (WESTERN AVENUE) between ACTON to the south and WEMBLEY to the north. At the beginning of the 20th century the area was selected by the Royal Agricultural Society as a permanent venue for its show ground, and the somewhat grandiose name 'Park Royal' was bestowed on it. Unfortunately the scheme did not work out, the Society moved on in 1905 and Park Royal was left in limbo. Munitions factories were built here in the First World War, and later housing development turned it into a standard suburb. It is the site of the Central Middlesex Hospital and of Guinness's vast London brewery (due to close in 2005).

Park Royal 'Underground' station, on the Piccadilly line, opened in 1931 (it replaced a previous station called Park Royal and Twyford Abbey, which had opened in 1903).

Parliament Hill Origin uncertain; legend has it that Guy Fawkes's co-conspirators gathered on the hill to watch the result of their plot to blow up Parliament in 1605 (hence its former alternative name, *Traitors' Hill*).

A hill at the southern edge of Hampstead Heath (*see under* HAMPSTEAD). It is 97 m (319 ft) high. It affords fine views of London, and eagerly taken-up opportunities for kite-flying. Leading up to it from the east is the homonymically named road where the writer George Orwell used to live, at number 77.

Parliament Square From its situation next to the Houses of *Parliament*.

A square in the City of WESTMINSTER (SW1), at the southern end of WHITEHALL and the western end of Westminster Bridge. It was laid out in 1868, after the completion of the new Houses of Parliament. It is dominated by BIG BEN and other parliamentary buildings, and contains many statues of national leaders (including Robert Peel, Benjamin Disraeli and Winston Churchill). Of late it has been liberally obstacled with concrete blocks to deter terrorist attacks.

Parrett A pre-English river name of unknown meaning.

A river in Somerset, formed from the confluence of the rivers ISLE and YEO[1] just to the south of Langport. It flows about 50 km (30 miles) northwest through the Somerset Levels (*see under* SOMERSET) and BRIDGWATER into the Bristol Channel (*see under* BRISTOL) at BURNHAM ON SEA.

Parson and Clerk. A pair of sandstone rocks on the shore at DAWLISH in Devon. The story is that an inland parson used to visit a certain Bishop of Exeter who was in ill health in the hope that he might gain the see on the bishop's death. One winter's night, when on his now customary errand guided by the parish clerk, they lost their way, but with the help of a country fellow eventually found shelter at Dawlish. They passed the night in carousal among rough company, and in the morning heard that the bishop was dead. In haste the parson pushed his clerk into the saddle, but the horses refused to budge. 'I believe the Devil is in the horses', said the parson. 'I believe he is', answered the clerk, only to be greeted with laughter from the company, who had now turned into jeering demons. The house disappeared and they found themselves on the seashore. The horses still ignored the whip and they both lost consciousness. Neither parson nor clerk ever returned to their parish, but two strange rocks now stood on the shore.

Parsons Green 'village green where the parson lives' (referring to Fulham parsonage, which stood to the left of the old village green).

A district of West London (SW6), in the borough of HAMMERSMITH AND FULHAM, at the southwestern end of the KING'S ROAD. It was once a well-to-do residential suburb, with fine houses gathered around the village green (on which an annual pleasure fair was held until it was suppressed in 1823), but now it is indistinguishable from the surrounding areas of FULHAM.

Parsons Green 'Underground' station, on the District line, opened in 1880.

Parson's Pleasure Perhaps from its use by local clergy, or alternatively an alteration of *Patten's Pleasure*, its name until the 19th century.

A bathing enclosure on the bank of the River CHERWELL at Oxford. It was acquired by Oxford University in 1865. It was a 'men only' enclosure, and bathing, and sun-bathing, in the nude became the common practice here. Up until the latter part of the 20th century it was customary for ladies to disembark from their punts and walk round behind rather than continue boldly past. It was closed down in 1991, when made part of the public area of the University Parks.

Its female equivalent, not far away, was DAMES' DELIGHT.

The name *Parson's Pleasure* was given to a satirical student magazine briefly published in Oxford in the late 1950s. Founded in 1958 by Adrian Berry, it was a direct ancestor of *Private Eye*, which inherited several of its contributors (e.g. Richard Ingrams and Willie Rushton). *See also* MESOPOTAMIA[1].

Parsonstown. The former name (from 1620 until 1922) of BIRR in County Offaly.

Partick Possibly OCelt *perthog* 'wood, bush'.

A district of Glasgow, just beyond where the salubrious WEST END[2] drops its pretensions. The comedian Billy Connolly grew up here.

before the Lord left Partick. A very long time ago. Michael Munro, author of that estimable work of urban lexicography, *The Complete Patter* (1996), surmises that the expression may derive from 'the area's high density of Glasgow University students'. (The present author was also once resident here, contributing to the area's general lack of sanctity.)

Partick Thistle FC. The team supported by Glaswegian romantics. Its ground is at Firhill (not in Partick), and its nickname (for botanically obvious reasons) is the Jags. It draws its support from deluded romantics and trendy West-Endies (*see under* WEST END[2]), as celebrated in the following old Glasgow joke:

> 'Are you going to see the Thistle this weekend, Torquil?'
> 'I'd love to, Farquar, but there's a Fassbinder season on at the Glasgow Film Theatre.'

The comedian Billy Connolly has alluded to the heartache of supporting the club:

> The years I thought the club's name was Partick Thistle Nil.

Partraí. The Irish name for PARTRY.

Partry Irish *Partraí*, etymology unknown.

A village in County Mayo, between LOUGH CARRA and LOUGH MASK. To the southwest are the **Partry Mountains**, whose peaks include DEVILS MOTHER and the highest in the range, MAUMTRASNA (673 m / 2207 ft). The hills saw some action in the Anglo-Irish War (1919–21):

> Along the Partry Mountains we had a dreadful day,
> In wars we were surrounded all upon the 3rd of May,
> My mind it was completely gone, it seemed to me a
>   dream
> That bullets flew like hailstones at Bealamoondian
>   stream.
>
> Michael Heneghan: 'The Partry Mountains' (1921)

War in Partry, the (1860). The name given in the press to the dispute between Father Patrick Lavelle, the Catholic parish priest of Tourmakeady at the foot of the northeastern end of the Partry Mountains, and Church of Ireland missionaries proselytizing in the region with the blessing of Thomas Plunket, Anglican Bishop of Tuam. The dispute came to a head when Lavelle accused Plunket of evicting tenants from his estate at Tourmakeady, leading to the latter's denunciation in the London *Times*.

Parts of Holland. *See* HOLLAND[1].

Parts of Kesteven. *See* KESTEVEN.

Parts of Lindsey. *See* LINDSEY.

Pas an Phointe. The Irish name for POYNTZPASS.

Passage West Referring to the channel that it overlooks, which is in CORK Harbour on the west side of Great Island.
A town in County Cork, just to the east of the city of Cork. In Irish it is **An Pasáiste** ('the passage').

Pass of Aberglaslyn. *See under* ABERGLASLYN GORGE.

Pass of Brander 'obstruction of the narrows', Gaelic *cumhang* 'defile, narrow pass' + *bhrannraidh* 'obstruction'.
A narrow and somewhat gloomy defile in Argyll and Bute (formerly in Strathclyde region), leading from the northwestern arm of LOCH AWE down to Loch Etive (*see under* ETIVE). BEN CRUACHAN forms the north side of the glen. It was described by John Barbour in *The Bruce* (14th century) as 'ane narrow place betuix a louchside and a bra'.

Here in 1306 Robert the Bruce fought Clan MacDougall, and it was either here or in the earlier engagement north of TYNDRUM that Bruce lost the Brooch of Lorne (*see under* LORNE). *Pass of Brander* was the name of a four-masted barque built in 1890 in Port Glasgow.

Pass of Killicrankie. *See under* KILLIECRANKIE.

Paston Perhaps 'Pæcci's farmstead', OE male personal name *Pæcci* + -TON; alternatively the first element may be from OE *pæsc(e)* 'muddy place, pool'.
A village near the north Norfolk coast, about 11 km (7 miles) southeast of Cromer. The Pastons, a well-to-do 15th-century merchant family responsible for the **Paston Letters**, a unique record of the life of the time, lived in the village. Their mansion no longer survives, but there are memorials to them in the local church.

Paternoster Row Probably 'row (of houses) occupied by rosary-makers', ME *paternostrer* 'maker of rosaries (beads used as an adjunct to prayer)' (from Latin *pater noster* 'our Father', the first words of the Lord's Prayer) + *rowe*. An alternative suggestion for its origin is that funeral processions on their way to St Paul's Cathedral began their *Pater noster* at the beginning of the Row.
A street in the City of London (EC4), to the north of St Paul's Cathedral. In the late Middle Ages several rosary-makers had their premises here (hence probably its name): in 1374 Richard Russell, a 'paternostrer', dwelt here, and there is a record of 'one Robert Nikke, a paternoster maker and citizen'.

By the end of the 16th century it was also the home of booksellers and publishers, and it remained a centre of the publishing business for over 300 years (its denizens knew it simply as 'The Row'), until it was devastated in an air raid on 28 December 1940. About 6 million books were destroyed.

See also AMEN CORNER, AVE MARIA LANE, CREED LANE.

Paternoster Square From PATERNOSTER ROW.
An area in the City of London (EC4) (*see under* LONDON), just to the northwest of ST PAUL'S Cathedral and within its precincts. From the 17th century until 1889 it was the site of a meat market, but this closed down when SMITHFIELD market opened. The area was very badly damaged in the air raid that destroyed much of PATERNOSTER ROW. In the 1960s it was redeveloped as a pedestrian precinct with shops and office blocks. This never found favour, however, with either the critics or the public – the precinct was not the only thing about it that was pedestrian, and its design jarred with the nearby cathedral – and in the 1990s it was demolished and a new, more harmonious (some would say blander) development put in train. Its frontage on to St Paul's is Juxton House, an office block tricked out with mock-classical features. The Temple Bar (*see under* TEMPLE) has been transferred here.

Pathfinder Village A 20th-century name, apparently from the Native American tribe 'Pathfinders'.
A 'village' in Devon, about 11 km (7 miles) west of Exeter. It is a purpose-built retirement community consisting of 'park homes', with all facilities laid on including a mobile library and residents' clubs.

Patland. A mildly offensive 19th-century name for Ireland, **Pat** being a slang term for an Irishman (also known as a **Patlander**), from the common Irish Christian name Patrick.

Patna Named in the early 19th century by William Fullarton, a local laird, who was born in the Indian city of Patna.
A former mining village on the River DOON, East Ayrshire, 8 km (5 miles) northwest of Dalmellington.

Patrick Street Presumably after St Patrick.

The main street in the city of Cork, comprising a great curving arc of shops. The street is locally known as **Pana**. Much of it was burnt down by Auxiliaries on 11 December 1920, during the Anglo-Irish War.

Doing Pana. The Cork equivalent of the Spanish *paseo* or the Italian *passeggiata*, in which groups of young friends parade up and down Patrick Street, discreetly eyeing up the opposite sex.

Patterdale 'Patric's valley', OCelt personal name *Patric* + OScand *dalr* 'dale'; *Patrichesdale c.*1180.

A village in the Lake District, Cumbria (formerly in Westmorland), 12 km (7.5 miles) north of Ambleside, at the foot of HELVELLYN and just short of the south end of ULLSWATER. It was formerly a centre of lead mining.

It was at Patterdale that, as a youth, Wordsworth (as he recalls in the first book of *The Prelude*) 'borrowed' a skiff one evening, launched himself onto Ullswater and was subsequently terrified by giant looming rocks:

> And, growing still in stature, the huge Cliff
> Rose up between me and the stars, and still,
> With measur'd motion, like a living thing,
> Strode after me.

Patterdale terrier. An alternative name for the Lakeland terrier (*see under* LAKELAND).

kings of Patterdale, the. The owners of the Mounsey estate in Patterdale, who, according to local tradition, had never paid homage to the Crown, nor paid rent to any lord or squire. The 'King' of his day is mentioned in Coleridge's journal (31 August 1800), tending his goats on Glenruddin Screes. Their home, **Patterdale Hall**, was referred to as 'the Palace'.

Paul '(church of St) Paul or Paulinus', from the dedication of the local church.

A hilltop village in western Cornwall, about 4 km (2.5 miles) south of Penzance. In the churchyard is the grave of Dolly Pentreath, who died in 1777 and is believed to have been the last native-speaker of Cornish.

Paulsgrove 'Pælli's grove', OE male personal name *Pælli* + *graf* 'grove'.

A northern suburb of PORTSMOUTH. In 2001 it was the scene of anti-paedophile riots.

Pauntley 'clearing in a valley', Welsh *pant* 'valley' + -LEY.

A village in Gloucestershire, in the valley of the River Leadon, about 14 km (9 miles) northwest of Gloucester. It was the birthplace of the cloth merchant Dick Whittington (d.1423), the four-times mayor of London (*see under* HIGHGATE). The poor boy of legend, who, according to the (17th-century) story, came to London with his cat, was in reality the son of a well-heeled, knightly family of late-medieval

Gloucestershire. His coat of arms can be seen on the west window of the tower of Pauntley's Norman church.

Pavey Ark Possibly 'Pavia's shieling' (i.e. temporary shelter), *Pavey* OFr female personal name *Pavia*; *Ark* OScand *erg* 'shieling' (*see* -ARY).

A mountain (698 m / 2289 ft) in the Lake District, Cumbria, on the north side of LANGDALE. The great crag on its south side rises above Stickle Tarn, a popular destination for walkers. The crag is split from bottom right to top left by Jack's Rake, a scramble.

Pays de Galles. The French name for WALES, meaning 'land of the Walliae', presumably showing French interchange of *g* and *w*, the Welsh being *les Gallois*. It is first recorded in the 12th century.

Peacehaven A coinage by the developer.

A small town on the East Sussex coast, about 11 km (7 miles) east of Brighton. Dating from the 1910s, it notoriously consists mainly of bungalows. Nikolaus Pevsner was suitably condemnatory:

> What is one to say? Peacehaven has been called a rash on the countryside. It is that, and there is no worse in England.
>
> *The Buildings of England: Sussex* (1965) (Peacehaven was fortunate that Ian Nairn was responsible only for the West Sussex part of the book: his opinion of the place would no doubt have burned through the page.)

It began life in the early years of the First World War. A local businessman, Charles Neville, bought a plot of land here and began to develop it as a resort. Having a good eye for publicity, he decided to run a competition to choose a name for it:

> £2,600 in prizes for a Name of a New South Coast Resort.
>
> *The Times* (10 January 1916)

The winning entry was **New Anzac-on-Sea**, intended as a tribute to the Australian and New Zealand (ANZAC) troops who had been stationed nearby at the beginning of the war. However it was later decided, particularly in the light of the carnage of Gallipoli (1915–16), of which ANZAC troops had borne the brunt, that this was not a happy choice, and in 1917 Charles Neville announced a new name: Peacehaven. This both denoted a 'haven of peace' for the town's fortunate residents and expressed the common desire for a swift end to the war. It also provided a suitable companion for nearby NEWHAVEN.

Peak District *Peak* 'hill', OE *peac* (in the 7th century the area was known as *Pecsætna lond* 'land of the Peak-dwellers').

An upland area at the southern end of the PENNINES, mainly in northern Derbyshire, which roughly speaking slots in between Derby in the south, Sheffield in the east, Huddersfield in the north and Manchester in the northwest (its northeastern corner is in South Yorkshire and West York-shire, its northwestern corner in Greater Manchester, and its southwestern edge in Cheshire and Staffordshire). Since at least the early medieval period its name has generally been simply **the Peak**. The alternative **Peakland** is a late 19th-century revival of an Old English formulation. 'Peak District' came on the scene in 1951, with the creation of the **Peak District National Park**, Britain's first such desig-nated conservation area. It has an area of about 1400 sq km (540 sq miles), and its highest points are KINDER SCOUT (637 m / 2088 ft) and Bleaklow Hill (628 m / 2060 ft) (*see under* BLEAKLOW).

The area divides fairly symmetrically into two portions. To the north is the HIGH PEAK, or Dark Peak, so called from the dark millstone grit rock of which it is formed and the peat and heather that overlays it. It is harsh, hard moorland, the flat tops of its mountains often shrouded in mist. More forgiving is the WHITE PEAK to the south, whose limestone hills are permeated with caverns and potholes.

Accessible from all sides, the Peak District provides a vital and much-used recreational outlet for the northern Midlands and the North, visited by hundreds of thousands of walkers, climbers, potholers and sightseers every year.

Peak Cavern. A cavern behind CASTLETON, in the Peak District. Its entrance, which is below the keep of Peveril Castle, is 18 m (60 ft) high, and once contained a small village. This, the tortuous cave which extends back from it (to a depth of 610 m / 2000 ft), and the flatulent noises produced by floodwaters forcing air out of narrow crevices in the cavern, earned it the alternative name of 'Devil's Arse'.

Peveril of the Peak. A novel (1823) by Sir Walter Scott. Its scene is set against the background of Peveril Castle in the Peak District (*see* CASTLETON) in the late 17th century, and its convoluted plot revolves around the love affair between Julian Peveril and Alice Bridgenorth, daughter of a neigh-bouring landowner.

Peak Forest From the medieval hunting forest in the vicinity. A village in Derbyshire, in the PEAK DISTRICT, about 8 km (5 miles) northeast of Buxton.

Pearse Station. One of Dublin's main railway stations, serving lines to the southeast. It is named in honour of the writer, educationalist and revolutionary Pádraic (or Patrick) Pearse (1879–1916), shot for his part in the Easter Rising (1916). It was formerly known as Westland Row Station, and Ireland's first railway line, opened in 1834, ran from here to DÚN LAOGHAIRE.

Peasedown St John *Peasedown* probably 'hill where peas grow', OE *pise* 'pea' + *dun* (*see* DOWN, -DON); *St John* from the dedication of the local church.

A village in Bath and North East Somerset (before 1996 in Avon, before 1974 in Somerset), about 8 km (5 miles) south-west of Bath. It developed from a 19th-century colliery settlement on the FOSSE WAY.

Pease Pottage From *pease pottage*, an old name for a dish of reconstituted dried peas of varying consistency between thick soup and porridge, often with a piece of salt pork in it. The allusion, first recorded in 1724 in the form *Peasepottage Gate*, was probably to the muddy condition of the local road.

A village in West Sussex, on the London–Brighton road (A23), about 3 km (2 miles) south of Crawley.

The notion about the derivation of its name (which has grown into a local legend), that the guards who pre-ceded George IV on his journeys from London to Brighton stopped off here for a bowl of the pottage, is chronologically untenable: George IV was not born until 1762. There is no evidence either to support the idea that the name was inspired by the use of the place as a stopping-point for prisoners to eat on their way to HORSHAM gaol.

Pebble Mill Road Apparently a modern name, presumably from a mill here.

A road in the EDGBASTON district of BIRMINGHAM. Since 1971 it was the location of the BBC's **Pebble Mill** studios, where such programmes as the lunchtime chatshow *Pebble Mill at One* (1972–86; 1991–96) and the rural radio-soap *The Archers* (1951–) were produced. They closed in 2004.

Peckham 'homestead by a peak or hill' (probably referring to a local elevation now known as 'Telegraph Hill'), OE *peac* 'peak, hill' + HAM.

A district of southeastern Inner London (SE15), in the bor-ough of SOUTHWARK, between Camberwell to the west and New Cross to the east. It was largely rural until well into the 19th century, but the arrival of the railway in the 1860s brought the usual rapid rash of tightly packed speculative housing. In the 20th century the small Victorian dwellings made way for fairly grim council estates.

Peckham had its 15 minutes of fame in the late 20th century as the setting of the BBC television sitcom *Only Fools and Horses* (1981–93, 1996, and subsequent 'specials'). The central character, 'Del Boy' Trotter, shares a high-rise council flat with his brother Rodney and his old grandad (and later their uncle) in Nelson Mandela House on the Nyerere estate in Peckham. On the side of the three-wheeled van from which he does his dodgy business is emblazoned the legend 'New York, Paris, Peckham' (*see also* SIDCUP).

Peckham Library (1999), a striking blue-green building shaped like an upturned 'L' supported on thin columns, won the Stirling Prize for its architects Alsop and Stormer in 2000. The hopes that it would provide a focus of regenera-tion for this run-down area were cruelly mocked when it appeared in video footage of the last moments of the 10-year-old schoolboy Damilola Taylor, stabbed and left to die nearby in November 2000.

The Manchester United and England footballer Rio Ferdinand (b.1978) was born in Peckham.

all holiday at Peckham. A 19th-century expression implying lack of appetite. For the rationale, *see* **go to Peckam**, *below*.

Fat Boy of Peckham, the. The sobriquet of Johnny Trunley or Trundley (b.*c*.1899), who at the age of five weighed 70 kg (11 stones) and was put on display as a freak at fairs, music halls, etc. The phrase was regularly invoked in the middle years of the 20th century when giving a dire warning about the dangers of obesity.

go to Peckham. An expression meaning 'to sit down to eat'. It is a little linguistic joke of the type which the 19th century was so fond of: 'peck ham'.

Peckham Rye *Rye* 'small stream', OE *rith*.

A district, open space and road to the south of Peckham. The name (first recorded in 1512) originally referred to a stream in the area (long since covered over). It became attached to an ancient local piece of common land: **Peckham Rye Common** (William Blake saw angels in an oak tree on the common as a child). This was, and is, widely referred to as simply Peckham Rye, or even just **the Rye**. The name came to be applied to the road that runs down the western side of the Common, and then to the whole local area (reinforced by the opening of a local railway station in 1866, originally called Rye Lane but subsequently renamed Peckham Rye).

Ballad of Peckham Rye, The. A novel (1960) by Muriel Spark. It creates a curious picture of the London underworld, with the odd suggestion of necromancy.

Peckham Rye. A 19th-century Cockney rhyming-slang phrase for 'tie' (of the sort worn around the neck). It was often shortened simply to 'Peckham'.

Peddar's Way *Peddar* probably 'pedlar', ME *peddere*.

An ancient trackway in west Norfolk, leading from the northeastern corner of the WASH southeastwards for about 70 km (43 miles) in almost a straight line to a point to the east of THETFORD, near the Suffolk border. Now a walkers' path, it was a trade route in ancient times.

Peebles 'tents, pavilions', OCelt *pebyll* (Gaelic *pobull*) + English plural *-s*.

A royal BURGH (1367) on the River TWEED, in Scottish Borders, 34 km (21 miles) south of Edinburgh. It was the county town of the former county of PEEBLESSHIRE, and the vast **Peebles Hydro** hotel bears witness to its one-time popularity as a spa and holiday destination for golfers and anglers – giving rise to the local motto, 'Peebles for Pleasure'. The Beltane Festival is held in June (Beltane being the

ancient Celtic spring festival), and includes the riding of the marches (a ceremonial tour of the burgh boundaries).

The explorer of the River Niger, Mungo Park (1771–1806), practised as a surgeon in Peebles from 1801 until he left for his last expedition in 1805. Peebles was the birthplace of William (1800–83) and Robert (1802–71) Chambers, who founded the famous Edinburgh publishing company of this name. The town library and museum are in a building presented to the town by William Chambers, and formerly known as the Chambers Institution.

Thre Prestis of Peblis, The. A long poem thought to be by John Reid of Stobo (?*c*.1430–1505; *see under* STOBO), in which the three priests each tell a tale. The Prologue begins:

> In Peblis town sum tyme, as I heard tell,
> The formest day of Februare befell
> Thrie Preists went unto collatioun
> Into ane privie plac of the said toun,
> Quhair that thay sat richt soft and unfutesair:
> They luifit not na rangald nor repair.

> (Scots *unfutesair* 'un-footsore', *luifit* 'loved', *rangald* 'disturbance', *repair* 'company')

Peeblesshire From PEEBLES + SHIRE.

A former county, once also known as Tweeddale (*see under* TWEED), which was bounded on the north by Midlothian, on the east by Selkirkshire, on the south by Dumfriesshire and on the west by Lanarkshire. The county town was PEEBLES. It was abolished in 1975 and became the district of Tweeddale in BORDERS region.

Peel A Manx name from ME *pele* 'fortification, palisade', referring to the castle on St Patrick's Isle.

A seaside town and fishing port on the west coast of the ISLE OF MAN. Offshore, linked to the town by a causeway, is St Patrick's Isle (the Norse name for Peel was *Holen*, meaning 'island'). A monastery was founded here in the 7th or 8th century, and the island is also the location of **Peel Castle**, the stronghold of the kings of Man until 1220, when they moved to CASTLETOWN. There is a tower called Fenella's Tower after the beautiful half-Moorish serving girl who jumps from it into a boat in Walter Scott's novel *Peveril of the Peak* (1823). The castle was once haunted by Moddey Dhoo ('black dog'), a spectral hound.

Pegwell Perhaps 'well or spring where pigs drink', ModE *pig* + *well* (the name is first recorded at the end of the 18th century).

A district of Ramsgate, in the ISLE OF THANET, Kent.

Pegwell Bay. A deep bay in Kent, immediately to the south of Ramsgate. The River STOUR[3] flows into it. It has been a magnet for Continental invaders over the centuries: the Romans landed nearby in AD 43 (*see* RICHBOROUGH); the Saxons arrived in the 5th century (*see* EBBSFLEET); and they were later followed by a force of Vikings (a replica Viking ship made the crossing in 1949, and is now on the cliffs above the bay). More peaceable comings and goings have been effected in the 20th century by commercial cross-Channel hovercraft, for which a terminal was built in the bay in the late 1960s.

The painting *Pegwell Bay, Kent* (1859–60) by William Dyce, which depicts women and children collecting shellfish, hangs in Tate Britain, London.

Pemberley. The ancestral pile of Jane Austen's Mr Darcy in *Pride and Prejudice* (1819), supposedly based on CHATS-WORTH. In the 1995 BBC television adaptation of the novel, other stately homes stood in for Pemberley: SUDBURY HALL in Derbyshire provided the interiors, while LYME PARK in Cheshire provided the exteriors.

Pembroke 'end land', Welsh PEN + *bro* 'land'; the original form *Pennbro* (mid-12th century) had become *Penbrocia* by 1231 and *Pembrok* by 1283; it is *Penfro* in Welsh. The name was presumably applied to the southwestern peninsula of Wales before becoming the name of the town.
A market town on an inlet of MILFORD HAVEN in Pembroke-shire (formerly in Dyfed), 15 km (9 miles) west of Tenby. It is pronounced 'pem-brook', and in Welsh it is **Penfro**. It was the county town of the pre-1974 county of Pembroke-shire.

The town, once an important port, grew up around **Pembroke Castle**, first built in the late 11th century, and rebuilt in the 12th and 13th centuries. It played a part in enforcing Anglo-Norman domination of the Welsh in this part of the country. In 1648, during the Civil Wars, it held out for 48 days against Cromwell. When the poet Samuel Taylor Coleridge visited in 1802 he wrote in his journal of:

> The half moon, the cavern a thoroughfare of the high tide, and the gull heaving on the waves.

The earldom of Pembroke was created in 1138, and an early holder of the title was Richard de Clare, known as Strongbow, who led the first Anglo-Norman invasion of Ireland in 1170. In 1452 the title was granted to Jasper Tudor, uncle of the future Henry VII, who was born here in 1457. **Pembroke College** in Oxford was named after William Herbert, 3rd Earl of Pembroke (1580–1630).
Pembroke. A breed of smaller, short-tailed corgi (*see also* CARDIGAN).

Pembroke Dock. A port on MILFORD HAVEN in Pembroke-shire (formerly in Dyfed), 3 km (2 miles) northwest of Pembroke. In Welsh it is **Doc Penfro**. A Royal Naval dock-yard was set up here in 1814 (having moved from the port of Milford Haven), and there is a ferry service to ROSSLARE in Ireland.

Pembrokeshire From PEMBROKE + SHIRE.
A former county and current unitary authority in southwest Wales. In Welsh it is **Sir Benfro**. The county town of the

pre-1974 county was PEMBROKE, and the county (and current unitary) is bordered to the north by Cardiganshire (Ceredigion), to the east by Carmarthenshire, and to the south and west by the Irish Sea. It became part of DYFED in 1974, and a unitary authority in 1996, with its seat at HAVERFORDWEST. Other town include TENBY, PEMBROKE DOCK, NEYLAND, MILFORD HAVEN, NARBERTH, ST DAVID'S and FISHGUARD.

In the Middle Ages the southwest of the county was colonized by English and Flemish settlers, with the so-called LANDSKER LINE separating them from the Welsh in the north of the county. This anglophone southwestern part of the county became known as LITTLE ENGLAND BEYOND WALES.

The **Pembrokeshire Coast National Park** was created in 1952 and is the only British national park to focus on the coastline (although in the north it also includes the PRESCELLY MOUNTAINS). The scenery takes in rugged lime-stone sea-cliffs, sandy beaches and quiet inlets. The **Pem-brokeshire Coast Path** stretches 293 km (186 miles) from Amroth in the south to St Dogmael's (near Cardigan) in the north.

The painter Graham Sutherland was greatly inspired by the landscapes of Pembrokeshire, which he first visited in 1934. His well-known, somewhat surreal *Entrance to a Lane* (now in Tate Britain) resulted from a visit in 1939.

> It was in this country that I began to learn painting … I wish I could give you some idea of the exultant strangeness of the place.
>
> Graham Sutherland: letter to Colin Anderson (1934)

Penarlâg. The Welsh name for HAWARDEN.

Penarth 'top of the headland', Welsh PEN + *garth* 'headland'.
A residential town and seaside resort built round **Penarth Head** in Vale of Glamorgan (formerly in Glamorgan, then South Glamorgan), some 4 km (2.5 miles) south of Cardiff. It was formerly an important coal-exporting port.

Pen Caer 'fort headland', Welsh PEN + *caer* (*see* CAHER).
The peninsula on the west side of Fishguard Bay on the north coast of Pembrokeshire (formerly in Dyfed). At its tip is STRUMBLE HEAD.

Pendennis Point *Pendennis* 'headland with a fort', Cornish *penn* 'headland' (*see* PEN) + *dinas* 'fort'.
A headland in Cornwall, just to the east of Falmouth and on the western side of the entrance to CARRICK ROADS. There is no sign of the ancient fortification that gave this pointed peninsula its name, but in the 16th century **Pendennis Castle** was built here. It was besieged by Parliamentarian forces for five months during the Civil Wars.

William Makepeace Thackeray appropriated the name for Arthur Pendennis, the central character of his semi-autobiographical *The History of Pendennis* (1848–50) and

---

❖ pen ❖

This is a Britonnic word occurring in England, Scotland and Wales. Some of the English names, such as PENDLE HILL (Lancashire), and PENDLEBURY (Greater Manchester), show that the Anglo-Saxons did not understand the word they used since they added the tautological Old English *hyll* (in the case of Pendle Hill the element was added twice). This usage also demonstrates that although *penn* properly means 'head, end', the Anglo-Saxons understood it to be a hill name and transferred it to that meaning.

Pen is one of the characteristic elements of Cornish names, found in PENTIRE, PENZANCE, PENDENNIS POINT and many another; but places in England from PENGE (Greater London) to PENRITH (Cumbria) and PEN-Y-GHENT (Yorkshire) contain the element, as well as the Welsh Penrhyn (Gwynedd, *see* PENRHYN CASTLE), PENARTH (Glamorgan) and PEMBROKE. Some of the Scottish names containing the element are slightly disguised: *see*, for example, KIRKINTILLOCH (Dunbartonshire) and COCKPEN (Midlothian).

---

narrator of *The Newcomes* (1853–55) and *The Adventures of Philip* (1861–62). Pendennis was a journalist – whence the use of 'Pendennis' as the title of the *Observer* newspaper's diary column.

Pendine 'end of the sand dunes', Welsh PEN + *tywyn* 'sand dunes'.

A small seaside resort on Carmarthen Bay in Carmarthenshire (formerly in Dyfed), 12 km (7 miles) northeast of Tenby. Stretching some 12 km (7 miles) to the east are **Pendine Sands**, eventually merging with Laugharne Sands (*see under* LAUGHARNE).

Pendine Sands were the setting for several attempts on the land-speed record in the 1920s. In 1926 J.G. Parry-Thomas twice broke the record in *Babs* (his specially adapted, chain-driven 400 h.p., 27-litre Liberty-engined Higham Special), raising it to 275.73 kph (172.331 mph). On 4 February 1927 Malcolm Campbell came down to Pendine with his *Blue Bird*, and attained 279.81 kph (174.883 mph). On 3 March Parry-Thomas set off once more along the beach in *Babs*, in an effort to top Campbell's speed and so restore Welsh honour. However, when *Babs* turned over and whipped off her driver's head with her chain, Parry-Thomas succeeded only in topping himself. *Babs* was buried on the beach, but exhumed in 1969. A restored *Babs* can be viewed at Pendine's Speed Museum (when not out racing); sadly the same cannot be said of J.G. The last time the record was broken at Pendine Sands was on 19 February 1928, when Campbell and *Blue Bird* reached 331.13 kph (206.956 mph).

Pendlebury 'stronghold on the hill', OCelt *penn* 'hill' (*see* PEN) + the tautonymous OE *hyl* 'hill' + *burh* (*see* BURY).

A town in Greater Manchester, 5 km (3 miles) northwest of Manchester's city centre.

Pendle Hill Pendle OCelt *penn* 'hill' (*see* PEN) + OE *hyl* 'hill'; the addition of ModE *hill* makes the name doubly tautonymous.

A prominent hill (557 m / 1829 ft) in Lancashire, 5 km (3 miles) east of Clitheroe, in the unwooded area known as the **Forest of Pendle**. It was on Pendle Hill that George Fox (1624–91) had the vision that inspired him to form the Society of Friends – the Quakers. Not all local associations have been so godly (*see below*). **Pendle** is a local authority district of Lancashire.

> … where [the] Ribble comes into Lancashire, Pendle Hill advanceth itself up to the sky, with a lofty head … But [it] is most notorious for the harm that it did long since to the country lying beneath it, by reason of a mighty deal of water gushing out of it; as also for a infallible prognostication of rain, so often as the top there is covered with mist.
>
> William Camden: *Britannia* (1596)

See also PEN-Y-GHENT.

Witches of Pendle, the. A group of ten alleged witches from the Forest of Pendle, who were hanged outside Lancaster on 20 August 1612. Their downfall may have been the result of an old feud between two families, who then proceeded to testify against each other – although the discovery on one woman of a third nipple (for suckling Satan), and the efficacy of a curse aimed by another at a tinker who then had a stroke, provided additional evidence. The charges included a number of murders and an unsuccessful attempt to blow up Lancaster Castle by magic. Among the convicted were Alice Nutter, Old Chattox, Mother Demdike and a number of her descendants. Mother Demdike cheated the hangman by dying in prison.

The story forms the basis of Harrison Ainsworth's novel *The Lancashire Witches* (1849), and is commemorated on the top of Pendle Hill every Hallowe'en.

Pendoggett '(place at the) head of two woods' (referring to its position at the head of two wooded valleys), Cornish *penn* 'head, top' (*see* PEN) + *dew* 'two' + *cuit* 'wood'.

A village in north Cornwall, about 14 km (9 miles) north of Bodmin.

Penfforddlas. The Welsh name for STAYLITTLE.

Penfro. The Welsh name for PEMBROKE.

Penge 'wood's end, top of the wood', OCelt *penn* 'head, end' (*see* PEN) + CED.

A district of southeast London (SE20), in the borough of BROMLEY (before 1965 in Kent, before 1888 in Surrey). In ancient and medieval times it was a wooded area (whence its name, which hints at a continuing Celtic population to the south of London in the Anglo-Saxon period), used for the pasturing of pigs. In the 1840s, with the coming of the railway, it became a distinctly upmarket London suburb, but house prices were badly hit by a notorious murder case here in 1877, and subsequent residential development was on a more modest scale.

The Rolling Stones' bassist Bill Wyman was born in Penge in 1936.

Penge Papers, The. A collection (1985) of gloomily humorous reflections on suburban life by Brian Wright, characterized as 'the confessions of an unwaged metropolitan househusband'.

Rumpole and the Penge Bungalow Murders. A novel (2004) by John Mortimer featuring his jobbing barrister Horace Rumpole (*see under* OLD BAILEY) and telling in 50-year flashback the story of how his involvement in the case of a young man accused of killing his father and his father's friend made his name. The affair was frequently referred to in the Rumpole stories over the years, as a sort of in-joke for aficionados, but the details (as with Sherlock Holmes and the giant rat of Sumatra) never emerged. All was revealed in this, the first full-length Rumpole novel.

Pengwern. The Welsh name for SHREWSBURY.

Penicuik 'cuckoo head', OCelt PEN 'head' (i.e. a prominent piece of land) + *y* 'the' + *cog* 'cuckoo'.

A town (pronounced 'penny-cook') in Midlothian, on the south side of the PENTLAND HILLS, 14 km (8.5 miles) south of Edinburgh. It was formerly a centre of paper-making. The fine 18th-century **Penicuik House** burned down in 1899, but its facade remains. The novelist Samuel Rutherford Crockett (1859–1914), whose works include *The Raiders* (1894; *see* GLEN TROOL), was a minister of the Free Church of Scotland in Penicuik from 1886 to 1895.

Penistone 'farm by a hill', OE *penning*, from OCelt *penn* 'hill' (*see* PEN) + OE -ING + -TON.

A small town on the River DON[2], South Yorkshire, 8 km (5 miles) southwest of Barnsley. Its name has given generations of Yorkshire schoolboys occasion to smirk, as has that of **Penistone Hill**, which rears proudly above the Brontë sanctum at HAWORTH.

> The wind meets me at Penistone.
> A hill
> Curves empty through the township …
>
> Donald Davie: 'The Wind at Penistone', from *A Winter Talent and Other Poems* (1957)

Penjerrick Perhaps 'head of the valley with the fierce stream', Cornish *penn* 'head' (*see* PEN) + *nans* 'valley' + an uncertain third element, perhaps *eyrik*, which may be an ancient stream name meaning 'fierce'.

A village in Cornwall, about 3 km (2 miles) southwest of Falmouth.

Penk A back-formation from PENKRIDGE.

A river in Staffordshire, which rises to the northwest of WOLVERHAMPTON and flows 38 km (24 miles) northwards through PENKRIDGE and STAFFORD to join the River TRENT[1].

Penkridge 'chief mound' (presumably referring to a burial-mound or tumulus, though none is evident in the locality), OCelt *penn* 'head, chief' (*see* PEN) + *crug* 'hillock, tumulus' (*see* CREECH, CROOK). The earliest record of the name is in the Latinized form *Pennocrucium*, applied to a nearby 4th-century Roman settlement.

A small town in Staffordshire, on the River PENK, about 10 km (6 miles) south of Stafford.

Penlee Point *Penlee* 'slab headland', Cornish *penn* 'headland' (see PEN) + *legh* 'slab stone'.

A headland to the north of MOUSEHOLE in southern Cornwall. The entire crew of eight from the Penlee lifeboat was lost in December 1981 while trying to reach survivors of the wrecked coaster *Union Star*.

Penllyn Possibly 'head of the lake', Welsh PEN + *llyn* 'lake' referring to Bala's situation at the head of Bala Lake.

An ancient area of northern Wales, centred on BALA. In 1202 Llywelyn ab Iorwerth (the Great) annexed the area and made it part of GWYNEDD.

There is a town called Penllyn in the USA (Pennsylvania).

Penmaenmawr 'big rocky headland', Welsh PEN 'headland' + *maen* 'rock' + *mawr* 'big, great'.

A seaside resort on CONWY BAY in Conwy unitary authority (formerly in Caernarvonshire, then in Gwynedd), North Wales, 7 km (4 miles) west of Conwy. The town takes its name from the rocky **Penmaenmawr Hill** (472 m / 1548 ft), to the west of the town, which in former times travellers from Bangor to Conwy had perforce to traverse. Daniel Defoe, in his *Tour Through the Whole Island of Great Britain* (1724–6), reports that 'Penmen-muir' had a terrifying reputation, but he reassures his readers that 'there is no danger of their falling', since 'there is now a wall built all the way, on the edge of the precipice, to secure them'. On the summit of the hill is a stone circle, and there was also an important Neolithic axe factory here.

The Liberal prime minister, W.E. Gladstone, holidayed at Penmaenmawr annually.

Penmaen Swatch *Penmaen* from PENMAENMAWR; *Swatch* ModE 'a channel between sandbanks'.

The stretch of water in CONWY BAY between the small village of Penmon on the eastern tip of Anglesey and Llanfairfechan and Penmaenmawr on the mainland. It is some 6 km (4 miles) across. The graveyard at Penmon is full of those who drowned in the Swatch.

Penn[1] '(place at the) hilltop', OCelt *penn* (*see* PEN).
A village in Buckinghamshire, in the CHILTERN HILLS, about 2.5 km (1.5 miles) north of Beaconsfield. The beech-clad Chilterns are particularly spectacular around here (that is, in a Home-Counties sense of 'spectacular').

Holy Trinity Church has a 14th-century 'doom painting' (portraying the Day of Judgement) which escaped the usual Reformation fate of such artefacts (destruction) by being hidden in the roof. It was rediscovered in 1938.

The village is the source of the Buckinghamshire family name 'Penn', and William Penn (1644–1718), founder of the colony (subsequently state) of Pennsylvania in the USA, is buried at nearby JORDANS.

Penn[2]. A southwestern suburb of WOLVERHAMPTON.

Pennan Possibly 'head of the water', OCelt *penn* 'head' (*see* PEN), 'headland' + *an* 'water'.
A picturesque fishing village in Aberdeenshire (formerly in Grampian region), 15 km (8 miles) west of Fraserburgh. Its name probably refers to the nearby **Pennan Head**. Pennan was the location for the village shots in Bill Forsyth's film *Local Hero* (1983), although the views out to sea from the village were filmed on the west coast, looking out to the SMALL ISLES rather than to the featureless North Sea. Nevertheless, the relevant pub and telephone box in Pennan may both be entered, and used.

Pennines, the The name is not recorded before the 18th century. It may be related to OCelt *penn* 'hill' (*see* PEN), or there may be some connection with the Apennine Mountains (*see* Defoe *below*) that form the spine of Italy, just as the Pennines form the spine of England, and/or to German *Pennin*, the Pennine Alps on the Swiss–Italian border, which include Monte Rosa and the Matterhorn.
A long north–south range of hills in northern England, also called the **Pennine Chain**. They stretch from the PEAK DISTRICT of Derbyshire and Staffordshire in the south, up through Lancashire, Yorkshire, eastern Cumbria, County Durham and Northumberland, to meet the Scottish Border at the CHEVIOT Hills. The highest peak is CROSS FELL (893 m / 2929 ft), and other peaks include KINDER SCOUT, BLEAKLOW, INGLEBOROUGH, PEN-Y-GHENT, WHERNSIDE and the Cheviot. The Pennine fells are generally rolling, and there is much tussocky or heather-clad moorland (the latter popular with grouse and their shooters). There are also long escarpments comprising limestone or gritstone edges, and many attractive dales. The limestone areas have their quota of dry river beds, show caves, pot holes, swallow holes and kettle holes, not to mention limestone pavements with their clints and their grikes. They are bleak, bare hills, but they have their millions of lovers.

> Like a dismayed girl undressed
> Briefly surprised, the hills clutch rags of reeds
> Close, and drag wind-dried bracken
> Over bare gipsy breasts.
>
> Carole Robertson: 'Pennine'

The Pennine Chain is often referred to as the **Backbone of England**. Daniel Defoe called the hills 'the English Appenine' and compared them to 'a wall of brass' dividing the country – although he was pleased to report that his simile might be literally true, in that it was suspected there was copper in them there hills; in fact, various metals have in the past been scraped out of the range's innards, and stone quarried from its flanks. During the Industrial Revolution, on either side of the chain and in some of the valleys penetrating it, grew great industrial towns and cities, initially, before the advent of steam, using the fast streams flowing off the hills to power their mills. For the industrial workers living here, the Pennines – 'the lungs of England' – became a weekend playground, although their right to roam the heights had to be fought for hard.

Pennine Way, the. Britain's oldest long-distance footpath, officially opened in 1965. Tom Stephenson of the Ramblers' Association had identified the route in the 1930s, but considerable negotiation was required with grouse-loving, rambler-hating landowners, not to mention direct action in the form of mass trespasses such as that on KINDER SCOUT in 1932. The route sticks mostly to high ground (some of it very remote), and stretches from EDALE below Kinder Scout in the Peak District to KIRK YETHOLM just over the Scottish border north of the Cheviot. It is some 400 km (250 miles) long and takes two to three weeks to complete.

Pennocrucium. A Roman settlement near present-day PENKRIDGE.

Pennycomequick Referring to a field, farm, etc. that is a source of rapid prosperity (effectively, 'Get rich quick!').
A hamlet in Devon, on the western edge of Dartmoor, about 5 km (3 miles) east of Tavistock.

Pennyghael 'pennyland of the Gael'; the *pennyland* was land held at a penny rental + tribal name *Gael*.
A small village on the Isle of MULL, on the south side of Loch Scridain at the neck of the Ross of Mull.

Penny Lane Possibly a reference to a toll charge.
A street in Liverpool that has also given its name to an area of the city. It is celebrated in the Lennon–McCartney (mainly McCartney) song of the same name, released by The Beatles in February 1967, which evokes a kaleidoscope

of images of life in the city. The actual street name-plate has often been stolen as a souvenir. On the other side of the double A-sided single was the similarly topographically inspired 'Strawberry Fields Forever' (*see* STRAWBERRY FIELDS).

> The bank was *there*, and *that* was where the tram sheds were … it was just reliving childhood.
>
> John Lennon: quoted by Ian MacDonald, *Revolution in the Head* (1994)

Penrhiwceiber Apparently 'top of the roof-beam hill', Welsh *pen* 'top' (*see* PEN) + *rhiw* 'wooded hill, slope' + *ceibr* '(trees suitable for making) roof-beams or joists'.

A village in Rhondda Cynon Taff (formerly in Glamorgan, then in Mid Glamorgan), situated on the southern edge of MOUNTAIN ASH.

Penrhyn Castle As for PENRYN.

A monstrously vulgar neo-Norman pile in Gwynedd (formerly in Caernarvonshire), 3 km (2 miles) east of Bangor. It was erected in 1827–40 by Thomas Hopper for George Dawkins, whose ancestor Richard Pennant, a slave-trader and owner of a Caribbean sugar plantation, had acquired the estate in 1765. Pennant also developed the Penrhyn slate quarries around BETHESDA, and established nearby **Port Penrhyn** for its export. Slate became the particular source of the family's wealth – celebrated in the masses of ornately carved slate in the interior of the castle. When Queen Victoria came to stay in 1859 as the guest of Dawkins's successor, she was even offered a slate bed (in fact, The Slate Bed) to sleep in, but opted for a more modest carved-oak four-poster. Seven years later she elevated her host to the peerage as Baron Penrhyn of Llandegai.

In 1940, during the Second World War, many of the masterpieces of the National Gallery were moved to Penrhyn Castle for safety to escape the Blitz. However, the authorities had not bargained for the antics of the elderly 4th Baron Penrhyn, who one night stumbled drunkenly into his Great Dining Room, creating the possibility that he would fall through a canvas such as Titian's *Bacchus and Ariadne*, or Velasquez's *Rokeby Venus*, or Van Eyck's *Arnolfini Marriage*, or Constable's *Hay Wain*. The assistant keeper, Sir Martin Davies, expressed some relief when Penrhyn put himself *hors de combat* by smashing up his car and 'himself a little'. However, the baron then threatened to let the castle to a girls' boarding school, with free access to the Great Dining Room – and the canvases. In the face of protests he withdrew this proposal in return for an annual rent of £250. Subsequently, at Churchill's urging, the paintings were moved to underground storage in caves at Manod (*see under* BLAENAU FFESTINIOG) near Snowdon.

On the 4th Baron's death in 1951, the castle was transferred to the National Trust in lieu of death duty.

Penrhyn Gwyr. The Welsh name for the GOWER PENINSULA.

Penrith 'hill ford', OCelt *penn* 'hill' (*see* PEN) + *rid* 'ford' (*see* FORD).

A market town and tourist centre in Cumbria (formerly in Cumberland), on the northeast edge of the LAKE DISTRICT National Park, 28 km (17 miles) south of Carlisle. **Penrith Castle**, built in the 14th century to provide protection against the Scots (who burned the town anyway), is but a bare ruin. **Penrith Beacon** (286 m / 937 ft) rises on its northeastern side, while to the south are the ruins of Brougham Castle, standing on the site of the Roman fort of **Brocavum** (the northern end of the Roman road over HIGH STREET). William Wordsworth's somewhat dour grandparents and uncle lived in Penrith, and as a boy he spent some unhappy holidays with them here.

Much of the cult film *Withnail and I* (1986) was filmed in and around Penrith; at one stage the anti-hero (played by Richard E. Grant) demands 'the finest wines available to humanity' – in a Penrith café.

There is a town called Penrith in Australia (New South Wales).

Penryn 'promontory', Cornish *penn* 'head, top' (*see* PEN) + *rynn* 'point of land'.

A town in Cornwall, about 3 km (2 miles) northwest of Falmouth. It stands on a ridge between two valleys, at the western extremity of FALMOUTH Harbour. Its main business is granite-processing.

Penshurst Perhaps 'Pefen's wooded hill', OE *Pefenes* possessive form of male personal name *Pefen* + *hyrst* 'wooded hill'.

A village in Kent, between the rivers Eden and Medway, about 8 km (5 miles) southwest of Tonbridge. The Tudor timber-framed houses at its centre prepare the way for **Penshurst Place** just to the northeast, the ancestral home of the Sidney family. Sir Philip Sidney (1554–86), poet, courtier, soldier and all-round Renaissance man, was born here, and it inspired his *Arcadia* (1581). Its oldest part, the Baron Hall, dates from the 1340s.

Pensilva Coined in the mid-19th century from the Cornish prefix *pen-* 'head, top' (*see* PEN) and the local name *Silva*.

A village in Cornwall, about 6.5 km (4 miles) northeast of Liskeard. It developed in the 19th century as a miners' settlement.

Pentire 'headland', Cornish *penn* 'head, top' (*see* PEN) + *tir* 'land'.

A village on the North Cornish coast, on the western outskirts of Newquay. A little further to the west is **West Pentire**.

Pentireglaze 'green headland', *see* PENTIRE + *glas* 'green'.

A village in north Cornwall, about 2 km (1.25 miles) southeast of PENTIRE POINT.

Pentire Point *See* PENTIRE.

A headland in north Cornwall, on the northeastern side of the mouth of the River CAMEL.

Pentland Firth 'sea inlet in the land of the Picts', *Pentland* OScand *Pettland* 'land of the Picts'; *Firth* OScand *fjorthr* 'fjord'.

The broad channel between the north coast of Scotland and ORKNEY. It is renowned for its dangerous rips, swirls and races, as at each tide the Atlantic comes heaving through into the North Sea, before pulling back again. Hazards for mariners include the **Pentland Skerries** (not the least of which is Muckle Skerry), some 8 km (5 miles) north of DUNCANSBY HEAD, the Merry Men of Mey (*see under* MEY), the SWELKIE and the Boars of Duncansby, while the particularly careless might find themselves banging into the islands of STROMA or Swona. It was so mariners could avoid this passage that the CALEDONIAN CANAL was built, and even today many ships too broad in the beam for the canal will seek a more northerly passage rather than risk their bulkheads here.

> ... the tides are so fierce, so uncertain, and the gusts and sudden squalls of wind so frequent, that very few merchants-ships care to venture through it ...
>
> > Daniel Defoe: *A Tour Through the Whole Island of Great Britain* (1724–6)

Pentland Hills 'land of heights', OCelt *pen* 'height, hill' + OE *land* 'land'.

Possibly the finest range of small hills in the world, extending from EDINBURGH southwestwards through MIDLOTHIAN and SCOTTISH BORDERS and then into SOUTH LANARKSHIRE.

> Look up to Pentland's towring taps,
> Buried beneath great wreaths of snaw,
> O'er ilk cleugh, ilk scar and slap,
> As high as ony Roman wa'.
>
> > Allan Ramsay (1684–1758): 'To the Phiz an Ode' (Phiz was a drinking club. Scots *ilka* 'every', *cleugh* 'hollow', *scar* 'crag', *slap* 'valley')

The skyline from Edinburgh presents a unique profile, and the northeastern peaks (for peaks these are) provide a wonderful ridge walk – Caerketton, Allermuir, Castle Law, Turnhouse Hill, Carnethy Hill, Scald Law (the highest point at 579 m / 1899 ft), East Kip and West Kip (beyond which the range loses its character to rough heather moorland). These were the hills of Robert Louis Stevenson's boyhood (*see* SWANSTON), and the view westwards along this ridge into a winter sunset is a sight that will stir many an Edinburgh mountaineer's heart more than the grandest vistas of the Greater Ranges.

> Be it granted me to behold you again in dying,
> Hills of Home! and to hear again the call;

> Hear about the graves of the martyrs the peewees crying,
> And hear no more at all.
>
> > R.L. Stevenson: 'To S.R. Crockett' (Scots *peewee* 'peewit, lapwing'; the 'martyrs' referred to are slain Covenanters – *see* Pentland Rising *below*)

On the southern slopes of Castlelaw is an Iron Age souterrain (underground dwelling), while on the northern flanks of Caerketton is Britain's largest dry ski slope, where the cries of the peewees are generally drowned by the whoops of the snowboarders.

Pentland Edition, the. The first collected edition of the works of Robert Louis Stevenson, edited by Edmund Gosse and published in 20 volumes 1906–7.

Pentland Rising. The name sometimes given to the short-lived revolt of the Covenanters against Charles II's religious policies in 1666. They met with defeat at RULLION GREEN, on the south side of the Pentlands. Robert Louis Stevenson's account, *The Pentland Rising*, written in his teens, was his first published work.

Pentonville Named after Henry *Penton*, MP for Winchester, who owned the land on which the area was developed.

A down-at-heel district of North London (N1), in the borough of ISLINGTON, to the east of King's Cross. It was one of London's earliest planned suburbs, laid out in the early 1770s by Henry Penton on a site of 54 ha (134 acres). By the 1840s it was a fully built-up residential area. It declined to a slum towards the end of the 19th century, and it was extensively redeveloped after the Second World War. Along its original southern boundary ran the New Road, renamed in 1857 as **Pentonville Road** (and valued at £120 on the Monopoly board).

Pentonville Prison. A prison in the CALEDONIAN ROAD, to the north of Pentonville, built in 1840–42 as a 'model prison', embodying new theories of penal treatment. To the criminal fraternity it is **the Ville**.

Penwith 'end district', Cornish *pennwedh*.

The local government district including LAND'S END in Cornwall. The name is also the old Cornish term for Land's End itself, and the **Penwith Peninsula** is the western tip of Cornwall, to the west of the waist of land between LELANT and MARAZION.

Pen-y-Bont ar Ogwr. The Welsh name for BRIDGEND.

Pen y Fan 'top of the peak' Welsh PEN + *y* 'the' + *fan* 'peak'.

The highest peak (886 m / 2906 ft) in the BRECON BEACONS, Powys (formerly in Brecknockshire), some 7 km (4.5 miles) southwest of Brecon. It is just a little higher than its nearby neighbour **Corn Du** (873 m / 2863 ft), and both have steep-sided north-facing cwms.

Penygadair. *See* CADER IDRIS.

Pen-y-Ghent OCelt *penn* 'hill' (*see* PEN) + *y* 'of the' + an uncertain element, possibly meaning 'borderland'.

A mountain (694 m / 2276 ft) in the Pennines of North Yorkshire within the YORKSHIRE DALES, 10 km (6 miles) north of Settle. It has a gritstone summit ridge (the poet Colin Speakman has called it 'this massy sphinx of black grit') on top of a limestone escarpment, and, together with INGLEBOROUGH and WHERNSIDE, forms part of the THREE PEAKS Walk.

The old saying –

Pendle-Hill and Pennigent
Are the highest hills between Scotland and Trent

– is wrong by a not inconsiderable margin. (For the correct answer, *see* the PENNINES).

Pen-y-Gwryd Possibly 'head of the welcome', Welsh PEN + *y* 'of the ' + *gwryd* 'length between the outstretched arms', and it is just possible that the word applies to the welcome implied by that gesture.

An old hotel at the junction of the Llanberis Pass (*see under* LLANBERIS) and the GWYNANT VALLEY, in Gwynned (formerly in Caernarvonshire), some 6 km (4 miles) westsouthwest of Capel Curig. Since the later 19th century the hotel – handily situated between SNOWDON and the GLYDERS – has been associated with the gentlemen-mountaineers who first explored the cliffs and gullies of SNOWDONIA. The successful Everest team of 1953 stayed here prior to the expedition, testing equipment, and some of their autographs are on the ceiling; they later brought back a small lump of the Himalayan mountain, which can be seen in the hotel bar. The hotel is often referred to simply as **the PYG**, and in this form it gave its name to the **Pyg Track** up Snowdon.

Pen-y-Pass 'head of the pass', Welsh PEN + *y* 'the' + ModE *pass.*

A small settlement at the top of the Llanberis Pass (356 m / 1168 ft) (*see under* LLANBERIS). There are a youth hostel and mountain-rescue base here, and it is the usual starting place for ascents of SNOWDON from the east.

And the wind from Cwm Idwal, Cwm Llydau, Cwm Glas,
    Comes whispering over the scree:
'Come back, mountain friends, to your youth on the pass;
    Come home, mountain climber, to me.'

Geoffrey Winthrop Young: 'The Pen-y-Pass Song'

Penzance 'holy headland' (alluding to the chapel of St Mary that once stood here), Cornish *penn* 'headland' (*see* PEN) + *sans* 'holy'.

A town in west Cornwall, on the western side of MOUNT'S BAY, about 14 km (9 miles) northeast of Land's End. It now incorporates the nearby seaport of NEWLYN, and is the most westerly town in England. It has always been an important port, in the past for the tin trade, more recently for ferries

to the SCILLY ISLES (there is also a helicopter service from the local heliport). It was practically demolished in the late 16th century by Spanish raiders, and the present-day town centre has a Georgian look. With the arrival of the railway in the middle of the 19th century it began to turn itself into a holiday resort, a role for which its exceptionally mild, Gulf-Stream-nurtured climate (palm trees along the promenade) well fits it.

Sir Humphry Davy (1778–1829), chemist and inventor of the miners' safety lamp, was born in Penzance.

Penzance hybrids. Various crosses between sweetbriar or eglantine (*Rosa eglanteria*) and Austrian briar (*R. foetida*). The flowers are pinkish with yellow centres.

Pirates of Penzance, The. A comic opera (1879) by Gilbert and Sullivan. Its subtitle is *The Slave of Duty*. Its flimsy plot centres on the romantic and other misadventures of a young man who had been apprenticed by mistake to a band of Cornish pirates (instead of the intended pilots). It received its first performance in PAIGNTON.

Peopleton Probably 'estate associated with Pyppel', OE male personal name *Pyppel* + -ING + -TON.

A village (pronounced 'pipəltən') in Worcestershire (before 1998 in Hereford and Worcester, before 1974 in Worcestershire), about 10 km (6 miles) southeast of Worcester. The Sussex and England fast bowler John Snow (b.1941) was born here.

Peper Harow Probably 'pipers' heathen temple' (perhaps alluding to birdsong, or to the music accompanying pagan ceremonies), OE *pipere* 'piper' + *hearg* '(heathen) temple'.

A village (*Peper* pronounced 'pepper') in Surrey, on the NORTH DOWNS, on the River Wey, about 3 km (2 miles) west of Godalming.

Pepperbox Hill Possibly a reference to the shape of the hill, a rounded dome.

A hill in Wiltshire, about 9 km (5.5 miles) southeast of SALISBURY. It is owned by the National Trust.

Perivale 'pear-tree valley', ME *perie* 'pear-tree' + *vale*.

A district of west London, in the borough of EALING (before 1965 in Middlesex), between Park Royal to the east and Greenford to the west (before the 16th century its name was Little Greenford). It is bisected by the A40 (Western Avenue), and it was the coming of this road in the 1920s that sparked off its growth: manifested first in industrial ribbon-development (the most notable example of which is the Art Deco Hoover Factory, built in 1932 to the design of Wallis Gilbert and Partners, and narrowly saved from destruction and restored by the Tesco supermarket chain in 1992) and later in speculative house-building.

Perivale 'Underground' station, on the Central line, opened in 1947.

Parish of enormous hayfields
Perivale stood all alone,
And from Greenford scent of mayfields
Most enticingly was blown.

> John Betjeman: 'Middlesex' (1958)

Perranarworthal '(parish of St) Piran in the manor of Arwothel', *Piran* the name of a 6th-century Irish (or possibly Welsh) saint who settled in Cornwall, and became the patron saint of tin-miners (*see further under* PERRANZABULOE) + *Arwothel* 'place beside the marsh' (Cornish *ar* 'beside' + *goethel* 'marsh').
A village in Cornwall, about 8 km (5 miles) northwest of Falmouth.

Perranporth 'cove or harbour of (the parish of St) Piran' (referring to PERRANZABULOE), *Piran* (*see* PERRANARWORTHAL) + ModE dialect *porth* 'cove, harbour' (*see* PORT).
A coastal village and resort in north Cornwall, about 11 km (7 miles) southwest of Newquay. It was established in the 19th century as a tin-mining village. It now earns its living mainly from its fine sandy beaches and dunes, beneath which lay the ruins of St Piran's Church (discovered in 1835 and enclosed in an unlovely concrete shell for preservation in 1910; there are, naturally, legends of ghostly bells ringing in the sand). Nearby is **St Piran's Round**, an earthwork amphitheatre where mystery plays were performed in the Middle Ages (and have been again in modern times).

The popular novelist Winston Graham moved to Perranporth in the 1930s, writing the *Poldark* series of novels featuring Ross and Demelza Poldark and set on Cornwall's north coast.

Perranuthnoe '(parish of St) Piran in the manor of Uthnoe', *Piran* (*see* PERRANARWORTHAL) + *Uthnoe*, of obscure meaning.
A village on the southwest Cornish coast, about 1.5 km (1 mile) southeast of Marazion.

Perranzabuloe '(parish of St) Piran in the sand', *Piran* (*see* PERRANARWORTHAL) + Latin *in sabulo* 'in the sand'.
A village in north Cornwall, about 2.5 km (1.5 miles) southeast of Perranporth. The St Piran from whom it gets its name is said to have been sent to Cornwall by St Patrick. According to another legend he was cast into the sea by his fellow Irishmen, bound to a millstone, and landed at Perranzabuloe. He set up a hermitage and discovered tin when he saw it streaming from the stone of his fireplace (hence his adoption by tin-miners as their patron saint).

Perry Bar 'pear-tree by a hill called Barr', OE *pirige* 'pear-tree' + an OCelt hill name (from *barr* 'hill').
A northern district (and parliamentary constituency) of BIRMINGHAM. It is the home of Oscott Roman Catholic Theological College.

Oscar Deutsch opened his first Odeon cinema in Perry Bar in 1930. By 1944 the Odeon chain had expanded to 318 cinemas.

Pershore 'slope or bank where osiers grow', OE *persc* 'twig, osier' + *ora* 'slope, bank'.
A town in Worcestershire (before 1998 in Hereford and Worcester, before 1974 in Worcestershire), on the River AVON[1], about 13 km (8 miles) southeast of Worcester. The impressive Norman **Pershore Abbey** (a Benedictine house) survived the Dissolution in better condition than most.

The town is surrounded by cornucopian orchards, which tempted the 17th-century poet Michael Drayton to hyperbole:

> Where full Pomona seemes most plentiously to flowe,
> And with her fruitery swells by Pershore in her pride.
>
> *Poly-Olbion* (1612)

The orchards are famous for their purple and yellow plums.

Perth 'copse' or 'thicket', OCelt *perth*. The Gaelic name is *Peart*.
A city and royal BURGH in central Scotland, on the River Tay, some 50 km (30 miles) north of Edinburgh. In the Middle Ages it was an important port. Until the 17th century the city was also known as **St John's Town** or **St Johnstoun**, as the first church in Perth was dedicated to St John the Baptist. The old name is reflected in Perth's association football club, St Johnstone, which was founded in 1884, is nicknamed the Saintees and has played at Mc-Diarmid Park since 1989.

> St Johnstoun is a merry toun
> Whaur the water rins sae schire;
> And whaur the leafy hill looks doun
> On steeple and on spire.
>
> William Soutar (1898–1943): 'St Johnstoun'

Perth was the capital of Scotland from the early 12th century until 1452 (*see* SCONE), the county town of the former county of PERTHSHIRE, and the seat of the former administrative authority of Perth and Kinross district, and is now the seat of the current unitary authority of PERTHSHIRE AND KINROSS.

To the north and south of the old city, and bordering the TAY, are two parks known as the North Inch and the South Inch, giving rise to the old chestnut that Perth is the smallest city in Scotland because 'it lies between two inches'. It is said that when Agricola's Roman legionaries first saw the Tay and the South Inch in *c*.AD 80 they exclaimed '*Ecce Tiberis, ecce Campus Martius*' ('Behold the Tiber, behold the Field of Mars', referring to Rome's river and a plain beside it).

Like STIRLING[1], Perth was formerly a strategic gateway between the HIGHLANDS and the LOWLANDS, and its position led to it being subjected to a total of seven sieges. It was notably recaptured from the English by Robert the Bruce in 1313. Perth became a burgh in 1106 and a royal burgh in 1210.

King James I of Scotland was assassinated in the city in 1437 in a conspiracy led by Walter, Earl of Atholl. When the murderers arrived where the King was staying, in the Blackfriars Monastery, Catherine Douglas attempted to prevent their entry by using her arm to bar the door. Her courage was in vain, and James was stabbed to death while attempting to escape down a privy. Catherine subsequently became known as Kate Barlass, and in Pre-Raphaelite poet Dante Gabriel Rossetti's 'The King's Tragedy' (1881) she relates the story of the king's murder.

In 1559 John Knox preached a famous sermon at the Church of St John in Perth, calling for the 'purging of the churches from idolatry'. This led to a fever of image-breaking throughout Scotland. Perth and nearby HUNTING-TOWER Castle witnessed two violent incidents involving King James VI, namely the Ruthven Raid and the Gowrie Conspiracy. In 1715 Perth came out for the Jacobite cause, and James, the Old Pretender, was proclaimed as King James III in the city. In 1745 the city again supported the Jacobites.

Perth's best-known appearance in literature is in Sir Walter's Scott's novel *The Fair Maid of Perth* (*see below*). Mention must also be made of '**The City of Perth**', a poem by William McGonagall (1825 or 1830–1902), in which the city is bathetically apostrophized:

> Beautiful Ancient City of Perth,
> One of the fairest on the earth,
> With your stately mansions and scenery most fine,
> Which seems very beautiful in the summer time ...

McGonagall was also responsible for a poem on 'The Fair Maid of Perth's House', which he described as 'magnificent to be seen'.

Perth was the birthplace of David Octavius Hill (1802–70), the pioneering photographer; John Buchan (1875–1940), the writer of popular adventure stories (including *Huntingtower*, after the nearby castle), and from 1935, as 1st Baron Tweedsmuir, governor general of Canada; and William Soutar (1898–1943), one of the leading poets, along with Hugh MacDiarmid, of the Scots Literary Renaissance of the 1920s and 1930s.

> There was a young person from Perth
> Who was born on the day of his birth.
> He was married, they say,
> On his wife's wedding day,
> And died when he quitted this earth.
>
> Anon.: limerick

There are towns called Perth in Australia (the capital of Western Australia), and Canada (Ontario). There is also the city of Perth Amboy, New Jersey, USA.

Fair Maid of Perth, The. A historical novel (1828) by Sir Walter Scott, based on an incident that took place in Perth in 1396. A bloody dispute had arisen between Clan Chattan and Clan Quhele, and King Robert III (reigned 1390–1406) resolved to decide the issue by a staged battle between 30 warriors from each clan (the Chattans were one man short, but Hal o' the Wynd, a Perth blacksmith, made up the numbers). In Scott's novel the Fair Maid is Catharine or Kate Glover, and her rival suitors, the hero Henry Smith and the villain Conachar, find themselves on opposing sides during the fight. Scott's novel provided the broad basis for Georges Bizet's opera *La Jolie Fille de Perth* (1867). The Fair Maid's House, in Blackfriars Wynd, is a rebuilt version dating from the later 19th century.

Five Articles of Perth, the. The Articles (1618) imposed on the Church of Scotland by James I and VI, enjoining kneeling at communion, the observance of Christmas, Good Friday, Easter and Pentecost, confirmation, communion for the dying and early baptism of infants. They were ratified by the Scottish Parliament on 4 August 1621, a day called Black Saturday, and condemned by the General Assembly at Glasgow in 1638.

Pacification of Perth (23 February 1573). An agreement between Regent Morton (representing the young Protestant king, James VI) and the Huntly-Hamilton action, supporters of the deposed Mary Queen of Scots, which helped to bring about the end of the civil war in Scotland

perthite. Any of a group of minerals, all of which are alkali feldspars. Varieties include cryptoperthite and microperthite. The first perthite to be identified was found near Perth, Ontario, and so is ultimately named after the Scottish city.

Treaty of Perth (1266). The treaty by which the HEBRIDES and the ISLE OF MAN were ceded to Scotland by the Norwegians following their defeat at the Battle of LARGS in 1263.

Perth and Kinross. A district of the former Tayside region created in 1975 out of most of PERTHSHIRE and all of KINROSS-SHIRE. It became the unitary authority of PERTHSHIRE AND KINROSS in 1996.

Perthshire From PERTH + SHIRE.
A traditional county of Scotland, containing parts of both the HIGHLANDS and the LOWLANDS. It was bounded on the west by Argyll, on the north by Inverness-shire and Aberdeenshire, on the east by Angus, and on the south by Kinross-shire, Clackmannanshire and Stirlingshire. Its county town was PERTH. The traditional county was abolished in 1975 (*see* PERTH AND KINROSS).

Perthshire Light Infantry, the. A former regiment, known under this name from 1815, but founded as the **90th Perthshire Volunteers** in 1794.

Perthshire and Kinross. A unitary authority created in 1996 out of the former PERTH AND KINROSS district of Tayside region. Its administrative centre is PERTH.

Peterborough 'St Peter's town', *Peter* from the dedication of the local abbey (later of the cathedral) + OE *burh* (*see* BURY).

A cathedral city and unitary authority in eastern central England, on the River Nene, about 60 km (38 miles) north-west of Cambridge and the same distance east of Leicester. Historically it was at the centre of an adminstrative area called the **Soke of Peterborough** (*soke* 'right of local juris-diction', from medieval Latin *soca*), which included the city and an area to the west between the rivers NENE and WELLAND and was under the jurisdiction of the abbot of the monastery (*see below*). It was within the boundaries of Northamptonshire, but in 1888 the Soke was given its own separate county council. In 1965 it was transferred to HUNTINGDONSHIRE, which became known as Huntingdon and Peterborough. In 1972 this county, including the city of Peterborough, was swallowed up by CAMBRIDGESHIRE, and the Soke disappeared. In 1996 Peterborough was desig-nated a unitary authority; this includes sizable areas to the east and west of the city.

Peterborough can trace its origins to a monastery that occupied the site from AD 650. At that time the site's name was *Medeshamstede* 'Mede's homestead' (OE male personal name *Mede* + *ham-stede*). The old monastery, dedicated to St Peter, was destroyed and all the monks slaughtered by the Vikings in 869. In 963 King Edgar granted the deserted land to Bishop Æthelwold, and the building of a new abbey, similarly dedicated to St Peter, led in due course to a change of the site's name to Peterborough. In 1118 the building of a cathedral began here, and it inherited the abbey's saint. **Peterborough Cathedral** contains the tomb of Catherine of Aragon. Mary Queen of Scots was also buried there, having been beheaded at nearby FOTHERINGHAY – Richard Fletcher, dean of Peterborough and father of dramatist John, officiated at her execution – but she was later removed to Westminster Abbey. The Bishop of Peterborough signs himself *Petriburg*.

Peterborough is on the edge of the FENS, and is an important centre for the processing of the agricultural produce of the surrounding area. Since the 19th century brick-making has also been a significant income-earner (*see also* OLD FLETTON). It is on the main East Coast line from London to Edinburgh, and forms an important junction with east–west lines. In 1967 it was declared a NEW TOWN[1].

The city's football club, **Peterborough United FC**, was founded in 1934 from the remnants of Peterborough and Fletton United. Its nickname is Posh. There are various accounts purportedly explaining the origin of this. The most widely accepted claims that supporters referred to the team as looking 'posh' when they kicked off in the Southern League against Gainsborough on 1 September 1934 wear-ing a new strip. According to another account, in 1921 the manager of Fletton United said that he wanted 'posh players for a posh new team', and the name stuck when Peterborough and Fletton United was established in 1923.

But on its formal founding in 1934 Peterborough United gained professional status, and *posh* may thus actually derive from *professional*. In 2003 the club was presump-tuously and successfully challenged by the singer 'Posh Spice' (Victoria Beckham) over its legal right to register the name as a trademark.

The churchman and theologian William Paley (1743–1805), author of the standard exposition in English theo-logy of the teleological argument for the existence of God, was born in Peterborough. The poet John Clare (1793–1864) (*see* HELPSTON) and the writer of *The Go-Between*, L.P. Hartley (1895–1972) (*see* WHITTLESEY), were born nearby.

There is a large city called Peterborough in Ontario, Canada (its name is used to designate a type of wooden canoe), a county called Peterborough in New Hampshire, USA and a town called Peterborough in South Australia.

Peterborough. Used adjectively to designate a Neolithic culture of a type identified archeologically from remains in the Peterborough area.

'Peterborough'. The name at the head of a diary column that appeared in the *Daily Telegraph* until February 2003, after which it was retitled 'London Spy' – whereupon the *Daily Mail*, with enterprising audacity, took over the name (and some of the former writers) for its own new diary column, its front-page headline proclaiming:

> Want to know where Peterborough is? It's the *Mail*'s new column about Middle England (what else?).
>
> *Daily Mail* (11 March 2003)

The original 'Peterborough' column was always the product of a variety of writers, and over the years they included A.N. Wilson, Auberon Waugh, and future *Telegraph* editors Bill Deedes and Charles Moore. The name comes from Peterborough Court, a small alleyway beside the *Telegraph* building in Fleet Street, which was so called because between the 14th and 19th centuries the site was owned by the bishops of Peterborough.

Peterborough Chronicle, The. A part of the Anglo-Saxon Chronicle written in Peterborough between 1121 and 1154 and covering the years 1070–1154. It is of great linguistic interest for the light it sheds on the transition from Old English to Middle English.

Peterculter 'St Peter's Church of Culter'; *Culter* is possibly 'back country', Gaelic *cùl* 'back' + *tìr* 'land'.
A village in Aberdeenshire (formerly in Grampian region), 13 km (8 miles) southwest of Aberdeen. The lands of Culter were divided in the 13th century: a church dedicated to St Peter was built on the north side of the Dee, while on the south side (formerly in Kincardineshire, but now also in Aberdeenshire), the village of **Maryculter**, or **Kirkton of Maryculter**, took its name from the church dedicated to the Virgin Mary.

Peterhead

Peterhead 'the headland with St Peter's Church', from the church built here in 1132.

A large fishing port in Aberdeenshire (formerly in Grampian region), 45 km (27 miles) north-northeast of Aberdeen. It is the most easterly town in Scotland, and Keith Inch, forming the northern arm of the big natural harbour (**Peterhead Bay**), is the most easterly point on the Scottish mainland. Peterhead was the seat of the former Banff and Buchan district council. The town was founded in 1593 by George Keith, the 5th Earl Marischal. During the 1715 Jacobite Rising, James Stuart, the Old Pretender, landed here (22 December 1715), only to depart again for the Continent a few weeks later, his demoralized army having melted away. Later in the 18th century Peterhead was briefly fashionable as a spa, but it is now better known for its high-security prison. '**The Peterhead Polka**' is a traditional fiddle tune.

> This
> Though a grey and quiet place
> Finds nothing much amiss.
> It keeps its stillness.
>
> Burns Singer (1928–64): 'Peterhead in May'

> Along the quay at Peterhead the lasses stand aroon,
> Wi' their shawls all pulled aboot them and saut tears runnin' doon;
> Don't you weep, my bonny lass, though you be left behind,
> For the rose will grow in Greenland's ice before we change our mind.
> *So it's cheer up, my lads, let your hearts never fail,*
> *As the bonnie ship the Diamond goes a-fishing for the whale.*
>
> Anon.: 'The Bonnie Ship, the Diamond' (19th-century song) (The *Diamond* sailed from Peterhead for the Davies Straits in 1812, and was lost in the ice in 1819.)

Peterlee After the local miners' leader *Peter Lee* (1864–1935), who became the first chair of Durham county council.

A NEW TOWN[1] in County Durham, 11 km (7 miles) north-west of Hartlepool. It was designated as a New Town in 1948, and Berthold Lubetkin, creator of the famous Penguin Pool at London Zoo, was appointed architect and planner. From 1955 the painter Victor Pasmore was consulting designer for the town.

Peterloo. *See under* MANCHESTER.

Petersfield Probably '(settlement at the) open land with a church dedicated to St Peter', *Peters* possessive form of *Peter* + OE *feld* (*see* FIELD).

A market town in Hampshire, on the River ROTHER, about 19 km (12 miles) north of Havant. It grew to prosperity in the Middle Ages on the wool trade. It is on the main London–Portsmouth road (now the A3), and in the era of the stagecoach it was an important stopping-place. The town centre retains much of its 18th-century feel. The coming of the railway in the 19th century sealed its fate as a future commuter town.

Peters Marland *Peters* from the dedication of the local church to St Peter; *Marland* 'cultivated land by a pool', OE *mere* 'pool' + *land* 'cultivated land'.

A village in Devon, about 13 km (8 miles) south of Bideford.

Peterstone Wentlooge 'farm belonging to St Peter in the territory of Glynwys', *Peter* + OE -TON + an anglicized version of Welsh *Gwynllwg*, a personal name with territorial affix -*wg*.

A village in Newport unitary authority (formerly in Monmouthshire, then in Gwent), some 9 km (5.5 miles) east of Cardiff, and 3 km (2 miles) southwest of **St Brides Wentlooge** (which has a church dedicated to St Bride/Bridget). The two are in the fenland of **Wentlooge Level**.

Peter Tavy *Peter* from the dedication of the local church to St Peter; *Tavy* from the River TAVY.

A village in Devon, on the western edge of DARTMOOR, about 4 km (2.5 miles) northeast of Tavistock.
See also MARY TAVY.

Petticoat Lane Probably because it was occupied by makers or sellers of ladies' petticoats.

The name between the early 17th century and the 1830s for the street in the City of London (E1) now officially known as MIDDLESEX STREET (before 1600 it was called Hog Lane). It is just to the east of LIVERPOOL STREET station. 'Petticoat Lane' (suppressed by 19th-century city fathers who did not want one of their streets named after women's underwear) survives as the designation of a well-known street market held here, which originated in the 18th century. It started off as an old-clothes market, and seconds and nearly-new items from the garment business are still its main stock-in-trade; but one can also get leather goods, watches and toys there (possibly not always off the front of the lorry). On weekdays the market now operates mainly in nearby Wentworth Street, but on Sunday mornings Middlesex Street itself fills with stalls and customers.

> Null Bazaar is … a big market … An interesting section … is the Chor Bazaar. Chor really means 'thieves.' Chor Bazaar, then, means the bazaar of thieves. Probably in the past thieves disposed of their stolen property here. In this bazaar – the Petticoat Lane of Bombay – you can buy secondhand articles of any description.
>
> B. Diqui: *Visit to Bombay* (1927)

Pettigo Irish *Paiteagó* 'lump, clod'.

A village straddling the border of Donegal and Fermanagh (and hence of the Republic and Northern Ireland), just north of Lower Lough Erne (*see under* ERNE).

Petty Cury 'small kitchen', OFr *petit curie*: a voguish medieval name for the old Cooks' Row here.

A street in CAMBRIDGE, linking Sidney Street with the market place.

Petty France 'little France'; perhaps so called because it was in an area once occupied by French merchants.

A street in the City of WESTMINSTER (SW1), just to the south of ST JAMES'S Park, linking Buckingham Gate with Tothill Street. John Milton lived here while he was writing his epic poem *Paradise Lost* in the 1650s. For many years the only occasion most people had to be aware of it was when they applied for a passport – it housed the headquarters of the Passport Office.

Petworth 'Peota's enclosure', OE male personal name *Peota* + *worth* 'enclosure' (*see* -WORTH, WORTHY, -WARDINE).

A small town in West Sussex, to the north of the SOUTH DOWNS, about 11 km (7 miles) east of Midhurst. Captivating and architecturally interesting as it is, it is dominated by the late 17th-century pile of **Petworth House** to the northwest, which stands in grounds laid out by 'Capability' Brown in 1751–64. The painter J.M.W. Turner stayed at the house many times, and produced some of his best work here. Several of his works now hang in the house, which also has canvases by Claude, Poussin and Van Dyck, and a room with limewood carvings by Grinling Gibbons (1648–1721). The building and grounds were donated to the National Trust by the 3rd Lord Leconfield in 1947.

The poet Wilfred Scawen Blunt (1840–1922) was born in Petworth.

Pevensey 'Pefen's river' (referring to the stream on which the village stands), OE *Pefenes* possessive form of male personal name *Pefen* + *ea* 'river' (*see* EA-).

A village in East Sussex, about 1 km (0.6 miles) from the sea and 8 km (5 miles) northeast of Eastbourne. Two thousand years ago it was on the coast, and around AD 340 the Romans built a fort here, called *Anderitum* (literally 'great ford', so it was evidently by a crossing of some coastal inlet), as a defence against Saxons with any thoughts of invasion (and thus part of the SAXON SHORE). It proved unequal to the task, however: in 491 King Ælle's South Saxons besieged and captured the fort and massacred its defenders. Its walls and towers are well preserved.

Pevensey Bay, the wide shallow bay at the centre of which Pevensey stands, continued to be an attractive target for invaders. William the Conqueror landed here in 1066, and gave the place to his half-brother Robert of Mortmain. The Normans built a massive castle on the ruins of the Roman fort. This was still in active service as recently as the Second World War, when camouflaged gun-emplacements were incorporated into it.

Pevensey became an important port, and by the 13th century it was one of the CINQUE PORTS, but gradually the sea retreated and marooned it inland. A new settlement on the coast has taken the name 'Pevensey Bay'.

Inland are the **Pevensey Levels**, a low-lying wet area between the SOUTH DOWNS and the end of the WEALD, watered by streams many of which are named 'haven' (e.g. **Pevensey Haven**, Hurst Haven, Waller's Haven).

Pewsey 'Pefe's island or well-watered land' (referring to a stretch of land along the bank of the Avon), OE *Pefes* possessive form of male personal name *Pefe* + *eg* 'island' (*see* -EY, -EA).

A small agricultural town in Wiltshire, on the River AVON[3], about 10 km (6 miles) south of Marlborough. Its centre is dominated by a statue of Alfred the Great. To the south is **Pewsey Down**, on which the figure of a white horse is carved: designed in 1937 by George Marples, a white-horse authority, it replaced one created nearby at the end of the 18th century, which had become hardly visible.

Vale of Pewsey. A wide fertile valley which runs in an arc from Devizes eastwards to beyond Pewsey. It is watered by the River AVON[3].

Philiphaugh Apparently 'dirty valley', OE *ful* 'dirty' + *hop* 'secluded valley' with tautological Scots *haugh* 'valley' (*see* HALE, -HALL).

A village in Scottish Borders (formerly in Selkirkshire), just southwest of Selkirk.

Battle of Philiphaugh (13 September 1645). An engagement in which the Marquess of Montrose's depleted Royalist forces were routed by the Covenanters under General David Leslie. Many Irish camp followers (mostly women and children) were summarily slaughtered, and the field where their skeletons were dug up in 1810 still bears the name Slain Men's Lea.

Phoenix Green *Phoenix* from the name of an 18th-century inn here.

A village in Hampshire, just to the north of the M3, about 5 km (3 miles) northwest of Fleet.

Phoenix Park 'park with the clear water', Irish *fionn* 'white, clear' + *uisce* 'water'.

A large park on Dublin's north side, formed as a deer park in 1662. The park includes Dublin's zoo and Áras an Uachtaráin (Irish, 'the abode of the president'), a building dating from 1751 and enlarged after 1782, when it became the residence of the lord lieutenants; after the foundation of the Irish Free State it became the residence of the governor-general (and was nicknamed Uncle Tim's Cabin, after the first governor-general, Tim Healy); it is now the residence of the Irish president – hence the expression **going for the Park**, meaning putting oneself forward as a candidate for the presidency.

Phoenix Park Murders (6 May 1882). The assassination of two high-ranking officials in Phoenix Park by a Fenian splinter group calling themselves the Invincibles. The victims, who were killed with surgical knives on the driveway of the lord lieutenant's residence, were the recently appointed chief secretary, Lord Frederick Cavendish, and the under-secretary, Thomas Burke. The leader of the attack was James Carey, who turned Queen's evidence, resulting in the public hanging of five of the eight-man assassination team. Carey attempted to escape to Australia, but was shot dead by another Invincible, Patrick O'Donnell, on board the liner *Melrose*. O'Donnell himself was hanged. The incident horrified Parnell, the leader of the Irish Nationalists at Westminster; he offered to resign his seat, but was persuaded to stay by Gladstone. *The Times* suggested that Parnell had in fact been involved, but when Parnell successfully sued it was shown that the newspaper had based its allegations on forged letters.

Piccadilly[1] From *Piccadilly Hall*, a facetious nickname given in the early 17th century to a house in this area belonging to Robert Baker, a tailor who had made his fortune from the sale of a type of lace-trimmed collar fashionable at that time and known as a *piccadill* or *piccadilly* (the word comes from French *piccadilles*, the ultimate source of which may be Spanish *picado* 'pierced').

A street in the WEST END[1] of London (W1), in the City of Westminster, running from PICCADILLY CIRCUS in the east to HYDE PARK Corner in the west. It was developed in the latter part of the 17th century and largely rebuilt a hundred years later. The northern edge of GREEN PARK runs along its western end.

Dividing the Court and Clubland enclaves of ST JAMES'S to the south from the aristocratic haunts of MAYFAIR to the north, Piccadilly became in the 19th century a highly fashionable street in which to own a town house (*see also* ROTHSCHILD ROW). And by the end of the century it had turned into high society's pleasure land (**the Dilly** was the place to find a toff, and also a prostitute):

> Oh, my name is Diamond Lily,
> I'm a whore in Piccadilly,
> And my father has a brothel in the Strand,
> My brother sells his areshole
> To the Guards at Windsor Castle,
> We're the finest fucking family in the land.
>
> Anon: 'Diamond Lily'

Wodehousian sprigs and clubmen would promenade up and down, seeing and being seen (P.G. Wodehouse titled one of his books *Piccadilly Jim* (1918)), perhaps popping into the Piccadilly Restaurant and Grill Room (**the Pic**) or the Ritz Hotel (opened in 1906). Piccadilly had its shops, too: the high-class grocers Fortnum and Mason; bookseller-royal Hatchard's; the outfitters Simpson's (now a bookshop); and the grocers Jackson's (their brand-name tea can still be found in airport shops all round the world, even though their own shop closed in 1980). Lyons opened its first tea shop in Piccadilly, in 1894.

As the 20th century moved on, the fine mansions were vacated (a reminder of them survives in Burlington House,

home since the 1860s of the Royal Academy), and Piccadilly's mystique came under threat. By the end of the century it was everyman's street, geared up for shopping and tourism. The Ritz survives (as do Fortnum's and Hatchard's, though the latter is no longer independent), but package-tour groups are more in evidence here than white ties and tiaras. Nevertheless, Piccadilly rates a respectable £280 on the Monopoly board.

> If you walk down Piccadilly with a poppy or a lily in your medieval hand.
>
> W.S. Gilbert and Arthur Sullivan: *Patience* (1881), Act I (The opera satirizes Oscar Wilde and the other Aesthetes)

> Goodbye, Piccadilly,
> Farewell, Leicester Square …
>
> Jack Judge and Harry Williams: 'It's a Long Way to Tipperary' (song, 1912)

There is a town called Piccadilly in Newfoundland, Canada.

piccadilly. A Cockney rhyming-slang term for 'silly'.

Piccadilly bushman. An Australian slang term applied in the early 20th century to a wealthy Australian who had left his native land for London. The Australian Ray Lawler wrote a play called *The Piccadilly Bushman* (1959).

Piccadilly Butchers, the. A former nickname for the Life Guards, due to their role in quelling the so-called **Piccadilly Riots** in 1810; one rioter was killed. The Piccadilly Riots were also called the Burdett Riots, as the occasion was the arrest of the radical politician Sir Francis Burdett on the warrant of the Speaker of the House of Commons.

Piccadilly cramp. An 18th-century slang expression for venereal disease.

Piccadilly crawl. An affected style of walking adopted by fashionable society during the 1880s.

Piccadilly daisy. A slang term in the first half of the 20th century for a prostitute. The allusion is to Piccadilly and PICCADILLY CIRCUS as notorious pick-up points in the era of street prostitution – for homosexuals as well as hetero-sexuals (the **dilly boys** serviced the formers' needs). In Second World War army slang, prostitutes were **Piccadilly commandos**.

Piccadilly fringe. A women's hairstyle popular in the late 19th century, in which the hair was cut short into a fringe and curled over the forehead.

'Piccadilly Johnny with the Little Glass Eye, The'. One of the best-known songs of Vesta Tilley (1864–1956), doyen(ne) of male impersonators in the music-halls.

Piccadilly line. A deep-level tube line on the London Underground system, running between Cockfosters in the east and Heathrow and Uxbridge in the west. It opened in 1906. It is known to those who work on the Underground as **'the Pic'**. The distance between LEICESTER SQUARE and COVENT GARDEN (0.25 km/0.16 miles) is the shortest between any two stations on the Underground.

Piccadilly percy. 1970s' rhyming slang for 'mercy'.

Piccadilly weepers. Long bushy side whiskers, worn without a beard and temporarily fashionable in the mid- to late 19th century.

Piccadilly window. A late 19th- and early 20th-century slang term for a monocle, as affected by the fashionable men promenading in Piccadilly.

> Nah I'm goin' to be a reg'lar toff …
> A Piccadilly winder in my eye.
>
> E. Graham: 'The Golden Dustman' (song, 1897)

Rake of Piccadilly, the. William Douglas, 4th Duke of Queensberry (1724–1810), a noted hellraiser also known as 'Old Q'. William Wordsworth referred to him as 'degenerate Douglas' (*see under* NEIDPATH CASTLE).

Piccadilly² Named after London's PICCADILLY¹.

A street in central Manchester, running southeast from the Arndale (shopping) Centre, past **Piccadilly Gardens** (and its eponymous bus station) to **Piccadilly Station**, the city's main railway station.

Piccadilly Circus From PICCADILLY¹.

An open crossroads in the WEST END¹ of London (W1), at the junction of PICCADILLY¹ and REGENT STREET. It was formed in 1819, when Regent Street was in the course of construction. It was originally circular (hence the name 'Circus'), but the northeastern part was demolished in the 1880s to admit the southern end of Shaftesbury Avenue, and in the late 20th century it was partially pedestrianized, eliminating its circular traffic flow.

Situated between the swells' Piccadilly and the more downmarket delights of SOHO, Piccadilly Circus became the hub of the West End. It used to be said, somewhat hyperbolically, that if you stood here for long enough, everyone you had ever known would walk past you. Modern developments may have driven out its human characters, from flower girls to prostitutes (often one and the same), but its physical aspect remains an icon of London. First and foremost there is its instantly recognizable statue, a boyish winged figure with a bow (pointing down Lower Regent Street), standing on one leg. Topping the Shaftesbury Memorial Fountain, erected in 1893 to commemorate the Earl of Shaftesbury, it was originally intended to represent the Angel of Christian Charity, but it rapidly became known as Eros. It was designed by Alfred Gilbert, and was the first statue in London to be made of aluminium. Since 1937 it has been boarded up on New Year's Eve and other such occasions, to deter revellers, and it spent the Second World War in Egham, Surrey. Visitors to London still seem to be seized with an irresistible desire to sit around its base (which has long since ceased to be a fountain).

Then there are the neon signs. The first electrically illuminated signs, advertising Bovril and Schweppes, were in place by 1910, and after the First World War these were followed by swathes of other winking, throbbing lights proclaiming the virtues of a whole range of products, from chewing gum to stout (the famous 'Guinness clock'). *The Times* in 1928 disapproved ('a hideous eyesore which no civilized community ought to tolerate'), but by then the neon had become a permanent and dominating feature of the northern side of the Circus (the free displays led Piccadilly Circus to be dubbed in the 1930s and 1940s the 'Scotsman's Cinema'). Like a little bit of Times Square, New York City, transplanted into London, it stands for London as pleasure city: this way for theatres, restaurants, nightclubs, bars, strip clubs, brothels. In the 21st century the products advertised are different, and digital screens have replaced neon, but the Circus retains much of its unique visual flavour.

The first Chinese restaurant in Europe opened in Piccadilly Circus in 1908, when Chung Koon, a Chinese ship's cook, left his vessel and, marrying an English girl, set up an eating establishment here called the Cathay.

Piccadilly Circus Underground station, on the Bakerloo and Piccadilly lines, was opened in 1906.

Piccadilly Corner Probably from London's PICCADILLY¹, perhaps ironically suggesting remoteness.

A village in Norfolk, about 8 km (5 miles) southwest of Bungay.

Pickering 'Picer's people's place', OE male personal name *Picer* + *-ingas* 'followers, family' (*see* -ING).

A market town in North Yorkshire, 25 km (16 miles) west of Scarborough. It is on the south side of the NORTH YORK MOORS, in the **Vale of Pickering**, a large flat area of fertile land. The castle (ruined but well-preserved) is said to have been used as a base for hunting by every English monarch up to 1400. Richard II was kept here shortly before his murder at PONTEFRACT.

Pickletillem Etymology unknown.

A hamlet in Fife, 4 km (2.5 miles) south of Newport-on-Tay.

Picts' Wall. *See* HADRIAN'S WALL.

Piddle 'marsh, fen', OE *pidele*.

A river in Dorset. It rises to the north of PIDDLEHINTON and flows 33 km (21 miles) south and then east through WAREHAM into a wide estuary and thence into POOLE Harbour.

In Thomas Hardy's novel *Far from the Madding Crowd* (1874), Bathsheba Everdene's home, Waterstone Manor, is by the Piddle.

The blatant suggestiveness of the name has led to the supposition that certain derived names (*see* PUDDLETOWN, TOLPUDDLE, TURNERS PUDDLE) have been bowdlerized, but in fact the change of 'i' to 'u' took place by perfectly normal phonological means in the early Middle Ages, when no need for euphemism would have been felt – *piddle* 'to urinate' did not come on the scene until the 18th century. And anyway, the local pronunciation of the 'puddle' places is still 'piddle'. Fortunately for those for whom it is all too much, the river has an alternative name – **the Trent**.

Piddlehinton 'estate on the River Piddle belonging to a religious community', PIDDLE + OE *hiwan* 'members of a religious community' + -TON.
A village in Dorset, on the River PIDDLE, about 6.5 km (4 miles) northeast of Dorchester. In the novels of Thomas Hardy it is fictionalized as **Longpuddle** or **Upper Longpuddle**.

Piddletrenthide 'estate on the River Piddle assessed at thirty hides', PIDDLE + OFr *trente* 'thirty' + OE *hid* 'hide' (an amount of land that would support one free family and its dependants, around 50 ha / 120 acres).
A village in Dorset, on the River PIDDLE, about 10 km (6 miles) north of Dorchester.

Pigeon Hugo Perhaps 'waterfall cave', *Pigeon* Cornish *pystill* 'waterfall'; *Hugo* Cornish *googoo* 'cave' (*ogo* in ModE dialect).
A high cliff (also known as **Pigeon Ogo**) to the northwest of KYNANCE COVE in Cornwall, on the western side of the LIZARD peninsula.

Pigeons, the Presumably self-explanatory.
A village in County Westmeath, just north of Auburn, 30 km (19 miles) west of Mullingar.

Pilgrims Hatch 'hatch-gate used by pilgrims (to the nearby chapel of St Thomas)', ME *pilegrim* 'pilgrim', with OE *hœcc* 'hatch, hatch-gate'.
A village in Essex, now effectively a northwestern suburb of BRENTWOOD.

Pilgrims' Way From its use by pilgrims; the name seems to have been bestowed on it in the 18th century.
The ancient route from WINCHESTER in Hampshire along the southern slope of the North Downs to CANTERBURY[1] in Kent, used in the Middle Ages by pilgrims visiting the shrines of St Swithin and Thomas Becket. The road followed by medieval pilgrims follows a much older trackway, probably a prehistoric trade route. Hilaire Belloc wrote of it in *The Old Road* (1904). Its original length was about 190 km (118 miles). Nowadays it forms part of the North Downs Way (*see under* NORTH DOWNS).

Pill 'creek', Somerset dialect.
A village in North Somerset (before 1996 in Avon, before 1974 in Somerset), on the south bank of the River AVON[2], about 5 km (3 miles) southeast of Avonmouth, now effectively part of EASTON IN GORDANO.

Pillar From the pillar-like crags below its summit.
A mountain (892 m / 2927 ft) in the western LAKE DISTRICT, Cumbria (formerly in Cumberland), rising above Ennerdale, some 15 km (9 miles) southwest of Keswick. The great cliff of **Pillar Rock** with its many fine rock climbs, is on the north side of the summit; it has two tops, High Man and Low Man. South of High Man is Jordan Gap, leading to the subsidiary summit called Pisgah. On the east side of Pillar Rock is the buttress called Shamrock.

> The mountains at the head of this Lake [Ennerdale Water] and Wastdale are the Monsters of the Country, bare bleak heads, evermore doing deeds of darkness, weather-plots, and storm-conspiracies in the clouds. Their names are Herd House, Bowness, Wha Head, Great Gavel [Great Gable], the Steeple, the Pillar and Seat Allian [Seatallan].
>
> Samuel Taylor Coleridge: letter to Sara Hutchinson (5 August 1802) (written at the top of Scafell)

Pilleth 'slope by the pool', OE *pull* 'pool' + *hlith* 'slope'.
A small village in Powys (formerly in Radnorshire), 6 km (4 miles) northwest of Presteigne.
Battle of Pilleth (June 1402). A battle in which Owain Glyndwr defeated the forces of Henry IV under Sir Edmund Mortimer. Mortimer was captured, and changed sides.

> ... the noble Mortimer,
> Leading the men of Herefordshire to fight
> Against the irregular and wild Glendower,
> Was by the rude hands of that Welshman taken,
> A thousand of his people butchered;
> Upon whose dead corpse there was such misuse,
> Such beastly shameless transformation,
> By those Welshmen done, as may not be
> Without much shame re-told or spoken of.
>
> William Shakespeare: *Henry IV, Part 1* (1597), I.i

For further examples of good cross-border relations, *see* OFFA'S DYKE.

Pilltown. An alternative spelling of PILTOWN.

Pilsdon Pen *Pilsdon* 'hill with a peak', OE *pil* 'pointed stake' + *dun* 'hill' (*see* DOWN, -DON); *Pen* 'hill'.
A hill in Dorset, to the north of the hamlet of Pilsdon, about 11 km (7 miles) northwest of BRIDPORT. At 303 m (909 ft) it is the highest in the county. There is an Iron Age earthwork on the summit.

Piltdown 'Pilca's hill', OE male personal name *Pilca* + *dun* 'hill' (*see* DOWN, -DON).
A hamlet in East Sussex, about 4 km (2.5 miles) northwest of Uckfield.
Piltdown Man. Skeletal remains found on **Piltdown Common**, once thought to be those of a fossil hominid. It was in 1908 and 1911 that Charles Dawson of Lewes 'discovered' two pieces of a highly mineralized human skull in a gravel bed here. By 1912 he and Dr Arthur Smith Woodward, Keeper of Geology at the British Museum

(Natural History), had unearthed a whole skull. This was thought to be that of a new genus of man, and was officially classified as *Eoanthropus dawsoni*. It came to be accepted as such by prehistorians, archaeologists and others, although a few were sceptical. In 1953 J.S. Weiner, K.P. Oakley and W.E. Le Gros Clark issued a report (*Bulletin of the British Museum* (Natural History), Vol. II, No. 3) announcing that the Piltdown mandible was a fake, in reality the jaw of a modern ape, the rest of the skull being that of *Homo sapiens*. Extinct animal bones and tools had also been placed in the site. The hoax, which duped most of the experts, was apparently planned by Charles Chatwin and Martin Hinton, two young palaeontologists working at the British Museum, to discredit their dictatorial boss Woodward.

Piltown Irish *Baile an Phoill* 'town of the pool or creek'.
A village, also spelt **Pilltown**, in County Kilkenny, 20 km (12 miles) northwest of Waterford.
Battle of Piltown (1462). An Irish engagement in the Wars of the Roses, in which Thomas, Earl of Desmond, defeated the Lancastrian Butlers, led by John, Earl of Ormond. Another Butler, Émonn mac Risderd, was captured and ransomed himself by handing over two valuable manuscript books.

Pimlico The ultimate source of the name is probably the *Pamlico* Indians of North America, who lived on the banks of the Pamlico river, near the settlements founded by Sir Walter Raleigh in Virginia in the 1580s. The colonists' lack of success, and the return of many of them to England, probably lent the name some familiarity, and at least one person seems to have taken it up as a personal name. This was Ben Pemlico or Pimlico, a brewer and tavern-keeper of Hoxton, who first appears in the records in a 1598 tract, *Newes from Hogsdon*. His alehouse was named after him, and it became famous for its Pimlico ale ('Have at thee, then, my merrie boys, and hey for old Ben Pimlico's nut-browne', to quote the tract). Ben eventually settled in the district that shares his name, and it seems likely that its name (first recorded in 1626) was copied from his original alehouse, or from Ben himself.
A district in southwestern Central London, in the City of WESTMINSTER (SW1), on the north bank of the River Thames to the south of VICTORIA[2] and to the west of CHELSEA. It was once noted for its pleasure gardens (pleasure in the euphemistic as well as the innocent sense), such as the Mulberry Garden (now the site of BUCKINGHAM PALACE) and Ranelagh Gardens, and for the pub Jenny's Whim. Much of the area was low-lying waste ground until the 1830s, when Thomas Cubitt began to develop it as a residential district. It was never quite as grand or fashionable as neighbouring BELGRAVIA (although useful as a stopping-off point for those aspiring in that direction), and after the Second World War it became a vaguely upper-crustish bedsitterland, ideal for the offspring of impoverished

aristocrats. At Pimlico's southern edge, on MILLBANK, there is the old Tate Gallery (now Tate Britain).
The composer Sir Michael Tippett (1904–98) was born in Pimlico.
The name 'Pimlico' has been used since 1991 as the name of a paperback non-fiction imprint of Random House UK, whose offices are in Pimlico.
Pimlico Underground station, on the Victoria line, opened in 1972. In the USA, Baltimore, Maryland has a Pimlico Race Course.
Passport to Pimlico. A film (1948) about a district of London that declares itself to be an independent state after the discovery of an ancient charter identifying the area as part of Burgundy. Starring Stanley Holloway and Margaret Rutherford among the citizens of the breakaway republic, it was the first of the so-called 'Ealing comedies' (*see under* EALING), and its title is still commonly quoted whenever a British village, town or city threatens to exert political independence in some form or other.
'that's gone to Pimlico'. A piece of 19th-century slang meaning 'that's ruined, that's smashed beyond repair', alluding to the reputation of Pimlico as a home of 'fallen women'.

Pimperne Perhaps 'five trees', OCelt *pimp* 'five' + *prenn* 'tree', or alternatively 'place among the hills', from a derivative of OE *pimp* 'hill'.
A village in Dorset, about 3 km (2 miles) northeast of Blandford Forum. To the north is **Pimperne Down**.

Pinchbeck 'minnow stream', OE *pinc* 'minnow' + *bece* 'stream in a valley' (influenced by OScand *bekkr*), or 'finch ridge', OE *pinca* 'finch' + *bæc* 'ridge'.
A village in Lincolnshire, close to the southwestern corner of the WASH, about 3 km (2 miles) north of Spalding.
pinchbeck. An alloy of copper and zinc, which resembles gold, and which takes its name from its creator Christopher Pinchbeck (d.1732), a watchmaker of Fleet Street: his family name would have derived from the Lincolnshire village.

Pinchinthorpe 'outlying farm of the Pinchun family', family name *Pinchun* + THORPE.
A hamlet in Redcar and Cleveland (formerly in the North Riding of Yorkshire, then in Cleveland), at the foot of the Cleveland Hills (*see under* CLEVELAND) just west of Guisborough. **Pinchinthorpe Hall**, now a country house hotel, dates from the 17th century.

Pineapple, the. A unique building in the garden of the Dunmore estate 9 km (5.5 miles) north of Falkirk. It was formerly in Stirlingshire, then in Central region, and is now in the unitary authority of Falkirk. The building (which is 14 m / 45 ft high) has a roof in the form of a giant stone pineapple. It was built in 1761 by an unknown architect, and pineapples were actually grown in the hothouse buildings on either side. It is now owned by the National Trust for Scotland, and leased to the Landmark Trust, which lets it as a holiday house.

Pinkie 'wedge-shaped valley', OCelt *pant* 'valley' + *cyn* 'wedge'; *Pontekyn* 12th century.

A battle site just south of MUSSELBURGH, in East Lothian (formerly in Midlothian), where on 10 September 1547 the English Protector during Edward VI's minority, the Duke of Somerset, defeated the Scots in the pursuit of his attempt to marry the young king to the infant Mary Queen of Scots. This policy was a continuation of the 'Rough Wooing' that had led to the earlier defeat of the English at Ancrum Moor (*see under* ANCRUM).

Pinkworthy Pond *Pinkworthy* perhaps 'Pinca's farm or enclosure', OE male personal name *Pinca* + *worthig* 'farm, enclosure' (*see* -WORTH, WORTHY, -WARDINE); alternatively the first element could be from OE *pinca* 'finch' or from the ModE plant name *pink*.

A pond (pronounced 'pinkery') on EXMOOR, about 7 km (11 miles) south of Lynton. It was created in the 19th century by local landowner John Knight, but its intended function is obscure.

Pinn Perhaps 'head, hilltop', OCelt PEN.

A village in south Devon, close to the coast, about 1.5 km (1 mile) west of Sidmouth.

Pinner 'peg-shaped or pointed flat-topped hill' (referring to an elongated ridge in the area), OE *pinn* 'point, peg' + *ora* 'elongated, flat-topped hill'.

A district of West London, in the borough of HARROW (before 1965 in Middlesex), between Harrow to the east and Ruislip to the west. Its very name seems to suggest middle-class neatness. It still has enough of the *rus in urbe* about it to qualify as part of METROLAND (Pinner 'Underground' station, on the Metropolitan line, opened in 1885).

> Early Electric! Sit you down and see,
> 'Mid this fine woodwork and a smell of dinner,
> A stained-glass windmill and a pot of tea,
> And sepia views of leafy lanes in Pinner, –
> Then visualize, far down the shining lines,
> Your parents' homestead set in murmuring pines.
>
> John Betjeman: 'The Metropolitan Railway' (1958)

Pinner was the birthplace of the novelist Ivy Compton-Burnett (1892–1969) and of the singer and songwriter Elton John (b.1947; real name Reg Dwight).

Sinner from Pinner, the. A name bestowed by the British media on the Pinner-bred teenager Jane March when she appeared as an 18-year-old in *The Lover* (1992), a film adaptation of a novel by the French writer Marguerite Duras. Such was the 'erotic authenticity' of March's love scenes with her co-star Tony Leung that rumours began to circulate that there was no 'acting' involved.

Pinvin 'Penda's fen' (despite local folklore, almost certainly not a reference to King Penda, the last great heathen king of Mercia (d. 654)), OE male personal name *Penda* + *fenn* 'fen'.

A village in Worcestershire (before 1998 in Hereford and Worcester, before 1974 in Worcestershire), about 13 km (8 miles) southeast of Worcester.

Pinxton Perhaps 'Penec's farmstead', OE *Peneces* possessive form of male personal name *Penec* + -TON.

A village in Derbyshire, about 19 km (12 miles) southeast of Chesterfield. Soft-paste porcelain ware was made here between 1796 and 1813, and the village's name is used to designate the factory's products. As G.A. Godden remarks, 'typical Pinxton porcelain is similar to puce-marked Derby porcelain of the 1790–1800 period' (*Illustrated Encyclopedia of British Pottery and Porcelain*, 1966).

Pipe and Lyde Originally two separate villages: *Pipe* 'pipe, conduit' (referring to a local stream, OE); *Lyde* from the name of the stream, literally 'the loud one', OE *Hlyde*.

A village in Herefordshire (before 1998 in Hereford and Worcester, before 1974 in Herefordshire), about 5 km (3 miles) north of Hereford.

Pipe Ridware *Pipe* denoting manorial ownership in the early Middle Ages by the Pipe family; *Ridware see* HAMSTALL RIDWARE.

A village in Staffordshire, on the River Blithe, about 8 km (5 miles) north of Lichfield.

See also MAVESYN RIDWARE.

Pipton 'Pippa's farm' or 'farm of the piper(s)', OE male personal name, or *pipere* 'piper', perhaps a musician or a bird name + -TON.

A village on the River WYE[1] (Gwy) in Powys, 8 km (5 miles) southwest of Hay-on-Wye.

Treaty of Pipton (19 June 1265). An agreement between Llywelyn ap Gruffydd of Gwynedd and Simon de Montfort, by which the latter was to receive £20,000 in return for recognizing Llywelyn as Prince of Wales (at this point Simon held Henry III prisoner). Two years later, after Simon's death, Henry III made a similar treaty with Llywelyn at MONTGOMERY.

Pirbright 'sparse woodland where pear-trees grow', OE *pirige* 'pear-tree' + *fyrhth* 'sparse woodland'.

A village in Surrey, about 8 km (5 miles) southwest of Woking. It is in the midst of northwest Surrey army country (Aldershot and Camberley are not far away), and before 1993 it was home to the Guards Depot. It now houses the Army Training Regiment. Its name no doubt inspired P.G. Wodehouse in his creation of the Jeeves-and-Wooster character 'Catsmeat' Potter-Pirbright.

Pisgah[1] The mountain overlooking Palestine on the summit of which Moses died, after having had his first sight of the Promised Land (Deuteronomy 3:27: 'Get thee up into the top of Pisgah, and lift up thine eyes westward, and northward, and southward, and eastward, and behold it with thine eyes: for thou shalt not go over this Jordan'); it is also called NEBO.

A hamlet overlooking the Vale of Rheidol in Ceredigion (formerly Cardiganshire, then part of Dyfed), some 12 km (7 miles) east of Aberystwyth.

Pisgah². A summit of PILLAR in the western Lake District.

Pisgah³. A village overlooking Dunblane in Stirling unitary authority (formerly in Stirlingshire, then in Central region).

Pishill 'hill where peas grow', OE *pise* 'pea' + *hyll* 'hill'.

A village (pronounced 'pishəl') in Oxfordshire, in the Chilterns, about 10 km (6 miles) northwest of Henley-on-Thames.

Pitcox 'a fifth portion', OCelt *pett* 'portion' + Gaelic *coig* 'one fifth', presumably one fifth of an original estate.

A hamlet in East Lothian, 5 km (3 miles) southwest of Dunbar.

Pitcur Probably OCelt *pett* 'portion' with an unidentified second element.

A small settlement in Perth and Kinross, on the north side of the SIDLAW HILLS, 4 km (2.5 miles) southeast of Coupar Angus. **Pitcur Castle**, now a ruin, dates from the 16th century, and was built by the Hallyburton family. **James Hallyburton of Pitcur** (1518–89) was provost of Dundee and one of the leading Protestant Lords of the Congregation who fought against Mary Queen of Scots.

Pitlochry 'stony place', OCelt *pett* 'portion, area' + *cloichreach* 'stony'.

A resort town in Perth and Kinross (formerly in Perthshire, and then in Tayside region), 18 km (11 miles) north of Dunkeld, now bypassed by the A9 Perth–Inverness road. It is regarded as the geographical centre of Scotland. The annual summer **Pitlochry Festival** of drama and music was founded in 1951.

> There was an old maid of Pitlochry
> Whose morals were truly a mockery,
> For under her bed
> Was a lover instead
> Of the usual porcelain crockery.
>
> Anon.: limerick

Nearby is Loch Faskally, with a spectacular salmon ladder bypassing its dam.

Pittenweem 'place of the cave', OCelt *pett* 'portion, area' + *na* 'of the' + *h-uamha* 'cave'.

A royal burgh (1542) and fishing port in Fife, on the north shore of the Firth of Forth, 15 km (9 miles) south of St Andrews. The name refers to St Fillan's Cave, supposedly the cell of the 9th-century missionary, which is still sometimes used for religious services. There are many well-preserved houses from the 16th and 17th centuries, when the town grew prosperous on trade with the Continent.

In 1704–05 Pittenweem was the setting of a notorious witch-hunt, in which a local youth, Patrick Morton, made wild allegations that led to the deaths of three people and the torture of many more. The last to die, Janet Bornfoot, was caught by a mob, beaten, stoned, and finally crushed under a door weighted down with rocks.

The Porteous Riots that took place in Edinburgh in 1736 had their origins in the robbery of an exciseman in Pittenweem by the smugglers Robertson and Wilson. (The riots feature in Sir Walter Scott's *Heart of Midlothian* – *see under* MIDLOTHIAN).

Pity Me First recorded in the 19th century, and originally a disparaging field name, as in 'pity me having to work this land'; a fanciful alternative etymology is 'small lake', OFr *petit* 'small' + *mere* 'lake' (there is no lake); also fanciful are the suggestions that when the monks were bringing St Cuthbert's coffin to DURHAM they dropped the coffin here, causing the saintly corpse to cry 'Pity me!'; and that the name represents the cries of the peewits or lapwings that are common hereabouts.

A village in County Durham, 4 km (2.5 miles) north of Durham itself.

Pixey Green A modern name, possibly referring to pixies.

A village in Suffolk, about 16 km (10 miles) west of Halesworth.

Plaistow 'place for play or sport' (probably referring to some sort of village-green-like public gathering place), OE *pleg-stow*.

A district (pronounced 'plasstow' or 'plahstow') of East London, in the borough of NEWHAM, between East Ham and West Ham. Its urbanization dates from the middle of the 19th century, when the railway arrived. Plaistow 'Underground' station, on the District and Metropolitan lines, opened in 1902.

The punk balladeer Ian Dury invented the character '**Plaistow Patricia**' for a song of the same name (1977). Plaistow Patricia is a seedy drug addict, killing herself through a life of excess:

> Well her tits had dropped, her arse was getting spread,
> She lost some teeth, she nearly lost the thread,
> 'Till she did some smack with a Chinese chap oh, oh,
> An affair began with Charlie Chan oh, oh.

Planet of the IRPS. A nickname of the DIVIS FLATS in the Lower Falls area of west Belfast.

Plas Newydd 'new mansion', Welsh *plas* 'mansion, park', with *newydd* 'new'.

A house and estate in ANGLESEY, 3 km (2 miles) southwest of Llanfairpwll. It has a notably scenic setting, overlooking the MENAI STRAIT and yielding excellent views of SNOWDONIA. The house's architecture offers an 18th-century classical-Gothic combination (its architect was James Watt).

Plas Newydd's chief artistic attraction lies in the works of Rex Whistler (1905–44), which populate the house. They were undertaken under the patronage of the 6th Marquess of Anglesey, and dominating them is the Italianate scene depicted in the enormous dining-room mural.

The garden contains a number of hybrid rhododendrons originally brought here from BODNANT.

Plaxtol 'place for play or sport', OE *pleg-stow* (*see also* PLAISTOW).
A village in Kent, about 8 km (5 miles) southeast of Sevenoaks.

Playing Place Originally the name of a circular area used for games.
A village in Cornwall, about 5 km (3 miles) southwest of Truro. It developed in the 20th century.

Plockton The Gaelic name is *Am Ploc*, Gaelic *am* 'the' + *ploc* 'lump, clod'; in *c*.1800 the local laird founded the village and added -TON.
An attractive village on the west coast of Highland (formerly in Ross and Cromarty), on a peninsula 8 km (5 miles) northeast of Kyle of Lochalsh. The place is popular with visiting yachtsmen, and many outsiders have settled here (the latter have objected to the local cows fouling the streets). The village and its environs formed the setting of the BBC television Sunday-night drama series *Hamish Macbeth* (1995–7), with Robert Carlyle in the title role as the local bobby. In the series Plockton was called 'Loch Dubh'.

Ploxgreen *Plox* 'small plots of land', ME *plocks* + ModE *green*; an upmarket name for an 18th-century housing estate.
A village in Shropshire, about 16 km (10 miles) southwest of Shrewsbury.

Plumbland 'plum-tree grove', OE *plume* 'plum-tree' + OScand *lundr* 'grove'.
A hamlet in Cumbria, 9 km (5.5 miles) northeast of Cockermouth. The church at Plumbland (a Victorian edifice that replaced a Norman church, itself replacing a Saxon foundation) is supposedly on the site where St Cuthbert's body rested during its long journey (*c*.870–90) from Lindisfarne to DURHAM. It is said that the beck at Plumbland turned red at the time of the execution of Charles I.

Plumpton 'farmstead where plum-trees grow', OE *plume* 'plum-tree' + -TON.
A village in East Sussex, on the SOUTH DOWNS, about 6 km (4 miles) northwest of Lewes. It is best known for its horse-racing track, whose sharp inclined bends have earned it the nickname 'the Wall of Death'.

Plumstead 'place where plum-trees grow', OE *plume* 'plum-tree' + *stede* 'place'.
A district in southeast London (SE18), in the borough of GREENWICH, between Woolwich to the west and Thames-

mead to the northeast. Until the middle of the 19th century it was largely riverside marshland, well drained, on which sheep grazed and fruit-trees were grown (as its name suggests); but thereafter urbanization took hold rapidly. However, after vocal demonstrations in the 1870s, local people won the right to have about 40 ha (100 acres) of common land preserved for public use – the current **Plumstead Common**.

The snooker-player Steve Davis (b.1957) was born in Plumstead.

Plumstead Peculiars, the. A London religious sect (more generally known as 'the Peculiar People') founded in 1838, and one of the more exotic forms of nonconformism that characterized the area. Its adherents refused medical aid, but not surgical, and relied on the efficacy of prayer and on anointing with oil by the elders. The sect's name was based on Titus 2:14: 'Who gave himself for us, that he might … purify unto himself a peculiar people' (*peculiar* in this context means 'belonging particularly to himself', not 'odd'). Their chapel closed in 1934.

Plumtree '(place at the) plum-tree', OE *plum-treow*.
A village in Nottinghamshire, about 10 km (6 miles) southeast of Nottingham.

Plungar 'triangular plot where plum-trees grow', OE *plume* 'plum-tree' + *gar* 'triangular plot'.
A village in Leicestershire, in the VALE OF BELVOIR, about 13 km (8 miles) west of Grantham.

Plush '(place at the) shallow pool', OE *plysc*.
A village in Dorset, about 17.5 km (11 miles) southwest of Blandford Forum.

Plusterwine Origin unknown.
A village in Gloucestershire, on the western side of the SEVERN estuary, about 5 km (3 miles) southwest of Lydney.

Plym A back-formation from PLYMPTON.
A river in Devon, which rises in the southwest of DARTMOOR, in the **Upper Plym Valley**, and flows 26 km (16 miles) southeastwards through **Plym Forest** and past the heritage **Plym Valley Railway** into the English Channel between PLYMPTON and PLYMOUTH.

Plymouth 'mouth of the River Plym', PLYM + OE *mutha* 'mouth'.
A seaport, city and unitary authority at the southwestern corner of Devon, at the mouth of the River Plym, on the eastern side of the HAMOAZE, about 60 km (37 miles) southwest of Exeter.

Its original English name was **Sutton** ('southern village'), which is preserved in 'Sutton Harbour', one of Plymouth's three harbours, and also in the name of one of its parliamentary constituencies (see SUTTON²). The adoption of the name 'Plymouth' seems to have been a 13th-century development.

By the end of the Middle Ages Plymouth was the pre-eminent port along this stretch of coast, and it was mainly from here that 16th-century English explorers and merchant venturers set out on their voyages of discovery around the world (Sir Francis Drake began his circumnavigation in the *Golden Hind* from Plymouth in 1577, and in 1581 he became mayor of the town). It was also the Pilgrim Fathers' starting-off point in 1620, Captain Cook's in 1772, Charles Darwin and the *Beagle*'s in 1831, and round-the-world yachtsman Francis Chichester's in 1966. Its strategic importance was established in 1588 when the English fleet sailed out from Plymouth to engage the Spanish Armada for the first time. Towards the end of the 17th century the Royal Naval Dockyard was constructed just to the west, at DEVONPORT, and since then Plymouth has had a continuous history as a Royal Navy port, guarding the WESTERN APPROACHES. It was very heavily bombed during the Second World War, and much of its present-day fabric is recent. The somewhat grim city centre is designed around two decidedly *Ostbloc*-style thoroughfares, named Armada Way and Royal Parade.

> Soft as the night and silent as the snow
> Rain pours her arrows on the open city
> The sailor and his fancy homeward go
> And evening draws its shutter, as in pity.
>
> Charles Causley (1917–2003): 'Plymouth'

Plymouth is also an international ferry port, maintaining services to Roscoff (France) and Santander (Spain). Shipping is guided into the harbour by the Eddystone Lighthouse (*see under* EDDYSTONE ROCKS).

The **University of Plymouth** was formed in 1992 from the Polytechnic of the South West (formerly Plymouth Polytechnic).

Sir John Hawkins (1532–95), old sea dog and mate of Sir Francis Drake, was born in Plymouth, as were William Bligh (1754–*c*.1817), commander of HMS *Bounty*, the historical painter and autobiographer Benjamin Haydon (1786–1846), the light versifier Austin Dobson (1840–1921), the literary critic and editor J.C. Squire (1884–1958), the Labour politician Michael Foot (b.1913), and the actors Richard Greene (1918–85; 'Robin Hood' on 1950s' television) and Donald Sinden (b.1923). David Owen (b.1938), who was born in PLYMPTON and represented two Plymouth constituencies in Parliament, took the title 'Lord Owen of Plymouth' when he was ennobled in 1992 (*see also* LIMEHOUSE). The artist Beryl Cook (b.1926) was once the landlady of a Plymouth boarding-house.

There are towns called Plymouth in the USA (California, Indiana, Iowa, Massachusetts (situated on Plymouth Bay and the first European settlement in New England, established by the Pilgrim Fathers in 1620), Nebraska, New Hampshire, Ohio, Pennsylvania, Utah, Vermont, Wisconsin) and in Tobago. It is also the name of the capital of Montserrat. There are towns called New Plymouth in the USA (Idaho) and New Zealand.

> Plymouth has given its name to some forty Plymouths all over the English-speaking world. What greater testimony is needed to the affection that it has inspired for the past 400 years? It is the mother of all Plymouths everywhere.
>
> W.G. Hoskins: *Devon* (1954)

See also EGGBUCKLAND *and* STONEHOUSE[2].

'Mystery of the Plymouth Express, The'. A short story by Agatha Christie. It first appeared in 1923, in *The Sketch*.

Plym. A colloquial name from the early part of the 20th century for an inhabitant of Plymouth. The expression has also been used for a member of the **Plymouth Brethren** (*see below*).

Plymouth. A sea area in the shipping forecast. It is in the English Channel, off the south coast of Cornwall and Devon, between SOLE to the west and PORTLAND to the east.

Plymouth. Used adjectivally to designate two types of ceramic ware made in Plymouth: hard-paste porcelain, the first such to be made in England, which was produced here in the later 18th century (manufacture moved to Bristol in 1774); and a coarse brown-and-yellow earthenware made in the 18th century.

Plymouth Argyll FC. Plymouth's Nationwide League football club (nickname: the Pilgrims). It was founded in 1886 as Argyle Football Club, and the reasons behind its name are not entirely clear. The Argyll and Sutherland Highlanders are said to have been stationed in the city at the time, and the locals seem to have admired their soccer skills. Then again, the club's first committee meeting was held in Argyle Terrace. It may be that both these factors came together with a general late 19th-century fashion for all things Scottish (inspired by Queen Victoria) to suggest the name. In the 20th century it was co-opted as Cockney rhyming slang for 'file' (the sort smuggled into prison in a cake).

Plymouth Brethren. An austere fundamentalist Protestant sect founded in Ireland around 1828 by a former Anglican priest, J.N. Darby (1800–82) (after whom its principles are sometimes called 'Darbyism'). They set up their first centre in England in 1830, in Plymouth – whence their name. In 1849 they split into Open Brethren and Exclusive Brethren. They have no organized ministry and lay emphasis on celebrating communion every Sunday. In its stricter form the sect allows its adherents little freedom of thought or action, and discourages close connections with non-members. This phenomenon was vividly described by auto/biographer Edmund Gosse in *Father and Son* (1907).

Plymouth cloak. A 17th-century term for a cudgel, as carried for self-protection. The idea behind the name is that the cudgel provides a defence for those without a cloak or other outer garment. A contemporary explains the Plymouth reference:

> *A Plymouth Cloak.* That is a cane or a staff, whereof this the occasion. Many a man of good extraction, coming home from far voyages, may chance to land here [at Plymouth], and being out of sorts, is unable for the present time and place to recruit himself with clothes. Here (if not friendly provided) they make the next wood their draper's shop, where a staff cut out, serves them for a covering.
>
> Thomas Fuller: *The History of the Worthies of England* (1662)

An alternative sometimes encountered is **Plymouth blade**.

Plymouth Company. A commercial trading company chartered by King James VI and I in April 1606 for the purpose of colonizing the eastern North American coast between parallels 38° and 45° N. Citizens of Plymouth were among its leading shareholders. It was not a conspicuous success: it established two colonies, but abandoned them two years later.

Plymouth gin. A variety and a brand name of English gin, as made in Plymouth, which has a more distinctive juniper flavour than London gin (*see under* LONDON). It is produced at England's oldest working gin distillery, which has been on the go since 1793.

Plymouth Hoe. An immense grassy esplanade in Plymouth, the higher parts of which offer splendid views of Plymouth Sound (*see below*). It was here that Sir Francis Drake was supposedly playing a game of bowls in 1588 when news came of the sighting of the Spanish Armada. In a defining moment of English *sang froid* he reputedly finished his game before departing to give Johnny Spaniard a seeing-to (the state of the tide would not have permitted him to sail straightaway, anyway). 'Hoe' comes from OE *hoh* 'projecting hill-spur, promontory'.

Plymouthism. The principles and practices of the Plymouth Brethren (*see above*). Its sectaries are sometimes known as **Plymouthites** or **Plymouthists**.

Plymouth of the West. A nickname of San Diego, California, bestowed because it was one of the first European settlements on the West Coast of the USA (as Plymouth, Massachusetts, was in the East). It was founded in 1769 by Father Junipero Serra.

Plymouth Rock. The place at which the Pilgrim Fathers landed in America in 1620, having set sail from Plymouth, England. The name has also been applied since the 1870s to a breed of large domestic fowl developed in the USA and widely used for meat production.

Plymouth Sound. A wide channel which leads from the confluence of the HAMOAZE and the River PLYM to the open sea. It is often known simply as **the Sound**. Its western side is guarded by Rame Head (*see under* RAME), from which the Spanish Armada was first sighted.

Plymouth Town. An early ballet score (1931) by Benjamin Britten. Its scenario concerns an innocent young sailor-boy who falls foul of a lady of the town on an evening ashore in Plymouth.

Plympton 'plum-tree farmstead', OE *plyme* 'plum-tree' + -TON. A village in Devon, once an important stannary (*see* the STANNARIES) and market town but now effectively an eastern suburb of PLYMOUTH. The painter Sir Joshua Reynolds (1723–92), who was educated at the local grammar school, was born here. In the 20th century the actor Paul Rogers (b.1917) was born here, as was the originally Labour politician David Owen (b.1938), who sat in Parliament for both the SUTTON[1] and DEVONPORT divisions of Plymouth and went on to be co-founder and leader of the Social Democratic Party.

Plymstock Probably 'outlying farmstead or hamlet associated with Plympton', PLYMPTON + OE *stoc* (*see* -STOCK, STOCK-, STOKE).

A southeastern district of PLYMOUTH, on the southern side of the River Plym.

Plynlimon George Borrow says 'Its proper name is Pum or Pump Lumon, signifying the five points, because towards the upper part it is divided into five hills or points.' He's (nearly) right: Welsh *pum(p)* 'five' + *llumon* 'chimney'.

A large, rounded mountain (752 m / 2467 ft) in Ceredigion (formerly in Cardiganshire, then in Dyfed), some 20 km (12 miles) east-northeast of Aberystwyth. In Welsh it is **Pumlumon**, and the highest of its five tops is **Pumlumon Mawr** (*mawr* 'great') or **Plynlimon Fawr**. It is noted for its wetness, mists and bogs; indeed, it is something of a giant sponge, and is celebrated as the source of the rivers Rheidol, WYE[1] (Gwy) and SEVERN (Hafren), the source of the last being known as Blaenhafren. (It is also the source of two less substantial rivers, the Dulas and Llyfant.)

> From high Plynlimmon's shaggy side
> Three streams in three directions glide;
> To thousands at their mouths who tarry
> Honey, gold and mead they carry.
> Flow also from Plynlimmon high
> Three streams of generosity;
> The first, a noble stream indeed,
> Like rills of Mona runs with mead;
> The second bears from vineyards thick
> Wine to the feeble and the sick;
> The third, till time shall be no more,
> Mingled with gold shall silver pour.
>
> Lewis Glyn Cothi: quoted by George Borrow, *Wild Wales* (1862)

Borrow sang the above-quoted lines on his ascent of the mountain; he also recorded that Plynlimon was the scene of two battles. The first, in the 10th century, saw the Danes and Welsh at blows on a spur of the mountain, the former sustaining 'a bloody overthrow'. The second, in 1401, arose when the Flemish settlers of Pembrokeshire pursued Owain Glyndwr and his men to one of the valleys at the foot of the mountain; there, although at one point almost victorious, the Flemings came off worse in the fight.

Pocklington 'Pocela's estate', OE male personal name *Pocela* + -ING + -TON.

A market town on the edge of the WOLDS in the East Riding of Yorkshire, 10 km (6 miles) northwest of Market Weighton. The grammar school dates back to 1515, and the anti-slavery campaigner William Wilberforce (1759–1833) was a pupil.

Point Lynas *Point* 'tapering land feature'; *Lynas* is thought to be a personal name.

The headland forming the northeastern corner of ANGLESEY, some 3 km (2 miles) east of Amlwch.

Point of Ayr OScand *eyrr* 'sandbank'.

The sandy headland on the western side of the mouth of the River DEE[2], in Flintshire (formerly in Clwyd), 7 km (4 miles) east of Prestatyn.

Point of Ayre OScand *eyrr* 'gravel bank'.

The northernmost tip of the ISLE OF MAN. To the southwest is the area called **the Ayres**.

Point of Stoer. *See* STOER.

Poisoned Glen, the There are various accounts of how this name came about. In legend, Balor of the Evil Eye (in Irish *Balor na Suíle Neimhe*) pursued the man who had ran off with his daughter, and he flung rocks after him, killing him. One of these rocks is now at the entrance to the glen, and is said to be the 'poisoned' or evil (Irish *neimhe*) eye of Balor. In another legend, Balor was slain here by his grandson Lugh, and blood from his single eye poisoned the land round about. In another account, Irish rebels poisoned the water in the glen as English soldiers made camp here, while in yet another it is said that the glen used to be full of Irish spurge (*see under* IRISH), which poisoned the fish in the river. The most widely accepted account, however, is that the locals called it *Glen Neamh* (Irish 'heavenly valley'), but the word *neamh* was transcribed phonetically by an English cartographer as 'Nev'; unfortunately, when this was later transcribed phonetically back into Irish it was interpreted as *nimhe* 'poisoned', and translated as such back into English.

A steep-sided glen in County Donegal, extending southwards from the village of Dunlewy into the DERRYVEAGH MOUNTAINS. Its granite cliffs have some fine rock climbs in between the vertical bog.

Pokesdown 'goblin hill', OE *poca* (ME *poke*) 'goblin' + *dun* 'hill' (*see* DOWN, -DON).

An eastern suburb of BOURNEMOUTH.

Pol A back-formation from POLPERRO.

A river in Cornwall, rising about 5 km (3 miles) inland and flowing southwards into the English Channel at Polperro.

Polapit Tamar *Polpit* perhaps 'pool in a hollow', OE *pol-pytt*, but an earlier spelling with *B-* suggests that the original name might have been *bula-pytt* 'bull-pit', perhaps a hollow for bull-baiting.

A village in Cornwall, on the Tala Water (a tributary of the River TAMAR), about 5 km (3 miles) north of Launceston.

Polchester. A fictionalized version of TRURO, which appears in the novels of Hugh Walpole (1884–1941), including *The Cathedral* (1922), *The Old Ladies* (1924) and *Harmer John* (1926).

Polden Hills *Polden* probably 'cow-pasture hill', OCelt name *Bouelt* (probably meaning 'cow pasture'; *see* BUILTH WELLS) + OE *dun* 'hill' (*see* DOWN, -DON).

A range of hills in Somerset, running roughly northwest–southeast to the northeast of Bridgwater.

Poldhu Cove *Poldhu* 'dark cove', Cornish *poll* 'pool, cove' + *du* 'black, dark' (*see* DDU, DUBH).

A cove in Cornwall, on the west coast of the LIZARD peninsula, about 9 km (5.5 miles) northwest of Lizard Point. At its southern extremity is **Poldhu Point**, from where in 1901 Guglielmo Marconi received the first transatlantic radio message in St John's, Newfoundland.

Pole of Itlaw, the The second element of Itlaw is most likely LAW, LOW 'hill' but the first is obscure; *Pole* is probably Gaelic *poll* 'pool'.

A low hill (135 m / 443 ft) west of the River DEVERON in Aberdeenshire, 7 km (4.5 miles) south of Banff.

Polesden Lacey *Polesden* 'Pal's valley', OE *Pales* possessive form of male personal name *Pal* + *denu* 'valley'; *Lacey* denoting ownership of the estate by the Lacey family (not recorded until the 1530s, so perhaps not genuinely manorial).

A country house in Surrey, about 5 km (3 miles) northwest of Dorking. It was built in the 1820s in Regency style to the designs of Thomas Cubitt (*see also* CUBITTOPOLIS), on the site of a previous house owned by the playwright Richard Brinsley Sheridan. It was extensively remodelled at the beginning of the 20th century, and now belongs to the National Trust.

Polesworth 'Poll's enclosure', OE *Polles* possessive form of male personal name *Poll* + *worth* (*see* -WORTH, WORTHY, -WARDINE).

A former coal-mining village in Warwickshire, on the River Anker, about 6 km (4 miles) east of Tamworth.

Polgooth 'goose pool' or 'pool of a watercourse', Cornish *poll* 'pool' + *goedh* 'goose' or *goeth* 'watercourse' (there was an ancient tin-works here).

A village in Cornwall, about 3 km (2 miles) southwest of St Austell.

Pollok Country Park 'little pool', OCelt *poll* 'pool' + diminutive suffix -*oc*.

A former country estate in southern GLASGOW, containing the Georgian mansion of **Pollok House** and the splendid modern gallery housing the Burrell Collection. The residential areas of **Pollokshaws** (OE *sceaga* 'wood') and **Pollokshields** (ME *schele* 'hut') are adjacent, the former to the north and the latter to the east; they are familiarly known respectively as **the Shaws** and **the Shields**.

Polmont Probably 'pool hill', Gaelic *poll*, 'pool' + Gaelic *monadh* 'hill'.

A large residential village about 4 km (2.5 miles) south of Falkirk and Grangemouth. It was formerly in Stirlingshire, then in Central region, and is now in the unitary authority of Falkirk.

Polomint City. A nickname for EAST KILBRIDE.

Polperro Probably 'Pyra's harbour', Cornish *porth* 'harbour' (*see* PORT) + male personal name *Pyra*.

A village and resort on the south coast of Cornwall, at the mouth of the River POL, about 5 km (3 miles) southwest of Looe. Its picturesque harbour was once home to a pilchard-fishing fleet, and also, in the 18th century, the location of extensive smuggling operations (the first Preventive Station in England was set up here in 1801). Now tourism has taken over, and the narrow winding streets near the harbour are crammed with souvenir shops.

Polstead 'place by a pool', OE *pol* 'pool' + *stede* 'place'.

A village in Suffolk, on the River Box, about 13 km (8 miles) southeast of SUDBURY[1]. In witch-hunting days women were immersed in the village pond here to find out if they were guilty (drowning signified innocence).

Polstead was the scene of an early 19th-century murder, which has become celebrated in legend, stage melodrama and ballad. Maria Marten was a local mole-catcher's daughter of loose morals who bore the child of Thomas Corder, the son of a prosperous farmer. Later William Corder, his younger brother, became enamoured of her with predictable consequences, but avoided marriage. In May 1827 an arrangement was apparently made for Maria to meet him at the Red Barn on his farm with the intention of going to Ipswich to be married. Maria was not seen alive again, but Corder went to London and married one Mary Moore, who kept a school. Eventually, Maria's body was discovered in the Red Barn and William Corder was hanged for her murder at Bury St Edmonds on 11 August 1828 at the age of 24.

The proceedings caused a sensation at the time (10,000 people turned out to watch the execution; the hangman sold the rope at a guinea an inch; and the trial record was bound in Corder's own skin), and the case was widely semi-fictionalized. The anonymous melodrama *Maria Marten; or, the Murder in The Red Barn* was a roaring success on the Victorian stage in the 1830s, and it is widely read and performed today, particularly by schools and amateurs, but occasionally professionally. Polstead has by now lived down its notoriety, but cottages in the village still frequently require exorcism.

Polyphant 'toad's pool', Cornish *pol* 'pool' + *lefant* 'toad'.

A village in Cornwall, on the River Inny, about 8 km (5 miles) west of Launceston. Its name has been applied to a type of greyish-green soapstone found in the locality.

Polzeath 'dry cove', Cornish *pol* 'pool, cove' + *sygh* 'dry'.

A village on the north coast of Cornwall, at the mouth of the River Camel, opposite Padstow. Its beaches are a magnet to surfers and wind-surfers.

Pom Apparently from *pomegranate*, which supposedly sounds like 'immigrant'.

A sometimes derogatory Australian and New Zealand term for a BRITON; an alternative is **Pommie**. Poms are usually whingeing and often bloody:

> Pass a law to give every single whingeing bloody Pommie his fare home to England. Back to the smoke and the sun shining ten days a year and shit in the streets. Yer can have it.
>
> Thomas Keneally: *The Chant of Jimmie Blacksmith* (1972)

Another derogatory Australian name for a Briton is a *kipper* (i.e. 'two-faced and with no guts').

Pomgolia. A jocular New Zealand name for BRITAIN, punning on Mongolia, and with a suggestion of the latter's remoteness and supposed godforsakenness. It was first recorded in the 1970s.

Pomfret. *See* PONTEFRACT.

Pomona. An alternative name for Mainland in ORKNEY.

Pompey. The nickname of PORTSMOUTH, applied particularly to the city as a Royal Navy base and (perhaps originally) to its football club. Various ingenious or fanciful suggestions have been made as to its origin, among them: that it was inspired by the captured French warship *Le Pompée*, which became the guardship of Portsmouth Harbour in 1811; that Portsmouth-based Royal Navy sailors climbed Pompey's Pillar on a visit to Alexandria in the late 18th century, and became known as the 'Pompey boys', a nickname which spread; that the local fire brigade, known as the Pompiers (from French *pompier*, literally 'pumper'), used to exercise on Southsea Common, closely adjacent to Portsmouth; and that Agnes Weston, the Victorian campaigner for sailors' welfare, was giving a lecture to sailors on a subject variously reported as Pompey (the Roman general) and Pompeii, and at a particularly affecting passage some tired and emotional members of the audience started calling out 'Poor old Pompey/Pompeii!'.

This last and rather far-fetched suggestion at least has the virtue of a connection with **Portsmouth FC**, to which the earliest known unequivocal application of the name to Portsmouth (in 1899) is attached: a few days later some of Miss Weston's audience were attending a Portsmouth home game when the goalkeeper fell over in attempting to get the ball, one of them shouted out 'Poor old Pompey!', and a nickname was born.

The more prosaic truth about the derivation of the name may be that *Pompey* is simply an erosion of *Portsmouth*, influenced by the name of the Roman general Pompey.

A complicating factor in the equation is **paws off, Pompey!**, a colloquial expression from between the early 19th century and the 1930s, meaning 'Hands off! Leave me alone!' It was coined around 1803, without the comma, and used as an anti-Napoleonic phrase, meaning 'keep your hands off Pompey'. *Pompey* here seems to have referred either to Lord Nelson (1758-1805) or to Portsmouth, but it is not clear which. By the 1830s the comma had been introduced and the phrase was generally used by women wishing to restrain an admirer's wandering hands.

The Portsmouth-born Charles Dickens put *pompey* into the mouth of Mrs Joe Gargery in *Great Expectations* (1861) as a verb, a dialectal or idiolectal transmogrification of 'pamper'.

Pompey. A novel (1993) of dystopian grotesquerie by Jonathan Meades, partially set in a town that bears a passing resemblance to Portsmouth.

Pompey whore. Early 20th-century bingo-callers' slang for the number 24. Portsmouth being a naval base, the collocation was far from a novelty.

Pomponian. A name sometimes bestowed on a native or inhabitant of Portsmouth.

Ponders End 'district (of the parish) associated with the Ponder family', ME *ende* 'end, quarter, district' + surname *Ponder*. A John Ponder is recorded at nearby Enfield in the 14th century.

A northern suburb of London, in the borough of ENFIELD (before 1965 in Middlesex), between Enfield Town to the west and the River LEA to the east.

The Conservative politician Norman Tebbitt (b.1931) was born in Ponders End.

Pons Aelius. A Roman settlement on the site of present-day NEWCASTLE UPON TYNE.

Pont Aberglaslyn. *See* ABERGLASLYN GORGE.

Pontardawe 'bridge over the River Tawe', Welsh *pont* 'bridge' + *ar* 'over' + river name meaning the same as TAFF.

A small town on the River TAWE in Neath Port Talbot (formerly in Glamorgan, then in West Glamorgan), some 13 km (8 miles) north of Swansea. The River TAWE, which rises in the hills of Forest Fawr, also gives its name to Abertawe, the Welsh name for SWANSEA[1].

Gareth Edwards, the legendary rugby union scrum-half for CARDIFF RFC, Wales and the British Lions, famed for his partnerships with outside-halves Barry John and Phil Bennett, was born here in 1947. Playing for the Barbarians against the All Blacks at Cardiff Arms Park in January 1973, Edwards scored what has been described as the greatest try ever – the culmination of a move that began with Bennett deep in the Barbarians half and passed through numerous pairs of hands before Edwards finished it by diving in to score in the corner.

Pontarfynach. The Welsh name for DEVIL'S BRIDGE[1].

Pontefract 'broken bridge', Latin *pons* 'bridge' + *fractus* 'broken'; *Pontefracto* 1090. The name is traditionally said to refer to the old Roman bridge over the River Aire, broken down by William I in 1069. Some now think it refers to a bridge over the small stream known as the Wash Dike, at the point where Bubwith Bridge is today, near the A645. Although the stream is small, the bridge over it would have been important, giving access to the main route north; it is not known when or how it was broken. There is also an OE version of the name, still sometimes used: *Pomfret*.

An industrial town in West Yorkshire, some 20 km (12 miles) southeast of Leeds. It is also called **Pomfret**, sometimes pronounced 'pumfr't'. The ruined Norman **Pontefract Castle** was the site of the final confinement and murder of Richard II in 1399:

> My lord, the mind of Bolingbroke is chang'd;
> You must to Pomfret, not unto the Tower.
>
> William Shakespeare: Northumberland in *Richard* II (1595), V.i

Pontefract was besieged three times during the Civil Wars before the Royalists surrendered in December 1644. More prominent today than the castle ruins are the vast modern cooling towers, visible from great distances to travellers on the A1.

Pomfret or **Pontefract cake.** A flat, round liquorice confection impressed with a castle. Local legend traces liquorice's connection with Pontefract to the 16th century, when a local schoolmaster, visiting the east coast, found a bunch of liquorice sticks washed up on the shore from a wrecked Armada galleon. He found these ideal for thrashing his charges, who would bite on other liquorice sticks to battle the pain – and thereby discovered a delicious new flavour. Thereafter, according to the story, liquorice was grown all around Pontefract (although it was probably the Romans who introduced the plant to Britain). Today, the plant appears on the badge of the local high school, and the town holds an annual liquorice festival. **Pontefract Museum** boasts the largest collection of liquorice-related items in the world.

Pontibus. A Roman settlement on the site of present-day STAINES.

Pontoon Etymology unknown.

A village and angling centre in County Mayo, between LOUGH CONN and Lough Cullin.

Pont Street *Pont* probably from Fr *pont* 'bridge' (probably referring to a bridge crossing the WESTBOURNE stream).

A street in BROMPTON, in southwest London (SW3), running from the eastern end of BEAUCHAMP PLACE eastwards across Sloane Street towards Belgrave Square (*see under* BELGRAVIA). It was laid out around 1830. Oscar Wilde was arrested on charges of homosexual practices in 1895 at the Cadogan Hotel, on the corner of Pont Street and Sloane Street.

> To the right and before him Pont Street
> Did tower in her new built red,
> As hard as the morning gaslight
> That shone on his unmade bed.
>
> John Betjeman: 'The Arrest of Oscar Wilde at the Cadogan
> Hotel' (1937)

Pont Street Dutch. A term coined by the cartoonist and architectural writer Osbert Lancaster (1908–86) for a 19th-century architectural style typified by the large gabled redbrick mansions that line Pont Street and nearby streets.

> Pseudish. This style which attained great popularity both
> in this country and in America (where it was generally
> known as Spanish-colonial), is actually our old friend
> Pont Street Dutch with a few Stockholm trimmings and a
> more daring use of colour.
>
> Osbert Lancaster: *Pillar to Post* (1938)

Ponty. A nickname given to both PONTYPOOL and PONTYPRIDD.

Pontypool 'bridge at the pool', Welsh *pont* 'bridge' + *y* 'the' + English *pool*; the pool is in the River Llwyd.

An industrial town and the administrative centre of Torfaen unitary authority (formerly in Monmouthshire, then in Gwent), bordered on the south by the New Town of Cwmbran. In Welsh it is **Pontypŵl**, and its nickname is **Ponty**. Pontypool has an old tradition of metal working, the first forge being in operation here in 1425, and iron smelting, beginning in 1577. The story goes that it was men from Pontypool who set up the first forge in North America (1682), and the town was certainly the first place in Britain to manufacture tinplate (1703).

Pontypool's rugby union club was founded in the late 1860s by members of the local cricket club. **Pontypool RFC's** golden era was in the 1970s and 1980s, when a clutch of talented players, including the legendary **Pontypool front row** of Bobby Windsor, Graham Price and Charlie Faulkner, played with distinction for Wales (and, in Windsor and Price's case, for the British Lions).

Pontypool japan. A type of heat-resistant japanned (varnished) tinplate manufactured in Pontypool from the 1730s. It is also known as **Pontypool ware**. The japanning technique involved a mixture of linseed oil, umber and litharge, while asphalt provided the dark ground. The technique was used for items such as teapots, trays and ornaments, and the motifs were largely Chinese. A factory established at USK[2] also produced Pontypool ware, and continued doing so for 40 years after the Pontypool factory closed in 1822.

Pontypridd 'bridge of the earth house', Welsh *pont* 'bridge' + *y* 'the' + *tŷ* 'house' + *pridd* 'earth'.

An industrial town at the confluence of the rivers TAFF and RHONDDA in Rhondda Cynon Taff (formerly in Glamorgan, then in Mid Glamorgan), 18 km (11 miles) northwest of Cardiff. There were bridges here from the Middle Ages, and one of these gave Pontypridd its name. A new bridge, comprising a beautiful single arch of 43 m (140 ft) over the River Taff, was built here in 1736 by the local stonemason William Edwards. This new bridge (now disused, and called the Old Bridge) led to Pontypridd being known as **Newbridge** into the 19th century, until it was realized that this was causing confusion with the town of NEWBRIDGE[1] in Monmouthshire.

It was a Pontypridd weaver and bard, Evan James, who wrote LAND OF MY FATHERS, the Welsh 'national anthem', in 1856 (translated by W.G. Rothery).

Pontypridd's rugby union club was founded in 1876 and is based at Sardis Road. The club's most celebrated player is probably the goal-kicking phenomenon Neil Jenkins, who scored more international points (1049) than any other Welshman. Under a new name, **Ponty Rugby**, Pontypridd is now a feeder team for the Cardiff Blues (*see under* CARDIFF).

Pontypridd was the birthplace of the singer and Welsh icon Tom Jones (b.1940; real name Thomas Jones Woodward). A rather different type of singer, the operatic baritone Geraint Evans (1922–92), worked for a time as a window-dresser in a Pontypridd dress shop after he left school at the age of 14.

Pontypŵl. The Welsh name for PONTYPOOL.

Pooksgreen Perhaps 'goblin's green', OE *puca* 'goblin' + ModE *green*, but a man called *Puke* is recorded here in the 13th century.

A village in Hampshire, at the mouth of the River TEST, about 5 km (3 miles) southeast of Totton.

Pook's Hill *Pook* 'mischievous demon, the Devil' (the same word as *Puck*), OE *puca* 'goblin'. The choice was probably influenced by the fact that *Pook* turns up elsewhere in Sussex in place names, but in those cases it comes from a family called *Pooke*.

A hill near BURWASH in East Sussex. It was originally called **Perch Hill**, but the success of Rudyard Kipling's *Puck of Pook's Hill* (1906) resulted in fiction becoming reality. Kipling wrote the book in his house, 'Bateman's', from the window of which he could see the hill. It is a collection of tales from English history: two children are acting out a scene from *A Midsummer Night's Dream* in a fairy ring in Sussex when they accidentally summon up Puck from the nearby Pook's Hill.

Pool, the. A nickname for LIVERPOOL and an abbreviated term for the POOL OF LONDON.

Poole '(place at the) pool' (referring to Poole Harbour), OE *pol* 'pool'.

A town and unitary authority on the Dorset coast, contiguous with BOURNEMOUTH to the east. The town is on the northern shore of a large (64 sq km / 24 sq miles), almost landlocked bay, **Poole Harbour**, which has one of Britain's most extensive shallow anchorages (it was the third largest embarkation point for US troops leaving Britain for the D-Day landings in the Second World War). The town itself began to develop as a port from the early Middle Ages, and centuries of use by fisherman, pirates and timber traders have left their mark on its heart, down by the quayside. Today, the facilities are more likely to be in use by oil prospectors or by the many thousands of recreational sailors and windsurfers who throng Poole Harbour every year.

The unitary authority was created in 1997 out of part of Dorset, with the town of Poole as its administrative headquarters.

Ceramic ware is a local speciality. **Poole Pottery**, on the Quay, was founded in 1875, and the designation 'Poole' has latterly become sought after by collectors.

The writer John le Carré (b.1931) was born in Poole. *See also* BROWNSEA ISLAND.

Poole Bay. A wide bay on the Dorset coast, stretching from Poole Harbour in the west to HENGISTBURY HEAD in the east.

Poolewe. *See* LOCH EWE.

Pool of London, the *Pool* 'deep stretch of a river', OE *pol* 'pool, creek, deep stretch of a river'.

A reach of the River THAMES[1] (often called simply **the Pool**) that extends eastwards from London Bridge to CUCKOLD'S POINT and LIMEHOUSE (about 3.5 km/2.25 miles). It is divided into a western section (the **Upper Pool**) and an eastern section (the **Lower Pool**). It is the farthest point up-river that large ships can find sufficient depth, and from Roman times until the 19th century, when enclosed docks began to

be built further downstream, it was London's main port, and this stretch of the river was always crowded with masts (or, latterly, funnels), its banks a seamless succession of wharves and cranes. As recently as 1894 Tower Bridge (*see under* TOWER OF LONDON) was built with raisable sections to allow shipping free passage, but today commerce has gone elsewhere, and they are seldom lifted.

> She had a gentle voice and that kind of London accent which is like the waters of the Thames at the Pool, by no means unpleasant but the least bit thick.
>
> Margery Allingham: *The Tiger in the Smoke* (1952)

Popham's Eau *Popham* presumably the name of the man who had the fen drained; *Eau* 'drainage canal', OE *ea* 'river' (influenced by Fr *eau* 'water'; *see* EA-).

An artificial waterway in Cambridgeshire and Norfolk, to the west of Downham Market, joining the River NENE (Old Course) with Well Creek. It is about 8 km (5 miles) long.

Poplar '(place at the) poplar-tree', ME *popler* (the place name, first recorded in 1327, predates (by some 30 years) the earliest known instance of the word as the name of the tree).

A district of East London (E3, E14), in the borough of TOWER HAMLETS, at the northern end of the ISLE OF DOGS. It grew with the development of the docks in the early 19th century (*see* DOCKLAND). Blighted by poverty and overcrowding in the second half of the century, it was an early nurturing-ground of socialism in Britain. It suffered severely in the Blitz of the Second World War: about half its houses were destroyed or damaged.

Poplar station on the Docklands Light Railway opened in 1987.

Arthur Morrison (1863–1945), author of *A Child of the Jago* (1896) (*see under* JAGO), was born in Poplar.

Poplarism. An early term of right-wing odium for what are viewed as excessive benefits for the needy, paid for by high taxes. It was inspired at the beginning of the 1920s by the pursuit of such a policy by the Poor Law Guardians of Poplar (George Lansbury, later leader of the Labour Party, was imprisoned for supporting a rates strike). A verb, *Poplarize*, soon followed:

> Those … will demand increased subsidies, allowances, and 'Poplarised' social services, to be paid for out of the proceeds of very high taxation.
>
> *Daily Telegraph* (6 November 1928)

Porlock 'enclosure by the harbour', PORT + OE *loca* 'enclosure'.

A village in Somerset, close to the coast, about 10 km (6 miles) west of Minehead. It is situated in a deep hollow, surrounded on three sides by the northern slopes of EXMOOR, and the road to it is by way of a very hairy 1-in-4-gradient hill (**Porlock Hill**) with strategically placed hairpin bends (in Victorian times visitors had to get out of their carriages and walk).

Even more than to this precipice, Porlock owes its notoriety to a reputed piece of unwitting literary sabotage: in 1797 Samuel Taylor Coleridge was staying at nearby NETHER STOWEY, in the Quantocks; he had been reading some materials relating to the Khan Kubla when (he claimed) he fell into a drugged sleep; when he awoke he found that two or three hundred lines of a poem about Kubla had come to him in his dreams; he

> ... instantly and eagerly wrote down the lines that are here preserved. At this moment he was unfortunately called out by a person on business from Porlock.
>
> S.T. Coleridge: Preliminary note to 'Kubla Khan; a Vision in a Dream' (1816)

... and when he finally got back to the poem an hour or so later, he had forgotten the rest of it. We have only Coleridge's word for this. The **person from Porlock** has since become metaphoricized into an agency of untimely – or perhaps timely – interruption:

> I long for the Person from Porlock
> To bring my thoughts to an end,
> I am growing impatient to see him
> I think of him as a friend.
>
> Stevie Smith: 'Thoughts about the "Person from Porlock"' (1962)

Porlock does have another literary connection, though: The Ship Inn in the High Street features prominently in R.D. Blackmore's *Lorna Doone* (1869).

On the coast about 3 km (2 miles) to the northwest, on **Porlock Bay**, is the small harbour called **Porlock Weir**, from which a busy trade with Wales was once carried on. Another 3 km (2 miles) further west is Culbone, whose church is the smallest in England.

Porrum-engreskey tem. The Romany name for WALES, according to George Borrow's *Romano Lavo-Lil* ('word book of the Romany', 1874). The name means 'leek-eaters' country'.

Portadown Irish *Port an Dúnáin* 'landing place of the little fort' (*see* PORT).
A town in County Armagh, just to the west of LURGAN, with which it was incorporated into the new town of CRAIGAVON in 1965. Portadown's residents are sometimes referred to as the 'Aberdonians of Ireland', on account of their supposed meanness (*see* ABERDEEN). Portadown developed as an industrial centre following the construction of the NEWRY canal in the 18th century. It is particularly famous for its roses – the mayor's chain is made up of gold medals won in many rose competitions by local growers such as Sam McGredy, whose great-grandfather founded the famous nursery (now transferred to New Zealand). In his memoirs, Anthony Powell recalls his battalion being stationed here and refers to it as

> ... a town politically reliable, if scenically unromantic.
>
> Anthony Powell: *To Keep the Ball Rolling* (1976–82)

See also DRUMCREE.

Portadown Saint, the. The poet and essayist Æ (George Russell, 1867–1935), known for his gentle mysticism. He was actually born in neighbouring Lurgan, the error deriving from Yeats's father John Butler Yeats (1839–1922), who called Russell 'a saint but born in Portadown'.

Port an Dúnáin. The Irish name for PORTADOWN.

Portarlington After Lord Arlington + ModE *port* (*see* PORT).
A market town on the River BARROW in County Laois, 15 km (9 miles) northeast of Portlaoise. Its Irish name is **Cúil an tSúdaire** ('nook of the leatherworker'). It was founded in the 17th century by Henry Bennett, Lord Arlington, and many Huguenot refugees settled here (the Protestant church here became known as 'the French church'). Portlarlington has Ireland's first peat-fuelled power station (1936).

Among the alumni of Portarlington school was Edward Carson (1854–1935), the 'Uncrowned King of Ulster' and leading opponent of Home Rule.

❖ port ❖

This element is widely represented in names in Britain and Ireland. Its general meaning is represented by the Latin word *portus* 'a harbour, a haven'. This gives many ancient and modern names. There is a cluster of *port* names around PORTSMOUTH (Hampshire), where the ancient name of the harbour was probably itself *port*: PORTCHESTER, PORTSDOWN and PORTSEA. The Irish PORTRUSH (County Antrim) and PORTSTEWART (County Derry), are both coastal, as is PORTSOY (Aberdeen). PORT ERIN (Isle of Man), PORT TALBOT and PORTHMADOG (Wales), and PORT ELLEN (Argyll and Bute) are more recent names. Somewhat disguised, the element appears in the first syllable of POLPERRO (Cornwall).

In some Gaelic names the *port* or *phort* element developed another sense, 'fort, embankment'. The clearest example of this is LONGFORD (Ireland), originally *longphort*, where the name means 'fortified house', while PORTLAOISE (County Laois), is an inland embanked settlement in bogland. In English names, another development for the element was the sense 'market town': most of the many Newport names here are towns that were given charters for holding markets, and the various Portways (such as PORTWAY, Hampshire and Wiltshire) are the roads used to transport goods to market (not necessarily to the new markets).

Port Bredy. The fictional name for BRIDPORT in the works of Thomas Hardy.

Port Charlotte Named after *Charlotte* Campbell + ModE *port* (*see* PORT).

A village on the east coast of the Rinns of ISLAY, in Argyll and Bute (formerly in Strathclyde region). It was founded in 1828 by Walter Campbell, laird of Islay and also a Gaelic scholar. He named it after his mother. The village is sometimes referred to as the **Queen of the Rinns**.

See also PORT ELLEN.

Portchester 'Roman fort by the harbour', PORT + OE *ceaster* (*see* CHESTER).

A town in Hampshire, on the north shore of Portsmouth Harbour (*see under* PORTSMOUTH), to the southwest of Portsdown. It is now effectively an eastern suburb of FAREHAM. As its name reveals, the Romans were here (they called it **Portus Adurni** or **Portus Ardaoni** – the second element adapted from an Old Celtic word meaning 'height' (*see* ADUR[1]), referring to PORTSDOWN), and in the 3rd century AD they built a massive fortification, with 20 bastions and walls more than 6 m (20 ft) high. Portchester formed part of the Romans' SAXON SHORE. **Portchester Castle** as it now exists was built by Henry II within the Roman precincts. Henry V assembled his forces here before sailing to France and victory at the Battle of Agincourt.

Port Ellen Named after *Ellen* Campbell, with ModE *port* (*see* PORT).

A large village on the south coast of ISLAY, in Argyll and Bute (formerly in Strathclyde region). It was founded in 1821 by Walter Campbell, laird of Islay and also a Gaelic scholar. He named it after his wife. The Port Ellen distillery, opened in 1825, closed in 1983.

See also PORT CHARLOTTE.

Port Erin Gaelic *Port Éireann* 'Irish port' (*see* PORT).

A small seaside resort on the west coast of the ISLE OF MAN, near its southern tip.

Port Eynon 'Einon's port or harbour', Welsh personal name *Einon*, with PORT.

A village on the southwest coast of the Gower Peninsula, Swansea unitary authority (formerly in Glamorgan, then West Glamorgan), 15 km (9 miles) west of Mumbles. South of the village is **Port Eynon Point**, location of the CULVER HOLE; the headland also forms the western enclosing arm of **Port Eynon Bay**.

Port Glasgow From GLASGOW, with ModE *port* (*see* PORT).

A port on the south shore of the Firth of Clyde (*see under* CLYDE), in Inverclyde (formerly in Renfrewshire and then in Strathclyde region). It is situated 7 km (4 miles) east of Greenock, and was built in the 17th century on the site of the fishing village of Newark by Glasgow merchants who wanted to take advantage of the new Atlantic trade, as at

that stage the River Clyde was too shallow to allow ocean-going ships to reach Glasgow itself. Port Glasgow's importance as a port declined after the Clyde was dredged in the later 18th century, allowing ships to sail further up the river. However, Port Glasgow continued as a shipbuilding centre, and it was here that the *Comet*, the first sea-going steam boat, was launched in 1812.

There is a local story that when the funeral of a girl who had died of consumption was passing the shore, a mermaid rose from the depths to offer the following advice:

> If they wad drink nettles in March,
> And eat muggins in May,
> Sae mony braw maidens
> Wadna gang to the clay.
>
> (*muggins* 'mugwort', *braw* 'beautiful')

Port Glasgow was the birthplace of the insomniac alcoholic poet James Thomson (1834–82), author of 'The City of Dreadful Night' (1874).

The Resurrection: Port Glasgow. A series of panels (1945–50) by the English painter Stanley Spencer (1891–1959). Spencer had gone to Port Glasgow during the Second World War as an official war artist to depict the stages of ship building in Lithgow's Kingston Yard, and these later, more clearly religious paintings derived from that experience.

Porthaethwy. The Welsh name for MENAI BRIDGE.

Porthcawl 'harbour of sea kale', Welsh *porth* 'harbour' (*see* PORT) + *cawl* 'sea kale', a plant (*Crambe maritima*) with fleshy leaves and edible shoots, gastronomically (although not taxonomically) comparable to asparagus.

A resort and former coal port in Bridgend unitary authority (formerly in Glamorgan, then in Mid Glamorgan), 15 km (9 miles) southeast of Port Talbot. With its Grand Pavilion, Coney Beach amusement park (modelled on New York's Coney Island) and one of the largest caravan sites in Europe, it is a traditional popular British seaside resort. **Merthyr Mawr Warren**, the area of sands and dunes to the east, was used to stand in for the Arabian Desert in David Lean's epic film *Lawrence of Arabia* (1962).

Porthia. *See* ST IVES[2].

Porthleven 'smooth harbour', Cornish *porth* (*see* PORT) + *leven* 'smooth'.

A town and port in western Cornwall, on MOUNT'S BAY, about 16 km (10 miles) east of Penzance. In former times it was the outlet for the tin ore mined in this part of the country, and routed through the Stannary town (*see* STANNARIES) of HELSTON.

Portleven Sands are to the southeast.

Porthmadog 'Madocks' port', Welsh *porth* 'port' (*see* PORT) + *Madog*, Welsh personal name, close to that of William Alexander Madocks MP (d.1828), who built the harbour and gave it his name. The original version was *Portmadoc*, but this was subsequently Welshified. In naming the place, Madocks also made a gesture towards commemorating the legendary Prince Madog (or Madoc), who supposedly sailed from near here to North America in the 12th century. Madocks also developed the nearby and onomastically related village of TREMADOG (Welsh *tre* 'hamlet, farm').

A resort town on Tremadog Bay in Gwynedd (formerly in Caernarvonshire), 33 km (20 miles) south of Bangor. It developed as a port to export slate from the now-disused quarries at BLAENAU FFESTINIOG, to which it is still linked by the Ffestiniog Railway. The harbour is now used only by pleasure craft.

Portishead 'headland by the harbour', OE *portes* possessive form of PORT + *heafod* 'head'.

A town and port in North Somerset (before 1996 in Avon, before 1974 in Somerset), to the west of the mouth of the River AVON². Its expansion to its present size was set in motion by the building of docks in the 19th century to supplement those of BRISTOL.

In the 1990s the town's name became more widely known thanks to the Bristol-based experimental music and dance group called **Portishead**. Fronted by singer Beth Gibbons, their best-known production was the album *Dummy* (1994).

Portknockie 'harbour of the little hills', Gaelic PORT + *cnoc* 'hill' (*see* KNOCK-) with a diminutive.

A large clifftop fishing village on the MORAY FIRTH, in Moray (formerly in Banffshire, then Grampian region), 8 km (5 miles) northeast of Buckie. It was founded in 1677. Offshore is the Bow Fiddle Rock, a sea stack with a natural arch.

Port Lách. The Irish name for PORTLAW.

Port Láirge. The Irish name for WATERFORD.

Portland 'estate by the harbour', PORT + OE *land* 'estate'.

A peninsula (in full the **Isle of Portland**) on the Dorset coast, just to the south of WEYMOUTH. It consists of a wedge-shaped island joined to the mainland by a narrow isthmus which is the southeastern end of CHESIL BEACH. The headland at its sharp southern tip is **Portland Bill**, 151 m (495 ft) high and guarded by a lighthouse. At the other end of the island is **Portland Castle**, a fortress built by Henry VIII, which overlooks **Portland Harbour**. This is the largest artificial harbour in Britain. Its 1800-m (6000-ft) breakwater was built of the local stone by convicts in the 19th century. It has a long history as a naval base.

Portland's flat spartan landscape is dotted with the quarries from which **Portland stone** (*see below*) is extracted.

There are towns and cities called Portland in the USA – Colorado, Indiana, Maine (an important petroleum port), Michegan, North Dakota, Oregon (the state's largest city), Tennessee, Texas – in Canada (Ontario), in Australia (New South Wales, Victoria) and in Barbados and New Zealand, and there is a parish called Portland in Jamaica.

Battle of Portland (18–28 February 1652). A naval engagement fought off Portland during the first Anglo-Dutch War, in which the English fleet under Admiral Blake defeated a Dutch fleet under Admiral Tromp.

Portland. A sea area in the shipping forecast. It is in the English Channel, off the south coast of Devon and Dorset, between PLYMOUTH to the west and Wight (*see under* WIGHT) to the east.

Portland beds. A series of limestone strata of the Upper Oolite, found on the Isle of Portland.

Portland cement. A cement that can set underwater, made by grinding lime and clay very finely together and roasting the resulting mixture in a kiln. It was patented in 1824 by Joseph Aspdin, a Leeds bricklayer, who named it 'Portland cement' because he thought that when set its colour resembled that of Portland stone.

Portlandian. A geologists' term denoting a subdivision of the Upper Oolite, developed in the Isle of Portland. It rests on KIMMERIDGE clay.

Portland Spies, the. Two clerks, Harry Houghton and Ethel ('Bunty') Gee, at the Underwater Weapons Establishment in Portland, who were discovered in 1961 to have been taking secret documents up to London and handing them to a man called Gordon Lonsdale near the Old Vic theatre. Lonsdale (in reality a Russian named Konon Trofimovich Modoly) passed the material to Peter and Helen Kroger of RUISLIP, where the documents were reduced to microdots that were then sent to the Soviet Union pasted over full stops in second-hand books. Houghton and Gee got 15 years in prison, Lonsdale 25 years, and the Krogers 20 years. Lonsdale was in the end exchanged for Greville Wynne in 1964 (Wynne was a British businessman jailed by the Russians for bringing out material from the Soviet double agent Oleg Penkovsky).

Portland stone. A hard white oolitic limestone characteristic of the Portland beds. It has been quarried as a building material for many centuries: St Paul's Cathedral is made of it, as is the external surface of the United Nations Building in New York. Lower grades of the stone are crushed for making cement.

Portland Vase, the. A Roman glass vessel of *c*.25 BC. Made of cobalt-blue glass decorated with opaque white figures in the manner of a cameo, it is one of the most exquisite surviving examples of ancient Roman glass-blowing skill. It was rediscovered near Rome in the 17th century and subsequently sold to the Duchess of Portland – whence its name. In 1810 it was lent to the British Museum, where in 1845 it was smashed by a vandal. It was successfully repaired, and is now one of the Museum's best-known and most prized exhibits.

Portland Place *Portland* in honour of the 2nd Duke of *Portland*, who owned land in the area.

A street in the centre of London (W1), running from Park Crescent (at the southern end of REGENT'S PARK) in the north to Langham Place in the south. Laid out around 1778 by the Adam brothers, it is unusually wide, an undertaking having been given at the time of building to Lord Foley, who lived at the southern end, that his view northwards would never be blocked. The buildings along either side now house embassies, legations and the offices of learned societies, but the street's most famous occupant is the BBC. Its headquarters, the curvilinear Broadcasting House, was constructed at the southern end in the late 1920s. Since then, 'Portland Place' has become almost synonymous with the BBC, and in particular with its higher management:

> If it is interventionist to work for a more powerful …
> Board of Governors, then an interventionist chairman I
> was at Portland Place.
>
> Charles Hill: *Behind the Screen* (1974)

Portlaoise Irish *Port Laoise* 'fort of Lugaid' (*see* PORT *and* LAOIS). The county town of County Laois, 75 km (47 miles) southwest of Dublin. It is pronounced 'port leash', and was formerly known as **Maryborough**, after Mary I (just as Laois itself was called Queen's County); it was during her reign that the plantation of Laois commenced. There is a large prison, nicknamed 'the Bog' (Laois being a peaty place).

Portlaw Irish *Port Lách* 'landing place of the hill' (*see* PORT). A village on the River Clodiagh in County Waterford, some 15 km (9 miles) west of Waterford itself. It was founded as a model village by the Quaker family of Malcolmson, to serve their cotton mill (1825) – a rare example of rural manufacturing industry in the South of Ireland.

Portmarnock Irish *Port Mearnóg* 'harbour of St Marnock' (*see* PORT); this contains the same personal name as that in KILMARNOCK, but the name does not necessarily refer to the same person.

A seaside resort in County Dublin, just south of Malahide. There are the remains of the church and well of St Marnock, after whom the place is named. There is also a championship golf course.

Port Meadow 'small island belonging to a city-dweller', ME *portman* 'citizen, burgess', with *eyt* 'islet'.

An area of flat open land in northwestern Oxford, about 138 ha (342 acres) in extent, on the eastern bank of the THAMES[1]. It is used largely for grazing, but there was an airfield here during the First World War. It has never been ploughed, and has been designated a Site of Special Scientific Interest.

Port Mearnóg. The Irish name for PORTMARNOCK.

Portmeirion 'port of MERIONETH', from the name of the then county (*Meirionydd*) in Welsh. Clough Williams-Ellis also chose the name partly to reflect that of Portofino, one of his inspirations, and partly to echo the name of nearby PORTHMADOG.

A small holiday village in Gwynedd (formerly in Caernarvonshire), on a headland 3 km (2 miles) southeast across the bay from Porthmadog. Portmeirion, built in the 1920s by the eccentric Welsh architect Clough Williams-Ellis (1883–1978), is an extraordinary Italianate fantasy, and has been described as 'the last nobleman's folly' and 'a Welsh Xanadu'. Williams-Ellis (who was knighted in 1972) purchased the old mansion of Aber Ia here, added Castell Deudraeth and its grounds to the property, then began the transformation of the site into something on the lines of Portofino in northwest Italy, building many Italianate buildings in pastel colours, some with distorted perspectives. He also rescued threatened architectural gems from Britain and the Continent and reconstructed them here (the place is also known as the **Home for Fallen Buildings**). The result is charmingly eclectic and it remains enormously popular as a tourist destination.

The dream-like atmosphere of the place made it an ideal set for 'The Village' in the cult television spy series *The Prisoner* (1967–8), and every year fans of the series hold a convention here.

Portobello[1] Spanish 'fine port'. It took its name from an 18th-century mansion here, itself named after Puerto Bello in Panama, captured by Admiral Edward Vernon in 1739 during the War of Jenkins's Ear.

A district of northeast Edinburgh, on the Firth of Forth (*see under* FORTH). Its sandy beaches once made it popular as a resort. It was the birthplace of the music-hall Scot Sir Harry Lauder (1870–1950), perpetrator of 'Roamin' in the Gloamin', 'End of the Road' and other hugely popular numbers.

Portobello[2] From PORTOBELLO[1], reputedly because, like Edinburgh's Portobello, it lies on a bed of rich clay that forms a valuable resource, and also because it was near a coal mine called Bunker's Hill, a name which, as with the Edinburgh Portobello, recalls a British military success (here, over the Americans at Bunker Hill, Boston, in 1775).

An eastern district of WOLVERHAMPTON, to the north of Bilston.

Portobello Road From its leading in the 19th century to *Porto Bello House*, later *Porto Bello Farm*, named after the British victory at Puerto Bello (*see* PORTOBELLO[1]).

A long road in West London (W10, W11), in the borough of KENSINGTON AND CHELSEA, running from North KENSINGTON southwards under the WESTWAY to NOTTING HILL GATE. It is famous for its street market. This dates from the 1870s, and some of the earliest traders were gypsies selling their wares. After the Second World War and the closure of the Caledonian Market (*see under* CALEDONIAN ROAD), the antique dealers moved into **Portobello Road Market**, and the serendipitous purchase here of wildly valuable *objets* for a tiny fraction of their worth became part of urban legend. Tourists flock here on Saturdays to participate (on other days of the week it is an ordinary general market, with a West Indian flavour appropriate to the community now in the area).

Port Omna. The Irish name for PORTUMNA.

Porton Down From *Porton*, the name of a village to the northwest, from an unknown first element (probably a river name, perhaps the former name of the River Bourne, on which the village stands) + -TON.

An area of downland in Wiltshire, at the southeastern edge of SALISBURY Plain, about 8 km (5 miles) northeast of Salisbury. In 1916 the Chemical and Biological Defence Establishment was set up here by the government to develop and manufacture chemical weapons (including poison gas) for use by the British Army in the First World War, and to devise methods of defence against them. This establishment soon became known simply as '**Porton Down**', which over the decades has developed into a flesh-creeping symbol of biological warfare: white-coated boffins poring over sinister retorts, one drop of whose contents could wipe out the entire population of the planet. That just about sums up the Porton Down public image. During the Cold War over 20,000 'volunteers' from the services took part in experiments here, many of them later allegedly resulting in illness and death, and at the beginning of the 21st century a debate raged as to whether the guinea-pigs could truly be said to have given their informed consent to participation.

With Britain having given up its chemical weapons programme in 1978, Porton Down became part of the Ministry of Defence's Defence Evaluation and Research Agency (1995) and then the Defence Science and Technology Laboratory (2001).

See also NANCECUKE.

Portpatrick From the dedication of the local church to St Patrick (*see also* PORT).

A small port on the west coast of the Rhinns of GALLOWAY, Dumfries and Galloway (formerly in Wigtownshire), 8 km (5 miles) southwest of Stranraer. There was a regular ferry service from here to DONAGHADEE in Northern Ireland until 1849, when the LARNE–STRANRAER route took over. In 1853 Sir Charles Tilston Bright laid the first submarine cable, from Portpatrick to Donaghadee.

Port Penrhyn. *See* PENRHYN CASTLE.

Portree 'harbour by the hillside', Gaelic *port* 'harbour' (*see* PORT) + *ruigheadh* 'of the slope'. It was formerly thought that the second element was *ríg* 'royal', from the visit here in 1540 by James V with a fleet of 12 ships.

The 'capital' of SKYE, situated halfway up the east coast, some 33 km (20 miles) northwest of Kyle of Lochalsh. It

was formerly in Inverness-shire, then from 1975 to 1996 it was the administrative seat of Skye and Lochalsh district (Highland region), and it is now in the unitary authority of Highland. Its excellent natural harbour led Martin Martin, the 17th-century traveller, to describe it as 'the fittest place'. It was in Portree (at McNab's Inn, which stood on the site of the present Royal Hotel) that Bonnie Prince Charlie is supposed to have said his last farewell to Flora MacDonald, having come with her 'over the sea to Skye'.

Port Rois. The Irish name for PORTRUSH.

Portrush Irish *Port Rois* 'landing place of the headland' (*see* PORT).

A seaside resort by the Ramore Peninsula on the north coast of County Antrim, 10 km (6 miles) southwest of the GIANT'S CAUSEWAY. An innovative electric tramway was built here by William Siemens in 1883, and there is a championship golf course. For Derek Mahon's unfavourable verdict on the place, *see under* PORTSTEWART.

Portsdown 'hill by the harbour' (referring to PORTSMOUTH Harbour), OE *portes* possessive form of PORT + *dun* 'hill' (*see* DOWN, -DON).

An area of chalky upland to the north of Portsmouth.

Portsea From PORTSEA ISLAND.

A western district of PORTSMOUTH, containing harbour facilities and naval and government offices. The area was originally known as **Portsmouth Common**, but its name was changed by Act of Parliament in 1792.

Arthur Conan Doyle practised as a doctor in Portsea between 1882 and 1889, and it was here that he conceived and first wrote about the character Sherlock Holmes.

Portsea Island *Portsea* 'island by the harbour' (referring to PORTSMOUTH Harbour), OE *portes* possessive form of PORT + *eg* 'island' (*see* -EY, -EA).

A bulbous peninsula on the south coast of Hampshire, at the eastern end of the Solent. It is taken up by the city of PORTSMOUTH and its close neighbour SOUTHSEA. The creek that separates it from the mainland is tidal, and it is joined to the mainland by three road bridges and a railway bridge, so the designation 'island' is tenuous (as well as being etymologically tautologous). To its west is Portsmouth Harbour, to its east Langstone Harbour (*see under* LANGSTONE).

Port Seton. *See under* COCKENZIE.

Portsmouth 'mouth of the harbour', OE *portes* possessive form of PORT + *mutha* 'mouth'.

A city, port and unitary authority on the Hampshire coast, on the eastern side of **Portsmouth Harbour** (*see below*), about 24 km (15 miles) southeast of SOUTHAMPTON. It was already a port in the days of King Alfred, but in 1194 Richard I recognized its strategic importance and created a settlement on PORTSEA ISLAND. By the beginning of the 13th century Portsmouth had become an important naval station accommodating the royal galleys, the docks enclosed by a strong wall. A royal dockyard was established here by Henry VII in 1496, and he also had the world's first dry dock constructed. Expanded considerably in 1698, Portsmouth consolidated its role over the centuries, and became the UK's main naval base. It was, as a consequence, heavily bombed during the Second World War (65,000 of its buildings suffered some damage in air raids, and 6650 were totally destroyed). Portsmouth was also a principal embarkation point in the D-Day operation. The naval dockyard was closed in 1981, although some naval facilities remain.

Notable reminders of British naval history can be viewed in Portsmouth, including Nelson's flagship HMS *Victory*, Henry VIII's prized *Mary Rose* (capsized 1545, raised 1982) and the Royal Navy's first 'ironclad' battleship HMS *Warrior* (1860). It was here in 1757 that Admiral John Byng (*see also* POTTERS BAR) was shot, '*pour*', as Voltaire observed in *Candide* (1759), '*encourager les autres*'. (Byng had been court-martialled for negligence after failing to attack with sufficient determination a French fleet defending Menorca.) Portsmouth is also an important commercial port, and ferries serve Bilbao, Caen, Cherbourg, Le Havre, St Malo, the CHANNEL ISLANDS and the ISLE OF WIGHT.

George Villiers, Duke of Buckingham, courtier and adviser to both James VI/I and Charles I, was assassinated in Portsmouth on 23 August 1628 by John Felton, a Puritan fanatic.

Portsmouth was made a city in 1926. The unitary authority, incorporating surrounding parts of HAMPSHIRE, came into being in 1997.

Much of Portsmouth's city-centre postwar rebuilding had a gloom-inducing quality. A notable icon was Owen Luder's 1966 Tricorn shopping centre, a grimly brutalist example of the architectural style known as 'rough concrete', which was regularly voted one of Britain's least loved buildings. Having been refused a preservation order, it was demolished in 2004. The decision is likely to have delighted Prince Charles, who once described the (long-derelict) building as 'a mildewed lump of elephant droppings'.

Portsmouth has an outstanding track record for the production of novelists: Charles Dickens (1812–70), George Meredith (1828–1909; he fictionalized the place as LYMPORT) and Olivia Manning (1911–80) were born here. In addition it was the birthplace of the philanthropist and traveller Jonas Hanway (1712–86), believed to have been the first Englishman to carry an umbrella, the engineer Isambard Kingdom Brunel (1806–59), the writer Walter Besant (1836–1901), the Labour politician and prime minister James Callaghan (b.1912), the poet Christopher Logue (b.1926), and the playwright Howard Brenton (b.1942). Charles Chubb (1779–1845), the inventor of the

famous lock, had an ironmonger's and ship's outfitter's shop in Portsmouth.

Portsmouth FC was founded in 1898 by a local solicitor called Pink. The club's nickname is one possible source for the city's nickname, **Pompey** (*see under* POMPEY). Bitter rivalry exists between fans of Portsmouth FC and those of nearby SOUTHAMPTON FC. In a competition to find an appropriate rebuttal for the term 'Scummer' with which Portsmouth fans have long derided them, Southampton fans chose 'skate' as their preferred term of stigmatization. An established Portsmouth slang word for a sailor, 'skate' appears to have been selected for its degrading sexual associations (it is claimed that sailors on long sea voyages had recourse to skate fish as a means of relieving sexual frustration).

Portsmouth University, formerly Portsmouth Polytechnic, was established in 1992.

A grittily realized contemporary Portsmouth is the setting for Graham Hurley's bleak series of detective novels featuring DI Joe Faraday, including *Angels Passing* (2002) and *Deadlight* (2003), of which one over-excited reviewer remarked: 'The Faraday series offers the key to an entire city. Read these books and you'll understand why Blair's Britain is falling apart.'

> The necessity of living in the midst of the diabolical citizens of Portsmouth is a real and unavoidable calamity. It is a doubt to me if there is such another collection of demons on the whole earth.
>> General James Wolfe (1758)

> Defence Secretary Geoff Hoon should have consulted the book [a guidebook to Britain] before opining in the House of Commons last week that 'Umm Qasr is a city similar to Southampton'. A British squaddie was quick to correct him, explaining: 'Umm Qasr has no beer, no prostitutes and people are shooting at us. It's more like Portsmouth.'
>> *The Observer* (30 March 2003)

There are towns and cities called Portsmouth in the USA (Iowa, New Hampshire (an important submarine base), North Carolina, Ohio, Rhode Island, Virginia (site of Norfolk Naval Yard)), Canada (Ontario) and Dominica in the West Indies.

See also PAULSGROVE *and* SOUTHSEA.

Duchess of Portsmouth. A title bestowed by Charles II on his French mistress (in the amatory rather than the pedagogical sense), Louise-Renée de Kéroualle (1649–1734). She was not popular among the king's subjects.

Portsmouth Harbour. A large natural harbour, about 1249 hectares (3086 acres) in area, formed by an inlet of the English Channel into the Hampshire coast. Its eastern side is bounded by PORTSEA ISLAND. Portsmouth is on the eastern bank of its entrance channel, GOSPORT on the western. It gives onto SPITHEAD, at the eastern end of the SOLENT, and opposite RYDE on the Isle of Wight.

Portsmouth Point. A rumbustious concert overture (1926) by William Walton. It was inspired by a print by the English artist and caricaturist Thomas Rowlandson (1756–1827) depicting a crowded scene at the quayside.

Portsoken 'district outside a city over which jurisdiction is extended' (referring to Portsoken's situation outside London's city walls), ME *portsoken* (from OE *port* 'town' (*see* PORT) + *socn* 'jurisdiction').

The most easterly of the ancient wards of the City of London (*see under* LONDON). It was the soke of the old *Knightenguild* outside the city wall in the parish of St Botolph, ALDGATE. The present-day **Portsoken Street** (E1) leads eastwards off the MINORIES.

Portsoy 'harbour of the worthy man', Gaelic PORT + *saoidh* 'good, brave, worthy man'.

A small resort and former fishing port in Aberdeenshire (formerly in Banffshire, then in Grampian region), 10 km (6 miles) west of Banff. There are many fine 17th- and 18th-century houses, and an annual traditional small boats festival. **Portsoy marble** was used in the construction of the Palace of Versailles.

Portstewart After the Stewart family, local landowners in the 18th century (*see also* PORT).

A seaside resort in County Londonderry, 5 km (3 miles) north of Coleraine. The Irish version of its name is **Port Stíobhaird**. The novelist Charles Lever (1806–72) worked as a physician in Portstewart, and the song lyricist Jimmy Kennedy (1902–84) was brought up here, the place inspiring songs such as 'Harbour Lights' and 'Red Sails in the Sunset':

> Red sails in the sunset, way out on the sea,
> Oh, carry my loved one home safely to me …

Others have taken a less rosy view of the place:

> Portstewart, Portrush, Portballintrae –
> *un beau pays mal habité,*
> policed by rednecks in dark cloth
> and roving gangs of tartan youth.
>> Derek Mahon: 'The Sea in Winter', from *Collected Poems* (1999)

Port Stíobhaird. The Irish name for PORTSTEWART.

Port St Mary *Port see* PORT; *St Mary* from the dedication of the 13th-century church.

A village near the southern tip of the ISLE OF MAN, on the east coast 5 km (3 miles) across the bay from Castletown.

Port Sunlight *Sunlight* from the brand-name of 'Sunlight' soap, made in the local factory, but also intended to suggest brightness, airiness and healthiness.

A garden village (now part of BEBINGTON) constructed from 1888 on the southwest bank of the estuary of the River MERSEY, within the metropolitan area of Merseyside (before 1974 in Cheshire), by William Hesketh Lever, 1st Viscount

Leverhulme (1851–1925) as a residential estate for the workers in his soap factory (his company, then called Lever Brothers, is now the giant Unilever). The original village had nearly 900 workers' cottages, set in a spacious and attractive environment, with a church, a civic hall, a hospital and a library. The Lady Lever Art Gallery (1922) here has an interesting Pre-Raphaelite collection.

Port Talbot *Port* ModE (*see* PORT); *Talbot* from the Talbot family, who became the local landowners in the 18th century; previously the place was known as *Aberavon* ('mouth of the River Afan'), still the name of part of the town.

An industrial port at the mouth of the River AFAN in Neath Port Talbot (formerly in Glamorgan, then in West Glamorgan), 9 km (5.5 miles) east of Swansea. The town grew up around the copper-smelting industry established here in 1770. Docks were built in 1837 for the export of local coal, but this trade declined in the earlier 20th century. However, steel-making took over: the massive Margam Abbey Works were built in 1947, and a deep-water port for giant ore-carriers was constructed in 1970.

From 1974 to 1996 Port Talbot and its surrounding area (including the Afan valley) formed the district of Port Talbot in West Glamorgan. The district was initially called Afan.

Port Talbot was the birthplace of Clive Jenkins (1926–99), the trade-union leader; the Conservative politician Geoffrey Howe (b.1926), whose resignation from Margaret Thatcher's government in 1990 ultimately led to her downfall; and the actor Sir Anthony Hopkins (b.1937). It is also home to Captain Beany, the orange-coloured would-be superhero who, in 1986, lay in a bath of baked beans for 100 hours to raise money for charity.

Portumna Irish *Port Omna* 'landing place by the tree trunk' (*see* PORT).

A small market town in County Galway, near where the River SHANNON enters the northern end of LOUGH DERG[2]. Just south of the town is the demesne of the ruined **Portumna Castle** (1609), seat of the Clanricarde Burkes; there is also a ruined Dominican friary (15th century) in the demesne, now a forest park. In 1659 the castle was captured by the Cromwellians, and in 1690 the Jacobite garrison surrendered to the Williamites. It was at Portumna in November 1886 that the Nationalist MPs John Dillon and William O'Brien first put into practice the Plan of Campaign against unfair rents and evictions of tenant farmers.

Portus Adurni. The Roman name for the settlement that is present-day PORTCHESTER. An alternative Roman designation was **Portus Ardaoni.**

Portus Dubris. A Roman settlement on the site of present-day DOVER.

Portway 'town way' (that is, the road to Salisbury), OE PORT 'town' + *weg* 'way'.

A Roman road in Hampshire and Wiltshire, which runs between SILCHESTER and OLD SARUM (Salisbury) via ANDOVER, a distance of about 59 km (37 miles).

Port Way 'ancient road' (a transferred sense of PORTWAY).
An ancient 11-km (7-mile) long trackway along the top of the LONG MYND in Shropshire. It was in use 3500 years ago by axe-traders.

Portwrinkle The first element is from Cornish *porth* 'cove' (*see* PORT); the second is obscure.
A village on the southern Cornish coast, about 10 km (6 miles) east of Looe.

Post-Mawr. The Welsh name for SYNOD INN.

Pothole County. A nickname sometimes given to County CAVAN, whose roads are particularly liable to subsidence due to the nature of the soil.

Potterhanworth Originally *Hanworth* 'Hana's enclosure', OE male personal name *Hana* + *worth* (*see* -WORTH, WORTHY, -WARDINE); the later addition of *potter* refers to pot-making here.
A village in Lincolnshire, about 11 km (7 miles) southeast of Lincoln.

Potterhanworth Booths *Booths* 'temporary shelter, herdsman's hut', OScand *both*.
A village in Lincolnshire, about 1.5 km (1 mile) northeast of Potterhanworth.

Potter Heigham Originally *Heigham,* perhaps 'homestead or enclosure with a hedge or hatch-gate', OE *hecg* 'hedge' or *hecc* 'hatch' + HAM; *Potter*, added in the 12th century, alludes to pot-making as a local occupation.
A village (pronounced 'heyəm' or 'highəm') in Norfolk, on the River Thurne, about 21 km (13 miles) northeast of Norwich. It is designated 'the capital of the BROADS'. It is a popular yachting centre, packed with visitors in the summer.

Potteries, the. A name (first recorded in 1825) for a district of northern Staffordshire, centred on STOKE-ON-TRENT (*see also* the FIVE TOWNS), which is the headquarters of the English china and earthenware industry. Clay has been worked here for centuries in the potbanks (the local word for 'pottery'), but it was the confluence of the development of local coalfields, the acquisition of reliable supplies of china clay from Cornwall (*see under* ST AUSTELL), and the construction of the Trent and Mersey Canal (*see under* TRENT[1]) that turned the area, in the 18th century, into an industrial site, its former rural acres covered with smoking factories. Josiah Wedgwood opened his works here in 1769. China manufacture continues to be the main local industry at the beginning of the 21st century.

Potters Bar 'potter's forest-gate', ME *barre* 'forest-gate'. Although some have cast doubt on it, the generally accepted theory is that *potter* is a family name, attested from the 13th century, and belonging to a man called Potter who owned a gate into Enfield Chase (*see under* ENFIELD) in the early 16th century. Alternatively, the name might refer to a toll-gate on a road leading to a pottery.
A town in Hertfordshire (before 1965 in Middlesex), just to the north of London, about 14 km (9 miles) southeast of ST ALBANS. It is a quintessential commuter dormitory. It is on the main railway line north from KING'S CROSS, and it achieved an unwanted notoriety on 10 May 2002 when a train crashed here, killing seven people and injuring over a hundred more.

Just south of Potters Bar, set in extensive parkland, is Wrotham Park, a privately owned mansion built in 1754 for Admiral John Byng, whose execution in 1757 (*see* PORTSMOUTH) thus left him little time to enjoy its Palladian elegance. Wrotham Park is now much favoured as a period location by film directors, and has appeared in such films as *Peter's Friends* (1992), *Princess Caraboo* (1994), *Gosford Park* (2001) and *Bridget Jones's Diary* (2001).

Potters Crouch Perhaps 'Potter's hill', family name *Potter*, with OCelt *crug* 'hill, mound' (*see* CREECH, CROOK).
A village in Hertfordshire, on the M10, on the southwestern outskirts of St Albans.

Potto 'mound by a deep hole', OE *potte* 'deep hole' + OScand *haugr* 'mound, hill'; *Pothow* 1202.
A hamlet in North Yorkshire, on the edge of the Cleveland Hills (*see under* CLEVELAND) 14 km (8.5 miles) northeast of Northallerton. **Potto Beck** is the local stream.

Pott Shrigley *Pott* 'deep hole', ME *potte*; *Shrigley* 'glade frequented by missel-thrushes', OE *scric* 'missel-thrush' + -LEY.
A village in Cheshire, on the western edge of the PEAK DISTRICT, about 11 km (7 miles) east of Wilmslow.

Poulnabrone The first element is Irish *poll* 'hole, hollow', and *nabrone* might mean something like 'of the breast or belly', i.e. a belly-button, which could refer to the shape of the site.
A Neolithic portal dolmen in the BURREN area of County Clare, 25 km (16 miles) north of Ennis. Between 3200 and 3000 BC the bodies of at least 23 people were placed in the burial chamber beneath. It attracts many visitors every year.

Poulton-le-Fylde 'farm by the pool in FYLDE', OE *pol* 'pool' + -TON, with the name of the local district.
A town in Lancashire, 5 km (3 miles) northeast of Blackpool. It was so named to distinguish it from **Poulton-le-Sands**, one of the villages out of which MORECAMBE grew, some 27 km (16 miles) to the north.

Poultry 'market where domestic fowls are sold, poultry market', ME *pultrie*.
A street in the City of London (EC2), essentially an eastward continuation of CHEAPSIDE to the BANK. It had acquired its name, from the poultry market held here, by the end

of the 13th century. As might be expected in a market street, there were plenty of taverns (including one appropriately called The Red Cock), and by the time of the Great Fire of London they were the street's main claim to fame.

The redevelopment of the site at No.1 Poultry, facing BANK, was much argued over in the latter part of the 20th century, a proposed design by the modernist architect Mies van der Rohe causing particular controversy. It was finally filled by a postmodern polychrome office block (1998) by Sir James Stirling.

The poet Thomas Hood (1799–1845) was born in a house in Poultry, and alludes to it in his famous lines in 'I Remember' (1802):

> I remember, I remember,
> The house where I was born,
> The little window where the sun
> Came peeping in at morn.

Poundbury 'Puna's fortification', OE male personal name *Puna* + BURY; the modern name re-uses that of the nearby Iron Age hill-fort, Poundbury Camp.

A model village on Duchy of Cornwall land (*see under* CORNWALL) in Dorset, about 1.5 km (1 mile) from Dorchester. It was set up in the 1980s at the instigation of the Prince of Wales (whose permission house-owners need to, for example, paint their front doors or park their cars in the street). It is planned eventually to cover 162 ha (400 acres) and to consist of new houses in traditional styles, along with parkland.

Powderham 'promontory in reclaimed marshland', OE *polra* 'reclaimed marshland' + *hamm* 'promontory' (*see* HAM).

A hamlet in Devon, on the western side of the estuary of the River Exe, about 8 km (5 miles) south of Exeter. Lord Halifax (1881–1959), the appeasing Conservative foreign secretary (1938–40), was born here. **Powderham Castle**, medieval in origin but dating in its present structure mainly from the 18th and 19th centuries, is the seat of the earls of Devon (and formerly home of Timothy Tortoise, thought to have been born in 1844 and until his death in 2004 Britain's oldest resident).

Powerscourt Probably originally from the *de Poer* family, who held lands here in the 13th century; the estate was granted to Richard Wingfield, 1st Viscount Powerscourt, in 1618 and remained in his family's possession until 1961.

A Palladian country mansion near Enniskerry, County Wicklow, some 20 km (12 miles) south of Dublin. In Irish it is **Cúirt an Phaoraigh** ('Power's mansion'). The house, designed by Richard Castle, dates from 1731–40, but was badly burnt in 1974 but has been partly restored. It is surrounded by magnificent gardens, and nearby is **Powerscourt Waterfall**, at 120 m (about 400 ft) the highest in Ireland, and the second highest in the British Isles after EAS A'CHÙAL ALUINN in the Scottish Highlands.

> Looping off feline through the leisured air
>   Water, a creature not at home in water,
>   Takes to the air. It comes down on its forepaws, changes
>   Feet on the rockface and again extended
> Bounds.
>
> Donald Davie: 'The Waterfall at Powerscourt' (1955–6)

There is a story that when George IV was visiting him, Viscount Powerscourt dammed the waterfall so that he could impress the monarch with a great cascade of water when the dam was breached. Luckily for the king (a known trencherman), he proved to be inseparable from his victuals at the banquet at Powerscourt House, and so avoided being washed away along with the proposed viewing point, a bridge below the waterfall.

Powerstock *Power-* perhaps from an old river name, as in *Porton* (*see* PORTON DOWN); *-stock* 'outlying farmstead' (*see* -STOCK, STOCK-, STOKE).

A hillside village in Dorset, about 6.5 km (4 miles) northeast of Bridport. On the summit of the nearby Eggardon Hill is an Iron Age fort.

Powys Possibly 'provincial place' from Latin *pagensis* 'of the outlying region (*pagus*)'; in Welsh, however, *powys* means 'quietness, rest'.

An ancient kingdom and modern administrative division of eastern central Wales. It is pronounced 'pow-iss', with 'pow' as in 'how'. The rulers of early medieval Powys also held lands in what is now England, in the counties of Herefordshire, Worcestershire and Shropshire (in the 5th and 6th centuries their capital was SHREWSBURY), but these lands were lost to the Mercians (*see under* MERCIA) in the 8th century, and by the end of the century OFFA'S DYKE had become the new frontier.

From 855 to 1063 Powys was ruled by the kings of GWYNEDD, and it was subsequently ruled by independent princes of Powys. Powys was at the peak of its power under Madog ap Maredudd (d.1160), who recovered some territory to the east of Offa's Dyke. After his death, Powys was divided into two lordships, **Powys Wenwynwyn** (South Powys) and **Powys Fadog** (North Powys). The former came under English rule in 1208, and the latter in 1269.

In the local government reorganization of 1974 Powys was revived as a new county, incorporating the former counties of BRECKNOCKSHIRE, MONTGOMERYSHIRE, and RADNORSHIRE (which all became districts of Powys). It survived the reorganization of 1996, as a unitary authority. It is bordered to the north by Flintshire and Denbighshire (formerly Clwyd), to the west by Gwynedd, Ceredigion and Carmarthenshire (formerly Dyfed), to the south by Neath Port Talbot, Rhondda Cynon Taff, Merthyr Tydfil (formerly West and Mid Glamorgan) and Blaenau Gwent (formerly Gwent), and to the east by Monmouthshire (formerly

Gwent), Herefordshire (formerly Hereford and Worcester) and Shropshire. The administrative seat is at LLANDRINDOD WELLS, and other towns include BRECON, BUILTH WELLS, WELSHPOOL, NEWTOWN[1] and LLANIDLOES. Rivers include the WYE[1] (Gwy) and SEVERN (Hafren), and there are many ranges of hills, the highest being the BRECON BEACONS in the south.

> There was a young caddy from Powys
> Who asked of his golfer, 'Just howys
>> It possible for you
>> To perform as you do?'
> Quoth he, 'An amalgam of ability and prowys.'
>
> Anon.: limerick

Vale of Powys. The upper valley of the River Severn.

Poyntzfield Originally known as *Ardoch*, Poyntzfield, like nearby JEMIMAVILLE, was named in the early 19th century after Jemima *Poyntz*, Dutch wife of the local laird.

A small settlement in the BLACK ISLE, Easter Ross, Highland, 8 km (5 miles) southwest of Cromarty.

Poyntzpass 'Poyntz's pass', after Lieutenant Charles *Poyntz*. A village in County Armagh, 15 km (9 miles) south of Newry on the border with County Down. It was founded in 1790, and in Irish it is **Pas an Phointe** (meaning the same). It takes its name from Lieutenant Charles Poyntz, commander of the garrison here, who in 1598 desperately fought off an attack by Hugh O'Neill. Poyntz, from Acton in Gloucestershire, was in 1609 granted 500 acres (about 200 ha) of land at nearby Brannock, and brought over a dozen families from Gloucestershire to settle there, calling his new village Acton.

The Ulster Robin Hood, Redmond O'Hanlon (1640–81), was born near Poyntzpass, and was buried near his birthplace after his head had been stuck on a spike in DOWNPATRICK.

Praa Sands From the name of the nearby beach, of uncertain origin: *Praa* perhaps 'hag's cove', Cornish *porth* 'cove' (*see* PORT) + *gwragh* 'hag', or 'hag's pool', Cornish *poll* 'pool' + *gwragh*.

A holiday village on the south Cornish coast, about 11 km (7 miles) east of Penzance.

Praed Street Named in honour of William *Praed*, chairman of the Grand Junction Canal Company.

A somewhat seedy road (pronounced 'prade') in western Central London (W2), in the City of WESTMINSTER, linking the EDGWARE Road in the east with PADDINGTON Station in the west. It was laid out by the Grand Junction Canal Company in the early 19th century to serve Paddington Basin (*see under* PADDINGTON). It contains St Mary's Hospital, where in 1928 Alexander Fleming discovered penicillin.

Pratt's Bottom 'valley associated with the Pratt family', *Pratt* + OE *botm* 'valley'. A family called Pratt is known of in this area from the 14th century.

A village on the southeastern edge of London, in the borough of BROMLEY (before 1965 in Kent), about 3 km (2 miles) south of Orpington. Its unsubtly humorous name on signposts enlivens the approaches to Junction 4 on the M25.

Prawle Point *Prawle* probably 'look-out hill', OE *praw* 'look-out' + *hyll* 'hill'.

A promontory in Devon, in the SOUTH HAMS, on the eastern side of the mouth of the KINGSBRIDGE estuary. It is the southernmost point in Devon. Just inland is the village of **East Prawle**.

Praze-an-Beeble 'meadow of the conduit', Cornish *pras* 'meadow' + *an* 'the' + *pibell* 'pipe, conduit'.

A village in Cornwall, about 3 km (2 miles) south of CAMBORNE.

Predannack Wollas 'lower headland of Britain' (the 'headland of Britain' is the LIZARD), *Predannack* Cornish *Predenn* 'Britain' + *-ek* 'place of'; *Wollas* Cornish *goles* 'lower'.

A village in Cornwall, on the west coast of the Lizard Peninsula, about 13 km (8 miles) south of Helston.

Preesall 'headland with brushwood', OCelt *pres* 'brushwood' + OScand *hofuth* or OE *heafod* 'headland'.

A village near the mouth of the River Wyre in Lancashire, 5 km (3 miles) east of Fleetwood.

Premier County, the. A nickname given to County TIPPERARY in the context of the Irish hurling championships. The reason for the name is obscure, but may refer to the fertility of the land.

Prescelly Mountains 'thicket of Selyf', Welsh *prys* 'thicket' + personal name *Selyf*, a Welsh version of Solomon.

A range of bare hills forming an inland salient of the Pembrokeshire Coast National Park (*see under* PEMBROKESHIRE), in northern Pembrokeshire (formerly in Dyfed), some 15 km (9 miles) east of Fishguard. Their Welsh name is **Mynydd Preseli**, and they are also referred to as the **Preseli** or **Preseley Hills**. The highest point is Foel Cwmcerwyn (536 m / 1758 ft), also called **Prescelly Top**, where, according to the Welsh literary classic *Mabinogion*, King Arthur and his knights fought the giant boar Twrch Trwyth; nearby are the Cerrig Meigon Arthur, the Stones of the Sons of Arthur who were killed by the boar.

Visitors to the area have found it one of the lands that time forgot. There are many prehistoric remains, including an ancient trackway, in use for four millennia, called the **Golden Road**. Blue stone quarried in the Prescelly Mountains was used in the construction of Stonehenge 3500–4000 years ago; how the stones (some weighing 4 tons) were transported the 225 km (140 miles) to Wiltshire is still the subject of speculation.

Prescot 'priests' cottage', OE *preost* 'priest', possessive plural *preosta* + *cot* (*see* -COT, COTE).

A town in Merseyside (formerly in Lancashire), between Liverpool and St Helens. It was the birthplace of the actor John Philip Kemble (1757–1853).

Preseli or **Preseley Hills.** *See* PRESCELLY MOUNTAINS.

Preseli Pembrokeshire *Preseli see* PRESCELLY MOUNTAINS; *Pembrokeshire see* PEMBROKE.

A former district (1974–96) of the former county of Dyfed, southwest Wales. The administrative seat was at Haverfordwest. In 1996 it and the former district of South Pembrokeshire were united and absorbed into the new unitary authority of PEMBROKESHIRE.

Prestatyn 'priests' farm', OE *preost* 'priest', possessive plural *preosta* + -TON.

A seaside resort in Denbighshire (formerly in Flintshire, then in Clwyd), 6 km (4 miles) east of Rhyl. It is the northern terminus of the Offa's Dyke Path (*see under* OFFA'S DYKE), and there are retirement homes, caravan sites and apparently boisterous holiday camps:

> Seven people were charged yesterday with criminal damage, public order offences, and possessing drugs after a 'seaside madness' weekend organized by Liverpool's Radio City at Pontin's holiday camp in Prestatyn, North Wales.
>
> *The Guardian* (18 March 2003)

Prestatyn was the birthplace of Sir Huw Weldon (1916–86), producer, broadcaster and senior executive at the BBC in the 1960s and 1970s; and of John Prescott (b.1938), syntactically challenged deputy prime minister in Tony Blair's New Labour government from 1997.

'Sunny Prestatyn'. An ironic but inescapably misogynistic poem in Philip Larkin's collection *The Whitsun Weddings* (1964). It begins

> Come to Sunny Prestatyn
> Laughed the girl on the poster,
> Kneeling up on the sand
> In tautened white satin.

The poem gave rise to Dr Edward Reiss's admired and delightfully titled paper, 'Sexual Politics in "Sunny Prestatyn"' (1999). Dr Reiss helpfully explains that the girl on the poster (who 'was slapped up one day in March' according to Larkin) is 'an icon of femininity and of the life beautiful, which is the lie beautiful and the lay beautiful'. Unpleasantly, this busty icon ends up drawn-on, mutilated and torn.

Presteigne 'priests' household', OE *preost* 'priest', possessive plural *preosta* + *hœmed* 'household'.

A small market town on the River Lugg in Powys (formerly in Radnorshire, of which it was the county town), on the English border 25 km (15 miles) east of Llandrindod Wells.

Its Welsh name is **Llandandras** ('church of St Andrew'). It was the home of John Bradshaw (1602–59), one of the signatories of Charles I's death warrant. There is an annual music and arts festival.

Preston 'priests' farm', OE *preost* 'priest', possessive plural *preosta* + -TON.

A market and industrial town in Lancashire (of which it is the administrative headquarters), 32 km (19 miles) south of Lancaster. It is at the highest navigable point on the River RIBBLE, and the docks carry out much trade with Ireland. The **Preston Bypass**, completed in 1958 and now part of the M6, was the first stretch of motorway in Britain. Locally, the town is known as **'Proud Preston'**.

The town grew by the site of a Roman fort, and it received its first charter in 1179. A battle was fought here during the Civil Wars (*see below*), and during the 1715 Jacobite Rising Thomas Forster and the Earl of Derwentwater (*see under* DERWENT[1]) led a Jacobite army south to Preston, where they were intercepted by Hanoverian forces and obliged to surrender (14 November 1715).

> Long Preston Peg to proud Preston went,
> To see the Scotch rebels it was her intent.
> A noble Scotch lord, as he passed by,
> On this Yorkshire damsel did soon cast an eye.
>
> Anon.: 'Long Preston Peg', a traditional ballad

Later in the 18th century Preston emerged as an important cotton-manufacturing town, and in the following century provided the inspiration for COKETOWN in Dickens's *Hard Times* (1854). In 1970 Preston was designated as part of CENTRAL LANCASHIRE, a NEW TOWN[1] entity.

Preston was the birthplace of Richard Arkwright (1732–92), inventor of the 'water frame' for spinning cotton; the poet Francis Thompson (1859–1907), author of 'The Hound of Heaven'; the girls-school story-writer Angela Brazil (1868–1947); Robert Service (1874–1958), the balladeer of the Canadian Arctic; the military commander Sir John Glubb ('Glubb Pasha'; 1897–1976); and the burly Lancashire and England cricketer Andrew Flintoff (b.1977). Henry 'Orator' Hunt was MP for Preston from 1831 to 1833.

Battle of Preston (17–19 August 1648). A battle in which Oliver Cromwell's Parliamentary army defeated an invading Scottish force under the Duke of Hamilton, intent on rescuing Charles I. Hamilton was captured and executed. Other Scots taken at Preston were sent to COVENTRY, where they were snubbed by the Parliamentarian populace, thus giving rise to the expression 'sent to Coventry'.

Battle of Preston (1715). *See* main entry *above*.

Brasseur de Preston, Le. A rarely performed three-act comic opera (1838) by the prolific French composer Adolphe Adam (1803–56). The 'Preston brewer' of its title is one Daniel Robinson. His wife Effie and twin brother George also feature in the opera.

Preston North End FC. Preston's senior football club, formed in 1881 and nicknamed the Lilywhites. In 1889 they won the first English Football League Championship and the FA Cup, thus the first team to win the double. David Beckham played for Preston North End for a month in the 1994–5 season before returning to Manchester United.

> Oh Lancashire is wonderful
> It's full of tits, fanny and Preston
>
> Anon.: Chant sung by Preston North End supporters

Preston Plumber, the. The many-capped Preston North End footballer Sir Tom Finney (b.1922), who scored 30 goals for England during his career. Finney, who made his professional and international debuts in 1946, was by trade a plumber, and the nickname was perhaps reinforced by his famous 1955 dash down the right side of a waterlogged Stamford Bridge to collect a loose ball; a photographer caught him dramatically avoiding a tackle in a spray of water to produce one of football's greatest images – known to PNE supporters as 'The Splash'. Finney retired from professional football in 1960. The road in which Preston North End's ground, Deepdale, is located has been renamed Sir Tom Finney Way.

Preston Bagot *Bagot see* MORTON BAGOT.
A village in Warwickshire, about 13 km (8 miles) north of Stratford-upon-Avon.

Preston Candover *Candover see* BROWN CANDOVER.
A village in Hampshire, about 17.5 km (11 miles) northeast of Winchester.

Preston Gubbals *Gubbals* denoting manorial ownership in the 11th century by a priest called Godebold.
A village in Shropshire, about 8 km (5 miles) north of Shrewsbury.

Prestonpans 'salt pans of the priests' farmstead', OE *preost* 'priest', in the possessive plural *preosta* + -TON + ME *pans*.
A small town on the Firth of Forth, 5 km (3 miles) east of Musselburgh, in Midlothian. It takes the first part of its name from the nearby village of Preston, and the second part from the fact that the monks of Newbattle Abbey panned salt here from the 13th century. **Prestonpans oysters** (called *pandours* in Scots) were once celebrated, for example in the poem 'Caller Oysters' by Robert Fergusson (1750–74) (*see also under* MUSSELBURGH).

Battle of Prestonpans (21 September 1745). A victory of Bonnie Prince Charlie's Jacobites – largely under the direction of Lord George Murray – over the forces of the Hanoverian government under Sir John Cope. The Highlanders charged at dawn, and it took only ten minutes to put the unprepared Hanoverians to flight. It was said that Cope was the first to bring the bad news to England, and he was mocked in a Jacobite song written by a local gentleman farmer, Adam Skirving (1719–1803), just after the battle:

> Oh Hey Johnny Cope, are ye waukin yet?
> Or are your drums a'beating yet?
>
> (Scots *waukin* 'waking')

Prestwich 'priest's farm', OE *preost* 'priest' + *wic* (*see* WICK).
A largely residential area of Greater Manchester, 6 km (4 miles) north of MANCHESTER city centre.
The comedienne Victoria Wood (b.1953) was born here.

Prestwick 'outlying farm belonging to the priests', OE *preost* (probably in the possessive plural *preosta*) + WICK.
A seaside town 4 km (2.5 miles) north of Ayr, with which it is contiguous. It is in South Ayrshire (formerly in Strathclyde region), and is home to a championship golf course, first laid out in 1851. The first 12 British Open golf championships, from 1860 to 1872, were played here. Prestwick hosted its last Open in 1925.
Prestwick was the birthplace of the golfer 'Young Tom' Morris (1850/1–75), who, like his father 'Old Tom', won the British Open four times.

Prestwick International Airport. A large airport between Prestwick and the village of Monkton to the north. Its origins can be traced to 1935, when the University of Glasgow Flying Squadron began training on a field here. During the Second World War the site was developed as an important base for transatlantic military flights, and in 1946 the British Overseas Airways Corporation began scheduled passenger flights to New York.

Pretty Corner. *See under* SHERINGHAM.

Prickwillow Probably 'willow-tree from which skewers or goads were made', OE *pricca* 'prick, skewer, goad' + *wilig* 'willow-tree'.
A village in Cambridgeshire (before 1974 in the Isle of Ely), about 5 km (3 miles) northeast of ELY[1]. Visitors to the village may inspect the Drainage Museum (concerned with drainage of the FENS, rather than more domestic matters).

Priddy Probably 'earth-house', OCelt *prith* 'earth' + *tigh* 'house'.
A village in Somerset, in the MENDIP HILLS, about 14 km (9 miles) southwest of Midsomer Norton.

Priestholm. *See* PUFFIN ISLAND.

Primrose Hill 'hill where primroses grow'.
A hill in North London (NW3, NW8), in the borough of CAMDEN, just to the north of REGENT'S PARK. It is 63 m (206 ft) high. It was covered by woods in the Middle Ages, but by Elizabethan times these had been replaced by meadowland (the poet Arthur Hugh Clough wrote in 1854 of 'the pastural eminence of Primrose Hill'). In the early 19th century it was a popular venue for duels. It was opened to the public as a park in 1842.
The residential district that grew up to the east of the hill in the 19th century has inherited its name, and eventually passed it on to the local railway station. The station was originally (1855) called Hampstead Road, and then

(1862) Chalk Farm, and did not become Primrose Hill until 1990. It closed in 1992.

> The fields from Islington to Marybone,
> To Primrose Hill and Saint John's Wood
> Were builded over with pillars of gold;
> And there Jerusalem's pillars stood.
>
> William Blake: *Jerusalem* (1815)

> Only last week, the place was dubbed Promiscuity Hill by the *Sun* … Promiscuity Hill!, where the pre-Raphaelite painter J.W. Waterhouse rigged up a boat in his backyard and painted his world-famous Ophelia; where W.B. Yeats and Sylvia Plath penned their poetry, and Kingsley Amis celebrated the sound of the wolves' howls rising on the wind from London Zoo.
>
> Genevieve Fox: 'Will Fame Kill the Hill?', in the *Evening Standard* (February 2005) (following rumours of wife-swapping among Primrose Hill's A-list celebrity residents)

Prince Charlie's Cave. *See* BEN ALDER.

Princes Risborough *Princes* denoting manorial ownership in the 14th century by Edward, the Black Prince (son of Edward III); *Risborough* 'hill(s) where brushwood grows', OE *hrisen* 'growing with brushwood' + *beorg* 'hill'.

A town in Buckinghamshire, in the CHILTERN HILLS, about 11 km (7 miles) south of Aylesbury.

Princes Street Named after George III's sons, the Prince of Wales and the Duke of York (the future George IV and William IV); the king had objected to the original proposed name St Giles Street, after the city's patron saint.

EDINBURGH's main shopping street, on the southern edge of the classical New Town, first planned in 1767. It is approximately 1.6 km (1 mile) long, and is unusual in that for most of its length there are buildings on only one side (Glaswegians say it is only half-finished); along the south side are **Princes Street Gardens**, leading steeply down to the hidden railway lines that run along what was once the bed of the long-drained sewer of the Nor Loch ('north lake'), nestling under the great precipitous mass of Edinburgh Castle Rock (*see under* EDINBURGH) and the tall tenements and spires of the Old Town. The gardens include the Gothic spike of the Scott Monument (1844) and the world's first floral clock (1903), complete with cuckoo every quarter of an hour, and are divided into two sections by the Mound, a steep ramp (made from rubble dug up during the construction of the New Town) carrying a road up to the Old Town and the ROYAL MILE; at the foot of the Mound are two Greek-style temples, housing the Royal Scottish Academy (1832) and the National Gallery of Scotland (1859). The prospect south from Princes Street is thus one of the finest from any city street in the world. Unfortunately, the south-facing façade of Princes Street has virtually nothing left of the original Georgian residential buildings, and even many of their Victorian replacements (department stores, hotels, etc.) were pulled down in the 1960s and 1970s to make way for some disastrously inferior concrete shop frontages, now housing a predictable range of high-street chains. However, at the eastern end there remains the very fine Adam-designed Register House (1772–92). In recent years Princes Street has become the venue (weather permitting) of the world's biggest and best Hogmanay party.

Princetown[1] Named in honour of the Prince Regent (later George IV), who as Duke of Cornwall owned the land it stood on. (There was a recent local history of sycophantic nomenclature: in 1780 a nearby farm was named Prince Hall).

A cheerless town in Devon, on Dartmoor, 400 m (1300 ft) above sea level, about 11 km (7 miles) east of TAVISTOCK. It grew up in the 1810s around Dartmoor Prison (*see under* DARTMOOR). Some of its rather spartan houses were built by the prison's original French and American prisoner-of-war inmates.

Princetown[2] The name dates from the same era as the Devon Princetown, so is presumed also to refer to the Prince Regent.

A village in Caerphilly unitary authority (formerly in Monmouthshire, then in Gwent), 2 km (1.2 miles) north of Rhymney, and 4 km (2.5 miles) west of Dukestown.

Principality, the. *See* WALES.

Prinknash 'Princa's ash-tree', OE *Princan* possessive form of male personal name *Princa* + *æsc* 'ash-tree'.

The site (pronounced 'prinnage') of a Benedictine abbey in Gloucestershire, about 9 km (6 miles) southeast of Gloucester. After the 16th-century Dissolution of the Monasteries the original abbey (the former residence of the abbots of Gloucester) was owned by a succession of families before returning to the Benedictines in 1928. An entirely new abbey has been built on the site, which has a pottery attached, famous for the manufacture of glazed earthenware with a finish like polished steel.

Printing House Square From its being occupied by many printers.

A former square in BLACKFRIARS (EC4), in the City of London. Originally part of Blackfriars monastery, it was occupied from the 17th century onwards by printers. They included the King's Printers, Norton and Bill. The *London Gazette* was first printed here, as was the infamous edition of the Bible that omitted the word 'not' from the seventh commandment (adultery). After the King's Printers moved out in the late 17th century their premises were acquired by John Walter. In 1785 he began printing the *Daily Universal Register* here, and in 1788 changed its name to *The Times*. Over the centuries the name of the square became synonymous with that newspaper's editorial staff, and particularly its editor and leader writers:

Is, indeed, anyone, anywhere, truly worthy of *The Times*? This was the awfully solemn thought which … sometimes oppressed Printing House Square.

Claud Cockburn: *In Time of Trouble* (1956)

When *The Times* moved in 1974 to Gray's Inn Road, its new offices were called **New Printing House Square**.

Probus From the dedication of the local church to the mysterious St Probus.

A village in Cornwall, in the valley of the River FAL, about 6 km (4 miles) northeast of Truro. Its church tower (38 m / 125 ft) is the tallest in Cornwall.

Prosen Water. *See* GLEN PROSEN.

Prosperous. A village in County Kildare, 30 km (19 miles) west of Dublin. It was founded and given its optimistic name in 1776 as a cotton-manufacturing centre, but the venture had failed by the end of the century. Its Irish name is **An Chorrcoill** ('the projecting wood').

Provinces, the. Those regions that lie well beyond the political and cultural centre. The word has its origins in Latin *provincia*, a conquered territory, and the Romans notably had their many, often far-flung, provinces, of which cold and northerly Britain was probably one of the least appealing. In an English context, province could mean SHIRE in the Middle Ages, and the island of Ireland was traditionally divided into its four provinces of CONNACHT, LEINSTER, MUNSTER and ULSTER. Today, however, the only remaining territory amongst these islands to be thus described is NORTHERN IRELAND, often referred to simply as **the Province** (notably by journalists).

More pervasive and insidious, however, is the adjective (and noun) **provincial**, which, while it can still carry a neutral status is more often loaded with cultural baggage: in this sense, to be provincial is to be decidedly unmetropolitan and uncosmopolitan. It is to be narrow-minded, unadventurous, more probably yokelly-rustic or suburban than urban, older rather than younger, ignorant or unsophisticated, sartorially drab, with low- to (at tops) middlebrow tastes, and possibly afflicted with the kind of regional accent as yet unacceptable to the modern media (other than comedically). In the British context one is at risk of being tarred with the brush for living anywhere outside the throbbing hub of (particularly Central) LONDON: too far out of earshot of the Hampstead Set (*see under* HAMPSTEAD), outside the political hothouse of WESTMINSTER, and beyond the lifestyles afforded by KNIGHTSBRIDGE or CHELSEA. Although there is a sense that the greater the remoteness the greater the level of provincial-ness, modern Little Englanders (*see under* ENGLAND) and the denizens of MIDDLE ENGLAND (wherever they dwell) would still qualify.

Prudhoe 'Pruda's spur', OE male personal name + *hoh* 'hill spur'.

A small town in Northumberland, 15 km (9 miles) west of Newcastle upon Tyne. The ruins of a Norman castle lie here. There is a Prudhoe Bay in northern Alaska.

Prussia Cove From the name of a local inn, The King of *Prussia*, whose landlord in the 18th century, John Carter, used the cove for his smuggling activities.

A cove on the southwest coast of Cornwall, about 5 km (3 miles) southeast of Marazion. It can be reached only on foot. The local seaside village has borrowed its name.

Pubic Triangle. A nickname for the red-light district of EDINBURGH. For other triangles, *see* BALTI TRIANGLE, Falkirk Triangle (*see under* FALKIRK), GOLDEN TRIANGLE and Rhubarb Triangle (*under* WAKEFIELD).

Puck. *See under* KILLORGLIN.

Puckoon Probably a version of Irish *pocán* 'little heap'.

A fictional Irish village in Spike Milligan's novel (1963) of the same name. In 1924 Puckoon comes to the attention of the Boundary Commission deciding the details of the border between NORTHERN IRELAND and the Irish Free State (*see under* IRISH), and ends up being split down the middle – even the chairs and the bar in the pub are on different sides of the border. *Puckoon* was turned into a film in 2003.

Pudding Lane 'offal lane' (referring to the use of the lane in the Middle Ages by the butchers of Eastcheap meat market to transport unwanted carcase-parts (including intestines) down to the Thames for loading on to the dung barges), ME *pudding* 'bowels, entrails, guts'.

A street in the City of London (EC3) (*see under* LONDON), just to the east of London Bridge, running from Eastcheap in the north towards Lower Thames Street in the south (in former times it led right down to the THAMES[1]). The Great Fire of London (1666) began in Farryner's baking shop in Pudding Lane on 2 September; from modest beginnings it went on to spread as far west as the TEMPLE, destroying 87 churches, including ST PAUL's[1] Cathedral, and 13,200 houses, but killing only 20 people.

Puddle Dock From the name of a former small inlet on the site with wharfage facilities, ME *puddel* 'small dirty pool'.

A street in the City of London (EC4), just to the east of BLACKFRIARS Bridge, running from Queen Victoria Street in the north to Upper Thames Street in the south. In 1959 the Mermaid Theatre, a project nurtured by the actor Bernard Miles, opened in Puddle Dock, the first new theatre in the City of London for 300 years.

On the Banks of the River Thames, are the Wharfs of Puddle Dock, used for a Laystall for the Soil of the Streets; and much frequented by Barges and Lighters, for taking the same away.

John Strype: *Stow's Survey of London* (1720)

Puddletown Earlier *Piddleton* 'farmstead on the River Piddle',

PIDDLE + -TON; the present-day version is first recorded in the 13th century.

A village (locally pronounced 'piddltən') in Dorset, on the River PIDDLE, about 8 km (5 miles) northeast of Dorchester. In Thomas Hardy's *Far from the Madding Crowd* (1874) it is fictionalized as **Weatherbury**. The open country to the southeast is the EGDON HEATH of his novels.

In 1956 Dorset County Council proposed to restore the 'original' *Piddle-* to its name, to bring it into line with other local names such as PIDDLEHINTON and PIDDLETRENTHIDE, but this met with great opposition – mainly on grounds of cost, but also because *Puddletown* was felt to be 'nicer' – and the proposal was not proceeded with.

Pudsey 'Pudoc's enclosure' or 'enclosure by the Wart', OE male personal name or *puduc* 'wart' (possibly the name of a hill) + *hæg* 'enclosure'.

An industrial town in West Yorkshire, 8 km (5 miles) west of Leeds, with which it is contiguous. It is thought that Pudsey might have been the site of the capital of ELMET, a Romano-British kingdom that resisted the Anglo-Saxons until the 7th century.

Pudsey has a peerless record as a producer of Ashes-winning England cricket captains, being the birthplace not only of the Yorkshire and England opening batsman Len Hutton (1916–90) – who regained the Ashes in 1953 (and whose earlier 364 against Australia at the Oval in 1938 was the world-record test-match score until Gary Sobers beat it in 1958) – but also of the Yorkshire and England all-rounder Ray Illingworth (b.1932), who took back the Ashes in 1970–1.

Puffin Island From its colony of puffins.

A small island less than 1 km (0.6 miles) off the eastern tip of ANGLESEY. The puffin population was reduced in the early 19th century, when many birds were culled for pickling and the production of lamp oil. In Welsh it is called **Ynys Seirol** ('isle of St Seirol') after the saint who lived in a cell on the island in the 6th century – hence also its former English name, **Priestholm** (from OScand *prestr* 'priest' + *holmr* 'island' (*see* -EY, -EA)).

Giraldus Cambrensis recorded in *Itinarium Cambriae* that if ever the monks on the island fell out with each other, 'a species of small mice, which abound on the island, consume most of their food and drink, and befoul the rest'. Once the monks kissed and made up, the plague of mice would disappear.

Pulborough 'hill or mound by the pool', OE *pol* 'pool' + *beorg* 'hill, mound'.

A small market town in West Sussex, on the River ARUN, about 17.5 km (11 miles) southwest of Horsham, at the point where the London–Chichester road crosses the Winchester–Brighton road. The older part of the town is on a hillside (whence its name).

Pullans, the Irish *pullán* 'small pool or hollow', referring here to lakes.

An area of little lakes in southern County Donegal, some 10 km (6 miles) south of Donegal town.

Pumlumon. The Welsh name for PLYNLIMON.

Punchestown. *See* NAAS.

Puncknowle Probably 'Puma's hillock', OE male personal name *Puma* + *cnoll* 'hillock'.

A village in Dorset, about 8 km (5 miles) southeast of Bridport.

Punnett's Town From the *Pannet* family, known in the locality in the 17th century.

A village in East Sussex, in the WEALD, about 5 km (3 miles) east of Heathfield. It has a windmill, moved here from Biddenden in Kent.

Pura Wallia. *See under* WALLIA.

Purbeck 'beak-shaped ridge frequented by the bittern or snipe' (referring to the Purbeck Hills), OE *pur* 'bittern, snipe' + *bic* 'beak-shaped ridge'.

An area in the southeastern corner of Dorset, now a local-government district. It takes its name from the **Purbeck Hills**, a range of chalk hills that traverse the central southern part of the area from east to west. The peninsula it occupies is called the **Isle of Purbeck**. A land of low hills and heath to the south of Poole Harbour (*see under* POOLE), this does have something of the self-contained feel of an island about it. Its main centres are WAREHAM and SWANAGE. It is dotted with quarries from which the celebrated local stone (*see below*) is extracted.

Purbeck beds. The three limestone strata that characterize the geology of the Isle of Purbeck and areas south and west.

Purbeck marble. Purbeck stone of the highest grade, much used in the past for ornamental architectural work.

Purbeck stone. Hard oolitic limestone of the sort extracted from the Purbeck beds. It is used for building and paving.

Purfleet 'Purta's creek or stream', OE male personal name *Purta* + *fleot* 'creek, stream'.

A district within the unitary authority of Thurrock (before 1998 in Essex), on the north bank of the River THAMES[1], at the northern end of the Dartford Tunnel (*see under* DARTFORD) and the QUEEN ELIZABETH II BRIDGE.

The lunatic asylum that features in Bram Stoker's *Dracula* (1897) is in Purfleet. The bloodsucking count buys an estate nearby.

Purley 'glade where pear-trees grow', OE *pirige* 'pear-tree' + -LEY.

A southern suburb of London, in the borough of CROYDON (before 1965 in Surrey), to the southwest of the town of Croydon. It is on the main road and railway from London to Brighton.

It is reasonably conventional leafy commuter-land – far from the lurid Gomorrah in Eric Idle's mind when he leered 'Purley – say no more!' on being told where mild-mannered clerk Michael Palin's wife came from in *Monty Python's Flying Circus*.

Purple Mountain From its coverage of heather.

A mountain (832 m / 2729 ft) on the west side of the lower Lakes of KILLARNEY, County Kerry. It is separated from MACGILLICUDDY'S REEKS by the craggy GAP OF DUNLOE.

Purse Caundle *Purse* probably denoting manorial ownership in the Middle Ages by a family of that name; *Caundle see* BISHOP'S CAUNDLE.

A village in Dorset, about 6 km (4 miles) east of SHERBORNE. The medieval **Purse Caundle Manor** has a noted ghost. *See also* STOURTON CAUNDLE.

Putney 'landing-place frequented by hawks' or 'Putta's landing-place' (perhaps alluding to a fishery here), OE *puttan* or *Puttan* possessive forms of *putta* 'hawk' or male personal name *Putta* + *hyth* 'landing-place'.

A district of southwest London (SW15), on the south bank of the River Thames, in the borough of WANDSWORTH, between the district of Wandsworth to the east and Barnes to the west. There may have been a settlement here in the Iron Age, and historically it has always been an important crossing point on the Thames. Ferries ran both cross-river and down to Westminster in the Middle Ages. The first modern bridge here, a wooden one, was built in 1729. In the 1880s the present stone structure replaced it. Since 1845 **Putney Bridge** has been the starting point of the annual Oxford-and-Cambridge Boat Race. Putney Bridge 'Underground' station (on the Fulham side) on the District line opened in 1880, originally under the name 'Putney Bridge and Fulham'; East Putney station (on the Putney side) on the same line opened in 1889.

Putney was heavily built up into a residential district over the course of the 19th and early 20th centuries, but the development was always of a fairly salubrious nature, and it remains – not grand, certainly – but comfortable and spacious, its demographic firmly middle-class. Perhaps its most celebrated resident was the poet Algernon Charles Swinburne (1837–1909), who lived with his friend Theodore Watts-Dunton at The Pines, 11 Putney Hill, described by Ford Madox Ford as the most lugubrious London semi-detached villa it was ever his fate to enter.

Thomas Cromwell (*c*.1485–1540), Henry VIII's chief minister, was born in Putney, as were the historian Edward Gibbon (1737–94) and the Labour politician and prime minister Clement Attlee (1883–1967). The last studio of the sculptor Henri Gaudier-Brzeska (1891–1915) was under a leaky railway arch in Putney.

In the 1997 general election the flamboyant entrepreneur James Goldmith stood unsuccessfully for the Referendum Party against the sitting Conservative candidate and former sports minister David Mellor in the constituency of Putney, delivering a memorably scabrous loser's speech.

There are towns called Putney in the USA (Georgia, South Dakota, Vermont).

go to Putney. An expression meaning 'go to blazes' or 'get drunk': in both senses, a piece of 19th-century euphemistic slang. There was also an extended version, **go to Putney on a pig.**

Putney Debates. A series of debates held in Putney parish church by the Parliamentarian Army Council in October 1647, during the Civil Wars, to discuss the 'Agreement of the People'. This was a document presented by the radical reformist Levellers (*see* SOUTHWARK) seeking a new social contract. The debates ended in deadlock.

Putsborough Probably 'Putt's hill or mound', OE *Puttes* possessive form of male personal name *Putt* + *beorg* 'hill, mound'.

A village on the northwest coast of Devon, on Morte Bay (*see under* MORTE POINT), about 14 km (9 miles) northwest of Barnstaple. Its broad sandy beach is **Putsborough Sand**.

Puttock End *Puttock* probably a family name, but ME *puttoc* 'hawk, kite' is possible.

A village in northern Essex, about 8 km (5 miles) west of SUDBURY[1].

Pwllheli 'saltwater pool', Welsh *pwll* 'pool' + *heli* 'brine'.

A small market town and resort on the south coast of the Lleyn Peninsula, Gwynedd (formerly in Caernarvonshire), 20 km west (12 miles) west of Porthmadog. It is pronounced, approximately, 'pool-thelly'. It was here, in August 1925, that members of the Army of Welsh Home Rulers and of the Welsh Movement met in the Maesgwyn Temperance Hotel (now a pet shop) to form Plaid Cymru, the Welsh national party. Nearby is a vast former Butlins holiday camp.

Pyg Track, the. *See* PEN-Y-GWRYD; SNOWDON.

Pyle Possibly '(place by) the stake', ME *pil* 'a stake'.

A small town in Bridgend unitary authority (formerly in Glamorgan, and then West Glamorgan), 12 km (7 miles) southeast of Port Talbot.

Pylle '(place by the) stream', OE *pyll* 'pool, stream'.

A village in Somerset, about 11 km (7 miles) east of GLASTONBURY.

Pytchley 'Peoht's glade', OE *Peohtes* possessive form of male personal name *Peoht* + -LEY.

A village (pronounced 'pie-chli') in Northamptonshire, about 4 km (2.5 miles) southwest of Kettering. The **Pytchley Hunt** (dating from around 1750) has been one of England's oldest and most exclusive fox hunts.

Pytchley (riding) coat. A double-breasted riding coat with full skirts that cover the saddle, worn for hunting.

Q

Quabbs 'muddy place', OE *cwabba*.
A village in Shropshire, near the Welsh border, about 32 km (20 miles) west of Ludlow.

Quadring 'muddy settlement of Hæfer's people' (referring to the surrounding Fens), OE *cwead* 'mud, dirt' + male personal name *Hæfer* + *-ingas* (*see* -ING).
A village in Lincolnshire, in the FENS, about 11 km (7 miles) north of Spalding.

Quadring Eaudike *Eaudike see* FRISKNEY EAUDYKE.
A village in Lincolnshire, about 1.5 km (1 mile) southeast of Quadring.

Quainton 'queen's farmstead or estate', OE *cwen* 'queen' + -TON.
A village in Buckinghamshire, about 11 km (7 miles) north-west of Aylesbury. On the northern edges of METROLAND, it was once served by the Metropolitan line from London: its station, Quainton Road, opened in 1891, but it was closed in 1948.

Quaker Island. Another name for the island of INCH-CLERAUN.

Quantock Hills *Quantock* an OCelt hill name, perhaps derived from *canto*- 'border, district' or possibly from *cantaco* 'a bend'.
A range of limestone and dark sandstone hills (pronounced 'kwontok') in North Somerset, extending about 19 km (12 miles) from near the coast at WATCHET southeastwards towards the **Vale of Taunton Deane** (*see under* TAUNTON). Their highest point is Wills Neck, at 384 m (1260 ft). Their slopes are heavily wooded (including, to the east, **Quantock Forest**), but the summits are bare heathland. It is red deer country, with stag hunts to prove it.

The **Quantocks'** moment in the literary spotlight came at the end of the 18th century, when William Wordsworth and Samuel Taylor Coleridge stayed in the area (at NETHER STOWEY) and wrote their ground-breaking *Lyrical Ballads* (1798), which included Coleridge's 'The Rime of the Ancient Mariner' (*see also* PORLOCK).

Eight springs have flown, since last I lay
On seaward Quantock's heathy hills,
Where quiet sounds from hidden rills
Float here and there, like things astray,
And high o'er head the skylark shrills.

S.T. Coleridge: 'Recollections of Love' (1807)

At the end of Book XIII (the last) of *The Prelude* (1805–50), Wordsworth addresses Coleridge, and remembers their time in Somerset:

That summer when on Quantock's grassy Hills
Far ranging, and among her sylvan Combs …

Quantoxhead 'projecting ridge of the Quantocks', *Quantocks* (*see under* QUANTOCK HILLS) + OE *heafod* 'head, projecting ridge'.
The name of a pair of villages, **East Quantoxhead** and **West Quantoxhead**, at the northwestern end of the Quantock Hills.

Quartershot. The fictional name for ALDERSHOT adopted by Thomas Hardy, as in *Jude the Obscure* (1895).

Quatt From an OE district name *Cwat(t)* of unknown meaning.
A village in Shropshire, near the River SEVERN, about 6 km (4 miles) southeast of Bridgnorth.

Quedgeley Perhaps 'Cweod's glade', OE male personal name *Cweod* + -LEY.
A village in Gloucestershire, about 5 km (3 miles) southwest of Gloucester.

Queen Adelaide From the name of a local pub, itself named after *Queen Adelaide* (1792–1849), wife of William IV.
A village in Cambridgeshire, in the FENS, about 3 km (2 miles) northeast of Ely.

Queenborough 'borough named after the queen' (referring to Queen Philippa (Philippa of Hainault; *c.*1314–69), wife of Edward III, during whose reign the town received its charter), OE *cwen* 'queen' + *burh* (*see* BURY).
A small town in Kent, on the west coast of the ISLE OF SHEPPEY, on the eastern side of the MEDWAY[1] estuary.

Founded in the 14th century as a bastion against French raids (there is a mid-14th-century castle), Queenborough was an important centre of the wool trade in the Middle Ages, but has since contracted in size and dignity.

Mayor of Queenborough, The. A comedy (1615–20) by Thomas Middleton. The play's title satirizes the presumptuousness of towns such as Queenborough that continued to elect mayors even though they had shrunk to mere villages.

Queen Camel *Queen* denoting manorial ownership in the Middle Ages by Queen Eleanor (1246–90), wife of Edward I; *Camel* perhaps an OCelt name from *canto-* 'border, district' + *mel* 'bare hill'.

A village in Somerset, about 10 km (6 miles) northeast of Yeovil.

Queen Elizabeth Forest Park Named in honour of Elizabeth II at the time of her coronation in 1953.

A large area (170 sq km / 66 sq miles) of conifer plantations, lochs and mountains around ABERFOYLE and the TROSSACHS in the southern Highlands. It was formerly in Perthshire and Stirlingshire, then in Central region, and is now nearly all in the unitary authority of Stirling. The Forestry Commission acquired its first land here in 1928.

Queen Elizabeth II Bridge. A bridge across the River Thames, about 27 km (17 miles) east of the centre of London. It carries M25 traffic from PURFLEET in THURROCK on the north bank to DARTFORD on the south. It was opened in 1991 by Queen Elizabeth II, in whose honour it was named. Also known as the **Dartford Bridge**, at the time it was the longest cable-stayed bridge in Europe (450 m / 1476 ft main span, 2.8 km / 1.74 miles total length including approach viaducts), and it is still a very prominent landmark in the flat landscape of the area. Together with the **Dartford Tunnel** it constitutes the **Dartford Crossing**.

Queenhithe 'queen's landing place' (referring originally to a dock belonging to Queen Matilda), OE *cwen* 'queen' + *hyth* 'landing place'.

A small street in the City of London (EC4), leading down from Upper Thames Street to the north bank of the River THAMES[1], just upstream of Southwark Bridge (*see under* SOUTHWARK). There was harbourage here in Anglo-Saxon times (a charter of Alfred the Great (898) refers to it as *Æthelredes hyd* 'Æthelred's harbour'), and up to the 15th century it was the most important dock in London, mainly handling corn and fish. By the early 12th century its name was Queenhithe, signifying that it belonged to Queen Matilda (1100–35), wife of Henry I, and in the later Middle Ages queens of England continued to exercise the right to charge tolls here. By the middle of the 16th century its name had been transferred to the street leading off it. The inlet where the harbour was can still be seen.

Queen of the Coast. A name by which SCARBOROUGH is sometimes known.

Queen of the Hebrides. A name by which ISLAY is sometimes known.

Queen of the Lakes. A name by which ULLSWATER is sometimes known.

Queen of the London Suburbs. A name sometimes used in the late 19th and early 20th centuries for EALING and SURBITON.

Queen of the North Isles. A name by which WESTRAY is sometimes known.

Queen of the Rinns. A name by which PORT CHARLOTTE is sometimes known.

Queen of the Scottish Peaks. A name by which BEN LOYAL in the far north of Scotland is sometimes known.

Queen of the South. A nickname for DUMFRIES and the name of the town's professional football club.

Queen of the South Coast. A nickname by which BOURNEMOUTH is sometimes known.

Queen of Watering Places. A 19th-century name sometimes given to SCARBOROUGH.

Queen o' the Borders. A name by which HAWICK is sometimes known.

Queensbury[1] From the name of the local Metropolitan line station, which was the winning entry in a newspaper competition (the contest did not greatly stretch entrants' onomastic skills – the next station down the line was already called 'Kingsbury').

A residential district of northwest London, in the borough of HARROW (before 1965 in Middlesex), to the southeast of Stanmore. It grew up around Queensbury station on the Metropolitan line, which opened in 1934.

Queensbury[2] The original village was called *Queen's Head*, after the inn here; it was renamed *Queensbury* in 1863 in honour of Queen Victoria.

A village in West Yorkshire, 6 km (4 miles) southwest of Bradford. The Black Dyke Band (a well-known brass band) was formed here in 1855, named after the local Black Dyke Mills where many of the players worked.

Queensbury[3] Probably 'hill thought to contain a queen's burial', OE *cwen* 'woman, queen' + *beorg* 'mound'.

A hill (697 m / 2286 ft) in Dumfries and Galloway (formerly Dumfriesshire), at the southern end of the LOWTHER HILLS, 12 km (7.5 miles) northeast of Thornhill. To its south is a subsidiary top, **Wee Queensbury** (512 m / 1680 ft). The dukes of Buccleuch, who had their seat at nearby Drumlanrig, were also marquesses of Queensberry, presumably taking the title (albeit with a variant spelling) from the hill.

It was the 9th Marquess, John Sholto Douglas, who sponsored the modern Queensberry rules (published 1867) governing boxing.

Queen's County. The name from 1556 to 1920 of County LAOIS.

Queensferry Named after *Queen* Victoria.
A small town near the mouth of the River DEE[2] in Flintshire (formerly in Clwyd), 8 km (5 miles) west of Chester. The first ferry was established as the Lower Ferry in 1726, and was renamed King's Ferry in 1828 after George IV. On the accession of Queen Victoria in 1837 it was renamed Queensferry. The ferry has long been replaced by bridges.

Queen's Ground A recent name, denoting royal ownership.
An area of fenland in Norfolk, about 13 km (8 miles) southeast of Downham Market.

Queen's Nympton Named (in conscious contrast with KING'S NYMPTON) in 1900 in honour of *Queen* Victoria, although the occasion is not known.
A village in Devon, now a southern district of SOUTH MOLTON.

Queen's Park Named in honour of *Queen* Victoria.
A residential district in West London (W10), in the borough of BRENT[2], to the north of the Harrow Road. It was developed as a unified project in the 1870s, and originally some of its roads were given names from A Street to P Street (an innovation soon quietly dropped). The area gave its name to **Queen's Park Rangers FC** (QPR), founded in 1885. Home games are played at Loftus Road ground.

The park just to the north, called **Queen's Park**, was named independently in 1887, also in honour of Queen Victoria. Queen's Park Underground station, on the Bakerloo line, opened in 1915.

Queenstown. The name between 1849 and 1922 of the port of COBH.

Queen's View. The name of two fine viewpoints in Scotland, named in honour of Queen Victoria. The first is on the north shore of Loch TUMMEL looking towards SCHIEHALLION, and was beheld by Queen Victoria in 1866. The second view, had by Victoria in 1869, is from Auchineden Hill, some 6 km (4 miles) northwest of Milnagavie, looking towards LOCH LOMOND.

Queensway So named, perhaps on the model of KINGSWAY, in 1938. Before that it was *Queen's Road*, a name adopted soon after Queen Victoria came to the throne in 1837, in acknowledgment, it was said, of the fact that as a young princess she used to ride along the road to Kensington Palace (at that time it was just a country track, called *Black Lion Lane*).
A street in BAYSWATER, in the City of WESTMINSTER (W2), running southwards from Westbourne Grove (*see under* WESTBOURNE) to HYDE PARK. It is now mainly inhabited by tourist hotels.

Queensway Underground station, on the Central line, opened in 1900, under the name 'Queen's Road'. This was changed to 'Queensway' in 1946.

Queenzieburn Possibly 'gentle stream', Gaelic *caoin* 'gentle' + *burn*.
A village in North Lanarkshire, 2 km (1.2 miles) west of Kilsyth.

Quenington 'women's farmstead' or 'farmstead associated with Cwen', OE *cwenena* possessive plural of *cwen* 'woman' + -TON or OE female personal name *Cwen* + -ING + -TON.
A village in Gloucestershire, about 13 km (8 miles) east of Cirencester.

Quethiock 'wooded place', Cornish *cuicdoc*.
A village in Cornwall, about 6 km (4 miles) east of Liskeard.

Quies '(islands of the) sow' (from the rocks' supposed piglike appearance), Cornish *gwis* 'sow'.
A small group of rocky islets to the west of TREVOSE HEAD in Cornwall.

Quilquox The first part is possibly Gaelic *coille* 'wood', but the second element is uncertain.
A small settlement in Aberdeenshire, 10 km (6 miles) northwest of Ellon.

Quinag Gaelic *cuinneag* 'milk pail, churn'.
A many-topped and craggily ramparted coxcomb of a mountain in northwest Highland (formerly in Sutherland), some 40 km (25 miles) north of Ullapool. The highest point is 808 m (2651 ft).

Quiraing Probably OScand *kvi-rong* 'crooked enclosure'.
A fantastical collection of large rock formations on the east side of the mountain called Meall nan Suireamach (542 m / 1778 ft) in northeast SKYE, Highland (formerly in Inverness-shire), 26 km (16 miles) north of Portree. The name is pronounced 'kweer-yng'. The rocks, made of decaying basalt, have names such as the Prison, the Table and the Needle.

> The Quirang is frozen terror and superstition.
>
> Alexander Smith: *A Summer in Skye* (1886)

Quoditch 'muddy or manured land', OE *cwæd* 'mud, dung' + *hiwisc* 'land supporting a family'.
A village in Devon, on the River Carey, about 19 km (12 miles) west of Okehampton.

Quoich, Loch. *See* LOCH QUOICH.

Quorndon 'hill where millstones are obtained', OE *cweorn* 'quern, millstone' + *dun* (*see* DOWN, -DON).
A village in Leicestershire, about 13 km (8 miles) north of Leicester. It is in the heart of fox-hunting country, and the

shortened form of its name, **Quorn**, is shared by one of the most famous and exclusive of all hunts.

> Above the fields of Leicestershire
> On arches we were borne
> And the rumble of the railway drowned
> The thunder of the Quorn.
>
>> John Betjeman: 'Great Central Railway, Sheffield
>> Victoria to Banbury' (1966)

There is also a Quorn in South Australia, north of Adelaide.

Quorn. The trade name of a type of textured vegetable protein made from an edible fungus and used as a meat substitute. It was launched on the market in Britain in 1984 (an appropriately suggestive date) and takes its name from its original manufacturers, Quorn Specialities Ltd, located in Quorndon. The provenance of a meatless product from a place associated precisely with the pursuit of live flesh has a somewhat unpalatable irony.

Quothquan Possibly OCelt CED 'wood' + *gwen* 'beautiful'.
A settlement in South Lanarkshire, 5 km (3 miles) northwest of Biggar.

Quoyloo Possibly 'sheltered pasture', *quoy* (OScand *kvi*) 'cattle fold, untaxed pasture' + *hle* 'shelter, lee'.
A settlement on Mainland, Orkney, 11 km (7 miles) north of Stromness.

Quy. *See* STOW CUM QUY.

R

Raasay Probably 'roe-deer ridge island', OScand *rar* 'roe deer' + *ass* 'ridge' + *ey* (*see* -AY).

A long thin island (pronounced 'raa-say') off the east coast of SKYE, in Highland (formerly in Inverness-shire). It is separated from Skye by the **Sound of Raasay**, which, at the **Narrows of Raasay**, is only 1 km (0.6 mile) wide.

The MacLeods of Raasay were Jacobites, and hid Bonnie Prince Charlie here for a while in 1746 following the disaster at Culloden (*see under* CULLODEN MUIR). The government's response was savage, including rape and murder, the sacking of the entire island and the destruction of every dwelling. However, by 1773, when Johnson and Boswell visited, the island had recovered, and MacLeod of Raasay entertained his visitors in a new **Raasay House** (now derelict thanks to the neglect of an absentee landlord in the 1960s and 1970s). Raasay (as the MacLeod laird was known) had ten daughters, who, much to Boswell's delight, danced every night – and as if this nightly exercise were not enough, one day, having attained the strangely flat summit of Raasay's highest hill, Dùn Caan (443 m / 1453 ft), Boswell was moved to dance a solo jig. This fit of 'sheer exuberance' was later immortalized in a caricature by Thomas Rowlandson, in *The Picturesque Beauties of Boswell* (1786). Johnson was later to recall that during their stay they found 'nothing but civility, elegance and plenty'.

The 'plenty' was to run out, however, and in 1843 the last MacLeod laird was forced to sell the island. Then the Clearances began, the people being evicted to make way for the more profitable sheep. The ghosts of this sad past are evoked in some of the poems of the great Gaelic poet Sorley MacLean (Somhairle MacGill-Eain, 1911–96), who was born on the island. Best known of these poems is the elegy 'Hallaig', whose title is the name of an abandoned township on the southeast side of the island:

> The window is nailed and boarded
> through which I saw the West

> and my love is at the Burn of Hallaig,
> a birch tree …

> Sorley MacLean: the poet's own translation of
> 'Hallaig', from *From Wood to Ridge: Collected Poems
> in Gaelic and English* (1989)

A further population decline occurred in the First World War. In 1914, at the outbreak of war, 36 young men gathered at the stables of Raasay House to volunteer. That day the clock on the stable tower stopped; and only 14 of the 36 men were to return.

Radcliffe 'red cliff', OE *read* 'red' + *clif* 'cliff, bank'.

A town in Greater Manchester, 7 km (4.5 miles) southeast of Bolton.

Radcliffe on Trent *Radcliffe* referring to the red soil along the banks of the Trent.

A town in Nottinghamshire, on the River TRENT[1], about 8 km (5 miles) east of Nottingham.

Radford Semele *Radford* 'red ford' (referring to the local red soil), OE *read* 'red' + FORD; *Semele* denoting manorial ownership in the early Middle Ages by the Simely family.

A village in Warwickshire, on the River LEAM and the GRAND UNION CANAL, about 5 km (3 miles) east of Warwick.

Radical Road, the. *See under* SALISBURY CRAGS.

Radipole 'reedy pool', OE *hreod* 'reed' + *pol* 'pool'.

A village in Dorset, on the River WEY[2], now a northern district of WEYMOUTH.

Radlett 'junction of roads', OE *rad* 'road' + (*ge*)*læt* 'junction, meeting'.

A town in Hertfordshire, about 8 km (5 miles) south of St Albans. It grew up around an important crossroads on WATLING STREET[1] – whence its name.

Radley 'red glade' (perhaps referring to the colour of leaves), OE *read* 'red' + -LEY.

A village in Oxfordshire (before 1974 in Berkshire), close to the River THAMES[1], about 3 km (2 miles) northeast of Abingdon. **Radley College**, a boys' public school, was founded in 1847; amongst its alumni are the cricketer Ted Dexter (b.1935) and the humorist Peter Cook (1937–95) – Dexter once had occasion as a prefect to cane Cook for drinking cider at Henley Regatta (see under HENLEY-ON-THAMES).

St James's Church is remarkable for its arcade consisting of four huge tree trunks.

Radley terraces. Areas of high ground above the flood plains of the River Thames at Radley.

Radnor. See NEW RADNOR and OLD RADNOR.

Radnorshire From Radnor (see OLD RADNOR), with SHIRE.

A former county of eastern-central Wales. Its Welsh name was **Sir Faesyfed** (from the Welsh name, **Maesyfed**, for NEW RADNOR). It was bordered on the east by Herefordshire and Shropshire, on the north by Montgomeryshire, on the west by Cardiganshire, and to the south by Brecknockshire. The county town was PRESTEIGNE. In 1974 it became a district of POWYS, with its administrative seat at LLANDRINDOD WELLS, and disappeared as an administrative unit in 1996 when Powys became a unitary authority. It is a generally hilly area, reaching to over 600 m (2000 ft) in the **Radnor Forest** west of Presteigne, and the highest peak is Great Rhos (660 m / 2165 ft).

Historically, the area that became Radnorshire was, in the early Middle Ages, part of the kingdom of Powys. It was taken by the Normans in the late 11th century, becoming part of the Welsh MARCHES. The area was eventually pacified by Edward I two centuries later, and became predominantly English-speaking.

John Bull (c.1562–1628), the composer, was born in Radnorshire (his exact birthplace is unknown).

Hill Radnor. A breed of woolly black-faced sheep found on the hills of Radnorshire, Herefordshire, Monmouthshire and Breconshire.

Radstock 'outlying farmstead by the road' (referring to the FOSSE WAY), OE rad 'road' + stoc (see -STOCK, STOCK-, STOKE).

A small town in BATH AND NORTH EAST SOMERSET (before 1996 in Avon, before 1974 in Somerset), about 12 km (7.5 miles) southwest of Bath. It was once the centre of the Somerset coalfield, now closed.

Raglan 'rampart', Welsh rhag 'before, against' + glan 'bank'.

A village in Monmouthshire (formerly in Gwent), 11 km (7 miles) southwest of Monmouth. The well-preserved **Raglan Castle** (mid-15th century) is said to be the last medieval castle built in Britain. In the Civil Wars it suffered a long siege at the hands of the Parliamentarians and surrendered in August 1647.

Lord Raglan. FitzRoy James Henry Somerset Raglan, 1st Baron Raglan (1788–1855), British commander in chief in the Crimean War (1854–6). After him is named the **raglan**

sleeve, a sleeve that continues to the collar, with no seam at the shoulder. A loose overcoat with such sleeves is called a **raglan**.

See also CARDIGAN.

Rainbow Corner A reference to the Rainbow Division (the 42nd Infantry Division, US Army, so called because it was composed of military groups from the District of Columbia and 25 states representing several sections, nationalities, religions and viewpoints) and to the rainbow in the insignia of SHAEF (Supreme Headquarters Allied Expeditionary Force).

A nickname during the Second World War for Lyons' Corner House in Shaftesbury Avenue, London (W1), which was taken over and turned into a large café and lounge for American service personnel, and became a general meeting place for Americans in London.

Rainhill 'hill of a man named Regna', OE personal name Regna + hyll, 'hill'.

A village in Merseyside, 5 km (3 miles) south of St Helens, famous only for being the the the location of the **Rainhill Trials** of 6–14 October 1829, this being the competition to choose the design of the locomotive for the Liverpool and Manchester Railway (see under LIVERPOOL). The contenders were Robert Stephenson's Rocket, John Braithwaite and John Ericsson's Novelty and Timothy Hackworth's Sans Pareil. The trains had to run 70 miles (113 km) in a day at an average of at least 10 miles (16 km) per hour on a flat surface over which they went back and forth. The Rocket did 2 miles (19 km) in 53 minutes on the first day and won a first prize of £500.

Raith Gaelic ràth 'enclosure' (see RATH).

A district of KIRKCALDY, Fife.

Raith Rovers. A football team, founded in 1883 in Kirkcaldy. On 27 November 1994 Raith Rovers acquired some kind of eternal glory by defeating Celtic in the Coca-Cola Cup.

Rake '(place at the) hollow or pass', OE hraca.

A village in West Sussex, about 11 km (7 miles) northwest of Midhurst.

Rame Perhaps '(place at the) barrier' (referring to the fortification on Rame Head), OE hrama.

A village on the south Cornish coast, just to the north of Rame Head.

Rame Head. A headland on the south Cornish coast, forming the western extremity of the mouth of Plymouth Sound (see under PLYMOUTH). There is an ancient fortress here.

In 1815 the HMS Bellerophon, with its infamous passenger Napoleon, was watched over from Rame while it was anchored in the neighbouring Cawsand Bay for a month. His presence was the talk of Devon and Cornwall … When the crew finally slipped anchor and set sail for St Helena … Rame Head and the Port Eliot and Anthony estates along the cliff were the last bit of England he set eyes upon. He turned to Captain Maitland and said quietly, '*Enfin, ce beau pays.*'

Candida Lycett Green: *England: Travels Through an Unwrecked Landscape* (1996)

Rampton Probably 'farmstead where the rams are kept', OE *ramm* 'ram' + -TON.

A village in Nottinghamshire, about 9 km (6 miles) southeast of Retford. A little to the southwest is **Rampton Hospital**, one of three prisons for the criminally insane in England (*see also* BROADMOOR).

Ramsbottom Disappointingly, 'valley of the ram' or 'of wild garlic', OE *ramm* 'ram' or *hramsa* 'wild garlic' + *bothm* 'valley'.

A town on the River IRWELL in Greater Manchester, 11 km (7 miles) northeast of Bolton

Ramsey¹ 'island where wild garlic grows' (referring to an area of dry ground in a marsh), OE *hramsa* 'wild garlic' + *eg* (*see* -EY, -EA).

A town in Cambridgeshire (before 1974 in Huntingdonshire), in the FENS, about 14 km (8.5 miles) north of Huntingdon. Of a Benedictine abbey founded here in 969 by Duke Ailwyn, 'Alderman of England', all that now remains is part of a 15th-century gatehouse, the 13th-century Lady Chapel (now part of the local grammar school) and a 12th-century guest-house or hospital (now the parish church).

Ramsey² 'stream where wild garlic grows', OScand *hramsa* 'wild garlic' + *a* 'stream'.

A seaside resort on the northeast coast of the ISLE OF MAN, some 20 km (12 miles) north of Douglas.

Ramsey Forty Foot *Forty Foot* from its proximity to the FORTY FOOT DRAIN.

A village in Cambridgeshire, about 4 km (2.5 miles) northeast of RAMSEY¹.

Ramsey Island Probably 'Hrafn's island', OScand personal name *Hrafn* + *ey* (*see* -AY), but *hramsa* 'wild garlic' is possible, and is known to have grown on the island.

A small island 1 km (0.6 miles) off St David's Peninsula, Pembrokeshire (formerly in Dyfed) – hence the contemporary Welsh name **Ynys Dewi** ('David's island'). There are colonies of red deer, seals and seabirds, and since 1992 it has been in the care of the Royal Society for the Protection of Birds. It is separated from the mainland by the narrow **Ramsey Sound**, which is half blocked by a line of jagged rocks known as **the Bitches**.

Traditionally, the first monastic foundation on Ramsey Island was established in the 2nd century by St Devynog. In the 5th century St Justinian, a nobleman from Brittany and a friend of St David, became a hermit here (although accompanied by his servants). Like many another hermit, he was much beset by demons, which eventually possessed the bodies of his servants who, thus rendered malevolent, cut off his head.

Ramsgate 'raven's gap' or 'Hræfn's gap' (referring to a way through the cliffs here), OE *hræfnes* or *Hræfnes* possessive forms of *hræfn* 'raven' or male personal name *Hræfn* + *geat* 'gap'.

A town, port and seaside resort in Kent, in the ISLE OF THANET, immediately to the south of Broadstairs. It was once one of the CINQUE PORTS, and today cross-Channel services run to Ostend and Dunkirk. It developed as a holiday town in the 19th century, having initially been popularized by a visit from George IV in 1827. The Victorian buildings on top of the cliff retain a certain faded grandeur (it always was a social cut above nearby MARGATE):

We leave Ramsgate, then, with its 'stuckuppishness' and stiff and formal society.

Chambers Journal (1853)

while the sands below provide the fun:

Ramsgate 'sands'... a rendezvous of Punch and Judy men, nigger minstrels, donkey-drivers, and the like.

C.E. Pascoe: *London of Today* (1886)

(In the 20th century, **Ramsgate sands** was rhyming slang for 'hands'.)

Immediately to the south is Pegwell Bay (*see under* PEGWELL), gateway to England for Romans, Saxons, Danes and (in the person of St Augustine) Christians. (*See also* EBBSFLEET.)

The architect and designer Augustus Welby Pugin built himself a house in Ramsgate in the 1840s. He also designed the Roman Catholic church here – St Augustine's (1846–51).

Ramsgate's literary connections include the poet and critic Samuel Taylor Coleridge, a regular summer visitor from 1816, the author R.M. Ballantyne, who researched some of his stories here, including *The Lifeboat* (1864), and Jane Austen, a visitor, probably in 1803, while her brother Frank was stationed here (Ramsgate is the setting for Wickham's attempt to elope with Darcy's sister in *Pride and Prejudice* (1813)).

The humorist Frank Muir (1920–98) and the mathematician and philosopher A.N. Whitehead (1861–1947) were born in Ramsgate.

Margate the shrimpy, Ramsgate the asinine, Canterbury the ecclesiastical.

George Sala: *Twice round the Clock* (1859)

Ramsgate Sands. A painting (1859) by William Frith, depicting the main beach at Ramsgate. He sold it to Queen Victoria.

Ramshorn 'ram's ridge' or 'ridge where wild garlic grows', OE *rammes* possessive form of *ramm* 'ram' or *hramsa* 'wild garlic' + *ofer* 'ridge'.

A village in Staffordshire, about 19 km (12 miles) east of STOKE-ON-TRENT.

Randalstown Irish *Baile Raghnaill* 'Randal's town', after *Randal* MacDonnell, a 17th-century Marquess of Antrim.
A small town in County Antrim, 5 km (3 miles) northwest of Antrim itself. **Randalstown Forest**, a wildlife reserve, is just to the south, bordering LOUGH NEAGH.

Rannoch 'region of bracken', Gaelic *raithneach.*
An area of the central HIGHLANDS north of GLEN LYON, in Perth and Kinross (formerly in Perthshire, and then in Tayside region). On its western edge, stretching across to GLEN COE, is **Rannoch Moor**, a heathery, lochan-studded, roadless wilderness, traversed on its east side by the Glasgow–Fort William railway line.

> Here the crow starves, here the patient stag
> Breeds for the rifle.
>
> T.S. Eliot: 'Rannoch, by Glencoe', from *Collected Poems 1909–1962* (1963)

Samuel Taylor Coleridge took a less bleak view than the pinched New England bank clerk, even though he had walked all the way from Tyndrum (where his spirits had been lifted by a bottle of Burton ale for lunch):

> ... eighteen miles of beautiful road, such as you may see in noblemen's pleasure grounds, through a wide wide moor, with rocky rivers, mountains of all shapes, scarr'd and lay'd open, but none craggy.
>
> Samuel Taylor Coleridge: journal (30 August 1803)

The shapely mountains he describes are the various peaks of the BLACK MOUNT.

In Robert Louis Stevenson's *Kidnapped* (1886), part of 'the flight in the heather' of David Balfour and Alan Breck takes them across Rannoch Moor:

> The mist rose and died away, and showed us that country lying as waste as the sea; only the moorfowl and the peewees crying upon it, and far over to the east a herd of deer, moving like dots. Much of it was red with heather; much of the rest broken up with bogs and hags and peaty pools; some had been burnt black in a heath fire; and in another place there was quite a forest of dead firs [they would have been Scots pines], standing like skeletons. A wearier-looking desert man never saw; but at least it was clear of troops, which was our point.
>
> chapter xxii

The remote **Rannoch Station** is on the east side of the moor, at the end of the road from **Loch Rannoch**. This road is part of the traditional 'Road to the Isles':

> Sure by Tummel and Loch Rannoch
> And Lochaber I will go
> By heather tracks wi' heaven in their wiles.
> If it's thinkin' in your inner heart

> The braggart's in my step,
> You've never smelled the tangle o' the Isles.
>
> Kenneth MacLeod: 'The Road to the Isles' (1917) (MacLeod was a native of Eigg)

At the east end of Loch Rannoch is the village of **Kinloch Rannoch**, while on the south side of the loch is the **Black Wood of Rannoch**, a fine remnant of the Old Caledonian Forest (*see under* CALEDONIA). Also on the south side of the loch is **Rannoch School**, a public school with a similar emphasis on outdoor activities to GORDONSTOUN.

rannoch. A Perthshire dialect word for fern or bracken, from the Gaelic word *raithneach* that gave the region its name.

Rannoch rush. *Scheuchzeria palustris*, a member of the arrow-grass family (Juncaginaceae). It grows in bog pools and is rare in Britain.

Rannoch Wall. A fine wall of red rock, popular with climbers, on the flank of the Crowberry Ridge (*see under* BUACH-AILLE ETIVE MÓR), overlooking **Rannoch Moor** (*see above*).

Raphoe Irish *Ráth Bhoth* 'ring fort of the huts' (*see* RATH).
A small market town in County Donegal, 8 km (5 miles) northwest of Lifford. St Columcille (Columba) founded a monastery here in the 6th century, and Raphoe became a diocese in the 12th century. Nothing much is left, and stone from the round tower was used to build the Protestant bishop's palace (now ruined) in the 17th century. The cathedral of the Catholic diocese of Raphoe is now at LETTERKENNY, while the Protestant diocese was joined to that of DERRY/LONDONDERRY in 1835. The Protestant St Eunan's Cathedral dates from the early 18th century.

Rasherhouse, the. A nickname for the women's section of MOUNTJOY PRISON.

Ratae Coritanorum. A Roman settlement on the site of modern-day LEICESTER.

Ratcliff 'red cliff' (referring to the colour of the soil on the bank of the Thames), OE *read* 'red' + *clif* 'cliff, bank'.
A district of East London (E1, E14), on the north bank of the River THAMES[1], in the borough of TOWER HAMLETS, between Whitechapel to the west and Limehouse to the east. From the 14th century it was a centre for building and refitting ships, and many Tudor voyages of discovery started from here – notably Sir Martin Frobisher's attempt in the mid-1570s to find the Northwest Passage. Later it became an overcrowded DOCKLAND residential area.

Ratcliff Highway. A road in Ratcliff running west to east from East SMITHFIELD to Limehouse Basin (*see under* LIME-HOUSE), along the northern edge of WAPPING. Its official name is 'The Highway', but the fuller form is kept in preservation by the notorious **Ratcliff Highway Murders**, a series of seven particularly brutal killings in the area within a few days in December 1811.

❖ rath ❖

In the early Middle Ages, Ireland was ruled by many chieftains, and most chieftains had a dwelling surrounded by a roughly circular earthen rampart for protection. This was the *rath*, and there are dozens of these in Ireland, most with the rampart still visible or traceable. Few became major towns. RAPHOE (County Donegal) and RATHFRILAND (County Down) are examples of the type. Curiously, there are relatively few of these place names in the north of Ireland, and RATHLIN ISLAND (County Antrim), despite appearances, is not a *rath* name. In Scotland the fortification was not always an earthen bank, but it was no less formidable for that: *see* BLAIRGOWRIE (Aberdeenshire) and REAY (Highland).

Rathad nan Eilean. The Gaelic name for the ROAD TO THE ISLES.

Ráth Bhoth. The Irish name for RAPHOE.

Ráth Caola. The Irish name for RATHKEALE.

Rathcroghan Irish *Ráth Cruachan* 'ring fort of the mound' (*see* RATH).
A historical site in County Roscommon, 20 km (12 miles) northwest of Roscommon itself. There is a large ring fort and tumuli scattered over a wide area, dating from the pre-Christian and early Christian eras. It was the seat of the kings of Connacht, and, in legend, the burial place of the goddesses Éire, Fodla and Banba (*see under* ÉIRE).

Ráth Cruachan. The Irish name for RATHCROGHAN.

Ráth Fraoileann. The Irish name for RATHFRILAND.

Rathfriland Irish *Ráth Fraoileann* 'Fraoile's ring fort' (*see* RATH).
A village in County Down, 13 km (8 miles) northeast of Newry. It is also spelt **Rathfryland**. The fort of its name was the seat of the petty kings of IVEAGH.

Rathkeale Irish *Ráth Caola* 'ring fort of Caola' (*see* RATH).
A small market town in County Limerick, 10 km (6 miles) northeast of Newcastle West. The ruined St Mary's Priory dates from the 13th century. There was a Desmond Fitzgerald castle here, burnt by the English in 1580.

Rathkeltair. The former Irish name for DOWNPATRICK.

Rathlin Island Irish *Reachlainn*, meaning unknown; in OCelt it was *Rechru*, and Ptolemy called it *Rikini* in the 2nd century AD.
An L-shaped island some 8 km (5 miles) off the north coast of County Antrim, in the Sea of MOYLE facing BALLYCASTLE. Most of the coastline consists of cliffs, providing a home for large numbers of seabirds. St Columcille (Columba) is said to have founded a monastery here in the 6th century, but in 795 the island was attacked by the Vikings – their first target in Ireland. Bruce's Cave at the northeast corner, by the lighthouse (one of three on the island), is supposedly where in 1306 Robert the Bruce, hiding from the English, watched the spider patiently rebuilding its web, so teaching him perseverance in the face of adversity (a similar but less convincing claim is made for a cave on ARRAN). In the Middle Ages the island was occupied by the MacDonnells from Scotland, who were massacred by the English in 1575 and 1584 (Francis Drake was involved on the former occasion). The island was not firmly assigned to Ireland until after a legal dispute in 1617. Irish-speaking survived among the inhabitants into the 1960s.

Rathlin O'Birne Island Irish *Reachlainn Uí Bhirn* 'O'Birne's *reachlainn*' (the meaning of which is unknown).
A tiny island off the west coast of County Donegal, some 10 km (6 miles) northwest of SLIEVE LEAGUE. It has a lighthouse.

Ráth Luirc Irish 'Lorc's ring fort' (*see* RATH).
A market town in County Cork, 32 km (20 miles) south of Limerick. It is also known by the simpler Irish name **An Ráth** ('the ring fort'), and, from its 17th-century foundation (by Richard Boyle, future Earl of Cork) up to the 1920s, was also known as **Charleville** (after Charles II). Éamon de Valera was educated at the Christian Brothers school in Ráth Luirc, while in 1922 Frank O'Connor, while fighting for the anti-Treaty Republicans during the Irish Civil War (1922–3), was briefly captured here.

Ráth Maonais. The Irish name for RATHMINES.

Rathmines Irish *Ráth Maonais* 'ring fort of the de Moenes' (*see* RATH), a family who acquired the land here in the 14th century.
A suburb of DUBLIN, incorporated into the city in 1930. The poet and essayist George Russell (Æ; 1867–1935) went to school in Rathmines.
Battle of Rathmines (2 August 1649). A victory for the Parliamentarian forces under Michael Jones, who made a sortie out of Dublin, where they had been besieged, and defeated the Irish Royalists under the Earl of Ormond.

Rathmore Irish *An Ráth Mhór* 'the big ring fort' (*see* RATH).
A battle site some 15 km (9 miles) south of Limerick, County Limerick, where in 1148 Turlough O'Brien achieved a victory over the Norse.

Rath of Mullaghmast. *See under* MULLAGHMAST.

Rat Island From its colony of black rats.
A small island at the southeastern corner of LUNDY. It shelters Lundy's one landing cove.

Rattray. *See under* BLAIRGOWRIE *and* RATTRAY HEAD.

Rattray Head *Rattray* 'headland of the fort settlement', OCelt
RATH (Gaelic *ràth*) 'circular fort' + *tref* (*see* TRE-).

A headland in BUCHAN, Aberdeenshire (formerly in Grampian region), 11 km (7 miles) north of Peterhead. Virtually
nothing remains of the old royal BURGH (1564) of **Rattray**,
west of the headland: its life as a port ended when in the
early 18th century the channel linking the Loch of Strath-
beg (northwest of the headland) to the sea was blocked in
a storm by sand from the neighbouring dunes.

Ravenglass 'Glas's share (of land)', OCelt *rann* 'share, lot'
+ personal name *Glas*; *Rengles c.*1180.

A village at the mouth of the Cumbrian ESK[4], 26 km
(16 miles) southeast of Whitehaven. It was formerly in
Cumberland. It is the site of the Roman port and fort of
Glannaventa. The **Ravenglass and Eskdale Railway**, with
its 15-in gauge track, was originally built to take ore from
the mines of Eskdale, but is now a tourist attraction. Near to
Ravenglass is MUNCASTER CASTLE.

> As Eske her farth'st, so first, a coy Cumbrian Lasse,
> Who cometh to her Road, renowned Ravenglasse ...
>
> Michael Drayton: *Poly-Olbion* (1619)

Ravenscar 'rock of the ravens', OScand *hrafn* 'raven' + *sker*
'rock'.

A village in North Yorkshire, 5 km (3 miles) south of Robin
Hood's Bay, at the terminus of the LYKE WAKE WALK.
George III in his madness was treated by Dr Willis of Raven
Hall at Ravenscar.

It was at Ravenscar in the early 17th century that
Thomas Challoner gave birth to the British chemical industry, when he used alum from the local quarries, seaweed
and stale human urine to make potassium ammonium
alum, a mordant used in dyeing wool. As the demand of
the Ravenscar works increased, urine was shipped in from
places such as Newcastle and London. The industry ended
in Ravenscar in the mid-19th century, after the discovery of
a technique for manufacturing alum synthetically (*see also*
Piss Willie of Yeadon *under* YEADON).

Rawmarsh 'red marsh', OScand *rauthr* 'red' + OE *mersc*
'marsh'.

A town in South Yorkshire, 4 km (2.5 miles) north of
Rotherham.

Raws of Strathbogie, the. *See under* STRATHBOGIE.

Rawtenstall 'rough cow pasture', OE *ruh* 'rough' + *tun-stall*
'cow pasture'.

A town in Lancashire, on the edge of the Forest of Rossendale (*see under* ROSSENDALE), some 15 km (9 miles) southeast of Blackburn.

Rayleigh 'glade frequented by female roe-deer or she-goats',
OE *ræge* 'female roe-deer, she-goat' + -LEY.

A town in Essex, about 10 km (6 miles) east of Basildon.

Rayners Lane From the name of the local Metropolitan line
station, which in turn was taken from that of an old lane leading northwards to Pinner, according to local tradition named
after an old shepherd called *Rayner* who lived in a cottage by
the lane in the 19th century.

A residential district of northwest London, in the borough
of HARROW (before 1965 in Middlesex). It grew up around
the Metropolitan line station (now also on the Piccadilly
line), which opened in 1906.

Raynes Park Originally the name of the local station, commemorating Edward *Rayne* (1778–1847), who owned farmland
that was developed in the mid-19th century by the London
and South Western Railway Company (there never was an
actual 'park' in the accepted sense of the term).

A residential and commuter suburb of southwest London
(SW20), in the borough of MERTON, between Wimbledon to
the northeast and New Malden to the southwest. It grew
up around the local railway station, which was opened in
1871.

Reach '(place at the) raised strip of land' (referring to a post-
Roman earthwork called DEVIL'S DYKE[1]), OE *ræc*.

A village in Cambridgeshire, about 13 km (8 miles) northeast of Cambridge.

Reachlainn. The Irish name for RATHLIN ISLAND.

Reachlainn Uí Bhirn. The Irish name for RATHLIN O'BIRNE
ISLAND.

Reading '(settlement of) Read(a)'s people', OE male personal
name *Read(a)* + -*ingas* (*see* -ING).

A market town and unitary authority (pronounced 'redding') within the historical county of Berkshire (of which
until 1998 it was the administrative centre), at the confluence of the rivers KENNET[1] and THAMES[1], about 60 km
(37 miles) west of London. In a key strategic position guarding the western approaches to the capital, there has long
been a settlement here. The Danes made an encampment
here in 870, and began marauding in the surrounding
countryside; they were taken on and defeated the following
year by Æthelred I and his brother Alfred at the battle of
ASHDOWN. In the Middle Ages Reading prospered thanks
to the wool trade. A great abbey was built here in 1121,
one of the richest in England. Now in ruins, **Reading Abbey**
contains the burial site of Henry I.

Apart from those ruins, little now remains of medieval
Reading (granted its town charter in 1253). It was very
badly knocked about in the Civil Wars. Reading is a modern
town, important formerly as a canal junction, latterly as a
railway junction, a business centre for surrounding agriculture and a manufacturer. It has a particular connection
with biscuits – Huntley and Palmer had their factory here
until 1974, in the 19th century the town was facetiously
dubbed 'Biscuitopolis', and the nickname of **Reading FC**,

the local professional football club (founded in 1871), is the Biscuitmen. (Since 1998 Reading FC have played their home games at the Madejski Stadium, which they have shared since 2001 with a professional rugby union club, London Irish RFC (*see under* LONDON).)

Sumer is icomen in, one of the earliest known English lyrics, was written in Reading Abbey (*see* **Reading Rota** *below*); and now the town hosts the annual WOMAD (World Music, Arts and Dance) Festival and also the much bigger **Reading Festival** (a general rock and pop festival). At the end of the 19th century comes Oscar Wilde's contribution: imprisoned here for homosexual offences between 1895 and 1897, he wrote the letter to Lord Alfred Douglas later published as *De Profundis* (1905), and after his release he wrote *The Ballad of Reading Gaol* (1898), based on his experiences there:

> Yet each man kills the thing he loves,
> By each let this be heard,
> Some do it with a bitter look,
> Some with a flattering word.
> The coward does it with a kiss,
> The brave man with a sword!

Reading University was established as a university college in 1892, and it became a fully-fledged university in 1926.

The prelate William Laud (1573–1645), the novelist Elizabeth Taylor (1912–75), the composer Mike Oldfield (b.1953), progenitor of the best-selling 1970s New Age album *Tubular Bells*, and the actress Kate Winslet (b.1975) were born here. Reading was also the birthplace of four famous Surrey cricketers: the bowler Alec Bedser and his twin brother Eric (b.1918), the former England captain Peter May (1929–94) and the gritty batsman Ken Barrington (1930–81).

It was on Reading station in 1919 that T.E. Lawrence's briefcase containing the first draft of his *The Seven Pillars of Wisdom* (1926) was stolen.

In response to Logan Pearsall Smith's well-known aphorism that 'People say that life's the thing, but I prefer reading', the poet John Betjeman is alleged to have remarked: 'What did he see in Reading? It's such a dull town.' The Victorians, who could never resist a pun, sometimes called Reading '**Scarlet-town**' ('red-ing').

There are towns called Reading in the USA (Michigan, Minnesota, Pennsylvania (an important industrial city and administrative headquarters of Berks County)) and in Jamaica.

Reading beds. A series of sand, clay and gravel strata which underlie the London clay in the London and Hampshire basins.

Reading onion. A type of maincrop onion developed in Reading in the early part of the 19th century by the seedsmen Sutton & Son.

Reading Rota. A name sometimes given to the Old English song *Sumer is icumen in* (*c*.1240), whose manuscript originated in Reading Abbey, and whose author is conjectured to be a monk named John of Forsete. (*Rota* means 'round', *Sumer is icumen in* being an early example of a vocal canon.)

Reading sauce. A piquant sauce flavoured with onions, herbs and spices. In the late 19th century its reputation was on a par with that of Worcester sauce.

> There are epithets
> That suit with any word–
> As well as Harvey's Reading Sauce
> With fish, or flesh, or bird.
>
> Lewis Carroll: *College Rhymes* (1862)

Reading wagon. A traditional type of Gypsy caravan, with a barrel-shaped upper part and large wheels. It was originally built by the Dunton family of Reading in the middle of the 19th century.

Thomas of Reading. A work of prose fiction (*c*.1599) by Thomas Deloney (?1560–1600), relating incidents in the lives of six master-clothiers of the West Country during the reign of Henry I. One of these incidents is the murder, at the Ostrich Inn, COLNBROOK, of a wealthy Reading clothier by the name of Thomas Cole. According to some accounts, 'Old Cole', as he seems to have been popularly known in the 17th century, may have been one of the originals of the 'Old King Cole' of nursery rhyme fame.

Readymoney Probably a complimentary comment on the quality of the land.

A hamlet on the southern coast of Cornwall, now a southwestern suburb of FOWEY[2].

Ready Token From the Ready Token inn known here in the 18th century: apparently it served drinks on a 'cash only' basis.

A hamlet in Gloucestershire, about 3 km (2 miles) southwest of Bibury. It lies on AKEMAN STREET.

Reay Probably Gaelic *ràth* 'fort' (*see* RATH).

A village on the north coast of Scotland, in Highland (formerly in Caithness), 15 km (9 miles) west of Thurso, and 3 km (2 miles) southwest of Dounreay. It is pronounced 'ray'. The chiefs of Clan Mackay have held the title **Lord Reay** since 1628, and large areas of Sutherland, formerly in their hands, became known as **Reay Country**; there is, for example, the **Reay Forest**, which is some 75 km (47 miles) southwest of the village, south of BEN STACK. The area includes the lovely FOINAVEN, one of whose peaks is called **Lord Reay's Seat**.

Wizard of Reay, the. Sir Donald Mackay (d.1649), who was elevated to the peerage as the 1st Lord Reay in 1628. He fought in Bohemia and Denmark for the Protestant cause in the Thirty Years War, and for Charles I during the English Civil Wars. Lord Reay supposedly studied the Dark Arts with the Devil in Rome, and it was this teacher's practice to claim the last pupil out of the door at the end of the course as his own. When the Wizard found himself in this unfortunate situation, he cunningly pointed behind him to his own shadow, with which, according to the principle of the Devil taking the hindmost (*Diabolus postremos capit* or, as some would have it, *Capit post diab*), the Devil had to be content. Thereafter it was noticed that Lord Reay never cast a shadow (although this may have had something to do with the Scottish climate). The Wizard's dealings with the Devil were not quite over, for still to come was the strange and geomorphologically consequential encounter with the Prince of Darkness in the depths of SMOO CAVE.

Rebel County, the. A nickname for County CORK, now used mostly in the context of Gaelic football and hurling championships. The name may go back to the time when the city of Cork came out in support of Perkin Warbeck's claim to the English throne in 1495. However, most people think of the nickname in relation to the Anglo-Irish War (1919–21), when the county witnessed many anti-British actions.

Recess An anglicized corruption of the Irish name *Sraith Salach* 'dirty river meadow'.
A village in Connemara, County Galway, 50 km (31 miles) northwest of Galway itself.

Rechrainn. The Irish name for LAMBAY ISLAND.

Reculver 'great headland' (probably referring to the Isle of Thanet), OCelt.
A village on the North Kent coast, to the west of the ISLE OF THANET and about 5 km (3 miles) east of HERNE BAY. In the path of invaders coming by way of Thanet, it has a long history of occupation. The Romans, who called it **Regulbium**, built a fort here in 200 (its walls can still be seen), and it formed part of the SAXON SHORE. The Saxons built a church in the 7th century, and its site was later occupied by a Norman church. This was demolished in 1809 (and much of its fabric removed to St Mary's in the nearby village of Hillborough), but its two towers (the 'Two Sisters') were left standing as a guide-mark for shipping on the Thames estuary.

It was off the coast near Reculver that much of the testing of Barnes Wallis's bouncing bomb (actually a spinning depth charge) was carried out prior to 617 Squadron's Dam Busters' raid on the Ruhr valley dams in 1943 (*see also* DERWENT[4].)
See also RICHBOROUGH.

Redbrick City. A nickname for BELFAST.

Redbridge From the *Red Bridge*, a bridge of red brick which carried a road (now the A12) across the River RODING at the point where it formed a boundary between Ilford and Wanstead. The bridge was demolished around 1922.

A borough of northeast London, created in 1965 by amalgamating the previous boroughs of ILFORD and WANSTEAD, and WOODFORD, with parts of DAGENHAM and CHIGWELL. It lies between Waltham Forest to the west and Barking and Dagenham to the east.

Its name, which was chosen to avoid any accusation of partiality towards one or other of the borough's constituents, had already been established locally by its application to the Underground station, on the Central line, which opened in 1947.

Redcar 'red or reedy marsh', OE *read* 'red' or *hreod* 'reed' + OScand *kjarr* 'marsh'.
A seaside resort in REDCAR AND CLEVELAND (of which it is the administrative headquarters), 13 km (8 miles) southeast of Hartlepool. It was formerly in the North Riding of Yorkshire, then in Cleveland. There is a well-known racecourse. Mo Mowlam, who as Northern Ireland secretary did much to bring about the 1998 Good Friday Agreement, was MP for Redcar until she retired from Parliament in 2001.

The inhabitants of Redcar are sometimes called (by the people of Middlesbrough) **Sandrakers**, referring to the old practice of collecting coal debris from the beach and selling it to householders.

Redcar and Cleveland. A unitary authority in northeast England, created in 1996 out of parts of CLEVELAND. It is bounded on the north by the mouth of the River Tees, on the east by the North Sea, on the south by North Yorkshire, and on the west by Middlesbrough. The administrative headquarters are at REDCAR, and other towns include SKELTON, GUISBOROUGH, BROTTON, LOFTUS, MARSKE-BY-THE-SEA and SALTBURN-BY-THE-SEA. The sea cliffs at BOULBY are the highest in England (203 m / 666 ft).

Red Cuillin. *See under* the CUILLIN.

Redditch 'red or reedy ditch' (if the former, probably referring to the colour of the soil), OE *read* 'red' or *hreod* 'reed' + *dic* 'ditch'.
A town in Worcestershire (before 1998 in Hereford and Worcester, before 1974 in Worcestershire), on the River ARROW[1], about 24 km (15 miles) northeast of Worcester and 24 km (15 miles) south of Birmingham. When makers of needles, fishhooks, etc. were forced out of London in the 17th century by plague and fire, many of them moved to Redditch, and the town became a centre for the production of such articles. It is also the home of the Anglepoise lamp (first made here in the early 1930s).

In 1965 Redditch was declared a NEW TOWN[1], to take the overspill from Birmingham.
See also CRABBS CROSS.

Blair Babe Jacqui Smith, MP for Redditch, a Midlands town consistently voted the most boring place to live in Britain, is in sunny mood. For the fourth year running, the town has published a powerfully enervating calendar – The Roundabouts of Redditch – which highlights some of its more exciting traffic islands. 'It's even better than ever,' purrs Smith.

The Observer (28 December 2003)

Red Down *Red* of uncertain origin: perhaps from OE *riht* 'straight' or *ric* 'strip of land'; *Down* 'hill', OE *dun* (*see* DOWN, -DON).

A hill in Cornwall, to the northeast of Bodmin Moor (*see under* BODMIN), about 6 km (4 miles) west of LAUNCESTON.

Redesdale 'valley of the River Rede', from an OE river name probably meaning 'red', due to the reddish tinge of the sand and gravel of its bed + OScand *dalr* 'valley, dale'.

The remote valley of the **River Rede** in northern Northumberland. It forms part of the route of the A68, which enters Scotland at CARTER BAR, the pass at the head of the valley; this is the only road route across the Cheviot Hills. The Rede itself (34 km / 21 miles in length) rises just on the English side of Carter Bar, and flows southeast to OTTERBURN, then south to join the North Tyne (*see under* TYNE[1]) near Bellingham.

> I'm a north countrie-man, in Redesdale born,
> Where our land lies lea, and grows ne corn …

> Anon.: 'Jack and Tom', a traditional Border ballad

Lord Redesdale. The 2nd Baron Redesdale, father of the Mitford sisters, who is portrayed as Uncle Matthew in Nancy Mitford's *The Pursuit of Love* (1945). Perhaps it was his ancestral proximity to the Scottish border that led 'Uncle Matthew' to utter such sentiments as 'Abroad is unutterably bloody and foreigners are fiends.'

Redeswire Fray (1575) OE *swire* 'col', 'hollow on the top of a ridge'.

A bloody fracas on CARTER BAR, at the head of Redesdale. Carter Bar was the traditional place where, every 40 days, the English and Scottish lords of the MARCHES, along with their attendants, met to attempt to resolve in a peaceable manner complaints of those either side of the Border. On this occasion a heated argument broke out between John Forster, the Warden of the English Middle March, and the Keeper of Liddesdale, and the altercation deteriorated into a skirmish. Just when the English thought they had the upper hand, a force from JEDBURGH arrived and won the day, taking many English prisoners. The event is remembered in Jedburgh's annual **Redeswire Ride**, and in the ballad 'The Raid of the Reidswire', a version of which is in Sir Walter Scott's *Minstrelsy of the Scottish Border*:

> The seventh of July, the suith to say,
> At the Reidswire the tryst was set;
> Our wardens they affixed the day,
> And, as they promised, so they met.
> Alas! that day I'll ne'er forgett!
> Was sure sae feard, and then sae faine –

> They came theare justice for to gett,
> Will never green to come again.

> (Scots *green* 'long')

Robin of Redesdale. The leader of a rebellion in Yorkshire in 1469 against Edward IV. It was possibly instigated by the Earl of Warwick, who captured the king that year.

Redhill 'red slope' (referring to an outcrop of red soil), OE *read* 'red' + *helde* 'slope'.

A town in Surrey, just to the south of the M25, now virtually contiguous with REIGATE to the west. It was just a village until the 19th century, when the coming of the railway began to transform it into a commuter town. It is now an important railway junction. It has its own airfield, which was an RAF Spitfire base during the Second World War. The painter Samuel Palmer (1805–81) died in Redhill.

Redhill Rococo. A wryly comic novel (1986) by Shena Mackay, evoking the frustrated atmosphere of suburban England 'during a gloriously hot summer' in the 1980s:

> Redhill was in essence a carpark, or a series of carparks strung together with links of smouldering rubble and ragwort, buddleia and willowherb.

Red Hills. *See under* the CUILLIN.

Red Island. *See under* SKERRIES.

Redmarley D'Abitot *Redmarley* 'glade with a reedy pond', OE *hreod* 'reed' + *mere* 'pond' (*see also* LAKE) + -LEY; *D'Abitot* denoting manorial ownership in the early Middle Ages by the d'Abitot family.

A village in Gloucestershire, about 15 km (9 miles) west of Tewkesbury.

Red Roses *Roses* probably Welsh *rhos* 'heath, hill'.

A village in Carmarthenshire (formerly in Dyfed), 13 km (8 miles) northeast of Tenby.

Redruth 'red ford', Cornish *rid* 'ford' (*see* FORD) + *rudh* 'red'.

A town in Cornwall, about 13 km (8 miles) west of Truro. Prosperity came in the 19th century, when the area around Redruth and nearby CAMBORNE produced two-thirds of the world's copper, but the 20th century found new and cheaper sources, many of the miners were forced to emigrate to find work and the town had to tighten its belt.

Redruth is now combined for administrative purposes with Camborne to form **Camborne-Redruth**.

The novelist and translator D.M. Thomas (b.1935) was born in Redruth.

See also GWENNAP.

redruthite. A naturally occurring sulphide of copper, also known as copper glance.

Red Wharf Bay Presumably self-explanatory.

A sandy bay on the east coast of Anglesey (formerly in Gwynedd), 6 km (4 miles) northwest of Beaumaris. The village of Red Wharf Bay is on the bay.

Reek, the. A familiar name for the CROAGH PATRICK mountain.

Reeks, the. A familar name for the MACGILLYCUDDY'S REEKS.

Regent's Canal Named in honour of the Prince *Regent* (*see* REGENT'S PARK).

A canal in north London, which runs 14 km (8.5 miles) from Paddington Basin (*see under* PADDINGTON) eastwards via CAMDEN TOWN, ISLINGTON and HACKNEY to LIMEHOUSE, where it joins the River THAMES[1]. Part of its course passes along the northern edge of REGENT'S PARK. It was opened in 1820. It forms a branch of the GRAND UNION CANAL.

Regent's Park Originally (1817) *The Regent's Park*, named in honour of the Prince *Regent*, afterwards King George IV (reigned 1820–30). Plain *Regent's Park* is first recorded in 1822.

A Royal Park in Central London, in the City of WESTMINSTER and the borough of CAMDEN (NW1), to the north of Marylebone Road. It was laid out in the 1810s and 1820s on land formerly occupied by Marylebone Park Fields, and opened to the public in 1838. It occupies an area of 197 ha (487 acres) and was designed by John Nash (1752–1835) for the Prince Regent, who had the ultimate intention (never realized) of building a palace here. Nash and Decimus Burton were the architects of the imposing stuccoed classical terraces that line the eastern and western sides of the park.

The park is circumscribed by a road called the Outer Circle. Within this is the much smaller Inner Circle, which contains Queen Mary's Gardens and the Open Air Theatre (opened in 1933). Close to the northern perimeter is London Zoo (*see under* LONDON), often referred to as **Regent's Park Zoo**. There is a large boating lake in the southwestern corner, and London Central Mosque is situated near the northwestern edge.

Between 1909 and 1985 Bedford College, a college of London University, was located in Regent's Park. It was then amalgamated with Royal Holloway College in EGHAM, and its buildings became the private **Regents College**, serving international students. Regent's Park Underground station, on the Bakerloo line, opened in 1906.

Regent's Park Bomb. An IRA bomb (20 July 1982), which exploded under Regent's Park bandstand while the Royal Green Jackets were giving a lunchtime concert. Six soldiers died. The Household Cavalry were targeted in HYDE PARK on the same day by a car bomb.

Regent's Park College. A college of Oxford University. It was founded in STEPNEY in 1810 to train men for the Baptist ministry. In 1856 it moved to premises in Regent's Park (whence its name), and in 1901 became incorporated into London University. In 1927 a gradual transfer to Oxford began, and in 1957 it became a fully-fledged Oxford college.

Regent's Park Explosion. An incident on 10 October 1874 in which a barge carrying gunpowder and petroleum along the REGENT'S CANAL blew up while passing through Regent's Park, killing the crew and badly damaging nearby houses.

Regent Street Named in honour of the Prince *Regent* (*see* REGENT'S PARK).

A street in the WEST END[1] of London (W1), in the City of WESTMINSTER, running from Langham Place southeastwards via OXFORD CIRCUS to PICCADILLY CIRCUS, and continuing, as **Lower Regent Street**, as far as Waterloo Place and PALL MALL. It was laid out in the 1810s to the design of John Nash (1752–1835). The original intention behind it was to form a royal drive between REGENT'S PARK and Carlton House, the Prince Regent's palace.

The central section, from Oxford Circus to Piccadilly Circus, ends in a broad eastward curve, originally known as 'the Quadrant' (redesigned in 1925–6 by Reginald Blomfield). It was planned as a shopping street, and continues to fulfil that function today. Among its various notable stores are Hamley's (the world's biggest toy shop) and Liberty's (designed, with its instantly recognizable mock Tudor facade, in 1924 by E.T. and E.S. Hall). More sybaritically, it is also home to the Café Royal, where leading artistic and literary figures of the late 19th and early 20th centuries (Augustus John, Aubrey Beardsley, Max Beerbohm, etc.) hung out, and to Veeraswamy's, one of London's earliest Indian restaurants.

Regent Street Polytechnic. A college in Regent Street, founded in 1839 as the Royal Polytechnic Institute. One of its leading figures during the 1880s was Quintin Hogg (1845–1903), grandfather of the Conservative politician Lord Hailsham. In 1966 it was combined with the Holborn College of Law, Language and Commerce to form the Polytechnic of Central London (*see under* LONDON).

The first public demonstration of cinematography was held by the Lumière brothers on 20 February 1896 in the Polytechnic, which also houses the earliest (1884) swimming bath in a public building in England.

Reigate 'gate for the female roe-deer' (probably referring to an entrance to a deer-park), OE *ræge* 'female roe-deer' + *geat* 'gate'.

A commuter town (pronounced 'rye-gate') in Surrey, at the foot of the NORTH DOWNS, just outside the M25, about 11 km (7 miles) east of Dorking. Redhill to the east is virtually contiguous with it. It is now part of the borough of **Reigate and Banstead**.

Beneath the mound where Reigate's Norman castle once stood are caves and tunnels, which during the Second World War were used as air-raid shelters. The castle itself was originally built after the Norman conquest of 1066 but fell into disrepair following the Civil Wars. **Reigate Priory**, to the west of the town, was founded in the 13th century.

The dancer Margot Fonteyn (1919–91) was born here. Reigate was also the birthplace of the only man both to captain England at cricket and to become an Anglican bishop – the Sussex and England cricketer and later Bishop of Liverpool (1975–97), the Rev. David Sheppard (1929–2005).

Rejerrah 'ford of Gorvoy', Cornish *rid, rys* 'ford' (*see* FORD) + male personal name *Gorvoy*.

A village in Cornwall, 6 km (4 miles) south of Newquay.

Relubbus Cornish *rid* 'ford' (*see* FORD) with an unknown second element.

A village in Cornwall, on the River Hayle, about 5 km (3 miles) northeast of Marazion.

Rendlesham 'Rendel's homestead', OE *Rendeles* possessive form of male personal name *Rendel* + HAM.

A village in Suffolk, about 19 km (12 miles) northeast of Ipswich. To the southeast is the extensive wooded area of **Rendlesham Forest**. In December 1980 this was the site of perhaps the most notable UFO sighting in Britain, by personnel from the nearby WOODBRIDGE US Air Force base.

Renfrew 'point of the current', OCelt *rhyn* 'headland' + *frwd* 'current', later Gaelicized as *Rinn-friú. Reinfry c.*1128.

A royal BURGH (1396) on the south side of the CLYDE, 9 km (5.5 miles) west of Glasgow. It is in Renfrewshire (formerly in Strathclyde region). Even though it was the county town of the traditional county of Renfrewshire, and gave its name to the former Renfrew district and the current unitary authority of Renfrewshire, the administrative headquarters of these local authority divisions were and remain in PAISLEY.

There is a Renfrew county in Canada (Ontario), and the Renfrew Millionaires are a Canadian ice-hockey team.

Baron Renfrew. A title awarded by the burgh of Renfrew in 1404 to the heir to the Scottish throne. The title is still borne by every Prince of Wales.

Battle of Renfrew (1164). An engagement in which Somerled (*c.*1113–1164), Lord of the Isles (*see* ISLES, LORD-SHIP OF THE), was defeated and killed by King Malcolm IV. The ending of Somerled's rebellion was attributed by contemporaries to St Kentigern acting in defence of Glasgow.

Renfrewshire From RENFREW + SHIRE.

A traditional county (created 1404) and current unitary authority of west-central Scotland, west of Glasgow and south of the Clyde. It was bounded on the east by Lanark-shire and on the south by Ayrshire. In 1975 it was split into the districts of INVERCLYDE to the west and RENFREW to the east; the latter was divided into the unitary authorities of Renfrewshire and EAST RENFREWSHIRE in 1996.

Repps Perhaps 'strips of land', OE *replas* plural of *reopul* 'strip of land'.

A village in the Norfolk BROADS, about 21 km (13 miles) northeast of Norwich.

Repton 'hill of the tribe called Hrype', *Hrype* tribal name of uncertain origin (*see also* RIPON) + *dun* (*see* DOWN, -DON).

A small town in Derbyshire, near the River TRENT[1], about 11 km (7 miles) southwest of Derby. In the 7th century it was the capital of MERCIA. Its church, St Wystan's, has a particularly fine 9th-century crypt, which probably held the tomb of King Ethelbald and became a pilgrimage shrine for St Wystan – making it one of the oldest unaltered places of worship in England. A Viking army captured and forti-fied the site in 873–4 and the bones of 250 of them were collected in a charnel house; it is not known how they died.

Repton School, a co-educational public school, was founded in 1557. The writers Christopher Isherwood (1904–86) and Roald Dahl (1916–90) went to the school, and William Temple (Archbishop of Canterbury 1942–4) was its headmaster from 1910 to 1914. Other **Old Reptonians** include the actor Basil Rathbone (1892–1967) and the sprinter Harold Abrahams (1899–1978), 100-metre cham-pion in the 1924 Summer Olympics and 'hero' of the 1981 film *Chariots of Fire*.

Republic of Ireland. *See under* IRELAND.

Rest and be Thankful. A pass (245 m / 804 ft) between Glen Croe and Glen Kinglass in the Arrochar Alps (*see under* ARROCHAR), Argyll and Bute (formerly in Strathclyde). The original military road was constructed in the wake of the 1745 Jacobite Rising, and works its way steeply up the head of Glen Croe (the present road takes a more gradual gradi-ent on the north flank of the glen). On the summit the soldiers who had laboured on the road inscribed a stone seat with the words 'Rest and be Thankful'.

Restormel Perhaps 'moor at the bare hill', Cornish *ros* 'moor' + *tor* 'hill' + *moyl* 'bald, bare'.

A location in Cornwall, above the River FOWEY[1], about 1.5 km (1 mile) north of LOSTWITHIEL. It is famous for **Restormel Castle**, first built around 1100, and with a strik-ing circular keep, with walls 3 m (10 ft) thick, dating from 1200. Now an empty shell, this last saw active service in the Civil Wars, when its Parliamentary garrison under the Earl of Essex was defeated and ejected. The name Restormel has now been adopted for the local council district.

Retew Cornish *rid* 'ford' (see FORD) with an uncertain second element, perhaps *du* 'dark, black'.

A village in Cornwall, about 11 km (7 miles) southeast of Newquay.

Retford 'red ford', OE *read* 'red' + FORD.

A market town in Nottinghamshire, on the River IDLE and the Chesterfield Canal, about 13 km (8 miles) east of Worksop. It is one of the oldest chartered boroughs in England. It is an important railway junction on the East Coast main line.

The novelist Catherine Gore (1799–1861), purveyor of high-society fiction to the middle classes, and the Nottinghamshire and England cricketer Derek Randall (b.1951) were born in Retford.

Rey Cross. *See* STAINMORE PASS.

Rhaeadr Gwy. The Welsh name for RHAYADER.

Rhayader Welsh *rhaeadr* 'waterfall'.

A small market town and holiday centre on the River WYE[1] (Welsh Gwy) in Powys (formerly in Radnorshire), 11 km (7 miles) northwest of Llandrindod Wells. The Welsh name is **Rhaeadr Gwy** ('waterfall on the Wye'). When the bridge across the Wye was built in 1780, the town's eponymous waterfall almost disappeared; prior to this it was listed among the SEVEN WONDERS OF NORTH WALES.

Rheged Etymology unkown.

An ancient British kingdom that flourished in GALLOWAY and CUMBRIA in the 6th century. Its capital was possibly at CARLISLE, and the legendary Welsh poet Taliesin (*see under* the village of TALIESIN) was a bard at the court of the king of Rheged.

Today Rheged is the name of Europe's largest grass-covered building, a tourist attraction in the northeast Lake District, some 3 km (2 miles) west of Penrith. This Rheged displays a number of 'giant movies' (on such themes as Everest and Antarctic exploration) and is also home to the National Mountaineering Exhibition.

Rhineland of Staffordshire, the. An occasional nickname for the area around ALTON[2] in Staffordshire.

Rhinns of Galloway, the. *See under* GALLOWAY.

Rhinns of Kells *Rhinns* probably OCelt *roinn* 'headland, promontory', the origin of Gaelic *rinn* 'sharp point'; *Kells* Gaelic *cealla* 'monastic cells'.

A line of remote moorland hills running north–south in Dumfries and Galloway (formerly in Kirkcudbrightshire), some 15 km (9 miles) northwest of New Galloway. Tops include CARLIN'S CAIRN, CORSERINE (the highest point, at 813 m / 2667 ft), Millfire and Meikle Millyea.

Rhinogs, the After the two main peaks, Welsh *rhinog* 'secret, mysterious'.

A range of hills in southern SNOWDONIA, Gwynedd (formerly in Merioneth), some 12 km (7.5 miles) northwest of Dolgellau. They take their name from the two central peaks, **Rhinog Fawr** (720 m / 2362 ft; Welsh *fawr* 'big') and **Rhinog Fach** (711 m / 2332 ft; Welsh *fach* 'little'). At the northern end of the range, beyond ROMAN STEPS, is Moel Ysgyfarnogod (623 m / 2043 ft), while at the southern end is Diffwys (750 m / 2460 ft). The **Rhinog National Nature Reserve** is in the centre of the range.

Rhisga. The Welsh name for RISCA.

Rhodesia A late 19th-century name, from *Rhodesia* (now Zimbabwe) in southern Africa.

A village in Nottinghamshire, on the River Ryton, now effectively a western suburb of WORKSOP.

Rhodes Minnis 'cleared common land', OE *rodu* 'clearing', with *gemœnness* 'common'.

A village in Kent, about 10 km (6 miles) northwest of Folkestone.

Rhondda Welsh *rhoddni* 'noisy, babbling'.

A river of South Wales, in the unitary authority of RHONDDA CYNON TAFF (formerly in Glamorgan, then in Mid Glamorgan). It is formed by the confluence at Porth of two rivers, **Rhondda Fawr** (Welsh *mawr* 'great') and **Rhondda Fach** (Welsh *bach* 'small'), and the high ridge between these two valleys is called **Cefn y Rhondda** ('ridge of the Rhondda', 481 m / 1578 ft). The Rhondda flows for approximately 20 km (12 miles) and joins the River TAFF at PONTYPRIDD.

> Greasy Rhondda
> River throws about the boulders
> Veils of scum to mark the ancient
> Degraded union of stone and water.
>
> Alun Lewis: 'The Rhondda'

The valleys of the two Rhonddas, built up with linear coal-mining settlements such as Treorchy, Ystrad, Clydach Vale, Tonypandy, Maerdy and Ferndale, are collectively referred to as '**the Rhondda**' (and, somewhat confusingly, sometimes as a single town called 'Rhondda').

> The Rhondda hills are tall and lean
> Like greyhounds stripped-down for speed,
> But the townships running close at their feet
> Are going all out to take the lead.
>
> Clifford Dyment: 'The Rhondda Hills are Tall and Lean',
> from *Experiences and Places* (1955)

Before the mid-19th century the Rhondda was barely populated. Then with the discovery of coal the place boomed. At its peak the Rhondda supplied one-third of the world's coal, and in the First World War 90 per cent of Royal Navy ships were powered by coal from the Rhondda.

> Circe is a drab ...
> Daily to her pitch-black shaft
> Her whirring wheels suck husbands out of sleep.
> She for her profit takes their hands and eyes.
>
> Alun Lewis: 'The Rhondda'

The industry suffered badly in the interwar years – one senior government official even suggested the valleys should be abandoned and turned over to a vast hydro-electric scheme – and there were many more pit closures before and after the 1984–5 Miners' Strike. The last pit closed in 1990, but despite Mrs Thatcher's efforts the spirit of the Rhondda did not die. There is now a **Rhondda**

Heritage Park at the Lewis Merthyr colliery (closed in 1983).

'Cwm Rhondda'. A hymn tune (the title meaning 'Rhondda Valley') by John Hughes (1873–1932), first published in 1907. There are various sets of words, but the most familiar are those by William Williams (1745), later translated from the Welsh by Peter Williams (1771):

> Guide me, O Thou great Jehovah,
> Pilgrim through this barren land.
> I am weak, but Thou art mighty;
> Hold me with Thy powerful hand.
> Bread of heaven, bread of heaven,
> Feed me now and evermore,
> Feed me now and evermore.

It is a favourite with Welsh male-voice choirs, and at Welsh rugby matches, and is one of the reasons, as Graham Mourie once pointed out, why, even though other teams may score more points, nobody ever beats Wales at rugby. In Italy, the tune is sung by Verona football supporters when they play AC Milan, with words along the lines of 'Just watch us do it again.'

Lord Rhondda. David Alfred Thomas (1856–1918), a South Wales mining magnate and Liberal MP, who introduced food rationing as a member of Lloyd George's government in the First World War. He was created Baron Rhondda in 1916, and Viscount Rhondda in 1918. His daughter, Lady Rhondda, inherited the viscountcy and in 1920 founded the notable independent news magazine *Time and Tide*.

Rhondda Cynon Taff From the rivers RHONDDA, CYNON and TAFF, all of which flow through it.

A unitary authority in South Wales. It is bordered on the south by Cardiff, Vale of Glamorgan and Bridgend, to the west by Neath Port Talbot, to the north by Powys and to the east by Merthyr Tydfil. The administrative seat is at CLYDACH VALE, and other towns include TREORCHY, ABERDARE, MOUNTAIN ASH, LLANTRISANT and PONTYPRIDD.

Rhos. An abbreviated name sometimes given to RHOSLLANERCHRUGOG.

Rhosllanerchrugog 'moor of the heather clearing', Welsh *rhos* 'moor' + *llannerch* 'clearing' + *grugog*, possessive of *grug* 'heather'.

A town in Wrexham unitary authority (formerly in Denbighshire, then in Clwyd), 5 km (3 miles) southwest of Wrexham. In the 16th century difficulties with its name led English speakers, who did not wish to be accused of hawking and spitting or reasonless sneezing, to dub it **Rose Lane Aghregog**, and it is now usually referred to simply as **Rhos**.

Rhos Mhic Thriúin. The Irish name for NEW ROSS.

Rhossili 'moor of St Fili', Welsh *rhos* 'moor' + personal name *Fili*. St Fili was possibly a son of the 6th-century St Cenydd who founded a priory at nearby Llangennith.

A village at the western end of the GOWER PENINSULA, in Swansea unitary authority (formerly in Glamorgan, then West Glamorgan), 20 km (12 miles) west of Mumbles. It was the birthplace of Petty Officer E. Evans, who died with Scott on the way back from the South Pole. The village, overlooking WORMS HEAD, is at the southern end of the long straight sands of **Rhossili Bay**, popular with surfers. The bay is backed by the steep **Rhossili Downs**, a favourite take-off point for hang-gliders. On the east side of the Downs are Sweyne's Howes (burial mounds), traditionally said to be the grave of Sweyn Forkbeard (d.1014), king of Denmark and father of King Cnut (Canute). Sweyn is also said to have given his name to SWANSEA[1].

Rhubarb Triangle, the. *See under* WAKEFIELD.

Rhuddlan 'red bank', Welsh *rhudd* 'red' + *glan* 'bank' (referring to the banks of the River CLWYD[1] here).

A small town in Denbighshire (formerly in Clwyd), 3 km (2 miles) south of Rhyl. The first **Rhuddlan Castle** was built in 1073, and a replacement was completed by Edward I in 1282. In the same year, while he was staying here, Edward was brought the head of Prince Llywelyn ap Gruffydd (also known as Llywelyn the Last), slain near BUILTH WELLS. In 1284 he summoned a meeting of Welsh leaders at Rhuddlan to sign the hated Statute of Rhuddlan (*see below*).

Battle of Rhuddlan (798). A battle in which Offa of Mercia routed the Welsh.

Statute of Rhuddlan (19 March 1284). A statute by which Edward I laid down the government for the newly conquered principality of Wales. The laws he imposed included the banning of the Welsh language in any official proceedings.

Rhum. A version of the name of the island of RUM.

Rhuthun. The Welsh name for RUTHIN.

Rhydaman. The Welsh name for AMMANFORD.

Rhyd-Ddu 'black ford or stream', Welsh *rhyd* 'ford, stream' (see FORD) + *ddu* (*see* DDU, DUBH).

A village in Gwynedd (formerly in Caernarvonshire), some 4 km (2.5 miles) southwest of the summit of SNOWDON. It was built to serve the local slate quarries in the 19th century, and became associated with the bard T.H. Parry-Williams (1887–1975). Just south of the village is the little lake of Llyn y Gadair, its shore

> Nothing but peat bog, dead stumps brittle and brown,
> Two crags, and a pair of quarries, both closed down.

> T.H. Parry-Williams: 'Llyn y Gadair', translated from the Welsh by Anthony Conran

This Llyn y Gadair is less prepossessing than the Llyn y Gadair that nestles in a cwm on the north side of CADER IDRIS, for the latter Llyn y Gadair, on a summer's evening, looking north to distant Snowdon, is one of the finest places on Earth.

Rhyl 'the hill', Welsh *yr* 'the' + ME *hull* 'hill'.

A seaside resort on the north coast of Denbighshire (formerly in Flintshire, then in Clwyd), 6 km (4 miles) west of Prestatyn. It is recommended by *The Rough Guide to Wales* (3rd edition, 2000) only to those who appreciate 'raw and raucous seaside shenanigans'. Others have been less charitable:

> A town only a man driving a crane with a demolition ball would visit with a smile.
>
> A.A. Gill: quoted in *The Observer* (20 October 2002)

Rhyl was the birthplace of the murderess Ruth Ellis (1926–55), the last woman to be hanged in Britain, and of the novelist Penelope Mortimer (née Fletcher; b.1918), author of *The Pumpkin Eater* (1962) and former wife of the writer and libertarian barrister John Mortimer.

> beach low and empty pale blue sky seagulls and one dog
>   near the horizon …
> David Cox's 'Rhyl Sands' a tiny gem burning quietly in
>   dirty Manchester
> ghostly echoes of last season's chip-papers in the drifting
>   sand
>
> Adrian Henri: *Autobiography* (1971), Part One 1932–51, 'Rhyl Sands' (David Cox (1783–1859) painted many vigorous landscapes in North Wales.)

Thrilla in Rhyla, the. The *Sun*'s leader headline on 17 May 2001 following a contretemps in Rhyl during the 2001 general election campaign in which the deputy prime minister John Prescott, infuriated at being struck by an egg thrown at point-blank range by Craig Evans, a farm worker protesting at Labour's rural policies, landed a well-aimed right hook on his assailant, with whom he then became entangled in an unseemly brawl. The headline played on the so-called 'Thriller in Manila', in which Muhammad Ali out-boxed Joe Frazier in the capital of the Philippines on 1 October 1975. Prescott, hitherto nicknamed 'Two Jags' Prescott for his two ministerial Jaguar cars, was promptly re-dubbed 'Two Jabs' Prescott. The phrase **Rumble in Rhyl** is also applied to the incident, playing on the 'Rumble in the Jungle', the epic heavyweight bout fought on 30 October 1974 in Kinshasa between Muhammad Ali and George Foreman.

Rhymney 'the auger-like river', Welsh *rhwmp* 'auger' (a boring tool) + *ni*, an adjectival suffix.

A river of south Wales. It rises on the southern slopes of Cefn Yr Ystrad in the Brecon Beacons and flows south through Caerphilly unitary authority to meet the sea just east of Cardiff (where it gave its name to the districts of Llanrumney and **Rumney**; the ruins of **Rumney Castle**, once a fine example of a Norman ringwork castle, are situated above a steep natural slope overlooking the river). In Welsh it is **Rhymni**. The river formerly formed the border between Glamorgan and Monmouthshire, and has a length of 58 km (36 miles). The industrial town of **Rhymney** is in the upper **Rhymney Valley**, 3 km (2 miles) west of Tredegar.

> Is his royal anger ferriaged
> where black-rimed Rhymni
>   soils her Marcher-banks …?
>
> David Jones: 'The Sleeping Lord', from *The Sleeping Lord and Other Fragments* (1974)

Rhymni. The Welsh name for Rhymney.

Ribble Probably from OE *ripel* 'boundary'.

A river in northwest England, with a length of 120 km (74 miles). It has its origins in the Pennines of North Yorkshire, where it is formed by the confluence of two streams, Cam Beck and the Gayle, between Ingleborough and Pen-y-Ghent. It then flows south through scenic **Ribblesdale** and Settle, before turning southwestwards into Lancashire. It enters its estuary at Preston, and the estuary in turn enters the sea at Lytham St Anne's.

Donald Davie, a Yorkshireman, imagined this largely Lancastrian river 'with awful interest':

> Dark gullies, sobbing alders
> Must surely mark its course;
> It rolls and rounds its boulders
> With more than natural force.
>
> Donald Davie: 'Lancashire', from *The Shires* (1974)

The Ribble Valley has associations with the novelist J.R.R. Tolkien, author of *The Lord of the Rings* (1954–5), who visited the area when his son was studying for the priesthood at St Mary's Hall near Stonyhurst. A 'Tolkien Trail', through places that may have been models for locations in Tolkien's Shire, has been created for visitors to follow.

The river is supposedly haunted by a water spirit called Peg o' Nell, possibly the ghost of a servant who slipped and broke her neck one winter night while fetching water. She is said to claim a life every seventh year.

Ribchester 'Roman fort on the River Ribble', OE river name + *ceaster* (see Chester); *Ribelcastre* 1086.

A village on the River Ribble, Lancashire, 13 km (8 miles) northeast of Preston. The remains of a Roman fort and settlement can still be seen.

Ribston Park *Ribston* 'rock where ribwort grows', OE *ribbe* 'ribwort' (*Plantago lanceolato*, a plant with ribbed, lance-shaped leaves and a spike of small white flowers) + *stan* (see Stone).

A historic park in North Yorkshire, between Knaresborough and Wetherby. The Knights Hospitallers founded a preceptory here in 1217. There is a walled and terraced garden dating from the late 17th century and pleasure grounds were developed here a century later.

Ribston pippin. A variety of dessert apple, the first pippins to be grown in England. They are strong-tasting and aromatic, and said to be the parent of the Cox's orange pippin. They were introduced from Normandy in 1707, when Sir Henry Goodriche planted three pips at Ribston Park; two died, but from the third came all the Ribston apple trees in England. The apple is also known as the Glory of York.

Richborough 'stronghold called Repta', *Repta* a reduced form of an ancient OCelt name probably meaning 'muddy waters' (referring to nearby Richborough Creek) + OE *burh* (*see* BURY).

A location in Kent, about 2.5 km (1.5 miles) northwest of SANDWICH. Two thousand years ago it was on the coast, and the Romans made it their chief port of entry into Britain. They called it **Rutupiae** (from the same Celtic source as provided the first syllable of the modern English name). They built a great fortress here (some of its 3.5 m / 12 ft thick walls survive), to guard both the port and the southern entrance to the WANTSUM Channel, which at that time separated the ISLE OF THANET from the mainland. Thus, it formed part of the defensive SAXON SHORE. They also constructed a massive free-standing arch, which would have served as both a landmark to shipping and an intimidation to the local populace (legend has it that the Emperor Claudius rode through it on an elephant when he visited Britain). From Richborough, WATLING STREET[1] led north-westwards to London and eventually to Chester.

Now marooned in salt marshes, Richborough was used as a military site in the First and Second world wars (it was an embarkation port for the invasion of Normandy in 1944).

See also RECULVER.

Richmond[1] 'strong hill', OFr *riche* 'strong' + *mont* 'hill'.

An attractive market town on the River SWALE[1], North Yorkshire, 21 km (13 miles) northwest of Northallerton. It is a tourist centre for the YORKSHIRE DALES, and its Theatre Royal (1788) is one of England's oldest theatres still in use.

The impressive **Richmond Castle** dates back to 1071, when Alan Rufus ('the Red') began building work, although the keep is 12th century. It was here that the Scottish king, William the Lion, was held after his capture at ALNWICK in 1174. There are said to be secret tunnels under the castle, and various stories have accumulated around them. In one, a potter called Thompson was exploring a tunnel when deep within he came across the sleeping forms of King Arthur and his knights. Nearby were a sword and a horn, and as Thompson was about to sound the horn the knights began to wake. In terror Thompson fled, as a voice behind him cried:

> Potter Thompson, Potter Thompson,
> If thou hadst drawn the sword or blown the horn,
> Thou hadst been the luckiest man e'er born.

Lewis Carroll (C.L. Dodgson) attended the grammar school here in 1844–6, and in 1989 William Hague, leader of the Conservative Party from 1997 to 2001, became MP for Richmond. J.M.W. Turner visited and painted the town and castle several times.

RICHMOND[2] in Greater London was named after the Yorkshire town by Henry VII, who, before defeating Richard III at BOSWORTH in 1485, was **Earl of Richmond**, and is referred to as 'Richmond' throughout Shakespeare's *Richard III*. An earlier Earl of Richmond was a Frenchman, Arthur, constable de Richemont (1393–1458), who fought the English alongside Joan of Arc, and who had been granted the English title in childhood.

Honour of Richmond, the. The name given in the Middle Ages to the area between the TEES in the north and the watersheds of the NIDD and WHARFE in the south. In 1399 the Honour was awarded to Ralph Neville, Earl of Westmorland, in return for his part in deposing Richard II and putting Henry IV on the throne.

Martha, oder der Markt zu Richmond. The best-known opera (in English *Martha, or Richmond Market*) (1847) of the German composer Friedrich von Flotow. It is the story of two girls who in jest disguise themselves as countrywomen and sell themselves as servants at a hiring fair in Richmond, only to find that they are legally bound to their new masters for a year. Flotow appropriated Thomas Moore's Irish melody 'The Last Rose of Summer', which is sung at one point in the opera by the aristocratic heroine as an English folk song.

'Sweet Lass of Richmond Hill'. A song by the Irish lawyer, playwright, United Irishman and government spy Leonard McNally (1752–1820), written in 1789 for Miss L'Anson of Hill House, Richmond, a lady who was afterwards to become his wife. McNally unsuccessfully defended the Irish rebels Napper Tandy, Wolfe Tone and Robert Emmet, probably because he was passing details of his defence in advance to the prosecution. His activities as a government spy only came to light after his death, when his son enquired whether his father's annual fee of £300 would pass to him.

> This lass so neat, with smile so sweet,
> Has won my right good will,
> I'd crowns resign to call thee mine,
> Sweet lass of Richmond Hill.

See also RICHMONDSHIRE.

Richmond[2] From RICHMOND[1]. The settlement was originally called *Sheen* ('Shene otherwise called Richemount' (1502); *see* EAST SHEEN). The name *Richmond* arrived at the beginning of the 16th century, when Henry VII named his new palace here after his earldom of Richmond in Yorkshire, and it was soon transferred to the neighbourhood.

A town in southwestern Outer London, on the south bank of the River THAMES[1], opposite TWICKENHAM, in the borough of RICHMOND-UPON-THAMES (before 1965 in Surrey). In the 13th century, when it was still a hamlet called Sheen, Edward I built a royal palace here. This burnt down in 1499 and Henry VII replaced it with an even grander building, which he called Richmond Palace. Elizabeth I died there.

The palace had mostly fallen down by the 18th century (only an archway, Wardrobe Court and the gatehouse now survive), but by then its presence had encouraged the growth of the hamlet into a prosperous and fashionable small town. In 1777 it was linked to Twickenham by **Richmond Bridge**, the oldest surviving crossing of the River Thames.

Richmond 'Underground' station, a terminus of the District line, opened in 1877.

Edward VIII (1894–1972) and the broadcaster Richard Dimbleby (1913–65) were born in Richmond. The actor Richard Attenborough took the title Lord Attenborough of Richmond-upon-Thames when he was ennobled in 1993.

The city of Richmond, state capital of Virginia, USA, and named after the London Richmond, was the capital of the Confederacy during the American Civil War. Other US Richmonds are to be found in California, Indiana, Kentucky and Rhode Island.

Richmond Hill. A hill to the south of Richmond. The pleasing view from its slopes, over the Thames, encouraged the building of houses, and many fine examples from the 18th century survive (along the road that has adopted the hill's name). At the top of the hill, where an inn called the 'Star and Garter' once stood, is the Star and Garter Home for disabled soldiers.

There is a Richmond Hill in Queens, New York and in Georgia, USA, and another in Ontario, Canada.

Richmond Park. A Royal Park to the southeast of Richmond, created by Charles I in 1635–7 to provide a convenient hunting ground (many deer – fallow and red – remain). With an extent of about 1000 ha (2500 acres) it is the largest urban park in Britain. The White Lodge, in the middle of the Park, is home to the Royal Ballet School. Amongst the Park's standard complement of memorial benches is one dedicated to the singer Ian Dury (1942–2000), which incorporates a solar-powered MP3 player.

Richmondshire. The traditional name for the area around the town of RICHMOND[1]. It became a local government district of North Yorkshire in 1974.

Richmond-upon-Thames. A southwestern London borough, formed in 1965 by joining RICHMOND[2] with BARNES, HAM[1], HAMPTON COURT, KEW, MORTLAKE, TEDDINGTON and TWICKENHAM. It lies between HOUNSLOW to the west and WANDSWORTH, MERTON and KINGSTON UPON

THAMES to the east. It is the only London borough that straddles the River Thames.

Rickinghall Superior *Rickinghall* 'Rica's people's nook of land', OE male personal name *Rica* + *-inga-* (*see* -ING) + *halh* (*see* HALE, -HALL); *Superior* 'higher', Latin.

A village in Suffolk, about 24 km (15 miles) northeast of Bury St Edmunds. Just to the west is **Rickinghall Inferior** (*Inferior* 'lower', Latin).

Rickmansworth 'Ricmær's enclosure', OE *Ricmæres* possessive form of male personal name *Ricmær* + *worth* (*see* -WORTH, WORTHY, -WARDINE).

A (former market) town in Hertfordshire, about 6 km (4 miles) south of Watford. It is here that the three rivers meet (the CHESS, the COLNE[2] and the Gade) that give THREE RIVERS district council its name. A branch links the town with the GRAND UNION CANAL.

Rickmansworth 'Underground' station, on the Metropolitan line, opened in 1887.

See also MOOR PARK[1].

Riddrie Possibly 'red hill-pasture', Gaelic *ruadh* 'red' + *airigh* 'hill-pasture' (*see* -ARY).

An area of northeastern Glasgow in which HM Prison BARLINNIE – the **Riddrie Hilton** – is situated.

> Grey over Riddrie the clouds piled up,
> dragged their rain through the cemetery trees.
>
> Edwin Morgan: 'King Billy', from *The Second Life* (1968)

Ridgeway 'road that follows the ridge (of the downs)', OE *hrycgweg*.

A prehistoric trackway and drovers' road in southern England, the western section of the ICKNIELD WAY, which runs along the top of the North Wessex Downs (*see under* WESSEX) and the Berkshire Downs (*see under* BERKSHIRE), above the KENNET[1] Valley, from near AVEBURY to STREATLEY, where it meets the River Thames. Its highest point is HACKPEN HILL. It passes many prehistoric sites along the way, including WAYLAND'S SMITHY and the UFFINGTON White Horse. It also crosses the site of the Battle of ASHDOWN (871), where Alfred the Great defeated the Danes.

In 1973 it was incorporated into the **Ridgeway National Trail**, a 137 km (85 mile) footpath opened by the Countryside Commission. This extends its route further northeastwards, along the Icknield Way as far as Ivinghoe Beacon (*see under* IVINGHOE).

Ridings of Yorkshire, the OE *thriding*, from OScand *thrithjungr* 'third part'.

The three parts into which the county of YORKSHIRE was divided until 1974: the NORTH RIDING, the WEST RIDING and the EAST RIDING OF YORKSHIRE. A fourth 'third part', *South Riding*, exists only as the title of Winifred Holtby's 1936 novel about provincial local government. The East

Riding of Yorkshire was revived as a unitary authority in 1996.

Rievaulx 'valley of the River Rye', OCelt river name probably meaning 'stream' + OFr *val* 'valley'.

A village on the southern edge of the NORTH YORK MOORS, North Yorkshire, 16 km (10 miles) east of Thirsk. It is pronounced 'ree-voe'. The impressive ruins of the great Cistercian **Rievaulx Abbey** date back to 1131; the abbot from 1147 was **St Aelred of Rievaulx**, also noted as a historian. Above the ruined abbey is the **Rievaulx Terrace**, an 18th-century landscaped promenade complete with temples and changing views, possibly designed by Sir John Vanbrugh. The abbey ruins were painted by, among others, John Sell Cotman and Turner.

The Labour politician, Harold Wilson, assumed the title **Baron Wilson of Rievaulx** after he resigned the premiership in 1976.

Rig of the Jarkness. *See under* GLEN TROOL.

Rillington Place Etymology unknown.

A former cul-de-sac in NOTTING HILL, West London (W11), where No.10, a shabby terraced house, was the location of the murders of at least eight women over the period 1943–53. John Christie had moved into the ground-floor flat with his wife in 1938 and ten years later Timothy Evans took the second-floor flat with his pregnant wife. In 1949 Evans, who was mentally retarded, confessed to the murder of his wife and baby girl and was hanged. In 1953 the mouldering bodies of three young women were found in Christie's kitchen cupboard by a new tenant. His wife's body was then discovered under the kitchen floorboards and the skeletons of two women buried some ten years earlier in the garden. Christie, a necrophiliac, confessed to these murders and to that of Mrs Evans, and was hanged. Evans was granted a posthumous pardon in 1966. The notoriety of the case led to Rillington Place being renamed, as Ruston Close. It still attracted unwelcome sightseers, however, and eventually it was demolished. The street which replaced it in the late 1970s, Bartle Road, has no No. 10.

The film *10 Rillington Place* (1971), based on a book by Ludovic Kennedy, offered a realistically sordid reconstruction of the *cause célèbre*, with Richard Attenborough in the role of the murderer and John Hurt as Evans.

Ringaskiddy Irish *Rinn an Scídigh* 'Scídioch's headland' or 'headland of the Skiddy family'.

A small town in County Cork, 10 km (6 miles) southeast of Cork itself, overlooking CORK HARBOUR. On the industrial estate is the Pfizer factory that manufactures Viagra (dubbed in Ireland 'the Pfizer riser'), much to everyone else's amusement.

Ring of Brodgar 'wide enclosure', OScand *breithr* 'wide, broad' + *garthr* 'enclosure'.

A megalithic stone circle on Mainland in Orkney, near to MAES HOWE and the STONES OF STENNESS. The circle is more than 100 m (328 ft) in diameter, and there are a total of 60 stones, although only 27 still stand; they vary in height from 2.1 m (6.9 ft) to 4.7 m (15.4 ft). The monument dates from the Neolithic period, and was probably erected some time between 2700 and 2500 BC.

> 'If those stones could speak –' Do not wish too loud.
> They can, they do, they will. No voice is lost.
>
>   Edwin Morgan: 'The Ring of Brodgar', from *Sonnets from Scotland* (1984)

Ring of Kerry. *See under* County KERRY.

Ringsend Irish *An Rinn* 'the headland', with the addition of English *end*.

An eastern part of Dublin, formerly a port.

> I will live in Ringsend
> With a red-headed whore,
> And the fan-light gone in
> Where it lights the hall-door …
>
>   Oliver St John Gogarty (1878–1957): 'Ringsend (After reading Tolstoi)'

It was in Ringsend that James Joyce first walked out with his future wife, Nora Barnacle, on 16 June 1904. The date became 'Bloomsday', the day on which all the action of *Ulysses* takes place.

Ringsend car. A one-horse hackney cab of a type that formerly brought the Dublin middle classes to bathe at Ringsend.

Ringsend uppercut. A kick in the groin; the connection of the phrase to the place is, however, obscure.

Ringwood Probably 'wood on a boundary' (perhaps referring to the edge of the New Forest, or to the Hampshire–Dorset boundary), OE *rimuc* 'boundary' + *wudu* 'wood'.

A town in Hampshire, on the River AVON[3], on the western edge of the NEW FOREST, about 14 km (8.5 miles) north of Christchurch. James, Duke of Monmouth stayed here (in a house now called Monmouth House) after his defeat at the Battle of SEDGEMOOR in 1685, prior to being taken to London to be executed.

There are towns called Ringwood in the USA (New Jersey, Oklahoma) and Australia (Northern Territory, Victoria).

Rinn an Scídigh. The Irish name for RINGASKIDDY.

Rinn Duáin. The Irish name for HOOK HEAD.

Rinns of Galloway, the. *See under* GALLOWAY.

Rinns of Islay, the. *See under* ISLAY.

Rinyo. *See under* ROUSAY.

Ripe '(place at the) edge or strip of land', OE *rip* 'edge or strip of land'.

A village in East Sussex, about 11 km (7 miles) east of Lewes.

Ripley 'woodland clearing in the form of a strip', OE *ripel* 'strip' + -LEY.

A town in Derbyshire, about 16 km (10 miles) northeast of Derby. The Midland Railway Centre museum is just to the northeast.

Ripon '(town in the land of) the Hrype tribe', OE *Hrypum*, dative plural of *Hrype*, a tribal name of obscure meaning; *Hrypis* c.715; *Ripum* 1086.

A market town and cathedral city in North Yorkshire, 35 km (22 miles) northwest of York. An abbey was founded here in the 7th century, and the Church of St Peter and St Wilfrid (12th–13th century; made a cathedral in 1836) has a crypt built by St Wilfrid, the first abbot, in 672. To this day St Wilfrid's Feast is celebrated annually with a big procession through the town. The market square has an obelisk 27 m (about 90 ft) high, erected in 1781 to celebrate the local MP's 60-year tenure of his seat. Every evening in the square, at nine o'clock, a horn is sounded by the Wakeman (nightwatchman), a tradition said to go back to 886 when Alfred the Great supposedly granted the town its first charter, along with the Charter Horn.

> Life doesn't get much better than Ripon – hearty solid farming folk; buttered teacakes in Foster's café; the sublime sight of the cathedral rising majestically in the mist against the backdrop on the noble Yorkshire Dales.
>
> Tom Dyckhoff: *The Guardian* (7 February 2004)

There is a town called Ripon in the USA (Wisconsin); the Ripon Falls (now submerged) are on the Victoria Nile, where it flows from Lake Victoria.

Earl of Ripon. Frederick John Robinson, 1st Earl of Ripon and Viscount Goderich of Nocton (1782–1859), Tory politician, briefly prime minister from August 1827 until his dismissal in January 1828. His son, the 2nd Earl, was viceroy of India from 1880 to 1884.

Ripon Jewel, the. An artefact dating from the time of St Wilfrid, found near the cathedral in 1976. It is a golden roundel set with garnets and amber, but the inlay in the middle is absent.

Treaty of Ripon (26 October 1640). A treaty that ended the second Bishops' War between Charles I and the Covenanting Scots. The Scots held on to Northumberland and County Durham, and received payments from the king, who had to summon the Long Parliament to ratify the treaty.

Ripple¹ '(place at the) strip of land', OE *ripel* 'strip of land'.

A village in Kent, about 3 km (2 miles) southwest of Deal. Sir John French (1852–1925), military commander on the Western Front in the First World War, was born in Ripple.

Ripple². A village in Worcestershire (before 1998 in Hereford and Worcester, before 1974 in Worcestershire), on the River SEVERN, about 8 km (5 miles) north of Tewkesbury.

Ripponden 'valley of the River Ryburn', OE river name *hrife* 'fierce' or *hreod* 'reed' + *burna* 'stream' + *denu* 'valley'; *Ryburnedene* 1307.

A town in West Yorkshire, 11 km (7 miles) northeast of Huddersfield.

Risca Possibly *rhisgau*, a suggested plural of Welsh *rhisg* 'bark', although this plural form is not known elsewhere. The name may have derived from a house with bark shingles, or a log cabin.

A (former mining) town in the valley of the Ebbw, Caerphilly (formerly in Monmouthshire, then in Gwent), 7 km (4.5 miles) northwest of Newport. In Welsh it is **Rhisga**.

Rishton 'rushy farm', OE *risc* 'rush' + -TON.

A small town in Lancashire, 5 km (3 miles) northeast of Blackburn.

Rivals, the An anglicized pronunciation of the highest peak, *Yr Eifl*.

A group of three small but elegantly pointed peaks on the north coast of the LLEYN PENINSULA, Gwynedd (formerly in Caernarvonshire), 10 km (6 miles) north of Pwllheli. The highest peak at 564 m (1850 ft) is **Yr Eifl** (Welsh 'the fork'), and on the easternmost peak, **Tre'r Ceiri** ('town of the giants') is a large Iron Age hillfort, said by some to have been one of the cities of Vortigern (the valley on the west side of the hills is called Nant Gwrtheyrn, meaning 'valley of Vortigern'). The lowest, northernmost peak is heavily quarried and has no name on the Ordnance Survey 1:25,000 map.

> There were giants in Llŷn in those days, and they lived on
>   this mountain
> Behind drystone walls piled high to keep secrets and
>   hutch holy
> Things from the god-searching singing wind off the sea
>   twelve fields below.
>
> Brian Morris: 'At Tre'r Ceiri', from *Stones in the Brook* (1978)

Roach A back-formation from ROCHFORD.

A river in Essex, which rises at Rochford and flows 14 km (9 miles) eastwards and then northwards to join the River CROUCH¹ near its mouth.

Roaches, the 'rocks', Fr *roches*.

A range of millstone-grit rocks near LEEK in Staffordshire. The wind and rain have weathered them into curious shapes. They are popular with rock-climbers, and at the start of the Second World War they also became home to a small herd of wallabies, released from a private collection (there is a stuffed specimen at Gradbach Mill Youth Hostel). *See also* HEN CLOUD.

Road, the. The name by which Charing Cross Road (*see under* CHARING CROSS) was known to booksellers and bibliophiles, in its heyday as the centre of the second-hand book trade in London.

Road to the Isles, the. The beautiful route through the Western HIGHLANDS from FORT WILLIAM to MALLAIG (from where there are ferries to the Outer Hebrides and Skye). In Gaelic it is **Rathad nan Eilean**. The route is taken both by the A830 and a single-track railway line, and passes by GLENFINNAN, ARISAIG and Morar (*see under* LOCH MORAR), with spectacular views across to the SMALL ISLES. This is the area where Bonnie Prince Charlie began and ended the 1745 Jacobite Rebellion.

'Road to the Isles, The'. A well-known song (1917) by Kenneth MacLeod, with music by Marjory Kennedy-Fraser. It belongs to the White-Heather-Club-Kenneth-McKellar school of tartanry (quotations may be found under RANNOCH and the CUILLIN). Note that MacLeod (not a man, incidentally, to be parted from his cromack) starts his itinerary much further east, passing 'by Tummel, Loch Rannoch and Lochaber'.

Roadwater Originally an alternative name of the River Washford, perhaps 'stream by a clearing', OE *rodu* 'clearing' + *wæter* 'stream'.

A village in Somerset, on the eastern edge of EXMOOR, about 10 km (6 miles) southeast of Minehead.

Roaringwater Bay A descriptive English name.

An inlet of the Atlantic in southwest County Cork, bounded by MIZEN HEAD to the west and CLEAR ISLAND to the east. Other islands in the bay include SHERKIN ISLAND, Hare Island, Horse Island, Castle Island (*see under* LOUGH KEY), the Calf Islands and Long Island.

Robertsbridge '(place at) Robert's bridge' (referring to Robert de St Martin, founder of the 12th-century abbey here). The earliest recorded form of the name, from the late 12th century, is Latin: *Pons Roberti*.

A village in East Sussex, on the River ROTHER[2], about 16 km (10 miles) northwest of Hastings. Cricket-bat-making is a noted local industry.

Robin Hood[1] From the name of a local inn, itself named after the legendary medieval outlaw-hero of SHERWOOD FOREST.

A village in Derbyshire, on the eastern edge of the PEAK DISTRICT, about 11 km (7 miles) west of Chesterfield.

Robin Hood[2] A modern name commemorating the outlaw of legend.

A village in West Yorkshire, on the southern outskirts of Leeds, about 3 km (2 miles) southwest of Rothwell.

Robin Hood's Bay The name is first recorded in 1532, but the connection with the legendary outlaw is the subject of a great range of unconvincing theories, including one that has him fleeing here and disguising himself as a fisherman.

A picturesque fishing village in North Yorkshire, 8 km (5 miles) southeast of Whitby. The locals call the place **Bay Town** or just **Bay**. It is situated where the NORTH YORK MOORS meet the NORTH SEA, and like all this coast is subject to coastal erosion: the main street was washed away in a storm in 1780 (and in another storm it is said that a ship's bowsprit broke through the window of the pub on the seafront). The remote village was once a great place for smuggling, and it is said that contraband could be taken from the seafront up through the closely packed houses to the top of the village without seeing the light of day.

The author Leo Walmsley (1892–1966) was brought up in Robin Hood's Bay, and his novel *Three Fevers* (1932), about a feud between two fishing families, was filmed on location here as *Turn of the Tide* (1935); other books of his set on this coast are *Phantom Lobster* (1933) and *Sally Lunn* (1937). Walmsley used the name 'Bramblewick' to refer to Robin Hood's Bay in these novels. (*See also* the Staithes Group *under* STAITHES.)

Robinson Etymology unknown.

A mountain (737 m / 2417 ft) in the LAKE DISTRICT, Cumbria (formerly in Cumberland), on the north side of BUTTERMERE.

Roby 'boundary farm', OScand *ra* 'boundary' + -BY.

A district of Liverpool, 9 km (5.5 miles) east of the city centre.

Rochdale 'valley of the River Roch', river name (back-formation from the old name *Recedham*, OE *reced* 'hall' + HAM 'homestead') + OScand *dalr* 'valley'.

A town in Greater Manchester, 17 km (11 miles) north of Manchester itself, at the confluence of the rivers Roch and Spodden. It was originally a market town specializing in wool, but in the 19th century grew as a centre of cotton-spinning. It was the home of the **Rochdale Pioneers** who founded the Cooperative Movement (*see below*).

Rochdale was the birthplace of Sir James Kay-Shuttleworth (1804–77), who was responsible for establishing a publicly funded elementary education system in England; of the reforming politician John Bright (1811–89), founder of the Anti-Corn Law League; and of the singer Gracie Fields (1898–1979), who made her first stage appearance in Rochdale in 1910 (and who described Capri, where she latterly lived, as 'like Rochdale with a sea coast'). Rochdale is also apparently the home town of the character Bet Lynch in the ITV soap *Coronation Street*. Among Rochdale's more notable MPs have been John Bright's fellow Anti-Corn Law campaigner Richard Cobden (from 1859 till his death in 1865); Arthur Henderson (1863–1935), leader of the Labour Party during the First World War, who was elected for Rochdale in 1903; and the corpulent

Rochdale-born Liberal 'Big' Cyril Smith (b.1928), Rochdale's MP from 1972 to 1992.

Rochdale Canal. A canal through the PENNINES between SOWERBY BRIDGE in West Yorkshire and the BRIDGEWATER CANAL in Manchester. It was opened in 1804.

Rochdale Hornets. The town's rugby league team.

Rochdale Pioneers. Properly, the Rochdale Society of Equitable Pioneers, a group of workers in Rochdale, who, inspired by the ideas of Robert Owen (*see* NEW LANARK), opened the first cooperative shop in 1844. It is in Toad Lane, and has been preserved. The Pioneers established the cooperative principle by sharing the profits among all the members of the cooperative.

Rochester Probably 'Roman town or fort called Rovi', *Rovi* a reduced form of *Durobrivae*, the Romans' name for the settlement (from an OCelt name meaning 'walled town with bridges') + OE *ceaster* (*see* CHESTER).

A town and port (in May 2002 it was demoted from the city status it had enjoyed since 1211 due to an administrative oversight by its councillors) within the unitary authority of MEDWAY[2], at the mouth of the River MEDWAY[1], in Kent, west of and adjacent to CHATHAM and GILLINGHAM[1] (the two other Medway Towns). Its strategic position, at the point where WATLING STREET[1] crosses the Medway, has made it an important place from earliest times. The Romans had a stronghold here, called **Durobrivae**; traces of its walls survive. The Saxons re-fortified the town around 600. The Normans guarded it with an impressive castle: all that remains today of **Rochester Castle** is the keep (five storeys high and with walls 3.5 m (12 ft) thick). They also provided it with its present-day cathedral: **Rochester Cathedral** is a small but impressive building (the original cathedral, founded by Æthelbert, King of Kent in 604, had been consecrated by St Augustine; the present one was rebuilt from 1077 by Gundulf, Bishop of Rochester). It has a splendid Romanesque facade.

Rochester is England's second oldest bishopric, and for a while in the Anglo-Saxon period it was an archbishopric. Not all of its incumbents have met happy ends: St John Fisher (1459–1535) was beheaded for denying the royal supremacy of Henry VIII; Nicholas Ridley (*c*.1500–55), burnt at the stake by Mary I, had been Bishop of Rochester under Edward V; and Francis Atterbury (1663–1732), a Jacobite, was accused of plotting against the Hanoverians in 1723 and obliged to flee abroad. John Knox (*c*.1514–72), offered the see after Ridley, was perhaps wise to refuse. The bishop at the beginning of the 21st century, Michael Nazir-Ali, was at one point favourite to succeed George Carey as Archbishop of Canterbury, but fell at the last hurdle. The Bishop of Rochester signs himself 'Roffen'.

Charles Dickens lived in Chatham when he was a boy, and was very familiar with Rochester. To judge by the names

under which he fictionalized it (**Dullborough** in *The Uncommercial Traveller* (1860) and **Mudfog** in *The Mudfog Papers* (1837–8)) he was not very impressed by it, but he evidently liked it enough to return to live here in later life. In 1856 he bought a house nearby called Gad's Hill Place (*see under* GADSHILL), which was his home for the rest of his life. His last book, the unfinished *Mystery of Edwin Drood* (1870), was largely set in Rochester (this time in the more agreeable guise of **Cloisterham**). Rochester is also Pip's home town in *Great Expectations* (1861) – Pip encounters Magwitch in the marshes outside the town – and is visited by the Pickwick Club in *Pickwick Papers* (1837): 'Glorious Pile!' they remark of **Rochester Castle** (*see above*). There is now a 'Charles Dickens Centre' in the town, and also a memorial to the author in the cathedral. The writer Enid Bagnold (1889–1981) was born in Rochester.

King's School, Rochester, a public school, was founded by Henry VIII in 1541. BORSTAL, location of the first borstal, is just 3 km (2 miles) to the southwest of the town.

There are towns and cities called Rochester in the USA (Illinois, Indiana, Michigan, Minnesota (home of the Mayo Clinic), New Hampshire, New York (two of them, one of them an important industrial city, home of Kodak), Ohio, Pennsylvania, Texas, Washington), Canada (Alberta) and Australia (Victoria).

Earl of Rochester. The most famous holder of this title was the 2nd Earl, the notoriously dissolute John Wilmot (1647–80). The openly sexual content of much of his poetry guaranteed it many centuries between plain covers in the libraries of gentlemen connoisseurs, but in recent decades it has undergone a critical revaluation and is very highly regarded.

Rochester portion. A colloquial euphemism from the late 17th to the early 19th centuries for *vagina*. 'B.E.' in *A New Dictionary of the Terms ancient and modern of the Canting Crew* (*c*.1698) defined it literally as 'two torn smocks and what Nature gave'. The expression originated in a Kentish proverb.

Rochford 'ford of the hunting dog', OE *ræcc* 'hunting dog' + FORD.

A town in Essex, on the River ROACH, about 5 km (3 miles) north of Southend-on-Sea. Anne Boleyn (*c*.1507–36), second wife of Henry VIII, is reputed to have been born here; her father, Sir Thomas Boleyn, was created Viscount Rochford in 1525.

See also ASHINGDON.

Rock Originally *Blacktor* 'black crag', OE *blæc* 'black' + *torr* 'crag, tor'. By the 18th century this had been altered to *Black Rock* (ME *roke* 'rock'), and in due course the *Black* was dropped.

A coastal village in Cornwall, on the north bank of the CAMEL estuary, opposite PADSTOW. After many centuries of blameless anonymity, it was suddenly dragged blinking into the spotlight of fashionability at the end of the 20th. The surfing beaches were the initial attraction, but by the 1990s it was the upper-crust resort of choice for those without the slightest leanings towards water sports.

Rockabill. *See under* SKERRIES.

Rockall Possibly a shortened form of the Gaelic name, *Sgeir Rocail, sgeir* 'skerry' + *rocail* 'hoarsely roaring'.

The furthest-flung part of the United Kingdom, some 385 km (about 240 miles) out in the North Atlantic from the west coast of HARRIS – of which it is officially a part, and is thus administered by the WESTERN ISLES authority. Rockall comprises a rock rising some 21 m (70 ft) out of the Atlantic, whose top measures 30 m (100 ft) by 24 m (80 ft).

The first recorded landing on the rock was in 1810, but before that the **Rockall Bank** fishing area was well known to the people of the Outer HEBRIDES. These were dangerous waters, and not all returned – as witness this lament by Rachel MacDonald of the Monach Islands, widowed in the mid-18th century:

> Devout was my prayer to Christ that you would return
> From the storm of the ocean and the roar of the blast,
> From Rockall fishing banks filled with harvest from the
> sea
> We'd see you in Cnoic here with heroes' reward.
>
> Rachel MacDonald: 'Lament for the *Canarag*', translated from the Gaelic by Donald A. Fergusson (*Canarag*, the name of the lost boat, is Gaelic for 'young dolphin'.)

The seas here continued to take lives. In 1904 the *Norge* foundered on the rock, with the loss of 600 lives.

Rockall acquired a significance to the Ministry of Defence in 1955 when the South Uist missile range was opened (*see under* UISTS), and on 18 September of that year a Royal Navy party landed by helicopter from HMS *Vidal* and annexed the rock for the Crown. It legally became part of the UK by the Island of Rockall Act (10 February 1972), which incorporated it into 'that part known as Scotland'. In the same year a navigation beacon was planted on the rock.

When territorial fishing rights came into question – and the possibility of oil or natural gas being found in the Rockall Bank arose – Ireland, Iceland and Denmark all questioned Britain's claim to sovereignty, arguing that an uninhabitable rock (as opposed to a habitable island) could not be sovereign territory. To establish its status as a habitable island, in the 1980s the adventurer and Atlantic rower John Ridgeway stayed on the rock for nearly a month, a feat later repeated by Tom MacLean, formerly of the SAS. Britain's claim is derided in the songs of Irish Republicans:

> Oh rock on Rockall, you'll never fall to Britain's greedy
> hands
> Or you'll meet the same resistance that you did in many
> lands,

> May the seagulls rise and pluck your eyes and the water
> crush your shell,
> And the natural gas will burn your ass and blow you all to
> hell.
>
> Anon.: 'Rock On Rockall' (The song suggests that Rockall was a pebble fallen from the clod hurled by the giant Finn MacCool that formed the ISLE OF MAN.)

In 1997 Greenpeace activists landed on Rockall, stayed a record 42 days and declared the rock to be the sovereign territory of Waveland.

Rockall. A sea area in the shipping forecast. It is north of Shannon, south of Bailey, and west of Malin and Hebrides.

> Darkness outside. Inside, the radio's prayer –
> Rockall. Malin. Dogger. Finisterre.
>
> Carol Ann Duffy: 'Prayer'

Rockall Times, The. 'Voice of the world's liveliest volcanic outcrop' – an anarchic website featuring satirical 'news' articles. In September 2002, for example, it announced Mel Gibson's plan to film *Finnegans Wake* in Hittite.

Rockingham 'Hroc(a)'s people's homestead', OE male personal name *Hroc(a)* + *-inga-* (*see* -ING) + HAM.

A village in Northamptonshire, about 2.5 km (1.5 miles) north of Corby. It is situated on the side of a hill, at the top of which dramatically stands **Rockingham Castle**, overlooking the WELLAND valley. Originally built by William the Conqueror, this has been much domesticated over the centuries. It played host to many medieval kings including Richard the Lionheart. A royal fortress for 450 years, the castle was taken by Cromwell's Roundheads during the Civil Wars. It was the setting of the 1980s BBC TV series *By the Sword Divided*, a period drama set in the 1640s during the Civil Wars. Charles Dickens frequently stayed in the castle, and modelled Chesney Wold, home of Sir Leicester Dedlock in *Bleak House* (1853), on it.

Rockingham chinaware and porcelain gets its name from the 2nd Marquis of Rockingham (*see below*), on whose Yorkshire estate it was made, at the Old Works, Swinton, from around 1745 to 1842. It is particularly associated with a type of purple-brown glaze.

Some 5 km (3 miles) to the east of here is Kirby Hall, the ruined shell of a large Elizabethan house originally begun in 1570 for Sir Humphrey Stafford, and with 17th-century additions (possibly by Inigo Jones).

There is a Rockingham County in New Hampshire, USA.

Council of Rockingham. A convocation of English bishops (also known as the **Synod of Rockingham**) held at Rockingham on 11 March 1095 to decide whether the king or the Pope had the primary right to invest an ecclesiastical authority. The question was given point by a dispute that had arisen between William II and Pope Urban II over the investiture of Anselm as Archbishop of Canterbury. The Council decided in favour of the king.

Rockingham Forest. An area of intermittently tree-covered land to the southeast of Corby. In the Middle Ages, when it was a royal hunting forest, it covered a vast area.

Rockinghamite. An adherent of the Whig statesman Charles Watson-Wentworth, 2nd Marquis of Rockingham (1730–82), prime minister 1765–6 and 1782. He supported the American claim to independence and was opposed to the American policy of successive governments of the 1770s and 1780s.

Rock of Cashel. *See under* CASHEL.

Rock of Dunamase. *See* DUNAMASE, ROCK OF.

Rock of Names, the. A rock on which are inscribed the names of S.T. Coleridge, Dorothy Wordsworth and Sara Hutchinson, William Wordsworth's sister-in-law. It is near Wythburn in the Lake District, and was submerged when THIRLMERE was dammed, although the inscribed fragments were at that point moved up the hillside.

Roding From the villages called *Roding* along part of its course (*see* the RODINGS). Its original name was *Hyle* (*see* ILFORD).

A river in Essex, which rises to the southeast of SAFFRON WALDEN and flows 48 km (30 miles) southwards through CHIPPING ONGAR, WOODFORD and Ilford into the River THAMES[1] to the south of BARKING (where it is known as Barking Creek).

Roding Valley 'Underground' station, on the Central line, opened in 1948. It lies between Woodford in the west and CHIGWELL in the east.

Rodings, the *Roding* '(settlement of) Hrotha's people', OE male personal name *Hrotha* + *-ingas* (*see* -ING).

A collective name for eight Essex villages in the valley of the River RODING, about 14 km (8.5 miles) to the east and northeast of Harlow. They are: **Abbess Roding** (from its ownership in the Middle Ages by the Abbess of Barking), **Aythorpe Roding** (from its manorial ownership in the Middle Ages by the Aitrop family), **Beauchamp Roding** (from its manorial ownership in the Middle Ages by the Beauchamp family), **Berners Roding** (from its manorial ownership in the Middle Ages by Hugh de Berners), **High Roding** (from its higher location), **Leaden Roding** (from the lead roof of its church), **Margaret Roding** (from the dedication of the local church) and **White Roding** (from the walls of its church, either made from pale-coloured stone or whitewashed).

Locally the name sometimes retains the Old English pronunciation 'roothings'.

Rodney Stoke *Rodney* denoting manorial ownership in the Middle Ages by the de Rodeney family; *Stoke see* STOKE BARDOLPH.

A village in Somerset, at the foot of the MENDIP HILLS, about 8 km (5 miles) northwest of Wells.

Roedean 'rough valley', OE *roh* 'rough' + *denu* 'valley'.

An eastern coastal suburb of BRIGHTON, within the unitary authority of Brighton and Hove. It is now best known for its girls' public school, founded in 1885, whose buildings look out over the English Channel, and which has come to stand for effortless superiority inculcated into females to almost the same extent as Eton has for males:

> A Roedean accent which could have flayed the skin off a waiter.
>
> F. Branston: *Up and Coming Man* (1977)

Roehampton 'home farm frequented by rooks', OE *hroc* 'rook' + *ham-tun* (*see* -TON).

A district of southwest London (SW15), in the borough of WANDSWORTH, to the southwest of Putney and the northeast of Richmond Park. In the 18th and early 19th centuries it developed from a country village into a highly select suburb, with several elegant mansions and villas. They have all now been demolished or converted to institutional or commercial use, and more modest housing covers many of their grounds, but the area retains an air of selectivity and modest prosperity.

The Alton West Estate, often referred to as the **Roehampton Estate**, is a famously opinion-dividing example of 1950s high-rise architecture. Nikolaus Pevsner notoriously loved it (he described its huge tower blocks as a natural progression upon 'Capability' Brown's picturesque landscapes); others, including some of the residents of the estate, have been less keen. Designed by Leslie Martin, it consists of twenty blocks with associated buildings and services.

The **Roehampton Institute** was founded in the 1970s from four existing colleges of education. In the early 1990s it became part of the University of Surrey, but in 2004 it split away to become the independent **Roehampton University**.

Queen Mary's Hospital, Roehampton (founded in 1915) pioneered the development of modern artificial limbs (the Battle of Britain pilot Douglas Bader had his legs fitted here, and there is now a Douglas Bader Foundation Centre). The Priory, a private clinic for recovering alcoholics and drug addicts, is in Roehampton.

The **Roehampton Club**, founded in 1901, has extensive sporting facilities (including polo grounds). Rosslyn Park Rugby FC plays its home games here.

Rogan's Seat OScand *sæti* 'high place, hilltop shaped like a seat', with the name *Rogan*, a local landowner.

A hill (671 m / 2201 ft) in the PENNINES of North Yorkshire, 25 km (16 miles) west of Richmond. It is the highest of the fells in the remote area between Swaledale (*see under* SWALE[1]) and STAINMORE PASS.

Roger Sand Presumably named after someone called *Roger*.

A sandbank in the southwestern corner of the WASH.

Róisín Dubh. A personification of IRELAND, who translates as 'Dark Roisin', and who first appears as **Mo Róisín Dubh** in an anonymous 16th-century Irish poem sometimes attributed to Owen Roe Mac Ward. The poem refers to the hope of Irish Catholics for help from abroad. Róisín Dubh was rendered as 'My Dark Rosaleen' by James Clarence Mangan in his 19th-century translation:

> O, my Dark Rosaleen,
>   Do not sigh, do not weep!
> The priests are on the ocean green,
>   They march along the Deep.
> There's wine from the royal Pope,
>   Upon the ocean green;
> And Spanish wine shall give you hope,
>   My dark Rosaleen! ...

In a different translation by the revolutionary and poet Padraic Pearse, Roisin ironically becomes the very English-sounding Little Dark Rose:

> Little Rose, be not sad for all that hath behapped thee:
> The friars are coming across the sea, they march on the main,
> From the Pope shall come thy pardon, and from Rome, from the East –
> And stint not Spanish wine to my Little Dark Rose.

In a rather different Irish version translated by Eleanor Hull, Roisin becomes **Ros geal dubh**:

> There's black grief on the plains, and a mist on the hills;
> There is fury on the mountains, and that is no wonder;
> I would empty the wild ocean with the shell of an egg,
> If I could be at peace with you, my Ros geal dubh.

See also KATHLEEN NI HOULIHAN *and* SHAN VAN VOCHT.

Rokeby Either 'Hroca's' or 'Hrokr's farm', OE or OScand male personal name *Hroca* or *Hrok* + -BY.

An estate (**Rokeby Park**) and mansion (**Rokeby Hall**) near Greta Bridge, County Durham (*see under* GRETA), pronounced 'roakby' or 'rookby'. It was while staying at the Hall with his friend, the scholar J.B. Morritt, that Sir Walter Scott began his *Rokeby* (1813), a long poem set after the Battle of Marston Moor (1644) during the Civil Wars. After this Scott realized that he was a better novelist than poet.

> The sound of Rokeby's woods I hear,
>   They mingle with the song:
> Dark Greta's voice is in mine ear,
>   I must not hear them long.
>
> Sir Walter Scott: *Rokeby* (1813), Canto V, Song: 'The Farewell'

Felon Sow of Rokeby, the. A ferocious pig belonging to Ralph of Rokeby (*fl.* early 16th century), who was the death of a number of swineherds. Finally Ralph offered her to the Grey Friars of Richmond, but, when three of the friars came to collect her, the Felon Sow reacted with such unreasonable violence that – despite a reading of the Gospels in Latin from the safety of a high branch – the friars were put to flight. The Sow's victory was short-lived, however, as the following day the friars sent out two armed men to dispatch the porcine heroine to the Great Sty in the Sky. A Te Deum was sung to mark her passing.

Maid of Rokeby, the. According to an 18th-century tale, the Maid of Rokeby was the ghost of a young woman stabbed to death in nearby Mortham Tower so that an unspecified Lord Rokeby could inherit her estate. Her bloodstains remained on the stairs of the tower for many years until she was exorcised by a priest. However, she still haunts the area, apparently with much wailing.

Rokeby Venus, The. The popular name for *The Toilet of Venus* (otherwise known as *Venus and Cupid*) by Velázquez (1599–1660), a rear view of a reclining nude painted *c.*1651 and now in the National Gallery in London. The popular name derives from the fact that until 1905 it hung in Rokeby Hall as part of the collection of the Morritt family. The postcard of the painting is apparently one of the most popular in the National Gallery shop (with male customers at least). On 10 March 1914 the painting itself was slashed with a meat chopper by a suffragette protesting at the re-arrest of Emmeline Pankhurst, but subsequently the damage was successfully repaired.

Rollright Probably 'Hrolla's property', OE male personal name *Hrolla* + *land-riht* 'land-rights, property'. An alternative explanation is that *Roll-* is a shortened form of *Rodland* 'wheel precinct' (referring to the stone circle), OCelt *roto* 'wheel' + *landa* 'precinct, church', and that *-right* comes from OCelt *rhych* 'groove' (referring to a small gorge nearby now called Danes Bottom).

Either of a pair of villages (**Great Rollright** and **Little Rollright**) in Oxfordshire, on the edge of the COTSWOLDS, about 16 km (10 miles) southwest of Banbury.

Rollright Stones. A Bronze Age stone circle (also known simply as the **Rollrights**) on the Warwickshire–Oxfordshire border, about 0.75 km (0.5 miles) northeast of Little Rollright. It is the third most important such circle in England after STONEHENGE and AVEBURY. It was probably used in funeral ceremonies, but an alternative legendary history has built up around it: a local king and his men supposedly met a witch on this spot; she promised him that if he could see Long Compton (a nearby Warwickshire village) from the top of a hill, he would become king of all England; he tried, but the witch raised up a mist, he failed and she turned him and his men to stone. The upright stones of the main circle (of which there are about 70) are known as the 'King's Men'; a solitary standing stone is the 'King Stone'; and a group of other stones a little way away are the 'Whispering Knights', supposedly a group of malcontents already plotting to overthrow the king.

Rolvenden 'Hrothwulf's woodland pasture', OE male personal name *Hrothwulf* + -ING + *denn* 'woodland pasture'.

A village in Kent, 5 km (3 miles) southwest of Tenterden. The children's author, Frances Hodgson Burnett, rented Great Maytham Hall here (now a retirement home) throughout the 1890s. Its overgrown high-walled garden, since tamed, is said to be the inspiration for her novel *The Secret Garden* (1911).

Rom A back-formation from ROMFORD.

A name given to the middle stretch of the River Beam, as it passes through Romford.

Romaldkirk 'St Rumwald's church', OE male personal name *Rumwald* + OScand *kirkja* 'church'.

A village in upper Teesdale, County Durham, 7 km (4.5 miles) northwest of Barnard Castle. According to a local ballad, '**The Last of the Lords of Romaldkirk**', the eponymous lord, while pursuing a white hart, met his end at a defile of the Tees called Percymere:

> He checked his steed, but 'twas too late,
> The tired beast reeled and fell,
> Rolled on its rider and both together
> Were plunged in that awful dell.

Romannobridge 'bridge of the fort of the monk', Gaelic *ràth* (see RATH) + *manaich* 'of the monk' + ModE *bridge*.

A village in Scottish Borders, 4 km (2.5 miles) south of West Linton.

Roman Steps. A stepped path, paved with large slabs, rising up the head of Cwm Bychan in the northern RHINOGS, Gwynedd (formerly in Merioneth), some 11 km (7 miles) southeast of Porthmadog. Despite their name, it is thought more likely that the steps were part of a medieval bridleway.

Rombalds Moor 'Rumbald's moor', Continental Germanic male personal name *Rumbald*, with OE *mor*.

A large extent of moorland in West Yorkshire, bounded by ILKLEY in the north, SKIPTON in the west, and KEIGHLEY and BINGLEY in the south. It includes Ilkley Moor. Rombalds Moor has many Neolithic and Bronze Age monuments, including the Twelve Apostles stone circle, the Pancake Stone, the Swastika Stone and the Great and Little Skirtfuls of Stones (both cairns marking burials).

Rome Hill Most likely a modern name.

A hill (565 m / 1854 ft) in South Lanarkshire, some 8 km (5 miles) west of the hills of Tweeddale (*see under* TWEED).

Romford 'wide ford' (referring to a place where the Roman road to Colchester crossed the River Beam), OE *rum* 'wide, spacious' + FORD.

A district of East London, in the borough of HAVERING (before 1965 in Essex), to the northwest of Hornchurch. It grew up where the Roman road to Colchester forded a stream, and there was a Roman camp called **Durolitum** nearby.

The poet Francis Quarles (1594–1622) was born in Romford.

ride to Romford. To get a new pair of breeches, or to get a new bottom put in an old pair. An expression dating from the late 18th and early 19th centuries, when Romford was known for producing high-quality leather breeches. Applied to a knife or similar implement, 'You may ride to Romford on it' indicated bluntness.

Romford lion. A jocular 17th-century term for a calf. In those days Romford was a cattle-market town.

Romiley 'spacious clearing', OE *rum* 'spacious' + -LEY.

A small town in Greater Manchester, 5 km (3 miles) east of Stockport.

Romney. *See* NEW ROMNEY *and* OLD ROMNEY.

Romney Marsh *Romney* originally probably a river name, 'Rumen's river', OE *Rumenes* possessive form of male personal name *Rumen* + *ea* (*see* EA-); alternatively perhaps '(place at the) broad river' (possibly because the marsh, with its many waterways, suggested a single broad river), OE (*æt thære*) *rumen ea* (*rumen* dative form of *rum* 'broad, spacious' + *ea* (*see* EA-)).

An area of reclaimed marshland in southeast England, on the Straits of Dover (*see under* DOVER), occupying about 104 sq km (40 sq miles) between WINCHELSEA, East Sussex, in the west and HYTHE, Kent, in the east. It is bounded to the north and west by the ROYAL MILITARY CANAL. Its seaward point is DUNGENESS. Its southwestern section is more specifically designated as WALLAND MARSH, its southeastern as DENGE MARSH.

Two thousand years ago it was largely under the sea, but the Romans began efforts at drainage and sea levels began to fall, and by Anglo-Saxon times human habitation was under way (by the 8th century the inhabitants were known as the *Merscware* 'marsh-dwellers'). Drainage was complete by the 17th century, and although the area was still infested with malaria, its pattern of land-use was already well established. The flat, rather bleak meadows are ideal for grazing sheep, and a recognized variety, the stocky, long-woolled **Romney Marsh** (or simply **Romney**) has been developed here. The Marsh also has its own distinctive style of church, small and intimate: at Ivychurch, for instance, or the isolated St Mary in the Marsh (near which E. Nesbit (1858–1924), author of *The Railway Children*, came to live late in life, in two army huts).

The mists which turn Romney Marsh into an eerie place, through which sheep or church may unexpectedly loom up, have also proved advantageous for smugglers. (The daring and mysterious Dr Syn, in Russell Thorndyke's eponymous novel (1915), carries out his smuggling activities on the Marsh – *see* DYMCHURCH.) Nowadays the Marsh has turned itself more law-abidingly to tulip-growing.

Cathedral of Romney Marsh, the. *See under* LYDD.

Romsey 'Rum's island or dry ground in a marsh', OE *Rumes* possessive form of male personal name *Rum* + *eg* (*see* -EY, -EA). A market town (pronounced 'romzi' or 'rumzi') in Hampshire, on the River TEST, on the eastern edge of the NEW FOREST, about 13 km (8 miles) northwest of Southampton. It grew up around its Norman abbey. **Romsey Abbey** had its origins in a Benedictine nunnery founded by Edward the Elder in 907, of which Alfred the Great's granddaughter Elfleda was the first abbess. Its wooden church was replaced in the middle of the 12th century by the surviving magnificent stone structure, which was bought by the townspeople of Romsey after the Dissolution of the Monasteries.

The nearby Palladian mansion called Broadlands was the birthplace and home of the statesman Lord Palmerston (1784–1865). A later occupant was Lord Mountbatten (1900–79), who amongst other titles styled himself 'Baron Romsey of Romsey'. He is buried in Romsey Abbey.

Romsey Psalter. A 15th-century illuminated manuscript containing the Psalms.

Rona Probably 'rough island', OScand *hraun* 'rough' + *ey* (*see* -AY).

A small, now uninhabited island just north of RAASAY, from which it is separated by the narrow **Kyle Rona** (Gaelic *caol* 'strait'). It is in Highland (formerly in Inverness-shire), 8 km (5 miles) off the east coast of SKYE. It was long in the hands of the MacLeods of Raasay, who had a reputation for piracy. In the 16th century the island was described by Dean Monro as a place of 'thieves, ruggars and reivers', and Acairseid Mhór – the fine, hidden natural harbour on the western side – was formerly known as Port nan Robaireann (Gaelic 'harbour of the robbers'). The island is sometimes called **South Rona**, to distinguish it from the remote NORTH RONA, far to the northwest.

Rona Raiders, the. A group of seven ex-servicemen who after the First World War, having been evicted from Rona, moved themselves and their families to Fearns on Raasay, where their ancestors had lived. They built themselves homes and began to cultivate the land. The public outrage that followed their subsequent arrest and custodial sentences obliged the government to step in and purchase both Rona and Raasay in 1922.

Ronin. A 'poetic' version of RUM used by Sir Walter Scott.

Rookhope 'valley of the rooks', OE *hroc* 'rook' + *hop* 'valley'.

A village in County Durham, in the valley of **Rookhope Burn**, a tributary of the WEAR, 19 km (12 miles) southwest of Consett. It was formerly a centre of lead and silver mining, and the extraordinary **Rookhope Chimney** took the noxious fumes from the smelting works a long way up the fellside. On the north side of the valley is Redburn Common, which gave its name to the Redburn Skulls –

eight mysterious skulls found some years ago in a quarry, all showing terrible tooth marks.

In Sir Walter Scott's epic poem *Harold the Dauntless* (1817), the outlaw Wulfstane has his home in Rookhope.

Rookhope Ryde, the (1569). A skirmish in 1569, when the invading Border reivers set about stealing the valley's sheep. The incident was commemorated in a ballad:

> Then in at Rookhope Head they came,
> They ran the forest but a mile,
> They gathered together in four hours
> Six hundred sheep within a while.

Roos OCelt *ros* 'promontory'; there is a low ridge protruding into the marsh here.

A village in the East Riding of Yorkshire, 6 km (4 miles) northeast of Withernsea.

Roosky Irish *Rúscaigh* 'marshy place'.

The name of a number of villages in Ireland, such as those in LEITRIM and MAYO.

Rosa, Glen. *See* GLEN ROSA.

Rosa Pinnacle. *See under* GLEN ROSA.

Rosbifs, les. A French slang term, meaning 'the roast-beefs', for the English and/or the British, derived from the English national dish. Americans have been known to call the British **Beefeaters** for similar reasons.

Ros Comáin. The Irish name for ROSCOMMON.

Roscommon Irish *Ros Comáin* 'St Comán's wood'.

The county town of County Roscommon, 25 km (16 miles) southwest of Longford. A monastery was founded here in the 8th century by St Comán (d.747), but nothing remains. However, there are the remains (mostly 15th century) of a Dominican friary founded in 1273 by Felim O'Conor, king of Connacht, who is buried here. On the west side of the town is a fine ruined castle built for the English king in 1269. It was held by the O'Conors in the 14th, 15th and 16th centuries, until retaken by the English in 1569. It was held by the Confederate Catholics from 1645 to 1652.

It was in Roscommon jail that 'Lady Betty' (*c*.1750–1810), a poor woman of 'dark disposition', was due to hang for the murder of a man (possibly her son returned from America). However, no one could be found to hang her until she herself volunteered for the job, thereby apparently securing her pardon. Thereafter she pursued a happy career as a hangwoman.

Roscommon, County. A pasture-rich county in the northwestern MIDLANDS of Ireland, in the province of CONNACHT. It is bounded on the east – across the SHANNON and LOUGH REE – by Leitrim, Longford and Westmeath, on the south by Offaly, on the west by Galway and Mayo, and on the north by Sligo. Roscommon became a county *c*.1580 and the county town is ROSCOMMON.

I married a man from County Roscommon
and I live in the back of beyond
with a field of cows and a yard of hens
and six white geese on the pond.

Gillian Clarke (b.1937): 'Overheard in County Sligo'

Ros Cré. The Irish name for ROSCREA.

Roscrea Irish *Ros Cré*, 'Cré's promontory', with *ros* referring to the land jutting into Lough Cré here.

A market town in County Tipperary, at the southern end of the SLIEVE BLOOM MOUNTAINS, 35 km (22 miles) southwest of Portlaoise. St Cronan founded a monastery here in the 7th century, and in the 8th century the monks produced *The Book of Dima*, an illuminated manuscript now in Trinity College Library, Dublin. On the site of St Cronan's foundation are the remains of a 12th-century Augustinian priory, and there is also a ruined 15th-century Franciscan friary. Within the remains of the 12th-century castle is a fine Queen Anne mansion. Today the town is renowned for its sausages and bacon.

Rose 'moorland', Cornish *ros*.

A village in Cornwall, about 8 km (5 miles) southwest of Newquay.

Rose Ash Originally *Ash* '(place at the) ash-tree', OE *æsc*; *Rose* denoting manorial ownership in the early Middle Ages by a man called Ralph.

A village in Devon, about 8 km (5 miles) southeast of South Molton.

Roseberry Topping 'Odin's hill', OScand *Othin* 'Odin' (the Norse war god) + *berg* 'hill', with the later addition of OE *topping*, from *top* 'hill'; the initial 'r' of Roseberry appears to have been borrowed from 'under' in the local village name Newton under Roseberry, first recorded as *Newton under Ouesbergh*.

A small but prominent summit (320 m / 1050 ft) in the Cleveland Hills (*see under* CLEVELAND), part of the NORTH YORK MOORS of North Yorkshire, 12 km (7.5 miles) southeast of Middlesbrough. It was formerly cone-shaped, but mining and quarrying led to a landslide that left the hill with the rocky profile it has today, a profile that has earned it the nickname of the **Cleveland Matterhorn**.

Rosedale 'valley of horses', OScand *hross* 'horse' + *dalr* 'valley'.

A valley in the NORTH YORK MOORS, North Yorkshire, some 15 km (9 miles) northwest of Pickering. Iron ore was mined here from the Iron Age, and there was a mining boom in the 19th century. The name of the small village of **Rosedale Abbey** is all that is left of the priory founded here in 1158.

Rosedale in Canada is an area of Toronto.

Rosehearty 'Abhartach's headland', Gaelic *ros* 'headland' + *Abhartaich* 'of Abhartach', an Irish clan name.

A town and former fishing port on the north coast of BUCHAN, in Aberdeenshire (formerly in Grampian region),

some 6 km (4 miles) west of Fraserburgh. It was founded in the 14th century by some shipwrecked Danes.

Roseland 'land by the headland', Cornish *ros* 'headland' + OE *land*.

A much holidayed-in peninsula on the southern coast of Cornwall, on the eastern side of CARRICK ROADS. It is noted for the semi-tropical vegetation that thrives in its mild climate and its National Trust-protected coastline. Its main centres are ST MAWES, Portscatho and ST JUST-IN-ROSELAND, and the peninsula culminates at St Anthony's Head, site of a lighthouse and a Second World War battery.

Rose Lane Aghregog. A name sometimes given to RHOSLLANERCHRUGOG.

Rosemarkie 'horse headland', Gaelic *ros* 'headland' + *marc* 'horse' with a suffix.

A village on the MORAY FIRTH in the BLACK ISLE, Highland (formerly in Ross and Cromarty), just northeast of Fortrose. The Irish monk St Moluag died here *c*.592.

Rosevear Probably Cornish *ros* 'promontory' (as in ROSELAND) with an unknown second element.

An uninhabited island in the SCILLY ISLES, the largest of the WESTERN ROCKS. Many species of seabird are found here.

Ros geal dubh. *See under* RÓISÍN DUBH.

Rosguill 'Goll's promontory', Irish *ros* 'promontory' + personal name of the legendary hero *Goll*.

A small peninsula on the north coast of County Donegal, between the FANAD peninsula (to the east) and SHEEP HAVEN (to the west). In Irish legend, Goll Mac Morna ('one-eyed son of Morna'), after whom the peninsula is named, was the leader of the Fianna before Finn MacCool. Subsequently he is involved in the death of Finn's son Cairell and throws a spear at Finn's grandson Oscar. After this he is trapped in Rosguill by his former comrades and dies of starvation.

Ros Láir. The Irish name for ROSSLARE.

Roslin Etymology obscure, but Gaelic *ros* 'promontory' + *linn* 'pool in a river' could be the elements, hence 'river pool by the promontory'.

A village in Midlothian, 11 km (7 miles) south of Edinburgh on the south side of the PENTLAND HILLS. An alternative spelling is **Rosslyn**. The **Roslin Institute** is a research establishment where Dolly, the first cloned sheep, was produced in 1997. Nearby is what Sir Walter Scott in *Rokeby* (1813) calls 'Roslin's magic glade' – **Roslin Glen**, a deep and picturesquely wooded red-sandstone gorge through which flows the North Esk (*see under* ESK[1]). At the east end of the glen is HAWTHORNDEN House, while at the west end is **Roslin Castle**, standing on a rocky promontory jutting out above the North Esk; access is by a bridge. The oldest parts, built by Sir William St Clair, 1st Prince of Orkney, are 14th-century, but mostly it is 16th–17th century.

Sir William's descendant, the third and last Prince of Orkney, also called Sir William St Clair, founded nearby **Roslin Chapel** in 1446. The chapel became the burial place of the St Clairs (or Sinclairs), and they were reputedly buried in their armour instead of coffins until 1650, when a Sinclair widow thought it 'beggarly to be buried in that manner'. In the ballad 'Rosabelle', Scott refers to the legend – and the belief that a red glow over the chapel would foretell disaster:

Seem'd all on fire that chapel proud,
Where Roslin's chiefs uncoffin'd lie,
Each Baron for a sable shroud,
Sheath'd in his iron panoply.

More remarkable than these stories is the interior of the chapel, which is full of some of the most ornate ecclesiastical carving in Scotland. Equally remarkable is the fact that the carving largely escaped the depredations of the Reformation, although an Edinburgh mob inflicted some damage in 1688. Restoration work was carried out in the 19th and 20th centuries. The most famous feature of the chapel is the Prentice Pillar, to which the legend attaches that the master mason went abroad to learn how to carve the pattern he had been given for the pillar. In his absence, an apprentice carved the present pillar, which is thought to be of superior design and craftsmanship to the other pillars in the chapel. The master was so furiously jealous on his return that he killed the apprentice. The story is probably apocryphal, as similar stories are told of several other buildings elsewhere. However, it is known that at one point the Bishop of St Andrews visited the chapel to reconsecrate it, presumably after it had witnessed some terrible dark doing.

In the 18th and 19th centuries Roslin Glen, Castle and Chapel proved a magnet for those in search of the picturesque. The Glen and Castle were painted by Alexander Nasmyth (1758–1840) and others, and notable literary visitors included Samuel Johnson, James Boswell, Robert Burns, Sir Walter Scott and William Wordsworth.

Battle of Roslin (1303). A substantial victory by a small Scots army under Sir John Comyn and Sir Symon Fraser. The battle comprised three separate engagements with three successive English forces. Guided by the local knowledge of one Prior Abernethy – who also inspired the Scots by building a giant cross on the highest of the nearby Pentland Hills – the Scots managed to drive thousands of English soldiers over the cliffs of Roslin Glen to their deaths in the river below.

Ros na Rún Irish, 'headland of the secrets or sweethearts'.
A fictional Connemara village, the setting of the Irish-language TV soap opera of the same name, first broadcast in 1996. Because of the violent goings-on here, sleepy Ros na Rún has been dubbed 'the murder capital of Ireland'.

Ross and Cromarty The first element is from Gaelic *ros* 'promontory', of which there are many on both coasts; the word can also mean 'moorland', which is also relevant to the topography, and gave a name to one of the prominent local clans, the Rosses; for the second element see CROMARTY.
A former county of northern Scotland, bounded on the north by Sutherland and Caithness, the North Sea in the east, Inverness-shire in the south and the Atlantic to the west. It also included LEWIS in the Outer Hebrides (*see under* the HEBRIDES). The county town was DINGWALL, and apart from the low, fertile strip in the east (including the BLACK ISLE), it is an area of wild rugged mountains and lochs, including some of the remotest fastnesses in Britain. Both coasts are heavily indented: on the west coast the sea lochs include LOCH BROOM, GRUINARD BAY, LOCH EWE, GAIR LOCH, Loch Torridon (*see under* TORRIDON), LOCH KISHORN, LOCH CARRON and Loch Alsh (*see under* KYLE OF LOCH-ALSH); on the east coast are the DORNOCH, CROMARTY, BEAULY and MORAY Firths. Notable mountains and ranges include AN TEALLACH, A'MHAIGHDEAN, SLIOCH[1], the giants of TORRIDON including BEINN EIGHE, LIATHACH and BEINN ALLIGIN, and the mountains of APPLECROSS and the FANNICHS. The best-known and most beautiful of the inland lochs is LOCH MAREE. The area is informally divided into **Easter Ross** and **Wester Ross**.

The earldom of Ross was established in the 12th century at the time that David I set about planting Anglo-Normans in the area. Ross became the county of **Ross-shire** in 1661, and was amalgamated with the county of CROMARTY in 1889. The county of Ross and Cromarty was abolished in 1975, when most of the mainland area became a district of Highland region. The latter became a unitary authority in 1996.

Ross County FC. A football club founded in 1929 and based at Victoria Park, DINGWALL. Admitted to the Scottish league in 1994, Ross County is the most northerly league club in Scottish football.

Rossan Point *Rossan* probably Irish *rosán* diminutive of *ros* 'promontory' or 'wood', here 'small promontory'.
The most westerly point in County Donegal, 8 km (5 miles) northwest of SLIEVE LEAGUE.

Ross Castle. *See under* KILLARNEY.

Rossendale Possibly 'valley in the moors', OCelt *ros* 'moor' + OE *dœl* 'valley'.
An upland area in southeast Lancashire, about 29 km (18 miles) north of Manchester. The valley of its name is that of the River IRWELL, and the name may refer to the moors of the Forest of Rossendale (*see below*). In 1974 Rossendale gave its name to a district and borough.

Forest of Rossendale. A moorland area , once referred to as the Royal Forest of Rossendale; it was for hundreds of years a royal hunting ground (what was known as 'deer forest', although this did not imply a forested area). In 1507 Henry VII opened up the area, and the towns of RAWTEN-STALL, HASLINGDEN and BACUP sprang up. The Forest is the source of the River IRWELL.

Rosses, the Irish *Na Rosa* 'the headlands'.

A heavily indented coastal area of northwest County Donegal, overlooking **Rosses Bay** and ARAN ISLAND. It is sometimes just referred to as **Rosses**. The main settlement is DUNGLOW.

> My sorrow that I am not by the little dún
> By the lake of the starlings at Rosses under the hill,
> And the larks there, singing over the fields of dew ...
>
>> Seumas O'Sullivan: 'The Starling Lake', from *Collected Poems* (1940)

For Rosses' appearance in William Allingham's 'The Fairies', *see under* SLIEVE LEAGUE.

The Irish-language novelist Fionn Mac Cumhaill (pseudonym of Maghnas Mac Cumhaill, 1885–1965) was born near Annagry in the Rosses, and his best-known work – for many years used as a set text in Irish schools – is *Na Rosa go Bráthach* (*The Rosses for Ever!*, 1939). The islands of the Rosses feature in some of the novels of Peadar O'Donnell, namely *The Storm* (1925), *Islanders* (1928) and *Proud Island* (1975), drawing on his experiences of teaching here. Another well-known native of the Rosses is the crooner Daniel O'Donnell (b.1953), who was born in Kincasslagh and whose popularity with ladies of a certain age has given rise to the riddle: 'What has 100 legs and no teeth? The front row of a Daniel O'Donnell concert.'

Rosses Point Irish *An Ros* 'the peninsula'.

A small resort on the sandy peninsula of the same name in County Sligo, 8 km (5 miles) northwest of Sligo itself. There is a championship golf course here.

Rosslare Irish *Ros Láir* 'middle headland'.

A seaside resort in County Wexford, overlooking **Rosslare Bay** some 8 km (5 miles) southeast of Wexford itself. George Bernard Shaw complained that:

> ... one cannot work in a place of such infinite peace.

Indeed it is (though this is perhaps not saying a lot) the sunniest place in Ireland, with an average of 4 hours 20 minutes of sunshine every day.

On the south side of the bay is **Rosslare Harbour**, founded by the English in 1210. There has been a regular ferry to FISHGUARD in Wales since 1906, and there are also ferries to PEMBROKE, Cherbourg, Le Havre and Roscoff.

Rosslyn. An alternative spelling of ROSLIN.

Ross-on-Wye *Ross* 'hill-spur, moor, heathy upland', OCelt *ros*.

A picturesque market town in Herefordshire (before 1998 in Hereford and Worcester, before 1974 in Herefordshire), on a steep cliff of red sandstone overlooking the River WYE[1], about 19 km (12 miles) southeast of Hereford.

John Kyrle (1637–1724), a local man and pioneer of town planning, initiated a lot of improvements in Ross (including a water-supply system), and laid out the public gardens known as 'The Prospect', which provide pleasing views of the river. The poet and satirist Alexander Pope bestowed on him the sobriquet '**Man of Ross**':

> Who taught that heaven-directed spire to rise?
> 'The Man of Ross', each lisping babe replies.
> Behold the market-place with poor o'erspread!
> He feeds yon almshouse, neat, but void of state,
> Where Age and Want sit smiling at the gate;
> Him portion'd maids, apprenticed orphans bless'd,
> The young who labour, and the old who rest.
>
>> Alexander Pope: *Moral Essays* (1731–5), Epistle iii

Samuel Taylor Coleridge, who stayed in Ross in 1794, also had a verdict on the man:

> Richer than a miser o'er his countless hoards,
> Nobler than kings or king-polluted lords,
> Here dwelt the man of Ross.

First held in 1996, the **Ross-on-Wye International Music Festival** attracts aficionados from all over the world to its annual August event.

Ross-shire. *See under* ROSS AND CROMARTY.

Rossville Flats. *See under* BOGSIDE.

Ros Treabhair. The Irish name for ROSTREVOR.

Rostrevor Irish *Ros Treabhair* 'Trevor's wood', after Edward *Trevor*, commander of the English garrison at Newry at the end of the 16th century.

A small resort on the north side of CARLINGFORD LOUGH, County Down, 12 km (7.5 miles) southeast of Newry.

Rostrevor was the birthplace of T.K. Whitaker (b.1916), the civil servant largely responsible for economic modernization in the Republic in the 1960s.

Rosyth 'landing-place headland', Gaelic *ros* 'headland, promontory' + OE *hyth* 'landing-place'. Despite the difficulty in accepting a hybrid Gaelic-English name, the present pronunciation of the name retains the sound found in some other *hyth* names like ROTHERHITHE; and the continuing use of the landing-place on the bank of the Firth of Forth also supports the etymology.

A town in Fife (pronounced 'ross-ithe', with the 'th' as in 'three'), on the north side of the Firth of FORTH, 5 km (3 miles) south of Dunfermline. It is best known for its large naval base and dockyard, particularly important in the First and Second World Wars. The government acquired the land for the base in 1903. Rosyth's naval activities have since declined, but there are now ferries to the Continent. Offshore is the anchorage of St Margaret's Hope[1].

> Rosyth guns sang, Sang tide through cable
> for Glasgow burning …
>
> Basil Bunting: *The Spoils* (1951)

Rothamsted 'rook homestead', OE *hroc* 'rook' + *hamstede* 'homestead' (*see also* HAM).

A location a little to the west of HARPENDEN in Hertfordshire. The mainly 16th- and 17th- century **Rothamsted Manor** is now a hall of residence. Work carried out by its owner at the end of the 19th century, John Bennett Lawes, led to the setting up of the **Rothamsted Experimental Station** for agricultural research.

Rothbury 'Hrotha's stronghold', OE male personal name *Hrotha* (or possibly OScand *rauthr* 'red') + *burh* (*see* BURY).

A small town in Northumberland, 18 km (11 miles) southwest of Alnwick. It is a tourist centre, and is surrounded by **Rothbury Forest**.

Rother[1] A back-formation from ROTHERBRIDGE. Its earlier English name was *Shire* 'bright one' (from OE *scir* 'bright, clear').

A river in Hampshire and West Sussex (also called the **Western Rother**), which rises to the north of LISS and flows 64 km (40 miles) eastwards via MIDHURST to join the River ARUN near PULBOROUGH.

Rother[2] A back-formation from ROTHERFIELD. Its earlier name was *Limen*, from an OCelt word meaning 'elm-tree'.

A river in East Sussex (also called the **Eastern Rother**), which rises near Rotherfield and flows 50 km (31 miles) eastwards, via ROBERTSBRIDGE and BODIAM, and then southwards into the English Channel at RYE. Until the 'Great Storm' of 1287, its mouth was several miles to the east, at NEW ROMNEY. For some distance it forms the boundary between Sussex and Kent.

Rother[3] 'chief river', OCelt river name.

A tributary of the DON[2] in South Yorkshire and Derbyshire. It rises southwest of CHESTERFIELD and joins the Don at ROTHERHAM.

Rother[4] From ROTHER[2].

A council district in East Sussex, about 520 sq km (200 sq miles) in extent, covering the southeastern corner of the county. Its administrative centre is BEXHILL. The council's website proclaims it the 'heart of historic 1066 country'.

Rotherbridge 'cattle bridge', OE *hryther* 'cattle' + *brycg* 'bridge'.

A hamlet in West Sussex, on the River ROTHER[1], about 2 km (1.2 miles) southwest of Petworth.

Rotherfield 'open land where cattle graze', OE *hryther* 'cattle' + *feld* (*see* FIELD).

A village in East Sussex, about 3 km (2 miles) east of Crowborough. Its large church, St Denys, has the remains of medieval mural paintings.

Rotherfield Greys *Greys* denoting manorial ownership in the Middle Ages by the de Gray family (the same family as owned the nearby GREYS GREEN).

A village in Oxfordshire, in the CHILTERN HILLS, about 4 km (2.5 miles) west of Henley-on-Thames. In the area is Greys Court, a fine Jacobean house with traces of a 14th-century predecessor.

Rotherfield Peppard *Peppard* denoting manorial ownership in the Middle Ages by the Pipard family.

A village in Oxfordshire, in the CHILTERN HILLS, about 5 km (3 miles) west of Henley-on-Thames.

Rotherham 'homestead on the River Rother', OCelt river name meaning 'chief river' + OE HAM.

An industrial town at the confluence of the DON[2] and the ROTHER[3] in South Yorkshire, 9 km (5.5 miles) northeast of Sheffield. The old **Rotherham Bridge** has one of the four surviving bridge chapels in England, dating from 1483. The town expanded considerably after the building of ironworks here in 1746.

Rotherham was the birthplace of the poet, Chartist and master-founder Ebenezer Elliott (1781–1849), known as the Corn Law Rhymer; of Sir Donald Bailey (1901–85), inventor of the Bailey bridge; and of the Arsenal, Manchester City and England goalkeeper David Seaman (b.1963).

Rotherham United FC, nicknamed the Merry Millers (after their Millmoor ground), was founded in 1870.

Rotherham plough. An improved form of plough, introduced from the Netherlands in the mid-18th century. The connection with the town is unclear.

Rotherhithe 'landing-place for cattle' (referring to a harbour from which cattle were shipped across the Thames for the market at Smithfield), OE *hryther* 'cattle' + *hyth* 'landing-place'.

A district of southeast London (SE16), on the south bank of the River Thames, in the borough of SOUTHWARK, between BERMONDSEY to the west and DEPTFORD to the southeast. It lies on a peninsula formed by a northward loop of the Thames, opposite WAPPING and LIMEHOUSE (Rotherhithe Street, which follows the peninsula's shoreline, is the longest street in London). From its beginnings it was a maritime settlement, looking towards the sea, its population a mélange of mariners, shipbuilders, dockers, smugglers, etc. London's first enclosed wet docks, the Howland, were built here in 1699, and Jonathan Swift made Rotherhithe the birthplace of his voyager Lemuel Gulliver. For over 150 years much of the eastern side of the area was covered by the Surrey Docks (*see under* SURREY). They were closed in 1970, and Rotherhithe has been extensively redeveloped since then.

Over a lengthy and often interrupted period up to the early 1840s Marc Isambard Brunel drove a tunnel between Rotherhithe and Wapping, the first to be constructed under the Thames (*see* Thames Tunnel *under* THAMES[1]). It now carries the East London line (*see under* EAST LONDON), and Rotherhithe Underground station, opened in 1884, is the first station south of the tunnel. In the first decade of the 20th century the **Rotherhithe Tunnel** was built, a single-bore road tunnel linking Rotherhithe and RATCLIFF, just downstream of the Thames Tunnel.

Over the centuries the pronunciation of *Rotherhithe* became eroded to 'redrif', and the name was conventionally spelt *Redriffe*:

> So walked to Redriffe, where I hear the sickness is, and indeed is scattered almost everywhere – there dying 1089 of the plague this week.
>
> Samuel Pepys: diary (20 July 1665)

The historical spelling has long since reasserted its sway over the pronunciation, but a reminder of the old way survives in the local street name Redriff Road.

Rothes Gaelic *ràth* 'ring-fort' (*see* RATH).
A small town and former BURGH on the River SPEY in Moray (formerly in Grampian region), 15 km (9 miles) southeast of Elgin. There are the scant remains of a medieval castle, but the town itself was established in the later 18th century. It is home to five whisky distilleries: Glen Grant, Glenrothes, Glen Spey, Speyburn and Capperdonich.

Rothesay 'Rother's island', male personal name *Roderick* + OScand *ey* (*see* -AY). The Roderick referred to in the name was the son of Reginald, to whom the island was granted in the 13th century. Its Gaelic name is *Baile Bhóid*, Gaelic *baile* 'settlement' + *Bhóid* 'Bute'.
A popular resort town, the main port and largest settlement on the island of BUTE, in the Firth of Clyde, Argyll and Bute (*see under* CLYDE). It is situated halfway up the east coast of the island, and was the county town of the old county of Buteshire, and from 1975 to 1996 was in Strathclyde region. **Rothesay Castle** goes back to at least the 13th century, when it was taken by Norsemen. In the later Middle Ages it was a royal residence (Robert III died here in 1406). During the Monmouth Rebellion of 1685 it was burnt down by the Duke of Argyll, but restoration work has subsequently been carried out. Argyll's men also burnt the town, but in the following century John Stuart, 3rd Earl of Bute (prime minister in 1762–3), rebuilt the town and encouraged industry. The first cotton mills in Scotland were built here. Rothesay has been a popular holiday destination for Glaswegians since the 19th century, although not all the facilities on offer are of the five-star variety:

> In search of lodgins we did slide,
> To find a place where we could bide,
> There was eighty-twa o' us inside
> In a single room in Rothesay, O.
>
> We a' lay doon tae tak our ease,

> When somebody happened for tae sneeze –
> An' he wakened hauf a million fleas
> In a single room in Rothesay, O.
>
> Anon.: 'The Day We Went to Rothesay, O'

There are towns called Rothesay in Australia (Victoria) and Canada (New Brunswick).

Duke of Rothesay. A title first given by Robert III to his eldest son, David, in 1398. This first Duke of Rothesay ruled in his father's stead from 1399 to 1402, when he was seized by his uncle, the Duke of Albany (*see under* ALBANY[1]), and died in the dungeons of Albany's castle at FALKLAND. His title survived, however, and is still the premier Scottish title borne by the Prince of Wales.

Rothesay (or **Rossy**) **docks.** Glaswegian rhyming slang for 'socks'.

Rothesay herald. One of the heralds in the Lyon Court (the Scottish Court of Heralds).

Rothiemurchus 'fort of Muirgus', Gaelic *ràth* (*see* RATH) + personal name *Muirgus*.
An area on the northern side of the CAIRNGORM MOUNTAINS, in Highland (formerly in Inverness-shire), some 5 km (3 miles) southeast of Aviemore. Its pronunciation is 'rothy-murchəs' ('ch' as in 'loch'). It is largely covered in Old Caledonian Forest (*see under* CALEDONIA), and the beauty of the place led John Buchan to write of the Scottish soldier in Iraq who described his camp as being 'twa miles on the Rothiemurchus side of Baghdad'.

The land has been in the possession of the Grants of Rothiemurchus for over 400 years. Elizabeth Grant of Rothiemurchus (1797–1886) was the author of the classic and witty *Memoirs of a Highland Lady* (posthumously published in 1898), and Rothiemurchus was the birthplace of Duncan Grant (1885–1978), the Post-Impressionist painter and member of the Bloomsbury circle.

'Rothemurche's Rant'. A traditional Scottish tune, for which Robert Burns wrote the words 'Fairest Maid on Devon Banks' (*see under* DEVON[2]).

Rothschild Row. A nickname (modelled on ROTTEN ROW) given in the late 19th and early 20th centuries to the western end of PICCADILLY[1], opposite GREEN PARK, on account of the large number of members of the Rothschild banking family who lived here then.

Rothwell[1] 'spring or stream by the clearing(s)', OE *roth* 'clearing' + *wella* 'spring, stream'.
A town in Northamptonshire, about 5 km (3 miles) northwest of Kettering. In the Middle Ages it was the second largest town in the county after Northampton, and it has the longest church.

Rothwell[2]. A town in West Yorkshire, 8 km (5 miles) southeast of Leeds.

Rotten Row Origin uncertain: the name is recorded as a medieval street name elsewhere in England, the first element apparently from ME *ratoun* 'rat', and denoting a rat-infested street; it may have been re-applied facetiously here, with a play on *rotten* alluding to the softness or looseness of the soil, suitable for horses and carriages. It is unlikely to be, as is often claimed, a direct alteration of *Route du Roi*, although that may have played some part in the pun.

A riding and carriage road in HYDE PARK, leading westwards from Hyde Park Corner to Kensington Gardens (*see under* KENSINGTON). It was once referred to as *Route du Roi* 'King's Route', alluding to its use by William III for riding across the park from ST JAMES'S to Kensington Palace. He had 300 lamps hung from the trees that lined it, creating the first road in England to be lit at night.

By the 19th century it was *the* quizzing ground of London high society: here Regency damsels would drive in their carriages, chaperoned by dowager dragons as hussars and grenadiers rode in attendance. For habitués it was now simply 'the Row'. The *haut monde* has long since taken itself off elsewhere, but horsemen and horsewomen continue to avail themselves of Rotten Row's compliant surface.

Rotten Row acquired the alternative name of **the Ladies' Mile**, which was first recorded in Mary Elizabeth Braddon's novel *Lady's Mile* (1866).

There is a similar riding-path in the northwestern part of Hampstead Heath (*see under* HAMPSTEAD) called Rotten Row, after the one in Hyde Park.

In its time *rotten row* has served as rhyming slang for both *bow* and *blow*.

Rottingdean Probably 'Rota's people's valley', OE male personal name *Rota* + -*inga*- (*see* -ING) + *denu* 'valley'.
A village on the East Sussex coast, about 8 km (5 miles) east of Brighton, and within the unitary authority of Brighton and Hove. It has a 13th-century church with stained glass by Edward Burne-Jones, who lived in the village, and a picturesque green and duck pond. Rudyard Kipling lived from 1897 to 1902 in a house, 'The Elms', overlooking the green, where he wrote *Stalky & Co* (1899), *Kim* (1901) and *Just So Stories* (1902).

The windmill on the outskirts of the village, on the SOUTH DOWNS, was the basis of the design for the colophon of the publishers William Heinemann.

Rough Castle Etymology unclear, but OE *ruh* 'rough (land)' is a possibility.
The remains of a large Roman fort on the ANTONINE WALL, some 4 km (2.5 miles) west of Falkirk. It was formerly in Stirlingshire, then in Central region, and is now in the unitary authority of Falkirk.

Roughley Probably 'rough clearing', OE *ruh* 'rough' + -LEY.
A northern suburb of SUTTON COLDFIELD, in the West Midlands.

Rough Tor[1] 'rough crag', OE *ruh* 'rough' + *torr* 'crag'.
A rocky hill on Bodmin Moor (*see under* BODMIN), 400 m (1312 ft) high, about 3 km (2 miles) northwest of BROWN WILLY.

Rough Tor[2]. A rocky hill in the middle of DARTMOOR, 546 m (1791 ft) high, about 6 km (4 miles) north of PRINCETOWN[1].

Roundway '(place by the) cleared way', OE *rymed* 'cleared' + *weg* 'way'.
A village in Wiltshire, about 3 km (2 miles) north of Devizes. **Battle of Roundway Down** (13 July 1643). A battle of the Civil Wars, fought on an area of rolling chalk downland to the north of Roundway, in which a Royalist army under Lord Wilmot defeated a Parliamentarian force under Sir William Waller.

Rousay 'Hrolf's island', OScand personal name *Hrolf* + *ey* (*see* -AY).
A hilly island in ORKNEY, 1 km (0.6 miles) across EYNHALLOW Sound from the northern part of Mainland. The island is noted for its prehistoric monuments, such as a number of brochs (circular dry-stone towers), and the burial cairns at Taversoe Tuick, Blackhammer, Knowe of Yarso and, largest of all, Midhowe. The Neolithic village at Rinyo (*c.*3700 BC) has given its name to the Rinyo-Clacton culture, represented by late Neolithic grooved ware found at the site, and at CLACTON-ON-SEA in Essex (as well as other places throughout Britain).

Rousham 'homestead of Hrothwulf', OE male personal name *Hrothwulf* + HAM.
An estate and house in Oxfordshire, 9 km (6 miles) west of Bicester. **Rousham House**, built around 1635 for Sir Robert Dormer, was redesigned in the 18th century by William Kent, who also laid out a celebrated landscape garden here (1738–40). The garden (picturesque in its 18th-century aesthetic sense) is a perfect example of the first phase of English landscaping and the only complete extant example of Kent's work as garden designer. Using the natural elements of the terrain, it features cascades, ponds, temples, a seven-arched portico above a bend in the River CHERWELL, and a touching memorial to 'Ringwood: an otter-hound of extraordinary sagacity'. The **Rousham Eyecatcher** is a sham ruin on the skyline opposite the house on the other side of the Cherwell.

Rous Lench *Rous* denoting manorial ownership in the Middle Ages by the Rous family; *Lench see* ATCH LENCH. (In the early Middle Ages the village was called *Bishop's Lench*, the manor being owned by the bishops of Worcester.)
A village in Worcestershire (before 1998 in Hereford and Worcester, before 1974 in Worcestershire), about 13 km (8 miles) north of Evesham.
See also CHURCH LENCH.

Rowardennan 'promontory of the hill of Eunan', Gaelic *rudha* 'promontory' + ARD + *Eonain* 'of Eunan'.

A small settlement on the east bank of LOCH LOMOND, in Stirling unitary authority, 3 km (2 miles) southwest of BEN LOMOND. The youth hostel is popular with those walking the West Highland Way.

Rowland's Castle Originally *Rolok's Castle*, OFr male personal name *Rolok* + ME *castel* (*see* CASTLE). The present-day version, first recorded in the 1360s, probably reflects a (would-be) association with Roland, one of Charlemagne's Paladins and a popular hero of medieval romance.

A village in Hampshire, about 5 km (3 miles) north of Havant. It has a station on the main railway line from London to Portsmouth.

Rowley Regis *Rowley* 'rough glade', OE *ruh* 'rough' + -LEY; *Regis* 'of the king' (denoting manorial ownership by the Crown in the early Middle Ages), Latin.

A district within the metropolitan borough of SANDWELL, to the west of Birmingham. It was one of the three boroughs joined together in 1966 to form WARLEY.

Roxburgh 'Hroc's fortified dwelling', *burgh* (*see* BURY) + OE personal name *Hroc* (meaning 'rook').

A small village 5 km (3 miles) southwest of Kelso, in the BORDERS (formerly in Roxburghshire), and the name of a local authority district between 1975 and 1996. The present village is some distance from the medieval royal BURGH of Roxburgh, which was a town of considerable importance in the Middle Ages, when, along with Edinburgh, Stirling and Berwick, Roxburgh formed the Court of the Four Burghs. At one point Roxburgh grew so large that some of the inhabitants were moved to the site of the present village.

The old royal burgh was dominated by **Roxburgh Castle**, a royal residence in the 13th century. Being situated near the Tweed and the English border, the castle was of considerable strategic importance. In 1313 Sir James Douglas (the Black Douglas) recaptured it from the English, having disguised his men as black cattle as they approached the walls. There is a story that just as the Black Douglas silently mounted the battlements an English mother was singing to her baby:

Hush ye, hush ye, little pet, ye,
The Black Douglas shall not get ye.

This turned out to be true, after a fashion, as Douglas spared both woman and child. However, in 1334 the castle returned to English hands, and it was not until the siege of 1460 – in which James II was killed when one of his cannons blew up – that the castle was retaken. This time the Scots levelled both castle and town.

There is a Roxburgh hydroelectric project in New Zealand (South Island).

Roxburghshire. A former county in southeast Scotland, bounded on the north by Selkirkshire, Midlothian and Berwickshire, on the east and south by the English county of Northumberland, and on the west by Dumfriesshire. It was abolished in 1975, becoming part of Borders region (*see under* the BORDERS), and, with some adjustments, became Roxburgh district until that too was abolished in 1996. It is now part of SCOTTISH BORDERS.

Royal Borough. A designation accorded to three English boroughs with royal connections, historically denoting that they have no overlord but the sovereign. They are: KENSINGTON (since 1965, KENSINGTON AND CHELSEA); KINGSTON UPON THAMES; and WINDSOR (since 1974, WINDSOR AND MAIDENHEAD). The last two are ancient: Kingston, the oldest, belonged to the Crown in Anglo-Saxon times. Kensington is much more recent (the status was granted by Edward VII in 1901, in recognition of the fact that Queen Victoria had been born and lived as a child in Kensington Palace), but, as is the way with parvenus, is much more likely than the other two to refer to itself openly as 'the Royal Borough'.

Other places have enjoyed the same status, including DORCHESTER[1], DUNSTABLE, SOUTHAMPTON and WARWICK.

Royal British Legion Village From its being established in 1921 as a rehabilitation centre by the *British Legion*, a British ex-service organization.

A village in Kent, about 4 km (2.5 miles) northwest of Maidstone. It was originally **British Legion Village**, and when the Legion was granted the right to add 'Royal' to its name in 1971, the village followed suit.

Royal burgh. *See* BURGH.

Royal Canal. A canal extending westwards from DUBLIN via MULLINGAR to the River SHANNON west of LONGFORD. It was planned as a northerly rival to the GRAND CANAL. Work began in 1790 and was completed in 1817, the total cost being a staggering £1,421,954. The town of Longford was linked to the main canal by a branch in 1830. The canal declined in importance after the coming of the railways, but since the 1980s there has been a programme of restoration for leisure users.

In the autumn of 1843 the Royal Canal witnessed a breakthrough that was to have a profound impact on modern science, for it was while walking by the canal with his wife that the mathematician and astronomer William Rowan Hamilton came up with the equation that was to form the basis of his theory of quaternions, a theory that allowed for the later development of quantum mechanics and nuclear physics. So anxious was Hamilton not to forget his inspiration that he scratched the equation on the parapet of Broom Bridge with his penknife.

Royal County, the. A nickname for County MEATH, deriving from the fact that TARA, seat of the ancient high kings, is in the county. The nickname is mostly used in association with the Gaelic football championship.

Royal Crescent. A road consisting of an arc of 30 terraced houses built in 1767 in the Palladian style, to the design of John Wood, which is the crowning architectural glory of Georgian BATH. It is one of the earliest and finest examples of its type in Europe. The houses are at the northern end of the Crescent only; to the south, lawns fall away down the hill, affording a magnificent vista both of and from the buildings.

Royal Dock. *See under* DEPTFORD.

Royal Docks. The collective name (officially **Royal Group of Docks**) given to a set of London docks built on the north bank of the River Thames, downstream of the ISLE OF DOGS, in what is now the borough of NEWHAM, and named after members of the British royal family. They were the last to be built in London, and at 99 ha (245 acres) covered the largest area of enclosed water of any docks in the world. The first of them to be constructed was the **Royal Victoria** (1855). This was followed by the **Royal Albert** (said to be the largest brick structure in the world), an eastward extension of the Royal Victoria, opened in 1880. Last came the **King George V**, completed in 1921. All closed in the 1970s. The runway of London City Airport (*see under* LONDON) was built on the narrow corridor of land that separates the Royal Albert from the King George V.

Royal Leamington Spa. *See* LEAMINGTON SPA.

Royal Mile, the. The long, relatively narrow road in the Old Town of EDINBURGH that runs from Edinburgh Castle down the crest of Castle Hill to the royal palace of Holyroodhouse (*see under* HOLYROOD). It incorporates sections of street officially called Castle Hill, Lawnmarket, High Street and Canongate, and is lined, for the most part, by tall tenements, broken by narrow alleys known as wynds, leading into courtyards. Among the many fine old buildings are John Knox's House, the High Kirk of St Giles, Parliament House (home of the old Scottish Parliament and of the present-day high court), the City Chambers, the Tron Kirk, Moray House and Canongate Church. The name 'Royal Mile' is first recorded in W.M. Gilbert's *Edinburgh in the Nineteenth Century* (1901), in which it appears in inverted commas, and was further popularized as the title of a 1920 guidebook by Robert T. Skinner. Be that as it may, Tobias Smollett in 1766 thought the street 'the hot-bed of genius' – it was here he met the leading figures of the Scottish Enlightenment, such as Adam Ferguson and David Hume.

Royal Military Canal. A canal in Kent and East Sussex built by the British government in the first decade of the 19th century in response to the threat of invasion during the Napoleonic Wars. It runs 31 km (19 miles) from HYTHE to RYE. It has regular dog-legs at which cannons would have been positioned, and the idea was that it would contain any troops that landed on the Kent coast. In the event the invasion threat faded, and it was never tested in the heat of battle. It fell into disuse in the early part of the 20th century, but it has recently been restored.

Royal Oak From the local Underground station, which in turn was named after a former inn, long since demolished.

A district of West Central London (W2), in the City of WESTMINSTER, just to the west of PADDINGTON station and close to the WESTWAY (A40(M)). It took its name from the Underground station, on the Hammersmith & City line, which opened here in 1871.

Royal Tunbridge Wells. *See* TUNBRIDGE WELLS.

Roy Bridge. *See under* GLEN ROY.

Royston[1] Originally (in the 12th century) called *Crux Roaisie* 'Rohesia's cross', female personal name *Rohesia* + Latin *crux* 'cross'. That became reduced to *Cruceroys* and eventually to simply *Roys*, and in the 13th century the suffix -TON was added. A town in Hertfordshire, about 21 km (13 miles) southwest of Cambridge. It grew up at the crossroads of the prehistoric ICKNIELD WAY and the Roman ERMINE STREET. A stone cross erected here by a woman called Rohesia gave the town its name. It is not certain who she was, but legend identifies her as the daughter of Henry I's Great Chamberlain Aubrey de Vere (d.1141) and wife of Geoffrey Mandeville, Earl of Essex (d.1144).

Royston's quadrivial position (today, on the A10 and the A505) has brought it business and prosperity – there are some fine Georgian houses and inns – but things are somewhat quieter now that the M11 bypasses it to the east. James VI and I had a palace here in the early 17th century. There is a town called Royston in Georgia, USA.

Royston crow. An alternative name in former times for the hooded crow (*Corvus cornix*).

Royston[2] 'Hror's or Roarr's farm', OE or OScand male personal name *Hror* or *Roarr* + -TON; *Rorestone* 1086. A former mining town in South Yorkshire, 5 km (3 miles) north of Barnsley.

Royston Vasey The real name of the English comedian Roy 'Chubby' Brown, who appeared as the foul-mouthed Mayor Vaughan in early episodes of the BBC radio programme. A fictional bleak northern town in which the surreal BBC radio comedy programme *The League of Gentlemen* (transferred to television in 1999) was set. Most of its inhabitants are barking mad in a distinctly sinister way. Its motto is 'You'll Never Leave'. In the television version it was played by the Derbyshire town of Hadfield, just to the northwest of GLOSSOP.

Royton 'rye farm', OE *ryge* 'rye' + -TON.

A town in Greater Manchester, on the north side of Oldham.

Ruan Lanihorne *Ruan* after the patron saint of the parish, St Ruan or Rumon (a Cornish saint of mysterious identity); *Lanihorne* the name of the local manor, 'Rihoarn's church-site', Cornish *lann* 'church-site' + personal name *Rihoarn*.

A village in Cornwall, on the River FAL, in the ROSELAND peninsula about 8 km (5 miles) southeast of Truro. Now decidedly off the beaten track, it used to lie on the main London–Penzance coach road.

Rubha Coigeach. *See under* COIGACH.

Rudyard Probably 'yard or enclosure where rue is grown', OE *rude* 'rue' + *geard* 'yard, enclosure'.

A village in Staffordshire, about 3 km (2 miles) northwest of Leek. To the northwest is **Rudyard Lake**, favoured by yachtsmen and windsurfers.

John Lockwood Kipling met his future wife, Alice, at a picnic organized by their employers on the shore of the lake, and they named their son (1865–1936) after the place. Funambulist *extraordinaire* Charles Blondin (1824–97) crossed the lake on a rope suspended 30 m (100 ft) above it.

Rugby Originally *Rocheberie*, probably 'Hroca's fortified place', OE male personal name *Hroca* + *byrig* dative form of *burh* 'fortified place' (*see* BURY); by the 13th century the original suffix had been replaced by the Scandinavian -BY. Alternatively the first element of the name may be from OE *hroc* 'rook'.

A market town in Warwickshire, close to the River AVON[1] and just to the west of the M1, about 17 km (11 miles) southeast of Coventry. It is an important railway junction, and came to prosperity in the 19th century on the back of the railways and engineering.

Rugby School, a (now) coeducational public school, was founded in 1567, but it really came to prominence during the reign of Dr Thomas Arnold, headmaster from 1828 to 1842. He had some revolutionary views on educational theory and practice (including the inculcation of the idea of the Christian gentleman and the importance of physical vigour, a combination that came to be known as 'muscular Christianity'), and he used Rugby as a test-bed for them. They became the cornerstone of British upper-class and upper-middle-class education for the next century and a half. The school also gave its name to **Rugby football** (*see below*).

Old Rugbeians (*see below*) include the poet and essayist Walter Savage Landor (1775–1864), the novelist Thomas Hughes (1822–96), the poet and critic Matthew Arnold (1822–88), son of Thomas Arnold, the children's writer Lewis Carroll (C.L. Dodgson; 1832–98), the novelist and critic Percy Wyndham Lewis (1882–1957) and the poet Rupert Brooke (1887–1915).

Thomas Hughes did more than most to evangelize the ethos of the Victorian public school in his book *Tom Brown's Schooldays* (1857), set in (a somewhat romanticized version of) his old school. In 1880 Hughes launched a utopian community in Tennessee, USA, which he called 'Rugby'. It was intended as a place where young English gentlemen could escape industrial Britain and work the land.

Rupert Brooke (*see* GRANTCHESTER) was also born in Rugby, as was the novelist and essayist Rose Macaulay (1881–1958). The fathers of both were masters at Rugby School.

There is also a town called Rugby in North Dakota, USA.

Rugbeian. A present or (**Old Rugbeian**) former pupil of Rugby School. In the 19th century the word was often spelt (with due deference to Latin) *Rugbæan*. The colloquial abbreviation is *Rug*.

Rugby fives. A form of fives (a court game involving hitting a small ball with the hand against a wall) developed at Rugby School, played in a four-walled court much like a squash court, and thus different from that of ETON and WINCHESTER fives.

Rugby football. A type of football (now commonly known simply as **rugby**) played with an oval ball and involving handling as well as kicking. There are two codes: **rugby union**, a 15-a-side game, which until the late 20th century was exclusively amateur; and **rugby league**, a 13-a-side game which has always been played professionally (*see under* HUDDERSFIELD). The game takes its name from Rugby School, and the story of how it began there is now well known: in 1823, during an ordinary game of football at the school, a boy called William Webb Ellis (after whom the trophy now played for in the Rugby Union World Cup competition is named) reputedly caught the ball or picked it up and started to run with it, against the rules though that was. It has now been demonstrated fairly conclusively that whatever it was that Ellis did, it did not precipitate the fully fledged emergence of Rugby football (carrying the ball seems still to have been technically forbidden at Rugby in 1828, three years after he left the school); but it is reasonably clear that handling and running with the ball had become a feature of football at Rugby by the 1830s. The new game's rules were officially codified in 1846.

The game is known, affectionately if old-fashionedly, as **rugger**, its (presumed to be) hearty exponents sometimes disparagingly called **rugger buggers**.

Rugeley 'glade on or near a ridge', OE *hrycg* 'ridge' + -LEY.

A market town (pronounced 'roodge-li' or, by local people in former times, 'ridge-li') in Staffordshire, near the northeastern edge of CANNOCK Chase, on the Trent and Mersey Canal (*see under* TRENT[1]), about 13 km (8 miles) southeast of Stafford. It was once a centre of a local mining industry (Lea Hall colliery, a large pit sunk as recently as the early 1960s, was closed in 1990).

Rugeley achieved a certain notoriety in the mid-19th century as the home town of the homicidal surgeon William Palmer (b.1824). He is said to have poisoned at least seven people, including his own brother. He was hanged in 1856. Palmer is the eponymous subject of Robert Graves's novel *They Hanged My Saintly Billy* (1957).

Ruislip Probably 'leaping-place where rushes grow' (referring to a point on the River Pinn where it was possible to jump across), OE *rysc* 'rush' + *hlyp* 'leaping-place'.

A residential district (pronounced 'rye-slip') of northwest London, in the borough of HILLINGDON (before 1965 in Middlesex), to the southwest of Pinner. It was largely rural until the railway and the Underground arrived at the beginning of the 20th century (on the Metropolitan and Piccadilly lines, Ruislip station opened in 1904 and Ruislip Manor in 1912; on the Central line, West Ruislip (a western terminus of the line) and Ruislip Gardens opened in 1948).

> Gaily into Ruislip Gardens
> Runs the red electric train,
> With a thousand Ta's and Pardon's
> Daintily alights Elaine.
>
> John Betjeman: 'Middlesex' (1954)

The locality is now probably best known for **Ruislip Lido**. Constructed in 1811 as a feeder for the Grand Junction Canal (now part of the GRAND UNION CANAL), it is now a boating lake and general outdoor leisure facility.

Ruislip leapt to unexpected prominence during the Cold War when an unassuming suburban bungalow here, hitherto believed to be the premises of a modest second-hand book business, was revealed to be a centre of Soviet espionage. Canadian-born spies Helen and Peter Kroger (real names Leoninta and Morris Cohen) operated a sophisticated radio station from the house, passing important defence information to Moscow (*see also* the Portland spies *under* PORTLAND). They were arrested, charged with espionage, and sentenced to 20 years' imprisonment in March 1961. They were released in 1969 in exchange for the British university lecturer Gerald Brooke, who had been imprisoned for spying in Moscow. The episode inspired Hugh Whitemore's successful play *A Pack of Lies* (1983).

The poet-scholar Peter Levi (1931–2000) was born here. *Tropic of Ruislip*. A novel (1974) by Leslie Thomas examining the fears, frustrations and lusts of a group of well-heeled executives on a luxury housing estate in Ruislip as they contemplate the approach of middle age.

Rullion Green The place was also once known as *Yorling's Green*: the name might represent OE, ME *æt thære Eorlinges grene* '(at) the green of a man called Erling', with the *-r-* of the definite article becoming attached to the personal name.

A slope below Turnhouse Hill, on the south side of the PENTLAND HILLS, 12 km (7.5 miles) south of Edinburgh, in Midlothian. It was the site of a battle in 1666 in which 'Bloody Tam' Dalyell (*see under* BINNS) led the Royalist forces to victory over the Covenanters.

> ... about the graves of the martyrs the whaups are
> crying ...
>
> Robert Louis Stevenson: 'To S.R. Crockett' ('Hills of Home')

Rum The name may be pre-Celtic and cognate with the word 'rhombus', i.e. lozenge-shaped; but it has clearly been interpreted historically as Gaelic and OScand *rum* meaning 'spacious (island)'. Some of the early spellings include OScand *ey* 'island' (*see* -AY).

An island of the Inner Hebrides, the largest of the SMALL ISLES, in Highland (formerly in Inverness-shire). It is 25 km (16 miles) west of Mallaig, and is separated from Eigg by the **Sound of Rum**. The mountains in the south of the island, collectively called the CUILLIN (like those on nearby Skye), mostly have Norse names, such as ASKIVAL.

In *The Lord of the Isles* (1815) Sir Walter Scott refers to the island as **Ronin**, explaining in a note that Rum is 'a name which a poet may be pardoned for avoiding, if possible' (modern opinion would veer to the position that no such pardon should be forthcoming).

Another equally unforgivable version of the name is the inauthentic **Rhum**, the spelling adopted by a previous owner, Sir George Bullough, and long perpetuated on maps. Bullough's father, John Bullough MP, a Lancashire industrialist, had bought the island in 1888 and turned it into a sporting estate. His son built the extravagant, luxurious and architecturally inappropriate Kinloch Castle (1900–2), and was also responsible for the equally inappropriate Bullough Mausoleum, a pseudo-Greek temple jarringly sited in the wilds of Glen Harris. This replaced John Bullough's previous resting place, a vault that a friend had described to Sir George as 'a public lavatory on the London Underground'. Sir George took this criticism to heart and blew it up. The Mausoleum now houses the remains not only of John Bullough but also of Sir George and his widow, who sold the island to the government in 1957.

The Nature Conservancy Council established Rum as a National Nature Reserve, and this is now run by Scottish Natural Heritage. Visitor access is strictly limited. Among the achievements of the naturalists here is the discovery that red deer can turn carnivore when faced with a tempting seabird chick. Another success has been the reintroduction to Scotland from Norway of the white-tailed sea eagle. Rum has the world's first wind-powered telephone exchange.

Rumbling Bridge. A village on the River DEVON[2], in Perth and Kinross, 6 km (4 miles) east of Dollar. It was formerly on the Tayside–Central boundary, and before that in Kinross-shire. It derives its name from the bridges (1713 and 1816) over the spectacular gorge, where the river makes a rumbling noise when in spate.

Rummidge An alteration of BRUMMAGEM.

A fictionalized version of BIRMINGHAM, and particularly of its university, which appears in the comic novels – notably *Changing Places* (1975) and its sequel *Small World* (1984) – of David Lodge (b.1935), former (now Emeritus) Professor of Modern English Literature at Birmingham University.

> Perhaps I should explain, for people who have not been there before, that Rummidge is an imaginary city, with imaginary universities and imaginary factories, inhabited by imaginary people, which occupies, for the purposes of fiction, the space where Birmingham is to be found on maps of the so-called real world.
>
> David Lodge: *Nice Work* (1988)

Rumps Point From the appearance of the headland.

A headland on the North Cornish coast, at the western end of Port Quin Bay, just to the north of the mouth of the River CAMEL.

Rumney. *See* RHYMNEY.

Runcorn 'wide bay or creek' (alluding to a former wide bay on the southern bank of the MERSEY), OE *rum* 'wide, spacious' + *cofa* 'bay, creek'.

An industrial town in the unitary authority of HALTON, within the county of Cheshire, on the south bank of the River Mersey, opposite WIDNES (to which it is linked by road and rail bridges).

The Manchester Ship Canal (*see under* MANCHESTER) and the BRIDGEWATER CANAL reach the Mersey at Runcorn. The River WEAVER also joins the Mersey here.

Runcorn was designated a NEW TOWN[1] in 1964. Its main business is chemicals:

> A wind ...
> ... blowing the chemical
> Reek out of Runcorn ...
>
> Donald Davie: 'A Liverpool Epistle', from
> *The Battered Wife & Other Poems* (1982)

There is an anonymous 1950s parody of the song 'Galway Bay', entitled 'Ditton Bay', that goes:

> If you ever go across the bridge to Runcorn,
> Then maybe at the closing of your day
> You will sit and watch the moon rise over Ditton
> And see the sun go down on Widnes Bay.

Another verse begins:

> For the breezes blowing o'er the track from Widnes
> Are perfumed by ICI's as they blow ...

(For the original, *see under* GALWAY.) ICI received its largest-ever fine in March 1998, after 150 tonnes of toxic chloroform gushed out of a pipe at its site at Runcorn, polluting groundwater for decades.

The popular novelist Hall Caine (1853–1931) was born in Runcorn.

Runnel Stone *Runnel* 'tidal stream, current', OE *rynel*.

A rocky islet about 1 km (0.6 miles) off GWENNAP HEAD, at the southern extremity of the LAND'S END peninsula.

Runnymede 'meadow at the island where councils are held', OE *run* 'council' + *eg* (*see* -EY, -EA) + *mæd* 'meadow'. (The locality is closely associated with horse racing, which led to the erroneous interpretation of the name as 'running meadow'.)

An area of meadowland on the south bank of the River THAMES[1], near EGHAM in Surrey, just to the west of the M25. As the history of its name indicates, its use as a meeting-place for deliberative assemblies dates back to Anglo-Saxon times, but its place in the annals of Britain was firmly secured in 1215 when it was the scene of the confrontation between King John and his barons, which culminated on 15 June in the king putting his seal to the Magna Carta, a charter defining and circumscribing royal powers and (at least as viewed in several centuries' retrospect) securing the political rights of the English people.

> Thou, who the verdant plain dost traverse here
> While Thames among his willows from thy view
> Retires; O stranger, stay thee, and the scene
> Around contemplate well. This is the place
> Where England's ancient barons, clad in arms
> And stern with conquest, from their tyrant king
> (Then rendered tame) did challenge and secure
> The charter of thy freedom.
>
> Mark Akenside: 'For a Column at Runnymede' (1758)

> And still when Mob or Monarch lays
> Too rude a hand on English ways,
> The whisper wakes, the shudder plays
> Across the reeds at Runnymede.
>
> Rudyard Kipling: 'The Reeds of Runnymede' (1911)

Since 1931 Runnymede has been owned by the National Trust. There is a memorial to US president J.F. Kennedy here and (on nearby Cooper's Hill) another to Commonwealth airmen who died in the Second World War. On the opposite bank of the Thames from Runnymede lies the archaeological site of Ankerwycke, acquired by the National Trust in 1998 and containing the remains of the 12th-century St Mary's Priory and the Ankerwycke Yew, a tree believed to be over 2000 years old.

Benjamin Disraeli signed his *Letters to Statesmen* (1836–9) with the pen name 'Runnymede'.

Runnymede Trust. An independent trust set up in 1968 as a think-tank on ethnicity and cultural diversity in Britain.

Rúscaigh. The Irish name for ROOSKY.

Rush Irish *An Ros* 'the promontory'.

A seaside resort and fishing port in County Dublin, 25 km (16 miles) north of Dublin itself.

Rushcliffe From the name of a former wapentake (administrative division of a shire) in the locality, 'slope where brushwood grows', OE *hris* 'brushwood, shrubs' + *clif* 'cliff, slope'.

An administrative district covering about 407 sq km (157 sq miles) of southeastern Nottinghamshire. Its administrative headquarters are in WEST BRIDGFORD, a leafy suburb of Nottingham, which is its largest centre of population.

The area's MP since 1970 has been the Conservative former cabinet minister and almost Party leader Kenneth Clarke.

Rushden 'valley where rushes grow', OE *ryscen* 'rushy' + *denu* 'valley'.

A town in Northamptonshire, close to the River NENE, about 8 km (5 miles) east of Wellingborough.

The football club **Rushden and Diamonds** was formed in 1992 from Rushden Town and Irthlingborough Diamonds. Its home ground is in IRTHLINGBOROUGH.

The writer H.E. Bates (1905–74), author of *The Darling Buds of May* (1958), was born in Rushden.

Ruskin's View. *See under* KIRKBY LONSDALE.

Russell Square From *Russell* the family name of the Dukes of Bedford, on whose estate the square was built.

A square in Central London (WC1), in BLOOMSBURY, just to the north of the British Museum. Laid out in 1800 by Humphry Repton, it is the second largest square in London (the largest is LINCOLN'S INN FIELDS). It was badly damaged in the Second World War. Many of its buildings are now occupied by departments of London University. Between 1925 and 1965 the publishers Faber & Faber had their offices here.

Russell Square Underground station, on the Piccadilly line, opened in 1906.

Rutherglen Possibly 'red glen', Gaelic *ruadh* 'red' + *gleann* (*see* GLEN).

An area of southeast Glasgow, formerly a royal BURGH in its own right – indeed, the oldest in Scotland (1126), leading the novelist John Galt to write of:

> The pure and immaculate royal burgh of Rutherglen.
>
> John Galt: *The Ayrshire Legatees; or, The Pringle Family* (1821)

A native of Rutherglen is a **Ruglonian**.

There is a town called Rutherglen in Australia (Victoria).

Ruthin 'red fortress', Welsh *rhudd* 'red' + *din* 'fortress'; the castle is built from red stone.

A market town and the administrative centre of Denbighshire (formerly in Clwyd), 23 km (14 miles) northwest of Wrexham. In Welsh it is **Rhuthun**. The red-stone **Ruthin Castle** that gives the town its name was built in 1280.

> It was at Ruthyn that the first and not the least remarkable scene of the Welsh insurrection took place by Owen [Owain Glyndwr] making his appearance at the fair held there in fourteen hundred, plundering the English who had come with their goods, slaying many of them, sacking the town and concluding the day's work by firing it; and it was at the castle of Ruthyn that Lord Grey dwelt, a minion of Henry the Fourth and Glendower's deadliest enemy, and who was the principal cause of the chieftain's entering into rebellion, having … poisoned the mind of Henry against him, who proclaimed him a traitor, before he had committed any act of treason …
>
> George Borrow: *Wild Wales* (1862)

In 1646, during the Civil Wars, the castle surrendered to the Parliamentarians after an 11-week siege and was then partially demolished. The castle, now heavily restored, incorporates a hotel specializing in medieval banquets.

Ruthin has an attractive market square with half-timbered buildings, some dating from the 15th and 16th centuries. In the square is the Maen Huail ('stone of Huail') commemorating an unchivalrous passage in the career of King Arthur. Huail, ruler of Edeirnion in North Wales, was often in revolt against Arthur, and the two also fought over a beautiful woman who lived in Ruthin. During the fight, Arthur was wounded in the knee, but obliged Huail to swear never to mention the fact. On a subsequent occasion Huail mocked Arthur's lop-sided dancing, at which Arthur had Huail taken outside, where he was summarily beheaded on the stone that bears his name.

Ruthven. *See under* HUNTINGTOWER *and* KINGUSSIE.

Ruthwell 'spring by a cross', OE *rod* 'cross' + *wella* 'spring'.

A small village (pronounced 'Rivvel') just north of the Solway Firth, 15 km (9 miles) southwest of Dumfries, formerly in Dumfriesshire and now in Dumfries and Galloway. Ruthwell was the site of the first savings bank, founded in 1810 by Dr Henry Duncan, the local minister.

Ruthwell Cross. A 5.5-m (18-ft) high ornately carved cross dating from the early 8th century. It is now housed in Ruthwell church. As well as relief sculptures of scenes from the Gospel and Christian tradition, the cross bears runic inscriptions of 18 verses of *The Dream of the Rood*, an Old English religious dream poem by an unknown author (once thought to have been Caedmon). The only manuscript of this poem was written in a southern English monastery at the beginning of the 11th century, but the runic inscription on the cross is clearly reproduced in the poem. In the poem the cross (*rood*) addresses the dreamer, telling how it suffered along with Christ. The Ruthwell Cross itself was toppled and partly defaced in 1642 by image-breaking Presbyterians, but was resurrected from under the floor of the church by Dr Henry Duncan (*see above*) in 1823.

Rutland 'Rota's estate', OE male personal name *Rota* + *land* 'estate'.

A unitary authority in eastern central England, bounded to the north and east by Lincolnshire, to the south by Northamptonshire (the boundary formed by the River WELLAND) and to the west by Leicestershire. Its other rivers are the Chater, the Eye and the Gwash. Its administrative centre is OAKHAM, and its other significant town UPPING-HAM; otherwise it is mainly rural. Historically it is a county, the smallest in England at 394 sq km (152 sq miles), but in 1974 it was absorbed into LEICESTERSHIRE. This state of affairs was never popular with Rutlanders, and in 1997 a measure of self-determination was restored to Rutland as a unitary authority. Its motto is *Multum in parvo* 'Much in little'.

Rutland is in the midst of the hunting shires, and the COTTESMORE hunt is based here.

Rutland is one of only two traditional counties of England not to appear in either the county cricket championship or the minor counties championship (the other being WESTMORLAND).

There are towns called Rutland in the USA (Illinois, North Dakota, Ohio, Vermont).

Rutland beauty. A name given in the USA to the larger bindweed (*Calystegia sepium*).

Rutland morocco. A proprietary name (registered in 1889) for a type of high-grade leather used in bookbinding.

Rutland panther. A mysterious large animal with black fur and a long tail glimpsed on several occasions in different parts of Rutland from 1994. It is probably a big cat released into the wild either because it grew too large or fierce to be kept as a pet or as a consequence of the Dangerous Animals Act 1976, which ruled that animals such as lynxes, panthers and pumas must not be kept as pets.

Rutland Water. An artificial lake in Rutland, about 3 km (2 miles) east of Oakham, in the valley of the River Gwash. Constructed in the 1970s to provide water for the East Midlands, it has the largest surface area (about 1200 ha / 3000 acres) of any man-made lake in Western Europe. It is popular with yachtsmen and windsurfers, and also attracts many wildfowl.

Rutland Weekend Television. A spoof television comedy (1975–6) created by and starring Eric Idle (of *Monty Python's Flying Circus*) about a television network supposedly based in Rutland (the name echoed that of the genuine London Weekend Television). One of its spin-offs, with musician Neil Innes, was a semi-real pop group called **The Rutles**, parodying The Beatles, who sang, among other things, 'A Hard Day's Rut'.

Ruyton-XI-Towns *Ruyton* 'farmstead where rye is grown', OE *ryge* 'rye' + -TON; *XI-Towns* because the parish originally consisted of eleven townships, which were amalgamated into one manor by the Earl of Arundel in 1301.

A village in Shropshire, about 16 km (10 miles) northwest of Shrewsbury. It is a straggly affair, strung out along a 1.5-km (1-mile) long main street. Its name is spoken as 'Ruyton (pronounced 'rye-tən') eleven towns'.

Rydal 'valley of rye', OE *ryge* 'rye' + OScand *dalr* 'dale'.

A small village in the Lake District, Cumbria, between Ambleside and Grasmere, and overlooking the small lake of **Rydal Water**.

> Where silver rocks the savage prospect cheer
> Of giant yews that frown on Rydale's mere …
>
> William Wordsworth: *An Evening Walk* (1793)

> Soft as a cloud is yon blue Ridge – the Mere
> Seems firm as solid crystal, breathless, clear,
> And motionless; and, to the gazer's eye,
> Deeper than Ocean, in the immensity
> Of its vague mountains and unreal sky!
>
> William Wordsworth: 'By the Side of Rydal Mere' (1835)

The house above the village called **Rydal Mount** was Wordsworth's home from 1813 until his death in 1850. Nab Farm on the north shore of Rydal Water was the home of the father of Thomas De Quincey's beloved Margaret Simpson, whom he married in 1817 after she had borne his child. The Wordsworths disapproved of this cross-class marriage, and relations between them and De Quincey were broken off. De Quincey became the owner of Nab Farm in 1829, but it had to be sold four years later.

Ryde 'small stream' (referring to Monktonmead Brook), OE *rith*.

A town and resort on the northeastern coast of the ISLE OF WIGHT, about 11 km (7 miles) southeast of Cowes. A major ferry terminal (fast catamarans call from Portsmouth), it also has much of the equipment of a traditional English seaside town, including a 0.8 km (0.5 mile) pier with its own railway track, along which run retired London Transport Underground trains. Built in 1814, it was the first such pier in Britain.

Offshore, **Ryde Roads** are a favourite beat for yachtsmen. The 'First Fleet', which carried the original British migrants (including convicts) to Botany Bay in Australia, set sail from Mother Bank, off Ryde, in 1787 under Arthur Phillip. There is now an industrial suburb of Sydney, Australia, named Ryde.

> Ryde … would be as nice a place as any … for dawdling, and getting health.
>
> W.M. Thackeray: letter (13 July 1849)

Ryder's Hill Probably from the surname *Ryder*.

A hill in the southeastern part of DARTMOOR, 516 m (1691 ft) high.

Rye '(place at the) island or dry ground in the marsh', OE *ieg* 'island, dry ground in a marsh' (*see* -EY, -EA). The place would originally have been described in OE as *æt thære iege* 'at the island'. In ME that became *atter ie*, and over time the *r* of *atter* migrated to *ie* – whence *Rye*.

A hill town at the extreme eastern end of East Sussex, on the River ROTHER[2], about 15 km (9 miles) northeast of Hastings and 3 km (2 miles) from the coast. Originally it was on the coast, and a major cross-Channel port – not one of the original five CINQUE PORTS, but the first of the later additions to the list (around 1336) – but in the 16th century the harbour silted up and the mouth of the Rother advanced southwards, leaving Rye marooned inland. Its picturesque buildings and cobbled streets, leading up to Church Square on top of the hill, bespeak the period of its pre-eminence and attract many visitors.

Rye's most famous resident was the novelist Henry James (1843–1916), who lived in Lamb House from 1898 until his death. He affectionately described Rye as 'the little old cobble-stoned, grass-grown, red-roofed town, on the summit of its mildly pyramidal hill'. Most of the writing of *The Wings of the Dove* (1902), *The Ambassadors* (1903) and *The Golden Bowl* (1904) took place in Lamb House, where James entertained a large number of contemporary writers as guests. The house's next occupant was the writer E.F. Benson (1867–1940), who made Rye (in the guise of TILLING) the backdrop of his 'Mapp and Lucia' stories. He rose to become Mayor of Rye in 1934–7. (There is a tradition, still observed every 23 May, that the annually elected Mayor of Rye throws hot new pennies to the waiting crowd from the Town Hall. This may echo past electoral bribery, or alternatively the time when the town had its own mint.) Lamb House had a third literary owner after the Second World War in the person of the novelist Rumer Godden (1907–98), author of *Black Narcissus* (1939).

The dramatist John Fletcher (1579–1625), who famously collaborated with Francis Beaumont in some 12 plays, and who allegedly collaborated with Shakespeare on *The Two Noble Kinsmen* (1613) and *Henry VIII* (1613), was born in Rye.

There is a town called Rye in New York state, USA.

> See you the windy levels spread
> About the gates of Rye?
> O that was where the Northmen fled,
> When Alfred's ships came by.
>
> Rudyard Kipling: 'Puck's Song', from *Puck of Pook's Hill* (1906)

Rye Bay. A bay on the East Sussex coast, to the south of Rye, into which the River ROTHER[2] flows. Much of it is lined by Camber Sands (*see under* CAMBER).

Rye Foreign '(place) outside Rye' (denoting that it was outside Rye's geographical boundary), RYE, with ME *forein* 'situated outside the district, parish, etc.'.

A village in East Sussex, about 3 km (2 miles) northwest of Rye.

Ryknild Street From a misdivision of OE *æt thære Ikenilde stræte* 'at the Icknield Street'.

An alternative form of ICKNIELD STREET.

Rylstone Possibly 'farm with a small stream', OE *rynel* 'streamlet' + -TON.

A village in North Yorkshire, 8 km (5 miles) north of Skipton. It is the home of Emily, the heroine of William Wordsworth's *The White Doe of Rylstone* (1815); *see* BOLTON ABBEY. In the 1990s members of the Rylstone Women's Institute created the then innovative but now much imitated *Alternative WI Calendar*, in which they posed naked behind strategically positioned jam jars and sundry other WI-ish items to raise money for a leukaemia charity. The efforts of these sterling Rylstonians are the subject of a feature film, *Calendar Girls* (2003), starring Helen Mirren and Julie Walters.

Ryme Intrinseca *Ryme* '(place at the) edge or border' (referring to the proximity of the Somerset boundary), OE *rima* 'edge, border, rim'; *Intrinseca* 'inner' (contrasted with the former manor of *Ryme Extrinseca* 'outer Ryme'), Latin.

A village in Dorset, about 6 km (4 miles) southeast of Yeovil. *See also* YETMINSTER.

Ryton 'rye farm', OE *ryge* 'rye' + -TON.

A town in Tyne and Wear (formerly in County Durham), 10 km (6 miles) west of Newcastle upon Tyne.

S

Sabhall. The Irish name for SAUL[1].

Sabrina. The Romano-British name of the River SEVERN.

According to Geoffrey of Monmouth (*Historia Regum Britanniae* (c.1136)), it was derived from *Sabre*, the name of the daughter of Locrinus, King of LOEGRIA, and his concubine Estrildis, whom he married after divorcing Guendoloena. The ex-queen gathered an army, and Locrinus was slain. Estrildis and Sabre were consigned to the waters of the Severn. The sea-god Nereus took pity on Sabre, or Sabrina, and made her the tutelary goddess of the river.

John Milton featured her in his masque *Comus* (1637) – Thyrsis invokes her in the song 'Sabrina Fair, Listen where thou art sitting'. Over 300 years later, ***Sabrina Fair*** became the British-release title (simply ***Sabrina*** in the United States) of a 1954 film by Billy Wilder, starring Humphrey Bogart, William Holden, and Audrey Hepburn as the heroine Sabrina Fairchild; the boat neckline, tied at the shoulders, worn by Hepburn in the movie became known in America as a **sabrina neckline**. (The film was remade as *Sabrina* in 1995 by Sydney Pollack.)

After its use by Milton, 'Sabrina' enjoyed an intermittent popularity as a female given name. The Scottish writer John Galt gave it to the new schoolmistress ('Miss Sabrina') in his *Annals of the Parish* (1821), and more recently it has adorned, in splendid isolation, a busty blonde (real name Norma Sykes; b.c.1931) who achieved a certain showbiz fame in the 1950s for being a busty blonde (*see also* the Hunchfront of Lime Grove *under* LIME GROVE).

Herbert Howells's *Missa Sabrinensis* ('Mass of the Severn') was first performed in 1954. Its name alludes to the course of the Severn through GLOUCESTERSHIRE, where Howells was born, and WORCESTER, where the premiere of the mass took place, and is also a tribute to a part of England that nurtured so many of its greatest composers – Elgar, Vaughan Williams, Holst, Gurney, Finzi and others.

Sackers Green *Sacker* probably the name of a landowner here.

A village in Suffolk, about 2.5 km (1.5 miles) southeast of SUDBURY[1].

Sackville Street. A former name for O'CONNELL STREET in Dublin.

Saddle, the From the saddle-shaped dip between its two tops. It is a direct translation of the Gaelic name, *An Dìollaid*. An elegant mountain (1010 m / 3314 ft) in the Western Highlands, rising on the south side of GLEN SHIEL, opposite the Five Sisters of Kintail (*see under* KINTAIL). The Forcan Ridge over Sgurr na Forcan to the summit is a classic mountain scramble.

Saddleback. An alternative name for the Lakeland fell BLENCATHRA.

Saddleworth Moor *Saddleworth* 'enclosure on a ridge shaped like a saddle', OE *sadol* 'saddle' + *worth* (*see* -WORTH, WORTHY, -WARDINE).

An area of Pennine moorland in Greater Manchester, some 10 km (6 miles) east of Oldham. Saddleworth Moor achieved grisly notoriety as it was here, between 1963 and 1965, that the child murderers Ian Brady and Myra Hindley (known as the '**Moors Murderers**') buried at least four of their five victims (aged 10–17) after raping and torturing them. In 1987, Hindley's information led to the recovery of the remains of the fourth body, Pauline Reade, on part of the moor known as Hollin Brow Knoll.

Sadgill Possibly 'cleft with a hunting hide', OScand *sat* 'hide for hunting' + *gil* 'ravine'.

A tiny settlement near the head of LONG SLEDDALE, in the eastern Lake District, Cumbria. In Mrs Humphry Ward's novel *Robert Elsmere* (1888), the farmhouse of Low Sadgill becomes 'High Gill'.

Sadler's Wells From the rediscovery of the water source here by Thomas *Sadler*.

Originally, a medicinal well in CLERKENWELL (E1), close to the top of what is now Rosebery Avenue. In the Middle Ages there had been a holy well here, belonging to St John's Priory, but it was blocked up at the time of the Reformation.

It was rediscovered by Thomas Sadler in 1683 when workmen were digging for gravel. The waters were pronounced to contain salts of iron, and the discovery was turned to immediate profit. However, when attendance at the well declined, music-hall entertainment was provided, and from the 1690s this became the chief attraction under James Miles.

In 1765 a builder named Rosoman erected a proper theatre here, which became famous for burlettas, musical interludes and pantomimes. The actor Edmund Kean, the actor–songwriter Charles Dibdin and the pantomime clown Joseph Grimaldi all appeared here. In 1844 Samuel Phelps took over and produced Shakespeare, but after his retirement the boom in West End[1] theatres cast **the Wells** into the shade and it eventually became a cinema, which closed in 1916.

A new theatre, built with the help of the Carnegie United Kingdom Trust, opened in 1931 under Lilian Baylis of the Old Vic, and it became one of the leading houses in London for the production of ballet and opera (in 1945 it staged the premiere of Benjamin Britten's *Peter Grimes*). In 1946 the ballet transferred to the Royal Opera House (*see under* Covent Garden); it retained its named link with the Wells, though, and in due course became the **Sadler's Wells Royal Ballet**. The **Sadler's Wells Opera Company** relocated to the London Coliseum in 1969 and in 1974 became known as the English National Opera Company. In 1996 the old Sadler's Wells theatre was effectively rebuilt; it reopened in 1998.

Sadler's Wells features in Tobias Smollett's *Humphry Clinker* (1771).

Trelawney of the Wells. A play (1898) by the comic dramatist and farceur Arthur Wing Pinero, which revolves around the travails of actress Rose Trelawney, contrasting thespian life at Sadler's Wells with the 'respectable' gentility of marriage. It is regularly revived by amateur groups, and has been produced by London's (Royal) National Theatre on two occasions (1965 and 1993).

Saffron Park. The fictional name for Bedford Park in G.K. Chesterton's *The Man Who Was Thursday* (1908).

Saffron Walden Originally *Walden* 'valley of the Britons', OE *wala* possessive plural form of *walh* 'Welshman, Briton' (*see* wal-) + *denu* 'valley'; *Saffron*, first recorded in the late 16th century, refers to the cultivation of saffron here.

A market town in Essex, close to the River Cam[2], about 21 km (13 miles) south of Cambridge. There was a Roman settlement here, and the Normans built themselves a castle when they arrived (only the keep survives). Its church, dating from the 15th century, is the largest in Essex.

The town prospered in the Middle Ages on the back of the wool trade, but it was for a more esoteric business that it became widely known: the cultivation of saffron. This was used extensively in medieval times as a dye and for its medicinal properties, and it was introduced at Walden in the mid-14th century. It did well, and in due course its name became combined with that of the town. The saffron crocus now figures in the civic coat of arms. For over 400 years, Saffron Walden was England's main saffron producer.

The Conservative politician R.A. ('Rab') Butler (1902–82), of Education Act (1944) fame, was MP for the Saffron Walden division of Essex from 1929 to 1965; he took the title Baron Butler of Saffron Walden when he was made a life peer.

Have with you to Saffron-walden; or, Gabriell Harveys Hunt is Up. A satire (1596) by Thomas Nashe, directed against Gabriel Harvey, a native of Saffron Walden, who had written slightingly of Nashe's work.

Saham Toney *Saham* 'homestead by the pool', OE *sæ* 'pool' + ham; *Toney* denoting manorial ownership in the Middle Ages by the de Toni family.

A village in Norfolk, about 13 km (8 miles) southeast of Swaffham.

St Abbs From OE female personal name *Ebbe* or *Æbbe*.

A small fishing village 4 km (2.5 miles) north of Eyemouth, in Scottish Borders (formerly in Berwickshire). Just north along the coast is **St Abbs Head** where in the 7th century a nunnery was founded by Ebba or Æbbe, daughter of King Æthelfrith of Northumbria. She had fled north on her father's death in 616 and survived a shipwreck here. The craggy coastline continues north of here to Fast Castle and beyond. St Abb's Head is also the name of a coastal station providing information for the shipping forecast.

St Agnes[1] From the dedication of the local church to the 4th-century child-martyr *St Agnes*.

A village and seaside resort on the north Cornwall coast, about 8 km (5 miles) north of Redruth. In the past it was a centre of the tin-mining industry, and the ruins of the old workings are still in evidence. Today it earns its living from its sandy beaches and fine clifftop views.

The portrait and historical painter John Opie (1761–1807) was born in St Agnes.

St Agnes Beacon. A hill 214 m (700 ft) high to the southwest of St Agnes, affording extensive views landwards (over Bodmin Moor) and seawards. A fire blazed from its summit in 1588 to warn of the approach of the Spanish Armada.

St Agnes Head. A headland about 1.5 km (1 mile) west of St Agnes. The cliffs are home to spectacular colonies of kittiwakes and other seabirds.

St Agnes[2] Originally *Agnes* 'pasture headland' (referring to a promontory on the island), OScand *hagi* 'pasture' + *nes* (*see* ness); the name was subsequently extended to the whole island, and the *St* added on the analogy of neighbouring islands such as ST MARTIN'S and ST MARY'S.

One of the SCILLY ISLES, to the southwest of St Mary's. It is 175 ha (433 acres) in area, and is the southernmost inhabited island of the group. The disused Old Lighthouse dates from 1680, making it one of the earliest in Britain.

St Albans From the dedication of the local abbey to *St Alban*, the first British Christian martyr, who at some time in the 3rd century was executed in the Roman amphitheatre outside the town for sheltering a Christian priest.

A cathedral city in Hertfordshire, on the River VER, about 31 km (19 miles) northwest of London. There was an important British settlement nearby, the capital of the Catuvellauni tribe, on the western bank of the Ver, when the Romans arrived. They took it over, under the name VERULAMIUM, and it became one of the most important centres of Roman Britain. It was the only Roman town to be declared a *municipium* (which meant that its inhabitants were officially Roman citizens). It stood on WATLING STREET[1] (whose name may be from the same source as 'Wæclingaceaster', an earlier Anglo-Saxon name for St Albans). STANE STREET[2] ran east from it. In AD 61 it was destroyed by the Iceni tribe under Queen Boudicca, but it was soon rebuilt.

After the Romans left it fell into ruin. In 793 a Benedictine abbey was founded by King Offa of Mercia on Holmhirst Hill, traditional site of the martyrdom of St Alban, on the opposite bank of the Ver. In recognition of his status as the first British martyr, it was given precedence over all other English abbeys. The original wooden building was replaced by a stone one in the late 11th century. At 159 m (521 ft), the nave of the **Cathedral and Abbey Church of St Alban** is the second longest in Europe after WINCHESTER Cathedral.

The abbey produced three outstanding medieval chroniclers: Roger of Wendover (*see under* WENDOVER); Matthew Paris (d.1259); and Thomas Walsingham (d. *c*.1422).

At the Dissolution of the Monasteries the abbey's lands were sold to the Bacon family (on his ennoblement, the philosopher and lawyer Francis Bacon (1561–1626) styled himself 'Baron Verulam, Viscount St Albans'). For the next three and a half centuries the abbey church served as the parish church, until in 1877 it was given cathedral status. Robert Runcie (later Archbishop of Canterbury) was Bishop of St Albans 1970–80.

The modern town of St Albans grew up around the abbey. During the Civil Wars it was the headquarters of the Parliamentarian army under the Earl of Essex. More prosaically, today St Albans is commuter territory for well-to-do expanding families who are, however, not well-to-do enough to afford bigger properties in the expensive leafy

areas of NORTH LONDON. It is the home of the Campaign for Real Ale.

The scholar and encyclopedist Alexander Neckham (1157–1217) was born in St Albans, as were John Ball (d.1381), one of the leaders of the Peasants' Revolt, and the 14th-century Sir John Mandeville, peddler of travellers' tales.

There are towns called St Albans in the USA (Vermont and West Virginia).

Battle of St Albans (22 May 1455). The first of two identically named battles in the Wars of the Roses. It was little more than an armed scuffle, but it launched the Wars with a success for the Yorkists.

Battle of St Albans (17 February 1461). The second battle, in which, in contrast to the first, the Yorkists were soundly defeated.

Book of St Albans, The. An anthology of treatises on hunting, hawking and heraldry, produced in the late 15th century. It was one of the last products of the press operated in St Albans between 1479 and 1486 by the so-called 'Schoolmaster Printer'. It contains the earliest example of colour printing in England.

St Albans clean shave. A late 19th-century colloquialism for a clergyman's beardless face, typical of the High Church.

St Alban's Head *Alban* an alteration (first recorded in the early 19th century, and presumably influenced by the place name ST ALBANS) of *Aldhelm*.

A high headland (alternatively named **St Aldhelm's Head**) on the southern coast of the Isle of Purbeck (*see under* PURBECK), about 8 km (5 miles) southwest of SWANAGE. Colonies of seabirds crowd the ledges of the cliffs.

St Aldhelm's Head Named in honour of *St Aldhelm* (*c*.640–709), the earliest English scholar of note and first Bishop of SHERBORNE.

An alternative (and the original) name of ST ALBAN'S HEAD.

St Andrews. A city and royal BURGH (1160) on the east coast of Fife, 17 km (10 miles) southeast of Dundee. It is an ancient university town, a mecca for golfers, and was once the ecclesiastical capital of Scotland.

The first religious community at St Andrews was probably founded by St Kenneth in the 6th century. The place was first known as **Mucross** (Gaelic *muc* 'boar' + *ros* 'headland'), then as **Kilrymont** ('church of the king's mount'; *see* KIL-, with Gaelic *rig* 'royal' + *monad* 'hill') or as **Kilrule** ('church of St Rule'). St Rule (also called St Regulus) was shipwrecked here in the mid-8th century, while accompanying some relics of the apostle St Andrew from Greece. Subsequently the Pictish king – who may have been converted by St Rule – established a church dedicated to St Andrew, who became the Picts' (and later the Scots') patron saint. Thus the settlement came to be called

St Andrews. In the early 10th century the bishops of Scotland moved here from DUNKELD, and St Andrews became an archbishopric in 1472, the archbishop becoming the primate of Scotland. The ruins of the medieval **St Andrews Cathedral**, priory and clifftop castle (the seat of the bishops) remain.

St Andrews inevitably became a focus of activity during the Reformation. Archbishop James Beaton burnt Patrick Hamilton here in 1528, creating Scotland's first Protestant martyr. Beaton's nephew, Cardinal David Beaton, 'that old limb of St Lucifer' (as Daniel Defoe called him), also became Archbishop of St Andrews, and on 1 March 1546 watched the popular reformer George Wishart burn at the stake from the battlements of St Andrews Castle. Before he died, Wishart predicted that Beaton would soon appear 'in as much shame as he now shows pomp and vanity'. On 29 May a band of local Protestant lairds took over the castle and killed the cardinal, hanging him over the battlements by an arm and a leg, so forming a St Andrews Cross. Wishart's prophesy had come to pass. During the siege of the castle by government forces that followed the rebels pickled Beaton's body in brine, inspiring the contemporary saying:

> For stickit is your cardinal, and salted like a sow.

In June 1547 the castle was forced to capitulate, and the rebels – who had been joined by John Knox – were sent off to the French galleys. Knox was released after some 19 months, and in 1559, back in St Andrews, he preached such a fiery sermon that the mob set about sacking the cathedral:

> Great bangs of bodies, thick and rife,
>   Gaed to Sanct Androis town,
> And, wi' John Calvin i' their heads,
> And hammers i' their hands and spades,
> Enrag'd at idols, mass, and beads,
>   Dang the Cathedral down.
>
> William Tennant (1784–1848): 'Papistry Storm'd'
> (Tennant was professor of oriental languages at
> St Andrews University.)

The cathedral soon fell into disrepair and became a quarry for local builders.

The **University of St Andrews**, founded as St Mary's College in 1411, is Scotland's oldest university. St Salvator's College was founded in 1450 and St Leonard's in 1512; they united in 1747, some of the latter's buildings later being taken over by St Leonard's, a private girls' boarding school. In the 17th and 18th century the university and town went into something of a decline:

> In the morning we arose to perambulate the city, which only history shows to have once flourished, and surveyed the ruins of ancient magnificence, of which even the ruins cannot long be visible, unless some care be taken to

> preserve them; where is the pleasure of preserving such mournful memorials?
>
> Samuel Johnson: *A Journey to the Western Islands of Scotland* (1775)

During his visit Johnson was lavishly entertained by the professors, leading the vernacular poet, Robert Fergusson (1750–74), an alumnus of the university, to pen a satire entitled 'To the Principal and Professors of the University of St Andrews, on their Superb Treat to Dr Samuel Johnson'. In this he proposed that, in response to the definition of oats in his dictionary that so insulted the Scots, 'Sam, the lying loun [fellow]' should have been fed such Scottish delicacies as haggis, sheep's head, black trotters and 'white and bloody puddins'.

Both town and university revived in the 19th century. Today the university is particularly popular with the products of English public schools, and was selected for the higher education of Prince William, the second in line to the throne. Notable alumni of St Andrews are too numerous to list, but include William Dunbar (1460/5–before 1530), the greatest of the Renaissance *makaris* (poets); the poet Sir Richard Maitland, Lord Lethington (1496–1586); John Napier (1550–1617), the inventor of logarithms; James 'the Admirable' Crichton (1560–82), man of many parts; the soldier James Graham, Marquess of Montrose (1612–50); John Arbuthnot (1667–1735), wit, satirist and friend of Swift and Pope; Adam Ferguson (1723–1816), the 'common sense' philosopher; the vernacular poet Robert Fergusson (1750–74); Andrew Lang (1844–1912), man of letters ...

> St. Andrews by the Northern sea,
> A haunted town it is to me!
> A little city, worn and grey,
> The grey North Ocean girds it round.
> And o'er the rocks, and up the bay,
> The long sea-rollers surge and sound.
>
> Andrew Lang: 'Almae Matres' (1884)

... Sir Robert Watson-Watt (1892–1973), the inventor of radar; and Sir James Black (b.1923), the pharmacologist and Nobel laureate. In 2002 Charles Paxton of St Andrews was presented with an 'IgNobel Prize' at Harvard University for his paper showing that sexual arousal in farmed ostriches is enhanced by the presence of humans. The great Trinidadian cricketer Learie Constantine was elected rector of the university in 1968, as was the philosopher John Stuart Mill a hundred years earlier, in 1867.

Golf has been played on the links at St Andrews since the Middle Ages, and the town is home to the Royal and Ancient Golf Club (the 'R and A'), founded in 1754 as the **Society of St Andrews Golfers**. The present name dates from 1834, and the club has become the ultimate world authority on the rules of the game. The four main courses – owned by the local authority, not the club – are the Old Course, the New Course, the Eden and the Jubilee. The golfer Nick Faldo is reported to have commented of St Andrews, 'when it blows there, even the seagulls walk', while a golfer of an earlier generation, the American Sam Snead, said:

> Until you play it, St Andrews looks like the sort of real estate you couldn't give away.

St Andrews hosted its first Open championship in 1873. In 2005 it will host its 27th.

The great golfers Old Tom (1821–1908) and Young Tom (1850/1–1875) Morris, both many times winners of the British Open, were born in St Andrews, where both also died. Robert Chambers (1802–71), the publisher, also died in St Andrews, as did Will Fyffe (1885–1947), the music-hall entertainer. It was the birthplace of Jo Grimond (1913–93), leader of the Liberal Party from 1956 to 1967.

There are towns called St Andrews in Canada (New Brunswick and Newfoundland), New Zealand (South Island) and the USA (South Carolina).

> I love how it comes right out of the blue
> North Sea.
>
> Robert Crawford: 'St Andrews', from *The Tip of My Tongue* (2003)

St Ann's Head From a lost chapel dedicated to *St Ann*.
The headland guarding the west side of the entrance to Milford Haven, Pembrokeshire (formerly in Dyfed), 18 km (11 miles) west of Pembroke. It was here that the oil tanker *Sea Empress* foundered in 1996, resulting in considerable ecological damage along the coast of south Wales.

St Anthony in Meneage *St Anthony* an alteration of *St Entenin*, the name of the Cornish saint to whom the local church was dedicated; *Meneage* '(land) of monks', Cornish *managh* 'monk' + adjectival suffix *-ek*.
An attractive village (the final syllable rhyming with *Haig*) in Cornwall, clinging snugly to the southern side of the mouth of the Helford River (*see under* Helford). Its Norman church is said to have been built in thanksgiving to the local saint for saving some seafarers from drowning.

St Asaph From the dedication of the cathedral to *St Asaph*.
A village on the River Elwy in Denbighshire (formerly in Clwyd), 7 km (4 miles) south of Rhyl. Its Welsh name is **Llanelwy** ('church on the River Elwy'). After St David's, it is the second smallest 'city' in Britain, and its cathedral (late 13th century) is Britain's smallest. A monastery was founded here in the 6th century by St Kentigern, who was succeeded as abbot by St Asaph in 570. St Asaph, who 'shone with virtue and miracles from the flower of his earliest youth', also became the first bishop. One of his greatest pieces of divinely sanctioned prestidigitation was the recovery of the ring traditionally worn by the queens of Gwynedd. The then queen had lost the ring while bathing

(a rare event, one suspects, in those dark days), and, fearing her husband's wrath, begged Asaph's aid. Asaph asked the couple to dine, and told the king of the loss. The king was furious, but after Asaph put in some triple-strength but silent prayers, was assuaged when the fish on his plate, freshly caught from the River Elwy, disgorged the ring.

Geoffrey of Monmouth was Bishop-Elect of St Asaph in 1151. William Morgan, who was largely responsible for the first translation of the Bible into Welsh (1588), was Bishop of St Asaph from 1601 until his death in 1604. Commemorated in the cathedral is the poet Mrs Felicia Hemans, who lived nearby and is now remembered only for 'Casabianca' ('The boy stood on the burning deck ...' *et cetera*). In 1920 the cathedral was the setting for the enthronement of Alfred Edwards, Bishop of St Asaph, as the first Archbishop of the newly disestablished Church in Wales.

Born illegitimate, the explorer Sir Henry Morton Stanley (1841–1904) was partly raised in St Asaph Workhouse. St Asaph was the birthplace of the Wales, Liverpool and Juventus footballer Ian Rush (b.1961).

St Austell From the dedication of the local church to the 6th-century monk and saint *Austol*, said to have been the godson of the Welsh saint Mewan.
A town in Cornwall, close to the southern coast, about 10 km (6 miles) west of the Fowey[1] estuary and 22 km (14 miles) northeast of Truro. Until the middle of the 18th century it was a relatively insignificant tin-mining village, but in 1755 William Cookworthy discovered deposits of kaolin, or china-clay, in the area. The exploitation of these, initially for the manufacture of porcelain, transformed St Austell's fortunes, and its appearance. The giant pock-marks of the quarries and the strange mountain ranges of conical green and white spoil heaps (a particular feature of nearby Hensbarrow Downs) combine to form a mysterious, almost lunar landscape. They are known locally as the Cornish Alps (*see* Cornish). The extraction of china-clay continues to make an important contribution to Cornwall's economy, although today its main use is in the manufacture of paper.

The local economy has received a boost from recent eco-tourism projects: a disused claypit 6 km (4 miles) to the northeast houses the Eden Project, while about 8km (5 miles) to the south are the Lost Gardens of Heligan.

St Austell Bay. A bay about 5 km (3 miles) wide on the south coast of Cornwall, immediately to the southeast of St Austell. Its extremities are Black Head, to the west, and Gribben Head, to the east. It includes Charlestown[1], from where much china-clay was exported.

St Bees After *St Bega*.
A village near the western coast of Cumbria (formerly in Cumberland), 6 km (4 miles) south of Whitehaven. Legend

has it that St Bega, the female Irish saint after whom the village is named, was shipwrecked here with some companions in the 7th century. (Alternatively, she was the daughter of an Irish king and was flown here by an angel on the day she was due to marry a Norse prince.) She was taken in at EGREMONT Castle by Lady Egremont, who persuaded her pagan husband to help the nuns to establish a convent here. He agreed to provide building materials, and any land that would be covered by snow the next morning. Although this was midsummer, the next morning dawned with snow on the ground between Egremont's castle and the sea, and the lord was obliged to cede it. The well-preserved **St Bee's Priory** dates from the 12th century.

> There was an old man of St Bees
> Who was horribly stung by a wasp.
>> When they said, 'Does it hurt?'
>> He replied, 'No it doesn't –
> It's a good job it wasn't a hornet!'
>
> W.S. Gilbert : limerick (after Edward Lear's
> 'There was an old man in a tree')

St Bees Head. A rocky headland some 5 km (3 miles) northwest of St Bees. Its 100-m (300-ft) red sandstone cliffs have enjoyed intermittent popularity with rock climbers.

> Men who write Tours and County histories I have by woeful experience found out to be *damned liars*, harsh words, but true! ... The St Bee's Head which I had read much of as a noble cliff, might be made a song of on the flats of the Dutch Coast – but in England 'twill scarcely bear a looking-at.
>
> Samuel Taylor Coleridge: letter to Sara Hutchinson (5 August 1802) (written at the top of Scafell)

St Blazey From the dedication of the local church to *St Blaise* (a 4th-century Armenian martyr).

A small town in Cornwall, about 5 km (3 miles) east of ST AUSTELL. The EDEN PROJECT is just to the west.

St Boniface Down From the dedication of the church in nearby Bonchurch to *St Boniface; Down see* DOWN, -DON.

An area of high downland at the southeast corner of the ISLE OF WIGHT. At 240 m (787 ft) it is the highest point on the island. It terminates in tall and somewhat crumbling cliffs, at the foot of which lie VENTNOR and BONCHURCH.

St Breock From the dedication of the local church to the 6th-century Welsh saint *Brioc*.

A village in Cornwall, on the western side of the River CAMEL, just to the west of WADEBRIDGE. The Royal Cornwall Showground is close by. To the southwest are the **St Breock Downs**, from which the clay hills of ST AUSTELL can be seen.

St Briavels From the naming of the local castle after *St Briavel*, an obscure Welsh saint.

A village in Gloucestershire, on the western side of the River SEVERN, close to OFFA'S DYKE, about 14 km (9 miles) north of Chepstow. Its medieval castle, now in ruins, was built as part of England's defences against Welsh incursions, and was once the administrative centre for the FOREST OF DEAN.

St Bride's Bay After the village of *St Brides* on the south side, itself named after St Bride/Bridget; there was probably an Irish missionary foundation here, and there is some evidence that it was called *Llansanffraid* (Welsh, 'St Bride', *b* becoming *ff*) from the 9th century, suggesting an early dedication.

A large bay on the west coast of Pembrokeshire (formerly in Dyfed), some 10 km (6 miles) west of Haverfordwest. ST DAVID'S Head and RAMSEY ISLAND are on the north side, and SKOMER Island on the south side.

St Brides Wentlooge. *See* PETERSTONE WENTLOOGE.

St Budeaux From the dedication of the local church to the 6th-century Celtic saint *Budoc*.

A northwestern district of PLYMOUTH, in Devon, by the mouth of the River TAMAR.

St Buryan From the dedication of the local church to *St Beryan*, a female saint of Irish origin.

A village in western Cornwall, about 5 km (3 miles) east of LAND'S END. The notoriously violent Sam Peckinpah film *Straw Dogs* (1971) – about a couple who are terrorized by brutish locals when they move to a remote part of rural Cornwall – was filmed in the locality.

St Catherine's Point From the dedication of a lost chapel to *St Catherine*.

A headland on the south coast of the ISLE OF WIGHT, the most southerly point of the island. It is guarded by a modern lighthouse, but on the Downs a short way inland is a medieval lighthouse, known locally as the 'Pepper Pot'. The story goes that it was built in 1325 as an act of penance by a certain Walter de Goditon, who had tried to steal a cargo of wine belonging to a local monastic community from a nearby shipwreck. An oratory dedicated to St Catherine once existed by the lighthouse, as a result of which it is known as **St Catherine's Oratory**.

St Clears From the dedication of the local church to *St Clear*, *fl*.9th century.

A village in Carmerthenshire (formerly in Dyfed), 14 km (8.5 miles) west of Carmarthen. In Welsh it is **Sanclêr**. Owain Glyndwr was defeated here in 1406 by the English and Flemings of Pembrokeshire.

St Cleer *See* ST CLEARS.

A village in Cornwall, on the southeastern edge of BODMIN Moor, 214 m (700 ft) above sea level, about 3 km (2 miles) north of Liskeard. Nearby are several prehistoric monuments, most notably The CHEESEWRING, the HURLERS and TRETHEVY QUOIT.

St David's From the cathedral dedicated to *St David, fl.*6th century.

A village in Pembrokeshire (formerly in Dyfed), 22 km (14 miles) northwest of Haverfordwest, and 4 km (2.5 miles) southeast of the rocky promontory of **St David's Head**, itself at the tip of **St David's Peninsula**, the northern arm enclosing St Bride's Bay. In Welsh the village is **Tyddewi** ('house of Dewi', i.e. St David). St David's is the smallest 'city' in Britain, although the magnificent **St David's Cathedral** (mostly 12th–14th centuries) is the largest church in Wales.

The city's ecclesiastical history goes back to *c.*550, when St David moved his monastery here, to the place called **Glyn Rhosyn** ('valley of roses'). According to legend, St Patrick had earlier intended establishing a monastery in the Glyn, but an angel told him the place was destined for St David, and that he must go on to Ireland. When St David himself arrived, he and his monks were faced with a posse of naked handmaidens, sent in as a weapon of last resort by the local pagans; needless to say, temptation was manfully resisted. The early monks called the place by the Latin name **Menevia** (from **Mynyw**, the early Welsh name for St David's, meaning 'a grove'), and it became a bishop's seat; Menevia is now the name of the Roman Catholic bishopric of Wales.

Edward III's lord chancellor, Houghton, was Bishop of St David's from 1361 to 1388, and, in an early deployment of the eschatologico-strategic doctrine of Mutually Assured Destruction, retaliated for his own excommunication by himself excommunicating the Pope from the steps of his cathedral; he may have calculated that, given a pilgrimage to remote St David's was worth two to Rome, he had the edge on the pontiff. Another bishop of St David's who sailed close to the wind was William Laud; he held the see from 1621 to 1626, but never visited the place, and is better known for being Charles I's Archbishop of Canterbury, and for losing his head four years before his sovereign lost his.

St David's was the birthplace of Richard Llewellyn (1906–83), author of *How Green Was My Valley* (*see* the VALLEYS).

St Day From the dedication of the local church to *St Day*, a popular Breton saint about whom little is known.

A village in Cornwall, about 3 km (2 miles) east of Redruth. In the days when copper mining was a thriving local industry it was accounted the mining capital of Cornwall, and evidence of the impact of mining on the local landscape can be viewed at GWENNAP Pit.

St Decumans From the dedication of an ancient church here to the Welsh *St Decuman*.

A southern district of WATCHET, on the Somerset coast.

St Devereux From the dedication of the local church to

St Dyfrig, a 6th-century Welsh monk and bishop who, according to legend, crowned Arthur 'King of Britain'.

A hamlet in Herefordshire (before 1998 in Hereford and Worcester, before 1974 in Herefordshire), about 10 km (6 miles) southwest of Hereford.

St Dogmaels From the dedication of the local church to *St Dogmael*, of whom nothing is known.

A village in Ceredigion (formerly in Cardiganshire, then in Dyfed), just across the River TEIFI from Cardigan. In Welsh it is **Llandudoc** (*llan* 'church' + name of an unknown saint *Tydoch*, the *-doch* part of whose name is possibly a contraction of 'Dogmael'). The original abbey was sacked by the Vikings, and the present ruins date from the 12th century. In the Middle Ages the monks said special prayers for the fish of the River Teifi before each fishing season, a practice that was revived in 1965. However, a disastrous season followed, many blaming this on an excess of men of the cloth at the ceremony.

St Dogwells From the same dedication of the local church as at ST DOGMAELS.

A village in Pembrokeshire (formerly in Dyfed), 9 km (5.5 miles) south of Fishguard. In Welsh it is **Llantydewi** ('church of the house of St David').

St Edmundsbury. The original name of BURY ST EDMUNDS in Suffolk. The diocese of which Bury is the centre is officially designated 'St Edmundsbury and Ipswich'; and 'St Edmundsbury' is now the name of the local council district.

Sainted Sod. A name given by St Senan to SCATTERY ISLAND.

St Edwardstowe. A former name for SHAFTESBURY.

St Endellion From the dedication of the local church to *St Endilient*, who according to Cornish legend was a daughter of the Welsh King Brychan of BRYCHEINIOG. She supposedly subsisted on cow's milk. When her cow was killed by a local lord, he in turn was slain by her godfather, none other than King Arthur. In demonstration of her saintliness, she brought both the lord and the cow back to life.

A hamlet in Cornwall, about 8 km (5 miles) northeast of Padstow. A music festival is held here every summer, and the **Endellion String Quartet** takes its name from the hamlet.

St Erth From the dedication of the local church to an Irish saint, *Ergh* or *Erc*: the saint was either the brother of St Euny (the dedicatee of the church of REDRUTH) or Bishop of Slane and protégé of St Patrick.

A village in western Cornwall, on the River Hayle, about 6 km (4 miles) southeast of ST IVES[2].

St Erth Praze *Praze* 'meadow', Cornish *pras*.

A hamlet in western Cornwall, about 3 km (2 miles) east of ST ERTH.

St George's Channel Etymology unkown, but perhaps from the patron saint of England.

The undiplomatically named stretch of water between Wales and Ireland, linking the Irish Sea (*see under* IRISH) with the CELTIC SEA and Atlantic Ocean to the southwest. It is some 160 km (100 miles) long. At its narrowest, between CARNSORE POINT in County Wexford and ST DAVID'S Head in Pembrokeshire, it is 80 km (50 miles) wide.

There is also a St George's Channel in the Bismarck Archipelago, Oceania, separating New Ireland from New Britain.

St Germans From the dedication of the local church to *St Germanus*, perhaps the 5th-century St Germanus of Auxerre, or a local saint of the same name.

A village in Cornwall, at the mouth of the River Tiddy, about 13 km (8 miles) west of PLYMOUTH. Just to the east the Tiddy is joined by the River Lynher, and their combined estuary is known as the **St Germans River**. It flows into the HAMOAZE. It is included in the TAMAR Valley.

The original church here was the seat of the Saxon bishops of Cornwall (the diocese of St Germans was created by King Athelstan in 931; its independent existence ceased in 1027). The present-day one is a Norman replacement.

St Giles From the dedication to *St Giles* of a leper hospital founded in the area in 1101 by Queen Matilda, wife of Henry I. A former district of Central London (WC1, WC2), at the western end of High Holborn (*see under* HOLBORN). It grew up outside London's city walls – whence the name of its parish church, **St Giles-in-the-Fields**, which reinforced the name of the area. As its population increased in the 17th and 18th centuries, it developed into one of the vilest and most congested slums in the capital, a hotbed of crime and prostitution (*see also* SEVEN DIALS). The Great Plague of 1665 started here.

> If poverty be a title to poetry, I am sure nobody can dispute mine. I own myself of the company of beggars; and I make one at their weekly festivals at St. Giles's. I have a small yearly salary for my catches and am welcome to a dinner there whenever I please, which is more than most poets can say.
>
> John Gay: *The Beggar's Opera* (1728), Beggar's 'Introduction'

Mid-19th-century redevelopment (particularly the cutting of New Oxford Street in 1847) destroyed the rookeries and robbed the area of its distinct and separate identity, but its name lives on in **St Giles Circus**, the crossroads at the junction of OXFORD STREET, TOTTENHAM COURT ROAD and Charing Cross Road (*see under* CHARING CROSS). It is the site of CENTRE POINT, a tower block of offices which caused controversy by remaining unoccupied for a long time after its opening in the mid-1960s.

St Giles rookery. A notorious 19th-century criminal slum, centred on the area now occupied by Centre Point tower. *Rookery* is an old slang word for a gambling-den or brothel.

St Giles's carpet. An ironic late-19th-century colloquialism for a sprinkling of sand on the street.

St Giles's Greek. A grandiose name, from the early 17th-century to the 19th, for 'slang' or 'cant'.

St Giles' From *St Giles* Church at its northern end.

A short, very wide street running north–south in central OXFORD. At its southern end is the Martyrs' Memorial, commemorating the burning at the stake of the Protestant martyrs Hugh Latimer and Nicholas Ridley (16 October 1555) and Thomas Cranmer (21 March 1556). St John's College is here, as is the Taylor Institution (the Taylorian), the Randolph Hotel, the Eagle and Child public house (where the literary coterie known as the Inklings – including J.R.R. Tolkien, C.S. Lewis, Neville Coghill and Charles Williams – used to meet), and also the quaintly nicknamed 'Ox and Cow' – a.k.a. the Oxford and County Secretarial College – alma mater to legions of sensible-skirted Sloane PAs. At its northern end St Giles' divides into the twin arteries of the Woodstock and Banbury Roads, which traverse the leafy, traditionally donnish, suburbs of North Oxford.

> The trees in St Giles', not yet autumnal yellow, were on the turn ... To the left, at the top of Beaumont Street, the façade of the Ashmolean in all its classical perfection was revealed in a Grecian blaze of bright light. The Martyrs' Memorial, built by Victorians to commemorate the courage of 16th-century Protestants, in fact awoke medieval pieties, seeming like an old Eleanor Cross and a throwback to that very religion which had consigned the heroes, sculpted round its base, to a heretics' death by burning.
>
> A.N. Wilson: *Iris Murdoch As I Knew Her* (2003)

St Giles in the Wood *St Giles* from the dedication of the local church to St Giles; *in the Wood* referring to its location in the wooded valley of the River TORRIDGE[1], and added to distinguish it from ST GILES ON THE HEATH.

A village in Devon, about 3 km (2 miles) east of Torrington.

St Giles on the Heath. A village in Devon, on the River Carey, about 6 km (4 miles) north of Launceston.

St Govan's Head From *St Govan*, who lived here as a hermit. A rocky headland forming the most southerly point of PEMBROKESHIRE (formerly in Dyfed), 9 km (5.5 miles) south of Pembroke. Situated in a ravine nearby is St Govan's Chapel, which dates from the 13th century (and in part may go back to the 6th century). St Govan is a somewhat mysterious figure: it has been suggested that he was a 6th-century follower of St David, or a reformed thief, or a 5th-century noblewoman called Cofen, or even the Arthurian Sir Gawain. However, it is most likely that he was an Irish follower of St Ailbe, who ended his days as a hermit in this remote spot; by tradition he died in 586.

There is a legend as to why St Govan chose to settle here: one day as he walked along the clifftop he was set upon by brigands, but he was saved when the rock swallowed him up, hiding him from his attackers, only opening up again when the danger had passed. The fissure can still be seen within the chapel, and if you make a wish there, facing the wall, and do not change your mind before turning around, your wish will apparently come true. Another curiosity of the place is the steps leading down to the chapel between the cliffs, which are allegedly more numerous on the way up than on the way down (or possibly vice versa).

St Helens[1] From the dedication of the local church to *St Helena* (the Empress Helen, mother of Constantine the Great, who in the Middle Ages was thought to be a native of Britain and who is reputed to have found the cross on which Christ was crucified).

A town in Merseyside, 18 km (11 miles) northeast of Liverpool. The town has long been famous for its flat glass manufacture (Pilkington), and has been dubbed **Glasstown**.

St Helens RFC, founded in 1873, was one of the northern defectors from the Rugby Football Union in 1895 (*see* HUDDERSFIELD). Nicknamed the Saints, the club has played in rugby league's Super League since 1996.

St Helens was the birthplace of the textile manufacturer and philanthropist John Rylands (1801–88), after whom Manchester University's library is named, and of the mischievously witty conductor, Sir Thomas Beecham (1879–1961).

> St Helens: a town so devastated by heavy industry it made Warrington look like an area of outstanding natural beauty.
>
> Pete McCarthy: *McCarthy's Bar* (2000)

St Helens[2] *see* ST HELENS[1].

A village on the ISLE OF WIGHT, about 13 km (8 miles) east of NEWPORT[2].

St Helens[3] From the dedication of a ruined chapel on the island; it is unclear whether the chapel was dedicated to *St Helena* (*see* ST HELENS[1]), or whether the name is an alteration of *St Illid* or *Eliduis*, as both of the latter occur in the early spellings of the name.

One of the SCILLY ISLES, to the north of Tresco. It is uninhabited, but it contains a mid-18th-century pest house in which plague-carriers were quarantined before being allowed into Britain.

St Helier Named after *St Helier*, a 6th-century martyr reputedly born in Belgium, who lived for 15 years as a hermit on Jersey before being killed by pirates.

A town on the south coast of JERSEY, the capital of the island and seat of the 'States of Jersey', the island's legislature. It is a market town, for the island's abundant agricultural produce, but nowadays its tone is set more by the numerous banks and trust companies that have opened offices in Jersey. It is also a popular holiday resort. Nearly one-third of the island's population lives in the town.

The Battle of Flowers takes place in St Helier every August. It dates from 1902 when it was first held to commemorate the coronation of King Edward VII and Queen Alexandra. It involves parades of floats ('the battle parade') decorated with exhibits made from fresh (and artificial) flowers. The main floats come from the 12 parishes of Jersey, but anyone can enter one. The 'battle' element arises from the fact that the crowd were formerly invited to rip up the exhibits and pelt each other with flowers.

The actor-manager Sir Seymour Hicks (1871–1949) was born in St Helier.

St Helier is also the name of one of the 12 parishes of Jersey.

St Ippollitts From the dedication of the local church to the 3rd-century Roman priest and martyr *Hippolytus*.

A village in Hertfordshire, about 2.5 km (1.5 miles) south of Hitchin.

St Ishmael From the dedication of the local church to the 6th-century saint *Isan* or *Ismail*, episcopal successor to St David, consecrated by St Teilo.

A village in Carmarthenshire (formerly in Dyfed), 13 km (8 miles) south of Carmarthen.

St Ishmael's. A village in Pembrokeshire (formerly in Dyfed), 7 km (4 miles) west of Milford Haven.

St Ive From the dedication of the local church to *St Ive* (*see* ST IVES[1]).

A village in Cornwall, about 6 km (4 miles) northeast of Liskeard.

St Ives[1] From *St Ive*, a Persian bishop whose relics are said to have been found there in 1001; before that it was called *Slepe* 'slippery place' (alluding to its location on the banks of the Ouse, OE *slæp*).

A market town in Cambridgeshire (before 1974 in Huntingdonshire), on the GREAT OUSE, about 8 km (5 miles) east of Huntingdon. It has strong associations with Oliver Cromwell (1599–1658), who had farming interests in the area; there is a statue of him in the Market Place.

The town's most notable architectural feature is its medieval bridge chapel, one of only four left in England. Still consecrated, it overhangs the six-arched stone bridge built across the Ouse in 1425.

Theodore Watts-Dunton (1832–1914), critic and constant companion of the poet Algernon Charles Swinburne, was born in St Ives.

The town features in an anonymous old rhyme (first recorded in a Harley manuscript of *c*.1730):

As I was going to St Ives,
I met a man with seven wives,
Each wife had seven sacks,
Each sack had seven cats,
Each cat had seven kits,
Kits, cats, sacks and wives
How many were going to St Ives?

The answer is 'one' – the rest were all going in the other direction (a similar riddle has been found in an ancient Egyptian papyrus).

St Ives² From the dedication of the local church to *St Ya*, a female Irish saint who is said to have floated across to Cornwall on an ivy leaf.

A town and port on the north coast of western Cornwall, in the district of Penwith, about 13 km (8 miles) west of Camborne. Its Cornish name was **Porthia**, 'harbour of Ya'. Pilchards were the original foundations of its prosperity (in the late 19th century the Rev. Francis Kilvert reported the local vicar as saying 'the smell of fish there is sometimes so terrific as to stop the church clock'; 75 million pilchards were said to have been landed here on a single day in 1864), and in the great 19th-century days of tin and copper mining it was an important shipping port.

By the end of the 19th century it had already begun to turn its attention to attracting holidaymakers. Many of them came to paint, and by the early 20th century professional artists were establishing themselves here. The leading figures of the **St Ives School**, from the late 1940s to the early 1960s, who put St Ives on the international abstract-art map, were Ben Nicholson (he lived here from 1939 to 1958), the sculptor Barbara Hepworth (she came here with Nicholson, and stayed for the rest of her life, eventually dying in a fire in her home, which is now the Barbara Hepworth Museum), Naum Gabo and the potter Bernard Leach (he established a pottery here in 1920, and '**St Ives**' is now the designation of a particular type of ceramic ware). (The Japanese potter Hamada Shoji, who was made a Living National Treasure in Japan in 1955, set up a kiln with Leach in the town in the 1920s.) A second wave, beginning in the 1960s, included Terry Frost, Patrick Heron, Peter Lanyon and Bryan Wynter. The Tate Gallery opened a branch museum in St Ives in 1993, showing examples of the art produced in the town.

Perkin Warbeck (1474–99), pretender to the English throne, was proclaimed king while his ship was anchored in St Ives harbour in 1497.

The composer George Lloyd (1913–98) was born in St Ives, as was the novelist Rosamunde Pilcher (b.1924). Her novel *The Shell Seekers* (1987) is set in St Ives' artists' colony.

No one departs,
No one arrives,
From Selby to Goole,
From St Erth to St Ives.

Michael Flanders and Donald Swann: 'The Slow Train' (1961) (St Ives station was actually reprieved from Dr Beeching's axe, the occasion for Flanders and Swann's song.)

St Ives³ Originally *Ives* 'place overgrown with ivy', OE *ifet* 'clump of ivy'. *St* was added in recent times, on the analogy of St Ives¹ and St Ives².

A village in Dorset, close to the Hampshire border, about 13 km (8 miles) north of Christchurch.

St James's From the Hospital of *St James*, a leper hospital for young women founded in the area in the 12th century.

A district in the West End¹ of London (SW1), in the City of Westminster, to the southwest of Trafalgar Square. At its heart is **St James's Palace**, a Tudor royal palace built by Henry VIII in the 1530s on the site of the former Hospital of St James. Charles I spent his last night here, before his execution. After Whitehall Palace (*see under* Whitehall) burned down in 1697 it became the monarch's main London residence. A relic of its 18th-century role is the accreditation of foreign ambassadors to the 'Court of St James'. The palace was badly damaged by a fire in 1809. Queen Victoria liked it and continued to use it, but its official status was ceded to Buckingham Palace in 1837, and it has since housed a changing cast of royal family members (Prince Charles made it his London residence until August 2003). Its main surviving Tudor portions are the imposing gatehouse, and the Chapel Royal, employer of such rich musical talents as Henry Purcell, William Byrd and Thomas Tallis, and venue of the weddings of Victoria and George V.

Abutting St James's Palace is Clarence House, designed by John Nash and built in the 1820s for the Duke of Clarence. It has housed most of the current royal family at one time or another, most notably Queen Elizabeth the Queen Mother from her premature monarchical retirement in 1953 to her death in 2002. Prince Charles made it his new London home from August 2003.

The gateway of St James's Palace commands the southern end of **St James's Street**, which links the southwestern end of Pall Mall with Piccadilly¹ to the north. Laid out in the early 17th century, this contains a mixture of first-division gentlemen's clubs (notably Boodles, Brooks's, the Carlton and White's – from whose bow-window Beau Brummell put on a show for the passing world in the 1810s) and shops dispensing the accoutrements of gentlemanly living (*see also* Jermyn Street). The latter include Lock's the hatters, J. Lobb the bootmakers, William Evans the gunsmiths, Justerini and Brooks the wine merchants, Davidoff and James J. Fox the cigar merchants and the wine merchants Berry Bros. and Rudd, whose carefully preserved 18th-century premises still contain the scales on which customers used to be weighed. Their presence has created a patina of discreet exclusivity around the name 'St James's' which other firms in a similar line of business have not been slow to cash in on if they are in a position to do so (for example, the wine merchants Grants of St James's).

St James's Park. A park created in the early to mid-16th century to the south of St James's Palace, on marshy land which had previously been pasturage for pigs. About 36.5 ha (90 acres) in extent, it is bounded to the north by the MALL, to the east by Horse Guards Road and to the south by BIRDCAGE WALK. Buckingham Palace is at its western end. It is the oldest of London's royal parks. Its long lake, known as the Canal, dates from Charles II's time; it is stocked with a wide range of aquatic birds, from the humble duck (which tourists and London office workers like to ply with the remains of their sandwiches) to the more exotic pelican. In the late 17th century the park boasted a crane with a wooden leg. Luckily the plan of George I to close the park and plant it with turnips never came to anything, but earned the king the nickname of 'Turnip-Hoer'. Restoration dramatist William Wycherley's first play (1671) was *Love in a Wood, or, St James's Park*, a comedy of intrigue.

In 1933, at the height of the Depression, the Chancellor of the Exchequer, Neville Chamberlain, took time off from the world economic crisis to write to *The Times* to report on a sighting of a grey wagtail in the park.

St James's Park Underground station, on the District and Circle lines, opened in 1868.

St John's Head. *See under* HOY.

St John's Town of Dalry. *See* DALRY.

St John's Wood *St John's* from the Knights Hospitallers of St John, who owned an area of woodland here in the Middle Ages.

A district of northwest London (NW8), in the City of Westminster, between REGENT'S PARK to the east and MAIDA VALE to the west. As its name suggests, it was once heavily wooded. Most of its trees were cut down in the mid-17th century, but it remained a rural area until the early 19th century. In the 1810s its development as a select up-market residential suburb began. Its elegant Gothic and Italianate villas attracted the professional middle classes, and were also favoured by artists and writers (George Eliot, Sir Edwin Landseer, Sir Lawrence Alma-Tadema and the poet Thomas Hood were among the area's 19th-century residents). But the occupants of Victorian St John's Wood who have left the most long-lasting mark on the memory are the courtesans:

> Ch Brane-Cantenac ... fully evolved 'biscuitty' bouquet; sweet, full, rounded, fleshy (sounds like the mistress of a wealthy Victorian gentleman, ensconced in a discreet villa in St John's Wood).
>
> Michael Broadbent: *Vintage Wine* (2002)

In the late 19th century the district was sometimes facetiously referred to as '**Sinjin's Wood**', a double pun on the 'sin' and 'gin' enjoyed in its environs, incorporated into the affectedly smart pronunciation of 'St John's'.

In 1814 Thomas Lord moved his cricket ground from Dorset Square (just to the south in MARYLEBONE) to St John's Wood (*see* LORD'S), and in the nearly two centuries since then the district's name has become a metonym for English cricket's ruling panjandrums:

> In March 1877 an Australian XI won a game that has retrospectively been celebrated as the first Test match, but in fact scarcely an eyebrow was raised in St John's Wood.
>
> Derek Birley: *The Willow Wand* (1979)

Brutal redevelopment in the early 20th century and Second World War bombing destroyed much of St John's Wood's Victorian charm, and parts of it are now dominated by blocks of luxury apartments (those with a view of play at Lord's command a particularly high price). It remained socially high-bracket, however, becoming a noted site for the upwardly mobile young wealth-creators of the 1960s: Beatle Paul McCartney lived in it, and Rolling Stone Mick Jagger sang about it:

> Your mother, she's an heiress,
> Owns a block in St John's Wood
>
> Mick Jagger and Keith Richards: 'Playing with Fire' (1965)

Yet its centre manages to retain a village feel. Locals tend to refer to the place affectionately as 'the Wood'. From the late 19th century to the early 20th, the punning nickname APOSTLE'S GROVE was current.

St John's Wood Underground station, on the Jubilee line (originally on the Bakerloo line), opened in 1939. There had been an earlier St John's Wood Underground station, on the Metropolitan line, which opened in 1868 (as St John's Wood Road); it was renamed Lord's in June 1939, but closed in November.

St John's Wood Clique. A group of artists who lived in the St John's Wood area in the late 19th century and influenced each other's styles. Their work became highly fashionable around the turn of the 20th century, but now few of their names ring bells (G.D. Leslie, H. Stacey Marks, G.A. Storey, W.F. Yeames ...). Probably the Clique's best-known product is Yeames's *And When Did You Last See Your Father?* (1878), a genre picture featuring a small Royalist boy being interrogated by Cromwellian soldiers.

St John's Wood dona. A late 19th-century term for an up-market prostitute or kept woman (alluding to the area's contemporary reputation – *see above*). *Dona* was 19th-century slang for 'woman', from Polari (theatrical and gay slang) *donah*.

St John's Wood vestal. A 19th-century euphemism for 'prostitute', punning ironically on *vestal virgin*.

St Juliot From the dedication of the local church to *St Julitta*.
A village in Cornwall, 5 km (3 miles) inland from Boscastle in the valley of the River Valency. It was here, in 1870, that the writer Thomas Hardy met his first wife, Emma Gifford, sister-in-law of the local rector, when he came to the village as a junior architect to restore the local church. The episode is reflected in Hardy's third novel, *A Pair of Blue Eyes* (1873), set on Cornwall's north coast (*see* Lyonesse). Its main character, Stephen Smith, is an assistant architect who surveys West Endelstow church to prepare for its restoration and falls in love with Elfride Swancourt, the vicar's daughter. Hardy returned to St Juliot in 1913, a year after Emma's death, placing a memorial plaque in the church.

> 'Why go to Saint-Juliot? What's Juliot to me?'
> Some strange necromancy
> But charmed me to fancy
> That much of my life claims the sport as its key.
>
> Thomas Hardy: 'A Dream or No' (1913)

See also Beeny.

St Just From the dedication of the local church to *St Just*, a 6th-century Celtic saint said to have preached the Gospel in England before the coming of St Augustine.
A town at the western extremity of Cornwall, in the district of Penwith (it is also known as **St Just-in-Penwith**), about 6 km (4 miles) northeast of Land's End. It has an amphitheatre, the Plain-an-Gwarry, where mystery plays used to be performed. Nearby is the **Land's End/St Just Airfield** (*see under* Land's End).

St Just-in-Roseland *Roseland see* Roseland.
A coastal village in Cornwall, on the eastern side of Carrick Roads, about 3 km (2 miles) north of St Mawes. The much-visited local church is remarkable for the almost tropical luxuriance of the vegetation in its sizeable churchyard, mostly planted in the late 19th and early 20th centuries, which rolls down to the tidal inlet; the church itself is surrounded by palm trees.

St Katherine's Dock From its originally belonging to the former Hospital of *St Katherine*.
A dock on the north bank of the River Thames[1], in Central London (E1), immediately to the east of the Tower of London and Tower Bridge. There was a dock or wharf here in the early Middle Ages. It belonged to the **Hospital of St Katherine**, which had been founded in 1148 by Queen Matilda (wife of King Stephen) as a hospital for the poor. Along with the associated church of St Katherine it became a 'royal peculiar', the personal property of the queens of

England and having its own jurisdiction. The direct present-day successor of the Hospital is the **Royal Foundation of St Katherine**.

In the 1820s all the buildings in the area were flattened and a new dock, St Katherine's Dock, was constructed on the site of the medieval wharf to the designs of Thomas Telford. It opened in 1828. Its total area of water was 3.8 ha (9.5 acres), closely overshadowed by tall yellow-brick warehouses. It closed down as a working dock in 1968. It was turned into a marina, the wharfside buildings adapting readily to their new roles as restaurants, nautical boutiques and upscale flats and serviced dwellings.

St Kevin's Bed. *See under* Glendalough.

St Kew From the dedication of the local church to *St Kew*, a female saint said to have come to Cornwall from Wales.
A village in Cornwall, to the west of Bodmin Moor, about 11 km (7 miles) northwest of Bodmin.

St Kew Highway *Highway* from its being on the main road (now the A39) to Wadebridge.
A hamlet in Cornwall, about 1.5 km (1 miles) southeast of St Kew.

St Keyne From the dedication of the local church to *St Keyn*, who, according to legend, was the daughter of the Welsh King Brychan of Brycheiniog.
A village (pronounced 'kane' or 'keen') in Cornwall, about 3 km (2 miles) south of Liskeard.

St Kilda There is no known saint of this name, and there are various theories as to its origin. The earliest record of the name is on a Dutch map of 1666. It may be from OScand *skildar* 'shields' (topographically appropriate). Another, less plausible, theory is that it arises from a misunderstanding of *Tobhar Childa*, the name of a well on Hirta; perhaps sailors landing here assumed that the well was named after a saint (as was common elsewhere), whereas in fact it is a tautonym: Gaelic *tobhar* 'well' + OScand *kelda* 'well'.
A remote and rocky archipelago 80 km (50 miles) west of Harris, described by the poet Douglas Dunn as 'this outcast of the Hebrides'. The main island is Hirta, and the others include Soay, Boreray, Stack an Armin and Stac Lee. Hirta was the only one of the islands to be inhabited (although there is some evidence of past cultivation on Borerary), and Soay[2] has given its name to a breed of sheep. The earliest settlement on Hirta may date back to the Bronze Age (*c.*1500 BC), but the earliest records of visits by outsiders are those of Dean Monro in 1549 and Martin Martin in 1697. A less willing and longer-term visitor was Lady Grange, who was confined on the island by her husband, MacLeod of Dunvegan (the owner of St Kilda), between 1734 until 1742 (having spent the previous two years on the Monach Islands). Her crime was to have overheard her husband and fellow Jacobites plotting in

their Edinburgh house, and then foolishly announcing that she would inform the authorities.

> 'They say I'm mad, but who would not be mad
> on Hirta, when the winter raves along
> the bay and howls through my stone hut …'
>
> Edwin Morgan: 'Lady Grange on St Kilda', from *Sonnets from Scotland* (1984)

The native people of St Kilda lived largely off seabirds, and the menfolk became adept rock climbers in order to harvest eggs and birds from the precipitous sea cliffs on Hirta and the other islands. At the top of the 425 m (nearly 1400 ft) cliffs on Hirta is the Lover's Stone, a rock that projects over the drop on which young men proved their nerve to their intended by performing a tricky balancing act.

The 17th-century traveller Martin Martin described the inhabitants as 'almost the only people in the world who feel the sweetness of true liberty', and indeed, although they paid a rent in kind to the MacLeod owners, they held all property in common, and made decisions collectively at the daily 'parliament'.

> But oh! o'er all, forget not Kilda's race,
>   On whose bleak rocks, which brave the wasting tides,
> Fair Nature's daughter, Virtue, yet abides.
>   Go, just, as they, their blameless manners trace!
> Then to my ear transmit some gentle song,
>   Of those whose lives are yet sincere and plain,
> Their bounded walks the rugged cliffs along,
>   And all their prospect but the wintry main.
> With sparing temp'rance, at the needful time,
>   They drain the sainted spring; or, hunger-prest,
> Along the Atlantic rock undreading climb,
>   And of its eggs despoil the solan's nest.
> Thus blest in primal innocence, they live,
>   Suffic'd and happy with that frugal fare
> Which tasteful toil and hourly danger give.
>   Hard is their shallow soil, and bleak and bare;
> Nor ever vernal bee was heard to murmur there!
>
> William Collins: 'Ode on the Popular Superstitions of the Highlands' (1784) (A solan or solan goose is a gannet.)

From the 18th century outside influences began to erode the independence and viability of life on St Kilda. Introduced diseases took their toll, and tourist visits were a cause of culture shock. A hell-fire minister who came to Hirta in 1865 and stayed for 25 years bullied the inhabitants into spending time in church when they should have been working to sustain themselves. Emigration further reduced the population until in 1930 the remaining 36 people were obliged to agree to resettlement on the mainland, at Lochaline in Morvern, Argyll.

> You can see they have already prophesied
> A day when survivors look across the stern

> Of a departing vessel for the last time
> At their gannet-shrouded cliffs …
>
> Douglas Dunn: 'St Kilda's Parliament: 1879–1979; the photographer revisits his picture', from *St Kilda's Parliament* (1981)

In 1957 St Kilda was presented to the National Trust for Scotland by the then owner, the 5th Marquess of Bute. In the same year the army set up a base on Hirta to track missiles from the South Uist range, and later established the only pub on the island, the Puff Inn. Access to the islands is restricted to National Trust working parties, who have restored many of the houses in the village. Day-to-day management is carried out by Scottish Natural Heritage; not only are the islands important breeding grounds for all kinds of seabirds, but they are also home to two unique subspecies, the **St Kilda field mouse** (*Apedemus sylvatica hirtensis*) and the **St Kilda wren** (*Troglodytes troglodytes hirtensis*), both larger than their mainland brethren. St Kilda is a UNESCO World Heritage Site.

St Kilda is also the name of a district in Melbourne, Australia.

St Leonards From the dedication of the original local church (destroyed by the sea in the 15th century) to the 6th-century hermit *St Leonard*.

A town and seaside resort on the East Sussex coast, to the west of and now contiguous with (and administratively linked to) HASTINGS. There was little to it until the late 1820s, when a London builder, James Burton, fired by the example of Brighton, decided there was money to be made here. He acquired land, built buildings, stuck on stucco and produced **St Leonards-on-Sea**, an elegant assemblage of Regency villas and terraces. Subsequent development has diluted and in some cases marred his vision, but St Leonards remains a civilized counterpoint to the more down-to-earth delights of Hastings (with which it shares a promenade).

St Leonards was the birthplace of the playwright David Hare (b.1947).

St Leonard's Forest From the dedication of a church in the forest to *St Leonard* (*see* ST LEONARDS).

An area of woodland in West Sussex, to the southwest of CRAWLEY and to the east of HORSHAM. It is one of the few remaining fragments of the huge forest which covered much of southeast England in ancient times.

St Margaret's Hope[1] 'the haven of St Margaret', *Hope* OScand *hop* 'landlocked bay'.

A sheltered anchorage in the Firth of Forth (*see under* FORTH), just south of the naval base at Rosyth. It takes its name from Queen (later Saint) Margaret (*see* SOUTH QUEENSFERRY).

St Margaret's Hope[2]. A village on a bay of the same name on SOUTH RONALDSAY, Orkney, 18 km (11 miles) south of

Kirkwall. There is a famous annual ploughing match on the beach for boys, prior to which the girls dress up as horses.

St Martin's From the dedication of the island's church to *St Martin* of Tours (d.397).

The third largest of the SCILLY ISLES, at the northeastern corner of the group, to the northeast of Tresco. Its chief town is Higher Town. It is noted for the beautiful shells that can be found on its beaches.

St Mary Axe From the former 12th-century church of *St Mary Axe* in the street (closed in 1560). This got its name from its claim to possess one of the three axes used by Attila the Hun to behead the 11,000 virgins said to have accompanied St Ursula on a mission to convert the heathen.

A street in the City of London (EC3), running from HOUNDSDITCH in the north to LEADENHALL STREET in the south. The Baltic Exchange (whose business was finding ships and aircraft for cargo, and vice versa), with its impressive Victorian marble Exchange Hall, was situated here, but was very badly damaged by an IRA bomb in 1992, and subsequently (and controversially) demolished to make way for the SWISS RE TOWER (usually referred to as the GHERKIN).

St Marylebone. *See* MARYLEBONE.

St Mary Mead. The fictional English village in which Agatha Christie's forensically gifted spinster Miss Marple lived. Like all such places, its body-count was alarmingly high.

St Mary's From the dedication of the parish church at Hugh Town to the Blessed Virgin *Mary* (the earliest known reference is to St Mary of Hennor, *Hennor* being the Cornish name of the landmass of Scilly before it was inundated and became the present islands).

The main island of the SCILLY ISLES, about 48 km (30 miles) west of Land's End. Its chief town is HUGH TOWN, which is capital of the whole island group.

St Mary's Hoo *St Mary's* from the dedication of the local church; *Hoo see* HOO.

A village on the peninsula that separates the estuaries of the THAMES[1] and the MEDWAY[1], within the unitary authority of Medway, in Kent. To the north are the **St Mary's Marshes**.

St Mary's Loch From the ruined *St Mary's* Kirk on the northwest side of the loch.

A beautiful loch, 20 km (12 miles) southwest of Selkirk in the mountainous upper Yarrow valley, which in turn is part of the Ettrick Forest (*see under* ETTRICK WATER) in Scottish Borders (formerly in Selkirkshire). At its southwest end a narrow strip of land, the site of TIBBIE SHIEL'S INN, separates it from the smaller Loch of the Lowes. The area is particularly associated with James Hogg, the Ettrick

Shepherd, and Sir Walter Scott, who describes the loch in *Marmion*:

> Thou know'st it well, – nor fen, nor sedge,
> Pollute the pure lake's crystal edge;
> Abrupt and sheer, the mountains sink
> At once upon the level brink;
> And just a trace of silver sand
> Marks where the water meets the land.
> Far in the mirror, bright and blue,
> Each hill's huge outline you may view;
> Shaggy with heath, but lonely bare,
> Nor tree, nor bush, nor brake, is there …
>
> Sir Walter Scott: *Marmion* (1808), Introduction to Canto II

The area is also the setting for Alasdair Gray's futuristic historical fantasy, *A History Maker* (1994). To the north of the loch is Dryhope Tower (*c*.1600), the home of Mary Scott, 'the Flower of Yarrow' (*see under* YARROW WATER).

St Mawes From the dedication of the local church to *St Maudyth*, a 5th-century Breton bishop.

A well-to-do harbour town in Cornwall, at the southern tip of the ROSELAND peninsula, on the northern side of the mouth of the Percuil River, about 5 km (3 miles) east of Falmouth. It has a castle, in an excellent state of preservation, built by Henry VIII to protect the eastern side of the FAL estuary and the CARRICK ROADS (its larger sister, Pendennis Castle in FALMOUTH, was intended to protect the western side). Poorly sited for defensive purposes, with a hill rising above it, the castle luckily never had to face foreign anatagonists, and its Royalist commander wisely surrendered to Parliamentarian forces without a fight during the Civil Wars. St Mawes, sleepy out of season, attracts the sailing fraternity (and sorority) and day trippers during the summer months.

St Mawgan From the dedication of the local church to *St Mawgan*, a Celtic saint of uncertain identity, venerated in Wales as St Meugan.

A village in north Cornwall, on the River Menalhyl (which flows through the **Vale of Mawgan** (also known as the Vale of Lanherne) into the sea at nearby **Mawgan Porth**). It is about 6 km (4 miles) northeast of Newquay, has a notable 13th-century (with later additions) church, and its RAF station (an important air-sea rescue centre for the eastern Atlantic) doubles as the airport for the NEWQUAY area.

St Mellion From the dedication of the local church to *St Melaine*, 6th-century Bishop of Rennes in France.

A village in Cornwall, a little to the west of the TAMAR estuary and about 15 km (9 miles) east of Liskeard.

St Michael Caerhays *St Michael* from the dedication of the local church to St Michael the Archangel; *Caerhays* is a local manorial name of unknown origin and meaning.

A village in Cornwall, a little way inland from Veryan Bay

(*see under* VERYAN) and about 5 km (3 miles) southwest of Mevagissey. The nearby **Caerhays Castle**, in fact a castle-esque stately home set in a beautiful woodland garden, was built by John Nash in the early 19th century, its expense ruining the family that commissioned it. Since 1840 it has been owned by a different family. The film version of Daphne du Maurier's *Rebecca* (1940) was partly shot here.

St Michael Penkevil *St Michael see* ST MICHAEL CAERHAYS; *Penkevil* a local Cornish manorial name probably meaning 'horse headland'.

A village in Cornwall, about 4 km (2.5 miles) southeast of TRURO.

St Michael's Island From the dedication of the 12th-century church to *St Michael*.

A small hammer-head peninsula in the southeast of the ISLE OF MAN, to which it is joined by a narrow isthmus.

St Michael's Mount From the supposed appearance of *St Michael* the Archangel to local fishermen in 495.

An island just off the south coast of Cornwall, in MOUNT'S BAY, opposite MARAZION. The designation 'Mount' is something of an exaggeration, but it does reach a height of 76 m (250 ft). Following the miraculous appearance of St Michael, which gave it its name, a church was naturally built here, and this was followed by the 8th century by a Celtic monastery. In the 11th century Edward the Confessor had a chapel constructed on the island. He handed it over to the Benedictine monks of Mont St Michel in Brittany (likewise named after a visit from St Michael), and they founded an abbey here. In the 14th century it was super-seded by a castle, which gives St Michael's Mount its present-day pinnacled and crenellated silhouette. After the Civil Wars it became the private residence of the St Aubyn family, and in 1954 it passed into the hands of the National Trust. At low tide it can be reached from the mainland by a narrow cobbled causeway.

According to Celtic legend, St Michael's Mount was built by the giant Cormoran. He supposedly forced his wife Cormelian to carry heavy granite boulders to the site. One day when he was sleeping, she substituted the easier-to-transport local greenstone. When he woke up and spotted her he was so furious that he kicked her. She dropped the boulder, and it can be seen on the causeway to this day.

> Saint Michaels Mount ... is a barren stony little wen or wart.
>
> John Taylor: *Wandering to see the Wonders of the West* (1649)

St Minver From the dedication of the local church to *St Minfre*, one of the legendary 24 children of King Brychan of BRYCHEINIOG.

A village in Cornwall, in the middle of the peninsula that forms the northeastern side of the CAMEL estuary, and about 5 km (3 miles) northeast of Padstow.

St Monans From the old Church of *St Monan* (a 6th-century Irish saint), said to have been dedicated by David II in *c.*1362 in gratitude for his recovery from a wound.

A small fishing port – also called **St Monance** – in eastern Fife, on the north shore of the Firth of Forth (*see under* FORTH), some 15 km (9 miles) south of St Andrews.

St Neot From the dedication of the local church to *St Neot*, a shadowy figure: according to medieval legend he was a monk of Glastonbury who became a hermit in Cornwall, and was related to or otherwise linked with Alfred the Great (the story of Alfred burning the cakes comes from a now lost *Life of St Neot*); moving further into the realms of fantasy, he is said to have been only 0.4 m (15 in) high and able to make crows obey him.

A village in Cornwall, in the wooded valley of **St Neot's River** (a tributary of the River FOWEY[1], which flows south-wards from DOZMARY POOL), on the southern edge of Bodmin Moor, about 8 km (5 miles) northwest of LISKEARD. Its church has one of the most stunning arrays of medieval stained glass to survive in England.

St Neots From the dedication of the local abbey to *St Neot*, whose relics are said to have been brought here in the 10th century from ST NEOT.

A town (pronounced 'nee-əts' or 'neets') in Cambridgeshire (before 1974 in Huntingdonshire), on the GREAT OUSE, about 30 km (19 miles) west of Cambridge.

St Nicholas Island. The original name of DRAKE'S ISLAND, in Plymouth Sound.

St Ogg's. The fictional name for GAINSBOROUGH in George Eliot's *Mill on the Floss* (1860).

St Osyth From the dedication of the local priory to *St Osgyth* (d.*c.*700), a granddaughter of King Penda of Mercia.

A village in Essex, on a small creek meandering off the estuary of the River COLNE[1], about 5 km (3 miles) northwest of Clacton-on-Sea. The eponymous St Osgyth was married to Sighere, king of the East Saxons, but the marriage was never consummated, and she withdrew to found a nunnery at a place then called Chich ('bend (in the stream)', OE *cicc*). A later, more blood-curdling version of her story has her beheaded by Viking raiders and carrying her head back to the priory before collapsing (but she would have to have reached a robust old age of about 150 for this to have actually happened). The priory from which the village takes its name is now a ruin.

Between the village and the sea is **St Osyth Marsh**.

St Pancras From the dedication of the local church to the 4th-century Roman boy-martyr *Pancras*.

A district in northern Central London (WC1, NW1), in the borough of CAMDEN, to the west of Finsbury. There was a settlement on the site, named after its church, in the 11th century, but its modern identity was fixed in the 1860s with the construction of the Midland Railway's London terminus here. The company chose a site just to the west of KING'S CROSS station, in an area of slums hitherto known as **Agar Town**. Their chosen designer was W.H. Barlow, who produced for them a single-span train shed 210 m (689 ft) long and 73 m (240 ft) across. The station still serves as the London terminus for rail services to Sheffield, Derby, Nottingham, Leicester and other Midland centres, and at the beginning of the 21st century it was being adapted to handle trains operating through the CHANNEL TUNNEL. It shares an Underground station (on the Circle, Hammersmith & City, Metropolitan, Northern, Piccadilly and Victoria lines) with King's Cross. The Northern line station opened as 'King's Cross for St Pancras' in 1907; the present-day designation 'King's Cross St Pancras' for the entire complex was first used in 1933.

The directors of the Midland Railway also required a hotel, which would provide both accommodation for travellers arriving in London and a facade for the station. They held a competition, and the winning design, by George Gilbert Scott, still looms over the Euston Road like a red-brick Rhineland castle, all Gothic pinnacles and crockets. It closed as a hotel in 1935 and since has been used for offices, storage, etc., but for most Londoners, Scott's **Midland Grand Hotel** is still what the name 'St Pancras' conjures up.

St Patrick's Bed. *See under* the MAUMTURK MOUNTAINS.

St Patrick's Island. *See under* SKERRIES.

St Paul's[1]**.** London's cathedral, situated at the top of LUDGATE HILL in the City of London (EC4). Its site has long been used for worship: there was a Roman temple here, and the first (probably wooden) cathedral was built here in 604 by St Ethelbert, king of Kent. Two more stone buildings followed it in the Anglo-Saxon period, and at the end of the 11th century a Norman cathedral rose here. With later medieval additions (including the tallest spire ever built) this became the largest church in England, and the third largest in Europe.

In the Middle Ages, Londoners generally knew their cathedral as plain 'Paul's'. Its precincts became something of a hang-out for loungers and gossips, and its nave was turned into a common thoroughfare (called **Paul's Walk**). After the Reformation its condition declined drastically:

> While you adorn your Churches there, we destroy them here: Among other, poor Pauls looks like a great Skeleton ... Truly I think nor Turk or Tartar ... would have used Pauls in that manner.
>
> James Howell: letter (*c*.1645)

Altogether it may have been a blessing in disguise when

'**Old St Paul's**' famously burned down in the Great Fire of 1666. (The only monument to survive was the one to the poet John Donne (1572–1631), who for the last ten years of his life had been Dean of St Paul's.)

The new cathedral was designed by Sir Christopher Wren and built under his direction between 1675 and 1710. Its most characteristic feature, its great dome (second in size only to St Peter's in Rome), has become almost an icon of London: it achieved a symbolical status during the Second World War, when it survived German bombs against all odds, and even at the beginning of the 21st century, when neighbouring upstarts surpass its height, it elegantly dominates London's skyline.

Many distinguished Britons are buried in St Paul's crypt (believed to be the longest in Europe), most notably national heroes Nelson and Wellington. It is also the last resting place of the cathedral's architect, above whose tomb is the inscription (composed by his son) *Lector, si monumentum requiris, circumspice* ('Reader, if you seek his monument, look around you'). St Paul's is used for great national occasions, such as thanksgivings for victory and monarchs' jubilee services, and Prince Charles married Lady Diana Spencer here.

When the monastery of the Abbey of St Peter at Westminster (*see under* WESTMINSTER) was dissolved in 1540, part of its revenues were transferred to St Paul's – whence the expression '**rob Peter to pay Paul**'.

St Paul's Underground station, on the Central line, opened in 1900, originally under the name 'Post Office' (the historic site of the General Post Office is just to the north, in King Edward Street).

> Upon Paul's steeple stands a tree
> As full of apples as may be;
> The little boys of London town
> They run with hooks to pull them down:
> And then they go from hedge to hedge
> Until they come to London Bridge.
>
> Anon.: 17th-century nursery rhyme, quoted in the *Oxford Dictionary of Nursery Rhymes* (1951)

Paul's Cross. An open-air pulpit within the precincts of Old St Paul's cathedral. It was used for making official announcements (e.g. royal proclamations and papal bulls) as well as delivering sermons. It was demolished in 1643 by order of Parliament.

St Paul's Churchyard. A street in the City of London which surrounds the western end of St Paul's cathedral. In the days of Old St Paul's, when it was still an actual churchyard, it was the centre of the London book trade (in those days, churchyards were not used as graveyards). All the major printers and booksellers of the 16th and early 17th centuries (including most notably Wynkyn de Worde) had premises there.

St Paul's School. A boys' public school founded in 1509 by John Colet, Dean of St Paul's and one of the most noted humanists in England. Its original premises (when it was the largest school in England) were next to Old St Paul's. The two burned down together, and the school moved several times over the succeeding centuries. It arrived at its present site, in BARNES, in 1968. Its sister academy **St Paul's Girls' School** was founded in 1904. It is in Brook Green (W6). The composer Gustav Holst was Director of Music there between 1905 and 1934; he composed his *St Paul's Suite* (a suite for string orchestra) for the school orchestra in 1913.

St Paul's² Probably from the dedication of the local church. A northeastern district of BRISTOL, home to many of the city's Afro-Caribbean residents. Every July there is the **St Paul's Carnival**, an event that began in the 1960s. Unfortunately though, the area is still best remembered nationally for the serious riots that broke out here in April 1980 after a period of racial tension, and it suffers from activities of the red-light variety too.

St Peter Port From the dedication of the local church to *St Peter*, perhaps in acknowledgement of the town's former association with fishing; *see also* PORT.

A town on the east coast of GUERNSEY, and the capital of the island. It has a large protected harbour. Many of its finest old houses were built with the profits of 18th-century smuggling.

The earliest surviving example of a pillar box in the British Isles is in Union Street, St Peter Port. It is made of cast-iron and dates from the 1850s.

The French poet and novelist Victor Hugo lived in the town (in exile from the regime of Napoleon III) from 1856 to 1870. His house is now the property of the city of Paris.

The town's French name is **St-Pierre-Port**.

St Pinnock From the dedication of the local church to *St Pinnuh*, of whom nothing is known.

A village in Cornwall, about 5 km (3 miles) west of LISKEARD.

St Ronan's Wells. *See under* INNERLEITHEN.

Saints' Road to Bardsey, the. A nickname for the B4417 which runs along the northern side of the LLEYN PENINSULA in Gwynedd. To the west of the peninsula is BARDSEY ISLAND, site of a 5th-century religious foundation and a former pilgrimage destination. The road's nickname probably derives from that of Bardsey Island, 'the Island of 20,000 Saints', referring to the number of monks buried on the island.

St Stephen's Green From the medieval church that formerly stood here, dedicated to *St Stephen*.

A large square in central DUBLIN, with a park in the centre. It was first laid out in 1663, although most of the grand classical mansions around it now date from the 18th and early 19th centuries; there are also some unfortunate interpolations from the 1960s. The doomed patriot Robert Emmet (1778–1803) was born in one of the mansions in the square, while another mansion, the Royal College of Surgeons, was the headquarters at Easter 1916 of a contingent of the Irish Citizen Army under Michael Mallin and Countess Markievicz (*see under* LISSADELL), who also held St Stephen's Green Park during the Rising. At the northwest corner of the square is a triumphal arch commemorating the Irish dead in the Boer War; it is known derisively to Nationalists as 'Traitor's Gate', while at the northeastern corner is the monument to Wolfe Tone (1967) by Edward Delaney, consisting of a sculpture of the man surrounded by standing stones, so earning it the nickname 'Tonehenge'.

There'll be wigs on the Green. A phrase meaning that trouble is anticipated. It originates in the 18th century, when it was customary to remove one's wig before fighting a duel. Many such encounters occurred on St Stephen's Green.

Saints' Way A modern coinage, honouring the peregrinations of the Cornish saints.

A walkers' path linking the north and south coasts of Cornwall. It goes from PADSTOW via the ST BREOCK Downs to FOWEY², a distance of about 50 km (30 miles). It follows a Bronze Age trade route (a safer alternative to the voyage around LAND'S END) that was later used by Irish and Welsh missionaries during the Dark Ages.

St Teath From the dedication of the local church to *St Tedda* or *Teth*, one of the legendary 24 children of King Brychan of BRYCHEINIOG.

A village in Cornwall, to the northwest of BODMIN Moor, about 15 km (9 miles) north of Bodmin.

St Tudy From the dedication of the local church to *St Tudy*, a 6th-century monk and bishop.

A village in Cornwall, to the west of BODMIN Moor, about 10 km (6 miles) north of Bodmin.

St Veep Probably from the dedication of the local church to *St Veep*.

A village in Cornwall, on the eastern side of the estuary of the River FOWEY¹, about 4 km (2.5 miles) northeast of the town of Fowey.

St Winifred's Well. *See under* HOLYWELL.

St Winnow From the dedication of the local church to *St Winnoc*, an 8th-century Welsh monk.

A village in Cornwall, on the eastern side of the estuary of the River FOWEY¹, about 5 km (3 miles) north of the town of Fowey.

Salcey Forest *Salcey* 'willow-copse, willow-wood', OFr *salceie* (from Latin *salicetum*).

An area of woodland in Northamptonshire, to the south of Northampton, on the eastern side of the M1.

Salcombe 'salt valley' (referring to the production of salt locally), OE *sealt* 'salt' + *cumb* (*see* -COMBE, COOMBE).

A town and resort in south Devon, on the western side of the KINGSBRIDGE estuary. It climbs picturesquely up the steep wooded side of the valley. There are still a few fishing boats here, but its main preoccupation nowadays is yachting: an annual regatta has been held here since 1857, and its calm waters and air of relaxed-but-keen competition attract many thousands of yachtsmen and their families in the summer (the social profile of its visitors has earned Salcombe the nickname **Kensington-on-Sea**).

Salcombe Regis *Regis* 'of the king', Latin, suggesting royal ownership, but the reason for the designation (first recorded in the 18th century) is not known; in the Middle Ages the manor was held by the Dean and Chapter of Exeter. Possibly it was inspired by a local field name such as *Kingsdown*.

A village close to the south coast of Devon, about 3 km (2 miles) northeast of Sidmouth. To its southwest is **Salcombe Hill** (*see under* SIDMOUTH).

Sale OE *sale*, dative of *salh* 'sallow-tree', a type of willow, especially *Salix cinerea*.

A town in Greater Manchester, 8 km (5 miles) southwest of Manchester city centre. Sale's rugby union club, originally founded in 1861 and now known as **Sale Sharks**, is one of the oldest rugby clubs in the world. The club is based at Edgeley Park in STOCKPORT.

There is also a town called Sale in Australia (Victoria).

Salem An abbreviation of Jerusalem found in the Bible.

There are villages of this name in Carmarthenshire, Ceredigion and Gwynedd. But none of these have achieved the fame of the Massachusetts Salem, site of mass witch trials in 1692, in which more than 20 of the accused were executed. 'Salem' is also evocative for English-speaking schoolchildren who have studied Arthur Miller's play *The Crucible* (1953), which draws on those events.

> In Judah is God known: his name is great in Israel. In Salem also is his tabernacle, and his dwelling place in Zion.
>
> Psalms 76:1–2

Salford 'ford by sallow-trees', OE *salh* 'sallow-tree' (*see* SALE) + FORD.

A city in Greater Manchester, some 3 km (2 miles) west of Manchester's city centre. It received its first charter in 1226, and exactly 700 years later, following expansion during the Industrial Revolution, it was made a city, underlining its sense of independence from MANCHESTER. At the old docks in **Salford Quays** is The Lowry (opened in 2000), an arts

centre that combines two theatres with a gallery displaying the works of the painter L.S. Lowry (1887–1976), who, although born in Manchester, lived for most of his life in Salford, working as a rent collector. **Salford University** (1966) was founded in 1896 as the Royal Technical Institute.

Salford was the birthplace of James Joule (1818–89), pioneer of the science of thermodynamics; the novelist Walter Greenwood (1903–74), author of *Love on the Dole* (1933); the broadcaster Alistair Cooke (1908–2004); the stage and screen actor Albert Finney (b.1936); the playwright Shelagh Delaney (b.1939, author of *A Taste of Honey* (1958)); the film director Mike Leigh (b.1943); and the footballer Paul Scholes (b.1974). Harold Brighouse set his famous play *Hobson's Choice* (1916) in Salford. From 1906 to 1910 the poet and essayist Hilaire Belloc was Liberal MP for South Salford.

Salford City Reds. Salford's rugby league club, originally founded in 1873. Salford defected from the Rugby Football Union to the Northern Rugby Union in 1896, a year after rugby's historic schism of 1895 (*see* HUDDERSFIELD). With the advent of rugby league's Super League in 1996 the club became Salford Reds, then Salford City Reds in 1999. The club was relegated from the Super League to the Northern Ford Premiership in 2003.

Salisbury 'stronghold at Sorvio', *Sorvio* a reduced form of *Sorviodunum*, the Roman name of the fort on the site of which the original city of Salisbury (*see* OLD SARUM) grew up (adapted from its OCelt name, probably from a personal name *Sorwjos* + *duno-* 'fort') + OE *byrig* dative form of *burh* 'stronghold' (see BURY). The Domesday Book form of the name is *Sarisberie*; the influence of Anglo-Norman changed the first *r* to *l*.

A city (pronounced 'sawlz-') in Wiltshire, on the rivers AVON[3], NADDER and Bourne, about 35 km (22 miles) west of Winchester. It grew up on the site of an Iron Age hillfort at OLD SARUM. The Romans settled here, and Saxon and Norman towns succeeded them. In the 1070s a cathedral was built here, which in the following century became an important intellectual centre.

By the beginning of the 13th century the lack of water on the site, and also friction between the military and ecclesiastical authorities, had convinced Bishop Poore of the need to move. A new site was chosen (according to legend, by shooting an arrow at random and seeing where it landed) on well-watered and fertile land about 2.5 km (1.5 miles) south of the original SARUM, near the confluence of the rivers Avon and Nadder. The foundation stone of the new **Salisbury Cathedral** was laid here on 28 April 1220. The bulk of the building work was completed by 1260, but around 1320 the cathedral's celebrated spire was added – at 123 m (404 ft) the tallest surviving medieval spire in Europe (though not mentioned by name, it was the inspiration for William Golding's novel *The Spire* (1964), which centres on the construction of a medieval cathedral spire; Golding himself had moved to Salisbury in 1939). The view of the cathedral across the Salisbury water meadows, iconicized in the paintings of John Constable, is world famous, and in 2002 readers of *Country Life* magazine voted it their 'favourite view' in Britain. Thomas Hardy preferred the cathedral close:

Upon the whole the Close of Salisbury under the full summer moon on a windless night, is as beautiful a scene as any I know in England

It is the largest such close in England, and residents have latterly included the former prime minister Sir Edward Heath. A clock in the cathedral nave, which dates from 1386, is said to be the world's oldest working clock. The cathedral has one of four original copies of the Magna Carta. The bishop of Salisbury signs himself 'Sarum'.

The grid pattern on which 'New Sarum' was originally laid out around the close remains in place, and Salisbury has managed to retain much of the aspect and the atmosphere of an ancient cathedral city.

In March 1655 Salisbury was the scene of 'Penruddock's Rising', a failed Royalist rising against the Protectorate, led by a Colonel Penruddock who, with 200 followers, entered Salisbury and seized members of the judiciary. The revolt was swiftly crushed and its leaders executed.

The playwright Philip Massinger (1583–1640) and the composer William Lawes (1602–45; *see* CHESTER) were born in Salisbury.

In Thomas Hardy's *Jude the Obscure* (1895), the city is fictionalized as MELCHESTER, and Jude works in the cathedral.

There are towns and cities called Salisbury in the USA (Connecticut, Indiana, Maryland, Missouri, New Hampshire, North Carolina, Pennsylvania, Vermont), Canada (New Brunswick) and Australia (South Australia). Until 1980, when it was changed to Harare, the capital of Zimbabwe (formerly Rhodesia, and before that Southern Rhodesia) was called Salisbury (after Lord Salisbury, British prime minister when the city was founded).

John of Salisbury. A philosopher and historian (*c.*1115–80), who became secretary to Thomas Becket and supported him against Henry II; he fled to France after Becket's murder, and became Bishop of Chartres in 1176.

Lord Salisbury. The 3rd Marquess of Salisbury, Robert Arthur Talbot Gascoyne-Cecil (1830–1903), three-time Conservative prime minister (1885–6, 1886–92, 1895–1902). He was the last British prime minister to sit in the House of Lords.

Oath of Salisbury. An oath that William I required all large landowners in England to take in August 1086 at Salisbury, swearing allegiance to him.

Roger of Salisbury. A cleric and politician (*c.*1065–1139),

who was a close adherent of Henry I. He was appointed chancellor under Henry in 1100 and Bishop of Salisbury in 1101. He was regent of England 1123–6. After Henry's death he fell from favour and power under Stephen.

St Osmund of Salisbury. A Norman priest (d.1099; canonized 1457; feast day 4 December) who was chancellor of England (*c.*1072–8) and Bishop of Salisbury (1078–99). He is said to have been William the Conqueror's nephew. He oversaw the completion of the Norman cathedral at Old Sarum, and his liturgical reforms were the basis for the Sarum Use (*see under* SARUM).

Salisbury Cathedral from the Meadows. A well-known painting (1831) by John Constable, in which cattle inhabit the rural watery foreground, with the cathedral behind. It was exhibited by the painter at the Royal Academy.

Salisbury Giant, the. A 4-m (12-ft) high pageant giant still used on special occasions. He is accompanied by morris dancers and Hob-Nob, a hobby horse. Both the Giant and Hob-Nob date back to the later Middle Ages, although their fabric has often been renewed since then. They live in Salisbury Museum when not out gallivanting.

Salisbury Plain. A largely uninhabited and uncultivated tract of chalk upland in Wiltshire, north of Salisbury. It is approximately 775 sq km (300 sq miles) in area. It was a busy place in prehistoric times, and it is rich in ancient earthworks and monuments. Easily the most famous is STONEHENGE, but there are also important sites at BADBURY, Chiselbury, DANEBURY, Figsbury, Ogbury, Scratchbury, Winkelbury, Yarnbury and Old Sarum. Nowadays large parts of the Plain are owned by the Ministry of Defence; they are used for military training, and are closed to the public.

Oh, Salisbury Plain is bleak and bare, –
At least so I've heard many people declare
For I fairly confess I never was there; –
Not a shrub, nor a tree, nor a bush can you see,
No hedges, no ditches, no gates, no stiles,
Much less a house or a cottage for miles; –
– It's a very sad thing to be caught in the rain
When night's coming on upon Salisbury Plain.

R.H. Barham: 'The Dead Drummer', *Ingoldsby Legends* (1840)

The poet Wordsworth *was*, however, 'there', and composed **'On Salisbury Plain'** (1793–4), subsequently published as **'Guilt and Sorrow; or, Incidents upon Salisbury Plain'** (1842):

The troubled west was red with stormy fire,
O'er Sarum's plain the traveller with a sigh
Measured each painful step, the distant spire
That fixed at every turn his backward eye
Was lost, tho' still he turned, in the blank sky
By thirst and hunger pressed he gazed around
And scarce could any trace of man descry,
Save wastes of corn that stretched without a bound,
But where the sower dwelt was nowhere to be found.

One of the more unusual later uses for the Plain was as the backdrop to The Beatles' performance of the surreal 'I am the Walrus' in their 1967 television film *Magical Mystery Tour*.

In 2004 an attempt was made to reintroduce the great bustard, the world's heaviest flying bird, to Salisbury Plain. It had been extinct in Britain since the last one was shot in 1832. It is the county bird of Wiltshire, and appears on the county council's coat-of-arms.

Shepherd of Salisbury Plain, The. A religious tract by the 'bluestocking' Hannah More, first published in *The Cheap Repository Tracts* (1795), a series of 'moral tales for the people'. It had enormous popularity. The story was based on the life of one David Saunders, who with his father had kept sheep on Salisbury Plain for a hundred years and who lived in a lonely cottage on Cheverell Down. He was noted for his homely wisdom and practical piety, and was turned by Miss More into a sort of idealized Christian peasant.

Treaty of Salisbury. An agreement reached in 1289 under which Margaret, 'Maid of Norway', granddaughter of the recently deceased Alexander III of Scotland, was to be brought to Scotland and not married without the consent of Edward I of England (his idea was to marry her to his son Edward, and so unify England and Scotland, but she died on the voyage over).

Salisbury Crags *Salisbury* said to be named after William de Montacute, Earl of Salisbury (1301–44), who accompanied Edward III on his Scottish expedition in 1327. However, the name is not recorded until the 15th century, and the commemoration itself seems unlikely.

A long, continuous line of cliffs, volcanic in origin, forming a band above a steep escarpment on the northwest side of ARTHUR'S SEAT in Edinburgh. This hill is often likened to a recumbent lion – in which case Salisbury Crags are its forepaws.

> If I were to choose a spot from which the rising or setting sun could be seen to the greatest possible advantage, it would be that wild path winding around the foot of the high belt of semicircular rocks, called Salisbury Crags, and marking the verge of the steep descent which slopes down into the glen on the south-eastern side of the city of Edinburgh. The prospect, in its general outline, commands a close-built, high-piled city, stretching itself out beneath in a form, which, to a romantic imagination, may be supposed to represent that of a dragon; now, a noble arm of the sea, with its rocks, isles, distant shores, and boundary of mountains; and now, a fair and fertile champaign country, varied with hill, dale, and rock, and skirted by the picturesque ridge of the Pentland mountains.
>
> Sir Walter Scott: *The Heart of Midlothian* (1818), Chapter 7

Scott goes on to complain about the state of the path, which the authorities shortly afterwards rectified by putting to work convicted radicals on constructing the so-called Radical Road along the base of the crags. This gave rise to the famous tongue twister:

> Round the rugged rocks the ragged rascals ran.

The 'ragged rascals' were, of course, originally, 'radical rascals'.

Scottish rhyming slangsters have adopted Salisbury Crag as a synonym for *scag* 'heroin'.

Salisbury Plain. *See under* SALISBURY.

Salle 'sallow or willow glade', OE *salh* 'sallow, willow' + -LEY, compare SAUL[2].

A village (pronounced 'sawl') in Norfolk, about 21 km (13 miles) northwest of Norwich. Its church is disproportionately large and splendid, thanks mainly to the munificence of various local cloth tycoons and landed families (including the Boleyns) in the late Middle Ages and early Tudor period. Local legend claims that Anne Boleyn is buried here (offically her body is in the chapel of St Peter ad Vincula in the TOWER OF LONDON).

Sallins Irish *Na Solláin* 'the willow groves'.

A village in County Kildare, on the main Dublin–Cork railway line, 3 km (2 miles) north of Naas.

Sallins Train Robbery (31 March 1976). An incident in which the mail train was held up at Sallins and over £200,000 stolen. The Gardaí suspected members of the Irish Republican Socialist Party, and eventually three men were imprisoned. Two were released on appeal, and the third was granted a state pardon in 1984.

Sally Gap A corruption of *saddle*, i.e. hill pass, from the Irish name *Bearnas na Diallaite* 'gap of the saddle'.

A road pass and fine viewpoint in the northern Wicklow Mountains, County WICKLOW, 12 km (7.5 miles) southwest of Bray.

Salop A contracted form of the Anglo-Norman version of the name *Shropshire* (with *l* substituted for English *r*).

An alternative version of the name *Shropshire*, used historically mainly for the sake of brevity (e.g. in addressing envelopes). In 1974 it was officially adopted as the name of the county, but it was disliked by many local people and was particularly unpopular with the Euro-MP for Salop and Staffordshire, who discovered when attending conferences in Continental Europe that *Salop* is uncomfortably close to French *salope* 'slut'. The official designation reverted to 'Shropshire' in 1980.

Salopian. (A person) of or from Shropshire. As a noun, the term commonly designates a present or ('Old Salopian') former pupil of Shrewsbury School (*see* SHREWSBURY), and locals also use it to refer to townspeople of Shrewsbury.

As an adjective, it has some specific applications: in particular, to a type of porcelain (similar to Worcester) made at the former Caughley factory (closed in 1814) near Broseley, Shropshire in the late 18th and early 19th centuries; and to a division of the Silurian period characterized by sedimentary rocks formed from consolidated clay.

Salt 'salt-pit, saltworks', OE *selte*.
A village in Staffordshire, about 5 km (3 miles) northeast of Stafford.

Saltaire A name coined in 1850, combining the name of the River AIRE with that of local industrialist Sir Titus *Salt*.
A town in West Yorkshire, 5 km (3 miles) northwest of Bradford. It was founded in 1853 by Sir Titus Salt as a model village for the textile workers in his factory, Salt's Mill, the largest in the world at the time of its opening in 1853. Salt's Mill is now given over to craft shops and a permanent exhibition of the work of the Bradford-born artist David Hockney. All the streets of the village (apart from Victoria and Albert) are named after members of Salt's family. In 2001 it was named as one of UNESCO's World Heritage Sites.
See also NEW LANARK.

Saltash Originally *Ash* 'ash-tree', OE *æsc*; the addition of *Salt-* (first recorded in 1302) reflects local salt production.
A hillside town and fishing port in Cornwall, on the opposite side of the TAMAR estuary from PLYMOUTH. It is linked to the eastern bank by Brunel's Prince Albert Bridge (1859), a railway bridge, and the Tamar Suspension Bridge (1961), carrying the A38. In former times tin was exported from the port.
Nearby, on the river, is the COTEHELE estate, now administered by the National Trust.
Saltash luck. A fruitless task that involves getting wet through. An expression in use, especially in the Royal Navy and Merchant Navy, since at least the early 20th century, and said to have been inspired by the persistently poor catches of people fishing off Saltash bridge – more succinctly summed up as 'a wet arse and no fish'.

Saltburn-by-the-Sea 'salt stream', OE *salt* + *burna* 'stream'.
A seaside resort in Redcar and Cleveland (formerly in the North Riding of Yorkshire, then in Cleveland), 17 km (11 miles) east of Middlesbrough.

Saltcoats 'salt cottages or huts', i.e. buildings of the saltworks, or houses of the saltworkers, ME *cotes* 'cottages, huts' (*see* -COT, COTE).
A resort town on the North Ayrshire coast (formerly in Strathclyde), south of and contiguous with Ardrossan. Saltworks were established here in the 16th century by James V. The Ayrshire novelist John Galt (1779–1839) described the people of Saltcoats as 'a sordid race'.

Saltdean 'salt valley' (referring to a gap in the Downs by the sea), OE *sealt* 'salt' + *denu* 'valley'.
A coastal village and resort within the unitary authority of Brighton and Hove, in East Sussex, about 8 km (5 miles) east of Brighton. Above it looms a Butlin's holiday camp in pre-Second World War *moderne* style. It also has a 1930s Lido.

Saltee Islands 'salt islands', OScand *salt* 'salt' + *ey* 'island' (*see* -AY).
Two small uninhabited islands some 5 km (3 miles) off FORLORN POINT on the south coast of County Wexford. In Irish they are **Ná Sailtí** ('salt islands'). It was to the Saltee Islands that Bagenal Harvey and John Colclough, two of the leaders of the 1798 United Irishmen's Rebellion, fled before being caught and beheaded. The islands have proved a safer refuge for a wide range of birdlife, and are owned by a person styling himself 'Prince Michael the First'.

Salter's Bank *Salter* probably either a surname or occupation (salt-maker or salt merchant), ME *saltere*.
The wide extent of sands off LYTHAM ST ANNE'S, Lancashire, on the north side of the mouth of the Ribble Estuary.

Saltfleetby St Clement *Saltfleetby* 'farmstead or village by the salt stream', OE *salt* + *fleot* 'stream' + -BY; *St Clement* from the dedication of the local church.
A village in northern Lincolnshire, about 13 km (8 miles) east of Louth.

Saltfleetby St Peter *St Peter* from the dedication of the local church.
A village in northern Lincolnshire, about 10 km (6 miles) east of Louth.

Salthill Irish *Bóthar na Trá* 'road of the strand', so the English presumably refers to sand dunes.
A southwestern suburb of GALWAY. It has been a popular seaside resort since the middle of the 19th century, and there is a curious tradition associated with the place called 'Kicking the Wall'; this involves doing just that at the end of the prom.

Saltmarket. A street in GLASGOW, south of Glasgow Cross, once a byword for poverty – hence the ironic expression **all the comforts of the Saltmarket**.

Saltram 'homestead or land in a river-bend belonging to the salters', OE *sealtere* 'salter' (someone who makes, sells, or works with salt) + HAM.
A Georgian house and gardens, 3 km (2 miles) west of PLYMPTON in Devon, on the banks of the estuary of the River Plym. Owned since 1957 by the National Trust, Saltram House was built in 1743 for Sir John and Lady Catherine Parker around the core of an existing Tudor mansion; the staterooms and salon, designed in 1768 by Robert Adam, are widely regarded as amongst Adam's finest

work. The adjoining gardens have attractive wooded walks along the River Plym.

Saltram House appeared in Ang Lee's 1995 film version of Jane Austen's *Sense and Sensibility*, playing the role of Norland Park, ancestral home of the Dashwood family.

Sampford Courtenay *Sampford* 'sandy ford' (referring to a ford on the nearby River Taw), OE *sand* + FORD; *Courtenay* denoting manorial ownership in the Middle Ages by the Curtenay family.

A village in Devon, to the north of DARTMOOR, about 21 km (13 miles) west of Crediton. With its thatched cottages and 15th-century church it is a natural for picture postcards. Things were less peaceful in 1549, though, when protests against the new Prayer Book in English led to riots, in which a member of the local gentry was killed.

Sampford Peverell *Sampford see* SAMPFORD COURTENAY (but here referring to a ford on the nearby River Lynor); *Peverell* denoting manorial ownership in the Middle Ages by the Peverel family.

A village in Devon, on the Grand Western Canal, about 8 km (5 miles) east of Tiverton.

Sampford ghost. An uncommonly persistent poltergeist which haunted a thatched house (destroyed by fire *c*.1942) in Sampford Peverell for about three years until 1810. In addition to the usual knockings, the occupants were beaten, curtains agitated and damaged, levitations occurred, and in one instance an 'unattached arm' flung a folio Greek Testament from a bed into the middle of the room. The Rev. Charles Caleb Colton, rector of the Prior's Portion, Tiverton (credited as author of these freaks), offered £100 to anyone who could explain the matter except on supernatural grounds. No one ever claimed the reward.

Sanclêr. *See* ST CLEARS.

Sanctuary, the. A hilltop stone circle in Wiltshire (its stones long gone, their positions now marked by concrete blocks), linked to AVEBURY by West Kennett Avenue (*see under* WEST KENNETT).

Sandaig 'sand bay', OScand *sandr* 'sand' + *vik* 'bay'.

The west Highland home of writer Gavin Maxwell, and the setting for his bestselling autobiographical story of life among otters and other flora and fauna, *Ring of Bright Water* (1960). He called the place Camusfeàrna ('bay of the alders'), but did not divulge its location until some years later. It is near **Sandaig Lighthouse**, on the Sound of Sleat, about 8 km (5 miles) south of GLENELG. The house burnt down in 1968, and Edal, one of the otters, was killed. Maxwell himself died a year later, and his ashes are buried at Sandaig.

Sanday 'sand island', OScand *sandr* 'sand' + *ey* (*see* -AY).

An island in Orkney, 27 km (16 miles) northeast of Kirkwall on Mainland. It is separated from Stronsay to the south by **Sanday Sound**, and is generally low-lying, the highest point

being the Wart (65 m / 213 ft). The island holds a few traces of the supernatural: the so-called Devil's Fingermarks are to be found on the ruins of Kirk of Lady near Overbister, while the 20-ton Saville Stone at Scar is said to have been thrown from the neighbouring island of EDAY by a witch at her daughter who had run off with a Sanday man. Another man from Sanday was troubled by a hogboon (a sort of elf), who was so annoyed that the man's wife had failed to leave out food that he made life a misery. The man and his family were so tormented that they decided to move to another farm – but as they drove their cart across the island they were dismayed when the hogboon's head popped out of a milk churn and declared: 'What a grand day for the flittin!'

Sandbach 'sandy valley-stream', OE *sand* + *bæce* 'valley-stream'.

A town (pronounced 'sandbatch') in Cheshire, on a tributary of the River Wheelock, about 8 km (5 miles) northeast of Crewe. There are two 7th-century Saxon crosses in the market place, and a grammar school was founded here in 1594. Sandbach Services are just to the south of Junction 17 on the M6.

I.A. Richards (1893–1979), poet, influential literary critic and mountaineer, was born in Sandbach.

Sandbourne. The fictional name for BOURNEMOUTH in several novels by Thomas Hardy.

Sandford Orcas *Sandford* 'sandy ford' (referring to a ford over a local stream called the Mill Stream), OE *sand* + FORD; *Orcas* denoting manorial ownership in the Middle Ages by the Orescuils family.

A village in Dorset, about 4 km (2.5 miles) northwest of Sherborne. It has attractive houses, built of golden Ham stone, and an Elizabethan manor.

Sandhurst 'sandy wooded hill', OE *sand* + *hyrst* 'wooded hill'.

A town within the unitary authority of BRACKNELL FOREST, in former Berkshire, on the River Blackwater, about 4 km (2.5 miles) northwest of Camberley and 14 km (9 miles) north of Aldershot.

It is pre-eminently an army town, defined by the presence, just to the southeast, of the Royal Military Academy, the British Army's training college for officers, which is popularly referred to as just '**Sandhurst**'. This was founded in the early 19th century as the Royal Military College. It was built by French prisoners of war during the Napoleonic Wars, and took in its first cadets in 1812. In 1947 it combined with the Royal Military Academy (Woolwich), and took the latter's name. Sandhurst is also home to the National Army Museum.

Those who have been trained at Sandhurst but who have not followed a primarily military career include Winston Churchill (1874–1965), King Alfonso XII of Spain

(1857–85), the Irish writer Lord Dunsany (1878–1957), the novelist Alec Waugh (1898–1991), the film star David Niven (1909–83), former British foreign secretary Lord Carrington (b.1919), Sultan Qabus ibn Sa'id of Oman (b.1940) and former Conservative Party leader Iain Duncan Smith (b.1954).

Sanditon. The name under which Jane Austen fictionalized BRIGHTON in her unfinished novel *Sanditon* (1817).

Sandown 'sandy enclosure or river-meadow', OE *sand + hamm* 'enclosure, river-meadow' (*see* HAM).

A town and seaside resort on the east coast of the ISLE OF WIGHT, in the centre of **Sandown Bay**, about 11 km (7 miles) southeast of Newport. Visitors are attracted in large numbers by its appropriately sandy beach (10 km / 6 miles long) and its record as one of the sunniest spots in Britain, and it rewards them with a range of traditional English seaside attractions (including the Island's only surviving pleasure pier).

Sandown Park *Sandown* 'sandy hill or down', OE *sand + dun* 'hill, down' (*see* DOWN, -DON).

A park and racecourse in ESHER, Surrey. Both the park (which also contains a golf course and a ski slope) and the track opened in 1875. Racing is both flat and National Hunt, and high-profile horse races run here include the Sandown Mile, the Classic Trial, the William Hill Handicap Hurdle and, most notably, the Coral-Eclipse Stakes ('Eclipse' after a famous 19th-century racehorse, great-great-grandson of the Darley Arabian). First run in 1886, the Eclipse was the first English horse race with a £10,000 prize.

Sandray 'sand island', OScand *sandr* 'sand' + *ey* 'island' (*see* -AY); this name has apparently retained the *-r* inflection where others, such as SANDAIG and SANDAY, have lost it. The modern Gaelic name is *Sanndraigh*.

A small uninhabited island in the southern Outer HEBRIDES. It is in Western Isles (formerly in Inverness-shire), 5 km (3 miles) south of Barra, and is separated from VATERSAY to the north by the **Sound of Sandray**. The last inhabitants left in the early 20th century.

Sandringham 'the sandy part of Dersingham' (referring to a nearby village), OE *sand +* DERSINGHAM.

A village in Norfolk, close to the southeastern corner of the WASH, about 11 km (7 miles) northeast of King's Lynn.

Its name is widely known thanks to **Sandringham House**, the British Royal Family's country residence. It was bought by Queen Victoria in 1861 for her eldest son, the future Edward VII (who set hard-to-meet standards for the mass slaughter of game birds there). In the 1870s it was converted in the Jacobean style. Twentieth-century British monarchs tended to prefer it to the somewhat oppressive splendours of BUCKINGHAM PALACE. But even Sandringham was too grand for George V (1865–1936); he spent as much

time as he could in the decidedly poky York Cottage in the grounds. George VI (1895–1952) was born – and died – here. Sandringham continues to be a favoured country retreat for Elizabeth II, who spends Christmas here with her family. King Olaf V of Norway (1903–91) was born on the estate, at Appleton House, as was Diana, Princess of Wales (1961–97), at Park House.

Sandwell 'sandy spring', OE *sand + wella* 'spring'.

A district of WEST BROMWICH, within the West Midlands (before 1974 in Staffordshire). In 1974 its name was conferred on a newly created metropolitan borough incorporating SMETHWICK and WEDNESBURY as well as West Bromwich, TIPTON, and ROWLEY REGIS. A new Sandwell and Dudley railway station, opened in the 1980s, made this part of the BLACK COUNTRY a regular stopping point for fast trains on the London–Stafford (and Manchester) routes.

Sandwich 'sandy harbour or trading centre', OE *sand + wic* (*see* WICK).

A town and former port in Kent, on the River STOUR[3], about 17.5 km (11 miles) east of Canterbury. In the Anglo-Saxon period and the early Middle Ages, when it was still on the coast, it developed into one of the most important ports in England (it was one of the original five CINQUE PORTS). It was via Sandwich that Thomas Becket fled to France and later returned to his martyrdom in Canterbury; Richard I landed here on his return from the Crusades; and the town was subject to continual French raids (in the worst, in 1457, it was partly burned down, and the mayor was killed; mayors of Sandwich still wear black robes in his memory). In the 16th century, however, the Stour silted up and the sea receded, and Sandwich's greatest days were over.

Its name, though, remains on everyone's lips, thanks to the fourth holder of the title Earl of Sandwich, John Montagu (1718–92). He was a gambling man, and he so resented time spent away from the tables that he had convenience meals prepared for him, which he could eat as he lost money. One of the most successful was a slice of cold roast beef between two pieces of toast, and its successors are to this day called '**sandwiches**'. (A less colourful account has it that the Earl, who was an assiduous politician and three times First Lord of the Admiralty – he sponsored Captain Cook's voyages of discovery, and the Hawaiian Islands were originally named the Sandwich Islands after him – ordered up the sandwiches so that he could work long hours at his desk without interruption.)

On the low sandy ground between the town and **Sandwich Bay** is the Royal St George's Golf Course, on which the Open Championship has been held 13 times, between 1894 and 2003. James Bond played Goldfinger here for a $10,000 stake (Bond's creator Ian Fleming was a member). P.G. Wodehouse, though, claimed he was put off his game here by 'the uproar of the butterflies in the adjoining meadows'.

There are towns called Sandwich in the USA (Illinois and Massachusetts (home of an important glass factory)) and a Sandwich Bay in Canada (Labrador).

Battle of Sandwich (24 August 1217). A sea-battle off Sandwich between the navies of Henry III of England and Prince Louis of France. Defeat for Louis put paid to his hopes of seizing the English throne.

Sandwich tern. A black, grey and white seabird (*Sterna sandvicensis*) of the tern family, found in Europe and Africa.

Sandwood Bay Possibly 'bay of sand-water', OScand *sand-vatn*, although it is also possible that the name is ModE and of much more recent coinage.

A bay in the far northwest of Scotland, in Highland (formerly in Sutherland), some 10 km (6 miles) south of Cape Wrath. The beautiful sandy beach can only be reached on foot, by a 6 km (4 mile) walk across the moors, past the freshwater **Sandwood Loch** and the ruined **Sandwood Cottage**. The latter is famously haunted by the ghost of a sailor who used to knock on the windows; he is said to have died when his galleon foundered here after the Armada. The area is also known as 'the land of mermaids', and several sightings were reported in the early years of the 20th century. Off the southwestern end of the bay is the sea stack called Am Buachaille (Gaelic 'the shepherd'); whether on a misty day this could be mistaken for a mermaid is a moot point.

Sandy 'sandy island' (referring to the elevated land on which the town stands), OE *sand* + *eg* (*see* -EY, -EA).

A town in Bedfordshire, on the River IVEL, about 13 km (8 miles) east of Bedford. The 19th-century **Sandy Lodge** houses the headquarters of the Royal Society for the Protection of Birds.

Sandycove. *See under* DÚN LAOGHAIRE.

Sannox. *See* GLEN SANNOX.

Sanquhar 'old fort', Gaelic *sean* 'old' + *cathair* 'fort' (*see* CAHER). A small town in Dumfries and Galloway (formerly in Dumfriesshire), 17 km (10 miles) northwest of Thornhill. It was once known for its knitting industry.

Sanquhar. Garments (such as gloves) knitted in an ornamental style using a double thread.

Saorstát Éireann. The Irish name for the Irish Free State (*see under* IRISH).

Sarehole Etymology unclear; the second part may be OE *hol* 'hollow'.

A southern suburb of BIRMINGHAM, in Hall Green, some 7 km (4 miles) from the city centre. The novelist J.R.R. Tolkien lived in a cottage here as a child with his widowed mother in the 1890s. Late Victorian Sarehole, then a rural

Warwickshire hamlet, seems to have been the model for Tolkien's SHIRE, the land of the hobbits in his novel *The Hobbit* (1937) and his trilogy *The Lord of the Rings* (1954–5). In 1967 Tolkien told a journalist from the *Scotsman* that the Shire 'was inspired by a few cherished square miles of actual countryside at Sarehole, near Birmingham', and in correspondence he spoke of the Shire as being based on a Warwickshire village around the time of Queen Victoria's Diamond Jubilee in 1897.

Like Bag End, Bilbo Baggins's home in the fictional village of Hobbiton, Tolkien's childhood home in Sarehole was close to a mill. **Sarehole Mill** retains a working watermill and museum, and is now open to the public.

Sark Etymology unknown.

One of the CHANNEL ISLANDS, about 11 km (7 miles) east of Guernsey (to whose bailiwick it belongs). At 5 sq km (2 sq miles) in area, it is the smallest of the four main islands. It consists of **Great Sark** and **Little Sark**, which are linked by a narrow isthmus called La Coupée. Off its northwestern corner is the much smaller island of BRECQHOU.

It is governed in semi-feudal fashion, as a 'Seigneurie' (established by Elizabeth I). The ruler is a hereditary Seigneur or Dame. The most celebrated recent incumbent of that post was Sibyl Hathaway, **Dame of Sark** from 1927 to 1974. The island has its own parliament, called the Chief Pleas.

Apart from agricultural vehicles, no motor vehicles are allowed on the island, and aircraft are banned too.

The novelist and artist Mervyn Peake (1911–68) spent three years on Sark with a group of other artists in the early 1930s, and it is the setting of his novel *Mr Pye* (1953).

The island's French name is *Sercq*.

Sarkese. Of or relating to Sark. Also a noun, denoting the people of Sark, or the variety of Norman French spoken on the island.

Sark lark. A colloquial term of the late 1980s for the lucrative exploitation of the virtual absence of company tax and company law on Sark. Any company could set up here provided it had a Sarkese on the board, and a lively cottage industry in directorships developed. It was estimated in 1988 that 10% of the island's population of fewer than 600 were company directors, and that Sark had the highest concentration of telex and fax machines in the world.

Sarn Helen Possibly Welsh *sarn heolen* 'paved causeway' or *sarn y lleng* 'causeway of the legion', although more fancifully it is said to be named after *Helen*, the Welsh wife of the Emperor Maximus (*see* CAERNARFON).

The road built by the Romans in western Wales, from their fort at Maridunum (CARMARTHEN) in the south to that at Segontium (Caernarfon) in the north. The road (segments of which survive) traverses some inhospitable upland terrain.

Sarnia. The Roman name for GUERNSEY.

Sarum From a misreading of the abbreviation *Sar'* in medieval documents. This was short for the Medieval Latin form of the name *Salisbury*, which was *Sarisberia* (*see* SALISBURY). The latter part of the word was represented by a symbol similar to a figure '4'. This was also the conventional manuscript representation of the ending *-um*, and anyone unfamiliar with *Sar'* might easily misinterpret it as *Sarum*.

The ecclesiastical name of SALISBURY. In modern usage the term mainly connotes the church practices and rituals prescribed in the pre-Reformation Sarum Use (*see below*), in whose prelapsarian simplicity and purity there was a revival of interest in the late 19th century.

> And there we'll sing the Sarum rite
> Tae English Hymnal airs.
>
>> John Betjeman: 'Perp. Revival i' the North',
>> *High and Low* (1966)

There have also been occasional literary uses of 'Sarum', though often these owe more to the historical connotations of OLD SARUM:

> A traveller on the skirt of Sarum's Plain
> Pursued his vagrant way, with feet half bare …
>
>> William Wordsworth: 'Guilt or Sorrow; or, Incidents
>> upon Salisbury Plain' (1842)

The present city of Salisbury was formerly called **New Sarum**, and the Bishop of Salisbury signs himself 'Sarum'.

Sarum. A colossal historical novel (1987) by Edward Rutherford, which tells the story of Salisbury and its area from prehistoric times to the late 20th century.

Sarum Use. The order of divine service used in the diocese of Salisbury from the 11th century to the Reformation (*see* St Osmund of Salisbury *under* SALISBURY).

Sassenach Gaelic *Sassunnach*, Irish *Sasanach* from medieval Latin *Saxones* 'Saxons'.

A derogatory term used by Highlanders for Scottish Lowlanders (*see under* the HIGHLANDS *and* the LOWLANDS), but more frequently used today by Scots in general for the English (who are sometimes also called Sassenachs by the Irish).

Sauchieburn Possibly 'burn of the willow copse', Gaelic *salchan* 'willow copse' (or possibly Gaelic *socach* 'projecting ground') + OE *burna* 'stream'; or possibly 'stream by the heathland growing with willows', OE *salh* 'willow' + *hæth* 'heathland' + *burna* 'stream'.

A battle site on the southwest side of STIRLING[1], where on 11 June 1488 James III was defeated and killed by rebel nobles. The site was in Stirlingshire, then in Central region, and is now in the unitary authority of Stirling; it is sometimes referred to as the **Field of Stirling**. At the battle the king's horse ran away with him and he was injured in a fall. Taking refuge at Beaton's Mill, near BANNOCKBURN, he was stabbed to death by a rebel dressed as a priest. On his death his 15-year-old son, who had accompanied the rebels at the battle but was no more than a pawn, became king as James IV. The young king was subsequently haunted by guilt, and his first Parliament produced an apologia to send to the princes of Europe, to explain the events at the battle in which his father 'happinnit to be slane'. From 1493 to 1513 James did penance by making an annual pilgrimage to the shrine of St Duthus in TAIN, in the far northeast of Scotland.

Sauchiehall Street 'willow valley', Gaelic *saileach* 'willow' + Scots dialect *haugh* 'valley, water-meadow' (*see* HALE, -HALL), with ModE *street*.

Glasgow's most famous street (pronounced 'sochiehall', with the first syllable pronounced to rhyme with 'loch') and one of its main shopping streets – hence the simile **like Sauchiehall Street** denotes a stramash, bustling crowd or brouhaha. In urban legend, at least, it is the centre of Saturday-night drunken revelry, as in the impersonation of the veteran rugby commentator Bill McClaren, who, when Scotland achieves a win, is supposed to say, with relish, 'They'll be breakin mony a windae doon Sauchiehall Street the night.' It is known familiarly as **Suckie**, and is linked to some of Glasgow's other main shopping streets via the phrase **up Suckie, doon Buckie an alang Argyle**, Buckie being Buchanan Street, and Argyle being, well, Argyle Street; the phrase is used to denote the approximate and meandering route of a Saturday afternoon of retail therapy.

Charles Rennie Mackintosh's Willow Tea Rooms (1904) are situated in Sauchiehall Street and his Glasgow School of Art (1896–1909) is on nearby Renfrew Street.

Saughall Massie *Saughall* 'nook of land where sallow-trees or willow-trees grow', OE *salh* 'sallow, willow' + *halh* 'nook of land' (*see* HALE, -HALL); *Massie* denoting manorial ownership in the Middle Ages by the de Mascy family.

A village (pronounced 'sawglə' or 'sawkəl') in the Wirral, now a western suburb of WALLASEY.

Saughton Prison 'willow farm', Gaelic *saileach* 'willow' + OE -TON.

Edinburgh's prison, in the west of the city. Four men were hanged here between 1928 and 1954.

Saul[1] Irish *Sabhall* 'barn'.

A village in County Down, just to the northeast of Downpatrick. It is traditionally the site where St Patrick established his first church in Ireland in 432, in a barn donated by a local chieftain, and the name is preserved from the 7th century as *Sabul Patricii* 'Patrick's *sabhall*'.

Tradition also has it that St Patrick returned to Saul to die in 461. There are the remains of a 12th-century abbey and a somewhat phoney replica of an early Irish church, built in 1932 on the 1500th anniversary of the first church.

Saul² 'sallow or willow glade', OE *salh* 'sallow, willow' + -LEY, compare SALLE.

A village in Gloucestershire, on the east bank of the River SEVERN, about 13 km (8 miles) southwest of Gloucester.

Saundersfoot 'foot of the cliff of the Saunders family', the family name being a version of *Alexander*, and the family was known here from the 13th century + ME *foot*.

A seaside resort in Pembrokeshire (formerly in Dyfed), 4 km (2.5 miles) north of Tenby. It overlooks **Saundersfoot Bay**, an inlet of Carmarthen Bay. The harbour, once used for the export of anthracite, is now used only by pleasure craft.

Savernake Forest *Savernake* 'district of the River Severn' (here perhaps referring to the River Bedwyn rather than the present-day Severn), SEVERN + OCelt -*og* 'district'.

An area of woodland (pronounced 'savvernack') in Wiltshire, immediately to the southeast of MARLBOROUGH. It covers 18 sq km (7 sq miles). It was a royal hunting ground as far back as the Anglo-Saxon period, but was sold off to private ownership in 1540. It was replanted with oaks and beeches in the 18th century, and the landscape designer 'Capability' Brown laid out the 6-km (4-mile) beech-lined Grand Avenue.

Savile Row After Lady Dorothy *Savile*, wife of Richard Boyle, 3rd earl of Burlington (1695–1753), who developed the estate in this area in the early 18th century.

A street in MAYFAIR, in the City of Westminster (W1), running north to south from Conduit Street to Vigo Street. At first, at the beginning of the 18th century, it was home mainly to military officers and doctors, but tailors soon began to open premises here, and the street in due course became famous as the heart of English tailoring, and particularly (from the latter part of the 19th century) for the making of stylish bespoke suits for gentlemen. 'Savile Row' came to connote apparel of discreet classiness:

> She took in the Savile Row cut of Edward's clothes.
>
> Agatha Christie: *The Hollow* (1946)

The oldest Savile Row tailor is Henry Poole & Co. (established in 1806). Other famous names include Gieves & Hawkes, Henry Huntsman & Sons, Hardy Amies Ltd, Kilgour French Stanbury (whose clients include Hugh Grant, Jude Law, Noel Gallagher and (for riding clothes) the Queen), Anderson and Sheppard, Richard James and Ozwald Boateng.

In the 1960s, however, the street shook off some of its fusty discretion to join the burgeoning nexus of fashion, music and youth culture, reaching its peak when

The Beatles opened the headquarters of their Apple company here, and famously gave an impromptu performance on the building's roof in 1969.

Savile Row also has its own police station, West End Central.

The playwright Richard Sheridan died in Savile Row in 1816.

Savoy, the After Peter of *Savoy*.

A precinct off the STRAND, in the WEST END¹ of London, centred on the former **Savoy Palace**. In 1245 Henry III granted it to his wife's uncle, Peter, Count of Savoy (whence its name). After he left, in 1263, it became the residence of Eleanor of Castile, wife of Prince Edward (afterwards Edward I). It was later given to Queen Eleanor's second son, Edmund of Lancaster. In the latter part of the 14th century it was the residence of John of Gaunt. On the accession of Henry IV in 1399, it was annexed to the Crown as part of the estates of the Duchy of Lancaster. Most of the original buildings had been destroyed by Wat Tyler's followers during the Peasants' Revolt in 1381, but Henry VII bequeathed funds for the reconstruction of the palace as a hospital for the poor under the name of St John's Hospital. It became a military hospital, then a barracks under Charles II, but this was demolished with the construction of John Rennie's Waterloo Bridge, which was completed in 1831. In the late 17th century, the Savoy precinct became a notorious rookery for evil-doers claiming rights of sanctuary. *See also* ALSATIA.

Savoyard. A term for a denizen or habitué of the Savoy, adapted from its original application to a native of Savoy in France. In the 17th and 18th centuries it denoted the desperadoes and outlaws who hid out in the Savoy at that time, and more recently it has been used for a performer in, or devotee of, the **Savoy Operas** (*see below*).

Savoy Chapel. A chapel in Savoy Street (WC2), originally within the precincts of the **Savoy Palace** (*see above*). It was built in 1505 and, after the destruction of St Mary le Strand by Protector Somerset (during Edward VI's minority), became known as St Mary le Savoy. It was repaired and restored several times in the 18th century and again by Queen Victoria in 1843 and 1864. In 1890 it became the first place of worship to be lit by electricity. In 1939 it was further refurbished, and designated the **King's Chapel of the Savoy**.

Savoy Conference. A conference held at the Savoy in 1661, after the Restoration of Charles II, between the bishops and the Presbyterian clergy to review the Book of Common Prayer. It resulted in only minor changes, which were included in the revised book of 1662. Most of the Presbyterian demands were rejected.

Savoy Hill. A street in the Savoy (WC2), leading down from the Strand to the Victoria Embankment (*see under*

EMBANKMENT). It was the site of the first studios of the BBC (1922) and until 1932 its headquarters, the original BBC call sign being 2LO (i.e. No. 2, London).

Savoy Hotel. A luxury hotel on the site of the old Savoy Palace (*see above*), between the Strand and the north bank of the Thames. Richard D'Oyly Carte had it built in the mid-1880s. It was one of the first hotels in London to be equipped with electric lifts and electric lighting. Its first manager was César Ritz (who went on to found the Ritz Hotel (*see under* PICCADILLY[1])) and its first chef Auguste Escoffier, who created the Pêche Melba here in honour of Dame Nellie Melba's visit in 1892. Its main restaurants, the **Savoy Grill** and the River Restaurant, are world-renowned. Its forecourt is the only street in the British Isles where traffic must keep to the right.

Arnold Bennett's *Imperial Palace* (1930), his last and longest novel, is set in the Savoy.

The Savoy features as the place of punishment of 'Godolphin Horne', the subject of one of Hilaire Belloc's *Cautionary Tales for Children* (1907) and a well-born child who is beset by the sin of pride:

> So now Godolphin is the Boy
> Who blacks the boots at the Savoy.

Savoy Operas. The comic operas with words by W.S. Gilbert (1836–1911) and music by Arthur Sullivan (1842–1900), produced by Richard D'Oyly Carte. Most of the operettas, from *Iolanthe* (1882) onwards, were first produced at the **Savoy Theatre** (*see below*).

Savoy Orpheans. A dance orchestra that regularly broadcast on the BBC from the Savoy Hotel between the First and Second World Wars. It made its debut in 1923, under Debroy Somers, but its most famous years were under the leadership of the pianist Carroll Gibbons.

Savoy Theatre. A theatre built by Richard D'Oyly Carte in the STRAND to stage his productions of the Gilbert and Sullivan operettas. It opened in 1881, with *Patience* (transferred from another theatre). The first original production here was *Iolanthe* (1882) and the last, *The Grand Duke* (1896 – a flop). At the beginning of the 20th century D'Oyly Carte sold the lease, and it turned into a general theatre. It became known for its Christmas productions of J.M. Barrie's *Peter Pan*.

'Stomping at the Savoy'. A song (1936: words, Andy Razaf; music, Benny Goodman, Edgar Sampson, Chick Webb), which was a hit in the late 1930s. The 'Savoy' referred to is the **Savoy Ballroom** in Harlem, New York City (where Ella Fitzgerald made her debut).

Sawbridgeworth 'Sæbriht's enclosure', OE *Sæbrihtes* possessive form of male personal name *Sæbriht* + *worth* (*see* -WORTH, WORTHY, -WARDINE). The -*bridge*- element arose as a folk-etymological alteration of -*briht* (locally the central syllable

eroded away completely, and the name was in the past generally pronounced 'sapsworth').

A small town in Hertfordshire, on the River STORT, about 5 km (3 miles) south of Bishop's Stortford. The fertile surrounding land supported the growth of the 19th-century nursery business, supplying plants for Victorian gardens and orchards. David and Victoria Beckham acquired a former orphanage near Sawbridgeworth after their marriage in 1999, and the extensively – and expensively – renovated property soon aquired a nickname suited to the Beckhams' status as media royalty – 'Beckingham Palace'.

Sawrey. *See* NEAR SAWREY.

Saxmundham 'Seaxmund's homestead', OE male personal name *Seaxmund* + HAM.

A town in Suffolk, about 30 km (19 miles) northeast of Ipswich. There are some pleasing Georgian houses along its strung-out main street, and the grounds of a late 19th-century mansion contain the largest dovecote in Suffolk. Bruisyard Vineyard is nearby.

Saxon Shore A translation of Latin *Litoris Saxonici*, a term used in the *Notitia dignitatum*, an early 5th-century administrative handbook concerned with the organization of Roman military units.

The coast of Norfolk, Suffolk, Essex, Kent, Sussex and Hampshire, from the WASH to the SOLENT, as fortified by the Romans against the attacks of Saxon and Frisian pirates, under the charge of the **Count of the Saxon Shore** (*Comes Litoris Saxonici per Britanniam*). His garrisons were at BRANCASTER (*Branodunum*) in Norfolk; BURGH CASTLE (*Gariannonum*) and Walton Castle in Suffolk; BRADWELL-ON-SEA (*Othona*) in Essex; RECULVER (*Regulbium*), RICHBOROUGH (*Rutupiae*), DOVER (*Dubris*) and LYMPNE (*Portus Lemanis*) in Kent; PEVENSEY (*Anderitum*) on the Sussex coast; and perhaps PORTCHESTER (*Portus Ardaoni*) near Portsmouth.

Scackleton 'valley by a summit', OE *scacol* 'point of land' + *denu* 'valley' (the latter element, rather than -TON, is suggested by the earliest recorded form, *Scacheldene* 1086).

A hamlet in the HOWARDIAN HILLS, North Yorkshire, 14 km (8.5 miles) west of Malton.

Scafell Pike 'peak of the hill with the shieling', *Scafell* OScand *skali* 'shieling, summer pasture' + *fjall* 'hill', with *pik* 'peak'.

A mountain (977 m / 3205 ft) in the Lake District, Cumbria (formerly in Cumberland), 18 km (11 miles) southwest of Keswick. It is the highest mountain in England, and is also called **Scafell Pikes**. The top called simply **Scafell** or **Sca Fell** (964 m / 3162 ft) is about 1 km (0.6 miles) to the southwest, and to reach it from Scafell Pike it is necessary to cross the col called Mickledore and to scramble up the rocks of Broad Stand. It is possible to climb Scafell Pike from Wasdale (*see under* WAST WATER), LANGDALE, Eskdale (*see under* ESK[4]) or BORROWDALE; this last is the Corridor Route, the oldest route, and that used by guides in the 19th century. Both tops, but particularly Scafell, are well-provisioned with mighty crags, which hold some of the oldest rock climbs in the Lakes, as well as some of the newest and hardest.

The poet Samuel Taylor Coleridge was a precursor to modern climbers of this peak:

> O my God! what enormous mountains these are close by me, and yet below the hill I stand on.
>
> Samuel Taylor Coleridge: writing to Sara Hutchinson (5 August 1802) from the summit – 'surely the first letter ever written from the top of Scafell!'

In his next letter to Sara, written the following day, Coleridge recounts how he had rashly decided to descend from the summit to Mickledore (not, from his description, following the conventional route), and thus embarked, somewhat to his terror, on perhaps the first attested rock climb undertaken in Britain for recreational purposes. Having reached safe ground (apparently via the fissure known as Fat Man's Agony), he looked back up as a thunderstorm approached at 'the enormous and more than perpendicular precipices and *bull's-brows* of Scafell!'

Another unwise summiteer was encountered by John Ruskin in 1859, as he walked from Borrowdale to Wasdale. This was:

> ... a young gentleman attired as though for a lounge in Bond Street; shirt-collar had he, an umbrella-parasol, and (if we do not exaggerate) straps! yes, he was bent upon ascending Scafell Pike in straps!! ... When we told one of the dalesmen what this superlatively dressed person was about to attempt, he pulled his pipe out of his contemptuous lips, and said 't' lad el dee', – meaning that it would be the death of him ... When mist came on that evening, in such thick folds that Wasdale might have been Salisbury Plain for all that we could see of the mountains, the good dalesman and some friends of his started to feel their way up those pikes. They found poor Straps, dead beat, but upon the very summit of the hill, lying down breathless upon his back, and watching the awful curtain of night and death descending upon him. It was so dark that even the dalesmen themselves lost their way in coming down, and carried the poor young gentleman into Eskdale.
>
> John Ruskin: *England's Lakeland: A Tour Therein*

In 1919 Lord Leconfield presented the summit of Scafell Pike to the National Trust as a war memorial. Among the names of the dead of the Great War whom one might remember on the summit is that of Siegfried Herford, who in April 1914, with George Sansom, pioneered a fierce and complex route up Scafell's *Central Buttress*, by far the most serious and difficult rock climb at the time on any British mountain.

Scagglethorpe 'Skakull's or Skakli's outlying settlement', OScand male personal name *Skakull* or *Skakli* + THORPE.
A village in North Yorkshire, 5 km (3 miles) east of Malton.

Scalby 'Skalli's village', OScand male personal name *Skalli* + -BY.
A town in North Yorkshire, 4 km (2.5 miles) northwest of Scarborough.

Scale Force 'waterfall by the shieling', *Scale* OScand *skali* 'shieling', with *fors* 'waterfall'.
A waterfall on **Scale Beck**, Cumbria (formerly in Cumberland), some 3 km (2 miles) west of Buttermere village, above CRUMMOCK WATER. It is the highest waterfall (38 m / 125 ft) in the Lake District.

Scalloway 'bay of the huts', OScand *skali* 'hut' + *vagr* 'bay'.
A small fishing port on Mainland, SHETLAND, some 8 km (5 miles) west of Lerwick. It was the 'capital' of Shetland until the later 18th century, and is the site of the ruins of the castle of Earl Patrick Stewart, whose tyrannous rule over Shetland and ORKNEY ended with his execution in the early 17th century. North of the village is Gallow Hill, the site of numerous witch burnings, including that of a fisherman who unwisely boasted that he could pull ready-cooked fish from the sea. Early in the 19th century the bay on which the village stands was reportedly visited by a Kraken, but no one dared investigate the matter further.

Scalp, the Irish *scailp* 'cleft of rock, chasm', referring to the feature here.
A pass through a ravine on the R111 road in County Dublin, between GOLDEN BALL and Enniskerry.

Scalpay¹ 'boat-shaped island', O Scand *skalpr* 'boat, ship' + *ey* (see -AY).
A small but well-populated island just off the southeast coast of North Harris, Western Isles (formerly in Inverness-shire). It is separated from Harris by the narrow **Sound of Scalpay**, over which there is now a bridge (opened in 1998). The lighthouse completed in 1789 was one of the first to be built on the west coast of Scotland. The inhabitants of Scalpay are called **Scalpachs**:

> ... a crofter tells me
> The Scalpay folk,
> Though very intelligent, are not Spinozas ...
>
> Norman MacCaig: 'Return to Scalpay', from *The World's Room* (1974)

Scalpay². A small, sparsely populated island off the east coast of SKYE, from which it is separated by the narrow **Caolas Scalpay** (Gaelic 'narrows of Scalpay'). On his 1773 tour Dr Johnson considered buying the island and improving its intellectual and spiritual life, until he discovered that the owner was expected to spend at least a quarter of the year there.

Scampton 'short farmstead', or 'Skammi's farmstead', OScand *skammr* 'short' or male personal name *Skammi* + -TON.

A village in Lincolnshire, about 8 km (5 miles) north of Lincoln. It is home to probably the most famous of all the RAF's Bomber Command air stations. During the Second World War it was the base of 617 Squadron, which flew the 1943 'Dam Busters' raid on the German Ruhr valley, using the famously innovative 'bouncing bomb'. (The events were rendered in suitably heroic fashion and with a memorable score in the 1955 film *The Dam Busters*, starring Michael Redgrave and Richard Todd.) In the Cold War Scampton was the first airfield where nuclear-armed Vulcan bombers went into service. It is no longer a fully active RAF base, but it is regularly used by the 'Red Arrows' formation-flying team.

Scapa Flow 'boat isthmus', *Scapa* OScand *skalpr* 'boat, ship' + *eith* 'isthmus, passage'; *Flow* OScand *floa* 'to flood'.

A large, sheltered anchorage in ORKNEY, between the islands of Mainland to the north, Hoy to the west and South Ronaldsay to the east. It opens out to the Pentland Firth to the south and to the Atlantic to the west via Hoy Sound. In 1912 the British government chose it as the main anchorage of the Grand Fleet, which was based here through the First World War. At the end of the war, the German fleet sailed into Scapa Flow and scuttled itself. It was on this occasion that many British sailors on board the flagship of the Grand Fleet heard an extended drumroll. Despite an extensive search of the ship, no drummer was found, and many said it was Drake's Drum that had been heard. (This legendary drum of Sir Francis Drake, the hero of the Armada, had also been heard at the outbreak of the war, and was again heard during the desperate evacuation from Dunkirk in 1940.) In 1918 Admiral Jellicoe, who had commanded the British fleet at Jutland in 1916, was made Viscount Jellicoe of Scapa.

Scapa Flow was also an important naval base during the Second World War, but in October 1939 a German submarine penetrated the defences and sank the battleship HMS *Royal Oak*, with the loss of 833 men. After this the CHURCHILL BARRIERS were built to block off the eastern approach channels. The base closed in 1956.

Fairway, a leading thoroughbred stud until his retirement in 1945, was foaled by a mare called Scapa Flow in 1925.

Scapa Flow. A Glaswegian rhyming-slang expression meaning 'Joe'.

Scara Brae. *See* SKARA BRAE.

Scarba Probably 'cormorant island', OScand *skarf* 'cormorant' + *ey* (*see* -AY).

A small island in the Inner HEBRIDES, 1 km (0.6 miles) north of Jura across the Strait of CORRYVRECKAN. It is in Argyll and Bute (formerly in Argyll, then in Strathclyde region). There are now no permanent inhabitants.

> And Scarba's isle, whose tortured shore
> Still rings to Corrievreken's roar …
>
> Sir Walter Scott: *The Lord of the Isles* (1815), Canto IV, xi

Scarborough 'Skarthi's stronghold', OScand male personal name *Skarthi* + OE *burh* (*see* BURY).

A seaside resort in North Yorkshire, 25 km (15 miles) northwest of Bridlington. It is situated where the NORTH YORK MOORS meet – and from time to time fall into – the NORTH SEA. The Normans built a castle on the headland that separates Scarborough's North and South Bays. During the Civil Wars the castle was besieged by the Parliamentarians, and the defenders surrendered to them in 1645, having been reduced to boiling their own boots for sustenance. George Fox, the founder of the Quakers, was imprisoned here in 1665–6.

Scarborough's martial history continued when in 1799 the American privateer John Paul Jones captured the British warship *Serapis* off the coast at Scarborough; more naval drama occurred on 16 December 1914, when German warships bombarded the town. A less likely nautical tale is that Robin Hood went out one day with the fishermen of Scarborough, and, being attacked by a French warship, boarded the vessel and seized a hoard of gold, distributing it among his poor shipmates.

Mineral springs were discovered at Scarborough in 1620, after a visitor, Mrs Elizabeth Farrow, sampled the local water and decided that something tasting quite so disgusting must be good for one. Scarborough subsequently thrived, its waters vaunted to cure almost all ills, including hypochondria. A local doctor built on this success by pronouncing on the health-giving properties of bathing in the sea – an activity that leads to an embarrassing incident for Matthew Bramble in Tobias Smollett's novel *Humphry Clinker* (1771). The town proclaimed itself as **the Queen of Watering Places** (although it is now more frequently referred to as **the Queen of the Coast**).

The novelist Anne Brontë, who set *Agnes Grey* here, died in Scarborough in 1849, and is buried in St Mary's Churchyard. The town was the birthplace of Sir George Cayley (1773–1857), pioneer of aerodynamics and designer of the first successful man-bearing glider; the painter Frederic, Lord Leighton (1830–96); and of the poets Edith (1887–1964) and Sacheverell (1897–88) Sitwell; Sacheverell set his novel *Before the Bombardment* (1926) in the town, and the family home is now a Sitwell museum. Scarborough was also the birthplace of the actor Charles Laughton (1899–1962) and of the novelist Susan Hill (b.1942). The playwright Alan Ayckbourn has long been artistic director of the Stephen Joseph Theatre here, and many of his plays have been premiered there.

There are towns called Scarborough in Canada (Ontario), New Zealand, Trinidad and Tobago, and the USA (Maine, Massachusetts).

'baby-killers of Scarborough'. The first lord of the Admiralty's description of the German navy after the bombardment of Scarborough on 16 December 1914:

> 'Whatever feats of arms the German Navy may hereafter perform, the stigma of the baby-killers of Scarborough will brand its officers and men while sailors sail the seas.'
>
> Winston Churchill: letter to the mayor of Scarborough (20 December 1914)

'Scarborough Fair'. A folk song, made known to an international audience in an arrangement by Simon and Garfunkel, which featured on the soundtrack to the film *The Graduate* (1967).

> Are you going to Scarborough Fair?
> Parsley, sage, rosemary and thyme.
> Remember me to the one who lives there,
> She once was a true love of mine.

'Scarborough Fair' is also a variety of new English rose, with pink flowers.

scarbroite. A clayey hydrous silicate mineral of alumina found near Scarborough.

Trip to Scarborough, A. A revised version (1777) by Richard Brinsley Sheridan of Sir John Vanbrugh's comedy *The Relapse* (1696), trading on the fashionable status of the town. It is characteristic of its late 18th-century context: all the bawdiness and cynical realism about money and marriage of the original is banished in favour of a suitably moral outcome.

Scarcewater Origin uncertain, but the name may be self-explanatory.

A village in Cornwall, about 11 km (7 miles) west of St Austell.

Scarlet-town. *See under* Reading.

Scartho 'mound near a gap, or associated with cormorants', OScand *skarth* 'gap' or *skarfr* 'cormorant' + *haugr* 'mound'.

A village in North East Lincolnshire (before 1996 in Humberside, before 1974 in Lincolnshire), now effectively a southern suburb of Grimsby.

Scattery Island A corruption of the Irish name *Inis Cathaigh* 'Cathach's island'.

A small island in the Mouth of the Shannon, County Clare, just offshore from Kilrush. St Senan (or Seanán or Senanus) founded a monastery here in the 6th century, and there are the remains of six medieval churches and a round tower. Pebbles from Scattery were believed to protect the bearer while at sea, and new boats were sailed sunwise round the island. St Senan himself apparently vowed that no woman should ever set foot on his 'sainted sod':

> 'Oh! haste and leave this sacred isle,
> Unholy bark, ere morning smile;
> For on thy deck, though dark it be,
>   A female form I see;
> And I have sworn this sainted sod
> Shall ne'er by woman's foot be trod.'
>
> Thomas Moore: 'St Senanus and the Lady', from *Irish Melodies* (1801–34)

Sceilig Mhichíl. The Irish name for Skellig Michael (*see under* the Skelligs).

Schiehallion 'fairy hill of the Caledonians', Gaelic *sith* 'fairy hill' + *chailleann* 'Caledonians'.

A mountain (1081 m / 3547 ft) in the central Highlands, in Perth and Kinross (formerly in Perthshire, and then in Tayside region), some 24 km (14.5 miles) west of Pitlochry. It is pronounced 'sheehalyan', and is at the geographical centre of Scotland. Its name may derive from the 'fairy well' on its slopes, which was formerly visited by local girls on May Day, dressed in white and bringing offerings of garlands to the fairies, who had the power to cure diseases and grant wishes.

The mountain has a distinctive conical shape when viewed from certain directions, and its symmetry led to it being selected in 1774 as the location of an experiment by the Astronomer Royal, Nevil Maskelyne (1732–1811), to determine the density of the earth (and also the value of Newton's universal gravitational constant) using a plumb line. Maskelyne spent four months on the mountain, and appears not to have been enchanted by the view:

> The Royal Society … made a point with me to go there to take the direction of the experiment, which I did, not without reluctance, nor from any wish to depart from my own observatory to live on a barren mountain, but purely to serve the Society and the public, for which I received no gratuity, and had only my expenses paid for me.
>
> Nevil Maskelyne: quoted in D. Howse, *Nevil Maskelyne, the Seaman's Astronomer* (1989)

There's a Schiehallion anywhere you go.
The thing is, climb it.

> Norman MacCaig: 'Landscape and I', from *The World's Room* (1974)

Other poets too have been lured by the sound of the hill. Edwin Morgan, for example, ends his catechistic celebration of Scottish place names thus:

> *and what was the toast?*
> Schiehallion! Schiehallion! Schiehallion!
>
> Edwin Morgan: 'Canedolia', from *Collected Poems* (1990)

Scholar Green *Scholar* originally *Scholehalc* 'nook of land with a hut', OScand *skali* 'hut, shieling' + OE *halh* (*see* Hale,

-HALL); by the middle of the 17th century it had become associated with ModE *scholar*, and *Green* had been added, in allusion to the village green.

A village in Cheshire, about 6 km (4 miles) east of Alsager.

Scilly Isles *Scilly* a pre-English name of unknown origin and meaning, first recorded in the 1st century AD: one suggestion links it (via a possible Roman name *Silina*) with the Celtic goddess who gave her name to the Romans' *Aquae Sulis* (*see* BATH). Until the 16th century it was standardly spelt *Silly*: the introduction of the *c* may have been suggested by *Sicily*, the name of another island at the 'toe' of a peninsula, or prompted simply by the desire to avoid the bathetic association with *silly*.

A group of about 140 granite islands and islets about 45 km (28 miles) off the southwest tip of Cornwall (also known as the **Isles of Scilly** or simply the **Scillies**). In the Middle Ages they belonged to the abbey of TAVISTOCK. They then passed into the possession of the Godolphin family, and since 1933 have been Crown property (with the exception of HUGH TOWN, St Mary's, the property there having been sold freehold to the occupiers in 1949). They are now part of the Duchy of Cornwall (*see under* CORNWALL). The archipelago covers about 12 sq km (4.7 sq miles). Only five of the islands are inhabited: BRYHER, ST AGNES[2], ST MARTIN'S, ST MARY'S (the largest, on which is situated the islands' capital, HUGH TOWN), and TRESCO. To the southwest of St Agnes is a small group of islets called the WESTERN ROCKS, and further west still is Bishop's Rock.

Arthurian legend associates them with the lost land of LYONESSE. They were certainly occupied in prehistoric times, as the large number of Bronze Age tombs and other remains attest. It is thought that the stone-chambered barrows found on the islands may have been the special home of the dead, known from Celtic mythology. The 16th-century antiquary William Camden identified the Scillies with the fabled islands called the Cassiterides, to which the Phoenician traders came, but there is no proof of this.

The islands sit in the path of the Gulf Stream, and the resulting exceptionally mild climate means not only that sub-tropical plants thrive here, but also that Scillonians (*see below*) can earn a significant proportion of their income from the cultivation of flowers. It ensures a steady flow of holidaymakers too. The sea is not always amiable, though: westerly gales have driven countless vessels onto the Scillies' rocks – a circumstance sometimes taken advantage of, or even connived at, in the past by local wreckers and pirates. Admiral Cloudesley Shovel's fleet was wrecked off the Scillies in 1707, and he was strangled for his emerald ring by an islander when he came ashore.

Scillonian. An inhabitant of the Scilly Isles. The term, perhaps modelled on *Devonian*, is first recorded in 1794.

Scone Possibly Gaelic *sgonn* 'mound', referring to the Mote Hill, a low mound associated with the early kings.

A village (pronounced 'skoon') in Perth and Kinross (formerly in Perthshire, and then in Tayside region), some 3 km (2 miles) north of Perth. The original village (now called **Old Scone**) was demolished to make way for the park of **Scone Palace** (1803–8), the seat of the earls of Mansfield, and the present village of **New Scone** was built 2 km (1.5 miles) away.

Scone succeeded FORTEVIOT as the Pictish capital in the 8th century. Kenneth MacAlpin, who united the Scots and Picts in the mid-9th century, brought the Stone of Scone (*see below*) here, and Scone became the site of the coronation of all Scottish kings until the 15th century. The tradition was revived by Charles II, who was crowned here as king of Scotland on 1 January 1651. Scone was also a centre of the early Celtic church, and an Augustinian monastery was founded in 1120. It was destroyed during the Reformation.

There is a town called Scone in Australia (New South Wales).

Stone of Scone, the. A rectangular block of reddish-grey sandstone measuring 66 cm (26 in.) by 41 cm (16 in.) by 28 cm (11 in), traditionally associated with the coronations of Scottish kings. Its only decoration is a simple cross. It is also known as the **Stone of Destiny** or the **Fatal Stone** (Gaelic *Lia Fail; see under* FÁL). Another name for it is **Jacob's Stone**, from the legend that the biblical Jacob used it as a pillow when he dreamt of the angels ascending and descending the ladder (Genesis 28:11). In another story, the stone was St Columba's pillow.

According to the first legend the stone was given to a Celtic king who married the daughter of an Egyptian pharaoh, and made its way to TARA in Ireland *c*.700 BC, where in ancient times the high kings were crowned. The Scots took it with them when they established the kingdom of DALRIADA in Argyll (although another story has Joseph of Arimathea bringing it to Scotland), and it was said that when the Dalriadan kings sat on the stone at their capital at DUNADD they took on royal power. Reputedly, the stone would 'groan aloud as with thunder' if anyone other than the rightful king sat on it. The stone was later kept at DUNSTAFFNAGE CASTLE, until Kenneth MacAlpin unified Scotland in the 9th century and moved it and his court to Scone. Subsequently, all Scottish kings were crowned while sitting on the stone until 1296, when Edward I of England seized the stone and took it back to London. In 1307 it was placed beneath Edward's new Coronation Chair in Westminster Abbey as a symbol of Scotland's supposed subjugation to the kings of England.

An ancient Latin saying associated with the stone goes:

Ni fallat fatum, Scoti quocunque locatum
Inveniunt Lapidem, regnare tenentur ibidem.

This was translated by Sir Walter Scott as:

> Unless the fates be faulty grown
> And prophet's voice be vain
> Where'er is found this sacred stone
> The Scottish race shall reign.

This prophecy was fulfilled in 1603 when James VI of Scotland was crowned as King James I of England on the Coronation Chair in Westminster Abbey.

On the night of 24–25 December 1950 Scottish nationalists stole the Stone of Scone from Westminster Abbey, and later placed it on the high altar of Arbroath Abbey, symbolically reminding the world of the Declaration of Arbroath (*see under* ARBROATH), Scotland's 'declaration of independence' of 1320. The stone was restored to its place in Westminster Abbey in February 1952, but officially returned to Scotland in 1996, when it was installed in Edinburgh Castle (*see under* EDINBURGH) on 30 November, St Andrew's Day.

Sco Ruston *Sco* 'wood', OScand *skogr*; *Ruston* 'farmstead near or among brushwood', OE *hris* 'brushwood' + -TON.
A village in Norfolk, about 16 km (10 miles) northeast of Norwich.

Scot For the etymology, *see* SCOTLAND.
A native of Scotland. In slang, a Scot is often a Jock (the Scottish version of Jack), or, in rhyming slang, a Sweaty Sock. More recently the Scots have unpleasantly been referred to by their benighted cousins south of the Border as Porridge Wogs, while in Australia and New Zealand they are sometimes, confusingly, known as Geordies. In 19th-century slang, a **scot** was a grumpy person worth teasing. The expression '**scot free**' does not refer to the Scots, but rather derives from OScand *skot* and refers to an old municipal tax; similarly the exclamation '**Great Scot!**' has nothing to do with Scotland, but rather refers to a famously pompous US soldier and politician, General Winfield Scott (1786–1866).
See also SCOTS *and* SCOTSMAN.

Scotch. An alternative to SCOTTISH, and also sometimes (especially formerly) applied to the SCOTS and to the Scots language. Although widely using the word themselves until the end of the 19th century, the Scots now dislike 'Scotch' except when applied to various foodstuffs (*see below*); unlike the English and the Americans, they never use the word Scotch to refer to Scottish whisky, which is quite simply 'whisky' as far as they are concerned. Someone who has a fondness for whisky has been described, since the earlier 20th century, as **Scotch by absorption**. Since the later 19th century, Scotch has also been a slang term for 'thrifty', 'mean', from the stereotype of Scottish financial probity. The verb *to scotch*, meaning to prevent or crush (something), is not related

to Scotland, although the etymology is obscure. Related to this (but again not to Scotland) is the word *scotch* for a marked line, as in the children's game *hopscotch*. However, it is possible but not certain that *butterscotch*, the brittle toffee-like confection, may be so named because first made in Scotland.

Scotch argus. A species of butterfly, *Erebia aethiops*, fairly widely distributed in Europe. It is largely brown, with red and black circular markings on the wings.

Scotch broth. A hearty soup made with beef or mutton stock, vegetables and pearl barley.

Scotch bun. Another name for black bun, a rich, spicy fruit cake often baked in a pastry case and eaten at Hogmanay.

Scotch casement. 18th- and 19th-century slang for the pillory.

Scotch catch. *See* Scotch snap *below*.

Scotch chocolate. A curious concoction from the later 18th and 19th centuries, comprising brimstone and milk. Similarly unpleasant, and from around the same period, is **Scotch coffee**, consisting of hot water cheered up by the addition of burnt biscuit.

Scotch collops. A traditional dish involving slices of meat (e.g. veal escalopes – hence 'collops') simmered in stock and seasonings.

Scotch convoy. The accompaniment of a guest back to his or her home.

Scotch cousin. A distant relative.

Scotch egg. A hardboiled egg encased in sausage meat, fried or baked, and served cold. It may be covered in breadcrumbs. Scotch egg is also rhyming slang for 'leg'.

Scotch fiddle. A slang term for venereal disease, current in the 18th and 19th centuries. **To play the Scotch fiddle** was to rub the index finger of one hand between the index finger and thumb of the other hand, a gesture implying to a Scotsman that he suffered from the affliction.

Scotch fir. A doubly erroneous former name for Scots pine (*see under* SCOTS).

Scotch flummery. A kind of steamed custard.

Scotch horses. A game in which a group of children run together with hands joined behind their backs.

Scotchie. A slang term for a Scotsman.

Scotch-Irish. In the USA, the name given to the Presbyterian Ulstermen (Scottish in origin) who emigrated to North America (principally Pennsylvania and the Carolinas) in the 18th century. It is said their way of speaking gave rise to the modern American accent.

Scotch laburnum. A species of laburnum, *Laburnum alpinum*, frequently found along roads in Scotland. It has much larger leaflets and longer flower-bearing racemes than the common laburnum, *Laburnum anagyroides*.

Scotch lick. An Irish slang term, current in the 20th century, for a poorly performed cleaning job.

Scotchman. A now-unacceptable word for a Scotsman. It was also formerly used as a slang word for a louse.

> In all my travels I never met with any one Scotchman but what was a man of sense: I believe everybody of that country that has any, leaves it as fast as they can.
>
> Francis Lockier (1668–1740): quoted in Joseph Spence, *Anecdotes* (1820)

In South Africa in the 19th century Scotchman was also used as slang for a florin (a 2-shilling piece), from the story that a Scottish farmer palmed off florins to his Black workers as half-crowns (worth 25% more).

Scotch mist. A dank, thick mist and/or drizzle, as may frequently be found clinging to the mountains of Scotland. Used figuratively, the phrase denotes woolliness of thinking, and is also used as rhyming slang for 'pissed', i.e. drunk. The cocktail called Scotch mist consists of whisky and crushed ice, served with a twist of lemon.

Scotch muffler. A drink of whisky taken to keep one warm.

Scotch nightingale. An old local name for the sedge warbler, *Acrocephalus schoenobaenus*.

Scotch ordinary. A slang term for lavatory around the turn of the 18th–19th century, at which time an ordinary meant an eating house.

Scotch pancake. A drop scone, a small round cake made from batter cooked on a griddle. In Scotland it is simply known as a pancake.

Scotch pint. A measure of 4 pints, i.e. half a gallon, used in the 19th century.

Scotch Plot. An alleged conspiracy, called the Queensberry Plot in Scotland, for a Jacobite rising and invasion of Scotland in 1703. After intriguing at St Germain-en-Laye (court of the Old Pretender) and Versailles, Simon Fraser, Lord Lovat (*c.*1667–1747), returned to Scotland with a letter from Mary of Modena (James II's widow) to be delivered to an unnamed nobleman. He addressed it to John Murray, Duke of Atholl, his personal enemy, and then took it to the Duke of Queensberry, Atholl's rival in the Scottish Ministry. This intrigue broke up the ministry and drove Atholl over to the Jacobites. It led to disputes between the English and Scottish Parliaments, but no punitive action was taken.

Scotch polo. An American slang term for golf.

Scotch screw. A slang term for a wet dream, referring to the Scottish reputation for meanness: in this case the 'screw' is free and not given to anyone else.

Scotch shout. Antipodean slang for a round of drinks in which everyone pays for their own.

Scotch snap or **catch.** A rhythmic figure consisting of a semiquaver followed by a dotted quaver, typical of such Scottish dances as strathspeys.

Scotch tape. An adhesive tape, the American equivalent of Sellotape. It was introduced in 1930 by the Minnesota Mining and Manufacturing Company of St Paul, Missouri, and was so named because 'a little went a long way' – a reference to the Scots' reputation for thriftiness.

Scotch warming pan. An archaic slang term for 'a she bed-fellow' (*Dictionary of Thieving Slang*, 1747); also for a fart.

Scotch woodcock. A culinary term for toast spread with anchovies or anchovy paste and covered with eggs scrambled with cream, or with finely chopped hard-boiled eggs in a white sauce. It is analogous in origin to Welsh rabbit (*see under* WELSH).

Scotch Corner. The junction of the A66 and the A1 in North Yorkshire, 12 km (7 miles) south of Darlington. The name, first recorded in 1860, comes from the fact that the A66 leads west over STAINMORE PASS towards southwest Scotland.

Scotch Corner in London is at the junction of Knightsbridge and the Brompton Road; the Scotch House tartan shop opened here in 1900.

Scotia Latin, 'land of the Scots', used after the amalgamation of the Scots and Picts in the 9th century.

Originally a Latin name for Ireland, in use up till the 12th century. The Irish themselves were known as **Scoti** or **Scotti**, and the term occurs, for example, in the name of the Irish scholar John Scottus Eriugena (*c.*810–*c.*877), whose work *De Preadestinatione* was dismissed by critics as '*pultes Scottorum*' ('Irish porridge'). It was the Gaelic speakers from Ulster who settled in Argyll who became the first Scots (*see under* DALRIADA).

Later, Scotia became a poetic name for Scotland:

> From scenes like these old Scotia's grandeur springs,
> That makes her loved at home, revered abroad:
> Princes and Lords are but the breath of kings,
> 'An honest man's the noblest work of God.'
>
> Robert Burns: 'The Cotter's Saturday Night' (1786)

Scotia today is generally pronounced as in Nova Scotia ('new Scotland'), the province of Canada so named in 1621 by the Scotsman William Alexander, who had been granted the territory by James VI and I.

Scotland From *Scoti* or *Scotti*, a Latinized medieval name for the Irish (the first Gaelic-speaking Scots were from northeastern Ireland); it is said that *scoti* originally meant 'bandits'.

One of the constituent countries of the United Kingdom, comprising the northern third or so of the island of BRITAIN, plus the numerous islands of the HEBRIDES, ORKNEY and SHETLAND. Geographically, the mainland of Scotland can be divided into three main parts: the HIGHLANDS, the LOWLANDS or the CENTRAL LOWLANDS, and the SOUTHERN UPLANDS. The patron saint of Scotland is St Andrew (*see under* St Andrews), and his flag (*see under* Athelstaneford) – a diagonal white cross on a blue ground – is the national flag (although the Scottish royal standard is a red lion rampant on a yellow ground). The national symbol is a Scottish thistle (*see under* Scottish), and the national motto the similarly prickly *Nemo me impune lacessit* (Latin, 'No one provokes me with impunity', rendered into Scots as 'Wha daur meddle wi me?'): it appears on the milled edge of the Scottish £1 coin.

At the time of the Romans, Scotland was inhabited by various Celtic tribes, and the Romans referred to the country as Caledonia after one of these tribes. In the so-called Dark Ages, the north of Scotland was dominated by the Picts, a Celtic people, while Strathclyde and Lothian were occupied by varieties of ancient Briton (Brittonic-speaking Celts). In the 5th–6th centuries Anglo-Saxons began to settle in Lothian, while Gaelic-speakers (called Scoti or Scotti) from Antrim in northeastern Ireland established the kingdom of Dalriada in Argyll and the Inner Hebrides. In the mid-9th century Kenneth MacAlpin, king of Dalriada, established his rule over the land of the Picts and also over Lothian. The country then became known as Alba, still the Gaelic name for Scotland (*see also* Albany[1]); in Latin it was known as Scotia. Strathclyde did not come under the rule of the Scots kings until the early 11th century. From this point the Scots kings began to refer to themselves as 'king of Scots' (*Rex Scotie*).

At this time the Hebrides, Orkney and Shetland were under Norse occupation. After the defeat of the Norwegians at the Battle of Largs (*see under* Largs) in 1263 the Hebrides were incorporated into Scotland, but it was not until 1472 that Orkney and Shetland came under the Scottish crown. The Scots also had to deal with the English threat, most potent in the reigns of Edward I and Edward II. Robert the Bruce's defeat of the latter at Bannockburn in 1314 largely put an end to English attempts to conquer Scotland, but warfare along the Border continued intermittently until in 1603 King James VI of Scotland succeeded his distant cousin, the childless Queen Elizabeth I, as James I of England. Although ruled by the same monarch, England and Scotland continued as two separate kingdoms, each with their own parliament, until the Act of Union of 1707 abolished the Scottish Parliament and unified the kingdoms. Thereafter there was a half-hearted attempt to call Scotland North Britain, but this never really caught on. In a referendum in Scotland in 1997 the Scots voted in favour of the devolution of certain powers from the Westminster Parliament, and in 1999 a reconstituted Scottish Parliament began to sit once more in Edinburgh.

Scotland has been awarded a number of sobriquets, including the Land of Cakes, the Land of the Mountain and the Flood, Haggisland and Marmalade Country.

In the 17th and 18th centuries is was derided as Louseland, Scratchland and Itchland, while George Borrow tells us that in Romany it is Juvlo-mengreskey tem ('lousy fellows' country'). The place has suffered its fair share of opprobrium through the ages, usually at the hands of the English:

> Had Cain been Scot, God would have changed his doom
> Not forced him wander, but confined him home.
>
> John Cleveland (1613–58): 'The Rebel Scot'

> God made it [Scotland], but we must remember that He made it for Scotchmen; and comparisons are odious, but God made Hell.
>
> Samuel Johnson: quoted in James Boswell, *The Life of Samuel Johnson* (1791)

> A Scotchman must be a very sturdy moralist who does not love Scotland better than truth.
>
> Samuel Johnson: *A Journey to the Western Islands of Scotland* (1775)

> A land of meanness, sophistry and mist.
> Each breeze from foggy mount and marshy plain
> Dilutes with drivel every drizzly brain.
>
> Lord Byron: 'The Curse of Minerva'

See also Scot, Scotch, Scots, Scotsman *and* Scottish.

Cold Shoulder of Scotland, the. A nickname for the lowland region of Buchan.

Company of Scotland. An overseas trading company set up in 1695. It came to grief shortly afterwards with the disastrous attempt to establish a trading settlement in Darien in Central America.

Curse of Scotland, the. In cards, the nine of diamonds. The phrase seems to be first recorded in the early 18th century, for Houston's *Memoirs* (1715–47) tell how Lord Justice Clerk Ormistone became universally hated in Scotland and was called the Curse of Scotland. As a result, when ladies encountered the nine of diamonds at cards they called it Justice Clerk. Among the suggested origins of the phrase are:

(1) It may refer to the arms of Dalrymple, Earl of Stair, that is, or ('or' is the heraldic term for 'gold') on a saltire azure, nine lozenges of the first. The earl was held in abhorrence for his role in the Massacre of Glen Coe (*see under* Glen Coe).

(2) The nine of diamonds in the old card game called Pope Joan is called the pope, the Antichrist of the Scottish reformers.

(3) In the game of comette, introduced by Mary Queen of Scots, it was the main winning card, and the game was the curse of Scotland because it was the ruin of many.

(4) The word *curse* is a corruption of *cross*, and the nine of diamonds is so arranged as to form a St Andrew's cross (but so are the other nines).

(5) It was the card on which the Butcher Cumberland (*see under* CUMBERLAND) wrote his cruel order after the Battle of Culloden (1746) (*see under* CULLODEN MUIR). The term was, however, apparently already current then.

(6) Francis Grose, in his *Dictionary of the Vulgar Tongue* (1811) has the following alternative propositions:

> Diamonds, it is said, imply royalty, being ornaments to the imperial crown; and every ninth king of Scotland has been observed for many ages, to be a tyrant and a curse to that country. Others say it is from its similarity to the arms of Argyle; the Duke of Argyle having been very instrumental in bringing about the union, which, by some Scotch patriots, has been considered as detrimental to their country.

'Flower of Scotland'. A song written and performed in the late 1960s by Roy Williamson of The Corries, a Scottish folk music duo, and taken up as an 'official' unofficial national anthem, sung by Scottish supporters at international football and rugby matches.

> O flower of Scotland
> When will we see
> Your like again
> That fought and died for
> Your wee bit hill and glen …

Some insist that the proper title is *'The* Flower of Scotland'.

Honours of Scotland. The Scottish crown jewels. They remained in Scotland following the union of the crowns in 1603, and were smuggled out of DUNOTTAR CASTLE during the Cromwellian invasion. After the Act of Union of 1707 they were sealed away in Edinburgh Castle (*see under* EDINBURGH), until 'rediscovered' in 1818 by Sir Walter Scott; they are now on display in Edinburgh Castle.

'Of the Realme of Scotland'. A section of *The Dreme*, a long poem by Sir David Lindsay (?1490–?1555), in which the narrator wonders why Scotland suffers from such 'Inprosperitie' given the virtues of its people and the richness of its natural resources:

> First, the haboundance of fyschis in our seis,
> And fructual montanis for our bestiall;
> And, for our cornis, mony lusty vaill;
>
> The ryche Ryueris, plesand and proffitabyll;
> The lustie loochis, with fysche of sindry kyndis;
> Hountyng, halkyng, for nobyllis convenabyll;
> Forrestis full of Da, Ra, Hartis and Hyndis;
> The fresche fontanis, quhose holesum cristel strandis
> Refreschis so the fair fluriste grene medis:
> So laik we no thyng that to nature nedis.
>
> (Scots *loochis* 'lochs', *da* 'does', *ra* 'roe deer')

It transpires that the root of Scotland's poverty and misery is 'Wantyng of Justice, polycie, and peace'.

'Scotland the Brave'. A traditional tune with words added in the 1950s by Glasgow journalist Cliff Hanley. It was something of an unofficial national anthem in Scotland until superseded by **'Flower of Scotland'** (*see above*).

> Land of my high endeavour,
> Land of the shining river,
> Land of my heart for ever,
> Scotland the brave.

Scotland Gate A modern colliery settlement, so presumably 'gateway to Scotland'.
A village in Northumberland, 6 km (4 miles) southeast of Morpeth.

Scotland in Miniature. A description sometimes applied to the island of ARRAN.

Scotlandwell From the springs here; the earliest reference (14th century) is in Latin: *Fontes Scotiae*.
A village in Perth and Kinross (formerly in Kinross-shire, and then in Tayside region), 7 km (4 miles) east of Kinross across LOCH LEVEN[1]. Agricola's Roman legionaries visited the springs in AD 84, and the water was for long thought to cure many diseases. The Red Friars built a hospital here in 1250, and among the distinguished visitors was Robert the Bruce, who was by then afflicted with leprosy, and Charles II, who no doubt suffered from the odd amorously inflicted itch.

Scotland Yard From its being the site of the London residence of the kings of Scotland from the 12th century.
Originally, a short street (in full, **Great Scotland Yard**) in London, leading off from the eastern side of WHITEHALL (SW1), towards its northern end. Its umbilical connection with the police began in 1827, when part of the precincts became the headquarters of the newly formed Metropolitan Police. The link with law enforcement was firmly established by the end of the century, and when in 1891 the Met moved to new premises at the southern end of Victoria Embankment (*see under* EMBANKMENT), it named them **New Scotland Yard**. Designed by Norman Shaw in somewhat baronial style, this was the building (phone: Whitehall 1212) that became familiar in film and television police dramas in the middle part of the 20th century. The granite with which it was faced was quarried by convicts on Dartmoor.

In 1967 the Metropolitan Police moved yet again, to a modern 20-storey headquarters in Victoria Street, taking the name 'New Scotland Yard' with them (a revolving three-sided name-board in front of the building is a frequently used television image). The old premises were renamed the Norman Shaw Building.

By then, 'Scotland Yard' (or often simply **'the Yard'**) had long been used as a metonym for the Metropolitan Police, and more particularly for its CID: if London's detectives were having difficulty with a case, the tabloid headline was sure to be 'Yard baffled'. High-profile detectives would have the sobriquet 'of the Yard' after their name – real ones, fictional ones and even combinations of the two (as in the case of *Fabian of the Yard*, a BBC police drama of the mid-1950s based on the real-life career of Detective Inspector Robert Fabian). *Private Eye* magazine styled its all-purpose bungling detective '**Inspector Knacker of the Yard**'.

Scots. As an adjective, pertaining to SCOTLAND or its people; as a noun, the people of Scotland (*see* SCOT), and also the version of English spoken there (in fact comprising a number of regional dialects). The Scots 'language' is also known as Lallans (*see under* the LOWLANDS) or, borrowing from the Greek, the Doric (i.e. a rustic vernacular). At the time of the Renaissance, Scots was capable a high literary flights, as in the work of such *makars* (poets) as William Dunbar (?1456–?1513) and Gavin Douglas (*c.*1475–1522). After the Act of Union of 1707, Scots was increasingly regarded as rude and uncouth in NORTH BRITAIN, although the popularity of the poems of Robert Burns helped to keep Scots alive as a literary language, albeit of an earthy variety. However, in prose literature, novelists such as Sir Walter Scott used Scots only to represent the speech of rustic characters.

In the 1920s Hugh MacDiarmid spearheaded the Scottish Literary Renaissance with the slogan 'Not Burns, but Dunbar', determined to use his 'synthetic Scots' (largely gleaned from Jamieson's *Etymological Dictionary of the Scottish Language*, 1808) for an intellectually elevated and internationalist poetry in the spirit of European Modernism. Despite such heroic efforts, the spoken dialects of Scots had, by the end of the 20th century, been considerably diluted by 'standard' English, largely under the influence of the broadcast media.

Pound Scots. English and Scottish coins were of equal value until 1355, after which the Scottish coinage steadily depreciated, and when James VI of Scotland became James I of England (1603) the pound Scots was worth 1s 8d, one-twelfth the value of an English pound. A pound Scots was divided into 20 Scots shillings each worth an English penny. The Scottish mint closed in 1709, two years after the Act of Union.

Queen of Scots' Pillar. A column in the Peak Cavern (*see under* PEAK DISTRICT), Castleton, Derbyshire, as clear as alabaster. It is said to be so called because on one occasion, when en route to throw herself on the mercy of Elizabeth I, Mary Queen of Scots proceeded thus far and then turned back.

Royal Scot. The name of a former train from Euston to Glasgow. The first forerunner of the service left London on 1 June 1862, and the name was officially bestowed in 1927,

when the journey took less than 5 hours – half an hour quicker than the fastest present-day Virgin train.

Royal Scots, the. A regiment of the British army, originally raised in 1625 as independent Scottish companies serving the king of France.

Royal Scots Fusiliers, the. A regiment of the British army, originally raised in 1678, and amalgamated in 1959 with the Highland Light Infantry to become the Royal Highland Fusiliers (*see under* the HIGHLANDS).

Scots Confession. The confession of faith of the reformed church in Scotland, published in 1560.

Scots ell. The Scottish yard, an obsolete measure equal to 37 in (92.5 cm). The **Scots acre** was equal to 5760 square ells or 1.3 imperial acres.

Scots Greys. A cavalry regiment of the British army, properly the **Royal Scots Greys**, founded in 1678 and so called because of their grey uniforms. They were nicknamed the Bubbly Jocks. In 1971 they were amalgamated into the Royal Scots Dragoon Guards (Carabiniers and Greys). In the 18th and 19th centuries, **Scots greys** was a slang term for lice, the Scots being supposedly an infested people.

Scots lovage. An umbelliferous plant, *Ligusticum scoticum*, with white flowers, purplish stems and a smell of celery. It is found in Britain, Germany and Scandinavia.

Scots mile. An obsolete measure of length, equivalent to 1980 imperial yards (the standard mile is 1760 yards).

Scots pebble. Any semi-precious stone, such as a garnet, found in the hills and rivers of Scotland.

Scots pine. A species of pine, *Pinus sylvestris*, found across Europe and northern Asia. It is one of the key components of the Old Caledonian Forest (*see under* CALEDONIA), and is only one of three conifer species native to Britain (the others being yew and juniper). It is also known (inaccurately) as 'Scotch fir'.

'Scots, wha hae'. A song, also known as 'Robert Bruce's March to BANNOCKBURN', by Robert Burns, celebrating the great Scottish victory of 1314:

> Scots, wha hae wi' Wallace bled,
> Scots, wham Bruce has often led,
> Welcome to your gory bed, –
> Or to victorie.

Scot's Dyke. An earthwork on the Anglo-Scottish border, running some 6 km (4 miles) east–west between the rivers ESK[2] and Sark, some 8 km (5 miles) north of Gretna. It was built in the later 16th century along a line determined in 1552 by Monsieur D'Oysel, the French ambassador to Scotland, to divide the DEBATABLE LANDS between England and Scotland; it is said to be the first man-made frontier in Europe.

> Ye ken Highlander and Lowlander, and Border-men, are a' ae man's bairns when you are over the Scots dyke.
>
> Sir Walter Scott: 'The Two Drovers' (1827)

Scots' Gap There is a tradition that this commemorates a Scottish raid in ancient times, but the name is first recorded in the 19th century. The village is near the A696/A68 route towards Redesdale, Carter Bar and the Scots Border – the only road route through the CHEVIOT Hills.

A village in Northumberland, 17 km (11 miles) west of Morpeth.

> … north to Scots Gap and Bellingham where the black rams defy the panting engine …
>
> W.H. Auden: *The Dog Beneath the Skin* (1935) (The village of Bellingham is 20 km / 12 miles west of Scots' Gap.)

Scotsman. A male native of SCOTLAND, the female of the species being a **Scotswoman**. The national stereotype encompasses thriftiness, Presbyterian dourness and dedication to hard work and career:

> It is never difficult to distinguish between a Scotsman with a grievance and a ray of sunshine.
>
> P.G. Wodehouse: *Blandings Castle and Elsewhere*, 'The Custody of the Pumpkin' (1935)

> The Scotsman is mean, as we're all well aware,
> And bony, and blotchy, and covered with hair,
> He eats salted porridge, he works all the day,
> And he hasn't got Bishops to show him the way.
>
> Michael Flanders (with Donald Swann): 'A Song of Patriotic Prejudice', from *At the Drop of Another Hat* (1964)

See also SCOT, SCOTCH *and* SCOTS.

Scotsman, The. One of Scotland's two national broadsheet newspapers, the other being *The Herald*, formerly *The Glasgow Herald* (*see under* GLASGOW). *The Scotsman* has been published in Edinburgh since its foundation in 1817 by William Ritchie and Charles MacLaren.

Scotstarvit Tower. A tower house in Fife, about 3 km (2 miles) south of Cupar. It dates from around 1579, and was the home of the geographer Sir John Scot (1585–1670), also the author of *Scot of Scotstarvit's Staggering State of Scots Statesmen*. The tower takes its name from its inhabitant, and from the nearby **Hill of Tarvit**, Tarvit deriving from Gaelic *tarbh* 'bull'. William Drummond of HAWTHORNDEN (1585–1649) penned a satire in macaronic Latin entitled '*Polemo-Middinia inter Vitarvam et Nebernam*' ('The Midden-Battle between Lady Scotstarvit and the Mistress of Newbarns').

The mansion at Hill of Tarvit dates from 1696, and was almost entirely rebuilt in 1906 by the noted Edwardian architect Sir Robert Lorimer. It is now owned by the National Trust for Scotland.

Scott Country. That area of the BORDERS associated with the life and work of Sir Walter Scott (1771–1832). It is centred on Sir Walter Scott's house at ABBOTSFORD and his eponymous viewpoint SCOTT'S VIEW, and takes in the valleys of the TWEED, ETTRICK WATER, TEVIOT and YARROW WATER, together with ST MARY'S LOCH, the GREY MARE'S TAIL, the EILDON HILLS and wilder heights, DRYBURGH ABBEY and such towns and villages as SMAILHOLM, JEDBURGH, KELSO, MELROSE and SELKIRK. Through *The Minstrelsy of the Scottish Borders* (1802–3), Scott brought the history and folklore of this once strife-torn, fairy-haunted area to life for a Romantic audience; he later revisited it in works such as *The Lay of the Last Minstrel* (1805; *see under* YARROW WATER), *The Black Dwarf* (1816; *see under* BLACK DWARF'S COTTAGE) and *The Monastery* (1820; *see under* MELROSE).

Compare CONSTABLE COUNTRY, BURNS COUNTRY, BRONTË COUNTRY *and* HARDY COUNTRY.

Scottish. An adjective pertaining to SCOTLAND and/or the SCOTS.

écossaise. A quick dance in 2/4 time, popular in the late 18th and early 19th centuries in both Britain and Europe. Both Beethoven and Schubert wrote examples. The word is short for *danse écossaise*, French for 'Scottish dance', although there is no known Scottish connection.

schottische. A round dance similar to the polka, but slower, popular in the 19th century (it was introduced into Britain in 1848). The word derives from German *der schottische Tanz* 'the Scottish dance', and the dance is also known as the Highland schottische, although its origins are more *mitteleuropäisch* than *schottisch*.

Scottish asphodel. *Tofielda pusilla*, a small member of the lily family with a cluster of greenish-yellow flowers on the end of a generally leafless stem. It is found in moist places in mountains.

Scottish blackface. A breed of hardy sheep with horns and a black face, common on the mountains of Scotland.

Scottish bluebell. The harebell, *Campanula rotundifolia*. It is unrelated to the common bluebell, and is celebrated in the traditional song 'The Bluebells of Scotland':

> Oh where, tell me where, did your Highland laddie dwell?
> Oh where, tell me where, did your Highland laddie dwell?
> He dwelt in bonnie Scotland where bloom the sweet bluebells,
> And it's oh! in my heart I rue my laddie well.

Scottish Chaucerians. A term traditionally given to the *makars* (poets) of the **Scottish Renaissance** (*see below*), such as King James I (1394–1437), Robert Henryson (?1424–?1506), William Dunbar (?1456–?1513) and Gavin Douglas (*c*.1475–1522). Scholars now believe they were in fact little influenced by Chaucer.

Scottish Colourists. A term coined in 1948 for a loose group of Scottish painters – S.J. Peploe (1871–1935), J.D. Fergusson (1874–1961), G.L. Hunter (1877–1931) and F.C.B. Cadell (1883–1937) – showing the influence of Cézanne, Matisse and the Fauves. They are now among the most admired British painters of the earlier 20th century.

Scottish dock. *Rumex aquaticus*, a member of the dock family similar to water dock, *R. hydrolapathum*, but with broader triangular leaves. It is rare in Britain.

Scottish Enlightenment. A term for the ferment of thought that took place in GLASGOW and EDINBURGH, two of the most important centres of the European Enlightenment of the 18th century. Leading thinkers of the Scottish Enlightenment included the economist Adam Smith, the philosophers David Hume, Francis Hutcheson, Adam Ferguson, Thomas Reid and Dugald Stewart, the chemist Joseph Black, the founder of modern geology James Hutton, and the inventors James Watt and John Loudon McAdam. One of the products of the movement was the *Encyclopaedia Britannica*, first published in Edinburgh in 1768–71. The movement was influential in America and France, Voltaire observing:

> We look to Scotland for all our ideas of civilization.

Scottish fold. A breed of cat originating in ANGUS in 1961, and characterized by ears that are folded forward and downward over the forehead.

Scottish Knight of Perfection. Said to be the 14th order in the hierarchy of Freemasonry, between the Royal Arch of Enoch and Knight of the Sword and of the East.

Scottish Martyrs. A group of Scottish political radicals who, in 1793–4, at the time of the French Revolution (of which they were ardent supporters), were convicted of sedition and transported to Australia. They were Thomas Muir (1765–99), William Skirving (d.1796), Thomas Palmer (1747–1802) and Maurice Margarot (1745–1815), and were all members of the **Scottish Friends of the People**, which campaigned for universal male suffrage and annual parliaments.

Scottish Orpheus, the. An epithet for James I, king of Scotland (1406–37), a noted musician and particularly remembered for his long poem *The Kingis Quair* (*c*.1424), a love-dream allegory in the Chaucerian manner.

Scottish Play, the. A propitiatory euphemism for Shakespeare's *Macbeth*, the acting profession believing it to be bad luck to give the play its proper title. Indeed, it is said to be courting disaster to stage the play, or even to quote from it. The superstition that the play is cursed is apparently based on a series of unfortunate incidents that have accompanied productions of *Macbeth* over the years, such as accidental injuries, sudden illnesses, attempted suicides, and even murders.

Scottish primrose. *Primula scotica*, a pink-flowered member of the primrose family, found on coastal turf and sand dunes in the north of Scotland.

Scottish terrier. A small thickset terrier with a square muzzle, upright ears and tail, and black wiry hair. It is also called a **Scottie** or **Scotty**.

Scottish thistle. The national badge of Scotland, although which species of thistle it is remains uncertain. The thistle was probably adopted as a heraldic emblem by James III (ruled 1460–88), and its origin as the symbol of Scotland lies in the legend recounting how the Scots were alerted to a surprise Viking raid when one of the invaders trod on a thistle and cried out in pain. The prickliness of the plant is said to reflect the Scottish character, as embodied in the national motto *Nemo me impune lacessit* ('Wha daur meddle wi me', in other words 'Who dares interfere with me').

The Scottish thistle plays a notable role in Hugh MacDiarmid's long poem in Scots, *A Drunk Man Looks at the Thistle* (1926), in which the plant, while remaining throughout as a symbol of Scotland, metamorphoses in the moonlight (and with the aid of whisky) to – among many other things – a skeleton to a pickled foetus to a crucifix to bagpipes to a tormenting labyrinth to the sail on Ahab's *Pequod* in pursuit of 'the muckle white whale' (the reference is to Melville's *Moby Dick*).

Scottish topaz. A type of transparent yellowish quartz, often originating in Brazil or Peru rather than in Scotland.

Scottish wormwood. *Artemisia norvegica* var. *scotica*, a British variant of Norwegian mugwort (known as mountain sagewort in North America), a low-growing tufted plant with yellowish flowerheads. It is found only on two mountains in Wester Ross in the Northwest HIGHLANDS, and was identified for the first time only in 1950.

Scottish Borders. A unitary authority created in 1996 to replace the former Borders region (*see under* BORDERS). The administrative centre remains at NEWTON ST BOSWELLS.

Scott's View. A viewpoint above the River TWEED looking towards the Eildon Hills from the B6356 some 4 km (2.5 miles) east of Melrose. Sir Walter Scott would stop his carriage here every time he rode this road; after his death, as his horses drew his hearse, they stopped here, unbidden, for one last time.

Scrabster 'rocky homestead', OScand *skjære* 'rocky' + *bolstathr* 'homestead'.

A small port on the north coast of Highland (formerly in Caithness), some 3 km (2 miles) across Thurso Bay from THURSO. From here ferries run to STROMNESS in Orkney.

Scrape, the. *See* DAWYCK.

Scratchland. A nickname for SCOTLAND, presumably for the same reasons as the country has been called ITCHLAND.

Scratch Wood *Scratch* perhaps 'Devil', early ModE, reflecting a reputation of the place as being haunted or unlucky.

An area of woodland to the north of EDGWARE, in the London borough of BARNET, close to the Hertfordshire border. Its rather chilling name reached a much wider public following the opening of the **Scratchwood Service Area**, just north of Junction 2 on the M1 (latterly rechristened as 'London Gateway Services', a much blander and less disconcerting proposition).

Screes, the. *See under* WAST WATER.

Scrooby 'Skropi's farmstead', OScand male personal name *Skropi* + -BY.

A village in Nottinghamshire, about 13 km (8 miles) northeast of Worksop.

Scrubs, the. *See* WORMWOOD SCRUBS.

Scullabogue The first element is probably Irish *scoil* 'school', but the remainder is uncertain.

The site of a massacre in County Wexford, near Carrigbyrne, during the 1798 United Irishmen's Rebellion. Retreating from their defeat at NEW ROSS, fleeing rebels brought stories of atrocities by government forces. In response, on 5 June 1798, rebels burned a barn at Scullabogue in which were held many loyalist prisoners, including women and children. With scant regard to either chronology or basic humanity, Michael O'Brien, the Wexford Bard (*see under* County WEXFORD), 'celebrated' the event a century later:

> 'Twas in 'ninety-six as the moon did fix
> Her beams o'er Scullabogue,
> The twinkling stars and the planet Mars
> Shone brightly o'er its grove;
> Where the Hessian brutes, they bit the dust,
> And Cromwell's crew were slain,
> Where the Yeomen fled and left their dead
> In the Ballyshannon Lane.
>
> 'Ballyshannon Lane'

Scunthorpe 'Skuma's outlying farmstead or hamlet', OScand male personal name *Skuma* + THORPE.

A town in North Lincolnshire (before 1996 in Humberside, before 1974 in Lincolnshire), beside the River TRENT[1], about 40 km (25 miles) west of Grimsby. Until the 19th century it was an insignificant little village, but then ironstone was discovered nearby. The first ironworks was opened here in 1864. Steel-making followed in the 1890s, and Scunthorpe mushroomed into an important industrial town (swallowing up four other villages in the process). It is the administrative headquarters of NORTH LINCOLNSHIRE.

The local football team, **Scunthorpe United FC**, were in the spotlight for a while when, in the early 1980s, the dual-sporting England cricketer Ian Botham played for them. The team's other noted alumnus is Kevin Keegan, who played for Scunthorpe United 1968–71 before finding fame with Liverpool FC.

The actress Joan Plowright (b.1929) was born in Scunthorpe, as was the golfer Tony Jacklin (b.1944).

'Scunthorpe' is one of those place names that have reputedly given rise to amusement or derision. Its fault may lie simply in its harsh and (to some ears) ugly sound, but the determinedly scabrous delight in pointing out that orthographically it contains a noted four-letter word. **Scunny** is a nickname for the football club and sometimes for the town.

Seaburgh. The fictional name for ALDEBURGH in M.R. James's ghost story 'A Warning to the Curious' (1925).

Seaford 'ford by the sea' (referring to a crossing at the mouth of the River Ouse, which formerly entered the sea here), OE *sæ* 'sea' + FORD.

A coastal town in East Sussex, about 13 km (8 miles) west of Eastbourne. Until the 16th century it was at the mouth of the River OUSE[3] and an important port (in 1229 it was made an auxiliary CINQUE PORT; it was the most westerly of the ports). In the 1570s, however, a violent storm sealed up the river's outfall with shingle, and Seaford was left high and dry (the Ouse now flows into the Channel at NEWHAVEN, about 3 km (2 miles) to the west). The SEVEN SISTERS[1] chalk cliffs are nearby to the east.

Seaforth. *See* LOCH SEAFORTH.

Seaham 'village by the sea', OE *sæ* 'sea' + HAM.

A port and former mining town in County Durham, 8 km (5 miles) south of Sunderland. Nearby is **Seaham Hall**, where Lord Byron married Annabella Milbanke in 1815. In 1922 Sidney Webb won **Seaham Harbour** for Labour. In 1935, after a notably bitter campaign, the then fiery socialist Manny Shinwell defeated ex-Labour man Ramsay MacDonald to win the constituency. He held the seat until 1950.

Seahouses A modern fishing settlement, 'houses by the sea'.

A village on an attractive stretch of the Northumberland coast, 5 km (3 miles) south of Bamburgh.

Seal Probably 'hall, dwelling', OE *sele*; alternatively 'sallow-tree copse', OE *sele*.

A village in Kent, about 3 km (2 miles) northeast of Sevenoaks.

Seale *See* SEAL.

A village in Surrey, about 5 km (3 miles) northeast of Farnham.

Seal Sand From the local prevalence of seals.

A sandbank in the seal-populated southeastern corner of the WASH. Female seals give birth on the various sandbanks in the area.

Sealyham 'farm or meadow on the River Sely', a river name found elsewhere in names of the region, but in Welsh known as *Anghof* (meaning unknown) + OE HAM.

An estate by Haverfordwest, Pembrokeshire (formerly in Dyfed), 11 km (7 miles) south of Fishguard.

Sealyham terrier. A breed of terrier with a coarse white coat and reaching a height of 30 cm (12 in). It was bred on the Sealyham estate in the later 19th century, by crossing Welsh terriers with Jack Russells.

Today I saw a Sealyham
Bite and shake a rat,
Drop it, bite and shake again
Until its neck broke.

Tod Thews: 'Dead Rat' (1961)

Seanchill. The Irish name for the SHANKILL ROAD in west Belfast.

Seanchua Dubh. The possible Irish name for SHANCODUFF.

Seandún. The Irish name for the area of SHANDON in Cork.

Sea of Moyle. *See* MOYLE, SEA OF.

Sea of the Hebrides. *See under* the HEBRIDES.

Sea Palling Originally *Palling* '(settlement of) Pælli's people', OE male personal name *Pælli* + *-ingas* (*see* -ING); the later addition *Sea* reflects its coastal position.
A village on the northeast Norfolk coast, about 26 km (16 miles) northeast of Norwich.

Seathwaite 'sedge clearing', OScand *sef* 'sedge' + *thveit* 'clearing'.
A small village at the head of BORROWDALE, in the Lake District, Cumbria (formerly in Cumberland), 12 km (7 miles) south of Keswick. It is the wettest inhabited place in England, with an average of 3225 mm (129 in) of rain per year. There is a local story that when one of the inhabitants commented that it was getting brighter, his neighbour replied: 'Hes tae been cleanin' thi winders?'

The village was formerly known for its poverty, and this was reflected in a number of sayings, for example, 'A Seathwaite candle's a greased seeve [rush]', and, referring to weak tea, 'It's hot and wet like Seathwaite broth'. However, the inhabitants were proud people. One Seathwaite lad, when sent on an errand to Coniston, was told at the front door of the house to go round to the service door at the back, to which he indignantly retorted: 'We've nay back doors i' Seathet.'

Seaton 'farmstead by the sea', OE *sæ* 'sea' + -TON.
A coastal town and seaside resort in Devon, in Lyme Bay (*see under* LYME REGIS), close to the mouth of the River AXE[1], about 13 km (8 miles) east of Sidmouth. Open-topped tramcars travel the **Seaton & District Electric Tramway** to the inland village of Colyford.

Seaton Delaval *Delaval* denoting manorial ownership by the de la Val family, resident here in the 13th century.
A small town in Northumberland, 12 km (7 miles) northeast of Newcastle upon Tyne. **Seaton Delaval Hall** (built 1720–9) is a Baroque mansion designed by the architect-playwright Sir John Vanbrugh.

Sebastopol Presumably after the Russian naval base in the Crimea that was the objective of British forces during the Crimean War.
A village in Torfaen unitary authority (formerly in Monmouthshire and then in Gwent), 3 km (2 miles) south of Pontypool.

Second Alexandria, the. A historical nickname for BERWICK-UPON-TWEED.

Sedbergh OScand *set-berg* 'flat-topped hill'.
A village in Cumbria, 15 km (9 miles) east of Kendal. There is a famous boys' public school here, founded in 1525; the lexicographer H.W. Fowler, author of *A Dictionary of Modern English Usage* (1926; often referred to simply as 'Fowler'), taught there until 1899.

Sedgefield 'Cedd or Secg's open land', OE male personal name + *feld* (*see* FIELD).
A town in County Durham, 16 km (9.5 miles) west of Hartlepool. Labour Party leader and prime minister Tony Blair has held the constituency since 1983. There is a racecourse nearby.

Sedgefield was home to the famous 'Pickled Parson'. In 1747 the local rector died, but his wife, anxious that the tithes should be paid as normal, preserved his corpse in salt to delay his burial and thus the news of his death. His ghost was said to haunt the rectory until it burned down in 1792.

Sedgemoor. The marshy site, on 5–6 July 1685, of a battle between the Catholic James II's army and the invading forces of the Duke of Monmouth, pretender to the British throne. It is situated in the northwestern part of KING'S SEDGE MOOR in Somerset, about 5 km (3 miles) east of Bridgwater.

Monmouth, Charles II's illegitimate son, had landed at LYME REGIS on 11 June intent on establishing himself at the head of a Protestant monarchy. He was declared king at TAUNTON on 20 June. From then on, however, things began to go rapidly downhill: he was pursued by the royal army under Lord Feversham, which caught up with him in the fens to the east of Bridgwater and fairly easily disposed of his untrained forces. He was taken to London and beheaded, and some 500 of his supporters were held prisoner in WESTONZOYLAND church, from the belfry of which a number were hanged. Others were left to the tender mercies of Judge Jeffreys' Bloody Assizes. It was the last battle to be fought on English soil.

Sedgley 'Secg's glade', OE male personal name *Secg* + -LEY.
An industrial and residential town in the West Midlands (before 1974 in Staffordshire), in the BLACK COUNTRY, about 5 km (3 miles) south of Wolverhampton.

Sedlescombe Probably 'valley with a house or dwelling', OE *sedl* 'house, dwelling' + *cumb* (*see* -COMBE, COOMBE).
A village in East Sussex, about 11 km (7 miles) north of Hastings. Nearby there is a Pestalozzi International Village (based on the ideas of Swiss educational theorist Johann

Heinrich Pestalozzi (1746–1827)) for the education of low-income or homeless children.

Seend 'sandy place' (referring to the local sandy soil), OE *sende*.
A village in Wiltshire, about 5 km (3 miles) southeast of Melksham.

Seend Cleeve *Cleeve* 'cliff, slope', OE *clif*.
A village in Wiltshire, on the Kennet and Avon Canal, immediately to the west of Seend.

Seething Probably '(settlement of) Sith(a)'s people', OE male personal name *Sith(a)* + *-ingas* (*see* -ING).
A village in Norfolk, about 16 km (10 miles) southeast of Norwich. It has its own airfield, which was the home of the US Army Air Force's 448th Bomber Group during the Second World War .

Sefton 'farm with rushes', OScand *sef* 'rush' + -TON.
A village in Merseyside, 10 km (6 miles) north of Liverpool. It gave its name to one of the borough councils to which many of the powers of Merseyside were devolved in 1986.

Segedunum. A Roman fort (meaning 'strong fort') at WALLSEND in Tyne and Wear. A large museum opened here in 2000.

Seil Modern Gaelic *Seile*, earlier *Saoil*, possibly from an Indo-European root *sal* 'stream, current' (there are various rivers called *Salia* or similar in Europe).
A small island in the Inner HEBRIDES, some 10 km (6 miles) south of Oban in Argyll and Bute (formerly in Strathclyde region). It is separated from the mainland by the narrow **Seil Sound**, which narrows further to the Clachan Sound, over which is the famous 'Bridge over the Atlantic' (properly called the Clachan Bridge), built in 1792. By the bridge is the inn called Tigh na Truish (Gaelic 'house of the trousers'), where, following the proscription of Highland dress in the wake of the 1745 Jacobite Rising, islanders would swap their kilts for trews before visiting the mainland. Part of the film of *Ring of Bright Water* (1969) was filmed in the village of Easdale on the western side of the island.

Séipéal Iosóid. The Irish name for CHAPELIZOD.

Seisyllwg 'territory of Sersyll', *Sersyll* the name of an ancient ruler with the territorial affix *-wg*.
A medieval kingdom in southwest Wales, formed in the 9th century by the union of CEREDIGION and YSTRAD TYWI (covering roughly Pembrokeshire, Ceredigion/Cardiganshire and Carmarthenshire, including the valley of the Towy). In the following century it became part of the kingdom of DEHEUBARTH.

Selborne 'stream by (a copse of) sallow-trees' (originally a river name, applied to what is now the Oakhanger Stream), OE *sealh* or *sele* 'sallow' + *burna* 'stream'.
A village in Hampshire, towards the western end of the SOUTH DOWNS, about 6 km (4 miles) southeast of Alton.

In the 18th century it had a curate called Gilbert White (1720–93), often referred to as **Gilbert White of Selborne**. Born in Selborne, he spent most of his life here, and devoted every spare moment to observing the natural world around him and describing it meticulously in his 'Naturalist's Journal'. This formed the basis of his *Natural History and Antiquities of Selborne* (1789), a pioneering work of ecology, which has made the name of Selborne famous around the world.

> The parish of Selborne lies in the extreme eastern corner of the county of Hampshire, bordering on the county of Sussex, and not far from the county of Surrey … The high part to the south-west consists of a vast hill of chalk, rising three hundred feet above the village; and is divided into a sheep down, a high wood, and a long hanging wood called *The Hanger*. The cover of this eminence is altogether beech, the most lovely of all forest trees, whether we consider its smooth rind or bark, its glossy foliage, or graceful pendulous boughs … The prospect is bounded to the south-east by the vast range of mountains called *The Sussex Downs* … At the foot of this hill, one stage or step from the uplands, lies the village, which consists of one single straggling street, three quarters of a mile in length, in a sheltered vale, and running parallel with *The Hanger*.
>
> Gilbert White: *Natural History and Antiquities of Selborne* (1789)

Selby 'farm with sallow-trees', OE *sele* 'sallow-tree' (a type of willow, especially *Salix cinerea*) + -BY.
A market town on the River OUSE[2], North Yorkshire, 21 km (13 miles) south of York. Exploitation of the **Selby Coalfield** – the largest in Europe – began in 1967 and ended in 2004.
   Selby was the birthplace of Henry I (1069–1135), king of England (1100–35).

Battle of Selby (11 April 1644). A Royalist defeat in the Civil Wars that led inexorably to the much greater defeat at Marston Moor later in the year.

Selkirk 'hall church', OE *sele* 'hall' + Scots *kirk* 'church'; the earliest spelling, *Selechirche c.*1120, suggests that the second element was originally OE *cirice* 'church'.
A royal BURGH (1113) above the lower reaches of ETTRICK WATER, in Scottish Borders, 9 km (5.5 miles) south of Galashiels. It was the county town of the former county of SELKIRKSHIRE.
   Of the 80 men of Selkirk who set off to fight the English at FLODDEN in 1513, only one returned – but he carried a captured standard. This figure is remembered in a statue in the town, and in the annual Common Riding. In 1645 the Marquess of Montrose stayed the night in Selkirk before his defeat at nearby PHILIPHAUGH. Sir Walter Scott, as sheriff of Selkirkshire from 1800 until 1832, administered justice in the Selkirk court house. There are statues both to

Scott, and to Mungo Park (1771–1806), the explorer of the Niger, who was born in nearby Foulshiels. Andrew Lang (1844–1912), the man of letters, was born in Selkirk.

Local legend tells the tale of the Selkirk soutar or souter (cobbler) Rabbie Henspeckle. One day a mouldy-smelling man came into his shop and bought a pair of shoes, paying with gold that he took from a purse full of worms and maggots. Suspicious, Rabbie followed the stranger to the churchyard, where the creature disappeared into a grave. Rabbie and some friends dug up the grave to find a corpse wearing the new pair of shoes. Next day Rabbie's wife heard him hammering in his workshop until there was a sudden scream. She rushed in to find her husband gone. When they dug up the grave again, they found the corpse clutching Rabbie's hat, but the soutar himself was never seen again.

Such cobblers appear to have played a prominent part in the burgh's civic and martial life, as recorded in the town war song:

> Up wi' the Souters o' Selkirk,
> And doon wi' the Earl o' Home.

There is a town called Selkirk in Canada (Manitoba), actually named after Thomas Douglas, 5th Earl of Selkirk, who founded the Red River Settlement nearby in 1812. Also in North America, the Selkirk Mountains stretch from British Columbia into Idaho and Montana; they were also named after the 5th Earl.

> A day oot o' Selkirk is a day wastit.
>
> Local saying

Selkirk bannock or **bannie**. A kind of flattened sweet bread containing dried fruit, a speciality of Selkirk since the 19th century.

'Selkirk Grace, The'. Another name for Robert Burns's 1793 'Kircudbright Grace' (*see under* KIRKCUDBRIGHT).

Selkirkshire. A former county, with Selkirk as its county town. It was bordered by Peeblesshire to the west, Midlothian to the north, Roxburghshire to the southeast and Dumfriesshire to the south. It was abolished in 1975, when it became part of ETTRICK AND LAUDERDALE district in the Borders region (*see under* BORDERS), and today is part of SCOTTISH BORDERS.

Sellafield 'land by the willow hillock', OScand *selja* 'willow' + *haugr* 'mound' + OE *feld* (*see* FIELD).

A nuclear power plant and reprocessing centre on the coast of Cumbria (formerly in Cumberland), 15 km (9 miles) southeast of Whitehaven. It was known as **Windscale** until 1971, when management of the site was transferred from the UK Atomic Energy Authority to British Nuclear Fuels Ltd. Calder Hall, the world's first industrial-scale nuclear power station, was opened here in 1956.

> The beautiful cooling-towers
> Of Calder Hall as strange
> As Zimbabwe, as the powers
> Of man to suffer change.
>
> Patric Dickinson: 'On Dow Crag', from *The World I See* (1960)

Britain's worst nuclear accident took place at Sellafield in 1957, when a fire destroyed the core of a reactor and released large amounts of radioactive iodine into the atmosphere. The activities at Sellafield continue to be controversial, provoking criticism from anti-nuclear campaigners, and from the Irish and Norwegian governments. However, the operation here is a major source of local employment.

> The toadstool towers infest the shore:
> Stink-horns that propagate and spore
>   Wherever the wind blows.
>
> Norman Nicholson: 'Windscale', from *Selected Poems 1940–1982*

Selly Oak Originally *Selly* 'glade on a shelf or ledge', OE *scelf* 'shelf, ledge' + -LEY; the later addition of *Oak* refers to an oak tree that stood here when the place was still a village.

A residential and studenty southwestern district of BIRMINGHAM, in the West Midlands, close to Birmingham University and Bournville. Its name predates any identifiably famous oaks in the area. An oak-tree was planted in the grounds of **Selly Oak House** as late as around 1830 by one John Rodway long after the area had come to be known as Selly Oak. Damaged by construction of nearby houses in the late 19th century, the (by now) dangerous tree was cut down in 1909 and its stump moved to **Selly Oak Park**, where it is commemorated with a plaque.

Selly Oak is renowned for Woodbrooke College, originally a Quaker foundation (1903), now part of Birmingham University; it is based in the house that used to belong to chocolate-manufacturer and Quaker Sir George Cadbury (*see under* BOURNVILLE).

Selmeston 'Sigehelm's farmstead', OE *Sigehelmes* possessive form of male personal name *Sigehelm* + -TON.

A village (pronounced 'selmstən' or 'simpsən') in East Sussex, at the foot of the SOUTH DOWNS, about 13 km (8 miles) southeast of Lewes.

About 2.5 km (1.5 miles) to the west is Charleston Farmhouse, home of the artist Vanessa Bell (Virginia Woolf's sister) from 1916 until her death in 1961. She shared it with her husband, Clive Bell, and her lover, the artist Duncan Grant, and other members of the Bloomsbury Group (*see under* BLOOMSBURY) were frequent visitors here, contributing to its unique decorative style.

Selsdon 'Sele's or Seli's hill', OE *Seles* or *Selis* possessive forms of male personal name *Sele* or *Seli* + *dun* 'hill' (*see* DOWN, -DON).

A southeastern district of CROYDON, in the London borough of Croydon (before 1965 in Surrey).

Selsdon Man. A nickname given to a supposed supporter of the proto-Thatcherite policies outlined at a conference of Conservative Party leaders at the Selsdon Park Hotel near Croydon in 1970. The policies included support for a market economy as opposed to state intervention, rejection of compulsory wage control and a refusal to rescue industrial 'lame ducks'. The coinage was based facetiously on Piltdown Man (*see under* PILTDOWN).

Selsey 'seal island', OE *seolh* 'seal' + *eg* (*see* -EY, -EA).

A coastal resort in West Sussex, on a headland between Chichester Harbour to the west and Bognor Regis to the east. In Anglo-Saxon times it was an important town, and had its own bishop. Over the centuries, though, coastal erosion gnawed away at it. In 1075 it lost its see (which had covered the whole of Sussex) to CHICHESTER, and there could well be the remains of a cathedral lying under the nearby waves. The modern settlement is a regrowth from a village a little inland.

The headland Selsey is on was once genuinely an island (whence the name), but by the early 19th century it had become attached to the mainland. The tip of the headland is called **Selsey Bill** (Modern English *bill* meaning 'beak, promontory'), a name first recorded in the 18th century (it may have been copied from Portland Bill (*see under* PORTLAND), as the headland itself is not particularly pointed or beaklike). It is sometimes referred to as the **Selsey Peninsula**.

According to tradition, Ælla and his army landed at Selsby Bill in 477, defeated the local inhabitants, and founded the kingdom of the South Saxons. That was absorbed by WESSEX in 825, but it formed the basis of what we now know as the county of Sussex.

Semer Water OE *sǣ* 'lake' + *mere* 'lake' (*see also* LAKE) + *wæter* 'lake', which suggests that the lake was originally called 'sæ', then 'sæ-lake' with *mere*, then 'Seamer lake' with *wæter*.

One of the largest areas of natural water in Yorkshire – which is not saying much, the lake being only 1 km (0.6 miles) in length. It lies about 3 km (2 miles) south of Wensleydale, in North Yorkshire. There is a story that in times past the lake was much smaller, until one day an angel disguised as a beggar called on the local villagers. He was turned away by all except an old couple in a hovel, who gave him hospitality. The next day the 'beggar' put a hex on the place:

> Simmer water rise, Simmer water sink,
> And swallow all the town
> Save yon little house
> Where they gave me food and drink.

The waters of the lake duly rose and swallowed as requested.

Send 'sandy place' (referring to the local sandy soil), OE *sende*.

A village in Surrey, on the River WEY[1], about 3 km (2 miles) southeast of Woking.

Senghenydd Probably 'territory of Sangan', Welsh personal name *Sangan* with territorial affix *-ydd*; the long-standing association of this place (since the 14th century) with the possibly 6th-century St Cenydd or Henydd (supposedly a son of Gildas) is probably mistaken.

A small town in Caerphilly unitary authority (formerly in Glamorgan, then Mid Glamorgan), 17 km (10 miles) north of Cardiff. It was also the name of a medieval district, the ruler of which, Ifor Bach, successfully stormed the Norman castle at CARDIFF in 1158.

The **Senghenydd colliery** was the scene of Wales's worst pit disaster in 1913, when an explosion caused the deaths of over 400 miners. The tragedy was heralded by the sighting of 'corpse birds' (robins and/or pigeons) flying around the pit head at Senghenydd – a sure sign of disaster to come, according to miners' lore.

Senlac. *See under* HASTINGS.

Senos. Ptolemy's name for the River SHANNON.

Sergeant Man Etymology uncertain, but there are several names with *Sergeant* in the Lake District. It may have referred to the feudal role of the sergeant in the Middle Ages or be a surname; *Man* may refer to a standing stone of approximately human size.

A mountain (736 m/ 2414 ft) in the LAKE DISTRICT, Cumbria, some 5 km (3 miles) northwest of Grasmere. It is a subsidiary top of High Raise (762 m / 2500 ft).

Serpentine From its winding shape.

A long curved lake in HYDE PARK and KENSINGTON Gardens. It was created when the small River WESTBOURNE was dammed in 1730, the idea originating with Caroline of Anspach (1683–1737), consort of George II. It has long been popular for swimming (the **Serpentine Lido** opened in the early 20th century) and boating in summer and for skating in winter, and has a less fortunate claim to fame as a chosen spot for suicides. It may have been in the Serpentine that Harriet Westbrook, deserted and pregnant wife of the poet Shelley, drowned in 1816.

In the mid-20th century its name was often shortened colloquially to 'the Serps'.

> I am hoping for a row … on the Serpentine, which is really almost as good as a lake.
>
> George Eliot: letter (22 October 1853)

Serpentine Gallery. An art gallery a little to the southwest of the Serpentine. It was originally built as a tea-house. Exhibitions of contemporary art are held here.

Settle OE *setl* 'house, dwelling'.

A market town on the River RIBBLE, North Yorkshire, 21 km (13 miles) northwest of Skipton. The **Settle-to-Carlisle railway line** is one of the most scenic in England, passing through the northwest PENNINES via Ribblesdale, Mallerstang and the EDEN[1] valley. It has been saved by enthusiasts from the depredations of many a would-be Beeching.

Settle was the birthplace of George Birkbeck (1776–1841), founder in 1823 of the London Mechanic's Institution, renamed Birkbeck College in 1907, and now part of the University of London.

Sheepless in Settle. The title of an apocryphal film, playing on the 1993 romantic comedy *Sleepless in Seattle*. The joke was apparently current in the Yorkshire Dales at the time of the 2001 foot-and-mouth epidemic.

Seven Dials From the dials (actually originally six in number) on top of a pillar in its centre.

Originally, a seven-road crossroads in the vicinity of HOLBORN in London (the roads were Great Earl Street, Little Earl Street, Great White Lion Street, Little White Lion Street, Great St Andrew's Street, Little St Andrew's Street and Queen Street). In the reign of Charles II a Doric pillar was placed in the centre, topped with a set of sundials pointing down each of the streets. One pair of streets had to make do with a single sundial, but this slight anomaly was brushed under the carpet when the dials came to give their name to the junction. The column and dials were removed in 1773 and in 1882 set up on WEYBRIDGE Green. In 1989 a new pillar with dials was erected on the original site and ceremonially unveiled by Queen Beatrix of the Netherlands. The four roads that meet here now are Earlham Street, Mercer Street, Monmouth Street and Shorts Gardens.

Meanwhile, the name of the crossroads had passed to the district around it, which came to be notorious for squalor, vice, crime and general degradation. It was long the headquarters of the ballad printers and balladmongers. Most of the slums were cleared away when the area was redeveloped in the 1870s and 1880s.

> Hearts just as pure and fair
> May beat in Belgrave Square
> As in the lowly air of Seven Dials!
>
> W.S. Gilbert: *Iolanthe* (1882)

It is now a modestly thriving area, with a mix of small traditional shops, boutiques and New Age-ish establishments.

Seven-road junctions in other towns have taken the name over: there is a Seven Dials in Brighton, for example.

In the second half of the 20th century *Seven Dials* was pressed into service as rhyming slang for 'piles' (in the 'haemorrhoids' sense).

Seven Dials raker. Late 19th- and early 20th-century slang for a prostitute whose home is in Seven Dials and who plies her trade elsewhere (as J. Redding Ware reported in his *Passing English of the Victorian Era* (1908), she 'never smiles out of the Dials').

Seven Hogs, the Presumably from the resemblance of the islands to pigs.

A group of small islets off the north coast of the DINGLE Peninsula, County Kerry. They are also called the **Magharee Islands** (Irish *Machairí* 'flat places'). On one of the islands St Seanach founded a monastery in the 6th century.

Seven Hunters, the. An alternative name for the FLANNAN ISLES.

Sevenoaks '(place by) seven oak trees', OE *seofon* 'seven' + *ac* 'oak-tree'. Presumably there was once an actual clump or copse of oak trees here that inspired the name, but its identity has not survived (a stand of seven oaks from Knole Park was planted in the eastern part of the town in 1955, but all but one were blown down in the freak storm of October 1987; they have been replaced by saplings).

A residential and commuter town in Kent, just outside the M25, about 24 km (15 miles) west of Maidstone. **Sevenoaks School** was founded in the 15th century.

The Vine in Sevenoaks is one of the oldest cricket grounds in England, dating back to the 18th century.

To the southeast of the town is KNOLE, one of the largest private houses in England.

Battle of Sevenoaks (18 June 1450). A battle in which a detachment of Henry VI's forces were routed by the Kentish rebels under Jack Cade. Henry was discomfited and Cade went on to briefly occupy London.

Seven Sisters[1] A long-established name for a set of seven similar or identical females or things. The original application was to the Pleiades, the seven daughters of Atlas and Pleione in Greek mythology, who were turned into stars. Among later recipients were a set of seven cannon cast by one Robert Borthwick and used at the Battle of FLODDEN (1513) and a group of seven US colleges (including Bryn Mawr, Radcliffe, Vassar and Wellesley) which are the female equivalent of what used to be the exclusively male Ivy League.

A set of seven dramatic undulating chalk cliffs on the East Sussex coast, between Cuckmere Haven (*see under* CUCKMERE) and BEACHY HEAD, to the west of Eastbourne, where the SOUTH DOWNS meet the sea. The names of the individual cliffs are Went Hill Brow, Baily's Brow, Flagstaff Point, Brass Point, Rough Brow, Short Brow and Haven Brow.

Behind the coast the **Seven Sisters Country Park** covers about 2.5 sq km (1 sq mile) of the Cuckmere Valley.

Seven Sisters[2]. An area of South TOTTENHAM, London, bordering SEVEN SISTERS ROAD.

Seven Sisters[3] From the name of the colliery opened here in 1872, and referring to the seven daughters of the colliery owner.

A village in Neath Port Talbot (formerly in Glamorgan, then in West Glamorgan), 14 km (8.5 miles) northeast of Neath.

Seven Sisters Road From *Seven Sisters*, a local nickname for a circle of seven elm trees which once stood by the road. According to legend they were planted outside a Tottenham tavern by seven local sisters on parting and going their separate ways.

A road in North London (N4, N7, N15), linking HOLLOWAY with TOTTENHAM. It was laid out in the 1830s. Over the years the district at the northeastern end of the road (in South Tottenham) began to be referred to as **Seven Sisters**, a development cemented by the opening of Seven Sisters Underground station, on the Victoria line, in 1968.

Seven Wonders of North Wales, the. An epithet given to seven northerly Welsh locations, as enumerated in an anonymous 18th-century poem:

> Pistyll Rhaeadr and Wrexham steeple,
> Snowdon's mountain without its people,
> Overton yew trees, Gresford bells,
> Llangollen bridge and St Winifred's well.

St Winifred's Well gives its name to HOLYWELL in Flintshire; for the Falls (Welsh *pistyll*) of Rhaeadr (which also means 'waterfall'), *see* RHAYADER. For the others, *see* GRESFORD, LLANGOLLEN, OVERTON[2], SNOWDON and WREXHAM[1].

Severn A pre-English (and possibly pre-Celtic) river name of uncertain origin and meaning.

A river in Wales and western England, which rises on PLYNLIMON (its source is called 'Blaenhafren' (Welsh *blaen* 'point, top')) and flows northeastwards, eastwards and then southwards via WELSHPOOL, SHREWSBURY, WORCESTER, TEWKESBURY and GLOUCESTER into the BRISTOL Channel. The Romans' version of its name was SABRINA, and the river's Welsh name, **Hafren**, is historically the same word.

At 354 km (220 miles) the Severn is the longest river in the United Kingdom. For much of its length it forms or follows the border between England and Wales. It is highly susceptible to flooding (notably at BEWDLEY, and the county cricket ground at Worcester is regularly turned into a small lake in winter). Its main tributaries are the AVON[1], STOUR[5], TEME, Vyrnwy (*see under* LAKE VYRNWY) and WYE[1].

The two sides of its estuary were linked in the late 19th century by a rail tunnel constructed between 1873 and 1885 about 6 km (4 miles) southwest of CHEPSTOW (where the river is about 3 km (2 miles) wide). In 1966 this was joined to the north by the **Severn Road Bridge**, a suspension bridge 988 m (3240 ft) long, carrying the M48. Now referred to as the 'old' Severn Bridge, it was reputedly the seventh-longest bridge in the world at its construction. A new road bridge, usually referred to as the **Second Severn Crossing**, more or less following the line of the rail tunnel and carrying the M4, was opened in 1996. Many of the earlier upstream bridges were destroyed in floods in 1795, but that event only hastened the building of Industrial Revolution-era iron bridges (*see below*). The former rail bridge at SHARPNESS no longer survives following the so-called **Severn Bridge Disaster** (25 October 1960), when two tanker-barges collided with it and five sailors died.

The Severn has been an active transport route since Roman times, and until the 1820s was navigable almost as far as Welshpool (today it can only be navigated 72 km (45 miles) upstream from Gloucester). Many inland ports grew up along its course (including BRIDGNORTH, Gloucester and Shrewsbury), and it is connected to many other waterways by canal (the first of which was the Droitwich Barge Canal of 1771). At IRONBRIDGE it is crossed by the first bridge in the world to be constructed of cast iron.
See also STOURPORT-ON-SEVERN; UPTON-UPON-SEVERN.

> The men that live in West England,
> They see the Severn strong
> A-rolling on rough water brown
> Light aspen leaves along.
>
> Hilaire Belloc: 'The South Country' (1910)

> And who loves joy as he
> That dwells in shadows?
> Do not forget me quite,
> O Severn meadows.
>
> Ivor Gurney: 'Severn Meadows' (1917)

Severn Bore. A tidal wave formed in the lower reaches of the River Severn (between LYDNEY and Gloucester) by the incoming Atlantic tide forcing its way into the rapidly narrowing river. It happens about 250 times a year, and in the spring and autumn can reach 3 m (10 ft) in height. It is popular with surfers.

Severn Suite, The. A suite (Opus 87) by Edward Elgar. It consists of an introduction, toccata and fugue, a minuet and a coda. He originally composed it as a test piece for the National Brass Band Contest at Crystal Palace in 1930. He made an orchestral arrangement (the form in which it is now usually heard) in 1932. It was dedicated to George Bernard Shaw. Its Severn background is focused particularly on Elgar's beloved Worcester: one section is entitled 'Worcester Castle', another 'The Cathedral'.

Severn Valley Railway. A (mostly) single-track preserved railway line running from BRIDGNORTH to KIDDERMINSTER.

Sewerby 'Sigvarth's farmstead', OScand male personal name *Sigvarthr* + -BY.

A coastal village in the East Riding of Yorkshire, on the northeastern outskirts of Bridlington.

Sexhow 'mound of a man called Sekkr', OScand male personal name *Sekkr* + *haugr* 'mound, hill'.

A settlement in North Yorkshire, 16 km (10 miles) northeast of Northallerton.

Sezincote 'gravelly cottages', OE *cisen* 'gravelly' + *cot* (*see* -COT, COTE).

A hamlet in Gloucestershire, in the COTSWOLDS, about 4 km (2.5 miles) southwest of Moreton-in-Marsh. **Sezincote House**, built between 1798 and 1805 by Samuel Pepys Cockerell, is a highly individual 'Indianized' building: its exterior combines Mughal and Hindu motifs, including a large turquoise 'onion dome', with Palladian style.

Sgùrr Alaisdair 'Alexander's peak', Gaelic *sgùrr* 'peak' (generally a rocky, pointed one) + Gaelic version of the first name of the first climber, *Alexander* Nicolson. This, and some of the other Skye Sgùrrs listed below, are among the few peaks in Britain named after known individuals.

The highest peak (993 m / 3258 ft) in the CUILLIN of Skye. Its striking summit pinnacle was first ascended in 1873 by Sheriff Alexander Nicolson of Skye, accompanied by a local shepherd called 'A. Macrae'; Nicolson recorded that 'one or two places were somewhat trying, requiring good grip of hands and feet'.

Sgùrr Mhic Choinnich 'Mackenzie's peak', Gaelic version of the surname of John *Mackenzie*, the famous Cuillin guide of the Victorian and Edwardian eras (*see* the CIOCH).

A rocky peak (948 m / 3110 ft) in the CUILLIN of Skye.

Sgùrr na Cìche. *See under* the CIOCH.

Sgùrr nan Gillean 'peak of the young men', Gaelic *nan* 'of the' + *gillean* 'young men'. Early in the last century it was half-jokingly suggested that this was 'from some idea of the enormous death-roll caused by mythical attempts to ascend it' (Colin B. Phillip, in *The Scottish Mountaineering Club Journal*, Vol. XIV).

A peak, at the northern end of the main CUILLIN Ridge in Skye, overlooking SLIGACHAN, from where its beautiful Pinnacle Ridge is seen in profile. The first ascent of the mountain, by the so-called Tourist Route, was made in 1836, by Professor J.D. Forbes, guided by the local gillie Duncan MacIntyre. The mountain has been memorably praised by the Gaelic poet Sorley Maclean:

> ... Sgùrr nan Gillean the best sgùrr of them,
> The blue-blacked gape-mouthed strong sgùrr,
> The sapling slender horned sgùrr,
> The forbidding great sgùrr of danger,
> The sgùrr of Skye above them all.

On its airy summit in the previous century, Sheriff Alexander Nicolson (after whom SGÙRR ALAISDAIR is named) was moved to piety:

The top of Sgurr nan Gillean is undoubtedly a very solemn place to be in, and the slight suggestion of danger gives it an awful charm. In such places there is no poet whom I prefer to King David, who, among his other fine qualities, must certainly have been an accomplished mountaineer. If he had not been accustomed to go up and down rocky hills, he would not have sung that glorious strain:

> I to the hills will lift mine eyes,
> From whence doth come mine aid,
> My safety cometh from the Lord,
> Who heaven and earth hath made.
> Thy foot He'll not let slide.

It was not a blind and fatal Force, but an intelligent Person, that did in the beginning create the heavens and the earth, that did in due time order the upheaval of Sgurr nan Gillean, and that does at this hour watch over every creature of His that goes up and down its craggy sides. If Professors Tyndall and Huxley should consider me an ass for this, I don't care. I back David against them both with great equanimity.

> Alexander Nicolson: in *Good Words* (an evangelical magazine), 1875

Sgùrr nan Spàinnteach. *See* GLEN SHIEL.

Sgùrr Thormaid 'Norman's peak', Gaelic version of the first name of the pioneering mountaineer Professor *Norman* Collie (*see* the Grey Man of Ben Macdui *under* BEN MACDUI *and see* the CIOCH).

A peak (927 m / 3041 ft) in the CUILLIN of Skye.

Shadwell 'shallow spring or stream', OE *sceald* 'shallow' + *wella* 'spring, stream'.

A district in East London (E1), on the north bank of the THAMES[1], immediately to the east of Wapping, in the borough of TOWER HAMLETS. It was only very sparsely inhabited until the 17th century, when the establishment of various riverside industries set population growth in train. **Shadwell Basin** was developed in the 1860s, as part of London Docks (*see under* LONDON); it closed for business in the 1960s.

See also CABLE STREET.

Shaftesbury 'Sceaft's fortified place' or 'fortified place on a shaft-shaped hill', OE *Sceaftes* or *sceaftes* possessive forms of male personal name *Sceaft* or *sceaft* 'shaft' + *byrig* dative form of *burh* 'fortified place' (*see* BURY).

A hill-town in Dorset, about 16 km (10 miles) north of Blandford Forum. It grew up around its abbey, a Benedictine nunnery founded in 888 by Alfred the Great. This housed the bones of Edward the Martyr, and was a great centre of pilgrimage (for a time the town became known as '**St Edwardstowe**'). King Cnut (Canute) died here in 1035.

The town's 213-m (700-ft) summit is reached by a number of very steep cobbled streets (notably Gold

Hill) of sufficient picturesqueness to have featured in several nostalgia-themed television advertisements for Hovis bread in the 1970s, featuring a delivery boy pushing a bread-laden bike up the hill. This wholesome image was dented in 2003 by the revelation of a brothel operating at the top of Gold Hill, prompting a local 'Hovis Hooker' joke:

> For £30, she'll show you her baps. For £60, you can have her buns. For £100, she'll offer you her bloomers. And for £150, she'll let you dip your little soldier in.
>
> 'A Spicy Roll in Hovis Country' in *The Observer* (27 July 2003)

From the top of the town's hill-spur (from which it may have got its name) there are stunning views over BLACKMOOR VALE.

In his fiction, including *Jude the Obscure* (1895), Thomas Hardy rendered Shaftesbury as SHASTON, an old alternative name for the town.

Shaftesbury Avenue Named in honour of the 7th Earl of *Shaftesbury* (1801–85), the philanthropist and social reformer whose work did much to improve working conditions in factories and mines.

A street in the WEST END[1] of London (W1, WC2), in the City of Westminster, running northeastwards from PICCADILLY CIRCUS across Charing Cross Road to New OXFORD STREET, and forming the northern border of London's CHINATOWN. It was laid out in the 1880s (at the cost of some of London's most noisome slums). By 1907 six theatres had opened here, and it has since become known as the heart of London's THEATRELAND. Ironically, the Shaftesbury Theatre itself was bombed in 1941, and subsequently demolished.

Shaggs Possibly from *shag*, the name of a cormorant-like bird, although the place is not especially close to its natural seashore habitat; alternatively perhaps from OE *sceacga* 'matted hair, wool, etc.', later 'tangled vegetation'.

A hamlet in Dorset, about 5 km (3 miles) northeast of LULWORTH.

Shakespeare Cliff From its being the cliff in Shakespeare's *King Lear* (1605) from which the blinded Gloucester thinks to throw himself. He is actually nowhere near it, but his disguised son Edgar describes its vertiginousness so vividly that he imagines himself at the brink:

> How fearful and dizzy 'tis to cast one's eyes so low!
> The crows and choughs that wing the midway air
> Show scarce so gross as beetles; half way down
> Hangs one that gathers samphire, dreadful trade!
> Methinks he seems no bigger than his head.
> The fishermen that walk upon the beach
> Appear like mice, and yond tall anchoring bark
> Diminish'd to her cock, her cock a buoy

> Almost too small for sight. The murmuring surge,
> That on the unnumber'd idle pebbles chafes,
> Cannot be heard so high. I'll look no more,
> Lest my brain turn, and the deficient sight
> Topple down headlong.
>
> William Shakespeare: *King Lear* (1605), IV.vi

A 107-m (350-ft) high chalk headland about 2.5 km (1.5 miles) southwest of Dover. The workings from an abortive 1880 attempt to construct a CHANNEL TUNNEL can still be seen at the foot of the cliff, as can spoil from the excavation of the present tunnel, which runs out to sea beneath the cliff.

Shakespeare Country. A touristic name widely exploited for the area of WARWICKSHIRE around and including STRATFORD-UPON-AVON, birthplace of William Shakespeare (1564–1616). It is first recorded as the title of a book (1900) by John Leyland.

Shakespeare villages. A group of villages near Stratford-upon-Avon that appear in a rhyme traditionally attributed to Shakespeare:

> Piping Pebworth, dancing Marston,
> Haunted Hillbro', hungry Grafton.
> Dudging Exhall, papist Wicksford,
> Beggarly Broom and drunken Bidford.

The verse was supposedly written after Shakespeare and a group of associates accepted a challenge to take part in a drinking competition with the men of BIDFORD-ON-AVON. They lost the challenge to Bidford's more seasoned topers, however, and were obliged to sleep off the effects of the carouse before returning to Stratford the next day.

Shambles, the OE *sceamol* 'butcher's stall'.

A medieval street in YORK, the city's oldest (mentioned in Domesday Book), lined with half-timbered houses. It was where the city's butchers did their business in the Middle Ages, hence the name. The butchers have gone, to be replaced with a variety of craft- and tourist-related shops, popular with visitors to the city.

Shancoduff Possibly Irish *Seanchua Dubh* 'old dark hollow'. A locality near the village of Iniskeen, County Monaghan, some 10 km (6 miles) west of Dundalk. The place gives a title to one of the poems of Patrick Kavanagh (1905–67):

> The sleety winds fondle the rushy beards of Shancoduff
> While the cattle-drovers sheltering in Featherna Bush
> Look up and say: 'Who owns them hungry hills
> That the water-hen and snipe must have forsaken?'

Shandon Irish *Seandún* 'old fort'.

An area in the centre of the city of Cork. The 18th-century St Ann's Church in Shandon, celebrated for its bells, is known jokingly as 'the Four-Faced Liar', as each of its four clock faces have been known to show different times.

'Bells of Shandon, The'. A celebrated poem by Francis Sylvester Mahony (Father Prout; 1804–66):

> On this I ponder, where'er I wander,
> And thus grow fonder, sweet Cork, of thee;
> With thy bells of Shandon,
> That sound so grand on
> The pleasant waters of the river Lee.

Mahony's lines, although originally intended as a squib, were mercilessly parodied by Anon.:

> But the bells of St Nicholas
> Sound so ridiculous
> On the dirty waters of Sullivan's Quay.

Shandy Hall After the fictional character, Tristram *Shandy*. The home of the novelist Laurence Sterne (1713–68), at Coxwold, North Yorkshire, 12 km (7 miles) southeast of Thirsk. Sterne was vicar of Coxwold from 1760 until his death in 1768, and here wrote both the anti-novel *The Life and Opinions of Tristram Shandy* (1759–67) and *A Sentimental Journey through France and Italy* (1768). He is buried in the churchyard.

Shankill Road Irish *Seanchill* 'old church' (*see* KIL-). An exclusively Protestant working-class street of industrial west Belfast. During the Troubles **'the Shankill'** – the road and its adjacent streets – became synonymous with hardline Unionism. In the same way 'the Falls' around the nearby Catholic FALLS ROAD became synonymous with hard-line Nationalism.

Shankill Butchers, the. The grimly appropriate name given to a loyalist gang responsible for a series of grisly sectarian murders of Catholics in the Shankill Road area in the mid-1970s. Eleven members of the gang were given life sentences for the murders by a Belfast court in 1979.

Shanklin 'bank by the drinking cup' (referring to the waterfall at Shanklin Chine), OE *scenc* 'drinking cup' + *hlinc* 'bank, ridge'. A town and seaside resort on the southeastern coast of the ISLE OF WIGHT, about 11 km (7 miles) southeast of Newport and just to the south of Sandown Bay. Cliffs 30 m (100 ft) high separate the town from the shore below, where many of the traditional ingredients of a Victorian coastal resort may be found.

John Keats stayed in Shanklin for over a month in 1819, and wrote the first part of his poem *Lamia* here.

PLUTO (Pipe Line Under The Ocean), the underwater oil-supply pipe which carried petrol from England to northern France after the D-Day landings (1944), had one of its two northern terminals in Shanklin; the other was at DUNGENESS.

Shanklin Chine. A deep narrow ravine (OE *cinu* 'fissure, cleft') in the cliffs at Shanklin, cut by a stream descending steeply to the sea. A path winds down, and the chine's natural mossy, ferny picturesqueness is augmented on summer nights by the provision of fairy lights. During the Second World War, Royal Marine commandos practised here for the disastrous Dieppe Raid of 1942.

Shannon In modern Irish it is *An tSionnainn* 'the old one', and the name probably originates in that of an ancient river goddess, *Sinann*. Ptolemy in the 2nd century AD recorded the name as *Senos*. However, in a folk tale the river is associated with a girl's name.

Ireland's longest river, with a length of 386 km (240 miles). It rises in the **Shannon Pot** (Irish **Log na Sionna** 'hollow of the Shannon'), a deep pool in the karst country of the CUILCAGH Mountains of County Cavan. A story associated with the place tells how a girl was tempted to eat the fruit from a sacred tree planted here by the druids. Immediately a great fountain of water jetted out of the ground, drowning the girl and forming a mighty river. The girl's name, Sionnán, is said to be the origin of the name of the river (not a theory upheld by modern philologists). Another belief associated with the river is recorded by Captain Francis Grose in his *Classical Dictionary of the Vulgar Tongue* (1785):

> It is said that a dipping in the River Shannon totally annihilates bashfulness.

From the Cuilcagh Mountains the Shannon flows generally southwards then southwestwards, and passes through a number of large lakes, including LOUGH ALLEN, LOUGH REE and LOUGH DERG². It also forms the boundaries between a number of counties: Roscommon, Leitrim, Longford, Westmeath, Offaly, Galway, Tipperary, Clare and Limerick. In its lower reaches, at ARDNACRUSHA, there is a major hydroelectric scheme, and there are many salmon farms along the river. Just beyond the city of LIMERICK (the upper limit of navigation) the Shannon enters its estuary, which forms an inlet some 80 km (50 miles) long, and it is to this stretch that James Joyce refers in the famous final passage of 'The Dead', in which he writes of

> the dark mutinous Shannon waves

The estuary at last opens out to the sea at **Mouth of the Shannon**, between LOOP HEAD and BALLYBUNNION. It was the parting of the waters of the Shannon estuary which, according to the legend, suggested the religious life to St Senan (*fl.*6th century).

> The Shannon and the Liffey and the tuneful Lee,
> The Boyne and the Blackwater sad music sing,
> The waters of the west run red into the sea –
> No matter what be trumps, their knave will beat our king.

> Egan O'Rahilly (1670–1726): 'Last Lines', translated from the Gaelic by Frank O'Connor (O'Rahilly was lamenting the breaking of the Treaty of Limerick in 1691.)

On the green banks of Shannon, when Sheelah was nigh,
No blithe Irish lad was so happy as I ...

Thomas Campbell: 'The Harper' (1799)

Shannon. A sea area in the shipping forecast. It is off the southwest coast of Ireland, between SOLE to the south and ROCKALL to the north.

Shannon Airport. A large airport for transatlantic flights in County Clare, on the north side of the Shannon estuary 20 km (12 miles) west of Limerick. A large industrial estate has grown up in the customs-free area around the airport, as has the new town of **Shannon** (Irish **Sionnainn**).

Shannon Callows Irish *caladh* 'water meadow'. The flood plains of the River Shannon, in Galway, Offaly and Westmeath.

Shannon–Erne Waterway. A canal for pleasure craft linking the rivers Shannon and ERNE in counties Cavan, Fermanagh and Leitrim.

Shanwick. The name of the air-control authority run by Shannon and PRESTWICK airports to cover the northeast Atlantic.

Shannonbridge Irish *Droichead na Sionainne* 'bridge of the Shannon'.
A village in County Offaly, near the confluence of the SUCK and the SHANNON, 15 km (9 miles) south of Athlone.

Shan Van Vocht Irish *An tSeanbhean Bhocht* 'the poor old woman'.
A personification of Ireland as a poor old woman, popular in the 18th and 19th centuries. It was adopted as the title of a Nationalist magazine published between 1896 and 1899. *Compare* KATHLEEN NI HOULIHAN *and* RÓISÍN DUBH.

Where will they have their camp?
Says the Shan Van Vocht;
On the Curragh of Kildare,
The boys they will be there,
With their pikes in good repair,
Says the Shan Van Vocht.

Anon.: 'The Shan Van Vocht' (a song written as the French fleet sailed for Ireland in 1796)

Shap 'pile of stones', OE *heap* 'heap, pile', referring to a prehistoric stone circle to the south of the village.
A village in Cumbria, 15 km (9 miles) south of Penrith. The ruins of **Shap Abbey**, on the west side of the village, date from the 12th century. The M6 and the main Glasgow–Euston railway line climb gradually over the pass of **Shap Summit** (316 m / 1036 ft) 3 km (2 miles) south of the village, while to the southwest are the **Shap Fells**, eastern outliers of the Lakeland Fells.

As on Shap Fell, the only time I was there,
Wind cutting over and snowflakes beginning to sail
Slantwise across, on haulage vans clashing their gears ...

Donald Davie: 'Lancashire', from *The Shires* (1974)

Shapinsay 'Hjalpandi's island', OScand *Hjalpandis*, male personal name in the possessive + *ey* (*see* -AY). The change of *hj-* to *sh-* is also found in the name SHETLAND.
An island in ORKNEY, 6 km (4 miles) north of Kirkwall on Mainland, across **Shapinsay Sound**. It was in Shapinsay Sound in 1910 that a man out shooting ducks supposedly saw a sea monster with a 5.5-m (18-ft) neck and the head of a horse. The **Fit o' Shapinsay** (Scots *fit* 'foot') is a headland on the east coast of the island. Shapinsay was the birthplace of the parents of 'the father of American letters', Washington Irving, author of 'Rip Van Winkle' and 'The Legend of Sleepy Hollow'; they emigrated to America in 1783, the year of his birth.

Shapwick 'sheep farm', OE *sceap* 'sheep' + *wic* (*see* WICK).
A village in Somerset, about 10 km (6 miles) northwest of STREET.

Shapwick Hoard. A hoard of early Roman coins, the largest ever found in Britain, which came to light in a field at Shapwick in 1999. They were discovered accidentally by Kevin Elliott, a dairy farmer's son, using a metal detector lent him by his cousin, Martin Elliott, a self-employed welder. The 9000 or so silver *denarii* date from between the time of Mark Antony (31 BC) and the emperor Severus Maximus (AD 222–235) and are calculated to have been buried in about AD 230 and to be the equivalent of 10 years' pay for a legionary soldier in the Roman army. The find is now in the British Museum.

Sharpenhoe 'sharp or steep hill-spur', OE *scearpan* dative form of *scearp* 'sharp, steep' + *hoh* 'hill-spur'.
A village in Bedfordshire, about 10 km (6 miles) north of Luton.

Sharpenhoe Clappers. A steep-sided wooded hill at the northern tip of the CHILTERN HILLS. It is now in the care of the National Trust. The origin of *Clappers* is uncertain: it could be from ME *clapper* 'land with rabbit burrows, rabbit-warren', but there may be some connection with OE *clop* 'hillock'.

Sharpness 'Scobba's headland', OE male personal name *Scobba* + *næss* (*see* NESS).
A seaport in Gloucestershire, on the eastern bank of the SEVERN estuary, about 25 km (16 miles) south of Gloucester. It is the highest point on the river navigable by larger vessels (of around 8000 tonnes). It is linked to Gloucester by a canal, constructed in 1827 to circumvent the Severn's treacherous riverbed.

Sharpness has one of the world's highest tidal ranges – up to 16 m (52 ft).

There was once an iron railway bridge across the Severn here, but it collapsed in 1960 and was never rebuilt (*see under* SEVERN).

Shaston Perhaps from Medieval Latin *Shaftonia* 'Shaftesbury', with *f* misread as *s*.

A former alternative name for SHAFTESBURY. Thomas Hardy used it in his fiction.

Shawfield Probably 'open land with a copse', OE *sceaga* 'copse' + *feld* (*see* FIELD).

An area of GLASGOW, on the South Side.

Shawfield Riots. Violent protests (1724) at a hike in malt tax, involving the looting of the house of Daniel Campbell, MP for Glasgow Burghs.

Shebbear 'grove where shafts or poles are obtained', OE *sceaft* 'shaft, pole' + *bearu* 'grove'.

A village (pronounced 'shebia') in Devon, about 13 km (8 miles) southwest of Torrington. Just outside the church-yard is a standing stone called the 'Devil's Stone', similar to the components of STONEHENGE. Apparently the Devil deposited it there, and every 5 November, in order to avoid ill fortune, the villagers turn it over with the aid of crowbars.

Sheefry Hills Irish *Cnoic Shiofra* 'Siofra's hills' (*see* KNOCK-).

A rugged massif in County Mayo, northeast across the Doo Lough Pass from MWEELREA. The highest point is Claschcame (772 m / 2532 ft).

Sheen. *See* EAST SHEEN.

Sheep Dyke. *See under* NORTH RONALDSAY.

Sheep Haven Irish *Cuan Na gCaorach* 'harbour of the sheep'; this is a translation of the original English name.

An inlet on the north coast of County Donegal, between HORN HEAD (to the west) and the ROSGUILL peninsula (to the east).

Sheep's Head Presumably 'headland grazed by sheep'.

A headland on the west coast of County Cork, at the end of the long, narrow **Sheep's Head Peninsula**, between Bantry Bay (*see under* BANTRY) and DUNMANUS BAY. Sheep's Head itself is also called **Muntervary** or **Montervary** (Irish *muintir* 'family of' + a family name). The climate is notably mild, with daffodils flowering in January. The **Sheep's Head Way** is an 88-km (55-mile) long-distance walk through the beautiful scenery of the peninsula.

Sheepwash[1] 'place where sheep are dipped', OE *sceap-wæsce*.

A hilltop village in Devon, about 13 km (8 miles) south of Torrington. Its original square plan, dating from Anglo-Saxon times, survives. There is a packhorse bridge across the nearby River TORRIDGE[1].

Sheepwash[2]. A village in Northumberland, 6 km (4 miles) east of Morpeth.

Sheepy Magna *Sheepy* 'island, or dry ground in a marsh, where sheep graze', OE *sceap* 'sheep' + *eg* 'island' (*see* -EY, -EA); *Magna* 'great', Latin.

A village in Leicestershire, about 15 km (9 miles) northwest of Hinckley. It is 'Magna' to distinguish it from the next-door (and somewhat smaller) village of **Sheepy Parva** (*Parva* 'small', Latin).

Sheerness Probably 'bright headland', OE *scir* 'bright' + *næss* (*see* NESS). Alternatively the first element could be from OE *scear* 'plough-share', referring to the shape of the headland.

A town and port in Kent, at the northwestern tip of the ISLE OF SHEPPEY, on the eastern side of the mouth of the River MEDWAY[1]. It was first put on the map by Charles II, who in 1665 had a dockyard built here. In the 19th century it became a naval coaling station, saving the new steam-powered vessels the trouble of negotiating the Medway down to CHATHAM. It remained a naval dockyard until 1960. It is now a busy container port, and there is also an international ferry service to Flushing.

At the age of 15 Edmund Kean (1787/90–1833) began his acting career in Sheerness, in Samuel Jerrold's theatre company.

Sheet 'projecting piece of land, corner or nook' (referring to its location in the angle of two streams), OE *sciete*.

A village in Hampshire, on the River ROTHER[1], on the northern outskirts of PETERSFIELD.

Sheffield 'open land by the River Sheaf', OE river name, from *sceath* 'boundary' + *feld* (*see* FIELD) (the Sheaf is a tributary of the Don); *Escafeld* 1086.

An industrial city and unitary authority on the River DON[2], Yorkshire, 55 km (33 miles) east of Manchester. It is on the edge of the Peak District, and, like Rome, is built on seven hills, many now graced with high-rise blocks.

The Norman baron, William de Lovetot, built a castle and church at Sheffield in the early 12th century, and Thomas de Furnival granted the town a charter in 1297. It was closely connected to the Talbot earls of Shrewsbury until 1616, when the manor passed to the Howard family (the dukes of Norfolk still have interests in the city). Mary Queen of Scots was held at Sheffield from 1569 to 1583 by the 6th Earl of Shrewsbury (and it was here that his page, Anthony Babington – of the unsuccessful Babington Plot against Elizabeth I – acquired his ardent devotion to Mary). Sheffield gained parliamentary representation only after the Great Reform Act of 1832, going on to become a borough in 1843, a city in 1893 and an Anglican bishopric in 1914. Despite heavy bombing in the Second World War, many of its grand civic buildings survived, and a millennium project is transforming the city centre. Many of the low-cost high-rise housing developments initiated by the local council in the 1960s, such as those in the Hyde Park area, have since been demolished.

Iron-working was carried out in the area from the Middle Ages, and the Sheffield cutlers found the local mill-stone grit excellent for grindstones. Sheffield was already known for its knives by the time of Chaucer (his Trumpington Miller bore a Sheffield whittle or short knife in his hose), and the Romany name for the city, according to George Borrow, is **Churi-mengreskey gav** ('cutler's town'). There was a major expansion of the metal industry during the Industrial Revolution, and Sheffield became particularly famed for **old Sheffield plate** (*see below*), and above all for steel (crucible steel, the Bessemer process and stainless steel were all invented here, and '**Sheffield**' is a trade mark). Sheffield now largely concentrates on specialist steels used for cutlery and precision tools. The cutlers have their own very grand guild, 'The Master, Wardens, Searchers, Assistants and Commonalty of the Company of Cutlers in Hallamshire in the County of York', incorporated in 1624, and the annually elected Master Cutler is the biggest wig in the city after the Lord Mayor. The non-specialist steel industry in Sheffield took something of a beating in the 1980s and 1990s, as reflected in the film *The Full Monty* (1997), in which unemployed Sheffield steel workers become male strippers to make ends meet.

> I've walked at night through Sheffield loin,
> 'Twas just like being in hell,
> Where furnaces thrust out tongues of fire
> And roared like the wind on the fell.
> I've sacked up coal in Barnsley pit
> With muck up to my knee –
> From Barnsley, Sheffield, Rotherham
> Good Lord deliver me.
>
>   Anon.: 'The Dalesman's Litany'

Sheffield has several museums, art galleries and theatres (the Crucible hosts the snooker World Professional Championship every April), plus two universities, the **University of Sheffield** (founded in 1897, chartered in 1905; among its alumni was the pioneer aviatrix Amy Johnson) and **Sheffield Hallam University** (1992, created from the former Sheffield Polytechnic). The Marriage Guidance Council (now called Relate) was first established in Sheffield, in 1947. The vast Meadowhall shopping centre attracts 30 million customers every year.

     Sheffield Wednesday FC is one of the city's main football teams, claiming descent from **Sheffield Wednesday Cricket Club**, founded in 1816 and so called because its players met to play on Wednesday half-holidays. The football club was founded in 1867, joined the Football League in 1893 and now plays at HILLSBOROUGH[2]; it is nicknamed the Owls. Sheffield's other main team is **Sheffield United** – nicknamed the Blades – which plays at Bramall Lane (once – in 1902 – also the host of a cricket test match). The city has been home to the National Sport Institute since 1997, and thinks of itself as the 'National City of Sport'.

     Sheffield was the birthplace of the composer and conductor Sir William Sterndale Bennett (1816–75); the novelist Malcolm Bradbury (1932–2000); Roy Hattersley (b.1932), former council-member and deputy leader of the Labour Party (1983–92); the novelist A.S. Byatt (b.1936) and her sister and fellow-novelist Margaret Drabble (b.1939); the Python and intrepid traveller Michael Palin (b.1943); and the boxer 'Prince' Naseem Hamed (b.1974). David Blunkett, populist New Labour Home Secretary until his resignation in 2004, became leader of Sheffield City Council in 1980, before being elected MP for Sheffield Brightside in 1987.

     There are towns called Sheffield in Canada (New Brunswick) and the USA (Alabama).

See also BEAUCHIEF *and* HALLAMSHIRE.

HMS *Sheffield*. A naval destroyer sunk by an Argentinian Exocet missile on 4 May 1982, during the Falklands War. An earlier HMS *Sheffield* was a cruiser that saw much service in the Second World War (including the sinking of the German battleships *Bismarck* and *Scharnhorst*). It also gave its name to a class of cruisers, one of which, HMS *Belfast*, is preserved as a museum at the Pool of London.

old Sheffield plate. A process of coating copper with silver, invented in 1742 by Thomas Boulsover. The method was used until the advent of electroplating in the 1850s.

Sheffield Eagles. Sheffield's rugby league team, founded in 1982. It played its first league game in 1984.

'Sheffield Grinders' Song'. A broadside ballad from the early 19th century, at a time when it was said every cutler in Sheffield possessed a copy of Thomas Paine's *The Rights of Man* (1791–2). The song begins:

> To be a Sheffield grinder it is no easy trade,
> There's more than you'd imagine in the grinding of a
>   blade,
> The strongest man among us is old at thirty-two,
> For there's few who brave the hardships that we poor
>   grinders do.

Sheffield handicap. A 20th-century rhyming slang word for 'crap'.

Sheffield Outrages. Various incidents sensationally recounted in the British press in 1866, in which trade unionists reportedly enforced rules and raised subscriptions by means of assaults, threats, seizure of tools and sabotage. At the same time trade unionists were campaigning for the end of discrimination between employer and employee in cases of breach of contract. The Royal Commission that followed resulted in the Trade Union Act, 1871, and the Criminal Law Amendment Act of the same year.

Sheffield plate. *See* **old Sheffield plate** *above*.

Sheffield Shield. The cricket trophy for which the Australian states play each other. It was first presented in the 1892–3 season by Lord Sheffield, who had taken an English side to Australia the previous year. In 1999 the Sheffield Shield was replaced by the Pura Milk Cup.

Sheffield Steelers. The city's ice-hockey team.

Sheffield Supertram. The city's super-modern light railway, opened in 1995.

Sheffield Park *Sheffield* 'open land where sheep graze', OE *sceap* 'sheep' + *feld* (*see* FIELD).

An estate in East Sussex, about 8 km (5 miles) east of HAYWARDS HEATH. At its heart is a large Gothic mansion that shares its name, designed in the 1770s by James Wyatt for the Earl of Sheffield. The surrounding gardens, famous for their rhododendrons and azaleas, were laid out by Humphry Repton.

A railway station was opened nearby in 1882, on the LEWES–EAST GRINSTEAD line. This fell to Dr Beeching's axe in 1960, but local rail enthusiasts resurrected a section in the middle, from Horsted Keynes to Sheffield Park. Steam services began in 1960 under the banner of the 'Bluebell Railway', and continue to be a popular tourist attraction as well as a location for period films and television dramas (including a television version of Edith Nesbit's *The Railway Children* in 1999).The line now extends northwards to Kingscote, near East Grinstead.

Shehy Mountains Irish *Cnoic na Seithe* 'hills of the fairies' (*see* KNOCK-).

A range of hills on the borders of counties CORK and KERRY, including the scenic GUAGÁN BARRA valley. The highest point is Carran (604 m / 1981 ft).

Shelf OE *scelf* 'shelving ground' or 'terrace of level ground on a slope'.

A village on the southwest edge of BRADFORD, West Yorkshire.

Shell Bay A self-explanatory modern coinage.

A bay at the northeastern tip of the Isle of Purbeck (*see under* PURBECK). Its sand is whiter than most in England.

Shellhaven Perhaps 'shelving inlet of the sea', OE *scylf* 'shelf, bank' + *hæfen* 'sea inlet, anchorage, harbour'.

An industrial anchorage on the north bank of the River THAMES[1], in Essex, now incorporated into CORYTON[2]. Coincidentally (for the name is an old one) the Shell Oil Company opened a refinery here in 1912.

Shell Ness 'shell headland', ModE *shell*, with NESS.

A headland at the far eastern tip of the ISLE OF SHEPPEY in Kent.

Shellow Bowells *Shellow* originally a river name, 'winding river' (referring to the river now known as the RODING), OE *Sceolge*, from *sceolh* 'twisted'; *Bowells* denoting manorial ownership in the Middle Ages by the de Bueles family.

A village in Essex, about 16 km (10 miles) east of HARLOW.

Shell Top 'hill resembling a limpet shell'.

A hill in the southern part of DARTMOOR, 475 m (1557 ft) high.

Shelsley Beauchamp *Shelsley* 'Sceld's glade', OE *Sceldes* possessive form of male personal name *Sceld* + -LEY; *Beauchamp* denoting manorial ownership in the Middle Ages by the Beauchamp family.

A village (pronounced 'beechəm') in Worcestershire (before 1998 in Hereford and Worcester, before 1974 in Worcestershire), on the River SEVERN, about 16 km (10 miles) northwest of Worcester.

Shelter Stone, the. A large granite boulder at the head of Loch Avon (*see under* AVON[5]) in the CAIRNGORM MOUNTAINS, Aberdeenshire (formerly in Grampian region). It is at an altitude of 760 m (2500 ft), some 3 km (2 miles) northeast of BEN MACDUI, and underneath the stone is a cave-like howf (rough shelter) for the hardy. Just west of the Shelter Stone, on the flanks of Ben Macdui, is the massive granite bastion of **Shelter Stone Crag**, with a number of very hard routes up to 275 m (900 ft) long, popular with climbers in both summer and winter. In the 19th century Sir Edwin Landseer painted a view across Loch Avon to the Shelter Stone Crag entitled *Lake Scene: Effect of Storm*. Another Victorian visitor described the mighty crag thus:

> The peak detached from Ben Muich Dhui shot forth from the snow as like the Aiguilles de Mont Blanc as one needle is like another.
>
> J.H. Burton: *The Cairngorm Mountains* (1864)

Shelve '(place on the) shelf', referring to an area of level ground among surrounding hills, OE *scelf* 'shelf'.

A village in Shropshire, about 21 km (13 miles) southwest of Shrewsbury. It is surrounded by the STIPERSTONES, and when lead was still being profitably mined in those hills in the early Middle Ages, Shelve was prosperous and populous enough to be granted a charter to hold a market.

Shenick's Island. *See under* SKERRIES.

Shepherd Market After Edward *Shepherd*, an architect and builder who set up a market here in 1735.

An area of small, narrow streets (including one itself named **Shepherd Market**) in the WEST END[1] of London, just to the north of PICCADILLY[1] at its southwestern end, in the City of Westminster. It is on the site of the original 'May Fair' (*see* MAYFAIR), which was suppressed more than once in the early 18th century for its licentiousness. Edward Shepherd built a two-storey market house here in the early 1730s, in which an entirely respectable meat market operated, but the area never lost its population of commercial ladies (in the Second World War its magnetic attraction for American servicemen earned it the nickname EISENHOWER PLATZ). It has always been the 'village' at the heart of Mayfair, and in the latter part of the 20th century it has developed into a more family-friendly area of restaurants, food shops, etc.

Shepherd's Bush Origin uncertain: *Shepherd* could be a family name, or could refer to actual shepherds; the term *shepherd's bush* denotes a bush from which a shepherd could keep watch on his flock, and there were farms in the area up to the 19th century.

A district of West London (W12), in the borough of HAMMERSMITH AND FULHAM, between Kensington to the east and Acton to the west. It is centred on **Shepherd's Bush Green**, officially Shepherd's Bush Common, a 3.25-ha (8-acre) triangular open space which nowadays is effectively a giant traffic island.

Shepherd's Bush has a long-standing association with the BBC. It acquired its television studios here in LIME GROVE in 1949, and in the 1950s constructed the BBC Television Centre on a 5.5-ha (13.5-acre) site acquired from the WHITE CITY. Broadcasting began from here in 1960. A significant proportion of radio production and transmission moved to the site from Broadcasting House in the 1990s. The BBC also had its own Television Theatre on Shepherd's Bush Green. The BBC sitcom *Steptoe and Son* (1962–5; 1970–4) was set in Shepherd's Bush (the Steptoes' scrapyard was in the fictitious Oil Drum Lane).

The open space known as WORMWOOD SCRUBS is in Shepherd's Bush (to the north of the WESTWAY), as is Loftus Road, Queens Park Rangers' home ground. **Shepherd's Bush Market** opened in 1914, beside the railway tracks; though not as high-profile as PORTOBELLO ROAD Market, it has a similar Caribbean flavour.

Shepherd's Bush Underground station, on the Central and Hammersmith & City lines, opened in 1864.

> Went to Shepherd's Bush. Oh, horror–stinking underground.
>
> L. Troubridge: *Life amongst the Troubridges* (1879)

Shepherd's Bush. A Cockney rhyming slang expression for the *push*, in the sense 'dismissal from one's job', and also for *mush* 'face'.

Shepperton Probably 'farmstead of the shepherd(s)', OE *sceap-hirde* 'shepherd' + -TON.

An urban area in Surrey, on the north bank of the River THAMES[1], now effectively a southwestern suburb of London, to the north of Weybridge and to the west of Walton-on-Thames. It owes its blip on the radar-screen to **Shepperton Film Studios**, opened in 1932 and in the early days known as 'Sound City'. The studios merged with Pinewood Studios near IVER in 2001, to form **Pinewood Shepperton**.

In H.G. Wells's *War of the Worlds* (1898), Shepperton was almost destroyed by the Martians, who had landed near what is now Junction 10 on the M25. Another sci-fi literary connection is J.G. Ballard's novel *The Unlimited Dream Company* (1979), in which the quiet dormitory suburb of Shepperton undergoes a startling transformation after a light aircraft crashes into the Thames here.

Sheppey. *See* ISLE OF SHEPPEY.

Shepton Mallet *Shepton* 'sheep farm', OE *sceap* 'sheep' + -TON; *Mallet* denoting manorial ownership in the early Middle Ages by the Malet family.

A market town in Somerset, in the MENDIP HILLS, about 8 km (5 miles) southeast of Wells. Appropriately enough, given its name, it came to prosperity in the Middle Ages through the wool trade; and after wool faded in importance, cider eventually took its place (it was the home of Showerings Ltd, makers of that quintessential 1950s pear-based tipple Babycham). Today Shepton Mallet still serves the agriculture of the surrounding country: farm machinery is made here, and it is the permanent site of the Bath and West Show.

The first armed clash of the Civil Wars occurred in Shepton Mallet, in 1642, when the town's Parliamentarian sympathizers tangled briefly with the Royalists of WELLS.

Shepway 'sheep track', OE *sceap* 'sheep' + *weg* 'way, track'. Originally the name of a lathe (one of the large administrative areas into which Kent was formerly divided) covering roughly the same area as the present district.

A council district of Kent, covering the southeastern corner of the county, from just north of Folkestone round to Dungeness. It includes ROMNEY MARSH and part of the NORTH DOWNS. It was formed in 1974. Its administrative centre is FOLKESTONE.

In former times the supreme court of the CINQUE PORTS was known as the **Court of Shepway**.

Sherborne Probably originally a river name, 'bright or clear stream', OE *scir* 'bright, clear' + *burna* 'stream' (the local river is now called *Yeo*).

A town in northern Dorset, close to the Somerset border, on the River YEO[1], about 26 km (16 miles) northwest of Blandford Forum. It has shrunk in status from Anglo-Saxon times, when it was the chief bishopric of WESSEX, but its abbey and two castles are striking reminders of its former importance. **Sherborne Abbey** was founded in 705, and was a cathedral until shortly after the Norman Conquest. It was largely rebuilt in the 15th century, and contains some of the most spectacular fan vaulting in England. Two of Alfred the Great's brothers, Æthelbert (king 860–5) and Æthelred (king 865–71), are buried here, as is the poet Sir Thomas Wyatt (1503–42). Since the 16th century part of the abbey buildings have been occupied by **Sherborne School**, a boys' public school (founded 1550). Its Old Boys include the novelists Alec Waugh, John Cowper Powys and David Cornwell (a.k.a. John le Carré), the poets C. Day Lewis and (at the prep school) Louis MacNeice, the mathematician and philosopher A.N. Whitehead and the father of the computer, Alan Turing. The school in James

Hilton's novella *Good-bye, Mr Chips* (1934) is based on Sherborne.

Of the two castles the earlier, now called the Old Castle, was built in the 12th century by Bishop Roger, Henry I's chancellor. It is now decidedly one of the ruins that Cromwell knocked about a bit. Elizabeth I gave it to Sir Walter Raleigh, but he seems to have found the accommodation rather basic, and in 1594 built himself a new, more comfortable castle, now called the New Castle or simply **Sherborne Castle**. It is said to have been here that a servant came across Walter smoking the new-fangled tobacco and threw a pot of ale over him to put him out.

In the Wessex novels of Thomas Hardy, Sherborne is fictionalized as **Sherton Abbas**, as in *The Woodlanders* (1887).

St Stephen Harding (*c*.1060–1134), one of the founders of the Cistercian order, and the astronomer James Bradley (1693–1762) were born in Sherborne.

Sherfield English *Sherfield* probably 'bright open land' (implying a lack of vegetation), OE *scir* 'bright' + *feld* (see FIELD); *English* denoting manorial ownership in the Middle Ages by the le Engleis family.

A village in Hampshire, about 5 km (3 miles) west of Romsey.

Sheriff Muir Possibly 'moor of the sheriff', Scots *muir* 'moor' – but the etymology is uncertain.

A stretch of moorland on the northwestern slopes of the OCHIL HILLS, about 5 km (3 miles) northeast of Dunblane. It was formerly in Perthshire, then in Central region, and is now in the unitary authority of Stirling. The megalithic **Sheriff Muir Stone Row** on the southeast side of the moor is sometimes referred to as the Wallace Stones, although in other accounts the Wallace Stone is the only one in the row still standing. It is said that William Wallace himself raised the stone after defeating the English.

Battle of Sheriffmuir (13 November 1715). An indecisive engagement in the 1715 Rising, in which the Jacobites under 'Bobbing John' Erskine, 6th Earl of MAR, confronted a Hanoverian force under John Campbell, 2nd Duke of Argyll. Although the battle was a draw, Mar's subsequent retreat to Perth marked the beginning of the collapse of the rebellion.

> Will ye gang to Sherramuir,
> Bauld John o' Innisture,
> There to see the noble Mar,
> And his Hieland laddies?
> 'A the true men o' the north,
> Angus, Huntly and Seaforth,
> Scouring on to cross the Forth,
> Wi' their white cockadies!
>
> James Hogg: *Jacobite Relics of Scotland* (1819)
> (The white cockade was the Jacobite badge.)

The absurdity of the enterprise is wryly commented upon in another traditional song, ascribed to the early 18th-century poet Murdoch McLennan:

> There's some say that we wan and some say that they wan
> And some say that nane wan at a' man,
> But one thing is sure that at Sheriff Muir
> A battle was fought on that day man.
> *And we ran and they ran and they ran and we ran*
> *And we ran and they ran awa' man.*

Sheringham 'Scira's people's homestead', OE male personal name *Scira* + *-inga-* (*see* -ING) + HAM.

A town on the north Norfolk coast, about 6 km (4 miles) west of Cromer. The original settlement (**Upper Sheringham**) is a village a little way inland. The main town was developed as a seaside resort in the later 19th century. To the southwest is **Sheringham Park**, a 312-ha (770-acre) woodland park laid out by Humphry Repton in the early 19th century. It is administered by the National Trust. Pretty Corner, an area of woodland, lies on the town's southern outskirts.

An inhabitant of Sheringham is known locally as a **Shannock** (some say that only those whose parents and grandparents were born in the town qualify for the designation). The origin of the term is unknown.

Sherkin Island Irish *Inis Arcáin* 'Arcán's island'.

An island off the southwest coast of County Cork, on the east side of ROARINGWATER BAY. There is a ferry from BALTIMORE on the mainland. There are the remains of a Franciscan friary founded in 1460.

Sherston 'stone or rock on a steep slope' (perhaps referring to a boundary marker at the nearby Gloucestershire border), OE *scora* 'steep slope' + *stan* (*see* STONE).

A village in Wiltshire, about 8 km (5 miles) west of Malmesbury.

Siegfried Sassoon – who was educated at nearby Marlborough College (*see under* MARLBOROUGH) – called his semi-fictionalized self George Sherston in *Memoirs of a Fox-Hunting Man* (1929), *Memoirs of an Infantry Officer* (1930) and *Sherston's Progress* (1936).

Battle of Sherston (June 1016). An encounter between the Saxons under Edmund Ironside and the Danes under Cnut. The Saxons won, but their triumph was short-lived; before the year was out, Cnut was king of England.

Sherton Abbas. The fictional version of SHERBORNE as found in the novels of Thomas Hardy, including *The Woodlanders* (1887).

Sherwood Forest *Sherwood* 'wood belonging to the shire', OE *scir* 'shire' + *wudu* 'wood'.

An area of ancient forest in NOTTINGHAMSHIRE. In the Middle Ages, when it was a royal hunting ground, it covered most of the northern part of the county with its oaks and birches. That was the era of by far its most famous denizen, the almost certainly legendary outlaw Robin Hood, who camped in the depths of the forest with his band of merry men and sallied forth to rob the rich and give to the poor. The earliest known reference to him, in William Langland's *Piers Plowman* (1377), postdates his supposed lifetime by nearly 200 years.

Much of the forest's 40,500 ha (100,000 acres) was cleared in the 18th century. The wooded area between NOTTINGHAM[1] and WORKSOP is now dominated by sporadic pine plantations, but many old oak trees survive in the more northerly part of the forest, particularly in the area of the DUKERIES. They include the Major Oak, a bit-part player in the Robin Hood legend (he hid from the Sheriff of Nottingham in it, and married Maid Marion there), which is one of the attractions of the **Sherwood Forest Country Park**, near EDWINSTOWE; and the Green Dale Oak, to the south of WELBECK ABBEY, which had a coach road 1.8 m (6 ft) wide driven through its trunk in 1724.

Trees from an earlier era have left a legacy of coal beneath the forest, and this was exploited from the middle of the 19th century onwards.

Sherwood Foresters, the. A British Army regiment, the 45th, which since 1970 has been combined with the 29th to form the **Worcestershire and Sherwood Foresters Regiment**. It was granted the title '**Royal Sherwood Foresters**' in 1813, abbreviated to just 'Sherwood Foresters' in 1867. Its long history since its late 18th-century origins includes most of Britain's military exploits, and the current combined regiment boasts a collective tally of 'no less than 23 Victoria Crosses'. Its colonel in chief is Princess Anne.

Shetland Before the Norse arrived, Shetland was known to the Irish chroniclers as *Inse Catt* 'islands of the Catt tribe' (who also gave their name to Caithness). The OScand name *Hjaltland* (from which Shetland derives) means 'hilt land', and is possibly a reference to the shape of Mainland.

A group of some 100 islands (of which fewer than 20 are inhabited) in the far north of the British Isles. Its southernmost tip, SUMBURGH HEAD, is 73 km (45 miles) northeast of Orkney, and 150 km (93 miles) northeast of the Scottish mainland. The most northerly point of Shetland, and thus of Britain, is Out Stack, a rock just north of MUCKLE FLUGGA: it is only some 600 km (400 miles) south of the Arctic Circle, and is nearly as far from the Scotland–England border as Land's End is. The islands are at the same latitude as southern Greenland.

Shetland is also referred to as **the Shetland Islands** or **Zetland**. It was formerly a county, and in 1975 became a unitary island authority. The main town and administrative seat is LERWICK, which took over from SCALLOWAY as the capital in the 18th century. Fishing and North Sea oil (for example, the terminal at SULLOM VOE) are the main staples

of the economy. The inhabitants of Shetland are known, at least to Orcadians, as **Shelties** (from Orkney dialect *sjalti*); Shetland ponies and Shetland sheepdogs (*see below*) are also known as shelties.

The largest island, on which Lerwick is situated, is **Mainland** (OScand *meginland*). Hence Scotland is never referred to in Shetland as 'the mainland', but simply as 'Scotland'. The other islands include UNST, YELL, FETLAR, WHALSAY, BRESSAY, PAPA STOUR, OUT SKERRIES, FOULA and FAIR ISLE. The islands are almost treeless, and are exposed to strong winds. The coastline is heavily indented with sea inlets called 'voes'.

In the 1st century AD, according to Tacitus, the Roman general Agricola sent a fleet around the north coast of Scotland, visiting the Orcades (Orkney), from where it was possible to see Thule – thought to be Shetland:

> Nowhere does the sea hold wider sway; it carries to and fro in its motions a mass of currents, and in its ebb and flow, it is not held by the coast but penetrates deep into the land and winds about in the hills, as if in its own domain.

> Tacitus: *De vita Julii Agricolae* (AD 94)

There are many prehistoric remains on Shetland, some dating back nearly 4000 years. Like ORKNEY, Shetland was under Norse rule from the 8th century until 1472, and thus many Shetland islanders do not consider themselves Scottish – and, indeed, geographically Shetland is closer to Bergen in Norway than to Aberdeen.

The action of Sir Walter Scott's novel *The Pirate* (1821) largely takes place in Shetland. Shetland was the birthplace of John Clunies Ross (1786–1854), the 'king' of the Cocos Islands (whose sovereignty was recognized by Queen Victoria); Sir Robert Stout (1844–1930), Liberal prime minister of New Zealand from 1884 to 1887; and Norman Lamont (b.1942), Conservative chancellor of the exchequer (1990–3).

The South Shetland Islands in the South Atlantic are part of British Antarctic Territory.

Shetland. A breed of sheep with a white face and curly horns. It produces **Shetland wool** (*see below*).

Shetland Bus, the. The collective name for the small fishing boats that ran between Shetland and Norway during the Second World War, in support of the Norwegian resistance movement. After heavy losses, the fishing boats were replaced in November 1943 by fast and heavily armed MTBs. The operation was run jointly by the SIS (Secret Intelligence Service) and SOE (Special Operations Executive), and its deputy commander, David Howarth, later wrote a book about it, entitled *The Shetland Bus* (1951).

Shetland mouse-ear. A species of chickweed, *Cerastium nigrescens*, found only on the island of Unst, and first identified in 1837.

Shetland pondweed. A rare pondweed, *Potamogeton rutilis*, with finely pointed leaves.

Shetland pony. A very small breed of pony, also called a sheltie.

Shetland reestit mutton broth. A hearty soup made with reestit (salted and dried lamb, a Shetland speciality), pearl barley, dried peas, potatoes, kale, etc.

Shetland shawl. A type of woollen shawl characterized by intricate lacework.

Shetland sheepdog. A small, long-haired breed of collie, also called a **sheltie**.

Shetland wool. A type of very fine wool, originally from the native sheep of Shetland. It is used in a variety of garments, such as Shetland shawls (*see above*), Shetland hose (stockings) and FAIR ISLE jumpers.

Shetland wren. A larger and paler subspecies, *Troglodytes troglodytes zetlandensis*.

Sheugh. A nickname sometimes given to the NORTH CHANNEL, from the Ulster-Scots word *sheugh* or *schuch*, meaning 'ditch' or 'water-filled drain'.

Shiant Isles 'the enchanted islands'. Gaelic *na h-eileanan* 'the islands' + *seunta* 'sacred, enchanted'.

A group of small islands 7 km (4 miles) off the southeast coast of Lewis, Western Isles (formerly in Ross and Cromarty), from which they are separated by the **Sound of Shiant** (formerly a favourite haunt of the Blue Men of the Minch; *see under* the MINCHES). The main islands are Garbh Eilean (Gaelic, 'rough island'), Eilean an Tigh ('home island') and Eilean Mhuire ('Mary's island'). The first two are joined by a natural pebble causeway, and have remarkable cliffs of columnar basalt, which at 150 m (500 ft) dwarf those of STAFFA. The last inhabitants left in the 18th century, although when Compton Mackenzie owned the islands (1925–36) he renovated a house and spent time during the summers writing there.

A sad story from 1786 tells how Captain Allan Morrison of Stornoway, called Ailein Duinn ('brown-haired Allan'), was drowned in a storm at sea and his body washed up on the Shiant Isles. His betrothed, Annie Campbell of Scalpay, died of grief, and when the boat taking her body across to Harris was struck by a storm, the crew jettisoned her coffin to save themselves. A few days after Captain Morrison's body was found, Annie's corpse washed up near where his had been discovered on the shores of the Shiant Isles. The tragedy is recalled in a Gaelic lament, still being sung in the early years of the 20th century:

> Brown-haired Allan, o hi, I would go with thee;
> Ho ri ri u ho, e o hug hoireann o,
> Brown-haired Allan, o hit, I would go with thee.

Shifnal 'Scuffa's nook of land', OE male personal name *Scuffa* + *halh* (*see* HALE, -HALL).

A market town in Shropshire, about 8 km (5 miles) southeast of TELFORD. It was largely destroyed by fire in 1591, and the aspect of its centre today is predominantly Georgian. It was formerly an important stopping-place for stagecoaches on the London–Holyhead road.

The town appealed strongly to Charles Dickens, and the description of the anonymous Shropshire town to which Little Nell and her grandfather made their laborious way in *The Old Curiosity Shop* (1841) owes much to Shifnal:

> In the streets were a number of old houses, built of a kind of earth or plaster, crossed and re-crossed in a great many directions with black beams, which gave them a remarkable and very ancient look. The doors, too, were arched and low, some with oaken portals and quaint benches, where the former inhabitants had sat on summer evenings. The windows were latticed in little diamond panes, that seemed to wink and blink upon the passengers as if they were dim of sight.

See also TONG.

Shilbottle 'building belonging to Shipley', Shipley is an adjoining village + OE *bothl* 'building'.

A former mining village in Northumberland, 5 km (3 miles) south of Alnwick. Mining started here in 1728 and the pit finally closed in 1981.

Shildon 'shelf hill', OE *scylfe* 'shelf' + *dun* (*see* DOWN, -DON).

A town in County Durham, 3 km (2 miles) southeast of Bishop Auckland. It was the birthplace of the miner and novelist Sid Chaplin (1916–86), who wrote about local mining life in books such as *The Leaping Lad* (1946) and *The Thin Seam* (1950).

Shillay. *See under* MONACH ISLANDS.

Shillelagh Irish *Síol Éalaigh* 'the descendants of Élathach', he being a warrior from the 9th century.

A village in County Wicklow, 25 km (16 miles) west of Arklow. It is in an area once covered in great oak forests, said to have supplied timber for the roofs of Dublin's St Patrick's Cathedral and London's Westminster Hall. The village name may be the origin of that of the traditional Irish cudgel, made from blackthorn or oak, popular in the faction fights of the early 19th century and with contemporary tourists of the more gullible sort. However, scholars believe the cudgel's name is more likely to derive from Irish *saill* 'willow' + *éille*, the genitive of *iall* 'thong, strap'. In the 1960s there was a US guided antitank missile called the Shillelagh.

Shining Tor A modern self-explanatory name.

A hill (559 m / 1834 ft) in the PEAK DISTRICT, on the Cheshire/Derbyshire border, about 17.5 km (11 miles) east of Macclesfield.

Shipley 'clearing for sheep', OE *scæp* 'sheep' + -LEY.
A town on the River AIRE in West Yorkshire, 5 km (3 miles) north of Bradford. The Leeds–Liverpool Canal runs through here. **Shipley Glen** has been a long-standing recreational area, and contains a tramway that has been running more or less consistently for over 100 years.
Shipley was the birthplace of the theatre and film director Tony Richardson (1928–91) and the novelist Leo Walmsley (1892–1966).

Shipston-on-Stour *Shipston* 'farmstead by the sheepwash', OE *sceap-wæsc* 'sheepwash' + -TON.
A market town in Warwickshire, on the River STOUR[4], about 16 km (10 miles) southeast of Stratford-upon-Avon. Some fine Georgian houses are a reminder of its days of wool-based prosperity.

Shipton Bellinger *Shipton* 'sheep farm', OE *sceap* 'sheep' + -TON; *Bellinger* denoting manorial ownership in the Middle Ages by the Berenger family.
A village in Hampshire, on the River Bourne, about 15 km (9 miles) west of Andover.

Shipton Moyne *Moyne* denoting manorial ownership in the Middle Ages by the Moygne family.
A village in Gloucestershire, in the COTSWOLDS, about 5 km (3 miles) northwest of Malmesbury.

Shipton-under-Wychwood *Wychwood see* WYCHWOOD.
A village in Oxfordshire, on the River EVENLODE[2], about 13 km (8 miles) northwest of Witney. **Ascott-under-Wychwood** (*see* ASCOT for etymology) lies a little to the northeast.

Shire, the. The fictional land of the hobbits in J.R.R. Tolkien's novels *The Hobbit* (1937) and *The Lord of the Rings* (1954–5). Situated in the northern part of Middle-Earth, and divided into four 'Farthings' (North, South, East and West), the Shire is a gentle, unspectacular country of fields, woods and downland. Beyond its borders stretches a wider – and wilder – world whose plains are broader, forests deeper, mountains higher and inhabitants more sinister. Its diminutive, furry-footed denizens, the hobbits, are wary of irruptions from outside: they prefer to keep themselves to themselves – tending their gardens, smoking their pipes, and drinking beer in public houses. Hobbits live in villages that either borrow their names from actual Old English place names of the English Midlands, West and South – BUCKLAND (Devon, Gloucestershire, Oxfordshire and Surrey), BUCKLEBURY (Berkshire), STOCK (Essex), WORMINGHALL (Buckinghamshire) – or, by dint of being made up of Old English place-name elements (Bywater, Deephallow, Frogmorton, Pincup, Scary, Tookbank, Whitfurrows), at least sound as though they do. The Shire and its inhabitants, in short, look suspiciously like a rose-tinted evocation of a pastoral England before suburbs, motorways, and out-of-town shopping centres encroached on its fields and hedgerows.
Tolkien obsessives have searched high and low for real-life English models for the fictional locations of the Shire and Middle-Earth, much of their attention focusing on the Berkshire Downs (rich in prehistoric and Saxon sites) and also on Oxfordshire and Warwickshire (counties where Tolkien spent much of his life and with whose MERCIAN heritage he felt a strong affinity). Tolkien himself said that the Shire was based on SAREHOLE, the Warwickshire village (now a suburb of Birmingham) where he lived as a child. Peter Jackson, director of the film version of Tolkien's trilogy (2000–2003), perhaps unsurprisingly steered clear of Sarehole when it came to filming the Shire scenes of the epic, which he shot in its entirety in his native New Zealand.

Shires, the. A collective term that seems to have got under way in the latter part of the 18th century as a designation for parts of England distant from the southeast. The main modern survivor of this usage is the political

---

❖ **shire** ❖

The OE word *scir* 'shire' was originally used much more widely than for the familiar counties of today. This can be seen from the '-shire' names for areas still in existence which are not counties, notably HALLAMSHIRE in South Yorkshire and RICHMONDSHIRE in North Yorkshire. Originating from the 10th century, following English unification, traditional county shires were administrative districts having their own courts and chief officers, respectively the *shire-moots* and the *shire-reeves* or sheriffs. Shires usually took their names from the chief town of the area (BUCKINGHAMSHIRE, NORTHAMPTONSHIRE), though older folk and tribal names are common in the south of England: KENT, ESSEX, SUSSEX, DORSET, SOMERSET and others.

Wales and Scotland had shires, and Irish counties acquired the '-shire' suffix in the 16th and 17th centuries; but in more recent times, administrative reorganization has tended to revive older district names such as POWYS and CEREDIGION (Wales), ANGUS (Scotland), and County CORK[2] and County KERRY (Ireland). The '-shire' suffix has now completely disappeared from Ireland. In England, the attempts in 1974 to merge RUTLAND into LEICESTERSHIRE and to combine parts of YORKSHIRE and LINCOLNSHIRE to form HUMBERSIDE, among other such reconfigurations, met with little favour: these novelties were relatively quickly abandoned, in 1996, and the shire-names were largely restored.

term **'knights of the Shires'**, referring to members of the English landed gentry (generally Conservative and stereotypically red-faced bufferish backwoodsmen) representing their local areas in Parliament.

In the middle of the 19th century the term took on a more specific application to that part of the EAST MIDLANDS (particularly Leicestershire and Northamptonshire) which is fox-hunting country. In that context, the Shires are the playground of the members of such celebrated hunts as the Belvoir, the Cottesmore, the Fernie, the Pytchely and the Quorn.

The Local Government Act of 1974 created a new category of **shire county**, denoting a non-metropolitan county. They are often collectively termed 'the Shires'.

shire horse. (Any of) a breed of large powerful draught horses with a fringe of long hair on the lower legs. The term (first recorded in the 1870s) originally denoted specifically a breed developed in the Midlands, but now it tends to be used as a cover term for various similar breeds (e.g. the Clydesdale (*see under* CLYDESDALE), the Percheron and the Suffolk punch (*see under* SUFFOLK)).

Shirley¹ 'bright glade', OE *scir* 'bright' + -LEY.

A residential district of southern Outer London, in the borough of CROYDON (before 1965 in Surrey), to the east of Croydon.

Shirley poppy. A cultivated poppy (*Papaver rhœas*) with large single or double red, pink, blue or white flowers. It was developed by William Wilks (1843–1923), vicar of Shirley and secretary of the Royal Horticultural Society.

Shirley². A western central district of SOUTHAMPTON, on the peninsula between the mouths of the rivers ITCHEN and TEST.

Shirley³. A southern suburb of BIRMINGHAM, near Solihull.

Shoeburyness Originally *Shoebury* 'fortress providing shelter' (perhaps alluding to a prehistoric camp here), OE *sceo* 'shelter' + *byrig* dative form of *burh* 'fortress' (*see* BURY). *Shoeburyness*, originally referring to the headland (*see* NESS), is first recorded in the 16th century; in due course the name spread to the town.

A promontory and town on the north bank of the THAMES¹ Estuary, in Essex, now essentially an eastern suburb of SOUTHEND-ON-SEA. It is popular with sailors and windsurfers. Shoeburyness is also a long-standing home to military firing ranges.

Shoe Lane Probably originally *Shoeland*, that is, 'land given (to a religious community – in this case the canons of St Paul's) so that shoes may be bought (out of the income from it)', OE *scohland*. Forms with *Lane* are not recorded before the latter part of the 13th century.

A road in the City of London (EC4), linking FLEET STREET with Holborn Circus (*see under* HOLBORN) to the north.

Until 1989 it housed the offices of the *Evening Standard*, since 1980 London's only major evening newspaper.

Shooters Hill 'hill or hill-slope of the shooter or archer', probably referring either to hunters who frequented the hill in the Middle Ages, or to armed robbers, OE *sceotere, scytere* 'shooter, archer' + *hyll* 'hill, hill-slope'.

A road and district in southeast London (SE18), in the borough of GREENWICH, between Charlton to the west and Bexleyheath to the east. The hill from which it takes its name is 133 m (432 ft) above sea level. It is a well-wooded area, but in the past it was even more densely covered in woodland, and extensively used for hunting (whence perhaps 'Shooters'). It was also fairly wild and remote: the road up the steep hillside, a stretch of WATLING STREET¹, the old London–Dover road (now the A207), was notorious for its highwaymen and footpads (another possible source of 'Shooters'). A gallows stood at a crossroads at the foot of the hill; the last execution there took place in 1805.

Its height and prominence have made it an important communications point: in the 16th century it was one of a chain of beacons, in the 18th there was a shutter telegraph on its summit, and it now has VHF radio transmitters.

shooter's hill. A 19th-century slang euphemism for *vagina*, punningly linking the place name with contemporary slang *shoot* 'to ejaculate, have sex'.

Shop¹ '(place with a) workshop', ModE.

A village in Cornwall, about 10 km (6 miles) north of Bude.

Shop². A village in Cornwall, about 3 km (2 miles) southwest of Padstow.

Shoreditch 'ditch by a steep bank or slope' (presumably referring to some local watercourse; not to the Thames, which is on the far side of the City of London), OE *scora* 'steep bank or slope' + *dic* 'ditch'.

A district of East London (N1, N2), in the borough of HACKNEY, immediately to the north of the City of London. A more romantic and popular (but untrue) derivation of its name than that given above is that it comes from Jane Shore (d.*c*.1527), Edward IV's mistress; the story comes from a ballad in the Samuel Pepys collection, a version of which is given in Percy's *Reliques* (1765):

> Thus, weary of my life, at length
> I yielded up my vital strength
> Within a ditch of loathsome scent,
> Where carrion dogs did much frequent:
> The which now since my dying day
> Is Shoreditch called, as writers say.

In the late 16th century Shoreditch was the birthplace of the first proper English theatre. In 1576 James Burbage opened a playhouse here called 'the Theatre'. It was the first of its type in the country, and survived until 1598, when it was moved south of the Thames and reopened as the Globe. Another theatre, the Curtain, opened here in 1577, and many actors lived in the vicinity.

Residential development proceeded apace from the end of the 17th century, and by the 19th Shoreditch was a densely populated and fairly rough area. At the beginning of the 21st, however, some of the trendiness of HOXTON was beginning to seep into it, as 'Britart' exponents appropriated the local lofts and factories for their studios and galleries: the White Cube, the Saatchi Gallery (before the move to County Hall), Tracey Emin, Gilbert and George, and so on.

The **bells of Shoreditch** parish church feature in the well-known 'Oranges and Lemons' rhyme:

> When will you pay me,
> Say the bells at Old Bailey.
> When I grow rich,
> Say the bells at Shoreditch.

Shoreditch Underground station, the northern terminus of the East London line, opened in 1913.

Duke of Shoreditch. A sobriquet said to have been bestowed on a local archer by Henry VIII for his success in an archery contest at Windsor. The title was long playfully applied to the captain of the Company of Archers of London.

Shoreditch fury. A 19th-century slang term for an aggressive woman.

'Shoreditch Toff, The'. A music-hall song composed and sung in the late 1860s by Arthur Lloyd. In it he took on the persona of 'Immensikoff', and wore a voluminous fur coat; these became very fashionable garments among men about town in the late 19th century, and were known as Immensikoffs.

Shoreham 'homestead by a steep bank or slope', OE *scora* 'steep bank or slope' + HAM.

A village in Kent, about 6 km (4 miles) north of Sevenoaks. The painter Samuel Palmer went to work here in 1826 with a group of other artists who, like him, were heavily influenced by William Blake. In the years up to 1837, when he returned to London, he produced his best and most glowingly visionary work.

There is a town called New Shoreham in Rhode Island, USA.

William of Shoreham. An early 14th-century cleric and poet, vicar of Chart near LEEDS[1]. Of his poetry, only seven lyrics survive, in a single manuscript. They are fairly typical of the religious verse of the time in their tender melancholy. His work is an important source for the understanding of the development of Middle English in Kent.

Shoreham-by-Sea. A town and port in West Sussex, at the mouth of the River ADUR[1], about 10 km (6 miles) west of Brighton. It has been a busy port since the late Middle Ages (it was the most important Channel port in the 16th and 17th centuries), and the construction of a basin here in the 1850s ensured it a healthy share of south-coast commercial traffic. It also has its own airfield (serving as Brighton's municipal airport): opened in 1910, it is the oldest licensed aerodrome in the United Kingdom. The chimneys of the nearby Portslade power station used to be a landmark for many miles around; only one remains.

Shoreham was a cradle of the British film industry: the Sunny South and Sealight Film Company was set up here, in 'Bungalow Town', in 1913, and the operation was taken over shortly afterwards by Sidney Morgan's Progress Film Company. The studios burned down in 1922, and Shoreham's chance of being a second Hollywood went with them.

Shortstown From its being built by *Short* Brothers.

A village in Bedfordshire, on the southeastern outskirts of Bedford. It was built in 1917 as a garden village by the aircraft-manufacturing firm Short Brothers. It was later taken over by the RAF.

Shotover 'steep slope' (referring to Shotover Hill), OE *sceot* 'steep place' + *ora* 'hill-slope'. Local ingenuity has come up with more colourful derivations: one candidate is the legendary shooting of an arrow over the local hill by one Sir Harry Bath; another, more specious but equally false, is Fr *château vert* 'green castle'.

A hamlet in Oxfordshire, immediately to the southeast of Oxford, just outside the ring road. **Shotover Hill** rises to about 150 m (445 ft). It is traversed by **Shotover Plain**, a grassy ride that was once the road from Oxford to London and a haunt of highwaymen.

Northeast of the hill, by the A40, is **Shotover House**, built by Sir James Tyrell in the 1710s, and set in formal gardens, part of which were landscaped by William Kent in the 1730s and remain much as they were in the 18th century.

Shotover Forest. A former royal hunting forest in Oxfordshire, to the southeast of Oxford. At its greatest extent, in the Middle Ages, it was over 39 sq km (15 sq miles) in area, and rich in deer and boar, but it dwindled owing to neglect, and in 1660 was disafforested. Its remnants are now **Shotover Country Park**, a mix of woodland, heath and grassland.

> There is a legend that a scholar of The Queen's College was walking in Shotover Forest reading Aristotle when a wild boar attacked him. The student rammed the volume down the boar's throat, uttering the words '*Graecum est*', and the boar expired.
>
> Christopher Hibbert: *The Encyclopædia of Oxford* (1988)

Shottery Either 'stream of the Scots' or 'trout stream', OE *Scota* possessive plural form of *Scot* or of *sc(e)ota* 'trout' + *rith* 'stream'.

A village in Warwickshire, now a western suburb of STRATFORD-UPON-AVON. Its fame rests on Anne Hathaway's Cottage, where Shakespeare's wife lived as a girl.

Shotton 'farm on the hill', OE *sceot* 'hill' + -TON.

An industrial town in Flintshire (formerly in Clwyd), near the mouth of the River DEE[2], 10 km (6 miles) west of Chester.

Shotts 'the slopes', OE *sceot* 'hillside, slope'.

An industrial town in North Lanarkshire (formerly in Strathclyde region), 12 km (7.5 miles) northeast of Motherwell. The hamlet of KIRK O' SHOTTS is 4 km (2.5 miles) to the northwest.

Shotts was the birthplace of the pioneering pathologist and royal physician Matthew Baillie (1761–1823). Kirk o' Shotts was the birthplace of the poet William Jeffrey (1896–1946).

Shottsford Forum. A fictional name for BLANDFORD FORUM in the novels of Thomas Hardy.

Shrewsbury 'fortified place of the Shrob district', district name (literally 'scrubland', OE *scrobb*) + OE *byrig* dative form of *burh* (*see* BURY).

A market town (pronounced 'shrowzbəri' or 'shrewzbəri') in Shropshire, situated in a loop of the River SEVERN, about 66 km (40 miles) northwest of Birmingham. It is the county town of SHROPSHIRE.

Shrewsbury's position close to the Welsh border gave it high strategic importance in former times. In the 5th and 6th centuries it was the seat of the Welsh princes of POWYS, and its name was **Pengwern**. In the late 8th century it was absorbed into the Anglo-Saxon kingdom of MERCIA. The Normans gave the town its first stone castle, and **Shrewsbury Castle** was enlarged and upgraded by Edward I in the late 13th century (he made Shrewsbury his seat of government between 1277 and 1283, while he was subduing the Welsh). It was a prosperous centre of the cloth trade in the Middle Ages, and reached its high-water mark when it became Charles I's capital for a short time at the beginning of the Civil Wars. Its centre retains a historic feel, with some particularly fine Tudor and Stuart timber-framed buildings.

The eastern and western bridges across the Severn to the town's suburbs are referred to respectively as the English Bridge and the Welsh Bridge.

Shrewsbury School, a boys' public school, was founded in 1552 by Edward VI. Its former pupils are known as 'Old Salopians' (*see* SALOP). Many of the early leading lights of *Private Eye* magazine, including Richard Ingrams, William Rushton, Christopher Booker and Paul Foot, were at the school together in the 1950s. Other alumni include the poet Sir Philip Sidney, the composer Edward German and the Conservative politician Michael Heseltine.

The naturalist and establisher of the theory of evolution Charles Darwin (1809–82) was born in Shrewsbury (and also attended Shrewsbury School), as was the musical historian Charles Burney (1726–1814). Robert Clive ('Clive of India'; 1725–74) was MP for the town from 1761 until his death (his house is now the Clive House Museum).

Shrewsbury provided the setting for George Farquhar's comic drama of army and country life *The Recruiting Officer* (1706). It is also the principal backdrop for Shropshire-born Ellis Peters's highly popular medieval crime stories revolving around the monk-detective Brother Cadfael, who lived at Shrewsbury Abbey. (Several stories were filmed for television from 1994, starring Derek Jacobi; unfortunately for lovers of local history, the filming took place outside Budapest.)

The mild controversy over the pronunciation of *Shrewsbury* is due to a misunderstanding of earlier centuries' spelling conventions. As the name's origin suggests (*see above*), the pronunciation 'shrowzbəri' is the historically 'correct' one, but in the past *shrew* and *shrewd* were often pronounced to rhyme with *show* and *showed*, which led to the introduction of the *-ew-* spelling for *Shrewsbury*. Pronounced as it looks, that became 'shrewzbəri' (the preferred local version).

Shelton, west of Shrewsbury, was the location of Owen Glendower's Oak. According to local legend it was from this tree, in full growth in 1403, that Owain Glyndwr (Glendower) witnessed the Battle of Shrewsbury (*see below*). The tree, whose girth was reported to be some 12 m (40 ft), was dead by the middle of the 20th century and was removed in the 1950s to make way for road improvements.

There are towns called Shrewsbury in the USA (Massachusetts, New Jersey), and a district of New Orleans, Louisiana, shares the same name.

> High the vanes of Shrewsbury gleam
> Islanded in Severn stream;
> The bridges from the steepled crest
> Cross the water east and west.
>
> A.E. Housman: *A Shropshire Lad* (1896)

See also MEOLE BRACE.

Battle of Shrewsbury (21 July 1403). A battle in which Henry IV, who had seized the throne in 1399, consolidated his power by defeating rebel forces under Henry Percy ('Hotspur'), who was killed in the battle. It features as the climactic setting of Shakespeare's *Henry IV Part 1* (1597).

by Shrewsbury clock. An expression used in former times with statements of duration, as an overt guarantee of exactness but, alluding to its original – a claim by Falstaff in *Henry IV Part 1* ('We rose both at an instant, and fought a long hour by Shrewsbury clock') – with an underlying implication of exaggeration.

Shrewsbury cake. A flat round crisp biscuit-like cake, as originally made in Shrewsbury.

Shrivenham 'river-meadow allotted by decree' (referring to land beside the River Cole allotted to the church after a dispute over ownership), OE *scrifen* 'allotted' + *hamm* 'river-meadow' (*see* HAM).

A village in Oxfordshire (before 1974 in Berkshire), in the VALE OF THE WHITE HORSE, about 32 km (20 miles) southwest of Oxford.

Shropshire From *Shrobsbury* (an early form of the name SHREWSBURY) + SHIRE.

A county in the western Midlands of England, on the Welsh border, bounded to the north by Cheshire, to the east by Staffordshire, the West Midlands and Worcestershire, to the south by Herefordshire and to the west by Powys. It contains the unitary authority of TELFORD AND WREKIN. Its administrative centre is SHREWSBURY, and other important centres include BRIDGNORTH, LUDLOW, MARKET DRAYTON and OSWESTRY. Its main rivers are the SEVERN and the TEME. The former divides the county into a relatively low-lying northern and eastern part and a higher southwestern section containing the **Shropshire Hills** (*see also* the LONG MYND *and* WENLOCK EDGE). It is one of England's least populated counties.

Shropshire is studded with Iron Age hillforts (*see* CAER CARADOC). Its pre-Roman British inhabitants were the Ordovices (*see under* GWYNEDD) and the Cornovii. It was settled by the Romans: WATLING STREET[1] ran through it, and WROXETER, capital of the *civitas* (self-governing tribal area) that the Romans granted the Cornovii, was the third-largest city in Roman Britain. Later Shropshire was a much disputed territory between Saxon MERCIA and Celtic POWYS (*see under* MARCHES). The Normans built several castles here.

Nowadays it is pre-eminently an agricultural county, its produce underpinning a flowering of local gastronomy in restaurants (notably in Ludlow) and country-house hotels. In the 18th century, however, it was at the cutting edge of the Industrial Revolution: it was the main iron-producing county in England, and the world's first cast-iron bridge was built at IRONBRIDGE in between 1778 and 1781.

In 1974 its name was officially changed to SALOP, but so great was the local outcry against this that in 1980 it was changed back to Shropshire.

In cricketing terms Shropshire is a 'minor county' (the club was founded in 1956) and plays in the minor counties championship.

Rural Shropshire and its landscapes were lyrically evoked in Mary Webb's famous novel of rustic life *Precious Bane* (1924), which was effusively praised by the then prime minister, Stanley Baldwin. Webb's earthy style of writing was less to the liking of the novelist Stella Gibbons, however, who parodied it skilfully and wittily in *Cold Comfort Farm* (1932) (*see* HOWLING).

Shropshire. A name given to either of two types of sheep associated with Shropshire: an old breed of horned sheep, and a modern variety of hornless black-faced sheep produced by crossing with the Southdown. The latter are now widely raised in America, mainly for their meat.

Shropshire Lad, A. A series of 63 poems by A.E. Housman (1859–1936), published together in book form in 1896. Mainly in ballad mode, they nostalgically conjure up the 'blue remembered hills' of his youth, an irrecoverable quasi-Salopian arcadia (Housman was actually born in FOCKBURY, Worcestershire, and at the time he started writing the poems he had never visited Shropshire):

> That is the land of lost content,
> I see it shining plain,
> The happy highways where I went
> And cannot come again.

At first the poems sank without trace, but at the time of the First World War their themes of parting and loss struck a chord, and they became hugely popular. Despite the author's disapproval, many English composers set them to music, the most memorable versions being those by Ralph Vaughan Williams and George Butterworth.

Shropshire Union Canal. A system of canals formed in the 1840s, running northwards from WOLVERHAMPTON through Shropshire to join the Manchester Ship Canal (*see under* MANCHESTER) and linked in with the River Severn. Canal-boating aficionados refer to it affectionately as the '**Shroppie**'.

Shudy Camps *Shudy* 'hovel, shed' (perhaps in studied contrast with nearby *Castle Camps*, which, as its name suggests, has its own castle), OE *scydd*; *Camps* 'enclosures', ModE.

A village in Cambridgeshire, about 21 km (13 miles) southeast of Cambridge. It is pronounced 'shoody'.

Shugborough 'wood, hill or fortification haunted by goblins', OE *scucca* 'goblin' + an indistinct element that may be *bearu* 'wood' or *beorg* 'mound', but most often reflects BURY.

A country house (in full **Shugborough Hall**) in Staffordshire, at the northern end of Cannock Chase (*see under* CANNOCK), about 9 km (6 miles) southeast of Stafford. It has been the home of the Anson family (now the earls of Lichfield) since 1624. George Anson (1697–1762), a naval commander who famously circumnavigated the globe between 1740 and 1744 during the War of Jenkins's Ear, attacking Spanish colonies and shipping as he went, was born here. The house is now owned by the National Trust, and the current photographer-earl's pictures are displayed.

Sí an Bhrú. The Irish name for NEWGRANGE.

Sibford Ferris *Sibford* 'Sibba's ford', OE male personal name *Sibba* + FORD; *Ferris* denoting manorial ownership in the Middle Ages by the de Ferrers family.

A village in Oxfordshire, about 11 km (7 miles) southwest of Banbury.

Sibford Gower *Gower* denoting manorial ownership in the Middle Ages by the Guher family.

A village in Oxfordshire, to the northwest of and now contiguous with SIBFORD FERRIS.

Sible Hedingham *Sible* denoting land ownership in the locality in the 13th century by a lady called Sibil; *Hedingham* probably 'homestead of Hyth(a)'s people, or of the dwellers at the landing-place', OE male personal name *Hyth(a)* or *hyth* 'landing-place' + *-inga-* (see -ING) + HAM.

A village (pronounced 'sibl') in Essex, on the River COLNE[1], about 11 km (7 miles) north of Braintree. It was the birthplace of Sir John Hawkwood (*c.*1320–94), a mercenary soldier who fought with the Black Prince at Poitiers (1356) and then moved on to Italy, where his services were much in demand. CASTLE HEDINGHAM lies just to the north of here.

Siccar Point Possibly 'point of safety', from Scots *siccar* 'safe, secure, sure'.

A rocky headland on the North Sea coast of Scottish BORDERS (formerly in Berwickshire), between COCKBURNSPATH and FAST CASTLE. Studying the various types of rock here (sandstones, breccia, greywackes and shales) in 1788 gave the pioneer geologist James Hutton (1726–97) an inkling of the processes by which sedimentary rocks are formed, and the processes by which they may subsequently be tilted and deformed; this in turn gave rise to the realization that the earth was much older than had hitherto been thought, and had not been created in the way described in Genesis.

Sicklinghall 'Sicel's corner of land', OE male personal name *Sicel* + -ING + *halh* (see HALE, -HALL).

A small village in North Yorkshire, 4 km (2.5 miles) west of Wetherby.

Sid 'the wide one', OE *sid* 'wide'.

A river in south Devon, which rises to the south of HONITON and flows about 9 km (6 miles) southwards into the English Channel at SIDMOUTH.

Sidcup Probably 'seat-shaped or flat-topped hill' (although this does not correspond particularly well with the local topography), OE *set-copp*.

A district of southeast London, in the borough of BEXLEY (before 1965 in Kent). The coming of the railway in the 1860s triggered its suburbanization, further intensified by electrification in 1926.

Sidcup was the birthplace of British plastic surgery. The surgeon Harold Gillies started to work on it in a hut here in the early years of the First World War, and by 1917 had developed his pedicle skin-graft technique (in which the graft is left temporarily attached to the site from which it was taken).

Edward Heath (prime minister 1970–4) was MP for Old Bexley and Sidcup (originally as Bexley) from 1950 to 2001 (latterly as Father of the House of Commons).

The district hit the headlines in spring 2004 when it was revealed that the mundane source of Dasani, Coca-Cola's exotically named 'lifestyle' bottled water, was Thames Water's mains supply to the Coca-Cola plant in Sidcup. The water was later withdrawn from the market after impurities were found to have been introduced in the production process. A delighted popular press had a field day, the *Daily Mail* commenting: 'Eau de Sidcup: Didn't Del Boy try that?' (The reference is to the character of 'Del Boy' Trotter from the popular BBC sitcom *Only Fools and Horses* (see under PECKHAM), one of whose schemes was to bottle tap water and market it as 'Peckham Spring'.)

> If only I could get down to Sidcup! I've been waiting for the weather to break. He's got my papers, this man I left them with, it's got it all down there, I could prove everything.
>
> Harold Pinter: Davies in *The Caretaker* (1960)

Sidlaw Hills *Sidlaw* possibly tautological, Gaelic *sidh* 'hill, fairy knoll' + Scots *law* 'rounded hill', but this is uncertain.

A range of low rounded hills running northeastwards from Perth to the north of Dundee, extending from Perth and Kinross into Angus. The range includes DUNSINANE (of Macbeth fame), and the highest point is Craigowl (455 m / 1493 ft).

Sidmouth 'mouth of the River Sid', SID + OE *mutha* 'mouth'.

A town and seaside resort on the south Devon coast, on Lyme Bay (see under LYME REGIS), at the mouth of the River SID, about 15 km (9 miles) northeast of Exmouth. It is bracketed by a pair of spectacular red sandstone cliffs, Salcombe Hill and Peak Hill.

It was a quiet fishing village until the late 18th century, but then it was discovered by a Jewish businessman called Emmanuel Lousada, who decided to turn it into the most elegant and genteel holiday resort in England. The well-to-do, denied their Continental watering holes by the Napoleonic Wars, flocked here and, as its fine Regency houses attest, it was for a time the height of fashion. Queen Victoria lived here as a baby, and the poet Elizabeth Barrett Browning lived here from 1832 to 1836, before moving to London.

Henry Addington (1757–1844), prime minister from 1801 to 1804, took the title Viscount Sidmouth when he was ennobled in 1805.

Sidney Street Origin unknown.

A street in STEPNEY, in East London (E1), between the MILE END Road to the north and the Commercial Road to the south.

Siege of Sidney Street. An incident on 3 January 1911 in which police and soldiers, on the orders of the home secretary Winston Churchill, who personally (and somewhat ostentatiously) attended the siege, surrounded 100 Sidney Street. Inside the house were three Latvian anarchists who had killed three policemen during a raid on a jeweller a few weeks earlier. Two of the gang were killed in the siege, but the leader, 'Peter the Painter' (a sign-painter by trade), escaped.

Sigingstone 'farm of the Sigin family', ME surname *Sigin* (known from the 13th century) + -TON.

A village in Vale of Glamorgan (formerly in Glamorgan, then South Glamorgan), 3 km (2 miles) north of Llantwit Major.

Silbury Hill *Silbury* perhaps 'hill by a hall', OE *sele* 'dwelling, hall' + *beorg* 'barrow, hill'. (It is unlikely that the hill gets its name from the legendary and otherwise unknown King *Sil*; the reverse is probably the case.)

An ancient earthwork in Wiltshire, to the south of AVEBURY, about 10 km (6 miles) west of MARLBOROUGH. It is the largest prehistoric man-made mound in Europe (about 40 m /130 ft high) and was probably made around 2600 BC. It has a surrounding ditch approximately 6 m (20 ft) deep, made by removing earth for the mound. When first built it was probably about a third higher than it is now, and the sides were terraced. Its original purpose is a mystery – the best guess may be a burial mound, the most romantic legend being that it is a repository of a life-size solid-gold statue of King Sil and/or his horse. It has been excavated three times, most recently when the BBC made a television documentary about it in the late 1960s, but nothing of any interest has ever been found.

Silchester Probably 'Roman station by a willow-copse', OE *siele* 'willow-copse' + *ceaster* 'Roman station' (*see* CHESTER). Alternatively the first element might be an eroded form of *Calleva*, part of the Latin name of the place.

A village in Hampshire, about 13 km (8 miles) north of Basingstoke. Before and during the Roman occupation of Britain it was an important town. It was the capital of the British tribe known as the Atrebates, at which time it was called **Calleva** (an Old Celtic name meaning 'place in the woods'). After the invasion it became for the Romans **Calleva Atrebatum**. By the 3rd century its site covered about 40 ha (100 acres), and the remains of many fine villas, amphitheatres, temples and baths from the 4th century have been excavated. There was also a Christian church here, the only one known to have been built in Roman

Britain. By the 5th century, however, the Romans had left, and gradually the town fell into decay. Today all that is left above ground is part of the walls and a gateway.

Silent Valley Presumably because silenced by the dammed waters.

The main valley penetrating the Mourne Mountains of County Down from the south. It contains two reservoirs created in the early 20th century to supply Belfast with water, and the border of their catchment area is marked by the Mourne Wall (*see under* MOURNE MOUNTAINS).

Silicon Fen. A nickname for CAMBRIDGE[1], echoing California's Silicon Valley (*see also* SILICON GLEN), and likewise indicating a preponderance of high-tech research and business activity, which developed in and around Cambridge from the later 1980s.

Silicon Glen. Scotland's answer to California's Silicon Valley, as the San José Valley was dubbed in the later 1970s, owing to the number of hardware and software industries established here. The name derived from the importance of the silicon-chip microprocessor to the computer industry (previously, when full of orchards, the San José Valley was known as the Valley of Heart's Desire). Scotland's Silicon Glen broadly coincides with that section of the Central Belt between Glasgow and Edinburgh, including such towns as STIRLING[1], LIVINGSTON, LINLITHGOW and EAST KILBRIDE, but also extending northeast to GLENROTHES and DUNDEE. More computers are made here per head of population than in any other country in the world.

The term 'Silicon Glen' is also applied more figuratively to that sector of the Scottish economy involved in computing, the internet and high technology.

Silk Willoughby *Silk* a reduced form of the name of a nearby place, *Silkby* 'Silki's farmstead' or 'farmstead near a gully', OScand male personal name *Silki* or OE *sioluc* 'gully' + -BY; *Willoughby* 'farmstead by the willow-trees', OE *wilig* 'willow-tree' + -BY.

A village in Lincolnshire, about 2.5 km (1.5 miles) south of Sleaford.

Silloth 'barn by the sea', OScand *saer* 'sea' + *hlatha* 'barn'. A small port and resort on the SOLWAY FIRTH, northwest Cumbria (formerly in Cumberland), some 30 km (20 miles) west of Carlisle.

Silsden 'Sigulfr's valley', OScand male personal name + OE *denu* 'valley'.

A town on the edge of Rombalds Moor, West Yorkshire, 6 km (4 miles) north-north-west of Keighley.

Silsoe 'Sifel's hill-spur', OE *Sifeles* possessive form of male personal name *Sifel* + *hoh* 'hill-spur'.

A village in Bedfordshire, about 5 km (3 miles) southeast of Ampthill.

Siluria after the *Silures*, an ancient British tribe.

A rare name for southeast WALES, possibly first coined in the title of a geological treatise by Sir Roderick Murchison (1854) regarding the **Silurian System** (430–395 million years ago). The Silures gave the Romans names for CAERLEON (**Isca Silurum**) and CAERWENT (**Venta Silurum**), and the 17th-century poet Henry Vaughan called himself '**the Silurist**'. *See also* GWENT.

Silurian Way. *See under* GRIZEDALE.

Silverdale 'silver-coloured valley', OE *seolfor* 'silver' + *dæl* 'dale'.

A village in Lancashire, overlooking MORECAMBE Bay, 13 km (8 miles) north of Lancaster. The novelist Elizabeth Gaskell was a frequent visitor, and wrote some of her books here; the village may have been the model for 'Abermouth' in *Ruth* (1853).

Silver End The name is first recorded in 1777; *silver* may refer to a smooth, grassy place.

A village in Essex, about 6 km (4 miles) southeast of Braintree. It was built on the site of the tiny hamlet of Silver End in the 1920s as a self-sufficient workers' village by the Braintree firm of F.H. Crittall, makers of metal window frames. When the company was taken over in the 1960s, the administration of the village passed to the local authority.

Silvermine Mountains From the silver mines here (zinc and lead are also mined).

A range of hills in County TIPPERARY, some 25 km (16 miles) east-northeast of Limerick. The highest point is Slievekimalta or Keeper Hill (694 m / 2276 ft), and the village of **Silvermines** is to the north.

Silverstone Probably 'Sæwulf's or Sigewulf's farmstead', OE *Sæwulfes* or *Sigewulfes* possessive forms of male personal names *Sæwulf* and *Sigewulf* + -TON.

A village in Northamptonshire, about 19 km (12 miles) southwest of Northampton. Its name has been put on the map by its motor-racing track, opened in 1948 on a disused airfield, and known simply as '**Silverstone**'. In that same year it staged the first British Grand Prix, and in 1950 it hosted the inaugural Grand Prix of the Formula One World Drivers' Championship. In 1987 it became the permanent home of the British Grand Prix (although out-of-date facilities and organizational hitches in the early 21st century cast some doubt on its continuation in that role). Major track features include the Becketts, Stowe and Club corners, the Abbey and Maggotts curves and the Hangar straight.

Silver Streak, the. A hyperbolic epithet sometimes applied in the 19th century to the ENGLISH CHANNEL.

> The silver streak, on the other side of which is dear England.
>
> J. Payn: *Myst Mirbridge* (1888)

Silvertown From S.W. *Silver* & Co., a local firm producing rubber goods, which built houses for its workforce in the area in the 1850s.

A district of East London (E16), in the borough of NEWHAM, on the north bank of the River Thames, to the southeast of Canning Town. In the past it was dominated by the vast ROYAL DOCKS, immediately to the north, and the Tate and Lyle sugar refinery. Both are now out of action, and Silvertown's main feature is London City Airport (*see under* LONDON). Silvertown station on the North London line, built in 1863 to serve the docks, has been renamed Silvertown & City Airport.

Silvertown Explosion. An incident in West Silvertown in 1917 in which about 60 tonnes (50 tons) of TNT exploded in a fire at Brunner Mond's chemical works. Large parts of the district were destroyed and 69 people were killed.

Simonsbath 'Simon's bathing-place'; a modern name, first recorded in the 16th century.

A village (pronounced 'simmonz-') in Somerset, on EXMOOR, on the River Barle, about 11 km (7 miles) southeast of Lynton. It was here in the early 19th century that a family called Knight cut down forests and introduced modern agriculture to Exmoor.

Simon's Seat[1] OScand *sæti* 'high place, hilltop in the shape of a seat', with the name of a local landowner.

A moorland top (485 m / 1591 ft) above the VALLEY OF DESOLATION in North Yorkshire, 12 km (7 miles) north of Ilkley.

Simon's Seat[2]. A hill (587 m / 1925 ft) in the northwest PENNINES, Cumbria, 16 km (10 miles) northeast of Kendal.

Sinclair's Bay. *See under* CAITHNESS.

Sinfin 'wide fen', OE *sid* 'wide' + *fenn* 'fen'.

A village in Derbyshire, now a southern suburb of DERBY within the unitary authority of Derby City.

Sinodun Hills. The official name for the WITTENHAM CLUMPS.

Síol Éalaigh. The Irish name for SHILLELAGH.

Sion Mills Not a biblical reference, but an anglicization of the Irish *Muileann an tSiáin* 'mill of the fairy mound'.

A village in County Tyrone, some 3 km (2 miles) south of Strabane. In 1969, Ireland defeated the mighty West Indies at the local cricket ground, bowling them out for 25.

Sionnainn. The Irish name for the new town of Shannon near Shannon Airport (*see under* SHANNON).

Sionnán. The girl's name said by some to be the origin of the name of the River SHANNON.

Sir Benfro. The Welsh name for PEMBROKESHIRE.

Sir Drefaldwyn. The Welsh name for MONTGOMERYSHIRE.

Sir Faesyfed. The Welsh name for RADNORSHIRE.

Sir Feirionnydd. The Welsh name for MERIONETH.

Sir Frycheiniog. The Welsh name for BRECKNOCKSHIRE.

Sir Gaerfyrddin. The Welsh name for CARMARTHENSHIRE.

Sissinghurst 'Seaxa's people's wooded hill', OE male personal name *Seaxa* + *-inga-* (*see* -ING) + *hyrst* 'wooded hill'.

A village in Kent, in the WEALD, about 10 km (6 miles) northwest of Tenterden. Nearby is **Sissinghurst Castle**, the remnants of an Elizabethan mansion (on the site of a medieval moated manor), restored and lived in by the poet-novelist and gardener Vita Sackville-West (*see also* KNOLE) and her diplomat husband Harold Nicolson. Around it in the 1930s they laid out **Sissinghurst Garden**. The fulsomely informal style of its planting (which owes much to Gertrude Jekyll) now attracts many thousands of visitors each year.

Sittaford Tor Origin unknown; first recorded in the 19th century as *Siddaford Tor*.

A tor in the middle of DARTMOOR, about 15 km (9 miles) west of Moretonhampstead. It is 538 m (1764 ft) high.

Sittingbourne Probably 'stream of the dwellers on the slope' (referring to Milton Creek), OE *side* 'slope' + *-inga-* (*see* -ING) + *burna* 'stream'.

A town in Kent, on Milton Creek (an inlet of the SWALE[2]), about 16 km (10 miles) east of Rochester. It is the administrative seat of Swale district. The gateway to the ISLE OF SHEPPEY, which is just to the north, it is essentially an industrial town. In the past, it was an important part of Britain's paper-making industry.

Siúr. The Irish name for the River SUIR.

Six Counties. A term sometimes applied to NORTHERN IRELAND, which consists of the counties of ANTRIM, ARMAGH, DOWN, FERMANAGH, LONDONDERRY (or Derry) and TYRONE, whose initials together produce the acronyms FATDAD or FATLAD. The use of the term Six Counties, like that of the TWENTY-SIX COUNTIES, is favoured by Republicans, and may imply non-acceptance of the separate existence of Northern Ireland.
See also THIRTY-TWO COUNTIES.

Six Mile Bottom From its being situated in a valley (OE *botm*) 6 miles from Newmarket.

A hamlet in Cambridgeshire, about 10 km (6 miles) southwest of Newmarket.

Sixpenny Handley *Sixpenny* an old Hundred name, 'hill of the Saxons', OE *Seaxe* 'Saxon' + OCelt *penn* (see PEN); *Handley* 'high wood or glade', OE *hean* dative of *heah* 'high' + -LEY.

A village in Dorset, in CRANBORNE Chase, about 14 km (9 miles) northeast of Blandford Forum. In the 18th century it was an early headquarters of Isaac Gulliver (1745–1822), Dorset's most famous smuggler.

Sixteen Foot Drain Because it was originally 16 ft (5 m) wide.

A canal in Cambridgeshire. Branching off the FORTY FOOT DRAIN at **Sixteen Foot Corner**, it extends 16 km (10 miles) northeastwards to the Norfolk border, where it becomes the Middle Level Main Drain.

Sizergh Castle 'Sigarith's summer pasture', OScand female personal name *Sigarith* + *erg* 'shieling or summer pasture' (*see* -ARY).

A house and gardens in Cumbria, formerly in Westmorland, 5 km (3 miles) south of Kendal. A Tudor mansion surrounding a 14th-century pele tower, Sizergh Castle was enlarged in the 18th century, and is now owned by the National Trust. The castle has a medieval female ghost. The story goes that her husband locked her in a room, left the castle, and she starved to death. Local tradition has it that her ghost can still be heard screaming.

Sizewell Probably 'Sigehere's spring or stream', OE *Sigeheres* possessive form of male personal name *Sigehere* + *wella* 'spring, stream'.

A coastal village in Suffolk, about 5 km (3 miles) north of Aldeburgh. Its fame, or notoriety, rests on its nuclear power stations, whose giant spheres dominate the landscape around. The original one, **Sizewell A**, a gas-cooled reactor, went on stream in 1966. Its controversial twin, the pressurized-water reactor **Sizewell B**, was the subject of a 340-day public enquiry before permission to build it was granted. It was completed in 1995. Plans to build Sizewell C were abandoned by the British government in December of the same year.

Skara Brae 'Skari's brae', OScand male personal name + Scots *brae* 'hill-slope' (from OScand *bra* 'brow').

A well-preserved stone-built Neolithic village on the west coast of Mainland, ORKNEY, some 24 km (14.5 miles) northwest of Kirkwall. An alternative spelling is **Scara Brae**. It was built some time before 3100 BC and was abandoned around 2600 BC. The site was covered with sand until revealed after a big storm in 1850. The lack of wood on the island meant that not only were the houses made of stone, but also pieces of furniture such as beds and lockers.

Skegness 'beard-shaped promontory' or 'Skeggi's promontory' (referring to a headland since removed by coastal erosion), OScand *skegg* 'beard' or male personal name *Skeggi* + *nes* (*see* NESS).

A town and seaside resort in Lincolnshire, on the northern side of the mouth of the WASH, about 30 km (19 miles) east of Horncastle. It was developed as a holiday town in the late 1870s by Lord Scarborough, who was quick to spot the potential of its long sandy beaches once the railway had arrived in 1875. It became very popular with Midlanders taking their annual break (Alfred Tennyson was an early fan too), and managed to stay ahead of the competition with various initiatives. Its 1908 slogan 'Skegness is so bracing', illustrated with the now famous John Hassall poster of the 'Jolly Fisherman' prancing light-heartedly along the sands, was the first successful modern advertising ploy for a seaside town, and secured the town's reputation for invigorating ozone-filled sea breezes (a.k.a. easterly winds blowing uninterruptedly from the Siberian steppes – in 1978, Skegness's 562-m (1843-ft) long pier was blown down in a gale). On Easter Monday 1936, Billy Butlin opened his first holiday camp here, on a site of a former sugar-beet field (it is now 'Butlins Funcoast World').

Skelligs, the Irish *Na Scealaga* 'the splinters'.
A group of jagged rocks in the Atlantic some 12 km (7.5 miles) off the IVERAGH peninsula of County Kerry. The group consists of Washerwoman's Rock (the smallest), **Little Skellig** and **Great Skellig** or **Skellig Michael** (Irish **Sceilig Mhichíl**), which has twin peaks of 218 m (715 ft) and 198 m (650 ft), separated by Christ's Saddle. Little Skellig is inhabited only by gannets, while Skellig Michael – one of a number of small mountainous islands on Europe's Atlantic coast associated with the Archangel Michael (others include Brittany's Mont St Michel and Cornwall's ST MICHAEL'S MOUNT) – has a lighthouse and near the top the spectacularly situated remains of an early Christian monastery, including beehive huts, reached by steps cut into the solid rock. The monastery is said to have been founded by St Finan in the 7th century and survived until the 13th century, when the monks moved to the mainland fleshpots of BALLINSKELLIGS. Prior to that the island was a place of pilgrimage, requiring a head for heights and some rudimentary rock-climbing skills to negotiate such features as the Needle's Eye and the Stone of Pain. Landings may only be made on Skellig Michael in the calmest of conditions, but this did not prevent the Vikings from sacking the place in 823. The Skelligs provided the last glimpse of Ireland to those forced to emigrate to America in the 19th century.

Skellig Michael was declared a UNESCO World Heritage Site in 1996.

Skellig. A novel (1998) for children by David Almond, in which a young boy called Michael finds a strange creature called Skellig in his garage, who turns out to be – perhaps – an angel.

Skelligs List, the. A traditional annual verse broadsheet making fun of those who the community considered should have got married for one reason or another. The broadsheet was pushed under doors on Ash Wednesday. The story behind the name (which does not fit well with the facts) is that the monks on Skellig Michael did not accept the Gregorian calendar reform of 1582, and hence Lent on the Skelligs came somewhat later than on the mainland – so that those in a hurry to wed could be married

on Great Skellig, while weddings were forbidden during the period of Lent on the mainland.

Skelmersdale 'Skjaldmarr's valley', OScand male personal name + *dalr* 'valley'.
A town in Lancashire, 10 km (6 miles) west of Wigan. It was designated a NEW TOWN[1] in 1961, and thereafter took in overspill from Liverpool.

Skelthwaite. The fictionalized version of SLAITHWAITE, West Yorkshire, used as the location for the long-running television soap opera *Where the Heart Is*.

Skelton 'farm on a ledge', OE *scelf* 'shelf, ledge' + -TON.
A town in Redcar and Cleveland (formerly in the North Riding of Yorkshire, then in Cleveland), 16 km (10 miles) east of Middlesbrough.

Skerries Irish *Na Sceirí* 'the skerries' (i.e. reefs or rocky islands).
A seaside resort and fishing port on the east coast of County Dublin, some 25 km (16 miles) north of Dublin itself. The name refers to a number of small offshore islands: St Patrick's Island, Red Island, Colt Island, Shenick's Island and, further out, Rockabill with its lighthouse. St Patrick's 'footprint' is on Red Island (which is linked to the mainland by a causeway), and the saint is said to have landed on St Patrick's Island on his voyage from Wicklow to Ulster; subsequently the locals stole his goat from the island and ate it, and to this day the inhabitants of Skerries are known as 'goats'.

Skerryvore 'big skerry', Gaelic *sgeir* 'skerry, sharp rock, reef' + *mhór* 'big'.
A low rock in the Atlantic 16 km (10 miles) southwest of Tiree, in Argyll and Bute (formerly in Strathclyde). In 1838–43 Alan Stevenson, an uncle of the novelist Robert Louis Stevenson, built the lighthouse here, which is 42 m (138 ft) high. It was a considerable feat of engineering, with over 4000 tons of granite being brought over from the Ross of Mull, and at one point the barracks for the workers on the rock – which is only 3 m (10 ft) above the sea at high tide – was swept away in a storm.

Skerryvore Edition. A 30-volume edition (1924–6) of the works of Robert Louis Stevenson, named after his house in Bournemouth, where he lived from 1885 to 1887, itself named in honour of his uncle's achievement. There is now a model of the lighthouse in the memorial garden to the author, at the end of R.L. Stevenson Avenue in Bournemouth.

> Eternal granite hewn from the living isle
> And dowelled with brute iron, rears a tower
> That from its wet foundation to its crown
> Of glittering glass, stands, in the sweep of winds,
> Immovable, immortal, eminent.
>
> Robert Louis Stevenson: 'Skerryvore: The Parallel', from
> *Underwoods* (1887)

Skibbereen Irish *An Sciobairín* 'the place of the little boats'.
A market town and fishing port on the south coast of
County Cork, some 65 km (40 miles) southwest of Cork
itself. It is affectionately known as **Skib**, and is the cathedral
town of the Catholic diocese of Ross. It is known inter-
nationally from the probably apocryphal story regarding
its local newspaper, said to have thundered:

> Let Herr Hitler be warned, the eyes of the *Skibbereen Eagle*
> are upon him.

However, an altogether older version has this:

> Let Lord Palmerston be warned, the *Skibbereen Eagle* has
> got its eye both upon him and on the Emperor of Russia.

Skibbereen saw some of the worst suffering during the
Great Famine, some 28,000 dying here, while another 8000
emigrated. Resentment at landlords, poverty, evictions and
hunger is embodied in the famous emigrants' ballad 'Old
Skibbereen' (or 'The Reasons I Left Auld Skibbereen'):

> Oh well I do remember the black December day
> The landlord and the sheriff came to drive us all away;
> They set my roof on fire with their cursed English spleen,
> And that's another reason why I left old Skibbereen.

The ballad ends with the rousing lines:

> And loud and high we'll raise the cry
> 'Revenge for Skibbereen!'

The Nationalist leader Michael Collins is said to have sung
the ballad at the Imperial Hotel in Cork the night before
his assassination on 22 August 1922.

Skiddaw Possibly 'overhanging hill', OScand *skuti* 'overhanging
crag' + *haugr* 'hill'.
A massy mountain (931 m / 3054 ft) in the northwestern
Lake District, Cumbria (formerly in Cumberland), overlooking BASSENTHWAITE LAKE and DERWENT[1] Water, 5 km (3
miles) north-northwest of Keswick. It is the lowest of the
three Lakeland Three-Thousanders (*see* LAKE DISTRICT) and
has been described by one guidebook writer as 'that heavy,
benevolent old giant', it being made of older rocks than
the volcanic heart of the Lakes. In the 19th century Charles
Lamb had similarly friendly feelings towards Skiddaw and
its neighbours, referring to them as 'fine old fellows …
broad-breasted brethren'.

> Thou ancient Skiddaw by thy helm of cloud
> And by thy many colour'd chasms deep,
> And by their shadows that for ever sleep,
> By yon small flaky mists that love to creep
> Along the edges of those spots of light,
> Those sunny islands on thy smooth green height …
>
> Samuel Taylor Coleridge: 'A Stranger Minstrel' (1800)

Coleridge made an ascent in August 1800, and was pleased
when another arrived at the summit and read his name

on a piece of slate, exclaiming (to Coleridge's immense
pleasure): 'Coleridge! I lay my life that is the *poet Coleridge*!'

> Sate in the sun. Coleridge's bowels bad, mine also. We
> drank tea at John Stanley's. The evening cold and clear. A
> glorious light on Skiddaw.
>
> Dorothy Wordsworth: journal (19 May 1802)

One of the sonnets of John Wilson (a.k.a. Christopher
North, 1785–1854) is entitled 'Written on Skiddaw, during
a Tempest'. Another poet who climbed the mountain was
John Keats, on his 1818 tour:

> It promised all along to be fair, & we had fagged & tugged
> nearly to the top, when at halfpast six [in the morning]
> there came a mist upon us & shut out the view; we did
> not however lose anything by it, we were high enough
> without mist, to see the coast of Scotland; the Irish sea;
> the hills beyond Lancaster; & nearly all the large ones of
> Cumberland & Westmorland, particularly Helvellyn &
> Scawfell: It grew colder & colder as we ascended, & we
> were glad at about three parts of the way to taste a little
> rum which the Guide brought with him … All felt on
> arising into the cold air, that same elevation, which a cold
> bath gives one – I felt as if I were going to a Tournament.
>
> John Keats: letter to Tom Keats (29 June 1818)

(For the poet's resort to strong liquor on his ascent of
another mountain, *see* BEN NEVIS.)

The summit of Skiddaw was long used for beacon fires,
as celebrated in these lines from Lord Macaulay's epic *The
Armada*:

> Till the proud Peak the flag unfurled over Darwin's rocky
>   dales,
> Till like volcanoes flared to heaven the stormy hills of
>   Wales,
> Till twelve fair counties saw the blaze from Malvern's
>   lonely height,
> Till streamed in crimson on the wind the Wrekin's crest of
>   light,
> Till Skiddaw saw the fire that burned on Gaunt's
>   embattled pile,
> And the red glare on Skiddaw woke the Burghers of
>   Carlisle.

In Victorian times a Scotsman, George Smith, lived as a
hermit on the flanks of the mountain, trading portraits of
passers-by for whisky.

Skiddaw grey. The tone of grey favoured for the jackets
of Lakeland huntsmen, such as the legendary John Peel
(1776–1854):

> D'ye ken John Peel with his coat so grey?
> D'ye ken John Peel at the break of the day?
> D'ye ken John Peel when's he's far far away
> With his hounds and his horn in the morning?
>
> J.W. Graves: 'John Peel' (1820)

Skipton 'sheep farm', OE *scip* 'sheep' + -TON; the pronunciation and spelling *Sk-* is Scandinavian.

A market town in Airedale, on the southern side of the Dales in North Yorkshire, 13 km (8 miles) northwest of Keighley. It is sometimes called **Skipton-in-Craven** (*see also* CRAVEN). The origins of **Skipton Castle**, rebuilt by Lady Anne Clifford after Civil War damage, are Norman.

Skipton was the birthplace of the moral philosopher Henry Sidgwick (1838–1900); and of Geoffrey Dawson (1874–1974), editor of *The Times* (1912–19, 1923–41), appeaser, and self-styled 'secretary-general of the Establishment'.

Skirrid, the An anglicized version of the Welsh name *Ysgyryd Fawr* 'great rough (hill)', *ysgyryd* 'rough' + *fawr* 'great'.

A hill in Monmouthshire (formerly in Gwent), some 5 km (3 miles) northeast of Abergavenny. Its Welsh name is **Ysgyryd Fawr**, and it is also often referred to as **Skirrid Fawr**. It was long a destination for pilgrims, owing to the great cleft in the peak said to have been made by the earthquake that followed Christ's death on the Cross. On the summit are the bare remains of St Michael's Chapel, built by persecuted Catholics in the 17th century.

> Kyrton-Beacon, Tumberlow, Blorench, Penvail and Skirridan, are some of the names of these horrid mountains ...; and I could not but fancy my self in view of Mount Brennus, Little Barnard, and Great Barnard, among the Alps.
>
> Daniel Defoe: *A Tour Through the Whole Island of Great Britain* (1724–6)

Skokholm 'island in the sound', originally identical with Stockholm, OScand *stokkr* 'stock', i.e. 'log, tree trunk', and here specifically 'a sound between land-masses' + *holmr* 'island' (*see* -EY, -EA); the *Sk-* arises from the common confusion of *c* and *t* in medieval manuscripts.

A small island 4 km (2.5 miles) off the west coast of Pembrokeshire (formerly in Dyfed). The first station in Britain for marking migratory birds was established here in 1933 by the naturalist R.M. Lockely, who had set up home on the island in 1927. The island is now managed by the Wildlife Trust for West Wales. To the north is the larger island of SKOMER.

Skomer 'cleft island', OScand *skalm* 'cleft' + *ey* (*see* -AY); two bays almost divide the island at the northeastern end, hence the 'cleft'.

A small island 1 km (0.6 miles) off the west coast of Pembrokeshire (formerly in Dyfed). There are many prehistoric remains, and the island is the largest seabird colony in southern Britain. It is managed by the Dyfed Wildlife Trust. To the south is the smaller island of SKOKHOLM.

Skomer vole. A subspecies (*Clethrionomys glareolus skomerensis*) of the bank vole. It provides a tasty snack for Skomer's short-eared owls.

> Today I saw a short-eared owl
> Bite and shake a Skomer vole,
> Drop it, bite and shake again
> Until its neck broke.
>
> Tod Thews: 'Skomer Vole' (1961)

Skull Irish *An Scoil* 'the school', referring to an ancient monastery.

A village overlooking **Skull Harbour**, on the western side of ROARINGWATER BAY, County Cork, 20 km (12 miles) west of Skibbereen.

Skye Possibly Gaelic *sgiath* 'winged': parts of the island are thought to protrude like wings.

The largest island of the Inner HEBRIDES, with an area of 1666 sq km (643 sq miles) and a maximum length of nearly 80 km (50 miles). It is in Highland (formerly in Inverness-shire), and is now joined by bridge to KYLE OF LOCHALSH on the mainland. Skye has a heavily indented coast (some say the coastline totals 1600 km / 1000 miles, but this no doubt depends on one's measuring technique), and no point on the island is more than 8 km (5 miles) from the sea. Among its many peninsulas are SLEAT in the south and VATERNISH and TROTTERNISH in the north. Its hills and mountains include the CUILLIN in the south (*see also* LOCH CORUISK), the STORR and QUIRAING in the north, and MACLEOD'S TABLES in the west. The 'capital' is PORTREE on the east coast. The climate is notoriously wet, earning Skye its nickname, **the Misty Isle**.

Back in the mists of time, Skye may have been the island home of the ancient Celtic amazon, Scáthach, who taught Cuchulain the arts of war. It was later taken over by the Vikings, but, like the rest of the Hebrides, it passed from the Norwegians to the Scottish Crown in 1266. Skye was thereafter dominated by the MacLeods of Dunvegan (*see under* DUNVEGAN CASTLE) and the Macdonalds of Sleat, who intermittently attempted to exterminate each other. After the failure of the 1745 Jacobite Rebellion, Flora Macdonald helped Bonnie Prince Charlie to escape his pursuers in the Outer Hebrides by disguising him as her maidservant, Betty Burke, and accompanying him to Skye (28–29 June 1746) in a small boat. The voyage became the stuff of legend, and is celebrated in the famous **'Skye Boat Song'** (*see below*). Less than 30 years later, Dr Johnson and James Boswell travelled to Skye as part of their Hebridean tour, and were much taken by the hospitality shown them at Dunvegan Castle. Skye suffered badly in the Highland Clearances, until in 1882 a group of Skye crofters took a firm stand against forced evictions at the Battle of the Braes (*see under* BRAES).

Skye has made a number of literary appearances, including:

> But I hae dream'd a dreary dream,
> Beyond the Isle of Skye;

I saw a dead man win a fight,
And I think that man was I.

> Anon.: 'The Battle of Otterbourne' (*see under*
> OTTERBURN; these lines from the old ballad are
> appositely quoted at the beginning and end of
> the 1955 film *The Man Who Never Was*.)

There was an old person of Skye
Who waltzed with a bluebottle fly
    They buzz'd a sweet tune
    To the light of the moon
And entranced all the people of Skye.

> Edward Lear: limerick

Seed of miraculous flowers lies cold in the bog,
Sun set in the beautiful land of the dead beyond the Isle
    of Skye.

> Kathleen Raine: 'Bheinn Naomh', from *The Hollow Hill*
> (1965)

The visit of Dr Johnson prompted the following:

A classical sanity considers Skye.
A huge hard light falls across shifting hills
            … But I hear
like a native dog notes beyond his range …

> Iain Crichton-Smith: 'Johnson in the Highlands',
> from *The Law and the Grace* (1965)

Leopard Man of Skye, the. Tom Leppard (originally
Woolridge), formerly a colour sergeant in the Rhodesia
Regiment, who has lived as a hermit in a remote part of
Skye since the late 1980s. He is reputed to be the most
tattooed man in the world, his whole body being covered
with leopard spots.

'Skye Boat Song'. A song written in 1908 by Harold Edwin
Boulton (1859–1935), evoking the voyage of Bonnie Prince
Charlie and Flora Macdonald (*see above*):

> Speed, bonnie boat, like a bird on the wing,
> 'Onward,' the sailors cry;
> Carry the lad that's born to be king,
> Over the sea to Skye.

Could Boulton have been influenced by some earlier lines?

> Sing me a song of a lad that is gone,
> Say, could that lad be I?
> Merry of soul he sailed on a day
> Over the sea to Skye.

> Robert Louis Stevenson: 'Sing me a song of a lad that is
> gone', from *Songs of Travel* (1896)

Skye terrier. A breed of terrier first bred in Skye some 400
years ago. It is characterized by a large head, long body,
short legs and long wiry hair. It was particularly popular
with the aristocracy in the 19th century.

Skye and Lochalsh. A former district (1975–96) of High-
land region, taking in parts of the old counties of Ross and
Cromarty (including Kyle of Lochalsh) and Inverness-shire.
The administrative seat was at PORTREE, on Skye.

Sky Road Presumably a reference to the wide open views.
A scenic route heading west along Clifden Bay from
CLIFDEN in Connemara, County Galway. There is both a
high road (up to 150 m / about 500 ft) and a low road, both
with fine views.

Slad 'valley' (referring to the Slad Valley), OE *slæd*.
A village in Gloucestershire, in the COTSWOLDS, about 3 km
(2 miles) northeast of STROUD. It lies in the **Slad Valley**,
between Stroud and Painswick.

Its most famous native son is Laurie Lee (1914–97), who
attended Slad Village School and later worked for a while in
an office in Stroud. In *Cider with Rosie* (1959) he richly
evoked the bygone rural life of village and valley:

> We chopped wood for the night and carried it in; dry
> beech sticks as brittle as candy. The baker came down
> with a basket of bread slung carelessly over his shoulder.
> Eight quartern loaves, cottage-size, black-crusted, were
> handed in at the door. A few crisp flakes of pungent crust
> still clung to his empty basket, so we scooped them up on
> our spit-wet fingers and laid them upon our tongues. The
> twilight gathered, the baker shouted goodnight, and
> whistled his way up the bank. Up on the road his black
> horse waited, the cart lamps smoking red.

Slaggyford 'ford at the muddy place', ME *slagging* 'muddy
place' + FORD.
A village in the upper valley of the South Tyne, North-
umberland, 29 km (18 miles) southwest of Hexham.
It is on the route of the Pennine Way (*see under* the
PENNINES).

Slain Men's Lea. *See under* PHILIPHAUGH.

Slains Castle Possibly Gaelic *sleamhuinn* 'smooth (place)'.
A castle originally situated on a promontory some 2 km
(1.2 miles) north of the village of Collieston and the
neighbouring hamlet of **Kirktown of Slains**, on the east
coast of Aberdeenshire (formerly in Grampian region). It
is now no more than a ruined tower. It was given by Robert
the Bruce to Sir Gilbert Hay, who had saved his life in battle.
The Hays later became earls of Erroll, and the Catholic 9th
Earl was involved in the pro-Spanish rebellion of 1594,
after which James VI blew up his castle.

On his return from exile in 1597 the 9th Earl began to
build a new castle some 7 km (4 miles) up the coast, on top
of the cliffs near Cruden Bay and Port Erroll. Subsequent
earls made various additions and rebuildings. Dr Johnson
and James Boswell visited in 1773, the former finding 'the
prospect here the noblest he had ever seen'. Among later
visitors was writer Bram Stoker, who used the castle as the
model for that of his vampire count in *Dracula* (1897). The
20th Earl was forced to sell in 1916, and the castle
subsequently fell into ruin.

Slaithwaite 'clearing where timber is felled', OScand *slag* 'blow, stroke' + *thveit* 'clearing'.

A small former textile town in the COLNE[3] Valley, in West Yorkshire, 7 km (4 miles) southwest of Huddersfield. Locals pronounce it 'slough'it' (Slough as in the town, not 'sluff' as in Brian Clough), though the pronunciation 'slath'wait' (as in the traditional Yorkshire pronunciation of 'bath' or 'path') is apparently permissible. The long-running television soap opera *Where the Heart Is* is filmed in Slaithwaite, in which it is known as **Skelthwaite**.

Slane Irish *Baile Shláine* 'town of Slanius', a ruler of ancient Meath; alternatively, 'town of fullness'.

A village in County Meath, on the River BOYNE 13 km (8 miles) west of Drogheda, and near to NEWGRANGE. Tradition has it that St Patrick lit a bonfire here at Easter 433 to proclaim the advent of Christianity to all Ireland. St Earc, whom Patrick made a bishop, is said to have founded a monastery here, and to have recited the psalms while immersed in the chilly waters of the Boyne.

Slane was the birthplace of the poet Francis Ledwidge (1891–1917), killed in action in Flanders.

Slaney Irish *Sleine* 'healthy one'.

A river of southeast Ireland, length 100 km (62 miles). It rises on LUGNAQUILLA in the Wicklow Mountains and flows south through County Carlow and then into County Wexford and through the **Slaney Gap** to ENNISCORTHY, the limit of navigation. After Enniscorthy the river becomes tidal and enters the sea at WEXFORD Harbour.

Slapton 'farmstead by a slippery or muddy place', OE *slæp* 'slippery muddy place' + -TON.

A village in Devon, not far from the seaside at Start Bay (*see under* START POINT[1]), about 10 km (6 miles) northeast of Kingsbridge. Caravanners and campers are well catered for here.

Slapton Ley. A lake to the south of Slapton, separated from the sea by a narrow bar of shingle. At about 1.3 sq km (0.5 sq miles) it is the largest natural lake in southwest England. The surrounding marshes (a nature reserve) are home to such rarities as Cetti's warbler and the strapwort.

Slapton Sands. A beach on Start Bay, just to the east of Slapton. It was here on the night of 27/28 April 1944 that a convoy of landing craft carrying US troops on a pre-D-day exercise came under attack, and suffered nearly 1000 casualties. The incident was not made public, and when it was finally revealed in the 1980s it was said to have been the result of an opportunistic attack by German E-boats. It had been hushed up supposedly in case the Germans realized that Normandy was the intended Allied landing place, rather than the Pas-de-Calais. Rumours persist, however, that it was a case of 'friendly fire', perpetrated by

British 'defending' troops who had been issued with live ammunition by mistake.

Slaugham 'homestead or enclosure where sloe grows', OE *slah* 'sloe, blackthorn' + HAM.

A village (pronounced 'slaffəm') in West Sussex (before 1974 in East Sussex), about 8 km (5 miles) east of Horsham. Its formerly fine Elizabethan country house, **Slaugham Place**, is now just a ruin (its staircase now graces LEWES Town Hall).

Slaughden Etymology uncertain, but possibly 'sloe valley', OE *slah* 'sloe, blackthorn' + *denu* 'valley'.

A location on the Suffolk coast, about 1.5 km (1 mile) south of ALDEBURGH, at a point where the River ALDE is only very narrowly separated from the sea. There is a Martello Tower here, built for defence against Napoleonic invasion but now offering holiday accommodation. The poet George Crabbe worked as a labourer at the docks at Slaughden Quay in 1767.

Slaughterford 'ford by the sloe-thorn', OE *slah-thorn* 'sloe, blackthorn' + FORD.

A village in Wiltshire, approximately 8 km (5 miles) west of Chippenham.

Slaughters, the. A collective name for the villages of LOWER SLAUGHTER and UPPER SLAUGHTER in the Cotswolds.

Slea 'muddy stream', OE *slio*.

A river in Lincolnshire, in the FENS. It rises near ANCASTER and flows 28 km (18 miles) eastwards through and beyond SLEAFORD before being linked by KYME EAU with the River WITHAM.

Sleaford 'ford over the River Slea', SLEA + FORD.

A market town in Lincolnshire, in the FENS, on the River Slea, about 30 km (19 miles) west of Boston. Its 13th-century church of St Denys, with its 44-m (144-ft) stone spire (one of the earliest of its type in England), its fine 17th- and 18th-century buildings (including the Carre Hospital, a group of almshouses founded in 1636 by Sir Robert Carre), and the massive late 19th-century Bass Maltings, over 300 m (1000 ft) long, attest to its prosperity over the centuries.

Slea Head Irish *Ceann Sléibhe* 'headland of the mountain'.

The southwestern point of the Dingle Peninsula (*see under* DINGLE), County Kerry. It is a fine viewpoint and is sometimes cited as the most westerly mainland point in Ireland, although this honour goes to GARRAUN POINT, 2.5 km (1.5 miles) to the northwest.

Sleap 'slippery place', OE *slæp*.

A village in Shropshire, on the **Sleap Brook** (a tributary of the River Roden), about 5 km (3 miles) southwest of Wem. It has its own airfield (once an RAF base).

Sleat OScand *sletta* 'smooth or level place'.

The southernmost peninsula of SKYE, once the stronghold of the Macdonalds, deadly enemies of the Macleods to the north. Their seat was at ARMADALE[1]. The **Sound of Sleat** runs between the Sleat peninsula and KNOYDART and MALLAIG on the mainland.

Sleeping Warrior, the. *See* ARRAN.

Sléibhte an Chomaraigh. The Irish name for the COMERAGH MOUNTAINS.

Sléibhte Cnoc Maol Réidh. The Irish name for MWEELREA.

Sléibhte Dhoire Bheitheach. The Irish name for the DERRYVEAGH MOUNTAINS.

Sléibhte Dhoire na Sagart. The Irish name for the DERRYNASAGGART MOUNTAINS.

Sleights OScand *sletta* 'smooth or flat field', with ME -*s* plural.

A large village on the River ESK[5], North Yorkshire, on the north side of the NORTH YORK MOORS, 5 km (3 miles) south of Whitby.

Sleine. The Irish name for the River SLANEY.

Slepe *See* SLEAP.

A village in Dorset, about 5 km (3 miles) north of Wareham.

Sliabh Ára. The Irish name for the ARRA MOUNTAINS.

Sliabh Ardachaidh. The Irish name for the SLIEVEARDAGH HILLS.

Sliabh Bearnach. The Irish name for SLIEVE BERNAGH[1].

Sliabh Bladhma. The Irish name for the SLIEVE BLOOM MOUNTAINS.

Sliabh Dónairt. The Irish name for the SLIEVE DONARD peak.

Sliabh Eachtgha. The Irish name for the SLIEVE AUGHTY MOUNTAINS.

Sliabh Eibhlinne. The Irish name for the SLIEVE FELIM MOUNTAINS.

Sliabh Gamh. The Irish name for the SLIEVE GAMPH range of hills.

Sliabh gCuillinn. The Irish name for the SLIEVE GULLION hill.

Sliabh Liag. The Irish name for the SLIEVE LEAGUE mountain.

Sliabh Luachra Irish 'mountain of the rushes'.

An area spanning eastern KERRY and northwestern CORK, and including such places as Kishkeam, BALLYDESMOND, Gneevguilla, Scarataglen and Knocknaboul. Sliabh Luachra is celebrated for its poets, its storytellers and particularly for its traditional musicians, famous for their polkas and slides; notable names include those of Denis Murphy, Julia Clifford, Tim Billy Murphy and Johnny O'Leary.

Sliabh Mis. The Irish name for the SLIEVE MISH MOUNTAINS.

Sliabh na mBan. The Irish name for the SLIEVENAMON mountain.

Sliabh na Muc. The Irish name for the SLIEVENAMUCK range.

Sliabh Speirín. The Irish name for the SPERRIN MOUNTAINS.

Sliabh Tuaidh. The Irish name for SLIEVETOOEY.

Slieve Anierin. *See under* the IRON MOUNTAINS.

Slieveardagh Hills Irish *Sliabh Ardachaidh* 'mountain of the high field'.

A range of hills rising to over 300 m (about 1000 ft) and straddling counties KILKENNY and TIPPERARY, some 15 km (9 miles) west of the town of Kilkenny. Coal was formerly mined here.

Slieve Aughty Mountains Irish *Sliabh Eachtgha* 'Eachtgha's mountain'.

A range of hills rising to over 300 m (about 1000 ft) in the south of County GALWAY and extending into CLARE.

Slieve Bernagh[1] Irish *Sliabh Bearnach* 'gapped mountain'.

A hill massif (530 m / 1738 ft) in eastern County Clare, rising on the west side of Lough Derg.

Slieve Bernagh[2]. A hill (727 m / 2385 ft) in the MOURNE MOUNTAINS of County Down, 6 km (4 miles) southwest of Newcastle.

Slieve Bloom Mountains Irish *Sliabh Bladhma* 'Bladhma's mountain', named after an ancient warrior who took refuge here; alternatively, 'flame or thunder mountain'.

A range of hills dramatically rising above the Irish MIDLAND bogs along the border of LAOIS and OFFALY. They are made of old red sandstone and quartzite, topped by large swathes of upland bog and great tracts of conifer plantation. The highest point is Arderin (528 m / 1732 ft), and the range is the source of the River BARROW. The **Slieve Bloom Way** is a footpath across the range, length 50 km (31 miles).

Slieve Donard Irish *Sliabh Dónairt* 'Dónart's mountain'; the eponymous Dónart or Domhangart was a disciple of St Patrick, and is said to have built a chapel on the summit and founded a local monastery.

The highest (850 m / 2788 ft) peak in Northern Ireland, in the MOURNE MOUNTAINS, County Down, 3 km (2 miles) southwest of Newcastle.

> I saw an old white goat on the slope of Slieve Donard ...
> Slieve Donard where the herbs of wisdom grow,
> The herbs of the Secret of Life that the old white goat has nibbled ...
>
> Patrick Kavanagh:'The Goat of Slieve Donard', from *Ploughman and Other Poems* (1936)

Slieve Felim Mountains Irish *Sliabh Eibhlinne* 'Eibhlinne's mountain'.

A range of hills rising to 462 m (1515 ft) in County LIMERICK, 20 km (12 miles) east of Limerick itself. The **Slieve Felim Way** is a 30-km (19-mile) walk from Moroe to the southwest of the range northwards through the SILVERMINE MOUNTAINS to Silvermines village. In 1601 Red Hugh O'Donnell, Lord of Tír Chonaill, to avoid Sir George Carew, led his army over the Slieve Felim Mountains en route to KINSALE, where he was to meet with disaster.

Slieve Gamph Irish *Sliabh Gamh* 'mountain of storms'.

A range of hills in western County SLIGO, extending over the border into MAYO. They are also called the **Ox Mountains**, a confusion arising from the similarity of *gamh* and *damh* 'ox'. The highest point is Knockalongy (545 m / 1788 ft), 20 km (12 miles) southwest of Sligo town.

Slieve Gullion Irish *Sliabh gCuillinn* 'mountain of the steep slope'.

A hill (575 m / 1886 ft) in south Armagh, 8 km (5 miles) southwest of NEWRY, on the west side of the GAP OF THE NORTH. It is the highest peak in County Armagh. On its summit is a prehistoric passage grave called Calliagh Birra's House, while on its slopes the 17th-century outlaw Redmond O'Hanlon took refuge.

At Slieve Gullion's Foot. A classic work (1941) on the folklore of Armagh by Michael J. Murphy.

Slieve League Irish *Sliabh Liag* 'mountain of flat stones'.

A mountain (595 m / 1952 ft) in southwestern DONEGAL, on the northwest side of Donegal Bay. On its southern, seaward side there plunges a great face, some 5 km (3 miles) wide, which, though not vertical and intermixed with scree and grass slopes, is sometimes cited as the biggest sea cliff in Europe. Actually, those on ACHILL ISLAND are higher.

> High on the hill-top
> The old King sits;
> He is now so old and grey
> He's nigh lost his wits.
> With a bridge of white mist,
> Columbkill he crosses,
> On his stately journeys
> From Slieveleague to Rosses ...
>
> William Allingham (1824–89): 'The Fairies' ('Up the airy mountain, / Down the rushy glen ...')

Slieve Mish Mountains Irish *Sliabh Mis* 'mountain of Mis'.

A range of hills at the eastern end of the Dingle Peninsula (*see under* DINGLE), County Kerry, some 5 km (3 miles) southwest of Tralee. The highest point is Baurtregaun (851 m / 2791 ft).

Slieve Miskish Mountains Possibly 'mountain of enmity'.

A range of hills rising to over 400 m (1300 ft) at the western end of the BEARA peninsula, County Cork.

Slievenamon Irish *Sliabh na mBan* 'mountain of the women' (referring to the tale of Finn's method of selecting a wife).

An isolated mountain massif (719 m / 2358 ft) in County Tipperary, overlooking the GOLDEN VALE, 10 km (6 miles) northeast of Clonmel. Near the summit is the Rock, a massive cairn thought to cover a prehistoric passage grave. There are many old tales about the mountain, the most famous being that the legendary hero Finn MacCool selected his wife by having all the women who fancied him race up the hill; however, favouring Grainne, he carried her secretly to the summit the night before.

'Maid of Slievenamon, The'. A song by Charles Kickham (1828–82), adopted as the 'national anthem' of Tipperary, and sung particularly when the county hurling and Gaelic football teams are in action.

> Alone, all alone, on a wave-wash'd strand,
> All alone in a crowded hall,
> The hall it is gay, and the waves they are grand
> But my heart is not there at all.
> It flies far away, by night and by day
> To the time and the joys that are gone!
> And I never can forget the sweet maiden I met
> In the valley near Slievenamon.

Slievenamuck Irish *Sliabh na Muc* 'pig mountain'.

A ridge rising to 368 m (1207 ft) in County Tipperary, 3 km (2 miles) south of TIPPERARY[1] itself. There are fine views south over the GLEN OF AHERLOW and the GALTEE MOUNTAINS, and north over the GOLDEN VALE.

Slievetooey Irish *Sliabh Tuaidh* 'mountain of the district'.

A hill (273 m / 895 ft) rising steeply above the cliffs on the south shore of Loughros Beg Bay, County Donegal, 15 km (9 miles) northwest of KILLYBEGS.

> this bare summit
> where fierce weathers pare
> heather and peat down
> to its skeletal bone ...
>
> Francis Harvey: 'Map Lichen on Slievetooey',
> from *In the Light on the Stones* (1978)

Sligachan 'place of shells', Gaelic *slige* 'shell' + *achadh* 'place, field'.

A small settlement on the island of SKYE, Highland (formerly in Inverness-shire), 14 km (8.5 miles) south of Portree, at the junction with the road to Dunvegan. There is little here apart from the **Sligachan Inn**, a traditional climbers' hostelry. It is situated at the foot of **Glen Sligachan**, which extends south along the east side of the main ridge of the CUILLIN. The **River Sligachan** flows into **Loch Sligachan**, a sea loch, a little north of the Inn.

> 'Tell me,' I said, 'where could I buy two pints of foaming shandy in shiny tankards?'
> 'Sligachan,' replied Ling.

'How far?'
'Ten miles.'
'Say it in hours.'
'Six hours.'
This 'free man of the hills' stuff has its tragic moments.

J.E.B. Wright: *Mountain Days in the Isle of Skye* (1934)

Sligeach. The Irish name for SLIGO.

Sligo Irish *Sligeach* 'shelly place'.
The county town of County SLIGO, some 50 km (31 miles) west of Enniskillen, at the head of **Sligo Bay**, an inlet of the Atlantic. Sligo is a seaport and manufacturing town, situated at the mouth of the short River Garavogue, which drains LOUGH GILL just to the east. The area round about has many prehistoric remains (*see*, for example, CARROWMORE *and* KNOCKNAREA).

The ford across the river at Sligo gave the town considerable strategic importance. The first castle was built by the Anglo-Norman Maurice Fitzgerald in 1245, and was destroyed four times that century by the local O'Donnells and O'Conors. In 1310 another Anglo-Norman, Richard de Burgo, the Red Earl of Ulster, built a new castle and rebuilt the town, but his castle was destroyed five years later by O'Donnell. The castle subsequently came into the hands of the O'Conors, until the O'Donnells took it in 1470. It was besieged by the English in 1595, and the town taken by the Parliamentarians in the Civil Wars. The Williamites captured the town in 1689, but it was retaken by the Jacobite leader Patrick Sarsfield.

Nothing remains of the medieval castles, but there are the ruins, largely 15th century, of a Dominican abbey founded by Maurice Fitzgerald in 1253. Many important local leaders were buried here. There are both Protestant and Catholic cathedrals, neither distinguished architecturally.

As a boy the poet W.B. Yeats spent much time in Sligo with his maternal grandfather Pollexfen that 'silent and fierce old man', and his kinder wife, Elizabeth. He later recalled how as a young man in London he

… longed for a sod of earth from some field I knew, something of Sligo to hold in my hand. It was some old race instinct like that of a savage …

The town was fictionalized as **Ballah** in some of Yeats's works, and the area round about is known as 'Yeats Country' (*see under* BENBULBEN, COLLOONEY, DRUMCLIFF, INNIS-FREE, *and* KNOCKNAREA). The poet's brother, the painter Jack Yeats, also spent much of his youth in Sligo.

In Teeling Street in Sligo there is a firm of solicitors with the improbable name of Argue and Phibbs.

Sligo, County. A county in the northwest of Ireland, bounded on the north by Donegal Bay, on the east by Leitrim, on the south by Roscommon and on the west by Mayo. The county town is SLIGO, and its lakes include LOUGH GILL, Lough Arrow and Lough Gara. Sligo is largely low-lying, apart from the SLIEVE GAMPH or Ox Mountains in the west and BENBULBEN in the north.

In Sligo the country was soft; there were turkeys
   Gobbling under sycamore trees
And the shadows of clouds on the mountains moving
   Like browsing cattle at ease.

Louis MacNeice: 'County Sligo'

Lord Sligo. The most colourful figure to hold this title was the 2nd Marquess (1788–1845), a friend of King George IV, Byron and De Quincey. While in Greece in 1812 he stole the columns guarding the entrance of the Treasury of Atreus at Mycenae, and persuaded a British warship to take them and other antique loot back to his home at WESTPORT, County Mayo; for his pains he was sent to jail for four months for bribing British seamen in time of war. On the day of his release his mother married the judge who sentenced him. The 6th Marquess found the pillars in the cellars of Westport House in 1906 and presented them to the British Museum in return for the replicas now at Westport.

Sligo, Leitrim and Northern Counties Railway. A defunct railway company, known as the SL and NC – an acronym interpreted by Sean O'Faolain in *An Irish Journey* (1941) as 'Slow, Lazy and Never Comfortable'.

Slíibhte Ghleann an Ridare. The Irish name for the GLANARUDDERY MOUNTAINS.

Slimbridge 'bridge or causeway over a muddy place', OE *slim* 'slime, mud' + *brycg* 'bridge, causeway'.
A village in Gloucestershire, in the Vale of Berkeley (*see under* BERKELEY), about 13 km (8 miles) west of STROUD. The wetlands between the village and the eastern bank of the SEVERN estuary are the home of the **Slimbridge Wildfowl Trust**, founded in 1946 by Sir Peter Scott. Covering about 48 ha (120 acres), it is Britain's largest wildfowl sanctuary, with huge flocks of geese, ducks and swans and the biggest collection of flamingos in captivity in Europe.

Slioch[1] Gaelic *sleigh* 'spear', but more prosaically it may be Gaelic *sliabhach* 'sloping place'.
An impressive mountain (980 m / 3215 ft) on the north side of LOCH MAREE, Highland (formerly in Ross and Cromarty). From across Loch Maree it appears like a great, square fortress, but its Gaelic name probably derives from the view across Lochan Fada to the northeast, where it appears as an elegant pointed peak.

Slioch and Sgurr Mor
Hang in the air in a white chastity
Of cloud and February snow …

Andrew Young: 'Loch Luichart', from *Winter Harvest* (1933)

Slioch[2]. A village in Aberdeenshire (formerly in Grampian), 4 km (2.5 miles) southeast of Huntly.

Battle of Slioch (December 1307). Two unsuccessful assaults (25 and 31 December) on Robert the Bruce's position here by his enemies, the earls of Buchan and Atholl.

Sloane Square Named in honour of the great physician and naturalist Sir Hans *Sloane* (1660–1753), whose collection of books, manuscripts and curiosities formed the basis of the British Museum (1749) and who owned the land on which the square was built (it was formerly known as *Great Bloody Field*, presumably after a battle here).

A square in southwest London (SW1), in western BEL-GRAVIA, in the borough of KENSINGTON AND CHELSEA, at the northeastern end of the KING'S ROAD. It was laid out in the last quarter of the 18th century. Its most notable present-day occupants are the Royal Court Theatre, home since 1956 of the English Stage Company and famous for its avant-garde and often controversial productions, and the quietly posh department store Peter Jones.

Leading north from the Square by way of Cadogan Square towards KNIGHTSBRIDGE is **Sloane Street**. In its upper reaches it is liberally populated with celebrated and expensive couture houses, and the Harvey Nichols depart-ment store is on its top right-hand corner.

The Square's situation, an elegant stone's throw from Eaton Square and the opulent purlieus of Belgravia and not much further from Chelsea, its demographic profile (*see* **Sloane Ranger** *below*) and the 'exclusivity' of its shops have given it and Sloane Street the unmistakable sheen of wealth and snobbery.

Sloane Square Underground station, on the District and Circle lines, opened in 1868. (Its rumbling trains below can be heard from the stalls of the Royal Court.) The River WESTBOURNE is carried across its platforms and tracks by means of a huge iron pipe.

Sloane, Sloanie. Colloquial abbreviations of *Sloane Ranger*.

> 'A Sloanie has a pony' is … ingrained in the Sloane mind.
>
> Peter York and Ann Barr: *Official Sloane Ranger Handbook* (1982)

Sloane Ranger. A British social stereotype of the late 1970s and 1980s: an upper-class or upper-middle-class and fashionable but conventional young person. The Sloane could certainly be male – clean-shaven, in the attire of a City gent or a slightly fogeyish country squire, and quite possibly called Henry or Toby – but for most people the name probably connoted chiefly the female of the species: resolutely trad., Hermès-scarfed or Alice-banded, invariably Conservative-voting and happier with dogs or horses than people. She might live in SW1, perhaps around Sloane Square (whence the name, punning on the US television righter-of-wrongs, *The Lone Ranger*), or SW3, or even south of the River if daddy's pockets were not quite deep enough,

but her spiritual home remained the country. (The young, ante-royal Diana Spencer was a model Sloane, and her nannying stint an archetype of pre-marital urban life for a Sloane Ranger.)

The term was reputedly coined by Martina Margetts, a sub-editor on *Harpers & Queen*, and introduced to a wider public by the style writer Peter York in an article in the magazine in October 1975. He and Ann Barr elaborated the concept in the *Official Sloane Ranger Handbook* in 1982.

Slochd Gaelic *slochd* 'deep hollow'.

A pass (405 m / 1328 ft) on the A9 Perth–Inverness road, in Highland (formerly in Inverness-shire). It is 12 km (7 miles) northwest of Aviemore, and links the valleys of the FINDHORN and the SPEY.

Slogarie Possibly 'moor of the sheep', Gaelic *sliabh* 'moor' + *g-caora* 'of the sheep'.

A hamlet some 6 km (4 miles) north of Lauriston, formerly in Kirkcudbrightshire, now in Dumfries and Galloway. Long ago a laird of Slogarie was known as 'the Earl of Hell'. According to the story, the laird sired two equally vice-ridden sons, after which his wife died of shame. One night the three of them sat up drinking and playing cards into the early hours of the Sabbath, when the laird capped his sins by burning his dead wife's Bible. The house was promptly struck by lightning and caught fire, and the laird was trapped trying to rescue his money chest. His two sons rode for help, while he burned slowly to death. One son fell over a cliff, and the other collided with a tree, both with fatal consequences.

Sloley 'glade where sloe grows', OE *slah* 'sloe, blackthorn' + -LEY.

A hamlet in Norfolk, about 17.5 km (11 miles) northeast of Norwich.

Slough 'miry place', OE *sloh* 'miry place, slough'.

A town and unitary authority within Berkshire (before 1974 in Buckinghamshire), on the M4, to the north of the River Thames, about 32 km (20 miles) west of London. Hitherto a comparatively small and insignificant village, it grew rapidly after a large trading estate of 280 ha (692 acres), containing some 290 factories, was built here in the 1920s, and it is now a thriving centre of commerce and light industry (the first Mars Bar was manufactured here in 1932). ETON is very nearby (just to the south of the M4) – whence the sarcastic name '**Slough Comprehensive**' for Eton College. Slough was accorded the status of unitary authority (the smallest in England at 26 sq km (10 sq miles)) in 1998. Most of its territory was taken from Buckinghamshire.

As if its lugubrious name and debilitatingly dull town-scape were not enough of a burden, Slough has around its neck the albatross of John Betjeman's now thoroughly hackneyed lines:

Come, friendly bombs, and fall on Slough
It isn't fit for humans now,
There isn't grass to graze a cow
Swarm over, Death!

'Slough', from *Continual Dew* (1937)

Later writers have been equally unimpressed:

Competing with Keats' 'And no birds sing' as the most
depressing phrase in the English language is that which
one hears as the train draws into the station: 'Slough, this
is Slough'.

Bill Murphy: *Home Truths* (2000)

And the observation of the 20th-century High Court
judge Melford Stevenson to a man accused of rape is of a
piece:

I see you come from Slough. It is a terrible place. You can
go back there.

No town could be quite as bleak (nor its inhabitants so
venal or vacuous) as Betjeman pictured them, and it has
some perfectly pleasant open spaces, but picturesqueness
is not on Slough's agenda. It seemed a fitting venue for
Wernham Hogg, David Brent's stationery firm in Ricky
Gervais and Stephen Merchant's groundbreaking BBC
television comedy series *The Office* (2001–3). It also served
as the backdrop for innumerable location scenes in the
Carry On films between 1958 and 1978.

In 2000 the local council announced plans to demolish
the whole of Slough's town centre and replace it with
something nicer. 'We have to admit John Betjeman had a
point', a spokesman said.

David Milsted: *Brewer's Anthology of England and the English*
(2001)

In a reply to a correspondent (15 January 1967)
Betjeman elaborated on the precise nature and cause of his
aversion:

The town of Slough was not, when those verses were
written, such a congestion as it is now and I was most
certainly not thinking of it but of the Trading Estate,
which had originated in a dump that now stretches
practically from Reading to London. The chain stores
were only then just beginning to deface the High Street,
but already the world of 'executives' with little
moustaches, smooth cars and smooth manners and
ruthless methods was planted in my mind along the
fronts of those Trading Estate factories.

John Betjeman: *Letters: Volume Two, 1951 to 1984* (1995)

The first public telegraph line in Britain was laid
between PADDINGTON and Slough in 1843.

It was in COLNBROOK, just to the southeast of Slough,
that the Cox's Orange Pippin apple was developed in the
1820s.

The astronomer Sir William Herschel (discoverer of
Uranus) lived in Slough from 1788 until his death in 1822;
it was here that his son, the equally famous astronomer Sir
John Herschel (1792–1871), was born.

Slug Road, the 'a hollow or pass between hills', Scots, a
variant of *sloc* or *slochd* (*see* SLOCHD).

The pass by which the A957 links Banchory and Stonehaven in Aberdeenshire (formerly in Grampian region). It
is also sometimes just called **the Slug**.

Slyne Head A corruption, with *s-* added, of the second half
of the Irish name *Ceann Léime* 'headland of the leap'.

A headland in County Galway, comprising a series of rocky
islets off the southwestern point of CONNEMARA. There is
a lighthouse on the islet of Illaunamid, established in 1836
and unmanned since 1990. In 1940 the crew of a torpedoed
Norwegian ship arrived at the lighthouse in their lifeboats
after four days at sea.

Sma' Glen, the 'the small valley', Scots.

A narrow, steep-sided defile through which the River
ALMOND[2] passes for some 6 km (4 miles), in the middle of
its course. It is in Perth and Kinross (formerly in Perthshire,
and then in Tayside region), and the pass is the route of
the road north from CRIEFF to ABERFELDY. Its strategic
importance is marked by the siting of a Roman signal
station at the south end of the glen, and General Wade
built a road through the glen in 1730.

The Sma' Glen is the traditional burial place of the
legendary Celtic bard Ossian (*fl.*3rd century AD), as recorded
by Wordsworth in 1803:

In this still place, remote from men,
Sleeps Ossian, in the Narrow Glen;
In this still place, where murmurs on
But one meek Streamlet, only one:
He sang of battles, and the breath
Of stormy war, and violent death;
And should, methinks, when all was past,
Have rightfully been laid at last
Where rocks were rudely heap'd, and rent
As by a spirit turbulent;
Where sights were rough, and sounds were wild,
And every thing unreconciled;
In some complaining, dim retreat,
For fear and melancholy meet;
But this is calm; there cannot be
A more entire tranquillity.

William Wordsworth: 'Glen-Almain, or the Narrow Glen'
(1803)

The massive rock called Ossian's Stone, at the northern end
of the glen, barred the route of Wade's road, and Wade's
men, when they moved it to its present position, found a
prehistoric burial underneath.

Smailholm 'narrow homestead', OE *smæl* 'narrow' + HAM; *Smalham* 1246. The second element has been assimilated to OScand *holmr*.

A small village 10 km (6 miles) east of Melrose, in Scottish Borders (formerly in Roxburghshire). Sir Walter Scott stayed here as a boy, at his grandfather's farm of Sandy Knowe. Nearby is **Smailholm Tower**, an impressive five-storey tower built in 1533 on a rocky outcrop. The place penetrated Scott's imagination:

> And still I thought that shatter'd tower
> The mightiest work of human power.
>
>   Sir Walter Scott: *Marmion* (1808)

Small Dole Originally a field name meaning 'narrow allotment', ME *small* 'narrow', with *dole* from OE *dal* 'allotment, share of land'.

A village in West Sussex, at the foot of the SOUTH DOWNS and close to the River ADUR[1], about 13 km (8 miles) northwest of Brighton.

Small Downs, the *See* the DOWNS.

An anchorage off the East Kent coast, towards the southern end of Sandwich Bay, to the north of the DOWNS.

Small Hythe 'narrow landing-place', OE *smæl* 'narrow' + *hyth* 'landing-place'.

A village in Kent, about 2 km (1 mile) south of Tenterden. In the Middle Ages it was a shipbuilding river port on the River ROTHER[2], but this silted up and Small Hythe dwindled to its present size. It is now on a stream called, unattractively, Reading Sewer.

The nearby early 16th-century **Smallhythe Place** is now a theatre museum. The actress Ellen Terry (1847–1928) once lived there.

Small Isles, the. The collective name for the Inner Hebridean islands of CANNA, RUM, EIGG and MUCK.

Smarden 'woodland pasture where butter is produced', OE *smeoru* 'butter' + *denn* 'woodland pasture'.

A village in Kent, on the River Beult, about 8 km (5 miles) north of Tenterden. It is a very small (and, with its black-and-white timbered houses, picturesque) village, but its church, St Michael's, is huge. Built in the 14th century, apparently after the granting of a market licence led to the anticipation of local economic growth, it is nicknamed 'the Barn of Kent'. Its wooden roof is 11 m (36 ft) high.

Smeeth 'smithy', OE *smiththe*.

A village in Kent, beside the M20, about 8 km (5 miles) southeast of Ashford.

Smerwick Possibly an OScand name, 'butter bay' *smjor* + *vik* (referring to the local produce), or 'small bay' *sma* + *vik*.

A village in County Kerry, some 50 km (31 miles) west of Overlee. It is on the west shore of **Smerwick Harbour**, a bay on the northwestern coast of the Dingle Peninsula (*see*

under DINGLE). In 1579 a force of 80 Spaniards landed here with a papal nuncio in support of the Desmond rebellion, and established a strongpoint within the ancient Dún an Óir (Irish 'golden fort'), known by them as Fort-del-Oro. The following year they were reinforced by 600 Italian soldiers, but on 10 November the fort was captured and its garrison (apart from the officers) was massacred by an English force under Lord Deputy Grey and Admiral Winter; Sir Walter Raleigh and Edmund Spenser are said by some to have been on the English side in this unpleasantness. The affair features in Charles Kingsley's Don-bashing adventure, *Westward Ho!* (1855), in which the author smugly writes:

> Many years passed before a Spaniard set foot again in Ireland.

Smethwick 'smiths' dwelling or building', OE *smeotha* possessive plural form of *smith* 'smith' + *wic* 'dwelling, building' (*see* WICK).

A town (pronounced 'smethick') within the metropolitan borough of SANDWELL, to the west of Birmingham (before 1974 in Staffordshire). In 1966 it became part of the conurbation of WARLEY. Begrimed by nearly two and a half centuries of industry (Matthew Boulton, James Watt and William Murdock the pioneers with their Soho Works of the second half of the 18th century, Guest, Keen and Nettlefold the big local firm), it is spiritually very much part of the BLACK COUNTRY.

Its name took a long time to recover from the political scandal of 1964 when, in the general election, the Conservative candidate Peter Griffiths took the local seat from Labour's Patrick Gordon Walker after an openly racist campaign carrying the slogan 'If you want a nigger for a neighbour, vote Labour'. The new prime minister Harold Wilson memorably and controversially described Griffiths, in a speech in the House of Commons (4 November 1964), as a 'Parliamentary leper', and government legislation to monitor racism began in this period.

The legendary seam and swing bowler Sydney Barnes (1873–1967), one of the greatest bowlers in cricket history (he took 189 test wickets at an average of 16.43 in just 27 test matches), was born in Smethwick. Barnes remains the only man to be picked for England whilst playing league and minor counties cricket (*see* STAFFORDSHIRE).

Smisby 'the smith's farmstead', OScand *smithr* 'smith' + -BY.

A village in Derbyshire, about 16 km (10 miles) south of Derby, close to the Leicestershire border.

Smithfield 'smooth field, level field', OE *smethe* 'smooth' + *feld* (*see* FIELD).

A district in the City of LONDON (EC1), to the north of ST PAUL'S[1] Cathedral, between Aldersgate Street to the east and Farringdon Street to the west. In the Middle Ages it was an area of flat, open land (whence its name) just outside the City Walls of London. Already by the late 12th century it was well known as the weekly venue of a horse market, and from 1133 the annual Bartholomew Fair was held here, originally as a cloth fair but later as a place of general (and fairly boisterous) entertainment – it was the setting of Ben Jonson's play *Bartholomew Fair* (1614); it was finally suppressed by the authorities in 1855, on account of its debauchery. The space was also used for tournaments, and in 1381 the fateful meeting between Richard II and the Peasants' Revolt leader Wat Tyler took place here (Tyler was stabbed by the Lord Mayor and later hanged nearby). Indeed Smithfield served as a place of public execution for over 400 years: the gallows were moved to TYBURN[2] in 1388, but heretics and 'witches' continued to be burned at Smithfield for a further 200 years and more. They include 200 victims in Mary Tudor's brief reign; they are often known as the **Smithfield Martyrs**, and there is now a 'Marian Martyrs' Monument' at Smithfield.

Smithfield's role as a livestock market had continued throughout (in the 18th century, cattle from as far away as the Scottish HIGHLANDS were driven hundreds of miles to Smithfield), but by the middle of the 19th century it was becoming impractical to bring live animals into the centre of London and slaughter them there. These operations were moved out to ISLINGTON, and Smithfield's new status was cemented with the opening of the London Central Meat Market here in 1868. It remains London's largest meat market, and the name '**Smithfield**' is now synonymous with it. The market's splendid premises, a Victorian palace of meat designed by Henry Jones, are situated by a street and square named **West Smithfield** (to distinguish them from **East Smithfield**, a completely separate entity, a street just to the east of the Tower of London). The sights and sounds of early-morning Smithfield, though a far cry from the stench and carnage of the 19th century, are not for vegetarians, or even faint-hearted meat-eaters. The rows upon rows of red-and-white carcases have sculptural qualities to give Damien Hirst pause; they are counterpointed by the red-stained white coats of their acolytes, the porters, whose gory exertions are recognized in the provision of licences for early-breakfast opening hours at the local pubs.

> And he hires a barrow and goes to Smithfield
> at dawn; at chill dawn sees the cold meat,
> shrouded in white nets borne on men's shoulders;
> meat from Argentines; from haired and red pelted
> hogs and bullocks. ...
>
> All in white like surgeons go the butchers of
> Smithfield, handling the shrouded cadavers;
> the stark and frozen corpses that shall lie like
> mummies in the ice house till the Sunday fire revives

them and they drip juice into the big plate to revive church goers.

> Virginia Woolf: 'Ode Written Partly in Prose on Seeing the Name of Cutbush Above a Butcher's Shop in Pentonville' (1934)

St Bartholomew's Hospital (Bart's), the oldest hospital in London, founded in 1123, is on West Smithfield square.

The architect Inigo Jones (1573–1652) was born in Smithfield.

There are towns called Smithfield in the USA (Nebraska, North Carolina (birthplace of the actress Ava Gardner (1922–90)), Pennsylvania, Texas, Utah, Virginia (source of Smithfield ham, a special local cure), West Virginia) and in South Africa (where it gives its name to a late Stone Age culture, the remains of which were found nearby).

Smithfield bargain. A slang term from the late 17th century to the mid-19th for a deal in which the buyer is cheated (the reputation of Smithfield vendors is confirmed by another contemporary expression, **sold like a bullock in Smithfield**, meaning 'badly cheated'). It subsequently came to be applied also to a marriage of convenience, based on financial interest (also known as a **Smithfield match**).

Smith's End 'area belonging to the smith or to the Smith family', occupational name *Smith* + ME *ende* 'end, district, area'.

A village in Hertfordshire, about 5 km (3 miles) southeast of Royston.

Smith Square Probably after Henry *Smith*, former owner of the land on which it was built.

A square in the City of Westminster (SW1), leading off the western side of MILLBANK and just to the south of the Houses of Parliament. It was laid out around 1726. It has long had contrasting political associations, and at one time held the headquarters of the Conservative, Labour and Liberal parties. Until 1980 the Labour Party was here at Transport House, the former headquarters of the Transport and General Workers' Union, and the Conservatives vacated their red-brick neo-Georgian premises at No. 32 in 2004.

St John's, Smith Square was originally a church – a magnificent Baroque one by Thomas Archer, built between 1713 and 1728. An early nickname for it was 'Queen Anne's footstool', after an apocryphal story that Queen Anne, when interviewing Archer, kicked over her footstool and said 'Make it like that', the four upturned legs representing the church's towers (in reality, the building began to settle during construction, and to stabilize it a tower and lantern turret were added at each corner; Lord Chesterfield likened the church to an elephant thrown on its back with its feet in the air). It was gutted in the Second World War, and subsequently resurrected as a concert venue.

Smoke, the. In colloquial and regional British English, a name applied to LONDON: in post-Clean Air Act days, when the capital is no longer choked by coal smoke, the force of the epithet may not seem so obvious, although the more insidious fumes of traffic do their best to preserve its relevance.

It appears to have had its beginnings (generally in the phrase 'the big smoke') in the English used by Australian Aborigines in the first half of the 19th century, applied to any large city, and it continues to be a characteristically Australian English usage, but it was well established in Britain too by the end of the century:

> Till that last awful winter! ... when the farmers had been mostly ruined, and half the able-bodied men of Mellor had tramped 'up into the smoke', as the village put it, in search of London work.
>
>   Mrs Humphry Ward: *Marcella* (1894)

For the earlier, Scottish equivalent, *see* AULD REEKIE.

Smoo Cave Probably from OScand *smuga* 'a narrow cleft', from the verb *smjuga* 'to creep', presumably reflecting how one might move in such a place.

A large cave on the north coast of Highland (formerly in Sutherland), 2 km (1.2 miles) east of DURNESS. There are three chambers, the largest of which is 60 m (200 ft) long by 35 m (120 ft) high. Into the second chamber a waterfall plunges through one of the holes in the roof, which were apparently made by the Devil and three witches. They had come to claim the 1st Lord Reay, the so-called Wizard of Reay (*see under* REAY), who was exploring the cave. He noticed that something was amiss when his dog returned from the inner chamber without any hair (a sure sign of devilry), and just as Auld Nick was about to claim him a cock announced the dawn, obliging the Prince of Darkness and his companions to make a rapid exit through the roof of the cave.

Snaefell 'snowy mountain', OScand *snær* 'snow' + *fjall* 'fell, mountain'.

The highest point (621 m / 2037 ft) on the ISLE OF MAN. Its dignity is compromised by the railway leading to its summit (built in 1895), where, even more regrettably, there is a café.

Snailbeach 'snail valley' (in contrast to nearby *Wagbeach* 'quaking valley'), ModE *snail* + OE *bæce* 'valley of a stream'.

A village in Shropshire, about 16 km (10 miles) southwest of Shrewsbury.

Snailwell 'spring or stream infested with snails', OE *snægl* 'snail' + *wella* 'spring, stream'.

A village in Cambridgeshire, about 3 km (2 miles) north of Newmarket.

Snáimh-dá-en. The Irish name for SWIM-TWO-BIRDS.

Snake Pass Presumably because it winds like a snake; a recent coinage.

A pass in Derbyshire, about 5 km (3 miles) east of GLOSSOP, which takes the traveller via the A57 into the valley of the River ASHOP, and down to LADYBOWER RESERVOIR in the heart of the HIGH PEAK. The steep winding road going up to the pass from Glossop is called **Snake Road**. To the north of the pass is Bleaklow, and to the south is Featherbed Top, on the south side of which, between it and KINDER SCOUT, is **Snake Path**.

Snape 'boggy piece of land', OE *snæp*.

A village in Suffolk, on the River ALDE, about 5 km (3 miles) west of Aldeburgh. Its small port still does a modest trade in grain, and its traditional business is the malting of barley: Elizabeth Garrett Anderson's father (*see* ALDEBURGH) was a Snape maltster, and the **Snape Maltings**, a 19th-century barley store, has since 1967 been the main concert hall for the Aldeburgh Festival (it was destroyed by fire in 1969, but subsequently rebuilt).

Snaresbrook The origin of the first part of the name is uncertain: it may be a personal name, or it may be from ME *snare* 'snare or trap for catching wild animals or birds'. The second part is from OE *broc* 'brook' (referring to a small stream flowing into the River RODING).

A district of northeast London (E11, E18), in the borough of REDBRIDGE, to the east of Walthamstow and to the north of Wanstead. It has some fine 18th- and 19th-century houses and verdant open spaces.

Its separate identity was preserved by the opening of a mainline railway station here in 1856, under the name 'Snaresbrook & Wanstead', and confirmed in 1947 when this began to be used by Central line trains and its name was changed to plain 'Snaresbrook'.

Snargate 'gate or gap where snares for animals are placed', OE *sneare* 'snare' + *geat* 'gate, gap'.

A village in Kent, at the western edge of ROMNEY MARSH, about 11 km (7 miles) northwest of Romney.

Snave Perhaps 'spits or strips of land', OE *snafa*.

A hamlet in Kent, on ROMNEY MARSH, about 8 km (5 miles) northwest of Romney.

Sneep, the. *See under* DERWENT[2].

Snetterton Perhaps 'Snytra's farm', OE male personal name *Snytra* + -TON.

A village in Norfolk, about 15 km (9 miles) northeast of Thetford. Just to the south, on the far side of the A11, is Snetterton motor-racing circuit.

Snettisham 'Snæt's or Sneti's homestead', OE *Snœtes* or *Snetis* possessive forms of male personal names *Snœt* or *Sneti* + HAM.

A village in Norfolk, on the eastern side of the WASH, about 8 km (5 miles) south of Hunstanton.

Snettisham Treasure. An Iron Age treasure-hoard discovered near Snettisham. A ploughman working in a field here in 1948 turned up a metal object which his foreman pronounced to be a bit of a brass bedstead. It turned out to be a gold torque and the beginning of the discovery of the richest hoard of its period in Britain. Further finds have been made over the years, including 50 torques and 70 bracelets, and in 1991 the site yielded a treasure trove of 1st-century BC Celtic coins. The reason for the location of the hoard is a mystery, as there is no sign of any contemporary settlement. The treasure is now in the British Museum.

Snig's End 'area belonging to the Snig family', ME surname *Snig*, with *ende* 'end, district, area'.
A village in Gloucestershire, to the west of the River SEVERN, about 11 km (7 miles) southwest of Tewkesbury.

Snitterby Probably 'Snytra's farmstead or village', OE male personal name *Snytra* + -BY.
A village in Lincolnshire, about 13 km (8 miles) northwest of Market Rasen.

Snitterfield 'open land frequented by snipe', OE *snite* 'snipe' + *feld* (*see* FIELD).
A village in Warwickshire, about 5 km (3 miles) north of Stratford-upon-Avon. It was the early home of John Shakespeare, father of William.

> Sir Silas looked red and shiny as a ripe strawberry on a Snitterfield tile.
>
> Walter Savage Landor: *Citation and Examination of William Shakespeare Touching Deer-Stealing* (1834)

Snodhill Probably 'snowy hill', OE *snawede* 'snowy' + *hyll* 'hill'.
A hamlet in Herefordshire (before 1998 in Hereford and Worcester, before 1974 in Herefordshire), about 21 km (13 miles) west of Hereford.

Snodland 'cultivated land associated with Snodd', OE male personal name *Snodd* + -ING + land.
A village in Kent, on the River MEDWAY[1], about 8 km (5 miles) southwest of Rochester.

Snoreham Probably 'homestead or enclosure by a rough hill', OE *snor* 'rough hill' + HAM.
A hamlet in Essex, about 8 km (5 miles) southeast of Maldon.

Snoring. *See* GREAT SNORING; LITTLE SNORING.

Snowdon 'snow hill', OE *snaw* 'snow' + *dun* (*see* DOWN, -DON).
The highest mountain (1085 m / 3560 ft) in England and Wales, and one of the SEVEN WONDERS OF NORTH WALES.

> Snowden Hill is a monstrous height, and according to its name, had snow on the top in the beginning of June; and perhaps had so till the next June, that is to say, all the year.
>
> Daniel Defoe: *A Tour Through the Whole Island of Great Britain* (1724–6)

Snowdon is in the heart of SNOWDONIA (to which it gives its name), in Gwynedd (formerly in Caernarvonshire), 19 km (12 miles) south of Bangor. Its Welsh name is **Yr Wyddfa** ('the tomb'), from the legend that the mountain is a cairn built over the grave of a giant killed by King Arthur. It is also known as ERYRI ('the high land'), although this name is also applied to all the mountains of SNOWDONIA collectively.

> I must not fail to tell you about the mountains which are called Eryri by the Welsh and by the English Snowdon, that is the Snow Mountains ... At the very top of these mountains two lakes are to be found, each of them remarkable in its own way. One has a floating island, which moves about and is often driven to the opposite side by the force of the winds ... The second lake ... abounds in three different kinds of fish, eels, trout and perch, and all of them have only one eye, the right one being there but not the left.
>
> Giraldus Cambrensis (Gerald of Wales): *Itinarium Cambriae* (12th century), translated by L. Thorpe

The lakes referred to are Glaslyn and Llyn Llydaw, and a number of other legends attach to them:

> Old wrinkled gossip says
> No bird dare fly across this craggy llyn,
> Fearing the anger of the doom-led queen
> Who to its black depth took her loneliness.
>
> Stanley Snaith: 'Lliddaw', from *Stormy Harvest* (1944)

The Snowdon massif consists of five peaks: the main summit, Yr Wyddfa Fawr ('the great tomb', 1085 m / 3560 ft), Crib-y-Ddysgl ('the bowl crest', Welsh *crib* 'crest, summit' + *y* 'the' + *ddysgl* 'dish, bowl'; 1065 m / 3493 ft; not regarded as a separate summit), CRIB GOCH (921 m / 3021 ft), LLIWEDD (898 m / 2946 ft), and Yr Aran ('the high place', 747 m / 2451 ft).

The **Snowdon Horseshoe**, a favourite route with the more energetic sort of hillwalker, starts at PEN-Y-PASS at the head of the LLANBERIS Pass, takes in a scramble over Crib Goch, then the main summit, and finally circles back round over Lliwedd. Other walking routes on this east/northeast side include the Pyg Track (*see* PEN-Y-GWRYD) and the Miner's Track, which passes by old copper workings. On the south side, from the GWYNANT VALLEY, is the Watkin Path, named after Sir Edward Watkin, a Victorian railway entrepreneur who constructed the path; this was opened by W.E. Gladstone in 1892, the event being commemorated on a plaque on an adjacent boulder (Gladstone's Rock). On the west side are the Pitt's Head Track from Pitt's Head Rock and the **Snowdon Ranger Track** (*see below*). The route from Llanberis is less popular and the least interesting, but is used by those heading for the impressive north-facing verticalities of Clogwyn d'ur Arddu ('the black cliff'), familiarly known as 'Cloggy', and the forcing ground of many generations of top British rock climbers. The route from Llanberis is also that taken by the narrow-gauge rack-and-pinion **Snowdon Mountain Railway** constructed in 1896 and taking tourists all the way to the summit to drink tea and eat buns in a concrete café; those who have reached the summit on foot would do well to avert their eyes (although in the early 21st century the excrescence was thankfully clad in native rock).

A more mysterious summit experience is recorded by the Rev. Francis Kilvert (noted diarist, and a curate in Wales from 1865 to 1872; *see under* CLYRO), who reported the belief that anyone spending a night on the summit of Snowdon 'will be found in the morning either dead or a madman or a poet' (the same was said of CADER IDRIS).

One poet who climbed Snowdon at night to see the dawn from its top and found himself moonstruck instead was Wordsworth. High on the mountain he had advanced 'with eager pace' ahead of his guide and friend …

> When at my feet the ground appear'd to brighten,
> And with a step or two seem'd brighter still;
> Nor had I time to ask the cause of this,
> For instantly a Light upon the turf
> Fell like a flash: I looked about, and lo!
> The Moon stood naked in the Heavens, at height
> Immense above my head, and on the shore
> I found myself of a huge sea of mist,
> Which, meek and silent, rested at my feet;
> A hundred hills their dusky backs upheaved
> All over this still Ocean, and beyond,
> Far, far beyond, the vapours shot themselves,
> In headlands, tongues, and promontory shapes,
> Into the Sea, the real Sea, that seem'd
> To dwindle, and give up its majesty,
> Usurp'd upon as far as sight could reach.
>
> William Wordsworth: *The Prelude*, Book XIII, Conclusion

In 2003 a Mr Paul McKelvey, 35, carried a full-sized fridge 160 km (100 miles) from Liverpool to the summit of Snowdon, in aid of a children's hospice.

Lord Snowdon. Anthony Armstrong-Jones (b.1930), photographer, who, having a Welsh name, was made 1st Earl of Snowdon on his marriage to the late Princess Margaret in 1960. They divorced in 1978.

Snowdon lily. A rare lily, *Lloydia serotina*, restricted to rocky places in the mountains of Snowdonia. Its delicate white flowers appear in May.

Snowdon pudding. A steamed pudding involving breadcrumbs, suet, raisins, lemon zest and marmalade. In Welsh it is **Pwdin Eryri**.

Snowdon Ranger. A title given to Snowdon mountain guides in the 19th century:

> 'And what profession does he follow?' said I; 'is he a fisherman?' 'Fisherman!' said the elderly gentleman contemptuously, 'not I. I am the Snowdon Ranger.' 'And what is that?' said I. The elderly man tossed his head

proudly, and made no reply. 'A ranger means a guide, sir,' said the younger man, 'my father-in-law is generally termed the Snowdon Ranger because he is a tip-top guide, and he has named the house after him the Snowdon Ranger. He entertains gentlemen in it who put themselves under his guidance in order to ascend Snowdon and to see the country.'

> George Borrow: *Wild Wales* (1862)

(Wordsworth also refers to his guide as '… the Shepherd, who by ancient right / Of office is the Stranger's usual guide'.) The term gave rise to the name of the **Snowdon Ranger Track**, this seeming to be the most popular route with the 19th-century guides.

Snowdonia From SNOWDON, the highest peak in the range. A mountainous area of northwest Wales, predominantly in Gwynedd (formerly in Caernarvonshire and Merioneth). The Welsh name for the range is **Eryri** ('the high land'), although sometimes this name is restricted to just the Snowdon massif.

In a narrow definition, Snowdonia is centred on SNOWDON, and also includes the CARNEDDAU, the GLYDERS, MOEL SIABOD, CNICHT, the MOELWYNS, MOEL HEBOG and the NANTLLE RIDGE. All the WELSH THREE-THOUSANDERS are contained within this area. However, the larger **Snowdonia National Park** (created in 1951) also incorporates mountains to the south and southeast, including the RHINOGS, CADER IDRIS, ARENNIG FAWR and the ARANS.

> These mountains are indeed so like the Alps …
>
> Daniel Defoe: *A Tour Through the Whole Island of Great Britain* (1724–6)

> It was so dismal and gloomy on these mountains, and so were my spirits. I felt as if we were wandering under the sea …
>
> Julius Rodenberg: 'Caernarvon and Llanberis' (1856)

In hospital in Poona, India, during the Second World War, the soldier-poet Alun Lewis imagined:

> … the great mountains, Dafydd and Llewelyn,
> Plynlimmon, Cader Idris and Eryri
> Threshing the darkness back from head and fin …
>
> Alun Lewis: 'In Hospital: Poona' (Carnedd Dafydd and Carnedd Llewelyn are the two highest peaks of the Carneddau; for the other names, see the relevant entries.)

Milk-white Snowdonian antelope, the. Percy Bysshe Shelley's description, in 'Letter to Maria Gisborne' (written in 1820), of Jane Gryffydh, daughter of the rector of Maentwrog in the Vale of Ffestiniog in southern Snowdonia. She had married his friend Thomas Love Peacock in 1819. Shelley described Peacock himself in the poem as 'this cameleopard'. In 1826, after the death of their third daughter, Jane suffered a mental breakdown and never fully recovered.

Snowdonia hawkweed. First identified by Caernarfon-born botanist John Griffith in the 1880s, the Snowdonia hawkweed (*Hieracium snowdoniense*) was declared a separate species in 1955, two years after its last sighting. It was thought extinct until 2002 (having proved particularly palatable to sheep), when it was rediscovered growing on a mountainside above BETHESDA.

Snowfield. The fictional town in George Eliot's *Adam Bede* (1859), thought to be based on WIRKSWORTH.

Snowshill 'hill where snow lies long', OE *snawes* possessive form of *snaw* 'snow' + *hyll* 'hill'.

A village in Gloucestershire, in the COTSWOLDS, about 5 km (3 miles) south of Broadway. The nearby **Snowshill Manor**, a Tudor manor house, once belonged to Charles Paget Wade, a magpie-like collector of anything and everything that took his fancy, including clocks, toys, bicycles, orientalia, musical instruments and craft tools. Wade left the house and its contents to the National Trust in 1951.

Soar An OCelt or pre-Celtic river name, perhaps meaning 'flowing one'.

A river in Warwickshire, Leicestershire and Nottinghamshire. It rises just within the borders of Warwickshire and flows 65 km (40 miles) through LEICESTER and LOUGHBOROUGH to just north of Ratcliffe-on-Soar where it joins the River TRENT[1] 14 km (9 miles) southwest of NOTTINGHAM[1]. It is navigable as far as Leicester.

Soay[1] 'sheep island', OScand *sauthr* 'sheep' + *ey* 'island' (*see* -AY).

A small island (pronounced 'so-ay' or 'soy') 1 km (0.6 mile) off the south coast of SKYE, Highland (formerly in Inverness-shire). It was bought by Gavin Maxwell (who later wrote *Ring of Bright Water*) in 1946 as the base for a shark fishery, an experience he wrote about in *Harpoon at a Venture* (1952). In 1953 all but one of the families asked to be moved from the island, and were resettled on MULL. Subsequently new settlers arrived on the island, which boasts the world's first solar-powered telephone exchange.

Soay[2]. A small island in the ST KILDA group.

Soay sheep. A goat-like feral sheep found only on Soay until some were brought to the mainland in the 1930s. The brown wool does not need to be shorn, but can instead be pulled out. The Soay sheep was common in Iron Age Europe, but was ousted by the so-called Roman sheep. It was probably introduced to Soay by the Vikings.

Soberton 'southern grange or outlying farm', OE *suth* 'south' + *bere-tun* 'grange, outlying farm' (*see* BARTON BENDISH).

A village in Hampshire, about 17.5 km (11 miles) northeast of Southampton.

Sodom and Begorrah. *See under* ABBEY THEATRE.

Sodor and Man 'southern isles and the ISLE OF MAN'; the addition of *Man* came about possibly as a mistranscription in the 17th century, as before then the name *Suthreys* – OScand *suthr* 'southern' + *ey* 'island' (*see* -AY) – denoted the Hebrides and the Isle of Man (southern in relation to Orkney and Shetland).

A diocese dating from perhaps the 11th century. Between 1152 and 1542 it was under the control of the Archbishop of Trondheim, but was then returned to the care of the Archbishop of York.

Sodor. A fictional British island (inspired by the name of the diocese), with a decidedly Celtic look, known to millions of children (and former children) as the setting for Thomas the Tank Engine and his adventures with his fellow trains on the Fat Controller's rail network. The stories, written from the mid-1940s by the Rev. W.V. Awdry, and then continued by his son Christopher in the 1980s, have become, under franchise, a worldwide phenomenon. They spawned, amid much else, a television series (narrated by ex-Beatle Ringo Starr) and a feature film.

Soho From the ME and early ModE hunting cry *soho*, from Anglo-Norman (the second element recurs in *tally-ho*). The derivation is either directly from the hunting field (hunting is recorded in the area from the mid-16th century) or perhaps via a public house of that name. The notion that the name came from the rallying cry of the Duke of Monmouth's supporters in the uprising of 1685 is chronologically untenable, as it dates from over 50 years before that (the fact that the duke had a mansion in Soho Square presumably lent credence to it).

A district in the WEST END[1] of London (W1), bounded to the north by OXFORD STREET, to the east by CHARING CROSS Road and to the southeast by LEICESTER SQUARE. In the Middle Ages it was farmland, but in 1536 it was sold to the Crown. It came to be used as a hunting ground, particularly for hares, and various grandees' houses arose in the area. Then in the 1670s residential development began to accelerate, accompanied by an influx of Huguenots after the revocation of the Edict of Nantes in 1685. By the middle of the 18th century it was almost exclusively a French quarter, a circumstance which attracted the artists and bohemians who have been part of Soho's scenery ever since (when the French poet Verlaine ran off with fellow poet Rimbaud in 1872, it was to Soho that they went). In the 1860s and 1870s Germans and Italians came to settle, followed by Swiss, Russians, Poles, Hungarians, Greeks and others, and the area cemented its reputation as a centre for foreign restaurants and delicatessen shops and a haunt of gastronomes. From the 1940s, Soho's sleazy Bohemianism attracted a rackety cast of frequently drunken writers, artists, etc. that included Francis Bacon, Dylan Thomas, Julian Maclaren-Ross, Rayner Heppenstall and Colin MacInnes (whose trilogy of London novels, *City of Spades*, *Absolute Beginners* and *Mr Love and Justice* (1957–60), captured the spirit and atmosphere of 1950s Soho). The pubs and drinking clubs that were their haunts included the Colony Club (run by 'the foul-mouthed and appropriately named Muriel Belcher' – Ed Glinert, *A Literary Guide to London* (2000)), the French House and the Coach and Horses (hang-out of the permanently sozzled journalist Jeffrey Bernard and the venue of the fortnightly lunches held by the Soho-based *Private Eye* magazine).

Soho also had its fair share of prostitutes, and after the Second World War organized crime moved in in a big way (with significant contributions from Maltese gangsters), running brothels, striptease parlours, sex cinemas, pornographic bookshops and clip-joints, operating protection rackets, and converting Soho into London's number-one red-light district. Westminster City Council did its unconvincing best to stamp out the vice, but it was not until the 1980s that market forces began to reclaim at least half of Soho, to the east of WARDOUR STREET (home of British film production), for a non-dirty-mac'd clientele. Restaurants and bars found a young market, and roads such as Old Compton Street, Dean Street, Frith Street and Greek Street (the last two leading northwards to **Soho Square** (*see below*)) attracted their own café society (with a notable gay component). Meanwhile to the south of Shaftesbury Avenue a Chinatown had established itself, centred on Gerrard Street. The relaxed Groucho Club (founded 1985, named in honour of Groucho Marx) in Dean Street has become the unofficial headquarters for the Soho, and indeed London-wide, publishing, artistic and media world.

To the west of Wardour Street, enlivened by the bustle of Berwick Street fruit and veg market and the pizzazz of Paul Raymond's Revue Bar (until 2003, when it went into administration), lies an unreconstructed Soho, its dingy doorways offering new 'models' up the stairs.

Among the area's more notable past residents are William Blake, William Hazlitt and Karl Marx. In 1925 John Logie Baird made the world's first successful transmission of true television from a building in Frith Street, Soho (opposite what is now Ronnie Scott's jazz club, which was founded in 1958).

Mid Manhattan, New York City, has a neighbourhood called *SoHo*, which originated as an artists' colony in the 1960s. Its name was presumably coined with *Soho* in mind, but is formally an acronym formed from '*s*outh of *Ho*uston Street'. (Its clone, *NoHo*, is appropriately to the north of Houston Street.)

Adrift in Soho. A novel (1961) by Colin Wilson about a young man's search for experience among the artists, beatniks, tarts and assorted deadbeats of 1950s Soho.

Gorilla of Soho, The. A German-made thriller (1968), set in London, about a gorilla-suited murderer whose victims end up in the Thames.

Soho Nailbomber, the. The epithet attached to the now-imprisoned David Copeland, who in 1999 planted nail bombs outside the Admiral Duncan, a Soho public house with a mainly gay clientele, killing three people. He also caused explosions in Brixton and Brick Lane. He was motivated by hatred of homosexuals and non-Whites.

Soho Square. The only formal square that lies within Soho. Constructed in the 1680s, it was first called King Square (the original stone statue of Charles II, now rather the worse for wear, still graces the square, albeit no longer in its central position). Originally the site of aristocratic town houses (almost all now gone), and later of embassies, today it is home to media groups (Paul McCartney's office, the *Harry Potter* publisher Bloomsbury, and film companies) and other offices. The gardens remain popular with the lunchtime *al fresco* sandwich-eaters and summer sunbathers, sometimes one and the same.

Soho tapestry. A type of tapestry produced in Soho in the late 17th and 18th centuries.

See also GREEK STREET.

Soke of Peterborough. *See under* PETERBOROUGH.

Soldier's Leap, the. *See under* KILLIECRANKIE.

Sole From the name of a submerged sandbank, Great *Sole* Bank.

A sea area in the shipping forecast. It is in the eastern Atlantic, to the south of Ireland, between SHANNON and FASTNET to the north and FITZROY to the south.

Sole Bay *Sole* probably 'muddy pool', OE *sol*.

The part of the Suffolk coast overlooked by SOUTHWOLD. It was a principal anchorage for the British navy in the 18th century.

Battle of Sole Bay (28 May 1672). The last naval engagement of the Third Anglo-Dutch war, in which a combined Anglo-French force commanded by James, Duke of York (later James II) fought its Dutch opponents under Admiral de Ruyter. The Dutch fleet was the more badly damaged, but the English also lost a lot of ships and had to retreat to port; neither side could claim decisive victory. It is sometimes known as the 'Battle of Southwold'.

Solent, the A pre-English name of uncertain origin and meaning: perhaps 'place of cliffs'.

The channel between the ISLE OF WIGHT and the coast of HAMPSHIRE:

> Betwixt the foreland and the firm [*terra firma*],
> She [the Isle of Wight] hath that narrow Sea, which we
>   the Solent term.
>
>   Michael Drayton: *Poly-Olbion* (1612–22)

At its widest it is 6 km (4 miles) across. In shape it is an inverted chevron, with Southampton Water (*see under* SOUTHAMPTON) at its apex; opposite it is COWES. Its eastern arm is dominated by Portsmouth Harbour (*see under* PORTSMOUTH), and contains the SPITHEAD naval roadstead. The shipyards on the creek-cut Hampshire shore of its western arm turned the oaks of the NEW FOREST into ships of the line for the Royal Navy.

The great ocean liners have navigated the Solent on their way to and from Southampton, and it is famous for its yacht races.

'Solent' Class. The standard type of motor lifeboat in service with the Royal National Lifeboat Institution in the middle and late 20th century.

Solent Breezes A poetical evocation of the local climate.

A holiday village on the east coast of Southampton Water (*see under* SOUTHAMPTON), about 2.5 km (1.5 miles) southeast of the mouth of the River HAMBLE. Developed in the 1960s, it is a permanent caravan site for yachtsmen and holidaymakers, inhabited only in the summer season.

Solihull Probably 'muddy hill', OE *sylig, solig* 'muddy' + *hyll* 'hill'. Alternatively the first element could represent OE *sulig* 'pigsty'.

A town and metropolitan borough in the West Midlands, on the GRAND UNION CANAL and just within the M42, now effectively a southeastern suburb of BIRMINGHAM. Before 1974 it was in Warwickshire.

Birmingham Airport and the National Exhibition Centre are in Solihull, and after the Second World War it became the home of Rover cars (and subsequently also of Land Rover).

The World Cup-winning England rugby union captain Martin Johnson was born here in 1970.

William Camden, author of *Britannia* (1596), a 16th-century historical guide to Britain, was dismissive of Solihull:

> I saw Solyhill; but in it, setting aside the church, there is nothing worth sight.

The poet Richard Jago, recalling his Solihull schooldays in the 18th century, was more deferential:

> Hail, Solihull! respectful I salute
> Thy walls; more awful once! when, from the sweets
> Of festive freedom and domestic ease,
> With throbbing heart, to the stern discipline
> Of pedagogue morose I sad return'd.
>
> Richard Jago: *Edge-hill*, Book III (1767)

Sollers Hope *Sollers* denoting manorial ownership in the Middle Ages by the de Solariis family; *Hope see* HOPE[1].

A village in Herefordshire (before 1998 in Hereford and Worcester, before 1974 in Herefordshire), about 13 km (8 miles) southeast of Hereford.

Soloheadbeg The last element is Irish *beag* 'small'; the remainder may be an English mining term, perhaps 'solo head', i.e. a single drift or gallery being worked here.

A quarry in County Tipperary, 4 km (2.5 miles) from Tipperary itself. It was the scene of the opening shots of the Anglo-Irish War (1919–21), when, on 21 January 1919, members of the South Tipperary Brigade of the IRA, led by Seán Treacy and Dan Breen, killed two constables of the Royal Irish Constabulary who were accompanying a consignment of gelignite to the quarry.

Solway Firth 'inlet of the pillar ford', OScand *sula* 'pillar' + *vath* 'ford' (see FORD), with *fjorthr* 'fjord, inlet'; the pillar in question is the LOCHMABEN STONE.

An inlet of the Irish Sea between Scotland (Dumfries and Galloway) and England (Cumbria). It is some 80 km (50 miles) long, and 60 km (40 miles) wide at its mouth. At its eastern end it is effectively the estuary of the rivers ESK[2] and EDEN[1]. The tides are rapid, and there is a tidal bore that travels at 16 kph (10 mph).

Battle of Solway Moss (24 November 1542). An English–Scots battle fought on the flat boggy ground just inside Cumbria at the eastern end of the Solway Firth, 4 km (2.5 miles) northeast of Gretna. The Scottish army under Oliver Sinclair had just entered England on a counter-attack, when it was defeated by Henry VIII's smaller English force under Sir Thomas Wharton. News of the defeat reached James V, who, exhausted and full of grief, died on 14 December, at the age of 30. A further disappointment had been the news of the birth of a daughter (Mary Queen of Scots), prompting the dying king to reflect on the fate of the Stuarts: 'It began wi' a lass, it'll gang wi' a lass' (referring to the fact that the Stuart royal line stemmed from Marjory Bruce).

Somerleyton 'Sumarlithi's farmstead', OScand male personal name *Sumarlithi* + -TON.

A village (pronounced 'summer-') in Suffolk, on the River WAVENEY[1], about 8 km (5 miles) northwest of Lowestoft. The present village takes its name from the nearby **Somerleyton Hall**, an Elizabethan mansion rebuilt in 1844 in the Italian style by Sir Samuel Peto (1809–89), property developer and MP for Norwich. He built the village for his employees to live in.

Somersal Herbert *Somersal* 'Sumor's nook of land', OE *Sumores* possessive form of male personal name *Sumor* + *halh* (see HALE, -HALL); *Herbert* denoting manorial ownership in the Middle Ages by the Fitzherbert family.

A village (pronounced 'summersǝl') in Derbyshire, about 24 km (15 miles) west of Derby.

Somersby Probably 'Sumarlithi's farmstead or village', OScand *Sumarlithis* possessive form of male personal name *Sumarlithi* + -BY.

A village (pronounced 'summersby') in Lincolnshire, about 8 km (5 miles) northeast of HORNCASTLE. The poet Alfred Tennyson (1809–92) was born here (his father was rector of Somersby and BAG ENDERBY).

Somerset '(district of the) settlers around Somerton', SOMER-TON + OE *sæte* 'settlers'. (The once current supposition that the name reflects the county's summery climate is wrong, but not entirely wide of the mark given the derivation of Somerton.) A county (pronounced 'summerset') of southwest England. It is bounded to the north by the Bristol Channel (*see under* BRISTOL) and by the unitary authorities of Bath and North East Somerset and North Somerset, to the east by Wiltshire, to the south by Dorset, and to the south and west by Devon. In 1974 it lost a northeastern portion of its territory (including its largest city, BATH) to the newly created county of AVON[7]. In 1996 this was reconfigured into the two above-mentioned unitary authorities. Somerset's largest town and administrative centre is TAUNTON. Its other main centres of population are BRIDGWATER, CHARD, CREWKERNE, FROME[2], GLASTONBURY, ILMINSTER, MINEHEAD, SHEPTON MALLET, STREET, WELLINGTON[3], WELLS and YEOVIL.

The bulk of the county is a flat plain, whose rich pastures support a thriving dairy industry. This is enclosed to the northwest and west by EXMOOR and the QUANTOCK HILLS, to the south by the BLACKDOWN HILLS and to the northeast by the MENDIP HILLS (including Cheddar Gorge (*see under* CHEDDAR)). Its main rivers are the FROME[1] (which forms part of the boundary with Wiltshire), the EXE and the PARRETT, with its tributaries the CARY, the ISLE, the TONE and the YEO[1]. The latter system drains the **Somerset Levels**, an extensive area of former marshland once frequently under water (2000 years ago people lived there on man-made islands in the lakes), but now successfully harnessed to agriculture (*see also* ATHELNEY *and* KING'S SEDGE MOOR).

Cider-production remains an important part of Somerset's economy, and in the 19th and early 20th centuries significant amounts of coal were mined in the northeast of the county (*see also* MELLS).

The punning thespian term MUMMERSET has tended to stereotype the county as yokelishly backward.

Somerset was part of the territory of the ancient British Belgae tribe, but was quickly subdued by the Romans, who mined for lead in the Mendips and built towns at AQUAE SULIS and ILCHESTER. The county abounds in associations, both historical and mythic, with native British resistance to the advancing Saxons in the post-Roman period. Its whole area seems to have become part of the Anglo-Saxon kingdom of WESSEX by the mid-7th century AD.

In cricketing terms Somerset is a 'first-class' county. Somerset County Cricket Club was founded in 1875 and has played in the county championship since 1891 but has never won the competition. Its most famous players are the big-hitting (but sadly depressive) Harold Gimblett, the England all-rounder Ian Botham (*see* HEADINGLEY), Andrew Caddick, Marcus Trescothick and the West Indians Sir

Vivian Richards and Joel Garner. Its home ground is the County Ground, Taunton.

'Green Hills o' Somerset, The'. A setting by Eric Coates of words by Fred Weatherly:

> Oh the green hills o' Somerset go rolling to the shore.
> 'Twas there we said that we'd get wed when spring came round once more ...

It was made famous in an early recording by Joan Hammond.

Protector Somerset. The epithet by which Edward Seymour, 1st Duke of Somerset (*c.*1506–52), was known when he was created Protector of England (and effective ruler) during the first two years of the minority reign of Edward VI (1547–9). He advanced Protestantism, defeated the Scots at PINKIE, but overreached himself and was deposed and executed. Before his demise, he had built the original **Somerset House** on London's STRAND: it was largely taken over by the Crown after Seymour's death, before being demolished in the late 18th century to make way for the current building, which retains the name.

Somerset Rhapsody, A. An orchestral work (Opus 21) by Gustav Holst, first performed in 1910. Dedicated to Cecil Sharp, it incorporates folk tunes collected by Sharp in Somerset: 'The Sheep-Shearing Song', 'High Germany' and 'The Lovers' Farewell'.

Somersetshire From SOMERSET. The name *Somersetshire* is first recorded in the 12th century.

An occasional alternative form of the name SOMERSET.

Somers Town From the *Somers* family, descendants of the 1st Baron Somers (1651–1716), lord chancellor of England, on whose land it was built.

A district (pronounced 'summers') of Central London (NW1), in the borough of CAMDEN, approximately between the present-day Euston and St Pancras stations. Building began here in the 1780s. It was planned as a salubrious urban development, but things soon began to go wrong, and its social profile dropped precipitously. Refugees from the French Revolution came to live here, and a large Spanish population also developed. By Victorian times it was a noisome slum. The 20th century saw extensive redevelopment, and in 1999 the new British Library building opened on the Euston Road.

Somerton 'farmstead used in summer' (alluding to pasturage which was too wet or marshy to be used in winter), OE *sumor* 'summer' + -TON.

A town (pronounced 'summertən') in Somerset, on the Somerset Levels (*see under* SOMERSET), on the River Carey, about 14 km (9 miles) northwest of Yeovil. It was once a most important place: in the Anglo-Saxon period it was the capital of Somerset, and in the Middle Ages it was the county town. Its former eminence is reflected in its elegant greyish-white limestone buildings and in its greatest legacy: the name of the county of Somerset.

Sompting '(settlement of the) dwellers at the marsh', OE *sumpt* 'marsh' + *-ingas* (*see* -ING).

A village (pronounced 'sompting' or 'sumpting') in West Sussex, on the northeastern outskirts of Worthing. It is best known for the unique Saxon tower of its church, St Mary's, the only surviving one in England with a gabled pyramidal cap (known as a 'Rhenish helm').

Sonning '(settlement of) Sunna's people', OE male personal name *Sunna* + *-ingas* (*see* -ING).

A village (pronounced 'sonning' or 'sunning') in Berkshire, within the unitary authority of Wokingham, on the River THAMES[1], on the northeastern outskirts of Reading. It is picture-postcard attractive, its arched bridge one of the oldest across the Thames. Deanery Gardens (1902), designed by Edwin Lutyens, is one of the finest works of the Arts and Crafts Movement.

> Sonning, a village prepensely picturesque.
>
> William Morris: as quoted in J.W. Mackail, *The Life of William Morris* (1899)

Sooside, the. *See* SOUTH SIDE.

Sorviodunum. The Roman name for OLD SARUM.

Soton. A conventional written abbreviation of SOUTHAMPTON.

Sots Hole Perhaps a humorous name for a place that only a *sot* (i.e. a drunkard) would attempt to farm; alternatively 'Soti's hollow', OScand male personal name *Soti* + OE *hol* 'hollow'.

A village in Lincolnshire, in the FENS, about 8 km (5 miles) west of Woodhall Spa.

Soutar, the Scots 'cobbler'.

A sea stack by the FAST CASTLE cliffs in Scottish Borders (formerly in Berwickshire). For other 'soutars' (or 'sutors' as they are also known) *see*, for example, under CROMARTY.

Souter Johnnie's Cottage. *See under* KIRKOSWALD.

South, the¹. A conventional term for the southern part of England. The broadest possible definition would probably leave it at 'anywhere that is not the NORTH¹', but in everyday usage there are further exemptions: it is to the south of the MIDLANDS, EAST ANGLIA is not included and there seems to be an unspoken consensus that the SOUTHWEST is not strictly or in all cases part of the South.

Such negative classifications avoid the awkward business of specifying a boundary. In the case of the broad definition, this is often boldly asserted to be a line drawn from the WASH to the River SEVERN. The narrower the focus, the closer the line sinks towards the crucial benchmark of Watford (as in the South being that which is not 'north of Watford' (*see under* WATFORD¹)). A catalogue that perhaps most would agree on is that the South includes, beyond the core of London and the SOUTHEAST, Hampshire, the

eastern parts of Dorset and Wiltshire, all of Berkshire and the southerly parts of Oxfordshire.

The 'north of Watford' line is a reminder that there is much more than geography at stake here. This is the 'favoured' part of England: the climate is balmier, the people are wealthier and healthier, things in general are easier. So the mixture of facts and stereotype goes. Northerners traditionally look askance on the **soft South**:

> Being not only a Londoner, but a central Londoner … I can breakfast and dine in my pansified quarters in the heart of the soft South, having spent most of the intervening time in the gritty, bracing, humorous, individualistic North.
>
> Alex Hamilton: *The Listener* (27 May 1976)

> There can hardly be a town in the South of England where you could throw a brick without hitting the niece of a bishop.
>
> George Orwell: *The Road to Wigan Pier* (1937)

Southerner. A native or inhabitant of the South.

South, the². *See under* IRELAND.

Southall 'southern nook of land' (distinguishing it from NORTHOLT, which was originally *Northall*), OE *suth* 'south' + *halh* (*see* HALE, -HALL).

A district of West London, in the borough of EALING (before 1965 in Middlesex). Until the 19th century the area was largely agricultural. The surviving legacy of the time is **Southall Market**, London's oldest horse auctions, which have been held on the same site since 1698. The arrival of the Great Western Railway in the 1830s precipitated urban development. The variety of pottery known as 'Martinware' (after its makers, the brothers Martin) was produced in Southall between 1877 and 1923.

Southall has a large population of Hindus and Sikhs, following waves of immigration from the Indian subcontinent in the 1950s and 1960s. Racial tensions caused serious riots here in July 1980, but that aberration aside, the area's communities live together most harmoniously. The Sri Guru Singh Sabha Gurdwara (2003) is one of the largest Sikh temples outside India.

Seven people died and 150 were injured when the Swansea–Paddington express crashed here in the **Southall Rail Accident** on 19 September 1997: it became the subject of a public enquiry.

Southampton Originally *Hamtun* 'estate on land hemmed in by water' (referring to the land between the Itchen and Test estuaries), whence HAMPSHIRE; OE *hamm* 'land hemmed in by water' (*see* HAM) + -TON. The *South-* (OE *suth*) was added around the 10th century to distinguish it from NORTHAMPTON.

A city, port and unitary authority on the Hampshire coast, at the confluence of the rivers ITCHEN and TEST, about

30 km (19 miles) northwest of PORTSMOUTH and 110 km (70 miles) southwest of London.

One of the great maritime cities of England, it has been a major port since the 11th century. A large proportion of England's trade with the Mediterranean during the Middle Ages was carried on through Southampton, and it was a key passenger port for France (Henry V embarked here on his way to Agincourt) and further afield (the Pilgrim Fathers set sail from here in the *Mayflower* in 1620). It lost business to LONDON in the 17th and 18th centuries, but in the 1840s new docks (now known as the 'Old Docks') were built and linked to London by railway, and Southampton resumed its premier position. Its status was confirmed in 1911 when the White Star Line moved its base there from Liverpool, making it the main port for transatlantic passenger traffic. The 'New Docks', facing the River Test, were completed in 1934. Southampton has the advantage of the SOLENT's double tides – four a day – which meant that it could accommodate the exceptionally large liners that were to dominate the North Atlantic in the first two thirds of the 20th century. One of the earliest, the *Titanic*, met an untimely and tragic end in 1912, but thereafter **Southampton Water**, the 11-km (7-mile) long channel between Southampton and the Solent, witnessed the regular passage of such ocean-going giants as the *Queen Mary*, *Queen Elizabeth*, *United States* and *QEII*; and CALSHOT was a base for long-distance passenger seaplane services. The seaplanes are long gone, and the liners now do cruise work, but Southampton remains the UK's principal passenger port.

> Yes, weekly from Southampton,
> Great steamers, white and gold,
> Go rolling down to Rio
> (Roll down – roll down to Rio!).
>
> Rudyard Kipling: 'The Beginning of the Armadilloes', *Just So Stories* (1902)

Because of its strategic importance Southampton was very heavily bombed during the Second World War, and most of it now has a fairly modern aspect.

The Supermarine company tested its seaplanes from Southampton Water. Its chief designer, R.J. Mitchell, went on to produce the Spitfire fighter, the prototype of which flew from what is now **Southampton Airport** – officially designated 'Southampton (Eastleigh)' – in EASTLEIGH on 5 March 1936. The airport now handles modest commercial traffic. The **University of Southampton** was established in 1952. Southampton is also home to the headquarters of the Ordnance Survey.

Southampton FC, founded in 1885, played their home games for many decades at a ground called 'the Dell'. In the 2001/2002 season they moved to a new ground, St Mary's. It is a reminder of their original name, **Southampton St Mary's** – as is their nickname, the Saints.

The historic rivalry between Southampton and nearby Portsmouth manifests itself in the decidedly sour relations between supporters of the towns' respective football clubs. For supporters of PORTSMOUTH FC, Southampton and its fans are 'Scummers'. According to one theory, this is an acronymic reference to the Southampton Company of Union Men (or South Coast Union Men) – dockers allegedly imported from Southampton to break a Portsmouth dock strike; according to another, it derives from the naval slang word 'scum', a term of abuse for merchant seamen who 'float on the water', and is thus a dismissal by the inhabitants of the historic royal naval station of Portsmouth of the denizens of the merely commercial port of Southampton.

The dramatist and scholar Nicholas Udall (1504–56), the hymnist Isaac Watts (1674–1748), the painter John Everett Millais (1829–96), the feminist Emily Davies (1830–1921), the critic and wine connoisseur George Saintsbury (1845–1933), the comedian Benny Hill (1925–92) and the film director Ken Russell (b.1927) were born in Southampton. Jane Austen lived here between 1805 and 1809.

There are towns called Southampton in Canada (Nova Scotia, Ontario) and the USA (on Long Island, New York – Jacqueline Kennedy Onassis was born there and the writer P.G. Wodehouse died there). There is a Southampton County in Virginia, USA, a Lower Southampton in Pennsylvania (it is a suburb of Philadelphia), and a Southampton Island at the mouth of Hudson Bay in Canada. *See also* SWAYTHLING.

South Ayrshire *See* AYRSHIRE.

A unitary authority created in 1996. It includes TROON, PRESTWICK, AYR[2] (its administrative headquarters) and GIRVAN. It is bordered to the south by Dumfries and Galloway, to the east by East Ayrshire and to the north by North Ayrshire.

South Bank[1]. A stretch of Thames-side land in London across the river from the Victoria Embankment (*see under* EMBANKMENT), from Westminster Bridge (*see under* WESTMINSTER) to London Bridge (*see under* LONDON). It was the site of the Festival of Britain, held on derelict land here in 1951, and now extends eastwards from the **South Bank Centre**, a composite of venues devoted to the arts, including the Royal Festival Hall (1951), Queen Elizabeth Hall (1967), Purcell Room (1967), Hayward Gallery (1968), National Film Theatre (1958 and 1970) and Royal National Theatre (1976). More recent additions, a little further east (making it more or less contiguous with BANKSIDE), are the Tate Modern (2000) art gallery in the disused Bankside Power Station and the new Globe Theatre (1996), a reimagined version of Shakespeare's theatre, and, at the western end, in the former County Hall (headquarters of the London County Council and the Greater London Council), the

London Aquarium and the Saatchi Gallery (2003). Jubilee Gardens, celebrating Elizabeth II's Silver Jubilee in 1977, are also here (on the site of the Festival of Britain's Dome of Discovery), as is the London Eye (*see under* LONDON).

The brutalist style of some of its buildings (notably Hubert Bennet and Jack Whittle's Queen Elizabeth Hall and Denys Lasdun's much criticized National Theatre, described by Prince Charles as 'a clever way of building a nuclear power station in the middle of London without anyone objecting') and its reputations as hotbed of avant-gardism and chattering-class grazing ground have meant that the wider British public have failed to take the South Bank and its arts complex to their hearts. In the 1980s it gained additional notoriety as a 'home for the homeless' in Cardboard City, an area of underpasses and railway arches near WATERLOO[1] Station in which the destitute devised makeshift residences in discarded cardboard cases and other packing materials. However, the down-and-outs have gone (or at least been forced elsewhere) by the conversion of the central underpass into the towering glass hatbox of the British Film Institute's IMAX Cinema, and there are continuing plans to renovate and redesign three of the main concrete offenders of the 1960s, the Hayward Gallery, Purcell Room and Queen Elizabeth Hall.

South Bank religion. A journalistic label for the religious activities in the diocese of SOUTHWARK in London, south of the Thames. It was associated with Mervyn Stockwood, Bishop of Southwark (1959–80), John Robinson, Suffragan Bishop of Woolwich (1959–69), author of *Honest to God* (1963), and some of their diocesan clergy. Characterized by outspokenness on moral and political issues, often from a socialist angle, and energetic attempts to bring the Church into closer relation with contemporary society and its problems, South Bank religion was not without its critics and the label was often applied disparagingly.

> That is rather the new idea inside the Church. I should definitely say you were a South Banker.
>
> Auberon Waugh: *Consider the Lilies* (1968)

South Bank Show, The. A television arts programme, presented since its inception in 1978 by Melvyn Bragg. The headquarters of London Weekend Television, which produces it, are on the South Bank.

South Bank University. A university founded in 1992, based on the former South Bank Polytechnic. Its headquarters are in Borough Road, SE1.

South Bank[2] From being on the south side of the River TEES. A town in Redcar and Cleveland (formerly in the North Riding of Yorkshire, then in Cleveland), 4 km (2.5 miles) east of Cleveland.

South Benfleet *Benfleet* 'tree-trunk creek' (probably referring to a rudimentary bridge), OE *beam* 'tree trunk' + *fleot* 'creek'.

A town in Essex, on an inlet of the River THAMES[1] called **Benfleet Creek**, to the north of Canvey Island.

In everyday usage it is generally referred to as **Benfleet**; the 'South' is to distinguish it from its smaller sibling, the nearby village of **North Benfleet**.

Southborough 'southern borough' (i.e. of TONBRIDGE), OE *suth* 'south' + *burh* (*see* BURY).

A commuter town in Kent, contiguous with and to the northwest of TUNBRIDGE WELLS. It developed with the coming of the railway in the 19th century.

South Bucks. An administrative district in the southernmost part of Buckinghamshire. Its main centre of population is BEACONSFIELD.

South Cave. *See under* NORTH CAVE.

South Cerney. *See under* CHURN.

South Circular Road. The A205, a road that runs in a roughly semicircular 32 km (20 mile) loop through the built-up areas of SOUTH LONDON and together with the NORTH CIRCULAR ROAD forms an annular traffic artery through the inner suburbs of the capital. It extends from KEW Bridge in the west to WOOLWICH in the east. Unlike the North Circular, it is not a purpose-built road; it utilizes existing thoroughfares.

South City. Estate agents' hyperbole for ELEPHANT AND CASTLE.

South Coast. The southern coast of England, where the land meets the ENGLISH CHANNEL. As the coastline in nearest proximity to the western parts of (an often hostile) Continental Europe, it has a rich history in terms of trade, travel, defence, and national self-definition: this is the history of the SAXON SHORE, the Battle of HASTINGS, the CINQUE PORTS and the great trading centre of SOUTHAMPTON, the defeat of the Spanish Armada, the naval bases of PORTSMOUTH and (further west) PLYMOUTH, the symbolically resonant White Cliffs of DOVER, and so on. In particular, though, and rather less dramatically, the name connotes that stretch of coast from Dorset eastwards through Hampshire and Sussex to Kent which, since the end of the 18th century, has been the holiday playground of southern England. It was the railway in the mid-19th century that really opened up the delights of the seaside to Londoners, and much of the characteristic paraphernalia of the major resort towns, from BOURNEMOUTH through BOGNOR REGIS, WORTHING, BRIGHTON, EASTBOURNE and HASTINGS to FOLKESTONE and DEAL – the piers, the promenades, the funfairs, the amusement arcades – are of that era. Later, in the early 20th century, came the bungaloid growth of holiday and retirement homes (*see* COSTA GERIATRICA) that disfigured many portions of the coast (typified for many by PEACEHAVEN). After the Second World War, cheap foreign package holidays deprived the south coast of its captive market, and many of its larger centres have diversified into the conference trade and other forms of commerce.

> All along the south coast
> the sea is sort of there
> the sun is sort of shining
> through a sort of salt sea air
> and all along the south coast
> can still be sort of seen
> a corner of sort of England
> that's forever sort of green.
>
> Jeremy Taylor: 'All Along the South Coast' (1971), from *Ag Pleeze Deddy!* (1992)

South Creake *Creake see* NORTH CREAKE.
A village in North Norfolk, about 11 km (7 miles) southwest of Wells-next-the-Sea. NORTH CREAKE is about 2.5 km (1.5 miles) to the north.

South Downs *Downs see* DOWN, -DON.
A range of low rolling chalk hills in southern England, extending from just to the east of WINCHESTER across eastern Hampshire and Sussex to the Channel coast, where they end spectacularly at the SEVEN SISTERS[1] cliffs to the west of BEACHY HEAD. Their highest point is BUTSER HILL.

At their western end they are fairly heavily wooded, but as they march eastwards their windswept grassy slopes more and more resemble the 'blunt, bowheaded, whalebacked downs' of which Rudyard Kipling wrote. These are Hilaire Belloc's 'great hills of the South Country', which 'stand along the sea':

> I never get between the pines
> But I smell the Sussex air;
> Nor I never come on a belt of sand
> But my home is there.
> And along the sky the line of the Downs
> So noble and so bare.
>
> Hilaire Belloc: 'The South Country' (1910)

Another artist to have been inspired by the South Downs was Eric Ravilious (1903–42), many of whose paintings and drawings seem to reveal their strong chalky bones.

The South Downs reminded T.H. Huxley (1825–95; 'Darwin's Bulldog') of a well-dressed carcase of mutton.

In prehistoric times the Downs were a hive of activity. People raised earthworks there, for military or religious purposes (*see* CHANCTONBURY RING *and* CISSBURY RING), and delved into the chalk for the flints they used as tools and weapons. Since the Elizabethan period the Downs' springy turf has been kept closely cropped by large flocks of sheep. By the 18th century they were a recognized breed, the **Southdown**, small and hornless, with medium-length wool but prized especially for their meat.
See also the DOWNS[1].

Southdown. A bus company that operated in the Sussex and Hampshire regions until being taken over by Stagecoach in 1992 and split up. Its vehicles had a distinctive livery of pale green and cream.

South Downs Way. A footpath that follows the ridge of the South Downs from Buriton near Petersfield to Beachy Head.

Southeast, the. The southeastern corner of England. Under the term's umbrella come SURREY, KENT and ESSEX (the core HOME COUNTIES) and also SUSSEX (East and West), the easterly part of BERKSHIRE and all but the northern extremities of BUCKINGHAMSHIRE and HERTFORDSHIRE. At its hub sits LONDON, although usages such as 'London and the Southeast' suggest that some people may view the capital as in the Southeast but not of it (as is often reflected in general election results). As the area of England with the highest levels of affluence, privilege and political power it is routinely envied and reviled in parts of the country further removed from the metropolis.

The Battle of Britain was fought out largely in the skies over the southeast of England in the late summer of 1940.

Southeast Iceland. A sea area in the shipping forecast. It is off the southeast coast of Iceland, between BAILEY to the south and FAEROES to the southeast.

Southend-on-Sea *Southend* 'southern end' (referring to the southern part of Prittlewell parish), ME *south* + *ende* 'end'. The suffix was not added until the 19th century.
A seaside resort and (since 1998) unitary authority in Essex, on the north bank of the THAMES[1] estuary, about 65 km (40 miles) east of London. For most of its existence it was an insignificant little hamlet at the southern end of the parish of Prittlewell (whence its name). Then, in the first decade of the 19th century, it was visited by Queen Caroline and her eight-year-old daughter Princess Charlotte. They thoroughly approved of it, and the royal imprimatur sparked its growth into one of England's leading holiday towns (in the process, its relationship with Prittlewell was reversed – the latter is now a district of Southend).

Southend offers the closest sandy beaches to London (11 km / 7 miles of them) and, before the 19th century was very old, paddle steamers were bringing trippers from London to sample its delights. Soon the railway and (in 1870) the introduction of bank holidays made access still easier, and the tradition of Southend – the Cockney leisuredrome, whelky, jellied-eelish East End-on-Sea – was well on the way to establishment:

> I had abided for a brief space at that paradise of cockneys, Southend.
>
> Miss Muloch: *Domestic Stories* (1862)

Most famous of the attractions on offer was and is its pier, originally designed to accommodate the steamers: at 2.1 km (1 mile 587 yards) it is the longest in the world, requiring an electric railway line to run along it (in the Second World War the pier was taken over by the Royal Navy, and renamed HMS *Leigh*). It has survived, despite periodic postwar fires and and other accidents. It is backed up by the full panoply of amusement arcades, funfairs, fast-food joints, parks and gardens, and the Germanically named Kursaal entertainment complex (originally built in 1901) to bring a whiff of 19th-century Continental watering-places.

Many of Southend's residents commute to London, and famously complain about the train service.

Southend Airport, to the north of the town, is perhaps best known for the car-ferry service that used to operate from here to the Continent, using the bizarre bulbous-nosed Carvair (a converted Douglas DC-4).

In 20th-century rhyming slang, *Southend-on-Sea* has stood for 'pee' or 'wee', and *Southend pier* for 'ear'.

Southern Ireland. *See under* IRELAND.

Southern Uplands. The rolling hills that occupy most of southern Scotland, south of the CENTRAL LOWLANDS. They are mostly in Dumfries and Galloway, and in Scottish Borders. The highest point is MERRICK (843 m / 2766 ft), in Galloway, and there are some 80 other hills over 610 m (2000 ft).

Southern Uplands Way, the. A long-distance footpath through the Southern Uplands, from Port Patrick on the Rhinns of Galloway to Cockburnspath on the North Sea coast. It is 341 km (212 miles) long.
See also DONALDS.

South Esk. *See* ESK[1] *and* ESK[3].

South Flobbets Etymology unknown.
A tiny settlement in Aberdeenshire, 7 km (4.5 miles) north of Oldmeldrum. **North Flobbets** is just to the north.

South Foreland. A chalk promontory on the coast of Kent, about 3 km (2 miles) northeast of DOVER, at the point where the northern edge of the NORTH DOWNS meets the sea. In 1899 Guglielmo Marconi set up a wireless station here, to communicate with Wimereux, 50 km (30 miles) away in France.

Southgate 'south gate' (referring to a southern entrance to ENFIELD Chase), OE *suth* 'south' + *geat* 'gate'.
A suburb of North London (N14), in the borough of ENFIELD, to the northeast of Friern Barnet. Until the latter part of the 19th century it was a small rural hamlet, but in the 1870s the railway arrived, and residential development got under way. The southwesterly part of the expanded area, which encroached on COLNEY HATCH, was named **New Southgate**. Development was greatly accelerated after 1933, when Southgate and nextdoor Arnos Grove Underground stations, on the Piccadilly line, were opened.

Several of Southgate's acres are covered by the Great Northern Cemetery (now officially the **New Southgate**

Cemetery), a privately run burial ground opened in 1861. The nearby cricket ground provides occasional suburban relief for Middlesex County Cricket Club from the fleshpots of ST JOHN'S WOOD.

South Glamorgan *See* GLAMORGAN.
A former county of south Wales, created in 1974 out of part of the old county of Glamorgan. Its Welsh name was the literal equivalent **De Morgannwg**. It was bounded to the south by the Bristol Channel, to the east by Gwent, and to the north and west by Mid Glamorgan. The administrative headquarters were in CARDIFF, and other towns included COWBRIDGE, BARRY and PENARTH. In 1996 it was divided among the unitary authorities of Cardiff and VALE OF GLAMORGAN.

South Gloucestershire *See* GLOUCESTERSHIRE.
A unitary authority in southwest England, on the eastern bank of the SEVERN estuary, formed in 1996 from the northerly segment of the county of AVON[7]. It is immediately to the north and east of BRISTOL, and it includes a western portion of the COTSWOLDS. Its main centres of population (apart from the eastern and northern suburbs of Bristol) are CHIPPING SODBURY and THORNBURY (its administrative centre).

South Hams 'southern enclosures, southern riverside land' (referring to the southern portion of the area between PLYMOUTH and the estuary of the River DART), OE *suth* 'south', with *hammas* plural of *hamm* 'enclosure, land by a river' (*see* HAM).
A council district in Devon, covering the area between the DART and PLYM estuaries, to the southeast of DARTMOOR. A rich agricultural area, it is networked by rivers running off Dartmoor, notably the AVON[4], the Erme and the Yealm. With its stunning coastal scenery (made accessible by the South West Coast Path), attractive villages and mild climate it is a great tourist draw (the main tourist centres are KINGSBRIDGE and SALCOMBE).

The name 'South Hams' was applied semi-officially to the area down to the 19th century, and revived as an official appellation in the 20th.
See also PRAWLE POINT.

South Kensington. A district of southwest Central London (SW5, SW7, SW10), in the borough of KENSINGTON AND CHELSEA, between Knightsbridge to the northeast, Chelsea to the southeast and Earl's Court to the west. The nucleus around which it grew and developed in the mid-19th century, and which remains its most characteristic feature, is the complex of museums, colleges and other forcing beds of the intellect to the south of HYDE PARK. It was Prince Albert in 1851 who suggested that the profits from the Great Exhibition should be put to such a purpose, and the area was informally dubbed ALBERTOPOLIS in his honour (it was also sometimes known as COLEVILLE, after Sir Henry Cole, who implemented much of Albert's plan). Its centre-pieces are probably the Natural History Museum, on Cromwell Road, built in the 1870s to the designs of Alfred Waterhouse; and the Royal Albert Hall, annual home of the BBC Promenade Concerts (the 'Proms') and venue for a whole range of other activities, from boxing to cookery exhibitions, which opened in 1870. Orbiting around them are (to name only the major institutions) the Victoria and Albert Museum (the 'V and A' opened in its present building in 1909), the Science Museum, Imperial College of Science and Technology, the Royal College of Art and the Royal College of Music. The forerunner of the Victoria and Albert, which opened in 1857, was known as the South Kensington Museum, and the name 'South Kensington' continued, into the 20th century, to connote the district's museums, collectively or individually:

> South Kensington has recently acquired a drug vase.
>
> *Burlington Magazine* (March 1933)

But there is more to South Kensington (or **South Ken**, as it is often affectionately known) than museums. To the west of Queen's Gate and to the south of Cromwell Road are street upon street of grand Victorian villas. Many of them are now broken up into flats, giving the area a bedsitterish quality which spills out into the bustle of Gloucester Road. Still others are now in service as embassies for various foreign countries. South of the Old Brompton Road, though, the *ton* tends to be a little more *haut* (in the BOLTONS, for example).

South Kensington Underground station, on the District, Circle and Piccadilly lines, opened in 1868.

The author Beatrix Potter (1866–1943) was born in South Kensington.

South Lanarkshire From LANARK + SHIRE.
A unitary authority created in 1996. It is bounded by West Lothian, North Lanarkshire and Glasgow to the north, East Renfrewshire and East Ayrshire to the west, Dumfries and Galloway to the south, and Scottish Borders to the east. Towns include HAMILTON[1] (the administrative centre), LANARK, BIGGAR and EAST KILBRIDE.

South London. That part of London to the south of the River THAMES[1]. In its broadest interpretation the term can be all-encompassing – so Wimbledon, for example, is in South London, and so is Croydon. But it tends to have a particular connotation: of those modest, slightly shabby inner suburbs that mushroomed with the spread of the railways in the second half of the 19th century, covering the fields of Surrey and Kent with serried ranks of scarcely distinguishable terraces – BALHAM, CAMBERWELL, CATFORD, CLAPHAM[1], KENNINGTON, LEWISHAM, PECKHAM, STREATHAM and their ilk. Give or take the odd pocket like BLACKHEATH

or DULWICH, and some patches of late 20th-century gentri-fication, it is not a land of grand houses and grand people: ordinary people live here (it is no accident that the 'man on the Clapham omnibus' (*see under* CLAPHAM[1]) comes from South London), for the most part working class or lower middle class, in two-up-two-downs or the council estates and tower blocks that succeeded them. 'Saaf Lunnon' ...

> Her drawl, which Peggie had known when it was pure South London, was now very Mayfair.
>
> Margery Allingham: *Mind Readers* (1965)

In many parts of South London (BRIXTON, for instance), the make-up of the community has been radically altered since the Second World War by immigration, but a train ride through the hinterland of VAUXHALL or LAVENDER HILL can still conjure up the all-but vanished pre-war South London suburbia, with its Englishmen's castle-homes and lovingly tended back gardens, so artfully sentimentalized in Noël Coward's *This Happy Breed* (1942).

> I have London in the marrow of my bones, and an inexpressible, almost immoderate love of it, but I have never felt South London to be a part of it. South London is for the most part a recently created dormitory, brought into being only in the last two centuries by the railways. Real London is nearly all north of the river: not only the whole, almost, of historic London but London as an exciting city to live in today, and the worlds of government and administration, the arts, the university, entertainment, the City, the various headquarters of the professions, even such things as good hotels and good shopping. South London is foreign to all this. At no time in my life would I have dreamt of living there.
>
> Bryan Magee: *Clouds of Glory: A Hoxton Childhood* (2003)

This feeling of South London being not really London is far from new. In the 19th century people jokingly nick-named it **Georgium sidus** 'the Georgian planet' (Latin *sidus* 'star'), the original name given by its discoverer, Sir William Herschel (1738–1822), to the planet now known as Uranus, in honour of George III: Uranus was then the furthest known planet from the Earth and thus from 'civilization'.

South Mimms *South* to distinguish it from *North Mimms*, now surviving only in the name of the nearby *North Mymms Park*; *Mimms* perhaps '(territory of the) *Mimmas*', a tribal name of unknown origin and meaning.
A village in Hertfordshire (before 1965 in Middlesex), about 2.5 km (1.5 miles) west of Potters Bar. Its name has reached a wide public thanks to South Mimms Services at the junction of the A1(M) and the M25.

South Molton *Molton* from an unknown first element (perhaps a pre-English hill name) + -TON.
A market town in Devon, on the River MOLE[2], at the south-western edge of EXMOOR, approximately 17.5 km (11 miles)

southeast of Barnstaple. It grew to prosperity in the Middle Ages on the back of the wool trade, and its fortunes were further bolstered by income from the BARNSTAPLE–BIDEFORD stagecoach, which stopped here, and from iron and copper mines in the area. Today its profile is more modest, but it has a fine legacy of Georgian buildings.

Henry Williamson, author of *Tarka the Otter* (1927), lived on the outskirts of the town for a while.

Southmoor. *See under* KINGSTON BAGPUIZE.

Southport A modern name, meaning self-evident, first coined in 1798. Prior to this it was called *South Hawes*.

A seaside resort in Merseyside (formerly in Lancashire), some 25 km (15 miles) north of Liverpool. The first hotel here was built in the 18th century, but major expansion (on land reclaimed from sand-dunes) occurred after the building of the railway from Liverpool in 1848, and from Wigan and Manchester in 1855. The pier (1859) was the first pleasure pier in Britain, and, at 1100 m (1200 yards), is the country's second longest. At low tide the sea goes out some 3 km (2 miles), leaving vast expanses of sand with names like Angry Brow and Horse Bank. Southport is also home to the Royal BIRKDALE golf course.

Southport was the birthplace of Lucy Boston (1892–1990), author of the Green Knowe books for children. George Nathaniel Curzon, Conservative politician and 'very superior person' (according to the anonymous rhyme), was MP for Southport from 1886 to 1898, and the novelist Mary Webb (1881–1927), author of *Precious Bane* (1924), went to school here.

South Queensferry. A small town in West Lothian, between the two Forth Bridges on the south side of the Firth of FORTH, 13 km (8 miles) west of Edinburgh. The town owes its name to Queen (later Saint) Margaret (1045–93), the Saxon wife of Malcolm III Canmore (ruled 1057–93). She was the sister of the English prince Edgar Ætheling and granddaughter of the English king Edmund Ironside, and had fled north after the Norman invasion. Margaret and Malcolm frequently used the narrow passage across the Firth from South to NORTH QUEENSFERRY on the Fife shore when travelling between EDINBURGH Castle and the royal palace at DUNFERMLINE. There may already have been a ferry of some kind before this time. After running for at least 900 years, the ferry service ended with the opening of the Forth Road Bridge in 1964, although recently a ferry service for foot passengers has recommenced. Opposite the old slipway is the 17th-century Hawes Inn, which is mentioned in Sir Walter Scott's *The Antiquary* (1816) and is where, in Robert Louis Stevenson's *Kidnapped* (1886), David Balfour is inveigled into boarding the brig *Covenant*, which, in his wicked uncle's plan, is to take him to slavery in the Carolinas (*see* EARRAID).

South Riding. An invention of the novelist Winifred Holtby (1898–1935); *see* RIDINGS OF YORKSHIRE.

South Rona. *See* RONA.

South Ronaldsay Ronaldsay 'Rognvald's island', OScand personal name *Rognvald* + *ey* (*see* -AY).

An island in southeast ORKNEY, about 6 km (4 miles) south of Mainland, to which it is linked by the CHURCHILL BARRIERS.

Southsea '(place in the) south by the sea' (referring to the location of Chaderton Castle), ModE.

A seaside resort on the south coast of PORTSEA ISLAND, within the unitary authority of Portsmouth. It originated in a castle (called Chaderton Castle, after its first governor) built here by Henry VIII in 1538 at the entrance to Portsmouth Harbour, at the southern tip of the island (hence a 'south sea castle'). Its development as a resort began in the early 19th century, and it still has some fine houses and terraces to prove it, but nowadays its main function is as a residential suburb of PORTSMOUTH. It is home to a D-Day Museum, which has an 83-m (272-ft) embroidery commemorating the Normandy landings of June 1944.

Rudyard Kipling spent five years in a foster home in Southsea, from the age of six; it was a horrible time for him, and he describes the experience in his story 'Baa Baa, Black Sheep' (1888).

The actor Peter Sellers (1925–80) was born in Southsea.

South Shields ME *schele* 'temporary shelter' (in this case for fishermen); *South* distinguishes it from NORTH SHIELDS across the Tyne.

A town on the south side of the mouth of the River TYNE[1], Tyne and Wear (formerly in County Durham), 12 km (7 miles) east of Newcastle. The Romans built a fort called **Arbeia** here, but the town owes its foundation in the 13th century to the Convent of Durham and developed as a river port in the Middle Ages. Shipbuilding was formerly important but has now declined. The inhabitants of South Shields are sometimes nicknamed **Sand-dancers**, after the bizarre, pseudo-Egyptian 'Sand Dance' of Wilson, Keppel and Betty, popular in the 1950s, the trio being natives of the town.

South Shields was the birthplace of: Sir William Fox (1812–93), who in the mid-19th century served four brief terms as prime minister of New Zealand; Ernest Thompson Seton (1860–1946), US naturalist and writer of animal tales such as *Lives of the Hunted* (1901); Elinor Brent-Dyer (1894–1969), author of the Chalet School stories; the actress Dame Flora Robson (1902–84); and Ridley Scott (b.1939), director of films such as *Alien* (1979), *Blade Runner* (1982) and *Thelma and Louise* (1991).

South Side, the. The area of GLASGOW on the south side of the River Clyde, known locally as **the Sooside**. Its inhabitants, known as **Soosiders**, traditionally view those living north of the river with suspicion, and vice versa.

South Town 'south estate' (denoting a southern part of the village of Medstead developed in the late Middle Ages), ME *suth* 'south' + *toun* (*see* -TON).

A village in Hampshire, about 8 km (5 miles) southwest of ALTON[1].

South Tyneside *See* TYNE[1].

A metropolitan borough in TYNE AND WEAR, formerly part of County Durham.

South Uist. *See under* the UISTS.

Southwark 'southern defensive work or fort' (referring to its position at the southern end of London Bridge, commanding the approach to the City), OE *suth* 'south' + *(ge)weorc* 'defensive work, fort'.

A district and borough (pronounced 'suthək') of SOUTH LONDON, on the south bank of the River Thames. As a district (SE1), it lies at the southern end of London Bridge (*see under* LONDON), between BERMONDSEY to the east and WATERLOO[1] to the west. It was an important settlement in Roman times. Two Roman roads met here (*see* STANE STREET[1] and WATLING STREET[1]), and it was, and remained throughout the Middle Ages and later, London's chief southern entry and exit point. There were travellers' needs to be met, and Southwark became famous for its inns: notably the Tabard, where Chaucer's pilgrims met, the White Hart and the George (the only one preserved today; dating from 1677, it is the last galleried inn in London). It also had a reputation as fun city: Southwark (and in particular BANKSIDE) was the place to go for theatres, brothels, bear-baiting, dog-fighting, etc. Not surprisingly, it also had seven prisons, including the Clink and the Marshalsea. It possessed two mints, and between the early 15th century and 1763 the annual **Southwark Fair** was held here (William Hogarth did a painting of it called *Southwark Fair* (1733)). On a more salubrious note, Guy's Hospital, one of London's major teaching hospitals, was opened in Southwark in 1725; its founder, Thomas Guy (1644/5–1724), was born in the borough.

The democratic Leveller movement (of those who would 'level all differences of position or rank between men') was founded in Southwark in 1645, during the English Civil Wars, by the republican agitator John Lilburne.

In 1550 most of Southwark was bought from the king by the City of London. It was officially constituted as a City ward (named 'Bridge Ward Without'), and came to be known as 'Southwark borough' (connoting a suburb, outside the City). Over four centuries later, the heart of Southwark is still 'the BOROUGH'.

In 1965 it was incorporated into the new London borough of Southwark (SE1, SE5, SE15, SE16, SE17, SE21, SE22,

SE24), which also includes BERMONDSEY, CAMBERWELL, DULWICH, ELEPHANT AND CASTLE, PECKHAM, ROTHERHITHE and WALWORTH. It lies between Greenwich and Lewisham to the east and Lambeth to the west. Apart from London Bridge, it is linked to the north bank of the Thames by **Southwark Bridge** (a road bridge built in 1912–21, replacing an earlier one of 1814–19, designed by the Scottish engineer John Rennie), BLACKFRIARS Bridge, Tower Bridge (*see under* TOWER OF LONDON), the Millennium Bridge and the ROTHERHITHE Tunnel.

The diocese of Southwark, covering sub-Thamesian London and part of Surrey, was created in 1905 (its territory was formerly part of ROCHESTER diocese). The ancient church of St Saviour and St Mary Overie (dating from the 12th century; *Overie* means literally 'over the river') was designated its cathedral. **Southwark Cathedral** contains monuments to the medieval poet John Gower and to William Shakespeare, whose youngest brother Edmund is buried here. (*See also* South Bank religion *under* SOUTH BANK[1].)

Southwark delftware. A type of tin-glazed earthenware made in Southwark during the 17th and 18th centuries.

South Warnborough. *See* NORTH WARNBOROUGH.

Southwell 'south spring' (referring to the Lady Well by the minster church), OE *suth* 'south' + *wella* 'spring'.

A town (generally pronounced 'suthəl', although the locals insist on pronouncing it as spelt) in Nottinghamshire, about 17.5 km (11 miles) northeast of Nottingham. It is dominated by its twin-towered collegiate church **Southwell Minster**, dating from 1108. Particularly noteworthy are an early Anglo-Scandinavian tympanum (door lintel) and some delicate late 13th-century foliate tracery in the Chapter House known as the **Leaves of Southwell**. The see of Southwell (roughly covering the area of Nottinghamshire) was created in 1884, and the minster is now a cathedral.

At the end of the first Civil War on 4 May 1647 Charles I went from The Saracen's Head inn in Southwell to surrender himself to the Scottish army.

A Southwell butcher by the name of Matthew Bramley is said to have developed the 'Bramley's seedling' cooking apple in the garden of his cottage in the mid-19th century.

Southwest, the. The southwestern extremity of England, comprising the counties of CORNWALL, DEVON[1] and SOMERSET and the western portion of DORSET. It therefore constitutes the southern part of the WEST COUNTRY.

Southwold 'south forest' (perhaps referring to forested land to the south of Lowestoft), OE *suth* 'south' + *wald* 'forest'.

A clifftop town and seaside resort on the Suffolk coast, overlooking SOLE BAY, just to the north of the mouth of the River BLYTH[1], about 16 km (10 miles) south of Lowestoft.

A pedestrian 'ferry' (man in a rowing boat) and, a little upstream, a footbridge connect it with neighbouring WALBERSWICK. By the 16th century it had become an important fishing port, but catering to holidaymakers has long since replaced fish as its main source of income. Not for Southwold, though, the amusement arcade and the kiss-me-quick hat. Its distinctive areas of lawn, the 'greens', were established as firebreaks following a disastrous conflagration in 1659, and have helped restrain ugly and high-volume urban development. Its clientele (bolstered in the 19th and 20th centuries by Brits returning to live in England from service in India – the historian Simon Schama has dubbed it 'Little Raj-by-the-Sea') has always been select, and its character might best be described as 'upmarket retro'. Its beach-huts are unfeasibly expensive.

> Southwold: the new Hampstead.
>
> Iain Sinclair: *London Orbital* (2002)

George Orwell lived in Southwold (in the house of his parents, returned ex-pats) in the late 1920s and early 1930s, and thoroughly loathed it. 'Knype Hill' in his second novel *A Clergyman's Daughter* (1935) is a thinly disguised portrait:

> One of those sleepy streets that look so intensely peaceful on a casual visit, and so very different when you live in them and have an enemy or creditor in every window.

And yet he continued to have his clothes cut by a Southwold tailor until the day he died.

Among the town's landmarks the most notable are the magnificent 15th-century St Edmund's church; the lighthouse, dating from 1890, which stands within the town; and Adnams brewery.

Battle of Southwold (28 May 1672). An alternative designation for the Battle of Sole Bay (*see under* SOLE BAY).

Southwold Jack. A brightly painted medieval wooden effigy of a man in armour, now to be found in St Edmund's church, but originally probably part of a clock, who struck the hours with his sword.

South Woodham Ferrers *South* to distinguish it from WOODHAM FERRERS.

A small town in Essex, on the River CROUCH[1], about 13 km (8 miles) northeast of Basildon. Until the 1970s it was a tiny village, but then it was designated a 'Riverside Country Town', and in the following two decades it spilled out into the surrounding countryside in waves of unprepossessing housing estates. It boasts no fewer than 25 roads with names inspired by J.R.R. Tolkien's *Lord of the Rings* trilogy, including Gandalf's Ride, Hobbiton Hill and Treebeard Copse.

South Yorkshire *See* YORKSHIRE.

A metropolitan county of northeast England. It is bordered on the south and west by Derbyshire, on the north by West Yorkshire, North Yorkshire and the East Riding of Yorkshire, on the east by Lincolnshire and Nottinghamshire. In 1986 much of its power was devolved to the metropolitan borough councils of BARNSLEY[1], DONCASTER, ROTHERHAM and SHEFFIELD.

Soutra 'house with a view' or 'house with a look-out place', originally *Soltre*, OCelt *sulw* 'viewpoint' + *tref* (*see* TRE-).

A pass (345 m / 1132 ft) in Midlothian 26 km (16 miles) southeast of Edinburgh where the A68 crosses the LAMMERMUIRS. There is a tremendous view north to EDINBURGH and FIFE. It was an old pilgrim route, and near the summit is **Soutra Aisle**, the bare remains of a hospice for travellers founded by Malcolm IV in 1164. More recently a wind farm has been built here.

Sowerby 'farm on sour ground', OScand *saurr* 'sour' + -BY.

A town in North Yorkshire, 13 km (8 miles) south of Northallerton. It merges with THIRSK to the north.

Sowerby Bridge. A town on the River CALDER[1], West Yorkshire, 5 km (3 miles) southwest of Halifax. To the west, on higher ground, is the old village of Sowerby.

Sow of Atholl, the. *See under* ATHOLL.

Spa Common *Spa* perhaps a reference to the river that passes nearby.

A village in Norfolk, about 1.5 km (1 mile) east of North Walsham.

Spade Town. A nickname for LURGAN.

Spa Fields The *Spa* was a chalybeate spring discovered in the fields in the 17th century, and developed later for medicinal purposes.

An open space – long since covered over – in CLERKENWELL, which on 2 December 1816 was the starting point of the **Spa Fields Riots**. A mass meeting was planned here to call for universal suffrage and reform of Parliament, but radical agitators led the crowd on the City of London. They were confronted by the lord mayor at the head of a force of police, and the ensuing riot was eventually broken up by troops. A surviving reminder of the venue is **Spafield Street** (EC1).

Spaghetti Junction. A wryly humorous nickname for the motorway interchange at GRAVELLY HILL near Birmingham, at which the M6 connects with the A38(M) and the A5127 in a maze of winding and intersecting roads, underpasses and overpasses which bears a more than passing resemblance to a bowl of spaghetti. (The analogy is best appreciated in aerial views.) It opened in 1971, and the name was firmly in place before the year was out. (It is now completely avoidable if through-traffic uses the new M6 Toll Road.) Since then the term has been applied more widely to other similar interchanges throughout Britain.

Spalding '(settlement of the) dwellers in Spald', *Spald* ancient district name (perhaps from OE *spald* 'ditch, trench') + *-ingas* (*see* -ING).

A town in Lincolnshire, on the River WELLAND, to the south of the WASH, about 37 km (23 miles) southeast of Grantham. It is the entrepôt for a wide area of rich agricultural land in the midst of the FENS: more than half the bulbs grown in Britain come from here, and it is also a prolific source of potatoes and other vegetables.

Spalding Gentlemen's Society, founded in 1710, is the oldest antiquarian society in England.

Spancil Hill 'hill of the tether', a translation of the Irish name *Cnoc an Urchaill*; *cnoc* 'hill' (*see* KNOCK-) + *an* 'of the' + *urchaill* 'hobble, tether'.

A locality 'just a mile' from Clooney, between Ennis and Tulla in eastern County Clare. There is now little more than a crossroads and a few ruins, but it was once the site of a famous horse fair, and the place gave its name to a well-known emigrant's ballad, beginning

Last night as I lay dreaming of pleasant days gone by
My mind being bent on ramblin' to Ireland I did fly.
I stepped on board a vision and I followed with a will
Till next I came to anchor at the cross near Spancil Hill.

Spanish Head First recorded in the 17th century, the name has been traditionally associated with wrecked ships of the Spanish Armada, but there is no clear evidence that any such ships came this way.

The southwesternmost tip of the Isle of Man.

Sparrowpit Perhaps 'sparrow hole' (referring to a deep valley), ModE *sparrow* + ME *pit* 'hollow, hole'.

A village in Derbyshire, in the PEAK DISTRICT, about 3 km (2 miles) east of Chapel-en-le-Frith.

Speakers' Corner. A small area near MARBLE ARCH in the northeastern corner of HYDE PARK, London, where a motley band of public speakers holds forth every Sunday. The name is relatively recent (it is first recorded in 1936), but the practice dates from 1855, when a large crowd gathered here to protest against Lord Robert Grosvenor's Sunday Trading Bill. There was no right of assembly then but it was granted in 1872 and anyone may now indulge in soapbox oratory on any subject they choose, so long as it is not obscene or blasphemous, or does not constitute an incitement to a breach of the peace. By the end of the 20th century most of the speakers were religious extremists. In 1999 the Home Secretary, Jack Straw, announced his intention to set up 'speakers' corners' in more than 250 British towns. Straw himself became something of an outdoor orator, frequently setting up his soapbox outside Marks & Spencer in his Blackburn constituency.

Speakers' Corner is a mixed grill of apostles and propagators, of oddities and crudities, of fanatics and eccentrics.

J.C. Goodwin: *One of the Crowd* (1936)

Spean Bridge From the bridge over the River *Spean* (etymology unknown). The first bridge was built here by General Wade in 1736, and the present one by Thomas Telford in 1819. A village at the junction of the roads linking Fort William, Inverness and Speyside, in Highland (formerly in Inverness-shire), 14 km (8.5 miles) northeast of Fort William. **Glen Spean** extends from here eastwards to LOCH LAGGAN.

Spean Bridge was the location of the first skirmish of the 1745 Jacobite Rising, when, on 16 August 1745 (three days before the raising of the standard at GLENFINNAN), a handful of MacDonalds took on two companies of Redcoats and forced them to retreat. During the Second World War the area round here was used for mountain-warfare training, as commemorated in the Commando Memorial a little to the west of the village.

Speedwell Cavern *Speedwell* probably 'succeed well' – a hopeful adjuration to 'get rich quick' from the cave's mineral proceeds.

A cavern in the PEAK DISTRICT, about 1 km (0.6 miles) west of Castleton. At 183 m (600 ft), it is the deepest cave accessible to the public in Britain. In the past lead was mined here, and 40,000 tons of rubble were dumped into the flesh-creepingly named 'Bottomless Pit', a pool at the bottom of the cavern, without raising the water level.

Speen[1] Probably 'place where wood-chips are found' (originally the name of a wood; apparently inspired by an older Latin name *Spinis* 'at the thorn-bushes'), OE *spene* 'wood-chip'.

A village in Berkshire, within the unitary authority of West Berkshire, now a western suburb of NEWBURY.

Speen[2]. A village in Buckinghamshire, about 6 km (4 miles) west of Great Missenden.

Speenhamland 'land of the people of Speen', SPEEN[1] + OE *hæme* 'dwellers' + *land* 'cultivated land'.

A former parish at SPEEN[1] in Berkshire.

Speenhamland System. A system of 'outdoor relief' (public aid administered to the needy not housed in workhouses or similar institutions) initiated by the magistrates of Speenhamland in 1795 to counter distress among the agricultural labourers of the district. Wages were to be supplemented by rate aid according to a minimum wage scale related to the price of bread and the size of the family. Outdoor relief was not new, but the Speenhamland system spread rapidly, particularly in the south. It tended to depress wages and demoralize its beneficiaries and sharply increased the poor rate (the local tax levied to pay for the aid). The Poor Law Amendment Act (1834) sought to terminate outdoor relief, but never wholly succeeded.

Speke Possibly OE *spec* 'brushwood'.

A suburb of LIVERPOOL, Merseyside, 15 km (9 miles) southeast of the city centre. It is the location of Liverpool's airport and of the 16th-century **Speke Hall**, in the care of the National Trust and noted for its half-timbering and plasterwork. As with TALKE in Staffordshire, there are inevitably jokes along the lines of 'Is this bus going to Speke?'

The former Beatles George Harrison (1943–2001) and Paul McCartney (b.1942) lived for part of their childhoods in Speke, where they became schoolfriends in the early 1950s; the McCartneys later moved to ALLERTON.

See also the DINGLE *and* WOOLTON.

Spelthorne 'thorn-bush where speeches are made' (referring to the meeting-place of one of the old Hundreds of Middlesex), OE *spel* 'speech' + *thorn* 'thorn-bush'.

An administrative district of Surrey, north of the River Thames, covering the area of ASHFORD², SHEPPERTON, STAINES, Stanwell, SUNBURY-ON-THAMES and the southern part of HEATHROW Airport. It was created in 1972 and named after an old Hundred (administrative unit) of Middlesex (before 1965 the area had been within the county of Middlesex).

Spennymoor 'hedged moor', OE *spenning* 'hedge, fence' + *mor* 'moor'.

An industrial town in County Durham, 8 km (5 miles) south of Durham itself.

Sperrin Mountains Irish *Sliabh Speirín* 'mountain of points'.

A range of gentle hills along the border of counties LONDONDERRY and TYRONE. The highest point is Sawel (678 m / 2224 ft). In 1609, at the beginning of the plantation of Ulster, when the 'Four Citizens' (businessmen from the City of London) were touring the province to assess its investment potential, the lord deputy of Ireland commanded their guide not on any account to let them see the Sperrins, as such barren uplands would, he was sure, put them off.

> The Derryman, I hope, is proud
> Of Sperrin tops that touch the cloud ...
>
> W.F. Marshall: 'The Hills of Home', from *Ballads*
> *and Verses from Tyrone* (1929)

Spey Origin unknown, possibly pre-Celtic.

Scotland's third-longest river, with a course of 157.5 km (98 miles). It rises in the MONADHLIATH MOUNTAINS of Highland (formerly Inverness-shire), and flows east then northeast through the wide valley west of the CAIRNGORM MOUNTAINS known as **Strathspey** (also called **Speyside**), famous for its malt whiskies. Towns and villages along the river include NEWTONMORE, KINGUSSIE, AVIEMORE, GRANTOWN-ON-SPEY and **Speybridge**; the river then crosses into Moray, past ABERLOUR to **Spey Bay**, where the river

meets the sea, the confluence being known as **Spey Mouth**. The river is famous for its salmon fishing.

strathspey. A stately Scottish country dance, the tunes for which, in four-four time, are typified by the rhythmic figure known as a 'Scotch snap' (a semi-quaver followed by a dotted quaver). The river also inspired a couple of fiddle tunes by J.S. Skinner: 'The Music o' Spey' (an air) and 'The Spey in Spate' (a reel).

Spiddal Irish *An Spidéal* 'the hospital' (*see* SPITAL), referring to an ancient hospice that once stood here.

A small seaside resort in County Galway, 18 km (11 miles) west of Galway itself. It is also spelt **Spiddle**. It is situated at the edge of the Connemara GAELTACHT, and there is an Irish college.

Spiddle. An alternative name for SPIDDAL.

Spike Island¹ Possibly from OE *spic* 'brushwood'.

A country park in Cheshire, within the unitary authority of HALTON. It was once covered by chemical works, but this industry declined here in the early 20th century, and in the late 1970s and early 1980s the area was restored as parkland, with grasslands, woods and waterways.

Spike Island². The nickname of the vast **Royal Victoria Military Hospital** built in the 1850s along the shore at NETLEY, near Southampton. Florence Nightingale called it 'a very expensive mistake'.

Spike Island³ Possibly self-explanatory.

A small island in Cork Harbour (*see under* CORK), about 1 km (0.6 miles) south of COBH. There was formerly a prison here and there is now a coastal defence station.

Spilsby 'Spillir's farmstead or village', OScand *Spillis* possessive form of male personal name *Spillir* + -BY.

A small market town in Lincolnshire, in the FENS, about 16 km (10 miles) west of Skegness. Sir John Franklin (1786–1847), who died in the Arctic while leading an unsuccessful expedition to discover the Northwest Passage, was born here.

Spital¹ 'hospital, religious house' (referring to a leper hospital here in the Middle Ages), ME *spitel* (*see* SPITAL) (from OFr *hospitale*).

A village in Berkshire, now effectively a southern suburb of WINDSOR.

Spital² Referring to a former hospital (*see* SPITAL) for lepers, associated with the chapel of St Thomas the Martyr.

A village in the Wirral, now a southern suburb of BEBINGTON.

Spitalfields 'land belonging to the hospital or religious house' (referring to the priory of St Mary in Shoreditch), ME *spitel* (*see* SPITAL) + *feld* (*see* FIELD).

An area in East London (E1), in the borough of TOWER HAMLETS, to the east of LIVERPOOL STREET station. It started

---

❖ spital ❖

Hospitals are found in most major towns these days, but were not common in medieval times. Middle English *spitel* was borrowed from Old French and Latin and referred initially to a place that gave hospitality, before developing the more modern sense. One of the social functions of early monasteries, and of the Knights Hospitallers religious foundation in particular, was the care of travellers and the sick, especially the dying and the outcast such as lepers. In medieval Latin this kind of establishment was the *hospitale* and it gives its name to SPIDDAL (County Galway), and SPITAL[1] (Berkshire and the Wirral). In Lincolnshire a small settlement grew up around the *spital* on the Roman road ERMINE STREET, hence SPITAL IN THE STREET; and in London SPITALFIELDS was land owned by or used to fund the 'hospital' of the local priory of St Mary Shoreditch. In Scotland the word appears in various SPITTALS.

---

to become built up in the middle of the 17th century, and by the end of the century had received a large influx of Huguenot refugees from France. Many of them brought their silk-weaving skills with them, and that trade characterized Spitalfields for the next two hundred years and more.

In 1682 Charles II granted a licence for a vegetable market here, and that too remained very much part of the local scene until quite recently. It finally moved out in 1991, leaving its distinctive 1890s red-brick market building and the streets around to a somewhat mobile population of organic-food outlets and craft shops.

Dominating the entire area is the austere form of Nicholas Hawksmoor's **Christ Church, Spitalfields**, built between 1714 and 1729. It is a brooding presence in Peter Ackroyd's novel *Hawksmoor* (1985).

In the 19th century Spitalfields descended into real poverty and slumdom. Jack the Ripper's second victim, Annie Chapman, was killed in a backyard off Hanbury Street, Spitalfields, in September 1888. The area's tradition as a haven for immigrants was continued in the late 19th century with a substantial Jewish influx, and after the Second World War the eastern part of Spitalfields, around BRICK LANE, became home to a sizeable Bangladeshi community.

The **Spitalfields Festival** in late June has become an established item on the classical music calendar.

The notorious thief (and prison escapologist) Jack Sheppard (1702–24) was born in Spitalfields, as was John Dolland (1706–61), progenitor of the opticians Dolland & Aitchison (as Dolland & Sons its original premises were in Spitalfields). The artists Gilbert and George bought a house in Fournier Street, Spitalfields, and an American, Dennis Severs, turned the early Georgian 18 Folgate Street into a 'living museum', by living an 18th-century life (complete with chamber pots, no gas or electricity, etc.) and occasionally opening the house for visitors to have similar experiences: it continues in this manner, although now with staff (who presumably don't live the life), after the owner died in 1999.

Spitalfields and Banglatown. A ward of TOWER HAMLETS borough council covering the area of Spitalfields and BRICK LANE. The recent coinage 'Banglatown' reflects the large size of the local Bengali population.

Spitalfields breakfast. 19th-century slang for no breakfast at all – i.e. going hungry. The contemporary lexicographer J.C. Hotten defined it laconically as 'a tight necktie and a short pipe'. The reference is, of course, to the area's poverty and deprivation.

Spital in the Street 'hospital or religious house on the Roman road', referring to an institution of uncertain early history, associated with the chapel of St Edmund the Martyr, on the section of Ermine Street between Lincoln and York: *Spital* (see SPITAL) with OE *strœt* (see STREET).

A hamlet in Lincolnshire, on the A15 (the old ERMINE STREET), about 16 km (10 miles) east of Gainsborough.

Spithead 'head of the spit of land' (referring to a sandy spit of land (today largely tarmacked over and built on) on the western side of the entrance to Portsmouth Harbour).

A roadstead or anchorage off the entrance to Portsmouth Harbour (*see under* PORTSMOUTH). Its name was originally that of a headland to the north, but since at least the early 18th century it has been applied to this stretch of the SOLENT. At that time the Royal Navy's Grand Fleet was based here, and it has been associated with the Navy ever since. It is the traditional venue for naval reviews. A notable one was held in 1897, for example, on the occasion of Queen Victoria's Diamond Jubilee, when the entire British fleet was drawn up here in the greatest display of naval power the world had ever seen. Somewhat less auspicious was the review of 20 May 1937: the BBC did a live outside broadcast from Spithead, and a tired and emotional Lieutenant Commander Tommy Woodrooffe offered as commentary: 'At the present moment the whole fleet's lit up. When I say "lit up", I mean lit up by fairy lamps. It's fantastic. It isn't a fleet at all … it's Fairyland. The whole fleet is in Fairyland,' and so on for a few more moments, during which the lights went off and Woodrooffe appeared to be convinced that the fleet had actually disappeared into thin air, at which point the broadcast cut to the studio announcer.

Spithead Mutiny. A mutiny in 1797 in which the crews of the Royal Navy's Channel fleet effectively went on strike over grievances about pay, promotion and leave. It lasted nearly a month, and ended after concessions were made by the government. Its relative success encouraged the outbreak of the more serious mutiny at the NORE the following month.

Spithead nightingale. An old Royal Navy slang term (inspired by the blowing of the boatswain's whistle) for a boatswain or boatswain's mate.

Spithead pheasant. A slang expression (again from the Royal Navy) for a kipper or bloater.

Spittal ME *spitel* (*see* SPITAL) from OFr *hospitale*.
There are villages of this name in Dumfries and Galloway (two), East Lothian, Northumberland and Pembrokeshire (the latter a foundation of St David's Cathedral). (For **Spittal of Glenshee** *see under* GLEN SHEE, and for **Spittal of Glenmuick** *see under* GLEN MUICK.)

Spofforth 'small plot of land next to a ford', OE *spot* 'small plot of land' + FORD.
A village in North Yorkshire, 5 km (3 miles) northwest of Wetherby. There are the remains of a medieval castle, the home of the Percy family before they moved to ALNWICK in the early 14th century.

Sporle Probably 'wood or glade where spars or shafts are obtained', OE *spearr* 'spar, shaft' + -LEY.
A village in Norfolk, about 3 km (2 miles) northeast of SWAFFHAM.

Sproatley 'clearing with new shoots', OE *sprota* 'new shoot', plural *sprotta* + -LEY.
A village in the East Riding of Yorkshire, 12 km (7.5 miles) northeast of Hull.

Sprotbrough 'Sprota's stronghold', OE male personal name *Sprota* + *burh* (*see* BURY); alternatively the first element may be *sprota* 'new shoot', plural *sprotta*.
A village in South Yorkshire, on a limestone edge above the River DON², 4 km (2.5 miles) southwest of Doncaster.

Spurn Head 'spur headland', OE *spurn* 'spur', from its shape.
The headland guarding the northern side of the mouth of the HUMBER. It is situated at the end of a long, curving, sandy spit in the East Riding of Yorkshire, some 35 km (20 miles) southeast of Hull. The area is an important nature reserve for seals and migrating birds. So dangerous are the waters hereabouts that there are two lighthouses, and the only permanently manned lifeboat station in Britain.
See also HOLDERNESS.

Square Mile, the. An epithet applied to the CITY of London (*see also under* LONDON), on account of its area (to

be precise, 274 ha (677 acres) – somewhat more than a square mile, which is 259 ha (640 acres)). First recorded in 1966, it is used mainly in the context of the City as a financial centre or of the City's governmental institutions:

> Prince Charles was made a Freeman of the City of London yesterday … It was the kind of traditional occasion that the square mile does so well.
>
> *The Guardian* (3 March 1971)

> Property groups and financial institutions in the Square Mile believe granting planning powers to the mayor of London will add an extra layer of bureaucracy to development.
>
> *The Times* (21 September 1998)

Sráid na Cathrach. The Irish name for MILLTOWN MALBAY.

Sraith Salach. The Irish name for RECESS.

Sròn na Cìche. *See under* the CIOCH.

Stab City. An unfortunate nickname for LIMERICK, deriving from the place's reputation for criminal violence in recent years.

Stac Pollaidh 'steep rock of the River Polly', OScand *stakkr* 'steep rock' (also applied to sea stacks) + Gaelic *pollaidh* 'of the little pool'.
A dramatic little mountain (613 m / 2011 ft) with a pinnacled summit ridge, in northwest Highland (formerly in Ross and Cromarty), some 17 km (11 miles) north of ULLAPOOL. Its anglicized spelling, which reflects its pronunciation, is **Stack Polly**. It is situated in the **Inverpolly Forest** (an unforested nature reserve). The **River Polly** meets the sea at **Polly Bay**.

Stadium of Light. The impressive home ground of Sunderland FC (*see under* SUNDERLAND), built in 1997 on the site of the former Wearmouth Colliery, which closed in 1993. It is the largest all-seater stadium in Britain built since the Second World War. Its name was not adopted from Benfica's Estádio da Luz in Portugal (where Luz is the suburb of that name, although also Portuguese for light), but rather reflects the fact that the whole stadium is illuminated every evening from twilight to midnight as a symbol of the regeneration of Sunderland itself.

Staffa 'pillar island', OScand *stafr* 'stave, pillar' + *ey* (*see* -AY).
A small island in the Inner HEBRIDES, some 12 km (7 miles) off the west coast of Mull, in Argyll and Bute (formerly in Strathclyde region). Staffa is one of the geological wonders of the world, its sea cliffs being made up of regular hexagonal (occasionally pentagonal) black basalt pillars (like those at the GIANT'S CAUSEWAY) up to 17 m (55 ft) high, topped by a bulging layer of amorphous lava of similar height. The Shetland poet Christine de Luca has aptly described this combination as 'a soufflé stiffening in a

crystal dish'. Cut into these formations at the southern tip of the island is the spectacular and much celebrated FINGAL'S CAVE, dubbed 'the Cathedral of the Seas'.

The first outsider to 'discover' the wonders of Staffa was the scientist Joseph (later Sir Joseph) Banks, soon after his return from Captain Cook's 1768–71 expedition, on which he had acted as naturalist. On 12 August 1772 Banks landed on Staffa, en route to Iceland, and published his findings in the *Scots Magazine* that autumn. That was to herald a flood of visitors, particularly to see Fingal's Cave.

Stafford 'ford by a landing-place', OE *stæth* 'landing-place' + FORD. (An alternative local explanation, that the river here can be forded with the aid of a staff, is without foundation.)

A market town in Staffordshire, on the River Sow and on the M6, about 25 km (15 miles) south of STOKE-ON-TRENT. It is the county town of STAFFORDSHIRE. It was founded by Æthelflæd, daughter of Alfred the Great. In the early Middle Ages it acquired two castles; only the ruins of one of them now remains. In the Civil Wars the town supported the Royalist cause and in consequence was fairly severely pummelled by the Parliamentarians, but one notable survivor is the High House, a four-storey timbered building where Charles I and Prince Rupert stayed in 1642. In the 18th century Stafford thrived as a shoe-making centre. Today it retains the air of a pleasant country town.

Izaak Walton (1593–1683), author of *The Compleat Angler*, was born in Stafford. The playwright Richard Brinsley Sheridan was MP for the town between 1780 and 1806.

There are towns called Stafford in the USA (Kansas, Nebraska, New York, Virginia) and a county called Stafford in Virginia.

Stafford. An alternative name for a Staffordshire bull terrier (*see under* STAFFORDSHIRE).

Stafford knot. *See* Staffordshire knot *under* STAFFORDSHIRE.

Stafford law. A 16th- and 17th-century term denoting the use of force to compel obedience. It is a pun on the more common contemporary synonym *club law* (*club* = staff).

Staffordshire From STAFFORD + SHIRE. The name *Staffordshire* is first recorded in the 11th century.

A county in the northwest Midlands of England. It is bounded to the west by Shropshire, to the north by Cheshire, to the west by Derbyshire and Leicestershire and to the south by Warwickshire and the West Midlands. Its county town is STAFFORD, and other important centres are BURTON UPON TRENT, CANNOCK, LEEK, LICHFIELD, NEWCASTLE UNDER LYME, RUGELEY, TAMWORTH and UTTOXETER and the unitary authority of STOKE-ON-TRENT. Its main river is the TRENT[1], and it is crossed by the **Staffordshire and Worcestershire Canal**. It includes part of the PEAK DISTRICT.

Roman-era Staffordshire was part of the territory of the Cornovii tribe (*see under* SHROPSHIRE). In the Anglo-Saxon period it was the heartland of the kingdom of MERCIA (*see also* TAMWORTH and LICHFIELD).

It is now predominantly an agricultural county, dairy farming being of particular importance. The coalfields of northern Staffordshire have gone, and the great industrial towns of the BLACK COUNTRY, to the south of the county, were hived off to the WEST MIDLANDS in 1974. Beer is still brewed at Burton upon Trent, though, and Staffordshire's signature industry, the earthenware- and china-making of the POTTERIES, remains very much in business (despite 21st-century closures at Wedgwood). Born in the 18th century, when the county was one of the first parts of England to feel the effects of the Industrial Revolution, and developed especially through the work of Josiah Wedgwood, it has ensured that Staffordshire's name has become synonymous with fine-quality ceramics (as in 'a Staffordshire figurine').

The **University of Staffordshire**, based in Stoke-on-Trent, was founded in 1992. It was formed from Staffordshire Polytechnic (formerly North Staffs Polytechnic).

In cricketing terms Staffordshire is a 'minor county' (the club was founded in 1871) and plays in the minor counties championship. Staffordshire were lucky enough, however, to be able to call on the services of the legendary bowler S.F. Barnes (*see also under* SMETHWICK) in the early part of the 20th century. Barnes took an incredible 1432 wickets for Staffordshire at less than 9 runs each, including 76 wickets at 8.21 each in his 56th year.

Staffordshire bull terrier. A sturdy, stocky breed of dog (also known as a **Staffordshire pit-bull**) developed as a bulldog-terrier cross. They are commonly black and white. These dogs usually wear studded collars and tend to be favoured by young men seeking extra machismo and random violence (they have been known to make unprovoked attacks on other dogs). The breed is often affectionately known by their owners as 'Staffs' (singular 'Staff').

Staffordshire cut. A colloquial term in cricket for a cut shot which sends the ball behind the wicket off the under edge of the bat, narrowly missing the stumps.

Staffordshire knot. A stylized figure of a half-knot. Originally called a 'Stafford knot', it apparently began life as the badge of the Stafford family, but it is now firmly associated with the county (it is the cap-badge worn by Staffordshire county cricketers, for instance). It is also used more widely as a decorative device.

Staffs. The standard written abbreviation of STAFFORDSHIRE.

Stags of Broad Haven. *See under* BROAD HAVEN.

Staindrop Probably 'stony valley', OE *stæner* 'stony land' + *hop* 'valley'.

A village in County Durham, 12 km (7.5 miles) southwest of Bishop Auckland.

Staines Originally *Stane* '(place at the) stone' (perhaps referring to a Roman milestone on the road from London to Silchester; a direct link with the present 'London Stone' is unlikely), OE *stan* (*see* STONE); the plural ending -*s* had been added by the end of the 11th century.

A town in Surrey, on the River THAMES[1], on the western edge of London, about 11 km (7 miles) southeast of Windsor. It was a settlement in Roman times, when its name was **Pontibus** '(place at the) bridges', reflecting its importance as a Thames crossing-place. Today it is best known for its reservoirs, the double **Staines Reservoirs** and the next-door King George VI Reservoir, which are familiar landmarks to travellers flying into or out of HEATHROW Airport. A rather more ancient local landmark is the so-called 'London Stone', marking the western limit of the jurisdiction of the City of London; it has been claimed as the origin of Staines's name, but the name is much older than the date (1285) on the stone.

'**Staines Massive**', an imaginary Black kids' gang, was part of the elaborate construct surrounding the comic persona 'Ali G', portrayed on television by Sacha Baron-Cohen (for those unfamiliar with the joke, Staines is an unlikely place for such an inner-city phenomenon).

Stainmore Pass 'stony moor pass', OE *stan*, replaced by OScand *steinn* (*see* STONE) + OE *mor* 'moor' + ModE *pass*.

The bleakest passage of the A66 through the northern PENNINES between APPLEBY-IN-WESTMORLAND and SCOTCH CORNER. It is not infrequently closed by snow in the winter. Sir Walter Scott described the place as 'Stanmore's lonely dell' (*Rokeby* (1813), I, xxvi), although it does not have the quaint and gentle dinginess usually associated with dells. To the north are the moorland hills of **Stainmore Common**, and to the south those of the generally treeless **Stainmore Forest**.

> Northumberland is … bounded by the mountains of Stainmore and Cheviot on the west, which are in some places inaccessible, in many unpassable.
>
> Daniel Defoe: *A Tour Through the Whole Island of Great Britain* (1724–6)

The high point of the pass, at 447 m (1466 ft), marks the boundary between CUMBRIA and County Durham (*see* DURHAM, COUNTY), and by the road here is the ancient Rey Cross (OScand *hrreyrr* 'cairn', here possibly marking the boundary).

> Allen-a-Dale is no baron or lord,
> Yet twenty tall yeomen will draw at his word;
> And the best of our nobles his bonnet will vail,
> Who at Rere-cross on Stanmore meets Allen-a-Dale.
>
> Sir Walter Scott: *Rokeby* (1813), III, xxx

Battle of Stainmore (954). The Rey Cross on the Stainmore Pass marks the spot where Erik (or Eric) Bloodaxe, Viking ruler of Jorvik (YORK) and king of NORTHUMBRIA, was killed in a battle with the English under King Edred.

> By such rocks
> men killed Bloodaxe.
> Fierce blood throbs in his tongue,
> lean words.
> Skulls cropped for steel caps
> huddle round Stainmore.
>
> Basil Bunting: *Briggflatts* (1966)

Stainton 'farmstead on stony ground', OE *stan* + -TON.

A village in South Yorkshire, 2.5 km (1.5 miles) east of Maltby. The Yorkshire, Derbyshire and England fast bowler F.S. ('Fiery Fred') Trueman, self-styled 'finest fast bowler that ever drew breath', was born here in 1931. There are further Staintons in Cumbria, Durham, Middlesbrough and North Yorkshire.

Staithes OE *stæth* 'landing place'.

A small fishing village on the coast of Redcar and Cleveland (formerly in the North Riding of Yorkshire, then in Cleveland), 28 km (17 miles) east of Middlesbrough. James Cook was apprenticed to a draper here at the age of 17 (1728–9), but the lure of the sea proved too great, and Cook left to begin his career as one of England's greatest sailors and explorers. The place gets a somewhat obscure mention in Basil Bunting's Poundian poem *The Spoils* (1951):

> Staithes, filthy harbour water,
> a drowned Finn, a drowned Chinee …

Staithes Group, the. A loose group of artists in the late 19th century, including Mark Senior (1864–1927) and Laura Knight (1877–1970). They based themselves along the coast between Staithes and ROBIN HOOD'S BAY.

Stalbridge 'bridge built on piles', OE *stapol* 'post, pile' + *brycg* 'bridge'.

A small market town in Dorset, about 11 km (7 miles) east of Sherborne, in the BLACKMOOR VALE. It has a 14th-century market cross. It made its reputation as a centre of glove-making.

The physicist Robert Boyle (1627–91) lived in Stalbridge.

Stalling Busk 'stallion's bush', *Stalling* ME *stalun* 'stallion'; *Busk* OScand *buskr* 'bush'.

A small settlement in North Yorkshire, 1 km (0.6 miles) south of SEMER WATER, and 6 km (4 miles) southeast of Hawes in Wensleydale.

Stalybridge 'bridge by the copse where staves are cut', OE *stæf* 'stave' + -LEY + *brycg* 'bridge'.

A former cotton town in Greater Manchester, some 13 km (8 miles) east of the city centre. The **Stalybridge Old Band**, founded in 1814, was one of the earliest brass bands in England.

Stamford 'stone ford' or 'stony ford', OE *stan* (*see* STONE) + FORD.

A market town in Lincolnshire, on the River WELLAND and on the A1, about 19 km (12 miles) northwest of PETER-BOROUGH. It dates back to Roman times, and during the period of Danish rule it was one of the FIVE BOROUGHS, and was designated the capital of the FENS. In the Middle Ages it prospered on the wool and cloth trades, Stamford cloth being famed throughout Europe for its strength and dur-ability (a particular PR coup was getting Cardinal Wolsey to use it for the tents at the celebrated 'Field of the Cloth of Gold' meeting between Henry VIII and Francis I of France in 1520). After the trade went into a decline Stamford con-tinued to earn a comfortable income as a staging point on the GREAT NORTH ROAD, but its increasing backwaterishness at least had the advantage of preserving its handsome 17th- and 18th-century aspect – an advantage not lost on 20th-century film-makers in search of a historical location (Stamford starred as MIDDLEMARCH, for instance, in a 1994 BBC television adaptation of George Eliot's novel). Many of its older buildings – which include medieval almshouses known as 'callises', founded by wealthy local merchants who conducted much of their business via the Channel port of Calais – are made of a grey limestone called Barnack Rag, quarried locally at Barnack. Stamford was the first town in England to be designated a Conservation Area (in 1967).

In St Martin's churchyard is the grave of Daniel Lambert, the 'biggest Englishman ever', who weighed 330 kilos (52 stone) when he died in 1809.

Stamford formerly hosted a well-known bull run, in which a bull was let loose in the streets and goaded into a rampage. The banning of this practice in Stamford follow-ing the Cruelty to Animals Act of 1835 was the first success-ful campaign of the Royal Society for the Prevention of Cruelty to Animals.

A little to the southeast of Stamford is Burghley House, ancestral home of the Cecils (*see also* HATFIELD[1]). It was built between 1555 and 1587 for William Cecil, the 1st Lord Burghley, Elizabeth I's long-serving advisor. (The Cecils played a major role in resisting the encroachments of the modern world on Stamford – largely in order to protect their own electoral interests. For instance, one of them was instrumental in ensuring that the main East Coast railway line went through Peterborough rather than Stamford.)

The conductor Sir Malcolm Sargent (1895–1967) was born in Stamford.

There are towns called Stamford in the USA (Connecticut, New York, South Dakota, Texas) and Australia (Queensland).

Stamford ware. A type of lead-glazed pottery of the late Anglo-Saxon and early Norman periods, made from estuarine clay obtained in the vicinity of Stamford.

Stamford Bridge *See* STAMFORD + *brycg* 'bridge'.

A village on the River DERWENT[3], on the border between York, the East Riding and North Yorkshire, 11 km (7 miles) east of York.

Battle of Stamford Bridge (25 September 1066). King Harold II of England was gathering an army in the south in anticipation of a Norman invasion when he heard the news that Harald Hardrada of Norway, together with Harold's exiled brother Tostig, had landed in Yorkshire. Harold marched his men north and confronted Harald's army at Stamford Bridge, where he offered the Norwegian safe passage home or seven feet of earth for his grave. Harald chose the latter, and ended the day needing it, for both he and Tostig were slain. The edge of Harold's victory was blunted a few days later with the news that William of Normandy had landed in Sussex, and Harold was forced to march his tired army south to take on the Normans near HASTINGS.

The victory at Stamford Bridge is celebrated annually in the village with the baking of a large pie in the shape of a wash-tub. This commemorates the Saxon who, seeing the bridge blocked by one huge and fearsome Viking, floated under the bridge in such a tub, and dispatched the giant from below with his spear.

Standard, Battle of the. *See* COWTON MOOR.

Standish 'stony pasture', OE *stan* (*see* STONE) + *edisc* 'pasture, enclosure'.

A town in Lancashire, 6 km (4 miles) north of Wigan.

Stanegate, the There are no early spellings, but the name ultimately derives from OScand *steinn* (*see* STONE) + *gata* 'road', referring to the Roman paved road.

A Roman road going from CORBRIDGE west to CARLISLE, built *c*.AD 85 by Agricola's troops, before the construction of HADRIAN'S WALL.

Stane Street[1] 'stone road' (that is, a paved road), OE *stan* (*see* STONE) + STREET.

A Roman road which led southwestwards from London Bridge (*see under* LONDON) through the NORTH DOWNS and on to CHICHESTER. The northermost part of its course is rep-resented today by Borough High Street (*see under* BOROUGH) and in Sussex sections of it are followed by the A29.

Stane Street[2]. A Roman road which led from ST ALBANS via BRAINTREE to COLCHESTER. Sections of it are now followed by the A120.

Stanford Dingley *Stanford* 'stone ford, stony ford', OE *stan* (*see* STONE) + FORD; *Dingley* denoting manorial ownership in the Middle Ages by the Dyngley family.

A village in Berkshire, within the unitary authority of WEST BERKSHIRE, on the River PANG, about 16 km (10 miles) west of Reading.

Stanford in the Vale From its situation in the VALE OF THE WHITE HORSE.

A village in Oxfordshire (before 1974 in Berkshire), on the River OCK, about 8 km (5 miles) northwest of Wantage.

Stanhope 'stony valley', OE *stan* (*see* STONE) + *hop* 'valley'.

A large village on the River WEAR in County Durham, 16 km (10 miles) southwest of Consett. It developed as a lead-mining centre in the 19th century, and is regarded as the 'capital' of Weardale.

See also WEAR.

Stanmore 'stony pool' (referring to a gravelly pool), OE *stan* (*see* STONE) + *mere* 'pool').

An outer suburb of northwest London, in the borough of HARROW (before 1965 in Middlesex), between Edgware to the east and Harrow Weald to the west. Bentley Priory, a fine late 18th-century house which was the headquarters of RAF Fighter Command during the Battle of Britain, is situated here.

Stanmore 'Underground' station opened in 1932 – originally on the Bakerloo line, now on the Jubilee, of which it is the northern terminus.

Stannaries, the From Medieval Latin *stannaria*, based on Latin *stannum* 'tin'.

The area of Cornwall and Devon formerly under the jurisdiction of the **Stannary courts**. Set up in 1201 under a charter of King John, these had the right and duty of trying cases involving tin- and lead-miners (except for assaults and murder, and land disputes). The system, which recognized the isolated and independent nature of the mining communities, survived until 1898. There were also **Stannary Parliaments** for Cornwall and Devon, with 24 representatives each; the Cornish one last met in 1752.

Stannary town. Any of four towns in Cornwall (HELSTON, LISKEARD, LOSTWITHIEL and TRURO) and four towns in Devon (ASHBURTON, CHAGFORD, PLYMPTON and TAVISTOCK) to which, in the past, tin was brought to be assessed and taxed.

Stanstead Abbotts Stanstead 'stony place', OE *stan* (*see* STONE) + *stede* 'place'; *Abbotts* referring to its early possession by the Abbot of Waltham.

A village in Hertfordshire, on the River LEA, about 6 km (4 miles) east of Hertford.

Stansted From STANSTED MOUNTFITCHET.

An airport (officially **London Stansted**) in Essex, about 3 km (2 miles) southeast of Stansted Mountfitchet and 3 km (2 miles) east of Bishop's Stortford, close to the M11. It began life as a US Army Air Force bomber base during the Second World War. Civilian operations began after the war, and in the 1950s the USAF returned and built a much longer runway, giving Stansted the potential to be developed as London's third airport (after HEATHROW and

GATWICK[1]). After much discussion and local opposition this duly happened. At first it was used mainly for cargo, but by the end of the 20th century, following the opening in 1991 of the striking new terminal building designed by Norman Foster, it was handling 5.5 million passengers a year. In December 2003 the Department of Transport announced plans for developing a second runway at Stansted, to be opened by 2011, much to the fury of local residents and environmental groups.

Stansted Mountfitchet Stansted 'stony place', OE *stan* 'stone' + *stede* 'place'; *Mountfitchet* denoting manorial ownership in the early Middle Ages by the Muntfichet family.

A village in Essex, on the River STORT, beside the M11, about 5 km (3 miles) northeast of Bishop's Stortford. The development of the nearby Stansted Airport has considerably boosted its economy.

The Normans built a castle here. It was destroyed by King John in 1215, but there is a modern timber-built replica, blending in with the village's suitably medieval-sounding name.

Stanton Drew Stanton 'farmstead by the stone(s)' (referring to ancient stone circles in the vicinity), OE *stan* (*see* STONE) + -TON; *Drew* denoting manorial ownership in the Middle Ages by someone called Drogo or Drew.

A village in Bath and North East Somerset (before 1996 in Avon, before 1974 in Somerset), about 10 km (6 miles) south of Bristol. There is an old toll-house at the approach to the village, and nearby are three Neolithic stone circles, with massive uprights. These stone circles are collectively known as 'The Wedding' or 'The Fiddler and the Maids'; the story associated with them tells how a wedding was being celebrated here late on a Saturday night, but when it came to midnight the musician refused to play on into the Sabbath. At this the bride swore she'd find another fiddler even if she had to go to hell to fetch him. The Devil duly arrived with his fiddle and the dancers danced so madly that by dawn they had all turned to stone.

Stanton Fitzwarren Stanton (*see* STANTON DREW) referring to a large standing stone in the vicinity; *Fitzwarren* denoting manorial ownership in the Middle Ages by someone called Fitz Waryn.

A village in Wiltshire, within the unitary authority of SWINDON, about 5 km (3 miles) north of the town.

Stanton Harcourt Stanton (*see* STANTON DREW) referring to nearby ancient stones known as the Devil's Quoits; *Harcourt* denoting manorial ownership in the early Middle Ages by the de Harecurt family.

A village in Oxfordshire, about 11 km (7 miles) west of Oxford. It was the seat of the Harcourt family from the 12th to the 18th century, when they moved to NUNEHAM COURTENAY. Their manor house has a 1540 gatehouse and a tower ('Pope's Tower') where Alexander Pope lived while translating Homer's *Iliad* in 1717 and 1718, and it also contains one of the most spectacular medieval kitchens to survive in England. After 1945 the Harcourt family returned, restored the house and planted gardens.

Stanton in Peak *Stanton* 'farmstead on stony ground', OE *stan* (*see* STONE) + -TON; *in Peak* referring to its location.
A village in Derbyshire, in the PEAK DISTRICT, close to the River DERWENT[1], about 5 km (3 miles) southeast of Bakewell.

Stanton Long *Stanton see* STANTON IN PEAK; *Long* referring to the way in which the village straggles out along its main road.
A village in Shropshire, about 16 km (10 miles) west of Bridgnorth.

Stanton St Bernard *Stanton see* STANTON IN PEAK; *St Bernard* denoting manorial ownership in the early Middle Ages by a man called Erebetus (later rationalized to *Bernard*; the *St* was perhaps suggested by the nearby STANTON ST QUENTIN; there is no connection with St Bernard of Clairvaux).
A village in Wiltshire, about 8 km (5 miles) east of DEVIZES.

Stanton St Quentin *Stanton see* STANTON IN PEAK; *St Quentin* denoting manorial ownership in the early Middle Ages by the de Sancto Quintino family.
A village in Wiltshire, about 6 km (4 miles) north of Chippenham.

Stanton upon Hine Heath *Stanton see* STANTON IN PEAK; *Hine Heath* 'heath of the domestic servants' (the reason for the curious specification is unknown), ME *hine* 'domestic servant' + *hethe* 'heath'.
A village in Shropshire, about 14 km (9 miles) northeast of Shrewsbury.

Stanwardine in the Fields *Stanwardine* 'enclosure made of stones, or on stony ground', OE *stan* (*see* STONE) + *worthign* 'enclosure' (*see* -WORTH, WORTHY, -WARDINE); *in the Fields* originally to distinguish it from a neighbouring settlement *Stanwardine in the Wood*.
A village in Shropshire, about 14 km (9 miles) northwest of Shrewsbury.

Staple Fitzpaine *Staple* '(place at the) pillar of wood or stone' (referring to a local marker post), OE *stapol* 'pillar of wood or stone'; *Fitzpaine* denoting manorial ownership in the Middle Ages by the Fitzpaine family.
A village in Somerset, among the BLACKDOWN HILLS, about 8 km (5 miles) southeast of TAUNTON.

Stapleford Tawney *Stapleford* 'ford marked by a post', OE *stapol* 'pillar of wood or stone' + FORD; *Tawney* denoting manorial ownership in the early Middle Ages by the de Tany family.
A village in Essex, close to the River RODING, about 13 km (8 miles) northwest of Brentwood.

Star[1] Perhaps dialect *star* 'rough grass'.
A village in Somerset, in the MENDIP HILLS, about 11 km (7 miles) east of Weston super Mare.

Star[2] From the name of an inn.
A village in Pembrokeshire (formerly in Dyfed), 13 km (8 miles) southeast of Cardigan.

Star[3] Probably OScand *storr* 'sedge'.
A village in Fife, 4 km (2.5 miles) northeast of Glenrothes.

Starcross Probably 'cross or crossroads where starlings gather', dialect *stare* 'starling' + CROSS.
A village in Devon, on the western shore of the estuary of the River EXE, opposite Exmouth.

Starling's Green 'green belonging to the Starlings'; a family called *Starling* is known here from the 15th century.
A village in Essex, about 11 km (7 miles) southwest of Saffron Walden.

Start Point[1] *Start* 'point of land', OE *steort*.
A headland on the North Cornish coast, on the broad bay to the south of TINTAGEL.
See also STERT POINT.

Start Point[2]. A headland in Devon, at the southeastern tip of the KINGSBRIDGE peninsula. It is the southern extremity of the 13 km (8 mile) wide **Start Bay**.

Staxigoe Etymology unknown.
A small settlement in northeast Highland (formerly in Caithness), 3 km (2 miles) northeast of Wick.

Staylittle Originally from the name of the *Staylittle Inn*, but popular tradition has created *Stay-a-little*, from the celebrated speed with which the local blacksmith brothers could re-shoe horses.
A hamlet in Powys (formerly in Montgomeryshire), 10 km (6 miles) northwest of Llanidloes. Its Welsh name is **Penfforddlas** ('top, end of the green road', *pen* + *ffordd* 'road' + *glas* 'green'), a name which reflects its remoteness, and may suggest that the English name is ironic.

Steel Cross A recent name of uncertain origin: it may be a reference to an iron signpost at a crossroads.
A village in East Sussex, on the northeastern outskirts of CROWBOROUGH.

Steep 'steep place', OE *stiepe*.
A village in Hampshire, on the northwestern outskirts of Petersfield.

Steep Holm *Steep* from its vertiginous sides; *Holm* 'island', late OE from OScand *holmr* (*see* -EY, -EA).
A barren rocky island in the mouth of the River SEVERN, about 8 km (5 miles) off Weston super Mare and about 4 km (2.5 miles) south of Flat Holm. It is privately owned. Several rare plants grow here.

Steeping From the name of two villages, *Great* and *Little Steeping* ('(settlement of) Steapa's people', OE male personal name *Steapa* + *-ingas* (*see* -ING)), along the river's course.

A river in Lincolnshire, in the FENS, which rises to the east of HORNCASTLE and flows 28 km (18 miles) southeastwards through WAINFLEET ALL SAINTS into the mouth of the WASH at GIBRALTAR. It is canalized in its lower reaches. From Wainfleet to the sea it is also known as 'Wainfleet Haven'.

Steeple From its appearance and the proximity of PILLAR.

A mountain (819 m / 2687 ft) in the LAKE DISTRICT, Cumbria (formerly in Cumberland), on the south side of Ennerdale, 1.6 km (1 mile) west of Pillar.

Steeple Bumpstead *Steeple* to distinguish the place from nearby Helions Bumpstead; *Bumpstead see* HELIONS BUMPSTEAD.

A village in northwestern Essex, about 14 km (9 miles) northeast of SAFFRON WALDEN.

Steeple Gidding *Steeple* to distinguish the village from nearby Great and Little Gidding; *Gidding see* LITTLE GIDDING.

A village in Cambridgeshire (before 1974 in Huntingdonshire), about 16 km (10 miles) northwest of Huntingdon.

Steeple Langford *Steeple* from the steeple of the local church, to distinguish it from Hanging Langford, on the other side of the river; *Langford see* HANGING LANGFORD.

A village in Wiltshire, on the River WYLYE[1], about 13 km (8 miles) northwest of Salisbury.

Stelling Minnis *Stelling* perhaps '(settlement of) Stealla's people', OE male personal name *Stealla* + *-ingas* (*see* -ING); *Minnis* 'common land', OE *mænnes*.

A village in Kent, just to the east of STANE STREET[1], near Lyminge Forest, about 14 km (9 miles) northeast of ASHFORD[1].

Stenhousemuir 'the moorland by the stone house', OE *stan* (*see* STONE) + *hus* 'house' + *moor*.

A small town on the River CARRON 4 km (2.5 miles) north of Falkirk, formerly in Stirlingshire, then in Central region, and now in the unitary authority of Falkirk. Until the late 19th century it was the site of the great cattle market called the Falkirk Tryst (*see under* FALKIRK[1]). Today the town is best known for **Stenhousemuir FC**, also called the **Warriors**, founded in 1884; at the time of writing they were languishing in Scottish League Division Two.

> Stenhousemuir, Glenrothes, Auchterarder, Renton
> – one way street to the coup of the mind.
>
>   Tom Buchan: 'Scotland the Wee', from *Dolphins at Cochin* (1969)

Stenness, Stones of. *See* STONES OF STENNESS.

Stepaside The name may refer to a narrow bridge where those crossing have to give way, or 'step aside'.

A village in Pembrokeshire (formerly in Dyfed), 7 km (4 miles) north of Tenby.

Stepney Probably 'Stybba's landing-place', OE *Stybban* possessive form of male personal name *Stybba* + *hyth* 'landing-place'. Alternatively the first element could be from OE *stybba* 'stump, pile', referring to the construction of the landing-place.

A district of EAST LONDON (E1, E3, E4), in the borough of TOWER HAMLETS, immediately to the east of the City of London. It has its own recognizable centre, around **Stepney Green** (E1), but the medieval **parish of Stepney** covered a huge area, from the City to the River LEA. By the end of the 17th century rapid population growth and consequent house-building was blurring its internal boundaries, creating an undifferentiated urban mass. The position was formalized in 1900 when the **Borough of Stepney** was created, one of London's largest, extending to BETHNAL GREEN in the north and POPLAR in the east. It was poor and overcrowded, dependent for its meagre prosperity on the docks and clothing manufacture, and with a large immigrant population. It suffered severely in the Blitz. Post-Second World War redevelopment has alleviated the worst of its deprivation, but it remains one of the poorer areas of London.

Cosmo Gordon Lang, later Archbishop of Canterbury, became Suffragan Bishop of Stepney in 1901, at the age of 37. Clement Attlee, later prime minister, was elected mayor of Stepney in 1919. The thief Jack Sheppard (1702–24), whose exploits in escaping four times from NEWGATE and other London gaols made him a popular hero, was born in Stepney.

Hamlet of Stepney Green, The. A play (1957) by Bernard Kops, who was one of the less well-remembered of the 1950s 'Angry Young Men'. The play relocates the lineaments of Shakespeare's plot to the EAST END.

Stepney wheel. An inflated tyre on a metal rim, which can be attached to the wheel of a vehicle with a punctured tyre, so that it can continue to be driven temporarily. Strictly speaking the name is not directly attributable to Stepney in London: it comes from Stepney Street in LLANELLI, where the device was originally made. The wheel did not catch on in Britain so the name died out there, but it found a ready market on the Indian subcontinent, and also in Malta, and **stepney** became a term in Indian and Maltese English for any spare tyre.

Stepony or **stipony.** A type of raisin-wine popular in the 17th and 18th centuries, made from raisins with added sugar and lemon juice, which may have got its name from Stepney.

Stert Point *Stert* 'point of land', OE *steort*; *compare* START POINT[1].

A point of land on the western side of the estuary of the River PARRETT, in Somerset. **Stert Island** is at the mouth of the river, opposite Burnham on Sea, and the sands of **Stert Flats** stretch out to the west of the river-mouth, as far as HINKLEY POINT.

Stevenage Probably '(place at the) strong oak-tree', OE *stithan* dative form of *stith* 'strong' + *æc* dative form of *ac* 'oak-tree'.
A market town in Hertfordshire, on the A1(M), about 8 km (5 miles) southeast of Hitchin. Its origins go back to the 9th century, and its centre preserves something of its early aspect, but it was transformed by its designation as a NEW TOWN[1] in 1946 (the first place in England to be so designated). The greatly enlarged Stevenage that emerged in the 1950s is one of the happier results of 20th-century town planning, spacious and with good modern architecture and the obligatory Henry Moore sculpture.

Edward Gordon Craig (1872–1966), the actor and theatre director-designer, was born in Stevenage.

Stevenston 'Steven's farmstead', personal name *Steven* (who owned the farm at least as early as the 13th century) + -TON.
A small industrial town in North Ayrshire (formerly in Strathclyde region), 3 km (2 miles) east of Saltcoats. It is dominated by the nearby Ardeer chemical works.

Steventon[1] 'estate associated with Stif(a)', OE male personal name *Stif(a)* + -ING + -TON, or perhaps 'farmstead at the tree-stump place', OE *styf(ic)ing* 'tree-stump place' + -TON.
A village in Hampshire, about 10 km (6 miles) southwest of Basingstoke. Jane Austen's father was rector here, and she was born in the rectory (now demolished) in 1775. She spent the first 25 years of her life here, and in that time wrote the first versions of *Sense and Sensibility*, *Pride and Prejudice* and *Northanger Abbey*.

Steventon[2]. A village in Oxfordshire (before 1974 in Berkshire), about 5 km (3 miles) northwest of DIDCOT. The route of the medieval causeway between the church and the village green, built by monks to save people getting their feet wet, can still be followed.

Stewartby From the name of the founder's father *Stewart* + -BY.
A village in Bedfordshire, about 8 km (5 miles) southwest of Bedford. It was built in 1926, on the site of an existing hamlet called WOOTTON PILLINGE, at the instigation of Sir Malcolm Stewart (1872–1951) as a model village for the employees of his brickworks. He named it in honour of his father Sir Halley Stewart (1838–1937), vice-chairman of the London Brick Company.

Stewarton 'Steward's farmstead', named after Walter, High Steward of King David + -TON.
A small town in East Ayrshire (formerly in Strathclyde region), 7 km (4 miles) north of Kilmarnock. It was the birthplace of the social reformer Robert Owen's father-in-law, David Dale, who built the mills at NEW LANARK.

Stewartry, the. *See* KIRKCUDBRIGHTSHIRE.

Stewponey From the name of the local public house, for which there are numerous explanations: the second element is probably ModE *pony* 'small horse', but the meaning of the first element could be anything from 'fishpond' to 'brothel', depending on the interpreter (though what a small horse might be doing in any of these situations is a moot question).
A village in Staffordshire, on the River STOUR[5], about 4 km (2.5 miles) west of STOURBRIDGE.

Steyning Perhaps '(settlement of) Stan's people' or '(settlement of) people who live at the stony place', OE male personal name *Stan* or *stæne* 'stony place' (*see* STONE) + -*ingas* (*see* -ING). Alternatively, the name could mean simply 'stony places', from the plural form of OE *staning* or *stæning*.
A small town (pronounced 'stenning') in West Sussex, on the River ADUR[1], about 8 km (5 miles) north of Worthing. In the early Middle Ages it was a thriving seaport, and from that period dates its very substantial church. Much of it, including its tower, was demolished after the Reformation, and what remains is more in keeping with the somewhat bijou, picturesque aspect of present-day Steyning.

M.C. Coles (1885–1954), the self-styled 'King of Lundy' (*see under* LUNDY), was born in Steyning.

Stibb '(place by the) tree stump', OE *stybb* 'tree stump'.
A hamlet in Cornwall, about 5 km (3 miles) northeast of Bude.

Sticker '(place by the) tree stumps', Cornish *stekyer* plural form of *stok* 'tree stump'.
A village in Cornwall, about 5 km (3 miles) southwest of St Austell.

Sticklepath 'steep path', OE *sticol* 'steep' + *pæth* 'path'.
A village in Devon, on the northern edge of Dartmoor, on the River TAW, about 5 km (3 miles) east of Okehampton. The Finch Brothers Foundry here, a working water-powered foundry between 1814 and 1960, is now an industrial museum.

Stickle Tarn. *See* PAVEY ARK.

Stiffkey[1] 'island with tree stumps', OE *styfic* 'tree stump' + *eg* (*see* -EY, -EA).
A village (pronounced as spelt or, formerly or locally, 'stewkey', 'stookey' or 'sticky') close to the north Norfolk coast, on the River Stiffkey, about 5 km (3 miles) east of Wells-next-the-Sea. Salt marshes (glowing with purple sea lavender in the summer) separate it from the sea.

Rector of Stiffkey, the. The Reverend Harold Francis Davidson (1875–1937), who achieved a certain notoriety as rector of Stiffkey in the early 20th century. He considered the most important part of his religious vocation to be saving the souls of fallen women, to which he devoted most of his energies. His neglected parishioners viewed his activities askance, particularly after, in the early 1930s, stories about him began to appear in the tabloid press and crowds of sightseers turned up in charabancs to hear him preach. He was defrocked in 1932, and he decided to become a music-hall entertainer. This turned out not to be a good career move, as in 1937 he was mauled by the partner in his act, a lion called Freddy, and died of his wounds.

Stiffkey² From STIFFKEY¹.

A river in North Norfolk, which rises to the east of FAKENHAM and flows 28 km (18 miles) westwards and then northwards into the North Sea just beyond STIFFKEY¹.

Stiletto in the Ghetto, the. A nickname for the Millennium Spire in Dublin's O'CONNELL STREET.

Stilton 'farmstead or village at a stile or steep ascent', OE *stigel* 'stile, steep ascent' + -TON.

A village in Cambridgeshire (before 1974 in Huntingdonshire), on the A1 (formerly ERMINE STREET), about 17.5 km (11 miles) northwest of Huntingdon.

Stilton cheese. A full-flavoured blue cheese, made from cows' milk. It is not and never has been made in Stilton. It was originally a Leicestershire cheese, made at Quenby Hall, and its manufacture is now legally restricted to Leicestershire, Derbyshire and Nottinghamshire. The Stilton connection is that the housekeeper at Quenby, Elizabeth Scarbrow, had an arrangement to supply the cheese to the Bell Inn in the village, and its fame was spread by travellers who encountered it on their journeys up and down the Great North Road. The name 'Stilton Cheese' was registered as a trademark in 1966.

> Coming south from [Stamford] we passed Stilton, a town famous for cheese, which is called our English Parmesan, and is brought to table with the mites, or maggots round it, so thick, that they bring a spoon with them for you to eat the mites with, as you do the cheese.
>
> Daniel Defoe: *A Tour Through the Whole Island of Great Britain* (1724–6)

White Stilton contains no spores of mould, and is very often combined with fruits to make a milder, sweeter version of the traditional blue. Its name is also protected.

Stinchcombe 'valley frequented by sandpipers or dunlins', OE *stint* 'sandpiper, dunlin' + *cumb* 'valley' (*see* -COMBE, COOMBE).

A village in Gloucestershire, beside the M5, about 13 km (8 miles) west of Nailsworth. The novelist Evelyn Waugh lived here between 1937 and 1956, in a house called Piers Court; his nickname for the village was 'Stinkers'.

Stinsford 'ford frequented by sandpipers or dunlins', OE *stint* 'sandpiper, dunlin' + FORD.

A village in Dorset, about 2.5 km (1.5 miles) east of DORCHESTER¹. The novelist Thomas Hardy sang in the local church as a boy, and his heart is buried in the churchyard.

The village is fictionalized as MELLSTOCK in his *Under the Greenwood Tree* (1872).

Stiperstones *Stiper*, of unknown origin + OE *stanas* (*see* STONE).

A range of hills in Shropshire, northwest of the LONG MYND, surrounding the village of SHELVE. Their jagged 536-m (1759-ft) summit results from shattering by frost during the last ice age. Witches are said to gather here, and one rocky outcrop is called the Devil's Chair.

The devilish associations of the place may have influenced the Shropshire-born novelist Mary Webb when she fictionalized the Stiperstones as the **Diafol Mountains** in her novel *The Golden Arrow* (1916).

Stirling¹ A document from the early 12th century has Stirling sited on a river called *Strevelin* (presumably an alternative name for the Forth), and it is possible that the town is named from the river.

A royal BURGH (*c*.1130) 50 km (31 miles) northwest of Edinburgh, on the River FORTH. It was the county town of the former county of STIRLINGSHIRE, and then the headquarters of Central region, and is now the HQ of the unitary authority of Stirling.

Stirling is dominated by a cliff-girt volcanic plug 75 m (250 ft) high on which stands **Stirling Castle**. This dates from at least the early 12th century, and there is evidence of earlier Pictish settlement; however, most of what can be seen today dates from the 15th and 16th centuries, and is regarded as a fine example of Scottish Renaissance architecture. The castle was often used as a royal residence. Alexander I died here in 1124, as did William I ('the Lion') in 1214 and Robert Stewart, the 1st Duke of Albany and virtual ruler of Scotland from 1388 until his death in 1420. James II was born here in 1430, and it was here, in 1452 that James, having invited the 8th Earl of Douglas (one of the Black Douglases) to the castle with a guarantee of safe conduct, killed Douglas with his own hands. James III was killed at the battle of SAUCHIEBURN, just south of Stirling, in 1488; his son, James IV, witnessed John Damian, alchemist, charlatan and abbot of Tongland Abbey near Kirkcudbright, attempt to fly off the castle walls:

> Damian, D'Amiens, Damiano --
> we never found out his true name, but there
> he crouched, swarthy, and slowly sawed the air
> with large strapped-on bat-membrane wings.
>
> Edwin Morgan: 'At Stirling Castle, 1507', from *Sonnets from Scotland* (1984)

(Needless to say, things went hard for this pioneer aviator, as the ground flew up to hit him.)

Mary Queen of Scots spent time here as a child, and the one-year-old James VI was crowned in the Church of the Holy Rude below the castle in 1567, while being preached at by John Knox. During this period Stirling shared with EDINBURGH the status of national capital, but its importance declined after the union of the Scottish and English crowns in 1603.

> Here Stuarts once in glory reigned,
> And laws for Scotland's weal ordained;
> But now unroof'd their palace stands,
> Their sceptre's sway'd by other hands;
> The injured Stuart line is gone,
> A race outlandish fills their throne –
> An idiot race, to honour lost;
> Who know them best despise them most!

> > Robert Burns: 'On the Window of an Inn at Stirling' (inscribed with a diamond, 27 August 1787) (The slur against the 'idiot race' – whose descendants are with us to this day – got Burns into a degree of trouble; two months later he returned and knocked out the offending pane, but travellers had already copied and circulated the lines.)

Stirling Castle is in what was for many centuries an important strategic position, guarding the narrowing of the Forth valley between the OCHIL HILLS and GARGUNNOCK Hills, making it not only the gateway to the HIGHLANDS, but also to FIFE, PERTH, and the whole of the northeast of Scotland. In the words of Alexander Smith, 'Stirling, like a huge brooch, clasps Highlands and Lowlands together'. The key to the route was the bridge over the River Forth at Stirling: the 'Auld Brig' (Scots 'old bridge') dates from the 14th century, but that fought over by William Wallace in 1297 (*see below*) was probably a little to the northwest. The strategic importance of the castle meant that it was subject to many sieges, and attempts to relieve sieges, such as the one that failed at BANNOCKBURN, just south of Stirling, in 1314.

The 'Old Town' on the sides of the hill beneath the castle has many notable buildings from the 16th to 18th centuries. One of these is the so-called Argyll's Lodging, built in 1632 by Sir William Alexander of Menstrie (later Earl of Stirling), the founder of Nova Scotia in Canada; when he died in debt the house passed to the Campbells of Argyll (as was so often the way). The house is now a youth hostel.

The **University of Stirling** was founded in 1967, Scotland's first completely new university establishment since Edinburgh in 1583 – although James VI and I had promised the town a 'free college' in 1617.

Battle of Stirling Bridge, the (September 1297). A battle in which the Scots under William Wallace and Sir Andrew de Moray defeated an English army led by John de Warenne, Earl of Surrey, and Hugh Cressingham. The Scots allowed the English to begin to cross the narrow wooden bridge over the Forth (possibly at Kildean, about 1.5 km / 1 mile northwest of Stirling Castle). The bridge was wide enough for only two mounted knights to cross abreast, and when the English vanguard under Cressingham had crossed

it the knights found themselves unable to manoeuvre on the marshy ground. At this point, as the old song relates:

> The Wallace gave a shout,
> Out his men came running,
> Stubbed the English host,
>   At the Brig o' Stirling …

> All the English men,
> Ran into each other,
> Nane could turn about,
>   Nane could go much further.

> Some fell o'er the side,
> In the Forth were drowning,
> Some were left to die,
>   On the Brig o' Stirling.

Following this victory, Wallace went on to ravage Cumberland, and was nominated guardian of the kingdom of Scotland in the name of King John Balliol.

Stirling Albion. A professional football club founded in 1945 as a replacement for an earlier Stirling-based football club, King's Park, whose ground had been obliterated by a Luftwaffe bomb during the Second World War. Nicknamed the Binos, Stirling Albion play home games at Annfield Park.

Stirling bomber. Properly the 'Short Stirling', a four-engined British bomber of the Second World War, which made its operational debut in 1941.

Stirling jug. An old liquid measure, equivalent to 3 pints (1.7 litres), used from the late 16th to the early 19th centuries.

Stirling[2]. A unitary authority created in 1996 out of much of the old CENTRAL region. It is bordered to the west by Argyll and Bute, to the north and east by Perth and Kinross, to the southeast by Clackmannanshire and Falkirk, and to the south by North Lanarkshire, East Dunbartonshire and West Dunbartonshire. It contains much of the Southern HIGHLANDS, as well as part of the CENTRAL LOWLANDS.

Stirlingshire From STIRLING[1] + SHIRE.
A former county of Scotland, bounded at the north by Perthshire, on the east by Clackmannanshire and West Lothian, on the south by Lanarkshire, and on the south and west by Dunbartonshire. The county town was STIRLING[1]. It was abolished in 1975, and most of it became Stirling district in CENTRAL region. In 1996 the unitary authority of STIRLING[2] was created, covering much of the old Central region.

East Stirlingshire. A professional football club, nicknamed the Shire. Founded in 1880, the club plays its home games at Firs Park in Falkirk.

Stithians From the dedication of the local church to *St Stithian*, a female saint unknown to history.
A village in Cornwall, about 5 km (3 miles) northwest of Penryn. The huge **Stithian's Reservoir**, to the west, is extensively used for sailing and other water sports.

Stivichall 'nook of land with tree stumps', OE *styfic* 'tree stump' + *halh* 'nook of land' (*see* HALE, -HALL).

A southern suburb of COVENTRY.

Stixwould 'Stigr's forest', OScand *Stigs* possessive form of male personal name *Stigr* + OE *wald* 'forest'.

A village in Lincolnshire, about 11 km (7 miles) southwest of Horncastle.

Stoak 'outlying farm(s)', OE *stoc* (*see* -STOCK, STOCK-, STOKE).

A village in Cheshire, close to the interchange of the M53 and the M56, about 8 km (5 miles) southeast of ELLESMERE PORT.

Stob Binnein Probably Gaelic *stob* 'peak' + *binnein* 'conical peak, pinnacle', although the second element may be Gaelic *innean* 'anvil', referring to the outline of the summit, a cone with a flattened top.

A lofty and shapely mountain (1165 m / 3822 ft) in the unitary authority of Stirling (formerly in Central region and before that in Perthshire). It is partner to the slightly higher BEN MORE[1].

Stobo 'heel of land with tree-stumps', OE *stobb* 'tree stump' + *hoh* 'hill-spur, heel of land'.

A hamlet in Scottish Borders (formerly in Peeblesshire), 7 km (4 miles) southwest of Peebles. The church may have originally been founded by St Kentigern (St Mungo). **John Reid of Stobo** (?*c*.1430–1505) is one of the poets whom William Dunbar (?1456–?1513) mourns in his *Lament for the Makaris*:

> And he [Death] has now tane, last of aw,
> Gud gentill Stobo et Quintyne Schaw,
> Of quham all wichtis hes pete:
> *Timor mortis conturbat me.*

Stock 'outlying settlement' OE *stoc* (*see* -STOCK, STOCK-, STOKE);

but the early spellings of *stock* in this name make possible a derivation from OE *stocc* 'tree stump'. The village was recorded as *Herewardestoc* ('Hereward's outlying settlement') in 1234, but the OE male personal name *Hereward* was later dropped.

A village in Essex, 5 km (3 miles) north of Billericay. *See also* the SHIRE.

Stockbridge 'bridge made of logs' (referring to a bridge across the Test), OE *stocc* 'log, tree trunk' (*see also* -STOCK, STOCK-, STOKE) + *brycg* 'bridge'.

An attractive large village in Hampshire, on the River TEST, about 14 km (9 miles) northwest of Winchester. Its wide main street is lined with former coaching inns, reflecting its former role as a stopping-place for travellers. It is still an important centre for anglers seeking the riches of the troutful Test.

Before the Reform Act of 1832, Stockbridge was notorious as one of the rottenest of all England's rotten boroughs.

Stocking Pelham *Stocking* 'made of logs' or 'by the tree stumps', OE *stoccen* (*see also* -STOCK, STOCK-, STOKE); *Pelham see* FURNEUX PELHAM.

A village in Hertfordshire, about 9 km (6 miles) northwest of Bishop's Stortford.

Stockleigh English *Stockleigh* probably 'glade with tree stumps', OE *stocc* 'tree stump' (*see also* -STOCK, STOCK-, STOKE) + -LEY; *English* denoting manorial ownership in the Middle Ages by the Engles family.

A village in Devon, about 6 km (4 miles) north of Crediton.

Stockleigh Pomeroy *Pomeroy* denoting manorial ownership in the Middle Ages by the de Pomerei family.

A village in Devon, about 5 km (3 miles) northeast of Crediton.

❖ -stock, stock-, stoke ❖

There are literally hundreds of names containing Old English *stoc*, which is something of a curiosity because the element appears only twice in the extant Anglo-Saxon documents independently of place names. The core meaning of *stoc* is 'outlying settlement or farm', and the fact that these *are* 'outlying' implies also that they were originally smaller and less significant than some central place.

The element appears as a name in simple form, as in STOAK (Cheshire) and frequently Stoke; it comes with family names as in STOGUMBER and STOGURSEY (Somerset), and STOKESAY (Shropshire); it appears with general words for settlements, as in STOCKPORT (with PORT) in Greater Manchester or in STOCKTON-ON-TEES (with -TON); it comes with woodland elements as in STOKESLEY (with -LEY) in North Yorkshire and in WOODSTOCK

(Oxfordshire); it appears with tribal names, as in BASINGSTOKE (Hampshire), and personal names, as in ODSTOCK (Wiltshire); it comes with bird names, as in LAVERSTOCK (Wiltshire), and with river names as in POWERSTOCK (Dorset) and TAVISTOCK (Devon). It is a truly versatile element.

There is a degree of overlap in meaning between *stoc* and Old Scandinavian *thorp* (*see* THORPE), but the latter element does not have the association that some *stoc* names have with monastic or religious sites: the aforementioned Tavistock and several other places are known to have had monasteries.

The association of *stoc* names with woodland naturally leads to potential confusion with *stocc(en)*: STOCKLEIGH ENGLISH and STOCKLEIGH POMEROY (Devon), and STOCKING PELHAM (Hertford-shire), contain *stocc* 'tree stump' and *stoccen* 'by the tree stumps'.

Stockport 'market place at an outlying hamlet', OE *stoc* (*see* -STOCK, STOCK-, STOKE) + PORT 'market place'.

A town and unitary authority in Greater Manchester, 10 km (6 miles) southeast of the centre of Manchester. The rivers GOYT and TAME² join at Stockport to form the MERSEY, which is here spanned by a 27-arch railway viaduct built in 1841, which, according to the novelist Richard Francis – many of whose novels, such as *Prospect Hill* (2003) are set in Stockport – takes 'an enormous bit out of the centre of the town'. (The town is also celebrated in the song 'Sunset over the Mersey' by the 1960s band The Purple Gang.)

Stockport's Church of St Mary has its origins in the 12th century, although much of it was rebuilt in the early 19th century following a collapse blamed on excessive bell-ringing in celebration of Nelson's victory at Trafalgar. The town received its first charter in 1220, and was a thriving market town. The cotton industry and hat manufacture became important in the 19th century; Stockport has Britain's only museum devoted to hats.

Stockport was the birthplace of John Bradshaw (1602–59), president of the court that tried Charles I; Joseph Whitworth (1803–87), engineer and arms manufacturer; the economist Clifford Douglas (1879–1952), originator of the once-popular theory of Social Credit; the tennis player Fred Perry (1909–95), the last Briton to win the men's singles at Wimbledon (1936); and of the burger-loving-turned-environmentalist Conservative politician John Selwyn Gummer (b.1939).

Stockport County FC was formed in 1883 by members of the local Congregational chapel. Nicknamed County, or the Hatters, the club is based at Edgeley Park (*see also* SALE).

Stocksbridge 'log bridge', OE *stocc* 'tree trunk' (*see also* -STOCK, STOCK-, STOKE) + *brycg* 'bridge'.

A town in South Yorkshire, on the edge of the PEAK DISTRICT, 11 km (7 miles) southwest of Barnsley.

Stockton-on-Tees 'farm at an outlying hamlet on the River Tees', OE *stoc* (*see* -STOCK, STOCK-, STOKE) + -TON, with river name TEES.

A town, port and unitary authority in northeast England, some 6 km (4 miles) west of, and now contiguous with, MIDDLESBROUGH. It was formerly in County Durham, and the unitary authority also includes some adjacent country-side. It received its first charter in the early 13th century, but its fame really stems from its connection to rail history and the Industrial Revolution. **Stockton Quay** was the terminus for the first section of the **Stockton and Darlington** company's new steam-powered railway (and its revolution-ary engine, *Locomotion*) in 1825, engineered by George Stephenson mainly for the purpose of transporting coal to the River Tees. (Initially passenger carriages were drawn by horses along the track.) The town can thus also claim the world's oldest railway station.

Stockton was the birthplace of the furniture maker Thomas Sheraton (1751–1806). Conservative politician and prime minister Harold Macmillan (1896–1986) was MP for Stockton for most of the time between 1924 and 1945, and took the title Earl of Stockton on his ennoble-ment in 1984.

Stockwell 'spring or stream by a tree stump', OE *stocc* 'tree stump' (*see also* -STOCK, STOCK-, STOKE) + OE *wella* 'spring, stream'.

A district of South London (SW9), in the borough of LAMBETH, between Clapham to the west, Brixton to the south and Camberwell to the east. It remained a rural village until the early 19th century. Large-scale residential develop-ment got under way in the 1830s, and was accelerated in the 1860s by the coming of the railway along Stockwell's southern boundary.

Stockwell Underground station, on the Northern and Victoria lines, opened in 1890. Stockwell bus garage, built in 1950, is remarkable for its huge barrel-vaulted reinforced-concrete roof, under which 200 buses can shelter.

Stockwell ghost. A supposed ghost that created a great sensation in Stockwell in 1772. The author of the strange noises turned out to be Anne Robinson, a maidservant.

Stoer Possibly OScand *staurr* 'stake', referring to the sea stack.

A small village on the northwest coast of Scotland, in Highland (formerly in Sutherland), 8 km (5 miles) north-west of Lochinver. It is at the neck of the peninsula leading northwest to the **Point of Stoer**. On the west side of this peninsula, just short of the Point, is the 60-m (200-ft) sea stack called the **Old Man of Stoer**, first ascended in 1966 by a party led by Dr Tom Patey of Ullapool.

Stogumber 'Gumer's outlying farmstead or hamlet', OE *stoc* (*see* -STOCK, STOCK-, STOKE) + personal or family name *Gumer*.

A village in Somerset, in the valley of Doniford Stream, between EXMOOR and the QUANTOCK HILLS, about 8 km (5 miles) south of Watchet. The chancel of the local church is strikingly decorated in William Morris style.

Stogursey 'Curci's outlying farmstead or hamlet', OE *stoc* (*see* -STOCK, STOCK-, STOKE) + de *Curci* family name of the manorial owners in the early Middle Ages.

A village in Somerset, in the shadow of the QUANTOCK HILLS, close to the coast and the estuary of the River PARRETT, about 13 km (8 miles) northwest of Bridgwater.

Stoke Bardolph *Stoke* 'outlying farmstead or hamlet, secondary settlement', OE *stoc* (*see* -STOCK, STOCK-, STOKE); *Bardolph* denoting manorial ownership in the Middle Ages by the Bardolf family.

A village in Nottinghamshire, about 10 km (6 miles) east of Nottingham.

Battle of Stoke (16 June 1487). A battle of the Wars of the Roses, in which the rebels supporting Lambert Simnel, pretender to the English throne, were defeated by the forces of Henry VII. Simnel was afterwards found a job in the royal kitchens, but his noble supporters were killed.

Stoke-Barehills. The fictional name for BASINGSTOKE in the novels of Thomas Hardy, including *Tess of the D'Urbervilles* (1891) and *Jude the Obscure* (1895).

Stoke Bliss *Stoke see* STOKE BARDOLPH; *Bliss* denoting manorial ownership in the Middle Ages by the Blez family.
A village in Worcestershire (before 1998 in Hereford and Worcester, before 1974 in Worcestershire), about 22 km (14 miles) northwest of Worcester.

Stoke Bruerne *Stoke see* STOKE BARDOLPH; *Bruerne* denoting manorial ownership in the Middle Ages by the Briwere family.
A village in Northamptonshire, on the GRAND UNION CANAL, about 11 km (7 miles) south of Northampton. It is close to a flight of seven locks, and within a few kilometres of the southern end of Blisworth Tunnel (*see under* BLISWORTH). It has a canal museum.

Stoke-by-Nayland *Stoke see* STOKE BARDOLPH; *-by-nayland* from its being close to (about 2.5 km/1.5 miles northeast of) NAYLAND.
A village in Suffolk, in CONSTABLE COUNTRY, about 11 km (7 miles) southeast of SUDBURY[1]. It is egregiously picturesque, and its church, with its massive 15th-century tower, was one of John Constable's favourite subjects.

Stoke Charity *Stoke see* STOKE BARDOLPH; *Charity* denoting manorial ownership in the Middle Ages by the de la Charite family.
A village in Hampshire, about 11 km (7 miles) north of Winchester.

Stoke D'Abernon *Stoke see* STOKE BARDOLPH; *D'Abernon* denoting manorial ownership in the early Middle Ages by the de Abernun family.
A village in Surrey, on the River MOLE[1], about 5 km (3 miles) northwest of Leatherhead. There was a Roman settlement here, and it was the scene of the first recorded honeymoon in English history, of Henry III's tutor with the daughter of the Earl of Pembroke in 1189. Since then it has largely succumbed to the creep of London suburbia, but an enclave of medieval manor house and parish church survives.
Stoke D'Abernon is the home of the Yehudi Menuhin Music School.

Stoke Dry *Stoke see* STOKE BARDOLPH; *Dry* 'dry land' (that is, above surrounding marshland).
A village in Rutland (before 1997 in Leicestershire, before 1974 in Rutland), about 3 km (2 miles) south of UPPINGHAM. Somewhat ironically, given its name, it is on the banks of the very large Eyebrook Reservoir.
Among the more improbable stories attaching to its parish church are that the Gunpowder Plot was hatched in a room over its porch (Sir Everard Digby, who financed

Guy Fawkes and his fellow plotters, did belong to a local Catholic recusant family); and that a rector locked a witch in it to die of starvation.

Stoke Mandeville *Stoke see* STOKE BARDOLPH; *Mandeville* denoting manorial ownership in the Middle Ages by the Mandeville family.
A village in Buckinghamshire, about 3 km (2 miles) southeast of AYLESBURY. It is famous for **Stoke Mandeville Hospital**, which specializes in spinal-cord injuries. Since 1948 it has hosted the **World Stoke Mandeville Wheelchair Games**, forerunner of the Paralympics (the original event was an archery competition held to coincide with the London Olympics of 1948).

Stokenchurch 'church made of logs', OE *stoccen* 'made of logs' (*see also* -STOCK, STOCK-, STOKE) + *cirice* 'church'.
A village in Buckinghamshire, on top of the CHILTERN HILLS, about 11 km (7 miles) northwest of HIGH WYCOMBE. It is on the M40, which cuts its way through the **Stokenchurch Gap** (also known as the 'Chiltern Gap') before descending to the Oxfordshire plain. A prominent landmark for travellers proceeding London-wards along the motorway is a television tower, visible for miles on the crest of the Chilterns, and looming over the village.

Stoke Newington Originally *Newenton* 'new farmstead or settlement', OE *niwan* dative form of *niwe* 'new' + -TON; the affix *Stoke* 'by the tree-stumps' or 'made of logs' (OE *stoccen*; *see also* -STOCK, STOCK-, STOKE) is first recorded in the late 13th century, as both *Newenton Stoken* and *Stoken Newenton*.
A district of North London (N16), in the borough of HACKNEY, between Dalston to the south and Tottenham to the north. It is on the line of the old Roman road to York, ERMINE STREET (the A10). Expanding London engulfed it in the middle of the 19th century, but a more ancient, almost rural aspect of the place survives in the vicinity of its old church. Indeed a village atmosphere pervades much of Stoke Newington Church Street, main thoroughfare now of a trendy multicultural community and dotted with above-average Indian restaurants.
In the 16th and 17th centuries Stoke Newington was a haven for Dissenters, who were forbidden to live in the City of London. The author Daniel Defoe (1660–1731), who was born here, is the best-known of its inhabitants from that period. The Nonconformist hymn-writer Isaac Watts (1674–1748) also lived and worked here.
See also ABNEY PARK.

Stoke-on-Trent *Stoke see* STOKE BARDOLPH; *Trent see* TRENT[1].
A city and unitary authority within Staffordshire, on the River Trent, about 23 km (14 miles) north of Stafford. The original Stoke-on-Trent was just a small village until the late 18th century. Pots had always been made here (early Bronze Age pottery has been found in the area), and

the new production and transportation methods of the Industrial Revolution transformed the village into a large Victorian industrial town, epicentre of the POTTERIES, with its smoking pot-banks and kilns and tightly packed houses. Many of the most resounding names in English pottery had their beginnings here, including Minton, Spode and pre-eminently Wedgwood (Josiah Wedgwood had his pottery works in ETRURIA).

Soon the towns surrounding Stoke – BURSLEM, FENTON, HANLEY, LONGTON and TUNSTALL[1] – had become drawn into a general conurbation. Arnold Bennett, a native of Hanley, referred to it as the FIVE TOWNS (although Stoke makes it six), and it forms the backdrop to much of his fiction (Stoke-on-Trent appears as 'Knype'). In 1832 they were grouped as a single parliamentary borough, called Stoke, and in 1910 they were constituted as a federated town, with a single council, under the name Stoke-on-Trent. It became a city in 1925 and a unitary authority in 1997.

> Finally ... there appeared, on paper, the mythical city of Stoke-on-Trent. But when you go there, you still see the six towns, looking like six separate towns. Unless you are wiser than I was, you will never be quite sure which of the six you are in at any given time.
>
> J.B. Priestley: *English Journey* (1934)

Jack Ashley was the (profoundly deaf) Labour MP for Stoke-on-Trent from 1966 to 1992.

Stoke City, the town's football team, has a number of celebrated alumni, including Stanley Matthews (from 1932 to 1946, and again from 1961 to 1965) and Gordon Banks, England's 1966 World-Cup-winning goalkeeper (signed in 1967).

In the 1970s, STOKE-ON-TRENT was co-opted as rhyming slang for *bent*, in the sense 'homosexual'.

Dinah Maria Craik ('Mrs Craik'; 1826–87), author of the novel *John Halifax, Gentleman* (1857), and the novelist and poet John Wain (1925–94) were born in Stoke-on-Trent. The pop singer Robbie Williams (b.1974) was brought up in Stoke, where his mother owned a pub.

Stoke Orchard *Stoke see* STOKE BARDOLPH; *Orchard* '(land for an) archer' (referring to a piece of land held from the king in return for supplying the services of an archer equipped with bow and arrows for 40 days a year), ME *archere*, later rationalized to ModE *orchard*.

A village in Gloucestershire, beside the M5, about 5 km (3 miles) north of Cheltenham.

Stoke Pero *Stoke see* STOKE BARDOLPH; *Pero* denoting manorial ownership in the Middle Ages by the Pyrhou family.

A hamlet (pronounced 'peeroh') in Somerset, on the northern part of EXMOOR, about 3 km (2 miles) northwest of DUNKERY HILL. It is set in a deep valley, and local people (when there were local people – the church and one farm are virtually all that remain of the parish) were said to have high voices from having to shout from one side to the other. To the south is the bleak and lonely **Stoke Pero Common**. It is about 396 m (1300 ft) above sea level.

Stoke Poges *Stoke see* STOKE BARDOLPH; *Poges* denoting manorial ownership in the Middle Ages by the le Pugeis family. A large village (pronounced 'pohjiz') in Buckinghamshire, in the THAMES[1] Valley, about 5 km (3 miles) northwest of Slough. It lies among the Chiltern Hundreds (*see under* CHILTERN HILLS), and indeed Stoke is one of the three Hundreds for the stewardship of which an MP can apply in order to resign his or her seat.

The poet Thomas Gray (1716–61) made the place famous. He often came here, to visit his mother, and it is here that he is thought to have begun (around 1742) his 'Elegy Written in a Country Churchyard':

> The curfew tolls the knell of parting day,
> The lowing herd wind slowly o'er the lea,
> The ploughman homeward plods his weary way,
> And leaves the world to darkness and to me.

He now lies in the churchyard, alongside his mother. (The church, the 13th-century St Giles's, has a curious 17th-century stained-glass window showing a naked man riding what looks like a bicycle and blowing a trumpet.)

Stokesay 'outlying farmstead or hamlet belonging to the de Say family', OE *stoc* (*see* -STOCK, STOCK-, STOKE) + family name *de Say* (denoting manorial ownership in the early Middle Ages). A village in Shropshire, on the River Onny, close to the southern end of WENLOCK EDGE, about 11 km (7 miles) northwest of Ludlow. It is famous for its 12th-century fortified manor house (**Stokesay Castle**), the earliest surviving one in England. Its two massive stone towers are joined by a remarkable 13th-century banqueting hall, with tall arched windows.

Stokesley 'clearing at an outlying hamlet', OE *stoc* (*see* -STOCK, STOCK-, STOKE) + -LEY.

A market town on the edge of the Cleveland Hills, North Yorkshire, 22 km (13 miles) northeast of Northallerton.

Stoke sub Hamdon *Stoke see* STOKE BARDOLPH; *sub* 'below', Latin; *Hamdon see* HAMDON HILL (referring to a local hill). A village in Somerset, about 8 km (5 miles) west of Yeovil. Most of its buildings, including the Norman church, are made of the local Ham stone (*see* HAM HILL). There is also a 15th-century priory. Behind the Fleur-de-Lys Inn is a court for the game of fives dating from the 1750s.

Stoke Talmage *Stoke see* STOKE BARDOLPH; *Talmage* denoting manorial ownership in the Middle Ages by the Thalemalche family.

A village in Oxfordshire, about 16 km (10 miles) southeast of Oxford.

Stoke Trister *Stoke see* STOKE BARDOLPH; *Trister* denoting manorial ownership in the Middle Ages by the Trister family. A village in western Somerset, close to the Dorset border, about 2.5 km (1.5 miles) east of Wincanton.

Stone '(place at the) stone or stones', OE *stan* (*see* STONE). A town in Staffordshire, on the River TRENT[1], about 11 km (7 miles) northwest of Stafford. Its name perhaps refers to a prominent stone building in the locality; a more circumstantial but unproven version is that it relates to a cairn of stones that marked the graves of two Christian Mercian princes murdered by their pagan father, King Wulfhere – there is a commemorative window in the parish church. But the name has also been linked with the so-called 'Petrifactions', plants that have been turned to stone by a local stream. The surrounding area is noted for its plant nurseries, where young trees and shrubs are produced.

John Jervis, Earl St Vincent (1735–1823), the English admiral who defeated the Spanish fleet at the Battle of Cape St Vincent in 1797, was born in Stone.

Stonehaven Possibly English 'stone haven'; earlier forms of the name such as *Steanhyve* and *Stonehive* suggest that an alternative for *haven* was OE *hyth* 'landing place'. A port 22 km (13 miles) south of Aberdeen. It was formerly the county town (from the 17th century) of the old county of KINCARDINESHIRE, then the administrative seat of KINCARDINE AND DEESIDE (in Grampian region), and is now in ABERDEENSHIRE. Stonehaven marks the northeastern end of the Highland Line (*see under* the HIGHLANDS). Every Hogmanay the young men of the town participate in the ceremony of 'Swinging the Fireballs', a typical mid-winter fire ceremony to see off evil spirits. Just down the coast are the ruins of DUNOTTAR CASTLE.

It was at Stonehaven that life first emerged from the oceans – at least, in 2003, a fossil was found on a nearby beach of a form of millipede with air holes, which turned out to be the oldest known (*c.*420 million years old) fossil of a land animal. Some commentators have asserted that life hereabouts has not advanced so very much since then, although more sober observers discount this assertion as entirely facetious.

Stonehenge 'stone gallows' (from the resemblance of two upright stones topped with a lintel to a gallows), OE *stan* (*see* STONE) + *hengen* 'gallows' (related to ModE *hang*). The name is first recorded around 1130. A megalithic structure in Wiltshire, on SALISBURY Plain, about 14 km (9 miles) north of Salisbury itself. It consists of a series of concentric stone circles, the most prominent of which, a ring of trilithons (two uprights crossed by a lintel), give the structure its immediately recognizable outline.

Stonehenge was constructed in several phases over a period of about 1400 years, beginning around 3000 BC. Two key elements are the forty or so huge blocks of dolerite (bluestone) erected around 2500 BC, having been brought (by means as yet unexplained) from the area of the PRESCELLY MOUNTAINS in Wales; and the sarsen stones, quarried from the nearby Marlborough Downs (*see under* MARLBOROUGH), from which the trilithonic circle was constructed around 1600 BC. Its axis is aligned with sunrise on the longest day of the year, 21 June (and with sunset on the shortest day, 22 December). Other notable features are the Heel Stone, a massive marker stone outside the entrance to the central enclosure (reputedly so named after the Devil hurled it at a monk he had caught spying on him, and pinned him to the ground by the heel); and the Aubrey

---

❖ **stone** ❖

Old English *stan* 'stone' is a very common element in English place names, but is rare in Wales, Scotland and Ireland, STENHOUSEMUIR (Falkirk) being one of relatively few. STAMFORD (Lincolnshire) and STANFORD DINGLEY (Berkshire) perhaps indicate a desirable firmness at the fording-place, but it is also possible that a marker stone was set up to indicate the whereabouts of the ford. This ambiguity about the precise meaning of the element persists in the many Stanton, Stanley and Stanste(a)d names – such as STANTON DREW (Bath and North East Somerset), LEONARD STANLEY (Gloucestershire) and STANSTED MOUNTFITCHET (Essex) – also in STAINES (Surrey) and STONE (Staffordshire). Where *stan* comes at the end of the name, however, as in BOSTON (Lincolnshire), BRIXTON (Greater London), BUXTON (Derbyshire), FOLKESTONE (Kent), LILLINGSTONE DAYRELL (Buckinghamshire) and LEYTONSTONE (Greater London), the reference is most likely to be to a particular stone, usually a territorial marker, or indicator of a meeting site, or even possibly a Roman milestone.

Some names, especially in the north of England such as STAINMORE PASS (Westmorland), show the influence of Old Scandinavian *steinn* 'stone': the original name was from Old English *stan* and *mor* 'stone moor', but the first element was pronounced in the Scandinavian fashion. The STANEGATE (Cumbria) also reflects a Scandinavian pronunciation, and possibly also the replacement of an Old English name: it refers to a Roman road and its original Old English name was probably something like STANE STREET[2] (Essex). But the influence is not all one way: KIRKSTONE PASS (Cumbria), from Old Scandinavian *kirkja* and *steinn* ('church stone'), has adopted an English pronunciation.

Holes, a circle of 56 holes named after the 17th-century antiquary John Aubrey, who discovered them.

Stonehenge's purpose remains a matter of speculation: a place of worship, a sacrificial arena, an astronomical calculator, a giant calendar – perhaps all of them at one time or another. It can at least be said that it had nothing to do with the druids, as it had been abandoned long before they arrived in Britain. Not that that deterred the modern druids and New Age travellers who flocked to Stonehenge in the 1970s and 1980s to celebrate the summer solstice (and sometimes came in for some rather heavy-handed treatment by the police).

Already by the early Middle Ages Stonehenge was a noted ancient monument (the chronicler Geoffrey of Monmouth mentioned it in the early 12th century, asserting that it was the burial place of King Constantine). It has remained ever since a powerful icon of prehistoric Britain. Those who approach it are sometimes underwhelmed by its apparent smallness against the vastness of Salisbury Plain and put off by the inadequacy of the arrangements for receiving visitors, but no one who has stood at its centre could deny the force of its atmosphere.

Stonehenge features at the end of Thomas Hardy's *Tess of the D'Urbervilles* (1891) – Tess is arrested here after having fled with Angel Clare following her stabbing to death of the caddish Alec.

Stonehenge was made a UNESCO World Heritage Site in 1986.

Stonehenge of the North. A nickname for Arbor Low.

Stonehouse[1] 'stone-built house', OE *stan* (*see* STONE) + *hus* 'house'.

A town in Gloucestershire, about 5 km (3 miles) west of Stroud. It was once a centre of the clothmaking industry.

Stonehouse[2]. A suburb of PLYMOUTH in Devon, between Devonport and central Plymouth. Stonehouse was incorporated into Plymouth in 1914 (having previously been a separate town).

Stones of Stenness *Stenness* 'stone promontory', OScand *steinn* (*see* STONE) + *nes* (*see* NESS).

A megalithic stone circle on the shore of Stenness Loch, on ORKNEY's Mainland near to MAES HOWE and the RING OF BRODGAR. The name is pronounced 'stane-is'. The circle has a diameter of 44 m (144 ft), and the tallest stone is 6 m (nearly 20 ft) high; only 4 of the original 12 stones are still standing, as a result of the actions of a local farmer who in 1814, tired of ploughing round them, embarked on a demolition exercise. The monument dates from *c*.3000 BC, in the Neolithic period. In historical times it is said that lovers would visit the stones at New Year and pray to the god Odin that they would keep their oaths. There is a tradition that the Stones of Stenness were once known as 'the Temple of the Moon', and the Ring of Brodgar as 'the Temple of the Sun', but it is conceivable that these names were bestowed by romantically inclined visitors in the 17th and 18th centuries.

Stonham Aspal *Stonham* 'homestead by a stone or with stony ground', OE *stan* (*see* STONE) + HAM; *Aspal* denoting manorial ownership in the Middle Ages by the de Aspale family.

A village in Suffolk, about 10 km (6 miles) east of STOWMARKET.

Stonyhurst. *See under* HURST GREEN.

Stony Stratford 'stony (place by a) ford on a Roman road' (referring to a place where the stony or gravelly bed of the River Ouse could be forded by travellers on Watling Street), OE *stanig* 'stony' + STRATFORD.

A town in Buckinghamshire, within the unitary authority of Milton Keynes, on the GREAT OUSE and on the A5 (the old WATLING STREET[1]), about 10 km (6 miles) northwest of the town of Milton Keynes. It has an Eleanor Cross (a cross commemorating Edward I's wife Eleanor of Castile, erected at his behest).

It was at Stony Stratford that the attendants of the 13-year-old Edward V, soon to become one of the 'Princes in the Tower', were arrested on the orders of the future Richard III while Edward was on his way to London in 1483 to be proclaimed king (*see under* TOWER OF LONDON).

Stopham 'Stoppa's homestead or river meadow' or 'homestead or river meadow by a hollow', OE male personal name *Stoppa* or *stoppa* 'hollow' + *ham* 'homestead' or *hamm* 'river meadow' (*see* HAM).

A village in West Sussex, close to the point where the River ROTHER[1] joins the River ARUN, about 3 km (2 miles) west of Pulborough.

Stormont A modern name, first recorded as *Storm Mount*, curiously appropriate for the place.

An eastern suburb of BELFAST, in County Down. The 19th-century baronial **Stormont Castle** came into state ownership in 1920 and is now the headquarters of the secretary of state for Northern Ireland. Nearby are the vast Parliament Buildings, or Parliament House, completed in 1932 to a forbidding neo-classical design by Sir Arnold Thorneley. Its austere facade rises above a mile-long approach drive and a strident statue of Sir Edward Carson, ultra-Unionist and 'Uncrowned King of Ulster' (*see under* ULSTER).

Parliament House, often referred to as 'Stormont', was home to the Northern Ireland Parliament until its suspension in 1972, and the word 'Stormont' was synonymous with that body, as 'Westminster' is for the UK Parliament. Parliament House is now home to the post-Good Friday Agreement Northern Ireland Assembly when it is not in suspension.

Stornoway Possibly 'steerage bay', OScand *stjorn* 'rudder, steerage' + *vagr* 'bay'. The modern Gaelic name is *Steornabhagh*.

A BURGH on the east coast of LEWIS, and the administrative seat of the WESTERN ISLES authority. It is the largest town in the Outer Hebrides. There is a fine natural harbour here, and the town developed as a fishing port in the 18th century. There is a ferry to ULLAPOOL on the mainland, and also air links. Bonnie Prince Charlie tried to obtain a boat here, but was thwarted by two local ministers (ancestors of the 19th-century historian Lord Macaulay).

Stornoway was the birthplace of the Canadian explorer Alexander Mackenzie (1755–1820), after whom the Mackenzie River is named.

> There was a young lady of Stornoway
> Who, through walking, her feet had quite worn away.
> Said she, 'I don't mind,
> For I think I might find
> A most troublesome corn will have gone away.'
>
> Anon.: limerick

Storr, the Gaelic *storr* 'buck tooth'.

A mountain (719 m / 2358 ft) in northeast SKYE, Highland (formerly in Inverness-shire), 11 km (6.5 miles) north of Portree. On its eastern side is an escarpment of sheer and crumbling basalt cliffs, 150 m (500 ft) high. At the foot of these cliffs is an area called the Sanctuary, which contains a number of striking pinnacles, including the Needle and the **Old Man of Storr**. The latter is 50 m (160 ft) high, and is undercut around the base. The Old Man was first climbed in 1955 by a party led by Don 'the Villain' Whillans, a small but gnarly Mancunian.

Stort A back-formation from BISHOP'S STORTFORD.

A river in Essex and Hertfordshire, which rises about 11 km (7 miles) southeast of ROYSTON[1] and flows 32 km (20 miles) southwards through STANSTED MOUNTFITCHET to Bishop's Stortford, from where, canalized as the **Stort Navigation**, it flows a further 22 km (14 miles) southwards and westwards past HARLOW to join the River LEA near HODDESDON.

Stour[1] 'the fierce one', OE *stur* 'violent, fierce'.

A river (rhyming with *hour*) in Dorset and Wiltshire, which rises near STOURHEAD and flows 88 km (55 miles) southwards and eastwards through STURMINSTER NEWTON, BLANDFORD FORUM and WIMBORNE MINSTER into the English Channel at CHRISTCHURCH. It is joined by the AVON[3] just before its mouth. Its southern reaches form part of Dorset's boundary with the unitary authorities of BOURNEMOUTH and POOLE.

Stour[2]. A river (rhyming with *tour*) in Essex and Suffolk, which rises to the south of NEWMARKET[1] and flows 75 km (47 miles) southwards and eastwards through SUDBURY[1]

and the Dedham Vale (*see under* DEDHAM) into the NORTH SEA. Over the latter part of its course it forms the boundary between Suffolk and Essex. Its estuary is 19 km (12 miles) long and 2.5 km (1.5 miles) across at its widest: MANNINGTREE is at its western end, and its mouth, where it is joined by the River ORWELL[1], is flanked by FELIXSTOWE to the north and HARWICH to the south.

Stour Valley. The valley of the River Stour, which marks the southern edge of EAST ANGLIA proper. It is markedly hillier than other parts of the region, a landscape of densely packed fields and woods that was John Constable's great inspiration ('All that lies on the banks of the Stour … made me a painter'; *see also* CONSTABLE COUNTRY). In the Middle Ages it was the centre of East Anglia's weaving trade: by the end of the 15th century the villages along its banks were producing more cloth than any other part of the country. Their subsequent rapid decline left them bypassed by the Industrial Revolution, and in consequence this is an area of high rural picturesqueness.

Stour[3]. A river (rhyming with *tour*) in Kent. Its source is the WANTSUM. The main river (also known as the **Great Stour**) rises near Lenham and flows 64 km (40 miles) southeastwards through ASHFORD[1] and then northeastwards through the NORTH DOWNS and CANTERBURY[1] and SANDWICH into the North Sea at Pegwell Bay (*see under* PEGWELL). It is joined at Ashford by the **East Stour**, and, 13 km (8 miles) east of Canterbury, by the **Little Stour** (after which it is known simply as the 'Stour').

Stour[4]. A river (rhyming with *hour* or *mower*) in Oxfordshire and Warwickshire, which rises about 10 km (6 miles) southwest of Banbury and flows westwards and northwards through SHIPSTON-ON-STOUR to join the River AVON[1] just to the west of STRATFORD-UPON-AVON.

Stour[5]. A river (rhyming with *hour*) in the West Midlands, Staffordshire and Worcestershire, which rises to the southwest of BIRMINGHAM and flows 32 km (20 miles) westwards through STOURBRIDGE and then southwards through KIDDERMINSTER to join the River SEVERN at STOURPORT-ON-SEVERN.

Stourbridge 'bridge over the River Stour', STOUR[5] + OE *brycg* 'bridge'.

An industrial town in the West Midlands (before 1974 in Worcestershire), on the River Stour, on the southern edge of the BLACK COUNTRY. It was incorporated into DUDLEY in 1974. Its specialism since the 16th century has been glassmaking (introduced by Hungarian refugees). Dr Johnson spent six months, probably as a teacher, at the local grammar school, which was founded in 1552.

Stourcastle. The fictional name for STURMINSTER NEWTON in Thomas Hardy's novel *Tess of the D'Urbervilles* (1891).

Stourhead '(place at the) head or source of the Stour', ModE. A country house in Wiltshire, about 1.5 km (1 mile) northwest of STOURTON, close to the source of the River STOUR[1]. Built in the early 18th century in the Palladian style, it is famous mainly for its gardens, designed and laid out in the middle of the century by the then owner, the banker Henry Hoare (1705–85). He dammed the Stour to make a lake, and around it created a classical fantasy-land (loosely based on the story of Virgil's *Aeneid*) of domed temples, bridges, grottoes, statues and magnificent trees.

When he was only 14 years old the historian Edward Gibbon is said to have been inspired by Stourhead's library to write *The Decline and Fall of the Roman Empire* (1776–88).

Stourport-on-Severn 'port (at the confluence of the rivers) Stour and Severn'. The name is a modern one, first recorded (as *Stourport*) in the 1770s.

An industrial town and port in Worcestershire (before 1998 in Hereford and Worcester, before 1974 in Worcestershire), at the point where the River STOUR[5] joins the River SEVERN, about 6 km (4 miles) southwest of Kidderminster. It was developed in the late 18th century, on the site of an existing settlement called **Lower Mitton**, around the basin linking the Stour with the Staffordshire and Worcestershire Canal (*see under* STAFFORDSHIRE). Opened in 1771, this connected the River Severn with the Trent and Mersey Canal (*see under* TRENT[1]). Stourport is probably the only significant town in Britain to have developed on a canal, and it remains an important inland-waterways centre. Its main industries have included carpet manufacture and the making of chains (in the biggest chain-works in Europe).

Stour Provost '(estate on the River) Stour (held by the Norman Abbey of) Préaux', referring to the manorial ownership of the place in the early Middle Ages. The second element was assimilated to ModE *provost* in the 15th century when the manor passed into the hands of the Provost of King's College, Cambridge (who sold it in 1925).

A village in Dorset, on the River STOUR[1], about 8 km (5 miles) southwest of Shaftesbury.

Stourton 'farmstead or village on the River Stour', *Stour* + -TON.

A village (pronounced 'stortən') in Wiltshire, on the River STOUR[1], about 14 km (9 miles) northeast of SHAFTESBURY. It is owned by the National Trust. STOURHEAD is 1.5 km (1 mile) to the northwest.

Stourton Caundle *Caundle see* BISHOP'S CAUNDLE.

A village in Dorset, in the BLACKMOOR VALE, on the River STOUR[1], about 8 km (5 miles) southeast of Sherborne.

See also PURSE CAUNDLE.

Stow Bardolph *Stow* 'place of assembly, holy place', OE; *Bardolph* denoting manorial ownership in the Middle Ages by the Bardulf family.

A village in Norfolk, about 3 km (2 miles) northeast of Downham Market. Its church contains a wax memorial effigy, dating from the mid-18th century, the only one of its type in England outside Westminster Abbey. It is of Sarah Hare, who died after pricking herself with a needle.

Stow cum Quy *cum* 'with', Latin; *Quy* 'cow island' (referring to a nearby raised area of pasturage), OE *cu* 'cow' + *eg* (*see* -EY, -EA).

A village (pronounced 'kwai') in Cambridgeshire, about 6 km (4 miles) northeast of Cambridge.

Stowe OE *stow* 'place, often a place for meeting or holy place'.

An estate in Buckinghamshire, about 5 km (3 miles) northwest of Buckingham, formerly the seat of the dukes of Buckingham and Chandos. The house was built and decorated in the 17th and 18th centuries by Robert Adam, Sir John Vanbrugh, William Kent and Grinling Gibbons, and its extensive landscaped gardens were laid out by Kent and 'Capability' Brown. Since 1923 the house has been a public school (**Stowe School**), while the gardens, **Stowe Park**, belong to the National Trust.

Stow Longa *Longa* 'long' (the village straggles along a hill), OE *lang*, Latin *longa*.

A village in Cambridgeshire (before 1974 in Huntingdonshire), about 5 km (3 miles) northwest of GRAFHAM WATER.

Stow Maries *Maries* denoting manorial ownership in the Middle Ages by the Mareys family (it is purely coincidental that the local church is dedicated to St Mary).

A village in Essex, just to the north of the estuary of the River CROUCH[1], about 16 km (10 miles) southeast of CHELMSFORD.

Stowmarket Originally *Stow* (*see* STOW BARDOLPH); the suffix was added, in recognition of the town's importance as a market, in the 13th century.

A market town in Suffolk, on the River GIPPING[2], about 19 km (12 miles) northwest of Ipswich. It has two notable poetical associations: with John Milton in the 17th century, who used to visit his tutor Thomas Young here; and with George Crabbe in the 18th, who spent some of his schooldays there.

The town's church of St Peter and St Paul boasts a rare 17th-century wrought-iron wig stand.

Stow-on-the-Wold *Wold* 'high ground cleared of forest', OE *wald*.

A market town in Gloucestershire, about 26 km (16 miles) east of Cheltenham. At 244 m (800 ft) above sea level it is the highest town in the COTSWOLDS. It stands at the meeting-point of eight roads, including the FOSSE WAY, and was at one time the most important wool town in England (at the beginning of the 18th century Daniel Defoe recorded 20,000 sheep being sold at Stow Fair in a single year). Nowadays, as a centre for Cotswold tourists, the majority of buying and selling done here is likely to be of antiques.

The town's St Edward's church (Norman in origin) was commandeered by Oliver Cromwell to imprison 1000 Royalist captives during the Civil Wars.

Strabane Irish *An Strath Bán* 'the white land by the river'.
A market town in County Tyrone, on the border with the Republic opposite Lifford, 20 km (12 miles) southeast of Derry/Londonderry. It is the administrative centre of the local authority district of the same name. Strabane is on the confluence of the rivers Mourne and Finn, which join to form the River Foyle. The land hereabouts was granted in the early 17th century to James Hamilton, who became 1st Earl of Abercorn. His successors developed Strabane as a linen town in the 18th century, but its fortunes subsequently declined, so that in the 1980s Paul Theroux reported that:

> Strabane was said to be the poorest town in Europe – it had the highest murder rate for its size, and the highest unemployment rate, and the fewest pigs, and the dimmest prospects.
>
> Paul Theroux: *The Kingdom by the Sea* (1983)

Strabane was the birthplace of the comic writer Flann O'Brien (Brian O'Nolan, 1911–66). Other notable natives include two former employers of Gray's printing works in Main Street: John Dunlap, who, having emigrated, was the first to print the American Declaration of Independence in 1776; and James Wilson, the grandfather of President Woodrow Wilson, who emigrated in 1807. Mrs Cecil Alexander, perpetrator of 'All Things Bright and Beautiful', lived in Strabane from 1833 until her marriage in 1850, and from 1860 to 1867 she lived with her clerical husband at Camus Rectory south of the town.

'Flower of Sweet Strabane, The'. A traditional song:

> If I were King of Ireland's Isle
> And had all things at my will
> I'd roam for recreation
> And I'd seek for comfort still,
> The comfort I would ask for
> So that you may understand
> Is to win the heart of Martha
> The Flower of Sweet Strabane.

Stradbally Irish *An Sráidbhaile* 'the street-town' (i.e. one without a fort or castle).
The name of a number of villages in Ireland, such as those in counties Laois and Waterford.

Stradbally Mountain Irish *Cnoc an Sráidbhaile* 'peak of the village' (*see* KNOCK-).
A mountain (824 m / 2703 ft) in the DINGLE Peninsula, some 12 km (7.5 miles) east of BRANDON MOUNTAIN.

Stragglethorpe *Straggle*, of unknown origin and meaning (it may be the name of an early owner, perhaps a man called *Straker*) + THORPE.
A village in Lincolnshire, on the River Brant, about 11 km (7 miles) east of Newark.

Straits of Dover. *See under* DOVER

Strand, the 'bank, shore' (referring to the bank of the River Thames), OE *strand*.
A road in Central London, running northeastwards from CHARING CROSS to the western boundary of the City of London (where it becomes FLEET STREET). Originally, when it was little more than a bridle path linking LONDON with WESTMINSTER, it ran (as its name suggests) along the north bank of the River THAMES[1]. As early as the 12th century noblemen were building houses here, and over the centuries the grand ducal mansion became a characteristic feature of the Strand (there is a sumptuous echo of it today in Somerset House, built in its present form as government offices in the late 18th century on the site of Lord Protector Somerset's mid-16th-century palace). Its nature began to change in the 17th century, when smaller houses appeared, and also shops; and by the 18th century it was the main parade-ground for London's prostitutes (as James Boswell several times bears witness in his journals). At this time roads still ran down from the south side of the Strand directly to the banks of the Thames (one of them, Villiers Street, was the site of Warren's Blacking Factory, which so seared itself into the memory of the young Charles Dickens in the 1820s), but in the 1860s the construction of the EMBANKMENT separated it decisively from the river. By the end of the 19th century the Strand had become pre-eminently a street of entertainment: it had more theatres than any other street in London (including the Gaiety and the Adelphi), several notable restaurants (such as Romano's and the Tivoli) and large numbers of music halls and pubs. It was the place where Londoners of all classes went for a good night out:

> Let's all go down the Strand (Have a banana!)
> Oh! What a happy land!
> That's the place fer fun and noise,
> All among the girls and boys.
> So let's all go down the Strand.
>
> Harry Castling: 'Let's all go down the Strand' (song, 1909)

> I'm Burlington Bertie
> I rise at ten thirty and saunter along like a toff,
> I walk down the Strand with my gloves on my hand,
> Then I walk down again with them off.
>
> W.F. Hargreaves: 'Burlington Bertie from Bow' (song, 1915)

Today only three theatres remain, and of the restaurants – unless you count the Savoy Grill (*see under* SAVOY) – only the time-capsuled Simpson's-in-the-Strand, where roasts are still carved at table from a trolley, retains any of the glories of the past. At the beginning of the 21st century, the main image conjured up by the Strand was for many people that of rough sleepers bedding down for the night in shop doorways.

To the east of Waterloo Bridge the character of the Strand changes markedly, due in no small part to the presence of two fine churches, the early 18th-century **St Mary le Strand** and Christopher Wren's later 17th-century St Clement Danes, now islanded in the middle of the road; of Somerset House (home to the Courtauld Institute's galleries); and of King's College, part of the University of London.

The Law Courts (properly the Royal Courts of Justice) at the eastern end of the Strand were built in Gothic style to the designs of G.E. Street between 1874 and 1882.

The house next to Northumberland House, which in the 17th century was the official residence of the secretary of state (the chief government minister), later became known as 'No.1, the Strand', and is said to have been the first house in London to be numbered. Modern usage tends to omit the *the* in quoting numbered addresses ('125 Strand'), but in all other circumstances it is retained.

The 'Strand' cigarette brand never really recovered from the notorious 1959 television advertisement for it, devised by John May of S.H. Benson, featuring a solitary Frank Sinatra lookalike in a trenchcoat lighting up in a deserted night-time London street. Its title, 'You're never alone with a Strand', became instantly recognizable and its music, by Cliff Adams, was issued on a record and called the 'Lonely Man Theme', but as an advertisement it was a disaster – the public evidently concluding that only miserable gits with no 'mates' or 'birds' smoke Strands. The brand was withdrawn shortly afterwards.

See also ADELPHI.

Handel in the Strand. A piece of music (1911), in the style of a jaunty clog dance, by the Australian composer Percy Grainger. Originally written for piano and cello, it later appeared in versions for various permutations of orchestral instruments. Grainger said of his piece: 'the music seemed to reflect both Handel and English musical comedy … – as if jovial old Handel were careening down the Strand to the strains of modern English popular music'.

Maypole in the Strand, the. A maypole erected, probably in the time of Elizabeth I, on a spot now occupied by the church of St Mary le Strand. It was destroyed by the Puritans in 1644, but another, 41 m (134 ft) high, was set up in 1661, reputedly by the farrier John Clarges to celebrate the marriage of his daughter to General Monck. By 1713 this was decayed, and another was erected, which was removed in 1718. It was bought by Sir Isaac Newton, who sent it to

a friend in Wanstead, where it was erected in the park to support the then largest telescope in Europe.

Strand Magazine, The. An illustrated monthly magazine published between 1891 and 1950. Sherlock Holmes first appeared in its pages, and latterly it featured innumerable short stories by P.G. Wodehouse.

Strangeways 'powerful stream', OE *strang* 'strong' + *gewæsc* 'stream'.

An area of Manchester, north of the centre, known particularly for **Strangeways Prison** – as celebrated, for example, in The Smiths' album *Strangeways, Here We Come* (1987). In 1990 a thousand inmates rioted, leading to the longest prison siege in UK history, lasting 25 days; several prisoners died in the course of the disturbance. There is a Strangeways Research Laboratory at Cambridge.

Strangford 'strong fjord', OScand *strangr* 'strong' + *fjorthr*, referring to the strong tidal current flowing through the narrows.

A small town in County Down, on the north side of the LECALE peninsula 10 km (6 miles) northeast of Downpatrick. Its Irish name is **Baile Loch Cuan** ('town of the lake of the harbours'). **Strangford Castle** is a much-altered 16th-century fortified town house.

The town overlooks the narrows linking **Strangford Lough** (Irish **Loch Cuan**) with the Irish Sea, through which there is a notable tidal race. The lough extends northwards for 20 km (12 miles) to NEWTOWNARDS. It has many islands and mud flats, and is an important wildlife habitat.

The lough and its riptides feature in Joseph Tomelty's novel *Red is the Port Light* (1948), a tale of passion and madness, and the area also provides the setting for Tomelty's best-known play *All Souls Night* (1948).

Stranraer 'broad point', Gaelic *sròn* 'point' + *reamhar* 'thick'. As Stranraer is not on a headland, the name may have originally applied to the northern point of the Rhinns of Galloway.

A port and seaside resort 35 km (21 miles) west of Newton Stewart at the head of LOCH RYAN, sheltered by the northern arm of the Rhinns of Galloway (*see under* GALLOWAY). Stranraer may have been the site of the Roman naval base called **Rerigonium** or **Rerigonus Sinus**. The town was formerly in Wigtownshire and is now in Dumfries and Galloway. It was the seat of Wigtown district from 1975 until its abolition in 1996. There is a regular ferry service to LARNE in Northern Ireland.

Stranraer FC (the Blues) is one of Scotland's oldest clubs, founded in 1870. Its varying fortunes saw it peaking in 1998 with promotion to the Scottish First Division, before sliding into Division Three.

Sir John Ross (1777–1856), the Arctic explorer, lived in Stranraer (he was born at the small village of Balsarroch, also in the Rhinns).

Strata Florida 'valley of flowers', Latin *strata* 'valley' + *florida* 'flowery', from the Welsh name of the valley, *Ystrad Fflur*.

A ruined 12th-century abbey on the upper reaches of the River TEIFI, Ceredigion (formerly in Cardiganshire, then in Dyfed), 24 km (14.5 miles) northeast of Lampeter. The Cistercian foundation established here in 1164 (possibly succeeding an earlier foundation) became one of the most important monasteries in Wales until abandoned during Owain Glyndwr's revolt at the beginning of the 15th century. In the next century it was pretty much destroyed during Henry VIII's Dissolution of the Monasteries, although it is said that at night candles still glimmer among the fallen stones. As with any self-respecting monastic ruin, there is also a spectral monk, who on Christmas Eve has been seen attempting to rebuild the high altar. The great poet Dafydd ap Gwilym died at Strata Florida *c*.1380, and is, according to tradition, buried under an ancient yew tree here.

See also DEVIL'S BRIDGE[1].

Stratfield Saye *Stratfield* 'open land by a Roman road' (referring to the Roman road from Silchester to London), OE *strǣt* (*see* STREET) + *feld* (*see* FIELD); *Saye* denoting manorial ownership in the Middle Ages by the de Say family.

A village in Hampshire, about 11 km (7 miles) northeast of Basingstoke. **Stratfield Saye House** is the home of the dukes of Wellington. The original was built in 1630. It was reconstructed in 1795 and in 1817 was presented by a grateful nation to the 1st Duke as a reward for his victory at Waterloo. His monstrous funeral carriage is on display there.

Stratfield Turgis *Turgis* denoting manorial ownership in the Middle Ages by the Turgis family.

A village in Hampshire, about 2.5 km (1.5 miles) southeast of Stratfield Saye.

Stratford 'ford on a Roman road', OE *strǣt* (*see* STREET) + FORD (referring to the place where the River LEA is forded by the road from London to Colchester).

A district of East London (E15), in the borough of NEWHAM, between West Ham to the east and Hackney to the west. Its industrial history stretches back to the early Middle Ages: ten mills are recorded in the area in Domesday Book, and over the succeeding centuries it was home to gunpowder-making, calico-printing, distilling and timber-milling, among other occupations. It was in the 1840s, though, that Stratford met its vocation: the railway. In 1839 the Eastern Counties Railway opened a station here, and in 1847 it established its main locomotive and rolling stock works here. Stratford never looked back: it became, and remains, a major rail junction and depot, and is now undergoing extensive redevelopment to host the Cross-Channel rail link. The 'Underground' station opened in 1946, originally on the Central line; it was joined in 1999 by the Jubilee line, as its eastern terminus.

The innovative theatre director Joan Littlewood brought her Theatre Workshop to the Theatre Royal, Stratford in 1953. It was disbanded in 1964, but she revived it in the 1970s. Among its most notable productions were her own *Oh! What a Lovely War* (1963), Brendan Behan's *The Quare Fellow* (1959) and Shelagh Delaney's *A Taste of Honey* (1958).

The poet Gerard Manley Hopkins (1844–89) was born in Stratford.

There are towns called Stratford in the USA (Connecticut, Iowa, New Hampshire, Oklahoma, South Dakota, Texas, Wisconsin), Australia (Victoria), Canada (Ontario – which has an annual Shakespearean Festival in emulation of STRATFORD-UPON-AVON – and Quebec) and New Zealand.

Stratford-atte-Bow. The name by which Stratford's neighbour BOW, across the River Lea, was known in the 13th and 14th centuries. It means 'Stratford at the Bow'.

Stratford Tony *Stratford see* STRATFORD (the ford in this case is where the Roman road between OLD SARUM and BADBURY RINGS crossed the River Ebble, a tributary of the AVON[3]; *Tony* denoting manorial ownership in the Middle Ages by the de Touny family.

A village in Wiltshire, on the River Ebble, about 6 km (4 miles) southwest of Salisbury.

Stratford-upon-Avon *Stratford see* STRATFORD (the ford in this case is where a minor local Roman road crossed the River Avon).

A market town in Warwickshire, on the River AVON[1], about 37 km (23 miles) southeast of Birmingham. It has a fine 15th-century bridge across the Avon (the 14-arched Clopton Bridge) and a unique annual Mop Fair dating from the Middle Ages, but frankly all other aspects of the town pale beside those connected with William Shakespeare (1564–1616), who was born here and died here. Little was made of the link until 1769, when the actor David Garrick organized Shakespeare Jubilee celebrations in the town. The event attracted attention, and ever since visitors (or pilgrims) have been coming to pay homage to the great poet and dramatist and see the places associated with his life. Stratford is now Heritage England's number-one destination outside London, and seethes with tourists every summer (and indeed every other part of the year).

What they can see includes the house where he was (probably) born (bought as a national memorial in 1847 for £3000); New Place, the house where he lived after he had retired from the theatre and returned from London to his home town; the grammar school where it is assumed he was educated; his tomb in Holy Trinity Church, with its famous inscription:

> Bleste be the man that spares the stones
> And curst be he that moves my bones

and, a little out of town at SHOTTERY, the cottage belonging to his wife, Anne Hathaway.

The first Shakespeare Memorial Theatre opened beside the River Avon in 1879. It burnt down in 1926, and in 1932 it was replaced by the present theatre, designed by Elisabeth Scott, which is the headquarters of the Royal Shakespeare Company (an early 21st-century proposal to pull it down and build a new one was defeated). Besides the Memorial Theatre the RSC has the Swan Theatre, built in the 1980s as an Elizabethan theatre-in-the-round, and the coyly named 'Other Place' (successor to 'The Place' in London), a studio theatre opened in 1974 where modern and experimental pieces are showcased.

The University of Birmingham's Shakespeare Institute is based in Stratford. It is housed in Mason Croft, once the home of Queen Victoria's favourite novelist, Marie Corelli (1855–1924).

Shakespeare's status as England's pre-eminent writer has helped spread the name 'Stratford' to towns around the English-speaking world (*see under* STRATFORD). In Stratford, Ontario, there is even an annual Shakespearean Festival in emulation of Stratford-upon-Avon.

Strathaven 'valley of the Avon', Gaelic *srath, strath* 'valley' + river name AVON[5].

A small town in South Lanarkshire (formerly in Strathclyde region), 11 km (6.5 miles) southeast of East Kilbride. It is on a minor River Avon, a tributary of the Clyde. Strathaven is pronounced 'strae-vən', as in:

> There once was a woman from Strathaven
> Who had as a pet a small rathaven.
>> Although small it was strong
>> And when she did wrong
> It knocked her down flat on the pathaven.
>
>> Anon.: limerick

Strath Avon. *See under* AVON[5].

Strathbogie 'valley of the River Bogie', Gaelic *srath, strath* 'valley' + *balg* 'bag-like, bulging'.

An area of northeast Scotland, in Aberdeenshire (formerly in Grampian region), centred on the **River Bogie** and the town of HUNTLY, built on the site of a settlement called the **Raws of Strathbogie** (Scots *raw* 'row of houses').

dance the reels o' Bogie, to. To engage in sexual intercourse; the expression was current in the 18th and 19th centuries, and plays on 'Old Bogey', a nickname for the devil.

Strathbogle. The fictional glen, village and Scottish baronial pile featured in BBC television's *Monarch of the Glen* (2000–).

See also ARDVERIKIE.

Strathclyde 'valley of the River Clyde', Gaelic *srath, strath* 'valley' + river name CLYDE.

Originally, an ancient kingdom of the Britons south of DALRIADA, with its capital at DUMBARTON. However, it was not known as 'Strathclyde' until the 9th or 10th centuries. Its origins lay in the Roman period, and by the 6th century (when the kingdom was converted to Christianity) it had extended beyond the Clyde valley to cover much of Ayrshire. Its power declined over the next few centuries, and in the early 11th century Duncan I brought it into the kingdom of Scotland.

The word was revived after the Second World War when the idea for a **Strathclyde Regional Park** was first mooted. This was subsequently established in a stretch of the CLYDE valley between HAMILTON[1] and MOTHERWELL. Its main feature is a new loch, especially designed for water sports.

In 1964 the Royal Technical College of Glasgow became the **University of Strathclyde**. A decade later, the local government reorganization of 1975 created the massive new **Strathclyde region**, which incorporated GLASGOW, RENFREWSHIRE, LANARKSHIRE, BUTESHIRE, DUNBARTONSHIRE, and parts of ARGYLL, AYRSHIRE and STIRLINGSHIRE. The region was abolished in 1996, being replaced by a number of unitary authorities.

Strathclyde Concertos. A series of ten concertos for various solo instruments (including oboe, cello, clarinet, horn, trumpet, double bass and flute) and orchestra, plus a concerto grosso and a concerto for orchestra (1987–96) by Peter Maxwell Davies.

Strathdon. *See under* DON[1].

Strath Earn. *See under* EARN.

Strath Finella Gaelic *srath, strath* 'valley' + *Finella* personal name.

A valley in Aberdeenshire (formerly in Kincardineshire and then in Grampian region), east of CLATTERIN BRIG and some 4 km (2.5 miles) southeast of the CAIRN O' MOUNT pass. It takes its name from Finella, daughter of the Earl of Angus, whose son had been executed by Kenneth II. In revenge, in 995, Finella killed the king at her castle, which was situated a little to the south, towards Fettercairn.

Strathkelvin 'valley of the River Kelvin', Gaelic *srath, strath* 'valley' + KELVIN (i.e. 'narrow stream').

A district of the former Strathclyde region, created in 1975 and abolished in 1996. It lay to the northeast of Glasgow, and consisted of parts of the old counties of DUNBARTONSHIRE, STIRLINGSHIRE and LANARKSHIRE. Its HQ was in KIRKINTILLOCH.

Strathmore 'the big valley', Gaelic *srath, strath* 'valley' + *mòr* 'big'.

A broad lowland valley extending northeastwards for some 70 km (43 miles) from just north of PERTH to BRECHIN in Angus, after which it merges with the Howe of the Mearns (*see under* the MEARNS). It is flanked by the Braes of Angus (*see under* ANGUS) on the north and the SIDLAW HILLS on the south, and includes stretches of the TAY, Isla and South Esk rivers.

Strathnaver 'valley of the River Naver', Gaelic *srath*, *strath* 'valley' + a pre-Celtic river name.

A long glen in northern Highland (formerly in Sutherland). The **River Naver** flows from **Loch Naver** northwards to meet the PENTLAND FIRTH at BETTYHILL. The glen was once well populated, but is now a bare, bleak place.

> The year that Patrick Sellar came to Strathnaver
> black smoke hung along its length
> from the homes so lately vacated by his tenants;
> too late for one young woman who would not leave,
> so perished in the flames, her unborn child within her.
> Old men, led out in time, were laid
> to die from frost instead of fire.
>
>> Gerald England: 'The Clearing of the Highlands' (Patrick Sellar was the estate factor of the Duke of Sutherland, who in 1816 was acquitted of culpable homicide and fire-raising while evicting the Duke's tenants in Strathnaver in 1814.)

Strathnaver is the setting for Iain Crichton Smith's novel about the Clearances, *Consider the Lily* (1968) (*see also under* SUTHERLAND).

Strath of Appin (Argyll). *See under* APPIN.

Strath of Appin (Perth and Kinross). *See under* DULL.

Strathpeffer 'valley of the River Peffery', Gaelic *srath*, *strath* 'valley' + river name *Peffery*. The river name is thought to be related to Welsh *pefr* 'radiant, beautiful'.

A small town in northeast Highland (formerly in Ross and Cromarty), 7 km (4 miles) west of Dingwall. It is in **Strath Peffer**, the valley of the short **River Peffery**, which enters the sea at Dingwall. Its mineral springs made Strathpeffer a popular spa from the later 18th to the early 20th century. It is said that the Devil washes his clothes in the sulphur springs, and there is no doubt that when the sulphurous water meets water from the chalybeate (iron salt) spring, the water turns black, a colour strongly suggestive of Satanic laundering.

The Brahan Seer (*see under* BRAHAN) predicted that in the future crowds seeking health and pleasure would flock to Strathpeffer. He also predicted that if five churches should be built in Strathpeffer, ships would anchor themselves to their spires. In the mid-19th century the locals strongly objected when a fifth church was proposed, but it was built anyway. Shortly after the First World War an airship flew over Strathpeffer, and its grapnel became entangled in one of the spires – much to the relief of the locals.

Battle of Strathpeffer (1411). A clan battle between Munros and MacDonalds. The Eagle Stone near the village is said to commemorate the battle (the eagle being the Munro crest), but the inscriptions are almost certainly older,

probably Pictish. The Brahan Seer predicted that if the stone should fall three times, ships would sail up the valley as far as Strathpeffer; so far the stone has fallen over twice, and it has now been concreted into the ground to ensure its stability.

Strathspey. *See under* SPEY.

Strathyre Possibly 'valley of the land', Gaelic *srath*, *strath* 'valley' + *tire* 'of the land'. The river in this strath is actually called the Balvag.

A valley (containing a small village of the same name) between LOCH LUBNAIG and BALQUHIDDER, in the heart of Rob Roy country. The west side of the valley is flanked by Beinn an t-Sithein (570 m / 1871 ft) – the 'hill of the fairy mound'.

> There's meadows in Lanark and mountains in Skye,
> And pastures in Hielands and Lowlands forbye;
> But there's nae greater luck that the heart could desire
> Than to herd the fine cattle in bonnie Strathyre.
>
>> Sir Harold Boulton: 'Bonnie Strathyre', sung to the traditional tune 'Taymouth'

Stratton Originally *Strœtneat* 'valley of the River Neat', Cornish *strad* 'valley' + OCelt river name, possibly from an Indo-European root meaning 'running water' (*see* NIDD), with the later addition of -TON.

A small hillside town in Cornwall, about 2 km (1.25 miles) inland from **Bude Bay**. It was the main settlement in the area until the seaside resort of BUDE grew up on its doorstep. It has some attractive thatched houses.

Battle of Stratton (16 May 1643). A battle (also known as the **Battle of Stamford Hill**) of the Civil Wars, fought about 0.75 km (0.5 miles) northwest of Stratton, in which Royalist forces under Sir Ralph Hopton heavily defeated the local Parliamentarians. The 'Cornish giant' Anthony Payne (1612–91), who was born in Stratton and is said to have been 2.2 m (7 ft 4 in) tall, fought on the Royalist side.

Stratton Strawless *Stratton* 'farmstead or village on a Roman road', OE *strœt* (*see* STREET) + -TON; *Strawless* 'lacking straw' (presumably implying agricultural infertility or unproductiveness), OE *streawleas*.

A village in Norfolk, about 12 km (7.5 miles) north of Norwich.

Strawberry Fields. The name of a girls' reform school in Woolton, LIVERPOOL, which inspired the Lennon–McCartney song (mainly by John Lennon) 'Strawberry Fields Forever', released as the alternative A-side of 'PENNY LANE' in February 1967.

Strawberry Hill From the house of the same name.

A district of TWICKENHAM in West London, in the borough of Richmond-upon-Thames, on the north bank of the River Thames opposite HAM[1]. It takes its name from a remarkable house owned by the writer Horace Walpole (1717–97), author of the influential Gothic novel *The Castle of Otranto* (1765). He bought it as a modest cottage in 1748, and over the next 44 years turned it into a whimsical Gothic extravaganza. Its name is pre-echoed in local field names from the late 17th century, and reflects the fact that strawberries had been grown in the area for the London markets from as far back as the 16th century. The attachment of the name to the district was strengthened by the opening of a railway station called 'Strawberry Hill' in the middle of the 19th century (at the instigation of Frances, Countess Waldegrave, a later owner of the house). The house is now home to St Mary's College, in the University of Surrey.

Strawberry Hill Gothic. The style of early Gothic Revivalist architecture inspired and epitomized by Strawberry Hill.

Stray, the ModE *stray* 'piece of unenclosed common land'.
A large open space of 80 ha (200 acres) in HARROGATE, North Yorkshire. It was created by Act of Parliament in 1770, which forbids building on this green space. The Stray is the site of several of the town's mineral wells.

Streatham 'homestead or village on a Roman road' (referring to the road from London to Brighton, close to the present A23), OE *stræt* (*see* STREET) + HAM.
A district (pronounced 'strettəm') of South London (SW16), in the borough of LAMBETH, between Tooting to the west and SYDENHAM to the east. Its character has been determined by the road on which it stands (and from which it gets its name): it was already by the Middle Ages an important resting point on the way to CROYDON, in the 18th century the stagecoaches to the developing SOUTH COAST stopped there, and **Streatham High Road** (the A23) continues to carry heavy north–south traffic (some of it of the kerb-crawling variety). It was the coming of the railway in the mid-19th century, though, which transformed Streatham into a sprawling suburb.

In the 20th century an unusually high density of cinemas and dance halls, not to mention a celebrated ice rink, helped to turn Streatham into South London's leisure capital.

To the south of the district is **Streatham Common**, now a mere 15 ha (36 acres), all that remains of a huge area of open land that once stretched all the way north to TULSE HILL.

Dr Johnson's friends Henry and Hester Thrale had a house in Streatham in the late 18th century, when it was still very much a village, and the great lexicographer was a frequent visitor between 1766 and 1782. Two hundred years later, another kind of hospitality was provided in the suburban Streatham house owned by Cynthia Payne, England's best-loved madam: as revealed at her 1980 trial, she famously accepted Luncheon Vouchers in part-payment for various non-culinary services at her establishment.

A mildly amusing word play, popular among upwardly mobile house-buying twenty- and thirty-somethings in the 1980s and 1990s, amended the mundane Streatham to the more genteel-sounding 'St Reatham'.

The composer Sir Arnold Bax (1883–1953), disc-jockey David Jacobs (b.1926), sometimes-Labour politician, former Greater London Council leader and later Mayor of London Ken Livingstone (b.1945), actor Simon Callow (b.1949) and supermodel Naomi Campbell (b.1970) were all born in Streatham.

Streatley 'glade by a Roman road' (referring to the ICKNIELD WAY), OE *stræt* (*see* STREET) + -LEY.
A village in Berkshire, on the River THAMES[1] opposite GORING (to which it is joined by an attractive bridge). It lies on the Icknield Way as it passes through the Goring Gap. There are wonderful views from the nearby **Streatley Hill**.

Street '(place by a) Roman road' (referring to the road from ILCHESTER to the Bristol Channel), OE *stræt* (*see* STREET).
A town in Somerset, about 17 km (11 miles) east of Bridgwater. At the beginning of the 19th century it was just a quiet village, but the seeds of expansion were sown in the 1820s when James Clark, an apprentice in a local sheepskin-rug firm, had the idea of making slipper-linings from the off-cuts of sheepskins. In 1825 he and his brother Cyrus

---

❖ **street** ❖

Old English *stræt* was borrowed from Latin *via strata* 'paved road' and was indeed commonly used to refer to the great roads the Romans laid in Britain: WATLING STREET[1], ERMINE STREET, ICKNIELD STREET, STANE STREET[1] and DERE STREET are some of these Roman roads. Settlements were named from their proximity to these roads, as with STREET (Somerset), Adwick Le Street (Yorkshire) and CHESTER-LE-STREET (County Durham); and where the roads crossed rivers the fords were characterized as *stræt* fords, as in STRATFORD and STRETFORD.

A later development occurred when people transferred this element to any kind of paved road, and particularly urban roads: the famous streets of London, REGENT STREET, OXFORD STREET and BOND STREET, reflect this usage. Another late development is the use of *street* to refer to a hamlet: STREET DINAS (Shropshire) and the STREET ENDS of Sussex and Kent refer to rather remote settlements, and the element seems to mean almost the opposite of what it meant originally: more 'off the beaten track' than 'paved road'.

founded a firm to meet the demand, and over the next century and a half it grew into the biggest shoe manufacturer in Britain, employing a third of Street's population. There is now a cluster of retail outlets known as Clark's Village, which contains the Clark's factory store.

Street is also home to Millfield School, a public school noted for its sporting excellence. It was founded in 1935 by Jack Meyer, and originally based in large house in Street which had belonged to the Clark shoe family.

Street Dinas *Dinas* 'fort', Welsh.

A village in Shropshire, close to the Welsh border, about 10 km (6 miles) northeast of OSWESTRY.

Street End[1] 'the end of the street' – probably in the sense that the metalled or Roman road runs out, although it could also be *street* in the early ModE sense 'hamlet', hence 'end of the cluster of buildings' forming the hamlet.

A village in Kent, about 4 km (2.5 miles) south of Canterbury.

Street End[2]. A village in West Sussex, about 5 km (3 miles) south of Chichester.

Strensham 'Strenge's homestead or enclosure', OE *Strenges* possessive form of male personal name *Strenge* + HAM.

A village in Worcestershire (before 1998 in Hereford and Worcester, before 1974 in Worcestershire), about 14 km (9 miles) southwest of Evesham. Strensham Services on the M5 are just to the north of Junction 8, where the motorway is joined by the M50.

Samuel Butler (1613–80), author of the long satirical poem *Hudibras* (1662–80), was born in Strensham.

Stretford 'ford on a Roman road', OE *stræt* (*see* STREET) + FORD.

A town on the southwestern outskirts of Manchester. Manchester United's ground at nearby Old Trafford has a **Stretford End**.

Stretton en le Field *Stretton* 'farmstead or village on a Roman road' (probably referring to an ancient salt-way (now lost) running from Grantham to Barrow on Soar), OE *stræt* (*see* STREET) + -TON; *en le* 'in the', OFr; *feld* (*see* FIELD).

A village in Leicestershire, on the River Mease, about 8 km (5 miles) southwest of Ashby-de-la-Zouch.

Stretton Grandison *Stretton see* STRETTON EN LE FIELD (the Roman roads in question were one running northwest from Gloucester (now the A417) and one running westwards from the village past Hereford); *Grandison* denoting manorial ownership in the Middle Ages by the Grandison family.

A village in Herefordshire (before 1998 in Hereford and Worcester, before 1974 in Herefordshire), on the River FROME[5], about 13 km (8 miles) northeast of Hereford.

Stretton Hills From their being close to such settlements as CHURCH STRETTON and Little Stretton.

A range of hills in Shropshire, between the LONG MYND to the west and WENLOCK EDGE to the east.

Stretton Sugwas *Stretton see* STRETTON EN LE FIELD (the Roman road in question was one running east–west to the north of Hereford); *Sugwas* 'alluvial land frequented by sparrows' or 'marshy alluvial land', OE *sugge* 'sparrow' or *sugga* 'marsh' + *wæsse* 'alluvial land'.

A village (pronounced 'suggəs') in Herefordshire (before 1998 in Hereford and Worcester, before 1974 in Herefordshire), on the River FROME[5], about 6 km (4 miles) northwest of Hereford.

Strid, the OE *stride* 'step, stride', here referring to a narrow channel, a place narrow enough to jump across.

A section on the River WHARFE, North Yorkshire, a little north of BOLTON ABBEY, where the mighty river is forced through a narrow, deep and tumultuous chasm. At its narrowest, the Strid is barely 2 m (6 ft) across, and many foolhardy people have attempted the jump. The consequences of failure are invariably fatal, as the victim is sucked down into underwater caverns from which there is no escape. It was here that the Boy of Egremont (*see under* EGREMONT) was drowned in 1157, while attempting the leap on horseback. More recently, in 1998, a couple on honeymoon drowned here, their bodies not being recovered for some weeks.

Striding Edge. *See under* HELVELLYN.

String, the. The road built across the middle of ARRAN in 1817 by Thomas Telford. It is now the B880, and links BRODICK and Blackwaterfoot. It was so named because sailors out at sea fancied it resembled a piece of string winding across the hills.

Stroat Originally '(place on the) Roman road', OE *stræt* (*see* STREET), but later influenced by Welsh *strat* 'valley' (referring to the valley of the Severn).

A village in Gloucestershire, on the west bank of the SEVERN estuary, to the south of the FOREST OF DEAN, about 5 km (3 miles) northeast of Chepstow.

Stroke City. A nickname for DERRY/LONDONDERRY.

Strokestown *Strokes* is apparently a reference to a battle, i.e. sword-strokes.

A village in County Roscommon, 23 km (14 miles) west of Longford. **Strokestown House**, a Palladian mansion designed by Richard Castle, was the family home of the Packenham Mahon family until 1979. It was built by Thomas Mahon MP (1701–82) on lands that had been granted to his grandfather, Nicholas, for his support of the Crown in what has become known as the Tudor Reconquest. Opened to the public in 1987, the house has a Famine Museum, situated in the stable ward, displaying original documents and letters relating to the years of the Great Famine on the Strokestown Park Estate.

Stroma 'island in the tidal stream', OScand *straumr* 'tidal stream' + *ey* (*see* -AY).

A small island in the PENTLAND FIRTH, some 6 km (4 miles) northwest of Duncansby Head. It is in Highland unitary authority (formerly in Caithness), rather than in Orkney. Legend has it that this territorial division was determined by the respective Earls of Orkney and Caithness by taking certain 'venomous animals' from Stroma and placing some in Orkney and some in Caithness; those taken to the latter thrived, whereas those taken to the former died.

The last of Stroma's permanent population left in the early 1960s, and the island was entirely depopulated in 1996, when the lighthouse was automated.

Stromeferry 'ferry at the promontory', Gaelic *sròn* 'promontory' + ModE *ferry*. The promontory is actually on the opposite side, at Stromemore ('big promontory', Gaelic *mòr* 'big').

A settlement on the south side of the narrows in LOCH CARRON, Highland (formerly in Ross and Cromarty), 13 km (8 miles) northeast of Kyle of Lochalsh. The small car-ferry here was the only route north until the road on the south side of Loch Carron was opened in 1970, when the ferry closed. The ruins of **Strome Castle** (not naturally ruined, rather blown up in 1602 and now owned by the National Trust for Scotland) are on the northern shore.

Stromness 'cape of the current', OScand *straumr* 'current' + NESS.

The second town of ORKNEY, on Mainland, some 20 km (12 miles) west of Kirkwall, the capital. It began to develop as a port in the 17th century, and until the end of the 19th century it was used by the Hudson's Bay Company and the Davis Strait whaling fleet. Sir John Franklin set off from here in 1845 on his doomed attempt to find the Northwest Passage. Today Stromness is the terminal for ferries from SCRABSTER and ABERDEEN on the Scottish mainland, from LERWICK in Shetland, and from HOY.

Stromness was the birthplace of John Rae (1813–93), the explorer of Arctic Canada who was involved in several attempts to find Franklin's party.

In the stories of George Mackay Brown (1921–96), Stromness is fictionalized as **Hamnavoe**.

Stronsay Possibly 'star island' or 'wealth island', OScand *stjarna* 'star' or *strjon* 'wealth' + *ey* (*see* -AY); if the latter is correct, it refers to the wealth produced by the fishery.

An island in ORKNEY, 20 km (12 miles) northeast of Kirkwall on Mainland. The main settlement of Whitehall (named after a house built by a retired pirate in the late 17th century) was once the centre of a major herring fishery, and at one time boasted 40 pubs. Initially the Dutch were the major players in the fishery, hence the name of 'Bay of Holland' in the south of the island. The **Stronsay Firth** lies between Stronsay, EDAY and SHAPINSAY.

Strontian 'promontory with a small hill' or 'promontory of the fairy hills', Gaelic *sròn* 'promontory, cape' + *tiahhean* 'with a small hill', or *t-sithean* 'of the fairy hills'.

A village on Loch Sunart (*see under* SUNART), Highland (formerly in Argyll, and then in Strathclyde), 32 km (19 miles) southwest of Fort William.

strontium. A radioactive element first found by Adair Crawford and William Cruickshank in a lead mine at Strontian in 1790, in its commonest ore **strontianite** (strontium carbonate).

Strood 'marshy ground overgrown with brushwood', OE *strod*.

A district of ROCHESTER, on the western side of the River MEDWAY[1], in Kent. The administrative headquarters of the unitary authority of MEDWAY[2] are situated here.

In past times it was said that the men of Kent were born with long tails, as a punishment for the murder of Thomas Becket in 1170, and the satirical poet 'Peter Pindar' (1738–1819; real name John Wolcot) fastened the legend on Strood:

> As Becket that good saint, sublimely rode,
> Thoughtless of insult, through the town of Strode,
> What did the mob? Attacked his horse's rump
> And cut the tail, so flowing, to the stump.
> What does the saint? Quoth he, 'For this vile trick
> The town of Strode shall heartily be sick.'
> And lo! by power divine, a curse prevails –
> The babes of Strode are born with horse's tails.
>
> *Epistle to the Pope* (1793)

Stroud 'marshy ground overgrown with brushwood', OE *strod*.

A town in Gloucestershire, on the River FROME[6], about 14 km (9 miles) south of Gloucester. For many centuries it was a cloth town, with 150 mills powered by the Frome turning COTSWOLD wool into fine broadcloth. A very small number remain active, specializing in the sort of felt used for billiard tables and tennis balls, but most have been turned to other industrial uses or converted into flats.

The writer Laurie Lee lived and worked in Stroud for some years in the early 1930s, and in his *As I Walked Out One Midsummer Morning* (1969) he describes setting out from Stroud and walking to London, on his way to take part in the Spanish Civil War. Another notable local was Edward Budding, who in 1830 invented the lawnmower (the idea came from a machine for cutting the nap of cloth).

Towards the end of the 20th century Stroud became something of an alternative-lifestyle centre, with a Green town council.

stroud. A term in use in North America from the 17th century for a blanket used for trading or bartering with the Native Americans, or for the cloth from which it was made. No decisive link with the town has, apparently, been established, but the coincidence of names is more than suggestive.

Stroudwater Scarlet. A scarlet-dyed cloth once made in Stroud for British Army uniforms.

Strubby Probably 'Strutr's farmstead or village', OScand male personal name *Strutr* + -BY.

A village in Lincolnshire, about 5 km (3 miles) southwest of Mablethorpe.

Strumble Head *Strumble* possibly 'storm hill', OE *storm* + *hyll*, with *storm* becoming *strom* and *b* added for ease of pronunciation.

The rocky headland at the tip of the PEN CAER peninsula on the north coast of Pembrokeshire (formerly in Dyfed) some 8 km (5 miles) northwest of Fishguard. It marks the southwestern edge of Cardigan Bay (*see under* CARDIGAN).

Studland 'cultivated land where a herd of horses is kept', OE *stod* 'herd of horses, stud' + *land* 'cultivated land'.

A village in Dorset, on the east coast of the Isle of Purbeck (*see under* PURBECK), about 3 km (2 miles) north of SWAN-AGE. It is situated towards the southern end of **Studland Bay** (which has a beach for nudists). To the north, **Studland Heath**, a nature reserve which shelters all six species of native British reptile (including the very rare smooth snake), extends into a peninsula which forms the southern part of the mouth of Poole Harbour (*see under* POOLE).

The village itself is predominantly red-brick, and has a particularly fine Saxon-Norman church. The village policeman in the mid-20th century was the model for P.C. Plod in Enid Blyton's 'Noddy' stories.

The eastern end of the South West Coast Path is at Studland Bay.

Sturmer 'pool on the River Stour', STOUR[2] + OE *mere* 'pool'.

A village in Essex, on the River STOUR[2], close to the Suffolk border, about 1.5 km (1 mile) southeast of Haverhill. It is mentioned in the Old English poem *The Battle of Maldon* (*see under* MALDON) in lines that make it clear that the place had a reputation for gossip as well as bravery: 'Steadfast warriors around Sturmer will have no need to accuse me of returning home lordless', says the noble Leofsunu before he fights to the death against the Vikings to avenge his lord Byrhtnoth.

Sturmer pippin. The name of a late-ripening variety of dessert apple developed here in the 1830s by S. and J. Dillistone. It has yellowish-green skin, sometimes with a russet tinge, and crisp, creamy-white flesh.

Sturminster Marshall *Sturminster* 'church on the River Stour', *Stour* + OE *mynster* 'church'; *Marshall* denoting manorial ownership in the Middle Ages by the Mareschal family.

A village in Dorset, on the River STOUR[1], about 8 km (5 miles) west of Wimborne Minster.

Sturminster Newton Originally the names of two separate places on opposite sides of the River Stour: *Sturminster* (*see* STURMINSTER MARSHALL) and *Newton* (*see* NEWTON ABBOT).

A market town in Dorset, in the BLACKMOOR VALE, on the River STOUR[1], about 13 km (8 miles) southwest of SHAFTES-BURY. It is famous for its six-arched medieval bridge across the Stour.

Thomas Hardy and his wife Emma lived here during 1876–8, a period he later described as 'idyllic' and during which he wrote his novel *The Return of the Native* (1878). In his *Tess of the D'Urbervilles* (1891) the town is fictionalized as **Stourcastle**.

The Dorset dialect poet William Barnes (1800–86) was born nearby.

See also MELBURY BUBB.

Sturry 'district by the River Stour', *Stour* + OE *ge* 'district'.

A village in Kent, on the River STOUR[3], about 5 km (3 miles) northeast of Canterbury.

Styal 'nook of land with a pigsty, or by a path', OE *stigu* 'pigsty' or *stig* 'path' + *halh* (*see* HALE, -HALL).

A village in Cheshire, on the southwestern outskirts of Greater Manchester, close to Manchester Airport (Ringway). The water-driven Quarry Bank Cotton Mill, on the River Bollin, was built in 1784, and the village grew up around it. The village was given to the National Trust in 1939, to be preserved as an example of an early industrial community. However, it is probably best known for **Styal Prison** for women, whose inmates have been known to refer to themselves ironically (picking up on the rhyme with *style*) as 'living in Styal' (also the title of a four-part television documentary in 1982). Just how ironic this description is was suggested by the spate of suicides at the prison between 2000 and 2003, which made national headlines.

Styhead Tarn. *See under* BORROWDALE.

Styrrup 'stirrup' (probably referring to the shape of a hill to the east of the village), OE *stig-rap*.

A village in northern Nottinghamshire, about 11 km (7 miles) north of Worksop.

Suck Irish *An tSuca* 'the calf'.

A river of west-central Ireland, rising in ROSCOMMON and flowing southwards along the Roscommon–Galway border to join the SHANNON at the junction of counties Galway, Roscommon and Offaly. It is 80 km (50 miles) long.

Sudbury[1] 'southern fortification' (the implied 'northern fortification' may have been BURY ST EDMUNDS), OE *suth* 'south' + *byrig* dative form of *burh* (*see* BURY).

A market town in Suffolk, on the River STOUR[2], close to the Essex border, 30 km (19 miles) west of Ipswich. It was an important cloth town (the making of woollen cloth was introduced by Flemings in the 14th century), and its centre still has some fine timber-framed houses from the medieval and early modern period. It practically doubled its size with new housing development in the last quarter of the 20th century.

St Gregory's church contains the preserved head of **Simon of Sudbury** (original surname Tybald or Theobald), a 14th-century Archbishop of Canterbury and chancellor of England who was blamed for unfair taxes and thus beheaded by the rebels during the Peasants' Revolt (1381).

Sudbury features as **Eatanswill** ('eat and swill') in Charles Dickens's *Pickwick Papers* (1837). When Mr Pickwick and his companions arrive it is in the throes of a parliamentary election, contested by the Blue Party and the Buff Party.

The painter Thomas Gainsborough (1727–88) was born in Sudbury. His house has been preserved as a museum dedicated to the artist.

There are towns called Sudbury in the USA (Massachusetts), Australia (Queensland) and Canada (Ontario).

Sudbury[2] 'southern manor house' (its implied counterpart was a now disappeared place called *Northbury* – perhaps the manor house of Harrow), ME *s(o)uth* + *bury* 'manor house'.
A western suburb of London, in the borough of BRENT[2] (before 1965 in Middlesex), between Harrow to the north and Perivale to the south. Sudbury Town and Sudbury Hills 'Underground' stations, on the Piccadilly line, opened in 1903.

Sudbury was the home of Wasps rugby union club (now London Wasps, *see under* LONDON) from 1923 until 1996. Wasps' Sudbury clubhouse still exists and is considered the club's spiritual home by diehards.

Sudbury Hall *Sudbury* 'south fortification', OE *suth* 'south' + BURY; its counterpart to the north is Norbury.
An Elizabethan house just inside Derbyshire, 8 km (6 miles) east of UTTOXETER. Its Grinling Gibbons wood carving, and the murals and plasterwork, are of a very fine quality, and it boasts a particularly grand 'Grand Staircase'. All these attractions were enough to tempt BBC producers, who cast the house's interiors as the inside of Mr Darcy's PEMBERLEY in the 1995 adaptation of Jane Austen's *Pride and Prejudice* (*see also* LYME PARK).

Sudbury Hall is now owned by the National Trust, and contains the Trust's Museum of Childhood.

Suffolk '(territory of the) southern people' (referring to the southern East Anglians, as contrasted with the northern East Anglians of NORFOLK), OE *suth* 'south' + *folc* 'people'.
A county (pronounced 'sufək') in East Anglia, forming the central part of the great bulge of land extending from the THAMES[1] estuary to the WASH. It is bounded to the north by Norfolk, to the east by the North Sea, to the south by Essex and to the west by Cambridgeshire. Its administrative centre is IPSWICH, and other towns of note are ALDEBURGH, BURY ST EDMUNDS, FELIXSTOWE, LOWESTOFT, SAXMUNDHAM, SOUTHWOLD, STOWMARKET and SUDBURY[1]. Its chief rivers are the DEBEN, the LITTLE OUSE, the ORWELL[1], the STOUR[2] (part of which forms the boundary with Essex) and the WAVENEY[1] (part of which forms the boundary with Norfolk). It consists of undulating lowlands (its highest point is a paltry 128 m (420 ft) at Rede, southeast of MILDENHALL[1]), with a small area of the FENS in the north, and heathland in the northwest (part of the BRECKLAND). Its coast is constantly subject to encroachment by the North Sea (for example, at DUNWICH).

Roman-era Suffolk was part of the territory of the ancient British Iceni tribe. BURGH CASTLE still stands as a reminder of Roman efforts to defend the SAXON SHORE. After the departure of the Romans, Suffolk lay within the Anglo-Saxon kingdom of East Anglia (the ship burial site of SUTTON HOO is the grave of a king of the East Angles). The area fell to the Danes in the late 9th century but was recovered by the Saxon king Edward the Elder in the early 10th.

Suffolk is mainly agricultural. In the Middle Ages it grew rich (like its neighbour Norfolk) on wool exports (to Flanders), and the fine 'wool churches', many of them almost cathedrals in miniature (*see* EYE[3], LAVENHAM, LONG MELFORD), which its merchants built on the proceeds bear witness to this prosperity. But as this declined, Suffolk, with no mineral resources or heavy industry to replace it, became something of a backwater. It is now popular territory with North London second-home owners.

The county has in the past gone by the nickname 'silly Suffolk', no doubt on account of its abundance of churches and religious houses (*silly* used to mean 'holy, blessed').

In cricketing terms Suffolk is a 'minor county' (the club was founded in 1932) and plays in the minor counties championship.

In the USA there is a town called Suffolk in Virginia, and Suffolk counties in Massachusetts and New York.

Six Folksongs from Suffolk. A collection (1932) of folksongs set to piano accompaniment by the composer E.J. Moeran, who had earlier published a similar collection of settings of Norfolk folksongs (*see under* NORFOLK).

Suffolk. Any of a breed of black-faced hornless sheep developed in East Anglia by mating Norfolk horned ewes with Southdown rams, and kept for meat. New Zealand has produced, since the 1930s, a **South Suffolk**.

Suffolk grass. A type of annual meadow grass (*Poa annua*).

Suffolk latch. A door-latch operated by a pivoted bar which lifts the latch when pressed down with the thumb.

Suffolk punch. A breed of short-legged, sturdy, thickset, chestnut-coloured draught horse. The term *punch* was formerly applied to any short barrel-bodied man, and may be short for *Punchinello*. The bloodline of all today's Suffolk punches can be traced back to one virile stallion, Crisp's Horse of Uffham, foaled in 1786.

Sugar Island. An area in NEWRY. Its name derives from the fact that in the 18th century the town imported sugar from the West Indies, via the Newry Canal linking it to Carlingford Lough.

Sugar Loaf From its shape.

A hill (596 m / 1955 ft) on the south side of the BLACK MOUNTAINS, just inside Monmouthshire (formerly in Gwent), 5 km (3 miles) northwest of Abergavenny. It is in the care of the National Trust. In 1807 the shoemaker-poet Robert Bloomfield ascended the hill, and composed an 'Invocation to the Spirit of Burns, at the summit of the Sugar-Loaf'.

The name also occurs in Ireland (*see* GREAT SUGAR LOAF), has been applied to the Scottish peak SUILVEN and is found around the world in relation to a number of similarly sugar-loaf shaped protuberances, most notably that in Rio de Janeiro, Brazil.

Suicide Valley. *See* LANGDALE.

Suilven Probably 'pillar mountain', OScand *sulr* 'pillar' + Gaelic *bheinn* 'mountain' (pronounced 'ven'; possibly a translation of the OScand *fjall* 'mountain').

A relatively small (at 731 m / 2398 ft) but spectacular mountain in ASSYNT, Highland (formerly in Sutherland), some 7 km (4 miles) southwest of Lochinver. It is pronounced 'silvən'. When viewed from the northwest it appears as a mighty sandstone pillar rearing up out of the hummocky, lochan-studded bogland, while from the southeast it appears as a steep-sided cone. From the sides (for example from the neighbouring peaks of CANISP or CUL MÒR) it can be seen to consist of a long, three-peaked ridge, somewhat like an ancient dinosaur. The end-on view prompted Thomas Pennant, the 18th-century traveller, to call it 'the Sugar Loaf', although the highest peak, at the northwest end, is more fittingly known in Gaelic as Casteal Liath, 'the grey castle'.

It is not surprising that the mountain has inspired poets:

> And Suilven, a great ruby shone ...
> The mountain in my mind burns on,
> As though I were the foul toad, said
> To bear a precious jewel in his head.

> Andrew Young: 'Suilven', from *Speak to the Earth* (1939)

For Norman MacCaig, Suilven and Cul Mòr were his 'mountains of mountains'. Suilven appears in a number of his poems, for example in 'Climbing Suilven' (1955), 'High up on Suilven' (1960):

> There are more reasons for hills
> Than being steep and reaching only high

and 'No Accident' (1965):

> Suilven's a place
> That gives more than a basket of trout. It opens
> The space it lives in and a heaven's revealed, in glimpses.

In 'Above Inverkirkaig' (1966) the poet imagines Suilven dragging itself across the plain to couple with Cul Mòr 'through human generations', and then

> indifferently
> observing on the bogs of Assynt
> a litter of tiny Suilvens ...

Suir Irish *Siúr* 'sister'.

A river of south-central Ireland; length 183 km (113 miles), one of the THREE SISTERS (the others being the BARROW and the NORE). It rises on DEVILS BIT MOUNTAIN some 15 km (9 miles) north of Thurles in County Tipperary, and in legend is said to have started to flow on the night that Conn of a Hundred Battles was born. The Suir flows south past CAHIR, then briefly north to CLONMEL (the upward limit of navigation), then east through CARRICK-ON-SUIR (the tidal limit) and WATERFORD town, to join the River Barrow just as it enters Waterford Harbour. The river forms the entire border between counties Waterford and Kilkenny, and most of that between Waterford and Tipperary.

> ... the gentle Shure that making way
> By sweet Clonmell, adornes rich Waterford ...

> Edmund Spenser: *The Faerie Queene* (1590–6), IV, xi

> How sweet 'tis to roam by the sunny Suir stream
> And hear the doves coo neath the morning's sunbeam
> Where the thrush and the robin their sweet notes
>   combine
> On the banks of the Suir that flows down by Mooncoin.
> *Chorus:*
> Flow on, lovely river, flow gently along,
> By your waters so sweet sounds the lark's merry song,
> On your green banks I'll wander where first I did join
> With you, lovely Molly, the Rose of Mooncoin.

> Watt Murphy (*fl.*1826; attributed): 'The Rose of Mooncoin' ('Molly', actually Elizabeth, was apparently the daughter of the Rector of Mooncoin (a village in County Kilkenny near the Suir); Murphy, a schoolteacher, is said to have fallen in love with her, but her father disapproved and sent her to England.)

Sula Sgeir 'gannet skerry', OScand *sula* 'gannet', with *sker* 'skerry'.

A remote rock in the North Atlantic, 60 km (37 miles) north of Lewis in the Outer Hebrides, and 18 km (11 miles) to the west-southwest of NORTH RONA. It has never been permanently inhabited, although men from northern Lewis used to make an annual trip to harvest young gannets (Gaelic *guga* 'fat silly fellow'), and their stone huts still stand. It is a National Nature Reserve.

Sule Skerry The second element is OScand *sker* 'skerry, rock outcrop'; the first might be OScand *sulr* 'pillar'.

A tiny islet some 60 km (37 miles) west of Orkney Mainland (*see under* ORKNEY). It has a lighthouse, the most remote in Scotland.

'Great Silkie of Sule Skerry, The'. A traditional ballad from Orkney, about a seal (*silkie*) who takes human form:

> I am a man upon the land,
> I am a Silkie in the sea,
> And when I'm far from every strand
> My home it is in Sule Skerry.

He takes a human lover, who bears him a child, but tragic consequences are predicted:

> It shall come to pass on a summer's day
> When the sun shines hot on every stone
> That I shall take my little young son
> And teach him for to swim the foam.
>
> And thou shalt marry a proud gunner
> And a proud gunner I'm sure he'll be
> And the very first shot that ever he'll shoot
> He'll kill both my young son and me.
>
> Alas, Alas, the maiden cried
> This weary fate's been laid for me
> And then she said and then she said
> I'll bury me in Sule Skerry.

Sulgrave 'grove near a gully or narrow valley' (probably referring to the valley of the River Tove), OE *sulh* 'plough, furrow, gully' + *graf* 'grove'.

A village in Northamptonshire, about 13 km (8 miles) northeast of Banbury. The 15th-century **Sulgrave Manor** was the ancestral home of George Washington's forebears. John Washington emigrated to Virginia in 1656, and his great-grandson George became the first president of the USA. The house is now open to the public, and contains portraits of Washington and some of his possessions (including a fragment of his wife's wedding dress).

Sullom Voe 'inlet or voe of the gannets', OScand *sulan* 'gannets' (gannets were once called solan geese) + *vagr* 'bay'.

A 12-km (7-mile) sea inlet almost cutting the northern part of Mainland, Shetland, from the rest of the island. The southern tip of the voe is some 30 km (18 miles) northwest of Lerwick. During the Second World War Sullom Voe was an important base for flying boats, and also an important deep-water anchorage for the Royal Navy. Today huge oil tankers call at the **Sullom Voe Oil Terminal**, which receives pipelines from the Ninian and Brent fields in the North Sea. The little village of **Sullom** on the western shore takes its name from the voe.

Sumburgh Head Possibly 'Sveinn's fortification', but more probably 'fortification of the pigs', OScand personal name *Sveinn*, or *svin* 'pig' + *borg* 'fortification' (*see also* BURY) + *hofthi* 'headland'; quite a few headlands are named after animals in Shetland.

The southernmost tip of Mainland, Shetland, some 35 km (21 miles) south of Lerwick and 73 km (44 miles) northeast of Orkney. A little to the north is the village of **Sumburgh** and the very busy **Sumburgh Airport**, which services many of the North Sea oil platforms. Offshore to the south is **Sumburgh Roost**, a fierce tidal current (from OScand *rost* 'fierce tidal current'). Sumburgh is also the name of a coastal station providing information for the shipping forecast.

Summerisle. The fictional Scottish island on which the cult film *The Wicker Man* (1972) was set. It was actually filmed in the small Kirkcudbrightshire village of DUNDRENNAN.

Summer Isles, the From their past and present use for summer grazing.

A group of small islands beyond the mouth of Loch Broom and COIGACH, in Highland (formerly in Ross and Cromarty), some 20 km (12 miles) northwest of Ullapool. There were a number of fishing stations established here during the 18th-century herring boom, but the islands are now uninhabited. The largest island is Tanera Mòr (Gaelic, 'large island of the pasture'), on which the naturalist Dr Frank Fraser Darling lived from 1938 to 1944, describing his experiences in his book *Island Farm*. The other islands include Tanera Beg, Isle Ristol, Priest Island, Bottle Island and Horse Island.

Isle Martin, 5 km (3 miles) northwest of Ullapool, is not regarded as one of the Summer Isles.

Summertown Apparently an alteration of *Somers Town*, a name put on his signboard by the first man to settle in the area, in the late 18th or early 19th century, a horse-dealer by the name of James Lambourn. When asked why he chose the name, he reportedly replied that it was because the place seemed so pleasant to him.

A northern suburb of OXFORD, dating from the 1820s. The BBC's Oxford studio is based here, and the place exudes gentility, albeit on a smaller scale than in some other parts of North Oxford.

Sunart 'Sven's fjord', OScand personal name *Sven* + *art*, corruption of *fjorthr*.

An area of the western HIGHLANDS bounded by Ardgour to the east, Moidart to the north, Ardnamurchan to the west and the long sea loch of **Loch Sunart** to the south. It is in Highland (formerly in Argyll).

Sunbury-on-Thames 'Sunna's stronghold', OE male personal name *Sunna* + *burh* (*see* BURY).

A market town in Surrey, on the River THAMES[1], about 22 km (14 miles) southeast of London. It is mainly residential. It is bisected by the M3, and dotted with several large reservoirs (landmarks on the approach to HEATHROW) which are extensively used for boating and windsurfing. Kempton Park racecourse is in its midst.

The rugby union club London Irish RFC (*see under* LONDON) used to be based here.

Sundaywell Etymology uncertain, but the name may refer to a well or stream of irregular output.

A tiny settlement in Dumfries and Galloway, 18 km (11 miles) northwest of Dumfries.

Sunderland OE *sundor-land* 'detached estate'.

A city, port and unitary authority at the mouth of the River WEAR, Tyne and Wear (formerly in County Durham), 17 km (10 miles) southeast of Newcastle upon Tyne. Inhabitants of Sunderland are known by the Geordies to the north as **Mackems** – they say 'mack 'em' for 'make them', and 'tack 'em' for 'take them'.

A monastery was founded on the north side of the mouth of the River Wear in 674, at a place later known as **Monkwearmouth**. It was here that the Venerable Bede, born locally, studied (he later lived at JARROW). On the opposite bank the settlement of **Bishopwearmouth** gained its name after being granted to the bishops of Durham in 930. The town of Sunderland – so called because 'sundered' by the River Wear – grew around these two places, and received its first charter in 1154. Its importance as a port, coal-mining town and shipbuilding centre began in the Middle Ages, and in the 19th century Sunderland was the largest shipbuilding town in the world. The 20th century witnessed a decline, and by the end of the century both shipbuilding and coal mining had ceased.

> Sunderland was not a lively nightmare of poverty. It was dark brown and depressed and enfeebled ... It had stopped believing there would be any end to this emptiness.
>
> Paul Theroux: *The Kingdom by the Sea* (1983)

However, new industries have arrived and Sunderland became a city in 1992; in the same year Sunderland Polytechnic became the **University of Sunderland**. The building of **Sunderland FC**'s STADIUM OF LIGHT in 1997 was another symbol of revival. Sunderland FC was originally founded by a Scottish schoolmaster in 1879 as Sunderland and District Teachers' Association Football Club. When the club moved to its new home, fans voted for a new nickname to replace the old Rokerites or Rokermen (after their previous ground at Roker Park), and came up with the Black Cats (referring to the name of a gun battery at the mouth of the River Wear in the 18th century, although there is also the story of a black cat appearing in the team's changing rooms, marking a turn-up in the club's fortunes).

In 1722 Sunderland was the setting for the last witch-burning in Britain.

Sunderland was the birthplace of Joseph Swann (1828–1914), inventor of the electric light bulb, and of Kate Adie (b.1945), one of BBC TV's top war reporters. In the 19th century, Sir Henry Irving began his professional acting career here as a 'walking gentleman'.

Short Sunderland. A large flying boat that entered service with the RAF in 1938. During the Second World War it was used extensively for coastal patrols, convoy escort duty and anti-submarine work.

Sun Hill. The fictional name for BLACKWALL in the popular television police series *The Bill*.

Sunk Island Sands From *Sunk Island*, an offshore sandbank in the 17th century, which is now part of the mainland.

A large sandbar near the mouth of the HUMBER, sheltered from the open sea by SPURN HEAD. The sands are an important area for birds.

Sunningdale Coined for a new parish formed in 1841, and apparently based on the name of the existing settlement (and part of the new parish) *Sunninghill* 'Sunna's people's hill', OE male personal name *Sunna* + -*inga*- (see -ING) + *hyll* 'hill'.

A residential district of Berkshire, within the unitary authority of Windsor and Maidenhead, about 3 km (2 miles) southeast of Ascot. It has long been associated with stockbrokers and similar CITY types. For their recreation they have the Sunningdale Golf Club (with its Old Course, opened 1901, and its new course, opened 1923), which has hosted the Dunlop Masters (1956), the Walker Cup (1987) and the European Open (1992), and for women players only the Weetabix British Open (1997 and 2001); with the WENTWORTH Championship golf courses just down the road, this is definitely Pringle sweater territory.

Nearby to the northeast is Fort Belvedere, former home of the Prince of Wales, later Edward VIII. It was here that he signed the instrument of abdication on 10 December 1936.

Sunningdale Agreement. An agreement reached by the British and Irish governments at the Civil Service College, Sunningdale in 1973 for the setting-up of a power-sharing executive in Northern Ireland. The main signatories were the British prime minister Edward Heath and the Irish *taoiseach* Liam Cosgrave. The power-sharing experiment was ended by a Protestant general strike in 1974.

Sunnyside A modern name, reflecting a south-facing aspect. A southern suburb of EAST GRINSTEAD in West Sussex.

Surbiton 'southern grange or outlying farm' (referring to its location relative to NORBITON, likewise a grange of the royal manor of KINGSTON), OE *suth* 'south' + *bere-tun* 'grange, outlying farm'.

A residential district of southwest Outer London (before 1965 in Surrey), between Kingston to the north and Chessington to the south, in the borough of KINGSTON UPON THAMES. Its development began in 1838 with the arrival of the railway (Kingston having declined to have the noisy interloper on its territory). Surbiton (or '**Kingston New Town**', or '**Kingston-on-Railway**', as it was at first called) was thus on the main line to London, and quickly began to grow as a dormitory suburb. It attracted the professional classes, filled up with prosperous villas, and earned itself the sobriquet '**Queen of the London Suburbs**'. Further rapid development after the opening of the Kingston bypass in 1927 was not on so grand a scale, but Surbiton has had no difficulty in maintaining its reputation for selectness and salubriousness – a reputation that made it the ideal setting for the BBC television sitcom *The Good Life* (1975–78), in which archetypal Surbitonians Margo and Jerry Leadbetter are outraged and bemused by the self-sufficiency project of their next-door neighbours, Tom and Barbara Good (in Surbiton, one does not keep a goat in the back garden).

The publisher William Heinemann (1863–1920), the round-the-world yachtswoman Clare Francis (b.1946) and the camp entertainer Julian Clary (b.1959) were born in Surbiton. F.R. Spofforth (1853–1926), the Australian 'Demon Bowler', died there.

Surrey 'southerly district' (referring to its location relative to Middlesex), OE *suther* 'southerly' + *ge* 'district'.
A county of southeast England, one of the HOME COUNTIES, bounded to the north by Berkshire and Greater London, to the east by Kent, to the south by Sussex and to the west by Hampshire. It originally extended northwards to the south bank of the River THAMES[1] (including SOUTHWARK), but over the centuries it has steadily lost territory to London (the last major readjustment being in 1965, after which London's southern boundary was 24 km (15 miles) south of the Thames). In 1974 it had to give up GATWICK[1] to West Sussex. Its administrative headquarters remain in KINGSTON UPON THAMES, despite this now being in Greater London (the umbilical is hard to cut – Surrey County Cricket Club (*see below*) plays its home matches at the OVAL, in the heart of SOUTH LONDON). The county's main centres are DORKING, FARNHAM, GUILDFORD (the county town), LEATHERHEAD, REIGATE, WALTON-ON-THAMES and WOKING. Its chief rivers are the MOLE[1] and the WEY[1], which drain into the Thames. It is mainly low-lying, but in the north the NORTH DOWNS cut across it from west to east, and its southern boundary with Sussex lies along the line of the WEALD.

Its shortage of spectacular scenery and the comfortable placidity of its townships have not earned Surrey many admirers. It is viewed as a land of limited horizons, small ambitions, conventional assumptions, conservative outlooks, self-satisfied uniformity – a bit like Switzerland without the Alps (although it does have BOX HILL[1]).

> Surrey is full of rich stockbrokers, company-promoters, bookies, judges, newspaper proprietors. Sort of people who fence the paths across their parks ... They do something to the old places – I don't known what they do – but instantly the countryside becomes a villadom ... Those Surrey people are not properly English at all. They are strenuous. You have to get on or get out. And they

play golf in a large, expensive, thorough way because it's the thing to do.
>
> H.G. Wells: *Mr Britling Sees It Through* (1916)

> If Kent is the garden of England, then Surrey is the patio.
>
> Jeremy Clarkson: *Sunday Times* (3 March 2003)

The **University of Surrey** was founded in 1966, based in Guildford; it used to validate the degrees of the Roehampton Institute (*see under* ROEHAMPTON), then briefly federating with it, until the latter achieved independent university status in 2004.

Surrey is, along with Yorkshire, traditionally one of the two strongest 'first-class' cricketing counties. The club was founded on 22 August 1845, and was a founder member of the county championship when that competition was officially constituted in 1890. It has won the championship 19 times (including seven seasons in a row in the 1950s), and a string of England's finest players, from Tom Hayward and Jack Hobbs in the early 20th century, through Peter May, Alec Bedser, Jim Laker, Tony Lock and Ken Barrington in the mid-20th century to Alec Stewart and Graham Thorpe today, have been Surrey cricketers. Its home ground is the OVAL, Kennington, London. Surrey took part in the earliest county cricket match on record, on 29 June 1709, playing Kent at Dartford Brent.

In the early Anglo-Saxon period Surrey may have formed part of a larger Anglo-Saxon kingdom with Middlesex and Essex, but there is no identifiable royal dynasty associated with the county. The area was controlled by MERCIA in the 8th century, then fell under the domination of WESSEX in the 9th (KINGSTON UPON THAMES was the place of coronation of Saxon kings from 899 to 979).

There have been several notable **earls of Surrey**: John de Warenne (*c*.1231–1304) won the Battle of DUNBAR, was appointed keeper of the realm of Scotland by Edward I, was defeated by William Wallace at Stirling Bridge (*see under* STIRLING[1]) and took part in the victory at FALKIRK[1]; Thomas Howard (1443–1524) led English forces to victory at FLODDEN in 1513, and was subsequently made 2nd Duke of Norfolk (*see under* NORFOLK); and his grandson Henry Howard (*c*.1517–47) was a poet of some note.

In 2002 the actress Penelope Keith (probably best known as Margo Leadbetter in the BBC sitcom *The Good Life*; *see under* SURBITON) was appointed High Sheriff of Surrey.

There is a city called Surrey in Canada (British Columbia) and a village of that name in the USA (North Dakota). Surrey is also the name of one of the counties of Jamaica.

> There was an old woman of Surrey,
> Who was morn, noon, and night in a hurry;
>   Called her husband a fool,
>   Drove her children to school,
> The worrying old woman of Surrey.
>
> *The History of Sixteen Wonderful Old Women* (1820)

Staircase in Surrey, A. A sequence of five novels (1974–9) by J.I.M. Stewart (an Oxford English don who also wrote detective stories under the name Michael Innes). The 'Surrey' of the title is a fictional Oxford college, and the staircase in question leads off one of its quadrangles. In *The Gaudy,* the first novel of the quintet, Duncan Patullo returns to his college for a gaudy (commemorative feast for former members), and is reacquainted with former friends and colleagues.

Surrey cart. A horse-drawn pleasure-cart with an open spindle seat, of a type originally built in Surrey. An adapted version was introduced into the USA in 1872 by J.B. Brewster & Co. of New York, and over the next 20 years this evolved into the familiar **surrey** (as in the 'surrey with the fringe on top' of Rodgers and Hammerstein's *Oklahoma!* (1943)), a two-seater four-wheeled carriage.

Surrey Docks. A complex of docks (in full **Surrey Commercial Docks**) in ROTHERHITHE, on the south bank of the River Thames. Their original nucleus was the Howland Great Dock, built in 1697 and later renamed Greenland Dock (it serviced the whaling ships that hunted the Greenland waters). The Grand Surrey Basin opened in 1807, and further enlargement took place in the mid-19th century. The timber trade with Scandinavia and the Baltic formed an important part of the Surrey Docks' business. They were closed in 1970 and extensive housing redevelopment later took place on their site. Surrey Docks station, on the East London line, opened in 1913 (having previously operated under the name Deptford Road); in 1989, reflecting the changed character of the area, it was renamed Surrey Quays. (*See also* DOCKLAND.)

In common with several other 'docks', *Surrey Docks* has proved admirably appropriate, both phonologically and semantically, as rhyming slang for *pox*.

Surrey fowl. A chicken specially fattened before being killed and prepared for cooking.

Surrey in the sun. An occasional nickname for the Chianti area of Tuscany in central Italy, a much-loved holiday destination of the English middle classes. The number of English visitors to the area has also led to the mildly humorous coinage of 'Chiantishire'.

Surrey loam. A type of soil dressing containing a clay base used for producing and renovating cricket wickets and other sports areas.

Surrey Puma, the. A beast, presumed to be an escaped big cat of some sort, sightings of which were reported between 1962 and 1966.

White Surrey. Richard III's favourite horse, presumably named for Thomas Howard, Earl of Surrey, who fought at BOSWORTH. It is mentioned in Shakespeare's play:

Saddle White Surrey for the field tomorrow.

Richard III (1592), V, iii

Surrey Heath. An administrative district of northwestern Surrey, formed in 1974, whose landscape is characterized by sandy heathland and scrub. It has been extensively colonized by the military (e.g. in BAGSHOT, CAMBERLEY and PIRBRIGHT).

Sussex '(territory of the) South Saxons', OE *suth* 'south' + *Seaxe* 'Saxons'.

A former county on the SOUTH COAST of England, bounded to the west by Hampshire, to the north by Surrey and to the east by Kent. According to tradition, Ælla and his army landed at Selsey Bill (*see under* SELSEY) in 477, defeated the local inhabitants, and founded the kingdom of the South Saxons. That was absorbed by WESSEX in 825, but it formed the basis of what we now know as Sussex. One of the largest of the historic English counties, it is about 130 km (80 miles) long from east to west. In the Middle Ages it was divided into six more-or-less parallel administrative units known as 'rapes'. These fell into a western section, based on CHICHESTER, and an eastern part, based on LEWES. In 1832 this conventional separation was formalized, and in 1888 EAST SUSSEX and WEST SUSSEX became distinct administrative areas with their own county councils. In 1974 they were constituted as separate counties.

Cut off from London by the NORTH DOWNS and the WEALD, with only two large harbours (Chichester and RYE), and itself divided by the SOUTH DOWNS, Sussex for most of the second millennium had a reputation as a remote, self-contained place, its population often unkindly caricatured as xenophobic illiterate brown-skinned farmers and yokels. Yet this was the Sussex whose soft yet stern beauty was romanticized by later residents such as Rudyard Kipling, who lived in BURWASH:

God gives all men all earth to love,
But, since man's heart is small,
Ordains for each one spot shall prove
Beloved over all.
Each to his choice, and I rejoice
The lot has fallen to me
In a fair ground – in a fair ground –
Yea, Sussex by the sea!

Rudyard Kipling: 'Sussex' (1902)

The Downs are sheep, the Weald is corn,
You be glad you are Sussex born!

Rudyard Kipling: 'The Run of the Downs', from
Rewards and Fairies (1910)

and Hilaire Belloc, who lived near HORSHAM:

I will gather and carefully make my friends
Of the men of the Sussex Weald,
They watch the stars from silent folds,
They stiffly plough the field.

By them and the God of the South Country
My poor soul shall be healed.

Hilaire Belloc: 'The South Country' (1910)

But if Sussex's communications were none too good in former centuries, it was far from being backward and behind the times. Indeed, medieval and early modern Sussex was one of the main industrial areas of England, the oak forests of its Weald fuelling the manufacture of massive amounts of iron.

By the end of the 18th century there were very few viable trees left, and the iron industry was on its last legs, but another part of the county was about to come to Sussex's rescue: the coast. A fashion for sea-bathing took hold in the 1770s, and Sussex, and in particular BRIGHTON, was the beneficiary. At first it was mainly the preserve of the well-to-do, but the coming of the railway in the 1840s, which put Brighton and other resorts within easy reach of London, turned the Sussex coast into the leisure capital of southern England. The price it had to pay for its popularity was an eczematous rash of bungalows and caravans.

The **University of Sussex** was founded in 1961 on a site in FALMER, to the north of Brighton. In its early years it was noted as a centre of radical thought and student dissent.

As with Suffolk, it was no doubt the abundance of churches and religious houses in the county that earned Sussex the nickname 'silly Sussex' (*silly* used to mean 'holy, blessed').

The time-honoured image of the Sussex Downs as the birthplace of cricket, with shepherds using their crooks to propel the ball over the sheep-cropped turf, is almost certainly wide of the mark – the earliest reliable evidence suggests that cricket had urban beginnings – but Sussex was certainly an early cradle of the game, and Sussex County Cricket Club was founded on 1 March 1839. It was a founder member of the county championship when that competition was officially constituted in 1890, but had to wait until 2003 to win it for the first time. Its famous players include C.B. Fry, K.S. Ranjitsinhji, Maurice Tate, Ted Dexter, John Snow and Tony Greig. Its home ground is the County Ground, HOVE.

There are counties called Sussex in the USA (Delaware, New Jersey, Virginia).

Can any county claim more curious surnames than Sussex? Pitchfork, Slybody, Devil, Lies, Hogsflesh, Sweetname, Juglery, Hollowbone, Stillborne, Fidge, Padge, Beatup, Wildgoose, and Whiskey are a few in the county archives that would certainly have interested Dickens.

Aytoun Ellis: letter to *The Times* (17 January 1953)

Sussex Carol. A traditional English carol whose tune and text ('On Christmas night all Christians sing / To hear the news the angels bring. / News of great joy, news of great

mirth, / News of our merciful King's birth') were collected by Cecil Sharp and Ralph Vaughan Williams from a Mrs Verrall of Monk's Gate, Sussex, in 1919 (the carol having been first published in a work by an Irish bishop, Luke Wadding, in *Small Garland of Pious and Godly Songs*, 1684).

Sussex marble. A type of marble that occurs in thin beds in the Wealden clay of Sussex and Kent. In former times it was widely used for pillars in churches.

Sussex pond pudding. A sweet suet pudding with butter and a lemon secreted in the middle. When the pudding is breached, buttery lemony juices form a pond around it.

Sussex spaniel. A breed of stocky long-coated spaniel with flat or slightly wavy golden hair, developed in Sussex and neighbouring counties.

Sussex weeds. A piece of early 20th-century hyperbole for 'oak trees', which grow in abundance in the Sussex Weald.

I will go north about the shaws
And the deep ghylls that breed
Huge oaks and old, the which we hold
No more than Sussex weed.

Rudyard Kipling: 'Sussex' (1902)

Sutherland 'southern land', as viewed by the Norsemen settled in Orkney and Shetland, OScand *suthr* 'south' + *land* 'territory'.

A former county in the far northwest of Scotland, bounded to the east by Caithness and the North Sea, to the south by Ross and Cromarty, to the west by the Atlantic and to the north by the Pentland Firth. The county town was DORNOCH. It became a district of Highland region in 1975 (with its seat at GOLSPIE), and was abolished in 1996 when Highland became a unitary authority. The area was long the homeland of the Mackay clan. The first **Duke of Sutherland**, George Granville Leveson-Gower (1758–1833), was responsible for the callous and extensive **Sutherland Clearances** of *c*.1810–20 (*see also under* STRATHNAVER).

Sutherland,
synonym for burnings, clearance,
the black aura of Castle Dunrobin,
stone cottages broken, like Auburn.

John Montague: 'Scotia: i.m. Hugh MacDiarmid' (AUBURN was Goldsmith's *Deserted Village*, and DUNROBIN CASTLE the home of the earls and dukes of Sutherland.)

Sutherland – its mountains streaming with pale scree, its black valleys of peat, its miles of moorland and bog, its narrow roads and surfy coast, and its caves. It was like a world apart, an unknown place in this the best-known country in the world.

Paul Theroux: *The Kingdom by the Sea* (1983)

Sutherland can
Heal me with space and silence.

Donald Davie: 'Strathnaver', from *The Battered Wife & Other Poems* (1982)

Kyle of Sutherland *kyle*, Gaelic *caol* 'strait'.

A long narrow loch just inland from the head of the Dornoch Firth, Highland (formerly in Sutherland), 20 km (12 miles) west of Dornoch.

Sutherland Highlanders, the. A regiment raised as the 93rd Regiment of Foot in 1799, and renamed the 93rd Sutherland Highlanders in 1861. They became part of the Argyll and Sutherland Highlanders (*see under* ARGYLL) in 1881.

Sutors of Cromarty, the. *See under* CROMARTY.

Sutton[1] 'south farmstead or village', OE *suth* 'south' + -TON.

A district and borough of southern Outer London (before 1965 in Surrey). The district is between CHEAM to the west and CARSHALTON to the east. Its development started in the second half of the 19th century, following the coming of the railway in 1847. By 1880 it was a substantial commuter town, and it continued to expand in the 20th century.

The London borough of Sutton (west of Croydon and east of Epsom and Ewell (*see under* EPSOM)) was formed in 1965 from (in addition to Sutton) Beddington, CARSHALTON, CHEAM and Wallington.

Sutton[2]. A central district of Plymouth. 'Sutton' was the original name of the settlement here, 'Plymouth' being reserved for its harbour. By the 16th century Plymouth had expanded and swamped its parent, but its main harbour, from where Drake sailed and the Pilgrim Fathers set out, still bears the name **Sutton Harbour.**

The US-born Lady Nancy Astor (1879–1964) became the first woman to take her seat in the House of Commons when she became MP for the Sutton division of Plymouth in 1919. Subsequent incumbents of the seat have included former Labour Foreign Secretary and Social Democratic Party leader David Owen (1966–74) and Conservative minister and notable diarist Alan Clark (1974–92).

Sutton Benger *Benger* denoting manorial ownership in the Middle Ages by a man called Berenger.

A village in Wiltshire, close to the M4, about 5 km (3 miles) northeast of CHIPPENHAM.

Sutton Coldfield *Coldfield* 'open land where charcoal is produced', OE *col* 'charcoal' + *feld* (*see* FIELD).

A town in the WEST MIDLANDS (before 1974 in Warwickshire), now effectively a northeastern outer residential suburb (the sort with a golf course) of BIRMINGHAM. It retains some fine 16th-century buildings for which it is indebted to Bishop Vesey, founder of the local grammar school.

The 970-ha (2400-acre) **Sutton Park** to the west of the town, one of the largest and finest of its type in the MIDLANDS, was the gift of Henry VIII. It is a remnant of an extensive forest that formerly covered much of the Midlands region. It includes woodland, lakes, heathland and wetland. *See also* ROUGHLEY.

Sutton Courtenay *Courtenay* denoting manorial ownership in the early Middle Ages by the Curtenai family.

A large sprawling village in Oxfordshire (before 1974 in Berkshire), on the River THAMES[1], about 13 km (8 miles) south of Oxford.

Sutton Courtenay was the birthplace of the Empress Matilda (or Maud) (1102–67), daughter of Henry I and claimant to the throne of England.

The Liberal prime minister H.H. Asquith (1852–1928) and the writer George Orwell (1903–50) are buried in the local churchyard.

Sutton Hoo Originally *Hoo*, probably 'spur of land', OE *hoe* dative form of *hoh*; later spellings add *Sutton* and change the *Hoo* to *Haugh* 'land in a river-bend'.

A hamlet in Suffolk, on the eastern side of the River DEBEN, opposite WOODBRIDGE.

Sutton Hoo Treasure. The contents of an Anglo-Saxon ship burial of the early 7th century (possibly the tomb of Rædwald, king of the East Angles), discovered beneath a mound near Sutton Hoo in 1939. It is one of the richest ever such finds and most of the treasure, consisting of a sword and sheath, gilt-bronze helmet, royal sceptre, silver bowls and other objects in precious metals, is now in the British Museum (some items are on show at Sutton Hoo itself). Further excavations were carried out on the site in the 1980s, and in 1991 a second undisturbed grave came to light. The site, on a 99-ha (245-acre) estate, was donated to the National Trust in 1998.

Sutton-in-Ashfield *Ashfield see* KIRKBY-IN-ASHFIELD.

A town in Nottinghamshire, in the former coalfield to the west of SHERWOOD FOREST, about 21 km (13 miles) northwest of Nottingham.

Sutton Mallet *Mallet* denoting manorial ownership in the Middle Ages by the Malet family.

A village in Somerset, about 8 km (5 miles) east of Bridgwater.

Sutton Mandeville *Mandeville* denoting manorial ownership in the Middle Ages by the de Mandeville family.

A village in Wiltshire, in the valley of the River NADDER, about 16 km (10 miles) west of Salisbury.

Sutton Montis *Montis* denoting manorial ownership in the Middle Ages by the Mons or Montacute family.

A village in southeastern Somerset, about 11 km (7 miles) northeast of Yeovil. Cadbury Castle (*see under* CADBURY) is just to the north.

Sutton Poyntz *Poyntz* denoting manorial ownership in the Middle Ages by the Poyntz family.

A village in Dorset, about 5 km (3 miles) northeast of Weymouth. A mounted image of George III, WEYMOUTH's benefactor, is cut into the chalk downs nearby.

Sutton Scotney *Scotney* denoting manorial ownership in the Middle Ages by the de Scotney family.

A village in Hampshire, about 11 km (7 miles) north of Winchester.

When ennobled, the industrialist and film magnate J. Arthur Rank (1888–1972) took the title Baron Rank of Sutton Scotney (with which, no doubt to his relief, nothing rude rhymes).

Sutton-under-Whitestonecliffe The affix refers to Whitestonecliff(e) (also called White Mare Crag) in the HAMBLETON HILLS, which consists of yellow limestone dating from the Upper Jurassic.

A village in North Yorkshire, some 3 km (2 miles) east of Thirsk, on the western side of the North York Moors. It reputedly has the longest village place name in England, but in comparison to Wales's LLANFAIRPWLLGWYN-GYLLGOGERYCHWYRNDROBWLLLLANDYSILIOGOGOCH it is a rather limp effort.

Sutton Valence *Valence* denoting manorial ownership in the Middle Ages by the Valence family.

A village in Kent, about 8 km (5 miles) southeast of MAIDSTONE.

Sutton Veny *Veny* 'marshy', OE *fennig*.

A village (pronounced 'venny') in Wiltshire, on the River WYLYE[1], at the southwestern edge of Salisbury Plain (*see under* SALISBURY), about 3 km (2 miles) southeast of Warminster.

Swadlincote Probably 'Sweartling's or Svartlingr's cottage(s)', OE male personal name *Sweartling* or OScand male personal name *Svartlingr* + OE *cot* (*see* -COT, COTE).

A town in Derbyshire, about 17.5 km (11 miles) southwest of Derby. There were coal mines in the area until the 1980s.

Swaffham 'homestead of the Swabians' (a North German people, some of whom presumably settled here), OE *Swæfe* 'Swabians' + HAM.

A market town in Norfolk, on the northern edge of the BRECKLAND, about 24 km (15 miles) southeast of King's Lynn. The triangular market place has some elegant Georgian houses, and at its centre is a market cross in the form of a domed rotunda.

Pedlar of Swaffham, the. Swaffham's local 'legend', generally identified with a merchant called (with suspicious appropriateness, *chapman* meaning 'merchant') John Chapman. The story goes that the pedlar went to London to seek his fortune. There he met a stranger (or shopkeeper, in another version) who told him that he would find it back in Swaffham, in the form of a pot of gold buried under a particular tree. He duly returned and unearthed the gold, which he used to finance the building of the north aisle of the town's church.

Swale[1] 'rushing water', OE *sw(e)alwe*.

A river in North Yorkshire, 96 km (60 miles) long. It rises on the Cumbrian border near NINE STANDARDS RIGG and flows east through **Swaledale** (the most northerly of the big YORKSHIRE DALES) to RICHMOND[1], then southeastward to meet the URE, with which it forms the OUSE[2].

Swaledale. A breed of horned sheep found in the north Pennines.

Swale[2]. A branch of the estuary of the River MEDWAY[1], which separates the ISLE OF SHEPPEY from mainland Kent. In the past it was a much more considerable river, but coastal changes have clipped its wings.

Swale[3] From SWALE[2].

An administrative district on the North Kent coast. It includes SITTINGBOURNE and the ISLE OF SHEPPEY.

Swallow Falls A mistranslation of the Welsh *Rhaeadr Ewynnol* 'foaming waterfall'. However, George Borrow, in *Wild Wales* (1862), records a local calling it 'Rhaiadr y Wennol', which he translates as 'Swallow Fall; called so from the rapidity with which the waters rush and skip along'.

An attractive, much-visited cataract on the River Llugwy in Conwy (formerly in Caernarvonshire, then in Gwynedd), 3 km (2 miles) west of Betws-y-Coed.

Swanage 'herdsmen's farm' or 'farm where swans are reared', OE *swan* 'herdsman' or *swan* 'swan' + *wic* (*see* WICK).

A town and seaside resort in Dorset, on the east coast of the Isle of Purbeck (*see under* PURBECK), approximately 14 km (9 miles) southeast of Wareham. It was a port in Anglo-Saxon times (King Alfred defeated a Danish fleet in **Swanage Bay** in 877, and his victory is commemorated by a curious column topped with cannon balls), and it was formerly the trading centre for Purbeck marble. It nowadays earns its living as a modest but agreeable holiday resort.

The limestone seacliffs to the west of the town are popular with rock-climbers, who refer to them collectively as '**Swanage**'. Among the names of individual cliffs are Boulder Ruckle, Subliminal Walls, Dancing Ledges, Blackers Hole, Cattle Troughs and Guillemot Ledge.

Two of Swanage's most notable architectural landmarks were borrowed from London: the facade of the Town Hall, designed by Christopher Wren in 1670 for the Mercers' Hall in London; and the Clock Tower, which until 1867 stood at the southern end of London Bridge.

Swanland 'Svanr's or Sveinn's grove', OScand male personal name *Svanr* or *Sveinn* + *lundr* 'grove'.

A village in the East Riding of Yorkshire, 10 km (6 miles) west of Hull.

Swanlinbar Unknown etymology, but the first element may be Irish *suan* 'sleep(y)'.

A village in County Cavan, on the east side of the Cuilcagh Mountains (*see under* CUILCAGH), 15 km (9 miles) south of Enniskillen. Its Irish name is **An Muileann Iarainn** ('Iarann's mill').

Swanscombe 'herdsman's enclosed land', OE *swanes* possessive form of *swan* 'herdsman' + *camp* 'enclosed land'. (The interpretation 'Sweyne's enclosed land', linking the name with the 11th-century Danish king who is said to have landed and set up winter quarters here, is chronologically impossible, as the name predates him by over 300 years.)
A town in North Kent, between Gravesend to the east and Dartford to the west.

Swanscombe skull. The fossilized remains of a hominid skull, fragments of which were found in a gravel pit near Swanscombe in 1935 and 1936. Its female possessor (nevertheless designated **Swanscombe man**) appears to be an early subspecies of *Homo sapiens* dating from about 200,000 years ago.

Swansea¹ 'island of Sveinn', OScand personal name *Sveinn* + *ey* (*see* -AY). Sveinn has not been identified, but is traditionally said to be King Sweyn Forkbeard of Denmark, who invaded England in 1013 (*see also* RHOSSILI).
A city and port in Swansea unitary authority (of which it is the administrative centre), some 55 km (33 miles) west of Cardiff. It was formerly in Glamorgan, then in West Glamorgan (of which it was also the administrative centre). It is situated at the mouth of the River TAWE – its Welsh name is **Abertawe** ('mouth of the River Tawe') – and it overlooks **Swansea Bay**, an inlet of the Bristol Channel (the whole built-up area around the bay, between MUMBLES and PORT TALBOT, is sometimes referred to as **Swansea Bay City**). Swansea, which was formerly made a city in 1970, is the second largest in Wales after Cardiff, with which there is some rivalry.

The Normans built a castle at Swansea, which developed as a market town. It grew as a coal port and metal-working centre during the 18th century (Nelson's ships were bottomed with copper from Swansea). Its importance as a port was increased with the opening of the **Swansea Canal** in 1798. The first oil refinery in Britain was built on the edge of town in 1918, and a branch of the University of Wales in 1920. Swansea suffered severe bomb damage during the 1941 Blitz, and some typically unfortunate redevelopment afterwards.

> Swansea was a vast cankered valley of sorrowful houses and grey churches and shut-down factories. I thought: No wonder the Welsh are religious!
>
> Paul Theroux: *The Kingdom by the Sea* (1983)

The poet and pardoned murderer Richard Savage (known mostly for his appearance in Dr Johnson's *Lives of the Poets*) fled to Swansea from his creditors in 1739, but

the following year was obliged to move on. Another (more permanent and prudent) poetic resident was Vernon Watkins (1906–67), who worked in a bank in Swansea for much of his life.

> Bright town, tossed by waves of time to a hill,
> Leaning Ark of the world, dense-windowed, perched
> High on the slope of morning ...
>
> Vernon Watkins: 'Ode to Swansea'

In literary circles the city is above all celebrated as the birthplace (in the district called Uplands) of Watkins's friend Dylan Thomas (1914–1953). Thomas spent much of his early life in Swansea, which he described as 'an ugly, lovely town'; he also wrote of the city having 'as many layers as an onion', any of which could make you cry. There is now a Dylan Thomas Theatre in the city. The leading Welsh painter Ceri Richards (1903–71) was born in Dunvant on the outskirts of Swansea, and the city has an art gallery named after him.

Swansea was also the birthplace of Richard 'Beau' Nash (1674–1762), the whimsical exquisite and master of ceremonies at fashionable Bath; and of the nearly-but-not-quite-so-dandyish Michael Heseltine (b.1933), the lion-maned 'lost leader' (in his own estimate, at least) of the Conservative Party. Sir William Hamilton inherited his first wife's estate at Swansea on her death in 1782; he patriotically lent his second wife, Emma Hamilton, to Admiral Nelson (whose ships, as noted above, were having their bottoms coppered in the town). Sir Arthur Brown, who made the first non-stop flight across the Atlantic with John Alcock in 1919, later became general manager of the Metropolitan Vickers Company in Swansea, where he died in 1948.

Swansea RFC, founded in 1874 and nicknamed the All Whites, is one of Wales's leading rugby union clubs. It plays its home games at St Helen's (also famous as a cricket ground). More than a hundred Swansea players have represented Wales, four of the most capped of these being Colin Charvis, Garin Jenkins, Robert Jones and Scott Gibbs. Swansea RFC now plays in the (semi-professional) Welsh premiership, and is a feeder club to the **Neath-Swansea Ospreys** (a regional team representing West Glamorgan), which plays in the (professional) Celtic League.

Swansea City FC is Swansea's professional football club, nicknamed the Swans. Founded as Swansea Town in 1912, the club plays its home matches at Vetch Field.

There are towns called Swansea in Australia (New South Wales and Tasmania) and the USA (Massachusetts), and part of Toronto in Canada is called Swansea (originally a village).

Swansea². A unitary authority formed in 1996 from part of the former county of WEST GLAMORGAN. The administrative centre is the city of Swansea, and it also includes MUMBLES and the GOWER PENINSULA. It is bordered on the south by the Bristol Channel, to the west and north by Carmarthenshire, and to the east by Neath Port Talbot.

Swanston 'Swein's farm', OScand male personal name *Swein* or *Sven* + -TON.

A hamlet beneath the northeast end of the PENTLAND HILLS, just south of Edinburgh. Its fame largely arises from the fact that writer Robert Louis Stevenson spent much time here as a boy, his father having begun renting Swanston Cottage in 1867. The cottage is described in *St Ives* (1897–8), and the hamlet also appears in the unfinished *Weir of Hermiston*.

Swanton Novers *Swanton* 'herdsmen's farmstead or village', OE *swan* 'herdsman' + -TON; *Novers* denoting manorial ownership in the Middle Ages by the de Nuiers family.

A village in Norfolk, about 11 km (7 miles) northeast of Fakenham.

Swanwick 'herdsmen's (dairy) farm', OE *swan* 'herdsman' + *wic* (*see* WICK).

A village (pronounced 'swonnik') in Hampshire, about 11 km (7 miles) southeast of Southampton. A new air-traffic control centre for England and Wales was completed here in 1995, but problems with the computer technology prevented it from becoming operational until 2002.

Sway Perhaps an OE river name meaning 'noisy stream' (OE *sweg* 'noise'), or from OE *swæth* 'swathe, track'.

A village in Hampshire, on the Little Avon, on the southwestern edge of the NEW FOREST, about 5 km (3 miles) northwest of Lymington. The action of Captain Marryat's novel *The Children of the New Forest* (1847) is set nearby.

Swaythling Probably a former name of the stream here (now called Monk's Brook), perhaps from OE *swætheling* 'misty stream'.

A northern suburb of SOUTHAMPTON. Southampton (Eastleigh) Airport is nearby.

Sweetheart Abbey. A ruined Cistercian abbey near the SOLWAY FIRTH, 10 km (6 miles) south of Dumfries. It was formerly in Kirkcudbrightshire, and is now in Dumfries and Galloway. Also known as **New Abbey**, Sweetheart Abbey was founded in 1273 and takes its name from a story relating to its founder, Dervoguilla, daughter of the last Celtic lord of Galloway and mother of John (de) Balliol, who was to be briefly king of Scotland. Her husband, also John, died in 1268, and thereafter she always kept his heart in a casket as her 'sweet, silent companion'. When she died in 1289 she was buried before the altar in the abbey church, with the casket placed on her bosom.

Swefling Probably '(settlement of) Swiftel's people', OE male personal name *Swiftel* + -*ingas* (*see* -ING).

A village in Suffolk, on the River ALDE, about 3 km (2 miles) northwest of Saxmundham.

Swelkie, the OScand *svelgr* 'whirlpool'.

A dangerous eddy that forms with the ebb tide to the north of the island of STROMA in the treacherous PENTLAND FIRTH. 'Lugless' Willie Lithgow describes the means of dealing with it thus:

> These distracted tides whirleth ever about, cutting in the middle circle a sloping hole which, if either ship or boat happen to encroach, they must either throw something into it, as a barrel, a piece of timber and such like, or that fatal euripus shall then suddenly become their swallowing sepulchre.
>
> William Lithgow: *Totall Discourse of the Rare Adventures and Painefull Peregrinations of Long Nineteen Years* (1632)

There is an old Norse legend as to how the Swelkie was formed (and how the sea became salt). King Frode of Denmark owned two magic quernstones that could make anything that you should wish. However, so vast were the quernstones that it took two giantesses to grind them. The greedy Frode gave these two giantesses no rest in producing more and more wealth for him. Resenting this, one night while Frode was asleep, the giantesses produced from the quernstones a Viking army led by one Mysinger. Mysinger killed the king, and then seized the quernstones and the giantesses, taking them aboard his ship, where he commanded them to grind out salt. Eventually so much salt was produced that the ship sank, just north of Stroma, and ever since, as the sea races past the giant quernstones it washes out more salt from the wreck and forms the Swelkie.

There is a traditional reel tune called '**The Stroma Swelkie**'.

Swell 'rising ground, hill', OE *swelle*.

A village in Somerset, about 14 km (9 miles) east of Taunton.

Swells, the. A collective name for the two COTSWOLD villages of LOWER SWELL and UPPER SWELL.

Swilly. *See* LOUGH SWILLY.

Swimbridge '(place at) Sæwine's bridge' (denoting an early tenant of the bridge), OE male personal name *Sæwine* + *brycg* 'bridge'.

A village in Devon, about 8 km (5 miles) southeast of Barnstaple. From 1832 to 1880 the local vicar was the Rev. Jack Russell, a founder member of the Kennel Club. He bred a new variety of small terrier for flushing foxes from their earths, which now bears his name.

Swim-Two-Birds. The English translation of the Irish *Snáimh-dá-en*, one of the resting-places of Mad Sweeney, hero of the early Irish legend *Buile Shuibne* ('The Frenzy of Suibne'). The name gave Flann O'Brien (Brian O'Nolan) the title of his idiosyncratic modernist novel *At Swim-Two-Birds* (1939), which parodies both popular fiction and the Celtic Twilight version of ancient Irish legends. Swim-Two-Birds itself is mentioned in *The Book of Armagh* (*see under* ARMAGH):

> *Venit ergo Patricius sanctus per alveum flumnis Sinnae per*
> *Vadum Duorum Avium (Snám Dá Én) in Campum Ai.*
> (So St Patrick came along the basin of the River Shannon
> through the Ford of Two Birds to the plain of Ai.)

Swim-Two-Birds has been identified as a spot on the right bank of the SHANNON opposite CLONMACNOISE; O'Nolan spent part of his childhood in the area. Jamie O'Neill adapted the title for his novel *At Swim Two Boys* (2001), a story of comradely love set at the time of the Easter Rising (1916).

Swinbrook 'brook where pigs drink', OE *swin* 'pig' + *broc* 'brook'.

A picture-postcard village in Oxfordshire, on the River WINDRUSH, about 3 km (2 miles) east of Burford, with numerous 17th- and 18th-century houses and cottages.

The sisters Nancy (1904–73) and Unity Mitford (1914–48) are both buried here (they had moved to the village in 1926).

Swindon 'hill where pigs are kept', OE *swin* 'pig' + *dun* (*see* DOWN, -DON).

A town and unitary authority in northern Wiltshire, just to the north of the M4, about 60 km (37 miles) west of Reading and 70 km (43 miles) east of Bristol. It was a modest country town until the 1830s, when the Great Western Railway arrived. A station was opened here, on the main line from London to Bristol, in 1835, and four years later it was chosen as the site of the company's main locomotive depot. Henceforth Swindon was first and foremost a railway town, in due course the home of British Railways' engineering works. Considerable expansion ensued, followed by a second phase after the Second World War, following its designation as a suitable site for development under the Town Development Act (1952). It was created a unitary authority in 1997, its territory extending widely to the north, east and south of the town (co-extensive with the former council district of THAMESDOWN).

On the A4259 Swindon boasts a pentagonal roundabout dubbed the 'Magic Roundabout' (after the children's television animated puppet programme (1965–77)). It inspired a song, 'English Roundabout', by Swindon pop group XTC.

The actress and blonde bombshell Diana Dors (1931–84; real surname Fluck) was born in Swindon, and the naturalist and author Richard Jefferies (1848–87) was born nearby.

Swinford Irish *Béal Átha na Muice* 'ford-mouth of the pigs' (*see* FORD).

A small market town in County Mayo, 25 km (16 miles) northeast of Castlebar.

Swingfield Minnis *Swingfield* 'open land where pigs are kept', OE *swin* 'pig' + *feld* (*see* FIELD); *Minnis* 'common land', OE *mœnnes*.

A village in Kent, about 6 km (4 miles) north of Folkestone.

Swinton¹ 'pig farm', OE *swin* 'pig' + -TON.

A town in Greater Manchester, 7 km (4.5 miles) northwest of Manchester city centre.

Swinton². A town in South Yorkshire, 16 km (10 miles) northeast of Sheffield. It was the home of Rockingham ware, manufactured at a pottery here from 1745 to 1842.

Swirral Edge. *See under* HELVELLYN.

Swiss Cottage From the name of a tavern in the locality resembling a Swiss chalet.

A district of NORTH LONDON (NW3), to the northwest of Regent's Park, in the borough of CAMDEN. Its eponymous epicentre, on the Finchley Road, is a public house built in the style of a Swiss chalet. The original version, erected on the site of a former tollgate keeper's cottage in 1803–4, was called the 'Swiss Tavern'. It was later renamed the 'Swiss Cottage'. By the middle of the 19th century the surrounding area was becoming fairly built up. In 1868 the Metropolitan Railway arrived and called its new station 'Swiss Cottage', and before long the name had attached itself to the district in general. That station closed in 1940, having been replaced in 1939 by an Underground station of the same name, originally on the Bakerloo line, but now the Jubilee line.

The current Swiss Cottage tavern was much rejigged after the Second World War. It claims to be the largest pub in London.

Swiss Re Tower From the name of the *Swiss Reinsurance Company*, which commissioned it.

A glass-clad tower office block shaped like a portly bullet, erected in ST MARY AXE in the City of London in 2001–3 to the design of Norman Foster. Built on the site of the former Baltic Exchange, the building is 180 m (590 ft) high. Its official name is the **30 St Mary Axe Tower**, but it much more commonly goes by its nickname '**the Gherkin**' – a tribute to the extent to which Londoners have taken its revolutionary appearance to their hearts (fortunately the tower does not curl to one side like a real gherkin). The GHERKIN won the 2004 RIBA Stirling award for building of the year. It is also nicknamed The Towering Innuendo.

Swnt Ennlli. The Welsh name for Bardsey Sound (*see under* BARDSEY ISLAND).

Swone-one A verbalization of *SW11*, the locality's postal district.

Society slang (pronounced 'swun-wun') in the 1970s and 1980s for BATTERSEA in South London, an area to which Sloanes and the like (*see under* SLOANE SQUARE) who could not afford BELGRAVIA had recourse. It made it sound a bit like SW1 (Belgravia's postal district).

Swords Irish *Sord* 'well', or 'sward'.

An industrial town in County Dublin, 12 km (7.5 miles) north of Dublin itself. By tradition St Columcille (Columba) founded a monastery here in the 6th century, and blessed the well that gives the town its name. He left the monastery in charge of St Finan the Leper, who, as a penance, had deliberately contracted leprosy. However, there are no records of a monastery here before the 9th century; that monastery was burned a number of times in the 11th and 12th centuries, and only a round tower remains. The pentagonal castle, originally built as the residence of the Archbishop of Dublin in the early 13th century, underwent many subsequent alterations.

Sybil Point Etymology unknown, but the female personal name Sybil is possible.

A headland on the northwest tip of the DINGLE Peninsula, County Kerry, 5 km (3 miles) west of SMERWICK Harbour. **Sybil Head** is just to the northeast.

Sydenham Originally *Chippenham* 'Cippa's homestead or enclosure', OE *Cippan* possessive form of male personal name *Cippa* + HAM. The *Ch-* changed to *S-* in the Middle Ages, probably due to Norman influence, but the *-p-* remained until the 17th century (its replacement by *d* perhaps the result of a copyist's error).

A district of southeast London (SE26), in the borough of LEWISHAM, between Dulwich to the northwest and Penge to the south. In common with much of the rest of SOUTH LONDON it became heavily built up in the middle of the 19th century: salubrious villas for the better-off on the heights of **Upper Sydenham**, more modest dwellings for the workers in **Lower Sydenham**. It received a considerable boost in 1854 when the CRYSTAL PALACE was re-erected here, and the area is dominated to this day by Crystal Palace Park. The newly formed London County cricket team played its home matches here from 1899, and from then until 1909 its star player, Dr W.G. Grace, lived and practised medicine in Sydenham.

Sydenham Damerel *Sydenham* 'broad or extensive enclosure', OE *sidan* dative form of *sid* 'broad, extensive' + *hamm* 'enclosure' (*see* HAM); *Damerel* denoting manorial ownership in the Middle Ages by the de Albemarle family.

A village in Devon, about 8 km (5 miles) west of Tavistock.

Sydling St Nicholas *Sydling* '(place on the) broad ridge', OE *sid* 'broad' + *hlinc* 'ridge'; *St Nicholas* from the dedication of the local church.

A village in Dorset, in the valley of **Sydling Water**, about 3 km (2 miles) southwest of CERNE ABBAS.

See also UP SYDLING.

Symonds Yat 'Sigemund's gap', OE *Sigemundes* possessive form of male personal name *Sigemund* + *geat* 'gate, gap'.

A hill pass (pronounced 'simmənz') in Herefordshire (before 1998 in Hereford and Worcester, before 1974 in Herefordshire), on the Gloucestershire border, about 11 km (7 miles) southwest of Ross-on-Wye. The River WYE[1] flows through it at the bottom of a narrow and spectacular gorge. **Symonds Yat Rock**, 152 m (500 ft) high, provides an excellent view of the loop which the river describes here. It is popular with rock-climbers.

There is a small village, also called **Symonds Yat**, on the east bank of the river.

Synge's Chair. A hollow cliffside rock on the island of Inishmaan in the ARAN ISLANDS, where the playwright J.M. Synge is reputed to have sat to look at the sea.

Synod Inn Named after an inn, itself presumed to be named after a *synod* (church council); there is a Synod Mill nearby, on the Afon Soden.

A hamlet in Ceredigion (formerly in Cardiganshire, then in Dyfed), about 6 km (4 miles) south of New Quay. Its Welsh name is **Post-Mawr** ('big post office', Welsh *post* 'post office' + *mawr*).

T

Table Mountain Named for its shape.

A hill (699 m / 2293 ft) in the Wicklow Mountains (*see under* County WICKLOW), some 6 km (4 miles) north of LUGNAQUILLA.

Tadcaster 'Tada's Roman fort', OE male personal name *Tada* + *ceaster* (*see* CHESTER).

A market town on the River WHARFE, North Yorkshire, 15 km (9 miles) southwest of York. The Romans called it **Calcaria** ('limestone place'), and stone quarried here was used to build the Roman fort at York and York Minster. Tadcaster has been known for its brewing since 1341, and today is home to Samuel Smith, Bass and John Smith breweries. After the Battle of TOWTON (1461), close to the town, the rout of the Lancastrians continued into Tadcaster.

Battle of Tadcaster (10 June 1487). A skirmish at the end of the Wars of the Roses, in which Lord Clifford (a Tudor) tried to intercept the Earl of Lincoln and sundry Yorkists (with Irish assistance).

Battle of Tadcaster (6 December 1642). An inconclusive battle during the Civil Wars, fought on and around Tadcaster Bridge over the Wharfe, between Sir Thomas Fairfax and his Parliamentarians and Royalists under the Earl of Newcastle.

Taf *See* TAFF.

A river in southwest Wales. It rises on the east side of the PRESCELLY MOUNTAINS in Ceredigion (formerly Cardiganshire, then part of Dyfed) and flows generally southwards then eastwards for 50 km (31 miles) through Carmarthenshire (also formerly part of Dyfed). The Taf estuary merges with that of the TOWY and enters the sea at CARMARTHEN Bay.

See also TAFF.

Taff A pre-Celtic river name from an Indo-European root meaning 'to flow' (*see also* THAMES[1], TAMAR).

A river in South Wales, formerly largely in Glamorgan (then Mid and South Glamorgan). In Welsh it is spelt **Taf**. It rises in the BRECON BEACONS of Powys and flows southwards

for 64 km (40 miles) through the unitary authorities of Merthyr Tydfil and **Rhondda Cynon Taff** (to which it contributes its name; the RHONDDA and CYNON are tributaries) via PONTYPRIDD and the village of **Taff's Well** (formerly noted for its waters) to enter the Bristol Channel at CARDIFF (to which it contributes the second syllable).

Contrary to the belief held in some quarters, the river name is not the origin of the term 'Taffy' for a Welshman (and hence 'Taffia' for the freemasonry of South Wales politicians); the onomastically disappointing truth is that Taffy derives from Welsh *Dafydd* 'David'.

Taff Trail. An 88-km (55-mile) cycle route from Brecon to Cardiff Bay.

Taff Vale Judgement, the. The verdict in a civil suit brought by the Taff Vale Railway Company in 1901 against the Amalgamated Society of Railway Workers. The judge granted the company £23,000 damages against the union as compensation for losses incurred by the company during a strike. The precedent established by the judgement potentially threatened the ability of unions to carry out industrial action, and resentment over this was a factor in the formation of the Labour Party in 1906. In the same year the Trades Dispute Act granted trade unions immunity from such actions.

Taff-Ely From the rivers TAFF and ELY[2].

A former district (1974–96) of Mid Glamorgan. The administrative centre was at PONTYPRIDD.

Tail o' the Bank, the. An anchorage in the upper Firth of CLYDE at the west end of the sandbanks (Pillar Bank and Cockle Bank) between DUMBARTON and GREENOCK. Formerly it was used by ocean liners to disembark passengers, and was an important assembly point for merchant convoys during the Second World War.

Tailtean. The Irish name for TELTOWN.

Tain Possibly a pre-Celtic river name from an identical Indo-

European root to TYNE[1], THAMES[1] and possibly TAY, and meaning 'to flow'.

An ancient royal BURGH in Easter Ross, on the south side of the DORNOCH Firth, Highland (formerly in Ross and Cromarty), 7 km (4.5 miles) south of Dornoch. It was Malcolm III Canmore who awarded Tain its first charter in the 11th century. Tain was the birthplace of St Duthus, who died in Armagh in 1065 and whose bones were brought back to Tain in 1253. The wife and daughter of Robert the Bruce sought sanctuary at the saint's shrine in 1307, but this was violated by the Earl of Ross, who captured them and turned them over to the English. Both St Duthus's Chapel (11th–12th century, now ruined) and St Duthus's Church (*c*.1360) became places of pilgrimage in the Middle Ages, James IV visiting every year from 1493 to 1513 as a penance for the death of his father at the Battle of SAUCHIEBURN. (This is the origin of the name of the road called the King's Causeway.)

Talbot Village From the name of its founders.

A village in Dorset, now a district within the unitary authority of BOURNEMOUTH. It was founded in the 1860s by two sisters, Georgina Charlotte Talbot and Mary Anne Talbot, as a model village for poor families who had been dispossessed by land enclosures around Bournemouth earlier in the 19th century.

Taliesin After the poet of the same name.

A village in Ceredigion (formerly in Cardiganshire, then in Dyfed), 6 km (4 miles) southeast of Aberdovey. The early and possibly legendary Welsh poet Taliesin (*fl*.550), the bard at the court of the king of RHEGED, supposedly died here, and the place was subsequently named after him. It is also called **Tre-Taliesin**.

Talisker Probably 'shelf rock', OScand *hjalli* 'shelf' + *sker* 'rock'.
A distillery on SKYE, producing a well-known single malt. It is at the village of Carbost, Highland (formerly in Inverness-shire), 16 km (10 miles) southwest of Portree. The small **River Talisker** actually rises some 2.5 km (1.5 miles) to the southwest, on the other side of the watershed, and flows westwards into **Talisker Bay**; all these features may take their name from the watershed itself.

Talke An OCelt name for the ridge here, related to Welsh *talcen* 'forehead'.
A hillside village in Staffordshire, now a southwestern district of KIDSGROVE, about 13 km (8 miles) northwest of Stoke-on-Trent.

Talke's name no doubt lays it open to puns of the 'Is this bus going to Talke?' variety (*compare* SPEKE), and folk-etymological speculation about its origins has been plentiful: it has been said to have been the venue of a council of war held by Charles I during the Civil Wars, or alternatively of a conference held by Charles Edward Stuart in 1745 (it predates both such 'events' by many centuries, of course).

Tallaght Irish *Tamhlacht* 'plague burial ground'.

A southwestern suburb of DUBLIN. In the 8th century St Maelruan founded a monastery here that later produced the *Martyrology of Tallaght* (10th century). A tower remains of the 14th-century castle built for the Archbishops of Dublin at Tallaght, which became a stronghold of the PALE.

Talla Water Possibly OCelt *talg* 'a brow'.

A small upland river in Scottish BORDERS (formerly in Peeblesshire), some 8 km (5 miles) west of ST MARY'S LOCH. It rises on the slopes of Molls Cleuch Dod and enters **Talla Reservoir** (part of Edinburgh's water supply) at the small settlement called **Talla Linfoots** (possibly 'pool at the foot of Talla', Gaelic *linne* 'pool' + English *foot*). Below the reservoir the river enters the TWEED.

Tâl Moelfre 'front of the bare hill', Welsh *tâl* 'front, end', with *moelfre* 'bare hill'.

A headland on the north coast of ANGLESEY (formerly in Gwynedd). It was the site of a battle in 1157 in which Owain Gwynedd defeated the forces sent against him by England's Henry II.

> At Tâl Moelfre a thousand war-cries
> Shaft on shining shaft, spear upon spear,
> Fear on deep fear, drowning on drowning.
>
> Gwalchmai ap Meilyr: 'The Battle of Tâl Moelfre' (12th century), translated from the Welsh by Joseph P. Clancy

The battle was also celebrated in a poem by Owain's illegitimate son, Hywel ab Owain Gwynedd (*c*.1140–70). This poem ends with what is thought to be a reference to his young self:

> And a thousand lords fled before
> A beardless champion at Menai.

Tamar Probably a pre-Celtic river name from an Indo-European root meaning 'to flow' (*see also* THAMES[1]).

A river in Cornwall and Devon, which for most of its course forms the boundary between the two counties, and hence has also been regarded as a cultural boundary between Celts and Anglo-Saxons. It rises at the northern tip of Cornwall, in the Hartland Peninsula (*see under* HARTLAND POINT), about 11 km (7 miles) northeast of Bude, and flows 97 km (60 miles) southwards into Plymouth Sound (*see under* PLYMOUTH). The **Tamar Bridge** (1961) carries the A38 between Plymouth and SALTASH. Below Saltash the river broadens out into an estuary known as the HAMOAZE. In the 19th century the Tamar was a vital artery of Cornwall's mining industry, and the detritus of this (in the form of, for example, old tin and lead smelting works) can be seen along its estuary to this day.

O spring has set off her green fuses
Down by the Tamar today,
And careless, like tide-marks, the hedges
Are bursting with almond and may.

> Charles Causley (1917–2003): 'The Seasons in North
> Cornwall'

The Tamar is rich in bird life, and the Tamar Otter Sanctuary (actually on the River OTTER) has done much to safeguard that engaging and endangered water mammal. The **Tamar Valley** is designated as an area of outstanding natural beauty. It covers the lower reaches of the river, from about 5 km (3 miles) south of Launceston, and also parts of the valleys of the TAVY and the St Germans River (*see under* ST GERMANS).

Two medieval bridges still survive along the Tamar's course: Greystone Bridge, near Dunterton, and Horsebridge, west of TAVISTOCK, both dating from the 1430s.

There is also a tidal estuary called the River Tamar in Tasmania.

Tamar Lake. A two-part lake (**Upper Tamar Lake** and **Lower Tamar Lake**) on the upper reaches of the River Tamar, near ALFARDISWORTHY.

Tame[1] A pre-Celtic river name from an Indo-European root meaning 'to flow' (*see* THAMES[1]).

A river in Warwickshire, the West Midlands and Staffordshire, which rises in WILLENHALL and flows eastwards to the north of Birmingham, and then, turning abruptly northwards, through TAMWORTH into the River TRENT[1] about 10 km (6 miles) southwest of BURTON UPON TRENT. It is about 40 km (25 miles) long. For part of its course within the West Midlands it is canalized as the **Tame Valley Canal**.

Tame[2]. A river in West Yorkshire, Greater Manchester and Cheshire, which rises on the moors to the northeast of OLDHAM and flows 35 km (22 miles) southwards to join the River GOYT at Stockport.

Tamerton Foliot *Tamerton* 'farmstead or village on the River Tamar', TAMAR + -TON; *Foliot* denoting manorial ownership in the Middle Ages by the Foliot family.

A village in Devon, on the east bank of the TAMAR estuary, within the unitary authority of PLYMOUTH.

Tameside 'by the side of the River TAME[2]'.

A unitary authority in Greater Manchester, on the east side of Manchester itself. It includes DENTON, DUKINFIELD and ASHTON-UNDER-LYNE (the administrative headquarters).

Tamhlacht. The Irish name for the Dublin suburb of TALLAGHT.

Tamworth Originally *Tamworthy* 'enclosure on the River Tame', TAME[1] + OE *worthig* (*see* -WORTH, WORTHY, -WARDINE). The second element had been replaced by the synonymous *worth* by the end of the 11th century.

A town in Staffordshire, on the River Tame and the Coventry Canal (*see under* COVENTRY), about 11 km (7 miles) southeast of Lichfield. It has a long history. In the 750s King Offa of Mercia had a palace here, and a mint. In 913 the Mercians under Æthelflæd, Alfred the Great's daughter, defeated the Danes at Tamworth, and fortified the town to prevent any counter-attack. After the Norman Conquest a great castle was built here; with many later additions it survives to this day.

The building of Tamworth's late-Jacobean town hall was financed by the local MP, Thomas Guy (c.1645–1724), who later founded Guy's Hospital in London.

Tamworth was the home of the Reliant Robin, the three-wheeled car that was the butt of many cruel jokes. The Reliant Motor Company was founded by a local car enthusiast, Tom Williams, in 1935, and the Robin was produced between 1973 and 2001. Reliant three-wheelers were the car of choice of television sitcom heroes Del Boy Trotter (*Only Fools and Horses*) and the eponymous Mr Bean.

> 'What do you call a Reliant Robin at the top of a hill?'
> 'A miracle.'

There are towns called Tamworth in the USA (New Hampshire), Canada (Ontario) and Australia (New South Wales).

Tamworth Manifesto. The manifesto issued to his constituents in 1835 by Sir Robert Peel (prime minister 1834–5, 1841–6), who was MP for Tamworth from 1830 until his death in 1850 (there is a statue of him in front of the town hall). Viewed as marking the point of transition from the old Tory party and as one of the cornerstones on which the modern Conservative Party was built, it made a commitment (albeit vague) to keep the changes of the 1832 Reform Act in place and maintain its spirit.

Tamworth pig. A large long-bodied red or brown pig developed in the Tamworth area, used mainly for bacon.

Tamworth Two. Two Tamworth pig siblings whose escape from Newman's Abbatoir in MALMESBURY in Wiltshire in January 1998 excited considerable media interest. The pair, christened 'Butch' and 'Sundance' by the *Daily Mail*, swam the River AVON[2] and hid out on a wooded hillside. Butch was swiftly recaptured, but Sundance managed to keep the media circus going until the end of the week. On capture, Butch was discovered to be female. The Two were naturally not returned to the abattoir, and were settled comfortably in a rare-breeds centre in Kent.

Tandridge Perhaps 'ridge with a pasture for pigs', OE *denn* 'woodland pasture for pigs' + *hrycg* 'ridge, hill'.

A village in Surrey, about 11 km (7 miles) east of Reigate. In 1974 its name was given to an administrative district of southeast Surrey.

Tanera Mór. *See under* the SUMMER ISLES.

Tangiers The earliest reference is in 1755; in 1662 Tangier had come under English rule, being part of the dowry of Catherine of Braganza of Portugal when she married Charles II.

A village in Pembrokeshire (formerly in Dyfed), 3 km (2 miles) north of Haverfordwest.

Tangley Perhaps 'glade at the spits of land', OE *tang* 'spits of land' + -LEY.

A village in Hampshire, about 8 km (5 miles) northwest of Andover.

Tangmere Perhaps 'tongs-shaped pool', OE *tang* 'tongs' + *mere* 'pool'.

A village in West Sussex, about 5 km (3 miles) northeast of Chichester. During the Second World War its RAF station was in the front line in the Battle of Britain. It was one of England's earliest airfields, opening in 1917, and it was in use until 1970. There is now a Military Aviation Museum here.

Tan Hill Inn Apparently a modern name, of uncertain origin. Britain's highest inn, at an altitude of 528 m (1732 ft). It is situated on the north side of the YORKSHIRE DALES, some 12 km (7.5 miles) east of Kirkby Stephen, just inside North Yorkshire (although exiled to County Durham from 1974 to 1987). In the past there was a coal mine at Tan Hill, and the inn is situated where a number of drovers' tracks met. There is still an annual sheep fair at Tan Hill, and the PENNINE Way finds its way past the door of the inn.

Tankerton 'Tancred's farmstead or estate', OGerman male personal name *Tancred* + -TON.

A village on the north coast of Kent, now an eastern district of WHITSTABLE. **Tankerton Bay** lies off Whitstable.

Tannochbrae. The fictional setting for *Dr Finlay's Casebook*; the two television series (1962–71; 1993–6) were shot in CALLANDER and AUCHTERMUCHTY respectively.

Tantallon Castle Possibly from OCelt *din talgwn* 'steep-fronted fort'.

A striking red-sandstone castle, now ruined, standing on a clifftop looking out to the BASS ROCK in the Firth of Forth, 4 km (2.5 miles) east of North Berwick in East Lothian. It was built in the later 14th century, and was a stronghold of the Douglases. It was not taken for three centuries, until 1651 when General Monck's Cromwellian forces destroyed it in a 12-day bombardment. The castle features in Sir Walter Scott's *Marmion* (Canto V, xv).

The poet Gavin Douglas (*c.*1475–1522), translator of Virgil's *Aeneid* into Scots, was born here.

ding doun Tantallon. To perform the impossible, to go too far (Scots *ding doun* 'knock down'). The phrase, current up to the early 20th century, refers to the supposed impregnability of the castle. However, Defoe tells a slightly different tale:

Tantallon Castle … was famous, in the Scots history, for being the seat of rebellion, in the reign of King James V. And hence came the old, and odd fancy among the soldiers, that the drums beating the Scots March, say, 'Ding down tan-tallon.' That beat or march being invented by King James the Vth's soldiers (or, perhaps, drummers).

Daniel Defoe: *A Tour Through the Whole Island of Great Britain* (1724–6)

Tantallon cake. A kind of biscuit similar to shortbread, but with scalloped edges.

Tantobie Possibly 'the part of the River Team associated with Toby', river name *Team* + personal or surname *Toby*; the village is a modern colliery settlement and the name is first recorded in the 18th century.

A village in County Durham, 3 km (2 miles) north of Stanley.

Tap o' Noth 'top of Noth' or 'hill of observation', Gaelic *taip a nochd*; if the former is correct, then *nochd*, Noth, became a district or farm name and was attached to other hills and bogs around.

A prominent hill (563 m / 1847 ft) in northern Aberdeenshire (formerly in Grampian region), with a vitrified fort on its summit, above the village of Rhynie some 12 km (7.5 miles) south of Huntly, on the edge of the Clashindarroch Forest. Its eastern shoulder is **Hill of Noth**, and roundabout are **Glen of Noth**, **Bogs of Noth**, **Raws of Noth**, **Oldnoth**, **Newnoth**, **Millton of Noth** and **Mill of Noth**.

Tara The Irish version of the name is *Teamhair* 'conspicuous place, hill of assembly', but scholars now think the name may derive from an earth goddess called *Temair*, possibly meaning 'dark one'; in one 12th-century Irish poem it is described as 'Temair noblest of hills'. Other versions of the name include *Temuri* and *Temrach*, and alternative traditions suggest that *Temuri* derives from the *muir* ('rampart') of Tea, daughter of Lugaid, son of Ith, in myth one of the Milesian invaders of Ireland, identified with the historical Celts.

A low hill (154 m / 505 ft) in County Meath, 10 km (6 miles) southeast of NAVAN, also called the **Hill of Tara**. It is one of the most important sites of ancient Ireland, and the oldest structure here, the Neolithic Dumha na nGiall ('Mound of the Hostages'), dates to *c.*2000 BC. It was at Tara, at least in legend, that the high kings of Ireland were crowned and had their palace. They bore the title *Rí Temro* (Irish 'king of Tara', or in Latin *Rex Temro*), and the tradition continued from at least the 3rd century AD up to the 10th century – although there is a legend that Tara was abandoned in the 6th century when two saints cursed the place, one having been obliged to hand over to King Diarmid I (d.565) a murderer who had sought sanctuary. Despite this double-whammy hex, Tara's great

reputation and significance continued to resonate down
the centuries:

> Temair noblest of hills
> Under which is Erin of the forays,
> The lofty city of Cormac son of Art,
> Son of mighty Conn of the Hundred Fights.

Anon.: 'Tara', from *The Dinnsenchas* (12th century),
translated by Edward Gwynn (In semi-legendary history,
Cormac MacArt established the Connachta dynasty at Tara
in the 3rd century, and here established schools of military
science, law and literature.)

> The harp that once through Tara's halls
> The soul of music shed,
> Now hangs as mute on Tara's walls
> As if that soul were fled.

Thomas Moore: 'The Harp that Once through
Tara's Halls', from *Irish Melodies* (1807)

There are various remains at Tara in addition to the
Mound of the Hostages. These include Bronze Age tumuli
and various earthworks, such as the Rath of the Synods,
the Ráth na Ríogh ('Fortress of the Kings'), the Forradh
('Royal Seat') and Teach Cormaic ('Cormac's House'). On
this last is a pillar stone said to be the coronation stone.
However, in an alternative tradition, the coronation stone
or FÁL was taken to Scotland, where it became known as
the Stone of Destiny or the Stone of Scone (*see under*
SCONE), which is now in Edinburgh Castle.

The rebels of 1798 suffered a defeat at Tara on 26 May.
In 1843, following in the wake of St Patrick, who preached
here in the 5th century, Daniel O'Connell, the Liberator,
addressed a mass meeting at Tara, calling for the repeal of
the Act of Union. Between 1899 and 1902 Tara somewhat
bizarrely became the focus of attention of the British-Israel
Association, which was convinced (a) that the Anglo-Saxon
race was descended from the Lost Tribes of Israel, and (b)
that the Ark of the Covenant was buried under the Hill of
Tara. When they started excavations, Nationalists flew into
a rage at this despoliation of a potent symbol of Irish
national identity, and pressure from the press and from
professional archaeologists eventually put a stop to the
nonsense.

In Margaret Mitchell's epic *Gone with the Wind* (1936)
Tara is the name of the O'Haras' mansion and plantation,
while *Tara Road* is the title of a 1998 novel by Maeve
Binchy.

Tara Brooch, the. A magnificent example of an 8th-
century ring-brooch, found on the shore near DROGHEDA;
the link with Tara is entirely fanciful.

Taransay Probably 'Taran's island', personal name *Taran*
+ OScand *-ey* (see -AY). In his *Life of St Columba* (7th century)
Adamnan mentions several people with the Pictish name
Tarain.

A small island in the Outer HEBRIDES, Western Isles
(formerly in Inverness-shire), 2 km (1.2 miles) off the west
coast of South HARRIS, from which it is separated by the
Sound of Taransay. The last permanent inhabitants left in
1942, but BBC TV's *Castaway 2000* series brought a wide
variety of people from all parts of Britain to live on the
island together for a year, their ups and downs being filmed
for the delectation of the viewing public.

Tarbat Ness Gaelic *tairbeart* originally 'place of portage' but
here weakened to 'neck of land', with OScand *nes* (see NESS).
A headland in Easter Ross (*see under* ROSS AND CROMARTY),
northeast Highland, between the DORNOCH Firth and the
CROMARTY Firth. Much of the Tarbat peninsula was
evacuated in 1943–4 to enable troops to practise landings in
advance of D-Day.

Tarbert Gaelic *tairbeart*, 'isthmus over which boats can be
drawn'.

There are several settlements called **Tarbert** or **Tarbet** in
Scotland, all situated where portage of boats is possible
across a neck of land between two stretches of water. These
settlements include:

Tarbert and **West Tarbert**, at either side of the isthmus
separating KNAPDALE and KINTYRE in Argyll and Bute, some
20 km (12 miles) south of Lochgilphead. Until 1266 all the
islands of the Hebrides came under the Norwegian Crown,
and there is a story that in the 11th century Magnus
Barefoot, son of King Olaf, demonstrated that Kintyre was
an island, and thus one of his father's Hebridean
possessions, by dragging his boats between West Loch
Tarbert and East Loch Tarbert.

Tarbert on the island of GIGHA, between **West Tarbert
Bay** and **East Tarbert Bay**, Argyll and Bute.

Tarbert halfway up the east coast of the island of
JURA, between **Tarbert Bay** and **Loch Tarbert**, Argyll and
Bute.

Tarbet 2 km (1.2 miles) east of Arrochar, Argyll and
Bute, at the east end of an isthmus between LOCH LONG
(a sea loch) and LOCH LOMOND. In 1263 Magnus, King of
Man and son-in-law of King Haakon of Norway, dragged
his 60 ships across here into Loch Lomond, where his
men pillaged and slaughtered along the shores. They carried
off hundreds of cattle to feed Haakon's last great expedition, which met with a decisive defeat at LARGS shortly
afterwards.

Tarbert at the east end of Ardnamurchan, Argyll and
Bute, at the south end of the isthmus between Loch SUNART
and Loch SHIEL.

Tarbet on LOCH NEVIS, at the narrows leading south to
LOCH MORAR, in Highland.

Tarbet on the Rubha Ruadh peninsula, between the
Sound of HANDA and Loch Laxford, northwest Highland.

Tarbert (An Tarbeart) on the neck of land between

North HARRIS and South Harris, between **West Loch Tarbert** and **East Loch Tarbert**, Western Isles.

Tarbolton Possibly 'main village on a hill', OE *bothl-tun* 'farm with buildings, chief village' (*see* -TON) + Gaelic *tòrr* 'hill'.

A village 10 km (6 miles) northeast of Ayr, in South Ayrshire (formerly in Strathclyde). Robert Burns worked on his father's farm at nearby Lochlea (1777–84), and then at Mossgiel (until 1789). In 1780 he founded the Bachelors' Club, a literary and debating society, in Tarbolton, and also joined the village Freemasons. A fellow Mason, John Wilson – the local schoolmaster who offered 'medical advice gratis' – so infuriated Burns with his 'Esculapian twaddle' that the poet was inspired to write his satirical 'Death and Dr Hornbook' (1785). Wilson's house still stands, near the churchyard. The young women of the town also featured in Burns's not entirely flattering poem **'The Tarbolton Lasses'**, in which Peggy is a snob, Sophy is easily won, Mysie is dour, and Jenny and Bessy are vain.

Tarn Hows 'tarn hills', *Tarn* OScand *tjorn* 'tarn'; *Hows* OScand *haugr* 'hill' in the plural.

A small lake in the LAKE DISTRICT, Cumbria, some 3 km (2 miles) northeast of CONISTON. Surrounded by pines and firs, and with views of the fells, it is one of the most picturesque and visited spots in the Lakes. It was presented to the National Trust by Beatrix Potter in 1930. On older maps it is named **The Tarns**, and in fact was originally two separate tarns until the 19th-century owners enlarged them and landscaped the surroundings.

Tarporley Perhaps 'peasants' or cottagers' glade', late OE *thorpere* 'peasant, cottager' + -LEY.

A small town in Cheshire, about 16 km (10 miles) northwest of Crewe. It has some attractive old gabled houses. The Manor House dates from 1586.

Tarr Perhaps 'rock, peak', OE *torr*.

A village in Somerset, about 13 km (8 miles) northwest of Taunton.

Tarrant[1] An OCelt river name probably meaning 'trespasser' (referring to its tendency to flood) (*see also* TRENT[1]).

A river in Dorset, which rises close to TARRANT GUNVILLE and flows 25 km (16 miles) southwards to join the River STOUR[1] to the southeast of BLANDFORD FORUM.

Tarrant[2]. The fictional setting of the glossy TV drama *Howards' Way* (1985–90), a Thatcherite saga of the business lives and tangled loves of upwardly mobile Hampshire boat-designing folk, launched as the BBC's big-budget answer to such US soap operas as *Dynasty*. Tarrant was based on the real-life village of Bursledon, on the River HAMBLE.

Tarrant Gunville TARRANT with *Gunville*, denoting manorial ownership in the Middle Ages by the Gundeville family.

A village in Dorset, on the River TARRANT, about 8 km (5 miles) northeast of BLANDFORD FORUM.

Tarring Neville *Tarring* perhaps '(settlement of) Teorra's people', OE male personal name *Teorra* + -*ingas* (*see* -ING). Alternatively the first element could be from OE *torr* 'rocky hill'; *Neville* denoting manorial ownership in the Middle Ages by the de Neville family.

A village (rhyming with the first two syllables of *Farringdon*) in East Sussex, about 2.5 km (1.5 miles) north of Newhaven.

Tarvit. *See under* SCOTSTARVIT TOWER.

Tattenham Corner From the name of an owner of the manor, Roger de *Tottenham*, whose surname probably came from TOTTENHAM in Greater London; originally the *Corner* was ME *corner* 'nook of land'.

A left-handed corner into the finishing straight at EPSOM racecourse, about 3.5 furlongs (700 m) from the winning post. It comes in the middle of a sharp descent, providing a stiff test for horses and riders (most famously in the Derby).

Tattershall 'Tathere's nook of land', OE *Tatheres* possessive form of male personal name *Tathere* + *halh* 'nook of land' (*see* HALE, -HALL).

A village in Lincolnshire, about 13 km (8 miles) southwest of Horncastle. The moated brick-built **Tattershall Castle** was the work of Ralph Cromwell, Lord High Treasurer of England in the mid-15th century; it was restored by Lord Curzon, Viceroy of India, in 1911–14. Cromwell was also responsible for the huge stone-built Holy Trinity church.

Tattingstone Perhaps 'Tating's farmstead', OE *Tatinges* possessive form of male personal name *Tating* + -TON; alternatively, 'farmstead associated with Tata', OE male personal name *Tata* + -ING + -TON.

A village in Suffolk, about 8 km (5 miles) southwest of Ipswich.

Tattingstone Wonder. A folly in the form of a medieval church, created in 1790 by the local squire, Edward White, out of three cottages, to improve the view from his house.

Tatton Dale *Tatton* 'Tata's farm', OE male personal name *Tata* + -TON.

A village in Cheshire, about 4 km (2.5 miles) north of Knutsford. It lies in **Tatton Park**, the former estate of the Egerton family, more than 400 ha (about 1000 acres) in extent. The house, **Tatton Hall**, dates from the late 18th and 19th centuries. Its formal gardens and woodland were laid out by Humphry Repton.

The Tatton parliamentary constituency achieved a certain notoriety in 1997 when its Conservative incumbent Neil Hamilton, who was under something of a cloud on account of accusations against his probity, was successfully challenged in the general election by the former BBC journalist Martin Bell, standing in a white suit on a ticket of moral uprightness. Bell remained its MP until 2001.

Taunton 'farmstead or village on the River Tone', TONE + -TON. A market town (pronounced 'tawntən', or locally 'tahntən') in Somerset, on the River Tone, about 14 km (8.5 miles) southwest of Bridgwater. It is the county town of SOMERSET. According to tradition, in the early 8th century King Ine of the West Saxons built a castle here, which was the basis of the place's later status and importance. The Normans replaced it with another castle, and it was here at the end of the 15th century that the trial of the royal pretender Perkin Warbeck was held. It now houses the County Museum. Taunton, strongly Parliamentarian during the Civil Wars, was also one of the main venues of the 'Bloody Assizes' in 1685, after the Monmouth Rebellion.

During the Middle Ages and beyond, Taunton was a great centre of the wool trade (**Taunton cloth**, or simply **Taunton**, was renowned for its quality). By the time the trade's best days had past, the town had already established other strings to its bow as the hub of the surrounding rich agricultural country: it has a very large cattle market, and cider-making is an important local industry.

Hugh Trenchard (1873–1956), first head of the Royal Air Force, was born in Taunton.

There is a town called Taunton in Massachusetts, USA.

Taunton Deane. An administrative district of Somerset. It revives the name of an ancient Hundred of the county, centred on the valley of the River Tone (*Deane* is from OE *denu* 'valley'), which is also preserved in the **Vale of Taunton Deane**, the fertile valley in the middle of Somerset, between the BLACKDOWN HILLS in the south and the QUANTOCK HILLS in the north, in which Taunton sits. Taunton Deane Services are between Junctions 25 and 26 on the M5.

Taunton turkey. A humorous name given in the 19th century to salt herrings, in which there was a lively trade in Taunton.

Tavernspite 'inn at the root of a dispute', Welsh *tafarn* 'inn' + *sbeit* 'dispute, spite'; the reason for the dispute is not known, but there are several other names that include *sbeit*. A village in Pembrokeshire (formerly in Dyfed), 13 km (8 miles) northeast of Tenby.

Tavistock 'outlying farmstead or hamlet on the River Tavy', TAVY + OE *stoc* (*see* -STOCK, STOCK-, STOKE). A market town in Devon, on the River Tavy, at the western edge of DARTMOOR, about 19 km (12 miles) north of Plymouth. It grew up around its great 10th-century Benedictine abbey, most of which disappeared at the time of the Dissolution of the Monasteries. In the Middle Ages it prospered as a tin-mining centre and became a stannary town (*see under* the STANNARIES). Then, from the 16th to

the 18th centuries, it earned its living mainly from cloth (at that time, the type of cloth made here was known as **Tavistock**). In the mid-19th century it returned to mining, but this time of copper: Tavistock became one of the world's most important copper-mining centres, and the nearby Great Consols mine was one of the world's largest. The prosperity of this period was responsible for the town's somewhat grey Victorian aspect. It is informally the 'capital' of western Dartmoor.

The 'Honour Oak' in Whitchurch Road was a boundary oak marking the Tavistock limit for French prisoners on parole from PRINCETOWN[1] prison in 1803–14, when England was at war with France, and also the place where money was left in exchange for food during the cholera epidemic of 1832.

Between 1539 and 1911 the town was owned by the Russell family, the dukes of Bedford, whose subsidiary title is 'Marquess of Tavistock'. Of the many thoroughfares given that name on the Russell Estates in London, the most notable is **Tavistock Square** in BLOOMSBURY, home of the British Medical Association, and venue between the two world wars of Leonard and Virginia Woolf's Hogarth Press. The **Tavistock Clinic**, which specializes in psychoanalytic treatment, originally opened nearby in 1920.

Sir Francis Drake (?1540–96) was born about 1.5 km (1 mile) to the south of Tavistock. Michael Heseltine was the town's MP from 1966 to 1974.

Tavistock Goosey Fair. A fair held in Tavistock on the first Wednesday in October originally, but no longer, for the selling of geese. It dates from 1105.

'Tis just a month come Friday next,
Bill Champernowne and me,
Us went across old Dartymoor
The Goosey Fair to see.
Us made usselves right vitty,
Us shaved and grazed our hair,
And off us goes in our Zunday clothes
Behind Bill's old grey mare.
Us smelt the zage and onion
'Alf a mile from Whitchurch Down,
And didn't us 'ave a blow out
When us put up in the town,
And there us met Ned Hannaford,
Jan Steer and Nicky Square,
I think that all the world must be
At Tavistock Goosey Fair.

Chorus:
And its oh, and where be a-going,
And what be a-doing of there,
Heave down your prong and stamp along,
To Tavistock Goosey Fair.

Anon.: 'Tavistock Goosey Fair'

tavistockite. A hydrous phosphate of aluminium and calcium, found near Tavistock in the mid-19th century.

Tavy A pre-Celtic river name from an Indo-European root meaning 'to flow' (*see also* TAW, THAMES[1] *and* TAMAR).

A river in Devon, which rises on western central DARTMOOR, at **Tavy Head**, and flows southwestwards via TAVISTOCK to join the River TAMAR at PLYMOUTH.

See also MARY TAVY *and* PETER TAVY.

Taw A pre-Celtic river name from an Indo-European root meaning 'to flow' (*see also* THAMES[1], TAVY *and* TAMAR).

A river in Devon, which rises to the west of Hangingstone Hill in northern DARTMOOR and flows northwestwards to BARNSTAPLE, where it broadens out into a 13-km (8-mile) estuary that debouches into Bideford Bay (*see under* BIDEFORD). The Taw is joined by the Rive TORRIDGE[1] at APPLEDORE[1].

Tawe *See* TAW.

A river in South Wales. It rises on the BLACK MOUNTAIN, Powys, and flows south for 48 km (30 miles) via PONTAR-DAWE ('bridge over the Tawe') to enter the Bristol Channel (*see under* BRISTOL) at SWANSEA[1] (whose Welsh name is **Abertawe**, meaning 'mouth of the Tawe').

Tay Possibly from the name of an ancient river goddess, meaning 'the silent one', but it may be an ancient pre-Celtic river name from an identical Indo-European root to TYNE[1] and THAMES[1], meaning 'to flow'. The Gaelic name is *Tatha*. It was called *Tanaus* or *Taus* by Tacitus, in his *Life of Agricola* (AD 98); in the following century Ptolemy called it *Tava*.

Scotland's longest river, 193 km (120 miles) long. It is also a noted salmon river, and its tributaries include the Lyon (*see under* GLEN LYON), the TUMMEL, the Isla (*see under* GLEN ISLA), the ALMOND[1] and the EARN. The course of the river was in the former Stirlingshire and Perthshire, then in the old TAYSIDE region, and is now in Stirling, and Perth and Kinross.

The Tay rises on the eastern slopes of BEN LUI in the western central Highlands as the Allt Coire Laoigh, which then becomes the River Cononish and then, south of TYNDRUM, the River Fillan. Between CRIANLARICH and Loch Tay it flows eastwards and is called the River Dochart. The narrow **Loch Tay** stretches 24 km (15 miles) northeastwards, dominated on its northern side by the massif of BEN LAWERS. At the northeastern end of the loch is **Taymouth Castle** (1801). From here the River Tay flows east past ABERFELDY, then south to DUN-KELD, east towards COUPAR ANGUS, then south to PERTH.

> All hail, ye scenes that o'er my soul prevail!
>> Ye spacious friths and lakes, which, far away,
>> Are by smooth Annan fill'd or past'ral Tay ...
>
>> William Collins: 'Ode on the Popular Superstitions of the Highlands' (1784)

East of Perth the river opens out into the estuary of the **Firth of Tay**, which extends some 40 km (25 miles) north-eastwards to the North Sea, past DUNDEE on the north shore and the dormitory village of **Tayport** on the south shore.

> O that yon river micht nae mair
>> Rin through the channels o' my sleep;
> My bluid has felt its tides owre sair,
>> Its waves hae drooned my dreams owre deep.
>
>> Lewis Spence (1874–1955): 'Great Tay of the Waves' (Scots *owre sair* 'overly painfully')

The 2.25 km (1.35 mile) **Tay Road Bridge** across the Firth of Tay from NEWPORT-ON-TAY to Dundee was opened in 1966. To the west is the older rail bridge (3.4 km / 2 miles long), opened in 1888, known simply as the **Tay Bridge**. This replaced the earlier rail bridge, destroyed in a storm in 1879 while a train was crossing, leading to the deaths of 90 people.

> Beautiful Railway Bridge of the Silv'ry Tay!
> Alas, I am very sorry to say
> That ninety lives have been taken away
> On the last Sabbath day of 1879,
> Which will be remember'd for a very long time.
>
>> William McGonagall: 'The Tay Bridge Disaster' (1880)

Tayside From the River TAY, which flows through it.

A former local authority region in Scotland, formed in 1975. It incorporated much of the old counties of PERTHSHIRE, KINROSS-SHIRE and ANGUS, together with the city of DUNDEE. It was bordered on the north by Grampian, on the north-west by Highland, on the southwest by Central and on the southeast by Fife. In addition to Dundee (the adminis-trative centre), it included PERTH, DUNKELD, ABERFELDY, PITLOCHRY, BLAIRGOWRIE, FORFAR, KIRRIEMUIR, ARBROATH, MONTROSE and BRECHIN. Tayside region was abolished in 1996, and its districts – PERTH and KINROSS, Dundee, and Angus – became unitary authorities.

Teamhair. The Irish name for the Hill of TARA.

Teapot Capital of North Wales, the. *See under* CONWY[2].

Tearaght Island Irish *An Tiaracht* 'rump, hindquarters' (usually of a horse).

A tiny island to the west of the BLASKET ISLANDS, County Kerry. It is 13 km (8 miles) west of GARRAUN POINT, the westernmost mainland point in Ireland, and is itself the most westerly point in Ireland, and indeed of Europe.

Tebay 'Tiba's island or water-meadow', OE male personal name *Tiba* + *eg* (*see* -EY, -EA), possibly referring to a small island in the River Lune, or to the water-meadows in the valley.

A village in Cumbria (formerly in Westmorland), 16 km (10 miles) northeast of Kendal. It is at the north end of the

Tebay Gorge, a dramatic and beautiful defile between the Howgill Fells to the east and the Lakeland Fells to the west. It provides the scenic highpoint for anyone travelling on the M6 or the main Glasgow–Euston railway line, both of which run through it.

Witch of Tebay, the. Mary Baynes (d.1811), a much-feared old woman, who is said to have predicted that 'fiery horse-less carriages' would one day run over Loups Fell; it became the course of the main railway line.

Teddington 'estate associated with Tuda', OE male personal name *Tuda* + -ING + -TON. The popular theory that the name means 'tide end town', referring to its position on the Thames, is neat but untrue.

A western outer suburb of London, on the west bank of the River Thames[1], in the borough of Richmond-upon-Thames (before 1965 in Surrey), to the northwest of Kingston upon Thames. **Teddington Lock** marks the highest point at which the Thames is tidal.

The National Physical Laboratory is situated in Teddington, as were the studios of Thames Television (*see under* Thames[1]).

The actor and dramatist Noël Coward (1899–1973) was born in Teddington, and the mystical Anglican poet Thomas Traherne (1637–74) ended his days here. The novelist R.D. Blackmore, author of *Lorna Doone*, lived in Teddington for much of his life (from the late 1850s until his death in 1900); he was invited to become Coward's godfather, but he declined.

Teddy Bear Country. The nickname given to the area around Ibrox Park in Glasgow.

Tedstone Delamere *Tedstone* probably 'Teod's thorn-tree', OE *Teodes* possessive form of male personal name *Teod* + *thorn* 'thorn-tree'; *Delamere* denoting manorial ownership in the Middle Ages by the de la Mare family.

A village in Herefordshire (before 1998 in Hereford and Worcester, before 1974 in Herefordshire), about 19 km (12 miles) east of Leominster.

Tedstone Wafre *Wafre* denoting manorial ownership in the Middle Ages by the le Wafre family.

A village in Herefordshire (before 1998 in Hereford and Worcester, before 1974 in Herefordshire), about 17 km (11 miles) east of Leominster.

Teermoyle Mountain Irish *Tír Maoile* 'district of the bare hill'.

A mountain (772 m / 2532 ft) in the Iveragh peninsula of County Kerry, some 20 km (12 miles) west of Macgilly-cuddy's Reeks.

Tees An OCelt or pre-Celtic name possibly meaning 'surging one'.

A river of northeast England 130 km (81 miles) long. It rises in the Pennines, on the eastern slopes of Cross Fell,

Cumbria, then passes through Cow Green Reservoir into County Durham and over Cauldron Snout and High Force waterfalls.

> Where Tees in tumult leaves his source
> Thundering o'er Cauldron and High Force …
> Sir Walter Scott: *Rokeby* (1813)

The Tees flows southeastwards through **Teesdale** to Barnard Castle. Upper Teesdale is celebrated for its alpine flora (*see* Teesdale sandwort *below*); in contrast, in the past, the poor of the area had to make a living by washing lead ore in the river, as recorded in a local song:

> My father was a miner, he lived down in the town,
> 'Twas hard work and poverty that always kept him down.
> He aimed for us to go to school, but brass he could not pay,
> So we had to go to the washing rake for just four pence a day.

After Barnard Castle, the Tees flows east through Darling-ton, before meandering northeastwards to the industrial area of **Teesside**, including Stockton-on-Tees and Middlesbrough (Teesside was a county borough 1968–74, then became part of Cleveland, itself split into unitary authorities in 1996). The last stretch of the Tees before it enters the North Sea at Tees Bay is called **Tees-Mouth**. Tributaries of the Tees include the Lune[2], the Balder and the Greta. The Tees is navigable up to Middlesbrough, and the **Tees Barrage** (completed 1985) provides a stretch of unpolluted, non-tidal water.

The river is said to be the home of a water spirit called Peg Prowler. Parents used to tell their children not to play on the banks of the river on Sundays, otherwise the green-haired Peg would pull them under the water and eat them.

Teesdale sandwort. An inconspicuous member of the pink family, *Minuartia stricta*, with small white flowers. It is found in wet, mountainous locations.

Teesdale violet. A rare member of the violet family, *Viola rupestris*, similar to, but smaller than, the common dog violet, with which it naturally hybridizes.

Teeswater. A breed of black-snouted, dreadlocked sheep, found in County Durham and other parts of northern England.

Teffont Evias *Teffont* 'boundary spring', OE *teo* 'boundary' + *funta* 'spring'; *Evias* denoting manorial ownership in the Middle Ages by the barons of Ewyas.

A village (pronounced 'ee-vye-əs') in Wiltshire, on the southern edge of Salisbury Plain (*see under* Salisbury), about 16 km (10 miles) west of Salisbury. It is a small and very attractive village with many thatched cottages. It was joined with the nearby village of **Teffont Magna** (Latin *magna* 'great') as a single parish in 1936.

Teifi A Welsh river name of unknown etymology.

A river in Ceredigion (formerly in Cardiganshire, then in Dyfed). It is 118 km (73 miles) long, and its anglicized form is **Teivy**. It rises at 455 m (1,493 ft) in **Llyn Teifi** (Welsh *llyn* means 'lake') near STRATA FLORIDA Abbey; this lake and its smaller neighbours are called the **Teifi Pools**. The Teifi flows southwest through LAMPETER and then west to CARDIGAN (whose Welsh name is **Aberteifi**, meaning 'mouth of the Teifi'), before its wide estuary enters Cardigan Bay.

Teigh 'small enclosure', OE *teag*.

A village (pronounced 'tee') in Rutland (before 1997 in Leicestershire, before 1974 in Rutland), about 8 km (5 miles) north of Oakham.

Teign An OCelt river name meaning 'sweeper, flooder'.

A river (pronounced 'teen' or 'tin') in Devon, which rises on northeastern DARTMOOR and flows 48 km (30 miles) eastwards and then southwards to NEWTON ABBOT, where it broadens out into a 6-km (4-mile) estuary that debouches into the English Channel at TEIGNMOUTH.

> By the wild sea-wall I wandered
> Blinded by the salting sun,
> While the sulky Channel thundered
> Like an old Trafalgar gun.
> And I watched the gaudy river
> Under trees of lemon-green
> Coiling like a scarlet bugle
> Through the valley of the Teign.
>
> > Charles Causley (1917–2003): 'Keats at
> > Teignmouth: Spring 1818'

Teignbridge 'bridge over the River Teign', TEIGN + OE *brycg* 'bridge'. Originally the name of the local Hundred (an administrative district), referring to a bridge over the Teign at Kingsteignton, 6 km (4 miles) west of Teignmouth.

A local-government district (pronounced 'tinbridge') in southwest Devon, including TEIGNMOUTH.

Teignmouth 'mouth of the River Teign', TEIGN + OE *mutha* 'mouth'.

A town and seaside resort (pronounced 'tinməth') on the south Devon coast, at the mouth of the River TEIGN, about 11 km (7 miles) southwest of Exmouth. It has a long history as a port (for both fishing and general trade – the Dartmoor granite to build London Bridge was shipped from here in 1821) and as a shipbuilding centre. It was also one of the first seaside resorts to be developed in Devon, in the mid-18th century.

Amongst the town's earliest visitors were the novelist Jane Austen (in 1802), the novelist and diarist Fanny Burney (on three occasions in 1773, 1778 and 1791), and the poet John Keats (in 1818), who visited his brother here. Elias Parish Alvars (1808–49), known as the 'King of Harpists',

was born here, as was Charles Babbage (1791–1871), regarded by some as the father of the computer.

Ransacked by the French in 1690, in the 19th century the town added some Victoriana to its Regency charm, and it has managed to retain some elegance.

Telford Named after the engineer Thomas *Telford* (1757–1834), who was appointed in 1786 surveyor of Shropshire, and in 1793 agent and engineer of the Ellesmere Canal Company (the canal linked SHROPSHIRE with the MERSEY). (Despite having the appearance of a place name with *ford*, the personal name *Telford* is from OFr *taille fer* 'iron-cutter', a name for a man who could cut through his opponent's armour; strangely appropriate for an engineer.)

A NEW TOWN[1] in Shropshire, in the shadow of the WREKIN, within the unitary authority of TELFORD AND WREKIN, about 19 km (12 miles) east of Shrewsbury. It is the administrative headquarters of the unitary authority. It was officially brought into existence in 1963, when it was named Dawley, after the village it was to be based on. It grew rapidly, absorbing existing settlements, and on 24 October 1968, after it had been decided to extend it further to the west and east, it was re-christened in honour of a Scottish engineer with notable Shropshire connections (*see above*). COALBROOKDALE and IRONBRIDGE are included within its conurbation.

See also DONNINGTON.

Telford and Wrekin. A unitary authority within Shropshire, based on TELFORD. It was created in 1998. It includes NEWPORT[3] within its territory.

Teltown Irish *Tailtean*, from the name of a Celtic goddess Taillte or Tailltiu.

A village in County Meath that gave its name to the **Aonach Tailteann** (Irish *Óenach Tailten*) or **Tailteann Games**, an annual week-long athletic gathering established, according to legend, in the 19th century BC by King Lugh of the Tuatha Dé Danaan. The games are thought to have continued until the Anglo-Norman invasion of the 12th century, and were revived in 1924, 1928 and 1932.

Teme Probably either an OCelt river name, perhaps meaning 'the dark one', or a pre-Celtic river name from an Indo-European root meaning 'to flow' (*see also* THAMES[1], TAVY, TAW *and* TAMAR).

A river (pronounced 'teem') in Powys, Shropshire, Herefordshire and Worcestershire, which rises about 4 km (2.5 miles) west of the Welsh–English border and flows 97 km (60 miles) southeastwards through KNIGHTON, LUDLOW and TENBURY WELLS to join the SEVERN just to the south of WORCESTER. For much of the early part of its course it forms the boundary between England and Wales.

> In valleys of springs of rivers,
> By Ony and Teme and Clun,

❖ temple ❖

In Ireland this is a commonly occurring name element from *teampall*, meaning 'church'. In England, however, the TEMPLE (Greater London) and the various other *temple* names (TEMPLE CLOUD and so forth) refer predominantly to property owned historically by the Knights Templars, a military order founded in the early 12th century to fight the Crusades. There also appears to be a Templar connection to TEMPLEMORE (County Tipperary).

> The country for easy livers,
> The quietest under the sun....
>
> A.E. Housman: *A Shropshire Lad* (1896)

Temple, the From the Knights *Templars*.

A site in the City of London (EC4) (*see* LONDON), on the north bank of the River Thames between Blackfriars Bridge and Waterloo Bridge. It was here that the Knights Templars established themselves around 1160 (having moved from HOLBORN), building their great house and a Round Church. (The Knights Templars belonged to a chivalric religious order founded in 1118 to protect pilgrims travelling to the Holy Land, and took their name from the Temple of Solomon in Jerusalem.) The Templars were suppressed in the early 14th century (on the grounds of heresy and general immorality) and all their property was confiscated, including their London headquarters. The premises were leased in the middle of the century to a group of lawyers, which in the early 15th century organized itself into two societies known as the **Inner Temple** and the **Middle Temple**. They survive to this day as two of the four Inns of Court. They occupy numerous buildings, ranging from medieval through Tudor and Victorian to modern, arranged in a maze of courtyards and alleyways on the site between FLEET STREET and the EMBANKMENT. The most notable of the buildings is **Middle Temple Hall**, opened by Elizabeth I in 1576; Shakespeare's *Twelfth Night* was premiered here in 1601.

The original 12th- and 13th-century **Temple Church**, with its circular nave, survives, albeit in heavily restored form. It suffered badly in the Blitz, as did the rest of the Temple.

Temple Underground station, on the Circle and District lines, opened in 1870 (originally as 'The Temple').

Temple Bar. A location at the point where FLEET STREET becomes the STRAND, marking the western limit of the City of London. A barrier is first recorded here in the late 13th century ('*barram Novi Templi*'). This seems to have been nothing more than a chain between two posts, but by the middle of the 14th century there was an arched gateway here, with a prison on top. This survived the Great Fire of 1666, but was nevertheless demolished, and a new one was erected in the 1670s to a design by Sir Christopher Wren. In the late 17th century it became the practice to display the heads of traitors impaled on spikes on top of the gate (it was quite a high gate, and those who wanted to get a better view could hire a telescope for a halfpenny). The last such exhibition was held in 1746. By the middle of the 19th century Temple Bar's central arch was becoming too much of an impediment to traffic, and in 1878 it was removed. It was later re-erected in THEOBALD'S PARK near Cheshunt, where it remained for more than a hundred years. At the beginning of the 21st century it was returned to the City, incorporated into the PATERNOSTER SQUARE redevelopment by ST PAUL'S[1] Cathedral.

While the arch itself has gone, its location retains its symbolic significance: a sovereign who wishes to enter the City of London via Fleet Street, typically on his or her processional way to St Paul's Cathedral, must stop here and ask permission of the Lord Mayor. The line is marked by a memorial in the centre of the road, erected in 1880, and surmounted by a griffin, the unofficial badge of the City.

temple-pickling. An underworld slang term from the late 17th century to the early 19th for the ducking of court officials beneath a pump; in the 17th century any bailiff caught within the precincts of the Temple was automatically punished in this way.

Temple Cloud *Temple* referring to lands in the vicinity held in the Middle Ages by the Knights Templars; *Cloud* '(rocky) hill', OE *clud*.

A village in Bath and North East Somerset (before 1996 in Avon, before 1974 in Somerset), about 6 km (4 miles) northwest of Midsomer Norton.

Temple Ewell *Ewell see* EWELL (the source referred to here is that of the Dour – *see* DOVER).

A village in Kent, now a northwestern suburb of DOVER. EWELL MINNIS is about 3 km (2 miles) to the southwest.

Temple Guiting *Guiting see* GUITING POWER.

A village (pronounced 'guy-ting') in Gloucestershire, in the COTSWOLDS and on the River WINDRUSH, about 16 km (10 miles) northeast of Cheltenham. The Knights Templars founded a preceptory here in the 12th century.

Templemore Irish *An Teampall Mór* 'the big church'.

A market town in County Tipperary, 14 km (8.5 miles) north of Thurles. The town takes its name from the preceptory founded at Templemore by the Knights Templars, who also built a castle here. The town also has a Gardaí training centre. George Borrow's father was stationed here in 1816 and the area features in Borrow's *Lavengro* (1851).

Tenbury Wells *Tenbury* 'stronghold on the River Teme', TEME + OE *burh* (*see* BURY); *Wells* referring to its status as a spa in the 19th century.

A market town in Worcestershire (before 1998 in Hereford

and Worcester, before 1974 in Worcestershire), on the River Teme, close to the Shropshire border, about 11 km (7 miles) southeast of Ludlow. Saline springs were discovered here in 1839, and, what with the town being a stopping-point on the coach-road from London to North Wales, it was soon doing reasonable business as a spa (hence the second part of its name). The water is no longer much of a revenue earner, but the townscape of Tenbury retains much of the feeling of that period.

Tenbury was one of Queen Victoria's favourites: she called it 'my lovely town in the orchard' (it is surrounded by orchards and hop fields).

Tenby 'little fort', from the Welsh name *Dinbych*, *din* 'fort' + *bych* 'small' (*see* BACH).

A seaside resort and fishing port on a promontory on the west side of Carmarthen Bay in Pembrokeshire (formerly in Dyfed), 14 km (8.5 miles) east of Pembroke. Its Welsh name is **Dinbych-y-Pysgod** ('little fort of the fish'; *y-Pysgod* was added in the 16th century, presumably to distinguish it from un-fishy DENBIGH, which is also *Dinbych* in Welsh).

There has been a fort or castle at Tenby from at least the early Middle Ages, as attested by the following:

> A splendid fort stands on the wide ocean,
> A sturdy stronghold, sea-encircled.
>
> Anon.: *'Edmyg Dinbych'* ('In Praise of Tenby'; 7th century),
> translated from the Welsh by Joseph P. Clancy

Giraldus Cambrensis (Gerald of Wales) was rector of the parish here from 1172 to 1175. Part of the Norman castle survives, as do most of the 13th-century town walls, and the town remained an important port until the end of the 16th century. It revived in the 19th century when the railway brought fashionable holidaymakers to savour its seaside delights.

Tenby has a unique New Year's Day ceremony in which the children of the town shower onlookers with raindrops from bunches of holly or box twigs. The recipients donate money as thanks for their good fortune. (The ceremony possibly originates in ancient winter fertility rites such as the Roman Lupercalia, in which every 15 February the priests of Lupercal sacrificed goats and a dog, and with thongs wrought from their victims' skins ran round the Palatine Hill whipping women, allegedly in order to render them fertile. In 494 Pope Gelasius IV hijacked the rite and turned it into the Feast of the Purification.)

Tenby was the birthplace of Robert Recorde (*c*.1510–58), mathematician, proposer of the = sign, and royal physician to Edward VI and Mary I; and of the painter Augustus John (1878–1961).

Tenby daffodil. A rare wild daffodil, *Narcissus obvallaris*, found only in Pembrokeshire. It has more erect, deeper-hued flowers than the better known *Narcissus pseudonarcissus* beloved of William Wordsworth.

Tendring Perhaps 'place where tinder or fuel is collected', OE *tynder* 'tinder, fuel' + -ING.

A village and administrative district in Essex. The village is about 14 km (8.5 miles) east of Colchester. The district covers the area between the estuaries of the COLNE[1] and the STOUR[2], to the east of Colchester, known as the **Tendring Peninsula**. Its southeastern coast, dubbed the 'Essex Sunshine Coast', contains the seaside resorts CLACTON-ON-SEA and FRINTON-ON-SEA.

Tennyson Down. An area of clifftop downland at the western tip of the ISLE OF WIGHT, between FRESHWATER Bay (near where the poet Alfred Tennyson lived in the mid-19th century) and the NEEDLES. It was given to the National Trust by the then Lord Tennyson in 1927 in memory of his father, the poet. It is about 6 km (4 miles) long, and at its highest point (148 m / 485 ft) there is a monument to Tennyson.

Tenterden 'Thanet-dwellers' woodland pasture' (for the feeding of pigs), *Thanet* (*see* ISLE OF THANET) + OE -*ware* 'dwellers' + *denn* 'woodland pasture'.

A market town in the WEALD of Kent, about 16 km (10 miles) southwest of Ashford. It came to prosperity in the Middle Ages on the back of the wool trade. Until the 17th century it was an inland port (*see* SMALL HYTHE), thanks to a channel from the River ROTHER[2], and it enjoyed associate status with the CINQUE PORTS, but then the channel silted up, cutting Tenterden off from the sea. The main street is notable for its white weather-boarded and bow-windowed Georgian shop-fronts.

Tenterden railway station is the terminus of the Kent and East Sussex Railway, Britain's first light railway.

William Caxton (1422–91), pioneer of printing in England, is thought to have been born in Tenterden.

Emma Hamilton's daughter by Lord Nelson, Horatia, married the vicar of Tenterden. They had nine children, and Horatia lived to the age of 80.

'Tenterden steeple was the cause of Goodwin Sands'. A satirical riposte made in former times when some ridiculous reason was given for a thing. The story, according to a sermon given by the 16th-century Protestant martyr Hugh Latimer, is that Sir Thomas More, being sent to Kent to ascertain the cause of the GOODWIN SANDS, called together the oldest inhabitants to ask their opinion. A very old man said, 'I believe Tenterden steeple is the cause', and went on to explain that in his early days there was no Tenterden steeple and there were no complaints about the sands. This reason seems absurd enough, but the fact seems to be that the bishops of Rochester applied to the building of Tenterden steeple moneys raised in the county for the purpose of keeping Sandwich haven clear, so that when they found that the harbour was becoming blocked up there was no money for the dredging work.

Tentsmuir Point *Tentsmuir* Scots *muir* 'moor' with an uncertain element that may be from temporary camps of fishermen here, or may be Scots *tent*, a unit of land derived from 'ten, tenth'.

A sandy headland in Fife, on the south side of the mouth of the Firth of Tay (*see under* TAY). To the south extends a great length of sand and the Forestry Commission's **Tentsmuir Forest**, largely consisting of pine trees. The forest is used for, among other things, husky racing.

Terrington St Clement *Terrington* 'Tir(a)'s people's farmstead', OE male personal name *Tir(a)* + *-inga-* (*see* -ING) + *-TON*; *St Clement* from the dedication of the local church.

A village in Norfolk, at the southeastern corner of the WASH, about 8 km (5 miles) west of King's Lynn. Dorothy L. Sayers's fictional village of FENCHURCH ST PAUL is partly based on it.

Terrington Marsh. An area of marshland between Terrington St Clement and the Wash.

Test An OCelt or pre-Celtic river name of unknown meaning.

A river in Hampshire, which rises near the southern edge of the North Wessex Downs (*see under* WESSEX), about 12 km (7.5 miles) southwest of Basingstoke, and flows 48 km (30 miles) southwestwards and southwards through STOCKBRIDGE and ROMSEY into Southampton Water (*see under* SOUTHAMPTON) at TOTTON. Along with its companion to the east, the ITCHEN, it is one of the premier trout streams in England.

The **Test Way** is a 70.5-km- (44-mile-) footpath, established in the 1980s, that crosses Hampshire from north to south. Starting at INKPEN Beacon on the North Wessex Downs, it follows the course of the Test as far as Totton in the river's tidal marshes on Southampton Water.

Tetbury 'Tette's fortified place', OE female personal name *Tette* + *byrig* dative form of *burh* (*see* BURY).

A small market town in Gloucestershire, in the COTSWOLDS, close to the Wiltshire border, about 8 km (5 miles) northwest of Malmesbury. Its attractive centre is dominated by modestly elegant grey stone houses, many of them from the 18th century, and a particularly fine pillared Elizabethan market hall.

About 2.5 km (1.5 miles) to the southwest is HIGH-GROVE, country home of the Prince of Wales.

Tetbury portion. A slang expression around the turn of the 19th century for sexual intercourse followed by a dose of venereal disease (or, as Francis Grose put it in his *Classical Dictionary of the Vulgar Tongue* (1796), 'A **** [cunt] and a clap'). Tetbury, as may be deduced, did not have a high reputation at that time.

Teviot A Celtic or pre-Celtic name, possibly meaning 'powerful one', and possibly related, like TWEED, to the Indo-European word found in Sanskrit as *tavás* 'to surge'.

A river in the Scottish BORDERS; length 60 km (37 miles). It rises in the hills on the border with Dumfries and Galloway, near the village of **Teviothead**, and flows northeastwards through **Teviotdale** and HAWICK to join the Tweed at KELSO. There is a traditional jig called '**Teviot Brig**'.

Flower of Teviot, the. In Scott's *Lay of the Last Minstrel* (1805), Lady Margaret of Bransome (or Branxholme) Hall in Teviotdale, who is wooed in the tale by Baron Henry of Cranstown.

> Sweet Teviot! on thy silver tide
> The glaring bale-fires blaze no more.
> No longer steel-clad warriors ride
> Along thy wild and willow'd shore.
>
> Sir Walter Scott: *The Lay of the Last Minstrel* (1805)

Teviotdale pie. A pie of minced beef, onions and Worcestershire sauce, with a suet batter topping. It is claimed to make a little meat go a long way, and may have originated as a wartime alternative to steak and kidney pudding. Its connection with Teviotdale itself is not clear.

Tewkesbury 'Teodec's fortified place', OE *Teodeces* possessive form of male personal name *Teodec* + *byrig* dative form of *burh* (*see* BURY). Teodec is popularly associated with a 7th-century missionary monk called Theocus, who is said to have built the first church here.

A market town in Gloucestershire, on the River AVON[1], close to its confluence with the SEVERN, about 16 km (10 miles) north of Gloucester. There is evidence that Benedictine monks had settled here by the early 8th century, and their successors were provided with a magnificent Norman abbey in the late 11th century. **Tewkesbury Abbey** has been dubbed 'one of England's most splendid churches' by Simon Jenkins (*England's Thousand Best Churches* (1999)). Its huge central tower is 40 m (132 ft) high. It escaped the usual fate of monastic buildings at the Dissolution of the Monasteries – demolition – thanks to the munificence of the local people: they bought it from Henry VIII for £453. Tewkesbury also has one of the earliest Baptist chapels in England, dating from the 1620s.

Just as providential as the survival of the abbey, Tewkesbury's failure to get involved in the Industrial Revolution means that many of its late medieval, Tudor and Georgian buildings survive to this day. They include some notable inns, such as The Black Bear, which claims to date from 1308, and The Royal Hop Pole, where the Pickwick Club dined in Dickens's *Pickwick Papers* (1836–7).

In the 16th and 17th centuries Tewkesbury was England's mustard capital ('His wit is as thick as Tewkesbury mustard', Shakespeare, *Henry IV, Part II* (1597), II.vi), but thereafter the centre of mustard production moved to NORWICH.

The novelist and essayist John Moore (1907–67) was born in Tewkesbury, and wrote of his concerns and love for the surrounding countryside in works such as *Portrait of Elmbury* (1945), based on the town, and *Brensham Village* (1946).

Battle of Tewkesbury (4 May 1471). The final battle of the first (and major) phase of the Wars of the Roses, in which the Lancastrian forces were decisively defeated, Margaret of Anjou (Henry VI's widow) was captured, Edward, the young Lancastrian prince of Wales, was subsequently killed and the throne was secured (until 1483) for the Yorkist king Edward IV. It was a particularly bloody encounter, and the field on which it was fought is to this day called Bloody Meadow.

Thame[1] An Indo-European river name, from a word meaning 'to flow' (*see also* THAMES[1]).

A river (pronounced 'tame') in Buckinghamshire and Oxfordshire. It rises to the north of AYLESBURY and flows 64 km (40 miles) southwestwards through THAME[2] to join the River Thames just to the south of DORCHESTER[2].

Thame[2] From THAME[1].

A market town in Oxfordshire, on the River THAME[1], about 19 km (12 miles) east of Oxford. Its unusually wide High Street is adorned by an attractive array of late medieval, Tudor and Georgian buildings, notable among them The Spread Eagle, at which, before the Second World War, the restaurateur and cookery writer John Fothergill pioneered the concept of the country inn as destination eating-place.

Thame has a late 16th-century grammar school, at which the poet John Milton and the parliamentarian John Hampden were pupils; Hampden was killed in a skirmish near Thame in the Civil Wars (*see* CHALGROVE).

James Figg (?1695–1734), the first recognized champion of England at fighting with bare fists, was born in Thame.

Thames[1] OE *Temese*, from Latin *Tamesa, Tamesis*. Ultimately from an Indo-European river name from a word meaning 'to flow'. The *Th-* spelling first appears in the 14th century, and derives from Anglo-Norman spelling convention; the modern form *Thames* is not recorded before the 16th century. Other English and Welsh river names, including TAFF, TAMAR, TAME[1], TAME[2], TAVY, TAWE, TAY, TEME and THAME[1], may well come from the same source.

A river (pronounced 'temz') in Gloucestershire, Wiltshire, Oxfordshire, Berkshire and London. The longest river entirely in England (and the second-longest in the United Kingdom, after the SEVERN), it rises at **Thames Head**, at the foot of the COTSWOLDS, about 6 km (4 miles) southwest of CIRENCESTER, and flows 338 km (210 miles) in a broadly southeasterly direction through LECHLADE (where its headstreams unite), OXFORD (between Lechlade and Oxford it is alternatively called the ISIS), ABINGDON, READING, MAIDENHEAD, WINDSOR and London, and along the **Thames Estuary** (whose northern and southern shores bound Essex and Kent respectively) into the NORTH SEA at the NORE. Its main tributaries are the WINDRUSH, EVENLODE[2], CHERWELL, THAME[1], COLNE[1], LEA (or Lee) and RODING; and from the south the KENNET[1], LODDON, WEY[1], MOLE[1], Darent (*see under* DARTFORD) and MEDWAY[1]. The Thames is navigable from CRICKLADE and tidal as far as TEDDINGTON. It has 47 locks (St John's Lock, Lechlade, being nearest the source), and there are 20 road and 9 rail bridges between HAMPTON COURT and the TOWER OF LONDON. From its mouth upstream as far as KEW the river is divided into 28 sections known as 'reaches' (*see* GALLIONS REACH).

In February 1937 the location of the source of the Thames became, briefly, a matter of parliamentary debate. The member for Stroud, a Mr Perkins, opined in the House of Commons that the true source of the Thames was at Seven Springs, southeast of Cheltenham. W.S. Morrison, member for Cirencester and Tewkesbury, and minister for agriculture, countered, correctly, that the Thames rises at Thames Head, southeast of Cirencester (*see under* KEMBLE). Seven Springs is in fact the source of the River CHURN, a Thames tributary.

From its source as far as Oxford the Thames is a quiet country river, its fishy fauna and numerous riverside pubs attracting anglers in large numbers. This is the 'stripling Thames' of Matthew Arnold's Scholar-Gipsy:

> For most, I know, thou lov'st retired ground!
> Thee at the ferry Oxford riders blithe,
> Returning home on summer nights, have met
> Crossing the stripling Thames at Bab-lock-Hithe,
> Trailing in the cool stream thy fingers wet
> As the punt's rope chops round;
> And leaning backwards in a pensive dream,
> And fostering in thy lap a heap of flowers
> Pluck'd in shy field and distant Wychwood
>   bowers
> And thine eyes resting on the moonlit stream.
>
> Matthew Arnold: 'The Scholar-Gipsy' (1853)

Arnold was an ardent devotee of the Upper Thames around and west of Oxford, remarking in 1885: 'I cannot describe the effect which this landscape always has upon me – The hillside with its valley, and Oxford in the great Thames valley below.'

Between Lechlade and Oxford the main channel of the Thames sends off numerous narrow branches, forming picturesque backwaters that only light pleasure craft can penetrate. From Oxford onwards the river broadens out as it flows through the flat fertile THAMES VALLEY. Downstream of GORING it comes into its own as a recreational waterway, plied by craft from river steamers through dinghies to skiffs: it was here that the three chums and Montmorency disported themselves in Jerome K. Jerome's *Three Men in a Boat* (1889). Prosperous riverside towns appear – HENLEY-ON-THAMES, MARLOW, MAIDENHEAD – their salubrious late-Victorian and Edwardian villas lining the banks.

From Windsor eastwards the river's surroundings become decidedly suburban – EGHAM, CHERTSEY, STAINES – and downstream of Teddington it begins its transformation into its second avatar: London's river. In many ways the Thames is the reason why London is where it is and became what it did – the first place upriver where the stream could be bridged, the highest point to which large cargo vessels could be brought – and it has always played a key role in the capital's – and hence the country's – life: the conduit for vital exports and imports; the gateway to a wider world (including a far-flung empire); a daily thoroughfare for all, from the lowest to the highest (Thames wherrymen were the cabmen of London from the Middle Ages to the early 19th century, and the Thames was the royal route from London to palaces upstream such as HAMPTON COURT); and witness to many of Britain's most significant moments of the past two millennia (the Romans bridged it during their period of occupation (*see* London Bridge *under* LONDON), and it provided the water to put out the fires of the Blitz):

> One saw this dirty commercial river as one came up, and he [Winston Churchill] was describing it as the silver thread which runs through the history of Britain.
>
> Queen Elizabeth II: quoted in Martin Gilbert, *Winston S. Churchill* (1988)

> I have seen the Mississippi. That is muddy water. I have seen the St Lawrence. That is crystal water. But the Thames is liquid history.
>
> John Burns, Labour politician (1858–1943): speech

The Thames in London has performed other less noble but no less important functions too: it was once the ultimate dumping ground for most of the capital's sewage, until the noisome years leading up to the 'Great Stink' of 1858 galvanized Parliament into having a modern sewerage system built (as part of the process, carried out by Sir Joseph Bazalgette, the river was embanked – *see* the EMBANKMENT). This was the Thames that figures so sinisterly in the novels of Charles Dickens: *Bleak House* (1853) begins with a chilling description of shrouding Thames fog ('Fog down the river, where it rolls defiled among the tiers of shipping'), and at the start of *Our Mutual Friend* (1865) a dead body is dragged

out of it. By the 1960s the river was so polluted that only eels could survive in it, but vigorous action thereafter cleaned it up to such an extent that in 1974 the first salmon was caught in the Thames for 150 years. Flash floods in London in the summer of 2004 overwhelmed the drainage system, however, flushing 100,000 tonnes of sewage into the Thames and killing thousands of fish.

In former times London could be so cold that the Thames froze over, and between the mid-16th century and the late 18th, in the so-called 'Little Ice Age', 'Frost Fairs' were regularly held on the ice, with stalls and booths, races, and even bull-baiting.

Until the 1960s the Thames was still busy with coalbarges, and cranes still bent over riverside wharves in the heart of the capital. Then, almost in the blink of an eye, it was over. The river's work evaporated, the docks closed (*see* DOCKLAND) and the Thames became, it seemed, the forgotten river, little more than an obstacle to be traversed in getting from one side to the other. Londoners appeared to have averted their eyes from their river: certainly, sporadic attempts to set up river-based transport links met with tepid support. Yet the sinuous looping Thames remains central to the idea of London – unmistakable alike to those who fly along its course on their way to Heathrow and to those who see it in the opening and closing credits of the BBC television soap *EastEnders*. So iconic is it that it has been used as the capital's logo.

Downstream of GRAVESEND the river begins to broaden out into its third great phase, the Thames Estuary. By the time it reaches its official end, at the Nore (where it is joined by the Medway), it is about 8 km (5 miles) wide, and there are 1.5-km (1-mile) wide sandbanks on either shore. To seaward of this it flares out further still, and the distance been the two extremities of FOULNESS in Essex and the NORTH FORELAND in Kent is no less than 40 km (25 miles). Down this funnel, with its treacherous sandbanks and mazy creeks, have come generations of traders and would-be invaders (the Dutch fleet continually harried the English here during the Anglo-Dutch wars of the 17th century, for instance).

> Thames, the most loved of all the Ocean's sons,
> By his old sire, to his embraces runs,
> Hasting to pay his tribute to the Sea,
> Like mortal life to meet eternity.
>
> John Denham: 'Cooper's Hill' (1642)

> Sweet Thames, run softly, till I end my song.
>
> Edmund Spenser: *Prothalamion* (1596) (The line is quoted, darkly, by T.S. Eliot in *The Waste Land* (1922).)

> Deep with the first dead lies London's daughter,
> Robed in the long friends,
> The grains beyond age, the dark veins of her mother,
> Secret by the unmourning water

Of the riding Thames.
After the first death, there is no other.

> Dylan Thomas: 'A Refusal to Mourn the Death, by Fire, of a
> Child in London' (1946)

There is a Thames (pronounced 'thaimes') River in Connecticut, USA, which flows through New London. There is also a river called Thames, and towns called Thamesford and Thamesville, in Ontario, Canada. There is also a town called Thames in the North Island of New Zealand, overlooking a wide gulf called the Firth of Thames.

Estuary English. A type of English accent identified as spreading out from London to the southeast of England, the area of the Thames Estuary, and containing a blend of received (standard) pronunciation and that of Cockney or London speech (*see under* LONDON). The term was coined in 1984 by the linguist David Rosewarne. The accent is regarded as typical of a (supposedly) increasing classless society, and observers have claimed to find traces of it as far afield as Glasgow.

> In contrast with Eliza Doolittle, who has to re-engineer her accent to become socially acceptable, the prime minister [Tony Blair] descended into estuary English in an attempt to reach out to the masses.
>
> *Sunday Times* (7 June 1998)

Father Thames. A male personification of the River Thames, which has become its modern quasi-tutelary deity. He appears in the works of Dryden and Pope and their contemporary Matthew Green, but was chiefly popularized by Thomas Gray, who apostrophizes him in his *Ode on a Distant Prospect of Eton College* (1747):

> Say, Father Thames, for thou hast seen
> Full many a sprightly race
> Disporting on thy margent green
> The paths of pleasure trace,
> Who foremost now delight to cleave
> With pliant arm thy glassy wave?

He appears in less fragrant guise in periodicals of the mid-19th century, the time of the Great Stink (1858), when the Thames was more sewer than river: a famous cartoon in *Punch* (21 July 1855), entitled 'Faraday giving his card to Father Thames', portrays the noisome old man arising slimily from the depths with an old kettle atop his trident.

> High in the hills, down in the dales,
>   Happy and fancy free,
> Old Father Thames keeps rolling along,
>   Down to the mighty sea. ...
>
> Kingdoms may come, kingdoms may go,
>   Whatever the end may be,
> Old Father Thames keeps rolling along,
>   Down to the mighty sea.
>
> R. Wallace and B. O'Hogan: 'Old Father Thames Keeps
> Rolling Along' (1933)

set the Thames on fire. To do something remarkable or distinctive. The expression, which dates from at least the 18th century, is usually used in the negative, implying a lack of any outstanding qualities or potential. There are parallel usages in other European countries (e.g. *den Rhein anzünden* 'to set the Rhine on fire'), which are enough to scotch the rather flaky theory, first advanced in 1865, that *Thames* in this context is a pun on *temse* 'corn sieve'.

> His second novel was successful, but not so successful as to arouse the umbrageous susceptibilities of his competitors. In fact it confirmed them in their suspicions that he would never set the Thames on fire.
>
> Somerset Maugham: *Cakes and Ale* (1930)

The phrase has occasionally been taken more literally, though: at a friend's stag party the writer Robert Byron poured 20 gallons of petrol on to the river and ended up setting fire to the party hotel.

'Song of the River Thames'. A song from John Dryden's opera libretto *Albion and Albanius* (1685).

> Old Father Ocean calls my Tyde:
> Come away, come away;
> The Barks upon the Billows ride,
> The Master will not stay ...

Sweet Thames. A novel (1992) by Matthew Kneale set in London in 1849 against the backdrop of the threat of a cholera epidemic, concerning the efforts of a civil engineer to improve the sewerage system. Its name is an ironic allusion to Edmund Spenser's characterization of the river (*see above*).

Thames & Hudson. A publishing house famous for its art books. It was founded in 1949 with offices in London and New York and it initially hoped to attract an English-speaking readership on both sides of the Atlantic: hence its name, from the rivers Thames and Hudson, on which London and New York respectively stand. The origin is also pictorially represented in its colophon of two dolphins, the upper one facing left or west, the lower right or east.

Thames barge. A type of round-bowed, flat-bottomed, massively strong sailing barge used on the River Thames in the 19th and early 20th centuries. Its most distinctive rig is a 'spritsail', a huge tarred canvas mainsail stretched diagonally by a spar. Thames barges are still kept and sailed recreationally by enthusiasts.

Thames Barrier. A movable barrier across the River Thames at WOOLWICH that forms part of London's flood defences. Completed in 1982, it consists of six massive flood-gates that can be raised when dangerously high tides are expected. The piers to which these are fixed are roofed with helmet-like metal shells, which give the Barrier its distinctive appearance.

Thames butter. Late 19th-century slang for totally rancid butter. The term seems to have arisen out of a garbled contemporary press report to the effect that a French chemist was making butter out of Thames mud at BATTERSEA. In fact he was extracting yellow grease from Thames mud-worms.

Thames Conservancy. A body set up by Act of Parliament in 1857 to be responsible for all aspects of the administration and control of the River Thames. It replaced the former Thames Commissioners. Powers relating to the tidal part of the river (downstream of Teddington) passed in 1909 to the Port of London Authority (*see under* LONDON), and its jurisdiction over the rest of the river was transferred in 1974 to the **Thames Water Authority.**

Thames Gateway. The region on the banks of the Thames downstream of London, from Tower Bridge (*see under* TOWER OF LONDON) eastwards to THURROCK and DARTFORD, designated as ripe for regeneration. Its powerhouse and exemplar is the DOCKLAND redevelopment, its grail the 2012 Olympic Games, for which STRATFORD is earmarked. A Thames Gateway Bridge is planned, linking BECKTON with THAMESMEAD.

Thames House. The headquarters since 1995 of MI5, situated on MILLBANK, near the Houses of Parliament. The building was originally owned by ICI, the chemical and paint manufacturer. The building is nowhere near as flamboyant as that of MI5's sister service, MI6 (*see under* VAUXHALL).

Thameslink. A railway service linking BEDFORD and BRIGHTON via London. It was started in 1989 following the reopening of the Snow Hill Tunnel beneath central London. Expansion of the service in the early 21st century is planned under the title **Thameslink 2000.**

Thames Path. A National Trail that runs alongside the Thames from its source to the **Thames Barrier** (*see above*), a distance of about 288 km (180 miles).

Thames Television. A television company that between 1968 and 1991 held the ITV weekday franchise for the London region. Amongst its biggest hits were *This Week*, *The Sweeney* and *Minder*. Its studios were at TEDDINGTON.

Thames Trains. A railway company that, until it lost its franchise in 2003, ran trains from the Thames Valley into PADDINGTON.

Thames Tunnel. A tunnel beneath the River Thames linking ROTHERHITHE with WAPPING. It was the first underwater tunnel in the world. Plans for it were produced at the beginning of the 19th century, but work did not get under way until the mid-1820s, under the direction of Marc Isambard Brunel. There were many delays due to flooding, and work was suspended altogether between 1828 and 1835 when the money ran out, but it was finally finished in 1843. At first it was used only by pedestrians, but in the 1860s it was converted into a railway tunnel. It now carries the East London line (*see under* EAST LONDON).

Thames[2] From THAMES[1].

A shipping-forecast area covering the southernmost part of the NORTH SEA, approximately as far north as northern Norfolk.

Thames Ditton *Thames see* THAMES[1]; *Ditton* 'farmstead by a ditch' (referring to a local drainage ditch), OE *dic* 'ditch' + -TON.

A small town in Surrey, on the south bank of the River THAMES[1], opposite HAMPTON COURT.

> There was an old man of Thames Ditton,
> Who called for something to sit on;
> But they bought him a hat,
> And said – 'Sit upon that,
> You abruptious old man of Thames Ditton!'
>
> Edward Lear: *More Nonsense, Pictures, Rhymes, Botany, Etc.* (1872)

Thamesdown A 20th-century coinage, incorporating the names of the area's northern and southern boundaries.

A former local-government district of northern Wiltshire, incorporating SWINDON and adjacent areas. It was bounded to the north by the River THAMES[1], and to the south by the line of the Marlborough Downs (*see under* MARLBOROUGH). In 1997 it was transformed into the unitary authority of Swindon.

Thameshaven A late 19th-century coinage, from THAMES[1] + ModE *haven* 'harbour'.

An industrial area adjacent to CORYTON[2] in Essex, within the unitary authority of THURROCK, on the north bank of the Thames estuary. It originated in the 1880s as a dock for the importation and handling of oil, and now its main business is oil storage.

Thamesmead A 20th-century coinage, from THAMES[1] + ModE *mead* 'meadow'.

A new town in southeast London (SE28), on the south bank of the River THAMES[1], spanning the boroughs of BEXLEY and GREENWICH, to the northeast of Plumstead. It was built between 1967 and the mid-1970s on reclaimed marshland. Several of its roads and buildings commemorate socialist heroes: Tawney Road, Titmuss Avenue, Raymond Postgate Court, Harold Wilson House and so on.

Thames Valley. The broad, low-lying valley of the River THAMES[1] to the northwest of London, particularly that part of it in Berkshire and Oxfordshire. It contains several large centres of population, notably HENLEY-ON-THAMES, MAIDENHEAD, OXFORD, READING and SLOUGH, but in between the river still winds its way through some unspoilt stretches of gentle countryside. This hinterland is home to innumerable members of the 4x4-owning classes. The landscapes where the southern CHILTERN HILLS meet the Thames are rather fine, especially as walking country, and are enhanced by the occasional stately pile nestling in the gentle folds of beech-clad hills.

Thames Valley Police Force (most famous fictional detective, Inspector Morse) covers Oxfordshire, Buckinghamshire and Berkshire. It has its headquarters in Kidlington, just north of Oxford.

Thames Valley Royals. A football club controversially proposed in 1983 by the crooked tycoon Robert Maxwell as a merged replacement for Oxford United and Reading FC. Opposition from Oxford United fans and Reading's chairman soon scuppered Maxwell's grand idea.

Thames Valley University. A university created in 1992 out of West London Polytechnic. It is sited in EALING. In the late 1990s it was branded in the press 'Britain's worst university'.

Thanet. *See* ISLE OF THANET.

Thankful villages. Those villages in England where all the men who went off to fight in the First World War came back alive. Arthur Mee, in his book *The Enchanted Land* (1936), lists 23 such villages, but more have since come to light. An expanded list (possibly not definitive) is given below, with the numbers of men involved:

> Bedfordshire: Stanbridge (33)
> Cambridgeshire: Knapwell (23)
> Derbyshire: Bradbourne (18)
> Gloucestershire: Brierley (14), Coln Rogers (25), Little
>   Sodbury (6), Upper Slaughter (44)
> Hertfordshire: Puttenham (15)
> Kent: Knowlton (12)
> Lancashire: Arkholme (59)
> Leicestershire: Saxby (unknown), Willesley (3)
> Lincolnshire: Bigby (10), High Toynton (14)
> Northamptonshire: Woodend (19)
> Nottinghamshire: Maplebeck (2), Wigsley (7),
>   Wysall (17)
> Norfolk: Ovington (14)
> Rutland: Teigh (11)
> Somerset: Aisholt (8), Chantry (not known), Chelwood
>   (4), Ilketshall St John (not known), Priddy (not
>   known), Rodney Stoke (17), Stanton Prior (4),
>   Stocklinch (19), Tellisford (3), Woolley (13)
> Suffolk: South Elmham (11)
> Wiltshire: Littleton Drew (22)
> Yorkshire: Catwick (20), Cayton (43; also a thankful
>   village after the Second World War), Cundall (12),
>   Norton-le-Clay (16)

Although SOMERSET had a somewhat disproportionate number of thankful villages (perhaps because many of the local units were posted to places such as India, out of the way of the fighting), Chris Howell's book *No Thankful Village* (2002) recounts the horrors that affected the men from the rural and mining communities between Bath and Wells, where there were no thankful villages.

Thatcham 'thatched homestead' or 'river-meadow where thatching materials are obtained', OE *þæc* 'thatch' + *ham* 'homestead' or *hamm* 'river-meadow' (*see* HAM).

A village in West Berkshire, on the A4 and the River KENNET[1], about 3 km (2 miles) east of Newbury.

Thaxted 'place where thatching materials are obtained', OE *þæc* 'thatch' + *stede* 'place'.

A small town in Essex, on the River CHELMER, about 11 km (7 miles) southeast of Saffron Walden. In the Middle Ages it prospered first as a manufacturer of cutlery and later as a centre of the cloth trade. Part of the proceeds went on a fine three-storeyed half-timbered guildhall, dating from the 15th century, and on the huge church of St John the Baptist, of similar date, whose 54-m (181-foot) tower and spire dominates the surrounding countryside.

In the 20th century the church was a hotbed of Anglo-Catholicism thanks to the energy and enthusiasm of the vicar, Conrad Noel. The composer Gustav Holst was organist for 12 years, and during his time there wrote some portions of *The Planets* (the broad tune in 'Jupiter', to which 'I Vow to Thee, My Country' was later set, is named 'Thaxted'). He also initiated the Thaxted music festival, which is still held every summer.

Another dominant feature of the Thaxted skyline is a tower windmill, built in 1804 by a local landowner and farmer, John Webb. Until 2000 it was open to the public as an example of a working mill.

The travel writer and anthologist Samuel Purchas (?1577–1626) was born in Thaxted.

Theale[1] 'planks' (referring to a bridge or building), OE *þelu* plural form of *þel* 'plank'.

A village in Berkshire, on the River KENNET[1], about 8 km (5 miles) west of Reading. It is on the A4, and in coaching days was a staging point on the London-to-Bath road.

Its church is virtually a 19th-century scale model of Salisbury Cathedral (*see under* SALISBURY), paid for by a local benefactress called Mrs Sophia Sheppard.

Theale[2] The planks (*see* THEALE[1]) referred to here were probably a plank-path across the local marshes.

A village in Somerset, 10 km (6 miles) west of Wells.

Theatreland. A term, first recorded at the beginning of the 20th century, for the district of a city where its theatres are concentrated, applied in Britain particularly to a segment of the WEST END[1] of London fanning eastwards from SHAFTESBURY AVENUE across LEICESTER SQUARE to Charing Cross Road (*see under* CHARING CROSS) and St Martin's Lane.

Theatre of Dreams. *See under* OLD TRAFFORD.

Theberton 'Theodbeorht's farmstead or village', OE male personal name *Theodbeorht* + -TON.

A village (pronounced 'thebbertən') in Suffolk, about 6 km (4 miles) northeast of Saxmundham. Charles Doughty (1843–1926), author of *Travels in Arabia Deserta* (1888), was born in Theberton Hall.

Theddingworth Probably 'Theoda's people's enclosure', OE male personal name *Theoda* + -*inga*- (*see* -ING) + *worth* (*see* -WORTH, WORTHY, -WARDINE).

A village in Leicestershire, about 8 km (5 miles) west of Market Harborough.

Theddlethorpe 'Theodlac's outlying farmstead or hamlet', OE male personal name *Theodlac* + THORPE.

Either of a pair of villages (**Theddlethorpe All Saints** and **Theddlethorpe St Helen**, distinguished by the dedication of their respective churches; pronounced locally 'thelthrəp') in Lincolnshire, close to the coast, about 8 km (5 miles) northwest of MABLETHORPE.

Thelnetham Perhaps 'river-meadow frequented by swans near a plank bridge', OE *thel* 'plank' + *elfitu* 'swan' + *hamm* 'river-meadow' (*see* HAM).

A village (pronounced 'thel-neethəm') in Suffolk, on the LITTLE OUSE, about 11 km (7 miles) west of Diss.

Themelthorpe Perhaps 'Thymel's or Thymill's outlying farmstead or hamlet', OE male personal name *Thymel* or OScand male personal name *Thymill* + THORPE; alternatively the first element could be from OE *thymel* 'thimble', referring metaphorically to the small size of the settlement.

A village in Norfolk, about 24 km (15 miles) northwest of Norwich.

Theobald's Park From the 16th-century *Theobald's* Palace (now demolished), where James VI and I lived for a time and died in 1625.

An estate in Hertfordshire, about 3 km (2 miles) southwest of Cheshunt. London's Temple Bar (*see under* TEMPLE) was removed from its original location in 1878, and re-erected at the entrance to the park (at the beginning of the 21st century it was returned to London).

The nearby mainline railway station is **Theobalds Grove**.

These Islands. A term coined by Irish Nationalists to replace the (to them) offensively hegemonic expression BRITISH ISLES. The term is widely used in Ireland, but its use would be confusing when employed by, for example, Irish-Americans in New York.

> I believe that by good fortune, hard work, natural talent and rich diversity, these islands are home to a great people …
>
> Michael Howard: New Year message (2004)

Was the leader of the British Conservatives giving a coded message to the many Unionists within his own party? Or was it a case of straightforward ignorance?
See also Hibernian Archipelago *under* HIBERNIA.

Thet A back-formation from THETFORD.

A river in Norfolk, which rises to the south of ATTLE-BOROUGH and flows 30 km (19 miles) southwestwards to THETFORD, where it joins the LITTLE OUSE.

Thetford 'people's or public ford' (referring to a ford across the Little Ouse), OE *theod* 'people' + FORD.

A small market town in Norfolk, in the BRECKLAND, at the confluence of the River THET and the LITTLE OUSE, about 21 km (13 miles) north of Bury St Edmunds. It has a long and distinguished history, but a comparatively low-key present. It stands on the ICKNIELD WAY, and there is evidence of Iron Age occupation; it was the capital of East Anglia under the Danes in the 9th century; and in the Middle Ages it was the cathedral city of East Anglia. By the 14th century there were no fewer than 20 churches in the town, and at least four monastic houses. However, the Dissolution of the Monasteries ripped the heart out of it, and little of great moment has happened here since. It tried to become a spa in the early 19th century, with conspicuous lack of success.

The writer and political theorist Thomas Paine (1737–1809), author of *The Rights of Man* (1791–2), was born in Thetford.

The external scenes for the BBC television sitcom *Dad's Army* (1968–77) were filmed in and around Thetford. (*See also* WALMINGTON-ON-SEA.)

There is a town called Thetford in the USA (Vermont).

Thetford Forest. A 32,400 ha (80,000 acre) forest (also known as **Thetford Chase**) planted immediately to the west of Thetford in the years after the First World War. It is the second largest in England. Much of it, to the southwest, is in Suffolk. It was for the most part planted in mind-numbingly straight rows, but the Forestry Commission is now endeavouring to introduce some notes of irregularity. It is now designated **Thetford Forest Park**. GRIMES GRAVES are situated in the northern part.

Thetford ware. A type of pottery made in Thetford and elsewhere in the early Middle Ages.

Theydon Bois *Theydon* probably 'valley where thatching materials are obtained', OE *thæc* 'thatch' + *denu* 'valley' (*see also* DOWN, -DON); *Bois* denoting manorial ownership in the Middle Ages by the de Bosco or de Bois family. There is no direct link with Fr *bois* 'wood', despite the presence nearby of Epping Forest.

A village (the *Th*- is as in 'thing'; *Bois* is 'boyz') in Essex, at the northeastern corner of Epping Forest (*see under* EPPING) and about 5 km (3 miles) northeast of Loughton. Theydon Bois 'Underground' station, on the Central line, opened in 1949.

Thiefrow. A rhyming nickname (first recorded in 1973) for London's HEATHROW Airport, from its former reputation for lax security and lost or purloined luggage. In the two years up to April 2003 there were 146 serious robberies at the airport, with a total haul of £74 million.

Thimbleby 'Thymill's or Thymli's farmstead or village', OScand male personal name *Thymill* or *Thymli* + -BY.

A village in Lincolnshire, about 1.5 km (1 mile) west of Horncastle. It is remarkable for the unique survival of three 16th-century so-called 'mud-and-stud' cottages, their walls made of posts and laths filled in with mud.

Thirlmere 'hole lake', OE *thyrel* 'hole' (referring to the manner in which the lake pierces the mountain terrain) + *mere* 'lake'.

A lake in the LAKE DISTRICT, Cumbria (formerly in Cumberland), on the west side of HELVELLYN, some 6 km (4 miles) southeast of Keswick. It was enlarged in 1894 to provide water for Manchester, and in the process drowned the village of Armboth and most of the village of Wythburn.

See also ROCK OF NAMES.

Thirsk OScand *thresk* 'marsh'.

A market town in North Yorkshire, 13 km (8 miles) south of Northallerton. It merges with SOWERBY to the south. There is a racecourse here. James Herriot, author of *All Creatures Great and Small* (1972), began his career as a vet in Thirsk.

Thirty-Two Counties. The whole of the island of Ireland, comprising the SIX COUNTIES of Northern Ireland and the TWENTY-SIX COUNTIES of the Republic. The term is mostly used by Republicans who do not accept the 1921 Partition, and provides a title for a popular Republican song, beginning:

> Here's to Donegal and her people brave and tall,
> Here's to Antrim, to Leitrim and to Derry,
> Here's to Cavan and to Louth, here's to Carlow in the
>   South,
> Here's to Longford, to Waterford and Kerry.

The song proceeds to enumerate and celebrate the remaining 22 counties.

Thirty-Two County Sovereignty Committee. A Republican organization critical of the Good Friday Agreement of 1998, and the revisions subsequently made to the Constitution of the Republic. It is sometimes abbreviated to **32CSC**, and is said to have links with the Real IRA, although both bodies deny this.

Thistleton 'farmstead or village where thistles grow', OE *thistel* 'thistle' + -TON.

A village in Rutland (before 1997 in Leicestershire, before 1974 in Rutland), about 11 km (7 miles) northeast of Oakham.

Thistley Green From the prickly nature of the village green.

A village in Suffolk, about 5 km (3 miles) northwest of Mildenhall.

Tholomas Drove 'Tholymer's cattle-road', ME surname *Tholymer* (known in the area from the 13th century), with *drove* 'road for driving cattle'.

A village in Cambridgeshire, in the FENS, about 8 km (5 miles) southwest of Wisbech.

Thomond Irish *Tuadh Mumhan* 'north Munster'.

An ancient kingdom of northern MUNSTER, covering what is now County CLARE, two-thirds of County TIPPERARY, most of County LIMERICK and the very north of KERRY. Up to the 12th century, the rulers of Thomond (the Dál gCais) and neighbouring DESMOND ('south Munster') took it in turns to be kings of Munster. The O'Briens became kings of Thomond in the 13th century, at a time when the kingdom was being encroached upon in the east by the Anglo-Norman Butlers, whose territory became known as ORMOND ('east Munster'). The O'Briens' kingdom of Thomond was gradually reduced to what is now County Clare, and in 1543, having submitted to the English Crown, the O'Briens became Earls of Thomond. Thomond still has its own identity, and **Thomond Park** in Limerick is home to Munster's rugby union team.

Bard of Thomond, the. The title given himself by the poet and wheelwright Michael Hogan (1832–99). His verse, much of it collected in *Lays and Legends of Thomond* (1865), is admired by some and derided by others. Here is an extract from 'The Grave of Sean Buidh MacNamara':

> Behold yon gray moss-covered stone
> Where Thomond's maids shed drops of sorrow
> There sleeps Sean Budh – cold, low and lone,
> The great and glorious MacNamara
> The heart and nerve that never shook
> The hand that left no mark unstruck.

Thompson 'Tumi's farmstead or village', OScand *Tumis* possessive form of male personal name *Tumi* + -TON.

A village in Norfolk, about 16 km (10 miles) northeast of Thetford.

Thong 'narrow strip of land', OE *thwang*.

A village in Kent, about 3 km (2 miles) southeast of Gravesend, close to the A2.

See also NETHERTHONG.

Thoor Ballylee 'the tower of Ballylee', from Yeats's phonetic rendering of Irish *túr*, referring to the tower of *Ballylee* Castle.

The name that the poet W.B. Yeats gave to a ruined 16th-century castle keep, near GORT in Galway. He bought the building in 1917 for £35 and restored it as a summer home, having the following lines inscribed on a tablet:

I, the poet William Yeats,

With old mill-boards and sea-green slates,

And smithy work from the Gort forge,

Restored this tower for my wife George;

And may these characters remain

When all is ruin once again.

In the title poem of *The Tower* (1928), which was mostly written here, Yeats climbs to the top of Thoor Ballylee to survey the landscape of a traditional, heroic way of life, now gone:

I pace the battlements and stare

On the foundations of a house …

And send imagination forth

Under the day's declining beam …

The Tower becomes an important symbol in several of Yeats's later poems, for example in Part II of 'Meditations in Time of Civil War':

An ancient bridge, and a more ancient tower.

A winding stair, a chamber arched with stone,

A grey stone fireplace with an open hearth,

A candle and written page.

In 1922, during the Civil War, the IRA blew up the bridge beside Thoor Ballylee, and the rubble damming the River Cloon caused a flood in the ground floor. The winding stair appears again in *The Winding Stair and Other Poems* (1933).

Yeats abandoned Thoor Ballylee in 1929, and it fell into disrepair until it was renovated as a Yeats Museum in 1965.

Thornaby-on-Tees 'Thormothr's farm', OScand male personal name *Thormothr* + -BY.

A town in Stockton-on-Tees unitary authority (formerly in Yorkshire), 5 km (3 miles) southwest of Middlesbrough.

Thornbury 'fortified place where thorn-trees grow', OE *thorn* + *byrig* dative form of *burh* (*see* BURY).

A small town in South Gloucestershire (until 1996 in Avon, until 1974 in Gloucestershire), in the Vale of Berkeley (*see under* BERKELEY), about 5 km (3 miles) east of the River SEVERN and about 17 km (11 miles) north of Bristol. The administrative headquarters of SOUTH GLOUCESTERSHIRE are located here. Its 16th-century church is a landmark for many miles around.

The cricketer W.G. Grace (1848–1915) lived in Thornbury as a boy.

Thorne OE *thorn* 'thorn-tree'.

A market town in South Yorkshire, 16 km (10 miles) northeast of Doncaster. Northeast of the town **Thorne Waste** (or **Thorne Moors**) has been heavily damaged by peat extraction. Thorne's colliery was closed in 1956, since when there have been intermittent plans to revive it.

Thorney 'thorn-tree island' (referring to a raised area of land in a fen), OE *thorn* + *eg* (*see* -EY, -EA).

A village within the unitary authority of Peterborough (before 1998 in Cambridgeshire, before 1974 in Huntingdonshire), in the BEDFORD LEVEL, about 10 km (6 miles) northeast of Peterborough. The most northerly of the Fenland islands, it was one of the last redoubts of Hereward the Wake in his rearguard fight against the invading Normans in the 1070s.

Thorney Island[1] From the village of *Thorney* (now West Thorney), on the east coast of the island; *Island* is tautonymous.

An island in CHICHESTER Harbour, in West Sussex.

Thorney Island[2] *Thorney see* THORNEY.

A former area of low-lying marshy land on the north bank of the River THAMES[1], where Westminster Abbey now stands. It appears to have been characterized as an 'island' on account of the ditches that surrounded and defined it, but its precise outline is no longer clear. It was an open, desolate area in Anglo-Saxon times (it is described in an 8th-century charter as *loco terribili* 'at the terrible place'), but after the 1060s, when Edward the Confessor re-established the abbey here and built himself a royal palace, it was gradually reclaimed and it came to be filled with smallholdings and market-gardens. There were still open fields here in the 18th century, but since then the buildings of Westminster have obliterated all trace of Thorney Island.

Thornfalcon Originally *Thorn* '(place at the) thorn-tree', OE; the suffix *-falcon* denotes manorial ownership in the Middle Ages by the Fagun family.

A village in Somerset, about 5 km (3 miles) east of Taunton.

Thorngumbald OE *thorn* 'thorn-tree', with the affix denoting manorial ownership in the Middle Ages by the Gumbaud family.

A village in the East Riding of Yorkshire, 12 km (7 miles) east of Hull.

Thornhill 'thorn hill', ME *thorn* + *hill*.

A town 22 km (14 miles) north of Dumfries, formerly in Dumfriesshire and now in Dumfries and Galloway. Kirkpatrick Macmillan (1813–78), the blacksmith who invented the bicycle in 1839, was born near the town.

Thornton[1] 'farm with a thorn-tree', OE *thorn* 'thorn-tree' + -TON.

A town in Lancashire, 6 km (4 miles) northeast of Blackpool. It now forms part of the town of Thornton CLEVELEYS.

Thornton[2]. A western suburb of BRADFORD, West Yorkshire. It was the birthplace of the Brontë sisters.

Thornton Heath. An outer southern commuter suburb of London (before 1965 in Surrey), in the borough of

CROYDON, to the southeast of Streatham. The heath from which it got its name was between Croydon and Streatham. The road across it was infested with highwaymen in the 17th and 18th centuries, and Dick Turpin is said to have operated here. A tiny vestige of the heath survives in Grangewood Park.

The railway arrived in the 1860s, but it was electrification of the line at the turn of the 20th century that transformed a still relatively rural area into a built-up suburb.

Thornton Hough *Hough* denoting manorial ownership in the Middle Ages by the del Hogh family.
A village (pronounced 'huff') on the WIRRAL, in Merseyside (before 1974 in Cheshire), about 3 km (2 miles) southeast of Heswall. Its present-day form, embellished by half-timbering, is the work of Lord Leverhulme, progenitor of PORT SUNLIGHT, who turned it into an estate village.

Thoroughbred County. A nickname for horsey County KILDARE, home of the national stud, and also known for its many training establishments and racing at the CURRAGH. The name is of relatively recent coinage, and the county has adopted a horse as its official symbol.

Thorpe 'outlying farmstead or hamlet, dependent secondary settlement', OScand *thorp* (*see* THORPE), or perhaps OE *throp*.
A village in Surrey, close to the intersection of the M3 and the M25, about 3 km (2 miles) south of Egham.

Thorpe Park. A theme park sited in an old gravel pit to the east of Thorpe. The accent is on water-based amusements.

Thorpe Arnold *Thorpe* 'outlying farmstead or hamlet, dependent secondary settlement', OScand *thorp* (*see* THORPE); *Arnold* denoting manorial ownership in the Middle Ages by a man called Ernald.
A village in Leicestershire, about 1.5 km (1 mile) northeast of Melton Mowbray.

Thorpe Bay *Thorpe see* THORPE.

❖ **thorpe** ❖

There are literally hundreds of English place names containing the Old Scandinavian element *thorp*. They occur predictably in the northern and eastern regions where the Scandinavian settlement and influence was most concentrated, but THORPE (Surrey) seems also to derive from this element, having only one early spelling that might indicate that the name came from the cognate Old English word *throp*. The word refers to a settlement dependent on a larger and more significant one, and even now most of the Thorpes are minor and outlying settlements.

A seaside resort in Essex, on the Thames Estuary, now an eastern suburb of SOUTHEND-ON-SEA.

Thorpe Constantine *Thorpe see* THORPE ARNOLD; *Constantine* denoting manorial ownership in the Middle Ages by the de Costentin family.
A village in Staffordshire, about 14 km (9 miles) east of Lichfield.

Thorpe Culvert *Thorpe see* THORPE ARNOLD; *Culvert* perhaps referring to a drainage channel.
A village in Lincolnshire, in the FENS, on the STEEPING River, about 11 km (7 miles) southeast of Skegness.

Thorpe Fendykes *Thorpe see* THORPE ARNOLD; *Fendykes* referring to a 17th-century drainage channel, ModE *fen* + *dyke*.
A village in Lincolnshire, about 1.5 km (1 mile) west of THORPE CULVERT.

Thorpe Langton *Thorpe see* THORPE ARNOLD; *Langton see* LANGTON HERRING.
A village in Leicestershire, one of the LANGTONS, about 5 km (3 miles) north of Market Harborough.

Thorpe le Fallows *Thorpe see* THORPE ARNOLD; *le Fallows* 'in the arable land', OFr definite article, short for *en le* 'in the' + OE *falh* 'ploughed land'.
A village in Lincolnshire, about 13 km (8 miles) northwest of Lincoln.

Thorpe-le-Soken *Thorpe see* THORPE; *-le-Soken* 'in the administrative district', OFr definite article *le* + OE *socn* 'district with special jurisdiction, soke'.
A village in Essex, about 8 km (5 miles) west of Walton-on-the-Naze.

Thorpe Malsor *Thorpe see* THORPE ARNOLD; *Malsor* denoting manorial ownership in the Middle Ages by the Malesoures family.
A village in Northamptonshire, about 3 km (2 miles) west of Kettering.

Thorpe Morieux *Thorpe see* THORPE ARNOLD; *Morieux* denoting manorial ownership in the Middle Ages by the Morieux family.
A village in Suffolk, about 16 km (10 miles) southeast of Bury St Edmunds.

Thorpeness From a local headland called *Thorpe Ness*, which itself got its name from the village of *Thorpe* (*see* THORPE ARNOLD).
A holiday village on the Suffolk coast, about 3 km (2 miles) north of Aldeburgh. It was constructed in the second and third decades of the 20th century.

Thorpe Satchville *Thorpe see* THORPE ARNOLD; *Satchville* denoting manorial ownership in the Middle Ages by the Sacheville family.

A village in Leicestershire, about 16 km (10) miles northeast of Leicester.

Thorpe Waterville *Thorpe see* THORPE ARNOLD; *Waterville* denoting manorial ownership in the Middle Ages by the Waterville family.

A village in Northamptonshire, about 16 km (10 miles) east of Kettering.

Thor's Cave Probably an example of the habit of attributing spectacular features to ancient gods.

A spectacular cavern perched on a hillside in the MANI-FOLD Valley in Staffordshire; the huge cave mouth, set in a great fang of limestone, can be seen from far away. The cave was inhabited from some 10,000 years ago until the Dark Ages, and more recently featured in Ken Russell's outrageously kitsch 1988 film adaptation of Bram Stoker's *The Lair of the White Worm* as the eponymous lair.

Threadneedle Street Probably from the thread and needle that appear in the coat of arms of the Merchant Taylors' Company, whose guildhall has been in the street since the 14th century.

A street in the City of London (EC2), connecting the junction at BANK with BISHOPSGATE to the east. The Bank of England has occupied much of the northern side of the street since 1734. Its present building, designed by Sir John Soane, with its massive windowless walls jealously guarding England's wealth, was begun in 1788. The first £5 note was issued from here in 1793.

The playwright and MP Richard Brinsley Sheridan, speaking in the House of Commons in 1797, made a somewhat coy allusion to 'an elderly lady in the City of great credit and long standing', meaning the Bank. The image struck a chord: there is a caricature by James Gillray, dated 22 May of the same year, depicting the Bank as an old lady with a dress made of paper money, seated firmly on the Bank's gold and ignoring the advances of the then prime minister, William Pitt the Younger. It was entitled *Political Ravishment: or the Old Lady of Threadneedle Street in Danger*, and it referred to Pitt's instruction that the Bank should not redeem its notes in gold and that it should issue £1 notes instead. Ever since the Bank of England has been known, more or less affectionately, as the **Old Lady of Threadneedle Street**.

The Royal Exchange (originally a stock exchange but now offices) is on the south side of Threadneedle Street. Its steps are one of the places from which a new sovereign is proclaimed.

Threapwood 'disputed wood' (alluding to its border position, which in the past placed it beyond normal jurisdiction and made it subject to claim and counter-claim), OE *threap* 'dispute, quarrel' + *wudu* 'wood'.

A village in Cheshire, on the Welsh border, about 24 km (15 miles) southwest of Nantwich.

Threave Castle Gaelic *treabh* 'farm, settlement'.

A castle on an island in the River DEE[3] in Dumfries and Galloway, just south of CASTLE DOUGLAS. It was built *c*.1370 by one of Scotland's most powerful nobles, Archibald the Grim, 3rd Earl of Douglas. It was taken by the Crown in 1455. In 1639 it was held by the hereditary keeper, the Earl of Nithsdale, against a siege by the Covenanters, until Charles I authorized him to surrender. The castle was subsequently dismantled, and is now in the care of Historic Scotland. Nearby **Threave Garden** has the National Trust for Scotland's school of practical gardening.

Three Bridges From three bridges crossing the River MOLE[1], which rises at Crawley.

A village in West Sussex, now a northeastern suburb of CRAWLEY. Its name dates back to the 16th century, but the settlement did not begin to develop until the middle of the 19th century, after the railway arrived in 1841 and a station was opened here (this is effectively now the station for Crawley on the London-to-Brighton line and is also an important junction).

> There was an old man of Three Bridges,
> Whose mind was distracted by midges,
> He sate on a wheel,
> Eating underdone veal,
> Which relieved that old man of Three Bridges.
>
> Edward Lear: *More Nonsense, Pictures, Rhymes, Botany Etc.* (1872)

Three Chimneys From a building here with three chimneys (the alternative explanation illustrated on the sign of a local pub with the same name – showing a French officer of the Napoleonic era looking at a three-armed signpost and musing on the *trois chemins* 'three ways' open to him – is a fine example of popular etymology).

A village in the WEALD of Kent, about 8 km (5 miles) northwest of Tenterden.

Three Cliffs Bay. *See under* OXWICH.

Three Cocks Named after a hotel, which took the emblem from the arms of the Williams family of Gwernyfed.

A village in Powys (formerly in Brecknockshire), 8 km (5 miles) southwest of Hay-on-Wye.

Three Cups Corner Perhaps referring to a place of refreshment, possibly a pub.

A village in East Sussex, about 18 km (11 miles) east of Uckfield.

Three Holes Referring to a local bridge with three arches.

A village in Cambridgeshire, in the FENS, about 11 km (7 miles) southeast of Wisbech.

Threekingham 'homestead of the Tricingas tribe', *Tricingas* an ancient tribal name of unknown origin + HAM (the extra *e* in the modern name is a popular *jeu d'esprit* with vaguely Yuletide overtones).

A village (pronounced 'threckingəm') in Lincolnshire, about 17 km (11 miles) east of Grantham.

Three Legged Cross[1] Origin uncertain. There are various possibilities, the most plausible (a three-way road junction) being also the least interesting; others include a gallows (also known popularly as a 'three-legged mare') and an elevated tripod with a cross on top erected to guide travellers across the moors.

A village in Dorset, about 8 km (5 miles) west of Ringwood.

Three Legged Cross[2]. A village in the WEALD of Kent, to the south of BEWL WATER, about 13 km (8 miles) southeast of Tunbridge Wells.

Three Mile Cross From a crossroads 3 miles from Reading. A village in Berkshire, 5 km (3 miles) south of Reading. It is the village depicted in *Our Village* (1832), a series of sketches and tales of rural life by Mary Russell Mitford (1787–1855), who lived here.

Three Peaks. This description can refer to three separate groups of mountains, each of which provides a tough day out. The **Three Peaks Challenge** is to climb the highest mountains in Scotland, Wales and England, respectively BEN NEVIS, SNOWDON and SCAFELL PIKE, within 24 hours (motorized transport is allowed in between). In the LAKE DISTRICT the phrase refers to the area's three mountains over 3000 ft (914.6 m), namely Scafell Pike, HELVELLYN and SKIDDAW, which form the course of the annual **Three Peaks Race** for fell runners. In the Yorkshire Dales the **Three Peaks Walk** takes in the summits of INGLEBOROUGH, WHERNSIDE and PEN-Y-GHENT.

Three Rivers From three rivers that traverse the district, the CHESS, the COLNE[2] and the Gade.

A local-government district in southwest Hertfordshire, created in 1974. Its headquarters are in RICKMANSWORTH, and it also includes CHORLEYWOOD and CROXLEY GREEN.

Three Shire Stone, the. *See under* WRYNOSE PASS.

Three Sisters, the. The collective name given to three rivers in southern Ireland, the SUIR, the BARROW and the NORE. The Nore joins the Barrow just north of NEW ROSS, while the Suir and the Barrow join at WATERFORD Harbour.

Three Sisters of Glen Coe. *See under* GLEN COE.

Thrigby 'Thrykki's farmstead or village', OScand male personal name *Thrykki* + -BY.

A village in Norfolk, about 8 km (5 miles) northwest of Great Yarmouth.

Throcking Perhaps 'place where beams are used or obtained', OE *throc* 'beam, post' + -ING.

A village in Hertfordshire, about 11 km (7 miles) south of Royston.

Throckmorton Perhaps 'farmstead by a pool with a beam bridge', OE *throc* 'beam, post' + *mere* 'pool' + -TON; alternatively the first element could be 'pond with a drain', OE *throcmere*.

A village in Worcestershire (before 1998 in Hereford and Worcester, before 1974 in Worcestershire), about 13 km (8 miles) southeast of Worcester.

Throgmorton Street Named after Sir Nicholas *Throckmorton* (1515–71), Elizabeth I's ambassador to France and Scotland (the family name comes from THROCKMORTON).

A street in the City of London (EC2), running to the north of and parallel to THREADNEEDLE STREET. The south side is occupied by the **Stock Exchange**, and the name of the street has become a metonym for the Stock Exchange or for the financial world of the City of London in general (the City column of the *Observer* is called 'Throg Street').

Thrumpton 'Thormothr's farmstead or village', OScand male personal name *Thormothr* + -TON.

A village in Nottinghamshire, about 13 km (8 miles) southwest of Nottingham.

Thrums. J.M. Barrie's fictional version of KIRRIEMUIR.

Thrupp[1] 'outlying farmstead or hamlet', OE *throp*.

A village in Gloucestershire, about 1.5 km (1 mile) southeast of Stroud.

Thrupp[2]. A village in Oxfordshire, on the Oxford Canal, about 4 km (2.5 miles) southeast of Woodstock.

Thundergay 'backside to the wind', Gaelic *ton re gaoithe*, a reference to its exposed position.

A tiny settlement in northwest ARRAN, 6 km (4 miles) southwest of Lochranza.

Thunderslap Hill. *See under* GLEN FIDDICH.

Thundersley 'sacred grove of Thunor' (the thunder god and war god of the pagan Anglo-Saxons, corresponding to the Thor of Norse mythology), OE *Thunres* possessive form of god name *Thunor* + -LEY.

A town in Essex, about 10 km (6 miles) northwest of Southend-on-Sea.

Thurles Irish *Durlas* 'strong ring fort'.

A market town on the River SUIR in County Tipperary, 38 km (24 miles) west of Kilkenny. It is pronounced 'thur-lez'. The Butlers of ORMOND seized the area from the Irish O'Fogartys, and in 1300 established a Carmelite monastery here. On the site of this stands the Catholic cathedral (1865–72) of the diocese of Cashel and Emly. There are also the remains of two Butler castles. In 1884 the Gaelic Athletic Association was founded at Hayes's Commercial Hotel in Thurles.

Synod of Thurles (1850). A meeting of the Catholic bishops of Ireland at which they discussed the Church's position vis-à-vis the new Queen's Colleges. These were secular universities established by the government in Ireland in 1845, and open to all denominations – and thus considered by many Catholics as atheistical. The synod narrowly voted to ban priests from taking up posts in the new institutions and to discourage Catholics from applying to study in them.

Thurloxton 'Thurlak's farmstead or village', ME *Thurlakes* possessive form of male personal name *Thurlak* (from OScand *Thorlakr*) + -TON.
A village in Somerset, about 6 km (4 miles) northeast of Taunton.

Thurnscoe 'thorn-tree wood', OScand *thyrnir* 'thorn-tree' + *skogr* 'wood'.
A town in South Yorkshire, 11 km (7 miles) east of Barnsley.

Thurrock 'place where filthy water collects', OE *thurruc* 'bilge'.
A unitary authority within Essex, on the north bank of the River THAMES[1], stretching from the eastern edge of London to CANVEY ISLAND. Its administrative centre is in GRAYS, and it also includes TILBURY. The great oil installations of CORYTON[2] and SHELLHAVEN are at its eastern end, but for many its chief claim to fame is its Lakeside Shopping Centre.

The name *Thurrock* originally denoted a stretch of marshland to the west of Tilbury (most of which was reclaimed by immigrant Dutch workers, but a portion remains as **West Thurrock Marshes**). It was inherited by the settlement now known as Grays, which in the early Middle Ages was *Grays Thurrock*, and by two other local villages: **Little Thurrock**, which is now a suburb of Grays, and **West Thurrock**, at the northern end of the Dartford Crossing (*see under* DARTFORD) (Thurrock Services, at Junction 30 of the M25, are nearby). The unitary authority of Thurrock was created in 1998.

Thurso From the River Thurso, which means 'river of the bull', connected with the name of the nearby promontory called *Tarvedunum* by the Romans and meaning 'bull fortress'. It used to be thought that the name derived from the Norse god Thor.
An attractive old BURGH on the north coast of Highland (formerly in Caithness), 30 km (19 miles) northwest of Wick. (The first syllable is pronounced as in 'third'.) It is the most northerly town on the British mainland, and forms the terminus of the railway line from Inverness. Thurso overlooks **Thurso Bay**, which is fed by the **River Thurso**. It was the main Norse port on the mainland until it was lost after the Battle of LARGS in 1263.

A number of witches were burnt in Thurso in 1718 as a result of the actions of a man called Montgomery. Someone had been helping themselves to the contents of his cellar, so one night he took up watch, armed with a sword. When he saw some cats lapping up his ale he killed two and cut the leg off a third. When two local women died suddenly and another lost her leg, it was plain that Satan was abroad in the town, and the application of torture resulted in the usual confessions.

Thurso was the birthplace of the philosopher Sir David Ross (1877–1971). The off-beat American poet Robinson Jeffers borrowed the name for the title of his volume *Thurso's Landing* (1932).

Battle of Thurso (1040). A battle in which the Norse under Thorfinn defeated an army commanded by the nephew of King Duncan.

Thurso Baker, the. Robert Dick (1811–66), a noted amateur geologist and naturalist who moved to Thurso in 1830 and set up a baker's shop. Among other achievements, Dick identified northern holy grass growing on the banks of the River Thurso, the only place it is known in Britain. His collection of fossils and botanical specimens is in Thurso town hall, and his biography (1878) was written by Samuel Smiles.

Tibbie Shiel's Inn After the name of the landlady.
An old inn at the south end of ST MARY'S LOCH in the Scottish Borders (formerly in Peeblesshire), originally established in her own cottage in the early 19th century by a young widow, Tibbie Shiel. The place soon acquired a reputation for hospitality in this remote spot on the road between SELKIRK and MOFFAT, and was frequented by Sir Walter Scott, James Hogg (the Ettrick Shepherd; *see under* ETTRICK WATER), De Quincey and other literary men. Tibbie's amiable ghost still apparently bustles about the still thriving (and now much enlarged) inn.

Tichborne 'stream frequented by young goats' (referring to the upper course of the River ITCHEN), OE *ticce* 'young goat' + *burna* 'stream'.
A village in Hampshire, on the upper reaches of the River ITCHEN, about 11 km (7 miles) east of Winchester.

Tichborne Claimant, the. The sobriquet applied to Arthur Orton, the central actor in the most celebrated impersonation case in English legal history. In March 1853 Roger Charles Tichborne, scion of the local landed family and heir to its ancient baronetcy, sailed for Valparaiso, Chile, and after travelling for a while in South America embarked on 20 April 1854 in a sailing ship called the *Bella*, bound for Jamaica. The ship went down and nothing more was heard or seen of Roger. In October 1865 'R.C. Tichborne' turned up at Wagga Wagga, in Australia, in the person of a man known locally as Tom Castro. On Christmas Day 1866 he landed in England as a claimant to the Tichborne baronetcy, asserting that he was the lost Roger. Lady Tichborne, the real Roger's mother, professed to recognize him, but the rest of the family could not be deceived. The case came to court, where the man's claims were proved to be false, and he was identified as Arthur Orton (1834–98), the son of a Wapping butcher. A further trial for perjury, lasting 188 days, ended in his being sentenced to 14 years' penal servitude. Orton confessed in 1884.

The case became so widely and incessantly talked about that for a time the colloquial expression 'No Tich!' was used to silence anyone holding forth at excessive length.

The dwarfish music-hall comedian Harry Relph (1868–1928) was given the nickname 'Little Tich' on account of his resemblance in babyhood to the rotund Orton. The name came to be applied to anyone of small stature, and by the middle of the 20th century *titchy* was a general British colloquialism for 'small'.

Tichborne dole. An ancient charity maintained by the Tichborne family and said to have been instituted by Lady Mabel Tichborne in 1150. The legend is that, when dying, she begged her husband to provide for the poor from the produce of the estate, and he promised to give the value of the land she could encircle while holding a burning torch. She rose from her deathbed, encompassed 23 acres of Tichborne Park (which came to be known, somewhat gruesomely, as 'the Crawls') and prophesied that if the charity were allowed to lapse, seven sons would be born to the family, followed by seven daughters, and the title would then lapse. The dole was stopped after 644 years and the then baronet had seven sons and his heir seven daughters. The third son changed his name to Doughty and revived the dole (in the form of bags of flour for needy local women), and escaped the full consequences of the curse. The title became extinct in 1968 with the death of Sir Anthony Doughty-Tichborne, the 14th baronet, who had three daughters but no son.

Tickhill 'Tica's hill', OE male personal name *Tica* (or *ticcen* 'young goats') + *hyll* 'hill'.

A village in South Yorkshire, 16 km (10 miles) east of Rotherham. There is a ruined Norman castle, and the remains of an Augustinian priory and the 15th-century hospital of St Leonard. The church is 14th century.

Tideswell 'Tidi's spring', OE *Tidis* possessive form of male personal name *Tidi* + *wella* 'spring, stream'.

A town in Derbyshire, in the PEAK DISTRICT, about 9 km (5.5 miles) east of Buxton. It has the so-called 'Cathedral of the Peak' (the large 14th-century church of St John the Baptist) and a noted well-dressing ceremony.

There were formerly lead mines in the area.

Tidpit Perhaps 'Tuda's pit or hollow', OE male personal name *Tuda* + *pytt* 'pit, hollow'.

A village in Wiltshire, about 13 km (8 miles) southwest of Salisbury.

Tidworth 'Tuda's enclosure', OE male personal name *Tuda* + *worth* (*see* -WORTH, WORTHY, -WARDINE).

A town in Wiltshire, on the eastern edge of Salisbury Plain (*see under* SALISBURY), about 14 km (8.5 miles) northwest of Andover. It consists of **North Tidworth** and the much smaller **South Tidworth**, which until boundary changes in 1991 was in Hampshire. It is an army town, with several barracks (the large army camp here was opened in 1902).

Demon of Tidworth, the. A monstrous supernatural dog with huge teeth and claws, which according to legend roamed nocturnally in the vicinity of Tidworth.

Tiger Bay Etymology unknown.

The area round the docks in Cardiff, now increasingly gentrified and referred to as Cardiff Bay (*see under* CARDIFF). During the 19th century it became Wales's first multiethnic community, as sailors from all round the world settled here and married locally. Among the ingredients of this rich ethnic mix were Irish, Yemenis, Somalis and refugees from the Spanish Civil War. Its most famous daughter is the cabaret singer Shirley Bassey (b.1937).

The film *Tiger Bay* (1959) is a crime melodrama in which Korchinsky (Horst Bucholz), a Polish sailor, returns to Cardiff and kills his girlfriend when he finds her living with another man. The murder is witnessed by tomboy Gillie (Hayley Mills). An intriguing relationship develops between the two, while Superintendent Graham (Hayley's father John Mills) investigates.

The name Tiger Bay (or Tiger's Bay) has been adopted by a Loyalist enclave in north BELFAST, between the Limestone Road and Duncairn Gardens

Tighnabruaich 'house of the bank', Gaelic *tigh* 'house' + *na bruach* 'the bank'.

A small village and popular sailing centre in southern Argyll, on the Kyles of Bute (*see under* BUTE) opposite the northwest end of the island of Bute. It is pronounced 'ti-na-brew-əch'. It was a traditional port of call for the old Clyde pleasure steamers going 'doon the watter', and the *Waverley* still visits twice a week during summer.

> Yet even in the brain o' Chaos
> For Scotland I wad hain a place,
> And let Tighnabruaich still
> Be pairt and paircel o' its will …
>
> Hugh MacDiarmid: *A Drunk Man Looks at the Thistle* (1926)

Tilbury Probably 'Tila's stronghold', OE male personal name *Tila* + *byrig* dative form of *burh* (*see* BURY). Alternatively, the first element could represent a lost stream name *Tila*, meaning 'useful one'.

A town and port in Essex, within the unitary authority of

THURROCK, on the north bank of the River THAMES[1], opposite GRAVESEND, about 42 km (26 miles) downstream from London Bridge. It has been a port since ancient times, and it was here in 1588 that Elizabeth I made her celebrated speech ('I know I have the body of a weak and feeble woman, but I have the heart and stomach of a king, and of a king of England too') to her forces about to embark to take on the Spanish Armada. The massive **Tilbury Fort** was originally built in 1539, and then rebuilt by Charles II in the late 17th century to guard against Dutch and French invasion; it saw service as recently as the Second World War.

> Of all the cursed roads that ever disgraced this kingdom in the very ages of barbarism, none ever equalled that from Billericay to the *King's Head* at Tilbury. It is for 12 miles so narrow that a mouse cannot pass by any carriage … The ruts are of an incredible depth.
>
> Arthur Young: *A Six Weeks' Tour Through the Southern Counties of Britain* (1768)

Large docks were built here in the 1880s. Run by the Port of London Authority, they did good business, and in the 1960s extensive roll-on-roll-off facilities were added, enabling Tilbury to deal with the containerized cargo that was rapidly becoming the industry norm. This was the most grievous nail in the coffin of the docks closer to the capital (*see* DOCKLAND), and by the 1970s Tilbury had taken over as the main port for London. It was at Tilbury that the ship *Empire Windrush* docked in June 1948, bringing some 500 West Indian immigrants, the first of many to arrive from the Caribbean in post-war Britain.

From the late 18th century to the mid-19th *Tilbury* was London slang for 'sixpence' (2½p), that being the fare on the ferry from Gravesend to Tilbury.

There is a town called Tilbury in Canada (Ontario).

Gervase of Tilbury (*c*.1150–*c*.1220). A cleric and lawyer, born in Tilbury, and the author of *Otia Imperilia* (Imperial Diversions), a miscellaneous compendium of history, natural history and geography, written for the Holy Roman Emperor Otto IV (d.1218). The work is an important source of medieval English folklore.

Tilbury docks. A late 19th-century London rhyming slang term for both 'pox' (in the sense 'venereal disease') and 'socks'.

Till From an Indo-European root meaning 'dissolve'.

A river in Northumberland, length *c*.70 km (43 miles). It rises on the southern slopes of the CHEVIOT, then flows east, north and northwest, joining the TWEED 4 km (2.5 miles) downstream of COLDSTREAM. In the old rhyme there is some rivalry between the two rivers:

> Says Tweed to Till –
> 'Wha gars ye run sae still?'
> Says Till to Tweed –

> 'Though ye rin wi' speed,
> And I rin slaw,
> For ae man that ye droon
> I droon twa.'
>
> Anon.: 'Two Rivers' (17th century)
> (Scots *gars* 'makes', *droon* 'drown')

Tillicoultry 'hillock in the back land', Gaelic *tulach* 'hillock' + *cul* 'back' + *tir* 'land'.

A small town at the foot of the OCHIL HILLS, 5 km northeast of Alloa, in Clackmannanshire (formerly in Central region).

Tilling From *Tillingham*, a local river name.

A fictionalized version of the East Sussex coastal town of RYE, used by E.F. Benson as one of the main backdrops of his 'Mapp and Lucia' stories. Its inhabitants are a caricatured cross-section of inter-war rentier society: the maiden ladies, the old India hand, the effeminate collector of bibelots, the endless bridge.

Tilly Whim Caves *Tilly Whim* 'Tilly's windlass', ModE surname *Tilly* + *whim* 'winding mechanism (for a mine-shaft), windlass'.

A set of caves in the cliffs near DURLSTON HEAD, to the south of SWANAGE in Dorset. They have been extensively quarried, and some important fossils have been found here. Smugglers have found them a useful place of concealment.

Tilstone Fearnall *Tilstone* 'Tidwulf's stone' (perhaps referring to a milestone), OE *Tidwulfes* possessive form of male personal name *Tidwulf* + *stan* (*see* STONE); *Fearnall* the name of a local place now lost, 'fern nook', OE *fearn* 'fern' + *halh* (*see* HALE, -HALL).

A village in Cheshire, close to the Shropshire Union Canal (*see under* SHROPSHIRE), about 17 km (11 miles) southeast of Chester.

Tiltups End *Tiltups* perhaps a dialect pronunciation of *hilltop*, but more likely from dialect *tiltup* 'covered wagon', hence *Tiltups End* 'the part of the country associated with wagons'.

A village in Gloucestershire, about 1.5 km (1 mile) south of Nailsworth.

Timberland 'grove where timber is obtained', OE *timber* or OScand *timbær* + *lundr* 'grove'.

A village in Lincolnshire, in the FENS, about 21 km (13 miles) southeast of Lincoln.

Tim Healy Pass. *See* HEALY PASS.

Tincleton 'valley of the small farms' (referring to the valley of the River FROME[1]), OE *tynincel* 'small farm' (a diminutive form of *tun; see* -TON) + *denu* 'valley'.

A village in Dorset, about 10 km (6 miles) east of Dorchester.

Tingewick Probably 'dwelling or (dairy) farm at the place associated with Tida or Teoda', OE male personal name *Tida* or *Teoda* + -ING + *wic* 'dwelling, (dairy) farm' (*see* WICK).

A village in Buckinghamshire, about 5 km (3 miles) west of Buckingham.

Tinopolis. A former nickname for LLANELLI.

Tin Pan Alley Probably from *tin pan*, late 19th-century US musicians' slang for a cheap, tinny piano.

A colloquial name (probably evolved in popular usage, although journalist/songwriter Monroe Rosenfeld claimed its coinage, *c*.1899) for a street inhabited by publishers of popular music, and hence applied metonymically to the pop-music industry in general. The original reference was to the area of Broadway and 14th Street in New York City, USA, but the nickname was soon adopted on the other side of the Atlantic for Denmark Street, a road in the WEST END[1] of London, off Charing Cross Road (*see under* CHARING CROSS). The 'Alley' is now largely deserted by song writers and music publishers, who have moved to bigger premises, but there are still several shops selling sheet music, musical instruments and so on.

In the old days 'Tin Pan Alley' song writers allegedly used to play their compositions to the 'old greys', the elderly doorkeepers and other employees in the offices of the music publishers. If the 'old greys' were still whistling the tunes after a week or so, then they were likely to be worth publishing. The phrase was adopted for the title of a weekly BBC television pop music programme: *The Old Grey Whistle Test* (1971–88).

Tintagel Probably 'fort by the neck of land', Cornish *din* 'fort' + *tagell* 'narrow neck, constriction'.

A village on the north Cornish coast, about 19 km (12 miles) northeast of Padstow. It takes its name from that of a clifftop castle on a peninsula at the 91-m (299-ft) **Tintagel Head**. This is actually a Norman castle, built in the 12th century and now in ruins, but legend assures us that a previous stronghold on the site was King Arthur's castle (excavations have revealed the remains of a Celtic monastery here). Already by the early Middle Ages the locality had a firm place in Celtic mythology – it was said to be the abode of King Mark of Cornwall, and serves as a backdrop to the tragic love story of Tristram and Iseult – and Geoffrey of Monmouth in his *Historia Regum Britanniae* (*c*.1139) declared that Arthur was born here. Tintagel features, of course, in Sir Thomas Malory's *Le Morte d'Arthur* (*c*.1478). Below the castle is 'Merlin's Cave', where the wizard is said to have made his home.

On the main street of Tintagel is King Arthur's Hall, built in 1933 as the headquarters of the Fellowship of the Round Table.

Originally, before it took the castle's name, the village was called *Trevena* ('farm on a hill', Cornish *tre* 'farm' + *war* 'upon' + *menydh* 'hill').

Tintagel. An orchestral tone poem (1917) by Arnold Bax. Celtic legend was one of the composer's main sources of inspiration, and the central section of the piece vividly conjures up the world of Arthur and Tristram (a musical reference to Wagner's *Tristan und Isolde* is included), but its most striking feature is probably the evocation of the Atlantic swirling and breaking at the foot of the Cornish cliffs with which it begins and ends. It is one of Bax's most popular and often-played works.

Tintern Abbey 'king's fortress', Welsh *din* 'fortress' + *teyrn* 'monarch, king', with ME *abbaye* 'abbey'.

A ruined Cistercian foundation situated on a bend of the River WYE[1] in Monmouthshire (formerly in Gwent), 6 km (4 miles) north of Chepstow. The abbey was founded in 1131 and dissolved in 1536, but its distance from nearby settlements saved its masonry (mostly dating from the 13th-century rebuilding) from excessive deconstruction at the hands of local builders. One of the nearest villages is **Tintern Parva** (Latin *parva* 'little'), 1 km (0.6 miles) to the north.

Tintern became popular with the Romantics following the publication in 1783 of *The River Wye and Several Parts of South Wales* by the Rev. William Gilpin, a work that commended and illustrated the picturesque qualities (bordering on the sublime) of the ruined abbey and its vale. Hot on the heels of the Rev. Gilpin came the Welsh poet Edward Davies, who trotted out such lines as these:

> Above Lancaut, in a sequestered dell,
> Where monks, in former days, were wont to dwell,
> Enclosed with woods and hills on every side,
> Stands Tintern Abbey, spoiled of all her pride,
> Whose mournful ruins fill the soul with awe ...
>
> [*et cetera*]
>
> Edward Davies: *Chepstow: A Poem* (1784)

J.M.W. Turner, following the likes of Edward Dayes and Thomas Hearne, visited and sketched in 1792, and again in 1798. In the latter year William Wordsworth and his sister Dorothy also visited the abbey, resulting in the immortal if prolixly titled '**Lines written a few miles above Tintern Abbey, on revisiting the banks of the Wye during a tour, July 13, 1798**'. Wordsworth had first been here five years before, and now recalled that then –

> The sounding cataract
> Haunted me like a passion: the tall rock,
> The mountain, and the deep and gloomy wood,
> Their colours and their forms, were then to me
> An appetite: a feeling and a love,
> That had no need of a remoter charm,
> By thought supplied, or any interest
> Unborrowed from the eye ...

Unfortunately, as the subsequent lines amply demonstrate, all that 'thought' supplies in the poet's vaunted maturity is a rag-bag of inchoate abstraction (the reader is referred to such phrases as 'the joy / Of elevated thoughts', 'a sense sublime / Of something far more deeply inter-fused', 'A motion and a spirit, that impels / All thinking things').

Perhaps of greater interest to the more practically minded visitor, who is nevertheless attuned to Words-worth's 'still, sad music of humanity', is the abbey's Great Drain (Latin *Cloaca Maxima*), an irregular channel that formerly ushered effluent from the *rere-dorter* (lavatories), kitchen and infirmary of the abbey to the ever-accom-modating Wye.

Tintinhull *Tintin-* from an OCelt name based on *din* 'fort', with an uncertain second element; *-hull* 'hill' (OE *hyll*) added later.

A village (locally pronounced 'tintnəl') in Somerset, close to the FOSSE WAY, about 6 km (4 miles) northwest of Yeovil.

Tinto Probably from Gaelic *teinntach* 'fiery', from its former use for beacon fires.

A large, isolated hill (707 m / 2320 ft) in South Lanarkshire, 10 km (6 miles) southwest of BIGGAR.

Tintown. The nickname for the former internment camp at the CURRAGH, County Kildare.

Tintwistle Probably 'prince's river-fork', OE *thengel* 'prince' + *twisla* 'river fork'.

A village (locally pronounced 'tinsəl') in Derbyshire, in LONGDENDALE, about 3 km (2 miles) northwest of Glossop.

The fashion designer Vivienne Westwood (b.1941) was born in Tintwistle.

Tiobraid Árann. The Irish name for TIPPERARY.

Tipperary Irish *Tiobraid Árann* 'well of the River Ara'; the river name derives from that of the local area and means 'ridged (place)'.

A market town in the GOLDEN VALE of County Tipperary, some 30 km (19 miles) northwest of Clonmel. The town was an Anglo-Norman foundation, built around a castle erected by the future King John, and there are the remains of a 13th-century Augustinian friary. The town figured little in Irish history until the late 19th century, when, during the Land War (the agrarian conflict be-tween landlords, the authorities and tenants), the tenants of the nearby Smith Barry estate set up the alternative, but unsuccessful, settlement of **New Tipper-ary.** Subsequently, in 1931, Tipperary witnessed the birth of Muintir na Tíre, a movement for the development of rural life in Ireland.

Tipperary was the birthplace of the Fenian leader John O'Leary (1830–1907).

In late 18th-century slang *Tipperary* was an adjectival synonym for 'drunk', the implication perhaps being that the afflicted party tends to 'tip' over.

I close my eyes and picture the emerald of the sea,
From the fishing boats at Dingle to the shores of
   Donaghadee,
I miss the River Shannon, the folks at Skibbereen,
The moorlands and the meadows and the forty
   shades of green.
But most of all I miss a girl in Tipperary town,
And most of all I miss her lips,
As soft as eiderdown …

> Johnny Cash: 'Forty Shades of Green' (1961)

Tipperary, County. A county (sometimes referred to as the PREMIER COUNTY) in south-central Ireland, in the province of MUNSTER. The county is said to have been created by King John in 1210, and was granted to the earls of ORMOND in 1328. It is bounded on the east by Laois and Kilkenny, on the south by Waterford, on the west by Cork, Limerick, Clare and Galway, and on the north by Offaly. With scant regard for etymology, it is divided, for admini-strative purposes, into two ridings, North and South (for the mathematical impossibility of such a division, *see* RIDINGS OF YORKSHIRE). The county town is CLONMEL, and other towns include TIPPERARY, CASHEL, THURLES and NENAGH. Part of the GOLDEN VALE is in the centre, while hills include SLIEVENAMON and the KNOCKMEALDOWN, GALTEE and SILVERMINE Mountains. The main river is the SUIR.

'It's a Long Way to Tipperary'. A popular song written in 1912 by Jack Judge and Harry Williams, which became a great hit with soldiers in the First World War, and whose enduring popularity has made Tipperary well known around the world.

> Goodbye, Piccadilly,
> Farewell, Leicester Square,
> It's a long, long way to Tipperary,
> But my heart's right there!

Rajah from Tipperary, the. The nickname of the adventurer George Thomas (1756–1802), who was born in Roscrea, County Cork. After deserting from the Royal Navy in India, he served a number of native rulers as a mercenary, and eventually himself became ruler of Meerut. He was deposed in 1802 and died before he could return to Ireland.

Tipperary fortune. In Ireland in the late 18th and early 19th centuries, an expression denoting a young woman with no assets apart from her physical attributes ('fortune' being Hiberno-English for 'dowry'). More earthily, the expression was also used to denote the latter collectively, specifically breasts, pudendum and anus (defined in Francis Grose's *The Classical Dictionary of the Vulgar Tongue* (1785) as 'two *town lands* [the breasts], *stream's town* [the pudend] and *ballinocack* [the anus].)

Tipperary lawyer. A mid- to late 19th-century expression used by the English and Anglo-Irish to denote a cudgel, reflecting the stereotype of the Irishman as a lover of fighting.

'Tipperary Recruiting Song'. An anonymous nationalist song from the later 19th century, demonstrating a reluctance to do JOHN BULL's 'dirty job':

> 'Tis now we'd want to be wary, boys,
> The recruiters are out in Tipperary, boys;
> If they offer a glass, we'll wink as they pass –
> We're old birds for chaff in Tipperary, boys …
>
> Then hurrah for the gallant Tipperary boys!
> Although 'we're cross and contrary', boys;
> The never a one will handle a gun,
> Except for the Green and Tipperary, boys.

'Tipperary So Far Away'. A Republican ballad about Sean Treacy (1895–1920), an organizer of the Gaelic League and Irish Volunteers in southern Tipperary. He was killed during the Anglo-Irish War (1919–21) in a gun battle in Dublin. The ballad ends:

> The soldiers of Erin bore him high
> On their shoulders, they solemnly tread,
> And many a heart with a tearful sigh
> Wept over our patriot dead.
> In silence they lowered him into the grave
> To rest till his reckoning day,
> Sean Treacy who died, his home to save
> In Tipperary so far away.

American President Ronald Reagan quoted a line from the ballad on his visit to his 'ancestral home' at BALLYPOREEN, on 3 June 1984.

Tippermuir 'big well' or 'Mary's well', Gaelic *tobor* 'well' + *mòr* 'big' or *Moire* 'Mary'.
A battle site in Perth and Kinross (formerly in Perthshire, and then in Tayside region), 10 km (6 miles) west-northwest of Perth. Here on 1 September 1644 the Marquess of Montrose, at the head of a Royalist army, won the first of a series of famous victories.

Tips End *Tips* of uncertain origin, but it may be a surname or ModE 'heaps'; *End* 'region, district'.
A village in Cambridgeshire, in the FENS, about 10 km (6 miles) east of March.

Tiptoe Probably denoting manorial ownership in the Middle Ages by the Typetot family.
A village in Hampshire, about 8 km (5 miles) northwest of Lymington.

Tipton 'estate associated with Tibba', OE male personal name *Tibba* + -ING + -TON.
A district within the metropolitan borough of SANDWELL, about 13 km (8 miles) northwest of Birmingham. Its parish registers, beginning in 1513, are the oldest surviving in

England. **Tipton Harriers**, a noted road and cross-country running club, was founded in 1910.

Tipton Three. A name bestowed by the media on Asif Iqbal, Ruhal Ahmed and Shafiq Rasul, three British Muslims from Tipton who were held in the US prison camp at Guantanamo Bay in Cuba, having been captured in Afghanistan in November 2001. They were returned to Britain in March 2004.

Tiptree Probably 'Tippa's tree', OE male personal name *Tippa* + *treow* 'tree'.
A small town in Essex, about 16 km (10 miles) southwest of Colchester. It is a notable fruit-preserving and jam-making centre ('Tiptree'® is a registered trademark of the jam-makers Wilkin and Sons Ltd).

Tír Chonaill. The Irish name for TYRCONNELL.

Tirconnell. An alternative spelling of TYRCONNELL.

Tiree 'land of Ith', Gaelic *tir* 'land' + the name of someone as yet unidentified, possibly a mythical leader of the Milesian invaders of Ireland.
The most westerly of the Inner HEBRIDES, lying 3 km (2 miles) southwest of COLL, in Argyll and Bute (formerly in Strathclyde region). It is pronounced 'tie-ree' and is some 80 km (50 miles) west of Oban. It is a fertile place, and in St Columba's time grain grown here helped to feed his monastery on Iona. It is also a flat island (the highest point being no more than 141 m / 462 ft), and is known as the windiest place in Britain, with an average wind speed of 27 kph (17 mph). To compensate, in the summer months it is also the sunniest place in Britain.

Because of its flatness Tiree is known by Gaelic nicknames meaning **the Land beneath the Waves** or **the Kingdom whose Summits are Lower than the Waves**. There is a rock on the island, called the Ringing Rock, which clangs if struck, but it is as well to show restraint, as it is said that if the rock is broken, Tiree will sink beneath the sea.

Tiree has a coastal station providing information for the shipping forecast.

Tír Eoghain. The Irish name for TYRONE.

Tír Maoile. The Irish name for the TEERMOYLE MOUNTAIN.

Tír na nÓg Irish 'the land of youth'.
The best of the otherworlds in Irish mythology, where the gods of the Tuatha Dé Danann (the Sidhe or fairies) and the most blessed of mortals stay for ever young. It is often described as an island, some placing it in the direction of the setting sun, far out in the Western Ocean. Time passes more slowly there; when the bard Oisín (Oisian) was taken to Tír na nÓg by his lover, the fairy woman Niamh, he found on his return after a twelvemonth that all his family and friends had been three hundred years dead.

Tír na nÓg is the title of a lyrical play for performance with music by the Welsh-language poet Thomas Gwynn Jones (1871–1949), while *Thompson in Tír na nÓg* is a satirical drama (1912) by Gerald MacNamara (Harry C. Morrow) in which an Orangeman finds himself in the company of the ancient Irish heroes. Inevitably, the name has also been given to a spattering of Irish theme pubs around the world, and even to a 'virtual Irish cybercafé'.

Tissington 'estate associated with Tidsige', OE male personal name *Tidsige* + -ING + -TON.

A village in Derbyshire, in the southern part of the PEAK DISTRICT, about 16 km (10 miles) southwest of Matlock. It has some fine limestone buildings, many of them donated in the 1830s by the local landed family, the Fitzherberts, as part of an improvement programme.

It is said to have been the village where the Derbyshire custom of well-dressing began, in the 14th century. This involves adorning the local wells (Tissington has five) with scenes and designs made out of flowers, feathers and other natural materials, and takes place each year on Ascension Day.

Titchfield 'open land where young goats are kept', OE *ticce* 'young goat' + *feld* (*see* FIELD).

A small town in Hampshire, on the western bank of the River MEON, opposite Fareham. It was once a seaport, but in the 18th century a sea-wall was built across the Meon to drain the nearby marshes, and that cut it off from the sea.

Titchfield also once had an abbey, founded in 1232. **Titchfield Abbey** suffered the usual fate at the Dissolution of the Monasteries, and was rebuilt as the family home of the earls of Southampton. The 3rd Earl was one of William Shakespeare's most noted patrons. It is believed that *Love's Labour's Lost* (1595) may have been written and first performed here.

Titchmarsh 'Tyccea's marsh', OE male personal name *Tyccea* + *mersc* 'marsh'.

A village in Northamptonshire, about 16 km (10 miles) east of Kettering.

Titfield A blend of *Titsey* and *Limpsfield*, the names of two adjacent Surrey villages.

A fictitious rural English village that is the setting of the 1953 Ealing comedy *The Titfield Thunderbolt*, starring Stanley Holloway and John Gregson, written by T.E.B. Clarke and directed by Charles Crichton. It concerns the villagers' attempts to thwart the closure of the local railway line, which involve the resurrection of an ancient locomotive (the 'Thunderbolt' of the title). It was filmed in the Cam Valley, to the south of Bath, and the part of Titfield station was taken by that of Monkton Combe.

Titsey 'Tydic's well-watered land', OE *Tydices* possessive form of male personal name *Tydic* + *eg* (*see* -EY, -EA).

A village in Surrey, on the NORTH DOWNS, just to the northwest of CLACKET LANE Services on the M25. On top of the 270-m (about 900-ft) **Titsey Hill** there was once a Roman villa.

Tittensor 'Titten's ridge', OE *Tittenes* possessive form of male personal name *Titten* + *ofer* 'ridge'.

A village (pronounced 'titənsaw') in Staffordshire, on the River TRENT[1] and on the A34, about 10 km (6 miles) south of Stoke-on-Trent.

Titterstone Clee Hill 'rocking stone on Clee Hill', ModE *titterstone* 'rocking, unstable stone' + place name *Clee Hill*.

A hill in the CLEE HILLS of Shropshire, about 8 km (5 miles) northeast of Ludlow. At 533 m (1749 ft) it is one of the highest in the county. On its flat top are the remains of an Iron Age fort.

Tiumpan Head The Gaelic name is *Rubha an t-Siumpain*. Both *Head* and *Rubha* mean 'promontory'; Gaelic *tiumpan* means 'hinder', and it is possible that the name might mean a promontory that is difficult to navigate around.

The headland at the northeast tip of the EYE PENINSULA, on the east coast of LEWIS, Western Isles (formerly in Ross and Cromarty), some 15 km (9 miles) northeast of Stornoway.

> I looked out across the water,
> a few ducks, miles and miles of sea,
> sparkling so coldly and so brilliantly
> I almost fell into their mineral laughter.
>
> Iain Crichton Smith: 'Tiumpan Head, Lewis', from
> *The Law and the Grace* (1965)

Tiverton 'farmstead or village at the double ford' (referring to its position at the confluence of the River Exe and its tributary, the Loman), OE *twi-fyrde* 'double ford' (*see* FORD) + -TON.

A market town in Devon, on the River EXE, about 22 km (14 miles) north of Exeter. It prospered in the 17th and 18th centuries as the main centre of the Devon cloth industry, and in the 19th century made a name for itself as a producer of lace.

Tiverton Castle, begun in 1066 and much restored, includes two original towers and a 14th-century gateway. Blundell's School, a public school, is in Tiverton. It was founded in 1604. One of its pupils was R.D. Blackmore, author of *Lorna Doone* (1869), and he sent its hero John Ridd to his old school.

William Bryant (b.1804), co-founder of Bryant & May matches, was the son of a Tiverton starch-maker.

There are towns called Tiverton in the USA (Rhode Island) and Canada (Nova Scotia, Ontario).

Tivetshall St Margaret *Tivetshall* probably 'nook of land frequented by lapwings', ModE dialect *tewhit* 'lapwing' + OE *halh* (*see* HALE, -HALL); *St Margaret* from the dedication of the local church.

A village in Norfolk, about 10 km (6 miles) northeast of Diss.

Tixover 'promontory where young goats are kept', OE *ticce* 'young goat' + *ofer* 'promontory'.

A village in Rutland (before 1997 in Leicestershire, before 1974 in Rutland), on the River WELLAND, about 15 km (9 miles) southeast of Oakham.

Toadmoor Originally 'toad pool', OE *tadige* 'toad' + *mere* 'pool', but OE *mor* 'marsh' was later substituted for the second element.

A village in Derbyshire, about 3 km (2 miles) north of Belper.

Tobar an Choire. The Irish name for TUBBERCURRY.

Tobercurry. An alternative spelling for TUBBERCURRY.

Tobermory 'Mary's well', Gaelic *tobar* 'well' + *Mhaire* 'Mary'. The main settlement on MULL, in the northeast corner of the island. It is in Argyll and Bute (formerly in Strathclyde region), and is one of the most attractive villages on the west coast of Scotland. The St Mary's Well after which it is named is just west of the town. Tobermory became important when in 1788 it was chosen by the British Fisheries Society as the site of a planned village and fishing station.

The town looks out on **Tobermory Bay**, and it was here in 1588 that the galleon *San Juan de Sicilia* (or the *Florida*, according to other sources), a refugee from the failed Spanish Armada, dropped anchor to take on provisions. When it appeared that the ship was about to leave without paying for the stores, either Maclean of Duart (*see* DUART CASTLE) or one of his men boarded the ship. It is said that he was confined by the Spanish, but managed to reach the powder store, which he set alight, sending the ship – along with a rumoured 30 million gold ducats – to the bottom. This treasure has never been recovered.

Tobermory features as the picturesque village of Bala-mory in the BBC television children's programme of that name, the first series of which was broadcast in 2003. The characters, such as Archie the Inventor, PC Plum and Miss Hoolie the Schoolteacher, live in the brightly painted houses that line Tobermory's sea front.

There is a town called Tobermory in Canada (Ontario), and also a Womble of Wimbledon Common of the same name. Tobermory, the eponymous hero of a short story by Saki (H.H. Munro, 1870–1916), is a cat who has apparently mastered human speech, but not the art of diplomacy.

Tobermory tottie. A confection, once popular in the west of Scotland, consisting of a chewy disc, dusted with powdered cinnamon, in which was contained a small plastic toy.

Todmorden 'Totta's boundary valley', OE male personal name *Totta* + *mære* 'boundary' + *denu* 'valley'.

A town on the River CALDER[1], West Yorkshire, 16 km (10 miles) west of Halifax. It was the birthplace of John Fielden (1784–1849), factory-owner, Radical politician and campaigner for the welfare of workers; Sir John Cockcroft (1897–1967), winner of the 1951 Nobel prize for physics for his work on particle accelerators; and of Sir Geoffrey Wilkinson (1921–96), winner of the Nobel prize for chemistry in 1973 for work in organometallic chemistry.

Toffeopolis. An occasional nickname of Goodison Park, the ground of EVERTON FC, on account of their nickname, the Toffees.

Toft[1] 'curtilage, homestead', OScand.

A village in Cambridgeshire, about 10 km (6 miles) west of Cambridge.

Toft[2]. A village in Lincolnshire, about 11 km (7 miles) northeast of Stamford.

Toft next Newton. A village in Lincolnshire, about 19 km (12 miles) northeast of Lincoln and 1.5 km (1 mile) northwest of NEWTON BY TOFT.

Tollard Royal *Tollard* probably from an OCelt hill name, a compound of *toll* 'hole, pit' and *ardd* 'height' (*see* ARD); *Royal* refers to the fact that King John had a feudal holding here.

A village in Wiltshire, about 19 km (12 miles) southwest of Salisbury. King John used to stay here while hunting in Cranborne Chase (*see under* CRANBORNE). His hunting lodge, now known as King John's House, still exists. It was restored by the 19th-century archaeologist Lieutenant-General Augustus Henry Lane Fox Pitt Rivers (founder of the Pitt Rivers Museum of ethnology in Oxford), who lived nearby.

Toller Fratrum *Toller* from the former name of the local river (now called the 'Hooke'), an OCelt river name meaning 'hollow stream'; *Fratrum* 'of the brethren' (referring to manorial ownership in the Middle Ages by the Knights Hospitallers), Latin.

A village in Dorset, on the River Hooke (a tributary of the FROME[1]), about 13 km (8 miles) northwest of Dorchester.

Toller Porcorum *Porcorum* 'of the pigs' (a joking reference to the local pig population, used to distinguish the village from its near neighbour TOLLER FRATRUM), Latin.

A village in Dorset, on the River Hooke (a tributary of the FROME[1]), about 1.5 km (1 mile) west of Toller Fratrum.

Toller Whelme 'source of the river Toller', river name *Toller* (*see* TOLLER FRATRUM) + OE *æwielm* 'spring, river-source'.

A village in Dorset, about 8 km (5 miles) northwest of Toller Fratrum.

Tolleshunt D'Arcy *Tolleshunt* 'Toll's spring', OE *Tolles* possessive form of male personal name *Toll* + *funta* 'spring'; *D'Arcy* denoting manorial ownership in the Middle Ages by the Darcy family.

A village in Essex, about 10 km (6 miles) northeast of Maldon. It is pronounced 'toalzhunt'. Margery Allingham (1904–66), the writer of crime novels and creator of the detective Albert Campion, lived at D'Arcy House from 1935 until her death.

It was on 7 August 1985 at White House Farm in Tolleshunt D'Arcy that Jeremy Bamber notoriously murdered five members of his adoptive family.

Tolleshunt Knights *Knights* apparently denoting that the parish originally comprised a knight's fee.

A village in Essex, about 3 km (2 miles) northwest of TOLLESHUNT D'ARCY.

Tolleshunt Major *Major* denoting manorial ownership in the early Middle Ages by someone called Malger.

A village in Essex, about 2.5 km (1.5 miles) west of TOLLESHUNT D'ARCY.

Tolpuddle 'Tola's estate on the River Piddle', OScand female personal name *Tola* + PIDDLE. The Tola in question was the widow of Urc, the royal bodyguard of Edward the Confessor, who around 1060 donated her lands, including Tolpuddle, to Abbotsbury Abbey.

A village in Dorset, on the River Piddle, about 13 km (8 miles) northeast of Dorchester.

Tolpuddle Martyrs, the. Six agricultural labourers of Tolpuddle who, under the leadership of George Loveless, formed a trade union to resist wage cuts. They were sentenced to seven years' transportation to Australia in 1834 on a concocted charge of administering illegal oaths. After continuous protests they were pardoned in 1836, returning home two years later. In 1934 the TUC built a set of six cottages in the village as a permanent memorial to them. According to tradition, the Martyrs held their meetings under a giant sycamore tree, now known as the 'Martyrs' tree'. All that remains of the sycamore today is a stump, the rest of the tree having been removed for safety reasons.

Tomb of the Eagles From the large numbers of bones of sea eagles found within; the animal may have been a tribal totem.

A large Neolithic chambered tomb at Isbister, near the south end of SOUTH RONALDSAY, Orkney. The remains of over 300 humans have been found in the tomb, which dates from *c.*3000 BC. The cairn covering the tomb was first uncovered by a local farmer, Ronald Simison, in 1958.

Tomintoul 'knoll of the barn', Gaelic *tom* 'knoll' + *an t-sabhail* 'of the barn'.

A village in Moray (formerly in Banffshire, then in

Grampian region), some 13 km (8 miles) northwest of COCK BRIDGE, and linked to it by the A939 over the pass of the LECHT, which is often blocked by snow in winter. It was founded by the Duke of Gordon in 1779, and at 354 m (1160 ft) it is the highest village in the HIGHLANDS. It was the home of the famous white witch Grigor Willox (*fl.*18th century).

Tomnahurich. *See under* INVERNESS.

Tom Thumb Stack. *See under* DUNCANSBY HEAD.

Tonbridge Probably 'bridge belonging to the estate or manor' (referring to a bridge across the River Medway), OE *tun* 'estate, manor' (*see* -TON) + *brycg* 'bridge'. Until the 18th century the name was generally spelt *Tunbridge* (as it is still usually pronounced), but it was then changed to *Tonbridge* to avoid confusion with nearby TUNBRIDGE WELLS (its offspring).

A market town (pronounced 'tunbridge') in Kent, at the highest navigable point of the River MEDWAY[1], about 17 km (11 miles) southwest of Maidstone. It is towards the southern edge of the borough of **Tonbridge and Malling** (*see* EAST MALLING), which lies between the NORTH DOWNS and the WEALD, and covers the middle reaches of the Medway. The town's origins may well go back to Roman times, and there was certainly an Anglo-Saxon settlement here. There are the remains of a Norman castle, some of whose stones found their way into the walls of Tonbridge's 18th-century houses.

Tonbridge School, a boys' public school, was founded in 1553. Its former pupils include the novelist E.M. Forster (1879–1970), the actor David Tomlinson (1917–2000), the cricketer Colin Cowdrey (1932–2000) and the novelist and poet Vikram Seth (b.1952). George Austen, father of the novelist Jane Austen, was a teacher here.

The lexicographer and usage guru H.W. Fowler (1858–1933) and the cricketer Frank Woolley (1887–1978) were born in Tonbridge. The poet Christopher Smart (1722–71) was born nearby, at Shipbourne.

Tone Perhaps an OCelt river name, possibly meaning 'roaring stream'; alternatively it could belong to the same Indo-European river name group as THAMES[1], TAME[1] and TAVY.

A river in Somerset, which rises about 20 km (12 miles) west of TAUNTON and flows eastwards through Taunton to join the River PARRETT about 8 km (5 miles) southeast of BRIDGWATER.

In Taunton, Somerset's county cricket ground is situated on the banks of the Tone, and the county's more vigorous hitters, such as Harold Gimblett, Ian Botham and Viv Richards, have regularly deposited cricket balls in it.

Tonehenge. *See under* ST STEPHEN'S GREEN.

Tong '(settlement on the) tongs' (referring to a piece of land between the two headstreams of the River Worfe, shaped

❖ -ton ❖

This is the most frequently occurring English place-name element, deriving from the Old English word *tun*. The earliest traceable meaning of the word is 'fence' or 'hedge' and it was applied to enclosed areas; but over the course of the Middle Ages it became the standard word for a farm, then more generally a settlement, until finally, in the Modern English word 'town', it refers to an urban area. In this last sense, the element is still in use, most often in district names such as 'Newtown' in many urban developments, but also in the names of 20th-century NEW TOWNS[1] such as NEWTOWN[1] (Powys) itself and NEWTON AYCLIFFE (County Durham).

Some names derived from *tun* retain its early sense of 'enclosure': Leighton, found in LEIGHTON BUZZARD (Bedford-shire), derives from the Old English *leac-tun* 'enclosure for growing leeks' or 'vegetable garden'. To make it clear when the *tun* contained a dwelling, the element HAM, meaning 'home-stead' was often added to create the compound element *ham-tun*: this gives names like NORTHAMPTON and SOUTHAMPTON.

In the north and east of England some *-tons* may derive from Old Scandinavian *tun*, which seems to have the same range of meanings in names as the Old English word. Places with Old Scandinavian personal names, such as Thormothr in THRUMPTON (Nottinghamshire), may originally have contained the Old Scandinavian *tun*, but the popularity of the element in English, and the availability of Old Scandinavian *by*, make it more likely that the element was borrowed by the Danish settlers from English, or that a previously English farm with a *-ton* name was taken over by a Dane. Names such as Thruxton (Hampshire and Herefordshire), not in areas conquered by the Danes, suggest that the eponymous Thorkell was a latecomer, perhaps one who bought the farm, or even possibly a man of mixed ancestry.

In the majority of cases, the element *tun* gives names with *-ton*. In Scotland and Ireland *-town* appears frequently, as in WIGTOWN (Wigtownshire). PRESTATYN (Flintshire) is the Welsh version of PRESTON 'settlement of the priests'. In English names about half of all place names containing *-ton* have a personal name as the first element, and when these have the possessive *-s* confusion with STONE is possible: SILVERSTONE

(Northamptonshire) and PETERSTONE WENTLOOGE (Newport) are respectively 'Sigewulf's or Sæwulf's farm' and 'farm belonging to St Peter's church' – the names have nothing to do with stones. Sometimes, as *tun* is so common an element, names that derive from other elements are assimilated to it: there are many examples of Langton 'long farm' (such as LANGTON HERRING, Dorset), but Langton (County Durham) and REPTON (Derbyshire) originally contained the Old English element *dun* 'hill' (*see* DOWN, -DON), not *tun*, and so originally meant 'long hill' and 'hill of the Hrype tribe' respectively; the last element of TINCLETON (Dorset) is not originally *tun* either, but *denu* 'valley'.

About one-fifth of -ton names are -*ingtons*. The -ING- element has a complex range of meanings, but for the most part -*ington* means 'farm associated with' the person or family whose name is the first element. Thus STEVENTON[1] (Hampshire) and STEVENTON[2] (Oxfordshire) mean 'farm associated with a man called Stifa'; and, though it is somewhat disguised, Sneinton (Nottinghamshire, *Notintone* in Domesday Book, 1086) is 'farm associated with Snot', the same person who gave his name to the much more important nearby settlement of NOTTINGHAM[1].

A very wide range of elements can be combined with *tun*, and those mentioned below all appear more than once. There are all kinds of vegetation (Ashton, as in ASHTON-IN-MAKERFIELD, and THORNTON[1] mean a farm characterised by ash or thorn trees respectively); landscape features (CLIFTON 'farm by a cliff or bank'); geographical positions (NORTON, SUTTON[1], ASTON and Easton (such as EASTON IN GORDANO), Weston (such as WESTON BEGGARD) and MIDDLETON); crops (Barton 'barley farm', as in BARTON BENDISH, and Whatton 'wheat farm'); and animals (Shepton, as in SHEPTON MALLET, Shipton as in SHIPTON BELLINGER, both 'sheep farm').

Of particular interest for settlement history are tribal or nationality names: some of the many Waltons, such as WALTON-ON-THAMES, refer to the settlements of Celtic peoples who remained after the Anglo-Saxon conquest (Old English *walh* 'Welshman, serf'; *see* WAL-); NORMANTON, of which there are many examples, refers to a farm or settlement belonging to Norwegians.

like the space between the arms of tongs), OE *tang* 'tongs, forceps'.

A village in Shropshire, close to Junction 3 on the M54, about 11 km (7 miles) southeast of Telford. It has no pub, but there is a magnificent 15th-century church, with some spectacular tombs. On the flimsiest evidence in the book, it advertises itself as the fictional burial-place of Little Nell in Dickens's *The Old Curiosity Shop* (1841), a claim appar-ently enthusiastically advanced by a recent verger, who showed visitors to a plausible-looking tombstone.

Tong Castle. An 18th-century folly in Moorish Gothic style, possibly designed by 'Capability' Brown. It was demolished in 1954.

Tonge '(settlement on a) tongue of land', OScand *tunga* 'tongue'.

A hamlet in Leicestershire, about 12 km (7.5 miles) north-west of Loughborough.

Tongue OScand *tunga* 'tongue', referring to the 'tongue' of land projecting here into the Kyle of Tongue.

A village on the north coast of Scotland, in Highland (formerly in Sutherland), some 55 km (34 miles) west of Thurso. It is situated on the long inlet called the **Kyle of Tongue** (Gaelic *caol* 'strait'), which opens out to the sea at **Tongue Bay**. A little to the north of the village is **Tongue House** (1714), seat of the Mackay chiefs until 1829.

Tonypandy 'fallow ground by the fulling mill', Welsh *ton* 'unploughed grassland' + *pandy* 'fulling mill' (one such existed here until the early 20th century).

A former mining town in the Rhondda, in RHONDDA CYNON TAFF unitary authority (formerly in Glamorgan, then in Mid Glamorgan), 8 km (5 miles) northwest of Pontypridd. It was the scene of rioting by miners in 1910, when Winston Churchill, then home secretary, sent in troops to aid the police.

> Would it not be better to stand on the corner in
>   Tonypandy
> And look up the valley and down the valley
> On the flotsam of the wreckage of men in the slough of
>   despair,
> Men and tips standing, a dump of one purpose with man
>
> > Saunders Lewis: 'The Deluge 1939', translated from the
> > Welsh by Gwyn Thomas (Lewis was leader of Plaid Cymru
> > in the 1930s, and in this extract he wonders whether this
> > bitter contemplation would not be 'better' than his life of
> > resolutions and committees.)
>
> You went down to Tonypandy for the Strike and the
>   General Strike,
> for the jazz carnival, and the football of strikers and
>   police,
> to the soup-kitchens and the cobbling,
> the jumble-sales for sore-ridden Lazarus …
>
> > J. Kitchener Davies: *The Sound of the Wind that is
> > Blowing* (written 1951–2), translated from the Welsh
> > by Joseph P. Clancy

Tonypandy was the birthplace of George Thomas (1909–97), Labour MP and Speaker of the House of Commons (1976–83), who became Viscount Tonypandy when he retired.

Tonypandy Terror, the. The Tonypandy-born boxer Tommy Farr (1914–86), who was British and Empire heavyweight champion in 1937–8. He lost on points in 1937 to the world champion, Joe Louis, in New York, and after the fight claimed his face looked 'like a dug-up road'.

Tooley Street Earlier *St Olave's Street*, from the former church here dedicated to St Olave (demolished in 1928). The much eroded form *Tooley* is first recorded in the early 17th century.

A street in southeast London (SE1), in the borough of SOUTHWARK, running parallel with the south bank of the Thames to the north and the arches beneath the approach to London Bridge station to the south. In the days when the POOL OF LONDON was still a working port most of the street's northern side was taken up with wharfside warehouses, and it enjoyed the nickname 'London's larder'.

Toon, the. A nickname for NEWCASTLE UPON TYNE.

Toot Baldon *Toot* 'look-out hill', OE *tot(e)*; *Baldon see* MARSH BALDON.

A village in Oxfordshire, about 5 km (3 miles) southeast of Oxford.

Tooting Probably '(settlement of) Tota's people', OE male personal name *Tota* + *-ingas* (*see* -ING); alternatively, the first element might represent OE *tot* 'look-out place' (although Tooting is inappropriately flat).

A district of southwest London (SW17), in the borough of WANDSWORTH, between BALHAM to the north and MERTON to the southwest. London began to send out its tentacles towards it in the 18th century, when mansions for City bigwigs began to be built here. Villas for the middle classes followed in the first half of the 19th century, and by the early 20th century Tooting was a well-built-up and fairly typical commuter suburb. In 1903 it became the southern terminus of London's first electric tram line.

Tooting Broadway Underground station (named from **Tooting Broadway**, once a large open stretch of road, now a small triangular area by the station) on the Northern line opened in 1926. The Granada, Tooting, is one of the more flamboyant examples of inter-war Art Deco cinema design, described by John Betjeman as 'a Spanish-Moorish-Gothic cathedral for the people of Tooting'.

Tooting Bec *Bec* denoting manorial ownership in the early Middle Ages by the Benedictine Abbey of St Mary of Bec in Normandy.

The northerly part of TOOTING (also known as **Upper Tooting**), representing the northern of the two manors into which the settlement was divided in the Middle Ages. Tooting Bec Common, in the eastern part of the district, covers about 60 ha (150 acres).

Tooting Bec Underground station, on the Northern line, opened in 1926. In the late 19th and early 20th centuries *Tooting Bec* (or simply *Tooting*) was used as rhyming slang for peck, in the sense of both 'a light kiss' and 'food'.

Topsham 'hilltop promontory', OE *toppes* possessive form of *topp* 'hilltop' + *hamm* 'promontory' (*see* HAM).

A town and port in Devon, on the eastern bank of the estuary of the River EXE, now effectively a southern suburb of EXETER. From Roman times until the 19th century it was Exeter's port. It did particularly well after 1282, when the Countess of Devon built a weir across the river, blocking access to Exeter (*see* COUNTESS WEAR). In 1567, however, things took a downturn when the new Exeter ship canal (the first in England) was opened, and in the 19th century Topsham's inability to accommodate large steamships hammered the last nails into its commercial coffin.

Toraigh. The Irish name for TORY ISLAND. The full form of the name is **Toraigh na dTonn**.

Tor Bay *Tor* from a hill called Torre (*see* TORQUAY).

A bay on the south Devon coast, about 22 km (14 miles) southwest of Exmouth. The northern part of its shore is occupied by TORQUAY. PAIGNTON is in the middle and BRIXHAM at the southern extremity.

Torbay From TOR BAY.

Originally a county borough, then an administrative district, now a unitary authority on the coast of south Devon. The last was formed in 1998, incorporating TORQUAY, BRIXHAM and PAIGNTON.

Torbay sole. A name devised by marketeers for witch sole (*Glyptocephalus cynoglossus*), the name of which was regarded as off-putting to British consumers, although the species had long been exported to France and Spain. As the Torbay sole is a sustainable species, its consumption is being encouraged by marine conservationists.

Torc Cascade. *See under* KILLARNEY.

Torfaen 'stone swelling', Welsh *tor*, a complex word meaning 'something cut or broken' or 'a swelling, protuberance' or 'river bank, mountain side' + *maen* 'stone'.

A unitary authority in southeast Wales, created in 1996 from the former Torfaen district of Gwent. It is bounded on the north and east by Monmouthshire, on the south by Newport, on the west by Caerphilly and Blaenau Gwent. Its administrative headquarters are at PONTYPOOL and the other main town is CWMBRAN.

Torquay '(place with a) quay near Torre' (referring originally to a jetty built by the monks of Torre Abbey, a late 12th-century Premonstratensian foundation (a Catholic religious order, from Prémontré in France) which itself took its name from a hill called Torre (from OE *torr* 'rocky hill') and parts of which survive in Torquay), *Torre* + ModE *quay*.

A seaside resort on the south Devon coast, overlooking TOR BAY, in the unitary authority of TORBAY, to the southeast of DARTMOOR, 32 km (20 miles) south of Exeter. The headquarters of Torbay unitary authority are here. A settlement seems to have developed around the monks' quay here in the 17th century. At first it was called *Fleet*, but before long the name of the jetty had become attached to it.

Torquay began to expand and develop in the 19th century – at first during the Napoleonic Wars, when naval families began to move in along this stretch of coast, and again in the 1830s, when word of its mild climate had spread. It attracted convalescents (Elizabeth Barrett in 1838, for example, although its beneficial effects were somewhat offset by the death of her brother in a boating accident here), and it also became a favourite place to retire to (the Irish playwright Sean O'Casey did so, for instance, as did the American sewing-machine magnate Isaac Merritt Singer,

the Arctic explorer William Scoresby and the physicist Oliver Heaviside of 'layer' fame: he predicted the presence of the ionosphere). If this population of the well-off elderly and sick suggests sedateness, that would not be too wide of the mark. Torquay's elegant hotels, its attractive harbour and marina, its palms and pines combine to produce an atmosphere that is at once Mediterranean and yet quintessentially English (this is the ENGLISH RIVIERA, after all).

The crime-writer Agatha Christie (1890–1976), the humorist Peter Cook (1937–95), the explorer Colonel Percy Fawcett (1867–?), who disappeared mysteriously in Brazil in 1925, and (probably) the explorer and writer Sir Richard Burton (1821–90) were born in Torquay.

> That atrabilious man from Torquay
> Was affected by melancholy,
> But his bile and his spleen
> And the bits in between
> Felt much better with wife number three.
>
> Peter Cook: *Tragically I Was an Only Twin* (2002)

The BBC television sitcom *Fawlty Towers* (1975–9) was set in Torquay; the character of Basil Fawlty, played by John Cleese, was based on a genuine Torquay hotelier, Donald Sinclair (1919–78), irascible proprietor of the Gleneagles Hotel.

There is a town called Torquay in Canada (Saskatchewan) and a village of that name in Tasmania.

See also KENT'S CAVERN *and* TORRE.

Torran Rocks *Torran* Gaelic *torrunn* 'rumbling, thunder'.

A group of half-submerged rocks scattered over a wide area in the sea some 6 km (4 miles) off the southwest tip of MULL. The named rocks include Na Torrain, Torran Sgoilte, Otter Rock and McPhail's Anvil.

Torre The name of a local hill (*see* TORQUAY).

A western suburb of TORQUAY.

Torr Head Irish *Cionn an Toir*, 'headland of the rocky height'.

A headland in County Antrim, 6 km (4 miles) southeast of FAIR HEAD. It is the closest point in Ireland to Great Britain, the distance across the North Channel to the Mull of Kintyre (*see under* KINTYRE) being a mere 20 km (12 miles).

Torridge[1] An OCelt river name meaning 'turbulent stream'.

A river in north Devon, which rises in the northwestern corner of the county and flows 64 km (40 miles) southeastwards past SHEEPWASH[1] and BLACK TORRINGTON and then, taking an abrupt turn, northwards through TORRINGTON and BIDEFORD into Bideford Bay at APPLEDORE[1] (where it is joined by the River TAW).

The rivers Torridge and Taw provide the setting for Henry Williamson's Devon-set classic of otter fiction, *Tarka the Otter* (1927). Williamson, who moved to the village of Georgeham, close to the north Devon coast, in 1921, called the area around here 'the Land of the Two Rivers'. Tarka's water-borne journeyings take him across both Exmoor and Dartmoor, and along the rivers Taw and the Torridge, before he is finally trapped and killed by hunters in a pool below Great Torrington Common.

Torridge² From TORRIDGE¹.

An administrative district of north Devon, of which the River Torridge forms the eastern boundary. Its main town is BIDEFORD.

Torridon Etymology obscure.

A mountainous area of Wester Ross, Highland (formerly in Ross and Cromarty), some 30 km (19 miles) north of Kyle of Lochalsh. **Glen Torridon** extends westwards from Kinlochewe near Loch Maree to the little village of **Torridon** on **Upper Loch Torridon**, a sea loch, which itself opens out into the wider **Loch Torridon**. The **River Torridon** flows through the western half of Glen Torridon. On the north side of the glen is the largely treeless area called the **Torridon Forest**, containing the spectacular serrated ridges of BEINN ALLIGIN, LIATHACH and BEINN EIGHE, sandstone mountains mostly capped with quartzite.

Torridonian sandstone. A type of hard red sandstone found in Torridon and other parts of the northwest Highlands, such as APPLECROSS, COIGACH and ASSYNT.

Torrington 'farmstead or village on the River Torridge', TORRIDGE¹ + -TON.

A hilltop town, more fully and officially **Great Torrington**, in north Devon, on the River Torridge, about 8 km (5 miles) southeast of Bideford. It is the home of Dartington Crystal (*see under* DARTINGTON). The village of **Little Torrington** is about 3 km (2 miles) to the south.

The Eton schoolmaster and poet William Johnson Cory (1823–92), who wrote the words of the 'Eton Boating Song' (1865), was born in Torrington.

There are towns called Torrington in the USA (Connecticut, Wyoming), in Canada (Alberta) and in Australia (New South Wales).

See also BLACK TORRINGTON.

Battle of Torrington (16 February 1646). A battle towards the end of the first Civil War in which Royalist forces under Sir Ralph Hopton were attacked by Sir Thomas Fairfax's much larger army and subsequently forced back into Cornwall. Hopton surrendered at TRURO the following month. The church at Torrington was then used to house 200 Royalist prisoners. Unfortunately it was doubling as a gunpowder store and it blew up, taking the prisoners with it. It was rebuilt in 1651.

Tor y Foel 'bare mountain side', Welsh *tor* (*see* TORFAEN) + *y* 'the' + *moel* 'bare, bald'.

A hill (551 m / 1808 ft) in the eastern BRECON BEACONS, in Powys (formerly in Brecknockshire), some 15 km

(9 miles) west of Abergavenny. The hill, visible from the home of the poet Henry Vaughan in LLANSANTFFRAED, inspired the opening of his poem 'The World':

> I saw Eternity the other night
> Like a Great Ring of pure and endless light …
>
> Henry Vaughan: 'The World', from *Silex Scintillans* (1650–5)

Tory Island Irish *Toraigh* 'place of towers', referring to the cliffs and isolated tors around the island.

An island some 10 km (6 miles) off the northwest coast of DONEGAL. There are two main settlements, East Town and West Town. In Irish mythology Tory Island was the home of the Fomorians, loathsome creatures defeated by the Tuatha Dé Danann and a dose of satire at the Second Battle of MOYTURA. Their king, Balor of the Evil Eye (said to be responsible for the POISONED GLEN), gave his name to Dún Bhalair (Irish 'Balar's fort'), a promontory fort at the east end of the island. Later, in the 6th century, St Columcille (Columba) founded a monastery here; there are a few scant remains. As there are no rats on the island, mainlanders are advised to avoid infestations by spreading some soil from Tory Island around the house.

Tory Island is separated from the mainland by **Tory Sound** – and by frequent storms, hence its fuller Irish name *Toraigh na dTonn* ('Tory of the breakers'). In 1974 a storm cut off the island for more than eight weeks and almost led to a permanent evacuation. However, the fortunes of the Irish-speaking islanders have since revived, and the people survive on tourism, lobsters and – surprisingly – painting.

Tory School. A school of naïve art that has its origin in the 1960s, when the English painter Derek Hill arrived on the island. A local man, James Dixon, watched Hill paint and declared that he could do better using the hairs from the tail of a donkey. Hill encouraged his efforts and soon others on the island took up painting; the results now have a worldwide audience. One of the most famous of the painters today is Patsy Dan Rodgers; he is also a musician and the **King of Tory Island**, a role that involves promoting the island and attracting visitors.

'Waves of Tory, The'. One of the most popular of Irish céilí dances.

Totland 'cultivated land or estate with a look-out place', OE *tot* 'look-out place' + *land* 'cultivated land, estate'.

A coastal village at the western end of the ISLE OF WIGHT, about 4 km (2.5 miles) northeast of the NEEDLES. It nestles behind **Totland Bay**, which is a popular traditional holiday resort.

Totnes 'Totta's headland', OE male personal name *Totta* + NESS.

A market town and port in south Devon, at the highest navigable point on the River DART, about 13 km (8 miles) northwest of Dartmouth. It is a town with a long past, though not quite as long as assigned to it by the legend of Brutus, great-grandson of Aeneas, who allegedly landed at Totnes at the end of his voyage from Troy and went on to found the kingdom of Britain. Corineus, one of Brutus's companions, is said to have killed the Cornish giant Gogmagog (*see under* GOGMAGOG HILLS) by hurling him from a cliff, a feat commemorated now in the name of a nearby cliff, Giant's Leap.

There was a mint at Totnes in Anglo-Saxon times, and in the late Middle Ages and the Tudor period the wealth it earned from the export of cloth and the import of wine made it the second most affluent town in Devon after Exeter. After the 16th century it went into a rapid decline, but some fine Elizabethan and Georgian buildings remain as a reminder of its high summer. It is still a working port in a small way, but at the beginning of the 21st century it is better known as a thriving 'New Age'-ish arts-and-crafts centre.

The well-preserved **Totnes Castle**, one of the oldest strongholds in Norman England, occupies a commanding position overlooking the town. Nearby lie the ruins of BERRY POMEROY castle.

The computing pioneer Charles Babbage (1791–1871) was a pupil at the King Edward VI Grammar School in Totnes.

Tottenham 'Totta's homestead or village', OE *Tottan* possessive form of male personal name *Totta* + HAM.

A district of northeast London (N15, N17), in the borough of HARINGEY, to the west of the River LEA, between EDMONTON to the north and STOKE NEWINGTON to the south. Until the early 19th century it was a rural community (the writer Izaak Walton stayed here on fishing trips), but by the 1830s urbanization was well under way, and it accelerated greatly in the 1870s after the LIVERPOOL STREET-to-ENFIELD railway arrived. Tottenham became a densely populated, mainly working-class area, with smatterings of light industry.

Thomas Hodgkin (1798–1866), the physician after whom Hodgkin's disease was named, was born in Tottenham. There is a Tottenham in Ontario, Canada.

Tottenham Hotspur FC. A Tottenham-based football club, founded in 1882. Its home ground is WHITE HART LANE (a name derived ultimately from that of a nearby tavern). Amongst its many achievements probably the most notable was the winning of the League and F.A. Cup double in 1960–1. The second part of its name (which is usually shortened to simply 'Spurs') was inspired by the area's connection with the dukes of Northumberland: in the 18th century a Tottenham man, Hugh Smithson, married into the Percy family, eventually becoming Duke himself; and Henry Percy (1364–1403), son of the first Earl of Northumberland (who features in Shakespeare's *Henry IV,*

Part I), acquired through his impulsiveness the nickname 'Hotspur'.

Tottenham is turned French. An expression current in the 16th and 17th centuries referring to an unlikely or remarkable change.

Tottenham pudding. A feed for pigs or poultry, consisting of sterilized kitchen waste. It was developed in Tottenham during the Second World War.

Tottenham Three, the. The collective name given to Winston Silcott, Engin Raghip and Mark Braithwaite, who were sentenced to life imprisonment in 1987 for 'having common cause' with the mob who murdered PC Keith Blakelock during the October 1985 Broadwater Farm riots in Tottenham. Their convictions were quashed in 1991 after tests revealed that Silcott's confession had been tampered with. Braithwaite and Raghip were released, though Silcott remained in jail until 2003 as he was serving a sentence for another murder as well.

Tottenham Court Road From *Tottenham Court*, earlier *Tottenhale Court*, the name of a manor house in the vicinity of present-day EUSTON: *Tottenhale* 'Totta's nook of land', OE *Tottan* possessive form of male personal name *Totta* + *halh* (*see* HALE, -HALL). Thus although the same OE personal name is involved, the origin of the road name is quite distinct from that of TOTTENHAM, and there is no reason to suppose that the Tottas concerned were one and the same. The name of the manor house had changed under the influence of *Tottenham* to *Tottenham Court* by the early 18th century.

A road in Central London (W1), in the borough of CAMDEN, linking OXFORD STREET with the Euston Road (*see under* EUSTON). It started life as a way across the fields from London to the ancient manor of Tottenham Court, and the earliest surviving record of it is as Tottenham Court Row, in 1708. Nowadays it is dedicated to shopping: the ever so slightly tacky southern end (loomed over by the great tower of CENTRE POINT) is given over almost entirely to computers, video and audio equipment and the like; the northern end is more varied but dominated by furniture shops, notably Habitat, (formerly) Maples and the decidedly upmarket Heals, which has been on the same Tottenham Court Road site since 1840.

Tottenham Court Road Underground station, on the Central and Northern lines, opened in 1900 (the Northern line station was originally called 'Oxford Street').

> Tottenham Court Road, the ugliest and most ludicrous street in London.
>
> V.S. Pritchett: *London Perceived* (1962)

Tottenham Hale *Hale* 'nook or corner of land', OE *halh* (*see* HALE, -HALL) (there is still a street in the area called 'the Hale').

An area of southeastern TOTTENHAM. Tottenham Hale

Underground station, on the Victoria line, opened in 1968.

Tottington 'Tota's farm', OE male personal name *Tota* (or *tot* 'look-out hill') + -ING + -TON.

A town in Greater Manchester, 5 km (3 miles) northwest of Bury.

Totton Probably 'estate associated with Tota', *see* TOTTINGTON.

A town in Hampshire, on the western side of the estuary of the River TEST, opposite SOUTHAMPTON, at the northeastern edge of the NEW FOREST.

Touchen-end 'road fork', OE *twicene*; the present form of the name may be a contraction of *Tuchin Lane End*, evidenced in the early 18th century.

A village in Berkshire, within the unitary authority of WINDSOR AND MAIDENHEAD, about 5 km (3 miles) south of Maidenhead.

Toutinna. *See under* ARRA MOUNTAINS.

Tove An OE river name meaning 'slow one'.

A river in Northamptonshire, which rises near SULGRAVE and flows 32 km (20 miles) eastwards through TOWCESTER and then southeastwards to join the GREAT OUSE to the northwest of Milton Keynes.

Towcester 'Roman station on the River Tove', TOVE + OE *ceaster* (*see* CHESTER).

A town (pronounced 'toaster') in Northamptonshire, on the River Tove, about 13 km (8 miles) southwest of Northampton. It originated as a Roman settlement on WATLING STREET[1] (now the A5), called **Lactodunum**, a name of Celtic origin apparently meaning 'milky fort' (apparently a reference to the cloudiness of the local river). The Anglo-Saxons fortified it, and it came under attack from the Danes. Its position on the road from London to Shrewsbury made it an important stopping-off point for travellers, and several old inns survive, including the mid-15th-century Talbot and the Saracen's Head, where Mr Pickwick lodged in Dickens's *Pickwick Papers* (1837). Most of the central townscape, however, is Victorian with a smattering of Georgian.

National Hunt racing is held at Towcester racecourse. The former airfield that once served Towcester is now SILVERSTONE racetrack.

Towednack '(parish of St) To-Winnoc', from the dedication of the local church to St Winwaloe (*see* GUNWALLOE), of whose name *To-Winnoc* (Cornish *to-* 'thy') is a pet-form.

A village in Cornwall, about 3 km (2 miles) southwest of St Ives.

Tower Hamlets. A borough of East London (E1, E2, E3, E14), immediately to the east of the City of London and bounded to the north by Hackney, to the east by Newham and to the south by the River Thames. It was created in 1965 out of the districts of BETHNAL GREEN, BOW, LIMEHOUSE, MILE END, POPLAR, RATCLIFF, SHADWELL, SPITALFIELDS, STEPNEY, WAPPING, WHITECHAPEL and the ISLE OF DOGS.

The name chosen for it is a revival of a term originally applied in the 16th century to the large area of East London from which the Lieutenant of the TOWER OF LONDON had the right to call men up for guard duty. By the 18th century it was the name of an administrative district covering 21 hamlets (including some in the eastern part of the City). This formed the basis of the parliamentary constituency of Tower Hamlets, created in 1832. In 1918 that was broken up into Bethnal Green, Hackney and Shoreditch, and the name 'Tower Hamlets' went out of use until its resurrection in 1965.

Tower of London. A fortress at the eastern edge of the City of London (E1), on the north bank of the River THAMES[1], in the borough of TOWER HAMLETS, on a site said once to have been occupied by Julius Caesar's fort. Its nucleus is a massive stone keep built in the latter part of the 11th century by Gundulf, Bishop of Rochester, in the reigns of William I and William II, with a view to intimidating the local populace and making it clear that the Normans were here to stay (most castles in that period were made of wood). In the *Anglo-Saxon Chronicle* for 1097 this is referred to as *thone tur* 'the tower', and to this day 'the Tower' in the context of London means the Tower of London. Its walls are 4.5 m (15 ft) thick in the lower part. On its second floor is the Chapel of St John, the oldest intact church building in London, completed in 1080. Around 1240 the tower was whitewashed, and ever since has been called the 'White Tower'.

Further fortifications were added to it over the centuries, and its great outer wall was completed in the reign of Edward I (1272–1307). Amongst its other features the most notable are the Bloody Tower (built in the late 14th century, and so named because the **Princes in the Tower** (*see below*) were thought to have been murdered here); the Byward Tower (built in the 1270s – a 'byward' is a subsidiary guard); and **Traitor's Gate** (a watergate beneath St Thomas's Tower through which prisoners were delivered to the Tower of London).

As well as being a fortress, the Tower has a special place in English history, both as a royal residence down to the time of James VI and I (reigned 1603–25) and as a state prison (being 'sent to the Tower' is a fate still only half-jokingly anticipated by those contemplating radical political action). It has also housed the Royal Mint (until 1810); a menagerie (its only remnants being the ravens, whose wings are clipped so that they cannot fly away, precipitating – so legend says – the fall of the kingdom); a notable collection of arms and armour (now removed to the Royal Armouries

Museum in LEEDS[1]), and the Public Records; and it is still the home of the Crown Jewels (they are kept in the Waterloo Barracks, to the north of the White Tower). Among the headsman's victims buried in its chapel of St Peter ad Vincula (see **Tower Green** below) are Edward Seymour, 1st Duke of Somerset (Protector Somerset, c.1506–52), Henry, 8th Earl of Northumberland (d.1585), Anne Boleyn (c.1504–36), Catherine Howard (d.1542), Lord Guildford Dudley (d.1554), Lady Jane Grey (1537–54), the Duke of Monmouth (1649–85) and Lords Kilmarnock, Balmerino and Lovat (supporters of the 1745 Jacobite rebellion). State prisoners confined here range from the turbulent Norman cleric Ranulf Flambard to Sir Thomas More, Sir Walter Raleigh (who wrote a lot of poetry while he was inside), Guy Fawkes, Sir Roger Casement and Rudolf Hess. During both world wars several German spies were executed here by firing squad.

The Tower is one of London's leading tourist sites, not the least of the attractions being the **Warders of the Tower of London** (popularly known as 'Beefeaters' – the name originally meant simply 'eater of beef', and connoted an overfed menial). They were designated Yeomen Extraordinary of the Guard in the reign of Edward VI, and still wear the somewhat flamboyant uniform of that period. Most of their time is taken up nowadays as tourist guides.

The ancient Ceremony of the Keys is still performed each night at the Tower, after the gates are locked at 10 o'clock by the Chief Yeoman Warder and his escort. The party is challenged on its return by the sentry with the words: 'Halt, who goes there?' The chief warder answers: 'The Keys.' The sentry asks: 'Whose keys?' 'Queen Elizabeth's keys,' is the reply. The guard presents arms and the chief warder removes his bonnet and calls: 'God preserve Queen Elizabeth!', to which the guard replies: 'Amen.' The keys are then deposited in the Queen's House.

> I find no glamour in the Tower. It appals ... The Tower means murder *now*, torture *now*, stranglings, treacheries, massacre, the solitary cell, the kick of the policeman's boot. The scratchings on the walls of the Tower are the scratchings of Auschwitz.
>
> V.S. Pritchett: *London Perceived* (1962)

The Tower was declared a UNESCO World Heritage Site in 1988.

All Hallows by the Tower. A church in Byward Street (EC3), close to the Tower of London, officially known as All Hallows Barking. Its origins can be traced back to Anglo-Saxon times. The nave was destroyed by German bombing in the Second World War, but has been reconstructed. William Penn, founder of Pennsylvania, was baptized here (1644). It is the guild church of Toc H, the community-action charity.

Liberty of the Tower. See **Tower Liberty** below.

preach on Tower Hill. 16th-century gallows humour for 'to be hanged' (see **Tower Hill** below).

Princes in the Tower, the. The boy king Edward V and his younger brother Richard, Duke of York, who were lodged in the Tower of London during May and June 1483, after which their uncle Richard, Duke of Gloucester, assumed the Crown as Richard III. The princes disappeared at this time and are generally presumed to have been murdered on their uncle's orders, but there is no conclusive evidence. Bones found during excavations near the White Tower in 1674 were transferred to Westminster Abbey. In 1933 experts proclaimed them to be bones of children of 12 or 13, the very ages of the princes.

Tower Bridge. A road bridge crossing the River THAMES[1] immediately downstream of the Tower of London. Designed by Sir Horace Jones in the Gothic style (a stipulation of the brief), it is a bascule bridge, which means that the roadway is in two counterbalanced sections that can be raised (originally hydraulically, now electrically) to allow large ships to pass through (vital originally, when the POOL OF LONDON was still a busy port, rather less useful now). It was opened in 1894 by the Prince of Wales (its high-level walkways were closed in 1910 after it was found that they attracted prostitutes). For nearly a hundred years (until the QUEEN ELIZABETH II BRIDGE opened) it was the only bridge below London Bridge (see under LONDON). Its unique outline, somewhat resembling conjoined BIG BENS, has become an icon of London. (It has been claimed that the gullible purchasers of London Bridge thought they were getting Tower Bridge.)

Tower Gateway. A station on the Docklands Light Railway (see under DOCKLAND), a little to the north of the Tower of London. It opened in 1987.

Tower Green. An open space immediately to the west of the White Tower, where highly placed traitors were executed to spare them the indignity of public beheading on **Tower Hill** (see below). Victims include Anne Boleyn, Catherine Howard and Lady Jane Grey. It is the site of the church of St Peter ad Vincula (literally 'St Peter in chains'), founded in the 12th century for the use of Tower prisoners. Many of them (including the above three) are buried here.

Tower Hill. A street on rising ground immediately to the north and west of the Tower of London. It occupies the site of what was formerly the principal place of execution of traitors held in the Tower. Among the 125 to have met their end here were Sir Thomas More, Thomas Cromwell, Archbishop Laud, the Duke of Monmouth and (in 1747) Lord Lovat, the last person to be executed by beheading in England. Up until the 1780s there was still a gallows here where criminals were hanged. The execution site is marked by a memorial plaque in Trinity Square Gardens.

The present Tower Hill Underground station, on the Circle and District lines, opened in 1967 on the site of what had been Tower of London Underground station (1882–4). It replaced the previous Tower Hill station (1946–67), originally named Mark Lane (1884–1946).

Tower Hill play. A slang term from the late 17th to the early 19th centuries, defined by Francis Grose in his *Classical Dictionary of the Vulgar Tongue* (1785) as 'a slap on the face and a kick on the breech', such eventualities being frequent in the rough-housing environs of Tower Hill.

Tower Liberty, Liberty of the Tower. The Tower of London with the fortifications and **Tower Hill** (*see above*). This formed part of the ancient demesne of the Crown, with jurisdiction and privileges distinct from and independent of the City of London. Its bounds are still beaten triennially by choirboys and children after a service in the Royal Chapel of St Peter ad Vincula. Governor, Chaplain, Warders and residents accompany them, and at each of the 31 boundary stones the Chaplain exclaims 'Cursed is he who removeth his neighbour's landmark.' The Chief Warder then says 'Whack it, boys, whack it!'

Tower of London, The. A novel (1840) by William Harrison Ainsworth, based loosely on the story of Lady Jane Grey. (*See also* the novel *Windsor Castle, under* WINDSOR.)

Tower Pier. A jetty on the north bank of the River Thames, at the western end of the Tower of London. It was a stopping-off point on the hydrofoil service introduced between CHARING CROSS and GREENWICH in the 1970s, and in former times paddle steamers plied between here and SOUTHEND-ON-SEA, taking Londoners on their seaside outings. The launch *Havengore* bore Sir Winston Churchill's body from here to the Festival Pier and Waterloo Station after his funeral in 1965.

Tower pound. The legal pound of 5400 grains (350 grams; 11¼ ounces Troy weight), used in England until the adoption of the Troy pound in 1526. It was so called from the standard pound kept in the Tower of London.

Tower Subway. A 412-m (1350-ft) tunnel beneath the River Thames linking the Tower of London on the north bank with TOOLEY STREET on the south bank. Opened in 1870, it was the first tube tunnel under the Thames. At first traversed by a steam-powered tramcar, it was later converted to pedestrian use. After **Tower Bridge** (*see above*) opened in 1894 it was closed down (although it still carries cables and water mains). Its northern entrance is marked by a kiosk at the foot of Tower Hill.

Tower weight. Weight expressed in terms of **Tower pounds** (*see above*).

Tow Law 'lookout hill', OE *tot* 'lookout' + *hlaw* (*see* LAW, LOW). A village in County Durham, 12 km (7.5 miles) northwest of Bishop Auckland.

Town of Books, the. A nickname for HAY-ON-WYE.

Town of the Four Masters. A name by which DONEGAL was once known.

Town With the Hole in the Middle, the. A nickname for BANBRIDGE in County Down.

Town Yetholm. *See under* KIRK YETHOLM.

Towton 'Tofi's farm', OScand male personal name *Tofi* + -TON. A village in North Yorkshire, 18 km (11 miles) southwest of York.

Battle of Towton (29 March 1461). A battle during the Wars of the Roses, a victory for the young Yorkist claimant, Edward IV. It was fought in a snowstorm, and was one of the bloodiest and most merciless battles ever fought on British soil (*see also* TADCASTER):

> I call it most cruel and bloody, because the animosity of the parties was so great, that though they were countrymen and Englishmen, neighbours, nay, as history says, relations; for here fathers killed their sons, and sons their fathers; yet for some time they fought with such obstinacy and such rancour, that, void of all pity and compassion, they gave no quarter ... here, at Towton, fell six and thirty thousand men on both sides, besides the wounded and prisoners (if they took any).
>
> Daniel Defoe: *A Tour Through the Whole Island of Great Britain* (1724–6)

Towy Possibly 'dark one' or 'water'; LLANDOVERY is at the confluence of the Towy, the Gwydderig and the Brân, and the Welsh version of its name, *Llanymddyferi* ('church by the waters', *llan* + *am* 'near' + *dyfri* 'waters') might reflect the ancient name of the Towy.

A river in southwest Wales. In Welsh it is the **Tywi**. It is 111 km (69 miles) long: it rises in the **Tywi Hills** between CEREDIGION (formerly Cardiganshire) and POWYS, and flows south through Llandovery and CARMARTHEN to enter the BRISTOL Channel at Carmarthen Bay.

In his poem *Grongar Hill* (1726) John Dyer (1699–1758) describes the **Vale of Towy** (Welsh *Dyffryn Tywi*), the broad valley of the river between Llandovery and Carmarthen; for an extract, *see* GRONGAR HILL.The poet Dylan Thomas spent childhood holidays in the valley of the Towy, a time recalled in 'Fern Hill' (1946).

> ... slowly the fishing holy stalking heron
> In the river Towy below bows his tilted headstone.
>
> Dylan Thomas: 'Over Sir John's Hill'

Toxteth 'Toki's landing-place', OScand male personal name *Toki* + *stoth* 'landing-place'. A district of Liverpool ('Liverpool 8') with a certain reputation for lawlessness. There were riots here in 1981. The Liverpool-born Liberal politician Herbert Samuel (1870–1963), the first high commissioner for Palestine, later took the title Viscount Samuel of Mount Carmel and of Toxteth.

blaze of trumpets from basement record players
loud guitars in the afternoon ...
bright green patches of mildew redpurple bricks stained
ochre plaster ...

Adrian Henri: 'Poem for Liverpool 8', from *Autobiography*
(1971)

Toyshop of Europe, the. A sobriquet applied by the Irish-
born politician and writer Edmund Burke (1729–97) to
BIRMINGHAM. In this context the word 'toy' refers not to
playthings for children but to trinkets, knick-knacks, etc.
in the manufacture of which Birmingham specialized.

Trafalgar From Cape *Trafalgar* in southwest Spain.
A sea area in the shipping forecast. It is in the eastern
Atlantic, off the southwest corner of Spain and the north-
west corner of Africa, to the south of FITZROY.

Trafalgar Square To commemorate the Battle of *Trafalgar*.
A square in Central London (WC2, SW1), in the City of
WESTMINSTER, at the northern end of WHITEHALL. It stands
on a site formerly occupied by the Royal Mews: originally,
in the 13th century, the place where the king's falcons were
kept, and later the royal stables. The buildings were
demolished in 1830, and the area was redeveloped over
the following decade as a public square, to a design by John
Nash. It was decided to use the square to honour Lord
Nelson (1758–1805), England's great naval hero and victor
over the French at the Battle of Trafalgar (1805; fought on
21 October about 19 km (12 miles) southwest of Cape
Trafalgar in southwestern Spain), and around 1835 it was
named Trafalgar Square. A competition was held in 1838
for a more specific monument to Nelson. This was won by
William Railton with a design for a 44-m (145-foot) column,
which was erected in the middle of the square and
surmounted in 1843 with a statue of Nelson. The ensemble,
officially 'the Nelson Column' but always referred to as
'Nelson's Column', has become one of the main icons of
London. The four bronze lions at its foot, designed by Sir
Edwin Landseer, were added in 1867.

On the northern side of Trafalgar Square is the National
Gallery, built in the 1830s, together with its 1980s
Postmodern addition the Sainsbury Wing, put up after a
previous design had been castigated by the Prince of Wales
as a 'monstrous carbuncle on the face of a much-loved and
elegant friend'. On the eastern side are James Gibbs's church
of St Martin-in-the-Fields (1722–4) and Herbert Baker's
South Africa House (1935), which saw many anti-apartheid
demonstrations in the second half of the 20th century. To
the west is Canada House.

In addition to Whitehall the main roads leading off
Trafalgar Square are the STRAND to the east, Northumberland Avenue (named after Northumberland House, belonging to the Percy family, dukes of Northumberland, which
once stood here) to the southeast, the MALL (by way of

Admiralty Arch), Cockspur Street and PALL MALL to the
west, and St Martin's Place (leading to the Charing Cross
Road (*see under* CHARING CROSS)) to the north.

Almost from the beginning the square has been a venue
for political demonstrations: the Chartists rallied here in
1848; in 1887 the so-called 'Bloody Sunday' encounter here
between radicals and Irish and the police left two people
dead; and in the late 1950s and early 1960s the Aldermaston Marches (*see under* ALDERMASTON) culminated in
a mass rally here. It has had its more light-hearted moments
too, though: it has become the traditional place for New
Year revellers to gather. In the shadow of the huge Christmas tree, donated annually since the Second World War
by Norway, they disport themselves in the fountains while
the police (mostly) look on indulgently.

At the beginning of the 21st century the northern side
of the square was pedestrianized, and public concerts and
similar entertainments have begun to be staged here. There
is no longer any (official) place for the pigeons, which have
always been part of the Trafalgar Square scenery; in 2003
it was made illegal to provide food for them.

In George Orwell's *Nineteen Eighty-four* (1949), Trafalgar
Square appears in the guise of 'Victory Square'. Traitors and
prisoners of war are executed there.

Trafalgar Square Underground station, on the Bakerloo
line, was opened in 1906. In 1979 it was combined with
the old Strand station to form 'Charing Cross'.

In the 20th century *Trafalgar Square*, or simply *Trafalgar*,
was used as rhyming slang for 'chair'.

SCARBOROUGH has its own Trafalgar Square, just beyond
the cricket ground: big-hitters of the past, such as C.I.
Thornton and Cec Pepper, were wont to deposit the ball
in it. There is also a Trafalgar Square in Bridgetown, Barbados (with a statue of Nelson).

Trafford 'ford on a Roman road', OE *strœt* (*see* STREET) + FORD;
Stratford 1206.
A metropolitan borough and unitary authority in Greater
Manchester, on the southwest side of Manchester. It
includes the area of **Trafford Park**.
See also OLD TRAFFORD.

Traitor's Gate (Dublin). *See under* ST STEPHEN'S GREEN.

Traitor's Gate (London). *See under* TOWER OF LONDON.

Tralee Irish *Trá Lí* 'strand of the River Lee' (which enters the
sea just south of the town).
The county town of County KERRY, 27 km (17 miles) northwest of Killarney. It is at the head of **Tralee Bay**, at the
northeastern end of the DINGLE Peninsula. Tralee was the
seat of the Fitzgerald earls of Desmond, and many of them
were buried in the Dominican friary founded by their
ancestor, John FitzThomas, in 1243 (little remains of his
foundation). After the failure of the second Desmond

rebellion (*see under* DESMOND) in 1583, Tralee was granted to an English soldier, Edward Denny. It was taken by Confederate Catholic forces in 1641, but fell in 1643 to the despised Murrough 'the Burner' O'Brien. In 1691 the Jacobites burnt the town rather than let it fall into the hands of the approaching Williamites. Tralee Workhouse was a focus of suffering during the Great Famine, some 25 people dying there every week, and the dead being buried in the Famine graveyard called God's Acre. At the time of the Easter Rising in 1916 the German ship *Libau* entered Tralee Bay with arms for the rebels, but was intercepted by the British, so failing to rendezvous with Sir Roger Casement, who had been put ashore nearby. During the subsequent Anglo-Irish War (1919–21) Tralee was a focus of activity. Today the town has little of architectural interest, although the otherwise workaday St John's Catholic church (1870) has a 60-m (about 200-ft) spire, reputedly the tallest in Ireland. There is a race course.

Tralee is said to have been the birthplace of St Brendan the Navigator (*c*.484–578), and was more certainly the birthplace of Dick Spring (b.1950), leader of the Irish Labour Party.

> A place like Tralee puts you in touch with a remembered but recently disappeared past, and makes you realize how long it is since you walked through a British town and thought, 'Oh good. There's a branch of Dixons.'
>
> Pete McCarthy: *McCarthy's Bar* (2000)

> There was a young girl of Tralee
> Whose knowledge of French was 'Oui Oui.'
>   When they said, 'Parlez-vous?'
>   She replied, 'Same to you!'
> She was famed for her bright repartee.
>
> Anon.: limerick

'Rose of Tralee, The'. A song by William Pembroke Mulchinock (?1820–64):

> The pale moon was rising above the green mountain,
>   The sun was declining beneath the blue sea,
> When I stray'd with my love to the pure crystal fountain
>   That stands in the beautiful vale of Tralee …
>
> She was lovely and fair as the rose of the summer,
>   Yet 'twas not her beauty alone that won me,
> Oh, no, 'twas the truth in her eyes ever beaming
>   That made me love Mary, the Rose of Tralee.

The story goes that Mulchinock was in love with Mary O'Connor, a servant in his mother's house. His love was thwarted not by class differences, but by a false accusation of murder, obliging him to flee to India for six years. He returned in 1833, just in time for Mary's funeral.

Mulchinock's words were set to music by Charles Glover (1806–63) and popularized by John McCormack (for example in the 1930 film *Song o' My Heart*); the song is also the anthem of the Kerry Gaelic football team. Since 1958 the Festival of Kerry held at Tralee has hosted an international Rose of Tralee contest for those of Irish extraction and startling (inner) beauty.

Trá Lí. The Irish name for TRALEE.

Trá Mhór. The Irish name for TRAMORE.

Tram Inn From the name of a local inn, which stood beside a coal-carrying tramline.

A village in Herefordshire (before 1998 in Hereford and Worcester, before 1974 in Herefordshire), about 8 km (5 miles) southwest of Hereford.

Tramore Irish *Trá Mhór* 'big strand'.

A popular seaside resort in County Waterford, 10 km (6 miles) south of Waterford itself. It takes its name from the great stretches of sand here, which have made Tramore popular for sea-bathing since Georgian times. There is also a race course. The town overlooks **Tramore Bay**, whose inner portion, Black Sand Lagoon, is separated from the sea by a sandy spit. The headlands on either side of the bay have pillars erected by Lloyds of London in the early 19th century, following a shipwreck, to warn sailors of its unwelcoming waters. On one of these pillars is the Metal Man, a giant cast-iron sculpture of a sailor pointing towards the safer waters of WATERFORD Harbour to the east. It is said that if a girl hops three times round the base of the statue she will be married within the year.

> Screams of girls and gulls
> Red-eyed in the Atlantic salt,
> Kicking over chip papers
> On the endless sands of Tramore.
>
> J.P. Macardle: 'On the Beaches', from *Loss
> and Lazy Longing* (1962)

Tranent OCelt *tref* 'farm' (*see* TRE-) + *nant* 'stream, valley'.
A former mining town in East Lothian, 6 km (4 miles) east of Musselburgh. Coal-mining began here in the 13th century, and subsidence from collapsed mines has caused the formation of a number of hollows in the ground. In 1722 a wooden railway was constructed to take coal to the nearby port of Cockenzie.

Clerk of Tranent. A poet of whom little is known apart from his appearance in William Dunbar's (?1456–?1513) elegy for dead poets, *Lament for the Makaris*:

> Clerk of Tranent eik he hes tane,
> That maid the Anteris of Gawane …
> *Timor mortis conturbat me*.

Massacre of Tranent (1797). The fatal shooting of a number of Tranent miners protesting about compulsory recruitment following the Militia Act.

Tranmere 'sandbank frequented by cranes' (the reference is of course to birds, although the docks of modern Birkenhead might make an alternative interpretation seem more appropriate), OScand *trani* 'crane' + *melr* 'sandbank'.

(Ingenious but unfounded alternative etymologies have been suggested: 'across the sea' (a Liverpudlian viewpoint), Latin *trans* 'across' + *mare* 'sea'; and 'village at the bare hill', pseudo-Welsh *Tre-yn-Moel*.)

A southeastern district of BIRKENHEAD, on the west bank of the MERSEY, in the WIRRAL. The local football club, **Tranmere Rovers FC**, was founded in 1884, as Belmont; it adopted its present name the following year.

Trap Etymology uncertain, but this is a modern, English name, perhaps relating to some industrial contrivance.

A village in Carmarthenshire (formerly in Dyfed), 5 km (3 miles) south of Llandeilo.

Traprain Law 'hill of Traprain', an old name meaning 'farm by the tree', *Traprain* OCelt *tref* (*see* TRE-) + *pren* 'tree, wood'; *Law* Scots from OE *hlaw* 'mound, conical hill' (*see* LAW, LOW). A striking, craggy, whale-backed hill (224 m / 734 ft) 7 km (4.5 miles) east of Haddington in East Lothian. Although not high, it dominates the land between the LAMMERMUIRS and the sea. The present name is thought to have been transferred to it from the name of a local farm. Its original name was **Dunpender** ('hillfort of the staves', OCelt *dun* (*see* DOWN, -DON) + *peledyr* 'staves', 'spear shafts'). The old name is found on documents as recently as the 15th century.

Traprain Law was first occupied in the Neolithic period. At the time of the Roman occupation it was the capital of the Votadini, the major Celtic tribe of the Lothians. However, around AD 500 they moved their capital to the Castle Rock in EDINBURGH. There is a legend about Princess Thenew or Enoch, unmarried daughter of Loth, the Votadani chief and king of the Lothians. He was so furious when he found out that she was pregnant that he had her thrown down the cliffs on the south side of Traprain Law. However, having prayed for foregiveness on her descent, she survived. The king, now believing her to be a witch, had her thrown into the sea near the ISLE OF MAY, where she managed to cling on to the rock still known as Maiden Hair Rock, before being swept up the Firth of Forth to the shore at CULROSS. Here she gave birth to her son, the future St Kentigern (or Mungo), the patron saint of Glasgow. Recent excavations on Traprain Law have opened the possibility that Kentigern may actually have been born here rather than in Culross.

Traprain Treasure, the. A hoard of battered Roman silver artefacts found only a little below the surface of Traprain Law in 1919. The objects, which are both ecclesiastical and secular, are thought to have been looted from the Rhineland by sea-raiders, or possibly acquired through trade, probably in the early 5th century. The treasure is now in the care of the National Museums of Scotland.

Traquair 'house on the River Quair', OCelt *tref* 'house, homestead' (*see* TRE-) + river name, perhaps derived from OCelt *Vedra* 'clear one'. The medieval spellings of the name indicate that the OCelt *tref* was replaced with Gaelic *treabhair* 'farmstead'.

A small village, little more than a hamlet, in the BORDERS (formerly in Peeblesshire), on the south side of the TWEED opposite Innerleithen. Nearby is **Traquair House**, claimed to be the oldest continuously inhabited house in Scotland. The oldest part is said to be 10th century, but much of what is visible dates from the early 17th century. The approach to the house was formerly through gates with statues of bears on either side, but these gates have remained closed since the 18th century. The story is that the 5th Earl of Traquair received Bonnie Prince Charlie here during the 1745 Jacobite Rising, and swore as the prince left through the Bear Gates that they would not be opened again until a Stuart regained the throne. An alternative story is that they were closed in 1796 by the 7th Earl, following the death of his countess. To the east of the village and house is **Elibank and Traquair Forest**, consisting of Forestry Commission plantations.

'Bush Aboon Traquair, The'. A song by Robert Crawford (1695–1732), celebrating a grove of birches near (Scots *aboon* 'above') the village, which subsequently attracted many visitors (including Robert Burns in 1787). Its fame led to its degradation, as people took away bits of wood to make such items as snuff boxes. The tune is employed in the trio sonata in D by the London-based composer Francesco Geminiani (*c.*1679–1762).

Trawden 'valley shaped like a trough', OE *trog* 'trough' + *denu* 'valley'.

A village in Lancashire, 3 km (2 miles) southeast of Colne. Above it rises the **Forest of Trawden**, an area of moorland rising to Boulsworth Hill (518 m / 1699 ft).

Trawsfynydd 'over the hill', Welsh *traws* 'across' + *mynydd* 'mountain'.

A village in Gwynedd (formerly in Merioneth), 11 km (7 miles) south of Blaenau Ffestiniog. The village was the home of the poet Ellis Evans (known as Hedd Wyn, 'beautiful peace'), killed on the Western Front in 1917, and a few weeks later awarded the Chair at the National Eisteddfod. The 1992 S4C (Channel 4 Wales) film *Hedd Wyn*, largely filmed in the village, was nominated at the 1994 Oscars for best foreign-language film. The village has a statue of the poet.

Next to the village is **Llyn Trawsfynydd**, created (1930) for a hydroelectric scheme. Also loomingly present is **Trawsfynydd Nuclear Power Station**, designed by Sir Basil Spence; it was completed in 1964 and decommissioned in 1995.

Treak Cliff *Treak* perhaps 'grief oak' (that is, a tree for hanging criminals), OE *trega* 'grief' + *ac* 'oak'.

A hillside in Derbyshire, close to Castleton in the PEAK DISTRICT. **Treak Cliff Cavern** is a source of Blue John, a rare

---

❖ tre- ❖

This Brittonic element, *tref, tre* – meaning 'house, homestead, farm, hamlet' – is one of the characteristic elements in Cornish names, occurring dozens of times, as in TREBETHERICK, TREGADILLETT, TRESCO. It also occurs in Scotland, in TRAQUAIR (Scottish Borders) and TRAPRAIN LAW (East Lothian). In Wales the element is found in (among others) Trefaldwyn and Trefylco (Powys), and Trefynwy (Monmouthshire), respectively the Welsh names of MONTGOMERY, KNIGHTON and MONMOUTH. The Welsh names clearly refer to larger settlements than the others, an indication that they were coined later than, and as alternatives to, the English names.

---

blue fluorspar, and also has some spectacular stalactites and stalagmites.

Trebetherick 'Pedrek's farm', Cornish TRE- + male personal name *Pedrek* (probably connected with St *Petroc* – see PADSTOW). A village in Cornwall, on the eastern side of the CAMEL estuary, opposite Padstow. The poet John Betjeman took his childhood holidays here, vividly recalled in *Summoned by Bells* (1960):

> As out of Derry's stable came the brake
> To drag us up those long, familiar hills,
> Past haunted woods and oil-lit farms and on
> To far Trebetherick by the sounding sea.

Betjeman now lies buried at the nearby church at St Enodoc (rescued from the sands in 1863).

Tredegar 'farm of Tegyr', Welsh TRE- + personal name *Tegyr*. The town took its name from the Tredegar family, on whose land the Tredegar Ironworks were built in 1800; the family themselves took their name from the small settlement of Tredegar near Newport.

A former mining town in Blaenau Gwent (formerly in Monmouthshire, then in Gwent), 3 km (2 miles) west of Ebbw Vale. It grew up around the Tredegar Ironworks built in 1800. In 1860 a New Tredegar Colliery was opened some 6 km (4 miles) to the south, and around this grew the small town known as **New Tredegar**.

Tredegar was the birthplace of the Labour politician Aneurin ('Nye') Bevan (1897–1960), inaugurator of the National Health Service; and of Neil Kinnock (b.1942), leader of the Labour Party from 1983 to 1992.

Tredrizzick 'farm covered with bracken', Cornish TRE- + *redenek* 'characterized by bracken'. A village in Cornwall, on the northeastern side of the CAMEL estuary, about 5 km (3 miles) northeast of Padstow.

Treen 'farm by a fort' (referring to the nearby Treryn Dinas), Cornish TRE- + *din* 'fort'.

A village in Cornwall, about 5 km (3 miles) southeast of Land's End. On a nearby headland are an Iron Age fort called Treryn Dinas and a 70-ton 'rocking stone' called Logan's Rock (*Logan* from Cornish *log* 'to move'); the rock was knocked off its pivot in 1824 by a nephew of the playwright Oliver Goldsmith and a gang of sailors; somehow they managed to get it back in place, but it has never rocked again since. There is a nudist beach at the foot of Treen cliff.

Trefaldwyn. The Welsh name for MONTGOMERY.

Trefdraeth. The Welsh name for NEWPORT[5].

Trefylco. The Welsh name for KNIGHTON.

Trefynwy. The Welsh name for MONMOUTH and MONMOUTHSHIRE.

Tregadillett 'Cadyled's farm', Cornish TRE- + personal name *Cadyled*.

A village in Cornwall, 3 km (2 miles) west of Launceston.

Tregaron Welsh TRE- + *Caron*, the name of the river, the parish and the dedication of the local church; it is impossible to say whether the hamlet is named directly from the saint (of whom nothing is known), or from the river name, but the lack of a marker such as *llan* ('church') might suggest the latter.

A small market town in the Teifi valley, Ceredigion (formerly Cardiganshire, then in Dyfed), 30 km (19 miles) southeast of Aberystwyth. Nearby is **Tregaron Bog** (Welsh *Cors Caron*), whose 10,000-year-old peat provides a valuable record of environmental and climatic change.

Tregaron was the birthplace of Henry Richard (1812–88), founder of the Peace Union, a precursor of the League of Nations.

Tregony Perhaps 'Rigni's farm', Cornish TRE + personal name *Rigni*.

A large village in southwest Cornwall, on the River FAL, about 10 km (6 miles) east of Truro. It is pronounced, unusually for a Cornish *Tre-* name, with the stress on the first syllable (and the *o* swallowed) – 'treg-ny'. Today Tregony is billed as the 'gateway to the ROSELAND' for touristic purposes, but in the Middle Ages, before tin streaming and silting made the Fal unnavigable around here, it was an important port. From here the local rough **Tregony cloth** would have been shipped.

Trelissick 'Ledik's farm', Cornish TRE- + personal name *Ledik*. A village in Cornwall, on the western side of the estuary of the River FAL, about 8 km (5 miles) northeast of Falmouth. **Trelissick Garden** (National Trust) features the sort of sub-tropical vegetation for which Cornwall is renowned, and also has a notable display of hydrangeas.

Trellick Tower Etymology unkown.

A tower block in North KENSINGTON, West London (W10), erected between 1968 and 1972 to the design of Erno

Goldfinger. Its distinctive outline, characterized by a separate lift-shaft connected to the main block by walkways, makes it an easily recognizable landmark to the north of the WESTWAY. In 2000 it was listed as Grade II*.

Tremadog *See* PORTHMADOG.

A village on the southern edge of SNOWDONIA, Gwynedd (formerly in Caernarvonshire), 1 km (0.6 miles) north of Porthmadog. The anglicized version of the name is **Tremadoc**. Like Porthmadog, it was developed and named after himself by William Alexander Madocks in 1810, but never grew into the town he had planned. The series of cliffs behind the village are collectively known to rock climbers as Tremadoc (although each crag has its own Welsh name), and the large bay overlooked by the village and flanked by the LLEYN PENINSULA to the west is called **Tremadoc Bay**.

Tremostyn. The Welsh name for MOSTYN.

Trent[1] An OCelt river name probably meaning 'trespasser, strongly flooding one'.

The chief river in the English MIDLANDS, and the third longest river in England. It rises in the South PENNINES, at Norton-in-the-Moors, near the Staffordshire–Cheshire border, and flows 275 km (170 miles), mainly northeastwards, through DERBYSHIRE, NOTTINGHAMSHIRE and NORTH LINCOLNSHIRE to join the OUSE[2], thus forming the HUMBER Estuary. For much of the latter part of its route it forms the boundary between Nottinghamshire and Lincolnshire. Its main tributaries are the Churnet, the DERWENT[4], the DOVE and the TAME[1]. It is tidal as far as Cromwell Lock, 5 km (3 miles) below NEWARK. Other major towns along its course are STOKE-ON-TRENT, BURTON UPON TRENT, NOTTINGHAM[1] and GAINSBOROUGH.

The Trent is subject to a tidal wave known as an 'eagre' (a word of unknown origin). When there is a tide of over 7.5 m (25 ft) at HULL, it forces a wave of between 0.3 and 1.5 m (1 and 5 ft) up the Trent as far as Cromwell Lock. The tidal Trent is the FLOSS of George Eliot's novel *The Mill on the Floss* (1860), whose flooding has such tragic results.

The Romans used the Trent as a transport route and the Danes used it as an invasion route, their means of access to Nottingham. Its navigation was improved in the 18th century, increasing its importance as a freight carrier. The **Trent and Mersey Canal**, constructed in the 1760s, connects it ultimately with the River MERSEY. Running along the valley of the River Trent, it is now little used, but in its heyday it transported the pots from the POTTERIES and the beer from Burton upon Trent. Near its northern end it is, or was, linked to the River WEAVER by the remarkable Anderton Boat Lift, built in 1875 and now a scheduled monument, which raised boats 15 m (50 ft) (*see also* **Harecastle Tunnels** *at* HARECASTLE). The Trent is also linked to the GRAND UNION CANAL.

There is also a river called the Trent in the USA (North Carolina) and a Trent Canal in Canada, which links Lake Huron with Lake Ontario.

There is no connection between the English Trent and that of the Council of Trent (the meeting of the Roman Catholic Church in the mid-16th century which promulgated the Counter-Reformation). There, *Trent* is the German version of *Trento*, the name of the northern Italian city where the Council was held.)

Trent Bridge. A cricket ground in WEST BRIDGFORD, Nottingham, the headquarters of NOTTINGHAMSHIRE County Cricket Club. It was opened in 1839 by the great early 19th-century entrepreneur of English cricket, William Clarke. It has been a test match ground since 1899. It had a reputation in the first half of the 20th century as something of a batsman's paradise: the cricket writer Neville Cardus mused that at Trent Bridge it was always 3 o'clock and the score was always 300 for 2. Just outside the ground was 'George Parr's tree', an elm tree so called because balls struck by Nottinghamshire's renowned hitter (1826–91) often sailed through its branches; it blew down in 1976 and small souvenir bats were made from its timber.

Trent Falls. The point at which the River Trent joins the Ouse and the Humber. It is an area of mudflats, favoured by waders and other estuary birds.

Trent[2]. An alternative name of the River PIDDLE.

Trent[3] From the name of a local stream called *Trent* (of the same origin as TRENT[1]).

A village in Dorset, about 5 km (3 miles) northeast of Yeovil. Charles II went into hiding for a fortnight in the local manor house after the Battle of Worcester (1651) (*see under* WORCESTER). Geoffrey Fisher, Archbishop of Canterbury 1945–61, became a curate in Trent after his retirement from Lambeth.

Treorchy 'village on the Orci or Gorci', Welsh TRE- + stream name of unknown meaning.

A former mining town in the Rhondda, in RHONDDA CYNON TAFF unitary authority (formerly in Glamorgan, then Mid Glamorgan), 13 km (8 miles) northwest of Pontypridd. In Welsh it is **Treorchi**. It is home to the oldest male voice choir in Wales, begun in 1883.

Tre'r Ceiri. *See under* the RIVALS.

Trerice. *See under* NEWQUAY.

Trerulefoot The first element is probably Cornish TRE- 'farm', but the remainder is obscure.

A village in Cornwall, about 10 km (6 miles) west of Saltash.

Tresco 'farm of elder-trees', Cornish TRE- 'farm' + *scaw* 'elder-tree'.

The second largest of the SCILLY ISLES, to the northwest of ST MARY'S. It was originally known as *Iniscaw* (Cornish, 'elder-tree island'), but the present name had been adopted from that of a local farm by the 14th century. It is famous for its subtropical Abbey Gardens.

Treshnish Isles Possibly 'Thrasi's cape', OScand personal name + *nes* (*see* NESS). The spelling *-nish* for *nes* is common in the Hebrides.

A group of small islands in the Inner HEBRIDES, some 15 km (9 miles) west of MULL. The islands include Cairn na Burgh More, Fladda, Lunga (which is a nature reserve) and Bac Mor or **Dutchman's Cap**, so named because from a distance it looks like a brimmed hat. The last inhabitants left Lunga in 1857. There is an old story that MacLean of Lochbuie was once imprisoned by his clan enemies in the now-ruined castle on Cairn na Burgh More, accompanied only by the ugliest woman on Mull. He nevertheless managed to sire an heir upon her, and this heir eventually reclaimed his father's inheritance. It is said that during the Reformation the monks of IONA buried their valuable library somewhere on Cairn na Burgh More.

Tre-Taliesin. An alternative name for TALIESIN.

Trethevy Quoit *Trethevy* 'Dewi's farm', Cornish TRE- + male personal name *Dewi*; *Quoit* a term used in Cornwall for a chamber-tomb or cist, from ModE *quoit* 'ring or disc used for throwing'.

A Stone Age chamber-tomb in Cornwall, about 5 km (3 miles) south of Minions. It is nearly 5 m (over 15 ft) high and surmounted by a massive capstone – Cornwall's largest Neolithic monument. Other names for it have been 'King Arthur's Quoit' and the 'Giant's House'.

Trevose Head *Trevose* originally a farm name, 'farm by the bank or dyke' (perhaps referring to an earlier fort), Cornish TRE- + *an* 'the' + *fos* 'bank, dyke'.

A headland in north Cornwall, about 8 km (5 miles) west of Padstow. Its cliffs are about 74 m (243 ft) high. The local lighthouse came into operation in 1847.

Trewassa 'Gwasso's farm', Cornish TRE- + personal name *Gwasso*.

A village in Cornwall, on the northwestern edge of Bodmin Moor (*see under* BODMIN), about 19 km (12 miles) west of Launceston.

Trewithen Probably 'farm of Gwethyen', Cornish TRE- + personal name *Gwethyen* or *Gwydhyan*.

A woodland garden about 8 km (5 miles) east of Truro in Cornwall. It was created over a period of 200 years by the descendants of the 18th-century owner Thomas Hawkins, who planted many of its trees himself. It features in particular magnolias, camellias, rhododendrons, maples and birches.

Trewoon 'farm on the downs', Cornish TRE- + *goen* 'downs'.
A village in Cornwall, about 3 km (2 miles) west of St Austell.

Triermain. *See* CASTLE ROCK OF TRIERMAIN.

Trim Irish *Baile Átha Troim* 'town of the ford of the elder tree' (*see* FORD).

A market town on the River BOYNE in County Meath, 14 km (8.5 miles) southwest of Navan. St Patrick is said to have founded a see here in the 5th century, with St Loman as its first bishop, and Trim is still the cathedral town of the Protestant diocese of Meath. Trim was a stronghold of the PALE, and **Trim Castle**, now a well-preserved ruin, is the largest Anglo-Norman castle in Ireland, dating from *c*.1200 (an earlier castle of Hugh de Lacey was destroyed by the Irish in 1174). Several parliaments were held in Trim Castle in the 15th century, including one that forbade the English to wear moustaches, a sure sign of Irishry. The future Henry IV was imprisoned here by Richard II, shortly before the latter's overthrow, and in 1536 Silken Thomas, the rebellious 10th Earl of Kildare, seized the castle. In 1647 the town was besieged, and in 1649 taken, by Confederate Catholics, but they were soon expelled by a Parliamentarian force under Sir Charles Coote.

Trim has another castle, built by Sir John Talbot in 1415. It was bought in 1717 by Esther Johnson, Swift's Stella, who sold it to Swift himself (Swift was earlier rector of nearby Laracor). The building later became a school, attended by the 1st Duke of Wellington before he went to the playing fields of Eton; he was later MP for the town.

Trim was the site of the first of the so-called 'monster meetings' held by the Irish nationalist leader Daniel O'Connell to campaign for repeal of the Act of Union. It attracted some 30,000 people on 9 March 1843.

Trimontium. The Roman name for the EILDON HILLS.

Tring 'wooded slope', OE *treow* 'tree' + *hangra* 'wood on a steep slope'.

A town in Hertfordshire, in the CHILTERN HILLS, about 16 km (10 miles) northwest of Hemel Hempstead. Its Zoological Museum, founded by Lionel Walter Rothschild in the late 19th century, houses the world's largest collection of fleas, together with (but not on) the stuffed remains of two renowned greyhounds, Mick the Miller and Ballyregan Bob (*see under* BALLYREGAN). Lionel Rothschild is also credited with having introduced into Tring from Europe the glis-glis or edible dormouse.

A certain inconsequentiality about its name has led to Tring being one of those places whose mention tends to raise a titter.

Trool. *See* GLEN TROOL.

Troon OCelt *trwyn* 'headland'.

A resort town on the coast of South Ayrshire (formerly in Strathclyde), 10 km (6 miles) north of Ayr. It derives its name from the prominent promontory where the harbour is located. There is a summer ferry service to Belfast. It is a major golfing centre, and the Old Course has hosted the Open on seven occasions between 1923 and 1997.

> There was a young golfer at Troon
> Who always played golf with a spoon.
> 'It's handy you see,
> For the brandy you see,
> Should anyone happen to swoon.'
>
> Anon.: limerick

Teenie fae Troon. A disparaging name applied by Glaswegians to any woman thought to be getting 'above her station' (Troon being regarded as a posh place).

Trossachs, the 'the cross-hills', Gaelic *na tròsaichean*.
The steep-sided wooded glen in the southern HIGHLANDS between Loch Achray and LOCH KATRINE. It is flanked by BEN VENUE to the south and BEN AN to the north, and is some 10 km (6 miles) west of Callander. By a looser definition, the name 'Trossachs' is applied to the whole area of mountains and lochs west of Callander, including Loch Venachar and LOCH ARD. The area was formerly in Perthshire, then in Central region, and is now in the unitary authority of Stirling.

When William Wordsworth and his sister Dorothy visited in 1803 he described the area as 'untouched, unbreathed upon', and found inspiration for 'The Solitary Reaper':

> Behold her, single in the field,
> Yon solitary Highland Lass!

The solitude of the place ended, however, after the tremendous success of Sir Walter Scott's *The Lady of the Lake* (1810), set here and round neighbouring Loch Katrine, and of his *Rob Roy* (1817), much of which is also set here. Hordes of tourists followed and continue to arrive in large numbers every summer. Few of them would echo the gloomy sentiments of the ageing Wordsworth, when he revisited the Trossachs in 1831:

> There's not a nook within this solemn Pass,
> But were an apt confessional for One
> Taught by his summer spent, his autumn gone,
> That Life is but a tale of morning grass,
> Withered at eve.
>
> William Wordsworth: 'The Trosachs' [sic] (1831)

The Trossachs are now part of the **Loch Lomond and Trossachs National Park**, opened in 2002.

Trotternish 'Thrond's headland', OScand male personal name *Thrond* + *nes* (*see* NESS).
The peninsula forming the northeastern tip of SKYE, Highland (formerly in Inverness-shire). It includes the STORR and QUIRAING.

Trottiscliffe 'Trott's cliff or hill-slope', OE *Trottes* possessive form of male personal name *Trott* + *clif* 'cliff, hill-slope'.

A village (pronounced 'trozly') in Kent, on the NORTH DOWNS, just to the north of the M20, about 14 km (8.5 miles) northwest of Maidstone. There is a Neolithic long barrow nearby called the 'Coldrum Stones'.

Trough of Bowland. *See under* FOREST OF BOWLAND.

Trowbridge 'tree-trunk bridge' (probably referring to a bridge over the River Biss), OE *treow* 'tree' + *brycg* 'bridge'.
A town in Wiltshire, about 14 km (8.5 miles) southeast of Bath. It is the administrative centre of WILTSHIRE. It came to prosperity in the late Middle Ages on the back of its cloth mills: the antiquary John Leland described it in the early 16th century as 'flourishing in drapery'.

Isaac Pitman (1813–97), the inventor of shorthand, was born in Trowbridge. The poet George Crabbe (1754–1832) died here.

Trowell 'tree stream' (perhaps referring to a tree-trunk used as a bridge), OE *treow* 'tree' + *wella* 'stream'.
A village in Nottinghamshire, about 8 km (5 miles) west of Nottingham.

Trowse Newton Originally two separate place names: *Trowse* 'wooden house', OE *treow* 'tree' + *hus* 'house'; *Newton see* NEWTON ABBOT.
A village in Norfolk, on the southeastern outskirts of NORWICH.

Troynovant. A name given by early chroniclers to London. It was an alteration of *Trinovant*, denoting the 'town of the Trinovantes', a British tribe inhabiting the area of Essex and southern Suffolk whose capital was probably at CHELMSFORD. This came to be interpreted as if it meant 'New Troy' (*Troy Novant*), in line with the legend, originally promulgated by Geoffrey of Monmouth in his *Historia Regum Britanniae* (*c*.1136) and widely accepted in the Middle Ages, that London had been founded by a Trojan called Brutus, a great-grandson of Aeneas, who travelled to Britain and established his kingdom here. According to the legend, the name *Britain* was derived from *Brutus*.

> For noble Britons sprong from Troians bold,
> And Troynouant was built of old Troyes ashes cold.
>
> Edmund Spenser: *The Faerie Queene* (1590–6)

Troy Town[1]. The guise under which the Cornish town and port of FOWEY[2] appears in the writings of Sir Arthur Quiller-Couch (1863–1944), and notably in his *The Astonishing History of Troy Town* (1888). Quiller-Couch, a Cornishman who lived in Fowey from 1892 until his death, was certainly well aware of the old Cornish usage *Troy town* for a labyrinthine maze of streets (from the name of the city in ancient Asia Minor), a particularly apt choice for the narrow streets of Fowey (pronounced 'foy', and hence rhyming with *Troy*). (On the island of ST AGNES[2] in the SCILLY ISLES there is a real, miniature maze, of indeterminate age, called **Troy Town Maze**.)

Troy Town[2] An allusion to a local maze (*see* TROY TOWN[1]).
A hamlet in Kent, close to the Surrey border, about 2.5 km (1.5 miles) northwest of Edenbridge.

Trull 'circular feature' (probably referring to a round hill or circular earthwork), OE *trendel*.
A village in Somerset, about 3 km (2 miles) southwest of Taunton.

Trumpet From the name of the local inn.
A village in Herefordshire (before 1998 in Hereford and Worcester, before 1974 in Herefordshire), about 5 km (3 miles) northwest of Ledbury.

Trumpington 'estate associated with Trump', OE male personal name *Trump* + -ING + -TON.
A village in Cambridgeshire, now a southern suburb of CAMBRIDGE[1]. The **Trumpington Road** is the main southwestern route into the city.

Trumpton. The fictitious rural setting of the eponymous children's puppet drama series devised by Gordon Murray as a spin-off from CAMBERWICK GREEN. It was first shown on BBC television in 1967. The most high-profile inhabitants of the small town, which is located in **Trumptonshire**, are Captain Flack and his intrepid team of firemen: Pugh, Pugh, Barney McGrew, Cuthbert, Dibble and Grubb.

Trunch Perhaps an OCelt name meaning 'wood on a spur of land' (*see* CED); alternatively, a name transferred from one of the French *Tronchets* (a name meaning 'wood').
A village in Norfolk, about 11 km (7 miles) southeast of Cromer.

Trundle, the OE *tryndel* 'circle'.
An Iron Age fort on a 206-m (676-ft) hill about 6 km (4 miles) north of Chichester in West Sussex. It was a stronghold of a British tribe called the Atrebates.

Truro Probably a Cornish name meaning '(place of) great water-turbulence' (Truro is at the confluence of two swift-flowing rivers and is liable to flooding in winter).
A cathedral city in Cornwall, about 14 km (8.5 miles) east of Redruth. It lies at the point where the rivers Allen and Kenwyn join to form a wider estuary, called **Truro River**, which in turn flows southwards into CARRICK ROADS. It is the administrative centre of CORNWALL.
In the Middle Ages it was one of the Stannary towns of Cornwall (*see* the STANNARIES), and it was also a very important port, exporting mineral ore. The river silted up in the 17th century, which considerably cramped its style, but kaolin is still exported from here. Prosperity returned in the early 19th century with the tin-mining boom, which has left Truro with a legacy of elegant Georgian buildings.
The diocese of Truro covers all of Cornwall and the western part of Devon. **Truro Cathedral**, the neo-Gothic Cathedral Church of Saint Mary, was constructed, to the design of John Loughborough Pearson, between 1879 and 1910; it was the first new Anglican cathedral to be built in England since ST PAUL'S[1]. Built of local granite and Bath stone, the cathedral surges dramatically from the heart of the city. Its interior boasts a particularly fine complement of Victorian stained glass.
The composer Giles Farnaby (*c*.1560–1640) and the actor Samuel Foote (1720–77) were born in Truro, as were the explorers Richard (1803–34) and John Lander (1807–39).
In a series of novels set in Cornwall (e.g. *The Cathedral*, 1922), Hugh Walpole (1884–1941) fictionalized Truro as POLCHESTER. He portrayed the town's beautiful late 18th-century Lemon Street (named after an 18th-century merchant called Mr Lemon who lived in a splendid house on Truro's Regent Street) under the name of 'Orange Street'.
There are towns called Truro in the USA (Iowa, Massachusetts), Canada (Nova Scotia) and Australia (South Australia).

Truskmore Etymology uncertain, but the second element is Irish *mhór* 'big, great'; the first element might be *trosc* 'a recess'.
A hill (647 m / 2122 ft) in the DARTRY MOUNTAINS, on the border of counties Leitrim and Galway, some 5 km (3 miles) east of BENBULBEN. Its summit is disfigured by an RTÉ transmission mast.

Trwyn y Gader. The Welsh name for CARMEL HEAD.

Tryfan Welsh *tryfan* 'pointed peak'.
An impressively rocky mountain (917 m / 3008 ft) in the GLYDERS of Snowdonia, Gwynedd (formerly in Caernarvonshire), some 7 km (4.5 miles) northeast of Snowdon. Not everyone has appreciated its spiky charms:

> Unbeautiful
> In a land of beautiful mountains, this giant, black,
> Barren, bleak, cloudgathering point
> Broods over the smaller water meadows, frowns
> On the windlashed, cold llyn …
>
> Frederic Vanson: 'Tryfan', from *Spring at Llyn Ogwen* (1972)
> (Welsh *llyn* 'lake')

There are many fine old rock climbs of not excessive difficulty such as *Grooved Arête* and *Belle Vue Bastion*, mostly on the East Face, which is traversed by Heather Terrace. The North Ridge is a popular scramble. In 1936 Herr Teufel and Herr Sedlmeyer, accompanied by a Mr Jenkins (who should have known better), scandalized the British climbing establishment by hammering a piton into a crack on a new route on Tryfan, subsequently known as *Munich Climb* (after the unsporting 'Munich Mechanists', who, in British opinion, engineered rock faces into submission). However, by 1970 British guidebook writers were stating that the piton was 'now considered proper'.

Freedom of Tryfan, the. The 'honour' granted those who have made the jump between Adam and Eve on Tryfan's summit. Adam and Eve are two upended, block-like boulders, and failure to achieve the leap between them would have unpleasant consequences.

Trym An OE river name, probably meaning 'strong one'.

A river in the unitary authority of Bristol, a tributary of the AVON². It is about 7 km (4.5 miles) long.

See also WESTBURY ON TRYM.

Tuadh Mumhan. The Irish name for THOMOND.

Tuaim. The Irish name for TUAM.

Tuam Irish *Tuaim* '(burial) mound'.

A town in County Galway, some 25 km (16 miles) east of LOUGH CORRIB. St Íarlaith founded a monastery here in the 6th century, and on the site in 1152 Turlough O'Connor, King of Connacht, built St Mary's Cathedral. Parts of this are incorporated into the 19th-century Protestant cathedral of the see of Tuam, KILLALA and Anchonry – the largest Anglican diocese in the British Isles, with the smallest number of worshippers. As well as being the seat of an Anglican bishop, Tuam also has the cathedral (1846) of the Catholic archdiocese of Tuam.

Tuam was the birthplace of the playwright and novelist Tom Murphy (b.1935). The Scottish poet George MacBeth died at Tuam in 1992.

Tubbercurry Irish *Tobar an Choire* 'well of the cauldron'.

A village in County Sligo, 30 km (19 miles) southwest of Sligo itself.

Tudeley Perhaps '(place at the) glade overgrown with ivy', from a misdivision of ME *atte Ivedeley*, from OE *ifede* 'ivy-covered' + -LEY.

A village in Kent, about 3 km (2 miles) southeast of Tonbridge. The church contains some spectacular stained-glass windows by Marc Chagall (1887–1985).

Tufnell Park Named in honour of William Tufnell, lord of the manor of Barnsbury in the mid-18th century and owner of the land on which Tufnell Park stands (there is no park in the area).

A residential district of North London (N7, N19), in the borough of ISLINGTON, between HAMPSTEAD to the west and HOLLOWAY to the east. In spite of permission to build having been acquired by William Tufnell in the 1760s, the area remained largely farmland until the 1830s, and its cows contributed significantly to London's milk supply. Then, however, the builders moved in, at first with substantial middle-class villas, later in the 19th century with more modest Victorian dwellings that gave Tufnell Park the rather drab aspect it retains to this day.

Tufnell Park Underground station, on the Northern line (High Barnet branch), opened in 1907.

Tulach Mhór. The Irish name for TULLAMORE.

Tulach Óg. The Irish name for TULLAGHOGUE.

Tullaghogue Irish *Tulach Óg* 'hillock of the youths'.

A village in County Tyrone, some 4 km (2.5 miles) south of Cookstown. It is also spelt **Tullyhogue**. The nearby ring fort was the site of the **Tullaghogue Stone**, a prehistoric standing stone that was used in the inauguration ceremony of each O'Neill chieftain for seven centuries, until it was destroyed in 1602 by Lord Mountjoy as he went about the destruction of Gaelic Ireland following the Battle of Kinsale (*see under* KINSALE).

Tullamore Irish *Tulach Mhór* 'big hill', referring to the hill on which St Catherine's Church now stands.

The county town of County OFFALY, 80 km (50 miles) west of Dublin. It is a market town and is situated on the GRAND CANAL. It was laid out by the Bury family in the mid-18th century, but in 1785 it suffered an early aeronautical disaster when a balloon crashed into the town and set it on fire, destroying many buildings (though the pub was saved). The town was subsequently rebuilt and enlarged, and became the new county seat. Today there is an annual (and appropriately named) Phoenix Festival, during which hot-air balloons fly over the town.

Tullamore Dew. A brand of whiskey first made at the Tullamore distillery (founded 1829) in the later 19th century. It takes the second part of its name from the initials of the general manager of the time, D.E. Williams, and was marketed with the slogan 'Give every man his dew.' Production has now moved elsewhere, but the town has a Tullamore Dew Heritage Centre.

Tullich. *See under* BALLATER.

Tullietudlescleugh. A CLARTYHOLE of a place imagined by T.W.H. Crossland in his regrettable diatribe *The Unspeakable Scot* (1902):

> He is the fine gentleman whose father toils with a muck-fork … He is the bandy-legged lout from Tullietudlescleugh, who, after a childhood of intimacy with the cesspool and the crab louse, and twelve months at 'the college' on moneys wrung from the diet of his family, drops his threadbare kilt and comes south in a slop suit to instruct the English in the arts of civilization and in the English language.

Tullochvenus The first element is Gaelic *tulach* 'knoll'; the second element is obscure, but has nothing to do with Venus, the Roman goddess of love (the first recorded reference has *-wyneys* as the second element).

A settlement in Aberdeenshire, 16 km (10 miles) northwest of Banchory.

Tullow Irish *An Tulach* 'the hillock'.

A town on the River SLANEY in County Carlow, 13 km (8 miles) southeast of Carlow itself. It was here that Father John Murphy, leader of the Wexford Rebellion (*see under* County WEXFORD), and his companion, James Gallagher, were captured by the Yeomanry on 3 July 1798. They were flogged, hanged and beheaded in the main square, where there is now a statue to Father Murphy. His body was subsequently burned in a barrel of pitch (cremation being then considered sacrilegious), although his remains were later secretly buried.

> And the Yeos at Tullow took Father Murphy
> And burned his body upon the rack.
>
> P.J. McCall (1861–1919): 'Boolavogue'

Tullyhogue. An alternative spelling of TULLAGHOGUE.

Tulse Hill Named from the *Tulse* family, local land-owners in the mid-17th century.

A residential district of South London (SW2), in the borough of LAMBETH, between STREATHAM to the west and DULWICH to the east. Building began here in a small way in the second decade of the 19th century, but it was the coming of the railway in 1869 that hastened and sealed the urbanization process.

Tumble From the name of an inn.

A village in Carmarthenshire (formerly in Dyfed), 12 km (7.5 miles) north of Llanelli.

Tumby Woodside *Tumby* perhaps 'Tumi's farmstead or village', OScand male personal name *Tumi* + -BY – alternatively, the first element could be from OE or OScand *tun* 'enclosure' (*see* -TON); *Woodside* referring to Tumby Wood, which was nearby in the 19th century.

A village in Lincolnshire, in the FENS, about 10 km (6 miles) southeast of Woodhall Spa.

Tummel 'gloomy river', Gaelic *teimheal* 'gloom, shade'. The Gaelic name of the river is *Abhainn Teimheil*, 'river of darkness'.

A river in Perth and Kinross (formerly in Perthshire, and then in Tayside region). Its source is Loch Rannoch (*see under* RANNOCH), from where it flows east through Dunalastair Reservoir and **Loch Tummel**. On the north side of Loch Tummel is the spectacular Queen's View, with a fine prospect westward along the loch to SCHIEHALLION; the viewpoint was so called from a visit by Queen Victoria in 1866. Loch Tummel was considerably enlarged by a hydroelectric dam in 1933. From Loch Tummel the river descends through a narrow wooded gorge, once the site of the spectacular **Falls of Tummel**; however, with the creation of Loch Faskally below the falls, the water level rose, diminishing the scale of the falls, which were renamed the **Linn of Tummel** (Scots *linn* 'deep narrow gorge'). Just above Loch Faskally the Tummel is joined by the River Garry (*see under* GLEN GARRY[1]). The Tummel re-emerges from Loch Faskally by PITLOCHRY and joins the River TAY some 8 km (5 miles) south of the town. The river's total length is approximately 60 km (37 miles).

Tunbridge Wells 'wells near Tonbridge' (*Tunbridge* is an earlier spelling of *Tonbridge* – *see* TONBRIDGE).

A spa town in the WEALD of Kent, on the East Sussex border, about 8 km (5 miles) southeast of Tonbridge (after which it was named). Medicinal springs were discovered here in 1606 by Lord North, and the town grew up around them. Word of the water's efficacy spread ('Tunbridgewater … Good for Splenitick distempers', Thomas Fuller, *The History of the Worthies of England*, 1662), and in the middle of the 17th century Tunbridge Wells began to blossom as a spa resort, notably satirized by the courtier-poet John Wilmot, 2nd Earl of Rochester:

> At five this morn when Phoebus raised his head
> From Thetis' lap, I raised myself from bed
> And mounting steed, I trotted to the waters
> The rendezvous of feigned or sickly praters
> Cuckolds, whores, citizens, their wives and
>   daughters.
>
> Earl of Rochester: 'Tunbridge Wells' (*c*.1673)

In 1700 the PANTILES, its oldest surviving street, was laid out. In the 18th century the town was *the* fashionable place of resort for London society, much easier of access than BATH, presided over by Beau Nash and visited regularly by the *beau monde*. The rise of BRIGHTON during the Regency period marked the end of its glory days, and it became something of a backwater, with a notoriously conservative populace (*see* **Disgusted of Tunbridge Wells** *below*). Yet if the nobility and the glitterati have long gone, Tunbridge Wells's elegant street and buildings continue to attract visitors in large numbers – and you can still take the waters.

In 1889 the town had the shot in the arm of being designated a royal borough, and in 1909 Edward VII allowed it to call itself **Royal Tunbridge Wells** in recognition of its many past royal visitors.

Tunbridge Wells cricket ground is the traditional venue for Kent to play Sussex in the County Championship, in June – rhododendron time:

> Parks takes ten off two successive balls from Wright,
> A cut to the rhododendrons and a hook for six.
>
> Alan Ross: 'J.M. Parks at Tunbridge Wells' (1951)

The sinologist Arthur Waley (1889–1966), the theatre director Tyrone Guthrie (1900–71), the poet Keith Douglas (1920–44) and the cricketer David Gower (b.1957) were born in Tunbridge Wells.

Disgusted of Tunbridge Wells. An ironic byname for a disgruntled resident of the worthy and respectable community of Tunbridge Wells, famed as a bastion of morality and decency. The name is supposedly used by those penning anonymous letters of complaint or objection to the press, especially on any matter relating to falling standards. It is uncertain where the phrase originated, but it is unlikely to have been in the Kentish town itself.

Disgusted of Tunbridge Wells would not have been pleased to hear that the South Bank is playing host to the world's most famous rabbit.

The Times (19 November 1999) (the reference is to a showing of Bugs Bunny cartoons with orchestral accompaniment)

Tunbridge ware. Wooden articles (tables, boxes, toys, etc.) made from cross-cut veneered woods arranged in a characteristic mosaic pattern. They were produced in Tunbridge Wells (and Tonbridge) from the late 17th century up to the 1920s.

Tunstall[1] 'farm site', OE *tun* (*see* -TON) + *stall* 'place, site'.
A town in Staffordshire, in the POTTERIES, now a northern district of STOKE-ON-TRENT. It is a centre for tile and earthenware manufacture. Under the guise of 'Turnhill' it is one of Arnold Bennett's FIVE TOWNS.

The first chapel of Primitive Methodism, an evangelical offshoot of Wesleyan Methodism, was founded in Tunstall in 1811.

Tunstall[2]. A village in Lancashire, 5 km (3 miles) south of Kirby Stephen. In Charlotte Brontë's *Jane Eyre* it is fictionalized as **Brocklebridge**, whither the pupils of Lowood (COWAN BRIDGE) walk every Sunday to church.

Turkey Street Originally *Tucke(y) Street* 'street associated with the Tucke(y) family'; the modern form of the name (presumably due to association with the Christmas bird) is not recorded before the early 19th century.
A road and a railway station in the northern part of ENFIELD, in North London. The station, on a western loop of the LIVERPOOL STREET-to-CAMBRIDGE[1] line, originally opened in 1891. It took its name from the road, but does not seem to have passed it on to the area around it.

Tur Langton Originally *Terlinton* probably 'estate associated with Tyrhtel or Tyrli', OE male personal name *Tyrhtel* or *Tyrli* + -ING + -TON, later remodelled under the influence of the nearby *Langtons*.
A village in Leicestershire, one of the LANGTONS, about 16 km (10 miles) southeast of Leicester.

Turnberry 'fortified place where thorn-trees grow', OE *thorn* + *burgh* (*see* BURY).
A village on the coast of South Ayrshire (formerly in Strathclyde region), 20 km (12 miles) southwest of Ayr. It is a world-famous golf centre, with a championship course that has hosted three Opens since 1977 (*see also* Ailsa Course *under* AILSA CRAIG). The village overlooks **Turnberry Bay**, and at the northern end of this are the remains of **Turnberry Castle**, where Robert the Bruce may have been born in 1274 (the other claimant is LOCHMABEN). Bruce returned here in 1307, after his sojourn in Arran, and shortly afterwards launched his military campaign against the English.

Turners Puddle 'estate on the River Piddle held by the Toners', *Turners* denoting manorial ownership in the early Middle Ages by the Toner family; *Puddle see* PIDDLE.
A village in Dorset, on the River Piddle, about 11 km (7 miles) northwest of Wareham.

Turnhill. A fictional name for TUNSTALL[1] in the novels of Arnold Bennett.

Turriff Possibly 'place at the mound', Gaelic *tor* 'mound, hill' + an unexplained ending.
A small town in BUCHAN, Aberdeenshire (formerly in Grampian region), 15 km (9 miles) south of Banff. As the locals say:

Turra, Turra, faur the sorra idder?
('Turriff, Turriff, where the devil else [is there]?')

Trot of Turriff, the (May 1639). A battle in which Royalists defeated a force of Covenanters. Fighting on the Royalist side was the notable translator of Rabelais, Sir Thomas Urquhart.

Turra Coo, the. A cow impounded in 1913 from a local farmer, Robert Paterson, for his failure to pay National Insurance contributions for his workers. When the authorities attempted to auction the cow, it escaped and made its way back to Paterson's farm at Lendrum, where it is commemorated by a granite slab.

Turville 'dry open land' (probably referring to Turville Heath, which is now also the name of a neighbouring hamlet), OE *thyre* 'dry' + *feld* (*see* FIELD).
A village in Buckinghamshire, in the CHILTERN HILLS, just to the south of the M40, about 10 km (6 miles) west of High Wycombe. It doubles as 'Dibley' in the BBC television sitcom *The Vicar of Dibley* (1994–2000), St Mary's Church being the sitcom's St Barnabas. Also filmed here was the 1998 television film *Goodnight Mister Tom*, based on the novel by Michelle Magorian.

Tutbury 'Tutta's (or Stut's) stronghold', OE male personal names *Tutta* or *Stut* + *byrig* dative form of *burh* (*see* BURY). If *Stut* was the original owner's name, the initial *S* would have been a casualty of Norman influence (as with the *Snot* of NOTTINGHAM[1] or the *s*- of TRAFFORD).
A small town in Staffordshire, on the River DOVE, about 6 km (4 miles) north of Burton upon Trent. It has a Norman church and the ruins of a 14th–15th-century castle in which Mary Queen of Scots was imprisoned.

Twatt[1] OScand *thveit* 'clearing', here a place cleared of brushwood.
A settlement on Mainland, ORKNEY, 22 km (14 miles) northwest of Kirkwall.

Twatt[2]. A settlement on Mainland, SHETLAND, 18 km (11 miles) northwest of Lerwick.

Tweed OCelt or pre-Celtic, possibly 'powerful one', and

possibly related, like TEVIOT, to the Indo-European word found in Sanskrit as *tavás* 'to surge'.

Scotland's fourth-longest river (after the TAY, CLYDE and SPEY). It flows northeast then east for 156 km (97 miles) through SCOTTISH BORDERS (formerly the counties of Peeblesshire, Selkirkshire, Roxburghshire and Berwickshire). In its lower reaches it forms the border with England for 27 km (17 miles), and its last 3 km (2 miles) are in England.

> Faire famous flood, which sometyme did devyde,
> But now conjoynes, two Diadems in one ...
>
>> Sir Robert of Aytoun: 'Sonnet: On the River Tweed'
>> (written around 1603, when James VI of Scotland
>> went south to ascend the throne of England)

Many of the main Border towns – including PEEBLES, INNERLEITHEN, GALASHIELS, MELROSE, KELSO and COLDSTREAM – are on its banks, as are several of the great Border abbeys. Its tributaries include Gala Water, YARROW WATER, ETTRICK WATER, the TEVIOT and the WHITEADDER. The Tweed is well-known as a salmon river, although, as elsewhere, the numbers of fish have declined in recent years.

The Tweed rises at **Tweed's Well**, just north of the DEVIL'S BEEF TUB, and near the sources of the Clyde and Annan, hence the old saying:

> Annan, Tweed an' Clyde
> Rise oot o'ae hillside.

Above Tweed's Well once stood **Tweed's Cross**, a wayside shrine destroyed during the Reformation; it was here that Sir James Douglas was said to have sworn fealty to Robert the Bruce in 1306.

The narrow upper valley of the Tweed, running northeast from its source to Peebles, is called **Tweeddale**. The village of **Tweedsmuir** lies in this steep-sided valley, giving its name to the **Tweedsmuir Hills** on either side, including GATHERSNOW HILL, BROAD LAW and Dollar Law. This area is closely associated with the novelist John Buchan (1875–1940), who adopted the title **Baron Tweedsmuir** when he was ennobled in 1935. The middle stretches of the Tweed between Peebles and NEWTON ST BOSWELLS are still surrounded by high hills, and this section, especially around Melrose, is associated with Sir Walter Scott, who built his home, ABBOTSFORD, overlooking the river. The lower reaches of the river run through a more lowland landscape, eventually reaching the North Sea at BERWICK-UPON-TWEED on the north bank and the village of **Tweed-mouth** on the south.

North of the Tweed. A phrase meaning Scotland. In fact, as pedants enjoy pointing out, quite a significant part of Scotland lies south of the Tweed, the river forming the border only in its lower reaches.

tweed. A kind of woollen cloth used for jackets, trousers and skirts. It is particularly favoured by the county set and, as long as the tweed jacket is patched at the elbow, by a certain sort of teacher. The origin of the name lies in a blunder. It should have been *tweel*, the Scots form of 'twill', but when the Scottish manufacturer sent a consignment to James Locke of London in 1826, the name was badly written and misread, and as the cloth was made on the banks of the Tweed, 'tweed' was accordingly adopted. In the 20th century, among a certain class of lady, the expression **to drop one's tweeds** meant to take one's clothes off and engage in sexual intercourse. (*See also* Harris tweed *under* HARRIS.)

Tweed kettle. A dish, also called salmon hash, popular in Scotland in the 19th century. It consists of chunks of salmon, simmered in white wine with onions, mushrooms and parsley.

Twelve Bens, the. An alternative name for the TWELVE PINS.

Twelveheads '(place with) twelve heads' (referring to the hammers in a set of tin-stamps).

A village in the former tin-mining area of Cornwall, about 6 km (4 miles) east of Redruth.

Twelve Pins, the A corruption of the alternative name, *the Twelve Bens*, from Irish *beinn* 'mountain'.

A fine many-peaked mountain massif in Connemara, County Galway, some 10 km (6 miles) east of CLIFDEN. Its Irish name is **Na Beanna Beola** or **Benna Beola** ('the peaks of Beola', referring to a chief of the legendary Firbolgs). They are made of a firm grey quartzite, and the highest point is Benbaun (727 m / 2385 ft).

> Down by the lough I shall wander once more
> Where the wavelets lap lap round the stones on the
>   shore:
> And the mountainy goats will be wagging their
>   chins
> As they pull at the bracken among the Twelve Pins.
>
>> Percy French: 'To the West'

Twenty Perhaps 'estate of 20 acres'.

A village in Lincolnshire, in the FENS, about 10 km (6 miles) southwest of Spalding.

Twenty-Six Counties, the. A term sometimes applied to the Republic of IRELAND as presently constituted. Its use may imply non-acceptance of the separate existence of NORTHERN IRELAND, referred to in this context as the SIX COUNTIES.

Twice Brewed. An inn and a collection of farms round about, on Hadrian's Wall in Northumberland, some 5 km (3 miles) northeast of Hexham. There are a number of (fairly unlikely) stories regarding the origin of the name. In one, Edward I, en route to Berwick, liked the tipple at the inn so much that he commanded the innkeeper to brew it again. In another, General Wade called by with his army in pursuit of Jacobites and complained that the ale was too weak and needed to be brewed again. The nearby **Once Brewed** Youth Hostel was opened in 1934 by the teetotal Lady Trevelyan, who declared, 'We will serve nothing stronger than tea, and I hope that even that will be only once brewed.' There is also now a Once Brewed National Park Visitor Centre.

Twickenham Probably 'Twicca's river-bend land' (referring to a bend in the River Thames here), OE *Twiccan* possessive form of male personal name *Twicca* + *hamm* 'land in a river bend' (*see* HAM); alternatively, the first element could be from OE *twicce* 'river-fork'.

A district of West London, in an eastward curve of the River THAMES[1], in the borough of RICHMOND-UPON-THAMES (before 1965 in Middlesex), between ISLEWORTH to the north and TEDDINGTON to the south. Its rural delights were discovered by Londoners in the 1700s, and by the end of the century it was the most fashionable suburb southwest of the capital. It attracted artists and men of letters. Amongst those who lived here, either permanently or temporarily, were Colly Cibber, Lady Mary Wortley Montagu, Horace Walpole (*see* STRAWBERRY HILL), Alfred Tennyson, Walter de la Mare, J.M.W. Turner and Vincent Van Gogh. The exiled Louis-Philippe of France also stayed here for a while. Its most famous poetical resident, however, was undoubtedly Alexander Pope (1688–1744), who lived here from 1718 until his death. He took a keen interest in landscape gardening and constructed a celebrated grotto in his garden. He was dubbed the **Bard of Twickenham**, but a frequent local alternative sobriquet, reflecting his acerbic wit and defective social skills (understandable in someone who was only 4 ft 6 in (1.3 m) tall and in constant pain from curvature of the spine), was the **Wasp of Twickenham**.

Twickenham became much more heavily built-up in the late 19th and early 20th centuries, but at its centre retains something of the feel of an 18th-century village. **Twickenham Bridge**, supplementing its road connection with RICHMOND[2] via Richmond Bridge, was opened in 1933.

A rugby ground was opened in Twickenham in 1909, on land bought in 1907 by William Williams (1860–1951) (part of it had been market gardens, whence the ground's early nickname, 'Billy Williams's Cabbage Patch'; the nearby Railway Tavern changed its name to The Cabbage Patch in the early 1970s). **Twickenham Stadium**, often known affectionately as **'Twickers'**, has undergone continual expansion and updating since the 1920s. It was extensively rebuilt in the 1990s and now has a capacity of 75,000. It is the venue for all of England's home matches (its first international match was staged in 1910), and is the headquarters of the English Rugby Football Union.

> A bomb under the West car park at Twickenham on an international day would end fascism in England for a generation.
>
> Philip Toynbee (1916–81)

Twickenham has another celebrated rugby ground in the form of the Stoop Memorial Ground, home of Harlequins RFC, founded in 1866.

The Royal Military School of Music is at Kneller Hall in Twickenham. **Twickenham Film Studios** opened in 1913. They were for long the headquarters of the London Film Company.

Louis-Philippe-Robert, duc d'Orléans (1869–1926), pretender to the French throne during the Third Republic, was born in Twickenham.

See also EEL PIE ISLAND.

Twiss Green *Twiss* 'fork in a road or river', OE *twis* (several Cheshire names derive from the surname *Twiss*, from the same root).

A village in Cheshire, within the unitary authority of WARRINGTON, about 8 km (5 miles) northeast of Warrington.

Twitchen[1] '(place at the) crossroads', OE *twicen*.

A village in Devon, at the southern edge of EXMOOR, about 8 km (5 miles) northeast of South Molton.

Twitchen[2]. A village in Shropshire, about 16 km (10 miles) northwest of Ludlow.

Two Tree Island. An island at the mouth of Benfleet Creek (*see under* SOUTH BENFLEET), between CANVEY ISLAND and the Essex coast.

Twycross '(place with) two crosses' (perhaps referring to a signpost with four arms), OE *twi-* 'two' + *cros* (*see* CROSS).

A village in Leicestershire, about 26 km (16 miles) west of Leicester. Its church, St James, contains French medieval stained glass, from the Sainte-Chapelle and from St-Denis, acquired after the French Revolution (one mid-12th-century panel from St-Denis may be the oldest example of stained glass in England).

Twycross Zoo Park, opened in 1963, has a notable collection of primates.

Twyford[1] '(place at the) double ford' (referring to fords across the rivers Loddon and THAMES[1]), OE *twi-* 'two' + FORD.

A town in Berkshire, within the unitary authority of WOKINGHAM, just to the south of the junction of the River Thames and the River Loddon, about 10 km (6 miles) southwest of Maidenhead.

Twyford[2] *See* TWYFORD[1] (the reference here is to the double channel in which the ITCHEN runs).

A village in Hampshire, on the River Itchen, about 5 km (3 miles) south of Winchester. About 2.5 km (1.5 miles) north of it is **Twyford Down**, the extreme western outpost of the SOUTH DOWNS. A proposal to cut through it with

the M3 motorway aroused extreme outrage among environmentalists, and activists' strategies to frustrate the road-
builders reached new and often confrontational heights,
but the road finally won in 1994.

Twynham. An old name for CHRISTCHURCH in Dorset.

Tyburn[1] 'boundary stream' (referring to the boundary between
the manors of Ebury and Westminster), OE *teo* 'boundary'
+ *burna* 'stream'.

A lost river of London, which is now contained within an
underground conduit. It rises at HAMPSTEAD and flows
southwards beneath REGENT'S PARK, GREEN PARK and
BUCKINGHAM PALACE into the River THAMES[1] to the west
of Vauxhall Bridge (*see under* VAUXHALL). It is carried in
huge metal pipes through the Underground stations at
BAKER STREET[1] and VICTORIA[2].

Tyburn[2] From TYBURN[1].

The former name of a district of western Central London, to
the east of PADDINGTON, through which the River Tyburn
flowed. The corner of the Edgware Road (*see under* EDG-
WARE) and the Bayswater Road (*see under* BAYSWATER), close
to where MARBLE ARCH now stands, was for 400 years the
main place of public execution for London and Middlesex.
The first hanging took place here in 1388 and a permanent
gallows was set up in 1571. Among those to meet their fate
here were Perkin Warbeck, pretender to the English throne
(1499), Oliver Plunket, the last Catholic martyr to die in
the British Isles (1681) and Jack Sheppard, highwayman
(1714, in front of a crowd of 200,000). After the Restoration
of Charles II the body of Oliver Cromwell was dug up, set
on a gibbet at Tyburn and later buried in a pit at the foot
of the gallows. The last criminal to be hanged here was
John Austin in 1783. After that, executions were carried
out at NEWGATE until its demolition. The site of the gallows
is marked by three brass triangles let into the pavement
here, recalling Tyburn's 'Triple Tree', a three-cornered
gallows that could dangle 21 persons at a time.

   The name of the district inevitably came to be tarnished
by its association with the gallows (not to mention the
various rather grisly colloquialisms that incorporated it),
and it was eventually changed to MARYLEBONE.

dance the Tyburn jig. Slang at the turn of the 19th
century for 'to be hanged'.

preach at Tyburn cross. Slang in the 16th century for 'to
be hanged'. The allusion is to the last words permitted to
the prospective suspendee.

Tyburn blossom.

   A young thief or pickpocket, who in time will ripen
   into fruit borne by the deadly never-green [i.e. the
   gallows].

   Francis Grose: *A Classical Dictionary of the Vulgar Tongue*
   (1796)

Tyburn check. Slang in the late 18th and early 19th
centuries for a hangman's noose.

Tyburn collar. A mid-19th-century term for a fringe of
beard worn under the chin. For the rationale, *see* Newgate
fringe *under* NEWGATE.

Tyburn face. A late 17th-century colloquialism for a
miserable, down-in-the-mouth look, as if expecting the
worst.

Tyburn foretop. A term around the turn of the 19th
century for a wig (also called simply a **Tyburn top**) with
the lock of hair at the front combed forwards over the eyes.
Such wigs were especially popular among the underworld
fraternity.

Tyburn piccadill. Slang in the 17th century for a hangman's noose; hence to 'put on a Tyburn piccadill' was to
be hanged – a piccadill was a type of lace-trimmed collar
fashionable at that time (*see under* PICCADILLY[1]).

Tyburn stretch. Slang from the late 17th to the early 19th
centuries for a hanging.

Tyburn string. Late 18th-century slang for a hangman's
noose.

Tyburn ticket. A certificate that, under a statute of
William III (1698), was granted to prosecutors who had
secured a capital conviction against a criminal, exempt-
ing them from all parish and ward offices within the
parish in which the felony had been committed. This,
with the privilege it conferred, might be sold once, and
once only, and the *Stamford Mercury* for 27 March 1818
announced the sale of one for £280. The Act was repealed
in 1818, but as late as 1856 a Mr Pratt of Bond Street
claimed exemption from sitting on an OLD BAILEY jury on
the strength of the possession of a Tyburn ticket and was
successful.

Tyburn tiffany. Slang in the 17th century for a hangman's
noose (a tiffany was a garment, especially a head- or neck-
scarf, made of sheer gauze muslin).

Tyburn tippet. Slang from the 16th to the 19th centuries
for a hangman's noose.

   And how many of our Popish Martyrs ... have worne the
   Tiburn-tippet, as Father Latimer phraseth it?

      John Trapp: *Commentary upon 1 Corinthians xiii 3*
      (1647)

Tyburn tree. Slang from the mid-18th century to the early
19th century for the gallows at Tyburn, and in particular
for the permanent gallows that had been erected in 1571
(*see above*). A large triangular structure capable of 'turning
off' 21 malefactors simultaneously, its first victim was the
'Romish Canonical Doctor' John Story.

   I wonder we han't better Company,
   Upon Tyburn Tree!

      John Gay: *The Beggar's Opera* (1728)

Tyburnia From Tyburn[2], on the model of Belgravia.

A somewhat literary name used in the second half of the 19th century for the residential district that had recently been built along the Bayswater Road (*see under* Bayswater) from Marble Arch (site of the former Tyburn gallows) to Lancaster Gate and northwards.

Tyddewi. The Welsh name for St David's.

Tydd Gote *Tydd* probably 'shrubs, brushwood', OE; *Gote see* Four Gotes.

A village in Lincolnshire, to the south of the Wash, about 8 km (5 miles) north of Wisbech.

Tyldesley 'Tilwald's clearing', OE male personal name *Tilwald* + -ley.

A town in Greater Manchester, 12 km (7.5 miles) southeast of Wigan.

Tyndrum 'house of the ridge' Gaelic *tigh* 'house' + *an* 'of' + *druim* 'ridge'.

A village 8 km (5 miles) northwest of Crianlarich, formerly in Perthshire, then in Central region, and now in the unitary authority of Stirling. The road and railway to Oban branch off west here from those leading to Fort William. Near the village Robert the Bruce fought Clan MacDougall in 1306, and it was either here or later at the Pass of Brander that he lost the Brooch of Lorne (*see under* Lorne).

Tyne[1] An OCelt or pre-Celtic word meaning 'river'.

A river in northern England. It is 72 km (45 miles) in length and for most of its course it flows through countryside. However, for its last few miles, before it disgorges into the North Sea, it is bordered by the heavily industrialized conurbation of Tyneside, including Newcastle upon Tyne, Gateshead, Jarrow, South Shields, North Shields and, finally, Tynemouth. For part of its course the river forms the traditional boundary between the counties of Northumberland and Durham, and Hadrian's Wall extends from the mouth of the Tyne to the Solway Firth. The Tyne is formed by the confluence, near Hexham, of the **North Tyne**, which has its source in Kielder Water (*see under* Kielder), and the **South Tyne**, which rises east of Cross Fell on the slopes of Bellbeaver Rigg in the high Pennines, near the source of the River Tees.

The river and its banks were celebrated in many poems by the poet and physician Mark Akenside (1721–70), the son of a Newcastle butcher, who features in Dr Johnson's *Lives of the Poets*.

'Banks of the Tyne, The'. A folk song in which the sailor gets his girl:

Come my lovely Nancy to church let us away
And we will quickly married be without the least delay
And afterwards my own true love we'll crown the day
with wine

And we'll have a joyful night my love all on the banks of Tyne.

'Fog on the Tyne'. A song by the Northumberland folk-rock group Lindisfarne; it was a chart success in the early 1970s, and has become something of a Geordie anthem.

Fog on the Tyne, you're all mine, all mine,
Fog on the Tyne, you're all mine.

Tyne. A sea area in the shipping forecast. It is situated south of Forth, west of Dogger and north of Humber.

Tyne Gap. The gap through the northern Pennines taken by Hadrian's Wall and the A69 between Hexham and Carlisle. The South Tyne flows along the eastern portion.

Tyne Tees Television. An ITV company serving the northeast of England. It was founded in 1959 and is now owned by ITV.

Tyne[2]. A river in southeast Scotland; length approximately 40 km (25 miles). It rises in Midlothian and flows north into East Lothian and then generally eastwards past Haddington to reach the North Sea between North Berwick and Dunbar.

Tyne and Wear. A metropolitan county in northeast England, formed in 1974, but whose administrative powers were devolved in 1986 to the metropolitan boroughs of Sunderland (which is on the River Wear), Newcastle upon Tyne, Gateshead, North Tyneside and South Tyneside.

Tynecastle Possibly Gaelic *tigh* 'house' with either *na caiseil* 'mound, rock' or *'n caisteil* 'fenced settlement'.

The stadium of Heart of Midlothian FC (*see under* Midlothian), on Gorgie Road, Edinburgh. There is also a Tynecastle High School in the city.

Tyneham Probably 'goat's enclosure', OE *tigan* possessive form of *tige* 'goat' + *hamm* (*see* Ham).

A deserted village in Dorset, close to the coast at Lulworth Cove (*see under* Lulworth). Its inhabitants were summarily ejected by the army in 1943, and it is now in the middle of an artillery range. It is the subject of Patrick Wright's *The Village that Died for England* (1995), subtitled 'The Strange Story of Tyneham'.

Tynemouth 'mouth of the river Tyne', Tyne[1] + OE *mutha* 'mouth'.

A seaside town on the north side of the mouth of the Tyne, in North Tyneside (formerly in Northumberland), 13 km (8 miles) east of Newcastle.

There is a traditional story regarding the old priory in Tynemouth, in which a monk steals a pig's head from a local manor. The lord of the manor fiercely beats the thief, who later dies. The other monks refuse the lord absolution until he grants them land and erects a cross (part of which can be seen in Newcastle's Museum of Antiquities). The inscription on the cross reads:

O horrid dede
To kill a man for a pigge's hede.

Henry Percy, 9th Earl of Northumberland (1564–1632), who was suspected of involvement in the Gunpowder Plot, was born in Tynemouth Castle. The American painter Winslow Homer (1836–1910) spent some time in Tynemouth in the 1880s, painting the fisherwomen.

Tynemouth, which has been described in the *Guardian*'s property pages (23 November 2002) as 'pretty, rugged and not too poncey', is home to Einstein the Incredible Football-Playing Octopus.

Tyneside. The industrial conurbation on either side of the lower reaches of the River TYNE[1]. It includes NEWCASTLE UPON TYNE, GATESHEAD, JARROW, SOUTH SHIELDS and NORTH SHIELDS. Natives of Tyneside are called **Tynesiders** or **Geordies**, and Geordie is also the name of the local dialect. *Geordie* is a local form of George, formerly a generic nickname for local miners, sailors and others. It is specifically associated with, if not actually derived from, the name of George Stephenson (1781–1848), the Newcastle engineer and railway pioneer. Sometimes Tyneside (or the whole of the northeast) is referred to as **Geordieland**.

See also NORTH TYNESIDE *and* SOUTH TYNESIDE.

Tynwald Hill 'hill of the field of the parliament', *Tynwald* OScand *thing* 'assembly of the people' + *vollr* 'field'.

An artificial mound near PEEL, Isle of Man, where the island's parliament, called the Tynwald, formerly met. The Tynwald claims to be the oldest parliament in the world in continuous existence and has two branches, the Legislative Council and the House of Keys. No British Act of Parliament applies to the island unless specifically stated. Every year, on 5 July (formerly on Midsummer Day), the parliament still holds a ceremony on Tynwald Hill, to announce new laws and the appointments of new officers. William Wordsworth described this ceremony in a sonnet entitled 'Tynwald Hill'.

Tyrconnell Irish *Tír Chonaill* 'Conall's land', after one of the sons of the semi-legendary Niall of the Nine Hostages; Conall conquered the area *c.* AD 400; *compare* TYRONE.

An old Irish territory, covering all of modern County DONEGAL apart from the peninsula of INISHOWEN. It is also spelt **Tirconnell**. It was ruled by the O'Donnells (the descendants of the eponymous Connell) until 1607, when Rory O'Donnell, Earl of Tyrconnell, left Ireland in the Flight of the Earls (*see under* LOUGH SWILLY).

Tyrconnell was the birthplace of St Columcille (Columba; *c.*521–597).

Earl of Tyrconnell. A new creation of the earldom was made by James II in 1685, when he awarded the title to the Irish politician Richard Talbot (1630–91). James made Tyrconnell his lord deputy of Ireland in 1687, and after the

Battle of the BOYNE Tyrconnell followed James to France. He returned to Ireland in 1691, but died of apoplexy two days after the Jacobite defeat at AUGHRIM. He was mocked in the anti-Jacobite song 'Lillibuléro':

Now that Tyrconnell is come ashore,
Lillibuléro, bullen a la,
And we shall have Commissions *go leor*
Lillibuléro, bullen a la.

Tyrone Irish *Tír Eoghain* 'land of Eoghan'; Eoghan was a son of the semi-legendary Niall of the Nine Hostages; Eoghan conquered the area *c.* AD 400; *compare* TYRCONNELL.

An ancient kingdom in central ULSTER and a county in western NORTHERN IRELAND. The ancient kingdom incorporated the modern county plus INISHOWEN (now part of Donegal), and was ruled by the O'Neills, descendants of its founder Eoghan, up until the Flight of the Earls in 1607 (*see under* LOUGH SWILLY). Prior to this the O'Neill chiefs were inaugurated near TULLAGHOGUE. After 1607 the area was subjected to the Plantation of Ulster.

County Tyrone is bordered on the north by County Londonderry, on the west by Donegal, on the south by Fermanagh and Monaghan and on the east by Lough Neagh and Armagh. The county town is OMAGH, and other towns include DUNGANNON, STRABANE and COOKSTOWN. The SPERRIN MOUNTAINS are in the north, shared with County Londonderry. In 1921 the county council was dissolved following its declaration of allegiance to the Irish Free State (*see under* IRISH), and in the 2001 Westminster elections the constituencies of West Tyrone, Fermanagh and South Tyrone, and Mid Ulster all returned Sinn Féin MPs.

The Derryman, I hope, is proud
Of Sperrin tops that touch the cloud;
Still, when I see, behin' the barn
The big, brown back of Mullagharn,
I'd let him keep, while she's our own,
The whole jingbang outside Tyrone.

W.F. Marshall: 'The Hills of Home', from *Ballads & Verses from Tyrone* (1929) (The reference is to Mullaghcarn (542 m / 1778 ft), 10 km (6 miles) northeast of Omagh.)

For 'the dreary steeples of Fermanagh and Tyrone', *see under* FERMANAGH.

Captain of Tyrone. The title by which Elizabeth I recognized the Ulster chieftain Shane O'Neill (*c.*1530–67).

Tyrone, County. *See under* TYRONE

Tyrrellspass Irish *Bealach an Tirialaigh* 'pass of Tyrell', referring to the road through the bogs and to Captain Richard *Tyrrell*.

A village in County Westmeath, 15 km (9 miles) south of Mullingar. The village was laid out as a crescent in the 18th century on the road through the bogs where in July 1597 Piers Lacy and Captain Richard Tyrrell ambushed and decimated a force of 1000 English troops under Christopher Barnewall.

Tyrrellspass was the home of Private James Joseph Daly, shot by the British in 1920 for his part in the Connaught Rangers' mutiny in the Punjab (*see under* CONNACHT). His body was brought back to Ireland for reburial in 1970.

Tytherton Lucas *Tytherton* 'estate associated with Tydre', OE male personal name *Tydre* + -ING + -TON; *Lucas* denoting manorial ownership in the Middle Ages by the Lucas family.
A village in Wiltshire, about 3 km (2 miles) northeast of Chippenham.

Tywardreath 'house on the beach', Cornish *ti* 'house' + *war* 'on' + *treth* 'beach'.
A village in Cornwall, to the north of Par Sands (*see under* PAR), about 5 km (3 miles) east of St Austell.

Tywi. The Welsh name for the River TOWY.

Tywyn Welsh 'sandy shore, sand dune'.
A coastal resort on Cardigan Bay (*see under* CARDIGAN), in Gwynedd (formerly in Merioneth), some 6 km (4 miles) north of Aberdovey. The Norman church contains a stone on which is inscribed the earliest known example of written Welsh (7th century).

U

Uckfield 'Ucca's open land', OE male personal name *Ucca* + *feld* (*see* FIELD).

A small town in East Sussex, in the valley of the River OUSE[3], on the southern edge of the WEALD, about 13 km (8 miles) northeast of LEWES.

> Uckfield is disappointing.
>
> Nikolaus Pevsner: *The Buildings of England: Sussex* (1965)

Uffington 'Uffa's estate', OE *Uffan* possessive form of male personal name *Uffa* + -TON.

A village in Oxfordshire (before 1974 in Berkshire), in the VALE OF THE WHITE HORSE, about 10 km (6 miles) west of Wantage. The chalk downland to the south is rich in prehistoric monuments, most notably the **White Horse of Uffington**, an elegantly elongated and stylized figure of a horse cut into the turf of a north-facing escarpment. It is 114 m (374 ft) long, and was made by digging trenches in the hillside and ramming chalk into them. The latest research suggests that it probably dates from the late Bronze Age, about 800 BC; despite a long-standing legend, it is highly unlikely that it was made to celebrate Alfred the Great's nearby victory over the Danes at the Battle of Ashdown in 871 (*see under* ASHDOWN). For G.K. Chesterton it existed 'before the gods that made the gods had seen their sunrise pass'. The hill across which it gallops, **White Horse Hill**, is the highest in the Berkshire Downs (*see under* BERKSHIRE) at 257 m (856 ft). At its summit, on the line of the RIDGEWAY, is **Uffington Castle**, an Iron Age hillfort dating from around 50 BC. A little to the northeast is the Blowing Stone, about 1.3 m (4 ft) high and pierced with holes, which is said to have been used in the past to sound the alarm at the approach of an enemy. Other near neighbours are DRAGON HILL and WAYLAND'S SMITHY.

The novelist Thomas Hughes (1822–96) was born in Uffington. In his *Tom Brown's Schooldays* (1857), the hero's pre-RUGBY boyhood is spent in Uffington, and the village and the surrounding district are lovingly described in its opening chapters:

> And then what a hill is the White Horse Hill! There it stands right up above all the rest, nine hundred feet above the sea, and the boldest, bravest shape for a chalk hill that you ever saw.

Hughes's *The Scouring of the White Horse* (1859) is centred on the process of cleaning the White Horse figure, removing weeds and the encroaching grass.

The poet John Betjeman and his wife lived in Uffington from 1934 to 1945.

> Despite a hideous colony of council houses at its east end … [Uffington] remains one of the loveliest villages in the Vale.
>
> John Betjeman and John Piper: *Murray's Berkshire Architectural Guide* (1949)

Ufton Nervet *Ufton* 'Uffa's farmstead or village', OE male personal name *Uffa* + -TON; *Nervet* denoting manorial ownership in the Middle Ages by the Neyrnut family.

A village in Berkshire, on the River KENNET[1], within the unitary authority of West Berkshire, about 11 km (7 miles) southwest of Reading.

Ugborough 'Ugga's hill', OE male personal name *Ugga* + *beorg* 'hill'.

A village in Devon, on the southern edge of DARTMOOR, about 19 km (12 miles) east of Plymouth. To the north of it is **Ugborough Moor**, surmounted by **Ugborough Beacon** (370 m / 1232 ft).

Ugglebarnby 'Uglubarthr's farmstead', OScand male personal name *Uglubarthr* + -BY.

A hamlet in North Yorkshire, on the north side of the NORTH YORK MOORS, 4 km (2.5 miles) south of Whitby.

Ugley 'Ugga's glade', OE male personal name *Ugga* + -LEY.

The name's embarrassing connotations gave rise in the 19th century to a euphemistic substitute *Oakley*, justified as being a translation of a spurious Latin original *Quercetum* (from *quercus* 'oak') and claimed as the historical precursor of which *Ugley* was a debased form.

A village in Essex, just to the east of the M11, about 10 km (6 miles) south of Saffron Walden. The members of the **Ugley Women's Institute** have a considerable cross to bear.

Uíbh Fhailí. The Irish name for OFFALY.

Uig '(place by the) bay', OScand *vik*.

A small port on the west side of the TROTTERNISH peninsula, northern Skye. It is in Highland (formerly in Inverness-shire), and is some 22 km (13 miles) northwest of Portree. It was here that Bonnie Prince Charlie landed when he sailed 'over the sea to Skye' from the Outer HEBRIDES with Flora Macdonald in 1746. Today there are car ferries to LOCHMADDY on North Uist and to TARBERT on Harris.

Uists, the 'inner dwelling', OScand *i vist*.

Two islands, **North Uist** and **South Uist**, in the southern Outer HEBRIDES, Western Isles (formerly in Inverness-shire). North Uist is some 12 km (7 miles) south of Harris, and the two Uists are separated by the island of BENBECULA, to which they are respectively joined by a causeway and a bridge; even before these were constructed, it was possible to cross over the sands between the three islands at low tide. There is now also a causeway to the little island of ERISKAY to the south. The main settlement on North Uist is LOCHMADDY, and that on South Uist is LOCHBOISEDALE. The population of North Uist is predominantly Protestant, while South Uist is largely Catholic (Benbecula is half and half).

The relation between the people of the Uists and the sea is intimate. The MacCodums of North Uist, for example, are known in Gaelic as *Sliochd nan Ron* ('offspring of the seals'), as it is said that they descend from the union of a man and a seal-maiden who was obliged to keep human form for all the years her lover hid her seal skin. A more recent animal settler is the hedgehog, first introduced in 1974. Hedgehogs have since proved a threat to the many rare wading birds that breed on the islands, leading the Royal Society for the Protection of Birds to propose a cull – much to the dismay of the British Hedgehog Preservation Society. As the cull began in 2003, the St Tiggywinkle Hedgehog Hospital of Buckinghamshire mounted a rescue mission.

Bonnie Prince Charlie spent some time on South Uist hiding from the Redcoats in the spring of 1746; it was here that he met Flora MacDonald (1722–90; *see under* SKYE), who was born on the island, at Milton. The British Army returned to South Uist in 1963 to set up a missile range.

In 2003 two Bronze Age mummies dating from around 3500 years ago were discovered at Cladh Hallan on South Uist, the only prehistoric mummies ever found in Britain. The bodies are of a man and a woman, who lived some two centuries apart. They were preserved by immersion in peaty water, then displayed for some 500 years before being buried around 1000 BC.

Birlinn Chlann-Raghnail (*The Birlinn of Clanranald*), the masterpiece of the 18th-century Gaelic poet Alasdair MacMaighstir Alasdair (Captain Alasdair MacDonald), tells of the voyage of Clanranald's galley (*birlin*) from South Uist to CARRICKFERGUS in Ulster.

UK. The standard abbreviation for UNITED KINGDOM.

Ulaidh. The Irish name for ULSTER.

Uley 'yew-tree clearing', OE *iw* 'yew' + -LEY.

A village in Gloucestershire, on the edge of the COTSWOLD escarpment, 4 km (2.5 miles) east of Dursley. Overlooking Uley and dominating its skyline is the Iron Age hillfort of **Uleybury**. A little further to the north is **Uley Long Barrow**, a Neolithic chambered burial mound that is better known as HETTY PEGLER'S TUMP.

Uley lies on the Cotswold Way (*see under* COTSWOLDS).

Ullapool 'Olafr's settlement', OScand personal name *Olafr* + *bolstathr* 'dwelling, settlement'.

A fishing port and tourist centre on Loch Broom, Wester Ross, in Highland (formerly in Ross and Cromarty), some 70 km (42 miles) northwest of Inverness. It was founded by the British Fisheries Society in 1788. There is a car ferry here to STORNOWAY on Lewis.

Ullswater 'Ulfr's lake', OScand male personal name *Ulfr* + OE *wæter* 'lake'.

A long, serpentine lake in the eastern LAKE DISTRICT, Cumbria (previously in Cumberland), some 12 km (7 miles) north of Ambleside. It is regarded by some as the most beautiful of Lakeland lakes, deserving its title '**Queen of the Lakes**'; the poet Wordsworth judged that it had 'the happiest combination of beauty and grandeur which any of the lakes affords'. In the 1790s, in furtherance, one supposes, of Wordsworthian tranquillity, tourist boats on the lake carried a cannon, which when fired apparently elicited a seven-fold echo from the surrounding fells. The poet himself saw his 'cloud of golden daffodils' (celebrated in 'I Wandered Lonely as a Cloud') in Gowbarrow Park, on the shores of Ullswater. He and his sister Dorothy came across them on 15 April 1802, and Dorothy recorded in her journal:

> They grew among the mossy stones about and above them; some rested their heads upon these stones, as on a pillow for weariness; and the rest tossed and reeled and danced, and seemed as if they verily laughed, with the wind that blew upon them over the lake; they looked so gay, ever glancing, ever changing.

Another favourite place of the Wordsworths was AIRA FORCE, on the north side of the lake.

Ulster 'land of the Ulaidh', Irish tribal name + OScand genitive -*s* + Irish *tír* 'land'. In Irish the name is simply *Ulaidh*.

One of the ancient kingdoms of Ireland (*see* the FIVE FIFTHS), and subsequently one of the island's traditional provinces. The ancient Ulaidh or Ulaid rulers of Ulster, with their seat at Emain Macha (NAVAN FORT), were pushed to the east of the River BANN by the Uí Néill dynasty in the 5th century; one group, the Dál Riata, sailed northeast to colonize Scotland (*see under* DALRIADA). Although there was a medieval Anglo-Norman earldom of Ulster, originating in the early 13th century, its power had fizzled out by 1461 when England annexed the province. Despite this nominal annexation, Ulster continued to be dominated by the O'Neill earls of Tyrone and the O'Donnell earls of Tyrconnell, and remained one of the most Gaelic areas of Ireland prior to the Flight of the Earls (*see under* LOUGH SWILLY) in 1607. After this it was subjected to plantation by English and Scottish settlers (the **Plantation of Ulster**). In the 17th century Ulster was divided into the counties of ANTRIM, ARMAGH, CAVAN, DONEGAL, DOWN, FERMANAGH, LONDONDERRY, MONAGHAN, TYRONE, but following Partition in 1921, Cavan, Donegal and Monaghan became part of the Free State (now the Republic of Ireland; *see under* IRELAND), while the remaining SIX COUNTIES remained part of the United Kingdom as NORTHERN IRELAND. Considerable bother has followed. The use of Ulster as a synonym for Northern Ireland is therefore inaccurate, although it is frequently used as such both by the press and by Unionists.

A native of Ulster is an **Ulsterman** (in Irish **Ultach**) or an **Ulsterwoman**. Ulster is sometimes referred to as the **Wee North** (*see under* the NORTH[2]), because of the popularity of that adjective in the province (*see also* the Wee City *under* DERRY/LONDONDERRY).

A representative Ulster team plays in rugby union's (professional) Celtic League.

> I found in Ulster, from hill to glen,
> Hardy warriors, resolute men;
> Beauty that bloomed when youth was gone
> And strength transmitted from sire to son.
>
> > Anon.: 'Aldfrid's Itinerary through Ireland' (12th century), translated by James Clarence Mangan

> So great and so long has been the misgovernment of Ireland, that we verily believe the empire would be much stronger if everything was open sea between England and the Atlantic, and if skates and cod-fish swam over the fair land of Ulster.
>
> > Sydney Smith: in the *Edinburgh Review*, 1820

> Down with the Ulster men!
> They don't know which from what.
> If Ireland sunk beneath the sea

> How peaceful everyone would be!
> You haven't said a word about the RUC?
> Down with the whole damn lot!
>
> > Noël Coward: 'Down with the Whole Damn Lot', song from *Co-optimists* (1920s). The RUC are the Royal Ulster Constabulary (*see below*).

> … Northward a far and fortified province
> Crouches under the lash of arid censure.
>
> > Donagh MacDonagh (1912–68): 'Dublin Made Me'

> Ulster folk seem forever on the boil, trying to swallow and be cruel at the same time. The accent seems full of strain and greed, and yet the people are relaxed and friendly.
>
> > Paul Theroux: *The Kingdom by the Sea* (1983)

Annals of Ulster, The. A 15th-century manuscript begun on the island of Senait (now called Belleisle) in Upper Lough Erne (*see under* ERNE), and also known as *Annála Senait*. It includes much material on the early medieval Uí Néill of Ulster. The original manuscript, begun by Cathal MacManus Maguire (d.1498) and completed by Ruaidhri Ó Luinín after his death, is in the library of Trinity College, Dublin, while Ó Luinín's copy is in the Bodleian Library in Oxford.

Enterprise of Ulster (1571–5). A failed and bloody English attempt to colonize Ulster. Sir Thomas Smith and his son Thomas attempted to take control of north DOWN and the ARDS PENINSULA[1], while Walter Devereux, Earl of Essex, focused his attention on ANTRIM. Smith and son found themselves fiercely opposed by Sir Brian O'Neill, and achieved little, while Essex was resisted by Sorley Boy MacDonnell, and despite ordering massacres of the O'Neills in Belfast and of the MacDonnells on RATHLIN ISLAND, he too had failed to secure a toehold in Ulster by the time of his death in 1576.

Famous Battle of the Catts in the Province of Ulster, The. A verse satire (1668) by the Dublin-born John Denham (1615–69).

Hound of Ulster, the. The legendary hero Cuchulain, Irish *Cú Chulainn*, meaning 'hound of Culann', who single-handedly defended Ulster from Queen Maeve of Connacht. Originally called Setanta, he gained his name because, having accidentally slain the watchdog of Cullan the smith, he was honour-bound to take the dog's place in penance.

Observe the Sons of Ulster Marching Towards the Somme. A play (1985) by Frank McGuinness concerning the experiences of the Ulster Division at the Battle of the Somme in 1916. By special dispensation the Ulster troops were allowed to wear their Orange Order collarettes over their uniforms as they headed across No Man's Land, an episode that forms the climax of the play. Their sacrifice is also commemorated in the **Ulster Tower** (*see below*).

Red Earl of Ulster, the. Richard de Burgh or Burgo (c.1259–1326), the Anglo-Norman Earl of Ulster and Lord of Connacht (*see also* SLIGO). He violently extended his power across both territories, and at one time was the most powerful man in Ireland. His daughter Elizabeth married Robert the Bruce in 1302, but he opposed Edward Bruce's invasion of Ireland in 1315. He was succeeded by his grandson William de Burgh, known as the Brown Earl. Red and brown probably refer to hair colour.

Red Hand of Ulster, the. An armorial device, originally part of the arms of the O'Neills of Ulster. It now constitutes part of the arms of Ulster and forms the centrepiece of the flag of Northern Ireland (which apart from the red hand and the Crown over it is the English cross of St George). The story behind the device is that O'Neill and a rival chieftain were sailing in a race towards Ulster, and the first to touch *terra firma* was to gain possession of the territory. With some élan, a smattering of cunning and a lump of blockheadedness, O'Neill won the day by cutting off his hand and hurling it onto the shore. Elements of the **Ulster Defence Association** and **Ulster Volunteer Force** (*see below*) have used the name 'Red Hand Defenders' when carrying out sectarian killings.

Royal Ulster Constabulary. The paramilitary police force of Northern Ireland from 1922, when it was formed out of part of the old Royal Irish Constabulary. The **RUC** was long regarded by Nationalists as a tool of Protestant Unionism, although it came under attack by Loyalists in the 1990s for the way it policed Orange marches, for example at DRUMCREE. In 2001, in the wake of the 1998 Good Friday Agreement, the RUC was reformed as the Police Service of Northern Ireland.

Save Ulster from Sodomy. A slogan devised by the Rev. Ian Paisley in 1977 in response to the recommendation by the Northern Ireland Human Rights Commission that the law banning homosexual acts in Northern Ireland be reformed. Gay rights activists responded with a 'Save Sodomy from Ulster' campaign. The Westminster Parliament eventually legalized homosexuality in Northern Ireland in 1982; it was only legalized in the Republic in 1993. Paisley was not yet done, however. Having in 1999 received an invitation to Gilbert & George's Naked Shit and Fundamental Pictures exhibition at Belfast's Ormeau Baths Gallery, Paisley declared that the pair had 'tainted the sacred soil of Ulster with their filth'.

ulster. A heavy double-breasted man's coat, belted at the back. They were first made in the province in the 19th century.

Ulster Canal. A canal linking LOUGH NEAGH and Lough Erne (*see under* ERNE) via MONAGHAN. It was built in 1841 and is now disused, although enthusiasts aim to restore it.

Ulster Covenant. An anti-Home Rule petition drafted in 1912 by Sir Edward Carson and James Craig (the future Lord Craigavon) on the model of the Solemn League and Covenant of the Scots Presbyterians of the 17th century. The Ulster Covenant was signed by 474,414 people.

> Being convinced in our consciences that Home Rule would be disastrous to the well-being of Ulster as well as the whole of Ireland, subversive of our civil and religious freedom, destructive of our citizenship and perilous to the unity of the Empire, we, whose names are underwritten, men of Ulster, loyal subjects of His Gracious Majesty King George V ... do hereby pledge ourselves in Solemn Covenant throughout this our time of calamity to stand by one another in defending for ourselves and our children our cherished position of equal citizenship in the United Kingdom, and in using all means which may be found necessary to defeat the conspiracy to set up a Home Rule Parliament in Ireland.

Ulster custom. The right of departing farm tenants to sell their interest in the land to the highest bidder, with the landlord's approval. It was also called 'tenant right' and was customary (although not universal) in Ulster. The right was incorporated into Gladstone's 1881 Land Act.

Ulster Cycle. A group of ancient Irish legends, also called the Red Branch Cycle. They were orally transmitted for nearly 1000 years, until written down in the 12th century. The best known epic is *The Cattle Raid of Cooley* (*see under* COOLEY).

Ulster Defence Association. A Loyalist paramilitary organization (abbreviated to **UDA**) in Northern Ireland, founded in 1971 and proscribed in 1992. Its military branch is the **Ulster Freedom Fighters** and its political wing the **Ulster Democratic Party**. It has been on ceasefire since the Good Friday Agreement. There have been violent feuds with its rival, the **Ulster Volunteer Force** (*see below*).

Ulster Defence Regiment. A regiment of the British Army established in 1970 to replace the B-Specials of the **Ulster Special Constabulary** (*see below*). It had both full-time and part-time members, and was regarded by Nationalists as dominated by Protestant extremists. In 1992 it was merged with the Royal Irish Rangers to form the Royal Irish Regiment.

Ulster fry. A cholesterol-rich breakfast comprising fried sausages, fried bacon and fried eggs (so far so English) with the essential accompaniment of soda bread and potato cakes. It is sometimes called 'a heart attack on a plate'.

Ulsterization. A name sometimes used for the process in the mid-1970s whereby the British passed control of operations against the IRA to the **Royal Ulster Constabulary** (*see above*): internment was phased out; more conventional judicial methods were used (processing IRA suspects through the (juryless) courts using draconian anti-terrorist legislation); special-category status for paramilitary prisoners was scrapped (leading eventually to the hunger strikes in the MAZE) – all an attempt to 'criminalize' the IRA. The term itself was coined on the model of Vietnamization, the process by which the Americans attempted to get the South Vietnamese to fight their own war prior to and after the US withdrawal from Vietnam in 1973.

Ulster King of Arms. The chief heraldic officer in Ireland until 1943, when the role was incorporated into the College of Arms in London, and its jurisdiction confined to Northern Ireland.

Ulster-Scots. A dialect of English spoken by some in Northern Ireland. It is also called **Ullans** and originated in Lallans, the Lowland Scots dialect brought to Ulster by Scottish settlers in the 17th century.

Ulster Special Constabulary. An armed auxiliary police force formed by the Northern Ireland government in 1922. It had three categories of member: As were full-time, Bs part-time and Cs reservists. The As and Cs were disbanded, but the B-Specials (as they became known) were reviled for their brutal treatment of civil rights marchers and the Catholic community in general at the beginning of the Troubles, and were disbanded following the 1969 Hunt Report. They were replaced by the **Ulster Defence Regiment** (*see above*), who came to be equally mistrusted by Nationalists.

Ulster Tower. A memorial at Thiepval Wood in the valley of the Somme to the men of the 36th Division – the **Ulster Division** – who fought at the Battle of the Somme in 1916. Their experiences are recalled in Frank McGuinness's play *Observe the Sons of Ulster Marching Towards the Somme* (*see above*). The tower, erected in 1921, is a replica of Helen's Tower on the estate of the Marquess of Dufferin at Clandeboye near Belfast, where the division had trained.

Ulster Unionist Council. A body created in 1904–5 to agitate for the maintenance of the union of Ulster with the UK. It continues to have political significance, and out of it developed the **Ulster Unionist Party.**

Ulster Unionist Party. The main Unionist party in Northern Ireland (at least until the electoral success of Ian Paisley's Democratic Unionist Party in 2003). The **UUP** originated in the Ulster Unionist Council formed in 1904–5, and formed successive governments of Northern Ireland from 1921 until devolved rule was suspended in 1972.

Ulster Volunteer Force. A Loyalist paramilitary grouping in Northern Ireland (often abbreviated to **UVF**). It was first established in 1913 by Sir Edward Carson to oppose Home Rule, and revived in 1966. During the subsequent Troubles it specialized in the sectarian killing of Catholics, often

under the guise of the Protestant Action Force. It declared a ceasefire in 1994, but there have been violent feuds with its rival, the **Ulster Defence Association** (*see above*).

Ulster will fight and Ulster will be right. An anti-Home Rule slogan first coined by Sir Randolph Churchill in a speech he made at Larne on 22 February 1886:

> Ulster at the supreme moment will resort to the supreme arbitrament of force. Ulster will fight and Ulster will be right.

Ulster Workers' Council. The Loyalist body that organized the strike of Protestant workers in May 1974, which brought an end to the power-sharing experiment in Northern Ireland set up by the Sunningdale Agreement (*see under* SUNNINGDALE).

Uncrowned King of Ulster, the. Sir Edward (later Baron) Carson (1854–1935), Anglo-Irish politician and lawyer. He represented the Marquess of Queensbury when he was sued by Oscar Wilde in 1895, and as leader of the Irish Unionist Party from 1910 orchestrated the movement in Ulster to resist Home Rule, by force if necessary. The byname derives from that of Charles Stewart Parnell, the Uncrowned King of Ireland (*see under* IRELAND).

Ulva 'wolf's island', OScand *ulfr* 'wolf', or personal name *Ulfr* + *ey* (*see* -AY).

A small island off the west coast of MULL, from which it is separated by the **Sound of Ulva**, which is less than 150 m (490 ft) across. At its opposite end it is connected by a causeway to the even smaller island of Gometra. It is in Argyll and Bute (formerly in Strathclyde region).

Ulva was long in possession of the MacQuarries, and Dr Johnson and James Boswell visited the chief in 1773:

> M'Quarrie's house was mean; but we were agreeably surprised with the appearance of the master whom we found to be intelligent, polite and much a man of the world … He told us his family had possessed Ulva for nine hundred years; but I was distressed to hear that it was soon to be sold for payment of debts.
>
> James Boswell: *The Journal of a Tour of the Hebrides, with Samuel Johnson, LL.D.* (1785)

Lachlan Macquarie (1761–1824), governor of New South Wales (1809–21) and 'father of Australia', was born on Ulva.

Thomas Campbell, who came to work as a tutor on Mull in 1795, wrote 'Lord Ullin's Daughter' during his stay, and had his eponymous heroine elope with the Chief of Ulva:

> A Chieftain, to the Highlands bound,
>   Cries, 'Boatman, do not tarry!
> And I'll give thee a silver pound
>   To row us o'er the ferry!' –

'Now, who be ye, would cross Lochgyle,
  This dark and stormy weather?'
'O, I'm the chief of Ulva's isle,
  And this, Lord Ullin's daughter.'

'Lochgyle' is Loch Na Keal, the sea loch on the south side of
Ulva. In the poem Lord Ullin, hot for vengeance, arrives
at the shore, only to see his daughter succumb to the
tempest:

'Come back! come back!' he cried in grief
  Across this stormy water:
'And I'll forgive your Highland chief,
  My daughter! – O my daughter!'

'Twas vain: the loud waves lash'd the shore,
  Return or aid preventing:
The waters wild went o'er his child,
  And he was left lamenting.

Ulverston 'Ulfarr's village', OScand male personal name *Ulfarr*
+ -TON.
A market town on the FURNESS peninsula, Cumbria (for-
merly in Lancashire), 14 km (8.5 miles) northeast of Barrow-
in-Furness. It is connected to Morecambe Bay (*see under*
MORECAMBE) by a short canal, built in the 1790s. St Mary's
Church is known as 'Four Ones Church', as it was founded
in the year 1111. In 1669 George Fox, the founder of the
Quakers, married the widow of Judge Thomas Fell of
Swarthmore Hall, Ulverston, and subsequently spent some
of his time here.

Ulverston was the birthplace of John Barrow (1764–
1848), founder of the Royal Geographical Society; and of
the comedian Stan Laurel (1890–1965); it is now home to
the Laurel and Hardy Museum.

There is a town called Ulverstone (with an 'e', though
named after Ulverston) in Australia (Tasmania).

Undercliff, the. An 11-km (7-mile) sloping clifftop stretch
of the Dorset and Devon coast between LYME REGIS in the
east and SEATON in the west, formed by the collapse of the
fragile limestone cliffs. It is subtropically overgrown with
trees, creepers and other plants, cut by deep chasms and
traversed by a single path. In 1955 it was designated a
National Nature Reserve.

It was the luscious trysting-place of Charles Smithson
and Sarah Woodruff in John Fowles's *The French Lieutenant's
Woman* (1969).

There is also an 'Undercliff' on the southwest-facing
coast of the ISLE OF WIGHT.

Union Canal Referring to the Union of 1707.
A canal completed in 1822, linking EDINBURGH with the
Forth and Clyde Canal (*see under* FORTH) near Falkirk.

United Kingdom. In full, the United Kingdom of Great
Britain and Northern Ireland, the official name of what is
often colloquially referred to as BRITAIN or GREAT BRITAIN,

although technically those expressions denote the island
comprising ENGLAND, WALES and SCOTLAND, and thus
do not include NORTHERN IRELAND. Neither the ISLE OF
MAN nor the CHANNEL ISLANDS are part of the United
Kingdom, but are rather Crown dependencies associated
with it.

The term 'United Kingdom' first came into use after
the Union of Great Britain and Ireland on 1 January 1801,
after which George III styled himself 'King of the United
Kingdom of Great Britain and Ireland'. With the establishment of the Irish Free State (*see under* IRISH) in 1921,
the name changed to its present form, often abbreviated
to **UK**.

UK plc. *See* Britain plc *under* BRITAIN.

United Kingdom Independence Party. A right-wing
political party formed in 1993, informally referred to as
UKIP. It campaigns on a platform of 'Five Freedoms': 'freedom from the European Union, freedom from crime,
freedom from overcrowding [i.e. freedom from 'mass
immigration'], freedom from bureaucratic politicians,
freedom from political correctness'. It is seen by some of
its opponents as a middle-class, *Daily Mail* version of the
British National Party (*see under* BRITISH).

Unst 'eagle's dwelling', OScand *orn* 'eagle' + *vist* 'dwelling'.
The most northerly of the larger islands in SHETLAND, 20 km
(12 miles) northeast of the northern tip of Mainland, and
1 km (0.6 miles) across Bluemull Sound from Yell. There
are ferry links to YELL and FETLAR, and also an air-strip.
Since the lighthouse on the small rocky island of MUCKLE
FLUGGA was automated in 1995, Unst has been Britain's
most northerly inhabited island. The northern tip of Unst,
Herma Ness (off which Muckle Flugga lies), is an important
bird reserve. Writer Robert Louis Stevenson visited Unst to
see his Uncle David's lighthouse on Muckle Flugga, and a
resemblance has been noted between the shape of Unst
and Stevenson's map of Treasure Island.

Unthank OE *unthanc*, a term used for land that is held without
permission, or that is ungratifyingly barren.
A village in Cumbria (formerly in Cumberland), 9 km
(5.5 miles) northwest of Penrith. In his masterpiece, *Lanark*
(1981), Alasdair Gray borrowed the name for the novel's
alternative GLASGOW.

Upavon '(place) higher up the Avon' (relative to NETHERAVON),
OE *upp* 'higher' + river name *Avon*.
A village in Wiltshire, on the River AVON³, in the northeastern part of Salisbury Plain (*see under* SALISBURY), about
6 km (4 miles) north of Netheravon.

Up Cerne '(settlement) higher up the River *Cerne*'.
A hamlet in Dorset, on the River CERNE, about 1.5 km
(1 mile) north of Cerne Abbas.

Uploders '(settlement) higher up the River Loders', OE *upp* 'higher up' + *Loders* an OCelt river name meaning 'pool stream', a former name of the River Asker.

A village in Dorset, on the River Asker, about 4 km (2.5 miles) east of Bridport.

Uplowman '(settlement) higher up the River Loman' (i.e. higher than TIVERTON), OE *upp* 'higher up' + *Loman* an OCelt river name, meaning 'elm-river'.

A village in Devon, on the River Loman, about 6 km (4 miles) northeast of Tiverton.

Upminster 'higher church' (reflecting its position on rising ground), OE *upp* 'higher up' + *mynster* 'large church, monastery, minster'.

An eastern suburb of London, in the borough of HAVER-ING (before 1965 in Essex), to the east of Hornchurch. It has a particularly fine 15th-century tithe barn and 19th-century windmill, reflecting its comparatively recent rural past.

Upminster 'Underground' station, the eastern terminus of the District line, opened in 1902, Upminster Bridge, on the same line, in 1934.

The singer and songwriter Ian Dury (1942–2000) was born in Upminster.

Upottery '(settlement) higher up the River Otter' (i.e. higher than Ottery St Mary), OE *upp* 'higher up' + *Ottery see* OTTERY ST MARY.

A village in Devon, on the River OTTER, about 8 km (5 miles) northeast of Honiton and 16 km (10 miles) northeast of Ottery St Mary.

Uppark 'upper park', ME *up* + *park*, distinguished from nearby Downpark.

A house and estate in West Sussex, dramatically situated on the crest of the SOUTH DOWNS, 8 km (5 miles) southeast of Petersfield. The house was built around 1690 by William Talman for Lord Grey, later Earl of Tankerton, and was the home of the Fetherstonhaugh family from 1747. Owned since 1954 by the National Trust, Uppark's elegant Georgian interior was extensively restored following a fire in 1989. The mother of the novelist H.G. Wells was housekeeper here between 1880 and 1893. Wells recollects his childhood at Uppark in his autobiography; the house also appears in his novel *Tono-Bungay* (1909) in the fictional guise of 'Bladesover'.

Upper Dicker *Upper*, ModE *upper; Dicker see* LOWER DICKER.

A village in East Sussex, close to the CUCKMERE river, about 13 km (8 miles) northwest of Eastbourne and 1.5 km (1 miles) south of LOWER DICKER.

Upper Hackney *Hackney* perhaps 'Haca's nook of land', OE *Hacan* possessive form of male personal name *Haca* + *halh* (*see* HALE, -HALL).

A village in Derbyshire, on the eastern edge of the PEAK DISTRICT, on the northwestern outskirts of Matlock.

Upper Hardres *Hardres* '(place at the) woods', OE *haradas* 'woods'.

A village (pronounced 'hardz') in Kent, about 8 km (5 miles) south of Canterbury.

Upper Heyford *Heyford* '(place by the) ford used at hay-making time', OE *heg* 'hay' + FORD.

A village in Oxfordshire, on the River CHERWELL, about 8 km (5 miles) northwest of Bicester. From the early 1950s to 1994 **RAF Upper Heyford** was a US air base; since then, part of the now-retired site been converted into the industrial **Heyford Park**.

Uppermill Self-explanatory.

A village in Greater Manchester, approximately 6 km (4 miles) east of Oldham.

Upper Sheringham. *See under* SHERINGHAM.

Upper Slaughter *Slaughter see* LOWER SLAUGHTER.

A quaint picture-postcardish village (despite its apparent mass-murderous connotations: *Slaughter* actually means 'muddy place') in Gloucestershire, on the River Eye, in the COTSWOLDS, about 5 km (3 miles) southwest of Stow-on-the-Wold and 1.5 km (1 mile) northwest of LOWER SLAUGHTER.

Its name is probably the best known among the distressingly small number of English villages (37 at one calculation) where all the men called up for the First World War came back safely. They are known collectively as the THANKFUL VILLAGES.

Upper Swell *Swell see* LOWER SWELL.

A village of great picturesqueness in Gloucestershire, in the COTSWOLDS, 1.5 km (1 mile) north of LOWER SWELL.

Upperthong. *See under* NETHERTHONG.

Upper Tooting. Another name for TOOTING BEC.

Upper Upham *Upham see* LOWER UPHAM.

A village in Wiltshire, about 12 km (7.5 miles) southeast of Swindon. It is a long way from LOWER UPHAM in Hampshire, but there is a Lower Upham Farm nearby.

Uppingham 'hill-dwellers' homestead or village' (probably referring to Castle Hill, to the west of the town), OE *yppe* 'raised place' + *-inga-* (*see* -ING) + HAM.

A small market town in Rutland (before 1997 in Leicestershire, before 1974 in Rutland), about 10 km (6 miles) south of Oakham.

Its most notable feature is **Uppingham School**, a co-educational public school founded in 1584. It was much expanded and its profile raised under the mid-19th-century headmastership of Edward Thring, and it has one of the largest school playing fields in England. A somewhat louche list of its old boys could be compiled including the writers

Norman Douglas and Ronald Firbank, the poet James Elroy Flecker, the cricket commentator Jonathan 'Aggers' Agnew and the humorist Stephen Fry. Rather more mainstream alumni were the folk-song collector Cecil Sharp and the Conservative politician Stephen Dorrell.

Upsettlington Possibly 'farm of Ulfketill', OScand male personal name (probably but not certainly *Ulfketill*) + -ING + -TON.
A small settlement by the River TWEED in Scottish Borders, 2 km (1.2 miles) southwest of Norham.

Up Sydling '(settlement) higher up Sydling Water'; *Sydling see* SYDLING ST NICHOLAS.
A village in Dorset, about 2.5 km (1.5 miles) north of Sydling St Nicholas.

Upton Cressett *Upton* 'upper farmstead', OE *upp* 'higher up' + -TON; *Cressett* denoting manorial ownership in the Middle Ages by the Cressett family.
A village in Shropshire, about 6 km (4 miles) west of Bridgnorth.

Upton Hellions *Hellions* denoting manorial ownership in the Middle Ages by the de Helihun family.
A village in Devon, about 3 km (2 miles) north of Crediton.

Upton Noble *Noble* denoting manorial ownership in the Middle Ages by the le Noble family.
A village in Somerset, about 5 km (3 miles) northeast of Bruton.

Upton Pyne *Pyne* denoting manorial ownership in the Middle Ages by the de Pyn family.
A village in Devon, about 6 km (4 miles) north of Exeter.

Upton Scudamore *Scudamore* denoting manorial ownership in the Middle Ages by the de Skydemore family.
A village in Wiltshire, about 3 km (2 miles) north of Warminster.

Upton Snodsbury Originally the names of two distinct places: *Upton see* UPTON CRESSETT; *Snodsbury* 'Snodd's stronghold', OE *Snoddes* possessive form of male personal name *Snodd* + *burh* (*see* BURY).
A village (pronounced 'snodgebəri') in Worcestershire (before 1998 in Hereford and Worcester, before 1974 in Worcestershire), about 10 km (6 miles) east of Worcester.

Upton-upon-Severn. A small market town in Worcestershire (before 1998 in Hereford and Worcester, before 1974 in Worcestershire), on the River SEVERN, about 14 km (9 miles) south of Worcester. It has some notable old inns, including The Anchor (17th century), The Bell and The White Lion (which appears in Henry Fielding's novel *Tom Jones* (1749)).

Urchfont 'Eohric's spring', OE *Eohrices* possessive form of male personal name *Eohric* + *funta* 'spring'.

A village (pronounced as spelt or, locally in former times, 'ushənt' or 'ershənt') in Wiltshire, at the northern edge of Salisbury Plain (*see under* SALISBURY), about 5 km (3 miles) southeast of DEVIZES. Its William-and-Mary manor house was once owned by William Pitt the Elder (prime minister, 1766–8).

Ure An OCelt or pre-Celtic name of unknown meaning.
A river in North Yorkshire, some 80 km (50 miles) long. It rises near the Cumbrian border and flows east through WENSLEYDALE then southeast through RIPON to join the SWALE[1] near Boroughbridge, thus forming the OUSE[2].

Uricon. A variant form of the name of the important Roman town VIRICONIUM, made familiar by the poet A.E. Housman in his *A Shropshire Lad*:

> The gale, it plies the saplings double,
> It blows so hard, 'twill soon be gone:
> Today the Roman and his trouble
> Are ashes under Uricon.
>
> A.E. Housman: 'On Wenlock Edge' (1896)

Urmston 'Wyrm or Urm's farmstead', OE male personal name *Wyrm* or *Urm* + -TON.
A suburban area in Greater Manchester, 9 km (5.5 miles) southwest of the city centre. It is part of the metropolitan borough of TRAFFORD.

Urney Irish *An Urnaí* 'place of vigil, oratory' (i.e. a small building for prayer).
A village on the Tyrone–Donegal border, 8 km (5 miles) southwest of Strabane. A former brand of chocolate, Urney Chocolate, was originally produced here as a cottage industry, hence the once famous slogan:

> Any time is Urney time.

Urr, Water of A pre-Celtic river name of which the etymology is obscure.
A river in what was Kircudbrightshire and is now Dumfries and Galloway; approximate length, 30 km (20 miles). It rises in **Loch Urr**, 16 km (10 miles) southwest of Thornhill, and in its course passes **Old Bridge of Urr**, **Haugh of Urr** (Scots *haugh* 'river meadow') and the **Motte of Urr**, the impressive remains of Norman earthworks (a *motte* is an artificial mound on which a castle is built), before flowing past DALBEATTIE and entering the SOLWAY FIRTH.

Usk[1] From an OCelt river name probably meaning 'abundant in fish'. The Roman name *Isca* derives from this; the Romans called CAERLEON *Isca Silurum*.
A river in South Wales. In Welsh it is **Wysg**. It is 137 km (85 miles) long, rising on the bleak marshy northern slopes of the BLACK MOUNTAIN and FFOREST FAWR. It first flows north to feed the **Usk Reservoir**, from where it runs

east then south through Powys and Monmouthshire, separating the BRECON BEACONS from the BLACK MOUNTAINS and passing the towns of BRECON, ABERGAVENNY, USK[2] and CAERLEON, before entering the Bristol Channel at NEWPORT[2].

Tennyson wrote of 'the full-tided Usk' in *Idylls of the King*, and W.H. Davies (1871–1940) remembered in his poem 'Days That Have Been' –

> When I would go alone at night to see
> The moonlight, like a big white butterfly
> Dreaming on that old castle near Caerleon,
> While at its side the Usk went softly by.

The river also appears in David Jones's litany of Welsh rivers:

> Is the Usk a drain for his gleaming tears
> who weeps for the land ... ?
>
>> David Jones: 'The Sleeping Lord', from *The Sleeping Lord and Other Fragments* (1974)

T.S. Eliot's short poem 'Usk' (1935) mysteriously begins:

> Do not suddenly break the branch, or
> Hope to find
> The white hart behind the white well.

For long these lines were held to be entirely symbolic, but in 2003 Philip Edwards, King Alfred Professor of English Literature at Liverpool University, announced that the white hart was actually the pub of that name in the village of Llangybi, in the valley of the Usk, 8 km (5 miles) east of Cwmbran; the overgrown, disused well – which Edwards believes was once a place of pilgrimage – lies about 100 m (330 ft) away.

Swan of Usk, the. The poet Henry Vaughan (1622–95), also known as the Silurist (*see* SILURIA). The name derives from the title of his 1651 volume *Olor Iscanus* (Latin, 'swan of Usk').

Usk[2] From the River Usk.
A small, attractive rural town on the River USK[1], in Monmouthshire (formerly in Gwent), 9 km (5.5 miles) east of Pontypool. Its Welsh name is **Brynbuga** ('hill of Buga', Buga being unidentified). The 12th-century Norman castle was partly destroyed during Owain Glyndwr's rebellion in the early 15th century.

Utsire From the name of a small rocky island about 24 km (15 miles) off the Norwegian coast, to the northwest of Stavanger.
The name of two sea areas, **South Utsire** and **North Utsire**, in the shipping forecast. They are off the southwestern coast of Norway, between VIKING to the west and FISHER to the south. They were introduced in 1984.

Uttlesford From the name of a former Essex Hundred (i.e. administrative district), 'Udel's ford', OE *Udeles* possessive form of male personal name *Udel* + FORD.

A council district in Essex, in the northeastern part of the county.

Uttoxeter Probably 'Wuttuc's heath', OE *Wuttuces* possessive form of male personal name *Wuttuc* + *hæddre* 'heath'.
A market town (pronounced 'yew-toxeter', 'uxeter' or, locally, 'utcheter' or 'uster') in Staffordshire, on the River Tean, close to the River DOVE and the Derbyshire border, about 19 km (12 miles) northeast of Stafford. In former times it was a staging post on the London–Liverpool road, and there are several old coaching inns here.

Dr Samuel Johnson's father, a LICHFIELD bookseller, had a stall in Uttoxeter market. On one occasion, remembered contritely for the rest of his life, the proud young Samuel refused to look after the stall when his father was ill. As an old man he returned to the town and stood for several hours in the rain on the spot where the stall had been. 'I trust,' he said, 'I have propitiated heaven for this only instance, I believe, of contumacy towards my father.' A ceremony commemorating the incident is held in Uttoxeter every September.

Uttoxeter has a notable National Hunt Steeplechase course (it stages the 'Midlands Grand National' in March). Flat racing is also held here.

Uxbridge 'bridge of the Wixan tribe', OE tribal name *Wixan* + *brycg* 'bridge'.
A district of West London, in the borough of HILLINGDON (before 1965 in Middlesex). It prospered considerably on the corn trade between the 12th and 19th centuries, due in no small part to its good communications – it was on the London–Oxford road (now the A40 WESTERN AVENUE – the M40 begins just to the west of Uxbridge), and in the early 19th century the Grand Junction Canal (now part of the GRAND UNION CANAL) was routed through Uxbridge. Thereafter, however, as the Great Western Railway was built further to the south and corn production in the surrounding area declined, the good times receded. The Tube arrived in 1904 (Uxbridge 'Underground' station is a western terminus of the Metropolitan and Piccadilly lines), and suburbia swiftly followed.

Uxbridge Magistrates' Court has HEATHROW Airport within its jurisdiction, so it has more than its fair share of such misdeeds as drug-smuggling to deal with. It is frequently cited by John Mortimer's Horace Rumpole as the epitome of juridical seediness:

> The Chancery Division is not to be found, as I must make clear to those who have no particular legal experience, in any of my ordinary stamping grounds like the Old Bailey or Snaresbrook. It is light years away from the Uxbridge Magistrates' Court.
>
>> John Mortimer: 'Rumpole and the Dear Departed', in *Rumpole for the Defence* (1981)

It was in Uxbridge that Charles I's advisor the Earl of Southampton attempted to negotiate peace with Parliament in 1645, on the basis of the so-called **Uxbridge Proposals** (also sometimes referred to, misleadingly, as the **Treaty of Uxbridge**). The negotiations were unsuccessful, largely owing to Charles's intransigence, and the final chance to end the Civil Wars by compromise was lost.

In the latter part of the First World War a Royal Flying Corps base was established in Uxbridge, and it has continued its military aviation connections ever since. During the Battle of Britain and the Blitz, most of Fighter Command's operations in southeast England were controlled from an underground bunker here.

Brunel University, founded in 1966, is in Uxbridge. It grew out of Acton Technical College (1928).

The actor and London theatre manager Sir Bernard Miles (1907–91) was born in Uxbridge.

There is a town called Uxbridge in Canada (Ontario).

Uzmaston 'Osmund's farm', OE male personal name *Osmund* + -TON.

A village in Pembrokeshire (formerly in Dyfed), 2 km (1.2 miles) southeast of Haverfordwest.

V

Valencia Island An anglicization, influenced by Valencia in Spain, of Irish *Béal Inse* 'estuary of the island', referring to the channel separating the island from the mainland.

An island off the northwest coast of the IVERAGH peninsula, County Kerry. It is also spelt **Valentia**, and its Irish name is **Dairbhre** ('place of oaks'). Valencia is now linked by road to the mainland at Portmagee, but there is still a ferry at Knights Town. The island was the terminus of the first transatlantic telegraph cable (1858), and has a coastal meteorological station providing information for the shipping forecast. The village of Knights Town is named after the 19th Knight of Kerry, the local landowner, who opened a slate quarry on the island in 1816 that provided much employment and the roof of the House of Commons at Westminster.

Valencia was the birthplace of Mick ('Micko') O'Connell (b.1937), the great Gaelic footballer, who played for his native county.

Vale of Avoca. *See under* AVOCA.

Vale of Aylesbury. *See under* AYLESBURY.

Vale of Belvoir From *Belvoir* Castle, so named from the fine and extensive view it commands, OFr *bel vedeir* 'beautiful view'.

A broad flat valley (pronounced 'beever') in northern Leicestershire and eastern Nottinghamshire, running southwest-to-northeast between NOTTINGHAM[1] to the west and GRANTHAM to the east. It is quintessential fox-hunting country, part of the SHIRES. The hunt known as the **'Belvoir'** actually meets in Lincolnshire, but the celebrated **Belvoir foxhound** was bred in the Vale in the 18th century.

William the Conqueror granted lands here to his standard-bearer, Robert de Todeni, who built a castle on an eminence – **Belvoir Castle**. Now the home of the dukes of Rutland, it has undergone numerous remodellings and renovations over the centuries. Its present-day egregiously medieval appearance is the work of the architect James Wyatt in the early 19th century.

The name 'Belvoir' has passed to a hamlet to the north of the castle.

Witches of Belvoir, the. Six women, including Joan Flower and her daughters Margaret and Philippa (servants at Belvoir Castle), who in the early 17th century were accused of witchcraft, and in particular of bewitching the Earl of Rutland and his wife and other relatives. Joan protested her innocence, requesting bread and saying that if she were guilty of witchcraft it would kill her. She was given some, and she choked to death on it. This so unnerved the others that they started incriminating each other. They were tried and convicted, and hanged at Lincoln prison on 11 March 1619.

Vale of Berkeley. *See under* BERKELEY.

Vale of Catmose *Catmose* 'marsh frequented by wildcats', OE *catt* 'wildcat' + *mos* 'marsh'.

An area of flat low-lying land in Rutland (before 1997 in Leicestershire, before 1974 in Rutland), to the west of Rutland Water (*see under* RUTLAND). Oakham lies in the Vale.

Vale of Clwyd. *See under* CLWYD[1].

Vale of Evesham. *See under* EVESHAM.

Vale of Glamorgan *See* GLAMORGAN.

A unitary authority of south Wales, created in 1996 out of the western part of SOUTH GLAMORGAN. The name was used for this area long before the creation of the unitary authority. It is bounded on the south by the Bristol Channel, to the northwest by Bridgend, to the north by Rhondda Cynon Taff and to the east by Cardiff. The administrative headquarters are at BARRY, and other towns include PENARTH and COWBRIDGE.

Vale of Gloucester. *See under* GLOUCESTER.

Vale of Health A commercial name bestowed by early 19th-century developers to counteract the area's well-earned reputation as a breeding ground of malaria.

A residential area at the western edge of the main eastern

part of Hampstead Heath (*see under* HAMPSTEAD). It was once a noisome, mosquito-ridden, sparsely populated marshland known as **Gangmoor**. The marshes were drained towards the end of the 18th century, and fashionable residences were built here, complete with a new and most salubrious name to attract customers. Building restrictions in the 1870s put a stop to further development, and it remains a small and select district.

Vale of Pewsey. *See under* PEWSEY.

Vale of Pickering. *See under* PICKERING.

Vale of Powys. *See under* POWYS.

Vale of Taunton Deane. *See under* TAUNTON.

Vale of the White Horse From the *White Horse* of Uffington (*see under* UFFINGTON), which is on its southern edge. The name dates at least from the middle of the 14th century.

A low-lying area running southwest to northeast from SWINDON to ABINGDON, between the River THAMES[1] to the north and the Berkshire Downs (*see under* BERKSHIRE) to the south. Its main town is WANTAGE.

Vale Royal 'royal valley', OFr *val* 'valley' + *roiale* 'royal'. The name was originally that of the site of St Mary's monastery near Northwich, which was founded by Edward I in the 13th century; the king himself bestowed the name, in the Latin form *Vallis Regalis*.

A council district within the county of Cheshire, which includes the towns of NORTHWICH and WINSFORD[1].

Valle Crucis Abbey 'abbey of the valley of the cross', Latin *valle* 'valley' + *crucis*, genitive of *crux* (*see* CROSS), a literal translation of the Welsh name of the valley, *Glyn y Groes*. The cross in question is possibly ELISEG'S PILLAR.

A ruined Cistercian abbey in Denbighshire (formerly in Clwyd), some 3 km (2 miles) north of LLANGOLLEN. It was founded in 1201 by Prince Madog ap Gruffydd of Powys, and was the first abbey in Britain built in the Gothic style. It was dissolved in 1535.

Owain Glyndwr came from GLYNDYFRDWY, a little to the west, and there is a story that after the failure of his rebellion in 1410 and his subsequent disappearance, the abbot of Valle Crucis met him early one misty morning near Llangollen. 'You are up early,' said Glyndwr to the abbot. 'No,' replied he, 'it is you who are early – by a hundred years.' This is said to refer to the accession of the Welsh Tudor dynasty (to whom Glyndwr was supposed to be related) to the throne of England. The abbey has another link to Glyndwr: his bard, Iolo Goch, is supposed to be buried here.

Valley From the cutting made nearby in the 1820s, from which material was extracted to build the causeway linking HOLY ISLAND[2] to ANGLESEY.

A village in Anglesey (formerly in Gwynedd), 5 km (3 miles)

southeast of Holyhead. In Welsh it is translated literally as either **Dyffryn** or **Y Fali**. RAF Valley, opened in 1941, hosts a flying school and a big search-and-rescue unit.

Valley of Desolation Named after a devastating flood here in the mid-19th century.

A picturesque little valley with attractive waterfalls in North Yorkshire, leading up towards SIMON'S SEAT[1], some 3 km (2 miles) north of Bolton Abbey.

Valley of the Rocks. A curving grassy valley alongside the coastal cliffs, and a sheer drop of 240 m (800 ft), about 2.5 km (1.5 miles) west of LYNTON in north Devon. It is punctuated by craggy rock formations and grazed by half-wild goats.

Valleys, the. The collective name for the series of deep, steep-sided north–south valleys cutting through the hills of central south Wales. The area is now covered by the unitary authorities of TORFAEN, BLAENAU GWENT, CAER-PHILLY[2], MERTHYR TYDFIL and RHONDDA CYNON TAFF (it was previously in Glamorgan, then Mid Glamorgan). Among the rivers enclosed by the Valleys are the RHONDDA, CYNON, TAFF, RHYMNEY and Ebbw and crammed along the valley floors (and sometimes creeping precipitously up the sides) are numerous towns and villages, including TREORCHY, MOUNTAIN ASH, Merthyr Tydfil, PONTYPRIDD, GELLIGAER, BARGOED, EBBW VALE, ABERTILLERY, CWMBRAN, PONTYPOOL and many more.

In the 18th century this was still a wild, barely populated place, a place, according to Daniel Defoe (*A Tour Through the Whole Island of Great Britain*, 1724–6), of 'horrid rocks and precipices ... a country ... full of horror'. The discovery of coal in the Valleys in the early 19th century attracted capital and thousands of impoverished people from rural Wales and further afield, who eked out a meagre and dangerous existence working down the mines. By 1920 a total of 620 pits employed 256,000 men, and the area had become a heartland of the Labour movement. There were many closures during the Depression of the 1930s, and many more in the postwar years. The Miners' Strike of 1984–5 heralded the end of coal mining in south Wales; following the strike, all but one of the pits (now worked as a cooperative) shut their gates for the last time. The Valleys have, however, survived: new industries have arrived, and much of the grimy detritus of the Industrial Revolution has been cleaned up and greened.

Life in a mining village in the Valleys from the turn of the 20th century to the 1970s is celebrated unsentimentally in Richard Llewellyn's tetralogy beginning with *How Green Was My Valley* (1939; Oscar-winning film version directed by John Ford, 1941), followed by *Up into the Singing Mountain* (1963), *Down Where the Moon is Small* (1966) and *Green, Green My Valley Now* (1975).

Vange 'fen or marsh district', OE *fenn* 'fen, marsh' + *ge* 'district'.

A village in Essex, now a southeastern suburb of BASILDON.

Vaternish 'water headland', OScand *vatr* 'water' + *nes* (*see* NESS).

A peninsula in northwest SKYE, Highland (formerly in Inverness-shire).

Vatersay Possibly an OScand personal name + *ey* 'island' (*see* -AY). The modern Gaelic name is *Bhatarsaigh*.

A small island in the southern Outer HEBRIDES, to the south of BARRA, to which it is attached by a causeway. It is in Western Isles (formerly in Inverness-shire). The causeway was completed in 1991; prior to that the crofters of Vatersay had to encourage their cattle to swim the channel, but when Bernie, a prize bull, drowned in 1986 (perhaps exhausted by procreative effort), there was such an outcry that the government was obliged to act. An earlier tragedy is recorded in a memorial on West Bay, erected to commemorate 350 men, women and children whose bodies were washed ashore when the *Annie Jane* went down in 1853, en route from Liverpool to Quebec.

Vauxhall 'Falkes' hall or manor house', OFr male personal name *Falkes* (referring to Falkes de Breauté, a supporter of King John who was granted the manor here in 1233) + ME *hall*.

A district (pronounced 'voxhall') of SOUTH LONDON (SE11), in the borough of LAMBETH, on the south bank of the River Thames to the southwest of Kennington. It was put on the map by **Vauxhall Gardens**, pleasure gardens opened in the area in the 1650s. Known officially until 1785 as '**New Spring Gardens**', they provided refreshments, musical entertainments (Thomas Arne, who wrote 'Rule, Britannia', was appointed 'composer to the Vauxhall Gardens' in 1745), fireworks, displays of pictures and statuary and the like, and at night were lit by over 1000 lamps. They also gave ample opportunity for amorous assignations, both amateur and professional. Samuel Pepys refers to them as '**Fox Hall**', and they crop up frequently in English literature down the centuries – for example, in Vanbrugh's play *The Provok'd Wife* (1697), Swift's *Journal to Stella* (1710–13), Dickens's *Sketches by Boz* (1836–7) and Thackeray's *Vanity Fair* (1847–8). One of Thomas Rowlandson's most famous paintings is *Vauxhall Gardens* (it was rediscovered in 1945, having for a long time been known only from an aquatint engraving).

Vauxhall Bridge, a road bridge linking Lambeth and PIMLICO, opened in 1816. Originally called the 'Regent's Bridge', it was the first iron bridge across the Thames in London. It was replaced by the present structure in 1906.

The northern end of the OVAL cricket ground is known as the **Vauxhall End**.

Vauxhall Underground station, on the Victoria line, opened in 1971.

Vauxhall Cross. A crossroads at the southern end of Vauxhall Bridge. The name has also been adopted for the nearby headquarters of MI6, an opulently – indeed theatrically – postmodern block designed by Terry Farrell and opened in the early 1990s.

Vauxhall Motors Ltd. A company that began life as the local marine-engineering company Vauxhall Iron Works Ltd. It made its first car in 1903. In 1905 it moved to LUTON, and was bought up by General Motors in 1925. The name 'Vauxhall' remains as a popular UK brand.

vokzal. The Russian word for 'railway station', and apparently deriving from *Vauxhall* but via an unclear route. Supposedly, Russian aristocrats' own pleasure gardens, being modelled on Vauxhall's (*see above*), acquired the generic name *vokzal*, and with the connection of such country estates by the new technology of railways the word eventually acquired its present meaning.

Vectis. The Roman name for the ISLE OF WIGHT.

Venantodunum. A Latinized form of the name HUNTINGDON coined (as if from Latin *venatio* 'hunting') by the 16th-century antiquary John Leland.

Venice of the Cotswolds, the. A nickname for the Cotswold village of BOURTON-ON-THE-WATER.

Venn Ottery 'marshy land by the River Otter', *Venn* OE *fenn* 'fen, marsh'; *Ottery see* OTTERY ST MARY.

A village in Devon, close to the River OTTER, about 5 km (3 miles) southwest of Ottery St Mary.

Venta Belgarum. The Roman name for present-day WINCHESTER.

Venta Silurum. A Roman town on the site of modern CAERWENT.

Ventnor Probably denoting manorial ownership by a family called le Vyntener. The name is first recorded in the early 17th century; before that, Ventnor was called *Holloway* 'hollow way' or 'way in a hollow' (referring to a road running northwards from Ventnor through the hills), OE *hol* 'hollow' + *weg* 'way'.

A town and seaside resort on the southeast coast of the ISLE OF WIGHT, about 5 km (3 miles) southwest of Shanklin. It was once a fishing port, but its mild climate attracted convalescents and winter holidaymakers, and it became a fashionable Victorian health spa. The town's steep terraces, climbing from the bottom of a 236-m (787-ft) cliff, contain many Gothic Revival buildings of the period. Beyond the clifftop is ST BONIFACE DOWN.

The poet Algernon Charles Swinburne (1837–1909) is buried in Ventnor.

There is a town called Ventnor in New Jersey, USA (near Atlantic City); Ventnor Avenue features in the original US Monopoly board, based on Atlantic City locations.

Ventongimps 'steadily flowing spring', Cornish *fenton* 'spring' + *compes* 'even'.

A village in Cornwall, about 2.5 km (1.5 miles) southwest of Zelah.

Venus Hill The early spellings have *Venis*; as the hill is in low-lying land, there is possibly a reference to a marsh (OE *fenn*), although it might equally be a discreet reference to a trysting-place.

A village in Hertfordshire, about 8 km (5 miles) southwest of Hemel Hempstead.

Ver From VERULAMIUM.

A river in Hertfordshire, which rises in the village of Redbourn (which was the earlier name of the river, OE *hreod* 'reed' + *burna* 'stream') and flows 18 km (11 miles) southeastwards through ST ALBANS to join the River COLNE[2].

Vercovicium. A Roman fort on HADRIAN'S WALL, on the site now known as HOUSESTEADS.

Vermuyden's Drain Named in honour of the Dutch engineer Cornelius Vermuyden (1595–?1683) who master-minded the reclamation of the FENS in the 17th century.

An alternative name for the FORTY FOOT DRAIN in Cambridgeshire.

Verney Junction *Verney* perhaps 'growing with ferns', OE *fearnig*.

A former northern terminus of the Metropolitan Railway (later the Metropolitan line), in Buckinghamshire, about 8 km (5 miles) southeast of Buckingham. Opened in 1891, it was intended to be a key link in a railway line that would one day connect Scotland and the North of England via London and a CHANNEL TUNNEL with the Continent. These grand plans, however, never came to fruition, and Verney Junction was closed in 1936. Its legacy is a small village that shares its name.

Vertis Etymology unknown.

The name probably used by the Romans for the town on the site of present-day WORCESTER.

Verulamium Etymology unknown.

A Roman city close to modern ST ALBANS.

On his ennoblement, the philosopher and lawyer Francis Bacon (1561–1626), who owned lands in St Albans, took an anglicized form of the name as his title: **Baron Verulam.**

Veryan From the dedication of the local church to *St Symphorian*, a 2nd- or 3rd-century Gaulish martyr.

A village in Cornwall, in a wooded valley just inland of the western end of **Veryan Bay**, about 17.5 km (11 miles) southwest of ST AUSTELL. It is notable for its five Round

Houses, two at each end of the village and one in the middle, supposedly built in the 19th century by a local vicar, the Reverend Jeremiah Trist, for his five daughters. He had them (the houses) made without corners so that the Devil could not hide in them.

At the western end of Veryan Bay is the tiny, white-washed village of Portloe. On the bay's eastern side are the sandy beaches of Hemmick Beach and Porthluney Cove, and the bay ends at the dramatic DODMAN POINT. Behind Porthluney is the battlemented Caerhays Castle (*see under* ST MICHAEL CAERHAYS).

Via Devana 'Chester road', Modern Latin, from Latin *via* 'road, way' + Modern Latin *Devana*, from *Deva* the Roman name for Chester. The name was coined by Dr Charles Mason, Woodwardian Professor of Geology at Cambridge University between 1734 and 1762.

The Roman road running from CHELMSFORD via CAMBRIDGE[1] to CHESTER and HOLYHEAD.

Via Gellia 'Gell's road', Modern Latin, from Latin *via* 'road, way' + the surname *Gell*.

A road (pronounced 'vy-ə jelliə') in Derbyshire, now a section of the A5012, between Cromford and Grangemill, about 5 km (3 miles) southwest of MATLOCK. A local man called Philip Gell had it constructed in the late 18th century and (not one to hide his light under a bushel) devised its name himself.

The trade name **Viyella** for a type of fabric (dating from the 1890s) was based on *Via Gellia*. The textile works of William Hollins of Nottingham, where the fabric was produced, was located on the road.

Vickerstown. *See under* BARROW-IN-FURNESS.

Victoria[1] An intended honour to Queen *Victoria* (1819–1901; reigned 1837–1901).

A new county planned for the East of England in the middle of the 19th century, between Lincolnshire and Norfolk. The intention was that it should be formed from land reclaimed from the WASH, but the plans never came to fruition.

However, given Britain's 19th-century imperial reach, the name 'Victoria' looms large globally. There are settlements of various sizes and types named after Queen Victoria in the USA (Kansas, Texas, Virginia), Canada (British Columbia (the capital city), Newfoundland), Argentina, Cameroon, Chile, Grenada, Hong Kong, the island of Mahé, Malta, the Philippines, and Sabah. There is a state called Victoria in Australia and a county of that name in Trinidad. There are rivers called Victoria in Argentina, Australia (Northern Territories) and Canada (Newfoundland), lakes in Australia (New South Wales), Canada (Newfoundland, Quebec) and East Africa (the second largest freshwater lake in the world; now called Victoria Nyanza), mountains and mountain ranges in Burma, New Zealand and Papua New Guinea and a waterfall (the Victoria Falls, named in 1855 by David Livingstone; local name *Mosi-oa-Tunya* 'smoke that thunders') in East Africa. There is a Victoriaville in Canada (Quebec), a Victoria Island in Canada (North Western Territories; the tenth largest island in the world), a Queen Victoria Spring in Australia (Western Australia) and a Victoria Land in Antarctica.

Victoria² From *Victoria* Station.

A southwestern district of Central London (SW1), in the City of WESTMINSTER, between Belgravia to the west, Westminster to the east and Pimlico to the south. It is an area largely of offices, shops and mansion blocks, dominated by the railway station at its western edge. Building development began here in the early 19th century, and around 1852 a new road, named **Victoria Street** in honour of the Queen, was laid out here, running westwards from Westminster. The London, Brighton and South Coast Railway opened a grand new terminus at its western end in 1860, and named it after the street: **Victoria Station**. And before long, the surrounding area had adopted the station's name.

The station serves southwest London, Surrey, Sussex and Kent. It handles huge numbers of commuters during the week, and has long been a holidaymakers' gateway to the SOUTH COAST (the Brighton Belle (*see under* BRIGHTON) departed from it). Its eastern side, once a separate station, serves DOVER; in the days of boat-trains it was the home of the Golden Arrow express, and known as the 'Gateway to the Continent':

> My foreign policy is to be able to take a ticket at Victoria station and go anywhere I damn well please.
>
> Ernest Bevin, Foreign Secretary: in *The Spectator* (20 April 1951)

Its links with Dover and GATWICK[1] mean that it has seen the arrival of more royalty and visiting heads of state than any other London terminus. (The other notable 19th-century Victoria Station is in MANCHESTER.)

In Oscar Wilde's *The Importance of Being Earnest* (1895), Jack Worthing describes how he had been found as a baby in a handbag in the left-luggage office at Victoria Station (the Brighton line). **Victoria Coach Station**, London's principal terminus for this mode of travel, lies a few hundred metres away on a three-acre site: it was opened in 1932, and was the responsibility of various private, then nationalized, coach companies until acquired by London Transport in 1988.

Victoria Underground station, on the Central, District and Victoria lines, opened in 1868. The **Victoria line**, a north–south link between WALTHAMSTOW and BRIXTON, opened in 1968.

Apollo Victoria. An Art-Deco cinema (1930) near Victoria Station, which was converted into use as a theatre in 1981. It is associated with big-scale musicals, notably Andrew Lloyd-Webber's roller-skating *Starlight Express*, which ran here from 1984 to 2002.

Victoria Palace. A theatre in Victoria Street, opened (as a music-hall) in 1911. Among the long-running shows it has been associated with are the Crazy Gang's comical extravaganzas (1947–62), the *Black and White Minstrel Show* (1962–70) and the Buddy Holly bio-musical *Buddy* (1989–95).

Victoria Embankment. *See under* EMBANKMENT.

Victorloo. A notional amalgam of the railway termini at VICTORIA² and WATERLOO[1], as featured in *The 5.52 from Victorloo*, a musical tribute to Southern Electric which formed the third movement of the *London Transport Suite* (1958), an orchestral suite by Sidney Torch.

Vidua. Ptolemy's name for Lough Foyle (*see under* FOYLE).

Vigo Village Named in commemoration of the capture of the Spanish port of *Vigo* by the British fleet in 1719.

A village (pronounced 'vye-go') in Kent, about 16 km (10 miles) northwest of Maidstone.

Viking From the name of a submerged sandbank, *Viking* Bank.

A sea area in the shipping forecast. It is to the northeast of Scotland, between FAIR ISLE to the west, FORTIES to the south and North and South UTSIRE to the east.

Vindolanda. *See* CHESTERHOLM.

Vinegar Hill An anglicized corruption of the Irish name *Cnoc Fiodh na gCaor* 'hill of the wood of the berries' (*see* KNOCK-).

A low hill (119 m / 389 ft) in County Wexford, across the River SLANEY from ENNISCORTHY. Vinegar Hill is also the name given to an Irish rebellion in Australia in March 1804, when some 250 Irish convicts (transported after the 1798 United Irishmen's Rebellion) marched on Paramatta. They made their last stand against British troops on a knoll subsequently known as Vinegar Hill. Eight of the ringleaders were hanged in chains and their bodies left to rot on the gibbets, and the rest were brutally flogged.

Battle of Vinegar Hill (24 June 1798). A battle in which the Wexford rebels under Father John Murphy, who were encamped on the hill, were routed by British troops commanded by General Gerald Lake. Lake's men proceeded to slaughter the camp followers left behind.

> Until, on Vinegar Hill, the fatal conclave.
> Terraced thousands died, shaking scythes at cannon.
> The hillside blushed, soaked in our broken wave.
> They buried us without shroud or coffin
> And in August the barley grew up out of the grave.
>
> Seamus Heaney: 'Requiem for the Croppies', from *Door into the Dark* (1969)

Vintry 'wine store' (referring to a large Thames-side wharf building occupied by Bordeaux wine-merchants where wine was unloaded, stored and sold), ME *viniterie*.

One of the 24 electoral wards of the City of London (*see under* LONDON), on the north bank of the River Thames in the area of QUEENHITHE. The local church of **St Martin Vintry** was destroyed in the Great Fire of 1665.

Virginia Like its American namesake, named after Queen Elizabeth I, 'the Virgin Queen'.

A small market town on Lough Ramor in County Cavan, 32 km (20 miles) northwest of Navan. Its Irish name is **Achadh an Iúir** ('field of the yew-trees'). The ruined Cuilcagh (or Quilca) House near Virginia was the home of the Rev. Thomas Sheridan, grandfather of the playwright (who spent much of his youth in Virginia), and friend of Jonathan Swift (who wrote much of *Gulliver's Travels* while staying with the Sheridans here).

Virginia Water From *Virginia* in the USA.

An artificial lake and residential district in Surrey, about 5 km (3 miles) southwest of EGHAM. The 57-ha (160-acre) lake, which occupies the southeastern corner of Windsor Great Park (*see under* WINDSOR), was laid out in 1746 at the instigation of William Augustus, Duke of Cumberland (best known as the bloody victor of CULLODEN in that same year), who had previously been Governor of Virginia in North America. His Virginia connection no doubt suggested the name, as apparently did the idea of carving the lake out of virgin territory, as the American colonies had been.

> Virginia Water: the name was a forecast of the forest wilds, the broad waters, and tranquil solitudes that were to be called forth by the waving of the magician's hand.
>
> James Thorne: *Handbook to the Environs of London* (1876)

The lake is surrounded by pleasant grounds, and on its margin is a Native American totem pole erected here in 1958 to commemorate the centenary of British Columbia.

The residential district of Virginia Water, to the southeast of the lake, is quintessential stockbroker belt and home to several celebrity golfing amateurs.

See also WENTWORTH.

Viriconium Perhaps 'Virico's town'.

A Roman town (also known as **Viroconium**) in Shropshire, on WATLING STREET[1], on the eastern bank of the River SEVERN, about 8 km (5 miles) southeast of present-day SHREWSBURY. It was the fourth largest town in Roman Britain, and the capital of the central region of the country (occupied by the tribe known as the Cornovii). It was once thought that it was sacked and burned by the Saxons, but it is more likely that it simply declined and withered as people moved to the up-and-coming Shrewsbury. Its modern descendant is the village of WROXETER.

See also URICON.

Vobster 'Fobb's rocky hill', OE *Fobbes* possessive form of male personal name *Fobb* + *torr* 'rocky hill'.

A hamlet in Somerset, about 8 km (5 miles) west of FROME[1].

Vord Hill. *See* WARD HILL.

Vowchurch 'coloured church' (probably referring to variegated stonework), OE *fah* 'multicoloured' + *cirice* 'church'; formally identical to FALKIRK[1] in Scotland.

A village in Herefordshire (before 1998 in Hereford and Worcester, before 1974 in Herefordshire), in the GOLDEN VALLEY[1], about 16 km (10 miles) southwest of Hereford.

Vyrnwy. *See* LAKE VYRNWY.

W

Waddesdon 'Weott's hill', OE *Weottes* possessive form of male personal name *Weott* + *dun* (*see* DOWN, -DON).

A village (pronounced 'wodzdən') in Buckinghamshire, on AKEMAN STREET, about 8 km (5 miles) northwest of Aylesbury. The nearby **Waddesdon Manor** was built for Baron Ferdinand de Rothschild in the 1870s and 1880s in the style of a French château. Now owned by the National Trust, it contains significant collections of paintings, furniture and china.

Wadebridge Originally *Wade* 'ford', OE *wæd* (*see* FORD); *-bridge* was added in the 15th century, after the bridge was built.

A town in Cornwall, on the River CAMEL at the point where it starts to broaden out into an estuary, about 8 km (5 miles) east of Padstow. It has a remarkable medieval bridge (from which it got the second half of its name), one of the finest surviving in England. About 100 m (320 ft) long, it has 14 arches (reduced from the original 17). It was built around 1468 at the instigation of Thomas Lovibond, vicar of neighbouring EGLOSHAYLE, who considered the ferry across the Camel too dangerous for his parishioners. The bridge, which was refurbished in 1994, is known as 'the bridge of wool' because, according to local legend, it was founded on sacks of wool.

Wade's Causey 'causeway of Wade'.

An old track extending across the NORTH YORK MOORS from Pickering Castle to Mulgrave Castle near WHITBY. In legend it was constructed by the Germanic giant Wade (father of Wayland the Smith) and his wife Bell, who are also held responsible for a number of other features in the region, including Pickering Castle, Mulgrave Castle, various earthworks and stone circles, and the HOLE OF HORCUM. Wade's Causey may, in reality, be a Roman road, though some argue for a later or earlier date.

Wadhurst 'Wada's wooded hill', OE male personal name *Wada* + OE *hyrst* 'wooded hill'.

A village in East Sussex, about 8 km (5 miles) southeast of Tunbridge Wells. In the past it was an important

small town, a wealthy centre of the Wealden iron industry. southeast England's last iron-ore mine closed at nearby Snape Wood in the 1850s. To the east is BEWL WATER.

Wainfleet All Saints *Wainfleet* 'creek or stream that can be crossed by a wagon', OE *wægn* 'wagon' + *fleot* 'creek, stream'; *All Saints* from the dedication of the local church.

A small market town in Lincolnshire, in the FENS, on the River STEEPING, about 8 km (5 miles) southwest of Skegness. In former times it was a port.

William of Waynflete (1395–1486), founder of Magdalen College, Oxford, was born here.

Wainfleet Haven. An alternative name of the River Steeping downstream of Wainfleet All Saints to the sea.

Wainscott 'shed for wagons', OE, ME *wægn, wain* 'wagon' + *cot* 'shed'.

A village in Kent, on the west bank of the MEDWAY[1] estuary, about 3 km (2 miles) northwest of Rochester.

Wainwrights After Alfred *Wainwright*.

The collective name for all the hills and mountains in the Lake District featured in the handwritten illustrated books of the late Alfred Wainwright, comprising the seven-volume series, *A Pictorial Guide to the Lakeland Fells*. There are 214 summits in this series, and a further 102 in an eighth volume *The Outlying Fells of Lakeland*.

See also MUNROS, CORBETTS, DONALDS, GRAHAMS, MURDOS, MARILYNS.

Wakefield 'open land where wakes are held', OE *wacu* 'wake' + *feld* (*see* FIELD), or possibly 'Waca's open land' with an OE male personal name *Waca*.

An industrial city and unitary authority in Yorkshire, 14 km (8.5 miles) south of Leeds. It was the county town of the former WEST RIDING of Yorkshire. Wakefield was an important centre in the Middle Ages and subsequently flourished on the cloth trade. It became a city in 1888 when the Church of All Saints (mostly 15th century) became **Wakefield Cathedral**, the cathedral of the new diocese of Wakefield; in 1895 the Bishop of Wakefield publicly burnt a copy of Thomas Hardy's novel *Jude the Obscure*. The grammar school was founded by Elizabeth I in 1591, and the town has one of the few bridge chapels in England (14th century, rebuilt 1847). In Wakefield Prison is the 'original' mulberry bush, brought to England in the 16th century, around which Wakefield's women prisoners once used to exercise, hence apparently the nursery rhyme –

> Here we go round the mulberry bush,
> The mulberry bush, the mulberry bush,
> Here we go round the mulberry bush
> On a cold and frosty morning.

Wakefield was the birthplace of the physician John Radcliffe (1652–1714); the writer George Gissing (1857–1903), in whose novel *A Life's Morning* (1888) it features as **Dunfield**; the sculptor Barbara Hepworth (1903–75); the playwright David Mercer (1928–80); and the novelist and playwright David Storey (b.1933), author of *This Sporting Life* (1960).

The area between Wakefield, Leeds and Bradford has been dubbed the 'Rhubarb Triangle', its heavy acidic soil being particularly conducive to the growth of such a crop. From Victorian times rhubarb was cultivated here in forcing-sheds and harvested by candlelight. Vast quantities were transported south to Covent Garden and Spitalfields on the so-called 'Rhubarb Express' train from Wakefield to London. The nightly rhubarb run is now but a distant memory: the last train ran in the 1960s, but the **Wakefield Festival of Rhubarb**, established in 1999, celebrates the past glories of this humble vegetable.

Battle of Wakefield (30 December 1460). A battle during the Wars of the Roses, in which Richard of York was defeated by Lancastrian forces. He was executed after the battle and his head displayed on the walls of York, wearing a paper crown.

Battle of Wakefield (21 May 1643). A battle during the Civil Wars in which Sir Thomas Fairfax defeated the Royalists and captured Wakefield.

Padfoot of Wakefield, the. A species of barghest, or supernatural monster-dog, which proves fatal to anyone who sees it.

Vicar of Wakefield, The. A novel by Oliver Goldsmith, recounting the adventures of the impoverished Dr Primrose and his family. It was published in 1766. Goethe was profoundly moved by what he called this 'prose idyll'.

Wakefield Plays. A cycle of 32 mystery plays performed at Wakefield in the late Middle Ages. Dating from the early 15th century, they dramatize Bible stories from the fall of Lucifer to the Last Judgement. The Wakefield Cycle is regarded as the finest of its kind, and the anonymous writer of some of the material is known as the **Wakefield Master**. (The cycle is also called the Towneley Cycle, after the family who long owned the manuscript.)

Wakefield Trinity Wildcats. Wakefield's rugby league team, originally founded as Wakefield Trinity in 1873 by young men from the local Holy Trinity Church. Wakefield Trinity was one of 22 northern rugby clubs that defected from the Rugby Football Union in 1895 to form the Northern Union (*see* HUDDERSFIELD). The club added 'Wildcats' to its name in 1998, when it was promoted to rugby league's Super League. Wakefield Trinity Wildcats play their home games at the Belle Vue stadium.

Wakes Colne *Wakes* denoting manorial ownership in the Middle Ages by the Wake family; *Colne see* COLNE[1].

A village (pronounced 'kohn') in Essex, in the Colne Valley (*see under* COLNE[1]), about 14 km (8.5 miles) northeast of Braintree.

See also COLNE ENGAINE *and* EARLS COLNE.

Walberswick 'Walbert's dwelling or (dairy) farm', *Walbertes* possessive form of OGerman male personal name *Walbert* + OE *wic* (*see* WICK) 'dwelling, (dairy) farm'.

A village in Suffolk, on the southern side of the mouth of the River BLYTH[1], opposite SOUTHWOLD (to which it is linked by a tiny ferry). In the 15th and 16th centuries it

---

❖ wal- ❖

The Old English element *walh, wealh* has a basic meaning of 'foreigner, Celt (or Briton), serf', terms more or less co-extensive in the Anglo-Saxon mind. The element is found in numerous names, and in the English name of WALES itself. It is hardly surprising that many Welsh people dislike the word, because of its original implication of servitude as well as ethnicity.

As the Anglo-Saxons drove westwards from the eastern coasts, many Britons fled to Wales, but a good many remained. Under the Anglo-Saxons their status was much reduced, but they could nevertheless still occupy land, and the settlements containing the element *walh* or *wealh* reflect this: many Waltons, Walcots

(*see* -COT, COTE) and some Walworths are dotted over the country. Examples include WALTON-ON-THAMES (Surrey) and WALWORTH (Greater London), An interesting number of water features belonged to Britons, as revealed in WALBROOK[1] in Greater London (brook), WALMER in Kent (pool) and WALPOLE in Suffolk (also pool).

Not all Waltons are derived from this element though: WALTON IN GORDANO (North Somerset) is probably 'forest farm', *weald tun*, or possibly 'farm by a wall', *weall tun*, and this example nicely illustrates the two main elements that can be confused with *walh*.

was a thriving port; now it is a relatively sedate resort village, popular with the sailing fraternity, and also with escapees from London. As early as 1880 *Punch* was noting its rural charms:

> O Walberswick's a village of very little tillage
> In the northern part of Suffolk, and it's very picturesque.
> And you fly from all the gritty, dirty bye-ways of the City
> To forget, in pleasant rambles, dreary duties at the desk.

An early 20th-century resident was the Scottish architect Charles Rennie Mackintosh. Sigmund Freud's daughter Anna set up home here before the Second World War, to be followed by other members of the clan in Sir Clement and latterly the journalist Emma and novelist Esther. Other local celebrities have included the film star Ann Todd, the writer and producer Richard Curtis and the disc jockey Simon Mayo.

Walberswick's picturesque qualities were extensively explored by the artist Philip Wilson Steer (1860–1942), who lived here from 1884 until the First World War and founded an artists' colony here.

Walbrook¹ 'brook of the Celts or Britons' (suggesting a British element in the population of London in the Anglo-Saxon period), OE *Wala* possessive plural form of *Walh* 'Celt, Briton' (*see* WAL-) + *broc* 'brook'.

A stream in the City of London, which rose in MOORFIELDS and flowed into the THAMES¹ a short distance upstream of London Bridge (*see under* LONDON). The Romans built their settlement around it. It was covered over around the middle of the 16th century and today it functions as a sewer (the London Bridge Sewer). Its name survives in that of a street (*see* WALBROOK²) and a ward of the City of London.

The Roman Temple of Mithras was discovered on its subterranean banks in 1954.

Walbrook² From WALBROOK¹.

A street in the City of London, running southwards from BANK to CANNON STREET. It is about 45 m (150 ft) east of the former river from which it got its name. The Wren church of St Stephen Walbrook is on its eastern side: the Samaritans were founded here in 1953, and the dramatist and architect Sir John Vanbrugh (1664–1726) is buried here.

Walbury Hill *Walbury* perhaps 'hill of Wal or of the Britons', OE male personal name *Wal* or *Wala* possessive plural form of *Walh* 'Celt, Briton' (*see* WAL-) + *beorg* 'hill'; the name is not recorded before the 18th century.

A hill in Berkshire, on the North Wessex Downs (*see under* WESSEX), about 13 km (8 miles) southwest of Newbury. At 297 m (974 ft) it is the highest chalk hill in England. It is linked by a ridge walk with the second-highest, Inkpen Hill (*see under* INKPEN).

Wales '(place of) the foreigners', OE *wealas*, plural of *wealh* 'foreigner', applied to the Britons by the Anglo-Saxons (*see* WAL-).

One of the constituent countries of the United Kingdom, comprising the peninsula stretching westwards from the English counties Shropshire, Herefordshire and Gloucestershire. The border often follows the rivers of the region, notably, north–south, the DEE², the SEVERN (Welsh *Hafren*), the TEME and the WYE¹. Wales is referred to (although not by nationalists) as a principality (and sometimes as **the Principality**) because the British monarch's eldest son bears the title **Prince of Wales** (*see below*). Wales's patron saint is St David, and its symbols are the leek and the daffodil. Wales is largely mountainous and rural, its hill ranges including the Cambrian Mountains (*see under* CAMBRIA), SNOWDONIA, the BRECON BEACONS and the BLACK MOUNTAINS. Industry is largely concentrated in South Wales, although the traditional heavy industries of iron, steel and coal have now almost disappeared from their heartlands in the VALLEYS. The Welsh language, resurgent in the 20th century, is widely spoken, especially in the centre and north.

Wales was one of the main strongholds of Brittonic-speaking tribes after the Anglo-Saxon invasions, and subsequently the border between Wales and MERCIA was defined by OFFA's DYKE. The present England–Wales border roughly follows it still. In the earlier medieval period Wales was divided into a number of kingdoms, such as POWYS, MORGANNWG, GWENT and GWYNEDD. The Normans made inroads into the Welsh MARCHES and areas such as PEMBROKESHIRE, and by 1283 Edward I of England had completed his conquest of Wales. In the early 15th century Owain Glyndwr (Owen Glendower) undertook a long and ultimately unsuccessful rebellion against English rule, and in 1536–43 English sovereignty was formalized in the Acts of Union. Welsh nationalism became a strong political force again in the 20th century, partly centred on Welsh-language issues. In 1997 the Welsh people voted in a referendum for a degree of devolution, and a new Welsh Assembly began to sit in the capital, CARDIFF, in 1999.

> First God made England, Ireland, and Scotland. That's when he corrected his mistakes and made Wales.
>
> Katharine Hepburn: quoted in *Time* (7 August 1978)

In the Welsh language Wales is CYMRU, in medieval Latin CAMBRIA or WALLIA, and in French PAYS DE GALLES. Slang terms for Wales include ITCHLAND and LEEKSHIRE. In Romany, according to George Borrow, Wales is PORRUMENGRESKEY TEM, meaning 'leek-eaters' country'.

By a peculiar quirk, a Wales cricket team has played in the English minor counties championship since 1988, while the former Welsh county of GLAMORGAN plays as a first-class county in the English county championship.

Although the English continue to be congenitally rude about the WELSH, they persist in liking Wales and moving (or at least purchasing second homes) here, despite the best efforts of the 'Sons of Glendower', a group responsible for fire-bombing English holiday cottages.

> When all else fails
> try Wales.
>
> Christopher Logue: 'To a Friend in Search of Rural Seclusion'

> Steal if possible, my reverend friend, one summer from the cold hurry of business and come to Wales.
>
> Percy Bysshe Shelley: letter (1812)

New South Wales (now a state) was the first British colony in Australia.

> There are still parts of Wales where the only concession to gaiety is a striped shroud.
>
> Gwyn Thomas: in *Punch* (18 June 1958)

See also LAND OF MY FATHERS.

Church in Wales, the. The name of the Anglican church in Wales since 1920, when the Church of England was disestablished here. This followed an Act of Parliament of 1914, passed despite the strident efforts of antidisestablishmentarians.

Green Bridge of Wales, the. A natural rock arch in the sea cliffs west of St Govan's Head, Pembrokeshire.

Mrs Wales. The account name that appeared on the cheques of the late Diana, Princess of Wales.

North Walian. As an adjective, of or relating to North Wales; as a noun, a denizen of the same. Use of the term is informal, and is largely limited to Wales itself.

Prince of Wales. A title first adopted in 1258 by Llywelyn ap Gruffydd of GWYNEDD, who had succeeded in uniting all of North Wales. His right to bear this title was recognized by Henry III in the Treaty of Montgomery (*see under* MONTGOMERY). However, Llywelyn was killed at BUILTH WELLS in 1282 during Edward I's invasion of Wales. Following the completion of the English conquest in 1282–3, Edward is popularly said to have presented Wales with a new prince in the form of his son Edward (the future Edward II), who was born at Caernarfon in 1284. The story is further embellished in Welsh tradition as follows: Edward I tricksily promised to provide Wales with a prince 'who could speak no word of English', and when his son Edward was born he presented him to the assembly, saying in Welsh *Eich dyn*, meaning 'your man'; this is said to be the origin of *Ich Dien*, the motto of the Prince of Wales – although in fact it is German, meaning 'I serve', and dates from the time of the Black Prince (1330–76).

In reality young Edward was created Prince of Wales in 1301. Since 1337 the monarch's eldest son has been born Duke of Cornwall, and the title 'Prince of Wales' has been conferred upon him subsequently. The last attempt to usurp this practice was on 16 September 1400, when, at GLYN-DYFRDWY, his supporters declared Owain Glyndwr to be the rightful Prince of Wales. A drawn-out rebellion against English rule followed.

The present title-holder, Charles, was invested at Caernarfon in 1969 in a pseudo-historical televised ceremony. (The *trompe-l'oeil* nature of the occasion is suggested by the golf-ball that was pressed into service as the spherical component of the newly designed coronet.) Charles has taken his responsibilities somewhat more seriously than other of the princes over the last 200 years.

> You're looking for topless sheep.
>
> Prince Charles: commenting on tabloid reporters' missing of the point as they accompanied him on a visit to a Welsh hill farm (1999)

'size of Wales, the'.

> … that phrase of English commentary used to describe somewhere remote and usually irrelevant …
>
> Hywel Williams: in *The Guardian* (6 August 2003)

Many London-based journalists seem only to have a very vague idea as to how large Wales actually is:

> The building [the SWISS RE TOWER] has 24,000 square metres of external glass, equivalent to five football pitches (or one-14,000th the size of Wales).
>
> Stephen Moss: in *The Guardian* (19 October 2004)

By this calculation Wales has an area of only 336 sq km, whereas the true figure is 20,767 sq km. It has been said that if Wales were to be ironed flat, it would be bigger than England.

South Walian. As an adjective, of or relating to South Wales; as a noun, a denizen of the same. Use of the term is informal, and is largely limited to Wales itself.

University of Wales. A federal higher-education institution, originating in 1872, with campuses at ABERYSTWYTH, BANGOR[1], CARDIFF, LAMPETER, NEWPORT[1] and SWANSEA[1].

Waleses, the. The collective name by which the family of the **Prince of Wales** (*see above*) is known, and thus currently applying to Charles and the princes William and Harry.

Wales and Monmouthshire. *See under* MONMOUTHSHIRE.

Walford. The fictional EAST LONDON borough (E20) in which the BBC television soap *EastEnders* (1985–), an ongoing chronicle of the complicated and miserable lives of East-End working folk, is set. Most of the action takes place in and around Albert Square and its local boozer, The Vic.

Its name may be a blend of such East and Southeast London place names as WALTHAM FOREST, WALTHAMSTOW, CATFORD and ROMFORD.

Walkden Possibly 'Walca's valley', OE male personal name *Walca* + *denu* 'valley'.

A town in Greater Manchester, 7 km (4.5 miles) northwest of Salford.

Wall¹ '(place by the) wall' (referring to its original location outside the walls of the Roman town of *Letocetum – see* LICHFIELD), OE.

A village in Staffordshire, about 3 km (2 miles) southwest of Lichfield. Once a Roman posting station on WATLING STREET¹, it has one of Britain's most complete Roman bathhouses.

Wall² '(place by the) wall', from its proximity to HADRIAN'S WALL.

A village in Northumberland, 5 km (3 miles) north of Hexham.

Walland Marsh *Walland* 'reclaimed marshland by the wall', OE *weall* 'wall' + *land* 'newly reclaimed or cultivated land'.

An area of marshland in Kent, to the southwest of ROMNEY MARSH and to the northeast of RYE.

Wallasey 'island of Waley', *Waley* former name of the area ('island of the Britons', alluding to the fact that the area was cut off at high tide and in floods), OE *Walh* 'Welshman, Briton' (*see* WAL-) + *eg* (*see* -EY, -EA) + *eg*. The second *eg* was tautologically added after the first had become obscured.

A residential and holiday town at the northeastern corner of the WIRRAL, within the metropolitan county of MERSEYSIDE. It includes NEW BRIGHTON, Egremont and Seacombe. Its long wide sandy beach faces the Irish Sea.

Wallasey is linked with LIVERPOOL by a tunnel under the Mersey:

> We dug the Mersey Tunnel, boys, way back in '33,
> Dug a hole in the ground until we found a 'ole called
> Wallasey.
> The foreman cried, 'Get on outside; the roof is falling
> down.'
> And I'm telling you, Jack, we all swam back to dear old
> Liverpool Town.
>
> Anon.: 'I Wish I Was Back in Liverpool'

The architect Maxwell Fry (1899–1987) and the film director Charles Crichton (1910–99) were born in Wallasey.

Wallia. A medieval Latin name for Wales. From the 12th century a distinction was made between **Pura Wallia**, the area of Wales dominated by the Welsh (GWYNEDD, POWYS and DEHEUBARTH), and **Marchia Wallia**, the area under Norman domination (*see* the MARCHES).

Wallingford 'ford of Wealh's followers', OE male personal name *Wealh* + -*inga*- (*see* -ING) + FORD.

A small market town in Oxfordshire (before 1974 in Berkshire), about 24 km (15 miles) southeast of Oxford.

Wallingford has an illustrious history. A Saxon fortified town, it was founded by King Alfred in the early 10th century. In 1066 William the Conqueror, marching north after victory at the Battle of HASTINGS, was forced to ford the THAMES¹ here on his way to London, where he was crowned king. The town's strategic importance as a Thames crossing-place convinced William to build a castle here in 1071. King Henry II held his first parliament in Wallingford in 1154 and the following year presented the town with a royal charter. **Wallingford Castle**, one of the most important royal castles in England, was a Royalist stronghold during the first Civil War before being captured following a 16-week siege by Oliver Cromwell. The castle was torn down stone by stone in 1652 on the order of Cromwell himself for fear of its becoming once again a bastion of Royalist support. Little remains of the castle today.

Despite the destruction wrought by a calamitious fire in 1675, Wallingford retains much of its medieval architecture. The 275-m (900-ft) stone bridge over the Thames here is of particular note.

The crime-writer Agatha Christie (1890–1976) lived in Winterbrook House in Wallingford from 1935 until her death (*see also* CHOLSEY).

Treaty of Wallingford (1153). A treaty between Stephen and the future Henry II, son of Matilda, which ended the civil wars between Stephen and Matilda over the royal succession. It followed the third siege of Wallingford Castle by Stephen's forces in 1152, which had been relieved by Henry. The treaty stated that Stephen could continue as king until his death, after which the throne would pass to Henry: conveniently for Henry, these events came to pass just a year later, in 1154.

Wallops, the. A collective name for the Hampshire villages of MIDDLE WALLOP, NETHER WALLOP and OVER WALLOP.

Wallop Brook. A stream in Hampshire on which Middle, Nether and Over Wallop stand. It is a tributary of the TEST.

Wallsend 'end of the wall', OE *wall* + *ende*.

A town in Tyne and Wear (formerly in Northumberland), 6 km (4 miles) east of Newcastle. It was the site of the Roman fort of **Segedunum**, at the eastern end of Hadrian's Wall. Wallsend was the home of the engineers George and Robert Stephenson, and developed as a shipbuilding centre. However, the last yard, Swan Hunter, closed in 1994.

The rock singer Sting (Gordon Matthew Sumner, b.1951) was born here.

Wallyford OE FORD with an uncertain first element.

A former mining village in East Lothian, 3 km (2 miles) east of Musselburgh. It is near the site of the Battle of PINKIE (1547). Wallyford was the birthplace of the prolific novelist Margaret Oliphant (1828–97).

Walmer 'pool of the Britons' (a water feature that has not survived the centuries), OE *Wala* possessive plural form of *Walh* 'Celt, Briton' (*see* WAL-) + *mere* 'pool'.

A village on the east coast of Kent, now a southern district of DEAL. Julius Caesar is reputed to have landed here in

55 BC. In the 1530s Henry VIII chose it as a site for one of the chain of coastal forts he had built to ward off French attack. In 1708 **Walmer Castle** became the official residence of the Lord Warden of the CINQUE PORTS. Amongst its most notable occupants in this capacity have been William Pitt the Younger, whose niece, the eccentric Lady Hester Stanhope, laid out the magnificent gardens, and the 1st Duke of Wellington, who died here in 1852 (the original Wellington boots are preserved in the castle).

The poet Robert Bridges (1844–1930) was born in Walmer and Joseph Lister (1827–1912), the founder of antiseptic surgery, died here.

Walmington-on-Sea Perhaps inspired by *Walmington* Fold, the name of a road in Woodside Park, North London, on an early 20th-century housing estate of which the other roads were named after genuine places in Sussex (e.g. Folkington, Lullington). Compare also WALMER and WILMINGTON, which may have been subliminal influences on the name.

A fictional seaside resort on the SOUTH COAST of England in which the BBC television sitcom *Dad's Army* (1968–77) was set. Its location was approximately halfway between DOVER and EASTBOURNE (in the direct path of the German invasion that the programme's protagonists were so comically ill-fitted to repel), and it has been variously identified with Littlestone-on-Sea (6 km / 4 miles north of DUNGENESS) and BEXHILL. The programme's extended success permitted familiarity with a wide range of Walmington landmarks, from Captain Mainwaring's branch of Martin's Bank and Jones the Butcher's to Timothy Whites and the Novelty Rock Emporium.

See also THETFORD.

Walney Island. *See* ISLE OF WALNEY.

Walpole 'pool of the Britons' (perhaps referring to a pool that appears here in the River Blyth at times of flooding), OE *Walh* 'Celt, Briton' (*see* WAL-) + *pol* 'pool'.

A village in Suffolk, about 3 km (2 miles) southwest of Halesworth. The Old Chapel here, converted around 1670 from a late 16th-century house, is said to be the second oldest Dissenting Chapel in England.

This and two synonymous villages in Norfolk are the source of the family name *Walpole*, shared by Sir Robert Walpole (1676–1745), England's first prime minister, his son Horace Walpole (1717–97) and the novelist Hugh Walpole (1884–1941).

Walsall 'Walh's nook of land or valley', OE *Walhes* possessive form of male personal name *Walh* + *halh* (*see* HALE, -HALL); alternatively, the first element could represent OE *walh* 'foreigner, Celt, Briton, Welshman' (*see* WAL-).

A manufacturing town and metropolitan borough in the West Midlands (before 1974 in Staffordshire), in the BLACK COUNTRY, about 13 km (8 miles) east of Wolverhampton

and to the east of the M6. Historically its main occupation has been the working of leather, including the making of saddlery and harness – a connection preserved in the nickname of **Walsall FC**: the Saddlers. It was noted, especially in the second half of the 19th century, for its manufacture of horse brasses. Coal was mined here until the 1930s.

The writer Jerome K. Jerome (1859–1927) was born in Walsall.

Walsingham 'Wæls's people's homestead', OE male personal name *Wæls* + *-inga-* (*see* -ING) + HAM.

Either of two neighbouring villages, **Great Walsingham** and **Little Walsingham**, in Norfolk, about 8 km (5 miles) south of Wells-next-the-Sea. The former was originally just Walsingham and Little Walsingham was named in relation to it. Walsingham then chose to emphasize its superior size with 'Great', but ironically it is Little Walsingham that is now somewhat the larger.

The reason for the smaller sibling's growth is the shrine of **Our Lady of Walsingham**. The original was built at Little Walsingham in 1061 by Lady Richeld, in response to a vision in which she was commanded to erect a replica of the House of Nazareth, where the Archangel Gabriel appeared to the Virgin Mary. It became a hugely popular place of pilgrimage during the Middle Ages, numbering Henry III and Edward I among its visitors. The pilgrims brought in revenue and by the 15th century Walsingham Priory was the second richest in Norfolk, after Norwich. It was destroyed at the Reformation, but in 1897 the cult was revived and the New Shrine was completed here in 1937. Modern pilgrims visit mainly the Anglican shrine in the village and the Roman Catholic Slipper Chapel a little way outside the village.

> OUR LADY OF WALSINGHAM
> There once the penitents took off their shoes
> And then walked barefoot the remaining mile;
> And the small trees, a stream and hedgerows file
> Slowly along the munching English lane,
> Like cows to the old shrine, until you lose
> Track of your dragging pain.
>
> Robert Lowell: 'The Quaker Graveyard in Nantucket', VI,
> from *Lord Weary's Castle* (1946)

Waltham Abbey From the nearby abbey, which itself was named from a settlement called *Waltham* 'forest estate' (referring to Waltham Forest – *see* WALTHAM FOREST), OE *wald* 'forest' + HAM 'homestead, estate'.

A town in Essex, on the River LEA, about 13 km (8 miles) southwest of Harlow and close to Junction 26 on the M25. The abbey, from which it gets the second part of its name, was founded in 1060 on the edge of Epping Forest (*see under* EPPING) by King Harold, and his body is said to have been buried here after his defeat at the Battle of Hastings.

It was considerably enlarged after the Conquest and, although much of it was destroyed at the Dissolution, what remains is one of the finest surviving examples of Norman ecclesiastical architecture in England. The composer Thomas Tallis (*c*.1505–85) had a post here before the Dissolution.

Waltham Cross 'cross near Waltham (Abbey)' (*see* Waltham Abbey) referring to an Eleanor Cross set up here in 1290 by Edward I in memory of his wife, Queen Eleanor (1245–90).

A village in Hertfordshire, now a southern district of Cheshunt, about 3 km (2 miles) west of Waltham Abbey and close to Junction 25 on the M25.

Waltham Forest Originally the name of the royal hunting forest now known as Epping Forest (*see under* Epping), from *Waltham* in Essex (*see* Waltham Abbey).

A borough in northeastern Outer London (E4, E10, E11, E15, E17), between Enfield to the west and Redbridge to the east. It was created in 1965 by combining Walthamstow with Chingford and Leyton.

Walthamstow Originally *Wilcumestowe*, probably 'place where guests are welcome' (alluding to a religious house that welcomes guests), OE *wilcuma* 'welcome visitor' + *stow* 'place' (alternatively the first element could represent the OE female personal name *Wilcume*). The modern version, recorded in the 1440s but not common until the 16th century, came about by association with Waltham Abbey, 10 km (6 miles) to the north.

A district of northeastern Outer London (E17), in the borough of Waltham Forest, between Leytonstone to the southeast and Tottenham to the northwest. It did not emerge significantly from Epping Forest (*see under* Epping) until the 15th century, and its growth was relatively slow until the 19th century, when it was transformed into a heavily populated and industrialized urban area. Its demographic profile was decidedly working-class poor, and early 20th-century slang stigmatized Walthamstow as 'the Shoot' (from *rubbish-shoot*). Its subsequent gropings towards gentility were mercilessly skewered in Mike Leigh's 1977 play *Abigail's Party*, set in Walthamstow.

Walthamstow has a well-known greyhound-racing track, and the longest street market in Europe (1.6 km / 1 mile). Its Town Hall (1937–42) finely presages the architectural spirit of Ceaucescu's Romania.

The first British car powered by an internal-combustion engine, the Bremer Car, was produced in Walthamstow (by local engineer Frederick Bremer) between 1892 and 1895.

The Labour leader and prime minister (1945–51) Clement Attlee was MP for West Walthamstow from 1950 to 1955, and on his retirement took the title **Earl Attlee of Walthamstow** (having earlier in his career joked that if he was ennobled he would take the title 'Lord Love-a-Duck of Limehouse' – his previous Commons seat).

Walthamstow Central Underground station, the northern terminus of the Victoria line, opened in 1968.

The craftsman, writer and social reformer William Morris (1834–96) was born in Walthamstow. The house to which he moved when he was 14 years old, the Georgian House in Lloyd Park (named in 1900 after a local benefactor, Edward Lloyd), contains the William Morris Gallery, which is the only public museum dedicated to Morris.

Walton in Gordano *Walton* 'farmstead in a forest or with a wall', OE *w(e)ald* 'forest' or *w(e)all* 'wall' + -ton; *Gordano see* Clapton in Gordano.

A village in North Somerset (before 1996 in Avon, before 1974 in Somerset), on the southwest bank of the River Avon[2], about 10 km (6 miles) from its mouth and 1.5 km (1 mile) northwest of Clevedon.

Walton-le-Dale *Walton* 'village of the Britons', OE *Walh* 'Briton', possessive plural *Wala* 'of the Britons' (*see* Wal-) + -ton; the affix means 'in the valley', OFr *le* '(in) the' + OScand *dalr* 'valley'.

A town in Lancashire, 2 km (1.2 miles) south of Preston. It was the site of the Battle of Preston (*see under* Preston) in 1648.

Walton-on-Thames *Walton see* Walton-le-Dale.

A town in Surrey, on the south bank of the River Thames[1], about 10 km (6 miles) southwest of Kingston upon Thames. It is solid bourgeois suburbia, with stockbrokerish highlights. The actress and singer Julie Andrews (b.1935) was born in Walton-on-Thames.

Walton-on-the-Naze *Walton see* Walton-le-Dale.

A small seaside resort in Essex, about 11 km (7 miles) northeast of Clacton-on-Sea and contiguous with Frinton-on-Sea, on the southeastern shore of the headland known as the Naze (*see* Ness). It was developed as a holiday destination in the early 19th century. Its somewhat garish pier is 244 m (800 ft) long.

Walworth 'enclosure of the Britons' (denoting a Celtic enclave amid a surrounding Anglo-Saxon population), OE *Wala* possessive plural form of *Walh* 'Celt, Briton' + *worth* (*see* -worth, worthy, -wardine).

A district of South London (SE17), in the borough of Southwark, to the east of Kennington. Its western boundary is formed by **Walworth Road**, leading southwards from the Elephant and Castle. The Labour Party had its headquarters here between 1980 and 1997, and 'Walworth Road' became a metonym for Labour's apparat. *See also* Millbank.

Wandle An apparent back-formation from *Wandlesworth*, an earlier form of the name Wandsworth (the name is not recorded in English until the early 17th century, long after the place name had become established as *Wandsworth*, so it may have been an artificial reconstruction; the earlier name of the river was probably *Lidburn*, perhaps 'stream called the loud one', OE *hlyde* 'loud one' + *burna* 'stream').

A river in southwest London. It rises near Croydon and flows 14 km (9 miles) northwards through MERTON and TOOTING into the River THAMES[1] to the west of Wandsworth Bridge (*see under* WANDSWORTH).

Wandsworth 'Wændel's enclosed settlement', OE *Wændeles* possessive form of male personal name *Wændel* + *worth* (*see* -WORTH, WORTHY, -WARDINE).

A district and borough in southwest London, on the south bank of the River THAMES[1]. The district (SW18) lies between PUTNEY to the west and CLAPHAM[1] to the east. The borough (SW11, SW12, SW15, SW17, SW18, SW19) was formed in 1965, incorporating also BALHAM, BATTERSEA, parts of CLAPHAM[1], PUTNEY, ROEHAMPTON and TOOTING.

Wandsworth supported several thriving industries from the Middle Ages onwards, from dying and bleaching, fur-making and hatting (Wandsworth hats became famous throughout Europe) to munitions-making and brewing (Young's Brewery continues the tradition to this day). Suburbia began to encroach in the 18th century, when wealthy Londoners built themselves houses around **Wandsworth Common**, a large area of open land in the southeast of the district, and the coming of the railways in the 19th century precipitated Wandsworth's residential transformation – comfortably genteel with some rough edges, never opulent but significantly gentrified in the latter part of the 20th century (it persisted in re-electing Tory councils, often in the teeth of a swing in the opposite direction in other parts of London).

Wandsworth Bridge, a road bridge across the Thames, links Wandsworth with FULHAM. The original was built in the early 1870s; its replacement opened in 1940.

Wandsworth Prison, opened in 1851 (originally under the name Surrey House of Correction), is the largest prison in England. In 1895 Oscar Wilde spent the first six months of his sentence for homosexual offences here (*see also* READING). One of its most noted 20th-century escapees was Ronald Biggs: sentenced to 30 years imprisonment for his role in the Great Train Robbery (*see* CHEDDINGTON), he escaped from Wandsworth Prison in July 1965 and fled, first to Australia and later to Brazil.

Wanlip 'lonely or solitary place', OE *anliepe*. (Local legend, of a giant called Bel who vowed to get to Leicester from Mount-sorrel (a distance of 11 km/7 miles) on his giant horse in three leaps, would have the name mean 'one leap' – Wanlip being the place where the first of Bel's ultimately unsuccessful three jumps landed.)

A village (pronounced 'wonn-', rhyming with *gone*) in Leicestershire, on the River SOAR, about 6 km (4 miles) north of Leicester.

Wanlockhead 'the head of (the stream with) the flat white stones', OCelt *gwyn* 'white' + *llech* 'flat stone'.

A village in the LOWTHER HILLS, at the head of **Wanlock Water**, 17 km (11 miles) north of Thornhill. It was formerly in Dumfriesshire, and is now in Dumfries and Galloway, near the border with Lanarkshire. The village, at a height of 467 m (1532 ft), claims to be the highest in Scotland. The area around the village and its neighbour, LEADHILLS, was for long a centre of lead-mining. The mines round Wanlockhead opened in 1680 and finally closed in 1959; Wanlockhead is now home to the Museum of Scottish Lead Mining. Gold was also found in the streams round about, and small quantities are still found by eager panners. Gold from the area was used in the crown of James V, in a ring for Queen Mary (spouse of George V) and in a brooch for Queen Elizabeth (spouse of George VI).

When William and Dorothy Wordsworth and Samuel Taylor Coleridge passed by Wanlockhead on their Scottish tour of 1803 they encountered some local bare-foot urchins, and were surprised to learn that they were studying Virgil and Homer in the originals (such was the universal state of Scottish education even then). They were also impressed by a giant lever-armed pump used at the mines, Coleridge comparing it to 'a giant with one idea'.

Wansbeck An old name of unknown meaning which has been assimilated to a name with OScand *bekkr* 'a stream' (the early spellings all have -*spic* or -*spike* or -*spyk*).

A river in Northumberland, with a length of 37 km (23 miles). It rises above Sweethope Loughs ('loughs' = lakes) and flows east through a wooded valley past MORPETH to meet the North Sea at ASHINGTON. Both the river and the town of Morpeth are celebrated in the following lines:

> O ye Northumbrian shades! which overlook
> The rocky pavement and the mossy falls
> Of solitary WENSBECK's limpid stream,
> How gladly I recall your well-known seats,
> Beloved of old; and that delightful time,
> When all alone, for many a summer's day,
> I wander'd through your calm recesses, led
> In silence, by some powerful hand unseen.

> Mark Akenside: *The Pleasures of Imagination* (1744)

Wansdyke 'Woden's dyke' (reflecting the belief that Woden, the principal god of the pre-Christian Anglo-Saxons, built the dyke or oversaw its construction), OE *Wodnes* possessive form of *Woden*, the name of the god otherwise known in Scandinavian mythology as Odin + *dic* 'dyke, ditch'.

An ancient earthwork in Berkshire, Wiltshire, Bath and North East Somerset and North Somerset, running some 96 km (60 miles) east to west from INKPEN, to the southeast of Marlborough, to near PORTISHEAD. It may have been built by Romano-Britons as a defence against Anglo-Saxon invaders.

Wansdyke is now also the name of a parliamentary constituency, covering the non-Bath portion of Bath and North East Somerset and also part of SOUTH GLOUCESTERSHIRE.

Wanstead Perhaps 'place by a tumour-shaped mound', OE *wænn* 'wen, lump' + *stede* 'place'; alternatively, 'place where wagons are kept', OE *wæn* 'wagon' + *stede* 'place'.

A district of northeast London (E11), in the borough of REDBRIDGE, between Leytonstone to the west and Ilford to the east. It lies at what was the southern extremity of Epping Forest (*see under* EPPING), and its footprint can still be seen at **Wanstead Flats** (known locally as 'the Flats'), a huge 135-ha (334-acre) open space (one third of which lies in Newham). In former times their name had a double life as rhyming slang for *spats*. Wanstead is a residential district, a mixture of elegant 19th-century villas and more modest recent housing. Wanstead Underground station, on the Central line, opened in 1947.

Wantage Originally *Waneting* '(place by the) fluctuating stream', from a derivative of OE *wanian* 'to decrease, wane' + -ING.

A market town in Oxfordshire (before 1974 in Berkshire), in the VALE OF THE WHITE HORSE, about 14 km (8.5 miles) southwest of Abingdon. Alfred the Great (849–99) was born here and is commemorated by a statue in the market place, the work of Count Gleichen (Queen Victoria's nephew), erected in 1877. In the novels of Thomas Hardy, Wantage is fictionalized as **Alfredston**. The town's late 18th-century reputation as a centre for pedlars and cut-throats earned it the nickname of **Black Wantage**.

Wantage's large, mostly 13th-century church of St Peter and St Paul is known as the 'Cathedral of the Vale'. Its bells were celebrated by John Betjeman (who lived here from 1951 until 1972 and wrote a number of poems inspired by the town and its surrounding area):

> Now with the bells through the apple bloom
>   Sunday-ly sounding
> And the prayers of the nuns in their chapel gloom
>   Us all surrounding ...
>
> John Betjeman: 'Wantage Bells' (1954)

The first steam tramway in England began operation in Wantage in 1873 and survived until 1948.

The moral philosopher Bishop Joseph Butler (1692–1752) and the jockey Lester Piggott (b.1935) were born in Wantage.

Wantage Code. The third law-code of King Æthelred II, issued at Wantage, probably in 997. Its provisions related to court proceedings, and contain the earliest known references in England to a sworn jury (with the function of accusing culprits rather than deciding guilt or innocence) and to the principle of majority verdicts.

Wantsum OE *wendsum* 'winding', referring to the sinuous course of the channel (*compare* WENSUM).

A river in Kent that is the source of the STOUR[3]. It joins the **Great Stour** and the **Little Stour** at the point where they combine to form the Stour, and it is part of the channel that in former times separated the ISLE OF THANET from the mainland.

Wapping Perhaps 'Wæppa's people's settlement' or 'Wæppa's place', OE male personal name *Wæppa* + -*ingas* or -*ing* (*see* -ING); alternatively, 'marshy or miry place', from a derivative of a word related to OE *wapol* 'pool, marsh, spring'.

A district (pronounced 'wopping') of East London (E1), on the north bank of the River Thames, in the borough of TOWER HAMLETS, between the City of London to the west and LIMEHOUSE to the east. It is linked to ROTHERHITHE by the Thames Tunnel (*see under* THAMES[1]).

Wapping's position by the POOL OF LONDON ensured that from medieval times it had close connections with seafaring. Its inhabitants included a large 'floating' population of seamen, and many local trades were connected with the sea: boat-builders, ship's chandlers and victuallers, navigational instrument makers and so on. A more chilling nautical link was EXECUTION DOCK, off Wapping High Street (a road that contained more than 30 sailors' taverns in the 18th century). It was not entirely coincidental that the district acquired a reputation for violence and criminality – a reputation considerably enhanced by the Ratcliff Highway Murders (*see under* RATCLIFF) of 1811. (*See also* LITTLE BARBARY.)

London Dock (*see under* DOCKLAND) opened here in 1805 and gradually the character of the area began to change. The narrow winding streets of houses and workshops were demolished, and replaced with wharves and warehouses. Wapping became part of Dockland. It suffered heavily from bombing during the Blitz.

Further radical changes followed the closing of the docks in the late 1960s. In 1984 Rupert Murdoch moved his News International organization, publishers of *The Times* and the *Sun*, from the Grays Inn Road to Wapping, against much opposition from the print unions: strenuous picketing of Murdoch's so-called **Fortress Wapping** during a year-long strike escalated into clashes in which heads and pride were severely bruised. Once News International and similar concerns were well-established, gentrification followed, Wapping's warehouses and factories proving readily adaptable to the needs of loft-dwellers.

The old, pre-Murdoch Wapping was the setting of Johnny Speight's BBC television sitcom *Till Death Us Do Part* (1966–8; 1972–5), featuring the irascible reactionary East Ender Alf Garnett.

The author W.W. Jacobs (1863–1943), best known for his chilling ghost story 'The Monkey's Paw' (1902), was born in Wapping, the son of a wharf manager, and used his intimate knowledge of the docks and their many colourful characters in his stories.

Wapping Underground station, on the East London line, opened in 1884.

Warborne. Thomas Hardy's fictionalized version of WIMBORNE MINSTER.

Ward Hill OScand *varth*, OE *weard* 'lookout, guard', i.e. a lookout position.

There are a number of Ward, Warth or Vord Hills in northern Scotland and the Northern Isles, including the highest points on SOUTH RONALDSAY (118 m / 387 ft), HOY (479 m / 1571 ft), Mainland, ORKNEY (268 m / 879 ft), FAIR ISLE (217 m / 712 ft) and FETLAR (158 m / 518 ft).

Wardle 'look-out hill', OE *weard* 'look-out, watch' + *hyll* 'hill'.
A village in Greater Manchester, 4 km (2.5 miles) north of Rochdale.

Wardour Street Named after the *Wardour* family, who owned the land on which it was laid out.
A street in SOHO, in the WEST END[1] of London (W1), running north to south from OXFORD STREET via SHAFTESBURY AVENUE to LEICESTER SQUARE. It was originally laid out in the 1680s.

In the latter part of the 19th century it became known for its antique shops, which specialized mainly in reproduction antiques of dubious quality and taste. In the early 20th century the furniture dealers were replaced by music publishers, and then after the First World War the film companies moved in, and Wardour Street became the centre of, and synonymous with, the British film industry:

> It amazes me how few films we manage to make in a year here: Wardour Street seems to have accepted defeat.
>
> *The Times* (20 December 1975)

''A' Bomb in Wardour Street'. A song (1978) by the Mod-inspired pop group The Jam, 'A' meaning 'Atomic'. It was released as the B-side of the single 'David Watts' and appeared on the album *All Mod Cons* in the same year.

Wardour Street English. The affected use of archaic words and phrases. The term was first applied by William Morris (1834–96) in 1888 to a translation of the *Odyssey* couched in language that reminded him of the pseudo-antique furniture that was in those days sold in Wardour Street.

Ware 'weirs' (probably referring to obstructions that frequently blocked the River Lea here in former times), OE *wær*.
A town in Hertfordshire, on the River LEA, about 5 km (3 miles) northeast of Hertford. It has an impressive array of old buildings dating back to the 14th century.

Lady Jane Grey was proclaimed Queen of England in Ware in 1553, and John Gilpin made an unplanned visit here (in William Cowper's 'The Diverting History of John Gilpin', 1785) when he lost control of his horse and was carried many miles beyond his intended destination, EDMONTON:

> Said John, It is my wedding-day,
>   And all the world would stare,
> If wife should dine at Edmonton,
>   And I should dine at Ware.

Great Bed of Ware, the. A fourposter bed 3.3 m (11 ft) square and capable of holding 12 people. It dates from the late 16th century and was originally at the White Hart Inn and then at the Saracen's Head Inn, Ware, but in 1931 it passed to the Victoria and Albert Museum in London.

> As many lies as will lie in thy sheet of paper, although the sheet were big enough for the bed of Ware in England.
>
> William Shakespeare: *Twelfth Night* (1599) III, ii

The bed is also mentioned in Lord Byron's *Don Juan* (1819–24), George Farquhar's *The Recruiting Officer* (1706) and Ben Jonson's *Epicœne* (1609).

Wareham Probably 'homestead by a weir', OE *wær* 'weir' + HAM.
A market town in Dorset, on the River FROME[3], at the western end of Poole Harbour (*see under* POOLE), about 24 km (15 miles) east of Dorchester. Its Saxon origins are betrayed by the grid pattern of its streets, and it was an important port until the Frome silted up in the Middle Ages.

The church of Lady St Mary contains a stone coffin said to be that of King Edward the Martyr, murdered at CORFE CASTLE in 978 by his stepmother. At St Martin's church is a statue to T.E. Lawrence ('Lawrence of Arabia'), who lived nearby at CLOUDS HILL (it was originally intended for Salisbury Cathedral, but the dean disapproved of Lawrence's homosexuality and put his foot down).

About 5 km (3 miles) south of the town is the so-called 'Blue Pool', a clay-pit lake with an intensely blue colour.

In the novels of Thomas Hardy Wareham is fictionalized as 'Anglebury'.

Warks. The standard written abbreviation of WARWICKSHIRE.

Warkworth 'Weorca's enclosure', OE male personal name *Weorca* + *worth* (*see* -WORTH, WORTHY, -WARDINE).
A village in a loop of the River Coquet, Northumberland, 10 km (6 miles) southeast of Alnwick. It is dominated by **Warkworth Castle**. Built on the site of a Norman castle, the present structure largely dates from the 12th century (with 19th-century restorations), and was the home of the Percy earls of Northumberland until the 16th century. Shakespeare describes it as

> ... this worm-eaten hold of ragged stone,
> Where Hotspur's father, old Northumberland,
> Lies crafty-sick.
>
> William Shakespeare: *Henry IV, Part 2* (1597), I.i

The castle's cellars stood in for the torture chambers in the 1998 film *Elizabeth* (directed by Shekhar Kapur), starring Cate Blanchett and Joseph Fiennes.

Nearby, cut out of a cliff above the River Coquet, is **Warkworth Hermitage**, where the Percys paid a series of hermits to pray for them until the Reformation.

> Then, scooped within the solid rock,
> Three sacred vaults he shows;
> The chief, a chapel, neatly arch'd,
> On branching columns rose.
>
> Bishop Percy: 'The Hermit of Warkworth' (1771)

Warley A re-application of a place name previously in use in the area: 'cattle pasture in a glade', OE *weorf* 'draught cattle' + -LEY.

A name adopted in 1966 for the conurbation in the West Midlands, to the west of Birmingham, consisting of OLD-BURY, ROWLEY REGIS and SMETHWICK.

Warminster 'church on the River Were' (a tributary of the Wylye), OE river name *Were*, meaning 'winding' + *mynster* 'large church, monastery'.

A market town in Wiltshire, situated on a hillside overlooking the valley of the River WYLYE[1], at the western edge of Salisbury Plain (*see under* SALISBURY), about 32 km (20 miles) northwest of Salisbury. Profits from the corn trade and the manufacturing of cloth built up its prosperity in the 17th and 18th centuries, and there are still some fine Georgian buildings from the latter part of that period.

Thomas Arnold (1795–1842), later headmaster of Rugby School, was a pupil for four years at the grammar school here (then Lord Weymouth Grammar School).

In the latter part of the 20th century Warminster became something of a UFO-spotting centre. The first sighting was reported at Christmas 1964, and it is claimed that curious objects then made repeated appearances in the skies over the town. Some suspected a connection with the nearby Army School of Infantry.

There is a town called Warminster in the USA (Pennsylvania).

Warningcamp Originally *Warnecamp* 'Wærna's enclosure', OE male personal name *Wærna* + *camp* 'enclosed piece of land'; the *-ing-* element did not appear until the 16th century, perhaps reflecting the local idea that the place could give early 'warning' of an attack on nearby Arundel Castle.

A hamlet in West Sussex, about 3 km (2 miles) east of Arundel.

Warninglid 'hill-slope associated with Wearda or Weardel', OE male personal name *Wearda* or *Weardel* + -ING + *hlith* 'hill-slope'.

A village in West Sussex, about 11 km (7 miles) south of Crawley.

Warrenpoint Apparently after an extensive rabbit warren hereabouts.

A seaside resort and port at the northwestern end of CARLINGFORD LOUGH, County Down, 10 km (6 miles) southeast of Newry. Its Irish name is **An Pointe** ('the point'). On 27 August 1979 two IRA bombs killed 18 British soldiers here (at Narrow Water), the worst loss of life suffered by the British Army in a single incident during the Troubles. On the same day, in County Sligo, the IRA blew up Lord Mountbatten's boat and him with it.

Warren Street[1] Named in honour of Anne *Warren*, wife of Charles Fitzroy, Baron Southampton, who owned the manor of Tottenham Court.

A road in Central London (W1), in the borough of CAMDEN, running east–west from TOTTENHAM COURT ROAD to Cleland Street, to the south of and parallel to the Euston Road (*see under* EUSTON). It was laid out in the early 1790s. In the early part of the 20th century it gained a slightly tarnished reputation as the centre of the secondhand-car trade.

Warren Street Underground station, on the Northern and Victoria lines, opened in 1907 (originally as 'Euston Road'; its name was changed in 1908).

Warren Street[2] Probably 'rabbit-warren hamlet', ModE *warren* + STREET 'hamlet'.

A village in Kent, on the NORTH DOWNS, about 17 km (11 miles) east of Maidstone.

Warrington 'farmstead or village by the weir or river-dam', OE *wering* 'weir, river-dam' + -TON.

A town and unitary authority in northwest England (before 1998 in Cheshire), on the River MERSEY and the Manchester Ship Canal (*see under* MANCHESTER), between LIVERPOOL to the west and Manchester to the east. It has some notable buildings dating back to the 18th century, when it was pre-eminently a clock-making centre. Other industries developed in the 19th and 20th centuries, from iron-founding to the manufacture of detergents. In 1968 Warrington was designated a NEW TOWN[1], precipitating considerable growth in size and population. It is now noted (jokingly as 'Varrington') for the production of Vladivar vodka.

Joseph Priestley, discoverer of oxygen in 1774, was a tutor at **Warrington Academy** (an institution for the sons of Dissenters) in the 1760s; and it is the source of justifiable municipal pride that in 1848 Warrington became the first town in England to have a public library supported by local rates.

In 1983 Eddie Shah anticipated the upheavals in the newspaper industry by defeating a long strike by the print unions over the use of non-union labour in his Messenger group of newspapers in Warrington.

> Warrington to-day observes its old-time festival known as 'Walking Day'. All the principal streets of the town ... will be given over entirely to the children attending the Sunday-schools.
>
> *Church Family Newspaper* (29 June 1906)

Warrington Bomb (20 March 1993). An IRA action in which two bombs hidden in litter bins in a busy Warrington shopping area exploded, killing a 3-year-old boy and injuring more than 50 other people; a 12-year-old boy died of his injuries five days later. The bad publicity accruing from the Warrington Bomb was arguably one of a number of factors that led to the first IRA ceasefire of 1994.

Warrington hammer. A type of joiner's hammer in which the peen (the sharp part of the head) runs crosswise to the handle.

Warrington Wolves. Warrington's rugby league team, probably founded in 1879. Warrington was one of 22 northern rugby clubs that defected from the Rugby Football Union in 1895 to form the Northern Union (*see* HUDDERSFIELD). The club was adorned from 1945 to 1962 by the Australian-born Brian Bevan, a try-scoring legend. Warrington's current name, adopted at the start of the Super League era in 1996, is less interesting (and rather less appropriate) than the club's historic nickname of the Wire, which arose from the fact that wirepullers from local factories were a mainstay of the team and its support in its early years.

Warsash 'ash-tree by the weir' or 'Wær's ash-tree', OE *weres* or *Wæres* possessive forms of *wer* 'weir' and male personal name *Wær* + *æsc* 'ash-tree'.

A village in Hampshire, on the eastern side of the mouth of the River HAMBLE, about 11 km (7 miles) southeast of Southampton.

Warsop 'Wær's valley', OE *Wæres* possessive form of male personal name *Wær* + *hop* 'enclosed valley'.

A town in Nottinghamshire, on the River Meden, about 8 km (5 miles) northeast of Mansfield. It lies in a former coal-mining district. To the west is **Warsop Vale**, which probably inspired the town's name.

Warth Hill. *See* WARD HILL.

Warwick 'dwellings by the weir or river-dam', OE *wæring* 'weir, river-dam' + *wic* (*see* WICK).

A town (pronounced 'worik') in Warwickshire, on the River AVON[1] and the GRAND UNION CANAL, just to the east of the M40, and about 32 km (20 miles) southeast of Birmingham. It is the administrative centre of WARWICKSHIRE.

It is virtually contiguous with LEAMINGTON SPA to the east.

Warwick has a long and distinguished history. It was originally fortified in 914 by Æthelflæd, a daughter of Alfred the Great (*see also* TAMWORTH), and by the time of the Norman Conquest it was a royal borough. In 1068 William the Conqueror had a castle built here on a cliff overlooking the Avon. In the 14th century this was much enlarged by the earls of Warwick (whose family in the following century were to play such an important part in the Wars of the Roses – notably in the person of Richard Neville (1428–71), dynastic manipulator *par excellence*, known as **Warwick the Kingmaker**). The rest of the medieval town was burnt down in 1694, but **Warwick Castle** survived and remained the home of the earls of Warwick until 1978. Its imposing medievalness (much of it actually the product of extensive 19th-century restoration) has been successfully turned to commercial account with artfully staged tournaments, waxwork displays and the like proving a magnet to tourists. Its grounds beside the Avon (**Warwick Castle Gardens**) were landscaped in the middle of the 18th century by 'Capability' Brown.

Blacklow Hill, just outside Warwick, was the scene of the murder on 19 June 1312 of Piers Gaveston, lover and favourite of King Edward II, by Edward's baronial opponents. A monument erected in 1821 marks the site of Gaveston's decapitation.

The **University of Warwick** was established in 1965. Its campus is close to COVENTRY. It developed something of a reputation, particularly in its early years, as a centre of avant-garde thought and radical action. Amongst its alumni is the rock singer Sting (birth name Gordon Matthew Sumner).

The poet Walter Savage Landor (1775–1864) was born in Warwick.

There are towns called Warwick in the USA (Georgia, New York, North Dakota, Rhode Island), Canada (Quebec) and Australia (Queensland).

Guy of Warwick. The eponymous hero of an anonymous medieval verse romance, part saint's life and part violent adventure story, composed originally in Anglo-Norman around 1300. It tells the story of Guy, son of the Earl of Warwick's steward, and the valorous deeds he performs in order to win the hand of Phelis, the Earl's daughter. These include fighting in the Holy Land, killing the Dun Cow of Dunsmore and slaying a dragon in Northumberland. After these feats he becomes a hermit near Warwick, begging bread of his wife at his own castle gate. On his deathbed he sends her a ring, by which she recognizes him, and she goes to close his dying eyes.

Warwick Vase. A vase found by Sir William Hamilton (1730–1803) in the grounds of the Emperor Hadrian's villa at Tivoli, near Rome, and now kept at Warwick Castle. It is thought to be the work of Lysippus.

Warwickshire From Warwick + shire. The name *Warwickshire* is first recorded in the 11th century.

A county in the Midlands of England. It is bounded to the north by Leicestershire and Staffordshire, to the east by Northamptonshire and Oxfordshire, to the south by Gloucestershire and to the west by the West Midlands (to which it lost much of its industrial northwestern corner, including Birmingham and Coventry, in 1974) and Worcestershire. Its administrative centre is Warwick, and other important towns include Kenilworth, Leamington Spa, Nuneaton, Rugby and Stratford-upon-Avon. Its main rivers are the Avon[1], the Stour[4] and the Tame[1].

Having given up its chunk of the Black Country, Warwickshire is now overwhelmingly agricultural, its fields supporting dairy farms and some arable farming.

In *Britannia* (1586), his county-by-county survey of Britain, the Tudor historian William Camden described pre-Roman Warwickshire as being part of the territory of the Cornovii tribe. Camden's account also divided the county into two areas – the Feldon and the Arden. The Feldon lies in the southeast of the county and is generally open country, while the Arden was, historically at least, the wooded area to the northwest of the River Avon[1]. Along with neighbouring Staffordshire, Warwickshire formed the heartland of the Anglo-Saxon kingdom of Mercia.

Most of Warwickshire is gently undulating countryside. Along its southeastern boundary with Gloucestershire, however, runs the northernmost section of the limestone Cotswolds. Ilmington Downs, above Ilmington, is the highest point in the county at 262 m (858 ft).

In cricketing terms Warwickshire is a first-class county. Warwickshire County Cricket Club was founded at the Queen's Hotel, Coventry, on 8 April 1882 and has played in the county championship since 1895, winning the competition on six occasions. Its famous players include S.F. Barnes (*see also* Staffordshire), M.J.K. Smith, Dennis Amiss, and the West Indians Rohan Kanhai, Alvin Kallicharran and Brian Lara (the latter's world record score of 501 not out was scored for Warwickshire against Durham at Edgbaston in 1994). Its home ground is the County Ground, Edgbaston, Birmingham.

> Warwickshire is the only county which Henry James called 'unmitigated England'.
>
> John Betjeman: *The Spectator* (30 August 1957)

Wasdale. *See under* Wast Water.

Wash, the Originally, in the mid-16th century, *the Washes*, referring to river estuaries fordable at low tide; from OE *wœsc* 'sandbank washed by the sea'. The plural form remained in use up to the 18th century.

An approximately rectangular inlet of the North Sea between Lincolnshire and Norfolk, at the point where the east coast of England meets the bulge of East Anglia. It is about 30 km (19 miles) long and 24 km (15 miles) wide. Several rivers flow into it, notably the Great Ouse, the Nene, the Welland and the Witham. Gibraltar Point (*see under* Gibraltar) is at its northwestern extremity, Hunstanton just to the south of its northeastern corner.

Flatness is the key concept here. The surrounding land is low-lying and featureless, the Wash itself a shallow expanse, half of which becomes mud and sand rather than water at low tide. Even when the Wash is full, its shifting sandbanks, ripping tides and swirling mists present an interesting challenge to anyone trying to navigate it. There are a myriad channels, banks and marker buoys, many of them with outlandish names (Teetotal Channel, Breast Sand, Thief Sand, Roaring Middle Buoy, Dolly Peg and so on).

It was the river estuaries merging flatly into the Wash that gave it its name (*see above*), and it was one of them in particular, the Nene, that famously caused King John the loss of his most treasured possessions. The road from Lincoln to Norfolk crossed the Nene, which was fordable at low tide but highly treacherous. John and his entourage attempted the crossing in 1205 but were caught by the rising tide. His baggage train, including his jewels, was lost in the quicksand, and is presumably still under there. A similar scene is recounted in Shakespeare's *King John* (1595; V.vi) by Philip the Bastard, illegitimate son of Richard I:

> I'll tell thee, Hubert, half my power this night,
> Passing these flats, are taken by the tide;
> These Lincoln Washes have devoured them:
> Myself, well-mounted, hardly have escaped.

However, many prefer the succinctness of the version by C. Sellar and R.J. Yeatman:

> John finally demonstrated his utter incompetence by losing the crown and all his clothes in the wash …
>
> *1066 and All That*

See also Victoria[1].

Washaway Perhaps ModE *washway* 'hollow road, or one crossed by a shallow stream'.

A village in Cornwall, 5 km (3 miles) northwest of Bodmin.

Washington[1] 'Hwæssa's farm', OE male personal name *Hwæssa* + -ing + -ton.

A town in Tyne and Wear (formerly in County Durham), 8 km (5 miles) southeast of Gateshead. It was designated a New Town[1] in 1964. From 1113 to 1613 **Washington Old Hall** was the home of the ancestors of George Washington, first president of the USA, and thus the place is the ultimate source of the federal American capital, and of Washington state.

Washington² 'Wassa's people's estate', OE male personal name *Wassa* + *-inga-* (*see* -ING) + -TON.

A village in West Sussex, at the foot of the SOUTH DOWNS, about 10 km (6 miles) north of Worthing. CHANCTONBURY RING is 1.5 km (1 mile) to the southeast.

Wast Water A shortened form of *Wasdale Water*, OScand *vatn* 'lake' + *dalr* 'valley', hence 'valley of the lake', with tautonymous OE *wæter* 'lake'.

A lake in the western Lake District, Cumbria (formerly in Cumberland), some 3 km (2 miles) southwest of SCAFELL PIKE. It is, at 78.5 m (258 ft), the deepest lake in England, but did not quite live up to Coleridge's high expectations of what a lake should be:

> The Lake itself seen from its foot appears indeed of too regular shape; exactly like the sheet of paper on which I am writing, except it is still narrower in respect of its length.
>
> Samuel Taylor Coleridge: letter to Sara Hutchinson (5 August 1802) (written at the top of Scafell)

The valley that Wast Water sits in is called **Wasdale**, from which the lake gets its name; however, there is no River Wast, the lake feeding instead the River Irt. On the eastern side of the lake are the gloomy crags and screes of the hill called the Screes:

> The screes are speeding down at perfect pitch
> before they tuck themselves in envelopes
> Wastwater seals and never means to post.
>
> William Scammell: 'The Screes'

Beyond the northern end of the lake is the small settlement of **Wasdale Head**. It is a tough country to farm:

> Every patch of pasture hard-won from the obdurate rock
> And held-fast to the earth by a net of walls …
>
> Tom Bowker: 'Wasdale Head'

Wasdale Head principally consists of the famously hospitable Wasdale Head Hotel. This hostelry was much favoured by the Victorian gentleman-mountaineers who came to explore the fine neighbouring peaks, described by Coleridge:

> The head of the Lake is crowned by three huge pyramidal mountains, Yewbarrow, Scafell, and the great Gavel [Great Gable].
>
> Samuel Taylor Coleridge: letter to Sara Hutchinson (5 August 1802)

To these one might add Haycock, Steeple, Pillar, Red Pike, Kirk Fell and, of course, the highest of them all, Scafell Pike. The Wasdale Head Hotel features prominently in Roger Hubank's novel *Hazard's Way* (2001), dealing with the political and social divisions among the cragsmen who frequented it at the time of the Boer War.

Watchet Probably '(place) under the wood' (referring to its location at the foot of cliffs that in former times were densely wooded), from OCelt CED 'wood'.

A town on the Somerset coast, about 11 km (7 miles) east of Minehead. It was once a busy and prosperous port – Samuel Taylor Coleridge's Ancient Mariner set sail from here – and its small and still active harbour adds to its attraction now as a modest resort town.

It is overlooked by the 13th-century hilltop church of St Decuman. Decuman was a Welshman who floated across the Bristol Channel to England; he was decapitated by a Danish invader, who was so impressed by his victim's *sang froid* in washing his head in a stream and putting it beside him as he lay down to die that he instantly converted to Christianity.

Water Referring to Whitewell Water nearby.

A village in the Forest of ROSSENDALE, Lancashire, 4 km (2.5 miles) northeast of Rawtenstall.

Waterbeach 'low ridge by water' (alluding to its location near the River Cam, in contrast to LANDBEACH), OE *wæter* 'water' + *bæc* 'low ridge'.

A village in Cambridgeshire, close to the west bank of the River CAM², about 8 km (5 miles) northeast of Cambridge.

Water-break-its-Neck. A waterfall in a ravine on the south side of Radnor Forest (*see under* RADNORSHIRE), Powys (formerly in Radnorshire), some 3 km (2 miles) north of Llanfihangel-nant Melan and 12 km (7.5 miles) west of Kington.

Waterfall 'place where a stream disappears under the ground' (referring to the local River Hamps, which does that), OE *wæter-gefall.*

A village in Staffordshire, on the eastern side of the PEAK DISTRICT National Park, about 12 km (7.5 miles) southeast of Leek. It is a little to the north of the similarly inspired WATERHOUSES.

Waterford 'inlet of the castrated rams', OScand *vethr* 'wether' (i.e. castrated ram) + *fjorthr* 'fjord, sea inlet', referring to a point on the Suir estuary where wethers were embarked for export.

A city and port on the River SUIR in County WATERFORD, of which it is the county town. Its Irish name is **Port Láirge** ('bank of the haunch', referring to the shape of the river bank). Waterford is 45 km (28 miles) west of Wexford, and situated shortly before the Suir enters the large natural inlet of **Waterford Harbour** (which also receives the waters of the BARROW and the NORE).

Waterford was founded by the Norse rulers of DUBLIN in 914. It was seized by the Anglo-Norman adventurer Strongbow (Richard de Clare, Earl of Pembroke) in 1170, who gave an indication of what the Irish were to expect over the centuries from their neighbours over the water by breaking the limbs of the leading citizens of the city and then throwing them into the sea. Waterford was soon after visited by Henry II, who took possession of the place, and subsequently the town became the second most important Anglo-Norman stronghold in Ireland after Dublin. King John gave the town its first charter when he visited in 1205, and Waterford developed as an important port in the Middle Ages, exporting wool and hides, and importing French wine. In 1495, during the reign of Henry VII, the town resisted the advances of the pretender Perkin Warbeck, and so gained its motto '*Urbs intacta manet Waterfordia*' (Latin, 'the city of Waterford remains intact'). It remained loyal to the English Crown through to the 17th century. In 1650 it was taken by Cromwellian forces under General Henry Ireton, and many Catholic merchants were expelled.

There are fragments of the medieval city walls, some Norman towers (such as Reginald's Tower, where Strongbow married the daughter of Dermot MacMurrough), and the remains of Greyfriars Monastery (13th century) and Blackfriars (1226), a Dominican monastery. The Protestant cathedral (belonging to the diocese of Cashel) dates from 1773 and the Catholic cathedral (of the diocese of Waterford and Lismore) from 1796. There are many fine 18th-century buildings, and the city experienced a bracing regeneration towards the end of the 20th century.

Waterford was the birthplace of Thomas Francis Meagher (1823–67), the Young Ireland leader and later governor of Montana; and of the actor-manager Charles Kean (1811–68). John Redmond, leader of the Irish Parliamentary Party, was MP for Waterford from 1891 until his death in 1918.

There are towns called Waterford in the USA (Connecticut, Maine and Pennsylvania).

Joffroi of Waterford. A medieval writer of romance, known for his retelling of legends associated with Troy, largely based on the pseudo-chronicles of Dares Phrygius.

Waterford glass. A type of hand-blown crystal glass manufactured in the city, with a higher-than-usual lead content. The Waterford factory was established by two Quaker brothers, George and William Penrose, in 1783, closed in 1851 and reopened exactly a century later. One of its best-known ranges, Lismore, was designed by the Czech émigré Mirek Havel and launched in 1952. In 1967 Jacqueline Kennedy visited the factory and ordered Waterford chandeliers for the Kennedy Center in Washington DC, so furthering the popularity of Waterford glass among Irish-Americans.

Waterford, County. A county in southeastern Ireland, bounded on the north by Kilkenny, Tipperary and Limerick, on the west by Cork, on the south by the Celtic Sea, and on the east by Waterford Harbour and Wexford. The county town is WATERFORD, and other towns include DUNGARVAN and LISMORE[2]. The COMERAGH MOUNTAINS and the River SUIR are in the north.

Watergrasshill Irish *Cnocán na Biolraí* 'little hill of the watercress'.
A village in County Cork, 20 km (12 miles) northeast of Cork itself.

Waterhouses 'houses by the stream' (referring to the River Hamps), ModE *water* 'stream' + *houses*.
A village in Staffordshire, on the eastern side of the PEAK DISTRICT National Park, about 0.8 km (0.5 miles) south of WATERFALL.

Waterloo[1] Probably from *Waterloo* Station, which itself got its name from Waterloo Bridge, which in turn was named in honour of the British and Allied victory over Napoleon's forces at the Battle of Waterloo on 18 June 1815. (Waterloo – etymologically probably 'wet marsh or wood', Old German – is in modern Belgium, about 12 km (7.5 miles) south of Brussels.) A district of South London (SE1), in the borough of LAMBETH, at the southern end of **Waterloo Bridge** (*see below*). In common with most areas in London (and elsewhere) around railway termini, it is somewhat scruffy and down-at-heel. Its most notable landmark, apart from the station, is the Old Vic Theatre, which opened in 1818 (as the Royal Coburg) and, in the early to mid-20th century under Lilian Baylis, became London's leading Shakespearean theatre and the first home of the National Theatre. It stands on the corner of The Cut, a street of small shops (originally, in the 1820s, called the New Cut, because it was 'newly cut' through Lambeth Marshes), and **Waterloo Road**, a dingy thoroughfare running southeastwards from Waterloo Bridge (Sidney Gilliat's film ***Waterloo Road*** (1944), starring John Mills as a squaddie with doubts about his wife's faithfulness, is set in the purlieus of Waterloo).

At the southern end of Waterloo Bridge there was for many years a well at the intersection of a series of pedestrian subways that came to be known as the Bull Ring. It became a notorious cardboard city and druggies' refuge. The site is now occupied by the British Film Institute's Imax Cinema, showing 3-D films. The area between here and the THAMES[1], containing such cultural landmarks as the Royal National Theatre and the Royal Festival Hall, has fastidiously distanced itself from the name 'Waterloo', being generally known as the SOUTH BANK[1].

There are towns and other settlements called Waterloo in the USA (Arkansas, Illinois, Indiana, Iowa, Montana, New York), Canada (Quebec, Ontario), Australia (Northern Territory) and Trinidad.

It has been speculated that *loo* 'lavatory' may be derived from *Waterloo*. No decisive evidence for this has ever been produced, but it may be more than a coincidence that in the early 20th century *Waterloo* was a British trade name for iron cisterns.

Waterloo Bridge. A road bridge across the Thames linking the area of the STRAND and ALDWYCH with LAMBETH. The original bridge, designed by the Scottish engineer John Rennie (*see* KELSO) and described by the sculptor Antonio Canova (1757–1822) as the finest in Europe, was opened by the Prince Regent in 1817. At first it was to be called the Strand Bridge, but before its opening it had been patriotically decided to link it with Wellington's recent glorious victory at Waterloo (*see above*). Its modern replacement (designed by Giles Gilbert Scott) dates from 1942. Until 1877 it was a toll bridge: the toll was a halfpenny, which led to that sum becoming known in 19th-century London slang as a 'waterloo'.

Waterloo Bridge is the title of a sentimental film melodrama (1931) starring Mae Clarke as a ballerina who marries an army officer (Kent Douglass) who is reported missing in action. Neglected by his family, she resorts to prostitution, offering her services on Waterloo Bridge. The superior 1940 remake stars Vivien Leigh and Robert Taylor. The real bridge was a favourite jumping-off point for suicides in the past, to such an extent that it came to be known as the 'Bridge of Sighs'.

Waterloo church. A name applied in the 19th century to churches built (many of them in Greek Revival style) with funds provided under an Act of 1821, to mark victory at the Battle of Waterloo and the nation's deliverance from invasion during the Napoleonic Wars. It was sometimes used specifically to refer to any of four churches dedicated to the evangelists in the old parish of Lambeth: St John, Waterloo Bridge Road; St Luke, Norwood; St Mark, Kennington; St Matthew, Brixton.

Waterloo Station. A railway station at the southern end of Waterloo Bridge. Opened in 1848, it is the terminus for suburban services to and from southwest London and Surrey, and for mainline services to and from southern and southwestern England (including, in the days of the great Transatlantic liners, the Ocean Terminal at SOUTHAMPTON). It grew somewhat by accretion: it once included the so-called 'Necropolis Station', to transport funeral traffic direct to Brookwood Cemetery near WOKING; Andrew Martin's novel *The Necropolis Railway* (2002) concerns a murder mystery on that line. In 1922 the whole, with the exception of the separate **Waterloo East**, became housed in a single brand-new building. Since 1993 its northwestern side, sumptuously reroofed to the design of Nicholas Grimshaw and renamed **Waterloo International**, has been the terminus for Eurostar trains operating through the CHANNEL TUNNEL. Waterloo has always been a stereotypically busy commuter station, the one sure landmark for rendezvous on its vast concourse being 'under the clock'.

Waterloo Underground station, on the Bakerloo, Jubilee and Northern lines, opened in 1906. In addition, the **Waterloo & City Railway**, operating a tube line between Waterloo and BANK, and known to its often disgruntled customers as 'the Drain', opened in 1898. Until 1994, when British Railways handed it over to them, it remained the only underground line in the capital not run by London Underground.

'Waterloo Sunset'. A song (1967) about loneliness, isolation and the consolations provided by the London scenes of its lyrics by the pop group The Kinks, written by Ray Davies. The song was originally intended to be titled 'Liverpool Sunset', but 'Waterloo Sunset' was chosen because the native North Londoner Davies had walked over Waterloo Bridge several times a week on his way to art school. The song appeared on the album *Something Else*.

Waterloo² Named after the *Waterloo* Iron Foundry, established in the mid-19th century.

A village in Dorset, within the unitary authority of Poole, now effectively a northern suburb of POOLE.

Waterloo³ After the battle (*see* WATERLOO¹).

A village in Norfolk, about 11 km (7 miles) north of Norwich.

Waterloo⁴ After the battle (*see* WATERLOO¹).

A tiny settlement in Aberdeenshire, 8 km (5 miles) west of Cruden Bay.

Waterloo⁵ After the Royal *Waterloo* Hotel, itself named after the battle (*see* WATERLOO¹).

An urban area, formerly a seaside resort, between Crosby and Bootle in Merseyside.

Waterloo⁶ After the battle (*see* WATERLOO¹).

A village in North Lanarkshire, 2 km (1.2 miles) southeast of Wishaw.

Waterloo⁷ After the battle (*see* WATERLOO¹).

A settlement in Perth and Kinross, 7 km (4 miles) southeast of Dunkeld.

Waterloo⁸ After the battle (*see* WATERLOO¹).

A village in Pembrokeshire, to the east of Pembroke Dock.

Waterlooville 'town of Waterloo', *Waterloo* + Fr *ville* 'town'. The name appears to have been inspired by The Heroes of Waterloo, a hostelry around which the town grew up in the 19th century. Local legend insists that the name of the inn commemorates soldiers and sailors who stayed here (or drank here) after disembarking at nearby Portsmouth on their way home from the Battle of Waterloo (*see under* WATERLOO¹).

A town in Hampshire, about 10 km (6 miles) north of Portsmouth.

Watermeetings. *See under* CLYDE.

Water of Girvan. *See under* GIRVAN.

Water Orton *Water* referring to its position by the River Tame; *Orton* 'farmstead by the riverbank or ridge', OE *ofer* 'bank, ridge' + -TON.

A village in Warwickshire, on the River TAME[1], between the M6 and the M42, about 11 km (7 miles) northeast of Birmingham.

Waterperry '(place with) pear-trees near the water' (referring to its location near the River Thame), OE *wæter* 'water' + *pirige* 'pear-tree'.

A village in Oxfordshire, on the River THAME[1], about 10 km (6 miles) east of Oxford. It is known principally for the very handsome **Waterperry Gardens** (which are a working nursery as well as being open to the public) laid out around a rather dull Georgian house, adjoining which is a church of Saxon origin with a 'wooden-hatted' belfry.

Watership Down *Watership* 'artificial watercourse' (referring to artificial ponds made on a nearby farm to preserve water in this chalky area), OE *wæterscipe*; *Down see* DOWN, -DON.

An area of downland in Hampshire, in the North Wessex Downs (*see under* WESSEX), about 5 km (3 miles) southwest of KINGSCLERE. Richard Adams (b.1920) used it as the setting of his eponymous and immensely popular animal novel *Watership Down* (1972). It concerns a community of rabbits who set out in search of a new home on the Downs when their Berkshire warren is destroyed by construction workers, and can also be read as a political or environmental allegory. Adams created a complete world and convincing speech for his animal characters, particularly memorable among whom are Hazel, Fiver and Bigwig. A two-dimensional cartoon film version (1978) was directed by Tony Guy.

Waterside From its riverside location.

An area of Derry/Londonderry on the east bank of the River FOYLE. It developed following the building of the first bridge across the Foyle in 1790, and many Protestants moved here, leaving the west bank, or **Cityside**, predominantly Catholic.

Watersmeet A descriptive name, probably recent.

A steep wooded gorge in North Devon, at the northern edge of EXMOOR, about 2.5 km (1.5 miles) east of Lynton. The **East Lyn** (*see* LYN) River is joined here by Hoar Oak Water, and after rain their combined forces cascade down in a peat-stained torrent to the sea (in 1952, with catastrophic results – *see* LYNMOUTH).

Waters of Moyle. An alternative name for the Sea of MOYLE.

Waterville From Waterville House (1844), whose name refers to the River Finglas.

A seaside and angling resort on BALLINSKELLIGS Bay in County Kerry, at the western end of the IVERAGH peninsula, some 50 km (31 miles) southwest of Killarney. Its Irish name is **An Coireán** ('the whirlpool'), referring to the confluence of the rivers Finglas and Currane.

Watford[1] 'ford used when hunting', OE *wath* 'hunting' + FORD.

A town (pronounced 'wotfəd') in Hertfordshire, on the River COLNE[2], between the M1 to the east and the GRAND UNION CANAL to the west, about 6 km (4 miles) northeast of Rickmansworth and 26 km (16 miles) northwest of London. At its heart is an old town, with a medieval church and a variety of other notable buildings from the late Middle Ages onwards, but in the 20th century it increased greatly in size, and its present-day aspect is decidedly modern.

Watford is the last outpost of the London conurbation that one leaves behind when travelling north on the M1, and it was probably that which led in the 1960s to the austral-centric notion of the town as the outer limit of urban-based civilization – expressed particularly in the phrase '**north of Watford**', implying a benighted cultural wilderness:

> City types who would not normally dream of venturing north of Watford were yesterday falling over each other in their scramble to join in the excitement and buy a little piece of Knutsford.
>
> *The Times* (4 November 1999)

Less forgivable prejudices are encapsulated in the southern White Trash formula 'Wogs begin at Watford' (an alliterative variation on the original 'Wogs begin at Calais').

The fortunes of **Watford FC**, founded in 1891, nicknamed the Hornets (from the team's black-and-yellow strip), and based at Vicarage Road, took an upturn in the early 1980s when the singer Elton John (a former local resident) became chairman and invested a chunk of his considerable wealth in the club. The golden era ended in the late 1980s when the club was relegated back to the old Second Division, and since then it has enjoyed an up-and-down existence. Since 1997 the club has shared Vicarage Road with Saracens, a professional rugby union club (*see under* ENFIELD). Saracens have contributed a number of players to the England national side in recent years, including Kyran Bracken and Richard Hill.

Watford was the birthplace of the screenwriter T.E.B. Clarke (1907–89), author of many of the Ealing comedies (*see under* EALING); of Joy Batchelor (1914–91), one half of the husband-and-wife team of film animators Halas and Batchelor; and of the pop singer and UN Goodwill Ambassador Geri Halliwell ('Ginger Spice'; b.1972).

There is a Watford City in the USA (North Dakota).

Watford². A village in Northamptonshire, beside the M1, about 8 km (5 miles) northeast of Daventry.

Watford Gap. A broad valley at the northern end of the COTSWOLDS, to the west of Northampton, where road, rail and canal routes run in parallel through the hills. It is sometimes regarded as the southern boundary of the MIDLANDS. Watford Gap Services are situated between Junctions 16 and 17 on the M1, just south of Watford.

Wath upon Dearne 'ford on the River Dearne', OScand *vath*, with river name *Dearne*, possibly OCelt or from OE *derne* 'hidden'.

A town on the Dearne and Dove Canal in South Yorkshire, 11 km (7 miles) southeast of Barnsley.

Watling Street¹ 'Roman road of Wacol's people', OE male personal name *Wacol* + *-ingas* (see -ING) + *strœt* (see STREET). (The Anglo-Saxons' name for the road, which is first recorded in the 9th century, appears to be based on the same folk-name as *Wœclingaceaster*, an early name for St Albans. It could well be, therefore, that *Watling Street* was originally just the road from London to St Albans, and that the name was only later applied to the rest of the Roman road.)

A Roman road that ran from DOVER northwestwards via CANTERBURY¹, London, ST ALBANS and DUNSTABLE to WROXETER in Shropshire. It was one of the most important strategic communications links in Roman Britain, connecting the port of Dover with the commercial centre of London, with Wroxeter, which was the chief town of a large area of central Britain, and (via a branch road) with the legionary fortress at CHESTER.

It is not clear whether the sections north and south of the River Thames formed a single continuous road in Roman times, but if they did they may well have been linked by a ford in the Westminster area. The northern section left London along the line of what is now the A5, past MARBLE ARCH and on up the Edgware Road (*see under* EDGWARE), through the MIDLANDS, along the boundary of Leicestershire and Warwickshire, to just beyond what is now TELFORD. In the 9th century it became the border between English and Danish territory (*see* DANELAW).

Watling Street² An alteration (no doubt under the influence of WATLING STREET¹) of earlier *Athelingstreet* 'street of the prince or princes', OE *œthelinges* or *œthelinga* possessive singular and plural forms of *œtheling* 'prince' + *strœt* (see STREET).

A street in the City of London (EC4), running east–west between CHEAPSIDE to the north and CANNON STREET to the south.

Wat's Dyke 'Wada's ditch', OE male personal name *Wada* + *dic* 'ditch, dike'.

A defensive earthwork along the Anglo-Welsh border parallel to and to the east of OFFA'S DYKE. It was built

around 700 and extends from Basingwerk on the DEE¹ estuary to the Morda Brook, south of Oswestry.

Wauchope Forest 'forest in the valley of the Britons', OE *Walh* 'Briton' + *hop* 'secluded valley', with ModE *forest*.

A remote and extensive area of coniferous plantation in the BORDERS (formerly in Roxburghshire), south of Jedburgh and west of CARTER BAR. It is pronounced 'wochəp' with the 'ch' as in *loch*. In 1787 Robert Burns wrote a rhyming 'Answer to the Gudewife of Wauchope-House', the lady having sent him a complimentary epistle in verse.

There is a town called Wauchope in Australia (New South Wales).

Waun Fach 'little moor', Welsh *gwaun* 'moorland, heath', with *fach* 'small' (*see* BACH), presumably in comparison to some other area of moorland.

The highest peak (811 m / 2661 ft) in the BLACK MOUNTAINS of Powys.

Waveney¹ 'river by a quagmire', OE *wagen* 'quagmire' + *ea* (*see* EA-).

A river in EAST ANGLIA, which for most of its course forms the eastern part of the boundary between Norfolk and Suffolk. It rises about 10 km (6 miles) west of Diss and flows 80 km (50 miles) eastwards and then northeastwards through DISS, BUNGAY, and BECCLES into the BROADS, where it broadens out into BREYDON WATER, to the west of GREAT YARMOUTH.

Waveney² From WAVENEY¹.

An administrative district in the northern part of Suffolk. Its northern boundary is formed by the River Waveney.

Waverley From *Waverley* Abbey, to the south of Farnham (from which Sir Walter Scott is said to have taken the title of his first novel, *Waverley* (1814), a dashing tale of the doings of young Edward Waverley at the time of the Jacobite uprisings in Scotland). Etymologically, *Waverley* is 'marshy glade' or 'glade by marshland', OE *wœfre* 'marsh' + -LEY.

An administrative district of southwestern Surrey. Created in 1974, its main centres of population are FARNHAM, GODALMING and HASLEMERE.

Waverley Station. Edinburgh's main railway station, at the east end of PRINCES STREET. Nearby is the gothic spike of the Scott Monument, and the station itself – opened in 1854 – is named after Sir Walter Scott's first novel, *Waverley* (1814). The title is the name of the hero, Edward Waverley, a name derived from the ruined Waverley Abbey, near FARNHAM, Surrey – the first Cistercian foundation in England (1128). Scott published all his subsequent novels as 'by the author of Waverley', remaining anonymous as the 'Great Unknown' until 1827. Thus the novels became known as the **Waverley Novels**. A number of other phenomena have taken their name from Scott's novel:

SS Waverley. The world's last sea-going paddle steamer, which still takes trippers 'doon the watter' on the Firth of Clyde, and offers other trips round Britain's coasts. It was built in 1947 to replace its predecessor, sunk off Dunkirk in 1940.

Waverley biscuit. A wodge of slushy nougat held between two wafers and a chocolate rim.

Waverley Notelets. A brand name of Woolworth stationery products.

Waverley Pen. A brand of pen manufactured by Mac-Niven and H. Cameron Ltd., immortalized by the jingle (*c.*1879):

> They come as a boon and a blessing to men,
> The Pickwick, the Owl and the Waverley pen.

This is thought to have derived from:

> It came as a boon and a blessing to men,
> The peaceful, the pure, the victorious PEN!
>
> > J.C. Prince: (1808–66), 'The Pen and the Press'

Wayland's Smithy So named by the Anglo-Saxons, who thought it must be the work of *Wayland*, the Teutonic equivalent of the Roman god Vulcan, a supernatural smith who forged chainmail for the gods.

A Neolithic passage grave (burial in a central chamber reached along a low passage) on the Berkshire Downs (*see under* BERKSHIRE), about 1.5 km (1 mile) east of the White Horse of Uffington (*see under* UFFINGTON). It is at least 5000 years old.

It was traditionally said that if a traveller tied up his horse here, left sixpence for a fee and retired from sight, he would find the horse shod on his return.

Wayland Wood Etymology uncertain.

An area of woodland in Norfolk, just southeast of Watton in the east of the county, associated with the legend of the Babes in the Wood. The story runs that the master of Wayland Hall left a little son and daughter to the care of his wife's brother. Both were to have money, but if the children died first the uncle was to inherit. After 12 months the uncle hired two ruffians to murder the babes. One of the men relented and killed the other, leaving the children in a wood. They died of exposure during the night, and Robin Redbreast covered them with leaves. All now went wrong for the wicked uncle: his sons died, his barns were fired, his cattle perished and he himself finally died in gaol. After seven years the ruffian was arrested for highway robbery and confessed the whole affair.

The ballad 'The Children in the Wood' appears in *Percy's Reliques* (a collection of old ballads published in 1765) and also in a crude melodrama, printed in 1601 and attributed on the title page to Rob Yarington, called *Two Lamentable Tragedies; the one of the murder of Maister Beech, a chandler in Thames-streete, etc. The other of a young child murthered in a wood by two ruffians, with the consent of his unkle.* It is uncertain which is earlier, the play or the ballad.

Norfolk tradition has long identified Wayland Wood (or Wailing Wood) as the scene of the tragedy, and nearby Griston Hall is described as the home of the wicked uncle.

There used to be an oak tree in Wayland Wood that was said to be where the children perished, but it was destroyed by lightning in 1879. Local lore has it that the sound of children sobbing can be heard by those who walk in the woods at dusk.

Babes in the Wood has become a familiar title to pantomime audiences, the grimness of the original story ameliorated by the usual comic and musical accoutrements of the pantomime genre. The expression 'babes in the wood' retains currency to denote innocence under threat; and in Irish history, the insurrectionists who lived in the mountains of WICKLOW and the woods of ENNISCORTHY in the later 18th century were known as 'babes in the wood'.

Weald, the 'woodland, forest', OE *weald* (related to German *Wald* 'forest'). The name is a shortening of *Andredesweald* 'forest of Andred', an anglicization of Romano-British *Anderida*.

An area of land in southeast England, lying between the NORTH DOWNS and the SOUTH DOWNS, in Sussex, Kent and Surrey. As its name suggests, it was once heavily wooded (the Romans called the forest here **Anderida**), but between the Middle Ages and the early modern period swathes of its great oaks and other trees were felled to fuel the Wealden iron industry and also to build ships for the Royal Navy. The land beneath the forest was rich in iron ore, the trees could be incinerated into charcoal to smelt the ore, and the forest streams provided power for forges and mills, so from the 14th to the 18th centuries the Weald was the site of England's first Industrial Revolution.

> Out of the Weald, the secret Weald,
> Men sent in ancient years,
> The horse-shoes red at Flodden Field,
> The arrows at Poitiers!
>
> > Rudyard Kipling: 'Puck's Song' from *Puck of Pook's Hill* (1906)

Thereafter industry moved northwards (the last Wealden iron-foundry closed in 1765), and the Weald reverted to agriculture: sheep-farming and, particularly in Kent, the growing of fruit and hops. Patches of its original woodland still survive, notably in ASHDOWN FOREST in Sussex.

> I … was born and lerned myn Englissh in the Weeld, where I doubte not is spoken as brode and rude Englissh as is in ony place of Englond.
>
> > William Caxton: Prologue to his translation of *Recuyell of the Historyes of Troye* (1473–4)

I will gather and carefully make my friends
Of the men of the Sussex Weald,
They watch the stars from silent folds,
They stiffly plough the fields.
By them and the God of the South Country
My poor soul shall be healed.

    Hilaire Belloc: 'The South Country' (1910)

Wealden. Of or relating to the Weald. The term is applied particularly to a style of timber house built in the Weald in the late medieval and Tudor periods, with a single roof covering a central hall and two-storeyed ends. It is also used as a noun to denote the series of Lower Cretaceous deposits of sand and clay characteristic of the Weald.

Wealden. An administrative district covering a large area of rural East Sussex. Its centres of population include CROWBOROUGH, HAILSHAM, Heathfield and Polegate.

Wealdstone 'stone at (Harrow) Weald' (referring to a sarsen stone here that probably originally marked the boundary between Harrow Weald and the rest of Harrow).
A district of northwest London, in the borough of HARROW (before 1965 in Middlesex), between the district of Harrow to the south and HARROW WEALD to the northwest. Its development as a residential London suburb followed the opening of Harrow and Wealdstone station by the London and Birmingham Railway in 1837. The Underground station on the Bakerloo line (now its northern terminus) followed in 1917.

The stone from which it gets its name can be seen embedded in the pavement outside The Red Lion in Harrow Weald.

Wear Probably a OCelt or pre-Celtic river name, related to Welsh *gweir* 'bend', referring to the river's winding course.
A river (pronounced 'weer') in northeast England, 107 km (66 miles) long. It rises in the PENNINES of northwest County Durham, near the Cumbrian border, and flows east through **Weardale**, long the hunting ground of the prince bishops of Durham, who preserved their game rights fiercely. The local lead-miners, however, were not intimidated, and often went poaching for grouse – 'the bonny moor hen'. In 1818 a group of them were caught by the bishop's keepers and kept in a locked room at an inn at the village of Stanhope before onward transport to court in Durham. In those days, poaching was still a capital offence and some of the miners' colleagues, hearing of their plight, mounted a successful rescue, leaving the keepers with black eyes and bloody noses. Their victory is celebrated in a local song:

You brave lads of Weardale, I pray you lend an ear,
The account of a battle you quickly shall hear,
That was fought by the miners, so well you may ken,
By claiming a right to their bonny moor hen.

Beyond Weardale the river winds generally northwards through the lowlands, passing BISHOP AUCKLAND, DURHAM and CHESTER-LE-STREET, before turning east to join the sea at SUNDERLAND, a city that early in its history absorbed the settlements of Monkwearmouth (site of a 7th-century monastery) and Bishopwearmouth.
See also TYNE AND WEAR.

Weatherbury. The name under which PUDDLETOWN is fictionalized in Thomas Hardy's *Far from the Madding Crowd* (1874).

Weatherfield. The fictitious MANCHESTER suburb in which the long-running television soap-opera *Coronation Street* is set.

Weaver Probably 'winding stream', OE *wefer*, but a possible alternative is that it is an OCelt river-name meaning 'amber-coloured stream'.
A river in Cheshire, which rises about 8 km (5 miles) west of NANTWICH and flows 72 km (45 miles) southwards and then northwards via CREWE and NORTHWICH to join the River MERSEY at RUNCORN. For most of its lower reaches it is canalized, and near its northern end it is linked to the River Trent by the Anderton Boat Lift (*see under* TRENT[1]). For many centuries it has been a 'salt' river, used for transporting the product of Cheshire's salt industry to Liverpool and Manchester for worldwide export.

Wedding, The. *See under* STANTON DREW.

Wedmore 'marsh used for hunting', OE *wæthe* 'hunting' + *mor* 'moor, marsh'.
A small town in Somerset, about 13 km (8 miles) west of Wells. It stands on an eminence above the open flat landscape that surrounds it.

Treaty of Wedmore. An accord reached at Wedmore around 878 between Alfred the Great and the Danish leader Guthrum. Under its terms Guthrum agreed to embrace Christianity and withdraw his forces northeastwards. It led in due course to the division of England into an Anglo-Saxon southwest and a Danish northeast (*see* DANELAW; *see also* the FIVE BOROUGHS).

Wednesbury 'Woden's stronghold', OE *Wodnes* possessive form of *Woden*, the name of the principal god of the pre-Christian Anglo-Saxons, otherwise known in Scandinavian mythology as Odin + *byrig* dative form of *burh* (*see* BURY).
An industrial town (pronounced 'wenzbəry' or, locally, 'wedgebəry') in the West Midlands (before 1974 in Staffordshire), in the BLACK COUNTRY, in the metropolitan borough of SANDWELL, about 5 km (3 miles) southwest of Walsall.

The poet and novelist Henry Treece (1911–66) was born in Wednesbury.

Wednesfield 'Woden's open land', OE *Wodnes* (*see* WEDNESBURY) + *feld* (*see* FIELD).

An industrial town (pronounced 'wenzfield' or, locally, 'wedgefield') in Wolverhampton metropolitan borough, West Midlands (before 1974 in Staffordshire), in the BLACK COUNTRY, about 3 km (2 miles) northeast of Wolverhampton itself.

Wee City, the. A nickname for DERRY/LONDONDERRY.

Weedon Bec *Weedon* 'hill with a heathen temple', OE *weoh* 'heathen temple' + *dun* (*see* DOWN, -DON); *Bec* denoting manorial ownership in the early Middle Ages by the Benedictine Abbey of St Mary of Bec in Normandy (as at TOOTING BEC).

A village in Northamptonshire, about 6 km (4 miles) southeast of Daventry. During the Napoleonic Wars it was designated as the capital of the country in the event of a French invasion.

Weedon Lois *Weedon see* WEEDON BEC; *Lois* perhaps referring to a well of St Loys or Lewis, or alternatively denoting manorial ownership in the Middle Ages by a family called Lois.

A village (pronounced 'loy') in Northamptonshire, about 10 km (6 miles) west of Towcester. The poet and eccentric Edith Sitwell (1887–1964) is buried in the churchyard here, a sculpture by Henry Moore marking her grave (Weston Hall, a Sitwell family home, is nearby).

Week 'dwelling, settlement, trading place', OE *wic* (*see* WICK). A village in Devon, about 10 km (6 miles) south of South Molton.

Weekley Probably 'wood or clearing near an earlier Romano-British settlement', OE *wic* 'earlier Romano-British settlement' (*see* WICK) + -LEY.

A village in Northamptonshire, about 2.5 km (1.5 miles) northeast of Kettering.

Wee North, the. A nickname for Northern Ireland (*see* the NORTH[2]).

Weeping Cross Referring to a standing cross erected at a place where weeping might be appropriate (e.g. near a place of execution or a leper house, or at a resting-place for funeral processions, or at a place for penitential devotion).

A village in Staffordshire, now effectively a southeastern suburb of STAFFORD.

There are also places called Weeping Cross in Oxfordshire, Shropshire, Suffolk and Wiltshire.

Wee Queensbury. *See under* QUEENSBURY[3].

Welbeck Abbey *Welbeck* '(place by the) stream', from the name of a local stream originally called *Wella* 'stream' (OE), to which *beck* 'stream' (OE *bæce* or OScand *bekkr*) was later tautologically added.

A country house and village in Nottinghamshire, in the DUKERIES, about 6 km (4 miles) southwest of WORKSOP.

There was a Premonstratensian monastery on the site from the late 12th century. After the Dissolution it became a private house, which by the mid-18th century (and after extensive alterations and expansions) had passed into the possession of the dukes of Portland. The most notable contributor to its subsequent development was the weirdly eccentric 19th-century 5th Duke, who had such an intense phobia about being seen that he had several miles of tunnels and suites of rooms built under the Abbey where he could skulk out of public view (the story of the last six months of his life is told in a novel, *The Underground Man*, by Mick Jackson, which was shortlisted for the Booker Prize in 1997). The house is now an Army college.

The village of Welbeck Abbey grew up in the vicinity of the house.

Welcombe 'valley with a spring or stream', OE *wella* 'spring, stream' + *cumb* (*see* -COMBE, COOMBE).

A village in Devon, on the Hartland Peninsula (*see under* HARTLAND POINT), about 27 km (17 miles) west of Torrington.

Welland Probably an OCelt or pre-Celtic river name of unknown meaning.

A river in Northamptonshire, Leicestershire, Rutland and Lincolnshire. It rises to the west of MARKET HARBOROUGH, and flows 110 km (68 miles) eastwards via STAMFORD, MARKET DEEPING and SPALDING through the Fenland bulb fields into the southwestern corner of the WASH. It forms the northern boundary of Northamptonshire.

Wellbridge. The fictional name for WOOL adopted by Thomas Hardy, as in *Tess of the D'Urbervilles* (1891).

Wellingborough 'stronghold of Wændel's people', OE male personal name *Wændel* + -*inga*- (*see* -ING) + *burh* (*see* BURY).

A market town in Northamptonshire, in the valley of the River NENE, about 16 km (10 miles) northeast of Northampton. It made its name in the 19th century mainly through the manufacture of boots and shoes, although it was also a centre of ironworking.

The church of St Mary's, Knox Road (1904–40), is one of the best examples of the work of the architect and restorer Ninian Comper (1864–1960), and was described by Sir John Betjeman as the 'finest modern parish church in England'.

Oliver Cromwell stayed in Wellingborough at the inn called The Hind (now the Hind Hotel) on his way to the Battle of NASEBY in June 1645.

The town of Willingboro in New Jersey, USA, derives its name from Wellingborough.

Wellington[1] Probably 'estate associated with Weola', OE male personal name *Weola* + -ING + -TON.

A village in Herefordshire (before 1998 in Hereford and Worcester, before 1974 in Herefordshire), about 8 km (5 miles) north of Hereford.

Wellington². A town in Shropshire, within the unitary authority of TELFORD AND WREKIN, on the northwestern edge of TELFORD.

Wellington³. A town in Somerset, on the M5, about 11 km (7 miles) southwest of Taunton. It has long prospered on the woollen industry and has some fine Georgian houses to show for it.

The 1st Duke of Wellington (1769–1852) took his title from the town (for reasons that are unclear; he only visited the place once, in 1819), and he is commemorated here today by the Wellington Monument, a 53 m (175 ft) obelisk erected in 1817 to the south of the town, on the BLACK-DOWN HILLS.

Wellington School, a private school dating from 1841, alma mater of the disgraced author and former Tory chairman Jeffrey Archer, is not to be confused with the prestigious Wellington College (*see* CROWTHORNE).

There are towns and cities called Wellington in the USA (Alabama, Colorado, Illinois, Kansas, Nevada, Ohio, Texas, Utah), Canada (Newfoundland, Nova Scotia, Ontario, Prince Edward Island), Australia (New South Wales, South Australia), New Zealand (the capital city) and South Africa. The great majority of them, including the New Zealand capital, were named in honour of the 1st Duke.

Wells 'the springs' (referring to natural springs here, at what is now the east end of the cathedral), ME plural form of OE *wella* 'spring'.

A city in Somerset, at the foot of the MENDIP HILLS, about 10 km (6 miles) northeast of Glastonbury. It is the smallest city in England (population around 10,000). There was a monastery here in the 8th century, but Wells's present-day glory is its three-towered cathedral. **Wells Cathedral**, seat of the bishops of Bath and Wells (*see under* BATH), was built in the late 12th and 13th centuries. It is notable for the 386 carved figures of saints and kings that adorn its west front; its elaborate 14th-century clock, with moving figures that strike the hours; and the astonishing and dramatic 'scissor arch' in its nave, which looks like an example of modern architecture but was added in the early 14th century. One of the many buildings that nestle around the cathedral, forming the largest medieval ecclesiastical precinct in England, is the Bishop's Palace, whose moat is fed by the springs from which the city gets its name. The cobbled Vicars' Close, dating from the middle of the 14th century, is the oldest complete medieval street in Europe.

The rest of the city centre's narrow streets, market place and ancient pubs reinforce the impression of a time capsule in brick and stone.

Wells-next-the-Sea. A small town and seaport on the North Norfolk coast, about 32 km (20 miles) west of Cromer. As a fishing port it has traditionally specialized in sprats and whelks, but latterly it has relied for its livelihood more on netting holidaymakers. In fact it used to be one of the most important trading ports in eastern England, but the coastline has retreated, belying the town's name and leaving it a good 1.5 km (1 mile) from the open sea. In the middle of town is a green called the Buttlands, used in the 16th century for archery practice.

Welsh OE *Welisc*, from *wealh* 'foreigner' (*see* WALES).

As an adjective, of or relating to Wales; as a noun, the Welsh language (belonging to the South Celtic branch of the Indo-European family), or (as **the Welsh**), the people of Wales. A largely but not completely obsolete variant is **Welch**, as in the **Royal Welch Fusiliers** (*see below*). The verb 'to welsh' (as on a deal) is unrelated and of obscure origin.

A number of slang terms have been applied to the Welsh. They were once known as leeks (*see* LEEKSHIRE) or Welsh goats, while **Welshies**, **Taffies** (from Dafydd, the Welsh form of David) and **Taffs** are still current. *Taffs* gave rise to the rhyming slang *Riff-raffs* and to the Taffia, the collective noun for the movers and shakers of modern Wales.

> Taffy was a Welshman, Taffy was a thief,
> Taffy came into my house and stole a side of beef.
> Anon.: English nursery rhyme

> 'We can trace almost all the disasters of English history to the influence of Wales.' … 'The Welsh,' said the Doctor [Fagan], 'are the only nation in the world that has produced no graphic or plastic art, no architecture, no drama. They just sing,' he said with disgust, 'sing and blow down wind instruments of plated silver.'
> Evelyn Waugh: *Decline and Fall* (1928)

> An impotent people,
> Sick with inbreeding,
> Worrying the carcase of an old song.
> R.S. Thomas: 'Welsh Landscape' (1955)

See also North Walian *and* South Walian under WALES.

Royal Welch Fusiliers, the. A regiment formed as Lord Herbert's Regiment of Foot in 1689; it went through a number of a number of name changes until the present one was fixed in 1921. They are nicknamed the Nanny Goats, the Royal Goats or the Royal Welch.

Welch Regiment, the. A regiment founded as the Welsh Regiment and redesignated the Welch Regiment in 1921. In 1969 it was amalgamated with the South Wales Borderers to form the Royal Regiment of Wales.

Welsh. A breed of pig with a long body and floppy ears.

Welsh bait. An archaic term for a short stop for a bite to eat during a journey; the second element survives in Northern English dialect *bait* 'snack', 'packed lunch'.

Welsh cake. A small flat cake or griddle cake cooked on a bakestone or in an iron pan. It is made from flour, fat, currants, egg, milk, salt and sugar.

Welsh comb. A former slang term (18th–19th century) for the fingers used as an implement to tidy one's hair.

Welsh corgi. A breed of small, sturdy, long-bodied, short-legged dogs, usually referred to as just corgis; there are two varieties, the CARDIGAN and the PEMBROKE. The breed is notable for being the dog of choice of the current monarch.

Welsh cricket. A former slang term (16th–17th century) for a louse.

Welsh dresser. A sideboard with open shelves above the cupboard.

Welsh ejectment. Getting rid of a tenant by taking off the roof of his or her house. The term was current in the earlier 19th century.

Welsh fiddle. A former slang term (18th–19th century) for any sexually transmitted disease.

Welsh harp. The musical instrument of the ancient Welsh bards. It is a large harp with three rows of strings, two tuned diatonically in unison, the third supplying the chromatic sharps and flats. The name is also applied to the Brent Reservoir (see WELSH HARP).

Welsh main. In cockfighting, a form of battle royal in which eight pairs were matched, next the eight winners, then four, and finally the last two, until only one was left alive.

Welshman's button. A species of caddis fly, *Sericostoma personatum*, so named by fishermen.

Welsh mile. Like a country mile, a Welsh mile is supposedly longer than its measure suggests, hence the expression **long and narrow like a Welsh mile**.

Welsh mortgage. A pledge of land in which no day is fixed for redemption.

Welsh mountain. A small, hardy breed of sheep.

Welsh mountain pony. A small, sturdy breed of pony.

Welsh mudwort. A rare waterweed, *Limosella australis*, with orange-tubed white flowers.

Welsh onion. A member of the lily family, *Allium fistulosum*, with a long, fat, hollow stem and a large round flower head bearing numerous small yellowish-white flowers. In Britain it is a garden-escape that has naturalized in places.

Welsh parsley. A 17th-century slang term for the hemp used in a hangman's rope.

Welsh poppy. An attractive, yellow-flowered member of the poppy family, *Mecanopsis cambrica*.

Welsh rabbit. Cheese melted with butter, milk, Worcester-shire sauce and the like, spread on buttered toast. 'Rabbit' is not a corruption of 'rarebit', as often supposed; rather the term is comparable to Scotch woodcock (see under SCOTCH), mock turtle soup, Bombay duck and so on,

indicating that the dish is a substitute for 'the real thing'. Given the proverbial fondness of the Welsh for cheese, toasted mostly, the substitute in this case may have been no penance:

> There was in heaven a great company of Welshmen which with their cracking and babbling troubled all the others. Wherefore God said to Saint Peter that He was weary of them and that He would fain have them out of heaven. To whom Saint Peter said, 'Good Lord, I warrant you, that shall be done.' Wherefore Saint Peter went out of heaven-gates and cried with a loud voice, '*Caws pob*' – that is as much to say 'roasted cheese' – which thing the Welshmen hearing, ran out of heaven a great pace. And when Saint Peter saw them all out, he suddenly went into heaven and locked the door, and so sparred all the Welshmen out.
>
> Anon.: *Merry Tales, Wittie Questions and Quicke Answers* (1567)

See also Caerphilly cheese *under* CAERPHILLY[1].

Welsh springer spaniel. A variety of springer spaniel that is smaller than the English springer spaniel, and which always has a red and white coat.

Welsh terrier. A wire-haired, black-and-tan breed of terrier. *See also* the WELSH THREE-THOUSANDERS.

Welsh Bicknor *Welsh* because it is on the Welsh side of the River Wye (although not actually in Wales), in contrast with ENGLISH BICKNOR; *Bicknor see* ENGLISH BICKNOR.

A village in Herefordshire (before 1998 in Hereford and Worcester, before 1974 in Herefordshire), in a loop on the western side of the River WYE[1], about 6 km (4 miles) south of Ross-on-Wye.

Henry V spent much of his boyhood and early youth in Welsh Bicknor.

Welsh End 'the district [of Whixal parish] towards the Welsh border', ModE.

A village in Shropshire, close to the Welsh border and the Shropshire Union Canal (*see under* SHROPSHIRE), about 16 km (10 miles) west of Market Drayton.

Welsh Harp From The *Old Welsh Harp*, a nearby inn on the Edgware Road (*see under* EDGWARE) which was a popular excursion destination in the 19th century; it was demolished and rebuilt in 1937.

A reservoir (officially named Brent Reservoir) in northwest London (NW2, NW9), in the boroughs of BARNET and BRENT[2], just to the north of Neasden and to the west of the southern end of the M1. It was created in the late 1830s by damming the River BRENT[1].

The reservoir (along with its pub) has provided a wide range of recreational activities. It is heavily used for sailing and other water sports, and in the late 19th century there was a greyhound-racing track on its banks (at which in 1876 the first mechanical hare was tried out).

Welsh Hook 'spur of land owned by a Welshman or a man called Wal', OE *hoc* 'spur of land', with possessive of personal name *Wal* or adjective *Welsh*.

A village in Pembrokeshire (formerly in Dyfed), some 10 km (6 miles) south of Fishguard.

Welshpool 'the Welsh pool', referring to the pool where the Lledin stream joins the SEVERN.

A small market town near the English border in Powys (formerly in Montgomeryshire), 26 km (16 miles) west of Shrewsbury. In Welsh it is **Y Trallwng** ('the very wet place', *y* 'the' + *tra* 'very' + *llwng* 'marsh, pool').

> This is a good fashionable place, and has many English dwellings in it, and some very good families ...
>
> > Daniel Defoe: *A Tour Through the Whole Island of Great Britain* (1724–6)

Welsh Three-Thousanders, the. The 14 mountains in Wales over 3000 ft (914.6 m). All of them are in SNOWDONIA, in the massifs of SNOWDON, the GLYDERS and the CARNEDDAU. They are (proceeding broadly from south to north):

> Snowdon (1085 m / 3560 ft)
> Crib Goch (921 m / 3021 ft)
> Eilidyr Fawr (923 m / 3027 ft)
> Y Garn (946 m / 3103 ft)
> Glyder Fawr (999 m / 3277 ft)
> Glyder Fach (994 m / 3260 ft)
> Tryfan (917 m / 3008 ft)
> Pen-yr-oleu-wen (978 m / 3208 ft)
> Carnedd Dafydd (1040 m / 3411 ft)
> Carnedd Llyewelyn (1064 m / 3490 ft)
> Yr Wlen or Yr Elen (962 m / 3155 ft)
> Foel Grach (976 m / 3201 ft)
> Foel Fras (942 m / 3090 ft)
> Garnedd Uchaf (926 m / 3037 ft)

The first known traverse in a single day was made in 1919 by Eustace Thomas, 'the greyhound of the groughs', in about 22.5 hours. Since then it has been done in less than 5 hours, and double and even triple traverses have been made.

See also CRIB GOCH *and* TRYFAN.

Welwyn '(at the) willow-trees', OE *weligum* dative plural form of *welig* 'willow-tree'.

A small town (pronounced 'wellin') in Hertfordshire, on the A1(M), about 8 km (5 miles) northwest of Hertford and just to the north of WELWYN GARDEN CITY. The majority of the buildings in its centre are Georgian.

Welwyn Garden City. A town in Hertfordshire, on the A1(M), about 13 km (8 miles) northeast of St Albans. It was created immediately after the First World War, to plans drawn up by Ebenezer Howard (1850–1928), the pioneer of the 'garden city' movement. Like his previous projects (*see* HAMPSTEAD GARDEN SUBURB, LETCHWORTH), it is

somewhat prodigal in its use of space, but the result is a harmonious and well-proportioned urban environment. Originally a privately run concern, it was taken over in 1948 by the Ministry of Town and Country Planning as a NEW TOWN[1], linked in with HATFIELD[1] to the south.

Its inhabitants generally refer to it simply as 'Welwyn', but although it is contiguous with the original WELWYN to the north, the two retain their separate identities.

Welbike. A folding motorbike developed during the Second World War by the Special Operations Executive (SOE) at its centre in Welwyn Garden City, after which it was named. The Welbike was designed to be parachuted behind enemy lines, so agents could retrieve it and make it ready for use within 11 seconds. Several were used on D-Day.

Wem 'dirty or muddly place', OE *wemm*.

A small market town in Shropshire, on the River Roden, about 17 km (11 miles) north of Shrewsbury. It was almost completely destroyed by fire in 1667.

Wem was owned in the late 17th century by the notorious Judge Jeffreys. In 1685, the year of the Bloody Assizes in which he dispatched so many of Monmouth's rebels to the gallows, he was made Baron of Wem.

The essayist and critic William Hazlitt (1778–1830) lived in Wem as a boy, and met Samuel Taylor Coleridge here.

Wem has long been renowned throughout Shropshire for the quality of its beer. The **Wem Brewery** closed in the 1980s, but brewing has been revived in the town (Hanby Ales).

Wembley 'Wemba's glade', OE male personal name *Wemba* + -LEY.

A district of northwest London, in the borough of BRENT[2] (before 1965 in Middlesex), between Northolt to the west and Willesden to the east. Its growth as a residential suburb was relatively modest in the 19th century, but there was a foretaste of things to come in 1889 when the **Wembley Park** area in the north of the district, hitherto a private estate, was acquired by the Metropolitan Railway Company as the site for a leisure centre for northwest London. One of its first manifestations was the so-called 'Great Tower', London's answer to the Eiffel Tower, work on which began in the early 1890s. Unfortunately, when the first stage was opened the crowds stayed away in their droves and it lost money heavily; 'Watkin's Folly', as it came to be known (after Sir Edward Watkin, its begetter), was left to rust and was eventually demolished in 1907.

Wembley really sprang to life after the First World War, when the Wembley Park site was chosen for the British Empire Exhibition of 1924–5. A great weight of neo-imperial architecture was planted on it, perhaps typified by the austere and somewhat threatening British Government Pavilion, guarded by the famous stone **Wembley lions**. Most of it lasted no longer than the empire it was erected to celebrate, although some was kept to serve humbler functions (the Palace of Industry, for example, as a warehouse). By far the most notable of these Wembley buildings was **Wembley Stadium**, built in 1922–3 on the site where the 'Great Tower' had been. It hosted the opening ceremony of the Empire Exhibition, but even before that, in 1923, it had established itself in the role for which it became most famous: venue of the FA Cup Final (in 1923, Bolton Wanderers v. West Ham). It also served as England's main home ground for international football matches and (since 1929) as the venue for the Rugby League Cup Final, and it staged the Olympic Games in 1948 and the World Cup Final in 1966. By the end of the 20th century its age was beginning to show, but plans for its refurbishment or complete redevelopment became so mired in political and financial difficulties that it was not until 2002 that the old stadium, with its celebrated 'Twin Towers', was pulled down and rebuilding began. The new stadium is planned to open in 2006. By 2004 the giant **Wembley Arch** of the structure was visible. In the interim, FA Cup Finals are being held in Cardiff's Millennium Stadium.

The stadium was joined in 1933–4 by the Empire Pool, now known as the **Wembley Arena** and used for entertainments as diverse as ice shows, pop concerts and boxing promotions, and in 1973–6 by the **Wembley Conference Centre**.

These developments became in the 1920s and 1930s the hub of a house-building orgy that transformed Wembley into the archetypal interwar London residential suburb.

The travel writer Robert Byron (1905–41) was born in Wembley, as was Keith Moon (1947–78), drummer for The Who. Walter Citrine, general secretary of the TUC 1926–46, was ennobled as Baron Citrine of Wembley.

Wembley Park 'Underground' station, on the Metropolitan and Jubilee lines, opened in 1894, and Wembley Central and North Wembley, on the Bakerloo line, in 1917.

Wembley Way. The informal name for the straight road leading from Wembley Park station to Wembley Stadium, which on Cup Final day is a seething mass of fans. Its official designation is Olympic Way. The rebuilding of the stadium will cut its length in half.

Wemyss Bay Gaelic *uaimh* 'cave, hollow' + English plural *-s* has been suggested (*compare* PITTENWEEM), although no caves are known here. Alternatively, it was from Bob Wemyss who lived in a hut on the shore in the early 19th century.

A village (pronounced 'weems bay') on the west coast of North Ayrshire (formerly in Strathclyde region), 11 km (7 miles) southwest of Greenock. It overlooks the eponymous bay and the Firth of CLYDE south of **Wemyss Point**, and there is a ferry to ROTHESAY on Bute.

See also EAST WEMYSS.

Wen, the. London. The old word *wen*, literally meaning 'a sebaceous cyst', has a long history of being applied metaphorically to any unsightly excrescence, particularly (in the same vein as Prince Charles's notorious 'monstrous carbuncle') to a new building, but it was the plain-speaking polemicist William Cobbett (1763–1835) who established it as a term for an urban blot on the landscape:

> Croydon is a good market-town; but is, by the funds, swelled out into a wen.
>
> *Rural Rides* (1830)

He reserved his especial scorn for London, which he denounced as the **Great Wen**, or simply the Wen:

> But what is to be the fate of the great wen of all? The monster, called … 'the metropolis of the empire'?
>
> (*ibid.*)

Wendens Ambo *Wendens* probably 'winding valley' (referring to the valley of the River Cam), OE *wende* 'winding' + *denu* 'valley'; *Ambo* 'both' (alluding to the union of the parishes of Great and Little Wenden in 1662), Latin.

A village in Essex, on the eastward branch of the River CAM[2], about 3 km (2 miles) southwest of Saffron Walden.

Wendover From the name of a local stream, an OCelt river name meaning 'white waters'.

A small town in Buckinghamshire, in the CHILTERN HILLS, close to the old ICKNIELD WAY, about 8 km (5 miles) southeast of Aylesbury. It has a wealth of venerable buildings, including the half-timbered Lion Hotel where Oliver Cromwell stayed in 1643. In the past it was a pocket borough, returning two members to parliament (a 'pocket borough' was a parliamentary constituency whose votes were controlled by a single patron).

To the east is HADDINGTON HILL and to the west COOMBE HILL, respectively the highest and second highest points in the Chilterns. There are forest trails through **Wendover Woods** to the east of the town.

There are towns called Wendover in the USA (Utah, Wyoming).

Roger of Wendover. A monk and historian (d.1236) of St Albans, author of *Flores Historiarum*, a chronicle of world history from the Creation to 1235, which was continued by Matthew Paris's *Chronica majora*. It was Roger who first told the tale of Lady Godiva.

Wendy 'island at a river-bend' (referring to its location in a bend of the North Ditch), OE *wende* 'river-bend' + *eg* (*see* -EY, -EA). (There is no connection with the coincidently homographic female name *Wendy*, which was invented by J.M. Barrie for his play *Peter Pan* (1904).)

A village in Cambridgeshire, in a bend of the North Ditch (close to the point where it joins the westward branch of the River CAM[2]), about 18 km (11 miles) southwest of Cambridge. It lies just to the west of ERMINE STREET.

Wenlock Edge *Wenlock see* MUCH WENLOCK.

A limestone escarpment in Shropshire, running for about 28 km (17 miles) from southwest to northeast between Apedale to the west and Corvedale to the east, about 27 km (17 miles) south of Shrewsbury. **Much Wenlock** is at its northern end.

For all the splendid views from its ridge, it no doubt would not have become so celebrated without the advocacy of A.E. Housman, who showcased it in one of the best-known poems in his *A Shropshire Lad* (1896):

> On Wenlock Edge the wood's in trouble;
> His forest fleece the Wrekin heaves;
> The wind it plies the saplings double,
> And thick on Severn snow the leaves.

It provides the basis of the first of Vaughan Williams's 1909 settings of six Housman poems for voice, piano and string quartet. He also named the whole cycle *On Wenlock Edge*. *See also* IPPIKIN'S ROCK.

Wensleydale From the village of Wensley, meaning 'Wændel's clearing', OE male personal name *Wændel* + -LEY, with the addition of OScand *dalr* 'valley'.

A long, steep-sided east–west valley in the YORKSHIRE DALES, North Yorkshire. It forms the upper valley of the River URE. The main town is HAWES, although the valley takes its name from the village of **Wensley** at its eastern end.

Wensleydale. A breed of sheep with long wool, found in the Dales, northern Lancashire, Cumbria and Scotland.

Wensleydale cheese. A type of white crumbly cheese, originally made by the monks at JERVAULX ABBEY, near Masham in North Yorkshire. It is a particular favourite of Wallace and Gromit, the animated creations of Nick Park, depicting a NORTH[1]-countryman and his dog.

Wensum 'the meandering one', OE *wende* 'winding' + adjective suffix *-sum* (*compare* WANTSUM).

A river in Norfolk, which rises in the fenlands to the east of the WASH and flows 48 km (30 miles) northwards past FAKENHAM and then southeastwards through NORWICH, where it joins the River YARE.

Went 'pleasant stream', OCelt *ueneto* 'pleasant'.

A tributary of the DON[2], along the border between North and South Yorkshire. It has been identified as the Anglo-Saxon Winwæd, where in 655 Penda of MERCIA was defeated and killed by Oswiu (or Oswy) of BERNICIA, the latter thereby taking over DEIRA; however, this identification is now doubted, as Winwæd is now considered to derive from OE *gewinn* 'battle' + *wæd* 'ford'.

Wentlooge Level. *See under* PETERSTONE WENTLOOGE.

Wentworth From *Wentworth* House, a large house in the district, built on an area of land formerly known as *Wentworth Waste*, after its owner, a Mrs Elizabeth *Wentworth* (d.1816).

A residential district to the northwest of VIRGINIA WATER in Surrey. At the heart of it is Wentworth Golf Club, on the site of Wentworth House, whose course hosts several important championships (notably the World Matchplay in October). The residences on the **Wentworth Estate**, surrounding the course, are for the seriously rich only. The Chilean ex-dictator Augusto Pinochet was housed here when he was detained in England in 1998–2000 (thereby becoming a neighbour of such luminaries as the entertainer Bruce Forsyth and Sarah Ferguson, aka the Duchess of York). *See also* SUNNINGDALE.

Weobley 'Wiobba's glade', OE male personal name *Wiobba* + -LEY.

A village (pronounced 'webly') in Herefordshire (before 1998 in Hereford and Worcester, before 1974 in Herefordshire), about 17 km (11 miles) northwest of Hereford. It has some very fine black-and-white timber-framed buildings. It was once quite a prosperous place (gloves and beer were its specialities), and returned two MPs to Parliament before the 1832 Reform Act put an end to such things. The neighbouring village of **Weobley Marsh** is just to the southwest.

Weobley had a reputation in the past as a centre of black magical activity – there were once said to be more than 50 witches within a 3 km (2 mile) radius of the village.

Wergs 'willows', OE *withiges* 'withies, willows'.

A northwestern suburb of WOLVERHAMPTON.

Wervin 'cattle fen' or 'quaking fen', OE *weorf* 'draught cattle' or *wifer* 'quaking' + *fenn* 'fen'.

A village in Cheshire, beside the M53, about 5 km (3 miles) north of Chester.

Wessex '(territory of the) West Saxons', OE *west* + *Seaxe* 'Saxons'.

An Anglo-Saxon kingdom in southwest England. Its origins can be traced to the latter part of the 6th century, in the area corresponding to modern GLOUCESTERSHIRE, WILTSHIRE, DORSET and HAMPSHIRE. Two powerful 7th- and 8th-century kings, Cædwalla and Ine, extended its territory into SOMERSET and DEVON, and in the 9th century, by the reign of Egbert, it controlled all the lands to the south of the THAMES[1]. Under Alfred the Great, in the second half of the 9th century, it was effectively coextensive with the southern, non-Danish-ruled part of England. Its capital was at WINCHESTER and its cathedral city was DORCHESTER[2].

Unlike other territories with similar 'Saxon' names, such as Essex and Sussex, Wessex never became a county, presumably because of its great size, but its name has lived on in various official and non-official roles. Of the latter, the earliest and best known is its fictional elaboration into the landscape of Thomas Hardy's novels:

It was in the chapters of *Far From the Madding Crowd*, as they appeared month by month in a popular magazine, that I first ventured to adopt the word 'Wessex' from the pages of early history, and give it a fictitious significance as the existing name of the district once included in that extinct kingdom ... Finding that the area of a single county did not afford a canvas large enough for this purpose, and that there were objections to an invented name, I disinterred the old one.

Thomas Hardy: *Far From the Madding Crowd*, Preface (1874)

The heart of Hardy's Wessex is in Dorset (he was born near DORCHESTER[1] in 1840), but it spreads out over much of the territory of the old Anglo-Saxon kingdom, to Oxfordshire in the north, Devon in the west and Hampshire in the east, and its topography and largely fictionalized toponymy match those of the real landscape. He renamed most places – for example, CASTERBRIDGE, MELCHESTER and SANDBOURNE for Dorchester, SALISBURY and BOURNEMOUTH – but he also used a smattering of real names, such as STONEHENGE, the River FROME[3] and Nettlecombe Tout. One of Hardy's collections of short stories was **Wessex Tales** (1888), and he called his first volume of poetry **Wessex Poems** (1898); he also had a terrier named 'Wessex' (a fox terrier, and according to its owner it 'bit bad poets and nuzzled good ones').

In the 20th and 21st centuries, 'Wessex' has proved a useful designation for commercial operations and regional bodies covering more than a single county: for example, Wessex Water.

Prince Edward took the title Earl of Wessex on his marriage to Sophie Rhys-Jones in 1999.

North Wessex Downs. An extensive area of chalk downland in West Berkshire, Wiltshire, northern Hampshire and southern Oxfordshire. At their northeastern corner they merge into the CHILTERN HILLS. The RIDGEWAY makes its way across the northern part of the Downs, and there are many prehistoric landmarks (*see* AVEBURY, SILBURY HILL, WAYLAND'S SMITHY, WINDMILL HILL).

Wessex. A term used to designate an early Bronze Age culture in southern England, *c.* 2000–1500 BC, represented by grave goods (objects placed in a grave with the dead) of native and European provenance.

Wessex saddleback. A breed of medium-sized black pig with a white band crossing the back.

Westland Wessex. A British helicopter developed by the Westland company from the American Sikorsky S-58 and first flown in 1958. It was a stalwart of the British armed forces for many decades, its most high-profile role being air-sea rescue.

West, the. The western part of central and southern England. The territory implied by the term is no more precisely defined than in the case of 'the SOUTH' or 'the

NORTH[1]', but it is at least clear that anywhere north of the MERSEY is not included: Lancashire and Cumbria are in the NORTHWEST, not the West. When the name appears in semi-official contexts – for example, on road signs pointing to 'Wales and the West' – the underlying assumption seems to be that the heartland of the area stretches northwards from BRISTOL up the Welsh border, taking in GLOUCESTERSHIRE, HEREFORDSHIRE, WORCESTERSHIRE and SHROPSHIRE. If pressed, areas further to the south can be included too, notably Somerset and Devon; but as these have their own regional name – 'the SOUTHWEST' – it may be felt that they are not so intrinsically part of 'the West' as their more northerly neighbours. (*See also* WEST COUNTRY.)

Great Western Railway. A railway company serving the west of England and South Wales, founded in 1833. Its London terminus was at PADDINGTON. Much of the early engineering work for it was undertaken by Isambard Kingdom Brunel (1806–59); he built more than 1600 km (1000 miles) of track, using a broad (7 ft/2.13 m) gauge rather than the standard (4 ft 8.5 in / 1.44 m) gauge. After the amalgamations following the 1921 Railways Act it became one of the four British railway companies. It was one of England's most high-profile companies, with a proper pride in its achievements, and its abbreviation GWR was often (half-)jokingly interpreted as 'God's Wonderful Railway'. It disappeared with nationalization in 1947, but was revived in name only when the railways were privatized in the mid-1990s, in the new company First Great Western.

University of the West of England. A university in Bristol, founded in 1992 on the basis of the former Bristol Polytechnic. Its campus is at FRENCHAY.

Western Daily Press. A daily newspaper published in Bristol.

Western Mail. A daily newspaper published in Cardiff.

West Bagborough *Bagborough* probably 'Bacga's hill', OE male personal name *Bacga* + *beorg* 'hill'.
A village in Somerset, in the QUANTOCK HILLS, about 13 km (8 miles) southwest of Bridgwater.

West Berkshire *See* BERKSHIRE.
A unitary authority in the western part of the historic county of BERKSHIRE, formed in 1998 when Berkshire was broken up into separate administrative units. It covers the northeastern part of the North Wessex Downs (*see under* WESSEX), and includes the towns of HUNGERFORD, NEWBURY (its administrative centre) and THATCHAM.

West Bletchley. A fictional name for HAYES used by George Orwell in his novel *Coming Up for Air* (1939).

Westbourne From *Westbourne* '(place) west of the stream' (the name of a former hamlet in the vicinity), OE *westan* 'to the west' + *burna* 'stream'.
A river (also known as **Westbourne Brook**) in West London, which rises in HAMPSTEAD and flows 19 km (12 miles)

southwards into the Thames at Chelsea. Most of it had been covered over by the middle of the 19th century, but a portion of it can still be seen above ground in the form of the Serpentine in Hyde Park, which was created by damming the Westbourne, and it can also be viewed crossing the tracks at Sloane Square Underground station in a huge iron conduit.

The same original hamlet name also lies behind **Westbourne Green** (W2), a district loured over by the Westway at the boundary between the City of Westminster and the Royal Borough of Kensington and Chelsea; the nearby road called **Westbourne Grove**; and the local railway station called **Westbourne Park**, opened in 1871.

West Bridgford *West* to distinguish it from East Bridgford, 11 km (7 miles) to the northeast (*see* Newark); *Bridgford* 'ford by the bridge', OE *brycg* 'bridge' + Ford.
A town in Nottinghamshire, on the River Trent[1], on the southeastern edge of Nottingham[1] (and now effectively a suburb of it). It is the administrative centre of the borough of Rushcliffe and of the county of Nottinghamshire. Trent Bridge cricket ground (*see under* Trent[1]) and Nottingham Forest's City Ground are within its boundaries.

West Briton. A contemptuous term for a person living in Ireland but adopting British mores and professing loyalty to the British Crown. The term was coined by the Nationalist D.P. Moran in his newspaper *The Leader*, which he established in 1900. The ironic term **West Britain** is sometimes also heard for Ireland considered as a British colony. *Compare* North Britain.

West Bromwich *West* to distinguish it from Castle Bromwich, 16 km (10 miles) to the east; *Bromwich see* Castle Bromwich.
An industrial town (pronounced 'brommidge' or – less commonly nowadays – 'brummidge') in the West Midlands (before 1974 in Staffordshire), in the metropolitan borough of Sandwell, in the Black Country, about 11 km (7 miles) southeast of Wolverhampton. Ironworks plus newly discovered local coal propelled it into the heat of the late 18th-century Industrial Revolution, and it grew rapidly in the 19th century as it sucked in the necessary workforce for its forges, furnaces and foundries.

The local football team is **West Bromwich Albion** (founded 1879), the name usually shortened to simply **West Brom**; its nicknames are the Baggies – said to refer to the baggy working clothes worn because of the heat by supporters from the local ironworks – and the Throstles, from the *throstles* (thrushes) that reputedly flocked around the area of bushy heathland known as the Hawthorns where the team's ground is. That ground, which has inherited the name 'the Hawthorns', is, at 168 m (551 ft) above sea level, the highest Football League ground in England.

Westbury 'western fortified place' (probably indicating that it was thought of as the westernmost such place on Salisbury Plain), OE *west* + *burh* (*see* Bury).
A small market town in Wiltshire, on the western edge of Salisbury Plain (*see under* Salisbury), about 8 km (5 miles) southeast of Trowbridge. A palace of the kings of Wessex is thought to have been situated here. It has traditionally made its living from the wool trade and the manufacture of gloves.

Carved into the chalk on a nearby hillside, Bratton Down, is the figure of a huge white horse. The original is thought to have been placed here to mark the victory of Alfred the Great over the Danes at Edington (about 5 km / 3 miles to the northeast) in 878. It was remodelled around 1778 by a man called Gee, steward to Lord Abingdon, who presumably thought he was enhancing its elegance, but in truth it cuts a slightly comical figure, with none of the vigour and stylishness of the White Horse of Uffington (*see under* Uffington). The contemporary who referred to the perpetrator as 'a wretch by the name of Gee' evidently shared that judgement.

There are towns called Westbury in the USA (Connecticut) and Tasmania, and a district of Johannesburg, South Africa, shares the name.

Westbury on Trym. A northwestern district of Bristol, on the River Trym. St Oswald of York founded a monastery here around 961.

West Calder. *See under* Calder[3].

Westcliff on Sea A coinage of the 1880s, referring to its position on cliffs to the west of Southend and alluding to the name Southend-on-Sea.
A seaside resort in Essex, on the north bank of the Thames Estuary, now mainly a western residential suburb of Southend-on-Sea. Created in the latter part of the 19th century, it was always intended that it should be more refined than its somewhat downmarket neighbour to the east (in the early 20th century there were serious moves to rename it 'Kensington-on-Sea'), and it remains decidedly the posh end of town.

West Country. The southwestern part of England, encompassing Cornwall, Devon, Somerset, Gloucestershire, Herefordshire and probably also the southwestern corner of Worcestershire and the western parts of Dorset and Wiltshire. The term therefore covers the Southwest and the southern part of the West – but there is much more to it than geographical boundaries. It is a marker of culture, of language, almost of ethos. This is a separate land, quintessentially rural and agricultural, a holiday destination, a land of (with notable dramatic exceptions, such as Dartmoor) quiet rolling hills and small valleys, where people speak with a characteristic burr (*see also* Zedland) and (heaven forfend the stereotype) a merry twinkle in their eye. Its name prefaces particularly the rich agricultural products of the region: West Country cider, West Country cheeses, West Country beef and so on.

West Curry Perhaps from a pre-English river name *Cory* of unknown meaning, also found in CORYTON[1] and CURRY RIVEL.
A village in Cornwall, about 11 km (7 miles) northwest of Launceston.

West Dereham. *See under* EAST DEREHAM.

West Drayton *West* to distinguish it from *Drayton Green*, 11 km (7 miles) to the east; *Drayton* 'farmstead or estate by a portage' (alluding to its location by the River Colne, from which loads would have been dragged across land, perhaps to avoid a bend), OE *dræg* 'portage, sledge' + -TON.
A residential district of West London, in the borough of HILLINGDON (before 1965 in Middlesex), on the River COLNE[2], between UXBRIDGE to the north and HEATHROW Airport to the south. It was the first stop west of PADDINGTON when the Great Western Railway opened in 1838.

It has long been the home of Heathrow Air Traffic Control, but in January 2002 responsibility for area control operations was transferred to SWANWICK.

West Dunbartonshire *See* DUNBARTONSHIRE.
A unitary authority created in 1996. It is bounded on the west by Argyll and Bute, on the north and east by Stirling unitary authority, on the east by East Dunbartonshire and Glasgow, and on the south by the Firth of Clyde. The main towns are DUMBARTON and ALEXANDRIA.

West End[1]. The western district of Central London, noted for its fashionable shopping, theatres, clubs, hotels and restaurants. The term, first recorded in 1773, connotes no precise boundaries, but broadly speaking it could be said to cover the area west of Charing Cross Road (*see under* CHARING CROSS), including SOHO, the theatreland around SHAFTESBURY AVENUE, the shops and clubs of PICCADILLY[1] and ST JAMES'S, the somewhat humbler department stores of OXFORD STREET, the expensive residences of MAYFAIR, and the Parks (St James's, GREEN PARK, etc). This, then, is the part of London that the wealthy and privileged inhabit, and which the rest of us (including East Enders (*see under* EAST END) from the far side of the City of London (*see under* LONDON), who historically have lived in the West End's smoke and smells thanks to the prevailing westerly winds) visit to have fun (to have a night out in style, you go **up West** – an expression first recorded in 1970, but no doubt in circulation long before that). Stereotypically, the poshest restaurants are here, the classiest prostitutes, the latest and most exclusive fashions and, of course, the best theatres (at the beginning of the 21st century there are 40 of them within a 3 km / 2 mile radius). The cliché is that

the highest achievement for a play is to have a long West End run, but latterly the district's theatrical connotations have become more equivocal: glitzy pinnacle on the one hand, but also commercial as opposed to subsidized theatre, putting on a diet of populist productions, relying largely on big-name stars and increasingly on musicals, whose audiences typically comprise overseas tourists and grannies bussed in from the provinces.

Reality has skewed the West End's white-tie-and-tiara image since it was laid down in the 19th and early 20th centuries, but the name retains much of its allure.

West End[2]. The smarter end of inner GLASGOW, largely consisting of elegant terraces of late Georgian and Victorian tenement blocks. This is the location of Glasgow University, Kelvingrove Park, Glasgow Museum and Art Gallery, and the BBC, and the area is supposedly dominated by student, artistic and media types – the **trendy West-Endies**. As in London, the West End is contrasted to the poorer East End, while the SOUTH SIDE (Glasgow south of the Clyde) is largely *terra incognita*. (EDINBURGH has a West End too, but it is really just a geographical designation without cultural resonances.)

> Where no names stay long, no families meet
> In Observatory Road and Clouston Street
> Where Harry and Sally who want to be 'free'
> And Morag who works in the BBC ...
>> William McIlvanney (b.1936): 'Bless This House: A Sampler for Glasgow Bedsits'

Western Approaches. The seas immediately to the west of Britain, and in particular those used by shipping approaching the ENGLISH CHANNEL, the Irish Sea (*see under* IRISH), the NORTH CHANNEL and the west coast of Scotland. The name, which is mainly used in naval and military contexts, dates from the immediate post-First World War period, when the area was set up as a Royal Navy Command: Admiral Sir Reginald Tupper was appointed Commander-in-Chief, Western Approaches, Queenstown, in 1919.

The Western Approaches were the scene of crucial encounters in the Battle of the Atlantic during the Second World War, and their name became familiar to many from the speeches of Winston Churchill and from radio news bulletins and newspaper reports.

The film *Western Approaches* (1944), played to great documentary effect by men of the Allied navies, was a fictional story, telling how torpedoed merchantmen in the Atlantic were used by a U-boat as decoys. The name also inspired the title of Sir Fitzroy Maclean's memoir *Eastern Approaches* (1949), dealing with his pre-war diplomatic life in the USSR and with his mission to the Partisan leader Tito in Yugoslavia during the Second World War.

Western Avenue. An arterial road (A40) in West London built in the 1920s, 1930s and early 1940s as a straighter and wider replacement for the initial section of the existing London-to-Oxford road. Starting at SHEPHERD'S BUSH, it runs more or less directly westwards to just west of UXBRIDGE, where it now links up with the M40. In its early days it proved irresistible to ribbon-developers, who lined it with not only houses but also factories (most notably the Hoover building – *see under* PERIVALE). In the late 1960s its route was extended by the WESTWAY into Central London.

The stretch of the road from HANGER LANE to WHITE CITY was appropriately dubbed 'Leadville' by Edward Platt in his eponymous history of Western Avenue and the unfortunates who have lived along its length from its construction to its partial demolition in the 1990s:

> The worst times are the summer afternoons, when the flood of traffic on Western Avenue thickens and congeals into a fetid stew of metal which clogs the road and gums up the air.
>
> Edward Platt: *Leadville* (2000)

Western Isles, the. A unitary authority that came into existence in 1975, and continued to exist after the local-government reorganization of 1996. The Gaelic name for the Western Isles is **na h-Eileanan an Iar**, and for the authority is **Comhairle nan Eilean Siar**. The administrative seat is at STORNOWAY, Lewis. It comprises the Outer HEBRIDES, formerly divided between the old counties of Inverness-shire and Ross and Cromarty, and also covers remote ST KILDA and ROCKALL. Informally the name (alternatively the **Western Islands**) is applied to all the Hebrides, both Inner and Outer, as in the title of Samuel Johnson's *A Journey to the Western Islands of Scotland* (1775).

In 1922, having bought LEWIS and HARRIS four years before, Lord Leverhulme, the soap man and already a baron, took the title Viscount Leverhulme of the Western Isles.

Western Rocks. A group of uninhabited rocky islets at the southwestern edge of the SCILLY ISLES. The largest is ROSEVEAR. Others include Daisy, Gilstone and Jacky's Rock.

Wester Ross. *See under* ROSS AND CROMARTY.

West Ginge. *See* EAST GINGE.

West Glamorgan *See* GLAMORGAN.

A former county in South Wales, created in 1974 out of part of the old county of Glamorgan. Its Welsh name was **Gorllewin Morgannwg** ('West Glamorgan'). It was bounded to the south by the Bristol Channel, to the west by Dyfed, to the north by Powys and to the east by Mid Glamorgan. The administrative headquarters were in SWANSEA[1], and other towns included NEATH[2] and PORT TALBOT. In 1996 it was divided into the unitary authorities of SWANSEA[2] and NEATH PORT TALBOT.

West Ham *West* reflecting its location relative to East Ham; *Ham see* EAST HAM.

A district of EAST LONDON (E7, E13, E15, E16), in the borough of NEWHAM, between STRATFORD to the west and EAST HAM to the east. It was a populous parish in the Middle Ages, and by the end of the 19th century it was a large borough with well-developed municipal institutions. It played an important role in the development of the socialist movement in Britain: the first ever Labour MP, Keir Hardie, was elected for West Ham South in 1892, and West Ham had the first Labour local administration in the country, from 1898 to 1900.

The local football team, **West Ham United**, was founded in 1895. It is generally known by its nickname, the Hammers. (Its reserve team provided a rhyming-slang synonym for *nerves*, usually abbreviated to simply **West Hams** – as in 'You don't half get on my West Hams'.)

West Ham 'Underground' station, on the District, Jubilee and Metropolitan lines, opened in 1902.

Westhoughton 'western farm in a nook of land', OE *west* + *halh* 'nook of land' (*see* HALE, -HALL) + -TON.

A former cotton town in Greater Manchester, 7 km (4.5 miles) east of Wigan.

West Kennett *West* to distinguish it from nearby East Kennett; *Kennett* from the River KENNETT[1].

A village in Wiltshire, on the River KENNET[1], on the North Wessex Downs (*see under* WESSEX), about 8 km (5 miles) west of Marlborough and 2.5 km (1.5 miles) southeast of Avebury. Its twin **East Kennett** lies a little further to the southeast.

SILBURY HILL and **West Kennett Long Barrow**, a chamber tomb dating from about 3250 BC, are to the west, and **West Kennett Avenue**, an ancient stone-lined trackway, leads from the monumental henge at Avebury south-eastwards to a small concentric stone circle known as 'The Sanctuary'.

West Kilbride *See* EAST KILBRIDE.

A small town in North Ayrshire (formerly in Strathclyde region), some 7 km (4.5 miles) north of Ardrossan.

West Knoyle. *See under* EAST KNOYLE.

Westley Waterless *Westley* 'westerly wood or glade', OE *west* + -LEY; *Waterless* 'wet glades', OE *wæter* 'water' + *leas* plural form of *leah* 'glade, clearing' (*see* -LEY once more).

A village in Cambridgeshire, about 8 km (5 miles) south of Newmarket.

West Linton *See* EAST LINTON.

A village on the south side of the PENTLAND HILLS, just inside Scottish Borders (formerly in Peeblesshire), 12 km (7.5 miles) southwest of Penicuik.

Linton. A breed of black-faced sheep originating in West Linton and popular on the hills of the upper Tweed valley.

West Lothian *See* LOTHIAN.

A former county and present unitary authority in eastern-central Scotland. It was part of Lothian region from 1975 to 1996. It is bounded on the north by the Firth of Forth, on the west by Falkirk (formerly Stirlingshire) and North Lanarkshire, on the south by South Lanarkshire, and on the east by Edinburgh and Midlothian. The county town of the old county was LINLITHGOW, and the county was at one time known as Linlithgowshire. The administrative headquarters of the unitary authority are at LIVINGSTON. Other towns include ARMADALE[2], BATHGATE, BROXBURN and WHITBURN. West Lothian is generally low-lying and there is much post-industrial landscape.

West Lothian Alps. An ironic name for the shapely red-coloured bings (spoil heaps) that dominate parts of West Lothian. They were thrown up by the extraction of shale oil, begun here by James 'Paraffin' Young (1811–83) in the 19th century – the world's first oil industry. The mines have long been closed, and the bings – where they have not been reduced to provide hard core for road building – are gradually greening over and being reabsorbed into the natural landscape. *See also* Cornish Alps *under* CORNISH.

West Lothian Question. The question first raised by Tam Dalyell, Labour MP for Linlithgow in West Lothian, when the prospect of Scottish devolution initially raised its head in the 1970s. The question was this: should Scottish MPs in Westminster be allowed to vote on legislation that does not affect Scotland, because a devolved Scottish parliament has its own powers in that area? Since Scotland achieved its own parliament in 1999 the question has been asked more frequently, for example in January 2004 over the issue of university top-up fees in England and Wales. In this case, even though the Scottish Parliament had already legislated to have no tuition fees for Scottish students at Scottish universities, many Scottish Labour MPs voted at Westminster for the government's bill for England and Wales.

West Malling *Malling see* EAST MALLING.

A village (pronounced 'mawling') in Kent, about 8 km (5 miles) west of Maidstone. Its (rebuilt) abbey, known as **Malling Abbey**, now occupied by Benedictine nuns, dates back to Norman times. (It was founded *c.*1090 by Gundulf, Bishop of Rochester.) The village also once had a Norman castle, of which all that now remains is St Leonard's Tower (also built by Gundulf).

A specimen of a particular type of late 16th-century tin-glazed earthenware jug was found in West Malling church, and is now known as a **Malling jug**.

Westmeath 'western MEATH'.

A county in central Ireland, in the province of Leinster, created by an act of 1542. Its Irish name is **An Iarmhí** ('western Meath'). It is bounded to the east by Meath, to the south by Offaly, to the west by Roscommon, to the northwest by Longford and to the north by Cavan. The county town is MULLINGAR, and the other main town is ATHLONE. The SHANNON and LOUGH REE are in the west, and other lakes include LOUGH DERRAVARAGH. Westmeath is generally low-lying and given over to pasturage.

West Meon. *See under* MEON.

West Mercia. *See under* MERCIA.

West Midlands. A county in the industrial western MIDLANDS of England. It was created in 1974 as a metropolitan county out of the southern part of the BLACK COUNTRY, including the northwestern corner of WARWICKSHIRE (with BIRMINGHAM, COVENTRY and SOLIHULL), the southeastern part of STAFFORDSHIRE (with SANDWELL, WALSALL, WEST BROMWICH and WOLVERHAMPTON) and a small chunk of northeastern WORCESTERSHIRE (including DUDLEY and HALESOWEN). Its administrative centre was Birmingham. Its status as an administrative county was abolished in 1986, and its powers were devolved to its constituent boroughs. It is now simply a geographical county, with no administrative authority.

The name chosen for it was a specific application of a term that had long been in use as a much more general designation for the westerly half of the Midlands, covering Warwickshire, Worcestershire, Herefordshire, Shropshire and western and southern Staffordshire. Owing to the clear danger of confusion this usage has been officially discouraged since the formation of the new county, but it is too well-established and obvious to disappear altogether (the dialect of Middle English characteristic of this area, for instance, is known as '**West Midland**').

> The roads of West Somerset are jammed as never before with caravans from Birmingham and the West Midlands. Their horrible occupants only come down here to search for a place where they can go to the lavatory free. Then they return to Birmingham, boasting in their hideous flat voices how much money they have saved.
>
> Auberon Waugh: in *Private Eye* (11 June 1976)

Westminster 'west monastery' (referring to the monastic foundation to the west of the City of London), OE *west* + *mynster* 'monastery'.

A city and borough in Central London, to the west of the City of London (*see under* LONDON). Its core area (SW1) lies on a southward bulge of the north bank of the River Thames to the south of ST JAMES'S and to the east of VICTORIA[2]. Together with areas further north and east towards the City (WC2), it was officially designated a city in 1900. In 1965 it was combined with districts to the north and west, including BAYSWATER, MARYLEBONE and PADDINGTON, to form the borough known as the **City of Westminster** (NW8, SW1, WC2, W1, W2, W9, W10).

A place called *Westmunster* is referred to in an Anglo-Saxon charter dated to 785, but the trustworthiness of that document is questionable, and the first reliable evidence we have of Westminster is from the late 10th century as the site of a Benedictine monastic foundation on what was at that time known as THORNEY ISLAND[2]. In the 1040s the pious King Edward the Confessor, unable to make a pilgrimage to Rome, vowed instead to found an abbey dedicated to St Peter. It was built on Thorney Island and consecrated on 28 December 1065. Eight days later Edward died; he was buried in front of the high altar. Within the year William I (William the Conqueror) had been crowned here. Since that time, the coronations of all English monarchs except Edward V and Edward VIII have taken place in **Westminster Abbey**, and between the reigns of Henry III and George II most were buried here too. It has become the nation's mausoleum, where many of those who have distinguished themselves in British national life are interred and memorialized. (Horatio Nelson is said to have remarked, before the Battle of the Nile (1798), 'Before this time tomorrow I shall have gained a peerage, or Westminster Abbey' – although in the event he ended up in ST PAUL'S[1] Cathedral.) A notable niche is Poets' Corner, replete with dead geniuses and poetasters. The Tomb of the Unknown Warrior is immediately inside the West Door. The Abbey remains a 'royal peculiar' – that is to say, it is directly under the jurisdiction of the sovereign, who appoints its dean and clergy. (In the 20th century *Westminster Abbey* was used as rhyming slang for *cabbie* 'taxi driver' and also (usually shortened to simply *Westminster*) for *shabby*.)

Edward the Confessor decided to move his main royal residence from the City of London to Westminster to oversee personally the construction of his abbey, and since then Westminster has been a key seat of political power in England, Britain and the United Kingdom. No trace remains of Edward's palace, but **Westminster Hall**, built by William II at the end of the 11th century, survives. Its late 14th-century hammer-beam roof has the widest unsupported span in the country. From the 13th century to 1882 it housed the law courts: Charles I was tried here. It now serves as a venue for grand parliamentary occasions, and also for the lying-in-state of British kings and queens and of distinguished statesmen (e.g. Gladstone and Churchill).

The Lords, meeting as a parliament, from the first sat in the **Palace of Westminster**. The Commons met in the Chapter House of the Abbey, but after a fire forced Henry VIII to decamp to WHITEHALL they moved into St Stephen's

Chapel in the palace, and ever since the palace has been the home of both houses of the British Parliament.

In 1834 the old palace, with the exception of Westminster Hall, burnt down. The competition to reconstruct it as purpose-built parliamentary premises was won by Charles Barry. The outline of the pinnacled neo-Gothic structure he provided, with the Victoria Tower at the southern end and the Clock Tower (formally St Stephen's Tower, popularly known as BIG BEN) at the north, has become recognizable all over the world, an icon of the British parliamentary system. The House of Commons was destroyed by a bomb in 1941 and rebuilt after the Second World War by Sir Giles Gilbert Scott (who somewhat toned down A.W. Pugin's lushly Gothic interior decor).

St Margaret's, Westminster, Parliament's church, stands in the shadow of Westminster Abbey. It was founded in the mid-12th century. Samuel Pepys and later Winston Churchill were married here; the printer William Caxton and the courtier, navigator and poet Sir Walter Raleigh are buried here.

In 1987 Westminster Abbey, Westminster Palace and St Margaret's Church all became UNESCO World Heritage Sites.

Since at least the early 19th century *Westminster* has been synonymous with 'Parliament' (as contrasted with WHITEHALL, which stands for the executive branch of government). A 'Westminster correspondent', for instance, reports on the debates (and less public goings-on) in the Palace of Westminster.

The **University of Westminster**, located on various sites within the City of Westminster, was established in 1992 on the basis of the former Polytechnic of Central London.

Westminster Underground station, on the District, Circle and Jubilee lines, opened in 1868, originally under the name 'Westminster Bridge'.

There are towns called Westminster in the USA (Maryland, South Carolina, Vermont).

'In Westminster Abbey'. A poem (1940) by John Betjeman, satirizing casual self-serving prayer:

> Gracious Lord, oh bomb the Germans,
> Spare their women for Thy Sake …
> But, gracious Lord, whate'er shall be,
> Don't let anyone bomb me.

Long Meg of Westminster. A noted Westminster virago in the reign of Henry VIII, around whose exploits a comedy (since lost) was performed in London in 1594:

> *Lord Proudly*: What d'ye this afternoon?
> *Lord Feesimple*: Faith, I have a great mind to see *Long Meg* and *The Ship* at the Fortune.

> Nathan Field: *Amends for Ladies* (1610), II, i

Her name has been given to several articles of unusual size. Thus, the blue-black marble in the south cloister of Westminster Abbey, over the grave of Gervase de Blois, is called 'Long Meg of Westminster'. Thomas Fuller, *History of the Worthies of England* (1622), says the term is applied to things 'of hop-pole height, wanting breadth proportionable thereunto', and refers to a great gun in the TOWER OF LONDON, so called, taken to Westminster in troublesome times. The *Edinburgh Antiquarian Magazine* (September 1769) tells of Peter Branan, aged 104, who was 1.9 m (6 ft 3 in) tall and commonly called 'Long Meg of Westminster'.

Provisions of Westminster. A programme of legal reforms agreed in Westminster Hall in 1259 between Henry III and his baronial opponents led by Simon de Montfort.

Statute of Westminster. Any of four statutes promulgated by the Westminster Parliament. Of the first three, dating from Edward I's reign, two (1275, 1285) were wide-ranging revisions of English law and the third (1290) related to feudal rights. The latest, and by far the best-known, was enacted in 1931, and laid down the legal and constitutional basis of the (British) Commonwealth.

Treaty of Westminster. Either of two treaties signed at Westminster. The first (1462; also known as the **Treaty of London**) was an underhanded and abortive attempt by Edward IV to gain control of the Scottish throne (*see under* ARDTORNISH POINT). The second (5–15 April 1654) concluded the first Anglo-Dutch War.

Westminster Assembly. An assembly set up in 1643 by the Long Parliament to reform the English church. It consisted of 30 laymen and 121 clergy (of varying shades of opinion), and met in the precincts of Westminster Abbey for ten years. Its most important achievement was the **Westminster Confession** (*see below*).

Westminster Bank. A former English clearing bank, founded in the City of London in 1834 as the London and Westminster Bank. In 1968 it merged with the National Provincial Bank and the District Bank to form the **National Westminster Bank**, now known by the abbreviated name **NatWest**.

Westminster Bridge. A road bridge across the River Thames linking PARLIAMENT SQUARE in Westminster with LAMBETH on the south bank. The original was opened in 1750. It was this bridge that inspired William Wordsworth's celebrated lines:

> Earth has not anything to show more fair:
> Dull would he be of soul who could pass by
> A sight so touching in its majesty:
> The City now doth, like a garment, wear
> The beauty of the morning; silent, bare,
> Ships, towers, domes, theatres, and temples lie
> Open unto the fields, and to the sky;
> All bright and glittering in the smokeless air ...

> Dear God! the very houses seem asleep;
> And all that mighty heart is lying still!
> 'Composed upon Westminster Bridge' (1807)

On a less elevated plane:

> As I was a-walking on Westminster Bridge,
> I met with a Westminster scholar;
> He pulled off his cap, an' drew off his gloves,
> Now what was the name of this scholar?

The answer to this not very taxing old nursery rhyme-cum-riddle is 'Andrew'.

The old bridge was replaced by the present structure in 1854–62. At its Westminster end is a statue of Boudicca (Boadicea) by Thomas Thorneycroft, on the south bank the figure of a lion in Coade stone (an artificial stone made in LAMBETH).

Westminster Cathedral. A brick-built Roman Catholic cathedral in Westminster, a little to the east of VICTORIA[2] Station, erected between 1895 and 1903 in neo-Byzantine style to the designs of J.F. Bentley. It is the seat of the Archbishops of Westminster, a post first held by Cardinal Wiseman (1850–65).

Westminster chimes. The pattern of chimes struck at successive quarters by BIG BEN in the Palace of Westminster, and used for other clocks and now also for door chimes. It uses four bells struck in five different four-note sequences, each of which occurs twice in the course of an hour. It is also known as **Westminster quarters**.

Westminster Confession. The Presbyterian Confession of faith adopted by the **Westminster Assembly** (*see above*) in 1646 and approved by Parliament in 1648. It became a standard definition of Presbyterian doctrine.

Westminster Hospital. A former leading London hospital, the first in the capital to be founded by voluntary contributions. It was established in 1720 as Westminster Infirmary, and became Westminster Hospital in 1760. It moved into its most famous premises, in Broad Sanctuary, near Westminster Abbey, in 1834; it was there that Dr John Snow pioneered the use of anaesthesia. It transferred to a new building in Horseferry Road just before the Second World War, and the old one was demolished in 1950 (the site is now occupied by the Queen Elizabeth II Conference Centre). Towards the end of the 20th century it was amalgamated with other hospitals to form the Chelsea and Westminster Hospital, which is situated in the Fulham Road.

Westminster School. A public school situated close to Westminster Abbey. Founded in 1560 by Elizabeth I, it was originally for boys only, but since 1972 it has admitted girls. It was created as the Abbey's school, but the formal connection was severed in 1864. King's scholars (the holders of special scholarships) have the privilege of acclaiming sovereigns at their coronation with the cry '*Vivat rex!*' or

'*Vivat regina!*' The school's old boys include the poets William Cowper (1731–1800), John Dryden (1631–1700) and Robert Southey (1774–1843), the philosopher John Locke (1632–1704), the historian Edward Gibbon (1737–94), the dramatists Ben Jonson (1572–1637) and Simon Gray (b.1936), the actor Peter Ustinov (1921–2004) and the architect Sir Christopher Wren (1632–1723). Former pupils are known as **Old Westminsters**.

> Proceed, great days! 'till learning fly the shore,
> 'Till birch shall blush with noble blood no more,
> 'Till Thames see Eton's sons for ever play,
> 'Till Westminster's whole year be holiday,
> 'Till Isis' elders reel, their pupils' sport,
> And Alma mater lie dissolved in port!
>
> Alexander Pope: *The Dunciad* (1742)

West Molesey. *See under* MOLESEY.

Westmorland 'territory of the people west of the moor' (i.e. the Pennines), OE *west* + *mor* 'moor' + *-inga-* (*see* -ING) 'people' + *land* 'territory'.

A former county in northwest England, including the southeastern part of the LAKE DISTRICT and part of the northwestern PENNINES. It was absorbed into CUMBRIA in 1974.

> Westmorland, a county eminent only for being the wildest, most barren and frightful of any that I have passed over in England, or even in Wales it self …
>
> Daniel Defoe: *A Tour Through the Whole Island of Great Britain* (1724–6)

Westmorland was bounded to the north by Cumberland, to the west by an exclave of Lancashire, to the south by Morecambe Bay, Lancashire and the West Riding of Yorkshire, and to the east by the North Riding of Yorkshire. The county town was APPLEBY-IN-WESTMORLAND, and other centres included AMBLESIDE, Windermere (*see under* Lake WINDERMERE) and KENDAL.

> The Sands of Westmorland, the Creeks and Bays
> Of Cumbria's rocky limits, they can tell
> How when the Sea threw off his evening shade
> And to the Shepherd's huts beneath the crags
> Did send sweet notice of the rising moon …
>
> William Wordsworth: *The Prelude* (1805–50), Book I

Westmorland is one of only two traditional counties of England not to appear in either the county cricket championship or the minor counties championship (the other being RUTLAND).

Westmorland wrestling. The same as Cumberland and Westmorland wrestling (*see under* CUMBERLAND).

West Mouse. *See under* MOUSE ISLANDS.

Weston Beggard *Weston* 'westerly farmstead or village' (that is, to the west of another settlement), OE *west* + -TON;

Beggard denoting manorial ownership in the Middle Ages by the Beggard family.

A village in Herefordshire (before 1998 in Hereford and Worcester, before 1974 in Herefordshire), about 6 km (4 miles) east of Hereford.

Weston Coyney *Coyney* denoting manorial ownership in the Middle Ages by the Koyne family.

A village in Staffordshire, within the unitary authority of STOKE-ON-TRENT, now effectively a southeastern suburb of Stoke.

Weston in Gordano *Gordano see* CLAPTON IN GORDANO.

A village in North Somerset (before 1996 in Avon, before 1974 in Somerset), about 2.5 km (1.5 miles) west of Clapton in Gordano.

Weston Jones *Jones* denoting manorial ownership in the Middle Ages by a man called John.

A village in Staffordshire, near the Shropshire border, about 16 km (10 miles) west of Stafford.

Weston Longville *Longville* denoting manorial ownership in the Middle Ages by the church of Longueville, France.

A village in Norfolk, about 14 km (8.5 miles) northwest of Norwich. The Reverend James Woodforde, whose journal, published in the early 20th century as *The Diary of a Country Parson*, paints a wonderfully detailed picture of rural society in England in the Georgian period, was rector of Weston Longville from 1774 until his death in 1803.

Weston Rhyn *Rhyn* 'peak, hill', Welsh.

A village in Shropshire, near the Welsh border, about 5 km (3 miles) north of Oswestry.

Weston Subedge *Subedge* 'beneath the edge or escarpment' (referring to the edge of the Cotswolds), Latin *sub* 'beneath' + OE *ecg* 'edge'.

A village in Gloucestershire, near the Worcestershire border, at the northwestern edge of the COTSWOLDS, overlooking the Vale of Evesham (*see under* EVESHAM), about 3 km (2 miles) northwest of Chipping Campden.

Weston super Mare *super Mare* 'on the sea', Latin (first recorded in the mid-14th century).

A town and seaside resort in North Somerset (before 1996 in Avon, before 1974 in Somerset), in **Weston Bay**, near the mouth of the River AXE[2], about 32 km (20 miles) southwest of Bristol. In 1800 it was still a tiny fishing village, but it developed very rapidly over the subsequent 150 years to become the largest town on the southern shore of the Bristol Channel (*see under* BRISTOL). It is now the administrative centre of North Somerset. It has most of the traditional appurtenances of an English seaside town, including two piers, a 3-km (2-mile) long promenade and extensive sands (at low tide these are supplemented by mud, but this is said to give off the ozone for which Weston is renowned).

The first Pontin's holiday camp was opened by Fred Pontin just to the south at Brean Sands in 1946.

The comic actor John Cleese (b.1939) and the television presenter Jill Dando (1961–99) were born in Weston super Mare, and the astrophysicist Sir Arthur Eddington (1882–1944) grew up here. The author, Tory politician and charlatan Jeffrey Archer (b.1940) was born and brought up in the town, and when he was ennobled in 1992 took the title Baron Archer of Weston super Mare.

Westonzoyland Originally *Westonzoy* 'westerly farmstead or manor of Sow' (that is, to the west of Middlezoy), OE *west* + *-TON* (*see* WESTON BEGGARD) + *-zoy* 'river Sow' (*see* MIDDLEZOY); the addition of *land* 'land, estate' is first recorded in the 19th century.

A village in the Somerset Levels (*see under* SOMERSET), about 5 km (3 miles) southeast of Bridgwater. The Battle of SEDGEMOOR (1685) was fought just to the north, and many of the Duke of Monmouth's defeated supporters were afterwards held prisoner and executed in Westonzoyland church.

Westport From its position on the west coast.

A market town and port on the Atlantic coast of County Mayo, overlooking CLEW BAY, 15 km (9 miles) southwest of Castlebar. Its Irish name is **Cathair na Mart** ('fort of the cattle'). The town was laid out by the architect James Wyatt in 1780. Nearby is the home of the Marquesses of Sligo, **Westport House**, a fine Georgian mansion dating from 1731, with additions dating from the early 19th century (for the doings of the 2nd Marquess, *see* Lord Sligo *under* County SLIGO). Thackeray visited the town in 1842, and was delighted with the comfortable inn and public pleasure grounds supplied by Lord Sligo:

Nature has done much for this pretty town of Westport; and after Nature, the traveller ought to be grateful to Lord Sligo, who has done a great deal too.

W.M. Thackeray (as Michael Angelo Titmarsh): *Irish Sketch-Book* (1843)

The house now has a zoo and theme park in the grounds.

Matt Molloy of The Chieftains has a bar in Westport, famous for its music sessions and craic.

There is a town called Westport in Connecticut, USA.

Westray 'west island', OScand *vestr* 'west' + *ey* (*see* -AY).

The most northwesterly island in ORKNEY, some 28 km (17 miles) north of Kirkwall on Mainland. It is separated from ROUSAY to the south by **Westray Firth**, and is sometimes called the **Queen of the North Isles**. In the 16th century Gilbert Balfour, Master of the Household to Mary Queen of Scots, built Noltland Castle on Westray, where Mary and Bothwell (the latter having become Duke of Orkney and Shetland) intended to stay after their marriage. However, after Mary was deposed Bothwell was obliged (less triumphantly) to flee to Westray, but Balfour would

not let him stay (Bothwell ended up dying, pox-gnawed and mad, in a Danish dungeon). A spectre called the Boky Hound used to announce deaths in the Balfour family at Noltland, while on the occasion of births and marriages the castle would be lit up by a mysterious light.

Dark-haired inhabitants on Westray are thought by their neighbours to be descendants of Spaniards shipwrecked after the Armada. They are known locally as 'Dons'.

The most northwesterly point on this most northwesterly Orkney island is Noup Head. Just short of this is Gentleman's Cave, where local Jacobite lairds hid following the failure of the 1745 Rebellion.

See also PAPA WESTRAY.

West Riding *See* the RIDINGS OF YORKSHIRE.

A former division of the county of Yorkshire. It was bounded to the east by the East and North Ridings, to the north by Westmorland, to the west by Lancashire and Cheshire and to the south by Derbyshire, Nottinghamshire and Lincolnshire. The county town was WAKEFIELD. In 1974 it was abolished and redistributed among NORTH YORKSHIRE, WEST YORKSHIRE and SOUTH YORKSHIRE.

To airs and graces
Equally the West Riding gave no houseroom
When I was young.

Donald Davie: 'Yorkshire', from *The Shires* (1974)

West Riding Regiment, the. A regiment formed in 1881, now the Duke of Wellington's Regiment (West Riding).

West Sussex *See* SUSSEX.

A county on the SOUTH COAST of England, formed in 1974 from the western part of the historic county of SUSSEX (which itself had been constituted as a separate administrative unit with its own county council in 1888, also called 'West Sussex', but with an eastern border somewhat further west than the present West Sussex's). It is bounded to the east by EAST SUSSEX, to the north by Surrey and to the west by Hampshire. Its county town is CHICHESTER, and other main centres are BOGNOR REGIS, CRAWLEY, HAYWARDS HEATH, HORSHAM, LITTLEHAMPTON, MIDHURST, SHOREHAM-BY-SEA and WORTHING. It also includes GATWICK[1] Airport. Its main rivers are the ADUR[1], the ARUN and the ROTHER[1].

It is bisected from west to east by the SOUTH DOWNS, and its northeastern corner is occupied by the western end of the WEALD. Inland it is a largely agricultural county, but on the coast tourism is important.

Westward Ho! A re-application of the title of Charles Kingsley's novel *Westward Ho!*

A seaside resort on the north Devon coast, about 3 km (2 miles) northwest of Bideford and 5 km (3 miles) south of the joint mouth of the TAW and TORRIDGE[1] rivers.

Charles Kingsley was staying in Bideford in the early 1850s when he completed a novel set in the Elizabethan period. Its plot centres on the repelling of the Spanish Armada. It contains vivid and romantic descriptions of the country around Bideford, where much of the action takes place. It was published in 1855, under the title *Westward Ho!* (an injunction to journey westwards, no doubt inspired by *Westward Hoe*, the name of a 1607 comedy by John Webster and Thomas Dekker; the resemblance to *hoe* 'promontory', as in *Plymouth Hoe*, is coincidental).

The gung-ho style of Kingsley's novel struck a patriotic chord at the time of the Crimean War and it was a great commercial success. One of the results of this success was the publicizing of the area around Bideford as a potential holiday destination. Developers were not slow to follow up the opportunity. In the early 1860s a group of local businessmen invested in the building of a hotel on the coast 3 km (2 miles) northwest of Bideford and, with a lively appreciation of fame by association, called it the Westward Ho! Hotel at the suggestion of a friend of Kingsley's, a Dr Acland of Bideford; Kingsley was not consulted and apparently was none too pleased. By the early 1870s other developments were mushrooming around the hotel, and the place was turning into a resort village – at the same time inheriting the name Westward Ho! It remains the only place name in Britain that ends with an exclamation mark.

Rudyard Kipling spent four years of his youth at United Services College in Westward Ho!, and the resort and its environs figure in his collection of school stories, *Stalky & Co* (1899).

Westway, the. The eastern end of the A40 in West London, including the raised motorway section – the A40(M) – constructed in late 1960s. Beginning at the Marylebone Flyover over the Edgware Road (*see under* Edgware), it runs westwards for about 5.5 km (3.5 miles) to the boundary between Hammersmith and Fulham and Ealing, where it becomes Western Avenue.

Westwell Leacon *Westwell* 'westerly spring or stream', OE *west* + *wella* 'spring, stream'; *Leacon* 'wet common land', Kentish dialect.
A village in Kent, beside the M20, about 8 km (5 miles) northwest of Ashford.

West Wellow *Wellow* the former name of the local river (now called the Blackwater), an OCelt river name perhaps meaning 'winding one' or 'pale blue one'.
A village in Hampshire, on the western side of the River Blackwater[4], towards the northern edge of the New Forest, about 6 km (4 miles) west of Romsey. The smaller neighbouring village of **East Wellow** is on the eastern side of the river.

West Wittering *Wittering see* East Wittering.
A resort village on the West Sussex coast, at the western corner of the Selsey peninsula, on the eastern side of the mouth of Chichester Harbour, opposite Hayling Island. It is decidedly more up-market than its near neighbour East Wittering.

The August 1999 issue of *The Tatler* magazine somewhat unexpectedly nominated West Wittering as the English answer to the Hamptons (a summer retreat on Long Island for the rich and famous of New York) but 'without its pretentiousness'.

West Wycombe *West* from its location in relation to High Wycombe; *Wycombe see* High Wycombe.
A picturesque village in Buckinghamshire, on the River Wye[3], in the Chiltern Hills, now effectively a western suburb of High Wycombe. All the houses, which range in period from the 15th century to the 19th, are the property of the National Trust.

Nearby is **West Wycombe Park**, an 18th-century country house built for the notorious hell-raiser Sir Francis Dashwood (*see also under* Medmenham). He was very keen on follies, and the grounds contain a massive mausoleum, a sham lodge, a Temple of Music and St Crispin's Cottages, built to look like a church from the house – not to mention the Hellfire Caves, quarried around 1750, which were used for Hellfire Club orgies. Dashwood also instigated the rebuilding of St Lawrence's Church, which on its rededication in 1763 was described as 'the most beautiful country church in England'. The large golden ball on top of its tower is a notable local landmark.

West Yorkshire *See* Yorkshire.
A metropolitan county of northern England, formed in 1974. In 1986 most of its powers were devolved to the metropolitan borough councils. Towns and cities include Leeds[1], Bradford, Wakefield, Halifax and Huddersfield. To the south is South Yorkshire, to the west Greater Manchester and Lancashire, and to the north and east North Yorkshire.

Wetherby 'farm of wether-sheep', OScand *vethr* 'wether' (castrated male sheep) + -by.
A market town on the River Wharfe, West Yorkshire, 21 km (13 miles) west-southwest of York. In the Middle Ages the lands round about were owned by the Knights Templar, who in 1240 obtained a charter for a weekly market at Wetherby. In 1824 the Duke of Devonshire sold all of the town (barring one house) to fund work at Chatsworth. There is a local saying that Wetherby avoids the snow storms that affect neighbouring areas because 'The weather goes by.' There is a racecourse near the town.

The Cowthorpe Oak near Wetherby can hold 70 persons in its hollow and is said to be over 1600 years old.

Wetherden 'valley where wether-sheep are kept', OE *wether* 'castrated male sheep' + *denu* 'valley'.

A village in Suffolk, about 5 km (3 miles) north of Stowmarket.

Wetheringsett Probably 'fold of the people of Wetherden', OE *Wetheringas* (reduced form of WETHERDEN + -*ingas* (*see* -ING)) + *sett* 'sheep-fold'.

A village in Suffolk, about 11 km (7 miles) northeast of Stowmarket and 11 km (7 miles) east of Wetherden. Richard Hakluyt, chronicler of the Elizabethan age of discovery, was rector here from 1590 until his death in 1616.

Wetwang Probably OScand *vætt-vangr* 'field used for law trials'.

A village in the East Riding of Yorkshire, 9 km (5.5 miles) west of Driffield. The name crops up in the fictional context of Middle-Earth in J.R.R. Tolkien's trilogy *The Lord of the Rings* (1954–5), where it denotes an area of marshland where the River Entwash joins the River Anduin. As can be seen above, the meaning of the real-life Wetwang is unlikely to have anything to do with bogginess.

Wexford 'sea inlet by the ridge', Irish *eiscir* 'ridge of mounds' + OScand *fjorthr* 'fjord, sea inlet'.

A port at the mouth of the River SLANEY on the east coast of County WEXFORD (of which it is the county town), 110 km (68 miles) south of Dublin. Its Irish name is **Loch Garman** ('lake of the River Garman'), Garman being a former name for this part of the River Slaney. The River Slaney opens out into the bay of **Wexford Harbour**, on the north side of which are the mud flats and sand dunes known as the **Wexford Slobs**, a haven for wildfowl. Wexford Harbour itself is guarded by a long sand spit and is too shallow for big ships, which use ROSSLARE Harbour down the coast. North of Wexford Harbour is the shallow **Wexford Bay** (also called North Bay). Wexford is the seat of the diocese of FERNS.

Wexford was founded in the 9th century by the Vikings, and seized by the Anglo-Norman Robert FitzStephen in 1169, becoming the first part of Ireland to be colonized from England. It received its first charter in 1318. Cromwell seized the town in October 1649 and slaughtered many of the inhabitants – by tradition in the BULLRING (an open area in the centre of the town used for bull-baiting from 1621 to 1770).

> They prayed to the English for humanity, and Cromwell slaughtered them ... Three hundred of the grace, the beauty, the virtue of Wexford slaughtered by those English ruffians.
>
> Daniel O'Connell: the famous 'Mallow Defiance' speech (11 June 1843)

Wexford was held for a month by Irish pikemen in the 1798 United Irishmen's Rebellion, and the Bullring was

turned into an armaments factory. Before they left they massacred a hundred of the Protestant inhabitants, but after their defeat at VINEGAR HILL many of them were executed in the town.

Fragments of the 14th-century town walls survive, as do the ruins of Selskar (Holy Sepulchre) Abbey, site of the signing in 1169 of the first Anglo-Irish Treaty, and where Henry II spent Lent in 1172 in penance for the murder of Thomas Becket. Henry also presented the town to Strongbow (Richard de Clare, Earl of Pembroke), who settled it with his compatriots.

Since 1951 Wexford has hosted an annual opera festival, held in the town's 18th-century opera house.

Wexford was the birthplace of the Arctic explorer Sir Robert McClure (1807–73), who in 1850 attempted to find Sir John Franklin's missing party by entering the Northwest Passage from the Bering Strait; and of the illustrator and political cartoonist Harry Furness (1854–1925). The Irish Nationalist leader Tim Healy (1855–1931) became MP for Wexford in 1880.

Wexford, County. A county in southeast Ireland, in the province of LEINSTER. It is nicknamed the MODEL COUNTY, and is bounded to the south by the Celtic Sea, to the east by the Irish Sea, to the north by Wicklow and to the west by Carlow, Kilkenny and Waterford Harbour. The county town is WEXFORD, and other towns include ENNISCORTHY, FERNS, NEW ROSS and ROSSLARE. The River BARROW and the BLACKSTAIRS MOUNTAINS are in the west, and the River SLANEY is in the centre of the county. There are many long sandy beaches. The Wexford hurling team (triumphant in 1996) is nicknamed the Yellowbellies, from its purple and gold strip.

It was in the Wexford baronies of Forth and Bargy, between Wexford Harbour and Bannow Bay in the southeast of the county, that the old dialect of English known as Yola was formerly spoken. This area was one of the earliest parts of the country to be colonized by the Anglo-Normans, and the inhabitants stayed exclusive, marrying only with their own kind and remaining unaffected by the re-Gaelicization of the county in the 14th and 15th centuries. They were steadfastly Catholic and Royalist, and lost much of their estates to the Cromwellians in the 1650s.

'Disused Shed in County Wexford, A'. One of the best-known poems of Derek Mahon (b.1941), in which the poet meditates on the secret life of fungi:

> And in a disused shed in Co. Wexford,
> Deep in the grounds of a burnt-out hotel,
> Among the bathtubs and washbasins
> A thousand mushrooms crowd to a keyhole.

'Ould Woman from Wexford, The'. An Irish variant on the folk song 'The Old Woman of Yorkshire' (*see under* YORKSHIRE). It begins:

Well, there was an old woman from Wexford
And in Wexford she did dwell,
She loved her old man dearly
But another one twice as well.

Wexford Bard, the. The ballad writer Michael O'Brien, author of such perennials as 'Ballyshannon Lane' and 'The Alfred D. Snow'. He sold his ballad sheets for a penny at fairs and sporting events across the county around the turn of the 19th and 20th centuries.

Wexford Carols. A collection of carols dating from the 17th century, some by Luke Wadding (*c*.1628–91), Bishop of Ferns, and others by Father William Devereux. The one most commonly referred to as 'The Wexford Carol' begins:

Good people all, this Christmas-time
Consider well and bear in mind
What our good God for us has done
In sending His beloved Son.

Wexford Rebellion (1798). Part of the 1798 United Irishmen's Rebellion. The Wexford Rebellion was sparked off by the burning of a Catholic chapel in BOOLAVOGUE, and the rebel leader, Father John Murphy, found himself at the head of an undisciplined host of peasants. He failed to link up with rebels elsewhere, and his force suffered defeats at NEW ROSS and finally at VINEGAR HILL.

And if for want of leaders, we lost at Vinegar Hill,
We're ready for another fight, and love our country still!
We are the boys of Wexford, who fought with heart and
hand,
To burst in twain the galling chain, and free our native
land.

R.D. Joyce: 'The Boys of Wexford', from *Ballads, Romances and Songs* (1861)

Wey[1] An ancient pre-English river name, from a root meaning 'water'.
A river in Hampshire and Surrey, which rises to the south of ALTON[1] and flows 55 km (34 miles) northeastwards via FARNHAM, GODALMING, GUILDFORD and WEYBRIDGE into the River Thames between CHERTSEY and WALTON-ON-THAMES.

Wey[2]. A river in Dorset, which rises just to the east of CHESIL BEACH and flows 19 km (12 miles) southeastwards into Weymouth Bay (*see under* WEYMOUTH).

Weybridge 'bridge over the River Wey', WEY[1] + OE *brycg* 'bridge'.
A town in Surrey, on the River Wey, about 5 km (3 miles) southwest of Walton-on-Thames. It is on the south bank of the River THAMES[1], and according to tradition Julius Caesar and his forces crossed the river here in 55 BC. Henry VIII had two houses, Ashley Park and Oatlands Park, in Weybridge, and married Catherine Howard here. (*See also under* SEVEN DIALS.)

Britain's first aerodrome was in Weybridge, as was the world's first air-travel booking office. The former motor-racing circuit of BROOKLANDS is nearby.

Richard Hughes (1900–76), author of *A High Wind in Jamaica* (1929), and the conductor Sir Colin Davis (b.1927) were born in Weybridge. The writers Thomas Love Peacock (1785–1866) and his son-in-law George Meredith (1828–1909) both lived here, the latter helping the former out in his financial difficulties.

Barnes Wallis (1887–1979), of bouncing bomb fame, was chief of aeronautical research and development at Vickers, later the British Aircraft Corporation, at Weybridge from 1945 to 1971.

Weymouth 'mouth of the River Wey', WEY[2] + OE *mutha* 'mouth'.
A seaside resort and port in Dorset, at the mouth of the River Wey, about 14 km (8.5 miles) south of Dorchester. It has a long history as a port – John Endicott sailed from here in 1628 to found Salem in Massachusetts, and back in the Middle Ages it may well be that the Black Death arrived in England via Weymouth – but it was its success as a seaside resort in the late 18th century that really put the town on the map, and for that it has George III largely to thank. He took a great liking to Weymouth, and it was here in 1789 that he became the first reigning monarch to bathe in the sea from a bathing machine (a device pioneered in Weymouth in 1763). His immersion, to the sound of the band playing 'God Save the King', was greeted with a mixture of awe and admiration ('The King bathes, and with great success,' noted Fanny Burney in her diary), and a fashion had been set which others were eager to follow. The town showed its gratitude in the form of an image of the king on horseback carved into a chalk hillside to the northwest.

Another, later admirer of Weymouth was Thomas Hardy, who stayed here often. In his novel *The Trumpet-Major* (1880), the town is fictionalized as **Budmouth**.

In 1857 the railway reached Weymouth, greatly increasing its importance as a port. Ferries serve the CHANNEL ISLANDS and Cherbourg.

The writer Thomas Love Peacock (1785–1866) was born in Weymouth.

The type of riding bit known as a 'weymouth', which is fixed rigidly to long cheekpieces, was presumably named after the town, but the precise connection is not known.

There are towns called Weymouth in the USA (Massachusetts) and Canada (Nova Scotia).

Weymouth Bay. A bay on the Dorset coast, with Weymouth approximately in its middle. Its southern corner is largely taken up by Portland Harbour (*see under* PORTLAND)

There is also a Weymouth Bay in Australia, on Cape York Peninsula in the northern part of Queensland.

Weymouth pine. An alternative name for the American white pine (*Pinus strobus*), commemorating the 1st Lord Weymouth, by whom the tree was extensively planted after its introduction into England in 1705.

Weymouth Sands. A novel (1934) by John Cowper Powys, set against a background of Portland and the sea. It had to be revised and released under the title *Jobber Skald* in 1935 following a libel action, but was republished in its original form and with its original title in 1963.

Whale Island Self-explanatory, perhaps from its rounded, hump-backed contour.

An island on the eastern side of Portsmouth Harbour (*see under* PORTSMOUTH). There is a road connection with Portsmouth.

Whalsay 'whale island', OScand *hvals* 'whale' + *ey* (*see* -AY).

An island 3 km (2 miles) off the east coast of Mainland, SHETLAND, some 20 km (12 miles) north of Lerwick. The comparatively large population mostly lives by fishing, and it is said that there are some 20 millionaire owners of deep-ocean trawlers on the island. The Bremen Böd, a 17th-century Hanseatic trading booth in the southwest of the island, is a reminder of the strong links the Northern Isles once had with mainland Europe.

The poet Hugh MacDiarmid (C.M. Grieve) went to live in a small cottage without running water on Whalsay with his family in 1933, at a place called Sudheim (OScand 'south home'), which has been turned into 'Sodom' on Ordnance Survey maps. No one on the island would live in the cottage, as the previous occupier had died of an 'infectious disease'. Among the poems inspired by Mac-Diarmid's stay are 'On a Raised Beach' (1934), 'With the Herring Fishers' (1934) and 'Island Funeral' (1939). MacDiarmid left in 1941 to work in a munitions factory in Clydebank. His son recalls following him the next year:

> The sweetest memories of childhood sank below the
> horizon and Whalsay, all love, and sorrow, and longing,
> became a miniaturized circuit imprinted on the memory …
>
>   Michael Grieve: 'Hugh MacDiarmid: The Man', from
>   Michael Grieve and Alexander Scott, eds, *The Hugh*
>   *MacDiarmid Anthology* (1972)

Whaplode 'watercourse or channel where eelpouts are found', OE *cwappa* 'eelpout' (a type of eel-like fish) + *lad* 'channel'.

A village in Lincolnshire, in the FENS to the south of the WASH, about 8 km (5 miles) east of Spalding.

Wharfe An OCelt river name meaning 'winding one'.

A river in Yorkshire; length 97 km (60 miles). It rises on the slopes of Cam Fell and flows east down into LANGSTROTHDALE in the Yorkshire Dales. At HUBBERHOLME Langstrothdale merges into **Wharfedale**, through which the Wharfe flows southwards past BOLTON ABBEY and ILKLEY and on eastwards to WETHERBY, eventually joining the OUSE[2] south of York. Both Thomas Girtin and Turner

painted scenes on the river, Turner transforming a thunderstorm at Farnley into his gigantic canvas of *Hannibal Crossing the Alps* (1812).

See also the STRID.

Wharram Percy *Wharram* 'place by the pots', dative of OE *hwer* 'pot, cauldron, kettle'; *Percy* denoting manorial ownership in the Middle Ages by the de Percy family.

The best known of thousands of now deserted medieval villages – because it was extensively excavated over a period of 40 years (1952–92). It lies about 10 km (6 miles) southeast of Malton and Norton, North Yorkshire, and is managed by English Heritage. The village's life ended in the 16th century, with the eviction of the remaining occupants to make way for grazing sheep.

Whatstandwell '(place belonging to) Wat Stonewell', personal name *Wat* (familiar form of *Walter*) *Stonewell*. A man of that name owned a house here, near a ford over the River Derwent, in the 14th century.

A village in Derbyshire, on the River DERWENT[4], at the eastern edge of the PEAK DISTRICT, about 8 km (5 miles) southeast of Matlock.

Wheathampstead 'homestead where wheat is grown', OE *hwǣte* 'wheat' + *ham-stede* 'homestead'.

A village in Hertfordshire, about 8 km (5 miles) northeast of St Albans. The nearby 16th-century farmhouse of Mackery End was visited by Charles Lamb and is described in his essay of the same name (1820).

Whernside 'hillside where millstone is found', OE *cweorn* 'millstone' + *side* 'hillside'.

A mountain (736 m / 2414 ft) in North Yorkshire, one of the THREE PEAKS of the YORKSHIRE DALES. It is 20 km (12 miles) north of Settle. Some 30 km (19 miles) to the east, above Wharfedale (*see under* WHARFE), are the mountains of **Great Whernside** (703 m / 2306 ft) and **Little Whernside** (605 m / 1984 ft).

Wherwell Probably 'bubbling stream' (referring to the River Test, well known for its whirlpools), OE *hwer* 'cauldron, kettle' + *wella* 'spring, stream'.

A village (pronounced 'werrəl' or 'orrəl') in Hampshire, on the River TEST, about 5 km (3 miles) south of Andover. Thatched and timbered cottages give it a high score on the picturesqueness scale. **Wherwell Priory**, destroyed at the Dissolution, was founded in 986 by Queen Ælfthryth, King Æthelred's mother, in expiation of the murder of her stepson Edward the Martyr in 978 (she was popularly supposed to have had him killed to secure the throne for Æthelred; *see also* CORFE CASTLE).

Wherwell cockatrice. A cockatrice (a fearsome mythical creature with the head, wings and feet of a cock and the tail of a serpent) said to have been hatched out of a cock's egg in Wherwell Priory, perhaps in the early 16th century.

According to the story, several people tried to kill it and perished in the attempt, until a local man called Green lowered a mirror into its lair, and it exhausted itself trying to fight its own reflection. Green then calmly speared it.

Whickham 'homestead or enclosure with a hedge grown from cuttings', OE *cwic* 'quick-set hedge' + *ham* or *hamm* (*see* HAM).

A town in Tyne and Wear, 6 km (4 miles) southwest of Newcastle upon Tyne.

Whiddy Island. *See under* BANTRY.

Whimple From the name of the local stream, an OCelt name meaning 'white pool or stream'.

A village in Devon, about 13 km (8 miles) northeast of Exeter.

Whinlatter Pass 'gorse-covered slope', OScand *hvin* 'gorse' + dialect *later* from Gaelic *lettir* 'hill-slope', with ModE *pass*.

A road pass (300 m / 984 ft) in the northwestern Lake District, Cumbria (formerly in Cumberland). It links Keswick and Lorton Vale to the west, passing through **Whinlatter Forest Park**.

Whipsiderry Origin unknown.

A village on the north coast of Cornwall, about 1.5 km (1 mile) northeast of Newquay.

Whipsnade 'Wibba's detached plot', OE male personal name *Wibba* + *snæd* 'detached plot'.

A village in Bedfordshire, on the edge of the CHILTERN HILLS, about 3 km (2 miles) south of Dunstable. To the south is **Whipsnade Zoo**, officially named Whipsnade Wild Animal Park, set up in 1931 by the Zoological Society of London as the country branch of London Zoo (*see under* LONDON). Its animals are kept in large open paddocks, where they can roam relatively freely and be easily seen by visitors. To the northeast, on **Whipsnade Downs**, is **Whipsnade Tree Cathedral**, a plantation of trees laid out in the 1930s by the then-owner of the land, Mr E.K. Blyth, as a memorial to his friends killed in the First World War. It has been in the ownership of the National Trust since 1960 and is open to the public.

Whissendine Perhaps 'valley of Hwicce's or Wic's people', OE male personal name *Hwicce* or *Wic* + *-inga-* (*see* -ING) + *denu* 'valley'; alternatively, 'valley of the Hwicce tribe', OE *Hwiccan* possessive form of tribe name *Hwicce* + *denu*.

A village in Rutland (before 1997 in Leicestershire, before 1974 in Rutland), in traditional fox-hunting country, about 6 km (4 miles) northwest of Oakham.

Whitburn 'white stream', OE *hwit* 'white' + *burna* 'stream'.

A town in West Lothian, some 12 km (7.5 miles) west of Livingston.

Whitby 'Hviti's village or farm', OScand male personal name *Hviti* + -BY. The Anglo-Saxons called this place *Streonzeshalch*, possibly 'nook of wealth', OE *(ge)streon* 'wealth' + *halh* 'nook of land' (*see* HALE, -HALL), before it was renamed by the Vikings.

A port and resort at the mouth of the River ESK[5] in North Yorkshire, 28 km (17 miles) up the North Sea coast from Scarborough. An abbey was founded here in 657 by **St Hilda of Whitby** (614–680) and became known as the Lantern of the North. In 664 it hosted the **Synod of Whitby** (*see below*), and it was here, in the same century, that an illiterate shepherd called Caedmon is said to have miraculously translated passages from the Bible into Old English – the earliest Christian poetry in English. St Hilda's abbey was destroyed by Vikings in 867. It was succeeded by a Benedictine foundation in 1078 and the ruins seen today near St Mary's Church (accessed by 199 steps) date from 1220.

In 1159 the Abbot of Whitby imposed an unusual penance on three local men who had killed a hermit. To avoid execution they and their descendants were to build a hedge on the shore every year that was capable of holding back the tide. To this day the ceremony of the Planting of the Penny Hedge or Horngarth is carried out annually in Whitby on the day before Ascension Day.

Captain James Cook served his nautical apprenticeship in Whitby (having previously worked as a draper's apprentice up the coast at STAITHES); his ship *Resolution* was built here and it was from here that he set sail in 1768 for the South Seas. Whitby was also an important whaling port in the 18th and 19th centuries, and was shelled by German warships on 16 December 1914.

Mrs Gaskell holidayed in Whitby in 1859 and used it, under the name of Monkshaven, as the setting for her novel *Sylvia's Lovers* (1863), concerned with the activities of press gangs in the Napoleonic Wars. A decade later it was while walking on the sands between Whitby and Sandsend to the west that Lewis Carroll had the idea for 'The Walrus and the Carpenter':

> The Walrus and the Carpenter
> Were walking close at hand;
> They wept like anything to see
> Such quantities of sand:
> 'If this were only cleared away,'
> They said, 'it would be grand!'

> Lewis Carroll: *Through the Looking-Glass* (1872), Chapter 4

Whitby's most famous literary appearance, however, is in Bram Stoker's *Dracula* (1897). When writing the book Stoker heard the true story of a Russian sailing ship, the *Demeter*, wrecked off Whitby, from which only a huge dog survived, swimming to shore. In his novel Stoker made the dog (or wolf) a disguise for Count Dracula as he landed on English shores at Whitby and then scampered up the 199 steps to a vampire-befitting residence in the local churchyard (based on Whitby's St Mary's Church). Visitors may now sample the Dracula Experience.

The novelist Leo Walmsley, who was brought up in nearby ROBIN HOOD'S BAY, used the name 'Burnharbour' to refer to Whitby.

Whitby was the birthplace of the biologist William Bateson (1861–1926), who founded and named the science of genetics, and of the novelist Storm Jameson (1897–1986); the philosopher Gilbert Ryle (1900–76) died here.

> Dark ages, calm and merry
> Beside the sea of my boyhood
> Sparkled on a Whitby
> Of cricketers in August.
>
> Donald Davie: 'The North Sea, in a Snowstorm', from
> *Collected Poems 1950–1970* (1972)

There is a town called Whitby in Canada (Ontario).

Synod of Whitby (664). A church council summoned by King Oswiu (or Oswy) of Northumbria to determine whether his territory (which included much of England) should stay with the rule of the Celtic Church, which differed from the Church of Rome in matters such as the determination of the date of Easter and the type of tonsure monks should wear. The Synod opted in favour of Rome, so setting the course of English ecclesiastical history for the next thousand years. St Colman of Lindisfarne, defeated leader of the Celtic faction, retreated to the remote island of INISHBOFIN, off the west coast of Ireland.

Whitchurch¹ 'white church' (probably referring to the white limestone of which the church was built, or alternatively to its being whitewashed), OE *hwit* 'white' + *cirice* 'church'.

A market town in Shropshire, close to the Welsh border, about 32 km (20 miles) north of Shrewsbury. It was a settlement of some importance in Roman times and today it still retains some pleasing 16th- and 17th-century buildings. The church of St Alkmund was founded in the 10th century by Queen Æthelfleda, daughter of Alfred the Great. Its 14th-century successor collapsed in 1711 and was rebuilt the following year.

The composer Sir Edward German (1862–1936), begetter of the operetta *Merrie England* (1902), was born in Whitchurch, as was John Talbot, 1st Earl of Shrewsbury (*c*.1387–1453), who was killed in France fighting in the English army against Joan of Arc.

Whitchurch². A village in Hampshire, on the River TEST, about 11 km (7 miles) east of Andover. In the days of the stagecoach it was a place of some importance, being on the road from NEWBURY to WINCHESTER, but since then it has retired into obscurity.

The judge Lord Denning (1899–1999) was born in Whitchurch.

Whitchurch Canonicorum *Canonicorum* 'of the canons' (referring to possession in the Middle Ages by the canons of Salisbury), Latin. (The local church is dedicated to St Candida (*anglice* St Wite) – a saint otherwise unknown to hagiology, so probably her name was inspired by that of the village rather than vice versa.)

A village in Dorset, about 8 km (5 miles) west of Bridport.

Whitcott Keysett *Whitcott* 'Hoda's cottage or shed', OE male personal name *Hoda* + *cot* 'cottage, shed' (*see* COT, -COTE); *Keysett* 'legal officer, sergeant', Welsh *ceisiad*.

A village in Shropshire, about 25 km (16 miles) northwest of Ludlow.

Whiteadder 'the White River Adder'; *White* distinguishes it from its tributary the Blackadder; *Adder* is an OCelt or pre-Celtic name possibly meaning 'flowing one'.

A river in southeast Scotland, approximately 50 km (31 miles) long. It rises in the Lammermuir Hills of East Lothian (*see under* the LAMMERMUIRS) and feeds the **Whiteadder Reservoir** before flowing generally southeastwards through the Scottish BORDERS, meeting the TWEED inside England, just west of BERWICK-UPON-TWEED.

White Calf, the. *See under* BROWN COW HILL.

Whitechapel 'white chapel' (that is, a chapel built of white limestone). The name, first recorded in 1340, refers to a 13th-century chapel in the area that in the early 14th century became the parish church (St Mary's).

A district of East London (E1), to the east of the City of London and to the north of WAPPING, in the borough of TOWER HAMLETS. Through it from southwest to northeast runs the **Whitechapel Road** (valued at a paltry £60 on the Monopoly board), which might be regarded as the EAST END's main street. It is the western end of the main route from London to Essex, and an overspill settlement outside the walls of London began to form around it in the early Middle Ages. Factories moved out here from the City, and trades became established that in many cases survived for centuries – notably the founding of bells, which is still carried on in Whitechapel. BIG BEN and Philadelphia's Liberty Bell were cast here.

French Huguenots were attracted to the district in the 17th century, establishing a pattern of multiethnic demography that survives to this day. There was a large Jewish population in Whitechapel in the latter part of the 19th century and in the first half of the 20th century, vividly chronicled in Israel Zangwill's *Children of the Ghetto: A Study of a Peculiar People* (1892), and in the second half of the 20th century Bengali immigrants brought a fresh ingredient to the mix.

The 19th century brought overcrowding, slum conditions, poverty and criminality, and Whitechapel's reputation nosedived (in Charles Dickens's *The Pickwick Papers* (1837), Sam Weller's verdict on it is 'not a wery nice neighbourhood'). As if to confirm its status as a place beyond the pale of respectable civilization, it was the venue of two major outbursts of headline-grabbing crime. In 1888 Jack the Ripper began his killing spree just off the Whitechapel Road. Within the next three months, in what became somewhat sedately known as the **Whitechapel Murders**, five more women, all save one prostitutes, were killed within a one-square-mile area. In late 19th-century slang a 'Whitechapel' was a sex murder. The Ripper's identity was never discovered, and has been the subject of ingenious and outlandish speculation ever since (candidates have ranged from members of the royal family to the painter Walter Sickert, the latter touted with much publicity by the US crime-writer Patricia Cornwell at the beginning of the 21st century). More than 70 years later Whitechapel became the Kray brothers' criminal playground: it was in The Blind Beggar pub at the eastern end of the Whitechapel Road in 1966 that Ronnie Kray shot a rival gangland boss, George Cornell, for calling him a 'fat poof'.

In 1865 William Booth founded in Whitechapel the Christian Mission, which became (in 1878) the Salvation Army. Toynbee Hall, a residential establishment providing a range of welfare and educational services, opened in Whitechapel in 1884; it was named after the historian and social reformer Arnold Toynbee (1852–83), who died serving the poor.

The Royal London Hospital is on the southern side of the Whitechapel Road.

Whitechapel 'Underground' station, on the District, Metropolitan and East London lines, opened in 1884, originally under the name 'Whitechapel (Mile End)'.

In the middle of the 19th century a 'Whitechapel' was (for reasons unknown) a score of two out of three wins in the game of coin-tossing; and in the 20th century it was Cockney rhyming slang for *apple*.

See also BANKER CHAPEL HO.

Whitechapel Art Gallery. An art gallery at the western end of the Whitechapel Road, in a *fin-de-siècle* Art Nouveau building designed by C.H. Townsend. It specializes in exhibitions of contemporary art.

Whitechapel beau. In late 18th-century slang, a man 'who dresses with a needle and thread, and undresses with a knife' (Francis Grose, *A Classical Dictionary of the Vulgar Tongue*, 1785).

Whitechapel breed. In late 18th-century slang, a woman who is 'fat, ragged and saucy' (Francis Grose, *A Classical Dictionary of the Vulgar Tongue*, 1785).

Whitechapel brougham. An ironic 19th-century colloquialism for a donkey, the horse-drawn brougham being well beyond the means of most Whitechapel residents.

Whitechapel cart. A type of light two-wheeled horse-drawn spring cart. In the 19th century they were generally known colloquially as simply 'Whitechapels'.

Whitechapel oner. Late 19th-century slang for an East End dandy.

Whitechapel play. A condescending term implying that East Enders lack the skill and subtlety to play sophisticated middle-class games. From the 18th century it was applied in whist to gauche play such as leading with all one's best cards, with no attempt to finesse one's opponent, or leading from a one-card suit in order to trump; in the 19th, to the potting of an opponent's ball in billiards.

Whitechapel portion. Around the turn of the 18th century, according to the anonymous compiler of *The New Dictionary of the Terms ancient and modern of the Canting Crew* (*c*.1698), the vagina, 'two torn smocks and what Nature gives'; in the 19th century, according to J.C. Hotten's *Dictionary of Modern Slang* (1864), 'a clean gown and a pair of pattens'. Also known as a **Whitechapel fortune**.

Whitechapel shave. In mid-19th-century slang, whitening applied to the face to lighten the 'five o'clock shadow' (the poor of Whitechapel could not afford to pay a barber to shave them).

Whitechapel warriors. A late 19th-century facetious colloquial name for the Aldgate militia (local part-time soldiers; ALDGATE is at the western end of Whitechapel).

White City From the white stucco with which the walls of the original stadium and exhibition buildings were adorned. A district in West London (W12), between WESTWAY (A40(M)) to the north and SHEPHERD'S BUSH to the south, in the borough of HAMMERSMITH AND FULHAM. In 1908 57 ha (140 acres) of land here were laid out with gleaming white pavilions and 0.8 km (0.5 miles) of waterways for the Franco-British Exhibition, held to cement the *Entente cordiale* of 1904. It was the biggest such event yet staged in Britain and attracted over eight million visitors. There was also a stadium here, which was used later the same year for the 1908 Olympic Games. It was here that the modern length of the marathon was fixed at 26 miles 385 yds (42.195 km) – it was originally planned at 26 miles exactly (41.84 km), but the extra yards were added to bring the finishing line in front of the royal box.

The exhibition buildings were taken over for government use during the First World War and afterwards fell somewhat into dereliction. Some continue to be used for storage. The stadium continued to be a major athletics venue until more modern facilities were opened at CRYSTAL PALACE in the 1960s. From 1927 greyhound races and motorcycle races were also held here, and until its demolition in the 1980s the stadium was the venue of the Greyhound Derby.

In the later 20th century the BBC began to colonize the area. It opened its Television Centre in Wood Lane in 1960, and in the 1990s many elements of BBC Radio moved there from Broadcasting House (on REGENT STREET).

White City Underground station opened in 1908, originally under the name 'Wood Lane (Exhibition)'. The original Metropolitan line station closed in 1959, but the Central line station, which opened a short distance away in 1947, remains in service.

White Cliffs of Dover. See under DOVER.

Whitefield 'white open land', OE *hwit* 'white' + *feld* (*see* FIELD).

A town in Greater Manchester, 4 km (2.5 miles) south of Bury.

Whitehall From the former *Whitehall* Palace.

A street in Central London (SW1), in the City of WEST-MINSTER, running north to south between TRAFALGAR SQUARE and PARLIAMENT SQUARE. Its route, linking CHARING CROSS and WESTMINSTER, existed in early medieval times, but when it got the name Whitehall in the 16th century this applied only to the northern part, by Whitehall Palace. It was extended further southwards in the early 18th century.

To begin with it was largely a residential street, but now it is almost entirely monopolized by government offices, and since the early 19th century the name *Whitehall* has been synonymous with the executive branch of the British government (as contrasted with Westminster, the legislative branch) and with the central power-base of the Civil Service:

> Whitehall is mesmerised by a phrase worthy of the Nixon White House, 'damage limitation'.
>
> *The Economist* (26 February 1977)

On the eastern side are the Ministry of Defence and the Department of Environment, Food and Rural Affairs; on the western side, Horse Guards, the Cabinet Office, the Treasury, the Foreign and Commonwealth Office and, at the northern end, the old Admiralty building. DOWNING STREET is a turning off the western side. In the middle of the road stands Sir Edwin Lutyens's Cenotaph, Britain's war memorial, erected in 1919–20; every November, on Remembrance Sunday, a remembrance service and parade are held here.

See also SCOTLAND YARD.

> In the case of nutrition and health, just as in the case of education, the gentleman in Whitehall really does know better what is good for people than the people know themselves.
>
> Douglas Jay: *The Socialist Case* (1939)

Q-Whitehall. A secret government communications facility in tunnels 30 m (100 ft) beneath Whitehall, extending, according to some reports, as far north as HOLBORN. Its size and scope have long fascinated investigative journalists and conspiracy theorists, and surface evidence is keenly sought: particular favourites are an extractor fan outside the Institute of Contemporary Arts in the MALL, with no obvious internal connection, and a mysterious doorway at the foot of the nearby Duke of York's Steps, both of which have been linked with a purported tunnel extension from Whitehall to BUCKINGHAM PALACE.

Whitehallese. A derogatory term for the sort of constipated jargon regarded as typical of the Civil Service.

Whitehall farce. A name given to any of a series of bedroom farces produced at the Whitehall Theatre, at the top end of Whitehall, in the middle years of the 20th century, and in particular to the ones presented by Brian Rix between 1950 and 1967.

Whitehall Palace. A former royal palace on the eastern side of Whitehall. It began life as the London residence of the Archbishops of York and was named York Place. The name *Whitehall* first appears in the 1530s, and may have been inspired by the pale-coloured stone of the Great Hall that was added to the original house in 1528 by Cardinal Wolsey, who was Archbishop of York at that time (alternatively it may have been a reappropriation of the name of the White Hall in the Palace of Westminster). In 1529 the building was confiscated by Henry VIII and was used as a royal palace from then until the reign of William III.

> You must no more call it York-place, that's past:
> For, since the cardinal fell, that title's lost:
> 'Tis now the king's, and call'd Whitehall.
>
> Shakespeare: *King Henry VIII* (1612), IV.i

The palace was mostly destroyed by fire in 1698 and only the Banqueting Hall, built 1619–22 by Inigo Jones, still stands. It was from an upper window of the Banqueting Hall that Charles I walked out on to a scaffold specially erected in Whitehall for his execution in 1649.

Whitehall warrior. A somewhat derisive colloquialism, dating from the 1960s, either for a civil servant, or more specifically for an officer in the armed forces employed as a civil servant, typically on retirement, rather than on active service – his 'battle' is thus with administrative matters rather than military ones.

White Hart Lane From a 16th-century tavern here called The *White Hart* (a white hart with a golden chain was the badge of Richard II).

A road between WOOD GREEN and TOTTENHAM, in North London (N17), in the borough of HARINGEY. Its name has popular resonance because, beyond its eastern end on the farther side of Tottenham High Road, is Tottenham Hotspur FC's ground, also called **White Hart Lane**.

The humanities campus of Middlesex University is in White Hart Lane.

Whitehaven 'white harbour', although the earliest known form *Qwithofhavene c.*1135 indicates 'harbour by the white headland', OScand *hvitr* 'white' + *hofuth* 'headland' + *hafn* 'harbour'.

A port and market town on the Irish Sea coast of Cumbria (formerly in Cumberland), some 45 km (28 miles) northwest of Barrow-in-Furness. It was laid out on a grid plan in the 17th century by the local Lowther family as a port to export coal from their mines. In the 18th century Whitehaven was the third busiest port in England, after London and Bristol, thriving on the slave and tobacco trades, which helped to finance the town's many elegant Georgian buildings. In the early years of the 19th century George Stephen Kemble, of the famous acting family, ran a theatre company in Whitehaven. Whitehaven's importance as a port has since declined and the last local coal mine closed in 1986, although the place continues to thrive as a local centre.

On 23 April 1778, during the American War of Independence, the American privateer John Paul Jones, on board his sloop *Ranger*, destroyed the shore battery at Whitehaven. In 1915 the town again became the subject of foreign attack, when a German U-boat surfaced and began shelling the place.

> There was an old man of Whitehaven
> Whose whiskers had never been shaven.
> He said, 'It is best,
> For they make a nice nest
> In which I can keep my pet raven.'
>
> Anon.: limerick

In the USA a suburb of Memphis, Tennessee, is called Whitehaven.

Whitehead Irish *An Cionn Bán* 'the white headland'.

A small seaside resort at the northeast end of BELFAST Lough, County Antrim, 5 km (3 miles) northeast of Carrickfergus. It takes its name from the white chalk cliffs here. The headland called **Black Head**, with its lighthouse and dark-coloured cliffs, is just up the coast.

White Ladies Aston *White Ladies* from its possession in the Middle Ages by the Cistercian nuns of Whitstones; *Aston see* ASTON.

A village in Worcestershire (before 1998 in Hereford and Worcester, before 1974 in Worcestershire), about 8 km (5 miles) southeast of Worcester.

Whiteley Village Named in honour of William *Whiteley* (1831–1907), founder of Whiteley's Stores, a former department store in BAYSWATER, London, whose will provided the

funds for the building of the 'village'. (Whiteley was shot dead in his office by a young man claiming to be his illegitimate son.)

A residential estate in Surrey, to the southeast of Weybridge. It was laid out in 1911 as a model village with almshouses, in accordance with the wishes of William Whiteley, and building was complete by 1924. It was designed by Frank Atkinson, who was also responsible for Selfridge's store in OXFORD STREET, London.

White Mounth. *See under* LOCHNAGAR *and* the MOUNTH.

White Peak *White* ModE, presumably from the white limestone; *Peak see* PEAK DISTRICT.

The central and southern part of the PEAK DISTRICT, in Derbyshire and Staffordshire. Less forbidding than the dark moors of the HIGH PEAK (or Dark Peak) to the north, it consists of limestone uplands cut through by the rivers DERWENT[4], DOVE, GOYT, MANIFOLD, NOE and WYE[2]. The action of water over the millennia has left its mark not just in deep forested ravines but also in a myriad caves and potholes. This is the area of the Derbyshire Dales: DOVEDALE[1], Miller's Dale, Monk Dale and so on.

The main towns in or on the margin of the area are ASHBOURNE[1], BAKEWELL (CHATSWORTH is nearby), BUXTON, CASTLETON, MATLOCK and WIRKSWORTH.

White Roding. *See under* the RODINGS.

Whitesand Bay Self-explanatory.

A sandy bay at the western tip of Cornwall, just to the north of LAND'S END. It is popular with surfers.

White Sheet Hill[1] Probably descriptive of a snowy or chalky hillside; *Sheet* is probably ModE *sheet*, but it could be from OE *sceot* 'slope, steep place'.

A hill in Wiltshire, about 13 km (8 miles) northwest of SHAFTESBURY. It is 245 m (802 ft) high. It is surmounted by an Iron Age hillfort.

White Sheet Hill[2]. A hill in Wiltshire, about 8 km (5 miles) east of SHAFTESBURY. It is 240 m (789 ft) high.

White Waltham *White* from the chalky soil in the neighbourhood; *Waltham see* WALTHAM ABBEY.

A village in Berkshire, within the unitary authority of WINDSOR AND MAIDENHEAD, about 5 km (3 miles) southwest of Maidenhead. The local airfield opened in 1935 as the de Havilland School of Flying. The Duke of Edinburgh learnt to fly here.

Whitford Point 'white or bright ford', OE *hwit* 'white, bright' + FORD.

A sandy headland in the northwest of the GOWER PENINSULA, in Swansea unitary authority (formerly in Glamorgan, then West Glamorgan), 6 km (4 miles) southwest of Llanelli across Burry Inlet (*see under* BURRY PORT). South of Whitford Point are the sand dunes of the **Whitford Burrows**.

The area (where there is a danger of unexploded shells off the paths) is a bird reserve and is in the care of the National Trust.

Whithorn 'white building', OE *hwit* 'white' + *ærn* 'building'.
A village in the MACHARS of Wigtownshire, now in Dumfries and Galloway, 14 km (8.5 miles) south of Wigtown. Whithorn was one of the most important early Christian centres in Britain, St Ninian having built a white-plastered stone church here in *c*.397. This was at a time when Britain was still ruled by the Romans (they left shortly afterwards), and his foundation was initially known by the Latin name *Candida Casa* ('white house', to mark it out from the usual wattle-and-daub huts), which became the Anglo-Saxon *Huitaern*. The remains of the priory that can be seen today date from the 12th century. St Ninian's shrine at Whithorn was for long a popular pilgrimage destination, and among those who visited were Robert the Bruce (who made it a royal BURGH), James IV and Mary Queen of Scots. The pilgrimage was made illegal in 1581 during the Reformation. A little to the southeast of Whithorn, on the coast (but not an island), is **Isle of Whithorn**, a village with a harbour and a 12th-century chapel dedicated to St Ninian. Pilgrims from overseas may have arrived at this harbour.

There is also a Whithorn in Jamaica.

Whitley Bay 'bay of the white clearing', OE *hwit* 'white' + -LEY + ModE *bay*.
A seaside resort in Tyne and Wear (formerly in Northumberland), 13 km (8 miles) northeast of Newcastle upon Tyne.

Whitstable 'white post' or 'councillors' post' (probably referring to a post marking a meeting place or, in the case of 'white post', a suitable landing-place), OE *hwitan* dative form of *hwit* 'white' or *witena* possessive plural form of *wita* 'councillor, member of the *witan* or king's council' + *stapol* 'post'.
A town in Kent, on the southern coast of the Thames estuary, at the mouth of the River SWALE[2], about 13 km (8 miles) north of Canterbury. Its name instantly conjures up oysters: they have long been cultivated here (Charles Dickens contributed a detailed description of the Whitstable oyster fishery to his magazine *All the Year Round* in 1859).

There is more to the town than molluscs, though: it is a modest, low-key seaside resort, and there is much sport for yachtsmen and windsurfers off its shingly shore.

A spit of land called 'the Street' juts out about 2.5 km (1.5 miles) into the sea, and can be walked along at low tide.

The first passenger-carrying railway in the world was opened between Whitstable and CANTERBURY in 1830. It ran through another first, a railway tunnel at nearby Tyler Hill. The line, known locally as the Crab and Winkle line, was finally closed down in 1953, and has been developed as a cycling and walking route. Not content with these pre-eminencies, Whitstable also lays claim to the oldest golf club-house in England.

Somerset Maugham (1874–1965) lived in Whitstable as a boy, and it appears thinly disguised as **Blackstable** in his largely autobiographical novel *Of Human Bondage* (1915) and in his satirical novel *Cakes and Ale* (1930). The actor Peter Cushing (1913–94) bought a seafront home here in 1959 and lived here until his death. Whitstable is also the home town of the heroine of Sarah Waters's *Tipping the Velvet* (1998), recounting the adventures of a Victorian lesbian; part of the 2002 BBC television adaptation was filmed here.

Whittlesey 'Wittel's island' (referring to an area of raised land in the Fens), OE *Wittles* possessive form of male personal name *Wittel* + *eg* (*see* -EY, -EA).
A small town in Cambridgeshire, in the FENS, between two branches of the River NENE, about 24 km (15 miles) southwest of Wisbech. Its church, St Mary's, has a very impressive spire.

At 2.7 m (9 ft) below sea level the nearby Holme Fen is the lowest point in Britain.

Sir Harry Smith (1787–1860), soldier and colonial administrator, after whose wife the South African town of Ladysmith (famously besieged during the Boer War in 1899–1900) was named, was born in Whittlesey, as was the novelist L.P. Hartley (1895–1972).

Whittlesey Mere. An area of fenland to the southwest of Whittlesey.

Whittlewood Forest *Whittlewood* 'Witla's wood', OE *Witlan* possessive form of male personal name *Witla* + *wudu* 'wood', or 'white-glade wood', OE *hwit* 'white' + -LEY + *wudu* 'wood'.
An area of mixed woodland and open land in Northamptonshire and Buckinghamshire, to the west of MILTON KEYNES. SILVERSTONE is to the northwest of the Forest.

Whyke Shortened from an earlier district name *Rumboldswhyke*: *Rumbolds* from the dedication of a local church to St Rumbold, added to an original *Whyke* 'dairy farm', OE *wic* (*see* WICK). (Rumbold, or Rumwald, was reputedly the precocious grandson of Penda, the heathen king of Mercia in the first half of the 7th century. Rumbold died at the grand old age of 3 days, but not before having proclaimed his Christian faith and preached learnedly on sundry difficult doctrinal and ethical matters. He was (not surprisingly) widely venerated in Anglo-Saxon England.)
A southern district (pronounced 'wik') of CHICHESTER in West Sussex.

Whyle Origin uncertain: the second element may be OE *leah* 'clearing, glade' (*see* -LEY).
A village in Herefordshire (before 1998 in Hereford and Worcester, before 1974 in Herefordshire), about 6 km (4 miles) northeast of Hereford.

Whyteleafe Adapted from a local field name, *White Leaf* Field, so called from the aspen trees that grew there. The coinage, which dates from the second half of 19th century, betrays its modernity by its Olde Englishe spelling (*y* for *i*, and the final *-e*).

A residential district in Surrey, within the M25 and close to the southern boundary of Greater London, about 3 km (2 miles) northeast of CATERHAM. Its development began in the mid-19th century in a field known as White Leaf Field, hitherto the property of a Mrs Glover. This was bought in 1855 by the company that owned the London–Uckfield railway, which built a station here and bestowed the name *Whyteleafe* on it.

Wiches, the. A collective name for the towns of MIDDLE-WICH, NANTWICH and NORTHWICH, on or near the River WEAVER in the central salt-producing area of Cheshire. Their common suffix (from OE *wic* (*see* WICK) in the specialized sense 'saltworks') reveals their shared industrial specialization, and how old that specialization is.

Wick OScand *vik* '(place by the) bay' (*see* WICK).

A royal BURGH (1589) and fishing port in the far northeast of Scotland, Highland, 22 km (14 miles) south of John o'Groats. It was the county town of the old county of CAITHNESS, and then the administrative seat of the former Caithness district. It overlooks **Wick Bay**, where the **River Wick** meets the sea. Some 3 km (2 miles) to the south is the ruined **Castle of Old Wick** (14th century), a landmark for sailors, who refer to it as **the Auld Man o' Wick**.

> Wick … the meanest of men's towns, set on what is surely the baldest of God's bays.
>
> Robert Louis Stevenson: letter to his mother (1868)

Wicken 'the dwellings, the specialized farm or trading settlement', either OE *wicum* dative plural form of *wic* (*see* WICK) or the ME plural form *wiken*.

A village in Cambridgeshire, about 10 km (16 miles) south of Ely.

Wicken Fen. A small area of fenland to the west of Wicken. It was donated to the National Trust in 1899 by a group of entomologists (making it the oldest nature reserve in the UK), and is one of the few remaining pieces of undrained fenland. It contains a wealth of rare and interesting wetland plants, including hemp agrimony, southern marsh orchid, great fen sedge and marsh fern.

Wicken Bonhunt Originally two separate names: *Wicken* see WICKEN; *Bonhunt* probably 'place where people were summoned for hunting', OE *bann* 'summons' + *hunte* 'hunting' (a possible alternative is 'bone spring' (referring to an ancient spring with remains of votive animal offerings), OE *ban* 'bone' + *funta* 'spring' – *see* BOARHUNT for the *f-* of *funta* changing to *h-*).

A village in Essex, about 6 km (4 miles) southwest of Saffron Walden.

❖ **wick** ❖

The Old English element *wic* 'farm, dwelling, settlement' has a wide range of forms in modern names, and an exceptionally interesting range of meanings. WIX, WICKEN, WICK RISSINGTON, WICKEN BONHUNT, WYKE and WEEK are among the names that have *wic* on its own; to these may be added forms such as *-wich*, as in DROITWICH (Worcestershire) and OXWICH (Glamorgan), and *-wig*, as in Wigwig (Shropshire). (For an explanation of the variations in pronunciation of *wic*, *see* Introduction.)

The thing that distinguishes a *wic* from a HAM or a *-TON* is an element of specialization of some sort. A *-ham* or a *-ton* is usually a farm or settlement of a general kind, whereas a *wic* has particular functions or features. One of these is that many *wicks* are at places where Romans had buildings or roads. This is sometimes signalled in the name – Adwick le Street (Yorkshire) is on the *stræt* or Roman road (*see* STREET) – but where it is not a glance at a map will show how many can be found in the vicinity of Roman occupation: for example, ALNWICK (Northumberland) is on the Roman road that is now the A1. Nearly all the places called Wickham or Wykeham, where these names derive from *wic-ham*, are within 2 miles of a Roman road.

Another specialized function of the *wic* is salt-making, an important medieval industry. DROITWICH and the Cheshire towns NORTHWICH, MIDDLEWICH and NANTWICH are examples of places with salt works. Making specialized goods merges into selling them, and many *wicks* were also trading places or places that shipped materials elsewhere: SMETHWICK (West Midlands) was a place renowned for ironsmiths and their products, and WOOLWICH (Greater London) for transport of woollen goods. Ownership or occupation was also an area of specialization: HARWICH (Essex) was an army camp occupied by the Vikings (from OE *here* meaning 'Viking army'), and PRESTWICK (Ayrshire) was a farm owned by priests.

Perhaps the most common kind of specialization in *wic* names, though, is that of dairy or pasture farming. Frequent names such as Butterwick 'butter farm' and Hardwick 'herd farm' show this; but so also do names such as the aforementioned Oxwich, or SHAPWICK (Somerset), which specify the kind of animals – oxen and sheep – farmed.

Not all *wick* names are from Old English *wic*, however. WICK in the Scottish Highlands, and LERWICK (Shetland) are among many names in the north that derive from Old Scandinavian *vik* 'bay'.

Wickhambreaux Originally *Wickham* 'homestead associated with an earlier Romano-British settlement', OE *wic* 'place associated with a *vicus* or Romano-British settlement' (*see* WICK) + *ham* 'homestead' (*see* HAM); -*breaux* denoting manorial ownership in the Middle Ages by the de Brayhuse family.

A picturesque village in Kent, about 6 km (4 miles) east of Canterbury.

Wickham Skeith *Wickham see* WICKHAMBREAUX; *Skeith* 'racecourse', OScand.

A village in Suffolk, about 11 km (7 miles) northeast of Stowmarket.

Wicklow 'meadow of the Vikings', OScand *vikingr* 'viking' + *lo* 'meadow'.

A coastal resort at the mouth of the River Vartry in County WICKLOW (of which it is the county town), 45 km (28 miles) south of Dublin. Its Irish name is **Cill Mhantáin** ('St Mantán's church'), after the saint who landed here with St Patrick in 431; their attempted conversion of the locals was unsuccessful, and appears to have resulted in the loss of some saintly teeth. Wicklow was later settled by the Vikings, and after the Anglo-Norman invasion the area was granted to the Fitzgeralds, who built a castle here in 1176 and also founded the 13th-century Franciscan friary. Subsequently the O'Byrnes and the O'Tooles attempted to dominate the town and extorted rents from the English settlers up to the 16th century. The ruins of Black Castle, which succeeded Maurice Fitzgerald's 12th-century castle, can still be seen on a rock near the harbour. It was taken by the Confederate Catholics in 1641, and by Cromwellian forces under Sir Charles Coote in 1649.

Wicklow, County. A county in eastern-central Ireland, in the province of LEINSTER. It is known as the **Garden County**, because of the many fine gardens attached to its big houses (such as POWERSCOURT). Wicklow is bounded on the east by the Irish Sea, on the north by Dublin, on the west by Kildare and on the south by Carlow and Wexford. The county town is WICKLOW, and other towns include ARKLOW and BRAY[2]. The county is dominated by the magnificent **Wicklow Mountains**, whose highest point, LUGNAQUILLA, is 925 m (3034 ft). The range – mostly of granite – is traversed by two east–west road passes, the SALLY GAP and, further south, the **Wicklow Gap**, while nestled in their arms are many fine glens, such as GLENMALURE and GLENDALOUGH, and the headwaters of a number of rivers, including the LIFFEY. The scenic Vale of AVOCA is to the southeast of the hills. Because of its remote fastnesses Wicklow was for long a place of refuge for fugitives and brigands.

> Still south I went and west and south again,
> Through Wicklow from the morning till the night,
> And far from cities, and the sites of men,

Lived with the sunshine and the moon's delight.
I knew the stars, the flowers, and the birds,
The grey and wintry sides of many glens,
And did but half remember human words,
In converse with the mountains, moors, and fens.

> John Millington Synge (1871–1909): 'Prelude' (His first play, *In the Shadow of the Glen* (1903), is set in Glenmalure in the Wicklow Mountains; Synge's *The Tinker's Wedding* (1909) also has a Wicklow setting.)

And the mist on the Wicklow hills
Is close, as close
As the peasantry were to the landlord,
As the Irish to the Anglo-Irish,
As the killer is close one moment
To the man he kills,
Or as the moment itself
Is close to the next moment.

> Louis MacNeice (1907–63): 'Dublin'

In December in Wicklow:
Alders dripping, birches
Inheriting the last light,
The ash tree cold to look at.

> Seamus Heaney: 'Exposure', from *North* (1975)

Wick Rissington *Wick* 'specialized farm', OE *wic* (*see* WICK); *Rissington* 'hill where brushwood grows', OE *hrisen* 'growing with brushwood' + *dun* 'hill' (*see* DOWN, -DON).

A village in Gloucestershire, in the COTSWOLDS, about 1.5 km (1 mile) northeast of Bourton-on-the-Water.

Wickwar *Wick see* WICK RISSINGTON; -*war* denoting manorial ownership in the Middle Ages by the la Warre family.

A village (pronounced 'wickwor') in South Gloucestershire (before 1996 in Avon, before 1974 in Gloucestershire), about 8 km (5 miles) north of Chipping Sodbury. In the late medieval and early modern periods it throve on the clothing industry, and it has a fine straight high street lined with Georgian buildings.

Widecombe in the Moor *Widecombe* 'valley where willow-trees grow', OE *withig* 'willow' + *cumb* (*see* -COMBE, COOMBE).

A village (pronounced 'widdykəm') in Devon, just to the east of the middle of DARTMOOR, about 16 km (10 miles) west of Newton Abbot. It lies at the heart of the moor, surrounded by high granite-strewn ridges and tors. The granite-built St Pancras Church is known as the 'Cathedral of the Moor'. On the second Tuesday in September the village green is the setting for **Widecombe Fair**, inspiration of a popular ballad that has made Widecombe's name famous (usually in the spelling **Widdicombe**) throughout the English-speaking world:

> Tom Pearse, Tom Pearse, lend me your grey mare
> All along, down along, out along lee,
> For I want for to go to Widdicombe Fair,

Chorus
With Bill Brewer, Jan Stewer, Peter Gurney,
Peter Davy, Daniel Whiddon, Harry Hawk,
Old Uncle Tom Cobleigh and all.

Unfortunately the mare dies and it can still be seen haunting the moor at night. The words and music of the song (which has become virtually the county song of Devon) probably date from the late 18th century.

Old Uncle Tom Cobleigh continues to appear in the modern carnival, dressed in an old linen smock astride an old grey mare that gives rides to children.

Widemouth Bay Self-explanatory: there is a gap of about a mile in the cliffs here.

A bay and coastal village in Cornwall, about 4 km (2.5 miles) south of Bude. It is the English end of the transatlantic cable that goes to Canada and the USA.

Wide Open A reference to the exposed position of this modern colliery village.

A village in Northumberland, 8 km (5 miles) north of Newcastle.

Widmerpool Originally *Widmere*, probably 'wide lake', OE *wid* 'wide' + *mere* 'lake', with *pol* 'pool' added when the name *Widmere* lost its meaning; alternatively, the first element could represent OE *withig* 'willow'.

A village in Nottinghamshire, about 13 km (8 miles) southeast of Nottingham. It owes such renown as it possesses to the use of its name by Anthony Powell for the enigmatic and somewhat sinister Kenneth Widmerpool, a character who pops up from time to time in his sequence of novels *A Dance to the Music of Time* (1951–75).

Widnes 'wide promontory', OE *wid* 'wide' + *næss* 'promontory' (*see* NESS).

An industrial town within the unitary authority of HALTON (before 1998 in Lancashire), on the north bank of the River MERSEY, opposite RUNCORN. It is the administrative centre of Halton.

It was while waiting on a platform at Widnes station for the milk train back to London in 1964 that a homesick Paul Simon began writing the song 'Homeward Bound'. A plaque (stolen but now replaced) marks the spot.

> Widnes, the Cheshire chemical town so unloved by so many that Paul Simon famously wrote Homeward Bound as he waited for the train out of it, would not be described by many outsiders as 'fantastic'.
>
> *The Guardian*

Many of the carcases from the foot-and-mouth epidemic of 2001 were incinerated in Widnes.

Widnes Vikings. Widnes's rugby league club. It plays in rugby league's Super League, playing its home matches at the Halton stadium, built on the site of its former ground, Naughton Park.

Widow McCormick's Cabbage Patch. The site of the humiliating end of William Smith O'Brien's Young Ireland rebellion in 1848, which afterwards mockingly became known by the name of the patch. On 29 July of that year O'Brien led 100 men to surround the house of Widow McCormick at Ballingarry in County Tipperary, 20 km (12 miles) southwest of Kilkenny. In the house were 46 members of the Royal Irish Constabulary, and the two sides proceeded to fight over the cabbage patch. (O'Brien surrendered; his life sentence was commuted to transportation and he returned to Ireland under the general amnesty of 1856.)

Wigan Thought to have been originally *Tref Wigan* 'Wigan's homestead', Welsh male personal name *Wigan* + *tref* (*see* TRE-).

An industrial town and unitary authority in Greater Manchester (formerly in Lancashire), 27 km (17 miles) northwest of Manchester. The Romans called it **Coccium** and had a garrison here. Wigan was granted a charter as a borough in 1246. It was an important trading centre from the Middle Ages and the centre of a coal-mining area from the 15th century. It expanded as a cotton-manufacturing town in the 19th century, but both coal and cotton industries have since declined. The natives of Wigan are known as **Pie-eaters**, apparently because during the miners' strike of 1926 the Wigan colliers were among the first to cave in to the employers (thus 'eating humble pie'); however, the name has since become a badge of honour. Wigan is also known for its own style of pie, consisting of meat, gravy and potato in crispy pastry. The town had a formerly famous fair:

> As I were going to Wigan Fair
> I see'd the gaffer on his grey mare,
> For his grey mare and his grey hat
> Was worse than my old factory brat.
>
> Anon.: folk song 'The Factory Doll'

In 2004 Sue Nelson, assistant chief executive of Keep Britain Tidy (which is based in Wigan), got into hot water for describing the town as the 'arse end of the world'.

Wigan was the birthplace of the entertainer George Formby (1904–61; *see below*); the comedian Roy Kinnear (1934–88); and the actor Sir Ian McKellen (b.1939). It was also the home town of the rock group The Verve, formed in 1989.

Road to Wigan Pier, The. George Orwell's account of poverty during the Depression in the industrial NORTH[1], specifically Barnsley, Sheffield and Wigan. It was commissioned by the Left Book Club and published in 1937. In it Orwell writes of:

> Labyrinths of little brick houses blackened by smoke, festering in planless chaos round miry alleys and little

cindered yards where there are stinking dustbins and lines of grimy washing and half-ruinous w.c.'s.

George Orwell: *The Road to Wigan Pier* (1937)

Wigan Alps. A recreation area created from old slag heaps, now used for dry ski slopes and water sports.

Wigan Athletic. Wigan's professional football club, nicknamed the Latics and based at Springfield Park. Founded in 1932, the club was admitted to the Football League in 1978. The former Soviet leader Mikhail Gorbachev was once rumoured to be a fan of the club.

Wigan Nightingale, the. The nickname of George Formby senior (James Booth; 1875–1921), music-hall performer and singer, father of the more familiar George Formby, the cheekie chappie in a host of comedy films of the 1930s and 1940s. Some say that it was George senior who coined the phrase '**Wigan Pier**' (*see below*). He was also called the **Wigan Sprinter**, on account of one of his sketches. George junior sang a number of songs involving Wigan, such as 'Bits Fra Wigan', 'In My Little Wigan Garden' and 'On the Wigan Boat Express'.

Wigan Pier. An area of Wigan on the Leeds–Liverpool Canal, taking its ironic name from the remains of a gantry, now little more than a few iron girders, protruding from a wall. The story goes that the name arose when a trainload of miners was delayed in Wigan next to a coal-wagon gantry. The area was flooded at the time and, when a miner asked a local where they were, the facetious reply came: 'Wigan Pier'. The tale spread and was soon picked up by music-hall performers (such as George Formby senior, the **Wigan Nightingale**; *see above*), who used it to mock the middle classes and their holidays at resorts that had proper piers. In the 1990s the area was redeveloped as a tourist attraction.

Wigan Warriors. Wigan's rugby league club, one of the most famous and successful in England. Originally founded as Wigan FC in 1872 by members of the town's cricket club, Wigan seceded from the Rugby Football Union in 1895 (*see* HUDDERSFIELD) to became founder members of the Northern Rugby Union. From 1902 until 1999 Wigan played at Central Park, during which time the club won 17 League Championships. Wigan now plays in rugby league's Super League, playing its home matches at the JJB stadium.

Wiggenhall St Germans *Wiggenhall* 'Wicga's nook of land', OE *Wicgan* possessive form of male personal name *Wicga* + *halh* 'nook of land' (*see* HALE, -HALL); *St Germans* from the dedication of the local church.

A village in Norfolk, about 5 km (3 miles) southwest of King's Lynn. Just to the south are three sister villages, their names likewise distinguished by the dedicatees of the local churches: **Wiggenhall St Mary Magdalen**, **Wiggenhall St Mary the Virgin** and **Wiggenhall St Peter**.

Wiggonholt 'wych-elm wood', OE *wicna* possessive plural form of *wice* 'wych-elm' + *holt* 'wood'.

A village in West Sussex, about 3 km (2 miles) southeast of Pulborough. It looks over Amberley Wild Brooks (a grazing marsh in a former floodplain) towards the SOUTH DOWNS.

Wight. A sea area in the shipping forecast. It is in the English Channel, off the coast of Hampshire and Sussex, between PORTLAND to the west and DOVER to the east.

Wight, Isle of. *See* ISLE OF WIGHT.

Wigton 'Wicga's village', OE male personal name + -TON.

A small town in Cumbria (formerly in Cumberland), 16 km (10 miles) southwest of Carlisle. It was the birthplace of Sir William Bragg (1862–1942), who, along with his son Sir Lawrence Bragg, won the 1915 Nobel prize for physics for their pioneering work on crystallography.

Wigtown 'Wicga's farm', OE personal name *Wicga* + -TON.

A royal BURGH (1457), formerly the county town of WIGTOWNSHIRE, now part of Dumfries and Galloway. It is some 25 km (16 miles) west of Kirkcudbright, and lies on the west side of **Wigtown Bay**, a wide inlet of the Solway Firth. Wigtown, with its many second-hand bookshops, is becoming a sort of Caledonian HAY-ON-WYE.

Wigtown Martyrs, the. Two Covenanters, Margaret McLauchlan (a woman of 62) and Margaret Wilson (aged 18), who on 11 May 1685 were tied to a stake and drowned by the incoming tide, during the religious upheavals of the 17th century. The place is marked by the so-called Martyrs' Stake, and there is also a Martyrs' Monument above the town.

Wigtownshire WIGTOWN + SHIRE.

A former county in southwest Scotland, comprising the western part of GALLOWAY, including the Rhinns of Galloway and the MACHARS. The area became part of DUMFRIES AND GALLOWAY in 1975. Wigtown continued as the name of a local authority district until the reorganization of 1996.

Wildboarclough 'deep valley frequented by wild boars', OE *wilde-bar* 'wild boar' + *cloh* 'deep valley'.

A village in Cheshire, on the western edge of the PEAK DISTRICT, about 16 km (10 miles) northeast of Congleton.

> A nut-brown maid whom he cannot remember
> Sold him herb beer, a farmhouse brew,
> One day above Wild Boar Clough, whose peat-sieved brown
> Waters were flecked below them.
>
> Donald Davie: 'Wild Boar Clough', from *Three for Water-Music* (1981)

Wild Boar Fell. A hill (708 m / 2322 ft) in the northwest PENNINES, Cumbria, 25 km (16 miles) northeast of Kendal. It takes its name, according to legend, from the last wild boar hereabouts, killed on the fell by Sir Richard Musgrave of Hartley Castle, who, when he was buried in 1409, was accompanied by a tusk from his quarry. On the summit of Wild Boar Fell are upright cairns leading to a Celtic burial place. Daniel Defoe describes it as 'a monstrous high mountain', and gives **Mowill Hill** as an alternative name.

Wilderness, the. A remote peninsula in southwest MULL, north across Loch Scridain from the Ross. The Gaelic name is **Ardmeanach** ('middle height', Gaelic *aird* 'height' + *meadhonach* 'middle'). The area consists of great basaltic lava flows, and among the geological marvels is Mc-Culloch's Tree, a 12-m (40-ft) 50-million-year-old fossil tree at Burg (in the care of the National Trust for Scotland).

Wildmore Fen *Wildmore* 'wild or uncultivated marshland', OE *wilde* 'uncultivated' + *mor* 'marshland'.
An area of fenland in Lincolnshire, about 14 km (8.5 miles) northwest of Boston.

Willenhall 'Willa's nook of land', OE *Willan* possessive form of male personal name *Willa* + *halh* (*see* HALE, -HALL).
A town in the WEST MIDLANDS, within the metropolitan borough of WALSALL (before 1974 in Staffordshire). The River TAME[1] rises nearby.

Willesden 'hill with a spring or by a stream', OE *wielles* possessive form of *wiell* 'spring, stream' + *dun* (*see* DOWN, -DON). *Wilsdon* had become the established spelling by the early 19th century; the historically inauthentic *Willesden* was introduced by the London & Birmingham Railway.
A district of northwest London (NW10), in the borough of BRENT[2], between WORMWOOD SCRUBS to the south and CRICKLEWOOD to the north. Its rural seclusion was rudely curtailed in the middle of the 19th century by the arrival of the railway: **Willesden Junction** opened in 1866 and is now a major hub of railway tracks in the western part of London. Its Underground counterpart, on the Bakerloo line, opened in 1915. Willesden Green Underground station, on the Jubilee line (originally the Metropolitan), opened in 1879. With the stations in place, developers were not slow to fill the spaces in between with cheap housing.

Willey[1] 'willow-tree glade', OE *wilig* 'willow' + -LEY.
A village in Warwickshire, 11 km (7 miles) north of Rugby.

Willey[2]. A hamlet in Shropshire, about 14 km (8.5 miles) south of Telford.

Willington 'Wifel's estate', OE male personal name *Wifel* + -ING + -TON; *Wyvelintun c.*1190.
A town in County Durham, 5 km (3 miles) north of Bishop Auckland. There is also a town called Willington in the USA (Connecticut).

Wilmington 'Wilma's farm or estate', OE *Wilman* possessive form of the male personal name *Wilma* + -TON (the *-ing-* here is a late adaptation of the original possessive ending *-an*).
A village in East Sussex, at the foot of the SOUTH DOWNS, about 8 km (5 miles) northwest of Eastbourne. Its fame rests on the **Long Man of Wilmington**, the 69-m (226-ft)

high figure of a man flanked by the two staffs that he is holding, cut into the chalk on Windover Hill. It is visible from the nearby A27. Speculation as to his age and provenance has ranged over the Roman, Anglo-Saxon and early medieval periods, but stylistically he is modern and probably dates from the mid-16th century.

In the local churchyard is an ancient yew tree, said to be the oldest in England. The girth of its trunk is 7 m (23 ft).

The largest city in Delaware, USA, is named Wilmington, after Spencer Compton, Earl of Wilmington (1673–1743), who was briefly a prime minister.

Wilmslow 'Wighelm's mound', *Wighelmes* possessive form of OE male personal name *Wighelm* + *hlaw* 'mound' (*see* LAW, LOW).
A town at the northern edge of Cheshire, about 8 km (5 miles) northwest of Macclesfield. It serves as a dormitory for Greater Manchester just to the north, with which it is now virtually contiguous. The affluence of its shopping-orientated populace has contributed to its central position in Cheshire's GOLDEN TRIANGLE. It has been said that there are more back-garden swimming pools in Wilmslow than anywhere else in Britain, and the town has been dubbed the 'Knightsbridge of the North'.

Wilton 'farmstead or village on the River Wylye', WYLYE[1] + -TON.
A town in Wiltshire, at the confluence of the River NADDER and the River Wylye, about 6 km (4 miles) northwest of Salisbury. It is one of the oldest boroughs in England, and it used to be the county town of Wiltshire. Alfred the Great founded an abbey here in 871.

Just to the southeast, on the site of the former abbey, is **Wilton House**, since Tudor times the home of the earls of Pembroke. The poet Edmund Spenser and the dramatists Ben Johnson and Christopher Marlowe all visited the house, and Sir Philip Sidney wrote part of his *Arcadia* (1581) here. Scenes from *Arcadia* are represented in the 17th-century panels around the Single Cube Room. The house was redesigned in the mid-17th century by Inigo Jones, and his most notable innovation was the Double Cube Room – which appeared as the ballroom in Ang Lee's film of *Sense and Sensibility* (1995), as well as in many other films, including Stanley Kubrick's *Barry Lyndon* (1975) and Nicholas Hytner's *The Madness of King George* (1994). During the Second World War the house was the headquarters of Southern Command, and the D-Day invasion of Normandy was planned here.

Around the world the name *Wilton* now connotes carpets. They have been made here since Elizabethan times, and the Royal Wilton Factory is over 300 years old. The earls of Pembroke were always strong supporters of the industry and one of them is even said to have secretly imported some French carpet weavers hidden in a wine barrel. The term *Wilton* now technically specifies a carpet in which the pattern is woven in loops of cut or uncut pile, rather than being (as with AXMINSTER) inserted in a backing.

There are towns called Wilton in the USA (Arkansas, Iowa, New Hampshire, North Dakota, Wisconsin).

Wilton Diptych, the. A portable medieval altarpiece painted on two hinged oak panels, portraying Richard II (to whom it probably belonged) with the Virgin and Child and an array of saints and angels, including Edward the Confessor and John the Baptist. It once hung in Wilton House (whence its name) but is now in the National Gallery.

Wilts. The standard abbreviation of WILTSHIRE.

> There was a young lady from Wilts,
> Who walked up to Scotland on stilts;
>   When they said it was shocking
>   To show so much stocking,
> She answered 'Then what about kilts?'
>
> Anon: limerick

Wiltshire From WILTON + SHIRE.

A county in southern England, bounded to the east by Berkshire and Hampshire, to the south by Dorset, to the west by Somerset, Bath and North East Somerset and South Gloucestershire and to the north by Gloucestershire and Oxfordshire. Its administrative centre is TROWBRIDGE, and other important towns are CALNE, CHIPPENHAM, DEVIZES, MALMESBURY, MARLBOROUGH, MELKSHAM, SALISBURY, WARMINSTER and WILTON. It also contains the unitary authority of SWINDON. Its main rivers are the AVON[2], the AVON[3] and the KENNET[1]. To the north are the Marlborough Downs (*see under* MARLBOROUGH) and SAVERNAKE FOREST, but the central and southern part of the county is dominated by the vast expanse of Salisbury Plain (*see under* SALISBURY).

Wiltshire is a largely agricultural county, with extensive arable acreage. It is also well known for its bacon and other pig products.

Wiltshire is notable for its prehistoric sites, in particular at AVEBURY, SILBURY HILL and STONEHENGE. When the Romans arrived here the area was populated by two ancient British tribes, the Atrebates and Durotriges, but neither put up much resistance to the newcomers. In the early 9th century Wiltshire was fought over by MERCIA and WESSEX, and it later became a focus of the struggle between Saxons and Danes.

In the past natives of Wiltshire were often called 'Moonrakers', with an underlying implication of learning difficulties. The story goes that some Wiltshire rustics, having seen the moon's reflection in a pond, were observed trying to fish it out with a rake, suggesting some deficiency in the IQ department. A more favourable local gloss, indicative of low cunning rather than mental limitation, is that the men were caught raking the pond for kegs of smuggled brandy and put off the customs men by inventing a silly excuse. Local lore links the tale with the pond known as the Crammer at Devizes.

In cricketing terms Wiltshire is a 'minor county' (the club was founded in 1893) and plays in the minor counties championship.

Wiltshire Horn. A breed of sheep with very light short hairlike wool.

Wimbish 'Wine's bushy copse', OE male personal name *Wine* + *bysce* 'bushy copse'.

A hamlet in Essex, about 6 km (4 miles) east of Saffron Walden.

Wimbledon 'Wynnmann's hill', OE male personal name *Wynnmann* + *dun* (*see* DOWN, -DON).

A residential district of southwest Outer London (SW19), in the borough of MERTON, between TOOTING to the east and KINGSTON UPON THAMES to the west. It grew up as a modest village on top of the hill from which it gets its name, and did not start to expand significantly until the railway arrived in 1838 (one of its earliest conquests in South London). Housing proliferated around the station and to the southeast (**South Wimbledon**), and a distinct apartheid developed between these lowlier residents and those who dwelt 'up the hill'. Still today this latter is the decidedly nobbier part of Wimbledon, with the more spacious roads and larger houses. Here live those who pay the 'Common rate'. The common in question is **Wimbledon Common**, a 450-ha (1110-acre) open space to the northwest of Wimbledon that is first recorded in the late 15th century. Large parts of it are now given over to golf, but there is more than enough left for the horse-rider and dog-walker. Like most such urban expanses, it seems to attract deviance: it is said that the politician Leslie Hore-Belisha (begetter of the Belisha beacon) was once arrested for proceeding across it naked on horseback, and on a more sombre note the Common saw the brutal and still unsolved murder of Rachel Nickell in 1992. At the centre of the Common is a famous windmill, built in 1817. (*See also* CAESAR'S CAMP.)

For two weeks every summer Wimbledon becomes global property when the international tennis circus arrives in town. The **Wimbledon Championships** have been held here since 1877. Men's and ladies' singles and doubles and mixed doubles titles are fought for in what is the only Grand Slam tournament still played on grass. It is run by the All England Lawn Tennis and Croquet Club (founded in 1877 as the All England Croquet and Lawn Tennis Club) and was first played at their Worple Road ground. It moved to its present site in Church Road in 1922. It is firmly part of the English sporting and social summer season, each year reigniting the frail and usually swiftly extinguished hope of British victory, and is rich with associations: the

Virginia-creeper-covered Centre Court, the overpriced strawberries and cream, the Robinson's Barley Water, the rain breaks (on one apparently memorable occasion serenaded by Cliff Richard), the voice of former BBC commentator Dan Maskell ('Oh, I say!'). The club has also hosted British home Davis Cup ties, and the outside courts are available to members when not in use for the Championships. Wimbledon is also the headquarters of the Lawn Tennis Association. (*See also* HENMAN HILL.)

Wimbledon FC, nicknamed the Dons, was founded in 1889, and elevated to the Football League in 1977. In a remarkable rise-and-fall story its finest hour came in 1988, when it beat Liverpool to win the FA Cup. Thereafter its fortunes went into a sharp decline, as it slid down the League and went into financial administration. The club managed to alienate supporters by relocating its ground to faraway MILTON KEYNES in 2003, before finally, as the renamed Milton Keynes Dons, disconnecting itself from its history in 2004. Angry former supporters founded a new local club, **AFC Wimbledon**, owned by the fans.

In the late 1960s a rival arose to tennis in the word-association response to *Wimbledon*: the Womble. This rather tiresome creature was invented by Elisabeth Beresford, who described it thus:

> The Wombles are a bit like teddy bears to look at but they have real claws and live underneath Wimbledon Common and devote their lives to 'tidying up' all the things those untidy Human Beings leave behind.
>
> *The Wombles* (1968)

Her books, and the television adaptations, cuddly toys, etc. based on them, achieved considerable popularity in the 1970s (capturing the conservationist Zeitgeist) and are still remembered, albeit not with universal fondness. The main Womble is Great Uncle Bulgaria, and others include Orinoco and Tobermory. Their cult was raised to greater heights by a pop group of the same name who dressed the part and took the charts by storm in 1974 with hits such as 'The Wombling Song' ...

> Underground, overground, wombling free,
> The Wombles of Wimbledon Common are we.

... and 'Remember You're a Womble'. The name *Womble* is said to have been derived from *Wombledon*, a fanciful variation on *Wimbledon*.

The painter John Bratby (1928–92) and the actor Oliver Reed (1938–99) were born in Wimbledon.

There are also towns called Wimbledon in the USA (North Dakota) and New Zealand.

Wimbledon. A romantic film comedy (2004) starring Paul Bettany and Kirsten Dunst in which an ageing British tennis player, inspired by his ongoing relationship with a successful US woman player, achieves a highly implausible victory

in the Wimbledon men's singles final. The real-life US tennis player Serena Williams, twice a Wimbledon ladies' singles champion, remarked a little ungenerously: 'It must be a comedy if a British player is winning at Wimbledon.'

Wimbledon Poisoner, The. A comic novel (1990) by Nigel Williams recounting the chaotic travails of a would-be suburban murderer. Williams returned to the same Wimbledon locale for *They Came from SW19* (1992) and *Scenes from a Poisoner's Life* (1994).

Wimblehurst. H.G. Wells's fictionalized version of MIDHURST.

Wimborne Minster *Wimborne* originally the name of the local river (now called the Allen), 'meadow stream', OE *winn* 'meadow' + *burna* 'stream'; *Minster* referring to a nunnery founded here in the late 8th century, OE *mynster* 'monastery (church)'.

A market town in Dorset, on the River Allen, close to its confluence with the STOUR[1], about 13 km (8 miles) northwest of Bournemouth. It is dominated by the Minster of St Cuthberga, a Norman mini-cathedral built on the site of the nunnery (destroyed by the Danes) that gave the town the second half of its name. It contains a Chained Library dating from 1686, one of the oldest public libraries in England, and also the only known royal brass in England, put up to the memory of Æthelred the Unready in the 15th century.

Thomas Hardy, who lived in Wimborne from 1881 to 1883, fictionalized it in his novel *Two on a Tower* (1882) as **Warborne**.

Wimpole 'Wina's pool', OE male personal name *Wina* + *pol* 'pool'.

A village in Cambridgeshire, about 16 km (10 miles) southwest of Cambridge. At **Wimpole Hall**, a rambling 17th-century country house much enlarged in the 18th, the original 'pool' of the name is now an ornamental lake. One of the improvements made to the Hall was to build a 'book room' in 1719 to house the magnificent collection of books and manuscripts of Edward Harley, 2nd Earl of Oxford, diligently catalogued by one of the finest early modern scholars, Humfrey Wanley. In the 20th century the house became the property of Rudyard Kipling's daughter and it is now administered by the National Trust. The grounds also accommodate **Wimpole Home Farm**, a model farm developed from 1794 and now dedicated to rare breeds.

Wimpole Street From WIMPOLE: Edward Harley, 2nd Earl of Oxford, who owned the land the street was built on, was also the owner of Wimpole Hall. *See also* HARLEY STREET.

A street in MARYLEBONE (W1), in the City of WESTMINSTER, running north to south from Devonshire Street to Wigmore Street. It was laid out in the 1720s. Notable past residents include the Tory politician and thinker Edmund Burke, the novelist Wilkie Collins and, most famously, the poet Elizabeth Barrett. She lived here in her father's house from 1838 to 1846. The story of her and her siblings' life under Edward Barrett's tyrannical regime, and of her escape to marry Robert Browning, is told in Rudolph Besier's play *The Barretts of Wimpole Street* (1930; filmed in 1934, with Charles Laughton as Barrett *père*).

Professor Henry Higgins lives at 27A Wimpole Street in Bernard Shaw's *Pygmalion* (1916).

Wincanton 'farmstead by the white (river) Cale', OCelt *winn* 'white' + *Cale* an OCelt river name of uncertain meaning + -TON.

A town in Somerset, close to the Dorset and Wiltshire borders, on the River Cale, about 16 km (10 miles) north-west of Shaftesbury. It is best-known for its National Hunt racecourse, which opened in its present location in 1925.

Winchcombe 'curved valley', OE *wincel* 'corner' + *cumb* (*see* -COMBE, COOMBE).

An attractive small market town in Gloucestershire, in the COTSWOLDS, on the River Isbourne, about 11 km (7 miles) northeast of Cheltenham. In the Anglo-Saxon period it was an important Mercian regional centre, and it once had its own abbey (destroyed at the Dissolution), but it declined in importance from the early Middle Ages, and it is now a quiet and modest place. The sumptuous mid-15th-century St Peter's Church, with its impressive array of gargoyles, bears witness to the prosperity the town formerly drew from the wool trade.

A little to the southeast is Sudeley Castle. Catherine Parr, who married its owner after the death of her previous husband, Henry VIII, was buried in its chapel. It was all but demolished by the Parliamentarians, having been a Royalist headquarters during the Civil Wars, and the present building is a 19th-century reconstruction. It is said to have been the model for Blandings Castle, Lord Emsworth's home in P.G. Wodehouse's comic novels (*but see also* CLEOBURY MORTIMER), and an annual Wodehouse festival is held here.

Winchelsea 'island by a river bend', OE *winceles* possessive form of *wincel* 'corner' + *eg* (*see* -EY, -EA).

A town on the EAST SUSSEX coast, on high land overlooking the River Brede, about 5 km (3 miles) south of Rye. It was originally a port on the eastern side of the ROTHER[2] estuary, and by the end of the 12th century it was one of the CINQUE PORTS. In 1288 it was all but destroyed in a great storm, but already by that time royal plans had been laid to build a new Winchelsea, on its present site, with a view to creating an up-to-date port to serve the Gascon wine trade. The result was a town laid out on a regular grid pattern. It retains that to this day, but its buildings are Georgian and modern rather than medieval. In Elizabethan

times its harbour silted up, and without its *raison d'être* it rather shrank in on itself. Daniel Defoe in *A Tour Through the Whole Island of Great Britain* (1724–26) characterized it as 'rather the skeleton of an ancient city, than a real town', and in 1697 Celia Fiennes wrote:

> I rode up a middle street and saw the others run across of good breadth …, but … there are but very few houses and … grass grows now where Winchelsea was, as was once said of Troy.
>
> Christopher Morris (ed.): *The Journeys of Celia Fiennes* (1947)

Winchester 'Roman town called Venta', pre-Celtic place name *Venta*, perhaps meaning 'favoured or chief place' + CHESTER.

A cathedral city in Hampshire, on the River ITCHEN, about 19 km (12 miles) north of Southampton. Its site was occupied in the Iron Age, and in Roman times it was the capital of a British tribe called the Belgae, and thus went by the name of **Venta Belgarum** ('chief place of the Belgae'). It was identified by Sir Thomas Malory (d.1471) and other early writers with the Camelot of Arthurian romances (in Castle Hall, all that remains of William I's **Winchester Castle**, can be seen 'King Arthur's Round Table', a medieval pastiche refurbished in Henry VIII's time).

Winchester became Alfred the Great's capital in the 9th century, and it was probably he who had the town newly laid out and fortified within the old Roman walls. There is a statue of Alfred on the Broadway. Winchester continued as joint capital of England with London after the Norman Conquest, and William the Conqueror had a second coronation in the Old Minster in 1068. By the beginning of the 12th century it was, jointly with NORWICH, the second largest city in the country. However, over the course of the Middle Ages London consolidated its position as England's main city and royalty's connections with Winchester loosened, and by the 15th century it had settled down to the more modest status of a historic provincial town.

Winchester had been a bishopric since 662, and after the Conquest it was decided to build a grand new cathedral. Building began in 1079, using stone from Quarr on the ISLE OF WIGHT. **Winchester Cathedral** has the longest medieval nave in Europe (170 m / 556 ft). It contains the remains of various Saxon kings, of King Cnut (Canute) and of William II, and a shrine of St Swithun. Swithun was Bishop of Winchester in the mid-9th century. He desired to be buried in the churchyard of the minster so that the 'sweet rain of heaven might fall upon his grave'. At his canonization the monks thought to honour the saint by transferring his body into the cathedral choir and fixed 15 July 971 for the ceremony, but it rained day after day for 40 days, thereby, according to some, delaying the proceedings – whence the superstition encapsulated in the old rhyme:

St Swithun's day, gif ye do rain, for forty days it will
    remain;
St Swithun's day an ye be fair, for forty days 'twill rain nae
    mair.

The shrine was destroyed during the Reformation and a
new one was dedicated in 1962. Izaak Walton (1593–1683),
author of *The Compleat Angler* (1653), and the novelist Jane
Austen (1775–1817) are also buried in the cathedral. Its
library has the oldest book room in Europe. The Bishop of
Winchester signs himself 'Winton'.

The earliest documented 'seld' – that is, a multiply
occupied shop building, as opposed to open-air stalls – is
recorded in Winchester in 1148.

In the novels of Thomas Hardy Winchester is fictionalized as **Wintoncester**. In *Tess of the D'Urbervilles* (1891)
Tess is hanged in the city gaol.

There are towns called Winchester in the USA (Idaho,
Illinois, Indiana, Kentucky, Massachusetts, New Hampshire,
Ohio, Tennessee, Texas, Wyoming), Canada (Ontario) and
New Zealand.

(The Winchester rifle, scourge of the American Wild
West, has no direct connection with the city of Winchester:
it was named after its inventor, Oliver F. Winchester
(1810–80); and the 'Winchester disk', an IBM computer
storage disk, was so called because it was originally intended
to contain the equivalent of two 30-megabyte disks, and
the Winchester rifle used a 0.30 calibre cartridge containing
0.30 grains of powder.)

Battle of Winchester (14 September 1141). A battle in
which forces loyal to King Stephen scattered his rival
Matilda's army, which was besieging Winchester.

Statute of Winchester. A law of 1285 embodying various
measures intended to improve the enforcement of law and
order (e.g. highways had to be widened and cleared of
shrubbery to reduce the risk of mugging).

Treaty of Winchester. A treaty of 1153 in which King
Stephen agreed to recognize his rival Matilda's son Henry
(in due course Henry II) as his heir.

Winchester Bible. A large, elaborately decorated bible
produced between 1160 and 1170, probably to the commission of Henry of Blois, Bishop of Winchester and brother
of King Stephen. It is kept in Winchester Cathedral.

Winchester bottle. A term (often shortened to simply
'Winchester') once used in the chemical and pharmaceutical industries for a bottle with the capacity of
one **Winchester quart** (*see below*).

Winchester bushel. An old British unit of measurement
equivalent to 2150 cubic inches and less than the current
imperial bushel of 2218 cubic inches.

'Winchester Cathedral'. A pop song (1966) by the British
songwriter-producer Geoff Stephens, which enjoyed chart
success in The New Vaudeville Band's version:

Winchester Cathedral
You're bringing me down
You stood and you watched as
My baby left town.

(*See also* 'Finchley Central' *under* FINCHLEY.)

Winchester College. A public school for boys, founded
in Winchester in 1382 by William of Wykeham, Bishop of
Winchester, and also founder (in 1379) of New College,
Oxford. It was intended for poor scholars, but modern **Old
Wykehamists** (as the school's old boys are called, after their
original benefactor) have usually avoided having indigent
parents. The College has the reputation of a rigorous intellectual forcing-house in contrast to the more relaxed, sport-
orientated regime of some other public schools. Alumni
include the writer and physician Sir Thomas Browne
(1605–82), the clergyman and essayist Sydney Smith
(1771–1845), the novelist Anthony Trollope (1815–82), the
poet and critic Matthew Arnold (1822–88), the Labour
politician Richard Crossman (1907–74) and the historian
Arnold Toynbee (1899–1975).

Winchester fives. A form of fives (a court game involving
hitting a small ball with the hand against a wall) developed
at Winchester College, played in a four-walled court. It is
similar to Rugby fives (*see under* RUGBY), but its court is
narrower at the back than at the front.

Winchester goose. A slang term from the 16th to the 18th
century for venereal disease. Why 'goose' is not entirely
clear (perhaps from the large egg-like buboes in the groin),
but 'Winchester' is an allusion to the fact that the brothels
of SOUTHWARK came under the jurisdiction of the Bishop
of Winchester.

Winchester hoard. An important cache of Iron Age
objects, dating from 75 to 25 BC, found in a field near
Winchester in 2000. It includes two matching sets of gold
jewellery, a man's and a woman's, with a necklace, a bracelet
and two brooches.

Winchester measure. Dry and liquid measures in use in
former times. The standards on which they were based were
originally deposited at Winchester.

Winchester quart. In pharmacology, a measure of liquid
capacity originally equal to 4 imperial pints (about 2.273
litres), and now 2.5 litres. The origin of the name is not
known.

Winchester School. A southern English style of manuscript
illumination of the 10th and 11th centuries, originating
in Winchester.

Winchester Three, the. Three young Irish people, Martina
Shanahan, Finbar Cullen and John McCann, who in 1988
were sentenced at Winchester Crown Court to 25 years'
imprisonment on charges of conspiracy to murder Tom
King, then Secretary of State for Northern Ireland. They
were freed on appeal in 1990.

Wincle Probably 'Wineca's hill', OE male personal name *Wineca* + *hyll* 'hill'; alternatively the first element could represent OE *wince* 'pulley, winch'.

A hamlet in Cheshire, on the western edge of the PEAK DISTRICT, about 11 km (7 miles) east of Congleton.

Windermere 'Vinandr's lake', OScand male personal name + OE *mere* 'lake' (*see also* LAKE).

A long, narrow lake in the southern LAKE DISTRICT, Cumbria, 12 km (7.5 miles) west of Kendal. It was still being referred to as **Winander Mere** in the 1720s by Daniel Defoe (who compared it to the Mediterranean Sea) and by John Keats in 1818 (*see below*). Windermere was formerly in Westmorland, with its southeastern and western shores in Lancashire. Windermere is the longest lake in England, stretching 16.8 km (10.5 miles) south from AMBLESIDE, and also the largest, at 14.7 sq km (5.67 sq miles). There are a number of attractive wooded islands in the central section of the lake, which provided a playground for the youthful Wordsworth:

> When summer came
> It was the pastime of our afternoons
> To beat along the plain of Windermere
> With rival oars, and the selected bourne
> Was now an Island musical with birds
> That sang for ever ...
>
> William Wordsworth: *The Prelude* (1805–50), Book I

On his summer tour in 1818 Keats visited and wrote:

> ... the Lake and Mountains of Winander – I cannot describe them – they surpass my expectation – beautiful water – shores and island green to the marge – mountains all round up to the clouds.
>
> John Keats: letter to Tom Keats (26 June 1818)

The small town of **Windermere** (which merges with **Bowness-on-Windermere** on its southern edge) is a major tourist centre. It was originally known as Birthwaite, but grew considerably around the Windermere Hotel after the North-West Railway line from Kendal was opened in 1847 – despite the protests of Wordsworth, who apparently believed that the restorative effect of Nature should not be shared with the hoi polloi. In 1844 he had written a 'Sonnet on the Projected Kendal and Windermere Railway', beginning:

> Is there no nook of English ground secure
> From rash assault?

Apparently there wasn't. The railway brought the trippers and the trippers wanted steam-powered nautical fun. The first fare-taking pleasure craft on the lake was the paddle-steamer *Lady of the Lake*, launched in 1846; many more were to follow. On Friday 13 June 1930 Sir Henry Seagrave and W. Hallwell of Rolls Royce were killed on the lake while attempting the world water speed record in *Miss England II*; the third member of the crew, the engineer Michael Willcocks, survived. For 2005 a speed limit of 10mph on the lake was announced.

A century before, in 1825, the lake witnessed a gaily painted regatta, organized by John Wilson (who, as Christopher North, is best known for *Noctes Ambrosianae*) to celebrate the birthday of Sir Walter Scott. Scott was visiting Wilson in his house at Elleray, on the north side of what is now the town of Windermere.

Arthur Ransome wrote *Swallows and Amazons* (1930) while staying at the Newby Bridge Hotel in Windermere, having been inspired by the sight of two girls sailing a dinghy on the lake. Although the lake in the story is based on Windermere, the fictional Wild Cat Island is based on Peel Island in CONISTON WATER. Less pleasantly, Aleister Crowley, 'the Great Beast', had a house on the shore of the lake where he tried to summon demons.

Windmill Hill A modern name; ModE *windmill + hill*.

A rounded hill in Wiltshire, about 2.5 km (1.5 miles) northwest of AVEBURY. On its summit is a causeway camp consisting of three concentric lines of earthwork, constructed around 2500 BC. The hill's name has been adopted to characterize the culture, artefacts, etc. of the Neolithic farming people who colonized southern England from the Continent about 5000 years ago (as in 'Windmill Hill pottery').

Windrush An OCelt river name perhaps meaning 'white fen'.

A river in Gloucestershire and Oxfordshire. It rises in the COTSWOLDS and flows 54 km (34 miles) through BOURTON-ON-THE-WATER and WITNEY to join the THAMES[1] at Newbridge about 16 km (10 miles) southwest of Oxford.

A village 8 km (5 miles) south of Bourton-on-the-Water shares the name of the river it stands on.

Windscale. *See* SELLAFIELD.

Windsor 'bank or slope with a windlass' (probably referring to a winch for hauling carts up the muddy bank of the Thames), OE *windels* 'windlass' + *ora* 'bank, slope'.

A town in Berkshire, on the south bank of the River Thames (opposite ETON), within the unitary authority of WINDSOR AND MAIDENHEAD, about 35 km (22 miles) west of London. The original settlement, a little to the southeast, is now called **Old Windsor**. The modern town, which grew up around the castle, was at first known as **New Windsor**, but it is now plain Windsor. Its main non-royal attraction is its Legoland, a theme park based on plastic building bricks.

There are towns called Windsor in the USA (Colorado, Connecticut, Illinois, Massachusetts, Missouri, New York, North Carolina, South Carolina, Virginia), Canada (Newfoundland, Nova Scotia, Ontario (Canada's main port of entry to the USA), Quebec), Australia (New South Wales) and New Zealand.

brown Windsor. A type of soup commonly served in English restaurants, train dining-cars, etc. in the 19th and early 20th centuries. Basically a fairly thin meat broth, it was one of the many dishes that gave English cookery a bad name.

Duke of Windsor. *See* **House of Windsor** *below*.

Early Windsor. A sweet and juicy variety of English apple that appears from August, and in appearance is similar to a Cox.

Edward of Windsor. A byname of Edward III (1312–77), who was born at Windsor.

Half Windsor. Not a semi-detached relation of the **House of Windsor** (*see below*) but the more modest configuration of the **Windsor knot** (*see below*).

House of Windsor. The British royal family. Its name dates from 17 July 1917 when, in a climate of hostility to all things German, George V (1865–1936) changed his family name, Saxe-Coburg-Gotha, inherited from his grandfather, Prince Albert (1819–61), consort of Queen Victoria, to the more British-sounding Windsor. He adopted this name partly because Edward III (1312–77) had used it, but chiefly as a symbolic reflection of the royal importance of Windsor Castle. (Of the various alternatives suggested, Tudor was rejected because of the unfortunate reputation of Henry VIII and FitzRoy because of its whiff of bastardy.) In 1960 Queen Elizabeth II declared that those of her descendants not entitled to the style of 'Royal Highness' or 'Prince' or 'Princess' would in future use the surname Mountbatten-Windsor, so linking the surname of her husband (before their marriage the Duke of Edinburgh was known as Lieutenant Philip Mountbatten) with their descendants without changing the name of the house established by her grandfather. The first use of the new name on an official document was at the marriage of Princess Anne to Captain Mark Phillips on 14 November 1973.

Edward VIII was granted the title **Duke of Windsor** in 1936 after he abdicated to marry Wallis Simpson, later the **Duchess of Windsor**. (For his tie, *see* **Windsor knot** *below*.)

Knights of Windsor. Originally a small order of knights founded by Edward III (reigned 1327–77) in 1348, after the wars in France, to assist English knights who had been held prisoner in France and become impoverished through having to pay heavy ransoms. It comprised 26 veterans, but under the will of Henry VIII (reigned 1509–47) their number was reduced to 13, with a governor, a post that has since remained. The members are meritorious military officers who are granted apartments in Windsor Castle with a small stipend in addition to their army pension. They take part in all ceremonies of the Order of the Garter and attend Sunday morning service in St George's Chapel as representatives of the Knights of the Garter. Their present uniform of scarlet tailcoat with white cross sword-belt, crimson sash and cocked hat was designed by William IV, who changed their name to the Military Knights of Windsor.

Because of their reduced circumstances they have also been known as the **Poor Knights of Windsor**, a name preserved in 'poor knights' pudding', an economical dessert made by sandwiching French toast with jam, fruit, etc. In the 19th century the blade-bone of a shoulder of mutton, eaten as leftovers, was known jocularly as a **poor knight of Windsor**.

Merry Wives of Windsor, The. A comedy (1597) by Shakespeare, based on the amorous misadventures of Sir John Falstaff. The fat knight pays court to Mistress Ford and Mistress Page, two married ladies of Windsor, and gets thoroughly discomfited for his presumptuousness – once by being hidden in a dirty-linen basket and tipped into a ditch, and again by being seized and pinched by mock fairies at a supposed assignation in **Windsor Forest** (*see below*). The play forms the basis of three operas: Nicolai's *Die lustigen Weiber von Windsor* (1849), Verdi's *Falstaff* (1893) and Vaughan Williams's *Sir John in Love* (1929).

Widow at Windsor, the. A name applied to Queen Victoria after her husband Albert, the Prince Consort, died at the end of 1861. Her remaining 39 years were largely spent in seclusion and she never ceased to mourn her loss. The epithet 'the Widow at Windsor' was applied by Rudyard Kipling in his *Barrack-Room Ballad* of that name (1892):

> Then 'ere's to the Widow at Windsor,
> An' 'ere's to the stores an' the guns,
> The men an' the 'orses what makes up the forces
> O' Missis Victorier's sons.

Windsor bean. An alternative name for the broad bean.

Windsor brick. A type of red fire-resisting brick formerly made at Hedgerley, near Windsor.

Windsor Castle. A castle on a steep chalk bluff overlooking the town of Windsor. England's premier castle and the largest inhabited castle in the world, its quintessentially castle-like outline has become a symbol of English history and of the monarchy whose ancestral abode it is. It was built in 1070 by William the Conqueror to guard the western approaches to London. It has been much altered and enlarged since then: William II had its first stone buildings put up (including the familiar central Round Tower); Henry III was responsible for most of its external defences; and the extensive developments by Sir Jeffry Wyatville in the reign of George IV produced the castle's now instantly recognizable skyline. It now covers 5.25 ha (13 acres). St George's Chapel, home of the Order of the Garter, was built in the late 15th century; Henry VIII and Charles I are buried here. The castle contains the sumptuous Royal Art Collection, and also Queen Mary's Doll's House, designed by Sir Edwin Lutyens in 1924.

Windsor Castle has always been a favourite royal residence. Edward III and Henry VI were born here. The present Queen is known to prefer it to BUCKINGHAM PALACE, and spends the weekend here when in London. She was present when a serious fire broke out here in 1992. It was successfully contained and the affected parts of the castle have since been completely restored.

To the east of the castle is the 162-ha (400-acre) Home Park, which contains the Royal Mausoleum at FROGMORE.

In 20th-century rhyming slang *Windsor Castle* denoted 'arsehole'.

Windsor Castle. A novel (1843) by William Harrison Ainsworth in which he popularizes the legend of Herne the Hunter (*see* **Windsor Forest** *below*). (*See also under* TOWER OF LONDON.)

Windsor chair. A wooden chair with a back of turned rods or rails, legs that slant outwards and, usually, a slightly concave seat. It can have arms.

Windsor Forest. An area of woodland at the western edge of **Windsor Great Park**. It is the legendary domain of Herne the Hunter, a phantom figure with antlers growing from his forehead who is said at times of national crisis to appear with his ghostly hounds on the site of a great oak tree that once grew in the forest ('Herne's Oak', cut down in 1796 and replanted in 1906). The story is that he was once a royal huntsman who had saved the king's life but hanged himself after falling from royal favour. Vaughan Williams's cantata *In Windsor Forest* (1931) was adapted from his opera *Sir John in Love* (*see* **The Merry Wives of Windsor** *above*).

Windsor Forest. A topographical poem by Alexander Pope, mixing landscape description with musings on philosophy, literature, politics, etc. It was published in 1713 to celebrate the Treaty of Utrecht, which ended the War of the Spanish Succession.

Windsor Great Park. A 1940-ha (4800-acre) area of wooded parkland to the south of Windsor Castle. It is crossed by the Long Walk, created by Charles II, and by Queen Anne's Ride, along which Queen Elizabeth drives on her way to ASCOT racecourse; both are 5 km (3 miles) long. At the southern end of the park is VIRGINIA WATER.

The Watch Oak in Windsor Great Park is said to be 800 years old and so called because the Duke of Cumberland (third son of George II), who defeated the Jacobites at Culloden in 1746, reportedly stationed a lookout in its branches during target practices to signal the accuracy of the cannon shots.

Windsor knot. A large loose knot in a tie, as sported in the 1950s by the Duke of Windsor. It is thus the full-blown version of the **Half Windsor** (*see above*).

Windsor Red. A commercial cheese made by mixing Cheddar cheese with red wine to give a marbled effect. It was launched in 1969.

Windsor soap. A translucent scented soap of a type ubiquitous in England in the 19th and early 20th centuries. It was usually brown.

Windsor tie. An American term for a broad bias-cut tie or scarf.

Windsor uniform. A uniform introduced by George III, consisting of a blue coat with red collar and cuffs, and a blue or white waistcoat. It is worn on certain occasions at Windsor Castle by members of the royal household and by guests by permission of the sovereign.

Windsor and Maidenhead. Originally, a borough created in 1974 by combining WINDSOR and MAIDENHEAD (it inherited the former's status as a ROYAL BOROUGH). Since 1998, a unitary authority formed from the northeastern part of Berkshire and a small slice of southern Buckinghamshire. It is 198 square km (76.5 miles) in extent, and its administrative headquarters are in Maidenhead.

Windsor of the North, the. A nickname sometimes applied to Alnwick Castle (*see under* ALNWICK).

Windy Gyle Probably 'windy ghyll', ModE *windy*, with OScand *gil* 'ravine'.

A hill (619 m / 2031 ft) in the Cheviot Hills, straddling the border, 7 km (4.5 miles) southwest of the CHEVIOT itself.

Windy Standard *Standard* possibly ME *standard* 'tree stump' or *standing* 'a place for shooting game'.

A hill (698 m / 2290 ft) in Dumfries and Galloway, 15 km (9 miles) east-southeast of DALMELLINGTON.

Wine City. *See under* GREENOCK.

Winfarthing 'Wina's quarter' (denoting ownership of a quarter of an estate), OE male personal name *Wina* + *feorthung* 'fourth part'.

A village in Norfolk, about 6 km (4 miles) north of Diss.

Winfrith Newburg *Winfrith* from the original name of the local river (now the Win), an OCelt river name meaning 'white or bright stream', OCelt *winn* 'white, bright' + *frud* 'stream'; *Newburgh* denoting manorial ownership in the Middle Ages by the Newburgh family.

A village in Dorset, about 13 km (8 miles) west of Wareham. A little to the north is **Winfrith Heath**, site of Winfrith Technology Centre. This was developed on the site of Winfrith Nuclear Research Station, opened in the late 1950s to test prototype reactors and decommissioned at the beginning of the 21st century.

Wing¹ Probably 'Wiwa's people's settlement', OE male personal name *Wiwa* + -*ingas* (*see* -ING); alternatively, the first element could represent OE *wig, weoh* '(heathen) temple'.

A village in Buckinghamshire, about 5 km (3 miles) southwest of Leighton Buzzard. It is notable for its 10th-century church, All Saints, with one of only eight Anglo-Saxon crypts remaining in England, and also for one of the few surviving medieval turf mazes in the country. MENTMORE is nearby.

Wing² 'field', OScand *vengi*.

A village in Rutland (before 1997 in Leicestershire, before 1974 in Rutland), about 6 km (4 miles) southeast of Oakham.

Win Green Earlier *Wingreen Hill*, but the origin of the name is obscure.

A hill in Wiltshire, approximately 5 km (3 miles) southeast of SHAFTESBURY. At 277 m (910 ft) it is the highest point of Cranborne Chase (*see under* CRANBORNE), and affords spectacular all-round views. It is crowned by a circle of trees.

Winnard's Perch Perhaps originally a humorous house name.

A village in Cornwall, about 11 km (7 miles) northeast of Newquay.

Winnats Pass *Winnats* 'pass through which the wind blows', OE *wind-geat* 'wind-gap'.

A pass between the craggy hills of the PEAK DISTRICT in Derbyshire, about 3 km (2 miles) just to the west of Castleton.

Winsford¹ 'Wine's ford', OE *Wines* possessive form of male personal name *Wine* + FORD.

A town in Cheshire, on the River WEAVER, about 13 km (8 miles) northwest of Crewe. Chemicals and salt are produced, and the town also serves as a dormitory for LIVERPOOL and MANCHESTER.

See also OVER².

Winsford². A village in Somerset, towards the southeastern part of EXMOOR, about 14 km (8.5 miles) southwest of Minehead. It is at the confluence of several rivers, including the EXE and the Winn (the name is a back-formation from *Winsford*), and it has seven bridges. A little to the west is **Winsford Hill** (428 m / 1405 ft).

The Labour politician Ernest Bevin (1881–1951) was born in Winsford.

Winterborne Came *Winterborne* from the name of the local river, 'winter stream' (denoting that it flows only or mainly in winter), OE *winter* + *burna* 'stream'; *Came* denoting manorial ownership in the Middle Ages by the abbey of St Stephen at *Caen* in Normandy.

A village in Dorset, about 2.5 km (1.5 miles) southeast of Dorchester.

Winterborne Herringston *Herringston* denoting manorial ownership (*see* -TON) in the Middle Ages by the Herring family.

A village in Dorset, about 2.5 km (1.5 miles) south of Dorchester.

Winterborne Zelston *Zelston* denoting manorial ownership (*see* -TON) in the Middle Ages by the de Seles family.

A village in Dorset, about 10 km (6 miles) south of Blandford Forum.

Winterbourne Abbas *Winterbourne see* WINTERBORNE CAME; *Abbas* denoting manorial ownership in the Middle Ages by the abbey of Cerne (*see* CERNE ABBAS).

A village in Dorset, about 8 km (5 miles) west of Dorchester.

Winterbourne Dauntsey *Winterbourne* from the former name (now *Bourne*) of the local river (*see* WINTERBORNE CAME); *Dauntsey* denoting manorial ownership in the Middle Ages by the Danteseye family.

A village in Wiltshire, about 6 km (4 miles) northeast of Salisbury.

Winterbourne Earls *Winterbourne see* WINTERBOURNE DAUNTSEY; *Earls* denoting manorial ownership in the Middle Ages by the earls of Salisbury.

A village in Wiltshire, about 5 km (3 miles) northeast of Salisbury.

Winterbourne Gunner *Winterbourne see* WINTERBOURNE DAUNTSEY; *Gunner* denoting manorial ownership in the Middle Ages by a lady called Gunnora.

A village in Wiltshire, about 6 km (4 miles) northeast of Salisbury.

Wintoncester. A fictionalized version of WINCHESTER in the novels of Thomas Hardy.

Winwæd. *See under* WENT.

Wirksworth 'Weorc's enclosure', OE *Weorces* possessive form of male personal name *Weorc* + worth (*see* -WORTH, WORTHY, -WARDINE).

A small town in Derbyshire, about 6 km (4 miles) southwest of Matlock. It is an old town, with steep terraces of stone houses, and it used to be an important centre for the mining of lead.

The town of **Snowfield** in George Eliot's *Adam Bede* (1859) is thought to have been based on Wirksworth.

> Wirksworth, a small rather hard-bitten town nestling between hills and quarries.
>
> Matthew Parris: *Chance Witness* (2002)

Wirral, the Probably 'nook of land where bog-myrtle grows', OE *wir* 'bog-myrtle' + *halh* 'nook of land' (*see* HALE, -HALL).

An oblong peninsula between the estuaries of the DEE² and the MERSEY, at the point where Wales meets England. Originally all in Cheshire, the northeastern part, on the south bank of the Mersey, was hived off in 1974 to become part of MERSEYSIDE, The Wirral becoming a metropolitan borough.

Industrial areas such as BIRKENHEAD, HESWALL and ELLESMERE PORT contrast strongly with the green countryside of the interior and the sandy beaches of resorts such as NEW BRIGHTON and WALLASEY.

The Wirral was made into a hunting forest in the 12th century by Ranulph le Meschin, 4th Earl of Chester, and remained a fairly wild place until well into the 15th century, with a reputation for harbouring outlaws (the anonymous author of the late 14th-century *Sir Gawain and the Green Knight* describes it as 'the wilderness of Wirral').

Wisbech Probably 'ridge by the marshy meadow', OE *wisse* 'marshy meadow' + *bæc* 'ridge'; alternatively, the first element might be *Wissey*, the name of a river in the vicinity, which is of OE origin and means 'marshy stream'.

A town (pronounced 'wizbeach') in Cambridgeshire, on the River NENE, about 19 km (12 miles) southwest of King's Lynn and 21 km (13 miles) south of the WASH. It was once only 6 km (4 miles) from the sea, and served as the port for PETERBOROUGH. Since then shifting river flows have pushed it further inland and, although it still functions as a port, its main role now is as the centre for the surrounding flower- and fruit-growing area: it specializes in Bramley apples and soft fruit such as strawberries, raspberries and blackberries. Fruit-canning is an important local industry.

Octavia Hill (1838–1912), co-founder of the National Trust, was born in Wisbech.

Wishaw¹ Possibly 'copse by river bend', OE *wiht* 'a river bend, winding valley' + *sceaga* 'copse'; the first element is disputed.

An industrial town 23 km (14 miles) southeast of Glasgow, in North Lanarkshire (formerly in Strathclyde). It was amalgamated with neighbouring MOTHERWELL in 1920. It was the birthplace of J.G. Lockhart (1794–1854), son-in-law and biographer of Sir Walter Scott.

Wishaw² Probably 'willow copse' or 'copse by a bend', OE *withig* 'willow' or *wiht* 'bend' + *sceaga* 'copse'.

A village in Warwickshire, about 5 km (3 miles) southeast of Sutton Coldfield and close to the M42. A little to the north is the BELFRY golf course.

Wisley 'clearing by a marshy meadow', OE *wisse* 'marshy meadow' + -LEY.

A village in Surrey, beside the River WEY¹, just outside the M25, about 5 km (3 miles) east of Woking. The (300 acre) **Wisley Gardens** were established by the Royal Horticultural Society in 1904. They have a wide variety of trees, shrubs and other plants, and also house the Society's research station.

Witch's Step, the An English translation of the Gaelic name *Ceum na Caillich*.

A deep nick in the rocky ridge east of Caisteal Abhail, ARRAN. It is also called **Carlin's Leap** (Scots *carlin* 'witch').

Witham A OCelt or pre-Celtic river name of uncertain meaning.

A river in Lincolnshire, which rises about 24 km (15 miles) south of Grantham and flows northwards through GRANTHAM and LINCOLN and then southeastwards through BOSTON into the WASH.

Withernsea 'lake by the thorn-tree', OE *with* 'towards' + *thorn* 'thorn-tree' + *sæ* 'lake'.

A small coastal town in HOLDERNESS, East Riding of Yorkshire (formerly in Humberside), 25 km (16 miles) east of Hull.

Withiel Florey *Withiel* 'glade where willows grow', OE *withig* 'willow' + -LEY; *Florey* denoting manorial ownership in the Middle Ages by the de Flury family.

A small village in Somerset, at the eastern edge of EXMOOR, about 11 km (7 miles) northwest of Wiveliscombe.

Withycombe Raleigh *Withycombe* 'valley where willows grow', OE *withig* 'willow' + *cumb* (*see* -COMBE, COOMBE); *Raleigh* denoting manorial ownership in the Middle Ages by the de Ralegh family.

A village (pronounced 'rawli') in Devon, now a northern suburb of EXMOUTH.

Witney 'Witta's island' (alluding to the high ground on which the town stands), OE *Wittan* possessive form of male personal name *Witta* + *eg* (*see* -EY, -EA). (The notion that the name derives from *white*, based on the town's blanket specialism and the fact that ModE *blanket* comes from Fr *blanc* 'white', is ingenious but false.)

A small market town in Oxfordshire, on the River WINDRUSH, at the eastern edge of the COTSWOLDS, about 16 km (10 miles) west of Oxford. With its access to Cotswold wool and plentiful water to power mills, it is not surprising that it became a world-famous centre for the making of blankets. Their manufacture goes back over 600 years and the name *Witney* became almost a generic term for the sort of heavy loose woollen cloth of which they are made, but, in an early example of name-protection, in 1909 a successful action was brought under the Merchandise Marks Act to limit the term to the products of Witney itself.

The town's old centre contains many handsome 17th- and 18th-century buildings in Cotswold stone, including the Old Blanket Hall (1720), with its curious one-handed clock, where the wool merchants used to meet.

Wittenham Clumps 'Witta's land in a river bend', *Wittan* possessive form of OE male personal name *Witta* + *hamm* 'land in a river bend' (*see* HAM), with ModE *clump*.

Two cone-shaped hills (Castle Hill and Round Hill), crowned with clumps of trees, about 7 km (4 miles) northeast of Didcot in Oxfordshire. Known officially as the **Sinodun Hills**, Wittenham Clumps were Iron Age hill-forts, possibly used by the Atrebati, an ancient British people living in the Thames Valley. They are now part of the Little Wittenham Nature Reserve. The view of the Clumps, rising prominently but unspectacularly from the Thames Valley, has inspired artists such as Paul Nash and Paul Kessling.

The villages of **Long Wittenham** and **Little Wittenham** are nearby.

Local nicknames for the Clumps include the 'Berkshire Bubs' (they were in Berkshire until 1974) and 'Mother Dunch's Buttocks' (after the wife of an unpopular local squire).

The startling discovery in 2003 of the chopped-up remains of an Iron Age woman at Castle Hill led archaeologists to speculate whether Wittenham Clumps were once a centre for human sacrifice.

> As up the hill with labr'ing steps we tread
> Where the twin Clumps their sheltering branches spread
> The summit gain'd, at ease reclining lay
> And all around the wide spread scene survey
> Point out each object and instructive tell
> The various changes that the land befel.
> Where the low bank the country wide surrounds
> That ancient earthwork form'd old Murcia's bounds.
>
> > Joseph Tubbs: poem carved on the 'poem tree' on Castle Hill, Wittenham Clumps, 1844

Wittering '(settlement of) Wither's people', OE male personal name *Wither* + *-ingas* (*see* -ING).

A village in Cambridgeshire, within the unitary authority of PETERBOROUGH (before 1974 in Huntingdonshire), about 5 km (3 miles) southeast of Stamford. Its main *raison d'être* is military aviation. In 1924 the RAF opened its Central Flying School here, and during the Second World War it was a base for Hurricanes and Spitfires. In 1953 Britain's first operational atomic bomb, codenamed 'Blue Danube', was delivered here, and from the late 1950s a huge V-bomber base was developed. Later Wittering became the home of the RAF's first Harrier jump-jets.

See also EAST WITTERING and WEST WITTERING.

Wiveliscombe Probably 'Wifel's valley' (alluding to the town's position in a valley between high hills), OE *Wifeles* possessive form of male personal name *Wifel* + *cumb* (*see* -COMBE, COOMBE); alternatively the first element could represent OE *wefil* 'weevil', denoting a beetle-infested valley.

A small town (pronounced as spelt, and locally also 'wilzkəm') in Somerset, in the Vale of Taunton Deane (*see under* TAUNTON), about 16 km (10 miles) west of Taunton.

Wivelsfield Probably 'Wifel's open land', OE *Wifeles* possessive form of male personal name *Wifel* + *feld* (*see* FIELD); alternatively the first element could represent OE *wefil* 'weevil', denoting open land infested with beetles.

A village in East Sussex, about 16 km (10 miles) north of Brighton. It is on the London-to-Brighton railway line, just north of BURGESS HILL, and is something of a commuter dormitory.

Wivenhoe 'Wife's hill-spur', OE *Wifan* possessive form of female personal name *Wife* + *hoh* 'hill-spur'.

A town in Essex, on the River COLNE[1], just to the southeast of Colchester. The local oysters, from the Colne estuary, have long had a high reputation.

The actress Joan Hickson (1906–98), Agatha Christie's Miss Marple in the BBC television series (1984–92), lived in Wivenhoe (as Joan Butler) for many years until her death.

> Wivenhoe … is at present a very pretty, clean town … There is a good sea-bath.
>
> > John Phillips: *A Treatise on Inland Navigation* (1785)

Wivenhoe Park. A mid-18th century house and park between Wivenhoe and Colchester. The park is now the home of the Essex University campus, whose 1960s tower blocks dominate the skyline.

Wix 'dwellings', ME *wikes* plural of *wike*, from OE *wic* 'dwelling, specialized farm' (*see* WICK).

A village in Essex, about 16 km (10 miles) northeast of Colchester.

Wixoe 'Widuc's hill-spur', OE *Widuces* possessive form of male personal name *Widuc* + *hoh* 'hill-spur'.

A village in Suffolk, about 16 km (10 miles) west of Sudbury.

Woburn 'winding stream', OE *woh* 'crooked' + *burna* 'stream'; *compare* WOOBURN.

A village (pronounced 'woe-' or 'woo-') in Bedfordshire, about 8 km (5 miles) southeast of Milton Keynes, just to the west of the M1.

Woburn Abbey. A palatial 18th-century mansion near Woburn, converted from a medieval abbey, which is the ancestral seat of the dukes of Bedford. It contains a notable collection of old masters and its extensive park was landscaped by Humphry Repton. The dukes have always been energetically innovative in their use of the house and grounds: in 1825, for example, a salicetum (a collection of willows) was planted here; at the beginning of the 20th century the 11th Duke established a herd of rare Père David's deer; and after the Second World War the 13th Duke was a pioneer in the commercial exploitation of stately homes, opening the house to the public and creating the **Woburn Safari Park**, the largest drive-through wildlife reserve in Britain.

Near Woburn Abbey is the Abbot's Oak, so called because the Abbot of Woburn was hanged on one of its branches in 1537, by order of Henry VIII.

Woburn Place and **Woburn Square** on the Bedford estate in BLOOMSBURY, London, take their names from Woburn Abbey.

Woking '(settlement of) Wocc(a)'s people', OE male personal name *Wocc* or *Wocca* + *-ingas* (*see* -ING).

A residential town in Surrey, about 10 km (6 miles) north of Guildford. Its expansion to its present size began with the coming of the railway line from Waterloo Station (*see under*

WATERLOO[1]) in the 1830s, and its major role now is as a commuter dormitory. Its most notable landmark is the onion-domed Shah Jehan Mosque, founded in 1889 by a Dr Leitner, a noted Orientalist. Its orientation towards Mecca was ascertained by a P&O captain with a naval compass.

The nearby Brookwood Cemetery, also dating from the late 19th century, is one of the world's largest. It was established to accommodate London's considerable overspill, and at one time had its own special railway service from Waterloo. Britain's first crematorium opened here in 1885.

In H.G. Wells's *The War of the Worlds* (1898) the Martians land in a sandpit on Horsell Common near Woking (Wells was living in the town when he wrote the book). In a letter Wells described with some relish his plans for the fictional destruction of the West Surrey bourgeoisie:

I completely wreck and sack Woking – killing my neighbours in painful and eccentric ways – then proceed via Kingston and Richmond to London, selecting South Kensington for feats of particular atrocity.

The television cook Delia Smith (b.1941) was born in Woking. The pop group The Jam was formed here in 1973.

There are some places which have always been dreadful ... Woking ... is one of them.

Bill Murphy: *Home Truths* (2000)

Wokingham 'Wocc's people's homestead', OE male personal name *Wocc* + *-inga-* (*see* -ING) + HAM.
A market town and unitary authority within Berkshire. It prospered modestly over the centuries, thanks to its bell-foundry and its silk manufacture, but did not grow to any great size. Then, after the Second World War, it was visited by planned expansion and had its own population explosion. When Berkshire was broken up into four independent unitary authorities in 1998, Wokingham was one of them.

Wolds, the From OE *wald* 'woodland', the word *wold* is now usually applied to areas of higher ground that have been cleared of forest; *see also* the COTSWOLDS and the WEALD.
An area of low, rolling, once wooded hills on the border between North Yorkshire and the East Riding of Yorkshire, starting some 30 km (19 miles) east of York and extending northeastwards towards the coast at Bridlington and FLAMBOROUGH HEAD. There is a **Wolds Way** long distance footpath. The Wolds are sometimes called the **Yorkshire Wolds** to distinguish them from the similar **Lincolnshire Wolds** to the south, also often referred to simply (but confusingly) as the Wolds.
Local author Winifred Holtby (1898–1935) described the Yorkshire Wolds thus:

Fold upon fold of the encircling hills, piled rich and golden.

Wolfpits 'pit(s) for trapping wolves', ME *wolf* + *pit*.

A tiny settlement in Powys (formerly in Radnorshire), some 3 km (2 miles) west of Old Radnor.

Wolf Rock Probably an allusion to either the fierce roar of the waves breaking on it or its reputation for 'devouring' ships.
A rocky islet off the southern tip of Cornwall, about 14 km (8.5 miles) southwest of LAND'S END. There is a lighthouse on it.

Wolf's Castle ME personal name and surname *Wolf*.
A village in Pembrokeshire (formerly in Dyfed), 10 km (6 miles) south of Fishguard.

Wolsingham 'Wulfsige's people's homestead', OE male personal name *Wulfsige* + *-inga-* (*see* -ING) + HAM.
A large village on the River WEAR in County Durham, 8 km (5 miles) east of Stanhope. It calls itself 'the Gateway to Weardale', and there is a steam railway linking it to STANHOPE.

Wolverhampton Originally *Hampton* 'high farmstead', OE *hean* dative form of *heah* 'high' + -TON; the initial element comes from OE *Wulfrun*, the name of the lady to whom King Æthelred II granted ownership of the manor in 985. (Despite conjecture, the name has nothing to do with *wolf*.)
A city and metropolitan borough within the WEST MIDLANDS (before 1974 in Staffordshire), about 22 km (14 miles) northwest of Birmingham. There was an abbey here in Anglo-Saxon times, and it was refounded in 994 by Wulfrun, a Mercian lady and sister of King Edgar, who owned the manor at the end of the 10th century and who gave Wolverhampton its name (*see above*). Her monastery does not survive, and her modern memorial is dedicated to Mammon rather than God: the Wulfrun Centre, a shopping precinct.

In the Middle Ages Wolverhampton was a prosperous wool-trading town. Then in the 18th century it became an iron-making centre. As the Industrial Revolution progressed, Wolverhampton grew and throve, and it became known as the 'Capital of the BLACK COUNTRY'. Times have been harder since, as a consequence of the decline in manufacturing industries. In the second half of the 20th century it attracted many immigrants from the Caribbean and South Asia. Formerly one of the largest towns in England, it was finally designated a city in 2000.

The other town-centre shopping mall, the Mander Centre, is named after a local entrepreneurial family, who also had Wightwick Manor (late 19th century) built to the west of the town. It is a good example of Arts and Crafts and William Morris designs, and is now in the possession of the National Trust.

Wolverhampton University was established in 1992, upgraded from the former Wolverhampton Polytechnic.

Wolverhampton Wanderers FC was founded in 1877. Their nickname, by which they are almost universally known, is **Wolves**. They play their home games at the Molyneux ground. Their greatest days were perhaps in the 1950s and 1960s, when they possessed players of the calibre of Billy Wright and Derek Dougan; success since then has been elusive.

The criminal and 'Thief-Taker General of England' Jonathan Wild (c.1682–1725), as celebrated in literature by Henry Fielding, the poet Alfred Noyes (1880–1958) and the singer Maggie Teyte (1888–1976) were born in Wolverhampton.

See also PENN[2] and WERGS.

Wulfrunian. An inhabitant of Wolverhampton (for etymology, *see above*). Former pupils of Wolverhampton Grammar School (founded 1512) are **Old Wulfrunians**.

Wolverton 'estate associated with Wulfhere', OE male personal name *Wulfhere* + -ING + -TON.

A town in Buckinghamshire, within the unitary authority of Milton Keynes, on the A5. In its modern form it was founded in 1838 as a railway town: it is halfway between London and Birmingham on the railway, and also on the GRAND UNION CANAL. Until recently the royal train was kept in a train shed here.

Wombleton 'Wynnbald's settlement', OE male personal name *Wynnbald* + -TON.

A village in North Yorkshire, 13 km (8 miles) west of Pickering, and some 300 km (186 miles) north of WIMBLEDON Common.

Wombwell 'spring in a hollow', OE *wamb* 'hollow' + *wella* 'spring' (or alternatively 'spring of Wamba', a male personal name).

A former mining town in South Yorkshire, 6 km (4 miles) southeast of Barnsley.

Wonastow 'holy place of St Gwnwarwy', Welsh saint's name + OE *stow* 'holy place'; Gwnwarwy is probably Welsh for Winwaloe, the 6th-century Breton saint commemorated in the names Landewednack and Gunwalloe in Cornwall.

A village in Monmouthshire (formerly in Gwent), 3 km (2 miles) southwest of Monmouth.

Wooburn Probably 'winding stream', OE *woh* 'crooked' + *burna* 'stream' (*see* WOBURN); a possible alternative is 'stream with a dam', with a first element from OE *wag* 'dam'.

A village in Buckinghamshire, about 3 km (2 miles) southwest of Beaconsfield.

Woodbine Woodbine is the wild honeysuckle with fragrant yellow flowers, *Lonicera periclymenum*.

A village in Pembrokeshire (formerly in Dyfed), 3 km (2 miles) south of Haverfordwest.

Woodbridge 'wooden bridge' or 'bridge near a wood', OE *wudu* 'wood' + *brycg* 'bridge'.

A market town in Suffolk, on the River DEBEN, about 11 km (7 miles) northwest of Ipswich. It used to be a thriving seaport. Now its main water traffic is pleasure yachts, but some elegant Georgian buildings attest to its former status. The SUTTON HOO treasure was discovered nearby in 1939. After the Second World War the surrounding area of Suffolk was rich in US Air Force bases, and Woodbridge's streets boasted as many well-sprung American limousines as anywhere in the UK. (*See also* RENDLESHAM.)

The poet George Crabbe (1754–1832) lived in Woodbridge in the 1770s as did Edward Fitzgerald (1809–83), translator of *The Rubáiyát of Omar Khayyám*, from 1860 until his death. (*See also* ALDEBURGH *and* BREDFIELD.)

Woodchester 'Roman camp in the wood', OE *wudu* 'wood' + *ceaster* (*see* CHESTER).

A village in Gloucestershire in the Nailsworth Valley, 3 km (2 miles) south of Stroud. Just to the north are the remains of a Roman villa. **Woodchester Park**, a secluded valley with a chain of five lakes, owned by the National Trust, lies to the southwest.

Woodford 'ford in or by the wood' (referring to a ford across the River RODING), OE *wudu* 'wood' + FORD.

A district of northeast London (E18), in the borough of REDBRIDGE, to the west of Epping Forest (*see under* EPPING). In the 18th and early 19th centuries it was a select area, scattered with the country houses of wealthy London merchants. Then, in 1856, the railway reached Woodford and suburbanization advanced on its tracks.

Winston Churchill was MP for Woodford from 1945 to 1964. There is an imposing statue of the great man in **Woodford Green**, the main central part of the district. The suffragette Sylvia Pankhurst lived here (mainly in Charteris Road) between 1924 and 1956. Woodford 'Underground' station, on the Central line, opened in 1947, as did **South Woodford**, the next station down the line.

Wood Green 'village green in or near woodland' (alluding to its original proximity to Enfield Chase), ME *wode* 'wood', with *grene* 'green'.

A district of North London (N22), in the borough of HARINGEY (of which it is the administrative centre), to the north of Hornsey. Its growth from a semi-rural hamlet to an Inner London suburb was precipitated by the arrival of the railway in 1859. It is now highly multicultural and multiracial. The application of the name to the district was consolidated by the opening of Wood Green Underground station, on the Piccadilly line, in 1932. Alexandra Palace (*see under* MUSWELL HILL[1]) was constructed, and its park laid out, at the western edge of Wood Green in 1873.

The first true self-service supermarket in Britain, in the food department of Marks & Spencer, opened in Wood Green in 1948. The district's love affair with retailing continued, and now it is dominated by the huge multi-outlet Shopping City, inaugurated by the Queen in 1981.

Woodhall Spa *Woodhall* 'hall in the wood' (perhaps referring to the place where a forest court met), OE *wudu* 'wood' + *hall*.

A town in Lincolnshire, on the edge of the FENS, about 24 km (15 miles) northwest of Boston. The second part of its name dates from the early 19th century, when a spring rich in iodine and bromine was discovered in an abandoned coalpit. The fashionable world made its way to Woodhall to imbibe, and has left its legacy in the form of some imposing Victorian and Edwardian villas (John Betjeman described the town as 'that unexpected Bournemouth-like settlement in the middle of Lincolnshire'). One of the houses, now a hotel, was taken over by the RAF in the Second World War as the officers' mess of 617 Squadron, the 'Dam Busters', based at nearby SCAMPTON.

In the Kinema, which opened in 1922, Woodhall Spa possesses one of the very few remaining cinemas in Britain in which the film is projected from behind the screen.

Woodham Ferrers *Woodham* 'homestead by a wood', OE *wudu* 'wood' + HAM; *Ferrers* denoting manorial ownership in the early Middle Ages by the de Ferrers family.

A village in Essex, about 1.5 km (1 mile) north of SOUTH WOODHAM FERRERS.

Woodham Mortimer *Mortimer* denoting manorial ownership in the Middle Ages by the Mortimer family.

A village in Essex, about 10 km (6 miles) east of Chelmsford.

Woodham Walter *Walter* denoting manorial ownership in the Middle Ages by the Fitzwalter family.

A village in Essex, about 10 km (6 miles) east of Chelmsford.

Wood Quay. An area on the south side of the River LIFFEY in DUBLIN. It was the site of a Viking fort, and subsequently developed in the Middle Ages as a centre of maritime trade. There were demonstrations by historians, archaeologists and others when building developments commenced on the site in the 1970s, continuing into the 1990s.

> It was old but it was beautiful
> And its structure was of wood,
> It was stratified by the Liffeyside
> Where the Viking fortress stood.
> These men of old were brave and bold
> And they shared out forefathers' blood,
> But we will fight for the Wood Quay site
> And the banks of Viking mud.
>
> Paddy Healy: 'The Ballad of Wood Quay'

Woodstock 'place in the woods', OE *wudu* 'wood' + *stoc* 'settlement' (*see* -STOCK, STOCK-, STOKE).

A market town in Oxfordshire, on the River Glyme, about 13 km (8 miles) northwest of Oxford. From Anglo-Saxon times it was a royal demesne and until the 17th century there was a royal residence here, latterly known as **Woodstock Manor**. Henry I kept his private zoo here, and Henry II is said to have set up his mistress Rosamund

Clifford ('The Fair Rosamund') here in a maze-like house where only he could find her (the story goes that his queen, Eleanor of Aquitaine, traced her whereabouts by following a thread and 'so dealt with her that she lived not long after'). Princess Elizabeth was held prisoner here by her sister Mary. The house, during the Civil Wars when it was a Royalist base, serves as the setting of Sir Walter Scott's *Woodstock; or, The Cavalier* (1826), a romantic tale revolving around the concealment of Charles II at Woodstock after his flight from the Battle of Worcester (*see under* WORCESTER). By the end of the Civil Wars the house was virtually destroyed. BLENHEIM PALACE now stands in what were its grounds.

The town is now a well-off commuter dormitory for Oxford and also a caravanserai for visitors to Blenheim. Its most notable hostelry is The Bear, an old coaching inn complete with its own stuffed bear.

There are towns called Woodstock in the USA (Illinois, New York, Vermont), Canada (New Brunswick) and Australia (Queensland). The best-known of them, a small town near Albany in New York state, gave its name to a huge rock festival held nearby in the summer of 1969. In 1994 a 25th anniversary restaging of the original event, commercially sponsored, attracted some 350,000 young (and not so young) people.

Edward of Woodstock. A byname of Edward the Black Prince (1330–76), who was born here.

Last Bus to Woodstock. The first (1975) in the series of detective novels by Colin Dexter featuring the Oxford-based Inspector Morse. In it Morse solves the murder of a young woman hitchhiker whose bludgeoned body is found in a pub car park in Woodstock. It was dramatized for television in 1988.

Woodstock Slop *Woodstock see* WOODSTOCK; *slop* 'gap in a hedge', Pembrokeshire dialect.

A village in Pembrokeshire (formerly in Dyfed), 13 km (8 miles) southeast of Fishguard.

Woofferton 'Wulfhere's or Wulffrith's farmstead', OE male personal names *Wulfhere* or *Wulffrith* + -TON.

A village in Shropshire, on the River TEME, about 5 km (3 miles) south of Ludlow.

Wookey 'trap or snare for animals' (perhaps referring to one set in Wookey Hole), OE *wocig*.

A village in Somerset, about 3 km (2 miles) west of Wells.

Wookey Hole. A large complex of caverns to the northeast of Wookey, carved by the River AXE[2] out of the southern limestone slopes of the MENDIP HILLS. The first three chambers contain many colourful stalactite and stalagmite formations, including, in the biggest, the Great Cave, a huge stalagmite known as the **Witch of Wookey**. With a generous measure of imagination this can be said to resemble the figure of the witch who is said to have lived in the cave in former times with her familiars, a goat and its kid (the caves were inhabited in the Iron Age and the early Roman period). Her legendary repulsiveness led to her directing her spells against 'the youth of either sex' as well as blasting every plant and blistering every flock. She was turned into a stone by a 'lerned wight' from Glastonbury but left her curse behind, since the girls of Wookey found (in the words of the ballad printed by Bishop Percy in his *Reliques of Ancient English Poetry*, 1765) 'that men are wondrous scant'. Another legendary denizen of the caves is a giant conger eel, about 10 m (30 ft) long, said to have got stuck here after chased in by angry fishermen whom it had deprived of their catch.

The nearby **Wookey Hole Paper Mill** is one of the oldest paper mills in Britain, dating from 1610.

Wool '(place by) the springs', OE *wiella* 'spring, stream'.
A village in Dorset, on the River FROME[3], about 8 km (5 miles) west of Wareham. In Thomas Hardy's *Tess of the D'Urbervilles* (1891) it is fictionalized as **Wellbridge**, an adaptation of the name of the local Jacobean manor house, Woolbridge Manor; and the name of the house's former owners the Turbervilles served as the model for *D'Urberville*.

Woolacombe 'valley with a stream', OE *wiella* 'spring, stream' + *cumb* (*see* -COMBE, COOMBE).
A seaside village in north Devon, about 6 km (4 miles) southwest of ILFRACOMBE, at the northern end of Morte Bay (*see under* MORTE POINT). To the south extends the wide expanse of **Woolacombe Sand**, launching pad for both swimmers and surfers.

Wooler 'ridge with a spring', OE *wella* 'spring' + *ofer* 'ridge'.
A small market town in Northumberland, at the northeast end of the CHEVIOT Hills, 24 km (15 miles) northwest of Alnwick. It is known locally as 'the Gateway to the Cheviots'.

Wooler is not overwhelmed with tourist attractions.
Nicholas Crane: *Two Degrees West* (1999)

Woolfardisworthy[1] 'Wulfheard's enclosure', OE *Wulfheardes* possessive form of male personal name *Wulfheard* + *worthig* (*see* -WORTH, WORTHY, -WARDINE).
A village (pronounced 'woolzery') in Devon, about 8 km (5 miles) north of Crediton.

Woolfardisworthy[2]. A fuller version of WOOLSERY.

Woolpack Corner Originally recorded (in 1545) as *Woolsack*, and probably from the name of a local inn called either The Woolsack or The Woolpack.
A hamlet in Kent, about 5 km (3 miles) northwest of Tenterden.

Wool Packs From their shape.
An outcrop of wind-sculpted rocks to the southeast of KINDER SCOUT, in the PEAK DISTRICT.

Woolpit 'pit for trapping wolves', OE *wulf-pytt*.
A village in Suffolk, about 14 km (8.5 miles) east of Bury St Edmunds.

Woolsery A reduced form of *Woolfardisworthy* (which is also still used).
A village in north Devon, about 16 km (10 miles) southwest of Bideford.

Woolsthorpe 'Wulfstan's outlying farmstead or hamlet', OE *Wulfstanes* possessive form of male personal name *Wulfstan* + OScand *thorp* (*see* THORPE).
A village in Lincolnshire, about 8 km (5 miles) west of Grantham. The mathematician and natural philosopher Isaac Newton (1642–1727) was born in Woolsthorpe, and it is said that it was while he was sitting under a tree in his mother's garden here in 1666 that the apple fell on his head which led to the train of thought that resulted in his formulation of the law of gravitation. The story originated with the French writer and philosopher Voltaire, who said that he got it from Mrs Conduit, Newton's niece.

Wooltack Point *Wooltack* 'overgrown spur of land', OE *wild* 'wild, overgrown' + *hoc* 'spur of land'.
The rocky headland marking the southern side of the entrance to St Bride's Bay on the west coast of Pembrokeshire (formerly in Dyfed), 15 km (9 miles) west of Milford Haven. It faces Skomer Island.

Woolton 'Wulfa's farm or estate', OE male personal name *Wulfas* + -TON.
A southeastern suburb of LIVERPOOL. Former Beatle John Lennon (1940–80) grew up here in 'Mendips', Menlove Avenue, the relatively comfortable home of his Aunt Mimi. The house is now cared for by the National Trust. Not far away, in ALLERTON, the Trust also administers Paul McCartney's parents' old house. It was supposedly after performing at St Peter's Church in Woolton, in 1957, that Lennon asked McCartney to join The Quarry Men, i.e. the embryonic Beatles.
See also The DINGLE *and* SPEKE.

Woolwich 'trading centre or harbour for wool', OE *wull* 'wool' + *wic* (*see* WICK).
A district (pronounced 'wool-idge' or 'wool-itch') in southeast London (SE18), in the borough of GREENWICH (formerly in Kent), on the south bank of the THAMES[1] opposite London City Airport (*see under* LONDON), between THAMESMEAD to the east and CHARLTON to the west. There is evidence of settlement here from Roman times, and by the Anglo-Saxon period that valuable commodity wool was evidently being traded through Woolwich. By the 14th century at the latest it had been established as the site of a cross-Thames ferry; the present **Woolwich Free Ferry** made its debut in 1889. (In the 20th century *woolwich ferry*

enjoyed some currency in London as rhyming slang for *sherry*, not exactly the regular tipple of the rhyming classes.) In 1512 Henry VIII opened a royal dockyard in Woolwich to build his new flagship, the *Great Harry*; several other ships were constructed here, but it was closed down in 1869.

By then, however, the character of Woolwich had been firmly determined as military rather than naval: an establishment for the manufacture and testing of guns and other weapons was in operation here in Tudor times, and in the early 18th century the main government weapons factory moved here from MOORFIELDS. It was originally called the Warren, but George III renamed it the Royal Arsenal in 1805. It is more generally known as **Woolwich Arsenal** (which is also the name of a local mainline railway station). It continued to produce munitions for the British armed forces until after the Second World War and, although it is now inactive and much of its site has been turned over to housing, many of its fine 18th- and early 19th-century buildings (by, among others, Vanbrugh and Wyatt) can still be seen. In 1721 the Royal Military Academy (known to its inmates as 'the Shop') was established in Woolwich (in 1947 it moved to SANDHURST), and the Royal Artillery Barracks are here.

In 1886 a soccer club was founded here called Royal Arsenal. In 1913 it moved its home north of the Thames to HIGHBURY, where it became somewhat better known under the name ARSENAL.

The **Thames Barrier** (*see under* THAMES¹), part of London's flood defences, lies across the River Thames at **Woolwich Reach**.

Thanks to innovative advertising campaigns and a memorable slogan ('We're with the Woolwich!') which has been going since the 1970s, the main connotation of the name *Woolwich* for most English-speakers at the beginning of the 21st century is the Woolwich Building Society (founded in 1847; since 1997 a bank under the name Woolwich plc; and now part of Barclays Bank plc).

On the north bank of the Thames opposite Woolwich is a small area called **North Woolwich** (E16). The name is not recorded until 1847, when a railway station was opened here, but the place is a relic of a 900-year-old Kentish enclave on the Essex coast – presumably where the ferry operated from.

Of the suffragan bishops of Woolwich the best-known have been John Robinson (1919–83), whose controversial *Honest to God* (1963) galvanized radical theological discussion in the 1960s, and the former England cricket captain David Sheppard (1929–2005).

Charles George Gordon (General Gordon) (1833–85) was born in Woolwich.

woolwich and greenwich. Rhyming slang for *spinach*.

Woolwich infant. A facetious 19th-century slang name for a type of heavy artillery piece.

Woore '(place by the) swaying tree', OE *wœfre* 'unstable'. A village in Shropshire, about 11 km (7 miles) northeast of Market Drayton.

Wootton Bassett *Wootton* 'farmstead in or near a wood', OE *wudu* 'wood' + -TON; *Bassett* denoting manorial ownership in the Middle Ages by the Basset family. A small hilltop town in Wiltshire, about 8 km (5 miles) west of Swindon and just to the south of the M4.

Wootton Courtenay *Courtenay* denoting manorial ownership in the Middle Ages by the Courtenay family. A village in Somerset, in the northern part of EXMOOR, about 5 km (3 miles) southwest of Minehead.

Wootton Fitzpaine *Fitzpaine* denoting manorial ownership in the Middle Ages by the Fitz Payn family. A village in Dorset, about 5 km (3 miles) northeast of Lyme Regis.

Wootton Pillinge *Pillinge* probably 'Peola's people's settlement', OE male personal name *Peola* + -*ingas* (*see* -ING); the *Wootton* was added much later, in the 16th century. A former hamlet in Bedfordshire, on the site of which STEWARTBY was built.

Wootton Wawen *Wawen* denoting manorial ownership in the early Middle Ages by a man called Wagen (OScand *Vagn*). A village (pronounced 'warn') in Warwickshire, about 11 km (7 miles) northwest of Stratford-upon-Avon. Its church is of Anglo-Saxon origin.

Worbarrow Tout *Worbarrow* 'look-out hill', OE *weard* 'watch, look-out' + *beorg* 'hill'; *Tout* 'look-out hill' (added tautologically after the meaning of *Worbarrow* had become forgotten), OE *tote*. A headland on the Dorset coast, about 16 km (10 miles) west of Swanage. To the west is **Worbarrow Bay**.

Worcester 'Roman town of the Weogora tribe', *Weogora* a pre-English folk name (perhaps from an OCelt river name meaning 'winding river') + OE *ceaster* (*see* CHESTER). A cathedral city (pronounced 'wooster') in WORCESTERSHIRE (before 1998 in Hereford and Worcester, before 1974 in Worcestershire), on the River SEVERN, about 40 km (25 miles) southwest of Birmingham. It is the county's administrative centre.

It was the river that drew the Romans to the place (their name for the city was probably *Vertis*), and there has been a settlement here ever since. The original cathedral church was built here around 680, but the present imposing edifice dates from the 1080s. **Worcester Cathedral** contains the tombs of King John and of Prince Arthur, Henry VIII's elder brother. Its sandstone bulk (with heavy Victorian restorations) dominates the city, not least as seen from the cricket ground, headquarters of Worcestershire County Cricket Club and one of the most visually appealing of all English grounds. The propensity of the Severn to burst its banks in the winter often finds graphic illustration in an underwater cricket pitch.

Worcester suffered considerably during the Civil Wars. Strongly Royalist in sympathies, it was the first English city to declare for the King and the last to surrender in 1646. Charles II had his headquarters here in 1651. (*See also* **Battle of Worcester** *below*).

Worcester's early prosperity was based on the manufacture of fine cloth, and by the middle of the 17th century it was the 12th largest town in England, but business declined in the early 18th century. A local citizen called Dr Wall had an idea to revive the city's economy: in 1751 he opened a porcelain factory to produce copies of the best Oriental and Continental wares, and also its own original designs. Two and a half centuries later **Royal Worcester** porcelain (the royal imprimatur was bestowed by George III) has a worldwide reputation.

Edward Elgar's father kept a music shop in Worcester, and the city was close to the composer's heart throughout his life. There is now a statue of him near the cathedral and there are invariably performances of his works at the Three Choirs Festival, for which the city rotates as host with Gloucester and Hereford.

Postwar city-centre development (dubbed locally the **'Sack of Worcester'**) has had a more than usually deleterious effect on the built environment.

The Bishop of Worcester signs himself 'Wigorn'.

The novelist Mrs Henry Wood (1814–87) was born in Worcester, as was the music-hall singer and comedienne Vesta Tilley (1864–1952; real name Matilda Powles). Many of the novels and stories of Francis Brett Young (1884–1954) are set in the neighbourhood of the city.

There are a city and county called Worcester in Massachusetts, USA, another county of that name in Maryland, and a town called Worcester in South Africa.

Battle of Worcester (3 September 1651). The final battle of the English Civil Wars, in which the numerically superior armies of Oliver Cromwell decisively defeated and effectively wiped out Charles II's forces. After the battle Charles made a romantically dramatic escape to France, which at one point is said to have involved hiding himself in an oak tree (*see under* BOSCOBEL HOUSE).

Berrow's Worcester Journal. A newspaper that bills itself as the 'oldest continually published newspaper in the world'. The British Library describes it as Britian's 'oldest surviving non-official newspaper'. Its origins were in 1690, but it began publishing regularly from 1709, when it was known as the *Worcester Post-Man*. It changed its name first to *The Worcester Journal*, and subsequently (in 1753)

to *Berrow's Worcester Journal* after the then-owner (this move being an attempt to distinguish it from an audacious competitor also calling itself *The Worcester Journal*). For much of its history it was filled with national and even international news, but today it is a free newspaper about things local.

Florence of Worcester. A monk and annalist (d.1118) whose *Chronicon ex chronicis* is a valuable source for late Anglo-Saxon and early post-Conquest English history. Sadly, in recent years it has been discovered that his real name was probably the (to modern ears) less sensational John.

Treaty of Worcester. A treaty concluded at Worcester in 1218 in which the Welsh prince Llywelyn ab Iorwerth was officially recognized as the 11-year-old Henry III's lieutenant in Wales and given the royal castles of CARMARTHEN and CARDIGAN. The agreement soon broke down.

Worcesterberry. A small black North American variety of gooseberry. It was once believed to be a hybrid of the blackcurrant and the gooseberry, and was sold as such by a Worcester nurseryman called Richard Smith – hence the name.

Worcester College. A college of Oxford University (*see under* OXFORD), established in 1714 on the site of and incorporating the buildings of Gloucester Hall, which had been founded in 1283 as Gloucester College. Funds for the foundation were provided by Sir Thomas Cookes, a Worcestershire baronet – hence the name. Alumni include Thomas de Quincey and Rupert Murdoch.

Worcester pearmain. A type of red-skinned eating apple introduced to cultivation about 1875 by Richard Smith, a Worcester nurseryman. In everyday parlance it is nowadays usually called simply a 'Worcester'.

Worcester sauce. *See under* WORCESTERSHIRE.

Worcester woman. A hypothetical psephological woman, identified in the run-up to the 2001 British general election as a 30-something school-run mother from a reasonably well-off part of southern England, married to a plumber or an electrician, and likely to buy the children computer games for Christmas. She had voted Labour (perhaps for the first time) in 1997, but was now having second thoughts, so the two main political parties courted her assiduously. Worcester was a Labour seat vulnerable to such vacillations (the city had reverted to Conservative control in the local-government elections of May 2000) – hence the name.

Worcester Park From *Worcester* House, residence of the Earl of Worcester who in 1606 was appointed keeper of NONSUCH PARK in Cheam.

A district partly in the London borough of SUTTON[1] and partly in EWELL, Surrey, between CHEAM to the southeast and NEW MALDEN to the northwest.

Holman Hunt executed his famous painting *The Light of the World* (1854) in Worcester Park, with John Everett Millais as the model for Christ.

The railway arrived in Worcester Park in 1865, and it was the signal for the start of steady development and expansion that by the middle of the 20th century had covered most of the area in concrete and bricks.

Worcestershire From WORCESTER + SHIRE. The name *Worcestershire* is first recorded in the 11th century.

A county in the southwest MIDLANDS of England. It is bounded to the east by Warwickshire, to the south by Gloucestershire, to the west by Herefordshire and Shropshire and to the north by the West Midlands. In 1974 it was combined with Herefordshire in a new county called HEREFORD AND WORCESTER, at the same time losing a northern industrial segment, including DUDLEY, HALESOWEN and STOURBRIDGE, to the West Midlands. However, this arrangement proved satisfactory to neither party, and in 1998 Hereford and Worcester were separated, with Worcestershire resuming its former county status. Its county town is Worcester, and other main centres are BROMSGROVE, DROITWICH, GREAT MALVERN, KIDDERMINSTER, REDDITCH and STOURPORT-ON-SEVERN. Its chief rivers are the AVON[1] and the SEVERN.

Worcestershire is chiefly agricultural (the Vale of Evesham (*see under* EVESHAM) being a notable fruit-growing area), but with a swathe of industry in the north, where it is contiguous with the West Midlands. Along its western boundary lie the MALVERN HILLS.

Dark Age Worcestershire was part of the territory of the Anglo-Saxon dynasty of the Hwicce, five generations of whose kings ruled an area corresponding to the diocese of Worcester in the 7th and 8th centuries AD. The kingdom of MERCIA controlled the area thereafter.

In cricketing terms Worcestershire is a 'first-class' county. Worcestershire County Cricket Club was founded at the Star Hotel, Worcester, on 11 March 1865 and has played in the county championship since 1899, winning the competition on five occasions. In the past, touring sides played the first game of their tour of England against Worcestershire at the County Ground at New Road, WORCESTER (spring showers permitting), but the tradition has now lapsed.

Worcestershire Beacon. A hill a little to the west of GREAT MALVERN, which at 425 m (1394 ft) is the highest point in the MALVERN HILLS.

Worcestershire sauce. A proprietary liquid condiment (more usually called simply 'Worcester sauce') sold in small bottles with a distinctive orange label. The recipe for it – vinegar, molasses, garlic, shallots, tamarinds and assorted spices – was devised by a Worcestershire man, Sir Marcus Sandys, an Indian Army veteran with time on his hands. He took it along to the Worcester grocers Lea and Perrins and got them to make up a large quantity. They made much more than he could use, and a lot got left in storage. When they came to examine it a few years later, they found it had benefited from the maturation and in 1838 they decided to put it on the market. It remains in popular use today for adding a certain pungency to stews, sauces, vinaigrettes, etc. and as an essential ingredient in Bloody Marys.

Worcs. The standard written abbreviation of WORCESTERSHIRE.

Worgret 'gallows', OE *wearg-rod*.

A village in Dorset, about 1.5 km (1 mile) southwest of Wareham.

Workington 'Weorc's village', OE male personal name *Weorc* + -ING + -TON.

A port and former mining town on the west coast of Cumbria (formerly in Cumberland), at the mouth of the River DERWENT[1], 10 km (6 miles) north of Whitehaven. Mary Queen of Scots landed here when she fled Scotland for good in 1568 after her defeat at LANGSIDE. A wild and rule-less form of football called Uppies and Downies is played in the town every year.

Workington is an industrial suburb of Harare, in Zimbabwe.

Worksop 'Weorc's valley', OE *Weorces* possessive form of male personal name *Weorc* + *hop* 'enclosed valley'.

An industrial town in Nottinghamshire, on the edge of the former Nottinghamshire coalfield and at the northern end of SHERWOOD FOREST, about 24 km (15 miles) southeast of Sheffield. It claims to be the 'capital' of the DUKERIES.

The church of the former priory survives, with a very long Norman nave and a 20th-century east end.

See also RHODESIA.

World's End[1] Presumably from its location on a boundary or its remoteness, although the latter is relative.

A hill (492 m / 1614 ft) on the border between Denbighshire and Wrexham unitary authority (formerly in Clwyd), 7 km (4.5 miles) north of Llangollen.

World's End[2] A suggestion of remoteness.

There are villages of this name in Berkshire, about 10 km (6 miles) north of Newbury; West Sussex, now a northeastern district of BURGESS HILL; Hampshire, about 4 km (2.5 miles) southwest of Hambledon; Suffolk, about 6 km (4 miles) southwest of Stowmarket; and Buckinghamshire, about 1.5 km (1 mile) northwest of Wendover (and disconcertingly close to CHEQUERS).

The name has also been given to a southeastern suburb of BIRMINGHAM and a district of the London borough of ENFIELD (N21). Perhaps its best-known application is to a district of CHELSEA (SW10), in the London borough of

KENSINGTON AND CHELSEA, at the western end of the KING'S ROAD: a notable local landmark here is a pub of the same name.

Worle Probably 'glade frequented by wood-grouse', OE *wor* 'wood-grouse' + -LEY.

A village in North Somerset (before 1996 in Avon, before 1974 in Somerset), now a northeastern suburb of WESTON SUPER MARE.

Worm, the. *See* WORMS HEAD.

Wormegay 'Wyrma's people's island' (referring to an area of high ground), OE male personal name *Wyrma* + *-inga-* (*see* -ING) + *eg* (*see* -EY, -EA).

A village in Norfolk, about 10 km (6 miles) southeast of King's Lynn.

Worminghall 'Wyrma's nook of land', OE personal name *Wyrma* + *halh* (*see* HALE, -HALL).

A village in Buckinghamshire, 7 km (4 miles) northeast of Thame.

See also the SHIRE.

Wormleighton 'Wilma's herb garden', OE male personal name *Wilma* + *leac-tun* 'herb garden'.

A village in Warwickshire, close to the Northamptonshire border, about 17 km (11 miles) southeast of Warwick.

Worm's Ditch. Another name for BLACK PIG'S DYKE.

Worms Head OE *wyrm* 'snake, worm, serpent', from its resemblance to the back of a sea serpent or dragon; the blow-hole at the western end of the Worm completes the picture. Two steep, sharp rocky islets forming the most westerly section of the GOWER PENINSULA, in Swansea unitary authority (formerly in Glamorgan, then West Glamorgan), some 3 km (2 miles) west of the village of Rhossili. The feature is also called **the Worm**, and in Welsh it is **Ynysweryn** ('cattle-worm island'). It is accessible for two and a half hours either side of low tide. Among those who have mis-calculated and found themselves cut off on the Worm was Dylan Thomas, who had to keep himself warm for many hours by running about and clapping his hands. He characterized the terrain leading to the Head as 'rubbery, gull-limed grass, the sheep-pilled stones, the pieces of bones and feathers'.

Wormshill Probably 'Woden's hill', OE *Wodnes* possessive form of *Woden*, name of the Anglo-Saxons' war-god + *hyll* 'hill'; alternatively, 'shelter for a herd of pigs', OE *weorn* 'band, herd' + (*ge*)*sell* 'animal shelter' (often applied to pig pasturage).

A village in Kent, about 11 km (7 miles) east of Maidstone.

Wormwood Scrubs *Wormwood* originally *Wormholt* 'snake-infested wood', OE *wyrm* 'snake' + *holt* 'wood'; *Scrubs* '(area of) low stunted trees and brushwood', ModE *scrub*.

A large open space in West London (W12), in the borough of HAMMERSMITH AND FULHAM, just to the north of the A40 (WESTWAY), between WHITE CITY to the south and WILLESDEN to the north.

By far its best-known feature is its eponymous prison, built between 1874 and 1890 by prison labour. Situated next to Hammersmith Hospital, it is the largest prison in Britain, able to accommodate over 1000 inmates. To habitués it is always simply **'the Scrubs'** (a name first recorded in the 1910s); and Scrubs Lane is a road not far to the east.

Worsbrough 'Wyrc's stronghold', OE male personal name + *burh* (*see* BURY).

An area on the south side of Barnsley, South Yorkshire.

Worstead 'site of an enclosure, farmstead', OE *worth* (*see* -WORTH, WORTHY, -WARDINE) + *stede* 'place'.

A village (pronounced 'wurstid' or, like the cloth, 'woostid') in Norfolk, about 19 km (12 miles) northeast of Norwich, which has given the English language one of its main cloth names. In the Middle Ages it was a thriving industrial town, the prosperity it derived from cloth-making being reflected in its fine late 14th-century church. Another tangible reminder of those days is the term *worsted*, which denotes a smooth closely woven woollen cloth without a nap, made from tightly twisted yarn, of a type originally manufactured in Worstead (the slightly nuanced spelling finally won out over *worstead* in the 19th century after hundreds of years

---

❖ -worth, worthy, -wardine ❖

The root meaning of these elements is 'an enclosure'. The most common is *worth*, with dozens of examples scattered all over England: from WARKWORTH (Northumberland), through CUDWORTH, HAWORTH and DODWORTH (all in Yorkshire) and FARNWORTH, FAILSWORTH and Saddleworth (*see under* SADDLE-WORTH MOOR) (all in Greater Manchester), into the Midlands, with HUSBANDS BOSWORTH and KEGWORTH (all in Leicester-shire), MOLESWORTH (Cambridgeshire), NAILSWORTH (Gloucester-shire), RICKMANSWORTH (Hertfordshire), down to London, with WANDSWORTH and ISLEWORTH, and thence to the south with LULWORTH (Dorset) and PETWORTH (West Sussex).

There are fewer *worthy* names then *worth* names: TAMWORTH (originally *Tamworthy*) in Staffordshire, MARTYR WORTHY (Hamp-shire) and CLATWORTHY (Somerset) are examples. The *-wardine* names are restricted to the West Midlands and the Anglo–Welsh border: Hawarden (Flintshire) at the western edge, STANWARDINE IN THE FIELDS (Shropshire) and Breadwardine (Worcestershire) represent these.

orthographic chaos, including such forms as (influenced by *wool*) *woolsted* and, in Scotland and northern England, *worset* and *wusset*).

Worthing '(settlement of) Weorth's people', OE male personal name *Weorth* + *-ingas* (*see* -ING).

A town and seaside resort on the West Sussex coast, about 16 km (10 miles) west of Brighton. Until the middle of the 18th century it was a tiny fishing hamlet, but then the enthusiasts for the new sea-bathing began to discover it. It got a great boost in 1798 when George III sent his youngest daughter here. Speculative builders moved in, and over the 19th century Worthing became what it essentially still is today, a more genteel and respectable (but not strait-laced) version of Brighton. It is also a bastion of the COSTA GERIATRICA, with a high proportion of elderly residents.

Worth Matravers *Worth* 'enclosure' (*see* -WORTH, WORTHY, -WARDINE), OE; *Matravers see* LANGTON MATRAVERS.

A village in Dorset, on the Isle of PURBECK, about 5 km (3 miles) west of Swanage and 1 km (0.6 miles) from the sea. The second part of the name is pronounced 'mətravəz'. In the past it was one of the main quarry villages for the extraction of Purbeck marble. It was also a smuggling centre.

On the nearby clifftop is a singular mid-12th-century chapel erected, according to legend, by a local man whose daughter and son-in-law had been drowned at sea. Its corners are at the four points of the compass, and so it is the only chapel in England with no east wall.

Wotter 'wood tor', OE *wudu* 'wood' + *tor*.

A village in Devon, on the southwestern edge of DART-MOOR, about 14 km (8.5 miles) southeast of Tavistock.

Wotton-under-Edge *Wotton see* WOOTTON BASSETT; -*under-Edge* referring to its location at the foot of the Cotswold escarpment.

A small town in Gloucestershire, on the western edge of the COTSWOLDS, about 10 km (6 miles) southwest of Nailsworth.

Wrabness 'Wrabba's headland', OE male personal name *Wrabba* + *næss* 'headland' (*see* NESS).

A village in Essex, on the south bank of the estuary of the River STOUR[2], about 8 km (5 miles) west of Harwich.

Wrangle 'crooked place' (perhaps referring to a crooked stream), OE *wrængel* or OScand *vrengill*.

A village in Lincolnshire, about 13 km (8 miles) northeast of Boston and 3 km (2 miles) from the coast.

Wrangway 'crooked road', OE *wrang* 'crooked' + *weg* 'road'.

A village in Somerset, about 3 km (2 miles) south of Wellington and just to the south of the M5.

Wraxall¹ 'nook of land frequented by buzzards or other birds of prey', OE *wrocc* 'buzzard or other bird of prey' + *halh* (*see* HALE, -HALL).

A village in North Somerset (before 1996 in Avon, before 1974 in Somerset), about 11 km (7 miles) west of Bristol. A much-turreted Gothic Revival mansion, Tyntesfield, was built here in the mid-19th century for the merchant William Gibbs, and was acquired, with its 200-ha (500-acre) garden, by the National Trust in 2002.

Wraxall². A village in Somerset, about 11 km (7 miles) east of Glastonbury.

Wraysbury 'Wigred's stronghold', *Wigredes* possessive form of OE male personal name *Wigred* + *burh* (*see* BURY).

A village in Berkshire, within the unitary authority of WINDSOR AND MAIDENHEAD, about 2.5 km (1.5 miles) north of Egham.

The local Ankerwyke yew is about 2500 years old. Overlooking the Thames near RUNNYMEDE, it was standing when King John signed Magna Carta in 1215. Henry VIII is said to have wooed Anne Boleyn beneath its boughs in the 1530s.

Wreake An OScand river name meaning 'twisted, winding'.

A river in Leicestershire, which rises to the east of MELTON MOWBRAY and flows 29 km (18 miiles) through Melton Mowbray and FRISBY ON THE WREAKE to join the River SOAR to the northeast of LEICESTER.

Wrecsam. The Welsh name for WREXHAM¹.

Wrekin, the An OCelt name which was also the source of VIRICONIUM.

A hill in Shropshire, about 407 m (1334 ft) high, 8 km (5 miles) west of TELFORD. It is an isolated lump of volcanic lava about 900 million years old. On its summit, from which on a clear day 17 counties can be seen, is an Iron Age hillfort, whose defenders, the Cornovii, were the last British tribe to hold out against the Romans (the Romans resettled them at nearby VIRICONIUM).

Wrekin College, at WELLINGTON[2], is a co-educational public school founded in 1880.

> On Wenlock Edge the wood's in trouble;
> His forest fleece the Wrekin heaves.
>
> A.E. Housman: *A Shropshire Lad* (1896)

See also TELFORD AND WREKIN.

Wrexham¹ 'water meadow of Wryhtel', OE personal name *Wryhtel* + HAM. The identity of Wryhtel is unknown.

A market and industrial town in WREXHAM[2] unitary authority, of which it is the administrative centre. In Welsh it is spelt **Wrecsam**. The town was formerly in Denbighshire, then in Clwyd, and is 18 km (11 miles) south of Chester.

The 16th-century Gothic Church of St Giles in Wrexham has a five-tiered tower topped by a steeple (1520), which was listed among the SEVEN WONDERS OF NORTH WALES; it is 41 m (135 ft) high. The tower is copied at Yale

University in the USA, and Elihu Yale (1648–1721), its founder, is buried in the churchyard of St Giles.

Thomas Pennant (1726–98), the traveller and zoologist, was educated at Wrexham School before going to Oxford, and the distinguished archaeologist Dame Kathleen Kenyon (1906–78) died in Wrexham. In 1990 Wrexham suffered an earthquake measuring 5.1 on the Richter Scale. It is the seat of the Roman Catholic bishopric of Menevia (Wales); see ST DAVID'S.

Wrexham². A unitary authority created in 1996 from the Wrexham Mealor district of Clywd, itself created in 1974. It is bordered by Cheshire to the east, Flintshire to the north, Denbighshire and Powys to the west and Shropshire to the south. The administrative seat is the town of WREXHAM¹.

Wreyland Probably 'newly cultivated land on the river Wray', ModE *land* with river name *Wray*, of unknown origin and meaning.

The name once given to a very small area (the **Manor of Wreyland**) within the picturesque village of LUSTLEIGH in east Devon. Wreyland's chief claim to fame is in the title of Cecil Torr's *Small Talk at Wreyland* (1918), an account of everyday life in the 19th and early 20th centuries in Wreyland and in the surrounding areas, based partly on the diaries of the author's father and grandfather. Research had been carried out by Torr using the original Latin texts pertaining to the old Manor of Wreyland, which his family is said to have owned.

Wrington 'farmstead on the Wring', *Wring* an earlier or alternative name (perhaps meaning 'winding stream') for the River Yeo + -TON.

A village in North Somerset (before 1996 in Avon, before 1974 in Somerset), on the River YEO¹, about 16 km (10 miles) east of Weston super Mare. The philosopher John Locke (1632–1704) was born here.

Wroughton 'farm on the River Worf', OCelt river-name meaning 'winding stream' (the river is now called the River Ray) + -TON.

A village in Swindon unitary authority, formerly in Wiltshire, 5 km (3 miles) south of Swindon city centre. It has been identified as the site of the Battle of Ellendun (825), in which King Egbert of WESSEX defeated Beornwulf of MERCIA. Many historians regard the battle as marking the shift from Mercian to West Saxon dominance of England.

Wroxeter 'Roman fort at or near Viriconium', VIRICONIUM + OE *ceaster* (see CHESTER).

A village in Shropshire, on the ancient highway of WATLING STREET¹ and close to the River SEVERN, about 8 km (5 miles) southeast of Shrewsbury. It is almost on the site of the Roman town of **Viriconium**, the remains of which were excavated from the 1860s onwards.

Wrynose Pass Wrynose is probably 'twisted headland', OE *wreo* 'twisted' + *nes* (see NESS).

A high road pass (390 m / 1281 ft) in the LAKE DISTRICT, linking Little LANGDALE with the head of the DUDDON valley. Like the HARD KNOTT PASS to its west, which carries the road on over to Eskdale, it is notorious for its hairpin bends and 1-in-3 gradients. At the summit of the Wrynose Pass is the **Three Shire Stone**, marking the spot where the boundaries of the old counties of Cumberland, Westmorland and Lancashire met. The Three Shires pub in Little Langdale greets and fortifies those who have made the strenuous passage of the pass from the west.

Wychavon Coined from an 'Old Englyshe' spelling of -*wich* (as in DROITWICH) + AVON¹.

An administrative district of Worcestershire (before 1998 of Hereford and Worcester), created in 1974 in the eastern part of the county (containing Droitwich and the River Avon).

Wychwood 'wood of the Hwicce' (an Anglo-Saxon people who occupied a region approximately covered by present-day Gloucestershire, Worcestershire and western Warwickshire), OE *Hwicce* + *wudu* 'wood'.

An ancient forest on the borders of Gloucestershire, Oxfordshire and Warwickshire, at the eastern edge of the territory of the Hwicce people. In the Middle Ages it was a favourite royal hunting ground. Fragments of it, watered by the River EVENLODE², remain to the east of SHIPTON-UNDER-WYCHWOOD.

> And fostering in thy lap a heap of flowers
> Pluck'd in shy fields and distant Wychwood bowers.
>
> Matthew Arnold: 'The Scholar-Gipsy' (1853)

Wycombe As in HIGH WYCOMBE and WEST WYCOMBE.

An administrative district of southern Buckinghamshire.

Wyddial 'nook of land where willows grow', OE *withig* 'willow' + *halh* (see HALE, -HALL).

A village (pronounced 'widgəl' or 'widyəl') in Hertfordshire, about 14 km (8.5 miles) east of Letchworth.

Wye¹ An Indo-European name from a root meaning 'water'.

The sixth-longest river in Britain, some 215 km (133 miles) long. It is largely in Wales and in Welsh it is called **Gwy**. It rises on the slopes of PLYNLIMON just inside Ceredigion before flowing generally southeastwards through Powys, past RHAYADER and BUILTH WELLS, before turning eastwards through HAY-ON-WYE and into Herefordshire, where it flows through the city of HEREFORD, then turns south through ROSS-ON-WYE and cuts a meandering gorge past the FOREST OF DEAN and SYMONDS YAT. It then briefly re-enters Wales, passing through MONMOUTH. Between Monmouth and the sea it forms the Anglo-Welsh border, and flows by TINTERN ABBEY and CHEPSTOW. Just below

Chepstow it enters the SEVERN estuary at the original Severn Road Bridge.

> All the water in Wye cannot wash your Majesty's Welsh plood out of your pody, I can tell you that.
>> William Shakespeare: Fluellen addressing the king in *Henry V* (1599), IV.vii

William Wordsworth visited the Wye valley in 1793, and again in 1798, famously commemorating the latter visit:

> Five years have passed; five summers, with the length
> Of five long winters! and again I hear
> These waters, rolling from their mountain-springs
> With a sweet inland murmur ...
> How oft, in spirit, have I turned to thee,
> O sylvan Wye! Thou wanderer through the woods,
> How oft has my spirit turned to thee!
>> William Wordsworth: 'Lines written a few miles above Tintern Abbey, on revisiting the banks of the Wye during a tour, July 13, 1798'

The shoemaker-poet Robert Bloomfield (1766–1823) toured the Wye valley in 1807, and in 1811 published *The Banks of Wye*.

There are rivers called Wye in Canada (Ontario) and the USA (Maryland).

Wye² *See* WYE¹.

A river in the PEAK DISTRICT of Derbyshire, which rises to the east of BUXTON and flows 28 km (18 miles) eastwards and southeastwards through BAKEWELL to join the River DERWENT⁴.

Wye³ A back-formation from *Wycombe* (as in WEST WYCOMBE). It is said to have been coined in the early 19th century by cadets of the Royal Military College at Great Marlow when map-making.

A river in Buckinghamshire, which rises in West Wycombe and flows 14.5 km (9 miles) southeastwards through HIGH WYCOMBE into the THAMES¹ near BOURNE END.

Wye⁴ 'heathen temple', OE *wig*.

A small town in Kent, in the NORTH DOWNS, on the River STOUR³, about 5 km (3 miles) northeast of Ashford. **Wye College**, now an agricultural and horticultural college affiliated to the University of London, originated as a college of priests founded by the Archbishop of Canterbury in 1447.

The dramatist Aphra Behn (1640–89) was born in Wye.

Wyke 'dwelling, specialized farm', OE *wic* (*see* WICK).

A village in Surrey, about 2.5 km (1.5 miles) east of Aldershot. It is pronounced to rhyme with 'like'.

Wyke, The. A village in Shropshire, about 8 km (5 miles) southeast of Telford. It is pronounced as for WYKE.

Wyke Champflower *Champflower* probably denoting manorial ownership in the Middle Ages by the Champfleur family.

A village in Somerset, about 5 km (3 miles) west of Bruton. It has a tiny early 17th-century church attached to the manor house.

Wyke Regis *Regis* 'of the king', Latin (denoting manorial ownership in the Middle Ages by the Crown).

A village in Dorset, opposite the southeastern end of CHESIL BEACH, now a southwestern district of WEYMOUTH.

Wylfa Head Welsh *gwylfa* 'look-out place, observation post'.

A headland on the north coast of Anglesey (formerly in Gwynedd), some 9 km (5.5 miles) west of Almwech. It is dominated by the giant box of Wylfa nuclear power station, whose managers have tried to mitigate its brooding presence by providing nature trails and a picnic and play area.

Wylye¹ A pre-English river name of uncertain origin; it may mean 'tricky stream', although it has no etymological connection with ModE *wily*.

A river (pronounced 'wily') in Wiltshire, which rises about 4 km (2.5 miles) west of KINGSTON DEVERILL and flows 35 km (22 miles) northeastwards and then southeastwards along the southwestern edge of Salisbury Plain to join the River NADDER just to the west of SALISBURY.

Izaak Walton, author of *The Compleat Angler* (1653), delighted to fish in the **Wylye Valley**, and John Constable painted here in the early 19th century.

Wylye² From WYLYE¹.

A village in Wiltshire, in the **Wylye Valley**, about 16 km (10 miles) northwest of Salisbury. Its 17th-century houses are characterized by attractive flint-and-stone chequerwork.

Wymeswold 'Wigmund's forest', OE *Wigmundes* possessive form of male personal name *Wigmund* + *wald* 'forest'.

A village in Leicestershire, about 8 km (5 miles) northeast of Loughborough. It was probably the partial inspiration for *Lymeswold*, the invented name given to a newly developed variety of French-style English soft cheese with restrained blue veining that was put on the market in 1982. The cheese, which was actually made in Cheshire, never really achieved commercial lift-off and was quietly withdrawn in the early 1990s.

Wymondham 'Wigmund's homestead', OE male personal name *Wigmund* + HAM.

A market town (pronounced 'windəm') in Norfolk, about 14 km (8.5 miles) southwest of Norwich. It was almost completely destroyed by fire in 1615. Among the few surviving pre-fire buildings are The Green Dragon, one of the oldest inns in England, and the Abbey Church (established as a priory in 1107), which is unusual in having a tower at each end: in the middle of the 14th century there was a bitter dispute over its ownership between the townspeople and the monks; the Pope awarded one half to each, and in due course the townspeople built their own new tower at their end. New (post-fire) is the octagonal half-timbered market cross, which was once used as a courthouse.

Robert Kett, leader of Kett's Rebellion in 1549 (*see* MOUSEHOLD HEATH), was a landowner in Wymondham.

Wynford Eagle *Wynford* an OCelt river name, 'white or bright stream', *winn* 'white, bright' + *frud* 'stream'; *Eagle* denoting manorial ownership in the Middle Ages by the del Egle family.

A hamlet in Dorset, about 11 km (7 miles) northeast of Bridport.

Wyre An OCelt or pre-Celtic river name probably related to WEAR.

A river in northwest Lancashire, length 45 km (28 miles). It rises east of LANCASTER and flows generally southwestwards to enter a long estuary that meets the sea at FLEETWOOD.

Wyre Forest *Wyre* perhaps from an OCelt or pre-Celtic river name meaning 'winding river'.

An area of woodland on the Shropshire–Worcestershire border, immediately to the west of BEWDLEY. Once a mighty forest, it now covers about 23 sq km (9 sq miles). Dowles Brook flows through it and the River SEVERN is at its eastern edge.

Wyre Forest is now also the name of a local parliamentary constituency (roughly corresponding to the old KIDDERMINSTER constituency) and of an administrative district of Worcestershire.

Wyre Piddle *Wyre* probably from WYRE FOREST; *Piddle* from the local Piddle Brook, from OE *pidele* 'marsh, fen' (*compare* PIDDLE).

A village in Worcestershire (before 1998 in Hereford and Worcester, before 1974 in Worcestershire), on the River AVON[1], about 3 km (2 miles) northeast of Pershore. *See also* NORTH PIDDLE.

Wysg. The Welsh name for the River USK[1].

Wytham 'homestead in a river bend' (referring to the nearby curve of the River Thames), OE *wiht* 'curve' + HAM.

A village (pronounced 'wy-təm') in Oxfordshire (before 1974 in Berkshire), close to the River Thames, about 8 km (5 miles) northwest of Oxford. It is owned by Oxford University (*see below*).

Wytham Abbey, built in the late 15th century on the site of a Saxon nunnery, was formerly the seat of the Earls of Abingdon.

Wytham Woods. A beautiful and ecologically important area of ancient semi-natural woodland, grassland and experimental farmland to the west of Wytham, encompassed by a loop of the River THAMES[1] and rising from the Thames floodplain to a height of 165 m (541 ft) at the top of **Wytham Hill**. The Wytham estate was given to Oxford University in 1943 by its last owner, Raymond ffennell, and the Woods are now managed by the university for ecological research. The Woods' sizeable badger population is believed to be the most studied in the world, and great tits, wood mice and bank voles are also closely monitored. Wytham Woods feature in Colin Dexter's Inspector Morse novel *The Way Through the Woods* (1993, dramatized for television 1995). Members of the public may walk in Wytham Woods with a permit from the University. *See also* 'Berkshire Tragedy' *under* BERKSHIRE.

XYZ

XMG. The abbreviation used by British soldiers serving in Northern Ireland, during the Troubles, for the Republican stronghold of CROSSMAGLEN.

Yar A back-formation from YARMOUTH[1].
A river towards the western end of the ISLE OF WIGHT, at the mouth of which stands Yarmouth. It is 4.8 km (3 miles) long.

Yard, the. *See* SCOTLAND YARD.

Yardley 'copse where rods are cut', OE *gyrd* 'rod, spar' + -LEY.
An eastern lower-middle-class/skilled-working-class suburb of BIRMINGHAM. Yardley is also one of Birmingham's parliamentary constituencies, within whose boundaries Birmingham Airport and the National Exhibition Centre are situated.

Yardley Gobion *Gobion* denoting manorial ownership in the early Middle Ages by the Gubyun family.
A village in Northamptonshire, on the GRAND UNION CANAL (served by **Yardley Wharf**) and just to the east of WATLING STREET[1], about 11 km (7 miles) northwest of Milton Keynes.
See also HIGHAM GOBION.

Yardley Hastings *Hastings* denoting manorial ownership in the early Middle Ages by the de Hastinges family.
A village in Northamptonshire, about 13 km (8 miles) southeast of Northampton.
Yardley Chase. An area of woodland and open land to the southwest of Yardley Hastings.

Yare An OCelt river name, probably meaning 'babbling stream'.
A river in Norfolk, which rises to the northwest of WYMONDHAM and flows 80 km (50 miles) eastwards through NORWICH (where it is joined by the River WENSUM) to the BROADS, where it feeds into BREYDON WATER. At the eastern end of this, having absorbed the waters of the BURE and the WAVENEY[1], it turns southwards through GREAT YARMOUTH and enters the North Sea at Gorleston.

Yarmouth[1] 'gravelly or muddy estuary', OE *earen* 'gravelly, muddy' + *mutha* 'mouth, estuary'.

A town and port on the northwestern coast of the ISLE OF WIGHT, on the eastern side of the mouth of the River YAR. It was the island's first purpose-built port. It was destroyed by French invaders in 1377, but after Henry VIII had **Yarmouth Castle** (now a ruin) built for its protection it began to prosper again. A ferry service plies to and from LYMINGTON.

Not to be confused with GREAT YARMOUTH on the Norfolk coast.

Yarmouth[2]. *See* GREAT YARMOUTH.

Yarrow Water 'rough river', OCelt *garw*; *Gierwa c.*1120.
A river in the Ettrick Forest (*see under* ETTRICK WATER) in Scottish Borders; length 38 km (24 miles). It rises above ST MARY'S LOCH, flows through the small settlements of **Yarrow Feus**, and joins the Ettrick Water just above Selkirk, near the site of the Battle of PHILIPHAUGH (1645), before the merged rivers join the TWEED a little below the town. John Ireland (*c.*1435–*c.*1500), chaplain to James III and James IV and the author of *The Meroure of Wyssdome* (1490), the first notable work of Scots prose, was rector of Yarrow, and Mungo Park (1771–1806), the explorer of the River Niger, was born at Foulshiels in the valley. Sir Walter Scott refers to Yarrow, 'Where erst the outlaw drew his arrow', in *Marmion* (1808), and set the framing narrative of *The Lay of the Last Minstrel* (1805) in Newark Castle, which remains as an impressive ruin in the lower part of the valley.

There is an old folk tale in which the Yarrow blacksmith's apprentice is troubled by a witch, who every night comes to his bed, slips a bridle on him and rides him to her coven. One night the apprentice's older brother takes his place, succeeds in swapping places with the witch and takes her to the smithy to be shod. The next day the witch is found with horseshoes on each of her hands and feet.

'Dowie Houms o' Yarrow, The' ('the doleful banks of Yarrow'). A traditional ballad from the time of the bloody Border reivers (raiders). It tells of the death of a knight who takes on nine men on 'yon high, high hill'. He is found by his beloved:

> She kiss'd his cheek, she kam'd his hair,
>   As oft she did before, O,
> She drank the red blood frae him ran,
>   On the dowie houms o' Yarrow.

Flower of Yarrow, the. Mary of Dryhope (Dryhope Tower is in the Yarrow valley), carried off by Wat Scott of Harden. The affair is the subject of a Border ballad, and she is referred to in Scott's *Marmion*:

> Then gaze on Dryhope's ruin'd tower,
> And think on Yarrow's faded Flower.

> Sir Walter Scott: *Marmion* (1808), Introduction to Canto II

'Rare Willie Drowned in Yarrow'. Yet another doleful Border ballad set in the Yarrow valley:

> She sought him east, she sought him west,
>   She sought him braid and narrow;
> Sine, in the lifting of a craig,
>   She found him drown'd in Yarrow.

> (Scots *sine* 'then')

'Yarrow Unvisited'. The first of three poems by William Wordsworth celebrating the river and its valley. On his tour with his sister Dorothy in 1803 he eagerly anticipated visiting the valley of the Yarrow, but never made it. Thus 'Yarrow Unvisited' looks forward to a future visit:

> Should life be dull, and spirits low,
> 'Twill soothe us in our sorrow
> That earth hath something yet to show,
> The bonny Holms of Yarrow!

Another eleven years passed before he was able to write **'Yarrow Visited'**, in which, among other things, he speculates as to the location of the death of the knight in the old ballad (*see above*). On this visit – which lived up to expectations – the poet was accompanied by his wife, son and sister-in-law. The party was guided by the local poet James Hogg, the 'Ettrick Shepherd':

> And is this – Yarrow? – *This* the Stream
> Of which my fancy cherish'd,
> So faithfully, a waking dream?

The third poem, **'Yarrow Revisited'**, was written after a visit in 1831, accompanied by his daughter and Sir Walter Scott.

Yarsop 'Eadred's remote valley', OE male personal name *Eadred* + *hop* 'remote valley'.

A village in Herefordshire (before 1998 in Hereford and Worcester, before 1974 in Herefordshire), about 13 km (8 miles) northwest of Hereford.

Yate '(place at the) gate or gap', OE *geat*.

A town in South Gloucestershire (before 1996 in Avon, before 1974 in Gloucestershire), about 16 km (10 miles) northeast of Bristol. It was once a village, but in the 1960s it was turned into an overspill town for Bristol. Uninspiring identikit housing estates sprawled over the countryside, and the obligatory concrete shopping centre was built. At one point its suicide rate was the highest in Western Europe.

Yazor 'Iago's ridge', Welsh male personal name *Iago* + OE *ofer* 'ridge'.

A village in Herefordshire (before 1998 in Hereford and Worcester, before 1974 in Herefordshire), about 1 km (0.6 miles) southwest of Yarsop.

Y Bont-Faen. The Welsh name for COWBRIDGE.

Y Drennewydd. The Welsh name for NEWTOWN[1].

Yeading 'settlement of Geddi's people', OE personal name + *-ingas* (*see* -ING).

A district of West London, in the borough of HILLINGDON (before 1965 in Middlesex), between the district of Hillingdon itself (to the west) and Greenford (to the east). It is pronounced 'Yedding'.

Yeadon 'steep hill', OE *gæh* 'steep' + *dun* (*see* DOWN, -DON).

A town in West Yorkshire, 12 km (7.5 miles) northwest of Leeds. Leeds Bradford International Airport is located on the eastern side of the town. It is pronounced 'yeedən'.

There is a Yeadon in the USA, a suburb of Philadelphia.

Piss Willie of Yeadon. A person who, before the Second World War, would take his cart round the town collecting people's urine (taking their 'piss') for the local woollen mill. The urine was fermented to ammonia, and used for bleaching the fat out of wool and in dyeing processes (*see also* RAVENSCAR).

Yealmpton 'farmstead on the River Yealm', OCelt or pre-Celtic river name of uncertain meaning + -TON.

A village in south Devon, on the River Yealm, about 10 km (6 miles) southeast of Plymouth. It was the reputed home of Old Mother Hubbard, the nursery-rhyme character created by Sarah Martin at nearby Kitley in 1805: a small thatched cottage here is claimed to have belonged to the real Mother Hubbard, a housekeeper.

Yeats Country. *See under* SLIGO.

Yell Possibly OScand *geldr* 'dry, barren' (the island is mostly bleak peat moorland).

A large island in northern SHETLAND, between Mainland and UNST. It is separated from the northeast coast of Mainland by **Yell Sound**, which is some 6 km (4 miles) across. The main settlement is **Mid Yell**, on **Mid Yell Voe** halfway up the east coast. On 20 July 1881, 58 Yell fishermen were lost at sea in a terrible storm.

> Grain o' wind now, boys, and the auld boat
> In through its blasts like a greyh'und courses
> Doon the tricky tideways o' Yell Soond, fu'
> O' sunshine noo – on white horses!

> Hugh MacDiarmid: 'Off the Coast of Fiedeland',
> from *A Kiss of Whistles* (1947)

Yellow Ford From the Irish name *Béal an Átha Bhuí* 'mouth of the yellow ford' (*see* FORD), apparently so named from the sandy river bed here.

A battle site close to the River BLACKWATER³, County Armagh, some 5 km (3 miles) north of Armagh itself. Here, on 14 August 1598 Hugh O'Neill, Earl of Tyrone, defeated a large English force under Henry Bagenal, en route to relieve the Blackwater Fort. Bagenal and hundreds of other English troops were killed. O'Neill's victory led to the saying among English soldiers waiting to embark for Ireland and contemplating desertion: 'Better hang at home than die like a dog in Ireland.' The battle is also known as the Battle of the Blackwater.

Yelverton Originally *Elleford* 'elder-tree ford', OE *ellen* 'elder-tree' + FORD; the suffix -TON is first recorded in the 18th century. The modern *Y*-spelling, reflecting local pronunciation, was introduced by the Great Western Railway in 1859.

A small town in Devon, at the southwestern edge of DART-MOOR, about 8 km (5 miles) southeast of Tavistock. It boasts a Paperweight Centre.

> We've a nice little place here at Yelverton
> And although it's a bit chilly in winter
> There's plenty of room on the moor for the kiddies
> And we have nice little outings to Princetown.
>
> Charles Causley (1917–2003): 'Yelverton'

Buckland Abbey (*see under* BUCKLAND MONACHORUM) is a little to the west.

Yeo¹ See YEOVIL.

A river (pronounced 'yo') in Somerset, which rises just over the Dorset border, about 5 km (3 miles) southeast of CREW-KERNE, and flows 39 km (24 miles) northwards (for some of its distance forming the Somerset–Dorset border) through YEOVIL and YEOVILTON and then westwards to join the River PARRETT near HUISH EPISCOPI.

Yeo² An OE river name perhaps meaning 'yew-stream'. Its form has been influenced by OE *ea* 'river' (*see* EA-).

A river in Somerset and North Somerset, which rises in the MENDIP HILLS and flows 32 km (20 miles) northwards through CONGRESBURY (from which its gets its alternative name, the **Congresbury Yeo**, distinguishing it from the YEO¹) into the SEVERN estuary between CLEVEDON and WESTON SUPER MARE.

Yeovil '(place on the) River Gifl or Ivel' (referring to YEO¹), OCelt river name *Gifl* meaning 'forked river'. The English form of the name was influenced by OE *ea* 'river' (see EA-).

A market town in eastern Somerset, on the River YEO¹, about 34 km (21 miles) southeast of Taunton. It services a rich agricultural area, processing dairy products and turning skins into leather, and for 300 years its particular specialization was the making of gloves. In the second half of the 20th century, however, it turned to industry and it became home to Westland Aircraft, the largest helicopter manufacturer in Europe.

Paddy Ashdown, the former leader of the Liberal Democrats, was MP for Yeovil from 1983 to 2001.

Yeovilton 'farmstead on the River Gifl or Ivel', *Gifl* (*see* YEOVIL) + -TON.

A village in Somerset, on the River YEO¹, about 6 km (4 miles) north of Yeovil. Its air base is the historic home of the Fleet Air Arm (its museum is here), from which the Navy currently operates helicopters and Sea Harrier units.

Yes Tor 'eagle's hill', OE *earnes* possessive form of *earn* 'eagle' + *torr* 'tor, hill'.

A high granite outcrop towards the northern edge of DART-MOOR in Devon, about 5 km (3 miles) south of OKEHAMP-TON. At 619 m (2030 ft) it is the second highest point on the Moor after nearby HIGH WILLHAYS.

Yetholm. *See* KIRK YETHOLM.

Yetminster 'Eata's church', OE male personal name *Eata* + *mynster* 'large church, monastery'.

A village in Dorset, about 6 km (4 miles) southeast of Yeovil.

The Yetties, a folk group formed in the 1960s, drew its members from here and nearby RYME INTRINSECA.

Yetts o' Muckhart 'gates of Muckhart', *Yetts* 'gate', Scots (probably referring to the tollhouse established here in the early 19th century); *Muckhart*, the local parish, meaning 'pig enclosure', Gaelic *muc* 'pig' + OScand *garthr* 'enclosure'.

A small settlement in Clackmannanshire, 11 km (7 miles) west of Kinross. It is at an important junction at the mouth of Glen Devon (*see under* DEVON²). Just to the south is the hamlet of **Pool of Muckhart**.

Y Fali. The Welsh name for VALLEY.

Y Fenni. The colloquial Welsh name for ABERGAVENNY.

Y Gelli. The Welsh name for HAY-ON-WYE.

Yidsbury. An offensive nickname applied in the 1970s to FINSBURY because of its large Jewish population.

Y Mynydd Du. The Welsh name for the BLACK MOUNTAIN.

Ynys Dewi. The Welsh name for RAMSEY ISLAND.

Ynys Enlli. The Welsh name for BARDSEY ISLAND.

Ynys Gybi. The Welsh name for HOLY ISLAND².

Ynys Môn. The Welsh name for ANGLESEY.

Ynys Seiriol. The Welsh name for PUFFIN ISLAND.

Ynysweryn. The Welsh name for WORMS HEAD.

York First recorded by Ptolemy in c.AD 150 as *Eborakon* 'place of yew-trees' or 'estate of a man called *Eburos*', an early British personal name that also means 'yew-tree'. Ptolemy's *Eborakon* was latinized by the Romans as *Eboracum*, anglicized by the Anglo-Saxons to *Eoforwic* 'wild boar town' and Scandinavianized by the Vikings to *Jorvik*. The Normans turned this into *Yerk* or *Yarke*, and by the 13th century *York* was established. A city and unitary authority on the River OUSE², formerly in YORKSHIRE (of which it was the county town) then in North Yorkshire. It is 36 km (22 miles) northeast of Leeds. The unitary authority, created in 1996, takes in a small area of surrounding countryside. The **University of York** was established in 1963.

Before the Romans arrived, the Brigantes had a settlement here. In AD 71 the Romans built on the site the provincial capital of **Eboracum**, which became the base for the northern campaigns of Hadrian. The Emperor Septimus Severus died in the city in AD 211, as did the Emperor Constantine Chlorus in 306, whereupon his son Constantine the Great was proclaimed emperor. The Romans withdrew in 407, but their influence lives on: the Archbishop of York still signs himself 'Ebor'.

After the Roman withdrawal in 407, York was known to the Saxons as **Eoforwic**. The Roman missionary Paulinus established the diocese of York in 625 and in 627 baptized King Edwin of Northumbria here. The metropolitan diocese of York, comprising the 14 dioceses of northern England, was founded in 735. At this time York was a famous centre of learning, and Charlemagne summoned Alcuin, head of St Peter's School in York, to set up a school at his capital Aix-la-Chapelle (Aachen).

York fell in 867 to the Danes, who called it **Jorvik** and developed it as a trading centre. The last Viking king of York, Eric Bloodaxe, was killed by the English at Stainmore in 954 (*see under* STAINMORE PASS). In 1066 at FULFORD INGS in York, King Harald Hardrada of Norway defeated the English, only to be defeated shortly afterwards by Harold of England at STAMFORD BRIDGE.

At the time of the Norman Conquest, York was the biggest city in England after London, with an estimated population of 8000. In the Middle Ages it continued to develop as a trading city, exporting wool to the towns of the Hanseatic League in northern Europe. However, as ships grew larger the Ouse was unable to accommodate them and the trade declined. York nevertheless maintained its importance as the centre of an archdiocese, and the English kings also held parliaments here and used the city as a base for campaigns against the Scots. In the 15th century Richard, Duke of York founded the **House of York** (*see below*), although after the Battle of Wakefield in 1460 (*see under* WAKEFIELD) he ended up dead with his head displayed on York's city walls, wearing a paper crown.

At the height of the Pilgrimage of Grace, the failed rebellion against Henry VIII's religious reforms, the rebels took over York, but after the rebellion was suppressed in 1537 their leader Robert Aske was executed in the city. In the same year the Council of the North, which implemented

Henry's Reformation in northern England, was established with its headquarters in York. During the Civil Wars the city was held by the Royalists until it fell in 1644 after the nearby Battle of MARSTON MOOR. In the 18th century York became a fashionable place to live:

> There is abundance of good company here, and abundance of good families live here, for the sake of the good company and cheap living; a man converses here with all the world as effectually as at London ...
>
> Daniel Defoe: *A Tour Through the Whole Island of Great Britain* (1724–6)

In the 19th century the city began to change somewhat in character, becoming more industrial, in particular developing as a railway centre. The Quaker family of Rowntree also founded their chocolate-making business here (and it was in York that B. Seebohm Rowntree carried out his pioneering studies of poverty in 1897–8).

York's long and colourful history is matched by its physical fabric. Visible from miles around is **York Minster**, the largest medieval cathedral in England (hence, according to George Borrow, the Romany name for York, BORI-CON-GRIKEN GAVE 'great church town'). The Minster was built 1220–1480, and badly damaged by fire in 1984 but since restored (in its honour **York City FC** are nicknamed the Minstermen). On closer inspection the visitor will marvel at the virtually complete city walls, the half-timbered medieval streets such as the SHAMBLES and the Georgian terraces along the Ouse and elsewhere. All that remains of York's castle is Clifford's Tower, where, during anti-Semitic riots in 1190, York's Jewish community burnt themselves alive rather than fall into the hands of the mob. York also has the Jorvik Viking Centre (with authentic smells), the Castle Museum and the National Railway Museum.

All this attracts some three million tourists to the city every year. Some of these visitors come in search of less substantial manifestations of heritage, for York has been officially declared by the Ghost Research Foundation to be the Most Haunted City in Europe. Among York's spectres are Mad Alice, executed in 1825 for the then capital offence of dangerous insanity; the Grey Lady, the wraith of a lady bricked up after an illicit love affair; and a cohort of Roman legionaries, only visible from the knee up (the old Roman road ran 40 cm / 16 in below the floor of the cellar where they have been seen). There has been some attrition, however: the ghost of a Second World War US pilot that used to haunt The Golden Fleece pub returned to the States with an American tourist in 1994, and now haunts her home in Quincy, California.

In February 2004 York's Asda store at Monk's Cross became the first British supermarket to hold a wedding ceremony. The couple had met at a checkout.

The Catholic conspirator Guy Fawkes (1570–1606) was

born in York; he went to St Peter's School, which does not celebrate on 5 November. York was also the birthplace of the neo-classical sculptor John Flaxman (1755–1826); of William Etty (1787–1849), painter of female nudes (many in York's City Art Gallery); of the poet W.H. Auden (1907–73); and of Daniel Defoe's Robinson Crusoe. Dick Turpin, the highwayman, was hanged here (on the KNAVE'S MIRE in 1739); his legendary ride from London to York on Black Bess was probably based on a spectacular ride completed in 15 hours by another highwayman, John Nevison, in 1676.

There are cities called York in Australia (Western Australia) and the USA (Montana, North Dakota, Nebraska, Pennsylvania, South Carolina). The Cape York Peninsula is the northeasternmost part of Australia, with Cape York at its tip. In Canada there is a York Factory (Manitoba), York Harbour (Newfoundland), Point York (Labrador) and a York River (Quebec). The York Mountains are in Alaska. Yorktown in Virginia, USA, is where in 1781 British forces under Lord Cornwallis finally surrendered to the Americans under George Washington, so effectively ending the American War of Independence. The city of New York, USA, was so named in honour of James, **Duke of York** (*see below*), after the English captured it from the Dutch in 1664; it was previously known as New Amsterdam. There are somewhat smaller New Yorks in Tyne and Wear and Lincolnshire, not to mention the diminutive NEWYORK in Argyll.

Archbishop of York. The 'Metropolitan' of the northern province of the Church of England. The archbishopric was established in 735 and the first archbishop was Egbert. The Archbishop of York is styled 'Primate of England'; the primacy of the Archbishop of Canterbury over that of York was only established by Pope Innocent VI (1352–62), and now Canterbury is styled 'Primate of All England'.

Duke of York. The title traditionally borne by the monarch's second son. Prince Andrew has held the title since 1986 (his then not insubstantial wife, Sarah, being dubbed by the tabloids 'the Duchess of Pork'); George VI held the title until his elder brother, Edward VIII, abdicated; James II was Duke of York while his brother Charles II was still alive. (*See also* **Grand Old Duke of York** *below*.)

Elizabeth of York. English queen consort (1465–1503), the daughter of Edward IV, who married Henry VII in 1486, so uniting the houses of York and Lancaster.

Glory of York, the. An alternative name for the Ribston pippin (*see under* RIBSTON PARK).

'Grand Old Duke of York, The'. A nursery rhyme commemorating the inconclusive British expedition to Flanders in 1794–5, during the French Revolutionary Wars. The duke in question was the commander of the expeditionary force, Frederick Augustus, Duke of York and Albany

(1763–1827), second son of George III, who became Commander-in-Chief in 1798.

> The grand old Duke of York
> He had ten thousand men,
> He marched them up to the top of the hill
> And he marched them down again.

In fact, this being Flanders, there was no hill, the Duke was barely over 30 and his army was 30,000 strong. In other versions of the rhyme the Duke is 'rare' or 'noble'. He is commemorated in the Duke of York's Column (completed 1833), between Waterloo Place and the Mall, London.

House of York. A dynasty founded by Richard, Duke of York (1411–60), a descendant of John of Gaunt's brother. Richard rebelled against Henry VI of the House of LANCASTER, so starting the War of the Roses between Yorkists and Lancastrians (whose badges were white and red roses respectively). Although Richard was killed, his son Edward IV took the throne in 1461; Edward in turn was succeeded by his son Edward V (one of the Princes in the Tower, *see* TOWER OF LONDON) and his brother Richard III, killed at BOSWORTH in 1485, so ending the Yorkist line.

St William of York. William Fitzherbert (c.1154), chaplain to King Stephen and Archbishop of York from 1142. He was canonized in 1227.

Statute of York (1322). A statute issued by a parliament summoned by Edward II at York. It stated that Parliament should debate issues that concerned the king and the kingdom, with the assent of the barons and 'the community of the realm'.

Treaty of York (1237). A treaty between Alexander II of Scotland and Henry III of England, by which the former gave up his claims to Northumberland, Cumberland and Westmorland. In return he received estates in northern England, in regard to which Henry was to be his feudal overlord.

Vale of York. The flat, characterless plain in which York sits. Donald Davie, in his poem 'At Knaresborough', describes the Yorkshire accent as having

> Vowels as broad as all the plain of York.

york, to. In cricket, to bowl a **yorker**, i.e. to deliver a ball that pitches directly beneath the bat, and so is likely to be missed by the batsman. The term is thought to have derived from a Yorkshire bowler.

York Buildings Company, the. A speculative venture established in 1675 to run a waterworks off the Strand, in London.

York Cycle. A cycle of nearly 50 medieval 'mystery' plays, and thus one of only four such surviving cycles. Different plays were performed by different guilds, usually with some connection with the subject matter – for example the Shipwrights performed the story of Noah.

yorkie. An informal name for a Yorkshire terrier (*see under* YORKSHIRE).

Yorkie Bar. A brand of thick chocolate bar, much favoured by lorry drivers (at least in the minds of marketing executives). It was created by the city's Rowntree company.

Yorkist. A supporter of the **House of York** (*see above*) during the Wars of the Roses.

York stone or **Yorkstone.** A type of stone much used for paving slabs (**York paving**). It is actually gritstone (a type of sandstone), also called Yorkshire stone, found in the Pennines to the west of York. It was used to pave much of London and other cities in the UK into the 20th century.

Yorkletts OE *geocled*, a measure of land equal to half a hide. A village near the North Kent coast, about 5 km (3 miles) southwest of Whitstable.

Yorks. The standard abbreviation for YORKSHIRE.

Yorkshire From YORK + SHIRE.

Formerly the largest county in England, bounded on the north by the Tees and County Durham, to the east by the North Sea, to the south by the Humber, Lincolnshire, Nottinghamshire and Derbyshire, and to the west, over the Pennines, by Cheshire, Lancashire and Westmorland. After the Danes invaded in the 9th century they divided Yorkshire into three 'ridings' (*see* the RIDINGS OF YORKSHIRE), and the administrative divisions of the NORTH RIDING, the WEST RIDING and the EAST RIDING OF YORKSHIRE continued up to the local government reorganization of 1974. Yorkshire was then divided into the counties of NORTH YORKSHIRE, WEST YORKSHIRE and SOUTH YORKSHIRE, with most of the East Riding being lumped, along with northern LINCOLNSHIRE, into HUMBERSIDE. In 1996 Humberside was abolished and the East Riding restored.

Throughout all these changes Yorkshire has kept its own strong identity, its badge of the white rose (*see* House of York *under* YORK) – although in a 2004 poll the people of Yorkshire treacherously voted for the harebell as their county flower – and above all its county cricket club, perhaps the most ardently followed in England (Yorkshire fathers have been known to drive mothers in labour great distances so that their sons are born in the county and therefore entitled to play for its club).

> In an England cricket eleven, the flesh may be of the South, but the bone is of the North, and the backbone is Yorkshire.
>
> Sir Len Hutton (1916–90)

Yorkshiremen, more than other Northerners, are known for their forthrightness and taciturnity, although their great rivals over the Pennines have their own opinions as to the virtues of their neighbours:

> Shake a bridle over a Yorkshireman's grave and he will rise and steal a horse.
>
> Lancashire saying

While Yorkshiremen are more than content with their geographical situation, it has not always appealed to the pampered metropolitan soul, the Rev. Sydney Smith famously remarking:

> My living in Yorkshire was so far out of the way, that it was actually twelve miles from a lemon.

Even today, there are those who share Smith's sense of disorientation when finding themselves in the county:

> A huddle of cows are gloating in front of me. A gaggle of chickens is shrieking with laughter behind me. I am in hell. I am in a place called Yorkshire.
>
> Johann Hari: in *The Independent* (1 October 2004)

A native of Yorkshire is sometimes referred to as a **tyke** (or **tike**), a long-established nickname (deriving from the OScand *tik*, meaning a 'dog' or 'cur'), that appears formerly to have specifically denoted a clownish rustic of the county. The term has now mostly shed its derogatory implications, and appears to be mainly used by Yorkshiremen themselves with a certain suggestion of pride in their county and its gritty, no-nonsense character. Thus it is encountered (in plural form) in sporting contexts to refer to teams representing Yorkshire, especially its county cricket club (but *see also* BARNSLEY[1] *and* LEEDS[1]). A headline such as 'Tykes snatch last-gasp victory in Roses match' would be certain to gladden the heart of any Yorkshireman.

The ongoing debate as to whether Robin Hood hailed from Nottinghamshire or Yorkshire resurfaced in the press in early 2004, with one correspondent handing down a decisive verdict:

> As Robin Hood wore bright green clothes, had a band of merry, not gruff, men and gave his money away, there is no way he could have hailed from Yorkshire.
>
> Steve Little: letter to *The Guardian* (24 January 2004)

Yorkshire itself remains untroubled by such barbs. Its attitude is summed up in an editorial of *The Fryer*, the organ of the Yorkshire Federation of Fish Fryers, which reacted to the proposed rationing of dripping in 1918 thus:

> Animal fat for the dominant race. Animal fat for the dominant county within that race.

In cricketing terms Yorkshire is a 'first-class' county. Yorkshire County Cricket Club was founded at the Adelphi Hotel, Sheffield, on 8 January 1863, and was a founder member of the county championship when that competition was officially constituted in 1890. It is traditionally regarded as one of the two strongest county sides, along with Surrey, having won the competition on 31 occasions, but 30 of these successes came between 1895 and 1968, with one solitary championship (2001) since that date. Its famous players have included George Hirst, Wilfred Rhodes, Percy Holmes, Herbert Sutcliffe, Hedley

Verity, Len Hutton (*see* PUDSEY), Fred Trueman (*see* STAINTON), Ray Illingworth, Geoffrey Boycott (*see* FITZWILLIAM), Darren Gough (*see* BARNSLEY[1]) and Michael Vaughan (the latter in fact a Lancastrian by birth). Yorkshire's home ground is HEADINGLEY Cricket Ground, Leeds. *See also* NORTH YORK MOORS *and* YORKSHIRE DALES.

come Yorkshire over someone, to. A 19th-century slang term meaning to cheat someone which derives from the stereotyping of Yorkshire people (*see* **Yorkshire bite** *below*).

Number One, Yorkshire. A nickname for the first house on the Great North Road in BAWTRY.

'Old Woman in Yorkshire, The'. A folk song beginning:

> There was an old woman in Yorkshire, in Yorkshire
>   did dwell,
> She loved her husband dearly and another man twice
>   as well.

In order to have her way with the latter she makes a concoction out of marrowbones to make her husband lose his sight. Apparently overwhelmed with grief at his blindness, the old man begs his wife to lead him to the river so that he can drown himself. Once there he begs her to push him in, but dodges out of the way at the last minute, so pitching her into the water:

> She swam until she floated unto the river's brim.
> The old man took his walking stick and shoved her
>   further in.

Yorkshire Association. An association formed in 1779 to petition Parliament to reduce political patronage. Conservatives regarded it as dangerously seditious.

Yorkshire bite. A 19th-century slang term for a greedy person, deriving from the stereotyping of Yorkshire people as mean and grasping.

Yorkshire compliment. A 19th-century slang term for a useless gift (and one that costs the donor nothing).

Yorkshire Day. 1st August. The day was established in 1975 by the Yorkshire Ridings Society in reaction to the local government reorganization of the previous year that abolished the Ridings of Yorkshire and handed part of the county to Humberside.

Yorkshire Feast Song. An ode to music by Henry Purcell (1690), with a text by Thomas D'Urfey. It was written for the annual feast of eminent Yorkshiremen (many of them cloth merchants) resident in London, and the words celebrate the superiority of Yorkshire grit over metropolitan languor. Among other things the lyrics recount the birth of the Emperor Constantine in York and the role of Yorkshiremen in bringing over William of Orange in the Glorious Revolution.

Yorkshire fog. A species of grass, *Holcus lanatus*, with pink or white branched flower heads in spikes and downy leaves.

It is tolerant of acid conditions and unpalatable to grazers except when young.

Yorkshire hog. An 18th-century term for a castrated ram.

Yorkshireman's toast. A traditional toast in the county:

> Here's tiv us, all on us; may we never want nowt,
> noan on us; nor me nawther.

Only pampered metropolitan souls (*see above*) should require a translation.

Yorkshire mixtures. A mixture of boiled sweets of different kinds, said to have come about when confectioner Joseph Dobson slipped and dropped a mixture of boiled sweets on the floor.

Yorkshire motto.

> Hear all, see all, say nowt,
> Eat all, sup all, pay nowt,
> And if tha' ever does owt for nowt,
> Do it for thissen.
>
>   (*thissen* 'thyself')

Yorkshire penny bank. A 20th-century rhyming-slang term meaning 'an act of masturbation' (*Yorkshire penny bank* = *wank*).

Yorkshire pole. A unit of measurement equivalent to 7 yards, as opposed to the normal pole (or rod or perch), measuring 5½ yards.

Yorkshire Post, The. A daily newspaper founded as the *Leeds Intelligencer* on 2 July 1754. It adopted its present title in 1866. In November 1939 it absorbed the even older *Leeds Mercury*, which was founded in 1718. It is the second oldest daily newspaper in the United Kingdom, after the *Belfast News-Letter* (*see under* BELFAST) which first appeared in 1737.

Yorkshire pudding. A small puffy, light pudding made by baking batter, usually served with roast beef and gravy, and so comprising an essential element of England's national dish. George Borrow would have us believe that the Romany name for Yorkshire is **Guyo-mengreskey tem**, meaning 'pudding eaters' country'.

Yorkshire Rasputin, the. A nickname given to Bernard Ingham (b.1932), former journalist and Labour candidate, who was press secretary to Margaret Thatcher throughout her premiership. The name refers to the 'Mad Monk' who had such a sinister influence over the last Tsar and Tsarina of Russia, and was applied to Ingham (a Yorkshireman) because of his mastery of the 'black arts' of spin-doctoring.

Yorkshire Ripper, the. The media nickname for Peter Sutcliffe (b.1946), murderer of some 13 women over a five-year period from 1975. The name was based on that of Jack the Ripper, the unknown murderer of several prostitutes in the East End of London in the late 1880s, the term relating to the gross mutilation of the bodies. In contemporary rhyming slang, *Yorkshire rippers* denotes 'slippers'.

Yorkshire stone. Another name for York stone (*see under* YORK).

Yorkshire terrier. A miniature long-haired terrier, with a 'blue' and tan coat. They are known familiarly as yorkies.

Yorkshire Tragedy, A. A Jacobean domestic tragedy, published in 1608 with Shakespeare's name on the title page, but more likely to have been written by Thomas Middleton. It is based on a real-life crime in which a man, repenting his depraved life, for some reason proceeded to murder his innocent wife and children.

Yorkshire tyke or **tike.** *See above.*

Yorkshire way-bit. A slang term, in use from the mid-17th to the mid-19th century, denoting a distance in excess of one mile. *Way-bit* means 'wee bit' (i.e. a short distance).

Yorkshire window. A type of sash window that opened horizontally, and not requiring counterweights. It is thought to have been invented by a Yorkshireman in the 17th century.

Yorkshire Witch, the. Another name for the Witch of Leeds (*see under* LEEDS[1]).

Yorkshire Dales, the OScand *dalr* 'valley'.

A scenic area of northwestern North Yorkshire, comprising many deep, steep-sided dales intersecting the high PENNINES. The area is largely limestone. The deep green valleys are often topped with white limestone cliffs known as 'scars' (*see* GORDALE SCAR). Above the cliffs are plateaux of bare rock known as 'limestone pavements' (in no way suitable for walking along, however). Numerous well-preserved drystone walls, originally built by sheep farmers, crisscross the hillsides throughout **the Dales** (as they are often more simply known), seemingly blending in with the limestone scenery.

The Dales are Britain's largest area of karst scenery, and beneath the surface lies a hidden (and partially unexplored) world of caverns, potholes and passages (*see* GAPING GHYLL), not to mention underground rivers and waterfalls, of which Thornton Force near Ingleton (sketched by J.M.W. Turner in 1816), with its drop of 14 m (46 ft) is the most spectacular. Other features include the natural rock amphitheatre of Malham Cove (*see under* MALHAM) and the gritstone outcrops of BRIMHAM ROCKS.

The Dales include CRAVEN, Airedale (*see under* AIRE), Ribblesdale (*see under* RIBBLE), Wharfedale (*see under* WHARFE), WENSLEYDALE, Swaledale (*see under* SWALE[1]), GARSDALE, Niddersdale (*see under* NIDD) and Littondale. Most of the area lies in the **Yorkshire Dales National Park**, created in 1954 and covering an area of about 1760 sq km (680 sq miles). Three of Yorkshire's highest mountains, WHERNSIDE, INGLEBOROUGH and PEN-Y-GHENT lie within the Park.

The Dales have been used as the backdrop for a number of films and television series, including most memorably the dramatizations of James Herriott's veterinary tales, *All Creatures Great and Small* (1978–90), based on the author's life as a rural vet in the 1940s (*see under* ASKRIGG); Britain's second-longest running television soap *Emmerdale*, formerly *Emmerdale Farm* (*see under* ARNCLIFFE); and the feature film *Calendar Girls* (2003) (*see under* KILNSEY).

The 2001 census revealed that the Yorkshire Dales has the highest number of males per female in Britain.

See also THREE PEAKS.

Dalesman. A Yorkshireman living in the Yorkshire Dales. *The Dalesman* magazine, the country's biggest regional magazine, was founded in 1939 in the village of CLAPHAM[2]. 'The Dalesman's Litany' with its repeated injunction 'From Hull and Halifax and Hell, good Lord deliver me', is a traditional song dating from the Industrial Revolution though based on an earlier Yorkshire poem (*see under* HALIFAX).

York Town Named in the early 19th century in honour of Frederick, Duke of *York*, who founded the nearby Royal Military College.

A western district of CAMBERLEY in Surrey, close to the Hampshire border. The Royal Military College (now the Royal Military Academy), which indirectly inspired its name, is just to the north in SANDHURST.

Youghal Irish *Eochaill* 'wood of yew-trees'.

A town, resort and fishing port at the mouth of the River BLACKWATER[2], County Cork, some 40 km (25 miles) east of Cork itself. It is pronounced 'yoogle' and sometimes spelt **Youghall**. The estuary of the Blackwater here is called **Youghal Harbour**, which opens out into **Youghal Bay**.

Youghal was founded by the Anglo-Normans in the 13th century, and later came into the hands of the Desmond Fitzgeralds. Many are buried in the 13th-century St Mary's Church. The medieval town walls and towers survive, as do the remains of a Benedictine and a Dominican abbey, despite the town being burned in 1579 during the Desmond Rebellion. This was followed by the plantation of MUNSTER, during which Sir Walter Raleigh was granted estates round Youghal, and he lived for a time in the town at Myrtle Grove (the house can still be seen).

Raleigh was Mayor of Youghal in 1588–9, but sold Myrtle Grove and his estates in 1602 to Richard Boyle, who was to become Earl of Cork (the latter is buried in Youghal). Local legend purports to have Raleigh planting the first Old World potato here, and being dowsed with water by a maid as he lit his first pipe.

By Raleigh 'twas planted at Youghal so gay
And Munster potatoes are famed to this day;
Ballinamora ora
A laughing red apple for me.

Anon.: in Thomas Crofton Croker, *The Popular Songs of Ireland* (1839)

However, WESTMEATH has a better claim on the potato, and the tobacco tale is likely to be apocryphal.

In John Huston's film of *Moby Dick* (1956), with Gregory Peck as Captain Ahab, Youghal plays the part of Nantucket.

> One Sunday morning, into Youghal walking,
> I met a maiden upon the way;
> Her little mouth sweet as fairy music,
> Her soft cheeks blushing like dawn of day!
>
> Anon.: 'Youghal Harbour' (18th century), translated from the Irish by Samuel Ferguson

Youghal needle lace. A very fine type of lace, originating in the 19th century and using cotton thread finer than human hair.

Yr Aran. *See under* SNOWDON.

Yr Eifl. *See under* the RIVALS.

Yr Wyddfa. The Welsh name for SNOWDON.

Yr Wyddgrug. The Welsh name for MOLD.

Yr Ynys Dywell. A former Welsh name for ANGLESEY.

Ysgyryd Fawr. The Welsh name for the SKIRRID.

Ysolglion Duon. *See* the BLACK LADDERS.

Ystrad Welsh 'valley'.

Part of the linear urban development in the valley of the River Rhondda Fawr (*see under* RHONDDA), in Rhondda Cynon Taff (formerly in Glamorgan, then in Mid Glamorgan). It is 4 km (2.5 miles) southeast of TREORCHY.

Ystrad Tywi 'valley of the River Towy', Welsh *ystrad* 'valley' + *Tywi*, the Welsh form of TOWY.

An early medieval kingdom in south Wales, broadly corresponding to Carmarthenshire and western Glamorgan (the latter now comprising Swansea and Neath Port Talbot unitary authorities). In the 9th century it united with CEREDIGION to form the kingdom of SEISYLLWG.

Ystwyth. *See under* ABERYSTWYTH.

Ythan 'chattering stream', OCelt *iaith* 'chattering' with suffix *-ona* forming a river name.

A river of Aberdeenshire; length approximately 60 km (37 miles). It rises near the small settlement of **Ythanwells** in STRATHBOGIE, and flows generally eastwards via ELLON, before entering the North Sea. Its estuary is an important habitat for wildfowl.

Y Trallwng. The Welsh name for WELSHPOOL.

Zeal Monachorum *Zeal* 'hall, manor house', OE *sele*; *Monachorum* 'of the monks' (referring to early possession by Buckfast Abbey), Latin.

A village in Devon, about 11 km (7 miles) northwest of Crediton.

Zeals '(place by the) willow trees', OE *salh* 'sallow, willow'.

A village in Wiltshire, 4 km (2.5 miles) west of Mere.

Zedland *Zed-* representing the West Country pronunciation of initial *s-* as *z-*.

A name applied humorously in the 18th and 19th centuries to the southwestern counties of England: SOMERSET, DEVON[1], CORNWALL and DORSET.

Zelah 'dwelling', OE *sele* 'dwelling, house, hall'.

A village in Cornwall, about 8 km (5 miles) north of Truro.

Zennor '(church of St) Sinar' (referring to a female saint of unknown origin and history).

A village on the north coast of the Penwith Peninsula (*see under* PENWITH) in Cornwall, about 17 km (11 miles) northeast of LAND'S END. It is said of Zennor (as of many other places in England) that its inhabitants once attempted to build a wall around a cuckoo to prevent it (and hence the season of spring) from flying away.

D.H. Lawrence and his German wife, Frieda, took a cottage nearby in 1916, but they were regarded suspiciously by the locals, who thought they were German spies, and were virtually hounded out in October 1917. Lawrence recounts this humiliating experience in Chapter 10, 'The Nightmare', of his novel *Kangaroo* (1923). The episode also forms part of the subject of Helen Dunmore's novel *Zennor in Darkness* (1993), which won the Orange Prize in 1996.

> I stand on the high Zennor
> Moor with ling and sour
> Grass and the loose stone walls
> Keeping the weasel's castle.
>
> W.S. Graham: 'Two Poems on Zennor Hill', from *Collected Poems 1942–1977* (1979)

Zennor Quoit. A Neolithic dolmen 3 km (2 miles) southeast of Zennor. Its huge roof slab, one of the largest in England, covers two burial chambers rather than the usual one.

Zetland. *See* SHETLAND.

APPENDICES, MAPS AND GLOSSARY

Investigating Place Names

The place names of Britain and Ireland have as rich a heritage as any part of the culture of these islands. All our significant native peoples as well as the successful invaders – the Romans, the Anglo-Saxons, the Scandinavians and the Normans – have, together, woven a complex multicultural and multilingual tapestry of names. It is one that presents challenges for those wanting to untangle its threads.

The entries in *Brewer's Britain and Ireland* often begin with an etymology, the derivation of the place name. And this book is full of confident statements about etymologies, that place name 'x' derives from elements 'y' and 'z'. But how do we know that this is so? How did we get here, to our modern place names, from a past that, in L.P. Hartley's well-known phrase, is 'another country'. It is a journey that is fascinating, surprising, sometimes mysterious and even amusing.

Constructing an etymology: a London case study

When those who study place names say that the London names Hornsey and Haringey derive from the same language elements and that they were originally the *same* name, the obvious question is: 'Why are the modern forms so different from one another?' The explanations given are not always absolutely conclusive because names change in many ways as they are used. But these two names – and to further confuse matters, the variant form Harringay – can serve to illustrate how we get to an etymology.

The different forms of these names are present in the written record from the 13th century, and appear as (among other forms) *Haringeie, Harengheye, Haringesheye* and *Harynsey* from 1201 to 1401. The individual elements that make up the versions of the name are from Old English, and are apparently *haring*, meaning 'a grey wood', or possibly the personal name *Hæring*, combined with *hæg* 'an enclosure'. The ending of both names (Haring*ey* and Horns*ey*) is what is left of *hæg*; this is confirmed by spellings with *-heye* alongside other medieval forms of *hæg* (*-eie, -aye, -ey* and others). Other names containing this element often lose the *-h-* pronunciation – as in Broomy (Kent) or Limbersey (Bedfordshire)

– but nevertheless have it in medieval spellings of the name.

There is very little difference in pronunciation between the two elements *haring* and *Hæring* proposed as the first part of such names. The main difference in the medieval names is the presence (or lack of it) of the possessive *-s*. Where the *-s* is present (e.g. *Haringesheye*), it is most likely that the early users of the name thought it meant 'Hæring's enclosure', because the possessive *-s* form is most often used with reference to people. This is a kind of rule of thumb in place-name study. Where the *-s* is not present (e.g. *Harengheye*), however, it is probable that the early users of the name thought it meant 'enclosure in or by a grey wood' with the element *haring*.

Since both types are present in the record, sometimes even given as alternatives, as for example in *Haringay alias Hornesey* in the 16th century, we cannot settle on one as the 'correct' etymology, but have to give both. This shows roughly how we arrive at the etymology of a name. But it's not the whole story.

Are these real words?

Neither *haring* 'a grey wood' nor the personal name *Hæring* are independently attested in Old English. We have in fact 'read back' here, using the forms of place names to suggest the existence of otherwise unknown personal names or elements. This might strike the reader as an intellectual sleight of hand. However, the process is far from one of 'making it all up'. In this case, the reasoning is as follows:

The element *har* 'grey' is very often used in relation to woodland, as in several places called Harwood (and compare Old Celtic *letocetum* 'grey wood' in Lichfield, Staffordshire); so is the element *-ing*, which, when added to a noun, makes it specify a place *characterized by* the feature in question, as in Stubbins (Manchester), from the noun *stubb* 'a tree stump' combined with *-ing* making 'a place characterized by tree stumps'. Similarly, Stockingford (Warwickshire) means 'ford by a place characterized by tree stumps', being derived from *stocc* 'tree stump' with the *-ing* element and *ford*. Many more examples of this kind of formation could be added, but these are sufficient to indicate that an element *haring* 'place characterized by grey (trees)' is not a wild stab in the dark.

Another example of 'reading back' is the Old English word *stoc*, quite different from the *stocc* just mentioned. It occurs only twice in ordinary Old English prose, where it means 'monastery'. But as a name element it is found literally hundreds of times as Stoke or *Stock-*, *-stoke* and *-stock*, most often meaning 'a secondary farm', though it does also refer to places belonging to monasteries. The point here is that even if we did not have the two Old English texts that use the word *stoc* (and we should not underestimate the randomness of the preservation of old manuscripts), we would nevertheless know what it meant from the way it is used in place names. To be scrupulous we have to refer to it as 'not independently attested'.

Personal names

One of the main differences between Celtic (Welsh, Gaelic, Cornish, etc.) and Germanic (English, Scots, etc.) names is that the latter use personal names far more frequently. We have noted that the personal name *Hæring* posited for Hornsey is not independently recorded, and the same is true for possibly half of the personal names thought to occur in place names. It is true, for example, of some of the most obvious place names of this type, like Hastings (Sussex) and Reading (Berkshire), where the personal names *Hæsta* and *Read(a)* are not otherwise recorded. The *-ing* element in these last two names means 'son of' or (in the plural) 'descendants or dependants of' *Hæsta* or *Read(a)*, and it is generally thought that Hastings and Reading were originally the areas controlled by these men. There is no serious alternative to this interpretation, even though *Hæsta* and *Read(a)* are not names independently mentioned anywhere in Old English sources. The sparseness of records of Old English personal names is a fact that can be attributed to many accidents of history: many names were given before the English could write; the records that were kept were mostly royal or ecclesiastical; the manuscripts were destroyed by violence and neglect (by Henry VIII in the Dissolution of the Monasteries as much as by the Vikings – and these among many other depredations).

Another difficulty with personal names is that sometimes we have to posit a *form* of the name that is not independently known. There are numerous place names beginning Raven-: some of these, like the various Ravensthorpes (Northamptonshire, Yorkshire) can be explained as deriving from the well-attested Old Scandinavian personal name *Hrafn*; some – like Ravendale (Lincolnshire), with Old Scandinavian *dalr*, and Ravenscar (Yorkshire), with Old Scandinavian *sker* – can be explained as 'valley of the ravens' and 'rocks of the ravens' respectively, with the Old Scandinavian possessive plural *hrafna* 'of the ravens'. But Ravenstone (Leicestershire and

Buckinghamshire) uses the Old English *tun* 'farm, estate' with a personal name (as identifiable by the possessive *-s* again). Since there are not many Scandinavian names in Buckinghamshire, it is quite possible in at least the case of the Buckinghamshire Ravenstone that the personal name is Old English *Hræfn*, which is unknown outside place names. As with Old Scandinavian *Hrafn* and *hrafn* and Old English *hræfn*, this means 'raven'; but it happens that the Old English personal name is not recorded other than in place names like this one, where the interpretation is uncertain.

The vicissitudes of grammar

So far, most of the grammatical forms we have mentioned have been what we might expect in modern English. The possessive form of the personal names Old English *Hæring* and Old Scandinavian *Hrafn* have both appeared as *-s* in Hornsey and Ravensthorpe. But many male personal names in Old English end in *-a*, and adjectives and common nouns end in *-a* or *-e*. The singular possessive and dative of these words is *-an*. This grammatical marker was very frequently lost later on, in Middle English, but place names preserve it in some circumstances, for example when the name, noun or adjective precedes an element beginning with a vowel or *h-*. Examples of names where this happens include the Fakenhams (East Anglia), Beckenham (Greater London), Bardney (Lincolnshire), Tutnall (Worcestershire): in each of these cases, the possessive *-n* (*Faccan, Beohhan, Beardan, Tottan*, meaning 'belonging to *Facca, Beohha, Bearda, Totta*') is retained despite all the other changes in spelling and pronunciation that have occurred. Similarly, a noun like *scucca* 'demon' combined with *hill* gives Shucknall (Herefordshire).

In the dative, where the name means 'at –', adjectives also have the *-n*, as in Longney (Gloucestershire), from *langa* 'long' in the dative form *langan*, with *eg*, and hence meaning '(at) the long island'. The same applies to the many Newnhams, from *niwe* 'new' in the dative form *niwan*, with *ham* and hence '(at) the new homestead'. The Newnhams supply a good contrast with the Newtons: the early spellings of many of the Newtons show an *-n* that was lost in the Middle English period; a survivor of the spelling with *-n* is North Newnton (Wiltshire). The various Newington names preserve the *-n* as a separate syllable in a false *-ing* form.

Sounds and spellings

Already we have seen that the modern spellings do not always give a reliable indication of what the etymology of a name might be. Hornsey and Haringey, with which we started out, are prime examples. Names are usually given by people who attach a meaning to the words they make into the name. The earliest spellings are important: they are the most reliable guides to the etymology of names because the people who wrote them down usually also knew also knew what they meant. But the majority of names are cited by people who simply think of them as names — not as having meaning, but as simply a way of specifying a certain place. This gives rise to frequent confusion of elements that sound similar or are common. The *-n* inflection of *niwan* in Newington becomes an *-ing* not only because both contain the *-n-* sound, but also because *-ington* is a common formation, as in Beddington (Surrey), Bovington (Dorset), Islington (Norfolk) and so on.

Shucknall and Tutnall, already mentioned, are spelt as if the final element were Old English *halh* 'a corner of land' instead of Old English *hyll* 'a hill', a frequent confusion of vowels in unstressed syllables. The element *-ton* is not infrequently confused with another word for 'hill', *-don*: Hambleton (Rutland) is composed of the same elements as Hambledon (Hampshire and Surrey), namely *hamel* 'crooked' and *dun* 'hill', but similar-sounding *-ton* has become the standard pronunciation and spelling. The Grendons (Buckinghamshire, Northamptonshire and Warwickshire) are from Old English *grene* 'green' and *dun* 'hill', but Grendon in Herefordshire is from *grene* and *denu* 'valley': quite the opposite of a hill.

Particularly in northern England we find Old English *ham* and Old Scandinavian *holmr*, and Old English *ford* and later *forth* being confused or interchanging. Durham, for example, is made up of the elements *dun* 'hill' and *holmr* 'island', and the name is precisely descriptive. The old county and university abbreviation, *Dunelm.*, retains the etymological elements in slightly modified form, but the usual spelling has substituted the English *-ham* for the Scandinavian *holmr*. The change has gone the other way in Bloxholm (Lincolnshire), which was originally identical with Bloxham (Oxfordshire), meaning 'Blocc's homestead', with Old English *ham*. The development of *ford* into *forth* is a sporadically occurring North Country dialect feature and we can compare Rufford (Lancashire) and Rufforth (Yorkshire), both made up of the elements Old English *ruh* 'rough' and *ford*. Stanford (Kent, Herefordshire, Essex, Berkshire, Oxfordshire, etc.) and two Yorkshire Stainforths are all originally from Old English *stan* 'stone' and *ford*, with the Stain- reflecting the Old Scandinavian variant and pronunciation *steinn* 'stone'.

Sound-changes

This last interchange of Old English *stan* and Old Scandinavian *steinn* is not properly a confusion, but rather one of a set of sound-changes that occurred in parts of Britain under the influence of Scandinavian speakers. (See the section in the Introduction on 'Scandinavian Names'.) There are many other sound-changes that occurred in the course of the history of English which are variously reflected in place names. Long vowels in Old English changed significantly in the Early Modern period, *c.*1500–1700. By way of illustration, Old English *tun* changed to *town* in normal usage, and while more

recent names in Scotland, Wales and Ireland like Newtown and Gordonstown follow exactly the pattern of older English names like Newton ('new') and Alfriston (with the Old English male personal name *Ælfric*), they reflect the later spelling and pronunciation of the element. The same change of vowel affected Old English *dun* 'hill', thus producing the pleasing linguistic oddity of many well known areas of high ground (particularly in southern England) being known as 'downs'.

Similarly, Old English *ham* changed to *home* in normal usage, but since this element apparently fell out of use in place names quite early on, there are very few *home* forms in major names because the names in question were already fixed (and in most cases *-ham* was pronounced something like *-um*) well before the change in vowel occurred; but in minor names we have many a Home Farm or Home Field. One of the posited first elements in Haringey and Hornsey, *haring*, contains the base word *har* 'grey', and the *Horn-* spelling of the name reflects the same change of vowel as *home* from *ham*. (Compare Old English *har* with modern English *hoar*.) The many Actons show the old spelling and pronunciation of Old English *ac* 'oak', which as an ordinary word has undergone the same basic change from a long *a* vowel to *oa* or *o* + consonant + *e* (such as is found in OE *stan* changing to modern *stone*: see Stanford, discussed above).

The influence of dialect

Some words were pronounced differently according to where they were spoken. The Old English word for a spring or well was pronounced *will* in the southwest, *wall* in the west Midlands and *well* in most of the rest of the country. Will (Devon), Wall (Shropshire) and Well (Kent and Yorkshire) all derive from this root. Heswall (Cheshire) and Haswell (County Durham) both come from Old English *hæsel* 'hazel' and *well*. There was similarly a difference between the southwestern half of England and the rest in the pronunciation of the word borrowed from Latin that comes into modern English as *street*. This is shown in the variants Stratford and Stretford, and Stratton and Stretton, where the first member of each pair is found predominantly (but not uniformly) in the southwestern half of England, and the second member in the northern and eastern parts.

More sound differences

A slightly more complex variety of sound results from the position of consonants in relation to vowels in Old English. Before an *i* or an *e*, for example, *c* is pronounced 'ch' and *g* is pronounced 'y', but in most other contexts they are pronounced 'k' and 'g'. So Old English *ceorl* 'churl, peasant' gives rise to the many Charltons, and Old English *cild* 'child' to the many Chiltons; Old English *geat* 'gate' gives names like Yateley (Hampshire), Yate (Gloucestershire) and Kirk Yetholm (Scottish Borders); and Old English *gield* 'tax' gives the

Yeldhams (Essex). At the end of a word, and preceded by *i*, the letter *c* is once again pronounced 'ch': hence the many names like Northwich, Nantwich and Middlewich (Cheshire) and Sandwich (Kent), which contain the element *wic* 'farm, dwelling, settlement'. However, the situation changes when there is a plural ending on *wic* like the dative *-um*, or when another element like *ham* is added: the various places called Wick, many place names ending in *-wick* and the various Wickhams result from this pronunciation.

'Lazy' pronunciation?

These examples demonstrate that variations in place names are the result of developments in the spoken language. Most of the interchanges and variations discussed above have occurred through a long evolution in the mouths of those using the names. This leads us to consider the fact that historically people have found certain combinations of sounds easier to pronounce than others. The *-p-* in Hampstead and *-hampstead* (*compare* Hamstead), Hampton, Burpham and Bumpstead was added to make the pronunciation easier, as was the *-d-* in Bewdley (*compare* Beaulieu) and Beadlow. Compare the pronunciation 'awlz-fəd' of Alresford (Hampshire), from Old English *alor* 'alder tree' with *ford*, with Alderford (Norfolk) and it will be evident that some names are easier to pronounce than others. And this is true not only in English, since Cumbernauld has an intrusive *-b-* (Gaelic *comar-nan-allt* 'meeting of the waters').

Another pronunciation change is called 'metathesis', and this is where the order of letters is altered. Old English *gærs* and *cærse* often became 'grass' and 'cress' before the Norman Conquest. Garsdon (Wiltshire) shows the old spelling and pronunciation of *gærs* with *-don*, but most place names containing the element *gærs* have the spelling *gr-*. With *cærse* we can compare Creswell (Derbyshire, Northumberland and Staffordshire) with Carswell (Berkshire and Gloucestershire). Some changes of this nature never became 'official' as such, but nevertheless appear in place names: Old English *cran* 'a crane or heron' appears in several Cranfords, but also in Cornforth (County Durham), both names containing *cran* and *ford*; and Birgham-on-Tweed contains the same elements as the Brighams in Cumbria and Yorkshire, namely Old English *brycg* 'bridge' and *ham*. The second element of Dumbarton is Gaelic *Breatann* 'Britons', also showing metathesis, or the interchange of original *brea-* with modern *bar-*.

One more sound change is worth illustrating: it is called 'dissimilation'. Many people pronounce 'February' by swallowing either the first or the second *r*, turning it into something like *Febury* or *Febry*. This occurs because it is harder to pronounce some consonants twice in certain combinations (here, the *-r-r* in February). The early spellings of Lincoln show that the second *-n*, at the end of the name, was often omitted because of the echo effect. But a whole range of spellings of the name between the 12th and the 14th centuries turn the name inside-out, with forms of the type *Nicoll* or *Nichole*. Less dramatically, *Sodbury* in Chipping Sodbury (Gloucestershire) was originally *Soppanbyrig* meaning '*Soppa*'s fortified place', and has had a *-d-* substituted because of the echo of *-p-* and *-b-* in the elements of the name.

Perhaps we cannot really talk of 'lazy' pronunciations. But it is clear that over the centuries, names have changed as the people using them have allowed their tongues to pronounce easier, rather than more difficult, combinations of sounds. The vast majority of place names in modern English contain fewer syllables than their originals, and shortening is the most obvious example of this simplification. Few names are as open about their abbreviation as Bo'ness (Falkirk), which was originally *Beornweardes-tun-næss* 'the promontory on Beornweard's estate'; but there are relatively few place names that do not drop a syllable or two.

Spellings again

The early spellings of names show us how the present-day spellings have evolved from the meaningful elements that made them up. But clearly it is the *sounds* that have become the names, as we have seen above. This development leads to the highly entertaining disparity between spelling and pronunciation in many names. Cholmondeley (Cheshire) is a curiosity that became fossilized in spelling while its pronunciation continued to change: the spelling is little different from the 13th-century form *Chelmundeleia*, meaning '*Ceolmund*'s clearing or glade' (with *ley*), but the pronunciation, famously, is 'Chumley'. The Devon Chulmleigh, made up of the same elements, shows how the spelling might have developed.

Meaning lost and regained

A few names have been mentioned that show how the original meaning of elements was lost, and how other elements were substituted. 'Tautonyms' – names that contain elements originally meaning the same thing – demonstrate this very nicely. Pendle Hill (Lancashire), contains the Brittonic element *penno* 'a hill', to which has been added Old English *hyll* 'a hill', with the consonant *-d-* inserted to make pronunciation easier, and then, for good measure, somewhat later Hill has been added. The name thus means 'hill, hill, hill'! There is a Pen Hill in Yorkshire too. Likewise, Breedon on the Hill (Leicestershire) contains Brittonic *bre* 'a hill', Old English *dun* 'a hill', and *on the Hill* to make it all obvious. And while we're on the subject of 'hill', another Brittonic word for 'hill' is *cruc*, occurring in names like Creech, Crich, Cruck and Crook. But the Anglo-Saxons did not recognize the word as meaningful, and thus Churchdown (Gloucestershire, with Old English *dun*), Church Hill and Churchill (Somerset and Worcestershire, with Old English *hyll*) replace *cruc* with a word the English recognized, namely *church*. In terms of etymology, these names mean 'hill hill'. These are just some of the more amusing tautonyms. But tautonyms remain strong evidence of the need for place names to describe topography, invaluable to people travelling before an age of road signs or motorized vehicles.

And finally, there are some names that are simply wholesale replacements. The Hampshire name Boarhunt is a delightfully macho, poetic replacement for the pleasant but hardly thrilling *Byrhfunt*. And thus the spring (*funta*, ultimately from Latin) by the fortified place (Old English *burh*) becomes a place of danger and excitement in this inspired reinterpretation.

Back to the present: modern name spellings

Much ink is spilled in local and national newspapers about the spelling of modern names. If you drive through the delightful village of Thornton near Pickering (North Yorkshire), you will be able to see signposts giving the name as 'Thornton-le-dale', 'Thornton le Dale' and 'Thornton Dale'. Which is correct? And should it be 'King's Norton' or 'Kings Norton', 'Bishop's Castle' or 'Bishops Castle'? There are many views on these matters. But there are two points we should note.

The first is that punctuation, such as the possessive apostrophe with *s*, started to be used in the modern fashion only around the 17th century, so hyphens and possessives in names are relative latecomers in terms of the history of names. The second is that, legally speaking, local authorities in Britain and Ireland are responsible for the place-name conventions used in their areas, and consequently there is no single rule that can be applied to all names. If one area uses an *'s* possessive in names, it is no guarantee that the same goes for 'identical' names in other areas.

Local convention has nearly always been a determining factor in all aspects of place-name spelling, pronunciation and meaning. But that is not to say that local people never get things wrong. The signs on the outskirts of Beeston (Nottinghamshire) proudly display a honey-bee. Like most of the other Beestons in Yorkshire and Norfolk, however, the name has nothing to do with bees, but comes from the Old English word *beos*, a type of long, rough grass, and means 'farm where bent-grass grows'. So, local convention notwithstanding, we have to go back to original languages to find out what a name 'really' means. Which is where we began, with Haringey and Hornsey ...

Paul Cavill

Administrative Names

The modern map of Britain and Ireland with its patchwork of neatly defined units of territory – each with perhaps an administrative or religious centre, or with a local legal jurisdiction and rights of taxation – represents the accumulated convenience of centuries. Many modern place names reflect the growth of administrative systems designed to regulate and delimits rights over territories. But names also preserve the record of ancient territories that have passed away. Some of the names of secular units, ancient and modern, appear in today's name elements or constitute names themselves.

The element *ge* in the English names Ely (Cambridgeshire), Margaretting (Essex), Sturry (Kent) and the county name of Surrey appears to refer to a territory something like a later county. In Wales, Brycheiniog or Brecon preserves the name of the territory of the 5th-century King Brychan, and Ardudwy, Mawddwy and Fawddwy are ancient tribal territories. Similarly in Scotland, Blairgowrie (Perth and Kinross), Fife and the area of Kyle (East and South Ayrshire) record the names of ancient chieftains and their territories, as Caithness does for an old tribal area. In Ireland, *tír* names, as in Tirconnell, Munster, Leinster and Ulster, record similar territorial divisions, although these divisions have greater importance today than those elsewhere so far mentioned.

The name of the larger territorial division in Britain and Ireland, and one of the oldest, is the *shire*, from Old English *scir*. After the unification of the English kingdoms in the 10th century, kings gave jurisdiction in their territories to *shire-reeves* (or sheriffs) and local noblemen, for the purposes of administering the law. The shire was originally a unit composed of smaller districts, with legal and other responsibilities; but in due course the name was applied far more widely, as the Norman, and later the English, kings found it useful for administrative purposes. Shires still exist in Wales and Scotland as well as England, and the name *shire* was also used for the counties of Ireland in the 16th and 17th centuries. The apparently more neutral, and certainly less English, *county*, deriving from Latin via French, is widely used for these same

districts. In Scotland, *stewartry* is also occasionally used (as for Kirkcudbrightshire).

The shire was made up of smaller units, the names of which vary enormously. In Kent the sub-divisions of the shire are *lathes* (the Shepway district was one), in Sussex they are *rapes*, and in many other counties there are, or were, *wards* (such as the London wards of Aldgate, Cornhill and Southwark); several modern unitary authorities are based on ancient wards, e.g. Stockton-on-Tees.

Smaller than these were the *hundreds* and *wapentakes*, the latter being the Scandinavian equivalent of the *hundred*, found in the area of the Danelaw, namely Northamptonshire, Leicestershire, Nottinghamshire, Lincolnshire, Derbyshire and Yorkshire. The *hundred* was in origin an area of land supporting 100 families, but it must soon have become a conventional sub-division of the shire. The Chiltern Hundreds retain the old name, but Brixton (London) and Sixpenny Handley (Dorset) were also old *hundred* names. Rushcliffe (Nottinghamshire) is the name of one of the old *wapentakes*. The equivalent in Wales is the *cantref*, or anglicized *cantred*, literally 'one hundred households or townships'; for much of the period from the 14th to the 18th centuries this word was used indiscriminately of British and Irish regions, but nowadays it is hardly used at all. One other sub-division of the shire was the *soke*, from Old English *socn* 'an area with its own jurisdiction': this is found today in several names – the Soke of Peterborough, and the Essex names Kirby le Soken and Thorpe-le-Soken.

Smaller yet were the areas of land contributing to the sub-divisions of the shire. In Ireland, the word *baile* is used both of early farmsteads and of modern townlands (the smallest administrative divisions of counties), and it is one of the most frequently occurring names, not least because there are some 60,000 townlands in the country. The *ceathrú* is a 'quarter-land', that is, a quarter of a townland, and this element is found in Carryduff (County Down) and Carrowmore (County Sligo); the last of these hints that 'quarter' is not a precise measurement, since it means 'big quarter'. The same element in Scots Gaelic is *ceathramh* 'quarter', and a precise parallel to Carrowmore is Kirriemuir (Angus), also meaning 'big quarter'. Here the quarter is a fraction of the *dabhach*, the davach or davoch, that being an area averaging some 400 English acres or 200 Scots acres. This element is found possibly in Dawyck (Scottish Borders) and certainly in Findochty (Moray) and Daugh of Invermarkie (Aberdeenshire).

The English equivalent of the Irish *baile* is the *hide*. The *hide* was the land necessary to support a single family and was approximately 120 acres in extent, although this must have varied a great deal according to the type of land. A *hundred* was so called because it was made up of 100 *hides*. Hyde Park (London) and Piddletrenthide (Dorset) contain the *hide* element in a recognizable form, but two other Dorset names

disguise it as -*head*, namely Combeteignhead and Fifehead. In Wales, the term *tref*, which appears in *cantref*, is one of the common words for town – as in Trefyclo and Y Drenewydd, the Welsh names for Knighton and Newtown (both in Powys) – and so is the Cornish equivalent *tre* in Treen, Trebetherick and many another name.

Two curiosities may be mentioned in conclusion. Arrochar (Argyll and Bute) derives its name from Latin *aratrum*, an ancient Scots land measure of approximately 100 Scots acres, or the land a team of oxen could plough in a year. Another land measure ultimately derived from the Latin is the *mile*, appearing in 'the Square Mile' as the City of London is known – one of the more recent coinages for an administrative area.

Paul Cavill

Church and Ecclesiastical Names

The church and various ecclesiastical institutions played a central role in society in earlier times throughout Britain and Ireland. This is everywhere evident from place names. To list all the Christian elements that come into place names would be too lengthy an endeavour here; however, a review of some of the religious elements involved may give the reader a sense of the possibilities and the variety. So here we will illustrate the influence of church buildings and sites, monastic buildings and sites, and ecclesiastical personnel on place names.

Saints' churches

Perhaps the dominant religious feature throughout Britain and Ireland is the site or church dedicated to a saint. English parish churches are customarily dedicated thus, and the names are occasionally used to distinguish different parts of a given place, e.g. Gussage All Saints and Gussage St Michael (both in Dorset). In Wales and Cornwall especially, the saint's name is prefixed by *llan-* or *lan-*, as in Llanelli 'church of St Elli' or Launceston 'church of St Stephen'. In Scotland and Ireland, *kil-* names proliferate, e.g. Kilmacolm 'church of my Columba' or Kilbride 'church of St Bridget'. Also in Scotland and the Isle of Man are names with *kirk* (Old English *cirice* or Old Scandinavian *kirkja*), such as Kirkmichael or Kirk Andreas. Some early church names in Ireland have the element *donagh* 'church', either on its own or in a compound such as Donaghpatrick 'St Patrick's church'; later church names frequently use the element *temple*, as in Templepatrick; a Gaelic variant of the same word occurs in Teampuill Chaon in Scotland, 'church of St Comgall'. Saints' burial-places are marked by the element *merthyr* in Wales, as in Merthyr Tydfil, and in Cornwall as *merther*, found in the parish name Merther.

Other churches

There are numerous *church* place names, too, of course, e.g. Church Stretton (Shropshire) and Christchurch (Dorset). Some original church names are disguised, as in the examples of Cheriton ('village with a church', Old English *cirice* + *tun*) in the south of England. Further north, *kirk* (Old Scandinavian *kirkja*) names become more common, with Kirbys and Kirkbys dotting the landscape, along with Kirtons and Kirkhams (all meaning 'village with a church'). The element we recognize as *chapel* occurs in England, Ireland and Wales, as in Capel (Surrey and Suffolk), Chapeltown (Yorkshire and County Down) and Capel Curig (Conwy). Another element that originated in late Latin *ecclesia* 'church' can be found in varying forms in Britain and Ireland: Aghlish and Eglish (Ireland), Eccles, Eccleshall, Ecclesfield and Eccleston (in various parts of England), Egloskerry and Egloshayle (both in Cornwall) and Ecclefechan (Scotland): *see* the place-name element entry on *eccles*. Yet another word, *basilica* 'church', borrowed from Greek into Latin, and from Latin into Middle Irish as *baslec*, seems to be the origin of Paisley in Scotland.

Monastic sites

Many early Christian sites were monastic, built for those dedicated to the pursuit of the religious life. Some foundations were obviously large and often prosperous communities; others were places occupied by hermits. Abbeys owned or occupied land, and these types of establishment provide a place-name element that appears particularly in Irish and English names: Abbey and Abbeygormacan (County Galway), Abbey Hulton (Staffordshire) and Abbeystead (Lancashire). Appin in Argyll also has the *abbey* element. The Irish *abbey* names usually translate Irish *mhainistir*, which is recognizable as originally the same word that came into English as *monastery* and *minster*. This element comes into Irish names like Monasterboice (County Louth), Minster (Kent and Oxfordshire) and Minsterworth (Gloucestershire). An English element not readily recognizable today is *hiwan* 'a household or religious community': it is found in many of the Hintons and in Clyst Honiton (Devon).

Other names referring to monasteries or their landholdings more or less directly include Charterhouse (Somerset), 'a house of Carthusian monks', and Brotherhouse (Lincolnshire); Ystradmynach (Glamorgan) is literally 'valley of the monk', although there is no known monastery nearby, and in Cornwall, Bodmin seems to contain the element *meneghi* 'church or monastic land'. English names containing the element *spitel* 'hospital' often refer to the foundations of the Knights Hospitallers, but they can have a more general reference to religious establishments for the care of the needy: Spitalfields (London), Spittle or (in many counties) Spital are examples. English and Scottish names containing *temple* usually refer to properties of the Knights Templars, for example Templand (Dumfries), Templeton (Devon), or Temple (Cornwall and Midlothian). Blackfriars (London) refers to the Dominican order, whereas Whiteabbey (County Antrim) refers to the Premonstratensian 'White Canons'. *White* in general can have a religious connotation: Whitland or Hen-dŷ-gwyn ar Daf (Carmarthenshire), 'white glade' or 'old white house on the River Taf', probably refers to an old monastic establishment.

An interesting range of names refers to hermits or the places where they lived. Kells in Ireland (there are several examples) refers to the groups of cells occupied by hermits; the names of more remote places occupied by hermits contain an element we recognize as 'deserted' from Latin *desertum*, which comes into Irish and Welsh names, e.g. Desertmartin (County Londonderry) and Diserth (Flintshire). In England, Armitage (Staffordshire), Armathwaite (Cumbria) and Hermitage (various counties) all refer to hermitages. Small chapels or oratories possibly used by hermits, but also with wider use, may be found in place names too: Bedern, a name found several times in Yorkshire, derives from Old English *bed-ærn* 'prayer-house'; Betws-y-coed, and other *betws-* names in Wales, are from Old English *bed-hus*, also 'prayer-house'; Rador (Glamorgan) seems to derive from the Latin word *oratorium*.

Some place-name elements that have a general meaning also apparently have specific reference to monastic foundations. The Newsteads (Lincolnshire and Nottinghamshire) both contain Old English *stede* 'place, site', and both had monastic houses, hence their meaning of 'new monastic site or foundation'; another Old English element, *stoc* 'outlying site, place', also has this reference, e.g. Tavistock (Devon), 'site on the River Tavy', and Stoke St Milborough (Shropshire), 'outlying place belonging to St Mildburh'. Less specific to monastic foundations, but having the sense 'holy place', are names with Old English *stow*, such as Halstow (Devon) and Hastoe (Hertfordshire) – both of which also contain *halig* 'holy' – Churchstow (Devon), with *cirice* 'church', and many places with saints' names, like Felixstowe (Suffolk) or Hibaldstow (Lincolnshire). Numerous other holy sites include water features such as *well* 'spring' in Holywell, Holwell, Halliwell (all found more than once, and containing *halig* 'holy') and *burna* 'stream' in Marylebone (London; 'St Mary's stream') and Holybourne (Hampshire).

Steeples and crosses

The most visible physical feature of religion in Britain and Ireland is usually the church. Many English churches have towers or steeples (both architectural features referred to by Old English *stiepel*): Steeple Ashton (Wiltshire), Steeple Bumpstead (Essex), Steeple Gidding (Cambridgeshire) and many another name results.

Less obvious, perhaps, but even more common in names is a monumental cross. Holyrood (Edinburgh and Staffordshire) contains the Old English element *rod* 'a cross', and Ruthwell (Dumfries), 'stream by a cross', appears to be named after its magnificent Northumbrian cross, now inside the village church. Radstone (Northamptonshire) and Rudston (East Yorkshire) both refer to a 'stone cross'. Another word for a cross in Old English is *mæl*, and it is likely that New Malden (Greater London) and Maldon (Essex) are hills with crosses; Trimdon (County Durham) had a wooden cross, *treo-mæl*, on or near the hill. Old English *cristel-mæl* 'crucifix' gives its name to a ford in Christian Malford (Wiltshire). Gaelic *crois* is found in Crossmyloof (Glasgow). But in Ireland crosses were so familiar that the Scandinavian settlers borrowed the word, and then the English followed suit. Irish *cros* is found in dozens of names, such as Crosspatrick (County Kilkenny) and Crossdoney (County Cavan). The enthusiasm with which the idea and its monumental and onomastic trappings were imported is evident throughout the north of England in the numerous examples of Crosby, Crosthwaite in various forms (Crostwick, Crostwight), Crosland, Crossrigg and so on. Staincross (West Yorkshire) is another form of 'stone cross', and Twycross (Leicestershire) apparently had two crosses.

The parish

The parochial (i.e. parish) system has left many evidences of its presence in minor names, but *parish* has replaced *church* in Whiteparish (Wiltshire), formerly *Whytechyrch*. Parish boundaries were important, and were walked around by priest and people annually at Rogationtide, with readings and prayers at appropriate places: this has given us Gospel Oak (London), on the parish boundary between Hampstead and St Pancras. Cressage (Shropshire), 'Christ's oak', was probably where sermons were preached. The parish name Deiniolen (Gwynedd), from Llandeiniolen 'church of little St Deiniol', has replaced the Nonconformist chapel name Ebeneser, but many of these biblical names remain in Wales, for example Bethesda (Gwynedd).

Ecclesiastical personnel

The sheer number of names involving ecclesiastical offices is bewildering, and the picture is made even more confusing by variants in different languages: for example, the word 'bishop' is found as Old English *biscop* in many Bishoptstones, as

Old Scandinavian *biskup* in Biscathorpe (Lincolnshire) and in the Latin form *episcopus* in Huish Episcopi or Kingsbury Episcopi (Somerset). 'Abbot' and 'abbess' come in numerous forms, too, although their modern forms are not always distinguishable. Abbotsford (Scottish Borders) and Abbotsbury (Dorset) refer to abbots, as do Thorpe Abbots (Norfolk), and Cerne Abbas and Milton Abbas (Dorset); whereas Compton Abbas and Melbury Abbas (Dorset) refer to abbesses (Latin *abbatisse*) and, more obviously, so does Abbess Roding (Essex). Monks and nuns also appear in various languages. There are many Monktons and places with *Monks* as an affix, such as Monks Risborough (Berkshire); but there is also Buckland Monachorum (Devon), from Latin *monachus*. The normal Old English word for a nun is *myncen*, and this gives names like Minchinhampton (Gloucestershire) and Minchington (Dorset), but this word is later replaced by Old English *nunne* and gives names such as Nuneaton (Warwickshire) and Nunburnholme (East Yorkshire), as well as the potentially confusing Nun Monkton (North Yorkshire).

Monks and nuns are also called 'brothers' and 'sisters', and thus we have Buckland Sororum (Somerset), 'of the sisters', and Toller Fratrum (Dorset), 'of the brothers', both from the Latin. But the Latin word for brother is most commonly found in the French derivative *frère* (Middle English *frere*) or English *friar*, as in Friern Barnet (London) or Fryerning (Essex). Canons belong to communities associated with cathedrals, and have given their name in Latin to Whitchurch Canonicorum (Dorset) and in English to Canonbury (London) and Canon Frome (Herefordshire); slightly different is Gaelic *chanain* 'priest', derived from the same Latin word, and found in Buchanan (Stirlingshire), although Canonbie (Dumfries and Galloway) refers to Augustinian canons. Other monastic or church officials include the sacristan, found in Sacriston (County Durham); the novices, as in Childer Thornton (Cheshire), from Old English *cildra* 'of the boys', here those of St Werburgh's Abbey; the prior, as in Priors Hardwick (Warwickshire); the almoner, as in Hinton Ampner (Hampshire); and the clerics, as in Clerkenwell (London).

Finally, there is the parson or priest. Parson Drove (Cambridgeshire) and Parsons Green (London) were both named after the parson. But far more frequent in settlement names are priests: they are found in the many Prestons (England and Scotland) and in the Welsh version, Prestatyn, as well as in Prestwick and Prestonpans (Scotland), Priestholm (Anglesey), Priestgill (Cumbria) and Priest Weston (Shropshire). The Old Scandinavian word for a priest or a hermit, *papi*, is found in many Scottish names, particularly Pabay, Pabbay, and Papa Stour and Papa Westray. Although we have generally translated these as 'hermit island' rather than as 'priest island', in these remote areas perhaps the distinction between a priest and a hermit was not as obvious as it would have been further south.

Paul Cavill

Britain: cities, major towns and other features

Britain: traditional counties

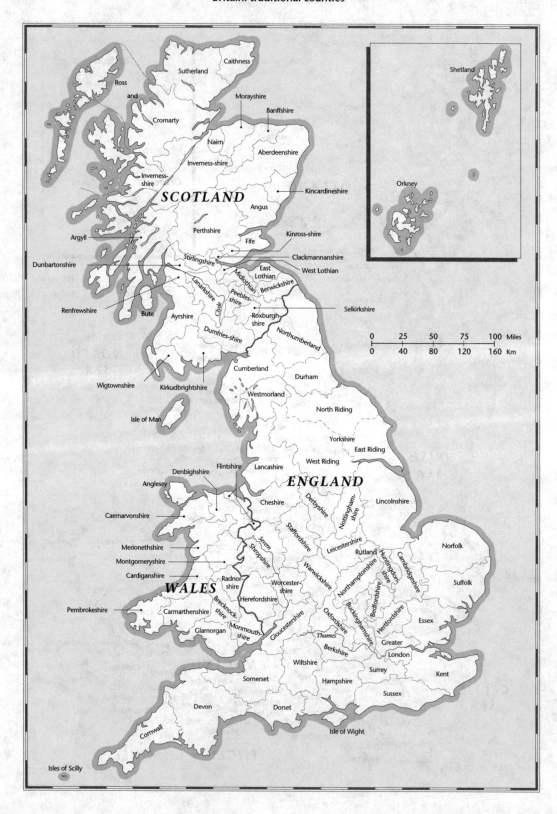

SCOTLAND

Caithness
Sutherland
Ross
and
Cromarty
Morayshire
Banffshire
Nairn
Inverness-shire
Aberdeenshire
Inverness-shire
Kincardineshire
Angus
Perthshire
Argyll
Kinross-shire
Fife
Dunbartonshire
Stirlingshire
Clackmannanshire
East Lothian
West Lothian
Lanarkshire
Midlothian
Berwickshire
Peebles-shire
Renfrewshire
Bute
Clyde
Roxburghshire
Selkirkshire
Ayrshire
Dumfries-shire
Northumberland
Wigtownshire
Kirkudbrightshire

Shetland
Orkney

ENGLAND

Cumberland
Durham
Westmorland
North Riding
Yorkshire
East Riding
West Riding
Isle of Man
Lancashire
Flintshire
Denbighshire
Cheshire
Derbyshire
Nottinghamshire
Lincolnshire
Anglesey
Caernarvonshire
Staffordshire
Leicestershire
Rutland
Cambridgeshire
Norfolk
Merionethshire
Severn
Shropshire
Warwickshire
Northamptonshire
Huntingdonshire
Montgomeryshire
Suffolk
Cardiganshire
Radnorshire
Worcestershire
Bedfordshire
WALES
Pembrokeshire
Herefordshire
Hertfordshire
Essex
Carmarthenshire
Brecknockshire
Gloucestershire
Oxfordshire
Buckinghamshire
Glamorgan
Monmouthshire
Thames
Greater London
Berkshire
Wiltshire
Surrey
Kent
Somerset
Hampshire
Sussex
Devon
Dorset
Isle of Wight
Cornwall
Isles of Scilly

0   25   50   75   100 Miles
0   40   80   120 160 Km

Britain: 1974 reorganization of the counties

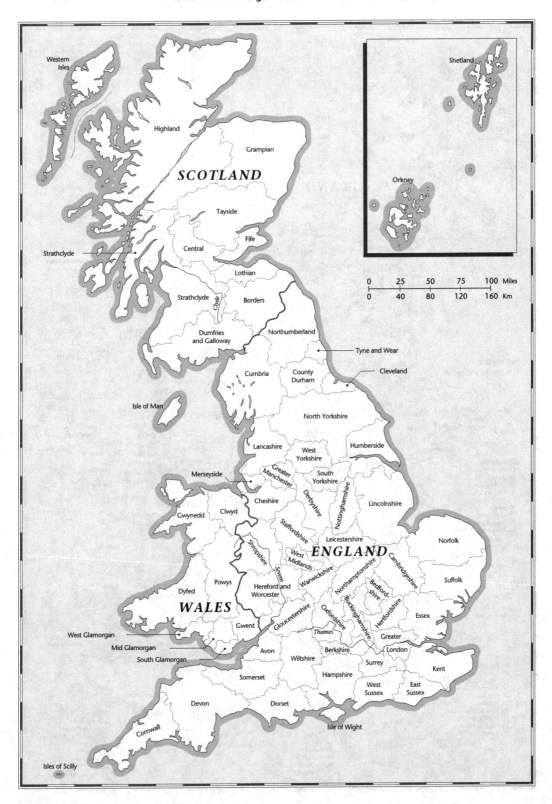

Britain: counties, metropolitan boroughs (extracted) and unitary authorities in the 21st century

Western Isles (Eilean Siar)

Shetland

Foula

Orkney

Fair Isle

Highland

Moray

Aberdeenshire

Aberdeen City

SCOTLAND

Angus

Perth & Kinross

51

Fife

Stirling

50

49

Argyll & Bute

46 47 48
45 44 41 40
43 42 39

East Lothian

North Ayrshire

East Ayrshire

South Lanarkshire

South Ayrshire

Scottish Borders

Dumfries and Galloway

44. Glasgow City
45. Renfrewshire
46. Inverclyde
47. West Dunbartonshire
48. East Dunbartonshire
49. Falkirk
50. Clackmannanshire
51. Dundee City

36. Darlington
37. Stockton-on-Tees
38. Middlesbrough
39. Midlothian
40. City of Edinburgh
41. West Lothian
42. North Lanarkshire
43. East Renfrewshire

Northumberland

Cumbria

Durham

36 37 38

Tyne & Wear

Hartlepool

Redcar and Cleveland

North Tyneside

Tyne & Wear

Newcastle upon Tyne

Gateshead

South Tyneside

Sunderland

Merseyside & Greater Manchester

Rochdale
Bolton **Bury** **Oldham**
Sefton **Wigan** **Salford** **Tameside**
St. Helens **Trafford** **Stockport**
Liverpool **Knowsley**
Manchester

Blackpool

Lancashire

North Yorkshire

West Yorkshire

York

East Riding of Yorkshire

City of Kingston upon Hull

North East Lincolnshire

West & South Yorkshire

Bradford **Leeds**
Calderdale
Kirklees **Wakefield**
Barnsley **Doncaster**
Sheffield **Rotherham**

26. Wrexham
27. Stoke-on-Trent
28. Derby
29. Nottingham
30. Leicester
31. Peterborough
32. Halton
33. Warrington
34. Merseyside
35. Blackburn with Darwen

Denbighshire
Flintshire
Isle of Anglesey

Conwy

Gwynedd

Greater Manchester

35

34 33
32

Cheshire

27

South Yorkshire

Derbyshire

North Lincolnshire

Lincolnshire

Nottinghamshire

28 29

Leicestershire

30

Rutland

31

Staffordshire

25

West Midlands

Wolverhampton
Walsall
Dudley **Sandwell**
Solihull **Coventry**
Birmingham

West Midlands

Shropshire

Powys

Ceredigon

WALES

Herefordshire

Worcestershire

Warwickshire

Northamptonshire

Norfolk

Suffolk

Cambridgeshire

15

Bedfordshire

14

Buckinghamshire

Hertfordshire

Essex

Oxfordshire

Gloucestershire

Severn

Carmarthenshire

23 22
19 20 21 24
17 16
18

Swansea

Pembrokeshire

Neath Port Talbot

Bridgend

16. Newport
17. Cardiff
18. Vale of Glamorgan
19. Rhondda Cynon Taff
20. Caerphilly
21. Torfaen
22. Blaenau Gwent
23. Merthyr Tydfil
24. Monmouthshire
25. Telford & Wrekin

5
4
2 3

West Berkshire

6

8 9
10
11

Greater London

12

13

Southend-on-Sea

Kent

Surrey

Wiltshire

Somerset

Hampshire

West Sussex

East Sussex

ENGLAND

Devon

Dorset

Isle of Wight

Portsmouth

Brighton & Hove

Cornwall & Isles of Scilly

Torbay

Poole

Bournemouth

Plymouth

1. Southampton
2. North Somerset
3. Bath & North East Somerset
4. City of Bristol
5. South Gloucestershire

6. Swindon
7. Reading
8. Wokingham
9. Bracknell Forest
10. Windsor & Maidenhead
11. Slough
12. Thurrock
13. Medway
14. Luton
15. Milton Keynes

Ireland: traditional provinces, modern counties, cities, major towns and other features

Glossary

Frequently Used Elements
in the Place Names of Britain and Ireland

KEY

aber	actual place-name elements in their *original* languages
aber	the forms ('reflexes') and mutations of elements that commonly occur in modern place names. A hyphen before the name means it normally appears as a suffix; a hyphen after the word means it normally appears as a prefix.
ABER	cross-references to boxed entries in the A–Z sequence of *Brewer's Britain and Ireland*

Abbreviations used

Co	Cornish
G	Gaelic
I	Irish
L	Latin
ME	Middle English
ModE	Modern English
OCelt	Old Celtic
OE	Old English
OFr	Old French
OScand	Old Scandinavian
S	Scots
W	Welsh

a (OScand) river

abbas (L) of the abbot or abbess

aber (W) estuary, confluence *see* ABER

abh, abhainn (I) river *see* AVON

ac (OE) oak tree

achadh (G, I) field *see* ACHADH

æcer (OE) cultivated land *see* FIELD

æl (OE) eel

æppel (OE) apple tree

ærgi (OScand) shieling, summer hill-pasture *see* -ARY

ærn (OE) house, building

æsc (OE) ash tree

æspe (OE) aspen tree

æwell, æwelm (OE) river-source

afon (G, W) river *see* AVON

agha- *see* ACHADH

aglish *see* ECCLES

aird (G, I) height, high place, promontory *see* ARD

àirigh (I) shieling *see* -ARY

allt (G) stream

allt (W) wooded slope

alor (OE) alder tree

amhainn (G) river *see* AVON

anna- *see* **eanach**

anstey *see* **anstig**

anstig (OE) narrow track

apuldor (OE) apple tree

ard *see* ARD

àrd (G, I), **ardd**, **arth** (W), **ardh** (Co) height, high place, promontory *see* ARD

-ary *see* -ARY

ast- *see* **east**

ash- *see* **æsc**

askr (OScand) ash tree

ath (I) new

áth (I) ford *see* FORD

auchen-, auchin- *see* ACHADH

auchter (S) *see* **uachdair**

austr (OScand) east

avon *see* AVON

-ay *see* -AY

-bach *see* **bæce**

bach (W) small *see* BACH

bæc (OE) back, ridge

bæce (OE) stream in a valley

bae (W) bay

bærnet (OE) land cleared by burning

bæth (OE) bath

baile (G, I) farm, settlement *see* BAL-, BALL-, BALLY-

bal- *see* BAL-, BALL-, BALLY-

bala (W) lake outlet

ball-, bally- *see* BAL-, BALL-, BALLY-

bán (I) white

bangor (W) stake in a wattle fence

banke (OScand) bank, hill-slope

bann (W) mountain

bar (OE) boar

bar (Co), **barr** (G) top

barnet *see* **bærnet**

barrow *see* **bearu**

barton *see* **bere-tun**

-batch *see* **bæce**

bay (ME) bay

beacen (OE) beacon, signal

-beach *see* **bæce**

beag (G, I) small

béal (I) estuary, mouth *see* BAL-, BALL-, BALLY-

bealach (G) pass

bealach (I) road *see* BAL-, BALL-, BALLY-

beam (OE) tree-trunk, beam

bean (OE) bean

bearu (OE) grove, wood

beau, bel (OFr) fine, beautiful

bece (OE) beech tree

bedd (W) grave

-beg *see* **beag**

beinn (G) mountain

beithe (G) birch tree

bekkr (OScand) stream

bel (OE) funeral pyre, beacon fire

ben *see* **beinn**

beo (OE) bee

beonet (OE) bent-grass, coarse grass

beorc (OE) birch tree

beorg (OE) hill, mound, tumulus *see* BURY

beos (OE) bent-grass, coarse grass

bere (OE) barley

bere-ærn (OE) barn, store for barley

bere-tun (OE) barley farm, outlying grange farm

bere-wic (OE) barley farm, outlying grange farm

berg (OScand) hill, mound tumulus *see* BURY

berth (W) hedge, wood

betws (W) chapel, oratory

big (W) peak

bigging (ME) a building

bile (I) tree, meeting-place

birki (OScand) birch tree

-bister *see* **bolstathr**

bla(r) (OScand) dark, exposed

black *see* **blæc**

blæc (OE) black, dark-coloured

blaen (W) highland, upper reaches of a river

blair *see* **blàr**

blàr (G) a plain, cleared land

boc (OE) beech tree

boc-land (OE) land granted by charter

bod (G) a clump

bod, bed (W) dwelling, settlement, church

bog (G) bog

boga (OE) bow, arch, bend

bol, bolstathr (OScand) homestead

bold (OE) house or building

bondi (OScand) free peasant

bont (W) bridge

bool- *see* **buaile**

borough *see* BURY

borth (W) harbour

both (OScand) booth, temporary shelter

bóthar (I) road

bothl, botl (OE) house or building

bothm, botm (OE), **botn** (OScand) broad river valley

bottom, -botham *see* **bothm**

bourne *see* **burna**

bow *see* **boga**

-boy *see* **buidhe**

bra (OScand) brow

brad (OE) broad, spacious

brae (S) hillside

brân (W) dark

bre (W) hill

breac (G) speckled

brec (OE) land broken up for cultivation

brekka (OScand) hill-slope

brembel (OE, ME), **bremel** (OE) bramble, blackberry bush

brende (ME) burnt, cleared by burning

brenin (W) king

brent *see* **brende**

brer (OE) briars

Brettas (OE) Britons

bridge *see* **brycg**

brigg (S) bridge

broad *see* **brad**

broc (OE) brook, stream

brom (OE) thorny bush, broom

bron (W) hill slope

brook *see* **broc**

brycg (OE) bridge, causeway

bryn (W) mound, hill, bank

buaile (I) hill-pasture

bucc (OE) buck, stag

buckland *see* **boc-land**

bugail (W) shepherd

buidhe (G, I) yellow

bula (OE) bull

bun (I) bottom

bur (OE) cottage, dwelling

burh (OE) fortified place, stronghold, manor house, town *see* BURY

burn (S), **burna** (OE) stream

-burn *see* **burn**

bury *see* BURY

buth (OScand) booth, temporary shelter

buwch (W) cow

bwlch (W) mountain pass

by (OScand) farmstead, village, settlement *see* -BY

bychan (W) small *see* BACH

byrig (dative of **burh**) at the fortified place *see* BURY

cadair, **cadeir**, **cader** (W) seat, high place *see* CAHER

cae (W) enclosure, field

caer (W), **cair** (Co) fortified place *see* CAHER

cærse (OE) cress, water-cress

cæster (OE) Roman station or town, fortification *see* CHESTER

caher *see* CAHER

cairn (G) heap of stones, rocky hill, burial mound

caiseal (I) ring-fort

caisléan (I) castle *see* CASTLE

calc (OE) chalk, limestone

cald (OE) cold

caled (W) hard

calf (OE) calf

cam(m) (Co, G, W) crooked

camb (OE) hill-crest, ridge

camp (OE) field, uncultivated land around a Romano-British settlement

caol (G, I) strait (of sea), narrow

capel (G, W) chapel

carl- *see* **karl**, *see also* **ceorl**

càrn (G), **carn** (Co, I, W) heap of stones, rocky hill, burial mound

carnedd (W) cairn, heap of stones

carr, cars- *see* **kjarr**

carraig (G, I), **carreg** (W) rock, crag

carrick (I) *see* **carraig**

cashel (I) *see* **caiseal**

castel (Co), **castell** (W), **castle** (ModE) castle, stronghold *see* CASTLE

castle *see* CASTLE

cat (G), **cath** (W), **cat(t)** (OE) cat, wild-cat

cathair (G, I) fort *see* CAHER

cealc (OE) chalk, limestone

ceald (OE) cold

cealf (OE) calf

ceann (G, I) headland, promontory, hill summit

ceap (OE) trade, market

ceaster (OE) Roman station or town, fortification *see* CHESTER

ceathrú (I) quarter

ced *see* CED

cefn (W) ridge, back

cei (W) quay

celli (W) grove

celyn, **celynnen** (W) holly tree

ceorl (OE) free peasant *see* CHARL-, CHORL-

ceping, **cieping** (OE) market

cese, **ciese** (OE) cheese

chapel (ME) chapel

charl- *see* CHARL-, CHORL-

cheap *see* **ceap**

chesil-, chisel- *see* **cisel**

chester *see* CHESTER

chipping *see* **ceping**

chorl- *see* CHARL-, CHORLchurch *see* **cirice**

cild (OE) child, young nobleman

cill (G, I) church, monastery, burial place *see* KIL-

cirice (OE) church

cisel, **ceosol** (OE) gravel

clachan (G) church, hamlet

cladach (G) shore

clæfre (OE) clover

clæg (OE) clay

clawdd (W) embankment

clay *see* **clæg**

cledd (W) sword

clif (OE) cliff, slope, river-bank

cliff(e), **clive** *see* **clif**

cloch, **clochàn** (I) stone, rocky ruin

clon- *see* **cluain**, *see also* ACHADH

cluain (I) pasture, meadowland, *see also* ACHADH

cniht (OE) young man, servant

cnoc (G, I) rounded hill, hillock, mountain *see* KNOCK-

cnoll (OE) hill-top, hillock

cnwc (W) rounded hill, hillock, mountain *see* KNOCK-

coal *see* **col**

cocc (OE) (1) hillock, (2) woodcock

coch (W) red

coed (W) wood *see* CED

cofa (OE) chamber, cave, cove

coill, **coillte** (I), **coille**, **coilltean** (pl), **coillteach** (G) wood *see* KIL-, *see also* CED

coire (G) hollow in mountainside, corrie

col (OE) (1) cool, (2) coal, charcoal

cold *see* **cald**, **kaldr**

-combe *see* -COMBE, COOMBE

-coombe *see* -COMBE, COOMBE

cool- *see* **cúil**

copp (OE) hill-top

corr (G, I) rounded hill

corrach, **currach** (G) marsh

corrie *see* **coire**

cors (W) bog, fen, marsh

cot (OE) cottage, hut, shelter *see* -COT, COTE

-cot, cote *see* -COT, COTE

cove *see* **cofa**

craig (W) crag, rock

cran (OE) crane, heron

craobh (G) tree, wood

crawe (OE) crow

creag (G) crag, rock

creech *see* CREECH, CROOK

cress- *see* **cærse**

crib (W) crest, summit

croes (W) cross, crossroads *see* CROSS

crois (I) cross *see* CROSS

croft (OE) enclosure, small enclosed field

crom (G) bend

cron (W) round

crook *see* CREECH, CROOK

cros (OE) cross *see* CROSS

cross *see* CROSS

cruach (G) heap, stack

cruc (OE) cross *see* CROSS

cruc, **crug** (OCelt) hill, mound, tumulus *see* CREECH, CROOK

crwn, **cryn** (W) round

cu (OE) cow

cúil (I) secluded place, nook

cùl (G) back

cul- *see* **cúil**

cum (L) with

cumb (OE) coomb, short valley *see* -COMBE, COOMBE

Cumbre (OE) the Cymry, the Cumbrian Britons

currach (I) bog, marsh, moor

curragh, curry, *see* **currach**

cwen (OE) queen

cwene (OE) woman

cweorn (OE) quern, hand-mill

cwm (W) round hollow in mountainside, glen, valley *see* -COMBE, COOMBE

cyln (OE) kiln

cymer (W) confluence

Cymry (W) the Welsh

cyne- (OE) royal

cyning (OE) king

cyta (OE) kite

dà (G) two

dabhoch (G) unit of land measurement (192 acres)

dæl (OE) pit, hollow, valley

dail (G) field

daingean (I) stronghold

dale *see* **dalr**, **dæl**, **dail**

dalr (OScand) valley

dâr, **derwen** (W) oak tree

darach (G) oak

dau (W) two

ddu (W) black, dark *see* DDU, DUBH

de (W) south, southern

dean *see* **denu**

dearg (G, I) red

deep *see* **deop**

deer *see* **deor**, **djur**

deg, **teg** (W) beautiful

-den *see* **denn**, **denu**

denn (OE) woodland swine pasture

denu (OE) narrow valley, *see also* DOWN, -DON

deop (OE) deep

deor (OE) animal, deer

derne (OE) hidden, overgrown with vegetation

derry *see* **doire**

dic (OE) ditch, dyke, embankment

dierne (OE) hidden, overgrown with vegetation

din (Co, W) fort

dinas (W) large town, fortress

díseart (I) hermitage

-dish *see* **edisc**

ditch *see* **dic**

djur (OScand) animal, deer

dobhar (G) water

doire (G, I) grove, oak wood

dôl (W) water meadow

domnach (I) an early church *see* KIL-

-don *see* DOWN, -DON

donagh *see* **domnach**

donn (G) brown

doon *see* **dún**

dour (Co) water

dove- *see* **dobhar**

down (G) fort *see* CASTLE, *see also* DOWN, -DON

down *see* DOWN, -DON

dræg (OE) slope used for dragging loads, dray, sledge

draeth (W) beach

-dre *see* **tre(f)**

droichead (I) bridge

droim (I) ridge, mountain crest

drom *see* **droim**

druim (G) ridge, mountain crest

drum *see* **droim**

drum (W) ridge, mountain crest

dry *see* **dryge**

dryge (OE) dry

dubh (G) black, dark *see* DDU, DUBH

duin (G) fort *see* CASTLE, *see also* DOWN, -DON

dùn (G) fort *see* CASTLE, *see also* DOWN, -DON

dún (I) fort *see* CASTLE, *see also* DOWN, -DON

dun (OE) hill, down *see* DOWN, -DON

dwfr (W) water

dyffryn (W) valley

dyke *see* **dic**

dyserth (W) hermitage

ea (OE) river see EA-

ea- river *see* EA-

-ea land partly surrounded by water *see* -EY, -EA

eaglais (I) church *see* ECCLES

eald (OE) old

eanach (I) marsh

èar (I) east

earn (OE) eagle

eas (G, I) waterfall

east (OE) east, eastern

eccles *see* ECCLES

ecg (OE) edge, escarpment

edge *see* **ecg**

edisc (OE) enclosure, park

eg (OE) island, dry ground in marsh, water meadow, land protruding into water *see* -EY, -EA

eglais (G) church *see* ECCLES

egland (OE) island *see* ISLE

eglos (Co), **eglws** (W) church *see* ECCLES

eik (OScand) oak tree

eilean (G) island

eithin (W) furze

elfitu (OE) swan

elle(r)n (OE) elder tree

elm (OE) elm tree

-en (W) small

ende (OE), **endi** (OScand) end, part of an area or estate

Engle (OE) the Angles, English

enis (Co) island *see* INIS

eochail (G) yew wood

eofor (OE) wild boar

eorl (OE) nobleman

eow (OE) yew-tree

eowestre (OE) sheep-fold

erg (OScand) shieling, summer hill-pasture *see* -ARY

eski (OScand) place of ash trees

ey (OScand) island *see* -AY

-ey land partly surrounded by water *see* -EY, -EA

fach (W) small *see* BACH

fada (G, I) long

fæger (OE) fair, pleasant

faen (G, W) stone

fæsten (OE) stronghold

fair (ModE) *see* **fæger**

-**fair** (W) St Mary

fàire (G) hill

fald (OE) fold, enclosure for animals

farn- *see* **fearn**

faur (W) big *see* **beag**

fearn (I) alder tree

fearn (OE) fern, bracken

fechan (W) small *see* BACH

feld (OE) open country, tract of land cleared of trees *see*
   FIELD

felin (W) mill

fell *see* **fjall**

fenn (OE) fen, marshy ground

ferja (OScand) ferry

ffin (W) boundary

field *see* FIELD

fin- *see* **fionn**

fionn, fhionn (G, I) white

firth *see* **fjorthr**

fjall (OScand) hill, fell

fjorthr (OScand) fjord, inlet

fleet *see* **fleot**

fleot (OE) estuary, inlet, creek, also stream

foel (W) bare (hill)

fola (OE) foal

folc (OE) folk, tribe, people

foli (OScand) foal

ford (OE) ford, river-crossing *see* FORD

fothach (G) lake

fothair, fothir (G) terrace, slope

foul- *see* **fugol**

fox (OE) fox

fowl- *see* **fugol**

frith *see* **fyrth(e)**

fugol (OE) (wild)fowl, bird

ful (OE) foul, dirty

funta (OE) spring (from Latin *fons, fontis*), spring with
   Roman brick or stonework

fyrhth(e) (OE) woodland, often sparse woodland or scrub

gærs (OE) grass

gall (G) foreign(er)

gar- *see* **garbh**

gara (OE) triangular plot of ground, point of land

garbh (G, I) rough

gardd (W), **garrdha** (I) garden

garry- *see* **garrdha**

gart (G) garden

garthr (OScand) enclosure

garv- *see* **garbh**

gat (OE), goat

gat-, gate- *see* **gat, geit**

gata (OScand) road, street

-**gate** *see* **gata, geit**

ge (OE) district, region

geard (OE) yard, enclosure

geat (OE) gate, gap, pass

gehæg (OE) enclosure

geit (OScand) goat

gelad (OE) river-crossing

gemænnes (OE) land held in common

gemære (OE) boundary

gemot (OE) meeting-place

gemythe (OE) confluence of rivers

geset (OE) dwelling, stable, fold

gewæd (OE) ford, crossing-place

geweorc (OE) building, fortification

gil (OScand) deep narrow valley, ravine

glais (W), **glaise** (Co, G) stream

glan (W) river bank, shore

glas (G, I, Co) grey, green, blue (or any mixture of these hues)

glas (Co, G) stream

gleann (G, I) glen *see* GLEN

glen *see* GLEN

glyn (W) valley *see* GLEN

goch (W) red

goen (Co) down, heathland

gors (W) bog, fen, marsh

gort (I) field *see* ACHADH

gos (OE) goose

græf (OE) pit, trench

græfe (OE) thicket, brushwood, grove

graf (OE) grove, copse

grave *see* **græf**

great (ME) large, big, an English equivalent for Latin
   major, magna

-**greave** *see* **græfe**

green *see* **grene**

grene (OE) (adj.) green-coloured, (noun) grassy place,
   village green

greot (OE) gravel

gres (OScand) grass

griss (OScand) young pig

grove *see* **graf**

gwawn (W) moorland

gwen (W) white, fair

gwern (W) marsh, alder trees

gwydh (Co) trees

gwyn (W), **gwynn** (Co) white, fair

hæg (OE) enclosure

hæme (OE) inhabitants, dwellers

hæm-styde (OE) homestead, site of a dwelling

hær (OE) rock, heap of stones

hæsel (OE) hazel tree

hæth (OE) heath, heather, uncultivated land overgrown
with heather

hafn (OScand) haven, harbour

haga (OE), **hagi** (OScand) hedged enclosure

hagu-thorn (OE) hawthorn

hale *see* HALE, -HALL

halh (OE) nook or corner of land, often used of land in
a hollow or river-bend *see* HALE, -HALL

halig (OE) holy

-hall *see* HALE, -HALL

ham (OE) homestead, village, manor, estate, *see* HAM

ham *see* HAM

hamble-, hamel- *see* **hamol**

ham-stede (OE) homestead, site of a dwelling *see* HAM

ham-tun (OE) home farm or settlement, enclosure in
which a homestead stands *see* HAM *and* -TON

hamm (OE) enclosure, land hemmed in by water or
marsh or higher ground, land in a river-bend,
river-meadow, promontory *see* HAM

hamol, **hamel** (OE) mutilated, crooked

han- *see* **heah**

-hanger *see* **hangra**

hangra (OE) wood on a steep slope

har (OE) grey, also boundary

hara (OE) hare

harrow *see* **hearg**

hart- *see* **heorot**

hat- *see* **hæth**

haugh *see* HALE, -HALL

haugr (OScand) hill, mound, tumulus

haven *see* **hafn**

haw *see* **haga**

head *see* **heafod**

heafod (OE) head, headland, end of a ridge, river-source

heah (OE) high, also chief

hearg (OE) heathen shrine or temple

heath *see* **hæth**

hecg(e) (OE) hedge

helde, **hielde** (OE) slope

hen (W) old

hen- *see* **heah**

hengest (OE) stallion

hen-lys (Co) old court

heorot (OE) hart, stag

here (OE) army

hid (OE) hide of land, amount of land for the support of one
free family and its dependants (usually about 120 acres)

higna *see* **hiwan**

hill *see* **hyll**

hind (OE) hind, doe

-hithe *see* **hyth**

hiwan (possessive **higna**) (OE) household, members of a
family or religious community

hiwisc (OE) household, amount of land for the support of
a family

hlaw, **hlæw** (OE) tumulus, mound, hill

hlinc (OE) ridge, ledge, terrace

hlith (OE, OScand) hill-slope

hlose (OE) pigsty

hoc (OE) hook or corner of land, land in a bend

hofuth (OScand) headland, promontory

hoh (OE) heel of land, projecting hill-spur

hol (OE) hole or hollow, deep

hole *see* **hol**

holegn (OE) holly

holmr (OScand) island, raised ground in marsh, river
meadow *see* -EY, -EA *and* HALE, -HALL

holt (OE) wood, thicket

hook *see* **hoc**

hop (OScand) land-locked bay, inlet

hop (OE) small enclosed valley, enclosure in marsh or moor

hope *see* **hop**

horn (OE, OScand), **horna** (OE) horn, horn-shaped hill or
piece of land

hors (OE) horse

horu (OE) filth, dirt

house *see* **hus**

how(e) *see* **haugr**

hræfn (OE), **hrafn** (OScand) raven

hramsa (OE, OScand) wild garlic

hreod (OE) reed, rush

hris (OE, OScand) brushwood, shrubs

hrither (OE) ox, cattle

hroc (OE), **hrokr** (OScand) rook

hrycg (OE), **hryggr** (OScand) ridge

hund (OE) dog

hunig (OE) honey

hunta (OE) huntsman

hurst *see* **hyrst**

hus (OE, OScand) house

hvals (OScand) whale

hvitr (OScand) white

hwæte (OE) wheat

hwit (OE) white

hyll (OE) hill

hyrst (OE) wooded hill

hyth (OE) landing-place or harbour, inland port

-hythe *see* **hyth**

ig (OE) yew-tree

inbhear (I), **inbhir** (G) estuary *see* ABER

-**ing** (OE) place characterized by, place belonging to
    see -ING

-**ing**- (OE) place associated with or called after *see* -ING

-**inga**- (OE) possessive case of -**ingas** *see* -ING

-**ingas** (OE) (plural suffix) people of, family or followers
    of, dwellers at *see* -ING

inis (G, I), **inish** (I) island *see* INIS

inch *see* INIS

innis (I) island *see* INIS

innis- *see* INIS

inver (G) estuary *see* ABER

íochtar (I) lower

-**iog** (W) an adjectival affix, as in Brycheiniog (*see* BRECON)
    or Blaenau Ffestiniog, here possibly 'territory of'

isle *see* ISLE

iw (OE) yew-tree

juxta (L) next to

kaldr (OScand) cold

kalfr (OScand) calf

karl (OScand) freeman, peasant *see* CHARL-, CHORL-

keith (G) wood *see* CED

kelda (OScand) spring

ken-, kin- *see* **ceann**

kil- *see* KIL-

king *see* **cyning**

kirk *see* **kirkja**

kirkja (OScand) church

kjarr (OScand) marsh overgrown with brushwood

knock- *see* KNOCK

krok (OScand) bend, land in a river bend

kross (OScand) cross *see* CROSS

kyle *see* **caol**

lacu (OE) stream, water-course *see also* LAKE

lad (OE) water-course

-lade *see* **lad**

læcc, **læce** (OE) stream, bog

lag (I) hollow

lairig (G) pass between hills

lake *see* LAKE

lamb (OE) lamb

lanark *see* **llanerch**

land (OE) tract of land, estate, cultivated land

lang (OE), **langr** (OScand) long

lann (G, Co) site of a church, burial ground, church

larg- *see* **lairig**

law *see* LAW, LOW

lawerce (OE) lark

leac (OE) leek, garlic

leah (OE) wood, woodland clearing or glade, later pasture,
    meadow *see* -LEY

leaht (G) cairn

leas (OE) pasture, meadow-land

leck- *see* **leac**

leiter (G), **leitir** (I) hillside, mountain slope

letter *see* **leiter**

-ley *see* -LEY

lin (OE, OScand) flax

lind (OE) lime-tree

linne, **llyn** (G, W) lake, pool

lios (I) fortified enclosure, fort

lis- *see* **lios**

little *see* **lytel**

llan (W) site of a church, burial ground, church

llanerch (W, G) clearing, glade

llyn (G, W) lake, pool

loc, **loca** (OE) lock, fold, enclosure

loch (G and I) lake *see* LOCH, LOUGH

-lode *see* **lad**

logaidh (G) hollow

logie *see* **lag**

long *see* **lang**

longphort (I) camp, stronghold, fort

lough *see* LOCH, LOUGH

-low(e) *see* LAW, LOW

lower (ModE) lower

lytel (OE) little

machair (G), **machaire** (I) plain

machar *see* **machair**

mæd (OE) meadow

mægden (OE) maiden

mæl (OE) cross, crucifix *see* CROSS

maen (G, W) stone

mæne (OE) land held in common

mære (OE) boundary

maes (W) field, open land

magh (G, I) plain

magher- *see* **machair**

magna (L) great

maid(en) *see* **mægden**

major (L) larger

maol (G) bare (hill)

mapel, **mapul**, **mapuldor** (OE) maple tree

mar- *see* **mære**, *see also* **mersc**

march, mark- *see* **mearc**

marsh *see* **mersc**

mawr (W) big *see* BACH

may- *see* **magh**

mead, meadow *see* **mæd**

meall (G) lump

mearc (OE) boundary

mel- *see* **methal**

melin (W) mill

melr (OScand) sand-bank, sand-hill

meos (OE) moss

mere (OE) pond, pool, lake *see also* LAKE

mersc (OE) marsh, marshland

methal (OScand) middle

mhór (G, I) big *see* BACH

micel (OE) great

mickle-, muckle- *see* **micel**, **mikill**

middel (OE) middle

middle *see* **middel**

mikill (OScand) great

mil-, mill- *see* **myln**

minster *see* **mynster**

mire *see* **myrr**

moel (W) bare (hill)

monach (G) monk

monadh (G) hill, moorland

monk *see* **munuc**

mont (OFr, ME) mount, hill

moor *see* **mor**

mór (G, I) big *see* BACH

mor (OE, OScand) moor, marshy ground, barren upland

-more *see* **mór**

mos (OE), **mosi** (OScand) moss, marsh, bog

moss *see* **mos**

mot (OE) meeting-place

mount- *see* **monadh**

muillean (I), **muilleann** (G) mill

muir *see* **mor**

mullin- *see* **muillean**

munuc (OE) monk

mus (OE, OScand) mouse

mutha (OE) river-mouth, estuary

mycel (OE) great

myln (OE) mill

mynster (OE) monastery, church of a monastery, minster
  or large church

mynydd (W) mountain

myrr (OScand) mire, bog, swampy ground

mythe (OE) confluence of rivers

næss (OE) promontory, headland *see* NESS

nant (W) valley, stream

nes (OScand) promontory, headland *see* NESS

ness *see* NESS

new *see* **niwe**

newydd (W) new

niwe (OE) new

north (OE), **northr** (OScand) north, northern

northman (OE), **northmathr** (OScand) a Norwegian

nua (I) new

nunne (OE) nun

oak *see* **ac**

ofer (OE) (1) bank, margin, shore, (2) flat-topped ridge,
  hill, promontory

old *see* **eald**

ora (OE) shore, hill-slope, flat-topped hill

oter (OE) otter

out, outer *see* **ut**, **utterra**

over *see* **ofer**, *see also* **uferra**

ox- *see* **oxa**

oxa (OE) ox

pailís (G) palisade, defensive enclosure

pallas *see* **pailis**

pant (G) bridge

papi (OScand) monk, hermit, priest

park (OFr, ME) enclosed hunting ground

parva (L) small

path *see* **pæth**

pæth (OE) path, track

peak *see* **pic**

peart (G) hedge, wood

peel *see* **pel**

pel (ME) palisade

pen (G, W), **penn** (OCelt) head, end, hill, also chief *see* PEN

penn (OE) pen, fold, enclosure for animals

perth *see* **peart**

perth (W) hedge, wood

peru (OE) pear

-peth *see* **pæth**

phort (G) port, fort *see* PORT

pic (OE) peak, point

pil (Scots) palisade

pirige (OE) pear tree

plega (OE) play, games, sport

plume (OE) plum, plum tree

pol (OE) pool, pond, creek

poll (Co, I, G) cove, pool, hollow

pont (W, G) bridge

port (G) port, fort *see* PORT

port (OE), **porth** (W) harbour, market *see* PORT

preas (G) brushwood, thicket

preost (OE) priest

pres (W) brushwood, thicket

prest- *see* **preost**

prys (W) brushwood, thicket

pwll (W) cove, pool, hollow

pyll (OE) tidal creek, pool, stream

pyrige (OE) pear tree

pytt (OE) pit, hollow

queen *see* **cwen**

ra (OScand) (1) boundary, (2) roebuck

ram- *see* **hramsa**

rath *see* RATH

ràth (G), **ráth** (I) circular fort *see* RATH

rauthr (OScand) red

raw- *see* **rauthr**

read (OE) red

red *see* **hreod**, **read**

refa (OE) reeve, bailiff

regis (L) of the king

rhinn (G) cape, promontory

rhos (G, W) moor, heath, promontory

rhyd (W) ford or stream

ribhach (I) grey, mottled

ric (OE) raised strip of land, ridge

ridge *see* **hrycg**

rig(g) *see* **hryggr**

rinn (I) cape, promontory

risc (OE) rush

rith, **rithig** (OE) small stream

rod (OE) cross, crucifix *see* CROSS

rod, **rodu** (OE) clearing

ros (OCelt, G, W) moor, heath, promontory

rother- *see* **hrither**

rough *see* **ruh**

row- *see* **ruh**

roy- *see* **ryge**

ruadh (I) red

rugr (OScand) rye

ruh (OE) rough

ruaidhe (G) red

rush *see* **risc**

ruy-, **ry-** *see* **ryge**

ryge (OE) rye

rysc (OE) rush

sal(e)- *see* **salh**

salh (OE) sallow, willow

salt (OE) salt, salty

sand (OE), **sandr** (OScand) sand

saurr (OScand) mud, dirt, sour ground

sæ (OE), **sær** (OScand) sea, inland lake

sæte (OE) plural dwellers, settlers

sæti (OScand) lofty place, hill-top

sætr (OScand) shieling, hill pasture, summer pasture

sceaga (OE) small wood, copse

sceap (OE) sheep

sceat (OE) corner or angle of land, projecting wood or piece of land

sceir (I) skerry

scela (OE) temporary hut or shelter, hill-pasture

scelf (OE) shelf of level ground, ledge

schele (ME) temporary hut or shelter, hill-pasture

scip (OE) sheep

scir (OE) (1) bright, clear, (2) district *see* SHIRE

scucca (OE) evil spirit, demon

sealt (OE) salt, salty

sean (G) old

Seaxe (OE) the Saxons

sele (OE) (1) dwelling, house, hall, (2) sallow or willow copse

seofon (OE) seven

set (OE) dwelling, stable, fold

sgeir (G) skerry

sgonn (G) mound

sgurr (G) peak

shan- *see* **sean**

-shaw *see* **sceaga**

she(e)r *see* **scir** (1)

shield *see* **scela**

shire *see* SHIRE

-shot(t) *see* **sceat**

sic (OE) small stream

sid (OE) large, extensive

side (OE) hill-side

skali (OScand) temporary hut or shed

sker (OScand) skerry

skogr (OScand) wood

slæd (OE) valley

slæp (OE) slippery muddy place

slakki (OScand) shallow valley

sliabh (I) mountain

slieve *see* **sliabh**

slige, **sligeach** (G, I) shell, shelly

sligo *see* **slige**

sloch (G) throat

smæl (OE) small

south *see* **suth**

spidéal (G, I) hospital, place of hospitality *see* SPITAL

spit(t)al *see* SPITAL

spitel (ME) hospital, place of hospitality *see* SPITAL

srath (G) valley bottom

sròn (G) promontory

stæth (OE) landing-place

stall (OE) stall for animals, fishing pool

stan (OE) stone, rock, boundary stone *see* STONE

stain-, stane- *see* STONE

staple- *see* **stapol**

stapol (OE) post, pillar of wood or stone

-stead, -sted *see* **stede**

steall (OE) stall for animals, fishing pool

stede (OE) enclosed pasture, place, site

steinn (OScand) stone, rock, boundary stone *see* STONE

steort (OE) tail or tongue of land

stig (OE), **stigr** (OScand) path, narrow road

stoc (OE) place, outlying farmstead or hamlet, secondary or dependent settlement *see* -STOCK, STOCK-, STOKE

stocc (OE) tree-trunk, stump, log *see also* -STOCK, STOCK-, STOKE

-stock, stock- *see* -STOCK, STOCK-, STOKE

stod (OE) stud, herd of horses

stoke *see* -STOCK, STOCK-, STOKE

stokkr (OScand), tree-trunk, stump, log

stone *see* STONE

stoth (OScand) landing-place

stow (OE) place, assembly place, holy place

stræt (OE) Roman road, paved road *see* STREET

stran- *see* **sròn**

strat-, stret- *see* STREET

strath (G) valley bottom

strath- *see* **srath**

straumr (OScand) current, tidal stream

street *see* STREET

strod (OE) marshy land overgrown with brushwood

stron- *see* **sròn**

sub (L) below

sumor (OE), **sumarr** (OScand) summer

suth (OE), **suthr** (OScand) south, southern

svin (OScand) swine, pig

swan (OE) (1) herdsman, peasant, (2) swan

swin (OE) swine, pig

tarbeart (G) place of portage, isthmus

teampall (I) church *see* TEMPLE-

temple- *see* TEMPLE-

thing (OE, OScand) assembly, meeting

thorn (OE, OScand) thorn-tree

thorp (OScand) secondary settlement, dependent outlying farmstead or hamlet *see* THORPE

thorp(e) *see* THORPE

threo (OE) three

throp (OE) dependent outlying farmstead, hamlet *see also* THORPE

Thunor (OE) heathen Germanic god

thveit (OScand) clearing, meadow, paddock

thwaite *see* **thveit**

thyrne (OE), **thyrnir** (OScand) thorn-tree

thyrs (OE) giant, demon

ticce(n) (OE) kid, young goat

tìr (G), **tír** (I), **tir** (W) land

tir-, -tir(e) *see* **tìr**

tobar (G, I) well, spring

tober- *see* **tobar**

toft (OScand) site of a house or building, homestead

tom (G) knoll

-ton *see* -TON

topt (OScand) site of a house or building, homestead

torr (OE) rock, rocky hill

tot(e) (OE) look-out place

trá(igh) (I, G) beach, shore

tra(w) *see* **trá(igh)**

tre- *see* TRE-

tre (Co), **tre(f)** (G, W) homestead, farm, town *see* TRE-

treabh (G) homestead, farm, town *see* TRE-

tree *see* **treow**

treo(w) (OE) tree, post, beam

tubber- *see* **tobar**

tulach (G, I) hill

tulla(gh), tulloch, tully *see* **tulach**

tun (OE) enclosure, farmstead, village, manor, estate *see* -TON

twi- (OE) double

twisla (OE) fork of a river, junction of streams

tywyn (W) shore

tyr-, -tyre *see* **tìr**

uachdair (G) upper part

uferra (OE) higher

uisce (I), **uisge** (G) water

ulfr (OScand) wolf

upp (OE) higher up

upper (ModE) upper *see also* **uferra**

ut, **uterra** (OE) outside, outer

vagr (OScand) bay

vath (OScand) ford

vatn (OScand) lake

vik (OScand) bay *see also* WICK

vithr (OScand) wood

vra (OScand) nook or corner of land

wad (OE) woad

-wade *see* **wæd**

wæd (OE) ford, crossing-place *see also* FORD

wælla (OE) spring, stream

wæsse (OE) riverside land liable to flood

wæter (OE) water, river, lake

wal- *see* WAL-

wald (OE) woodland, forest, high forest land later cleared

walh (OE) Briton, Welshman *see* WAL-

wall (OE) wall, bank

-wardine *see* -WORTH, WORTHY, -WARDINE

-**ware** (OE) dwellers (plural)

water *see* **wæter**

wath *see* **vath**

way *see* **weg**

weald (OE) woodland, forest, high forest land later cleared

wealh (OE) Briton, Welshman *see* WAL-

weall (OE) wall, bank

weard (OE) watch, ward, protection

weg (OE) way, track, road

well *see* **wella**

wella (OE) spring, stream

weoh (OE) heathen shrine or temple

weorc (OE) building, fortification

wer (OE) weir, river-dam, fishing-enclosure in a river

west (OE) west, western

wet (OE) wet, damp

wether (OE) wether, ram

whit-, white- *see* **hwit**

wic (OE) earlier Romano-British settlement; dwelling, specialized farm or building, dairy farm; trading or industrial settlement, harbour *see* WICK

wice (OE) wych-elm

wick *see* WICK

wid (OE) wide, spacious

wig (OE) heathen shrine or temple

wilig (OE) willow tree

-with *see* **vithr**

withig (OE) withy, willow tree

Woden (OE) heathen Germanic god

woh (OE) twisted, crooked

wold *see* **wald**

wood *see* **wudu**

worth, **worthig**, **worthign** (OE) enclosure, enclosed settlement *see* -WORTH, WORTHY, -WARDINE

-**worth**, worthy *see* -WORTH, WORTHY, -WARDINE

wudu (OE) wood, forest, also timber

wulf (OE) wolf

wyrm (OE) snake, dragon

y(r) (W) the (i.e. the definite article)

yard *see* **geard**

-**ydd** (W) indicator of possession

yea- *see* **heah**

ynys (W) island *see* INIS

ystrad (W) valley